THE OFFICIAL ENCYCLOPEDIA OF BRIDGE

NEWLY REVISED, FOURTH EDITION

CONTRIBUTING EDITORS

THE OFFICIAL ENCYCLOPEDIA OF BRIDGE

NEWLY REVISED, FOURTH EDITION

Authorized by the American Contract Bridge League

and Prepared by Its Staff

HENRY G. FRANCIS

Editor-in-Chief

ALAN F. TRUSCOTT

Executive Editor

RICHARD L. FREY

Editor Emeritus

DIANE HAYWARD

Editor, Fourth Edition

CROWN PUBLISHERS, INC. ● NEW YORK

EDITORIAL ADVISORY BOARD

Copyright © 1984 by American Contract Bridge League, Inc.
Copyright © 1976, 1971, 1964 by Crown Publishers, Inc.

All rights reserved. No part of this book may be reproduced or transmitted in any form or by any means, electronic or mechanical, including photocopying, recording, or by any information storage and retrieval system, without permission in writing from the publisher.

Published by Crown Publishers, Inc., One Park Avenue, New York, NY 10016 and simultaneously in Canada by General Publishing Company Limited. Manufactured in the United States of America.

Library of Congress Cataloging in Publication Data

Main entry under title:

The Official encyclopedia of bridge.

   Bibliography: p. 902
   1. Contract bridge—Dictionaries. I. Francis, Henry G. II. Hayward, Diane. III. American Contract Bridge League.
GV1282.22.O35   1984   795.41′5′03   84-1791
ISBN 0-517-55272-8

FOREWORD

This is the fourth occasion on which I am writing a Foreword since I proposed, in 1962, that the American Contract Bridge League compile this work. I now find I cannot do better than repeat a part of the first paragraph of the third edition: "*The Official Encyclopedia of Bridge* has become a living panorama of the game, combining past history with present kaleidoscopic change. Even while changing, its purpose remains: 'To provide an official and authoritative answer to any question a reader might ask about the game of contract bridge and its leading players.'"

However, due principally to the heroic efforts of the new editor-in-chief, Henry Francis, and the continuing contributions and revisions by Executive Editor Alan Truscott, Editor Diane Hayward and many others throughout the world, this magnificent fourth edition makes a quantum leap in the technical material which comprises Part I. Many new and intriguing methods and ideas have made their appearance in the past seven years, and some have been widely adopted.

Despite an increase of 64 pages, the new material and the new names in the biographical section (Part II) have made it necessary to adopt more stringent qualifications for listing, and some of the names that appeared previously have had to be omitted. Nevertheless, there are far more entries than ever before in Part II.

Alas, this edition also records the passing of important bridge personalities, many of whom served on the Editorial Board or on the panel of Contributing Editors. New authorities and new champions have assumed the vacant posts. But the efforts of those who have made their last contribution to bridge and to previous editors of this Encyclopedia will be long remembered — most notably those of the late Albert H. Morehead, whose title as chairman of the original editorial board does not begin to cover the contributions he made.

Among those deserving of special mention, too, are Thomas M. Smith, who supervised the second edition, and Amalya L. Kearse, now a Justice of the Federal Court of Appeals, who somehow managed the superb organization of the third edition, even while conducting a busy law practice.

Major articles, surviving with some updates, have been contributed by Eric Crowhurst, Monroe Ingberman, Albert Dormer, Marshall Miles, Edgar Kaplan and Jeff Rubens. To them, as to all contributors, bridge in general and this work in particular owe deepest thanks. Grateful recognition is also due to Edith Simon, now retired ACBL librarian; to Rhoda Barrow Lederer, whose work in producing a British version of our first edition is reflected in this one, and, of course, to Diane Hayward, who had the task of updating the entries for this edition.

Let us not forget the 200,000 members of the ACBL, and its Board of Directors who gave the project official sponsorship and authorized the use of the League's invaluable records. Also to those members of the International Bridge Press Association and to the officials of many of the non-U.S. bridge organizations for help in providing details of a great many of the entries concerning bridge outside the purviews of the ACBL.

Space does not permit listing all who contributed to making this the greatest compendium of bridge history and affairs. Let us hope that their part in accomplishing this will be its own reward.

—RICHARD L. FREY
Editor Emeritus

HOW TO USE THIS ENCYCLOPEDIA

For easy reference, this book is divided into four main parts: I. General Information (technical — bidding and play; historical; procedural — tournament organization, laws, etc.; geographical; and terminological); II. Biographies; III. Tournament Results; IV. Bibliography.

I. General Information.

Technical. When more than one name is in use for a specific system, convention, etc., the major entry is under the term most commonly used in America. A cross-reference will be found for alternative names.

Appearance of a term or name in small capitals indicates that a separate entry is to be found either in Part I or in the biographical section.

The reader who wishes to study a particular field of bidding or play is advised to consult one of the following major headings. In each case, a number of cross-references permit investigation of the subject in depth: ARTIFICIAL CALL; BIDDING; BIDDING SYSTEMS; COMPETITIVE BIDDING; COUP; DEFENSE; DEFENSIVE BIDDING; DOUBLES; DUMMY PLAY; ENTRY; 4 NOTRUMP CONVENTIONS; LIMIT; MATHEMATICS OF BRIDGE; NOTRUMP BIDDING; 1♣ SYSTEMS; OPENING BID; OPENING LEADS; RESPONDER'S REBID; RESPONSE; SIGNALS; SLAM CONVENTIONS; SQUEEZE; TWO-BID; 2♣ SYSTEMS.

Historical. Every effort has been made to record the history of the American Contract Bridge League and other major national and international organizations. Information of importance — some of it newly discovered — will also be found under HISTORY OF BRIDGE, HISTORY OF PLAYING CARDS, and the entries of historic figures in the biographical section.

Procedural. The Laws of Rubber Bridge (1981) and of Duplicate Bridge (1975) are given in full. Various aspects of tournament organization are presented or cross-referenced in the article DUPLICATE BRIDGE.

Geographical. National bridge organizations throughout the world are listed, and histories and descriptions of them are provided.

Terminological. An effort has been made to list and define all terms, both regular and colloquial, in common use throughout the English-speaking world.

II. Biographies. Under the heading "Leading Bridge Personalities" are listed more than twenty-five hundred bridge notables. Occupations given are not necessarily current ones but indicate that the individual was at some time primarily engaged in that vocation. Where an individual is given credit for a contribution to bridge in the main body of the encyclopedia, his name appears in small capitals to indicate that a separate entry for this person is in the biographical section.

Noteworthy achievements by an increasing number of players who have appeared on the scene since the first (1964) edition of this encyclopedia have imposed new and stricter criteria for including individual biographies. It has been necessary to omit many players who have won fewer than three major regional events, or whose failure to win recent events suggests that they have become inactive; to drop the recording of second place finishes in events of less than major national ranking; to omit the complete detailing of regional titles from the biographies of those who have to their credit many such triumphs, or whose national and international achievements overshadow such victories. However, all such successes are to be found recorded in the history of the event itself, as detailed in Part III.

III. Tournament Results. Except for WORLD CHAMPIONSHIPS and USBA GRAND NATIONALS results (listed under these headings in Part I), all North American and most of the important international tournament results have been divided into three Appendixes: Appendix I — North American Championships: the ABA tournaments, the three ACBL NAC tournaments, the Grand National Teams playoff, and the ACBL-wide and Intercollegiate Championships; Appendix II — ACBL Regional Championships; Appendix III — International Championships; European, Far East and South American Championships.

IV. Bibliography. Significant books on all aspects of bridge and its evolution are here listed according to subject.

The American Contract Bridge League, P.O. Box 161192, Memphis TN 38186, will endeavor to render library service to owners of this encyclopedia who send a request for information with a self-addressed stamped envelope.

A

ABA. See AMERICAN BRIDGE ASSOCIATION.

ABL. See AMERICAN BRIDGE LEAGUE.

ABP. See ASSOCIATION OF BRIDGE PROFESSIONALS.

ABPA. American Bridge Press Association.

ABTA. See AMERICAN BRIDGE TEACHERS' ASSOCIATION.

ACBL. See AMERICAN CONTRACT BRIDGE LEAGUE.

ACBL BULLETIN. See BULLETIN, THE CONTRACT BRIDGE.

ACBL CHARITY FOUNDATION. See CHARITY PROGRAM OF THE ACBL.

ACBL HANDBOOK. A handbook that sets forth under one cover the regulations and practices followed by the American Contract Bridge League in several important phases of its activities. Interested persons or groups may secure copies of the handbook or sections thereof from ACBL HEADQUARTERS.

ACBL HEADQUARTERS. 2200 Democrat Road, Post Office Box 161192, Memphis, Tennessee 38186–9982.

ACBL LAWS COMMISSION. See LAWS COMMISSION OF THE ACBL.

ACBL PLAYER NUMBER. See PLAYER NUMBER.

ACBL–WIDE GAMES. Four times annually, in conjunction with each North American Championship and during the month of May (formerly January), the ACBL conducts a game that is played at separate sites throughout the North American continent and elsewhere. All sections in each game are conducted virtually simultaneously, and the ACBL provides computer-dealt hands, one set for each section, so that all sections play identical hands. At the conclusion of the game the participants are provided with printed copies of the first 36 deals, accompanied by expert analyses. After comparing scores sent in from each game site, the ACBL determines a winner and a runner-up on a best percentage score basis for each of its 25 districts and an overall winner and runner-up for the entire ACBL. For results, see Appendix I. The record winning score in an ACBL-wide game is 82.95%, recorded in the March 1971 game. The low record for a winning score is 72.98% in the Fall 1966 game. The largest ACBL-wide game, 17,524 pairs, was held during the 1972 Spring NAC. The first ACBL-wide game was held at the Summer NAC in 1962.

Two of the four annual games are conducted for the benefit of the ACBL Charity Foundation and the Canadian Bridge Federation Charitable Fund (see CHARITY PROGRAM OF THE ACBL). Proceeds from the other two games are used to help cover the expenses of ACBL members who earn the right to represent either their country or the ACBL in international competitions such as the World Team Olympiad, the Bermuda Bowl, the Venice Trophy and the World Pairs Championships.

Each unit and affiliated club is invited to participate in the ACBL-wide game by conducting a section of the event in its own playing quarters.

Any unit or club may award prizes to the winners of its own game, if it so desires. See also OMNIUM.

APBP. See ASSOCIATION OF PROFESSIONAL BRIDGE PLAYERS.

AWL. See AMERICAN WHIST LEAGUE.

A POSTERIORI PROBABILITIES. See PROBABILITIES, A POSTERIORI.

A PRIORI PROBABILITIES. See PROBABILITIES, A PRIORI.

ABOVE THE LINE. A phrase denoting all scores in rubber bridge entered above a horizontal line on the score sheet, including penalties and the premiums for honors, slams, rubbers, overtricks, and fulfilling a doubled or redoubled contract. See PREMIUM SCORE.

ABSOLUTE FORCE. A bid which makes it incumbent on partner to guarantee that another bid can be made by the player making the absolute force. Unless the bid is overcalled or doubled immediately, the partner is under conventional obligation to make some call other than a pass. See DEMAND BID, FORCING BID.

ACCIDENTS. From time to time a player may suffer from some misfortune. He may miscount his points, missort his hand, mishear the bidding, or pull out a wrong card. In such circumstances he should be particularly careful not to react in any way when he discovers his error.

ACCORDING TO HOYLE. A phrase indicating that a procedure is sanctioned both legally and ethically; in addition, that it has the backing of custom. The prestige of EDMOND HOYLE was so great that the phrase "according to Hoyle" came to mean correct procedure in general.

ACE. The suit card with only a single pip. In most games, including all those of the bridge family, it is the highest ranking card; hence, a top performer in any field.

In England, the ace of spades was the card which indicated that the duty had been paid and its printing was controlled by the government. Ever since the wrapper carried the duty or tax notation, the card has remained ornate in England and the United

States, where each manufacturer developed an individual design to serve as a trademark.

In other countries, other aces have served to carry the trademarks: clubs in France, hearts in Germany. See: ACE-SHOWING RESPONSES; HONOR TRICKS; OPENING LEADS; POINT-COUNT.

ACE FROM ACE-KING. The traditional lead of the king from an ace-king holding has been abandoned by many players in favor of the ace lead. Some players lead the ace against notrump contracts only, because an ace lead against notrump is unlikely to be attractive if the king is not held.

The argument in favor of leading the ace is that it avoids certain ambiguities which arise if the king is led:

(1) After the lead of the king against a suit contract, the opening leader's partner is unsure whether to indicate a small doubleton combination. He would wish to do so if the lead is from ace-king, but not if it is from king-queen. The same would apply if the leader's partner holds a doubleton jack.

(2) After the lead of the king against any contract, the opening leader's partner is uncertain whether to signal with his second card holding the jack and two small cards. In this situation he would wish to signal if the lead was from king-queen but not if it was from ace-king. (It is assumed in all cases that dummy holds three worthless cards.)

Against this, the proponents of the king lead point out that the lead of an unsupported ace is not uncommon against a suit contract, and the leader's partner may wish to know whether the king is held.

Holding a doubleton ace-king, this special procedure is reversed: the king is led followed by the ace.

Whatever convention is being used, the ace lead is tactically advisable against a slam contract: the king is too revealing when the opposing hands have a singleton opposite a combination headed by queen-jack.

For an alternative method of avoiding the ambiguity arising from the king lead, see RUSINOW LEADS.

ACE AND KING SHOWING RESPONSES. A method of showing aces and kings in response to an opening two bid. Some combinations can be shown in one bid; others require more rounds of bidding. With no aces and no kings, the responder bids 2 NT. With one king and no aces, the first response is 2 NT, and then if his partner makes a bid below the game level, responder bids the suit with the king.

If responder has one ace and no kings, he bids the suit in which he has the ace. If he has two kings and no aces, he jumps to 3 NT. If he has two aces and no kings, he jumps to 4 NT. If he has one ace and one king, he first bids the suit in which he has the ace and later bids the suit in which he has the king.

ACE-GRABBER. A player who leads or takes his aces at his first opportunity, thereby sometimes making the play easier for the opponents.

ACE-HIGH. (1) A term dating from whist days indicating that the ace is the highest card in the suit or

the cut. Obsolescent in bridge because the alternative procedures associated with other games have been generally forgotten. (2) Descriptive of a suit held by one player in which the ace is the top card.

ACE IDENTIFICATION. An extension of the GERBER CONVENTION, devised by Norman Squire of England, to discover which ace a partnership is missing.

When responder has shown one or two aces in response to 4♣, 4 NT asks for further information. If responder has one ace, he bids the suit of the ace. If he has two aces, he bids:

5♣	with aces of the same color
5♢	with aces of the same rank
5♡	with mixed aces

This may assist in deciding whether to bid a small slam, and possibly a grand slam if the 4 NT bidder has a void. See also ROMAN GERBER.

ACE LEAD. Against notrump, by a convention of long standing, this lead requires partner to play his highest card of the suit led. This may be helpful if the opening leader has A-K-J-10-x-x, and his partner holds the queen, but these situations are not common. This is not applicable of course if a partnership uses ACE FROM ACE-KING as a standard lead.

ACE SHOWING. See CUEBIDS TO SHOW CONTROLS.

ACE-SHOWING RESPONSES. Answers to forcing opening bids that are based on the theory that the opener with a powerful unbalanced hand is more interested in his partner's first-round controls than in his long suit or general strength.

This is sometimes employed over FORCING TWO-BIDS, but is also common in conjunction with conventional 2♣ STRONG ARTIFICIAL OPENINGS, especially in Europe (see PIERRE ALBARRAN). A minimum response, other than a negative one, shows the ace of the suit bid. The responses to a conventional 2♣ bid would be:

2♢	negative
2♡ or 2♠	ace-showing
2 NT	8 points at least, but aceless
3♣ or 3♢	ace-showing
3 NT	two aces

French experts vary this scheme in two ways. A 2 NT response is permitted with two kings; and a hand holding two aces can make a more precise response:

3♡	two mixed aces (♠ and ♢, or ♡ and ♣)
3♠	two aces of the same color
3 NT	two aces, both major or both minor

The opening bidder can subsequently ask for kings by using the bid normally employed to ask for aces — 4 NT or 4♣ at choice.

A method suggested by CHARLES S. HOBLIT, of Detroit, for use over natural forcing two-bids, requires responder to show top trump honors, if any, along with his aces. The responses are:

single raise	one trump honor, no ace
double raise	two trump honors, no ace
new suit	ace in suit, no trump honor
jump in new suit	ace in suit, one trump honor
double jump in new suit	ace in suit, two trump honors
2 NT	no trump honors, no ace
3 NT	no trump honors, two aces

An alternative scheme is to respond according to the *step* principle, showing aces and kings simultaneously. See STEP RESPONSES. See also BLUE TEAM CLUB; CAB SYSTEM; DYNAMIC NOTRUMP; SCHENKEN SYSTEM (2 ◊); SKINNER TWO BIDS; TAM II 2♣ AND 2 ◊ OPENINGS.

ACE VALUES. A method of distributional valuation developed as part of the BARON SYSTEM.

When valuing a hand for a raise, the HONOR TRICK value of the hand is added to the following distributional values:

	with 3 trumps	with 4 trumps
void	2	3
singleton	1	2
doubleton	½	1

(But a second shortage counts at half value unless five trumps are held.)

The total is the level to which responder should raise playing LIMIT RAISES. For example:

$$♠Q J 3 2 \quad ♡K Q 6 \quad ◊K 6 5 2 \quad ♣9 6$$

In response to a 1♠ opening bid, this hand counts three ace values (two for honor tricks plus one for the club doubleton) and therefore justifies a raise to 3♠.

If the opening bidder is planning to raise his partner's response, he subtracts two from his ace values and raises to the level of the answer: *i.e.*, with four ace values he raises to the two level, with five to the three level, and so on. See DISTRIBUTIONAL COUNTS.

ACES OVER TWO-BIDS. See ACE-SHOWING RESPONSES.

ACES SCIENTIFIC SYSTEM. A detailed system formulated by the ACES TEAM with the aid of a computer for research and experimentation. Precise standards are set for all phases of bidding, including detailed methods for dealing with opponents' interference in constructive auctions. The main features of the system, as described by BOBBY GOLDMAN, are:

(1) 15½ to 18 point notrump openings. Responses of 2 ◊ and 2 ♡ are JACOBY TRANSFERS; 2♠ promises both minor suits and is a mild slam try; 3♣ and 3 ◊ are weak; 3 ♡ and 3 ♠, both artificial, are mild slam tries in clubs and diamonds respectively.

2♣ is non-forcing STAYMAN, following which responder may: rebid 3♣ to seek a 4-4 minor suit fit; or rebid 3 ◊ (artificial) to show a long minor suit and slam interest; or rebid three of the other major suit to show four-card support for opener's major, an unidentified singleton and slam interest.

(2) Major suit openings promise at least five cards; a 1 NT response is forcing for one round; two-level reponses are virtually forcing to game. Jump raises are limit, and forcing raises may be made in one of

six ways to show specific point ranges and hands with and without singletons. See UNBALANCED SWISS, VALUE SWISS.

Jump shifts into minor suits show solid suits with at least 6½ playing tricks; opener's rebids below 3 NT show stoppers rather than suits.

(3) Minor suit openings promise at least three-card suits. Immediate jump raises are limit; jumps to three of the *other* minor suit are forcing raises. These jump shifts and delayed jump raises are forcing to 3 NT or four of a minor. Jump shift responses into major suits promise either a solid suit, or an excellent suit in a notrump type hand, or a strong suit with strong support for opener.

(4) 2♣ openings (strong and artificial) are usually forcing to game. Responses of 2 ◊ are neutral; other suits are natural with good values in the suit; 2 NT and 3 NT deny any aces and show balanced hands with no suit worse than J-x-x. Two-level openings other than clubs are WEAK TWO-BIDS.

(5) Slam conventions include modern Roman responses to BLACKWOOD, GERBER, and SUPER GERBER, plus a fifth step to show two aces and a useful void, and additional steps to show one ace and a useful void. Further slam tries may be made after the ace-asking response. 5 NT, even after Blackwood, asks about trump quality whenever a fit has been agreed.

ACES TEAM. A full-time professional bridge team, organized in 1968 by Dallas financier IRA CORN for the express purpose of returning the world team championship to the United States.

Corn selected six players from among America's leading young experts, paying each a salary, plus tournament expenses, to undertake a full-time career of studying and playing bridge. He started with JAMES JACOBY and BOBBY WOLFF, and shortly thereafter added BILLY EISENBERG, BOBBY GOLDMAN and MICHAEL LAWRENCE. ROBERT HAMMAN joined the team in 1969. MONROE INGBERMAN, mathematician and bridge writer, worked with the Aces as their first coach. In mid-1968 retired Air Force Colonel JOSEPH MUSUMECI was added as trainer and coach. The team was incorporated as the U.S. Aces, but was popularly known as the Dallas Aces and later simply as the Aces.

Using a computer to analyze results and to generate specific sets of hands to provide practice in given areas of the game — slam hands, preemptive openings, etc. — the Aces spent 50 to 60 hours a week perfecting the bidding systems and discussing problems encountered at the table. Complete records of all hands played were compiled for critical analysis. From the intensive study and analysis emerged various bidding styles including the ORANGE CLUB, used by Wolff and Jacoby; the similar BLACK CLUB, used by Hamman and Eisenberg; and the ACES SCIENTIFIC SYSTEM, used by Goldman and Lawrence. Besides competing in North American Championships and Regional knockout team-of-four contests, the Aces also engaged many of America's top experts in practice matches in Dallas and staged a series of exhibition matches. See SHARIF BRIDGE CIRCUS.

In 1969, the team achieved the first major goal set

by Corn by winning the Spingold Knockout Teams and later a playoff match that earned the Aces the right to represent North America in the 1970 BERMUDA BOWL in Stockholm, Sweden. With the BLUE TEAM retired, the Aces returned the Bermuda Bowl to North America for the first time since 1954. The Aces successfully defended their world title in 1971. See WORLD CHAMPIONSHIPS.

In 1971 Eisenberg left the team and was replaced by PAUL SOLOWAY. By June of 1972 the team had become a part-time effort, with the players being paid only their expenses rather than salaries. Thereafter the makeup of the Aces began to change. In 1972 the Aces were runner-up to Italy in the Team Olympiad. Jacoby–Wolff played the Orange Club; Hamman–Soloway, the Green Club and Goldman–Lawrence, Standard American with special treatments. In early 1973 Soloway was replaced by MARK BLUMENTHAL. The Aces were second to Italy in the Bermuda Bowl, playing as two threesomes: Wolff–Hamman–Jacoby playing Aces Club and Goldman–Lawrence–Blumenthal playing Standard American with special treatments. Soon thereafter Lawrence and Jacoby left the team and were replaced by ERIC MURRAY and SAMMY KEHELA. In 1974 the Aces were second to Italy with Hamman–Wolff playing the Aces Club, Blumenthal–Goldman, Aces Scientific, and Kehela–Murray, Colonial Acol.

In 1975 EDDIE KANTAR and JOHN SWANSON made their first appearances in international play with the Aces and Soloway–Eisenberg were back on the team. The Aces were second to Italy in the Bermuda Bowl and the team was Hamman–Wolff (Aces Club); Eisenberg–Kantar, Soloway–Swanson (Standard American with special treatments).

The Aces won the 1977 Bermuda Bowl as Zone 2 representatives, and another team from North America finished second. Playing for the Aces once again were Hamman–Wolff, Soloway–Swanson and Eisenberg–Kantar. In 1979 four ex-Aces won the Bermuda Bowl in Rio on a team captained by MALCOLM BRACHMAN (Eisenberg, Goldman, Kantar, Soloway). The next year in the 1980 World Team Olympiad Corn captained the Aces to second place behind France. His team was Hamman–Wolff, still playing the Aces Club; Soloway–IRA RUBIN (Standard American with special treatments) and FRED HAMILTON–MIKE PASSELL (FIVE-CARD MAJORS, TWO-OVER-ONE GAME FORCE). In 1981 for the first time in many years no Ace or former Ace was present on the U.S. international team.

In the fall of 1981 Corn put together one more Aces team. He had great hopes for Hamman–Wolff (the only players to remain constantly with the Aces throughout a 13-year period), ALAN SONTAG–PETER WEICHSEL and MIKE BECKER–RONNIE RUBIN. Just three months after Corn's sudden death of a heart attack in April, 1982 — the Aces won the Spingold in Albuquerque and qualified for the International Team Trials in Minneapolis that November. Hamman, in summing up the history and the victory of this Aces team, reported, "Just say that we won one for big Ira." The Aces name stuck with them. In the Minneapolis trials which they won they were known as the *Aces* rather than as the *Spingold* and their nonplaying captain was Joe Musumeci.

ACOL DIRECT KING CONVENTION. A bid of 4 NT to ask about kings by a player whose partner has already made a bid specifically showing the number of aces he holds. This convention can be used with such conventions as GAMBLING 3 NT, when it has been agreed that this bid denies an outside ace, and STEP RESPONSES TO STRONG ARTIFICIAL TWO-BIDS.

ACOL 4 NT OPENING. A specialized bid asking for aces. The responses are:

5 ♣	no ace	5 ♠	♠ A
5 ♢	♢ A	5 NT	two aces
5 ♡	♡ A	6 ♣	♣ A

ACOL SYSTEM. The system which is *standard* in British tournament play, and widely used in other parts of the world. The originators were a group of players which included MAURICE HARRISON-GRAY, IAIN MAC LEOD, J. C. H. MARX, TERENCE REESE and S. J. SIMON. It was called Acol because it was first played in 1934 in the small North London bridge club on the street of the same name. Many of the ideas were derived from the early writings of ELY CULBERTSON.

The chief features of the system are:

(1) The weak notrump not vulnerable and the strong notrump vulnerable. The original ranges were 13–15 and 16–18, but 12–14 has become standard for the weak range, and 15–17 is often preferred to 16–18. The system is frequently used with a weak or strong notrump at all vulnerabilities (see also THREE-QUARTER NOTRUMP).

(2) LIMIT RAISES and notrump responses. Raises and notrump responses are never forcing in their own right. After an opening bid of 1 ♠, a response of 2 NT or 3 ♠ is encouraging but not forcing, showing about 11 points or the distributional equivalent.

(3) Jump rebids are not forcing unless in a new suit.

(4) Opening suit bids tend to be slightly weaker than in American methods, especially if a six-card major suit is held.

(5) TWO-OVER-ONE RESPONSES are made more freely than in American methods: 8 points with a five-card suit, or 7 points with a six-card suit may be sufficient.

(6) Fourth-suit bids are used conventionally by most Acol experts. See FOURTH SUIT FORCING.

(7) 2 ♣, artificial strong opening, forcing to 2 NT.

(8) ACOL TWO-BID, forcing for one round.

(9) GAMBLING 3 NT. A long strong minor suit with at least two other suits protected.

(10) 4 NT opening asks for specific aces. See ACOL 4 NT OPENING.

Other regular features of the system are listed separately: CULBERTSON 4-5 NT or BLACKWOOD; STAYMAN CONVENTION; GRAND SLAM FORCE; TRIAL BID. Optional features of Acol listed separately include: ACOL DIRECT KING CONVENTION; BARON SLAM TRY; BENJAMIN; CROWHURST; FLINT 3 ♢; FLINT 2 ♢; GERBER CONVENTION; INTEREST-SHOWING BIDS; KOCK-WERNER REDOUBLES; RESPONSIVE DOUBLE; ROMAN BLACKWOOD; ROMAN 2 ♢; SHARPLES; SHORT-SUIT GAME TRIES; STRONG NOTRUMP AFTER PASSING; SWISS; TEXAS; UNUSUAL NOTRUMP; VOID-SHOWING BIDS; WEISSBERGER.

ACOL TWO-BID. A type of intermediate two-bid, strong and forcing for one round. A strong distributional hand is required with at least eight playing tricks:

(a)	(b)
♠ A K Q 8 7 5 4	♠ 8
♡ A J 4	♡ A Q J 10 5 4
◇ 9 6	◇ A K 9 8 5
♣ 2	♣ 9
Bid: 2♠	Bid: 2♡

A suit of six or more cards is normal, but the bid can be used with two strong five-card suits.

The negative response is 2 NT (although some use the next highest suit by special partnership agreement), after which a simple rebid or a bid of a lower-ranking suit at the three level is non-forcing.

A suit takeout response approximates to a standard two-over-one takeout, but can be weaker at the level of two. A single raise is highly constructive, suggesting a slam, and virtually promising an ace. A double raise shows about 10 points but no ace. If responder has moderate strength but no marked distributional feature and no slam ambitions, he can make a negative reponse and then bid game. See BENJAMIN.

ACORNS. One of the suits in old-time PLAYING CARDS. See also PACK.

ACTIVE DEFENSE OVERCALLS. A competitive method devised by KRIS BHAVNANI of Carlisle MA. The following three actions in *immediate* position after an opening in one of a suit are the nucleus:

1) 1 NT is a weak takeout with two good or any three spades (Q–x or better, except over 1♠).

2) A cuebid over a 1♣, 1◇ or 1♡ opening is a weak takeout with four or more spades. A cuebid of 2♠ is no different from 1 NT over 1♠, but is best played as very weak and distributional.

3) A two-level overcall (jump or not) shows two suits — the suit bid and the next higher-ranking excluding the opened suit. Here clubs ranks over spades, so for example 1♠–2♡ shows hearts and clubs. There should be no more than a doubleton in the fourth suit.

Partner can expect nine cards in the two suits in case 3, and three or more cards in each takeout suit (except for the lower and higher spade lengths) in cases 1 and 2. Since partner knows your suit lengths to within one card in most cases, he can apply total-trick valuation based on his own hand and take the appropriate defensive or lead-directing action.

The remaining overcall options are:

a) Overcall at the one level for lead direction and limited competition.

b) Overcall at the three level — intermediate to preemptive with one predominant suit.

c) Double, even with defective distribution Italian style, to show a good hand with 14 + points and game prospects.

ADEQUATE TRUMP SUPPORT. See TRUMP SUPPORT.

ADJUSTED SCORE. A score assigned by the tournament director when either an infraction of the Laws or a procedural error has occurred and the director is so empowered. The adjusted score may take various forms. *e.g.*, exactly average for all concerned, above or below average, an assigned matchpoint or IMP score on a hand, a change in the number of tricks taken, the reshuffling and playing of a hand, a change in the overall score, etc. Any penalty assessed the offending side need not balance the indemnity awarded the non-offending side. See LAWS OF DUPLICATE (Laws 12, 64.C, 82, 84).

ADVANCE CUEBID. A cuebid of a first-round control (in rare cases, a second-round control) made before the cuebidder's partner knows the agreed trump suit. The purpose of this cuebid is to distinguish between a normal raise and a raise based on controls plus a good distributional fit that offers some hope for slam if partner has the right distribution or high-card structure.

For example the bidding goes:

SOUTH	NORTH
1♠	2♡
3♠	4♣

North holds:

♠ J 6 5
♡ A Q 9 7 3
◇ 9 2
♣ A 10 4

If South holds a solid spade suit, the ♡K and a diamond control, slam at spades will be a reasonable undertaking, but might not be reached unless North shows his slam interest by cuebidding the ♣A before supporting spades. From South's seat, however, the 4♣ bid is ambiguous. North could have a heart–club two-suiter or be making an advance cuebid.

The cuebid might also be used after a jump shift:

SOUTH	NORTH
1♠	1 NT
3◇	4♣

North holds:

♠ 7
♡ Q 10 6 4
◇ K 8 7 3 2
♣ A 5 2

North's hand has grown to slam proportions after South's jump shift, so he makes a slam try by cuebidding the ♣A *before* raising diamonds. Here also South is not yet certain whether North has a legitimate club suit or is cuebidding in support of diamonds, or possibly spades.

Variations of this cuebid occur in many notrump sequences, but cannot be considered *true* advance cuebids because the trump suit is set by implication. For example:

SOUTH	NORTH	SOUTH	NORTH	SOUTH	NORTH
1 NT	3♣	2 NT	3♡	1♠	1♠
4◇		4♣		2 NT	3♡
				4◇	

The logical interpretation of South's last bid in each of these auctions is that he has strong support for partner's last named suit, a maximum for his previous bid(s), a wealth of first- and second-round controls and, usually, a ruffing value and the ace of the cuebid suit. Without these features, South would support North's suit or rebid 3 NT, as North's bidding requested. See also RESPONSES TO 1 NT AND 2 NT.

ADVANCE SAVE. A sacrifice bid made before the opponents have reached their probable optimum contract. This may have two objectives: first, to leave the opposition in doubt about whether the sacrifice bidder expects to make his contract; second, to make the opponents guess at a high level without giving them full opportunity to exchange information.

For example, East–West are vulnerable and the bidding goes:

WEST	NORTH	EAST	SOUTH
1♣	1♡	2♡	6♡

South holds:

    ♠ 5 3
    ♡ Q 7 5 3 2
    ◊ J 7 5 3 2
    ♣ 6

It is highly probable that East–West are headed for a slam in a black suit, so South aims to set his opponents a problem. South is prepared to concede a penalty of 900 or thereabouts, which may prove an accurate sacrifice and also may goad East–West into attempting an impossible contract. See also SACRIFICE OR SAVE.

ADVANCED SENIOR MASTER. The second highest in the ranking of players in the AMERICAN CONTRACT BRIDGE LEAGUE. To achieve this rank, a player needs 200 master points, including at least 20 RED POINTS. See RANKING OF PLAYERS.

ADVERSARY. Either opponent of declarer, or, during the auction, a player on the other side. The laws of 1963 use *opponent* for the latter and *defender* for the former. Senior adversary was synonymous with declarer's left-hand opponent, and junior adversary with his right-hand opponent.

AFRICA. See the following areas and countries, listed separately as African Bridge Federations: CENTRAL AFRICA, EGYPTIAN BRIDGE ASSOCIATION, MOROCCO, SOUTH AFRICA.

AGGREGATE SCORE. See TOTAL POINT SCORING.

ALBERT TWO CLUBS. An artificial opening bid, used by the Venezuelan team in the 1966 and 1967 BERMUDA BOWL, that describes a powerful hand, generally forcing to game.

The responses are:

2 ◊ : 7 or more points
2 ♡ : 0–6 points
2 ♠ : five-card or longer spade suit
2 NT: five-card or longer heart suit
3 ♣ or 3 ◊ : natural
3 ♡ : 0–2 points, balanced hand
3 ♠ : six-card spade suit headed by three honors
3 NT: six-card heart suit headed by three honors
4 ♡ or 4 ♠ : solid six- or seven-card suit

ALCATRAZ COUP. A coup in contract bridge is a term applied to any strategic play. A few situations can come up which are not covered by the rules. The Alcatraz Coup is one of these; as the name suggests, it is considered a form of robbery that almost warrants a prison term for the perpetrator. The following is an example:

    DUMMY
    A J 10

    DECLARER
    K x

Declarer, to make three tricks in the suit, calls the jack from dummy and, receiving a small card from right-hand opponent, fails to follow suit. Fourth hand either produces the queen or a small card. If a small card, declarer corrects his revoke by substituting the small card, leads to his king, and has the ace in dummy for the third trick. If fourth hand produces the queen, declarer *corrects his revoke* by producing the king, sweetly permitting his left-hand opponent to change his play, and finesses the located queen on the next play.

Whenever the coup occurs, the defenders are entitled to redress and should receive an adjusted score in accordance with LAWS OF DUPLICATE (Laws 12A, 47F). No director would permit a declarer to gain an advantage of this type, and any such swindle attempted deliberately should meet with a serious penalty on ethical charges.

ALERTING. A method of drawing opponents' attention to the fact that a particular bid has a conventional or unusual meaning. In 1971 the ACBL adopted a CONVENTION CARD that provided boxes for a partnership to check off its basic bidding agreements, thereby eliminating the need to list all partnership understandings. In addition, the ACBL has made it mandatory for a player to Alert his opponents whenever his partner makes a bid that has a special partnership meaning and that is other than a "Class A" CONVENTION. The recommended procedure is that when such a bid occurs, the player announces to his right-hand opponent, "Alert". The opponent can request an explanation at that time by saying, "Please explain", or can reserve the right to inquire at any later time when it is his turn to call or play. See EXPLANATION OF CONVENTIONAL CALL OR PLAY. A player must use the Alert procedure unless his opponents specifically request him not to do so before the auction begins. See CONVENTION. A player who gains information from his partner's Alert should avoid taking advantage of it. However, if his partner has Alerted in error or has given a wrong explanation, it is improper for him to correct the error immediately or to indicate in any manner that a mistake has been made; and he is under no legal or moral obligation to offer a correction later. If, as a result of Alerting, whether or not an explanation is requested, a partnership either avoids a misunderstanding or becomes aware of a misunderstanding, an ADJUSTED SCORE may be awarded. See LAWS OF DUPLICATE (Laws 16, 40, and Proprieties II, IV).

Use of diagonal bidding SCREENS in national and (since 1975) world championship play has made it necessary in many cases for the bidder himself to point silently to an Alert sign for the benefit of his opponent. This procedure is then repeated by the partner for the benefit of the latter's opponent on his side of the screen. Occasionally the explanations of the two partners differ and it becomes necessary for the director, or a tournament committee, to decide on the need to adjust the score or replay a deal. In the absence of screens, an informal method of Alerting used in many international events is to tap on the table.

ALL-AMERICAN REGIONAL CHAMPION-SHIPS. A four-day event held annually in the Midwest, beginning in 1938. This tournament is usually staged in Cleveland or Akron (and in past years Toledo and Detroit) over Memorial Day. For past results, see Appendix II.

ALL INDONESIA BRIDGE ASSOCIATION (GA-BUNGAN BRIDGE SELURUH INDONESIA). This association was founded in 1953, and by 1968 had a membership of approximately 6,000. The Association is a member of the Far East Bridge Federation, and participates in the Far East Championships and World Olympiads. Indonesia won the Far East Championships in 1962, 1964, 1972, 1973, 1974, 1979 and 1980. National tournaments include an annual Intercity Championship and biennial events for Open Pairs, Mixed Pairs, and Women's Teams (odd-numbered years) and Open Teams and Women's Pairs (even-numbered years).

Officers, 1982:
President: Wisnu Djayengminardo
Secretary: Djanwar Dt. Madjolelo, c/o Koni Pusat – Senayan Jakarta, Indonesia

ALL-WESTERN CHAMPIONSHIPS. A Regional Championship held annually since 1935, originally held in May, subsequently held over Labor Day in San Francisco (alternate sites are Palo Alto and Oakland). From 1935 through 1947 it was also called BRIDGE WEEK and was the second segment of the Memorial Day tournament which began in Los Angeles. Players paid $8.00 to board the Wednesday *Daylight Special* train in Los Angeles bound for San Francisco; enroute the Team-of-Four event was played. Events in San Francisco were held Thursday through Sunday originally at the Whitcomb Hotel and subsequently at the Sheraton Palace Hotel, and more recently at the Hyatt Regency. The All-Western is one of the larger regionals, averaging more than 3500 tables over the six-day tournament. For past results see Appendix II.

ALLEN OVER NOTRUMP. A convention suggested by LARRY ALLEN of Summerville SC for use in conjunction with JACOBY TRANSFER BIDS to initiate a search for a 4-4 minor suit fit. After responder has bid 2♣ STAYMAN and opener has responded in a major suit, a rebid of the other major by responder asks opener to show another four-card suit if he has one. If opener has rebid 2◊ in response to Stayman, a 3♣ bid by responder is also a minor suit inquiry. Opener rebids 3◊ with 3-3-4-3 distribution, rebids 3 NT with 3-3-3-4 distribution, and rebids three of his shorter major suit if he has four cards in each minor suit. See also BARON COROLLARY.

ALLEN OVER 2♣. A method devised by ELLEN ALLEN of Summerville SC to describe three-suited hands of game-forcing strength. A 2♣ strong artificial opening is used, with an automatic 2◊ ARTIFICIAL RESPONSE; a jump rebid by opener to three of a major suit or four of a minor suit shows 4-4-4-1 or 5-4-4-0 distribution, with shortness in the suit bid.

ALPHA ASKING BIDS. (1) Asking bids in the ROMAN SYSTEM concerned with controls in a side suit. See ROMAN ASKING BIDS. (2) Asking bids in the SUPER PRECISION system concerned with responder's support for the 1♣ opener's suit. See SUPER PRECISION ASKING BIDS.

ALTERNATE THREAT SQUEEZE. See COMPOUND SQUEEZE.

ALTERNATIVE SQUEEZE (Either-Or Squeeze). A simple squeeze played as a double squeeze.

$$♠ \ A \ K \ Q \ x$$
$$♡ \ K$$
$$◊ \ —$$
$$♣ \ —$$

$$♠ \ x \ x$$
$$♡ \ x$$
$$◊ \ K$$
$$♣ \ A$$

Suppose that West has the ♡A, and East has the ◊A. Spades cannot be guarded by both opponents, so that North's small spade technically cannot be a DOUBLE MENACE because it is not possible for opponents to hold four spades each. However, when South leads the ♣A, whichever opponent is actually guarding spades must unguard that suit in order to keep his ace. If West keeps his ♡A, North discards the ♡K. If West started with four or more spades the squeeze has worked on him. Alternatively, if West started with fewer than four spades, East is now squeezed.

Monroe Ingberman

AMBIGUOUS BIDS. See PARTNERSHIP MISUNDERSTANDINGS.

AMERICAN AUCTION BRIDGE LEAGUE. See AMERICAN BRIDGE LEAGUE.

AMERICAN BRIDGE ASSOCIATION. The national organization founded in 1932 to encourage duplicate bridge among black players. It continued to develop steadily, reaching a total membership of about 4,000 in 1982 including 1,500 Life Masters. It conducts two annual National tournaments, a Spring National, usually held in April since 1969, and a Summer National, usually held in August since 1934, with pair championships for Open, Mixed, Men's and Women's Pairs, an Individual, and team championships for Open, Mixed, Men's and Women's Teams. The earliest National championships were held in New York, but since that time have been held in many major cities all over the U.S. For past results of the ABA Open Teams and Open Pairs, see Appendix I.

In the early days of contract bridge, blacks were excluded from most major tournaments. In 1932, a small group of black players in the greater New York area decided to foster and promote duplicate bridge among blacks. To that end, they conceived the idea of establishing a national organization and made contact with similar groups in other parts of the country. The result was the foundation of the American Bridge Association by Dr. M. E. DuBissette (President, 1932–35), Horace R. Miller (President, 1936), and L. C. Collins, with John W. Cromwell, Jr., of Washington, D.C.

In 1936 the ABA merged with the Eastern Bridge League, a group of New York City clubs headed by Morgan S. Jensen. There followed a period of steady expansion under the presidency of Dr. E. T. Belsaw (1936–49). Four geographical sections were formed, subsequently expanded to seven, which conducted sectional tournaments equivalent to ACBL Regional tournaments. A masterpoint system was established for rating players. The bi-monthly *ABA Bulletin*, edited by W. R. Tatem from 1944–53, became an outstanding publication, and its high standards were maintained under the succeeding editors, Clarence Farmer (1953–70), Bobbye Caldwell (1970–81), and Dr. William Furr (1982–).

Official recognition of the growing acceptance of black participation in tournaments came in 1952, when the ACBL passed an amendment proposed by GEN. ROBERT J. GILL by which each unit became the sole judge of membership qualifications in its territory.

Enactment of federal legislation which forbade the exclusion of blacks from hotels, etc., was speedily followed in 1964 by an ACBL regulation ensuring the right of any ACBL member to play in any National tournament no matter where held.

The last barrier to ACBL membership of blacks was removed in 1967 when the ACBL included in its bylaws the proviso that "no person shall be denied membership because of race, color, or creed".

An outstanding achievement of the ABA administration under VICTOR R. DALY, Washington, D.C. (President, 1949–64), was the conduct of negotiations leading to the building of mutual rapport and respect between the ACBL and the ABA. Hundreds of ABA members joined the ACBL, and several became Life Masters. The first black Life Master of the ACBL was MARION WILDY (1956), and the first ABA Life Master to achieve Life Master ranking in the ACBL was LEO BENSON (1962).

The close association of the ACBL and the ABA continued under the ABA presidency of MAURICE ROBINSON, New York City (President, 1964–69). At the suggestion of the ABA, representatives of the ABA and the Greater New York BA, a unit of the ACBL, met in two exhibition matches in New York in 1969 resulting in one win for each organization.

The leading masterpoint holder of the ABA in 1982 was Robert Price of Chicago. WILLIAM SIDES was the leading player on the West Coast. The leading ABA woman player was Joyce Williams of Chicago, who was also its second-ranking masterpoint holder.

Officers, 1982:

President: Dr. Arthur Reid

Executive Secretary: Ken Cox, 555 Kappock Street, Bronx NY 10463

AMERICAN BRIDGE LEAGUE. An organization founded in 1927 at Hanover NH (see HISTORY OF BRIDGE). The original title was "American Auction Bridge League," but the word "Auction" was dropped in 1929. The League amalgamated with UNITED STATES BRIDGE ASSOCIATION in 1937 to form the AMERICAN CONTRACT BRIDGE LEAGUE. ABL presidents are listed under PRESIDENTS, and ABL results are listed with ACBL results under Fall NAC and Summer NAC in Appendix I.

AMERICAN BRIDGE OLYMPICS. American winners of the WORLD PAR CONTESTS are listed under that title.

The Culbertson organization staged a national Olympic in 1932, distinct from the World event. The winners were: North-South, Dr. and Mrs. Monte F. Meyer; East-West, James M. Magner, Jr., and William C. Campbell.

AMERICAN BRIDGE TEACHERS' ASSOCIATION. A nonprofit professional organization composed primarily of bridge teachers, but also includes tournament directors and bridge writers, dedicated to promoting higher standards of bridge teaching and playing.

The ABTA was founded in 1957 by a charter membership of 150. At the initial meeting, held in New York City, the 14 members attending, including Deborah N. Glover, the organizing secretary, and GEORGE S. COFFIN, the organizing treasurer, proposed that the goal of the organization be "to provide and protect the standards of bridge teaching and its practitioners, to establish a code of ethics and minimal fees insofar as is practical, and to make known in the public and professional interest any information in the bridge profession."

The Association is divided into ten regions, each headed by a vice president, who, with the assistance of state chairmen, arrange frequent meetings where teachers learn new techniques and have an opportunity to examine the latest teaching equipment. In addition, there is an annual meeting, usually held in conjunction with the Summer North American Championships of the ACBL, where several days are spent listening to outstanding bridge teachers and players. Most of the leading bridge personalities have addressed this convention at least once and many have appeared on several occasions.

Applicants for membership in the ABTA are required to pass an entrance exam. Once accepted, members are rated according to experience, training, and attendance at teachers' seminars, with the highest rating being "Master Bridge Teacher."

The Association publishes a quarterly bulletin, which includes news of the organization's activities, articles on teaching techniques, and an exchange of ideas for promoting business. See BIBLIOGRAPHY, P.

Presidents of the ABTA have been:

1958–59	*Jo Woods
1960–61	Margaret M. Wales
1962	*Deborah N. Glover
1963	*George S. Gooden

1964	Dorothy Jane Cook
1965	Kenneth B. Turner
1966	Nellie Harrington
1967	Helen D. Albano
1968–69	Thelma Smith
1970–71	Helen Cale
1972–73	Effie Lindsay Long White
1974–75	*Edward L. Gordy
1976–77	Eloene Griggs
1978–79	Antha Mallander
1980–81	Dr. T. B. Lyons
1982–83	Frank Thomas, Jr.

*deceased

Secretary, 1982–83: Delanie Webb, P.O. Box 159 Macclesfield, NC 27852

AMERICAN CONTRACT BRIDGE LEAGUE. The NATIONAL AUTHORITY and governing body for organized bridge activities and promotion on the North American continent; it is by far the largest bridge organization in the world. The ACBL, as it is usually referred to in this book, traces its history from the organization of the American Auction Bridge League in Hanover NH at the 1927 congress (tournament) of the AMERICAN WHIST LEAGUE, by a group sparked by RALPH R. RICHARDS, Detroit, including E. J. TOBIN and ROBERT W. HALPIN, Chicago, HENRY P. PAEGER and CLAYTON W. ALDRICH, Cleveland. Tobin was named Executive Secretary. CONTRACT BRIDGE was introduced into the second congress held in Cleveland in 1928, during which year the infant organization acquired the services of WILLIAM E. MC KENNEY, whose originality, drive and organizational ability did much to establish the League. The increased popularity of contract bridge at the expense of the older game, auction bridge, led to the name change to AMERICAN BRIDGE LEAGUE in 1929. A merger of this group with the UNITED STATES BRIDGE ASSOCIATION was effected in 1937, with McKenney, first named Executive Secretary in 1929, remaining at the helm of the organization until 1947, shortly before his death in 1950.

In 1948–49 a major reorganization of the League was carried out by WALDEMAR VON ZEDTWITZ, as president and chairman, aided by the Steering Committee of ROBERT J. GILL, RALPH GRESHAM, LEE HAZEN, BERTRAM LEBHAR, JR., RAYMOND J. McGROVER, and ALBERT H. MOREHEAD and the Bylaws Committee headed by LAWRENCE WEISS of Boston.

McKenney was succeeded by RUSSELL J. BALDWIN, who was appointed Business Manager and remained so until his recall to active duty with the U.S. Army in 1951, at which time ALVIN LANDY was named acting Business Manager. In 1952, Landy was advanced to the position of Executive Secretary, remaining in that post until his death in 1967. TOM STODDARD, then Executive Administrator, served briefly as Executive Secretary pro tem until EASLEY BLACKWOOD was appointed to that post in 1968, retiring after three years, as he had planned, on March 1, 1971. RICHARD GOLDBERG, Assistant Executive Secretary under both Landy and Blackwood, was named as Blackwood's successor.

The membership of the League grew spectacularly from the 270 who joined the American Auction Bridge League to more than 15,000 at its 20th birthday in 1947; following merger in 1956 with the PACIFIC BRIDGE LEAGUE, which became the ACBL's Western Division, headed by Stoddard, growth ac-

celerated to 170,000 in 1970 and approached 190,000 in 1982.

During these years, the League moved to New York from the Midwest in 1934; then to its own building in Greenwich CT in 1967. This became sole national headquarters in 1968 when the Western office was closed. In 1972 the League erected its own building in Memphis TN, opened in late November at 2200 Democrat Road, with adequate space for its then needs and provision for anticipated expansion.

In addition to the growth in membership, there has been a tremendous increase in the scope and influence of the League's activities. Beyond the authorization and supervision of bridge tournament activities from the level of North American and Regional CHAMPIONSHIP TOURNAMENTS to the games run in some 5,000 affiliated duplicate bridge clubs, ACBL activities include: formulation and publication of the LAWS, both of CONTRACT (Rubber) BRIDGE and of DUPLICATE CONTRACT BRIDGE; conduct of charity games and other activities which raised approximately six million dollars through 1982 (See CHARITY PROGRAM); cooperation with other national bridge organizations, through membership in the WORLD BRIDGE FEDERATION for which it hosted two WORLD TEAM OLYMPIADS (1964, 1972), one WORLD PAIR OLYMPIAD (1978), and eight WORLD CHAMPIONSHIPS for the BERMUDA BOWL, following the inception of that event in 1950 in Bermuda.

Two major forces in the League's growth are the MASTERPOINT PLAN and the RANKING OF PLAYERS, both of which were important considerations in the League's consolidation with USBA and the Pacific Bridge League. In 1961, the huge task of issuing and recording members' master points was computerized. In 1975, when this service had grown to require mailing some 38,000 notification cards per semi-monthly cycle, it was streamlined to a once-a-month operation. In 1981 the ACBL installed an IBM System 3 Model 15D computer, which took the place of the computer service bureaus used by the League in previous years. As of 1982, the computer had taken over many tasks, including printing point confirmation cards, *Bulletin* mailing labels, new member welcome cards, membership cards, membership renewal notices, Unit report forms, special lists such as new Life Masters and Top 500 leaders, club sanction renewal forms, transaction journals, etc. The League plans eventually to add programs covering inventory control, sales, cash receipts and accounts payable, plus many others. The League's *Bulletin*, published monthly, is the most widely distributed and one of the most highly respected publications in its field. The League has also compiled and published records and selected hands of all world championships and team Olympiads since 1953. See BIBLIOGRAPHY, G.

In addition to units in the United States, the ACBL encompasses units in Bermuda, Canada and Mexico as well. The major championship tournaments conducted by the ACBL thrice annually are North American Championships, and are recognized by the World Bridge Federation as Zonal Championships. See WORLD BRIDGE FEDERATION PLAYER RANKINGS.

Members of the ACBL BOARD OF DIRECTORS and BOARD OF GOVERNORS are chosen by the membership. See DISTRICT, UNIT. The Board of Directors elects the PRESIDENTS, CHAIRMEN and HONORARY MEMBERS of the League. Copies of the BYLAWS and ACBL HAND-BOOK are available to members on request from ACBL HEADQUARTERS.

AMERICAN CONTRACT BRIDGE LEAGUE CHAMPIONSHIPS. Tournaments held three times a year in various North American cities, called North American Championships (NAC) rather than NATIONALS since 1976. Played over a 10-day period from Friday through a week from the following Sunday, they consist of six or seven major multi-session North American Championships, many two-session *regionally rated* events and single-session SIDE GAMES played two, three or four times daily. Certain of the more important championships have a bearing on ACBL representation in international events as high finishers in major pair games may earn qualifying points toward the next WORLD PAIR CHAMPIONSHIP and winning teams in the VANDERBILT, SPINGOLD, REISINGER and GRAND NATIONAL may qualify for Trials to select ACBL representatives in WORLD TEAM CHAMPIONSHIPS. Major NAC events at the three championship tournaments are (new events and the year each went on the calendar in italics):

SPRING NAC — Vanderbilt Knockout Teams, Women's Knockout Teams, Men's Board-a-Match Teams, Open Pairs, Men's Pairs, Women's Pairs. The 78-pair *Grand National Pairs (1979)* playoffs are held in conjunction with the Spring NAC with two qualifying rounds on the preceding Wednesday and two final rounds on the preceding Thursday.

SUMMER NAC — Spingold Master Knockout Teams, Life Master Pairs, Master Mixed Teams, *NA Men's Swiss, NA Women's Swiss, Non-Life Master Swiss. (1982)* The eight *Grand National Teams (1973)* quarterfinalists play off on the Thursday preceding the Summer NAC and on the first Friday and first Saturday in quarterfinal, semifinal and final knockout matches.

FALL NAC — Reisinger Board-a-Match Teams, Blue Ribbon Pairs, Life Master Men's Pairs, Life Master Women's Pairs, Mixed Pairs, *North American Swiss Teams (1977), Non-Life Master Pairs (1981). Rookie Grand National Pairs (1979).* The 26-pair Rookie GNP final is held in conjunction with the Fall NAC, played in two sessions on the first Saturday of the tournament.

AMERICAN LEADS. Leads devised at whist to give partner a count when a solid suit was being led. The lead of the jack followed by the queen, for example, showed a solid seven-card suit. The inventors were CAVENDISH of London, and Nicholas Browse Trist of New Orleans. Although they have been long obsolete, American leads were a milestone in the development of defensive signals.

AMERICAN WHIST LEAGUE. The AWL was founded in Milwaukee in 1891 as a central organiza-tion to control and promulgate the laws of WHIST. Its sponsorship of tournaments between representatives of member clubs did much to stimulate the com-petitive aspects of games of the bridge family. Within the first few years of the life of this League its members worked out official laws, rules, a code of ethics, boards, methods of scoring, and move-ments of boards and players for all sorts of games up to teams of sixteen.

The Tournaments of the American Whist League (called congresses) were contested for the Hamilton Trophy (Club Teams of Four), 1892-1934; the Min-neapolis Trophy (Club Pairs), 1895-1934; the Brooklyn Trophy (Auxiliary Association members), 1896-1911; Associate Members Trophy (Mixed Pairs), 1901-1934; Manhattan Trophy (Mixed or Women's Pairs), 1908-1934; the Congress Trophies (Men's Pairs), 1908-1934.

By the end of the Thirties, the League existed in name only, although whist congresses, attended by a few lifelong devotees, continued into the Fifties. The careers of many of the players prominent in whist continued into auction bridge and contract, in-cluding such names listed in this encyclopedia as ROBERT F. FOSTER, ROBERT W. HALPIN, NATHAN KELLY, SIDNEY S. LENZ, WINFIELD S. LIGGETT, JR., ANDREW J. MOUAT, CHARLES L. PATTON, RALPH R. RICHARDS, P. HAL SIMS, CHARLTON WALLACE, WILBUR C. WHITE-HEAD, MILTON C. WORK.

The AWL prolonged its life by adding an Auction Team event in 1924 and an Auction Pair event in 1930. A Contract Whist event in 1934 did not prove popular and was dropped, but the Contract Pair event began in 1930 and the Team event in 1932 con-tinued through 1937, with winners listed below:

	ALL-AMERICAN TEAMS OF FOUR
1932	David Burnstine, Willard S. Karn, Howard Schenken, P. Hal Sims
1933	Sam Fry, Jr., Charles S. Lochridge, Walter Malowan, Louis H. Watson
1934	A. Mitchell Barnes, H. Huber Boscowitz, Sam Fry, Jr., Louis H. Watson
1935	A. Mitchell Barnes, B. Jay Becker, Oswald Jacoby, Harold S. Vanderbilt
1936	Louis J. Haddad, Edward Hymes, Jr., Oswald Jacoby, Merwyn D. Maier
1937	M. N. Besser, M. S. Becker, Jr., Robert W. Halpin, H. Kempner

	ALL-AMERICAN OPEN PAIRS
1930	Dorothy Rice Sims, Waldemar K. von Zedtwitz
1931	Robert E. Smith, Frederick C. Thwaits
1932	Joseph E. Cain, Walter J. Pray
1933	Sam Fry, Jr., Louis H. Watson
1934	Sam Fry, Jr., Louis H. Watson
1935	B. Jay Becker, Waldemar K. von Zedtwitz
1936	Allyne Paris, Robert F. Rubel
1937	Arthur Glatt, Albert Weiss

AMERICAN WHIST MOVEMENT. A schedule for conducting duplicate contests between teams-of-four originated for tournaments at whist, later adapted to auction bridge and contract. See TEAM-OF-FOUR MOVEMENTS.

AMSTERDAM CLUB SYSTEM. Bidding system used mainly in The Netherlands. The main features of the system's opening bids:

1♣—17 or more HCP.
1◊—12-16 HCP with fewer than four hearts.
1♡—12-16 HCP, canape with clubs or diamonds possible.
1♠—12-16 HCP, canape with clubs possible.
1 NT—15-17 HCP.

2♣–12–16 HCP, solid suit, second suit possible.

2◊–Multi-colored.

2♡ or 2♠–Roman.

2 NT–Minors.

3♣ or 3◊–in first or second position shows a strong, solid six-card suit with outside stoppers.

3 NT–Solid suit, no outside entries.

4♣ or 4◊–Transfers respectively to 4♡ and 4♠.

In this system, many relays are used to get the opening bidder to clarify his holding.

ANALYSIS. The appraisal of a bidding or playing situation. It is generally used in reference to the play of the cards. A good analyst will recognize the possibilities inherent in a particular deal and act accordingly, so as to give his side the best mathematical or psychological chance in either dummy play or defense.

ANALYSIS SHEETS. Printed matter giving analyses of hands played in a specific contest, such as an ACBL-WIDE game. Since the hands are computer-dealt, and since they are the same at all sites, it is possible to arrange for an expert to be given a set of the deals months in advance. The expert then makes a thorough study of each deal before writing a short synopsis of what is likely to happen and what should happen. This material is typeset and printed in advance and sent to the persons in charge at each site where the hands will be played. The package of analysis sheets is opened immediately after the game and each player receives a copy, enabling him to check his results against what the expert considers to be par.

ANCHOR SUIT. See ASTRO.

ANGLO–AMERICAN MATCHES. Teams representing Great Britain (or England) and the United States (or North America) have met on many occasions. The official meetings in World Championship competition are given under WORLD CHAMPIONSHIP with these headings: WORLD TEAM OLYMPIAD, BERMUDA BOWL, VENICE TROPHY TEAMS, ROSENBLUM CUP TEAMS.

The following semi-official or unofficial matches have been played:

London, 1930. America (Ely and Josephine Culbertson, Theodore A. Lightner, and Waldemar K. von Zedtwitz) beat England (Lt. Col. Walter Buller, Alice G. Evers, Cedric Kehoe, and Nelson Wood-Hill) by 4,845 total points over 200 boards.

London, 1933. For the SCHWAB CUP. America (Ely and Josephine Culbertson, Theodore A. Lightner, and Michael T. Gottlieb) beat England (Lt. Col. Henry M. Beasley, Gerald G. Domville, P.V. Tabbush, George Morris, Graham F. Mathieson, and Lady Doris Rhodes) by 11,110 total points over 300 boards.

London, 1934. For the SCHWAB CUP. America (Ely and Josephine Culbertson, Theodore A. Lightner, and Albert H. Morehead) beat England (Richard Lederer, William Rose, Henry St. John Ingram, and Stanley Hughes; with Col. George G. J. Walshe

[capt.] and A. Frost as alternates) by 3,600 total points over 300 boards.

London, 1949. For the CROWNINSHIELD CUP. England beat America by 330 total points, the net result of two matches. England (Maurice Harrison-Gray [capt.], Kenneth W. Konstam, Terence Reese, and Boris Schapiro) beat America (Johnny R. Crawford, George Rapee, Samuel M. Stayman, and Peter A. Leventritt) by 2,950 total points. The same American team beat England (Ewart Kempson [capt.], Rixi Markus, Kenneth W. Konstam, Leslie Dodds, Edward Rayne, Jordanis T. Pavlides, and Graham F. Mathieson) by 2,620 total points. Both matches were of 96 boards.

London, 1954. England (Terence Reese, Boris Schapiro, Kenneth W. Konstam, Adam Meredith, and Edward Mayer) beat America (Clifford W. Bishop, Melton A. Ellenby, Douglas Steen, Lewis L. Mathe, and Don Oakie; William Rosen was absent) by 81 IMPs over 100 boards.

Miami, 1955. America (Waldemar K. von Zedtwitz, Harold Harkavy, William S. Root, Albert Weiss, Edward Burns, William Seamon, Harold Vanderbilt, Charles Goren, and Charles Whitebrook) beat Great Britain (Terence Reese, Kenneth W. Konstam, Leslie Dodds, Adam Meredith, and Jordanis T. Pavlides) by 150 total points over 100 boards.

London, 1956. England (Terence Reese, Boris Schapiro, Kenneth W. Konstam, Leslie Dodds, and Edward Mayer) beat America (Samuel M. Stayman, Charles Goren, Charles J. Solomon, Myron Field, Lee Hazen, and Richard Kahn) by 79 IMPs over 100 boards.

Philadelphia, 1976. Bicentennial challenge match. The U.S. (Colonists) (Edgar Kaplan, Norman Kay, Bobby Goldman, Mark Blumenthal, Robert Jordan, Arthur Robinson with Simon [Skippy] Becker as npc) defeated Great Britain (Redcoats) (Claude Rodrigue, Tony Priday, Barnet Shenkin and Michael Rosenberg) 90 IMPs to 65 over 40 boards.

See also JOSHUA CRANE.

ANTICIPATION. See PREPAREDNESS, PRINCIPLE OF.

ANTI-FRAGMENT BIDS. See SPLINTER BIDS.

APPEAL. An appeal may deal only with an illegal or improper act by a contestant or an action or decision of the director. The appeal must be joined by both members of a partnership or a majority of a team to receive consideration.

Should a player be dissatisfied with a ruling by a director as to a matter of fact that occurred at a table, the player, his partner agreeing, may ask for an appeal (sometimes termed a "protest") of the ruling. The director may act on the appeal himself, on his own initiative, or by consultation with others, overruling his own decision or that of one of his assistants. If he does not do so, and the appeal is pursued, he turns it over to the tournament committee for adjudication if it is a matter of fact. The director himself rules on any question of a decision on a point of law.

In hearing an appeal, the tournament committee

should give primary consideration to the director's statements of facts occurring in his presence.

An appeal from a ruling of law by the director or of fact by a tournament committee may be appealed further to the National Authority. If practical, the National Authority will hear the case on the spot; if impractical, the director is required to forward the appeal with a written statement of the facts as found by the committee or the director, and an expression of his views on the legal aspects of the case, as well as such written statements as the appellants may desire to make. See COMMITTEE; DIRECTOR; LAWS OF DUPLICATE (Laws 88, 89); PROTEST.

APPENDIX TABLE. A method of expanding sections to accommodate extra tables without increasing the number of boards in play; particularly useful for adding late pairs or tables to HOWELL MOVEMENTS. The result of adding appendix tables to the seven-table Howell game has led to the THREE-QUARTER MOVEMENT for eight, nine, and up to 12 tables.

The use of appendix tables in MITCHELL MOVEMENT games is possible, although infrequently employed, except as adapted into certain GUIDE CARD movements for two-session events. One use that is popular is that of a NOVICE TABLE appendix to a regular game where inexperienced players may be accommodated without delaying the regular game. The application of the appendix table principle by former National Tournament Director PAUL MARKS has made the RAINBOW INDIVIDUAL MOVEMENT adaptable for numbers of tables one or even two greater than a prime number (such as 7, 11, 13, 17, etc.)

The technique of handling an appendix table is simple. In a Howell movement, a table (or tables) may be appended to any table where there are two moving pairs. The North–South pair at the base table is instructed to remain stationary as is the East–West pair at the appended table. Boards are constantly relayed from the base table to the appended table, and as moving pairs arrive at the base table to sit North–South, they are instructed to play at the appended table, then to resume their regular progression. In a Mitchell game, a table (or tables) may be appended to any section that consists of a prime number of tables. Boards are placed on the base table (or tables) and are relayed with the appended table (or tables). Throughout the game the boards move regularly to the next lower table within the prime section. The East–West pair at the base table remains stationary, as does the North–South pair at the appended table. All other pairs move each round, East–West moving to the next higher table and North–South skipping one table to the next higher table.

APPROACH-FORCING SYSTEM. A term applicable to most standard methods of bidding, including GOREN or STANDARD AMERICAN. The CULBERTSON SYSTEM was the earliest of these, and was the basis on which many other systems were built. The original objective of ELY CULBERTSON was to emphasize the need for slow suit exploration, in preference to a precipitate excursion into notrump. See APPROACH PRINCIPLE.

APPROACH PRINCIPLE. The precept of ELY CULBERTSON favoring opening suit-bids and a slow exchange of information in preference to notrump opening bids and responses. He described it this way:

In view of the fact that in making an opening bid, the player is venturing into unknown territory, it is wise for him to proceed cautiously, to feel his way, and thus, protected by a network of approach suit-bids of one, act with care until he learns something about the distribution of honor strength held by both his partner and his adversaries.

The Approach Principle, as applied to contract, may be stated as follows: *Whenever a hand contains a biddable suit, even a shaded four-card minor, that suit and not notrump should usually first be bid.* The *notrump complex*, which suggests that the opening bid on a hand should be notrump even when the hand contains a biddable suit, is a disease especially prevalent among advanced players. The logical place for notrump bidding is after information has been exchanged as to suit lengths and distribution. Notrump bids in the early stages crowd the bidding too much and eliminate many valuable suit-bids, while the bid of a suit always leaves the alternative of notrump without increasing the contract. The use of the Approach Principle does not decrease, but, as a matter of fact, increases the number of safe notrump contracts undertaken.

Culbertson's dislike of indiscriminate notrump bids stemmed from experience. Too many of his contemporaries carried over from auction the phobia created by the scoring table (where if the opponents held three honors in a suit they might outscore the declarer who made only two-odd or three-odd). Thus they tended to bid 1 NT with almost any hand lacking a suit headed by three honors. Hampered by lack of a Stayman convention to discover a 4-4 fit after the notrump opening, far too often the wrong contract was reached.

In support of the approach idea, Culbertson quoted the following hands:

WEST (dealer)	EAST
♠ A Q x x	♠ J x x x
♡ A x	♡ x
◇ A J x	◇ K x x x
♣ A 10 x x	♣ K x x x

Culbertson's suggested bidding was:

WEST	EAST
1 ♣	2 ♣
3 NT	4 ♣
Pass	

A few years later, most good players — including Culbertsonites — would open with 1 ♣, and arrive at the same final contract. But in citing this example, he was shooting at the flaw of opening a notrump with more than the desirable strength, as well as the danger of missing the spade fit.

In the beginning, Culbertson recommended notrump openings on a range of three honor tricks not vulnerable to four-plus honor tricks vulnerable. His zeal for approach principles caused him to limit the bid to 4-3-3-3 distribution with an occasional exception for 4-4-3-2, including a strong doubleton — not less than Q-x.

Thus, analysis of the 1937 prototype World Championship reveals that the Culbertson team did not use a single opening bid of 1 NT. As methods of responding to 1 NT were improved so as to discover suit fits after the notrump opening, Culbertson gradually relaxed his strictures against opening notrumps on hands of the *wrong* distribution in order to use the bid on more hands of the *right* high-card strength. Thus, by 1949, 4-4-3-2 and 5-3-3-2 distributions (but not five-card majors) were officially included in the notrump family — no longer as exceptions. But while the distributional range was spread, the high-card range was narrowed, standardized at three and one-half to four-plus honor tricks which were later interpreted — by Culbertson as well as by others — as 16-18 high-card points, with even 6-3-2-2 distributions admitted to the notrump family on hands of proper high-card strength and strong doubletons.

In spite of these changes, over a span of more than 30 years the Culbertson Approach Principle remained, with but little alteration, a basic principle of bidding. A few more hands containing biddable suits were opened with 1 NT; the standards for biddable suits in the responder's hand were shaded down. But it remained standard practice to avoid indiscriminate notrump openings, and especially to avoid responses of 1 NT to partner's suit bid if a response could be given at the one-level in another suit. The notrump response may result in a suit fit being missed, and may lead to the weak hand becoming the declarer at notrump. Many experts play that a response of 1 NT to 1 ◊, for example, absolutely denies holding a four-card major suit. Others, however, would not choose to respond in a worthless four-card suit. See BIDDABLE SUITS.

ARABIA. See BRIDGE FEDERATION OF ASIA AND THE MIDDLE EAST.

ARGENTINE BRIDGE ASSOCIATION. (Asociación del Bridge Argentino). This Association was founded in 1934, the first on the South American continent. It is a member of the South American Bridge Confederation, with a membership that grew from 750 in 1969 to 2,300 in 1982. It is sponsor of the team that has won the South American Championships 14 times. Until Venezuela triumphed in 1965, Argentina was the only country to represent South America in the Bermuda Bowl, doing so on nine occasions, beginning in 1958. National competitions include Open Teams, Open Pairs, and Masters Individual; also the GABARRET CUP, given for the most master points in a year.

Officers, 1982:
President: Dr. Luis J. Perez Colman
Secretary: Gonzalo Araujo, Lavalle 1145 4° Piso "B"
   1048 Buenos Aires, Argentina

ARNO. See LITTLE ROMAN.

ARRANGEMENT OF CARDS. The act of sorting the cards in one's own hand or (by the declarer) in the dummy's hand, which includes the conventional

placing of trumps to the declarer's left in the dummy's hand. Most players sort their cards into suits, red and black alternately, and place the cards in each suit according to rank. It is regarded as an offense against the proprieties of bridge for any player to draw inferences about another player's hand by noting the position of the cards. But some players split suits and avoid singletons at the end of the hand to protect themselves against players with better eyesight than ethics.

ARRANGEMENT OF TABLES. At a duplicate tournament, the arrangement of tables depends on the size and shape of the playing space and the expected number of tables which must be accommodated (see TABLE SPACING). A hairpin type of arrangement is more desirable than a straight line arrangment for sections in order to bring the last table into proximity with the first in each section.

ARRANGEMENT OF TRICKS. In duplicate bridge, the act of turning a card face down on the edge of the table immediately in front of a player after four cards have been played to a trick, with the long axis of the card pointing to the players who won the trick; in rubber bridge, the act of collecting the cards played to a trick by a member of the side that won the trick and then turning them face down on the table so that the tricks are identifiable in proper sequence. See LAWS (Law 66); LAWS OF DUPLICATE (Law 65).

ARRANGING.
(1) A term having reference to the aligning of the cards of the dummy as that hand is being spread on the table just after the opening lead has been made. The declarer may arrange the cards to his own satisfaction when he states that he is doing so.
(2) A statement by a player before he has bid in the first round of bidding meaning that he has been lax in picking up his hand or looking at it, and is not in a position to act when it becomes his turn. A call of some sort should follow this remark with reasonable dispatch.
(3) The act of sorting one's own cards. See ARRANGEMENT OF CARDS.

ARROW. The symbol on the duplicate board which indicates the alignment required so that the North player receives the hand designated for him. Table cards have the compass points printed on the edges; the boards have the arrow symbol pointing to the North hand; the arrow point and the printed direction coinciding, each player's hand is directly in front of him in the board. See: ARROW SWITCH; SCRAMBLED MITCHELL MOVEMENT.

ARROW SWITCH. The right-angle turning of the table guide card between rounds of a Mitchell duplicate movement, to produce a SCRAMBLED MITCHELL MOVEMENT. The field is thus combined to one field instead of two for scoring purposes.

A single arrow switch does not provide balanced comparisons by any means, as adjoining North-South pairs play all but four boards in direct competition in a 13-table game, and all but two boards in a larger game. To secure balanced comparisons, an arrow switch should be made two to four times during the play, and the number of rounds in each position should be varied. ALEX GRONER, in his *Duplicate Bridge Direction*, offers a table for the arrow switch. See SCRAMBLED MITCHELL.

ARTIFICIAL CALL. An arbitrary call which can be correctly interpreted by partner only if agreement has been reached about its meaning in advance.

Certain artificial bids are now so standard that their apparent normal meaning would be considered as an *artificial* convention. For example: a takeout double; a 2 NT negative response to an opening two-bid, etc.

At the extreme of artificiality are *cipher* bids which bear no relation to the suit named or to any other suit. The most common examples are the STAYMAN responses of 2♣ and 3♣ over 1 NT and 2 NT respectively, and the responses to Blackwood. Other examples are the conventional 2♣ opening bid with a powerful hand, and the FLINT 3◊ convention.

Cipher bids are developed to the maximum by the RELAY SYSTEM, in which one player can make a series of artificial bids to discover the details of his partner's hand.

The multiplication of artificial bids of all kinds in the postwar years led to some objections. The AMERICAN CONTRACT BRIDGE LEAGUE, the FRENCH BRIDGE FEDERATION, and the ENGLISH BRIDGE UNION, among others, restrict the use of artificial systems and conventions, such as the Italian systems and others of similar complexity, in normal tournament play. It is considered that the users of such systems gain an unfair advantage against opponents unfamiliar with the methods employed. This is particularly true in pair tournaments and other events in which a small number of boards are played in each round.

Defensive bids take on a different meaning against artificial systems, and the meanings of doubles, notrump bids, and bids in the opponent's suit have to be carefully considered. A further point is that a defender can afford to pass over an artificial forcing bid holding a strong hand, knowing that he will get a further opportunity to bid.

At the international level the use of artificial systems often causes debate, but legislation against them is hardly possible: it would appear to discriminate against the successful European users of such methods.

In the early Thirties there was some doubt about the legality of certain artificial bids. In 1933 the Portland Club in London, one of the law-making bodies, ruled that the Culbertson 4–5 NT convention and others that could indicate the possession of specific cards were illegal. The decision was based on the idea that a bid that showed possession of a particular card amounted to the exposure of that card.

This ruling was quickly challenged in America, and the Whist Club gave an opposite verdict.

Many different articles are included in this book dealing with artificial bids. Those connected with SLAM BIDDING are listed under SLAM CONVENTIONS. Others include: ACE-SHOWING RESPONSES; ASPRO;

ASTRO; ASTRO CUEBIDS; BENJAMIN; BLUE TEAM 2◊; BROZEL; COMPETITIVE DOUBLE; DEFENSE TO STRONG ARTIFICIAL OPENINGS; DOUBLE FOR SACRIFICE; DRURY; DYNAMIC NOTRUMP; FLANNERY 2◊; FLINT; 4◊ CONVENTIONS; FOURTH SUIT, FORCING AND ARTIFICIAL; GLADIATOR; JACOBY TRANSFER BIDS; LANDY; LEBENSOLD; LIMIT JUMP RAISE TO SHOW SINGLETON; MEXICAN 2◊; MICHAELS CUEBID; OKUNEFF CONVENTION; ROMAN 2◊; RUBIN TRANSFERS; SOUTH AFRICAN TEXAS; SWISS CONVENTION; TEXAS CONVENTION; TRANSFER BIDS; TRANSFER OPENING THREE-BIDS; 2◊; TWO-SUITER conventions; TWO-WAY GAME TRIES; TWO-WAY STAYMAN; UNBID MINOR SUIT FORCE.

ARTIFICIAL CLUB BIDS. See 1♣ SYSTEMS.

ARTIFICIAL RESPONSES AND REBIDS AFTER NATURAL NOTRUMP. See NOTRUMP BIDDING.

ARTIFICIAL 2◊ AND 2♣ OPENINGS. The bids and responses as advocated by SAM STAYMAN are:

2◊ corresponds to the strong artificial 2♣ bid usually used with weak two-bids. 2◊ is the negative response. The bidding may die below game only after the sequences:

2◊ — 2♡	or	2◊ — 2♡
2 NT		2♣ — 2 NT
		3♣

When 2◊ is thus used, 2♣ shows a strong intermediate hand, usually based on one or both major suits. Responder almost always bids 2◊, after which opener bids:

Two, three or four of a major to show a single-suited hand with eight, nine or ten tricks respectively.

2 NT to show a 19–20-point hand.

3♣ and 3◊ (conventional) to show major two-suiters worth eight tricks and nine tricks respectively.

Four of a minor (conventional) shows a major two-suiter worth ten tricks, with a void in the minor bid.

Other responses to 2♣ are:

A minimum suit-bid to show a 3- or 4-point hand with a six-card major or a seven-card minor.

2 NT to show a weak minor two-suiter.

3 NT to show a strong minor two-suiter.

It follows that opening bids of 1♡ or 1♠ are limited, showing fewer than eight playing tricks and fewer than 19 points.

See also BENJAMIN, ROMEX.

ASBURY PARK. The scene of many of the most important national championships in the early years of contract bridge. The nine-day Summer championships of the ABL and later of the ACBL were held there from 1930 to 1941 inclusive, making it the focal point of the bridge tournament year. In the early Forties the Asbury Park Convention Hall became too small to accommodate a national championship. From 1958 through 1969 it was the scene of the annual regional tournament of the New York-New Jersey Conference.

See CITY OF ASBURY PARK TROPHY.

ASIA. See the following listed separately as Asian Bridge Federations: ALL INDONESIA BRIDGE ASSOCIATION; ASIA AND THE MIDDLE EAST, CHINA, FAR EAST, HONG KONG CONTRACT BRIDGE ASSOCIATION, INDIA, JAPAN, MALAYSIA, PAKISTAN, PHILIPPINES, SINGAPORE, TAIWAN, THAILAND.

ASIA AND THE MIDDLE EAST. See BRIDGE FEDERATION OF ASIA AND THE MIDDLE EAST.

ASKING BIDS. A method by which one player can discover specific information about DISTRIBUTION and CONTROLS held by his partner. These bids usually are used when exploring for a slam contract, but sometimes are used when checking the feasibility of a game contract. The original Asking Bids were devised by ALBERT MOREHEAD and developed by ELY CULBERTSON.

For many years Asking Bids fell into disuse — they were not a part of Standard American or any of the major systems used. However, in recent years various forms of Asking Bids have very much returned to favor. Many of the leading Italian players who consistently won world championships in the Fifties, Sixties and Seventies employed Asking Bids. All of the RELAY SYSTEMS now in vogue all over the world rely heavily on Asking Bids. Most of these relay systems have one member of a partnership asking a long series of questions by making relay bids and the other partner responding in a predetermined pattern. Using these sophisticated methods, it often is possible for the asking partner to announce his partner's exact distribution plus the location of all honor cards.

Several Asking Bids are commonly used by most partnerships. The 5 NT GRAND SLAM FORCE is an Asking Bid as ace-asking bids like BLACKWOOD and GERBER. The WEST COAST CUEBID is an Asking Bid, attempting to ferret out the possibility of a notrump game. A raise to five of a suit after an opponent has overcalled usually asks partner to bid the slam if he has first-round or second-round control of the opponents' suit. Even the STAYMAN 2♣ response to 1 NT is an Asking Bid.

However, the Asking Bids used by those employing relay methods go far beyond these simple applications.

ASOCIACIÓN DEL BRIDGE ARGENTINO. See ARGENTINE BRIDGE ASSOCIATION.

ASOCIACIÓN PARAGUAYA DE BRIDGE. See PARAGUAY BRIDGE ASSOCIATION.

ASOCIACIÓN PERUANA DE BRIDGE. See PERUVIAN BRIDGE ASSOCIATION.

ASOCIACIÓN URUGUAYA DE BRIDGE. See URUGUAY BRIDGE ASSOCIATION.

ASPRO. A method of defending against 1 NT openings based on ASTRO, devised by TERENCE REESE. (The name is borrowed from a popular British brand of aspirin.)

The term *astronaut* is used to designate the overcaller, and the term *relay* to describe the responses in the neutral suit. Astro is varied in three respects:

(1) *Major two-suiters* are bid differently. The 2♣ overcall is often used with a major two-suiter. With five spades and four or five hearts, the astronaut bids 2♣ and follows with 2♠ over the 2◇ relay.

With four spades and five hearts the treatment varies with the strength of the overcaller's hand. Normally he bids 2♣ followed by 2♡ giving responder the opportunity to show spades. With a stronger hand he bids 2◇ followed by 2 NT.

(2) *Pronounced two-suiters* (6–5 or 6–6 distribution). Specific bids are laid down for each two-suited hand:

2 NT	black suits
3♣	minor suits
3◇	red suits
3♡	major suits

With the odd two-suiters (spades–diamonds or hearts–clubs), bid two of the minor suit and follow with a jump in a six-card suit.

(3) *A redouble* by the astronaut or the responder is an SOS. For alternative methods of defending against 1 NT, see ASTRO, BROZEL, EXCLUSION BID, LANDY, and RIPSTRA.

ASSETS. A method of distributional valuation originated by ALAN TRUSCOTT and described by him in *Teach Yourself Basic Bidding*. It provides for automatic re-evaluation by opener and responder as the bidding develops.

For a long suit (5 or more cards)	count one asset
For a singleton	count one asset
For a void	count two assets

Each asset, or distributional point, is counted at the start, and may bring the high card points up to the 13-points required for an opening. This gives a sound result, for it distinguishes between 4-3-3-3 and 4-4-4-1, which the long-suit method does not, and between 5-4-2-2 and 5-4-3-1 which neither the long-suit method nor the short-suit method does.

Both opener and responder adjust their assets in the light of the auction:

If there appears to be no fit	assets disappear
If there is an 8-card fit	assets count normally
If there is a 9-card fit	assets double
If there is a 10-card fit	assets triple

Suppose that after a 1♠ opening showing a five-card suit responder holds:

    ♠ J x x x x
    ♡ x x x x x
    ◇ —
    ♣ x x x

Four assets triple, and the jack gives a total of 13 for a bid of 4♠.

ASSIGNMENT OF SEATS. At a duplicate tournament the seating assignments are made on the entry blank which is purchased by the contestants. In the second session of pair events, when there has been a qualifying session, this may be done by giving GUIDE CARDS to the players which show their seating assignment for all rounds. See SEED, SEEDING.

ASSIST. To raise a suit first bid by partner. See RAISE.

ASSOCIATION OF AMERICAN PLAYING CARD MANUFACTURERS TROPHY.

Awarded to the winners of the two-session Commercial and Industrial Team Championship held at the Summer NAC until 1965, donated by the Association of American Playing Card Manufacturers, an organization founded in 1939 to promote the playing of card games. Until it ceased to exist in 1964 it was managed by the J. Walter Thompson agency. Consultants on card games to the Association were: GEOFFREY MOTT-SMITH, 1939–60; ALBERT A. OSTROW, 1960–62; WILLIAM S. ROOT, 1962–64. In 1965 the trophy was replaced by the UNITED STATES PLAYING CARD TROPHY.

ASSOCIATION OF BRIDGE PROFESSIONALS (ABP).

An organization of professional bridge players formed in 1981 and recognized as an accredited professional organization by the ACBL in 1982.

ASSOCIATION OF PROFESSIONAL BRIDGE PLAYERS (APBP).

An organization of professional bridge players formed in 1981 and recognized as an accredited professional organization by the ACBL in 1981.

ASSUMPTIONS, IN PLAY.

When a contract depends on the positions of two or three key cards, it often helps to make a definite assumption about one of them. If you can afford to have it wrong, assume that it is wrong; if you must have it right, assume that it is right and build up your picture of the opposing hands on that basis.

The following is a difficult example of *second-degree* assumption:

```
              ♠ A K 10 6 3
              ♡ Q 5
              ◇ Q 4
              ♣ K Q 6 2
WEST
♡ K led
              ♠ Q J 9 4 2
              ♡ 7
              ◇ A J 6 3
              ♣ 8 7 4
```

West deals at game all and the bidding goes:

WEST	NORTH	EAST	SOUTH
1♡	Dbl	2♡	3♣
Pass	4♠	All Pass	

West leads the ♡K and continues with the ♡A. South ruffs and draws trumps in two rounds. What should he play next? The contract will fail only if South loses two tricks in clubs and one in diamonds. Suppose that he leads a club, which looks obvious. If East holds the ♣A, then surely West will hold the ◇K and South will be defeated. Playing a diamond first, on the other hand, South is completely safe. If West holds the ◇K, and puts it up, there will be two club discards on declarer's ◇A–J. But if East holds the ◇K, then assuredly West will hold the ♣A. It is a puzzling but instructive hand. This is the distribution against which South has to guard:

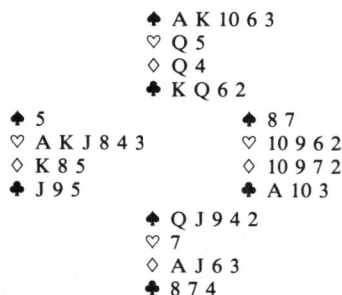

```
              ♠ A K 10 6 3
              ♡ Q 5
              ◇ Q 4
              ♣ K Q 6 2
♠ 5                      ♠ 8 7
♡ A K J 8 4 3            ♡ 10 9 6 2
◇ K 8 5                  ◇ 10 9 7 2
♣ J 9 5                  ♣ A 10 3
              ♠ Q J 9 4 2
              ♡ 7
              ◇ A J 6 3
              ♣ 8 7 4
```

Terence Reece. Quoted from *The Expert Game*.

ASSUMPTIONS, MATHEMATICAL.

See MATHEMATICAL ASSUMPTIONS.

ASTERISK BIDS.

Bidding conventions not in general use, though permitted.

The name derived from the format of the convention card adopted in 1960 by the American Contract Bridge League, on which these bids were marked by * with a footnote that the use of these bids must be called to opponents' attention. Later regulations require ALERTING to such bids.

ASTRO.

Over 1 NT, a specialized use of minor suit overcalls to show two-suited hands. The name of the convention is derived from the initial letters of the inventors' names: *A*llinger–*ST*ern–*RO*sler. After a strong or a weak notrump, in the direct or the reopening position:

2♣	shows *hearts* and a minor suit
2◇	shows *spades* and another suit

The Astro bidder promises at least nine cards in two suits; and his suits must have some solidity if he is vulnerable.

The Astro bidder's partner has a choice of these actions:

(1) Two of the anchor major (i.e., the particular major suit guaranteed by the overcaller): shows at least three cards in the suit and no game ambitions.

(2) Three of the anchor major: a game invitation with at least four-card support. The strength depends mainly on the vulnerability situation, and to a lesser extent on the strength of the notrump opening.

(3) Four of the anchor major: natural.

(4) Pass: a weak hand, and a long suit (probably of six cards) in the minor bid by partner.

(5) Two of the neutral suit (i.e., the next suit above the Astro bid): a negative action, denying the ability to make any other response. Indicates at least a doubleton in the neutral suit and usually fewer than three cards in the anchor suit.

(6) 2 NT: artificial and forcing. Shows some support for the anchor major, and suggests game prospects without guaranteeing a further bid.

(7) New suit takeout or jump (including a jump in the neutral suit and a *raise* of the takeout bid): shows a six-card or longer suit.

The Astro bidder has a choice of rebids after a neutral response. He may pass with five cards in the neutral suit, or show five cards in the anchor suit by *rebidding* it. He may show his second suit at the level of three, indicating a probable six-card suit and more than minimum playing strength.

In most sequences, 2 NT by either player is artificial and forcing. As responder's second bid, it is likely to be weak:

WEST	EAST
♠ A 5 2	♠ Q 4 3
♡ A J 10 5 4	♡ 6
◊ 6	◊ Q 8 5 3 2
♣ K 10 8 5	♣ Q 9 6 4

WEST	NORTH	EAST	SOUTH
			1 NT
2♣	Pass	2◊	Pass
2♡	Pass	2 NT	Pass
3♣	All Pass		

Astro Variations. Some partnerships use a variation of Astro similar to the BROZEL convention, called Pinpoint Astro, which is more explicit as to the two suits held.

2♣	Shows hearts and club
2◊	shows hearts and diamonds
2♡	shows hearts and spades
2♠	shows spades and a minor suit

A modification adopted by many ROTH-STONE players uses both two-level and three-level overcalls in order to show precisely which suits are held:

2♣	shows clubs and spades
2◊	shows diamonds and spades
3♣	shows clubs and hearts
3◊	shows diamonds and hearts
Double shows hearts and spades

Yet another variation, devised by MATTHEW GRANOVETTER, uses a double to show spades and another suit. 2♣ shows clubs and hearts; 2◊ shows diamonds and hearts.

Defense. The opening bidder's partner has several choices if his side appears to have the balance of strength. He can double with a defensive hand, usually with a good holding in the anchor major and the suit he doubles; cuebid the anchor major when his hand is unsuited to defense; or pass to await developments (remembering that there *might* not be any). A non-jump new-suit bid (including a *raise* in the Astro bidder's minor) would be unconstructive. 2 NT would be natural. For an alternative defense to Astro, see LEBENSOLD CONVENTION.

For alternative defensive conventions against notrump openings, see ASPRO, BROZEL, EXCLUSION BID, LANDY and RIPSTRA.

ASTRO CUEBID. Devised by the authors of the ASTRO convention, these are used to show certain two-suited hands.

An immediate cuebid in the suit bid by the opener shows a long minor together with a shorter major suit. The bid shows clubs and hearts unless one of these suits has been bid, in which case the next-higher suit is assumed.

(a)	(b)
♠ 5 3	♠ 5
♡ A K J 6	♡ K 10 6 5 2
◊ 7	◊ Q 10 9 7 4 3
♣ A Q 10 8 5 2	♣ 6

With hand (a), the cuebid would be used over 1◊ or 1♠. This is an inconvenient hand to bid with standard methods. Note that the problem is less acute if the minor suits are reversed. Over 1♠, for example, a double would then be appropriate, followed by a diamond bid over a club response.

With hand (b), 2♣ can be bid over 1♣ at favorable vulnerability. As clubs have been bid, the cuebid must show the red suits.

ATTACK. To take the initiative in bidding or play at some risk. Used particularly with reference to the opening lead.

ATTACKING LEADS. A risky lead away from a high-card combination such as A–Q, K–J or an unsupported high honor. This is common against a notrump contract, but less common against a suit contract when a PASSIVE LEAD is often called for. See OPENING LEADS.

The term *attacking lead* used to be applied to a lead from an honor sequence, but this meaning is obsolete.

Several situations deserve special mention:

(1) An attacking lead is desirable when the leader holds four or more trumps or can deduce that his partner holds four or more trumps.

(2) An attacking lead is desirable when the opponents have reached a suit game tentatively after bidding three suits. For example:

WEST	EAST
1♣	1♠
2♣	3♠
3♡	3♠
4♠	Pass

The opening leader can expect his partner to have any missing high diamond honor because both North and South have avoided notrump. It is probably desirable to take diamond tricks before declarer can get discards, and also to force the declarer, whose trump fit is likely to be 4–3.

(3) An attacking lead has to be considered against a contract at a high level, either in a suit or notrump, if the bidding suggests that declarer will have a long suit in his hand or the dummy.

(4) An attacking lead should not be made against a grand slam.

ATTITUDE. The interest or lack of interest of a defender in having a suit led or continued by his partner. The usual method of encouraging the lead or continuation of a suit is a HIGH LOW SIGNAL. See also ODD-EVEN DISCARDS and UPSIDE-DOWN SIGNALS.

AUCTION. The bidding by the four players for the contract. The dealer is the first bidder after the cards are dealt. He may pass or bid. The bidding proceeds clockwise around the table. Each player may pass, make a bid or raise a preceding bid, or double or redouble. The bidding ends when three players have passed in succession (or four players on the first round of bidding).

In the Midwest *auction* is sometimes used as a synonym for *final contract*: "4♠ was a fine auction."

AUCTION BRIDGE. The third step in the evolution of the general game of bridge. Its predecessors were WHIST and BRIDGE WHIST. The great innovation in auction bridge was the introduction of competitive bidding. It was first played in 1903 or 1904, but the precise circumstances are disputed. The first code of laws governing the play of auction was set forth in 1908, the product of a joint committee of the Bath Club and the Portland Club. The popularity of auction bridge increased enormously, and the activity in whist and bridge whist decreased proportionately. After the introduction of CONTRACT BRIDGE in 1926, auction bridge lost favor rapidly.

In auction bridge the aim was to keep the contract as low as possible because the declarer's side was credited with the number of tricks won, whether contracted for or not. For example, the declarer may have bid 2♠ and actually won six tricks over his book. He was credited with making a small slam. Penalties and premiums in auction are the same without regard to vulnerability. Honor scoring in auction bridge is different from contract bridge — so important, in fact, that it may distort the bidding, especially in duplicate auction.

Auction bridge scoring is as follows:

Scoring — Provided declarer has won at least the number of odd tricks named in his contract, declarer's side scores for each odd trick won:

	Undoubled	Doubled	Redoubled
With notrump	10	20	40
With spades trump	9	18	36
With hearts trump	8	16	32
With diamonds trump	7	14	28
With clubs trump	6	12	24

Game and Rubber. When a side scores, in one or more hands, 30 points or more for odd tricks, it has won a game and both sides start fresh on the next game. When a side has won two games it wins the rubber and adds to its score 250 points.

Doubles and Redoubles. If a doubled contract is fulfilled, declarer's side scores 50 points bonus plus 50 points for each odd trick in excess of his contract. If a redoubled contract is fulfilled, declarer's side scores 100 points bonus plus 100 points for each odd trick in excess of his contract. These bonuses are additional to the score for odd tricks, but do not count toward game.

Undertricks. For every trick by which declarer falls short of his contract, his opponents score 50 points; if the contract is doubled, 100 points; if it is redoubled, 200 points.

Honors. The side which holds the majority of the trump honors (A, K, Q, J, 10), or of the aces at notrump, scores:

For 3 honors (or aces)	30
For 4 aces in one hand at notrump	100
For 5 honors in one hand	100
For 4 trump honors in one hand	80
For 4 trump honors in one hand, 5th in partner's hand	90
For 4 aces in one hand at notrump	100
For 5 honors in one hand	100

Slams. A side which wins 12 of the 13 tricks, regardless of the contract, scores 50 points for a small slam. A side which wins all 13 tricks, regardless of the contract, scores 100 points for grand slam.

Points for overtricks, undertricks, honors and slams do not count toward game. Only odd tricks count toward games, and only when declarer fulfills his contract.

Contract Bridge for Auction Players. ELY CULBERTSON, gives the complete details of auction bidding contrasted, in parallel columns, with contract bidding. See also *Auction Bridge Complete* by MILTON C. WORK.

National championships at auction:

American Bridge League

MEN'S TEAM OF FOUR

1927	Ely Culbertson, Theodore A. Lightner, Ralph R. Richards, Waldemar K. von Zedtwitz
1928	Edward Baker, Sam L. Guggenheim, Morris Kastriner, Philip E. Leon
1929	Cmdr. Winfield Liggett, Jr., George Reith, P. Hal Sims, Sir Derrick J. Wernher
1930	Vincent F. Boland, John H. Law, Maurice Maschke, Carl T. Robertson
1931 1932	David Burnstine, Oswald Jacoby, P. Hal Sims, Waldemar K. von Zedtwitz

MEN'S PAIRS

1927	Carl Apthorp, Henry P. Jaeger
1928	Sam L. Guggenheim, Philip E. Leon
1929	Ely Culbertson, P. Hal Sims
1930	Frank S. Eaton, Ralph R. Richards
1931	P. Hal Sims, Waldemar K. von Zedtwitz
1932	P. Hal Sims, Waldemar K. von Zedtwitz
1933	Maurice Maschke, George Parratt

WOMEN'S TEAM OF FOUR

1927	Josephine Culbertson, Mrs. Owen Gilman, Mrs. A. O. Lynch, Louise G. Russ
1928	Margaret Beech, Mrs. Charles W. Nokes, Mrs. H. E. Parsons, Mrs. H. D. Stahl
1929	Millie K. Alexander, Emma Dafter, Rose Fleischer, Mrs. Sidney Lovell
1930	Mrs. Charles W. Nokes, Josephine Robertson, Mrs. E. P. Sawhill, Fannie Schryver
1931	Marguerite Hoffmeier, Josephine Robertson, Anne Rosenfeld, Matie White
1932	Mrs. Jay S. Jones, Jr., Elinor Murdoch, Olive Peterson, Marguerite Stengel

WOMEN'S PAIRS

1927	Hortense Evans, Mrs. Sidney Lovell
1928	Margaret Beech, Mrs. H. D. Stahl
1929	Mary Clement, Dorothy Rice Sims
1930	Josephine Robertson, Anne Rosenfeld
1931	Mrs. Jay S. Jones, Olive Peterson
1932	Elinor Murdoch, Marguerite Stengel

American Whist League

ALL-AMERICAN TEAM-OF-FOUR TROPHY

1924	Sidney S. Lenz, Cmdr. Winfield Liggett, Jr., P. Hal Sims, Edwin A. Wetzlar
1925	Ralph A. Amerman, H. E. Bidwell, Charles F. Snow, H. C. Wallace
1926	Ely Culbertson, Josephine Culbertson, Theodore A. Lightner, Ralph R. Richards
1927	Carl Apthorp, Henry P. Jaeger, Maurice Maschke, Carl T. Robertson
1928	Grace Buschmann, Mrs. A. R. Coffin, Josephine Robertson, E. J. Tobin
1929	C. L. Downs, Oswald Jacoby, Theodore A. Lightner, Dorothy Rice Sims
1930	Sam L. Guggenheim, Morris Kastriner, Philip E. Leon, Edward C. Wolfe
1931	David Burnstine, Oswald Jacoby, Willard S. Karn, P. Hal Sims
1932	David Burnstine, Willard S. Karn, P. Hal Sims, Waldemar K. von Zedtwitz
1933	H. Huber Boscowitz, David Burnstine, Oswald Jacoby, Edwin A. Wetzlar
1934	Anne Rosenfeld, Helene Scranton, George Unger, Sir Derrick J. Wernher

AUGUST CONVENTION. See TWO-WAY STAYMAN.

AUSTRALIAN ASKING BIDS. A slight modification of the original CULBERTSON ASKING BIDS. Holding a singleton in the asked suit and two aces, a jump is made in the suit of the lower-ranking ace. In some cases the asking bid can be made below the four-level: 2♠ in response to 1♡, for example, is used as an asking bid.

AUSTRALIAN BRIDGE. An independent bimonthly magazine, published from GPO 3805, Sydney, NSW 2001, established in 1970 with DENIS HOWARD as editor. He was succeeded in 1972 by RON KLINGER, a contributing editor, *Bridge Encyclopedia*.

AUSTRALIAN BRIDGE FEDERATION. This federation was founded in 1934 as the Australian Bridge Council, with New South Wales, Victoria, and South Australia as original members. Later the Australian Capital Territory, Queensland, Tasmania, and Western Australia joined the Federation, and associate members are the Northern Territory and the Territory of Papua and New Guinea. From 2,000 members in 1970 the Federation had grown to more than 12,000 members in 1982. Australia participates in the Far East Championships, winning the Open Teams in 1968 and 1970, the Women's Teams in 1973, 1974, 1975, 1977, and the Far East Pairs in 1971 and 1972. The WBF Zone 7 Championship has been held since 1970 (except for 1972), Australia winning in 1970, 1971, and 1974. Australia competes in the World Olympiads and participated in the Bermuda Bowl 1971 (placing third), 1976, 1977, 1979, 1981. It annually sponsors an Interstate Congress, consisting of Teams, Pairs, and Individual Championships, an annual Open Teams event, and Youth (under-30) Championships, and also sponsored a Par Point event for Pairs from 1956 to 1963. It awards the McCutcheon Trophy for most master points won in a year.

Officers, 1982:
President: Denis Howard
Treasurer: Mr. E.E. (Ted) Crichton, 50 Sir Thomas Mitchell Drive, Davidson 2085, New South Wales, Australia

AUSTRALIAN TRUMP–ASKING BID. A trump-asking bid initiated by either partner's use of the cheapest bid in notrump immediately after a major suit has been agreed. The inquiry, which could be made as low as the two level, focuses on the king and queen of trumps. Lacking both king and queen, the partner of the asking bidder signs off in the trump suit. The other responses are in steps, not counting the trump suit as a step:

1st step	queen
2nd step	king
3rd step	king and extra length
4th step	king and queen
5th step	king and queen and extra length

For alternative methods see TRUMP ASKING BID.

AUSTRIAN BRIDGE FEDERATION (ÖSTERREICHISCHER BRIDGE VERBAND). This federation was founded in 1928–29 by DR. PAUL STERN, inventor of the VIENNA (AUSTRIAN) SYSTEM, who became its first president. By 1982 it had 1200 members. The Federation is a member of the European Bridge League and participates in European Championships, organizing the events in Vienna in 1934 and 1957. Austrian teams recorded a double victory in the 1937 World Championships, winning both the Open and Women's Team events. Austria won the World Open Pair Olympiad in 1970. In the European championships, Austria won the Open Team in 1932, 1933, and 1936, and the Women's Team in 1935 and 1936. Among the many events which the Federation sponsors each year are tournaments at Loiben and Salzburg and the International Bridge Week at Velden in the spring.

Officers, 1982:
President: Dr. Otto Streichsbier
Vice President: Karl Rohan, Wasserfeldstr. 15 5020, Salzburg, Austria

AUSTRIAN SYSTEM. See VIENNA SYSTEM.

AUTOBRIDGE. A commercial device by means of which lesson hands can be used for self-teaching bidding and play. A deal sheet is inserted in a special board so that only the player's own cards are shown. As the deal progresses, the player finds that his own bids and plays are automatically corrected, and that the bids and plays of the other players are automatically revealed. The board and deal sheets are accompanied by a booklet, in which the hands are set out and the bidding and play explained by experts.

Experts who have composed Autobridge hands include ELY and JOSEPHINE CULBERTSON, ALBERT MOREHEAD, RICHARD FREY, CHARLES GOREN, ALFRED SHEINWOLD, and ALAN TRUSCOTT.

AUTOMATIC ACES. A way of showing the number of aces held in certain situations.

After an opening bid of 1 NT or 2 NT receives a forcing response in a new suit at the level of three, if the opener has a fit with responder's suit and slam ambitions, he shows the number of aces he holds by a step method.

NORTH	SOUTH
2 NT	3♠
4◇	

This shows good spade support and three aces (4♣ would show two aces; 4♡, four aces). If the opening bid was a weak notrump, the first step response would show one ace. If the opening bidder has no slam ambitions he raises responder's suit or bids 3 NT.

AUTOMATIC HAND REGISTERS. In original duplicate whist before 1883 each hand was written on a *register* (hand-record slip), then tricks were scooped in as usual. So the players had to reconstruct their hands from registers for replay at the next table. The four loose hands were carefully piled atop each other crosswise into a small box, a device too unstable to move without mixing up or scrambling the cards. So after every round *all* players had to move to new tables.

In 1883 James Alison invented the automatic hand register simply by having players keep all their played cards face down in front of themselves as today we still do. Each perpendicular card marked a trick won, a *live* soldier; else it was placed horizontally. But players still put their played hands in the little box *in stassis* on the table.

In order to correct this second problem special card trays were introduced, each equipped with rubber bands to hold each hand more securely for passing the boards to the next table. Soon a company in Kalamazoo MI manufactured the world's first duplicate board with card pockets sold as Paine's Whist Trays. These were cumbersome, but at least they aided the growing popularity of duplicate whist, especially in the great whist tournaments held 1894 through 1936 by the AMERICAN WHIST LEAGUE.

AUTOMATIC SQUEEZE. A simple squeeze which will operate against either opponent.

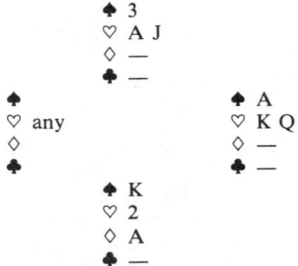

The lead of South's ◇ A squeezes East, and would also squeeze West if the defenders' hands were exchanged. Whatever West discards, the ♠ 3 is thrown from dummy.

This situation contrasts with a POSITIONAL SQUEEZE, when only the player who plays immediately after the squeeze card is under pressure, and the declarer's discard from the third hand varies with the defender's discard. See also SQUEEZE.

AUTOMATIC 2 ◇ RESPONSE. See 2 ◇ ARTIFICIAL RESPONSE TO FORCING 2♣ OPENER.

AUTOMATON CONTRACT BRIDGE PLAYER. An obsolete electric machine designed by William Patzer to play a specific bridge hand against anyone who would put a coin into the machine to start the proceedings. The machine would make winning plays against various stratagems used by the declarer — i.e., the paying customer. See also ROBOT BRIDGE PLAYER.

In the days of whist there were several very popular machines which it was claimed were able to play whist. The first, invented by an American named Balcom and adapted for exhibition by Maelzel, was exhibited *circa* 1829–31. An automaton called "Psycho" was exhibited by John Maskelyne at the Egyptian Hall, Piccadilly, London for several decades starting in 1875. The *New York Journal* exhibited an automaton whist player, named the "Yellow Kid," in New York in 1896.

AVERAGE EXPECTANCY. The term applied to the expected holding of the partner of the opening bidder; it may refer to one-third of the missing cards of a suit or one-third of the missing honor strength. The fraction will vary as the bidding progresses. It was much used in the CULBERTSON SYSTEM in his arguments for pre-emptive bids.

AVERAGE HAND. A hand that contains ten high-card points. An ace, king, queen, and a jack, or one-fourth of all the high honors, is the average expectation of each player before the hands are seen. This basic assumption furnishes the player with a simple yardstick for measuring the relative high-card strength of a given hand, and may assist materially in estimating the game potential or penalty expectancy of any bid. Hence, two or three points added to an average hand is the valuation of a hand with a minimum opening bid.

AVERAGE SCORE. One-half the matchpoints possible on a given hand or in a particular session of a matchpoint pairs tournament.

In IMP pair games *average* on a given board is the arithmetical mean of all scores on that board, usually excluding the highest and the lowest. This constructed *average* is called a *datum*. See INTERNATIONAL MATCHPOINTS.

The average score is usually the basis on which adjusted scores are awarded when a particular hand cannot be properly played. When the hand cannot be played through no fault of one pair, the adjustment is usually 20% of the average score added to the average score. Deduction from the average score is made by the tournament director when one of the pairs is at fault. These are referred to as Average-plus or Average-minus.

AVOIDANCE. A plan of play designed to prevent a particular opponent from gaining the lead.

There are two main reasons for pursuing such a plan. First, it may be necessary to prevent a defender with established winners from gaining the lead, especially at notrump. Second, declarer may have a suit combination which is vulnerable to a lead from a particular side. Both aspects of avoidance arise if either of these suit combinations is held:

	(a)	(b)
	DUMMY	DUMMY
	3 2	2
	DECLARER	DECLARER
	A J 4	K J 4 3

In each case South is playing 3 NT and West leads the 5 to East's queen. If South wins the trick, East becomes the dangerous hand, but if South holds up twice, West becomes the opponent to be feared. South's play at the first trick must therefore be determined by an examination of the whole hand to discover which opponent is more likely to secure the lead. If a vital king or queen is missing in a side suit, it is usually obvious which opponent may gain the lead. If the missing card is an ace, there will often be an inference available from the bidding. In the examples above, West would be likely to have a side ace if he has volunteered a bid, and unlikely to have one if he has passed throughout.

The suit combination which most commonly indicates the need for an avoidance play is a guarded king or the equivalent: a guarded queen when one top honor has been played, or, as in the examples above, a guarded jack when two top honors have been played; a guarded 10 would operate in the same way if three honors have been played.

But if declarer may have to lose the lead twice, the danger suit maybe one in which he has one sure guard and a partial guard:

(a)	(b)	(c)
DUMMY	DUMMY	DUMMY
J 4 3 2	A 3 2	K 3 2
DECLARER	DECLARER	DECLARER
A 10	Q 4	Q 4

In each case the right-hand opponent is the danger hand. In (a) and (b) there is a certainty of two stoppers if the suit is led from the left. In (c), suppose that the left-hand opponent holds the ace. Declarer then has two tricks if the suit is led from his left, but only one trick if it is led from the right.

The danger hand may suddenly change. Suppose that in (a) the danger hand secures the lead and plays a low card. The 10 loses to an honor, and the ace is knocked out. The left-hand opponent has suddenly become the danger hand: he may have one small card remaining, which he can lead to allow his partner to score two tricks.

Similarly, in (c), the right-hand opponent may gain the lead and play a low card. Declarer puts up the queen, which holds the trick. It is obvious that the left-hand opponent must not be permitted to gain the lead.

Avoidance play may require unusual handling of a suit which needs development.

(d)	(e)	(f)
DUMMY	DUMMY	DUMMY
K J 8	K 9 2	K 9
DECLARER	DECLARER	DECLARER
A 10 9 5 2	A J 4 3	A Q 4 3 2

The left-hand opponent is the danger hand. In (d) declarer runs the 10 or 9: it would be quite wrong to play the ace first, because the queen may have three guards. In (e) a deep finesse of the 9 is taken if South is trying for three tricks. The danger hand can secure the lead only if it has both the missing honors. In (f) the 9 is *finessed* with the virtual certainty that it will lose. (If the danger hand held both honors, he would play one.) This ensures four tricks against any normal break, and keeps the danger hand from the lead unless it has J–10–x–x.

Another type of avoidance play is possible in this situation:

```
              A K 3 2
Q 8 7                    J 10 9
              6 5 4
```

South needs three tricks in this suit, but must not permit East to gain the lead. Declarer leads twice from his hand, permitting West to win a trick with the queen if he plays it at any stage. If West is able to make a discard on the suit led from dummy back to declarer's hand, he can thwart South's plan by the spectacular discard of his queen.

Avoidance play can also be effected by LOSER-ON-LOSER technique or by DUCKING.

B

BA. Bridge Association.

BL. Bridge League.

BPRO. See BRIDGE PROFESSIONAL REGISTRATION ORGANIZATION.

BABY BLACKWOOD. The use of a 3 NT bid conventionally to discover the number of aces held by partner. The convention is usually applied after a forcing double raise in a major suit. For example:

SOUTH	NORTH
1♡	3♡ (forcing)
3 NT	

South's 3 NT bid is a request for aces. North bids 4♣ with no aces (or four aces), 4◇ with one ace, and so on. Similarly, an immediate jump to 3 NT in response to a 1♡ or 1♠ opening may be used as Baby Blackwood.

An alternative proposal is to have 2 NT to uncover the number of aces partner holds. Whenever either player bids 2 NT, partner bids 3♣ with no aces, 3◇ with one ace, etc. Subsequent bids of 3 NT, 4 NT and 5 NT can then be used to locate the number of kings, queens and jacks, respectively held by partner. See BLACKWOOD.

BACK IN. To make the first bid for one's side, after passing on a previous round, in the face of opposing bidding. See BALANCING.

BACK SCORE. The summary sheet on which the results of each rubber are credited to the winners and debited against the losers, in rubber bridge or Chicago. Results are entered in hundreds of points, with 50 points ignored in England but counted as 100 in the United States. The back score is referred to by more colorful names in England, as "flogger" or "washing list," while many American clubs refer to it as a "ledger."

BACKWARD FINESSE. An unnatural finessing maneuver which may sometimes be made for special reasons.

(a)
```
              ♠ A 3 2
♠ Q 5 4                    ♠ 10 8 7 6
              ♠ K J 9
```

(b)
```
              ♠ K 3 2
♠ A J 4                    ♠ 9 7 6 5
              ♠ Q 10 8
```

In (a), the normal play is to finesse the jack, which is an even chance. As the cards lie, it is easy to see that the winning play is to lead the jack. If this is covered, South finesses the 9 on the way back.

Similarly in (b), the normal play is to finesse the 10 after leading to the king, but the lead of the 10 is essential in the position given, with a finesse of the 8 to follow. (The position of the ace is irrelevant.)

There are three possible reasons for selecting the backward finesse. First, there may be a good reason to believe that the natural finesse will fail, based on an inference from an opening bid, for example, or a failure to open the bidding.

Second, the backward finesse may be an AVOIDANCE play. Suppose that in each of the above cases the declarer has an extra small card in his own hand and in the dummy, and needs three tricks without allowing West to gain the lead. His best play is the jack in (a) and the 10 in (b). It is doubtful whether this should be classified as a backward finesse, because South may well reject the finesse on the way back.

Third, the play may be selected when SHOOTING for a top in a pair event or playing for a SWING in a team-of-four match.

In defense the backward finesse can be a natural play dictated by cards visible in dummy. See SANDWICH DEFENSE.

BACKWASH SQUEEZE. A unique type of TRUMP SQUEEZE in which both menaces are in the same hand and the player sitting behind the hand with the menaces holds both guards plus a losing trump, and is caught in the *backwash* of a squeeze by means of a ruff taken in the hand holding the menaces. Analyzed and described by GÉZA OTTLIK in the February 1974 issue of *The Bridge World*, the backwash squeeze can have any of a number of other end game characteristics. Three such hands are used here by permission of *The Bridge World*.

Occasionally the backwash squeeze can be used as a DISCOVERY play. The following example requires a VIENNA COUP for the execution of the squeeze.

♠ A 10 8 5 4 2
♡ 10 7 3
♢ 9 2
♣ K J

♠ 6
♡ K Q J 8
♢ K Q 10 5
♣ A 10 9 3

South plays in ♡4 after having rested briefly in 3 NT until East doubled for a spade lead. West leads a heart and East plays low. South wins with the 8 and leads a club to the jack, which holds. So far, so good. Declarer leads a diamond to the king, which wins, a club to the king, and another diamond. East plays the ♢A and leads a trump. West plays the ace and another trump while East throws a spade. The lead is in the South hand, and declarer needs five of the last six tricks, in this position:

♠ A 10 8 5 4 2
♡ —
♢ —
♣ —

♠ 3
♡ 9
♢ J 6
♣ Q 7

♠ 6
♡ K
♢ Q 10
♣ A 10

If either minor-suit honor were unguarded the contract could be made by guessing which and dropping it, and drawing the last trump. But the bidding suggests that West has the hand shown. The solution is to lead a spade to the ace, and ruff a losing spade with the master trump, setting up an unnecessary trump trick for West (Vienna Coup), but squeezing him in the process. When the spade is ruffed, West is backwash-squeezed. South may, of course, misguess the position — he still has to read West's holding correctly. But he is no worse off than before; he will have seen another card played before making the decision and will have confirmed the exact spade count. No other play will work in the above ending.

The backwash squeeze can be used to strip a defender of his exit cards preparatory to a throw-in play.

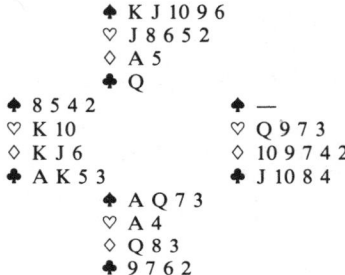

♠ K J 10 9 6
♡ J 8 6 5 2
♢ A 5
♣ Q

♠ 8 5 4 2   ♠ —
♡ K 10   ♡ Q 9 7 3
♢ K J 6   ♢ 10 9 7 4 2
♣ A K 5 3   ♣ J 10 8 4

♠ A Q 7 3
♡ A 4
♢ Q 8 3
♣ 9 7 6 2

South has arrived in 4♠ after a 13–15 notrump opening by West and an ASTRO ♢2 bid by North, showing spades and another suit. West led the ♣K and forced dummy with a second club. Planning to set up dummy, declarer led ace and another heart. West won and forced dummy again in clubs. Declarer ruffed a heart high, then led a low spade to dummy and discovered the unfortunate spade division. Suddenly a simple hand had become complicated. North was on lead, with declarer needing five of the last six tricks:

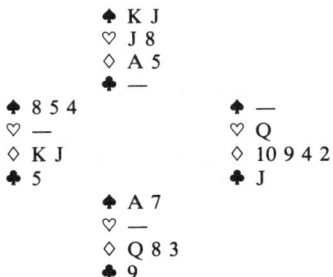

♠ K J
♡ J 8
♢ A 5
♣ —

♠ 8 5 4   ♠ —
♡ —   ♡ Q
♢ K J   ♢ 10 9 4 2
♣ 5   ♣ J

♠ A 7
♡ —
♢ Q 8 3
♣ 9

Declarer ruffed a heart with the ♠A — and the backwash caught West in its undertow. An underruff would let declarer draw trumps; and a diamond pitch would allow South to cash the ♢A and then lead the ♡J, throwing a club. Thus, West had to part with his club — is only exit card. South cashed the ♠K–J and led the last heart. West ruffed, but was endplayed.

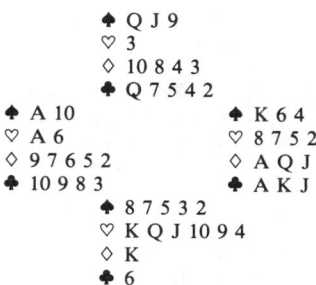

♠ Q J 9
♡ 3
◇ 10 8 4 3
♣ Q 7 5 4 2

♠ A 10	♠ K 6 4
♡ A 6	♡ 8 7 5 2
◇ 9 7 6 5 2	◇ A Q J
♣ 10 9 8 3	♣ A K J

♠ 8 7 5 3 2
♡ K Q J 10 9 4
◇ K
♣ 6

South has arrived in 2♡ doubled after a strong 1♣ opening by East showing 17 or more points, and a CARD SHOWING DOUBLE by West promising 6–8 points. Clubs were led and continued, with South ruffing the second round. South tried to slip the 9♡ through but West took his ace and shifted to the ace and another spade. When East won his trump king he cashed the ◇A and continued with the queen. Declarer had lost five tricks and apparently had one more to lose — if he drew the last trump he could not return to the closed hand to run the hearts. Because of the blockage in the North–South spades, East's ♠6 prevented ordinary suit-establishment. However, South ruffed the diamond queen and cashed three top hearts, East being forced to follow suit, leaving this position:

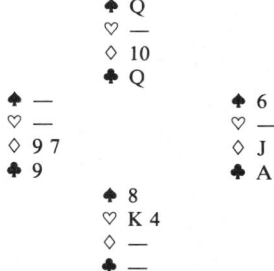

♠ Q
♡ —
◇ 10
♣ Q

♠ —	♠ 6
♡ —	♡ —
◇ 9 7	◇ J
♣ 9	♣ A

♠ 8
♡ K 4
◇ —
♣ —

South led a heart, ruffed it with dummy's ♠Q — and East was squeezed. If he underruffed, the South hand would be high. If he discarded a plain suit he would promote one of dummy's cards which would be led, forcing East to ruff and allowing South to overruff.

BAD CARD HOLDER. A player who seems consistently to hold less than his fair share of honor cards at rubber bridge. Although many losing players explain their losses by claiming to be bad card holders, lack of skill is a more likely explanation. Both mathematics and practical tests suggest that any given player and any given partnership will hold close to an average holding over a long period in terms of percentage.

BAD CARDS. (1) Consistently inferior cards in a session of rubber bridge.

(2) Cards that are expected, on the basis of the bidding, to be of little or no value to partner. If partner shows an unbalanced distribution with one very long suit or two long suits, minor honors in the other suits are unlikely to be of value to him. Similarly, tenace holdings or single honors other than the ace

deteriorate if the suit is bid by the left-hand opponent.

If partner has bid two suits, a holding of three small cards in the suit which is not going to be trumps represents a liability, and four small cards is almost as bad. See WORKING CARDS.

BAD HANDS. Hands containing little or no honor strength.

S. J. SIMON pointed out that underbidding with a bad hand is a common error of the average player. He gave this spectacular example of the need to bid with a weak hand:

♠ 4 3 2
♡ K 2
◇ 5 4 3 2
♣ 5 4 3 2

The bidding:

WEST	NORTH	EAST	SOUTH
	1 ◇	Pass	2 ♣
2 ◇	3 ♣	Pass	3 ◇
4 ♣	4 ◇	Pass	5 ♣
5 ◇	Pass	5 ♠	Pass
6 ♣	Pass	?	

East has been forced to express a choice between the major suits, and has shown no strength whatever. He has the vital ♡K, and West must be confident of making 12 tricks without that card. Therefore the ♡K must be the 13th trick, and East should bid the grand slam.

If partner shows great strength, a player should always ask himself whether his hand is better than it might be in the light of his earlier bidding.

BAD POINTS. See BAD CARDS (2).

BAHAMAS CONTRACT BRIDGE CLUB. Organized in 1965, it is a member of the CENTRAL AMERICAN AND CARIBBEAN BRIDGE FEDERATION. It joined the WBF in 1970 and participated in the 1972 World Team Olympiad.

Officers, 1982:
President: Fred C. Rubbra
Secretary: Eva Dugdale, P.O. Box 1036, Nassau, Bahamas

BAIRD TROPHY. Awarded for the Open Individual Championship, donated by JAMES C. BAIRD in memory of his wife in 1948; contested at the Fall NAC until 1957, then transferred to the Spring NAC under which heading the past results are listed.

BALANCE OF POWER. A concept first put forth by S. GARTON CHURCHILL involving the calculation of the safety of entering the auction based on actions taken by the opponents. See BALANCING.

BALANCE OF STRENGTH. The concept of calculating which side holds the majority of the high-card points. If a player adds his own point-count to the minimum shown by his partner, and the total is more than 20, he knows his side has the balance of strength. Sometimes he can infer that his side is likely to have the balance of strength by relying on the normal expectation of strength in his partner's hand.

BALANCED COMPARISONS. A principle embodied in most types of duplicate movement. If two pairs in competition play a given number of boards in the same direction (North–South or East–West), the movement is perfectly balanced if the same result is achieved by comparing either pair with a third pair.

Any full MITCHELL MOVEMENT is automatically balanced because the players do not change direction, and the stationary players, like the moving players, compare with each other throughout.

A SCRAMBLED MITCHELL cannot be completely balanced. Computers have been used to find the best set of arrow switches for each size game.

The original HOWELL MOVEMENTS were not balanced, nor were the later schedules prepared by COL. RUSSELL J. BALDWIN and WILLIAM C. McKENNEY. The first completely balanced Howell schedules were prepared by JACQUES ACH and CHARLES KENNEDY in 1935.

BALANCED DISTRIBUTION (or pattern). A hand that appears suitable for notrump rather than trump contracts. Standard types are 4-4-3-2, 4-3-3-3, and 5-3-3-2; 5-4-2-2 and 6-3-2-2 are borderline cases. See EXPECTED NUMBER OF CONTROLS IN BALANCED HANDS. The completely balanced 4-3-3-3 distribution can be described colloquially as flat, square or round, an example of the strangeness of bridge geometry.

Balanced distribution can also refer to an even division of one suit around the table, but this is a rare usage.

BALANCING (or protection, which is the normal term in England). Reopening with a bid or double when the opposing bidding has stopped at a low level.

After a suit opening.

WEST	NORTH	EAST	SOUTH
1 ◊	Pass	Pass	?

East's hand is known to be extremely weak, so South can balance with a hand of medium strength on the assumption that his partner has unrevealed strength.

The normal range for a simple suit bid by South in this situation would be 8–13 points in high cards. The spade suit is particularly significant: possession of spades favors balancing action, and lack of spades counts against it.

In more general terms, a shortage in an unbid suit, especially a major, militates against balancing, and a shortage in the opponent's suit favors it.

♠ 3
♡ A Q 6 4
◊ K J 5 3
♣ Q 6 4 2

South has sufficient strength to bid 1 ♡, but that would be dangerous. The opponents almost certainly have a spade fit, which they are likely to discover if given the opportunity. It is perhaps better policy to allow them to play 1 ◊, which may be a poor contract for them.

But if the opening bid had been 1 ♠, balancing action (in this case a double) would be automatic. It is now probable that East–West are in their best denomination, that North–South have a fit somewhere, and that North has some strength. North will frequently pass a strong hand with length and strength in the opponent's suit, but South can discount that possibility if he himself has the opponent's suit.

If South jumps in a new suit, he shows a hand too good for a simple balancing bid, probably a six-card or strong five-card suit and about 12–16 points.

A balancing double closely resembles a takeout double by the second player: there is virtually no upper limit, but with only moderate strength it should usually indicate a shortage in the opponent's suit and at least three-card support for each unbid suit. A balancing double may be slightly weaker (a minimum of about 10 points with ideal distribution) than an immediate takeout double. See also BALANCING 2♠ FOR TAKEOUT. A balancing double is unattractive with a void in the opponent's suit and 5-5-4-0 distribution because the second player will often pass for penalties. MARSHALL MILES suggests that the cuebid in the opponent's suit should be used freely in this position: it would not guarantee a game or even a second bid, and second hand bids as he would in response to a takeout double.

A balancing bid of 1 NT is a weakish action, but exactly how weak is a matter of opinion. Standard treatment suggests the equivalent of a weak notrump opening, with about 11–14 points. KAPLAN-SHEIN-WOLD indicates an 8–10 point range, because a stronger hand would double. Others advise a 12–16 point range, because hands of this strength may otherwise present problems: a double may not be convenient with three or four cards in the opponent's suit and a doubleton in an unbid suit.

After a suit opening and response.

The most important consideration is whether the opening side seems to have a fit. If the opening bid is raised to the two-level and the opener passes, balancing action is strongly indicated, especially if the opening bid was in a minor suit.

WEST	NORTH	EAST	SOUTH
1 ♣	Pass	2 ♣	Pass
Pass	?		

In this situation North should almost invariably balance. Holding:

♠ A J 5 3
♡ K J 4 2
◊ J 3
♣ 6 4 2

he doubles. If South bids 2 ◊, North corrects to 2 ♡, leaving South the option of continuing with 2 ♠.

When one side has a fit, their opponents are almost sure to have a fit also. If the opening bid was 1 ◊ raised to 2 ◊, balancing is usually called for. For this reason many players continue to three of the minor suit as a preemptive maneuver to forestall balancing action.

WEST	NORTH	EAST	SOUTH
1 ♣	Pass	2 ♣	Pass
3 ♣			

or

1◇	Pass	2◇	Pass
3◇			

See PREEMPTIVE RE-RAISE.

Balancing action is desirable in theory but more difficult in practice if a major suit has been opened and raised. The player who balances must be prepared for his side to land at the three-level, although a balancing bid of 2♣ over 2♡ can occasionally be risked with a four-card suit.

When a suit is raised directly, it is almost certain that the opening side has a combined eight-card or better fit. The same applies if the responder's suit is raised. Balancing action is strongly indicated after:

WEST	NORTH	EAST	SOUTH
1♣	Pass	1♡	Pass
2♡	Pass	Pass	?

There are other situations in which the opening side seems likely to have an eight-card fit:

(a)		(b)		(c)	
WEST	EAST	WEST	EAST	WEST	EAST
1♡	1 NT	1♡	1 NT	1◇	1♡
2♡	Pass	2◇	2♡	1 NT	2◇
			or Pass		

In each case North–South are likely to have a spade fit and should usually try to contest the auction, either with a spade bid or a balancing double.

In (a), (b), and (c) both North and South are in a position to take balancing action. Although North (South in case [c]) is not in the pass-out position, he knows that East–West will probably drop the auction at the level of two.

If the opening side bids three or four suits, or drops the bidding at 1 NT, balancing is less attractive. The hand will frequently be a misfit for both sides, and it will pay to defend rather than contest.

WEST	NORTH	EAST	SOUTH
1♡	Pass	1 NT	Pass
Pass	Dbl		

or

1♡	Pass	1♠	Pass
1 NT	Dbl		

In these sequences, North is implying that he passed originally on a strong hand because he holds strength and length in the opener's heart suit. He is hoping for a penalty, although South might choose to bid if his hand is very weak and he has a long suit.

After a 1 NT opening.

A 1 NT bid passed by the opener's partner produces a situation in which balancing is often not expedient. The probabilities are that the opening side has no good fit, and therefore that the defending side also has no good fit. The best policy, therefore, generally is to remain silent. To bid a five-card suit in the pass-out position may produce a double from opener's partner and a singleton trump in the dummy. However, some risks may have to be taken at board-a-match or pair scoring; conventional machinery such as ASTRO OR LANDY can prove helpful.

With an Unusual Notrump, see also UNUSUAL NOTRUMP.

BALANCING 2♣ FOR TAKEOUT. A convention

used in the ROTH-STONE SYSTEM in which a BALANCING bid of 2♣ is artificial and shows 6–9 points with support for the unbid suits. The balancing takeout double is reserved for hands worth 10 or more points.

BALDWIN MEMORIAL TROPHY. For the four-session Swiss Team event contested at the Summer North American Championships, presented by the widow of COLONEL RUSSELL J. BALDWIN in his memory. First awarded in 1970. Past winners are listed under Summer NAC, Appendix I.

BALTIC CONGRESS. An international bridge festival held annually in Gdánsk, Poland, since 1961. The main event is for Intercity Teams, restricted to selected city teams which compete for the Baltic Bowl, but there are also events for Open Teams, Open Pairs, Mixed Pairs and Individuals. The Baltic Bowl contest was first held in 1963, and in 1968 attracted teams from Norway, Sweden, Belgium, Italy, Czechoslovakia, Hungary and Russia.

BAMBERGER POINT-COUNT. See ROBERTSON POINT-COUNT and VIENNA SYSTEM.

BANGKOK CLUB. A system developed principally by SOMBOON NANDHABIWAT of Thailand and used by the Thai pairs in the 1966, 1967, and 1969 WORLD CHAMPIONSHIPS. The chief features are:

1♣ *opening* is a one-round force, denies possession of any five-card suit other than clubs, and shows 12–20 points. Responder bids 1◇ with 0–6 points or 7–8 points and no biddable suit, 1♡ or 1♠ with 7–10 points, 2♣ or 2◇ with 8–10 points, or 1 NT with 11 points or more, which is game-forcing. A jump response in a suit shows a six-card suit with 4–6 points, and a jump to 2 NT is made with 9–10 points with no four-card major and no five-card minor.

After a semi-positive response of 1♡ or 1♠, a new suit by opener on the two-level, other than clubs, is natural and forcing to game. Over a minor-suit response, a new suit asks for a control, with 2 NT as the positive response. After a 1 NT response, opener may show a suit naturally on the two-level, raise to 2 NT with a minimum balanced hand, or show various strengths of strong balanced hands by specialized rebids on the three-level.

If an opponent overcalls the 1♣ opening, responses are natural. If an opponent doubles, responses on the one-level are natural, equivalent to a positive response, jump responses are preemptive, and a redouble shows 11 points or more.

1◇, 1♡, or 1♠ *openings* guarantee a five-card suit with 11–17 points.

1 NT opening shows 18 points or more with a five-card suit, or 21 points and up with balanced distribution. 2♣ is the conventional negative response (0–6 points), over which opener may ask for a major by rebidding 2◇. With 7 points or more, responder may bid a five-card suit, or raise to 2 NT to deny a five-card suit, over which opener may ask for a major by rebidding 3♣.

Two-bids are natural, game-forcing, with 2 NT as the conventional negative response.

BANNING OF BRIDGE IN RUSSIA. See RUSSIA.

BAR, BARRED. (1) A bid out of rotation during the auction, or an insufficient bid if corrected in certain permissible ways, or exposure of certain cards has, as a penalty, the requirement that the partner of the offender must pass whenever it is his turn to call or at his next opportunity to do so.

(2) An ethical player, when his partner has hesitated and then passed at some point during the auction, is expected to bar himself from taking any action on his cards that is in any way questionable; that is, he will lean over backwards to avoid taking advantage of his partner's hesitation.

(3) A player may be technically *barred* from further bidding, especially if he has limited his hand previously. See, e.g., PREEMPTIVE RE-RAISE, SIGN-OFF BID.

(4) A player may be prohibited by the methods he is using from making a certain bid. For example, pairs using psychic responses to WEAK TWO-BIDS may agree that opener is barred from rebidding past three of his own suit. The opponents are entitled to know if this is the case, so such a sequence calls for an Alert.

BARBADOS BRIDGE LEAGUE. This league was founded in 1966. It competes annually with Trinidad and Tobago in Open and Women's teams, and in CENTRAL AMERICAN AND CARIBBEAN BRIDGE FEDERATION events. Its national events include two Interclub series, a Knockout Interclub event, and a four-session Open Pairs.

Officers, 1982:
President: E.L. (Jimmy) Cozier
Secretary: Eric G. Amory, P.O. Box 190, St. Michael's Row, Bridgetown, Barbados

BARCLAY BRIDGE SUPPLIES. The largest bridge supply firm in the world, selling books, teaching manuals and textbooks, duplicate supplies, trophies and gift items. The firm publishes teaching manuals and textbooks as well as other books on bridge, incuding *Duplicate Bridge Direction*, the official tournament director's manual by ALEX GRONER, and is the United States distributors for AUTO-BRIDGE. Presently owned by the Silvermans, Harry (president), Shirley (vice-president) and Murray (treasurer), the firm was founded by Charles Michaels in the late Forties and directed for many years by his daughter Ruth.

BARCLAY MOVEMENT. A movement designed by SHEPARD BARCLAY in the late Twenties so that competition between any two teams is completed in the same round of play. The necessity of relaying boards led to its early discontinuation as the size of the fields increased. LAWRENCE ROSLER, in 1963, designed a movement incorporating the good features of this movement for larger fields. See TEAM-OF-FOUR MOVEMENT.

BARCLAY TROPHY. Awarded for the North American Championship Master Mixed Teams, this trophy was donated by SHEPARD BARCLAY in 1929.

From 1946 through 1955 it was contested as a separate event held on the West Coast. In 1948 it was replaced by the LEBHAR TROPHY. Past results are listed under Summer North American Championships.

BARCO SQUEEZE. A triple-double squeeze, exerting pressure on both opponents in three suits.

The most famous example was played by Edward T. Barco, and described by him in *The Bridge World* (Dec. 1935).

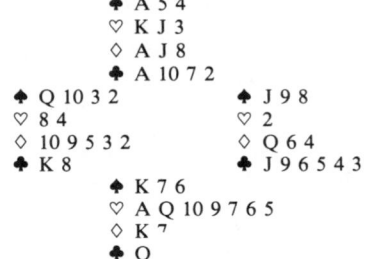

West led a trump against South's contract of 7♡, and declarer ran five trump tricks to reach this ending:

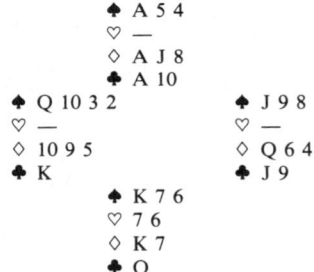

South led a further heart, on which West and North discarded a spade. East was squeezed, and had to discard a spade also. The last trump squeezed West in three suits. However, if he had discarded a diamond, declarer would have had to make the double-dummy play of entering dummy and leading the ♢ J. See HEXAGON SQUEEZE.

BAROMETER. A method originated in Sweden in which all groups of boards are played simultaneously. Running scores are posted on the Barometer shortly after the conclusion of each round, thus heightening the interest for both players and spectators. Toward the end of an event, the known positions of the pairs in contention often will influence the tactics they choose in attempting to win.

Barometer scoring was first used in world championship play in the WORLD OPEN PAIRS in 1970. In the United States it was first used on the national level at the 1974 Spring NAC tournament in the final session of a secondary event.

BARON BRIDGE SUPPLIES. One of the two major bridge supply companies in the United States, it was formed in 1975 by RANDY BARON and his wife Mary of Shelbyville KY. The firm's business is comprised of one-third mail order in the U.S., one-third in tournament sales and one-third in wholesale foreign trade.

BARON COROLLARY. An adjunct to TWO-WAY STAYMAN, of increasing popularity in Canada, that is designed to discover 4-4 minor suit fits. After responder has bid 2 ◇ (forcing to game), and opener has bid 2 NT, denying a four-card major or a five-card minor, a 3 ♣ rebid by responder asks opener's precise distribution. Opener rebids 3 ◇ with 3-3-4-3, 3 NT with 3-3-3-4, or three of his longer major if he has two four-card minors. See also ALLEN OVER NOTRUMP.

BARON NOTRUMP OVERCALL. An equivalent to a weak takeout double. It is usually made with a singleton or void in the opponent's suit, and the most likely distribution is 4-4-4-1. The maximum strength is 13 points, and the minimum depends on vulnerability, It has achieved little popularity because 1 NT is valuable as a natural overcall. For an alternative method of making a weak takeout double, see MICHAELS CUEBID.

BARON SLAM TRY. An invitation to a slam contract if partner holds good trumps.

A bid of the suit next below the agreed suit at the five or six level specifically asks partner whether he holds good trumps. So if spades are agreed, 5 ♡ invites 6 ♠, and 6 ♡ invites 7 ♠.

What constitutes good trumps depends on the previous auction. Partner must ask himself how much worse his trump holding might be in the light of his previous calls.

BARON SYSTEM. An English system developed in the Forties by LEO BARON, ADAM MEREDITH and others. Its exponents have had considerable success in British tournament play, and many of the system ideas have taken root in the general theory of the game. Examples are: (1) the weak notrump opening bid combined with a 1 NT constructive rebid; (2) bidding UP THE LINE with four-card suits; (3) relaxed requirements for BIDDABLE SUITS; (4) the five-card suit requirement for a response of 2 ♡ to an opening of 1 ♠; (5) the lead of ACE FROM ACE-KING.

Other distinctive features of the system are: (6) A bid of the third suit by the opener is forcing (e.g., 1 ♣-1 ♡-1 ♠; or 1 ♠-2 ♣-2 ◇). Some experts using standard methods follow this theory when the response is at the level of two. (7) An immediate raise requires at least four-card trump support. (8) Suit opening bids are highly prepared, with a four-card spade suit being opened ahead of a five-card heart suit regardless of quality. (9) Simple overcalls are strong and jump overcalls weak.

See also: ACE VALUES; BARON NOTRUMP OVERCALL; BARON SLAM TRY; 2 NT OPENING; 2 NT RESPONSE.

BARON 2 NT RESPONSE. See 2 NT RESPONSE.

BARRAGE. The French term for PREEMPTIVE BID. Sometimes used by English writers to describe a series of obstructive bids.

BARRICADE. An obsolete term for PREEMPTIVE BID or BARRAGE, coined by P. HAL SIMS.

BARTON 1 ♣. An English system popular in the Thirties. The 1 ♣ opening bid promised 3½ quick tricks or more.

BATH COUP. A simple hold-up of the ace when the jack is also held:

(a)

	4 3 2	
K Q 10 9 6		7 5
	A J 8	

(b)

	A 3 2	
K Q 10 9 6		7 5
	J 8 4	

In each case the king is led and is allowed to win. If declarer holds two small cards, as in (b), he should generally play the higher one. This play may cause West to think that East has begun a high-low, and induce him to continue the suit to South's advantage.

The play dates from the days of WHIST, and is presumably named after the English watering place of Bath.

BATTLE, SARAH. A character invented by Charles Lamb to embody his idea of what a perfect whist player should be. In his *Essays of Elia* he wrote: "She loved a thorough-paced partner, a determined enemy. She took and gave no concessions. She never made a revoke nor even passed it over in her adversary without exacting the utmost forfeiture. She fought a good fight — cut and thrust. She sat bolt upright, and neither showed you her cards, nor desired to see yours . . . I never in my life — and I knew Sarah Battle many of the best years of it — saw her take out her snuffbox when it was her turn to play, or snuff a candle in the midst of a game or ring for a servant until it was fairly over. She never introduced or connived at miscellaneous conversation during its progress. As she emphatically observed, 'cards were cards,' and if I ever saw mingled distaste in her fine last-century countenance, it was at the airs of a young gentleman of a literary turn, who had been with difficulty persuaded to take a hand, and who, in his excess of candor, declared that he thought there was no harm in unbending the mind now and then, after serious studies, in recreations of that kind! She could not bear to have her noble occupation, to which she wound up her faculties, considered in that light. It was her business, her duty, the thing she came into the world to do — and she did it. She unbent her mind afterwards over a book.''

BECHGAARD SIGNALS. A method of discarding to show the length of a suit, devised by Kai Bechgaard, South Africa.

With five cards, a *delayed* signal is used: three, four, and then two, for example.

With six cards, a *continued* signal is used: four, three, and then two.

With seven cards, a *double* signal is used: three, two, five and then four.

For alternative methods of treating this type of situation, see LENGTH SIGNALS.

BELATED SUPPORT. Support for the opener's original suit on the second round after opener has rebid 2 NT (as distinguished from PREFERENCE and JUMP PREFERENCE).

WEST	EAST
1♡	1♠
2 NT	3♡

A forcing sequence, which would show exactly three-card support if LIMIT RAISES are being used. If the opener then bids 3♠ he also shows three-card support.

BELGIAN ROYAL BRIDGE FEDERATION (FÉDÉRATION ROYALE BELGE DU BRIDGE, BELGISCHE BRIDGE FEDERATIE). This federation was founded in 1932 by a group of thirteen clubs headed by the Cercle Privé du Royal Automobile Club of Brussels. The Federation annually sends teams to the European Championships, organizing the 1935 event in Brussels and the 1965 and 1973 tournaments in Ostend. Among the events it sponsors are the Belgian Team Championship, played by teams of clubs, and an Open Pair event. The Federation had more than 5,000 members in 1982.

Officers, 1982:
President: Paul Carlier
Secretary: Robert de Coster, Avenue Louis Lepoutre, 57, 1060 Bruxelles, Belgium

BELONG. An expression to indicate which side can legitimately expect to buy the contract. A player who says he knew that "the hand belonged to the opponents" indicates that he judged the opposition could make the highest positive score on the deal. In such circumstances, it may pay to take an ADVANCE SAVE or other preemptive action. Alternatively, a player who judges that he will be outgunned in high cards may prefer to remain silent on the theory that he will end up as a defender and does not wish to give information that may help the declarer.

An alternative meaning of the word in modern bridge jargon, especially in a POST-MORTEM, is to indicate the most desirable contract for a side: "We belong in 5◇".

BELOW THE LINE. Points at RUBBER BRIDGE entered below the horizontal line on the score sheet. These points are solely those made by bidding and making partscores or games. All other points are scored above the line only. Points scored below the line count toward winning a game or rubber. At DUPLICATE BRIDGE or CHICAGO, the term may be used loosely to refer to trick score. See SCORING.

BENJAMIN. Convention permitting an Acol player to use weak WEAK TWO-BIDS in the major suits; invented by ALBERT L. BENJAMIN (Scotland). Opening bids of 2♣ and 2♡ are weak. An opening bid of 2◇ is equivalent to an Acol bid of 2♣ and almost

guarantees game. The negative response is 2♡ and the sequence 2◇–2♡–2 NT, showing 23–24 points, can be passed.

An opening bid of 2♠ shows a normal Acol one round forcing two-bid in an unspecified suit and promises at least eight playing tricks. The negative response is 2◇ and any positive response is forcing to game. With this method it is possible to use an Acol two-bid when clubs is the primary suit. See ACOL SYSTEM.

BENNETT MURDER. This historic tragedy took place in Kansas City MO on Sept. 29, 1929. The victim was 36–year–old John G. Bennett, a prosperous perfume salesman, who met his death as a result of a game of contract in which he played with his wife, Myrtle, against another married couple, Charles and Mayme Hofman. Mrs. Bennett became so infuriated at her husband's play that she shot him following a bitter quarrel. She was tried for murder in March of 1931 and was acquitted.

The alleged hand was as follows:

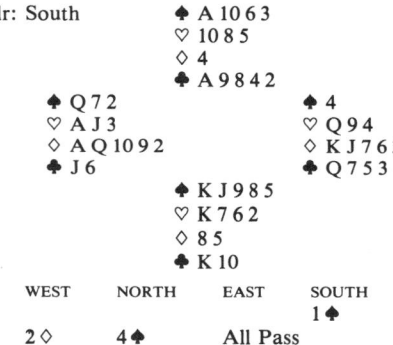

Dlr: South	♠ A 10 6 3
	♡ 10 8 5
	◇ 4
	♣ A 9 8 4 2

♠ Q 7 2　　　　　　　　♠ 4
♡ A J 3　　　　　　　　♡ Q 9 4
◇ A Q 10 9 2　　　　　◇ K J 7 6 3
♣ J 6　　　　　　　　　♣ Q 7 5 3

　　　　　♠ K J 9 8 5
　　　　　♡ K 7 6 2
　　　　　◇ 8 5
　　　　　♣ K 10

WEST	NORTH	EAST	SOUTH
			1♠
2◇	4♠	All Pass	

Bennett opened the bidding without sufficient values for an opening bid and suffered an unusually heavy penalty. However, 4♠ was not an impossible contract, given the actual distribution. West opened the ◇A and shifted to the ♣J. Bennett actually won this with the king and set about drawing trumps, ending his chances. Instead he should have ruffed a diamond, led a trump to his king and continued with his last club. When West followed, he should have gone up with the ace and led the ♣9, intending to discard a heart if it was not covered. If East covered with the queen, Bennett should ruff and let West overruff. If at this point West should lead either red suit, Bennett would have had his 10 tricks. Only a trump lead at this point could keep South from making his contract — and saving his life.

The episode was entertainingly described at length by Alexander Woollcott in *While Rome Burns*.

BERMUDA. ACBL Unit 198, it hosted the first of the present BERMUDA BOWL series held in 1950, and gave its name to the world championship trophy.
President: Charles Vaucrosson, P.O. Box 774, Hamilton 5, Bermuda.

BERMUDA BOWL. The annual World Team Championship; the trophy at stake therein.

The first postwar world contract bridge team championship was played in Bermuda in 1950 on the initiative of NORMAN M. BACH. The contest was a three-cornered match among teams representing the United States, Great Britain (the European champion), and Europe (a combined Sweden–Iceland team).

The next six Bermuda Bowl contests were two-team events between the United States and the winners of the European Championships.

In 1958, the contest became a three-cornered event with the inclusion of the South American champions.

In 1960, 1964, 1968 and 1972, which were Team Olympiad years, there was no Bermuda Bowl competition. In 1974 the WORLD BRIDGE FEDERATION voted to conduct the Bermuda Bowl in odd-number years only. To provide a transition, the Bermuda Bowl and the World Team Olympiad were played consecutively, in Monte Carlo in 1976.

Starting in 1961, the defending champion was invited to compete. This practice was discontinued after the 1977 Bermuda Bowl, when two teams from the United States met in the final. One was the team that qualified through the Trials method, the other was the defending champion. The executive council of the WBF decided it was not good for two teams from the same zone to compete in the final.

From 1950 to 1963 inclusive, the Bermuda Bowl was organized under the auspices of the ACBL and the EUROPEAN BRIDGE LEAGUE, with the collaboration of the South American Bridge Confederation starting in 1958. Since 1963, the Bermuda Bowl has been conducted by the WBF. In 1965 the WBF voted to expand the event to a five-team contest by including the Far East champions, who became eligible for the first time in 1966. The Bermuda Bowl became a six-sided affair for the first time in 1971 when Australia exercised its right to represent the South Pacific Zone. The Central American–Caribbean Zone was represented for the first time in the 1979 championship. And the BRIDGE FEDERATION OF ASIA AND THE MIDDLE EAST fielded a representative in the Bermuda Bowl for the first time in 1981. The European Zone was allotted a second spot in the competition in 1981.

The pattern for Bermuda Bowl competition was changed radically, starting with the 1983 competition. The winners of the North American Team Trials and the European champions advanced automatically to the semifinals. The North American runner-up and the second-place European team also qualified for Bermuda Bowl play, but they had to take part in a round-robin with the winners of the other zones to determine the other two semifinalists. Also eligible to play in the round-robin were the victors from South America, Far East, Central America-Caribbean, Australia-New Zealand and Asia-Middle East. In addition, the host country has the right to enter a team if that country has not already qualified as a Zonal representative.

In order to insure that two teams from the same Zone do not meet in the final, the WBF stipulated that if two teams from the same Zone reach the semifinals, they must oppose each other in a semifinal. If it ever should happen that three teams from the same Zone should qualify for the semifinals, there would be a three-cornered match among such teams to decide which would meet the fourth semifinalist, which would be given an automatic bye into the final.

The WBF also decided in 1981 that future Bermuda Bowls, starting in 1985, would not be held in either Europe or North America. World Team Olympiads and World Pair Championships would be held in even years in either North America or Europe, while Bermuda Bowls would be held elsewhere in odd years.

For a full listing of Bermuda Bowl results, see WORLD CHAMPIONSHIPS (II).

BERMUDA INCIDENT. In 1975, during the early qualifying stages of the WORLD CHAMPIONSHIPS, being played in Bermuda in celebration of the 25th anniversary of the Bermuda Bowl, GIANFRANCO FACCHINI, a member of the Italian team, was accused of giving foot signals to his partner, SERGIO ZUCCHELLI.

The first person to notice unusual foot movements was BRUCE KEIDAN, an American news correspondent monitoring the match between Italy and France. Keidan reported his observation to the North American npc, ALFRED SHEINWOLD, and to EDGAR KAPLAN, a member of the WBF Appeals Committee. Kaplan informed WBF president JULIUS ROSENBLUM. Rosenblum himself observed for a time, then he assigned special observers from the Appeals Committee, JOHANNES HAMMERICH of Venezuela and James O'Sullivan of Australia, to monitor the Italian pair.

According to Keidan, Hammerich and O'Sullivan, Facchini reached out with his feet on several occasions during auctions and before opening leads, and apparently touched Zucchelli on the toes once or more; Zucchelli's feet remained completely immobile, and Facchini did not move his feet at other times. Rosenblum, Hammerich and WBF vice president JAIME ORTIZ-PATIÑO of Switzerland therefore decided to monitor Italy's next qualifying match, using European observers. Before this plan could be implemented, however, the WBF was informed that the North American team would refuse to play against Zucchelli and Facchini in this next scheduled match. This, plus the fact that rumors of the foot-movement accusation were already rampant, caused the WBF to inform all team captains of what had transpired, to postpone the Italy–North American match, and to convene a hearing immediately.

The WBF Appeals Committee heard testimony from observers Keidan, Hammerich, O'Sullivan, Rosenblum and TRACY DENNINGER of Bermuda. Facchini did not deny moving his feet, but attributed his movements to nervous tension. Zucchelli testified that he was unaware of any foot actions by his partner. OSWALD JACOBY, who had analyzed some of the hands, was called as a witness, but the Committee was unable to find specific correlation between the foot movements observed and the bidding or play of the hands — a factor usually considered essential to conclusive proof of cheating. The WBF therefore resolved that Facchini and Zucchelli ". . . be severely reprimanded for improper conduct with respect to the actions of Mr. Facchini moving his feet unnaturally and touching his partner's feet during the auction and before the opening lead''. Coffee tables were thereafter placed beneath the card tables to block any possibility of further such movements.

Sheinwold promptly issued a statement: "The North American team endorses the verdict of guilty but deplores the failure of the World Bridge Federation to bar this pair from further international competitions". The word *guilty* had not appeared in the original verdict, but a later statement from Rosenblum corrected this omission by declaring that the accused pair "had been found guilty only of improper foot movements". The first meeting between the Italian and North American teams, postponed from Sunday afternoon, was played that evening. Italian npc SANDRO SALVETTI kept the suspect pair out of the lineup, saying that their nerves were frayed by the accusations. Two days later, the pair also sat out the second qualifying match against North America, although they had played in other matches in the interim.

On the morning of the first session of the final between Italy and North America, when Sheinwold learned that Facchini and Zucchelli were listed in Italy's starting lineup, he announced that the North American team would not play against this pair unless instructed to do so by the ACBL. ACBL representatives in Bermuda unanimously ordered the team to play. Italy fared poorly with the accused pair in the lineup, and it was only after they had been benched at the request of BENITO GAROZZO and GIORGIO BELLADONNA that her team staged an *impossible* rally to retain the world title.

The partnership of the accused players was broken up and the WBF advised Italian bridge officials that it would not welcome the nomination of either player to any event it conducted in the immediately foreseeable future. See BUENOS AIRES AFFAIR; CAPTAIN; CHEATING; CHEATING ACCUSATIONS.

BERMUDA REGIONAL CHAMPIONSHIPS. This regional was first played in 1962. For past results, see Appendix II.

BETA ASKING BIDS. (1) Asking bids in the ROMAN and SUPER PRECISION SYSTEMS concerned with responder's support for the suit bid by the 1♣ opener. After the negative response of 1♢, opener initiates the inquiry by jumping in a major suit (or, in Roman, by simply rebidding a minor suit). The responses are as set out in ROMAN ASKING BIDS.

(2) Asking bids in the SUPER PRECISION system concerned with the quality of a side suit after responder has made a positive response in notrump are also sometimes called Beta Asking Bids, although the difference in schedule of responses has led them to be designated Delta Asking bids in the version of Super Precision used by GIORGIO BELLADONNA and BENITO GAROZZO. See SUPER PRECISION ASKING BIDS.

BETS. Betting is illegal in tournament play sanctioned by the American Contract Bridge League or any of its affiliated groups.

Occasionally rather sizable bets have been made on the results of challenge bridge matches, notably the CULBERTSON-LENZ MATCH of 1931-32 and the CULBERTSON-SIMS MATCH of 1935.

Bets on the outcome of a rubber or match are based on the side winning the larger number of points rather than the rubber bonus or bonuses, and are thus distinguished from STAKES, which are based on the difference in points earned at so much per point.

BEYNON TROPHY. This trophy was donated by GEORGE W. BEYNON in 1947 and formerly awarded for the Senior Masters Individual Championship. This event was part of the Life Master Individual Championship and was played as an independent tournament. In 1958 it became part of the Fall NAC until 1960, when it was withdrawn. Past results are listed under Fall NAC. From 1965 to 1971 the trophy was returned to competition and awarded to the winners of a two-session event for non-qualifiers in the Flight B Master Pairs at the Summer NAC, under which past results are listed.

BIBLIOGRAPHY. See page 902.

BID. A call by which a player proposes a contract that his side will win at least as many odd tricks (one to seven) as his bid specifies, provided the hand is played at the denomination named. See LAWS (Law 38).

BID OF MORE THAN SEVEN. A call by a player contracting for more than seven-odd tricks, and one which is, therefore, inadmissible. See LAWS (Law 38).

BID OUT OF ROTATION. A call by a player, not in turn. See LAWS (Law 31).

BID-RITE TEAM. The team that won the Eastern Team-of-Four Championship in 1933. The members were HOWARD SCHENKEN, DAVID BRUCE (Burnstine), RICHARD L. FREY, and CHARLES S. LOCHRIDGE. Named for the Bid-Rite Playing Card Co., the first manufacturer of four-color cards. Clubs were blue and diamonds were orange.

BID WHIST. An outgrowth of whist somewhat similar to auction bridge in method of bidding but differing considerably in method of scoring. The bidding is opened by the player to the left of the dealer; highest bidder leads after he has named the trump suit. Seventeen points is the maximum score on a deal, each trick counting one and the four face cards of the trump suit counting one each to the player who takes them in a trick. Sometimes confused with BRIDGE WHIST, this game, now obsolete, was not a direct link in the chain between whist and contract. See HISTORY OF BRIDGE.

BIDDABLE SUIT. The minimum requirements for a bid in terms of the length and strength of the suit.

In the Thirties, the CULBERTSON SYSTEM laid down Q-J-3-2 as a minimum biddable suit, but permitted this to be shaded slightly in certain circumstances.

Modern writers tend to reject a generalized rule for biddable suits, recognizing that the requirements must depend on the circumstances in which the bid is made. Four main situations can be listed.

Opening bid. The higher the rank of the suit, the higher the suit requirements tend to be. 1♣ is often used as a prepared bid with a three-card suit, usually with 4–3–3–3 pattern and a minimum or near-minimum opening bid. Most authorities require that the three-card suit be headed by a high honor, but in an extreme case this requirement might be waived:

♠ A J 10 5
♡ A K J
◊ 5 4 2
♣ 8 4 3

Many players using standard methods would bid 1♣ and hope for the best.

If the red suits were reversed in this example, most experts would open 1◊, regarding the quality of the suit as of greater importance than the convenience of rebid provided by an opening of 1♣. But this is an exceptional case. A bid of 1◊ usually shows at least a four-card suit, but no guarantee is made about the quality of the suit. Four small cards may be sufficient in certain circumstances.

Standards are generally higher for major-suit openings (not taking into account players who favor FIVE-CARD MAJORS). Few experts are prepared to open with 1♡ or 1♠ unless the suit is biddable in the original Culbertson sense. A few players distinguish between hearts and spades, opening four-card heart suits more readily than four-card spade suits.

Responses to suit bids. A similar principle applies: the most economical bid may sometimes be made with a three-card suit, especially a minor suit, while the most space-consuming bid usually indicates a five-card or longer suit.

(a)	(b)	(c)
♠ K 7 5	♠ 9 7 5	♠ 9 7 5
♡ A 5 2	♡ A 5 4 2	♡ A K 4
◊ A 6 3	◊ K 6 3	◊ 6 4 3
♣ 9 6 4 3	♣ A 6 3	♣ 8 7 4 3

With hand (a), most experts would select a response of 1◊ to an opening bid of 1♣. This is a waiting bid which can come to little harm, and there is no good alternative unless a 2 NT response is being used as a limit bid.

Hand (b) presents a problem when responding to an opening bid of 1♣. 2♡ is clearly ruled out because nearly all experts reserve this space-consuming response for hands containing a five-card or longer heart suit. The hand is not strong enough for 2 NT (unless this is played as limit). So the general expert choice would be 2♣.

It is usually dangerous to bid a three-card major suit, but PIERRE JAÏS of France, recommends 1♡ in response to 1◊ with hand (c), or 1♠ in response to 1♡ if the major suits are reversed. This is an extreme treatment, but illustrates the general principle of striving to make the most economical bid.

Conversely, a response at the two-level in the suit ranking immediately below the opener's almost always shows a minimum of five cards, as with the response of 2♡ to 1♠.

The most controversial problem concerning biddable suits is whether a weak four-card major suit should be bid at the one-level in preference to 1 NT. The authorities who favor five-card majors require a four-card suit of any strength to be shown at the level of one, but other leading writers are divided or noncommittal on this point. See WALSH SYSTEM.

Rebids. This is similarly controversial when the choice lies between showing a weak four-card major suit and rebidding 1 NT. In 1959, a panel of American experts were asked whether they subscribed to the idea of "giving highest priority to finding a major-suit fit." There were 29 panelists who answered yes, without reservations; 38 panelists answered yes, with reservations; 17 replied that they would bid the four-card major suit only if it was worth showing. On this specific hand:

♠ 7 4 3 2
♡ 5 3
◊ A Q 7
♣ A Q J 7

the panelists were asked to choose between a rebid of 1♠ and a rebid of 1 NT after opening 1♣ and receiving a response of 1♡. There were 49 votes for 1♠ and 43 for 1 NT.

In a survey conducted by *Bridge World* magazine in 1967, 90 leading experts were asked whether a 1 NT rebid after an opening bid of 1♣ and a response of 1♡ denied a four-card spade suit. Sixty-five percent replied yes, indicating that the modern tendency is toward bidding major suits regardless of their quality.

The problem is slightly different at the level of two, when the choice lies between rebidding a five-card suit and introducing a weak four-card suit. A bid in the four-card suit, if lower ranking, would probably be the preference of the majority, in most situations.

Overcalls. In most situations, the overcaller can apply the standards of a rebiddable suit (see OPENER'S REBID), but standards must vary widely in accordance with such factors as vulnerability, level of the auction, and preemptive effect. See OVERCALL.

BIDDER. A player who states or indicates a BID. Occasionally the term is used to indicate a player who is prone to overbid, or one who will prefer trying a doubtful contact rather than defending in a competitive bidding situation. Also, any player during the auction period.

BIDDING. The period following the deal and ending after the third successive pass of any bid, double or redouble. Aspects of this phase of the game are listed under the following group headings: ARTIFICIAL CALL; BIDDING SYSTEMS; COMPETITIVE BIDDING; DOUBLES; NOTRUMP BIDDING; OPENING BID; SLAM CONVENTIONS; VALUATION. Other articles include: APPROACH PRINCIPLE; ARTIFICIAL CALL; BAD CARDS; BALANCE OF STRENGTH; BELATED SUPPORT; BIDDABLE SUITS; BIDDING SPACE; BORDERLINE OPENING BIDS; CANAPÉ; CHANGE OF SUIT; CHOICE OF SUIT; DELAYED GAME RAISE; DOUBLE RAISE; DRURY; FAST ARRIVAL, PRINCIPLE OF; FIVE-CARD MAJORS; FORCING SEQUENCES; GUARD; IMP TACTICS; IMPOSSIBLE BID; IN-

VERTED MINOR SUIT RAISES; INVITATIONAL BID; JUMP REBIDS BY RESPONDER; LIMIT BID; LIMIT JUMP RAISE; LIMIT JUMP RAISE TO SHOW SINGLETON; MATCHPOINT BIDDING; 1 NT RESPONSE; ONE-OVER-ONE RESPONSE; OPENER'S REBID; PARTSCORE BIDDING; PASSED HAND; PREEMPTIVE BID; PREEMPTIVE RE-RAISE; PREEMPTIVE RESPONSE; PREFERENCE; PSYCHIC BIDDING; PSYCHIC CONTROLS; RESPONDER'S REBIDS; SHOOTING; SHORT CLUB; SHORT SUIT GAME TRIES; SIGNOFF BID; SINGLE RAISE; SKINNER PSYCHIC CONTROLS; SLAM BIDDING; STRENGTH-SHOWING BIDS; STRONG NOTRUMP AFTER PASSING; SWISS CONVENTION; THREE-CARD SUITS, BIDS IN; 3 NT RESPONSE; TRAP BID; TRIAL BID; TRIPLE RAISE; TRUMP SUIT; TRUMP SUPPORT; 2 NT RESPONSE; TWO-OVER-ONE RESPONSE; TWO-WAY GAME TRIES; UP THE LINE; VALUE OF GAME; WAITING BID; WEAK JUMP SHIFT RESPONSES; WEAK SUIT; WEAK TWO-BIDS; WEAKNESS RESPONSE; WORKING CARDS.

BIDDING BOX. A device that permits silent bidding. First used in Scandinavian countries. To make a bid, the player takes the appropriate card from a box attached to the corner of the table on his right and places it in front of him on the table. All bidding cards remain on the table until the auction is concluded, thus avoiding the need for a review of the bidding. The possibility of mishearing or misunderstanding a bid also is eliminated. Bidding boxes were used for the first time in World Championships during the World Pair Championships in Sweden in 1970. Beginning in the World Championships at Las Palmas in 1974, bidding boxes have been used exclusively at World Championships. Bidding boxes also are used during late rounds of ACBL championships. The concensus of those who have used bidding boxes is that they are a great improvement over verbal bidding, especially in international matches.

Jannersten Förlag AB - Bridgeakademin, Box 45 77401 Avesta, Stockholm, Sweden

BIDDING CONTESTS. See INTERNATIONAL BRIDGE ACADEMY.

BIDDING SCREEN. See SCREEN.

BIDDING SPACE. The amount of room used in terms of bids which have been skipped. A response of 1 ♡ to 1 ◇, for example, uses no bidding space, but a response of 2 ♣ would use up all the possible bidding space. The general theory is that the length of a suit tends to increase as the bidding space consumed in bidding it increases.

(1) In opening the bidding, 1 ♣ is not infrequently a three-card suit, and the length expectancy increases up the line. 1 ♠ is usually a five-card suit, even for players who do not require five-card majors.

(2) Similarly in responding, a response using no bidding space, e.g., 1 ♠–1 ◇, may occasionally be a three-card suit. A response using all the bidding space (e.g., 1 ♠–2 ♡) is nearly always a five-card suit.

(3) In rebidding by the opener, a rebid in the original suit is most likely to be a five-card suit if it consumes no space (1 ♡–2 ◇–2 ♡), but almost sure

to be a six-card suit if all the bidding space has been used (1 ♡–1 ♠–2 ♡).

(4) Overcalls represent exceptions, for tactical reasons. 1 ♠ over an opposing bid of 1 ♣ is slightly more likely to be a four-card suit than it would be over 1 ♡. In the former case the overcaller may be taking a calculated risk in the hope of shutting the opponents out of a heart fit.

BIDDING SYSTEMS. Specific methods of bidding are discussed under the following headings: ACES SCIENTIFIC; ACOL; BARON; BIG DIAMOND; BISSELL; BLUE TEAM CLUB; BULLDOG; CAB; CANARY CLUB; CULBERTSON; EFOS; FOUR ACES; FRENCH CLUB; GOREN; KAPLAN-SHEINWOLD; LEVINREW; LITTLE MAJOR; LITTLE ROMAN; MARMIC; NEW SOUTH WALES; NOTTINGHAM CLUB; OFFICIAL; PRECISION CLUB; REITH'S ONE OVER ONE; RELAY; ROMAN; ROMEX; ROTH-STONE; SCHENKEN; SIMS; STANDARD AMERICAN; STAYMAN; TREFLE SQUEEZE; VANDERBILT CLUB; VIENNA; WALSH; WINSLOW.

BIDDING TO THE SCORE. See PARTSCORE BIDDING.

BIFF. Colloquial for trumping the led suit, particularly a winning card on an early lead.

BIG CLUB. See SCHENKEN SYSTEM.

BIG DIAMOND SYSTEM. A method introduced by G. ROBERT NAIL and ROBERT STUCKER, the cornerstone of which is a forcing 1 ◇ opening, promising an unbalanced hand with at least 17 points. 1 ♡ is the negative response (0–9), and 1 NT shows a positive response in hearts. After a negative response, minimum rebids by opener show 17–21 points; jump rebids ask responder to define his support and strength by steps, or to jump to game with good support and a void or singleton. Double jump rebids by opener are game forcing, and responder shows his support by steps. Opener may then bid a new suit to ask for controls in that suit. After a positive response, opener jumps to show a self-sustaining suit, or rebids 2 NT (18–20) or 3 NT (21–23) with no fit for responder's suit and all unbid suits stopped.

Other openings include:

(1) 1 ♣, forcing, showing a balanced hand not suitable for a 1 NT opening (14–16) or a 2 NT opening (20–21). A 1 ◇ response is negative (0–10).

(2) 2 ♣, non-forcing, showing 12–15 points with 4-4 or better in the minor suits. Over a 2 NT response, opener rebids three of a minor suit if he has five cards in the suit, or three of a major with three cards in that suit.

(3) 2 ◇, showing 14–16 points and 4-4 or 5-4 in the major suits. Responses of 3 ◇, 3 ♡, and 3 ♠ are invitational; 2 NT is game forcing and opener rebids 3 ♣ or 3 ◇ with 4-4 in the majors and three cards in the minor suit bid, or rebids 3 ♡ or 3 ♠ with five cards in the major bid.

BIG TOP. The highest matchpoint score on a board when two or more sections are scored together.

Common big tops are 25 and 38. See SCORING ACROSS THE FIELD.

BIOGRAPHIES. See Section II.

BIONIC BRIDGE. A plan to use computers to play bridge without cards. It was conceived by C. C. WEI and developed in Taiwan by PATRICK HUANG and others. Each player sits at a computer terminal with a keyboard. He is shown his own cards and then a bidding diagram to which he contributes as necessary. When the bidding is over and the opening lead has been made, he is shown his hand and the dummy in correct relationship, and makes his play in correct turn. The computer prevents all the standard misdemeanors — it is impossible to make an insufficient bid, to bid out of turn, to play out of turn or to revoke.

The prototype versions were designed for head-to-head match play, and the computer calculates the IMPs. However, it can be readily adapted for matchpoint play, and it will be possible to play long-distance matches using a telephone hook-up.

BIRITCH, or Russian Whist. The historic four-page pamphlet, thought to be the earliest publication of the rules of bridge. Authorship has now been traced to John Collinson of London, in whose name copyright was entered July 14, 1886. A reproduction, made available through the courtesy of Cambridge University Library, is in the ACBL library. The principal innovations from short whist are described as follows:

...No card is turned up for trumps.

The dealer, after the cards have been looked at, has the option of declaring the suit he elects for trumps, or of saying "Pass," in which latter case his partner *must* declare trumps.

In either case, the one declaring may, instead of declaring trumps, say "BIRITCH," which means that the hands shall be played *without* trumps.

... Either of the adversaries may say "Contre," in which case the value of all tricks taken is *doubled*, the dealer or his partner may however thereupon say "Sur contre," in which latter case the value of all tricks taken is *quadrupled*, and so on *ad infinitum*.

... The person to the left of the dealer leads a card. Then the partner of the dealer exposes all his cards, on the table, which are played be as at *Dummy Whist.*

GAMES AND RUBBERS

A game is won by the first side which scores *in play* 30 points. The honours do not score towards the game.

The *Rubber* consists ... of two games out of three.

SCORING

The *odd tricks* count as follows:

If "Biritch" is declared........................ each 10 points
If "Hearts" are made trumps .... " 8 "
If "Diamonds" are made trumps .... " 6 "
If "Clubs" are made trumps .... " 4 "
If "Spades" are made trumps .... " 2 "

If *all* the tricks are taken by one side they add 40 extra points. This is called "GRAND SLAMM."

If *all the tricks but one* are taken by one side they add 20 extra points. This is called "PETIT SLAMM."

The *winners* of each rubber add 40 points to their score. This is called "CONSOLATION."

There are *four honours* if "BIRITCH" is declared, which are the *four aces*.

Equality in aces counts nothing.
3 aces...................... 3 tricks
4 aces...................... 4 tricks
4 aces in one hand .... 8 tricks

There are *five honours*, viz: Ace, King, Queen, Knave, and Ten, if *trumps* are declared.

Simple honours (3) .... 2 tricks
4 simple honours .... 4 tricks
4 simple honours in one hand... 8 tricks

5 simple honours in one hand... 1 trick additional to the score for four honours

If one hand has *notrumps* (trumps having been declared), his side, in case of it scoring honours, adds the value of simple honours to its honour score, or, in case of the other side scoring honours, the value of simple honours is deducted from the latter's honour score. This is called "CHICANE."

Despite existence of this pamphlet, derivation of the name *bridge* from *biritch* was long disputed on the ground that no such word existed in Russian. Research by ROBERT TRUE in the early Seventies found that earlier Russian dictionaries did include the term, defined as *herald, town crier, announcer*, making it a logical name for a game which introduced the new idea of announcing the declaration at which the hand was to be played. It is interesting to observe the designation of *biritch* for the declaration of notrump, a feature never part of whist. Use in the pamphlet of the French terms for double and redouble would tend to confirm that bridge was played earlier in France, or in those diplomatic circles where French was the prevailing language. See also HISTORY OF BRIDGE.

BISSELL. An original method for showing distribution with the first bid, devised by Harold Bissell of New York and published in 1936. It attracted favorable attention from B. JAY BECKER, LOUIS WATSON and EDWARD HYMES, and anticipated some modern European systems, such as ROMAN and RELAY.

Valuation. This was by a distributional point-count which ingeniously took into account the strength of combined honors as well as suit lengths. Honor cards were valued at 3, 2 and 1 point respectively if there were 0, 1 or 2 higher honors missing in the same suit.

To these were added distributional points: 1 for the fourth card in any suit; and 4 for the fifth and succeeding cards in any suit.

The grand total bore a direct relation to the playing-trick strength of a hand (three times the number of playing tricks) and was therefore an accurate measure of the power of the hand.

BLACK CLUB. A modified version of BLUE TEAM CLUB used by BILLY EISENBERG and BOB HAMMAN in the 1971 Bermuda Bowl.

The 1♣ opening promises 17 or more points; all other openings are limited. The opening bid style is mildly CANAPÉ. The 1 NT opening shows 16–17 HCP, or 13–15 points and a 3-3-3-4 or 3-3-2-5 distribution.

Other methods include FLANNERY 2♦, weak two in the majors, GLADIATOR over 2 NT openings, and cuebids for slam exploration, with first- and second-round controls treated as equals and shown up-the-line.

BLACK POINTS. Master points won other than in regional or national championships. See GOLD POINTS; RANKING OF PLAYERS; RED POINTS; REGIONAL AND NATIONAL POINTS.

BLACK AND RED GERBER. A variation of the GERBER convention devised by Irving Cowan, Shedden ON, which uses 4♣ as the ace-asking bid only when a red suit has been agreed on as trumps. When clubs or spades are to be trumps, the ace-asking bid is 4 ◊. This modification retains a lower-level ace-asking bid than BLACKWOOD, while avoiding the ambiguity of using 4♣ as Gerber, with clubs as the agreed suit.

BLACKPOOL MOVEMENT. A movement popular in England in which 10 tables play 24 boards. Two boards are played in each round, and byestands are placed between tables 1 and 10, and between 5 and 6. Players and boards move as in a normal MITCHELL MOVEMENT for 11 rounds, so that in the eleventh round original opponents are again in opposition. For the twelfth round East–West pairs deduct their pair number from 11 and move to the indicated table.

BLACKWOOD. A convention in which a 4 NT bid is used to discover the number of aces held by partner. It was invented by EASLEY BLACKWOOD of Indianapolis IN in 1933 and has attained worldwide popularity.

The conventional responses to the 4 NT bid are:

5♣	no ace or four aces
5◊	one ace
5♡	two aces
5♠	three aces

If the 4 NT bidder continues by bidding 5 NT he is asking for kings in a similar fashion. As this must be an attempt to reach a grand slam, the 5 NT bid guarantees that the partnership holds all four aces.

Requirements. There are no specific requirements, but the 4 NT bidder should feel safe at the level of five and have an expectation of 12 playing tricks in the combined hands. He should expect to be able to make a successful decision on the basis of his partner's response and should therefore usually be well provided with second- and third-round playing tricks in the combined hands. It is seldom wise to use the convention when holding a void suit or a worthless doubleton.

If the intention is to play in a minor-suit slam, discretion must be exercised if the 4 NT bidder has fewer than two aces. Blackwood may be used with one ace if the intended trump suit is diamonds, but not if it is clubs.

In some circumstances it may be possible to play in 5 NT. If the Blackwood bidder next bids an unbid suit at the five-level, he is requesting responder to bid 5 NT.

Void suits. Void suits may not be counted as aces, but there are several methods in which voids can be indicated.

(1) Make the normal response, but at the level of six, to show the indicated number of aces and an unspecified void. Thus 6♣ shows no ace and a void; 6◊ shows one ace and a void, etc.

(2) Bid 6♣ to show one ace and a void; 6◊ to show two aces and a void. (Used by the GARDENER-ROSE partnership.)

(3) Bid 5 NT to show two aces and a void; six of a suit ranking below the agreed trump suit to show a void in that suit and one ace; six of the agreed trump suit to show one ace and a higher-ranking void. (In-

troduced by the JORDAN-ROBINSON partnership.)

(4) Holding two aces, make the response that normally shows no aces; holding three aces, make the response that normally shows one ace. When the 4 NT bidder signs off, the responder does not pass, but now bids the suit of his void. Responses at the six level show one ace and a void, as in (3) above. (Devised by JEFF RUBENS.)

(5) Using a three step set of normal responses to Blackwood in which 5♣ shows 0 or 3 aces, 5◊ shows 1 or 4, and 5♡ shows two aces, make a bid higher than 5♡ to show a void. 5♠ shows a spade void and one ace; other responses are as in (3) above. (Used in ROMEX.)

Interference bidding. See BLACKWOOD AFTER INTERFERENCE.

Non-conventional. There are a number of situations in which 4 NT should be treated as a natural bid. Experts sometimes disagree on specific situations, but there is general agreement on the following rule:

A 4 NT bid is a natural bid whenever the partnership has not bid a suit genuinely. For example:

SOUTH	NORTH	SOUTH	NORTH	SOUTH	NORTH
1 NT	4 NT	2♣	2◊	1 NT	2♣
		2 NT	4 NT	2◊	4 NT
		(using an			
		artificial			
		2♣ bid)			

But there are other circumstances in which the 4 NT bid should be treated as natural. Careful partnership agreement is needed. The following rule is generally valid: If, during the auction, one player bids 3 NT and his partner bids four of a minor suit as a slam suggestion, a subsequent 4 NT bid by either player should be a natural sign-off bid. For example:

SOUTH	NORTH	SOUTH	NORTH
1♠	2♡	1♠	2♣
3 NT	4◊	3 NT	4♣
4 NT		4 NT	

In these sequences the final bid rejects the slam invitations and expresses a desire to play in 4 NT.

A more general rule is recommended by TERENCE REESE; 4 NT is natural when no suit has been agreed, either directly or by inference.

This covers a wide range. For example:

SOUTH	NORTH
1♠	2♡
3 NT	4 NT

Many players would regard this as conventional, but on Reese's rule it would be natural.

SOUTH	NORTH
1♡	2 NT
4 NT	

This type of 4 NT bid is listed as conventional by Blackwood himself, but would be natural on Reese's rule. If South wishes to bid 4 NT conventionally, he can make a forcing bid at the level of three and follow with 4 NT on the next round.

By agreement, a raise from 2 NT to 4 NT at any stage can be regarded as natural: a conventional 4 NT can always be postponed. But judgement may be required when 3 NT is followed by 4 NT.

	SOUTH	NORTH
	1 ♠	3 ♡
	3 NT	4 NT

This is clearly conventional. North may be planning to play in either major suit, but has had no opportunity to fix a suit below game level.

Also, any sudden jump from a suit bid to 4 NT is of necessity conventional.

See also: BABY BLACKWOOD; BOWERS; BYZANTINE BLACKWOOD; CULBERTSON 4-5 NT; DECLARATIVE-INTERROGATIVE 4 NT; GERBER CONVENTION; NORMAN 4 NT; ROMAN BLACKWOOD; ROMAN GERBER; SAN FRANCISCO CONVENTION; SUPER BLACKWOOD; SUPER GERBER; and SUPPRESSING THE BID ACE.

BLACKWOOD AFTER INTERFERENCE. The traditional method for dealing with opponents who overcall a BLACKWOOD bid has been to double when-ever the size of the prospective penalty is attractive, and otherwise to pass with no aces and bid the cheapest suit with one ace, and so forth up the line. Modern conventions recognize that the penalty will rarely be sufficiently lucrative to warrant a double, and therefore give that call an artificial meaning related to the number of aces held by the Blackwood responder. The most common such conventions are:

(1) DEPO, which stands for Double Even, Pass Odd. A double shows zero, two, or four aces; a pass shows one or three.

(2) DOPI, which stands for Double Zero, Pass 1. A double shows no aces, pass shows 1, and two or more aces are shown by bidding up the line.

(3) PODI, which stands for Pass Zero, Double 1. The double and the pass have the reverse of the meanings they have using DOPI; other bids are the same. Similarly, DOPE is the reverse of DEPO.

DOPI is more widely used than PODI. A number of experts agree to use DOPI when the overcall is below the trump suit at the five-level, allowing room for bidding two or more aces up the line, and to use DEPO when the overcall is at five of the trump suit or higher and space is scarce.

It is also possible to use Roman responses with DOPI or PODI. The first step shows 0 or 3 aces, the second step shows 1 or 4 while the first bid other than pass or double shows 2. Pairs that play KEY-CARD BLACKWOOD would be well advised to discuss whether or not the trump king counts in responding after interference.

Some experts play a variation of DOPI when 4 NT is doubled. ROPI (redouble zero, pass one) or its reverse, RIPO can be used. This can lead to occasional misunderstandings, and the more popular choice is to act as if the double had not taken place.

BLACKWOOD THEORY OF DISTRIBUTION. A formula applied when missing four cards including the queen.

♠ K J 10 7 4

♠ A 8 6 2

South lays down the ace and both defenders play low. On the second round West plays low, and South has to decide whether to finesse or play for the drop.

Mathematically is is extremely close. EASLEY BLACKWOOD suggests a rule based on the LAW OF SYMMETRY: If the combined North-South holding in their shortest suit is:

(a) five cards, or four cards divided 2-2: play for the drop

(b) four cards divided 3-1 or 4-0, or fewer than four cards: finesse

This formula was tested on a large number of published hands and produced excellent results. However, it can apply only when there are no indications from the bidding and play, which is rarely the case.

BLANK. A VOID. Used as an adjective, it indicates lack of a protecting small card for an honor, as a *blank* king. As a verb, it means to discard a protecting small card, as to *blank* a king.

Blank honors, whether singleton or doubleton, are slightly devalued in most POINT-COUNT methods.

BLANK HAND. A hand with seemingly no trick-taking potential (see YARBOROUGH).

BLANK SUIT. See VOID.

BLIND LEAD. The first lead on any hand, so called because the opening leader has not seen the dummy. Particularly is this term applied when the leader's partner has not bid, and the declarer's side has bid only one denomination.

TERENCE REESE, noted English bridge player, is quoted as saying, "Blind leads are for deaf players." See OPENING LEAD.

BLIND PLAYERS. Blindness is not an insurmountable obstacle to bridge playing. The cards are marked with Braille symbols, and sighted players in turn call the card played to each trick. A blind player may at any time ask that the remaining cards in the dummy be called off. Early Braille markings were not standardized and often players could not read one another's Braille.

J. PATRICK DUNNE and DR. ARTHUR DYE were the first blind players to participate in major American Contract Bridge League tournaments. DR. LOIS ZWART (now WILEY) commenced playing a few years later, accompanied by her Seeing Eye dog. Dr. Dye and Dr. Wiley both earned the LIFE MASTER rating as have other blind players — JOHN LARSEN of Minneapolis, Anne Cunningham of Charlotte NC, Sarah Howard of Newport News VA and MICHAEL ANDREW LEVINSON of Daly City CA who, though legally blind, won the Life Master Men's Pairs at the Fall 1981 North American Championships.

The Metrolina Association for the Blind provides transportation for blind players who play in a special section of the Charlotte (NC) Bridge Association game.

An organization devoted to teaching is *Bridge for the Blind*, 248 Elwood Ave., Newark NJ 07106. This nonprofit corporation, founded and directed by HELEN D. ALBANO, purchases and distributes Brailled lessons and cards, enrolls and trains teachers of the blind, certifies qualified teachers and issues diplomas to students who have attended the required bridge courses.

BLOCK. A situation in which entry problems within a particular suit make it difficult or impossible to cash winners or possible winners in that suit. This occurs when both members of a partnership (the declaring side or the defense) hold significant honor cards, and one of them has no accompanying small cards. For example:

NORTH	NORTH
K Q J 10	Q J 3 2
SOUTH	SOUTH
A	A K

In these cases the block is complete, and the honor cards in dummy cannot be utilized unless a side entry is available. Sometimes the block may be less embarrassing:

NORTH	NORTH
A J 4 3 2	A 4 3 2
SOUTH	SOUTH
K Q	K Q J

If there is no side entry to dummy, South must sacrifice an honor by overtaking the last honor in his own hand. He needs a 3–3 division of the defenders' cards to make more than three tricks.

The general rule for resolving blocked situations, or for avoiding unnecessary blocks, is that high cards must be played from the shorter hand as quickly as possible. See also UNBLOCKING and INTERNAL BLOCK.

BLOCKBUSTER. A bridge hand of seemingly tremendous trick-taking potential. Frequently, however, these hands have a weakness and give rise to very large sets when the partner's hand contains no protective features and the trump suit divides unfavorably. See also MONSTER and ROCK-CRUSHER.

BLOCKED SQUEEZE. See CRISS-CROSS SQUEEZE, under SIMPLE SQUEEZE. For other types of blocked squeeze, see ENTRY SQUEEZE and STEPPINGSTONE SQUEEZE.

BLOCKING. Playing so as to create a block in the opponent's suit. For example:

♠ A 5 2

♠ K 10 8 6 3   ♠ Q 9

♠ J 7 4

West leads the ♠ 6 against 3 NT. The normal play is to hold up the ace twice, but this is useless if West rather than East is likely to gain the lead. In that case South should put up dummy's ace, abandoning the chance that the lead is from king-queen. Whenever East holds a doubleton honor the spade suit is blocked for the defense.

Notice that if the defensive entry was held by East, he would need to unblock with the queen on the first trick.

Another position:

♠ A 6 4

♠ Q 9 8 5 3   ♠ K J

♠ 10 7 2

In this position West leads the five and South puts up dummy's ace, hoping for East to hold two honors doubleton. When the defenders gain the lead, they can cash only one spade trick.

♠ 8 6

♠ A 9 4 3 2   ♠ K J 10

♠ Q 7 5

When East wins the lead of the three with the king, and returns the jack, South should cover and so block the suit. He assumes that West's three is an honest fourth-best lead, in which case West cannot have six spades, and East cannot have a doubleton. If there were two small spot cards missing, suggesting a six-card suit with West, South should play low on the jack.

♠ A 3

♠ K J 7 5 4   ♠ Q 8

♠ 10 9 6 2

On the lead of the five, South blocks the suit by putting up dummy's ace. This permits a triumph for the rare player who underleads K–Q–J–x–x (see OPENING LEADS).

♠ 7 5

♠ Q 6 2   ♠ A 10 9 8 4

♠ K J 3

West leads the two to East's ace, and the 10 is returned. If South judges that West had led from an honor, he puts up the king and achieves a block.

See also UNBLOCKING.

BLUE PETER. A humorous term for a high-low signal invented in 1834 by LORD HENRY BENTINCK. This was probably the first defensive signal in any game of the whist family. The name is nautical in origin, referring to a signal hoisted in harbor to denote that a ship is ready to sail. Bentinck's signal was used in a side suit to indicate to partner a desire to have trumps led. For uses of the high-low or echo in contract, see SIGNALS, SIGNALING and PETER.

BLUE RIBBON PAIRS, NORTH AMERICAN CHAMPIONSHIP. A championship event contested annually at the Fall NAC, under which heading past results are listed. Entry is limited to (1) players who, within a specified period of time, have finished high in North American Championship events, or have finished first or second in regional-rated events, (2) the top 100 masterpoint holders, (3) members of current official teams representing the ACBL or any of its member countries in international competition, and (4) winners of Grand National District championships.

BLUE TEAM. The popular name of the Italian international bridge team which gained a remarkable series of successes beginning in 1956. The name is apparently derived from the 1956 Italian Trials, when the Blue Team defeated the Red Team.

FEDERICO ROSA, the late Secretary of the Italian Bridge Federation, explained that the successes of the Blue Team were closely connected with the name of CARL ALBERTO PERROUX, the Technical Commissioner of the Italian Bridge Federation. He undertook this duty in 1950, and scored his first success in the following year when the team which he had selected won the European Championship in Venice. But the subsequent World Championship encounter with the United States at Naples showed that the young Italian champions were lacking in experience and team discipline.

But this did not cause Perroux to lose heart. He wrote then that the Italians had wished to reach the moon too quickly. This was a promise and a threat. From that day, two groups of enthusiasts, under the paternal leadership of the Technical Commissioner, dedicated themselves to a profound and detailed study of the game. As a result the two schools—the Neapolitan and the Roman—gave birth not only to the most accurate bidding systems ever devised, including ARNO (LITTLE ROMAN), an offshoot of the ROMAN SYSTEM, but also to the great story of the Blue Team, made up of men such as WALTER AVARELLI, GIORGIO BELLADONNA, EUGENIO CHIARADIA, MASSIMO D'ALELIO, PIETRO FORQUET, BENITO GAROZZO, CAMILLO PABIS-TICCI, and GUGLIELMO SINISCALCO.

The Italians did not have to wait too long before avenging the 1951 defeat. From 1956 the Blue Team, captained by Perroux through 1966, GUIDO BARBONE in 1967, and Angelo Tracanella in 1968–69, went from victory to victory, and finally reached the moon. They set an international record which will probably never be equalled: four consecutive European Championship wins, ten consecutive World Championship victories in the Bermuda Bowl, and three consecutive World Team Olympiad victories.

With the universe theirs, the Blue Team announced its retirement after winning the 1969 World Championship. After the ACES' victories in the 1970 and 1971 Bermuda Bowls, the Blue Team briefly returned to world competition for the 1972 World Team Olympiad. With UMBERTO BARSOTTI as their nonplaying captain and using modifications of the PRECISION CLUB system, the Blue Team won the round robin and went on to defeat the Aces in the finals 203–138. Italy continued its domination of the Bermuda Bowl in 1973, 1974, and 1975 with SANDRO SALVETTI as npc, but with only two or three members of the traditional Blue Team in the lineup.

BLUE TEAM CLUB. An increasingly popular offspring of the NEAPOLITAN system, developed principally by BENITO GAROZZO. See BIBLIOGRAPHY C. The chief features of the Blue Team Club are:

1 ♣ opening is forcing and normally shows 17 or more points (4-3-2-1 count). Occasionally distributional factors may dictate a 1 ♣ bid with slightly less than 17, or a weaker opening with exactly 17.

Responses show controls by steps, counting an ace as 2 controls and a king as 1. 1 ◇ shows 0–2 controls, less than 6 points; 1 ♡ shows 0–2 controls, 6 points or more; 1 ♠ shows 3 controls, and so on up to 2 ◇, which shows 6 controls and 2 NT showing 7. Jump responses of two of a major show a six-card suit headed by two honors but less than 6 points.

If 1 ♣ is overcalled at the one-level, a pass is equivalent to the first step response and a double to the second. Other responses are control-showing, except that two hearts and two spades retain the same meaning as if there were no intervention. After a jump overcall the responses follow a similar pattern: pass is the weakest bid, double shows 6 or more points, suit responses are forcing for a round, a response in notrump shows 3 or 4 controls, and a cuebid shows 5 or more controls.

1 ♣ is generally forcing to 1 NT if the response is one diamond, or to 2 NT if the response is 1 ♡. The partnership is committed to game after any other control-showing response.

The opener can force to game by a jump rebid in a suit. If he rebids 1 NT or 2 NT, the responder can use STAYMAN. Responder usually makes his first rebid in his best suit, and subsequently shows significant features.

1 ◇, 1 ♡, and 1 ♠ openings are natural limited bids, showing 12–16 points and at least a four-card suit. Occasionally 1 ◇ may be opened on a three-card suit. With two suits of equal length, opener bids the higher-ranking. With two suits of unequal length, the shorter suit is bid first unless the hand is a minimum and the long suit is higher-ranking.

Most responses are normal. Jump raises are limited. A 2 NT jump response is invitational, showing 11–12 points and 4-3-3-3 distribution. Jump shifts show solid or near-solid suits and 13 points or more. Strong hands are bid according to the CANAPÉ principle. Responder's first suit may not be a real suit if his second is higher-ranking.

A response at the two-level is forcing for one round, or to 2 NT. Opener must rebid a five-card suit if he has one. After a 1 ♡ or 1 ♠ opening, a second-round jump by responder to 4 ♣ or 4 ◇ agrees opener's suit as trump and shows a control in the bid suit. See BLUE TEAM 4♣-4◇ CONVENTION.

If opener has a maximum opening, usually 14–16 points, he may make a jump rebid or reverse. Concentration of points in the bid suits favors the selection of a strong rebid.

1 NT opening shows a balanced hand, either 13–15 points with a club suit and exactly three cards in each major, of 16–17 points. Minor-suit responses are artificial. 2 ♣ normally shows 8–11 points and requests opener conventionally to rebid 2 ♣ with the strong notrump, or make some other two-level bid to describe the strength and club length of the 13–15 notrump. After a 2 ♣ rebid, 2 NT by responder asks for majors; minor-suit rebids are nonforcing. After any other rebid by opener, responder's rebids are mostly nonforcing, though encouraging in some cases.

A 2 ◇ response shows a minimum of 12 points and is forcing to game. With a strong notrump, opener bids a four-card major or bids 3 ♣ with no major, after which 3 ◇ by responder inquires about the minors. With a weak notrump, opener rebids 2 NT, after which 3♣ by responder requests opener to describe his strength and number of clubs in four steps.

Jump responses to the three-level show six-card suits headed by two of the top three honors with 6-7 points. Jump responses of 4♣ and 4♦ are transfers to 4♡ and 4♠ respectively.

2♣ *opening* shows a good club suit of at least five cards and 12-16 ponts. If a second suit is held, opener will usually have a minimum of 15. A response of 2♦ is artificial and asks opener to bid a secondary suit. If he does not have one, he rebids either 2 NT with stoppers in two of the outside suits, or 3♣ with a stopper in only one outside suit. 3♦ by responder then requests opener to pinpoint his stoppers. Other two-level responses are natural and non-forcing. Jump responses are forcing to game.

2♦ *opening* shows a powerful three-suited hand (4-4-4-1) with 17-24 points. See BLUE TEAM 2♦.

2♡ *and* 2♠ *openings* are WEAK TWO-BIDS with a normal range of 8-11. 2 NT is the only forcing response.

3♣ *opening* is a natural preempt and shows a minimum of seven playing tricks, including one outside the club suit.

GAMBLING 3 NT.

Other opening bids are standard.

Blackwood is used on the first and second rounds of bidding, or in later rounds if a jump bid. Responses are ROMAN BLACKWOOD style, with 5♣ showing one ace or four, and 5♦ showing none or three. In other situations 4 NT is a natural slam invitation. Partner can cooperate by showing an additional feature. He may pass, but more often signs off in the agreed suit. See DECLARATIVE INTERROGATIVE 4 NT.

Defensive bidding is normal, but overcalls are made freely, especially at the one-level. Jump overcalls are intermediate. In response to takeout double, the cheapest bid may be a HERBERT NEGATIVE.

BLUE TEAM 4♣-4♦ CONVENTION. A delayed game raise used in the BLUE TEAM CLUB system to describe responder's minor suit controls. When opener bids and rebids a major suit or opens a major suit and rebids in notrump and responder has excellent support for opener's suit, he responds as follows:

(1) 2♣ followed by 4♣ shows first- or second-round control of clubs and denies first- or second-round control of diamonds;

(2) 2♦ followed by 4♦ shows first- or second-round control of diamonds and denies first- or second-round control of clubs;

(3) 2♣ followed by 4♦ shows either first-round control of both clubs and diamonds or second-round control of both suits;

(4) 2♦ followed by 4♣ shows first-round control of one minor and second-round control of the other.

See also NEAPOLITAN 4♦ CONVENTION.

BLUE TEAM 2♦. A bid showing a hand worth 17-24 high-card points, with 4-4-4-1 distribution.

An integral part of the BLUE TEAM CLUB system, this convention can also be used with standard methods. Responses fall into one of four categories:

(1) *Immediate sign-off:* with a very weak hand (about 0-5 points) and three or more spades, responder bids 2♠. Opener will normally pass unless he has either a singleton spade or a maximum hand with four spades. With a singleton spade, opener rebids 2 NT, allowing responder to select one of the other three suits.

(2) *Discouraging response with long broken suit:* with a hand worth 5-6 points containing a broken six-card suit, responder bids three of his suit. If that suit is opener's singleton he will pass unless he has a maximum. If opener has four cards in responder's suit he may either bid game or try for slam by cue-bidding his singleton. After the cuebid, responder bids in steps to show whether he has the ace or king of his suit, and whether or not he has any singleton.

(3) *Encouraging response with long good suit:* with a hand worth about 6-7 points containing a six-card suit headed by any three honors or two of the top three honors, responder bids 2 NT. This bid asks opener to bid the suit *below* his singleton. At his next turn responder bids his suit (or bids 3 NT if his suit is clubs and opener has shown a singleton club by rebidding 3♠). If opener's singleton is in responder's long suit, opener may pass with a minimum, or may bid game in notrump or in responder's suit with a maximum. If opener has four cards in responder's suit the partnership is committed to game, and opener may try for slam by cuebidding. Responder then cuebids a singleton if he has one.

(4) *Relay response:* with a hand unsuitable for any of the above responses, responder bids 2♡, an artificial bid that asks opener for information. With a minor suit singleton and/or a maximum (21-24), opener bids the denomination below his singleton; rebids of 2 NT and 3♣ show minimum hands and rebids of 3♦ through 3 NT show maximums. If opener has instead a minimum (17-20) and a major suit singleton, he rebids 2♠; responder then rebids 2 NT asking opener to bid 3♣ with a singleton heart, 3♦ with a singleton spade and 17-18 HCP, or 3♡ with a singleton spade and 19-20. Responder may then cuebid opener's known singleton to ask about various features of opener's hand such as point count, controls, and queens.

BLUFF. A bid or play made with deceptive intent. See PSYCHIC BID and DECEPTIVE PLAY.

BLUFF FINESSE. See CHINESE FINESSE.

BOARD. (1) A duplicate board. (2) The table on which the cards are played. (3) The dummy's hand, so called because it lies on the table. See LAWS OF DUPLICATE (Law 2).

BOARD, DUPLICATE. An oblong or square board used in various forms of duplicate bridge, slotted with four sections, each deep enough to hold one quarter of a standard deck of playing cards.

The face, or top, of each board has listings appropriate to the board's use, as follows: numbered so that it can be quickly distinguished from companion boards of the same set, one slot marked to indicate the dealer, vulnerability conditions marked both in the slot itself (usually in red) and on the face of the board.

Sometimes the cards to be placed in the slots are shuffled by the players and dealt at the beginning of each contest, but for larger tournaments organizers usually obtain preshuffled or machine-prepared hands to be put into play instead of player-dealt hands.

As adapted for use in contract bridge, the boards are usually packed in sets of 32 or 36 in a carrying case designed for them. Dealer and vulnerability follow a standardized pattern, with North dealing the first board, East the second, South the third, and West the fourth with the same rotation repeated for every subsequent set of four. Vulnerabilty is arranged in a 16-board pattern as follows:

Board	1	2	3	4	5	6	7	8
Dealer	N	E	S	W	N	E	S	W
Vulnerability	No	N-S	E-W	Both	N-S	E-W	Both	No
Board	9	10	11	12	13	14	15	16
Dealer	N	E	S	W	N	E	S	W
Vulnerability	E-W	Both	No	N-S	Both	No	N-S	E-W

Thus every player deals in each of the four possible vulnerability situations. George Beynon notes that this pattern can be put into a magic square, in which N means N-S vulnerable; E, E-W; B means Both; and O for no vulnerability thus:

O N E B
N E B O
E B O N
B O N E

In England the boards in use have the deal 180° out of phase, South dealing on board #1.

The first duplicate boards (then called trays) were devised by Cassius M. Paine and J. L. Sebring in 1891. They were square boards, called Kalamazoo after the company that manufactured them. The first oblong boards were produced by WILLIAM Mc KENNEY in 1928 using paper, and the first metal boards were manufactured in 1931 by F. DUDLEY COURTENAY. The first plastic boards were used by the ACBL at the North American Championships in Salt Lake City in 1976. The ACBL now uses plastic boards exclusively.

Square and circular boards are also used, and paper, cardboard, wood, and plastic are alternative materials. Wallets made of plastic and foldable when not in use are popular in Europe and South America.

BOARD OF DIRECTORS OF THE ACBL. The body that manages and controls the business and activities of the ACBL. The Board is composed of one director elected by each DISTRICT for a three-year term. The terms of the directors are staggered, with approximately one-third of the directors being elected each year. There are three regular meetings each year, usually just preceding North American Championships.

BOARD OF GOVERNORS OF THE ACBL. A body that has the power to make recommendations to the BOARD OF DIRECTORS OF THE ACBL, and to receive reports from and to ratify certain actions taken by that Board. It is composed of five members from each DISTRICT and, in addition, all past Presidents of the ACBL and all past Chairmen of the Board of Governors. Three regular meetings a year are held, usually during North American Championships.

BOARD-A-MATCH SCORING. A method of scoring multiple team matches where each team plays against a variety of opponents, in which each board has exactly the value of 1 matchpoint. The highest matchpoint score among those in direct competition is the winner. Although this method used to be prevalent, it has been replaced in large part by INTERNATIONAL MATCHPOINTS with SWISS MOVEMENT pairing.

The movement is so arranged that if the North–South pair of a given team plays a board against the East–West pair of an opposing team, the East–West pair of the given team plays the same board against the North–South pair of the same opposing team. If the total of a team's North–South and East–West scores on the same board is positive, that team receives 1 matchpoint. If it is negative, the team receives 0 matchpoints. If the total is exactly zero (that is, if both teams achieve the same score), both teams receive ½ matchpoint.

This type of event has made somewhat of a comeback in the past few years. Some sectionals now schedule a board-a-match event as a one-session contest instead of a mixed pairs, which in many areas has lost its popularity. Each board in a match is scored board-a-match, and the total score is the basis for pairings in the next round of the Swiss. Such an event usually is scheduled only in the top flight of a flighted Swiss Teams.

BOARD-A-MATCH TEAMS. A team event in which scoring is done on a board-by-board basis. A team earns one point for each algebraic plus for the two pairs, a zero for an algebraic minus, and a half for an exact tie. This form of team competition used to be the common last-day event at sectional and regional tournaments, but it fell from favor soon after Swiss Teams made its debut. Now the REISINGER TEAMS, the NORTH AMERICAN MEN'S PAIRS and the NORTH AMERICAN MIXED TEAMS are the only national events still run on board-a-match scoring. Board-a-match events seldom are scheduled at regional and sectional tournaments. Top-flight players claim board-a-match is the toughest type of bridge event, requiring intense concentration for every card played. The event's popularity diminished over the years when it became apparent that the skill involved is so high that the same teams were winning almost all the time.

Board-a-match is virtually unknown in Europe, where it is sometimes termed "point-a-board." For movements employed see AMERICAN WHIST; NEW ENGLAND RELAY; PATTON; ROSLER. For other forms of teams events see AGGREGATE; DOUBLE ELIMINATION; KNOCKOUT; HYBRID SCORING; QUOTIENT; ROUND-ROBIN; SWISS.

BODY. A term used to describe a hand with useful intermediate cards such as 10s, 9s, and 8s. Some authorities advocate counting a 10 as half a point, sometimes only for notrump purposes. The 10 is of greatest value in combination with one or two higher honors, such as K–10–x, Q–10–x, or K–Q–10. It has least value when isolated (10–x–x) or in a solid suit (A–K–Q–J–10). Similarly a 9 may be valuable in combination (Q–10–9) but almost worthless in isolation.

Body may be a decisive factor in making a bidding decision:

♠ K 10 5 4
♡ A Q 9
◊ Q 10 9
♣ K J 8

This hand counts 15 points in high cards, but the intermediate cards make it a "good" 15, and most experts would treat it as a 16-point hand, and open with a standard 16–18 notrump.

Body is a factor to consider when making BORDERLINE OPENING BIDS. As the bidding proceeds, a player can often revalue his intermediate cards. A hold of 10–9–x is certainly worthless if the bidding marks partner with a singleton or a void, and very probably worthless opposite a doubleton. But there is a good chance that the 10–9 will be valuable opposite a probable three card suit: partner may have something like A–J–x, K–J–x, or Q–8–x.

BOLAND CLUB SYSTEM. An early (1931) system devised by Vincent F. Boland of Shaker Heights OH. The 1♣ bid was *either* an artificial bid promising between three and five honor tricks *or* a normal club bid. In the latter case the clubs were rebid on the second round. Other one-bids showed that the opening was about a minimum in honor strength. Two bids were strong and forcing. The system was popular in the Cleveland area.

BOLAND CONVENTION. A method of slam exploration after a natural raise to 4 NT, devised by M. M. Miller and Corti Boland, Toronto. After the bidding:

WEST	EAST
1 NT	4 NT

West declines the invitation by passing if he has a minimum. With an average hand in terms of point count (i.e., 17 points using a standard 16–18 notrump) he bids five of his lowest ranking biddable suit. Responder acts accordingly, and may jump to the six-level in another suit without excluding other contracts. A 5 NT rebid would deny a biddable suit.

With a maximum hand, the opener jumps to the six-level in his lowest ranking biddable suit in similar fashion.

The covnention can be used in the same way after any natural jump from 2 NT to 4 NT.

BOLS BRIDGE TIPS. A series of annual contests invented by the late HERMAN FILARSKI and subsidized by the Bols Company of The Netherlands in which players of international stature submitted bridge tips for publication in periodicals all over the world. A panel of judges voted each year to decide the winner. The tips were distributed to members of the INTERNATIONAL BRIDGE PRESS ASSOCIATION and became a popular feature in most bridge magazines and many newspaper columns worldwide. The articles appeared in 19 languages. Later the tips were gathered together, expanded and made into a book, *Bridge Tips by World Masters*, with TERENCE REESE as editor.

BOLS BRILLIANCY AWARDS. Outstanding writeups of spectacular plays. The Bols Company of The Netherlands offers prizes annually to the writers who chronicle the most brilliant plays and to the players who perform the brilliancies. Journalists from all over the world compete, and winners are chosen by an international panel of experts.

BONNEY'S SQUEEZE. A triple squeeze against one opponent combined with a simple squeeze against the other. Analyzed by Norman Bonney (d. 1939) of Boston.

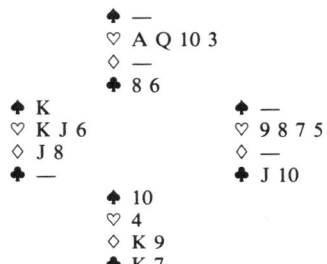

South leads the ◊ K on which he throws a club from dummy. East is squeezed and must discard a heart. Now the lead of the ♣ K squeezes West in three suits.

At the start South has all but *two* of the remaining tricks, but he manages to win all six by means of the squeeze.

　　　　　　　　　　　　　　　　Monroe Ingberman

BONUS. A term used in all types of bridge to describe various premiums given under the scoring rules to sides or partnerships who accomplish specified aims, to wit: In rubber bridge, bonuses are awarded for the winning of the rubber by scoring two games before the opponents have scored two games. A bonus of 700 points is credited to the side winning a two-game rubber before the opponents have won even one game. If the opponents have won a game, the bonus becomes 500 points. A bonus of 50 points is paid any side scoring a successful doubled or redoubled contract. A bonus is scored above the scoring line for a side which, in the given hand, has held honors in trump, or all the aces in one hand at notrump. This bonus is either 100 or 150 points. (See HONORS.) Bonus scores are given to sides who successfully bid and make any slam contract. (See SLAM.) If a rubber of bridge has to be terminated before its regular conclusion, a bonus of 300 points is given to a side that is a game ahead, and a partscore earns a 50-point bonus. In CHICAGO bridge, bonuses can occur on each of the four hands, inasmuch as in this type of contest each deal is really almost a separate game of itself. A nonvulnerable side scoring a game in Chicago is credited with 300 points immediately, and a vulnerable side, 500. Slam bonuses are the same as in rubber bridge, and honors are likewise scored. A partial score achieved on the fourth or final deal, however, acquires an extra bonus in Chicago of 100 points. This bonus, however, is awarded only for partials actually acquired on the last deal — there is no premium for a partial remaining open at the conclusion of a four-deal CHUKKER. In duplicate bridge, a bonus is awarded for the making of any partial score (a below-game score) on a given deal. The bonus is 50 points. The regular slam premiums apply in duplicate scoring as explained above, but there are no bonuses for honors, except in total-point scoring. In duplicate, the regular Chicago bonuses for games bid and made apply, e.g., 300 for making a nonvulnerable game and 500 for making a vulnerable game.

BOOK. The tricks won by a side which have no value in the score; a whist term with little significance at contract bridge. For the declarer, the first six tricks taken constitute his book; for the adversaries, the amount of the declarer's bid subtracted from seven, or the maximum number of tricks the adversaries may take without defeating declarer's contract. The origin of the term apparently lies in the old practice of forming the first six tricks into a "book" by placing them all in one stack.

BOOK GAME. Style of a player who is acquainted with the situations described in the books about bridge, and rigorously follows this pattern of bidding and play. It features theoretical knowledge, but implies lack of skill from practice and lack of versatility.

BOOK PLAYER. A player who plays a BOOK GAME. "The book player is a safe partner, but is not very dangerous as an adversary." (A. W. Drayton: *Art of Practical Whist*).

BOOKS. See BIBLIOGRAPHY.

BORDERLINE OPENING BIDS. When the decision seems to be close between opening the bidding with one of a suit and passing, a number of considerations may influence a good player.

Position at the table. The third player can open relatively freely, with a point or two less than he would normally require. This is partly because there is no necessity to rebid, and partly because the opening may inconvenience the fourth player, who is likely to have the best hand at the table. The fourth player may also open, especially at matchpoint scoring, with one point below the normal requirements in the hope of snatching a part-score; but in this situation the spade suit is crucial; if the fourth player is weak in spades he should usually refrain from opening a doubtful hand.

Vulnerability. This may sway a borderline decision, especially at matchpoints. With a 5-3-3-2 hand, for example, when the five-card suit is weak, there is a distinct possibility of playing a part-score down two to save an opposing part-score. The vulnerabilty would then make the difference between a good score and a bad one.

Location of honors. In general, a hand with honors in its long suits is well placed in attack, while a hand with honors in its short suits is more effective in defense. This factor is allowed for to some extent in most point-count systems, which devalue singleton kings, queens, and jacks, and doubleton queens and jacks.

Consider the following two hands:

	(a)		(b)
♠	9 4 3	♠	A J 4
♡	A J 7 5 3	♡	J 7 5 3 2
◇	A Q 5 4	◇	J 5 4 3
♣	3	♣	A

The distribution and point-count are the same, but hand (a) has a sound opening bid, and hand (b) does not—although it could have an acceptable opening bid in some situations. The difference lies in the location of the honor cards.

Rebid prospects. The ease or difficulty of the rebid will often be a determining factor.

Majors or minors. The possession of a major suit, and particularly spades, favors an opening bid. An opening bid in a major has some obstructive value, and the prospects of outbidding the opponents and of scoring a game are slightly improved.

BOSTON CHESS CLUB. This club, founded in 1857 in Boston MA, was the oldest club devoted to games in the United States. In 1926, bridge playing replaced chess as the chief activity at the club. In modern times contract was played almost exclusively. When the club encountered severe difficulties in 1981, the interests in the club were sold to the Cavendish Club in Brookline MA.

BOTTOM. In tournament play, the lowest score on a particular hand in the group in direct competition. It is extended to indicate an excruciatingly bad result.

BOWERS VARIATION OF BLACKWOOD. A method of responding to BLACKWOOD credited to Stewart Bowers of New York. A response of 5 ◇ shows an ace of a suit bid by the partnership, and 5 ♡ shows an unbid ace. 5 ♠ shows two aces, and 5 NT three aces.

BOX A CARD. To place a hand in a duplicate board with a card, usually not the top card, turned face up.

BRAZILIAN BRIDGE CONFEDERATION (CONFEDERAÇAO BRASILEIRA DE BRIDGE). This confederation was founded in 1955, and formed of the bridge leagues of Guanabara, São Paulo, Bahia, Rio Grande do Sul, Pernambuco, Minas Gerais, and Rio de Janeiro. By 1982 it had a membership of more than 3,100 competing in local championships and an annual National Championship for Open Teams and Open Pairs. Brazil participates in South American Championships and World events. The Confederation won the South American Championships 1949, 1955, 1956, 1967-1975, 1977, 1978, the SAC Women's Teams 1954, 1955, 1956, 1958, 1959, 1965, 1966, 1972, 1973, 1975, 1980, 1981, and represented the South American Confederation in the Bermuda Bowl in 1969, 1970, 1971, 1973, 1974, 1976, 1979.

Officers, 1982:
President: Fernando S.G. Frota
Secretary: Sergio M. Barbosa, Rua Raul Pompeia 12, 20000 Rio de Janeiro, Brazil

BREAK. The distribution of the outstanding cards in a suit in a manner favorable to the declarer. This may imply that a suit was divided evenly or nearly so, or that an adversely held honor was positioned so that it did not develop into a winning trick. The term "break" is also used to indicate the actual distribution of the cards outstanding in the suit; or with the adjective "bad" to indicate unfavorable distribution from the declarer's standpoint.

In most contexts, "split" may be used as a synonym for "break," both as a noun and a verb: "the suit *split* (or broke) badly (or well)." "There was a bad *split* (or break) in spades." For expectations as to how a suit will break, see MATHEMATICAL TABLES 4, 4A.

BREAKAGE. A rubber bridge term for rounding off the score to the nearest 100 points.

BREAKING TIES. The breaking of ties in duplicate contests, when it is a question of the winner, is done for the purpose of awarding of trophies when it is not feasible to award duplicates to the tying pairs or teams. Masterpoint awards in ACBL tournaments are awarded equally to each tying group, the amount being one-half the sum of the awards for first and second places. The main occasion for breaking of ties during the course of the competition is to determine which of two or more pairs, tied for the last qualifying position or positions, is entered into the final session. In either case, for pair events, the method is similar. All boards played by all tying groups are considered, and 1 point awarded for an above average score and ½ point awarded for an average score if the board or boards were not played in direct comparison. If the tying pairs are in direct comparison on any board, 1 point is awarded to the pair with the better matchpoint result on that board, ½ point if their matchpoint result is a tie. In team events, the result of the match between the two tying teams is used with BOARD-A-MATCH SCORING. In head-to-head team competition, such as knockout events, additional boards are played, In SWISS TEAMS, ties usually are broken by means of SWISS POINTS. The total of scores of all opponents are tallied for the tied teams, and the winner is the team with the highest total. Sometimes only matches played in the second half of the event are used to compute Swiss Points. The method of breaking ties should be approved by the SPONSORING ORGANIZATION or announced in the CONDITIONS OF CONTEST, before being used.

BRIDGE. A partnership game of cards derived from WHIST and played by four persons. The term can refer to three distinct games, which are listed under BRIDGE WHIST, AUCTION BRIDGE, and CONTRACT

BRIDGE. All these games have been referred to simply as *bridge* during their periods of dominance, and the term "bridge whist" was not used when the game was in vogue (1894–1904). It was coined subsequently to distinguish the game from its successors.

The earliest printed mention of *bridge* appears to be in a pamphlet published in 1886 entitled "Biritch, or Russian Whist." Although there is no certainty that the game is Russian, the fact that it was christened "Russian Whist" gave weight to the idea that it originated in Russia. It does, as a matter of fact, bear a close resemblance to Vint, Preference, and similar games; and Vint certainly is of Russian origin. See also BIRITCH; HISTORY OF BRIDGE; RUSSIA.

BRIDGE BATTLE OF THE CENTURY. See CULBERTSON-LENZ MATCH.

BRIDGE BUFF'S BULLETIN. A bulletin published quarterly since 1973 by BILL SACHEN of Waukegan IL, in the interests of bridge book collectors. New and old books and periodicals are reviewed, master lists of all known bridge and whist books have been published, and subscribers can publicize lists of books they wish to purchase or sell. See BIBLIOGRAPHY, O.

BRIDGE CHALLENGER. A computer game. It is possible to play bridge with this machine with the computer taking one, two, three or even all four hands. The game is reasonably sophisticated — it can finesse, play logically, postpone drawing trumps, etc. It also announces bids and plays verbally.

BRIDGE COLUMNS. Ever since the game of auction bridge became popular, newspapers and periodicals have had columns in which bridge is featured. These columns are quite varied, frequently containing local bridge news including results of local duplicate contests, anecdotes, interesting results; other columns are of a didactic nature such as quizzes and problems; while others feature outstanding and unusual bridge hands with explanations of bidding and play and sidelights on the personalities involved. Some are distributed to newspapers through national syndicates, appearing in hundreds of papers; others are produced locally for one, two or three papers.

The popularity of bridge columns is attested to by the fact that very few papers have ever dropped one permanently because every such attempt met with violent protest from the readers of the paper.

BRIDGE D'ITALIA. A monthly magazine published by the Italian Bridge Federation. GUIDO BARBONE is the magazine director, and he is assisted by the following editorial committee: Dino Mazza, Salvatore Modica and Gregorio Medugno. See BIBLIOGRAPHY, O.

BRIDGE FEDERATION OF ASIA AND THE MIDDLE EAST. This federation was formed in 1980 by P. C. GOENKA who is its founder president. Its members include India, Pakistan, Bangladesh, United Arab Emirates, Mauratius, Sri Lanka and Nepal.

Officers, 1982:
President: P. C. Goenka
Secretary: Mazhar Jafri, Shaukat Law Associates, 217–218 Central Hotel Annexe, Abdullah Haroon Road, Karachi, Pakistan

BRIDGE FEDERATION OF INDIA. This federation was formed in 1958 by RAMNIWAS R. RUIA who was its president from founding until 1970. It has been a member of the WORLD BRIDGE FEDERATION since 1959, FAR EAST BRIDGE FEDERATION since 1972 and BRIDGE FEDERATION OF ASIA AND THE MIDDLE EAST since 1980. The principal National tournaments sponsored yearly include Team of Four (Ruia Gold Trophy), Open Pairs (Holkar Trophy), Open Teams (Singhania Trophy), Mixed Pairs (Lalbhai Trophy), National Masters (Sundaram Trophy) and Interstate Championship (Guru Dutt Trophy).

Officers, 1982:
President Emeritus: P. C. Goenka
President: S. G. Bose Mullick
Secretary: Y. Kamalakara Rao, 3-6-190 Himayat nagar, Hyderabad–500 029, India

BRIDGE GOLF. See GOLF.

BRIDGE HEADQUARTERS. Name given to an organization formed in the Thirties to exploit the OFFICIAL SYSTEM. It turned out to be abortive, perhaps because the only binding force among its individual members was an ambition to emulate the success of ELY CULBERTSON.

BRIDGE HISTORY. See HISTORY OF BRIDGE.

BRIDGE JOURNAL, THE. A bi-monthly magazine intended for the edification of and exchange of ideas by serious players, founded and first published in 1963 by PAUL HEITNER and JEFF RUBENS and aimed at improving technical and mechanical aspects of the game, especially at tournament level. Some of the regular features of this publication were a *Spotlight on Bidding* match between experts, a problem forum on bidding and play, and a *Systems Corner*. When Rubens became Associate Editor of *The Bridge World* in 1967, the *Journal* ceased independent publication and merged with *The Bridge World*. See BIBLIOGRAPHY, O.

BRIDGE MAGAZINE. An English monthly with an international reputation published in Leeds. It was founded in 1926 by A. E. MANNING-FOSTER, and is therefore the oldest bridge periodical (as of 1964). Publication was suspended, however, during the war years, and in number of issues *Bridge Magazine* is therefore exceeded by *The Bridge World*. EWART KEMPSON became the editor when publication was resumed in 1946, and continued in that capacity after the merger with the *British Bridge World* in 1964. After Kempson's death ERIC C. MILNES assumed the post of editor. PHILLIP ALDER has been the editor since November 1980. See BIBLIOGRAPHY, O.

BRIDGE MATHEMATICS. See MATHEMATICS OF BRIDGE.

BRIDGE-O-RAMA. A method of displaying bridge competition to a large audience. The technique was devised in Italy, and first used in the 1958 Bermuda Bowl. The forerunner of this development was used in the Thirties when an electric display board was used in exhibitions in department stores. The features of Bridge-O-Rama include a large display board on which the hands can be placed in frames, so that the representations of the actual cards are lighted, along with devices for indicating the winning card, tricks won by declarer or defender, the contract, and other information. In addition to the display board there is a *console,* or bank of light switches, by which the lights of the display board are controlled. Explanations and comments on the bidding and play are provided by an expert panel.

The largest audience for a Bridge-O-Rama showing was the crowd of 1,500 that attended the finals of the 1964 Olympiad in the Hotel Americana in New York City. The size of the crowd made necessary the simultaneous VUGRAPH screening of the hands for spectators too far away to see the Bridge-O-Rama board.

Because setting up the deals for Bridge-O-Rama slowed up the play and required a large staff, exhibitions since the 1971 Bermuda Bowl in Taiwan have been almost exclusively by means of vugraph, enhanced in some cases by closed circuit television of the play in the open room.

BRIDGE OLYMPICS. See WORLD PAR CONTESTS.

BRIDGE IN PRISON CAMPS. The absorbing character of duplicate bridge to such an extent that one is unaware of the passage of time has made it an ideal activity for prisoners of war confined in military prison camps. A POW returning in 1973 from a Vietnamese prison camp described the materials improvised to run a duplicate game twice a week for three years: porcelain covered metal plates sometimes served as both the duplicate board and the traveling score sheet — the hands, each wrapped with a scrap of paper showing its compass position, were stacked atop an upside down plate for passing from one *table* (a folded blanket) to another; the eating side of the plate carried the traveling score diagram; when pencils were not available for scoring on the plates, toilet paper was used for score sheets, with scores entered by use of cotton-tipped bamboo sticks dipped in homemade ink.

While American hostages were being held in Iran (Nov. 4, 1979–Jan. 20, 1981) many of them learned to play bridge to help pass the time. One hostage in solitary confinement dealt out thousands of hands and got quite upset because East–West were getting most of the high cards — he identified with North–South.

BRIDGE IN PRISONS. In 1972, recognizing that bridge is such an absorbing and constructive activity that it might assist in the rehabilitation of the prisoners, the ACBL Board of Directors and the ACBL Charity Foundation instituted a policy of encouraging the playing of duplicate bridge in penal institutions.

The League and various member units have donated cards, boards, bridge books, and other instructional materials to prison duplicate clubs. In 1973 the ACBL Charity Foundation made a $5,000 contribution to the Foundation for the Advancement of Inmate Rehabilitation and Recreation. The American Bridge Teachers' Association has assisted the program by waiving its initiation fees and dues for prison inmates who qualify as bridge teachers and pass the ABTA examination. Local clubs have encouraged their players to participate in prison duplicate games. By early 1982 there were some two dozen duplicate clubs in penal institutions.

It is perhaps fitting that bridge be encouraged in prisons since the idea of playing with one hand exposed as the dummy may have originated in NEW-GATE Prison, where whist was played in this manner as a three-handed game prior to 1820.

BRIDGE PROFESSIONAL REGISTRATION ORGANIZATION (BPRO). An organization of professional bridge players formed in 1981 and recognized as an accredited professional organization by the ACBL in 1982.

BRIDGE TOURNAMENT FOR CLUBS IN CO-PENHAGEN. The world's oldest yearly bridge event, played every year since 1927. Invitations are issued to all clubs in Copenhagen, of any sort, including clubs promoting relations between countries, clubs of doctors, engineers, women's liberation, etc. Each year the Tournament is played on the second Monday of each month from November through April.

BRIDGE WEEK. A Regional Championship held annually since 1935, originally held over Memorial Day weekend in Los Angeles, later held in July, and since 1975 played in Pasadena CA. From 1935 through 1947 the tournament was also called the ALL-WESTERN. It was played over two weekends, Saturday through Tuesday in Los Angeles at the Biltmore; later sites were the Elks Temple and the Ambassador Hotel. Players paid $8.00 to board the Wednesday *Daylight Special* train bound for San Francisco for the second segment; enroute the Team-of-Four event was played. Events in San Francisco were held Thursday through Sunday originally at the Whitcomb Hotel and subsequently at the Sheraton Palace Hotel. From 1948 through 1955 the name Bridge Week was also given to the annual San Francisco tournament, which is now called the All-Western. Bridge Week has always been the biggest Regional Championship, and the 1965 figure of 10,948 tables set a world attendance record for regionals. Since 1973 the STODDARD TROPHY has been awarded to the player winning the greatest number of master points during the tournament. For past tournament results see Appendix II.

BRIDGE WHIST. The game which succeeded WHIST in popularity until AUCTION BRIDGE became the vogue early in the twentieth century. Chief differences between bridge whist and whist are the manner of selection of the trump suit, the introduc-

tion of play at notrump, the exposure of the dummy hand, and the innovation of the double and redouble calls, which could continue indefinitely. This re- and re-doubling feature introduced the element of gambling for very high stakes into the staid game of whist, which caused a storm of disapproval. The *Whist Reference Book*, published in 1898, called doubling "the most objectionable feature of the game." Instead of the trump suit being selected by the turn of the last card dealt, the dealer or his partner has the privilege of naming the trump suit or notrump. It was a requirement of the game that the leader ask, "Partner, may I lead?" to which his partner, if he did not plan to double, was required to respond, "Pray do." The play then proceeded as in auction or contract bridge. The scoring is different from whist, in which each trick counted only one point. In bridge whist, the four suits and notrump have varying values. Spades are the lowest of the suits in value, followed in ascending order by clubs, diamonds, hearts, and notrump. Honors, games, rubbers, and slams are also scored. The greatest exponent of the strategy and tactics of bridge whist was JOSEPH B. ELWELL, who wrote many books on the subject, chief among them, *Advanced Bridge,* published in 1904.

Contemporary players and writers referred to the game simply as "bridge." As the shorter term was also used later to refer to auction bridge and contract bridge, card historians invented the term "bridge whist" to identify the original form of bridge.

BRIDGE WORLD, THE. The oldest *continuously* published magazine dealing with contract bridge, founded and first published by ELY CULBERTSON in October, 1929. Published monthly, it was a comparative success from the start, and such events as the CULBERTSON-LENZ MATCH of 1931–1932 and the CULBERTSON-SIMS MATCH later did much to further interest.

Culbertson, who held the post of editor in chief until September of 1943, founded it with the idea of making it a widely popular publication, and for a short time it was placed on newsstand sale, but this proved uneconomical. It soon became what it has remained: a magazine for better than average players, and a sounding board for new and improved theories (having been first to present such ideas as the STAYMAN CONVENTION; the ROTH-STONE and KAPLAN-SHEINWOLD systems; LAVINTHAL suit-preference signals; UNUSUAL NOTRUMP bids, and many other ideas). *The Bridge World's* "Master Solvers' Club," featuring a panel of experts who vote for and explain why they chose what they consider the correct bid in a monthly series of problems, has been copied by almost every bridge publication.

Publication was taken over from Culbertson in 1943 by ALBERT H. MOREHEAD, who edited it in association with RICHARD L. FREY, JOSEPHINE CULBERTSON, ALPHONSE MOYSE, JR., and others until 1946 when it was taken over by Moyse who ran it under the Culbertson aegis until the death of the Culbertsons, December 1955–March 1956, when he became sole owner and editor. In November 1963, the magazine was bought by the McCall Corporation, with Moyse retained as editor. When Moyse retired at the end of 1966, McCall's divested itself of the magazine. EDGAR KAPLAN and JEFF RUBENS became sole owners, with Kaplan assuming the role of editor and Rubens associate editor. Much of the material that Rubens had been publishing in *Bridge Journal* appeared in *The Bridge World*, including a highly popular series of bidding matches between expert partnerships. The list of sometime editors and contributing editors includes, in addition to the Culbertsons, Morehead, Frey, and Moyse, many of the famous bridge writers: B. JAY BECKER, SAM FRY JR., CHARLES H. GOREN, WILLIAM J. HUSKE, OSWALD JACOBY, THEODORE A. LIGHTNER, WALTER MALOWAN, GEOFFREY MOTT-SMITH, ALFRED SHEINWOLD, ALEXANDER M. SOBEL, ALAN F. TRUSCOTT, BOBBY WOLFF, WALDEMAR K. VON ZEDTWITZ, and others.

BRIDGE WORLD STANDARD. A *system* arrived at largely by consensus of experts and other subscribers through a series of polls conducted by *The Bridge World*. It provides the standard for the bidding problems posed to the Master Solvers' Club, a monthly feature in the magazine, and is as well a useful frame of reference for casual partnerships. The principal elements are:

(1) *Opening bids:* strong notrumps (15 to a *bad* 18), with nonforcing STAYMAN, and preemptive jump responses to three of a minor suit; strong four-card major suits may be opened if a convenient rebid is available; WEAK TWO-BIDS; 2♦ is strong and artificial, with natural positive responses;

(2) *Responses and rebids:* limit jump raises, with 3 NT response and SWISS used as forcing raises; up-the-line responses with four-card major suits; a response of 1 NT to 1♣ shows 8–10 points; reverse rebids by opener forcing; jump rebids by responder not forcing except in opener's minor or in a new suit; responder's nonjump rebids of new suits over opener's 1 NT rebid are not forcing; opener's bid of a new suit after a single raise is a natural game try;

(3) *Slam conventions:* Blackwood over suit bids; Gerber over notrump bids; grand slam force;

(4) *Competitive conventions and treatments;* negative doubles through 3♠; responsive doubles after takeout doubles; nonforcing nonjump responses after an overcall over partner's 1 NT opening; preemptive re-raises; 2 NT response over opponent's double shows a limit raise of opener's suit, with other changes of suit and jump shifts nonforcing; preemptive jump overcalls; unusual 2 NT overcall for the two lower unbid suits; LANDY; takeout doubles of preempts through 4♡, with penalty doubles of higher preempts; jump responses to partner's 1 NT overcall are invitational, with a cuebid the only force.

BRIDGE WORLD TEAM. A name applied to several teams in the early Thirties whose members were particularly associated with *The Bridge World*. The most famous of these teams comprised ELY and JOSEPHINE CULBERTSON, WALDEMAR VON ZEDTWITZ, and THEODORE LIGHTNER. Their successes included the VANDERBILT CUP of 1930 and the first of the ANGLO-AMERICAN MATCHES.

BRIDGERAMA. The European term for BRIDGE-O-RAMA.

BRIDGESAMBANDS ISLANDS. See ICELANDIC BRIDGE UNION.

BRIDGETTE. A bridge game for two players invented by Prince JOLI KANSIL (the former Joel D. Gaines), with the assistance of WALDEMAR VON ZEDTWITZ, and acclaimed by many experts as the best of all two-handed bridge games. It is played with a 55-card deck — the standard pack plus three extra cards called *colons*. The *colons* are used in the play to force the opponent to discontinue the suit he is leading. In an advanced version of Bridgette, *cuebids* are used to elicit specific information about the opponent's distribution.

BRING IN. To establish a suit and make effective use of the established winners. The ability to bring in a suit may be affected by considerations of ENTRIES, TEMPO, CONTROLS, or DUCKING, or by the SUIT COMBINATION in the suit being established.

BRITISH BRIDGE. Direct methods of bidding advocated in the Thirties by a group of English players headed by WALTER BULLER and EWART KEMPSON, as opposed to the approach-forcing methods popularized by ELY CULBERTSON.

BRITISH BRIDGE LEAGUE. This League was founded in 1931 by ALFRED E. MANNING-FOSTER. Since 1938 it has been a federal body, with the English Bridge Union, the Northern Ireland Bridge Union, the Scottish Bridge Union, and the Welsh Bridge Union as its chief constituents. Among other bodies affiliated to the League are India, New Zealand, and South Africa.

The League selects British teams for European Championships and World events. Their successes include the Bermuda Bowl 1955, and European Championship 1948, 1949, 1950, 1954, 1961, 1963. The British Women's Team won the World Women's Team Olympiad in 1964, the Venice Trophy in 1981, and the European Women's Championship on numerous occasions.

The League organizes the CAMROSE TROPHY for home international competition, the GOLD CUP for Open Teams, the Portland Cup for Mixed Pairs, and the Lady Milne Cup for Women's Team-of-Four.

Officers, 1982:
President: L. Shenkin
Secretary: A.F. Moon, 146 St. James Avenue, Thorpe Bay, Essex SS1 3LN

BRITISH BRIDGE WORLD. An English monthly publication (1932–1939) founded by HUBERT PHILLIPS. It was revived in 1956 as a successor to the *Contract Bridge Journal*, and continued until 1964 when it merged with *Bridge Magazine*. See BIBLIOGRAPHY, O.

BRITISH PARLIAMENT MATCHES. Matches between the House of Commons and the House of

Lords held annually since 1975. This unique event was founded by RIXI MARKUS with the assistance of the Right Honourable Harold Lever, MP, and is staged by *The Guardian*, national daily newspaper for which Markus is bridge editor. The matches are played under the conditions of rubber duplicate: that is, the same hands are played at each of the two tables in the match but the scoring is rubber-bridge scoring. The winners:

1975	House of Lords
1976	House of Commons
1977	House of Commons
1978	House of Commons
1979	House of Lords
1980	House of Lords
1981	House of Lords
1982	House of Lords

BROZEL. Developed by Bernard Zeller of West Orange NJ as a defense against an opposing 1 NT opening, and may be used either in the direct or balancing position.

A double shows a one-suited hand. If partner does not wish to defend, he bids 2♣ and passes the doubler's next bid. All overcalls on the two-level show two suits as follows:

2♣	shows hearts and clubs
2♦	shows hearts and diamonds
2♡	shows hearts and spades
2♠	shows spades and a minor
2 NT	shows clubs and diamonds

An overcall on the three-level shows a singleton or void in the bid suit and support for the other three suits.

After a weak response to a 1 NT opening, a double again describes a one-suited hand. Without suitable defense, partner bids the next higher-ranking suit, then passes the doubler's next bid. All simple overcalls shows the bid suit and the next higher-ranking unbid suit. 2 NT is a takeout for the three unbid suits, and a cuebid is a stronger takeout, implying game possibilities.

For alternative defensive conventions against notrump openings, see ASPRO: ASTRO; EXCLUSION BID; LANDY; and RIPSTRA.

BUDAPESTI BRIDZS EGYESÜLET. See HUNGARIAN BRIDGE ASSOCIATION.

BUENOS AIRES AFFAIR. In 1965, the international bridge world was rocked by a widely publicized charge that TERENCE REESE and BORIS SCHAPIRO, representing Great Britain in the BERMUDA BOWL at Buenos Aires, Argentina, had transmitted information about the heart suit by finger signals.

The accusers, B. JAY BECKER and DOROTHY HAYDEN, members of the North American team, and ALAN TRUSCOTT, bridge editor for *The New York Times*, testified that the British pair were observed to be holding their cards in a varying manner, with a different number of fingers, either closed or spread, showing at the back of their hands from deal to deal. After comparing findings, it was suggested that Reese and Schapiro were signaling the number of hearts they held (two fingers for two or five hearts, depending on whether the fingers were closed or spread, three fingers for three or six hearts, and so forth). The evidence was presented to JOHN GERBER, (npc, North American team), who, in turn brought it to the attention of RALPH SWIMER (npc, British team), and GEOFFREY BUTLER, chairman of the BRITISH BRIDGE LEAGUE and member of the WORLD BRIDGE FEDERATION executive committee and chairman of its Appeals Committee. After an independent investigation, Butler called a meeting of the Appeals Committee to present his observations, to study the evidence further, and to inform Reese and Schapiro of the charges against them. Both denied the allegations. The matter was then brought to the attention of the WBF Executive Committee. On the last day of the World Championship, by a vote of 10–0 (CARL'ALBERTO PERROUX abstaining, one absentee), The Executive Committee found Reese and Schapiro guilty of using illegal signals, and the evidence was turned over to the British Bridge League for final disposition. Swimer conceded the Great Britain-Argentine match, which Great Britain had won 380–184, and the Great Britain–North American match, in which Great Britain was leading 288–242 with twenty boards to play.

After receiving the WBF report, the British Bridge League set up an independent inquiry to study the charges, headed by Sir John Foster, Queens Counsel, and General Lord Bourne, assisted on the technical aspects of the case by Alan Hiron and RICHARD ANTHONY PRIDAY. The Foster report, released after more than ten months' consideration, found Reese and Schapiro "not guilty" of the cheating allegation. In the opinion of Sir John Foster, the technical evidence appeared to indicate that Reese and Schapiro had not profited in the bidding or play from a foreknowledge of the heart suit, and thus failed to substantiate the testimony of the prosecution's witnesses.

After learning of this verdict, which was released after the 1966 WBF meeting, WBF President CHARLES SOLOMON stated, "It is doubtful that the WBF can accept the decision of the London hearing . . ." His position was that the WBF had rendered the verdict in Buenos Aires and had submitted its report to the British Bridge League to determine what punitive action would be taken.

At its annual meeting in 1967, the WBF Executive Committee reaffirmed its earlier guilty verdict and passed a resolution that the chairman of the Credentials Committee refer applications of any player found guilty of irregular practices in WBF-sponsored tournaments to the Executive Council. The implication was that applications by Reese and Schapiro would not be accepted, and the implication became fact in 1968 when the Executive Council so answered a query from the British Bridge League concerning possible entry of Reese and Schapiro in the 1968 WORLD TEAM OLYMPIAD. As a result, the British Bridge League elected not to participate in the Olympiad.

In 1968, the Executive Council restored Reese and Schapiro to good standing on the ground that the three-year ban that had been in effect since 1965 constituted adequate punishment.

The repercussions of the episode during the years of controversey spanned the American and European continents. An article by RIXI MARKUS defending Reese that appeared in *The Bridge World* resulted in a libel suit by Swimer, and the reluctance of Reese and Swimer to play against each other created problems in the 1968 British Team Trials. The evidence for both sides was presented in books by two of the controversy's leading figures: Reese's *Story of an Accusation* and Truscott's *The Great Bridge Scandal*. See BIBLIOGRAPHY, P. See also BERMUDA INCIDENT, CHEATING ACCUSATIONS.

BULLDOG SYSTEM. Devised by WILLIAM HANNA and DOUGLAS STEEN. The name is derived from the first names of the authors: Bill–Doug.

Features of the system include:

(1) A variable 1 NT opening: 12–14 not vulnerable, 17–19 vulnerable.

(2) KIVI convention: 1 NT–4 ◊ asks for precise point-count; opener bids 4 ♡ with minimum, 4 ♠ with average hand, and 4 NT with maximum.

(3) Artificial JUMP SHIFT to 3 ♣ on powerful hands, permitting other jump shifts to be made preemptively.

(4) OKUNEEF convention. After a cuebid used to invite 3 NT if partner holds a stopper, the lowest possible bid in an unbid suit shows a partial stopper in the opponent's suit. If this is not possible below 3 NT, a bid suit may be utilized.

(5) STAYMAN on the second round, after notrump rebids.

Other conventions listed separately include RESPONSIVE DOUBLES and RUSH ASKING BIDS.

BULLETIN, THE CONTRACT BRIDGE. A monthly magazine, official organ of the AMERICAN CONTRACT BRIDGE LEAGUE, with by far the largest circulation of any bridge periodical, since it goes to all members of the League, totaling nearly 200,000. Published originally as *The Bulletin of the American Bridge League* in 1934; the word "Contract" was added when the name of the League was changed in 1937. It became *The Contract Bridge Bulletin* in 1962.

Earliest issues, edited by GEOFFREY MOTT-SMITH and WILLIAM HUSKE, consisted of a four-page tabloid newspaper listing tournament results and facts concerning upcoming tournaments. In subsequent years it was edited by GEORGE BEYNON and then ALFRED SHEINWOLD.

In May 1958, editorship was assumed by RICHARD L. FREY, who instituted radical changes in format and content. In June of 1958 the directory of bridge clubs was included in the *Bulletin* for the first time. In June 1959, increasing circulation made possible a switch to offset printing. In 1960, the publication went from 10 issues a year to a full 12-issue monthly. Pages jumped from 408 in 1958 to 968 in 1969. A Master Pointers section was begun in February 1964.

In 1970, Frey retired and his duties were assumed by three of his assistants. STEVEN BECKER was appointed Executive Editor; TANNAH HIRSCH became the Editor; and THOMAS SMITH was named Business Manager.

Major changes in the top editorial positions took place again in 1972, when the ACBL moved its headquarters to Memphis. In 1973 HENRY G. FRANCIS became Executive Editor; SUE EMERY was appointed Editor; RICHARD OSHLAG became Business and Advertising Manager.

Under Francis, the *Bulletin* again made major strides. In addition to extensive coverage of major bridge events around the world, the Master Pointers section was expanded, in-depth personal interviews were introduced, and The Mailbox became the springboard for all sorts of high-spirited discussions, from smoking to GOLD POINTS, from ALERTS to professionalism. In addition, the *Bulletin* now features special inserts geared to specific geographic areas — Mid-Atlantic, Midwest, Midsouth, Northwest, Canada, New England and New York. The *Bulletin* has continued its growth — in 1981 *Bulletin* pages numbered 1304. See BIBLIOGRAPHY, O.

BULLETINS. Daily Bulletins are issued at all World Championships and at most international championships. Daily Bulletins at World Championships are enhanced by contests which draw interesting contributions from outstanding journalists present at the tournament. Daily Bulletins also are issued at all ACBL North American Championships and at many ACBL Regionals. Daily Bulletins from the World Championships and from the ACBL are available on subscription. In addition, many ACBL Districts and Units issue Bulletins on a regular basis giving local news and including some technical material.

BUMBLEDOG AND BUMBLEPUPPY. Humorous terms applied to bad players or bad play in whist.

BUMP MITCHELL. An adaptation of the MITCHELL MOVEMENT invented by Forrest Sharpe for the accommodation of a half table. The game is set up as if there were no half table (extra pair) and boards are distributed to all the full tables only. If the number of full tables is even, a skip at the normal time will be necessary.

The extra pair plays North–South, sitting out the first round and taking the highest North–South number. At round two this pair replaces the North–South pair at Table 1 and stays at Table 1 for the rest of the session. The North–South pair originally at Table 1 sits out the second round and bumps the North–South pair originally at Table 2 on the third round, remaining at Table 2 for the rest of the session. In like fashion pair 2 bumps pair 3, pair 3 bumps pair 4, etc., until the end of the session. It is convenient and logical, but not necessary, to actually change the number of a table to match the number of the North–South pair that is sitting there. It also is not necessary for the pair that was sitting out to physically supplant another pair. The pair with the highest North–South number keeps their own table. At round 2 the North–South pair at Table 1 sit with no opponents and no boards (as if they did not exist). On round 3 the North–South pair at Table 2 sit with no opponents and no boards, etc.

The pairs that sit out must be factored up the proper amount so that their scores may be compared with those of the ones who did not sit out.

All boards are in play every round, so all have the same matchpoint top, no matter how many rounds are played. A complete movement is not required.

The total number of rounds possible is one fewer than the number of full tables. For example: nine rounds are possible with 10½ tables.

This movement is not acceptable if 7½, 9½ or 13½ tables are in play and one desires to play seven rounds of four boards, nine rounds of three boards and 13 rounds of two boards, respectively.

BURNER. A colloquialism used in bridge tournaments to refer to a photocopying machine by means of which raw scores (i.e., not matchpointed) are made available to players a few minutes after the end of a session.

BUSINESS DOUBLE. See PENALTY DOUBLE.

BUSINESS PASS. See PENALTY PASS.

BUST. Bridge slang term for a seemingly valueless hand. See YARBOROUGH.

BUSY CARD AND IDLE CARD. These terms were originated by ELY CULBERTSON, and used in his *Red Book on Play* (see BIBLIOGRAPHY, D). His definitions are:

A busy card is one which will have a definite duty in the play of the hand, either as a trick winner or as a guard to a card which will or may eventually win a trick. The idle cards have no such function; they serve the holder only in that he may discard them and save his busy cards for a better purpose.

If a suit is distributed as shown in the diagram, then West's small card is idle, but both the king and queen are busy.

A J 10

K Q x   x x x x

x x x

The terms arise in connection with squeeze play, whose object is to force the discard of a busy card by an opponent.

Monroe Ingberman

BYE. (1) In team-of-four competition, an advance to a later round without the necessity of winning or playing a match. This occurs at some point in the play in order to reduce the field to a power of two.

(2) In pair contests, a BYESTAND is used as a temporary resting place for boards not in play during a particular round.

(3) In pair matches, when an uneven number of pairs compete, there is one table, a bye table, at which traveling pairs find no opponents, or where a stationary pair has no opponents come to them.

(4) A slang term, unsanctioned by law, for "I pass". Sometimes also "Bye me," or "I go bye". Such terms are to be avoided since, unless they are always used, they infringe the warning against different designations for the same call. See LAWS OF DUPLICATE, PROPRIETIES IIIA3.

BYESTAND. A stand (it may be a chair or small side table) where one or more sets of boards rest dur-

ing rounds in which they are not in play. The bye stand is usually placed in such position that the boards will be conveniently available to the table where they will be in play next.

The most common use of a byestand is described under MITCHELL MOVEMENT. A pamphlet (available on request from the ACBL office) instructs the tournament director what procedure to follow to correct the omission or misplacement of the byestand in a Mitchell movement. The use of a byestand in a Mitchell game is necessary only when it is desired to play all the boards. (See EIGHT TABLES; TWELVE TABLES.) If one or more sets of boards are not to be played, the SKIP MOVEMENT eliminates the need for the byestand.

Byestands also are common in all HOWELL and THREE-QUARTER movements as well as some team movements.

BYLAWS OF THE ACBL. The ACBL Bylaws govern principally such matters as the elections, meetings, and powers of the BOARD OF DIRECTORS, BOARD OF GOVERNORS, and officers. With respect to membership in the ACBL, the Bylaws provide as follows:

A. Any person of good moral character is eligible to membership in the American Contract Bridge League (hereinafter called ACBL). No person shall be denied membership because of race, color, or creed. Upon application, favorably acted upon by a Unit with jurisdiction, such applicant shall become and remain a member unless:

(1) He has failed to pay his dues in accordance with regulations established by the Board of Directors.

(2) He is suspended or expelled in accordance with paragraph "E" hereof.

B. A member may belong only to the Unit within whose jurisdiction he resides, unless there are District Regulations creating exceptions.

C. Each Unit may determine the qualifications for membership, but such qualifications for membership shall not contravene any provision of these Bylaws or the Certificate of Incorporation.

D. Honorary members may be elected by the Board of Directors. They shall be exempt from payment of dues and shall be honorary members for life.

E. A member of the ACBL may be censured, suspended, expelled, or otherwise disciplined in accordance with regulations established by the Board of Directors.

F. Life membership may be awarded to members who meet such qualifications and requirements as the Board of Directors may establish. Life members shall be subject to the same disciplinary regulations and procedures as other members. They shall not be required to pay dues but may be required, in order to maintain an active status and receive services from the ACBL, to pay such annual service charges as the Board of Directors may impose from time to time. These service charges shall be less than the annual dues and they may be imposed with such exceptions as the Board of Directors shall determine.

BYZANTINE BLACKWOOD. A complex modern variation of the 4 NT ace-asking convention, devised by J. C. H. MARX of Great Britain, in which the responses are given in the style of ROMAN BLACKWOOD and may be based on a *key suit* king instead of one of the aces normally shown. Key suits include the trump suit, any genuine side suit that has been bid and supported, and any suit bid by a player whose partner's first bid was in notrump. Byzantine is not used when there are more than two key suits. If there is only one key suit, a king of a *half-key* suit, i.e., a genuine suit that has been bid but not supported, may be shown.

When there is only one key suit the Byzantine responses to 4 NT are:

5 ♣   No ace, or three aces, or two aces plus the key suit king

5 ♦   One ace, or four aces, or three aces plus the key suit king

5 ♡   Two aces, or the ace, king and queen of the key suit, or the ace-king of the key suit plus the king of the half-key suit

5 ♠   Two aces plus the king and queen of the key suit, or three aces plus the king of the half-key suit

5 NT   Three aces plus the king and queen of the key suit, or all the aces plus the king of the key suit

When there are two key suits, half-key kings are not shown and the higher Byzantine responses are expanded as follows:

5 ♡   Two aces or the ace, king and queen of a key suit, or one ace and both key suit kings

5 ♠   Two aces plus the king and queen of a key suit, or two aces and both key suit kings, or one ace plus the king of one key suit and the king and queen of the other key suit

5 NT   Three aces plus the king and queen of a key suit, or three aces and both key suit kings, or all the aces plus one key suit king, or two aces plus the king of one key suit and the king and queen of the other, or one ace and the kings and queens of both key suits.

See also CULBERTSON 4-5 NT, KEY CARD BLACKWOOD, ROMAN BLACKWOOD.

C

CACBF. See CENTRAL AMERICAN AND CARIBBEAN BRIDGE FEDERATION.

CBA. CONTRACT BRIDGE ASSOCIATION.

CBAI. See CONTRACT BRIDGE ASSOCIATION OF IRELAND.

CBL. CONTRACT BRIDGE LEAGUE.

CBPU. See CONCERNED BRIDGE PLAYERS UNION.

CAB. A British system of bidding which incorporates some of the features of the STANDARD AMERICAN style:

(1) Strong notrump opening bids, with GLADIATOR responses. (But responses of 2 ♦, 2 ♡ and 2 ♠ are constructive and nonforcing.)

(2) Jump raises and 2 NT responses are forcing except in competition.

(3) Suit opening bids are unprepared. 1 ♠ is bid with:

     ♠ A K 10 6
     ♡ A 5 3
     ♦ 5 2
     ♣ Q 9 7 2

After a response at the level of two (10 points or more), the opener can rebid 2 NT with a minimum hand.

(4) A conventional 2♣, with ACE-SHOWING RESPONSES. A subsequent 4 NT bid asks for kings on the BLACKWOOD principle.

(5) CUEBIDS TO SHOW CONTROLS are used extensively, and in some situations are compulsory.

(6) ACOL TWO-BIDS: a suit response at the two-level may consist of no more than a fair five-card suit.

(7) Opening three-bids in a minor suit invite 3 NT: either the suit is solid, or it is nearly solid and there is an outside entry.

The initials CAB stand for two Clubs, Ace-showing, and Blackwood. The chief contributions to the development of the system were made by LESLIE DODDS.

CADDY. An assistant at a bridge tournament. Duties of the caddy are to *dress* the tables (putting pickup slips, pencils and private scores on the tables); picking up the completed entry blanks; assembling the boards at the conclusion of play, and otherwise making himself useful. In pair events or team events scored by BOARD-A-MATCH, the caddy picks up the score slips at the completion of each round and assists the scorer in checking doubtful slips. In a KNOCKOUT TOURNAMENT or a team game with a SWISS MOVEMENT there are no score slips to be picked up, and the caddy's chief duty during the session is to transport the boards played at one table of each match to the other table of the same match.

Assignment of caddies to work various sessions of a duplicate tournament is the responsibility of the local tournament committee. Generally selection is made from interested high-school boys and girls.

CALCUTTA. A duplicate tournament with a feature making possible a fair-sized financial gain to any player or other participant. After the entries have been made, an auction is held at which players, spectators and others bid for and *buy* the contesting pairs. The total of the moneys bid for the players is put into a POOL which is distributed to the purchasers of the winning entries. In addition, cash prizes or other worthwhile stimuli are provided so that the contestants themselves have a stake in the results. It is usually a proviso that a contestant may purchase from the buyer up to a 50% interest in his own partnership at the original price.

Because of the gambling feature involved in the auctioning of the participants, the AMERICAN CONTRACT BRIDGE LEAGUE does not sanction a Calcutta, and master points are not awarded. See GAMBLING AT BRIDGE.

CALIFORNIA CUEBID. See WESTERN CUEBIDS; CUEBIDS IN OPPONENT'S SUIT.

CALIFORNIA SCORING. A method of computing the East–West pairs' matchpoint score by assigning them the same score as their North–South opponents, rather than the reciprocal. Using this method the East–West pair with the lowest score is then the winner. Alternatively, each East–West score may be subtracted from the maximum possible matchpoint total to produce the same score that would have been achieved using regular matchpoint scoring methods. California Scoring derived its name from its popularity primarily in California and other Western clubs. See TRAVELING SCORE SLIP.

CALL. Any bid, double, redouble or pass. See LAWS OF CONTRACT BRIDGE.

CALL AFTER THE AUCTION IS CLOSED. See LAWS (Law 39).

CALL IN ROTATION AFTER AN ILLEGAL CALL. See LAWS (Law 34).

CALL OUT OF TURN. See LAWS (Laws 28–35).

CALLING A CARD OR A SUIT. The privilege of compelling an opponent to lead or play a certain card or a certain suit, to play his highest or lowest, or to win or lose a trick. See LAWS (Laws 26, 27c, 30b, 31b, 32a, 36a, 37, 38, 39b, 50, 52, 56b, 57, 73). See LAWS OF DUPLICATE (Laws 46, 51).

CAMROSE TROPHY. Competed for annually by England, Scotland, Northern Ireland, Wales, and formerly Eire, under the auspices of the BRITISH BRIDGE LEAGUE. It was presented by Lord Camrose in 1936, and won on every occasion by England until Scotland succeeded in 1964.

CANADIAN-AMERICAN REGIONAL CHAMPIONSHIPS. A four-day event held annually during the spring. Beginning in 1951, the tournament has usually been staged in Montreal, Ottawa, Quebec or upstate New York. It was the successor of a historic tournament which began in the Thirties. For past results, see Appendix II.

CANADIAN–ATLANTIC REGIONAL CHAMPIONSHIPS. A six-day event held annually at the start of summer. Beginning in 1968, the tournament has been staged in Halifax in Nova Scotia as well as in Moncton, Saint John and Fredericton in New Brunswick. For past results, see Appendix II.

CANADIAN BRIDGE FEDERATION. The official National Contract Bridge Organization, as recognized by the WORLD BRIDGE FEDERATION, for the 24 Canadian Units of the ACBL. Founded in 1967 for the purpose of promoting a national identity and union of Canadian bridge players, it designates Canada's representatives to WBF Olympiad events, publishes a magazine, *The Canadian Bridge Digest,* and promotes the ACBL Canadian Charitable Fund, whose trustees are executive members of the Federation. Canadian players are eligible to compete for places on the North American team for the BERMUDA BOWL. ERIC MURRAY achieved this honor in 1962, 1966, 1967, and 1974; SAMMY KEHELA in 1966, 1967, and 1974.

Officers, 1982:

President: Mrs. Helen Shields

Secretary: Dr. F.A. Baragar, 6608 84th Street, Edmonton, Alberta, T6E 2W9 Canada

CANADIAN NATIONAL REGIONAL CHAMPIONSHIPS. A six-day event held annually in Toronto since 1951. For past results, see Appendix II.

CANADIAN NATIONAL TEAMS. In 1980 the GRAND NATIONAL TEAMS that involved Canadian players was separated to become the Canadian National Teams championships. This premier event on the country's bridge calendar begins in the fall on a grass-roots basis at clubs throughout the Dominion. In 1980, 13 teams qualified for a national round-robin playoff in Toronto with the four top teams qualifying for the semifinal and final knockouts. The winners represented Canada in the World Team Olympiad in 1980 and participated in Memphis Trials to select ACBL representative for 1981 Bermuda Bowl.

In 1981 the playoff in Ottawa was the culmination of a multi-stage elimination process reducing the field to 13 qualifiers from the six Canadian Bridge Federation zones plus defenders from the previous year who were awarded a bye into the playoff. The winners represented Canada in the Rosenblum Cup Teams in Biarritz in 1982.

In 1982 a grass-roots team qualified handily for the Zone final and played steadily to win the Zonals, besting enroute the CNT champions of the two previous years. They were one of four teams to survive the 14-team round-robin, they won a 64-board semifinal match and eventually won the 72-deal final by exactly 1 IMP. The winners qualified for the Minneapolis Trials held in November 1982 to select Zone 2 representatives for the 1983 Bermuda Bowl.

The following were the Canadian National Teams in the first three years of the competition: (*italics, augmented*)

1980	1981	1982
Allan Graves	Allan Graves	Gordon Crispin
Sammy Kehela	Sammy Kehela	Nick Gartaganis
Eric Kokish	Eric Kokish	Zygmunt Marcinski
George Mittelman	George Mittelman	Voyteck Pomykalski
Eric Murray	Eric Murray	*Keith Balcombe*
Peter Nagy	Peter Nagy	*Ross Taylor*
Gerald Charney (npc)	Doug Andrews (npc)	George Retek (npc)
		Eric Kokish, coach

CANAPÉ. A bidding method in which the long suit

is usually bid on the second round. This was developed by PIERRE ALBARRAN in France, where it has had a considerable following. By contrast, standard methods are described in France as *la longue d'abord* (long suit first). Canapé has influenced Italian bidding theory, and is incorporated in both the BLUE TEAM and ROMAN systems.

Albarran's definition of canapé was: "With a two-suited hand of more than minimum strength, the higher-ranking suit must be bid on the first round if it has four cards, and on the second round if it has more than four cards."

Four-card major suits are usually bid ahead of any minor suit; five-card major suits are bid on the first round if the hand is a minimum. Normal reverse sequences are inverted (*inversés*):

♠ A Q 10 x x
♡ K Q x x
◊ K x
♣ x x

Using canapé, the opening bid is 1 ♡, and 2 ♠ is bid on the next round. A heart preference is highly improbable, so the canapé player can stay safely at the level of two.

Canapé is admittedly in difficulty with certain minimum hands, such as those with four spades and five clubs. 1 ♠ followed by 3 ♣ would exaggerate the strength, and 1 ♣ followed by 1 ♠ would imply a five-card spade suit.

A modified version called "canapé tendency" (*tendance canapé*) has been used successfully in international competition by PIERRE JAÏS and ROGER TRÉZEL. They bid minimum hands in normal fashion, but adopt the canapé principle for hands of maximum strength and some hands of intermediate strength.

CANARY CLUB. An artificial bidding system developed in 1964 by JOHN LOWENTHAL and PAUL HEITNER. The name of the system is derived from its chief features — CANAPÉ, RELAY bids, and 1 ♣ FORCING.

1 ♣ opening shows 17 points or more, or a strong distributional hand. Responses tend to follow the BLUE TEAM control-showing pattern with certain exceptions, and after the initial response the auction tends to develop naturally with a variety of asking bids available once the trump suit is agreed.

1 ◊, 1 ♡, and 1 ♠ openings are natural according to the canapé principle, but do not guarantee any defensive strength. Major-suit raises or jump raises are limited bids. 2 ♡ over 1 ♠ is nonforcing, and jump shifts are preemptive with the exception of 3 ♡ over 1 ♠.

1 NT opening shows a balanced hand with 12–16 points.

2 ♣ opening is natural, at least a six-card club suit, no four-card major, with 11–16 points.

2 ◊ opening is equivalent to a ROMAN 2 ♣ bid. A response of 3 NT shows a solid suit, and jumps in a suit are specialized asking bids.

2 ♡ and 2 ♠ openings are similar to the ROMAN system; clubs cannot be longer than the major. If responder jumps in a suit, it is an asking bid with the major the agreed trump suit.

CANNIBAL SQUEEZE. See SUICIDE SQUEEZE.

CAPPELLETTI CUEBIDS. Devised by A. MICHAEL CAPPELLETTI of Alexandria VA. When the opponents have bid two suits, the lower-level cuebid shows both unbid suits with greater length in the lower-ranking suit. The higher-level cuebid shows both unbid suits with greater length in the higher-ranking suit.

CAPPELLETTI OVER NOTRUMP. Devised by A. MICHAEL CAPPELLETTI of Alexandria VA. Over opponents' opening 1 NT in either first or balancing seat,

2 of a major shows two-suiter with that major plus a minor.

2 ◊ shows both majors.

2 ♣ shows any one-suited hand (partner usually responds 2 ◊).

CAPTAIN. Teams representing major bridge countries in international play normally have a nonplaying captain (although Great Britain won three successive European Championships 1948–50 with MAURICE HARRISON-GRAY as playing captain). The captain's chief function is to decide who shall play at each stage in the contest, taking into account such factors as the ability and stamina of the players at his command, the caliber of the opposition, the closed and open room, and VUGRAPH. In addition, the captain represents the team in discussions relating to the conditions of play, and in protests and appeals. He also acts as the team's spokesman on all social occasions.

The importance of the captain's role has been recognized in recent years, and it is usual for a World Championship contestant to appoint an experienced player whose decisions will be respected and accepted by the players in his charge. At one time the president of the ACBL was automatically designated nonplaying captain of its international team, but this practice was discontinued after 1961. With the inception of the playoff method of selection from the winners of the four major team championships, each team was required to select a nonplaying captain from a panel of eligible captains selected by the ACBL BOARD OF DIRECTORS, and the captain of the winning team was virtually an automatic selection for the World Championship, although subject to Board confirmation.

CARLO ALBERTO PERROUX, of Italy, who made a considerable contribution to the remarkable series of victories compiled by the BLUE TEAM, earned a reputation as one of the most powerful and successful nonplaying captains in the history of bridge.

CAPTAINCY. The control of the auction assumed by one partner in certain situations. For example, in BLACKWOOD auctions the 4 NT bidder is the captain, and his partner simply follows instructions in making the agreed responses. But captaincy may shift from one partner to the other in a single auction. For example, if the Blackwood bidder continues with 5 NT, indicating his side's possession of all the aces, in some circumstances the responder may take responsibility for a grand slam contract. In many auctions there is no captain and both players simply use their judgment in arriving at what they hope will be the best contract.

The term also applies to the player in charge of the affairs of a team. The captain can be either a player or a non-player. The captain makes the key decisions for his team — who will sit out, who will play with whom, what table which players will sit at, whether to appeal a director's decision, etc.

CARANSA TOURNAMENT. Founded in 1971 by MAURITS CARANSA, this International Swiss Teams tournament is held annually at the Amsterdam Hilton. The event is open to all Dutch players and to international star teams sponsored by commercial firms.

CARD, DAMAGED OR MARKED. See DAMAGED CARD.

CARD COMMITTEE. In private clubs it is customary that a committee of two or more members is charged with the responsibility of order and decorum in the club's card room. Referred to this committee are disputes which arise in the play that cannot be settled by reference to the rules of the game in question. Also under the jurisdiction of this committee come such questions as what games will be permitted, rules of procedure for forming tables, maximum stakes and unpaid wagers. With respect to contract bridge tournaments, see COMMITTEE.

CARD FEE. See ENTRIES.

CARD PLAYED. See PLAYED CARD.

CARD READING. Drawing correct inferences about the nature of the opponent's holdings and distribution from information disclosed by the fall of the cards.

♠ A 8
♡ K Q J 7 6
◇ J 8 7
♣ 6 5 3

♠ Q J 10 4 3 2
♡ A 5 3
◇ A K
♣ 10 7

South plays in 4♠ after East has opened the bidding with 1♣. West leads the ♣2 and East wins with the ace, and shifts to the ♡9. A seemingly secure contract is now in some jeopardy. East clearly has a singleton heart, and very likely three trumps including the king. Obviously his play is to win the second trump lead and put partner in with a club honor for a heart ruff. Declarer can foil this defense by playing East for the ◇Q (not unlikely on the bidding). Winning the heart in dummy, he plays off the ◇A-K before crossing to the ♠A. The ◇J is led from dummy, East covering and South discarding his last club, thus effectively severing communication between the defenders. The complete deal:

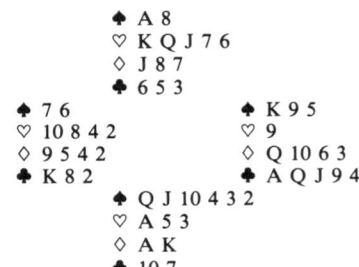

Combining accurate card-reading with counting often provides valuable clues for the defense. Careful examination of the evidence provided East with the opportunity to defeat the contract on this hand:

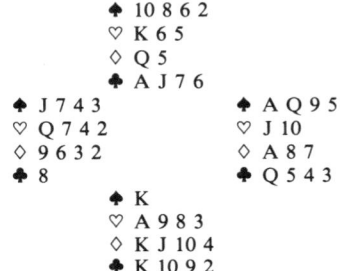

The bidding has been:

SOUTH	NORTH
1♣	1♠
1 NT	2 NT
3 NT	

West leads the ♡2, and East's 10 loses to declarer's ace. A club is led to dummy's ace, and the jack run, West discarding the ◇2. The ◇Q is taken by East, and he reviews the situation.

He knows that South has four club tricks, and at least two in hearts. What about the diamonds? West's diamond discard on the second club is revealing: he is unlikely to have parted with one from 10-x-x-x or J-x-x-x. Could West have started with five diamonds? Not very likely, for in that case he might have led one. South can therefore be assumed to have three diamond tricks, enough for his contract, should he regain the lead. The only hope for the defense seems to lie in spades. If East's estimate of the situation is correct, then West had started with a 4-4-4-1 distribution, marking declarer with a singleton spade — very likely the king, considering his bidding.

Declarer's play of the club suit seems to bear this out; having a two-way finesse, he chose to take it into the hand that was less likely to shift to spades, if it lost. On this reasoning East lays down the ♠A, dropping declarer's king, and continues with a small card to his partner's jack. A third round of spades permits East to score the Q-9 to defeat the contract. See also COUNTING THE HAND and INFERENCE.

For full discussions of card reading, see *Card Reading* by ERIC JANNERSTEN, *The Art of Card Reading at Bridge* by FRED KARPIN, and *How To*

Read Your Opponent's Cards by MIKE LAWRENCE.
(BIBLIOGRAPHY, D.)

Sammy Kehela

CARD SENSE. A special aptitude for playing card games, specifically (in this context) bridge.

Until psychological research and Army selection procedures satisfactorily demonstrated the existence of special aptitudes, there was considerable controversy about whether card sense existed.

Although he changed his mind later, ELY CULBERTSON was originally among the skeptics, commenting as follows: "One hears a good deal about that elusive something called 'card sense.' It is spoken of as though it were some mysterious, deeply inborn faculty which cannot be taught. Lack of 'card sense' is always said to be the great bugaboo blocking the prospective bridge player's path to improvement. As a matter of fact, 'card sense' — whatever those who use the term mean — is a certain facility at cards shown by some players and entirely lacking in others."

Among good bridge players, it is virtually impossible to distinguish between what is the result of card sense and what is the result of experience. Card sense is more easily distinguishable among beginners, when it appears to be a compound of various elements: intelligence, interest and youth.

There is probably a high correlation between ability to learn the elements of bridge and mathematical aptitude, and a rather lower correlation with intelligence quotient. See also INTUITION.

CARD-SHOWING DOUBLE. A double that does not promise any particular distribution but instead shows general high card strength. The amount of strength promised by a double that shows *cards* obviously varies according to the circumstances in which the double is made. For example, the DOUBLE OF 2♣ RESPONSE to a WEAK NOTRUMP would show strength equivalent to that of a double of a 1 NT opening; the double of interference with a PRECISION CLUB opening bid, however, promises about 5-8 points.

CARDS. Used in a colloquial sense, usually in describing the meaning of certain doubles, to mean high card strength. See CARD-SHOWING DOUBLE.

CARDS, NEUTRAL AND POSITIVE. The only information disclosed by the play of a neutral card is the obvious point that the player has that particular card. The essence of this is that the player is not void of the suit, and even this knowledge will generally have little or no effect on problems of probability.

A card may be said to have positive value when: (1) the holder was deemed certain to have played it, or; (2) it indicates the position of one or more other specified cards, or suggests their probable location, or; (3) it indicates the distribution of all the outstanding cards of a suit.

```
          NORTH
          ♠ 5 4 3
          ♡ A K 2
          ◇ A J 8 6 5
          ♣ K 3
```

```
          SOUTH
          ♠ A J 2
          ♡ Q 8 4 3
          ◇ K 10 7
          ♣ A J 5
```

South plays in notrump, and West leads the ♣K. South assumes that West holds the ♣K-Q-10. If he also assumes that West was certain to make this lead, there will be odds of 13 to 10 that East has the ◇Q:

(a) If East follows with a low spade, these odds are only very slightly altered. East's card is neutral, and indicates only that West does not have seven spades. The elimination of all distributions where West holds seven spades removes more cases favorable to East's holding the ◇Q than unfavorable cases. The odds are a very little less than 13 to 10, and the difference may be disregarded.

(b) If East plays a heart at trick one, there will be positive significance in the fact that he has played a nonspade, though the card itself is neutral. The odds are 13 to 6 that East holds the ◇Q. We know now that East is not void of hearts, but we cannot say that he was certain to play a heart whatever cards he holds.

(c) If East discards a club at trick one, the odds are again 13 to 6 that he has the ◇Q.

CARDS OF A SUIT IN OPPONENT'S HAND. See SUIT, NUMBER OF CARDS IN.

CARIBBEAN CHAMPIONSHIPS. Organized in 1964 as an informal international championship for countries in the Caribbean area. The first Caribbean Championshp was held in Curaçao, Netherlands Antilles, and the two subsequent tournaments were staged in Barranquilla, Colombia, and Caracas, Venezuela, respectively. Venezuela won the first two events and Colombia won the championship in 1968. There were four participating nations in the 1968 event: Colombia, Ecuador, Netherlands Antilles and Venezuela. See CENTRAL AMERICAN-CARIBBEAN CHAMPIONSHIPS.

CARRYOVER SCORES. Under the regulations of the AMERICAN CONTRACT BRIDGE LEAGUE, certain events in tournaments of sectional or higher rating are conducted in more than one session. These events may or may not involve elimination of some of the contestants from the main event (see CONSOLATION EVENT).

If no players are eliminated from the event, their matchpoint score is carried over from one session to the succeeding session, and the event decided upon the total score in all sessions. Regulations require that if a later session of a playthrough multi-session event has a different top score on a board, provision is made for adjusting to the top score in the first session. See FACTORING.

When the original starting field is reduced for later sessions, regulations provide that scores in the early (qualifying) round or rounds be carried over into the final session on the basis of a formula.

$$\text{carryover} = \frac{M\ Q^2 a\ B}{E\ S}$$

where M represents the number of match points in the qualifying round or rounds which a contestant scores, Q^2 is the square of the number of pairs in the final session, a is the average on a board in the finals, B the number of boards in the qualifying round or rounds, E the number of pairs entered in the event, and S is the sum of all qualifying scores of pairs eligible for the finals.

If there is one qualifying round and one final, the total spread from top to bottom score is reduced to twice the top score on a board in the finals; if there are two qualifying rounds and one final, the total is reduced to three boards; and for two qualifying rounds and two final rounds, four boards. The formula may give a smaller spread.

The carryover method also is used in some ACBL team events. In board-a-match events at North American Championships, such as the Reisinger Teams and the Men's Board-a-Match Teams, a carryover formula along lines similar to the ones outlined above is applied. In the North American Swiss Teams event, different carryover formulas are applied from qualifying to semifinal and from semifinal to final. Half of any score greater than 5 is carried over from qualifying to semifinal. However, Victory Points are used in the final. Each finalist is given a carryover equivalent to 1 Victory Point for each full quarter over 5 a team scores in the semifinal.

At the world level, a special carryover formula was applied in BERMUDA BOWL competition in 1977, 1979 and 1981. Half the IMP difference from the round-robin was carried over to the final or semifinal if the team that finished higher in the round-robin had the plus; only one-third of the IMP difference was carried over if the team that finished lower in the round-robin had the plus. The Bermuda Bowl plan adopted for championships from 1983 on will not require a carryover plan.

Carryover also is applied from the qualifying to the semifinal and from the semifinal to the final of the World Open Pairs and from the qualifying to the final of the World Women's Pairs. A special carryover formula also is used in the Swiss Teams portion of the ROSENBLUM TEAMS. Another special carryover plan was used in the semifinals of the 1980 World Team Olympiad.

CASH. To play a winning card and win the trick.

CASH IN (also CASH OUT). To take a series of tricks by playing winning cards one after another. The term is usually applied to a situation where a player realizes that he is on lead for what is probably going to be the last time during that particular hand, and while in control, he will now take his tricks. The term can be applied to a declarer as well as defenders.

CAVALIER. A fourth COAT CARD, which is still maintained in some playing cards as an alternative for the JACK. See PACK.

CAVENDISH CLUB (New York City). Founded in 1925 by WILBER C. WHITEHEAD, in association with GRATZ M. SCOTT, and EDWIN A. WETZLAR, the Club was housed for the first eight years at the Mayfair House, and then moved to the Ambassador Hotel. From 1950–65 it was at the Ritz Tower Hotel. From 1965 to 1974 it occupied premises on Central Park South. In 1974 it moved to the Carlton House.

Since 1941 the Cavendish Club has been a nonprofit membership corporation, managed by the Club secretary, B. JAY BECKER 1941 to 1947, Rudolf Muhsam from 1947 to 1973 and subsequently THOMAS M. SMITH Director of Activities since 1979. The presidents have been GRATZ M. SCOTT 1925–35, FRANK CROWNINSHIELD 1935–47, NATE SPINGOLD 1948–58, SAMUEL STAYMAN 1958–62, HOWARD SCHENKEN 1963–64, HAROLD OGUST 1965–67, Leonard Hess 1968–70, EDWARD LOEWENTHAL 1971–73, Roy V. Titus 1976, Archie Brauer 1976–79, Yehnda Koppel 1979–80, Roy V. Titus 1980–81, SAM M. STAYMAN 1981–82. Members have included very many players of international reputation: B. JAY BECKER, JOHN R. CRAWFORD, BILLY EISENBERG, PHILIP FELDESMAN, MYRON FIELD, HARRY FISHBEIN, RICHARD L. FREY, SAM FRY, JR., CHARLES H. GOREN, WILLIAM P. GRIEVE, EDWARD HYMES, JR., OSWALD JACOBY, RICHARD KAHN, EDGAR KAPLAN, NORMAN KAY, EDITH KEMP, BORIS KOYTCHOU, PETER A. LEVENTRITT, THEODORE A. LIGHTNER, ADAM MEREDITH, ALBERT H. MOREHEAD, ALPHONSE MOYSE, JR., HAROLD OGUST, GEORGE RAPÉE, ALVIN ROTH, IRA S. RUBIN, ALFRED SHEINWOLD, HELEN SOBEL SMITH, CHARLES SOLOMON, Sylvia Stearns, TOBIAS STONE, ALAN TRUSCOTT, DOROTHY HAYDEN TRUSCOTT, HAROLD S. VANDERBILT, WALDEMAR K. VON ZEDTWITZ. Honorary members include GENERAL ALFRED GRUENTHER, BARON ROBERT DE NEXON, GEORGE S. KAUFMAN, Rose Loewenthal, Waldemar K. Von Zedtwitz.

CAVENDISH TROPHY. Awarded for the NAC Open Pair Championship; donated by the Cavendish Club of New York in 1928; contested at the Fall NAC, under which heading past results are listed. Since 1963 awarded to the winners of the BLUE RIBBON PAIRS CHAMPIONSHIP.

CELEBRITIES. Many persons who are outstanding in their own spheres of activity also find much enjoyment playing bridge. Heads of state whose bridge-playing activities have received considerable publicity include U. S. President DWIGHT D. EISENHOWER and Chinese Premier DENG XIAOPING. Many top-flight performers of stage, screen and television have been and are avid players. OMAR SHARIF has played in top-level competition and is acknowledged world-wide as an accomplished competitor. Telly Savalas, TV's Kojak who is a look-alike of ACBL tournament director BILL SCHODER, enjoys a strong rubber or two, as do Ronnie Cox, Dick Yarmy, Cara Williams, Don Addams, Robert Quarry and Ray Walker. George Burns finds the game exciting, and playwright GEORGE S. KAUFMAN has even contributed magazine articles about the game. The Marx Brothers also were bridge players. Movie and TV cameraman George Clemmens met his wife while they were playing in a bridge game on the movie lot.

The sports world has many bridge enthusiasts — it

is one of the favorite games when clubs are making long trips. The list includes the likes of Tom Seaver, Jim Bunning, Tim McCarver, Richie Ashburn, Pinky Higgins, Norm Cash and Dizzy Dean. Life Master Pauline Betz Addie, the former tennis great, also enjoys a good game of duplicate, and chess expert Bent Larsen probably would be a bridge expert if bridge was his game instead of chess.

Folks in the world of music also find relaxation playing bridge. Sonya LaUnica, a world-famous singer, once said "It's easier to sing than to bid these computer hands!" Concert pianist Leonard Pennario has achieved Life Master rating even though he constantly hears great pieces of music while trying to concentrate on a hand. Robert Helps also has turned to bridge for relaxation. IGNACE PADEREWSKI and opera conductor WALTER HERBERT had great appreciation for the intricacies of bridge.

Carl Albert, former speaker of the House of Representatives, and Justice John Stevens of the U. S. Supreme Court find pleasure in a good bridge game. Federal Judge CARL RUBIN is a former president of the American Contract Bridge League, and Federal Judge AMALYA KEARSE not only is a bridge expert — she also was editor of the Third Edition of the *Bridge Encyclopedia* and is a bridge author. Bridge enthusiast Abe Drasin is mayor of Grand Rapids MI.

In the world of literature, SOMERSET MAUGHAM not only played the game — he managed to inject bridge situations into some of his works, as did IAN FLEMING, creator of James Bond, AGATHA CHRISTIE and CHARLES DICKENS. Author Terry Quinn is much interested in the game, and one of his works, *The Great Bridge Conspiracy*, is entirely about bridge. Novelist DON VON ELSNER is the well-known creator of the bridge character, Jake Winkman.

Every year there is a bridge match in Great Britain between members of the House of Lords and the House of Commons.

This should in no way be construed to be a complete list of celebrities interested in bridge — it is only the tip of the iceberg. However, it gives an indication of how bridge is part of the life of folks in all professions and vocations.

CENTRAL AMERICAN AND CARIBBEAN BRIDGE FEDERATION (Federación Centroamericana y Del Caribe De Bridge).

Founded in 1971, the federation received full recognition in 1976 from the WORLD BRIDGE FEDERATION as a zonal conference (Zone 5). In 1982 there were 14 participating nations. Annual tournaments are held. See CENTRAL AMERICAN–CARIBBEAN CHAMPIONSHIPS.

Officers, 1982:
President: David A. Berah
Secretary: John Maduro, c/o Punte Chame Turistica S.A., Apartado 10520 Panama 4, Republic of Panama

CENTRAL AMERICAN–CARIBBEAN CHAMPIONSHIPS.

Formerly CARIBBEAN CHAMPIONSHIPS. Held annually for the 14 member nations of the CENTRAL AMERICAN AND CARIBBEAN BRIDGE FEDERATION. The winners of the National Team event were:

1971	Jamaica	1977	Venezuela
1972	Jamaica	1978	Results not available
1973	Venezuela	1979	Mexico
1974	Jamaica	1980	Colombia
1975	Colombia	1981	Results not available
1976	Panama	1982	Results not available

CENTRAL STATES REGIONAL CHAMPIONSHIPS.

Held annually in Chicago, originally a 10–day tournament which was first staged in 1935. The addition of a Knockout Team Championship in 1962 brought the total of events to nine, reduced to eight in 1965 when the Life and Senior Master Teams was discontinued. In 1971 this tournament was split into two Regionals, Central States Part I and Central States Part II. For past results, see Appendix II.

CHAIRMAN.

The chief elected official of the AMERICAN CONTRACT BRIDGE LEAGUE prior to the reorganization in 1949. Subsequently the title was revived, in the form of Chairman of the BOARD OF DIRECTORS. Since 1963 the title has generally been accorded to the immediate Past-President of the ACBL.

Past holders of the title include:

1938–42	*Nate Spingold	1967	*Eilif B. Andersen
1943–45	*Albert H. Morehead	1968	John W. Norwood, Jr.
1946–47	*Brig. Gen. Robert J. Gill	1969	Joseph J. Stedem
1948–49	Waldemar von Zedtwitz	1970	Ed Theus
1950–52	*Curt Reisinger	1971	*William A. Baldwin
1953	*Peter Leventritt	1972	Hon. Carl B. Rubin
1954	*Julius Rosenblum	1973	Percy X. Bean
1955	*Charles Solomon	1974	Jerome R. Silverman
1956	*J. G. Ripstra	1975	Ruth McConnell
1957	*Charles J. Solomon	1976	Lewis L. Mathe
1958	Winslow H. Randall	1977	*Donald A. Oakie
1959	*Frank T. Westcott	1978	Louis S. Gurvich
1960–61	*Max Manchester	1979	Walter O'Loughlin
1962	*Jerry Lewis	1980	Leo J. Spivack
1963	*James P. Ferguson	1981	*Ira G. Corn, Jr.
1964	*Jerry Lewis	1982	James Zimmerman
1965	Leo J. Seewald	1983	Sydney A. Levey, Jr.
1966	Robin B. Mac Nab		

*Deceased

CHALLENGE.

A declaration proposed by SIDNEY LENZ in 1929 to replace the TAKEOUT DOUBLE. It was used experimentally in one New York club, but received little support.

In the Fifties the term was revived in a different sense, as an attempt to check artificial bidding. When any one player has made two bids, a positive bid can be *challenged*. The bidding then ends, and the contract reached is played redoubled. This plan, originated by Col. Cyril Rocke, also received little support.

CHALLENGE TROPHY.

The CITY OF ASBURY PARK TROPHY, originally awarded for a special challenge TEAM-OF-FOUR EVENT.

CHAMPIONSHIP TOURNAMENTS.

The principal function of the ACBL and other governing bodies is to provide interesting bridge competition for its members, and to record accurately the achievements made by each member in competitive play. To this end the ACBL sponsors and conducts a large number of tournaments at which MASTER POINTS are awarded. They are divided into several classes depending on the importance of the event, the territory represented, the movement employed, the conditions of sponsorship, and the total of entries. Classification of each event is published in advance, and master points are awarded according to printed schedules.

(1) *North American Championships.* These North American championship events are conducted by the ACBL itself. Each major event is held only once a year, split among the three ten-day tournaments, a spring date in March, a summer date late in July or August, and a fall date late in November or December. See NORTH AMERICAN CHAMPIONSHIP. To facilitate entry by players in various parts of the country, it is customary to hold one in the East, one in the Central, and one in the Western part of the country.

(2) *Regional Championships.* ACBL membership is divided into 25 geographical districts, each strictly limited as to territory. These events are conducted by ACBL districts under the supervision of a rated director appointed by the ACBL. At least two Regional tournaments are allocated to each district annually, ranking next in importance to the North American Championships and offering the players of the area an opportunity to earn a substantial number of GOLD and RED POINTS. Thus credit toward Life Master status is given to specified events at each Regional tournament. In addition, at each North American Championships a number of secondary events are conducted which are given regional championship status.

(3) *Sectional Championships.* These events are conducted by ACBL units under the supervision of a rated director appointed by the ACBL. Each unit is expected to conduct at least one Sectional tournament a year, and additional tournaments are allocated on the basis of membership and history of previous sectional tournament scheduling.

(4) *Unit Championships.* Each unit may conduct 16 sessions of Unit Championship-rated events annually. (These events may be run simultaneously throughout the unit. Additionally a unit is allocated one Unitwide event for each 200 members. Two Charity Sectionals and an extended IMP–team event fill out the unit schedule of special events.) If a unit does not hold a Sectional tournament during the calendar year, it may conduct one local tournament not to exceed three consecutive days (six consecutive sessions).

Further information can be obtained in the *ACBL Handbook*, latest copies of which are available from ACBL HEADQUARTERS.

Championship tournaments are staged in countries throughout the world. Many determine national championships, and many decide area or continental championships, such as the South American Championships, the European Championships, etc. Such tournaments also are held at the world level — BERMUDA BOWL, VENICE TROPHY, TEAM OLYMPIAD, etc.

CHANCE. The element of luck or hazard present in almost all card games but materially reduced in potency as a feature in bridge. Chance in bridge is usually concerned with the quality of the cards dealt one in rubber contests, but even this should become

relatively equal to both sides over a long period of time. The number of points held by a player or partnership tends to approach the theoretical expectation over a long period, although the absolute difference may increase. In play situations chance can be a factor, but the expert player will tend to be able to reduce its influence by applying skill and mathematical deliberation to situations where a lesser player would merely play on and attribute any failure to luck of the bad variety.

Even in duplicate bridge, chance can be a considerable factor in the short run. Good contracts fail and bad contracts succeed; hands which represent borderline games and slams are likely to favor one side at the expense of the other. Less obvious, but equally important, is the chance of playing the right opponents at the right moment. With luck you will play against good opponents when they have no control of the bidding and play, and against weaker players when the bidding and play are slightly too difficult for them. See also FORTUNE.

CHANGE OF SUIT. The first mention of a suit not previously bid by any player; used on a wide variety of hands in which exploration is called for. In standard methods, the general rule is that a change of suit by the responder is forcing for one round; a change of suit by the opener is nonforcing. This is subject to many exceptions.

Changes of suit by the responder are nonforcing in the following cases:

(1) If responder passed originally. But a jump shift by a passed hand is a doubtful case. Most authorities treat this bid as forcing for one round, implying a fit with the opener's suit. But some players reserve the right to pass, especially if the jump is from a minor suit to a major.

(2) If the second player doubled or bid 1 NT. (But some play a change of suit over a double as forcing.)

(3) If the opener rebid 1 NT, for example:

WEST	EAST
1 ♣	1 ♠
1 NT	2 ◇

(But in ROTH-STONE this sequence retains its forcing character. See also UNBID MINOR SUIT FORCE.)

(4) In response to 1 NT at the level of two.

(5) A jump shift below the game level.

(6) At the level of three on the second round, for example:

WEST	EAST		WEST	EAST
1 ♠	2 ♡	or	1 ♠	2 NT
3 ♣			3 ♣	

CHANGING A CALL. The act of substituting a call for a call made previously at the same turn. See LAWS (Law 25).

CHANGING PROBABILITIES DURING PLAY. See PROBABILITIES A POSTERIORI and PROBABILITIES A PRIORI.

CHARITY FOUNDATION. See CHARITY PROGRAM OF THE ACBL.

CHARITY GAMES FOR OTHER BENEFICIA-

RIES. See CHARITY PROGRAM OF THE ACBL.

CHARITY PAIRS. A one-session event held at the Summer NAC for the MID-ATLANTIC CUP. The proceeds from this event, as well as the Senior Pairs, held at the same time as the Charity Pairs, and two ACBL-WIDE GAMES for charity, are donated to the ACBL Charity Foundation for distribution to selected beneficiaries. See CHARITY PROGRAM OF THE ACBL.

CHARITY PROGRAM OF THE ACBL. The ACBL devotes a substantial part of its effort and activity to its charity program. Charity funds are turned over to the ACBL Charity Foundation, which is administered by an elected Board of Trustees. Members of the Board of Trustees are unpaid, and include persons who have had experience in administering charity funds. Under approved Bylaws, the Trustees may make grants to any local or national charity deemed worthy.

It is the policy of the Trustees to select, as beneficiaries, national organizations functioning in many areas, and devoting a large part of their funds to medical research from which lasting benefits are expected. The charity program has two purposes. The first, obviously, is to make an important contribution to worthy charities. The second is to foster good public relations for the League, and to provide its units and clubs with a promotional tool by which they can stimulate interest and extend their activities.

The program includes many types of games at the club, unit and National levels.

Every ACBL sanctioned club that meets at least 18 time a year is required to hold at least one game annually, the proceeds of which must be contributed to the ACBL Charity Foundation or the Canadian Charitable Fund. An ACBL club that holds a weekly game is entitled to hold two one-session charity club championships annually, which receive 70% of sectional rating. The first such event each year must benefit one of the League charities and while it is hoped that the club will select the Foundation as the beneficiary of the second game, the club may instead contribute the proceeds to a local charity of its choice, provided that the selected charity is tax exempt according to the Internal Revenue Service. When a local charity is selected, the Charity Tournament Report form must include the name of the charity and the amount contributed. Regardless of the recipient, the proceeds contributed must amount to at least $1.00 per player per session. A club may substitute one or more sessions of Charity club tournaments for one or more sessions of its club tournaments. However, such substitutions earn only club championship rating.

Similar regulations apply to the ACBL units. Each unit may conduct two charity events annually of one or two sessions; each event receives sectional rating. This is in addition to the two annual Continentwide Charity games, which are normally run by the unit and which also are sectionally rated. The amount contributed from a Unit Charity game must amount to at least $1.50 per player per session, while for the Continentwide events a minimum donation of $1.75 per player is required.

Applications for unit charity tournaments must be submitted to the office of the ACBL Charity Department prior to scheduling. The need to apply well in advance and on the appropriate form cannot be emphasized too strongly. The very minimum is 60 days in advance of the requested date, and even more time should be allowed if possible. It frequently happens that the requested date conflicts with some other activity in the vicinity and cannot be used for the charity game. Sufficient time is then necessary for selection of a new date. Clubs, however, do not have to make advance application for their charity tournaments.

A number of sectional and regional tournaments have added a charity game to the regular schedule of events. This practice is encouraged, provided the charity game is *added* to the regular events, and not *substituted* for one of them. In such a case, the charity game receives sectional rating, and is usually scheduled on the evening before the start of the tournament proper.

Experience has proved that attendance at a charity game can be greatly increased, even doubled or more, by advance planning and thorough promotion. This, of course, reacts to the advantage of the beneficiary, but it also has important benefits for the sponsoring organization.

A big problem for any bridge group is to make new contacts, to interest new people, and the charity game is the best opportunity to do it. A good charity campaign will make contacts with scores of potential new members, people who like bridge but haven't yet taken up duplicate. Every duplicate player knows the fascination of the game, and if a new person can be induced to play it even once, he is likely to become a regular player and a club member.

The Charity Program has very great advantages in attracting favorable attention to the ACBL, providing additional master points for its members, and enabling its local groups to expand their activities and membership. However, these benefits can be realized only if fully exploited at the local level. They accrue directly to the members, clubs and units, but only to the extent that they take advantage of the opportunities. See ACBL-WIDE GAMES.

The earliest charity games of the ABL and ACBL began in 1934 on the initiative of WILLIAM McKENNEY, and these efforts were continued in subsequent years, especially in New York City. The chief beneficiaries were various children's organizations, including the Children's Cancer Fund, Inc., and the WAR ORPHANS SCHOLARSHIP, INC.

From 1951 to 1964 one or two charities were nominated annually as the beneficiaries of the ACBL's national charity program:

1951–52	Damon Runyon Memorial Fund	$ 25,713.21
1952–53	American Heart Association	38,846.64
1953–54	March of Dimes	53,345.68
1954–55	American Cancer Society	60,469.48
1955–56	National Society for Crippled Children	76,431.71
1956–57	American Heart Association	85,831.76
1957–58	American Cancer Society	104,809.61
1958–59	Arthritis and Rheumatism Foundation	136,814.67
1959–60	Red Cross Disaster Fund	163,540.01
1960–61	National Association for Mental Health	173,395.82
1961–62	Family Service Association of American National Kidney Disease Foundation	157,632.76
1962–63	National Multiple Sclerosis Society, Institute of Logopedics	229,541.46
1963–64	American Cancer Society, United	

Cerebral Palsy Association	221,493.00

The desire to aid less well-known but thoroughly worthwhile causes with smaller contributions, rather than to make one or two very large contributions, to a national group each year, led the Board of Directors of the ACBL to establish its own Charity Foundation on July 1, 1964. From 1964 to 1981, the Foundation approved grants totaling more than $2.8 million to the following organizations:

Albany Medical College	$ 10,000.00
Allergy Foundation of America	48,000.00
American Cancer Society	323,600.00
American Diabetes Association	255,500.00
Arthritis Foundation	406,500.00
Child Welfare League of America	40,000.00
Family Service	7,500.00
Foundation for Advancement of Inmate Rehabilitation and Recreation	5,000.00
Homemaker Services	7,500.00
Howe Laboratory of Ophthalmology	56,000.00
Leader Dogs for the Blind	10,000.00
Le Bonheur Children's Medical Center	8,835.00
Muscular Dystrophy Association of America	25,000.00
Myasthenia Gravis Foundation	12,500.00
National Association for Mental Health	273,000.00
National Association for Retarded Children	30,000.00
National Cystic Fibrosis Foundation	125,500.00
National Foundation for Neuromuscular Diseases	43,000.00
National Jewish Hospital at Denver	6,800.00
National Kidney Foundation	66,000.00
National Multiple Sclerosis Society	83,000.00
National Society for Crippled Children and Adults	20,000.00
National Tuberculosis Association	73,000.00
St. Jude Children's Research Hospital	32,000.00
Salk Institute for Biological Studies	65,000.00
United Cerebral Palsy Research Foundation	222,200.00
Local Charity Grants	400,000.00
Minor Grants	185,418.00

The League appointed as original trustees of the Foundation a group composed of: GENERAL ALFRED M. GRUENTHER (President), BENJAMIN O. JOHNSON, JOHN E. SIMON, JERRY M. LEWIS, and Sidney B. Fink. Presidents following Gruenther's retirement in 1965 have been Fink (1965-1967), Johnson (1968-1973), JOSEPH J. STEDEM (1973-1974), PERCY X. BEAN (1975–1980) and JEROME R. SILVERMAN (1981-1982). The Treasurer is LEE HAZEN. In 1982 the Trustees of the Foundation, who are responsible for disbursing the funds raised, were:

Joan DeWitt	Nate Silverstein
Ruth McConnell	Katherine Wei
Jerome Silverman	

Trustees Emeriti are:

Percy X. Bean	Leo J. Seewald
Gen. Alfred M. Gruenther	John E. Simon
Lee Hazen	Samuel M. Stayman
Robin B. Mac Nab	Joseph J. Stedem
John W. Norwood	Edgar Theus
Abner Parker	Joseph Weintraub
Hon. Carl B. Rubin	

CHARLES GOREN FOUNDATION. See INTERCOLLEGIATE BRIDGE TOURNAMENT.

CHEAPER MINOR. See DEFENSE TO OPENING THREE-BID; SECOND NEGATIVE RESPONSE AFTER ARTIFICIAL FORCING OPENING.

CHEAPEST BID. The most economical bid available at any particular point in the auction, such as 1 ◇ in response to 1 ♣. Many conventional bids and systems make use of this principle of economy by attaching special meanings to club bids at various levels, and occasionally to diamond bids. The same principle of economy is followed in making natural opening bids and responses. See CHOICE OF SUIT and UP THE LINE.

CHEATING. Throughout history, card cheats have always been held in contempt. It is so with bridge.

The LAWS OF CONTRACT bridge are not designed to prevent cheating or to provide redress. The lawgivers have presumably taken the view that it would be wrong to accord cheats a status by providing legal remedies against their activities. This also is the policy of the ACBL; exclusion from membership is the penalty for premeditated cheating, but a case of momentary weakness might be dealt with by temporary suspension. ("The penalty of cheating is exclusion from society", wrote the great whist authority, CAVENDISH.)

Cheating at Rubber Bridge. At rubber bridge, cheating is not a problem. Short of actually manipulating or marking the cards, it is impracticable for a lone player to cheat effectively. The fact that good bridge is so exact an art militates against cheating, for a player who makes bids or plays which are against the odds but which prove consistently successful soon excites suspicion. Cheating in clubs is therefore rare.

Traditional forms of cardsharping are unrewarding in bridge because each deal is almost equally important. A sharper can hardly make a killing by awaiting a suitable opening as in such games as poker, and if he just *happened* to pick up good cards every time he dealt, his career would be shortlived. The dealing of *seconds*, therefore, the classic technique of the cardsharping aristocracy, is not an effective means of winning. (An accomplished sharp, dealing from a marked pack, sees when a high card is about to go to an opponent, and deals that opponent the next card instead, keeping the high card for himself or his partner.) For the same reason, another time-honored device of sharps, ringing in a cold deck, will not yield a reward commensurate with the risk.

Cheating at Duplicate. The fact that duplicate is a game for fixed partnerships as opposed to the cut-in style of rubber bridge makes dishonesty more practicable. Fortunately, in duplicate there is a powerful safeguard; success gained otherwise than by fair combat is empty to a true bridge player, and cheating presents no attraction to a normal person. It is happily true that to most competitors their own self-respect is at least as important as the kudos to be gained from tournament successes.

Cheating at duplicate is by no means easy to define. Although the Laws do not recognize cheats, the section called "The Proprieties" defines two main types of improper conduct: breaches of ethics and breaches of etiquette. Breaches of ethics are commonly thought of as unfair practices which fall short of deliberate cheating, but it is possible for the difference to be one of degree only. For example, a pair who take note of inflections in bidding would be considered unethical, while a pair who set out to impart similar information by secret signals would be considered cheats. (See also ETHICS, ETIQUETTE and PROPRIETIES.)

The following are some of infringements peculiar to the tournament world. By their aggravated nature they can be classified as cheating and have been dealt with as such by the ACBL.

Spying on upcoming boards. Disciplinary action

has been taken against players who have been observed taking note of play at other tables. One player who cheated too discreetly to be detected by ordinary surveillance was found out when an observant tournament director noticed he seemed to score consistently better on even-numbered boards than on odd-numbered boards. Observation over a period of time proved he made a practice of listening to conversations at adjoining tables when he had finished a set of boards, making notes on his private scorecard.

Altering scoresheets. This practice all but disappeared at ACBL tournaments when the practice of posting BURNER copies of the recap sheet began. These burners showed every player's score on every board as well as the matchpoints earned on most of them. The risk of detection became far too great.

Secret signals. Various forms of signaling, usually by the defenders, have been attempted. Generally the purpose is either to suggest an opening lead or to convey the hand pattern held — i.e., 4–5–3–1, etc. The result of such cheating, if attended by any degree of success, is inevitable. The suspicions of competent players are soon aroused, and in a short time the offenders are marked men.

Many tournament procedures have been devised that are unobtrusive but effective safeguards against cheating. Thus, in the LAWS OF DUPLICATE, some of the examples cited as irregularities are anticheating safeguards. These are:

"86 B.3. Any discussion of the bidding, play or result of a board, which may be overheard at another table.

"86 B.4. Any comparison of scores with another contestant during a session.

"86 B.5. Any touching or handling of cards belonging to another player."

See BERMUDA INCIDENT, BUENOS AIRES AFFAIR, CHEATING ACCUSATIONS.

Harry Goldwater and Albert Dormer

CHEATING ACCUSATIONS. Accusations of CHEATING are rare in serious tournament bridge, and substantiated accusations are even rarer. It is generally recognized that an allegation that is not supported by solid evidence should not be made, and that *accusation by rumor* is highly improper.

At the international level there have been very few cases of charges being brought. Most of these were disposed of, without widespread publicity, by the national or international committees concerned. The notable exceptions occurred in the 1965 and 1975 BERMUDA BOWL. See BERMUDA INCIDENT, BUENOS AIRES AFFAIR.

Several suggestions have been made, aimed at preventing cheating and forestalling accusations of cheating. Screens called FRANCO BOARDS were introduced in Italian events years ago, but did not find general acceptance. In 1974, the proposal of WORLD BRIDGE FEDERATION president JULIUS ROSENBLUM to use bidding SCREENS in the 1975 Bermuda Bowl in order to eliminate accusations of cheating met with a sharp division of opinion, with many taking the position that such screens would be demeaning to the players and to bridge itself. Nevertheless, in 1975

bidding screens were used for the first time in World Championship play, and their use in combination with BIDDING BOXES virtually eliminated any problems relating to the inadvertent exchange of unauthorized information and the ethical problems resulting from hesitations. The response of the players to the screens and boxes was overwhelmingly positive. The irony of the 1975 Bermuda Bowl was, however, that while the screens designed to eliminate cheating accusations were being enthusiastically received, an Italian pair were accused of cheating by using foot signals under the tables. See BERMUDA INCIDENT and HOUSTON AFFAIR.

Another accusation of cheating was leveled at two members of Italy's 1973 and 1974 Bermuda Bowl champions. Leandro Burgay, who was passed over by the ITALIAN BRIDGE FEDERATION (FIB) as a choice for the 1976 Bermuda Bowl and World Team Olympiad team, presented a tape to the FIB. Burgay claimed the tape contained a telephone conversation between him and BENITO BIANCHI in which Bianchi had openly discussed illegal signaling methods. According to the tape, Bianchi explained how he and PIETRO FORQUET had used cigarettes to convey signals during the 1973 and 1974 Bermuda Bowl. The case came to the attention of the WBF, but nothing ever came of it because it was never proven that the tapes were authentic.

CHESS PLAYERS. Nobody has ever reached the highest levels at both chess and bridge, but many have been expert at one game and near-expert at the other. High-ranking bridge players who are also strong chess players include OSWALD JACOBY and ALAN TRUSCOTT. Among chess players, two former world champions, Emanuel Lasker and José Raoul Capablanca, once were contributing editors of *The Bridge World*. GUILLAUME le BRETON DESCHAPELLES was acknowledged as the finest player of his day at both games.

CHICAGO (Four Deal Bridge). A form of the game much played in clubs and well suited to home play. Its effect is to avoid long rubbers of uncertain duration; a member never need wait longer than the time (about twenty minutes) required to complete four deals. The game is called "Chicago" for the city in which it originated, and sometimes "club bridge."

Basic rules. The LAWS OF CONTRACT BRIDGE and rules for CLUB PROCEDURE are followed, except as modifed by the following rules.

The rubber. A rubber consists of a series of four deals that have been bid and played. If a deal is passed out, the same player deals again and the deal passed out does not count as one of the four deals.

A fifth deal is void if attention is drawn to it at any time before there has been a new cut for partners or the game has terminated; if the error is not discovered in time for correction, the score stands as recorded. A sixth or subsequent deal is unconditionally void and no score for such a deal is ever permissible.

In case fewer than four deals are played, the score shall stand for the incomplete series and the fourth deal need not be played unless attention is drawn to the error before there has been a new cut for partners or the game has terminated.

When the players are pivoting,* the fact that the players have taken their proper seats for the next rubber shall be considered a cut for partners.

Vulnerability. Vulnerability is not determined by previous scores but by the following schedule:

first deal:　　　　neither side vulnerable

second and　　　　dealer's side vulnerable, the
third deals:　　　　other side not vulnerable

fourth deal:　　　　both sides vulnerable

Premiums. For making or completing a game (100 or more trick points), a side receives a premium of 300 points if on that deal it is not vulnerable or 500 points if on that deal it is vulnerable. There is no additional premium for winning two or more games, each game premium being scored separately.

The score. As a reminder of vulnerability in Four-Deal Bridge, two intersecting diagonal lines should be drawn near the top of the score pad, as follows:

The numeral "1" should be inserted in that one of the four angles thus formed that faces the first dealer. After play of the first deal is completed, "2" is inserted in the next angle in clockwise rotation, facing the dealer of the second deal. The numerals "3" and "4" are subsequently inserted at the start of the third and fourth deals, respectively, each in the angle facing the current dealer.

A correctly numbered diagram is conclusive as to vulnerability. There is no redress for a bid influenced by the scorer's failure to draw the diagram or for an error or omission in inserting a numeral or numerals in the diagram. Such error or omission should, upon discovery, be immediately corrected, and the deal or deals should be scored or rescored as though the diagram and the number or numbers thereon had been properly inserted.

Partscores. A partscore or -scores made previously may be combined with a partscore made in the current deal to complete a game of 100 or more trick points. The game premium is determined by the vulnerability, on that deal, of the side that completes the game. When a side makes or completes a game, no previous partscore of either side may thereafter be counted toward game.

A side that makes a partscore in the fourth deal, if the partscore is not sufficient to complete a game, receives a premium of 100 points. This premium is scored whether or not the same side or the other side has an uncompleted partscore. There is no separate premium for making a partscore in any other circumstances.

Deal out of turn. When a player deals out of turn, and there is no right to a redeal, the player who should have dealt retains his right to call first, but such right is lost if it is not claimed before the actual

dealer calls. If the actual dealer calls before attention is drawn to the deal out of turn, each player thereafter calls in rotation. Vulnerability and scoring values are determined by the position of the player who should have dealt, regardless of which player actually dealt or called first. Neither the rotation of the deal nor the scoring is affected by a deal out of turn. The next dealer is the player who would have dealt next if the deal had been in turn.

Optional rules and customs. The following practices, not required, have proved acceptable in some clubs and games.

(i) Since the essence of the game is speed, if a deal is passed out, the pack that has been shuffled for the next deal should be used by the same dealer.

(ii) The net score of a rubber should be translated into even hundreds (according to American custom) by crediting as 100 points any fraction thereof amounting to 50 or more points: e.g., 750 points count as 800; 740 points count as 700 points.

(iii) No two players may play a second consecutive rubber as partners at the same table. If two players draw each other again, the player who has drawn the highest card should play with the player who has drawn the third-highest, against the other two players.

(iv) To avoid confusion as to how many deals have been played: Each deal should be scored, even if there is no net advantage to either side (for example, when one side is entitled to 100 points for undertrick penalties and the other de is entitled to 100 points for honors). In a result that completes a game, premiums for overtricks, game, slam, or making a doubled contract should be combined with the trick score to produce one total, which is entered below the line; for example, if a side makes 2 ♠ doubled and vulnerable with an overtrick, 870 should be scored below the line, not 120 below the line and 50, 500, and 200 above the line.

In some clubs, notably the Cavendish (New York City), the vulnerability on the second and third deals is reversed. The objective is to give the nonvulnerable side an opportunity to preempt as dealer.

CHICAGO TROPHY. Awarded for the North American Open Team Championship (board-a match scoring) until 1965 when it was replaced by the REISINGER MEMORIAL TROPHY; contested at the Fall NAC (under which heading past results are listed). The Chicago Trophy was donated by the Auction Bridge Club of Chicago in 1929. (In 1928, the open team competition was for the Harold S. Vanderbilt Cup.)

CHICANE. A term from BRIDGE WHIST referring to a hand that is void of trumps. It was scored the same as three honors. In contract bridge, the term is obsolete in its original sense, though it is occasionally used to describe a void suit, as "chicane in hearts."

CHICO 2 ◊ . A simplified version of the MULTI 2 ◊ . An opening bid of 2 ◊ shows either a weak two-bid in a major or a strong (20 +) 4-4-4-1.

---

*In a pivot game, partnerships for each rubber follow a fixed rotation.

CHILEAN BRIDGE FEDERATION (FEDERA-

CIÓN CHILENA DE BRIDGE). Founded in 1951, it had a membership of more than 300 in 1982 in 17 affiliated clubs. Chile participates in all South American Championships, hosting the 1951, 1957, 1965, and 1972 events in Santiago, and occasionally in World Olympiads. National events held annually are for Men's and Women's Championships.

Officers, 1982:
President: Erwin Lips Mendoza
Secretary: Mrs. Adriana Villaseca Escobar, Avenida Los Leones No. 927, Santiago, Chile

CHINA. See CHINESE BRIDGE ASSOCIATION.

CHINESE BRIDGE ASSOCIATION. This association was founded in June 1980 as the National organization governing bridge activities with 30 provincial, municipal and other bridge societies as its members. Recognized by the WORLD BRIDGE FEDERATION in 1980, CBA has a total membership of 8,000 players. Bridge in China dates back to the 1930s and was prevalent in the cities of Beijing, Shanghai, Tianjin and Guangzhou mainly in the form of rubber bridge. From 1978 duplicate bridge has been popularized. CBA organizes two National championships every year, in Spring and Autumn. Each province also organizes its regular tournament on the provincial and municipal level. With promotion of bridge in China, some tourist cities like Shanghai and Hangzhou have hosted international invitational tournaments in 1980 and 1981 involving 13 cities with 150 participants and 17 cities with 120 participants respectively.

Officers, 1982:
President: Rong Gaotang
Secretary: Mrs. Li Wei,9, Tiyuguan Road, Beijing, China

CHINESE FINESSE. An attempt to win a trick by leading an unsupported honor.

♣ A 5
♣ K 8 6 2   ♣ J 10 7
♣ Q 9 4 3

If South needs to avoid a loser in this suit, he may dismiss the remote chance of dropping the singleton king, and try the effect of leading the queen from his hand. In the diagrammed situation West may well decide to duck, fearing that South has Q–J–10, with or without the 9.

CHINESE TAIPEI BRIDGE ASSOCIATION. This association was founded in 1950 at Taipei, Taiwan (Formosa), and by 1982 had an approximate membership of 2,800. It participates in World Olympiads and Far East Championships, hosting the latter events in Taipei in 1959, 1963 and 1969, and hosting the Bermuda Bowl in 1971. Taipei won the Far East Championship in 1967, 1969 and 1971, and finished second in 1968. When Australia could not represent the Far East Bridge Federation in the 1969 World Championships, Taipei was named as alternate and succeeded in making the best showing of a Far East team by finishing second, a feat it repeated in 1970. The chief National Championship is for the Governor's Cup.

Officers, 1982:
President: Sam S. F. Tung
Executive Secretary: Mr. C.K. Tou, 11/F, 212 Chung, Hsiao E. Road, Section 4, Taipei, Taiwan

CHOICE, RESTRICTED. See RESTRICTED CHOICE.

CHOICE OF PACKS AND SEATS. The winner (or highest card) of the cut for first deal has the choice of which seat he will take and which of the two packs he wishes to deal. Presumably, unless the wrong player deals at some subsequent point, the cards will continue to be dealt by this player and his partner, the other pack by their opponents.

CHOICE OF SUIT. In opening the bidding and responding, a long suit is normally bid ahead of a short one, but a few exceptions should be noted:

(1) A three-card minor suit, particularly clubs, is often bid ahead of a four-card major suit. Using FIVE-CARD MAJORS, the prepared minor-suit bid is made in all situations. In standard methods the major suit will usually be preferred if the suit is biddable and there will not be any rebid difficulty. In practice a four-card major is rarely bid with a 4–3–3–3 distribution: a minimum hand needs to keep the bidding at a low level; a hand of medium strength normally opens 1 NT; and a maximum hand bids 1♣ in order to make it easy for partner to respond.

(2) A strong four-card suit is often bid ahead of a five-card suit ranking immediately below it. This is necessary with a minimum or near-minimum hand; with hands of intermediate strength, a REVERSE from the long suit into the short suit becomes possible. There can be an acute problem if both suits are of poor quality:

♠ A x x x
♡ A x x x x
◇ A J x
♣ x

It would be risky to bid 1♠ followed by 2♡. The least evil is perhaps to bid 1♡, and rebid 2◇ if responder bids 2♣.

(3) A five-card suit may be bid ahead of a six-card suit ranking immediately below it if the hand is a minimum:

♠ x
♡ A J x x x
◇ A Q x x x x
♣ x

1◇ followed by a heart bid would not be justified by the strength of the hand, and opposing bidding might shut out the heart suit. Most players will bid 1♡, treating the hand as a 5–5 distribution.

(4) In response to 1♠, a three-card club suit is sometimes bid in preference to a four-card heart suit.

(5) In response to an opening bid in a red suit, a major suit is sometimes bid at the one-level in preference to a five- or six-card minor suit at the two-level. This may be because the hand is not strong enough to bid at the level of two, or to avoid concealing the major suit when the hand is not worth two constructive bids.

See also BIDDABLE SUITS; CANAPÉ; THREE-CARD SUITS, BIDS IN; WALSH.

With two or three suits of equal length, the choice is more complicated:

(6) With five-card suits (or six-card suits) the opener normally bids the higher-ranking unless he has both black suits. Some players bid 1♣ with two five-card black suits if the hand is strong enough to make a rebid at the level of three.

An exception can arise when a player holds a minimum hand and a void. With 5–0–5–3 or 3–5–0–5, some players bid the minor suit for reasons of preparedness.

(7) With two or three four-card suits the opener's choice is usually the suit below the shortage, or most nearly below it. But if this rule produces a weak four-card major suit, most players would search for another bid. This may provide particularly difficult if the hand is a minimum and it includes a doubleton club:

♠ J x x x	♠ J x x x	♠ A K x
♡ J x x x	♡ A K x	♡ J x x x
◊ A K x	◊ J x x x	◊ J x x x
♣ A 10	♣ A 10	♣ A 10

Many players would open these hands with 1◊, and would hope not to be faced by the problem of finding a rebid over a response of 2♣.

If the opener's hand is strong, there is rarely a rebid problem. In that case a minor suit is often bid in preference to a major, with the idea of keeping the bidding low and giving partner the maximum opportunity to respond with a weak hand.

If the opener holds both minor suits, he usually has a free choice, and may be guided by tactical or lead-inhibiting considerations; he will hardly ever wish to bid both suits. However, 1◊ is clearly preferable holding a worthless trebleton heart:

♠ A J
♡ 10 x x
◊ K J x x
♣ K J x x

1♣ would leave the opener with an impossible rebid after an overcall of one heart and a response of 1♠.

With three four-card suits, the "middle" suit may sometimes fare better than the suit below the shortage:

♠ K Q x x
♡ K Q x x
◊ A x x x
♣ x

Players who require responder to show a four-card major at the one-level if possible, often prefer to bid 1♡ rather than 1♠. This avoids the awkward rebid decision which faces the opener if he opens 1♠, and receives a response of 1 NT or 2♣.

(8) With five-card suits, responder invariably prefers the higher-ranking for his response. For responder's choice with four-card suits, see UP THE LINE.

CHUKKER. A term for four deals of CHICAGO. It is also used in a long team match for a group of boards followed by comparison of scores. The term is borrowed from polo.

CHURCHILL STYLE. The methods of bidding advocated by S. GARTON CHURCHILL of New York. The main features are:

(1) A weak notrump opening. Churchill was among the first leading American theorists to advocate this bid and his followers were the exclusive advocates of it for many years. In this style, however, not all weak balanced hands are opened with 1 NT. 1♡ would be bid with

♠ x x
♡ A Q x x
◊ A J x x
♣ Q 10 x

Hence, the 1 NT rebid might be made with as little as 2½ HONOR TRICKS.

(2) A "utility" 1 NT response with a wide variety of weak hands. 1 NT would be the response to 1♡ with any of the following:

♣ Q x x	♣ Q x x	♣ Q x x x x	♣ Q 10 x x x x
♡ K x x	♡ K x x x	♡ K x	♡ x x
◊ x x x	◊ x x x x	◊ x x x	◊ x
♣ x x x x	♣ x x	♣ x x x	♣ 10 x x x

On the last example, responder would bid spades at his next opportunity. The corollary is that all other responses, including a single raise in the opener's suit, imply a forward-going response.

After the "utility" 1 NT response, the opening bidder, unless his holding is inflexible, will normally rebid a suit lower in rank, although, with a reasonably good balanced hand, he is allowed to pass, and oftentimes does. This was the forerunner of the forcing ROTH-STONE 1 NT response.

(3) Light opening bids with distributional patterns such as 5–4–3–1, 5–4–4–0, 4–4–4–1, 6–4–3–0, 5–5–3–0, 6–5–1–1, etc.

(4) Frequent bids in short suits; Churchill was well before his time in using such bids as all-purpose bids for exploring for games and slams, or steering the contract into a particular hand, etc.

(5) Constructive overcalls; forcing jump overcalls.

(6) Four-card openings in suits of any strength.

(7) "Picture Bidding"; jump rebids and responses used essentially to describe solid or near-solid suits as well as slam aspirations.

(8) No strength-showing forcing opening bid.

(9) Sparing use of pre-emptive bids.

(10) BALANCE OF POWER bidding (see BALANCING).

CIPHER BID. See ARTIFICIAL BID.

CIRCUS. See SHARIF BRIDGE CIRCUS.

CITY OF ASBURY PARK TROPHY. Awarded for the Challenge Team-of-Four Championship, an event held from 1930 until 1937 at the Summer NAC, under which the results are reported. The trophy was a statuette carved and cast by DOROTHY RICE SIMS, and donated by her and her husband, P. HAL SIMS.

The conditions of the event made it unique in that the runners-up could challenge the winners to play for the championship; on the few occasions when this happened, however, the winners retained the title. The championship was equivalent in status to the SPINGOLD event which took its place in 1938.

Thereafter the trophy was turned over to the New York–New Jersey Conference, which awarded it annually from 1958 through 1969 to the winner of the most master points at their summer regional. When the conference regional was moved from Asbury Park, that city which had originally presented the trophy, requested its return.

CLAIM OR CONCESSION. Declarer makes a claim whenever he announces that he will win or lose one or more of the remaining tricks, or suggests that play may be curtailed, or intentionally faces his hand. Declarer makes a concession when he announces that he will lose all of the remaining tricks, or when he agrees to a defender's claim. The declarer is required to state his proposed line of play when he claims, and the defenders must give him a reasonable amount of time to make a statement. If the claim is questioned, the director must be called whether or not declarer stated a line of play. If no line was stated, the director should ask for one, not allowing declarer to make a statement that requires a particular defender to hold a particular card unless that fact was established before the claim. Following a claim or concession, play ceases. The director must void any play that occurred after the claim or concession but before he arrived at the table.

Defender makes a concession when he announces that he will lose one or more of the remaining tricks or agrees to declarer's claim. Defender makes a claim when he announces that he will win one or more of the remaining tricks or shows any or all of his cards to declarer for this purpose. The same basic ideas that pertain to declarer's claim or concession are true of a defender's claim or concession. It is up to the director to decide the fate of the remaining tricks as equitably as possible to both sides. He will award to the declarer any trick that the defenders could lose by normal (this includes careless or inferior) play. If part of the defender's claim requires independent action by his partner that is not clearcut, this probably creates a doubtful point which may have to be resolved in favor of the declarer.

When a director is adjudicating the results on a board on which the defenders have contested a claim, his goal is to restore equity — to restore the result which most probably would have been obtained had there been no claim. Any doubtful points are resolved in favor of the defenders.

There is no pat solution on how to rule on claims. A degree of judgment is required since the intent of the Laws is to resolve each individual case as equitably as possible to both sides.

Under certain conditions, a concession may be canceled by the director. The situations are as follow:

(1) If a trick has been conceded that has already been won. For a concession to be canceled under these circumstances, the error must be reported to the director within the established correction period.

(2) If declarer concedes defeat of a contract he has already made. Once again, for this to be applied, the error must be reported to the director within the established correction period.

(3) If a defender concedes the making of a contract that has already been defeated. The correction period rule applies here as well.

(4) If a trick is conceded that cannot be lost by any reasonable line of play, and attention is drawn to it before all four hands are returned to the board.

(5) If a defender concedes one or more tricks and his partner objects at once.

CLARAC SLAM TRY. A feature of the PRO SYSTEM based principally on a 4♣ bid to ask about aces and other controls. The name CLARAC is an acronym for CLub Asking, Respond Aces and Controls.

Responses to the 4♣ bid vary according to whether or not the partner of the 4♣ bidder has shown a good hand. By a limited hand, the responses to 4♣ are: 4◊ with no aces and no king-queen combinations; 4 NT with no aces but with reasonable king-queen values; 4♡, 4♠, or 5♣ with one ace plus first- or second-round control in the suit named; 5◊, 5♡, 5♠, or 6♣ with two aces plus second-round control in the suit named; 5 NT with three aces and no other control. By a good hand, the responses to 4♣ show one ace more than they do by a limited hand.

Over any response but 4◊, a suit bid by the 4♣ bidder is an asking bid in that suit. Responses are: cheapest suit to deny first- or second-round control; cheapest notrump to show second-round control; raise to show two of the top three honors; any other suit to show the ace of the asked suit plus second-round control in the bid suit. More asking bids may follow.

CLASH SQUEEZE. A squeeze in three suits, distinguished by the presence of a special type of long menace called a *clash menace*, analyzed and named by Chien-Hwa Wang (in *Bridge Magazine* articles 1956–57).

A2

K   J 10

Q

South's queen is a clash menace against West's king.

A x x

Q J   9 x x

K 10

South's 10 is a clash menace against West's queen and jack.

The following are the basic positions for a clash squeeze.

(1) Simple Squeeze

Positional

♠ A 2
♡ A J
◊ —
♣ —

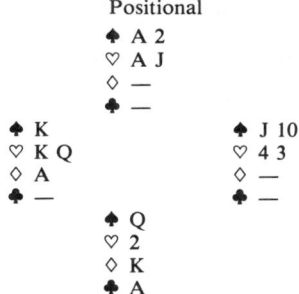

♠ K   ♠ J 10
♡ K Q   ♡ 4 3
◊ A   ◊ —
♣ —   ♣ —

♠ Q
♡ 2
◊ K
♣ A

South leads the ♣A, which squeezes West in three suits (if West discards a spade, South cashes the queen and then crosses to the ♡A in order to take the ♠A).

Delayed (secondary)

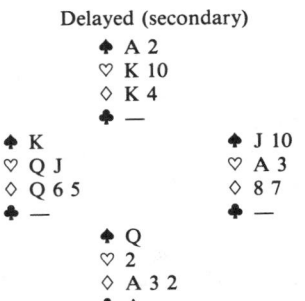

```
            ♠ A 2
            ♡ K 10
            ◇ K 4
            ♣ —
♠ K                    ♠ J 10
♡ Q J                  ♡ A 3
◇ Q 6 5                ◇ 8 7
♣ —                    ♣ —
            ♠ Q
            ♡ 2
            ◇ A 3 2
            ♣ A
```

South leads the ♣A, which squeezes West in three suits. West must discard a heart, and North throws a spade. Now South can lead a heart and establish a trick in that suit. See also VICE SQUEEZE.

(2) Double Squeeze (nonsimultaneous and positional). A double clash squeeze consists of two parts: a clash squeeze against one opponent, then a simple squeeze against the other.

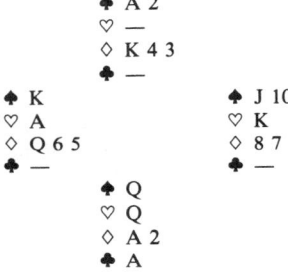

```
            ♠ A 2
            ♡ —
            ◇ K 4 3
            ♣ —
♠ K                    ♠ J 10
♡ A                    ♡ K
◇ Q 6 5                ◇ 8 7
♣ —                    ♣ —
            ♠ Q
            ♡ Q
            ◇ A 2
            ♣ A
```

South leads the ♣A, and West is clash squeezed. He must discard a heart, after which South plays the ◇K then ◇A to squeeze East in the majors.

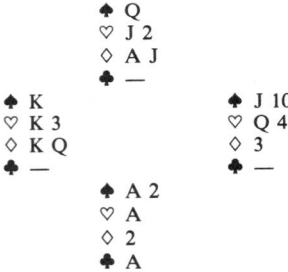

```
            ♠ Q
            ♡ J 2
            ◇ A J
            ♣ —
♠ K                    ♠ J 10
♡ K 3                  ♡ Q 4
◇ K Q                  ◇ 3
♣ —                    ♣ —
            ♠ A 2
            ♡ A
            ◇ 2
            ♣ A
```

The ♣A lead by South clash squeezes West, and forces him to discard a heart. South cashes the ◇A (VIENNA COUP), then crosses to the ◇A, squeezing East in the majors.

(3) Double Squeeze (simultaneous)

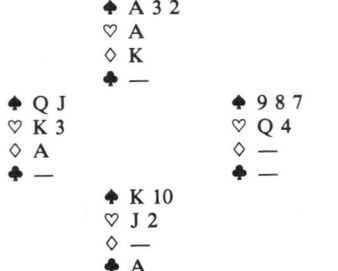

```
            ♠ A 3 2
            ♡ A
            ◇ K
            ♣ —
♠ Q J                  ♠ 9 8 7
♡ K 3                  ♡ Q 4
◇ A                    ◇ —
♣ —                    ♣ —
            ♠ K 10
            ♡ J 2
            ◇ —
            ♣ A
```

On the lead of the ♣A West must discard a heart, North throws a diamond, and East is squeezed in the majors.

This is a positional squeeze.

Secondary

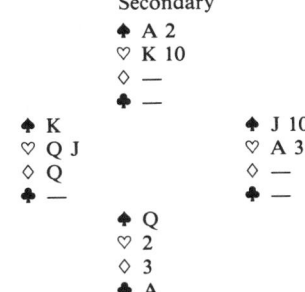

```
            ♠ A 2
            ♡ K 10
            ◇ —
            ♣ —
♠ K                    ♠ J 10
♡ Q J                  ♡ A 3
◇ Q                    ◇ —
♣ —                    ♣ —
            ♠ Q
            ♡ 2
            ◇ 3
            ♣ A
```

South leads the ♣A. If West discards a heart, North throws a spade, and East throws a heart. South leads a heart to establish a trick in that suit, with the ♠A for an entry. If West throws a spade, North throws a heart as does East. South cashes the ♠Q and leads a heart to throw in East who must give the last trick to North's ♠A.

(4) Trump Squeeze

Single

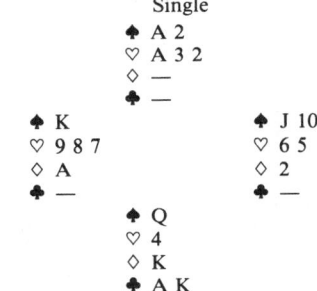

```
            ♠ A 2
            ♡ A 3 2
            ◇ —
            ♣ —
♠ K                    ♠ J 10
♡ 9 8 7                ♡ 6 5
◇ A                    ◇ 2
♣ —                    ♣ —
            ♠ Q
            ♡ 4
            ◇ K
            ♣ A K
```

With clubs as trumps, South leads the king of that suit. West can do no better than discard a heart, but now South can ruff out that suit, using the ♠A as a re-entry. This squeeze is positional.

Double

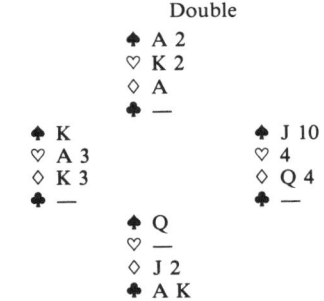

```
            ♠ A 2
            ♡ K 2
            ◇ A
            ♣ —
♠ K                    ♠ J 10
♡ A 3                  ♡ 4
◇ K 3                  ◇ Q 4
♣ —                    ♣ —
            ♠ Q
            ♡ —
            ◇ J 2
            ♣ A K
```

Clubs are trumps. South leads the trump king, and West must throw a diamond. North and East discard hearts. South cashes the ◇A, and ruffs a heart which squeezes East in spades and diamonds.

Monroe Ingerman

CLEAR A SUIT. At notrump play, to clear a suit is to force out, by continued leads of the suit, adversely held high cards so that the remainder of the cards in that suit are winners. At suit play, the term is used also to indicate a line of play which cashes winners in one side-suit and trumps out the balance of the cards in that suit so as to eliminate all cards of the suit from both the declarer's and dummy's hand. Then if a trick is lost to the defense later, a further lead of this suit gives declarer the option of trumping in one hand while discarding a potential loser in the other. See also ELIMINATION and STRIP PLAY.

CLOCKS. Devices used at tournaments to indicate to the players how much time is left in the round and when the round is ended. The clocks usually are large display boxes with the time indicated by lights. A sound usually is emitted when two minutes remain in the round, and a second sound occurs when the round is over.

Clocks also are used to time pairs in a team event. Since are there are penalties for slow play, it becomes necessary to determine who was responsible for the slow play. The only realistic way to do this is to time the individual pairs with clocks such as chess clocks.

CLOSED HAND. The hand of the declarer, as distinct from the OPEN HAND, which is now legally referred to as the DUMMY. The terms date from auction bridge, the first of the predecessors of contract bridge to make declarer's partner's hand visible to all, and under the direction of the declarer.

CLOSED ROOM. In team-of-four matches, particularly in knockout matches, the two pairs of a team play in different rooms or different areas of the same room. One of these rooms is designated the open room, one the closed room. Normally, spectators are permitted in the open room, and these spectators are free to come and go, without hindrance. However, if spectators are permitted in the closed room, they are restricted to one table and are not permitted to leave until the match they are watching is terminated. As soon as one of the matches in the closed room has been terminated, the original open room becomes a closed room to which no other spectators are permitted entrance, and to which no contestant or spectator may be readmitted after leaving until the last open room contest has terminated.

In important matches where arrangements are made for play-by-play relaying of information to a large group of spectators, the boards are originally played in a closed room with a starting time appreciably earlier than that for the replay. Thus information may be kept from the players in the replay but made available to spectators, who can contrast the results of the first play with what is going on in the replay. Spectators thus are more fully informed of what has gone on than are any of the actual contestants.

In some major events such as the European Championship, the open room is always open, but players are not permitted to leave the closed room until the open half of their match is completed. See BRIDGE-O-RAMA.

CLOTHESLINE. An arrangement by which travel-

ing score slips can be displayed for study by the players when the recapitulation sheet does not show information beyond the matchpoint score itself.

CLUB. (1) The symbol ♣, which appears on the 13 cards of the lowest ranking of the four suits in a bridge deck, stems from the French (*trèfle*), but the name seems to be of Spanish or Italian origin as a translation of *basto* or *bastone*. (2) The club suit consists of the 13 cards bearing this symbol. Since the club suit as trump is the least likely final declaration when a choice of trump suits is available, many systems make use of the naming of this suit to show conventional holdings. See CLUB CONVENTIONS.

CLUB BRIDGE. See CHICAGO.

CLUB CHARITY GAMES. See CHARITY PROGRAM OF THE ACBL.

CLUB CONVENTIONS. The low-ranking club suit is particularly well suited for conventional uses of various kinds. The VANDERBILT CLUB was the original "club convention" and has had many successors (see 1♣ SYSTEMS and 2♣ SYSTEMS). Conventional club bids at higher levels include 2♣ STRONG ARTIFICIAL OPENING, STAYMAN and GERBER.

CLUB PROCEDURES. See HOUSE RULES. Each bridge club will find that there are situations in its operation that are not covered by the LAWS or where the laws do not agree with the desire of the members of the club on such points as precedence in entering a table, complement of a table, personal dislikes of certain players, methods of settling games for stakes and like problems. Procedures used in such cases should always be consistent and definitely formulated for future reference.

CLUB SYSTEMS. See 1♣ SYSTEMS, 2♣ SYSTEMS.

CLUBS. Organizations or groups of bridge players who form units acting as centers of interest for players in a particular community. ¹All over the world may be found clubs catering to the needs and wishes of people in all walks of life who have one common interest, contract bridge.

Clubs are today so diversified as to type of premises and rules of membership that a comprehensive description is impossible. Large cities all over the world have at least one and often many more such clubs. Those who prefer to play for stakes can usually be accommodated, providing they pass whatever standards are set up. Those who prefer duplicate can usually find an open-game club devoted to such purposes. In smaller towns throughout America, the emphasis has shifted to duplicate bridge, and a club for that purpose is almost always available to the players of the community. The ACBL issues annual directories of the 5000-plus clubs operating under its auspices. Games usually occur at regular periods, with specially scheduled Club championship events every calendar quarter. Fees are charged for each participation, and in some cases annual dues as well. In North

America, many owners have banded together into the Club Owners Association for the group's mutual benefit.

CLUBS FOR TAKEOUT. A variation of CHEAPER MINOR TAKEOUT. The bid for takeout is always made in clubs. Even when the preempt is in clubs, the next higher club bid shows a hand worth a takeout double.

COAT CARDS. The original term in English for the three cards of each suit which represent costumed human figures: the king, queen and jack. In some countries a fourth coat card, variously the valet or courtier, is included in the deck. The term has been superseded by a corruption, "court cards." See FACE CARDS.

COFFEE-HOUSE BRIDGE. Card playing in European coffee houses frequently featured conversational or other gambits designed to mislead opponents, and the term "coffee-house bridge" became a synonym for legal but unethical gambits. Such questions as "Did you bid a *spade?*" with a rising inflection to inform partner of a sound spade holding in one's own cards, or "What did you bid first over 1 ◊ ?" to right-hand opponent when one wants his partner to lead that suit against a notrump contract, are gambits that are easily caught.Such a player is ostracized at rubber bridge, and the offense is adjudicated in duplicate bridge when a director is present. Action on a doubtful hand after a slow pass by partner is somewhat harder to classify, but the ethical player will pass all such doubtful hands after such a slow pass by partner.

Conversational gambits, even when made without any devious intent, have no place at the bridge table among serious, ethical players.

COFFEE-HOUSING. Indulging in unethical actions with full intent to mislead opponents. See COFFEE-HOUSE BRIDGE.

COFFIN TROPHY. Awarded for the NAC Women's Teams (since 1976 a knockout event), donated by Charles E. Coffin in 1933, contested at the Fall NAC until 1963, when it was transferred to the Spring NAC, under which heading past results are listed.

COLD. Bridge slang term describing an easily makable contract. In post-mortem heat, players tend to exaggerate the degrees of coldness.

COLLECTION AND ARRANGEMENT OF TRICKS. See LAWS OF CONTRACT BRIDGE (Law 66); LAWS OF DUPLICATE (Law 65).

COLLECTIONS OF PLAYING CARDS. These collections, public and private, are fairly numerous; quite a few museums have cards as part of their material on graphic arts.

The largest collection in the United States, a gift of the United States Playing Card Company to the Museum of Art, is in Cincinnati OH . In New York City, the Morgan Library has a few of the oldest and most valuable cards. Yale University has a collection of more than 3000 packs, uncut sheets, and card printers' woodblocks acquired by the late Melbert and Mary Cary and willed to Yale University in 1967.

The French collection is in the Bibliothèque Nationale in Paris; London has two collections, one in the British Museum, the other in the Guildhall; others are in Vienna, Nuremberg, Dresden, Munich, and Budapest.

COLLEGE BRIDGE. See INTERCOLLEGIATE BRIDGE TOURNAMENT.

COLLOQUIALISMS. Bridge has evolved or adopted its share of colloquialisms. For example, see the following: BIFF; BLOCKBUSTER; DEATH HOLDING; DUB; FIXED; FRAME; GAME HOG; GOULASH; HOOK; HORSE AND HORSE; JUNK; KIBITZ; KICK IT; KILLED; LAY-DOWN; LOCK; MAMA-PAPA BRIDGE; MAYONNAISE; PALOOKA; PHANTOM SACRIFICE; PIANOLA; PUMP; PUNCH; QUACK; RAGS; RIDE; SHAKE; SOCK; STIFF; SUCKER'S DOUBLE; TANK; UNDER THE GUN; and UPPERCUT.

COLOMBIAN BRIDGE FEDERATION (FEDERACIÓN COLOMBIANA DE BRIDGE). This federation was founded in 1963 by Jorge Ospina, Ivan Hoyos, Francisco Soto Pombo, Rodolfo Segovia, and Jorge Combariza, representing the various clubs of Bogotá, Medellín, Barranquilla, Cali, and Pereira; by 1982 there were more than 1,300 members. The Federation participates in South American Championships and Caribbean Championships, and its international successes include South American Women's Teams 1968, 1970, 1976, second 1964, and the Caribbean Championship 1968. National Championships for Open Teams, Open Pairs, and Masters Pairs, and Regional tournaments are held annually.

Officers, 1982:

President: Joaquin Prieto Isaza

Secretary: Rafael Morales Paris, Calle 61 No. 13-23 Of. 201, Bogota D.E., Colombia

COLONIAL ACOL. A version of ACOL popular in Canada; its basic elements were used by all three Canadian pairs in the 1972 World Team Olympiad. Major features include four-card major suit openings (1 ♣ opening may be prepared). Jump raises are usually limit, with either SWISS, JACOBY 2 NT or SPLINTERS used to show a strong raise. 1 NT opening is 16–18, although some shade it to 15–17, with TWO-WAY STAYMAN. Opening bids of 2 ◊ , 2 ♡ , or 2 ♠ are ACOL TWO-BIDS; some partnerships use FLANNERY 2 ◊ .

COLOR. A term occasionally used to distinguish suit-play as opposed to notrump play. In the bidding, to "change the color" means to bid a new suit. The term is virtually synonymous with "suit."

COLORFUL CUEBID. Devised by DOROTHY HAYDEN TRUSCOTT, this is an immediate overcall in the opponent's major suit to show two unbid suits of the same color. See also CUEBIDS IN OPPONENT'S SUIT; MICHAELS CUEBID.

COLUMNS. See BRIDGE COLUMNS.

COMBINATION TEAM SCORING. A method of scoring team-of-four events that permits comparison of pair scores as well as team scores. After award of team scores on a win-half-loss basis, the North–South scores are matchpointed on the basis of the number of times the board was played, and the East–West scores also matchpointed on the same basis.

In theory this combination team scoring permits a team to analyze its game as to which of the pairs contributed to the winning or losing of boards by securing a less-than-average result.

This is also the method by which team scores are computed on a board that has been fouled between the times that the two halves of the team play it; the fields resulting from the fouling are matchpointed separately, and the combination of the percentages of the possible matchpoints totaled for the two team halves; such a total of less than 70 losing the board, exceeding 130 winning it, and between these percentages being awarded a half on the board.

COMBINATIONS. The idea of a combination is fundamental to bridge calculations. Examples where we use this conception are in calculating the probability of a specified hand pattern or the division of a suit among the four players. We also use it very frequently in calculating the respective probabilities of (or the ratio between) the division of the combined holding of the defenders in a specified suit or with specified honor holdings.

Our general expression for a combination is nCr, which we read as 'the number of combinations of n things taken r at a time'. For example, 4C2 means the number of ways in which we can select two articles out of a total of four articles.

We note that if r = n we can write nCn in place of nCr. Whatever the number n represents nCn is equal to 1. After all, there is only one way in which we can select n articles out of a total of n articles. There is also only one way in which we can select no (0) articles.

The values of a selected number of combinations are given in Table 5 (p. 279).

If we wish to calculate the value of a combination we need to understand the concept of the 'factorial'. For bridge purposes the factorial of a number is the product of all numbers from 1 up to and including the specified number, e.g., five factorial (written 5!) is $1 \times 2 \times 3 \times 4 \times 5$. When using factorials in our calculations we often find it simpler to reverse the above order, setting out 5! as $5 \times 4 \times 3 \times 2 \times 1$. Conventionally the value of 0! is taken as 1.

Let us consider the number of ways in which we can select 13 cards from a pack of 52 cards. Our first can be any one of the 52 cards, our second any one of 51 cards, etc. We have the following calculation

$$52 \times 51 \times 50 \ldots \ldots \times 41 \times 40$$

which is the same as multiplying all the numbers from 52 down to 1 and dividing the answer by the product of all the numbers from 39 down to 1. We can express this calculation by the formula

(mathematical shorthand)

$$\frac{52!}{39!}$$

However, this is not the whole of the story. The answer we obtain would be correct if we were interested in the order in which we select the 13 cards. This is not the case. The order in which the cards are selected is irrelevant for our purpose. Let us take one of the 13 cards at random. It could have been selected on any one of our 13 draws. A second of these cards could have been selected on any one of the remaining twelve draws, and so on. In other words, we have $13 \times 12 \times 11 \ldots \times 1$ (or 13!) ways in which those 13 cards could be selected. This means that the total number of ways in which 13 cards can be selected from a pack of 52 cards is

$$\frac{52!}{39! \; 13!}$$

(See "Number of Possible Hands, Deals at p. 304). Our general formula for this type of calculation is

$$nCr = \frac{n!}{r! \times (n\text{-}r)!}$$

Let us now look at a simple example where the defenders have a combined holding of four cards in a specified suit. This means that they hold 22 cards in the other three suits. A named player can have a holding in the specified suit of

0 cards in 4C0 × 22C13 ways.
1 card in 4C1 × 22C12 ways.
2 cards in 4C2 × 22C11 ways.
3 cards in 4C3 × 22C10 ways.
4 cards in 4C4 × 22C9 ways.

Bearing in mind that 26 cards can be divided between the two defenders in 26C13 (or 10,400,600) ways, we obtain the following table

		%.
4C0 × 22C13	= 1 × 497 420	
	= 497 420 =	4,782 6
4C1 × 22C12	= 4 × 646 646	
	= 2 586	
	584 =	24,869 6
4C2 × 22C11	= 6 × 705 432	
	= 4 232	
	592 =	40,695 7
4C3 × 22C10	= 4 × 646 646	
	= 2 586	
	584 =	24,869 6
4C4 × 22C9	= 1 × 497 420	
	= 497 420 =	4,782 6
	10 400 600	100.000 1

The extra 0.000 1% is, of course, due to approximating.

We note that nCr = nC(n-r). In other words, 4C1 is equal to 4C3. This is obvious, for if one player can hold r cards in a specified number of ways his partner must be able to hold the remainder of the partnership cards in exactly the same number of ways.

Now let us examine the problem of a holding of specified cards. Let us assume that the four cards held by the defense in a named suit consist of

K–Q–x–x. What is the probability that a named defender, *e.g.*, West, holds both the king and the queen? He can hold

$$
\begin{aligned}
\text{K–Q–x–x} &= 4C4 \times 22C9 \\
&= 1 \times 497\,420 \\
&= 497\,420 \\
\text{K–Q–x} &= 2C2 \times 2C1 \times 22C10 \\
&= 1 \times 2 \times 646\,646 \\
&= 1\,293\,292 \\
\text{K–Q} &= 2C2 \times 22C11 \\
&= 1 \times 7705432 \\
&= 705\,432 \\
\hline
& 2\,496\,144
\end{aligned}
$$

The respective percentages are 4.782 6; 12.434 8 and 6.782 6, the total being exactly 24%.

When we compare the probability of his holding the doubleton K–Q with the probability of his holding the singleton K half our work is already done. We have

$$
\begin{aligned}
\text{K–Q} &= 2C2 \times 22C11 = 1 \times 705\,432 \\
&= 705\,432 \qquad\quad = 6.782\,6 \\
\text{K} &= 1C1 \times 22C12 = 1 \times 646\,646 \\
&= 646\,646 \qquad\quad = 6.217\,4
\end{aligned}
$$

We find that 705 432 and 646 646 have a highest common factor (HCF) of 58 786, giving us a ratio of 12:11.

As 2C2 and 1C1 are both equal to 1 we are really comparing 22C11 and 22C12. This comparison can be made without the above calculations if we note that

$$
nC\,(r+1) = \frac{nCr \times (n-r)}{r+1}
$$

In our above example we have n = 22 and r = 11, so

$$
22C12 = \frac{22C11 \times (22-11)}{11+1} \text{ or } \frac{22C11 \times 11}{12}
$$

giving us a ratio of 22C12 to 22C11 of 11:12.

Alternatively we can use the formula

$$
nC(r-1) = \frac{nCr \times r}{n-(r-1)} \qquad \text{or}
$$

$$
22C11 = \frac{22C12 \times 12}{22-(12-1)}
$$

giving us the ratio of 22C11 to 22C12 as 12:11.

This method may be used to draw other comparisons, *e.g.*, which has the greater probability, and by how much, that a named player will hold two out of four missing cards or that he will hold three of such cards? We have a comparison between

$$
4C2 \times 22C11 \text{ and } 4C3 \times 22C10.
$$

We know that

$$
22C11 = 22C10 \times \frac{12}{11}
$$

and that

$$
4C2 = 4C3 \times \frac{3}{2}
$$

so

$$
4C2 \times 22C11 = \left(4C3 \times \frac{3}{2}\right)\left(22C10 \times \frac{12}{11}\right)
$$

The ratio is thus

$$
4C2 \times 22C11 : 4C3 \times 22C10 :: 18 : 11.
$$

This means that the chance of a named player holding two of four missing cards is higher than his chance of holding three of such cards. However, the overall chance of a 3–1 or 1–3 break is 22 : 18 (or 11 : 9) as there are two different (and equal) ways in which the defenders' cards can be divided so that one of them holds three cards, but only way in which each of them holds two cards.

There are many other problems in which we can use this method of calculating the ratios between two (or more) different probabilities.

Alex Traub

COME-ON, COME-ON SIGNAL. A defensive maneuver by which one player indicates to his partner that he wishes a suit, led by his partner, to be continued. The usual come-on is a HIGH-LOW SIGNAL, called also an "echo," and in England, a PETER. An alternative is the UPSIDE-DOWN SIGNAL.

COMIC NOTRUMP OVERCALL. An overcall of 1 NT to show a weak hand with a long suit. Partner bids 2♣ to locate the long suit. See also GARDENER NOTRUMP OVERCALL.

COMM. & IND. Commercial and Industrial.

COMMAND BID. A term suggested by GEORGE ROSENKRANZ to describe a bid which compels partner to make a specific response but which: a) Does not promise a holding of the commanded suit (compare TRANSFER BID); b) does not promise any particular strength (compare DEMAND BID); c) does not ask about the holding in any suit (compare ASKING BID), *e.g.* FLINT 3♦ over 2 NT; ROMEX 2♡, 2♠, or 2 NT over 2♦.

COMMERCIAL AND INDUSTRIAL TEAMS. See UNITED STATES PLAYING CARD TROPHY.

COMMITTEE. In tournaments of the American Contract Bridge League of sectional or higher rating, a committee from the sponsoring organization is charged with the responsibility of making necessary arrangements. This is known as the tournament committee. The work of this committee is divided into two parts, before and during the tournament. Among the pre-tournament duties are arrangements for location, dates, securing of sanctions, arrangements for services to the players, prizes, obtaining the services of a director, publicity and financing.

During the course of a tournament, the director may be called on to make a ruling where he is unable to secure agreement on the facts under question. In such cases, and in cases where the director uses his discretionary powers, a player may, through the director, appeal to the tournament committee. Such an appeal is based on questions of fact, not of law. See Chapter XI, LAWS OF DUPLICATE CONTRACT BRIDGE.

Appeals to the national authority on matters of conduct, deportment or ethics can be taken to the National Conduct, Deportment and Ethics Committee, and on questions of law to the National Laws Commission.

Occasionally, the tournament committee delegates to a subcommittee (known as an appeals committee) its duties at a particular tournament. See NATIONAL APPEALS COMMITTEE.

At world championships, a specially appointed appeals committee is on duty during and after every session of play.

COMMON MARKET CHAMPIONSHIPS. A biennial tournament held in Western Europe starting in 1967 for member countries of the European Common Market. The tournament consists of several team events, in which each country may enter one team, and several pair events, in which each country may be represented by a number of pairs.

COMMON-SENSE SYSTEM. See CRANE SYSTEM.

COMMUNICATION BETWEEN PARTNERS. The act of conveying information within a partnership. It is a breach of ethics when information is conveyed intentionally by a remark, gesture or mannerism. See LAWS (Proprieties, I). Information can of course be conveyed legitimately by bids and defensive plays.

COMMUNICATION PLAY. A play intended to preserve or establish communication (transfer of the lead) between partnership hands to make it possible at a strategic time to lead from a certain hand; or a play to destroy such means of communication between the opponents. Various plays of this nature are discussed in the following articles: DESCHAPELLES COUP; DUCKING; ENTRY; ENTRY-KILLING PLAY; HOLD-UP; MERRIMAC COUP; SCISSORS COUP.

COMMUTER BRIDGE. A set-to at bridge on trains, popular in Boston, Chicago, New York, Philadelphia and other cities. Players who regularly use the same train for commuting arrange to have the first player to enter the train reserve a double seat, and the other players use the same car, joining the game as soon as they board the train. In New York, the cards are dealt as the last player boards, and play is continued until the train reaches the Newark or 125th Street station, after which no further hands are dealt.

Originally, running scores in the form of rubbers prevailed, continuing from day to day with settlement of the wagers made monthly, but in the Sixties four-deal bridge (CHICAGO) gained ground.

COMPARING SCORES. Discussion of results already achieved by contestants in a duplicate competition. Making such comparisons with other contestants playing the same board in tournament play before the session's play has been completed has long been held to be unethical. Since 1963 these comparisons have been declared illegal, and the director is authorized to assess penalties for them.

The private scores kept by many tournament players furnish material for long and involved discussions of what might have been, and are very useful for later study and as a reminder of holdings.

In club games where traveling score slips are used to facilitate the scoring of the game, knowledge of previous results on an individual board is legitimately available to the players after the board has been played. Courtesy requires that the player responsible for scoring the result make the slip available to the other players who are entitled to see it; discussion of previous results should be held in abeyance until both (or all) the boards of the current round have been completed. Score comparison is not regarded with disfavor in Europe. Players may compare scores on boards already played by both partnerships unless specifically instructed to the contrary. See ESTIMATION.

COMPARISONS. At duplicate, comparisons are made between pairs (or players) who played a board in the same direction, and consequently under similar conditions of dealer, vulnerability, and holding. See BALANCED COMPARISONS.

COMPASS POINTS. In discussing bridge hands, columnists describe the four players by using the points of the compass to distinguish the players. Thus North and South compete against East and West. In tournament play, too, the table markers designate the seating of the players for the original deals by compass directions at designated tables. In the usual MITCHELL type of tournament competition, the North and South players remain in the same seats throughout, doing the scoring and passing the boards, while the East and West players move from table to table in a direction opposite that in which the boards are passed. In other types of competition, a pair of players may occupy either the North–South or the East–West seats for a portion of the session.

COMPETITION. (1) Any duplicate bridge contest. See TOURNAMENT. (2) A bidding situation in which both sides are active.

COMPETITIVE BIDDING. Bidding sequences in which both partnerships enter the auction. Doubling situations are listed under DOUBLE. Other articles dealing with competitive bidding include: BALANCING; CUEBIDS IN OPPONENT'S SUIT; DEFENSE TO DOUBLE OF 1 NT; DEFENSE TO 1 NT; DEFENSE TO OPENING FOUR-BID; DEFENSE TO OPENING THREE-BID; DEFENSE TO STRONG ARTIFICIAL OPENINGS; DEFENSE TO TWO-SUITED INTERFERENCE; DEFENSIVE BIDDING; DIRECTIONAL ASKING BID; DOUBLE JUMP OVERCALL; FORCING PASS; FREE BID; GARDENER NOTRUMP OVERCALL; JUMP OVERCALL; KOCK-WERNER REDOUBLE; LEAD-DIRECTING BID; LEBENSOLD; 1 NT OVERCALL; OVERCALL; OVERCALL IN OPPONENT'S MAJOR SUIT; OVERCALL IN OPPONENT'S MINOR SUIT; PHANTOM SACRIFICE; POSITIONAL FACTOR; PRESSURE BID; PUSH; REDOUBLE; ROMAN JUMP OVERCALLS; RULE OF TOTAL TRICKS; S O S REDOUBLE; SAFETY LEVEL; SAVE; 2 NT OVERCALL; UNUSUAL NOTRUMP; WEAK JUMP OVERCALL; WEAK NOTRUMP OVERCALL.

COMPETITIVE DOUBLE. A double in a competitive auction which invites partner to bid game but gives him the option of signing off in a partscore or passing for penalties. One increasingly popular example is the MAXIMAL OVERCALL DOUBLE. Competitive doubles can be useful in contested auctions where the enemy suit has been bid and raised at a low level:

WEST	NORTH	EAST	SOUTH
			1♡
2♣	2♡	3♣	Pass
Pass	?		

North may hold

♠A 7 4 3   ♡J 6 2   ◊A 10 9 4   ♣8 3

He is too strong to pass and his holding in clubs is too weak to make either a penalty double or a cooperative double, but his aces are useful for either offense or defense. Since South will usually not have sufficient values in the opponents' suit to double for penalties in such an auction, and since any unilateral action could easily be wrong, some experts prefer to use this double as competitive. It says: "Partner, I have a good hand with two-way values and don't know what to do; *you* decide."

Another typical competitive double occurs when the doubler's previous bidding shows that he cannot possibly be strong in the suit he is doubling.

WEST	NORTH	EAST	SOUTH
			1◊
Pass	1 NT	2♠	Pass
Pass	?		

North cannot have as many as four good spades in view of his original 1 NT response, and his location in front of the spade bidder is hardly ideal for defensive purposes. Thus a double is competitive, showing a hand such as:

♠A 6 3   ♡J 6 4   ◊A 6   ♣10 9 7 4 3

Partner is asked to decide whether to play for the penalty, or bid on in notrump.

COMPLEMENTARY SCORES. When two contestants play against each other in a matchpoint contest, their combined matchpoint scores add up to the matchpoint top available on that board, and the two scores are complements of each other. For example, if top score is 12 points and the North–South pair earns 8 points, the opposing East–West pair earns 4 points. Similarly if one pair earns 2½ points, the opposing pair earns 9½ points.

COMPLETE THE CUT. See CUT (2).

COMPLETE TABLE. In rubber bridge, four or more players. In club bridge, club rules sometimes specify six players as constituting a complete table. When a table is complete, no other player may cut in until or unless one of the players withdraws.

The alternative procedure, common in England, is for players to cut into any table which has completed a rubber, provided only that three players may not cut in unless there is only one table in play. This arrangement produces a greater circulation of players.

COMPOUND SQUEEZE. A preparatory triple squeeze, followed by a double squeeze, analyzed exhaustively by CLYDE E. LOVE. This ending requires two double menaces (guarded by both opponents) and a one-card menace. The one-card menace must be placed to the left of the opponent threatened.

Declarer has all remaining tricks but one.

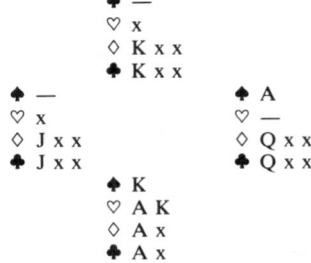

South leads the ♡A, and East is squeezed in three suits. In order to avoid giving declarer a trick directly, East must unguard a minor suit. South cashes the king and ace of that suit, leaving West with the sole guard in that suit. Now the lead of South's remaining heart effects a double squeeze. Each of the double menaces must be accompanied by a winner in its suit to provide an entry.

The alternate threat squeeze is a hybrid form of compound squeeze with very special requirements.

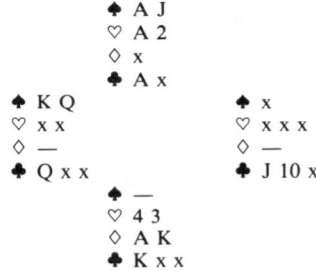

South leads the ◊A, and West must discard one of his guards. Since a spade would give up a trick directly, West must throw a heart or a club. If he chooses a heart, the low heart is discarded by North on the ◊K continuation. Meanwhile, East has thrown a heart and a spade. Now a heart lead squeezes West (in spades and clubs), and the ♠A which follows squeezes East (in hearts and clubs). If West chooses to discard a club on the ◊A, declarer leads a club to the ace and cashes the ♠A and returns to his hand with the ♣K. Now the lead of the ◊K brings about a simultaneous double squeeze.

From this, the special requirements for this squeeze are: (1) a one-card menace accompanied by a winner and placed to the left of the threatened opponent; (2) a double menace (the alternate threat suit) accompanied by a winner and any two cards of that suit in the hand opposite.

In addition, the usual requirements for a compound squeeze must be present.

Monroe Ingberman

COMPOUND TRUMP SQUEEZE. A COMPOUND SQUEEZE in which at least one opponent is subject to a TRUMP SQUEEZE. The following ending was posed as a double dummy problem by William Whitfeld before 1900.

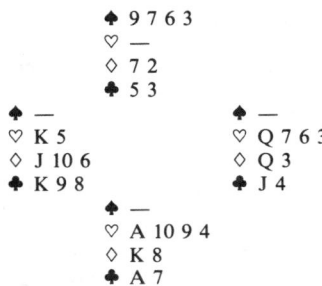

♠ 9 7 6 3
♡ —
♢ 7 2
♣ 5 3

♠ —   ♠ —
♡ K 5   ♡ Q 7 6 3
♢ J 10 6   ♢ Q 3
♣ K 9 8   ♣ J 4

♠ —
♡ A 10 9 4
♢ K 8
♣ A 7

South has the lead with spades as trumps and needs all the tricks.

South leads a low heart and trumps in dummy. A trump is led from dummy and East must discard a club or a diamond to avoid letting declarer establish an extra heart trick by ruffing. South discards whichever suit East discards, and leads that suit from dummy, winning in his hand. Declarer now cashes the ♡ A, discarding a diamond from dummy, and leads a small heart, ruffing. When dummy's last trump is led, East obviously must keep his last heart and discard whichever minor suit he has retained. South discards his heart and West is squeezed in the minor suits.

Robert True

COMPUTER GAMES. Several manufacturers have produced bridge games that are powered by computers. Some have deals pre-programmed into them, others require cassettes. See BRIDGE CHALLENGER and BIONIC BRIDGE.

COMPUTER HANDS. First used in the Eastern States Regional tournament in 1963. Hand records prepared from the computer's random shuffle provide a practical, quick, inexpensive method of producing twinned hands in a multi-section event.

The rules of Contract Bridge require that a precise series of operations be performed in dealing a hand. This process is specified (1) to guarantee that any particular deal is completely random and (2) to ensure that no player has any clue as to the nature of the deal before he picks up his cards. The computer is capable of dealing in the same manner as humans, but it is hardly practical. Instead the computer is programmed to use a very simple technique. In the computer memory, 52 locations are set aside, each one representing a card. The sequence in which the cards are initially arranged is immaterial. Let us assume the order to be spades, hearts, diamonds and clubs each arranged in natural order. For the first card (♠A) the computer selects a series of eight random digits. The same random generation process is used to fill the remainder of the 52 positions. This process generates a completely unpredictable and unrelated sequence of digits. The computer now arranges or *sorts* these random numbers into arithmetic sequence. After this is done, the first 13 cards are assigned to North, the second 13 to East, etc. Other methods of distributing the cards could be used, but this works as well as any. After this is done, the computer must arrange the hands in suits in sequence and prepare to have them printed out.

The use of computer hands has become widespread at tournaments from the Sectional level up. In addition to the usual hand records, where one hand is printed per sheet, the computer now also produces a printed record on which 16 hands appear. These can be used as a master for printing at tournaments, so that at the end of each session a set of hand records is available to every contestant.

Computer hands cause no problems in the conduct of the game. Of course the players who actually duplicate hands from a hand record cannot play those particular hands, so the movement cannot be complete. But this is a small price to pay for the ability to have the same hands played at every table throughout a large tournament.

Over the years, there have been frequent complaints concerning the distribution and unusual or unfortunate suit breaks. These are regularly blamed on computer hands. However, many studies have been made in an attempt to determine whether the random deals performed by the computer match the odds for distribution. The patterns of the 3,080 computer hands used in the round-robin qualifying rounds of the 1972 World Team Olympiad were analyzed by *The Bridge World*, and the incidence of each hand pattern was found to be very close to mathematical expectations (see mathematical tables, Table 1). Suits were found to have broken evenly slightly more often than would be expected. Tournament Director Sid Kilsheimer decided to do a similar check of computer hands. He chose the hands that have been played from 1964 through 1981 in the ACBL-Wide Charity, Olympiad Fund and International Fund games. These are hands that were played all over the American Contract Bridge League. He checked 60 sets of hand records (8,024 hands), and the predicted occurrence of various distributions was extemely close to the expected occurrence. Said Kilsheimer in an article in the *ACBL Bulletin* (November 1981), "I for one as a director and player am firmly convinced that the computer hands *do* represent a truly fair set of deals."

COMPUTER SCORING. The first serious attempt to score a bridge tournament with computer assistance was in Ostend, Belgium, in the early Fifties. The players used sensitized pencils to enter the scores on punched cards which were fed directly into a machine. Besides calculating the overall standings, the machine furnished each pair with a virtual reproduction of their personal score card, with the matchpoints awarded on each board.

Other pioneering efforts were made in Denver in 1957, in New York in 1962 and through the late Sixties and early Seventies at various North American Championships. Boeing developed a program that worked satisfactorily in 1970 and RICHARD FREEDMAN wrote one that was used in NAC's in 1977 and 1978 and in the World Pair Championships in New Orleans in 1978. Computers have been used to score the World Pair Championships every four years since Cannes in 1962. Sweden's program, used in Stockholm in 1970 and Las Palmas in 1974, was received very favorably. Some problems were encountered during the 1982 World Pair Championships in Biarritz, France, but in general computer scoring was well received. However, a common complaint is that no RECAP SHEETS, only FREQUENCY SHEETS, are provided against which a player can compare his score.

The first NAC event to be scored by computer was the Life Master Pairs in Los Angeles from July 28–August 2, 1963. All the early experiments used a large, off-site computer that had to be fed information through telephone lines. There were two problems with this. Because of the high cost of short term rental of terminals and telephone lines and the cost of long distance telephone transmission time and the cost of *connect time* (when the scores were being entered in the computer), these efforts were far more costly than doing the scoring manually. Also, because of the logistical problem of taking the scores to a remote area, the need to enter every score before the machine could start working and the long trip back to the playing area to hang the sheet, there was no improvement of service to the players. In fact, many players who had previously watched directors score their section felt that there was a disservice because now they had nothing to do until their scores came out.

Current plans are to use small microcomputers to do the scoring for a small number of sections (3–6). These will be easily portable from site to site and should eliminate many of the logistical problems previously encountered. The first NAC to be scored primarily by computer was the 1982 Fall NAC at Minneapolis.

COMPUTERS (in their application to bridge organization). From 1961 to 1963 the ACBL used unit record equipment and a staff of eight to maintain masterpoint and membership records for 140,000 bridge players by a punch card method. This was superseded in January 1964 by more efficient magnetic tape equipment. In 1981 the ACBL purchased its own computer (IBM System 3/Model 15D) and began processing all membership and masterpoint award transactions in house. The sole remaining service produced outside of the ACBL consisted of computer-dealt hand records for tournaments.

CONCEDE. To yield one or more of the remaining tricks to the opponents. See LAWS (Laws 70, 73, 74); LAWS OF DUPLICATE (Laws 68, 70, 71).

CONCERNED BRIDGE PLAYERS UNION (CBPU). An organization of professional bridge players formed in 1981 and recognized as an accredited professional organization by the ACBL in 1982.

CONCESSION. See CLAIM OR CONCESSION.

CONDITIONS OF CONTEST. A statement governing the competition in an event. In general there should be a preliminary statement as to the masterpoint requirements or other prerequisites for entry into the event, the number of sessions the event will run, the entry fee, how many qualifying sessions and how many final (or semifinal) sessions. In knockout team games there should also be a statement as to

such matters as the number of boards to be played in each match; the seeding rights, *i.e.*, the rights exercisable by the higher-ranked team with respect to the choice of seats and opponents; any restrictions on the right to have two pairs who played each other in the first half of the match play against each other in the second half; the method of resolution of the match in the event of a tie, and so forth. In SWISS MOVEMENT team games the conditions of contest must include statements as to the form of scoring used, including the scale of VICTORY POINTS, if any. In a pair event a final statement, made up after the event is under way, includes the setup of the game, number to be qualified and method of qualification, whether at-large pairs will be qualified, and computation of the carryover, and the setup of the final (or semifinal) session(s).

CONDONING. An action immediately following an irregularity by the opposition which would have been a proper one if the preceding action had been proper.

At rubber bridge, an irregular bid can be condoned in this way unless the non-offending side has drawn attention to the irregularity. In duplicate such a bid can be condoned as a matter of law. In both forms of the game an irregular lead can be condoned in all circumstances. If a declarer leads from the wrong hand, a defender may follow in proper sequence, either on his own initiative or if his partner so requires. See LAWS 34, 53, 60; LAWS OF DUPLICATE (Laws 27, 53, 60).

CONDUCT. See ETHICS AND CONDUCT.

CONFEDERAÇAO BRASILEIRA DE BRIDGE. See BRAZILIAN BRIDGE FEDERATION.

CONFEDERACIÓN SUDAMERICANA DE BRIDGE. See SOUTH AMERICAN BRIDGE CONFEDERATION.

CONFERENCE. A voluntary association of neighboring ACBL units or districts organized to further the purposes of the ACBL and of its member units. The powers of a Conference are limited to those delegated to it by the member units. Among the reasons for organizing an ACBL Conference are the promotion of matters of mutual interest, such as tournament attendance and the reduction of interunit and inter-district frictions.

CONGLOMERATE MAJOR RAISES. An extension of the SWISS CONVENTION designed to allow responder to make a forcing raise of a major suit opening while specifying whether it is based on a singleton somewhere in the hand, on great high card strength, on very good trumps or merely on general strength. Using the bids just beyond a jump raise (starting with 3♠ over 1♡, or 3 NT over 1♠), responder bids as follows:

First step	shows a singleton (unidentified)
Second step	shows 17–18 HCP
Third step	shows four trumps headed by at least two of the top three honors,

Fourth step

or more than four trumps headed by at least the ace or king shows any hand worth a strong raise that does not meet the above criteria.

After responder has shown a singleton, opener can ask where it is by making the cheapest bid. Responder bids the suit of his singleton if he can do so without going past four of the trump suit; otherwise he bids four of the trump suit.

For alternative methods see SUPER SWISS, UNBALANCED SWISS RAISE, VALUE SWISS RAISES.

CONGRESS. Term for tournament, dating back to the days of whist. The term no longer is used in North America but still is common as a synonym for tournament in other sections of the world.

CONOT 2 NT. See 1 NT OPENING (Responses).

CONSOLATION EVENT. In most SECTIONAL and higher rated TOURNAMENTS, the OPEN PAIR event and occasionally other events are held in two or more SESSIONS, one or more of which may be QUALIFYING SESSIONS. The players who do not qualify for the last session or sessions are eligible for competition in a secondary event played at the same time as the final of the main event, which event is known as a CONSOLATION. In REGIONAL and NORTH AMERICAN CHAMPIONSHIPS where GOLD and RED POINTS are awarded for the main event, the consolation event awards are also partially in red points, and the balance in regular master points. See also SECONDARY EVENT. The World Open Pairs also features a consolation event.

CONSTRUCTIVE. A description applied to a bid that suggests game prospects but is not forcing. The partner will take further action more often than not. See ENCOURAGING (1).

CONSULTATION. This practice between partners regarding a penalty is forbidden under Law 11, LAWS OF DUPLICATE, and any such discussion cancels the right to penalize.

CONTESTANT. One or more players competing for a combined score. In an individual contest, each player enters as an individual, changing partners as the movement requires and receiving credit for his own score on each board he plays. In a pair contest, players enter as pairs, playing with the same partner throughout for a common score on all boards played. In a team contest, players enter as a team of four or more, changing partners among their own teammates as permitted by the CONDITIONS OF CONTEST, but competing for a common score.

CONTESTED AUCTION. See COMPETITIVE BIDDING.

CONTRACT. (1) The undertaking by declarer's side to win, at the denomination named, the number of odd tricks specified in the final bid, whether undoubled, doubled or redoubled. (2) The game of contract bridge, loosely. See TRUMP SUIT.

CONTRACT BRIDGE. Fourth in the succession of partnership card games that began with WHIST and continued with BRIDGE WHIST and AUCTION BRIDGE. The essential point of difference from its predecessor is that no tricks won in the play are counted toward game except those which are contracted for in the bidding. A declarer contracting for and making 100 points in trick score has made a game and becomes vulnerable. Game contracts are: 3 NT (first trick worth 40, and subsequent tricks 30 each); four of a major suit, hearts or spades, worth 30 each; five of a minor suit, diamonds or clubs, worth 20 each. The lowest bid in the auction is 1 ♣, followed by one of diamonds, hearts, spades or notrump, and so on up to seven of any suit or notrump. It must be noted that a call of a higher number of tricks outranks a bid of a lower number, even though the lower number bid may be valued at a higher trick count. Contracts may be doubled and redoubled to increase premiums and penalties. There are bonuses for contracts of six and seven, called small and grand slams. See SCORING; MAJORITY CALLING.

Sides may be predetermined if two partnerships are pre-established. Otherwise the cards are CUT to establish partnerships and, in any case, to determine the first dealer. Partners face each other in seats arbitrarily named for compass points, North and South opposing East and West. The player at the dealer's left shuffles the cards and presents them to the dealer, who offers them to the player at his right for a cut. Normally, two decks of 52 cards are used, the dealer's partner shuffling the second deck and placing them after shuffling at his right, from where the next dealer offers the cards to the previous dealer for a cut. The dealer distributes the cards one at a time to each player in a clockwise manner beginning with the player on his left, and taking the last card himself, ending with each player having before him a hand of 13 cards. The players study their hands, and the bidding period begins.

The dealer has the opportunity to open the bidding, or he may pass. During the bidding, correct procedure requires that bids be made in a uniform manner, as, "pass," "1 ♣," "double," etc. Any variation from the standard formula is improper, as also are any gestures, remarks, mannerisms or grimaces. See PROPRIETIES. The auction proceeds until three players have passed in succession following the last bid, double or redouble. If all four players pass, the deal is abandoned and the next player deals. (In CHICAGO, the same dealer redeals.) At the end of the bidding, the declarer is determined as that player of the partnership who first named the denomination, suit or notrump, of the final bid. This completes the bidding phase of the hand.

The player to the left of the declarer has the duty of making the OPENING LEAD. After he has led a card, declarer's partner places his hand face up on the table, and the play of his cards is at the management of the declarer. See ARRANGING.

The play consists of 13 tricks, to each of which each player contributes one card in proper clockwise sequence. To each trick each player must play a card of the suit led, if able. If unable, he may play any card. Any trick containing a trump is won by the highest trump; any trick not containing a trump is won by the highest card of the suit led. The winner of each trick has the right and duty of leading to the next trick.

The declarer then attempts to make his contract, by taking as many tricks in excess of six as his final contract specified he would take. If he succeeds, he enters his trick points BELOW THE LINE and any extra tricks or bonuses he may have earned ABOVE THE LINE. When a partnership's total of trick points exceeds 100, that partnership is vulnerable, and a new GAME is started from a zero trick score on each side. The side first winning two games gets the bonus for winning the RUBBER. See SCORING.

If the declarer fails to make his contract, his opponents score points above the line for each UNDERTRICK. These points are increased if the contract has been DOUBLED or REDOUBLED during the period of the auction.

The game grew out of its predecesor, auction bridge, rather slowly and obscurely, with the idea of trick score bonuses for contracted tricks deriving from the French game of PLAFOND. In his slightly fictionalized memoirs of World War I entitled *Ashenden*, SOMERSET MAUGHAM, who took bridge very seriously, reported a game in Switzerland: "The game was contract, with which I was not very familiar." In the early Twenties, two booklets entitled *Contract Bridge* were published, and an unsuccessful application was made to the Knickerbocker Club to prepare a code of contract rules.

It was not until 1925, however, that contract bridge reached its full development. HAROLD S. VANDERBILT practiced with and perfected a new scoring system, including the vulnerability feature, while on an ocean cruise from Los Angeles to Havana. Changes in the scoring since 1925 were fairly frequent in the early days, but minor in character.

Vanderbilt's contract bridge caught on very rapidly with many players of the game, but for several years there was no formal regulation of bridge, and in many clubs both auction and contract bridge were played. Rules adopted by the card committee of the WHIST CLUB (NYC) were probably the most widely used. Earlier laws produced by ROBERT F. FOSTER and the Knickerbocker Whist Club were withdrawn in favor of the Whist Club version.

The first issue of *The Bridge World* magazine, edited by ELY CULBERTSON, in October 1929, advocated the promulgation of an international Code of Laws for Contract Bridge. Subsequently, committees representing the United States, England and France were appointed, and the first International Code became effective Nov. 1, 1932. See LAWS OF CONTRACT BRIDGE.

In September 1930, Ely Culbertson published his *Contract Bridge Blue Book*, which became a best seller and which appeared in annual revisions for four years (see BIBLIOGRAPHY). It was Culbertson, through his writings, his personality, his lectures and his organization, who was most responsible for the wide vogue the game quickly attained. The international publicity resulting from the famous CULBERTSON-LENZ MATCH in 1931 and the ANGLO-AMERICAN MATCHES in 1930, 1933, and 1934 made the new game of Contract Bridge a household word. Although Culbertson's was the first widely accepted

system of bidding in Contract Bridge, it became outmoded, and numerous other systems of bidding have come to the fore since his day. The GOREN methods, based on POINT-COUNT valuation, which became standard in the United States after 1950, are based firmly on the foundations laid by Culbertson.

CONTRACT BRIDGE ASSOCIATION OF IRELAND. Founded in Dublin in 1932, this association controls the game in the 26 southern counties of Ireland. A group of individuals managed it until 1937 when numerical and geographical growth made it necessary to change to affiliated club membership, and the association became a purely organizing body. In 1982 there were more than 330 clubs divided into 10 regions, with a membership of over 20,000. Ireland hosted the 1967 European Championships in Dublin. For international participation, see IRISH BRIDGE UNION. Competitions include Open Teams and Pairs Championships, with 20 open Congresses held annually at different times of the year.

Officers, 1982:
President: Mrs. J. Britton
Secretary: Marie Gleeson, 17 Beechpark,
     Athlone, Westmeath, Ireland

CONTRACT BRIDGE ASSOCIATION OF POLAND (POLSKI ZWIAZEK BRYDZA SPORTOWEGO). This association was founded in 1956 and known until 1962 as the Polish Bridge Union. By 1982 it had a membership of 6,200 in 547 clubs. The Association participates in European Championships, hosting the 1966 event in Warsaw and finishing second in 1970, annually sponsors the Baltic Bowl competition (see BALTIC CONGRESS), and took part in the World Olympiad 1962, 1964, 1966, 1970, 1972, 1974 and won the Rosenblum Teams in 1978. National championships are held annually for Open Teams (a league event, divided into divisions, with automatic promotion and relegation of the winning and losing teams), Open Pairs, Mixed Teams, Mixed Pairs, and an Individual. Except for the Open Teams, national events are conducted on a multistage elimination method, also used to select Poland's international team. In 1968, more than 500 teams participated in the Open Teams event, and 3,500 players contested for the Open Pairs title. The Association also awards master points and publishes a monthly magazine, *Brydz*.

Officers, 1982:
President: Marian Frenkiel
Secretary: Leonard Michniewski, ul. Kniewskiego
     9 m 4, 00-019 Warszawa, Poland

CONTRACT BRIDGE FORUM, THE. Monthly bridge publication of the ACBL Western Conference, which appears in newspaper form. Orginally it was published privately by TOM STODDARD beginning in 1935 and subsequently on behalf of the PACIFIC BRIDGE LEAGUE. Editor: KEN MONZINGO, P.O. Box 20626, San Diego CA 92120.

CONTRACT BRIDGE LAWS. For rubber bridge, see LAWS OF CONTRACT BRIDGE; for duplicate bridge, see LAWS OF DUPLICATE; for Chicago, see CHICAGO.

CONTRACT BRIDGE LEAGUE OF THAILAND.
Founded in 1947 by Lt. William Howard Hunter, in 1982 it numbered more than 100 members. The League participates in World Team Olympiads and Far Eastern Championships, winning the event in 1961, 1963, 1965, and 1966. In 1966 Thailand became the first representative of the Far East Bridge Federation to participate in the Bermuda Bowl, and also represented the FEBF in the 1967 World Championships.

Officers, 1982:
President: Somboon Nandhabiwat
Secretary: Boonserm Weesakul, 19 Sukumvit, 23 Bangkok, Thailand

CONTRACT WHIST. A cross between WHIST and CONTRACT BRIDGE. The four players bid in turn for the contract, but the play is that of whist, with all four hands concealed. The principles of the game were set forth in *Contract Whist*, by HUBERT PHILLIPS, published in 1932. Although played only occasionally, it is considered by some to be a game requiring high skill.

CONTRACTING. A word which signifies the act of agreeing to take a certain number of tricks in a deal of bridge.

CONTRACTING SIDE. Declarer and his partner. The opponents are the defending side.

CONTROL ASKING BIDS. See ASKING BIDS.

CONTROL MAINTENANCE. A strategy aimed at preventing a defender from gaining the mastery of a particular suit. In notrump hands, HOLD-UP PLAY is the key to control. In trump play, control usually refers to the struggle against a defender holding trump length. The following example is from *Reese On Play* by TERENCE REESE.

A fairly well-known stratagem to avoid losing control of trumps is to refuse to ruff until dummy can cope with the suit which the opponents have led:

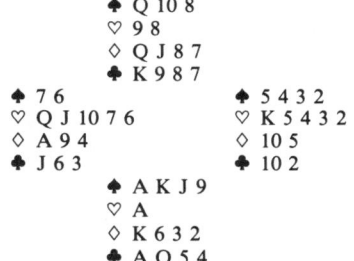

The ♡ Q is led against 4♠. If declarer draws three or four rounds of trumps, the 4–2 split is fatal for him. The right play is to draw two rounds of trumps and then clear diamonds. West wins with the ace and plays a second heart; South discards a club from his hand and any further heart leads can be dealt with in dummy.

In the play of this hand declarer used two stratagems to protect himself from losing control; one was to clear the side suit before drawing trumps, and the other was to refuse to ruff the second heart.

CONTROL SWISS CONVENTION. See SWISS CONVENTION.

CONTROLLED PSYCHICS. See PSYCHIC CONTROLS.

CONTROLS. (1) Generally, holdings that prevent the opponents' winning one, two or conceivably three immediate tricks in a specified suit.

First-round control: ace, or a void in a trump contract.
Second-round control: king, or a singleton in a trump contract.
Third-round control: queen, or a doubleton in a trump contract.

Controls may be discovered or revealed by means of ASKING BIDS or CUEBIDS.
(2) Specifically, aces and kings. An ace is normally counted as two "controls," and a king as one. See BLUE TEAM CLUB.
See also EXPECTED NUMBER OF CONTROLS IN BALANCED HAND.

CONVENTION. A call that, by agreement, not inference, gives or requests information unrelated to the denomination named, as defined by the ACBL for its convention classification system. For example, if a bid of 1♣ is understood to mean possession of general strength not necessarily in the club suit, or perhaps not in the club suit at all, that is a convention, for ordinarily the bid of 1♣ implies the bidder's willingness to play the hand at a club contract — that is, it implies the possession of general strength with either length or strength in the club suit. See ARTIFICIAL CALL and LAWS OF DUPLICATE (Law 40). In addition, a play by a defender that conveys a meaning by agreement rather than by inference is a convention.

The ACBL lists bidding conventions that are acceptable in tournament play. Prior to 1969, these were listed in two general categories: Class I, those automatically allowed in all tournaments, and Class II, those dependent on the discretion of the tournament committee. With the increasing proliferation of conventions, the ACBL adopted new regulations in 1969 and 1970. All conventions were placed in six general classes, A, B, C, D, E and F, and, effective January 1, 1971, a new CONVENTION CARD and an Alert procedure were introduced. Emphasis shifted from listing all partnership agreements to checking the most common understandings, writing in uncommon conventions and ALERTING the opponents to special conventions and treatments. For this purpose, bids were classified as follows:

CONVENTION: A call that, by agreement, not inference, gives or requests information unrelated to the denomination named.

TREATMENT: A call that indicates desire to play in the denomination named (or promises or requests values in that denomination) but that also, by agreement, gives or requests information on which further action can be based.

NATURAL CALL: A call that suggests itself as the final contract, without giving additional information on which further action could be based.

All natural calls and treatments are allowed in every class game; only conventions are subject to regulation. However, every player is responsible for Alerting his opponents whenever his partner uses an unusual treatment or convention, not checked off on the convention card. In addition, a player must use the Alert procedure unless his opponents specifically request him not to do so before the auction begins.

In 1982 the following bidding conventions were listed:

CLASS A

(Must be allowed in all local or higher-rated events except at sanctioned clubs.)

4 NT ace and 5 NT king-asking conventions and responses to handle interference.

Gerber.

Grand Slam Force.

Stayman Club response to notrump.

Lightner Double.

Takeout Double.

Unusual Notrump (by unpassed hand must be at two-level or higher).

SOS Redouble.

Cuebid for strong takeout.

2 ♣ opening, forcing, strong, and artificial.

2 ◇ negative response to forcing 2 ♣ opening.

2 NT negative response to natural, strong opening two-bid.

CLASS B

(Must be allowed in sectional or higher-rated championship events.)

Negative Double.

4 ♣ slam conventions (Gerber variations, etc.).

2 NT over opponent's takeout double as a conventional raise.

Stayman diamond response to notrump.

Takeout bids over opponents' preempts.

Transfers (Jacoby and Texas).

Gambling 3 NT (maximum one side stopper).

Over opponent's 1 NT opening: 2 ♣ for majors; 2 ♣ for minors, 2 ◇ for majors; better minor for major-suit takeout.

1 NT response to major forcing.

Defenses after opponents' conventional calls.

1 ♣ forcing.

1 ◇ artificial negative response to 1 ♣ opening.

2 ◇ artificial response to natural 2 ♣ opening.

Second negative response after artificial forcing opening bid.

Limited 2 ♣ opening — forcing, strong and artificial.

CLASS C

(Must be allowed in regional or higher-rated championship events.)

Asking bids (suit control and trump quality asking).

Flint (3 ◇ or 3 ♣).

Jump to 2 NT or 3 NT as forcing raise.

Jump and double-jump shift to show forcing raise.

Cuebid for light takeout or two-suit takeout.

Responsive doubles.

Conventional responses and rebids after weak two-

bids. (A 2 NT response requires no Alert.)

Conventional responses to natural, strong two-bids.

Checkback or delayed Stayman.

Astro.

Brozel.

Calls which by agreement reveal a psych.

Drury.

Flannery 2 ◇ opening.

Impossible negative.

Gambling 3 ♣.

CLASS D

(Must be allowed in national championship events.)

Weak two-bids with point count range of 8 HCP or more and conventional responses and rebids.

Strong ace asking other than 4 ♣ or 4 NT, and king asking other than 5 NT.

Other artificial responses and rebids after natural notrump.

2 ◇ opening – forcing, strong and artificial.

2 ◇ openings: Roman, Schenken, Precision, Stayman, Mexican.

Dynamic 1 NT.

3 ♣ opening – forcing, strong and artificial with intermediate two-bids.

Transfer jump responses to opening bids.

Other defenses over opponent's notrump opening.

Double of 3 NT for lead of specified suit.

Negative Slam Double.

Opening 2 NT or higher for minors.

1 NT overcall for takeout.

Balancing 2 ♣ for takeout.

Competitive doubles.

Opening 4 ♣ and 4 ◇ transfers.

Artificial first-round responses to artificial forcing opening bids.

Roman two-suit jump overcalls.

2 ♣ or 2 ◇ opening (three-suiter) at or near minimum opening.

Gambling 2 NT – one outside stopper.

Jump to 2 NT or jump shift as limit raise.

Flannery 2 ♡ opening.

CLASS E

(May be used only if approved in advance on Form 505 or approved by the Tournament Committee for extended team play.)

Herbert responses to takeout doubles and one-bids.

Strong artificial 1 ◇ opening bid.

TAM II 2 ◇.

Opening two-bids which show two suits, at least one of which is known.

Conventional balancing calls.

Omnibus 2 NT response to 1 ♡ or 1 ♣ opening bid.

Preemptive opening transfers.

Strong 1 NT response to 1 ◇, 1 ♡, 1 ♣ opening.

Cuebid to show solid or near-solid suit.

CLASS F

(May not be authorized for use in other than extended team play — matches of 16 boards or more.)

Big Diamond System, Pro System, Lea System, Roman System, Chico 2 ◇, Simplified Multi-Color 2 ◇.

For descriptions and evaluations of these and

other conventions see Kearse, *Bridge Conventions Complete,* Kantar, *Bridge Conventions,* and Root and Pavlicek, *Modern Bridge Conventions,* BIBLIOGRAPHY, E.

CONVENTION CARD. In tournament bridge, all players are entitled to know the meaning of all calls and plays made by opponents. If any call or play conveys a meaning to a partner that the opponents could not be expected to recognize, or that is not the standard meaning the call or play would have, it is a *conventional call or play.* See CONVENTION and ARTIFICIAL BID. See also ALERTING. In order to facilitate such exchange of information, a card, on which generally used conventions and treatments may be checked off and which provides space to list other conventional bids, is provided. This convention card is often on the back of the card on which a partnership can keep a record of their scores on the boards played. In 1982, the WORLD BRIDGE FEDERATION introduced its own four-sided convention card for use in all world championships.

CONVENTIONS, Guide to ACBL Classifications. Following are the conventions that were classified by the ACBL, together with their 1982 classifications. Class A conventions can be used in any game from club through North American Championship. Each subsequent class has a narrower sphere, ending with Class F conventions, which can be used only in extended team events under specific circumstances.

NONSTANDARD SIGNALS*
Bechgaard Signals (to show length of a suit)
Odd-Even Discards - (includes Roman Discards - Require Verbal Alert)
Odd-Even Signals
Revolving Discards (Lavinthal Signals - Require Verbal Alert)
Signals to Show Specific Honor Cards
Upside-Down Signals - (Require Verbal Alert)

CONVENTIONS FOR THE DEFENDERS
Fisher Doubles - (Class D)
Lightner Slam Doubles - (Class A)

MAKING INQUIRIES
Ace Identification - (Class C)
Acol 4 NT Opening - (Class C)
Baby Blackwood - (Class D)
Baron Slam Try - (Class C)
Black and Red Gerber - (Class B)
Blackwood - (Class A)
Byzantine Blackwood - (Class A)
Control Asking Bids - (Class C)
Culbertson Asking Bids - (Class C)
Culbertson 4-5 NT - (Class A)
Culbertson Trump Asking Bids - (Class C)
Culwood - (Class A)
D.I. ("Declarative Interrogative" or "Declarative Informatory") - (Class C)
Depo - (Class A)
Extended Gerber - (Class B)
Fane 4♣ Convention - (Class B)

* 1982, Sponsoring Organization has the authority to designate the nonstandard defensive signaling that will be allowed, including the above.

4♣ Asking Bid - (Class C)
Fulwiler Asking Bids - (Class C)
Gerber - (Class A)
Gerber After 2 NT and 3 NT Openings - (Class A)
Grand Slam Force - (Class A)
Key Card Blackwood - (Class A)
Key Card Gerber - (Class B)
Lebovic Asking Bid - (Class C)
Malowan (Grand Slam Force After Blackwood) - (Class C)
Responding to Blackwood Over Opponent's Interference - (Class A)
Roman Asking Bids - (Class C)
Roman Blackwood - (Class A)
Roman Gerber - (Class B)
Romex Trump Asking Bids - (Class C)
San Francisco - (Class A)
Super Precision Asking Bids - (Class C)
Super Gerber - (Class D)
The R/H 4 NT Convention - (Class C)
Wang Trump Asking Bids - (Class C)

TOP LEVEL AND HIGHER and FORCING OPENING BIDS AND RESPONSES
Ace and King Showing Responses - (Class C)
Ace-showing Responses - (Class C)
Ace-showing Responses to 2♣ Openings - (Class D)
Artificial 2♣ Opening - (Class A)
Automatic 2◇ Response - (Class B)
Big Diamond System - (Class F)
Blue Team Club (*Conventions within system are classified)
Blue Team 1♣ Opening - (Class B)
Cheaper Minor as a Second Negative - (Class B)
Clarac Slam Try - (Class D)
Dynamic 1 NT - (Class D)
Herbert Negative (To a Two Bid, - Class C)
Herbert Second Negative - (Class B)
Impossible Negative - (Class C)
Lea System - (Class F)
Little Roman Club (Arno) - (*see below)
Mexican 2◇ - (Class D)
Multi 2◇ Opening - (Class F)
Precision Ace-asking Bids - (Class C)
Precision Club System - (Class B)
Precision Control Asking Bids - (Class C)
Precision Trump Asking Bids - (Class C)
Pro System (Pattern Relay Organized System) - (Class F)
Roman Club - (*System is Class F)
Rubin Opening Transfers - (Class D)
Schenken Club - (Class B)
Schenken 2◇ - (Class D)
Stayman 2♣ and 2◇ Openings - (Class D)
Step Responses to 2♣ Openings - (Class D)
Tam II 2♣ and 2◇ Openings - (Class E)
2◇ Negative - (Class A)
2◇ as the Only Positive Response - (Class D)
2◇ Negative, 2♡ Neutral - (Class D)
2 NT as a Negative Response - (Class A)

OFFENSIVE PREEMPTIVE CONVENTIONS
4♣ and 4◇ as Strong Transfers - (Class D)
4♣ and 4◇ as Weak Transfers - (Class D)
4 NT as Weak Minor Preempt - (Class D)

* Conventions within the System are classified

Gambling 3 NT (Maximum One Side Stopper) - (Class B)

Kantar 3 NT - (Class B)

3 NT as Weak Minor Preempt - (Class D)

TWO AND THREE-SUITED OPENING BIDS

Flannery 2 ◊ - (Class C)

Flannery 2 ♡ - (Class D)

Neapolitan 2 ◊ - (Class D)

Precision 2 ◊ - (Class D)

Roman 2 ♣ - (Class D)

Roman 2 ◊ - (Class D)

2 ♣ Opening for Minors - (Class E)

2 ◊ Opening as Minimum Three-Suiter - (Class D)

2 ◊ Opening for Majors - (Class E)

2 NT Opening for Minors - (Class D)

COMPETITIVE BIDDING

Astro - (Class C)

Astro Cuebid - (Class C)

Balancing 2 ♣ Bid (for takeout - (Class D)

Brozel - (Class C)

Cheaper Minor Takeout - (Class B)

Clubs for Takeout - (Class B)

Colorful Cuebids - (Class C)

Competitive Doubles - (Class D)

Cooperative Doubles - (Class D)

Copenhagen - (Unclassified Convention)

Cuebid as a Light Takeout - (Class C)

Defense Against Opponents Two-Suited Calls - (Class B)

Exclusion Overcalls - (Class B)

Fishbein - (Class B)

Herbert Negative Response to a Takeout Double or One-bid - (Class E)

Kock Werner Redouble - (Class B)

Landy - (Class B)

Lebensold - (Class D)

Leghorn Diamond Takeouts - (Class B)

Michaels Cuebids - (Class C)

Modified Astro - (Class D)

Negative Doubles - (Class B)

Negative Slam Doubles - (Class D)

Notrump for Takeout - (Class B - Fishbein variation)

Optional Doubles - (Class B)

Pinpoint Astro - (Class D)

Positive Slam Doubles - (Extension of Negative Slam Double -Class D)

Redoubles for Takeout Over 1 NT Doubled - (Class D)

Responsive Doubles - (Class C)

Ripstra - (Class B)

Ripstra Against Gambling 3 NT - (Class B)

Roman Jump Overcalls - (Class D)

Roth-Stone Astro - (Class D)

Simplified Takeout Over Strong Artificial Openings - (Class B)

S.O.S. Redoubles - (Class A)

Stayman After Notrump Overcalls - (Class A - may require an alert . . .)

Stayman Over Opponent's Notrump Overcall - (Unclassified)

Strong Cuebids - (Class A)

Takeout Doubles - (Class A)

Takeout Doubles of Preempts - (Class B)

Takeouts Against Four-level Preempts - (Class B)

Top and Bottom Cuebids - (Class C)

Transfers Over Doubles of 1 NT - (Class D)

Truscott Over Strong Artificial Openings - (Class B)

2 ♣ for Minors, 2 ◊ for Majors - (Class B)

2 NT as a Limit Raise Over Opponent's Takeout Double - (Class B)

2 NT as a Preemptive Raise Over Double of Minor Suit Opening - (Class B)

Two-suited Takeouts Over Preempts - (Class B)

Two-way Exclusion Bids - (Class D)

Unusual Notrump and Minors - (Class F)

Unusual Notrump and Minors Over Notrump - (Class D)

Unusual Notrump Overcall - (Class A)

Unusual 1 NT Overcall - (Class D)

Unusual-over-Unusual - (Class B)

Upper Suits Cuebids - (Class C)

Weiss - (Class B)

RESPONSES TO NOTRUMP OPENING BIDS

August 2 ◊ - (Class D)

Automatic Aces - (Class D)

Boland - (Class D)

Conot 2 NT - (Class D)

Double-Barreled Stayman - (Class B, 2D)

Flint - (Class D)

Flint 3 ♣ - (Class D)

Flint 2 ◊ - (Class D)

Forcing Stayman - (Class A)

Gladiator - (Class D)

Jacoby for the Minor Suits - (Class D)

Jacoby Over 2 NT Openings - (Class B)

Jacoby Transfers - (Class B)

Murray 2 ◊ - (Class D)

Nonforcing Stayman - (Class A)

Sharples - (Class D)

Slam-try Stayman - (Class B)

Smolen Transers Over Notrump Openings - (Class D)

South African Texas - (Class D)

Stayman for Stoppers - (Class B)

Stayman Over a 3 NT Opening - (Class A)

Stayman Over a 2 NT Opening - (clubs = Class A, diamonds = Class B)

Texas Transfers - (Class B)

2 NT Response as a Relay to 3 ♣ - (Class D)

Weissberger - (Class D)

RESPONSES AND REBIDS AFTER NATURAL OPENING BIDS IN A SUIT

Baron 2 NT - (Natural, Alertable)

Conglomerate Major Suit Raises - (Class C)

Control Swiss - (Class C)

Delayed Stayman - (Class C)

Drury - (Class C)

Fragment Bids - (Class C)

Inverted Minor Raises - (Alertable Treatment)

Jacoby 2 NT - (Class C)

Jump Shift by Passed Hand - (Alertable Treatment)

Jump Shift Showing a Singleton - (Class C)

Jump Shift to 3 ♣ - (Class C)

Limit Raises to Show Singletons - (Natural, Alertable)

McCabe Adjunct - (Class C)

Ogust Rebids - (Class C)

1 NT Forcing - (Class B)

Relays Over Weak Two Bids - (Class C)
Short Suit Game Tries - (Alertable Treatment)
Snap (strong notrump after passing) - (Unclassfied)
Soloway Jump Shifts - (Treatment)
Splinter Raises, - (Class C)
Swiss - (Class C)
Trump and Control Swiss - (Class C)
Trump Swiss - (Class C)
2♣ as the Only Force After a One Notrump Rebid - (Class D)
2 NT Forcing Response to Weak Two Bids - (Class C)
Two Relays and a Transfer - (Class C)
Two-way Game Tries - (Unclassified)
Unbalanced Swiss Raises - (Class C)
Unbid Minor as Delayed Stayman - (Class C)
Unbid Minor as the Only Force After a 1 NT Rebid - (Class D)
Value Swiss Raises - (Class C)
Wolff Over 2 NT Rebid - (Class D)

CONVERSATION. Conversation is carried on at the bridge table in the LANGUAGE of the bidding and the play of cards. Any other conversation during the bidding or play of the hand is either distracting (and therefore discourteous), revealing (and therefore improper and even illegal), or misleading. (See COFFEE-HOUSING, legal at poker but not at bridge.) Although bridge is a social game, any socializing or gossiping should be confined to the short period of the deal, or prior to the start of the game or during a refreshment intermission.

COOPERATIVE DOUBLE. A double that leaves partner the option of passing for penalities or bidding further. (A special type is the OPTIONAL DOUBLE.) Originally used by ELY CULBERTSON to describe a double of an opening three-bid, the term is now better reserved for some more complicated situations:

WEST	NORTH	EAST	SOUTH
			1♡
1♠	2♡ or	2♠	Pass
	1 NT		
Pass	Dbl		

As North's first bid showed limited strength, he is unlikely to have a hand on which he can be confident of defeating 2♠. The double is a suggestion which leaves the final decision to South.

WEST	NORTH	EAST	SOUTH
			1♣
Pass	Pass	Dbl	1♠
2♢	Pass	Pass	Dbl

In the light of his previous bidding, South can hardly have any positive assurance of defeating 2♢. He obviously has a maximum one-bid, perhaps 20 high-card points and 4-3-1-5 distribution. North has to consider whether he can contribute anything to the defense, and may decide to bid 2♠, 3♠, 2♡ or pass.

This type of double can occur in many disguises, but the doubler has always limited his hand in such a way that he cannot be in a position to guarantee a penalty. See also COMPETITIVE DOUBLE; DOUBLE; MAXIMAL OVERCALL DOUBLE; OPTIONAL DOUBLE.

COPENHAGEN CONVENTION. A defensive bid designed by JOHN TRELDE of Denmark to show a two-suited hand. After an opening bid, a jump to 2 NT shows the two lowest unbid suits, 3♣ the lowest and highest unbid suits, and 3♢ the two highest unbid suits.

CORRECT THE COUNT. See RECTIFYING THE COUNT.

CORRECT PACK. See PACK.

COUNT. A term used in three distinct senses, referring to: (1) the number of cards held in a suit, see COUNTING THE HAND, FOSTER ECHO, LENGTH SIGNALS, TRUMP ECHO; (2) the strength of a hand, see DISTRIBUTIONAL COUNTS, POINT-COUNT; (3) the number of tricks that must be lost for the operation of a squeeze; see RECTIFYING THE COUNT, SQUEEZE WITHOUT THE COUNT.

COUNT SIGNALS. See FOSTER ECHO, LENGTH SIGNALS, TRUMP SIGNALS.

COUNT SQUEEZE. A squeeze that operates on a player who does not guard a crucial suit in such a way as to give declarer a count of the suit, allowing him to drop an honor off-side instead of taking a losing finesse.

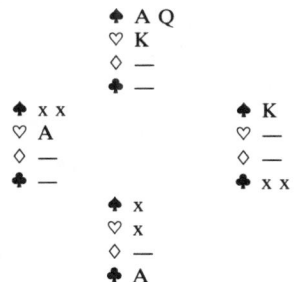

Suppose that West is known to have the ♡A, South leads the ♣A and West discards a spade. North can safely discard the ♡K. South leads a spade, and West follows low. North's ace must be played for it is known that West's remaining card is the ♡A. If West had guarded spades, he would have been caught in a SHOW-UP SQUEEZE.

                                        Monroe Ingberman

COUNT, SQUEEZE WITHOUT THE. See SQUEEZE WITHOUT THE COUNT.

COUNTING CARDS. It is each player's responsibility to determine that the hand he is about to play contains exactly 13 cards. This determination should be made before he looks at the face of any card. The LAWS (Law 7) OF DUPLICATE BRIDGE also require that the cards be recounted before being replaced in the board at completion of play.

COUNTING THE HAND. Deducing the distribution of the hidden hands from information gained during the bidding and early stages of play.

On many hands, the crucial play depends on the distribution of one particular suit. By observing or projecting the distributions of the other three suits, a player may be able to deduce how the key suit splits, *even if that suit has not yet been led.*

The procedure used is simple arithmetic, based on two facts: each suit has 13 cards; each player started with 13 cards in his hand.

The following is an elementary illustration of the basic technique of counting the hand: A decision which at first glance is a pure guess reduces to a certainty as a result of the play of the other suits.

WEST	EAST
♠ A Q 7	♠ K 5 3
♡ K Q 6	♡ A 4 2
◇ A K J 3	◇ Q 8 4 2
♣ A J 5	♣ K 10 3

West plays 7 NT, with the ♣ J led. He should delay his decision in clubs to the very end, by first cashing all his winners. South follows twice to each major, but discards clubs on the third round of each. He then follows to three rounds of diamonds, while North discards a heart on the third round. Now, by subtraction, North is known to have started with five cards in each major and two diamonds, hence only one club. So West cashes dummy's ♣ K, and (unless North drops the queen) finesses through South with certainty.

In the above example, counting the hand made declarer's final play a sure thing. More often, counting will indicate which play has the highest probability of success.

Suppose South had followed to four diamonds. Now it would be known that he started with five clubs, and North with two clubs. Then West should finesse through South as before, this time with odds of five to two that South has the missing queen. (When declarer finally takes the finesse, each defender has only one unknown card, but the odds determined from the count of the *initial* distribution are unchanged.) See PROBABILITIES, A POSTERIORI and A PRIORI.

In the illustration above, declarer's problem was simply which way to take a finesse. Sometimes counting the hand will help declarer decide between a squeeze and a finesse. Sometimes it will point up the necessity to handle a problem suit in a way radically different from what he would otherwise have attempted.

WEST	EAST
♠ A K Q	♠ 7 5 3
♡ A K Q	♡ 6 4 2
◇ A Q 8	◇ K 7 3
♣ K Q 7 3	♣ A 10 4 2

Again West plays 7 NT, with the ♣ J led. Apparently West must cash king and queen of clubs, hoping that North has two or more clubs or that the jack is singleton. But before playing clubs, West should cash his major-suit winners. On the third round of each, South discards diamonds. West then cashes the ◇ A-Q, and both opponents follow. Counting North's hand — five spades, five hearts, and two diamonds — shows that he has at most one club, which must be the 8, 9, or jack if West is to make the contract. So West abandons the normal play in

clubs, and instead leads the 3 to dummy's ace. If North follows with the 8 or 9, declarer leads a club from dummy and covers South's card, using the carefully preserved ◇ K as a re-entry for a second finesse if South splits his holding.

The preceding examples were played at notrump, so declarer could count the hand by cashing his winners, and noting when the opponents showed out. In a suit contract, this type of play runs the risk of the opponents gaining a ruff. However, in a suit contract, declarer may be able to count the hand by using *his own* trumps for ruffing. For example, if dummy has A-K-x-x in a side suit, and declarer has two small, declarer may be able to ruff the suit twice in his hand. He does not gain any tricks by doing this, as his long trumps were winners anyhow. In fact, in the process of ruffing he destroys any squeeze or throw-in threat in the suit. But he is sure to obtain the count of the suit, if that is the crucial factor in the play of the rest of the hand.

So far, we have considered only cases where declarer's information on the count was gained during the play. Inferences about suit lengths may also be drawn from the opponents' bidding (or failure to bid), from the opening lead, or from defenders' plays or signals (see DISCOVERY). These inferences are, of course, not as firm as when a player fails to follow suit.

Defensive Play. Counting the hand is as important for the defenders as for the declarer.

NORTH (Dummy)
♠ K J
♡ 10 5 3
◇ A 8 6 3
♣ A 8 7 2

EAST
♠ A Q 6
♡ J 9 7 6
◇ Q J 10
♣ J 9 5

South plays in 5 ◇, no other suits have been bid. West leads the ♠ 5. East wins and leads a second high spade, which South ruffs. South cashes ◇ K-A; West follows once, then discards a spade. South now cashes the ♡ A-K-Q (West following three times), then leads a diamond. East wins and counts declarer's hand — one spade, three hearts, five diamonds, therefore four clubs. So East does not fall for declarer's trap, and return a club, jeopardizing West's doubleton king or queen. Instead he leads a major, yielding a useless sluff-ruff, and eventually sets the hand with a club trick.

In addition to absolute counts, as in the above example, and inferential counts from the bidding, the defenders have a counting aid not available to the declarer — the LENGTH SIGNAL. Most experts use such signals sparingly, to help partner in the play of one specific suit. The policy of some experts is to signal length in all suits, when they think partner will profit more than declarer from a complete count of the hand.

In general, when partner is unlikely to be misled, a defender should make it as difficult as possible for declarer to count the hand. For instance, if a suit has gone around three times, the defender should retain the thirteenth card as long as possible, to keep declarer in doubt as to its location. It is usually wrong for a defender's first discard to be a worthless card in a suit where he has five cards and dummy has four cards — an astute declarer may be able to use this inference in counting the hand.

For a full discussion of counting. see *All Fifty-Two Cards (How to Reconstruct the Concealed Hands at the Bridge Table)* by MARSHALL MILES (BIBLIOGRAPHY, D). See also CARD READING.

Lawrence Rosler

COUNTING TRUMPS. This does not present problems for the expert, but the inexperienced player sometimes has trouble. There are three methods, which in increasing order of efficiency are:

(1) Wait until you need to know and then add the cards played to the cards remaining in view and subtract from 13. This means a lot of effort and often produces the wrong result.

(2) a. As declarer, note at the start how many trumps the defenders have, and mentally reduce that total as the cards appear.

b. As defender, make a guess from the bidding about the length of declarer's trumps. See how many this gives your partner. Then adjust your thinking if required.

(3) Think in terms of distributional patterns, which are of course the same as the patterns of a particular hand. If you have a 4-4 trump fit you are thinking of the patterns 4-4-3-2 or 4-4-4-1. If one defender shows out on the second round you know automatically that the other defender began with four and has two more. Players who are used to thinking in terms of patterns are able without difficulty to count all the suits. Two elements of the pattern are known at the start. When the bidding or play reveals a third, the fourth element is known automatically.

This is the expert method, and intermediate players should take the trouble to acquire the knack. A conscious effort to note the pattern of any 13-card hand improves familiarity with the patterns.

COUP. A special maneuver by declarer in the play of the hand. More specifically, without further designation, it refers to an endplay situation in which a defender's finessable trumps are trapped without a finesse. This may arise when there is no entry to take a finesse, or when there is no trump to lead for a finesse. Often the coup has to be prepared by shortening the trump length, reducing it to not more than the same length as the defender's. For example (see top of right column for hand):

South plays in 4♡ after West has shown minor suits by an unusual notrump overcall. The ◊ A is led and ruffed, and a heart is led to the king. South cashes the ◊ K, ruffs a diamond, and plays three rounds of spades ending in dummy. A spade is ruffed, and a club is played. South must eventually make his two remaining trumps.

When the preparation of the coup makes it necessary to ruff a winner, the term GRAND COUP is used. Single, double and triple grand coups refer to

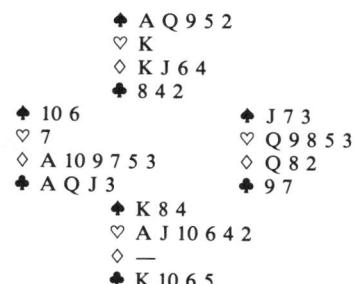

situations in which one, two, and three winners are ruffed respectively.

For the term coup applied in other special contexts, see ALCATRAZ; BATH COUP; COUP EN PASSANT; DESCHAPELLES COUP; MERRIMAC COUP; MORTON'S FORK COUP; PITT COUP; ROBERT COUP; SCISSORS COUP.

COUP EN BLANC. A term formerly used by some writers instead of DUCK.

COUP EN PASSANT. The lead of a plain suit card to promote a low trump behind a higher trump to a winning position. The term is taken from chess. See also ELOPEMENT.

In the following position, spades are trump. The lead is in the North hand.

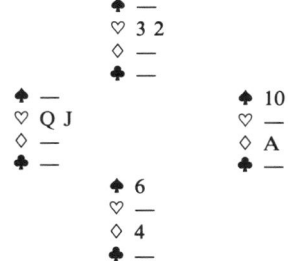

Declarer (South) holds no more winning cards. However, when a heart is led from the North hand, South makes a trick with the ♠6. If East discards, South ruffs the heart. If East ruffs with his master trump, the ♠6 wins the final trick. In the above example, if East held ♠10-5, South would score the ♠6 *en passant* in a similar manner, overruffing if East ruffed low and discarding if East ruffed high.

COUP WITHOUT A NAME. See SCISSORS COUP.

COURT CARDS. The king, queen and jack of each suit are represented by coated figures rather than pips, giving rise to the expression *coat card.* This term was corrupted to court card and extended to include the ace, probably due to the association with the figures in a royal court.

COURTESY. Any bridge player should, at all times, maintain a courteous attitude toward his partner and his opponents. See LAWS OF DUPLICATE, Proprieties, Section III. Also, see ETIQUETTE.

COURTESY BID. A response made on a very weak

hand to allow for the possibility that the opener has great strength.

COURTESY OF THE TABLE. A feature of the laws of auction bridge and the first laws of contract bridge. If dummy left the table, the defenders were required to take over dummy's duty of guarding declarer against the possibility of revoking. No penalty could be exacted against a declarer who revoked if the defenders had failed to ask the routine question, "Having no more?"

It was customary, although not legally necessary, for the dummy to ask for the Courtesy of the Table on leaving the table. This served to remind the defenders of their obligation in the matter.

This requirement was omitted from the first International edition of LAWS, published in 1932.

COVER CARDS. A method of valuation devised by GEORGE ROSENKRANZ as part of the ROMEX SYSTEM, but applicable in any method.

Aces and kings are cover cards — also queens if they are likely to be effective. If the opener's hand is measured in terms of losers, responder can judge how many of the losers he covers:

```
                  RESPONDER
               ♠ Q x
               ♡ K Q x x
               ◇ K x x x
               ♣ x x x
       OPENER              RESPONDER
       1 ♠                 1 NT
       2 ♡                 4 ♡
```

The opening bidder should have at most seven losers, and responder has four cover cards: ♠Q, ♡K-Q and ◇K. Four of opener's losers are covered, leaving three, and game can be bid. If the ♣Q were the ♣Q it could not be counted as a cover card, and a raise to 3♡ would be sufficient. See LOSING TRICK COUNT.

COVERING HONORS. When an honor is led and the next player follows with a higher honor, he is said to have covered an honor with an honor. Second hand should usually cover an honor if he might establish a trick in that suit for himself or partner in the process.

If an honor is led from a sequence of touching honors, it is seldom proper to cover until the last of the sequentials is led. The following examples are typical:

```
(a)               A x x
       K x x                  10 x x
                  Q J 9 x
```

The queen is led. If West covers, then South can take a finesse against the 10. West must duck the first honor lead but cover at the second opportunity.

If West does cover, he can be expected to hold K, K-x, or K-10.

```
(b)               K x x
       Q x x                  A 9 x x
                  J 10 8
```

South leads the jack and makes two tricks if West covers. If West ducks, East can win or duck, and

South is held to one trick provided the defenders avoid leading the suit subsequently.

```
(c)               A x x
       Q 9 x                  K 8 x x
                  J 10 x
```

If West covers the jack he gives South two tricks.

The decision about whether to cover is generally more difficult when the honor is led by declarer. Generally, if dummy does not have the honor directly below declarer's card, it should be assumed that declarer has it, and the defender should wait and cover the next honor. If dummy has the honor below the card led by declarer, it is often proper to cover unless declarer is believed to have a TWO-WAY FINESSE. When in doubt, the best policy is usually to duck quickly. An exception to the rule about not covering a sequence occurs when the opposing suit can be blocked:

```
(d)               A K x x x
       Q 9 x                  x x x
                  J 10
```

If dummy has no entry, West must cover the jack or 10 to prevent declarer from making five tricks.

```
(e)               Q J 10 9 x
       x x x                  K x x x
                  A
```

If the queen is led and covered, the remainder of the suit is established in the North hand.

```
(f)               A x
       K x x                  x x x
                  Q J 10 x x
```

If the queen is led West must not cover. He can ensure a trick in the suit because the ace must be played on the second round.

There are numerous exceptions to this rule, and a clever declarer can pose the defenders many problems, as in the following examples:

```
(g)               A x
       K x x                  J 10 x x
                  Q x x x
```

If South needs to steal a trick in the suit, he can lead the queen and West may duck.

```
(h)               A x x
       K x                  10 9 x
                  Q J x x x
```

If South leads the queen, West must cover with a doubleton king; otherwise South can continue with a small card and drop the king.

```
(i)               Q J 10 8 x
       A x x x                  K 9 x
                  x
```

At a trump contract, North leads the queen in a side suit. East must play the king. If he ducks, the king may be ruffed out eventually.

Jeff Rubens

CRACK. An expert player, partnership or team. As a verb, there are three meanings: (1) to obtain bad results after a period of success; (2) to double; (3) to open a new suit during the play of the hand. The latter two meanings are bridge colloquialisms.

CRANE SYSTEM. An obsolete bidding system

devised by JOSHUA CRANE, in which the full value of the hand was bid immediately in accordance with its point-count. A hand counting to 12–15 was bid at the one level; a hand worth 16–19 was bid at the two level, etc. This may have been the earliest published system to include a distributional point-count: both opener and responder counted three points for a singleton and six points for a void once the trump suit had been agreed. Also called, somewhat optimistically, the *common-sense system*.

CRASH. A method of bidding defensively against an artificial forcing 1♣ opening bid. The word CRASH is an acronym for *Color–RA*nk–*SH*ape. After an opening 1♣ forcing bid, a double or an overcall of 1◊ or 1 NT show various types of two-suited hands. Double shows color — both suits are red or both are black. 1◊ shows rank — both suits are majors or both are minors. 1 NT shows shape — both suits are pointed (spades and diamonds) or both are rounded. These bids are usually made on weak distributional hands — usually at least nine cards in the suits pinpointed. Bids of 1♡, 1♠, 2♣ and 2◊ show single-suited hands. Partner of the CRASH bidder usually responds as high as possible in the lowest suit possible. Overcaller passes if this is one of his suits, but bids the next higher suit in his own two-suiter if the overcaller has chosen the wrong pair of suits. For example:

WEST	NORTH	EAST	SOUTH
1♣	Dbl	Pass	3♣
Pass	3◊	Pass	?

If South is 4–4 in clubs and hearts, he will correct to hearts because he knows partner has a heart-diamond hand. If North had a black hand, he would have passed 3♣.

The original version of this convention had 1◊ for color, 1♡ for rank and 1 NT for shape, with a double reserved to show a hand of some strength and with all two-level overcalls showing one-suited hands.

CRASHING HONORS. The deceptive play of a suit by declarer resulting in the defense wasting two high honors on one trick.

The most common situation in which the declarer can crash honors occurs when the declarer holds concealed length in his own hand. The lead of an honor from dummy may cause second hand to cover with an honor, crashing still a third honor in the other defender's hand. For example:

```
              ♠ J 8 5 3
    ♠ A                   ♠ K 4
              ♠ Q 10 9 7 6 2
```

If the ♠ J is led from dummy (North), East may play the king in the hope that West holds ♠ 10–x, 10–9, or 10–x–x.

Declarer may also crash honors with a lead from his own hand toward the dummy. This play is most likely to work if dummy is apparently (or actually) short of entries, as the defenders may believe declarer did not have the option of taking a finesse. Thus:

```
              ♡ 9 8 7 6
    ♡ K 4                   ♡ A
              ♡ Q J 10 5 3 2
```

With dummy (North) barren of entries, South leads the ♡ Q. If West believes declarer is trying to avoid a loser in the suit by leading the queen from A–Q–J, he may play the king.

More subtle examples of crashing honors can be found in holdings in which the declarer is missing several top cards. The choice of card to lead might not seem too important in this suit:

```
              ◊ J 8 5 3

              ◊ 10 9 7 6 4
```

If possible, declarer (South) should start the diamond suit by leading the jack from dummy. East may play the ace from A–Q–2, or may split honors from K–Q–2.

Sometimes, it helps declarer's plan if the defenders know about his length in a suit. In the example below, South has indicated a six-card club suit.

```
              ♣ J 8
    ♣ Q 5 3                 ♣ A K
              ♣ 10 9 7 6 4 2
```

South leads the ♣ 2 toward dummy's jack. As he would make the same play with A–K–7–6–4–2 of clubs in his hand, West is faced with a guess. If West takes the wrong view, the defense will crash honors in clubs.

In a slightly different sense, declarer may sometimes crash a single honor by making it fall on a trick with low cards, so it will not interfere with the trick-taking potential of declarer's honor cards.

```
              ♠ —
    ♠ A 5                   ♠ J 10 9
              ♠ K Q 8 7 6 4 3 2
```

South, who has opened with 4♠, can afford to lose only one spade trick. His only chance is to lead the ♠ Q from the closed hand. West may suspect that South has an even longer suit than he actually holds (or may make a mistake), and so play low. South can now crash the ♠ A with one of East's minor honors by leading a low spade, preserving his king for the third round of the suit.

Jeff Rubens

CRISSCROSS SQUEEZE. A blocked squeeze described under SIMPLE SQUEEZE.

CROCHET. See WINKLE SQUEEZE.

CROCKFORD'S CLUB. In London, England, a famous proprietary club descending from a gambling club founded by Willian Crockford in 1827. In modern times it has been primarily a bridge club. In December 1961, Crockford's reverted to its gambling traditions by becoming the headquarters of *chemin-de-fer* in England.

CROCKFORD'S CLUB. Founded by ELY CULBERTSON in New York in 1932 and named after the English club of the same name. The club was famous for its high-quality cuisine and for its luxurious appointments, as was its sister club in Chicago. Many famous American players of the Thirties were members of Crockford's including: Ely Culbertson, JOSEPHINE CULBERTSON, RICHARD FREY, SAM FRY., MICHAEL GOTTLIEB, OSWALD JACOBY, THEODORE LIGHTNER, ALBERT MOREHEAD, ALPHONSE MOYSE, SIDNEY RUSINOW, HOWARD SCHENKEN, DOROTHY SIMS, P. HAL SIMS, HELEN SOBEL, SHERMAN STEARNS, HAROLD VANDERBILT and WALDEMAR VON ZEDTWITZ. Many members were drawn from high society rather than from the tournament bridge world. The club was in operation from 1932 to 1938.

CROSSRUFF. A method of play whereby ruffing tricks are made in each of a partnership's hands, thus using the trumps separately.

When a crossruff is played, ruffing tricks are being taken in two side suits. It is usually a good idea to cash winners in the remaining suit at an early stage.

```
              ♠ A Q 5
              ♡ 3
              ◇ A J 8 5 3
              ♣ K Q 10 5
  ♠ 6 4 3 2                  ♠ 10 9 8
  ♡ K Q 10 6 4               ♡ J 9
  ◇ 4                        ◇ K Q 10 7 6 2
  ♣ 6 4 3                    ♣ 7 2
              ♠ K J 7
              ♡ A 8 7 5 2
              ◇ 9
              ♣ A J 9 8
```

After East opens 3◇, West leads a trump against South's 6♣ contract. South can count only five top tricks outside of clubs and must therefore make all his remaining trumps separately. He must be careful to cash his three spade tricks immediately, else the defenders will discard spades when failing to follow to red suit tricks. If this happens, declarer will lose his good spades to opposing ruffs. If the spades cannot be cashed at once, there is no hope for the contract.

CROWHURST CONVENTION. A secondary STAYMAN inquiry after a 1 NT rebid by opener, devised by ERIC CROWHURST of Reading, England, and widely used by British tournament players. Opener is assumed to have 12–16 HCP; the 2♣ rebid by responder asks for further clarification. If opener has 15–16 he rebids 2 NT (game forcing) regardless of his distribution; with 12–14 opener either (1) rebids a five-card major suit, (2) shows three-card support for responder's major suit, (3) shows an unbid four-card major suit, or (4) bids 2◇. See also STAYMAN ON SECOND ROUND.

CROWNINSHIELD TROPHY. Presented by FRANK CROWNINSHIELD for British-American competition. Contested only once, in 1949, when an unofficial U.S. team (JOHN CRAWFORD, PETER LEVENTRITT, GEORGE RAPÉE, SAMUEL STAYMAN) played matches against two British teams. The result was a win for Britain by 330 aggregate points. See ANGLO-AMERICAN MATCHES.

CUDGELS. The club suit.

CUEBID. A forcing bid in a suit in which the bidder cannot wish to play. It is applied to (1) bids in the opponents' suit at any level; (2) bids to show controls at a high level after a suit has been agreed directly or by inference.

CUEBID AS A LIGHT TAKEOUT. An immediate cuebid of an opponent's opening bid is a weak takeout bid for the other three suits. This method reserves the takeout double for stronger hands having greater defensive values.

CUEBIDS IN OPPONENT'S SUIT. When a player bids a suit which has originally been called by his opponents, he is said to make a cuebid. A cuebid is not made in the expectation of actually playing in the relevant suit; it is made for exploratory or control-showing purposes.

In the early days of contract bridge, a cuebid could be made in only two situations: The immediate overcall in the opponent's suit guaranteed a void (or at any rate, no losers) in the suit. This was later extended to strong hands with a singleton in the suit. At *later stages* in the auction, opposite a partner who had already bid, the cuebid in the opponent's suit was used to show control of the suit, and suggest slam.

In the above form, the opportunity to make a cuebid rarely occurred. Modern bidders, therefore, particularly in California and in England, developed methods on the basis that any cuebid below the game level is simply a forcing bid. This concept has not been accepted by GOREN and some other conservative authorities, but has gained wide acceptance in expert circles.

Cuebids are used much more extensively by experts than by others. In studying the meaning of various cuebids, the subject is considered (1) from opener's viewpoint, (2) from responder's viewpoint, and (3) from defenders' viewpoint.

Cuebids by Opener. The level at which the cuebid is made is a vital consideration. The meaning changes according to whether game has been reached.

Above the game level, there can be no doubt that the cuebid is a slam try. The same is true in this sort of situation:

WEST	NORTH	EAST	SOUTH
			1♠
2♡	3♠	Pass	4♡

North–South are already committed to playing in at least a game in spades, so 4♡ must be a slam try, showing control of the heart suit. First-round control of hearts (ace or void) is virtually guaranteed.

But when partnership is still searching for the *safest* game contract, the cuebid by opener is much less precise. He may or may not have slam ambitions. He may or many not have a control in the cuebid suit. Time will tell:

WEST	NORTH	EAST	SOUTH
			1♣
1♡	1♠	Pass	2♡

All North can tell at this stage is that South has an

enormous hand, and wants to be in at least a game. North must make the most helpful bid he can think of, which is likely to be notrump if he has a heart stopper. If he has a double heart stopper and a *weak* hand he should jump to 3 NT. This should serve as a warning to South that duplication is present.

South may have any of the following hands:

(a)

♠ A Q 7 4
♡ 6
◇ A 6 3
♣ A K J 5 4

South's hand offers good slam prospects, and it would be wrong to raise immediately to 4♣. He plans to bid 4♣ on the next round, whatever rebid he gets from North. A delayed raise to game always promises more than an immediate game bid. See FAST ARRIVAL, PRINCIPLE OF.

(b)

♠ A 4
♡ 7 5
◇ A J 5
♣ A K Q J 5 4

Here the cuebid is made, not as in slam try, but as a means of reaching the *best* game contract.

Although he has no spade fit and no heart control, South must insist on reaching game. He is too strong to bid 3♣, which could be passed. If North bids 2 NT, South raises to 3 NT. If North rebids 2♠, South simply bids 3♣, and awaits developments.

(c)	(d)
♠ A J 6	♠ A 6 5
♡ 5	♡ 5 4
◇ A J 7	◇ K Q J 6
♣ A K Q 9 5 4	♣ A K Q

On both these hands South will bid 3♣ if North bids 2 NT in response to South's 2♡ cuebid. In each case, the best contract may turn out to be 4♣, which North will bid if the has a five-card suit or a strong four-card suit.

Notice that in no case does South have a void heart. With a void it will usually be better to make a *jump cuebid*. This pinpoints a void specifically.

In some circumstances, a cuebid is not even completely forcing to game. Consider the following:

WEST	NORTH	EAST	SOUTH
			1♣
Pass	Pass	1♡	2♡

or

WEST	NORTH	EAST	SOUTH
			1♣
1♡	Pass	2♡	3♡

South cannot be insisting on game here because he did not open with a forcing bid, and his partner's hand may be completely worthless. He may have either of these hands:

♠ A Q 5 4	♠ A K 3
♡ —	♡ —
◇ A K 7 2	◇ A J 8
♣ A Q J 8 6	♣ K Q J 8 7 3 2

This particular cuebid, even without a jump, suggests a void in hearts. (With a singleton heart, a takeout double would be the normal action: South

would then be less reluctant to hear his partner pass the double for penalties.)

The following example shows the advantage of playing the low-level cuebid as a vague forcing bid, without any guarantee of control in the suit.

WEST	NORTH	EAST	SOUTH
			1♣
2♣*	3♡	Pass	3♠

*weak

South holds:

♠ 7 5
♡ J 3
◇ Q 8 3
♣ A K Q 7 4 3

This use of the cuebid to ask about stoppers is prevalent in the West and is called a WESTERN CUEBID. It is the only way for South to steer the contract into 3 NT if North has a spade guard. (If South had a spade stopper he could simply bid 3 NT himself.) Unless the partnership has this understanding, South is forced to bid 4♣, or even 4♡, when the notrump game may easily be best (see DIRECTIONAL ASKING BID).

A cuebid must always be considered within the framework of the bidding. If the cuebidder and his partner have limited their hands by the earlier auction, the cuebid may be made even in a partscore situation, when there is no intention of reaching game.

This is illustrated by the following example:

WEST	NORTH	EAST	SOUTH
			1♣
1◇	Pass	1 NT	Pass
Pass	Dbl	Pass	2◇

South's hand was:

♠ Q J 10 6
♡ A 7 5 4
◇ 6
♣ K J 8 4

As he had passed over 1 NT and then refused to stand the double, it was clear that South was weak. With North also limited by his original pass, the cuebid was simply a useful maneuver to find a major-suit fit.

Cuebids by Responder

WEST	NORTH	EAST	SOUTH
			1♣
1♠	2♠		

Classically this would have shown a club fit with no losers in spades, and a desire to reach at least game. In the modern style, North could have any of the following hands:

(a)	(b)	(c)
♠ A 6	♠ 7 4 2	♠ K J
♡ A K J	♡ K J 7 3	♡ A J 7 4
◇ 9 6 5 3 2	◇ A 10 5	◇ A J 6
♣ J 4 2	♣ K Q 7	♣ 10 6 4 2

These examples are taken from Reese and Dormer's *Blueprint for Bidding* (English title: *The Acol System Today*).

All three hands would present problems without

the use of the cuebid. A bid of 2♡ on (b) or (c) would suggest a five-card suit, and a bid of 2◊ on (a) is misleading with such a weak suit. In each case North raises to 3 NT if South's rebid is 2 NT, showing a spade stopper.

This usage in no way bars responder from making the cuebid with its classical meaning. He follows with a club raise or a clear-cut slam move, and the situation becomes clear to opener.

When North has a spade void, he can show this unequivocally by a jump cuebid of *3♠*. (Unusual jump bids which have no normal meaning can often be useful to show a specific void.)

The responder can cuebid with great freedom on the second round of bidding:

WEST	NORTH	EAST	SOUTH
			1♣
Pass	1◊	1♠	Pass
Pass	2♣		

North holds:

    ♠ Q 8
    ♡ A 10 5
    ◊ A J 8 7 4
    ♣ J 5 2

In this case South is limited by his failure to bid over 1♠, which strongly suggests that his hand is minimum. North intends to pass if he gets a discouraging bid of 3♣ or 3◊ from South. This is one case in which the bidding can die short of game after a cuebid. If South has any game ambitions, he must make some more constructive bid.

Counter-cues and redoubles. If South has ♠A–x–x or ♠K–x–x, for example, he can make a counter-cuebid of 3♠, which steers 3 NT into the North hand.

Having the contract played from the right side of the table is a consideration also on this deal:

Dlr: S   ♠ Q 5
Vul: N–S   ♡ 6 2
             ◊ K Q 3
             ♣ A Q 8 7 6 4

♠ J 10 9 8 6 2   ♠ K 7 4
♡ A K 10 3   ♡ 9 8
◊ 7 4   ◊ J 9 8 5
♣ 5   ♣ J 10 9 2

             ♠ A 3
             ♡ Q J 7 5 4
             ◊ A 10 6 2
             ♣ K 3

WEST	NORTH	EAST	SOUTH
			1♡
Pass	2♣	Pass	2◊
2♠	3♣	Dbl	Redbl
Pass	3 NT	All Pass	

If the cuebid were not available, North would be in trouble over 2♠. 3♣ or 3◊ would be substantial underbids, likely to lead to a missed game.

East's double of 3♠ strongly suggests that he has a top spade honor, so North–South are able to play 3 NT from the North position. When a cuebid (in the opponent's suit or otherwise) is doubled, a redouble shows control of the suit; whether it is first- or second-round control is a matter for partnership agreement.

There are often opportunities for using the cuebid after an original pass by the cuebidder:

WEST	NORTH	EAST	SOUTH
			1◊
1♠	2♠	Pass	

This shows a near opening bid, a balanced distribution, and insufficient spade strength to bid 2 NT. For example:

       (a)   (b)
     ♠ 7 4 3 2   ♠ A 6 4
     ♡ A Q 6   ♡ A K J
     ◊ Q 8 5   ◊ 10 9 8
     ♣ K 10 7   ♣ 10 9 7 3

Holding a fit with the opener's suit, the responder will rarely wish to look further than a raise of partner's suit. With the hands given, North would have an impossible bid to make. In each case he is hoping for 3 NT, but with his partner to play it.

In the event of North wishing to make a cuebid because he has a powerful diamond fit, he can still do so. But until North clarifies the situation on the next round, South must bid on the assumption that North's hand is balanced. Any simple bid by South on the second round, such as 3♣ or 3◊, may be passed. So if South wants to be in game he must make a counter-cuebid of 3♠ or take some other strong action.

A Cuebid in notrump. A cuebid in notrump is both rare and rarely understood. Suppose the bidding goes:

WEST	NORTH	EAST	SOUTH
			1◊
1 NT	2 NT		

What does North's bid mean? It cannot be a balanced hand trying for a notrump game, because any such hand would simply double 1 NT and take a penalty. 2 NT in this situation should be regarded as a cuebid, simply forcing to game. It shows an unbalanced hand which does not wish to defend against notrump. A two-suiter is likely, such as:

         ♠ A Q 6 5 4 2
         ♡ A J 6 5 3
         ◊ 9
         ♣ 4

There should be game in one of the major suits, but a double will not work out well if, as is likely, West has a strong club suit.

Once the game level has been reached, the cuebid becomes simply control-showing. Almost invariably it will show the ace or a void, but might occasionally be made with a second-round control. This can be ventured if the cuebidder's trump holding is strong, as there is then no danger that partner will race for a grand slam missing a trick in the enemy suit.

Negative inferences. The failure to cuebid can be very significant:

    WEST   EAST
    ♠ A Q 7 5 4 3   ♠ K J 8 5
    ♡ A K J 6 3   ♡ 7 2
    ◊ —   ◊ A Q 10 8 3
    ♣ 9 4   ♣ 10 6

WEST	NORTH	EAST	SOUTH
1♠	4♣	4♠	Pass
5♠	Pass	Pass	Pass

This asks only for control of clubs. If West had any other worries he would make a suitable cuebid.

Similarly, a player who holds

♠ 5 2
♡ A Q 7 6 4 2
◇ —
♣ A K 8 7 3

can bid 5♡ when his partner's 1♡ has been over-called with 1♠.

There are numerous possibilities for cuebidding after partner's opening bid of 1 NT. Frequently the cuebid has to take the place of a STAYMAN inquiry which has been frustrated by the intervening bid.

♠ A K 7 3
♡ Q 6
◇ A 10 6 2
♣ K J 6

South holds this hand and the bidding goes:

WEST	NORTH	EAST	SOUTH
			1 NT
2♡	3♡	Pass	3♠
Pass	3 NT	Pass	?

North's bid of 3♡ could have any of three meanings. He could be paving the way for a slam; he could be trying to find a 4–4 spade fit to play in 4♠; or he could be worrying about the presence of a heart guard for 3 NT.

The 3 NT bid makes it clear that he has not got spades, nor is he seeking a slam. His only reason for not bidding 3 NT directly was because he has no heart guard.

In these circumstances, West would enjoy 3 NT, so South must bid 4◇. He expects to play a game in spades, diamonds, or clubs.

Another curious cuebid can arise after a 1 NT opening bid:

WEST	NORTH	EAST	SOUTH
			1 NT
Dbl	2 NT		

This cannot be a natural bid, because a hand which is ready to suggest 3 NT would prefer to redouble. The redouble is almost sure to produce a good score, probably from a penalty when the opponents play in some doubled contract at the two-level. So 2 NT must be a forcing bid with a very unbalanced distribution — probably a two-suiter on which game seems feasible. Over West's double, a jump to 3♠ for example, should be preemptive, not forcing, so 2 NT is the only forcing bid at North's disposal.

Cuebids by the Defenders. Cuebids by the side which did *not* open the bidding are considered under two headings; cuebids by second hand and cuebids by fourth hand.

Cuebids by second hand. The immediate overcall in the opponent's suit has been the subject of experiment in recent years. There are no fewer than five varieties:

(1) *Classical* (Culbertson-Goren). The equivalent of an opening forcing bid, guaranteeing a game. Goren insists that the cuebid shows first-round control in the cuebid suit, without explaining what to do if that feature is not present. Culbertson is less rigid, permitting the cuebid with a singleton, and allowing

for the possibility that the bidding may die short of game if the responding hand is very weak. Modern bidders contend that these interpretations weaken the value of the bid, since there is so rarely an opportunity to use it.

(2) *Modern* (Reese and Dormer). Here the cuebid is used for most powerful hands with game prospects, when a takeout double is unsuitable because a penalty pass would be unwelcome. *Blueprint for Bidding* gives these three examples of 2◇ after an opening 1◇:

♠ A K 10 8 4 3 2	♠ A Q 10 7 4
♡ K 4	♡ K J 8 7 5
◇ 7	◇ —
♣ A J 6	♣ A Q 5

♠ K Q 9 5 4
♡ A
◇ 9
♣ A K J 8 3 2

In (a), the spades are bid and rebid, and the bidding can die at 3♠. If (b) gets a 3♠ response, a repeat cuebid of 3◇ is used to ask for a major suit. The bidding can stop at 3◇ or 3♠. If (c) gets a 2♡ response, which is likely, the rebid is 3♣, which can be passed.

(3) *Hypermodern* (the MICHAELS CUEBID). Here there is a two-suited hand, usually less than opening bid strength. Over a minor suit it shows major suits; over a major suit it shows the unbid major and an unspecified minor. In the latter case the hand may be stronger. See also KANTAR CUEBID.

It is generally true that two-suited hands are difficult to bid in defense, and this has given rise to various attempts, such as the unusual notrump, to show two suits with one bid. An alternative two-suiter cuebid:

(4) *Artificial* (the ASTRO CUEBID). This method is described by its inventors, LARRY ROSLER, ROGER STERN and PAUL ALLINGER. It shows a minor-major two-suiter — the lower unbid minor and the lower unbid major. The minor suit is always long, and the distribution is likely to be 6–5, 6–4, or 5–4. The strength will vary wildly. At favorable vulnerability, it might be a 5-point hand hoping for a sacrifice, while at unfavorable vulnerability the cuebidder must have a sound hand able to play safely at the three-level. See also COLORFUL CUEBID.

(5) *Natural.* There is a strong argument for playing an immediate overcall in an opponent's minor suit as a natural bid to show a suit, especially if the opponents do not open four-card major suits. In that case they will frequently bid a three-card minor suit, and the second player may want to bid the suit naturally.

Against opponents who open freely with weak four-card major suits, or even three-card major suits, the cuebid may be used naturally at all times.

Of the five different methods listed above, the tendency in expert circles is to veer toward the second method, i.e., modern. Under this method, the second player may make delayed cuebid in a variety of circumstances. A common situation follows a takeout double:

WEST	NORTH	EAST	SOUTH
			1 ♡
Dbl	Pass	2 ♣	Pass
2 ♡			

Many years ago this bid was used as a natural bid to show a strong heart suit, and it was not forcing. This treatment has been abandoned, partly because such hands usually pass the opening heart bid, and partly because it is needed as a cuebid with a variety of strong hands.

The precise meaning of the cuebid is influenced by the type of *immediate* cuebid being used. If this has the normal strong meaning, then the delayed cuebid is certain to be less than a game-forcing hand. Using a specialized cuebid — (3), (4), or (5) above — the delayed cuebid has no upward limit. In either case the minimum should be a hand with about 20 points.

A cuebid following partner's double is, of course, very different:

WEST	NORTH	EAST	SOUTH
			1 ♠
Pass	Pass	Dbl	Pass
2 ♠			

It would be unprofitable to reserve this cuebid for a hand which can guarantee game, because West's original pass makes it unlikely that he has such a hand. The cuebid here simply suggests a game, and West could have as little as:

♠ 8 7 4
♡ J 10 8 5
◊ A Q 10
♣ K 9 2

If East's next bid is 3♣ or 3◊, West can and should pass. Over 3♡, he can just afford to continue to game, because all his points are *working*. If East has a good sound double, he will either bid a game directly or make a further cuebid of 3♠.

A pass followed by a bid in the opponent's suit may need a little study. Usually it is a natural bid, based on a strong suit which the opponent has stolen. For example:

WEST	NORTH	EAST	SOUTH
			1 ♠
Pass	1 NT	Pass	Pass
2 ♠			

This indicates a good six-card spade suit. South and North may well have only four spades and one spade respectively, so West cannot allow himself to be talked out of playing in spades. He would be less inclined to bid 2♠, perhaps, if the opening bid promised a five-card suit. See OVERCALL IN OPPONENT'S MAJOR SUIT.

The same would apply if the opening bid was in hearts, but the situation is different when the opening bid was in a minor suit:

WEST	NORTH	EAST	SOUTH
			1 ◊
Pass	1 NT	Pass	Pass
2 ◊			

Now it is much less likely that West will want to bid 2◊ naturally, because North–South will almost always have six diamonds between them and usually more. It is more useful, therefore, to use the bid in the opponent's minor suit as a cuebid for a major-suit takeout on this type of hand:

♠ K 8 5 3
♡ A 10 6 3
◊ 7 5 4
♣ K 2

West could not afford to make an original double with this hand, partly because his strength is insufficient, and partly because he is not prepared for a club response. It is highly probable after this auction that East–West have a 4–4 fit or better in one of the major suits, and the 2◊ cuebid is an effective way for East–West to balance themselves into a major suit.

If West makes a cuebid of this type, and East is in any doubt about its significance, he can usually come to the right conclusion by considering his own holding in the cuebid suit. If he has a misfit in the cuebid suit, the bid is likely to be natural. If not, it is likely to be for a takeout.

To complete the picture as far as cuebids by the second player are concerned, there is the rare notrump cuebid. A bid of 2 NT over an opening bid of 1 NT is not simply an unusual notrump asking for minor suits. It shows a freak two-suited hand on any kind, and could be based on K–Q–x–x–x–x in both major suits.

Cuebids by fourth hand. Here there is much more variety, and six common cases need consideration.

(1) After two passes. If South bids 1◊ and East bids 2◊ in the pass-out position, the cuebid should mean the same as if made by second hand. East bears in mind that West and North are limited by their original passes.

(2) *After a pass and a suit response*

WEST	NORTH	EAST	SOUTH
			1 ◊
Pass	1 ♠	2 ◊	

This is clearly forcing to game, but there is some difference of opinion about the meaning of a bid of 2◊ instead of 2♠. The usual American interpretation is that this would also be a cuebid, of a different order of strength. This is hardly necessary because a double is available as a request for a takeout, and 1 NT can be given a similar meaning by agreement. The British treatment is different: if the opponents bid two suits, a bid in their original suit is natural. This applies more frequently when second hand has overcalled.

(3) *After an overcall and a pass*

WEST	NORTH	EAST	SOUTH
			1 ◊
1 ♠	Pass	2 ◊	

This is back to the earlier pattern: a strong hand which expects to go to game but does not know where to go. East might hold:

♠ K 3
♡ Q J 6 2
◊ 10 3
♣ A K 7 5 4

East expects to reach game, but this could be in any denomination except diamonds. West may show any additional feature: a second suit if he has one; a diamond guard by bidding notrump; or a good overcall including a six-card spade suit by jumping to *3♠*. If he can do no more than rebid 2♠, East raises to 3♠, which can be passed. If East–West are vulnerable, East might go to 4♠ over 2♠. This depends on the partnership's overcalling standards.

Alternatively, East may hold a hand which is worth a raise to 4♠, but offers some slam chances. If he bids 2◇, and follows with 4♠ West may be able to continue.

Another treatment that has become increasingly popular among modern players is to use this cuebid as responder's only strong bid, usually equivalent to a limit raise of the overcaller's suit.

For example, the bidding goes:

WEST	NORTH	EAST	SOUTH
1♡	1♠	Pass	2♡

South holds:

♠ K 9 5
♡ A 7 2
◇ K J 9 8 3
♣ 10 6

In standard methods, South would express the value of his hand by jump raising to 3♠, but this may get his side too high. Employing the cuebid as an invitational measure permits South to explore accurately for game without endangering the partial contract. If North rebids 2♠, South passes, while if North shows additional values above a minimum overcall by jumping to 3♠ or introducing a new suit, South supports spades as cheaply as possible to describe the limited nature of his cuebid. With a stronger hand, South would again cuebid, but would take some further action over a minimum rebid by North. As a corollary, a double raise of an overcall is freed for use as a preemptive tactic. See also RESPONDING TO OVERCALLS.

(4) After a double and a pass

This is very common:

WEST	NORTH	EAST	SOUTH
			1◇
Dbl	Pass	2◇	

East can hold any hand on which he expects to get to game, but does not know where. A typical hand would be:

♠ K 7 6 3
♡ K 7 6 3
◇ 9 3 2
♣ A K

Over 2◇, West is almost sure to bid a major, which East raises to game. A raise to 3♠ would not be forcing, and would be appropriate if the ♣K were turned into the jack or a small card.

This last point involves an important principle. In general, a cuebid is not completely forcing to game. It loses its forcing quality when a limited position is reached. A raise is always limited, so the bidding can die below game. A minimum double and a minimum cuebid may not have enough combined values for game. This allows East to make the cuebid freely on hand which would otherwise present a problem.

(5) After a double and a bid

WEST	NORTH	EAST	SOUTH
1◇	Dbl	1♡	2♡

This is similar to (2), in that the opponents have bid two suits. 2♡ is a normal cuebid, with no interest in

a heart contract. Holding four hearts or more, he would certainly double. But the only way to show diamonds at this point is to bid them, so 2◇ should simply mean a desire to play in that contract.

(6) After a notrump overcall

WEST	NORTH	EAST	SOUTH
1◇	1 NT	Pass	2♣

There are two schools of thought about this position. The normal interpretation is that it is a cuebid, which can be used as a Stayman substitute.

Alternatively, 2♣ can be retained as a Stayman bid, in which case 2◇ is a weak hand that wants to play in diamonds. This is not too unlikely because the notrump bidder has promised a good diamond holding.

The situation changes to some degree when the opening bid is 1♣.

WEST	NORTH	EAST	SOUTH
1♣	1 NT	Pass	2♣

Obviously this presents a dilemma. If 2♣ indicates a weak hand that should play in clubs, how does the partnership look for a major suit fit? Many players use CHEAPER MINOR, which means that 2♣ would show the weak club hand while 2◇ would probe for the major suit fit.

Jump cuebids. Another form of cuebid that has been adopted by many players. A jump cuebid is used to show a strong raise in the overcaller's suit. When this is used, a simple cuebid usually indicates a limit raise, while a jump in the overcaller's suit is preemptive. The use of the regular and jump cuebids also can be reversed, with the jump cuebid showing the limit raise and the immediate cue the strong rise. The jump cuebid also can be used to show a singleton in the opponent's suit.

Conclusion. Cuebidding is an extremely broad subject. There are hundreds of situations in which low-level cuebids can be used effectively, and most of them are impossible to classify because they occur on the second or third round of bidding. In these situations, cuebids may provide an answer to bidding problems which would otherwise be insoluble. See also DOUBLE OF A CUEBID and COLORFUL CUEBID.

CUEBIDS TO SHOW CONTROLS (see also

CUEBIDS IN OPPONENT'S SUIT). A bid in a suit in which the partnership cannot wish to play is usually a control-showing cuebid if the partnership is already committed to a game contract. A slam invitation is implied:

(a)		(b)	
NORTH	SOUTH	NORTH	SOUTH
1♠	3♠	1♠	1♡
4◇		3♡	4◇

In each case the side is committed to game, and a suit has been firmly agreed. The final bid is a slam suggestion, and the cuebidder's partner acts accordingly. If his hand is completely unsuitable for slam purposes, he signs off in the agreed trump suit at the lowest level. If he is willing to cooperate in a slam venture, he can bid a slam directly, or take some other strong action which will take the bidding past the game level. When in doubt, he can sometimes make a further cuebid below the game level; in case (a), South can make cuebid of 4♡ in his turn without taking the bidding past 4♠.

The first cuebid is assumed to show first-round

control (usually the ace, but occasionally a void), although a hand which is known to be very weak might make a cuebid with a king. Later cuebids by either player may show second-round controls.

It is usual (and in some systems compulsory) to make the cheapest possible cuebid. Therefore in case (a) above, North denies first-round club control, and in case (b), South denies first-round spade control.

An alternative recommended by JEREMY FLINT is to cuebid first the higher ranking of two touching aces and the lower of two nontouching aces. (The trump suit is excluded in determining which suits are touching.) The intent is to create extra room for the partnership to show all its controls. A hand given in illustration by HUGH W. KELSEY in his book on Slam Bidding (see BIBLIOGRAPHY, C) is:

WEST	EAST
♠ A 7	♠ 3
♡ A 5 4	♡ K 8 6
◇ J 10 9 6 5 2	◇ A K Q 7
♣ K 4	♣ A Q 8 5 3

Using standard methods of bidding all controls as cheaply as possible, the auction would start:

WEST	EAST
1 ◇	3 ♣
3 ◇	4 ◇
4 ♡	5 ♣
5 ♠	?

East cannot be sure his partner has the ♣ K and cannot find out without committing himself one way or not. Using the Flint style, however, the auction would be:

WEST	EAST
1 ◇	3 ♣
3 ◇	4 ◇
4 ♠	5 ♣
5 ♡	5 ♠
6 ♣	7 ◇

West's cuebid of his aces in reverse order has created just one bit of extra space, but that one step is enough. The Flint method has its disadvantages, however, when the hand that initiates the cuebidding has only one ace, for there will be second-round controls that the hand cannot show without promising first-round control.

A bluff cuebid is made not infrequently to inhibit a lead:

NORTH	SOUTH
1 ♣	3 ♣
4 ♣	4 ♠
6 ♣	Pass

It is possible that North had a grand slam in mind, but abandoned that possibility when South made the discouraging return to 4 ♠. But it is more likely, if North is a good player, that he was bent on 6 ♣ and bid 4 ♣ on the way to inhibit a club lead. If East is also a good player he will see through the maneuver and lead a club, which opens the way for a double-cross genuine cuebid.

Certain bids may at first sight appear to be cuebids, but on inspection do not conform to the defintion:

(a)		(b)	
NORTH	SOUTH	NORTH	SOUTH
1 ♡	2 ♣	1 ♡	2 ♣
3 ♣	3 ♠	4 ♣	4 ♡

In case (a), North–South are not committed to a game contract, because the bidding can die in 4 ♣. 3 ♠ is not a cuebid suggesting a slam, but a STRENGTH-SHOWING BID suggesting 3 NT, the spade holding could be Q-J-x.

In case (b), South's bid of 4 ♡ is quite unconstructive. It simply suggests that 4 ♡ may be a better contract than 5 ♣, and the heart support may be as little as a doubleton honor.

The above treatment should be regarded as standard unless a partnership agrees otherwise. For alternative treatments see: ASKING BID; INTEREST-SHOWING BID; and ROMAN ASKING BID. For related topics see also: DOUBLE OF A CUEBID; OUT-OF-THE-BLUE CUEBID; TRIAL BID; and VOID-SHOWING BID.

In the early years of contract, various authorities, including ROBERT F. FOSTER, SIDNEY LENZ, GEORGE REITH, and E. V. SHEPARD devised complex systems of cuebidding. These were intended to offer alternatives to the CULBERTSON 4-5 NT CONVENTION and other devices for locating aces, but they did not achieve any popularity.

CULBERTSON ASKING BID. See ASKING BID.

CULBERTSON 4-5 NT. A slam convention showing aces and kings as well as asking for them. The 4 NT bid promises either:

three aces, or
two aces and a king of a suit genuinely bid by the partnership.

The responses

Holding two aces, or one ace and all the kings of genuinely bid suits, bid: 5 NT.
Holding no ace, bid: five of lowest genuinely bid suit.
Holding one ace, usually bid the ace suit (but if this is the lowest bid suit, a jump to six is necessary).

Notice that the signoff is not in the agreed trump suit, but in the lowest suit which the partnership has genuinely bid. Responder can exercise some discretion when he holds one ace and no additional values. If his normal response would take the bidding above the five level in the agreed trump suit, he may invent some lower bid.

Holding two aces *and* a king, the responder is often interested in a grand slam. Provided his king is not in the agreed trump suit, he may bid the suit in which he holds a king. This may be temporarily misleading, but he can clarify the situation by making a constructive bid on the next round.

This convention was generally superseded by BLACKWOOD and other conventions, but retained popularity among some leading British players. See BYZANTINE BLACKWOOD.

CULBERTSON–LENZ MATCH. The *Bridge Battle of the Century*, as it was called when it took place between December 1931 and January 1932, was a genuine milestone in the history of the development and promotion of bridge as it is known today. Combining as it did every feature designed to capture and hold the interest of the then bridge-mad multitudes, and starring the greatest celebrities then prominent in bridge, it was predestined to be an exciting and long-remembered event. These were the years when bridge was making its impact felt keenly in the United States for the first time. During the previous decade, many new styles of bidding and play had come to the forefront, and most prominent among these was the CULBERTSON SYSTEM. Conceived and popularized by a man who was a born molder of opinions and customs, and who was a superbly able practical psychologist as well, the Culbertson System took the nation by storm, and was indeed original in concept and, as practiced by its leading exponents, a successful and highly practical method of bidding in bridge. Naturally its success caused many rivalries and feuds among those players who were at the very top rungs of the bridge ability ladder. This resulted in a strange war — a Systemic War in which 12 leading authorities (including SIDNEY LENZ, MILTON WORK, WILBUR C. WHITEHEAD and EDWARD V. SHEPARD) got together and organized a corporation, Bridge Headquarters — all forces joined to combat Culbertson's domination of contract bridge.

The principal leader of the various groups in opposition to the Culbertson methods was Lenz, a veteran of auction bridge. In his camp were other great luminaries of the game who also felt that their methods were superior to the Culbertson System. The name by which the Lenz forces' system was called was the OFFICIAL SYSTEM. A book on this system, which acknowledged its debt to Culbertson in that much of it was derived from his concepts, was later to be written by Work. The actual match was the result of a challenge made earlier in 1931 by Culbertson to the Lenz faction. There were many complications to be ironed out before agreement as to conditions could actually be achieved, but essentially the match was finally played on a pair-against-pair basis, with Culbertson wagering $5,000 against Lenz's $1,000 on the outcome, with the money going to charity no matter who won. Culbertson promoted the match as the struggle of a young, loving married couple against the forces of adversity — 12 jealous authorities, the establishment, combined against them. Of course it was also billed as a grudge fight and a battle of systems. As a result the match was a topic of conversation at every bridge table and at many dinner tables long before it began. In all, 150 rubbers were played, and during 88 of them Culbertson played with his wife, JOSEPHINE. His partners for the balance of the encounter were THEODORE A. LIGHTNER, WALDEMAR VON ZEDTWITZ, HOWARD SCHENKEN, and MICHAEL GOTTLIEB. Lenz played the first 103 rubbers with OSWALD JACOBY, who then resigned because of a difference of opinion on the play of a defensive situation. Lenz's partner for the remainder of the session was CMDR. WINFIELD LIGGETT. ALFRED GRUENTHER, then a lieutenant instructor at West Point, was chief referee of the match. The Culbertson team won by a margin of 8,980 points. Careful and accurate records of cards held for each deal were kept, and at the conclusion it was determined that each side had held fairly much the same number of high cards as the other. The first half of the match was held at New York's Chatham Hotel, and the second part at the newly opened Waldorf-Astoria. The conditions of play and of protocol in general were governed by an agreement to

which both Culbertson and Lenz were signatory, and the bridge laws under which the match was conducted were those published by the WHIST CLUB of New York. Coverage by the press of the nation was stupendous. Stories about the match were on the front pages of newspapers all over America. Regular correspondents were dispatched to the scenes of play, and some of the great newspaper personalities of the time wrote articles for their papers and for syndicates. The Associated Press laid heavy cables right into the Culbertson apartment at the Chatham Hotel, assigned reporters to the match and gave play-by-play coverage while Western Union and Postal Telegraph established branches in a spare room. A continuous line of the rich and famous moved into the drawing room and out of it, viewing the action through cracks in a large leather screen, and trying to catch a glimpse of the players' faces or the flash of a card being played. Culbertson called it the greatest peep-show in history. A 438-page book (*Famous Hands of the Culbertson–Lenz Match*) was published in three sections with bidding and play analyzed by Culbertson and his partners, Jacoby and Lt. Gruenther. Complete statistics were collated, and records of every phase of the match carefully kept. However, the single most significant feature of the entire proceedings was the enormous impetus it gave bridge when the game's popularity was already great.

	CULBERTSON	LENZ
Points won	122,925	113,945
Rubbers won	77	73
Number of two-game rubbers	37	32
Size of average rubber won	934	866
Largest rubber won	2,580	2,825
Games	195	186
Small slams bid and made	9	8
Small slams defeated		
(not including sacrifices)	9	5
Grand slams defeated	0	1
Opening suit bids of one	366	289
Opening 1 NT bids	43	45
Opening forcing bids	5	5
Small slams made but not bid		
(many owing to lucky breaks)	20	19
Games made but not bid		
(many owing to lucky breaks)	15	13
Successful contracts	273	273
Defeated contracts	142	162
Number of (exact) game contracts		
voluntarily bid and defeated	48	49
Number of penalties of 600 or more	7	14
Points lost in penalties of 600 or more	5,900	11,500
Aces	1,745	1,771
Kings	1,775	1,741
Honor tricks	3,649½	3,648
Points (4-3-2-1)	18,091	17,898
Value of average rubber	899	
Hands dealt	879	
Hands passed out	25	

CULBERTSON NATIONAL STUDIOS. An organization of bridge teachers which flourished in the Thirties. Some 4,000 bridge teachers passed examinations in the CULBERTSON SYSTEM and were granted certificates attesting their fitness to teach the Culbertson methods. A similar organization was developed later by CHARLES GOREN. See also AMERICAN BRIDGE TEACHERS' ASSOCIATION.

CULBERTSON–SIMS MATCH. A 150-rubber pair match held in March and April of 1935 with ELY and JOSEPHINE CULBERTSON on one side against P. HAL and DOROTHY SIMS. On the next-to-last day of the match, Culbertson played with ALBERT H. MOREHEAD and Sims with B. JAY BECKER, while the ladies took a holiday. The match was won by the Culbertsons by a margin of 16,130 points. In this match, which took place as a result of a challenge issued by Sims, accurate records were kept of the proceedings and of the cards and deals held by the participants. Publicity for the contest was not as widespread as in the CULBERTSON-LENZ MATCH three years earlier, but the nation's interest was aroused. Both sides took to the airwaves on weekly radio broadcasts to describe various features of the games, and hands of particular merit were discussed. The match served to whet the public's already keen appetite for bridge and anything about it, as well as to reinforce the position of authority held by the Culbertson group.

CULBERTSON SYSTEM. The system of bidding developed by ELY CULBERTSON, revised periodically to incorporate new developments. For example, in 1930 Culbertson regarded a response in a new suit as nonforcing, which was a departure from his 1925 auction principles. He adhered to this in the 1933 *Blue Book*, which listed a one-over-one response as "99 44/100% forcing", but abandoned the idea in 1935 when it became clear that the mass of bridge players would not be converted.

Other nonforcing bids were featured in the early *Blue Books*, abandoned shortly afterward, and revived by others as "modern" innovations. Examples are: LIMIT RAISES; limit 2 NT response; and WEAK NOTRUMP openings, nonvulnerable. All these became features of the ACOL style; and limit raises and weak notrumps regained some popularity among American tournament players in the sixties. The 1933 *Blue Book* also included the WEAK JUMP OVERCALL.

The Culbertson System, influenced both by the methods of the successful FOUR ACES and by pressure of public opinion, was crystalized in the 1936 *Gold Book*. The bidding set out in the *Gold Book*, with one notable exception, became standard practice in America for the next 15 years, and was only slightly modified by the GOREN SYSTEM, which won the allegiance of the bridge-playing masses in the Fifties. The chief features were:

(1) Valuation by HONOR TRICKS.

(2) Uniform standards for BIDDABLE SUITS, with Q-J-x-x a minimum four-card suit. This applied to the opening bidder, irrespective of whether the suit was a major or a minor. The responder could bid a shaded or conditional biddable suit.

(3) The APPROACH PRINCIPLE, emphasizing suit opening bids and responses in preference to notrump bids.

(4) The FORCING TWO-BID; any opening suit bid of two requiring the partnership to reach game. (Later modified, 1952–53, so that responder could pass after a sequence such as 2♠–2 NT–3♠.)

(5) The forcing takeout (or JUMP SHIFT) showed 3½ honor tricks (or about 16 points). This requirement was raised by Goren and later authorities.

(6) STRONG NOTRUMP (4–4½ honor tricks) preferably limited to 4–3–3–3 distribution in accordance with the approach principle.

(7) Jump rebids by opener or responder (see OPENER'S REBIDS) not forcing unless in a new suit. (This principle was modified by later writers: see GOREN SYSTEM and STANDARD AMERICAN.)

(8) ASKING BIDS were introduced in 1936, and reintroduced in 1953 with amplifications, but never gained substantial support.

In 1952–53 Culbertson also introduced his own DISTRIBUTIONAL COUNT.

CULBERTSON TROPHY. Any of a number of trophies donated by ELY and JOSEPHINE CULBERTSON, all of them for minor events. In 1962 the name was given to the World Pair Championship trophy, first contested at Cannes, France.

CULWOOD CONVENTION. (Thomas Bigelow): Responses to 4 NT:

> no aces – 5♣
> one ace – 5♢
> two aces – 5♡

In order to bid 4 NT the bidder must have three aces or two aces and a king of a bid suit.

The response of 5♠ shows that the partnership holds all aces and the kings of all bid suits.

The response of 5 NT shows that in addition to holding all the aces, the partnership holds two of the three top honors of the trump suit in the responding hand.

CUMBERLAND HAND. See DUKE OF CUMBERLAND'S HAND.

CUMULATIVE SCORE. In tournament bridge, when an event is scheduled for more than one session of play and there is no elimination of players from the event, the winner of the event is decided by cumulative score; that is, the total of the scores made in each of the sessions. However, should there be a different *average score* for the two or more sessions (owing to playing a different number of boards, a no-show for the second session, or other reason), the later sessions' scores are factored by a multiplier that makes the sessions comparable to the first session, so that a particularly high score in any session would carry the same weight as in any other session.

In rubber bridge, where the partnerships change from rubber to rubber, a cumulative score of points won or lost in each rubber is kept so that each player's status of winnings or losses is shown at the termination of each rubber.

In progressive or party bridge, the cumulative score is the totality of points won at all tables at which the player played. Generally, only plus scores are considered, and losses are not deducted before being entered onto the cumulative score sheet.

In knockout team-of-four matches, all points are scored both plus and minus for both pairs of both teams, and the team with a greater plus total than minus total is the winner. This is referred to as AGGREGATE SCORE and has been generally supplanted in head-to-head matches by International Match Points.

CUPS, SWORDS, MONEY, WANDS. Names of

suits in Tarot. Tarot was a special deck of cards used in ancient Italy and elsewhere for various games and for fortunetelling. Tarot cards are still in use today, mostly for parlor games.

CURIOSITIES. See FREAK HANDS.

CURSE OF SCOTLAND. A term applied to the ◇ 9, for which various explanations are given, none completely authoritative. *The Bridge Magazine* once listed six possible origins for the term as follows:

1. That in the once popular round game *Pope Joan*, the ◇ 9 was called *the Pope*, the antichrist of Scottish Reformers.

2. That the ◇ 9 was the chief card in the game *cornette*, introduced into Scotland by the unhappy Queen Mary.

3. That *Butcher* Cumberland wrote the orders for the Battle of Culloden, 1746, on the back of the card. This is very doubtful.

4. That the order for the Massacre of Glencoe was signed on the back of this card.

5. That the dispositions for the fatal field of Flodden (1513) were drawn up on it by James IV of Scotland. Both these last have only the slightest authority.

6. That it is derived from the nine lozenges that formed the arms of the Earl of Stair, who was especially loathed for his connection with the Massacre of Glencoe and the union with England (1707).

CURT REISINGER TROPHY. See REISINGER MEMORIAL TROPHY; REISINGER TROPHY.

CURTAILING MOVEMENT DURING PLAY. A method of terminating a game at a given time, without playing all of the boards scheduled under the movement in use. It is accomplished by omitting one or more of the rounds normally scheduled by the movement.

In general, any movement in which all boards in play at each round may be terminated at the end of any round, with no other defect than disturbance of balanced comparisons.

In a pair or individual movement involving either bye boards or relays, early termination also disrupts the scoring, for some boards will be played more often than others. This will result in a different top on certain boards, and a different possible score for some or all contestants. See TRUNCATED HOWELL MOVEMENT. See also NINE TABLES for an unusual cutting procedure in a MITCHELL game.

CURTAIN CARD. A record of a hand in a duplicate board. The curtain card is placed in the tray with the hand; the player is thus able to determine that the hand he has taken from the board is the one that was to have been there. Use of curtain cards is rare in the United States, but still found elsewhere. An advantage of curtain cards is that fouled boards are discovered immediately. See FOULED BOARD; HAND RECORD; MISSING CARD.

CUT. (1) At the commencement of rubber bridge play, a pack of cards is spread out, face downward,

and each player draws one, turning it face up. Rank and suit of these cards determine the makeup of the first partnerships, and the original dealer. (2) At the conclusion of each hand, the cards are gathered together and reshuffled for the next deal. The new dealer presents the shuffled deck to the right-hand opponent, who cuts the pack by removing more than four but fewer than 48 cards from the top of the deck, and places the cards removed alongside the balance of the deck, nearer to the dealer. The dealer then completes the cut by placing the part of the pack which was originally on the botton above the part originally on the top. (3) A colloquial term for the verbs "trump" or "ruff," used commonly in Scotland. (4) To terminate a movement before the scheduled completion.

CUT IN. To assert the right to become a member of an incomplete table, or to become a member of a complete table at such time as it may become incomplete.

CUTTHROAT BRIDGE. 1. A name applied to a traditional three-handed game (described under THREE-HANDED BRIDGE) and to a four-handed game with flexible partnerships.

In the four-handed version originated by S. B. Fishburne, Tulsa OK, and sometimes called "Reject" or "Let's Pick Partners," the opening bid must be natural and honest (at least 13 points in high cards, and at least four cards in the suit bid). The auction closes when a bid is followed by three passes; doubling and redoubling takes place later. No partscore contracts are played: the cards are thrown in, and the deal passes.

The player who makes the final bid is always declarer, and after the final pass he nominates one of the other three players as his partner. That player becomes the dummy, and moves into the seat opposite the declarer. Declarer's partner has the option of rejecting the partnership, in which case he scores with the defenders instead of with the declarer. Either defender may double and declarer (or dummy if he has not rejected) may redouble.

A separate score is kept for each player, using normal contract scoring as far as possible. The rubber bonus is only 500 if either defender has a game. Only plus scores are recorded, so no entry is made on the score of the one, two, or three players who are on the losing end of a deal. In the final scoring, each player has a reckoning with each other player.

Honors are scored only by the player holding them. A player becomes vulnerable in the usual way. A non-vulnerable player scores 300 if his vulnerable partner scores rubber points.

A weak point in this version of the game was the rejection of partscores. 3 NT was seldom played, because a player with a weak hand could bid 4♣ or 4 ◇ without risk; unless someone made a higher bid, the hands were thrown in.

This gave rise to another version which gained considerable popularity in New York clubs: After the (natural) opening bid, the next player must make a bid of 4 NT or higher. Some games include a GOULASH feature.

2. A term also used to describe the manner in

which some bridge players play: To go after every possible trick, whether as declarer or defender.

CUTTING FOR DEAL, PARTNERS. At the beginning of each rubber, in order to establish partnerships and determine the original dealer, the four participating players each draw a card from an unfaced deck. The two players drawing the highest ranking cards play as partners, and the player with the higher of these two is the dealer on the first hand. An alternate method of determining deal and partners for second and subsequent rubbers is pivoting (see PIVOT BRIDGE).

At CHICAGO, a method combining both the CUT and the pivot is frequently used, the cut establishing partnerships and deal for the first round, the highest cut card determining the pivot player. After the first round, the pivot player remains stationary and plays with his original right-hand opponent for the second round, and then with his original left-hand opponent for the third round. The pivot player, who deals the first hand of each of the three rounds, is often termed the wheel. See LAWS (Law 3).

CUTTING OUT. It is frequently impractical to have exactly four players. When five players form a table, an order of omission from the table is established by drawing. The player with the lowest card sits out the first rubber, and other players sit out in their turn in the order thus established.

Alternatively, a fresh draw can be made after each rubber, with the lowest to sit out; only players who have not sat out participate in the draw. This is a matter of club procedure.

The draw for participation in the rubber is usually quite distinct from the draw, or cut, for partners. But see PIVOT BRIDGE.

CYCLIC MOVEMENT. A movement in which contestants follow each other in a regular sequence or series. When a move is called, each contestant moves to a position previously occupied by a given other contestant, whose name or number is known in advance. The HOWELL MOVEMENT for pairs is a typical cyclic movement. Many other movements for pairs, teams or individuals use the cyclic feature in some form.

CZECHOSLOVAK BRIDGE ASSOCIATION (CESKOSLOVENSKY BRIDZOVY SVAZ). Founded in the early Thirties by Dr. F. Rieger, a high-ranking government official, it merged local bridge clubs which had been existing in most larger urban centers since the middle of the Twenties. Yearly national team championships were held in the High Tatra mountains. Teams representing Czechoslovakia participated in European Championships from their inception in 1933. Other international events were hosted by the Association in various places. Among the leading players of that period were Karl Stein (he evolved the *Prague Forcing*, elements of which have been incorporated in other later systems), Hanus Eisler, BERNARD BORAK, Frank Joles, and Victor Glaser. After the events of 1938/1939, all of these players fled the country or were incarcerated. However, after the end of WWII

many of them (except Stein who perished in France — he missed evacuation along with his comrades in the Czechoslovak Forces abroad due to illness) returned to Czechoslovakia and the Czechoslovak Bridge Association was resurrected. Joles brought the Limit System back from his "sojourn" at a concentration camp, and a National League competition was held as early as the Fall of 1945. In 1946 a Czechoslovak team was invited to go to Britain to play the first international matches after WWII there. In 1947, two British teams came to play return matches at Marianske Lazne. In this period Joles, Kewan (Kuhn), Eisler, Ladislav, Vajda, and DR. JOHN PRESSBURGER represented Czechoslovakia in these meets. However, after a Communist government had taken over in Czechoslovakia in 1948, bridge again mostly withdrew to private homes, but even then enthusiasts kept the game alive. In 1961 the Czechoslovak Bridge Association was reestablished officially, joined the EUROPEAN BRIDGE LEAGUE in 1968, and hosted the first Junior European Championship in the same year. In addition to national team and pair competitions, the International Bridge Week of Marianske Lazne has become a regular event. After 1948 the members of the "old guard" left Czechoslovakia (with only a few exceptions): Joles went to Chile where he helped to promote our sport in that country. Borak and Glaser are in the United States, Eisler emigrated to Austria which country he also represented internationally, Kewan collects impressionist paintings, and Pressburger (a British subject) lives in and occasionally plays for West Germany. Presently the leading Czechoslovak players are Karel Textor, Dr. Miroslav Hanke and Ing. Frantisek Leitner.

Officers, 1982:

Chairman: Ing. Václav Hejduk

Vice Chairman: Vladimir Krása, Mánosova 24, CS 120 00 Prague 2, Czechoslovakia

D

D.I. See DECLARATIVE-INTERROGATIVE 4 NT.

DEPO. See BLACKWOOD AFTER INTERFERENCE.

DOPI. See BLACKWOOD AFTER INTERFERENCE.

DAMAGED CARD. According to the LAWS, Law 7: A pack containing a card so damaged or marked that it may be identified from its back must be replaced if attention is drawn to the imperfection before the first card of the current deal is dealt.

DANGER HAND. The declarer often strives to prevent one opponent, the danger hand, from obtaining the lead. This may be because that player has established winners, or because he will be able to make a damaging lead through a vulnerable honor holding. See AVOIDANCE.

DANISH BRIDGE LEAGUE (DANMARKS BRIDGE FORBUND). This League was organized in 1939 as a consolidation of the "Dansk Bridge

Union'' and the ''Dansk Bridge Liga,'' which had been functioning one east and one west of the Great Belt since 1933. As of 1982, there were approximately 270 clubs throughout Denmark, with a membership of 14,500. The League participated in the 1960, 1964, 1968, 1972, 1976 and 1980 World Team Olympiads, and annually sends teams to the European Championships; it sponsored the first post-war event in Copenhagen in 1948 at the urging of the late HERMAN DEDICHEN. The record of the Women's Teams in the European Championships is particularly noteworthy — they have won the title on six occasions, 1938, 1948, 1949, 1955, 1957 and 1958. The Danish Bridge League sponsors Open Teams and Pairs Championships, the Danish Cup, adult education, and the magazine *Dansk Bridge*, and introduced a masterpoint program in 1970.

Officers, 1982:

President: Bent-Lehde Pedersen

Secretary: Inge Keith Hansen, Skovledet 95A,
  DK-3400 Hillerød, Denmark

DATUM. A reference score from which the number of IMPs won or lost in an IMP pair game can be computed. See AVERAGE SCORE.

DEAD. Bridge jargon to describe a player in a hopeless situation. It usually refers to the play of the hand, as in, ''North made a killing shift, and I was dead.'' Also said of a hand, especially dummy, which has been robbed of (or never had) a re-entry.

DEAL. (1) To distribute the 52 cards at contract; (2) the privilege of thus distributing the cards; (3) the act of dealing; (4) the cards themselves when distributed.

The dealer distributes the cards face down, one at a time in rotation into four separate hands of 13 cards each, the first card to the player on his left and the last card to himself. If he deals two cards simultaneously or consecutively to the same player, or fails to deal a card to a player, he may rectify the error, provided he does so immediately and to the satisfaction of the other players. The dealer must not allow the face of any card to be seen while he is dealing. Until the deal is completed, no player but the dealer may touch any card except to correct or prevent an irregularity. See LAWS (Laws 8, 9, 10), LAWS OF DUPLICATE BRIDGE (Law 6).

DEALER. The player who distributes the cards at a hand of bridge. At the start of a rubber of regular bridge or of CHICAGO, a cut is made for partners and for the deal privilege, the player who receives the highest card becoming dealer. After the entire deck has been given out one by one in turn to each player starting at the left of the dealer, each fourth card going to the dealer himself, the dealer speaks first in the auction by either bidding or passing, subsequent calls proceeding normally clockwise from his position.

The term *dealer* is also a specialized slang word applying to a person who knows how to cheat at cards by arranging or *stacking* the pack in such fashion as to give himself and/or his partner by far the best of the cards continuously.

DEALING DEVICE. (1) a crank-operated machine which distributes the cards. (2) An electrically operated card table which accepts the used pack, shuffles it, and distributes the cards for the next deal. Neither has gained wide acceptance.

DEATH HOLDING. A holding in a suit which seems an *a priori* certainty to kill the partnership's chances of playing or defending successfully. The most common examples are (1) a holding of x-x in the opponents' suit in a hand with slam possibilities; with a small doubleton in one hand it is likely that neither partner can adequately control the opponents' suit for slam play; (2) a defensive holding of Q-x in front of a long suit headed by A-K in the dummy's or declarer's hand; such a holding gives little hope of a trick on power, and no hope that declarer will misplay or misguess.

DECEPTION, MATHEMATICS OF. The rule of multiplication of probabilities (see PROBABILITY OF SUCCESSIVE EVENTS) is applicable when declarer has to decide whether a card is a DECEPTIVE PLAY. The probability that a suspected card is true is the probability that the player holds a distribution that leaves him no choice but to play it. The probability that it is false is the probability that he has a distribution from which the deceptive play would be attractive, multiplied by the probability that he would in fact decide to play the falsecard.

A 8 3 2

K Q 10 4

After winning the opening lead, South plays the king. West follows low, and East plays the 9. The probability that this is a singleton is approximately 2.8%. However, East may hold J-9-x-x, and the probability of this holding is about 8.4%. Consequently, if the probability that East would play the 9 from J-9-x-x is greater than ⅓, that distribution would be more likely than the singleton 9. ALBERT DORMER and TERENCE REESE have postulated that the play of the 9 from J-9-x-x is obligatory, in order to present South with a choice of plays on the second round. If South accepts this view, he must play the ace next time. (For simplicity, the assumption has been made that, if West held J-7-6-5, he would play the low cards indiscriminately.)

The problem should be pursued a little further. Suppose that the only deception envisaged is the play of the 9 from J-9-x-x, that is to say that East holds either J-9-x-x or the singleton 9 when he plays the 9. With a side entry to dummy, South can now give himself a better chance. He enters dummy and leads low toward the Q-10. If East shows out, South plays the queen, and has a marked finesse against West. To counteract this, East must not merely play the 9 from J-9-x-x, but also from 9-x-x and 9-x. If he is deemed capable of this, there is little attraction for declarer in the play just described, since if East follows to a low card from dummy, declarer will have to guess whether to finesse the 10 or play the queen. As 9-x-x and 9-x each have a probability of about 10.2%, South would do better to play dummy's ace on the second round, unless he estimates only a very small probability of the 9 being played from a doubleton or tripleton.

A detailed explanation of this case is as follows: It is assumed that East will always play the 9 from J–9–x–x. The possible plans for South are:

A. Low to the ace, so as to be able to finesse against East if West shows out.

B. Enter dummy with a side-suit, lead toward Q–10, and finesse the 10 if East follows.

C. Enter dummy with a side-suit, lead toward Q–10, and play the queen if East follows:

The probabilities that the relevant distributions were dealt to East are: 9–x or 9–x–x, 64%; J–9–x–x, 27%; singleton 9, 9%. Let p = the probability that East will play the 9 if he has 9–x or 9–x–x. Then the chance of plan A succeeding is .64 times p + .27, and of plan B succeeding, .09 + .27. Therefore if p is less than 14%, plan A is preferable. That is, plan A should be preferred unless it is thought that West would not play the 9 from 9–x or 9–x–x at least seven times in fifty. The chance of plan C succeeding is .64 times p + .09, and plan C is thus clearly inferior to plan A. If entries permit, the two should be led from North's hand on the first round of that suit. It is now more difficult for East to play the 9 from J–9–x–x. West may hold the 10 and the play of the 9 could concede a trick unnecessarily.

Alex Traub and Robert True

DECEPTIVE BID. See LEAD-INHIBITING BID and PSYCHIC BIDDING.

DECEPTIVE LEAD. See OPENING LEAD.

DECEPTIVE OPENING LEAD. See FALSE-CARDING and OPENING LEAD.

DECEPTIVE PLAY. The term deceptive play could well be used of any play that aims to mislead an opponent. Discriminating writers, however, tend to restrict the use of the term to plays by the declarer. Deceptive play by the defenders is more suitably described as FALSECARDING, and is dealt with under that title.

Deceptive plays by the declarer are analyzed under these headings:

(1) Weakness-concealing plays.
(2) Strength-concealing plays.
(3) Honor-crashing plays.
(4) *Scrambling* plays that interfere with the defenders' signals.
(5) Miscellaneous deceptive plays.

Weakness-concealing plays. Bluff is the basis of most of these plays; the declarer deliberately does something which is not correct technique, in the hope that the deceptive effect of his play will outweigh its mathematical shortcoming.

♠ 8 6 3
♡ 9 2
♢ Q J 10 6 4
♣ K Q 7

♠ A K 9 4
♡ A J
♢ K 9 8 3
♣ A 8 2

West leads a small heart against South's 3 NT contract, and East puts up the queen. If perfect defense were to be assumed, South's best play would be to duck. After winning the next trick he would play diamonds, hoping that the defender with the ♢ A had no more hearts to play.

This plan has a slight but legitimate chance of success. In practice it is very much better to win the *first* trick, and drive out the ♢ A. If West has it, and the ♡ K as well, he may not find the right continuation. East's play of the ♡ Q on the opening lead has made it plain to West that declarer has the jack, but he does not know that it is bare. West may conclude that his best chance of defeating the contract is to find East with a black ace, so that he can lead hearts through declarer's jack.

On other ocasions the declarer tries to bluff his way through by opening up a weak suit himself.

♠ J 6 2
♡ A K 10
♢ 8 6 3
♣ A 10 9 7

♠ Q 7 3
♡ Q 8 3
♢ A 10 2
♣ K Q 4 3

West leads the ♡ 4 against South's 3 NT contract. Declarer's ninth trick can come only from spades, and then only if both ace and king are in one hand. Further, if declarer attacks spades himself, and is lucky enough to find the cards suitably placed, the defender will probably shift to diamonds.

Declarer's best plan is to take the opening lead in dummy, and lead diamonds himself, inserting the 10 if East plays low and ducking if East puts up an honor. There is a reasonable chance that the defenders will attack spades.

Many weakness-concealing plays involve releasing a high card earlier than need be. Against a notrump contract, West leads the two of a suit in which dummy holds J–x–x and declarer Q–x. If East plays the ace, it can do no harm for declarer to drop the queen. East will probably recognize that this is not a singleton, and he may assume that declarer's other card is the king. There are many variations of this theme.

Sometimes bluff is needed to extract tricks from an unpromising holding. A declarer who is reduced to the necessity of attempting to make two tricks with K–x–x in dummy and J–x–x in the closed hand does best to lead the king from the table. If the cards are distributed as follows:

```
                K x x
    A 10 x                  Q x x x
                J x x
```

West may conclude that South is trying to establish a suit headed by the queen and jack in the closed hand. If West seeks to molest declarer's communications by holding up the ace, South has every chance of two tricks, for East is unlikely to put up the queen on the second round and West may hold up the ace a second time.

Strength-concealing plays. These are resorted to most frequently in notrump contracts. The usual occasion is when declarer wants the defenders to continue a suit which they have opened, rather than shift to a suit which he fears more.

```
          ♠ K J 7 3
          ♡ 10 7 2
          ◇ Q J 10 5
          ♣ 8 7

          ♠ A Q 2
          ♡ J 8
          ◇ A 9 7 4 3
          ♣ A Q 6
```

West leads a small club against 3 NT and East plays the jack. Declarer can afford to win with the ace rather than the queen. He crosses to dummy with a spade and takes the diamond finesse, hoping that if it loses West will continue clubs rather than shift to hearts. The stratagem is a familiar one but can be effective.

Following is a play to conceal strength which can occur equally at a suit contract or at notrump:

```
          Q 5 2


          A 10 9 8
```

South needs to develop a second trick in the suit, but entry difficulties make it necessary to lead from the closed hand. He has no indication of where the king is located.

Some players will lead the 10 in the hope of putting pressure on West, but actually the 8 is better, especially if West can be expected to realize that South has the ace. By leading the 8, declarer conceals the fact that he has a possible finesse against the jack. Hence, if West has the king, he is more likely to put it up, for from his viewpoint the declarer may have no option but to play dummy's queen. It is, therefore, sound psychology to lead the 8, and run it if West plays low.

Honor-crashing plays. Plays aimed at persuading the defenders to spend two honors — usually trumps — on one trick range from the simple to the subtle. Some examples are given under the title CRASHING HONORS, but others are more deceptive flavor.

```
          Q 7 x x


          10 8 x x x
```

The usual way of playing this suit is by leading small toward the queen. Declarer loses only two tricks provided that the suit divides evenly, that West has the lone jack, or that West has A-K-x or A-K-J.

The fact that the defenders would expect declarer to play thus can make the lead of the queen from dummy effective. If the bidding rules out the possibility that East has a singleton, the queen lead cannot cost and may tempt a cover from East if he has K-J-x or A-J-x.

Sometimes the best way of crashing the defenders' honors is to induce them to ruff with a small trump before the trump suit has been touched. (See hand at top of right column.)

In a pairs contest South plays 4♠ after West has made a preemptive bid in hearts. When West opens the ♡J, South's best deceptive play is to win in hand, cross to the ♣A, and continue hearts, throw-

```
                    ♠ Q 9 8 6
                    ♡ A K 8
                    ◇ K Q 7 6 4
                    ♣ A
  ♠ K              ♠ A 2
  ♡ J 10 9 7 5 4 3  ♡ 6 2
  ◇ 10              ◇ 9 8 3 2
  ♣ Q J 9 6        ♣ 7 5 4 3 2
                    ♠ J 10 7 5 4 3
                    ♡ Q
                    ◇ A J 5
                    ♣ K 10 8
```

ing a diamond from hand. If East ruffs in small on the third round, South overruffs and drops the enemy trumps together for a high matchpoint score.

Scrambling plays. When the declarer has pronounced views as to whether he wants the defenders to continue a suit or shift, he may be able to cut in on their signals. The general rule for declarer is to put out the same signals as he would if he were defending — a high card to encourage a continuation, a low card to discourage. The following is a basic position:

```
          9 7 4
  A K J 3          10 8 5
          Q 6 2
```

When West leads the king against a suit contract, South drops the 6 to make East's 5 look like the beginning of an echo.

If the declarer has more than two cards to signal with, it does not necessarily follow that he should play the highest.

```
          9 3 2
  A K J            10 8 5
          Q 7 6 4
```

When West leads the king and East plays the 5, South should drop the 6, not the 7. If he played the 7, West would realize that some deception was afoot, for it is a basic rule of defensive signaling that encouraging signals should be as high as is safely possible. East, therefore, would not start an echo with the 5 if he also held the 6. So, if South dropped the 7 in the above diagram, West would suspect that he held the 6 as well. Similarly:

```
          8 3
  Q J 10 5          9 7
          A K 6 4 2
```

South is playing a notrump contract, having concealed this suit in the bidding. West leads the queen, and South, needing to develop the suit, encourages in the hope that West will continue. In this diagram, both the 4 and the 6 are apt to be effective, but against players who themselves always falsecard as high as possible the 4 is best; if West reasons that South would play the 6 to encourage, West will be all the more convinced that East's 7 is the beginning of a signal.

It can be good policy for declarer to scramble the signals even when he has no immediate objective in mind.

```
          K Q 4
  J 9 5 2          10 8 6
          A 7 3
```

Suppose South wants to enter dummy to lead another suit. By leading the 7, rather than the 3, he may confuse West's count of the hand. East's 6 may appear to West as the beginning of an echo; it may even suggest to him that East is holding up the ace.

There are some more advanced situations where the declarer has not only to play the right card — he has to know also which hand to lead from.

```
                K Q J 8 2
        9 6 5               A 10 4
                7 3
```

South is playing a notrump contract, and has no entries to dummy. He needs two tricks from the suit.

If South starts by playing the 3 toward dummy's king, West will play the 5, and East will know that his partner has either three cards in the suit or a singleton. In neither case can it cost East to play his ace on the second round, so South will be thwarted in his endeavor.

Suppose instead that South leads the 7 from hand; now, from East's angle his partner's 5 could be the beginning of an echo, showing a doubleton. In any case, East allows dummy to win the first trick, but the critical point comes on the second round: provided that the second lead comes from *dummy*, East will have to make his decision without any sure guidance from partner.

On other occasions it can be better to make both leads from the closed hand:

```
                K Q J 2
        A 8 6               10 9 4
                7 5 3
```

This time South is playing a suit contract, and will be inconvenienced if the ace is held up until the third round. He leads the 5 from hand and dummy wins. Now he must re-enter the closed hand in another suit and lead the 7; West may place his partner with two or four cards, and in either event may release the ace. The principle followed is to make the defender with the stop card play *second* to the vital trick.

Also coming broadly under the heading of scrambling plays are those where the declarer has to follow suit with a particular card in order to make it more difficult for the defenders to gauge his holding.

```
                K J 6
        8 5               A Q 10 7 4 2
                9 3
```

South is playing a suit contract, and West leads the 8 of this side suit, which East has bid. Dummy plays the jack, East the queen, and South drops the 9. If he plays the 3 instead, East knows that it is safe to continue with ace and another (unless the partnership is playing MUD leads). After the play of the 9, however, East has to take account of the possibility that declarer has a singleton.

In general, in such situations as above, the declarer follows suit with a card higher than the one led, but sometimes only a certain card will do.

```
                K 7 4 3
        2               A Q 8 6 5
                J 10 9
```

Again West leads a suit bid by his partner, and this time declarer wants to lose only one trick. (Discards are available elsewhere.) His best chance is to play

low from dummy and drop the 10 from hand. East may still read the situation correctly, but his task would be easier if declarer played either the jack or the 9; he would then be able to infer that partner would not have opened the 2 from either J-10-2 or 10-9-2.

Miscellaneous deceptive plays. One group of situations which does not fall readily under any other heading, and which has been little explored is the following:

	WEST	EAST
(a)	10 7 3 2	A K Q 6 4
(b)	J 6 5 4	A K 10 7 3
(c)	10 5 4 3	A K 8 6 2

In each case East is declarer, and these are his trump holdings. It costs nothing to lead the high card from West each time, intending, if North plays low, to overtake and play normally for the drop. Occasionally the deceptive precaution will pay dividends, as where North covers the 10 with the jack from J-9-8-5 in example (a), enabling his cards to be picked up by subsequent finesses. Example (b) is similar, while in (c) East improves his chances not only when North has all four outstanding cards but also when he covers from J-9-7 or Q-9-7.

There are many similar positions, and the field is widened when account is taken of inferences from the bidding. For example:

	WEST	EAST
	10 4 3 2	A K 8 6

The 10 lead costs only when North has the lone queen or jack. If the bidding precludes this possibility, the 10 is liable to prove doubly effective, since North will be expecting declarer to play him for trump length. Further, North may not care to outbluff the declarer by playing low from a holding headed by queen and jack, since declarer may well run the 10 in this situation.

The basis of another group of miscellaneous plays is that the lead should be made from dummy toward the closed hand:

```
                A Q x x

                x x x
```

South has to develop this suit at notrump but does not need immediate tricks. Best play is to lead small from dummy on the first round. East may put up the king from a variety of holdings which would have ruined the declarer had he played any other way. Similarly:

```
                K x x x

                Q x
```

At a suit contract, South leads from dummy on the first round, and the queen holds. Ordinary technique is to play low from both hands on the next round, and hope to ruff out the ace on the third. Entries permitting, however, it is better to re-enter dummy after the queen, and to lead again toward the closed hand. East may put up the ace, fearing that declarer started with both queen and jack.

Albert Dormer

DECK. (1) The pack; a synonym used regularly in

America but not in England. (2) A colloquial term for a big hand. "Holding the deck" refers to a hand with a disproportionate number of high cards, or to a session in which a player holds a number of such hands. See PACK.

DECLARATION. (1) Contract, e.g., a heart declaration. (2) A statement of intent as to further line of play made by the declarer at some point previous to the play of the last trick of any given hand. See also CALL.

DECLARATIVE-INTERROGATIVE (D.I.) 4 NT. The use of 4 NT as a general slam investigation, rarely as BLACKWOOD; developed originally as part of the NEAPOLITAN system. 4 NT is Blackwood if it is a jump bid, or bid at the first opportunity after a sudden leap to game. Otherwise, it promises two aces if bid by an unlimited hand, or one ace by a limited hand, and requests partner to show an undisclosed feature (a first- or second-round control, or even a key queen) by bidding the suit containing the feature. The reply does not promise extra values unless it goes past five of the agreed trump suit. Responder may also answer by jumping to six of the agreed suit to deny interest in a grand slam, or by bidding 5 NT to announce a complete maximum and strong interest in a grand slam. Over any normal five-level reply, a rebid of 5 NT again asks for additional features in an effort to reach a grand slam and promises one more ace than originally guaranteed.

In several systems such as KAPLAN-SHEINWOLD and BLUE TEAM CLUB, D. I. 4 NT asks for features without promising a specific number of aces. In Blue Team when 4 NT is bid in the course of a series of cuebids it is a generalized slam try indicating that all suits are controlled, unless the player who bids a 4 NT bypasses a suit in which control has not been shown. Some expert partnerships have agreed that after a Blackwood 4 NT and the ace-showing response, 5 NT is always declarative-interrogative, asking for features rather than for the number of kings.

DECLARER. The player who first bid the denomination of the final bid. If the final bid is hearts, the player on the side making the final bid that first named hearts is the declarer. The declarer controls the play of his own hand and the dummy as a united force.

DECLARER'S CLAIM OR CONCESSION OF TRICKS. See CLAIM or CONCESSION and LAWS (Law 70); LAWS OF DUPLICATE (Laws 68–71).

DEEP FINESSE. A finesse when three or more cards are missing higher in rank than the card finessed. This is often made in order to execute a DUCK or AVOIDANCE play, but can be a genuine play necessary to achieve the best result. Well-known situations are:

(a)	(b)	(c)
Q 10 x	A J 9	A Q 9
x x x	x x x	x x x

With (a) the 10 is finessed, although it might be right to put up the queen if West leads a low card: it would be unusual to lead from A-J or K-J with Q-10-x visible in dummy.

With (b) and (c) the 9 is finessed to give the maximum chance.

A rarer deep finesse can occur when a singleton is held opposite a five-card suit including J-10-8:

(d)	(e)	(f)
A J 10 8 x	K J 10 8 x	Q J 10 8 x
x	x	x

In each case the best chance of developing three tricks is to finesse the 8 on the first round.

See also FINESSE and SUIT COMBINATIONS.

DEFEAT THE CONTRACT. To prevent the declaring side from making as many tricks as required by the final contract.

DEFECTIVE TRICK. A trick that contains fewer or more than four legally played cards. See LAWS (Law 68); LAWS OF DUPLICATE (Law 67).

DEFENDER. An opponent of the declarer; one who attempts to prevent the declarer from making his contract. The secondary objective of preventing overtricks is of major importance at duplicate.

DEFENDER'S CLAIM OR CONCESSION OF TRICKS. See CLAIM OR CONCESSION and LAWS (Law 73); LAWS OF DUPLICATE (Laws 70, 71).

DEFENDING HAND. Either opponent of the declarer; occasionally used in the bidding to refer to an opponent of the player who opened the bidding.

DEFENSE, DEFENSIVE PLAY. The play by the opponents of the declarer. The primary object of defensive play is normally to defeat the contract, even at the expense of presenting declarer with overtricks if the chosen line of defense is unsuccessful. At duplicate, however, particularly at matchpoint play, holding declarer to a minimum number of tricks can be important, indeed. Articles dealing with defensive play that should be consulted are: COVERING HONORS; DESCHAPELLES COUP; DISCARDING; DISCOVERY; DUCK; ENTRY-KILLING PLAY; FALSECARDING; FORCING DECLARER TO RUFF; JETTISON; MATCHPOINT DEFENSE; MERRIMAC COUP; OVERRUFF; PLAY FROM EQUALS; RULE OF ELEVEN; SECOND HAND PLAY; SPOT CARDS; THIRD HAND PLAY; THROUGH STRENGTH; TRUMP PROMOTION; UNDERRUFF; UP TO WEAKNESS; UPPERCUT. For all topics relating to OPENING LEADS, see that heading.

DEFENSE TO DOUBLE OF 1 NT. In standard practice the double of a 1 NT opening bid is for penalties. The usual means of escape is for opener's partner to bid a suit, and the traditional meaning of a redouble is to penalize the doubler. See DOUBLES OF NOTRUMP BIDS (Third hand problems). However, several alternatives are designed either to locate the partnership's best escape suit or to place the notrump opener as declarer, or both.

One suggested method is to use TRANSFER BIDS. Responder bids the suit next below his long suit. If responder's suit is clubs he redoubles to ask opener to bid clubs. If responder has no long suit but has seven or eight cards in the major suits, he can redouble, ostensibly transferring to clubs; but, after opener bids 2♣, responder bids 2◊, asking opener to choose between hearts and spades.

In a simpler method, suggested by MARTIN J. COHN of Atlanta, suit bids by responder remain natural, and the redouble itself is used as a STAYMAN-type inquiry for the majors.

A third possibility is to use a response of 2◊ to ask opener to bid his better major suit, and to redouble to ask him to bid his better minor suit. In this method, responder's immediate run-out to 2♡ or 2♠ would be natural, and his bid of 2♣ would promise a long minor suit. If responder's suit is diamonds he runs to that suit over the double of 2♣ that will presumably be forthcoming.

Finally, a method proposed by ALAN TRUSCOTT. A redouble forces 2♣ and may show club length. If the redoubler follows with two of a red suit he shows a four-card suit with at least one other four-card suit higher in rank. A direct 2♣ bid shows a four-card club suit with at least one other four-card suit in reserve. Direct bids of 2◊ and higher are natural. Unlike other methods, this enables the partnerships to find 4–4 fits in the minor suits with assurance. The method works equally well when a 1 NT overcall is doubled.

DEFENSE TO INTERFERENCE WITH BLACKWOOD. See BLACKWOOD AFTER INTERFERENCE.

DEFENSE TO 1 NT. Specialized actions after an opposing opening bid of 1 NT are discussed under other headings: ASPRO; ASTRO; BROZEL; DOUBLES OF NOTRUMP BIDS; EXCLUSION BID; LANDY and RIPSTRA.

The general rule of the defenders is to pass when in doubt. An overcall is far more dangerous after a notrump opening than after a suit opening because the opening bidder has defined his hand precisely. The opener's partner is therefore in a position to judge the defensive prospects accurately.

This caution applies equally in the pass-out position. Although the fourth player has the advantage of knowing that the opposing strength has an upward limit of about 23 points, he should be discouraged by knowing that his side is unlikely to have a good suit fit. The opening bid and the pass by the opener's partner imply that those two hands are balanced. If the fourth player has a long suit, his partner is likely to be short in the same suit.

An overcall should therefore be assumed to be a six-card suit, although a nonvulnerable player might sometimes venture into the auction with a strong five-card suit. Even with a six-card suit and a good hand, it may be advisable to pass if the distribution is defensive (e.g., 6 3 2 2) rather than attacking (say, 6 4 2 1).

If the opening bid is a strong notrump, the opponents are unlikely to head for game and make it. But this is not so against a weak notrump, and responding to an overcall needs consideration. Some experts regard a bid of 2 NT by the overcaller's partner as a forcing bid – a type of cuebid in the opener's

denomination. Suit takeouts of the overcall are then nonforcing.

DEFENSE TO OPENING FOUR-BID. Against an opponent's opening bid at the four level it is standard to use the calls of double and 4 NT in a variety of ways, depending on the suit of the opening bid.

Against an opening preempt of 4♣ or 4◊, a double is for takeout. Some partnerships use a bid of 4 NT as a natural bid; some use it as BLACKWOOD.

Against a 4♡ opening, a double is for takeout and guarantees spade support. The prevailing agreement is that a 4 NT bid is takeout for the minor suits.

Against a 4♠ opening a double is used for penalties. Hence a 4 NT bid is for takeout.

DEFENSE TO OPENING THREE-BID. The following methods can be used as a defense against WEAK TWO-BIDS also:

(1) Standard. A double is primarily for takeout, but is sometimes described as "cooperative" or "optional" because the doubler's partner may sometimes decide to pass in the expectation of a penalty. A normal minimum for the double would be 16 points in high cards, or 13 points in the pass-out seat. The double implies support for the unbid major or majors unless the doubler has considerable reserve strength.

Other bids would be natural, including 3 NT, which would be a minimum of 18 points. Desirable features for this bid would be a double stopper in the opener's suit and a good minor suit.

(2) Fishbein. Devised by HARRY FISHBEIN. A double of a three-bid is for penalties, and the doubler's partner should rarely take any action. A bid in the cheapest available suit is a conventional bid to replace a takeout double. 3♡ over 3◊, for example, would show a minimum of 16 points in high cards and a three-suited hand, or possibly a two-suited hand. The Fishbein takeout bid over 3♠ would be 4♣. The takeout bid is unconditionally forcing because it might be based on a two-suited hand. The convention does not apply in the pass-out position.

(3) Cheaper (or lower) minor. The use of the cheaper available minor suit as a takeout bid: 3◊ over 3♣, and 4♣ over other three-bids. As in the Fishbein convention, a double is for penalties, and the convention does not apply sitting under the three-bidder (although it can apply by partnership agreement). This convention is standard among English tournament players. A variation is known in America as the SMITH CONVENTION, devised by CURTIS SMITH. He recommends the use of 4♣ as the takeout bid in all circumstances, even over 3♣.

(4) Optional double. A double that promises a balanced hand with both support for the unbid suits and some strength in the opener's suit. It invites the doubler's partner to pass for penalties.

(5) Weiss. The use of the cheaper minor for takeout as in (3) above, with the double used as an optional double as in (4).

(6) 3 NT for takeout. Rare in America, but combined with a double for penalties, this is standard procedure in England at rubber bridge. A disadvantage is that 3 NT is often needed as a natural bid.

(7) Reese. 3 NT for a takeout over major-suit three-bids only, with a double for penalties. Double for takeout over minor suits and in fourth seat.

(8) Two-suiter takeouts. Overcalls of four in a minor suit after a major-suit three-bid can be used to show that suit and the unbid major. In combination with standard takeout doubles, this solves some difficult two-suiter problems. The single-suited minor-suit hand is often suitable for a 3 NT overcall or a jump to the five-level. The two-suiter bids can be applied in both second and fourth seats. (A minor two-suiter can be shown by a jump to an "unusual" 4 NT.)

(9) Cheaper minor over the blacks. 3 ◊ over 3 ♣ and 4 ♣ over 3 ♠ are for takeout. Double over these bids is therefore for penalties. Double over 3 ◊ and 3 ♡ is cooperative.

DEFENSE TO PREEMPTIVE BIDS. See DEFENSE TO OPENING FOUR-BID; DEFENSE TO OPENING THREE-BID and WEAK TWO-BIDS.

DEFENSE TO A SQUEEZE. The prerequisites for a true squeeze are: menace cards, properly located and oriented; sufficient entries to these menaces; and correct timing. Unless all these elements are present, the squeeze will not be effective unless the opponents misdefend. There are several principles which can assist the defenders to discard correctly.

(1) If one defender guards a two-card menace and two isolated menaces, then he should unguard the long menace when a choice must be made among the three suits.

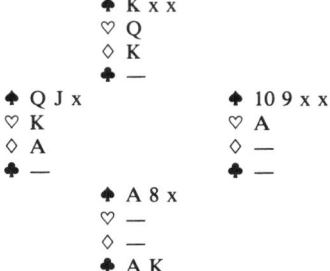

The lead of the ♣A squeezes West in three suits. If he discards a diamond, the North's king becomes established. If he discards a heart, the ending leads to a twin-entry DOUBLE SQUEEZE. West must discard a spade, his guard to the long menace.

(2) When a defender guards two long menaces and one isolated menace, then he should unguard the long menace placed to his left.

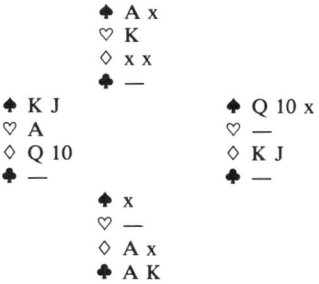

South leads the ♣A, which squeezes West in three suits. If he discards the ♡A, then North's king becomes established. If he discards a diamond, then South cashes the ace of that suit, which leads to a positional double squeeze. West must discard a spade, the guard to the long menace situated to his left.

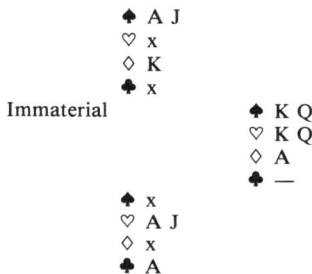

Immaterial

PROGRESSIVE SQUEEZE defense. In this example, South leads the ♣A, which squeezes East in three suits. Any discard costs a trick, so that East's objective must be to protect himself from a progressive squeeze, which would cost him two tricks. A heart is the only discard which will achieve this end.

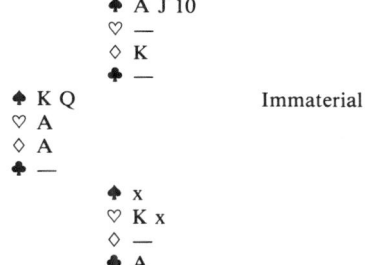

Immaterial

This resembles an automatic REPEATED SQUEEZE position, but it is faulty in that a one-card menace (the ◊K) is misplaced in the North hand. When South leads the ♣A, West must discard the ◊A. Otherwise South can win all the remaining tricks.

(3) On rare occasions an underruff (see UNDERRUFF) proves to be a defender's only safe play. The following hand from a par contest illustrates the point. (ROMANET).

    ♠ Q 7 5 3
    ♡ Q J 10
    ◊ K
    ♣ J 10 9 6 5
♠ A J 10 4   ♠ K 9 8 6 2
♡ A K 9   ♡ 7 5 2
◊ 7   ◊ J 4
♣ A K Q 7 4   ♣ 8 3 2
    ♠ —
    ♡ 8 6 4 3
    ◊ A Q 10 9 8 6 5 3 2
    ♣ —

East is declarer in 6♠. South leads the ◊A, followed by the queen. West ruffs the second diamond with the ace and North must underruff. Any other discard would enable declarer to establish a trick. When the trumps are run off, North cannot be squeezed since he discards after West, which hand contains all the menace cards.

Sometimes correct discarding will not save the

defenders; an early attack against one of the basic elements of the squeeze may be the only means to break it up.

(a) Destruction of the menace. This can be effected in two ways: (1) by leading the suit at every opportunity, thus forcing declarer to play the menace card prematurely; and (2) by making it impossible to ISOLATE THE MENACE. This latter occurs usually at a trump contract. TERENCE REESE provides this example to illustrate the attack on menace cards.

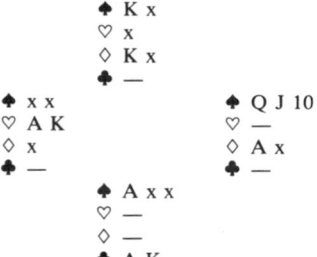

South is declarer at 6 ◊. West leads the ♡ K. If West continues with another heart, South ruffs, and after drawing trumps, enters dummy with the ♣ A to ruff a third heart, thus leaving West alone with the burden of guarding that suit as well as the spade suit. However, if West refrains from leading the second heart, then the heart menace cannot be isolated; East's jack cannot be ruffed out, West can discard all his hearts, relying on East to guard that suit.

(b) Attack on entries. This defense consists of playing the suit where declarer has a long menace. In this way a two-card menace may become an isolated menace, a twin-entry menace may be transformed into an ordinary two-card menace, etc.

```
              ♠ K x
              ♡ x
              ◊ K x
              ♣ —
 ♠ x x                    ♠ Q J 10
 ♡ A K                    ♡ —
 ◊ x                      ◊ A x
 ♣ —                      ♣ —
              ♠ A x x
              ♡ —
              ◊ —
              ♣ A K
```

Clubs are trumps, and West has the lead. If West leads a heart or a diamond, South can ruff and play his last trump, and East will be squeezed in diamonds and spades. The ending is a twin-entry simple squeeze. However, if West leads a spade, the twin-entry menace is reduced to a two-card menace of the usual sort and the squeeze must fail.

(c) Failure to rectify the count. Many times declarer must lose one or two tricks to the opponents in RECTIFYING THE COUNT for a squeeze. Defenders can withhold their cooperation in this maneuver, either by failure to cash established winners or by refusing to win a trick offered by the declarer. The example below, if permitted to succeed, is known as a SUICIDE SQUEEZE.

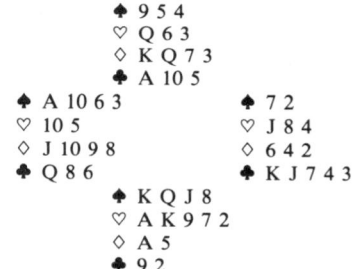

South is declarer at 3 NT, and West leads a spade. South wins the second round, and returns the suit. If West cooperates with declarer and cashes all his spades, then East can discard his clubs, but the second club lead won in dummy later squeezes him in the red suits. West cannot even cash the fourth spade without putting pressure on his partner. East can let go of two clubs on the third and fourth spades, but when declarer cashes his ♣ A–K, East must either unguard the diamonds or discard a heart, whereupon declarer will be able to set up dummy's fourth heart for his ninth trick. West can cash only two spades, but then he must switch and declarer cannot make his contract.

BERTRAND ROMANET gives the following hand:

```
              ♠ 9 5 4
              ♡ Q 6 3
              ◊ K Q 7 3
              ♣ A 10 5
 ♠ A 10 6 3              ♠ 7 2
 ♡ 10 5                  ♡ J 8 4
 ◊ J 10 9 8              ◊ 6 4 2
 ♣ Q 8 6                 ♣ K J 7 4 3
              ♠ K Q J 8
              ♡ A K 9 7 2
              ◊ A 5
              ♣ 9 2
```

South is declarer at 6 ♡, and receives the lead of a diamond. After drawing trumps, he leads from North up to the ♠ K. If West ducks two rounds of spades, the contract is unmakable. On the other hand, if he wins either of the first two rounds of spades, South can execute a spade-diamond squeeze against West.

Monroe Ingberman

DEFENSE TO STRONG, ARTIFICIAL OPENINGS. With the modern trend toward strong artificial opening bids, it becomes increasingly necessary for the defending side to have some conventional understanding about how to enter the auction, either to prepare for a possible sacrifice or to prevent the opponents from finding their best contract. Several methods are in current use, most of them based on the theory that the defending side will usually not find it profitable to enter the auction except with preemptive-type hands, containing either a long suit or two suits.

(1) The simplest defense, employed by the majority of tournament players, uses a double to show length in the major suits, and a 1 NT overcall to show length in the minor suits. This treatment would ap-

ply directly over an artificial 1♣ opening, or over an artificial 1◇ response. Single suit bids are natural and show long suits; jump overcalls are preemptive. This method can be used over strong artificial 2♣ and 2◇ openings as well, but few pairs do so.

(2) Truscott defense. Devised by ALAN TRUSCOTT, this method allows the defense to show all two-suited and one-suited hands. After a strong artificial opening, such as 2♣ or SCHENKEN or BLUE TEAM 1♣, or the artificial negative diamond response, one-suited hands are shown by a jump overcall. All simple overcalls show a two-suiter, the bid suit and the next higher-ranking. The two nontouching suit combinations are shown by a double (the doubled suit and the nontouching suit) or a notrump overcall (the other two suits). For example, after an artificial 2♣ opening, a 2◇ overcall shows diamonds and hearts, 2♠ shows spades and clubs, double shows clubs and hearts, and 2 NT shows diamonds and spades. The only alteration after a negative 2◇ response is that the double shows diamonds and spades and 2 NT shows clubs and hearts.

A possible weakness with this convention occurs in the rare case where the defender holds a strong hand (either a balanced strong notrump or a strong one-suiter) and has no convenient way to enter the auction after a Schenken or Blue Team 1♣ opening. A modification that would cover this eventuality is to use a double to show a strong hand, approximately equivalent to the minimum strength shown by the opening bid, and a notrump overcall to show the two nontouching suit combinations.

(3) Defense to PRECISION CLUB. A method developed by THE PRECISION TEAM to defend against Precision Club openings allows the defense to show either a preemptive one-suited or two-suited hand, or a strong hand. The double is used to show 16 or more points in a hand that may be balanced; it is roughly the equivalent of a standard double of a 1 NT opening. A 1 NT overcall of 1♣ shows length in the major suits; a 2 NT overcall shows length in the minor suits. This defense could be used against other 1♣ SYSTEMS, but is most valuable against the Precision system because that system reduces the minimum high-card requirement for 1♣ openings to 16 points. Hands in which the opener has only 16 points may well belong to the *defense*, and the incidence of 16-point hands is more than 80% as high as the total incidence of 17- and 18-point hands.

(4) EXCLUSION BIDS. (5) CRASH. (6) IDAK (or IDAC). (7) WONDER BIDS.

DEFENSE TO TWO-SUITED INTERFERENCE.

When an opponent makes a two-suited cuebid such as a MICHAELS CUEBID or a two-suited overcall such as the unusual 2 NT OVERCALL or the ROMAN JUMP OVERCALL, the partner of the opening bidder has available several countermeasures to advance his side's cause: the double, the raise, the cuebid, and the bid of the new suit not shown by the opponent's interference.

Standard practice: Responder doubles with a hand which would have been worth a redouble of a takeout double and which is interested primarily in defense. Responder makes a simple raise in opener's suit with a hand worth a traditional free single raise after an overcall. A cuebid in either of the suits shown by the interference is a general force, with the more expensive cuebid logically promising a stronger hand than the cheaper cuebid.

"Unusual over Unusual". When the interference is in the form of an unusual 2 NT overcall, some partnerships retain the standard meanings of the double and the raise, but assign a specific meaning to each cuebid. Each cuebid shows the strength of a limit raise or better, and each shows length in one of the suits not promised by the overcall. The lower cuebid shows length in the lower suit, and the higher cuebid shows length in the higher suit that was not shown by the overcall. For example:

WEST	NORTH	EAST	SOUTH
	1♠	2 NT	3◇

South's 3◇ bid shows a hand worth at least a limit raise in spades. Free bids are forcing to game.

For a convention dealing in part with two-suited interference over 1 NT openings, see LEBENSOLD.

DEFENSIVE BIDDING.

All the bidding by a side after the opponents have opened the auction. (However, the bidding by the opener's side can sometimes be "defensive.") Specific defensive actions are discussed under various other headings including: BALANCING; CUEBIDS IN OPPONENT'S SUIT; DEFENSE TO OPENING THREE-BIDS; DEFENSE TO 1 NT, DEFENSE TO STRONG ARTIFICIAL OPENINGS; DOUBLE; DOUBLE FOR SACRIFICE; JUMP OVERCALL; OVERCALLS; PENALTY DOUBLE; SACRIFICE; TAKEOUT DOUBLE; TWO-SUITER CONVENTIONS. Some specialized defensive methods are listed under various systems, such as ROTH-STONE and KAPLAN-SHEINWOLD.

Accurate defensive bidding requires considerable judgment and experience. In this department of the game, the expert has a much greater advantage over the average player than he has in normal constructive bidding. Some of the many factors which have to be taken into account are:

(1) *The risk involved.* Is there a real danger of being doubled and losing more than the opponents could score if left to their own devices? This may vary with the type of scoring, and with a psychological estimate of the opponents. Are they likely to be quick doublers?

(2) *The prospects* of achieving something by action. Possible goals are: (a) bidding and making a part-score, game, or slam; (b) saving effectively against a contract the opponents could make (see SAVE); (c) pushing the opponents to a level at which the defense may have a chance; (d) disrupting the opponents' bidding so that they reach the wrong contract. In general, the holding in the opponent's suit is a determining factor: a shortage favors action, and length and/or strength indicate passivity.

(3) *Vulnerability*, a paramount factor. Favorable vulnerability often generates aggressive action by the defenders, especially at duplicate. Both sides are very conscious of the fact that a three-trick defeat is a triumph for the defenders if it saves a vulnerable game, with the extra possibility that the opening side may permit itself to be pushed to a dangerous level. This situation becomes exaggerated at the slam level: a nonvulnerable pair can afford to go down seven

tricks to save a vulnerable small slam, and 11 tricks to save a vulnerable grand slam.

(4) *Level of the auction.* If a bid has to be made at a higher level, it is obviously more dangerous, and it may also offer poorer prospects. A side that bids 1 ♠ over an opposing 1 ◊ is more likely to buy the final contract than a player who bids 2 ◊ over 1 ♠. For both these reasons a bid at a higher level indicates a better hand. Similarly a double of 1 ♠ can be made more freely than a double of 1 ♠, because the latter offers fewer prospects and is less safe.

(5) *Estimate of partner's hand.* Simple addition of the minimum point-counts shown by the opponents and the points held by a defender will often reveal that partner's hand is virtually worthless. If you hold 16 points and a balanced hand, and an opening bid of 1 ♠ on your left gets a response of 2 ◊, partner's probable range is 0–3 points, and the lower end of that scale is the more likely. To bid in such a situation, which the Europeans call "in sandwich," is clearly dangerous. It would be less dangerous if the response was 1 NT, and least dangerous if the opener's suit had been raised. If the opener's side has established a fit, the chance that the defending side has a good fit is increased.

(6) *Honor wastage.* Queens and jacks in suits bid by the opponents are not only worthless for attacking purposes but should be rated as a minus quantity: they increase the defensive prospects, and therefore the danger of a PHANTOM SAVE. Conversely, queens and jacks in a suit held by the defending side are probably worthless in defense. Queens and jacks in side-suits are likely to play a part in any contract.

(7) *Honor position.* Most honor holdings increase in value when the suit is bid by the right-hand opponent, and decrease in value when the suit is bid on the left. (The exceptions are solid sequences such as king-queen-jack, and an ace not backed by another honor.) Similarly, three small cards is a poor holding if the suit was bid on the right, but rather better if the suit was bid on the left; any honor holding which partner may have has lost or gained value as a result of the bidding.

(8) *Length of suit.* An immediate overcall of an opening suit bid is normally at least five cards. In most other situations, a suit bid by the defending side is likely to be based on six-card length; e.g., after a notrump opening, or after two suit bids by the opener's side.

(9) *Raise your partner.* The need to support partner freely increases as the auction becomes more competitive. For example, if both sides are vulnerable and the bidding goes:

WEST	NORTH	EAST	SOUTH
			1 ♡
1 ♠	4 ♡	?	

If East has some honor strength, it might be right for him to bid 4 ♠ holding a singleton spade honor: the chance that West has a very substantial spade suit is greatly increased by the North-South bidding.

(10) *Preparation.* The defending side may have to prepare its bidding in the same way that the opener does. A minimum takeout double would be unprepared if the doubler has a doubleton in an unbid suit. Consider this hand after right-hand opponent has bid 1 ♡:

♠ A Q 6 4 3
♡ 7
◊ 5
♣ A 10 9 8 6 3

At favorable vulnerability there are excellent chances of an effective save over an opposing 4 ♡ bid, so 2 ♣ followed by a spade bid at the lowest available level on the next round is the indicated procedure. At unfavorable vulnerability, it is sufficient to overcall 1 ♠. Unless partner can support spades there is no great future, and it would be too dangerous to make a second bid at a high level. At equal vulnerability the decision would be closer.

(11) *Fit in side-suit.* When a good fit has been established in one suit, the degree of fit in another suit may be an important consideration. In a competitive auction a player who has overcalled and found a fit should sometimes bid a second suit in order to help his partner judge the right action at a high level. If the overcaller's partner bids a side-suit after finding a fit, it is more likely to be for lead-directing purposes.

(12) *Holding in the opponent's suit.* Three small cards in the opponent's suit is usually a bad holding, but it becomes better than a doubleton if the suit has been strongly bid and supported: partner can be expected to have a singleton or void.

(13) *Push.* The defenders frequently have to make "push" bids:

WEST	NORTH	EAST	SOUTH
			1 ♠
2 ♣	2 ♠	3 ♣	

East's club support may be only a doubleton honor. The bid is worthwhile if he thinks that each side can make about eight tricks. The risk is not great, and East gives his side the chance of a plus score if the opponents allow themselves to be pushed to 3 ♠.

DEFENSIVE TRICK. A card or card combination that may be expected to win a trick if an opponent becomes the declarer.

In some situations a player with a solitary defensive trick may need to take positive action. If 6 ♡ is reached voluntarily and the bidding has indicated that 6 ♠ is a possible SACRIFICE, a hand that is known to be very weak should usually double if it has one defensive trick. This should help partner to make the right decision (which may still be to bid 6 ♠), and avoid a PHANTOM SACRIFICE. For artificial uses of doubles and passes to reveal whether or not the partnership has enough defensive tricks to defeat the slam, see DOUBLE FOR SACRIFICE.

DELAYED DUCK SQUEEZE. A particular form of SECONDARY SQUEEZE.

DELAYED GAME RAISE. A bidding sequence equivalent to a standard jump raise.

♠ K J 5 4
♡ A 5 3
◊ 8 2
♣ A Q 9 7

This hand is too strong to raise an opening 1 ♠ to 4 ♠ in any normal bidding style. Using LIMIT RAISES, a substitute for the forcing double raise is necessary, and 2♣ followed by 4♠ is the usual device. This is not completely satisfactory if the opener's rebid is 2♦ because the nature of responder's hand is not clarified; but in that case the slam prospects are remote.

For alternative solutions to this problem, see SWISS convention, 3 NT RESPONSE, and 2 NT RESPONSE. These devices would be used on relatively balanced hands, in which case the delayed game raise can be reserved for markedly two-suited hands.

DELAYED RAISE. See BELATED SUPPORT; PREFERENCE.

DELAYED STAYMAN. See STAYMAN ON SECOND ROUND.

DELTA ASKING BIDS. See SUPER PRECISION ASKING BIDS.

DEMAND BID. A forcing bid. A term used occasionally to refer to a FORCING TWO-BID but otherwise obsolete.

DENIAL BID. A bid that indicates lack of support for partner's bid (an obsolescent term).

DENMARK. See DANISH BRIDGE LEAGUE.

DENOMINATION. The suit or notrump specified in a bid. See LAWS (Law 18).

DEPO. See BLACKWOOD AFTER INTERFERENCE.

DESCENDING ORDER. The order of the rank of the denominations: notrump, spades, hearts, diamonds and clubs.

DESCHAPELLES COUP. The lead of an unsupported high honor in order to establish an entry to partner's hand. This sacrificial play was invented by GUILLAUME DESCHAPELLES at whist.

```
              ♠ A Q 10 4
              ♡ A J
              ◇ 8 7 5 4
              ♣ 8 6 3
    ♠ 3 2                      ♠ 9 8 7 6 5
    ♡ Q 8 6                    ♡ K 10 7 5
    ◇ K Q J 9 6 3              ◇ A
    ♣ 7 5                      ♣ A 4 2
              ♠ K J
              ♡ 9 4 3 2
              ◇ 10 2
              ♣ K Q J 10 9
```

The blocked diamond position makes it very difficult for the defense to defeat South's highly optimistic 3 NT contract. East overtakes the ◇K lead with his ace, and must hope that his partner has a queen outside diamonds. If West has the ♣Q, the contract will be defeated automatically, so East assumes that his partner holds the ♡Q. The return of the ♡K is the key play. Whether or not South ducks, West's ♡Q is established as an entry, and South can be held to five tricks. Any other play by

East at the second trick permits South to make his contract. Note that the play of the ♡K cannot give South his contract if West has the ♣Q: South's maximum would then be four spade tricks, three heart tricks, and one club trick.

For a similar defensive play aimed at destroying an entry instead of creating one, see MERRIMAC COUP.

DESPERATION LEAD OR PLAY. A lead or play made in defiance of the dictates of safety when defensive prospects seem poor. A tactic usually reserved for rubber bridge, not duplicate. For example, after this bidding:

WEST	NORTH	EAST	SOUTH
	Pass	1♠	Pass
3♠	Pass	4♠	Pass
Pass	Pass		

South has to lead from:

```
              ♠ 8 7
              ♡ K 4
              ◇ J 8 5 4 2
              ♣ 9 7 4 3
```

The lead of the ♡K is a desperation lead trying to promote a heart ruff in South's hand. North may hold ♡A, or ♡Q and ♣A.

DEUCE. The two-spot, the lowest card, so named from the French *deux* coming from the Latin *duo*. The name is also applied to the two spots on a die, in gaming with dice, whence it is naïvely held that the imprecation "What the deuce!", meaning distaste for an unexpected and unfortunate turn of events, was derived.

In defensive play the deuce has definite meanings. When led against a notrump or suit contract it usually indicates the leader holds four cards in the suit led, or perhaps three, headed by at least one honor. Some partnerships lead the deuce from four small cards. When a defender leads the deuce in a suit in which he is presumably short, it most likely indicates a singleton. When defender discards a deuce, he wishes to discourage the continuation of that particular suit or a subsequent switch to it.

DEUTSCHER BRIDGE-VERBAND. See GERMAN BRIDGE LEAGUE.

DEVIL'S BEDPOSTS. The ♣4.

DEVIL'S COUP. Often called the disappearing trump trick; defenders' seemingly certain trump winner vanishes owing to a certain lie of the cards:

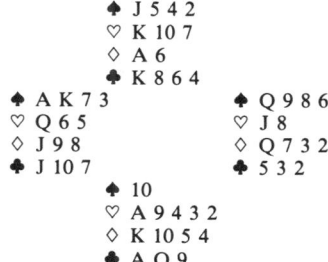

```
              ♠ J 5 4 2
              ♡ K 10 7
              ◇ A 6
              ♣ K 8 6 4
    ♠ A K 7 3                   ♠ Q 9 8 6
    ♡ Q 6 5                     ♡ J 8
    ◇ J 9 8                     ◇ Q 7 3 2
    ♣ J 10 7                    ♣ 5 3 2
              ♠ 10
              ♡ A 9 4 3 2
              ◇ K 10 5 4
              ♣ A Q 9
```

Declarer (South) reaches an optimistic ♡ 6 contract, apparently off a spade and a trump trick. However, West leads two rounds of spades. South ruffs the second, plays three rounds of clubs ending in dummy, and ruffs a spade. Ace, king, and a small diamond ruffed in dummy is followed by a ruff of dummy's last spade, arriving at the following end position:

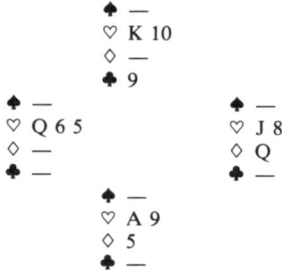

South leads his diamond and East-West are helpless to prevent him from taking the remainder of the tricks. If West trumps low, North overtrumps and makes the last two tricks with high trumps. If West ruffs with the queen, dummy overruffs with the king, and East's jack is finessed on the return.

For another type of disappearing trump trick, see SMOTHER PLAY.

DEVIL'S PICTURE BOOK, DEVIL'S TICKETS. Names given to playing cards by New England Puritans. From the time of their introduction in Europe, gambling at cards had been opposed: in 1397, John I, King of Castile, forbade dice and cards; in 1397, the Provost of Paris forbade playing at dice or cards on workdays; in 1404, the Synod of Langres forbade clergymen to play at dice or cards; in 1423, St. Bernardino preached against cards and persuaded the people of Bologna to throw their cards into a fire; and in 1541, the Parliament of Paris forbade play at dice or cards in the homes of the town and suburbs.

The objections were usually against gambling or against workingmen wasting their time; but the Puritans, for example, held that the Second Commandment (graven images) was violated by face cards. Hence, some churches permitted games using decks without court cards.

The opposition to cards has dwindled steadily, and the term is used humorously today except in a few isolated communities.

DEVYN PRESS. Formed in 1979 by RANDY BARON, Shelbyville KY, and ANDREW BERNSTEIN, Atlanta, the firm re-publishes important bridge books that are out of print, as well as new titles, most of which are written by bridge professionals.

DEVONSHIRE CLUB CUP. Awarded to winners of the RUBBER DUPLICATE tournament at the Devonshire Club, London, England.

DIAMOND. (1) The suit second lowest in rank, next above the club suit, represented by the symbol ◇ ; (2) the symbol. The suit originated in France in the sixteenth century; its name obviously comes from the diamond-shaped lozenge used for the pips.

DINK. To shorten the trumps of either dummy or declarer by forcing him to ruff; a rarely used colloquialism.

DIRECT COMPETITION. Such competition exists between two contestants when they play hands which are identical with respect to cards, relative location, dealer, and vulnerability. See BALANCED COMPARISONS.

DIRECTION. The designation of North, South, East, West, or the hand held by these players.

DIRECTIONAL ASKING BID. A specialized use of a low-level CUEBID IN OPPONENT'S SUIT to invite partner to bid notrump. Partner must bid notrump if he holds Q-x, J-x-x, or better in the opponent's suit. The directional asking bidder may have two objectives. First, he may wish to discover whether his side has a combined stopper in the opponent's suit when he himself holds Q-x, J-x-x, or a singleton king. Second, he may wish to steer the contract into his partner's hand. A player with A-x-x or K-x-x should wish to be dummy if the right-hand opponent has bid the suit. The lead should come up to partner's possible Q-x or J-x-x.

However, the low-level cuebid is regularly used on the West Coast and in England as a general-purpose forcing bid (or Western cuebid). The cuebidder will often have no stopper of any kind in the opponent's suit, and his partner bids notrump if, and only if, he has a full stopper in his own right. (In general, the Western cuebid "asks" if opponents have bid only one suit, but shows a stopper if they have bid more than one.)

Each partnership must decide whether the low-level cuebid shows a guard (East-Coast style), no guard (West-Coast style), or half a guard (directional asking bid). The last methods can be combined to some extent by regarding a repeat cuebid below the game level as a directional asking bid:

WEST	NORTH	EAST	SOUTH
			1 ♣
Pass	1 ◇	1 ♡	2 ♡
Pass	3 ♣	Pass	3 ♡

South holds:

♠ A 4
♡ J 7 3
◇ 9
♣ A K Q 9 7 6 2

3 NT can still be reached if North has as little as a singleton heart king or queen.

DIRECTOR. (1) Tournament director, the person designated to supervise a bridge tournament and to apply and interpret the LAWS OF DUPLICATE BRIDGE. These duties are outlined in Laws 77-87, and his responsibilities set forth. (2) Director of ACBL governing body at national or lower level. Throughout this encyclopedia, Director (capitalized) is used in sense (2). Tournament director is not capitalized.

DIRECTOR CLASSIFICATION. See TOURNAMENT DIRECTORS.

DIRECTOR'S INSTRUCTIONS. See INSTRUC-
TIONS, DIRECTOR'S.

DISAPPEARING TRUMP TRICK. See DEVIL'S
COUP; SMOTHER PLAY.

DISCARD. (1) To play a card which is neither of the
suit led, or of the trump suit, or (2) the card so
played. Colloquialisms for discard include ditch,
pitch and shake, Defenders can and do convey information to each other by the specific nature of certain
discards. See DEFENSE; DISCARDING; SIGNALING.

DISCARDING. Deciding what cards to keep in the
late stages of the play is one of the basic arts of the
game. Although there are no absolute rules, and
each case must be considered on its merits, a number
of general considerations are worth remembering.

(1) It is usually desirable to retain four cards in a
useful side-suit held in the dummy:

NORTH
♠ A K 8 2

WEST
♠ 9 7 6 4

If South has a doubleton queen, West's anemic
holding consitutes a vital stopper. In order to retain
his spades, West should not hesitate, for example, to
unguard a queen in another suit in which dummy is
weak. In the unlikely event that declarer has A–K–J,
he is likely to finesse.

Notice that West's spade, holding could be significant with the 5 instead of the 9: if South then held
J–9–3 or 10–9–3 he would need a side entry to dummy to make four tricks.

The same consideration applies when the declarer
is known to have or may have a four-card side-suit.

(2) Attention to the bidding will usually locate for
the defender missing aces and kings, and sometimes
queens and jacks. This is relatively easy when the
declarer has made a notrump bid showing a specific
point-count range, but may be possible in other
situations. The defender should mentally reconstruct
declarer's original hand, and decide whether his
bidding would be consistent with or without a particular honor card. Suppose this is the position:

NORTH
♠ K J 5

EAST
♠ Q 8 6 3

When discarding, East must make up his mind who
holds the ace. If South holds it, East must retain
three clubs. If West has the ace, East should keep a
doubleton.

If East held small cards only in the same situation,
he should be careful to retain three cards if he
believes that declarer holds the ace.

(3) A defender should usually discard established
winners for which he has no conceivable entry. One
exception arises in this common position:

NORTH
♠ A Q

WEST
♠ K 2

At the twelfth trick South is in a position to try for
an overtrick by taking a finesse. If East has kept two

clubs, the finesse can be taken safely. But if East has
kept one club and a *useless* winner, South may not
choose to jeopardize his contract.

(4) Signaling may help your partner to discard accurately, and attention to his signals should help
you. Except in obvious cases, one need not worry
about informing declarer. Declarers dislike being
deceived and many do not place any reliance on the
defenders' plays.

A valuable rule is to signal with the highest card
that can be spared. It then follows that any high encouraging discard denies the next higher card, and
promises the next lower.

NORTH
♣ 4 3 2

WEST
♣ A 8 5

If East has discarded the ♣K, declarer's clubs must
be worthless, and West can lead the suit happily. If
East has thrown the jack, West should lead the 5,
not the ace. East must have started with K–J–10–9 or
possibly J–10–9–x. But if East throws the queen,
West must leave clubs alone. South's king can be
trapped later.

(5) A player discarding from a worthless hand
should do his best to help his partner, who may need
information. If a defender has worthless holdings in
two suits, he should normally be careful to discard
from both suits as soon as possible. The discarding
of two or three small cards from one suit only would
raise a presumption that he had something to look
after in the other suits.

If partner is likely to be interested in length rather
than strength, one possible maneuver is to discard
one suit completely. Alternatively, with a regular
partner, it is possible to give LENGTH SIGNALS at each
stage. With 9-7-5-3-2, the sequence would be 2, 7,
3, 9, 5. The first discard is discouraging. Subsequently, a low card means an odd number of cards
remaining, and a high card means an even number.

(6) It will often be clear that, unless partner has
certain cards, there is nothing to be done. Discards
can then be made on the assumption that partner has
those cards.

John Brown gives this example in his *Winning
Defense.*

        ♠ A K J 6
        ♡ 10 6 5
        ◇ 8 3
        ♣ 9 4 3 2

♠ 9 8 7 5   ♠ 10 3 2
♡ J 8 3   ♡ K 9 4 2
◇ J 9 2   ◇ K 10 5 4
♣ Q J 10   ♣ 7 6

        ♠ Q 4
        ♡ A Q 7
        ◇ A Q 7 6
        ♣ A K 8 5

South played in a wildly optimistic 6 NT, and made
it as a result of bad discarding. The ♣Q was led and
won by the king, and South returned a low club.
West won and shifted to a spade, taken by South's
queen.

South crossed to the ♣J, finessed the ♡Q, and
cashed two club tricks and one more spade, leaving
this position:

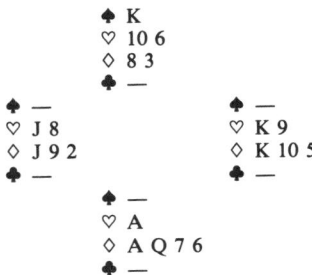

On the last spade everyone discarded a diamond, and South finessed the ◊ Q to make his contract. The fault lay primarily with East, for South's play had clearly marked him with at least three diamonds. Even if declarer held A-Q-J◊, he wouldn't be able to get back to dummy to repeat the diamond finesse and East's king would score a trick at the end. After East's error, however, West could still have saved the defense by realizing that his partner must be guarding hearts, and unless East also held a diamond honor, the contract was unbeatable. West would then discard a heart and all would have been well.

DISCIPLINARY CODE.

DISCIPLINARY CODE. The ACBL Disciplinary Code, approved in 1975, provides that every member charged should have a fair hearing. Disciplinary bodies in the ACBL are Units, Districts, the National Board of Directors and Tournament Committees. The jurisdiction of these bodies, grounds for discipline, sanctions which may be imposed, appeal procedures and procedural principles for the conduct of hearings are covered by the Code.

DISCIPLINE. The ability of both members of a partnership to follow an agreed system when partnership action is called for.

The ROTH-STONE SYSTEM was the first to stress partnership discipline as a requirement for use of the system, although all systems had implied its necessity without actually stressing it. Selection committees for teams in international competition have more and more stressed the importance of discipline under the heading of established partnerships.

DISCOURAGING BID. A bid indicating that game is unlikely but not impossible. Examples are: responder's raise of opener's suit from one to two, as a first response or as a rebid; responder's bid of 1 NT as a first response or as a rebid; opener's minimum rebid of his suit after a one-round forcing response at the two level; and in some styles a suit takeout in response to an overcall.

The bidder expects a combined point-count in the range of 18–22, or the distributional equivalent, and partner continues only if he has considerable additional strength in terms of high cards, distribution or fit.

DISCOURAGING CARD. A card which denotes a lack of interest in a suit's being continued or led. Usually a low card, the 6 or lower, it may be played either when following suit or when discarding upon another suit. See also DISCARD and SIGNALS.

DISCOVERY. The process of maneuvering the play in order to learn vital information about the hidden hands.

TERENCE REESE gives this example in *The Expert Game*.

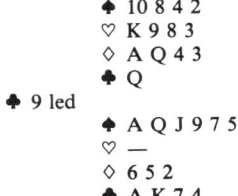

With neither vulnerable, South opens 1♠ in fourth seat. North raises to 4♠, and South bids 6♠.

South will look first to see if there is any reason for cashing the ♠A and play for some elimination position. The chances of this are obscure, so he may judge that the hand depends on one of two finesses and lead a spade for a finesse of the queen.

It is possible to improve on that play. At the second trick declarer should lead the ♡K from dummy. If East covers with the ace, South ruffs and finesses the ◊Q. East wins with the king and leads the ♠6. Now South has discovered for sure that East holds the ♡A and ◊K. Since West opened the ♠9 it is probable also that East holds ♠J-10; if South wants to look further, he can place East with intermediate cards in both hearts and diamonds, for had West held a solid sequence in either suit he would presumably have led it.

In short, South has built up for East a hand on which, if it contained the ♠K as well, he might well have opened the bidding third hand. Having reached this point, South may decline the spade finesse and play for the drop of the singleton king.

A different type of discovery play can be aimed at determining a suit division.

```
               ♠ Q 8 3
               ♡ 8 4
               ◊ 8 7 2
               ♣ K Q 8 4 3
  ♡ 3 led                    ♡ 10 played
               ♠ A K 5
               ♡ K 9 6
               ◊ K Q J 10 5
               ♣ A 6
```

South opens 2 NT and is raised to 3 NT. He wins the first trick with the ♡K, and has to choose between playing diamonds and clubs. The diamond play wins if the heart suit is split 4–4; the club play wins if the clubs split 3–3.

The even club split is slightly more likely mathematically, and the heart lead increases the chance that West has a five-card suit. But instead of plunging on clubs, South can give himself both chances if the defenders are good players. At the second trick he leads the ♣6 to dummy's king, followed by a low club to the ace. West is likely to signal his club length (see LENGTH SIGNALS) by playing low from a three-card holding or high from two or four. If West's club plays indicate that the suit will not break, South abandons clubs, and tries diamonds. This preserves the chance of making the contract if the hearts are split evenly, and avoids a possible two-trick defeat.

Discovery plays by the defenders are very rare. The following example is from the 1961 British International Trials with ALAN TRUSCOTT sitting West.

```
                    ♠ 9 3
                    ♡ A 8 7 2
                    ◊ 7 6 4 2
                    ♣ K J 7
    ♠ A Q 10 7                  ♠ 8 4
    ♡ K Q 9 4                   ♡ J 10 6 3
    ◊ Q J 3                     ◊ K 10
    ♣ A 2                       ♣ 10 8 6 5 3
                    ♠ K J 6 5 2
                    ♡ 5
                    ◊ A 9 8 5
                    ♣ Q 9 4
```

Both sides vulnerable; dealer East.

WEST	NORTH	EAST	SOUTH
			Pass
1♡	Pass	2♡	2♠
Dbl	2 NT	Pass	3◊
Dbl	Pass	Pass	Pass

West led the ♡K, captured by dummy's ace. South led a spade to his jack, and West won with the queen. It was clearly necessary for the defenders to lead trumps, but the lead of the queen would have blocked the suit, and prevented the defenders from playing three rounds advantageously. West judged that his partner must have a high diamond honor or the ♣Q. To learn which, he led the ♣A to get an ATTITUDE signal. When East dropped the ♣3 it was clear that he did not hold the ♣Q, so West shifted to the ◊3. South was held to six tricks, losing 800.

DISCRETIONARY POWERS. See ADJUSTED SCORE and Laws 9–12 and 80–87 of the LAWS OF DUPLICATE.

DISQUALIFICATION. Law 87, LAWS OF DUPLICATE BRIDGE, provides that a director is specifically empowered to suspend a player for the balance of a session, or subject to the approval of the tournament committee or the sponsoring organization, to disqualify a player, pair or team for cause in order to maintain discipline or order.

DISTRIBUTION. The manner in which the cards of a suit are dispersed among the four hands of a deal, or the manner in which the number of cards in the four suits are distributed in one hand. Variations in distribution are the basis of various bidding systems in use. See BIDDING.

DISTRIBUTIONAL COUNTS. Distributional points added to high-card points are used to arrive at an overall hand valuation. There are various ways in which the standard 4–3–2–1 POINT-COUNT can be supplemented:

Goren count, devised by WILLIAM M. ANDERSON of Toronto, and adopted and developed by CHARLES H. GOREN.

void	counts 3 points
singleton	counts 2 points
doubleton	counts 1 point

This applies to the opener's hand, and these points are added to the high-card POINT-COUNT (subject to the usual corrections).

If the responding hand plans to raise the opener's suit, he applies a different count:

void	counts 5 points
singleton	counts 3 points
doubleton	counts 1 point

In addition, the responder makes certain corrections, deducting a point for each of the following; (a) a raise with 3 trumps; (b) a 4–3–3–3 distribution; (c) an insufficiently guarded high-card. Also, a point is *added* for a king, queen, or jack in the trump suit provided this does not bring the total number of high-card points in the trump suit to over 4.

Karpin count, popularized by FRED KARPIN of Silver Spring MD, who was the first to achieve a large following with a distributional point-count method. Distributional points are assigned for length, one point for each card over four in any suit. Thus any five-card suit counts 1 point, any six-card suit 2 points, and so on.

Short suits are counted in raising partner according to the following schedule:

	with 4 or more trumps	with 3 trumps
void counts:	3	2
singleton counts:	2	1
doubleton counts:	1	0

These are in addition to points for length.

A simple version of the Karpin idea was published in 1947 by the late RICHARD A. MILLER. An even earlier pioneer of distributional point-count was Victor Porter of Boston. His method, published in 1938, allowed 4 points for each singleton and void, and 2 points for a doubleton in both hands.

Culbertson count, published by ELY CULBERTSON in 1952. For an opening suit bid, count each card over three in any suit as one point except that the fourth card does not count in the trump suit. When declarer's opening bid has been raised, he counts the fourth trump as a point, and adds 2 points when he holds six or more trumps. Responder also counts 2 points for holding six or more trumps when giving a raise and makes some minor correction: (a) 1 point is deducted for three-card trump support or 4–3–3–3 distribution; (b) 1 point is added for holding a void or two singletons.

Prior to Culbertson's adoption of point-count, he advocated a distributional count. Honor winners and long-suit winners were added, and the total of the combined hands represented the level to which the side could bid. A supporting hand counted ruffing values, but did not count length in side suits.

Roth count, devised by ALVIN ROTH to quantify the POINT-COUNT adjustments in hand evaluation which experts make in light of the bidding. The Roth system retains the 4–3–2–1 WORK POINT-COUNT for honor cards and the basic 3–2–1 Goren count for shortness. It adds points for long suits: one point for any six-card major or for a good-six-card minor; two points for any seven-card major or for a good seven-card minor.

Adjustments to shortness and length points are made in light of the degree of fit shown by one's partner's bidding. With 0–2 cards in partner's suit, no points are counted for shortness in a side suit; with 3 cards in partner's suit, the normal 3–2–1 scale of shortness count should be used; with 4 cards in partner's suit one extra point should be added for each singleton, plus one extra point if there are any doubletons. If one's own suit is raised by partner or if partner makes a notrump bid showing a balanced hand, one point is added for each card in the suit in excess of four.

Combination count, devised in England, uses lengths and shortages immediately. Karpin length points are supplemented by 2 for a void and 1 for a singleton. This is applied to both opener and responder in all situations with two provisos: (a) the opening bidder may not count more than 3 distributional points; (b) in responses and rebids no player may count more distributional points than he has cards in his partner's suit.

All distributional counts are an attempt to reach by formula the bid which an expert will make on the basis of experience. Their chief value is in giving guidance to inexperienced players; experts seldom make any conscious calculation of distributional points. See VALUATION AND ASSETS.

DISTRIBUTIONAL POINT-COUNT. For the distributional value of certain short suit holdings translated into point-count, see DISTRIBUTIONAL COUNTS, DISTRIBUTIONAL VALUES.

DISTRIBUTIONAL VALUES. The trick-taking possibilities of a hand that depend on the distribution of the cards in the other three hands rather than on the rank of the cards in their respective suits; low-card tricks in general, including long-suit tricks and ruffing tricks (short-suit tricks).

The classic example of the power of distribution *versus* points is the DUKE OF CUMBERLAND'S HAND. A slight variation, given below, has been immortalized by IAN FLEMING in his *Moonraker*.

The famous James Bond, sitting North and partnering *M*, sets out to teach a lesson to the cheat *Drax*.

Having pre-arranged the pack, Bond sees to it that the evil Drax gets the West hand and it will be clear that, no matter which of his three suits East chooses to lead, the final contract of 7♣ doubled and redoubled by Bond cannot be defeated. Playing for enormous stakes, this costs Drax something like 15,000 pounds—a salutary lesson indeed!

```
                 ♠ —
                 ♡ —
                 ◊ Q 8 7 6 5 4 3 2
                 ♣ A Q 10 8 4
♠ A K Q J                    ♠ 6 5 4 3 2
♡ A K Q J                    ♡ 10 9 8 7 2
◊ A K                        ◊ J 10 9
♣ K J 9                      ♣ —
                 ♠ 10 9 8 7
                 ♡ 6 5 4 3
                 ◊ —
                 ♣ 7 6 5 3 2
```

DISTRICT, DISTRICT ORGANIZATION. The territory of the ACBL is divided into 25 geographic Districts. East District is represented on the ACBL BOARD OF DIRECTORS by one Director, and on the ACBL BOARD OF GOVERNORS by five representatives. Areas included within each District are shown in Appendix II at the beginning of the recapitulation of the District Tournament results.

Each District is governed by a District Organization, whose functions include the organization of the REGIONAL TOURNAMENTS assigned to the District, the conduct of a District-wide contest to select a team to represent the District in the GRAND NATIONAL team playoffs, to select pairs to represent the District in the Grand National pair playoffs, the coordination of the scheduling of SECTIONAL TOURNAMENTS within the District and with neighboring Districts, and the establishment of a DISTRICT JUDICIARY COMMITTEE.

DISTRICT CHAMPIONSHIP. See GRAND NATIONALS CHAMPIONSHIPS (2).

DISTRICT JUDICIARY COMMITTEE. A committee of the DISTRICT ORGANIZATION whose rights and responsibilities include hearing appeals from disciplinary action imposed on a member by a unit board of directors, and conducting disciplinary hearings *ab initio*, which may result in censure, suspension or expulsion of a player.

DITCH. A colloquialism for DISCARD.

DOOP. A device developed by RONALD ANDERSEN which permits "one table duplicate games," so that hands previously played in tournaments can be played in the home.

DOPE. See BLACKWOOD AFTER INTERFERENCE.

DOPI. See BLACKWOOD AFTER INTERFERENCE.

DOUBLE. A call that increases the scoring value of odd tricks or undertricks on an opponent's bid. See DOUBLES and LAWS (Law 19).

DOUBLE ACTION. In some bidding situations, a player will pass after some hesitation, squirming, gesture or other mannerism that will alert his partner to the idea that he has some other possible action than a pass in mind. Such a hesitation on the part of one's partner should not deter a player from taking whatever action his own holdings might justify. However, it is unethical to re-open the bidding with a double to encourage partner to take whatever action he was considering. For a player who has so hesitated to take action after a double by his partner is highly questionable ethically.

DOUBLE AGAINST SLAM. See DOUBLE FOR SACRIFICE; LIGHTNER DOUBLE.

DOUBLE-BARRELED STAYMAN. A method of combining forcing and non-forcing STAYMAN. See TWO-WAY STAYMAN.

DOUBLE COUP. A trump coup in which two ruffs are necesary to achieve the required end position.

DOUBLE OF A CUEBID. At a high level, a double of a suit bid in which there is no intention of playing can be used for lead-directing purposes, or perhaps to suggest a save. It is an indiscreet action if there is no positive purpose other than intimidation, because it gives the left-hand opponent the possibility of a pass or a redouble. There is no general agreement about the meaning of a redouble in this situation: in one style the redouble shows second-round control of the suit.

A double of a cuebid at a low level would be lead-directing by a side which is on the defensive. But a double of a normally preemptive cuebid such as a MICHAELS CUEBID would, in standard practice, show a strong defensive hand. See DEFENSE TO TWO-SUITED INTERFERENCE.

DOUBLE DUMMY. (1) Play of a hand that could not be improved upon, as though declarer were looking at all four hands as in DOUBLE DUMMY PROBLEMS. It can also be used to refer to perfect play by the defenders.

Originally, Double Dummy was a two-handed form of whist in which each player had a dummy. Some players exposed all four hands, thus giving rise to the modern usage.

(2) Trademark of a two-hand contract game, introduced in 1975, in which each player has a dummy. Since each player already sees two hands, no dummy hand is put down on the table.

DOUBLE DUMMY PROBLEMS. Problems in the play of the hand in which the solver knows the holdings in all four hands. In attempting to discover the solution, the solver is usually required to make an unusual play such as losing a trick early in the play, discarding a high card, or unprotecting his own suit; the finish is usually a SQUEEZE or END PLAY. Since the solver must contend with perfect defense, the correct solution must include the best play by both sides, any other plays that are just about as good; a second or third line of play is called a variation, and not a solution. A solution must include all variations.

DOUBLE ELIMINATION. A method used in the VANDERBILT and SPINGOLD knockout team events in the annual ACBL spring and summer tournaments from the mid-Fifties until 1966 and 1965 respectively, and occasionally in other knockout team events.

As is implied in the name, a knockout tournament is one in which a team that loses a head-on match is eliminated from further competition. In a double knockout, the usual procedure is modified to provide that no team is eliminated until it has lost two matches.

The first competition between teams thus results in a group of losers and a group of winners (usually termed winners' bracket and losers' bracket). Matches continue in the winners' bracket, with half the competing teams continuing in the winners' bracket in the next round, the balance joining the losers' bracket. Eventually there is one surviving team from the winners' bracket.

In the losers' bracket, head-on play continues between one-time losers. Winners of these matches continue play in the next round, with losers in this bracket being eliminated as they have then lost their second match. In each round of the losers' bracket, the winners of the previous round are joined for the next round by the losers in the preceding round from the winners' bracket. This can often lead to a possible rematch between two teams that have previously competed against each other, and the CONDITIONS OF CONTEST are usually designed to provide as few as possible of such rematches.

Special provisions must usually be made in the conditions for the last few matches, depending on whether the losers' bracket ends up in a round of two, three, four, or five.

See REPECHAGE.

DOUBLE FINESSE. A finesse against two outstanding honors. The classic situation is:

A Q 10

x x x

The only serious chance of making three tricks is to finesse the 10. A more difficult situation is:

A J 4 3 2

10 9 6 5

With this holding some players would play the ace, hoping for an honor to fall or for a 2–2 division. But the better percentage play is to take two finesses. See also DEEP FINESSE, FINESSE, and SUIT COMBINATIONS.

DOUBLE GRAND COUP. A play by which declarer twice ruffs winning cards in order to reduce the hand which is long in trumps to the same length as that of an opponent, in preparation for a COUP.

DOUBLE JUMP. A bid two levels higher than necessary. This may refer to a RAISE (1 ♡ –4 ♡), a RESPONSE (1 ♡ –3 ♠ or 4 ♠) or an OVERCALL (1 ♡ –3 ♠ or 4 ♠). The term is obsolescent, partly because it is frequently misunderstood or misused by inexperienced players who confuse a DOUBLE RAISE (1 ♡ –3 ♡) with a DOUBLE JUMP RAISE (1 ♡ –4 ♡).

DOUBLE JUMP OVERCALL. A preemptive jump after an opposing opening bid. As with all preemptive actions, the bidder must allow for the vulnerability and the level at which he has to bid. The bid normally requires a suit of at least seven cards, but some liberties may be taken at favorable vulnerability. Over 1 ♣, a jump to 3 ♠ may be tried with a hand as weak as:

♠ K Q J 10 3 2
♡ 3
♢ 10 9 7 5
♣ 8 4

This offers a definite possibility of shutting out the heart suit. In other situations the RULE OF TWO AND THREE should be applied. See PREEMPTIVE BID; PREEMPTIVE OVERCALL; and WEAK JUMP OVERCALL.

DOUBLE JUMP RAISE. A triple raise, such as 1♡–4♡; sometimes confused with a jump raise such as 1♡–3♡. See TRIPLE RAISE.

DOUBLE JUMP SHIFT REBID. See OPENER'S REBID.

DOUBLE JUMP TAKEOUT. A preemptive response one level higher than a JUMP SHIFT, such as 1♡–3♠, or 1♠–4♡. See PREEMPTIVE RESPONSES.

DOUBLE KNOCKOUTS. See DOUBLE ELIMINATION.

DOUBLE MENACE. In a double squeeze situation, the threat card in the suit guarded by both opponents.

DOUBLE MITCHELL. A form of duplicate tournament competition to permit comparison between a greater number of pairs that can be had in direct competition in a single section. The boards are carefully twinned (either at the table or beforehand) and a MITCHELL MOVEMENT used. In scoring the event, all North–South scores from both sections are entered on the same recapitulation sheet, and the matchpoints are awarded across the pairs in both sections as one field. Similar treatment is accorded the East–West scores. Thus top score is increased from 12 to 25 on a board.

Double Mitchell is also used to describe a movement for two small sections which can be linked together to permit half of the boards to be played by the midway point. For example, suppose two parallel six-table sections in which the tables are numbered 1 through 6 and 11 through 16, are sharing boards, 1 with 11, etc., on each round. Both sections move within themselves for three rounds using the normal Mitchell progression. The moving pairs then move to the adjoining section without progressing, i.e., from table 1 to 11, 2 to 12, etc. After a further three rounds of normal Mitchell progressions, all pairs have played all the boards then in play. New boards are then introduced in play and twinned. Players then take their positions for what would normally be the fourth round (add three or subtract three from their original pair number in the section they started in), and play three rounds in that section. After these three rounds, they make a move similar to that after the third round, and complete the last three rounds in the adjacent section. If all sections in a big tournament are thus subdivided, it becomes possible to commence the matchpointing in the middle of the play. In Europe, where all sections are matchpointed against the whole field, with top score occasionally in the hundreds, this is a distinct advantage.

DOUBLE NEGATIVE. A bid or rebid by responder after opener has opened with a strong two-bid or an artificial strong 2♣ bid, that denies a hand worth more than 0–3 points. Several such double negatives are in current use:

(1) 2◇ ARTIFICIAL RESPONSE TO FORCING 2♣ OPENING when using STEP RESPONSES (Kaplan modification), or a 2♡ ARTIFICIAL RESPONSE as neutral.

(2) HERBERT NEGATIVE (touching suit) rebid after a negative response has previously been made to the forcing opening.

(3) Cheaper minor rebid after a negative response has previously been made to the forcing opening.

When the double negative is made by responder's rebid as in (2) and (3), it is sometimes called a SECOND NEGATIVE.

DOUBLE RAISE. A jump raise of opener's suit from one to three (1♠–3♠, or 1◇–3◇). The standard meaning is a hand with 13—15 points and at least four-card trump support, and the bid is forcing to game.

In accordance with an idea put forward by MARSHALL MILES, the responder may make the bid with a much stronger hand of similar distribution, with the intention of making a slam effort on the next round.

Many tournament players prefer to make the double raise encouraging but not forcing (see LIMIT JUMP RAISES). Some use the limit jump raise only when the suit is a minor, or only after an opponent has overcalled.

INVERTED MINOR SUIT RAISES are an alternative treatment. For substitutes for the standard forcing jump raise, see DELAYED GAME RAISE; SWISS CONVENTION; 2 NT RESPONSE, and 3 NT RESPONSE.

DOUBLE RAISE IN MINOR, PREEMPTIVE. See INVERTED MINOR SUIT RAISES.

DOUBLE OUT OF ROTATION. See LAWS OF DUPLICATE, Law 32.

DOUBLE FOR SACRIFICE. A double of an opponent's voluntary slam bid after the doubler's side has bid and raised a suit preemptively, designed to help the defenders decide whether they have enough tricks to defeat the slam or should sacrifice. The double indicates how many tricks the doubler expects to take. There are two variations of the convention.

One method, called the Negative Slam Double, played by IRA RUBIN, requires the left-hand opponent of the slam bidder to double only if he has no defensive tricks. If his partner has fewer than two such tricks, he sacrifices. If the slam bidder's LHO has one or two tricks he passes and his partner doubles only if he has no tricks, allowing the slam to be played doubled if the pass was made with two tricks, or the sacrifice to be taken if the pass was made with one trick. For obvious reasons, RICHARD L. FREY originally christened this convention the "Undouble."

An alternative method, called the Positive Slam Double, requires the slam bidder's LHO to double only if he has two defensive tricks. If instead he passes, his partner will sacrifice with no tricks, pass with two tricks, or double with one trick, allowing the slam to be played doubled if the pass was made with one trick, or the sacrifice to be taken if the pass was made with no tricks.

DOUBLE SHOWING ACES. See DEFENSE TO INTERFERENCE WITH BLACKWOOD.

DOUBLE IN SLAM-GOING AUCTION. See DEFENSE TO INTERFERENCE WITH BLACKWOOD; DOUBLE FOR SACRIFICE; DOUBLE OF A CUEBID; LEAD DIRECTING DOUBLE; LIGHTNER DOUBLE.

DOUBLE SQUEEZE. A squeeze of both opponents. It involves three suits, which may be labeled A, B, and C; then one opponent is squeezed in suits A and B while the other is squeezed in suits B and C. Thus a double squeeze is a combination of two simple squeezes, one against each opponent. Every double squeeze requires a squeeze card, a double menace, and two isolated menaces, guarded by only one opponent. Declarer must have all but one of the remaining tricks. The following classifications are based on analysis by BERTRAND ROMANET.

(1) Simultaneous. In a simultaneous double squeeze both opponents are squeezed on the same trick. There are three basic positions:

(a) Balanced

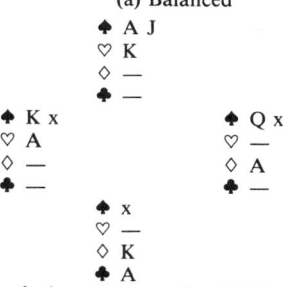

South leads the squeeze card, which is the A♣. West is squeezed in the majors, and he must discard a spade. North throws a heart, and East is squeezed in spades and diamonds. This is a positional squeeze.

(b) Automatic

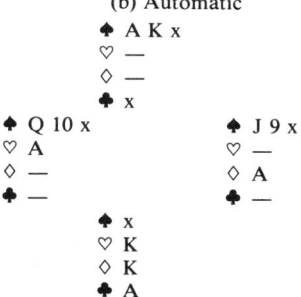

South leads the ♣A, squeezing West in the majors. West must discard a spade, and now East is squeezed in spades and diamonds.

(c) Twin Entry

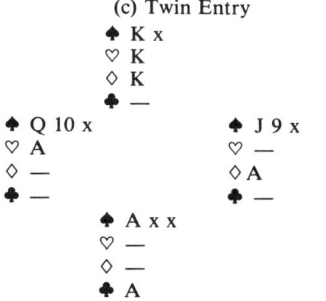

South leads the ♣A, West must throw a spade, North discards a heart, and East is squeezed in spades and diamonds. This is a positional squeeze.

(2) Nonsimultaneous. In a nonsimultaneous double squeeze there are two separate squeeze cards. Declarer's last established trick in the fourth suit squeezes one opponent; a trick or more thereafter, the second squeeze card disposes of the other opponent. The second squeeze card lies opposite the first squeeze card, and it accompanies the isolated menace guarded by the opponent who was squeezed initially. There are four basic positions (Romanet):

(a) Inverted Left

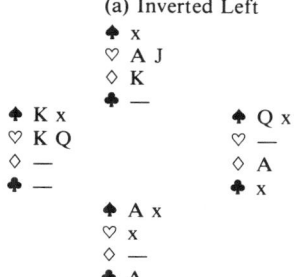

South leads the ♣A, forcing West to discard a spade, and North throws a low heart. Now South leads a heart to the ace which squeezes East in spades and diamonds. This is a positional squeeze.

The term *inverted* refers to the fact that the double menace accompanies the squeeze card, which is unusual since the double menace ordinarily lies opposite the squeeze card. *Left* indicates that the isolated menace guarded on the left is accompanied by a winner.

(b) Inverted Right

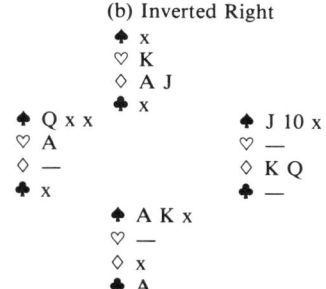

South leads the ♣A, forcing East to discard a spade. Now North wins the ♢A, squeezing West in spades and hearts. This is an automatic squeeze.

For this squeeze an ordinary two-card menace against both opponents does not suffice; a recessed menace is required.

(c) Twin Entry Left

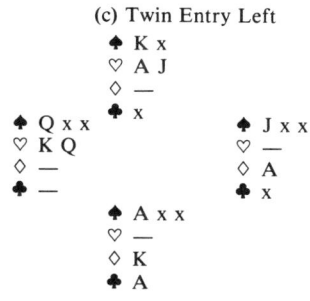

South leads the ♣A, which forces West to discard a spade. Now a lead to the ♣K, followed by the ♡A squeezes East in spades and diamonds. This is a positional squeeze.

This ending combines elements of the balanced and twin-entry positions discussed above.

(d) Inverted Left Recessed

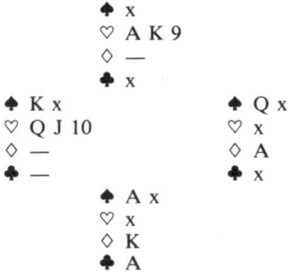

South leads the ♣A, which forces West to discard a spade. Now North wins two top hearts, the last of which squeezes East in spades and diamonds. This is a positional squeeze.

The isolated menaces are arranged as in a balanced double squeeze, but the double menace is inverted. As compensation, North must have two winners, one of which is an entry. The last two positions illustrate the available endings.

See also BARCO SQUEEZE; BONNEY'S SQUEEZE; CLASH SQUEEZE; HEXAGON SQUEEZE; RECIPROCAL SQUEEZE.

Monroe Ingberman

DOUBLE TENACE. A tenace in which the sequence is broken in two places, such as A-Q-10, K-J-9.

DOUBLE OF 3 NT. See LEAD-DIRECTING DOUBLE.

DOUBLE TOP. In some individual tournaments it is not practical to maintain direct comparison within a group on all of the boards played. Thus every score will be duplicated to each of the two players who were partners on the board. In matchpointing the scores, thus, there are two identical entries for each score, and each award is entered twice, once to each of the players. Thus there are two top scores on each board; and a game so scored is referred to as scored with a double top.

The term is also used to refer to a scoring method more in use in other countries, whereby each matchpoint score is obtained by counting two points for each poorer score and one point for each equal score. This eliminates the half points in matchpointing. Thus with 13 pairs in competition, top score would be 24 rather than 12, amounting to a double top. See STANZA MOVEMENT.

DOUBLE OF 2♣ RESPONSE TO NOTRUMP. The 2♣ response to an opening bid of 1 NT is usually used as the STAYMAN convention. When 2♣ is bid in response to a strong notrump, a double by the LHO of the 2♣ bidder is normally a lead-directing bid showing concentrated strength in clubs, but not pro-

mising overall strength. See DOUBLES OF ARTIFICIAL BIDS FOR PENALTIES.

When the opening notrump bid is of the weak variety, however, the responder sometimes has a very weak hand with which he wishes to escape into a suit. See WEAK NOTRUMP. The escape is frequently initiated by a 2♣ response. Consequently for most expert partnerships the double of the 2♣ response to a weak opening notrump simply shows general strength. The double does not promise any particular distribution, but suggests that the doubler has a hand with which it would have been appropriate for him to double the notrump opening had he been sitting over the opener.

DOUBLER. A player who has doubled.

DOUBLES. The two main categories are PENALTY DOUBLES and TAKEOUT DOUBLES, which are listed separately. Distinguishing between the two types is not always easy. The following is a sound general rule: *A double of a suit bid below the game level is for a takeout if partner has not bid.*

Conversely, a double is for penalties if:

(1) The bidding is at the game level or above; or

(2) The bid doubled is in notrump; or

(3) The doubler's partner has already bid.

But these generalities require some qualification in particular cases.

(1) Even at the game level, a double may have a takeout flavor. If the bidding goes 1♡–pass–4♡–double, the doubler is unlikely to be loaded with hearts. He indicates a hand with considerable high-card strength, and expects a takeout, although partner will often exercise his option of passing for penalties. If the suit were spades, the penalty aspect would be more dominant.

(2) A double of a response of 1 NT is a special case (1♡–pass–1 NT–double). This is primarily for takeout, although responder will often exercise his option to pass.

(3) Doubles on the second round have to be considered on their merits, and are sometimes ambiguous. The old theory was that a double of a suit rebid is for penalties when the same suit could have been doubled on the first round. This is true in cases like:

WEST	NORTH	EAST	SOUTH
			1♠
Pass	2♣/1 NT	Pass	2♠
Dbl			

West must have spade length and strength, and was lying in wait. The situation would not be so clear in a minor suit:

WEST	NORTH	EAST	SOUTH
			1◇
Pass	1 NT	Pass	2◇
Dbl			

West may have diamond strength, but equally, since both opponents are limited, he may be looking for a major suit. East's diamond length will usually enable him to interpret the double correctly.

If another takeout action is available, a double is clearly for penalties. The following sequences only look similar:

(a)

WEST	NORTH	EAST	SOUTH
			1♣
Pass	1♢	Pass	2♣
Dbl			

(b)

WEST	NORTH	EAST	SOUTH
			1♢
Pass	2♣	Pass	2♢
Dbl			

Sequence (a) is clearly for penalties: West would make a cuebid of 2♢ holding the majors.* In sequence (b) the cuebid is not available, so the double is ambiguous: it is likely to be for a takeout, but East must inspect his hand.

Experts disagree about the meaning of this sequence:

WEST	NORTH	EAST	SOUTH
			1♡
Pass	1 NT	Pass	2♣
Dbl			

The doubler can be expected to have some heart strength, but whether he has clubs is not clear.

A double is always for penalties if three suits have been been: there are no longer two or more suits between which the responder can choose. However, if made at a low level, some expert partnerships nevertheless use such doubles as takeout, and some treat the double as a COOPERATIVE DOUBLE.

Doubles other than penalty doubles and takeout doubles may be used in a variety of situations to give information. In slam auctions, for example, doubles may be used offensively as a DEFENSE TO INTERFERENCE WITH BLACKWOOD. Defensively, doubles may be used to exchange information as to when to sacrifice against a slam. See DOUBLES FOR SACRIFICE. See also CARD SHOWING DOUBLE, COMPETITIVE DOUBLE, DOUBLE OF 2♣ RESPONSE TO NOTRUMP, MAXIMAL OVERCALL DOUBLE.

Other doubling situations are discussed under: BALANCING; COOPERATIVE DOUBLE; DOUBLE OF CUEBID; DOUBLES OF NOTRUMP BIDS; FREE DOUBLE; INHIBITORY DOUBLE; LEAD-DIRECTING DOUBLES; LIGHTNER DOUBLE; NEGATIVE DOUBLE; OPTIONAL DOUBLE; PENALTY PASS; RESCUE; RESPONSES OVER OPPONENT'S TAKEOUT DOUBLE; RESPONSIVE DOUBLE; STRIPED-TAIL APE DOUBLE; SUCKER'S DOUBLE; as well as PENALTY DOUBLES and TAKEOUT DOUBLES.

DOUBLES OF ARTIFICIAL BIDS FOR PENALTIES.

At a high level the situation is clear-cut. A player who doubles a response to BLACKWOOD, or a GERBER 4♣ bid, for example, is showing strength in the suit he has doubled in the hope of directing his partner to the right opening lead. There is a negative inference which is sometimes overlooked: the player who does *not* double a conventional bid on his right usually does not want that suit led.

At a low level, other considerations come into play. The double for business is the standard treatment when the hand seems sure to *belong* to the side that is doubled. This would apply if the bid doubled

*The same would apply to the sequence 1♢–pass–1 NT–pass–2♣–double.

is: a conventional 2♣; a conventional response (negative or ace-showing) to a conventional 2♣; or a STAYMAN response to 2 NT or a standard (strong) notrump. See also FISHER DOUBLE.

When the doubling side may well have the majority of the high-card strength, the double may be put to better use by partnership agreement — either to show general strength or in some more specialized way. Each situation needs examination in relation to the convention used by the opponent. See DOUBLE OF 2♣ RESPONSE TO NOTRUMP; JACOBY TRANSFER BIDS; 1♣ SYSTEMS; ROMAN SYSTEM; TEXAS, and WEAK NOTRUMP. For an alternative treatment of all such situations, see TWO-SUITER conventions.

DOUBLES OF NOTRUMP BIDS.

In principle, such doubles are for penalties, and partner is not expected to take out the double unless he has a very poor defensive hand with a long suit. There is one important exception:

WEST	NORTH	EAST	SOUTH
1♡	Pass	1 NT	Dbl

It is probably more useful to reserve South's double for a hand which would make a takeout double of 1♡ than for the rarer hand which would wish to punish 1 NT, although North may often choose to pass for penalties.

A number of situations deserve separate comment:

(1) *Doubles of strong notrump openings.* A very rare action, seldom justified unless a long strong suit is held together with side entries. Partner should hardly ever take out the double. A play with a balanced 17-point hand should usually pass a notrump opening, because the possible losses exceed the possible profits. The meaning of the double does not vary in fourth seat, and the opening leader tends to lead a short suit. For alternative treatments, see ASTRO, BROZEL.

(2) *Doubles of weak notrump openings.* A double by second hand should be at least as strong as the opening bid, and a good suit to lead is desirable but not essential. To pass a weak notrump with a balanced 15-point hand runs a serious risk of missing a game; to double with less leads to trouble when the opener's side has the balance of strength.

The double by fourth hand is a theoretical problem. Apparently the fact that opener's partner has passed should encourage the fourth player, but this is deceptive. Experienced players do not pass very weak hands when their partners have opened with 1 NT, instead they scramble out into a suit at the level of two in an attempt to avert disaster. So when 1 NT has been passed, the opener's side is more likely than not to hold the balance of strength, and the fourth player should be cautious about doubling. (But this sort of thinking might permit the third player to try a double cross by passing with a near-Yarborough.) Conversely, the fourth player should double a two-level suit takeout by third hand with any hand with which he would have doubled an opening weak notrump on his right. Many players extend this treatment to a double of a STAYMAN response to allow for the possibility that third hand is taking evasive action (see DOUBLE OF 2♣ RESPONSE

TO NOTRUMP); this gives up the lead-directing double of a Stayman bid based on clubs.

The doubler's partner should takeout only with a long suit and a very weak hand.

(3) *Double of a 1 NT overcall.* By third player this is a simple indication that he has at least 8–9 points, and therefore expects his side to have the balance of strength. This principle applies to most notrump doubles: the double is made when the doubler thinks it more likely than not that his side has more than 20 high-card points. If the opener doubles 1 NT, either by second or fourth hand, he shows a maximum one-bid, probably 19–21 in high cards.

(4) *Doubles of 3 NT* are often lead-directing. See LEAD-DIRECTING DOUBLE.

(5) *Double of a notrump rebid.*

WEST	NORTH	EAST	SOUTH
			1 ♣
Pass	1 ♡	Pass	1 NT
Dbl			

or

WEST	NORTH	EAST	SOUTH
			1 ♣
Pass	1 ♡	Pass	1 NT
Pass	Pass	Dbl	

In both sequences the double is intended for penalties. In the first case West has club strength, and in the second case East has heart strength.

Third hand problems. When an opening 1 NT bid is doubled, the opening bidder's partner has four standard options.

(a) *Redouble.* A call indicating that the opener's side has the majority of the high-card strength, and that a penalty should be available if the doubling side escapes into a suit. A frequent action holding 9 points or opposite a weak (12–14) notrump. Opposite a standard (16–18) notrump, 5 points is theoretically sufficient, but slightly more is desirable in view of the likelihood that the doubler has a good suit to lead.

(b) *2 NT.* A bid with no natural meaning, because a strong balanced hand would always redouble. It is therefore treated as a type of cuebid, and is likely to be based on a strong two-suited hand.

(c) *2 ♣.* Not Stayman after a double. It is normally a natural bid with a long club suit, and should be assumed to be so by the opener. However, the bid is often made on a weak unbalanced hand with the intention of making an S O S redouble when doubled. This would be an appropriate action with a 4-4-4-1 distribution, for example.

(d) *Three of a suit.* An unlikely action opposite a standard notrump. Opposite a weak notrump it would be preemptive, with a six-card suit and no game ambitions.

For other options available to the partner of the opening notrump bidder, see DEFENSE TO DOUBLE OF 1 NT.

DOUBLETON. An original holding of two cards in a suit. If an opening lead is made from a doubleton, the top card is customarily led first. For evaluation of a doubleton, see DISTRIBUTIONAL POINT-COUNT.

DOUBLY IMPROPER CALL. A call which is ir-

regular in two respects, such as an insufficient bid out of rotation. See LAWS (Law 31).

DOWN. Defeated; said of a declarer who has failed to make a contract. The term is used in various ways, such as "We are down two" or "down 700," meaning the side has failed to make a contract by two tricks, or has incurred a penalty of 700 points.

DRAW FOR PARTNERS. See LAWS (Law 3).

DRAWING TRUMPS. The action of removing the trumps from the opponents' hands. When he first gains the lead, declarer should usually draw trumps, provided that in doing so he does not remove cards from his own hand or dummy which are necessary for some other purposes. There are various considerations which may persuade declarer to postpone drawing trumps.

Ruffs. Declarer may need to ruff some of his losers in the dummy. It may be necessary to give the lead to the opponents in the process of establishing and taking the ruffs, and they may lead trumps at every opportunity. Declarer must leave at least enough trumps in dummy to take care of his losers while allowing for such trump leads by the defense (see CROSSRUFF).

Entries. Often declarer can use dummy's trumps as entries. These entries may be required for finesses or development of a side suit in declarer's hand. If no other entries are available, these plays must be made while drawing trumps.

Sometimes declarer plans to establish dummy's suit. Once it has been established, the trump suit may provide the only entry to dummy. If this delayed entry would not be available after drawing trumps and taking ruffs in dummy, then either play must be postponed, and dummy's suit established first. Eventually the dummy may be entered by drawing the last trump, or by means of a ruff.

Stoppers. Dummy's trumps may serve as stoppers in a certain suit. However, it may not be expedient for declarer to ruff all his losers in that suit; instead he plans to establish discards, which may entail losing the lead to the opponents. Declarer seeks to leave one trump in dummy (to stop the opponents' suit) for each time he must lose the lead in this fashion.

Declarer may be able to use his trumps or dummy's trumps as stoppers. He may be unable to ruff in his hand lest he lose trump control. Therefore he must leave enough trumps in the dummy to cope with the opponents' suit while he proceeds with the development of the hand.

Timing. Declarer may put off drawing trumps because his play for the hand as a whole requires him to deal first with other matters:

(1) Declarer may seek to establish a quick discard for a potential loser before the defenders can establish and cash their trick in that suit.

(2) Declarer has a side-suit which is not solid. Unless he has abundant trumps it is best to test the side-suit before all the trumps are drawn. This is important if the trump suit is broken.

(3) Declarer has a choice between the ruffing game and the long suit plan (particularly if the long

suit is in dummy). By leading the long suit at once, declarer can vary his plan according to circumstances.

Weakness. If the trump length and strength is shared about equally between the two sides, declarer should usually avoid trump leads:

NORTH
J 5 4

SOUTH
K 9 7 2

In such situations South can hope to collect two or three trump tricks by leaving his holding intact for the end game.

With extreme weakness in trumps, declarer is on the defensive. He may need to lead trumps to avoid opposing ruffs.

Master Trump. Declarer usually ceases to draw trumps when one defender has one or two master trumps. But a trump continuation may still be desirable to achieve a throw-in, or simply to get rid of the lead; and it may be necessary to drive out a master trump which would otherwise interrupt the run of dummy's established suit at a time when dummy has no remaining entry.

DRIVE OUT. To force the play of a high card, i.e., to lead or play a card sufficiently high in rank to force the play of an adverse commanding card to win the trick, or to continue until this result is achieved.

DROP. To capture an adverse potential winning card by the direct lead of a higher card or series of higher cards, as to drop an unguarded king by the play of an ace; also, the play which endeavors to capture an adverse card, as to "play for the drop," instead of finessing.

Whether to finesse or play for the drop is generally a case of determining the correct mathematical probabilities. However, this preference is considerably modified by information derived from the bidding and play, and it is the policy of good players to obtain as much information as possible, inferential as well as exact, before committing themselves. For example:

WEST	NORTH	EAST	SOUTH
1♣	Pass	Pass	1 NT
Pass	3 NT	Pass	Pass
Pass			

If during the play, East shows up with an ace or king, it is highly unlikely that he will hold another high honor, since he passed his partner in 1♣. It would therefore be indicated for South to disregard the mathematical probabilities, and arbitrarily place all missing honors in the East hand.

DRURY. A convention that uses an artificial 2♣ response by a PASSED HAND in response to a major suit opening.

(a)		(b)	
SOUTH	NORTH	SOUTH	NORTH
Pass	1♠	Pass	1♡
2♣	2♦	2♣	2♦

In both cases the 2♣ bid asks the opener to clarify his strength, and the 2♦ rebid is in principle negative, showing a sub-minimum opening.

In (a) South might hold:

♠ K 9 7 3		♠ 10 9 3
♡ K 6 4 2	or	♡ 6 5
♦ Q 7		♦ A J 7 4
♣ K J 8		♣ A 10 9 7

South continues with 2♠, showing a stronger hand than would have been indicated by an immediate raise to 2♠.

The responder in no way guarantees a fit with opener's suit. He would bid 2♣ in response to 1♠ with:

(c)		(d)
♠ J 5		♠ 3
♡ K J 10 7	or	♡ 9 3 2
♦ A J 7 5		♦ K J 9
♣ Q 7 3		♣ A J 10 9 6 5

With hand (c) responder avoids the routine 2 NT response, partly because there may be a fit in hearts, and partly because 2 NT may be too high opposite a light opening bid. He follows with 2♡, showing a four-card suit, if the rebid is 2♦. Any other rebid would show a full opening bid.

With hand (d) the responder bids 2♣ followed by 3♣. In this case the Drury player may end up one level higher than other players — usually the converse is true — but these hands are not common because a good six-card club suit will often justify an original 1♣ or 3♣ bid.

The 2♦ rebid by the opener is not necessarily negative, and cannot be passed. He may hold a hand worth a full opening bid or more on which diamonds is his natural rebid. In that case he follows with a constructive bid of 2 NT or a bid at the three-level, which makes the position clear to the responder.

The convention works similarly after an opening bid of 1♡, but the frequency is much lower because responder will bid 1♠ if he can.

The inventor of the convention, the late DOUGLAS DRURY, used a response of 2 NT to show a balanced 11–12 points with a doubleton in partner's major and a trebleton in the unbid major. But his leading supporters never use the 2 NT response, preferring to have the chance of playing at the level of two in a major suit.

If the 2 NT response is ruled out for natural purposes, it can be used to show a balanced hand with a good major suit fit and about 11 points. The jump raise to the three-level would be unbalanced and semi-preemptive. See also REVERSE DRURY.

For an alternative device with a similar object, see SNAP.

DUB. At bridge, a dub is a player whose game is below the standards of the players with whom he competes.

DUCK. To play a small card, and surrender a trick which could be won, with the object of preserving an ENTRY. When the suit has been led by an opponent, the duck is mechanically identical to a HOLD-UP, in that a master card (or cards) is retained, but the objective is different. A play ducks in order to pursue his own aims, but holds up in order to thwart the opponents.

A *coup en blanc* is a ducking play for the purpose of winning a later trick.

Apart from a considerable number of situations listed under SAFETY PLAY, ducking plays may be listed under five main headings:

(1) *Suit combinations*

To make the maximum number of tricks in notrump with no side entry to dummy:

(a)	(b)
A K x x x	A Q x x x
DUMMY	DUMMY
x x or x x x	x x or x x x

In (a) the first trick is ducked and the declarer hopes for an even split to make four tricks; with three small, he may duck twice to make three tricks. The situation in (b) is similar, but declarer finesses on the second round; if declarer has three small cards, the first-round duck is slightly better than a finesse followed by a duck because right-hand opponent might hold a singleton king.

(c)	(d)
K Q 10 7 x x	K J 8 x x x x
DUMMY	DUMMY
x x	x x

These are harder, and declarer needs more optimism. In each case he must duck the first trick completely in the hope of finding the right-hand opponent with a singleton ace. If the required situation does exist, it would be brilliant play for the left-hand opponent to play his highest card in an attempt to deflect declarer from his purpose.

(2) *Trap combination*

In notrump with no side entry in dummy:

(e)	(f)	(g)
A Q J x x x	A Q J x x	A Q 10 x x x
DUMMY	DUMMY	DUMMY
x x	x x x	x x x

In each case a small card is led, and left-hand opponent plays the king. A duck ensures the loss of only one trick, and is essential in (e): if left-hand opponent has brilliantly played the king from a doubleton or tripleton, he has gained a trick for his side.

In (f) and (g) declarer does slightly better to win the first trick, return to his hand, and plan to duck the second round if the king was singleton; but he requires a convenient entry, and there may be an AVOIDANCE consideration.

(h)	(i)
A K x x x	A Q x x x
DUMMY	DUMMY
J 10	J 10

If declarer's lead is covered, he must duck and hope for a 3–3 division. The only hope of five tricks is for left-hand opponent to fail to cover holding Q–x–x (or K–x–x). It is therefore better to lead the 10, following the principle of leading low from a sequence when you wish to avoid a cover.

(j)	(k)
A x x x x	A x x x x
DUMMY	DUMMY
Q J x	J 10 9

In both cases declarer leads a high card and must duck if left-hand opponent covers. In (k) the jack is the best lead: declarer plans to follow with the 9. If left-hand opponent is left with a doubleton honor, he may make the mistake of playing low, and declarer makes four tricks.

(3) *Double and triple*

Again in notrump with no side entry to dummy:

(l)	(m)
A x x x x	A 9 x x x
DUMMY	DUMMY
x x x	x x x x

With (l) two ducks and a 3–2 split are needed to make three tricks. (m) requires one duck if the suit splits 2–2, giving four tricks; a 3–1 split requires two ducks, and gives three tricks; a 4–0 split requires three ducks and gives two tricks. This is the only possible situation for a tripleduck.

(4) *Control*

In a trump contract:

(n)	(o)	(p)
x x	A x	A x x
DUMMY	DUMMY	DUMMY
A x x	x x x	x x x

Declarer usually ducks with (n) unless there is a possibility of a 7–1 division. This prepares for a ruff in dummy without the need for a side entry, and retains control of the suit if the opponents shift: this may be most important if they are able to draw dummy's trumps.

Declarer would not duck with (o) if a ruff is the only consideration, but it may be right to duck for control reasons. If the defenders can prevent a ruff, declarer is better placed with the ace still in dummy.

The duck with (p) could also be described as a hold-up. It interferes with the defensive communications, and may prevent the defense taking a second trick if the suit is divided 5–2.

(5) *Defensive*

A defender in a trump contract often ducks to prepare for a ruff by his side or in order to prevent a ruff by declarer:

(q)		(r)	
WEST	EAST	WEST	EAST
x x	A x x x	x x	A x x

In (q) West leads a doubleton in a side suit in the hope of getting a ruff. East ducks if he can judge that the lead is more likely to be a doubleton than a singleton, and if he thinks that West is more likely to secure the lead.

The objective is reversed in (r), although the mechanics are the same. West leads a doubleton trump aiming to prevent a ruff in the dummy. Again East ducks if he judges that West has a doubleton and the likely entry.

The suit combination plays described above for the declarer are also available for the defenders, almost always in notrump contracts. Some ducks that are simple for the declarer are very much harder for the defense:

		(s)		(t)	
		x x		J x x	
K x x	A x x x x	K x x x x		A x x	
		Q J 10		Q x	

In (s) West leads low and an entryless East must duck. In (t) the duck can be on the first or second round. The first-round duck may have the advantage of depriving dummy of an entry, because declarer can drop the queen under the ace. This would only lose if the lead was from Q–x–x–x specifically. See also THIRD-HAND PLAY.

DUEL. A two-handed form of bridge invented by Norman B. Hasselriis, and described by him in *The Bridge World* magazine for February 1950.

DUFFER. A bridge player of inferior ability.

DUKE OF CUMBERLAND'S HAND. A phenomenal hand at whist. The Duke of Cumberland, son of George III, King of England, was an inveterate gambler for high stakes. One day, at the notorious gaming rooms in Bath, it is said that he was dealt the following hand:

♠ A K Q   ♡ A K Q J   ◇ A K   ♣ K J 9 7

The game being whist, the last card, a club, was turned to set the trump suit. The Duke, sitting at dealer's left, had the opening lead. In accordance with sound whist precepts, he opened the ♣7. Obviously it was to his interest to knock out all the opponents' trumps as quickly as possible to avoid the ruffing of any of his solid top cards.

The Duke's opponents proceeded to assert that he would not win a single trick, and to infuriate him into a bet.

The complete deal was:

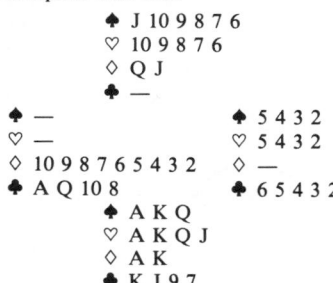

West won the ♣7 with the 8, and led a diamond which was trumped by his partner. East returned a club, the Duke's 9 being taken by the 10, and a second diamond was trumped by East. East led his last trump into his partner's tenace over the Duke, and West won and led the final trump from his hand, felling the Duke's king. West's seven established diamonds won the last seven tricks.

This display of virtuosity by East-West cost the Duke the sum of 20,000 pounds or nearly $100,000.

Such is the story of the *Duke of Cumberland's Hand* as related by Professor Richard A. Proctor in

How to Play Whist (1885). One wonders why the Duke, an experienced whist player, did not speculate on how his opponents could foretell the outcome. (Remember that no hand is exposed in whist.) A more plausible version of this legendary episode suggests that the South hand was given to the Duke, who knew that it was manufactured and ventured to bet in the face of that knowledge.

The victim may have been an earlier duke, "Butcher" Cumberland, son of George II, but the scant evidence favors the later duke.

DUMB BIDDER. A device to permit silent bidding. It consists of a small board placed in the center of the table on which the four suits, notrump, numbers from 1 to 7, double, redouble, and pass are inscribed. Each player makes his bid by tapping the appropriate secions with a pencil. This avoids any possible revealing inflections. For alternative silent methods see BIDDING BOX, SLIDING BOX, WRITTEN BIDDING.

DUMMY. (1) The declarer's partner after he has placed his cards face up on the table, which is done immediately after the opening lead is made by the opponent on the declarer's left; (2) the cards held by the declarer's partner, also called the dummy's hand. The name originated in dummy whist, in which there were only three players, the fourth hand being exposed as the "dummy," an imaginary and silent player (see HISTORY OF BRIDGE). The dummy in bridge takes no part in the play; he may not suggest by word or gesture any lead or play, but he may call attention to errors of play or violations of law. The dummy may ask his partner if he has any or none of the suit led, to prevent a revoke. If the dummy looks at his partner's hand or the hand of either adversary, he forfeits his right to protect his partner from revoking. See LAWS (Laws 42, 43).

DUMMY BRIDGE. A form of bridge for three. Player cutting low plays as dummy's partner for the entire game or rubber. Usually only single games are played before a new cut, the winner scoring a bonus of 50 points. Dealer or his partner names the trump suit. Dummy deals first and partner declares, having looked only at the dummy hand. When an opponent deals, however, he may pass to his partner the right to name trumps. Dealer's left-hand opponent is the only player who may double. The dummy is not exposed until after the opening lead. Otherwise, play is as in BRIDGE WHIST.

One theory of the origin of AUCTION BRIDGE attributes it to a game in which three British officers in a post in India remote from any fourth player evolved the idea of bidding for the dummy.

DUMMY PLAY. The management of the assets of the declarer and the dummy; synonymous with "declarer's play." The subject is dealt with under the following general headings: COUPS; END PLAY; MATHEMATICS OF BRIDGE; SQUEEZE. Also under the following particular titles: AVOIDANCE; BACKWARD FINESSE; BLACKWOOD THEORY OF DISTRIBUTION;

BLOCKING; CARD READING; CONTROL; COUNTING THE HAND; CRASHING HONORS; CROSSRUFF; DECEPTIVE PLAY; DEEP FINESSE; DISCOVERY; DRAWING TRUMPS; DUCK; DUMMY REVERSAL; ENTRY; FINESSE; GAMBIT; HOLD UP; IMP TACTICS; JETTISON; LOSER ON LOSER; MATCHPOINT PLAY; NEGATIVE INFERENCE; OBLIGATORY FINESSE; OPTIONS; OVERTAKE; PERCENTAGE PLAY; PLAY FROM EQUALS; RUFF AND DISCARD; RUFF AND RUFF; RUFFING FINESSE; RULE OF ELEVEN; SAFETY PLAY; SHOOTING; SINGLETON KING; SMOTHER PLAY; SPOT CARDS; SUIT COMBINATIONS; THROW-IN; TRUMP PICK-UP; TRUMP SUIT MANAGEMENT; TWO-WAY FINESSE; UNBLOCKING; UNDERRUFF.

DUMMY REVERSAL. A procedure by which the dummy is made the master hand. Generally speaking, it is advantageous to ruff only in the hand that contains shorter trumps, but in a dummy reversal extra tricks may sometimes be developed by ruffing in the long hand and later using dummy's trumps to extract those of the opponents.

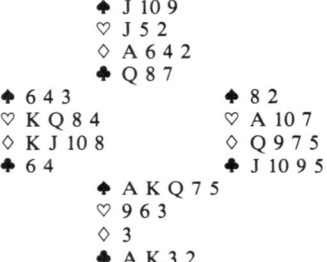

South plays in 4♠, and the defense cash their three heart tricks before shifting to a diamond. Superficially it seems that declarer must bank on an even division in clubs or alternatively draw two rounds of trumps and then attempt to ruff the fourth club in dummy in case they divide unevenly. Both these lines are inferior to the dummy reversal which requires only a 3-2 break in trumps. Dummy wins the diamond, and a low diamond is ruffed with the ♠A. Dummy is re-entered twice in spades—declarer conserving his small trumps for that purpose—to ruff the remaining diamonds with the king and queen, leaving this position:

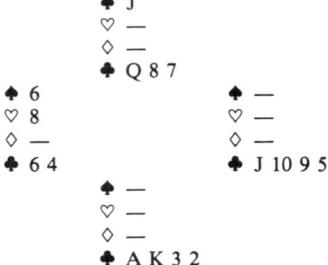

Declarer now crosses to dummy's ♣Q, and leads the ♣J, extracting the last trump upon which he discards his losing club, and takes the last two tricks with the ♣A-K.

Sometimes the decision to "reverse," or establish the dummy in preference to his hand, is forced upon declarer by the character of his trump suit.

```
              ♠ A K J
              ♡ 10 2
              ◇ A J 8 7 3
              ♣ A 9 8
♠ 3 2                          ♠ 10 9 4
♡ 7 5 4                        ♡ Q J 9 3
◇ Q 9 5 4                      ◇ K 10 6
♣ Q J 10 2                     ♣ 6 5 4
              ♠ Q 8 7 6 5
              ♡ A K 8 6
              ◇ 2
              ♣ K 7 3
```

The contract is 6♠, and West leads the ♣Q. If declarer attempts to ruff his losing hearts in dummy he will promote a trump trick for East which together with the club loser would spell defeat. However, by ruffing three of dummy's diamonds in his hand—establishing the fifth diamond in the process—he can utilize dummy's trumps for drawing purposes, and loses only a club trick.

Sammy Kehela

DUMMY WHIST. A variety of WHIST for three. The player who draws the lowest card plays with the dummy as his partner. The last card dealt is turned as trumps. Dummy is not exposed until after the opening lead is made. Each trick over book (6) counts as one point. Seven points are game.

DUMMY'S FIRST TRICK PLAY. Most of the problems concerning the choice of plays from dummy at the first trick relate to doubleton honors. An interesting rule, suggested by M. D. Macdonald of Wyckoff NJ, covers the play with Q-x and J-x:

Play low from dummy if the opponents have exactly two significant honors. In table form:

doubleton queen

declarer has	significant honors	play
A-10-x	K-J	low
K-10-x	A-J	low
J-x-(x)	A-K	low
A-x-(x)	K	high
A-9-x	K-J-10	high
10-x-x	A-K-J	high
A-J-x	K	high
K-x-(x)	A	high

(Exception: x-x-x; doubtful case K-9-x, in which the right play varies with circumstances.)

doubleton jack

declarer has	significant honors	play
A-10-x	K-Q	low
Q-x-(x)	A-K	low
K-10-x	A-Q	low
A-K-x	Q	high
A-Q-x	K	high
A-9-x	K-Q-10	high
K-9-x	A-Q-10	high

(Two obvious exceptions: A-x-x and K-x-x.)

When dummy has more than two cards, it is usually right to play low at the first trick, but there are some obvious exceptions. Play high, for example, with Q-x-x facing nothing, or J-x-x facing A-K-x.

Special circumstances may call for special plays:

A-x-x	K-10-x
Dummy	Dummy
J-x-x	Q-x-x
(a)	(b)

In (a) the play of the ace may block the suit. East would have to have a doubleton king or queen. But if he has a quick entry he can unblock effectively.

In (b) it is sometimes right to play the king from dummy. If East has A-J-9-x-x he will have to win and cannot continue. If dummy plays low East can play the nine, ready to run the suit if West gains the lead.

DUMMY'S FORFEITURE OF RIGHTS.
Invoked if the player whose hand is the dummy intentionally looks at his partner's or an opponent's hand. He then forfeits his privileges in protection of his partner against revokes or leading from the wrong hand. See LAWS (Laws 42, 43).

DUMMY'S HAND.
It is the responsibility of all the players equally that dummy's hand shall be a proper one. No revoke can be claimed as a result of an improper play from the dummy. See DUMMY.

DUMMY'S RIGHTS AND LIMITATIONS.
Dummy has certain absolute and limited rights as described in LAWS OF DUPLICATE (Laws 42, 43). In a rubber bridge game, particularly under social conditions in the home, the old rule of *courtesy of the table* required that the opponents inquire of the declarer whether a play to a trick constituted a revoke, and failure to so inquire waived the right to a penalty for such a revoke. Normally, however, such courtesy should be granted to the hostess or host who, as dummy, engages in cleaning ashtrays, replenishing drinks and otherwise servicing the table.

DUOBRIDGE.
A four-handed bridge game for two players invented by ART KAPLAN of Merrick NY in 1977. The game is played with a regular 52-card deck. It is unique for a two-player bridge game in that the players play as *partners* against imaginary *opponents*. The key to the game is the DuoBridge Deal, a semi-random deal of the cards based on mathematical principles that enable the players to feel they are actually participating in a four-handed game.

DUPLICATE.
A term applied to the playing of the same deal of cards by more than one table of players; successively applied to whist, auction bridge and contract bridge. See DUPLICATE BRIDGE and HISTORY OF BRIDGE.

DUPLICATE, MATHEMATICS OF MATCH-POINT.
See MATHEMATICS OF MATCHPOINT PLAY.

DUPLICATE BOARD.
See BOARD, DUPLICATE.

DUPLICATE BRIDGE.
The form of bridge in which the same hand is played more than once. Each competing unit (which may be an individual, pair or team) seeks to perform better than one or more other units playing the identical deals in similar circumstances. The luck of the deal, so important in rubber bridge, is therefore eliminated to a large extent, and bridge becomes a satisfactory test of skill. (But see CHANCE.)

The first application of the duplicate idea dates from whist. The pioneer in this field was JOHN T. MITCHELL, who invented the first pair movement and whose book on duplicate whist was published in 1891. The long series of American Whist League Championships began in the same year. (See HISTORY OF BRIDGE.)

The duplicate principle was never applied to the original game of bridge (see BRIDGE WHIST) which flourished in the decade 1894-1904. It was generally believed that bridge, unlike whist, was not a suitable game for serious competition. This was perhaps partly because at this stage of its development bridge permitted unlimited redoubles, which emphasized the gambling element in the game and gave it a pokerlike character.

The first games of duplicate auction bridge were apparently held in 1914 under the auspices of the American Whist League, but another 10 years elapsed before a national auction tournament was staged.

The application of duplicate to contract bridge was a rapid development, and the first national championship was held in 1928, when the game was less than three years old, under the auspices of the AMERICAN (auction) BRIDGE LEAGUE.

The most popular form of duplicate is the weekly club game. This usually consists of a pair event of 21 to 28 boards, lasting some 3½ hours. The number of tables varies widely. Usually the players pay a card fee. Many clubs run several games a week, and a few clubs in large metropolitan areas run games each afternoon and evening throughout the year.

Players wishing to join a club can obtain free copies of a booklet entitled "Easy Guide to Duplicate" and of a Directory of Clubs by applying to ACBL HEADQUARTERS.

Duplicate bridge can be a satisfying home game for eight players. (See TWO TABLES.) It is also very popular as part of the recreation program of commercial and industrial organizations.

For the more complex organization of tournaments above the club level, see AMERICAN CONTRACT BRIDGE LEAGUE and CHAMPIONSHIP TOURNAMENTS.

The mechanics of play at duplicate are covered in LAWS OF DUPLICATE BRIDGE, Laws 2-8. In order to make replay of the hand possible, some modification of the mechanics of the deal, shuffle and gathering of tricks from those of RUBBER BRIDGE or CHICAGO is necessary.

Essentially, the mechanics of duplicate require the following steps:

(1) Getting the right boards and correct opponents to the table. See MOVEMENTS.

(2) Withdrawal of the hand to be played from the board, counting the cards to ascertain the correctness of the hand.

(3) Determination of vulnerability and dealer on the board (see BOARD, DUPLICATE). The bidding then proceeds as in rubber bridge.

(4) The play to the trick. Instead of playing to the center of the table, each player faces his contribution or lead face up, in front of him, in turn. When the four cards have been played to the trick, each player turns his card face down, in a line, in front of him. The card is pointed toward his partner if they have won the trick, but placed with the length from right to left if the trick was won by the opposition.

(5) Determination of and agreement about the result. All four players should, as a result of the preceding paragraph, agree as to the number of tricks won by the declarer; if disagreement exists, the cards should not be disturbed, but the result determined by the director, who should be summoned.

(6) Recounting the cards and replacing them in the pockets of the duplicate board.

At duplicate every deal is scored separately. Neither part scores nor games bid and made carry over to the next deal. Whenever one side scores a game or a part score they collect, in addition to the trick score, an immediate bonus:

For making a vulnerable game	500
For making a nonvulnerable game	300
For making a part score	50

Honors do not count at duplicate. In all other respects the scoring is the same as at rubber bridge.

Articles dealing with various aspects of handling duplicate tournaments are: TWO, THREE, FOUR, etc., to FIFTEEN TABLES; movements: AMERICAN WHIST, BARCLAY, BLACKPOOL, BUMP MITCHELL, CYCLIC, HOWELL, INDIVIDUAL, MCKENNEY–BALDWIN, RAINBOW INDIVIDUAL, ROVER, SCRAMBLED MITCHELL, SHORT HOWELL, SWISS, TEAM-OF-FOUR MOVEMENTS, BOARD-A-MATCH TEAMS, THREE-QUARTER HOWELL; ADJUSTED SCORE, APPENDIX TABLE, ARROW, ARROW SWITCH, ASSIGNMENT OF SEATS, BALANCED COMPARISONS, BREAKING TIES, BYESTAND, CALIFORNIA SCORING, CARRY-OVER SCORES, CONVENTION CARD, CURTAILING, MOVEMENT DURING PLAY, DUPLICATE SCORING, ENTRIES, FACTORING, FOULED BOARD, HALF TABLE, HAND RECORDS, HYBRID SCORING, INTERNATIONAL MATCHPOINTS, TABLE, COMPUTER HANDS, MATCHPOINT, POSTING THE SCORE, PRIVATE SCORECARD, RECTIFICATION, ROUND-ROBIN, SCORING CORRECTIONS, SEED/SEEDING, SLOW PLAY, STARTING TIME, SUBSTITUTE, SUSPENSION, TRAVELING SCORE, TOURNAMENT DIRECTOR.

DUPLICATE BRIDGE LAWS. See LAWS OF DUPLICATE.

DUPLICATE SCORING. The scoring of each deal is covered by the provisions of Laws 73 and 74 of LAWS OF DUPLICATE. The following scoring table lists all possible duplicate results:

Bid	Made	Not Vulnerable			Vulnerable		
		Undbld	Dbld	Redbld	Undbld	Dbld	Redbld
1♣-1◇	1	70	140	180	70	140	180
	2	90	240	380	90	340	580
	3	110	340	580	110	540	980
	4	130	440	780	130	740	1380
	5	150	540	980	150	940	1780
	6	170	640	1180	170	1140	2180
	7	190	740	1380	190	1340	2580

Bid	Made						
1♡-1♠	1	80	160	470	80	160	670
	2	110	260	670	110	360	1070
	3	140	360	870	140	560	1470
	4	170	460	1070	170	760	1870
	5	200	560	1270	200	960	2270
	6	230	660	1470	230	1160	2670
	7	260	760	1670	260	1360	3070
1 NT	1	90	180	510	90	180	710
	2	120	280	710	120	380	1110
	3	150	380	910	150	580	1510
	4	180	480	1110	180	780	1910
	5	210	580	1310	210	980	2310
	6	240	680	1510	240	1180	2710
	7	270	780	1710	270	1380	3110
2♣-2◇	2	90	180	510	90	180	710
	3	110	280	710	110	380	1110
	4	130	380	910	130	580	1510
	5	150	480	1110	150	780	1910
	6	170	580	1310	170	980	2310
	7	190	680	1510	190	1180	2710
2♡-2♠	2	110	470	590	110	670	790
	3	140	570	790	140	870	1190
	4	170	670	990	170	1070	1590
	5	200	770	1190	200	1270	1990
	6	230	870	1390	230	1470	2390
	7	260	970	1590	260	1670	2790
2 NT	2	120	490	630	120	690	830
	3	150	590	830	150	890	1230
	4	180	690	1030	180	1090	1630
	5	210	790	1230	210	1290	2030
	6	240	890	1430	240	1490	2430
	7	270	990	1630	270	1690	2830
3♣-3◇	3	110	470	590	110	670	790
	4	130	570	790	130	870	1190
	5	150	670	990	150	1070	1590
	6	170	770	1190	170	1270	1990
	7	190	870	1390	190	1470	2390
3♡-3♠	3	140	530	710	140	730	910
	4	170	630	910	170	930	1310
	5	200	730	1110	200	1130	1710
	6	230	830	1310	230	1330	2110
	7	260	930	1510	260	1530	2510
3 NT	3	400	550	750	600	750	950
	4	430	650	950	630	950	1350
	5	460	750	1150	660	1150	1750
	6	490	850	1350	690	1350	2150
	7	520	950	1550	720	1550	2550
4♣-4◇	4	130	510	670	130	710	870
	5	150	610	870	150	910	1270
	6	170	710	1070	170	1110	1670
	7	190	810	1270	190	1310	2070
4♡-4♠	4	420	590	830	620	790	1030
	5	450	690	1030	650	990	1430
	6	480	790	1230	680	1190	1830
	7	510	890	1430	710	1390	2230
4 NT	4	430	610	870	630	810	1070
	5	460	710	1070	660	1010	1470
	6	490	810	1270	690	1210	1870
	7	520	910	1470	720	1410	2270
5♣-5◇	5	400	550	750	600	750	950
	6	420	650	950	620	950	1350
	7	440	750	1150	640	1150	1750
5♡-5♠	5	450	650	950	650	850	1150
	6	480	750	1150	680	1050	1550
	7	510	850	1350	710	1250	1950
5 NT	5	460	670	990	660	870	1190
	6	490	770	1190	690	1070	1590
	7	520	870	1390	720	1270	1990
6♣-6◇	6	920	1090	1330	1370	1540	1780
	7	1020	1330	1810	1470	1880	2460
7♣-7◇	7	1440	1630	1910	2140	2330	2610
7♡-7♠	7	1510	1770	2190	2210	2470	2890

	Not Vulnerable			Vulnerable		
Down	Undbld	Dbld	Redbld	Undbld	Dbld	Redbld
1	50	100	200	100	200	400
2	100	300	600	200	500	1000
3	150	500	1000	300	800	1600
4	200	700	1400	400	1100	2200
5	250	900	1800	500	1400	2800
6	300	1100	2200	600	1700	3400
7	350	1300	2600	700	2000	4000
8	400	1500	3000	800	2300	4600

9	450	1700	3400	900	2600	5200
10	500	1900	3800	1000	2900	5800
11	550	2100	4200	1100	3200	6400
12	600	2300	4600	1200	3500	7000
13	650	2500	5000	1300	3800	7600

After the score on any hand has been determined according to this table, a comparison of results becomes possible.

Most pair events and all individual events are scored on a matchpoint basis. After all the scores have been determined on a board, 1 matchpoint is awarded to a team, pair or individual for every score that they have bettered, and ½ matchpoint for every score that they have duplicated. Totaling of the matchpoint scores determines the winner for the session. When an event is held in two or more sessions without elimination, the total score is carried forward and the event winner determined by the largest total score.

Scores for a multi-session event where elimination is involved, however, do not carry over totals from the qualifying round. Carryover depends on the number of qualifying rounds and the number of final rounds and is provided for by conditions of contest. For details of the formula used in ACBL tournaments, see CARRYOVER SCORES.

For team-of-four play, there are three methods of scoring in use: BOARD-A-MATCH; TOTAL POINTS, and INTERNATIONAL MATCHPOINTS. (Other methods in use in Europe include COMBINATION TEAM SCORING and QUOTIENT SCORING.)

In board-a-match, the most common type of team competition in the United States until the introduction of the enormously popular SWISS MOVEMENT in 1967, each board is scored as 1, ½ or 0 match points, depending on whether the total score on the two plays is greater than zero, zero, or less than zero. This system of scoring over-emphasizes the extra trick, the notrump versus suit play, the hair-trigger partscore double. An alternative, particularly in longer matches, is total-point scoring, which, however, has the defect of being able to determine the outcome of a match on two or so major SWING hands. The International Matchpoint method, which has gained considerable currency, is designed to eliminate the defects of both board-a-match and total-point scoring methods. In the present IMP scale (see Law 74), the small swings are rewarded with fewer points than larger swings, but the award to a large swing hand is still great in comparison.

IMP scoring may be used for pair events, where a pair's score on a board is determined by its reference to a mean score on the board (by averaging all except the upper and lower scores made) with an IMP award based on the difference. (See INTERNATIONAL MATCHPOINTS; INTERNATIONAL OPEN TEAM SELECTION.)

In Swiss Teams, scoring is based on International Matchpoints. Sometimes the win–tie–loss method is used; sometimes the IMP total is converted to Victory Points.

DUPLICATE TECHNIQUE. See IMP TACTICS; MATCHPOINT BIDDING; MATCHPOINT PLAY.

DUPLICATE TOURNAMENT. See DUPLICATE BRIDGE and CHAMPIONSHIP TOURNAMENTS.

DUPLICATE TRAY. See BOARD, DUPLICATE.

DUPLICATE WHIST. The oldest form of duplicate competition, in which movements such as the MITCHELL and HOWELL were developed.

DUPLICATING BOARDS. See TWINNING.

DUPLICATION OF DISTRIBUTION. This occurs where the suit lengths in a partnership's hands are evenly matched. A distributional flaw that limits the trick-taking potential of a pair of hands, it manifests itself in the absence of a long suit that can be developed.

♠ A Q 10	♠ K J 9
♡ K Q J 9	♡ A 10 6 2
◇ A 10 3	◇ 9 7 6
♣ 6 4 2	♣ Q 7 3

The presence of a long card in either hand would permit the development of an additional trick, but with the above distribution, no game contract is likely to be fulfilled, though sufficient values are held.

DUPLICATION OF VALUES. A concentration of strength and control in the same suit between two partners. When too much of the combined strength of the partnership is concentrated at one point there are likely to be serious weaknesses elsewhere and an unsound contract is often reached.

WEST	EAST
♠ A K	♠ Q J
♡ K Q J 10 4	♡ A 9 7 5
◇ A 7 5	◇ K 6 4 3
♣ 4 3 2	♣ 8 6 5

The above hands contain sufficient values to warrant a game contract in hearts, which has to fail owing to the poor division of strength in the black suits.

Another form of duplication:

WEST	EAST
♠ 6	♠ A K Q 8 7
♡ A J 10 4 3	♡ K Q 7 6
◇ K Q 8 5	◇ 9
♣ 9 7 5	♣ 6 4 2

A contract of 4♡ would be almost impossible to avoid, though declarer has four quick losers. Both hands contain, in effect, second-round control in spades and diamonds, leaving a glaring weakness in clubs. If West's ◇K–Q (5 points) were changed to the ace (4 points), the game would be a lay-down, for now East's singleton diamond would be pulling its weight.

Certain sequences have been devised to identify duplication of values at the slam level, for example, keeping out of six where there is a prospect of two immediate losers in a suit:

WEST	EAST
1♠	3♠
4◇	4♡
5♠	

Here the opener's last bid asks partner to bid a slam if he has as good as a second-round control in the unbid suit, clubs.

In a general way, duplication can be detected

when a player has a void or singleton in a suit in which his partner has indicated some strength, for example:

	WEST	NORTH	EAST
	1 ♡	1 ♠	1 NT

West holds:

♠ —
♡ K Q 8 6 2
◇ A Q 9 3
♣ K J 7 4

and must tread warily, for his partner's values (in spades) seem to be misplaced for purposes of a suit contract.

DUTCH BRIDGE LEAGUE. See NETHERLANDS BRIDGE LEAGUE.

DYNAMIC NOTRUMP. A 1 NT opening bid to show an unbalanced hand with 18–21 points. Developed by GEORGE ROSENKRANZ as a cornerstone of the ROMEX SYSTEM.

Responses are control-showing as in the BLUE TEAM style, counting an ace as two controls and a king as one. 2 ♣ shows no more than one control with 0–6 points; 2 ◇ shows less than two controls with 7 or more points; 2 ♡ shows two controls: 2 ♠ shows three controls, etc.

Opener's rebids are natural except that after a 2 ♣ response, 2 ◇ asks responder to bid a major. A notrump rebid describes a minor two-suiter.

With a balanced hand of less than 19 points, opener opens in a suit, then rebids either 1 NT with 12–16 points or 2 NT with 17–18 points.

E

EBL. See EUROPEAN BRIDGE LEAGUE.

EFOS. Economical Forcing System. See EFOS SYSTEM.

EAST. One of the four hands at the bridge table. East is the partner of West and the left-hand opponent of North.

EASTERN SCIENTIFIC. A style of bidding in which the principal features are strong notrump openings with non-forcing Stayman and Jacoby Transfer bids, five-card major-suit openings with a forcing 1 NT response and limit raises. Two-over-one responses are strong but not necessarily forcing to game. Other elements are weak two-bids, with a strong artificial 2 ♣ opening forcing to 2 NT or three of a major suit; also negative and responsive doubles.

EASTERN STATES REGIONAL CHAMPION-SHIPS. A ten-day tournament held annually in New York City, usually in May, since 1929. In its early years it was organized by the Knickerbocker Whist Club under the title of Eastern Championships, and had the prestige of a National championship. The most important of the nine major events are the REIS-

INGER TROPHY for Knockout Teams and the GOLDMAN TROPHY for Open Pairs. For past results, see Appendix II.

EASY ACES. In auction bridge, at notrump, no honors were scored when aces were divided 2–2 among the pairs.

Also, the name of a popular radio show in the Thirties associated with Goodman Ace and his wife Jane. It was a comedy series which began with a bridge theme.

ECHO. See HIGH-LOW SIGNAL.

ECONOMY OF HONORS. A playing technique intended to preserve honor cards from capture by opposing honors or trumps. The opponents can sometimes be encouraged to give up their high cards in exchange for low ones.

K Q x x

J x x

South leads twice from his own hand in order to make three tricks when West holds A–x. See ACE-GRABBER , which illustrates the opposite principle.

MICHAEL J. SULLIVAN gave these examples of economy of honors.

(1)

	♠ 10 6 3 2	
	♡ K 6	
	◇ K 9 6	
	♣ 8 6 4 3	
♠ K J 9 4		♠ Q 7
♡ Q J 8 5		♡ 10 4 3 2
◇ J 8 5 2		◇ Q 10 3
♣ A		♣ J 10 9 7
	♠ A 8 5	
	♡ A 9 7	
	◇ A 7 4	
	♣ K Q 5 2	

South plays 1 NT and receives the lead of the ◇ 2 from West. Needing two club tricks and holding actual or potential stoppers in all other suits, South wins the ◇ A and, as insurance against the bare ♣ A in the West hand, leads a low club. The ace drops and all is well, but even if it hadn't, the entries and tempos are available for two subsequent leads toward the ♣ K–Q–x.

(2)

	♠ K 9 6 3	
	♡ A 10	
	◇ A 5	
	♣ A 6 5 3 2	
♠ J		♠ 10
♡ Q 8 3		♡ K J 7 6 4 2
◇ 10 8 4 2		◇ K Q 9 7 6 3
♣ K Q J 9 7		♣ —
	♠ A Q 8 7 5 4 2	
	♡ 9 5	
	◇ J	
	♣ 10 8 4	

West leads the ♣ K against South's contract of 4 ♠. Unless the ♣ A is ruffed, South has 10 certain tricks. To guard against that lone possibility, declarer ducks the first round of clubs and subsequent club leads until West either shifts to another suit or permits South to ruff the fourth round of clubs. Eventually declarer gets to discard his losing heart on the carefully preserved ♣ A.

ECUADOR BRIDGE ASSOCIATION (ASOCIACION DE BRIDGE DEL ECUADOR).

The Association is a member of the South American Confederation and participates in South American Championships.
Officers, 1982:
President: Ing. Enrique Alarcon San Miguel
Secretary: Asthol J. Grunauer, P.O. Box 503, Guayaquil, Ecuador

EFOS SYSTEM. The "economical forcing system" used in international championships by leading Swedish players such as JAN WOHLIN, Nils Olaf Lilliehöök, and Gunnar Anulf. A minimum suit response, such as 1♠ in reply to 1♡, is treated artificially. The object is to give the opener every opportunity to make a natural descriptive rebid. A single raise of responder's artificial suit response is a strong bid indicating reversing values. For a similar idea, see RELAY SYSTEM.

EGYPTIAN BRIDGE ASSOCIATION (ASSOCIATION EGYPTIENNE DE BRIDGE).

Founded in 1934, the Association participates in the World Olympiads and formerly participated in European Championships. National events include Open Teams and Pairs and an Inter-Club tournament. The 1960 World Women's Team Olympiad was won by Egypt.
Officers, 1982:
President: Ahmed Hani Garranah
Secretary: Mohsen Kamel, 8, Gawad Hosni Street, Cairo, Egypt

EHAA (Every Hand An Adventure) is a highly natural system developed in the early Sixties, which became quite popular during the Seventies and is still in widespread use today. Its salient features are four-card majors, sound opening bids, weak two-bids in all four suits and an opening bid of 1 NT that shows less than an opening bid of one of a suit (most players use a 10–12 HCP range). In general, EHAA players tend to use a minimal number of conventions, relying heavily on bidding judgment rather than a scientific approach. Most forego the use of any artificial forcing opening bid, although some use a 3♣ opening as an artificial game force.

The heart of the system is an undisciplined weak two-bid, showing almost any kind of hand pattern, promising 6–12 HCP and a minimum of five cards, possibly as little as x-x-x-x-x, in the suit bid. All responses are rebids are natural, with a single raise or 2 NT response played as constructive but not forcing.

EIGHT or EIGHT–SPOT. The seventh highest ranking card in each suit, having eight pips of the suit to which it belongs on the face. See: DISCARD;

HIGH-LOW SIGNALS; OPENING LEADS; RULE OF ELEVEN.

EIGHT TABLES. At Duplicate, eight tables provide for competition among 32 players as individuals, 16 pairs or eight teams-of-four. For team-of-four competition the best movement is a Swiss Team event. Board-a-match play requires special movements of the boards and the East-West pairs.

Study of the chart below will show that this is a seven-table RAINBOW MOVEMENT, with the addition of stationary players numbered 29, 30, 31 and 32. All other players move. East moves to the next higher numbered table, South skips a table in the same direction, North skips two tables in the same direction; the boards move to the next lower numbered table, and West skips a table to the next lower numbered. However, the movement of each group is interrupted as a player goes to a seat occupied by a stationary player; the four players thus affected play instead, for that round only, at table 8, where the boards remain stationary. After playing at table 8, each player goes to the table determined by the seat from which he was displaced.

As a pair game, eight tables may be either MITCHELL or THREE-QUARTERS MOVEMENT. If the former, tables 1 and 2 relay boards, and a bye stand is placed between tables 5 and 6; the full eight rounds should be played to eliminate factoring. If three-quarters movement cards are used, 13 rounds of two boards are played; if the SHORT HOWELL MOVEMENT is used, 11 rounds of two boards are provided. It is also possible to play a Mitchell, four boards to a round, with a skip after the fourth round, for a 28-board movement.

As a team-of-four contest the best movement, as stated above, is the Swiss Team movement. (See SWISS TEAMS.) For board-a-match play there are irregularities. To start the game distribute four boards per table, starting with 1 to 4 on table 1, 5 to 8 on table 2, etc. Have each East-West pair skip a table in the lower direction. East-West 1 goes to table 7, East-West 2 goes to table 8, etc.

Following the first round the boards move to the next lower table but the East-West pairs skip two tables instead of one. East-West 1 skips from table 7 to table 4; East-West 2 skips from 8 to 5; etc. Following the second, third and fourth rounds the East-West pairs skip a table in the lower direction and the boards move to the next lower table. After the fifth round the East-West pairs skip two tables and the boards skip one table. East-West pair 1 skips from 6 to 3; East-West 2 skips from 7 to 4; etc. To save confusion the director can pick up the boards, put them in order, and redistribute them, four to a table, starting with 25 to 28 on table 1.

If a seventh round is advisable, have East-West pairs 1 to 4 add 4 to their number and go to that table. East-West 5 to 8 will subtract 4 from their number and go to that table. Boards in play will be reshuffled. This is the only time during the game the boards are reshuffled. Tables 1 and 5 will relay boards 1 to 4, tables 2 and 6 will relay boards 5 to 8, tables 3 and 7 will relay 9 to 12 and 4 and 8 will relay 13 to 16.

For 7½ or 8½ tables, see HALF TABLE MOVEMENTS.

THIRTY-TWO PLAYER INDIVIDUAL MASTER SHEET
Based on Appendix Rainbow, devised by PAUL N. MARKS

Sets		1		2		3		4		5		6		7		8
Round																
1 N/S	T1	29–15	T2	2–16	T3	3–31	T4	4–18	T5	5–19	T6	6–20	T7	7–21	T8	1–17
E/W		8–22		30–23		10–24		11–32		12–26		13–27		14–28		9–25
2 N/S	T7	4–19	T1	29–20	T2	6–21	T3	7–31	T4	1–16	T5	2–17	T6	3–18	T8	5–15
E/W		13–23		14–24		30–25		9–26		10–32		11–28		12–22		8–27
3 N/S	T6	7–16	T7	1–17	T1	29–18	T2	3–19	T3	4–31	T4	5–21	T5	6–15	T8	2–20
E/W		11–24		12–25		13–26		30–27		8–28		9–32		10–23		14–22
4 N/S	T5	3–20	T6	4–21	T7	5–15	T1	29–16	T2	7–17	T3	1–31	T4	2–19	T8	6–18
E/W		9–25		10–26		11–27		12–28		30–22		14–23		8–32		13–24
5 N/S	T4	6–17	T5	7–18	T6	1–19	T7	2–20	T1	29–21	T2	4–15	T3	5–31	T8	3–16
E/W		14–32		8–27		9–28		10–22		11–23		30–24		13–25		12–26
6 N/S	T3	2–31	T4	3–15	T5	4–16	T6	5–17	T7	6–18	T1	29–19	T2	1–20	T8	7–21
E/W		12–27		13–32		14–22		8–23		9–24		10–25		30–26		11–28
7 N/S	T2	5–18	T3	6–31	T4	7–20	T5	1–21	T6	2–15	T7	3–16	T1	29–17	T8	4–19
E/W		30–28		11–22		12–32		13–24		14–25		8–26		4–27		10–23

EIRE. See CONTRACT BRIDGE ASSOCIATION OF IRELAND.

EITHER-OR SQUEEZE. See ALTERNATIVE SQUEEZE.

ELEVEN, RULE OF. See RULE OF ELEVEN.

ELEVEN TABLES. At duplicate, 11 tables afford excellent competition for either 44 individuals, 22 pairs or 11 teams-of-four. Eleven tables is not an excellent movement for 11 Swiss Teams, but it is possible to run a Swiss Team game with 11 tables. (See SWISS MOVEMENT.)

As an individual tournament, 11-table (11 being a prime number) games are conducted under the RAINBOW MOVEMENT. Twenty-two boards are in play for 11 rounds, and top is 10, average 110. It is also possible to extend the number of partnerships and boards to 24 or 27 by playing eight or nine rounds of three boards each. An interchange of partnerships by an exchange of seats between East and South, for two-board rounds, or by a counterclockwise movement by West in a three-board round, increases the number of partnerships, but usually slows down the speed with which the game can be conducted.

As a pair contest, 22 boards in 11 rounds complete either a MITCHELL or SCRAMBLED MITCHELL MOVEMENT. If more boards are desired, eight or nine rounds of three boards can be played. The THREE-QUARTERS HOWELL MOVEMENT provides for 26 boards in 13 rounds with nine stationary pairs.

Standard teams-of-four movement requires 10 rounds. At 30 boards, it is too long, at 20 boards, too short for most sessions. Usually 24 boards are played, with the two middle rounds eliminated. After four rounds, traveling pairs return the boards just played to their home table and subtract three (or add eight) to their number to get their fifth-round assignment. If it's advisable to play 10 rounds of three boards each, distribute three boards to a table with 1–3 on table 1, 4–6 on table 2, going around to

31–33 on table 11. The boards are shuffled before the first round and not shuffled again during the game. To start the game have the East–West pairs skip a table in the lower direction. East–West 1 skips to 10, East–West 2 skips to 11, etc. After each round the East–West players skip a table in the lower direction and the boards move one table in the lower direction.

For 10½ tables or 11½ tables, see HALF TABLE MOVEMENTS.

ELIMINATION. A type of endplay in which (1) neutral suits are all played from both declarer's and dummy's hand, the last of such plays (2) saddling a defender with the lead in order to force the defender to make a lead desired by the declarer. The play of the neutral cards is referred to as a STRIP PLAY, the saddling of a defender with the lead as a THROW-IN PLAY. See the latter for a discussion of various types and illustrations. See also PARTIAL ELIMINATION.

ELOPEMENT. A term coined by GÉZA OTTLIK of Budapest, Hungary, in a series of *Bridge World* articles to describe coups by which a player scores a trick with a trump that would not ordinarily have sufficient rank to take a trick. The simplest type of elopement is a COUP EN PASSANT. In the following elopement spades are trump:

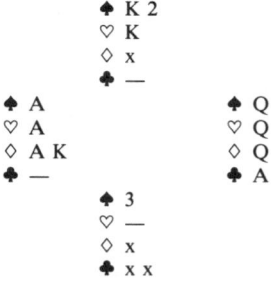

South leads a club and, remarkably, takes three

tricks. If West ruffs, a diamond is discarded from dummy. If West throws a diamond, the club is ruffed in dummy and a heart is ruffed in the South hand, and the lead of South's last club is a coup en passant. If West instead throws the $\heartsuit$ A, the club is ruffed and the $\heartsuit$ K provides a discard for South's losing diamond while West ruffs with his master trump.

ENCRYPTED SIGNALS. Discovered by PETER WINKLER of Atlanta. Using such signals, information can be passed both covertly and legally between partners, adding a new dimension to the theory of the game.

Of the three major activities — bidding, defense and dummy play — that comprise the game of bridge, the first two require cooperation between partners. It is thus desirable in both cases to communicate as much information as possible to one's partner, while giving as little as possible to the opponents. This objective is made difficult to achieve by two laws of the game: (1) all communication must be done via legal bids and card play; and (2) partnerships may not have private agreements (e.g., about the meaning of some bid or play.)

It is thus not too surprising that, until recently, secret communication with one's partner was generally regarded as solely the province of cheaters. Ethical bridge players concentrated on communicating whatever information seemed to be more likely to help partner than the opponents, and withholding the rest.

Suppose, for example, that in the course of bidding toward a slam South wishes to tell his partner (North) that he holds the $\clubsuit$ A. He can usually do this by making an appropriate bid (e.g., a cuebid of 4$\clubsuit$), but the opponents also may benefit from this information. For South instead to write a note and pass it under the table to North would obviously be a violation of law (1). Alternatively, the North-South partnership might have made a prior agreement that in the present auction a bid of 4$\heartsuit$ shows the $\clubsuit$ A; but then law (2) requires that the agreement be made known to the opponents.

Nonetheless, the information that South has the $\clubsuit$ A is sometimes passed to North in unwittingly covert fashion; if North, holding the other three aces, employs an ace-asking convention (such as Blackwood) and South gives the one-ace reply. North can then see that his partner's ace is in clubs, but no law requires North to reveal to the opponents what he can deduce from looking at his own hand. This instance is of no practical importance, since when North-South hold all the aces the opponents are not likely to care who holds which.

On the other hand, once one piece of information has been passed covertly, it can be used as key for another; e.g., conceivably South's next bid might carry the message "I hold the king of the suit ranking one below the suit in which I hold the ace."

To clarify the situation consider the following gross simplification. Suppose that there are only three players, A, B and C, and each is randomly dealt a card from a deck which consists only of the three cards x, y and z. A wishes to communicate a single bit of information (e.g., whether or not he

dyes his hair) to B but not to C. Suppose that A holds x and he "guesses" that B holds y; A then makes the following public announcement: "I hold either x or y." If B responds "So do I," then key is established. If A dyes his hair he is now in a position to say "I dye my hair if my card is x, otherwise I do not." C remains in the dark.

On the other hand if A misguesses and B holds z, B will respond "Sorry; I have neither x nor y"; the key is now blown and A cannot attain his objective. It thus appears that the situation is worth, on the average, ½ bit of key to A and B. It should be noted, however, that if C had for some reason revealed his holding, then no guessing by A would have been necessary.

Using a similar strategy at the bridge table, with four players and 52 cards, suggests an average of 4⅓ bits of key available for covert partnership communication. That may not sound like much to a cryptographer, but to a bridge player the ability to transfer even a single bit of information covertly to his partner could be crucial.

Of course, the guessing needed to establish key at the bridge table has to be coded by legal bids. Since there are barely enough of these for sufficient communication to arrive at a good contract, bids cannot be wasted solely for the purpose of establishing key. Hence we attempt to establish key only when the attempt simultaneously passes information valuable in the selection of a contract. Key established in this manner will be termed *active*.

When the opponents are doing the bidding we must be content to listen; frequently they will reveal a piece of information which establishes our key "for free." This *passive* key can then be used to encrypt defensive signals.

Here is a simple example of an active crypto-convention. A jump raise of partner's opening suit traditionally shows a strong hand with trump support; suppose we require in addition either the ace or king of trumps. (With both or neither some other response, e.g., 3 NT, can be employed.) This is useful by itself, since trump quality is important in slam bidding, but it is also an attempt to establish key. If opener is missing both top trumps he rebids 3 NT and key is lost, but otherwise, if interested in slam, he rebids as follows: with the ace of trumps, he cuebids normally (i.e., bids a suit in which he has control); but with the king of trumps, he cuebids a suit in which he *lacks* control. Responder can tell which by looking at this own top trump, but the opponents have not been tipped off as to the killing opening lead. This could be especially important in duplicate bridge where overtricks are often crucial.

Certain modern conventions which guarantee specific holdings make key establishment an easy second step. An example is disciplined weak two-bids, in which an opening two-bid in first or second position guarantees two of the top three honors in the trump suit. Why not have some response (say, 2 NT) guarantee the missing honor? This provides key for a three-way encryption of opener's "feature" rebid; e.g., the sequence 2$\clubsuit$ – 2 NT – 3$\heartsuit$ might be used to show "either A–K of trumps and a high heart or A–Q of trumps and a high club or K–Q of trumps and a high diamond." Only partner knows for sure!

In another example, a variation of a convention sometimes called "Rosenkranz" enables the partner of an overcaller to show the ace or king of the overcaller's suit (to show him that a lead in that suit is safe). Add a way for overcaller to confirm the other card and a scheme for utilizing the key, and "Rosenkranz" becomes "Rosenkrypt."

To take advantage of passive key one needs at least two different opening lead agreements (e.g., fourth-best, and third/fifth best) and at least two signaling systems (e.g., low card encourages, high card encourages.) One of the systems is selected for use whenever no key is obtained.

Key is obtainable whenever the opponent who eventually becomes declarer gives an *exact count* of some quantity. Examples: declarer answers the STAYMAN convention, showing four cards of a certain suit, or uses the splinter convention, showing one card; declarer shows his aces or kings in a BLACKWOOD reply; declarer shows his exact point-count in a notrump sequence; declarer shows out of a suit early in the play. In each case the exposure of the dummy will enable each defender to count the number of the objects in question which is held by his partner. The opening leader can, for example, use one lead agreement when holding an odd number of "objects" and the other when holding an even number. His partner can "read" the lead as soon as dummy is spread, but hopefully the declarer cannot until too late in the play.

When key is obtained because declarer has shown out of a suit, it is too late to encrypt the opening lead but perhaps not too late to encrypt the defensive signals. Here a fancy encryption scheme can be used because the defenders may have a lot of key; they, and only they, know the exact spot-card distribution of the suit in question.

It should be noted that although passive key is more easily obtained than active key, it must be used with discretion. Some forms are not completely reliable (e.g., Stayman, point-count). Opening leads can be blown and repeated defensive signals present declarer with depths. Worse, it may occasionally happen that the key can be "turned"—declarer determines during the play what system is in use and takes advantage of deductions concerning the location of cards involved in the key. On balance, though, most forms of passive key are safe and effective.

Peter Winkler

EN PASSANT. See COUP EN PASSANT.

ENCOURAGING. (1) A term applied to a bid which strongly urges partner to continue to game. The bid is usually one trick short of game (2 NT, 3 ♡ or 3 ♠), and indicates that the combined hands are known to total 23—24 points (or the distributional equivalent), and that therefore game is in view. If partner has an unpromising hand with no values in reserve for his previous bidding, he may pass, but will usually continue to game.

The following bids are all encouraging in standard theory:

SOUTH	NORTH		SOUTH	NORTH
1 ♣	1 ♡		1 ♣	1 ♡
2 NT			3 ♡	

WEST	NORTH	EAST	SOUTH
			1 ♠
1 ♡	Pass	3 ♡	

The last sequence, with a jump raise of an overcall, is treated as preemptive by some theorists.

In many other sequences, opinions are divided. For example, a jump bid by responder is always treated as forcing in STANDARD AMERICAN, especially as interpreted on the East Coast. But a jump by responder in notrump or in a suit already bid by the partnership is simply encouraging in the style of experts in other areas such as the West Coast, the Midwest, Texas, and England. See JUMP REBIDS BY RESPONDER.

CONSTRUCTIVE and *forward-going* are almost synonymous terms for encouraging.

(2) A term applied to a defensive signal by which a player urges his partner to continue playing the suit led. See COME-ON, HIGH-LOW SIGNAL, UPSIDE-DOWN SIGNALS.

END GAME FALSE-CARDING. See FALSE-CARDING.

ENDPLAY. A play taking place usually toward the end of the hand, though sometimes earlier. The preparation for an endplay may begin as early as the first or second trick; its object is to win an additional trick. They are essentially of three types; the forced lead or throw-in play, the coup or trump-reducing play, and the squeeze play. Many variations of each type occur. Articles dealing with various endplays are listed under the general headings COUP and SQUEEZE, and under the particular headings RUFF AND DISCARD, RUFF AND RUFF, SMOTHER PLAY, THROW-IN, TRUMP PICK-UP, UNDERRUFF.

ENGLISH BRIDGE UNION. This union was founded in 1938 as the successor to the Duplicate Bridge Control Board. It is a constituent member of the British Bridge League, and its players have achieved many international successes representing Great Britain. The EBU was host to the European Championship at Brighton in 1950 and 1975, at Torquay in 1961 and at Birmingham in 1981. It had a membership of more than 29,000 in 1982, and organizes many National events, of which the most important are the Life Masters Pairs, National Pairs, and Crockford's Cup.

Officers, 1982:
Chairman: M. Blank
Executive Secretary: Peter Briggs, 15B High Street, Thame, Oxon. OX92BZ

ENTRIES. Sold for events at a bridge tournament to provide a control of seating assignments. Each entry blank designates an individual's, pair's or team's original seating assignment as to table number (and direction if appropriate) and section.

Particular seating assignments are usually separated from others at multi-sectioned events for assignment to known expert players to distribute such players equitably throughout the field. See SEED, SEEDING and ASSIGNMENT OF SEATS.

ENTRY. A means of securing the lead in a particular hand. Careful and effective use of entries is one of the basic arts of card play. In most situations it is sound strategy to maintain entries in both hands, which means preserving entries in the weaker hand where possible.

When both hands hold high cards, and there are more high cards than tricks, declarer should try to preserve a flexible entry situation:

♠ A Q 10

♠ K J 9

Suppose the first spade trick is won with the ace. If South will need entries to dummy, he should drop his king; if he needs entries to his hand, he should drop the 9. The jack is definitely a bad play. Declarer should aim to have the sequence of cards alternate from hand to hand: dropping the jack would leave dummy's Q 10 in effective sequence.

Similarly when drawing trumps, declarer may leave himself with two low trumps in one hand and one in the other. He should try to arrange that the single trump ranks between the trumps in the opposite hand.

A 4-4 fit will often provide an entry with a spot-card if the suits divides 3-2.

♠ A Q 10 3

♠ K J 9 2

If dummy needs every possible entry, South should start by overtaking any high card as economically as possible. Later he repeats the process, and if the suit splits 3-2, he does so a third time, giving dummy a fourth-round entry with the three.

The same is true if the defenders have one, two, or three winners in the suit. If declarer has four small cards in each hand, he can arrange to win the fourth round in either hand, except in the rare case when the spotcards do not overlap at all.

Some special situations involving entries are dealt with under the following headings. DESCHAPELLES COUP; ENTRY-SHIFTING SQUEEZE; ENTRY SQUEEZE; GAMBIT; HOLD UP; MERRIMAC COUP; SCISSORS COUP; STEPPINGSTONE SQUEEZE; UNBLOCKING; UNBLOCKING SQUEEZE.

ENTRY-KILLING PLAY. A play made with the object of cutting the opponents' entry to a particular hand. Special varieties of this are discussed under MERRIMAC COUP (by the defense) and SCISSORS COUP (by the declarer).

The following are typical maneuvers by second hand when dummy is entryless:

♠ A J 10 x x

♠ Q x x   ♠ K x x

♠ x x

When South leads the suit, West must play the queen to hold South to one trick in the suit. If he plays low, East must allow the 10 or jack to hold to prevent South making four tricks.

♠ A J 9 x

♠ K 10 x   ♠ Q 8 x x

♠ x x

When South leads, West must again play high. If he plays low, South can make a second trick in the suit by finessing the nine.

Similarly, plays can be made by the declarer. If East were declarer in these two cases, he would play high from dummy on a lead from South if he could judge the situation accurately.

ENTRY-SHIFTING SQUEEZE. An entry-shifting squeeze is a positional squeeze in which the squeeze card is a winner accompanied by additional winners in the same suit that provide communication between declarer's hand and dummy. Declarer manages his entries in the suit of the squeeze card so that he can take advantage of the discards chosen by the defender under pressure.

I. Trumps
A. One opponent guards two suits

1.
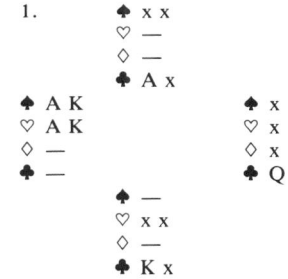

Clubs are trumps, and South leads. If East's trump were the deuce, declarer could claim the remaining tricks on a crossruff. In the actual end position, South leads the ♣K and West is squeezed in the majors: If West discards a heart, South retains the lead, and a heart ruff establishes a long card in that suit; if West discards a spade, declarer overtakes with dummy's ♣A, and he ruffs a spade to establish a winner in dummy.

2.
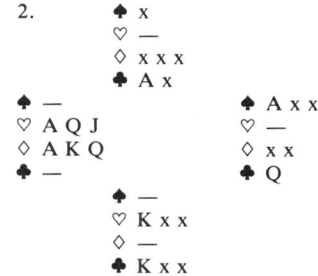

With clubs as trumps, the lead of the ♣K squeezes West in two suits: If West discards a heart, then South retains the lead to ruff a heart, a diamond is ruffed, and a heart is conceded; if West discards a diamond, North overtakes in order to ruff a diamond and exit with a heart, endplaying West, and forcing him to establish a red suit for declarer.

B. One opponent guards three suits

1.

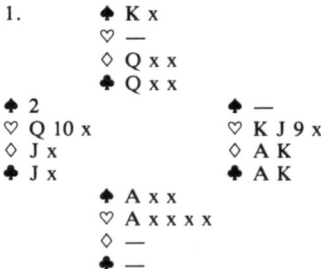

```
        ♠ K x
        ♡ —
        ◇ Q x x
        ♣ Q x x
♠ 2                    ♠ —
♡ Q 10 x               ♡ K J 9 x
◇ J x                  ◇ A K
♣ J x                  ♣ A K
        ♠ A x x
        ♡ A x x x x
        ◇ —
        ♣ —
```

With spades as trumps, North leads the ♣K, and East is squeezed in three suits: If East discards a club or a diamond, North retains the lead to ruff out the remaining honor in that suit; if East discards a heart, then South overtakes with the ♣A in order to establish hearts.

2.

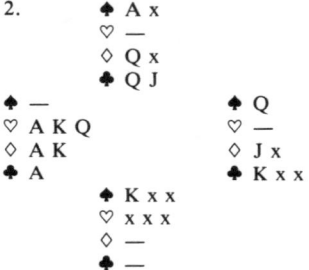

```
        ♠ A x
        ♡ —
        ◇ Q x
        ♣ Q J
♠ —                    ♠ Q
♡ A K Q                ♡ —
◇ A K                  ◇ J x
♣ A                    ♣ K x x
        ♠ K x x
        ♡ x x x
        ◇ —
        ♣ —
```

With spades as trumps, South leads the ♣K, and West is squeezed in three suits: If West discards a club or a diamond, then the ♠A is played from dummy, and a ruff establishes a trick in the suit discarded by West; if West discards a heart, then South retains the lead in order to establish a long heart.

3.

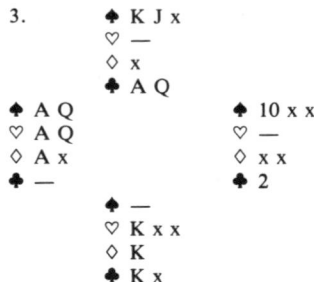

```
        ♠ K J x
        ♡ —
        ◇ x
        ♣ A Q
♠ A Q                  ♠ 10 x x
♡ A Q                  ♡ —
◇ A x                  ◇ x x
♣ —                    ♣ 2
        ♠ —
        ♡ K x x
        ◇ K
        ♣ K x
```

With clubs as trumps, the lead of the ♣K squeezes West in three suits: If West discards a spade, then North wins the ♣A and establishes spades; if West discards a heart, then South retains the lead to establish hearts; if West discards a low diamond, then South retains the lead, and exits with the ◇K, forcing West to establish one of the majors for declarer; finally, if West pitches the ◇A, South retains the lead in order to cash the ◇K, and throw West into the lead with a low heart, again forcing him to establish one of the majors for declarer.

4.

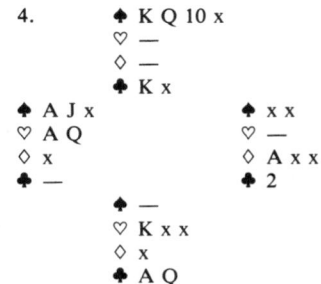

```
        ♠ K Q 10 x
        ♡ —
        ◇ —
        ♣ K x
♠ A J x                ♠ x x
♡ A Q                  ♡ —
◇ x                    ◇ A x x
♣ —                    ♣ 2
        ♠ —
        ♡ K x x
        ◇ x
        ♣ A Q
```

With clubs as trumps, the lead of the ♣Q squeezes West in three suits: a spade discard allows South to overtake and establish spades; if West pitches a heart, then South retains the lead to ruff out the ♡A; finally, if West discards a diamond, then North overtakes in order to play the ♣K, ditching his diamond, and throwing West into the lead (if West ducks, a low spade endplays him on the next trick) in order to establish one of the majors for declarer.

5.

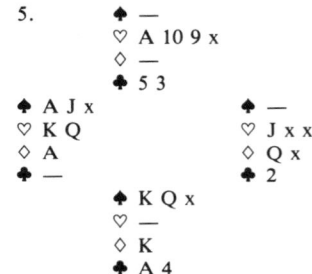

```
        ♠ —
        ♡ A 10 9 x
        ◇ —
        ♣ 5 3
♠ A J x                ♠ —
♡ K Q                  ♡ J x x
◇ A                    ◇ Q x
♣ —                    ♣ 2
        ♠ K Q x
        ♡ —
        ◇ K
        ♣ A 4
```

With clubs as trumps, the lead of the ♣4 squeezes West in three suits: If West discards a spade, then South retains the lead to ruff out the spades; if West discards a heart, then North wins the ♣5 in order to cash the ♡A and take a ruffing finesse against the ♡J; if West pitches the ◇A, then South retains the lead to cash the ◇K, ruff out the ♣A, and cash the ♡A discarding the losing spade.

The two-suit squeezes require a balanced trump holding (equal length in both hands) when declarer has all but one of the remaining tricks, but they require an unbalanced trump holding if a trick must be lost after the squeeze.

The three-suit squeezes require an unbalanced trump holding, unless a throw-in menace is involved, in which case a balanced trump holding is needed.

II. Notrumps

  A. One opponent guards two suits

1.

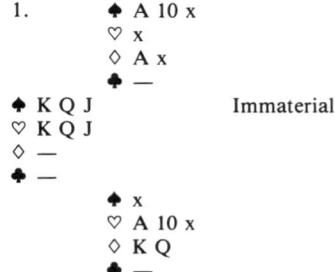

```
        ♠ A 10 x
        ♡ x
        ◇ A x
        ♣ —
♠ K Q J              Immaterial
♡ K Q J
◇ —
♣ —
        ♠ x
        ♡ A 10 x
        ◇ K Q
        ♣ —
```

South is declarer in a notrump contract. When the ◇ K is led, West is squeezed in the majors: If West discards a heart, declarer overtakes with the ◇ A and then plays ace and another heart, establishing the long heart in his hand, with the ◇ Q as entry to cash it; if West discards a spade, dummy's low diamond is played, retaining the ◇ A as entry to the long spade; this is established by playing Ace and another spade.

2.

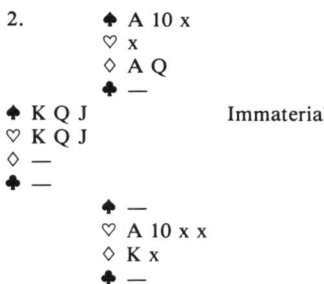

In a notrump contract, South leads a low diamond, squeezing West in the majors: If West discards a heart, then the ◇ A wins the trick, and hearts are established; if West discards a spade, then the ◇ Q is played from dummy, and spades are established.

3.

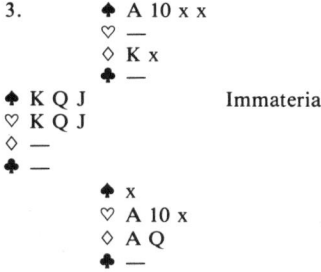

In a notrump contract, the lead of the ◇ A squeezes West in the majors: If West discards a heart, then dummy unblocks the ◇ K, and hearts are established; if West discards a spade, then dummy retains the ◇ K as an entry, and spades are established.

4.

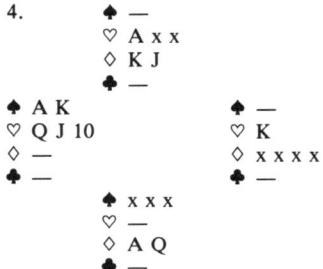

In a notrump contract, the lead of the ◇ Q squeezes West in the majors: after a spade discard, South retains the lead and concedes a spade; after a heart discard, North overtakes with the ◇ K in order to play a low heart to East's ♡ K, South discarding the ◇ A.

B. One opponent guards three suits

1.

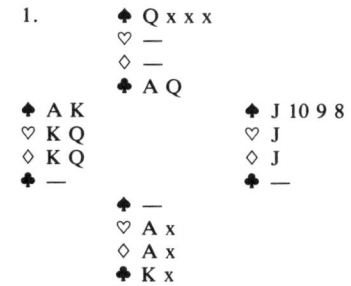

In a notrump contract, South leads a low club, squeezing West in three suits: If West unguards a red suit, North wins the ♣ A, and returns a club to the ♣ K, allowing South to cash the red Aces, and the long card in the suit unguarded by West; after a spade discard by West, North wins the ♣ Q, concedes a spade to West, wins the forced return of a red suit, cashes the other red Ace, and returns a club to the ♣ A in order to cash the ♣ Q.

2.

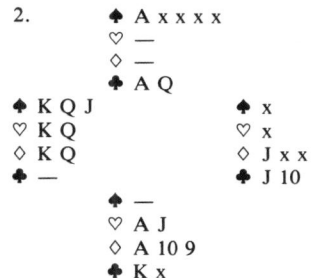

In a notrump contract, the lead of a low club squeezes West in three suits: after a major suit discard, South proceeds as in the previous diagram; When West discards a diamond, North wins the ♣ A, cashes the ♠ A for a discard of the ♡ J, returns to hand with the ♣ K to cash the red Aces and exit with a diamond, forcing East to concede a diamond at the finish.

3.

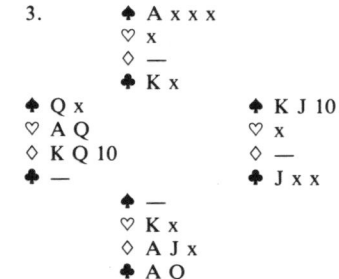

To win five tricks at notrump, South leads the ♣ Q, squeezing West in three suits: after a spade discard, North wins the ♣ K, cashes the ♠ A, (assuming West comes down to ♡ A-Q; ◇ K-Q) plays ◇ A and another diamond, forcing West to concede a trick to South's ♡ K; after a heart discard, South plays a low heart to the bare ♡ A, and ducks the ◇ K continuation, forcing West to concede a trick to North's stranded ♠ A or concede a trick to South's ◇ J; if West discards a diamond, South retains the lead to play ◇ A and another diamond, forcing West to concede an extra trick in one of the majors.

4.

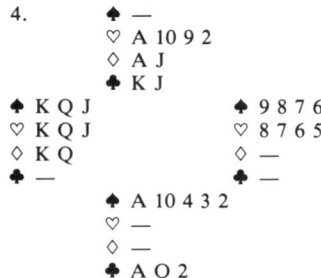

```
                  ♠ —
                  ♡ A 10 9 2
                  ◇ A J
                  ♣ K J
    ♠ K Q J                   ♠ 9 8 7 6
    ♡ K Q J                   ♡ 8 7 6 5
    ◇ K Q                     ◇ —
    ♣ —                       ♣ —
                  ♠ A 10 4 3 2
                  ♡ —
                  ◇ —
                  ♣ A Q 2
```

Needing seven tricks at notrumps, South leads the ♣Q to squeeze West in three suits: after a spade discard, South retains the lead and plays ♣A and a low spade; after a heart discard, North wins the ♣K to play ♡A and a low heart, and a diamond discard establishes North's ◇J for the seventh trick (North wins ♣K, ◇A, ◇J, and ♡A before returning a club to the South hand).

5. (Stepping-Stone)

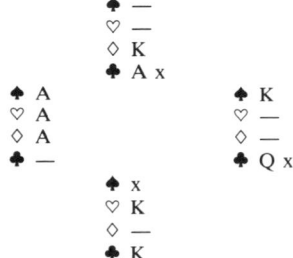

```
              ♠ —
              ♡ —
              ◇ K
              ♣ A x
    ♠ A                 ♠ K
    ♡ A                 ♡ —
    ◇ A                 ◇ —
    ♣ —                 ♣ Q x
              ♠ x
              ♡ K
              ◇ —
              ♣ K
```

Needing two tricks at notrump, South leads the ♣K, and West is squeezed in three suits: discarding a red ace establishes the corresponding king for declarer, so West discards the ♣A. (If South held the ♣K, this discard would concede a trick directly.) South retains the lead and exits with a spade to East's ♣K, forcing him to lead a club to North's ♣A.

6. (Stepping-Stone)

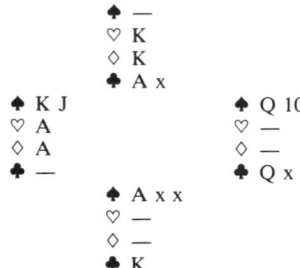

```
              ♠ —
              ♡ K
              ◇ K
              ♣ A x
    ♠ K J               ♠ Q 10
    ♡ A                 ♡ —
    ◇ A                 ◇ —
    ♣ —                 ♣ Q x
              ♠ A x x
              ♡ —
              ◇ —
              ♣ K
```

Needing three tricks at notrumps, South leads the ♣K, squeezing West in three suits: after a spade discard, South retains the lead to play ♣A and another spade, forcing East to play a club to North's ace; after the discard of a red ace, North wins the ♣A to cash the established king, exits with a club or the remaining red king to win the ♣A at the finish.

Monroe Ingberman

ENTRY SQUEEZE. A squeeze that is aimed at forcing a defender, or both defenders, to discard from a seemingly worthless holding so that declarer can create an extra entry to one hand or the other by overtaking a card of winning rank. Analyzed and described by GEZA OTTLIK in the December 1967 issue of *Bridge World*. His article, entitled "The Quest," won the first INTERNATIONAL BRIDGE ACADEMY "Article of the Year" award in 1968, and three of the hands from this article have been used herein by permission of *Bridge World*.

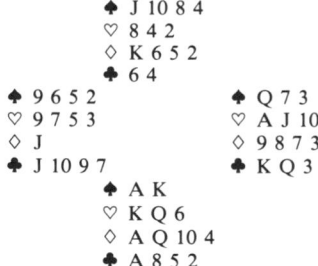

```
              ♠ J 10 8 4
              ♡ 8 4 2
              ◇ K 6 5 2
              ♣ 6 4
    ♠ 9 6 5 2             ♠ Q 7 3
    ♡ 9 7 5 3            ♡ A J 10
    ◇ J                   ◇ 9 8 7 3
    ♣ J 10 9 7           ♣ K Q 3
              ♠ A K
              ♡ K Q 6
              ◇ A Q 10 4
              ♣ A 8 5 2
```

South declares 3 NT after East has opened the bidding, and West leads the ♣J. East overtakes with the queen and continues with the king and a third club as declarer holds up the ace until the third round. The ◇A-Q reveal the 4-1 division, but South can still get home if he concedes a club to West, which crushes East in three suits. Clearly East cannot let go of a spade, and if he discards a heart, one heart lead from dummy suffices to establish two tricks in that suit for declarer. So East is forced to discard one of his "useless" diamonds. Now declarer has two diamond entries to dummy by overtaking the 10 with the king and can lead twice toward his heart honors. As Ottlik noted in his article: "Those silly little diamonds in East's hand have a function after all. Nondescript, irrelevant, or immaterial as they maybe called, by their sheer existence they also serve. They stand and wait, in the way, blocking traffic, hindering enemy lines of communication. And having his value, however silent, taciturn and hidden, they are subject to the pressure of a squeeze."

Occasionally it may be necessary for declarer to unblock a spot card to create the position for an entry squeeze.

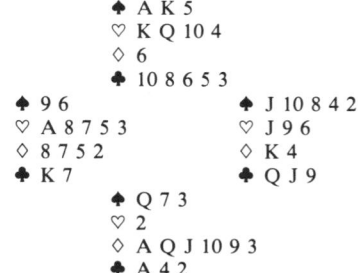

```
              ♠ A K 5
              ♡ K Q 10 4
              ◇ 6
              ♣ 10 8 6 5 3
    ♠ 9 6                ♠ J 10 8 4 2
    ♡ A 8 7 5 3          ♡ J 9 6
    ◇ 8 7 5 2            ◇ K 4
    ♣ K 7                ♣ Q J 9
              ♠ Q 7 3
              ♡ 2
              ◇ A Q J 10 9 3
              ♣ A 4 2
```

After an aggressive auction, in which West has overcalled in hearts and has been raised by East, South lands in a near-hopeless contract of ◇6. West's spade lead, however, gives declarer a chance, providing he wins the spade in dummy and carefully unblocks the 7 from his hand. After a successful diamond finesse, South runs all his trumps but one, discarding four clubs from dummy, and on the fifth round East is squeezed. He cannot discard a heart; otherwise declarer plays a heart to the queen and returns the king, smothering East's jack. Nor can East let go of a club, which would allow South to lead a heart to the queen (West must duck), then concede a club. Thus, East is forced to come down to a singleton spade. This merely postpones the inevitable though, for South leads a heart to the queen, ruffs a heart, and returns to dummy by overtaking the ♠Q with the ace. The ♡K crashes the jack and ace and declarer's carefully preserved ♠3 allows him entry to dummy's high heart.

The entry squeeze can also operate against both opponents in the form of a double squeeze.

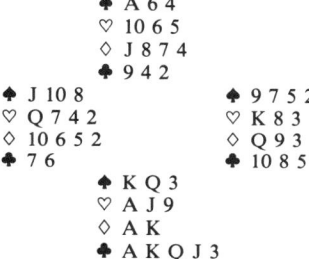

♠ A 6 4
♡ 10 6 5
♢ J 8 7 4
♣ 9 4 2

♠ J 10 8
♡ Q 7 4 2
♢ 10 6 5 2
♣ 7 6

♠ 9 7 5 2
♡ K 8 3
♢ Q 9 3
♣ 10 8 5

♠ K Q 3
♡ A J 9
♢ A K
♣ A K Q J 3

West leads the ♣J against South's contract of 6 NT. Rather than bank everything on finding East with both heart honors, or guessing which opponent might hold a doubleton honor, declarer wins the spade in hand and cashes five rounds of clubs, discarding a diamond and a heart from dummy. On the last club West is in some difficulty. If he holds fewer than three hearts, South can lead a heart from his hand to establish two tricks in that suit. Alternatively, if West comes down to fewer than three diamonds, declarer can cash the ♢A–K, the ♠K–A, then take the heart finesse; West, marooned with nothing but hearts, must then return a heart into declarer's tenace. So West is "squeezed" down to a singleton spade. East, in turn, is squeezed on the last club, for he must also hold three cards in each red suit and can hold no more than one spade. South has thus squeezed both opponents in a suit in which he started with three top winners and now makes his slam by overtaking the ♠K with the ace for a heart finesse. The ♠6 provides entry to dummy for the second heart finesse.

A squeeze that is required because a blocked suit prevents declarer from cashing one of his "sure" winners has also been called an entry squeeze, but these squeezes are more properly categorized under different headings. See UNBLOCKING SQUEEZE. (See top of right column for hand.)

Also described as an overtaking squeeze, South leads the ♡A, discarding a club from dummy, and East is squeezed in two suits. If he discards a spade, South can play the ♠A, which establishes his low spade. If East discards his ♣A, South leads a low spade to North's king, which enables him to cash the ♣K.

The blocked menace contains two winners, with the length of the master card accompanying the

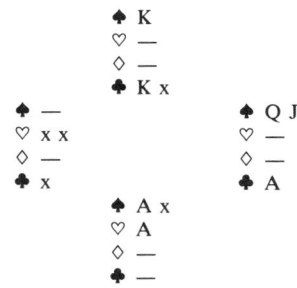

♠ K
♡ —
♢ —
♣ K x

♠ —
♡ x x
♢ —
♣ x

♠ Q J
♡ —
♢ —
♣ A

♠ A x
♡ A
♢ —
♣ —

squeeze card. The other hand contains a one-card menace against the same player who controls the blocked suit. Since the East and West cards could be interchanged and the squeeze would remain effective, the squeeze is automatic.

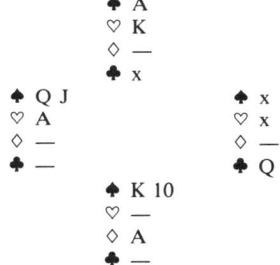

♠ A
♡ K
♢ —
♣ x

♠ Q J
♡ A
♢ —
♣ —

♠ x
♡ x
♢ —
♣ Q

♠ K 10
♡ —
♢ A
♣ —

Also known as a jettison squeeze, South leads the ♢A. If West discards the ♡A, South leads a spade to the ace and cashes the ♡K. If West discards a spade, North discards (jettisons) the ♠A and plays the king of that suit, establishing the 10.

These squeezes are sometimes called STEPPING-STONE SQUEEZES (Reese).

Monroe Ingberman

EQUALS. Cards that are in sequence, or cards that are in effect in sequence because all cards of intervening rank have been played. See PLAY FROM EQUALS.

EQUITY. The *equity rule* for adjusting scores. See LAWS OF DUPLICATE (Law 12).

ERRORS IN SCORING. See LAWS OF DUPLICATE (Law 75) and SCORING CORRECTIONS.

ESCAPE SUIT. A long suit held in reserve by a player making a gambling or psychic bid. An overcall of 1 NT by a player with a weak hand and a long broken suit is a well-worn tactic. It is not difficult to expose the maneuver by doubling and forcing the overcaller to escape into his suit, but the tactic has some positive value: a weak hand with a long suit might otherwise be shut out of the auction unless WEAK JUMP OVERCALLS are being used.

Psychic bids in a short suit with an escape suit in reserve are seldom met with because they tend to be more dangerous to partner than to the opponents. For a regular systemic use of a bid with an escape suit, see GAMBLING 3 NT.

ESTABLISH. To make a suit or an individual card good by forcing out the opponent's guards or winners. Thus one may establish K–Q–J–10–9 of a suit for four tricks after conceding one to the ace.

ESTABLISHED CARD. A card that has been promoted to winning rank after all higher-ranking cards in the other hands have been played.

ESTABLISHED ENTRY. An entry developed by driving out a higher card.

ESTABLISHED REVOKE. A revoke which may not be corrected. A revoke becomes established as soon as the revoking player or his partner leads or plays to the next trick, or, if the revoke is made in leading, as soon as the revoking player's partner plays to the trick on which the revoke is made; or by the act of making a claim. A revoke made on the 12th trick never becomes established. See LAWS (Law 63).

ESTABLISHED SUIT. A long suit in which a player holds all the remaining high cards, which at notrump or after trumps have been drawn at a suit contract will all be winners when the suit is led and run. The object of notrump play is essentially to establish one or more long suits by drawing or forcing out whatever high cards the opponents may hold in that suit.

ESTIMATION. The attempt to judge the score that one is likely to have earned in a duplicate game. Generally a player estimates by comparing his result on a hand with those likely to be obtained elsewhere. As a result of this procedure, one can often alter one's tactics toward the end of a session, playing a somewhat chancier game if one is behind and needs "tops" to win, or playing "down the middle" if one is way ahead and can afford to coast. See SHOOTING.

ETHICS AND CONDUCT. The term "ethics" is commonly used in relation to the observance of fair play. Breaches of ethics are generally thought of as unfair practices which fall short of deliberate cheating.

The Laws deal with the whole question of proper behavior at bridge under the general heading, "Proprieties." In popular thought, however, there is a distinction between unethical conduct and bad manners and this distinction is followed here. Thus the provisions of the Proprieties which relate to good behavior are dealt with under a separate entry, ETIQUETTE.

Of the five sections of the Proprieties in the LAWS OF DUPLICATE BRIDGE, those dealing with ethics are Nos. I (General Principles), II (Improper Information) and IV (Partnership Agreements).

ETIQUETTE. Much of the popularity of contract bridge is attributable to the high standards of etiquette which are observed by the players. No other modern game leans so heavily on the expectation that participants will conduct themselves in a highly civilized manner.

In tournament bridge, violations of proper etiquette are to be expected from inexperienced players, either through ignorance or inadvertence. A well-mannered opponent who is the victim of such a violation will, if he considers that comment is called for, be at pains to make it clear that his comment is intended to be helpful rather than admonitory.

At the other end of the scale is the noxious violation by the experienced player who complains loudly — but unofficially — of a violation of ethics or etiquette committed against him. "I wuz robbed!" is never heard from a player of high standards of etiquette; he either makes an official protest or says nothing.

The LAWS OF CONTRACT BRIDGE deal with the whole question of proper behavior under the heading, "Proprieties." Matters of etiquette, as distinct from questions of ethics, are dealt with in Part III of the Proprieties.

Among the breaches of good manners frequently observed are the following: discussion between two partners of a board just played when there is another board to play; looking at an opponent's hand after it has been placed in the board without asking permission; criticism of an opponent's bidding or any implication of bad faith on the part of the opponents without having previously called the director to the table. Appearing at a bridge tournament dressed carelessly or sloppily is an insult to the ladies and gentlemen against whom such a player competes.

Among the examples of good manners at the table are these items summed up by J. S. Weller, printed in the *Bridge Bulletin* of Johannesburg, South Africa.

(1) Good temper. Bring pleasure with you to this amusement. Take every event in good humor, and by no means incite ill humor.

(2) Silence. Never talk or twitch when someone is thinking — most rigidly enforced during the auction when no questions are to be tolerated.

(3) Smooth action. Smooth flow of action without aggravating chitchat enhances the joy of the game and gets hands finished faster. Have your bid ready before it is your turn.

(4) Advice. Don't give advice. Just think.

(5) Visitors. Visitors must remain still in one place until the hand is completed. They are bound by all proprieties even more strictly than the players. They are not even allowed to be careless, such as leaving a hand they feel is dull. They may never point out any infraction or impulsively correct a player.

(6) Sportsmanship. Feel that others are doing the best they can, considering the effect on them of your presence. No grown person, much less a bridge player, ever makes a condescending, belittling or humiliating remark. Once in a while you will be gratified to observe an act deserving of a compliment. Give it.

(7) Winning. Winning makes a prize player feel very good indeed. It makes a child exult.

(8) Losing. Losing is accompanied by a grim, cheerful, determined, hopeful, anxious, patient demeanor; never by a complaint or a grumble.

(9) Facts. When two cannot agree on what has occurred, the child is right. The bridge player will agree

that he possibly could be. If a referee gives a decision, be gracious; don't talk back.

(10) Women. Women don't exist in a bridge game, nor do men; only bridge players. All are equally bound by etiquette. Courtesy exists, favors because of sex do not.

EUROPEAN BRIDGE LEAGUE. Founded in 1947 at Copenhagen, by delegates from the bridge federations of eight countries (Belgium, Denmark, Finland, France, Great Britain, The Netherlands, Norway, and Sweden). All were members of the INTERNATIONAL BRIDGE LEAGUE, which they voted to dissolve to form a new league, in a new setting, Denmark. A. J. E. Lucardie was elected President, and HERMAN DEDICHEN (at whose instigation the meeting was called) was named Honorary Secretary. Congresses of the league have always been combined with the European Championships. In 1948 the League was a member of the group of three, with the PORTLAND CLUB and ACBL, that issued the International Laws of Bridge. Membership of the EBL numbers a total of 25 countries, the original eight plus Austria, Czechoslovakia, Germany, Greece, Hungary, Iceland, Ireland, Israel, Italy, Lebanon, Monaco, Poland, Portugal, Spain, Switzerland, Turkey and Yugoslavia.

The European Championship results, listed in Appendix III, include the prewar events held under the auspices of the International Bridge League. In 1937 the championship in Budapest was a World Championship as well as a European Championship, and the results are listed under WORLD CHAMPIONSHIPS. Similarly, there were no European Championships in 1960, 1964, 1968, 1972 and 1976 because World Team Olympiads took place in those years. When the WBF decided to hold the BERMUDA BOWL competition in the odd-numbered years only, starting in 1977, the European Championships also became a biennial event, to be held shortly prior to each Bermuda Bowl.

Some of the many contributions of the European Bridge League and its constituent bodies to bridge on the international level include: European Match Points (later called INTERNATIONAL MATCH POINTS); procedure for recording in detail a large number of matches played simultaneously; the development of BRIDGE-O-RAMA; and the custom of using English as the international bridge language.

Considerable contributions to the development of international bridge in Europe have been made by: A. J. E. Lucardie (IBL President 1933–34 and 1938–39); Sir A. Noel Mobbs of England (EBL President 1948–50); BARON ROBERT DE NEXON (EBL President 1950–65); COUNT CARL BONDE (EBL President 1965–69); MARCHESE SILVIO CARINA-MAZZACCARA (EBL President 1969–73); ANDRÉ LEMAÎTRE (1973–80); HERMAN DEDICHEN (EBL Secretary 1947–58); ERNST HELDRING (EBL Secretary 1958–71); Wolf Achterberg (1971–). Because of their impressive contributions to the EBL, Baron R. de Nexon was elected President Emeritus upon his retirement in 1965, and GEOFFREY BUTLER was elected President Emeritus in 1974.

Officers, 1982:

President: Nils E. Jensen
Secretary: David Bardach, 62, La Guardia Street, P.O. Box 19703, Tel Aviv, Israel

EUROPEAN BRIDGE REVIEW. See BIBLIOGRAPHY, O..

EUROPEAN JUNIOR CHAMPIONSHIPS. A biennial event for players under the age of 25, first officially held in Delft, The Netherlands, in 1972. Two previous events had been held in Prague, Czechoslovakia, in 1968 and Dun Laoghaire, Dublin, in 1970, won by Sweden and Denmark, respectively.

Winners and runners-up in the official events have been:

	SITE	WINNERS
1972	Delft, The Netherlands	1. Poland
		2. Israel
1974	Copenhagen, Denmark	1. Sweden
		2. Ireland
1976	Lund, Sweden	1. Austria
		2. Sweden
1978	Stirling, Scotland	1. Great Britain
		2. Sweden
1980	Tel Aviv, Israel	1. Norway
		2. Spain
1982	Salsomaggiore, Italy	1. Poland
		2. Great Britain

EVEN. A term applying to the equal distribution of the outstanding cards in a suit, as a 3–3 division of six outstanding cards.

EVENT. A contest of one or more sessions in duplicate bridge played to determine a winner.

EXCESS POINTS. When cumulative scoring was used in pair competition, the limit placed on the number of points that could be scored was, for the defenders, 600 if not vulnerable, 900 if vulnerable; for the declarer, 800 if not vulnerable, 1,000 if vulnerable. No limitation was placed if the contract was for a slam. Losers lost total points, winners were credited only with the maximum and the balance carried to a special "excess points" column used only for breaking ties. In England, the 600 maximum for defenders was 700. Since matchpoint scoring has almost totally replaced total-point scoring, this provision was omitted from the Laws of 1943 and subsequently.

EXCLUSION. A Unit board of directors may vote to exclude a member of another Unit from its tournaments for cause. See also SUSPENSION.

EXCLUSION BID. A bid which shows a holding in every suit *except* the one named. This is a feature of the ROMAN SYSTEM. After an opening bid of 2♣ or 2♦, showing a three-suited hand, the opener rebids in his short suit if he receives the conventional positive response of 2 NT (see ROMAN 2♦). Similarly, the Roman System prescribes a bid in the shortest unbid suit in response to a takeout double; this has a transfer effect, permitting the stronger hand to become declarer. A takeout double is itself an exclusion call in a wide sense: it implies support for all suits except the one already bid.

Exclusion bids have been adopted by some partnerships as a defense against strong artificial opening bids. This device is useful for competing on three-suited hands in which no suit has been bid naturally. An extension of this convention devised by ANDREW BERNSTEIN, which he calls the "Super Convention," is to use an overcall of an opponent's notrump opening as a two-way exclusion bid. The overcall thus shows either length in the suit bid, or shortness in the suit bid and support for all other suits. The partner of the overcaller is expected to treat the overcall as natural if he has fewer than three cards in the suit. Otherwise he is expected to take his choice of the other suits.

EXCLUSION OVERCALLS. See EXCLUSION BID.

EXHAUST. To draw all cards of a suit from the hand of any player. A player becoming void of a suit during the play is said to be exhausted of that suit, as distinguished from holding no cards of that suit originally.

EXHIBITION MATCHES. At certain major championship tournaments, advance arrangements are made for exhibition matches before a considerable audience. In such events, all contestants must agree, as a condition of entry, that they will, if required, participate in the exhibition matches at the announced time and place. The right of the governing body to impose this condition has been vigorously contested by some players, but without success. Since a considerable number of spectators are involved, the starting time must be rigidly observed, taking precedence over the convenience of the contestants. See BRIDGE-O-RAMA and VUGRAPH.

EXIT. To "get out of one's hand," particularly when it is undesirable to lead from one's hand, usually by making a lead which is not likely to jeopardize the value of any partnership holding.

EXIT CARD. A card by which one can exit from one's hand, offering an escape from an opponent's attempted throw-in or elimination play.

EXIT PLAY. A defensive unblocking maneuver executed in order to avoid a throw-in.

```
            ♠ K Q 10 9
            ♡ Q 10 3
            ◇ K 4 2
            ♣ 9 4 3
♠ 7 2                    ♠ 6 5
♡ A K 8 5                ♡ 7 6 2
◇ Q J 9                  ◇ 10 8 7 5
♣ K J 8 6                ♣ 10 7 5 2
            ♠ A J 8 4 3
            ♡ J 9 4
            ◇ A 6 3
            ♣ A Q
```

South is in 4♠ after an opening bid on his left, and West leads three rounds of hearts. Declarer wins, draws trumps, and plays ace, king, and another diamond, hoping to throw West in for a favorable club lead. West, however, makes an exit play, disembarrassing himself of the queen and jack on the first two

diamond leads, and retaining the 9, which his partner overtakes on the third round to play a club, defeating the contract

EXODUS. A method of responding after partner's opening 1 NT bid has been doubled. A redouble forces opener to rebid 2♣. The redouble indicates that responder has a suit he wishes to play at the two level. If it is clubs he passes partner's forced 2♣. If he bids another suit, declarer passes.

If responder bids a suit at the two level over the double, he is asking opener to choose between the suit bid and the suit immediately higher, i.e., opener's choice over 2♡ would be either hearts or spades. If responder's suits are not touching, he bids two of his lower-ranking suit. If opener bids the next higher suit, responder bids his higher-ranking suit, allowing opener to make a choice.

If responder, after redoubling, bids 2 NT over opener's forced 2♣, he is using a form of FORCING STAYMAN. If responder bids 2♠ over the double, opener must rebid 2 NT, and responder now bids his minor, guaranteeing a hand good enough for 3 NT or at least four of the minor.

EXPECTANCY. What a player is entitled to expect in various circumstances governed by mathematical probabilities. (1) In the deal, a player's expectancy is one ace, one king, one queen and one jack. (2) After looking at his hand and before any bidding has taken place, a player may expect his partner to hold one-third of the outstanding honor cards. (3) In some bidding situations, a player's expectation of partner's strength may be clear-cut. If a player with 17 points hears a bid of 1 NT (16-18) bid on his right, the expectation of his partner's hand is three points. (4) In the play, expectancy depends on more complex mathematical calculations. (See MATHEMATICAL TABLES.) The trick expectancy from the most promising line of play in many situations is given under SUIT COMBINATIONS. See also EXPECTATION.

EXPECTATION. The average result which would be achieved over a long trial period. In order to compute the expectation of a particular play, it is necessary to consider not only the frequency of gain or loss but the *amount* that is being risked. For example, let us compute the expectation of a pair that reaches a contract of 4♠, not vulnerable, at rubber bridge. This contract, we will say, depends on winning one of two finesses (a 75% chance). Assuming the contract will either make or fail by one trick and that the pair will receive 300 points for making the game. The pair's expectation is:

(75%)	×	(+420)	+	(25%)	×	(−50)
chance		result		chance		result
of		of		of		of
success		success		failure		failure

This sum is 315 − 12.5 = 302.5. In making this computation we take into account that 75% of the time the pair will score + 420 and 25% of the time the pair will score − 50.

Let us contrast this expectation with that of a pair with the same cards that stops in 3♠. The expectation of the latter is (assuming 50 points for a part score):

(75%) × (+170) + (25%) × (+140)
chance   result   chance   result
of an   of just   of   when just
overtrick overtrick making   making

This sum is 127.5 + 35.0 = 162.5. Thus, the expectation of the pair bidding game is higher. This indicates that it is favorable to attempt the game under these conditions. By bidding the game, a pair will win an average of 302.5 points whereas by stopping short it will win an average of only 162.5. A similar calculation will indicate that it is not profitable (in the long run) to bid such a game which depends on two successful finesses (only a 25% chance).

In the play of the hand, the declarer may sometimes be unable to determine the correct play without resorting to (at least a rough) calculation of the expectation of different lines.

WEST   EAST
♠ A K 6 2   ♠ 5 4
♡ A K 6 2   ♡ 5 4
♢ A K 2   ♢ 5 4
♣ 3 2   ♣ A K Q 7 6 5 4

West plays 6 NT against the opening lead of the ♢Q. East-West are vulnerable. How should West play?

A safety play for the contract is available. West needs only six club tricks for his contract. By ducking the first round of clubs (when North follows), he ensures his contract without an overtrick (+1440). By trying to run the clubs, he will make an overtrick (+1470) unless North holds all four clubs. If declarer fails to make the safety play and North has four clubs, he will be down three tricks (−300).

The expectation of the safety play is:

(100%) × +1440 = 1440

The expection of trying to split the clubs is:

(5%) × (−300) + (90%) × (+1470)
chance   chance
North has   clubs are

four clubs
        + (5%) × (1440)
        chance
        South has
        four clubs
        (West ducks
        when North
        shows out)

This expectation is only 1380. Therefore, the safety play is the superior play.

WEST   EAST
♠ Q 5 4 3   ♠ J 2
♡ Q 5 4 3   ♡ J 2
♢ A K 2   ♢ 5 4
♣ 3 2   ♣ A K Q 7 6 5 4

West plays in 1 NT against an opening lead of the ♢Q. East-West are not vulnerable. Once again the safety play guarantees the contract (with an overtrick) for +120. If West fails to employ the safety play and North has all four clubs, he will be set two tricks for −100.

The expectation of the safety play is

(100%) × +120 = 120

while the expectation of trying to run the clubs without loss is

(5%) × (−100) + (90%) × (+150)
        + (5%) × (+120) = 136

(assuming the defenders will discard correctly on the run of clubs).

In this case, the safety play is *not* the superior play. (This does not take into account the fact that if the clubs were 4–0 there might have been some North-South bidding. Such a consideration makes the safety play even less desirable.)

Jeff Rubens

EXPECTED NUMBER OF CONTROLS IN BALANCED HANDS. A table of the number of controls statistically predictable in balanced hands of varying strength, analyzed and described by

EXPECTED NUMBER OF CONTROLS IN BALANCED HANDS

HCP	Relative Frequency	0	1	2	3	4	5	6	7	8	9	10	11	12
3	1216	67	33											
4	1891	40	39	21										
5	2505	23	48	29										
6	3129	12	41	47										
7	3795	5	30	46	19									
8	4192	2	19	44	28	7								
9	4377	*	10	35	44	11								
10	4379	*	5	24	44	27								
11	4179	*	2	14	40	33	11							
12	3755	*	1	8	30	42	17	2						
13	3242		*	3	20	39	34	4						
14	2687		*	1	11	33	38	17						
15	2115		*	*	5	24	42	23	6					
16	1596		*	2	14	36	37	10	1					
17	1155		*	1	8	27	39	24	1					
18	799		*	*	3	18	39	30	10					
19	526		*	1	10	32	40	15	2					
10	333		*	*	5	22	38	31	4					
21	201		*	*	2	13	35	35	15					
22	115		*	1	6	26	43	20	4					
23	62.9		*	*	3	17	38	35	7					
24	32.6		*	*	1	9	31	38	21					
25	16.0		*	*	*	4	21	43	26	6				
26	7.32			*	1	12	37	41	9					
27	3.21			*	*	6	28	41	25					
28	1.28			*	2	18	44	32	4					
29	0.48			*	1	9	35	49	6					

GEORGE ROSENKRANZ in the December 1974 issue of *Bridge World* and reprinted here with their permission. Knowledge of the average expectations of numbers of aces and kings for the strength point-count already shown is useful in determining whether or not to bid aggressively.

The table shows the approximate frequencies of specific numbers of controls (Ace = 2, King = 1) in all hands with 4-3-3-3, 4-4-3-2 or 5-3-3-2 distribution. Blanks indicate zero frequency; asterisks indicate usually less than one-half of 1 percent frequency.

EXPERT. A player of conceded skill. The caliber of the player accorded this title will vary with the circles in which he regularly plays; expertise cannot be measured by MASTERPOINTS or in any other mechanical way, such as by having won one tournament or even by having played in international competition.

The title of expert will probably be recognized as valid only when it has been awarded by a verdict of the expert's peers. It is, however, loosely used to characterize anyone who plays better than the usual level of the game in which the player plays.

EXPLANATION OF ANY CALL OR PLAY. Whenever a player makes a conventional call that is not a Class A CONVENTION, his partner should alert the opponents so that they may inquire as to its meaning. See ALERTING, PRIVATE CONVENTION. During the auction and before the final pass any player may, at his own turn to call, ask for a full explanation of any call made by an opponent. After the final pass and throughout the play, any player except dummy may, at his own turn to play, ask for an explanation of opposing calls or card play conventions. See FACE DOWN LEADS; LAWS OF DUPLICATE (Laws 20, 40.).

A player who asks for an explanation of a bid should beware of giving information to his partner by his question. For example, a player who asks the meaning of a normal 1♣ opening bid when he holds great club strength may be subject to penalty under Law 16. It is better to ask a question in general terms, rather than draw attention to one particular suit-bid and so expose oneself to the suggestion that the question may be lead-directing.

When the auction is over, it is recommended that dummy volunteer any explanation about his side's bidding which he may think necessary. Voluntary explanations during the auction are not advisable because they may enlighten partner (or appear to enlighten him). If a player gains information as a result of his partner's explanation, he must carefully avoid taking advantage of it. However, it would be improper for him to offer an immediate correction of his partner's incorrect explanation of the partnership understanding, and he has no obligation to offer a correction at a later time. See LAWS OF DUPLICATE (Proprieties II, IV).

A tournament director may direct a player to leave the table while his partner gives an explanation; and it may be proper for him to depart voluntarily (at his partner's request or of his own volition) if a possibility of a misunderstanding exists.

EXPOSED CARD. For cards exposed during the bidding, see Law 23. Cards exposed during the play are covered by Laws 48, 49, and 73; LAWS OF DUPLICATE (Laws 48, 49, 70).

EXPOSED HAND. A hand placed in full view of all the players. This usually refers to dummy's hand, but it may also apply to the hand of declarer or a defender, which may become exposed by accident or in the process of making a claim. See LAWS 48, 49, 62, 64, 73; LAWS OF DUPLICATE (Laws 48, 49, 62, 64, 70).

EXTENDED GERBER. A method of pinpointing certain key cards in slam bidding, devised by Jerold A. Fink of Cincinnati.

After a trump suit is established, a bid of 4♣ requests partner to show controls (ace—2 controls, king—1 control). 4♦ shows 0 or 1; 4♥ shows 2; 4♠ shows 3; 4 NT shows 4. With 5 or more controls, responder subtracts 5 and bids accordingly. After the conventional 4♦ response, a 4♥ bid asks responder to clarify whether he holds 0 or 1 controls by bidding 4♠ with 0 controls (or 5 or 10), or 4 NT with 1 control (or 6 or 11).

Other four-level bids by the asking bidder are sign-offs. The asking bidder may also sign off by bidding 5♣ and passing partner's forced 5♦ response, or by bidding 5♦ and passing partner's forced 5♥ response or correcting it to 5♠. Other combinations of rebids on the five level are conventional, asking partner to show points (king—2 points, queen—1 point) in two specific suits by seven steps, ranging from 0 points for the first step to 6 points for the seventh step.

EXTENDED LANDY. The LANDY convention is a 2♣ takeout for the major suits over an opponent's notrump opening. An extension suggested by MARTIN COHN of Atlanta is to use a 2♣ bid as a takeout for the majors over any call of 1 NT by the opponents, whether it be a response, a rebid or an overcall.

EXTRA TRICK. A trick scored in excess of the number of tricks required to fulfill a contract. Such tricks are scored above the line and do not count toward game at their trick value. Extra tricks carry premium values if the contract has been doubled or redoubled. See OVERTRICK and SCORING.

F

FABER CUP. Awarded for the AWL National Auction Team Championship, it was donated by EBERHARD FABER in 1927; contested as an Open Team event at the Summer NAC until 1952, when it was withdrawn from competition and replaced by the MARCUS CUP.

FACE (of a card). The front of a playing card, containing the suit and rank of the card.

FACE CARDS. The cards which have a representation of a human figure, called orginally coat cards, later court cards. Their design is virtually the same for all manufacturers in America and Britain, deriving from eighteenth century French patterns.

Earlier designs depended on the skill of the artists who carved the wood blocks, and gradually degenerated from representation of recognizable people and objects into meaningless figures. It has been said that Henry VIII was the model for all four kings; the oldest extant English cards have the same curling moustache and divided beard on the four kings, and legend has it that the queens were likenesses of Elizabeth of York, Henry VII's queen. The remainder of the design is clearly derived from cards made in Rouen, France; the faces differ, but the costumes, position of the hands, and weapons all show similarities.

The French packs developed along their own lines until 1813, when an official design was promulgated; the cards were all named, and even today the names appear on many packs:

	SPADES	HEARTS	DIAMONDS	CLUBS
KING	David	Charles	César	Alexandre
QUEEN	Pallas	Judith	Rachel	Argine
JACK	Hogier	Lahire	Hector	Lancelot

All represent real or mythical figures except Argine, an anagram of Regina.

In the Hungarian pack, eight of the face cards represent characters in Schiller's drama, *Wilhelm Tell*, laid in Switzerland:

SUITS	OBER	UNTER
Acorns	Wilhelm Tell	Rezsö Harras
Leaves	Ulrich Ruden	Walter Fürst
Bells	Vadász Stüssi	Itel Reding
Hearts	Herman Gezler	Pásztor Kuoni

But an oddity exists; the cards were never used in Switzerland.

The usual German packs do not have a queen, but have two jacks (or knaves), the Ober and the Unter. Some German packs, however, have four face cards, king-queen-jack-jack. The trappola pack (Spain and Italy) uses a mounted cavalier in place of the queen.

FACE–DOWN LEADS.

A procedure first introduced experimentally by the WBF in 1972 and adopted by the ACBL in 1975, requiring the opening leader to place his opening lead face down on the table, following which his partner may ask questions about the auction. This ensures that the partner of the leader will have the opportunity to ask questions about the auction before dummy is tabled, and that his questions will not influence the opening leader in his choice.

FACED CARD.

A card exposed to all the players, which may be a card in the dummy, a penalty card, or a card exposed by a player making a claim or his opponent. No revoke penalty can be exacted for failure to play a faced card. See also PLAYED CARD.

FACT.

A happening at a bridge table. When the facts are in dispute, or their interpretation is a matter of judgment, the matter may be referred to the tournament committee. This includes the significance or otherwise of hesitations. The committee may not overrule the director on a point of law, although an appeal may lie to the NATIONAL LAWS COMMISSION.

FACTORING.

The process of adjusting matchpoint scores to the same base to make them comparable for ranking purposes. Percentage is a special type of factoring in which scores are adjusted to a basis of 1.000 or 100%.

When scores are to be compared for ranking within a group of contestants, it is necessary that the comparison be on the same base. For instance, in a 12½ table MITCHELL game, the usual procedure is to have a phantom pair 13 in the East–West field. Consequently all of the North–South players have a bye round, and play 24 boards only, whereas the East–West players would play all 26 boards (in 13 rounds of play). Top on a board in such a case is 11, and the possible for East–West players is 286, but only 264 for the North–South players. To make the scores comparable, the North–South scores must be multiplied by the fraction 286/264 (13/12). To facilitate the computation, add 1/12 of the score obtained to the North–South scores.

There are several principles of factoring that should be observed. Scores should be factored up to the highest average rather than down to the lowest average, even if this means more scores are to be factored. There is a good reason for this: a winner must be .5 of a matchpoint above the second-place finisher or the event is declared a tie. Factoring up will give a winner where factoring down may produce a technical tie (less than ½ matchpoint difference) for first place.

In some half-table movements, certain boards are played more or less frequently than other boards, resulting in a higher top score on certain boards. In these cases, the possible score for each team should be computed and the percentage of this possible for each team found. To determine what percentage constitutes a clear win (equivalent to ½ matchpoint), the percentage that constitutes ½ point should also be computed, and this used as a guide to determine technical ties; e.g., assume team A has 76.5 points out of a possible 132, and team B has 75 points out of a possible 129; team A's percentage is 57.95; team B's is 58.14, a difference of .19% which may or may not be a clear win. One-half point out of a possible 132 is .38%. The difference is less, and therefore the two teams are in a technical tie for first place. Team B would win the prize, but team A would share equally in any masterpoint award.

For one-session events in more than one section where there is a different top score in each section (an example would be one 14-table Mitchell section, top 12, average 156, and one 7-table three-quarters movement, top 6, average 78), the scores in the section with the lower top score would be factored up to those of the larger section (in this case, by simply doubling, 312/156 or 2 being the factor applied).

If the smaller section were an 11-table game with a three-quarters movement, 10 top, 130 average, the factor would be 312/260 or 6/5, one-fifth of their score being added to the scores in the smaller section.

In two-session events (without elimination) in which there are more or less contestants in the second session, and consequently the top score on a board is different, the second session is always adjusted to the possible score of the first session; in this case the factor to be used may be more or less than 1, and the factoring can be up or down.

For further information, the AMERICAN CONTRACT BRIDGE LEAGUE has a pamphlet entitled "Factoring" which explains the method in more detail.

FAILURE TO COMPLY WITH A LEAD OR PLAY PENALTY.

The act of playing an INCORRECT CARD when a player is able to lead or play from an unfaced hand a card or suit required by law or specified by an opponent in accordance with an agreed penalty. See LAWS OF DUPLICATE, Law 52.

FALL, FALL OF THE CARDS.

The play of a card or cards on a trick; the order in which they are played.

FALL NATIONALS.

See FALL NORTH AMERICAN CHAMPIONSHIPS.

FALL NORTH AMERICAN CHAMPIONSHIPS.

Formerly called the Winter Nationals. This annual tournament held since 1927 takes place in November or early December. These championships were originally under the auspices of the AMERICAN BRIDGE LEAGUE, and since 1937 have been controlled by the AMERICAN CONTRACT BRIDGE LEAGUE. The Fall North American Championships began as a four-day tournament and were enlarged to eight days four years later. Nine-day tournaments became standard in postwar years. In 1963, the addition of the International Fund Pairs lengthened the tournament to nine and one-half days and the Fall NAC became a full ten-day tournament when the ACBL rescheduled the major events in 1969. The largest Fall NAC was the 1980 tournament in Lancaster PA, when 13,521 tables participated.

In 1928 the major event of the ABL's "winter congress" was the Open Pairs played for the CAVEN-DISH TROPHY, presented by the CAVENDISH CLUB (New York City).

The CHICAGO TROPHY (now the REISINGER) for Board-A-Match Teams-of-Four was put in play in 1929, and the HILLIARD TROPHY for Mixed Pairs, presented by OLGA HILLIARD of New York, was introduced at the 1931 Fall NAC. For past results of Fall North American Championships, see Appendix 1.

FALL NORTH AMERICAN CHAMPIONSHIPS

Year	Site	Tables	Year	Site	Tables
1927	Chicago		1950	New Orleans	
1928	Cleveland		1951	Detroit	
1929	Chicago		1952	Miami	2,017
1930	Cleveland		1953	Dallas	1,798
1931	Philadelphia		1954	Atlanta	1,775
1932	New York		1955	Miami	2,359
1933	Cincinnati		1956	New Orleans	2,777
1934	New York		1957	Los Angeles	6,154
1935	Chicago		1958	Detroit	4,046
1936	Chicago		1959	Coronado CA	5,838
1937	Washington		1960	New York City	6,391
1938	Cleveland		1961	Houston	4,967
1939	Pittsburgh		1962	Phoenix	6,468
1940	Philadelphia		1963	Miami	7,129
1941	Richmond		1964	Dallas	8,686
1942	Syracuse		1965	San Francisco	11,198
1943	New York		1966	Pittsburgh	8,896
1944	Atlantic City		1967	New Orleans	8,904
1945	Atlantic City		1968	Coronado CA	7,858
1946	Hollywood FL		1969	Miami Beach	9,069
1947	Atlantic City		1970	Houston	7,994
1948	Philadelphia		1971	Phoenix	7,080
1949	Philadelphia		1972	Lancaster PA	11,545
1973	Las Vegas	13,464	1981	San Francisco	11,377
1974	San Antonio	8,419	1982	Minneapolis	7,465
1975	New Oreans	11,705	1983	Bal Harbour FL	
1976	Pittsburgh	8,787	1984	San Diego	
1977	Atlanta	10,701	1985	Winnipeg	
1978	Denver	9,467	1986	Atlanta	
1979	Cincinnati	9,262	1987	Anaheim CA	
1980	Lancaster PA	13,521	1988	Nashville	

FALSECARDING.

A defender is said to falsecard when he plays a card other than his lowest with the intention of deceiving the declarer. (Thus, a high card played as the beginning of an echo is not a falsecard because there is no intention to deceive.)

The term falsecard derives from the fact that defenders normally play *true* cards in order to provide each other with information. The declarer, with no partner to worry about, is not obliged to play true cards, so for him there is no such thing as a falsecard.

Deceptive play by the declarer may extend to the conduct of the whole hand, whereas in practical play the defenders are usually limited to the play of a single falsecard to one trick. It is, therefore, convenient to treat the subject of deceptive play by the defenders under the title "Falsecarding," dealing with declarer play under the title DECEPTIVE PLAY.

The defenders' advantage. Although the defenders are usually restricted to the choice of a single card, rather than a complete tactical play, they have many more opportunities for skillful deception than the declarer, a fact which is not generally realized. Consider this situation:

$$\begin{array}{c}
K\ 7\ 3 \\
J\ 9\ 6\ 2 \qquad\qquad A\ Q\ 4 \\
10\ 8\ 5
\end{array}$$

East is the declarer, and clearly there is no way for him to bring in the suit without loss. If dummy's jack is lead, North covers and South's 10 is promoted.

Now suppose instead that the declarer is South and that West is on lead. If West leads the jack, the declarer cannot be sure whether or not it is right to cover; he cannot see the defenders' cards. In the diagram, the king must be put on to make the 10 a guard; but it may turn out that West has made a clever play from the Q–J, the true position being:

$$\begin{array}{c}
K\ 7\ 3 \\
Q\ J\ 9\ 2 \qquad\qquad A\ 6\ 4 \\
10\ 8\ 5
\end{array}$$

Now if the king is played on the first lead from West, East wins with the ace and returns the suit through South's 10; the defenders take all the tricks.

Suppose that in diagram (b) the declarer is East once more, and that he again leads an honor from dummy. If North covers, he allows declarer all the tricks, but North has no difficulty in playing low; seeing the Q–J in dummy, he ducks the first lead, following the maxim that a defender should cover the last of touching honors — a complete answer to problems of this sort.

Clever falsecarding aims at exploiting the defenders' advantage in situations of that kind. Falsecarding is analyzed under these headings: Playing a Known Card; Trump Suit Falsecarding; Random Falsecards Which Cannot Deceive Partner; False Signals; Deceptive Opening Leads; False-Carding in the Middle or End Game.

Playing a known card. A well-established principle of defensive play is that in a critical position the defender should play a card which he is known to hold, if he can do so without sacrificing a trick. Example:

```
            A J 5
Q 10 3                   8 6 2
            K 9 7 4
```

South leads low, finesses dummy's jack, and continues with ace and another. When the ace is played, West can follow suit with two cards of equal value, the queen and 10. He should play the card he is known to hold, the queen, offering declarer the possibility of finessing the 9 on the third round.

Such maneuvers are common in a keen game, even when the defender has no specific objective in mind.

```
            A K J 6
Q 5 4                   10 8 3 2
            9 7
```

South finesses dummy's jack. West should play the queen on the next round, for until he releases the queen, declarer knows that the suit cannot possibly be ruffed on his left. Similarly:

```
            A Q 7 5
K J 10 3                8 6 4 2
            9
```

Playing a crossruff, South finesses dummy's queen and continues with ace and another, ruffing. Until West parts with the card he is known to hold, the king, declarer can safely ruff low.

More difficult to gauge is the early release of a high card whose position is not marked but soon will be. It may be necessary to have a grasp of the strategy of the entire hand before this sort of play is safe.

```
                ♠ Q 4
                ♡ K J 10 8 3
                ◇ Q 8 6
                ♣ A 3 2
♠ 9 2                           ♠ J 3
♡ 9 6 4                         ♡ A Q 7 5
◇ 10 7 5 2                      ◇ A K J 4
♣ J 10 6 4                      ♣ K 7 5
                ♠ A K 10 8 7 6 5
                ♡ 2
                ◇ 9 3
                ♣ Q 9 8
```

South plays in 4♠ after East has opened the bidding. Diamonds are led and South ruffs the third round. Needing to establish two heart tricks, he finesses dummy's 10.

East wins with the ace, not the queen, and returns a trump. East judges that declarer will expect him to have the ace for his opening bid, so if he wins the first trick with the queen, declarer will take a ruffing finesse against the ace on the next round and make his contract. After East's deceptive play of the ace, however, declarer may try to bring down the queen in West by ruffing the second round. If he tries that,

shortage of entries prevents him establishing a second heart trick.

The following hand illustrates a different reason for releasing a high card whose location will soon be known to the declarer.

```
                ♠ A K 5
                ♡ 7 2
                ◇ A Q J 8 3
                ♣ 9 5 2
♠ 9 8 2                         ♠ J 6 4 3
♡ A 10 8 6 3                    ♡ Q 9 5
◇ K 2                           ◇ 10 7 4
♣ Q 7 4                         ♣ J 10 6
                ♠ Q 10 7
                ♡ K J 4
                ◇ 9 6 5
                ♣ A K 8 3
```

In a pairs contest, West leads a small heart against 3 NT, and the queen is topped by the king. South returns a diamond, and West, knowing that his king is lost, plays it immediately. Now South has a problem, even if he knows West as a guileful player. If he takes the trick, and it turns out that the king is singleton, he makes only nine tricks when he could have made 10 by ducking, establishing the long card without letting East into the lead.

Trump suit falsecarding. The suit combinations illustrated below can exist in any suit, whether trumps or not, but it is best to consider them as being trump. The fact that in every case the declarer has the majority of cards means that the suit usually will be trumps; also, the deceptive maneuvers require an exact appreciation of the layout of the suit, and in practical play this condition is seldom met unless the suit is trumps.

The essence of most of the following plays is that failure to falsecard would leave the declarer no option but to adopt a winning line of play. The falsecard presents him with the possibility of following an alternative line, which will lose. This type of falsecard is still purposeful even if the declarer is unlikely to fall into the trap set for him. Had the falsecard not been played, there would have been no possibility of declarer's going wrong; after the falsecard there is such a possibility, however slight.

```
            A J 8 3
K 2                     10 9 6
            Q 7 5 4
```

South leads small and finesses dummy's jack. If East plays the 6, declarer has no choice but to play the ace on the next round, making all the tricks. If East plays the 9 or 10, declarer may enter the closed hand to lead the queen, which would be the winning play if East had 10-9 doubleton or a singleton.

There are some plays which appear dangerous at first sight but which in fact are obligatory if a high standard of play is to be assumed.

```
            A Q 6 2
4                       K 10 8 3
            J 9 7 5
```

When declarer leads small and finesses dummy's queen, only the 8 from East offers hope of a second trick. If East wins with the king, the ace will be played on the next round, and a third-round finesse will pick up the suit. After the play of the 8, declarer may come to hand and lead the jack, which would be a good play if East held 10-8 alone, but costs a trick in the actual diagram. Following is one of many variations of the theme.

<pre>
           K Q 9 4
10 8 6 3   A
           J 7 5 2
</pre>

Unless West plays the 8 when a low trump is led toward dummy's king, he has no chance of a second trick.

This next position also has variations:

<pre>
           J 9 3
8 5 4   Q 10
           A K 7 6 2
</pre>

Whether South lays down the ace from hand or leads the 3 from dummy, East can probably read the position well enough to gauge that it is safe to drop the queen.

The following play is liable to score:

<pre>
           Q 2
J 10   A 7 3
           K 9 8 6 5 4
</pre>

When South leads small to the queen, East ducks smoothly and the declarer probably continues by finessing the 9 in his own hand. Had East taken the queen with the ace, South would have played to drop the jack on the next round, recognizing that there would be no purpose in finessing against A-J-7-3 in East's hand. A similar position:

<pre>
           7
J 10 6   A 5
           K Q 9 8 4 3 2
</pre>

Dummy's 7 is led and the king wins. Unless West plays the 10 or jack, declarer has no choice but to lead a low card to the next trick.

Many falsecards have a better chance of succeeding in a pairs contest, where declarers are willing to take measured risks for an extra trick.

<pre>
           J 8 6 2
Q 10 9 5   3
           A K 7 4
</pre>

When South plays the ace, West drops the 9 or 10. If declarer can afford to lose one trick, he does best to play small toward the jack, which preserves the position against any lie of the defenders' cards, but in a pairs contest he may decide instead to cross to dummy and lead the jack. This is equally safe against four cards in East's hand, and nets a big match-point score if West holds 10-9 alone.

Occasionally it is possible to forestall these defensive wiles.

<pre>
           Q 8 4 2
3   J 9 6 5
           A K 10 7
</pre>

When declarer plays the ace from hand, the standard falsecard for East is the 9. If he fails to play the 9, declarer is bound to continue by leading toward the queen, discovering the finesse against the jack. After the play of the 9, declarer may continue with the king from hand, with the idea of finessing against West if he has J-6-5-3.

Entries permitting, declarer in the above situation should make the first lead from dummy. Now it is dangerous for East to drop the 9, for partner could have the singleton 10.

There is another type of falsecard which, though not occurring in the trump suit, is associated with suit contracts. This is the play of a high card — perhaps setting up winners for declarer — to dissuade declarer from following a line of play which the defender knows must win. A bold player may sacrifice a high card in this way even though he may be unable to envisage the likely effect; it is sufficient for him that the declarer must be deflected from the course which he has apparently set. A classic hand of this kind was defended by the British player, TERENCE REESE, in his Oxford days.

<pre>
                 ♠ Q 9 6 3
                 ♡ K J 5
                 ◇ 9 7 4 2
                 ♣ J 3
  ♠ J 10 4   ♠ 5
  ♡ Q 8 7 2   ♡ 10 4 3
  ◇ A K J   ◇ 10 8 6 5 3
  ♣ 8 5 4   ♣ Q 9 6 2
                 ♠ A K 8 7 2
                 ♡ A 9 6
                 ◇ Q
                 ♣ A K 10 7
</pre>

West led diamonds against South's 6♠ contract. Having ruffed the second round, South played three rounds of clubs, ruffing in dummy. Since it was evident that the fourth club could be ruffed with impunity, Reese dropped the queen on the third round. The declarer continued with the ♠ Q-A. When East showed out on the second trump, it appeared safe to lead the ♣ 10, intending to discard a heart in dummy and subsequently ruff a heart. When the ♣ 10 was led, West made his trump jack to defeat a contract which would have been made routinely had not East falsecarded.

Random falsecards which cannot deceive partner. The previous situations have been mainly those where an immediate purpose could be discerned, justifying the defender in breaching his duty to play true cards. There are, however, situations where it is permissible for a defender to falsecard with the more general aim of harrying the declarer, and spoiling his count of the hand. The most common is where declarer has shown out of a suit; now, since both defenders know the exact distribution of the suit, they may falsecard with no specific aim in mind.

<pre>
                 ♠ K J 8 7 2
                 ♡ A K 5
                 ◇ K 6
                 ♣ A 6 3
  ♠ 9 5   ♠ 4
  ♡ Q J 10 8 6   ♡ 7 3 2
  ◇ J 9 5 3   ◇ Q 10 8 4 2
  ♣ 9 4   ♣ Q 8 7 5
                 ♠ A Q 10 6 3
                 ♡ 9 4
                 ◇ A 7
                 ♣ K J 10 2
</pre>

West leads the ♡ Q against 6♠. South's only problem is to locate the ♣Q for the overtrick and, though the hand does not lend itself to maneuver, declarer should endeavor to extract what information he can before putting himself to the club guess. After drawing trumps, he plays a second and third round of hearts, ruffing. West must play his cards circumspectly; if he follows thoughtlessly with the 6 and 8, declarer will reflect that West probably had a five-card heart suit, since the lead of the queen is more attractive when both jack and 10 are behind it. So slight a consideration as this would be enough to sway declarer's play of the clubs; South would play East for the ♣Q since, holding shorter hearts than West, he may hold longer clubs.

On the second and third round of hearts, West does best to play the 10 and jack, seeking to create the impression that East is the player with long hearts, but if declarer notices that East has played the 7 on the third round although the 6 is still missing, he may begin to wonder.

If, in a situation like that, West really held the doubleton ♣Q, it is doubtful whether he would be well advised to play his hearts in such a way as to give declarer a true count of the suit, in the expectation that declarer would take the losing play in clubs. Such maneuvers fall into the category of pure bluff rather than tactics, and in a keen game the defenders usually do best to play accurately and let declarer guess.

Falsecards of that type are more effective if made before declarer actually shows out of the suit, since he is then more inclined to take them at face value.

```
                    ♠ K 10 7
                    ♡ A 5
                    ◇ K 4 3 2
                    ♣ 10 8 6 5
        ♠ Q 9 8                 ♠ 6 5 3 2
        ♡ Q 10 4 3              ♡ J 6 2
        ◇ 9 5                   ◇ J 6
        ♣ J 9 7 3               ♣ A K Q 2
                    ♠ A J 4
                    ♡ K 9 8 7
                    ◇ A Q 10 8 7
                    ♣ 4
```

South plays 6◇ after East has dealt and passed. When West leads the ♣3, East falsecards, winning with the king rather than the queen. (If the ace stands up on the next round, West will not be critical of the falsecard; if it doesn't, West knows all.) Declarer ruffs the ace, and has to guess the spade position to make his contract. Had East won the opening lead with the queen, South would have reflected (after finding the red jacks in East) that East might have opened the bidding had he held the ♣Q and 13 points in all.

False signals. The defenders labor under the disadvantage that most of their signals are sent "in clear" and so are liable to enemy interception. On a hand like the following, the declarer's task is easier if his opponents are known as conscientious signalers. (See top of right column for hand.)

South plays 6♣ in a pairs contest. Having won the club lead with the king and drawn trumps, South's problem is whether to try to ruff out the hearts for

```
                    ♠ 8 7
                    ♡ K 8 7 5 4
                    ◇ 8 6 2
                    ♣ A 9 5

                    ♠ A K Q 10 6 5
                    ♡ A 2
                    ◇ A Q J
                    ♣ K 7
```

two discards or to finesse diamonds; shortage of entries means that he cannot try both. But, if the defenders echo to show two or four cards, declarer knows what to do after playing ace and another heart.

Best results are obtained by defenders who keep up with the game and at a given time are conscious whether a false signal could mislead partner. Very often it can be recognized that partner will not be misled. In such cases, defenders should vary their signals between true and falsecards rather than try to outsmart the declarer.

False signals can be used to persuade the declarer to ruff unnecessarily, or to ruff high, in a critical trump situation.

```
                    ♠ A Q 9
                    ♡ J 10 8 2
                    ◇ J 7
                    ♣ K Q 10 6
        ♠ K J 6 3               ♠ 10 7 5 4
        ♡ 6                     ♡ Q 9 7 5
        ◇ A K Q 8 6             ◇ 9 3 2
        ♣ J 5 3                 ♣ 9 4
                    ♠ 8 2
                    ♡ A K 4 3
                    ◇ 10 5 4
                    ♣ A 8 7 2
```

South plays 4♡ after West has opened 1◇. On the ◇A-K, East echoes with the 9 and 2. Since it is quite possible that East has a doubleton diamond, declarer may judge to ruff with the 10 when West plays the third round. If he does so, he loses two trump tricks instead of one.

Deceptive opening leads. Defenders should seldom depart from the accepted conventional leads. To underlead an ace against a suit contract, or to lead an honor from the middle of a sequence, may score on a particular hand, but if it is done frequently, the loss in partnership accuracy will outweigh the gain thus made.

Because that is generally recognized as true, the occasional deceptive lead can be all the more effective. Some leads, such as the jack from Q–J doubleton, are so well known as to lack any element of surprise. The following is also far from fresh:

```
                    J 6 4
        10 9 2                  Q 3
                    A K 8 7 5
```

Left to himself, the declarer loses no tricks in this trump suit when he plays to drop the doubleton queen. Some authorities have commended the opening lead of the 9, the theory being that declarer may put on the jack and play East for Q–10–3–2 or Q–10–x.

Declarer's protection against being duped too often is the knowledge that a good defender seldom leads a trump other than his lowest. To lead the 9 from 9-2, for example, can never gain as compared with leading the 2, and can cost in more than one way. Since most defenders are averse to leading a singleton trump, the declarer should look suspiciously at the lead of a 9 or card of similar rank; particularly when, as in the above diagram, he himself holds the card of next lower rank, and knows that the card led cannot be the top of a sequence.

The deceptive lead of fifth-best instead of fourth-best against notrump is a more persuasive maneuver. It is liable to gain in many situations like the following:

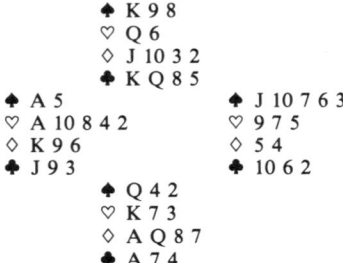

```
              ♠ K 9 8
              ♡ Q 6
              ◊ J 10 3 2
              ♣ K Q 8 5
♠ A 5                        ♠ J 10 7 6 3
♡ A 10 8 4 2                 ♡ 9 7 5
◊ K 9 6                      ◊ 5 4
♣ J 9 3                      ♣ 10 6 2
              ♠ Q 4 2
              ♡ K 7 3
              ◊ A Q 8 7
              ♣ A 7 4
```

West's own wealth of high cards makes it unlikely that his partner can contribute to the defense, so he leads the ♡2 against 3 NT. Dummy wins, the ◊ J runs to West's king, and a small heart comes back. Declarer cashes his diamonds, and both defenders discard spades. Now South has to decide whether to set up a spade or to seek his ninth trick in clubs. After chasing two rounds of clubs he is none the wiser and, taking the opening lead at its face value, he may think that hearts are 4–4 and that it is safe to play a spade.

No less effective is the lead of third-best in an attempt to create the impression that a five-card suit is held. This is the other side of the picture from the previous deal:

```
              ♠ Q 10 9
              ♡ Q 6 2
              ◊ A K 6
              ♣ Q 9 7 5
♠ A 7 3 2                    ♠ 8 5 4
♡ A 9                        ♡ 7 5 4 3
◊ J 10 5 3                   ◊ 7 4
♣ A 8 4                      ♣ J 6 3 2
              ♠ K J 6
              ♡ K J 10 8
              ◊ Q 9 8 2
              ♣ K 10
```

Again West knows that partner has little to fight with, so he leads the ♠3 against South's 3 NT contract. After driving out the ♡A and receiving the return of the ♠2, South has only eight tricks, and has to decide whether to play a club or test diamonds. If he knew that West had only four spades, he could safely play a club; after the deceptive lead, however, he may decide to try for the diamond break, in which case he establishes a setting trick for the defenders.

Other opportunities for a deceptive lead are sometimes missed. Suppose the declarer in a notrump contract opened the bidding with 1 NT, and subsequently showed a spade suit in response to STAYMAN; since both defenders have a count of the spades, expecting declarer to have precisely four, there is no reason why the defender, if he decides to open up the suit, should give declarer free information by leading a conventional fourth-best; he can simply lead his lowest card.

Falsecarding in the middle or end game. At the opening lead, the defender is restricted in his deceptive maneuvers by the necessity of not misleading partner, and by a general lack of information. In the middle game, however, it is possible for both defenders to know the exact lie of the cards while declarer is still in doubt. When this is the case, defenders can deceive declarer without deceiving each other.

The position illustrated under the heading The Defenders' Advantage is a basic one to which there are many variations. Example:

```
              K 7 3
A Q 8                  J 9 6 2
              10 5 4
```

Judging in the middle game that three tricks are needed from this suit, West leads the queen. Declarer may duck twice, playing him for Q–J.

```
              A J 9 4
Q 10 5                 K 8 6
              7 3 2
```

South leads low, intending to follow the percentages by finessing the 9 the first time and the jack the second. By putting up the queen, West may persuade declarer that he has the king as well, and deflect him from his course. Similar positions arise when West is on lead:

```
              J 9 6
K 10 5 2              Q 8 3
              A 7 4
```

If circumstances compel West to open this suit, the king is the card. Conversely, in a position such as the following, it may be best to lead small:

```
              J 9 7
K Q 3                10 6 5 2
              A 8 4
```

There are a number of miscellaneous positions in the middle game where the play of a high card may alter declarer's whole plan of campaign:

```
              A Q 10 9
7 4 3                 K J 8
              6 5 2
```

When declarer finesses dummy's 10, East wins with the king instead of the jack. If declarer assumes that the jack is with West, and that he has three certain tricks by finessing the 9 on the next round, he may fall into indiscretion.

In the end game there are occasions when a desperat e lead offers the only hope of escaping from an elimination.

```
              A 9 7
Q 8 2                J 6 4 3
              K 10 5
```

If South has staged an elimination which compels West to open this suit, the queen is best, offering declarer the possibiltiy of winning in hand, and finessing against the jack. If West leads small instead, declarer can play only for split honors. Similarly:

```
              Q 9 5
    J 8 4              K 10 6 2
              A 7 3
```

If West leads small, declarer may play low in dummy, and capture the 10 with the ace; on the next round he probably finesses the 9. If West leads the jack on the first round, declarer may cover on the assumption that the 9 sits behind the 10.

Suppose that in the above example the declarer is on lead, and plays small toward the table. Suppose also that East is marked with the king, and the declarer intends to insert dummy's 9, forcing East to lead away from the king or concede a ruff-sluff. On South's lead, West puts in the jack to make it appear that he has the 10 as well, in which case declarer's play would be to duck in dummy.

For declarer's counterweapon, see DECEPTION, MATHEMATICS OF.

Albert Dormer

FALSE PREFERENCE. A return to partner's original suit at the lowest level when holding greater length in the second suit. See PREFERENCE BIDS.

FAMILY (bridge playing). Brothers B. JAY BECKER and SIMON BECKER can form perhaps one of the strongest family bridge teams in the world. B. Jay's two sons Steve and Michael are both North American champions and the latter represented North America in Bermuda Bowl competition. Other powerful family combinations include the JACOBYS—Oswald, his wife Mary Zita, his son Jim, and Jim's wife Judy are all Life Masters—and Oswald and Jim are world champions; WILLIAM SEAMON, his sisters EDITH KEMP and ANNE BURNSTEIN, his wife Rita and his son and daughter Michael and Janet are all Life Masters; the CROSSLEYS, a three-generation bridge-playing family whose youngest generation includes 1974 Vanderbilt winners David and Robert; the KASLE family consists of Gaylor, North American Champion who is ninth on the ACBL list of members with the greatest total points; his wife Sharon, his brother Dennis and his mother Lee, all of whom are Life Masters with regional wins to their credit; Lee was a national champion in 1959. Sidney Kasle, Gaylor's father, who died in 1960 at the age of 45, was LM #525 with many wins and a record of service to the Central Indiana Unit of the ACBL; Great Britain's GARDENERS; and Italy's BENITO and MARISA BIANCHI, ANNA VALENTI, the latter's sister-in-law and partner in many international titles, and Anna's husband (Marisa Bianchi's brother), PAOLO VALENTI, a former nonplaying captain of the BLUE TEAM. Other family groups to make a mark in bridge during the last decade include the KAUFMANS, Warren and Marliese, and their sons Chris and Andrew, the latter reigning as the youngest Life Master for a few months in 1981; the HSIEH family with father George and three sons

David, Billy and Dougie, all Life Masters. Billy was the youngest Life Master at the age of 13 in 1980, and Dougie, now the youngest LM, ascended to the title in September 1981 at the age of 11; the COHEN family with father Ralph, assistant executive secretary of the ACBL, as a world-class player who represented Canada, son Billy who has won a North American Swiss Teams championship and placed second in the Vanderbilt, wife Joan and son Jordan who are both Life Masters, and youngest son Mitchell who is fast closing in on Life Masterhood.

FANE 4♣ CONVENTION. A method devised to determine how many aces responder holds, and which ones they are. The responder to the 4♣ bid starts by bidding his lowest ranking ace. The responses are as follows:

```
    4◇   = ◇ A
    4♡   = ♡ A
    4♠   = ♠ A and no other ace
    4 NT = ♣ A
```

If the responder to 4♣ has either no aces or four aces, he must bid 5♣. After the response to 4♣, if the 4♣ bidder rebids 5♣, he asks how many aces are held. The responses are

```
    5◇   = 1 ace
    5♡   = 2 aces
    5♠   = 3 aces
```

After a 4♠ response to 4♣, showing only the ♠A, a 5♣ bid can be used as a cuebid, asking the responder to show his lowest-ranking king. If the player who has bid 4♠ and 5♣ rebids 5 NT, he asks how many kings are held. The responses are

```
    6♣   = 0 kings
    6◇   = 1 king
    6♡   = 2 kings
    6♠   = 3 kings
    6 NT = 4 kings
```

FAR EAST BRIDGE FEDERATION. The Far East Bridge Federation was formed in 1957 before the WORLD BRIDGE FEDERATION and has held tournaments amongst its member countries for 25 years. Fourteen countries are members of this federation. It includes Australia and New Zealand who are outside Zone 6, the area defined by the WBF as Far East for representation in the BERMUDA BOWL. It also includes India and Pakistan who are also outside the zonal area. It is of significance that three member countries, Australia, Indonesia and Pakistan, participated in the 1981 Bermuda Bowl in Westchester NY. The total membership consists of: Australia, People's Republic of China, Hongkong, India, Indonesia, Japan, Malaysia, New Zealand, Pakistan, Philippines, Singapore, South Korea, Chinese Taipei Bridge Association and Thailand.

It annually sponsors a Far East championship, played for the possession of the Rebullida Trophy, and an International Pairs Championship, first held jointly with the 1959 Far East Championship. (For past results of the Far East Championships, see Appendix III.) In 1958, the delegates to the Federation's annual convention decided to adopt WRITTEN BIDDING as the official method in all future tournaments. The Far East Bridge Federation was admitted to participate in the World Team Championships in 1966 and was represented by the holders of the Far East Championship, Thailand. In 1969 and 1970 the Far East representatives, Republic of China, finished second in the World Championships. Pakistan placed second in the Bermuda Bowl 1981.

Officers, 1982:
President: Raymond Chow
Secretary: Benno Gimkiewicz, Hamlet & Co. Ltd., P.O. Box 122, Bangkok, Thailand

FAST ARRIVAL, PRINCIPLE OF. The principle that the greater the speed with which a contract is reached, the weaker the hand that placed the contract and, conversely, that the more gradual the approach, the greater the suggestion that a higher contract may be appropriate. The most commonplace example is the obvious difference between North's bidding in examples (a) and (b):

	(a)		(b)
SOUTH	NORTH	SOUTH	NORTH
1 ♠	4 ♠	1 ♠	3 ♠ (forcing)

Similarly North's bidding in (c) below is more encouraging that it is in (d):

	(c)		(d)
SOUTH	NORTH	SOUTH	NORTH
1 NT	2 ♣	1 NT	2 ♣
2 ♠	3 ◇	2 ♠	4 ♠
3 NT	4 ♠		

FAST PASS. A lightning action which may improperly convey weakness. The prevention of a fast pass is one of the reasons for the SKIP-BID WARNING. See also RHYTHM.

FEATURE, FEATURE SHOWING. A feature is a particular holding of an ace or king (occasionally a queen) which may be of particular importance in a given hand. Showing of features in a hand through the bidding commences only when a suit is agreed on and a game is assured. Among the conventions that are in common use to determine features are ACE-SHOWING RESPONSES, ASKING BIDS, GERBER, BLACKWOOD, and other 4 NT bids, the GRAND SLAM FORCE, CUEBIDS, and various combinations or modifications thereof. See also WEAK TWO-BIDS.

FEDERAÇAO PORTUGESA DI BRIDGE. See PORTUGUESE BRIDGE FEDERATION.

FEDERACIÓN CHILENA DE BRIDGE. See CHILEAN BRIDGE FEDERATION.

FEDERACIÓN VENEZOLANA DE BRIDGE. See VENEZUELAN BRIDGE FEDERATION.

FÉDÉRATION BELGE DU BRIDGE. See BELGIAN BRIDGE FEDERATION.

FÉDÉRATION FRANÇAISE DE BRIDGE. See FRENCH BRIDGE FEDERATION.

FÉDÉRATION LIBANAISE DE BRIDGE. See LEBANESE BRIDGE FEDERATION.

FÉDÉRATION ROYAL MAROCAINE DE BRIDGE. See MOROCCO BRIDGE FEDERATION.

FEDERATION SUISSE DE BRIDGE. See SWISS BRIDGE FEDERATION.

FEDERAZIONE ITALIANA BRIDGE. See ITALIAN BRIDGE FEDERATION.

FICTION. See LITERATURE AND BRIDGE.

FIFTEEN TABLES. At duplicate, 15 tables provide for competition among 60 players, 30 pairs, or 15 teams-of-four. It is a very good movement for 15 teams-of-four for board-a-match. It is reasonably difficult to direct for 15 tables of Swiss Teams. (See SWISS MOVEMENT.)

As an Individual tournament, a group of 60 players used to be extremely awkward. The movement usually used was a 52-player RAINBOW with a double appendix. However, Tournament Director MAURY BRAUNSTEIN devised a movement that allows for 26 boards to be played in 13 rounds, with a top of 12. The movement through most rounds is similar to that used in other Individuals: South up one table, East up two tables, West down two tables, boards down one table, North stationary. After Rounds 5 and 7, East and West skip an extra table. After Round 12, South, West, East and the boards all move an extra table. If hand record duplication is used, then the duplication round is counted as the first round and only 24 boards are played, with a top of 11. This duplication round counts as a playing round as far as when the irregular moves take place.

As a pair game, the usual and simple solution is a MITCHELL, either straight or scrambled. There are guide cards available for treating 14 to 20 tables as appendix movements using only 26 boards. This is standard in many countries where direct comparison on all the boards in play is desired. It is also sometimes used as the last session of multi-session events, although twinned seven-, eight-, or nine-table sections give comparable results with proper seeding of the sections.

As a team game, 28 boards are required to complete the movement. When 24 boards are desired, either the middle two, or the first and last rounds can be conveniently omitted.

For 14½ or 15½ tables see HALF TABLE MOVEMENTS.

FIFTH HONOR. The ten-spot of the trump suit.

FINAL BID. The last bid in the auction, followed by three consecutive passes. There can be no further bidding. The final bid becomes the contract.

Note that it is bad practice for a player to lead instead of making the final pass, since unless he makes a FACE-DOWN LEAD, he will deprive his partner of the right to review the bidding or ask questions about it.

FINESSE. The attempt to gain power for lower-ranking cards by taking advantage of the favorable position of higher-ranking cards held by the opposition.

The most common uses of the finesse are:

(1) *To avoid losing a trick.*

♣ A Q

♣ 3 2

South cannot afford to lose a club trick. He therefore leads a club to North's queen, finessing against the king. If West has the king, the queen will win, and South will avoid a club loser.

♠ Q 10 6 2

♠ J 9 3   ♠ K 8 7 5

♠ A 4

West leads the ♠ 3, and South must avoid a spade loser. If South reads the position correctly, he will play the ♠ 10 from dummy, finessing against the ♠ J. This enables South to avoid a spade loser.

(2) *To gain a trick with low-ranking cards*

♡ A 3 2

♡ Q 6 5

Needing two heart tricks, South cashes North's ace and leads toward his queen. If East holds the king, the queen will score a trick for South.

◇ Q 3 2

◇ 7 6 5

South needs one diamond trick. His best chance is to find West with both the A-K. He therefore leads toward the queen in the North hand, in an attempt to finesse against the A-K, thereby creating a trick for the queen.

(3) *To prepare for a second finesse in the same suit.* A finesse can often be used to create a second finesse. When this is done successfully, the second finesse usually results in the direct gain of a trick.

♣ A J 10

♣ 4 3 2

Needing two club tricks, South leads low to dummy's 10. If this finesse loses to an honor in the East hand, declarer is in position to take two tricks via a second finesse if West has the remaining high honor.

♠ A J 9

♠ 4 3 2

Needing two spade tricks, South leads low toward the North hand. When West follows low, he finesses the 9. If West started with K-10 or Q-10, this will drive a high honor from the East hand and a second finesse of the jack will result in two tricks for South.

(4) *To prepare for a pinning play in the same suit.* A finesse can also be preparatory to a different form of trick-gaining play in a suit. By taking an early finesse, it may be possible to reduce the length of the suit in one enemy hand.

♡ Q 9 8 7

♡ J 5   ♡ K 10 6

♡ A 4 3 2

Needing three heart tricks, South leads low, and finesses dummy's 7. East wins with the 10, but declarer later enters the North hand, and pushes the queen through East, blotting out the entire defensive holding.

◇ Q 10 8 3 2

◇ J 9 4   ◇ A K 7 6

◇ 5

With some other suit as trump, South must develop two diamond tricks. He leads low from his hand, finessing North's 8. Later, the queen is led from the North hand to ruff away East's remaining honor. The suit will now fall after the second ruff (see FALSECARDING).

(5) *As an avoidance play.* A finesse may prove useful for keeping a particular opponent off lead.

♠ Q J 9
♡ A 10 9
◇ 10 7 5 4 2
♣ 3 2

♠ 3   ♠ A 6 5
♡ 5 4 3 2   ♡ 8 7 6
◇ Q 9 8   ◇ K J 6 3
♣ A Q 10 9 5   ♣ J 7 6

♠ K 10 8 7 4 2
♡ K Q J
◇ A
♣ K 8 4

Against South's 4♠ contract, West leads the ♠ 3. East plays two round of spades.

South now leads a club from dummy. If East follows low, South should finesse the 8! This is an avoidance play, designed to keep East off lead and avoid the killing play of the third trump.

If East has the ♣ A, the next club lead will score the ♣ K, and produce the game-going trick. However, if West has the ace, East can be prevented from leading the third round of trump. South later enters dummy with a heart, and leads a club to his king. This loses to West's ace, but declarer cannot be prevented from ruffing his third club in dummy.

(6) *As a safety play.* A finesse is often part of a safety play.

♣ K 9 2

♣ A J 5 4 3

South wishes to avoid losing two spade tricks. He cashes the ace and then leads toward dummy. If West follows with a small card, he finesses dummy's 9 to guard against West having started with Q-10-x-x (see SAFETY PLAY).

♣ A 10 9 8

♣ K 7 6 5 4

South wishes to avoid losing two spade tricks. He leads from either hand, and finesses by playing low from the opposite hand. In this way, Q-J-x-x in either hand can be picked up with only one loser.

(7) *To gain one or more entries*

♠ K 7 4
♡ J 8 7
◇ A 9 7 6 5
♣ J 10

♠ 8 5 2   ♠ —
♡ A K 10 9   ♡ Q 6 5 4 2
◇ Q 2   ◇ J 10 3
♣ A Q 9 8   ♣ 7 6 5 3 2

♠ A Q J 10 9 6 3
♡ 3
◇ K 8 4
♣ K 4

This hand demonstrates many techniques in the play of the cards. With best play on both sides, it hinges on repeated finesses to gain entries. South opens 4♠ in third position, and all pass. West leads the ♡K which holds. West cannot continue with the ♡A, for declarer will discard a diamond from his hand, later establishing the diamond suit by ruffing (see LOSER-ON-LOSER), preventing a lead through the ♣K. If West leads a lower heart, declarer will play the ♡J to force East's queen. He will later pass the ♡8 to West while discarding a diamond and will thereby make his contract (see AVOIDANCE).

Nor can West shift to diamonds, for whereas declarer cannot establish diamonds without allowing East one lead if he must start the suit (see UNBLOCK-ING), if West leads a diamond, he can be forced to win a trick with the queen. Declarer can force this by leading low from his hand toward the dummy, but if West ducks, dummy must win and declarer must duck the next diamond. Now the diamonds cannot be unblocked before trump is drawn (see BLOCKING). However, if West shifts to the ◊Q, declarer will allow him to hold the trick. If West leads a low diamond, declarer will top East's honor with his king, and after drawing trump will allow West to hold the second diamond.

Since West cannot profitably lead clubs, his only chance is to shift to a trump. Because of the recurring finesse for entry position in the trump suit, it makes no difference which trump West plays.

Suppose West leads the ♠2. Declarer finesses dummy's 4, which holds. The ♡J is played from dummy, East covers with the queen, and declarer ruffs with an honor. Now the ◊K and ◊A are cashed, West unblocking the ◊Q under the ◊K to avoid being thrown in with that card. The ♡8 is played. When East cannot cover, declarer's last diamond is discarded.

West wins and cannot lead a club or a heart, so he plays another trump. Declarer finesses the 7 (or wins the king while unblocking from his hand if West plays the 8), underplaying with his 6, ruffs a diamond to establish the suit, re-enters dummy with the remaining spade, and runs the diamonds.

On this deal, two finesses were taken against West's trump cards to obtain a third entry to dummy. Notice that if South must lead spades himself, he can enter dummy only twice against best defense by West. See also BACKWARD FINESSE; CHINESE FINESSE; DOUBLE FINESSE; SUIT COMBINATIONS.

FINESSING AGAINST PARTNER. See THIRD-HAND PLAY.

FINESSING PROBABILITIES. These and all finessing situations are listed under SUIT COMBINATIONS.

FINLANDS BRIDGEFORBUND. See FINNISH BRIDGE LEAGUE.

FINNISH BRIDGE LEAGUE (SUOMEN BRIDGELIITTO or FINLANDS BRIDGEFOR-BUND). This League was founded in 1936 by Helsingfors Bridge Club and Bridge Club Spades, the two clubs then in existence. In 1982 there were approximately 1,850 active members in 50 clubs. Participants in European Championships since 1936, all Scandinavian Championships and the 1960, 1968, and 1972 World Olympiads. The European Championships were held in Helsinki in 1953 and the Scandinavian Championships in 1949 and 1957.

Officers, 1982:
President: Pentti Uusivirta
Secretary: Leo Neimo, Linnustajankuja G-H-44, 02940 EsPoo 94, Finland

FIRST HAND. The dealer, who is the first player to have the opportunity to bid or pass, has the first hand. Should the first hand make a call other than a pass, he becomes the opening bidder. If the first hand passes, the opportunity to become the opening bidder passes to the opponent on his left.

FISHBEIN CONVENTION. See DEFENSE TO OPEN-ING THREE-BID.

FISHBEIN TROPHY. This award is given to the player with the best overall individual performance record in the Summer North American Championships. The trophy, in memory of Sally Fishbein, was donated by the ACBL in recognition of the untiring efforts of HARRY J. FISHBEIN who served as Treasurer of the ACBL and refused to accept the customary compensation. The winners from 1952 through 1962 are:

1952 John R. Crawford	1958 Helen Sobel
1953 Milton Q. Ellenby	1959 Ira S. Rubin
1954 David Carter	1960 Boris Koytchou
1955 Paul H. Hodge	1961 Marshall Miles
1956 Tobias Stone	1962 Ira S. Rubin
1957 John R. Crawford	

The following are the Fishbein Trophy winners since 1962, together with their point totals. An asterisk indicates the record was broken that year.

1963 Alvin Roth	191.5	1973 Dr. Richard H. Katz	199.49
1964 Percy E. Sheardown	222.5*	1974 Richard Shepherd	161.84
1965 Alvin Roth	209.7	1975 Grant S. Baze	176.
1966 Alvin Roth	185.5	1976 Dr. Richard H. Katz	219.44
1967 Phil Feldesman	176.85	1977 Ken Cohen	198.10
1968 George Rapee	182.05	1978 Mike Passell	215.45
1969 Robert D. Hamman	179.75	1979 Bobby Wolff	179.48
1970 David Strasberg	154.97	1980 Peter Weichsel	194.
1971 Barbara Rappaport	186.79	1981 Ralph Katz	236.*
1972 B. Jay Becker	178.92	1982 Mike Smolen	221.41

FISHER DOUBLE. A lead directing double of a notrump contract asking for a minor-suit lead, developed by DR. JOHN FISHER of Dallas. After an opening bid of 1 or 2 NT, if there have been no legitimate suit bids, a double of the final notrump contract asks for a club lead if STAYMAN has not been used and a diamond lead if it has.

FIT. A term referring to the effectiveness or ineffectiveness of two partnership hands in combination commonly used to refer specifically to the TRUMP SUIT, under which heading various trump fits are discussed.

When the hand as a whole is considered, the fit may be distributional. With a sound trump fit, a shortage in each hand in different suits is likely to lead to an effective CROSSRUFF. (For an unsatisfactory fit, see DUPLICATION OF DISTRIBUTION.)

Fit can also be considered in terms of honor cards, which may or may not be effective in play (see GOOD CARDS).

FIVE or FIVE SPOT. The tenth ranking card in a suit, having five pips of the suit to which it belongs.

FIVE-ACE BLACKWOOD. See KEY-CARD BLACK-WOOD.

FIVE-BID. Any bid at the five level, to take 11 tricks if it becomes the final contract. As an opening bid, it indicates a hand of unusual power. As a bid made during the auction, it may be a slam invitation or part of a specialized slam convention. To play voluntarily 5♠ or 5♡ and fail is one of the most ignominious results possible at the bridge table. Experts prefer to estimate slam possibilities below the game level.

See: ADVANCE SAVE; BLACKWOOD; FIVE OF A MAJOR OPENING; 5 NT OPENING; PREEMPTIVE BID; SUPER GERBER.

FIVE-CARD MAJORS. The concept according to which an opening bid of 1♠ or 1♡ guarantees at least a five-card suit. Many tournament players graft this rule onto standard bidding methods, although it is not usually applied after partner has passed. There are arguments for and against this procedure.

The knowledge that the opening bidder has a five-card suit often simplifies responder's problems, especially if there is competitive bidding. If the opening bid promises a five-card suit, a jump raise to three (either forcing or limit) can be made readily with three-card support, and a single raise can even be made with a doubleton. With this hand:

♠ K 2
♡ 8
♢ 10 8 6 4 3
♣ K 8 5 4 2

there is no sensible response to an opening bid of 1♠. But 2♠ is attractive if the spade bidder has promised a five-card suit, and it may help to shut out an opposing heart contract.

There are two main arguments against the five-card rule. First, it forces the opening bidder to make frequent prepared, and slightly unnatural, bids in minor suits. Problems arise especially with two four-card majors and a club shortage (4-4-4-1 or 4-4-3-2 distributions) when the opening bid has to be 1♢, and a response of 2♣ causes difficulty. It is true that a major-suit fit can always be found if the opponents are silent; but a heart fit often remains undiscovered if there is an overcall of 1♠.

Second, the extended use of the minor-suit opening gives more freedom to the opposition. A major-suit opening has distinct preemptive value, and may make it difficult for the opponents to enter the auction.

A possible compromise worth consideration is to bid four-card heart suits but not four-card spade suits. It is the 1♠ opening which commonly sets responder problems, and a spade fit, unlike a heart fit, seldom goes undiscovered after a minor-suit opening.

Grafting of the five-card requirement onto otherwise standard methods creates bidding problems with certain kinds of hands, most notably those with 4-4-4-1 distribution, those with two four-card majors and three bad diamonds, and those with a good four-card major ranking directly above a bad five-card suit. Those who opt for five-card majors tend to be most successful when playing a system which integrates that factor with forcing notrump responses and negative doubles.

FIVE OF A MAJOR OPENING. Shows a hand missing both top honors in the trump suit, but with no outside losers. Partner is invited to raise accordingly with one or both of the missing key cards. Probably the rarest bid in bridge.

5 NT OPENING. A very rare opening bid, showing a balanced hand which can guarantee 11 tricks. Responder is asked to raise the bidding one level for each ace, king, or queen which he holds.

FIVE-ODD. A term indicating five tricks over the book, or 11 tricks in all.

FIVE OR SEVEN. A phrase indicating the type of partnership holdings on which a successful play makes a grand slam, but if the play is not successful, the opponents can cash a second trick immediately, holding the result to five-odd. For a hand of this type, see MATCHPOINT BIDDING. In rubber bridge, probably the grand slam contract should be preferred, but there may be situations at duplicate where a six-odd contract is tactically better, even though this is neither the maximum nor the safest contract.

FIVE-SUIT BRIDGE. This game, devised in 1937 by Dr. Walter H. W. Marseille, a Viennese psychologist and mathematician, used a special 65-card deck. There were five suits of 13 cards and each of the four players was dealt 16 cards. The remaining card was called the "widow" and placed face upwards on the table. After the dummy was exposed the declarer was entitled to exchange any card in his own hand or the dummy for the widow.

The fifth suit was green in color (except in England where it was blue) and was called "leaves" in Austria, "crowns" or "royals" in England and "eagles" in America. Public interest was aroused when George VI bought some decks at an exhibition and several books were written about the game, but it did not achieve lasting popularity.

FIVE TABLES. At duplicate five tables provide competition for 20 players, 10 pairs, or five teams-of-four. Board-a-match scoring is very good for five teams-of-four. You can also score by International Match Points or Victory Points, but Swiss Team movements are impractical with this few teams and the odd number.

As an Individual, the 20-player RAINBOW movement is recommended. Begin the game by putting five boards on each table. 1–5 go on table 1, 6–10 go on table 2, right around to 21–25 on table 5. The boards are shuffled before the first round only.

Rd.	N	S	E	W	Bd.	N	S	E	W	Bd.	N	S	E	W	Bd.	N	S	E	W	Bd.	N	S	E	W	Bd.
	Table 1					Table 2					Table 3					Table 4					Table 5				
1	20	1	10	12	1	19	5	9	11	2	18	4	8	15	3	17	3	7	14	4	16	2	6	13	5
2	20	2	7	15	2	19	1	6	14	3	18	5	10	13	4	17	4	9	12	5	16	3	8	11	1
3	13	9	20	3	3	12	8	19	2	4	11	7	18	1	5	15	6	17	5	1	14	10	16	4	2
4	4	20	11	6	4	3	19	15	10	5	2	18	14	9	1	1	17	13	8	2	5	16	12	7	3
5	8	14	5	20	5	7	13	4	19	1	6	12	3	18	2	10	11	2	17	3	9	15	1	16	4
6	20	6	15	2	6	18	10	14	1	7	17	9	13	5	8	16	8	12	4	9	19	7	11	3	10
7	20	7	12	5	7	18	6	11	4	8	17	10	15	3	9	16	9	14	2	10	19	8	13	1	6
8	3	14	20	8	8	2	13	18	7	9	1	12	17	6	10	5	11	16	10	6	4	15	19	9	7
9	9	20	1	11	9	8	18	5	15	10	7	17	4	14	6	6	16	3	13	7	10	19	2	12	8
10	13	4	10	20	10	12	3	9	18	6	11	2	8	17	7	15	1	7	16	8	14	5	6	19	9
11	20	11	5	7	11	17	15	4	6	12	16	14	3	10	13	19	13	2	9	14	18	12	1	8	15
12	20	12	2	10	12	17	11	1	9	13	16	15	5	8	14	19	14	4	7	15	18	13	3	6	11
13	8	4	20	13	13	7	3	17	12	14	6	2	16	11	15	10	1	19	15	11	9	5	18	14	12
14	14	20	6	1	14	13	17	5	15	15	12	16	9	4	11	11	19	8	3	12	15	18	7	2	13
15	3	9	15	20	15	2	8	14	17	11	1	7	13	16	12	5	6	12	19	13	4	10	11	18	14
16	20	16	19	17	16	5	1	4	2	17	6	7	10	8	18	11	12	15	13	19					
17	20	17	18	19	17	4	5	3	1	18	10	6	9	7	19	15	11	14	12	20		Out			
18	20	18	17	16	18	3	4	2	5	19	9	10	8	6	20	14	15	13	11	16		Of			
19	20	19	16	18	19	2	3	1	4	20	8	9	7	10	16	13	14	12	15	17		Play			
20	18	17	19	16	20	1	2	5	3	16	7	8	6	9	17	12	13	11	14	18					

North at table 1 is #1, North at table 2 is #2, etc. West at table 1 is #6, West at table 2 is #7, etc. South at table 1 is #11, table 2's South player is #12, until you reach #15 at table 5 South. East is 16 to 20, starting with #16 at table 1.

You can, if you choose, have them play the first two hands of a round in their original seats, then have South and East change places for the third and fourth boards, then have West move to the South position for the fifth board. This allows everyone to play with everyone else.

When the first round is completed the boards go to the next lower table, North remains at the table, the original West skips a table in the lower direction, the original South moves to the next higher table, and East skips a table in the higher direction. Each player follows the same moves following each round.

As a pair event, five rounds of five boards each as a MITCHELL game with a top of four and an average of 50 is sometimes used. The HOWELL MOVEMENT is available with nine rounds of three boards. For four and one-half tables, this is much preferable, with pair 10 as the phantom.

For team-of-four contests, see TEAM-OF-FOUR MOVEMENTS; the standard team-of-four progression (pairs skip a table down while boards move one table down) completes the game in four rounds, usually of six boards each. TOTAL POINT, BOARD-A-MATCH, or IMP scoring can be used.

For 4½ tables or 5½ tables, see HALF TABLE MOVEMENTS.)

FIXED. A colloquial term to designate a pair who have received a bad score through no fault of their own. Usually applied to a situation in which a player has made a technical error or suffered a legal misadventure, and gained a good result thereby. His innocent opponents, who suffered, but probably not in silence, can say that they have been fixed.

FLAG-FLYING. An obsolete colloquialism for a bid made with full consciousness of its failure if allowed to stand, in the hope of avoiding a greater loss if the opponents are permitted to play the contract. The term was used to describe a bid made after the opponents had apparently reached their final contract, rather than one interjected during the auction. In this way it is distinguished from preemptive action (see PREEMPTIVE BID). *Sacrifice* and *save* are the modern terms.

FLANNERY 2 ◊. Developed by WILLIAM FLANNERY of Pittsburgh, formerly of McKees Rocks PA, to show an 11–15 point hand with five hearts and four spades. Eleven-point hands must contain 2½ defensive tricks.

Major-suit responses on the two-level are signoffs, though opener may raise with a maximum and a minor-suit void. Jump responses in the majors are invitational, and jumps to 4♣ and 4 ◊ are transfers to 4♡ and 4♠ respectively. If responder bids a minor on the three-level, opener bids 3 NT with a fit (ace or king doubleton, or queen third). A 2 NT response asks opener to clarify his strength and distribution. Opener rebids 3 ♡ with 11–13 points or 3♠ with 14–15 points and two cards in each minor (or 3 NT with 14–15 if his strength is concentrated in his minor suit doubletons), 3♣ or 3 ◊ with three cards in the bid suit, or 4♣ or 4 ◊ with four cards in the bid suit.

The standard defense to Flannery 2 ◊ is to play that a 2 ♡ overcall is a three-suited takeout (with shortness in hearts). Double of 2 ◊ shows the equivalent of a strong notrump opener and is penalty oriented. A 2 NT overcall is unusual for the minors, while suit overcalls other than 2♡ are natural. See also FLANNERY 2♡.

FLANNERY 2♡. An opening bid of 2♡ to show a hand worth 11–15 points with five hearts and four spades. Responses and rebids are the same as for the FLANNERY 2◊ convention, except that to sign off in hearts responder simply passes.

The Flannery 2♡ bid is not as easy to defend against as its 2 ◊ counterpart. The usual practice is to play that the double of 2♡ shows the strong notrump and that 2♠ shows a three-suited takeout. The assumption (not always valid) is that the long spade suit is the least likely hand one might hold.

FLAT. (1) Hand: A hand without distributional

values, particularly one with 4-3-3-3 distribution. "Square" and "round" are also used to describe this type of hand.

(2) Board: A deal on which no variations in result are expected in the replays.

FLINT 3♣. A modification of the FLINT 3◊ convention designed to allow the partnership to rest in 3◊ after a 2 NT opening bid, as well as in three of a major suit. The 3♣ response to 2 NT is a relay requiring opener to rebid 3◊. Responder may pass if his suit is diamonds, or may bid a long major suit, which opener is expected to pass.

Using this variant, a response of 3◊ to the 2 NT opening is used as a STAYMAN-type inquiry for major suits.

FLINT 3◊. Devised by JEREMY FLINT of England to permit a partnership to stop below game in a suit contract after an opening bid of 2 NT. Although there is a FLINT 3♣ convention with the same goal, and a FLINT 2◊ convention for use with weak 1 NT openings, the 3◊ convention is the one that is commonly known simply as Flint.

Over 2 NT, a response of 3◊, rarely needed as a natural bid, is artificial and demands a rebid of 3♡ by the opener. If responder's suit is hearts he passes 3♡, otherwise he bids 3♠, 4♣, or 4◊, expecting opener to pass.

The opener may choose to continue to game if his hand is particularly suitable.

3◊ can still be bid in a natural sense, if followed by a bid other than a minimum suit bid. 3◊ followed by 3 NT, for example, shows a genuine diamond suit and mild slam possibilities.

FLINT 2◊. A convention devised by JEREMY FLINT of England to invite game in notrump or a minor suit after a WEAK NOTRUMP opening. A 2◊ response promises either a hand with a long solid minor suit or an unbalanced hand with at least four cards in each minor. With the former hand, responder rebids 3♣ with a solid club suit or with a solid diamond suit and club stopper; or he rebids 3◊ if he has a solid diamond suit and no club stopper. If responder has the unbalanced hand with both minors, he rebids his stronger major suit.

The 2◊ response is forcing to 3 NT or four of a minor suit. Opener is requested to bid a four-card major suit if he has one; otherwise he bids 2 NT. After responder clarifies his hand opener can either bid 3 NT if he knows all suits are guarded, show an unbid stopper if he has one, sign off in four of a minor, or bid game in a minor.

FLOGGER. See BACK SCORE.

FLOWER MOVEMENT. The Flower (or Endless Howell) movement is an adaptation of the HOWELL MOVEMENT so that the apparently haphazard movement of the players is replaced by an orderly progression by which one pair (North-South at table 1) is anchored, and remains stationary throughout. All other pairs progress, East-West moving toward the higher numbered table, until they reach the highest

numbered table. After that round they merely switch directions at that table, and thereafter move to the next lower numbered table. As the players reach table 2, North-South, their next progression is to table 1, where they will sit East-West, then to table 2, East-West.

There are two major disadvantages when using the Flower Movement or Endless Howell. One disadvantage is that highly unbalanced comparisons result. Another is the movement of the boards. A complicated movement, including many bye-stands, must be worked out before the game starts. However, the movement works well in extended team events where indirect comparisons do not occur. This type of movement is popular in Europe for BAROMETER SCORING. Over a given number of rounds it permits each pair to play against every other pair. The Barometer, however, requires preduplication of the boards. (See BAROMETER SCORING.)

FLUKE. A fortuitous profit. An extreme case would be represented by a player dropping a card that appears disastrous but produces a brilliant result.

FORCE. (1) Noun: Any bid making it incumbent upon the bidder's partner to bid at least once more. (2) Verb: To cause to ruff; to cause a player to use a high card.

FORCED BID. When a player makes a FORCING BID, his partner is required systemically to make some sort of response. The response may be a WEAKNESS RESPONSE, or a STRENGTH-SHOWING BID. It is possible that a PASS is a correct response (see PENALTY PASS) to a bid normally forcing.

FORCING BID. A bid which, because of system or convention, requires the partner to "keep the bidding open," by making some call other than a pass if there is no intervening call. Examples can be found under FORCING SEQUENCES and FORCING PASS.

Perhaps the most widely used forcing bids are the JUMP SHIFT by an unpassed hand and the ONE-OVER-ONE or TWO-OVER-ONE responses by an unpassed hand.

FORCING CLUB. See 1♣ ARTIFICIAL AND FORCING.

FORCING DECLARER TO RUFF. A method of defensive play, usually sound strategy when other forms of defense seem inadvisable or doubtful. When a defender, by the play of an established side-suit, forces declarer to use his valuable trumps, it sometimes causes the declarer to lose control of the play. Sometimes called *pumping declarer*. In the following deal the insistent forcing of the declarer's strong trump hand enabled the defending partnership to defeat an otherwise sure game contract: (See hand at top of next page.)

West's opening lead is the ♠K, which East wins with the ace to unblock his partner's suit. East returns the ♠7, which West wins with the queen. West continues the suit, forcing South to ruff. South now leads a heart, which is won by West with the ace, and again West leads a spade, forcing South to ruff a second

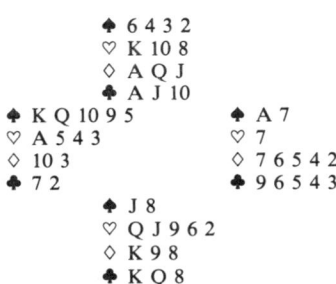

```
            ♠ 6 4 3 2
            ♡ K 10 8
            ◇ A Q J
            ♣ A J 10
♠ K Q 10 9 5            ♠ A 7
♡ A 5 4 3              ♡ 7
◇ 10 3                 ◇ 7 6 5 4 2
♣ 7 2                  ♣ 9 6 5 4 3
            ♠ J 8
            ♡ Q J 9 6 2
            ◇ K 9 8
            ♣ K Q 8
```

With West the dealer, the bidding went:

WEST	NORTH	EAST	SOUTH
1♠	Dbl	Pass	3♡
Pass	4♡	All	
		Pass	

time. South leads a second round of hearts. At this point, it is obvious that South cannot make his contract, for West's greater length in trumps gives him a trump winner. This was brought about by West's continued forcing, which battered down the declarer's trump fortress.

Sammy Kehela

FORCING LEADS. Plays by the opening leader aimed at weakening the declarer's trump suit. The lead is most effective when the leader has four trumps, and can visualize the declarer being forced to ruff prematurely and perhaps lose trump control.

Generally a forcing lead is made from a long suit, as in notrump, for should the attack succeed, the declarer may have to exhaust his attenuated trump suit in extracting the defender's trumps. Subsequently, if the defense regains the lead, they will be in a position to cash the established cards in their suit, for the hand will have been reduced to notrump.

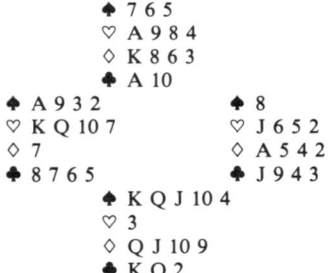

```
            ♠ 7 6 5
            ♡ A 9 8 4
            ◇ K 8 6 3
            ♣ A 10
♠ A 9 3 2              ♠ 8
♡ K Q 10 7            ♡ J 6 5 2
◇ 7                   ◇ A 5 4 2
♣ 8 7 6 5             ♣ J 9 4 3
            ♠ K Q J 10 4
            ♡ 3
            ◇ Q J 10 9
            ♣ K Q 2
```

The contract is 4♠ by South. If the singleton diamond is led, the declarer has an easy ride, but holding four trumps, West should resist this temptation and attack in hearts. Declarer wins and forces out the ♣A. West continues hearts, reducing South's trump length to his own. Declarer is now in a cleft stick: if he draws West's trumps and plays diamonds, East wins, and the defense secures two heart tricks. Alternatively, if he abandons trumps after discovering the bad break, West will score two of his small trumps.

Often the opening leader can diagnose the proper occasion for a forcing lead from the auction: (See top of right column for hand.)

South's bidding has pinpointed a singleton or void in hearts; East almost certainly has at least four

SOUTH	NORTH
1♠	2♣
2◇	2 NT
3♣	3♠
4♣	

West holds: ♠ 4
                  ♡ K J 6
                  ◇ 10 5 3 2
                  ♣ Q 7 6 3 2

trumps. A forcing game should be initiated by leading the ♡K (pinning a possible singleton queen in the South hand).

NORTH	SOUTH
2♣	2 NT
3♣	3♡
4♡	

West holds: ♠ 9 8
                  ♡ Q J 10
                  ◇ A J 8 2
                  ♣ Q J 10 8

In this situation, the dummy can be visualized as having ♡ A-K-x and a singleton diamond. Accordingly, West should eschew the *normal* club lead in favor of the ◇ A, a forcing lead against dummy's trumps, in order to promote his trump holding.

See also ATTACKING LEADS.

Sammy Kehela

FORCING 1 NT. Opening bids: see DYNAMIC NOTRUMP, LITTLE ROMAN CLUB SYSTEM. Overcalls: see COMIC NOTRUMP, GARDENER NOTRUMP OVERCALL, LEA SYSTEM, UNUSUAL 1 NT OVERCALL. Responses: see 1 NT RESPONSE TO MAJOR, FORCING.

FORCING PASS. A pass which forces partner to take further action, and informs him not to pass out the present contract. Such a pass may be made in the following situations:

(1) The opponents have taken an obvious sacrifice. A forcing pass denotes the desire to bid toward a higher contract if partner is willing.

(2) The opportunity for a sacrifice has arisen. A forcing pass denotes the desire to sacrifice, and asks partner to do so if he cannot double the opponents, and defeat their contract.

(3) A safety level has been established below which the contract cannot be sold. A forcing pass denotes inability to find a suitable call, or the desire to see if partner can double the enemy bid.

(4) After a slam-level sacrifice, a forcing pass sometimes denotes control of the enemy suit, and requests partner to bid a slam if he has the necessary outside values.

FORCING RAISE. Perhaps nothing in bidding has changed as much in recent years as the way in which responder makes a forcing raise of opener's suit. Until recently, a DOUBLE RAISE was practically the only way to indicate a forcing raise. Today, however, the double raise usually is a LIMIT BID. Diverse methods of showing the forcing raise have been developed, including JACOBY 2 NT, SPLINTERS, MINISPLINTERS, and various forms of the SWISS CONVENTION.

FORCING REBID. See OPENER'S REBIDS.

FORCING SEQUENCES. A series of bids by a partnership that require the bidding to continue. Some sequences cannot be passed by virtue of the strength shown by the last bid; certain others are considered to be forcing when the partnership has shown values for a game or slam while still bidding at a modest level. Again, some sequences commit the partnership to continue bidding until game is reached (or a worthwhile penalty extracted, should the opponents interfere); while others are merely forcing for one round.

Some common examples of forcing sequences follow, with the forcing bid underlined. (There is no unanimity of opinion as to the nature of many sequences. With the plethora of bidding systems and styles that abound, most sequences lend themselves to varying interpretations, not only from system to system, but from partnership to partnership.)

Sequences that are forcing for one round.

1 . New suit by responder:

    a)   1 ♡   1 ♠

    b)   1 ♡   2 ♣

    c)   1 ♣   1 ♠
         2 ♣   2 ♡

    d)   1 ♣   1 ♡
         1 NT   2 ♠

        but not: 1 ♡—1 ♠—1 NT—2 ♡

    e)   1 ♣   1 ♡
         1 ♠   2 ♦

        (see FOURTH SUIT FORCING)

2 . Reverse bids by opener after a two-level response:

    a)   1 ♣   2 ♣
         2 ♠

    b)   1 ♠   2 ♡
         3 ♣

3 . New suit by opener after the trump suit has been agreed:

    a)   1 ♠   2 ♠
         3 ♣

Game-forcing sequences.

1 . First-round jumps by responder:

    a)   1 ♠   2 NT

    b)   1 ♠   3 ♠
        and
        1 ♠   3 ♠

        (see LIMIT RAISE)

    c)   1 ♡   2 ♠

        (see WEAK JUMP-SHIFT RESPONSES)

2 . Jump rebids by opener:

    a)   1 ♡   2 ♣
         3 ♡

        (but not: 1 ♡—1 ♠—3 ♡)

    b)   1 ♡   1 ♠
         3 ♣

3 . Miscellaneous sequence:

    a)   1 ♡   1 ♠
         3 ♡   3 ♠

    b)   1 ♡   2 ♦
         2 NT   3 ♡

    c)   1 ♠   2 ♡
         3 ♦   3 NT
         4 ♣

4 . JUMP REBIDS by responder:
    This is a controversial topic, and is treated separately.

The above discussion has centered on forcing sequences that stem from opening bids of one of a suit. For other forcing sequences, see FORCING TWO-BID and ONE NO TRUMP OPENING.

                                    Sammy Kehela

FORCING STAYMAN. See STAYMAN.

FORCING TAKEOUT. See JUMPSHIFT.

FORCING TWO-BID. The traditional use of an opening two-bid in a suit to show a hand which can virtually guarantee game, or even slam. (Also referred to as Culbertson two-bid, DEMAND BID or STRONG TWO). It was a cornerstone of the CULBERTSON system and remained standard practice in the U.S. and many other parts of the world. In postwar years many experts abandoned the Forcing Two in favor of the WEAK TWO-BID, the ACOL TWO-BID, and other treatments. A variety of formulas have been put forward to determine whether a hand is worth a forcing two. Goren gives this schedule:

With a good five-card suit	25 high-card points.
With a good six-card suit	23 high-card points.
With a good seven-card suit	21 high-card points.

With a second good five-card suit, one point less is needed. If the game is to be in a minor suit, two points more are needed. Two more formulas were devised by HY LAVINTHAL: (a) More honor tricks than possible losers. (This rule was incorporated into the Culbertson System.) (b) Rule of 24: add to the high-card point count two points for every card over four in any suit; then subtract a point for any king or queen not in sequence with a next-ranking honor; bid two if the answer is 24 or more. However, the expert does not normally use such rules; he employs the forcing two-bid if he has reasonable game prospects opposite a worthless or nearly worthless hand. Another consideration is that a hand may be slightly too weak for a forcing two, but at the same time distinctly too strong for an opening bid of one in a suit. In such circumstances, a lightly shaded two-bid may be a lesser evil than an overstrength one-bid.

However, the likelihood that a one-bid may be passed out is a further consideration. Highly distributional hands may safely be opened with a bid of only one, because if opener's partner passes it is most unlikely that both opponents will do so. Lacking controls of three suits therefore, the expert will tend to open with a one-bid and jump later to show distribution.

Culbertson later modified the *unconditionally*

game-forcing character of the bid to permit partner to pass a bust hand if opener's call after a 2 NT response was a simple rebid of his first suit, i.e.:

$$2\heartsuit - 2 \text{ NT} - 3\heartsuit$$

Responses. The conventional negative response is 2 NT. Other responses are positive and natural, showing at least 7–8 points and seldom less than one quick trick (i.e., an ace, a king-queen, or two kings)

However, other responding treatments are used, including ACE-SHOWING RESPONSES and HERBERT NEGATIVE.

FORESIGHT. Looking ahead in the bidding or play. Examples of this are the prepared minor-suit opening bid to provide a convenient rebid over partner's or opponents' action, the early loss of a trick in order to set up a squeeze position, and a switch by defenders to a new suit in order to break up a possible throw-in play. See BIDDING; ENDPLAY; PREPAREDNESS, PRINCIPLE OF.

FORFEIT. To cancel a right or turn to call. See LAWS OF RUBBER BRIDGE (Law 15), LAWS OF DUPLICATE (Law 11).

FORK. See FOURCHETTE.

FORTUNE. Chance may play an important role at the card table, but fortune can be significant in bridge events away from the table. There are three recorded instances of players achieving international honors as a result of fortuitous circumstances.

In 1937 the United States Women's team at the World Championship at Budapest found itself one short. An American lady whose name has not been recorded was brought in to complete the team. She was a player with social bridge experience only who happened to be staying in Budapest at the time.

In 1961 at the Fall North American Championships in Houston, ROBERT STUCKER and JACK BLAIR formed an impromptu partnership in order to complete a section in the Open Pairs and oblige the tournament director. They finished second in the event and subsequently represented the United States in the World Open Pairs in Cannes, 1962, in consequence of their success.

MARY EDWARDS of Esher, England, was brought in as a substitute in the 1959 British international women's trials to replace a player who had fallen ill. From an apparently hopeless position, trailing the rest of the field by a substantial margin, she qualified for the British team in partnership with Mrs. G. R. Higginson, St. Annes-on-Sea, England. Subsequently they became European champions when their team won in Palermo, Italy.

FORTUNETELLING. Predicting the future of an individual by giving *significance* to a pattern of playing cards spread before him. Standard packs can, of course, be used, but the TAROTS, with their individuality, provide a greater opportunity for imaginative divination.

FORWARD GOING. See CONSTRUCTIVE.

FOSTER ECHO. A third-hand unblocking play

against notrump, intended at the same time to show count. With a four-card holding, the first play is the second highest, followed by the third highest, reserving the lowest card for last. With a three-card holding, the first play is the second highest, then the lowest.

FOULED BOARD. A board into which a card or cards or hands have been interchanged to incorrect pockets. Usually a fouled board occurs when the board is being discussed after the play, and various hands are interchanged across the table.

Fouling a board is perhaps the most heinous sin in bridge competition, because the scores prior to and after the fouling cannot be compared. When a board has been reported as fouled, the director must determine at what point in the competition the fouling occurred, and must matchpoint the results in some fair manner in the two fields thus created.

In pair play, one method is based on a formula devised by COL. RUSSELL BALDWIN. To use his formula, top on a board must be more than 9 and each group must have at least 4 scores. If both conditions are met the scores in the two fields are matchpointed as though the field were complete; i.e., with a 7-point top if the field has eight pairs. This is the X in the formula. A is the normal average (without any foul), N is the number of times the board was played in the group under consideration, and M is the award in match points to be given for the score.

$$M = \frac{A}{N} (2X + 1)$$

Many tournament directors have announced automatic penalties against both pairs at the table where the fouling of the board occurred, usually of the top score on a board for the session. To guard against the possibility of fouling a board, no more than one hand should be removed from the board at a time during discussions. This is particularly true when the opponents are not at the table.

In board-a-match team play, the correct manner of handling a fouled board is a matter of regulation, which has been changed from time to time. Under 1976 regulations of the ACBL, the scores, both North-South and East-West, are divided into two fields, before and after the fouling, each field is matchpointed independently, and the percentage of possible match points for each pair then is determined. For each team that played the board in different positions, the percentages are added and the board is won if the total is 120 or more, halved from 80 to 120, and lost with 80 or less. Results for teams that played the board in identical form are computed in the usual way, since the fouling occurred either before both halves of the teams had played it, or after both halves of the teams had played it.

A board with two hands having an incorrect number of cards, for example 12–14 is not fouled since no result can be achieved on this deal. The Law: "Incorrect Number of Cards" applies and the pair(s) who looked at their incorrect hands should receive average minus. The player(s) who caused the cards to be misplaced may be assessed ¼ of a board penalty, unless they are habitual offenders in which case the penalty can be more.

FOUR or FOUR-FOUR SPOT. The eleventh ranking card of each suit, designated by four pips of the suit symbol on the face.

FOUR ACES POINT-COUNT. See FOUR ACES SYSTEM and POINT-COUNT.

FOUR ACES SYSTEM. methods used by the FOUR ACES TEAM in winning many championships during the Thirties. The main features of the system were:
(1) POINT COUNT of ace = 3; king = 2; queen = 1; jack = ½. This makes a total of 26 points in the pack, and 6½ represent an average hand; 9½ points represent a mandatory opening bid.
(2) *Limited 1 NT* opening with a range of 11½–13 points. (Hands with less than seven honor cards are devalued by ½ point for each honor, and hands with more than seven honors similarly increased in value.) Establishment of this notrump range solved major rebidding headaches; in combination with point-count and rigidly prescribed responses, it precluded many of the notrump bidding faults that plagued inexpert players.
(3) *Minor-suit bids*, if need be in a three-card suit, as exploring maneuveers, either by the opener or the responder.
(4) WEAK JUMP OVERCALLS.
(5) PSYCHIC BIDS by third hand and occasionally first hand showing some high-card strength in the suit bid and little else.
(6) JUMP SHIFT to the level of two or three as a psychic control. The opener rebids 2 NT with a psychic, and with any other rebid a slam is reached.

The Four Aces' book included a number of other original ideas, many of which have become standard practice.

FOUR ACES TEAM. The team that dominated tournament competition in the mid-Thirties. The first appearance of this team was at the Summer NAC in Asbury Park in 1933, when DAVID (BURNSTINE) BRUCE, RICHARD FREY, OSWALD JACOBY, and HOWARD SCHENKEN won the CITY OF ASBURY PARK TROPHY in the teams event that was later to be superseded by the SPINGOLD. Burnstine and Jacoby had been original members of THE FOUR HORSEMEN. Burnstine, Schenken, and Frey (with CHARLES LOCHRIDGE) played as the BID-RITE TEAM earlier in 1933, when Jacoby and MICHAEL T. GOTTLIEB were members of Culbertson teams. Gottlieb joined the team immediately afterward, and during 1934 the Four Aces' major wins included the Vanderbilt, the Spingold, the GRAND NATIONAL (the top team event of the United States Bridge Association), and the Reisinger. They successfully defended the Grand National in Feb. 1935, and also repeated in the Vanderbilt, with SHERMAN STEARNS replacing Frey, who had resigned from the team when he became an executive in the Culbertson organization. Gottlieb retired in 1936 and was replaced by MERWIN D. MAIER. B. JAY BECKER and other experts played occasionally as members of the team, which did not play after Dec. 1941 but continued as an entity for purposes of book and newspaper publication until 1945.

The Four Aces played their own system, and wrote a book, *The Four Aces System of Contract Bridge* (see BIBLIOGRAPHY, C) which presented their original expert methods. Though the system was widely followed by tournament players, the book was not a commercial success.

FOUR-BID. A bid at the four-level, to take 10 tricks if it becomes the final contract.

FOUR-CARD MAJORS. Opening bids of 1♠ or 1♡ holding a four-card suit. The old auction bridge idea of requiring a five-card suit for an opening bid has found a place in several modern systems such as ROTH-STONE and KAPLAN-SHEINWOLD. In the Seventies the pendulum swung so far that a majority of experts and tournament players were using five-card majors. To what extent they have been followed by the bridge public at large remains doubtful, but the tendency has been for bridge teachers to recommend the five-card style. (see BIDDABLE SUITS).

FOUR-CARD SUIT BIDS. See BIDDABLE SUITS.

4♣ ASKING BID. See 4♣ CONVENTIONS.

4♣ BLACKWOOD. See ACE IDENTIFICATION, BLACK AND RED GERBER, GERBER CONVENTION, EXTENDED GERBER, KEY CARD GERBER, ROMAN GERBER, and SUPER BLACKWOOD.

4♣ CONVENTIONS. See CLARAC SLAM TRY, 4♣ BLACKWOOD, 4♣ AND 4♦ OPENING TRANSFERS, RUBIN TRANSFERS, SOUTH AFRICAN TEXAS, SWISS CONVENTION. See also SPLINTER BID, VOID-SHOWING BIDS.

An alternative usage, devised by Howard Robinson of New York City, is to use 4♣ as a three-stage asking bid to determine singletons, aces, and trump honors.

When 4♣ is a jump bid, or immediately follows a jump raise of another suit, partner is requested to bid a suit in which he holds a singleton or revert to the agreed trump suit with no singleton. The next ranking suit by the asking bidder then requests partner to show the number of aces he holds. If the asking bidder again bids the next ranking suit, responder shows his trump honors (ace, king, or queen) by three steps. The asking bidder signs off whenever he bypasses the asking denomination or reverts to the agreed trump suit.

4♣ AND 4♦ OPENING PREEMPTS. Such bids usually are based on an eight-card minor in a poor hand. If the partnership is using a GAMBLING 3 NT to show a solid minor, then an opening of 4♣ or 4♦ would show a broken suit.

4♣ AND 4♦ OPENING TRANSFERS. An opening bid of 4♣ promising a long heart suit or an opening of 4♦ promising a long spade suit. As most frequently used, opener promises a hand stronger than the normal direct opening of four of a major suit. This convention is called NAMYATS. Some pairs use the four-of-a-minor opening to show a weaker hand, or a hand with a solid major suit and nothing else.

Responder usually accepts the transfer by bidding four of opener's major. However, the bid of the next higher suit is available without getting the partnership beyond game, and can be used either as a re-transfer, making opener the declarer, or as an asking bid.

For an alternative treatment see RUBIN TRANSFERS.

FOUR-DEAL BRIDGE. See CHICAGO.

4 ◇ CONVENTIONS. See BLUE TEAM 4♣–4◇ CONVENTION; 4♣ AND 4◇ OPENING TRANSFERS; NEAPOLITAN 4◇ CONVENTION; RUBIN TRANSFERS; SOUTH AFRICAN TEXAS; TEXAS CONVENTION.

4 ◇ OPENING TRANSFER. See 4♣ AND 4◇ OPENING TRANSFERS, RUBIN TRANSFERS.

4–5 NT CONVENTION. See CULBERTSON 4-5 NT.

FOUR HORSEMEN. A champion team of the early Thirties. It was formed by P. HAL SIMS in 1931 to challenge the earlier success of the Culbertson team. The other "horsemen" were WILLARD S. KARN, DAVID BURNSTINE (Bruce) and OSWALD JACOBY. They won the two major team championships in 1932, the VANDERBILT and the ASBURY PARK, by large margins, and won the REISINGER convincingly in 1933. Sims' efforts to develop and promote his own system in opposition to Culbertson did not suit Jacoby and Bruce, who successively left the team (see FOUR ACES TEAM).

4 NT CONVENTIONS. Since a 4 NT bid is the lowest bid possible above the game level, it is a bid that is frequently used to initiate inquiries to lead either to a slam bid, or to stay below the slam level if the partnership hands cannot make a slam. Among the specialized uses of this bid are the following, dealt with in the following articles: ACOL 4 NT OPENING, BLACKWOOD, BOLAND CONVENTION, BOWERS VARIATION BYZANTINE BLACKWOOD, CULBERTSON 4-5 NT, CULWOOD, DECLARATIVE-INTERROGATIVE 4 NT, DEFENSE TO OPENING FOUR-BID, KEY-CARD BLACKWOOD, KING CONVENTION, NORMAN, ROMAN BLACKWOOD, SAN FRANCISCO, SUPPRESSING THE BID ACE.

For a discussion of the distinction between the quantitative and conventional uses of 4 NT, see BLACKWOOD.

4 NT OPENING. In standard methods, shows a balanced hand too strong to open 3 NT. It should be a ten-trick hand with perhaps 28–30 points. This rare bid is in disuse in standard practice, because an opening 2♣ bid followed by 4 NT will serve equally well.

For alternative treatments, see ACOL 4 NT OPENING; 4 NT OPENING PRE-EMPT; RUBIN TRANSFERS.

4 NT OPENING PRE-EMPT. Devised by TERENCE REESE and JEREMY FLINT as part of the LITTLE MAJOR SYSTEM and subsequently adopted by several American experts to distinguish between a strong and weak minor-suit game pre-empt.

An opening bid of 4 NT shows a weak pre-empt of 5♣ or 5◇ with less than five controls, counting an ace or void as two controls and a king or singleton as one control. Consequently, an opening bid of 5♣ or 5◇ would show a stronger pre-empt, five or more controls. For an alternative treatment see RUBIN TRANSFERS.

4 NT OVERCALL. A bid of 4 NT after an opposing opening bid is usually a form of the UNUSUAL NO TRUMP, calling for a minor suit. This could not apply after an opening bid of 3♣, 3◇, or a weak 2◇, in which case the bid would be BLACKWOOD. For treatment of 4 NT overcall after an opening bid at the four level see DEFENSE TO OPENING FOUR-BID.

FOUR-ODD. Four tricks over the book, or ten tricks in all.

FOUR OF A SUIT OPENING. A natural opening bid of four to show a long, strong suit with little side strength. A typical hand would contain a seven- or eight-card suit, but a six-card suit is possible.

$$
\begin{array}{l}
♠ \; — \\
♡ \; K\,Q\,J\,6\,5\,4 \\
◇ \; K\,Q\,J\,8\,7 \\
♣ \; 3\,2
\end{array}
$$

If this is the dealer's hand, 4♡ has a lot to recommend it. An opening four in a minor would seldom be based on a solid suit, because of the possibility of 3 NT. For alternative treatments, see 4♣ AND 4◇ OPENING TRANSFERS, LITTLE MAJOR, RUBIN TRANSFERS.

FOUR TABLES. At duplicate, four tables provide for competition among 16 (or 17) players as individuals, eight pairs of players, or four teams of four.

As an individual tournament, it has the difficulty of being very short (15 or 16 boards) or too long (30 or 32 boards). Player assignments to seats and distribution of boards are shown under INDIVIDUAL MOVEMENT.

As a pair game, the HOWELL MOVEMENT, with seven rounds, is preferable to the MITCHELL MOVEMENT, with only four rounds. With seven pairs, the phantom should be pair 8. Either three or four boards may be played per round.

If the Mitchell movement is used, tables 1 and 2 should relay boards throughout, with a bye stand between tables 3 and 4. Boards move from 1 to 4 to bye stand, to 3, to 2 where they are shared with table 1. Traveling pairs move from 1 to 2 to 3 to 4 to table 1 after each round. Three is top score on a board and average is one and one-half times the number of boards in play.

As a team-of-four event, three stanzas are required; in the first stanza, traveling pairs of teams 1 and 2 exchange places, as do the traveling pairs of 3 and 4; boards are relayed between tables 1 and 2 and between tables 3 and 4; in the second stanza, traveling pairs of teams 1 play at 3 and of team 3 at 1; similarly with teams 2 and 4; in the third stanza, teams 1 and 4 and teams 2 and 3 interchange traveling pairs, and relay the boards. Boards are reshuffled at the end of each stanza, and the six matches are scored individually. BOARD-A-MATCH, TOTAL POINT, or INTERNATIONAL MATCHPOINT SCORING can be used, and ties broken with summation from the three matches at board-a-match or total point or by quotient of points won divided by points lost at International Match Points.

For 3½ and 4½ tables see HALF TABLE MOVEMENTS.

FOUR-THREE-TWO-ONE COUNT. See POINT-COUNT.

FOURCHETTE. A tenace; and obsolete term for A–Q, K–J, or Q–10.

FOURTEEN TABLES. At duplicate, 14 tables provide competition among 56 players, as individuals, 28 pairs, or 14 teams. The team-of-four can be board-a-match or Swiss team competition – either is a good contest.

As an individual tournament, twinned RAINBOW sections of seven tables can be used with a 13 top. This provides 21 boards with the same number of partnerships. Also possible is an Appendix Rainbow as described in EIGHT TABLES and TWELVE TABLES, where the *bumped* players will play boards 27 and 28 at table 14, with all other players moving and all players playing 13 rounds, 26 boards, top 12, average 156. The Appendix Rainbow movement could be cut at 11 or 12 rounds if desired.

As a pair game, 14 tables has become the basic unit for a section where there are many sections. When it is desired to pre-duplicate the hands from prepared hand records, the players who do the duplicating do not play the hand they duplicate; therefore it is necessary to have at least 14 tables in each section in order to play the standard 26 boards.

As a board-a-match team game there are irregularities in the movement. To start the game you distribute the boards with 1 and 2 on table 1, 3 and 4 on table 2, going around the room until you have 27 and 28 on table 14. To start the game the East-West pairs skip a table in the lower direction and the boards are shuffled. After the first and second round the boards move to the next lower table and the East-West pairs skip a table in the lower direction. After the third round the boards move normally but the moving pairs skip an extra table, or, if you prefer, skip two tables. The East-West pairs move normally for the next six rounds. After the ninth round the moving pairs skip an extra table and the boards skip a table. For the remaining rounds the moving pairs make the regular team-of-four move.

To give you an idea, East-West #1 plays at the following tables: 13, 11, 9, 6, 4, 2, 14, 12, 10, * 7, 5, 3. North-South #1 plays 3, 5, 7, 10, 12, 14, 2, 4, 6, * 9, 11, 13. * = Boards skip.

If a 13th round is advisable the moving pairs 1 to 7 add 7 to their table number and go to that table. Moving pairs 8 to 14 subtract 7 from their table number and go to that table. Tables 1 and 8, 2 and 9, 3 and 10, 4 and 11, 5 and 12, 6 and 13, and 7 and 14 relay boards for that round. For the 13th round the boards are reshuffled.

For 13½ or 14½ tables see HALF TABLE MOVEMENTS.

FOURTH BEST. See FOURTH HIGHEST.

FOURTH HAND. The fourth player to have the opportunity to make a call, the player to the dealer's right.

FOURTH-HAND BIDS. For a discussion of minimum openings in fourth seat, see BORDERLINE OPENING BIDS.

The idea that the fourth player must have additional strength to open the bidding is now quite obsolete, and at duplicate a player may open slightly light in the hope of snatching a partscore.

Opening three-bids and weak two-bids in fourth position show maximum values, close to an opening bid, but rarely occur. Other opening bids are not affected by the positional factor. See also PASSED HAND.

FOURTH HIGHEST. Traditionally the fourth highest card of a long suit is led to develop long card tricks in a suit or to give partner the count in the suit led. The application of the RULE OF ELEVEN when the card led is the fourth highest is a determining factor in play by third-hand and declarer.

FOURTH-SUIT ARTIFICIAL. A convention in which the bid of the only unbid suit by responder at his second turn is a waiting move promising nothing about the suit named. This is popularly called "fourth-suit forcing", but this is an unsatisfactory term since nobody plays such a bid as nonforcing. The question is whether or not the bid shows length and/or strength in the fourth suit.

When used artificially, as it is by a majority of experts, the responder usually has two or three losers in the fourth suit. The opener should not bid notrump unless he has a stopper in the fourth suit, which is in effect an unbid suit.

Examples of the bid are:

NORTH	NORTH	NORTH
♠ 7 5 4	♠ A 3	♠ 8 4
♡ A 6 2	♡ 7 5 4	♡ K 6
◊ A K Q 4	◊ 9 7 2	◊ A K Q 6 4 2
♣ 8 4 3	♣ A K J 6 5	♣ 7 5 3

SOUTH	NORTH	SOUTH	NORTH	SOUTH	NORTH
1♣	1◊	1♠	2♣	1♠	2◊
1♡	1♠	2◊	2♡	2♡	3♣

The fourth suit is forcing for one round only, and promises a minimum of 10-11 points if made at the two-level or higher. Responder seldom wishes to bid the fourth suit in a natural sense, because he would then be able to bid notrump. See OUT-OF-THE-BLUE CUEBID.

FOURTH-SUIT FORCING. A popular misdescription of FOURTH-SUIT ARTIFICIAL.

FRACTIONAL MASTERPOINT CERTIFICATES. See RATING POINTS.

FRAGMENT. A term describing a suit of two or more cards that is not long enough to bid naturally; usually a three-card holding. The bid of a fragment is designed to imply shortness in an unbid suit. See FRAGMENT BID.

FRAGMENT BID. An unusual bid — usually a double jump — in a new suit on the second round of bidding, showing a fit with partner's suit and a shortage in the fourth suit (devised by MONROE IN-GBERMAN). The last bid in each of the following sequences is a fragment bid:

(a)	(b)	(c)
NORTH SOUTH	NORTH SOUTH	NORTH SOUTH
1♣ 1♡	1♣ 1♡	1♣ 1♡
3♦	1♠ 4◇	1♠ 4♣

The fragment bidder usually has two or three cards in the fragment suit, and must have a singleton or void in the fourth suit — clubs in (b).

The fragment idea can be extended to this situation:

NORTH	SOUTH
1♡	2♣
2◇	3♣

Here the bid shows a fit with hearts and a diamond shortage. (The more orthodox treatment is to use this sequence to show a fit with diamonds, because South's hand has been improved by North's rebid.)

For alternative treatments of such sequences, see ASKING BIDS, SPLINTER BIDS, SWISS CONVENTION, and VOID-SHOWING BIDS.

Although fragment bids were originally devised as a use for the double jump shift, which was otherwise usually an IDLE BID, when a player has made a bid that denies a two-suited hand, a fragment bid may be made in a suit without jumping. The implication of the fragment bid is that the bidder has support for his partner's suit and a singleton in the remaining suit. See SOLOWAY theory of JUMP SHIFTS.

FRAME. A colloquialism for a game. The term probably came from the appearance of the scoring pad used in rubber bridge: the vertical and horizontal lines, the edge of the single column pad, and the line drawn underneath the score when the game is completed "frame" the trick-score constituting the game.

FRANCE. See FRENCH BRIDGE FEDERATION.

FRANCO–AMERICAN MATCHES. Teams representing France and the United States (or North America) have met on many occasions. There have been 16 official meetings in world championship competition.

(Details of teams and scores are given under WORLD CHAMPIONSHIPS).

The following semiofficial or unofficial matches have been played:

(1) Paris 1930. United States (Ely and Josephine Culbertson, Theodore Lightner, Waldemar von Zedtwitz) drew with France (Pierre Bellanger, Pierre Albarran, A. B. de Puchesse, Robert de Nexon, Georges Rousset, Emanuel Tulumaris, Sophocles Venizelos). The match was played at PLAFOND, the forerunner of contract bridge, and, after a dispute, was abandoned as a draw shortly before the end when the scores were almost level.

(2) Paris 1954. France beat the United States (Cliff Bishop, Milton Ellenby, Lewis Mathe, Don Oakie, Doug Steen) by 17 IMPs.

FRANCO BOARD. A screen invented by Italian international MARIO FRANCO, and at one time used in major Italian events. It is placed diagonally across the table so that each player cannot see his partner and can see only one opponent. A trap in the center of the screen is raised before the start of the play so that all players can see the dummy. Combined with WRITTEN BIDDING, the board virtually removes any possibility of inadvertent exchange of illicit information, and greatly reduces the ethical problems resulting from hesitations. See BIDDING BOXES, BIDDING SCREEN, ROLLING BOX.

FREAK. A single hand or a complete deal of abnormally unbalanced distribution. Usually a hand in which one player has more than seven cards in one suit, or more than eleven cards in two suits.

FREAK HANDS. In the field of bidding, there is no doubt that the expert has a tremendous advantage over the great majority of bridge players, for he has come across virtually every conceivable bidding situation, and has learned how to handle it. There is one type of bidding situation, however, that even the veriest of tyros handles as well (or as badly) as the expert. This is in the field of freak hands, hands that contain eight, nine or ten-card suits, plus a void or two. (See DUKE OF CUMBERLAND'S HAND, MISSISSIPPI HEART HAND, and SWING HAND.) These hands defy scientific evaluation, and past experiences are of no help in appraising these anomalies. So the expert, like the average player, has to guess what he should bid; and when it comes to guessing, anybody is as good as anybody else.

Consider a few freak hands. The three deals which follow were all taken from North American Championships events. The first one arose in the Master Mixed Teams Championship of 1961.

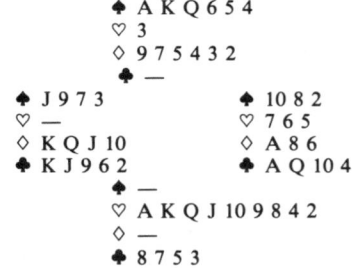

As is readily apparent, South can take 13 tricks at hearts against any defense. When the board was played, East, as dealer, passed, and South either passed, bid 1♡, bid 4♡, or bid 6♡. As to what the proper bid on the South hand was, there is no answer.

How freak hands can be wrecked on the rocks of distribution is evidenced in the following deal, which came up in the Master Mixed Teams Championship of 1949.

```
              ♠ K Q J 5 4 3 2
              ♡ 3
              ◇ —
              ♣ A Q 10 7 4
   ♠ 9                        ♠ A 8 7
   ♡ 10 8 6 5                 ♡ K Q 9 4
   ◇ Q 10 8 4 2               ◇ A K J
   ♣ 9 8 3                    ♣ K 5 2
              ♠ 10 6
              ♡ A J 7 2
              ◇ 9 7 6 5 3
              ♣ J 6
```

Neither side vulnerable. North dealer. The bidding at every table was identical.

WEST	NORTH	EAST	SOUTH
	1♠	Dbl	Pass
2◇	4♠	Dbl	All Pass

Eleven tricks were made at every table, declarer's only losers being the ace of trumps and the ♣K. Is there an authority, an expert, or an average player who would dare to say that East's business double of 4♠ was an improper bid?

We have all run into situations comparable to the one contained in this final deal, and there isn't a thing we can do about it in preparing ourselves to handle it in the future.

```
              ♠ 5
              ♡ 7 4
              ◇ 10 8 4
              ♣ J 10 7 6 4 3 2
   ♠ K Q J 7 6 3 2            ♠ 10 9 8 4
   ♡ K Q 3                    ♡ A J 10 9 5 2
   ◇ —                        ◇ 6 5 3
   ♣ 9 8 5                    ♣ —
              ♠ A
              ♡ 8 6
              ◇ A K Q J 9 7 2
              ♣ A K Q
```

North–South vulnerable, South dealer, the bidding:

WEST	NORTH	EAST	SOUTH
			2◇
2♠	Pass	4♠	5◇
5♠	6◇	6♠	Dbl
All Pass			

It will be observed that West's only loser was the ace of trumps. Did South do something wrong when he doubled the slam contract?

Fred Karpin

FREE BID. A bid made by a player whose partner's bid has been overcalled by right-hand opponent. In such circumstances partner will have another chance to bid, so it would seem unnecessary to bid with minimum values. Traditional theory therefore pre-

scribed elevated standards for all "free" actions, equivalent to perhaps an additional king.

However, experts have long since abandoned this requirement except when the bid is 1 NT.

There are three separate categories.

(1) 1 NT (e.g., 1♣–1♡–1 NT). The traditional range is 10–12 or 9–12, but many players reduce this by partnership agreement, sometimes to as little as 7–10. In that case the minimum would apply only when holding a double stopper in the opponent's suit.

(2) Suit response (e.g., 1♣–1♡–1♠). A minimum of 9 points according to old textbooks, but the modern expert style is to bid as if there has been no interference. There is a strong tendency for the free response to show a five-card suit (especially playing NEGATIVE DOUBLES), or at least a strong four-card suit. But in the ROTH-STONE SYSTEM, added values are necessary for a free bid; a negative double is used with weaker hands.

A free two-over-one response (e.g., 1♣–1♡–2◇) is usually held to show 11 points, or even 12; the standard should be slightly higher when the opener cannot rebid his suit at the level of two.

(3) Raises. In this category (e.g., 1◇–1♠–2◇), almost all experts have abandoned the idea that the raise shows greater strength than it would without the overcall. There is no disadvantage in raising exactly as if there had been no overcall, and there is a considerable tactical loss in adopting a waiting policy.

Free rebids by the opener follow similar principles. Any obviously suitable action should be taken, even with a minimum hand on which no desirable action is available.

FREE DOUBLE. A double of a contract which represents a game if undoubled. Usually confined to rubber bridge, when a partscore will convert an earlier partscore into game. If both sides have a partscore, judgment of a high level is required; all players may be straining their resources.

Doubles of game and slam contracts connot properly be described as free. See PENALTY DOUBLE and SUCKER'S DOUBLE.

FREE FINESSE. A defensive lead which allows declarer to take a finesse without the risk of losing the trick, or a finesse which could not normally be taken at all.

FREE RAISE. A single raise of opener's suit after an overcall. The classical theory that a free raise implies extra strength (8–10 points) has been generally abandoned; most experts maintain the normal range (6–9 points) irrespective of the overcall. However, the overcall may make it necessary to relax the requirements for trump support, especially if the overcall is in the suit ranking immediately below opener's:

(a)	(b)
♠ A x	♠ x x
♡ x x	♡ A x x x
◇ x x x x	◇ Q x x x
♣ A J x x x	♣ K x x

In (a), a raise to 2♣ would be appropriate when 1♣ has been overcalled by 2♡. In (b), 1♣ should be raised to 2♣ after an overcall of 1♠. In each case the trump length is one card below standard. These examples assume that NEGATIVE DOUBLES are not being used.

FRENCH BRIDGE FEDERATION (FÉDÉRA-TION FRANÇAISE DE BRIDGE). Founded in 1935, this federation had a membership of more than 38,000 in 1982. French victories in international events include the Bermuda Bowl 1956, World Team Olympiad 1960 and 1980, Rosenblum Teams 1982, World Pair Olympiad 1962, European Championship 1953, 1955, 1962, 1966, 1970, 1974, European Women's Team Championship 1939, 1953, 1954, 1956, 1965, 1969. France hosted the World Championship in Monte Carlo in 1954, the World Pair Olympiad in Cannes 1962, the World Team Olympiad in Deauville 1968, and the European Championships in Paris 1949. National events held annually include Open Teams and Open Pairs.

Officers, 1982:
President: Jose Damiani
Secretary: Robert Fehr, 53, Avenue Hoche, 75008, Paris, France

FRENCH CLUB. A simple 1♣ forcing system once in common use in France and other parts of the world.

FRENCH SCORING. In tournaments sanctioned by the French Bridge Federation, the value of the fourth odd trick in no trump contracts is reduced to 20 points. Thus ten or more tricks will be scored the same in either no trump or a major suit.

If it is assumed that a major game should be prefered to a notrump game, this scoring eliminates the edge given to the notrump contract when both will produce the same ten or more tricks.

FREQUENCY CHARTS. Informational sheets produced for the players when computer scoring is used on across-the-field tops. The charts tell the number of times each score is achieved on each deal and also list the matchpoints each score is worth. Players use these charts to check their scores, but one drawback is that a player cannot tell whether or not he was credited with the correct result on any given board.

FULFILLING CONTRACT. Taking as many tricks, in the play of the hand, as contracted for in addition to the book of six, i.e., eight tricks in a contract of two. A bonus of 50 points is awarded for a less-than-game contract in duplicate, 300 for a non-vulnerable game, and 500 for a vulnerable game.

FULWILER CONVENTION. A form of asking bid. After the trump suit has been established, any bid by either partner at the lowest range in another suit asks for control in that suit. Responses are in steps:

no control	1 step
singleton	2 steps
void	3 steps
king	4 steps
ace	5 steps
ace and king	6 steps

for example:

WEST	EAST
1♠	2♠
3♣	3 NT

(four steps, showing the ♣K).

Subsequently, the opener can *ask* about trump honors. See ROMAN ASKING BIDS.

G

GABARRET CUP. This Argentine award donated in memory of ADOLFO GABARRET is the equivalent of the ACBL McKENNEY TROPHY. The winners are:

1956	Carlos Ottolenghi	1969	Egisto Rocchi
1957	Alejandro Castro	1970	David Zanalda
1958	Alberto Berisso	1971	Alberto Berisso
1959	Arturo Jaques	1972	Carlos Cabanne
1960	Arturo Jaques	1973	Augustín Santamarina
1961	Luis Attaguile	1974	Augustín Santamarina
1962	Alberto Berisso	1975	Martín Monsegur
1963	Egisto Rocchi	1976	Egisto Rocchi
1964	Marcelo Lerner	1977	Agustín Santamarina
1965	Marcelo Lerner	1978	Egisto Rocchi
1966	Eduardo Díaz	1979	Héctor Camberos
1967	Ricardo Calvente	1980	Pablo Lambardi
1968	Alberto Berisso	1981	Agustín Santamarina

GABUNGAN BRIDGE SELURUH ASSOCIATION. See ALL INDONESIA BRIDGE ASSOCIATION.

GADGET. An artificial bidding device which can be grafted on to standard bidding methods but is not an integral part of any system. The term applies to nearly all the articles listed under ARTIFICIAL BIDS and SLAM CONVENTIONS.

GAMBIT. A deliberate sacrifice of a trick in order to gain additional tricks. The term is borrowed from chess.

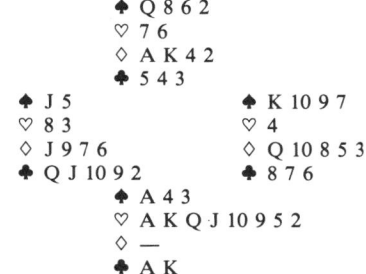

West leads the ♣Q against South's contract of 6♡. Declarer, at trick two, must play one of his two small trumps and concede an otherwise unnecessary trick to the 8. This forces a trump entry to the dummy, and permits South to discard his two spade losers on dummy's diamond winners. A spade lead would have defeated the contract.

GAMBLING AT BRIDGE. Playing for stakes is quite common in regular rubber bridge circles. In duplicate, however, it is prohibited in contests sponsored by the American Contract Bridge League. See CALCUTTA, POOL.

GAMBLING 3 NT. An opening bid based on a long, solid minor suit, a feature of the ACOL SYSTEM that has been adopted by many players using an artificial 2♣ forcing opening bid.

(a)	(b)
♠ A 5	♠ 7
♡ K 2	♡ Q 8 3
◇ J 3	◇ A K Q 8 4 3 2
♣ A K Q J 7 4 3	♣ J 3

The amount of outside strength required to make this bid varies with the individual partnership. In its original form stoppers were needed in at least two side-suits, as in (a). The modern tendency is to make the bid (except in fourth position) with little or no outside strength, as in (b).

Responses:

(1) 4♣ shows extreme weakness and a desire to play at the four-level in opener's suit.

(2) 4◇ is usually used artificially. A common arrangement is to use it as a singleton inquiry. Opener bids a major-suit singleton, bids 4 NT without a singleton, and bids his minor with a singleton in the other minor.

(3) 4♠ and 4♡ are natural, with a self-sufficient six-card suit or better.

(4) 4 NT is conventional, with responses downgraded because the opener has already shown an ace. A 5◇ rebid would therefore show *two* aces.

(5) 5♣ shows a desire to play in five of opener's suit — possibly for pre-emptive reasons.

(6) 5◇ is natural, implying that responder has a club honor and has therefore deduced that opener's suit is diamonds.

(7) 6♣ shows a desire to play a minor-suit slam.

Defenses:

The most effective method of bidding against a gambling 3 NT opening bid is to use the RIPSTRA convention. Assuming adequate high-card strength, the bid of four of the better minor suit as a take-out for the majors gives the partnership the best chance of finding its best suit.

If 3 NT has become the final contract, the best chance to defeat the contract is usually for the opening leader to cash a winner in order to take a look at dummy and to obtain information from his partner as to which hand controls which side suits.

GAME. The winning of 100 points below the line in bridge. Game can be attained by bidding and winning a succession of two or more partscores, or can be bid in one contract after it is determined that the partnership has sufficient values in the combined hands. The first team to win two such games wins the rubber and the premium. In CHICAGO, a game may be bid and scored on each of four deals and it is theoretically possible for a side to win four games in one CHUKKER.

GAME ALL. The situation when both sides are vulnerable. The term is rare in the United States but standard in England.

GAME BID. A bid for just enough odd tricks to complete the requirement for game in a particular suit or notrump. In duplicate bridge this is a bid for 3 NT, four of a major suit or five of a minor suit. In rubber bridge if a pair has a partscore, a game bid usually requires fewer tricks; a partscore of 40 points, for example, would make 2 NT, two of a major or three of a minor into game bids.

GAME CARDS. There are many games that are played with cards that are not the PACK of playing cards. Authors, Rook, and Old Maid are examples of games designed principally for children. Flash cards, such as those used in teaching word recognition and foreign languages in schools, are other types. Dominoes and Mah-Jongg can also be played with cards in place of the blocks and tiles.

Major manufacturers of card games are located in Salem and Springfield MA, but games are produced by a wide variety of individual manufacturers, and most are covered by patents.

GAME CONTRACT. An undertaking of a contract which, if successful, will earn enough points in TRICK-SCORE to make or complete the 100 required for a game. In notrump, three-odd, in hearts or spades, four-odd, in clubs or diamonds, five-odd tricks produce at least the 100 points necessary from a LOVE score. With a PARTSCORE, lower contracts become game contracts. Some rubber bridge players will DOUBLE a game contract more freely than below-game contracts, although such tactics are misconceived. See SUCKER'S DOUBLE.

GAME DEMAND BID. A bid which, once made, imposes an obligation upon the partnership to keep the bidding alive until game is reached or a satisfactory penalty inflicted upon the opponents. An obsolescent term. See FORCING TWO-BID.

GAME-FORCING BID. A bid which announces that the partnership should reach a game contract or higher, and thereby establishes a GAME-FORCING SITUATION.

GAME-FORCING SITUATIONS. A sequence of bidding which has committed both members of a partnership to reach a game contract. Many of these are listed under FORCING SEQUENCES.

GAME-GOING. A term applied to any hand or bidding situation which promises to develop a game for the partnership.

GAME HOG. A player who habitually distorts his own bidding in the expectation that all hands should be played at a game contract.

GAME IN. A colloquial expression meaning vulnerable.

GAME INVITATION. See COMPETITIVE DOUBLE; DRURY; INVITATIONAL BID; JUMP RAISE BY RESPONDER; LIMIT JUMP RAISE; LIMIT JUMP RAISE TO SHOW SINGLETON; MAXIMAL OVERCALL DOUBLE; SHORT-SUIT GAME TRIES; TWO-WAY GAME TRIES; WEAK-SUIT GAME TRY.

GAMMA TRUMP ASKING BIDS. Asking bids in

the ROMAN and SUPER PRECISION systems concerned with the quality of responder's suit, which is inferentially agreed as trumps. The Roman responses are as follows:

1st step	— Queen or worse
2nd step	— King
3rd step	— Ace
4th step	— Two top honors
5th step	— Three top honors

For responses in the SUPER PRECISION system, which are identical to the trump-asking responses in standard PRECISION CLUB, see PRECISION ASKING BIDS.

GARBAGE. A colloquial term for a minimum type of holding whose majority values are in unsupported queens and jacks.

GARDENER NOTRUMP OVERCALL. A two-way bid which may be either a natural notrump overcall with 16–18 points or a weak hand with a long suit. Partner usually bids 2♣ to find out which type of overcall was made, and the overcaller rebids 2 NT if he has the natural strong type. There is a technical reason for this procedure if strong jump overcalls are being used: a weak hand with a long suit has no convenient way to enter the auction. Devised by NICO GARDENER, London. If the bid is always weak, it is referred to by the French as the *Sans Atout Comique*. See COMIC NOTRUMP.

GATHERING TRICKS. The taking in of tricks won by a side. The tricks taken by a side should be arranged in such a way that their number and sequence are apparent. See LAWS (Law 66).

GERBER CONVENTION. A 4♣ bid to ask partner how many aces he holds. The responses are:

4♦	no ace
4♡	one ace
4♠	two aces
4 NT	three aces
5♣	four aces

By analogy to the BLACKWOOD convention, 4♦ can be used instead of 5♣ to show the rare holding of four aces. As originally written, the 4♣ bidder uses the next available bid to ask for kings on the same principle, but cannot use the agreed trump suit for this purpose. For example, 4♠ asks for kings over a response of 4♡, unless spades is the agreed trump suit, in which case 4 NT becomes the king-asking bid. The modern tendency is to use 4♦ to show four aces along with 5♣ to ask for kings rather than the next higher bid. This helps remove ambiguity.

There may often be difficulty in distinguishing a conventional 4♣ bid from a natural one. Some players restrict the use of the convention to situations in which no suit has been genuinely bid (e.g., after a 1 NT or 2 NT opening, or a conventional 2♣ bid followed by 2 NT or 3 NT).

If 4♣ is to be used more generally, there are three possible rules a partnership can adopt:

(1) 4♣ is conventional unless it is a direct club raise.

(2) 4♣ is conventional unless clubs have been genuinely bid by the partnership.

(3) 4♣ is conventional if it is a jump bid, or if a suit has been specifically agreed. This is perhaps the best of these rules.

A partnership also has to consider how responder should act holding a void, or when there is interference bidding.

Treatment of similar situations is discussed under BLACKWOOD convention.

This convention, invented in 1938 by the late JOHN GERBER of Houston, is sometimes referred to as 4♣ Blackwood. See also ACE IDENTIFICATION; BLACK AND RED GERBER; CLARAC SLAM TRY; EXTENDED GERBER; KEY CARD GERBER; ROMAN GERBER; SUPER GERBER.

GERMAN BRIDGE LEAGUE (DEUTSCHER BRIDGE VERBAND). Founded in 1932, by 1982 it had approximately 11,400 members. The League participates in Olympiads and European Championships, hosting the 1963 event in Baden-Baden. The League also sponsors teams that compete in the Common Market Championships and the major European International Bridge Festivals. In the past, German teams contested for the Mitropa Cup, held annually in Austria, and have won the open division once and the women's event twice. The League awards master points and publishes a monthly magazine, *Deutsches Bridge Verbands-Blatt*.

Officers, 1982:
President: Vacant
Secretary: Detlev Piekenbrock, P.O. Box 2453, D-4900 Herford, Germany

GESTURE. A mannerism that suggest a call, lead, play, or plan of play. See LAWS (Law 16).

GET A COUNT. To determine during the play the number of cards held in one or more suits by one of the hidden hands. See COUNTING THE HAND.

GHOULIES. See GOULASH.

GIVE COUNT. As a defender, to give a LENGTH SIGNAL to one's partner.

GLADIATOR. A method of responding to 1 NT, devised in New Zealand, and used in slightly modified forms in the ROMAN and CAB systems.

A response of 2♣ is a relay, requiring the opener to bid 2♦. A minimum suit bid by responder then shows weakness, and the opener passes. Other rebids by the responder are limited.

A response of 2♦ is a STAYMAN-type inquiry for major suits, and is forcing to game. A response of 2♡ or 2♠ is forcing, and higher suit responses are slam suggestions.

GO DOWN. Synonym for failure to make a contract.

GO UP. To play a high and possibly winning card when faced with a choice of playable cards.

GODDARD TROPHY. Awarded to the winners of the Men's and Women's Pairs contested at the Summer North American Championships. It was donated by the ACBL in 1937 and named after Ed Goddard, the organizing chairman of the series of Summer championships held at Asbury Park. For past results see Appendix I.

GOLD CUP. The Knock-out Team Championship of Great Britain, contested under the auspices of the BRITISH BRIDGE LEAGUE. (See also VON ZEDTWITZ GOLD CUP.)

GOLD POINT. Effective January 1, 1969, the ACBL added as a requirement for advancement to LIFE MASTER status the proviso that all players who had zero RED POINTS as of that date needed 25 gold points of the required 50 red points in order to achieve Life Master rank. These points are awarded for overall placing or for winning a section top in regional or higher-rated events that are not restricted by an upper masterpoint limit. Gold points count toward the required red point total.

GOLDER CUP. This trophy was presented in memory of BENJAMIN M. GOLDER in 1947 by his widow, Peggy, subsequently Mrs. Charles J. Solomon. The Ben Golder Memorial Trophy originally was contested for a single-session event intended principally for team-of-four players who had drawn byes or who had been eliminated in the first round. It was also open to other players with 20 or more master points. In 1951 the masterpoint requirement was 30–50. In 1963 it became a two-session event with a minimum masterpoint requirement of 100, and no longer open to a member of a team still remaining in the Spingold. Since 1976 only one member of the partnership must meet the 100-MP requirement. Results are listed under Summer North American Championships.

GOLDMAN TROPHY. For the Open Pair Championship at the Eastern States Regional. Presented by Julian Goldman in 1929, it had the status of a North American Championship during the Thirties.

GOLDSCHMIDT. A convention used in response to an opening 16–19 notrump. A 2♣ response asks the notrump bidder to clarify his point holding: 2◇ = 16, 2♡ = 17, 2♠ = 18, 2 NT = 19. After this exchange, a 3♣ bid asks opener to bid a four-card major if he has one, 3◇ otherwise. This convention once was popular in the southern New England area.

GOLDWATER RULE. The satirical suggestion by Tournament Director HARRY A. GOLDWATER that an opening lead out of turn should generally be accepted (see LAW 56 for declarer's other options). The rationale is that a player who does not know whose turn it is to lead probably doesn't know the right lead either.

GOLF. As many bridge-players also play golf, combined golf and bridge events are sometimes popular. An English plan conceived by D. Garfitt Clowes is to matchpoint the golf in the same way that a bridge event is scored (ten or more strokes on a hole counts as an automatic *bottom* or shared *bottom*). These

scores are then divided by two, and the same pairs play a HOWELL or SCRAMBLED MITCHELL event to determine the winner on the combined scores.

GOOD. An adjective used to describe a hand which is better than the simple POINT-COUNT would suggest, as in "a good 18". This may be owing to distributional factors, to the presence of BODY, to the location of honors in long suits, or to a combination of these items.

GOOD CARDS. Cards which have been established during the play and which are winners that can be cashed.

In a wide sense, a player of a partnership holding good cards has more than a fair share of the honor strength.

But the term is sometimes used in a more precise technical meaning, referring to honor cards which have improved in value as a result of the auction. In a competitive auction, the improvement may arise because the significant honors are over the opponent who has bid the suit (see POSITIONAL FACTOR).

GOODWILL COMMITTEE. This committee was organized by the ACBL in 1955 with JOHN E. SIMON as chairman and LOUISE DURHAM as co-chairman. In 1957 the committee was made permanent, with two members, one man and one woman, being appointed from each District by the District Director to hold permanent membership in the Committee. In 1959 gold lapel pins were approved for all members of the Committee. In 1963 three assistant chairmen were designated: ETHEL KEOHANE (East), LOUISE DURHAM (Central) and EVELYN PIRO (West). In 1972 JOHN T. MURPHY (Canada) was added as another assistant chairman. The present make-up of the Committee consists of eight assistants—five in the United States, two in Canada (East and West) and one in Mexico.

In 1975 JEROME SILVERMAN succeeded John Simon as chairman, who became Honorary Chairman Emeritus. In 1977 Kay Moody became chairman. In 1979 DR. JOHN M. PRATT was named chairman.

GOREN AWARD. Endowed by Charles H. Goren, this award for the Bridge Personality of the Year is presented annually by the INTERNATIONAL BRIDGE PRESS ASSOCIATION. It is made to the person deemed most worthy of recognition as an outstanding bridge personality. The Award is made annually but it is not restricted to achievement during the period in question: account may be taken of the entire bridge career of the nominee. For a list of winners see INTERNATIONAL BRIDGE PRESS ASSOCIATION AWARDS.

GOREN POINT-COUNT. See POINT-COUNT and DISTRIBUTIONAL POINT-COUNT.

GOREN SYSTEM. The bidding methods advocated by CHARLES H. GOREN in his many books since 1944. The method incorporated the GOREN POINT COUNT in which an ace equals 4 points, a king 3, a queen 2 and a jack 1. In addition, a void counts for 3 points, a singleton for 2 and a doubleton for 1. The value of a hand is determined by adding the high card point total to the distributional total. 13–point hands are optional in the system, but 14–point hands *must* be opened. A third-hand opening can be made with as few as 11 points if the hand contains a fairly good suit. A four-hand opening bid should be made on 13 points, even though no good rebid is available. A different valuation system is used for the hand that figures to be dummy. High cards are counted at face value, and honors in partner's suit are promoted by a point each. One point is added for each doubleton, 3 for a singleton and 5 for a void if a fit has been established. A point should be deducted if dummy holds only three trumps, and another point should be subtracted if the dummy hand has a 4-3-3-3 distribution.

Using these methods, Goren determined that 26 points usually will produce game in a major, 29 game in a minor, 33 a small slam and 37 a grand slam.

The Goren System advocates opening 4-card majors as long as the suit is biddable—at least Q–x–x–x. When holding biddable touching suits of equal length, the higher-ranking should be the opening bid. When the two biddable suits of equal length are spades and clubs, the opening bid should be 1♣. In other combinations, the suit below the short suit should be the opening bid.

With balanced hands, responder should bid 1 NT with 6–10 points, 2 NT with 13–15 and 3 NT with 16–18. Responder should have the unbid suits stopped for the 2 NT and 3 NT bids. When responder has trump support, he should raise partner's suit to 2 with 7–10 points, to 3 with 13–16 points. Responder should jump shift with 19 or more points. He should respond in a new suit at the one level with 6 or more points. A two-level response in a new suit requires 10 points. With hands containing 11 or 12 points, responder should find two bids without forcing partner to game.

Opening two-bids in a suit should be made with a good five-card suit and 25 points, with a good six-card suit and 23 points, and with a good seven-card suit and 21 points.

Openings in notrump should be based on the following: 1 NT, 16–18 points; 2 NT, 22–24 points; 3 NT, 25–27 points. When evaluating for an opening notrump bid, a player should count only his high card values. A 2♣ response to 1 NT (also a 3♣ response to 2 NT) asks the opening bidder about his biddable major suits. With no four-card major, opener should rebid 2◊; with a four-card heart suit, 2♡; with a four-card spade suit or two four-card majors, 2♠.

GOREN TROPHY. Awarded for the North American Championship Men's Teams, donated by CHARLES H. GOREN in 1946. It was contested at the Fall NAC until 1963 and then transferred to the Spring NAC, under which heading past results are listed.

GOULASH. A deal in which the cards are not shuffled, and are dealt five to each player for two circuits, and finally three to each player. The name is apparently derived from Hungarian goulash, a highly spiced mixture of meat and vegetables, and is intended to suggest a spicy and unusual mixture.

Players sometimes agree to play goulash when a hand has been passed out, particularly in private or commuter games. Goulashes are standard in CUT-THROAT BRIDGE and TOWIE.

A more extreme form, known as the *passing goulash*, achieved some popularity in the Twenties and Thirties. Each partner was permitted to pass six cards to his partner after the conclusion of the deal, usually three cards followed by two cards followed by one card.

A goulash is sometimes referred to as *mayonnaise* or *hollandaise*.

GRAND COUP. A play by which declarer deliberately shortens his trump holding by ruffing a winner in order to achieve a finessing position over an adverse trump holding in an end position.

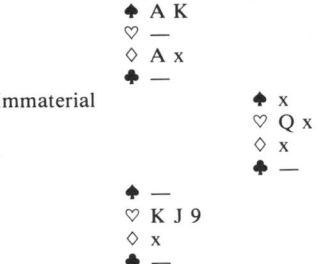

Declarer, in a heart contract, has discovered West to be void of hearts. With the lead in the dummy, declarer leads the ♠A and trumps it. He re-enters dummy with the ◊A to lead any card at trick 12. East must ruff and declarer overruffs.

GRAND MASTER. See WORLD BRIDGE FEDERATION PLAYER RANKINGS.

GRAND NATIONAL CHAMPIONSHIPS. (1) A series of annual championships first held in 1934 by the UNITED STATES BRIDGE ASSOCIATION and continued annually until 1937. For results, see USBA GRAND NATIONALS.

(2) See GRAND NATIONAL PAIRS, GRAND NATIONAL ROOKIE PAIRS, GRAND NATIONAL TEAMS. See also CANADIAN NATIONAL TEAMS.

GRAND NATIONAL PAIRS. This has been a major ACBL open pair championship since 1979. The initial stages of the GNP are conducted over the course of several months of competition at the club, unit and district levels. Each district qualifies three or four pairs for the final held prior to the Spring North American Championships under which heading results are listed. The number is determined by the total entry in the district at the unit level. In August 1978 more than 61,000 pairs entered at the grass roots level for the 1979 championships. In 1981 the total grew to more than 72,000 pairs.

GRAND NATIONAL ROOKIE PAIRS. This has been a major ACBL pair championship since 1979. Competition is limited to ACBL members who have fewer than 20 master points. The initial stage of the GNRP is conducted at the club level for a one-week period in September. Each district qualifies one pair and the 26th pair is qualified from the district which has the greatest participation as a percentage of total ACBL membership in the district. The 26 pairs compete in the two-session final which is held during the Fall North American Championships under which heading the results are listed.

GRAND NATIONAL TEAMS. This major ACBL team championship, contested since 1973 for the MOREHEAD TROPHY, is patterned in many respects after the USBA's earlier event. The initial stages of the GNT are conducted over the course of several months in each ACBL district in the United States, Mexico and Bermuda, for members of units within the district, to produce a district championship team. Canada originally participated in this event, but in 1980 Canada began conducting its own national team championship parallel to the GNT. In 1973 approximately 1,500 teams entered at the grass roots level. In 1980, 6,032 teams entered. The district champions compete within eight Grand National Zones for the Zonal Championship. The final playoffs are contested as knockouts by the eight zonal champions at the Summer North American Championships, under which heading the results are listed. The winning team is entitled to compete against the winners of the SPINGOLD TROPHY, REISINGER TROPHY and VANDERBILT CUP (I) for the right to represent North America or the United States in the WORLD CHAMPIONSHIP two years hence. See INTERNATIONAL OPEN TEAM SELECTION.

GRAND OLD MAN OF BRIDGE. A term applied in the Twenties and early Thirties to MILTON C. WORK and in later years to SIDNEY LENZ.

GRAND SLAM. The winning of all thirteen tricks by the declarer. The bonus for a grand slam, 1,000 points when not vulnerable and 1,500 when vulnerable make a grand slam, bid and made, one of the best rewarded accomplishments at rubber bridge, and one of the more effective methods of SHOOTING at duplicate. While the general tendency among rubber bridge players is to avoid bidding grand slams except in ironclad situations, the mathematics of the game suggest rather freer acceptance of the risks involved in view of the large rewards.

See SLAM BIDDING for an explanation of methods of exploration suitable to bidding grand slams, and the percentage or odds that justify such bids. For a brief period (1932–35) the grand slam bonuses were higher than they are now: 1,500 non-vulnerable, 2,250 vulnerable.

GRAND SLAM FORCE. A method of locating the top trump honors when a grand slam is in view. It was devised by ELY CULBERTSON in 1936, was first described in a *Bridge World* article by JOSEPHINE CULBERTSON, and is often in consequence referred to in Europe as a Josephine.

A bid of 5 NT asks responder to bid a grand slam if he holds two of the top three trump honors. (This clearly does not apply if 5 NT is a natural notrump raise, or if it is used as part of another slam convention.) A jump to 5 NT fixes the last bid suit as trump unless another suit has been specifically agreed.

It is sometimes necessary to know whether responder has one of the top three honors. If the agreed trump suit is not clubs, one or more intermediate bids are available at the six-level for this purpose.

If diamonds are agreed, 6 ◇ should show one top honor. If a major suit has been agreed, several methods are in use, designed to permit a partnership to reach a grand slam missing Q–x–x in the trump suit.

One method is to divide the responses into four steps. The first step would show the weakest trump holding for the previous bidding (three or four small), the second step would show the queen, the third step the ace or king and the fourth step the ace or king with extra length. If hearts are agreed, the first and second steps are combined into one. If diamonds are the agreed suit, the first and second steps and the third and fourth steps are combined. For example,

```
                 NORTH
                 ♠ K 5 3 2
                 ♡ 6 5 4
                 ◇ 8 5 3
                 ♣ 10 7 2

                 SOUTH
                 ♠ A 10 9 8 6 4
                 ♡ A K
                 ◇ A K Q 9 7
                 ♣ —

        SOUTH            NORTH
        2 ♠              4 ♠
        5 NT             6 ♡
        7 ♠
```

North's jump raise shows four spades, and his step response to the grand slam force shows the king. Since there is unlikely to be a trump loser, South bids the grand slam.

An alternate expert method, perhaps superior theoretically, is to sign off in the trump suit with the worst trump holding; other responses at the six-level are made inversely, the higher the bid the weaker the trump holding. In order to retain all four steps to show gradation of trump quality even when a suit other than spades has been agreed, some partnerships use jumps to five of the suit above the agreed trump suit, rather than to 5 NT as the grand slam force.

The grand slam force can also be used in conjunction with Blackwood. The ROMEX system uses a bid of 5 NT as the grand slam force even after 4 NT has been used as Blackwood. It is more common, however, for partnerships to use the MALOWAN SIX CLUB CONVENTION to ask about trump honors. After the conventional response to Blackwood a bid of 6 ♣ is the grand slam force, providing clubs are not agreed.

In some systems, such as SCHENKEN, it is possible to agree on a trump suit and cue-bid first- and possibly second-round controls before 4 NT is reached. RICHARD P. REED, Boulder CO, suggests that 4 NT should then be used to pinpoint trump honors. Partner returns to the agreed trump suit with none of the top three honors, bids the lowest-ranking side suit with the king or queen, the next ranking side suit with the ace, the highest-ranking side suit with two of the top three honors, and 5 NT with full control of the trump suit. See also BYZANTINE BLACKWOOD; TRUMP ASKING BIDS.

GREECE. See HELLENIC BRIDGE FEDERATION.

GREEN SUIT. The fifth suit in the American version of FIVE-SUIT BRIDGE, called Eagles. Prior to the introduction of five-suit bridge, the green suit was a nonexistent fifth suit. See HIPPOGRIFFS.

GROSVENOR GAMBIT. A humorous psychological ploy described by Frederick Turner of Los Angeles in *The Bridge World* in June 1973. A defender deliberately makes a clear error, giving the declarer an opportunity which he will refuse to take because he expects rational defense. The hope is that the declaring side will be demoralised on later deals. For example:

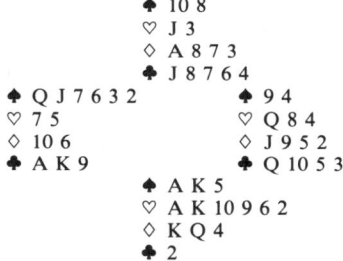

Two top clubs are led against 6 ♡. South ruffs and plays spades, ruffing the third round in dummy. Instead of overruffing East discards. His trick comes back because South plays top trumps, sure that West has the queen.

GROUP SCORE. The score made by all the pairs in a group on a set of hands constituting a match. Competition between clubs and cities is sometimes based on a team of eight, twelve, or an even larger number of players. In such a game, each pair from one side meets each of the pairs on the competing side, all playing the same set of boards. The net score (plus and minus) of all pairs is included in the group score.

Also, in total point pair contests, the net score on a set of boards on which two particular pairs are in opposition.

GUARD (or Stopper). An honor holding in a particular suit which will or may prevent the opponents running the suit.

A guard may be:
(1) Positive: A, K-Q, Q-J-10, J-10-9-8.
(2) Probable: K-J-x, K-10-x, Q-J-x.
(3) Possible: Q-x-x, J-9-x-x.

(4) Positional: K-x.
(5) Partial: K, Q-x, J-x-x, 10-x-x-x.

GUARD SQUEEZE. A squeeze in three suits, in which an opponent holds guards in two suits, and his holding in a third suit prevents declarer from taking a winning finesse.

There are five basic endings, each of which resembles the basic double squeeze position. By contrast with the double squeeze, the guard squeeze takes place when the same opponent controls both isolated menaces, but as compensation the double menace contains finesse possibilities.

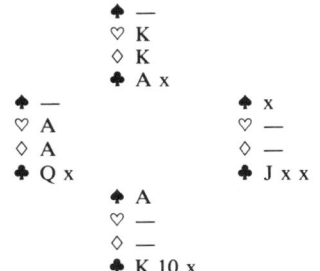

South leads the ♣ A, and West is squeezed in three suits. He must discard a club, but South leads a club to the ace (dropping the queen) and finesses the 10 on the way back.

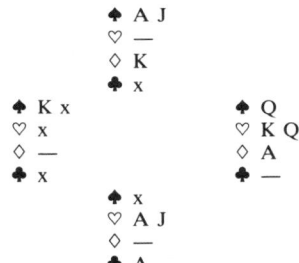

South leads the ♣ A, and East is squeezed in three suits. If he discards a spade, South can lead that suit, and finesse the jack.

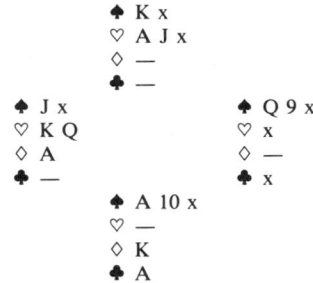

South leads the ♣ A and West is squeezed in three suits. If he discards a spade, South leads a spade to the king (dropping the jack) and finesses the 10 on the way back.

In each of the above positions the squeeze retains its effectiveness even if one of the isolated menaces is guarded by both opponents. This leads to a *double guard squeeze* whose constituents are a guard squeeze against one opponent and a simple squeeze against the other.

There are two other double guard squeeze positions:

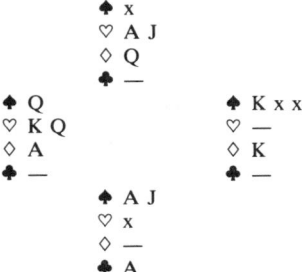

South leads the ♣A, and West is squeezed in three suits. He must discard a diamond. Now the ♡A squeezes East in spades and diamonds.

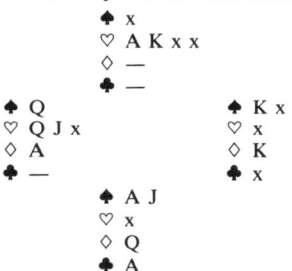

South leads the ♣A, and West is squeezed in three suits. He is forced to discard a diamond. South takes two top hearts, squeezing East in spades and diamonds.

See HEXAGON SQUEEZE; HEXAGON TRUMP SQUEEZE; TRUMP SQUEEZE.

Monroe Ingberman

GUARDED HONOR or GUARDED SUIT. See GUARD.

GUIDE CARD. A card, usually printed, with prearranged instructions to each contestant, telling him which seat to occupy and which boards to play at each round. The guide card may also enable a contestant to check the positions and identities of his opponents.

Guide cards may be in the form of printed instruction cards remaining permanently at each table (suitable only for cyclic movements); or they may be in the form of separate cards to be hand-carried by each contestant (suitable for either cyclic or noncyclic movements).

Guide cards are used for HOWELL MOVEMENT pair games, team games, and individual contests.

H

HALF TABLES. An extra pair at a duplicate game. To accommodate the pair and still keep the game a fair contest requires a choice of methods by the director. The choice is based on the size of the game, the movement in use, and the time when it becomes

known that a half-table situation exists. Two major possibilities exist for HOWELL or THREE-QUARTER MOVEMENT games. If it is known in advance that a half-table situation exists, the director will consider that he has a full table and run the movement with a PHANTOM pair. Any pair scheduled to play the phantom pair will have a sit-out for that round. If the half-table situation evolves after the game is underway, it is best to use an APPENDIX TABLE. If the MITCHELL MOVEMENT is being used, several options usually are available.

If the game is being run as a Mitchell movement, the director is likely to make different choices based on whether or not he knows about the half-table situation prior to the start of the game. For example, if the director knows he has 8½ tables as the boards are being distributed, he probably will run the game on a nine-table movement with pairs in the opposite direction sitting out when they play the phantom #9. However, if the extra pair arrives during the first round when a nine-table game already is in progress, then the director no doubt will use a ROVING PAIR. Few problems are caused if an extra half table is added during the first round, but it is strongly recommended that no additional pairs be added once the first move has been made.

The ACBL has guide cards for half-table games which are available upon request. Following are suggestions for half-table movements. No attempt has been made to include all the possibilities. However, it will be pointed out when one movement is clearly superior to the others.

2½ tables — Run a three-table Howell. If the game has already started, let the late pair sit out the first round and bump all the other pairs in order.

3½ tables — Run a four-table Howell. This is one time, and the only time we know of, that it is advisable to stop the game and restart if the half table comes in late. A regular appendix won't work.

4½ tables — Run a five-table Howell. If the half table comes in during the first round, use an appendix at any table other than Table 1.

5½ tables — Use the six-table Three-Quarter. If the half table comes in late, append any table where there is no stationary pair. If you have a Mitchell movement, a Roving pair will work well, or set up a relay between Tables 1 and 6 with bye boards between Tables 3 and 4. The phantom pair should be North–South 6; East–West pairs sit out when they reach Table 6.

6½ tables — The best movement is the seven-table Howell. If the half table comes in late, append the pair to any table in the six-table Three-Quarter movement where there is no stationary pair. With a Mitchell movement, put out four boards at each table and have the pair at Table 7 sit out the first round. If the phantom pair is North–South, the East–West pairs will sit out when they arrive at Table 7. If the phantom pair is East–West, the North–South pairs will sit out when they are scheduled to meet East–West 7. If the game already has started when the extra pair arrives, use the Roving Pair method.

7½ tables — Use the eight-table Three-Quarter. If the pair comes in late, append the half table to any table not having a stationary. If a Mitchell movement is planned, use the eight-table movement with a relay between Tables 1 and 8 with bye boards between Tables 4 and 5. The phantom pair should be North–South 8. A Roving Pair probably is best if a seven-table Mitchell is already in progress.

8½ tables — Use the nine-table Three-Quarter or append to any table not having a stationary pair. If you know before the game starts that you have a half table, the best movement is a nine-table Mitchell. Put out boards on all tables and have one of the pairs sit out at Table 9. If the phantom pair is North–South 9 the East–West pairs will sit out when they reach Table 9. If the phantom pair is East–West, the North–South pairs will sit out when they are scheduled to play East–West 9. If the extra pair arrives after the game is underway, use the Roving Pair method.

9½ tables — Use the 10-table Three-Quarter movement with a phantom pair or the nine-table Three-Quarter with an appendix at any table having two moving pairs. If the Mitchell movement is used, the best alternative, if time permits playing 10 rounds, is a relay between Tables 1 and 10 with bye boards between Tables 5 and 6. The phantom should be pair 10 North–South. The ACBL has a guide card movement for an East–West Roving Pair movement. A 10-table Mitchell with the phantom pair at North–South 10 and a skip after the fifth round, also is feasible, but boards and pairs must be factored.

10½ tables — A Three-Quarter movement is uncommon with this many tables but it is possible to set up for an 11-table Three-Quarter with a phantom pair or append a 10-table Three-Quarter at any table where there is no stationary pair. The best movements are a 10½ table Roving Pair or BUMP MITCHELL.

11½ tables — It's possible to use the 12-table Three-Quarter with a phantom or to append a pair to the 11-table Three-Quarter. Best is the Roving Pair or Bump Mitchell. A good alternative is a 12-table game with a relay between Tables 1 and 12. The phantom pair is North–South 12. Put bye boards between Tables 6 and 7.

12½ tables — It is possible to append a 12-table Three-Quarter. The best movement is to set up a 13-table Mitchell with a phantom pair at Table 13. If the phantom pair is North–South the East–West pairs sit out when they reach Table 13. If the phantom pair is East–West the North–South pairs sit out when they are scheduled to play against East–West 13. A Roving Pair will work very well and should be used if the half table comes in late.

13½ tables — The best movement is a Roving Pair. A Bump Mitchell will work but the game will have to be curtailed. For 14 rounds set up a relay between Tables 1 and 14 and bye boards between Tables 7 and 8. The phantom pair should be North–South 14. East–West pairs sit out when they reach Table 14.

14½ tables — The best movement is the Roving Pair or Bump Mitchell. Either will work easily and well.

15½ tables — The best movement is a Bump Mitchell. The Roving Pair requires special movements after certain rounds.

HALF TRICK. An original holding in a suit that will win a trick by virtue of being a high card about half the time. A queen held in company with an ace of the same suit, or a king with a guard, is a half trick on original valuation. The position of adverse bids as the bidding progresses may add to or detract from such a valuation.

HALL OF FAME. A plan for commemorating the achievements of outstanding bridge personalities, suggested by LEE HAZEN, New York NY, and inaugurated in 1964 by *The Bridge World*. The first three members elected were ELY CULBERTSON, CHARLES GOREN, and HAROLD VANDERBILT; the next three were OSWALD JACOBY, SIDNEY LENZ, and MILTON WORK. The plan is no longer in effect.

HAMILTON CLUB (London). One of the leading English card clubs, founded by COL. HENRY M. BEASLEY, 1939, in association with Carl Repelaer, who continued to manage the club after Beasley's death in 1949. The club was closed in the early Seventies; it had included among its members leading English players, such as LESLIE W. DODDS, JORDANIS T. PAVLIDES, and RIXI MARKUS, who contributed to the development of the CAB SYSTEM. The club was regularly visited by American experts.

HAND. (1) A particular deal of 52 cards. (2) The cards held by one player. The term is also used to indicate the order in bidding rotation, as in "second hand" or "fourth hand."

HAND DISTRIBUTIONS. See HAND PATTERNS for general and specific distributions. See MATHEMATICAL TABLES for percentage frequency and distributions.

HAND HOG. A player who (often mistakenly) feels that he is the best qualified to manage the hands as declarer. The usual method of operation is to pass with minimum opening bids but to respond with jumps in notrump.

HAND PATTERNS. There are 39 possible hand patterns, ranging from the most balanced, 4-3-3-3, to the most unbalanced, 13-0-0-0. A player can hold specifically four spades, three hearts, three diamonds and three clubs in 13C4 × 13C3 × 13C3 × 13C3 different ways, which computes to 16,726,464,040 or 2.634% of the 635,013,559,600 hands he could hold (see NUMBER OF POSSIBLE HANDS). This, of course, is not the percentage probability that he will have a 4-3-3-3 hand, because the four card length need not be in spades, but could be in any of the four suits, so the chance of a 4-3-3-3 hand is 10.536%.

A rearrangement of the suits in a particular distributional pattern is termed a *permutation* of the pattern; 4-3-4-2 is a permutation of a 4-4-3-2 pattern. If we use the same letter of the alphabet to indicate the same length in a suit, there are three classes of hands:

AAAB, such as 4-3-3-3 or 4-4-4-1, etc.,
which has 4 permutations

AABC, such as 4-4-3-2 or 5-5-2-1, etc.,
which has 12 permutations
ABCD, such as 5-4-3-1 or 7-3-2-1, etc.,
which has 24 permutations
Thus, the probability of five spades, four hearts, three diamonds and one club is .539%, but the probability of some 5-4-3-1 distribution is 24 times as great, or 12.931%. For all possible hand patterns, see MATHEMATICAL TABLES, Table 1.

Alec Traub and Roy Tefler

HAND RECORDS. (1) Diagrams set up by the players after a deal in a major match is completed; (2) the sheets on which individual computer-dealt hands are printed for distribution to players for duplication; (3) the sheets distributed to players at the conclusion of a game on which all the hands from that session are printed.

In some tournaments, particularly in Europe, the players make a record of each hand after they have played it on the first round. This card is then placed with the hand in the pocket, and can be used by succeeding players to check whether the cards they hold are the ones that were originally dealt into that hand. Such hand records are known as CURTAIN CARDS.

HANDBOOK, ACBL. See ACBL HANDBOOK.

HANDICAPPED PLAYERS. A number of bridge players have overcome serious physical handicaps to become high-ranking players. There are a number of BLIND PLAYERS who have earned LIFE MASTER status. The late FRED SNITE played from an iron lung. Polio victim Robert Penn was transported to a Honolulu tournament in his wheelchair with a mechanical respirator attached. Morris Ribyat earned his LM Gold Card in 1962, 15 years after he became a victim of multiple sclerosis. Paralyzed from the neck down since a car accident in 1959, Life Master Walter Lewis of Pascagoula MS won all four events at an Alabama sectional in 1976. Martha Newbill, longtime Life Master from New Port Richey FL, plays from a wheelchair.

But most outstanding among the players who participate from wheelchairs is HERMINE BARON, who twice won the McKenney Trophy, setting a record in 1964. She represented the United States in international competition in 1968, 1978 and 1982 and is second on the list of ACBL members with the greatest total points, having achieved 20,490 by 1983.

Born armless, Life Master MIKE WILSON of Vancouver plays bridge using his toes. BILLY GOUGH of Oreland PA, a Life Master with 6400 points and a qualified director, is a muscular dystrophy victim. PAT O'BRIEN a Life Master with 3000 points and a certified director, is a hemophiliac.

A victim of kidney disease, Roberta Runion became a Life Master at a Wichita KS regional while taking three dialysis treatments a week. John Helfrich, born with only one kidney, also underwent dialysis treatments and eventually had a transplant. He became a Life Master in 1983 at a Jackson MS regional where he also served as tournament chairman.

ACBL member Athan Cosmas devised card holders to assist players with arthritic fingers and those who may have been injured.

HANDICAPPING. A method of scoring in which each contestant is given a handicap (either plus or minus) based on previous performance or degree of competence. In the past in the ACBL, handicaps were used only to determine who won the JACKPOT — master points were never based on handicaps. However, this was changed in 1980. At that time, the League strongly urged its member clubs to consider using a handicap method in order to create more interest among the less experienced and less talented players. The plan most often used divides the master points available for a club game into two, with half going to those who have the best raw scores and the other half going to those who have the best handicap scores. The most common form of handicap used is one based on an average of past performances matched against an almost unattainable par of .650. This method requires additional work on the part of the club manager or director, but it is more equitable because the handicaps are based on results, avoiding claims of favoritism. This system is similar to the computation of averages in bowling, providing for a rapid change in handicap, up or down on the basis of recent result. The handicap is computed on the basis of 90% or 100% of the difference between the player's average performance and an artificial par established at 65% of possible.

It is also possible to handicap according to rank. Using this system, the sum of the handicaps of the partners constitutes the handicap for the pair. Because some players in such games do not hold ACBL rank, the ACBL recommends that the club manager or director arbitrarily assign such players to the MASTER classification.

Handicapping also is frequently used to make the sale of weaker teams more productive in a CALCUTTA tournament.

HANDLING CARDS. The handling of cards other than a player's own is improper. At duplicate, a player may ask to see his opponent's (or his partner's) card, and the player involved will turn it for him. There are some players who take a hand belonging to another player out of the board after play has been completed in order to discuss a matter of bidding or play. This practice is officially discouraged and is illegal if the opponents are not present. It is the cause of most fouled boards.

HANDS NOT PLAYED OUT. Hands can be concluded before the last trick for various reasons. Frequently declarer will table his hand and make a CLAIM, even as early as after the opening lead. He should then make a statement of how he would play if he actually continued the physical motions of doing so, and if the line he intends to follow seems reasonable to the opposition and is not susceptible of any challenge by them, then the cards can be thrown in. See CLAIM OR CONCESSION.

HEAD-TO-HEAD. A term used to describe any match in bridge of pre-arranged set opposition; that is, one team of four or more against another of the same number. Use of the term is restricted to two-team contests only.

HEART. The symbol ♡ for the second-ranking suit in bridge. Hearts are between spades and diamonds in value. The suit designation originated in France in the sixteenth century and takes its name from the shape of the pips used in designating card rank.

HEART SUIT. The second-ranking suit, with scarlet pips on each card in the shape of a heart. The suit ranks just below spades in bidding, and above diamonds.

HEARTBREAKER. A term applied to a hand that fails in a big way to live up to one's original expectations of it. It can be a defensive hand where one has, for example, been dealt cards that enable one to double a certain final contract with the assurance of setting the opponents badly. If, because of the distributional situations or highly expert card play by declarer, the contract is made, then surely the "heartbreaker" term would follow, If, on the other hand, one is declarer at a contract that seems sure of success, and especially if the contract is a slam or a doubled or redoubled game bid, and is unable to make the hand or to avoid a large set in the process, then that hand is often called a "heartbreaker," too. Also applied to a session of duplicate which promises more than it achieves: in a head-to-head team match a pair may outplay their immediate opponents only to find their team score is negative.

HEDGEHOG SQUEEZES. Hedgehog squeezes were named and analyzed by Hugh Darwen in the *(British) Bridge Magazine*, March 1968 and April 1968. A hedgehog squeeze is a squeeze of one opponent in two or three suits and a squeeze of the other opponent in three suits. These are the basic endings:

I. Single hedgehogs

　1. Non-Simultaneous guard hedgehog

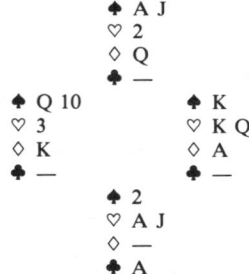

On the lead of the ♣A, West and North discard hearts, and East is squeezed out of the ◇A. Now the lead of the ♡A squeezes West in spades and diamonds.

　　2. Simultaneous guard hedgehog
(See hand at top of right column.)

The lead of the ♣A squeezes West out of the ◇A, North discards the ♡K, and East is squeezed in spades and diamonds.

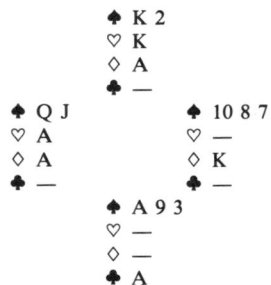

3. Blocked guard hedgehog

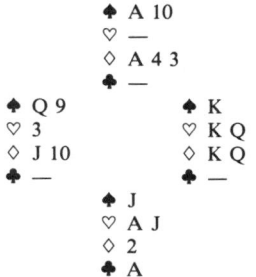

On the ♣A lead, West discards a heart, North discards a diamond, and East is squeezed out of a diamond. Now the lead of the ◇A squeezes West in spades and diamonds.

4. Automatic clash hedgehog

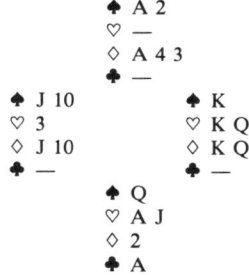

On the ♣A lead, West discards a heart, North discards a diamond, and East is squeezed out of a diamond. Now the lead of the ♡A squeezes West in spades and diamonds.

5. One-way clash hedgehog

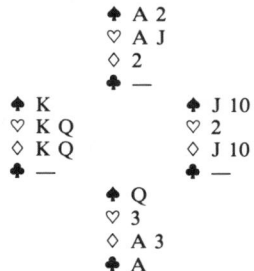

The lead of the ♣A squeezes West out of a diamond, while North and East discard hearts. Now the lead of the ♡A squeezes East in spades and diamonds.

II. Double hedgehogs (also known as "hexagon squeezes")

    1. Double guard hedgehog

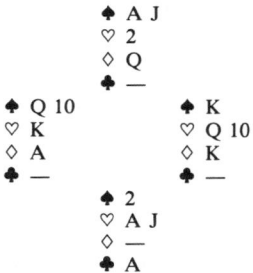

    The lead of the ♣A squeezes West out of the ◊A, North discards the ♡2, and East is squeezed in three suits.

    2. Double clash hedgehog

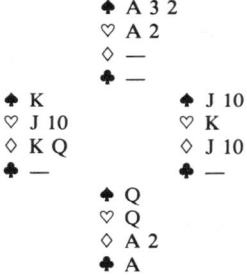

    The lead of the ♣A forces West to discard a diamond, North discards the ♠2, and East is squeezed in three suits.

    3. Hybrid double hedgehog

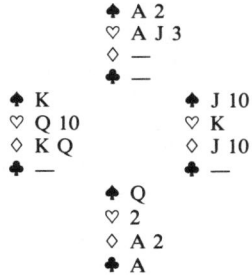

    The lead of the ♣A forces West to discard a diamond, North discards the ♡3, and East is squeezed in three suits.

III. Progressive hedgehogs

    1. Guard/guard progressive hedgehog

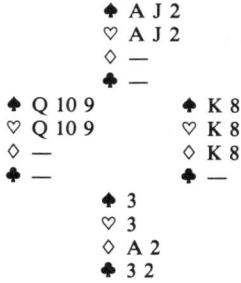

When South cashes his clubs, West, North, and East must discard one card from each major. Now the ◊A squeezes West in the majors.

    2. Clash/clash progressive hedgehog

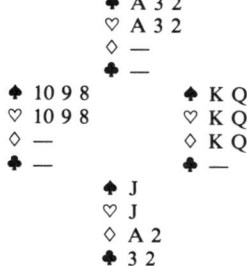

The play is the same as in diagram 1.

    3. Clash/guard progressive hedgehog (type 1)

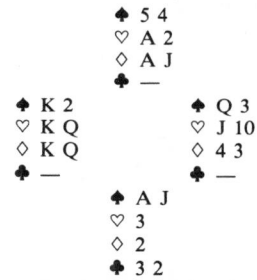

When South cashes his two clubs, West must discard a card in each major, North discards a spade then a diamond (unless West discards a diamond), and East discards two diamonds. Now the lead of a diamond to the ◊A squeezes East in the majors.

    4. Clash/guard progressive hedgehog (type 2)

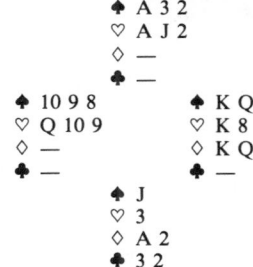

When South cashes his clubs, East is compelled to discard a card in each major. Now the lead of the ◊A squeezes West in the majors.

HELLENIC BRIDGE FEDERATION. The national bridge organization of Greece, it was founded in 1965 by two clubs with approximately 320 members; in 1975 it had nine clubs as members, and three as affiliated organizations. The Federation participates in the European Championships, hosting the 1971 event in Athens, and participated in the 1968 World Team Olympiad. National events include Open Pair and Team Championships.

Officers, 1982:
President: Evangelos C. Glykis

Secretary: J. Kavadias, 6 Evripidou Street, Athens 122, Greece

HELP SUIT GAME TRY. See WEAK SUIT GAME TRY.

HERBERT NEGATIVE. The idea that a negative response in a variety of situations can be made by making the cheapest possible suit response. It was advocated by WALTER HERBERT when he was a member of the Austrian national team, and was applied in many ways in the VIENNA SYSTEM. Some of its many possible applications include: response to FORCING TWO-BID; response to TAKEOUT DOUBLE; response to ACOL TWO-BID; as a SECOND NEGATIVE response to a strong forcing opening.

HERMAN TROPHY. This trophy, awarded to the player with the best overall individual performance record at the Fall North American Championships, was donated by Sally Lipton (formerly Mrs. Lou Herman) of New York, in 1952, in memory of her husband. The recipients of this award 1952 through 1962 were:

1952 Alvin Roth	1958 Sylvia Stein
1953 John R. Crawford	1959 Morton L. Rubinow
1954 Paul H. Hodge	1960 Oswald Jacoby
1955 Milton Q. Ellenby	1961 Philip Feldesman
1956 Paul H. Hodge	1962 Marshall Miles
1957 Lewis L. Mathe	

The following are the Herman Trophy winners since 1962, together with their point totals.

1963 Eric R. Murray	211	1972 Steve W. Robinson	181
1964 Dr. Harold Rockaway	180	1973 Larry Cohen	207
1965 Michael S. Lawrence	211	1974 Fred Hamilton	202
1966 Charles Coon	144	1975 Walter J. Walvick	171
1967 Sammy R. Kehela	155	1976 Paul Soloway	199
1968 Henry Bethe	144	1977 John A. Mohan	160
1969 Sylvia Stein	150	1978 Robert D. Hamman	165
1970 Ira S. Rubin (tied		1979 Bobby Levin	233
with) Chuck Burger	154	1980 Jeff Meckstroth	225
1971 John M. Grantham	150	1981 Chip Martel	224

HESITATION. See HUDDLE.

HEXAGON SQUEEZE. A double guard squeeze in which each of the three menaces is protected by both opponents. (Analyzed and named by GEORGE COFFIN.)

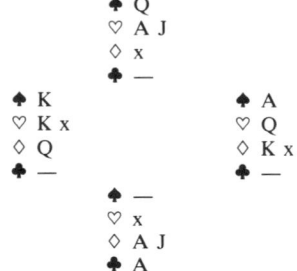

South leads the ♣A, and West must discard a spade. North discards a diamond, and East is squeezed in three suits. Once West discards his spade, East is caught in a standard guard squeeze. See also BARCO SQUEEZE.

HEXAGON TRUMP SQUEEZE. A HEXAGON SQUEEZE in which both of the opponents are trump squeezed.

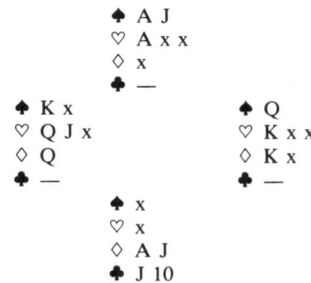

South is on lead needing all the tricks; clubs are trumps. South leads the ♣J. West must discard a heart, dummy can discard a diamond, and East is squeezed in three suits. If East discards a spade, West can be finessed. East obviously cannot discard a diamond, and if he lets go a heart, the ♡A and a heart ruff will establish an extra heart trick.

Alternatively, when West discards a heart on the ♣J, suppose North and East both discard spades. South leads to the ♡A and ruffs a heart. A spade to the ace then squeezes East in hearts and diamonds. In this variation the squeeze of East occurs three tricks later than the squeeze of West.

Robert True

HIDDEN ENTRY. A low card, usually in the dummy hand, by which an entry may be made, usually established as such through the play of unnecessarily high cards by the declarer. Thus, if dummy has A-Q-10-6 and declarer K-J-9-5, the 6 may be set up as an entry by playing the king to the same trick as the ace, the jack to the same trick as the queen, and the 9 to the same trick as the ten.

HIGH CARD. A ranking card; an honor card; a card that wins a trick by virtue of its being higher in pip value than the other three cards in the trick. A spot card which becomes the master card in the suit is said to be high.

HIGH CARD POINT PROBABILITIES. Average High Card Point (HCP) counts are easy to calculate. Before any cards are seen, the average HCP count for any one hand is 10 and the average HCP count for a partnership is 20. (This is based on the popular count of ace = 4, king = 3, queen = 2, jack = 1.) If a player has seen that his hand has X HCPs but has no information about the strength of any other hand, then on the average the remaining high card points are split equally among the other three hands, giving an average HCP count of $(1/3)(40 - X)$ for each. However, averages do not say very much because hands so often vary from the averages. Probabilities can be calculated for the various possible HCP counts, and the appended tables present the results of these calculations.

Table 1 is largely self-explanatory, but it is important to note that its probabilities apply only when there is no information about the strength of any hand. Many bridge players complain that it is hard to get a decent hand. Table 1 shows that the probability of 11 or fewer HCPs is 65.183%, so about 2/3 of all hands are too weak to open at the one level. Those opening 1 NT on 15-17 HCPs can see from Table 1 that the probability of an HCP count in this range is 4.424% + 3.311% + 2.362% = 10.097%.

Table 2 is largely self-explanatory, but it is important to note that its probabilities apply only when there is no information about the strength of any hand. Table 2 shows that the probability of 26 or more HCP in a partnership's hands is 100.000% -87.354% = 12.646%, or about one deal in eight. Similarly, the probability of 33 or more HCP in a partnership is 100.000% - 99.652% = .348%, or about one deal in 300. Also, the probability of 37 or more HCP in a partnership is 100.000% - 99.991% = .009%, or about one deal in 10,000. Readers can calculate the probabilities of other numbers of HCP for game or slam after allowing for their judgments of how many distributional points are present.

Table 1
Probabilities of High Card Point Counts for One Hand

HCP	Percentage	HCP	Percentage
0*	.364	19	1.036
1	.788	20	.644
2	1.356	21	.378
3	2.462	22	.210
4	3.845	23	.112
5	5.186	24	.056
6	6.554	25	.026
7	8.028	26	.012
8	8.892	27	.0049
9	9.356	28	.0019
10	9.405	29	.00067
11	8.945	30	.00022
12	8.027	31	.00006
13	6.914	32	.00002
14	5.693	33	.000004
15	4.424	34	.0000007
16	3.311	35	.0000001
17	2.362	36	.000000009
18	1.605	37**	.0000000006

Table 2
Probabilities of High Card Point Counts for a Partnership

HCP	Percentage	HCP	Percentage
0	.00005		
1	.0005	21	8.047
2	.002	22	7.566
3	.006	23	6.831
4	.018	24	5.907
5	.043	25	4.892
6	.093	26	3.883
7	.186	27	2.943
8	.341	28	2.124
9	.588	29	1.463
10	.955	30	.955
11	1.463	31	.588
12	2.124	32	.341
13	2.943	33	.186
14	3.883	34	.093
15	4.892	35	.043
16	5.907	36	.018
17	6.831	37	.006
18	7.566	38	.002
19	8.047	39	.0005
20	8.222	40	.00005

Bertrand N. Bauer

*The probability of a yarborough (no card higher than a 9) is 0.054703%. The probability of a square yarborough (4-3-3-3 suit distribution and no card higher than a 9) is 0.007744%.

HIGH CARD POINTS. A basis for determining the relative strength of a hand, especially for notrump contracts. The most common method for figuring high card points is as follows: Ace = 4, king = 3, queen = 2, Jack = 1. Many authorities also count an extra point for holding all four aces and a half a point for each 10. Most of the schemes for opening notrumps are based on this count.

The total of high card points, taking into consideration suit lengths, often is used as a basis for opening the bidding with a suit bid. Usually a hand that contains a total of 13 points in combined high card plus distributional points is considered an opening bid; a 12-point hand usually is considered optional.

CHARLES GOREN is credited with popularizing the point-count method of bidding. Bridge players everywhere suddenly found that they could estimate the strength of their hand reasonably accurately by using this method. Nowhere has this been more apparent than in notrump bidding. Goren told his students that 26 high card points in the partnership hands usually would be enough to produce game, and statistical studies have proved him correct.

The 4-3-2-1 method of evaluating high cards is not the only one that has been promulgated. Since it is acknowledged that the ace is somewhat undervalued using this count, there also have been adherents of a 6-4-2-1 count. Another that has had its share of popularity is the 3-2-1-½ count. But the method used by the vast majority of players all over the world is the 4-3-2-1. Although it may not be the most accurate, it certainly is easy to use and is accurate enough to get a partnership to the correct bidding level the vast majority of the time.

HIGH-CARD TRICK. A term originally used to denote a trick won with an honor. The phrase had some currency in the OFFICIAL SYSTEM.

HIGH-LOW SIGNAL. Known also as echo or come-on, the high-low signal is probably the most important single weapon that the defenders possess in their arsenal of aggressive warfare. In its normal, recurring application, the high-low signal in a suit expresses the desire for a continuation of that suit, or an interest in that suit being played when partner obtains the lead. For example:

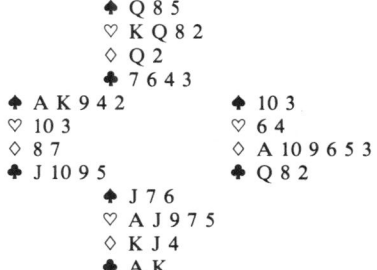

**A hand cannot have more than 37 high card points without exceeding 13 cards.

Against South's 4♡ contract, West opens the ♠K, dummy plays the 5-spot, and East puts up the *10*, South dropping the 6. West then continues with the ♠A, upon which East drops the 3-spot. Observing that East has played high-low, urging the continuation of the spade suit. West plays a third round of spades, East trumping. The ◇A is then cashed, for the setting trick.

Where the high-low signal is initiated by an unusually high card — such as the ♠10 in the above deal — it is of course rather simple for partner to recognize. But, on frequent occasions, one is not dealt an unusually high card as the top half of the doubleton and is forced to originate the signal with a low card. However, on the continuation of the suit, when a lower card is played, the high-low signal becomes unmistakable. Here is an illustration, taken from a tournament.

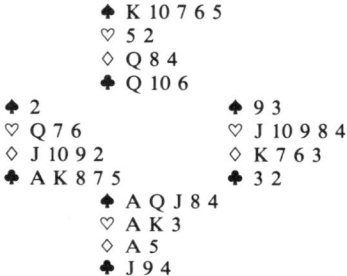

```
        ♠ K 10 7 6 5
        ♡ 5 2
        ◇ Q 8 4
        ♣ Q 10 6
♠ 2                    ♠ 9 3
♡ Q 7 6                ♡ J 10 9 8 4
◇ J 10 9 2             ◇ K 7 6 3
♣ A K 8 7 5           ♣ 3 2
        ♠ A Q J 8 4
        ♡ A K 3
        ◇ A 5
        ♣ J 9 4
```

Against South's 4♠ contract, West leads the ♣K, East playing the 3-spot. On this trick South drops the jack.

An unobservant West would probably now shift to the ◇J, thereby allowing declarer to fulfill his contract. But our actual West defender observed that the ♣2 was missing. Either declarer still had that card, or third-hand had initiated a high-low signal with the 3-spot. So West now led the ♣A, upon which East played the missing 2-spot. A third round of clubs was of course ruffed by East, and the 4♠ contract was ultimately defeated.

From East's point of view, it would have been nicer to have held, let us say, the ♣8–2 instead of the 3–2, so that a more violent signal could have been given with the 8-spot. But a high-low signal with the 3–2 nevertheless accomplished the purpose, thanks to West's observation. For alternative methods of signaling, see ODD-EVEN DISCARDS; UPSIDE-DOWN SIGNALS.

Unfortunately, as with all conventions, the high-low signal is often applied promiscuously, or misapplied, and is given merely because it is the "orthodox" thing to do. One sometimes forgets that the signal is given to get partner to continue the suit led *only* if it will attain an objective for the defenders. Here is an example of the misuse of the high-low signal.

West opened the ◇K against South's 4♠ contract, and East mechanically played the 8-spot. West then continued with the ace, East dropping the 2, after which a third diamond was led, East ruffing. From here in declarer had no problem. He drew trumps, and discarded his ♣J on dummy's high ◇Q.

On the opening lead of the ◇K, East should have

played the discouraging 2, not the 8. What did East have to gain by ruffing the third round of diamonds? Not a thing, since he possessed a natural trump trick which could never be taken away. Had he played the ◇2, West, at trick two, would unquestionably have shifted to a club. East would then have made his ♣K, and declarer would have lost his contract.

There is a conventional situation in which a high-low signal is given not to denote an interest in the suit, but to indicate an *even number* of cards in that suit. This convention is discussed and illustrated in the section entitled LENGTH SIGNALS, but a passing illustration at this point would not be out of order.

It is a rather simple convention, and is most useful when a defensive holdup play must be employed. The setup to which it is applicable is the following:

When it is obvious that declarer is trying to establish a long suit in dummy (which has no outside entries), and that second hand's partner (or second hand himself) is going to have a problem as to when he should take his ace, second hand (or his partner) gives a high-low signal when holding *two or four* cards of that suit; where second has *three* cards of that suit (say, 7-4-2), he plays his lowest card (the 2) on the first lead, and then follows up by playing the next highest (the 4). In this latter case, partner will know that the signaler has exactly three cards in that suit, since with two or four he would have given a high-low signal. Here is a practical application of this high-low convention:

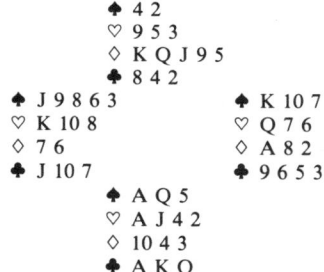

```
        ♠ 4 2
        ♡ 9 5 3
        ◇ K Q J 9 5
        ♣ 8 4 2
♠ J 9 8 6 3           ♠ K 10 7
♡ K 10 8             ♡ Q 7 6
◇ 7 6                ◇ A 8 2
♣ J 10 7             ♣ 9 6 5 3
        ♠ A Q 5
        ♡ A J 4 2
        ◇ 10 4 3
        ♣ A K Q
```

Against South's 3 NT contract, West opened the ♠6, East's king falling to declarer's ace. South then led the ◇10, West played the *7-spot*, and North and East followed with low diamonds. Declarer then led the ◇4, West played the *6-spot*, and dummy's 9 captured the trick when East properly declined to take his ace. Declarer now went down a trick, being unable to establish and cash dummy's diamonds.

West's high-low signal (7, 6) had told East that West had either two or four diamonds. That he had four became an impossibility when South led a second diamond, for if West had four diamonds then there were fourteen in the deck. Therefore East knew that West originally held precisely two diamonds, and that declarer still had a diamond left after the second diamond lead. See LORD HENRY BENTINCK.

HIGH REVERSE. A non-jump bid in a third suit at the level of three. For example, 1 ♡ —2 ◊ —3 ♣. (This term is English usage, not current in the United States.) See OPENER'S REBID.

HIGHER BID. A bid higher in rank than the last previous bid; a sufficient bid. Usually a higher bid refers to a bid that is merely sufficient, i. e., does not use as much as a full level of bidding space. Where one or more levels of bidding space are used, it is termed a jump, skip, or pre-emptive bid.

HIGHEST SCORE. In AMERICAN CONTRACT BRIDGE LEAGUE competition, several pairs have produced remarkable scores in major North American Championship events. S. GARTON CHURCHILL and CECIL HEAD held the single-session record with a 77.4% game in the 1948 Life Master Pairs until 1963, when ERIC MURRAY and AGNES GORDON scored 77.9% (506½ match points on a 325 average) in the final session of the Fall NAC Mixed Pairs. This was subsequently beaten by ANDREW BERNSTEIN and GENE NEIGER, who totaled 244 on a 156 average in the first session of the 1968 Spring NAC Open Pairs for 78.2%. For consistency in scoring, it is unlikely any pair can match the performance of BARRY CRANE and DR. JOHN FISHER in the 1970 Spring NAC Open Pairs. Averaging 69.5% in the two qualifying rounds and 63.4% in the two final sessions, their winning total of 924 was the highest ever for a four-session pair championship.

In regional competition, PAUL STERN and BOB WEBBER, scored 257 (82.3%) in the Open Pairs at Great Lakes in 1973, only slightly below the 260 (83.3%) — highest on record for a 156 average game — scored by C. C. WEI and RON ANDERSEN in a single-session at the 1974 New York Winter Regional.

HILLIARD TROPHY. Awarded for the North American Championship Mixed Pairs. Donated by OLGA HILLIARD In 1931, it was contested at the Fall NAC until 1946, then transferred to the West Coast and played as part of BRIDGE WEEK until 1957, while retaining the status of a championship event. Since 1958 it has been contested as a two-session event at the Spring NAC, under which heading past results are listed.

HINDSIGHT. Most bridge players are able to find the perfect bid, the correct line of play, and the killing defense after the hand has been misbid, misplayed, or misdefended at the table. Players who regularly indulge in long discussions of this sort are known as RESULT PLAYERS or second-guessers.

HIPPOGRIFFS. Sometime humorous name of a mythical suit; chiefly used in a celebrated anecdote about a man who dreamed he held a perfect no-trump hand with thirteen sure winners against a stranger (Satan), who was in the lead. The Devil then proceeded to run a 13-trick set against declarer by cashing all the cards of a weird greenish suit called hippogriffs.

HISTORY OF AMERICAN BRIDGE ASSOCIATION. See AMERICAN BRIDGE ASSOCIATION.

HISTORY OF BRIDGE. Bridge can trace its ancestry at least to the early 16th century in England (first reference 1529 in a published sermon by Bishop Latimer) and through succeeding centuries when prototype forms of whist were played under such names as triumph, trump, ruff, slamm, ruff and honours, whisk and swabbers, whisk, and whist. "Whist" may have referred to the rapid action of sweeping up the cards after winning a trick, or "whist" to a call for silence. The game was popular under its modern name of whist by the middle of the 17th century, but it was not until 1742 that the first book devoted to whist appeared: EDMOND HOYLE's famous "Short Treatise" (see BIBLIOGRAPHY, A). This rapidly became a best seller, and many pirated editions appeared immediately afterwards.

Whist maintained its popularity as a fashionable amusement, and in 1834 LORD HENRY BENTINCK invented the HIGH-LOW SIGNAL. This was the forerunner of much research and writing by authorities on the game such as JAMES CLAY, CAVENDISH, DESCHAPELLES and many others.

The first game of duplicate whist was apparently played in London in 1857 under Cavendish's direction. It was intended to demonstrate the advantage accruing to skillful play, and a team of supposedly good players was deliberately pitted against supposedly poor opposition (there having been no previous criterion for judging them). The "good" players won easily. Cavendish observed that this procedure all but eliminated the luck of the deal, but his pioneering effort was not followed for nearly a quarter of a century.

The United States was slightly ahead of England in extending the duplicate method. A duplicate whist game was played privately in Chicago in 1880 and in a club in New Orleans in 1882. The first interclub match was played in Philadelphia in 1883. The first duplicate match in the Old World was probably in Glasgow, Scotland, in 1888.

Duplicate offered the possibility of replacing private play by public contest. Major steps forward in 1891 were the foundation of the AMERICAN WHIST LEAGUE, the invention of the Kalamazoo tray (first duplicate board) and the first book on tournament organization, written by JOHN T. MITCHELL who devised the first movement for pair play and described the method of matchpointing which has been used ever since.

Although the American Whist League was to flourish for some 40 years, BRIDGE, the game which eventually led to its decline and fall, had come on the American scene early in the 1890s, at about the time it was also introduced in England. As chronicled by J. B. ELWELL and R. F. FOSTER, the game reached New York in 1893, thanks to HENRY I. BARBEY, whose privately printed Laws of Bridge are dated 1892.

In London, the Portland Club began to play bridge in 1894 at the instance of Lord Brougham who had learned it in India from some army officers. (W. Dalton in *Auction Bridge Magazine* of September 1927 states that Lord Brougham brought the game from Cairo.) But, according to a letter published in *Bridge Magazine* in 1932, Frank J. Nathan had played in the "first" English game in 1892 at St. George's Club, Hanover Square. It was introduced by a Colonel Studdy who said it was of Levantine origin and that he had learned it in the trenches at Plevna during the Russo-Turkish War of 1877–1878.

This earlier dating of the game and the probability that it was of Turkish or Russian origin is strongly supported by evidence uncovered in 1974–1975 by ROBERT H. TRUE, who quotes from a 1904 issue of *Notes and Queries*, a letter from A. M. Keiley (nationality unknown): "I was in 1886...a member of the Khedival Club in Cairo, and bridge was the principal card game played there at my entry and, as members told me, had long so been." One of the names by which bridge was first known on the Riviera was *Khedive*, presumably because players had met it in Cairo. Turkey held Egypt almost without interruption from the early 16th century until World War I and "Khedive" was the official title held by the Turkish viceroy.

Further new evidence confirming Levantine origin and earlier dating of the game was presented by Bob van de Velde of The Netherlands in IBPA *Bulletin #222*. Sources for this evidence are *Daily Telegraph* (England, November 1932), *La revue du bridge* (France, December 1932) and *Bridge* (The Netherlands, February 1933). The primary source, *Daily Telegraph*, carried an article by a Mr. O. H. van Millingen who lived in Constantinople in 1879 or 1880 and remembered "a very interesting game called Britch, a game that became very popular in all clubs and dethroned the game of whist." He included a letter, dated January 7, 1922, of his friend Edouard Graziani who at that time worked for the Italian Embassy as a translator and was one of the best bridge players of the *Cercle d'Orient*. In August 1873 Graziani played the game of bridge for the first time at the home of Mr. Georges Coronio, manager of the Bank of Constantinople. Also present at that game "in Buyukdere along the bank of the Upper-Bosphorus" were Mr. Eustache Eugenidi and a Mr. Serghiadi, "a Rumenian financier" who taught the principles of bridge to the foursome. "After Constantinople", Graziani wrote, "bridge came first to Kairo, from where it conquered the Riviera, Paris, London and then New York".

A claim of even earlier existence of the game appears in the introduction to *Modern Bridge* by "Slam" published in London in 1901: "Bridge, known in Turkey as 'Britch,'...has been played in South-Eastern Europe...ever since the early sixties."

Although there are combinations of Turkish words pronounced somewhat similarly to "biritch," from the evidence thus far uncovered the origin of the name if not of the game seems clearly to be Russian. Both "vint" and another Russian game called

"yeralash" include the notrump feature introduced by bridge, and, according to the rules in the 1886 pamphlet, "biritch" meant the declaration of notrump, with honor bonuses for the holding of three or four aces.

All this makes less plausible than ever the suggestion that the name of the game comes from the fact that the dealer "bridged" the bid when he passed his right of choice to his partner. It seems more likely that the term "I bridge it" when dealer did not wish to say "I make it—" derived from the name of the game, rather than vice versa.

The pattern of the progress of the game, slow until it reached America and England, suggests that, unlike Whist, which began a "below-stairs" game played by the serving class, bridge spread through diplomatic circles in such capitals as Constantinople and Cairo.

The origin of the word *bridge*, until recently characterized as "obscure," is often traced to an 1886 pamphlet in the British Museum entitled, "BIRITCH, or Russian Whist." But the clue that was earlier described as "slender"—on the ground that there was no such Russian word nor any game of that name played in Russia—has since gained considerable weight. The word *Biritch* is chronicled in Russian histories from the 10th through the 17th centuries; it meant, among other things, the town crier whose official duty it was to announce government edicts. It appears as "biritch" (accented on the second syllable) in dictionaries of Imperial days. In French, *annoncer* means to bid. Of course one of the major innovations of bridge was that the dealer or his partner had the right to announce or declare the trump suit, or to make it notrump.

An important change from whist was the exposure of one hand (dealer's partner) as the dummy, following the precedent of DUMMY WHIST, originated as a game for three players. According to one popular theory, this idea evolved from a game played first in India by three British officers so isolated they were unable to find a fourth. See THREE-HANDED BRIDGE; NEWGATE.

Another innovation was the introduction of the double and redouble. There was no limit to the number of redoubles, and this "gambling" feature of the new game, soon to be eliminated by the change to Auction Bridge, was one of the strong arguments against bridge adduced by whist devotees.

The prototypical game of bridge, or bridge whist, had a short life. A great step forward was taken in 1904, when the auction principle was introduced, traditionally in India, possibly in England. Auction bridge grew steadily in popularity until 1927, though only toward the end of this peirod were auction bridge tournaments organized. For some reason it was believed that the duplicate principle, long popular among whist players, was not suitable for bridge.

The next major change may have been developed in France, where the game of PLAFOND was played in 1918 and perhaps earlier. A similar game, S.A.C.C., was described by SIR HUGH CLAYTON as having been "invented" in India in 1912, and similar games had been tried in the United States before 1915. In all such games each side had to bid to its "plafond" or ceiling: only tricks bid and made counted toward game. This variation rapidly became the standard French game, but did not succeed elsewhere in spite of occasional experiments.

Up to this point whist, bridge, auction, and plafond had simply grown, which is generally the way with card games. No individual can be given credit for inventing the dummy, the idea of bidding, the auction principle, or the ceiling principle of plafond. But in 1925 HAROLD S. VANDERBILT perfected a new form of the game, embodying the plafond principle but including the element of vulnerability and producing a socring table that corrected the major faults in plafond. He succeeded so well that his game of "contract bridge' became the staple diet of card players everywhere. Afterward, he wrote:

Many years of experience playing games of the Whist family were, I think, a necessary prelude to acquiring the background and knowledge needed to evolve the game of Contract Bridge. Starting as a young boy about 70 years ago, I have played successively over the years Whist, Bridge, Auction Bridge, and Plafond.

...I compiled in the autumn of 1925 a scoring table for my new game. I called it Contract Bridge and incorporated in it, not only the best features of Auction and Plafond, but also a number of new and exciting features; premiums for slams bid and made, vulnerability, and the decimal system of scoring which by increasing both trick and game values and all premiums and penalties was destined to add enormously to the popularity of Contract Bridge.

An ideal opportunity to try out my new game presented itself while I was voyaging shortly after completing my scoring table with three Auction Bridge playing friends on board the steamship *Finland* from Los Angeles to Havana via the Panama Canal, a nine-day trip.

...At first, we were at a loss for a term, other than "game in," to describe the status of being subject to higher penalties because of having won a game. Fortunately for us, a young lady on board the *Finland* solved that problem by suggesting the word "vulnerable."...

We enjoyed playing my new game on board the *Finland* so much that, on my return to New York, I gave typed copies of my scoring table to several of my Auction Bridge playing friends. I made no other effort to popularize or publicize Contract Bridge. Thanks apparently to its excellence, it popularized itself and spread like wildfire.

No world-popular game in history — certainly none in the Whist family — can so accurately pinpoint its conception and the first time it was ever played. Recent research has established that the *Finland* reached Balboa on October 31, 1925, too late to proceed through the Canal or for passengers to go ashore. FRANCIS BACON III, in 1975 the then sole surviving member of Vanderbilt's foursome, recalled that on that night the lady who suggested "vulnerable" was allowed to join their game of plafond and attempted to suggest some exotic and impractical changes based on a game she said she had played in China. This so irritated Vanderbilt that the next day,

while the *Finland* passed through the Canal, he worked out the scoring table for contract which, except for notrump tricks then being valued at 35 points each, remained virtually unchanged half a century later. On that night, November 1, the game became Contract Bridge, scored under Vanderbilt's new rules.

Within two years, three codes of laws had been produced for the new game. Those of Robert F. Foster and the Knickerbocker Whist Club (both 1927) were withdrawn in favor of the more authoritative code issued by the WHIST CLUB of New York. In 1928 the game was adopted in the major New York clubs, and late that year the first National Championship was held, with the VANDERBILT CUP as the prize.

In 1929 the American Auction Bridge League dropped the word "Auction" from its title and it became clear that contract had supplanted auction. The established auction authorities struggled to achieve expertise in the field of contract, but for the most part unsuccessfully. Leadership in the new game went to ELY CULBERTSON, who founded the first contract magazine in 1929 (*The Bridge World*) and wrote his celebrated *Blue Book* in 1930. This revolutionary work set out the principles of approach-forcing bidding which became the nucleus of all modern standard systems.

Thanks to a thriving organization which exploited every phase of bridge activity and to his natural flair for publicity exhibited notably in the CULBERTSON-LENZ MATCH, Culbertson retained his leadership throughout the Thirties, untroubled by the tournament successes of the FOUR ACES.

Culbertson's interest and enthusiasm declined, and in the Forties the leadership passed to CHARLES H. GOREN, who achieved great success by adapting Culbertson's methods to point-count valuation.

The growth of tournament bridge was hampered in the Thirties by the simultaneous activity of three separate organizing bodies, the AMERICAN BRIGE LEAGUE, the AMERICAN WHIST LEAGUE, and the UNITED STATES BRIDGE ASSOCIATION. But from 1937 onward the AMERICAN CONTRACT BRIDGE LEAGUE had the field to itself, and there followed a period of steady growth stimulated by the masterpoint plan.

1935 became the year of the first recognized World Championship, although several semiofficial international matches had been played earlier. Later landmarks on the international scene were the first of the postwar World Championship series in 1950, the foundation of the WORLD BRIDGE FEDERATION in 1958, and the first team Olympiad in 1960.

The only major innovation in contract bridge during its first 40 years of existence was the development of CHICAGO, the four-deal game which displaced traditional rubber bridge in many clubs during the early Sixties. But this, like contract bridge itself, was a change in scoring rather than in structure, and there have been few radical changes in the game nor do any seem likely in the immediate future.

HISTORY OF PLAYING CARDS. The earliest known cards were used in China, at least as long ago as 979 A. D. The pack was divided into four suits, 14 cards in each, and was used for paper money as well as for games. This discredits the pleasant story that they were invented in 1120 A. D. to amuse the concubines of the Emperor Suen-ho. There is a tradition that a Venetian carried cards from China to his native city, the first place in Europe where they were known. This traveler may have been Niccolo Polo, who returned from China about 1269 with his brother Matteo, or it may have been Niccolo's son, the famed Marco, who accompanied his father and uncle on their second trip to that empire.

Some authorities favor India over China as the original source. A tenuous link has been suggested between early European cards and Ardhanari, the goddess of Hindu mythology. She was represented holding in her four hands a wand, a cup, a sword, and a ring (symbolizing money). Similar symbols appeared on some early European playing cards. One discredited theory suggests that cards were brought to Europe by the Gypsies, who may have belonged originally to an Indian race. They have been traced through Persia and Arabia into Egypt and then to Europe, and a body of over 100 entered Paris in August 1427 (Pasquier: *Recherches Historiques*).

However, this date is too late to be significant. Cards were manufactured in many parts of Europe, notably in Nuremberg, Augsburg, and Ulm, in the fourteenth century, and perhaps even earlier. The Italian TAROT cards may have predated the German cards: they are mentioned in an Italian manuscript dated 1299. Johanna, Duchess of Brabant mentions cards in the Netherlands in 1379, and cards were known in Spain at least as early as 1371. The Moors or Saracens may have brought cards to Spain and Italy, but the attempt to show a resemblance between the Spanish word for cards (naipes) and the Arabic word (nabi, "a prophet"), is not well founded.

In 1392 in France, the monarch Charles VI ordered a hand-painted deck to be made by Jacquemin Gringonneur, and this historical fact gave rise to the idea that cards originated in France. However, it seems clear that this order was for cards similar to others already in use. The royal treasurer, accounting for moneys paid out, mentions three packs of cards, painted "in gold and diverse colors, ornamented with many devices, for the diversion of our Lord, the King." Seventeen of these cards are on exhibition at the Bibliothèque Nationale (see COLLECTIONS OF PLAYING CARDS).

Cards probably reached England later than the other European countries. Chaucer, who died in 1400, never mentions cards, although he enumerates the amusements of the day: "They dance and they play at chess and tables." The reference to playing with four kings in the Wardrobe Rolls of Edward I in 1278 ("ad ludendum ad quattuor regis") almost certainly refers to some other game, perhaps a form of chess. The earliest clear-cut reference to playing cards in England dates from 1465, when manufacturers of playing cards petitioned Edward IV for protection against foreign imports, and were favored by an appropriate edict.

"There is a legend telling how the sailors with Columbus," writes Catherine Perry Hargrave in *A History of Playing Cards*, "who were inveterate gamblers, threw their cards overboard in superstitious terror upon encountering storms in these vast and mysterious seas. Later, on dry land they regretted their rashness and in the new country made other cards out of the leaves of the copys tree, which greatly interested the Indians." This seems to be more than a legend, for Garcilaso de la Vega (*Historia de la Florida*, Madrid, 1723) tells that the soldiers of Spain played with leather cards in the 1534 expedition. Cards were known to the early Mexicans as *amapatolli*, from *amatl* meaning paper and *patolli* meaning game.

The present pack of 52 cards, arranged in two black and two red suits, probably derived from the early Italian TAROT packs, in which there were four suits with 10 SPOT CARDS and four COURT CARDS— KING, QUEEN, CAVALIER, and KNAVE. The queen was not included in early packs, and the chevalier still holds her position in some modern packs (see PACK). The knave has been variously represented by a VALET, and still carries this name, although modern usage changes it to the JACK. The chevalier, as apart from the queen, has been dropped from the 52-card pack.

The Chinese playing cards differ considerably from the occidental; they are long and narrow, usually 2 to 2½ inches long and ½ to 1 inch wide, early cards longer and even narrower. In number of suits and cards, both the Chinese and Hindu decks differ markedly from ours. One Hindu deck includes 144 cards with eight suits of 18 cards, another has 120 cards with 10 of 12 cards; one Chinese deck has only 30 cards, three suits of nine cards and three extra cards of supreme value, but four suits were normal.

Long before bridge was heard of, playing cards were used in many forms of gambling and in fortunetelling, and acquired an unsavory reputation, being associated with all vices. The DEVIL'S PICTURE BOOK and other names indicate the horror with which they were regarded by the virtuous and religious.

Playing cards, as a luxury, provided a source for much revenue in TAXES, first levied on them in England in 1615.

For information about the MANUFACTURE OF PLAYING CARDS at the present time, see that heading.

HIT. Slang used as two distinct transitive verbs: (1) To double. (2) To ruff.

HOLD. (1) To possess (a certain card or cards). (2) To win or guarantee the winning of a trick (by the play of a certain card). Thus, if partner plays the king when you hold the ace, and no ruff is impending, the king is said to hold the trick unless you decide to overtake it.

HOLD OFF. To refuse to play a winning card. See DUCK and HOLD UP.

HOLD UP. The hold-up play is the refusal to win a trick in order to maintain control of the suit which an opponent has led until such time as the control can be relinquished with comparative safety.

Although there can be various reasons for the desire and necessity of maintaining control, one practical motive stands out above all others: to break the communication between the opponents' hands — that is, to eliminate from one of the opponents' hands the suit which has been led, so that if the devoided one obtains the lead subsequently, he will be unable to play back his partner's suit.

In this section, the hold-up play is discussed from the viewpoint of the declarer only. The play is also utilized by the defensive side, e.g., dummy, at a 3 NT contract, possesses ♠5-2, ♡6-3, ◇6-3-2, ♣K-Q-J-10-9-2, and a defender, holding, for example, the ♣A-7-6, holds up his ace long enough to prevent the establishment and cashing of dummy's club suit. See LENGTH SIGNALS.

The hold-up play is most frequently employed by declarer at notrump contracts, although there are many situations where it is also used to good advantage in suit contracts.

Let us examine a few illustrations of the hold-up play in action.

```
              ♠ Q 6 5
              ♡ K 8 4
              ◇ A J 9 8 3
              ♣ 8 3
  ♠ 10 7 2                    ♠ J 9 8 2
  ♡ Q 10 6 5                  ♡ J 9 3
  ◇ 7                         ◇ K 6 5
  ♣ K J 9 5 4                 ♣ Q 10 2
              ♠ A K 4
              ♡ A 7 2
              ◇ Q 10 4 2
              ♣ A 7 6
```

Against South's 3 NT contract, West opens the ♣5, East puts up the queen, and South employs the hold-up play, declining to take the ace. East continues with the ♣10, and once again South plays low, East overtaking with the jack. West then leads a third round of clubs, declarer winning with the ace. Clubs have now been eliminated from the East hand.

The diamond finesse is then tried, East taking the trick with the king. Whatever East returns, declarer will win and capture the remainder of the tricks.

It is apparent that if declarer had taken the first or second club trick, he would have been defeated. From this deal, it will be observed that the hold-up play is actually the counterattack to the normal opening lead (against notrump contracts) of the fourth-best in the longest suit. The hold up is based on the assumption that the leader usually has more cards in the suit led than does his partner; and each time declarer declines to win successive leads in that suit, the leader's partner, who started with few cards in that suit, must play another and another, until he finally has none left; and is *nondangerous* when he later obtains the lead.

In a nontrump contract, the hold-up play is designed to protect in all situations where the adversely led suit is divided in such a fashion that the opening leader has the greater number. When the suit that is led is divided evenly, say 4-4, the declarer requires no protection, since only three tricks will be lost in that suit (whether he captures the first, second, or third lead), plus one trick in the suit which

he is going to establish (diamonds in the above deal). In this deal, had the eight adverse clubs been divided 4-4, any player would have fulfilled the 3 NT contract. And if the ◇K were favorably located, again everybody would have made his contract whether he held up or not.

Thus, the hold-up play is what one might call comprehensive insurance; it takes care of everything; a bad division of the suit led, and a key card being adversely located.

Against a suit contract, especially when an opponent has overcalled, declarer sometimes has to guess whether or not to employ the hold-up play. For example:

```
          ♠ 9 5 2
          ♡ A J 10 6
          ◇ 8
          ♣ K Q 7 5 3


          ♠ A 7 3
          ♡ Q 9 3
          ◇ A 4
          ♣ A J 10 6 4
```

The bidding:

WEST	NORTH	EAST	SOUTH
			1♣
1♠	2♡	Pass	2 NT
Pass	4♣	Pass	4♡
Pass	5♣	All Pass	

West, having overcalled in spades, opens the ♠K and South has a rough problem. Shall he take the king, or shall he hold up? If West has the ♡K, then no matter what declarer elects to do, he will come out all right, since he will in this case have no losers in hearts, diamonds or clubs. But if East has the ♡K, then the success of declarer's contract depends on his ability to diagnose whether East started with one or two spades.

If West has six spades, then if declarer wins the opening lead, draws trumps, and takes a heart finesse which loses to East, the latter will have no spade to playback. Declarer will now be able to discard one of his losing spades on dummy's fourth heart. Of course, if West has six spades, and declarer declines to win the opening lead, East will ruff the second spade — and East's ♡K will ultimately become the setting trick.

But if West started with five spades (and East with two), then it becomes imperative for declarer to refuse to win the opening lead. If he doesn't, then when East wins the ♡K, he will return his remaining spade, and West will make two spade tricks. If declarer does hold up, then when he wins the spade continuation at trick two, East will have no more spades. Declarer will now fulfill his contract.

As is obvious, it is a pure guess as to whether to win the first spade lead or hold up instead.

In duplicate bridge, the issue of whether to hold up or not can be a most difficult one to decide. Here is an example: (See hand at top of next page.)

With no adverse bidding, South arrives at a 3 NT contract. West leads the ♣6, and East puts up the queen.

In rubber bridge, there would be no problem

♠ 9 7
♡ A 8 3
◇ K Q 10
♣ A J 10 9 5

♠ A 4 3
♡ K 6 5
◇ A J 8 3
♣ Q 8 7

whatsoever. The ace would be held up until the third round, and this would just about guarantee the contract, regardless of the location of the ♣K.

But at matchpoints, the decision as to whether to hold up or not is not an easy one to make. If West has the ♣K, 12 tricks are there for the taking. If one plays safe, and holds up the ♣A for two rounds, then only 11 tricks will be made if the club finesse is successful. And if other North–South pairs choose to gamble on this deal for 12 tricks, the hold up will get a bad matchpoint score.

However, if the ♣K is held by East, then by taking the first or second club declarer might well go down at 3 NT.

Probably the best course of action is to hold up on the first spade lead, and see what East plays back. This hold up cannot prove costly, since declarer can't ever make 13 tricks. If East should return, let us say, the ♠2, then declarer should take it, for if the ♡ is East's fourth best, then declarer will make 9 tricks, since the eight adversely held spades will then be divided 4–4. And if the ♠2 is East's remaining spade, then declarer will make either 11 or 12 tricks, depending on which opponent has the ♣K.

If, at trick two, East plays back, let us say, the ♠10, probably declarer should hold up again. In this case, there is a real danger that West started with five spades, and East with three spades. And, in this latter situation, while holding up twice, declarer hopes that the club finesse loses, so that his technically correct rubber bridge play may receive its just deserts.

Fred Karpin

HOLDING. (1) The cards one is dealt in a particular suit, as in the expression, "a club holding of king, queen, and two little." (2) A descriptive term used in reckoning one's entire hand, and often used in the question, "What would you bid holding five spades to the ace-queen, etc.?"

HOLLAND. See NETHERLANDS BRIDGE LEAGUE.

HOLLANDAISE. See GOULASH.

HOME STYLE BRIDGE. In the early 1970s NATE SILVERSTEIN of Memphis devised a movement for a one-winner pair game. It is usually called a "Swiss Pair" game. The game gained popularity in some of the country clubs in Memphis. In 1979 the ACBL adopted most of the ideas and converted the game into an experimental Home Style bridge program.

The basic method of scoring is Chicago or "Four-Deal Bridge". Pairs are assigned seats at random by the director. When the game starts, and at the start of each round, the players cut for deal. Each round

they play four hands. On the first hand no one is vulnerable, the second and third hands the dealer's side is vulnerable, and the last hand everyone is vulnerable. Partscores carry over, honors are scored. If you complete a hand when your side is vulnerable you score a bonus of 500, if you complete a game on a hand where your side is not vulnerable your bonus is 300 points. If you score a partscore on the last hand, and it does not complete a game, you receive a bonus of 100. All other scoring, overtricks, undertricks, doubles, redoubles, etc., are scored the same as in all other forms of bridge.

The only exception to playing four hands is if you have three or four tables. In this instance the director may opt to play six hands a round. In this instance no one would be vulnerable on the first two hands, the dealer's side vulnerable on the third and fourth hands, and both sides vulnerable on the last two hands.

At the end of the round the players total their points. The pair with the fewer points deduct their total from the greater. The difference is then coverted into Victory Points. Following is a Victory Point schedule.

Difference in total points	Victory Points
0–40	10–10
50–140	11–9
150–240	12–8
250–340	13–7
350–540	14–6
550–740	15–5
750–940	16–4
950–1240	17–3
1250–1540	18–2
1550 or more	19–1

This is the ACBL Home Style formula. In the original method 1550–1940 was 19–1, and 1950 or more was 20–0. However, players in this type of game are discouraged by zeroes — hence the change.

The easiest way to assign pair numbers is the pair starting at Table 1 North-South is assigned Pair #1, East-West at Table 1 is Pair #2, North-South at Table 2 is Pair #3, and so forth.

When the first round is completed and the Victory Point totals have been entered, the director gives each pair their second-round assignment. This is Swiss pairing where each pair plays against a pair with a score as close to theirs as is possible. The pair with the most Victory Points plays the pair with the next most Victory Points and so on. The one exception is that no pair can play another pair more than once. If the two pairs with the most Victory Points could not play because they had already played, the pair with the greatest total would play the pair with the third most points. This continues until all pairs have received a new assignment.

This is usually a fun kind of game and attracts players who aren't interested in braving the rigors of duplicate bridge with the attendant restrictions and many conventions. It also appeals to the newcomer to competitive bridge. For these reasons Home Style Bridge is usually limited to the very basic conventions and understandings. Blackwood and Stayman are frequently the only conventions permitted. The use of understandings such as weak two bids, weak notrumps and preemptive jump overcalls is almost always barred. This is up to the director or, more specifically, up to those playing in the game. Any conventions could be permitted as long as they are determined beforehand.

Home Style Bridge is an interesting and enjoyable contest and has a strategy all its own. Once the players become familiar with the game they frequently become as devoted to the game as followers of other forms of bridge.

Home Style Bridge can be sanctioned for clubs and rating points issued on the same scale as for duplicate clubs. For more information contact The American Contract Bridge League, P.O. Box 161192, Memphis TN 38116.

HONG KONG CONTRACT BRIDGE ASSOCIATION.
Founded in 1951 by J.M. Remedios, E.M. Marchetti, and Victor Zirinsky, with a nucleus of Hong Kong social clubs, by 1982 its membership was approximately 290. The Association was one of the original members of the Far East Bridge Federation and annually sends teams to compete in the Far East Championships. Hong Kong hosted the event in 1960, 1965, and 1973, and won the Far East Championships in 1959 and 1960. National events held annually are Open Teams, Master Teams, Open Pairs, Master Pairs and Mixed Pairs.

Officers, 1982:
Chairman: Leslie L. Sung
Vice-Chairman: Victor Zirinsky, 1122 Princess
    Building, Hong Kong

HOME TOWN RULING.
An action by the director which accepts the credibility of players personally known to him as opposed to others from distant parts; the type of ruling sometimes given by club directors in favor of regular participants in the games as opposed to occasional drop-ins comes in this category and is even less defensible. Application of the published rules from the rule book for any and all players must in the long run provide the fairest competition and the most enjoyable game.

HONOR.
One of the five top cards in a suit at bridge. An ace, king, queen, jack or 10 can properly be described as an honor.

HONOR CRASHING PLAYS.
See CRASHING HONORS and DECEPTIVE PLAY.

HONOR LEAD.
The lead of an honor, usually the top one of a sequence. The lead of an honor conventionally indicates possession of one or more lower touching honors, the exception being the lead of the king, which may be made from an A–K or K–Q holding. The purpose of the honor lead is usually to establish the cards directly beneath it. In the middle game the lead of an unsupported honor card is often correct.

Spades are trump, and West is on lead and forced to open up the hearts. The queen is the proper play, for if he leads a low card, South simply plays the 8 from dummy, forcing the jack from East. On the next

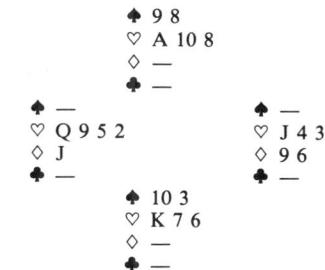

round he has a simple finesse position with dummy's A–10 over West's queen.

DUMMY (N)
K 9 8
WEST
J 6 4 3

West is on lead and has no further card of entry. Requiring three tricks from this suit, he must lead the jack, hoping that his partner has A–Q–10.

See also INTERIOR SEQUENCE; JOURNALIST LEADS; OPENING LEAD; RUSINOW LEAD; ZERO OR TWO HIGHER LEADS.

HONOR SCORE.
An extra bonus in rubber bridge and in CHICAGO scored above the line when claimed by a player (declarer, dummy, or defender) who held during the current deal any of certain honor card holdings in the trump suit as follows: For holding any four of the five top trump honors — 100 points. For all five trump honors — 150 points. For all the aces at notrump — 150 points. Honors are not scored at duplicate except in total-point team-of-four play. See LAWS OF CONTRACT BRIDGE (Law 84), LAWS OF DUPLICATE (Law 73).

HONOR STRENGTH.
The trick-taking value of a hand in honor tricks. This was of great importance as a basis for calculation of the power of a hand in the CULBERTSON SYSTEM.

HONOR TRICK.
A unit of defensive valuation of honor cards and combinations. It is, of course, a combination which may also be expected to win a trick on the offensive. Valuations of combinations were made in accordance with the following table in the CULBERTSON SYSTEM:

2 HT	A–K
1½ HT	A–Q
1 HT	A, K–Q, K–J–10
½ HT	K–x, Q–J–x
+ values	any queen (but not a singleton)
(about ¼ HT)	any jack combined with another honor (but no singleton or doubleton, and not A–K–Q–J) any singleton or void (not more than one)

See DEFENSIVE TRICK and QUICK TRICK.

HONORARY MEMBERS.
A title awarded by the American Bridge League and American Contract Bridge League. This title is awarded for long and meritorious service to the League.

ABL

1927	*Milton C. Work	1932	*E.J. Tobin
1928	*Wilbur C. Whitehead	1933	*A.E. Manning-Foster
1929	*Maurice Maschke	1934	*P. Hal Sims
1930	*Eberhard Faber	1935	*Nathan S. Kelly
1931	Waldemar K. von Zedtwitz	1936	*Nate B. Spingold

ACBL

1937	Philip Steiner	1959	Charles H. Goren
			*Dr. A.M. Dye
1938	*Ely Culbertson	1960	*Tom Stoddard
1939	*Henry P. Jaeger	1961	*Charles J. Solomon
1940	*Cmdr. W.A. Corley	1962	John E. Simon
1941	*Harold S. Vanderbilt	1963	*Max M. Manchester
			*Bertram Lebhar, Jr.
1942	*Maj. Clarence Wyatt	1964	Jeff Glick
1943	*Russell J. Baldwin	1965	*Sidney B. Fink
1944	*Gen. Alfred M. Gruenther	1966	*Harry J. Fishbein
1945	Gen. Robert J. Gill	1967	Oswald Jacoby
1946	*Albert H. Morehead	1968	*Frank T. Wescott
	*Maureen O'Brien Bailey	1969	Samuel M. Stayman
1947	*Benjamin M. Golder	1970	*Julius L. Rosenblum
	*Mrs. James C. Baird	1971	Joseph J. Stedem
1948	*Shepard Barclay	1972	Phyllis Smith
1949	*Alexander M. Sobel	1973	Kate Buckman
1950	*Dr. Louis Mark	1974	Louise Durham
1951	*James C. Baird	1975	*Kay Moody
1952	R.L. Miles, Jr.	1976	*Charles S. Landau
1953	*Curt H. Reisinger	1977	*Fred B. Ensminger
1954	*Fred Snite, Jr.	1978	*William A. Baldwin
1955	*George W. Beynon	1979	Margaret Wagar
1956	*George Alderton II	1980	Easley Blackwood
1957	*Alvin Landy	1981	Hon. Carl B. Rubin
1958	Lee Hazen	1982	Ethel Keohane

*Deceased

HONORS. The five highest ranking cards in each suit; specifically, for the purpose of scoring honor premiums, the ace, king, queen, jack, and ten of the trump suit, or the four aces at no trump, are honors. See LAWS (Law 84), LAWS OF DUPLICATE (Law 73).

HOOK. Colloquialism for FINESSE.

HORSE AND HORSE. Slang term for both sides vulnerable.

HOSPITALITY. The general term for efforts by a host unit at a bridge tournament to make the players feel more comfortable and welcome. Among the forms that hospitality takes are souvenir programs and pencils; free orange juice (at Florida tournaments), coffee, or cokes; after-game refreshments; between-sessions buffets and even dinners; after-session dancing; morning tours to places of local interest; style shows and brunches; panel discussions; daily bulletins, etc.

HOUSE OF COMMONS. See BRITISH PARLIAMENT MATCHES.

HOUSE OF LORDS. See BRITISH PARLIAMENT MATCHES.

HOUSE PLAYER. A player at a bridge club who is available for making up tables and for joining tables when a member wishes to leave. Generally house players receive some compensation for their services to the club, but arrangements vary from club to club regarding winnings or losings at play. Some clubs have a few regular players who make themselves available to help in forming tables in exchange for remission of fees for their play.

HOUSE RULES. Additions or amendments to the LAWS as required to meet conditions of play in a club or group. Proper subjects for house rules would be the posting of deposits to guarantee losses in rubber bridge games, clothing or dress rules, rules for cutting in to existent games, eligibility to play, pivoting regulations when time for play is limited, termination time of the game, etc.

HOUSTON AFFAIR. The January 1977 North American Team Trials competition that ended when the team captained by JOHN GERBER was forced to forfeit when two members of his five-player team, LARRY COHEN and DR. RICHARD H. KATZ, resigned from both the team and the American Contract Bridge League with 32 deals of the 128–board final still to be played. As a result, the 1976 Grand National Teams victors — PAUL SOLOWAY, BILLY EISENBERG, EDDIE KANTAR, JOHN SWANSON, BOB HAMMAN and BOBBY WOLFF — were declared the Trials champions and became eligible to represent North America in the 1977 Bermuda Bowl in Manila, The Philippines. This sextet went on to win the Bermuda Bowl in one of the most exciting World Championship finals in history.

The Gerber team, which also included GEORGE ROSENKRANZ, ROGER BATES and JOHN MOHAN, had a 40-IMP lead, 221–181, after the 96th deal of the final concluded Saturday evening's play. However, the start of the last 32-board set was held up on Sunday because the Tournament Committee was studying some charges concerning irregularities involving Katz and Cohen. Closed-door conferences consumed much of the day until an announcement was made by ACBL President LOUIS GURVICH that Katz and Cohen has resigned from their team and from the ACBL. This reduced the Gerber team to three members, forcing a forfeit.

In the following days, there was much media conjecture concerning the reasons for the sudden unexpected resignations. Various newspaper articles quoted "reliable sources" as saying that Katz and Cohen had been guilty of serious infractions against the Proprieties of bridge.

Soon after these accusations appeared in print, Katz and Cohen filed a $44 million lawsuit against the ACBL, Gurvich, LEW MATHE and DON OAKIE. The suit alleged defamation of character, interference with business interests, false accusations of cheating, coerced withdrawal from the Houston Trials, and forced resignation from the ACBL. The suit demanded that Katz and Cohen be reinstated as ACBL members and that the Trials continue from the point where they were terminated. Gurvich, Mathe and Oakie all were members of the Tournament Committee at Houston, and all three were present during the events that took place on the final day.

Katz and Cohen later filed another suit in which they accused the ACBL of violation of federal antitrust actions. Discontinued with prejudice.

The action finally was settled on February 23, 1982. The settlement consisted of the following:

1. Dr. Richard H. Katz and Lawrence Cohen are each readmitted, effective immediately, to member-

ship in the ACBL with all privileges of full membership, except that they agree not to play together as a partnership.

2. Should Katz and Cohen desire to play together as a partnership, their request will be submitted to the National Board of the ACBL, to be decided under the rules and regulations of the ACBL. The ACBL will not entertain such an application prior to March 1, 1984.

3. The parties will be compensated by Commercial Union Assurance Company, insurer of the ACBL, for costs and attorneys' fees incurred with respect to this lawsuit: Katz and Cohen will receive the sum of $75,000 and the ACBL will receive an amount yet to be determined.

4. The lawsuit is dismissed. Katz, Cohen and the ACBL shall exchange mutual releases of all claims.

In an explanation of the settlement in the April 1982 *ACBL Bulletin*, ACBL President JAMES ZIMMERMAN wrote:

"This case was unique in that Katz–Cohen resigned from membership in the ACBL rather than face charges of improper communication and certain ejection from the ACBL should these charges be sustained. No matter how one may feel as to whether there was or was not improper communication, the fact remains that because of their resignations no evidentiary presentation of this charge was ever made.

"Those who were of the opinion that Katz and Cohen were guilty of exchanging information improperly have retained that opinion. I doubt that a resolution by a trial would have changed it, especially since that question would not have been the most relevant issue in the trial. Those who were on the other side were also vehement on behalf of Katz and Cohen — it is equally likely that their opinion would not have been changed by a trial.

"This matter has been before the ACBL Board of Directors for five years. Management has been continually required to furnish information to all lawyers. Katz and Cohen, by their resignations, have not been members of the ACBL nor have they played in ACBL-sanctioned events for five years.

"Estimates were that the trial would take five to eight weeks. A judge in Los Angeles County, therefore, made a most strenuous effort to dispose of this case without a trial.

"The basic position of the ACBL through all negotiations was that Katz and Cohen should not play together as a pair. Katz and Cohen would not accept this restriction. When there was movement by Katz and Cohen toward acceptance of restriction, this basic concession made it possible to find a ground whereby they could be considered for re-admission. On February 23, 1982, Katz and Cohen were re-admitted, but they agreed not to play together.

"The Katz-Cohen lawsuit alleged a number of causes of action, all of which were terminated by this settlement. Payment of the plaintiffs' legal fees was made by the insurance company alone, a result of negotiations between the insurance company and the plaintiffs. No payments to the plaintiffs were made by the ACBL. (The amount of remuneration to the ACBL for legal fees is in litigation at this writing.)

"Is this settlement a precedent-setting case for any future law suit' Absolutely not! Each case will be dealt with individually."

HOWARD TROPHY. See PRESIDENT'S CUP.

HOWELL MOVEMENT. A method of producing one winner from a field at duplicate in which all pairs play each of the boards in play, with comparison in direct competition with other pairs on approximately half of the boards, and adverse comparison on the other boards. Because of the requirement that all pairs be met in head-on competition, the movement is not practical for many of the possible number of tables.

The four-table, five-table, and seven-table movements (requiring seven rounds of four boards, nine rounds of three boards, and 13 rounds of two boards, respectively) provide excellent competition. Starting assignments for these movements are given below, and positions and boards for each round subsequent can be got by the following rules: the highest numbered pair remains stationary throughout; each other pair replaces the pair with the next lower number for their next seat, with number 1 replacing the pair with the next to the highest number. Boards progress so that each table plays the boards in ascending order.

There are as many sets of boards in play during the session as there are rounds to be played. The extra sets are on a byestand behind the highest numbered table. From here they are fed ino the last table, and the boards at the byestand are replenished from table 1. Note the special byestand layout with four tables.

For six tables, as well as eight to 12 tables, see THREE-QUARTER MOVEMENT. See also SHORT HOWELL.

At the bottom of the page is a chart showing the starting positions for four tables (1st line), five tables (second line) and seven tables (third line).

HUDDLE. A longer-than-usual pause preceding an action in the bidding (usually) or the play of a hand. If the huddle is followed by a positive action, usually no harm is done to the opponents. However, the ethics of the game (all information is to be conveyed

Table 1		Table 2		Table 3		Table 4		Table 5		Table 6		Table 7	
Prs.	Bds.	Prs.	Bds.	Prs.	Bds.	Prs.	Bds.	Prs.	Bds.	Prs.	Bds.	Prs.	Bds.
8v1	1	3v6	4	2v7	6	5v4	7						
7v3	1	5v2	2	10v1	3	9v8	4	4v6	5				
5v12	1	2v4	2	9v10	3	14v1	4	8v13	5	7v11	6	6v3	7

by the bids made, not the manner of making them) require that the partner of the huddler not take cognizance of the information that the huddler "had a problem." See SLOW PASS.

One of the situations that used to cause difficulties was the problem that a player had after a pre-emptive bid on his right. Many hands seemed too good to pass but did not offer a clear-cut alternative action. A huddle followed by a pass created an ethical problem for the partner. Should he take action on some sort of miscellaneous holding or not? Partner's huddle has reduced the danger that the right-hand opponent holds a powerful defensive hand. This frequently recurring problem was answered in the United States by the "skip-bid warning rule", which puts the player following the pre-empter under the obligation to take a huddle at all times when a skip-bid has been made so that his partner will have no ethical problem in connection with a valid huddle holding.

Players should strive for a rhythm in the tempo of bidding in order to obviate the necessity of huddling.

In the play, a hesitation by one defender will often reveal that he holds a key card. In that case his partner is not necessarily barred from making the indicated play, but should satisfy himself before doing so that he would have had sound technical reasons for playing in the same way without any hesitation.

A hesitation in the play when there is no possible reason to think (e. g., when playing a singleton, or when following suit with insignificant small cards) is an offense against the Proprieties. In such cases the director may award an adjusted score under Law 12. See RHYTHM and SKIP-BID WARNING.

HUNGARIAN BRIDGE ASSOCIATION (BUDAPESTI BRIDZS EGYESÜLET).

This association was revived in 1963 for organizing National Championships and tournaments with a wide international participation. In 1981 there were 740 regular and 750 associate members. In prewar years Hungary was one of the dominating teams in European Championships, winning the title in 1934 and 1938 and finishing second in 1935 and 1936. Not active in this competition 1939 to 1969, in 1968 the Association joined the EUROPEAN BRIDGE LEAGUE and has since taken part in all European Championships, in the 1976 and 1980 World Team Olympics, frequently in Juniors and sporadically in Ladies European Championships. The Association is holding annual competitions for National Championships in Open Teams, Open Pairs and Mixed Pairs, as well as three major international events: the Budapest Bridge Festival (IBBF) in January, the Budapest Summer Bridge Festival in July and the Lake Balaton Bridge Week in September. The Association publishes a monthly magazine *Bridzsélet* (editor Peter Zánkay).

Officers, 1982:
President: György Antal
Secretary: Gábor Salgó, 1015 Budapest,
  Hattyu utca 1, Hungary

HYBRID SCORING.

To combine the best features of IMP scoring and BOARD-A-MATCH scoring in team games where only short matches occur between two teams, a form of scoring has been developed by the ENGLISH BRIDGE UNION.

Three-board matches. A total of 10 points at stake in each match, divided as follows: 2 points for winning the board (ties on a board are awarded 1 each) for a total of 6 points. The additional 4 points to be awarded based on aggregate score, divided as follows:

$$
\begin{aligned}
&0\text{-}240 \text{ divide } 2\text{-}2\\
&250\text{-}490 \text{ divide } 3\text{-}1\\
&500 \text{ and over, } 4\text{-}0
\end{aligned}
$$

Four-board matches. A total of 13 points at stake in each match, divided as follows: 2 points for winning the board, for a total of 8 points. The additional 5 points based on aggregate score:

$$
\begin{aligned}
&0\text{-}340 \text{ divide } 2\frac{1}{2}\text{-}2\frac{1}{2}\\
&350\text{-}590 \text{ divide } 3\ \ \text{-}2\\
&600\text{-}990 \text{ divide } 4\ \ \text{-}1\\
&1{,}000 \text{ and over, } 5\ \ \text{-}0
\end{aligned}
$$

Five-board matches. A total of 16 points at stake, in each match, divided as follows: 10 points for boards won at 2 points per board, the additional 6 points based on aggregate score:

$$
\begin{aligned}
&0\text{-}440 \text{ divide } 3\text{-}3\\
&450\text{-}740 \text{ divide } 4\text{-}2\\
&750\text{-}1{,}240\\
&\qquad\text{divide}\qquad 5\text{-}1\\
&1{,}250 \text{ or over, } 6\text{-}0
\end{aligned}
$$

A difference of 10 points on a board is considered to be a tie, as in IMP scoring, rather than a win, as in board-a-match scoring.

An alternate method of dividing the extra points based on aggregate score, when not all boards are played by all contesting teams, is as follows:

Add the net score on each of the boards to obtain total aggregate score (this is without regard to whether the score is plus or minus).

Compute the net aggregate score as a percentage of the total aggregate score, and convert to VICTORY POINTS on the basis of:

$$
\begin{aligned}
&0\text{-}5\% &&2 &&\text{-}2\\
&\text{over } 5\text{-}10\% &&2\frac{1}{2}\text{-}1\frac{1}{2}\\
&\text{over } 10\text{-}15\% &&3 &&\text{-}1\\
&\text{over } 15\text{-}25\% &&3\frac{1}{2}\text{-}\frac{1}{2}\\
&\text{over } 25\% &&4 &&\text{-}0
\end{aligned}
$$

This scale was used in four-board matches in competition for the English Bridge Union's Pachabo Cup.

I

IBL. See INTERNATIONAL BRIDGE LEAGUE.

IBM NUMBER. See PLAYER NUMBER.

IBPA. See INTERNATIONAL BRIDGE PRESS ASSOCIATION.

IBPA AWARDS. See INTERNATIONAL BRIDGE PRESS ASSOCIATION AWARDS.

IDAK (or IDAC). A defensive bidding system against strong artificial club sequences. IDAK stands for Instant Destroyer and Killer, while IDAC means Instant Destruction Against a Club. The system is used when not vulnerable. WONDER BIDS are used when vulnerable.

The system works this way. If RHO opens an artificial club or responds artificially to a 1♣ opening:

1. If you have a long suit, bid the suit immediately below it at whatever level you deem appropriate (notrump shows clubs). This is not a transfer bid per se, for responder can pass the suit you bid but not the one you've shown. With two suits, "transfer" in one and rebid in the other.

2. 1♠ shows a 4-3-3-3 pattern (any) *or* a string of spades. Responder assumes you have the first type and bids his best suit at whatever level he wishes. If you really have a string of spades, you can always rescue him.

3. A *jump* in spades at any level shows the minor suits. Responder can ask for your better minor by bidding notrump.

4. A double shows a three-suited hand (any). If responder has: (a) a one-suited hand, he responds *two suits below his real suit* (i.e., spades shows diamonds) at any level. The original doubler bids the suit shown with support, and passes without it. (b) With both majors and an interest in preempting, responder bids 2 NT, for the doubler guarantees a major. (c) With both minors and interest in preempting, he bids three or more notrump. (d) With a constructive hand (9 + points) and two suits, responder bids 1 NT. The doubler now bids his suits up the line if there is no interference. If there is interference, the doubler should double again if short in the interference suit, and pass otherwise. (e) With specifically spades and diamonds, or hearts and clubs, responder can jump in either suit (which shows the other one), knowing that the doubler will have support for one of the suits.

ICELANDIC BRIDGE UNION (BRIDGE-SAM-BAND ISLANDS).

Founded in 1948 by six of the leading bridge clubs in Iceland, in 1982 there were approximately 1,500 members. The Union participates frequently in European Championships, finishing third in the 1950 event in Brighton, and also in the Scandinavian Championships, finishing third in 1966. In its first appearance in a World Team Olympiad 1968, Iceland finished tenth.

Officers, 1982:
President: Thorgeir Eyjolfsson
Secretary: Gudmundur Hermannsson, Lauavegur 28, 101 Reykjavik, Iceland

IDIOT COUP. A defensive play with an indelicate name which works only if the declarer is naive. Consider this position:

```
              A K 10 x x
  J x                      Q x
              x x x x
```

In normal circumstances the top honors are played. But if South leads from his hand and West plays the jack, South may have to think after winning in dummy. Since it would be bad play for West to split with Q–J–x, South should not be tempted to take a second round finesse. If he does so his partner may address him by the name of the Coup. If South continued with the ace, as any good player would, and finds that West began with Q–J–x, he has become the victim of a GROSVENOR GAMBIT.

This devious play requires more imagination when it is East who must attempt to divert declarer from an obvious winning line:

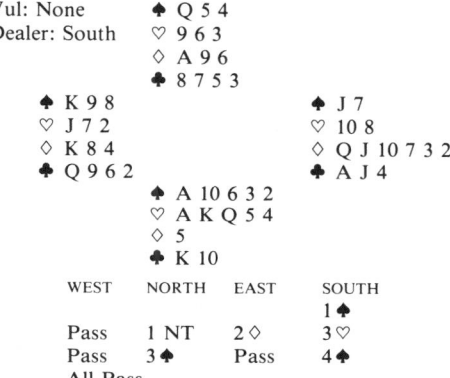

Vul: None   ♠ Q 5 4
Dealer: South ♡ 9 6 3
              ◇ A 9 6
              ♣ 8 7 5 3

♠ K 9 8   ♠ J 7
♡ J 7 2   ♡ 10 8
◇ K 8 4   ◇ Q J 10 7 3 2
♣ Q 9 6 2   ♣ A J 4

              ♠ A 10 6 3 2
              ♡ A K Q 5 4
              ◇ 5
              ♣ K 10

WEST	NORTH	EAST	SOUTH
			1♠
Pass	1 NT	2◇	3♡
Pass	3♠	Pass	4♠
All Pass			

South won the diamond lead, led to the ♠A and misjudged by ducking a trump to East's jack. Another diamond was ruffed, and South cashed three heart winners. To reach the dummy he ruffed a heart winner in order to lead to the ♣K. But MIKE SMOLEN as East confused the issue by throwing the ♣J. South fell into the trap by finessing the ♣10 to go down. Obviously East would not have thrown an honor from a queen–jack holding.

IDLE BIDS. Bids which have little or no natural function in a standard method of bidding, and which are therefore available for specialized use.

Bidding is a language with a limited vocabulary. If more bids can be added to a player's vocabulary without affecting other situations, efficiency tends to be increased. Theoreticians therefore search for idle bids, and try to assign useful meanings to them.

One example is a jump to 2 NT when the opener's suit bid has been doubled. This is idle because a player with a strong balanced hand would automatically redouble. Many players therefore use this bid conventionally to show a useful hand, probably 10-11 in high cards, with at least four-card support for the opener' suit. The immediate jump raise over the double can then be reserved for preemptive use. See 2 NT RESPONSE (OVER OPPONENT'S TAKEOUT DOUBLE).

Another example is a response of 5 NT to a 1 NT opening. As 4 NT is a natural invitation to 6 NT, 5 NT is not needed for that purpose. Some players therefore use it as an invitation to 7 NT, guaranteeing six. The same idea would apply to 2 NT-5 NT. See also IMPOSSIBLE BID.

IDLE CARD. See BUSY CARD and IDLE CARD.

ILLEGAL CALL. A call out of rotation, insufficient, or otherwise improper, during the bidding period of a hand.

ILLOGICAL BID. See IMPOSSIBLE BID.

IMP. Abbreviation for INTERNATIONAL MATCH-POINT. It is frequently used either as the three letters, or as the word *imp* in conversation.

IMP SCORING. See INTERNATIONAL MATCHPOINTS.

IMP TACTICS. Bidding and play at IMPs is an intermediate stage between match points and rubber bridge. It is important to understand the mathematical factors that influence the bidding of games and slams.

The Odds. Bidding a close, non-vulnerable game can gain a swing of 250 points, 6 IMPs. If you go down, you may lose a swing of 190 points, 5 IMPs. So the odds are only 6 to 5 in your favor, without allowing for the badly splitting hand on which you get doubled. It is about even money.

Vulnerable games, though, gain 10 IMPs and lose only 6. Here the odds are much more favorable. So, bid any vulnerable game that seems faintly possible; but bid a non-vulnerable game only with solid expectation of making it.

For example, suppose you hold:

♠ K 8 4
♡ A 10 2
◇ K 7 3
♣ Q J 10 5

After two passes, you open 1♣. Partner jumps to 2 NT. Push on to 3 NT if vulnerable, but pass if you are not.

Small slams are even-money bets at IMPs; you stand to gain or lose the same amount. However, tend to assume that any touch-and-go slam will not be bid at the other table. That's a fact of life. Thus, if you are comfortably ahead in the match, or playing a team you rate to beat easily, hold back; but if you are the underdog, play for the swing and bid. Actually, the best chance a weak team has to beat a stronger one is to bounce into slam whenever there seems to be a possibility of making.

Grand slams appear to have odds against them of only 15 to 11 non-vulnerable, or 17 to 13 vulnerable. These are not nearly so prohibitive as the 2 to 1 total-point odds — IMP scoring always reduces the big swing compared to the little one. But there is a hidden factor: at the other table, your opponents may not bid even a small slam. Then, going down in a grand slam vulnerable costs you 26 IMPs, the 13 you lose, plus the 13 you could have won: and making your grand slam gains only four IMPs extra. Perhaps you think it is next to impossible for the enemy to miss a small slam when you are thinking of a grand slam, but it has happened many, many times. So avoid grand slams unless you can count 13 tricks.

How does all this compare to matchpoint du-

plicate? There it probably pays to bid any game with a 45% chance. (You never get a tremendous score for staying out of a close game even when it should go down, for the defense is too often poor; and, after all, you are trying to get a big score and win the tournament.) This means that a duplicate buff playing at IMP scoring should be less willing than usual to bid a non-vulnerable game, but more ready to bid a vulnerable game. Slam bidding is much the same at IMPs as at pairs, but you are a little readier to bid a doubtful small slam at pairs, since you are more likely to need points urgently. In pairs, as at IMPs, you steer clear of doubtful grand slams, for a small slam bid and made is usually a good score.

One- and Two-IMP Swings. One major difference between IMPs and pair scoring is in the relative insignificance of tiny swings; overtricks, and the extra points for notrump or major suits. Play these North–South hands at 3 NT against the lead of the ◇2:

♠ 6 4
♡ 7 4
◇ A 8 3
♣ A K Q 7 5 2

♠ A K 10 5 2
♡ A J
◇ J 10 6 5
♣ 6 3

At matchpoint play, you should duck; this will probably allow you to make 11 tricks. Of course you will get a heart shift and will go down if clubs do not split, but you must try for the extra tricks. At IMP scoring, you rise with the ◇ A and concede a club, playing safe for your contract.

Now, suppose you ducked the diamond. Your heart stopper is knocked out; you test the clubs and they split 4–1. At matchpoints you take a diamond finesse and cash out for down one; it may even be a good score, for everyone is in the same spot. At IMPs, if you neglected to play safe, you would play a spade to your 10, trying desperately to make your contract, because an extra undertrick does not bother you. Defense is very much simpler at IMPs than at matchpoint pairs, for your objective is always to defeat the contract, never to stop overtricks. For example:

♠ A J 4 2
♡ 10 6 3
◇ 5
♣ K Q J 9 5

♠ 8 5
♡ A Q 2
◇ 10 8 6 3
♣ A 8 7 2

South opened 1♠, North bid 3♠, South 4♠. You are East, and your partner leads the ◇ K, won by declarer. Trumps are drawn and your ♣A is knocked out. At matchpoints you cash your ♡A, or, if hungry for a good score, you lead the ♡2, hoping that declarer has ♡ K-x-x and will duck to ensure his contract.

At IMPs you have no choice; you lead the ♡Q. Clearly, your best chance to defeat 4♠ (not to hold it to four, but to defeat it) is to find declarer with king-third or fourth in hearts and partner with J-9. Declarer is then likely to go wrong, playing you for Q-J. Of course, most of the time you will lose your ace, declarer will hold K-J or K-x, or K-9; but then you never could have defeated the contract.

In bidding, also, you ignore tiny differentials at IMPs keeping your eye on the main chance, making your contract. Suppose you hold:

$$♠ \ Q \ 5$$
$$♡ \ Q \ 8 \ 6 \ 3$$
$$◊ \ 8 \ 7$$
$$♣ \ A \ 10 \ 7 \ 4 \ 2$$

Partner opens 1♣, you respond 1♡, partner rebids 1 NT. At matchpoints, you might pass, hoping to make 120; at IMPs you bid 2♣. This must be safer, and you simply score 90 or 110 instead of 120 or 150.

Suppose you have the same hand when partner opens 1♦. You bid 1 NT; partner rebids 2♣. At matchpoints it is surely right to give a false preference to 2♦; at IMPs, it is surely better to raise clubs. Plus 110 and plus 140 are, in effect, the same at IMPs, and you look for the safest, not the largest, plus. Obviously, this applies even more forcibly to game and slam contracts. You are perfectly willing to play in a minor suit if it is safer; you never strain to play notrump or major suit contracts simply for the few extra points. Of course, whatever the scoring, it is hard to make 5♣ and 5◊, so these are not common contract. However, they should be played at IMPs much more often than at matchpoint pairs. The answer is: never even consider swings of one or two IMPs. Ignore them in your thinking about dummy play, defense or bidding. Of course, when your contract is secure (or when, on defense, you see that it is impossible to defeat the declarer), you can give yourself the pleasure of battling over the extra trick or tricks. But this is a frill. The business of IMP playing is making or setting contracts. The tiny swings almost always even out over a long match. And if your team goes out to win all the one-IMP and two-IMP swings, you are likely to lose the match.

Competing for Partscores. In many respects the fierce competition over partscore hands which characterizes matchpoint pairs should be carried over into IMPs. That is, you must do a lot of balancing; or, if you prefer, you must get into the auction early and very "lightly." One way or the other, you must not let the enemy buy a lot of contracts peacefully at the two level. The difference between 2♡, making two, and 3♡ down one, may be five IMPs, and a few swings like this can cost you a match.

Now, duplicate-oriented players usually do compete or balance at the two-level when playing IMPs. Where they tend to go wrong is in competing at the three-level. Here there is a big difference between the two games. This is a common dilemma in pairs.

WEST	NORTH	EAST	SOUTH
			1♠
Pass	2♣	Dbl	Pass
3♡	Pass	Pass	

You, South, hold:

$$♠ \ A \ Q \ 8 \ 6 \ 4$$
$$♡ \ A \ 8 \ 5$$
$$◊ \ K \ 10 \ 4$$
$$♣ \ J \ 8$$

If the cards lie favorably for your side, you might well make 3♠; you cannot get a good result defending. Likewise, if the lie is unfavorable, the opponents might make 3♡; then you might do better to go down at 3♠. So at matchpoints you should consider bidding.

At IMPs though, you should certainly pass. Whether you are + 140 or + 100 is a matter of one IMP; the same is true of − 100 or − 140. However, if both 3♡ and 3♠ go down, not at all unlikely, the swing can be five IMPs. If your distribution were unbalanced, so that both contracts might make, then six IMPs might be gained by bidding. But with a flat hand you should expect that only one contract or the other can be made, according to whose finesses work. You cannot lose much by passing, only by bidding.

The key is to think about plus scores on partscore hands, not how big a plus or how small a minus. If both pairs can be plus on three-quarters of the small hands, the team can win almost any match.

Sacrifice Bidding. One area of difference between the matchpoint and the IMP approach is in sacrificing against game contracts. Sacrificing can be very rewarding at matchpoints — it is a triumph to lose 300 rather than 420, or 500 rather than 620. At IMPs, though, for the swing of 120 points you earn three IMPs. And this is not a very good return on your investment, that is, for your gamble that the opponents could make their game. True, you are spared the worry of going for too much (losing 700 to save 620, for example); this costs only two IMPs. But if you take a PHANTOM SACRIFICE of 500 points against an unmakable game, you lose 12 IMPs. So the odds are not nearly as good as at duplicate.

The other side of this picture is that you are much more prone at IMPs than you are at duplicate to double an enemy sacrifice, rather than push on to five in a major. In a pair game you are reluctant to accept 500 points in exchange for a vulnerable game; it can almost be a zero. Playing IMPs though, you double a sacrifice bid unless you are a cinch for 11 tricks; the odds are greatly against bidding on.

Of course, this refers to the "matchpoint" type of sacrifice. In any game it pays to go for 100 or 300 against a vulnerable game. At any scoring it pays to bid on to five of a major on the chance you will make it when you feel that you may not beat the opponents by more than a trick. One should not say "never sacrifice" or "always double a sacrifice"; merely remember that the odds are quite different from those at matchpoints, so your normal tendencies must be different also.

Actually, one type of sacrifice is popular among experienced IMP competitors; this is a premature sacrifice made in the hope of stampeding the opponents to the five-level. Thus, it aims at a 12-IMP, not a three-IMP profit.

Suppose partner opens 3♡, not vulnerable against vulnerable, right-hand opponent doubles, and you hold:

♠ K 6
♡ A J 7 4
◇ Q 7 2
♣ 8 5 4 2

Jump to 5♡. You are likely to have to make this bid over 4♠, so bid it immediately. Your left-hand opponent, under pressure, may bid 5♠, down one.

Another time when a sacrifice aims at a large number of IMPs is when you save against a slam. Down six doubled, 1100, can gain eight IMPs if your partners make 1430.

Penalty Doubles. In almost all doubling situations at IMPs, the odds favor the coward, not the hero. Consider the position in which vulnerable opponents have crept up to 4♠ on a shaky auction. You can see that they are running into bad breaks and probably will go down, perhaps even two tricks. Then a double stands to gain 300 points for a two-trick set or lose 170 should the contract make; but the IMP odds are only 7 to 5. And if the opponent's contract is a silly one, your partners probably have stopped at a partscore; then a double stands to gain only an IMP or two, for you would have a handsome swing in your favor anyway.

This, actually, is quite similar to matchpoint thinking; why double the opponents if they have overbid when you are getting most of the points anyway? And maybe they have not overbid; and perhaps your double will allow them to make a contract which otherwise would go down; this is particularly disastrous at IMPs.

An entirely different situation is the one in which you are debating whether to double an enemy overcall or to bid your own game contract. At matchpoints the critical consideration is the vulnerability; can you score in penalties more than the value of your game? For example, suppose you hold:

♠ 7 2
♡ A Q 8
◇ K 9 8 3
♣ K 7 5 4

Partner opens 1♠, right-hand opponent overcalls 2◇. In a pair game you would certainly double if non-vulnerable against vulnerable; a two-trick set seems sure if partner stands the double. You would be reluctant to double at equal vulnerability, for fear that a two-trick set would not equal the score for the game which your side could probably make. At IMPs, in contrast, you should double at all but the most unfavorable vulnerability. If you lose 100 or 120 points (300 against 420, or 500 against 600), that is only three IMPs. But on the one deal in three when your cards will not produce game, you will win from 8 to 12 IMPs. So you will gain heavily in the long run, assuming that your own game contract is merely likely, not certain.

However, suppose you hold:

♠ Q J 6
♡ K 9 5
◇ K J 8 4
♣ A 10 3

With neither side vulnerable, partner opens 1♠ and right-hand opponent overcalls 2◇. At matchpoints you might double, hoping to collect 500 (when all you could make was 430 or 460). But at IMPs this

swing is worth only 1 or 2 IMPs; and if you score 300 (against 430 or 460 at the other table) you lose four IMPs. So you will lose in the long run by doubling. Suppose this situation comes up three times in an evening. On each occasion you double the enemy when you have a laydown game yourself, and twice you beat them 500, once 300. At matchpoints you would have two-thirds of the points, a winning percentage. At IMPs you would be minus.

The key question at IMPs, then, is whether or not your game is sure. With the first example, you can feel only that game is probable, so you are anxious to play for penalties. Holding the second example, you can hardly imagine a hand that partner can have which will not produce 10 or 11 tricks at notrump, so you are reluctant to double. In short, at IMPs, go for the surest, not the most sizable, plus score.

One big difference between proper matchpoint and IMP approach is in doubling enemy partscores on competitive auctions. If you have bid up to 3♡ in a pair game and vulnerable opponents contest with 3♠, you are likely to double any time you feel sure that your contract would make; you must try to get 200 instead of 100. Obviously, this is suicidal at IMPs. If you score 100 when 140 is made at the other table, you lose 1 IMP, and 200 would gain you only 2 IMPs. For this 3-IMP pickup, you are risking a loss of 12 IMPs when the doubled contract is made (and your teammates play it undoubled). At matchpoints, you would gain considerably by doubling such contracts even if one in three is made against you; at IMP scoring you would be a big loser.

Speculative lead-directing doubles (i.e., calling for a lead which does not ensure a set but merely increases your chances) are slightly better bets at IMPs than at total points. For example, suppose you double a non-vulnerable 3 NT contract to get a favorable lead. At matchpoints you are gambling a top against a bottom, instead of settling for slightly below average; the odds are a little better than even money. To figure the odds at IMPs, assume that the game is bid and made at the other table. If you beat the contract, you gain 500 while if it makes, you lose 150; these total-point odds become 11 IMPs to 4. The chance of overtricks reduces this to about two to one in your favor. That is, you will break even if the lead you direct beats one game in three.

The odds become most attractive when it is a slam which you are doubling. Superficially, this does not seem to be so. If you double a non-vulnerable 6♠ contract you gain 1080 (15 IMPs) when you beat it, while you lose 230 (6 IMPs) if you do not. But this assumes that the contract is the same at the other table, and this is an unwarranted assumption in the case of a close slam (as distinct from a touch-and-go game which probably will be bid). If only game is reached at the other table, your loss from doubling a makable slam is 1 IMP; and when your double was necessary to defeat the slam, your gain is 22 IMPs. (You gain 11 instead of losing 11.) At odds of 22 to 1, it is hard to go wrong.

General Tactics. There is another area of difference, though, caused not so much by the scoring as by the objectives of the two games. At matchpoints, you are trying to beat some huge (and ever increasing) number of competing pairs. At IMPs, you are trying to beat one team (at a time). And, in a pair contest, the huge field usually means that a great number of poor and inexperienced players are your direct or indirect opponents. But in an IMP team game you are not likely to meet any really bad opponents. What this means is that it is probably the winning style at matchpoints to try to beat par, to try for unusually good results; in contrast, at IMP scoring, this is not the winning style (unless you are far behind or a decided underdog).

Par bridge, i.e., taking everything which is yours without trying to steal what belongs to the enemy will win almost any IMP match. Of course, you and your teammates are bound to make a few errors, but if you play a steady game, and make fewer mistakes than your opponents, you will win. A 51% game is good enough. At matchpoints, 51% is a disaster; even 60% games will not win tournaments. You must take more chances (and this means make more bad bids) to win a pair game. One illustration of this is in preemptive bidding.

> ♠ 6
> ♡ K Q 10 8 6 4
> ◇ A J 10 6 3
> ♣ 2

At matchpoints one might open 4♡ as dealer with neither side vulnerable. At IMPs better heart spots would be desirable, and there is a greater chance that the hand should be played in diamonds, so open 1♡. At IMPs, there is less incentive to "steal."

Another illustration is in balancing in risky positions, i.e., when the opponents have not found a fit. Suppose that the auction goes as follows:

WEST	NORTH	EAST	SOUTH
1 NT*	Pass	Pass	?

With neither side vulnerable, you hold, sitting South:

> ♠ K 10 8 4 3
> ♡ 5
> ◇ A 10 6 5
> ♣ Q 7 4

At matchpoints, bid 2♠. If you pass, you are settling for a normal, under-average score; it would be better to try to beat par with an unsound overcall. At IMPs, you should pass, accepting the fact that it is "wrong" to overcall. The risk of a disastrous result is one you do not have to take when trying to beat one team instead of 200 pairs.

In the bridge world there are quite a few famous players whose great strength is their tactical bidding. (A "tactical" is a bad bid which gets a good result.) These experts do very well at matchpoints, winning far more than their share of tournaments, killing the weak fields. But they do poorly in team games.

So, save your bad bids for matchpoints. When you play IMPs, try a cautious, cowardly style: leave the heroics to your opponents. Then, at the end of the match you can compliment them for some brilliant bid while they are congratulating you for winning. (Reprinted by permission from *The Bridge World*, Nov.-Dec. 1963.)

Edgar Kaplan

---
*16–18

IMPS FOR PAIR GAMES. Used for some pair events, particularly for team trials. There are two methods. (1) Set up a norm for each deal, usually arrived at by taking the average of all the results on the deal, excluding the top and bottom scores. Then each pair's result is IMPed against the norm. The winner is the pair with the highest plus. (2) Two expert pairs play all the deals against each other, and their results become the norms. Using this method, however, it is necessary to have two sets of winners, one North–South and one East–West. See INTERNATIONAL MATCHPOINTS.

IMPERFECT PACK. A pack of playing cards which is incomplete or in which one or more cards are duplicated. See LAWS (Laws 11, 12), LAWS OF DUPLICATE (Laws 13, 14).

IMPOSSIBLE BID. Legally, an "inadmissible call" (see LAWS 36-39). A bid of eight is one example. A historic case was the double of "two cokes" ordered by the right-hand opponent. (It was suggested that this required a minimum holding of two Scotches.)

Technically, a bid which is inconsistent with previous bidding by the same player, and which therefore reveals that he is ignorant of bidding principles or has made a mistake.

For example, the bidding 1 NT—3 NT—4 NT is impossible. If made by a good player, it would imply that the first bid was a mistake: probably there was an ace hidden when he counted his hand originally.

However, some impossible bids become possible on closer examination. A bid which is forcing but limited can often be employed in a sense which appears impossible. MARSHALL MILES suggested a response of 2 NT to a suit bid with a balanced hand counting about 19 points. The idea was to follow with a natural 4 NT bid, so describing accurately a hand which is difficult to define by normal methods. See also IDLE BIDS.

IMPOSSIBLE NEGATIVE. A method of responding over a PRECISION CLUB opening in order to show 4-4-4-1 distribution. Responder first makes the negative response of 1 ◇, then jumps in his short suit in order to show that he did not have a negative hand after all.

IMPROPER CALL. A bid or double during the auction when the caller is under obligation to pass.

IMPROPER REMARK. Any statement or question by a player during the play or bidding of a hand which refers to a possible holding or interpretation of an action of the current hand. The proprieties of the game state that any information must be exchanged between partners by proper calls at a steady rhythm, or by the order of play of cards when a choice of possible plays is present. See PROPRIETIES and COFFEE-HOUSE.

IMPROPRIETY. A violation or breach of ethical conduct; also the failure to observe proper etiquette. See ETHICS; ETIQUETTE; LAWS (Proprieties, I–III).

IN BACK OF. A term describing the relationship of

a player to the opponent on his right; i. e., a player who plays after the player on his right is said to be "in back of" that player. An equivalent term is "over."

IN FRONT OF. The phrase used to describe the relationship between a player and his left-hand opponent; i.e., the player who plays before another player is said to be "in front of" that player. An equivalent term is "under."

IN THE RED. A seeming paradox in bridge terminology: in rubber bridge or CHICAGO it would mean being a loser, but in duplicate it describes a score good enough to earn master points, because rankings that qualify for points are indicated in red on the recap sheet.

INADMISSIBLE CALLS. See LAWS (Laws 36–39).

INADMISSIBLE DOUBLE OR REDOUBLE. See LAWS (Law 36).

INADVERTENT CALL. See LAWS (Law 24).

INADVERTENT INFRINGEMENT OF LAW. A violation of the proper procedure without deliberate attempt to do so. It is assumed that all infringements of laws are inadvertent, and the penalties prescribed for such infringements are designed to indemnify the non-offenders against potential loss as a result of such inadvertence.

INCOMPLETE HAND. An original holding of less than thirteen cards. Any missing card or cards are presumed to have been a part of the original hand, no matter where it or they may be found, unless attention is called to the imperfection. It is the responsibility of each player to count his cards at each deal. See LAWS (Law 11); LAWS OF DUPLICATE (Laws 13, 14).

INCOMPLETE PACK. A pack of cards from which one or more cards are missing. If a deal is made from an incomplete pack, the deal is void, if discovered within the legal time limits, and a new pack is substituted.

INCOMPLETE TABLE. (1) In club play, a table of four or five players in which there is room for a new comer to cut in. Some clubs designate five players, some six, as a full complement of players. (2) In home play, two or three players in search of one or two. (3) In duplicate play, see HALF TABLE.

INCORRECT CARD. Any card played which is improper in that it may become a revoke, or is played out of turn. See LAWS OF DUPLICATE (Laws 52, 61–63.)

INDEMNIFY. To give redress to a side that has been injured by an infraction of the rules by the other side. In duplicate bridge it is the duty of the tournament director to impose penalties for infractions. See LAWS OF DUPLICATE (Law 10). In rubber bridge a penalty may be imposed by agreement of

the players, or by either member of the non-offending side (except dummy) so long as he does not consult his partner. See LAWS OF CONTRACT BRIDGE (Law 14).

INDIA. See BRIDGE FEDERATION OF INDIA.

INDICATOR. Gadget by which the final contract can be indicated on the table, to aid bridge players with memory lapses. However, players who forget the final contract during the play of the hand also forget to set the indicator. It has not proved popular.

INDICES. Small identifying marks in the corners of playing cards, printed above the suit symbol.

The first use of indices is difficult to determine. Special packs of the seventeenth and eighteenth centuries (educational, heraldic, political, etc.) had so much of the card taken up with pictures and words that the identification consisted of a number or letter beside one pip in an upper corner. No one seems to have adapted this for use with regular playing cards for a long time. In the 1870s three American card makers tried different solutions to the problem. One put miniature cards in two corners (calling the style *Triplicate*); another used merely a letter or number and a small pip (called *Squeezers*, because they did not need to be fanned); the third put these in all four corners (*Quadruplicate*).

The use of double indices permits a hand to be fanned either right or left, and European cards today are usually so made; English and American players chose the single index at each end which is current today. In 1893 some packs were issued with a large corner pip, with a white index within it. Today some Swiss packs use no index pip, but put the index as a white numeral in the pip nearest the corner. Spanish and some Italian (trappola) packs have indices from 1 to 13, including both suit and court cards.

INDIVIDUAL MOVEMENT. A method of competition in which each contestant plays with many different partners. The movement most often used is the RAINBOW MOVEMENT, in which all players are in direct competition only with those players who began play in the same direction. The movement works as follows: North players are stationary, South players progress each round to the next higher numbered table, East players skip a table toward the higher numbered table, West players skip a table toward the lower numbered table, and the boards are passed to the next lower numbered table.

The movement is especially effective when the number of tables in play is a prime number — 5, 7, 11, 13, 17, 19. In a five-table game, five boards are put out at each table. After the second board, East and South switch positions, and after the fourth board, the original East sits West and the original West moves to the South position. In this way, each player plays with three different partners each round — a total of 15 partners during the session. In a seven-table game, three boards are put out at a table. After the first board, East and South switch positions, and after the second board, the original East sits West and the original West moves to South. For the other prime numbers, two boards are put out at each table. After the first board, South and East switch positions. All players resume their original directions at the start of each round.

Workable Rainbow movements have been invented for nine tables (21-board game) and 15 tables (24-board game). Appendix Rainbow movements are available for eight, 10, 12, and 14 tables. However, it is often preferable to break some of the larger games into two sections — 10 tables becomes two five-table sections, 12 tables becomes a seven and a five, 14 tables becomes two sevens, 16 tables becomes a nine and a seven, 18 tables becomes two nines, etc.

The SHOMATE MOVEMENT also is possible for some games, but it is not recommended although it does provide for balanced comparisons of a sort. The Shomate involves many movement irregularities and is a major chore to score. Modern-day directors almost never use the Shomate.

Two tables with eight, nine and 10 players can be accommodated in an Individual tournament. The boards of each round are relayed between the two tables, with one less round than there are players. The game can be curtailed at any point, as all boards are completed after each round. In all cases, the players are assigned numbers. They replace the player with the next lower number at the end of each round. (In the eight-player movement, player #8 is stationary, and #1 replaces #7.) Starting assignments are as follows:

	Table 1				Table 2			
	N	S	E	W	N	S	E	W
8 players	8	1	6	2	5	7	3	4
9 players	2	4	3	7	6	5	8	9
10 players	1	5	4	6	3	8	9	10

Three tables (12 or 13 players) can also compete. For 12 players the boards are relayed among the three tables, making a minimum of three boards per round. Complete play thus requires 33 boards, but it may be curtailed after any set of boards has been finished. Original assignment at tables (in order, North, South, East, West) are: table 1: 12, 1, 5, 11; table 2: 4, 3, 10, 7; table 3: 2, 9, 6, 8. Player #12 is stationary, each player replacing the player with next lower number, #1 replacing #11 at the end of each round.

The 13-player movement runs 13 rounds, two boards to a round. The tables play the boards in ascending order, the first set starting at table 1, sixth set at table 2 and 12th set at table 3. Seating assignments are as follows: table 1: 1, 3, 5, 6; table 2: 7, 12, 13, 4; table 3: 2, 9, 8, 11. All players replace the next lower numbered player for the next round, player #1 replacing player #13.

Sixteen players play 12 rounds of two boards with boards 1 and 2 at table 1 for the first round, boards 3 and 4 shared between tables 2 and 3, and boards 5 and 6 at table 4. Tables 2 and 3 share boards throughout. Additional boards feed in at table 4, and are out of play after three rounds. With 17 players, the relay is unnecessary. Thirteen rounds are played, the first three sets of boards on tables 1 to 3 and the sixth set on table 4, progressing to

lower-numbered tables. In the original seating diagrams below, players with the four highest numbers remain stationary throughout; other players replace the player with the next lower number (#1 following #12 in the 16-player game, and sitting out one round and replacing #13 in the 17-player game).

16-Player						17-Player				
	N	S	E	W	Bds		N	S	E	W	Bds
Table 1	16	1	6	10	1–2	17	8	1	3	1–2
Table 2	4	5	13	3	3–4 RELAY	10	16	6	5	3–4
Table 3	8	15	12	9	3–4 RELAY	9	13	15	12	5–6
Table 4	7	2	11	14	5–6	11	4	7	14	11–12

Boards go to the next lower table in order until boards 25–26 have been played at table 3. Then boards 1–2 follow 25–26.

Boards follow in order. Players sitting out are factored up.

INDIVIDUAL TOURNAMENT. A bridge competition in which each contestant plays with many different partners, playing one or two hands with each. Obviously it is impractical to have partnership understandings with so many players in the limited time available for discussion, so that bidding systems are kept simple, and conventional bids held to a minimum. In order to eliminate a certain amount of the luck involved in indiscriminate partnerships, it is frequently desirable to break the field by masterpoint holdings into two or more flights. For movements used, see RAINBOW, APPENDIX (Rainbow) TABLE, and others discussed under the appropriate number of TABLES and INDIVIDUAL MOVEMENTS.

INDONESIA. See ALL INDONESIA BRIDGE ASSOCIATION.

INFERENCE. A conclusion drawn from a call or play made by partner or an opponent. Though the ability to gather and assimilate the most delicate clues is the hallmark of a fine player, the bidding and play of many hands abound with inferences that can be drawn by the average performer provided that he is alert and knows what to look for. Note than an inference implies uncertainty. An inference leaving no room for doubt would be a deduction.

A declarer's task is frequently lessened when the opponents have been in the auction; apart from yielding specific information about the enemy suit(s), interference bidding generally assists the declarer to *guess* better in the play of a critical suit. For example in playing a common combination such as:

K J 10 9

A 8 7 6

Declarer has to catch the queen, and with nothing to guide him, he must sometimes guess wrong. See TWO-WAY FINESSE. Suppose, however, that in the course of the auction West has made a preemptive bid marking himself with shortages elsewhere; the odds now clearly favor a finesse against his partner.

In taking advantage of the information provided by the bidding, a declarer frequently must resort to unusual plays: (See hand at top of next page.)

South is declarer in 4♠ after East has opened the bidding with 1 NT. West leads a trump, and South,

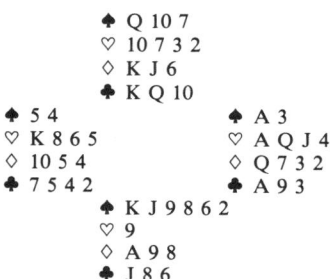

```
                ♠ Q 10 7
                ♡ 10 7 3 2
                ◊ K J 6
                ♣ K Q 10
    ♠ 5 4                      ♠ A 3
    ♡ K 8 6 5                  ♡ A Q J 4
    ◊ 10 5 4                   ◊ Q 7 3 2
    ♣ 7 5 4 2                  ♣ A 9 3
                ♠ K J 9 8 6 2
                ♡ 9
                ◊ A 9 8
                ♣ J 8 6
```

faced with three certain losers, has to avoid losing a diamond. The standard play of this combination is to finesse the jack, but in this instance declarer is fairly sure that East has the queen from his bid. His best chance is to take a backward finesse, leading the jack through East, and if covered, finessing against West for the 10 on the second round.

Sometimes the defenders' side find themselves in the unhappy position of guiding declarer's play through not bidding:

```
                ♠ K Q 4
                ♡ Q 6
                ◊ Q J 4 3
                ♣ A J 10 5
    7 5                        ♠ J 9 2
    ♡ A K 4 3                  ♡ J 9 7 5 2
    ◊ K 7 6                    ◊ 10 9 8 5
    ♣ 8 7 4 2                  ♣ K
                ♠ A 10 8 6 3
                ♡ 10 8
                ◊ A 2
                ♣ Q 9 6 3
```

The bidding:

WEST	NORTH	EAST	SOUTH
Pass	1♣	Pass	1♠
Pass	2♣	Pass	4♠
All Pass			

West cashes two hearts, and shifts to a trump, declarer drawing three rounds ending in dummy in order to take the diamond finesse. West wins and exits with a heart, South ruffing. The ♣K is now marked with East, for in the play West has shown up with the ♣A, ♡K and ◊K, and if he also held the ♣K he would have opened the bidding. Declarer's only chance is that the king is singleton. Accordingly, he plays a club to the ace, dropping East's lone king, winning both the contract and suspicious looks from the opposition.

Declarer has an even greater scope for making educated guesses based upon the play of the opponents' cards. This is particularly true when the defenders are forced to discard on a long suit, the order of their discards being most helpful to declarer. The accuracy of the inferences thus drawn varies with the skill of the opposition, for good players generally plan ahead in these situations, often leaving the declarer with little to go on. Nevertheless, it is the mark of a good player that he *guesses* the right play more often than not.

On rare occasions, the defenders are helpless to prevent declarer from gaining an inference.

```
                ♠ A 10
                ♡ J 4 3
                ◊ K Q 2
                ♣ A K Q 9 3
    ♠ 5 3 2                    ♠ K
    ♡ Q 7                      ♡ A K 10 9 6 5
    ◊ 9 7 6 3                  ◊ A 5 4
    ♣ 10 8 6 4                 ♣ 7 5 2
                ♠ Q J 9 8 7 6 4
                ♡ 8 2
                ◊ J 10 8
                ♣ J
```

The bidding:

WEST	NORTH	EAST	SOUTH
	1♣	1♡	3♠
Pass	4♠	All Pass	

West leads the ♡Q and continues the suit, East winning the king. After cashing the ◊A, East is in a cleft stick: if he returns a third heart, South will ruff high and West's failure to overruff will mark the ♠K. On the other hand, if he does not continue hearts, South's suspicions will be aroused and he is bound to diagnose the position.

The defending side is sometimes better placed to make deductions, for they have the advantage of being able to gather clues from both declarer's and partner's actions.

In a general way, the defenders can make certain assumptions about the nature of declarer's holding by his approach. For example, at a suit contract, if he plays a side-suit before broaching trumps, he probably has a shaky trump suit. On the other hand, if trumps are drawn immediately, it is safe to infer that declarer intends to utilize a side-suit to dispose of his losers. At notrump, when declarer makes no attempt to establish a strong suit, it is reasonably certain that the suit is ready to run.

```
                ♠ 8 7 6
                ♡ A 2
                ◊ K J 10 4 3
                ♣ Q 4 3
        ♠ K Q 10 9 4
        ♡ J 4 3
        ◊ 9 2
        ♣ A J 10
```

The bidding:

WEST	NORTH	EAST	SOUTH
			1 NT
Pass	3 NT	All Pass	

West leads the ♠K, which declarer wins with the ace. To the second trick, South leads a club; West plays the ace and then the ♠Q, dropping declarer's jack, and takes three further spade tricks to defeat the contract.

South held:

```
                ♠ A J
                ♡ K 9 7
                ◊ A Q 8 7
                ♣ K 9 5 2
```

West made two unusual plays: he rose with the ♣A in a position where it is customary to play low, and he continued spades at the risk of establishing the jack for declarer. The question is: how did he know? West reasoned that declarer could not have started with A-J-x of spades, for with that holding he would have surely refused the first spade, rendering the defense helpless. Either partner had the jack or, more likely, declarer had A-J alone. Further, declarer's failure to play on diamonds surely meant that the suit was solid, in which case, if declarer was permitted to steal a club, he would almost certainly have 9 tricks: one spade, five diamonds, one club, and two hearts (he was likely to have the ♡ K for his bid).

Defenders are often misled into committing a blunder, basing their defense on the assumption that a declarer has adopted a reasonable line of play. Similarly, in deciding his play at a crucial point in a hand, a defender has to assume that his partner has played well. TERENCE REESE gives this example:

```
              ♠ Q 6
              ♡ A Q J 9 5
              ◊ J 9 4
              ♣ Q 7 4
♠ 10 5                    ♠ J 9 4
♡ 8 6 2                   ♡ 7 3
◊ A 5 2                   ◊ K Q 10 7
♣ K 10 6 5 3             ♣ A 9 8 2
              ♠ A K 8 7 3 2
              ♡ K 10 4
              ◊ 8 6 3
              ♣ J
```

South plays in 4♠ and West leads the ♣5 to his partner's ace. East shifts to the ◊ K and continues with the 7, declarer falsecarding with the 8. West is now faced with the problem of *guessing* whether to attempt to cash the third diamond or the ♣K. From his point of view, declarer might have well dropped the ♣J at trick one from J-x, and with apparently nothing to guide him he played the ♣K, giving declarer the contract. West failed to draw the proper inference from his partner's play: if East had held five diamonds, leaving declarer with two, he would have realized that the defense could take only two diamond tricks and would have played the ◊ Q to hold the lead before shifting back to clubs. See also CARD READING and COUNTING THE HAND.

Sammy Kehela

INFERENTIAL PROBLEM. A problem which requires the deduction of the lie of hidden cards through the use of information of a form not found in ordinary play.

Two examples of inferential problems follow. The first problem is of moderate difficulty and provides a good introduction to inferential problems. The second problem is a harder nut to crack with only one clue given as to the makeup of the concealed hands.

Big Casino and Little Casino*

by Jeff Rubens

Contract: 6 ◊ by South
Clues: (See hand at top of next column.)

*Reprinted from *The Bridge Journal*, Jan.-Feb. 1964.

```
              ♠ 3
              ♡ 9 6 4
              ◊ A 7 6
              ♣ K Q 9 5 4 2

              ♠ A Q 9 5 4
              ♡ 3 2
              ◊ K 9 5 3
              ♣ A 10
```

(1) After the lead of any black card, South can make his contract by perfect play. However, after the lead of any red card, perfect defense can defeat the contract.

(2) (A "spot card" is any card from 2 through 10.) The sum of East's spot cards in hearts subtracted from the sum of his spot cards in diamonds is exactly one third of the sum of all his black spot cards.

(3) Neither defender is void of hearts, and neither defender holds both big casino (◊ 10) and little casino (♣ 2).

What are the exact East-West hands and how does South fulfill his contract after a favorable lead?

Solution to "Big Casino and Little Casino"

As neither defender is void of hearts, South must discard all his hearts before losing the lead. Further, he cannot lose a trick to one of the three missing low trumps. If diamonds are 3-3, no discards can be taken. Therefore, diamonds must be 4-2 with West holding two blank honors. In this way, declarer can obtain two discards on the clubs in dummy. These discards must be taken after two trumps are drawn, therefore one ruff must establish the spade suit. This places East with ♠ K-J-10 and four clubs. East's four clubs must include the jack as the lead of a black card must help declarer by providing an entry for a black suit finesse. Since the sum of East's black spot cards is divisible by three, East must hold ♣ J-8-6-3. Since West holds the ♠ 2, East's diamond honor is the 10. Therefore, East holds two hearts with a spot total of 15 and the East-West hands are:

```
♠ 8 7 6 2            ♠ K J 10
♡ A K Q J ? ?        ♡ ? ?
◊ Q J                ◊ 10 8 4 2
♣ 7                  ♣ J 8 6 3
```

After a black suit lead, declarer wins cheaply. He cashes the ◊ K and ◊ A, takes the remaining black suit finesse, clears all the black suit tops in the South hand, ruffs a spade in dummy and discards two hearts on good clubs. Clubs are now continued until East ruffs. If East ruffs low, South overruffs and leads good spades. If East ruffs high, South takes the balance easily. If East never ruffs, he is trump couped at trick 12.

East's two hearts must be 10-5, not 8-7, for if East held ♡ 8-7, the opening lead of ♡ 5 would not defeat the contract!

Inferential Problem*

By Terence Reese

*Reprinted from *The Bridge World*. Feb. 1950.

♠ 8 5 2
♡ J 6
♢ K 6 5 3 2
♣ 8 6 5

♠ K J 9 6
♡ K 7
♢ J 9 4
♣ Q 9 4 2

South played a contract of 3 NT. West led the ♣ 6. East won with the ace and returned the 4. West won with the jack and played the king, on which East played the 3, and all followed. West then cashed the thirteenth spade. The contract was just made.

"Nicely played," said West to declarer at the end of the hand. "There was nothing we could do, was there, partner?"

"Well, yes," said East. "If, at the fourth trick, you had played any card except the thirteenth spade we could have put them one down."

Assuming that East was right, what was South's hand?

Solution to "Inferential Problem"

The key lies in realizing that the last spade, in addition to making the timing right for a squeeze, gives South a chance to unblock in diamonds. The diamond holding is A-Q-8-7, and the suit is blocked unless South can discard one of them. (The diamonds cannot be A-Q-10-8 or A-Q-10-7, for then a diamond lead by West would resolve the difficulty.)

Declarer has, at most, eight tricks on top. The ninth can come only from a squeeze in hearts and clubs. The hearts must be A-Q alone — if A-Q-x, the lead of ♡ K would be fatal to the defense — and the clubs A-K-7-3, for if they are as good as A-K-10-x, the lead of ♣ Q gives South three tricks in clubs, an enables him to endplay West. So the whole hand is:

♠ Q 10 7   ♡ A Q   ♢ A Q 8 7   ♣ A K 7 3

The play, when West leads the last spade, is to discard a heart from dummy and a diamond from declarer's hand. West exists with a diamond; declarer cashes the ♣ A-K, and runs off the diamonds. The last diamond squeezes West in hearts and clubs.

Jeff Rubens

INFORMATION, UNAUTHORIZED. See UN-AUTHORIZED INFORMATION.

INFORMATORY DOUBLE. An early name for the TAKEOUT DOUBLE. More recently used by ROBERT EWEN in his book on doubles to encompass doubles designed to give the partner of the doubler a variety of options or information, such as the COMPETITIVE DOUBLE.

INFORMATORY PASS. See PENALTY PASS.

INHIBITORY DOUBLE. A psychic maneuver in a competitive auction aimed at intimidating the opponents. It usually takes the form of a double of a forcing bid after partner has made an overcall. For example:

WEST	NORTH	EAST	SOUTH
			Pass
1♡	2♣	2♠	Dbl

East's 2♠ bid is clearly forcing, and if South held a good hand with spades he would be well advised to wait for better things. The doubler, in fact, usually has a bad hand with support for his partner's suit, to which the latter retreats at his turn.

INITIAL BID. The first bid of any deal. See OPENING BID.

INITIAL LEAD. The first lead of any deal. See OPENING LEAD.

INNER SEQUENCE. A sequence of which the top card is not the top card of the suit holding. In a holding Q-10-9-8, the inner sequence is the 10-9-8. See INTERIOR SEQUENCE.

INSPECTION OF TRICKS. (1) A trick may be inspected by any player until such player has turned his play to the trick face down. (2) Until play ceases, QUITTED TRICKS may not be inspected except at the director's specific instruction. (3) After play ceases, the played and unplayed cards may be inspected to settle, e. g., a claim of a revoke or of the number of tricks won and lost; but no player should handle cards other than his own. See LAWS OF DUPLICATE, Law 66.

INSTINCT (or intuition). A term loosely applied to one's inherent feeling about the right play, or less often the right bid, to make during a deal of bridge. Some players are said to be totally devoid of instinct or card sense (really sensitivity), and have to make calculations either rapid or involved for any play involving percentages. The concept of "instinct" as such has been challenged by many authorities, but those who possess it or claim to possess it maintain its definite existence. See TABLE PRESENCE.

INSTRUCTIONS (director's). The announcements by the director by which a movement in a session of duplicate bridge is completed. At the end of each round, the director instructs the players as to their movement and the movement of the boards in play. At determined times, this movement may vary for one or more rounds. The ARROW SWITCH, SKIP, and redistribution of boards are examples of such variations. Instructions are also given to the contestants for twinning of boards, methods of qualification, starting times for succeeding sessions, and other conditions of contest.

INSUFFICIENT BID. A bid which is lower in rank than a bid previously made in the same auction. For the penalties involved, see LAWS (Law 27).

INSULT. The 50-point penalty that the doubling side pays for doubling a contract that the declaring side makes.

INTERCITY MATCH. Many intercity matches have been played in various parts of North America.

Notable among these were the series between New York and Philadelphia which the latter won regularly.

The first matches to have official status were those for the *Sports Illustrated* Trophy, subsequently for the Congress Playing Card Trophy when the United States Playing Card Company assumed chief sponsorship of the series in 1966 which it withdrew after the 1968 matches. These two-day events preceded the Summer North American Championships from 1960 to 1973, and the city acting as host for the NAC was the contender against the defending champions. The first contest was held in California in 1960. It was held twice that year, at the Summer NAC and again in the fall, and also in 1968 when New York hosted the Spring NAC. Results are listed as follows:

YEAR	WINNER	LOSER
1960	Los Angeles	New York
1960	Los Angeles	New York
1961	Houston	Los Angeles
1962	Twin Cities	Houston
1963	Los Angeles	Twin Cities
1964	Los Angeles	Toronto
1965	Chicago	Los Angeles
1966	Chicago	Denver
1967	Montreal	Chicago
1968	Montreal	New York
1968	Minneapolis	Montreal
1969	Los Angeles	Minneapolis
1970	Boston	Los Angeles
1971	Boston	Chicago
1972	Boston	Denver
1973	Boston	Washington

INTERCOLLEGIATE BRIDGE TOURNAMENT. An annual event formerly contested by universities and colleges throughout the United States and Canada, organized by GEOFFREY MOTT-SMITH, 1949–1960, WILLIAM ROOT, 1961–1965, LAWRENCE ROSLER and JEFF RUBENS, 1966–1967, and subsequently by representatives of the Association of College Unions—International and the American Contract Bridge League. When the Charles Goren Foundation offered financial assistance in 1969 the tournament became known as the Charles Goren Intercollegiate Bridge Tournament. One year—in 1974—the Celanese Corporation assumed full financial responsibility for the tournament.

A feature of the tournament in the early years was the use of par hands. The earliest matches were conducted as a face-to-face contest for 16 finalists, but in 1953 the procedure was changed to a mailing of par hands to each campus with the scorecards rated in New York. Under this plan, titles were awarded to the highest-scoring pair on the North-South hands and on the East-West hands. In 1965, the face-to-face final was restored and par hands were used in the qualifying round. Initially, the final was scored by matchpoints, but international matchpoint scoring was adopted in 1967, and the conversion of IMPs to Victory points was introduced in 1968. Par hands were eliminated in 1969, and the tournament became a three-stage contest, with an on-campus qualifying round and a regional semifinal in addition to the final. The national final had the reputation of being a showcase tournament and a number of national champions emerged from these contests. The 37th and final contest was held in Memphis in April, 1979 after which the ACBL withdrew technical and financial support. For a list of Intercollegiate winners, see Appendix I.

INTEREST-SHOWING BIDS. Bids which can be used as an alternative to CUEBIDS when the opener and responder have agreed on a major suit at the level of three or four. Having been often suggested and played in the United States without achieving popularity, they were developed in 1948 by some Cambridge University, England, players (E.M.L. and J.R.A. Beale, and H. Peter F. Swinnerton-Dyer), and are an optional part of the ACOL SYSTEM.

If the bidding goes 1♠–3♠; 1♠–4♠; 2♠–3♠; or 2♠–4♠; or similarly in hearts, a change of suit which would normally be a cuebid is made in a suit in which some support is needed. For example:

(a)	(b)
♠ A K 10 5 3	♠ K Q 9 5 4
♡ Q J 7 3	♡ A K J 6
◇ A	◇ Q 7 3
♣ K Q 7	♣ A

The opening bid of 1♠ is raised to 3♠, an Acol limit raise showing about 11 points or the equivalent counting distribution.

On hand (a) the interest-showing bid would be 4♡, indicating that the opener needs some help in the form of heart honors or a heart shortage.

The interest-showing bid may well be made in a three-card suit. On hand (b) the opener rebids 4◇ to ask for support in that suit.

In each of these cases a normal cuebid would leave the responder in doubt about how to evaluate his hand for slam purposes.

For an alternative treatment, see ASKING BIDS.

INTERFERENCE BID. Any defensive overcall which is not attacking or strength-showing, but is designed to obstruct somewhat the path of the opponents, who have already opened the bidding. Sometimes interference is made with pre-emptive or jump-bid tactics. See NUISANCE BID and OVERCALLS.

INTERIM RESPONSE. See WAITING BID.

INTERIOR CARD. An intermediate card; formerly, the second card in sequence, as the jack in a holding of queen, jack, and others.

INTERIOR SEQUENCE. A sequence within a suit such that the top card of the suit is not a part of the sequence, as the Q–J–10 in a holding of A–Q–J–10, or the J–10–9 in a holding of A–J–10–9. Some experts play that the lead of the jack against notrump denies a higher honor, and therefore lead the 10 from A–J–10 and K–J–10. By extension, a lead of the 10 can promise a higher honor by partnership agreement. The 9 would then be led from a holding headed 10–9. See JOURNALIST LEADS; RUSINOW LEADS; ZERO OR TWO HIGHER LEADS.

INTERMEDIATE CARDS. See BODY and SPOT CARDS.

INTERMEDIATE JUMP OVERCALL. A jump overcall promising a good six-card suit and a hand approximately the strength of an opening bid. An ideal hand with which to make an intermediate jump overcall in hearts would be ♠x–x ♡A–K–J–9–x–x

◊ A-x ♣ J-x-x. For alternative uses of the jump overcall see JUMP OVERCALL, ROMAN JUMP OVERCALL, WEAK JUMP OVERCALL.

INTERMEDIATE TWO-BID. An opening bid of two in a suit to show a strong hand somewhat short of game strength. In the original version, introduced about 1930, responder could pass the intermediate two-bid with a worthless hand, and some experts still play it in this fashion. Most, however, play it as a one-round force, with 2 NT the required weakness response. See ACOL TWO-BID.

INTERNAL BLOCK. See UNBLOCKING.

INTERNATIONAL BRIDGE. There have been international tournaments and challenge matches since the earliest years of bridge. The first officially sponsored international tournament was held in Vienna in June 1930 under the auspices of the AUSTRIAN BRIDGE FEDERATION. The first international organization was the INTERNATIONAL BRIDGE LEAGUE, founded in 1932 by a small group of European countries, which conducted European championships until 1939. After World War II, the EUROPEAN BRIDGE LEAGUE was formed to replace the IBL. Today there are a large number of regional international organizations or tournaments. See BALTIC CONGRESS; CENTRAL AMERICAN AND CARIBBEAN BRIDGE FEDERATION; COMMON MARKET CHAMPIONSHIPS; FAR EAST BRIDGE FEDERATION; NORDIC CHAMPIONSHIPS; SOUTH AMERICAN BRIDGE CONFEDERATION; SOUTHERN AFRICAN BRIDGE FEDERATION; BRIDGE FEDERATION OF ASIA AND THE MIDDLE EAST.

The first official world championship was held in New York in 1935 between France, reigning European champions, and a team representing the AMERICAN BRIDGE LEAGUE. The only other pre-war world championship was held in 1937 in Austria, hosted by the IBL. World championship play resumed in 1950 with the first of a series of contests for the BERMUDA BOWL. Since 1963 the Bermuda Bowl has been conducted by the WORLD BRIDGE FEDERATION, formed in 1958. The WBF also conducts WORLD PAIR CHAMPIONSHIPS, WORLD TEAM OLYMPIADS, VENICE TROPHY matches and ROSENBLUM CUP matches.

INTERNATIONAL BRIDGE ACADEMY. Formed in 1965 at Ostend at the urging of JEAN BESSE and Pierre Collet for the purpose of fostering the study of bridge as a science. The Academy holds biennial Congresses in conjunction with the World Team and Pair Olympiads and publishes journals in French and English after each Congress, which include a report on the meeting as well as articles on the scientific and technical aspects of bridge. The Academy awarded its first literary prize in 1968 to GÉZA OTTLIK of Hungary for his *Bridge World* article "The Quest." Since 1966 it has staged a world bidding contest for the Marcel Peeters Challenge Cup, which has attracted wider international participation each year since its inception. Members of the Academy's Council of Directors are Jean Besse, President; Pierre Collet, General Secretary, BP 111, 1040 Brussels, Belgium, Charles Monk, Secretary; Ton Schipperheyn, Deputy Secretary; Edgar Kaplan and J. R. Vernes.

INTERNATIONAL BRIDGE LEAGUE. A forerunner of the WORLD BRIDGE FEDERATION, founded on June 10, 1932, at Scheveningen, The Netherlands, by a small group of European countries. During the years 1932–39, the IBL organized annual championships, including a WORLD CHAMPIONSHIP in Budapest in 1937. The other tournaments ranked as European Championships.

Presidents of the IBL were:

1932–3	Alfred E. Manning-Foster	Great Britain
1933–4	Anthony J. E. Lucardie	Holland
1934–5	R. Delhaye van Gransberghe	Belgium
1935–6	Dr. Emil Henriques	Sweden
1936–7	H. E. Tibor de Kallay	Hungary
1937–8	Johannes Brun	Norway

In 1936 and 1937 the IBL was subdivided into a European Division and an American Division. ALBERT MOREHEAD was president of the American Division.

INTERNATIONAL BRIDGE PRESS ASSOCIATION (IBPA). A worldwide organization of some 500 bridge writers, mostly professionals, whose reports and articles appear in newspapers and magazines and other periodicals in most countries where tournament bridge is played. Authors and radio and TV lecturers also are eligible for membership. The European Bridge Press Association, the father of the IBPA, was formed at the Oslo 1958 European Championships by the journalists present. At the first Olympiad, played in 1960 in Turin, many non-European bridge writers joined, so the name was changed to International Bridge Press Association. The first president, GUY RAMSEY, died in office and was succeeded by RAINIK HALLE, (1960–1964). JACK KELLY then served as president from 1964 until his death in 1970. RICHARD FREY then became president and served until he resigned the position in 1981. ALAN TRUSCOTT is the present president.

ERIC JANNERSTEN was executive secretary-treasurer from the foundation of the organization until he resigned that post in 1975. At that time he was named senior vice president for life. He was editor of the IBPA monthly bulletins until 1967, when RHODA BARROW (LEDERER) assumed the editorial duties. ALBERT DORMER took over the editorship in 1973 and retained that position until he resigned in 1981. He was succeeded by PATRICK JOURDAIN as editor and DAVID REX-TAYLOR as managing editor.

HERMAN FILARSKI took over as executive vice president in 1975 and was responsible for many promotions in which the IBPA was involved. These included the BOLS TIPS, which bridge writers throughout the world incorporated in their columns; the BOLS BRILLIANCY AWARDS, which are given at World Championships for outstanding articles by bridge writers about outstanding plays by competitors in the World Championships; the Philip Morris tournaments in Europe, which lead to a Grand Final in Monte Carlo each year; and the Heineken Fluke Award, which was given to the bridge writer who wrote the best story about a fluke during the 1980 World Team Olympiad in Valkenberg. The Bols Tips later were gathered together and expanded in a book for which TERENCE REESE was the editor.

Vice presidents for the IBPA have included JO VAN DEN BORRE, LEON SAPIRE, ARTURO JAQUES, HAROLD FRANKLIN, ALBERT MOREHEAD, ALFRED SHEINWOLD, JOSÉ Le DENTU, HENRY FRANCIS, Herman Filarski, Alan Truscott, CARLOS CABANNE, STEEN MØLLER, SVEND CARSTENSEN, and Albert Dormer.

The IBPA's functions have embraced negotiations with tournament organizers to improve working conditions and accessibility of information to the press; closer cooperation with national and international bridge organizations; publication of anthologies, such as *Bridge Writers Choice* (1964 and 1968) and *Bols Tips*; establishment and presentation of annual awards for accomplishments in various fields of bridge; the dissemination of news bulletins to members and associate members, and the sponsorship of bridge promotions.

1982 officers are: Alan Truscott, president; JEAN BESSE, first-vice president; ELOENE GRIGGS, secretary; BERL STALLARD, treasurer; DENIS HOWARD, counsel; and Anne Staveley, membership chairman. See INTERNATIONAL BRIDGE PRESS ASSOCIATION AWARDS.

INTERNATIONAL BRIDGE PRESS ASSOCIATION AWARDS.

Personality of the Year (Charles H. Goren Award)

1973	André Lemaître
1974	Julius L. Rosenblum
1975	Rixi Markus
1976	Herman Filarski
1977	Jaime Ortiz-Patiño
1978	Edgar Kaplan
1979	Amalya L. Kearse
1980	Deng Xiaoping
1981	Albert Dormer

Sportsman of the Year (John E. Simon Award)

1973	Omar Sharif
1974	Alan Sontag
1975	Donald A. Oakie
1976	Lord Glenkinglas, Sir Timothy Kitson, Rt. Hon. Harold Level MP
1977	Maurits Caransa
1978	Not Awarded
1979	Steve Landen
1980	Not Awarded
1981	Not Awarded

Best Article or Series on a System or Convention (C. C. Wei "Precision" Award)

1973	Charles H. Goren
1974	Eric Kokish
1975	George Rosenkranz
1976	Jeff Rubens
1977	Kit Woolsey
1978	Jeff Rubens
1979	Ed Manfield *and* Kenneth Lebensold
1980	Eddie Kantar
1981	Jeff Rubens

Best Played Hand of the Year (Charles J. Solomon Award)

1973	José le Dentu
1974	Benito Garozzo
1975	Tim Seres
1976	Harold Ogust
1977	Dominique Pilon
1978	Maurizio Sementa
1979	Benito Garozzo
1980	Andrzej Wilkosz
1981	Lajos Linczmayer

Best Bid Hand of the Year (George Rosenkranz "Romex" Award)

1975	Matt Granovetter, Ron Rubin
1976	Gabino Cintra, Christiano Fonseca
1977	Eric Kokish, Peter Nagy
1978	Chip Martel, Lew Stansby

1979	Kyle Larsen, Ron Von der Porten
1980	Knud-Aage Boesgaard, Peter Schaltz
1981	Not Awarded

The five annual awards serve a number of useful purposes: To confer distinction upon outstanding personalities in the world of bridge; to recognize excellence in bridge and to improve the standard of bridge journalism; to provide useful cash sums in addition to the distinction conferred; to gain publicity for IBPA and for bridge.

INTERNATIONAL CHAMPIONSHIPS. See WORLD CHAMPIONSHIPS; Appendix III for European Championships, Far East Championships, South American Championships; Appendix I for North American Championships.

INTERNATIONAL CODE. The Laws of Rubber Bridge or of Duplicate Contract Bridge.

INTERNATIONAL FUND PAIRS. One-session pair events held at the Spring and Fall North American Championships. These are in addition to the International Fund ACBL-WIDE GAMES held in May and July. The proceeds are used to defray the expense of North American participation in Bermuda Bowl competition.

INTERNATIONAL MASTER. See WORLD BRIDGE FEDERATION PLAYER RANKINGS.

INTERNATIONAL MATCH. A contest between two (or more) countries. See ANGLO-AMERICAN MATCHES; FRANCO-AMERICAN MATCHES; WORLD CHAMPIONSHIPS. For European Championships, Far East Championships, South American Championships, see Appendix III.

INTERNATIONAL MATCHPOINTS. A method of scoring used frequently in team events, and occasionally in pair events.

The procedure appears to have been invented in Vienna, and was first used at the international level in the 1938 European Championship in Oslo. IMPs were first used in the 1951 Bermuda Bowl.

The original name was EMP, or European Match Points. The original scale provided for a maximum gain of 12 points, as follows:

Point Diff.	EMP	Point Diff.	EMP
10– 30	1	400– 490	7
40– 60	2	500– 590	8
70–100	3	600– 740	9
110–180	4	750–1490	10
190–290	5	1500–1990	11
300–390	6	2000 and up	12

A revised scale was adopted for the 1948 European Championships in Copenhagen, with a maximum of 15 points. A further revision in 1961, devised by a subcommittee of the World Bridge Federation, brought the maximum to 25 points. This had the effect of increasing the relative award to large gains, and brought the scale slightly nearer to total-point scoring. A further revision was made effective September 1, 1962. That scale is still in use.

1948 Scale		1961 Scale	
Point Diff.	IMPs	Point Diff.	IMPs
0– 10	0	0– 10	0
20– 60	1	20– 40	1

		50– 80	2
70– 130	2	90– 120	3
140– 210	3	130– 160	4
		170– 210	5
220– 340	4	220– 260	6
350– 490	5	270– 310	7
		320– 360	8
500– 740	6	370– 420	9
750– 990	7	430– 490	10
		500– 590	11
1000–1240	8	600– 690	12
1250–1490	9	700– 790	13
		800– 890	14
1500–1990	10	900–1040	15
2000–2490	11	1050–1190	16
		1200–1340	17
2500–2990	12	1350–1490	18
3000–3490	13	1500–1740	19
		1750–1990	20
3500–3990	14	2000–2240	21
4000 and up	15	2250–2490	22
		2500–2990	23
		3000–3490	24
		3500 and up	25

1962 Scale

Total Points	IMPs	Total Points	Imps
20– 40	1	750– 890	13
50– 80	2	990–1090	14
90–120	3	1100–1290	15
130–160	4	1300–1490	16
170–210	5	1500–1740	17
220–260	6	1750–1990	18
270–310	7	2000–2240	19
320–360	8	2250–2490	20
370–420	9	2500–2990	21
430–490	10	3000–3490	22
500–590	11	3500–3990	23
600–740	12	4000–up	24

The purpose of introducing International Matchpoints was to eliminate the inherent defects of other methods: total-point scoring accented one or two big swing boards; board-a-match reduced all boards to equal status. The general effect of the graduated scale of International Matchpoints is to flatten the value of high scores and to heighten the value of partscore contracts.

In team games, the International Matchpoints are awarded after the net score of the team (North-South and East–West) has been computed. The points are awarded to the team with a positive net score.

In pair events, each pair is compared with an *average* score, and the International Matchpoints awarded may be positive (for a score better than average) or negative (for a score below the average). The *average* score is the arithmetic mean of all scores, except that the best and worst scores are usually omitted in computing the comparison value. The purpose of this is to prevent one unusual result influencing scores at other tables. The best and worst scores, however, are used in computing the difference for that pair from the average. The net IMP scores on each *match* may be converted into victory points on a graduated scale.

This use of IMP scoring in pair events was originated by the British Bridge League under the Chairmanship of GEOFFREY BUTLER, and is sometimes called the Butler Method.

The most logical use of International Matchpoint scoring in pair competition is in connection with qualifying events for pairs to compete in team events, as it adapts pair play to team scoring results. However, this method of scoring has been used successfully at the club level.

INTERNATIONAL OPEN TEAM SELECTION.

Many methods have been tried for selection of the North American team for Bermuda Bowl contests or of the United States team for World Olympiads. No method has proved satisfactory, but the following have been tried:

1950–60 — Team Performance:

From 1950 to 1960, the ACBL selected the winners of the SPINGOLD, or the victors in a play-off between the Spingold and VANDERBILT winners. This had the advantage of producing a well-knit team, but it sacrificed the theoretical objective of fielding the "best" team: it is unlikely that the best six players, or the best three pairs, will form themselves into a voluntary team.

In 1960 the United States was entitled, by virtue of the size of the ACBL membership, to send four teams to the first World Team Olympiad. Two of the teams sent were the winners of the Vanderbilt and the Spingold. Each of the other teams consisted of three pairs selected by a committee (the five most recent ACBL Presidents attending the 1959 Fall Nationals) from among the contestants remaining in the seventh or eight round of the Vanderbilt and Spingold respectively. The four teams were:

Spingold Winners	Vanderbilt Winners
Oswald Jacoby	John Crawford
Ira Rubin	Sidney Silodor
Victor Mitchell	B.J. Becker
William Grieve	Norman Kay
Morton Rubinow	Tobias Stone
Samuel Stayman	George Rapee
Benjamin O. Johnson (npc)	Julius Rosenblum (npc)
Spingold 2	*Vanderbilt 2*
Charles H. Goren	Leonard Harmon
Helen Sobel	Sidney Lazard
Howard Schenken	William Hanna
Harold Ogust	Meyer Schleifer
Lewis L. Mathe	Donald Oakie
Paul Allinger	Ivar Stakgold
R.L. Miles, Jr. (npc)	Harry Fishbein (npc)

1961 - Direct Selection:

The ACBL International Team for 1961 consisted of three pairs selected by the ACBL Board of Directors from among the winners and runners-up in major national events. The direct selection method suffers from the disadvantage that it is virtually impossible to find selectors who are: technically competent; objective and unattached to particular players; not themselves candidates for the team. Italy solved this problem by appointing CARLO ALBERTO PERROUX as "dictator" in charge of selection, but most countries would not accept this solution, even if a Perroux were available.

1962–69 Trials by Pairs:

In an effort to be fair and just, and to select pairs that are in effective current form, pairs trials were instituted in 1961 for the selection of the 1962 Team. From 1961 to 1966, the first three pairs in each trial were nominated as the international team for the following year, and the fourth-place pair became the alternate pair. Beginning with the 1967 trials, this automatic selection method was dropped and the nonplaying captain was permitted to select any two of the top four pairs, and the third and alternate pair from among the remaining finalists. JULIUS ROSENBLUM exercised this option in 1967 when he named EDGAR KAPLAN and NORMAN KAY, who had finished fourth in the trials, to the team and PHILLIP FELDESMAN and IRA RUBIN, the third-place pair, as alternates, the only time the top three pairs were not selected as the international team.

The scoring method used in the trials is that described under INTERNATIONAL MATCH POINTS.

1961 (Houston)	1. Charles Coon, Eric Murray
	2. G. Robert Nail, Mervin Key
	3. Lewis Mathe, Ron Von der Porten
	4. Norman Kay, Sidney Silodor
1962 (Phoenix)	1. James Jacoby, G. Robert Nail
	2. Robert Jordan, Arthur Robinson
	3. Howard Schenken, Peter Leventritt
	4. Gerald Michaud, David Carter
1963 (Miami)	1. Robert Hamman, Don Krauss
	2. Sam Stayman, Victor Mitchell
	3. Robert Jordan, Arthur Robinson
	4. Lewis Mathe, Edward Taylor
1964 (Dallas)	1. Howard Schenken, Peter Leventritt
	2. Ivan Erdos, Kelsey Petterson
	3. B. Jay Becker, Dorothy Hayden
	4. Robert Hamman, Don Krauss
1965 (San Francisco)	1. Phillip Feldesman, Ira Rubin
	2. Lewis Mathe, Robert Hamman
	3. Eric Murray, Sammy Kehela
	4. B. Jay Becker, Dorothy Hayden
1966 (Pittsburgh)	1. Eric Murray, Sammy Kehela
	2. Edgar Kaplan, Norman Kay
	3. Al Roth, William Root
	4. B. Jay Becker, Dorothy Hayden
1967 (Atlantic City)	1. Robert Jordan, Arthur Robinson
	2. Al Roth, William Root
	3. Phillip Feldesman, Ira Rubin
	4. Edgar Kaplan, Norman Kay
1968 (Atlantic City)	1. George Rapee, Sidney Lazard
	2. Billy Eisenberg, Bobby Goldman
	3. Robert Hamman, Eddie Kantar
	4. Ira Rubin, Jeff Westheimer

1970 — Vanderbilt-Spingold Play-off:

The Pair-Team trials were discontinued in order to allow selection of an entire team rather than individual pairs to comprise a team. The 1970 International Team was selected by a direct 180-board play-off between the winners of the 1969 Vanderbilt and Spingold. However, this did not prove entirely satisfactory since it limited the number of teams that could challenge for international representation and reduced the prestige of the Fall North American Championships, which previously had two events that qualified pairs for the trials.

1971-72 — Placing-Points Play-offs:

Beginning with the 1969 Fall NAC, the ACBL adopted a play-off among the teams with the best records over the course of a year. Teams placing high in the three major team championships (Reisinger, Vanderbilt, and Spingold) were awarded points according to the following scale:

Vanderbilt and Spingold		Reisinger	
1st	— 10 points	1st	— 6 points
2nd	— 4 points	2nd	— 4 points
3rd–4th	— 2 points	3rd	— 2 points

If a team accumulated 20 points it was to be automatically designated the International Team; otherwise teams with lesser numbers of points were to play off.

1973 — Vanderbilt, Spingold, Reisinger, Grand Nationals Winners Play-off:

With the introduction of the GRAND NATIONAL CHAMPIONSHIPS (2) in 1972, the selection of the North American international team became a simple matter of a four-team play-of among the winners of the ACBL's four major team events: the Vanderbilt, Spingold, Reisinger, and Grand Nationals.

1980 — Vanderbilt, Spingold, Reisinger, Grand National, Canadian National Winners Playoff:

At the request of the CANADIAN BRIDGE FEDERATION, that section of the Grand National Teams that involved Canadian players was separated from the main event and changed into a Canadian National Teams Championship. The Canadian champions became a fifth entry in the trials in those years when a Bermuda Bowl team was being chosen. The trials start with a round-robin, with one team being eliminated. The usual knockout format is used from that point on, with a carryover formula applied.

INTERNATIONAL PAIR EVENTS. See COMMON MARKET CHAMPIONSHIPS; INVITATIONAL PAIRS CHAMPIONSHIP; PAN AMERICAN INVITATIONAL CHAMPIONSHIPS; WORLD PAIR CHAMPIONSHIPS; CAVENDISH PAIRS.

INTERNATIONAL PALACE OF SPORTS. See KING OR QUEEN OF BRIDGE.

INTERNATIONAL POPULAR BRIDGE MONTHLY. A magazine published in Great Britain dealing with bridge happenings around the world with emphasis on Great Britain. TONY SOWTER is managing editor, and JOE AMSBURY is consultant editor.

INTERNATIONAL TEAM PLAY-OFF MATCHES. See INTERNATIONAL OPEN TEAM SELECTION.

INTERNATIONAL TEAM TRIALS. See INTERNATIONAL OPEN TEAM SELECTION

INTERNATIONAL WOMEN'S TEAM SELECTION. The United States has sent women's teams to each of the World Women's Team Olympiads, each selected by a different method. For the 1960 event, a committee consisting of the five most recent ACBL Presidents attending the 1959 Fall Nationals selected the team, by choosing three pairs of women who finished first or second in any national championship event during 1959.

For 1964, a trial by pairs was held, similar to the trials held during that period for the INTERNATIONAL OPEN TEAM SELECTION. For 1968 a round-robin was held, for which four pairs qualified. Each pair played a 32–board match in partnership with each of the other pairs, and npc MAGARET WAGAR was empowered to select any three of the four pairs.

For 1972, women's teams were to earn points in the major national team championships and play off to determine the U.S. 1972 women's team. However, one team amassed so many points that it was designated without a play-off. The following were the U.S. women's teams in the first four Olympiads:

1960	1964
Agnes Gordon	Agnes Gordon
Dorothy Hayden	Muriel Kaplan

Malvine Klausner	Alicia Kempner
Helen Portugal	Helen Portugal
Sylvia Schwartz	Stella Rebner
Jo Sharp	Jan Stone
Charles J. Solomon (npc)	Paul Hodge (npc)
1968	1972
Hermine Baron	Mary Jane Farell
Nancy Gruver	Emma Jean Hawes
Emma Jean Hawes	Marilyn Johnson
Dorothy Hayden	Jacqui Mitchell
Suzanne Sachs	Peggy Solomon
Rhoda Walsh	Dorothy Hayden Truscott
Margaret Wagar (npc)	Margaret Wagar (npc)

For 1976, women were permitted to earn "selection points," either as teams or as pairs, on all-women teams in the Vanderbilt, Spingold, Reisinger, and Spring National Women's Team events. Available points ranged from 1 point for being runner-up in the Spring Women's teams to 28 for winning the Vanderbilt or Spingold. To be selected intact, a team must have won more qualification points than any individual pair, except that if there were only one higher pair, a four-person team plus the high-ranking pair would form the six-member team. See also VENICE TROPHY.

INTERVENING BID. An overcall.

INTERWOVEN HOWELL. Two HOWELL games of equal size, so arranged that each plays (at each round) the boards which are not in play in the other.

Since a Howell game of X tables requires $2X - 1$ sets of boards, $X - 1$ sets are out of play at a given time. By proper arrangement these boards may be used in a parallel or "interwoven" Howell game; except that there must be one pair of relay tables at which the same set of boards is in play simultaneously in both games.

INTUITION. See INSTINCT.

INVERTED MINOR SUIT RAISES. The combination of the following two procedures:

(1) *Single raise in minor strong:*

♠ K 6 4
♡ 5 3
♢ Q J 4
♣ K 10 5 4 2

With this hand, bid 2♣ in response to 1♣. In KAPLAN-SHEINWOLD this is forcing, with a range of 9–20 points.

Also used in BARON, when it is simply constructive with a range of 7–10 points.

(2) *Double raise in minor pre-emptive:*

Used on hands on which the opponents may well hold the majority of the high-card strength, and are likely to have a major-suit fit:

♠ 6 5 3
♡ 8 2
♢ 9 3
♣ J 9 7 6 4 3

This would be sufficient for a nonvulnerable jump from 1♣ to 3♣. If vulnerable, the bidder should have a singleton.

INVITATION. A bid which encourages the bidder's

partner to continue to game or slam, but gives him the option of passing if he has no reserve values in terms of high-card strength or distribution.

In nearly all cases such bids are one level below the game or slam which is being suggested, so bids of 2 NT or three of a major suit often come in this category.

INVITATIONAL BID. Bid indicating strong game prospects, which requests partner to continue if he has some reserve strength. The bidder announces that he can count about 23–24 points in the combined hands (including distribution).

A bid of 2 NT is normally invitational:

WEST	EAST	or	WEST	EAST
1 NT	2 NT		1 ♡	2 ♣
			2 ♡	2 NT

but a jump by responder (response or rebid) is an exception, being forcing, in standard methods.

A jump rebid by the opener is invitational:

WEST	EAST
1 ♡	1 ♠
3 ♡	

and so is a single raise from two to three in the later stages of the auction:

WEST	EAST		WEST	EAST
1 ♠	2 ♠		1 ♠	2 ♠
2 ♠	3 ♠		2 ♡	3 ♡

For other sequences which are invitational in some styles but forcing in others, see JUMP REBIDS BY RESPONDER. See also conventions listed in GAME INVITATION.

INVITATIONAL PAIRS CHAMPIONSHIP. An invitational pair event that until January 1981 was sponsored by the London *Sunday Times* and called LONDON SUNDAY TIMES PAIRS. The field is usually limited to 16–22 leading pairs from many countries. The winners:

1963	Pierre Jaïs, Roger Trézel (France)
1964	Terence Reese, Boris Schapiro (England)
1965	No contest
1966	Gérard Desrousseaux, Dr. Georges Théron (France)
1967	Claude Rodrigue, Louis Tarlo (England)
1968	Claude Delmouly, Leon Yallouze (France, Egypt)
1969	Jean Bessé, John O. Collings (Switzerland, England)
1970	Nico Gardener, Richard Anthony Priday (England)
1971	Bob Slavenburg, Léon Tintner (The Netherlands, France)
1972	Lukasz Lebioda, Andrezej Wilkosz (Poland)
1973	Steven Altman, Alan Sontag (U.S.A.)
1974	Gianfranco Facchini, Sergio Zucchelli (Italy)
1975	Alan Sontag, Peter Weichsel (U.S.A.)
1976	Michael Rosenberg, Barnett Shenkin (Scotland)
1977	Jean-Michel Boulenger, Henri Svarc (France)
1978	Sven-Olov Flodqvist, Per Olof Sundelin (Sweden)
1979	Pedro Paulo Assumpção, Gabriel Chagas (Brazil)
1980	Victor Goldberg, Barnett Shenkin (Scotland)
1981	Sven-Olov Flodqvist, Per Olof Sundelin (Sweden)

IRELAND. See CONTRACT BRIDGE ASSOCIATION OF IRELAND; IRISH BRIDGE UNION; NORTH OF IRELAND BRIDGE UNION.

IRISH BRIDGE JOURNAL. Bridge periodical published six times yearly and edited by Patrick F. Walsh. It covers all major events, bidding and play competitions and receives contributions from VICTOR MOLLO and PETER PIGOT. It also carries an official bulletin of the CONTRACT BRIDGE ASSOCIATION OF IRELAND. See BIBLIOGRAPHY, O.

IRISH BRIDGE UNION. Founded in 1955, the union consists of representatives from both the CONTRACT BRIDGE ASSOCIATION OF IRELAND and NORTH OF IRELAND BRIDGE UNION. It is responsible for selecting teams to represent the whole of Ireland in World Olympiads and European Championships (but not for CAMROSE TROPHY matches), and for organizing All-Ireland events for Teams-of-Four and Pairs. Membership, comprising the total of both integral bodies, was about 21,500 in 1982.

Officers, 1982:
President: J.J. Murphy
Secretary: Marie Gleeson and W.M. Kelso,
  17 Beachpark, Athlone, Westmeath, Ireland

IRON DUKE, NOT THROUGH THE. An expression indicating that the user holds a very strong hand. The remark is an improper one, and is usually made when the player splits cards of equal value to prevent a finesse.

IRREGULAR LEAD. A calculated departure from normal procedure occurring in the play of the first card to any trick by a defender.

IRREGULARITY. A deviation from correct procedures set forth in the LAWS and PROPRIETIES.

ISOLATING THE MENACE. A maneuver in squeeze-play technique

A menace may be controlled by both opponents, in which case it is usually advantageous to have the full burden of guarding that suit imposed on one opponent. The term "isolating the menace" refers to declarer's efforts in that direction: he seeks to have the menace isolated so that it is protected by only one opponent.

```
            A K x x
  Q J x x              10 x x
            x x
```

If the diagram illustrates the distribution of a side suit at a trump contract, then North's menace can be isolated by playing off the ace and king followed by a ruff on the third round. At any contract a first-round duck would ensure that the menace was isolated.

                              Monroe Ingberman

ISRAEL BRIDGE FEDERATION. Revived in 1960, the Federation had close to 3,000 members in 1982 in seven main branches: Tel Aviv, Haifa, Jerusalem, Netanya, Savyon, Beersheba, and Eilat. In 1963 Israel became a member of the European Bridge League, and has participated in European Championships since 1965, hosting the 1974 event, and in Olympiads since 1964. Israel was runner-up in the 1975 European Championships, thereby winning the right to represent Europe in the 1976 Bermuda Bowl. The Federation sponsors an International Bridge Festival, held annually in Tel Aviv since 1966, and National Championships, which are held in the main branches throughout the year. The growth of popularity of bridge in Israel is attested to by the fact that in 1967 an official Hebrew bridge terminology was submitted to the Israeli Academy of Language for approval; since then, bridge columns in Israeli papers, formerly printed in English, German, or French, have appeared in Hebrew. The Federation also awards master points.

Officers, 1982:
Chairman: David Bardach
Secretary: Pinchas Herschberg, P.O. Box 29703,
  61 296 Tel Aviv, Israel

ITALIAN BRIDGE FEDERATION (FEDERAZIONE ITALIANA BRIDGE). Founded in 1936 in Milan by PAOLO BARONI, FREDERICO ROSA and E. Pontremoli. Reactivated after World War II, with CARL' ALBERTO PERROUX as President, the Federation became an official body organizing regular National contests, which gave impetus to a national interest in the game. By 1982 there were more than 17,000 members in 130 affiliated bodies and 160 clubs. About 50 tournaments are organized annually, including Open and Mixed Teams and the Knockout Teams for the Italian Cup, which attract an entry of 400 teams. The record of the Italian BLUE TEAM is an extraordinary one that is unlikely to be equaled. The first Italian team to compete in the European Championships in 1938 was the predecessor of the invincibles who became European Champions 1951, 1956, 1957, 1958, 1959, 1965, 1967, 1969, 1971, 1973, 1975, 1976, 1979 and 16 times World Champions (Bermuda Bowl 10 times from 1957–69, 1973–75, and World Olympiad winners 1964, 1968, 1972).

Officers, 1982:
President: Guido Barbone
Secretary: Dino Mazza, Largo Augusto, 3,
  20122 Milano, Italy

ITALIAN SYSTEMS. See BLUE TEAM CLUB; LEGHORN DIAMOND; LITTLE ROMAN CLUB; MARMIC SYSTEM; ROMAN SYSTEM; SUPER PRECISION.

J

JACK. The fourth ranking card in a suit. Aslo called knave. See COAT CARDS; COURT CARDS; VALET.

JACK, TEN, OR NINE SHOWING ZERO OR TWO HIGHER HONORS. See ZERO OR TWO HIGHER LEADS.

JACKPOT. Extra money beyond the entry fee collected from players for special prize purposes. Usually the pair or team taking part in the jackpot that places highest collects the jackpot money.

JACOBY INDIVIDUAL MOVEMENT. See RAINBOW INDIVIDUAL MOVEMENT.

JACOBY TRANSFER BIDS. Used in responding at the two-level to 1 NT opening bids, or in responding at the three-level to 2 NT openings. These transfers were introduced to the American bridge public by OSWALD JACOBY in a *Bridge World* article in 1956, although they had been used in Sweden as early as

1953–54 as a result of a series of articles in *Bridge Tidningen* written by Olle Willner.

2 ◇ shows hearts and asks opener to bid 2 ♡.

2 ♡ shows spades, and asks opener to bid 2 ♣.

This convention greatly increases the chance that the strong hand will be the declarer in a suit contract. It also solves the problems created by many hands of intermediate strength:

(a)	(b)
♠ Q 10 8 7 6 4	♠ 8
♡ K 6 3	♡ A 10 9 5 4
◇ 4 3	◇ 10 5
♣ 7 5	♣ K Q 10 5 3

On hand (a) the response is 2 ♡, and the rebid of 2 ♠ is raised to 3 ♠. This is a game invitation which the opener can pass if he wishes.

On hand (b) the response of 2 ◇ shows the heart suit, and responder continues with 3 ♣. This shows his two-suited hand, and leaves the next move to the opener. 3 ♣ is forcing, but might be made on a slightly weaker hand.

There are methods for extending transfers to the minor suits. One is to use a 2 ♠ response to transfer to 3 ♣ and a 3 ♣ response to transfer to 3 ◇. Another is to use the 2 ♠ response as a minor two-suiter in a game-going hand with slam interest (see MINOR SUIT STAYMAN). A third alternative is to use the 2 ♠ response to show a game-going hand with one long minor suit and slam interest.

JACOBY 2 NT. A method of increasing the accuracy of slam bidding, developed by OSWALD JACOBY, and used in conjunction with limit major suit raises.

After a 1 ♡ or 1 ♠ opening, a jump to 2 NT by an unpassed hand is a forcing raise of unlimited strength. As revised, opener's conventional rebids to clarify his strength and distribution are as follows: a new suit on the three-level shows a singleton or void in the bid suit, a new suit at the four-level shows 6-5-1-1 distribution (with a minimum 1 ♡ opening, opener should not show a spade suit); four of the agreed trump suit shows a minimum opening bid, no slam interest; three of the agreed trump suit shows 16 points or more, strong interest in slam; and 3 NT describes a sound opening bid (14–15 points), but no distributional feature.

JAMAICA BRIDGE ASSOCIATION. An original member of CACBF founded in 1944, it had a total of 16 affiliated clubs in 1982, with a membership of 130. National events held annually are the Open Teams and Open Pairs.

Officers, 1982:
President: Ryan Peralto
Secretary: Felicity Cronk, 30 Commodore, Devon Road, Kingston 10, Jamaica, WI

JAPAN CONTRACT BRIDGE LEAGUE. Founded in Tokyo in 1953 with 11 members, by 1982 the membership had grown to more than 3,100 in 55 affiliated clubs, with branches in Osaka, Nagoya and Sapporo. Participates in the Far East Championships, hosting the 1958, 1964 and 1979 events, and in the World Par Championships; sent a team to the

1972 World Team Olympiad. National tournaments of importance include the Double Knockout Teams for the Prince Takamatsu Cup, Round Robin Teams for the Japan Times Cup, Teams-of-Four (modified board-a-match scoring) for the Fujiyama Cup, and Open Pairs for the Okazaki Club.

Officers, 1982:
President: Fumio Watanabe
Secretary: Titsuji Hikawa, Room No. 705, Fudosankaikan Bldg., 5-ban Yotsua 3-chome, Shinjuku-ku, Tokyo 160, Japan

JETTISON. The discard of a high-ranking honor, usually an ace or a king. The term was originated by GEOFFREY MOTT-SMITH.

A typical example is the following:

```
            A 10 8 6 4 3
    Q 2                   J 9 5
            K 7
```

In a notrump contract, South leads the king in a position in which East needs an entry. West must drop the queen, for otherwise South will allow the queen to hold on the next round.

The play may be necessary to effect an unblock, to create an entry or to avert a ruff. See also ENTRY SQUEEZE.

JETTISON SQUEEZE. A form of ENTRY SQUEEZE.

JOKER. A fifty-third card in decks of cards, sometimes used as a substitute or "wild" card, but not used in bridge. See TAROT.

JORDAN. See RESPONSES OVER OPPONENT'S TAKEOUT DOUBLE and 2 NT RESPONSE (Over opponent's takeout double).

JOSEPHINE. The GRAND SLAM FORCE, associated in Europe with the name of JOSEPHINE CULBERTSON, and therefore named after her. (Mrs. Culbertson was the first to write about the convention; it was devised by her husband, ELY CULBERTSON.)

JOURNALIST LEADS. A method of opening leads advocated by the *Bridge Journal* in 1964–1965. The details are as follows:

Against notrump contracts:

A usually from A-K-J-x (x-x) or A-K-10-x (x-x). Third hand is requested to unblock a high honor if he can afford it, otherwise to give a length signal (high with an even number, low with an odd number of cards in the suit).

K from A-K or K-Q (assuming a high honor should be led).

Q from Q-J (or K-Q-10-9; third hand is requested to play the jack if he has it).

J from J-10. The jack denies a higher honor.

10 from A-10-9, K-10-9, Q-10-9, A-J-10, K-J-10. The 10 guarantees a higher honor (Q, K or A).

9 from 10-9. The 9 promises the 10 and no higher honor.

Second highest or highest from lower spot cards to discourage suit continuation.

Usually lowest card from a long suit headed by

one or two honors to encourage suit continuation.

The purpose of these leads is to make it easier for third hand to know whether to continue the attack on the suit led or to shift. The following hand shows what can happen when Journalist leads are not used.

Dlr: North
Vul: Both
IMPs

```
                    ♠ A J 10 6 3
                    ♡ 5
                    ◊ 7 4
                    ♣ A K 10 7 2
                                    ♠ Q 9 5 2
                                    ♡ Q J 10 4
                                    ◊ A 6 3
                                    ♣ Q 5
```

WEST	NORTH	EAST	SOUTH
	1♣	Pass	1♡
Pass	1♠	Pass	3 NT
All Pass			

Using standard leads, West led the ◊ 10 to East's ace, South playing the 2. Now if South started with a hand like: ♠K–x ♡A–K–x–x–x ◊Q–J–2 ♣–x–x–x, East must continue diamonds. But if the 10 was West's highest diamond, a heart shift is called for. East actually continued diamonds and found South with: ♠K–x ♡K–x–x–x ◊K–Q–J–x ♣J–x–x. Declarer won the diamond, cashed ♣A–K (because he could hardly afford to lose a finesse to East and get a heart through) and made 10 tricks.

Using Journalist leads, West would have led the ◊9, and East would have shifted to a heart, defeating the contract.

Against suit contracts Journalist Leads follow a different pattern. From two touching honors the second highest is led; from spot cards the highest card below the 9 may be led to indicate a weak holding: otherwise, the third highest is led from an even number of cards or the lowest from an odd number of cards.

JUMP BID. A call of more than is necessary to raise the previous bid and made at any point after the auction has been opened. Bids of two or more than necessary are termed *double jumps*, etc. SKIP BID is a more general term, embracing jumps to any level.

JUMP OVERCALL. A suit overcall at a level one higher than necessary:

SOUTH	WEST	SOUTH	WEST
1◊	2♣	or 1♠	3◊

In traditional methods this bid shows a strong six-card suit or a seven-card suit, and about 15–17 points in high cards. The jump in a minor suit is a strong invitation to 3 NT, and the suit should be solid or nearly solid. With a still stronger hand the usual procedure is to double and bid the suit, perhaps with a jump, on the second round. For other uses of this jump, see INTERMEDIATE JUMP OVERCALL; ROMAN JUMP OVERCALL and WEAK JUMP OVERCALL.

One of the primary reasons for ELY CULBERTSON'S initial introduction of the jump overcall as a strong bid was to take care of good two-suited hands, with

which the player would not welcome a bid in a third suit or a penalty pass in response to a takeout double; many experts consider this to be of greater value than using the single-jump overcall as a weak preempt.

JUMP PREFERENCE. Returning to partner's original suit at a level one higher than necessary:

WEST	EAST
1♡	1♠ or 2♣ or 1 NT
2◊	3♡

In CULBERTSON and ACOL such bids are nonforcing. Many experts take an intermediate position, regarding them as forcing if the first response was at the two-level, and nonforcing otherwise. See also JUMP REBIDS BY RESPONDER.

If the opener gives jump preference, it is sometimes nonforcing:

WEST	EAST
1♠	1♡
2♣	2◊
3♡	

JUMP RAISE. See DOUBLE RAISE.

JUMP RAISE IN RESPONDER'S SUIT. See OPENER'S REBID.

JUMP REBID BY OPENER. See OPENER'S REBID.

JUMP REBIDS BY RESPONDER. These are jump bids short of game by responder at his second turn. The meanings of such bids vary widely. In STANDARD AMERICAN all such jump bids are considered forcing, whether or not responder rebids his own suit, supports partner's suit or names a new suit. In ACOL, however, jump rebids in responder's own suit or declarer's suit are not forcing, although jump rebids in a new suit are forcing. Partnership discussion and agreement are a must in this area. (See chart on page 204.)

JUMP SHIFT. A new suit response at a level one higher than necessary:

WEST	EAST		WEST	EAST
1♡	2♠	or	1♡	3♣

In standard methods this shows a hand of great strength which can almost guarantee a slam (19 points or more including distribution). The hand is usually one of four types: a good fit with opener's suit; a strong single-suiter; a strong two-suiter; or a balanced hand with more than 18 points. However, the last type is not easy to handle with a jump shift, and an alternative method is described under IMPOSSIBLE BIDS.

Many experts have less elevated standards for a jump shift, making the bid with about 17 points including distribution; in ACOL, 16 points or less with a good fit or a good suit. In this last case the response may be made in a three-card suit, either because the hand is balanced or because there is a fit with opener but no side suit.

A theory advanced by PAUL SOLOWAY that is gain-

JUMP REBIDS BY RESPONDER

Two Notrump	Forcing Style	Nonforcing Style
1♠ – 1♡ 1♠ – 2 NT	13–15, as an original 2 NT response. (An 11–12 point hand remains a problem.)	11–12. A 13–15 hand bids 3 NT, or makes a fourth-suit bid.
Jump Preference 1♠ – 1♡ 1♠ – 3♣	13 or more.	11–12; perhaps only three-card support, but four or five is probable.
1♠ – 2♣ 2♡ – 3♣	13 or more. Probably three-card support, because of the failure to bid 3♣ originally.	11–12; three-card support if used in combination with limit raises.
1♡ – 1♠ 1 NT – 3♡	Shows game values, with the exact strength depending on the range of the 1 NT rebid.	Forcing — a special case. The strength depends on the strength of the 1 NT rebid.
1◊ – 1♠ 1 NT – 3◊	Ditto.	10–12, probably four-card support; weaker if the 1 NT rebid was constructive.
Jump Raise 1♠ – 1♡ 1♠ – 3♠	13–15 and four-card support; equivalent to 1♠ – 3♠.	10–12 and four-card support; equivalent to a limit raise of 1♠ – 3♠. A stronger hand bids 4♠, or bids the fourth suit followed by 4♠ as a mild slam suggestion.
Jump Rebid 1♠ – 1♡ 1♠ – 3♡	Games values and a six-card suit.	10–11 points and a six-card suit.
Jump Shift 1♠ – 1♡ 1♠ – 3◊	Game values; usually a hand with a fit in opener's second suit, which has therefore improved to the point of slam prospects. But a two-suiter is possible.	As forcing style.

ing adherence among experts is that jump shifts should be limited to three types of hands: (1) one-suiters, (2) semi-balanced hands, and (3) hands with a good fit for opener's suit. Responder clarifies his hand by his rebid. If he has a one-suited hand he rebids his suit. If he has a semi-balanced hand his next bid is in notrump. If he has a good fit for opener, he can made a FRAGMENT bid in a new suit to show a singleton in the fourth suit, or he can return to opener's suit to deny having a singleton. This method of showing a singleton and support for opener's suit is workable only if it is agreed that the jump shift cannot be made with a two-suited hand; under this agreement responder's bid of a new suit at his second turn cannot show a real suit.

Another method, proposed by RICHARD P. REED of Boulder CO, is to use a jump shift to show 19 or more points in support of opener's suit and the bid suit shows the lowest first-round control in responder's hand.

Perhaps the most unusual treatment of the jump shift is that used by WILLIAM L. PASSELL and DAVID STRASBERG. Their idea is that a jump shift shows a solid suit in the next higher-ranking suit, opener's suit excepted. For example, after a 1♠ opening, a jump to 2♣ shows a solid diamond suit. Opener normally accepts the transfer, which permits responder to cuebid his other controls. If responder is unable to cuebid, he supports the agreed suit, and a subsequent bid of 4 NT by opener is not BLACKWOOD, but asks about the length of responder's suit.

Rebids by the opener after a jump shift are not standardized, but the opener should usually make the rebid he was planning after a nonjump response, only, of course, one level higher. There are two exceptions to this principle: a nonjump rebid of 3 NT would not promise extra values, nor would a reverse.

This idea was originated by ELY CULBERTSON, who called it "jump takeout" or "forcing takeout".

For a preemptive use of this response, see WEAK JUMP SHIFT RESPONSES. See also PASSED HAND.

JUMP SHIFT REBID. See OPENER'S REBID.

JUMP SHIFT TO 3♣. In order to keep the forcing raise at as low a level as possible, while reserving the jump to 2 NT for notrump type hands, some partnerships use a jump shift to 3♣ as a forcing major suit raise. The jump says nothing about the responder's clubs. Opener rebids 3◊ if he has a singleton or a void. Without a singleton or void, opener should rebid as follows to describe his trump holding.

3♡ shows two of the top three trump honors.

3♠ shows one of the top three trump honors.

3 NT shows none of the top three trump honors.

JUMP TAKEOUT. See JUMP SHIFT.

JUMP TO GAME IN MAJOR SUIT. See OPENER'S REBID for jump to game in responder's major suit or in opener's major suit. See also TRIPLE RAISE.

JUNIOR MASTER. An ACBL player who has won at least one master point but fewer than 20. See RANKING OF PLAYERS.

JUNK. A contemptuous term used to describe a hand or a holding felt to be particularly valueless by the person describing it. See BAD CARDS.

K

KAMIKAZE NOTRUMP. A bidding system devised by John Kierein of Boulder CO. The cornerstone of the system is a first- or second-seat opening of 1 NT with 9–12 HCP. In addition, weak two-bids show 9–11 HCP and can be bid on a five-card suit. Frequent psychs are employed by third hand after two passes.

The ACBL Board of Directors passed regulations which barred the use of special conventions in conjunctions with the super-weak 1 NT opener. Naturally this limits its effectiveness.

KANTAR CUEBID. A specialized cuebid after an opponent's overcall suggested by EDDIE KANTAR. After, for example,

WEST	NORTH	EAST	SOUTH
1♠	2♦	3♦	

In this specialized usage, 3♦ shows a 5-4-4-0 or 4-4-4-1 hand with a shortage in the opponent's suit. The strength may be as little as 8–9 high-card points, but there is no upward limit.

For other uses of the cuebid, see CUEBID IN OPPONENT'S SUIT.

KANTAR 3 NT. See 3 NT OPENING.

KAPLAN-SHEINWOLD. A system devised by EDGAR KAPLAN and ALFRED SHEINWOLD, based on the WEAK NOTRUMP and aimed at more precisely limiting the strength shown by all bids. The features of the system are:

(1) Weak notrump with 12–14 points. An 11-point hand may be opened with 2½–3 QUICK TRICKS, or a 15-point hand with less than two quick tricks. Responses of 2♦, 2♥, 2♠, 3♣ and 3♦ are weak sign-off bids. A bid of 2♣ followed by a minor-suit rebid is strong and forcing. Other responses are standard, with nonforcing STAYMAN. A bid of 2♣ followed by 3♥ or 3♠ is forcing, and shows a more balanced pattern than an immediate jump. Whether doubled or not, responder runs from 1 NT with fewer than 5 points, often into 2♣ or 2♦.

After an overcall, a double is negative and a new suit bid at the three level is forcing.

(2) Minor-suit openings are sound (but any hand with three quick tricks must be opened). If balanced, 15–20 points and possibly a three-card suit: 1 NT

rebid shows 15–17; and 2 NT rebid shows 18–20. A single raise of responder's major shows 15–17; a double raise shows 18–19; a triple raise shows 20–21 (in each case the requirements are reduced as distribution improves). A maximum unbalanced hand reverses or jump shifts before raising.

Responder bids a major in response whenever possible. Opener's reverse is a one-round force, and 2♣ following 1♦ is treated as a reverse. A 3 NT rebid shows a solid minor with outside stoppers.

For single and double raises, see INVERTED MINOR SUIT RAISES. Single raises are forcing and double raises are preemptive. A response of 1 NT shows 5–8, and 2 NT 12–15. A balanced 9–11 point hand may respond in the other minor.

If the opening is doubled, takeouts retain their meaning, but all raises are preemptive (redouble is the strong raise).

Opener may raise responder's major with three-card support in competition.

(3) NEGATIVE DOUBLE.

(4) Jump shift by responder is preemptive in competition.

(5) FIVE-CARD MAJORS, which can be light: a 9-point hand with quick-trick and playing-trick strength is possible. Exceptionally, a strong four-card suit may be bid, with a balanced minimum honors concentrated in two suits, or a touching lower-ranking, weak five-card suit. 1 NT RESPONSE FORCING, but opener passes with the rare balanced minimum hand.

LIMIT JUMP RAISES are used. The jump raise preceded by 1 NT shows three-card support and a more balanced hand. A 3 NT response is used instead of the standard (strong) jump raise. A 2 NT response is standard. A minor-suit response is 12–13 minimum unless followed by a rebid in the minor, showing only a semi-solid suit headed by the ace; a delayed raise for opener or a 2 NT rebid is game-forcing.

After 1♥–1♠, opener rebids 1 NT, 2♥ or 2♠ with a minimum. A bid of 2♣ or 2♦ would be more constructive. After 1♠–2♥ (minimun 10 and a five-card suit), minimum hands bid 3♥ or 2♠; maximum hands (18 or more) bid 3♣ or 3♦, which are the only forcing bids; other bids show 15–17, including 2 NT, which shows a singleton heart.

(6) Opening psychics are lead-directing, containing a legitimate suit with a high honor (2–6 points). A jump shift forces the opener to rebid in his suit or notrump, whichever is cheaper. Psychics are recommended only when nonvulnerable; at IMPS, only nonvulnerable versus vulnerable; at BOARD-A-MATCH, never.

(7) WEAK TWO-BIDS need one and one-half to two quick tricks and a semi-solid suit in first and second position. A single raise is preemptive, and other responses by an unpassed hand are forcing: 2 NT asks the opener to bid a side honor.

(8) 2♣ is the only forcing opening. After a 2♦ negative response, the bidding can stop short of game if the opener rebids 2 NT or bids and rebids one suit.

(9) 3 NT opening shows a 2 NT hand (20–22) with a long solid minor.

(10) CUEBIDS are used under game to suggest a slam and over game to ask about an unbid suit. A subsequent 4 NT bid is a natural slam invitation, as in BLUE TEAM CLUB.

(11) GERBER over notrump bids.

(12) BLACKWOOD in other situations.

(13) GRAND SLAM FORCE.

(14) ROMAN ASKING BIDS.

(15) TAKEOUT DOUBLES emphasize distribution: there should be not fewer than three cards in each unbid suit. A cuebid is the only forcing response.

(16) OVERCALLS have the same range as an opening bid. Responder should seldom pass if he would have responded to an opening bid.

(17) WEAK JUMP OVERCALLS, usually with a maximum of one and one-half tricks.

(18) 1 NT OVERCALL shows 17–19. A two-level takeout is a signoff, and a cuebid is Stayman.

(19) Optional features of the system include: SHORT-SUIT GAME TRIES; FLINT 3 ◊; UNUSUAL NO-TRUMP; LANDY; FRAGMENT BIDS; MICHAELS CUEBID; ROMAN 2 ◊; WEAK JUMP SHIFT RESPONSES by passed hand; 3 ♣ as "prelude to signoff" over a jump rebid of 2 NT; 2 ◊ as forcing Stayman; 2 NT over opposing takeout double as semi-preemptive raise; 3 NT after limit jump raise of major to ask for short suit.

Edgar Kaplan

KEEPING SCORE. The process by which a record is kept of the activity during a rubber of bridge or of CHICAGO, and of the result on a board in duplicate. There can be more than one scorekeeper among a group of rubber bridge players, but in duplicate the score is usually kept by North.

KEEPING THE BIDDING OPEN. For the strength needed to make a response, see ONE OVER ONE RESPONSE. For opening action by the fourth player see BALANCING.

KELLY SOLID SUIT SIGNAL. Devised in the days of whist by NATHAN KELLY. The play of the second highest or highest card of a suit (originally led) to the second trick of the suit to show that the balance of the suit (five cards originally or longer at notrump play) is now established and will run.

KEM CARD TROPHY. For the Non-Master Pair Championship, donated by the Kem Card Company in 1937; originally the National Amateur Pair Championship; contested at the Fall North American Championships until 1966 and subsequently at the Spring North American Championships under which headings past results are listed.

KEM CARDS. The first successful plastic cards, manufactured in America since 1934. Each year several new designs are introduced. Lost or damaged cards will be replaced by the manufacturer. See PLASTIC CARDS.

KENYA BRIDGE ASSOCIATION. A group formed in 1963 with approximately 130 members.

Officers, 1982:

President: Ahmed Hani Garranah

Secretary: Amir Juma, P.O. Box 42914, Nairobi, Kenya

KEOHANE TROPHY. For the Open Individual Championship, contested at the Summer North American Championships donated by ETHEL KEOHANE in 1973 in memory of her husband, William H. Keohane. Past winners are listed under Summer North American Championships.

KEY CARD BLACKWOOD. A form of BLACK-WOOD in which the king of trumps is counted as a fifth ace. Responder bids 5 ♣ with no aces or four aces, 5 ◊ with one ace or five aces, 5 ♡ with two aces, and 5 ♠ with three aces. A subsequent bid of 5 NT by the Blackwood bidder may be used in various ways. It may ask for kings in the normal manner, except that the king of trumps would not be shown. Or it may ask for an additional feature in the Blackwood responder's hand. See also BYZANTINE BLACKWOOD; CULBERTSON 4-5 NT; KEY CARD GERBER; ROMAN KEY CARD BLACKWOOD.

KEY CARD GERBER. A modification of the GER-BER CONVENTION in which trump honors may be counted as aces. When only the trump king is to be counted as an ace, responder bids 4 ◊ with no aces or four aces, 4 ♡ with one ace or five aces, 4 ♠ with two aces, and 4 NT with three aces. Some partnerships agree to count both the king and queen of trumps as aces. Using this agreement responder's 4 ♠ bid would show two or six aces. See BYZANTINE BLACKWOOD; ROMAN GERBER.

KHEDIVE. An early name for bridge as played on the French Riviera, which lends support to the belief that the game is of Turkish origin. (See HISTORY OF BRIDGE.)

KIBITZER. An onlooker at bridge or other games.

KIBITZER'S MAKE. A hand which seems to have sufficient controls, enough high-card winners, and sufficiently few losers to be successful in a contract, but which for reasons of entry problems, duplication of values, or lie of the cards is doomed. The term comes from the habit of some poorly trained kibitzers to indulge in analyses that careful scrutiny shows to be fallacious.

KIBITZING. The act of watching a game from the sidelines. In serious play at top clubs and at tournaments in America and in Europe, the level of play is usually high, so there are unwritten, as well as written, rules concerning the deportment of any onlooker. See LAWS (Law 11, Proprieties, V). These onlookers know that it is extremely important for them not to give away any information about the nature of the hand or the holding that they are watching. In ACBL tournaments, kibitzers usually are permitted. However, one kibitzer may be removed at a player's request without cause. Any kibitzer can be removed for cause (failing to observe the proprieties for kibitzers). There are numerous stories and legends that have sprung up over the years about kibitzers and, although many of them are apocryphal, some are true, and others contain more than a germ of truth. Many of these tales are based on situations where the players are arguing vehemently about a bid or play, and it is decided that the matter be referred to the kibitzer for his opinion, with many varied and humorous endings.

The word "kibitzer" itself derives from the German word for a green plover, a highly inquisitive bird. The role of the kibitzer grew somewhat in stature and story as bridge itself expanded and progressed. In H. T. WEBSTER's regular series of bridge cartoons drawn for the New York *Herald Tribune*, the artist's attention was often turned to kibitzers, and the resulting drawings were among his most amusing. Some of the great humorists of the Thirties and Forties occasionally did pieces about kibitzers, and one of the wittiest was GEORGE S. KAUFMAN's "The Great Kibitzers' Strike." All the comic and semi-serious articles reflected the general mores and customs of the times regarding kibitzers and attitudes toward them. A classic story, and one of the few completely true ones, involved the players at a well-known New York club and their one kibitzer. The contract was 5 ◊ doubled, and with the opponents on lead to the tenth trick, declarer spread his hand, claiming the balance, just making the contract. The opposition agreed, and the cards were just about to be thrown in, when the kibitzer pointed out a defensive lead which would have defeated the contract at that point. Bitter harangue and confusion then ensued and the matter was at length referred to the card committee. The final decision was that declarer be credited with making 5 ◊ doubled, the defense be credited with defeating the contract one trick, and the kibitzer be ordered to pay the difference.

KICK IT. Colloquial term for "I double". Also a colloquialism for boosting the contract as a preemptive measure.

KILLED. (1) Captured, as in "The king was killed by the ace". (2) The fate of a player or pair playing well but scoring badly. At duplicate the term implies that the opponents have played luckily and well on a group of boards. At rubber bridge it would refer to a session of poor cards and bad breaks. The term is always born of frustration and frequently of a desire to avoid admissions of poor play to one's teammates or oneself. (3) Denuded of whatever entries it may have had, as "The spade lead killed the dummy".

KING. The second highest ranking card in a suit in bridge. See COAT CARDS and COURT CARDS.

KING OR QUEEN OF BRIDGE. This honorary title is bestowed each year by the International Palace of Sports, Inc., on the high school senior having the highest number of ACBL master points to his or her credit. As a part of the Kiwanis International Youth Career Awards Program, the International Palace of Sports, located in North Webster IN, each year presents a plaque to the King or Queen of Bridge and awards a $1,000 scholarship to the alma mater of the winner, to be granted to a deserving student selected by the high school. The program is designed to inspire young people to better citizenship. Past holders of the title and their winning masterpoint totals are:

1973	Jay Merrill	470
1974	Jeff Meckstroth	480
1975	Bobby Levin	964
1976	Warren Spector	420
1977	Marc Franklin	315
1978	Matt Franklin	456
1979	Regina Barnes	441
1980	Tony Marks	505
1981	Doug Levene	664*
	Steve Cochran	622*
1982	Steve Weinstein	1019

KING CONVENTION. A variation of the CULBERTSON 4-5 NT convention in which responder with two aces and a king may sometimes bid the suit in which he holds the king.

KING LEAD. See JOURNALIST LEADS; OPENING LEADS; RUSINOW LEADS.

KISS OF DEATH. A penalty of 200 points on a partscore deal in a pair contest; usually down two vulnerable, or down one doubled vulnerable.

KIVI CONVENTION. See BULLDOG SYSTEM.

KNAVE. The jack, the fourth highest ranking card of a suit. This term is obsolete in American usage, and obsolescent elswhere, although it had considerable currency in England and Continental Europe until the Forties. One reason for the quick acceptance of the term "jack," instead of "knave" is that in reporting hands or in any abbreviated diagram or description of play the initial J can be used, whereas previously Kn had to be used, since a plain K would have been ambiguous. See COAT CARDS and COURT CARDS.

KNOCK. (1) An action, of doubtful propriety, consisting of hitting the table lightly instead of speaking the word "pass". While it is true that bridge laws technically condone passes executed in irregular style, provided the offender at least is consistent in passing that way all the time, the best practice and that most approved by top tournament directors remains the spoken word "pass." (2) An informal method of ALERTING.

KNOCK TOGETHER. See CRASHING HONORS.

KNOCKOUT SQUEEZE. A knockout squeeze is a squeeze in three suits, one of which is the trump suit. Declarer ruffs the fourth suit in the long trump hand, forcing the threatened defender to choose between establishing declarer's side suit or allowing him to score an extra trump trick.

Example: (See top of next page.)

---

*Note: A tie was declared when 53 master points earned by Doug Levene before the deadline did not make the April 10 computer list which that year was used to determine the winner of this award.

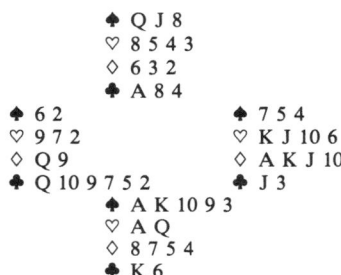

♠ Q J 8
♡ 8 5 4 3
♦ 6 3 2
♣ A 8 4

♠ 6 2   ♠ 7 5 4
♡ 9 7 2   ♡ K J 10 6
♦ Q 9   ♦ A K J 10
♣ Q 10 9 7 5 2   ♣ J 3

♠ A K 10 9 3
♡ A Q
♦ 8 7 5 4
♣ K 6

South is declarer in 4♠ after East opened the bidding and West showed club length. West leads a trump won by the ♠8 in dummy. A heart is led for a finesse of the ♡Q, and declarer continues with three rounds of clubs, ruffing the third round with the ♠K. On the third club, East is squeezed in three suits: a spade "discard" allows declarer to score an eventual diamond ruff in dummy, a heart discard allows declarer to establish and cash a long heart in dummy, while a diamond discard enables declarer to score a diamond ruff in dummy or establish and cash a long diamond in his hand, depending on the defense.

Monroe Ingberman

KNOCKOUT TOURNAMENT. An event (usually for teams of four or more) in which one team plays against only one opposing team in a given session. The losers are eliminated. The winners remain in the contest, and meet new opponents at later sessions, until only one winning team remains.

In a DOUBLE KNOCKOUT event, a team must lose twice before being eliminated. After its first loss, a team is transferred to the "loser's bracket," from which teams are eliminated after each round, and to which teams losing in the second or later rounds in the winner's bracket are added. See also REPECHAGE.

KOCK-WERNER REDOUBLE. A rescue device invented by the Swedish partnership of Rudolf Kock and Einar Werner. When partner's low-level overcall has been doubled, a redouble calls for a takeout. For example:

WEST	NORTH	EAST	SOUTH
			1♣
1♡	Dbl	Rdbl	

East shows that he has a singleton or void in hearts, and requests a takeout into another suit. The possibility of playing in 2♣ is not excluded: the best escape is often to a suit bid by the opposition.

Such redoubles are almost useless in a natural sense. If East is satisfied to play in 1♡ doubled, he simply passes.

(The treatment of the redouble needs special consideration if North–South are using NEGATIVE DOUBLES.)

See also S O S REDOUBLE.

L

LHO. Left-hand opponent, or the player on declarer's left.

LOL. An expression designating innocent-appearing bridge players who unexpectedly bid and play against you as though they were world champions. The letters originally designated "little old ladies", and were used as a term of some opprobrium, but the frequency with which little old ladies secured excellent results by simple common-sense action against pseudo-experts has caused the connotation to become more one of amusement and respect rather than of belittlement.

LANCIA TOURNAMENTS. In 1975 a team sponsored by Lancia Division of Fiat and consisting of WALTER AVARELLI, GIORGIO BELLADONNA, PIETRO FORQUET, BENITO GAROZZO, OMAR SHARIF, with assists from Antonio Vivaldi and Antonio Saladino, played four challenge matches in the United States against teams that had each earned the right to challenge the Lancia team by winning a qualifying Swiss tournament. The tour was organized by Goren International; the tournaments were sanctioned and conducted by the ACBL.

The prizes for any team that beat the Lancia team were five Lancia cars; if no team beat the Lancia team, the team with the best losing score would receive the five cars; the prizes for the team with the best score in losing to the Lancia team without winning any cars were steamship cruises.

The matches were played in New York, Los Angeles, Chicago and Miami. The Lancia team was defeated in every match except Chicago. Thus every challenging team won prizes. Participants were: New York — MATT GRANOVETTER, RON RUBIN, ALAN SONTAG, PETER WEICHSEL; Los Angeles — LARRY COHEN, BILLY EISENBERG, EDDIE KANTAR, DR. RICHARD KATZ; Chicago — WILLIAM ROSEN, MILTON ROSENBERG, LES BART, George O'Neill, Miami — ROGER BATES, JOHN MOHAN, GEORGE ROSENKRANZ, Sol Dubson.

LANDY. A conventional overcall of 2♣ after an opposing notrump opening as a request for a takeout with emphasis on the major suits, devised by ALVIN LANDY of New York. The overcaller promises at least four cards in each major suit, and is probably short in one or both minors. (A player with balanced distribution would normally double or pass.) The Landy bidder seldom has more than 15 high-card points.

Many players limit the convention to an immediate overcall of a weak notrump, but it can also be extended by agreement to the fourth position, and/or to strong notrump bids.

Responses to the Landy bid are not standardized, but the following scheme had the endorsement of the inventor of the convention:

(1) 3♣ is a forcing response unrelated to clubs, and asks the Landy bidder to describe his hand further. The responder may have equal length in the major suits. This is the *only* forcing response.

(2) 3♣ and 3♡ are game invitations, and might be based on a three-card suit.

(3) *2 NT* and *3 ♦* are natural and encouraging but not forcing.

(4) *2 ♦* shows a weak hand with diamond length.

(5) *Pass* shows a weak hand with club length.

Defense. A double of the Landy bid by the third player is often reserved for a good defensive hand which sees prospects of a good penalty (although one authority uses the double to show clubs). As a corollary, 3♣ is natural and unconstructive with a long club suit.

Some of the other bids available to the opener's partner need careful consideration. 2♠ and 2♡ are unlikely to be needed as natural bids in the face of an announced major two-suiter, so a partnership can give these bids a specialized meaning.

A response of 2 NT can be employed as *unusual*, asking opener to bid a minor suit. A hand which would raise 1 NT to 2 NT without interference can double and bid 2 NT on the next round.

(For alternative conventional defenses to 1 NT opening bids, see ASPRO; ASTRO; BROZEL; EXCLUSION BID; RIPSTRA.)

LANDY TROPHY. A trophy awarded in memory of ALVIN LANDY to the winners of the Spring ACBL-WIDE charity game since 1969.

LANGUAGE. (1) Symbolic: The art of communication between partners; as, "the language of bidding" and "the language of signals". (2) Verbal: English is the official language of WBF tournaments and other international tournaments.

LATE PAIR. A pair desiring to enter an event after it has started. An ingenious director can usually add one or more pairs to a game during the first round (or even later) without disrupting play for those who have already started. See APPENDIX TABLE; HALF TABLE.

LATE PLAY. Play, after completion of a session, of one or more boards which would normally have been played during an earlier round.

A late play arises when the director observes that a given table has one or more boards to play in a given round when the rest have finished and are ready to move. The director may instruct the contestants not to start another board, but to return at the end of the contest to play the board then.

LAVINTHAL SIGNAL. See SUIT PREFERENCE.

LAW OF BALANCED DISTRIBUTION. A general principle relating to suit distributions, stated as follows by JOHN A. TIERNEY, Annapolis: The more symmetrical of two specific holdings is the more probable. Two equally symmetric holdings are equally probable.

This does *not* mean that an even suit split is more likely than an uneven one, which is untrue with four cards (or a higher even number). It refers to specific layouts. If five cards are missing, the Q-J-4-3-2, all the following are equally probable: Q-4; 3-2; Q-4-3; 4-3-2. The following are less symmetric, and therefore less probable: Q; 2; Q-J-4-3; Q-4-3-2.

LAW OF TOTAL TRICKS. A theory described by Jean-Rene Vernes of Paris in *The Bridge World*, designed to assist in competitive bidding situations.

The rule is that in each deal, if each side played in its own trump suit, the total number of tricks theoretically available to both sides is approximately equal to the total number of trumps held by both sides, each in its respective suit. The rule of thumb suggested by this theory is that it is usually relatively safe to bid for as many tricks as your side has trumps. Factors that increase the safety of further competition include the existence of a double fit and the possession of all the honors in the trump suit.

LAW OF SYMMETRY. A theory of distribution suggested by ELY CULBERTSON. His idea was that imperfect shuffles tend to produce a suit pattern equivalent to a hand pattern in the same deal. A player with 5-4-3-1 distribution should expect the outstanding cards in his long suit to be divided 4-3-1 more frequently than the mathematical odds would suggest. There is no mathematical or empirical basis for this theory.

LAWS. See LAWS OF CONTRACT BRIDGE. In this encyclopedia "LAWS" refers to the Laws of both Contract and Duplicate unless separate reference is made to "LAWS OF DUPLICATE".

LAWS OF BRIDGE. In 1743, EDMOND HOYLE published *A Short Treatise on the Game of Whist, Containing the Laws of the Game.* The laws as codified there became so universally accepted that they guided whist players for over 100 years. The Arlington and Portland clubs revised the code in 1864, and the Portland Club remained as the recognized authority in the newer game of bridge, the laws of this newer game appearing under the pen name of Boaz in 1895. Other clubs adopted their own versions, until in 1902 a committee representing many card clubs promulgated an American code. This set of laws was not received with universal acclaim, and gradually the laws of the Whist Club (New York) became standardized.

Bridge, which had succeeded in surpassing whist, was itself superseded by auction bridge, and in 1909 the Portland and Bath clubs in England framed a Code of Laws of Auction Bridge; the Whist Club followed with its Laws of Auction Bridge in 1910. These were revised in 1911, 1912, 1915, 1917, and 1920, and in 1926 the most recent code was adopted. In the Twenties auction bridge began to be succeeded by the then new game of contract bridge, and in 1927 the Whist Club adoted a code based essentially on the 1926 Laws of Auction Bridge. This time the American clubs were ahead of their British counterparts, the Portland and other clubs adopting a code in 1929.

For several years thereafter, the Whist Club, the Portland Club, and the Commission Française du Bridge worked through their committees to make a code that would be international in scope, finally agreeing on one on October 19, 1932. This code was revised by equivalent groups in 1935, 1948 and 1963.

Meanwhile, the peculiar requirements of duplicate bridge, which was sweeping the country and much of the world, pointed up the necessity for a code to cover duplicate. The first such code was the result of a committee of the American Bridge League, adopted in November 1928. The 1932 revision of the *Laws of Contract Bridge* necessitated a 1933 revision of the duplicate laws. In America a further revision in 1943 of the laws of duplicate led to an international effort (1948–49 by the Portland Club, the European Bridge League, and the National Laws Commission for America) that revised the *Laws of Contract Bridge* and the *Laws of Duplicate Contract Bridge*. These laws remained in vogue throughout the world until the revision of both, under the same international groups, which became effective July 1, 1963.

The duplicate laws were further revised in 1975 under the auspices of the ACBL (with major contributions by EDGAR KAPLAN, DON OAKIE, and ALFRED SHEINWOLD) and the WORLD BRIDGE FEDERATION and thus became the first truly worldwide code. The rubber bridge laws were further revised in 1981 (with major contributions by B. JAY BECKER, EDGAR KAPLAN and ROGER STERN). Representing the promulgating bodies were the following:

LAWS COMMISSION
of The American Contract Bridge League
Edgar Kaplan, *Chairman*

B. Jay Becker	Easley Blackwood
John Gerber	Richard L. Goldberg
Charles H. Goren	Oswald Jacoby
Thomas F. McCarthy	Donald Oakie
Carl B. Rubin	Edgar Theus

DRAFTING COMMITTEE
FOR DUPLICATE BRIDGE
Alfred Sheinwold, *Chairman*

John Gerber	Edgar Kaplan
Donald Oakie	Edgar Theus

WORLD BRIDGE FEDERATION
LAWS COMMITTEE

Geoffrey L. Butler, *Chairman* (Great Britain)
Julius Rosenblum, *Ex-Officio* (United States)
Carlos Cabanne (Argentina)
Silvio Carini Mazzaccara (Italy)
Johannes Hammerich (Venezuela)
Edgar Kaplan, (United States)
André LeMaître (Belgium)
Dr. Ralph Mizroch (South Africa)
Donald Oakie (United States)
George Rosenkranz (Mexico)
Leslie Schneideman (New Zealand)
Alfred Sheinwold (United States)
Gunnar Zabel (Norway)
Victor Zirinsky (Hong Kong)

LAWS COMMISSION OF THE AMERICAN CONTRACT BRIDGE LEAGUE. A committee of the AMERICAN CONTRACT BRIDGE LEAGUE charged with formulating and promulgating the official laws of Rubber and Duplicate Contract Bridge.

In the preparation of international codes, the Commission collaborates with other bodies, which have included the WHIST CLUB of New York, the PORTLAND CLUB of London, the EUROPEAN BRIDGE LEAGUE and the WORLD BRIDGE FEDERATION.

Former members of the Commission, now deceased, who have made substantial contributions to the development of the Laws include: WALTER

BEINECKE, EDWARD HYMES, JR., WILLIAM E. Mc KEN-NEY, GEOFFREY MOTT-SMITH, GEORGE REITH and Harold Richard.

In 1983 the members of the Commission were: EDGAR KAPLAN, chairman; B. JAY BECKER, EASLEY BLACKWOOD, RICHARD L. GOLDBERG, CHARLES H. GOREN, OSWALD JACOBY, THE HON. AMALYA KEARSE, GEORGE ROSENKRANZ, JEROME R. SILVERMAN, ROGER STERN, ED THEUS, KAREN R. ALLISON, NANCY GRUVER, JEFFREY D. POLISNER and LEE HAZEN, Member Emeritus.

LAWS COMMITTEE OF THE WORLD BRIDGE FEDERATION. See WORLD BRIDGE FEDERATION LAWS COMMITTEE.

LAWS OF CONTRACT BRIDGE

THE SCOPE OF THE LAWS

The Laws are designed to define correct procedure and to provide an adequate remedy whenever a player accidentally, carelessly or inadvertently disturbs the proper course of the game, or gains an unintentional but nevertheless unfair advantage. An offending player should be ready to pay a prescribed penalty graciously.

The Laws are not designed to prevent dishonorable practices and there are no penalties to cover intentional violations. In the absence of penalty, moral obligations are strongest. Ostracism is the ultimate remedy for intentional offenses.

THE OBJECT OF THE PROPRIETIES

The object of the Proprieties is twofold: to familiarize players with the customs and etiquette of the game, generally accepted over a long period of years; and to enlighten those who might otherwise fail to appreciate when or how they are improperly conveying information to their partners — often a far more reprehensible offense than a violation of a law.

When these principles are appreciated, arguments are avoided and the pleasure that the game offers is materially enhanced.

Part I

DEFINITIONS

[For definitions, see definitions under LAWS OF DUPLICATE BRIDGE.]

Part II

PRELIMINARIES

1. THE PLAYERS — THE PACK

Contract bridge is played by all four players with a pack of 52 cards of identical back design and color, consisting of 13 cards in each of four suits. Two packs should be used, of which only one is in play at any time; and each pack should be clearly distinguishable from the other in back design or color.

2. RANK OF CARDS

The suits rank downwards in order — Spades (♠), Hearts, (♡), Diamonds (♢), Clubs (♣). The cards of each suit rank in descending order: Ace, King, Queen, Jack, 10, 9, 8, 7, 6, 5, 4, 3, 2.

3. THE DRAW

Before every rubber, each player draws a card from a pack shuffled and spread face down on the table. A card should not be exposed until all the players have drawn.

Unless it is otherwise agreed, the two players who draw the highest cards play as partners against the other two players. When cards of the same rank are drawn, the rank of suit determines which is higher.

The player with the highest card deals first and has the right to choose his seat and the pack with which he will deal. He may consult his partner, but having announced his decision must abide by it. His partner sits opposite him. The opponents then occupy the two remaining seats as they wish, and having made their selection must abide by it.

A player must draw again if he draws more than one card, or one of the four cards at either end of the pack, or a card adjoining one drawn by another player, or a card from the other pack.

Part III

THE DEAL

4. THE SHUFFLE

Before the first deal of a rubber, the player to the dealer's left should shuffle the pack thoroughly, without exposing the face of any card, in full view of the players and to their satisfaction. Thereafter, as each player deals, the dealer's partner shuffles the other pack for the next deal, and places the pack face down on his right.

A pack properly prepared should not be disturbed until the dealer picks it up for his deal, at which time he is entitled to the final shuffle.

No player other than the dealer and the player designated to prepare the pack may shuffle.

5. THE CUT

The pack must be cut immediately before it is dealt. The dealer presents the pack to his right-hand opponent, who lifts off a portion and places it on the table toward the dealer. Each portion must contain at least four cards. The dealer completes the cut by placing what was originally the bottom portion upon the other portion.

No player other than the dealer's right-hand opponent may cut the pack.

6. NEW CUT — NEW SHUFFLE

There must be a new cut if any player demands one before the first card is dealt. In this case, the dealer's right-hand opponent cuts again.

There must be a new shuffle, followed by a cut:

(a) If any player demands one before the dealer has picked up the pack for his deal. In this case, the player designated to prepare the pack shuffles again.

(b) If any player demands one after the dealer has picked up the pack but before the first card is dealt. In this case only the dealer shuffles.

(c) If a card is turned faced up in shuffling. In this case the player who was shuffling shuffles again.

(d) If a card is turned face up in cutting. In this case only the dealer shuffles.

(e) If there is a redeal (see Law 10).

7. CHANGE OF PACK

The two packs are used alternately, unless there is a redeal.

A pack containing a card so damaged or marked so that it may be identified from its back must be replaced* if attention is drawn to the imperfection before the last card of the current deal has been dealt.

A pack originally belonging to a side must be restored on demand of any player before the last card of the current deal has been dealt.*

8. THE DEAL

The dealer distributes the cards face down, one at a time in rotation into four separate hands of thirteen cards each, the first card to the player on his left and the last card to himself. If he deals two cards simultaneously or consecutively to the same player, or fails to deal a card to a player, he may rectify the error, provided he does so immediately and to the satisfaction of the other players.

The dealer must not allow the face of any card to be seen while he is dealing. Players should not look at the face of any card until the deal is completed.**

9. ROTATION OF THE TURN TO DEAL

The turn to deal passes in rotation, unless there is a redeal. If a player deals out of turn, and attention is not drawn to the error before the last card has been dealt, the deal stands as though it had been in turn, the player who dealt the cards is the dealer, and the player who missed his turn to deal has no redress; and the rotation continues as though the deal had been in turn, unless a redeal is required under Law 10.

10. REDEAL

A redeal cancels the faulty deal; the same dealer deals again, unless he was dealing out of turn; the same pack is used, unless it has been replaced as provided in Law 7; and the cards are shuffled and cut anew as provided in Laws 4 and 5.

There must be a redeal:

---

*See Footnote to Law 8.
**A player who violates this provision forfeits those rights to a change of pack (Law 7) or redeal (Law 10) marked with an asterisk (*).

(a) If, before the last card has been dealt, it is discovered that

    (i) a card has been turned face up in dealing or is face up in the pack or elsewhere;

    (ii) the cards have not been dealt correctly;*

    (iii) a player is dealing out of turn or is dealing with a pack that was not shuffled or not cut, provided any player* demands a redeal.

(b) If, before the first call has been made, it is discovered that a player has picked up another player's hand and has seen a card in it.

(c) If, before play has been completed, it is discovered that

    (i) the pack did not conform in every respect to the requirements of Law 1, including any case in which a missing card cannot be found after due search;

    (ii) one player has picked up too many cards, another too few;

    (iii) two or more players on opposing sides have allowed any cards from their hands to be mixed together, following a claim that a redeal is in order.

11. MISSING CARD

When a player has too few cards and a redeal is not required by Law 10 (c), the deal stands as correct, and:

(a) If he has played more than once to a previous trick, Law 67 applies;

(b) If a missing card is found elsewhere, not in a previous trick, that card is deemed to have belonged continuously to the deficient hand and must be restored to that hand; it may become a penalty card, as provided in Law 23 or 49, and failure to have played it may constitute a revoke.

12. SURPLUS CARD

When a player has too many cards and a redeal is not required by Law 10 (c), the deal stands as correct, and

(a) If the offender has omitted to play to a trick, Law 67 applies.

(b) If the offender has picked up a surplus card from a previous trick, or from dummy's hand, or from the other pack, or elsewhere, such surplus card shall be restored to its proper place; and

    (i) If the surplus card is in the offender's hand when it is discovered, there is no penalty.

    (ii) If the surplus card had been led or played, or had been played to a previous trick, the offender must substitute for it a card of the same suit as the surplus card. The non-offending side wins that trick. When attention is drawn to the offense before the lead to the next trick, either member of the non-offending side may, without penalty,

withdraw a play made subsequent to the offense, and substitute any legal play.

Part IV

GENERAL LAWS
GOVERNING IRREGULARITIES

13. PROCEDURE FOLLOWING AN IRREGULARITY
(Club Law 13)

When an irregularity has occurred, any player — except dummy as restricted by Law 43 — may draw attention to it and give or obtain information as to the law applicable to it. The fact that a player draws attention to an irregularity committed by his side does not affect the rights of the opponents.

After attention has been drawn to an irregularity, no player should call or play until all questions in regard to rectification and to the assessment of a penalty have been determined. Premature correction of an irregularity on the part of the offender may subject him to a further penalty (see Law 26).

14. ASSESSMENT OF A PENALTY
(Club Law 14)

A penalty may not be imposed until the nature of the irregularity to be penalized has been determined and the applicable penalty has been clearly stated; but a penalty once paid, or any decision agreed and acted upon by the players, stands and should not be corrected even though at some later time it may be judged incorrect, except by agreement of all four players.

15. WAIVER OR FORFEITURE OF PENALTY

The right to penalize an offense is forfeited if a member of the non-offending side

(a) waives the penalty;

(b) calls (Law 34) or plays (Law 60) after an irregularity committed by the opponent to his right.

16. UNAUTHORIZED INFORMATION
(Club Law 16)

A player may be subject to penalty if he conveys information to his partner other than by a legal call or play.

Information conveyed by an illegal call, play or exposure of a card is subject to the applicable law in Part V or VI.

If a player conveys information to his partner by means of a remark or question or by an unmistakable hesitation, special emphasis, tone, gesture, movement, mannerism or any other action that suggests a call, lead or plan of play; and if attention is drawn to the offense immediately, (penalty) either member of the non-offending side (dummy excepted) may prohibit any call or play so suggested.

Part V

THE AUCTION

Correct Procedure

---

17. DURATION OF THE AUCTION

The auction begins when the last card of a correct deal has been placed on the table. The dealer makes the first call, and thereafter each player calls in rotation. When three passes in rotation have followed any call (but see Law 34), the auction is closed.

18. BIDS

Each bid must name a number of odd tricks, from one to seven, and a denomination. A bid supersedes the previous bid if it names either a greater number of odd tricks, or the same number of odd tricks in a higher denomination. A bid that fulfills these requirements is sufficient; one that does not is insufficient. The denominations rank in descending order: notrump, spades, hearts, diamonds, clubs.

19. DOUBLES AND REDOUBLES

A player may double only the last preceding bid, and then only if it was made by an opponent and no calls other than pass have intervened.

A player may redouble only the last preceding double, and then only if it was made by an opponent and no calls other than pass have intervened.

A player should not, in doubling or redoubling, state the number of tricks or the denomination; but, if he states either or both incorrectly, he is deemed to have doubled or redoubled the bid as it was made.

All doubles and redoubles are superseded by a subsequent legal bid. If there is no subsequent bid, scoring values are increased as provided in Law 81.

20. REVIEW AND EXPLANATION

A player who does not hear a call distinctly may forthwith require that it be repeated.

During the auction and at his own turn to call, a player (unless required by law to pass) may require a restatement of the auction in its entirety.

After the final pass, declarer before playing from dummy, or either defender at his first turn to play, may require a restatement of the auction in its entirety.

A request to have calls restated should be responded to only by an opponent (dummy, or a player required by law to pass, may so respond). All players should promptly correct errors in restatement.

A player may require an explanation of the partnership understanding relating to any call made by an opponent, but only at that player's own turn to call or play. A request for an explanation of a call should be responded to by the partner of the player making the call (see Proprieties 4).

21. CALL BASED ON MISINFORMATION

A player has no recourse if he has made a call on the basis of his own misunderstanding.

A player may, without penalty, change any call he may have made as a result of misinformation given him by an opponent, provided his partner has not subsequently called. If he elects to correct his call,

his left-hand opponent may then, in turn and without penalty, change any subsequent call he may have made.

22. PROCEDURE AFTER THE AUCTION IS CLOSED

After the auction is closed:

(a) If no player has bid, the hands are abandoned and the turn to deal passes in rotation.

(b) If any player has bid, the final bid becomes the contract and play begins.

Irregularities

23. CARD EXPOSED OR LED DURING THE AUCTION
(Club Law 23)

Whenever, during the auction, a player faces a card on the table or holds a card so that it is possible for his partner to see its face, every such card must be left face up on the table until the auction closes; and (penalty) if the offender subsequently becomes a defender, declarer may treat every such card as a penalty card (Law 50).

In addition:

(a) If it is a single card below the rank of an honor and not prematurely led, there is no further penalty.

(b) If it is a single card of honor rank, or any card prematurely led, or if more than one card is so exposed, (penalty) the offender's partner must pass when next it is his turn to call.

24. IMMEDIATE CORRECTION OF A CALL

A player may substitute his intended call for an inadvertent call, but only if he does so, or attempts to do so, without pause for thought. If legal, his last call stands without penalty; if illegal, it is subject to the applicable law.

25. CHANGE OF CALL
(Club Law 25)

A call substituted for a call made previously at the same turn, when it is too late for correction as provided in Law 24, is cancelled; and:

(a) If the first call was illegal, the offender is subject to the applicable law.

(b) If the first call was a legal one, the offender must either

    (i) allow his first call to stand and (penalty) his partner must pass when next it is his turn to call; or

    (ii) make any legal call and (penalty) his partner must pass whenever it is his turn to call.

The offender's partner will also be subject to a lead penalty as provided in Law 26 if he becomes a defender.

26. CHANGE OF CALL — LEAD PENALTIES
(Club Law 26)

When a player makes a call and subsequently

changes it to another legal call (except as permitted under Law 24), then if he becomes a defender:

(a) if the changed call was in a suit, and the substituted call did not repeat that suit, declarer may* either require the offender's partner to lead, or prohibit him from leading, such suit when first the offender's partner has the lead (including the opening lead). A prohibition continues for as long as offender's partner retains the lead. When the irregular call artificially relates to a denomination other than the one actually named, "such suit" is the suit or suits to which the call relates.

(b)if the changed call was

(i) in notrump, and his final call at that turn was not,

or

(ii) pass, double or redouble, other than an out-of-rotation call repeated in turn in accordance with Law 30 (a) or 32 (b)(i),

declarer may* prohibit offender's partner from leading any one specified suit when first the offender's partner has the lead (including the opening lead). This prohibition continues for as long as offender's partner retains the lead.

27. INSUFFICIENT BID
(Club Law 27)

An insufficient bid made in rotation must be corrected by the substitution of either a sufficient bid or a pass**, unless the irregular bid is accepted. Any insufficient bid may be accepted (treated as legal) at the option of the opponent on offender's left, and is accepted if that opponent calls.

If the call substituted is

(a) the lowest sufficient bid in the same denomination, the auction proceeds as though the irregularity had not occurred.***

(b) any other sufficient bid, or pass, (penalty) the offender's partner must pass whenever it is his turn to call, and the lead penalties of Law 26 will apply if he becomes a defender.

If the offender attempts to substitute a double or redouble, it is cancelled; he must pass at that turn and the offense is subject to the penalty provided in subsection (b) above.

If a player makes an insufficient bid out of rotation, Law 31 applies.

Call Out of Rotation

28. CALLS CONSIDERED TO BE IN ROTATION

A call is considered to be in rotation

(a) when it is made without waiting for the right-hand opponent to pass, if that opponent is required by law to pass.

(b) when it is made by the player whose turn it was to call, before a penalty has been imposed for a call out of rotation by an opponent; it waives any penalty for the call out of rotation and the auction proceeds as though that opponent had not called at that turn.

29. PROCEDURE AFTER A CALL OUT OF ROTATION

After a call out of rotation, the opponent to offender's left* may either:

(a) make any legal call; if he chooses to do so, the call out of rotation stands as if it were legal (but if it is an inadmissible call, see Law 35), and the auction proceeds without penalty;

or,

(b) require that the call out of rotation be cancelled. The auction reverts to the player whose turn it was to call. The offender may make any legal call in proper turn but is subject to penalty under Law 30, 31 or 32.

30. PASS OUT OF ROTATION
(Club Law 30)

When a player has passed out of rotation

(a) before any player has bid, or when it was the turn of the opponent to his right** to call, (penalty) the offender must pass when next it is his turn to call.

(b) after any player has bid and when it was the turn of the offender's partner to call, (penalty) the offender must pass whenever it is his turn to call; the offender's partner may make a sufficient bid or may pass, but may not double or redouble at that turn. The offender's partner will be subject to the lead penalties of Law 26 if he becomes a defender.

31. BID OUT OF ROTATION
(Club Law 31)

When a player has bid out of rotation

(a) at the turn of offender's partner to call, or before any player has called when the opponent on the offender's left was the dealer, (penalty) the offender's partner must pass whenever it is his turn to call, and the lead penalties of Law 26 will apply if he becomes a defender.

(b) at the turn of the opponent on the offender's right*** to call,

(i) if that opponent passes, the bid out of rotation must be repeated, and there is no penalty (if the bid out of rotation was insufficient, it must be corrected as provided in Law 27);

(ii) if that opponent makes a legal**** bid, double or redouble, the offender may in turn make any legal call. If such call repeats the denomination of the bid out of rotation, (penalty) the offender's

---

*Declarer specifies the suit at the time that offender's partner first has the lead.

**The offender is entitled to select his final call at that turn after the applicable penalties have been stated, and any call he has previously attempted to substitute is cancelled, but the lead penalties of Law 26 will apply if he becomes a defender.

***Offender's partner must not base any subsequent calls or plays on information gained from such a withdrawn bid.

---

*He alone exercises the option, although any player may draw attention to the irregularity.

**After any player has bid, a call at offender's left-hand opponent's turn is a change of call; Law 25 applies and not this section.

***After any player has bid, a call at offender's left-hand opponent's turn is a change of call; Law 25 applies and not this section.

****An illegal call by that opponent may be penalized in the usual way, after which this sub-section, (b)(ii), applies.

partner must pass when next it is his turn to call. If the substituted call does not repeat the denomination, (penalty) the offender's partner must pass whenever it is his turn to call, and the lead penalties of Law 26 will apply if he becomes a defender.

32. DOUBLE OR REDOUBLE OUT OF ROTATION
(Club Law 32)

When a player has doubled or redoubled out of rotation,*

(a) If it was the offender's partner's turn to call, (penalty) the offender's partner must pass whenever it is his turn to call; the offender may not thereafter, in turn, double or redouble the same bid he doubled or redoubled out of turn; and the lead penalties of Law 26 (b) will apply if he becomes a defender.

(b) If it was the turn of the opponent on the offender's right* to call:

(i) If the opponent on the offender's right passes, the double or redouble out of rotation must be repeated and there is no penalty.

(ii) If the opponent on the offender's right bids, the offender may in turn make any legal call, and (penalty) the offender's partner must pass when next it is his turn to call, and the lead penalties of Law 26 (b) will apply if he becomes a defender.

33. SIMULTANEOUS CALLS

A call made simultaneously with one made by the player whose turn it was to call is deemed to be a subsequent call.

34. RETENTION OF THE RIGHT TO CALL

A player may not be deprived of any turn to call by one or more passes following a pass out of rotation, when there has been no subsequent bid.** All such passes — the pass out of rotation, plus the subsequent passes that would serve to end the auction — are cancelled. The bidding reverts to the player whose turn it was to call before the pass out of rotation, and the auction continues as though there had been no irregularity.

Inadmissible Calls

35. INADMISSIBLE CALL CONDONED
(Club Law 35)

When, after any inadmissible call specified below, the opponent to the offender's left makes a call

---

*After any player has called, a call at offender's left-hand opponent's turn is a change of call; Law 25 applies and not this section.
**After a pass out of rotation that has been accepted by a pass from the player to offender's left (it thus stands as legal), three passes in rotation may follow a call; apparently, this would end this auction, as provided by Law 17. However, a player would then be deprived of an opportunity to call, and this is not permitted.

before a penalty has been assessed, there is no penalty for the offense (the lead penalties of Law 26 do not apply). If the inadmissible call was

(a) a double or redouble not permitted by Law 19, that call and all subsequent calls are cancelled; the auction reverts to the player whose turn it is to call and proceeds as though there had been no irregularity;

(b) a bid, double or redouble by a player required by law to pass, that call and subsequent legal calls stand; but if the offender was required to pass for the remainder of the auction, he must still pass at subsequent turns;

(c) a bid of more than seven, that call and all subsequent calls are cancelled; the offender must substitute a pass, and the auction proceeds as though there had been no irregularity;

(d) a call after the auction is closed, that call and all subsequent calls are cancelled without penalty.

36. INADMISSIBLE DOUBLE OR REDOUBLE
(Club Law 36)

Any double or redouble not permitted by Law 19 is cancelled, and the offender must substitute a legal call: and (penalty) the offender's partner must pass whenever it is his turn to call, and the lead penalties of Law 26 (b) will apply if he becomes a defender. Further, if the bid that was inadmissibly doubled or redoubled becomes the final contract, either member of the non-offending side may specify that the contract be played undoubled.

If the right of the non-offending side to penalize is forfeited, Law 35 applies.

37. BID, DOUBLE OR REDOUBLE IN VIOLATION
OF THE OBLIGATION TO PASS

A bid, double or redouble by a player who is required by law to pass is cancelled, and (penalty) both members of the offending side must pass during the remainder of the auction, and the lead penalties of Law 26 will apply if they become defenders.

38. BID OF MORE THAN SEVEN
(Club Law 38)

No play or score at a contract of more than seven is ever permissible. A bid of more than seven by any player is cancelled, and (penalty) both members of the offending side must pass during the remainder of the auction; and the lead penalties of Law 26 will apply if they become defenders.

39. CALL AFTER THE AUCTION IS CLOSED
(Club Law 39)

A call after the auction is closed is cancelled, and:

(a) If it is a pass by a defender or any call by declarer or dummy, there is no penalty.

(b) If it is a bid, double or redouble by a defender, the lead penalties of Law 26 apply, unless the call has been condoned (see Law 35 (d)).

40. CONVENTIONS AND PSYCHIC BIDS
(Club Law 40)

A player may make any call or play (including an intentionally misleading call such as a 'psychic bid,' or a call or play that departs from commonly accepted or previously announced conventional practice) without prior announcement, provided that it is not based on a partnership understanding. But a player may not make use of a bidding or play convention unless,

(a) his side has disclosed its use of such a call or play beforehand, or

(b) it has been agreed beforehand that the use of partnership understandings be disclosed at the time they are used, and his partner does so disclose it. In this case, partner's disclosure must be confined to an indication that a convention has been used; he should not offer any explanation unless requested to do so.

Any group may, by agreement, restrict the use of conventions in its games.

Part VI

THE PLAY

Correct Procedure

41. OPENING LEAD, REVIEW, QUESTIONS

After the auction closes, the defender on declarer's left makes the opening lead.* After the opening lead, dummy spreads his hand in front of him on the table, face up and grouped in suits with the trumps on his right. Declarer plays both his hand and that of dummy.

Declarer, before he plays from dummy, or either defender at his first turn to play, may require a restatement of the auction in its entirety.

After it is too late to have previous calls restated, declarer or either defender is entitled to be informed what the contract is and whether, but not by whom, it was doubled or redoubled.

Either defender may require an explanation of the partnership understanding relating to any call made by an opponent (see Proprieties 4), but only at that defender's own turn to play. Declarer may at any time require an explanation of the partnership understanding relating to any call or play made by a defender.

42. DUMMY'S RIGHTS

Dummy is entitled to give or obtain information as to fact or law; and provided he has not forfeited his rights (see Law 43) he may also:

(a) question players regarding revokes as provided in Law 61;

(b) try to prevent any irregularity;**

(c) draw attention to any irregularity, but only after play is concluded.

43. DUMMY'S LIMITATIONS

Dummy may not participate in the play (except to

---

*After the final pass, either defender has the right to ask if it is his opening lead.

**He may, for example, warn declarer against leading from the wrong hand.

---

play the cards of dummy's hand as directed by declarer), or make any comment on the bidding, play, or score of the current deal; and if he does so, Law 16 may apply. Dummy may not call attention to an irregularity during play except to try to prevent an irregularity before it occurs.

Dummy forfeits the rights provided in (a), (b) and (c) of Law 42 if he exchanges hands with declarer, leaves his seat to watch declarer play, or, on his own initiative, looks at the face of a card in either defender's hand; and if, thereafter,

(a) He is the first to draw attention to a defender's irregularity, declarer may not enforce any penalty for the offense.

(b) He warns declarer not to lead from the wrong hand, (penalty) either defender may choose the hand from which declarer shall lead.

(c) He is the first to ask declarer if a play from declarer's hand constitutes a revoke, declarer must substitute a correct card if his play was a revoke, and the penalty provisions of Law 64 apply.

44. SEQUENCE AND PROCEDURE OF PLAY

The player who leads to a trick may play any card in his hand.* After the lead, each other player in turn plays a card, and the four cards so played constitute a trick.

In playing to a trick, each player must follow suit if possible. This obligation takes precedence over all other requirements of these Laws. If unable to follow suit, a player may play any card.*

A trick containing a trump is won by the player who has contributed to it the highest trump. A trick that does not contain a trump is won by the player who has contributed to it the highest card of the suit led. The player who has won the trick leads to the next trick.

45. CARD PLAYED

Each player except dummy should play a card by detaching it from his hand and placing it, face up, on the table where other players can easily reach and see it. Dummy, if instructed by declarer to do so, may play from his hand a card named or designated by declarer.**

A card must be played:

(a) If it is a defender's card held so that it is possible for his partner to see its face.

(b) If it is a card from declarer's hand that declarer holds face up, touching or nearly touching the table, or maintains in such a position as to indicate that it has been played;

(c) If it is a card in dummy deliberately touched by declarer except for the purpose of arranging dummy's cards or of reaching a card above or below the card or cards touched.

---

*Unless he is subject to restriction after an irregularity committed by his side.

**If dummy places in played position a card declarer did not name, the card must be withdrawn if attention is drawn to it before each side has played to the next trick, and a defender may withdraw (without penalty) a card played after the error but before attention was drawn to it (see Law 47).

(d) If the player who holds the card names or otherwise designates it as the card he proposes to play. A player may, without penalty, change an inadvertent designation if he does so without pause for thought; but if an opponent has, in turn, played a card that was legal before the change of designation, that opponent may, without penalty, withdraw any card so played and substitute another.

(e) If it is a penalty card, subject to Law 50.

(f) If it is a card in dummy's hand that dummy has illegally suggested as a play, unless either defender forbids the play of such card, or an equal of it, or a card of the same suit, as provided in Law 16.

A card played may not be withdrawn except as provided in Law 47.

46. PARTIAL DESIGNATION OF A CARD TO BE PLAYED FROM DUMMY'S HAND

When declarer instructs dummy to play a card from dummy's hand, as permitted by Law 45, but names only a suit or only the rank of a card, or the equivalent, without fully specifying the card to be played, declarer must complete his partial designation. Dummy must not play a card before declarer has completed his partial designation, and if dummy prematurely plays a card, Law 16 applies on that trick only, unless a defender has subsequently played.

47. RETRACTION OF A CARD PLAYED
(Club Law 47)

A card once played may be withdrawn only:

(a) to comply with a penalty, or to correct an illegal play, or to correct the simultaneous play of two or more cards (see Law 58);

(b) after a change of designation as permitted by Law 45 (d);

(c) after an opponent's change of play, to substitute a card for one played;*

(d) to correct a play* after misinformation by an opponent. A lead out of turn may be retracted without penalty if the leader was mistakenly informed by an opponent that it was his turn to lead.

Penalty Card

48. EXPOSURE OF DECLARER'S CARDS

Declarer is not subject to penalty for exposing a card, and no card of declarer's or dummy's ever becomes a penalty card. Declarer is not required to play any card dropped accidentally.

When declarer faces his cards after an opening lead out of turn, Law 54 applies.** When declarer faces his cards at any other time, he may be deemed to have made a claim or concession of tricks, in which case Law 68 applies.

49. EXPOSURE OF A DEFENDER'S CARDS

Whenever a defender faces a card on the table, holds a card so that it is possible for his partner to see its face, or names a card as being in his hand, before he is entitled to do so in the normal course of play or application of the law, (penalty) each such card becomes a penalty card (Law 50).*

50. DISPOSITION OF A PENALTY CARD

A card is a penalty card when prematurely exposed. It must be left face up on the table until it is played or until an alternate penalty has been selected.

A single card below the rank of an honor and exposed inadvertently (as in playing two cards to a trick, or in dropping a card accidentally) becomes a minor-penalty card. Any penalty card of honor rank, or any card exposed through deliberate play (as in leading out of turn, or in revoking and then correcting) becomes a major-penalty card; when one defender has two or more penalty cards, all such cards become major-penalty cards.

When a defender has a minor-penalty card, he may not play any other card of the same suit below the rank of an honor until he has first played the penalty card. (However, he is entitled to play an honor card instead of the minor-penalty card.) There is no further penalty, but the offender's partner must not base any subsequent play on information gained through seeing the penalty card.

When a defender has a major-penalty card, such card must be played at the first legal opportunity, whether in leading, following suit, discarding or trumping. If a defender has two or more penalty cards that can legally be played, declarer may designate which is to be played. The obligation to follow suit, or to comply with a lead or play penalty, takes precedence over the obligation to play a penalty card, but the penalty card must still be left face up on the table and played at the next legal opportunity.

When a defender has the lead while his partner has a major-penalty card, declarer may choose to impose a lead penalty at this point: he may require that defender to lead the suit of the penalty card, or may prohibit that defender from leading that suit (a prohibition continues for as long as he retains the lead). If declarer does impose a lead penalty, the penalty card is picked up at once. If declarer does not, the defender may lead any card; but the penalty card remains a penalty card. The defender may not lead until declarer has indicated his choice.

51. TWO OR MORE PENALTY CARDS

When a defender has two or more penalty cards in one suit, and declarer requires the defender's partner to lead that suit, the defender may pick up every penalty card in that suit and may make any legal play to the trick.

When a defender has penalty cards in more than one suit, declarer may prohibit the defender's partner from leading every such suit; but the defender may then pick up every penalty card in every suit

---

*The offending side must not base any subsequent plays on information gained from such a withdrawn play.
**Declarer should, as a matter of propriety, refrain from spreading his hand.

---

*Exposure of a card or cards by a defender who is making a claim or concession of tricks is subject to Law 70.

prohibited by declarer and may make any legal play to the trick.

52. FAILURE TO LEAD OR PLAY A PENALTY CARD

When a defender is required by Law 50 to play a penalty card, but instead plays another card, he must leave that illegally played card face up on the table; and

(a) declarer may accept the defender's lead or play, and declarer must accept such lead or play if he has thereafter played from his or dummy's hand, but the unplayed penalty card remains a penalty card; or

(b) declarer may require the defender to substitute the penalty card for the card illegally led or played. Every card illegally led or played by the defender in the course of committing the irregularity becomes a penalty card.

Lead Out of Turn

53. LEAD OUT OF TURN ACCEPTED

Any lead out of turn may be treated by an opponent as a correct lead. It becomes a correct lead if an opponent accepts it by making a statement to that effect, or if that opponent next to play plays a card to the irregular lead.*

However, the player whose proper turn it was to lead — unless he is the offender's partner — may make his proper lead subsequent to the infraction without his card being treated as played to the irregular lead. The proper lead stands, and all cards played in error to this trick may be withdrawn without penalty.

54. OPENING LEAD OUT OF TURN

When a defender makes the opening lead out of turn:

(a) Declarer may accept the irregular lead as provided in Law 53. Dummy's hand is spread in accordance with Law 41, and the second card to the trick is played from declarer's hand; but if declarer first plays to the trick from dummy's hand, dummy's card may not be withdrawn except to correct a revoke.

(b) Declarer must accept the irregular lead if he could have seen any of dummy's cards (except cards exposed during the auction, subject to Law 23). He is deemed to have accepted the irregular lead if he begins to spread his hand as though he were dummy** and in so doing exposes one or more cards; declarer must spread his entire hand, and dummy becomes declarer.***

(c) Declarer may require the defender to retract his irregular lead (except as provided in (b) above), and then Law 56 applies.

---

*When such a play is made by a defender who is not next to play after the irregular lead, Law 57 applies.

**Declarer should, as a matter of propriety, refrain from spreading his hand intentionally.

***However, if cards are so exposed from both declarer's and dummy's hands, the player who was regularly to become declarer remains declarer.

55. DECLARER'S LEAD OUT OF TURN

When declarer leads out of turn from his or dummy's hand;

(a) Either defender may accept that lead as provided in Law 53.

(b) Either defender may require declarer to retract that lead. Then,

(i) if it was a defender's turn to lead, declarer restores the card led in error to his or dummy's hand, without penalty;

(ii) if declarer has led from the wrong hand when it was his turn to lead from his or dummy's hand, he withdraws the card led in error; he must lead a card from the correct hand, and, (penalty) if able to do so, a card of the same suit. Failure to observe this obligation in playing from his own hand is a revoke (see Law 64).

56. DEFENDER'S LEAD OUT OF TURN

When a defender leads out of turn:

(a) Declarer may accept that lead as provided in Law 53.

(b) Declarer may require the defender to retract that lead; the card illegally led becomes a major-penalty card (see Law 50 — note that lead penalties are provided).

Irregular Leads and Plays

57. PREMATURE LEAD OR PLAY BY A DEFENDER

When a defender leads to the next trick before his partner has played to the current trick, or plays out of turn before his partner has played, (penalty) declarer may require the offender's partner to play:

(a) his highest card of the suit led; or

(b) his lowest card of the suit led; or

(c) a legal card of another suit specified by declarer.

Declarer must select one of these options, and if the offender's partner cannot comply with the penalty selected he may play any card, as provided in Law 59.

When, as a result of the application of the penalty, the offender's partner wins the current trick, he leads to the next trick; and any card led or played out of turn by the other defender becomes a penalty card (Law 50).

A defender is not subject to penalty for playing before his partner if declarer has played from both hands; but a singleton or one of two or more equal cards in dummy is not considered automatically played unless dummy has played the card or has illegally suggested that it be played (Law 45 (f)).

58. SIMULTANEOUS LEADS OR PLAYS

A lead or play made simultaneously with another player's legal lead or play is deemed to be subsequent to it.

If a defender leads or plays two or more cards

simultaneously, and if only one such card is visible, he must play that card; if more than one card is exposed, he must designate the card he proposes to play and each other card exposed becomes a penalty card (Law 50.)

If declarer leads or plays two or more cards simultaneously from either hand, he must designate the card he proposes to play and must restore any other card to the correct hand. If declarer withdraws a visible card and a defender has already played to that card, such defender may, without penalty, withdraw his card and substitute another.

If the error remains undiscovered until both sides have played to the next trick, Law 67 applies.

59. INABILITY TO LEAD OR PLAY AS REQUIRED

A player may play any correct card if he is unable to lead or play as required to comply with a penalty, either because he has no card of the required suit, or because he has only cards of a suit he is prohibited from leading, or because of his obligation to follow suit.

60. PLAY AFTER AN ILLEGAL PLAY

A play by a member of the non-offending side after the opponent on his right has led or played out of turn prematurely, and before a penalty has been imposed, forfeits the right to penalize the offense. The illegal play is treated as though it were legal, (except as provided in Law 53 for a play by the proper leader), unless it constitutes a revoke. If the offending side had a previous obligation to play a penalty card or to comply with a lead or play penalty, the obligation remains at future turns.

When a defender plays after declarer has been required to retract his lead out of turn from either hand, but before declarer has led from the correct hand, the defender's card becomes a penalty card (Law 50).

A play by a member of the offending side before a penalty has been imposed does not affect the rights of the opponents and may itself be subject to penalty.

The Revoke

61. FAILURE TO FOLLOW SUIT — INQUIRIES CONCERNING A REVOKE

Failure to follow suit in accordance with Law 44, or failure to lead or play, when able, a card or suit required by law or specified by an opponent in accordance with an agreed penalty, constitutes a revoke. Any player, including dummy,* may ask a player who has failed to follow suit whether he has a card of the suit led, and may demand that an opponent correct his revoke. (A claim of revoke does not warrant inspection of quitted tricks, except as permitted in Law 66.)

62. CORRECTION OF A REVOKE

A player must correct his revoke if he becomes aware of the occurrence of the revoke before it becomes established. To correct a revoke, the offender withdraws the card he played in revoking and follows suit with any card. A card so withdrawn becomes a penalty card (Law 50) if it was played from a defender's unfaced hand. The card may be replaced without penalty if it was played from declarer's or dummy's hand* or if it was a defender's faced card. Each member of the non-offending side may, without penalty, withdraw any card he may have played after the revoke but before attention was drawn to it. Except as provided in the next paragraph, the partner of the offender may not withdraw his card unless it too constituted a revoke.**

After the eleventh trick, a revoke, even if established, must be corrected if discovered before the cards have been mixed together. If the revoke was committed by a defender before his partner has played to the twelfth trick, and if offender's partner holds cards of more than one suit, (penalty) declarer may then require the offender's partner to play to that trick either of the two cards he could legally have played.

63. ESTABLISHMENT OF A REVOKE

A revoke becomes established when the offender or his partner leads or plays (whether legally or illegally) to the following trick, or names or otherwise designates a card to be so played, or makes a claim or concession of tricks orally or by facing his hand. The revoke may then no longer be corrected (except for a revoke after the eleventh trick — see Law 62), and the trick on which the revoke occurred stands as played.

64. PROCEDURE AFTER ESTABLISHMENT OF A REVOKE (Club Law 64)

When a revoke has become established,

(a) if the trick on which the revoke occurred was won by the offending side, (penalty) after play ceases, the trick on which the revoke occurred plus one of any subsequent tricks won by the offending side are transferred*** to the non-offending side (if no subsequent trick was won by the offending side, only the revoke trick is transferred).

(b) if the trick on which the revoke occurred was won by the non-offending side, (penalty) after play ceases, one of any subsequent tricks won by the offending side is transferred*** to the non-offending side;

(c) there is no trick penalty for the established revoke if,

    (i) the offending side did not win either the trick on which the revoke occurred or any subsequent trick; or if,

    (ii) the revoke was a subsequent revoke in the same suit by the same player; or if,

---

*Unless he has forfeited his rights, as specified by Law 43.

*Subject to Law 43. A claim of revoke does not warrant inspection of quitted tricks except as permitted in Law 67.
**In such case, the card withdrawn becomes a penalty card if it was played from a defender's unfaced hand.
***For the scoring of transferred tricks, see Law 77.

(iii) the revoke was made in failing to play any card faced on the table or belonging to a hand faced on the table, including a card from dummy's hand; or if,

(iv) attention was first drawn to the revoke after all players had abandoned their hands and permitted the cards to be mixed together; or if,

(v) the revoke was made after the eleventh trick.

N.B. When any established revoke, including one not subject to penalty, causes damage to the non-offending side insufficiently compensated by this law, the offending side should, under Proprieties 1, transfer additional tricks so as to restore equity.

Tricks

65. COLLECTION AND ARRANGEMENT OF TRICKS

The cards constituting each completed trick are collected by a member of the side that won the trick and are then turned face down on the table. Each trick should be identifiable as such, and all tricks taken by a side should be arranged in sequence in front of declarer or of one defender, as the case may be, in such manner that each side can determine the number of tricks it has won and the order in which they were taken.

66. INSPECTION OF TRICKS

Declarer or either defender may, until a member of his side has led or played to the following trick, inspect a trick and inquire what card each player has played to it. Thereafter, until play ceases, quitted tricks may be inspected only to account for a missing or surplus card. After play ceases, the tricks and unplayed cards may be inspected to settle a claim of a revoke, of honors, or of the number of tricks won or lost. If, after a claim has been made, a player on one side mixes the cards in such a way that the facts can no longer be ascertained, the issue must be decided in favor of the other side.

67. TRICK EITHER APPROPRIATED IN ERROR OR DEFECTIVE

A trick appropriated by the wrong side must, upon demand, be restored to the side that has in fact won the trick by contributing the winning card to it. The scoring value of the trick must be credited to that side.*

A trick containing more or fewer than four cards is defective. When one player is found, during play, to have fewer or more cards than all the other players, the previous tricks should be forthwith examined, face down; if a defective trick is discovered, the player with a correspondingly incorrect number of cards is held responsible. The defective trick is inspected, face up, and —

(a) Unless all four hands have played to a sub-

---
*If calls have been made on a subsequent deal, see Law 78.

sequent trick, the defective trick is rectified as follows:

(i) If the offender has failed to play a card to the defective trick, he adds to that trick a card he can legally play:

(ii) If the offender has played more than one card to the defective trick, he withdraws all but one card, leaving a card he can legally play;

(iii) The non-offending side may, without penalty, withdraw any cards played after the irregularity and before attention was drawn to it; but the offending side may not withdraw cards that constitute legal plays, and any cards they withdraw may become penalty cards (Law 50).

(b) After all four hands have played to a subsequent trick, (penalty) the defective trick, if won by the offending side, is transferred to the non-offending side; and

(i) If the offender has failed to play a card to the defective trick, he forthwith faces and adds a card to that trick, if possible one he could legally have played to it.

(ii) If the offender has played more than one card to the defective trick, he withdraws all but one card, leaving the highest card he could legally have played to that trick. A withdrawn card may become a penalty card (Law 50); such a card is deemed to have belonged continuously to the offender's hand and failure to have played it to an earlier trick may constitute a revoke.

Claims and Concessions

68. DECLARER'S CLAIM OR CONCESSION OF TRICKS

Declarer makes a claim or a concession whenever he announces that he will win or lose one or more of the remaining tricks, or suggests that play may be curtailed, or faces his hand. Declarer should not make a claim or concession if there is any doubt as to the number of tricks to be won or lost.

69. PROCEDURE FOLLOWING DECLARER'S CLAIM OR CONCESSION
(Club Law 69)

When declarer has made a claim or concession, play is temporarily suspended and declarer must place and leave his hand face up on the table and forthwith make a comprehensive statement as to his proposed plan of play, including the order in which he will play the remaining cards.

Declarer's claim or concession is allowed, and the deal is scored accordingly, if both defenders agree to it. The claim or concession must be allowed if either defender has permitted any of his remaining cards to be mixed with another player's cards; otherwise, if either defender disputes declarer's claim or concession, it is not allowed. Then, play continues.

When his claim or concession is not allowed,

declarer must play on, leaving his hand face up on the table. At any time, either defender may face his hand for inspection by his partner, and declarer may not impose a penalty for any irregularity committed by a defender whose hand is so faced.

The objective of subsequent play is to achieve a result as equitable as possible to both sides, but any doubtful point must be resolved in favor of the defenders. Declarer may not make any play inconsistent with the statement he may have made at the time of his claim or concession. And if he failed to make an appropriate statement at that time, his choice of plays is restricted thereby :

(a) If declarer made no relevant statement, he may not finesse* in any suit unless an opponent failed to follow in that suit before the claim or concession, or would subsequently fail to follow in that suit on any conceivable sequence of plays.

(b) If declarer may have been unaware, at the time of his claim or concession, that a trump remained in a defender's hand, either defender may require him to draw, or not to draw, the outstanding trump.

(c) If declarer did not, in his statement, mention an ususual plan of play, he may adopt only a routine line of play.

If declarer attempts to make a play prohibited under this law, either defender may accept the play, or, provided neither defender has subsequently played, require declarer to withdraw the card so played and substitute another that conforms to his obligations.

70. DEFENDER'S CLAIM OR CONCESSION OF TRICKS
(Club Law 70)

A defender makes a concession when he agrees to declarer's claim, or when he announces that he will lose one or more of the remaining tricks.

A defender makes a claim when he announces that he will win one or more of the remaining tricks, or when he shows any or all of his cards for this purpose. If:

(a) the claim pertains only to an uncompleted trick currently in progress, play proceeds normally; cards exposed or otherwise revealed by the defender in making his claim do not become penalty cards, but Law 16, Unauthorized Information, may apply to claimer's partner.

(b) the claim pertains to subsequent tricks, play is temporarily suspended; the claimer must place and leave his hand face up on the table and make a comprehensive statement as to his proposed plan of defense. The claim is allowed, and the deal scored accordingly, if declarer agrees to it. If declarer disputes the claim, the defenders must play on with the claimer's hand face up on the table. Those cards do not become penalty cards. However, declarer may prohibit claimer's partner, under Law 16, from making any play that could be suggested to him by seeing the faced cards.

---

*For these purposes, a finesse is a play the success of which depends on finding one defender rather than the other with or without a particular card.

71. CONCESSION WITHDRAWN

A concession may be withdrawn:

(a) If a player concedes a trick his side has, in fact, won; or if declarer concedes defeat of a contract he has already fulfilled; or if a defender concedes fulfillment of a contract his side has already defeated. (If the score has been entered, see Law 78).

(b) If a trick that has been conceded cannot be lost by any probable sequence of play of the remaining cards, and if attention is drawn to that fact before the cards have been mixed together.

(c) If a defender concedes one or more tricks and his partner immediately objects, but Law 16 may apply.

Part VII

THE SCORE

72. POINTS EARNED

The result of each deal played is recorded in points, which fall into two classes:

1. *Trick Points.* Only declarer's side can earn trick points, and only by winning at least the number of odd tricks specified in the contract. Only the value of odd tricks named in the contract may be scored as trick points (see Law 81). Trick points mark the progression of the rubber toward its completion.

2. *Premium Points.* Either side or both sides may earn premium points. Declarer's side earns premium points by winning one or more overtricks; by fulfilling a doubled or redoubled contract; by bidding and making a slam; by holding scorable honors in declarer's or dummy's hand; or by winning the final game of a rubber.* The defenders earn premium points by defeating the contract (undertrick penalty) or by holding scorable honors in either of their hands (see Law 81).

Each side's premium points are added to its trick points at the conclusion of the rubber.

73. PARTSCORE — GAME

The basic units of trick scores are partscore and game. A partscore is recorded for declarer's side whenever declarer fulfills a contract for which the trick score is less than 100 points. Game is won by that side which is the first to have scored 100 or more trick points either in a single deal or by addition of two or more partscores made separately. No partscore made by either side in the course of one game is carried forward into the next game.

74. THE RUBBER

A rubber ends when a side has won two games. At the conclusion of the rubber, the winners of two games are credited with a premium score of 500 points if the other side has won one game, or with 700 points if the other side has not won a game. The trick and premium points scored by each side in the

---

*For incomplete rubber, see Law 80.

course of the rubber are then added. The side with the larger combined total wins the rubber, and the difference between the two totals represents the margin of victory computed in points.

75. METHOD OF SCORING

The score of each deal must be recorded, and it is preferable that a member of each side should keep score.

Scores are entered in two adjacent columns separated by a vertical line. Each scorer enters points earned by his side in the left-hand column, and points earned by his opponents in the right-hand column.

Each side has a trick score and a premium score, separated by a horizontal line intersecting the vertical line. All trick points are entered, as they are earned, in descending order below the horizontal line, all premium points in ascending order above that line.

Whenever a game is won, another horizontal line is drawn under all trick scores recorded for either side, in order to mark completion of the game. Subsequent trick scores are entered below that line.

76. RESPONSIBILITY FOR THE SCORE

When the play of a deal is completed, all four players are equally responsible for ascertaining that the number of tricks won by each side is correctly determined and that all scores are promptly and correctly entered.

77. TRANSFERRED TRICKS

A trick transferred though a revoke penalty is reckoned for all scoring purposes as though it had been won in play by the side to which it had been awarded.*

78. CORRECTION OF THE SCORE

When it is acknowledged by a majority of the players that a scoring error was made in recording an agreed-upon result (e.g., failure to enter honors, or incorrect computation of score), the error must be corrected if discovered before the net score of the rubber has been agreed to. However, except with the consent of all four players, an erroneous agreement as to the number of tricks won by each side may not be corrected after all players have called on the next deal.

In case of disagreement between two scores kept, the recollection of the majority of the players as to the facts governs.

79. DEALS PLAYED WITH AN INCORRECT PACK

Scores recorded for deals played with an incorrect

*Declarer plays in 3 ♡ and makes eight tricks. A revoke by a defender is found to have been established, with the defenders having won both the trick in which the revoke occurred and a later trick. Two tricks are transferred from the defenders to declarer, who therefore has ten tricks. Since he bid only 3 ♡, he scores 90 trick points, which count toward game, and 30 premium points for the overtrick.

pack are not subject to change by reason of the discovery of the imperfection after the cards have been mixed together.

80. INCOMPLETE RUBBER

When, for any reason, a rubber is not finished, the score is computed as follows:

If only one game has been completed, the winners of that game are credited with 300 points; if only one side has a partscore or scores in a game not completed, that side is credited with 50 points; the trick and premium points of each side are then added, and the side with the greater number of points wins the difference between the two totals.

81. SCORING TABLE

TRICK SCORE
Scored below the line by declarer's side, if contract is fulfilled:

| | IF TRUMPS ARE | | | |
	♣	♦	♡	♠
For each trick over six bid and made				
Undoubled	20	20	30	30
Doubled	40	40	60	60
Redoubled	80	80	120	120

| | AT A NOTRUMP CONTRACT | | |
	UNDBL	DBL	REDBL
For the first trick over six, bid and made	40	80	160
For each additional trick over six, bid and made	30	60	120

The first side to score 100 points below the line, in one or more hands, wins a GAME. When a game in won, both sides start without trick score toward the next game. First side to win two games wins the RUBBER POINTS.

PREMIUM SCORE
Scored above the line by declarer's side

RUBBER, GAME, PART-SCORE, CONTRACT FULFILLED

For winning the RUBBER, if opponents have won no game	700
For winning the RUBBER, if opponents have won one game	500
UNFINISHED RUBBER — for having won the only game	300
For making any DOUBLED or REDOUBLED CONTRACT	50

81. SCORING TABLE (continued)
SLAMS

	NOT VULNERABLE	VULNERABLE
For making a slam		
Small Slam (12 Tricks) bid and made	500	750
Grand Slam (all 13 tricks) bid and made	1000	1500

OVERTRICKS

	NOT VULNERABLE	VULNERABLE
For each OVERTRICK (tricks made in excess of contract)		
Undoubled	Trick Value	Trick Value
Doubled	100	200
Redoubled	200	400

HONORS
Scored above the line by either side:

For holding four of the five trump HONORS (A, K, Q, J, 10) in one hand	100
For holding all five trump HONORS (A, K, Q, J, 10) in one hand	150
For holding all four ACES in one hand at a notrump contract	150

UNDERTRICK PENALTIES

Tricks by which declarer fails to fulfill the contract; scored above the line by declarer's opponents if contract is not fullfilled:

	NOT VULNERABLE		
	UNDBL	DBL	REDBL
For first undertrick	50	100	200
For each additional undertrick	50	200	400
	VULNERABLE		
	UNDBL	DBL	REDBL
For first undertrick	100	200	400
For each additional undertrick	100	300	600

Part VIII

ALTERNATIVE CLUB LAWS

When bridge is played at a club, it is often practicable to designate an impartial and experienced person as "Arbiter" for the game. The Arbiter interprets and applies the Laws after an irregularity occurs, and generally assumes the role assigned to the "Director" in duplicate bridge. When such an Arbiter is available, certain laws can be modified so as to produce greater equity.

The "Club Laws" prescribe a somewhat different procedure after attention is drawn to an irregularity, and there is a different disposition for disputed claims. The principal changes, however, lie in the authority given to the Arbiter, after specified types of irregularity, to "adjust the score" of a deal once play is over. In adjusting a score, the Arbiter assigns a new result, the result he judges would likely have been achieved had the irregularity not occurred. The Arbiter should resolve any substantial doubt in favor of the non-offending side.

The alternative laws are in force only upon advance agreement by the players, or in accordance with the standing and published policy of a club. Any game may play under these Club Laws, so long as an Arbiter is nominated in advance; when there are more than four members of a table, a non-playing member can act as Arbiter.

CLUB LAW 13

The Arbiter must be called as soon as attention is drawn to an irregularity. Calling the Arbiter does not forfeit any rights to which a player may otherwise be entitled. Any player except dummy may draw attention to an irregularity and call the Arbiter. The fact that a player draws attention to an irregularity committed by his side does not affect the rights of the opponents.

After attention has been drawn to an irregularity, no player should call or play until the Arbiter has determined all matters in regard to rectification and to the assessment of a penalty. Premature correction of an irregularity on the part of an offender may subject him to further penalty.

CLUB LAW 14

The Arbiter assesses penalties when applicable. When these Club Laws provide an option among penalties, the Arbiter explains the options available. The Arbiter may assign an adjusted score, but only when these Club Laws empower him to do so, or when the Law provides no indemnity to a non-offending contestant for the particular type of violation of law or propriety committed by an opponent. He may not assign an adjusted score on the ground that the penalty provided in the Law is unduly severe or unduly advantageous to either side.

CLUB LAW 16

If a player conveys information to his partner by means of a remark or question, or by an unmistakable hesitation, special emphasis, tone, gesture, movement, mannerism or any other action that suggests a call, lead or plan of play; and if attention is drawn to the offense and the Arbiter is called, the Arbiter should require that the auction or play continue, reserving the right to assign an adjusted score if he considers that the result could have been affected by the illegal information.

After play ends, he should award an adjusted score to redress damage caused to the innocent side, when an opponent chose from among alternative logical actions one that could reasonably have been suggested by his partner's tempo, manner, remark, etc.

CLUB LAW 23

(Regular Law 23 stands intact but with the following addition, which applies as well to a change of call, an insufficient bid, a call out of rotation and an inadmissible call.)

When the penalty for an irregularity, under this or any other Law, would compel the offender's partner to pass at his next turn, and when the Arbiter deems that this enforced pass will necessarily* damage the innocent side, the Arbiter may reserve the right to assign an adjusted score.

CLUB LAW 25

The penalties in Club Law 23 apply.

CLUB LAW 26

Regular Law 26 stands intact, but with the following additions as sub-section (c).

(c) If the changed call related, by convention, to a denomination other than one named in the call, it is the particular denomination to which the conventional call relates, rather than the one actually mentioned, that determines which subsection the Arbiter will apply — (a) or (b) — as well as the suit to which he will apply sub-section (a).

CLUB LAW 27

Regular Law 27 stands intact but with the following addition to sub-section (a).

If the insufficient bid conveyed such substantial information as to damage the non-offending side, the Arbiter may assign an adjusted score.

---

*The score should not be adjusted merely because the penalty happened to result in good fortune for the offending side. The word "necessarily" restricts score adjustment to those instances in which the offender could have known, at the time of his infraction, that it would be to his advantage to require partner to pass.

LAWS OF CONTRACT BRIDGE

CLUB LAW 30

The provisions of Club Law 23 may apply.

CLUB LAW 31

The provisions of Club Law 23 may apply.

CLUB LAW 32

The provisions of Club Law 23 may apply.

CLUB LAW 35

The provisions of Club Law 23 may apply.

CLUB LAW 36

The provisions of Club Law 23 may apply.

CLUB LAW 38

The provisions of Club Law 23 may apply.

CLUB LAW 39

The provisions of Club Law 23 may apply.

CLUB LAW 40

If the Arbiter decides that a side has been damaged through its opponents' failure to explain the meaning of a call or play, he may award an adjusted score.

CLUB LAW 47

If a card retracted under sections (c) or (d) above gave substantial information to an opponent, the Arbiter may award an adjusted score.

CLUB LAW 64

Regular Law 64 stands, except that, when after any established revoke, including those not subject to penalty, the Arbiter deems that the non-offending side is insufficiently compensated by this Law for the damage caused, he should assign an adjusted score.

CLUB LAW 69

When declarer has made a claim or concession, play ceases (all play subsequent to a claim or concession must be voided by the Arbiter). Declarer must place and leave his hand face up on the table and forthwith make a comprehensive statement as to his proposed plan of play, including the order in which he will play his remaining cards.

Declarer's claim or concession is allowed, and the deal is scored accordingly, if both defenders agree to it. The claim or concession must be allowed if either defender has permitted any of his remaining cards to be mixed with another player's cards; otherwise, if either defender disputes declarer's claim or concession, the Arbiter must be called to adjudicate the result of the deal.

The Arbiter should adjudicate the result of the deal as equitably as possible to both sides, but any doubtful point should be resolved in favor of the defenders. He should proceed as follows:

(a) He should require the declarer to repeat the statement he made at the time of his claim. The Arbiter should then require all players to put their cards face up on the table and should hear the defenders' objections to the claim.

(b) When a trump is outstanding, he should award a trick to the defenders if

    (i) in making his claim declarer made no statement about that trump, and

    (ii) it is at all likely that declarer was unaware, at the time of his claim, that a trump remained in a defender's hand, and

    (iii) a trick could be lost to that trump by any normal play (an inferior or careless play can be normal, but not an irrational play).

(c) He should not accept from declarer any proposed line of play inconsistent with his statement. If declarer did not make an appropriate announcement at the time of his original claim, the Arbiter should not accept from declarer any unusual line of play, or any proposed play that requires a finesse* in a suit, unless an opponent failed to follow in that suit before the claim or concession, or would subsequently fail to follow in that suit on any conceivable line of play.

CLUB LAW 70

A defender makes a concession when he agrees to declarer's claim or when he announces that he will lose one or more of the remaining tricks.

A defender makes a claim when he announces that he will win one or more of the remaining tricks, or when he shows any or all of his cards to declarer for this purpose. If

(a) the claim pertains only to an uncompleted trick currently in progress, play proceeds normally; cards exposed or otherwise revealed by the defender in making his claim do not become penalty cards, but Club Law 16, Unauthorized Information, may apply to claimer's partner.

(b) the claim pertains to subsequent tricks, play ceases (all play subsequent to the claim should be voided by the Arbiter). The defender must place and leave his hand face up on the table and make a comprehensive statement as to his proposed plan of defense. The claim is allowed, and the deal scored accordingly, if declarer agrees to it. If declarer disputes the claim, the Arbiter must be called to adjudicate the result of the deal. He does so as equitably as possible to both sides, but should award to the declarer any trick that the defenders could lose by normal play (an inferior or careless play can be normal, but not an irrational play).

---

*For these purposes, a finesse is a play the success of which depends on finding one defender rather than the other with or without a particular card.

CLUB APPEALS COMMITTEE

Whenever possible, a club should establish an Appeals Committee to review decisions of the Arbiter; and any game may designate a Committee to which appeals may be taken. If such a procedure has been agreed to or published in advance, any player may appeal any decision by the Arbiter. The Appeals Committee exercises all powers assigned by these Laws to the Arbiter, and may overrule any of his decisions.

When an Arbiter's decision is overruled on appeal, only the scoring of the particular deal is affected; subsequent scores stand as recorded. If the Committee's decision results in fulfillment of a contract originally recorded as defeated, or defeat of a contract recorded as fulfilled, then,

(a) for a contract now fulfilled: in addition to the other trick score and premium score, declarer's side received a premium of 50 points for a partscore that would not then have increased the below-the-line score to 100; and for any other contract, declarer's side received a premium according to vulnerability — 300 points if declarer's side was non-vulnerable, 400 points if declarer was vulnerable and the defenders not, 500 points if both sides were vulnerable.

(b) for a contract now defeated, when the original scoring resulted in a game: in addition to the other premium score, the defenders receive a premium of 50 points if they alone had scored a partscore in that game; plus a premium of 500 points if declarer's side originally won two of two games, or 200 points if the defenders side originally won two of three games.

PROPRIETIES

1. GENERAL PRINCIPLES

These Laws cannot cover every situation that might arise, nor can they produce equity in every situation covered. Occasionally, the players themselves must redress damage. The guiding principle: The side that commits an irregularity bears an obligation not to gain directly from the infraction itself; however, the offending side is entitled to profit after an infraction, as an indirect result, through subsequent good fortune.*

To infringe a law of propriety intentionally is a

---

*Two examples may clarify the distinction between direct gain through an infraction and indirect gain through good luck.

(a) South, declarer at 3 NT, will have nine tricks available if the diamond suit — ace-king-queen-sixth in dummy opposite declarer's singleton — divides favorably; and the six missing diamonds are in fact split evenly, three-three, between East and West. However, West, who holds jack-third, shows out on the third round of diamonds, revoking. Thus, declarer wins only three diamond tricks instead of six, for a total of six tricks instead of nine. The established revoke is later discovered, so one penalty trick is transferred after play ends. But declarer is still down two.

Here, East-West gained two tricks as a direct consequence of their infraction. The players should adjudicate this result, scoring the deal as 3 NT making three. (Note, declarer is not given a penalty trick in addition; the object is to restore equity, to restore the result likely to have occurred had the infraction not been committed.)

serious breach of ethics, even if there is a prescribed penalty that one is willing to pay. The offense may be the more serious when no penalty is prescribed.

There is no obligation to draw attention to an inadvertent infraction of law committed by one's own side. However, a player should not attempt to conceal such an infraction, as by committing a second revoke, concealing a card involved in a revoke or mixing the cards prematurely.

It is proper to warn partner against infringing a law of the game: for example against revoking, or against calling, leading or playing out of turn.

2. COMMUNICATION BETWEEN PARTNERS

Communication between partners during the auction and play should be effected only by means of the calls and plays themselves, not through the manner in which they are made, nor through extraneous remarks and gestures, nor through questions asked of the opponents and explanations given to them. Calls should be made in a uniform tone without special emphasis or inflection, and without undue hesitation or haste. Plays should be made without emphasis, gesture or mannerism and so far as possible at a uniform rate.

Inadvertently to vary the tempo or manner in which a call or play is made does not in itself constitute a violation of propriety, but inferences from such variation may properly be drawn only by an opponent, and at his own risk. It is improper to attempt to mislead an opponent by means of a remark or a gesture, through the haste or hesitancy of a call or play (such as hestitation with a singleton) or by the manner in which the call or play is made.

Any player may properly attempt to deceive an opponent through a call or play (so long as the deception is not protected by concealed partnership understanding). It is entirely proper to avoid giving information to the opponents by making all calls and plays in unvarying tempo and manner.

When a player has available to him improper information from his partner's remark, question, explanation, gesture, mannerism, special emphasis, inflection, haste or hesitation, he should carefully avoid taking any advantage that might accrue to his side.

3. CONDUCT AND ETIQUETEE

A player should maintain at all times a courteous attitude toward his partner and opponents. He should carefully avoid any remark or action that might cause annoyance or embarrassment to another player or might interfere with the enjoyment of the game. Every player should follow uniform and correct procedure in calling and playing, since any departure from correct standards may disrupt the orderly progress of the game.

As a matter of courtesy, a player should refrain from:

(i) Paying insufficient attention to the game (as when a player obviously takes no interest in his hand, or frequently requests a review of the auction).

(ii) Making gratuitous comments during the

play as to the auction or the adequacy of the contract.

(iii) Detaching a card from his hand before it is his turn to lead or play.

(iv) Arranging completed tricks in a disorderly manner, thereby making it difficult to determine the sequence of plays.

(v) Making a claim or concession of tricks if there is any doubt as to the outcome of the deal.

(vi) Prolonging play unnecessarily for the purpose of disconcerting the other players.

Furthermore, the following are considered breaches of propriety:

(a) Using different designations for the same call.

(b) Indicating approval or disapproval of a call or play.

(c) Indicating the expectation or intention of winning or losing a trick that has not been completed.

(d) Commenting or behaving during the auction or play so as to call attention to a significant occurrence, or to the state of the score or to the number of tricks still required for success.

(e) Volunteering information that should be given only in response to a question.

(f) Looking intently at any other player during the auction or play, or at another player's hand as for the purpose of seeing his cards or of observing the place from which he draws a card (but it is not improper to act on information acquired by inadvertently seeing an opponent's card).

(g) Varying the normal tempo of bidding or play for the purpose of disconcerting another player.

(h) Mixing the cards before the result of a deal has been agreed upon.

4. PARTNERSHIP AGREEMENTS

It is improper to convey information by means of a call or play based on special partnership agreement, whether explicit or implicit, unless such information is fully and freely available to the opponents.

It is not improper for a player to violate an announced partnership agreement, so long as his partner is unaware of the violation (but habitual violations within a partnership may create implicit agreements, which must be disclosed). No player has the obligation to disclose to the opponents that he has violated an announced agreement; and if the opponents are subsequently damaged, as through drawing a false inference from such violation, they are not entitled to redress.

When explaining the significance of partner's call or play in reply to an opponent's inquiry, a player should disclose all special information conveyed to him through partnership agreement or partnership experience; but he need not disclose inferences drawn from his general bridge knowledge and experience. It is improper for a player whose partner has given a mistaken explanation to correct the error immediately or to indicate in any manner that a mistake has been made. (He must not take advantage of the unauthorized information so obtained).

5. SPECTATORS

A spectator, including a member of the table not playing, must not display any reaction to bidding or play while a hand is in progress (as by shifting his attention from one player's hand to another's). He must not in any way disturb a player. During the hand, he must refrain from mannerisms or remarks of any kind (including conversation with a player). He may not call attention to any irregularity or mistake, nor speak on any question of fact or law except by request of the players.

RULES FOR CLUB PROCEDURE

The following rules, governing membership in new and existing tables, have proven satisfactory in club use over a long period of years.

A. DEFINITIONS

Member — An applicant who has acquired the right to play at a table either immediately or in his turn.

Complete Table — A table with six members.

Incomplete Table — A table with four or five members.

Cut In — Assert the right to become a member of an incomplete table, or to become a member of a complete table at such time as it may become incomplete.

B. TIME LIMIT ON RIGHT TO PLAY

An applicant may not play in a rubber unless he has become a member of a table before a card is duly drawn for the selection of players or partners.

C. NEWLY FORMED TABLES

Four to six applicants may form a table. If there are more than six applicants, the six highest-ranking ones become members. The four highest-ranking members play the first rubber. Those who have not played, ranked in their order of entry into the room, take precedence over those who have played; the latter rank equally, except that players leaving existing tables to join the new table rank lowest. Precedence between those of equal rank is determined by drawing cards, the player who draws the higher-ranking card having precedence.

D. CUTTING IN

An application establishes membership in a table either forthwith or (if the table is complete) as soon as a vacancy occurs, unless applications in excess of the number required to complete a table are made at the same time, in which case precedence between applicants is established by drawing cards, as provided in the preceding rule.

E. GOING OUT

After each rubber place must be made for any member who did not play that last rubber, by the member who has played the greatest number of consecutive rubbers at that table. Cards are drawn for precedence if necessary. A member who has left another existing table must draw cards, for his first rubber, with the member who would otherwise have played. A player who breaks up a game by leaving three players at a table may not compete against them for entry at another table until each of them has played at least one rubber.

F. MEMBERSHIP LIMITED TO ONE TABLE

No one can be a member of more than one table at the same time, unless a member consents, on request, to make a fourth at another table and announces his intention of returning to his former table as soon as his place at the new table can be filled. Failure to announce such intention results in loss of membership at his former table.

FOUR-DEAL BRIDGE

Four-Deal Bridge is a form of Rubber Bridge much played in clubs and well suited to home play. Long rubbers are avoided; extra players need wait no longer than the time (about twenty minutes) required to complete four deals. The game is also called Club Bridge or Chicago (for the city in which it originated).

For complete laws of Four-Deal Bridge, see CHICAGO.

LAWS OF DUPLICATE BRIDGE. See LAWS OF DUPLICATE CONTRACT BRIDGE.

LAWS OF DUPLICATE CONTRACT BRIDGE. In 1975 the Laws of Duplicate Contract Bridge were revised under the auspices of the World Bridge Federation. This was the first revision since 963. In many respects the changes in the new Laws are merely changes in language or terminology. In the American edition,* as set forth below, substantively new provisions are indicated by italics.

LAWS OF DUPLICATE CONTRACT BRIDGE

THE SCOPE OF THE LAWS

The Laws are designed to define correct procedure and to provide an adequate remedy whenever a player accidentally, carelessly or inadvertently dis-

---

*Although considerably different in arrangement, the American version is substantively identical to the International edition.

turbs the proper course of the game, or gains an unintentional but nevertheless unfair advantage. An offending player should be ready to pay graciously any penalty or accept any adjusted score awarded by the Tournament Director.

The Laws are not designed to prevent dishonorable practices, but rather to redress damage inadvertently done.

THE OBJECT OF THE PROPRIETIES

The object of Proprieties is twofold: to familiarize players with the customs and etiquette of the game, generally accepted over a long period of years; and to enlighten those who might otherwise fail to appreciate when or how they are improperly conveying information to their partners—often a far more reprehensible offense than a violation of a law.

When these principles are appreciated, arguments are avoided and the pleasure that the game offers is materially enhanced.

CHAPTER I

DEFINITIONS

Adjusted Score—An arbitrary score assigned by the Tournament Director (see Law 12).
Auction—1. The process of determining the contract by means of successive calls. 2. The aggregate of calls made. 3. The period during which calls are made.
Average—The arithmetic median between the greatest and least awarded scores available.
Bid—An undertaking to win at least a specified number of odd tricks in a specified denomination.
Board—A duplicate board as described in Law 2; or the four hands as originally dealt and placed in a duplicate board for play during that session.
Call—Any bid, double, redouble, or pass.
Contestant—In an individual event, a player; in a pair event, two players playing as partners throughout the event; in a team event, four or more players playing as teammates.
Contract—The undertaking by declarer's side to win, at the denomination named, the number of tricks specified in the final bid, whether undoubled, doubled, or redoubled.
Convention—A call that serves by partnership agreement to convey a meaning not necessarily related to the denomination named. 2. Defender play that serves to convey a meaning by agreement rather than inference.
Deal—1. The distribution of the pack to form the hands of the four players. 2. The cards so distributed considered as a unit, including the auction and play thereof.
Declarer—The player who, for the side that

makes the final bid, first bid the denomination named in that bid. He becomes declarer when the auction is closed.

Defender—An opponent of declarer.

Denomination—The suit or no trump specified in a bid.

Director—A person designated to supervise a duplicate bridge contest and to apply these Laws.

Double—A call over an opponent's bid increasing the scoring value of fulfilled or defeated contracts (see Law 73).

Dummy—1. Declarer's partner. He becomes dummy when the auction is closed. 2. Declarer's partner's cards, once they are spread on the table after the opening lead.

Event—A contest of one or more sessions.

Follow Suit—Play a card of the suit that has been led.

Game—100 or more trick points scored on one deal.

Hand—The cards originally dealt to a player, or the remaining portion thereof.

Honor—Any Ace, King, Queen, Jack, or ten.

International Match Point [IMP]—A unit of scoring awarded according to a schedule established in Law 74 B.

Irregularity—A deviation from the correct procedures set forth in the Laws and Proprieties.

Lead—The first card played to a trick.

Match Point—A unit of scoring awarded to a contestant as a result of comparison with one or more other scores.

Odd Trick—Each trick won by declarer's side in excess of six.

Opening Lead—The card led to the first trick.

Opponent—A player of the other side; a member of the partnership to which one is opposed.

Overtrick—Each trick won by declarer's side in excess of the contract.

Pack—The 52 playing cards with which the game of Contract Bridge is played.

Partner—The player with whom one plays as a side against the other two players.

Part-Score—90 or fewer trick points scored on one deal.

Pass—A call specifying that a player does not, at that turn, elect to bid, double, or redouble.

Penalty—An obligation or restriction imposed upon a side for violation of these Laws.

Penalty Card—A card prematurely exposed by a defender.

Play—1. The contribution of a card from one's hand to a trick, including the first card, which is the lead. 2. The aggregate of plays made. 3. The period during which the cards are played.

Premium Points—Any points earned other than trick points (see Law 73).

Rectification—Adjustment made to permit the auction or play to proceed as normally as possible after an irregularity has occurred.

Redeal—A second or subsequent deal by the same player to replace his first deal.

Redouble—A call that increases the scoring value

of odd tricks or undertricks of a bid of one's own side that an opponent has doubled.

Revoke—The play of a card of another suit by a player who is able to follow suit or to comply with a lead penalty.

Rotation—The clockwise order in which the right to call or to play progresses.

Round—A part of a session played without progression of players.

Section—A group of contestants playing independently of any other group insofar as movement of boards and players is concerned.

Session—A period of play during which a specified number of boards is scheduled to be played.

Side—Two players who constitute a partnership against the other two players.

Slam—A contract to win twelve tricks, six odd tricks (called Small Slam), or to win all thirteen tricks, seven odd tricks (called Grand Slam); also the fulfillment of such a contract.

Specified Suit—Any suit that a player, in exacting a penalty, requires to be led or not to be led.

Suit—One of four groups of cards in the pack, each group comprising thirteen cards and having a characteristic symbol: spades (♠), hearts (♡), diamonds (◇), clubs (♣).

Team—Two pairs playing in different directions at different tables, but for a common score (applicable regulations may permit teams of more than four members).

Trick—The unit by which the outcome of the contract is determined, regularly consisting of four cards, one contributed by each player in rotation, beginning with the lead.

Trick Points—Points earned by declarer's side by fulfilling the contract (see Law 73).

Trump—Each card of the suit, if any, named in the contract.

Turn—The correct time when a player may call or play.

Undertrick—Each trick by which declarer's side falls short of fulfilling the contract (see Law 73).

Vulnerability—The condition of being exposed to greater undertrick penalties and entitled to greater premiums (see Law 73).

CHAPTER II

PRELIMINARIES

◆ ◆ ◆ ◆ ◆

1. THE PACK—RANK OF CARDS AND SUITS

Duplicate Contract Bridge is played with a pack of 52 cards, consisting of 13 cards in each of 4 suits. The suits rank downward in the order— Spades (♠), Hearts (♡), Diamonds (◇), Clubs (♣). The cards of each suit rank downward in the order—Ace, King, Queen, Jack, 10, 9, 8, 7, 6, 5, 4, 3, 2.

2. THE DUPLICATE BOARDS

A duplicate board containing a pack is provided for each deal to be played during a session. Each board is numbered and has four pockets to hold the four hands, designated North, East, South, and West. An arrow indicates the North hand. The dealer and vulnerability are designated as follows:

North Dealer	Boards 1	5	9	13
East Dealer	Boards 2	6	10	14
South Dealer	Boards 3	7	11	15
West Dealer	Boards 4	8	12	16
Neither Side Vulnerable	Boards 1	8	11	14
North-South Vulnerable	Boards 2	5	12	15
East-West Vulnerable	Boards 3	6	9	16
Both Sides Vulnerable	Boards 4	7	10	13

The same sequence is repeated for Boards 17–32, and for each subsequent group of 16 boards.

3. ARRANGEMENT OF TABLES

Four players play at each table, and tables are numbered in a sequence established by the Director. He designates one direction as North; other compass directions assume the normal relationship to North.

4. PARTNERSHIPS

The four players at each table constitute two partnerships or sides, North-South against East-West. In pair or team events the contestants enter as pairs or teams, and retain the same partnerships throughout a session (except in the case of substitutions authorized by the Director). In individual events each player enters separately, and partnerships change during a session.

5. ASSIGNMENT OF SEATS

A. Initial Position
The Director assigns an initial position to each contestant (individual, pair, or team) at the start of a session. Unless otherwise directed, the members of each pair or team may select seats, among those assigned to them, by mutual agreement. Having once selected a compass direction, a player may change it only upon instruction or permission of the Director.
B. Change of Direction or Table
Players change their initial compass direction or proceed to another table in accordance with the Director's instructions. The Director is responsible for clear announcement of instructions; each player is responsible for moving when and as directed, and for occupying the correct seat after each change.

CHAPTER III

PREPARATION AND PROGRESSION

◆◆◆◆◆◆

6. THE SHUFFLE AND DEAL

A. The Shuffle
Before play starts, each pack is shuffled. *There must be a cut if either opponent so requests.*
B. The Deal
The cards must be dealt face down, one card at a time in rotation, into four hands of thirteen cards each; each hand is then placed face down in one of the four pockets of the board.
C. Representation of Both Pairs at Deal
A member of each side must be present during the shuffle and deal unless the Director instructs otherwise.
D. New Shuffle and Redeal
1. Cards Incorrectly Dealt or Card(s) Exposed
There must be a new shuffle and a redeal if it is ascertained before the last card is dealt that the cards have been incorrectly dealt, or that a player has seen the face of a card.
2. At Director's Instruction
There must be a new shuffle and a redeal when required by the Director for any reason he deems sufficient.
E. Director's Option of Shuffling and Dealing
1. By Players
The Director may instruct that the shuffle and deal be performed at each table immediately before play starts.
2. By Director
The Director may perform the shuffle and deal in advance, himself.
3. By Agents or Assistants
The Director may have his assistants, or other appointed agents, perform the shuffle and deal in advance.
4. Different Method of Dealing or Pre-dealing
The Director may require a different method of dealing or pre-dealing.
F. Duplication of Board
If required by the conditions of play, one or more exact copies of each original deal may be made under the Director's instructions.

7. CONTROL OF BOARDS AND CARDS

A. Placement of Board
When a board is to be played it is placed in the center of the table. The board remains in the center of the table until play is completed.
B. Removal of Cards from Board
After the four players are seated, each player takes a hand from the pocket corresponding to his compass position.
1. Counting Cards in Hand before Play
Each player must count his cards face down, before looking at the face of any card, to be sure he has exactly thirteen.

2. Control of Player's Hand

During play each player retains possession of his own cards, not permitting them to be mixed with those of any other player. No player should touch any cards other than his own (but declarer may play dummy's cards in accordance with Law 45) during or after play except by permission of the Director.

3. Counting Cards in Hand after Play

Each player should count his cards again after completion of play, just before returning them to the board.

C. *Returning Cards to Board*

Each player restores his original 13 cards to the pocket corresponding to his compass position. Thereafter no hand should be removed from the board unless a member of each side, or the Director, is present.

D. *Responsibility for Procedures*

The North player is responsible for the proper observance of these procedures, and for maintaining proper conditions of play at the table. However, if the East-West pair alone is stationary, the responsibility becomes East's.

8. SEQUENCE OF ROUNDS

A. *Movement of Boards*

1. Director's Instructions

At the start of each session, the Director instructs the players on the proper movement of board from table to table at each round.

2. Responsibility For Moving Boards

The North player at each table is responsible for moving the boards just completed at his table to the proper table for the following round, unless the Director instructs otherwise.

B. *End of Round*

In general, a round ends when the Director gives the signal for the start of the following round; but if any table has not completed play by that time, the round continues for that table until play has been completed and the score of the final board of the round has been agreed upon and entered on the proper scoring form.

C. *End of Last Round and End of Session*

The last round of a session, and the session itself, ends for each table when play of all boards scheduled at that table has been completed, and when all scores have been entered on the proper scoring forms.

CHAPTER IV

GENERAL LAWS
GOVERNING IRREGULARITIES

◆◆◆◆◆◆◆

9. PROCEDURE FOLLOWING AN IRREGULARITY

A. *Calling Attention to an Irregularity*

1. During the Auction Period

Any player may call attention to an irregularity during the auction, whether or not it is his turn to call.

2. During the Play Period

(a) Declarer or Either Defender

Any of the three active players may call attention to an irregularity that occurs during the play period.

(b) Dummy (dummy's restricted rights are defined in Laws 42 and 43).

(1) Dummy may not call attention to an irregularity during the play but may do so after play of the hand is concluded.

(2) Dummy may attempt to prevent an irregularity from occurring (Law 42B2).

B. *After Attention is Called to an Irregularity*

1. Summoning the Director

(a) When to Summon

The Director must be summoned at once when attention is drawn to an irregularity.

(b) Right to Summon

Any player may summon the Director after attention has been drawn to an irregularity during the auction. Any player except dummy may summon the Director during the play.

(c) Retention of Rights

Summoning the Director does not cause a player to forfeit any rights to which he might otherwise be entitled.

(d) Opponents' Rights

The fact that a player draws attention to an irregularity committed by his side does not affect the rights of the opponents.

2. Further Bids or Plays

No player should call or play until the Director has explained all matters in regard to rectification and to the assessment of a penalty.

C. *Premature Correction of Irregularity*

Any premature correction of any irregularity by the offender may subject him to a further penalty (see Law 26).

10. ASSESSMENT OF A PENALTY

A. *Right to Assess Penalty*

The Director alone has the right to assess penalties when applicable. Players do not have the right to assess or waive penalties on their own initiative.

B. *Cancellation of Payment or Waiver of Penalty*

The Director may allow or cancel any payment or waiver of penalties made by the players without his instructions.

C. *Choice between Two or More Penalties*

1. Explanation of All Options

When these laws provide an option among penalties, the Director explains all the options available.

2. Declarer's Choice of Penalties

If the declarer has a choice of penalties he must make his selection without assistance from dummy.

11. FORFEITURE OF THE RIGHT TO PENALIZE

A. *Action by Non-Offending Side*

The right to penalize an irregularity may be

forfeited if either member of the non-offending side takes any action before summoning the Director.

B. Action by Player to Offender's Left
1. Call before Imposition of a Legal Penalty
The right to penalize an irregularity is definitely forfeited if the player to offender's left calls, after an irregularity by his right hand opponent, and before a legal penalty has been stated and imposed (Law 34).
2. Play before Imposition of a Legal Penalty
The right to penalize an irregularity in play is definitely forfeited if the player to the offender's left plays, after the irregularity by his right hand opponent, before a legal penalty has been stated and imposed (Law 60).

C. Consultation between Non-Offending Partners
1. Consultation Not Permitted
Consultation between partners regarding the imposition of a penalty is not permitted.
2. Consultation Has Taken Place.
When the Director considers that the non-offending partners have consulted regarding the imposition of a penalty, the partnership forfeits its right to penalize.

D. Irregularity Called by Spectator
1. Spectator Responsibility of Non-Offending Side
The right to penalize an irregularity may be forfeited if attention is first drawn to the irregularity by a spectator for whose presence at the table the non-offending side is responsible.
2. Spectator Responsibility of Offending Side
The right to correct an irregularity may be forfeited if attention is first drawn to the irregularity by a spectator for whose presence at the table the offending side is responsible.

E. Penalty after Forfeiture of the Right to Penalize
Even after the right to penalize has been forfeited under this law, the Director may assess a penalty under his exercise of discretionary powers.

12. DIRECTOR'S DISCRETIONARY POWERS

A. Right to Assign an Adjusted Score
The Director may assign an adjusted score (or scores), either on his own initiative, or on the application of any player, but only when these Laws empower him to do so (see Law 84), or:
1. Laws Provide No Indemnity
The Director may award an adjusted score when he judges that these Laws do not provide indemnity to the non-offending contestant *for the particular type of violation of law or propriety committed by an opponent.*
2. Normal Play of the Board is Impossible
The Director may assign an adjusted score if no rectification can be made that will permit normal play of the board.
3. Incorrect Penalty Has Been Paid
The Director may assign an adjusted score if an incorrect penalty has been paid.

B. No Adjustment for Undue Severity of Penalty
The Director may not assign an adjusted score on the ground that the penalty provided in these Laws is either unduly severe or advantageous to either side.

C. Assignment of Adjusted Score
1. How Assigned
An adjusted score is assigned by altering the total-point score on the board prior to match-pointing, or by the assignment of zero or more match points (see Law 84).
2. Point Assignment in Proportion to Irregularity
    (a) Point Award to Non-Offending Side
        The number of points assigned to the non-offending side should not exceed the number required to offset the irregularity.
    (b) Points Assigned to Offending Side
        The number of points assigned to the offending side to offset the irregularity may be reduced by penalty points.
3. Balance in Assigned Scores
The indemnity points awarded the non-offending side need not balance the penalty points assessed against the offending side.

13. INCORRECT NUMBER OF CARDS

A. No Player Has Seen Another Player's Card(s)
When the Director decides that one or more pockets of the board contained an incorrect number of cards, he should correct the discrepancy as follows and require that the board then be played and scored normally.
1. Hand Records
When hand records are available, the Director should distribute the cards in accordance with the records.
2. Consult Previous Players
If hand records are not available, the Director should correct the board by consulting with players who have previously played it.
3. Require a Redeal
If the board was incorrectly dealt, the Director should require a redeal (Law 6).

B. A Player Has Seen Another Player's Card(s)
When the Director determines that one or more pockets of the board contained an incorrect number of cards, and after restoration of the board to its original condition a player has seen one or more cards in another player's hand, if the Director deems:
1. The Information Gained is Inconsequential
That such information will not interfere with normal bidding or play, the Director should require that the board be played and scored normally.
2. The Information Will Interfere with Normal Play
That the information gained thereby is of sufficient importance to interfere with normal play, the Director should award an adjusted score and may penalize an offender.

14. MISSING CARD

A. Hand Found Deficient Before Play Commences
When three hands are correct and the fourth is

found to be deficient before the play period begins, the Director makes a search for the missing card, and:

1. Card Is Found

If the card is found, it is restored to the deficient hand.

2. Card Cannot Be Found

If the card cannot be found, the Director reconstructs the deal, as near to its original form as he can determine, by substituting another pack.

B. Hand Found Deficient During Play

When three hands are correct and the fourth is found to be deficient during play, the Director makes a search for the missing card, and:

1. Card is Found

(a) If the card is found among the played cards, Law 67 applies.

(b) If the card is found elsewhere, it is restored to the deficient hand, and penalties may apply (see 3., following).

2. Card Cannot Be Found

If the card cannot be found, the deal is reconstructed as nearly as can be determined in its original form by substituting another pack; and penalties may apply (see 3., following).

3. Possible Penalties

A card restored to a hand under the provisions of Section B of this Law is deemed to have belonged continuously to the deficient hand. It may become a penalty card (Law 50), and failure to have played it may constitute a revoke.

15. PLAY OF A WRONG BOARD

A. Players Have Not Previously Played Board

If players play a board not designated for them to play in the current round:

1. Designate a Late Play

The Director may require both pairs to play the correct board against each other later.

2. Score Board as Played

The Director should allow the score to stand if none of the four players have previously played the board.

B. One or More Players Have Previously Played Board

If any player plays a board he has previously played, with the correct opponents or otherwise, his second score on the board is cancelled both for his side and his opponents, and the Director should award an adjusted score to the contestants deprived of the opportunity to earn a valid score.

16. UNAUTHORIZED INFORMATION

A. Definition

1. Accidental Unauthorized Information

Any extraneous information a player receives about a board he is playing or has yet to play is accidental. This unauthorized information encompasses information received by looking at the

wrong hand; by overhearing calls, results or remarks; by seeing cards at another table, or by seeing a card belonging to another player at one's own table before the auction begins.

2. Illegal Unauthorized Information

Any information conveyed by a player, other than declarer, to his partner by means of a remark, *question, unmistakable hesitation, special emphasis, tone,* gesture, *movement,* mannerism, *or any other action* that *may* suggest a call, lead or plan of play, is illegal unauthorized information.

B. Report of Accidental Unauthorized Information

The Director shall be notified forthwith of the accidental receipt of any unauthorized information, preferably by the recipient.

1. Director's Action

(a) Board Can Be Played Normally

If the Director judges that the unauthorized information accidentally received is not of sufficient importance to interfere with normal bidding or play, he should require that the board be played and scored normally.

(b) Board Cannot Be Played Normally

If the Director judges that the board cannot be played normally:

(1) Award Adjusted Score

The Director may assign an adjusted score to the pairs involved or:

(2) Substitute Player

The Director may appoint a temporary substitute to replace the player who received unauthorized information.

C. Report of Alleged Illegal Information

1. Calling the Director

Any player *except dummy* may call the Director if it appears that illegal information has been conveyed by another player.

2. Director's Action

If attention is drawn to the offense and the Director is summoned forthwith, the Director *should require* that the auction or play continue, reserving his right to assign an adjusted score if he considers that the result *could have been* affected by the illegal information.

CHAPTER V

THE AUCTION
◆◆◆◆◆◆

PART I

Correct Procedure

Section One

Auction Period

17. DURATION OF THE AUCTION

A. Auction Period Starts

The auction period begins for each player

when he looks at his hand after removing it from the board.

B. The First Call

The player designated by the board as dealer makes the first call.

C. Successive Calls

The player to dealer's left makes the second call, and thereafter each player calls in turn in a clockwise rotation.

D. End of Auction Period

The auction period ends when three passes in rotation have followed any call (but see Law 35).

18. BIDS

A. Proper Form

A bid must name a number of odd tricks, from one to seven, and a denomination. (Pass, double and redouble are calls but not bids.)

B. To Supersede a Bid

A bid supersedes a previous bid if it names either the same number of odd tricks in a higher-ranking denomination, or a greater number of odd tricks in any denomination.

C. Sufficient Bid

A bid that supersedes the immediately previous bid is a sufficient bid.

D. Insufficient Bid

A bid that fails to supersede the immediately previous bid is an insufficient bid.

E. Rank of the Denominations

The rank of the denominations in descending order is: no trump, spades, hearts, diamonds, clubs.

19. DOUBLES AND REDOUBLES

A. Doubles

1. Legal Double

A player must double only the last preceding bid. The bid must have been made by an opponent and no calls other than pass may have intervened.

2. Proper Form for Double

In doubling, a player should not state the number of odd tricks or the denomination. The only correct form is the single word "Double."

3. Double of Incorrectly Stated Bid

If a player, in doubling, incorrectly states the bid, or the number of odd tricks or the denomination, he is deemed to have doubled the bid as it was made. (*Law 16—Unauthorized Information—may apply.*)

B. Redoubles

1. Legal Redouble

A player may redouble only the last preceding double. The double must have been made by an opponent and no calls other than pass may have intervened.

2. Proper Form for a Redouble

In redoubling a player should not state the number of odd tricks or the denomination. The only correct form is the single word "Redouble."

3. Redouble of an Incorrectly Stated Bid

If a player, in redoubling, incorrectly states the doubled bid, or the number of odd tricks or the denomination, he is deemed to have redoubled the bid as it was made. (Law 16—Unauthorized Information—may apply.)

C. Double or Redouble Superseded

Any double or redouble is superseded by a subsequent legal bid.

D. Scoring a Doubled or Redoubled Contract

If a doubled or redoubled bid is not superseded by a subsequent legal bid, scoring values are increased as provided in Law 73.

20. REVIEW AND EXPLANATION OF CALLS

A. Call Not Clearly Heard

A player who does not hear a call distinctly may forthwith require that it be repeated.

B. Review of Auction during Auction Period

Before the auction closes, a player is entitled to have all* previous calls restated when it is his turn to call, unless he is required by law to pass.

C. Review after Close of Auction

1. Opening Lead Inquiry

After the final pass either defender has the right to ask if it is his opening lead (see Laws 47E and 41).

2. Review of Auction

Declarer or either defender may, *at his first turn to play,* require all* previous calls to be restated.

D. Who May Review the Auction

A request to have calls restated should be responded to only by an opponent.

E. Correction of Error in Review

Any player, including dummy or a player required by law to pass, may and should promptly correct an error in restatement.

F. Explanation of Conventional Meaning of Calls

1 During the Auction

During the auction and before the final pass, a full explanation of *any* call made by an opponent may be requested by any player, but only at that player's turn to call.

2. During the Play Period

After the final pass and *throughout the play period,* declarer or *either defender*** *may request such an explanation of opposing calls,* and declarer may request an explanation of the defenders' card play conventions, but only at his own turn to play (N.B.: Law 16 may apply).

21. CALL BASED ON MISINFORMATION

A. Call Based on Caller's Misunderstanding

A player has no recourse if he has made a call on the basis of his own misunderstanding.

---

* A player may not ask for a partial restatement of previous calls and should not halt the review before it has been completed.

** Sponsoring organizations are specifically authorized to establish different regulations applying to the defenders' questions before the first trick has been completed.

B. Call Based on Misinformation from an Opponent

1. Change of Call

A player may, without penalty, change a call he may have made as a result of misinformation given to him by an opponent (*failure to alert promptly to a conventional call or special understanding, where such alert is required by the sponsoring organization, is deemed misinformation*), provided that his partner has not subsequently called.

2. Change of Call by Opponent Following Correction

When a player elects to change a call because of misinformation (as in 1., preceding), his left hand opponent may then in turn change any subsequent call he may have made, without penalty (*unless his withdrawn call conveyed such substantial information as to damage the non-offending side, in which case the Director may assign an adjusted score*).

3. Too Late to Change Call

When it is too late to change a call, Law 40C may apply.

Section Two

Auction Is Closed

22. PROCEDURE AFTER THE AUCTION IS CLOSED

A. No Player Has Bid

After the auction is closed, if no player has bid, the hands are returned to the board without play. There *may not* be a redeal.

B. One or More Players Have Bid

If any player has bid, the final bid becomes the contract and play begins.

PART II

Irregularities in Procedure

Section One

Exposed Card, Auction Period

23. CARD EXPOSED OR LED DURING AUCTION

A. Director's Action

When the Director determines, during the auction, that a player has faced a card on the table, or held a card so that it is possible for his partner to see its face, he must require that every such card be left face up on the table until the auction closes; and (penalty) if the offender subsequently becomes a defender, declarer may treat *every* such card as a penalty card (Law 50). In addition:

1. Low Card Not Prematurely Led

If it is a single card below the rank of an honor and not prematurely led, there is no *further* penalty.

2. Single Card of Honor Rank, or Card Prematurely Led

If the card is a single card of honor rank, or is any card prematurely led, (penalty) offender's partner must pass when next it is his turn to call.

3. Two or More Cards are Exposed

If two or more cards are so exposed, (penalty)

offender's partner must pass when next it is his turn to call.

B. Enforced Pass May Damage Innocent Side

When the penalty for an irregularity, under this or any other Law, would compel the offender's partner to pass at his next turn, and when the Director deems that this enforced pass will *necessarily* damage the innocent side:

1. Direct That the Auction Continue

The Director may direct that the auction and play continue, reserving the right to assign an adjusted score if he considers that the result was affected by the illegal information, or:

2. Assign an Adjusted Score

The Director may forthwith assign an adjusted score.

Section Two

Changes of Calls

24. IMMEDIATE CORRECTION OF CALL

A. Correcting Inadvertent Call

A player may substitute his intended call for an inadvertent call but only if he does so, *or attempts to do so,* without pause *for thought*. If legal, his last call stands without penalty.

B. Correction to an Illegal Call

If the substituted call is an illegal call, it is subject to the applicable Law.

25. CHANGE OF CALL

A. Attempt to Change Illegal Call

A call substituted for an illegal call made previously at the same turn, when too late for correction as provided in Law 24, is cancelled. The offending side is subject to the applicable law for the illegal call, and may also be subject to Law 26.

B. Attempt to Change Legal Call

A call substituted for a legal call made previously at the same turn, when Law 24 does not apply, is cancelled. The legal call stands and (penalty):

1. Auction Period Penalty

The offender's partner must pass whenever it is his turn to call.

2. Lead Penalties

Offender's partner may be subject to the lead penalties of Law 26.

26. UNAUTHORIZED INFORMATION GIVEN BY CHANGE OF CALL

When a player illegally names a denomination not selected as his final call at that turn (as in changing a call except as permitted by Law 24, or in making or correcting a legal call), then if he becomes a defender:

A. Illegal Call Is a Suit Bid

If the illegal call is a suit bid:

1. Illegally Named Suit Is Not Conventional

When the illegally named suit is not conventionally related to another suit or suits, declarer may either (penalty):

(a) Require Lead of Illegally Named Suit

Require the offender's partner to lead the illegally named suit at his first turn to lead (includng the opening lead); or

(b) Prohibit Lead of Illegally Named Suit
Prohibit the offender's partner from leading the illegally named suit at his first turn to lead (including the opening lead) and for as long as the offender's partner retains the lead.

2. Illegally Named Suit Is Conventional
When the illegally named suit is conventionally related to another suit or suits, declarer may either (penalty):

(a) Require Lead of Conventionally Related Suit
Require the offender's partner to lead a card of a specified suit thus conventionally related at his first turn to lead (including the opening lead); or

(b) Prohibit Lead of Conventionally Related Suit
Prohibit the offender's partner from leading any card of any thus related suit at his first turn to lead (including the opening lead) and for as long as the offender's partner retains the lead.

B. *Illegal Call is No Trump Bid*
If the illegal call was a no trump bid,

1. No Trump Bid Is Not Conventional
When the illegal no trump bid is *not conventionally related to a suit or suits,* and if the offender's partner is to make the opening lead, (penalty) declarer may require the offender's partner to make the opening lead in a specified suit.

2. No Trump Bid Relates to Suit or Suits
When the illegal no trump bid conventionally relates to a suit or suits, Law 26A2 applies.

C. *Illegal Double or Redouble*
If another call has been substituted for an illegal double or redouble, the penalties provided in Law 27B3 apply.

Section Three

Insufficient Bid

27. INSUFFICIENT BID

A. *Insufficient Bid Accepted*
Any insufficient bid may be accepted (treated as legal) *at the option* of the opponent to offender's left. It is accepted if that player calls.

B. *Insufficient Bid Not Accepted*
If an insufficient bid made in rotation is not accepted, it must be corrected by the substitution of either a sufficient bid or a pass (the offender is entitled to select his final call at that turn after the applicable penalties have been stated, and any call he has previously attempted to substitute is cancelled, but Law 26 may apply).

1. Corrected by Lowest Sufficient Bid in Same Denomination

(a) No Penalty
If the insufficient bid is corrected by the lowest sufficient bid in the same denomi-

nation, the auction proceeds as though the irregularity had not occured (but see (b) following).

(b) Award of Adjusted Score
If the Director judges that the insufficient bid conveyed such substantial information as to damage the non-offending side, he may assign an adjusted score.

2. Corrected by Any Other Sufficient Bid
If the insufficient bid is corrected by any other sufficient bid, (penalty) the offender's partner must pass whenever it is his turn to call (and Law 26 may apply).

3. Corrected by a Pass
If the insufficient bid is corrected by a pass, (penalty) the offender's partner must pass whenever it is his turn to call; and if the offender's partner is to make the opening lead:

(a) Require Lead of Specified Suit
Declarer may require the offender's partner to lead a specified suit; or

(b) Prohibit Lead of a Specified Suit
Declarer may prohibit the offender's partner from leading a specified suit; this prohibition to continue for as long as offender's partner retains the lead.

4. Attempt to Correct by a Double or Redouble
If the offender attempts to substitute a double or redouble for his insufficient bid, the attempted call is cancelled; he must pass and the offense (penalty) is subject to the penalties provided in (3) preceding.

C. *Insufficient Bid Out of Rotation*
If a player makes an insufficient bid out of rotation, Law 31 applies.

Section Four

Call out of Rotation

28. CALLS CONSIDERED TO BE IN ROTATION

A. *Right Hand Opponent Required to Pass*
A call is considered to be in rotation when it is made by a player at his right hand opponent's turn to call, if that opponent is required by law to pass.

B. *Call by Correct Player Cancelling Call Out of Rotation*
A call is considered to be in rotation when made by a player whose turn it was to call, before a penalty has been assessed for a call out of rotation by an opponent; the call thus made waives any penalty for the call out of rotation and the auction proceeds as though the opponent had not called at that turn.

29. PROCEDURE AFTER A CALL OUT OF ROTATION

A. *Out of Rotation Call Cancelled*
A call out of rotation is cancelled (but see B following) and the auction reverts to the player whose turn it was to call. Offender may make any legal call in proper rotation, but may be subject to penalty under Laws 30, 31, or 32.

B. Forfeiture of Right to Penalize

Following a call out of rotation, the opponent next in rotation to the offender *may elect* to call, thereby forfeiting the right to penalize.

30. PASS OUT OF ROTATION

A. Before Any Player Has Bid

When a player has passed out of rotation before any player has bid, (penalty) the offender must pass when next it is his turn to call.

B. After Any Player Has Bid

1. At Offender's Right Hand Opponent's Turn to Call

After any player has bid, for a pass out of rotation made at the turn of offender's right hand opponent to call, (penalty) offender must pass when next it is his turn to call (*if the pass out of rotation relates by convention to a specific suit, or suits, thereby conveying information, Law 26 may apply*).

2. At Offender's Partner's Turn to Call

(a) Action Required of Offender

After any player has bid, for a pass out of rotation made at the offender's partner's turn to call, (penalty) the offender must pass whenever it is his turn to call (and Law 26 may apply).

(b) Action Open to Offender's Partner

Offender's partner may make any sufficient bid, or may pass, but may not double or redouble at that turn.

(c) Offender's Partner Passes

If offender's partner passes and subsequently is to make the opening lead:

(1) Require Lead of a Specified Suit

Declarer may require offender's partner to lead a specified suit; or

(2) Prohibit Lead of a Specified Suit

Declarer may prohibit offender's partner from leading a specified suit, such prohibition to continue for as long as he retains the lead.

3. At Offender's Left Hand Opponent's Turn to Call

After any player has bid, a pass out of rotation at offender's left hand opponent's turn to call is treated as a change of call and Law 25 applies.

31. BID OUT OF ROTATION

When a player has bid out of rotation (and the bid is cancelled, as the option to accept the bid has not been exercised—see Law 29):

A. Before Any Player Has Called

1. Offender's Right Hand Opponent's Turn to Call

(a) Right Hand Opponent Passes

When his right hand opponent passes, offender must repeat the bid out of rotation and there is no penalty.

(b) Right Hand Opponent Bids

If his right hand opponent bids, offender

may pass, double,* or make any legal call; if his call

(1) Repeats Denomination of Bid Out of Rotation

Repeats the denomination of his bid out of rotation, (penalty) offender's partner must pass when *next* it is his turn to call (see Law 23B).

(2) Does Not Repeat Denomination of Bid Out Of Rotation

Names a denomination other than that named in his call out of rotation, (penalty) offender's partner must pass whenever it is his turn to call (see Law 23B) and Law 26 must apply.

2. Offender's Partner's or Left Hand Opponent's Turn to Call

When a player has bid out of rotation, and it was the turn of either his partner or his left hand opponent to call, (penalty) offender's partner must pass whenever it is his turn to call (see Law 23B), and Law 26 may apply.

B. After Any Player Has Called

1. At Offender's Partner's Turn to Call

When a player has bid out of rotation, after any player has called, and when it was offender's partner's turn to call, (penalty) offender's partner must pass whenever it is his turn to call (see Law 23B), and Law 26 may apply; and if offender's partner is to make the opening lead:

(a) Requiring the Lead of a Specified Suit

Declarer may require offender's partner to lead a specified suit; or

(b) Prohibiting the Lead of a Specified Suit

Declarer may prohibit offender's partner from leading a specified suit, such prohibition to continue for as long as he retains the lead.

2. At Offender's Right Hand Opponent's Turn to Call

(a) Right Hand Opponent Passes

(1) Out of Rotation Bid Was Sufficient

If the bid out of rotation was sufficient, and offender's right hand opponent now passes, offender must repeat his bid and there is no penalty.

(2) Out of Rotation Bid Was Insufficient

If the bid out of rotation was insufficient, and offender's right hand opponent now passes, offender's insufficient bid must be corrected as though it had been made in rotation, as provided in Law 27.

(b) Right Hand Opponent Makes a Legal Bid, Double or Redouble†

If offender's right hand opponent makes a legal bid, double or redouble, (penalty) *the penalty provisions of A1(b) preceding apply.*

---

* Law 23B may apply.

† An illegal call by that opponent may be penalized in the usual way, after which this subsection B2(b) applies.

3. At Offender's Left Hand Opponent's Turn to Call

Offender's bid out of rotation is treated as a change of call and Law 25 applies.

32. DOUBLE OR REDOUBLE OUT OF ROTATION

A. Inadmissible Double or Redouble Out of Rotation

An inadmissible double or redouble out of rotation is subject to Law 36.

B. Double or Redouble Out of Rotation, in Violation of Obligation to Pass

A double or redouble out of rotation when in violation of a legal obligation to pass, is subject to Law 37.

C. Doubles or Redoubles Out of Rotation Not Subject to Laws 36 or 37.

1. Made at Offender's Partner's Turn to Call

If a double or redouble out of rotation has been made when it was the offender's partner's turn to call, the offender's partner must pass whenever it is his turn to call (see Law 23B); the offender may not thereafter, in turn, double or redouble the same bid he doubled or redoubled out of turn; and if the offender's partner is to make the opening lead:

  (a) Requiring the Lead of a Specified Suit
     Declarer may require the offender's partner to lead a specified suit; or

  (b) Prohibiting the Lead of a Specified Suit
     Declarer may prohibit the offender's partner from leading a specified suit, such prohibition to continue for as long as the offender's partner retains the lead.

2. Made at Offender's Right Hand Opponent's Turn to Call

If a double or redouble out of rotation has been made at offender's right hand opponent's turn to call, then:

  (a) Offender's Right Hand Opponent Passes
     If offender's right hand opponent passes, offender must repeat his out of rotation double or redouble and there is no penalty.

  (b) Offender's Right Hand Opponent Bids
     If offender's right hand opponent bids, the offender may in turn make any legal call and the penalty provisions of 27B3 apply.

33. SIMULTANEOUS CALLS

A call made simultaneously with one made by the player whose turn it was to call, is deemed to be a subsequent call.

34. CALL IN ROTATION AFTER AN ILLEGAL CALL

A. Forfeiture of Penalty For Illegal Call

A call by a member of the non-offending side, after an illegal call by the opponent to his right, and before a penalty has been assessed, forfeits the right to penalize the offense.

B. Illegal Call Legalized

The illegal call is treated as though it were legal, *except that:*

1. Illegal Call Was a Bid of More Than Seven

A bid of more than seven is treated as a pass.

2. Illegal Call Was an Inadmissible Double or Redouble.

If the illegal call was an inadmissible double or redouble, *that call and all subsequent calls are cancelled; the auction reverts to the player whose turn it was to call and proceeds as though there had been no irregularity.* Law 35 or 37 may apply.

35. RETENTION OF RIGHT TO CALL

A. Player Retains Right to Call

A player may not be deprived of his right to call by one or more passes following a pass out of rotation, when there has been no subsequent bid.

B. Passes Cancelled

The Director should cancel all such passes, and the bidding reverts to the player who had missed his turn. The auction proceeds as though there had been no irregularity.

Section Five

Inadmissible Calls

36. INADMISSIBLE DOUBLE OR REDOUBLE

A. Definition

An inadmissible double or redouble is one not permitted by Law 19.

B. Inadmissible Double or Redouble Cancelled

Any inadmissible double or redouble is cancelled, and the offender must substitute a legal call; *Law 26 applies.*

C. Inadmissibly Doubled or Redoubled Bid Becomes Final Contract

If the bid that was inadmissibly doubled or redoubled becomes the final contract, either member of the non-offending side may specify that the contract be played undoubled.

D. Right to Penalize Inadmissible Double or Redouble is Forfeited

If the right of the non-offending side to penalize is forfeited, Law 34 applies.

37. BID, DOUBLE OR REDOUBLE IN VIOLATION OF OBLIGATION TO PASS

A. Bid, Double or Redouble Cancelled

If a player required by law to pass bids, doubles or redoubles, his call is cancelled, and:

1. Auction Penalty

Both members of the offending side must pass during the remainder of the auction.

2. Lead Penalties

If the offender's partner is to make the opening lead,

(a) Require Lead of Specified Suit
Declarer may require offender's partner to lead a specified suit; or

(b) Prohibit Lead of Specified Suit
Declarer may prohibit offender's partner from leading a specified suit, such prohibition to continue for as long as offender's partner retains the lead.

B. Right To Penalize Forfeited

If the right of the non-offending side to penalize is forfeited as provided in Law 11, the offender's bid, double or redouble, if otherwise legal, stands at that turn; but if the offender was required to pass for the remainder of the auction, he must still pass at subsequent turns.

38. BIDS OF MORE THAN SEVEN

No play or score at a contract of more than seven is ever permissible.

A. Bid of More Than Seven Cancelled

A bid of more than seven by any player is cancelled, and (penalty) both members of the offending side must pass during the remainder of the auction.

B. Lead Penalty

If a player bids more than seven, and his partner is to make the opening lead, declarer may either:

1. Require Lead of a Specified Suit
Require offender's partner to lead a specified suit; or

2. Prohibit Lead of Specified Suit
Prohibit offender's partner from leading a specified suit, such prohibition to continue for as long as offender's partner retains the lead.

C. Right to Penalize Forfeited

If the right to penalize is forfeited as provided in Law 11, the offender must substitute a pass; any call that may have been made subsequently is cancelled; and the auction proceeds as though there had been no irregularity.

39. CALL AFTER THE AUCTION IS CLOSED

A. Call after Auction Ends

A call made after the auction is closed is cancelled.

B. Pass by Defender

If a defender passes after the auction is closed there is no penalty.

C. Any Call by Declarer or Dummy

If declarer or dummy makes any call after the auction is closed there is no penalty.

D. Bid, Double or Redouble by a Defender

If a defender bids, doubles or redoubles after the auction is closed, declarer may either:

1. Require Lead of Specified Suit
Require offender's partner, when first it is his turn to lead, to lead a specified suit; or

2. Prohibit Lead of Specified Suit
Prohibit offender's partner, when first it is his turn to lead, from leading a specified suit, such

prohibition to continue for as long as the offender's partner retains the lead.

E. Right to Penalize Forfeited

If the right of the non-offending side to penalize is forfeited, as provided in Law 11, all calls made after the close of the auction are cancelled without penalty.

Section Six

Conventions and Agreements

40. PARTNERSHIP UNDERSTANDINGS

A. Right to Call

A player may make any call or play (including an intentionally misleading call—such as a 'psychic' bid—or a call or play that departs from commonly accepted, or previously announced, conventional practice), without prior announcement, provided that such call or play is not based on a partnership understanding.

B. Concealed Partnership Understandings Prohibited

A player may not make a call or play based on a partnership understanding, unless an opposing pair may reasonably be expected to understand its meaning, or unless his side discloses the use of such call or play in accordance with the regulations of the sponsoring organization.

Director's Option

If the Director decides that a side has been damaged through its opponents' failure to explain the meaning of a call or play, he may award an adjusted score.

D. Regulation of Conventions

The sponsoring organization may regulate the use of bidding or play conventions.

E. Convention Card

1. Right to Prescribe
The sponsoring organization may prescribe a convention card on which partners are to list their conventions, and may establish regulations for its use.

2. Referring to Opponents' Convention Card
During the auction *and play, any player except dummy may refer to his opponents' convention card at his own turn to* call or *play.*

CHAPTER VI

THE PLAY

◆◆◆◆◆◆

PART I

Procedure

Section One

Correct Procedure

41. COMMENCEMENT OF PLAY

A. The Opening Lead

After the auction closes, the defender on declarer's left makes the opening lead.

B. Spreading Dummy's Hand

After the opening lead has been made*, dummy spreads his hand in front of him on the table. The cards are face up, sorted in suits, with trumps to dummy's right.

C. Playing Dummy's Hand

Declarer plays both his hand and that of dummy.

D. Inquiry as to Final Contract

After it is too late to have previous calls restated, as provided in Law 20, declarer or either defender is entitled to be informed as to what the contract is and whether, but not by whom, it was doubled or redoubled.

42. DUMMY'S RIGHTS

A. Absolute Rights

1. Give or Obtain Information

Dummy is entitled to give or obtain information, *in the Director's presence,* as to fact or law.

2. Keep Track of Tricks

He may keep count of tricks won and lost by each side and may draw attention to the fact that another player's card, played to any preceding trick, has been pointed in the wrong direction.

3. Play as Declarer's Agent

He may play the cards of the dummy as declarer's agent and only as directed by him (see Law 16).

B. Qualified Rights

Dummy may exercise other rights subject to the limitations provided in Law 43.

1. Revoke Inquiries

Dummy may question players regarding revokes as provided in Law 61 (he may ask a player who has failed to follow suit to a trick whether he has a card of the suit led).

2. Attempt to Prevent Irregularity

He may try to prevent any irregularity (he may, for example, warn declarer against leading from the wrong hand).

3. Draw Attention to Irregularity

He may draw attention to any irregularity, *but only after play of the hand is concluded.*

43. DUMMY'S LIMITATIONS

A. Limitations on Dummy

1. General Limitations

    (a) Calling the Director

        Dummy should *not* call the Director *during play.*

    (b) Calling Attention to Irregularity

        Dummy may *not* call attention to an irregularity *during play* except to try to prevent an irregularity before it occurs (Law 42B2).

    (c) Participate in or Comment on Play

        Dummy may not participate in the play or make any comment on the bidding or play.

---

* The sponsoring organization may specify a delay (see footnote to Law 45).

2. Limitations Carrying Specific Penalty

    (a) Exchanging Hands

        Dummy *may not* exchange hands with declarer.

    (b) Leave Seat to Watch Declarer

        Dummy *may not* leave his seat to watch declarer's play of the hand.

    (c) Look at Defender's Hand

        Dummy *may not,* on his own initiative, look at the face of a card in either defender's hand.

B. Penalties for Violation

1. General Penalties

Dummy is liable to penalty under Law 86 for any violation of the limitations listed in A1 or A2 preceding.

2. Specific Penalties

If dummy, after violation of the limitations listed in A2 preceding:

    (a) Draws Attention to Defender's Irregularity

        Is the first to draw attention to a defender's irregularity, declarer may not enforce any penalty for the offense.

    (b) Warns Declarer on Lead

        Warns declarer not to lead from the wrong hand, (penalty) either defender may choose the hand from which declarer shall lead.

    (c) Asks Declarer About Possible Irregularity

        Is the first to ask declarer if a play from declarer's hand constitutes a revoke or failure to comply with a penalty, declarer must substitute a correct card if his play was illegal, and the penalty provisions of Law 64 apply.

44. SEQUENCE AND PROCEDURE OF PLAY

A. Lead to a Trick

The player who leads to a trick may play any card in his hand (unless he is subject to restriction after an irregularity committed by his side).

B. Subsequent Plays to a Trick

After the lead, each other player in turn plays a card, and the four cards so played constitute a trick. (For the method of playing cards and arranging tricks see Law 65.)

C. Requirement to Follow Suit

In playing to a trick, each player must follow suit if possible. This obligation takes precedence over all other requirements of these Laws.

D. Inability to Follow Suit

If unable to follow suit, a player may play any card (unless he is subject to restriction after an irregularity committed by his side).

E. Tricks Containing Trumps

A trick containing a trump is won by the player who has contributed to it the highest trump.

F. Tricks Not Containing Trumps

A trick that does not contain a trump is won by the player who has contributed to it the highest card of the suit led.

G. Lead to Tricks Subsequent to First Trick
The player who has won the trick leads to the next trick.

45. CARD PLAYED

A. Play of Card from a Hand
Each player except dummy plays a card by detaching it from his hand and facing* it on the table immediately before him.

B. Play of Card from Dummy
Declarer plays a card from dummy by naming the card, after which dummy picks up the card and faces it on the table, In playing from dummy's hand declarer may, if he prefers, pick up the desired card himself.

C. Compulsory Play of Card
1. Defender's Card
A defender's card held so that it is possible for his partner to see its face must be played to the current trick (if the defender has already made a legal play to the current trick, see Law 45E).
2. Declarer's Card
Declarer must play a card fom his hand held face up, touching or nearly touching the table, *or maintained in such a position as to indicate that it has been played.*
3. Dummy's Card
A card in the dummy must be played if it has been deliberately touched by declarer except for the purpose of arranging dummy's cards, or of reaching a card above or below the card or cards touched.
4. Named or Designated Card
  (a) Play of Named Card
    A card must be played if a player names or otherwise designates it as the card he proposes to play.
  (b) Correction of Inadvertent Designation
    A player may, without penalty, change an inadvertent designation if he does so without pause *for thought;* but if an opponent has, in turn, played a card that was legal before the change in designation, that opponent may withdraw without penalty the card so played and substitute another (see Law 47F).
5. Penalty Card
A penalty card must be played, subject to Law 50.

D. Card Misplayed by Dummy
If dummy places in. the played position a card that declarer did not name, the card must be withdrawn if attention is drawn to it before *each side* has played to the next trick, and a defender may withdraw (without penalty) a card played after the error but before attention was drawn to it (see Law 47F).

E. Fifth Card Played to Trick
1. By a Defender
A fifth card contributed to a trick by a defender

becomes a penalty card, subject to Law 50, unless the Director deems that it was led, in which case Laws 53 or 56 apply.
2. By Declarer
When declarer contributes a fifth card to a trick from his own hand or dummy, there is no penalty unless the Director deems that it was led, in which case Law 55 applies.

F. Dummy Indicates Card
After dummy's hand is faced, dummy may not touch or indicate any card (except for purpose of arrangement) without instruction from declarer. If he does so, the Director should be summoned forthwith. The Director should rule whether dummy's act did in fact constitute a suggestion to declarer, and if it did (penalty) he may forbid declarer to make any play predicated upon the suggestion.

G. Turning the Trick
No player should turn his card face down until all four players have played to the trick.

Section Two

Irregularities in Procedure

46. INCOMPLETE OR ERRONEOUS CALL OF CARD FROM DUMMY

A. Proper Form for Designating Dummy's Card
When calling a card to be played from dummy, declarer should clearly state both the suit and the rank of the desired card.

B. Incomplete or Erroneous Call
In case of an incomplete or erroneous call by declarer of the card to be played from dummy the following restrictions apply:
1. Incomplete Designation of Rank
If declarer, in playing from dummy, calls "high," or words of like import, he is deemed to have called the highest card of the suit indicated (*or if dummy is last to follow suit to the trick, the lowest winning card*); if he calls "low," or words of like import, he is deemed to have called the lowest.
2. Name of Suit but Not Rank
If declarer names a suit but not a rank, he is deemed to have called the lowest card of the suit indicated (*unless this was incontrovertibly not his intention*).
3. Name of Rank but Not Suit
If declarer names a rank but not a suit:
  (a) In Leading
    Declarer is deemed to have continued the suit in which dummy won the preceding trick, provided there is a card of the named rank in that suit.
  (b) All Other Cases
    In all other cases, declarer must play a card from dummy of the named rank if he can legally do so; but if there are two or more such cards that can be legally played, declarer must designate which is intended.

---

* *Sponsoring organizations may require an opening lead face down.*

4. Designated Card Not in Dummy

If declarer calls a card that is not in dummy, the call is void and declarer may designate any legal card.

5. No Suit or Rank Designated

If declarer indicates a play without naming either a suit or rank (as by saying, "play anything," or words of like import), either defender may designate the play from the dummy except when such play was incontrovertibly not declarer's intention.

47. RETRACTION OF CARD PLAYED

A. To Comply with Penalty

A card once played may be withdrawn to comply with a penalty (but see Law 49).

B. To Correct an Illegal Play

A played card may be withdrawn to correct an illegal play (but see Law 49).

C. To Change an Inadvertent Designation

A played card may be withdrawn without penalty after a change of designation as permitted by Law 45C4(b).

D. Following Opponent's Change of Play

After an opponent's change of play, a played card may be withdrawn without penalty to substitute another card for the one played.

E. Change of Play Based on Misinformation

1. Lead Out of Turn

A lead out of turn may be retracted without penalty if the leader was mistakenly informed by an opponent that it was his turn to lead.

2. Declarer's Retraction of Play

   (a) Defender Has Not Subsequently Played

      Declarer may retract a card played from his own hand or dummy after a mistaken explanation of a defender's conventional play and before a corrected explanation, but only if no card was subsequently played to that trick.

   (b) One or More Subsequent Plays Made

      When it is too late for declarer to correct a play, under (a) preceding, Law 40C applies.

F. Exposure of Retracted Card by Damaged Side

If a card retracted under sections D or E preceding gave substantial information to an opponent, the Director may award an adjusted score.

G. Illegal Retraction

Except as provided in A through E preceding, a card once played may not be withdrawn.

PART II

Penalty Card

48. EXPOSURE OF DECLARER'S CARDS

A. Declarer Exposes a Card

Declarer is not subject to penalty for exposing a card, and no card of declarer's or dummy's hand ever becomes a penalty card. Declarer is not required to play any card dropped accidentally.

B. Declarer Faces Cards

1. After Opening Lead Out of Turn

When declarer *inadvertently* faces his cards after an opening lead out of turn, Law 54 applies (*but it is a violation of propriety to spread his hand when he knows he is declarer*).

2. At Any Other Time

When declarer faces his cards at any time other than immediately after an opening lead out of turn, he *may be* deemed to have made a claim or concession of tricks, and Law 68 then applies.

49. EXPOSURE OF A DEFENDER'S CARDS

Whenever a defender faces a card on the table, holds a card so that it is possible for his partner to see its face, or names a card as being in his hand, before he is entitled to do so in the normal course of play or application of law, (penalty) each such card becomes a penalty card (Law 50); but see Law 70 (Defender's Claim or Concession of Tricks).

50. DISPOSITION OF PENALTY CARD

A. Definition of Penalty Card

A card prematurely exposed by a defender is a penalty card *unless the Director designates otherwise.*

B. Penalty Card Remains Exposed

A penalty card must be left face up on the table immediately before the player to whom it belongs, until it is played or until an alternate penalty has been selected.

C. Leader's Partner Has Penalty Card

1. Lead Must Be Held for Declarer's Option

When a defender has the lead while his partner has a penalty card, he may not lead until declarer has stated which of the options open to him he is selecting. If the defender leads prematurely, he is subject to penalty under Law 49.

2. Declarer's Options

   (a) Require or Prohibit Lead of Penalty Card Suit

      The declarer may require that defender to lead the suit of the penalty card, or may prohibit him from leading that suit for as long as he retains the lead. If declarer exercises this option, the penalty card may be picked up.

   (b) Penalty Card to Remain Penalty Card

      If declarer does not exercise the option provided in (a) preceding, the defender may lead any card, but the penalty card remains a penalty card.

   (c) Two or More Penalty Cards

      See Law 51.

D. Play of Penalty Card

A penalty card must be played at the first legal opportunity, whether in leading, following suit, discarding or trumping. If a defender has two or more penalty cards that can legally be played, declarer may designate which is to be played. The obligation to follow suit, or to comply with a lead or play penalty, takes precedence over the obligation to play a penalty card, but the penalty card must still be left face up on the table and played at the next legal opportunity.

51. TWO OR MORE PENALTY CARDS

A. Defender's Turn to Play
(See Law 50: If a defender has two or more penalty cards that can legally be played, declarer may designate which is to be played at that turn.)
B. Leader's Partner Has Two or More Penalty Cards
1. Penalty Cards in Same Suit
   (a) Declarer Requires Lead of That Suit
   When a defender has two or more penalty cards in one suit, and declarer requires the defender's partner to lead that suit, the defender may pick up every penalty card in that suit and may make any legal play to the trick.
   (b) Declarer Prohibits Lead of That Suit
   If the declarer prohibits the lead of that suit, the defender may pick up every penalty card in that suit and may make any legal play to the trick.
2. Penalty Cards in More Than One Suit
   (a) Declarer Requires Lead of a Specified Suit
   When a defender has penalty cards in more than one suit, declarer may require the defender's partner to lead any suit in which the defender has a penalty card (but B1(a) preceding then applies).
   (b) Declarer Prohibits Lead of Specified Suits
   When a defender has penalty cards in more than one suit, declarer may prohibit the defender's partner from leading every such suit; but the defender may then pick up every penalty card in every suit prohibited by declarer, and make any legal play to the trick.

52. FAILURE TO LEAD OR PLAY A PENALTY CARD

A. Defender Fails to Play Penalty Card
When a defender fails to lead or play a penalty card as required by Law 50, he may not, on his own initiative, withdraw any other card he may have played.
B. Defender Plays Another Card
1. Play of Card Accepted
   (a) Declarer May Accept Play
   If a defender has led or played another card when he could legally have led or played a penalty card, declarer may accept such lead or play.
   (b) Declarer Must Accept Play
   Declarer must accept such lead or play if he has thereafter played from his own hand or dummy.
   (c) Penalty Card Remains Penalty Card
   If the played card is accepted under either (a) or (b) preceding, the unplayed penalty card remains a penalty card.
2. Play of Card Rejected

Declarer may require the defender to substitute the penalty card for the card illegally played or led. Every card illegally led or played by the defender in the course of committing the irregularity becomes a penalty card.

PART III

Irregular Leads and Plays

Section One

Lead out of Turn

53. LEAD OUT OF TURN ACCEPTED

A. Lead Out of Turn Treated as Correct Lead
Any lead faced out of turn may be treated as a correct lead. It becomes a correct lead if declarer or either defender, as the case may be, accepts it (*by making a statement to that effect*), or if the player next in rotation plays* to the irregular lead. (If no acceptance statement or play is made the Director will require that the lead be made from the correct hand.)
B. Wrong Defender Plays Card to Declarer's Irregular Lead
If the defender at the right of the player from whose hand the lead out of turn was made plays* to the irregular lead, the lead stands and Law 57 applies.
C. Proper Lead Made Subsequent to Irregular Lead
If it was properly the turn to lead of an opponent of the player who led out of turn, that opponent may make his proper lead to the trick of the infraction without his card being deemed played to the irregular lead. When this occurs, the proper lead stands, and all cards played in error to this trick may be withdrawn without penalty (see Law 47F).

54. OPENING LEAD OUT OF TURN

A. Declarer Accepts Lead
When a defender faces the opening lead out of turn declarer may accept the irregular lead as provided in Law 53, and dummy is spread in accordance with Law 41.
1. Declarer Plays Second Card
The second card to the trick is played from declarer's hand.
2. Dummy Has Played Second Card
If declarer plays the second card to the trick from dummy, dummy's card may not be withdrawn except to correct a revoke.
B. Declarer Must Accept Lead
If declarer may have seen any of dummy's cards (except cards that dummy may have exposed during the auction and that were subject to Law 23), he must accept the lead.
C. Declarer Begins to Spread His Hand
If declarer inadvertently† begins to spread his

---

* But see C below.
† Declarer should, as a matter of propriety, refrain from spreading his hand when he knows that he is declarer.

hand as though he were dummy, and in so doing exposes one or more cards, and if subsection B preceding does not apply, the lead must be accepted, declarer must spread his entire hand and dummy becomes declarer.

D. Declarer Refuses Opening Lead

When declarer requires the defender to retract his opening lead out of turn, Law 56 applies.

55. DECLARER'S LEAD OUT OF TURN

A. Declarer's Lead Accepted

If declarer has led out of turn, either defender may accept the lead as provided in Law 53.

B. Declarer Required to Retract Lead

1. Defender's Turn to Lead

If declarer has led when it was a defender's turn to lead, and if either defender requires him to retract such lead, declarer restores the card led in error to the proper hand without penalty.

2. Lead in Declarer's Hand or Dummy's

If declarer has led from the wrong hand when it was his turn to lead from his hand or dummy's and if either defender requires him to retract the lead, he withdraws the card led in error. He must lead from the correct hand and, (penalty) if able to do so, a card of the same suit.

C. Failure to Comply with Penalty

Failure by declarer to comply with the lead penalty may subject him to penalty under Law 64.

56. DEFENDER'S LEAD OUT OF TURN

A. Declarer Accepts Lead

See Laws 53 and 54.

B. Declarer Requires Retraction of Lead

When declarer requires a defender to retract his lead out of turn, the card illegally led becomes a penalty card, and Law 50 applies.

Section Two

Other Irregular Leads and Plays

57. PREMATURE LEAD OR PLAY BY DEFENDER

A. Premature Lead or Play to Next Trick

When a defender leads to the next trick before his partner has played to the current trick, or plays out of turn before his partner has played, (penalty) the card so led or played becomes a penalty card, and declarer must select one of the following options. He may require the offender's partner:

1. Follow Suit with Highest Card

To play the highest card he holds of the suit led, or

2. Follow Suit with Lowest Card

To play the lowest card he holds of the suit led, or

3. Play Card of Another Suit

To play a legal card of another suit specified by declarer.

B. Offender's Partner Cannot Comply with Penalty

When offender's partner is unable to comply with the penalty selected by declarer, he may play any card, as provided in Law 59.

C. Declarer Has Played from Both Hands before Irregularity

A defender is not subject to penalty for playing before his partner if declarer has played from both hands; but a singleton, or one of two or more equal cards (cards of the same suit adjacent in rank) in dummy, is not considered automatically played unless dummy has played the card or has illegally suggested that it be played (see Law 45).

58. SIMULTANEOUS LEADS OR PLAYS

A. Play Made Simultaneously with Legal Play

A lead or play made simultaneously with another player's legal lead or play is deemed to be subsequent to it.

B. Defender Plays Two Cards Simultaneously

1. Only One Card Visible

If a defender leads or plays two or more cards simultaneously, and if only one such card is visible, he must play that card.

2. More Than One Card Exposed

If more than one card is exposed, he must designate the card he proposes to play, and each other card exposed becomes a penalty card (Law 50).

C. Declarer Plays Two or More Cards Simultaneously

1. Declarer Must Designate Correct Card

If declarer leads or plays two or more cards simultaneously from either hand, he must designate the card he proposes to play, and must restore any other card to the correct hand.

2. Declarer Withdraws Visible Card

If declarer withdraws a visible card and a defender has already played to that card, such defender may, without penalty, withdraw his card and substitute another (see Law 47F).

D. Error Not Discovered

If the error remains undiscovered until both sides have played to the next trick, Law 67 applies.

59. INABILITY TO LEAD OR PLAY AS REQUIRED

A player may play any correct card if he is unable to lead or play as required to comply with a penalty, whether because he holds no card of the required suit, or because he has only cards of a suit he is prohibited from leading, or because of his obligation to follow suit.

60. PLAY AFTER AN ILLEGAL PLAY

A. Play of Card after Irregularity

1. Forfeiture of Right to Penalize

A play by a member of the non-offending side after the opponent on his right has led or played out of turn or prematurely, and before a penalty has been assessed, forfeits the right to penalize that offense.

2. Irregularity Legalized

Once the right to penalize has been forfeited, the illegal play is treated as though it were legal (except as provided in Law 53) unless it constitutes a revoke.

3. Other Penalty Obligations Remain

If the offending side had a previous obligation to play a penalty card, or to comply with a lead or play penalty, the obligation remains at future turns (see Laws 52 and 64).

B. *Defender Plays before Required Lead by Declarer*

When a defender plays a card after declarer has been required to retract his lead out of turn from either hand, but before declarer has led from the correct hand, the defender's card becomes a penalty card (Law 50).

C. *Play by Offending Side before Assessment of Penalty*

A play by a member of the offending side before a penalty has been assessed does not affect the rights of the opponents and may itself be subject to penalty.

Section Three

The Revoke

61. FAILURE TO FOLLOW SUIT—INQUIRIES CONCERNING A REVOKE

A. *Definition of Revoke*

Failure to follow suit in accordance with Law 44, or failure to lead or play, when able, a card or suit required by law or specified by an opponent in accordance with an agreed penalty, constitutes a revoke (but see Law 59).

B. *Right to Inquire about a Possible Revoke*

Any player, including dummy (subject to Law 43), may ask a player who has failed to follow suit whether he has a card of the suit led (but a claim of revoke does not warrant inspection of quitted tricks, except at the Director's specific instruction—see Law 66).

62. CORRECTION OF A REVOKE

A. *Revoke Must Be Corrected*

A player must correct his revoke if he becomes aware of the irregularity before it becomes established.

B. *Correcting a Revoke*

To correct a revoke, the offender withdraws the card he played in revoking and follows suit with any card.

1. Defender's Card

A card so withdrawn becomes a penalty card (Law 50) if it was played from a defender's unfaced hand.

2. Declarer's or Dummy's Card, Defender's Faced Card

The card may be replaced without penalty if it

was played from declarer's or dummy's hand*, or if it was a defender's faced card.

C. *Subsequent Cards Played to Trick*

1. By Non-offending Side

Each member of the non-offending side may, without penalty, withdraw any card he may have played after the revoke but before attention was drawn to it (see Law 47F).

2. By Partner of Offender

Except as provided in subsection D following, the partner of the offender may not withdraw his card unless it too constituted a revoke (in which case, the card withdrawn becomes a penalty card if it was played from a defender's unfaced hand).

D. *Revoke after Eleventh Trick*

1. Must Be Corrected

After the eleventh trick, a revoke, even if established, must be corrected if discovered before all four hands have been returned to the board.

2. Offender's Partner Had Not Played to Trick Twelve

If the revoke occurred before it was the turn of the offender's partner to play to the twelfth trick, (penalty) declarer or either defender, as the case may be, may then require the offender's partner to play to that trick either of two cards he could legally have played.

63. ESTABLISHMENT OF A REVOKE

A. *Revoke Becomes Established*

A revoke becomes established:

1. Offending Side Leads or Plays to Next Trick

When the offender or his partner leads or plays to the following trick (any such play, legal or illegal, establishes the revoke).

2. A Member of Offending Side Indicates a Lead or Play

When the offender or his partner names or otherwise designates a card to be played to the following trick.

3. Member of Offending Side Makes a Claim or Concession

When a member of the offending side makes a claim or concession of tricks orally or by facing his hand (or in any other fashion).

B. *Revoke May Not Be Corrected*

Once a revoke is established, it may no longer be corrected (except as provided in Law 62D), and the trick on which the revoke occurred stands as played.

64. PROCEDURE AFTER ESTABLISHMENT OF A REVOKE

A. *Penalty Assessed*

1. Offending Side Has Won Revoke Trick

When a revoke is established, and the trick on which the revoke occurred was won by the offending side, (penalty) after play ceases, the trick on which the revoke occurred, plus one of any

---

* Subject to Law 43. A claim of revoke does not warrant inspection of quitted tricks except as permitted in Law 67.

subsequent tricks won by the offending side, are transferred to the non-offending side.

2. Offending Side Did Not Win Revoke Trick
When a revoke is established and the trick on which the revoke occurred was not won by the offending side (penalty) after play ceases, *one* of any subsequent tricks won by the offending side is transferred to the non-offending side.

B. No Penalty Assessed

1. Offending Side Fails to Win Revoke Trick or Subsequent Trick
The penalty for an established revoke does not apply if the offending side did not win either the revoke trick or any subsequent trick.

2. Second Revoke in Same Suit by Offender
The penalty does not apply to a subsequent revoke in the same suit by the same player.

3. Revoke by Failure to Play a Faced Card
The penalty does not apply if the revoke was made in failing to play any card faced on the table or belonging to a hand faced on the table, including a card from dummy's hand.

4. After Non-offending Side Calls to Next Deal
The penalty does not apply if attention was first drawn to the revoke after a member of the non-offending side has made a call on a subsequent deal.

5. After Round Has Ended
The penalty does not apply if attention was first drawn to the revoke after the round has ended.

6. Revoke after Eleventh Trick
The penalty does not apply to a revoke that was made after the eleventh trick.

C. Director Responsible for Equity
When, after any established revoke, including those not subject to penalty, the Director deems that the non-offending side is insufficiently compensated by this Law for the damage caused, he should assign an adjusted score.

PART IV

Tricks

65. ARRANGEMENT OF TRICKS

A. Completed Trick
When four cards have been played to a trick, each player turns his own card face down on the edge of the table before him.

B. Keeping Track of the Ownership of Tricks

1. Tricks Won
If the player's side has won the trick, the card is pointed lengthwise toward his partner.

2. Tricks Lost
If the opponents have won the trick, the card is pointed lengthwise toward the opponents.

C. Orderliness Required
Each player should arrange his own cards in an orderly overlapping row in the sequence played, in order to permit review of the play after its completion, if necessary to determine the number of tricks won by each side or the order in which the cards were played.

D. Agreement on Results of Play
A player should not disturb the order of his played cards until agreement has been reached on the number of tricks won.

E. Noncompliance

1. Rights Placed in Jeopardy
A player who fails to comply with the provisions of this Law may jeopardize his right to claim ownership of doubtful tricks or to claim a revoke.

2. Cards Incorrectly Pointed
Any player may request that a card incorrectly pointed be turned in the proper direction.

66. INSPECTION OF TRICKS

A. Current Trick
So long as his side has not led or played to the next trick, declarer or either defender may, *until he has turned his own card face down on the table,* require that all cards just played to the trick be faced for his inspection.

B. Quitted Tricks
Thereafter, until play ceases, quitted tricks may not be inspected (except at the Director's specific instruction, for example, to verify a claim of a revoke).

C. After the Conclusion of Play
After play ceases the played and unplayed cards may be inspected to settle a claim of a revoke, or of the number of tricks won or lost (or of honors in total point play); but no player should handle cards other than his own. If, after a claim has been made, a player mixes his cards in such a manner that the Director can no longer ascertain the facts, the issue must be decided in favor of the other side.

67. DEFECTIVE TRICK

A. Irregularity Detected before Both Sides Have Played to Next Trick
When a player has omitted to play to a trick, or has played too many cards to a trick, the error must be rectified if attention is drawn to the irregularity before a player on each side has played to the following trick.

1. Player Failed to Play Card
To rectify omission to play to a trick, the offender supplies a card he can legally play.

2. Player Contributed Too Many Cards
   (a) Offender Withdraws Surplus Card(s)
   To rectify the error of playing too many cards, the offender withdraws all but one card, leaving a card he can legally play. Each card so withdrawn becomes a penalty card (Law 50) if it was played from a defender's unfaced hand.

   (b) Change of Play by Non-offenders
   After a card has been so withdrawn, each member of the non-offending side may, without penalty, withdraw any card he played after the irregularity but before attention was drawn to it (see Law 47F).

B. Irregularity Discovered after Both Sides Play
When attention is drawn to a defective trick after

both sides play to the following trick, or when the Director later determines that there was a defective trick, from the fact that one player holds too few or too many cards and a corresponding improper number of played cards on the table before him, the defective trick stands as played and:

1. Player with Too Few Cards

A player with too few cards plays the remainder of his hand with fewer cards than the other players; he does not play to the final trick (or tricks), and if he wins a trick with his last card the lead passes in rotation.

2. Player with Too Many Cards

A player with too many cards *plays the remainder of his hand with more cards than the other players; all cards remaining unplayed after the final trick are added to that trick (but no card so contributed changes the ownership of that trick).*

3. Penalty on Offending Player

When it is no longer possibly to rectify a defective trick, failure to play a card to that trick, or the play of more than one card to that trick, is penalized as an established revoke. The Director should apply the penalty provisions and exemptions of Law 64. For this purpose the Director should attempt to determine the exact trick at which the irregularity took place, but should he be unable to do so with certainty, the defective trick is deemed to be the earliest one possible.

PART V

Claims and Concessions

68. DECLARER'S CLAIM OR CONCESSION OF TRICKS

A. Concession by Declarer

Declarer makes a concesssion when he announces that he will lose all the remaining tricks, or when he agrees to a defender's claim.

B. Claim by Declarer

Declarer makes a claim whenever he announces that he will win or lose one or more of the remaining tricks, or suggests that play be curtailed, or *intentionally* faces his hand.

C. Required Statement by Declarer

In making his claim declarer *is required* to state his proposed line of play.

D. Play Ceases

Play Ceases. When declarer has made a claim questioned by either defender the Director *must* be summoned immediately. *No action of any kind may be taken pending the Director's arrival (all play subsequent to a claim or concession must be voided by the Director). See Law 69.*

69. DIRECTOR'S RULING ON DECLARER'S
CONTESTED CLAIM

A. General Objective

In ruling on a contested claim by declarer, the Director should adjudicate the result of the board as equitably as possible to both sides, but any doubtful points should be resolved in favor of the defenders. He should proceed as follows:

B. Investigatory Steps Director Should Follow

1. Require Declarer to Repeat Claim Statement

The Director should require declarer to repeat the statement he made at the time of his claim.

2. Require All Hands to be Faced

Next, the Director should require all players to put their remaining cards face up on the table.

3. Hear Defenders' Objections

The Director should then hear the defenders' objections to the claim.

C. There Is an Outstanding Trump

When a trump remains in one of the defenders' hands, the Director should award a trick or tricks to the defenders if:

1. Failed to Mention Trump

Declarer, in making his claim, made no statement about that trump, and

2. Was Probably Unaware of Trump

It is at all likely that declarer at the time of his claim was unaware that a trump remained in a defender's hand, and

3. Could Lose a Trick to the Trump

A trick could be lost to that trump by any normal play (including the careless or inferior but not the irrational).

D. Declarer Proposes a New Line of Play

The Director should not accept from declarer any proposed line of play inconsistent with his statement.

E. Declarer Failed to Make Appropriate Announcement

If declarer did not make an appropriate announcement at the time of his original claim, the Director should not accept from him any proposed line of play the success of which depends upon finding either opponent with or without a particular card, unless an opponent failed to follow to the suit of that card before the claim was made, *or would subsequently fail to follow to that suit on any conceivable line of play.*

70. DEFENDER'S CLAIM OR CONCESSION OF TRICKS

A. Defender's Claim

A defender makes a claim when he announces that he will win one or more of the remaining tricks, or when he shows any or all of his cards to declarer *for this purpose.*

1. Claim Pertains Only to Current Trick

If the claim pertains only to an uncompleted trick currently in progress, play proceeds normally; cards exposed or otherwise revealed by the defender in making his claim do not become penalty cards, but Law 16 may apply; and see Law 57.

2. Claim Pertains to Subsequent Tricks

(a) Play Ceases

If the claim pertains to subsequent tricks, play must cease (any play subsequent to a claim or concession must be voided by the Director), and the defender is required to state his proposed line of defense.

(b) Claim Questioned

When the claim is questioned by declarer, the Director must be summoned immediately and no action of any kind may be taken pend-

ing his arrival. The Director should adjudicate the result of the board as equitably as possible to both sides, but should award to the declarer any trick that the defenders could lose by normal (including the inferior or careless but not the irrational) play.

B. Defender's Concession

A defender makes a concession when he agrees to declarer's claim, or when he announces that he will lose one or more of the remaining tricks. (Concession cancelled, see Law 71.)

71. CONCESSION CANCELLED

A concession may be *cancelled by the Director:*

A. Illegal Concessions

1. Trick Side Has Won

*If any player concedes a trick his side has, in fact, won.

2. Contract Fulfilled

*If declarer concedes defeat of a contract he has already fulfilled.

3. Contract Defeated

*If a defender concedes the fulfillment of a contract his side has already defeated.

B. Concession of Trick That Cannot Be Lost

If a trick that has been conceded cannot be lost by any *probable* play of the remaining cards, and if the Director's attention is drawn to that fact before all four hands have been returned to the board.

C. Concession Disputed by Other Defender

If a defender concedes one or more tricks and his partner immediately objects, but Law 16 may apply.

CHAPTER VII

PROPRIETIES
◆◆◆◆◆◆◆

I. GENERAL PRINCIPLES

A. Observance of Laws

1. General Obligation on Contestants

Duplicate bridge tournaments should be played in strict accordance with the Laws.

2. Waiving of Penalties

In duplicate tournaments it is improper to waive a penalty for an opponent's infraction even if one feels that one has not been damaged.

3. Non-offender's Exercise of Legal Options

When these Laws provide the innocent side with an option after an irregularity committed by an opponent, it is proper to select that action most advantageous.

4. Offenders' Options

After the offending side has paid the prescribed penalty for an inadvertent infraction, it is proper for the offenders to make any call or play advantageous to their side, even though they thereby appear to profit through their own infraction.

---

* For a concession to be cancelled under this clause, the error must be reported to the Director within the correction period established under Law 75.

---

5. Responsibility for Enforcement of Laws

The responsibility for penalizing irregularities and redressing damage rests solely upon the Director and these Laws, not upon the players themselves.

B. Infraction of Law

1. Intentional

To infringe a law intentionally is a serious breach of propriety, even if there is a prescribed penalty that one is willing to pay. The offense may be the more serious when no penalty is prescribed.

2. Inadvertent Infraction

There is no obligation to draw attention to an inadvertent infraction of law committed by one's own side.

3. Concealing an Infraction

A player should not attempt to conceal an inadvertent infraction, as by committing a second revoke, concealing a card involved in a revoke, or mixing the cards prematurely.

II. IMPROPER INFORMATION

A. Proper Communication between Partners

1. How Effected

Communication between partners during the auction and play should be effected only by means of the calls and plays themselves.

2. Correct Form for Calls

Calls should be made in a uniform tone without special emphasis or inflection, and without undue haste or hesitation. (However, sponsoring organizations may require mandatory pauses, as on the first round of the auction, or following a skip bid.)

3. Correct Form for Plays

Plays should be made without emphasis, gesture, or mannerism, and so far as possible at a uniform rate.

B. Improper Communication between Partners

1. Gratuitous Information

It is improper for communication between partners to be effected through the manner in which calls or plays are made, through extraneous remarks or gestures, or through questions asked of the opponents or explanations given to them.

2. Prearranged Improper Communication

The gravest possible offense against propriety is for a partnership to exchange information through prearranged methods of communication other than those sanctioned by these Laws. The penalty imposed for infraction is normally expulsion from the sponsoring organization.

C. Player Receives Improper Information from Partner

When a player has available to him improper information from his partner's remark, question, explanation, gesture, mannerism, special emphasis, inflection, haste, or hesitation, he should carefully avoid taking any advantage that might accrue to his side.

D. Variations in Tempo

1. Inadvertent Variations

Inadvertently to vary the tempo or manner in which a call or play is made does not in itself constitute a violation of propriety, but inferences from such variation may properly be drawn only by an opponent, and at his own risk.

2. Intentional Variations

It is grossly improper to attempt to mislead an opponent by means of remark or gesture, through the haste or hesitancy of a call or play (such as a hesitation before the play of a singleton), or by the manner in which the call or play is made.

E. Deception

Any player may properly attempt to deceive an opponent through a call or play (so long as the deception is not protected by concealed partnership understanding). It is entirely proper to avoid giving information to the opponents by making all calls and plays in unvarying tempo and manner.

F. Violation of Proprieties

When a violation of the proprieties described in this part results in damage to an innocent opponent:

1. Player Acts on Improper Information

If the Director determines that a player chose from among logical alternative actions one that could reasonably have been suggested by his partner's tempo, manner or remark, he should award an adjusted score (see Law 16).

2. Player Injured by Deliberate Improper Deception

If the Director determines that an innocent opponent has drawn a false inference from deliberately and improperly deceptive information, he should award an adjusted score (see Law 12).

III. CONDUCT AND ETIQUETTE

A. Proper Attitude

1. Courtesy Toward Partner and Opponents

A player should maintain at all times a courteous attitude toward his partner and opponents.

2. Etiquette of Word and Action

A player should carefully avoid any remark or action that might cause annoyance or embarrassment to another player, or might interfere with the enjoyment of the game.

3. Conformity to Proper Procedure

Every player should follow uniform and correct procedure in calling and playing, since any departure from correct standards may disrupt the orderly progress of the game.

B. Etiquette

As a matter of courtesy a player should refrain from:

1. Lack of Attention

Paying insufficient attention to the game (as when a player obviously takes no interest in his hand, or frequently requests a review of the auction).

2. Making Gratuitous Comments

Making gratuitous comments during the play as to the auction or the adequacy of the contract.

3. Prematurely Detaching a Card

Detaching a card from his hand before it is his turn to lead or play.

4. Disorder in Played Cards

Arranging the cards he has played to previous tricks in a disordered manner, or mixing his cards before the result of the deal has been agreed upon.

5. Questionable Claims or Concessions

Making a claim or concession of tricks if there is any doubt as to the outcome of the deal.

6. Prolongation of Play

Prolonging play unnecessarily for the purpose of disconcerting the other players.

7. Disrespectful Summoning of the Director

Summoning the Director in a manner discourteous to him or to the other contestants.

C. Breaches of Propriety

It is a breach of propriety:

1. Variations in Calls

To use different designations for the same call.

2. Displaying Reaction to Calls or Plays

To indicate any approval or disapproval of a call or play.

3. Revealing Expectation of Trick Result

To indicate the expectation or intention of winning or losing a trick that has not been completed.

4. Pertinent Comment or Act during Auction or Play

To comment or act during the auction or play to call attention to a significant incident thereof, or to the state of the score, or to the number of tricks still required for success.

5. Volunteering Information

To volunteer information that should be given only in response to a question.

6. Staring at Other Players

To look intently at any other player during the auction or play, or at another player's hand as for the purpose of seeing his cards or observing the place from which he draws a card (but it is not improper to act on information acquired by inadvertently seeing an opponent's card).

7. Deliberate Variation of Tempo

To vary the normal tempo of bidding or play for the purpose of disconcerting the other players.

8. Unnecessary Departure from Table

To leave the table needlessly before the round is called.

IV. PARTNERSHIP AGREEMENTS

A. Concealed Partnership Agreements

It is improper to convey information to partner by means of a call or play based on special partnership agreement, whether explicit or implicit, unless such information is fully and freely available to the opponents (see Law 40).

B. Violations of Partnership Agreements

It is not improper for a player to violate an announced partnership agreement, so long as his partner is unaware of the violation (but habitual violations within a partnership may create implicit agreements, which must be disclosed). No player has the obligation to disclose to the opponents that he has violated an announced agreement; and if the opponents are subsequently damaged, as through drawing a false inference from such violation, they are not entitled to redress.

C. Answering Questions on Partnership Agreements

When explaining the significance of partner's call or play in reply to an opponent's inquiry (see Law 20), a player should disclose all special information conveyed to him through partnership agreement or partnership experience; but he need not disclose inferences drawn from his general bridge knowledge and experience.

D. Correcting Errors in Explanation

1. Explainer Notices Own Error

If a player subsequently realizes that his own explanation was erroneous or incomplete, he should immediately call the Director (who will apply Law 21 or Law 40C).

2. Error Noticed By Explainer's Partner

It is improper for a player whose partner has given a mistaken explanation to correct the error immediately, or to indicate in any manner that a mistake has been made (he must not take any advantage of the unauthorized information so obtained). He is under no legal or moral obligation at any later time to inform the opponents that the explanation was erroneous. *

V. SPECTATORS

A. Conduct During Bidding or Play

1. Personal Reaction

A spectator must not display any reaction to the bidding or play while a hand is in progress (as by shifting his attention from one player's hand to another's).

---

* Two examples may clarify responsibilities of the players (and the Director) after a misleading explanation has been given to the opponents. In both examples following, North has opened one no trump and South, who holds a weak hand with long diamonds, has bid two diamonds, intending to sign off; North explains, however, in answer to West's inquiry, that South's bid is strong and artificial, asking for major suits.

Example 1—Mistaken Explanation

The actual partnership agreement is that two diamonds is a natural sign-off; the mistake was in North's explanation. This explanation is an infraction of law, since East-West are entitled to an accurate description of the North-South agreement (when this infraction results in damage to East-West, the Director should award an adjusted score). If North subsequently becomes aware of his mistake, it is to his advantage immediately to notify the Director—this may serve to minimize the damage caused by his infraction. South must do nothing to correct the mistaken explanation during the auction period; if he becomes declarer or dummy, he may then volunteer a correction of the explanation.

Example 2—Mistaken Bid

The partnership agreement is as explained—two diamonds is strong and artificial; the mistake was in South's bid. Here there is no infraction of law, since East-West did receive an accurate description of the North-South agreement; they have no claim to an accurate description of the North-South hands. (Regardless of damage, the Director should allow the result to stand.) South must not correct North's explanation (or notify the Director) immediately, and he has no responsibility to do so subsequently.

In both examples, South, having heard North's explanation, knows that his own two diamond bid has been misinterpreted. This knowledge is "improper information" (see Proprieties, Part II), so South must be careful not to base subsequent actions on this information (if he does, the Director should award an adjusted score). For instance, if North rebids two no trump South has the improper information that this bid merely denies a four-card holding in either major suit; but South's responsibility is to act as though North had made a strong game try opposite a weak response, showing maximum values.

2. Mannerisms or Remarks

During the round, a spectator must refrain from mannerisms or remarks of any kind (*including conversation with a player*).

3. Consideration for Players

A spectator must not in any way disturb a player.

B. Spectator Participation

A spectator may not call attention to any irregularity or mistake, nor speak on any question of fact or law except by request of the Director.

CHAPTER VIII

THE SCORE
◆◆◆◆◆◆

72. DUPLICATE CONTRACT BRIDGE SCORING

A. Authorized Scoring

The Rubber Bridge scoring table applies to Duplicate Bridge with exceptions noted as follows:

B. Exceptions

1. Trick Points

Trick points scored on one board do not count toward making game on a board subsequently played.

2. Premium Points

Premium points are scored for making a part-score or game, not for winning a rubber.

3. Honors

Honors are not scored in match-point or international match-point play.

73. DUPLICATE BRIDGE SCORING TABLE

TRICK SCORE

Scored by declarer's side, if the contract is fulfilled:

		IF TRUMPS ARE		
For each odd trick	♣	◇	♡	♠
bid and made				
Undoubled	20	20	30	30
Doubled	40	40	60	60
Redoubled	80	80	120	120

	AT A NO TRUMP CONTRACT		
	Undoubled	*Doubled*	*Redoubled*
For the first odd trick			
bid and made	40	80	160
For each additional			
odd trick	30	60	120

A trick score of 100 points or more, made on one board, is GAME. A trick score of less than 100 points is PART-SCORE.

PREMIUM SCORE

Scored by declarer's side:

SLAMS

For making a SLAM	*Not vulnerable*	*Vulnerable*
Small Slam (12 tricks)		
bid and made	500	750
Grand Slam (all 13 tricks)		
bid and made	1,000	1,500

OVERTRICKS

For each OVERTRICK	*Not vulnerable*	*Vulnerable*
(tricks made in		
excess of the contract)		
Undoubled	Trick Value	Trick Value
Doubled	100	200
Redoubled	200	400

PREMIUMS FOR GAME, PART-SCORE, FULFILLING CONTRACT

For making GAME, vulnerable 500
For making GAME, not vulnerable 300
For making any PART-SCORE 50
For making any doubled or redoubled contract 50

HONORS

Scored by either side at total-point play, not at match-point play:
For holding four of the five trump HONORS
  (A, K, Q, J, 10) in one hand 100
For holding all five trump HONORS
  (A, K, Q, J, 10) in one hand 150
For holding all four ACES in one hand
  at a no trump contract 150

UNDERTRICK PENALTIES

Scored by declarer's *opponents* if the contract is *not* fulfilled:

UNDERTRICKS
(tricks by which declarer falls
short of the contract)

	NOT VULNERABLE		
	Undoubled	Doubled	Redoubled
For first undertrick	50	100	200
For each additional undertrick	50	200	400
	VULNERABLE		
	Undoubled	Doubled	Redoubled
For first undertrick	100	200	400
For each additional undertrick	100	300	600

74. METHODS OF SCORING

A. Match-Point Scoring

In match-point scoring each contestant is awarded, for scores made by different contestants who have played the same board and whose scores are compared with his: two scoring units (match points or half match points) for each score inferior to his, one scoring unit for each score equal to his, and zero scoring units for each score superior to his.

B. International Match-Point Scoring

In international match-point scoring, on each board the total point difference (not including honors) between the two scores compared is converted into IMPs according to the following scale:

Difference in points	IMP	Difference in points	IMP
20– 40	1	750– 890	13
50– 80	2	900–1090	14
90–120	3	1100–1290	15
130–160	4	1300–1490	16
170–210	5	1500–1740	17
220–260	6	1750–1990	18
270–310	7	2000–2240	19
320–360	8	2250–2490	20
370–420	9	2500–2990	21
430–490	10	3000–3490	22
500–590	11	3500–3990	23
600–740	12	4000 and up	24

C. Total Point Scoring

In total point scoring, the net total point score (including honors) of all boards played is the score for each contestant.

D. Special Scoring Methods

Special scoring methods are permissible, if approved by the sponsoring organization. In advance of any contest the sponsoring organization should publish conditions of contest detailing conditions of entry, methods of scoring, determination of winners, breaking of ties, etc.

75. TRICKS WON

A. Agreement on Tricks Won

The number of tricks won should be agreed upon before all four hands have been returned to the board.

B. Disagreement on Tricks Won

If a subsequent disagreement arises, the Director must be called. No correction may be made unless the Director is called before the round has ended (see Laws 8 and 71).

C. Error in Score

1. Correction Period Specified

An error in computing or tabulating the agreed-upon score, whether made by a player or scorer, may be corrected until the expiration of the period specified for such corrections by the sponsoring organization.

2. Correction Period Not Specified

Unless otherwise specified by the sponsoring organization, the correction period expires 30 minutes after the official score has been completed and made available for inspection.

CHAPTER IX

TOURNAMENT SPONSORSHIP

◆◆◆◆◆◆

76. SPONSORING ORGANIZATION

A sponsoring organization conducting an event under these Laws has the following duties and powers:

A. Tournament Director

To appoint the tournament Director. If there is no tournament Director, the players should designate one of their own number to perform his functions.

B. Advance Arrangements

To make advance arrangements for the tournament, including playing quarters, accommodations, and equipment.

C. Session Times

To establish the date and time of each session.

D. Conditions of Entry

To establish the conditions of entry.

E. Supplementary Regulations

To publish or announce regulations supplementary to, but not in conflict with, these Laws.

CHAPTER X

TOURNAMENT DIRECTOR

◆◆◆◆◆◆
Section One

Responsibilities

77. DUTIES AND POWERS

A. Official Status

The director is the official representative of the sponsoring organization.

B. Restrictions and Responsibilities
1. Technical Management
The director is responsible for the technical management of the tournament.
2. Observance of Laws and Regulations
The director is bound by these Laws and by supplementary regulations announced by the sponsoring organization.
C. Director's Duties and Powers
The director's duties and powers normally include the following:
1. Assistants
To appoint assistants, as required to perform his duties.
2. Entries
To accept and list entries.
3. Conditions of Play
To establish suitable conditions of play, and to announce them to the contestants.
4. Discipline
To maintain discipline and to insure the orderly progress of the game.
5. Law
To administer and interpret these Laws.
6. Errors
To rectify any error or irregularity of which he becomes aware.
7. Penalties
To assess penalties when applicable.
8. Waiver of Penalties
To waive penalties, at his discretion, upon the request of the non-offending side.
9. Disputes
To adjust disputes, and to refer disputed matters to the appropriate committee when required.
10. Scores
To collect scores and tabulate results.
11. Reports
To report results to the sponsoring organization for official record.
D. Delegation of Duties
The Director may delegate any of the duties listed in C to assistants, but he is not thereby relieved of responsibility for their correct performance.

78. RECTIFICATION OF ERRORS OF PROCEDURE

A. Director's Duty
It is the duty of the Director to rectify errors of procedure and to maintain the progress of the game in a manner that is not contrary to these Laws.
B. Rectification of Error
To rectify an error in procedure the Director may:
1. Assignment of Adjusted Score
Assign an adjusted score as permitted by these Laws.
2. Specify Time of Play
Require or postpone the play of a board.
3. Reservation of Decision
Reserve his decision on any point of fact or law.

79. NOTIFICATION OF THE RIGHT TO APPEAL

If the Director believes that a review of his decision on a point of fact or exercise of his discretionary power might be in order (as when he assigns an adjusted score under Law 12), he should advise a contestant of his right to appeal.

Section Two

Rulings

80. RULINGS ON AGREED FACTS

When the Director is called to rule upon a point of law, procedure, or propriety, in which the facts are agreed upon, he should rule as follows:
A. No Penalty
If no penalty is prescribed by law, and there is no occasion for him to exercise his discretionary powers, he should direct the players to proceed with the auction or play.
B. Penalty Under Law
If a case is clearly covered by a law that specifies *a* penalty for the irregularity, he should assess that penalty and see that it is paid.
C. Player's Option
If a law gives a player a choice from among two or more penalties, the Director should explain the options and see that a penalty is selected and paid.
D. Director's Option
If the law gives the Director a choice between a specified penalty and the award of an adjusted score, he should attempt to restore equity, resolving any doubtful point in favor of the non-offending side.
E. Discretionary Penalty
If an irregularity has occurred for which no penalty is assessed by law, the Director may award an adjusted score.

81. RULINGS ON DISPUTED FACTS

When the Director is called upon to rule upon a point of law, procedure, or propriety, in which the facts are not agreed upon, he should proceed as follows:
A. Director's Assessment
If the Director is satisfied that he has ascertained the facts, he should rule accordingly.
B. Facts Not Determined
If the Director is unable to determine the facts to his satisfaction, he must make a ruling that will permit play to continue, and notify the players of their right to appeal.

Section Three

Correction of Irregularities

82. ADJUSTED SCORE IN TEAM PLAY

A. Normal Play Possible
When an irregularity occurs in team play, if these Laws provide a rectification that will permit normal play of the board, the Director should rule acordingly.
B. Normal Play Impossible
When no rectification will permit normal play of the board:
1. Time Available

If time permits, the Director should substitute a new board to be played at both tables:

(a) Equal Fault

When neither team is at fault or if both teams have contributed to the error, or

(b) Board Not Played

When the teammates of the players involved have not yet played the board.

2. No Time Available

When time will not permit the substitution of a new board, the Director should assign an adjusted score.

3. Board Played at Other Table

When the board has been played at the other table, the Director should assign an adjusted score, taking into consideration in his adjustment any unusually favorable result obtained by the non-offending team.

83. FOULED BOARD

A. Definition

A board is considered to be 'fouled' if the Director determines that one or more cards were misplaced in the board, in such manner that contestants who should have had a direct score comparison did not play the board in identical form.

B. Scoring the Fouled Board

In scoring a fouled board the Director determines as closely as possible which scores were made on the board in its correct form, and which in the changed form. He divides the score on that basis into two groups, and rates each group separately as provided in the regulations of the sponsoring organization.

Section Four

Penalties

84. AWARD OF INDEMNITY POINTS

In a pair or individual event, when a non-offending contestant is required to take an adjusted score through no fault or choice of his own, such contestant should be awarded a minimum of 60% of the match points available to him on that board, or the percentage of match points he earned on boards actually played during the session, if that percentage was greater than 60%.

85. PENALTIES IN INDIVIDUAL EVENTS

In individual events, the Director should enforce the penalty provisions of these Laws, and the provisions requiring the award of adjusted scores, equally against both members of the offending side, even though only one of them may be responsible for the irregularity. But the Director, in awarding adjusted scores, should not assess procedural penalty points against the offender's partner, if, in the Director's opinion, he is in no way responsible for the violation.

86. PROCEDURAL PENALTIES

A. Director's Authority

The Director, in addition to enforcing the penalty provisions of these Laws, should also assess penalties for any offense that unduly delays or obstructs the game, inconveniences other contestants, violates correct procedure, or requires the award of adjusted scores.

B. Offenses Subject to Penalty

Offenses subject to penalty include but are not limited to:

1. Tardiness

Arrival of a contestant after the specified starting time.

2. Slow Play

Any unduly slow play by a contestant.

3. Loud Discussion

Any discussion of the bidding, play, or result of a board, which may be overheard at another table.

4. Comparing Scores

Any comparison of scores with another contestant during a session.

5. Touching Another's Cards

Any touching or handling of cards belonging to another player (Law 7).

6. Misplacing Cards in Board

Placing one or more cards in an incorrect pocket of the board.

7. Errors in Procedure

Any error in procedure (such as failure to count cards in one's hand, playing the wrong board, etc.) that requires an adjusted score for any contestant.

8. Failure to Comply

Any failure to comply promptly with tournament regulations, or with any instruction of the Director.

9. Improper Behavior

Any improper or discourteous behavior.

87. SUSPENSION AND DISQUALIFICATION OF PLAYERS

A. Director's Power to Suspend

In performing his duty to maintain order and discipline, the Director is specifically empowered to suspend a player for the current session or any part thereof (the Director's decision under this clause is final).

B. Director's Right to Disqualify

The Director is specifically empowered to disqualify a player, pair, or team for cause, subject to approval by the Tournament Committee or sponsoring organization.

CHAPTER XI

APPEALS

88. RIGHT TO APPEAL

A. Contestant's Right

A contestant may appeal for a review of any ruling made by the Director or by one of his assistants.

B. Time of Appeal

Any appeal of a Director's ruling must be made not later than thirty (30) minutes after the conclusion of the session during which the ruling was made.

C. How to Appeal

All appeals must be made through the Director.

D. Concurrence of Appellants

An appeal shall not be heard unless both members of a pair (except in an individual contest), or *the* captain of a team, concurs in appealing. An absent member shall be deemed to concur.

89. PROCEDURES OF APPEAL

A. No Appeals Committee

The Chief Director should hear and rule upon all appeals if there is no Tournament or Appeals committee, or when a committee cannot meet without disturbing the orderly progress of the tournament.

B. Appeals Committee Available

If a committee is available:

1. Appeal Concerns Law

The Chief Director should hear and rule upon such part of the appeal as deals solely with the law. His ruling may be appealed to the committee.

2. All Other Appeals

The Chief Director must refer all other appeals to the committee for adjudication.

3. Adjudication of Appeals

In adjudicating appeals the committee may exercise all powers assigned by these Laws to the Director, except that the committee may not overrule the Director on a point of law or regulations, or on exercise of his disciplinary powers.

C. Appeal to National Authority

After the preceding remedies have been exhausted, further appeal may be taken to the national authority (on a point of law in the ACBL, the Laws Commission of the ACBL, P.O. Box 161192, Memphis TN 38186).

For home play, see also HOME STYLE BRIDGE, PARTY CONTRACT BRIDGE, PIVOT BRIDGE, PROGRESSIVE BRIDGE.

LAY DOWN. Verb: (1) to put the dummy's cards on the table; (2) to play a (high) card with the assurance of winning that particular trick.

LAY-DOWN. A colloquialism for a hand that can, virtually, be claimed for a successful contract as soon as the dummy is exposed. However, surprising things happen to lay-down hands with disconcerting frequency. PIANOLA is a synonym.

LEA SYSTEM. A 1♣ system devised by Robert H. Lea of Denver. 1♣ is bid with nearly all hands with 12 or more points. Responses are on a step system: 1◊, 0–5; 1♡, 6–8; 1♠, 9–11, etc. 1 NT openings are weak. Other one openings show a six-card suit and 15 or 16 points including distribution.

Notrump and minor suit overcalls show two-suited hands in all circumstances. Notrump shows the two low-ranking unbid suits. Diamonds shows the two high-ranking unbid suits. Clubs shows the high-ranking suit and the low-ranking suit. If 1 NT is overcalled, the opener is assumed to have clubs. Therefore 2♣ over 1 NT, for example, would show diamonds and spades.

LEAD. The first card played to a trick. See LAWS (Law 44).

LEAD-DIRECTING BID. A bid made primarily for the purpose of indicating a desired suit for partner to lead initially against an impending adverse contract. North holds, for example,

    ♠ 10–x–x
    ♡ x–x
    ◊ A–K–x–x
    ♣ x–x–x–x

and the bidding has proceeded:

WEST	NORTH	EAST	SOUTH
	Pass	1♡	1♠
2♡			

A bid of 3◊ by North in this position is a lead-directing bid. He has no intention of playing a diamond contract, and will retreat to 3♠ if doubled. He is merely maneuvering to secure a diamond opening lead if the final contract is in hearts.

LEAD-DIRECTING DOUBLE. The most frequent case is a double of a voluntarily bid contract at 3 NT by the player not on lead. In current practice the double requests in order of priority: (a) the lead of the opening leader's suit; (b) the lead of the doubler's bid suit; (c) the lead of the first suit bid by dummy. However, it may not be right to lead dummy's suit if it has been rebid; and some authorities leave to judgment the situation in which both defenders have bid a suit. See also FISHER DOUBLE.

The lead-directing double may occur at the part-score level:

		(a)	
WEST	NORTH	EAST	SOUTH
			Pass
Pass	1◊	Pass	2 NT
Pass	Pass	Dbl	

		(b)	
WEST	NORTH	EAST	SOUTH
			1◊
Pass	1 NT	Pass	Pass
Dbl			

In each case the double is suggesting the lead of a diamond.

A double of 3 NT when neither side has bid a suit implies that the doubler has a solid suit which can be run immediately. The opening leader will tend to lead a short major suit in which he has no honor.

The double of a voluntarily bid suit game often has the same implications as a LIGHTNER DOUBLE of a slam contract:

WEST	NORTH	EAST	SOUTH
			1♠
Pass	1♠	Pass	4♠
Dbl			

West probably has a void club, and is gambling that he will be able to get two club ruffs and defeat the contract.

A double of a conventional bid such as a response to BLACKWOOD has obvious lead-directing implications. There is also a negative inference: a player who does not double such a bid is likely to prefer another lead. See DOUBLES OF ARTIFICIAL BIDS FOR PENALTIES.

LEAD-INHIBITING BID. A tactical bid, in the nature of a semi-psychic call, which is designed to prevent the opponents from leading a specific suit. For example:

♠ K Q 6
♡ K J 7
♢ 8 5 2
♣ A Q 7 5

The normal opening bid should be 1 ♣ followed by a rebid of 1 NT. An opening bid of 1 ◇, made with the idea of discouraging a diamond lead against notrump, would be a lead-inhibiting bid.

Another common form of a lead-inhibiting bid:

♠ —
♡ K 7 6 5 2
♢ 9 5
♣ A K 8 5 3 2

After an opening bid of 1 ◇ by partner, one immediately thinks in terms of six or seven. A bid of 3 ◇ with this hand might stop the opponents from cashing the first two diamond tricks.

LEAD OUT OF TURN. An irregularity in play. See LAWS (Law 54 for opening lead out of turn. Law 55 for declarer's lead out of turn, and Law 56 for defender's lead out of turn).

LEAD OUT OF WRONG HAND. (by declarer). A lead out of turn by declarer, leading either from his or dummy's hand incorrectly. See LAWS (Law 55).

LEAD THROUGH. To lead through a particular opponent is to initiate the lead in the hand to the right of that opponent, forcing that opponent to play to the trick before the leader's partner plays to it. See THROUGH STRENGTH; UP TO WEAKNESS.

LEAD THROUGH STRENGTH. See THROUGH STRENGTH.

LEAD UP TO. To lead with the object of enabling partner's hand to win a trick because of weakness in the hand on the leader's right. Occasionally, a strong hand may be led up to, when the object is not necessarily to win the trick. A lead is always "up to" the hand on the leader's right. To "lead up to" is always leading "up to" the fourth hand. See UP TO WEAKNESS.

LEAD UP TO WEAKNESS. See UP TO WEAKNESS.

LEADER. The person or player who first plays to any given trick, "as opening leader."

LEADING FROM HONORS. See ATTACKING LEAD, JOURNALIST LEADS, OPENING LEADS, THIRD HIGHEST LEAD.

LEAGUE. An organized association, which may be on a local, regional, national, or international scale. Members of the league may be individuals, clubs, teams, or other groupings. In this volume "the League" normally refers to the American Contract Bridge League. In England, "league" is commonly used as a synonym for ROUND-ROBIN.

LEAP. A bid missing several levels, generally to

game or slam, either in support of partner or in a new suit, inviting partner to pass at his next opportunity. Alternatively, a leap to a slam convention may be made.

LEAVE IN. See PENALTY DOUBLE.

LEAVES. One of the suits in early European PLAYING CARDS (a translation of German and Slavic words). See PACK.

LEBANESE BRIDGE FEDERATION (FÉDÉRATION LIBANAISE DE BRIDGE). Founded in 1949 by three Beirut bridge clubs, in 1982 the federation had approximately 280 members. The Federation usually sponsors teams to compete in the European Championships and acted as host for the 1962 event in Beirut.

Officers, 1982:
President: George Fayad
Secretary: Gaby Merhy, P.O. Box 54,
  Beirut, Lebanon

LEBENSOHL CONVENTION. See LEBENSOLD CONVENTION.

LEBENSOLD APPLICATIONS. The Lebensold idea can be used, and often is, in two important situations.

(1) *Responding to double of weak two-bids:* If a weak 2 ♠ bid is doubled, a suit response at the three-level has an uncomfortably wide range in standard bidding:

WEST	NORTH	EAST	SOUTH
2 ♠	Dbl	Pass	3 ♡

North cannot tell whether his partner has eight points or none at all. With a good hand he must guess whether to continue to game. Using Lebensold the responder promises moderate values, perhaps 6–9 points or the equivalent. With a very weak hand he must bid 2 NT, forcing a 3 ♣ bid from opener. Responder can pass 3 ♣ with length in that suit, or pick another suit. If the doubler is so strong that he hopes for game opposite a very weak South hand, he can disregard the instruction to bid 3 ♣.

(2) *Responding to a reverse:* In modern versions of Standard American the reverse after a one-level response is forcing:

NORTH	SOUTH
1 ♣	1 ♠
2 ♡	

The Lebensold idea allows a 2 NT bid to be used on all weak responding hands, showing a desire to play at the three level. North must bid 3 ♣, and South passes or corrects according to the nature of his hand. Other responses are forcing, allowing a natural development of the bidding to game or slam. If the opener has bid both minor suits, the fourth-suit bid can be used instead of 2 NT to show weakness.

LEBENSOLD CONVENTION. A convention first described by GEORGE BOEHM of New York and attributed by him, wrongly, to KEN LEBENSOLD of New York. It deals with the problem created for the partner of an opening notrump bidder following an overcall. The mechanism varies depending on whether the overcall shows one suit or two and whether it is made at the two level or three level.

Over a natural two-level overcall, a double is for penalties, a two-level suit bid is non-forcing, a three-level suit bid is forcing and a 2 NT bid forces opener to rebid 3 ♣. Responder can pass opener's 3 ♣ bid if he has a weak hand with long clubs or can rebid; if he rebids a suit below the rank of the suit overcalled, it is a signoff; if he rebids a suit above the rank of the suit overcalled, it is invitational to game.

A cuebid is Stayman while a relay to 3 ♣ followed by a cuebid is also Stayman! The difference is that one shows a stopper in the opponent's suit and the other denies it. Direct jumps to 3 NT and 3 NT following a relay to 3 ♣ are similar — raises to game with or without a stopper. It is up to the individual partnerships to decide which sequence shows the stopper and which denies.

Over a two-suited overcall such as LANDY, the double is penalty-oriented in at least one of the suits shown by the overcall. The two-level bid of a suit not shown by the overcall is not forcing, while the three-level bid of such a suit is forcing to game. Cuebids are generally forcing to game. Only when the overcall shows two specific suits and responder cuebids the cheaper may the partnership stop below game.

Over a three-level overcall the double is a takeout for any suits not shown by the overcall. Suit bids at the three level are forcing to game.

Lebensold has been modified to extend its use to bidding over opponents' weak two-bids. After a takeout double of a weak two, a new suit at the three level is forward-going. With a bad hand responder can bid 2 NT, forcing 3 ♣. If responder corrects to a suit below the weak two-bid suit, it is a signoff. This is especially helpful when the takeout doubler holds a hand which is good enough to raise a fair hand to game but not good enough to make game opposite a bad one.

LEBHAR TROPHY. For the NAC Mixed Team Championship. Donated by Bertram Lebhar, Jr., in 1948, in memory of his wife Evelyn; a replacement for the BARCLAY TROPHY. Contested at the Summer NAC, under which heading past results are listed.

LEBOVIC ASKING BID. A convention devised by WOLF LEBOVIC of Toronto, and publicized by SAMMY KEHELA of Toronto; when two or three suits have been bid and a minor suit has been agreed as trumps, a double jump in an unbid suit asks about control in that suit. The last bid in each of the following auctions would be a Lebovic asking bid.

(a)		(b)	
SOUTH	NORTH	SOUTH	NORTH
1 ♣	1 ♡	1 ♠	2 ◇
1 ♠	3 ♣	3 ◇	4 ♡
4 ◇			

The responder to the asking bid answers as follows: with a singleton in the asked suit he bids six of the trump suit, with king doubleton or longer he bids 4 NT, with the ace or a void he bids the asked suit, and with none of the above he makes the minimum bid in the trump suit.

LEDGER. See BACK SCORE.

LEFT-HAND PLAYER. The player on declarer's left. In assessing penalties there has been a differentiation between left- and right-hand opponents as respects power or right to invoke penalties. Generally, however, the term is restricted to use in describing situations on play.

An alternative term is left-hand opponent, abbreviated to LHO.

LEG. A colloquial rubber bridge term to indicate a game already won. Partners who have a leg are vulnerable.

LEGAL. Applied to any call or play not in contravention of the mechanics of the game as set forth in the laws. A legal convention is one that is listed properly on the convention card that is either approved by the tournament committee or by the tournament director for use in that event. See LAWS, Sections I, II, and III, and PROPRIETIES.

LEGAL OPPORTUNITY. See LAWS (Law 50).

LEGHORN DIAMOND (LIVORNO) SYSTEM. Similar to the ROMAN SYSTEM, developed by BENITO BIANCHI and Giuseppe Messina and used successfully in many EUROPEAN CHAMPIONSHIPS. The chief features are:

1 ♣ opening is forcing and may show any of four different types of hand: (1) 12–15 points, balanced distribution and no five-card major; (2) unbalanced with a long minor, 12–20 points, possibly with a side four-card major if the point range is 12 or 13; (3) unbalanced with a long major and no side four-card major or five-card minor, 16–20 points; or (4) a three-suiter with a singleton or void in a major, 12–13 points.

2 ◇ (natural) and 1 ◇ are both negative responses, showing less than 8 points. 1 ♡ and 1 ♠ responses are positive, 8 points or more, and 1 and 2 NT deny a four-card major and are limited to 8–10 and 11–12 points respectively. Jump suit response are natural and game forcing, except 3 ♣, which is forcing for only one round and suggests 3 NT. A jump to 2 ◇ may be made on a four-card suit if responder intends to CANAPÉ into a major.

If 1 ♣ is doubled, a pass is equivalent to the negative response and shows four-card support for clubs, although responder may have 8–11 points with three clubs in which case he will double, cuebid or bid notrump at his next turn; nonjump suit responses are limited to a maximum of 9 points; 1 NT shows 10–11; and a redouble or a jump response shows 12 points or more. If 1 ♣ is overcalled, a raise to 2 ♣ shows a five-card suit and 5–7 points; a cuebid is strong and asks for a stopper; one-level suit responses show 8–11; and two-level suit responses normally show 12 points or more.

The auction tends to develop naturally after the initial response. Minimum major-suit rebids by opener usually describe the weak balanced hand, but he may have the minimum major-minor two-suiter or the three-suiter. With either of the unbalanced hands, opener makes a simple rebid in a minor with

12-17, jumps to the two-level in a major with 16-17, or jumps to the three-level in any suit with 18-20. After a positive response, a jump rebid by opener to 2 NT shows exactly 15 points. After responding in a major, responder's second suit is his long suit.

1 ◊ opening is forcing and shows either a balanced hand with 19 points or more, or an unbalanced hand that is about a trick short of game, possibly a three-suiter with at least 20 points.

Suit responses show controls by steps (king = 1 control; ace = 2 controls). 1 ♡ shows no controls; 1 ♠ shows 1 control, and so on. With no controls but scattered queens and jacks, responder bids 1 NT with 5-6 points or 2 NT with 7 or more. If 1 ◊ is doubled or overcalled, a pass is substituted for the first step and redouble or double for the second step.

A simple notrump rebid by opener describes a balanced hand with 19-21 points and a jump notrump rebid shows 22 points or more. If opener is unbalanced, he usually makes a minimum rebid in a suit, over which responder rebids conventionally by eight steps to show support. A new suit by opener is then a second asking bid, and the responses are on the same scale for that suit. After responder has made his support-showing step response to opener's second suit, a bid of the cheapest denomination by opener is a relay asking responder to choose between opener's suits.

1 ♡ and 1 ♠ openings are natural but show two different types of hand: (1) less than 16 points with a five-card or longer major; or (2) a two-suiter, usually a four-card major and a five-card or longer side suit, with 14-19 points. To distinguish between the two types, opener normally rebids his major with the first type of hand, even if he has a side four-card suit, and bids his second suit (jumping with 17-19 points) with hand type two.

1 NT opening is standard (16-18) and denies a five-card major. A 2 ♠ response is STAYMAN and other two-level responses are weak transfers to the next higher-ranking suit. The transfers to 2 ♡ and 2 ♠ are presumed to be weak unless responder rebids. A rebid of 2 NT by responder is BLACKWOOD. 2 ♠ is ostensibly a transfer to 3 ♣, but may be preparatory to a sign-off in diamonds. Jump suit responses are strong and show interest in slam, and direct jumps to 4 ◊ and 4 ♡ are transfers to 4 ♡ and 4 ♠ respectively. A jump to 4 ♠ shows 7 or more points with at least 5-5 distribution in the major suits. If opener has three or four aces and kings in the major suits his rebid is 4 ◊, allowing responder to decide whether to sign off or to develop the auction with special asking bids. This structure of responding is also used after a 1 ◊ opening and a 1 NT rebid.

2 ♣ and 2 ◊ openings show three-suited hands (4-4-4-1 or 5-4-4-0 distribution) with 12-16 and 17-19 points respectively. Responses and rebids are similar to the Roman System.

2 ♡ and 2 ♠ openings show two-suited hands, the bid major and a four- or five-card minor, with 9-12 points. 2 NT is the only forcing response and compels opener to bid his minor, after which a new suit by responder asks opener to define his hand pattern. Opener rebids his major with a six-card suit, rebids his minor with 5-5 distribution, bids a three-card

fragment or bids 3 NT with 5-4-2-2 distribution.

2 NT opening shows at least five cards in each minor with 14-16 high card points. 4 ♣ and 4 ◊ are the only strong responses and request opener to bid a six-card minor if he has one, or (with 5-5 distribution) to bid 4 ♡ with a minimum and 4 ♠ with a maximum.

3 NT opening is BLACKWOOD. During the auction 3 NT is also Blackwood whenever it is an illogical bid, such as 1 ♠-3 NT, or 1 ◊ -1 ♠-3 NT.

Defensive bidding follows the general Italian style. Overcalls are made freely, and a takeout double shows opening bid strength but no particular distribution. In response to a double, the next suit may be a HERBERT NEGATIVE. With the perfect distribution for a takeout double (4-4-4-1 or 5-4-4-0), the overcaller cuebids with 12-16 points, or jump cuebids with more than 16, except over a 1 ♠ opening; a 2 ♠ overcall over 1 ♠ is equivalent to a 2 ♠ opening. If an opponent preempts at the three-level, a 3 NT overcall shows two suits of the same rank and a double shows two suits of different rank. Jump overcalls are intermediate. See UNUSUAL NOTRUMP.

LENGTH. The number of cards held in a particular suit, usually referring to five or more; as opposed to STRENGTH, the high card values held in a suit. See DISTRIBUTIONAL VALUES.

LENGTH OF SESSION. A session is generally 13 rounds of two boards each, and experienced players should complete this in about 3½ hours. In no case may a tournament of the ACBL consist of less than 22 or more than 30 boards in pair competition. One board to a round may be used only in certain one-session team events or in individual contests; in some team events, particularly in head-on knockout competition, late rounds may be more than 30 boards. See ACBL HANDBOOK.

LENGTH SIGNALS (also called count signals). A method by which one defender can indicate to his partner the length held in a particular suit. The standard procedure is to play high-low with an even number of cards, and play the lowest with an odd number of cards. (The reverse procedure, called UPSIDE-DOWN-SIGNALS, has come strongly into favor in recent years.)

The normal application occurs when the declarer attacks a suit in which he is strong, but a signal can be made in a suit which is both led and dominated by the defenders. (See FOSTER ECHO.) In a high-level contract, the opening leader may need to know his partner's length in order to judge which tricks can be cashed quickly.

Accurate suit-length signals are the key to a golden treasury of defensive plays, seemingly brilliant, but in fact within the compass of everyone who is willing to count the cards. After a few tricks have been played, good defensive signalers may know nearly all about the unseen hands and should be able to play just as accurately as declarer, if not more so.

Everyone agrees that when a defender *does* echo, he shows an even number of cards. And when he does not? Does that necessarily mean an odd number? Or has he decided not to echo for fear of giving information to the declarer? And why, if at all, is it permissible to try to mislead declarer by issuing a false signal?

It is possible for players to agree about every conceivable situation, but such an agreement is unethical if not explained to the opponents, and time-wasting if it is. Best is a commonsense approach which need not be announced at all.

When following a suit played by the declarer, always echo to show an even number of cards *unless it appears that this may help declarer*; then, don't echo at all. But occasional false signals should be made in situations where it will not matter that partner is misled. See also TRUMP SIGNAL.

In this connection, there are two valid psychological points. First, it is not wise to try to outsmart the declarer continually by making false signals. The declarer usually comes out of a guessing game better than the defenders, and the reason is not hard to see. When the declarer has the lead, he has command of the play; he can come out of a huddle with a "rap-rap" which leaves the defenders no time for thought — and of course, a false signal has to be made smoothly and urbanely, if it is not to boomerang. So, false signals should be avoided unless the play has been thought out well in advance. But some false signals *must* be made: it is essential not to become typed as a player whose echoes are always dependable.

The second psychological point arises when a defender is afraid to signal for fear of tipping his hand to a declarer. If it seems a borderline case, it is better to signal. Declarers are desperately afraid of looking silly in a situation like this:

```
              K 9 5 3
  10 8 6 2                J 7
              A Q 4
```

South plays the ace and queen, and West, caught on the wrong foot, echoes with the 6 and 2. Vain declarers, and those with critical partners, will not finesse dummy's 9 on the third round. (Although the finesse is the percentage play; see RESTRICTED CHOICE.) They would rather be wrong five times in a situation like this than suffer the ignominy of letting East make a trick with J-10-x. In a world of bluff and double-bluff, this human failing is something tangible to hold onto.

Usually the defenders have to cooperate if declarer is to be led astray. In a situation like the following, declarer is more likely to go wrong if both players false-card:

```
              ♠ J 10 2
              ♡ J 9 8 3
              ◇ 9 3
              ♣ 9 5 4 3
  ♠ A 9 4              ♠ 3
  ♡ A 10 7             ♡ K 6 5 4 2
  ◇ Q J 6 2            ◇ 10 7 4
  ♣ K Q 10             ♣ J 8 6 2
              ♠ K Q 8 7 6 5
              ♡ Q
              ◇ A K 8 5
              ♣ A 7
```

West's 1 ◇ opening is passed to South, who lands in 4 ♠. West leads the ♣ K and South holds off in order to create a ruffing communication between dummy and the closed hand. South wins the second club and plays diamonds, intending to ruff the third round low and the fourth high. If East is awake, he will try to persuade declarer to ruff both diamonds high and rely on a 2-2 trump break. When South plays the ◇ A and ◇ K, East plays high-low with the 10 and 4. But West must keep up with the ball too, and withhold his normal suit-length signal; he should play the 2 followed by the 6, supporting the theory that the diamonds are 5-2.

For a method by which declarer can plan to take advantage of length signals, see DISCOVERY.

Albert Dormer

LENZ TROPHY. For the World Par-Point Championships of the WBF, donated in memory of SIDNEY LENZ by his long-time secretary, Mrs. Adele Hess. See WORLD PAR CONTESTS for results.

LESSON HANDS. Bridge teachers regularly offer prepared deals to their pupils, illustrating points in bidding and play covered by their lessons.

LEVEL. The "odd-trick" count in excess of the book, that is, each trick over six. Thus an overcall of 2 ♣ is a bid made at the two level and a contract to make eight tricks. A 4 ♠ opening bid is said to be made at the four level. See OVERCALLS.

LEVENTRITT TROPHY. For the Life Master Pairs consolation event; donated by PETER A. LEVENTRITT of New York in 1950. It was contested until 1972 at the Summer NAC under which heading past results are listed.

LEVINREW. A system devised by GEORGE LEVINREW of Jerusalem, Israel, formerly of Brooklyn NY. The chief features are:

(1) Weak two-bids with a range of 9-12 points. New suit responses are forcing. 2 NT and single raises are encouraging.

(2) Major-suit openings promise five cards. 1 ♠, 1 ♡ and 1 ◇ show 15-23 points, including distribution. One-level rebids normally show 15-17, two-level rebids 18-20 and three-level rebids 21-23, but a single raise counts as a one-level rebid, and so on.

(3) A response to a suit-bid may have as little as 4 high-card points and can be artificial. A jump raise or a jump in a new suit is preemptive. 1 NT response is weak, showing a lower-ranking suit of at least six cards.

(4) 1 ♣ shows at least 12 points including distribution. A one-over-one response is not forcing.

(5) Weak notrump.

LIFE MASTER. The highest rank of player in the AMERICAN CONTRACT BRIDGE LEAGUE. (For qualification for this rank, see RANKING OF PLAYERS.) The category was created by the AMERICAN BRIDGE LEAGUE in 1936, and selection of the first Life Masters was based on national tournament successes, although a masterpoint program had been in effect since 1934. Initially, the rank was conferred on a group of 10 players, ranked in order according to the number and importance of their national victories, and an eleventh player was made Life Master shortly thereafter. The first 100 players to achieve the rank were:

1.	David Bruce	1936	47.	M. A. Lightman	1945
2.	Oswald Jacoby	1936	48.	Samuel Stayman	1945
3.	Howard Schenken	1936	49.	Edward N. Marcus	1945
4.	Waldemar K. von		50.	Charles A. Hall	1945
	Zedtwitz	1936	51.	Emily Folline	1946
5.	P. Hal Sims	1936	52.	Joseph E. Cain	1946
6.	B. Jay Becker	1936	53.	Harry Feinberg	1946
7.	Theodore		54.	Ambrose Casner	1946
	A. Lightman	1936	55.	Samuel Katz	1946
8.	Richard L. Frey	1936	56.	Jack Ehrlenbach	1946
9.	Michael T.		57.	J. Van Brooks	1946
	Gottlieb	1936	58.	Simon Rossant	1946
10.	Sam Fry, Jr.	1936	59.	Edward G.	
11.	Merwin D. Maier	1936		Ellenbogen	1946
12.	Charles S.		60.	Sidney B. Fink	1946
	Lochridge	1937	61.	Bertram	
13.	Charles H. Goren	1938		Lebhar, Jr.	1946
14.	A. Mitchell Barnes	1938	62.	Meyer Schleifer	1947
15.	Harry J.		63.	Louis Newman	1947
	Fishbein	1939	64.	Elinor Murdoch	1947
16.	Charles J.		65.	Paula Bacher	1947
	Solomon	1939	66.	Florence Stratford	1947
17.	Sally Young	1939	67.	Jules Bank	1947
18.	Fred D. Kaplan	1939	68.	William McGhee	1947
19.	John R.		69.	Maynard Adams	1947
	Crawford	1939	70.	Edith Kemp	1947
20.	Walter Jacobs	1939	71.	David Carter	1947
21.	Morrie Elis	1939	72.	Jack Cushing	1947
22.	Phil Abramsohn	1940	73.	Dr. A. Steinberg	1947
23.	Edward		74.	Jane Jaeger	1947
	Hymes, Jr.	1940	75.	Cecil Head	1947
24.	Alvin Landy	1940	76.	S. Garton	
25.	Helen Sobel Smith	1941		Churchill	1947
26.	Sherman Stearns	1941	77.	Edward S. Cohn	1947
27.	Robert A.		78.	John Carlin	1947
	McPherran	1941	79.	Lawrence Welch	1947
28.	Jeff Glick	1942	80.	Frank Weisbach	1947
29.	Arthur Glatt	1942	81.	Charlton Wallace	1944
30.	Dr. Richard		82.	Dr. Louis Mark	1947
	Ecker, Jr.	1942	83.	Edward Taylor	1947
31.	Albert Weiss	1942	84.	Dan Westerfield	1947
32.	Lee Hazen	1942	85.	Tobias Stone	1947
33.	Peggy Solomon	1942	86.	Mark Hodges	1947
34.	Alvin Roth	1942	87.	Leo Roet	1947
35.	Sidney Silodor	1943	88.	Sol Mogal	1947
36.	Olive Peterson	1943	89.	Herbert Gerst	1947
37.	Margaret Wagar	1943	90.	Lewis Mathe	1947
38.	Peter A.		91.	Ludwig Kabakjian	1947
	Leventritt	1943	92.	Gratian Goldstein	1947
39.	Edson T. Wood	1944	93.	Allen P. Harvey	1947
40.	Ralph Kempner	1944	94.	Lewis Jaeger	1947
41.	Arthur S.		95.	Mildred	
	Goldsmith	1944		Cunningham	1947
42.	Simon Becker	1944	96.	Elmer J. Schwartz	1947
43.	Stanley O. Fenkel	1944	97.	Linda Terry	1947
44.	George Rapee	1944	98.	Maurice Levin	1948
45.	Ruth Sherman	1944	99.	Dave Warner	1948
46.	Robert Appleyard	1945	100.	Ernest Rovere	1948

As of December 10, 1982 the ACBL had issued 35,162 Life Master cards. Of this number 31,630 were living, and the top 100 masterpoint holders were:

1.	Barry Crane	29,170	51.	Leslie Tsou	8,732
2.	Hermine Baron	20,396	52.	Lew Mathe	8,719
3.	Paul Soloway	19,214	53.	Erik Paulsen	8,716
4.	Ron Andersen	17,583	54.	G. Robert Nail	8,573
5.	Jim Jacoby	17,478	55.	Gunther Polak	8,553
6.	Mary Jane Farell	17,381	56.	Meyer Schleifer	8,538
7.	Alan Bell	16,773	57.	Paul Ivaska	8,523
8.	John Fisher	16,160	58.	Joan Remey	8,447
9.	Gaylor Kasle	15,938	59.	Marc Jacobus	8,438
10.	Mike Passell	15,247	60.	Eric Murray	8,410
11.	Mark Lair	13,910	61.	Jan Janitschke	8,324
12.	Morris Portugal	13,804	62.	Peter Pender	8,295
13.	Fred Hamilton	13,474	63.	Hugh MacLean	8,293
14.	Oswald Jacoby	12,412	64.	Victor Mitchell	8,285
15.	Gerald Caravelli	12,325	65.	Edith Kemp	8,225
16.	Al Roth	12,193	66.	Don Oakie	8,208
17.	Mike Lawrence	12,189	67.	Harold Guiver	8,186
18.	Kerri Shuman	12,071	68.	Michael Moss	8,178
19.	Bobby Wolff	12,028	69.	Sidney Lazard	8,102
20.	Mike Shuman	11,709	70.	Tom Hodapp	8,095
21.	Mark Blumenthal	11,510	71.	Jim Bennett	8,073
22.	Edgar Kaplan	11,316	72.	Alan Sontag	8,053
23.	Norman Kay	11,066	73.	David Berkowitz	8,032
24.	Eddie Wold	10,744	74.	Jo Morse	8,025
25.	Bob Hamman	10,639	75.	Gerald Bare	8,012
26.	Steve Robinson	10,555	76.	Jim Zimmerman	7,955
27.	Richard Henderson	10,521	77.	Betty Ann Kennedy	7,874
28.	Curtis Smith	10,384	78.	William Passell	7,832
29.	Carol Sanders	10,242	79.	Eddie Kantar	7,750
30.	Mike Smolen	10,127	80.	John Zilic	7,726
31.	Helen Portugal	10,055	81.	Paul Swanson	7,719
32.	Lou Bluhm	9,945	82.	Roger Bates	7,705
33.	Tom Sanders	9,804	83.	Chet Davis	7,676
34.	Garey Hayden	9,716	84.	Evan Bailey	7,644
35.	Jeff Meckstroth	9,599	85.	Chuck Lamprey	7,643
36.	Ethel Keohane	9,596	86.	Rhoda Walsh	7,596
37.	Mike Cappelletti	9,575	87.	Richard Walsh	7,560
38.	Peter Rank	9,498	88.	Ron Smith	7,544
39.	Cliff Bishop	9,362	89.	Billy Rosen	7,530
40.	Peter Weichsel	9,222	90.	Bobby Goldman	7,430
41.	Charles Coon	9,109	91.	Jon Wittes	7,411
42.	John Mohan	9,029	92.	Malvine Klausner	7,340
43.	V. Craig Janitschke	8,972	93.	Emma Jean Hawes	7,317
44.	Clarence Goppert	8,940	94.	Robert Morris	7,290
45.	Robert Sharp	8,900	95.	David Siebert	7,281
46.	Kathie Wei	8,879	96.	B. Jay Becker	7,279
47.	David Treadwell	8,868	97.	J. David King	7,236
48.	Kit Woolsey	8,855	98.	David Ashley	7,221
49.	Robert Lipsitz	8,838	99.	Richard Pavlicek	7,201
50.	Phil Leon	8,783	100.	Dorothy Hayden	
				Truscott	7,172

LIFE MASTER MEN'S PAIRS, NORTH AMERICAN CHAMPIONSHIP. See MOUSER TROPHY.

LIFE MASTER PAIRS, NORTH AMERICAN CHAMPIONSHIP. See VON ZEDTWITZ GOLD CUP.

LIFE MASTER WOMEN'S PAIRS, NORTH AMERICAN CHAMPIONSHIP. See SMITH TROPHY.

LIFT. A term meaning "raise."

LIGHTMAN TROPHY. For the charity event at the Spring NORTH AMERICAN CHAMPIONSHIPS, under which heading results are listed; presented in memory of M. A. LIGHTMAN of Memphis TN. First contested, under different circumstances, in 1958.

LIGHTNER DOUBLE. A lead-directing double of a slam contract. If competent opponents bid a slam voluntarily, it may be expected that they will fulfill their contract or fail by one trick. Thus a normal penalty double is unlikely to gain much. In 1929 the late THEODORE LIGHTNER of New York devised a more useful interpretation of this bid. A double by the hand not on lead is conventional. Partner is requested to choose an unusual lead which may result in the defeat of the slam. A conventional double of this sort excludes the lead of a trump, a suit bid by the defenders, or an unbid suit. The player who doubles expects to ruff the lead of a side suit mentioned by the opponents, or else to win two top tricks in that suit.

Some experts treat this double quite rigidly. They define the double to mean that partner must lead dummy's first-bid side suit. Other good players, including Lightner, interpret the bid more loosely. An unusual lead is requested and partner must deduce from the context which suit is required.

♠ A J 9 8
♡ A K J 7 4
◇ Q 7
♣ 9 7

♠ 10 7		♠ 4 3 2
♡ 10 8 6 5 3		♡ —
◇ J 10 9 8		◇ A K 5 4 3 2
♣ 10 8		♣ 5 4 3 2

♠ K Q 6 5
♡ Q 9 2
◇ 6
♣ A K Q J 6

South plays 6♣, after opening 1♣ and getting a response of 1♡. East doubles for an unusual lead. West leads a heart, East ruffs and cashes the ◇ A for the setting trick. Without the double West would have led a diamond which declarer would have covered from dummy. East would be forced to win the only trick the defense could take. See also LEAD-DIRECTING DOUBLES. For an alternative use of the double of a slam when the defenders have bid and raised a suit of their own, see DOUBLE FOR SACRIFICE.

LILIES. See ROYAL SPADES.

LIMIT. (1) The highest stake permitted in a bridge club. Most bridge clubs set a limit of one or two cents per point (in England, per 100 points, where a stake of a pound per 100 is about the U.S. equivalent of three cents a point).

(2) A bid which shows a maximum as well as a minimum range of values in the bidder's hand. Various limit bids are discussed in the following articles: DELAYED GAME RAISE; DOUBLE RAISE; INVERTED MINOR SUIT RAISES; INVITATIONAL BID; LIMIT BID; LIMIT JUMP RAISE; NOTRUMP BIDDING; 1 NT RESPONSE; SINGLE RAISE; STRONG NOTRUMP AFTER PASSING; 3 NT RESPONSE; TRIPLE RAISE; and 2 NT RESPONSE.

LIMIT BID. A bid with a limited point-count range, usually fewer than 4 points. Although a standard jump raise (1♠–3♠) is limited in the wide sense of the term, limit is normally applied only to nonforcing bids below the game level.

With some exceptions, a bid is limited and nonforcing if it is in notrump, if it is a raise, if it is a preference, or if it is a minimum rebid in a suit previously bid by the same player. Opening notrump bids are invariably limited.

Once we have decided that a certain bid is limited, the vital question arises: how wide can the limits be? *The nearer the bidding is to game, the closer the limits must be.* When the bidding reached 2 NT with the possibility of 3 NT; or when the bidding reaches

3♠, there is no longer any margin for exploration. So to give partner the chance of making an accurate decision, all such bids must have a range of only 2 points. Thus 1♡–2 NT by a passed hand shows 11–12, and 1♡–1 NT–2 NT shows 17–18; similarly 1♠–3♠ by a passed hand shows 10–11, or the equivalent, and 1♡–1♠–3♠ shows 17–18, or the equivalent. All these are typical *encouraging* bids, indicating that the partnership has a minimum of 23–24 points and urging partner on to game if he has a little more than his promised minimum.

Conversely, any bid of 1 NT and any limited bid of two of a suit can afford a range of 3 or 4 points: there is still time for partner to make an encouraging bid below the game level. So 1♡–1 NT or 1♡–2♡ are each 6–9 (and may have to stretch a little further at that), and 1♡–1♠–2♠ is 13–16, or the distributional equivalent. In the same way, opening 1 NT bids always have a range of 3 points (e.g., 16–18), but these could even be a point wider still without any disastrous loss of accuracy. See OPENER'S REBID, RESPONDER'S REBID, and RESPONSE.

LIMIT JUMP RAISE. A feature of the ACOL and KAPLAN-SHEINWOLD systems, among others. A raise from 1♡ to 3♡, for example, is nonforcing but strongly encouraging. It shows a hand with about 11 high-card points or the distributional equivalent.

If the opening bidder has a minimum, he normally passes. If the nine-trick contract fails, it will often turn out that the opponents could have made a part-score or even a game.

Limit jump raises were a part of the original CULBERTSON SYSTEM (to 1934) and were revived for minor suits only in 1948. Some players use limit jump raises in competition only — that is, after a suit overcall by an opponent; and nearly all players ascribe to them quite a low limit, over an opponent's takeout double.

LIMIT JUMP RAISE TO SHOW A SINGLETON. A part of the WALSH SYSTEM, using an immediate jump raise of opener's major suit opening to show three or four trumps, 10–12 points, and a singleton somewhere in the hand. If opener is interested in locating responder's singleton, he makes the cheapest bid over the limit raise (See MATHE ASKING BID.)

This device can be used with other bidding styles if the partnership uses a forcing 1 NT response to opening bids of 1♡ or 1♠. The forcing notrump followed by a jump to three of opener's suit can be used to show a balanced limit raise.

LIMIT RAISE. A raise with closely defined limits of strength. Many such bids are limited in this way in standard methods, such as the single raise of opener's suit.

The chief application is the jump raise from one to three (see LIMIT JUMP RAISE). The bid would indicate at least four-card trump support with 10–11 points or the distributional equivalent.

The corollary is that a jump raise on the second round is invitational but nonforcing:

WEST	EAST		WEST	EAST
1♣	1♠		1♣	1♡
3♠			1♠	3♠

The second of these sequences is not clearly defined in standard methods. See JUMP REBIDS BY RESPONDER.

LIMIT RESPONSES. The combination of LIMIT RAISES with limit responses in notrump, so that responses of 2 NT and 3♣ to an opening bid of 1♠, for example, are both encouraging but not forcing.

LINE. The dividing horizontal marking on a score pad below which game and partial scores (trick scores) are written. See ABOVE THE LINE and BELOW THE LINE.

LITERATURE AND BRIDGE. Several full-length novels have focused on bridge. *Tickets to the Devil*, by RICHARD POWELL, deals with the activities at a Spring North American Championship, both at the tables and away from them. *Yarborough* by B. H. Friedman outlines the adolescence and young manhood of two precocious heroes. In one AGATHA CHRISTIE mystery, *Cards on the Table*, the murder takes place during a bridge game and Hercule Poirot solves it by analyzing the score pad. Another British mystery and suspense writer, Georgette Heyer (1903-1974), also wrote about murder at a bridge game in *Duplicate Death*. A series of paperbacks by DON VON ELSNER (*The Ace of Spies, The Jack of Hearts, The Jake of Diamonds, Kona Contract,* etc,) features a fictitious bridge pro, Jake Winkman, in a variety of adventures in tournament settings, in which the quality of the bridge hands is highly professional. Similarly, FRANK THOMAS, a veteran actor of stage, movies, radio and television, now a bridge teacher and editor of the ABTA Quarterly, has written two books about "Sherlock Holmes, Bridge Detective," which combine good storytelling with excellent bridge hands. Author TERRY QUINN relates the adventures of a strange foursome caught up in the world of tournament bridge and international intrigue in *The Great Bridge Conspiracy*. In Sinclair Lewis's *Main Street* the local bridge club is a barometer of the protagonist's and accommodation to the social life in Gopher Prairie MN. In IAN FLEMING's *Moonraker*, James Bond rigged a variation of the DUKE OF CUMBERLAND'S HAND in dealing with the villain of that book. (See DISTRIBUTIONAL VALUES.)

Among famous writers who have used a bridge theme for short story purposes are: SOMERSET MAUGHAM ("The Three Fat Women of Antibes", "The Facts of Life"); Roald Dahl ("My Lady Love, My Dove"); RING LARDNER ("Contract", "Who Dealt"); and GEORGE S. KAUFMAN ("The Great Kibitzers' Strike of 1926"). See Cole and Edwards, eds., *Grand Slam*, BIBLIOGRAPHY, B.

In his long short story, "The Death of Ivan Ilych", completed March 25, 1886, LEO TOLSTOY made "vint", a Russian variation of bridge whist, the favorite leisure activity of his central character.

S. J. SIMON, a European champion and bridge writer, made some minor references to the game in the delightful series of novels he wrote with Caryl Brahms. C. S. Forester made his naval hero, Horatio Hornblower, a whist expert. JULES VERNE's whist expert, Phileas Fogg, begins his incredible journey in *Around the World in Eighty Days* as a result of a wager made with his whist-playing associates.

For Charles Lamb's view of whist players, see BATTLE, SARAH.

LITTLE MAJOR SYSTEM. An artificial system of bidding devised by TERENCE REESE and JEREMY FLINT, London, in the early sixties and now obsolete. In principle, an opening of 1♣ denotes a heart suit and 1◇ denotes a spade suit. Strong hands are opened with 1♡, and minor suit hands with 1♠.

LITTLE ROMAN CLUB (ARNO) SYSTEM. Developed by CAMILLO PABIS-TICCI and MASSIMO D'ALELIO, and first used successfully in the 1965 BERMUDA BOWL. The system is patterned closely on the principles of the ROMAN SYSTEM, especially the opening two-bids and structure of defensive overcalls. Its chief features are:

1♣ opening is forcing and shows either a balanced hand with 12-16 points, or a 17-20 point hand with a club suit or a two-suiter with at least four clubs. After a negative response of 1◇ (less than 10 points), opener rebids on the one-level to the balanced minimum opening. If responder makes a positive response of 1♡ or 1♠, opener describes the minimum opening by raising with four-card support or rebidding 1 NT with 12-14 points, or conventionally rebidding 2♣ with 15-16 points. After a positive response in a minor, opener bids a suit on the two-level with 12-14 points or 2 NT with 15-16 points. A response of 1 NT is forcing to game, showing 12 points or more, over which opener bids a suit on the two-level with 12-13 points or raises to 2 NT with 14-16 points. Jump responses are also forcing to game, and request opener to rebid conventionally by four steps to describe his strength and support for responder's suit.

With a strong distributional hand, opener bids his longest suit at a higher level than with a balanced hand.

1◇, 1♡, 1♠ openings are forcing and natural according to the CANAPÉ principle with 12-20 points. The opening bid may be made in a three-card suit with a minimum of 15 points or if opener's longest suit is clubs. The next higher suit by responder (1 NT over 1♠) is the conventional negative, after which opener makes a simple rebid with 12-16 points or a jump rebid with a stronger hand. After a positive response, a normal rebid by opener is forcing for one round, and responder creates a game-force if his rebid is a reverse, a jump in a new suit, a raise of opener's second suit if it is a major, or a jump raise of opener's first suit. A 1 NT response, if it is not a negative, shows a balanced hand with at least 12 points and is forcing to game.

If opener rebids in notrump after opening 1◇, he has a balanced hand with 17-20 points. Responder may then bid 2♣, forcing opener to rebid 2◇ and pass responder's next bid, or he may bid 2◇ to inquire about opener's major-suit holding and exact high-card strength.

1 NT opening is forcing and shows either a balanced hand with 21-24 points, or a powerful distributional hand that is forcing to game. Responder shows the number of aces he holds by steps, and opener rebids 2 NT with the balanced hand, or canapés in a suit with the unbalanced hand. After a 2 NT rebid, 3♣ by responder is STAYMAN and 3 ◇ requests opener to rebid 3 ♡ with a minimum and 3 ♠ with a maximum. This conventional treatment also applies to an auction of 1 ◇, 1 NT, 2 NT.

2 ♣, 2 ◇, 2 ♡, and 2 ♠ openings are as in the ROMAN SYSTEM with certain variations in opener's rebids.

2 NT opening shows a minimum of five cards in both minors with 12–16 points.

Jump overcall in the opponents' suit is equivalent to a strong takeout double.

Jump overcall of a 1 NT opening describes a strong two-suiter, the bid suit and the next higher ranking suit. The nontouching combinations (spades and diamonds, or hearts and clubs) are shown by a 2 NT overcall. Responder bids 3 ♣ to allow the overcaller to define which combination he holds.

Takeout doubles may be made on either a balanced hand or a strong one-suited hand.

For other bidding treatments, see ROMAN SYSTEM.

LITTLE SLAM. See SMALL SLAM.

LIVORNO SYSTEM. See LEGHORN DIAMOND.

LOCAL TOURNAMENTS. See CHAMPIONSHIP TOURNAMENTS.

LOCK. A colloquial term, used principally in post mortems, to mean a 100% sure play or contract. For example, "4 ♠ was a lock." In certain ethical situations the term has a similar meaning: "After his partner's HUDDLE he had a lock to double."

LOCKED (IN OR OUT OF A HAND). To win a trick in a hand from which it is disadvantageous to make the lead to the next (or some later) trick is to be locked in. It usually refers to an endplay against a defender (see THROW IN) or to a declarer who is forced to win a trick in the dummy hand, when he has high cards established in his own hand which he is unable to enter. Locked out refers to situations in which established cards in the dummy cannot be cashed because an entry is not available.

LONDON SUNDAY TIMES PAIRS. See INVITATIONAL PAIRS CHAMPIONSHIP.

LONG CARDS. Cards of a suit remaining in a player's hand after all other cards of that suit have been played.

LONG HAND. The hand of the partnership which has the greater length in the trump suit, or, in notrump play, the hand which has winners that are or may be established. See AVOIDANCE.

LONG SUIT. A suit in which four or more cards are held. Frequently it is used in connection with a hand of little strength but with great length in a particular suit. For bidding on such a hand, see PREEMPTIVE BID.

LONG TRUMP. Any card of the trump suit remaining after all other players' cards of the suit have been played.

LOSER. A card that must lose a trick to the adversaries if led, or if it must be played when the suit is led by an adversary. At notrump, all cards below the ace and not in sequence with it are possible losers, but may become winners if the play develops favorably. At a suit contract, the same may be said with the exception that losers may possibly be ruffed if the suit is short in one hand. A distinction must be made between possible losers and sure losers. The former may be discarded on a setup suit, or ruffed, or perhaps discarded on a setup card cashed by an adversary. If a loser cannot be disposed of, it must, of course, lose a trick to the opponents.

LOSER ON LOSER. The act of playing a card that must be lost on a losing trick in some other suit. This technique can be valuable in many situations, the most common of which are:

(1) *To allow a safe ruff to produce a trick:*

```
              ♠ 4 3 2
              ♡ A J 6 5 2
              ◇ 5 3
              ♣ A 7 4
   ♠ 6 5                    ♠ 8 7
   ♡ Q 3                    ♡ K 10 8 7 4
   ◇ K Q J 9 8 6            ◇ A 2
   ♣ Q 10 8                 ♣ J 5 3 2
              ♠ A K Q J 10 9
              ♡ 9
              ◇ 10 7 4
              ♣ K 9 6
```

WEST	NORTH	EAST	SOUTH
2 ◇	Pass	3 ◇	3 ♠
Pass	4 ♠	All Pass	

West leads the ◇ K. East overtakes with the ace, and continues the suit. West wins and plays a third diamond. South realizes that East will be able to over-ruff dummy. He therefore plays a loser on a loser by discarding a club from dummy. Declarer can later ruff a club in dummy safely.

(2) *To allow a safe re-entry:*

```
              ♠ 5 4 3 2
              ♡ A 3
              ◇ 6 5
              ♣ A 7 6 4 2
   ♠ A K 10                  ♠ Q J 9 6
   ♡ Q 5                     ♡ J 8 6
   ◇ Q 10 7 4 2              ◇ J 9 8
   ♣ K J 10                  ♣ Q 5 3
              ♠ 8 7
              ♡ K 10 9 7 4 2
              ◇ A K 3
              ♣ 9 8
```

West leads three rounds of spades, and declarer ruffs. Two rounds of diamonds are cashed and the third round is trumped in the North hand. After cashing the ♡ A, declarer must now re-enter his hand to continue drawing trump. If he leads ace and another club, East will win and his spade continuation will create two trump tricks for the defense. Instead, declarer cashes dummy's ♣ A and then leads a fourth round of spades, playing a loser on a loser by discarding his remaining club. The defense is now helpless. Declarer is fortunate in the distribution of the East-West minor suit cards but has nothing to lose by attempting this play.

(3) *To prevent a later overruff threat:*

```
              ♠ —
              ♡ A K Q 7
              ◇ 10 7 6 5 3
              ♣ J 7 4 3
   ♠ J 4                    ♠ A 5 3 2
   ♡ J 9 4                  ♡ 10 8 6 5
   ◇ K Q J 4                ◇ 9 8
   ♣ K 10 8 2               ♣ A 9 5
              ♠ K Q 10 9 8 7 6
              ♡ 3 2
              ◇ A 2
              ♣ Q 6
```

With East–West vulnerable, South opens 4♠, and buys the contract. West leads the ◇K, which declarer wins. An immediate discard is necessary, so South takes three rounds of hearts, discarding his losing diamond. If South now fails to play the last heart, careful defense will obtain two clubs and two trump tricks. East will lead his last heart at a later stage, promoting West's jack of trump (see TRUMP PROMOTION).

Instead, South uses the loser-on-loser technique. He leads dummy's remaining heart, discarding a club loser. East wins this trick, but the contract cannot be defeated.

(4) *To prevent a particular opponent from gaining the lead* (see AVOIDANCE):

```
              ♠ K J
              ♡ A K 4
              ◇ A 7 4 3 2
              ♣ J 10 6
   ♠ A 6 4 2                ♠ 7
   ♡ —                      ♡ J 10 9 8 7 6 5
   ◇ J 10 9 8               ◇ K Q
   ♣ A K Q 8 3              ♣ 5 4 2
              ♠ A 10 9 8 5 3
              ♡ Q 3 2
              ◇ 8 6
              ♣ 9 7
```

WEST	NORTH	EAST	SOUTH
		3♡	Pass
Pass	Dbl	Pass	3♠
All Pass			

West leads the ♣K and (erroneously) continues with the A-Q. South observes that the bidding suggests West is void of hearts. He therefore plays a loser on a loser by discarding a diamond on the third club. If South ruffs the third club, West will shift to diamond after winning the second round of spades. South will then be unable to enter his hand without surrendering a heart ruff.

After South's discard on the third trick, his contract is safe.

(5) *To establish one or more tricks in the suit played:*

WEST	EAST
♠ A K J	♠ 5 4 3
♡ —	♡ K Q 4
◇ A 3	◇ 10 7 6 5
♣ A K J 10 9 8 7 3	♣ Q 6 2

Against West's contract of 6♣, North leads the ◇K.

West wins and draws two trumps ending in the East hand. He should now lead the ♡K from dummy, throwing a loser on a loser by discarding his diamond if East does not cover. If North wins the ♡A, the ♡Q will provide a discard for the ♠J. (Naturally, West has retained an entry to the East hand in clubs!) If South has the ace, either the ♡K will win or the ace will be ruffed out. Declarer can now try the spade finesse for an overtrick.

(6) *To help establish a side suit* (see AVOIDANCE):

```
              ♠ K Q 3
              ♡ J 9 7
              ◇ A 7 6 3 2
              ♣ 6 4
   ♠ 10                     ♠ J 9
   ♡ A K 10 8 5             ♡ Q 6 4 3
   ◇ 10 5                   ◇ Q J 9
   ♣ A Q 10 9 2             ♣ J 8 7 3
              ♠ A 8 7 6 5 4 2
              ♡ 2
              ◇ K 8 4
              ♣ K 5
```

WEST	NORTH	EAST	SOUTH
1♡	Pass	2♡	2♠
3♣	3♠	Pass	4♠
Pass	Pass	Pass	

West leads the ♡K, and all follow. West, who has been reading this article, realizes that if he leads the ♡A, declarer will play a loser on a loser by discarding a diamond. This will allow the diamond suit to be established by ruffing and prevent East from gaining the lead to annihilate the ♣K.

West therefore shifts to a trump (a diamond has the same effect).

Declarer wins in dummy, playing the four from his own hand. Anxious to execute the loser-on-loser play, he leads the ♡9 from dummy. East shakes off a yawn and rises with the queen to prevent the diamond discard. Declarer ruffs with the 5, returns to dummy by leading the ♠6 to the remaining honor in dummy. The ♡J is led from dummy. East cannot cover, and declarer sheds a low diamond. West wins and grudgingly cashes the ♣A to prevent an overtrick. Despite the best defense after the opening lead, declarer triumphs by continuing after his loser-on-loser play and careful unblocking in the spade suit (see UNBLOCKING.)

(7) *To avoid a force:*

WEST	EAST
♠ A K Q J	♠ 10 8 5
♡ 3	♡ 9 8 7
◇ A 4 3	◇ 10 7 5
♣ A K J 9 5	♣ Q 10 8 2

Against West's 4♠ contract (Don't ask me how he got there! It's a good contract, isn't it?), the defense begins with two rounds of hearts. To avoid weakening his trump holding, West should discard losing diamonds on the next two rounds of hearts. A fourth round of hearts can be ruffed in the East hand. If the trumps break 3-3 or 4-2, declarer romps home.

If declarer ruffs a heart too early, a 4-2 trump break may defeat him, the defense taking four hearts and one trump trick.

(8) *To execute an endplay by creating a throw-in card:*

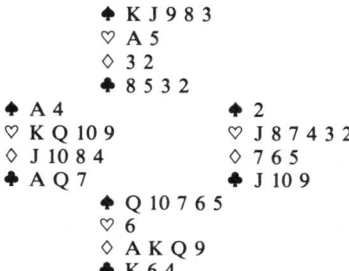

```
          ♠ K J 9 8 3
          ♡ A 5
          ◇ 3 2
          ♣ 8 5 3 2
♠ A 4                        ♠ 2
♡ K Q 10 9                   ♡ J 8 7 4 3 2
◇ J 10 8 4                   ◇ 7 6 5
♣ A Q 7                      ♣ J 10 9
          ♠ Q 10 7 6 5
          ♡ 6
          ◇ A K Q 9
          ♣ K 6 4
```

Against South's 4♠ contract, West leads the ♡K. Declarer wins with the ace, ruffs a heart, and leads a trump. West cautiously rises with the ♠A, and exits with a spade. Declarer wins and tries to drop the ◇J, 10. On the third diamond, a club is discarded from dummy. South then leads the fourth round of diamonds. When West covers, declarer makes use of loser-on-loser technique by discarding another club from dummy. West is in, and must give away a trick.

(9) *To execute an endplay by forcing an opponent to remain on lead* (see RUFF AND DISCARD).

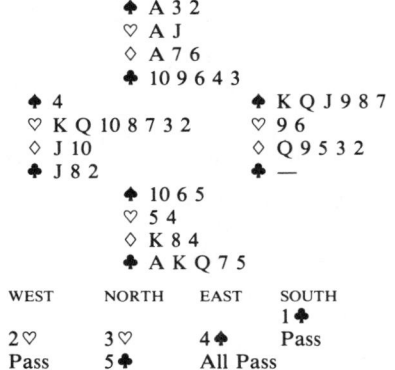

```
          ♠ A 3 2
          ♡ A J
          ◇ A 7 6
          ♣ 10 9 6 4 3
♠ 4                          ♠ K Q J 9 8 7
♡ K Q 10 8 7 3 2             ♡ 9 6
◇ J 10                       ◇ Q 9 5 3 2
♣ J 8 2                      ♣ —
          ♠ 10 6 5
          ♡ 5 4
          ◇ K 8 4
          ♣ A K Q 7 5
```

WEST	NORTH	EAST	SOUTH
			1♣
2♡	3♡	4♠	Pass
Pass	5♣	All Pass	

West leads the ♠4, which is won by North's ace. Declarer draws three rounds of trump and, placing West with seven hearts, cashes the two top diamonds and plays the ♡A–K.

West is stuck on lead with all hearts remaining and must give up a ruff-and-discard. When he leads a heart, a diamond is thrown from dummy. South tosses a loser on a loser by discarding a spade from his own hand. West is forced to remain on lead. On the next heart, declarer ruffs in dummy and discards his last spade. He then crossruffs the balance of the tricks, having turned four losers into only two! West could counter brilliantly by permitting dummy's ♡J to win, after which declarer would have no recourse.

(10) *To rectify the count for a squeeze.* This use of the loser-on-loser technique has many variations. Some of the most esoteric play problems revolve around declarer's attempt to correct the count for a squeeze by losing a trick in the correct suit. The following hand illustrates the method in a fairly complex setting.

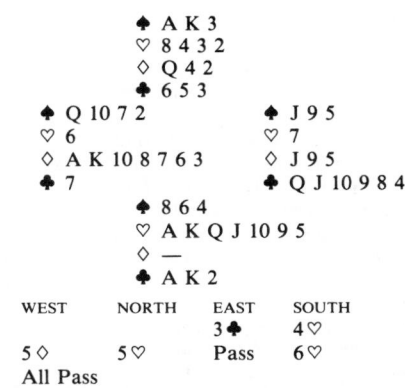

```
          ♠ A K 3
          ♡ 8 4 3 2
          ◇ Q 4 2
          ♣ 6 5 3
♠ Q 10 7 2                   ♠ J 9 5
♡ 6                          ♡ 7
◇ A K 10 8 7 6 3             ◇ J 9 5
♣ 7                          ♣ Q J 10 9 8 4
          ♠ 8 6 4
          ♡ A K Q J 10 9 5
          ◇ —
          ♣ A K 2
```

WEST	NORTH	EAST	SOUTH
		3♣	4♡
5◇	5♡	Pass	6♡
All Pass			

West leads the ◇K, and South surveys the situation. He realizes that if neither opponent is short of spades (a reasonable assumption on the bidding) an elimination will fail, and the only chance for the contract is a double squeeze. The ◇Q is a menace against West, and declarer's third club threatens East. But the count is wrong. Declarer must lose a trick before the squeeze will operate.

Where can this trick be lost? Certainly not in spades or clubs, for the loss of a trick in either of these suits will destroy the essential menace cards. Therefore, a trick must be lost in diamonds. Furthermore, this trick must be lost *at once*. If declarer attempts to give up a diamond trick later on, the defense will play a third diamond, quashing the diamond menance. Therefore, declarer must throw a loser on a loser on the first trick. He discards a spade.

West has no effective defense. His best play is a spade. Declarer wins and runs winners until this ending is reached.

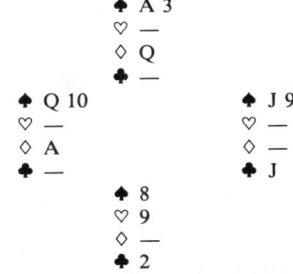

```
          ♠ A 3
          ♡ —
          ◇ Q
          ♣ —
♠ Q 10                       ♠ J 9
♡ —                          ♡ —
◇ A                          ◇ —
♣ —                          ♣ J
          ♠ 8
          ♡ 9
          ◇ —
          ♣ 2
```

When South leads the ♡9, West must surrender a spade. Dummy discards the ◇Q, and East is squeezed in spades and clubs.

Jeff Rubens

LOSERS. A method of valuation for unbalanced hands used in the ROMAN and ROMEX Systems. Every missing ace, king or queen is counted as a loser unless shortness compensates. A doubleton king is one loser, but a doubleton queen is two losers. See LOSING TRICK COUNT and COVER CARDS.

LOSING-TRICK COUNT. A method of hand valuation. In 1934 the principle of assessing a hand in terms of "losers" was put forward by F. DUDLEY COURTENAY in his book, *The System the Experts*

Play. The general idea was this: when a suit fit came to light, you added the number of worthless cards in your hand to the number of losers revealed by your partner's bidding; the total was subtracted from 18, and the answer would tell you how many odd tricks the combined hands were likely to take.

After years of semi-obscurity the LTC was revived by MAURICE HARRISON-GRAY and is now accepted as a reasonably accurate ready reckoner which pays due regard to the features that really matter.

This method of valuation is no longer treated with disdain by the expert. For instance, it is an integral part of the ROMAN SYSTEM, which has helped Italy to win seven world championships.

The Losing-Trick Count applies only to trump contracts. When a notrump contract is contemplated, the standard yardstick is the Milton Work Count.

Basic count of losers. With a void or singleton ace, count no loser in that suit; with any other singleton, or with A–x or K–x, count one loser; with any other doubleton, count two losers.

In each suit of three or more cards, including the trump suit, count one loser for each missing high honor (A, K, or Q).

Do not count more than three losers in any one suit.

Count one loser only in a suit headed by A–J–10.

Some distinction must obviously be made between A–x–x, K–x–x, and Q–x–x. The first is a better two-loser holding than K–x–x, and three losers must be counted in a queen-high suit unless: (a) it is the proposed trump suit; (b) the suit has been bid by the partner; (c) the queen is supported by the jack; (d) the queen is "balanced" by an ace in another suit.

The initial count. An opening bid of one is made with: (a) not more than seven losers; (b) adequate high-card values, including two defensive tricks; (c) a sound rebid.

A response in a new suit is made with: (a) at the one-level — not more than 9 losers (sometimes 10 with compensating values); (b) at the two-level — not more than 8 losers (sometimes 9 with compensating values).

The count on the second rounds. Neutral rebids by opener (e.g., 1♡–1♠–2♡, or 1♠–2♠–2◊ or 1♠–1♡–2♠) do not promise fewer than 7 losers.

A jump rebid by the opener in his original suit (e.g., 1♠–1♠–3♠) shows 7 winners and (in most cases) only 5 losers.

A reverse rebid by the opener at the two-level (e.g., 1♠–1♠–2◊) shows five losers (sometimes six with a high point-count). A reverse at the three-level (e.g., 1♠–2♠–3♠) whows not more than five losers.

A jump rebid by the responder in his original suit (e.g., 1♡–1♠–2♠–3♠) shows 6 losers.

A responder's reverse at the two-level (e.g., 1◊–2♠–2◊–2♡) shows 6 to 7 losers. A reverse at the three-level (e.g., 1♡–1♠–2♡–3♠) shows not more than 6 losers.

It soon becomes second nature to adjust the original count of losers in the light of the bidding. Trump control is an important factor, and a loser should be deducted whenever the quota of aces and

other key features, such as a king or a singleton in the right spot, is better than it might be on the bidding. The LTC will put a nonexpert player on the right track in a case like the following:

South dealer
Vul: E-W

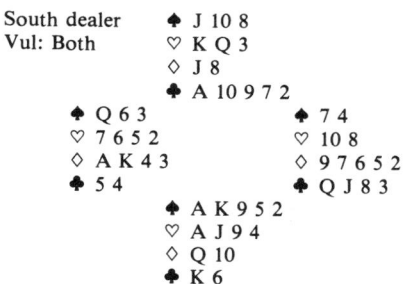

The bidding:

SOUTH	WEST	NORTH	EAST
Pass	1♡	Pass	2♡
2♠	3♠	Pass	4♡
Pass	Pass	Dbl.	Pass
Pass	Pass		

West had six losers, and East was marked with nine; 15 from 18 suggested that even 3♡ might fail through a dearth of top cards, but one of West's losers could be deducted for trump control, and a game try was in order. 3♡ would sound like mere contention, so he made a TRIAL BID in the spot where help was most needed. The onus was then on East, who saw two good reasons for jumping to game — his fourth trump and an ideal holding in the trial suit. The ♠Q was led and West could not go wrong, in view of South's initial pass, when he came to tackle diamonds.

Application of the LTC would have averted an inelegant result on the deal below:

South dealer
Vul: Both

```
            ♠ J 10 8
            ♡ K Q 3
            ◊ J 8
            ♣ A 10 9 7 2
  ♠ Q 6 3                ♠ 7 4
  ♡ 7 6 5 2              ♡ 10 8
  ◊ A K 4 3              ◊ 9 7 6 5 2
  ♣ 5 4                  ♣ Q J 8 3
            ♠ A K 9 5 2
            ♡ A J 9 4
            ◊ Q 10
            ♣ K 6
```

The bidding:

SOUTH	WEST	NORTH	EAST
1♠	Pass	2♣	Pass
2♡	Pass	3♣	Pass
4♣	Pass	4♡	Pass
5♣	Pass	Pass	Pass

West could sit back and relax after cashing two diamonds. South made two common mistakes: his 17 points went to his head, and he read too much into a nonforcing preference bid. The LTC should serve as a halt sign. South has six losers, and his partner should have eight; if he deducts 14 from 18, he will see the futility of looking beyond 4♣.

Maurice Harrison-Gray

LOU HERMAN TROPHY. See HERMAN TROPHY.

LOVE. The state of the game, in rubber bridge, where there is as yet no score.

LOVE, TO PLAY FOR. To play rubber bridge without stakes.

LOVE ALL. A term, borrowed from tennis, used in some countries to describe that situation where neither side has made any score. Used in England at duplicate to indicate that neither side is vulnerable, but not used in the United States.

LOVE SCORE. Zero score; neither side vulnerable and no part-score.

LOW CARD. A card in a suit that is not an honor; any card from the deuce to the 9, usually represented by an x in card or hand descriptions.

LOW LEVEL TEXAS. See JACOBY TRANSFER BIDS.

LOWER MINOR. See DEFENSE TO OPENING THREE-BID; SECOND NEGATIVE RESPONSE AFTER ARTIFICIAL FORCING OPENING.

LOWEST SCORE. The lowest score in major team-of-four play occurred in 1957, in the first Far East Team Championship at Manila. On the third set of eight boards in the match between Hong Kong and the Philippines, not one IMP was scored by either side. On each of the eight hands, both teams arrived at the same contract and made the same number of tricks. In a board-a-match team held at a Greater New York BA sectional tournament in 1975, one of the 74 teams entered scored only one-half board out of 26 — a record that is unlikely to be broken, and if it is, it won't be by much. In pair play, the lowest recorded score is 13% (by opera star Lauritz Melchior). In head-to-head team play the record can be claimed for EDDIE KANTAR, BILLY EISENBERG, ALAN SONTAG, FRED HAMILTON and JIM CAYNE. In the first 16 deals of the 1983 Vanderbilt Knockout final in Hawaii they were outscored 68–2 by BILL ROOT, RICHARD PAVLICEK, EDGAR KAPLAN and NORMAN KAY, and were then penalized 10 IMPs for slow play. So they began the second quarter of the match with a score of minus 8 IMPs.

LUCK. A basic reason for the success of duplicate bridge is that it incorporates the optimum degree of luck. Although this means that the best players do not invariably win, it adds greatly to the fascination of the game and to the interplay of psychological factors. Par contests, where the luck element is removed, are much less popular.

Individual contests contain by far the largest element of luck and are less highly regarded as a test of skill than other forms of duplicate. The hazardous

nature an individual contest derives partly from the constant change of partners. Good luck may take the form of being teamed with a strong and compatible partner on critical deals which require accurate bidding or play; it would be bad luck to be teamed with an incompatible partner on such deals, and a player would prefer to reserve such a partner for a set of flat boards. Similarly, being teamed against incompatible players on swingy deals could be good luck, and a player might pick up a high matchpoint score without taking an active part.

After individual contests, pair events contain the next highest proportion of luck. In a single-session event, a pair who are measurably stronger than the field will probably win less than half the time; but they will nearly always finish in the leading group. The greater the importance of a pair event, the greater the number of boards played, thus reducing the effect of luck.

Another facet of luck in pairs events is that toward the end of a contest an experienced pair who estimate that they have less than a winning score may adopt unusual tactics in an attempt to improve dramatically. Such tactics may take the form of bidding poor slams or games, or declining to bid good slams, in the hope that an improbable distribution of the cards will favor an unusual contract. Thus it is theoretically possible for a pair to have a comfortable lead with a few boards to go, to continue to bid and play perfectly, and yet be passed by a pair who have deliberately bid their way to faulty contracts or made imperfect plays. (See SHOOTING.) The fact that this is so has given rise to the misconception that the structure of pairs scoring is necessarily faulty; an alternate view is that it adds to the excitement and affords more scope for judgment and opportunism.

It is in team-of-four games — particularly those where the scoring is by International Match Points — that luck is reduced to a minimum; consequently these events carry most prestige and are the accepted medium for international competition.

At the same time, the structure of team games is such that luck, when it does occur, is both more recognizable and more dramatic than in pairs contests. This adds greatly to the ways in which skill may be manifested. For example, a player who at a critical stage of a close match is faced with the decision whether to bid an even-money slam may bring into the reckoning such factors as the personal idiosyncrasies of his counterpart at the other table, the bidding systems being played there, whether the players there will be able to judge the score as accurately as he and so on. Dramatic strokes of misfortune can also exert a profound psychological effect on the players and provide a stern test of character in the face of adversity.

Aside from close decisions, luck in team play may result in correct play being penalized by an unfortunate lie of the cards, while less sound play succeeds.

In team play an admitted but small mistake in technique can sometimes be penalized to an extent altogether out of proportion to the degree of error. Following were the cards in the crucial semifinal match between Britain and Italy in the second World Team Olympiad, held in New York City in 1964.

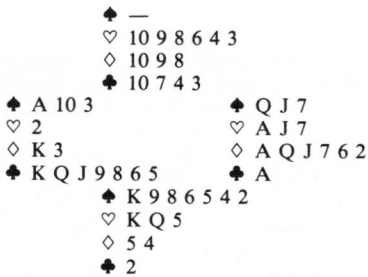

```
              ♠ —
              ♡ 10 9 8 6 4 3
              ◇ 10 9 8
              ♣ 10 7 4 3
   ♠ A 10 3              ♠ Q J 7
   ♡ 2                   ♡ A J 7
   ◇ K 3                 ◇ A Q J 7 6 2
   ♣ K Q J 9 8 6 5       ♣ A
              ♠ K 9 8 6 5 4 2
              ♡ K Q 5
              ◇ 5 4
              ♣ 2
```

In the closed room the British bid to the best contract as follows:

WEST	EAST
Harrison-Gray	*Flint*
	2 NT
4 ♣	4 NT
7 NT	Pass

7 NT was a spread, and the British scored 2220. When the deal was replayed on Bridge-O-Rama, the bidding was:

WEST	NORTH	EAST	SOUTH
Avarelli	*Reese*	*Belladonna*	*Schapiro*
	Pass	1 ◇	1 ♠
3 ♣	Pass	4 ◇	Pass
4 NT	Pass	5 NT	Pass
6 ◇	Pass	7 ◇	All Pass

This contract would be made unless North could ruff the opening lead or unless trumps were divided 5–0, the latter being only a 4% chance. Since 7 ◇ bid and made gives a score 2140, normal expectation would be a swing of 2 International Match Points to the team which had bid 7 NT. In fact the British South opened a low spade against 7 ◇ and his partner ruffed. The swing to Britain was thus 2320, or 20 IMPs. Although the Italian bidding was imperfect, one might say that they suffered ill luck to the extent of perhaps 18 IMPs. See also FORTUNE.

LUNCH-TIME BRIDGE. Popular, especially in large corporations that have teams belonging to the various commercial bridge leagues. In lunchrooms where there is sufficient space, one may find occasional foursomes of a serious or semi-serious nature, and these develop into groups of decent ability from time to time. If a person is willing to take a good chunk of time away from his rest or eating period to play a card game, it stands to reason there must be keen interest. In larger luncheon groups, there are even lunchtime matches, consisting of 6–board contests and lasting about 40 minutes.

M

MACCABIAH GAMES. Games which celebrate athletic achievement held quadrennially in Israel and sometimes called "Israel Olympics". The Games were named after Judah Maccabeus, a Hebrew religious zealot who fought against the encroaching Hellenization of Jewish life symbolized by the Greek Olympic-style games and the cult of the physical.

The Games are open to amateur Jewish participants, all of whom must have Jewish mothers. Since its inception in 1932, the Games have included athletics, gymnastics, football, tennis and cricket. In 1977, for the first time, bridge and chess were accepted as competing sports. Gold medalists in bridge are:

1977	(Israel) David Birman, Michael Hochzeit, Capt. Kaufman, Yeshayahu Levit, Adrian Schwarz, Mori Stampf, Reubin Kunin (npc)
1981	(United States) Jim Cayne, Billy Eisenberg, Alan Greenberg, Eddie Kantar, Don Krauss, Neil Silverman

MACHINE-PREPARED HANDS. See COMPUTER HANDS.

MACHLIN TROPHY. Donated by the Machlin family in memory of Sadie Machlin, long-time ACBL employee, and awarded to the winners of the Charity Game at the Fall North American Championships, under which heading past results are listed.

MAGAZINES. See BIBLIOGRAPHY, O.

MAGNETIC CARDS. Cards made from a very thin sheet of metal. Though not themselves magnetic, the cards are attracted to and held onto a magnetized board which is part of the set.

The principal advantage of these cards is that play can take place alongside outdoor pools, on breezy patios, or at the beach. Manufacture began in 1962, and prices are comparable to those of plastic cards and bridge tables.

MAJOR. A major suit, i.e., hearts or spades.

MAJOR SUIT. Either of the two highest-ranking suits, hearts and spades, so characterized because they outrank the third and fourth suits in the bidding and scoring.

MAJOR TENACE. An original holding of ace-queen (without the king) of a suit. After one or more rounds of a suit have played, the highest and third highest remaining cards of the suit in the hand of one player are called major tenace (when the second highest remaining card is not held by the same player).

MAJORITY CALLING. The principle by which any bid outranks any other bid at a lower level, regardless of scoring value. The opposite principle, numerical calling, was standard in auction bridge, although abandoned in the United States in 1913. In this procedure 4 ♣, for example, could follow a bid of 5 ♣ because its scoring value was higher.

MAKE. Used in bridge in four different senses. As a verb, it may mean (1) to shuffle the deck; (2) to succeed in a contract; (3) to win a trick by the play of a card. As a noun, it means a successful contract, but usually a hypothetical one in the POST-MORTEM: "5 ◇ would have been a make."

MAKE UP. To shuffle the cards.

MAKE UP A TABLE. A player who, with at least three others, forms a table for play at rubber, or CHICAGO bridge, is said to make up a table.

MALAYSIAN CONTRACT BRIDGE ASSOCIATION. Founded in 1961 as the Malayan Contract Bridge Association, it subsequently changed to its present title in 1964. It has a membership of about 150 with headquarters in Kuala Lumpur and branches in Penang and Selangor, and also in Singapore until that territory became a separate state in 1965. The Association participates in the FAR EAST BRIDGE FEDERATION championships hosting the 1968 event in Kuala Lumpur, and annually sponsors National Championships for the Tunku Abdul Rahman Trophy (Open Pairs), Malaysia Cup and various Interstate Team-of-Four contests.

Officers, 1982:
President: Mrs. Norella Mohar
Secretary: David Law, P.O. Box 568, 33 Jalan
    Klyne, Kuala Lumpur, Malaysia

MALOWAN 6♣ CONVENTION. A variation of the GRAND SLAM FORCE originated by WALTER MALOWAN. After BLACKWOOD has been used, a 5 NT bid is not available as a grand slam force because it would be a conventional bid asking for kings. 6♣ is therefore used as a substitute grand slam force unless clubs is the agreed trump suit.

The responses to 6♣ must be influenced by the fact that the ace of trumps is already known. MARSHALL MILES suggests that the cheapest available bid should be used at the six level to show the best possible trump holding, with increasingly strong bids showing increasingly worse holdings.

MALTAIS CONVENTION. See STAYMAN AFTER OVERCALL.

MAMA–PAPA BRIDGE. A term applied to a simple bidding style uncluttered with conventions.

MANUFACTURE OF PLAYING CARDS. After the establishment of papermaking in America, several printers, including Benjamin Franklin, seem to have produced packs of cards as a sideline. The first man specifically listed as a manufacturer of playing cards was Jazaniah Ford of Milton MA, about 1800, followed by Thomas Crehore of Dorchester.

The fundamental principle of manufacture has changed little over the century. The standard "poker" card measures 2½ × 3½ inches, but bridge cards are a little narrower, 2¼ × 3½, to facilitate the holding of 13 cards in a player's hand. The stock on which the cards are printed consists of two thin sheets of paper pasted together with a black paste. (A single sheet of heavier paper would not suffice; if a player had a lamp at his back, the light would show what he had in his hand, to the player across from him. The black paste makes the paper properly opaque.) Hence playing cards are sometimes called *pasteboards*.

One or two full packs of cards are printed at a time on large sheets of pasteboard. The individual cards are then stamped out, one at a time, with a sharp die that works like a housewife's biscuit cutter, but one that cuts about 36,000 cards per hour. Simultaneously, and synchronized to the infinitesimal fraction of a second in which the die descends, the edges of the cards are pressed into a knife-edge, almost invisible to the naked eye, but enough to permit each card to slip between two other cards during a shuffle, and this retards the fraying of the edges.

Delicate operations like this require special machinery, designed for this specific purpose. Modern refinements on traditional processes have not been disclosed in patents, and rate among the world's most jealously guarded trade secrets.

The demand for playing cards is not likely to outrun supply. It has been said that the largest playing-card plant could, without effort, supply the wants of the card-playing world.

Modern cardplayers are accustomed to the *double-head* card, which can be read from either end, and to the INDICES in the two corners, which permit one to recognize the card without seeing its entire face. Cards of this type did not become standard until the late 1870s. Until then a player had to look at a full face of the card, and hold it right-side up, to know what the card was.

Either superstition or habit prevents major changes in playing-card design. Unsuccessful attempts have been made to print the suits in four colors; to redesign the pips; to clothe the face cards in modern dress; and to introduce circular cards. Soviet Russia tried to replace the "anachronistic kings and queens" with revolutionary heroes, but so many packs were smuggled in that the conventional royalty cards were reinstated. (See also FIVE-SUIT BRIDGE.)

A more modest change reintroduced in 1964 and embodied in special decks used in the World Team Olympiad was to use a very pale blue-green tint instead of white for the background of the faces. This has been show to reduce eyestrain.

For information on early cards and different packs, see HISTORY OF PLAYING CARDS; PACK; TAXES; TAROT. See also PLASTIC CARDS.

MARCUS CUP. A board-a-match open team award, donated by friends in memory of EDWARD N. MARCUS, of Boston, 1953. This event replaced the FABER CUP and was contested until 1978 at the Summer North American Championships, under which heading past results are listed.

MARK MEMORIAL TROPHY. A trophy donated in memory of DR. LOUIS MARK. It is presented annually at the Spring North American Championships, as part of the ACBL charity program, to the ACBL unit which has raised the largest amount of money in proportion to the size of its membership.

MARKED CARD. See DAMAGED CARD.

MARMIC SYSTEM. An Italian system, apparently obsolete, whose name is derived from the first names of the inventors (MARio FRANCO and MICHele GIOVINE). It is probably the most unusual system ever played in serious international competition by a major bridge country, and in some respects was a forerunner of the ROMAN SYSTEM. The chief feature was that a player was expected to pass in first or second position with balanced distribution and 16½–19 points. The same principle applied after an opponent's opening bid, and in each case the passer's partner was expected to balance with 5 points or more. This opened the possibility for trap passing by the opponents, and the system was amended to provide an opening 1 NT bid, instead of the strong pass, at unfavorable vulnerability.

MARX 2♣. An alternate name, especially in England, for the STAYMAN convention. Originated by JACK MARX approximately at the same time as the American counterpart devised by GEORGE RAPÉE.

MASTER. A player in the AMERICAN CONTRACT BRIDGE LEAGUE with at least 20 masterpoints but fewer than 50. See RANKING OF PLAYERS.

MASTER CARD. The highest unplayed card of a suit. It can also be thus characterized while actually being played.

MASTER HAND. The hand which controls the situation — more particularly, the one which controls the trump suit, leading out high trumps to prevent adverse ruffs, and retaining a trump or two to prevent the adverse run of a long side suit. It is usually the declarer's hand, but sometimes, when the declarer's trumps are more valuable as ruffers, the dummy is made the master hand. See DUMMY REVERSAL.

MASTER INDIVIDUAL, NORTH AMERICAN CHAMPIONSHIP. Formerly called World Master Individual or Life Master Individual. See STEINER TROPHY.

MASTER KNOCKOUT TEAMS, NORTH AMERICAN CHAMPIONSHIP. See SPINGOLD TROPHY.

MASTER MIXED TEAMS, NORTH AMERICAN CHAMPIONSHIP. See BARCLAY TROPHY and LEBHAR TROPHY.

MASTER POINT. The unit which measures bridge achievement in tournament play.

The term first arose when eligibles for the ABL's 1934 von Zedtwitz Master Pairs (later Life Master Pairs) were chosen from a list of players credited with masterpoints for winning tournaments run by the ABC and the AWL, as well as the Vanderbilt and Eastern Championships which at that time were independent events. In the following year, winners of many smaller tournaments that had applied for ABL sanction became eligible. To offset this rapid and somewhat haphazard inflation of *masters*, in 1936 the League created the rank of LIFE MASTER, then awarded only to those who had won their points in national championships or the equivalent. These point awards were tiny. At the outset, 10 points was the qualifying minimum, and a scheme for deducting points each year made it necessary for Life Masters to continue successful competition in order to retain their status. Deductions were discontinued in 1944.

Meanwhile, the USBA announced its own masterpoint program and appears to have been the first to extend the idea to the club level. Effective Sept. 1, 1935, City Masterpoints were awarded for duplicate games in USBA-affiliated clubs. These were convertible at 10 for 1 into State Masterpoints, awarded for citywide tournaments, which were in turn convertible at 10 for 1 into National Masterpoints, awarded for State tournaments. A legal dispute over the ABL's claim of exclusive right to award master points was not resolved until 1937, when the USBA was merged into the ABL, becoming the ACBL. The ACBL introduced Rating Points (later called Fractional Master Points), worth $1/100$ of a master point, into club games effective Jan. 1, 1938. The result was a rapid acceleration in the growth of League membership, but it also led to the eventual need to distinguish among points won at local, regional, and national levels.

Master points are awarded at ACBL tournaments in amounts proportional to the size and classification of the event and the rating of the tournament. The basic point structure is based on open pairs. Since such events as mixed pairs, men's pairs, women's pairs and unmixed pairs are restricted to some extent, point awards for them are lower than for open pairs. Since team games are considered to be a truer test of skill, point awards for them are slightly higher than for open pairs.

In general, awards at a sectional tournament are approximately double those at a local, and awards at a regional tournament are approximately triple those at a local. Awards for most North American Championships are fixed, and they are substantially higher than regional awards. Both the Vanderbilt Teams and the Spingold Teams award 150 master points to the winners — this is the highest masterpoint award given by the ACBL.

Masterpoint awards at local, sectional and regional tournaments are given according to a formula in which the principal ingredient is the size of the event. In general, awards climb arithmetically up through 60 tables, and thereafter they follow a logarithmic curve which very much slows down the rate of increase.

England adopted a masterpoint scheme in 1956, and was followed by many other countries. In most of these schemes the scales of awards are less generous, and the achievement of high rank is usually slower. Points won in foreign bridge leagues may be converted to ACBL Masterpoints under certain conditions. See GOLD POINTS; MASTERPOINT PLAN; RED POINTS; REGIONAL AND NATIONAL POINTS.

MASTERPOINT CERTIFICATE. See RATING POINTS.

MASTERPOINT PLAN. The method of awarding masterpoints in bridge tournaments at club, sectional, regional and national levels. Creation of the Masterpoint Plan in 1936 must be credited to WILLIAM McKENNEY and RAY EISENLORD, with many others contributing to later developments. The details of the method by which the plan operates at the club level are set out in the ACBL HANDBOOK.

Any club or group in the United States, Canada,

Bermuda or Mexico may apply for a franchise to issue masterpoints at regularly scheduled duplicate games. The clubs are of three types: Open (to all comers); Invitational (restricted to members of the group and invited guests); and Novice (restricted to players with not more than a stipulated number of masterpoints).

The ACBL publishes an annual directory of clubs, which enables members to find bridge activity in any city they may visit.

Rating points must be awarded at every duplicate game conducted by a franchised club. Rating points are hundredths of a full point. The scale for invitational clubs is slightly lower; and novice clubs (or games) score at an even lower scale.

Once each calendar quarter a weekly club is entitled to a Club Tournament game with greatly increased rating point awards. Those clubs meeting less frequently are entitled to a Club Tournament for every 12 regular scheduled sessions.

At club tournament level and higher, events can be of various types: Open Pair; Mixed Pair; Men's Pair; Women's Pair; Individual; and team events of various kinds. The scale of awards increases steadily through the various levels — club, sectional, regional and national. The highest award for any single event is given to the winners of the VANDERBILT and SPINGOLD championships (150 points), and to the winners of the Blue Ribbon Pairs Championship and Life Master Pairs Championship (125 points). See also AMERICAN CONTRACT BRIDGE LEAGUE; DUPLICATE BRIDGE; DUPLICATE TOURNAMENT; FRANCHISED CLUBS; MASTER POINT; RANKING OF PLAYERS.

Many other countries have adopted a masterpoint plan along similar lines. The WORLD BRIDGE FEDERATION also has such a plan, with GRAND MASTER as the premier rank.

MASTER TOURNAMENT. An event or series of events at a bridge tournament where the requirements for entry into the competition include the holding of a high masterpoint rating. For most of the championship events in the Spring North American Championships of the American Contract Bridge League, a rating of National Master is required; in the Summer North American Championships, that of Senior Master. In the Open Pairs events, the top flight is frequently limited to Life Masters. See RANKING OF PLAYERS.

MASTER TEAMS CHAMPIONSHIP. See MARCUS CUP.

MATCH. A session or event of head-to-head competition between two pairs or two teams-of-four or more players.

The shortest matches in international competition were the 18-board qualifying round matches in the 1964 WORLD TEAM OLYMPIAD. The longest matches were played for the BERMUDA BOWL, from 1951 to 1957, when there were only two teams in competition, and 224 to 256 boards were played. Even longer matches (300 boards) have been played on semi-official occasions. See ANGLO-AMERICAN MATCHES. The most famous of the nonofficial challenge *pair*

matches of the Thirties were longer still. Both the CULBERTSON-LENZ MATCH (Dec. 1931–Jan. 1932) and the CULBERTSON-SIMS MATCH (March–April, 1935) were 150 rubbers. In the former 879 hands were dealt, only 25 of which were passed out.

MATCH PLAY. A team-of-four contest in which two teams are competing for an appreciable number of boards. Tactics at match play are described in IMP TACTICS and STATE OF MATCH.

MATCHPOINT. A credit awarded to a contestant in pair or individual events for a score superior to that of another contestant in direct competition.

The number of matchpoints available to a contestant is normally one less than the number of contestants in direct competition. For example, in a game of 13 rounds there are 13 North-South scores in direct competition and 13 East-West scores in direct competition. The highest score in each group beats the other 12 scores in that group and receives 12 match points, the greatest number available to it.

Other pairs receive 11, 10, 9 points, etc., according to the number of pairs beaten in direct competition. The lowest pair in each group beats no pair in direct competition and receives 0 matchpoints.

When two or more pairs achieve identical scores, each pair receives ½ matchpoint for each pair with which its score is tied (see Law 74, LAWS OF DUPLICATE).

When matchpoint scoring is used in team games, the score that is obtained by a team on a board is 1 matchpoint if the combined score is plus, 0 is the score is minus, and ½ if the team score is neither plus nor minus. (Each board is thus scored as a match in itself, hence "board-a-match" scoring.)

In tournaments in other sections of the world and in WORLD BRIDGE FEDERATION play, matchpoints are doubled to eliminate halves. A pair receives two matchpoints for each pair it beats and one for each pair it ties. See also DOUBLE TOP; SCORING ACROSS THE FIELD.

MATCHPOINT BIDDING. If bridge were played double-dummy (if one could see all four hands whenever one had to make a decision), the bidding and play would be exactly the same at matchpoint duplicate as at rubber bridge. A minor exception is caused by the scoring of honors at rubber bridge. If one could see only partner's hand, the bidding would usually be the same. The objective on any one hand is the same for both forms of bridge: to score the maximum number of points or to allow the opponents to score a minimum number. Yet successful matchpoint tactics are quite different from successful rubber bridge tactics. For example, suppose the bidding, with both sides vulnerable, has gone as follows:

WEST	NORTH	EAST	SOUTH
			1 ♡
Pass	2 ♡	Pass	Pass
?			

West holds: ♠ Q 9 8 x x
            ♡ x
            ◇ A x x x
            ♣ Q 10 x

The opponents' lack of enterprise marks East with at least 8 points, perhaps as many as 14. He may or may not fit West's hand. At either rubber or duplicate, West should bid 2♣ when East holds:

♠ K J x x
♡ x x x
◇ K J x
♣ K x x

West should pass when East holds:

♠ x
♡ K J 10 x
◇ J x x x
♣ K x x x

Since West does not know which type of hand his partner has, he must consider what he has to lose or gain by bidding. The best probable result from bidding is that East–West, instead of North–South, will make a partscore. This is equivalent to approximately a 250-point gain. A partscore is worth an additional 50 points at rubber bridge, the same as at duplicate. The worst likely result is a 500- or 800-point penalty. Which is more likely to occur? Surely the former.

A reopening 2♣ bid would probably work out as follows: Four times in ten the opponents would bid and make 3♡, in which case the reopening bid would have neither lost nor gained.

Four times in ten it would gain. Perhaps East–West would be + 140 instead of + 100, + 110 instead of − 110, − 100 instead of − 110, or + 100 instead of − 110 (because the opponents bid again).

The other two times the reopening bid would lose, perhaps quite heavily. The net loss from these two occasions would be greater than the gain from the other four.

In rubber bridge, it would not pay to reopen with a weak suit because, in the long run, a reopening bid would lose points. In duplicate, a reopening bid is advisable. This is true whether most of the other West players would bid or not, but it is easier to demonstrate if the potential reopener were a lone wolf. Passing would result in an average score, 6 matchpoints out of 12. Whenever the reopening bid should gain, it would result in a top; whenever it should lose, it would result in a bottom. At rubber bridge, it is necessary to weigh the *amount* of gain against the *amount* of loss when considering any action. In duplicate, the main consideration is the *frequency* of gain or loss. The following hand illustrates a similar principle, except that the mystery is in regard to the opponents' holdings rather than partner's.

WEST	EAST
♠ A 10 x	♠ K Q x x
♡ 10 x	♡ x x
◇ A K J x	◇ Q 9 x x x x
♣ Q 10 9 x	♣ A

At rubber bridge, the bidding might well be as follows:

WEST	NORTH	EAST	SOUTH
			Pass
1◇	Pass	1♠	Pass
2♣	Pass	4◇	Pass
5◇	All Pass		

East has a good enough hand to be almost certain that 5◇ will be safe. Besides, a slam is still possible from his point of view. Consequently, he shows his excellent diamond support while still allowing West to return to spade with four-card spade support.

At duplicate, the bidding should start the same way, but East would probably bid 4♠ over the raise to 2♣. A slam is unlikely, and with such a good four-card spade suit, East would not want to 'risk' a final diamond contract. Perhaps the word "risk" seems unusual here, but at duplicate 5◇ is a much poorer gamble, hence a greater risk, than is 4♠. At least 75% of the time, East–West will do better in spades than in diamonds; they cannot afford to "play safe" when the odds favor the more dangerous contract. This is true despite the fact that the gain in playing spades cannot exceed 20 to 50 points, while the loss, when the spades break badly, or the opening diamond lead is ruffed, can be several hundred points.

It has been stated that the same contract usually would be chosen at duplicate as at rubber bridge if one could see partner's hand. The following is an exception. Even the reason for the exception is that bridge is not a double-dummy game.

WEST	EAST
♠ A x	♠ x x
♡ A x x	♡ x x
◇ K Q J x x	◇ A x x
♣ 10 8 x	♣ A Q J 9 x x

The ideal contract at rubber bridge is 7♣ — despite the fact that the odds are slightly *against* making it! To simplify this discussion, assume that the diamonds are not 5-0, and the slam depends merely upon the club finesse. Normally two-to-one odds are needed to justify a grand slam bid, but these odds are based on the assumption that a small slam is safe. In this case, with a major suit lead, declarer will take either 11 or 13 tricks, never 12. By bidding seven, half the time declarer will score 1440 or 2140 points. At rubber bridge, a nonvulnerable game is worth approximately 300 points, even though no points are scored till the rubber is completed. When the club finesse fails, he will score − 100 or − 200. By bidding seven, he will average + 670 not vulnerable or + 970 vulnerable. This is better than he can score at any other contract.

Why is 7♣ not the ideal contract for duplicate also? The reason is that it will be very difficult, if not impossible, to get to *any* slam. The best contract is 6♣. Just bidding six, and making seven, will be good for a top board when no one else is in a slam. If the club finesse fails, down one may still be worth some points since the 3 NT bidders may also be down one.

It is time to move on from theory to some practical applications.

WEST	NORTH	EAST	SOUTH
			1♡
Pass	1 NT	Pass	2◇
Pass	?		

What should North bid with the following?

♠ Q 10 x
♡ 10 9 x
◇ J 10 x x
♣ Q J x

At rubber bridge, the answer is clear cut. Pass, for two reasons. 2♦ should be safer than 2♥ especially if South has only four hearts. Also, if North bids 2♥, South may bid again, while a pass will prevent him from doing so. Surely 2♦ will be safer than 3♥. Since game is out of the question, one should stop in the safest contract.

With   ♠ x x x   or   ♠ A x x
              ♥ Q x x   ♥ Q 10
              ◊ K Q x x   ◊ K x x
              ♣ x x x   ♣ x x x x x

a false preference for 2♥ would be sound tactics at rubber bridge because game is still fairly likely.

At duplicate, a return to 2♥ is advisable on all three hands. In the last two cases, the reason is the same as for rubber bridge: Game is still possible, and if opener has to pass, the hand may play as well (or within one trick as well) as hearts as at diamonds. In the first case, the reason is different. The hope is that opener will pass, and that he will pick up an extra 10 or 20 points in hearts. Quite frequently he will get too high or be defeated by a bad break, but the risk is justifiable because the odds are right.

WEST	NORTH	EAST	SOUTH
			1♥
Pass	1♠	Pass	?

What should South bid with:

         ♠ K x x
         ♥ A K x x x
         ◊ A 10 9 x
         ♣ x

At rubber bridge, the correct bid is surely 2◊. Unless North can bid again, there will be no game. If he does bid again, the delayed spade support will describe this hand perfectly: a pretty good hand, three-card spade support, and a singleton club. This sequence has the best chance to indicate whether the two hands fit, whether they belong in game, and what the best game (or slam!) contract will be. For example, with:

         ♠ A x x x x
         ♥ 10 x
         ◊ K J x
         ♣ x x x

North would pass a raise to 2♠, but would gladly bid four over the more descriptive sequence. Furthermore, responder would keep the bidding open by taking a false preference of 2♥ over 2◊ with the hand just described — at rubber bridge.

At duplicate, South should raise to 2♠ immediately. North might have to pass either a 2♠ or a 2◊ bid, and if so, 2♠ would surely be the better duplicate contract. The superior results at partscore contracts compensate for less efficient game and slam bidding since partscores are just as important as games or slams at duplicate. When each hand is worth as much as another, one cannot afford to adopt a style of bidding, which is bad for the partscore hands and good only for games and slams. Besides, there are hands such as the last example when responder would pass a 2◊ rebid *at duplicate* (rather than risk an inferior partscore contract by giving a false preference) even though he would always bid again at rubber bridge. Competitive bid-

ding is more competitive at duplicate. The first hand of this article illustrated a situation where it was advisable to reopen at duplicate and advisable to sell out at rubber bridge. It would be just as disastrous to let the opponents play 2♥ when one could make 2♠ as it would be to take an 800-point set.

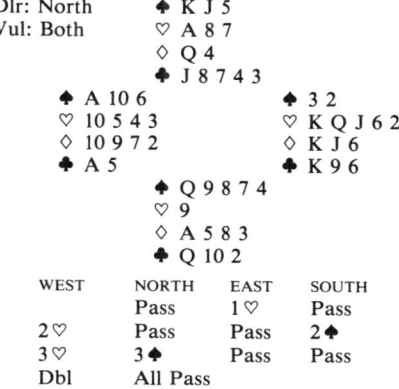

Dlr: North
Vul: Both

	♠ K J 5	
	♥ A 8 7	
	◊ Q 4	
	♣ J 8 7 4 3	

♠ A 10 6   ♠ 3 2
♥ 10 5 4 3   ♥ K Q J 6 2
◊ 10 9 7 2   ◊ K J 6
♣ A 5   ♣ K 9 6

         ♠ Q 9 8 7 4
         ♥ 9
         ◊ A 5 8 3
         ♣ Q 10 2

WEST	NORTH	EAST	SOUTH
	Pass	1♥	Pass
2♥	Pass	Pass	2♠
3♥	3♠	Pass	Pass
Dbl	All Pass		

East–West must defend carefully to defeat 3♠. As the cards lie, they can make 4♥. There are several interesting features about the bidding. The opening bid and raise were routine. So was the 2♠ bid — at duplicate. West properly bid 3♥ since he had a maximum raise. The first questionable bid was North's raise to 3♠. Usually, when the opponents are pushed one trick higher by a reopening bid, the percentage bid is to pass in all close situations. The reopener has already inferred from the opponents' bidding that his partner has high cards, and his partner has no business bidding again to show these same high cards. He should bid again only with good distribution or cards exceptionally well placed. The result from passing should be no worse than at other tables where someone failed to reopen, and it will be better than when the opponents have been pushed beyond their depth. However, North's questionable bid would have gained him a top if West had not doubled. West knew that he would get a very poor score, perhaps 2 matchpoints out of 12, if North–South should make exactly 3♠. Consequently a double could not cost more than 2 matchpoints. On the other hand, if North–South should make exactly eight tricks, it would be extremely costly not to double. West actually a good defensive hand, and is tempted to double anyway; he would double with a poorer hand than he actually has. At rubber bridge a double which could convert a partscore into game would need about seven-to-one odds in its favor.

In duplicate, a double is sometimes the percentage bid even when the odds are *against* defeating the contract. Suppose, for example, that East–West were to bid 4♥ over 3♠. North–South are doomed to get a bottom anyway, since presumably other pairs will not bid game. So a double won't cost them a thing. If the hands were changed slightly so that 4♥ could be defeated, a double would gain a few points, since +200 is better than North–South could do in spades. With nothing to lose and everything to gain, a double must be the right bid. If a double can lose only 2 points and may gain 9 or 10, it is a good gamble, even when one expects the contract to be made.

Another way it pays to be more competitive in duplicate is taking sacrifices. For example, suppose the bidding has gone as follows:

WEST	NORTH	EAST	SOUTH
			1 ♡
Pass	3 ♣	Pass	3 ◇
Pass	3 ♡	Pass	4 NT
Pass	5 ♡	Pass	7 ♡
Pass	Pass	?	

Only North–South are vulnerable, and East holds

```
♠ Q J 10 9
♡ x x
◇ x x x
♣ J 10 x x
```

At rubber bridge, he has no problem. It would be foolish to take a deliberate 2100-point sacrifice to save a measly 110 points. The opponents are not infallible, and partner may win a trick with the ◇ Q. At duplicate it is very tempting, and probably correct, to bid 7 ♣. North–South are unlikely to bid 7 NT with their unbalanced hands, and if they do, there is a good chance of setting them. The real problem is whether most North–South pairs will bid a grand slam. If not, −2100 would be a bad result, and it is better to gamble on defeating 7 ♡, just the same as at rubber bridge.

The more common dilemma is whether or not to take a sacrifice against a game contract. In rubber bridge, it is losing tactics to take deliberate 500-point sacrifice against a vulnerable game when there is any reasonable hope of defeating it. In duplicate, the sacrifice is correct if the contract is a normal one and a favorite to make.

Marshall Miles

MATCHPOINT DEFENSE. Defense at duplicate is often more difficult than at rubber bridge. In the latter, the objective is clear-cut: try to set the contract. It makes little difference when declarer makes an overtrick through an unsuccessful attempt to defeat him. At duplicate, the overtrick makes a great deal of difference.

```
            ♠ K J 5
            ♡ 9 3 2
            ◇ A Q J 8 5
            ♣ Q 6
♠ Q 8                    ♠ 7 6 3
♡ A 8 7 4                ♡ K J 10
◇ 9 7                    ◇ 10 3 2
♣ K 9 7 5 2              ♣ J 10 8 3
            ♠ A 10 9 4 2
            ♡ Q 6 5
            ◇ K 6 4
            ♣ A 4
```

WEST	NORTH	EAST	SOUTH
			1 ♠
Pass	2 ◇	Pass	2 ♠
Pass	4 ♠	All Pass	

West leads a small club, won by dummy's queen. Declarer plays the ♠ K, then takes a losing trump finesse to West's doubleton queen. What should West do? At rubber bridge, he should lead a low

heart. This play will set the contract whenever it can be set — when East has ♡ K-Q-x or K-J-10; also when he has ♡ J-10-9 and the ◇ K. At duplicate the right play is not clear-cut, but cashing the ace is probably correct. It loses in only two situations, and it gains (a trick) much more frequently — whenever declarer has the two red kings.

Suppose that West is on lead with:

```
♠ Q J 10 9
♡ A 8 7
◇ 9 5 3
♣ 7 5 2
```

After the following bidding:

WEST	NORTH	EAST	SOUTH
	1 ♣	Pass	2 ◇
Pass	2 NT	Pass	3 ♣
Pass	3 ♠	Pass	5 ◇
Pass	6 ◇	All Pass	

North apparently has the ♡ K; South probably has two hearts. The best chance to set the contract is to lead a low heart, and hope that East has the queen and that either North or South has the jack. If that situation exists, declarer may misguess. The low heart lead is not correct at duplicate because it stands too good a chance of giving away an overtrick. The opponents may have both the ♡ K-Q, or they may be missing the queen *and* jack (in which case declarer would have to play dummy's king).

The defense against unusual contracts may be just as interesting as the play of unusual contracts.

```
Vul: N-S        ♠ Q 8 7 5 4 2
                ♡ 10 7
                ◇ K J 9 8
                ♣ 9
  ♠ 9                      ♠ A J 10 3
  ♡ A J 8 6 3              ♡ K Q 9 2
  ◇ A 6 5 3                ◇ Q 10 7
  ♣ Q 10 6                 ♣ 8 5
                ♠ K 6
                ♡ 5 4
                ◇ 4 2
                ♣ A K J 7 4 3 2
```

WEST	NORTH	EAST	SOUTH
		1 ♠	2 ♣
Dbl	All Pass		

West's double is a gambling bid made only because of the favorable vulnerability. West leads his singleton spade and ruffs the low spade return. At this point West can reconstruct the unseen hands almost card for card. Since East opened a four-card spade suit, he also surely has four hearts. The ◇ Q is necessary for the opening bid, and besides, East would have returned the ♠ J or 10 as a suit preference signal if his diamonds were 10-high. West can see that 4 ♡ is cold and easy to reach. Therefore he must gamble on a two-trick set. He does so by underleading the ◇ A. This play risks letting declarer make his contract, but the risk must be taken since +200 would be a poor result anyway. After stripping declarer's red cards, East will lead another spade to promote West's queen of trumps.

Suppose the hands were the same, but with neither side vulnerable, South overcalls 4 ♣. West doubles, of course, and the defense starts out the same way.

This time West should not risk underleading the ◇ A. Plus 500 will be almost as good as +700, but +300 would be a bottom.

Another way in which the defense at duplicate varies from the defense at rubber bridge is that the defenders can take advantage of declarer's greed.

```
                ♠ 10 9
                ♡ 9 8 4
                ◇ A Q J 5
                ♣ A K J 7
     ♠ J 7                      ♠ 8 5 4 2
     ♡ Q 10 7 6 2               ♡ A J 5
     ◇ 8 6                      ◇ K 10 7
     ♣ 10 8 4 2                 ♣ 6 5 3
                ♠ A K Q 6 3
                ♡ K 3
                ◇ 9 4 3 2
                ♣ Q 9
```

WEST	NORTH	EAST	SOUTH
			1 ♠
Pass	2 ◇	Pass	3 ◇
Pass	3 ♠	Pass	4 ♠
All Pass			

The bidding is not recommended, but that is the way it went. West led the ♣2, won by declarer's 9. He cashed three top spades and took the diamond finesse, which won. Dummy's clubs were now cashed for heart discards; East also discarded a heart on the last club. Declarer then ruffed a heart with his next-to-last trump in order to repeat the diamond finesse. This time the finesse lost. East cashed the good ♠8, and the defenders took the remaining tricks. Down one!

Did East make the right play in refusing the first diamond finesse, or was he just lucky? By playing cautiously, declarer could have made an overtrick after East's duck. However East had a psychological factor working in his favor. Declarer risked his contract when he took the diamond finesse. If he wanted to play safe, he would have cashed his clubs first for heart discards. He did not play the hand this way because he was afraid of being stuck in the dummy, unable to take the diamond finesse. Since declarer has risked his contract to take the diamond finesse, it would be inconsistent for him not to play to repeat the finesse, so as to make his apparently successful gamble pay off.

Marshall Miles

MATCHPOINT DUPLICATE, MATHEMATICS OF. See MATHEMATICS OF MATCHPOINT PLAY.

MATCHPOINT PLAY. In duplicate play, the test for deciding between various alternatives is not how much (in total points) a given play could gain or lose, but how many match points it could gain or lose. (But see IMP TACTICS for a discussion of this specialized branch of duplicate play.) When the contract is a normal one, this means, "Does the play have better than a 50% chance of success?" (See hand at top of right column.)
The opening lead is the ♡4 to East's king. West ducks the ♡7 return, playing the deuce. It is almost certain that three more heart tricks will be run by the

```
                ♠ 10 9
                ♡ J 5
                ◇ K Q 10 9 6 2
                ♣ A K 4

                ♠ A K J 8
                ♡ Q 10 9
                ◇ J 3
                ♣ J 10 9 6
```

WEST	NORTH	EAST	SOUTH
	1 ◇	Pass	1 ♠
Pass	2 ◇	Pass	2 NT
Pass	3 NT	All Pass	

opponents as soon as the lead is lost. Combined with the trick already lost and the ◇ A, that is one too many. At rubber bridge, the proper play would be to try for four spade tricks and four club tricks without touching the diamonds. Declarer's chances would not be good, but it would be worth a try with so much to gain, so little to lose. In duplicate there is much more to lose. Down one should be almost an average board, while down two would surely be a cold bottom. The odds are greater than three to one that attacking the black suits will lose a trick rather than gain a trick, which means that playing to make the hand will result in three bottom boards for every top. When the odds are so unfavorable, it is better to play safe for eight tricks. The fact that the contract is for nine tricks is immaterial, since it is the contract everyone will reach.

Following is another example illustrating the same principle. In this case, however, declarer does not deliberately refuse to try to make his contract. He merely adopts a risky line of play which gives him a good opportunity for overtricks.

```
                ♠ 7 5
                ♡ K 4
                ◇ A K 10 9 7 6
                ♣ A J 4

                ♠ A 10 8
                ♡ A 10 7
                ◇ J 5
                ♣ 10 8 7 5 2
```

WEST	NORTH	EAST	SOUTH
	1 ◇	1 ♠	1 NT
Pass	3 NT	All Pass	

A spade is led, and declarer holds up until the third trick, upon which West discards a heart. The correct rubber bridge play would be to attack the diamonds by cashing the ace and king. If West has the queen, it is unnecessary to finesse, since West has no spade to return, and only five diamond tricks are needed. On the other hand, a losing finesse to East's singleton or doubleton queen would be disastrous. In duplicate, the better play is to take a first-round diamond finesse. This play will gain (a trick) approximately twice as often as it will lose (several tricks).

The finesse gains if West holds Q-8-4-3, Q-8-4-2, Q-8-3-2, Q-4-3-2, Q-8-4, Q-8-3, Q-8-2, Q-4-3, Q-4-2, Q-3-2 (10 distributions). The finesse loses if East holds Q, Q-8, Q-4, Q-3, Q-2 (5 distributions). Each 3-2 division is slightly more likely than each 4-1 distribution.

Both the contracts shown were quite normal. It is proper to jeopardize one's normal contract when the odds are favorable. When a contract is exceptionally good, it is proper to play safe, just as at rubber bridge.

A hard-to-reach game or slam, or a doubled contract, would be an example of a good contract. When just making the contract will be worth 10 matchpoints out of 12, only exceptionally good odds would justify jeopardizing the contract for an overtrick.

Some of the most interesting problems arise in the play of unusual contracts at duplicate.

```
Dlr: North      ♠ A 10 6 4 2
Vul: N–S        ♡ 8 5
                ◊ Q 2
                ♣ Q 5 3 2

                ♠ K J 9 5
                ♡ 4 2
                ◊ A K 10 9 3
                ♣ 6 4
```

WEST	NORTH	EAST	SOUTH
	Pass	1♡	1♠
4♡	4♠	Pass	Pass
Dbl	All Pass		

North's 4♠ bid was a bit odd, considering the vulnerability, and many South players would fail to overcall with a four-card suit. It is safe to say that 4♠ doubled will not be played at any other table, and down two will be a bottom, not even a tie for bottom. West leads the ♡Q, followed by the jack. Next he plays the ♣A followed by the ♣J to East's king (dummy playing low). East returns the ◊2, and West does not cover the 10. The only problem is how to play the trump suit for no losers. If the spades are split 2–2 and the diamonds no worse than 4–2 the opponents cannot make 4♡; consequently – 200 would be a bottom. Declarer must base his play on the assumption that 4♡ can be made, and a singleton spade is more likely than a singleton diamond. It appears that West has five clubs to his partner's two, so if anyone has a singleton spade, it will be West. The proper play is to lead to the ace and finesse East for the queen. This works, since the four hands are as follows:

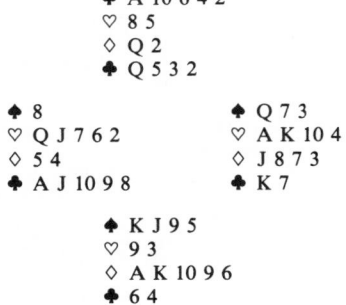

```
                ♠ A 10 6 4 2
                ♡ 8 5
                ◊ Q 2
                ♣ Q 5 3 2

  ♠ 8                       ♠ Q 7 3
  ♡ Q J 7 6 2               ♡ A K 10 4
  ◊ 5 4                     ◊ J 8 7 3
  ♣ A J 10 9 8              ♣ K 7

                ♠ K J 9 5
                ♡ 9 3
                ◊ A K 10 9 6
                ♣ 6 4
```

Suppose that the four hands and bidding were changed slightly. The only difference in the bidding is that the 4♠ contract is not doubled.

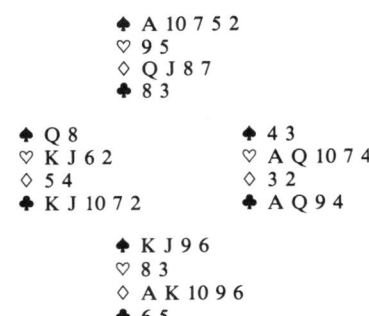

```
                ♠ A 10 7 5 2
                ♡ 9 5
                ◊ Q J 8 7
                ♣ 8 3

  ♠ Q 8                     ♠ 4 3
  ♡ K J 6 2                 ♡ A Q 10 7 4
  ◊ 5 4                     ◊ 3 2
  ♣ K J 10 7 2              ♣ A Q 9 4

                ♠ K J 9 6
                ♡ 8 3
                ◊ A K 10 9 6
                ♣ 6 5
```

The defenders take the first four tricks in hearts and clubs, then exit with a diamond. Should declarer play the same as before? The fact that he is not doubled enables him to make an unusual type of safety play. He should bang down the ♠A–K. If the queen does not fall, he doesn't care, because he knows that 4♡ is cold, and – 200 will be a good sacrifice. What he does not want to risk is a – 200 when, as here, the opponents can only make 3♡. Minus 100 will beat all the – 140 scores.

```
Dlr: South      ♠ 7 6 5
Vul: E–W        ♡ K 7 6 2
                ◊ K 5 4 2
                ♣ 5 2

                ♠ K 3
                ♡ A Q 4 3
                ◊ Q J 3
                ♣ J 8 6 3
```

South opens with a weak notrump, and the other players pass. West leads the ♠4 to East's ace. East returns the jack, and West plays the deuce. Before planning the play, declarer should evaluate his contract, and try to determine what other pairs in direct competition will be doing. If they buy the bid, most of them will be playing hearts. They will score 110 or 140, depending upon how the hand breaks. It is impossible to do as well at notrump as at hearts, no matter how badly the opponents defend, so the only hope to salvage the board is that the opponents can make something. Sure enough, North–South have a maximum of five defensive tricks against spades, and perhaps only three or four, depending upon the distribution. Since it is not possible to beat the pairs playing in hearts, the proper attitude is to forget about them and to concentrate on beating the pairs defending against spades. If North–South were vulnerable, it would be necessary to steal a diamond trick somehow — minus 200 would be no good at all. But not vulnerable, North–South can afford a two-trick set. Minus 100 should be just as good as – 50. The proper play is not to try to steal anything, but just to hope that the hearts will break so that five tricks can be cashed. The whole hand is as follows:

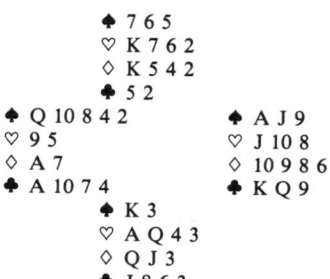

```
              ♠ 7 6 5
              ♡ K 7 6 2
              ◇ K 5 4 2
              ♣ 5 2
♠ Q 10 8 4 2              ♠ A J 9
♡ 9 5                    ♡ J 10 8
◇ A 7                    ◇ 10 9 8 6
♣ A 10 7 4               ♣ K Q 9
              ♠ K 3
              ♡ A Q 4 3
              ◇ Q J 3
              ♣ J 8 6 3
```

At most tables, South opens with a suit bid, and West plays 2♠ or 3♠, after an overcall and a raise by his partner. Minus 100 is an excellent result for North–South, but −150 would be a bottom.

```
              ♠ 5 4 2
              ♡ A Q 6 4 3
              ◇ 10 9 3
              ♣ 4 2

              ♠ A J
              ♡ K J 10 7
              ◇ A K J 7
              ♣ Q 6 5
```

WEST	NORTH	EAST	SOUTH
			1♡
Pass	2♡	Pass	3 NT
All Pass			

West leads the ♠K. How should declarer play this contract? The first question is what will happen at the other tables. It seems quite likely that most of the field will be playing at 4♡. With the same spade lead, the declarers in 4♡ will either make five by discarding a club on the fourth diamond, or be down one if the diamond finesse fails. What are the prospects in notrump? To make four or be down several if the diamond finesse fails. That is, down several if the finesse *is attempted* and fails. The only chance for a decent board is not to take the diamond finesse, and to hope that it does not work. It it does not work, down at 3 NT will tie the field, which will be down one at 4♡. If the queen happens to be a doubleton, offside, refusing the finesse will result in an overtrick and a top.

```
              ♠ K 6 5
              ♡ K 7
              ◇ 7 5 3 2
              ♣ 8 5 4 3

              ♠ A J 10 9 3
              ♡ A 8 4
              ◇ A Q
              ♣ A 10 6
```

The opening lead against 3 NT is a small diamond, East playing the jack. At this point, nine tricks are cold, and an overtrick is made if declarer guesses the spades right. How many tricks will the 4♠ bidders take? Presumably they will not get a diamond lead, and they will take nine or ten tricks, depending upon how they guess the spades. Nine or ten tricks can be taken at notrump, depending upon the spade guess. Nine tricks at notrump beat nine tricks at spades; ten tricks at notrump beat ten tricks at spades. If declarer can guess the spades the same way as the declarers playing 4♠, he will automatically get a

good result. The normal play in spades is to ruff the third round of hearts, then play the ♠K and finesse the jack on the next round. Playing at notrump, declarer should also finesse through East by playing the king and finessing the jack.

Suppose that East had played the ◇K at the first trick. Declarer would have the same nine or ten tricks at notrump as before, but with the diamond finesse working the 4♠ bidders would take 10 or 11 tricks, depending upon how they guess spades. The only chance for a good result at notrump would be to guess the spades right while the spade bidders guess wrong. Their normal play in spades would be the same whether the diamond finesse works or not. Since they will play East for the ♠Q, the notrump declarer should play West for the queen.

In the last example, the proper play depended upon what happened at the first trick. When the opening lead gave declarer a trick, he played one way. When it did not, he played another way. It happened that declarer was more concerned about beating declarers in another contrat than beating declarers in his own contract. However, the opening lead also has an important influence upon the play of *normal* contracts.

```
              ♠ J 10 5 2
              ♡ 6 3 2
              ◇ K Q 10 6
              ♣ A 3

              ♠ A Q 7 4 3
              ♡ A 7 4
              ◇ J 3 2
              ♣ Q 2
```

WEST	NORTH	EAST	SOUTH
			1♠
Pass	2◇	Pass	2♠
Pass	3♠	Pass	4♠
All Pass			

West leads a club, a small card is played from dummy, and when East produces the jack, declarer wins with the queen. How should declarer play the spades? Normally he would take a finesse. However, the lead was very favorable. It gave declarer a trick he could never have won by himself. With a heart lead, declarer would have to be lucky to make four, and he would have no chance for more. Now he has a virtual cinch for contract and an overtrick. Rather than risk a losing spade finesse and a heart return before the diamonds are established, declarer should cash the ♠A, and knock out the ◇A. After the favorable lead, declarer should not jeopardize his advantage.

```
              ♠ 8 3 2
              ♡ 7 6 3
              ◇ A J 10 5 4
              ♣ Q 6

              ♠ A 7 6
              ♡ A K
              ◇ Q 9 3
              ♣ A K J 10 5
```

WEST	NORTH	EAST	SOUTH
			2 NT
Pass	3 NT	All Pass	

Surely every pair in the room will arrive, somehow, at 3 NT. West goes into a long study, and finally leads the ♠4. Apparently West had no clear-cut lead, but he made a good guess. Without a spade lead, declarer would be cold for 12 or 13 tricks, depending upon the diamond finesse. Should declarer hold up two rounds so as to shut out the thirteenth spade if the diamond finesse loses? He should not! If the diamond finesse loses, South is doomed to a poor result by West's fortunate lead. On the other hand, if South wins immediately and if the diamond finesse works, he will still take thirteen tricks. For that matter, the correct play at duplicate is probably to win the first trick even when West leads the king. Winning the first trick will always be worth a top or tie for top when the ◊K is on side. Therefore it is clearly the best play half the time. Even when the diamond finesse loses, declarer may tie with pairs who have held up, but not long enough. Holding up one round is best only when the finesse is off and East has a doubleton spade; holding up two rounds will lose to all other lines of play when the diamond finesse works, and it will be worth a top only East has three spades with the ◊K.

Marshall Miles

MATCHPOINT SCORING.

In duplicate tournaments matchpoint scoring makes each board of equal importance with any other board, whether the hand involved is a partscore competitive bidding situation or a grand slam. Most pair tournaments are scored by matchpoints. Most team contests and occasional important pair events are scored by IMPs, which make larger swings possible on big hands, and approach the tactics of rubber bridge. See DUPLICATE SCORING for the details of scoring procedures. For a fuller discussion of the effect of matchpoint scoring on bidding and play tactics, see MATCHPOINT BIDDING; MATCHPOINT PLAY; SHOOTING. See DUPLICATE BRIDGE for a full listing of the technical aspects of tournament organization. For the origins of the duplicate method, see HISTORY OF BRIDGE. See also LAWS OF DUPLICATE, Laws 72-76.

MATCH RECORDS.

See HAND RECORD; BIBLIOGRAPHY, G.

MATHE.

A defense against strong 1♣ openings covered under DEFENSE TO STRONG ARTIFICIAL OPENINGS.

MATHE ASKING BID.

A method of locating a singleton in a hand that has responded with a LIMIT jump major RAISE, devised by LEW MATHE of Los Angeles. Used principally by partnerships that use limit jump raises to promise a side singleton, the Mathe Asking Bid is opener's rebid of the cheapest denomination after responder's limit raise. If the suit that has been established is spades, responder simply bids four of the suit in which he has a singleton. If hearts is the agreed suit, responder rebids 3 NT if he has a singleton spade, or bids his minor suit singleton.

Mathe Asking Bids may also be used where the limit raise has not guaranteed a singleton.

MATHEMATICAL APPROXIMATIONS.

When we deal with a quantity which can be expressed as a whole number we can express it exactly, so that we do not need to approximate. This does not mean that we never approximate. An example of an approximation is when we give the number of possible deals as 5.36×10^{28}. Rather than write out all 29 digits we express the quantity briefly with an error of less than 0.1% (itself an approximation).

When we cannot express a quantity as a whole number we can adopt one of two forms, vulgar fractions or decimal fractions.

If we use vulgar fractions we can always express a quantity (or number) precisely, e.g., ½, 5-5/13, ⅔, etc. We have, however, the disadvantage that when calculating with numbers of which two or more contain vulgar fractions we have to find the common denominator of such fractions, e.g.,

$$5 \frac{5}{13} \times \frac{2}{3} = \frac{70}{13} \times \frac{2}{3} = \frac{140}{39} = 3 \frac{23}{39}$$

Further disadvantages are the space occupied and the greater possibility of error in calculating or writing down the numbers.

When we use decimal fractions we frequently are able to express a number precisely, e.g., ½ = 0.5. When we have a recurring decimal the number is still expressed precisely, e.g.,

$$\frac{1}{7} = 0.142857 = \frac{142857}{999999} = \frac{1}{7}$$

However, the great advantage when calculating with decimals is that we have a constant common denominator — the appropriate power of 10. When we have recurring decimals we may lose this advantage and either have to approximate or revert to vulgar fractaions.

When our number is one which cannot be expressed precisely in decimal fractions we are forced to approximate. The most widely quantity which can only be expressed as an approximation is the relationship (or ratio) between the circumference of a circle and the diameter of that circle, which is expressed by the Greek letter *Pi*. We give this with the first 10 decimal places, i.e.,

3.14159 26535*

It is customary to 'round up' the last decimal figure we decide to use by increasing it by 1 if the following figure is 5 or more, e.g., our approximations for *Pi* would be

3.14   3.142   3.1416   3.14159   etc.

Out next problem is to decide how many decimal places we need in order to achieve our required degree of accuracy.

If we wish to express a simple number the choice is easy. We can choose quite arbitrarily and anyone who is given that number knows that it is accurate to within one-half either way of the last digit, e.g.,

3.142 must lie between 3.1415 and 3.142499 . . . .

Our difficulty arises when we have to perform mathematic operations on one or more approximations. We may not achieve the degree of accuracy we require, e.g., we have

3.14 × 4 = 12.56
3.142 × 4 = 12.568 (or 12.57).

If we wish our answer to be accurate to n places of

decimals it will usually be sufficient if we approximate to n + 1 decimal places. If we want to be extra careful we can use n + 2 decimal places — no real problem if we have access to a modern calculator or computer. However, if we multiply by large numbers any approximation error will be magnified and we should increase our number of decimal places when we make our original approximations.

We should try to use standard methods for similar problems. Failing this we may find ourselves embarrassed by discrepancies. An instructive example appears in this encyclopedia. Although the articles we mention were first published in the encyclopedia in 1964 it was only in 1982 that the discrepancy was pointed out to the author by his friend, Dott. Ing. Bruno Burian, the well-known Italian bridge mathematician.

Under the heading 'Mathematic Assumptions' the defenders hold Q–J–x–x of a suit. A comparison is made between the probabilities of a named defender holding the doubleton Q–J or the singleton J. These are given as

Q–J	52.17%	22C11
J	47.83%	22C12

Under the heading 'Probabilities a Posteriori' we compare the equivalent holding of a doubleton K–Q or the singleton K when the opponents have a combined holding of K–Q–x–x. The comparison is given as

K–Q	6.8%
K	6.2%

The percentages are based on 100% representing all possible divisions of the four cards, but the comparison is K–Q doubleton = 53.31% and singleton K = 47.69%.

In the first case our approximate ratio is 52 : 48 or 13 : 12, while in the second case it is 34 : 31. The discrepancy is shown more clearly if we use a common base

13:12 = 442:408   34:31 = 442:403

There is a discrepancy of over 1%.

In fact the precise ratio between the holding of the doubleton K–Q (or Q–J) and the holding of the singleton K (or J) is the very simple one of 12:11. A comparatively easy method of making the calculation is given in the heading COMBINATIONS.
* With the advent of computers it has been possible to calculate *Pi* to any number of decimal places within the range of the computer used. It is interesting to note that in 1596 Ludolph van Ceulen, a German mathematician who lived in Holland, calculated *Pi* to 35 decimal places. At his request this number (known in Germany as 'the Ludolphian number') was inscribed on his tombstone.

Alec Traub

MATHEMATICAL ASSUMPTIONS. In all calculations of odds or probabilities, certain assumptions are made. The accuracy of an answer depends upon the validity of the assumptions. A condition that is taken for granted is that the pack has been sufficiently shuffled so that all possible deals are equally probable. Under the heading ODDS GOVERNING SPECI-

FIED CARDS, paragraph 7(b), is an example of another assumption that is specifically mentioned in the discussion.

Many controversies arise because the parties fail to mention the assumptions they make. By listing these clearly, the cause of dispute is often immediately apparent. An example is the following:

NORTH
5 4 3 2

SOUTH
A K 10 9 8

On the play of the ace, West plays the jack, and East the 6. Dummy is entered and the 3 is led, East playing the 7. Should the king be played or the finesse taken? Only two cases have to be considered:

(a) Where West originally held
Q–J   52.17%   22C11

(b) Where West originally held
J   47.83%   22C12

(the notation 22C11 can be read: the number of combinations of 22 things taken 11 at a time).

We can make any of the following assumptions:

(1) With Q–J, West will always play the jack. In this case, playing for the drop is a 52% chance.

(2) With Q–J, West will always play the queen. In this case, the finesse is a 100% chance (a sure thing).

(3) With Q–J, West will play either honor indiscriminately. This means that in the 52.17% of the cases when he held the Q–J, he will have played the queen 26% of the time, and the jack 26% of the time. When he has the singleton jack, he is bound to play it all 48% of the times. The odds are thus 24 to 13 in favor of the finesse.

Assumption (3) is based on a postulate to Bayes's Theorem, published over two hundred years ago, providing that in the absence of knowledge to the contrary, we assume that all prior probabilities are equal. It is the assumption a player should make in normal circumstances. See OPTIMUM STRATEGY; RESTRICTED CHOICE; SUIT COMBINATIONS.

Roy Telfer and Alec Traub

MATHEMATICAL TABLES. The tables below give a variety of information. When a percentage given is less than 1/10,000 of 1% , the number of zeros before the first significant figure is indicated in parentheses. Thus 0.(6)3 should be read as .0000003.

TABLE 1

Probable Percentage Frequency of Distribution Patterns

This table may be used to determine percentages of various distribution patterns, both for hand patterns and suit patterns. Figures are expressed in percentage of hands. The percentage expectation of a particular pattern with the suits identified is given in the last column. For example, the chance that a given player has four spades, four hearts, three diamonds, and two clubs is 1.796%.

Pattern	Total	Specific
4–4–3–2	21.5512	1.796
4–3–3–3	10.5361	2.634
4–4–4–1	2.9932	0.748
5–3–3–2	15.5168	1.293
5–4–3–1	12.9307	0.539
5–4–2–2	10.5997	0.882
5–5–2–1	3.1739	0.264
5–4–4–0	1.2433	0.075
5–5–3–0	0.8952	0.075
6–3–2–2	5.6425	0.470
6–4–2–1	4.7021	0.196
6–3–3–1	3.4482	0.287
6–4–3–0	1.3262	0.055
6–5–1–1	0.7053	0.059
6–5–2–0	0.6511	0.027
6–6–1–0	0.0723	0.006
7–3–2–1	1.8808	0.078
7–2–2–2	0.5129	0.128
7–4–1–1	0.3918	0.033
7–4–2–0	0.3617	0.015
7–3–3–0	0.2652	0.022
7–5–1–0	0.1085	0.005
7–6–0–0	0.0056	0.0005
8–2–2–1	0.1924	0.016
8–3–1–1	0.1176	0.010
8–3–2–0	0.1085	0.005
8–4–1–0	0.0452	0.002
8–5–0–0	0.0031	0.0003
9–2–1–1	0.0178	0.001
9–3–1–0	0.0100	0.0004
9–2–2–0	0.0082	0.0007
9–4–0–0	0.0010	0.(4)8
10–2–1–0	0.0011	0.(4)4
10–1–1–1	0.0004	0.0001
10–3–0–0	0.00015	0.(4)1
11–1–1–0	0.(4)2	0.(5)2
11–2–0–0	0.(4)1	0.(5)1
12–1–0–0	0.(6)3	0.(7)3
13–0–0–0	0.(9)6	0.(9)2

TABLE 1A

Probable Frequency of High Card Content

This table gives the expectancies of having specific point counts, using the 4–3–2–1 count. Note that the chances of holding exactly one-fourth of the points — 10 — is the most probable, but only by a slight margin over 9. The chart also shows why many players prefer to use a lower range for an opening notrump, say 12–14, rather than the usual 15–17 or 16–18. The chance to use notrump as an opening bid comes up far more often. The chance of holding 12–14 points comes to 20.6345%, or one hand in five. The chance of holding 15–17 is only 10.0963%, or one hand in 10 — only about half as often as 12–14. Of course most of the hands with these counts will not be opened 1 NT for one reason or another — usually distribution.

Point Count	%	Point Count	%
0	.3639	16	3.3109
1	.7884	17	2.3617
2	1.3561	18	1.6051
3	2.4624	19	1.0362
4	3.8454	20	.6435
5	5.1862	21	.3779
6	6.5541	22	.2100
7	8.0281	23	.1119
8	8.8922	24	.0559
9	9.3562	25	.0264
10	9.4051	26	.0117
11	8.9447	27	.0049
12	8.0269	28	.0019
13	6.9143	29	.0007
14	5.6933	30	.0002
15	4.4237	31–37	.0001

TABLE 2

Probability of Holding an Exact Number of Cards of a Specified Suit

This table gives the probability (a priori, before dealing) of holding an exact number of cards in a specified suit. The number of times the specified number of cards can be expected in any suit in the course of 100 deals is four times as great.

Number of Cards	%
0	1.279
1	8.006
2	20.587
3	28.633
4	23.861
5	12.469
6	4.156
7	0.882
8	0.117
9	0.009
10	0.0004
11	0.(5)9
12	0.(7)8
13	0.(9)16

TABLE 3

Probability of Distribution of Cards in Three Hidden Hands

This table gives probability of distribution of the remaining cards in a suit for a one-hand holding in column (a) among the other three hands, column (b) expressed as a percentage column (c). For brevity, probabilities of less than half of 1% are omitted.

(a)	(b)	(c)	(a)	(b)	(c)
0	6–4–3	25.921		3–3–3	11.039
	5–4–4	24.301		4–4–1	9.408
	5–5–3	17.497		6–2–1	4.927
	6–5–2	12.725		5–4–0	2.605
	7–4–2	7.069		6–3–0	1.390
	7–3–3	5.184	5	3–3–2	31.110
	8–3–2	2.121		4–3–1	25.925
	7–5–1	2.121		4–2–2	21.212
	6–6–1	1.414		5–2–1	12.727
	8–4–1	0.884		5–3–0	3.590
1	5–4–3	40.377		4–4–0	2.493
	6–4–2	14.683		6–1–1	1.414
	6–3–3	10.767		6–2–0	1.305
	5–5–2	9.911	6	3–2–2	33.939
	4–4–4	9.347		4–2–1	28.282
	7–3–2	5.873		3–3–1	20.740
	6–5–1	4.405		4–3–0	7.977
	7–4–1	2.447		5–1–1	4.242
	8–3–1	0.734		5–2–0	3.916
	8–2–2	0.601		6–1–0	0.870
2	4–4–3	26.170	7	3–2–1	53.333
	5–4–2	25.695		2–2–2	14.545
	5–3–3	18.843		4–1–1	11.111
	6–3–2	13.704		4–2–0	10.256
	6–4–1	5.710		3–3–0	7.521
	5–5–1	3.854		5–1–0	3.077
	7–3–1	2.284	8	2–2–1	41.211
	7–2–2	1.869		3–1–1	25.185
	6–5–0	0.791		3–2–0	23.247
3	4–3–3	27.598		4–1–0	9.686
	5–3–2	27.096		5–0–0	0.671
	4–4–2	18.817	9	2–1–1	48.080
	5–4–1	11.290		3–1–0	27.122
	6–3–1	6.021		2–2–0	22.191
	6–2–2	4.927		4–0–0	2.608
	7–2–1	1.642	10	2–1–0	66.572
	6–4–0	1.158		1–1–1	24.040
	5–5–0	0.782		3–0–0	9.388
4	4–3–2	45.160	11	1–1–0	68.421
	5–3–1	13.548		2–0–0	31.579
	5–2–2	11.085			

TABLE 4

Probability of Distribution of Cards In Two Hidden Hands

This table gives the probability of distribution of cards in two given hands. Column (a) shows number of cards in the two known hands; column (b) shows the number of outstanding cards in the two hidden hands; column (c) the ways in which these cards may be divided; column (d) shows the percentage of cases in which the distribution in column (c) occurs, followed by a bracketed figure showing the number of cases applicable. By dividing the percentage in column (d) by the bracketed figure, the probability that one opponent will hold particular specified cards of that remainder can be obtained.

(a)	(b)	(c)	(d)	
11	2	1-1	52	(2)
		2-0	48	(2)
10	3	2-1	78	(6)
		3-0	22	(2)
9	4	3-1	49.74	(8)
		2-2	40.70	(6)
		4-0	9.57	(2)
8	5	3-2	67.83	(20)
		4-1	28.26	(10)
		5-0	3.91	(2)
7	6	4-2	48.45	(30)
		3-3	35.53	(20)
		5-1	14.53	(12)
		6-0	1.49	(2)
6	7	4-3	62.17	(70)
		5-2	30.52	(42)
		6-1	6.78	(14)
		7-0	0.52	(2)
5	8	5-3	47.12	(112)
		4-4	32.72	(7)
		6-2	17.14	(56)
		7-1	2.86	(16)
		8-0	0.16	(2)
4	9	5-4	58.90	(252)
		6-3	31.41	(168)
		7-2	8.57	(72)
		8-1	1.07	(18)
		9-0	0.05	(2)
3	10	6-4	46.20	(420)
		5-5	31.18	(252)
		7-3	18.48	(240)
		8-2	3.78	(90)
		9-1	0.35	(20)
		10-0	0.01	(2)
2	11	6-5	57.17	(924)
		7-4	31.76	(660)
		8-3	9.53	(330)
		9-2	1.44	(110)
		10-1	0.10	(22)
		11-0	0.002	(2)
1	12	7-5	45.74	(1584)
		6-6	30.49	(924)
		8-4	19.06	(990)
		9-3	4.23	(440)
		10-2	0.46	(132)
		11-1	0.02	(24)
		12-0	0.0003	(2)
0	13	7-6	56.62	(3432)
		8-5	31.85	(2574)
		9-4	9.83	(1430)
		10-3	1.57	(572)
		11-2	0.12	(156)
		12-1	0.003	(26)
		13-0	0.(4)2	(2)

TABLE 4A

Probability of Distribution of Two Residues between Two Hidden Hands

A residue is said to be favorably divided when it is divided as evenly as possible, e.g., 8 cards divided 4-4 or 7 cards divided 4-3. In this table, column (a) shows the number of cards outstanding in each of the two suits in the two hidden hands; column (b) shows the percentage of cases in which both residues will divide as evenly as possible; column (c) shows the percentage of cases in which at least one residue will divide favorably.

(a)	(b)	(c)
8-8	11.87%	53.57%
8-7	21.77	73.13
8-6	12.44	55.81
8-5	23.10	77.45
8-4	13.86	59.56
7-7	40.42	83.93
7-6	23.10	74.60
7-5	43.31	86.69
7-4	25.99	76.88
6-6	13-20	57.86
6-5	24.75	78.61
6-4	14.85	61.37
5-5	46.75	88.90
5-4	28.05	80.47
5-3	53.29	92.53

TABLE 5

Tables of Combinations (Values for nCr)

In making mathematic computation involving bridge (see MATHEMATICS OF BRIDGE), the formula nCr appears frequently. Since the formula involves factorial numbers, the computation is tedious (13! means $13 \times 12 \times 11 \times 10 \times 9 \times 8 \times 7 \times 6 \times 5 \times 4 \times 3 \times 2 \times 1$). Values of nCr appear in the table below.

TOTAL NUMBER FROM WHICH COMBINATIONS CAN BE TAKEN

r	2	3	4	5	6
2	1				
3	3	1			
4	6	4	1		
5	10	10	5	1	
6	15	20	15	6	1
7	21	35	35	21	7
8	28	56	70	56	28
9	36	84	126	126	84
10	45	120	210	252	210
11	55	165	330	462	462
12	66	220	495	792	924
13	78	286	715	1287	1716
14	91	364	1001	2002	3003
15	105	455	1365	3003	5005
16	120	560	1820	4368	8008
17	136	680	2380	6188	12376
18	153	816	3060	8568	18564
19	171	969	3876	11628	27132
20	190	1140	4845	15504	38760
21	210	1330	5985	20349	54264
22	231	1540	7315	26334	74613
23	253	1771	8855	33649	100947
24	276	2024	10626	42504	134596
25	300	2300	12650	53150	177100
26	325	2600	14950	65780	230230

r	7	8	9	10
7	1			
8	8	1		
9	36	9	1	
10	120	45	10	1
11	330	165	55	11
12	792	495	220	66
13	1716	1287	715	286
14	3432	3003	2002	1001
15	6435	6435	5005	3003
16	11440	12870	11440	8008
17	19448	24310	24310	19448
18	31824	43758	48620	43758
19	50388	75582	92378	92378
20	77520	125970	167960	184756
21	116280	203490	293930	352716
22	170544	319770	497420	646646
23	245157	490314	817190	1144066
24	346104	735471	1307504	1961256
25	480700	1081575	2042978	3268760
26	657800	1562275	3124550	5311735

22C11	= 705432	25C11	= 4457400
23C11	= 1352078	25C12	= 5200300
23C12	= 1352078	25C13	= 5200300
24C11	= 2496144	26C11	= 7726160
24C12	= 2704156	26C12	= 9657700
24C13	= 2496144	26C13	= 10400600

TABLE 6
Sundry Odds

Various odds have been of interest to bridge players for many years. Below are a number of different possibilities, with odds computed.

Number of different hands a named player can receive

52C13   635,013,559,600

Number of different hands a second named player can receive

39C13   8,122,425,444

Number of different hands the third and fourth players can receive

26C13   10,400,600

Number of possible deals

$52! \div 13!^4$
53,644,737,765,488,792,839,237,440,000

Number of possible auctions with North as dealer, assuming that East and West pass throughout

$2^{36} - 1 = 68,719,476,735$

Number of possible auctions with North as dealer, assuming that East and West do not pass throughout

$(4 \times 22^{35} - 1) \div 3 = 128,745,650,347,030,683,$
120,231,926,111,609,371,363,122,697,557

Odds against each player having a complete suit

2,235,197,406,895,366,368,301,559,999 to 1

Odds against each player receiving identical hands except for difference of suit

♠ A K Q	♠ J 10 9	♠ 8 7 6	♠ 5 4 3 2
♡ J 10 9	♡ 8 7 6	♡ 5 4 3 2	♡ A K Q
◇ 8 7 6	◇ 5 4 3 2	◇ A K Q	◇ J 10 9
♣ 5 4 3 2	♣ A K Q	♣ J 10 9	♣ 8 7 6

Approximately: 55,976,427,337,829,109,025 to 1

Odds against receiving a hand

AKQ AKQ AKQ AKQJ
the J being in any of the four suits:
158,753,389,899 to 1

Odds against receiving a perfect hand, a hand that will produce 13 tricks in notrump irrespective of the opening lead or the composition of the other three hands:

169,066,442 to 1

Odds against a YARBOROUGH

Approximately 1,827 to 1

Odds against both members of a partnership receiving Yarboroughs

546,000,000 to 1

Odds against a hand with no card higher than 10

274 to 1

Odds against a hand with no card higher than jack

52 to 1

Odds against a hand with no card higher than queen

11 to 1

Odds against a hand with no aces

slightly more than 2 to 1

Odds against being dealt four aces

Approximately 378 to 1

Odds against being dealt four honors in one suit

Approximately 22 to 1

Odds against being dealt five honors in one suit

Approximately 500 to 1

Odds against being dealt at least one singleton

Slightly over 2 to 1

Odds against having at least one void

Approximately 19 to 1

Odds that two partners will be dealt 26 named cards between them, e.g., all the red cards.

495,918,532,948,103 to 1 against

Odds that no players will be dealt a singleton or void

Approximately 4 to 1 against

Odds that four specified cards will be cut by the four players

270,724 to 1 against

MATHEMATICAL VALUE OF GAME. See VALUE OF GAME.

MATHEMATICAL VALUE OF PARTSCORE. See PARTSCORE BIDDING.

MATHEMATICS OF BRIDGE. The mathematics of bridge runs the gamut from simply counting the number of cards in one's hand up to involved problems of probability theory. Some examples of the application of mathematics to bridge are:

(1) Bidding systems, methods, and conventions. Use may be made of the frequency with with various patterns occur (see MATHEMATICAL TABLES, Table 1).

A bidder will also find it valuable to know the ways in which the outstanding cards are likely to be divided among the three hidden hands. We may wish to determine the probability that a trick will not be lost in a suit in which we have a particular holding. It can be determined from Table 3 that with A-K-Q-J-x-x there is a nearly 94% probability that no trick will be lost, but with A-K-Q-x-x-x-x, the probability is only 84%.

(2) Sacrifice bidding.

(3) Choice among part-score, game, and slam. These are dependent on EXPECTATION, and of course, on correctly estimating the value of the players' hands.

(4) Percentage play. This is shown in MATHEMATICAL TABLES, Table 4.

(5) Safety play. This is governed by expectation. See SUIT COMBINATIONS.

(6) Countering false cards (see DECEPTION, MATHEMATICS OF; FALSECARDING).

To express and solve such mathematic problems are used the ordinary arithmetic symbols, and also the following two.

n! (read, n factorial), meaning that one multiplies all the numerals starting at 1, up to and including the number represented by n.

nCr (read, the number of combinations in which n things can be selected r at a time). Thus 52C13 is the number of different hands of 13 cards that can be dealt to a single player from a pack of 52 cards. The formula for finding this is:

$$\frac{n!}{(n-r)! \times r!} \quad \text{or} \quad \frac{52!}{39! \times 13!}$$

Applications of this formula are, among others,

(a) NUMBER OF POSSIBLE HANDS. DEALS

(b) The number of cards held in a suit

(c) Hand patterns

(d) ODDS GOVERNING SPECIFIED CARDS

The following headings also cover facets of mathematics of bridge: CARDS, NEUTRAL AND POSITVE; DECEPTION, MATHEMATICS OF; EXPECTATION; HAND PATTERNS; MATHEMATIC ASSUMPTIONS; BIBLIOGRAPHY, M; MATHEMATICS OF MATCH-POINT PLAY; NUMBER OF POSSIBLE HANDS, DEALS; ODDS, IN BRIDGE; OPTIMUM STRATEGY; PERCENTAGE PLAY; PROBABILITIES, A POSTERIORI; PROBABILITIES, A PRIORI; PROBABILITY OF SUCCESSIVE EVENTS; SUIT, NUMBER OF CARDS IN; VALUE OF GAME.

Alex Traub and Roy Telfer

MATHEMATICS OF DECEPTION. See DECEPTION, MATHEMATICS OF.

MATHEMATICS OF MATCHPOINT PLAY. The values of a game do not apply to duplicate at matchpoints. A nonvulnerable game is always worth 300, a vulnerable game, 500, and a partscore 50 points, as opposed to the generally assumed values of 350, 500, or 700, and 100 points at rubber bridge.

This is particularly applicable to SAFTEY PLAYS. In matchpoint duplicate, a safety play is used only if the distribution to be guarded against has a probability of more than 50%. Of course, if the contract is an excellent one that only a few other competitors will arrive at, any safety play that will ensure it is used; similarly if the contract is a very bad one, the best chance to make a good score is that better contracts will be defeated by unusual distribution, so any possible safety play is used. For other considerations at matchpoint play, see MATCHPOINT BIDDING, MATCHPOINT PLAY and MATCHPOINT DEFENSE.

MAX or MAXIMUM. The greatest number of tricks which can be made with any holding. However, "to play for the maximum" may be used technically to indicate the line of play which will produce the maximum average number of tricks in the long run. The term is used in this sense in the article on SUIT COMBINATIONS. The word also can be used to describe a holding in high card strength or to justify a bid, e.g., "I had a maximum."

MAXIMAL OVERCALL DOUBLE. A type of COMPETITIVE DOUBLE used to invite game when the auction is too crowded for any other approach. The following situation is typical:

WEST	NORTH	EAST	SOUTH
			1♠
2♡	2♠	3♡	?

South may have a hand with which he wishes to signoff in 3♠ or a hand worth a game invitation. Either hand can be described if the maximal overcall double is used as a conventional bid inviting game and the 3♠ bid is reserved for use as a signoff.

If the enemy competition is not in the *maximum* suit (the one just below South's), however, maximal overcall doubles are not needed if the partnership has agreed that opener's bid in the available side suit consitutes a general game try:

WEST	NORTH	EAST	SOUTH
			1♠
2♢	2♠	3♢	?

Here South can bid 3♡ (conventional, forcing) to invite game in spades and bid 3♠ to sign off, so some advocates of maximal overcall doubles prefer to use this double for penalties. See also COMPETITIVE DOUBLES.

MAYONNAISE. Variant of GOULASH.

McCABE ADJUNCT. See WEAK TWO-BIDS.

McKENNEY. Standard term in Great Britain for the SUIT PREFERENCE signal, named for WILLIAM E. McKENNEY of the AMERICAN CONTRACT BRIDGE LEAGUE, who helped popularize it.

McKENNEY–BALDWIN MOVEMENT. One of a series of pair movements planned by WILLIAM E. McKENNEY and worked out by RUSSELL J. BALDWIN, then respectively secretary and tournament director of the AMERICAN BRIDGE LEAGUE.

The most widely used were two-session pair movements for 16 to 32 pairs, in which each pair played against each of the others in the course of two sessions, with approximately BALANCED COMPARISONS. One session consisted of a MITCHELL MOVEMENT using the APPENDIX TABLE concept, and the other of an INTERWOVEN HOWELL.

McKENNEY SIGNAL. See SUIT PREFERENCE.

McKENNEY TROPHY. This trophy is presented to the ACBL member who has accumulated the most master points during the calendar year. The trophy was put into play on January 1, 1938 by WILLIAM E. McKENNEY, ACBL executive secretary. The previous year the AMERICAN BRIDGE LEAGUE awarded a trophy to CHARLES H. GOREN for winning the greatest number of master points in one year, hence this competition dates back to 1937. Goren dominated the picture in the early years, winning eight times. The winners from 1937 through 1947 are:

1937	Charles H. Goren	1943	Charles H. Goren
1938	Morrie Elis	1944	Helen Sobel
1939	Merwyn D. Maier	1945	Charles H. Goren
1940	Morrie Elis	1946	Sidney Silodor
1941	Helen Sobel	1947	Charles H. Goren
1942	Helen Sobel		

The following are the McKenney victors since 1947, together with their point totals. An asterisk indicates the record was broken that year.

1948	Charles H. Goren	377½	1965	Peter C. Rank	1141
1949	Charles H. Goren	440*	1966	Peter A. Pender	1282
1950	Charles H. Goren	398½	1967	Barry Crane	1309
1951	Charles H. Goren	457*	1968	Paul Soloway	981
1952	Barry Crane	604*	1969	Paul Soloway	1434*
1953	William Rosen	470	1970	Hermine Baron	1399
1954	David C. Carter	468	1971	Barry Crane	1443*
1955	Norman Kay	519	1972	Dr. John Fisher	1387
1956	Tobias Stone	791*	1973	Barry Crane	1562*
1957	Edgar Kaplan	807½*	1974	Kerri Shuman	1619*
1958	Leonard B. Harmon	767½	1975	Barry Crane	1547
1959	Oswald Jacoby	784	1976	Mike Passell	1815*
1960	Robert F. Jordan	872½*	1977	Ron E. Andersen	2009*
1961	Oswald Jacoby	735	1978	Barry Crane	1790
1962	Oswald Jacoby	713	1979	Clarence Goppert	2118*
1963	Oswald Jacoby	1034*	1980	Ron E. Andersen	2725*
1964	Hermine Baron	1370*	1981	Mel Skolnik	2421

MEAN SCORE. A score computed for a board at duplicate play, from which IMPs can be determined. See INTERNATIONAL MATCHPOINTS (for pair games).

MECHANICS OF BRIDGE. Described in sections I, II, and III of the LAWS.

MEDIUM CARDS. The lower honor cards and the higher spot cards. Those which provide BODY in long suit holdings or in support of a partner's bid suit.

MEMBER. (1) Of a table: one of the players constituting a table at rubber bridge, whether actively playing or awaiting re-entry to the table for the next rubber, or round of CHICAGO; (2) of a team: a player whose name was listed on the official entry blank whether actively playing or not (see RESERVE PLAYER); (3) of the ACBL: a person who has joined one of the geographical units chartered by the ACBL; see BYLAWS OF THE ACBL; (4) of a club: a player who is eligible to compete in duplicate play at clubs that are not open to all members of the ACBL.

MEMBERSHIP LIMIT. Table membership is limited to six players, unless exactly seven players are present (LAWS, "Rules for Club Procedure," Section F), and no player may be a member of two tables simultaneously. In order to make up tables with greater flexibility, many of the larger bridge clubs use HOUSE PLAYERS in order to be able to accommodate members as they arrive. For precedence in play at a table, see CUT IN.

MEMORY DUPLICATE. See REPLAY DUPLICATE.

MENACE. See THREAT CARD.

MEN'S BOARD-A-MATCH TEAMS, NORTH AMERICAN CHAMPIONSHIP. See GOREN TROPHY.

MEN'S PAIRS. An event at duplicate competition between pairs of players, all of whom are men. Masterpoint awards are 20% lower than those for events of comparable size and duration open to all players. At most sectional tournaments, the men's pair event is held on Friday afternoon.

MEN'S PAIRS, NORTH AMERICAN CHAMPIONSHIP. See WERNHER TROPHY.

MEN'S SWISS TEAMS, NORTH AMERICAN CHAMPIONSHIP. See Appendix I, Fall NAC.

MENTAL PLAY. Hand valuation is mental play. To estimate the trick-winning value of his hand, the player must foresee the conditions that will obtain when the cards are actually played. The better the player, the more accurate his valuation; for he can foresee only those plays which he can actually execute.

MERRIMAC COUP. The deliberate sacrifice of a high card with the object of knocking out a vital entry in an opponent's hand, usually the dummy. Named after the *Merrimac*, an American coal-carrying ship sunk in 1898 in Santiago Harbor in an attempt to bottle up the Spanish fleet (often misspelled Merrimack, in confusion with the Civil War ironclad that fought the Monitor).

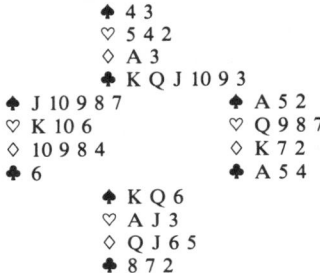

```
              ♠ 4 3
              ♡ 5 4 2
              ◇ A 3
              ♣ K Q J 10 9 3
  ♠ J 10 9 8 7           ♠ A 5 2
  ♡ K 10 6               ♡ Q 9 8 7
  ◇ 10 9 8 4             ◇ K 7 2
  ♣ 6                    ♣ A 5 4
              ♠ K Q 6
              ♡ A J 3
              ◇ Q J 6 5
              ♣ 8 7 2
```

South is the declarer at a contract of 3 NT. West leads the ♠J which East wins with the ace. East at this point sees that the ◇A is dummy's only entry after the ♣A is knocked out, and East, realizing that this entry must be destroyed immediately, effectuates this by playing his ◇K to trick two. This defense holds declarer to eight tricks and defeats the contract.

MEXICAN NATIONAL REGIONAL CHAMPIONSHIPS. A five-day tournament held in Mexico City, Mexico, beginning in 1955. This tournament became an annual event in 1964 when it acquired permanent Regional status. For past results, see Appendix II.

MEXICAN 2◇. A bid showing a balanced hand with 19-21 high-card points and 4-6 losers. A weak five-card major is permitted. Devised by GEORGE ROSENKRANZ as a cornerstone of the ROMEX SYSTEM.

Negative responses (0-4 points) are: pass with diamond length; 2♡ — transfer to 2♠ preparatory to a sign-off in clubs, hearts or spades (2♡ may also be a semi-positive with 5-6 points); 2♠ — transfer to 2 NT.

Positive responses (7 points or more and game forcing) include: TEXAS TRANSFERS; 2♣ — transfer to 2 NT with 7-9 points, balanced distribution; 2 NT — 10 points or more, normally balanced; three of a suit — at least 10 points with a broken six-card suit. Responder's high-card requirements are reduced by 1 point for each five-card suit and by 2 points for a six-card major.

In the modern version (1982) the bid is used differently. If balanced the opener must have 23–24 points, but he may also have an ACOL TWO-BID in a major suit or a strong three suited hand.

MEXICO. An independent member of the WORLD BRIDGE FEDERATION whose teams compete separately in the World Bridge Olympiad. Nationally and locally, however, Mexico's organized tournament bridge is conducted by two Units of the ACBL, and Mexican players are eligible to compete to represent North America on ACBL teams for the BERMUDA BOWL.

Officers, 1982:

President: Dr. George Rosenkranz

Mexican National Federation of Bridge, A.C., Parque Via Reforma 1730, Mexico 10, D.F., Mexico

MICHAELS CUEBID. The use of an immediate cuebid in the opponent's suit as a takeout double. Devised by the late MICHAEL MICHAELS of Miami Beach.

The bid is usually made with a two-suited rather than a three-suited hand:

♠ J 10 9 4 3	♠ K Q 6 4
♡ A J 10 6 2	♡ J 10 7 6 4
◇ 6	◇ A 4
♣ 8 7	♣ 8 7

If an opponent opens with a minor suit, the cuebid is recommended with either of these hands unless the vulnerability is unfavorable. Over a minor suit the emphasis is on the major suits; there should be at least nine cards in the major suits and 6–11 points.

Over a major suit the cuebid shows the unbid major suit and an unspecified minor suit:

♠ 7	♠ —
♡ Q J 10 9 5	♡ 10 9 8 7 4
◇ 7 5	◇ A K J 6 2
♣ A J 10 6 2	♣ Q 6 4

On each of these hands, 2♣ would be bid over 1♠. If partner does not fit the unbid major, he can bid notrump as a request to the cuebidder to show his minor suit.

The major-suit cuebid is unlimited in point-count: the cuebidder may have a strong hand, and plan to take further action.

Over either type of cuebid, partner will usually bid the full value of his hand if there is a known fit; and in some circumstances he may put pressure on the opponents by making an advance sacrifice. He can also make use of a second cuebid to ask for further definition of the cuebidder's hand.

As with other devices which are partly obstructive, both the cuebidder and his partner have to watch the vulnerabilty. At unfavorable vulnerability, freakish distribution is needed to make the cuebid.

MID-ATLANTIC CUP. For the charity event at the Summer North American Championships. Presented by the Mid-Atlantic Bridge Conference in 1951.

MIDDLE CARD. The middle card of an original three-card holding. Generally referred to in connection with opening leads. See THREE SMALL CARDS, LEAD FROM.

MIDDLE GAME. The play, usually referring to the declarer's play, after the original lead or first few tricks won by the defenders, during which the plan of the play is developed, frequently leading to END PLAY positions or preparation for them. Aspects of the middle game are discussed in a number of articles listed under DEFENSE and DUMMY PLAY.

MIDDLE GAME FALSE-CARDING. See FALSE CARDING.

MIDDLE SUIT. See DOUBLE MENACE.

MID-SOUTH SPRING REGIONAL CHAMPION-SHIPS. A five-day tournament held annually since 1941 in Western Tennessee or Alabama (and in past years Louisiana, Mississippi and Arkansas). For past results, see Appendix II.

MILES CONVENTION. A convention devised by MARSHALL MILES using a response of 2 NT to a suit bid, followed by a natural rebid of 4 NT to show a balanced hand with about 19 high-card points. Such a hand is difficult to describe using ordinary methods.

MILES RESPONSES TO 2 NT OPENINGS. A method of responding to opening bids of 2 NT devised by MARSHALL MILES to facilitate safe exploration for slams, games, or partscores in any suit. The principal responses are as follows: 3♣ is STAYMAN; following a Stayman sequence, a 4♣ rebid by responder is GERBER, and a 4◇ rebid is a slam try that may be wholly artificial; JACOBY TRANSFER BIDS; jumps to the four level are natural, showing a broken suit with slam interest; 3 NT transfers to 4♣ and promises a good suit, after which responder may show a second suit if he has one; 3♠ transfers to 3 NT, which responder may pass if he merely wanted to raise to game, or over which he may bid (1) 4♣ to show a good diamond suit or a diamond-major two-suiter, (2) four of any other suit to show 4-4-4-1 distribution with shortness in the suit bid, or (3) 4 NT to show 5-5 or longer in the minor suits.

MILES TROPHY. For the Master Pairs Championship (senior and advanced senior) at the Summer North American Championships donated by R. L. MILES JR., in 1950, for the Master Pairs, an event discontinued in 1975. Past winners are listed under Summer North American Championships.

MILLER SLAM CONVENTION. On stronger hands there is an adjunct to the BOLAND CONVENTION advocated by M. M. Miller, Toronto, whereby 1 NT—5♣ asks for precise point-count, 5◇, 5♡, and 5♠ showing 16, 17 and 18 points respectively. It is forcing to a small slam, and a rebid by the 5♠ bidder of 5 NT requires the opener to show his lowest four-card suit headed by a queen, or any five-card suit.

MINI MCKENNEY: In November 1974 the ACBL Board of Directors established a series of annual awards on a *National* basis and a *Unit* basis similar to the McKenney for the categories of Rookie of the Year, Master of the Year, National Master of the Year, Senior Master of the Year and Advanced Senior Master of the Year. This was implemented by management for the calendar year 1975 and suitable medallions, first known as ''little McKenneys'' were earned by ACBL members in the five classifications below that of Life Master.

ACBL-wide winners in the various categories include:

Rookie of the Year (0–5 MPs)

1975	Robert Blanchard, New York City NY	164
1976	Carolyn Behr, Orlando FL	176
1977	Dr. Jim Sternberg, Fort Lauderdale FL	377
1978	Bob Rosen, North Miami FL	216
1979	Cameron R. Cotton, Sacramento CA	190
1980	Alan Kieist, Cheverly MD	262
1981	Rick Purdy, Duluth MN	123

Non-Master of the Year (5–20 MPs)

1975	Jim Prentice, Santa Monica CA	161
1976	Janice Seamon, Gainesville FL	153
1977	Craig Harrison, Seattle WA	265
1978	Marc Arbour, Scarborough ON	201
1979	Elisabeth Brenhouse, Newport Beach CA	255
1980	Mary Wolf, Philadelphia PA	183
1981	George Landreth, Blackduck MN	388

Master of the Year (20–50 MPs)

1975	Jeff Overby, St. Augustine FL	231
1976	Milton Stern, Dallas TX	306
1977	John D. Jones, Redondo Beach CA	364
1978	Ross Taylor, Hamilton ON	282
1979	Bruce Rogoff, Great Neck NY	223
1980	Bill Weakley, Nashville TN	237
1981	Robert Bobker, Wheeling IL	262

National Master of the Year (50–100 MPs)

1975	Claudia Zucker, Atlanta GA	214
1976	Stasha Wroblewski, Garnerville NY	365
1977	Lynn Deas, Norfolk VA	360
1978	Mark Bartusek, Anaheim CA	479
1979	Dan Jacob, Vancouver BC	296
1980	Keith Woolf, Mentor OH	422
1981	Andrew Kaufman, Bowie MD	304

Senior Master of the Year (100–200 MPs)

1975	Allan Feineman, St. Petersburg FL	508
1976	Shirley Boice, Cheyenne WY	359
1977	Jeff Corbin, Wichita KS	427
1978	Keith Balcombe, Oshawa ON	426
1979	Juanita Skelton, Dallas TX	628
1980	Chris Kaufman, Bowie MD	305
1981	Mary Wolf, Philadelphia PA	363

Advanced Senior Master of the Year (200–Life Master)

1975	Troy Horton, Beaverton OR	493
1976	Claudia Zucker Feagin, Atlanta GA	442
1977	Fran Dolmage, Clovis NM	380
1978	Mike Hansen, Vancouver WA	342
1979	Ken Chen, Charlotte NC	401
1980	Elisabeth Brenhouse, Newport Beach CA	781
1981	Chris Hough, Ann Arbor MI	342

MINIMUM. A holding which justifies an original bid, response, or rebid with no high-card strength or distributional values in reserve. See BORDERLINE OPENING BIDS.

MINI-SPLINTERS. The use of a jump shift to show a raise with shortness in the bid suit. Many players who use mini-splinters play them only by passed hands. Others use the bid to show limit-raise strength only. See also SPLINTER BIDS.

MINOR. A minor suit.

MINOR SUIT. Either of the two lower-ranking suits, diamonds or clubs.

MINOR SUIT STAYMAN. An artificial bid in response to an opening bid in notrump to explore for a minor suit game or slam or to determine whether or not notrump is playable. One such convention uses a 2◇ response to initiate the exploration. See TWO-WAY STAYMAN (2). An alternative is to use a 2♣ bid to ask about minor suits. If opener has four cards in one minor suit he bids that suit; if he has four cards in both minors he bids a major suit control; if he has no four card minor, he bids 3 NT if he has no interest in a minor suit slam, or bids 2 NT if he can tolerate further investigation. If responder rebids in a major suit he shows a singleton in that suit.

MINOR SUIT SWISS. A method devised by ALBERT DORMER and TERENCE REESE for use in conjunction with nonforcing minor suit jump raises, to show a strong hand in support of opener's minor suit without going past 3 NT. In response to a 1♣ opening, a jump to 3◇ would show a very good club raise, and a jump to 3◇ would show a moderately good club raise. In response to a 1◇ opening, a jump to 3♣ would show the very good raise and a jump to 3♡ would show the moderately good raise. All these jumps are forcing either to 3 NT or to four of opener's minor suit.

In determining which jump to make, principal emphasis is placed on the richness of responder's controls.

(a)	(b)
♠ x x	♠ A x
♡ K Q x	♡ x x x x
◇ K Q x x x	◇ K 10 x x x
♣ K x x	♣ A Q

Opposite a 1◇ opening, responder would jump to 3♡ with hand (a), and to 3♣ with hand (b). An alternative recommended by H. W. KELSEY is for responder not to attempt to distinguish between moderate and very good strength, but to choose among all three unbid suits and jump in the suit in which he holds the most secure stopper.

MINOR SUIT TEXAS. See SOUTH AFRICAN TEXAS.

MINOR TENACE. An original holding of king-jack (without the ace or queen) of a suit. After one or more rounds of a suit have been played, the second and fourth highest remaining cards of the suit in the hand of one player are also called a minor tenace. See TENACE.

MIRROR MITCHELL. See TEAM-OF-FOUR MOVEMENTS.

MISCUT. An illegal cut; a cut that leaves fewer than four cards in either portion of the deck.

MISDEAL. An imperfect deal, owing to an incorrect number of cards being dealt to any player, a card being exposed during the deal, etc. See LAWS (Laws 8–12); LAWS OF DUPLICATE (Laws 6, 13, 14).

MISFIT. A term used to describe a situation where two hands opposite each other in any given deal are unbalanced, each containing two long suits and extreme shortages or voids in its third and fourth suits, and further, where these lengths are met by shortages in the partner's hand and the short suits correspondingly met by lengths in the reverse hand. Where not even one 4–4 or better trump fit can be found in a set of 26 cards, the deal may be said to be a misfit as respects those two hands.

MISHEARING. For mishearing of a bid or called card there is no recourse. If a player is not sure what a previous bid was, he may and should ask for a review of the auction when it becomes his turn to bid. If left-hand opponent bids 1 ♦, partner passes, and right-hand opponent bids 4 ♦, a call of 3 ◇ is insufficient, even though the caller may have thought that right-hand opponent had bid 2 ♦.

In the play, dummy should not put a card in the played position until he has ascertained that the card was specifically named by the declarer, and it is the declarer's duty to see that any card he has named is the one actually placed in the played position by the dummy. See ACCIDENTS.

MISNOMER. A bid or play improperly called. If a player bids 1 ♡, for instance, when he meant to bid 1 ♦, he may substitute his intended call if he does so without pause for thought; otherwise his call, if legal, stands, and if illegal, is subject to penalty. Should a player change a call after a pause, he is giving information to his partner to which his partner is not entitled, and a penalty under this provision should be enforced.

If a card is called by declarer from dummy in error, he may change the call if he does so without pause for thought , otherwise the called card, if a legal play, stands as the card played.

MISPLACED BYE STAND. A bye stand in a MITCHELL game with even number of tables placed at a position other than equidistant from the sharing tables. Adjustment can be made for a bye stand too near the head table or too far from it.

If the bye stand is too near, the game can proceed without change until the halfway mark; the next round is the correction round, and players should be warned of an unusual move. The first set of boards is placed on the bye stand, which is then placed in the proper spot. The highest set of boards does not move, but all other boards move down one table. East-West players make their normal move. The North-South players who have just finished playing the highest numbered boards, and the North-South players at the highest numbered table interchange for this round only (keeping their original table number after the correction round). During the correction round, and all subsequent rounds, the last two tables relay boards instead of the first and last tables. (During the correction round, the two interchanging North-South players play against the pair they met on the first round, unavoidably.)

If the bye stand is too far, the adjustment is fairly simple. After half the rounds have been played, Table 1, which has been sharing boards with the highest-numbered table, shares boards with Table 2 for all but the last round. That is the only change during these rounds. The final round is an "adjustment" round. Table 2 and the table just beyond the halfway mark (for instance, Table 5 in an eight-table game) share the lowest-numbered set of boards. There will be two tables at which opponents will meet pairs they have played earlier—this cannot be avoided. For additional information, see *Bridge Director's Manual* by GEORGE BEYNON.

MISSING CARD. A card which is not in any of the four hands. If three of the four hands have a correct number of cards, and the fourth is deficient, and the fact is determined before play ends, a search for the card is conducted; if the card is located, it is deemed to have been in the hand which is deficient. In rubber bridge, if the card cannot be found, the hand is thrown out and a new deck of cards substituted. In duplicate, the director consults players who have played the hand, and a new deck is used to supply the board. When the missing card has either been found, or its denomination established, it is deemed to have been a member of the deficient hand, and may either be an exposed card or establish a discard on a previous trick as a revoke. See LAWS, (Law 11); LAWS OF DUPLICATE (Law 14).

MISSISSIPPI HEART HAND. A famous trick hand dating from the days of whist:

```
              ♠ 10 5 4 3 2
              ♡ —
              ◇ 5 4 3 2
              ♣ 5 4 3 2
♠ —                        ♠ J 9 8 7 6
♡ 8 7 6 5 4 3 2            ♡ —
◇ A K Q J 10 9             ◇ 8 7 6
♣ —                        ♣ 10 9 8 7 6
              ♠ A K Q
              ♡ A K Q J 10 9
              ◇ —
              ♣ A K Q J
```

It will be seen that a diamond lead holds South to six tricks in a heart contract, and a game cannot be made in any denomination. South can make nine tricks in a spade contract, or 10 tricks in a club contract.

An equivalent hand was given by Hoyle in 1747, and the modern version was given by Thomas Matthews in 1804. It was probably used by the cardsharps of the Mississippi River steamboats during the Civil War period, who hoped to persuade South to make a heavy bet on the odd trick with hearts as trumps. It grew in favor among the professional cheaters in the days of BRIDGE WHIST. As doubling and redoubling could continue indefinitely, the odd trick in a low-stake game could become worth $10,000 (or as much as the client was considered good for) with the help of sufficient redoubles. CHARLES M. SCHWAB is reported to have paid off not less than $10,000 on this hand. See IAN FLEMING.

MISSORTING HAND. See ACCIDENTS.

MR. AND MRS. An event at a bridge tournament in which entries are limited to married couples, playing together. In England such a tournament has the name FLITCH. When held, this event has been quite popular, particularly at tournaments held around St. Valentine's Day.

MITCHELL DIAMOND. A bidding system devised by SAMUEL M. STAYMAN and named for his frequent partner, VICTOR MITCHELL. A 1 ◊ opening is used for most strong hands worth 17–18 or more points. Other features are five-card major suit openings of limited strength, 16–17-point 1 NT opening, a natural 2 ◊ opening showing a five-card or longer diamond suit, and weak two-bids in the major suits. The 2 ♣ opening shows either a balanced hand worth 20–22 points or a hand worth an ACOL TWO-BID in a major suit. The 2 NT opening shows a minor two-suiter. The 1 ♣ opening is an all-purpose bid used for any hand of opening strength that does not fit any of the above bids.

MITCHELL–HOWELL MOVEMENT. A two-session pair movement, in which one session is played as a SCRAMBLED MITCHELL and the other as a twin or INTERWOVEN HOWELL.

MITCHELL–HOWELL movements are available at the ACBL office for 16 to 38 pairs, and for 42 pairs. Twinned 20's are used for 40.

Mitchell–Howell movements are especially valuable for two-session games up to 15 tables. For instance, with 10 tables it's fairly simple to run a 10–table Mitchell in the first session and for the second session to put first-session North–South pairs into one five-table section and the East–West pairs from the first session into another section. Duplicate the boards and run two five-table Howells with a nine top.

Since there is an eight top in the first session and a nine top in the second, the second session must be factored down 1/9 to produce an overall winner. ACBL regulations require that the first session be used as the basis for factoring. Another possibility — use a Relay Mitchell in the first session, producing a nine top in both sessions. This also provides a perfect contest — three-board matches against all 19 of the other competing pairs.

The same movement could be used with nine tables. In the first session run a Mitchell movement. In the second session you would have two 4½-table Howells. Let the sitout pairs play each other and avoid a sitout. Top in both sessions is eight so no factoring is involved. The only problem here is that pairs will play one pair they played in the first session.

With 16 tables or more it's usually practical to play two Mitchell sections with a crossover for the second session.

MITCHELL MOVEMENT. A method of play for duplicate whist originated by JOHN T. MITCHELL which has been continued through auction and contract. In the Mitchell movement, the North–South players remain stationary while the boards progress from table to next lower numbered table, and the East–West pairs move to next higher numbered tables at the completion of each round of play. The result of this type of movement is to divide each section in play into two fields which do not compete against each other but play separate contests. To produce one winner using this movement, see SCRAMBLED MITCHELL MOVEMENT.

In a Mitchell movement game, each pair takes as its number the table number at the table where they commence play for the first round, and boards are distributed, one set to each table for an odd number of tables. When there is an even number of tables in play, and it is desired to have as many rounds in play as there are tables in play, no boards are put on table 1, and a set of boards is left between tables after exactly half of the boards have been distributed. (For a 12-table game, the extra set of boards is between tables 7 and 8; for an eight-table game, between 5 and 6; for a six-table game, between tables 4 and 5.) See BYESTAND. The balance of the boards are then distributed with the last set of boards on the highest numbered tables. Through the entire play, the boards at table 2 are relayed between tables 1 and 2, and at the end of each round, are passed to the highest numbered table. The boards at the table with the higher number above the byestand are moved to the byestand, and the lower numbered table gets its new boards from those previously at the byestand.

If the game is not to play as many rounds as there are tables, and the game has an even number of tables, no byestand is used. After half the rounds have been completed, the East–West players SKIP one table in their progression, with normal movement resumed after succeeding rounds have been played.

MIXED PAIRS. An event at duplicate competition between pairs, each of which has one man and one woman member. It is usually the most sociable of the events, and is held on Friday evening at most sectional tournaments. See HILLIARD TROPHY.

MIXED PAIRS, NORTH AMERICAN CHAMPIONSHIP. See ROCKWELL TROPHY.

MIXED TEAM EVENTS. In tournaments in the United States, a mixed team is composed of four (occasionally five or six) players, who are obligated to compete at all times as two mixed pairs, one member of each partnership being of each sex. In the U.S. formerly, and in some other countries still, a team is a mixed team if it has at least one member of the opposite sex.

MIXING CARDS AFTER PLAY. Illegal if a claim has been made to inspect the cards for a revoke, or to ascertain honors or the number of tricks won or lost. See LAWS (Law 67).

MNEMONIC DUPLICATE. See REPLAY DUPLICATE.

MONACO SYSTEM. A prototype relay system devised by PIERRE GHESTEM of France, and used by him very successfully in world championships in partnership with RENÉ BACHERICH.

The 1♣ opening bid was not necessarily strong. The artificial relay bids available, usually by responder but sometimes by opener, were almost always in diamonds.

After major-suit openings the minimum action (1♡–1♠, or 1♠–1 NT) was a relay. Most responses at the two-level were transfers. See RELAY SYSTEMS.

MONITORS. Persons assigned to handle specialized chores at the table during high-level team events, occasionally at high-level pair events. Sometimes the monitor keeps track of how long each pair takes to make its bids and plays so that the tournament committee can make an informed decision concerning penalties for slow play. More often the monitor is the liaison between players on either side of the BIDDING SCREEN. The monitor notes the bids made on his side of the table, then calls them aloud for the benefit of the players and monitor on the other side of the screen. The monitor also frequently is called upon to keep complete bidding and play records of the action at his table. See ROLLING BOX.

MONSTER. A bridge hand of great trick-taking potential either because of a preponderance of high-card winners or because of concentrated strength in long suits and extreme shortness in weak suits. Also, a very big one-session score — a *big game*.

MOREHEAD TROPHY. Donated by *The New York Times* in memory of its long-time bridge editor ALBERT H. MOREHEAD. The trophy was originally awarded to the winners of a special knockout team event that followed the REISINGER team contest at the Fall NORTH AMERICAN CHAMPIONSHIPS in 1967, but was withdrawn when the event proved unpopular. The winners and runners-up were:

1967	1.	Steve Altman, Michael Becker
		Charles Peres, Daniel Rotman
	2.	Paul Deal, Noel Duvic, Frank Hoadley
		Gerald Kendal, Paul Munafo

Since 1973 the trophy has been awarded to the winners of the GRAND NATIONAL TEAMS.

MOROCCO BRIDGE FEDERATION (FÉDÉRATION ROYALE MAROCAINE DE BRIDGE). Founded in Casablanca by M. Tazi Mohamed, in 1957, after independence was achieved by Morocco, succeeding the Moroccan unit of the Fédération Française de Bridge. In 1982 there were approximately 850 members, of whom more than half were in Casablanca. The Federation sponsors annual contests for teams and pairs.

Officers, 1982:
President: Hamid Sebit
Secretary: Djerart, 10, rue Bendahan, Casablanca, Morocco

MORRIS TRANSFER. A transfer bid used by PRECISION CLUB partnerships. After opener bids 1♣, responder uses the conditional transfer when he holds 8 + high card points and 5 + card suit. The transfer asks opener to bid the transfer suit with three to an honor or any four; otherwise bid his own suit or notrump, as his hand suggests. The transfers are as follows: 1♡ to 1♠, 1 NT to 2♣, 2♣ to 2◊,

2◊ to 2♡. If opener fails to transfer, he denies a fit for the requested transfer suit.

If responder bids 1♠ over 1♣, this is a transfer to 1 NT and sets up a Morris Asking Notrump sequence. Responder then rebids as follows:

    2♣ — Stayman
    2◊ — 0 or 4 aces
    2♡ — one ace
    2♠ — two aces
    2 NT — three aces

If opener wishes to learn about kings, he bids the next higher suit, and responder bids up the line. If opener wishes to know about queens, he uses the next step bid and responder answers up the line.

MORTON'S FORK COUP. A maneuver by which declarer presents a defender with a choice of taking a trick cheaply or ducking to preserve an honor combination, only both decisions cost the defense a trick. If the defender wins the trick, he sets up another high card in the suit for declarer, while if he ducks, his winner disappears because declarer has a discard possibility. The name is derived from an episode in English history. Cardinal Morton, Chancellor under King Henry VII, habitually extracted money from wealthy London merchants for the royal treasury. His approach was that if the merchants lived ostentatiously, it was obvious that they had sufficient income to spare some for the king. Alternatively, if they lived frugally, they must be saving substantially and could therefore afford to contribute to the king's coffers. In either case, they were impaled on Morton's Fork.

DOROTHY TRUSCOTT gives this example of the coup:

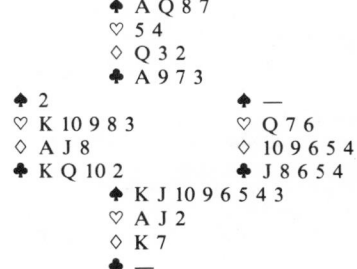

South plays 6♠ after West has opened the bidding with 1♡ and receives the lead of the ♣K. Since South cannot profitably discard on the ♣A, he ruffs the first round, draws the outstanding trump and leads a low diamond toward the queen. If West goes up with the ace, declarer subsequently discards two hearts on the ◊Q and ♣A, while if West withholds the ◊A, declarer discards his losing diamond on the ♣A and loses only one heart trick. Alternatively, had declarer judged that East held the ◊A, he could have couped that defender by leading a low diamond toward his king.

MOTT–SMITH TROPHY. This trophy is awarded every year to the player with the best overall individual performance record in the Spring NORTH AMERICAN CHAMPIONSHIPS. Donated by friends in memory of GEOFFREY MOTT-SMITH in 1961, it was made retroactive to 1958 in order to include all the winners. The winners from 1958 through 1967 are:

1958	Ivar Stakgold	1963	Sidney Silodor *tied*
			with Norman Kay
1959	Lewis L. Mathe	1964	Lewis L. Mathe
1960	Norman Kay	1965	Philip Feldesman
1961	Robert F. Jordan	1966	Philip Feldesman
1962	Robert F. Jordan	1967	Lewis L. Mathe

The following are the Mott–Smith Trophy winners since 1967, together with their point totals:

1968	Norman Kay	135	1976	Larry Cohen	225
1969	Sue Sachs	168	1977	Mark Blumenthal	200
1970	Barry Crane	155	1978	Mike Passell	250
1971	Barry Crane	135	1979	Jeff Meckstroth	215
1972	Paul Swanson *tied*		1980	Jeff Meckstroth *tied*	
	with Jack Blair	159		with Eric Rodwell	173
1973	Bobby Wolff	233	1981	Allan Stauber	166
1974	Ron E. Andersen	250	1982	David Berkowitz *tied*	
1975	Roger Bates	203		with Harold Lilie	198

MOUSER TROPHY. A trophy in memory of WILLIAM S. MOUSER, presented by his friends in 1964. It is awarded to the winners of the Fall North American Championships Life Master Men's Pairs.

MOVE. The change of seats in duplicate bridge after a round has been completed.

MOVEMENT. A schedule of PROGRESSION for players, indicating the seat to be occupied and the boards to be played by each player at each round. The TOURNAMENT DIRECTOR announces the movement to be followed, which is usually arranged to provide each contestant with different opponents at each round.

Specific movements in common use are listed under the following headings: AMERICAN WHIST MOVEMENT; HOWELL MOVEMENT; MITCHELL; SCRAMBLED MITCHELL; SHORT HOWELL; THREE-QUARTER (Howell) MOVEMENT; WEB MOVEMENT; SHOMATE; RAINBOW.

MOYSIAN FIT. A contract in which declarer's trump suit is divided 4-3, usually thus described when the selection is made deliberately. Named for ALFONSE MOYSE, JR., whose ardent advocacy of this choice was part of his case in favor of opening four-card majors and raising with three trumps.

MUD. A lead convention in which the original lead from three small cards is the middle one, followed in play by the higher. The name comes from the letters of middle, up, down, the order in which the cards are played. See THREE SMALL CARDS, LEAD FROM.

MULTI 2 ◇. A convention used widely in many areas of the world but not in North America. It is called the Multi because the 2 ◇ opening bid can have several different meanings, with subsequent calls indicating which type of hand the opener holds. In general, a 2 ◇ opening bid shows a balanced hand with 21–22 points, a 4-4-4-1 (any singleton) with 18–21 points, or a weak two-bid in hearts or spades (6–10 points and a six-card suit, except in fourth position where the opener is expected to be about a king stronger).

Here are the basic responses to 2 ◇ :

Responder Bids	Meaning
2 ♡	To play opposite a weak 2 ♡ bid
2 ♠	To play opposite a weak 2 ♠ bid, but interested in hearts
2 NT	Forcing inquiry, interested opposite either weak two
3 ♣	Natural, 6 + card suit, constructive but nonforcing
3 ◇	Natural, 6 + card suit, constructive but nonforcing
3 ♡	Preemptive in whichever major partner holds
3 ♠	6 + card spade suit, invitational
3 NT	To play, probably based on a long minor suit
4 ♣	Natural and game-forcing
4 ◇	Natural and game-forcing
4 ♡	To play in partner's major at the four-level
4 ♠	To play

To play in 4 ♡ , respond 2 ♡ and then bid 4 ♡ over partner's expected 2 ♠ rebid.

After 2 ◇ –2 ♡

Opener Rebids	Meaning
Pass	Weak two in hearts
2 ♠	Weak two in spades
2 NT	21–22, balanced
3 ♣	18–21, 4-4-1-4
3 ◇	18–21, 4-1-4-4 Opener's rebid is always in suit below his
3 ♡	18–21, 1-4-4-4 singleton
3 ♠	18–21, 4-4-4-1

This is the most common way to use the Multi, but many other methods are possible. It is up to the individual partnerships to decide what kind of hands a Multi can show and to further decide how to differentiate them.

MULTIPLICATING BOARDS. See TWINNING.

MURDER. See BENNETT "MURDER."

MURRAY CONVENTION. Devised by ERIC R. MURRAY, Toronto. See TWO-WAY STAYMAN.

N

NAC. See NORTH AMERICAN CHAMPIONSHIPS.

NAC APPEALS COMMITTEE. The committee appointed at each North American Championship by the ACBL Board of Directors to hear appeals from rulings of directors or complaints as to conduct or ethics. The power and jurisdiction of this committee end with the end of the national tournament for which its appointment is made. See also COMMITTEE.

NCBO. National Contract Bridge Organization. A WBF term for an organization of any independent or self-governing country with at least 250 members. The membership of the WORLD BRIDGE FEDERATION is comprised of approximately 78 NCBOs.

NPC. Nonplaying captain. See CAPTAIN.

NAMYATS. Name sometimes applied to 4♣ AND 4◊ OPENING TRANSFERS. These transfers are used by SAMUEL STAYMAN and some other experts to show strong 4♡ and 4♠ openings. Namyats is Stayman spelled backwards.

NATIONAL APPEALS COMMITTEE. The committee appointed at each North American Championship by the ACBL Board of Directors to hear appeals from rulings of directors or complaints as to conduct or ethics. The power and jurisdiction of this committee end with the end of the national tournament for which its appointment is made. See also COMMITTEE.

NATIONAL AUTHORITY. The body which, in each country, has responsibility for sponsoring and promoting bridge in that country. For the names of such organizations, see entry under each country. Most national authorities are members of the WORLD BRIDGE FEDERATION. See NCBO. The national authority has jurisdiction over all competition in that country and APPEALS on matters of law and fact are taken to the group designated by the national authority to hear them. In the ACBL the national authority on matters of law is the LAWS COMMISSION OF THE ACBL.

NATIONAL LAWS COMMISSION. See LAWS COMMISSION OF THE AMERICAN CONTRACT BRIDGE LEAGUE.

NATIONAL MASTER. A ranking among the players in the AMERICAN CONTRACT BRIDGE LEAGUE. A National Master must have at least 50 master points but fewer than 100. See RANKING OF PLAYERS.

NATIONAL POINTS. See REGIONAL AND NATIONAL POINTS.

NATIONAL TOURNAMENT. A tournament which determines the winners of various events on a nationwide basis. In the ACBL there are three such tournaments held yearly, each with a different schedule of major events. In 1975 these were renamed North American championships. See CHAMPIONSHIP TOURNAMENTS; NORTH AMERICAN CHAMPIONSHIP.

NATIONAL TRUMP. The establishing by a governing body of a particular suit as trump at whist.

NATIONALS. A term for one of the NATIONAL TOURNAMENTS, now titled NORTH AMERICAN CHAMPIONSHIPS.

NATIONWIDE CHARITY GAME. See ACBL-WIDE GAMES.

NATURAL CALLS. Calls which reflect the character of the hand and suggest a possible final contract. A natural call is contrasted with an ARTIFICIAL

CALL. However, some bids which have artificial meanings can be used as natural bids.

NATURAL 4 NT. See BLACKWOOD.

NEAPOLITAN. A system devised principally by EUGENIO CHIARADIA, and played in many World Championship events by a group of Neapolitan players, which has included PIETRO FORQUET, GUGLIELMO SINISCALCO, MASSIMO D'ALELIO and BENITO GAROZZO. Since 1965 Garozzo, as the leading Neapolitan theorist, has gradually revised the system, renaming it the BLUE TEAM CLUB system. It is this version that has become increasingly popular in the United States and was adopted as the official system of the SHARIF BRIDGE CIRCUS. See BLUE TEAM CLUB.

NEAPOLITAN 4◊ CONVENTION. A form of delayed game raise used in the NEAPOLITAN SYSTEM. It is a jump bid which applies when a forcing jump in the intended trump suit is not available:

WEST	EAST	WEST	EAST	WEST	EAST
1♠	2♣	1♠	2♣	1♡	1♠
2♠	4◊	2♡	4◊	2♣	4◊
agrees spades		agrees hearts		agrees hearts	

See BLUE TEAM 4♠-4◊ CONVENTION.

NEAPOLITAN 2◊. See BLUE TEAM 2◊.

NEAR-SOLID SUIT. See SEMI-SOLID SUIT.

NEDERLANDSE BRIDGE BOND. See NETHERLANDS BRIDGE LEAGUE.

NEGATIVE DOUBLE. The original name for a takeout double, in general use from 1915 to 1930, about which time the term "informatory" became current, later superseded by the more descriptive term takeout double. In 1957 ALVIN ROTH and TOBIAS STONE introduced a modern "negative double," in which what was formerly a penalty double of a suit overcall was used as a takeout bid. This feature of the ROTH-STONE SYSTEM was christened Sputnik because it was an important new device dating from the same period as that Russian space satellite.

NORTH	EAST	SOUTH
1◊	1♡	Dbl
	or 1♠	
	or 2♣	

The double shows a hand on which any normal bid is unsatisfactory; it can be made at the one-level with as little as 7 points:

    ♠ K x x x
    ♡ x x
    ◊ K J x x x

Double if partner's 1♠ opening is overcalled with 1♡. See also CARD-SHOWING DOUBLE.

It may also be made on a hand worth an opening bid:

    ♠ A Q 9 x
    ♡ J x x x
    ◊ K
    ♣ A J x x

Double if partner's 1 ◇ opening is overcalled with 1 ♡; follow with a cuebid if convenient. The double is preferred to a bid of 1 ♠ because a free bid is rarely made with a four-card suit (however, some experts prefer to bid a four-card spade suit and use the negative double to how length in the unbid minor. See NEGATIVE FREE BIDS).

The opening bidder responds to the double in accordance with his assessment of game prospects. A cuebid would be the only absolute force. With strengh in the opponent's suit, he can make a penalty pass.

The negative double treatment can be extended to the following situations:

(1) High-level overcalls, whether strong or preemptive, up to and including 4 ♠. The higher the overcall the more likely it is that the opener will decide to pass for penalties, so a shaded raise often should be given in preference to the double.

(2) A natural overcall at the two- or three-level in a minor suit after a notrump opening bid. The double would then show support for one or both major suits, but would not be forcing to game.

In KAPLAN-SHEINWOLD, negative doubles are used after nonjump overcalls only, and promise four cards in any unbid major. The strength is unlimited, and the opener rebids as though the indicated major had actually been bid. Free responses show no additional strength, but promise five-card suits when a negative double could have been made instead.

Defense. When the right-hand opponent has made a negative double, the situation is similar to a bid over an opposing takeout double. A redouble shows high-card strength, and may expose an opening psychic bid. A jump raise of the overcaller's suit would be preemptive. See also ROSENKRANZ DOUBLE.

NEGATIVE FREE BID. A modern solution to a common bidding problem. Consider this situation:

WEST	NORTH	EAST	SOUTH
	1 ♣	1 ♠	?

South has:

♠ x x
♡ A Q x x x x
◇ Q x
♣ x x x

This is not strong enough in standard methods for a 2 ♡ bid, so the usual solution is to make a negative double planning to bid hearts on the next round. But this may be difficult if spades are raised, and the negative double solution is not available if the suit is diamonds rather than hearts.

The alternative is to make a "negative free bid" of 2 ♡ on this hand, or of 2 ◇ if that suit is held. This is of course nonforcing. This obviously affects the use of the negative double. It is no longer needed for a hand that can make a negative free bid, but it is required for stronger hands that would normally make a forcing suit-response at a minimum level. Therefore a negative double followed by a new suit becomes forcing, indicating a hand with game values.

Negative free bids are not needed at the one level and are of dubious value at the four level. Many partnerships agree to use negative free bids at the two and three levels only.

NEGATIVE INFERENCE. Information deduced from a player's failure to take a specific action in the bidding or play. Though this type of inference is frequently available, it is often overlooked, the average player preferring to concentrate on more positive clues.

Here is a hand where the declarer was able to diagnose the location of a critical card based upon negative inferences gleaned from the bidding and play.

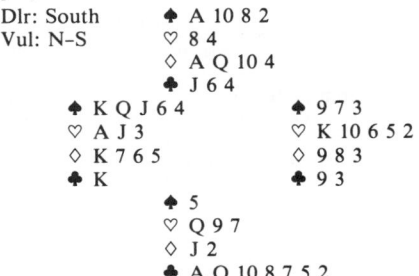

Dlr: South
Vul: N–S

```
              ♠ A 10 8 2
              ♡ 8 4
              ◇ A Q 10 4
              ♣ J 6 4
♠ K Q J 6 4              ♠ 9 7 3
♡ A J 3                 ♡ K 10 6 5 2
◇ K 7 6 5               ◇ 9 8 3
♣ K                     ♣ 9 3
              ♠ 5
              ♡ Q 9 7
              ◇ J 2
              ♣ A Q 10 8 7 5 2
```

The bidding:

WEST	NORTH	EAST	SOUTH
			Pass
1 ♠	Pass	Pass	2 ♣
2 ◇	3 ♣	3 ♠	4 ♣
Pass	5 ♣	All Pass	

West opened the ♠ K, and the declarer, ARTHUR ROBINSON, won with dummy's ace. With the ♡ A-K to lose, declarer had to pick up both minor suit kings. The percentages favor a finesse in the club suit; nevertheless he led a club to his ace at trick two, dropping West's king. A successful diamond finesse gave him 11 tricks.

Robinson *guessed* the club position well. He reasoned that if West had held both top hearts he would surely have led one in order to inspect the dummy and judge the best continuation. The absence of a heart lead therefore marked East with a high heart — if he held the ♣ K in addition he would have responded on the first round. The only hope, therefore, was that West held a singleton king. See also INFERENCE.

Sammy Kehela

NEGATIVE RESPONSES. Artificial responses that show weakness. Examples are: a 2 NT response to a FORCING TWO or an ACOL TWO; a 1 or 2 ◇ response to an artificial 1 ♣ or 2 ♣ opening; or a 2 ♡ response to an artificial 2 ◇ opening. See also DOUBLE NEGATIVE; HERBERT NEGATIVE; SECOND NEGATIVE RESPONSE AFTER ARTIFICIAL FORCING OPENING. For natural negative responses, see WEAKNESS RESPONSE.

NEGATIVE SLAM DOUBLE. See DOUBLE FOR SACRIFICE.

NET SCORE. The result of a rubber of bridge or of CHICAGO after the losing side's score is subtracted from the winning, or higher score. In rounding off to the nearest 100, 50 points counts as an extra 100 in the United States, but is dropped in England.

The term is also used in team matches to designate

the difference between the scores of two teams at the end of a session or a match; it can be expressed in total points or in INTERNATIONAL MATCHPOINTS.

NETHERLANDS ANTILLES BRIDGE ASSOCIATION (BRIDGE BOND NEDERLANDSE ANTILLEN).

Founded in 1963, by 1982 the association had approximately 225 members. It participated in the World Team Olympiad 1964, 1968, 1972, World Pair Olympiad 1966, South American Championships 1963, as well as several international matches in South America. The Association consists of five affiliated clubs in two districts, Curaçao and Aruba. A system of master points was introduced in 1965, and National Championships have been held annually for Open Teams and Open Pairs since 1961.

Officers, 1982:
President: E.H.M. Berend
Secretary: H. Beerman, Mgr. Kieckensweg 44-B, Willemstad, Curaçao, Netherlands Antilles

NETHERLANDS BRIDGE LEAGUE (NEDERLANDSE BRIDGE BOND).

Founded in 1930 by the late A.J.E. Lucardie, and in 1982 had approximately 42,000 members. The League participates in World Olympiads, finishing fourth in 1968, and European Championships, hosting the 1932, 1939, and 1955 events, the Netherlands 1980 World Team Olympiad finishing third. Holland finished second in the 1965 and 1966 European Championships and represented Europe in the 1966 Bermuda Bowl. It won the 1966 World Open Pair Olympiad. National events are held annually. Many of the League's activities are designed to stimulate participation by young players and grass roots players. (Official training-courses for tournament director and bridge teacher.)

Officers, 1982:
President: Henk Maaten
Secretary: Andre Boekhorst, Stadhouderslaan 62, 583 L Utrecht The Netherlands

NEUTRAL CARDS. See CARDS, NEUTRAL AND POSITIVE.

NEUTRAL LEAD. See PASSIVE LEAD.

NEUTRAL SUIT. See ASTRO.

NEW DEAL. A fresh deal to take the place of a misdeal or to replace a deal void for any reason.

NEW ENGLAND REGIONAL CHAMPIONSHIPS.

Originated in 1930 with the BOSTON CHESS CLUB under the sanction of ABL first and then ACBL. In 1937, in some events, the Cavendish Club of Boston ran a second regional for the same New England area. In 1948 the New England Bridge Association took over both sets of regionals and from that time on each event was held only once a year, with the exception of the Men's and Women's Pairs in 1964 and either a Team or Pair event run concurrently with the Knockout Teams. The two-day Individual Championship, held annually since 1945, was developed by the late William Keohane in-

to the largest event of its kind. For past results, see Appendix II.

NEW ENGLAND RELAY. A movement for team-of-four contests originally used for competition at whist. When the number of competing teams was odd, the American Whist League movement was used, but this required the use of a phantom table when the number of competing teams was even. A movement first used in Boston eliminated this necessity by placing two parallel rows of tables, with the lower numbered tables in one row, and the higher numbered tables in the other. Boards are distributed with the first set at the first table, second set at a BYESTAND, third set at the second table, fourth set at a byestand, etc., until all sets are distributed to half the tables and their byestands. Traveling pairs move to the next lower table, and the boards are put on the byestand toward the lower numbered table, and removed from the byestand toward the higher numbered table at the conclusion of each round. During the play, each of the lower numbered tables relays the boards with the table in the adjacent row.

The movement is still in use at some tournaments, but has been largely supplanted by other movements. See TEAM-OF-FOUR MOVEMENT.

NEW MINOR FORCING. See 2♣ REBID BY RESPONDER AS ONLY FORCE AFTER 1 NT REBID; CROWHURST CONVENTION: STAYMAN ON SECOND ROUND; UNBID MINOR SUIT FORCE.

NEW SOUTH WALES SYSTEM. A variation of the VIENNA SYSTEM used by RICHARD J. CUMMINGS and TIM SERES of Australia. The principal features are five-card openings in diamonds, hearts, and spades, strong 1 NT openings, weak two-bids in the major suits. The 2♣ opening, which is used sparingly, is game forcing; the 2 NT opening shows a strong minor two-suiter, and the 2♦ opening shows a balanced hand with at least 21 HCP. A forcing 1♣ opening is used for all other hands, e.g., long club suit, or a balanced hand worth 12–14 or 19–20, or a hand of any strength with 4-4-4-1 distribution.

All responses in new suits are forcing, and jump shifts are used as modified CULBERTSON ASKING BIDS.

NEW ZEALAND BRIDGE ASSOCIATION. Founded in 1936, by 1982 it had a membership of approximately 18,800 in 87 clubs. Based on New Zealand's total population of 3,000,000, this Association is probably relatively the largest in the world. The Association participates in the Far East Championships and in competitions with Australia, and sent teams to the World Team Olympiad 1972, Bermuda Bowl 1974. National events include Open Teams and Pairs Championships, and an Inter-Provincial Teams of Four.

Officers, 1982:
President: Mrs. D.N. Allen
Secretary: Mrs. S.G. Truman, P.O. Box 12. 116, Wellington, New Zealand

NEW ZEALAND RELAY SYSTEM. See SYM-

METRIC RELAY SYSTEM.

NEWGATE. A prison in England where, prior to 1820, whist was played as a three-handed game with one hand exposed as the dummy.

NEWLY FORMED TABLES. These can be created with four to six players ranking according to precedence, this generally being established by order of entry into the playing room. Players leaving an existing table to cut into the new table have lowest precedence. See RUBBER BRIDGE.

NINE or NINE-SPOT. That card ranking sixth highest in a suit, and being between the 10 and 8 in position.

NINE TABLES. At duplicate, nine tables provide for competition among 36 players as individuals, 18 pairs or nine teams-of-four.

As an individual tournament the RAINBOW MOVEMENT offers the best contest. Guide cards are available for this movement.

As a pair event, MITCHELL, THREE-QUARTER (Howell) MOVEMENT or SHORT HOWELL movements may be used. In the Mitchell game, either eight or nine rounds of three boards each can be played.

As a team-of-four event, nine tables provide an excellent movement for meeting each of the other teams in an uninterrupted team-of-four progression, boards going to the next lower numbered table, and players skipping a table toward the lower number. The SWISS TEAM movement does not work well for nine tables. It requires three-way matches, and bad pairings may become necessary in the late rounds. For 8½ or 9½ tables, see HALF TABLES.

NO BID. A term meaning "pass" standard in England and some other English-speaking countries such as Australia and New Zealand where there is some likelihood of confusion in the enunciation of *pass* and *hearts*. The term has been generally accepted by custom, but does not appear in the official laws and is subject to the warning (see LAWS OF DUPLICATE, Proprieties IIIA3) against use of different designations for the same call. Regulations for international play may specifically bar the term because it may be mistaken for another call, e.g., *double*.

NO CALL. An obsolete and inaccurate term occasionally used instead of PASS.

NONFORCING SEQUENCES. A sequence which permits either member of the partnership to drop the bidding. A sequence starting with a suit bid can be assumed to be nonforcing unless it is listed under FORCING SEQUENCES.

Before passing a nonforcing sequence, a player should satisfy himself that a game contract is unlikely to be a sound proposition. He should also be sure that he cannot convert safely to a superior partscore.

NONFORCING STAYMAN. See STAYMAN.

NONMASTER PAIRS. See KEM CARD TROPHY.

NONMATERIAL SQUEEZES. Nonmaterial squeezes are squeezes against strategic values, rather than material values such as winners or guards to winners. Nonmaterial squeezes operate against cards that are apparently idle, but actually perform a vital function, such as prevention of a throw-in, or protection of the defender's communications.

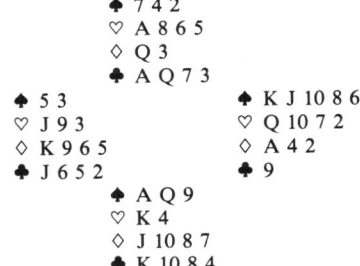

```
              ♠ 7 4 2
              ♡ A 8 6 5
              ◊ Q 3
              ♣ A Q 7 3
  ♠ 5 3                    ♠ K J 10 8 6
  ♡ J 9 3                  ♡ Q 10 7 2
  ◊ K 9 6 5                ◊ A 4 2
  ♣ J 6 5 2                ♣ 9
              ♠ A Q 9
              ♡ K 4
              ◊ J 10 8 7
              ♣ K 10 8 4
```

Neither side vulnerable

Dealer East

WEST	NORTH	EAST	SOUTH
		Pass	1 ◊
Pass	1 ♡	1 ♠	1 NT
Pass	3 NT	Pass	Pass
Pass			

Lead: ♠ 5

South wins the first spade, and he unblocks clubs by leading the ♣8 to dummy's ♣A. The ♣3 is returned to the ♣K, as East discards a diamond. Now the ♣10 is led and East is squeezed: If East throws a spade, it is safe to establish diamonds; a heart discard allows declarer to establish a long heart in dummy which can be reached with a fourth round club entry; and another diamond discard allows declarer to establish that suit, since East must take his now singleton ◊ A before the spades have been established.

Monroe Ingberman

NONPLAYING CAPTAIN. See CAPTAIN.

NONVULNERABLE. The condition of a side that has not won a game in a rubber of bridge. In CHICAGO or four-deal bridge, each pair is nonvulnerable twice; that is to say, on the first deal and on either the second or third deal depending on local rules as respects dealer's vulnerability. In duplicate, deals or "boards" are marked according to vulnerability so that each tray clearly displays the vulnerability conditions, whether they be all nonvulnerable, or either side or neither side. When a pair is not vulnerable, it can bid with slightly more freedom than when vulnerable, because the schedule of penalties for undertricks is set up so as to levy more severe punishment on vulnerable pairs that incur penalties. Frequently then, it will be found that a nonvulnerable pair will "take a save" rather than allow the opposition to make a game, the premium for which can be quite high, especially if, conversely, the team scoring the game is vulnerable. See LOVE ALL.

NORDIC CHAMPIONSHIPS. Organized in 1946 by delegates from the bridge federations of the three Scandinavian nations (Denmark, Norway, Sweden) and Finland, meeting at Copenhagen. The Nordic Championships represented one of the first postwar efforts to revive international bridge competition in Europe. The initial tournament was staged later the same year in Oslo, and the Championships were held on an annual basis until 1949. Iceland joined the competition in 1949 and has been a regular participant ever since. After the European Championships, the importance of a separate Nordic competition lessened, so the event became a biennial competition, except for a three-year lapse from 1959–62.

NORMAL EXPECTANCY. The holding in either high cards or distribution which a player might expect in partner's hand when he decides whether to open the bidding. This can be roughly approximated as one-third of the missing high cards or high-card points, and one-third of the remaining cards in the suit. Partner's responses and future actions modify this concept as the bidding progresses. See SUIT COMBINATIONS and TRUMP SUPPORT for further treatment.

NORMAN 4 NT. A slam convention in which kings and aces are shown with one bid. An ace is counted as 1 point and a king as ½ point, and responses are according to the following table:

5 ♣	less than 1½ points
5 ♢	1½ points
5 ♡	2 points
5 ♠	2½ points
5 NT	3 points, etc.

The 4 NT bidder can usually determine which aces and kings are held by responder.

This convention has been popular in England, where it is credited to NORMAN DE VILLIERS HART and Sir Norman Bennet, and was incorporated into the VIENNA SYSTEM. Several similar methods have been used in America, but only the SAN FRANCISCO convention achieved any substantial following.

Similar responding principles are used in the BLUE TEAM CLUB System and by some players after an artificial 2 ♣ opening.

NORSK BRIDGE FORBUND. See NORWEGIAN BRIDGE ASSOCIATION.

NORTH. A position in a bridge foursome or in a bridge diagram opposite South and to the left of West. In duplicate games the scoring is done by North. In newspaper columns North is usually the dummy.

NORTH AMERICAN AMATEUR PAIR CHAMPIONSHIP. See KEM CARD TROPHY.

NORTH AMERICAN AMATEUR TEAM-OF-FOUR CHAMPIONSHIP. See ROTHSCHILD TROPHY.

NORTH AMERICAN BLUE RIBBON PAIRS CHAMPIONSHIP. See CAVENDISH TROPHY; BLUE RIBBON PAIRS.

NORTH AMERICAN CHAMPIONSHIP. The awards in major events at the three principal tournaments of the AMERICAN CONTRACT BRIDGE LEAGUE, which embraces the United States, Canada, Mexico and Bermuda, are the NORTH AMERICAN CHAMPIONSHIPS. Prior to 1975 they were known as NATIONAL TOURNAMENTS, with National champions. See also GRAND NATIONAL CHAMPIONSHIPS. The major championship events were allocated as follows in 1982:

SPRING
OPEN KNOCKOUT TEAMS for the
 VANDERBILT CUP
MEN'S PAIRS
WOMEN'S PAIRS
MEN'S BOARD-A-MATCH TEAMS
WOMEN'S KNOCKOUT TEAMS
OPEN PAIRS
GRAND NATIONAL PAIRS
SUMMER
MASTER KNOCKOUT TEAMS for the
 SPINGOLD TROPHY
LIFE MASTER PAIRS
MASTER MIXED TEAMS
NON-LIFE MASTER SWISS TEAMS
MEN'S SWISS TEAMS
WOMEN'S SWISS TEAMS
GRAND NATIONAL TEAMS for the
 MOREHEAD TROPHY
FALL
OPEN BOARD-A-MATCH TEAMS for the
 REISINGER TROPHY
MIXED PAIRS
LIFE MASTER MEN'S PAIRS
LIFE MASTER WOMEN'S PAIRS
NON-LIFE MASTER PAIRS
BLUE RIBBON PAIRS
OPEN SWISS TEAMS
GRAND NATIONAL ROOKIE PAIRS

Winner of these events can be found under each tournament listing in Appendix I.

Other events are held at each of the North American Championships that do not have major championship status, but for which the competition is no less keen.

NORTH AMERICAN CHAMPIONSHIPS. Name given in 1975 to the three AMERICAN CONTRACT BRIDGE LEAGUE CHAMPIONSHIP tournaments held each year for North America. (Formerly known as "NATIONALS.") Results are reported in Appendix I.

NORTH AMERICAN GRAND NATIONAL PAIRS CHAMPIONSHIP. See GRAND NATIONAL PAIRS.

NORTH AMERICAN GRAND NATIONAL ROOKIE PAIRS CHAMPIONSHIP. See GRAND NATIONAL ROOKIE PAIRS.

NORTH AMERICAN GRAND NATIONAL TEAMS CHAMPIONSHIP. See MOREHEAD TROPHY.

NORTH AMERICAN LIFE MASTER MEN'S

PAIRS CHAMPIONSHIP. See MOUSER TROPHY.

NORTH AMERICAN LIFE MASTER PAIRS CHAMPIONSHIP. See VON ZEDTWITZ GOLD CUP.

NORTH AMERICAN LIFE MASTER WOMEN'S PAIRS CHAMPIONSHIP. See SMITH TROPHY.

NORTH AMERICAN MASTER INDIVIDUAL CHAMPIONSHIP. Formerly called World Master Individual or Life Master Individual. See STEINER TROPHY.

NORTH AMERICAN MASTER KNOCKOUT TEAMS CHAMPIONSHIP. See SPINGOLD TROPHY.

NORTH AMERICAN MASTER MIXED TEAMS CHAMPIONSHIP. See BARCLAY TROPHY and LEBHAR TROPHY.

NORTH AMERICAN MEN'S BOARD-A-MATCH TEAMS CHAMPIONSHIP. See GOREN TROPHY.

NORTH AMERICAN MEN'S PAIRS CHAMPIONSHIP. See WERNHER TROPHY.

NORTH AMERICAN MEN'S SWISS TEAMS CHAMPIONSHIP. See Appendix I, Fall NAC.

NORTH AMERICAN MIXED PAIRS CHAMPIONSHIP. See ROCKWELL TROPHY.

NORTH AMERICAN NON-LIFE MASTER PAIRS CHAMPIONSHIP. See Appendix I, Fall NAC.

NORTH AMERICAN NON-LIFE MASTER SWISS TEAMS. See Appendix I, Summer NAC.

NORTH AMERICAN OPEN BOARD-A-MATCH TEAMS CHAMPIONSHIP. See REISINGER MEMORIAL TROPHY.

NORTH AMERICAN OPEN KNOCKOUT TEAMS CHAMPIONSHIP. See VANDERBILT CUP.

NORTH AMERICAN OPEN PAIRS CHAMPIONSHIP. See CAVENDISH TROPHY; SILODOR TROPHY.

NORTH AMERICAN OPEN SWISS TEAMS CHAMPIONSHIP. See Appendix I, Fall FAC.

NORTH AMERICAN RUBBER BRIDGE CHAMPIONSHIPS. A form of nationwide bridge competition conducted in 1962 and 1963 by North American Van Lines of Fort Wayne IN, in connection with their sponsorship of the TV series *Championship Bridge with Charles Goren.*

Entrants formed groups for home play. High scorers in each game center area qualified for a knockout rubber bridge competition, the two finalist pairs meeting next evening to play the same hands (pre-dealt centrally) as played in every city. The highest scoring pair east of the Mississippi met the highest scoring Western pair, face to face, in a final

(played in 1962 in Chicago, in 1963 in New York City). Judges were CHARLES GOREN, ALVIN LANDY, and RICHARD L. FREY.

	WINNERS	RUNNERS-UP
1962	Mrs. Joe Garcia, Georgia Boone	John Steele, Stanley Stone
1963	Mrs. Burt Howe, Burt Howe	Martin Phillips, Ira Trivers

NORTH AMERICAN SENIOR AND ADVANCED SENIOR MASTER PAIRS CHAMPIONSHIP. See MILES TROPHY.

NORTH AMERICAN TEAM TRIALS. See INTERNATIONAL OPEN TEAM SELECTION.

NORTH AMERICAN WOMEN'S KNOCKOUT TEAMS CHAMPIONSHIP. See COFFIN TROPHY.

NORTH AMERICAN WOMEN'S PAIRS CHAMPIONSHIP. See WHITEHEAD TROPHY.

NORTH AMERICAN WOMEN'S SWISS TEAMS CHAMPIONSHIP. See Appendix I, Summer NAC.

NORTH OF IRELAND BRIDGE UNION. This organization, founded in 1932, is the controlling body of the six northern counties of Ireland. By 1982 there were more than 50 clubs affiliated, with a total membership of about 1,500. The Union belongs to the BRITISH BRIDGE LEAGUE, and competes annually with England, Scotland, and Wales for the CAMROSE TROPHY. For other international participation, see IRISH BRIDGE UNION. The NIBU hosted the European Championship at Dun Laoghaire in 1952.

Officers, 1982:
President: Mrs. M. Ninnoms
Secretary: W.M. Kelso, 9 Upper Malone Road, Belfast, Ireland

NORWEGIAN BRIDGE ASSOCIATION (NORSK BRIDGE FORBUND). Founded in 1932, in 1982 it had a membership of about 16,500 with 561 clubs. The Association embraces 45 districts of sparsely populated countryside, which compete for the Norwegian Team and Pairs Championships. The 1974 Open Pairs Championship drew more than 9,000 players, and a National team event attracted 394 teams. Norway annually participates in the European Championships, finishing second in 1938 and 1969, and hosted the 1938, 1958, and 1969 events in Oslo. It represented Europe in the 1970 Bermuda Bowl.

Officers, 1982:
President: Ole Smestad
Secretary: Rolp J. Olsen, Postboks 5261, Majorstua, Oslo 3, Norway

NOTRUMP. A denomination in which a player may bid at bridge. Notrump is the ranking denomination during the auction, being just above spades in precedence. One is required to take only nine tricks for game at notrump, since the first trick over book of six counts for 40 points and the subsequent tricks for 30 points each as in a major suit. As the name implies, contracts at notrump are played without a trump suit; the play therefore is entirely different from that of suit contracts, one of the chief differences being that declarer while planning his line of play attempts to count winners rather than losers. At notrump, a primary concern of the side contracting for game or partial is that there be stoppers in the suits bid or held by the opponents. More game contracts are played at notrump than at any other denomination. The two-word spelling "no trump" is standard in England. The hyphenated form, "no-trump" is a rare compromise.

NOTRUMP BIDDING. The standard point-count is particularly effective in its application to notrump bidding. A partnership aims to reach 3 NT with 26 points in high cards in the combined hands, and is prepared to play in game with 25. Similarly, 6 NT should be reached with 34 points, and 33 points will offer a fair play.

Different aspects of this subject are under: BOLAND CONVENTION; DYNAMIC NOTRUMP; EXPECTED NUMBER OF CONTROLS IN BALANCED HANDS; 5 NT OPENING; 4 NT OPENING; GERBER CONVENTION; GLADIATOR; JACOBY TRANSFER; 1 NT OPENING; 1 NT RESPONSE; OPENER'S REBIDS; RESPONDER'S REBIDS; SHARPLES; 6 NT OPENING; SOUTH AFRICAN TEXAS; STAYMAN; TEXAS CONVENTION; 3 NT OPENING; 3 NT RESPONSE; THREE-QUARTER NOTRUMP; 2 NT OPENING; 2 NT RESPONSE; TWO-WAY STAYMAN; WEAK NOTRUMP; WEISSBERGER; WOODSON TWO-WAY NOTRUMP.

NOTRUMP DISTRIBUTION. A hand distribution suited to notrump play rather than a suit because of its balanced pattern. The three most common distributions are: 4-3-3-3, 4-4-3-2, 5-3-3-2. Occasionally 5-4-2-2 or 6-3-2-2 can be considered as notrump pattern.

NOTRUMP OPENING. See 1 NT OPENING; 2 NT OPENING; 3 NT OPENING; 4 NT OPENING; 5 NT OPENING; 6 NT OPENING.

NOTRUMP OVERCALL. See 1 NT OVERCALL; 2 NT OVERCALL; 3 NT OVERCALL; 4 NT OVERCALL; UNUSUAL NOTRUMP.

NOTRUMP PLAY. Play and defense in notrump contracts are discussed in many of the headings listed under DEFENSE and DUMMY PLAY.

NOTRUMP RESPONSES TO SUIT OPENINGS. See 1 NT RESPONSE; 2 NT RESPONSE; 2 NT RESPONSE OVER OPPONENT'S TAKEOUT DOUBLE; 3 NT RESPONSE.

NOT VULNERABLE. See NONVULNERABLE.

NOTTINGHAM CLUB. A system popular in the English Midlands. The chief features are:

(1) 1 ♣ opening bid with 16-21; negative response, 1 ◊ with less than 8 points.

(2) 1 ◊ with 12-13 points and no four-card major suit. Minimum suit responses are nonforcing and show 0-11 points.

(3) 1 ♡ and 1 ♠, 12-15 with five-card suit.

(4) 1 NT, 13-15 points.

(5) 2 ♣, 12-15 with club length.

(6) 2 ◊, forcing opening with 22 or more.

(7) 2 ♡ or 2 ♠, 12-15 with eight playing tricks.

NOVELS. See LITERATURE AND BRIDGE.

NOVICE GAMES. A method of promoting duplicate bridge among inexperienced players that has proved very helpful in stimulating interest and building up membership in duplicate clubs and the ACBL. At sectional and higher-rated tournaments, the novice game is often conducted as a special event. It is normally limited to players with fewer than 20 masterpoints. Sometimes there is a pre-game talk on duplicate techniques.

The novice program received a boost in 1965 when the ACBL introduced analyzed sets of hands for novices with sufficient printed analysis sheets for distribution to all participants. The analysis sheet permits the novice to compare his result with what could have or should have beendone on the board, and is often used as a reference for an increasingly popular post-game show where four experts replay four, six, or eight of the novice deals on VUGRAPH. Analyzed novice sets are available from ACBL HEADQUARTERS at a nominal charge.

When the ACBL revised its club regulations in 1969, novice games became a regular feature of many of the ACBL franchised clubs. Each club that holds a novice game at least once a month is awarded a "bonus factor," which allows the club to increase its masterpoint awards to the top finishers in its regular game.

NOVICE TABLE. An appendix table at a duplicate contest, usually a club game, where inexperienced players remain stationary, getting their boards from a table in the regular competition, relaying with the table to which it is appended. The players at the novice table keep their own scores, which can be entered on the recapitulation sheet on a separate line, matchpoints being awarded in relation to the scores in the regular game. No harm is done if the novice table does not play all the boards, so the regular game is not appreciably slowed up. As players become more familiar with the techniques of duplicate, they join the regular game.

The pamphlet "Easy Guide to Duplicate Bridge," in which the use of novice tables and NOVICE GAMES is more fully described, is available from ACBL HEADQUARTERS.

NUISANCE BID. A bid made to hinder the opponents and dislocate the flow of their bidding.

NUMBER. Used as in *going for a number*. Number as used here refers to the high numerical value of a set that a competitor sustains (*e.g.*, 500, 700, 800 & 1100). A number usually represents a loss, because it exceeds the value of the score the opponents could have obtained on their own by declaring the contract plus any bonuses that might be connected to the fulfillment of their contract.

NUMBER OF POSSIBLE HANDS, DEALS.

(1) The number of hands any named player can have is

$$\frac{52!}{39! \times 13!} = 635{,}013{,}559{,}600$$

(2) The number of hands a second named player can have is:

$$\frac{39!}{26! \times 13!} = 8{,}122{,}425{,}444$$

(3) The number of ways the remaining 26 cards can be divided is:

$$\frac{26!}{13! \times 13!} = 10{,}400{,}600$$

(4) The total number of possible deals is the three above numbers multiplied together, or

$$\frac{52!}{(13!)^4} = 53{,}644{,}737{,}765{,}488{,}792{,}839{,}237{,}440{,}000$$

These rather simple-appearing mathematical formulas for the first three are the number of combinations in which 13 items can be combined from a supply of 52, 39 and 26 respectively. The fourth figure is, as mentioned, the product of the other three. In each case the symbol ! (read "factorial") means that the number preceding it is multiplied successively by each smaller number down to 1. A rather elementary "program" enables an electronic calculator of sufficient scope to handle the fantastic arithmetic problem in a matter of minutes.

Roy Telfer and Alec Traub

O

OBJECT OF THE GAME. The object of the game is to do the best one can with the cards one has been dealt on a particular deal, so that at the conclusion of the hand, one can feel the result well warranted by the efforts put into the planning and strategy of the hand. It is sometimes said that the immediate object when playing rubber bridge is to score game and rubber, so as to receive the scoring advantages thereto pertaining. Likewise, in CHICAGO, games should be bid, as there are substantial bonuses accruing as benefits. In duplicate, the object of the game is to score points on a particular deal or board, and various factors have to be weighed so as to determine the way to obtain the best score. Through the years, however, there has been one school of thought that has consistently maintained that the object of bidding in contract bridge should be to bid in such a way as to get the opponents into a contract they cannot make, and then double and set them. The points thus built up can attain significant proportions above the line. Of course this was largely a rubber bridge theory, and one that does not necessarily pertain to four-deal games or duplicate. Objectives may be affected by considerations of partnership psychology. See RUBBER BRIDGE TACTICS.

OBLIGATION TO PASS. When a player bids out of turn, the Laws may require as a penalty that his partner must pass when next it is his turn to call, or for the duration of the auction. This is an "obligation to pass". If a player under such an obligation to pass makes a bid, double, or redouble, then both members of the offending side must pass for the entire auction. For the conditions which bring an obligation to pass, see LAWS (Laws 30, 31, 32, 36, 37, and 38). Lead penalties may also apply.

OBLIGATORY. A term characterizing a play which cannot lose but may win a trick, when the situation is such that not to make the play will gain nothing and will lose the opportunity of making a trick that might otherwise be sacrificed, as an obligatory duck, an obligatory finesse, etc.

OBLIGATORY FINESSE. The play of a small card on the second lead of a suit in the hope that the adversary yet to play holds only the commanding card of the suit. The object of the play is to limit the number of losers in the suit when only two of the five honors are held. It is usually made when the position of the master card is marked, and the adversaries originally held five cards of the suit. Thus, in the following situation:

$$\spadesuit \text{ Q 7 4 2}$$
$$\spadesuit \text{ A 5} \qquad \spadesuit \text{ J 10 9}$$
$$\spadesuit \text{ K 8 6 3}$$

if South leads toward the North hand, and the ace is not played by West, he puts up the queen and wins the first spade trick, and leads a low spade from North. When East plays one of his equals, South must play a small card in the hope that West originally held only one guard to the ace. This play can lose nothing, since if the cards are otherwise distributed at least two tricks must be lost in spades in any event. Hence, an "obligatory" finesse is a play which cannot lose but may gain a trick.

ODD–EVEN DISCARDS. Methods of signaling which assign different meanings to odd-numbered and even-numbered spot cards. Some partnerships extend these discards to include following suit to partner's opening lead as in the ROMAN SYSTEM. As normally played, an odd-card discard encourages in the suit discarded. An even-card discard is discouraging and is suit preference as in LAVINTHAL SIGNALS. (A high card asks for a shift to the higher-ranking suit, a low card indicates a preference for the lower-ranking suit.)

ODD TRICK. A trick won by the declarer, in excess of the first six tricks. The term is a holdover from WHIST, in which the winning of the odd trick was paramount.

ODDS, IN BRIDGE. Odds describe a ratio between two probabilities, the probability that an event (such as a player holding a particular card) will occur to the probability that it will not occur. If such a probability is expressed as a decimal, the alternate probability is the difference between totality (1), and that decimal. MATHEMATICAL TABLES, Table 4, shows the probabilities of distribution of cards between two hidden hands. It shows, for instance, that the probability that three outstanding cards will divide 2–1 is 78%. Expressing this probability in terms of odds *on* a 2-1 division are 78-22 or 39-11. The odds *against* a 2-1 division is the opposite (converse) of these figures, or 11-39, (which is the odds *on* a 3-0 division). Odds represent what would be a fair bet.

Odds are often used to express the probability of two events that are mutually exclusive (cannot both happen at the same time, such as two winners in a prizefight). Thus in dealing with the division of four cards in a suit, Table 4 shows that the odds *against* a 2-2 division are 49.74 to 40.70 (approximately 5-4), provided that it is known that each opponent has at least one card of the suit. It should be noted that in this computation the possibility of a 4-0 split would be eliminated by one lead to test, and therefore odds could be expressed because there were left only two possible a priori divisions, 2-2 and 3-1.

Roy Telfer and Alec Traub

ODDS GOVERNING SPECIFIED CARDS. (For explanation of the notations used in this article, see MATHEMATICS OF BRIDGE, and SUIT, NUMBER OF CARDS IN.)

(1) A player can have 1C1 × 51C12 hands in which he holds the ♠A. He can have the ace and three other spades in 1C1 × 12C3 × 39C9 ways.

(2) If 26 cards are seen, of which n are spades, one of the other hands can have a singleton spade in (13-n) C1 × (26 = (13-n)) C12 ways; that is, if six spades are seen, a singleton in an unseen hand can occur in 7C1 ×19C12 ways; he can have a named singleton, such as the ♠Q, in 1C1 ×19C12 ways.

(3) A player can have n specified cards in nCn × (52-n) C (13-n) ways. He can, for instance, have the ♠A and the ♡K-Q in 3C3 × 49C10 ways.

(4) If 26 cards are known, the formula in (3) above, becomes nCn × (26-n)C(13-n).

(5) If there are an equal number of unknown cards in two closed hands, there is a 50% chance that a named card will be in one of those hands.

(6) When the entire distribution of a suit is known: (a) the probability that a named card in the suit is in a particular hand is proportional to the number of cards held in the suit; and (b) the probability that a named card of another suit is in a particular hand is proportional to the number of cards other than those of the suit whose distribution is known.

As an example, if 10 spades are held by East-West, and East is known to hold six, and West, therefore, four, the chance that a named spade is with East is 60% (6 to 4). The chance that East holds a named card in some other suit is 43.75% (7 to 9), since there are seven vacant places (non-spades) in East's hand as against nine such vacant places in West's.

(7) The vacant places method (see [6] above) can be used in only two cases: (a) where the entire distribution of one or more suits is known; then the odds governing any of the other cards are accurately shown by this method; (b) where the play of an opponent shows RESTRICTED CHOICE. An example would be: with no defense bidding and an opening lead of the ♡Q from West. If we assume (see MATHEMATICAL ASSUMPTIONS) that this is from the ♡Q-J, and that West was certain to lead it, the odds on any other named card being with West are 11-13.

(There are only 11 vacant places in the West hand, and 13 in East's.)

In the above case, the assumption was made that declarer's side held the ♡A-K. If only the ♡A is held, then it must be assumed that East holds the ♡K, and there are only 12 vacant places in the East hand and the odds become 11-12 instead of 11-13.

If East does not follow suit, the rule in (7)(a) applies because the exact distribution of hearts is known.

If East follows suit with an insignificant heart, the odds change only very slightly, because it is possible to exclude only those distributions in which East was void of hearts. This is so small that the vacant places method is still accurate. A fallacy to be avoided is to argue that since East followed with a nondescript heart, there are only 12 vacant places in his hand, and the odds are 11-12 that a missing card is with West. The fallacy ignores the difference between significant and insignificant cards, for which see CARDS, NEUTRAL AND POSITIVE.

Roy Telfer and Alec Traub

OFFENDER. The player who commits an irregularity. The laws assume that an offender commits the irregularity without doing so deliberately, and the penalties are devised in order to rectify such an error as equitably as possible. For a player to commit an irregularity, either with the intent of invoking a law to his advantage or with the intent of gaining or giving information improperly, is a violation of the proprieties of the game; it is unethical conduct and is not acceptable under any conditions. In duplicate bridge, Law 12 may be invoked.

OFFENSE. The attack. An offensive play or bid is an attacking move, as distinguished from a defensive play or bid. This is not to be confused with declarer or defender, since both of these must usually take offensive or defensive positions with certain suit holdings.

Also, a breach of law.

OFFICIAL LAWS. See LAWS OF CONTRACT BRIDGE and LAWS OF DUPLICATE.

OFFICIAL SCORE. In duplicate bridge, the account prepared by the director (or under his supervision) which sets forth each contestant's score for each board, and his score and rank for the session, and for the event. The basis for the official score is the set of traveling score cards on which all the results for each board are recorded, and sets of *pick-up slips*, each showing a result on a board, team score slips, or other primary source. These primary sources are recorded on a *recapitulation sheet*, from which matchpoints and rankings are computed. It becomes the official score after the expiration of the *correction period*. See LAWS (Law 77); PICK-UP SLIPS; RECAPITULATION SHEET; TRAVELING SCORE SLIP.

OFFICIAL SYSTEM. A system of contract bridge bidding devised and endorsed by a group of leading American authorities in 1931-32. They opposed themselves to ELY CULBERTSON, while acknowledging their debt to him in certain areas of theory. Prominent among the group were MILTON C. WORK, SIDNEY S. LENZ, WILBUR C. WHITEHEAD, WINFIELD LIGGETT, JR., and F. DUDLEY COURTENAY. Other members of the Advisory Council were: CHARLES T. ADAMS, SHEPARD BARCLAY, FRED G. FRENCH, HENRY P. JAEGER, MADELEINE KERWIN, Mrs. Guy Purdy, E.V. SHEPARD, Victor R. Smith, Charles S. Street, EDWARD C. WOLFE, Walter F. Wyman.

Three of the principles which the Official System advocated in opposition to Culbertson have their place in the modern game: (1) the employment of the 4-3-2-1 count for notrump bidding; (2) the incorporation of an intermediate game invitation (non-forcing) suit bid of two; (3) the employment of an original opening forcing bid — the (artificial) TWO CLUB CONVENTION, designed not only for game but also for slam bidding. See BRIDGE HEADQUARTERS.

OGUST REBIDS. See WEAK TWO-BIDS.

OKUNEFF CONVENTION. See BULLDOG SYSTEM.

OLYMPIAD. Worldwide team competition at contract bridge, conducted by the WORLD BRIDGE FEDERATION. Contests have been held ever four years since 1960. For results see WORLD CHAMPIONSHIPS.

OLYMPIC. A name first applied in bridge in the sense of a contest of skill at contract bridge in which anyone may participate. The first AMERICAN BRIDGE OLYMPIC and WORLD BRIDGE OLYMPIC were promoted, sponsored and originated by ELY CULBERTSON in 1932. For results of this and other Olympics, see WORLD PAR CONTESTS. The term was modified to OLYMPIAD to describe WORLD CHAMPIONSHIP events conducted by the WORLD BRIDGE FEDERATION.

OLYMPIC PAR EVENTS. See WORLD PAR CONTESTS.

OMNIUM. A nationwide French tournament with many novel features, first played in 1963. The organizer was IRÉNÉE BAJOS de HÉRÉDIA. Special decks with perforated edges were distributed to all playing centers, so that the players themselves could select the 13 cards needed for each deal by inserting a metal pin in the appropriate hole. The deals were pre-played but not "prepared". Scoring was on a basis similar to a PAR CONTEST, with awards for good and bad results in bidding and play according to the decisions of an expert panel.

ONE-BID. A bid contracting to win one odd trick, seven tricks in all. Articles appropriate to this heading are: BORDERLINE OPENING BIDS; CHOICE OF SUIT; 1 NT OPENING; OPENING SUIT BID.

1♣ ARTIFICIAL AND FORCING. Played in a variety of forms (see 1♣ SYSTEMS). The earliest in contract was HAROLD S. VANDERBILT'S "Club Convention," although ROBERT F. FOSTER advocated a similar idea in auction.

1♣ SYSTEMS. In an effort to reach the optimum

contract, many players use systems which use an artificial opening bid of 1♣. Such systems discussed in articles in this book are BANGKOK CLUB; BLUE TEAM CLUB; CANARY CLUB; FRENCH CLUB; LEA; LEVINREW; LITTLE ROMAN; MARMIC; NOTTINGHAM; ORANGE CLUB; PRECISION; RELAY; ROMAN; ROTH CLUB SYSTEM; TRÉFLE SQUEEZE; VANDERBILT; VIENNA.

1◇ NEGATIVE RESPONSE TO 1♣. In most bidding systems that use an artificial opening of 1♣ as a forcing bid, a 1◇ response is used to deny certain values. In some systems the 1◇ response denies certain point count; in others it denies a certain number of controls..

1◇ STRONG ARTIFICIAL OPENING. See BIG DIAMOND SYSTEM; LEGHORN DIAMOND; MITCHELL DIAMOND.

1 NT FORCING TAKEOUT. See COMIC NOTRUMP OVERCALL; GARDENER NOTRUMP OVERCALL; LEA SYSTEM; UNUSUAL NOTRUMP.

1 NT OPENING. The development of notrump bidding is discussed under APPROACH PRINCIPLE. Limit bidding and the STAYMAN convention combine to make 1 NT a cornerstone of modern bidding methods.

In considering an opening notrump bid, three aspects have to be reviewed.

(1) *Strength*. High-card points only are counted, but a five-card suit is worth a point, and the presence of tens can be taken into account. The standard range is 16–18, and alternatives are very rare at rubber bridge. In tournament play, on the other hand, many variations are met with. These include:

(a) 17–20. Used in the ROMAN SYSTEM.

(b) 15–18. A relaxation of the standard range.

(c) 15–17. A slight adjustment of the standard range. By including a 15-point hand the range for a 1 NT rebid is reduced. The 18-point hand is then dealt with by a 2 NT rebid (e.g., 1♣—1♡—2 NT).

(d) 14–16. Used in the LITTLE MAJOR SYSTEM, and now used in the modern style of Precision.

(e) 13–15. Originally used nonvulnerable in the ACOL SYSTEM (now obsolete), and presently an integral feature of PRECISION and some other BIG CLUB systems.

(f) 12–14. The usual range for a WEAK NOTRUMP, used by many players using standard methods as well as the followers of KAPLAN-SHEINWOLD and BARON systems. Some relax the requirements to include 11-point hands.

(g) 10–12. A very weak notrump used most often in duplicate pairs tournaments. Some players use it only at favorable vulnerability, but others use it regardless of vulnerability. It is also the lower range of the WOODSON TWO-WAY NOTRUMP.

(h) 8–10. This extremely low range is called the KAMIKAZE NOTRUMP, and the bid is used only in duplicate pairs play. It is highly preemptive in nature. The ACBL Board of Directors has ruled that it is a conventional bid, and, since it has not received approval, it cannot be used in ACBL tournament play.

(i) Combinations. Two ranges, one weak and one strong, may be employed, depending on vulnerability and position at the table. The most common is 12–14 not vulnerable and 15–17 vulnerable, used in the Stayman System, the Acol System, and with a different valuation method, in the original CULBERTSON SYSTEM. Some favor a weak notrump at all vulnerabilities in fourth position, because a double is virtually impossible. See THREE-QUARTER NOTRUMP; WOODSON TWO-WAY NOTRUMP.

(2) *Distribution*. An orthodox notrump opening bid has one of the following distributions: 4-3-3-3; 4-4-3-2; or 5-3-3-2 with the five-card suit a minor. However, good players sometimes allow themselves the following exceptions:

(a) 5-3-3-2 with a five-card major-suit. May be tried either because tenace holdings make a notrump contract particularly attractive, or because a 16-point hand is held. The latter is likely to create a rebid problem after a one-level response or a single raise.

(b) 5-4-2-2. Two doubleton major-suit kings and a 16-point hand would be typical:

♠ K x
♡ K x
◇ K J x x
♣ A Q x x x

An opening bid in a minor suit would lead to a rebid problem after a major-suit response.

(c) 6-3-2-2. In this case also the doubletons are likely to be strong, and the strength of the hand is likely to be a minimum or sub-minimum; 15 points is likely using a 16–18 range.

(3) *Location of strength*. There is a tendency to prefer a notrump bid holding tenaces, making it likely that the opening lead will be an advantage to declarer. Conversely, a notrump bid is unattractive with points concentrated in two suits:

♠ x x x
♡ x x x
◇ A K J
♣ A K Q x

The concentration of honors in the minor suits would count against 1 NT. On the other hand, a serious rebid problem will have to be faced after an opening of 1 ♣ and a one-over-one suit response.

There is also a tendency, which some authorities make a rule, to avoid a 1 NT bid holding a weak doubleton. The objection to this treatment is that it often creates a rebid problem:

♠ x x
♡ A J x
◇ A Q 10 x
♣ K Q x x

If the opening bid is 1 ◇ (or 1 ♣) the rebid will be difficult after any one-level response (except 1 ♣—1 NT). For reasons of this kind many players open 1 NT whenever the point-count and distribution are suitable, regardless of the location of the honor strength.

Responses to 1 NT. The structure of responses is independent of the range of notrump opening being used. There is one tactical exception when a weak hand faces a WEAK NOTRUMP opening. See WEAK NOTRUMP. The point-counts for various responses are based on a 16–18 notrump. When a lower range is in use, the range for various responding bids must be scaled up accordingly.

(1) 2 ♣. Almost invariably Stayman. Occasionally a 2 ♣ is natural when it is followed by a 3 ♣ after the Stayman response. This is one of the methods used to show a long club suit in a weak hand. See also GLADIATOR, PUPPET STAYMAN, and SKINNER RESPONSES TO A 1 NT OPENING.

(2) 2 ◇. This bid is used frequently in both the natural and the conventional way. As a natural bid, it is not constructive, showing at least a five-card diamond suit and no interest in game. As a conventional bid, the two most popular methods are JACOBY TRANSFER BIDS and TWO-WAY STAYMAN. In the WALSH SYSTEM, 2 ◇ also can be the beginning of a relay to show a strong minor.

(3) 2 ♡. A natural bid showing at least a five-card suit with no interest in game; but often used in tournament play as a JACOBY TRANSFER BID.

(4) 2 ♠. Another bid that can be either natural or conventional. In a natural sense, it shows at least a five-card suit and no interest in game. Conventionally 2 ♠ can be MINOR SUIT STAYMAN, BARON, a transfer to 2 NT or a transfer to 3 ♣.

(5) 2 NT. 8–9 points and relatively balanced if used naturally. The hand may contain a long minor suit, in which case the point-count requirement is reduced slightly. The 2 NT bidder is unlikely to have a four-card major unless his hand is perfectly flat. The BARON SYSTEM uses 2 NT as a conventional forcing bid, asking partner to bid four-card suits up the line. 2 NT also can be used as a relay, forcing opener to rebid 3 ♣. Responder can pass 3 ♣ with a weak hand and a long club suit, or he can bid 3 ◇ with a weak hand and a long diamond suit, in which case opener must pass. 2 NT also is used as a takeout for the minors.

(6) 3 ♣. As a natural bid, 3 ♣ can be used three different ways—forcing, invitational or preemptive. Conventionally 3 ♣ can be a transfer to 3 ◇ or an EXCLUSION BID, showing shortness in clubs and support in all other suits—usually a 4-4-4-1.

(7) 3 ◇. Like 3 ♣, this bid can have three meanings in a natural sense—forcing, invitational or preemptive. It also can be an EXCLUSION BID, probably showing a 4-4-1-4 distribution.

(8) 3 ♡ or 3 ♠. As natural bids, they can be either invitational or forcing, always showing at least a five-card suit. Opener usually bids game in either notrump or the major, choosing the major whenever he has three or more of the suit bid by responder. A rebid in a new suit at the four level is a slam try, showing an excellent fit for responder's suit, the ace of the suit bid and a maximum notrump. See also AUTOMATIC ACES; EXPECTED NUMBER OF CONTROLS IN BALANCED HANDS.

(9) 3 NT. If responder's hand is balanced, his range is likely to be 10–14. But often he holds a long minor suit and less high-card strength. A minor suit of A-Q-x-x-x-x would justify a 3 NT venture without any outside strength.

(10) 4 ♣. This bid has no natural meaning. Conventionally it usually is GERBER, but it could also be

SOUTH AFRICAN TRANSFER, requesting opener to rebid 4♡.

4◇. This bid also has no natural meaning. Conventionally it would be a TEXAS TRANSFER to hearts or a SOUTH AFRICAN TRANSFER to spades.

(11) 4♡ and 4♠. A bid closing the auction. Usually a six-card suit with at least 7-8 points, but might be a strong five-card suit if there is an outside singleton or void. 4♡ might be TEXAS.

(12) 4 NT. A balanced hand, usually 4-3-3-3 distribution, with 15-16 points. A natural slam invitation, and the opener may show suits at the five-level in the hope of locating a 4-4 fit (see BOLAND CONVENTION).

(13) 5♣ or 5◇. A freak hand with a long, broken minor suit, probably seven or eight cards in length, and little honor strength.

(14) 5 NT. An IDLE BID in standard methods. Used by some experts as an invitation to 7 NT, i.e., a hand slightly too strong to bid 6 NT with 19-20. With a minimum, the opener must bid 6 NT. Suits may be shown at the six level.

(15) 6 NT. A balanced hand, probably 4-3-3-3 with 17-18 points. Closes the auction.

1 NT OVERCALL. A direct overcall of 1 NT shows a hand approximately equivalent to a 1 NT opening bid in standard methods, and is therefore balanced with 16-18 points in high cards. Individual partnerships vary the range slightly, and may use 15-17, 15-18, or 16-19. Occasionally it may be expedient to overcall 1 NT with a singleton:

> ♠ 5
> ♡ A Q 5
> ◇ A Q 7 3
> ♣ K J 6 4 2

If the right-hand opponent opens 1♡ or 1◇, 1 NT is rather better than an overcall of 2♣ or a TRAP PASS.

Responses by Overcaller's Partner. Partnerships should agree on one of the following methods:

(1) The cuebid in the opener's suit is used as a STAYMAN-substitute. A response of 2♣ is therefore natural and weak unless clubs was the opener's suit. This should be assumed unless another agreement is made.

(2) Overcaller's partner ignores the opening bid, responding exactly as he would have done to a notrump opening bid. In this case 2♣ is always Stayman. The bid in the opponent's suit, other than clubs, is weak and natural. This is not unlikely if the opener's suit was diamonds.

(3) Combining methods (1) and (2) above, overcaller's partner bids 2♣ as nonforcing Stayman, and makes a cuebid in opener's suit, assuming it was not clubs, as forcing Stayman. This means that the overcaller's side will not be able to play in either 2♣ or opener's suit, but it has the advantage of giving the overcaller's partner the tools to sign off, to invite, or to force to game.

(4) Overcaller's partner ignores the opening bid, responding as he would have done to 1 NT except when the suit was clubs. In that case 2◇ is used as a Stayman substitute. This arrangement permits the overcaller's side to play in the opponent's minor

suit, which will often be desirable.

Action by Opener's Partner. After a 1 NT overcall, a new suit by the responder at the two-level is weak. He is likely to have a good five-card suit or a six-card suit, with less than 9 points in high cards. A jump to three-level in a new suit is a weak preemptive action with a six- or seven-card suit. With most strong hands (9 points or more) a double is appropriate. The only other strong action is a bid of 2 NT (see CUEBID IN OPPONENT'S SUIT) which suggests a freakish, unbalanced hand, probably a two-suiter, inadequate for defense.

When the overcall is doubled, the partnership should use whatever method has been agreed after a 1 NT opening has been doubled. See DEFENSE TO DOUBLE OF 1 NT.

For 1 NT bids by opener's right-hand opponent, see BALANCING, UNUSUAL NOTRUMP; UNUSUAL 1 NT OVERCALL.

1 NT REBID. A second call of 1 NT by the opening bidder after a suit bid of one by responder. See OPENER'S REBID. For conventional actions by responder after the 1 NT rebid see CROWHURST CONVENTION; STAYMAN ON SECOND ROUND; 2♣ REBID BY RESPONDER AS ONLY FORCE AFTER 1 NT REBID; UNBID MINOR SUIT FORCE.

1 NT RESPONSE. A bid of 1 NT when partner has opened the bidding with a suit. The normal range for the bid is 6-9, but 10 is possible, particularly by a passed hand which does not wish to bid a four-card suit at the level of two.

1♠ — 1 NT is the commonest situation, and covers a wide range of hands. The responding hand may be quite unbalanced, but be unable to respond at the level of two:

> ♠ 3
> ♡ K 7 6 4 3
> ◇ K 10 8 7 2
> ♣ J 3

If the opener's rebid is 2♣, showing presumably 5-4 distribution, responder should bid 2◇. This does not exclude a heart contract, because the opener will continue to 2♡ with 5-3-1-4 distribution.

If the opener rebids a lower-ranking suit at the two-level, responder should very rarely go beyond two of the original suit. When he does so, the reason is usually a fine fit for opener's second suit:

(a)	(b)	(c)
♠ 5	♠ 5	♠ 5
♡ A 8 5 4 2	♡ A 7 4 3	♡ K 7 5 3
◇ K 7 4 3	◇ K 8 6 2	◇ 8 7 3 2
♣ 10 7 6	♣ J 8 5 3	♣ K Q 7 4

After

1♠	1 NT
2♡	

hand (a) can jump to 4♡. The five-card trump support, combined with the singleton spade and two useful honors, is enormously powerful. With (b), 3♡ is sufficient. Ten tricks may be out of reach if the opener has a minimum with a four-card heart suit. With hand (c) it would not be wrong to pass. If a try is to be made, some players would make it in clubs, showing a heart fit and some side strength in clubs. This helps the opener to make the right decision: with 5-4-3-1 distribution, for example, he will tend to sign off with a singleton club and bid game with a singleton diamond. This is a matter of partnership agreement; for many partnerships 3♣ would simply show club length.

A 2 NT rebid by responder is just conceivable in standard methods, but would be barred by some partnerships.

As the sequence

1♠	1 NT
2♡ (or ◊ or ♣)	

has a very wide range (10–18 in high cards), some experts make a jump rebid of 3♡ or 3◊ nonforcing. 3♣ then becomes an artificial game-force, unrelated to the club suit. The result is that the rebid at the level of two is more limited, and there is less temptation to try for game. (The same principle would be applied to other jump shifts in a lower ranking suit, such as

1♡	1 NT
3♣	

encouraging but nonforcing).

Other strong rebids available to the opener include:

(1) 2 NT. Showing about 17–18 points and probably a five card or even six-card spade suit; the failure to open 1 NT is significant. If responder bids a new suit, it is long, weak and nonforcing

(2) A reverse:

1♡	1 NT
2♠	

Also encouraging with about 17–18 points. Shows four spades and five (or six) hearts.

(3) A jump rebid:

1♠	1 NT
3♠	

Encouraging but nonforcing, and roughly 16–17 points in high cards.

(4) Jump shift:

1♠	1 NT
3◊	

Game-forcing, more than 18 points in high cards. Usually five spades and four or five diamonds, with a singleton or void in an unbid suit. (But see the alternative treatment above.)

(5) 3 NT. Usually a balanced distribution with 19–20 points, but might be somewhat less with a solid six- or seven-card spade suit.

(6) Jump rebid to game:

1♠	1 NT
4♠	

An unbalanced hand with 8½ or more playing tricks, and at least a six-card suit.

The lower the rank of the opening bid, the lower the frequency of the 1 NT response. This is because minimum responding hands have alternative possibilities without going to the level of two. Over 1♡, 1 NT denies a four-card spade suit (although some experts are prepared to conceal a very weak four-card spade suit).

Similarly, the 1 NT response to a minor suit

denies a four-card major suit in principle, and strongly suggests a balanced hand. Over 1♣, 1 NT almost guarantees 4–3–3–3 distribution, and the four-card is normally a minor (see 1 NT RESPONSE TO MINOR SUIT).

See also DRURY; 1 NT RESPONSE TO MAJOR, FORCING; STRONG NOTRUMP AFTER PASSING.

1 NT RESPONSE TO MAJOR, FORCING. This response is used on a wide range of hands, including many which would qualify in standard systems for a single raise or a response at the two level in a new suit. The main purpose is to narrow the range for a single raise. In ROTH-STONE a single raise is strong (10–12 points), and 1 NT followed by a preference at the level of two is weak (6–9 points). In other systems, such as KAPLAN-SHEINWOLD, EASTERN SCIENTIFIC, WALSH and PRECISION, a single raise is constructive, usually with four trumps, while a preference after a 1 NT response is weaker, often with three-card support and occasionally with two-card support.

Since these systems usually guarantee five cards for a major-suit opening, it is assumed that the opener can take a further bid without strain. If he has a six-card suit, he rebids it. If not, he makes his rebid in another biddable suit or his lowest-ranking three-card suit.

There are some inconvenient possibilities. If the opener's distribution is 4–5–2–2, the systems do not provide him with a rebid, and he may end up playing with six trumps in the combined hands. (This can also happen, for example, when the opener's distribution is 5–3–3–2 and responder has 1–3–3–6. The final contract may be 2◊.) In this rare situation some players would break the rule and open 1♠ if the spade suit was a strong one.

1 NT RESPONSE TO MINOR SUIT. Most systems lay down 8–10 points as the requirement for a response of 1 NT to an opening of 1♣; in GOREN, 9–11 are needed. This is because a weaker hand can usually always find some other bid; which may be a suit at the level of one, a raise to 2♣, or if need be a response of 1◊ based on a three-card suit. Some players treat a response of 1 NT to 1◊ in the same way, but this creates problems when responder has a weak hand including a club suit.

A modern tendency is to relax these requirements and respond 1 NT to 1♣ with as little as 6 points. This has some pre-emptive value, because the fourth player cannot bid at the one level; but it loses slightly in constructive efficiency.

In KAPLAN-SHEINWOLD the range is 5–8 points.

ONE-ODD. One trick more than six, the book. A bid of one odd is a bid to win seven tricks.

ONE OVER ONE RESPONSE. A suit response at the level of one to an opening suit bid. For example, 1♠ — 1♡.

The minimum strength for this response is 6 points, but in some styles a response is permitted with 3 or 4 points and distributional features. The maximum is the level fixed for a JUMP SHIFT, i.e., about 17 points in standard methods and about 15 points in ACOL. For players using WEAK JUMP SHIFT responses, the one over one has no upper limit.

The longest suit is usually chosen for the response, and if two five-card suits are held, the higher-ranking is given preference. However, a four-card suit that can be bid at the one-level is often preferred to a five or six-card suit which has to be bid at the two level when the strength of the hand does not justify a two-over-one response.

For other aspects of this response, see CHOICE OF SUIT and UP THE LINE.

ONE-SPOT. A colloquial alternative for ACE.

ONE-SUIT SQUEEZE. A hybrid between a squeeze and a throw-in, described by PAUL LUKACS. Most squeeze situations involve two or more suits.

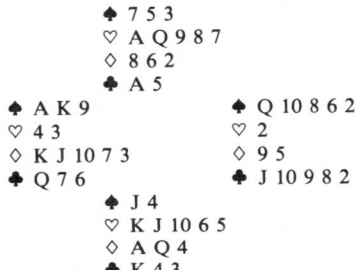

```
                ♠ 7 5 3
                ♡ A Q 9 8 7
                ◊ 8 6 2
                ♣ A 5
  ♠ A K 9                    ♠ Q 10 8 6 2
  ♡ 4 3                      ♡ 2
  ◊ K J 10 7 3               ◊ 9 5
  ♣ Q 7 6                    ♣ J 10 9 8 2
                ♠ J 4
                ♡ K J 10 6 5
                ◊ A Q 4
                ♣ K 4 3
```

The bidding:

WEST	NORTH	EAST	SOUTH
			1 ♡
2 ◊	3 ♡	Pass	4 ♡
All Pass			

Spades are led three times and South ruffs. After ace, king, and a ruff in clubs and three rounds of trumps the position is:

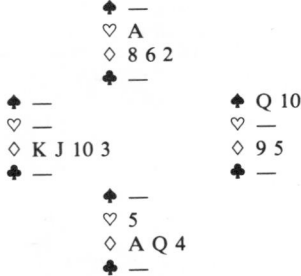

```
            ♠ —
            ♡ A
            ◊ 8 6 2
            ♣ —
  ♠ —                   ♠ Q 10
  ♡ —                   ♡ —
  ◊ K J 10 3            ◊ 9 5
  ♣ —                   ♣ —
            ♠ —
            ♡ 5
            ◊ A Q 4
            ♣ —
```

♡ A is led. If West discards the ◊ 3, South merely ducks a diamond. If West discards the 10, South leads the 6 from dummy. If East ducks, so does South. If East puts up the 9, South covers, creating a tenace position. For a related situation, see RUFF AND RUFF.

ONE-SUITER. A hand with a suit at least six cards long that contains no other suit with more than three cards.

ONE-TWO-THREE PRE-EMPTIVE. See PRE-EMPTIVE RE-RAISE.

OPEN. (1) To lead to the first trick in the play of the hand. (2) The bidding: to make the first bid in a given auction. (3) Teams, pairs: tournament contests in which any pair, whether mixed (man and woman) or not, or any team of whatever constituency may play. (4) Room: that room in a championship event in which spectators may be present in somewhat substantial numbers as opposed to a CLOSED ROOM that is limited as to both audience and accessibility. (5) Club: a game in which anyone may play.

OPEN BOARD-A-MATCH TEAMS CHAMPIONSHIP, NORTH AMERICAN CHAMPIONSHIP. See REISINGER MEMORIAL TROPHY.

OPEN HAND. The dummy's hand, exposed on the table, as distinguished from the "CLOSED" HAND of the declarer.

OPEN INDIVIDUAL CHAMPIONSHIP. See BAIRD TROPHY.

OPEN KNOCKOUT TEAMS, NORTH AMERICAN CHAMPIONSHIP. See VANDERBILT CUP.

OPEN PAIRS. An event of duplicate competition between pairs of players without regard to sex or masterpoint holding. When the event is scheduled for two or more sessions, there is often a qualifying and a final, with those eliminated eligible to compete in a consolation event. See CARRYOVER SCORES, QUALIFYING.

OPEN PAIR CHAMPIONSHIP, NORTH AMERICAN CHAMPIONSHIPS. See CAVENDISH TROPHY; SILODOR TROPHY.

OPEN SWISS TEAMS CHAMPIONSHIP. See Appendix I, Fall NAC.

OPENER'S REBID. The second bid by the opener who began with a suit-bid of one is frequently the crucial point in the auction. The following summary refers to standard methods (unless otherwise specified), and is limited to auctions in which responder made a nonjump bid in a new suit. Other rebids are dealt with separately under such headings as JUMP SHIFT; 1 NT RESPONSE; 2 NT RESPONSE; SINGLE RAISE and DOUBLE RAISE.

(1) *After a* ONE-OVER-ONE RESPONSE.
(a) *1 NT rebid.* 13–15 is the standard range using a 16–18 notrump opening, but 12 is possible. If the opening notrump is 15–17, the rebid is 12–14. For users of a weak notrump (12–14) the notrump rebid is a minimum of 15 (15–17 in KAPLAN-SHEINWOLD; 15–16 in ACOL).

The specific sequence 1 ♡ —1 ♠ —1 NT can be given distinct treatment. In Kaplan-Sheinwold it shows 12–14, equivalent to a 1 NT opening; and there is an argument for treating this sequence as strong when a strong notrump is being used.
(b) *Rebid in original suit.* These usually require a six-card suit, because the opener avoids rebidding a five-card suit if he can. A six-card suit is almost a certainty if the response was the most economical possible:

WEST	EAST	WEST	EAST
1♡	1♠	1♠	1◊
2♡		2♡	

In each case West had four other minimum rebids at his disposal, and chose to rebid his original suit. The opener is far more likely to rebid a five-card suit if the response used up bidding space:

WEST	EAST
1♠	1♠
2♣	

In these situations the opener may have an unbid four-card suit, or even a five-card suit, which he could not show without making a strength-showing reverse bid.

(c) *Rebid at the one level.* For example, 1♣–1♡–1♠. This is a most unrevealing rebid, covering a very wide range of hands. The only information responder has is that the opener is unlikely to have as many as 19 high-card points, because he would then presumably have made a jump shift rebid. The black suit lengths remain shrouded in mystery. More often than not the club suit will be longer; 5–4 and 6–4 would be common distributions, and 6–5 possible. Even 5–3 and 6–3 are conceivable:

♠ A K 5	♠ A K 5
♡ 6 2	♡ 6 2
◊ 5 4	◊ 5 4 3
♣ A K Q 7 5 4	♣ A K Q 7 5

With both these hands many experts would open 1♣, and rebid 1♠ over 1♡.

Equal black-suit lengths are common, 4–4, 5–5, or theoretically 6–6. In exceptional cases the spades may be longer than the clubs:

♠ 7 5 4 3 2	♠ A Q 6 4
♡ 7 5	♡ 7 6 2
◊ A 3	◊ 9 8 2
♣ A K Q 4	♣ A K 6

Both these hands are awkward to bid and in each case the lesser evil may be to bid 1♣ and rebid 1♠ over 1♡.

Similar considerations apply to the sequences 1♣—1◊—1♠, and 1♣—1◊—1♡, although in the latter case a 5–5 distribution is unlikely. 1◊—1♡—1♠ is slightly more precise: a three-card diamond suit is improbable and so is 5–5 distribution.

(d) *Rebid in lower-ranking suit at the two level.* Four sequences are possible, all consisting of a red-suit opening, a major-suit response, and a minor-suit rebid. For example:

WEST	EAST
1♡	1♠
2♣	

The most likely distribution for West is 5–4, but 5–5, 6–4, and 6–5 are all possible. 5–4 and 4–4 are possible in some styles, but should be avoided if possible because the responder may have to give preference to the original suit with a doubleton. When the rebid bypasses 1 NT in this way, the responder can reasonably assume that the opener's original suit was a five-carder.

These sequences have a wide range in standard methods (10–18 in high cards), and are therefore dif-ficult to handle. They are strong in ROTH-STONE and Kaplan-Sheinwold, and in the latter system the sequence is virtually forcing if the opener bids both minor suits. The alternative is to try to avoid such rebids with as many as 17–18 points.

(e) *Reverse.* Four sequences are possible, all consisting of a minor-suit opening, a major-suit response, and a red-suit rebid. For example:

WEST	EAST
1♣	1♠
2♡	

The most likely distribution for West is 5–4. His reverse bid promises more clubs than hearts, so obvious alternative distributions are 6–4 and 6–5. A three-card heart suit is possible:

♠ Q 7 5	♠ Q 3
♡ A K 4	♡ A K 4
◊ 7 2	◊ 7 2
♣ A K J 8 3	♣ A Q J 9 5 3

These untypical reverses are often provoked by a weakness in the fourth suit. This factor may even cause the opener to break the rule that the first suit must be longer:

♠ Q 7 5
♡ A K 7 3
◊ 6 2
♣ A K Q 4

Even a 5–5 distribution is conceivable if a player with 3–5–0–5 distribution chooses to open 1♣.

The high-card strength for this reverse is normally 16–18, and it is highly encouraging but not forcing. Some systems treat the bid as forcing (Roth-Stone, Kaplan-Sheinwold, and BARON).

(f) *Single raise in responder's suit.* For example, 1◊—1♠—2♠. Usually 12–16 points, and an expectation of four-card trump support. Five-card trump support is theoretically possible if the sequence is 1♣—1♠—2♠. Three-card trump support is common, and is usually appropriate unless the hand is completely balanced or has a six-card suit to rebid.

Some authorities indicate that this single raise promises more than a minimum opening bid, but such treatment does not work well if the opener has a minimum hand: he may then be forced to break the rule or make a distorted rebid of some other kind.

(g) *2 NT rebid.* The standard range is 19–20, i.e., a hand too strong to open a 16–18 1 NT. The responder continues to game unless he has made a subminimum response. The range is reduced to 18–19 for those using a 15–17 1 NT opening, and is 17–18 in ACOL. A simple rebid in his own suit by the responder is ambiguous in standard methods. It would be a sign-off in Acol, but forcing in Kaplan-Sheinwold (which uses 3♣ as preparatory to a sign-off). Other suit bids at the three level are clearly forcing, including a bid in the opener's suit. See WOLFF CONVENTION.

(h) *Jump rebid in opener's suit.* For example 1♣—1♡—3♣. This shows a good six-card suit or perhaps a seven-card suit and about 15–17 high-card points. The bid is encouraging, not forcing, and in a minor suggests 3 NT. A new suit bid by responder at the three level would show a notrump stopper and not necessarily length.

(i) *Jump raise in responder's suit.* For example, 1 ◇ —1 ♠ —3 ♠ . Usually indicates 16–18 high-card points and four-card spade support. Three-card support is possible if the high-card strength is concentrated in the bid suits:

♠ A K 5
♡ 5 4 2
◇ A K J 6 3
♣ Q 5

Responder usually continues to game or slam, but may pass if his response was minimum or sub-minimum.

(j) *Jump shift rebid.* For example, 1 ◇ —1 ♠ —3 ♣ or 3 ♡ . Shows an unbalanced hand and is forcing to game. The opener often has a fit for responder's suit which he plans to show later:

♠ A K 6 4
♡ 6
◇ A Q J 7 3
♣ A J 6

WEST	EAST
1 ◇	1 ♠
3 ♣	

Opener intends to support spades later and so indicate heart shortage.

(k) *3 NT rebid.* The standard range of 21–22 has been abandoned by virtually all experts, mainly as a result of the abandonment of the forcing two in favor of weak two-bids. The 3 NT rebid is therefore little used. It may be: (i) exactly 20 points and a balanced hand, if the opening notrump is 15–17 and a 2 NT rebid is 18–19, (ii) 19–20 in Acol; (iii) a hand strong in minor-suit playing tricks:

♠ 5
♡ A 5 2
◇ A 9 3
♣ A K Q 10 9 6

The bidding is 1 ♣ —1 ♠ —3 NT.

(l) *Jump to game in responder's major suit.* For example, 1 ◇ —1 ♠ —4 ♠ . This shows four-card support and sufficient values to justify game. The most common type of hand is relatively balanced with 19–20 points, because a powerful unbalanced hand is likely to prefer a jump shift rebid (see [j] above).

(m) *Jump to game in opener's major suit.* 1 ♡ — 1 ♠ —4 ♡ is the only possible sequence. Many powerful hands with a seven-card suit or even an eight-card suit would qualify. A six-card suit is possible:

♠ Q 5 4
♡ K Q J 10 7 3
◇ 6
♣ A K 3

In this case the opener's hand has been improved by the partial fit in spades. (The partial spade fit is automatically indicated in Acol, because other hands with sufficient playing strength would qualify for a 2 ♡ opening.)

(n) *Double jump rebid.* This can be a jump to four of opener's suit, or a double jump shift to the three level or the four level:

(a)		(b)		(c)	
WEST	EAST	WEST	EAST	WEST	EAST
1 ♠	1 ♡	1 ♠	1 ♡	1 ♠	1 ◇
4 ♣		3 ♠		4 ◇	

These sequences are virtually useless in a natural sense, although (b) could be used to show the rare 6–6 hand. Players using such bids normally do so as part of a slam convention. Auction (a) is normally used to show a hand worth a raise to game in hearts, but with a long and probably solid club suit. A typical hand would be:

♠ x ♡ K Q x x ◇ A x ♣ A K Q x x x

For other uses of these jump rebids see ASKING BID; FRAGMENT BID; SPLINTER BID; VOID-SHOWING BID.

(2) *After a* TWO OVER ONE RESPONSE.

(o) *2 NT rebid.* For example, 1 ♡ —2 ♣ —2 NT. This is 15–18 in standard practice, and is never passed. It is theoretically forcing in Roth-Stone (13–16) and Kaplan-Sheinwold (15–17). It may be passed in Acol (15–17) because responder may have only eight points.

(p) *Rebid in original suit.* For example, 1 ♠ —2 ◇ —2 ♠ . This shows a minimum opening bid with 10–14 or possibly 15 points in high cards. The suit will usually be a five-carder, but may be a good five-card suit if no alternative presents itself. The chance of a five-card suit is greatest if the response is in the suit ranking immediately below opener's: 1 ♠ —2 ◇ —2 ♠ ; 1 ♡ —2 ◇ —2 ♡ ; or 1 ◇ —2 ♣ —2 ◇ . On the other hand, the sequence 1 ♠ —2 ♣ —2 ♠ nearly always represents a six-card suit: with only five spades the opener would usually be able to find an alternative rebid of 3 ♣ , 2 NT, 2 ♡ or 2 ◇ .

If the opener's suit is a weak five-carder which will play badly opposite a possible singleton, many players would try to avoid rebidding it:

♠ J 6 4 3 2
♡ A 5
◇ A Q 5
♣ Q 4 2

If the response to 1 ♠ is 2 ♣ , some experts would raise to 3 ♣ . But this is ruled out by some authorities (see [r] below) in which case the choice lies between two diamonds, which is unlikely to come to harm, and rebidding the bad spades.

If the response to 1 ♠ is 2 ♡ , 2 NT and 3 ♡ are both better rebids than 2 ♠ if the style used permits these rebids with a minimum hand.

(q) *Rebid in lower-ranking suit.* For example, 1 ♠ —2 ♣ —2 ◇ . In standard practice this promises no additional strength and is not forcing: the opener may have 5–5 distribution and 11 high-card points. The opener should therefore try to avoid this minimum rebid with 16 points or more.

Some authorities treat the change of suit as forcing, in which case the bid has no upward limit of strength.

(r) *Single raise in responder's suit.* For example, 1 ♡ —2 ◇ —3 ◇ . There are two distinct schools of thought. Many textbooks class this bid as encouraging, with about 15–16 points in high cards; this makes it forcing in effect, and leaves unsolved the problem of minimum hands in which the natural action is to raise responder's suit. Other authorities therefore regard the single raise as a minimum rebid which does not promise extra strength and is in no way forcing.

(s) *Reverse at the two-level.* For example, 1♡—2♣—2♠. Forcing in standard methods, and virtually all nonstandard ones. Some players would regard the bid as game-forcing. The first suit must be longer than the second, so that 5-4 is the expected distribution with the possibility of 6-4 or 6-5. Players who raise the two-level response with a minimum (see [r] above) may reverse into a three-card suit:

♠ A Q 5
♡ A Q 8 6 4
◊ 7 2
♣ K J 6

If the response to 1♡ is 2♣, 2♠ is best if 3♣ would be a minimum. These sequences are strong (16 points or more) in all systems except Roth-Stone, in which the hand is likely to be a minimum and the distribution 4-4.

(t) *Second suit at the three level (sometimes called "high reverse").* For example, 1♡—2◊—3♣. Forcing in all methods, and game-forcing in most. Players who do not regard this bid as game-forcing should agree on the circumstances in which the bidding can stop short of game. (Possible are: simple rebid by responder; simple preference by responder; simple rebid by responder followed by rebid of opener's first suit.) The distribution is usually 5-5 or 5-4; 5-5 is less likely if the suits are spades and clubs, because many players open 1♣ with such hands. The opener's second suit will often be a three-carder:

♠ 5 2
♡ A Q 9 4 3
◊ A Q 8
♣ A Q 6

After 1♡—2◊, 3♣ would be the expert choice. If the clubs were K-J-2, 3♣ would still be chosen by those who do not regard 3◊ as encouraging (see [r] above).

(u) *Jump shift to the three level.* For example, 1♠—2♣—3◊. Game-forcing, and may conceal a good fit for partner's clubs. Players who regard a 2◊ rebid as forcing usually reserve the jump shift for a marked two-suited hand — 5-5 or better.

(v) *Jump rebid in opener's suit.* For example, 1♠—2◊—3♠. Forcing in standard methods (but not in Acol) and shows a good six-card suit.

(w) *Jump to game in opener's suit.* For example, 1♠-2◊-4♠. A strong six-card suit or better with values for game and no interest in a notrump contract. In Acol a moderate fit with responder's suit is implied because of the failure to open with a two-bid (compare [m]).

(x) *Jump raise in responder's suit.* Forcing in a minor suit, for example 1♠—2◊—4◊ and presumably four-card or five-card support (not forcing by definition in Acol, but some partnerships play it as forcing). 1♠—2◊—4♡ is a special case. It shows a hand slightly too good for 3♡ (according to style) and may be three-card support because responder has promised a five-card suit.

(y) *3 NT rebid.* For example, 1♠—2◊—3 NT. Equivalent to a 2 NT rebid over a one-level response, and therefore normally 19-20 points; but some experts would make this bid with 18 points or even 17.

(z) *Double jump shift.* For example, 1♠—2♣—4◊. As (n) above.

OPENING BID. The first call in the auction other than a pass. The treatment of opening bids is discussed in the following separate articles: BIDDABLE SUITS; BORDERLINE OPENING BIDS; CANAPÉ; CHOICE OF SUIT; FIVE-CARD MAJORS; FIVE OF A MAJOR OPENING; 5 NT OPENING; FORCING TWO; 4 NT OPENING; GAMBLING 3 NT; 1 NT OPENING; OPENING SUIT BID; PRE-EMPTIVE BID; SIX OF A SUIT OPENING; 6 NT OPENING; 3 NT OPENING; 2♣; 2 NT OPENING; WEAK TWO-BID.

OPENING BIDDER. The player at a deal of contract who makes the first bid of an auction.

OPENING CALL. The original call made by the dealer to start the auction. See OPENING BID.

OPENING LEAD. After the bidding has been concluded, the play of the hand commences by the declarer's left-hand opponent making an original or opening lead. For selection of opening leads, see OPENING LEADS.

OPENING LEADS. Defense is regarded as the most difficult aspect of bridge. Since the opening lead is the only defensive play made while the dummy is concealed, it requires a kind of *detective* reasoning and considerable analysis of the meaning of every call in the auction, as well as agreed conventional leads and plays to the first trick. The opening lead is frequently the source of substantial profits and losses.

Choosing the Card. The card chosen for the opening lead should help pave the way for the defeat of the contract, insofar as this is possible, and should convey information to partner about the leader's holding in the suit. Some typical card choices, once the suit has been selected, are summarized in the accompanying table.

The *standard* approach has a substantial number of critics, and one important controversy concerns the lead from a sequence of honors. With holdings like A-K-Q, K-Q-J, or Q-J-10, any of the honors can be led with equal trick-taking effect. The main concern is to inform partner about the opening leader's holding. The customary practice is to lead the king from A-K (unless it is doubleton, in which case the ace is led) and the top card from any other honor sequence. Similarly, the *standard* lead from holdings such as K-10-9-8 or Q-10-9-8 is the 10, the top of the *interior sequence.* However, standard leads create potentially costly confusion in certain instances. For example, the king is led from both A-K-4 and K-Q-4, so partner may have difficulty deciding whether to signal encouragement with J-8-2; and the 10 is led from both K-10-9-8 and 10-9-8-2, so partner may have difficulty deciding whether to return the suit when he gains the lead. Therefore, conventional *nonstandard* opening lead methods have become increasingly popular among experts, including ACE FROM ACE-KING; JOURNALIST LEADS; RUSINOW LEADS; and ZERO OR TWO HIGHER LEADS.

A second controversy has to do with the lead from three small cards against a suit contract. The top card is perhaps most common, but all three possibilities have been recommended. See THREE SMALL CARDS, LEAD FROM.

A third controversy concerns the standard fourth-best lead from a long suit. Against suit contracts, an increasing number of experts prefer to give count more accurately by leading the *third highest* card from an *even* number, and the *lowest* card from an *odd* number. Against notrump contracts, some use a low spot card lead to encourage the return of the suit and lead a high spot card to discourage a return; others object to this because the leader's partner can no longer use the RULE OF ELEVEN. These modifications are an integral part of JOURNALIST LEADS.

Choosing the Suit.

Clues from the bidding. Regardless of the carding method that is used, no table or convention can indicate the right *suit* to lead; judgment and deduction must be applied to each situation. In particular, the auction can provide the astute opening leader with valuable clues:

(1) If the opponents are strong in certain suits, the opening leader should look elsewhere for his selection.

(2) If the opponents are weak in a particular suit, the opening leader should attack it. See ATTACKING LEAD.

(3) If one opponent is likely to be void in a certain suit (as when he bids two suits several times and supports a third suit), the opening leader should not lead that ace if the enemy ends up in a suit contract.

(4) If dummy holds a long and strong side suit that will provide numerous discards (as when he has rebid it several times), the opening leader should be aggressive and try to take tricks in a hurry.

(5) If the opponents have staggered into their contract with little strength to spare, the opening leader should be cautious and avoid giving away the fulfilling trick.

(6) If the opponents have strength to spare, (at rubber bridge or IMPs) an aggressive lead has little to lose save an unimportant overtrick.

(7) If partner has indicated a good suit to attack by bidding it (see LEAD-DIRECTING BID), it is usually safe to lead it.

(8) If partner has denied length and strength in a suit by refusing to make a cheap one-level overcall when given the opportunity, the opening leader should not try to hit him in that suit.

(9) If partner has indicated general high-card strength by making a takeout double, it is relatively safe to lead away from an unsupported honor.

(1) If partner has denied general high-card strength by making a preemptive bid, it is not advisable to lead away from an unsupported honor.

(11) If partner has requested the lead of a specific suit by making a LEAD-DIRECTING DOUBLE or LIGHTNER DOUBLE, it is usually advisable to lead it.

Clues from the strength of the opening leader's hand. If the opponents bid game and the opening leader has 13 or 14 high-card points, he should visualize the near-YARBOROUGH in partner's hand and reject any lead that requires substantial high-card help (such as the lead from an unsupported honor). When the opening leader's strength is mediocre, however, it is reasonable to expect some useful aid from partner.

The location of the opening leader's strength is also important. If he holds finessable positions such as K–3–2 in front of suits bid by dummy, or a few small cards behind suits bid by declarer, the defenders are likely to be in trouble. Declarer's finesses rate to win, and the suits appear to be breaking well for the opponents. Holding length and weakness in dummy's long suit is also a bad sign, for declarer will probably be able to establish it with little difficulty. In such cases, an aggressive opening lead is often justified. But if the opening leader holds strength behind declarer's bid suits, and if he can see that important suits will be breaking badly for the enemy, a more conservative strategy is preferable.

Clues from the strength of the opening leader's suit. Other things being equal, it is frequently desirable to lead from stronger suits. Leading from Q–10–4–3 is preferable to Q–4–3–2 because less help is needed from partner to build tricks (and avoid a disaster), while Q–J–10–9 is superior to both holdings. However, as the preceding sections indicate, other things are often *not* equal; and many opening leaders go wrong by using the strength of one suit as their sole guide while ignoring valuable information available from other sources.

Leads against notrump contracts. Since declarer cannot ruff when he runs out of a suit, the defenders should usually try to establish length winners. Assuming that the bidding has not indicated the need for special action, the following guidelines apply:

(1) A five-card or longer holding in an unbid suit is usually an excellent choice, provided that the opening leader has at least one probable entry. For example, leading the three-spot from A–Q–6–3–2 is ideal; even if declarer gets an undeserved trick with the king, three or four winners are likely to be established while the high cards are retained for use as entries.

(2) From a completely entryless hand, the opening leader should reject his own (weak) long suit and try to build length winners in partner's hand. An unbid *major* suit containing three cards or a strong doubleton is likely to be a good choice.

(3) From holdings such as J–10–9–x–x, Q–J–10–x–x, K–J–10–x–x, or A–J–10–x–x in a suit bid by the enemy, the fourth-best card should be led. This avoids blocking the suit when partner has a useful doubleton, and is likely to tempt declarer into a fatal error in situations like this:

Q 2

J 10 9 4 3   ♠ K 5

A 8 7 6

After the jack lead, South has two stoppers by covering. If the 4 is led instead, South inevitably plays dummy's queen.

(4) If no five-card or longer suit is held, a solid or nearly solid four-carder (such as Q–J–10–9 or J–10–9–3) is likely to build some winners without giving anything away.

(5) Leading from broken four-card suits is less desirable. Attacking from Q-10-4-2 in an unbid suit is not unreasonable, since the lead has a good chance to pay off if partner has even one of the missing honors. However, a suit like A-Q-3-2 should be avoided because the potential for length winners is too limited to justify giving declarer an undeserved trick.

(6) Against 3 NT, leading an honor from A-K-2 in an unbid suit can be every effective (especially at rubber bridge or IMPs). Partner may turn up with five to the queen, or with five small cards and a side entry. Even the lead of an honor from A-Q-2 has at times paid similar dividends.

(7) If no attractive lead exists, a passive lead (as from three or four small cards) has the advantage of being relatively safe. Even the lead of a small doubleton may be correct (see SHORT-SUIT LEADS).

(8) In some instances, the opening leader may gain by disguising the length of his long suit. See FALSE-CARDING.

(9) After a 2 NT opening bid, a passive lead is more frequently correct. Declarer's hand contains most of his side's strength, so he may have entry problems if left to his own devices.

(10) Against notrump partials, a passive lead is more frequently correct. The strength is more evenly divided between the two sides, so the defenders are less likely to have to collect tricks in a hurry.

(11) After a GAMBLING 3 NT opening bid has been passed out, it is desirable to lead an ace. Declarer is trying to score nine fast tricks with the aid of a solid minor suit, so losing the lead even once may be fatal.

Leads against suit contracts. Here the defenders are less likely to gain by trying to build length winners, since declarer can simply ruff in when he runs out of a suit. Assuming that the bidding has not indicated the need for special action, the following guidelines apply:

(1) Leading from solid or nearly solid honor sequences, such as A-K-J-5, K-Q-J-7-3, Q-J-10-2, or J-10-9-5, is likely to be both constructive and safe. Leading from weaker honor holdings like K-Q-7-3 or Q-J-9-2 can also be effective, but may cost a trick when partner is weak in the suit.

(2) Leads from long suits are safer but less likely to establish several tricks, while leads from short side suits are riskier but more likely to establish several tricks. If the defenders must rush to collect their winners (as when dummy's bidding shows a long side suit that will provide numerous discards), it is better to lead from Q-7-5 in an unbid suit than from Q-8-6-5-4. When safety considerations are more important, however, leading from length is preferable.

(3) When holding four or more trumps, it is particularly desirable to lead from a long suit. If declarer can be forced to ruff several times, his trumps may run out before the defenders' do and cause him to lose control of the hand. See FORCING LEADS.

(4) When no attractive lead exists, a passive lead (as from three or four small cards) has the advantage of being relatively safe.

(5) A trump lead is desirable in several situations: when the bidding indicates that declarer will try to ruff losers in dummy or crossruff; when the defenders hold substantial strength in all side suits, as when the opponents sacrifice against a contract that the defenders expected to make on power; when a one-level contract is passed out; and when a passive lead is indicated and the opening leader holds a few small trumps. A trump lead is mandatory when a one-level takeout double is passed out. However, a trump lead should be avoided when the opening leader's holding is too precarious to lead from; when the bidding indicates that the defenders must take their tricks in a hurry; when the opening leader is very long in a suit declarer plans to ruff in dummy, indicating that partner will be able to overruff; when the opening leader has a singleton trump; and when the opening leader has four or more trumps, in which case the forcing game is preferable. See TRUMP LEADS.

(6) A side-suit singleton is likely to be effective when the opening leader has some extra low trumps to use for ruffing and a probable entry in trumps, so long as the leader's partner rates to have an entry or two. However, singleton leads should usually be avoided when the opening leader has no excess low trumps to ruff with (as when holding A-Q or Q-J-3); when he has four or more trumps, in which case the forcing game is preferable; or when the singleton is a king or queen.

(7) Side-suit doubletons are considerably less likely to produce ruffs than are singletons, and should be led for this purpose only when holding a quick entry *in trumps*. A small doubleton may be a satisfactory passive lead, however. In some infrequent cases, leading from K-2 or Q-2 may be justified because the opening leader is truly desperate (see DESPERATION LEAD OR PLAY).

(8) With an otherwise worthless hand, leading the king from K-7-4-3 in partner's bid suit can be effective. If the king holds the trick, the opening leader may now be able to make a profitable attack through dummy in a different suit; while if the opening lead is the normal small card and declarer has a singleton, no further leads through dummy will be possible.

(9) Underleading the ace is normally avoided, but can be a winning choice. The defenders may need tricks in a hurry, and declarer may also be missing the queen and misguess; or it may be urgent to put partner on lead for an attack through declarer's hand or to obtain a ruff. See UNDERLEAD.

Leads against slam contracts. If the opponents reach a small slam and the opening leader holds K-Q and an ace, it is obvious that the king should be led. However, fate usually does not conspire to deal all the defenders' high cards to the opening leader, so he often has to decide whether to lead away from an unsupported king or queen in an unbid suit. Fortunately, slam contracts often involve considerable amounts of bidding, which offer more clues to the opening leader. Normally, the following guidelines apply:

(1) Against a small slam, an attacking lead is preferable when dummy's bidding indicates a long, establishable suit. A passive lead is more appropriate if both declarer and dummy appear to have balanced hands, whether or not the contract is at notrump.

(2) Against suit small slams, an ace lead is desirable if it is in an unbid suit and the opening leader holds a probable second winner elsewhere, or if the bidding suggests that the opponents might be off two fast tricks. Otherwise the ace lead is more debatable, and should normally be avoided if it is in a suit bid by the enemy.

(3) Against suit small slams, singleton leads are often effective. However, they should be avoided if both opponents have bid the suit, in which case the lead may help them overcome a bad break; or if the opening leader has a sure winner (or a relatively strong hand), in which case the slam will be defeated anyway if partner can take a trick.

(4) Against suit small slams, a trump lead is dangerous; it may pick up partner's queen and save declarer a crucial guess. However, a trump lead may work well if the bidding plus the leader's holding indicates that partner has at most a singleton, the auction strongly suggests that declarer plans to do a great deal of ruffing in one or both hands, and the trump holding is safe to lead from.

(5) Against a grand slam, without an immediate winner to cash, it is usually desirable to make a safe lead. Only one trick is needed to defeat the contract, so building winners in unnecessary. Trump leads are frequently desirable against suit grand slams, but should be avoided if partner may have the queen of trumps and a safe selection is available elsewhere.

Board-a-match and matchpoint considerations. At board-a-match scoring, the opening leader must be careful to avoid losing a board that his teammates at the other table have all but won. At matchpoints, there are conflicting consideratons. Notrump contracts based on shaky stoppers are more common at this form of scoring, so the opening leader is more likely to gain by trying to run a long suit. Yet conceding even one undeserved trick can result in a bottom score, so care must be taken to avoid presenting declarer with a gift that his counterparts at other tables will not receive. Thus an unusual attempt to defeat a contract, correct at rubber bridge or IMPs, may be wrong at matchpoints because it is too likely to concede the overtrick. (See MATCHPOINT DEFENSE.) Opening leads at matchpoints are a source of considerable complexity (and headaches).

Robert Ewen

*Opening Leads: Some Typical Card
Choices Once the Suit Has Been Selected*

Suit Length	Holding in Suit	Lead vs. NT	Lead vs. Suits
Two Cards	Any nontrump doubleton	Top card	Top card
	Trumps: honor sequence or ace-any	—	Top card[1]
	Trumps: any other doubleton	—	Low card
Three Cards	9–8–7 or worse, not in trumps	Top card	Top card[2]
	Trumps: three small	—	2nd best[3]
	10–x–x, J–x–x, Q–x–x, K–x–x	3rd best	3rd best
	Q–10–x, K–10–x, K–J–x	3rd best[4]	3rd best
	10–9–x, J–10–x, Q–J–x, K–Q–x	Top card	Top card
	Trumps: J–10–x	—	3rd best
	A–x–x, A–10–x	3rd best[5]	Ace
	A–J–x, A–Q–x	2nd best[6]	Ace
	A–K–x or better	King	King
Four Cards	9–8–7–6 or worse	4th best[7]	4th best[7]
	10–x–x–x, J–x–x–x, Q–x–x–x, K–x–x–x	4th best	4th best
	10–9–x–x, J–10–x–x, Q–J–x–x	4th best	4th best[8]
	Q 10–x–x, K–10–x–x, K–J–x–x	4th best	4th best
	Q–10–9–x, K–10–9–x, K–J–10–x	2nd best	2nd best
	A–10–9–x, A–J–10–x	2nd best	Ace
	10–9–7–x, J–10–8–x, Q–J–9–x, K–Q–10–x	Top card	Top card
	10–9–8–x, J–10–9–x, Q–J–10–x, K–Q–J–x	Top card	Top card
	A–x–x–x, A–10–x–x, A–J–x–x, A–Q–x–x	4th best	Ace
	K–Q–x–x, K–Q–9–x, A–K–x–x, A–K–10–x	4th best	King
	K–Q–10–x, A–K–10–9, A–K–J–x, or better	King	King

Suit Length	Holding in Suit	Lead vs. NT	Lead vs. Suits
Five Cards	The rules for four-card suits are frequently correct. Against *notrump* contracts, however, the degree of solidity of an honor sequence is particularly important. Compare the following situations:		
	10–9–7–x–x, 10–9–8–x–x, J–10–8–x–x	4th best	
	10–9–7–6–x, 10–9–8–6–x, 10–9–8–7 x	Top card	
	J–10–8–7–x, J–10–9–7–x, J–10–9–8 x	Top card	
	Q–J–9–x–x, K–Q–9–x–x	4th best	
	J–10–9–x–x, Q–J–10–x–x, K–Q–10–x–x, K–Q–J–x–x	Top card or 4th best [9]	
	Q–J–9–8–x, K–Q–10–9–x	2nd best [10]	
	Q–J–10–8–x, Q–J–10–9–x, K–Q–J–9–x, K–Q–J–10–x	Top card	
	Q–10–9–x–x, K–10–9–x–x, A–10–9–x–x	4th best	
	Q–10–9–7–x, Q–10–9–8–x, K–10–9–7–x, K–10–9–8–x	2nd best	
	A–10–9–7–x, A–10–9–8–x	2nd best	
	K–J–10–x–x, A–J–10–x–x	2nd best or 4th best [10]	
	K–J–10–8–x, K–J–10–9–x, A–J–10–8–x, A–J–10–9–x		
	A–K–10–9–x	King or ten [12]	
	A–K–J–x–x	King or 4th best [12]	
	A–K–J–10–x	Ace [13]	

[1] An old chestnut is to lead the jack from Q–J or the nine from 10–9, hoping to induce declarer to misguess on the next round. However, this is unlikely to be necessary against a declarer familiar with RESTRICTED CHOICE.

[2] Middle and low are also popular. See THREE SMALL CARDS, LEAD FROM.

[3] Followed by the smallest, thus denying a doubleton.

[4] In some cases, the jack from K–J–x is proper in order to unblock.

[5] The ace is preferable if partner does not figure to have a side entry.

[6] The ace is correct is some cases.

[7] The top card or second best may be led to deny an honor; see text.

[8] The queen from Q–J–x–x is correct in some cases.

[9] Fourth best is preferable when the goal is to establish the whole suit, rather than play safe, and when an opponent is likely to have four cards in the suit.

[10] Partner is expected to play the immediately lower honor if he has it.

[11] King from K–J–10–9–x–x is correct in some cases.

[12] The king is preferable when a sure side entry is held.

[13] Partner is expected to play an honor if he has one, and to signal his count (high-low for even, low-high for odd) if he does not.

OPENING 1 NT BID. See 1 NT OPENING.

OPENING SUIT BID. An opening of 1♣, 1◊, 1♡, or 1♠ has a normal range of 10–20 high-card points. It may sink below 10 in some freak cases — with 6–6 distribution, for example. It may rise above 20 with unbalanced hands, usually 4–4–4–1 or 5–4–3–1 patterns, unsuited to a 2 NT opening and not quite strong enough for a forcing opening.

For special factors affecting the opening bid, see BIDDABLE SUITS; BORDERLINE OPENING BIDS; CHOICE OF SUIT.

OPPONENT. A member of the adverse team at bridge. An opponent can be a member of an opposing team of four, or five or six as well as merely a temporary adversary.

OPPONENT'S SUIT. A suit held or bid by one or both adversaries. In judging the bidding, a holding of three small cards in the opponent's suit is generally a danger signal. But if the opponent's suit is supported, a small tripleton may actually be better than a small doubleton because the chance of finding a singleton with partner is increased. For bids in the opponent's suit, see CUEBIDS IN OPPONENT'S SUIT.

OPPOSITION. (1) The opponents on a hand, set of hands or rubber; (2) The contestants in DIRECT COMPETITION; (3) The balance of the field; (4) The other team in a head-on team event.

OPTIMUM STRATEGY. Plans of play adopted by declarer or defender in the light of different tactics which may be adopted by the opposing side.

The following is one example of the complications which can arise in considering alternative strategies:

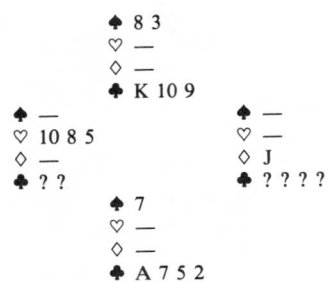

```
        ♠ 8 3
        ♡ —
        ◇ —
        ♣ K 10 9
♠ —                    ♠ —
♡ 10 8 5               ♡ —
◇ —                    ◇ J
♣ ? ?                  ♣ ? ? ? ?
        ♠ 7
        ♡ —
        ◇ —
        ♣ A 7 5 2
```

Spades are trumps. East is in.

Further conditions are that West is marked with three hearts and East with the ◇ J. Declarer knows, therefore, that the critical club suit is divided 2–4, but he doesn't know where the ♣ Q and J are. Clubs are therefore designated with question marks on the diagram. Lest he give a ruff and discard, East must obviously lead a club, and, of course, declarer's aim is to make all the tricks.

The problem is to analyze the optimum strategy both from declarer's and (more importantly) defender's point of view.

The defender's clubs may break:

(1) x–x — Q–J–x–x. . . . .   6 cases
(2) Q–x — J–x–x–x. . . . .
    or
    J–x — Q–x–x–x. . . . .   8 cases
(3) Q–J — x–x–x–x. . . . .   1 case
               TOTAL   15 cases

Let us examine East's possible tactics.

(a) The "naïve" tactic. East is a weak player. He leads queen or jack in (1). He leads small in (2) and, perforce, in (3).

Against such an opponent it is clear that South will lose only in (3). He will win 14 times out of 15.

(b) The "expert" tactic. East is a good player. He leads queen or jack whenever he has one (or both) of these cards.

Now declarer has to reverse his play. As (2) is more likely than (1), South should play for divided honors, i.e., cash the ace in hand and drop West's other honor next. So, South wins in (2) (8 cases) but loses in (1) (6 cases).

Declarer, however, takes a little revenge in case (3) as TERENCE REESE points out in his *Expert Game.* For South can easily divine case (3) from the very fact that East had led a small card (having no alternative). So South wins also in case (3) hence, in 9 cases out of 15.

To prevent this, East may lead sometimes small and sometimes high in case (2). Say 50% each. Which leads to:

(c) The shrewd tactic. East always leads an honor in (1), always small in (3), but in case (2) he leads half the time high and the rest small. Against this tactic, South does better to revert to his behavior against tactic (a), playing East for both honors whenever he leads high, and only then.

South thus wins the 6 cases from (1) and 4 of the 8 cases from (2), thus, on balance, 10 cases out of 15.

This shrewd tactic is therefore no improvement, but we may now figure out the correct optimum strategy as follows:

(d) The optimum strategy. East leads, of course, always an honor in (1), but in case (2) he leads exactly, but "at random,," a small card 12½% of the time, i.e., once out of 8 times.

It is clear that declarer now has to play for split honors whenever East leads high (7 cases against 6). But if East leads small, declarer may:

(i) play for split honors. He will win in 0 + (7 + 1) + 0 = 8 cases (out of 15).

(ii) play for Q–J with West. He will win in 0 + (7 + 0) + 1 = 8 cases (out of 15).

Thus according to whether his strategy is naïve, expert, shrewd, or optimum, the defender wins a trick in 14, 9, 10, or 8 cases out of 15. And declarer has no way to improve on those chances.

Jean Besse

(Reprinted by permission from *British Bridge World,* January 1960.)

OPTIONAL. A term applied to a bid, play or point of law in which a player may have two or more choices; as distinguished from compulsory action or procedure strictly regulated by law.

OPTIONAL DOUBLE. A COOPERATIVE DOUBLE showing a balanced hand with enough high cards to defeat the contract in all probability, and with support for any unbid suit. The partner of the doubler need not have a substantial trump holding in order to pass; he is expected to pass unless he has a good suit and unbalanced distribution. For example, the following hand would be appropriate for an optional double of a 3 ♡ opening pre-empt:

```
        ♠ A K 7
        ♡ A J 2
        ◇ 7 4 3
        ♣ A Q 6 5
```

See also DEFENSE TO OPENING THREE-BID; PENALTY DOUBLE; TAKE-OUT DOUBLE..

OPTIONS.

(1) Alternative actions available to a player in certain circumstances after an irregularity by the opposing side. An opening lead by the wrong defender is a case in which the declarer has four options. (See LAWS, Laws 54 and 56).

(2) Alternative play possibilities available to a declarer. He should usually adopt a sequence of play which will "preserve options." A play which retains the possibility of trying for other possibilities is usually better than one which stands or falls on immediate success, even if the second is a better percentage chance.

ORANGE CLUB. Strong club system used by JAMES JACOBY and BOBBY WOLFF in the 1970, 1971 and 1972 World Championships.

The 1 ♣ opening promises 17 or more points; responses show controls. Other opening bids are limited and natural according to the CANAPÉ principle. A 1 NT opening shows a balanced hand with 13–15 points with a 4- or 5-card club suit or 16–17 with any balanced distribution.

Other features include BLUE TEAM 2 ◇, FLANNERY 2 ♡, weak two-bid in spades only; singleton- and void-showing forcing raises by a passed hand.

ORIGINAL BID. The first bid made in an auction. Reference is frequently made by a partner to one's "original bid" as having been in spades, or notrump, etc., as for example: "I returned you to spades, since that was your original bid".

ORIGINAL HOLDING. The cards one has in a given suit at the beginning of play or at the beginning of the auction. Thus one might say, while describing the play of a hand, that one's original spade holding was five to the A–J–10, and that at a certain point one was down to the 10 and two little cards in the suit.

ORIGINAL LEAD. See OPENING LEAD.

ÖSTERREICHISCHER BRIDGE-VERBAND. See AUSTRIAN BRIDGE FEDERATION.

OUR HAND. A colloquial expression indicating that a player thinks his side can make the highest positive score on a deal in which both sides take part in the auction. See BELONG.

OUT. A player who is a member of a table at rubber bridge, but not actively participating. The order in which players are out is established by cutting, the holder(s) of the lowest card or cards cut sitting out for the first rubber, other players going out in order.

OUT-OF-THE-BLUE CUEBID. An unusual bid of a new suit which cannot be taken as a suit bid, indicating support for partner's last bid suit, strength in the cue-bid suit (often first-round control), and interest in reaching a high-level contract. The phrase was coined by NORMAN SQUIRE, England, in his *Theory of Bidding*. See BLUE TEAM 4♣-4◇ CONVENTION.

OUT OF TURN. Not in rotation. For a bid out of rotation, see LAWS (Laws 30–32), for a lead out of turn, see Laws 54–56, for a play out of turn, see LAW 57.

OUT ON A LIMB. A phrase used to describe a player who has taken unusual or precipitate action during an auction, and is in great danger of being doubled at a contract that is both risky and untenable and susceptible of great loss as to points. During the play of a hand, one may be said to be out on a limb as respects a situation, for example, when one is "wide open" in a suit at notrump, although the opposition may not be aware of this, or when one is playing at a trump contract and not only does not have control of the trump suit but is extremely vulnerable to attack in that area.

OVER. A term used to indicate one's position at the table in respect to one's right-hand opponent. One may be correctly said to be over that opponent if one is West to his South, for example. This term may be used in bidding situations as well as in play. See RIGHT-HAND PLAYER.

OVERBID. A call offering to undertake a contract for a greater number of tricks than is justified by the bidder's holding. Matters of system are often involved; a call may be an overbid in one system but an underbid in another.

In competitive auctions, or auctions that are likely to become competitive, an apparent overbid may be an ADVANCE SAVE.

The term overbid is sometimes erroneously used in referring to an OVERCALL. See SACRIFICE.

OVERBIDDER. A player who consistently bids higher than his high-card and distributional strength justify.

Playing with an overbidder, it is clearly necessary to be conservative, although this is no remedy holding extreme weakness. However, the overbidder must not be allowed to think that he is playing with an underbidder, or worse will follow. If the underbidder bids normally when he is due to be dummy he is little better off, because that is the situation in which the overbidder, vain of his dummy play, reaches for the moon. ELY CULBERTSON suggested a policy of overbidding with an overbidder in the hope of curing his excesses, but even if the overbidder were curable, life might be too short for a player trying to win.

OVERBOARD. The state of being (much) too high in a given auction. See SAFETY LEVEL.

OVERCALL IN OPPONENT'S MAJOR SUIT. 2♡ over 1♡, or 2♠ over 1♠, is most often used as a CUEBID IN OPPONENT'S SUIT, in which case it can have any of a number of agreed-upon meanings.

The natural use of an overcall in an opponent's major suit is most beneficial when the opponents use a CANAPÉ style of bidding, in which a major suit opening may frequently be made on a suit of only three cards.

OVERCALL IN OPPONENT'S MINOR SUIT. 2♣ over 1♣, or 2◇ over 1◇, is often used naturally instead of as a cuebid. Such treatment is most useful if the opponents are playing five-card majors, or any other method which requires frequent opening bids with prepared three-card minor suits. See also CUEBIDS IN OPPONENT'S SUIT.

OVERCALLS. In a broad sense, the term overcall refers to any positive action by the player on the left of the opening bidder. In this article, only minimum bids in a suit will be considered. (For other actions, see INTERMEDIATE JUMP OVERCALL, JUMP OVERCALL, 1 NT OVERCALL, PRE-EMPTIVE OVERCALL, 2 NT OVERCALL, WEAK JUMP OVERCALL, etc.).

There are eight factors which may influence a player in making an overcall. In roughly descending order of importance, these are:

(1) *Length.* An overcall is nearly always based on a five- or six-card suit. A strong four-card suit may sometimes be sufficient if nonvulnerable at the level of one, but an obstruction factor (see [6] below) might be a consideration. A seven-card or longer suit will usually, but not always, qualify for action at a

higher level. A vulnerable overcall at a two-level is more likely to be based on a six-card suit than a five-card suit.

(2) *Strength.* An average overcall is perhaps equivalent to a minimum suit bid, with perhaps 13 points in high cards. The maximum with a five-card suit is likely to be 15–16 points, i.e., a hand just short of the strength required to double and then bid the five-card suit. In favorable circumstances, not vulnerable at the level of one, a normal minimum is a hand with a king less than an opening bid. Even less is possible if the opponents are vulnerable, and the overcaller is visualizing a 4♠ save against 4♡. In other circumstances, i.e., when vulnerable or when bidding at the level of two, the overcaller's partner should assume that the overcaller has an opening bid.

(3) *Vulnerability.* A nonvulnerable player can afford to make "unsound" overcalls. The opponents will be less eager to double for penalties, and when they do so, may find that have a poor bargain. This is particularly true at match points·at the part-score level, when down two not vulnerable is a frequent source of profit against part-scores of 110 or more in the other direction.

(4) *Level.* One-level overcalls can obviously be made more freely than two-level overcalls. The latter are very much easier to double for penalties (see PENALTY DOUBLE).

(5) *Quality.* In borderline cases the texture of the suit can be important. Q-J-10-9-8-7 is sure to be four playing tricks, but Q-J-5-4-3-2 could turn out to be only one or two. Similarly, an overcall on a suit such as K-Q-10-9-6-5 can have lead-directing advantages if the opponents buy the contract and the overcaller's partner is on lead, whereas an overcall on a suit such as Q-9-7-5-2 is likely to result in embarrassment, or worse.

(6) *Obstruction.* An overcall which consumes the opponent's bidding space is always more attractive than one which does not. 1♠ over 1♣, 2♣ over 1♢, 2♢ over 1♡, and 2♡ over 1♠, all have a preemptive quality, leaving the opponents little room in which to maneuver. In each case a single raise is the only positive action open to the next opponent with a minimum responding hand.

(7) *Opponent's vulnerability.* At all forms of duplicate the overcaller must be sensitive to the opposing vulnerability. At favorable vulnerability he can show a profit by saving in 4♠ against 4♡ and making seven tricks. At unfavorable vulnerability great discretion must be exercised. If a 2♣ overcaller of 1♠ can be doubled and down two, he has met disaster with little prospect of gain. To overcall in such circumstances needs a solid six playing tricks, and even that may not be sufficient.

(8) *Opponent's methods.* Overcalls can be made slightly more freely against opponents using NEGATIVE DOUBLES. Overcalls of 1♠ over a minor suit should be made slightly more freely against opponents who do not open four-card major suits. There is then a greater chance that they can be prevented from finding a heart fit.

Responding to Overcalls

For action by the third player after an overcall, see

FREE BID. Actions by the overcaller's partner come under four headings.

(1) *Raises.* The traditional treatment is for a raise to the two-level to be mildly encouraging, a raise to the three-level to be strongly encouraging (but not forcing), and for a raise to four to be natural and strong.

Suppose an opening bid of 1♣ and a vulnerable overcall of 1♠. If the responder had three-card support and 4-4-3-2 distribution, he would raise to 2♠ with 8–10, to 3♠ with 11–12, and to 4♠ with 13–15. Note that overcalls are regularly raised with three-card support, and might be raised with lesser holdings, especially if the third player bids. If the bidding went:

WEST	NORTH	EAST	SOUTH
			1♡
1♠	4♡	4♠	

with both sides vulnerable, it is conceivable that East, might hold a singleton spade honor and considerable honor strength in the minor suits.

If the overcall is not vulnerable at the level of one, partner must use more discretion in raising. The ranges given above should then be increased by about 2 points.

An alternative treatment put forward by LAWRENCE ROSLER and ROGER STERN treats all raises of overcalls as pre-emptive, and uses a cuebid in the opponent's suit as a constructive raise to the appropriate level. So when 1♣ is overcalled with 1♠, 2♣, 3♣ and 4♣ would be constructive raises to two, three and 4♠ respectively.

A modification of the Rosler-Stern treatment, retaining all raises as pre-emptive, is to use the simple cuebid as the start of any sequence to describe a hand worth at least a limit raise of the overcaller's suit. In this variation, the cuebid is the only forcing response to the overcall; it allows the partner of the overcaller to clarify by his rebid whether he has a limit raise or a strong raise, or perhaps a strong hand with a good six-card suit of his own. His bid of a new suit after he has cuebid is forcing for one round, although not to game.

(2) *Notrump responses.* These are always constructive, but necessarily vary in strength with the vulnerability and level of the overcall.

After a one-level overcall the following ranges apply:

	NOT VULNERABLE	VULNERABLE
1 NT	9–12	9–10
2 NT	13–14	11–12
3 NT	15–16	13–16

The 2 NT ranges are reduced slightly if the overcall was at the two-level.

(3) *Suit takeouts.* Nonforcing, except by special partnership agreement.

WEST	NORTH	EAST	SOUTH
			1♣
1♡	Pass	1♠	

East has a substantial spade suit, a strong five-carder at worst, and a heart misfit. He expects West to pass, although game might still be reached if there is a fit in spades. If East had bid his suit at the two-level — 2♢ — he would have a good six-card suit.

The meaning of a jump shift is a matter or partnership agreement. It may be forcing to game, forcing for one round, strongly encouraging, or preemptive, according to choice.

(4) *Cuebid.* This is covered under CUEBID IN OPPONENT'S SUIT. Note the special usage given to the cuebid under *Raises* above.

OVERLEAD. The Australian term for the traditional opening lead: higher of touching honors. RUSINOW leads of the second-highest honor are called UNDERLEADS.

OVERRUFF. To trump higher than the right-hand opponent after a plain-suit lead. An overruff is almost always good policy. The main exceptions occur when there is a possibility of achieving a trump promotion. A player who holds a certain trump trick together with a possibility of a second trick should usually refuse to overruff. This is an obvious position with spades as trumps:

```
                ♠ 4 3 2
♠ A J                        ♠ 6 5
              ♠ K Q 10 9 8 7
```

If East leads a suit of which South and West are both void, South may elect to ruff high. West then ensures two trump tricks by refusing to overruff.

OVERTAKE. To play a higher card than the one already played by partner for entry reasons. The objective may be suit establishment:

```
NORTH
♣ A J 10 9 8 7
SOUTH
♣ K
```

If five tricks are needed from this suit in a notrump contract, and there is only one entry in the North hand, the king must be overtaken by the ace. The same would apply if South held the queen singleton and North's suit was headed by the ace or king.

An alternative reason for overtaking would be an urgent need for an entry for finessing purposes.

```
WEST                 EAST
♠ A 6                ♠ 7 3
♡ K                  ♡ A J 5 3
◇ A J 8 4            ◇ 9 7 3 2
♣ A Q J 6 5 3        ♣ 10 9 2
```

North leads a spade against West's 3 NT contract. The only hope is to run the club suit, so West overtakes his ♡K with the ace in order to take the club finesse. This sacrifices a heart trick, but makes the contract if the club finesse succeeds.

Another common reason for overtaking is dealt with under UNBLOCKING.

OVERTAKING SQUEEZE. A specialized form of triple squeeze in which the squeeze trick can be won in either hand.

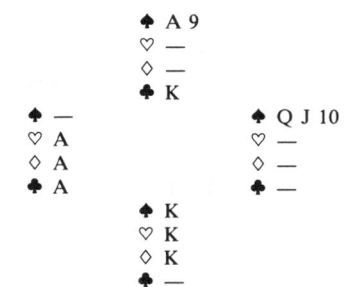

South leads the ♠K, and West is squeezed in three suits. If he discards a red ace, North plays low and South cashes the red king. If West discards the ♣A, North overtakes and cashes the K♣. South thus wins two tricks.

An analogous triple squeeze at a trump contract can give South all the tricks.

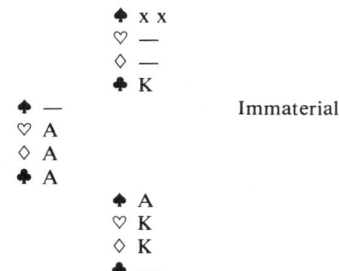

Spades are trump, and South leads the ace of that suit which squeezes West in three suits, enabling South to win the last three tricks.

Monroe Ingberman

OVERTRICK. A trick taken by declarer in excess of the number of tricks required for his contract. If a player is in 4♠ and takes 12 tricks, he is said to have made two overtricks. If a contract is doubled or redoubled, and an overtrick or overtricks are taken, the premium accruing to declarer's side can be substantial. Under certain conditions redoubled overtricks can be worth more than the corresponding slam premium. At duplicate, the making of an overtrick can be all-important — it can actually win a board or even an entire tournament. This situation cannot occur in rubber bridge unless, again, the redoubled feature comes into consideration.

OVERTRUMP. See OVERRUFF.

P

PBA. See PROFESSIONAL BRIDGE ASSOCIATION.

PODI. See DEFENSE TO INTERFERENCE WITH BLACKWOOD.

PRO. Pattern Relay Organized. Also refers to a professional bridge player. See PRO SYSTEM, PROFESSIONAL PLAYERS.

PTDA. See PROFESSIONAL TOURNAMENT DIRECTORS ASSOCIATION.

PACIFIC BRIDGE LEAGUE. An organization founded by TOM STODDARD in 1933, and developed by him through the 15 years of its existence. The League included the 11 far-western states, plus the territories of Hawaii and Alaska and the Canadian provinces of British Columbia and Alberta.

The League rapidly reached a four-figure membership, and promoted two major tournaments, in addition to many minor ones. The ALL-WESTERN tournament was started in Los Angeles in 1935, and BRIDGE WEEK in 1936. The latter was held half in Los Angeles and half in San Francisco.

Collaboration between the ACBL and the Pacific BL began in 1940, when uniform masterpoint systems were agreed. A closer affiliation was planned in 1948, when the great services of Tom Stoddard to the Pacific BL were recognized. He was named President Emeritus of ACBL Western Division, with permanent status on the Executive Committee. The final merger between the ACBL and the Western Division became effective Jan. 1, 1956.

PACIFIC NORTHWEST REGIONAL CHAMPIONSHIPS. A six-day tournament held annually since 1949 in Alaska, British Columbia, or Washington (and prior to 1967, in Oregon). Until 1958 this tournament was held over Washington's Birthday; then it was moved to early fall, and in 1968 it shifted to late April or early May. From 1963–67 the tournament was held twice annually, once in the spring and once in the fall. The spring event used various names including Polar-Canadian Regional, or Polar, Canadian, British Columbia Centennial, and Vancouver, but became known as the Pacific Northwest Regional in 1968 when the fall event was replaced by the Canadian and Puget Sound Regionals. For past results, see Appendix II.

PACIFIC SOUTHWEST REGIONAL CHAMPIONSHIPS. A six-day tournament held annually originally in Coronada CA (in Anaheim CA in 1968) and since 1972 held in San Diego (in Coronado in 1979), beginning in 1946. For past results, see Appendix II.

PACK. A group of a specific number of cards of consistent composition, sold and used as a unit.

The makeup of a pack depends on the date and the country. In the Western world they are composed of four suits, with three FACE CARDS and up to thirteen SPOT CARDS, and have an extra card (JOKER) or cards. The tables below describe some of the many packs that have been in use. When ace is included with the face cards, it ranks high; when included with the spot cards, it ranks low, and is called the ONE-SPOT.

(1) Pack with one of each card:

No. of cards	Game or Country	Face Cards	Spot Cards
62	500	A K Q J	*13 12 11 10 9 8 7 6 5 4 3 2
60	Fantan	K Q J	12 11 10 9 8 7 6 5 4 3 2 1
52	Bridge, Poker	A K Q J	10 9 8 7 6 5 4 3 2
48	Alouette	K C J †	9 8 7 6 5 4 3 2 1
48	Old German	K O U †	10 9 8 7 6 5 4 3 2

No. of cards	Game or Country	Face Cards	Spot Cards
40	Trappola	K C J †	7 6 5 4 3 2 1
36	Schwerter (Ger.)	K O U †	10 9 8 7 6 2
36	Russian	K Q J	10 9 8 7 6 1
36	Sixettes	A K Q J	10 9 8 7 6
32	Piquet	A K Q J	10 9 8 7
32	German	K O U †	10 9 8 7 2
24	Schnaps	A K Q J	10 9

(2) Packs with two of each suit:

No. of cards	Game or Country	Face Cards	Spot Cards
64	Bezique	A K Q J	10 9 8 7
48	Pinochle	A K Q J	10 9
48	Gaigel	A K Q J	10 7

(3) With a group of extra cards not a part of the four suits called in various countries, atouts or atutti:

97 Minichiate taroc (Florence) 41 atutti, and each suit has four face cards and ten spot cards.

78 Lombard tarot (Venice) 22 atutti, and each suit has four face cards and ten spot cards.

62 Tarocchino (Bologna) 22 atutti, and each suit has four face cards and six spot cards (10 9 8 7 6 1).

54 Tarok (German) 22 atutti, and each suit had four face cards and four spot cards, black suits 10 9 8 7 and red suits 4 3 2 1.

64 Sicilian 22 atutti, K Q C J 10 9 8 7 6 5 of four suits and the ace and 4 of coins.

For the 22 atutti, see TAROT.

For bridge purposes, the pack is a set of 52 standard playing cards divided into four suits (spades, hearts, diamonds and clubs) of 13 cards each, ranking in descending order from the ace to the deuce. See LAWS (Law 1).

In the U.S. term *deck* is often preferred. See also HISTORY OF PLAYING CARDS; PLAYING CARDS.

Albert Field

PACKET. A portion of the deck held together, as in gathering tricks, or in dividing the cards for shuffling purposes.

PAIR. A twosome or partnership of two players. All games at bridge come down to the basic competitive situation of pair versus pair, bridge being a partnership, or pair, game.

PAKISTAN BRIDGE ASSOCIATION. Formed in 1973, the association participates in Far East Championships and was represented in the 1981 Bermuda Bowl. It conducts national championship events.

Officers, 1982:
President: Syed Saeed Jafri
Secretary: Shams Quraishi, ^c/o Macquin & Co., Krishna Mansion, Iverity Road, Karachi, Pakistan

PALOOKA. A run-of-the-mill bridge player, a non-expert.

PANAMA. A defensive bidding system against the FORCING CLUB. Bids at the two-level show either a weak jump overcall in the suit bid or a three-suiter with shortage in the bid suit.

PANAMA BRIDGE ASSOCIATION. Founded in 1968, the association participates in CACBF, finishing second in Open Teams 1971, 1972, 1974. It also participated in the 1974 Olympiad.

Officers, 1982:

*Only two of the thirteen-spot cards are used.
† C = Cavalier, O = Ober, U = Unter.

President: John Maduro
Secretary: Luisa Bertoli, ^c/o Punte Chame Turistica S.A., Apartado 10520, Panama 4, Republic of Panama

PAN-AMERICAN INVITATIONAL CHAMPIONSHIPS. An invitational pair championship first held in 1974 in Mexico City, scored by IMPs. This competition was discontinued after 1977. The winners:

1974	Grant S. Baze, Peter A. Pender *(tied with)*
	Robert D. Hamman, Bobby Wolff
1975	Grant S. Baze, Peter A. Pender
1976	Robert D. Hamman, Bobby Wolff
1977	Robert D. Hamman, Bobby Wolff

PAR, PAR SCORE. See PAR CONTEST.

PAR CONTEST. A tournament using prepared hands, each of which embodies a predetermined optimum (par) result. The players' results are compared with par, rather than with each other.

In an ordinary duplicate tournament, how you fare depends to a large degree on how well or poorly your opponents play against you. In a par contest, your skill alone determines the result. You may not profit by an opponent's blunder if you have already erred.

World Championships on a par basis were held in 1961 and 1963 by the World Bridge Federation which prefer the term par-point, perhaps because par can easily be confused with pair. Until 1966 the Intercollegiate Bridge Tournament was the only par contest held annually in the United States. The National Industrial Recreational Association Tournament was conducted in 1963 and 1964 as a par contest but then adopted matchpoint scoring.

The following hand (from the 1963 National Industrial Recreation Association Par Tournament) illustrates the fundamental difference between a par contest and an ordinary duplicate.

Dlr: South
Vul: Both

```
                  ♠ Q 3
                  ♡ A 10 7
                  ◇ J 10 8 7 5
                  ♣ A Q 10
   ♠ 4 2                        ♠ K J 8 7 6 5
   ♡ K 9 5 3                    ♡ J 6
   ◇ Q 6                        ◇ A 4 3
   ♣ 9 6 4 3 2                  ♣ 8 7
                  ♠ A 10 9
                  ♡ Q 8 4 2
                  ◇ K 9 2
                  ♣ K J 5
```

WEST	NORTH	EAST	SOUTH
	1 ◇	1 ♠	2 NT
Pass	3 NT	All Pass	

Opening lead: ♠ 4.

To earn par, East must not play an honor on the first trick, no matter what dummy plays. Then when West wins the ◇ Q, he can play a spade, establishing East's suit while East still has the ◇ A for entry.

In a duplicate tournament, many defenders would defeat the contract after playing an honor on the first trick, because South would play incorrectly and win the trick. In a par contest, these defenders would not be awarded par.

In 1963, the World Bridge Federation adopted an International Par Point Contract Bridge Code, drafted by MICHAEL SULLIVAN and ROBERT WILLIAMS of Australia. This code deals with irregularities and penalties. The basic decisions about the format of the contest are left to the organizers. Some of the factors to be considered are discussed below.

Par-point scoring may be used for individual, pair, or team contest, (but only pair games are common). For a pair game, the par-setters should strive to ensure that the North–South pairs and East–West pairs will meet problems of equal difficulty. Such judgments are necessarily subjective, however, and it is better to choose the North–South and East–West winners separately.

(1) *The Bidding.* The bidding problems should be arranged so as not unduly to favor or penalize any common system or convention. As a rule, par points are awarded on the basis of the final contract reached, not on the actual auction. Minor awards may be given to inferior contracts.

On some deals, players may be instructed (by a slip accompanying the board) to make specified preemptive bids, so that all pairs holding the other hands will be presented with uniform bidding problems. Furthermore, players are instructed to refrain from psychics or other unwarranted or misleading bids. Nevertheless, all the vagaries of competitive auctions cannot be anticipated. Some players will inevitably face more difficult opposition bidding than others, and the par-setters may be called on to adjudicate. Despite this opportunity for redress, it is here that luck or the skill of one's opponent is most likely to affect one's score.

(2) *Before the Play.* So that all competitors face the same play or defense problem, it is usual to specify both the contract to be played and the opening lead. A traveling slip, accompanying the board for this purpose, is consulted after the bidding is over. The official contract need not be the same as the contract awarded maximum bidding par points, if a more interesting play problem is presented.

The par-setters may also provide a guidance auction, from which the players can derive information needed during the play. They are instructed to ignore the actual bidding at their table (but there again, some luck enters).

(3) *The Play.* At the discretion of the par-setters, the traveling slip may inform the players before the play begins whether the pair is for the declarer or the defenders. This saves time by eliminating long huddles by the non-involved side, but adds another artificial aspect to the event.

In addition to the opening lead, the play to one or more tricks may be directed, and declarer or defenders may receive public or private instructions. The primary purpose is to obviate the awarding of *automatic pars*, if the opponents should slip in advance of the anticipated problem. These instructions may also ensure the defeat of a misplaced contract or the fulfillment of a misdefended contract. This is of secondary importance, however, as the par would not be awarded in any case if the play at the table deviated from the prescribed line. Minor awards may be given for partially correct or slightly inferior lines of play or defense.

Note that an equitable two-way play par (that is, a separate par both for the declarer and the defenders on one deal) is almost impossible to arrange. For example, in the hand given above, South will not have a chance to make a par play (ducking the first trick) if East first makes *his* par play by ducking. Then that South would have to be awarded an unearned automatic par.

4. *Movements.* Every player must play all the boards. No movement is necessary — a pair could well play the entire session against one pair of opponents, sharing the boards with the other tables. This arrangement also saves time, as the faster players need not wait for the slower ones to finish their boards each round. Nevertheless, for social and other reasons, some limited movements of the players is desirable.

It is recommended that a time limit for each group of boards be imposed. In important tournaments, the use of chess clocks should be considered.

Lawrence Rosler

PAR HAND. A hand prepared for use in a PAR CONTEST. By extension, a randomly dealt hand suitable for inclusion in such a contest because a single technical aspect of play or defense is dominant.

PAR POINT BRIDGE. See PAR CONTEST.

PARAGUAY BRIDGE ASSOCIATION (ASOCIACIÓN PARAGUAYA de BRIDGE). The Association is a member of the South American Confederation and participates in South American Championships.

Officers, 1982:
President: Philippe L. deBourbon
Secretary: Moises Levy, Mariscal Lopez 140, "Casa Argentina", Asuncion, Paraguay

PARTSCORE. A partial; a trick-score of less than 100 points. In RUBBER BRIDGE, a partscore counts toward game, and enables a side, with the addition of further partscores or a single partscore, should it be of sufficient point value, to make game. Sometimes it may happen that a side in possession of a partscore will have to bid up to game level in order to buy the contract, and, when the game is made, the entry on the scoring pad for that frame simply includes the total of both the game score and the previous partscore or scores. In cases where the adversaries score a game while one's side is in possession of a partial, that particular frame is then ended, and the only value of the partscore is as a part of the full score of one's side containing all the points above and below the line when added together at the conclusion of the rubber, or, as in CHICAGO, at the end of the fourth deal.

In DUPLICATE BRIDGE, any partscore, vulnerable or not, carries with it a premium or bonus of 50 points in addition to the trick-score itself. In rubber bridge, a partial is worth much more. An arbitrary figure of 100 points is usually applied to a partscore. More realistically, however, the true worth of a partial may be 200 points, depending upon the respective vulnerability and certain other factors. See PARTSCORE BIDDING.

PARTSCORE BIDDING. Bidding by a side which possesses a partscore is a subject which is scantily treated by textbooks and produces considerable disagreement among experts. The following treatment is based on the opinion of a number of experts.

Forcing Bids. The most noticeable difference between partscore bidding and normal bidding results from the fact that many bids which would otherwise be forcing are no longer forcing when they complete the game. A new suit by responder, for example, is not forcing if it is sufficient for game. Similarly, a jump from one to three in a suit, or from one of a suit to 2 NT may be passed. The jump shift remains forcing, however, regardless of the partscore.

Suit Bids. Because so many bids become nonforcing if they complete a partial, it is difficult for a partnership to conduct any lengthy bidding investigation. It is therefore of primary importance that whenever a partial exists, all suit bids should stress quality. Thus it would be poor policy to open a three-card minor with a partial. With 60 on score, holding ♠ A-K-J-x, ♡ x-x-x, ◇ x-x-x, ♣ A-J-x, a player should open 1 ♠, and pass partner's response (unless it is a jump shift). Similarly, responder should ignore a suit of doubtful quality. With 70 on score, holding ♠ K-x-x, ♡ Q-9-x-x, ◇ x-x, ♣ A-x-x-x, the response to 1 ◇ should be 1 NT, bypassing the poor heart holding. However, with ♠ K-x-x, ♡ x-x, ◇ x-x, ♣ Q-J-10-9-x-x, the response to 1 ◇ should be 2 ♣, this response at the two level does not promise as much high-card strength as at love score. Rather, it stresses the quality of the club suit. The opening bidder is expected to pass unless he has good reason to continue.

Notrump Bids. All notrump bids tend to have a slightly wider range when the bidder has a part score. Using, normally, 16-18 point notrump bids, with 60 on the score, it would be correct tactics to open 1 NT holding either

♠ A J x	or	♠ A J x
♡ K J x		♡ K J x ·
◇ A Q x x		◇ Q x x x
♣ K J x		♣ K J x

Some experts allow themselves more latitude than others in the range of their opening notrump, but taking the average approach of the experts consulted, it can be stated that standard expert procedure is to widen the range for an opening 1 NT by about a point in either direction when a partscore is held.

There are two reasons for this increase in the notrump range. First, there is always a tremendous tactical advantage in opening with 1 NT. Partner is immediately in an excellent position either to place the contract or punish overzealous opponents. The opponents are unable to compete at the one level and may find it too dangerous to begin their search for a fit at the two level. To reopen in fourth seat after an opening notrump by opponents with a 60 partial is particularly dangerous, because opener's partner may pass with up to 13 high-card points, instead of being limited by his pass to seven or less.

Tactical advantages exist for opening 1 NT frequently at no score also, but in this case the problem of whether to reach game or settle for a partial is paramount; widening the range of the notrump would be against the interests of accuracy. With a substantial partial, the question of whether to reach game or not is already solved, and tactical considerations become more prominent. Naturally the prospect of missing a slam is a deterrent to increasing the upper limit unduly. With 60 on score, and a passed partner, it is surely good tactics to open 1 NT with 19 points regardless of the normal range, as slam can hardly be missed.

The second, and less obvious, reason for increasing the range, and thus the frequency of the notrump opening, goes back to the stress on quality for opening suit-bids. If the normal 1 NT range is 15 to 17 points, and a partial of 40 is held, it would be proper to open 1 NT holding ♠ K-x-x, ♡ A-x-x-x, ◇ A-x x-x, ♣ K-x. Ordinarily such a hand would be opened 1♡ or 1◇, depending on partnership attitude toward four-card majors. With the partscore, the suit-bid carries an added implication of quality. Partner will strain to raise the suit-bid, and the safer spot in notrump will be missed. If suit play is better, responder can choose the suit.

Other notrump bids are likewise affected by the partial. Most experts play 21–22 point opening 2 NT bids. They increase this range, particularly the upper limit, when a partial exists. By far the most frequently used range (and, therefore, logically, the standard range) for an opening 2 NT bid is 21–24 with a partial of 60 or more, and 20–24 with a lesser partial.

The opening strong 3 NT bid becomes almost extinct in a partscore holding of 30 or more. It is better to open with 2♣, and rebid 2 NT to a 2◇ response. Any other response, and a slam can be investigated with impunity. Using strong two-bids, a two-bid in the best suit and a pass to the negative 2 NT response are in order.

All of the notrump bids, the simple response of 1 NT is most affected by a partscore. Normally this bid shows 6–9 in STANDARD AMERICAN, but with a partial it tends to become 4–12. The lower limit is reduced because of the strain to keep the bidding open when game is so near; the upper limit is largely affected by distaste for bidding a weak suit.

The responses of 2 and 3 NT remain close to their usual ranges. The 13–15 range for a 2 NT response increases to 13–16 with a partial, and becomes nonforcing, of course. The 3 NT range moves from 16–17 to 17–18. It is a common practice among average players to avoid both these responses on some theory that it is unnecessary to *get so high* with a partial. This is a fallacy. There should be no danger at this level opposite an opening bid. More important by far is the fact that these bids are extremely useful when the opening bidder has slam aspirations.

Raising Partner's Suit. As responder, when holding a fit with partner, it is imperative to show it immediately. The fact that one side has a fit increases the chances that the opponents have a fit and a profitable sacrifice. With a 90 partscore and an opening 1♠ bid by partner, holding ♠ Q-J-x-x, ♡ K-x, ◇ Q-x-x-x, ♣ x-x-x, bid 2♠ immediately. If opener's hand is such that 1♠ is the partnership limit, fourth hand will take some action, and the necessary 2♠ bid on the next round will come after the opponents have found their fit. Immediate action may keep the opponents out altogether. With a partscore, it is standard to give a single raise with 6–12 points. The lower limit may be reduced as far as three points if the raise is necessary to complete the game. With 13–16 points it is still standard to give a jump raise from one to three in a suit. With a stronger hand, a jump shift is in order.

Stayman with a Partial. With a partscore of 60, the opening bid is 1 NT, and the response is 2♣. In standard practice this is STAYMAN, but a substantial minority of experts regard 2♣ as natural. Failing any partnership agreement, the opener should assume the bid is conventional. This can at worst lead to a contract of 3♣ instead of 2♣, while a pass of a conventional 2♣ bid could be a complete disaster.

Forcing Two-Bids. Bridge authorities agree that with a partscore a forcing two-bid may be made with less than the normal requirements—perhaps a full playing trick less. This makes sense. A slam can be missed if partner has a little something, and if the one-bid is kept open because of the partial, on very little, a forcing rebid may get the combined hands overboard. By opening with a strong two-bid, the strength of the hand is announced in one bid, and can be bid conservatively thereafter. The texts maintain that the strong two-bid is a one-round force. Although the experts consulted agree in theory with this, many confessed that if they held nothing, they might pass in practice.

Tactical Considerations. With a partscore, is is wise to open lighter or stronger than ususal? What about when the opponents have a partial? Or when both sides are on score? This is an area of wide disagreement. No standard approach exists, but the various schools of thought are presented so the reader may form his own opinions.

One school holds that as long as fewer tricks are required to make a game, opening bids may be slightly weaker with a partial. A second school recommends using stronger opening bids with a partial. This group reasons: If the bidding is opened with a partial, the opponents are very apt to compete. Responder will fight for the partscore on the strength of the opening bid; if this bid is subminimum, responder may push too high, presenting the opponents with a very attractive double, or, even worse, he may decide to *punish* competing opponents, and double them into game. A third school suggests opening light with spades, but normally or slightly over without spades. Obviously the side with spades has an advantage in any bidding battle. Still a fourth school feels that the advantages and disadvantages of either stronger or lighter bids just about cancel each other out, maintaining that normal bids will work out best in the long run. About half of the experts consulted recommended normal openings with a partial.

There are also various theories as to the best procedure when the opponents have a partial. A slight majority of the experts suggest opening light, believing that the best defense is an early offense. It is dangerous to overcall or balance against opponents who have a partial as they may have strength in reserve: hence the value of getting in first with the opening bid. Light takeout doubles and overcalls are also favored for the same reason. Many recommend the preemptive opening of 1 ♠ or 1 NT with a slightly lighter range than usual. ELY CULBERTSON, in his *Contract Bridge Complete*, says "Shade your bids downward if the opponents have a partscore and upward if you have the partscore." Then there are those who like to have stronger openings when the opponents have a partial; they would rather pass out a hand than open a minimum when they are at such a disadvantage in the score. Lastly there are those who stand steadfast for the normal opening.

A further point arising when the opponents have a partial is often overlooked. When in doubt whether to bid game or settle for a partscore, it is better to stretch a bit and bid game. The reason is that the value of success is substantially increased by the fact that the opponent's partial is wiped out.

When both sides have a partscore, the experts are split into two roughly equal camps: those favoring lighter openings and those favoring normal openings. Reasons given are various combinations of those above.

The Value of a Partial. Experts have long been aware that a partscore at rubber bridge is worth far more than the 50 points awarded in the rules for a partial in an unfinished rubber. Because of the many imponderable factors involved, including the identity of one's opponents, mathematicians cannot agree on the correct way to calculate the value mathematically. However, JEAN BESSE, kept a record or more than 1000 partscore situations ("Autour de l'Étoile," *British Bridge World*, p. 34, August 1959). He compared the scores when a partial had just been achieved and again when the partial had been completed. Allowing 300 for any first game, 400 for the second game, and 500 for any third game, his results were as follows:

Values (over and above the trick score) of a nonvulnerable partial of 40 or more	90
Value of a vulnerable partial (opponents not vulnerable) of 40 or more	110
Value of a partial of 40 or more at game all	220

The tremendous value of a partial at game all he attributes partly, of course, to the increased value of game, but mainly to the increased difficulty encountered by vulnerable opponents in trying to defend.

In many of the bridge clubs of this country today, four-deal bridge, CHICAGO, has taken the place of rubber bridge. A partial must be worth somewhat less in this form of bridge, due to the limited time in which to capitalize on it. Naturally, a partial on the fourth deal is worth exactly the 100 points awarded for it in the rules.

Dorothy Hayden Truscott

PARTSCORE BONUS. In duplicate competition, 50 points are scored as a bonus for fulfilling a partscore contract. In CHICAGO, a bonus of 100 points is

given for a partscore contract successful on the last hand. For the mathematical value of a partscore see PARTSCORE BIDDING.

PARTIAL DESIGNATION. Incomplete specification by declarer of the rank or suit of a card to be played from dummy's hand. See LAWS (Law 46).

PARTIAL ELIMINATION. A throw-in play depending on ruff-and-discard possibilities in which the stripping process is incomplete.

In a perfect elimination the declarer eliminates all the suits which a defender may safely lead and saddles him with the choice of conceding a ruff and sluff or leading into a tenace. A partial elimination, on the other hand, is so called because the declarer only partially eliminates the suits which a defender may safely lead; now, whether the defender will have to lead to the declarer's advantage will depend on distributional hazards.

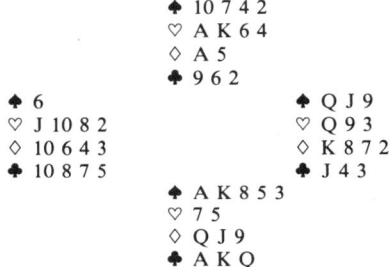

Playing in 6 ♠, South wins the heart lead and tests trumps. When West fails on the second round, South attempts an endplay to avoid taking the diamond finesse. He plays the second top heart, ruffs the third round in his hand, and takes his three top clubs before throwing the lead to East's master trump. East fortunately has no hearts or clubs left and has to lead away from the ◇ K.

South's maneuver is a *partial* elimination because he could only partially eliminate hearts. He did not have the entries to eliminate the hearts completely. This play had the added advantage that if East did have a club as an exit card he might have been unwilling to give declarer a ruff-sluff and led a diamond anyway. The ruff-sluff could not possibly help South because he had only one trump left and could not ruff both the club return and dummy's last heart.

In the above example the critical suit — hearts — was eliminated from two of the four hands. When the distribution is favorable, a partial elimination may succeed even though the critical suit be eliminated from only one hand: (See hand at top of next page.)

With hearts as trumps, South can make 12 tricks by means of partial elimination. He wins the spade lead, plays off the trump ace, and eliminates the black suits. He cashes the ◇ A–K and exits with a trump. West wins, but he is the only player without a diamond in his hand. He has to return a black suit, and South ruffs on the table, at the same time sluffing a diamond from the closed hand.

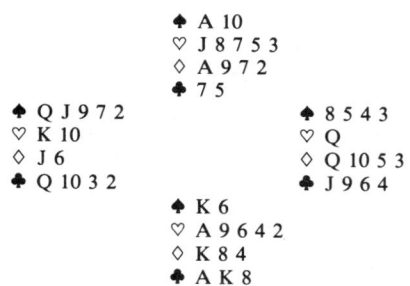

```
              ♠ A 10
              ♡ J 8 7 5 3
              ♢ A 9 7 2
              ♣ 7 5
♠ Q J 9 7 2              ♠ 8 5 4 3
♡ K 10                   ♡ Q
♢ J 6                    ♢ Q 10 5 3
♣ Q 10 3 2               ♣ J 9 6 4
              ♠ K 6
              ♡ A 9 6 4 2
              ♢ K 8 4
              ♣ A K 8
```

A partial elimination can also operate when one of the defenders still has a trump in his hand:

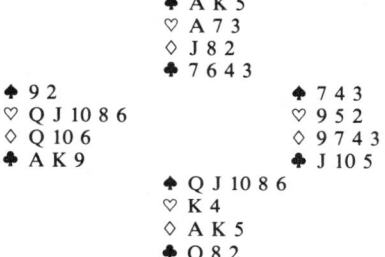

```
              ♠ A K 5
              ♡ A 7 3
              ♢ J 8 2
              ♣ 7 6 4 3
♠ 9 2                    ♠ 7 4 3
♡ Q J 10 8 6             ♡ 9 5 2
♢ Q 10 6                 ♢ 9 7 4 3
♣ A K 9                  ♣ J 10 5
              ♠ Q J 10 8 6
              ♡ K 4
              ♢ A K 5
              ♣ Q 8 2
```

West opens the bidding with 1♡, and South reaches a contract of 4♠ instead of 3 NT. After a heart lead, prospects are poor, but a partial elimination offers the best chance. However, it is essential to keep at least one trump in each hand to profit from a possible ruff and sluff; this means that South can afford to draw only two rounds of trumps, and must therefore rely on West's having no more than two trumps.

South wins the heart lead, plays off the ace and queen of trumps, and continues with a second and third round of hearts, ruffing. He then plays ace, king, and another diamond, throwing West into the lead. As expected, West has the outstanding high cards and has to offer a ruff and discard or concede a trick to the ♣Q.

PARTIAL SCORE. See PARTSCORES.

PARTNER. The player with whom one is paired in a game of bridge.

PARTNER'S SUIT. The suit bid or rebid by the player opposite one during an auction. It is usually advisable to support partner's suit when one can, as this builds firmness and reliability in a partnership. As respects defensive play situations, the leading of partner's suit raises many questions. Whether it should be led at all, and if so, which card of one's holding, etc., are all problems with which a good player constantly concerns himself.

PARTNERSHIP LANGUAGE. See SIGNALS and SYSTEMS.

PARTNERSHIP MISUNDERSTANDINGS. All partnerships have misunderstandings about the meaning of bids, although these should be infrequent in a well-established expert partnership. Some

advance consideration can reduce the frequency of such errors.

Such misunderstandings fall into four general categories:

(1) The strength of a bid. For example, the traditional strength of a 2 NT opening is 22–24 points, but a majority of experts prefer 21–22 points as the range for this bid, and open with an artificial 2♣ bid when they hold stronger hands.

(2) The nature of a bid: sign-off, discouraging, encouraging, or forcing (for one round or to game). A good example is a jump in a new suit over an opposing takeout double (see RESPONSES OVER OPPONENT'S TAKEOUT DOUBLE). According to the partnership understanding, this bid can be preemptive, encouraging, forcing for one round, or forcing to game.

(3) Artificial or natural quality of a bid. Confusion can occur when a partnership has not specifically agreed whether a particular artificial device is being employed, such as LANDY over opposing notrump bids, especially with an unfamiliar partnership. Both players may normally use a convention, and be aware that the partner normally uses it, but still be in doubt about whether it is in use because it has not been discussed.

A more common source of difficulty is doubt about whether a convention is applicable to a particular situation. It is sometimes difficult to diagnose, for example, whether 4 NT is natural or conventional; or whether a bid in the opponent's suit is a cuebid or an attempt to play in that suit.

(4) The nature of a double. There may be doubt about whether a double is for penalties or for takeout. A failure to agree on the use of RESPONSIVE or NEGATIVE DOUBLES would be an example of this problem. There are also situations, usually after the first round of bidding, in which the intentions of the doubler are not clear.

The nature of a pass may also be crucial, especially if a FORCING PASS is a possibility.

No partnership can avoid misunderstandings altogether, but the following suggestions may help to reduce the incidence of disaster.

First, a regular partnership should have a detailed understanding.

Second, a player should avoid making an ambiguous bid when an unambiguous alternative is equally satisfactory.

Third, when an ambiguous bid is made, a partnership should apply some automatic rule. A reasonable rule is to take the weaker interpretation in each case, that is: the lower point range; nonforcing against forcing; natural as against conventional; and takeout rather than penalty double. The opposite rule is also playable, and so are a variety of hybrid rules. In any case, it is advisable to have some rule. This often avoids impending trouble, provided both players are aware of the possibility of trouble.

PARTNERSHIP PSYCHOLOGY. The art of keeping partner happy is worth more in terms of results than much advanced technical knowledge; but it is an art which many players, including some at the highest level never learn.

At rubber bridge the player who encourages his partner instead of shouting at him, praising the occasional good plays instead of pointing out the obvious and frequent bad ones, earns large dividends. His partners then like to play with him, and play above themselves. On the other hand, a player who is subjected to a barrage of criticism is likely to play below his best not only for the remainder of the rubber but on subsequent occasions.

In tournament play, self-made partnerships ought in theory to be more compatible, but this is not always the case, and the same principles are applicable. Long-lived tournament partnerships usually consist of players who enjoy each other's company and have a genuine respect for each other. Egotists whose main concern is to prove how brilliantly they themselves play and how foolishly their partners perform may have temporary successes, but they have to find new partners regularly.

PARTNERSHIP RUBBER BRIDGE. A style of rubber bridge popular in England whereby two players play as partners throughout a session. Players agree in advance to play as partners, as they would in a duplicate event, and there is no game for unpaired individuals. This tends to raise the standard of the game by excluding those who, through inferior ability or character deficiency, find it difficult to get a partner.

PARTNERSHIP UNDERSTANDING. An agreement between partners which enables them to draw information or inferences from the bidding and play. It is not to be confused with PRIVATE CONVENTION, which is illegal and unethical. It is the duty of all partnerships to make sure that any understanding they may have on the meanings of bids or plays of which the opponents could not reasonably be expected to have knowledge be clearly and concisely stated on their CONVENTION CARD in tournament play, and announced to the opponents in rubber bridge. See ALERTING, EXPLANATION OF CONVENTIONAL CALL OR PLAY.

PARTNERSHIPS. Either or both of the two sets of the players at a table, North–South and East–West. Players who play together frequently are considered an established partnership; players who pair up for a particular event, having played together either seldom or never, have a more casual partnership. Most of the bidding and play conventions were established as successful tactics by established partnerships; it is noteworthy that the use of these bids was carefully explained to opponents by their developers, and they were quite well known even before their publication.

PARTY BRIDGE. Private games consisting of at least two tables. The CHICAGO or four-deal method is customary. It is usual to give prizes to the players with the best scores and the player with the worst score may receive a booby prize. The manner of mixing partnerships is manifold; some hostesses use commercial tallies which give seating assignments to players, by which players enjoy four hands with all

the other players or, alternately, all the other players of opposite sex. Another form, where excellence of bridge is to be rewarded, provides that, after each round, the winning pairs move to the lower numbered table, except at the head table, where the losing pair goes to the highest numbered table.

Other possibilities are outlined under PARTY CONTRACT BRIDGE, LAWS OF.

PARTY CONTRACT BRIDGE, LAWS OF
DUPLICATE FOR HOME PLAY, AND COMPETITION NOT IN DUPLICATE

The forms of Duplicate play described in the Laws are readily adapted to home play. Special games suitable to a small number of tables, or emphasizing the social above the competitive element, are described in the following pages.

For a single table, the available games are REPLAY DUPLICATE and PIVOT BRIDGE (non-Duplicate). For two or three tables there are INDIVIDUAL MOVEMENTS, and MITCHELL or HOWELL PAIR MOVEMENTS, and TEAM-OF-FOUR MOVEMENTS. For a larger number of tables, where it is desired to emphasize the social element, the popular game is PROGRESSIVE BRIDGE.

In general, the Laws of Duplicate Contract Bridge apply to all forms of Duplicate and multiple-table play — from the simplest Replay contest to the most elaborate championship tournament.

Even in simple home games, such as Replay Duplicate, it is advisable to appoint one participant as Supervisor and to invest him with all the authority of a Tournament Director. Experience has shown that without a guiding hand even a social game is likely to be delayed or deadlocked by trivial irregularities.

Replay Duplicate

Replay Duplicate is a contest between two pairs. It is played in two sessions, called the Original Play and the Replay.

The players take places, one being designated North. The trays (boards) are shuffled, and are played with the arrows pointing North. Any number of trays is feasible.

A separate scoreslip is kept for each tray. At the close of the session the trays and scoreslips are laid aside where they will be undisturbed.

At some later time, the same four players take the same relative positions about the table. The trays are replayed with the arrows pointing East. Again a separate scoreslip is kept for each board.

The scoring may be by matchpoints or total points. If the former method is used, each deal is treated as a separate match. The pair having the better net score on a deal is credited with 1 point. The final scores are the totals of these matchpoints.

If total point scoring is employed, the two slips for each deal are compared, and the pair having the greater plus or lesser minus is credited with the difference. The next scores for all deals, so determined, are totaled, and the pair having the larger total wins the difference.

Replay Duplicate is popular as a home game among foursomes that meet weekly for social bridge. It can easily be played in a continuous series of sessions. Half of the time in each session is devoted to the original play of new trays, and half to the replay of old trays.

The game tends to become a test of memory rather than of bridge skill. To check this tendency the following measures are recommended:

1. Do not play the trays in consecutive order. Choose the tray to be played next at random from the stack.

2. Avoid comment of any sort about the deal after its original play.

3. Allow at least a week to elapse between the original play and the replay.

It is sometimes desired to make the game a test of skill in play alone. The bidding during the original play is then recorded, and for the replay this bidding is read to fix the contract and declarer.

Individual Contests

In an individual game, each player plays once with every other as partner, and twice against every other as opponent.

The initial seating of the players in games for two or three tables is shown below:

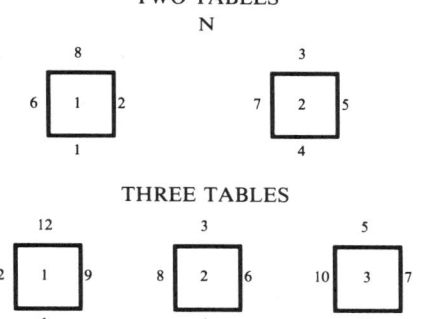

TWO TABLES

THREE TABLES

The game may be conducted without guide cards, thus:

1. Allow the players to take places at random. Reserve the North position at Table 1 for the Supervisor; this player is *anchor*, retaining his seat throughout the game.

2. From this schedule inform each player of his number, and tell him who is the player of next-lower number.

3. Announce that after each round, all players but the anchor will progress, each player taking the seat vacated by the player of next-lower number. (Player 1 follows Player 7 or 11, respectively.)

A new set of trays is played in each round. The set is played at all tables, the trays being circulated at convenience. The eight-player game requires seven rounds, with a total of 14, 21, or 28 boards. The twelve-player game requires eleven rounds, and the only feasible number of boards is 33.

The scoring of individual contests is explained in the Laws of Duplicate Contract Bridge.

Progressive Rubber Bridge

Progressive Rubber Bridge is a variation of the usual progressive game. It has proved increasingly popular, and may in time supplant the usual form. It follows the methods of progression and change of partners described in the preceding laws, but the scoring is somewhat different.

Under this arrangement it is preferable to play eight deals to a round, or to fix the length of a round by a definite time limit — say 30 minutes. If the length of a round is determined by a time limit, any deal which has been started before time is up may be completed, but no new hand may be dealt.

Rubber Bridge scoring is used. As many rubbers as possible are completed during the time allotted. A rubber completed in two games carries a bonus of 700 points. A three-game rubber carries a bonus of 500 points. If a side has won one game toward a rubber and the other side has not won a game, 300 points are allowed for the single game won. If one side only has a partscore (a trick-score totaling less than 100) in an unfinished game of an unfinished rubber, that side adds 50 points to its score.

Vulnerability is determined by the state of the score and not according to Section 9 of the Progressive Code. A side is vulnerable when it has won a game and remains vulnerable until the conclusion of that rubber. However, vulnerability lapses at the conclusion of a round and a new rubber is started at the beginning of each new round.

At the end of a round each player enters on his tally only his net gain or loss — not his total score. At the end of the session these net gains and losses are totaled and the player's final score, plus or minus as the case may be is entered at the bottom of his tally.

PASS. A call by which a player indicates that, at that turn, he does not choose to contract for a number of odd tricks at any denomination, nor does he choose, at that turn, to double a contract of the opponents or redouble a contract by his side that opponents have already doubled.

The proprieties require that only one term be used in passing. NO BID is an acceptable alternative (standard in England), but all calls must be made with uniform usage. See CALL, BID, PENALTY PASS, NO BID.

PASS or THROW IN. A deal in which all four players pass on the first round of bidding. The score is zero. In duplicate, the hand is scored and returned to the board; in rubber bridge, the deal passes to the next player, but in CHICAGO a redeal by the same dealer is required. The term "pass out" is also applied to the action of the player who, after two passes, declines to reopen the bidding at a comparatively low level. He is said to be in the "pass-out seat" or the "pass-out position."

PASS OUT OF TURN. This can occur under two different circumstances: when it is the turn of the opponent on the right, or when partner's turn to call precedes the offender's turn to call. In the first case, no damage has been done, and the penalty is that the offender must echo his pass when next it is his turn to bid; in the latter case, damage has been done to the opponents, and the penalty is correspondingly more severe. See LAWS (Law 30, a, b). See also OBLIGATION TO PASS.

PASSED HAND. When partner has opened the bidding in third or fourth seat, the problems of the responder may be rather special. There are two complicating factors: (1) a change of suit is no longer forcing, so responder must be prepared for a "sudden death" pass of his response; (2) partner may have opened a sub-minimum hand, to direct a lead or to try for a small plus score, and will then be annoyed if responder gets too high.

Since any response may be passed, one must be very wary of responding in anemic suits. In general, the higher the response the greater is the chance that it will be dropped. This means that the responder can answer 1 ◊ to 1 ♣ with a weakish suit (four to the jack), since someone at the table will bail responder out. But if one responds 1 ♡ or, more particularly, 1 ♠, one should have a respectable four-card suit (at least four to the queen-ten). And if the response is at the two-level, one must be prepared to play opposite a doubleton—partner is now even money to pass. So responder would want to have a six-card suit or at least a husky five-carder.

Suppose that one had passed this hand:

♠ K Q 2
♡ J 6 4 3
◊ A 9 6 3 2
♣ 7

If partner opens 1 ♣, respond 1 ◊. If, instead, he opens 1 ◊, respond 3 ◊ (not 1 ♡, as one might if it were forcing). If partner opens 1 ♡, one cannot temporized by answering 2 ◊, so 3 ♡ seems best. And if partner opens 1 ♠, one must still avoid the 2 ◊ response, for one belongs in spades, not diamonds—responder may choose between 2 ♠ or 3 ♠, and the jump raise is probably better in the long run.

Suppose that one had passed this hand:

♠ K 6
♡ Q 10 4 2
◊ K 10
♣ K 9 6 3 2

Again, one must be careful about bidding suits. Should partner open with 1 ◊ a 1 ♡ response is preferable to 2 ♣. True, the hand is strong enough for a two-level response and for two bids; but (1) partner may pass before the second bid, and (2) partner is more likely to find a rebid if he can do so at the one-level, and (3) if partner does pass, one would rather be in the higher scoring major suit. What would be the response with this hand if partner opened 1 ♠? Not 2 ♣, and certainly not 2 ◊. The best bet is 2 NT, and this jump response could easily be right over 1 ◊ or 1 ♣ as well.

In contrast, if responder passed a hand that does contain a strong suit, he can give himself a little more freedom in bidding at the two-level. For example, holding:

♠ Q 7 5 2
♡ 7 4
◊ 2
♣ K Q 10 8 6 3

one would respond 2 ♣ to a 1 ◊ opening if it was a passed hand, while 1 ♠ would be correct if it was not. What makes the difference? Once the responder passed, there is a fighting chance to play in 2 ♣ when the responder bids it: and if partner rebids 2 ◊, one can carry on with 2 ♠ without creating a forcing situation. What is more, it is dangerous to respond 1 ♠—if partner passes there is no reason to believe

that this is either the safest or most productive contract.

Since the requirements for a two-over-one suit takeout are shaded down, there is a worry about missing game when holding the normal solid values for this response. Consider these hands:

♠ 8 3   ♠ 7 4
♡ K Q 10 8 7 4 2   ♡ 6 2
◊ A 10 5   ◊ 8 5
♣ 5   ♣ A K Q 10 9 6 5

If, for some reason that appealed at the time, either hand has been passed, jump shift over partner's opening. 2 ♡ or 2 ♣ in response to 1 ♠ is no longer nearly enough; one must jump to three. This puts partner on notice that there are game ambitions even opposite the bare minimum opening bid with which partner would pass a simple response. (Some experts, especially in England, use the jump shift by a passed hand as a one-round force with support for opener's suit.)

Jump bids should be made sparingly opposite a passed hand, because partner can have spare values for his opening. The last two examples are safe enough at the three-level, for there are seven winners, and partner should have the decency to provide two. But passed hand jump raises and jumps to 2 NT entail considerable risk of a minus score. Consider these hands:

♠ K 8 6 2   ♠ A Q J 9
♡ J 10 4   ♡ 7 5 3
◊ A Q 7 5   ◊ 10 2
♣ 7 3   ♣ K 10 8 2

WEST	EAST
Pass	1 ♠
3 ♠	Pass

No one made a bad bid—East's third-hand opening is irreproachable, and West has the values for a passed-hand jump raise—but the final contract is dangerously high. Unless two finesses succeed, it will go down for a poor score. How do East-West get to 2 ♠? It is no solution for West to temporize with 2 ◊, as he might had partner opened in first seat, for he will be left in this unappetizing contract. Some players might bid only 2 ♠ with the West hand, fearing a light opening, but this risks missing game opposite a sound minimum, for the range of the single raise becomes impossibly broad (unless these players bid in delicately graded intonations; then they will get into a different kind of trouble).

Here is a similar problem:

♠ J 8 7 3   ♠ 9 6 2
♡ Q 10 4   ♡ A K J 2
◊ K J   ◊ Q 10 9 4
♣ A 9 4 2   ♣ J 6

WEST	EAST
Pass	1 ♡
2 NT	Pass

This contract is not likely to be a success. What went wrong? Surely, West could not bid only 1 NT or 2 ♡; 3 ♡ is a possible response, but it is almost certainly down one. A response of 1 ♠ would be passed, and declarer can develop ulcers playing in a trump suit like that. Perhaps light third- and fourth-hand openings are undesirable.

Not really. One will show a big matchpoint profit in the long run by opening these hands. When partner has a normal minimum count, one will earn a small plus or at least impede the opponents or direct a good lead. The examples above are unlucky, but there is an answer for them too.

A suggestion is to adopt the DRURY CONVENTION. When the bidding is opened in third or fourth seat with one of a major, the response of 2♣, by the passed hand, is artificial. It asks opener if he has a normal bid, or if he opened light. If opener has shaded his values, he answers 2◊; if he has a reasonable hand, he makes his natural rebid.

In the examples above, West would respond 2♣, Drury. East would rebid 2◊, and West would sign off safely at two of opener's major. Let us see an auction where opener has his full bid:

♠ K 7 2   ♠ A Q 10 8 4
♡ A Q J 3   ♡ K 10 6 2
◊ Q 7 6 2   ◊ 9 8
♣ 8 6   ♣ A 5

WEST	EAST
Pass	1♠
2♣	2♡
4♡	Pass

Here, the advantage of Drury is in making it easy to find the heart fit; without it, West would likely jump to 3♠. However, the principal use of this convention is in staying at the two-level in case East's hand is:

♠ A J 9 8 4
♡ 6 2
◊ 9 8 4
♣ A J 5

The bidding then would be:

WEST	EAST
Pass	1♠
2♣	2◊
2♠	Pass

Many experts play REVERSE DRURY. In this method, 2♣ still is the forcing response, asking opener about the strength of the opening bid. However, 2◊ no longer is the negative response—a rebid of two in the suit opened constitutes the negative. Any other response shows opener had full values for the opening bid. See also RULE OF SIXTEEN.

Edgar Kaplan

PASSIVE DEFENSE. A defense which aims principally to avoid establishing tricks for declarer, rather than principally to establish tricks for the defense. A defender's continuation of a suit already led either by declarer or the defense, rather than attacking a new suit, is a common type of passive defense.

PASSIVE LEAD. An opening lead which is unlikely to hurt the defending side, but is not expected to have a positive value. A lead from three or four small cards is a typical passive lead, but in certain circumstances a trump lead may be passive, or a lead in an opposing suit which is likely to be solid. See ATTACKING LEAD; OPENING LEAD.

PASTEBOARDS. A name given to playing cards because a coating of black paste between two paper layers gave the stock on which the cards were printed an opacity that made it impossible to see through them. See MANUFACTURE OF PLAYING CARDS.

PATTERN RELAY ORGANIZED SYSTEM. See PRO SYSTEM.

PEETERS, MARCEL CHALLENGE CUP. See INTERNATIONAL BRIDGE ACADEMY.

PENAL INSTITUTIONS. See BRIDGE IN PRISONS.

PENALTY. (1) An obligation or restriction imposed upon a side for violation of the Laws of Bridge. In the language of the lawgivers, penalties are designed "... to provide an adequate remedy whenever a player accidentally, carelessly or inadvertently disturbs the proper course of the game. An offending player should be ready to pay graciously any penalty or adjusted score awarded by a Tournament Director."

(2) An amount scored above the line by the declarer's opponents when the declarer fails to make a contract. The penalty provisions of the score table are gauged so as to make competitive bidding a fine art.

Many of the great stories in the anecdotage of the game are concerned with penalties. The biggest penalty in a championship tournament was reported from the Men's Pairs at the 1964 Summer North American Championships held at Toronto.

```
                    ♠ —
                    ♡ A K Q J 9 7 6 4 2
                    ◊ 7
                    ♣ K Q 5
♠ 10 8 6 2                      ♠ A K Q 7 5 4 3
♡ 10 3                          ♡ —
◊ 5 3                           ◊ 9 4
♣ J 10 9 8 7                    ♣ 6 4 3 2
                    ♠ J 9
                    ♡ 8 5
                    ◊ A K Q J 10 8 6 2
                    ♣ A
```

With both sides vulnerable, the par contract is a 7♠ sacrifice by East–West, which costs 1400 as compared with 2220 for the grand slam which North–South can make in hearts. (7◊ by South is defeated if West leads a heart.) At most tables the final contract was in fact 7♠ doubled, but at a number of other tables the North–South pairs refused to be outbid and overcalled 7♠ with 7 NT, which was of course doubled and was usually redoubled. The auction at one such table was:

WEST	NORTH	EAST	SOUTH
	2♡	2♠	3◊
Pass	4 NT	5♠	6♣
Pass	7♡	7♠	7 NT
Pass	Pass	Dbl	Redbl
All Pass			

Spades were led, and West did not fail to unblock with the 8 and 10. East thus took the first seven tricks for a penalty of 4000. At another table the bidding was:

WEST	NORTH	EAST	SOUTH
	2♣	3♦	4 NT
Pass	6♡	Pass	7 NT
Pass	Pass	Dbl	Redbl
All Pass			

West, doubtless attributing some unusual lead-directing significance to his partner's double, led a club and the contract was made for a score of 2930. The spread between top and bottom score was thus 6930.

PENALTY CARD. A card that has been prematurely exposed by a defender, and must be left face up on the table until legally played or permitted to be picked up. If it is a LEAD OUT OF TURN, the declarer has several options, some of which permit the penalty card to be picked up; if it remains a penalty card on a lead out of turn, or is prematurely exposed in any other condition, it must be played at the first legal opportunity that the player may have to play it. See LAWS, Laws 23, 49–53, 55, 57, 58, and 62: LAWS OF DUPLICATE (Laws 23, 49–52, 54, 56–58, 62).

PENALTY DOUBLE. The distinction between penalty doubles and takeout doubles is discussed under DOUBLES. Normal penalty doubles can be considered in three categories:

(1) Positive doubles. Suppose an opening bid is overcalled and doubled, and the opener's hand seems unsuited to defense. Should he stand the double or take it out?

If the opening bid was of a sort which describes the hand within narrow limits, stand the double. If the opening bid is 3♣ with this hand:

♠ K J 8 7 6 4 3 2
♡ 3
♢ 2
♣ J 5 4

pass a double by partner of an overcall of 4♡. He does not expect the opener to have defensive strength.

Having opened with a three-bid, a four-bid, and weak two-bid, or any notrump bid, pass partner's double of an overcall. These are all bids which describe a hand within narrow limits.

Opponents seldom argue with a forcing two-bid, but when they do, retaliation must be swift and sure and there must be no partnership misunderstanding. The responder should beware of doubling on hands which contain a feature outside the enemy suit.

♠ A J 6 5 ♡ Q 8 7 4 ♢ 5 4 3 ♣ 7 2

After a 2♣ opening by partner, do not double an overcall of 2♠. Too often the hand will belong in a heart contract. In any event, the hand must be useful in attack, and game must be there. Experience shows that the double is best reserved for hands like

♠ Q 10 7 6 5 ♡ 8 7 4 ♢ 5 4 3 ♣ 7 2

If this is the partnership understanding, opener will the double with

♠ 4 ♡ A K J 5 ♢ A K J ♣ K Q J 8 3

If the double is made on both hands above, the opener has a very tough decision. He will never

know, with the last hand, whether he is surrendering game or slam for poor recompense.

Having opened with a two-bid, opener should accept partner's double of an intervening call *unless holding game in hand with fewer than five defensive tricks.*

(2) Low-level doubles. Partner deals and opens 1♠, overcalled with 2♣. With equal vulnerability, consider

(a)		(b)
♠ 6 5	and	♠ Q J 8 4
♡ A 10 8 5		♡ 3 2
♢ K 10 4 3		♢ 8 7 4
♣ A K 6		♣ K Q 7 2

Here (a) holds no surprise for the overcaller, who knew that he was missing the ♣A–K. If the overcaller holds a seven-card suit and an outside trick, the double would score only 300, a poor substitute for the game.

The best doubles are made with unexpected trump tricks. J–10–6–5 with compensating outside values is a better double than A–K–6, since the overcaller may not be expecting to lose any trump tricks.

There is a further reason for not doubling on hand (b). Although it contains a jolt for the enemy in clubs, the spade holding is too long. Experience shows that it is not winning bridge to double with length in partner's suit; the opponents will be short, and opener's high cards may not take tricks.

True, at matchpoint duplicate, particularly with vulnerable opponents, a double can be the winning bid even with three or four cards in opener's suit. Certainly it should be possible to secure as good results as would have been obtained if the opponents had not overcalled, and, of utmost significance in a keen game, is the partnership understanding that the doubler is short in the opener's suit. See IMP TACTICS, MATCHPOINT BIDDING.

Another critical situation: Vulnerable against not vulnerable opponents, partner opens 1♡, overcalled by 2♢.

♠ K 2 ♡ 7 6 ♢ A 10 5 4 ♣ K J 9 7 3

With different vulnerability, the double might be winning action. But with unfavorable vulnerability, a four-trick set is needed to outweigh the game. Probably 2 NT is the most suitable call.

Supposing opener's bid was 1♠ instead of 1♡, the 2 NT bid is not as attractive. The absence of a heart stopper makes the double a more desirable action. When contemplating a tight double, consideration should be given to alternative actions. If they are happy alternatives, they should be preferred.

When the opponents overcall at the one-level, there are more alternatives to a double than when they bid at the two-level, so a double at the one-level should be based on better trumps. With

♠ A 10 8 4 ♡ 3 2 ♢ K J 8 2 ♣ J 5 4,

if partner opens 1♠, bid 1♠ over a diamond overcall. If partner opens 1♡, and the overcall is 2♢, double; the bid of 2♠ is not a happy alternative.

Summarizing the above: Never double with four or more cards in partner's suit, be slow to double with three; save the hair-trigger doubles for occasions when short in opener's suit, singleton or doubleton. Do not double low-level overcalls unless trump tricks are of the *unexpected* variety. If there is an action that could have been taken without the overcall, prefer it.

Against experienced opponents, close doubles are profitable only when it is understood that partner is free to pull the double if his hand is unsuitable. Thus a double is not a death sentence from which there is no appeal. Rather, it is the duty of the doubler's partner to review the sentence. To stand pat on an unsuitable hand does not show confidence in partner; it shows rather a dereliction of duty.

A low-level double is simply a proposition, like many other calls in bridge. Partners expect each other to exercise judgment. The opener should not automatically pass.

Vulnerable, against not vulnerable opponents, opener bids 1♠ on

♠ A K 6 2 ♡ A Q 10 ◇ A 9 8 7 ♣ 5 2.

Left-hand opponent overcalls 2♣, partner doubles. On no account should the double be pulled. *Partner knew opponents were not vulnerable when he doubled*, and his decision must be respected. If partner thinks 2♣ can be beaten opposite a minimum opening, this hand should make a holiday in opener's heart. The penalty must be greater than the value of 3 NT. But the double should be pulled with opener's holding

♠ J 9 8 7 4 ♡ A K 10 7 3 ◇ A 6 ♣ 2.

Partner, doubling 2♣, *does not know about that heart suit*. The risk of partner having length in the unbid suit is too great.

The best low-level doubles, by far, are made when the partnership hands do not fit well. A further reason for pulling the double on the last hand is the fact that partner will probably intend to open your bid suit, and an opening from K–x in spades could be horrible.

In deciding whether to pull a low-level double or not, quick tricks are as important as trumps. Doubler is entitled to expect a normal quota of defensive tricks implied by a sound opening bid.

♠ A K 7 6 5 3 ♡ Q 4 2 ◇ A 9 ♣ 6 4

Having opened 1♠, most experts would stand for a double of a 2♣ overcall; the doubler is expected to be short of spades, and that suit should produce two tricks; the ◇ A is the third, and there might even be a diamond ruff. If the hand were more unbalanced, the double should be pulled unless the clubs were better. Any hand that contains a void in the doubled suit is unsuited to standing a low-level double. Doubler does not *need* trump tricks from the opener, but there are many situations in play where even a single trump led up to the doubler will be very worthwhile.

The above can be summarized: Stand a low-level double with three quick defensive tricks; pull it with fewer unless there is compensation in trump strength; pull the double nearly always with an unbid five-card suit.In a close decision, decide whether a lead or your bid suit will be welcome or not.

(3) Game doubles. Doubles of game contracts in a competitive auction are usually aimed at taking the maximum penalty from opponents who have taken a

SAVE. However, the double may also act as a warning to partner not to proceed further. If a pass would be a FORCING PASS, then a double indicates a disinclination to go further. For this reason a player who anticipates disaster if his side bids further may double when his prospects of beating the opposing contract are not better than moderate.

Doubling a game contract which has been reached voluntarily without interference is very seldom good policy (unless the doubler suspects an advance save, for example, after 3♠–4♠).

Doubling a game on the basis of high cards only is a costly exercise. For the double to be worthwhile, both opponents must have limited their hands in such a way that it is clear that neither has any strength in reserve. For example:

WEST	EAST
1♣	1♡
2♡	2 NT
3 NT	

In this auction it is clear that both players are straining to reach game, and either opponent may double if the honor strength, especially in clubs and hearts, seems well placed for the defense.

If the contract is a suit, a double becomes attractive if the declaring side has run into a bad trump split. It is sometimes possible to double with a void because the other defender is marked by the bidding with five trumps. But it is still necessary for both opponents to be limited, so that all possibility of a redoubled overtrick is excluded.

DOUBLES OF NOTRUMP BIDS are listed separately. See also COOPERATIVE DOUBLE, DOUBLE FOR SACRIFICE, LEAD-DIRECTING DOUBLE, LIGHTNER DOUBLE, OPTIONAL DOUBLE.

Albert Dormer

PENALTY EXCESS. See EXCESS POINTS.

PENALTY LIMITS. In social or progressive bridge, in order to prevent one hand from assuming overwhelming importance, it is customary to limit the plus score in premium points for doubled and redoubled undertrick penalties. Generally, 1000 points is the limit. In TOTAL POINT SCORING for pair events, a method that is obsolescent if not obsolete, a similar though somewhat smaller limit was set. See EXCESS POINTS.

PENALTY PASS. A pass by a player after a TAKEOUT DOUBLE from his partner and a pass by right-hand opponent. For example:

WEST	NORTH	EAST	SOUTH
			1 ◇
Dbl.	Pass	Pass	

East's pass indicates considerable length and strength in diamonds; five cards headed by three honors would normally be the minimum diamond holding. Even holding five strong diamonds, a pass would be unwise with a two-suited hand, because the declarer would be likely to score ruffs. After such a pass, West has an obligation to lead a trump, because East will wish to draw South's trumps.

After a minor-suit opening, a penalty pass may

come into consideration with nothing but trump length at unfavorable vulnerability. If the contract succeeds, even with an overtrick, the resulting score may be less than the opener's side could have scored in other ways.

A penalty pass becomes more attractive if the doubler was in a balancing position. QJxx of trumps may be a sufficient trump holding.

PEOPLE'S REPUBLIC OF CHINA. After a 30-year ban, bridge suddenly became the intellectual game for the whole of China. Early in 1979, the All-China Sports Federation formed the All China Contract Bridge League. Within three months, bridge associations were established all over the country. Bridge is now being played at every level. Play is free — directors and other officials are volunteer workers. Within six months after the establishment of the ACCBL, an intercity tournament was staged. Later a team tournament was held in which there was a total entry of 176 teams. See CHINESE BRIDGE ASSOCIATION.

PERCENTAGE. A quotient obtained by dividing the actual matchpoint score of a contestant by the possible score of that contestant, which is then expressed as a percentage (of the possible score). Winning percentages tend to be higher (70 to 75%) in team games than in pair games (60 to 64%).

PERCENTAGE PLAY. A play influenced by mathematical factors when more than one reasonable line of play is available. See PROBABILITIES A POSTERIORI, SUIT COMBINATIONS, and MATHEMATICAL TABLES (Tables 4, 4A).

The following examples show how the above references can be used in bridge play.

(1) Neither the auction nor the play to the first trick has shown any marked UNBALANCED DISTRIBUTION in defenders' hands. Dummy has A–K–Q–J–4–3–2, and declarer is void in the suit. There is about 36% probability that the suit will be divided 3–3.

(2)

A K Q 10

4 3 2

The correct line of play, based solely on PROBABILITIES A PRIORI, is to play the A–K–Q unless East shows a singleton or void. From percentage play, probabilities are:

3–3 division	35.53%
J–x (J–9, J–8, J–7, J–6, J–5) in hand	16.15%
J singleton in hand	2.42%
J–9–8–7–6–5 with West	.74%
J–x–x–x–x with West	6.05%
	60.89%

The alternative play of taking a finesse on the third round, unless the jack has been played, has the following probabilities:

J in West's hand	50.00%
J–x with East	8.07%
J singleton with East	1.21%

To make four tricks in the suit, the odds are slightly

less than 61 to 59 on refusing the finesse.

(3)

A Q 10 7 3 2

9 8 5

Declarer disregards the safety play in favor of trying for the maximum number of tricks. He plans to finesse the queen and make six tricks if West holds both honors doubleton or if East holds the singleton jack. He may also have to decide on his action if West plays low and the finesse loses. Reference to Table 4 shows that the distribution

6–4 opposite K–J has a probability of 6.8%
J–6–4 opposite K has a probability of 6.2%

The odds are therefore 34 to 31 on playing the ace on the second round after the finesse has lost, as against taking a second finesse.

Percentage play often requires calculations which, though not too difficult, require more involved operations. This may be valuable in subsequent analysis but not practical at the table. In the following, two lines of play present themselves.

♠ —
♡ Q 3 2
◊ A K Q 10 4 3 2
♣ 7 5 4

♠ K Q J 6 3 2
♡ A K J 6 5 4
◊ —
♣ 3

South plays in 6♡. West leads the ♣Q, then a second club on which East plays the king. South ruffs. As West presumably has the ♣Q–J and East the ♣A–K, the play of this suit has not altered the ratio of the a priori odds, but in our more detailed calculations we must assume that East and West each originally held at least three clubs.

South's best line of play depends upon the probability of the divisions of the two red suits. To determine this accurately it is necessary to calculate the appropriate combinations as explained in SUIT, NUMBER OF CARDS IN. For a satisfactory approximate answer apply the rule of multiplying PROBABILITY OF SUCCESSIVE EVENTS. (This is an approximation because the distribution of the two suits is interdependent, not independent. We note the discrepancy when we give the result of our detailed calculations later.)

To the third trick South leads the ♡A, East and West both following. At the fourth trick South can
(a) lead the ♡K;
(b) lead a low heart to dummy's queen;
(c) lead the ♡J.
In each case we must consider the position if (i) West follows to the second round of hearts, and (ii) West does not follow.

(a) (♡K) will win whenever

hearts are 2–2	40%	
diamonds are 3–3		36%
or doubleton ◊ J		16%
		52%

The probability that both will occur (hearts 2–2 and diamonds come home) is 40% of 52%, which equals 20.8%. If hearts actually divide 2-2, South leads the ♠K, and if this is covered his troubles are over. Assuming that West will cover half the time he holds the ace this gives another 4.8% (50% of 50% of 19.2%), bringing our total to 25.6%.

If West has three hearts (25%), South leads to dummy's ♡Q and makes his contract with the above division of diamonds (52%). This gives another 13%. Similarly, we have a further 13% if East has three hearts and there is the above diamond division.

Our grand approximate total for (a) is thus 51.6%.

(b) (low heart) will win whenever

hearts are 2-2	40%
diamonds 4-2	48%
diamonds 3-3	36%
singleton ◇ J	2%
any other division provided West has the ♠A	7%
	93%

or

West has 3 hearts	25%
West has three or four diamonds and the ♠A	30%
East has 3 hearts	25%
diamonds are 3-3	36%
doubleton ◇ J	16%
East has five small diamonds and two low spades, or J-x-x-x and three low spades	2%
	54%

Our grand total for (b) is thus (40% of 93%) + (25% of [30% + 54%]), or 58.2%.

(c) (♡ J) is obviously inferior to (b). If West follows to the second round of hearts and we overtake the ♡ J we lose if West has three hearts and three diamonds even if he also has the ♠A, South has to return to his own hand twice — once to take the ruffing finesse in spades and once to draw West's last trump. One entry has to be the ruff of a fourth diamond, and West will overruff. If the ♡ J is not overtaken, the lead is not in dummy for the diamond suit to be led.

A more detailed calculation which takes account of the interdependence of the suit distributions gives us 48.99% for (a) and 52.62% for (b). We note that there is less difference between these two numbers than between our approximate calculations. This is due to the fact that (b) contains a larger number of unbalanced hands, the type on which approximate calculations give misleadingly high figures.

PERCENTAGES. Since chance plays considerable part in the distribution of cards at a bridge table, it is understandable that expert players are interested in the mathematical percentages applicable to different situations. Among the articles dealing with percen-

tage are: MATHEMATICS OF BRIDGE, PERCENTAGE PLAY, SLAM BIDDING, SUIT COMBINATIONS, VALUE OF GAME, and PARTSCORE. MATHEMATICAL TABLES also deals with various percentage situations. Bridge writers frequently use a variation of percentage, ODDS IN BRIDGE, in discussing situations yielding to mathematical treatment.

PERFECT BRIDGE HAND. A hand that will produce 13 tricks in notrump irrespective of the opening lead or the composition of the other three hands. A hand containing all 13 cards of a suit, therefore, does not qualify as a perfect hand, since such a hand will not take even a single trick if played in notrump. Although most players think of a hand containing four aces, four kings, four queens and a jack as the perfect hand, actually it is only one of many. Altogether there are 3,756 possible perfect hands, which break down as follows:

Hand Pattern				Number of Possible Hands
AKQJxxxxx	AK	A	A	1,512
AKQJ10xxx	AKQ	A	A	672
AKQJ10xxx	AK	AK	A	672
AKQxxxxxx	A	A	A	480
AKQJ109x	AKQ	AK	A	168
AKQJ109x	AKQJ	A	A	84
AKQJ109x	AK	AK	AK	28
AKQJ109	AKQJ	AK	A	24
AKQJ10	AKQJ	AKQ	A	24
AKQJ109	AKQJ10	A	A	12
AKQJ109	AKQ	AKQ	A	12
AKQJ109	AKQ	AK	AK	12
AKQJ10	AKQJ10	AK	A	12
AKQJ10	AKQJ	AK	AK	12
AKQJ10	AKQ	AKQ	AK	12
AKQJ	AKQJ	AKQ	AK	12
AKQJ	AKQJ	AKQJ	A	4
AKQJ	AKQ	AKQ	AKQ	4
				3,756

As there are 635,013,559,600 possible hands a player can hold, the odds against holding such a "perfect hand" are 169,066,442 to 1.

Alec Traub

PERIODICALS. See BIBLIOGRAPHY.

PERMANENT TRUMP. At WHIST, a variation in which club card committees or other governing bodies declared a suit to be trump for all games under their jurisdiction. The rules of Whist provided that the trump suit would be the suit of the last card dealt by the dealer to himself.

PERUVIAN BRIDGE ASSOCIATION (ASOCI-ACIÓN PERUANA DE BRIDGE). Founded in 1957, in 1982 it had approximately 170 members. Peru's representatives to the South American Championships are decided by annual tournaments, for both men's and women's events. The Association sent teams to the World Team Olympiad in 1972, hosted the 1956, 1961, 1967, and 1974 South American Championships in Lima, and won the Women's Team Championships in 1963 and 1969.

Officers, 1982:

President: Oscar Vidal

Secretary: Maria Delfina Alvarez-Calderon, Av. Orrantia 475, San Isidro Lima, 27, Peru

PETER. A term used in Great Britain, but rarely elsewhere, to describe a high-low made in discarding, such as high-low in any given suit. Originally, in whist, the use of the term was restricted to a high-low in the trump suit only. See HIGH-LOW SIGNALS and BLUE PETER.

PHANTOM PAIR. In a pair contest with an odd number of pairs, the pair which would (if present) complete the last table. The contestant scheduled to play against the phantom pair has a bye round.

PHANTOM SACRIFICE (or phantom save). A sacrifice bid against a contract which would have been defeated.

PHENOMENAL HANDS. See FREAK HANDS.

PHILIPPINE CONTRACT BRIDGE LEAGUE. Organized in 1954, by 1982 its membership was over 325. The League participates in the Far East Championships, hosting the 1957, 1962, 1967, 1974, and 1977 events in Manila, and World Olympiads. Philippine teams won the Far East Championship in 1957 and 1958 and the Women's Team Championship in 1967, 1968, and 1979. National events are held annually for Knockout Teams, Open Teams, Mixed Teams, and Masters Pairs.

Officers, 1982:
President: Mrs. Rina Milhomme
Secretary: Mrs. Majorie Leven, P.O. Box 65 MCC, Metro Manila, Philippines

PIANOLA. A hand at bridge which presents no problems to declarer, so easily playable that it almost plays itself. The name derives from the old player piano or "pianola" which would "play" itself.

PICK UP. To capture or drop an outstanding high card.

PICK-UP BOY (GIRL). See CADDY.

PICK-UP SLIP. A form devised for the recording of the result on the play of one board on one round. Information contained on the slip includes identifying numbers of the pairs, the board number, which pair was the declarer, the final contract and by whom, whether doubled, redoubled, or undoubled, the result, trick-score, extra tricks, game or doubled bonuses, partscore bonus, slam bonus, or undertrick score. Usually the North (or South) player has the responsibility of making out the score, the East-West pair having responsibility for checking the entries and verifying the slip. After each round the pick-up slips are collected and results of the round entered on the recapitulation sheet by the director or a designated scorer.

PIN. The lead of a high card when the right-hand opponent has an unguarded card slightly lower in rank. The play can be made either by declarer or by a defender.

A 9 8 7 6

Q 10 5

If South must have five tricks from this suit, his only chance, a faint one, is to lead the queen and hope the singleton jack is on his right.

The defenders can sometimes falsecard in an attempt to avert an impending pin:

```
              ♡ Q 10 3 2
   ♡ J 5 4                ♡ A K 8 7 6
              ♡ 9
```

South plays in a spade contract after East has bid hearts and West has raised them. If East plays in routine fashion by winning with the king and shifting to another suit, South can establish a heart trick in the dummy by ruffing a low heart and later leading the queen, or vice versa. But if East wins the first trick with the ace and returns a low heart, South is likely to conclude that West started with K-x-x.

PINK POINTS. An obsolete term for REGIONAL POINTS. It was used to distinguish points won at a Regional tournament from those won at a National tournament (red points).

PINPOINT ASTRO. See ASTRO.

PIP. A small design indicating the suit to which a particular card belongs. The SPADE suit is indicated by a spearhead, the HEART suit by a heart, the DIAMOND suit by a diamond-shaped tile, the CLUB suit by a clover leaf. The spot cards have as many pips as the rank of the card indicates, from 1 to 10 in the standard deck, in addition to two INDICES, the lower half of which is a pip.

In German cards, the pips of LEAVES and ACORNS usually have stems, and are often attached as if on a branch. In the trappola PACK, the pips often vary in size and design, and the SWORDS and CUDGELS are usually interlaced. See SUIT and INDICES.

PITCH. A colloquial term for DISCARD.

PITCH COUNT. An old name for the 4-3-2-1 POINT COUNT.

PITT COUP. A play by which the declarer places himself in a position to lead through his left-hand adversary in a suit in which the dummy holds a major tenace over the left-hand adversary's minor tenace. It frequently involves the unblocking of a trump suit in dummy, and also may include a deliberate higher-than-necessary ruff with an honor in the closed hand so as to be able to lead low through West.

```
              ♠ J 9 8 6
              ♡ 8 6 3
              ◇ 8 6 5 4 3 2
              ♣ —
  ♠ 10 4 3 2                ♠ Q
  ♡ 9 5                     ♡ A Q J 10 7 2
  ◇ K Q                     ◇ 10 7
  ♣ Q 9 8 5 2               ♣ A J 7 4
              ♠ A K 7 5
              ♡ K 4
              ◇ A J 9
              ♣ K 10 6 3
```

WEST	NORTH	EAST	SOUTH
			1 ♠
Pass	2 ♠	3 ♡	3 NT
Pass	4 ♠	All Pass	

West opened the ♡9, won by East who returned the suit. South won with the king. The ♠A was led, on which declarer called for the 8 from dummy (maintaining a two-way finesse situation against the 10). East's queen marked West with four spades to the 10. Declarer led ace and another diamond, hoping for and getting the 2–2 split in the suit. West won the second diamond, and returned a club, dummy discarding and East winning the ace. East returned the high heart, which declarer ruffed with the king. The lead of the ♠7 permitted South to take a finesse, playing dummy's 6; a further spade lead through West enabled declarer to unblock the high diamond from his hand on the fourth spade lead, and win the balance of the tricks in dummy.

The name is artibrary, resulting from the use of *Pitt, Chatham,* etc., in WHIST literature to designate particular players.

PIVOT BRIDGE, LAWS OF. (A form of social bridge played at home games where, instead of advancing from table to table as in party or progressive bridge, the players change or pivot among themselves at each individual table.)

Pivot bridge is played by four (or five and sometimes six) players at a table. This form may be used for a single table or for large gatherings in which it is desirable to have each table play as a separate unit without progression by the players.

The game is so arranged that each player plays with each other player at his table both as partner and opponent. There are two methods of play: first, four deals may be played to a round, one deal by each player, and the players change partners at the end of each four deals; second, rubbers may be played, and the players change partners at the end of each rubber.

If four deals to a round are played, the scoring is exactly the same as in Progressive Bridge; if rubbers are played, the scoring is exactly the same as in Rubber Bridge. The laws given below explain only the method of rotation in changing partners, not scoring, vulnerability, etc., which are covered elsewhere.

DRAW FOR PARTNERS

1. The players draw cards for partners and deal, and for a choice of seats and pack. The player who draws highest is the first pivot, and he deals first and has the choice of seats and packs. The player who draws second highest is the pivot's first partner; the player who draws third highest sits at the pivot's left during the first round; the player who draws fourth sits at the pivot's right; and if a fifth player is present, he does not participate in the first round or rubber.

CHANGING PARTNERS (FOR FOUR PLAYERS)

2. During the first three rounds or rubbers, the players change positions as indicated in the following diagram:

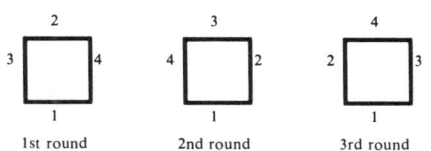

1st round   2nd round   3rd round

After the third round or rubber, the players again cut for position and partners.

CHANGING PARTNERS (FOR FIVE PLAYERS)

3. If five players desire to play at the same table, they may be accommodated in this manner:

For the first round or rubber, the players take the positions indicated by their draw for position under law No. 1. For rounds one to five, they take the positions indicated in the following diagram:

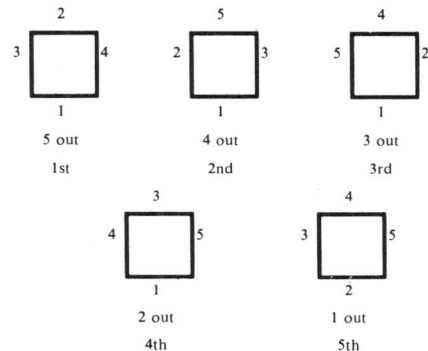

At the end of each five rounds, the players again draw for positions and partners.

COMMENT

This arrangement permits each player to play with each other player once as partner and twice as opponent, and each player sits out one round in turn.

SIX PLAYER PIVOT

4. With six players at the same table, a complete pivot enabling each player to play once as partner and twice against each combination of opponents other than the player who is cut out at the same time, may be arranged by following this sequence of partnerships:

3-4	1-5	1-3	3-5	1-6	1-4	3-6	1-2
v	v	v	v	v	v	v	v
5-6	2-6	2-4	4-6	2-5	2-3	4-5	5-6

The player numbers correspond to the order in which they are cut out, with 1-2, 3-4 and 5-6 out simultaneously. If more than eight rounds are to be played, the pivot is resumed at round 3, or a new order may be determined by cutting so as to have different players out at the same time.

DETERMINATION OF THE WINNER

5. At the completion of each round or rubber, the player enters on his tally both his own score and that of his opponents. Each player totals his own and his opponents' scores separately and records the difference, plus or minus as the case may be, at the bottom of his tally. The player having the highest plus score is the winner and the others rank in descending order according to their scores.

PLACE THE CARDS, PLACING CARDS. See ASSUMPTIONS, IN PLAY; CARD READING.

PLACING THE LEAD. See AVOIDANCE.

PLAFOND. A French card game which was the immediate predecessor of contract. HAROLD S. VANDERBILT, the originator of contract bridge, used *plafond* (which means "ceiling") as the basis for his approach to the new game.

PIERRE BELLANGER (*The Bridge World*, Sept. 1931) dates the origin of Plafond to 1918, where it was introduced at the Cercle Littéraire of Paris shortly after the Armistice. Only those tricks bid for and made were scored below the line and counted toward game. Tricks made above the bid scored 50 points above the line for each additional trick. Except for increasing the slam bonuses to 100 for a small slam and 200 for a grand slam, awarded whether the slam was bid or not, the trick scores and penalties were much as in auction. However, a bonus of 50 points was scored for making any contract successfully; the first game for either side received a bonus of 100; winning the rubber was worth an additional 400. Bellanger also claims authorship of the words, "Contract Bridge," an appendix to his 1914 edition of *Legislation du Bridge aux Enchères* mentioning *"Bridge avec Contrat"*. But contract, as it was introduced in 1914 at the Automobile Club de France, was only an embryonic form of Plafond.

GEORGE F. HERVEY, bridge correspondent of *The Field*, cites a letter to that publication, dated February 8, 1941, in which SIR HUGH CLAYTON records that the contract principle was invented by four players in Poona (India) in 1912. The game was developed out of auction and named S.A.C.C., an acronym of the four men who invented it. On July 15, 1914, the rules of this game were published by Sir Hugh in *The Times of India*, and there is evidence that the game was played in various parts of India from that date until some years after promulgation of the first official code of laws to govern contract bridge (December 1929).

MILTON C. WORK reported that similar games had been tried in the United States before 1914 but failed to become popular. Obviously, none of these games included the vulnerability feature and the scoring table devised by Vanderbilt, but it would appear that the "ceiling" principle of Plafond may have come to France from India or at least have originated there at an earlier date than reported by Bellanger.

There was a Franco-American Plafond Match in 1930 which ended about even, and which employed many of the newly established contract bridge methods, but most players essaying both games tended to prefer the more precise and demanding contract.

PLAIN SUIT. A suit other than the trump suit.

PLAN OF PLAY, PLANNING THE PLAY. The mental process by which DECLARER decides on how to use the assets of the combined hands to fulfill the contract, and, secondly, to develop OVERTRICKS or to minimize penalties. Among the things to be considered is the management of the trump suit, development of long cards in side suits, maintenance of communication between the two hands, if and how to FINESSE, development of ENDPLAYS, SAFETY PLAYS against adverse distributions, and others. Declarer should mentally review these and other problems before playing to the first trick, even though such play may be automatic. Original plans should frequently be changed as more information about adverse holdings is developed, but the declarer should not require time to consider each play, and thus delay the tempo of the game. See NOTRUMP PLAY.

PLASTIC CARDS. Cards made of acetate cellulose or a vinyl or polyvinyl compound.

Since the wearing qualities of paper are limited, inventors searched for years for a substitute that would be more enduring. Success depended on two inventions, a method of making the thin material opaque so that no card could be identified from the back, and a formula for making ink that would adhere firmly to the plastic surface.

In 1932, SIEGFRIED KLAUSNER registered in Austria and other European countries a patent for making non-inflammable opaque plastic sheets and for making playing cards from them by coating the printed surfaces with a lacquer derived from the basic plastic. After manufacturing the cards under the trade name Mirakel, he sold domestic rights to Piatnik, the S. E. Europe monopoly, which took the cards off the market; but he retained U.S. rights and in 1934 founded the Kem Company with ELY CULBERTSON and others. The resulting KEM CARDS outwear paper cards, are resistant to soiling, and are easily cleaned.

Plastic cards are made by three companies in the United States, and by several in Japan and Europe. In spite of their proven superiority in many ways, they represent only about 2½% of the number of packs sold yearly. See MANUFACTURE OF PLAYING CARDS.

PLASTIC VALUATION. One of the phrases popularized in the writings of ELY CULBERTSON to describe the mental processes of the bidder as he receives more information regarding the makeup of his partner's hand. REVALUATION, PROMOTION OF TRUMP HONORS, and DISTRIBUTIONAL COUNTS were all covered in the one phrase.

PLAY (of the hand). See NOTRUMP PLAY.

PLAY AFTER AN ILLEGAL PLAY. Such action forfeits (waives) any penalty incurred by the illegal play, unless the illegal play constitutes a revoke. This is in accordance with the principle that the non-offending side may "condone" an offense. Such a play may be made only by the player to the left of the hand making the illegal play, and such right is not affected by partner calling attention to the illegality of the play. See LAWS (Law 60).

PLAY FROM EQUALS. When holding cards of equal rank in a suit, it is often very important which card is chosen to be played to a particular trick. A defender's card may provide partner with important information, or it may deceive the declarer. A declarer's card may confuse the defense, or at least avoid giving away information unnecessarily.

Defensive play from equals. On the opening lead, there is a standard table which usually requires that the higher of two equal honors be led. The only exception to this is that the king is usually led from ace, king, and others (see OPENING LEADS). However, when the honor combination is bare (no small cards) the lower honor is sometimes led to inform partner of the situation. For example, the normal lead from A–K–x against a suit contract is the king. From A–K alone, the usual lead is the ace. When this is followed by the king, the partner of the leader will know that the opening leader has exhausted the suit led (otherwise, the normal lead of the king would have been made).

This reversing order of plays can also be used later in the defense. Consider, for example, the deal below:

```
              ♠ K 8 7
              ♡ A Q J 10 8
              ◇ Q 5
              ♣ J 9 8
♠ 9 6 4                      ♠ 3 2
♡ 9 3                        ♡ 7 5 2
◇ J 10 9 8                   ◇ A 7 6 4 3 2
♣ A 4 3 2                    ♣ K Q
              ♠ A Q J 10 5
              ♡ K 6 4
              ◇ K
              ♣ 10 7 6 5
```

SOUTH	NORTH
1♠	2♡
3♡	4♠
Pass	

Against South's 4♠ contract, West leads the ◇ J.

East wins the ◇ A and sees at once that the defense must look to clubs for the setting tricks. East should shift to the ♣ Q, not the king. After the ♣ Q wins and East continues with the ♣ K, West should overtake to give East a club ruff. If East has started with three clubs to the K–Q, he would have made the normal shift to the ♣ K. In this case, the deliberate play of the *wrong* honor from equals indicates no other cards in the suit led.

Sometimes, the lower honor is led from equal cards for the purpose of deceiving the declarer.

In many situations, a defender's play from equals should be the card he is known to hold. The most common situation in which this opportunity arises is:

```
              ♠ A J 2
♠ Q 10 4                     ♠ 8 7 6
              ♠ K 9 5 3
```

The declarer, South, leads the ♠ 3, and finesses dummy's jack. When the ♠ A is cashed, West should drop the queen. This card ranks equally with the 10, but the cards are not equivalent, as West is *known to hold the queen*. If West drops the 10 under the ace, South must make four tricks in the suit. If West drops the queen on the second round, South is

faced with a guess.

In some situations, the correct play from equals depends on the assumption of a possible distribution of the cards.

```
              ♡ A J 3
♡ K Q 4 2              Immaterial
              ♡ 7 led
```

When the declarer leads the ♡ 7, if West decides to split his honors, he should play the queen and not the king. It is possible that declarer is missing the 10, and can be put to a difficult guess on the second round of hearts. For example, the suit might be distributed:

```
              ♡ A J 3
♡ K Q 4 2              ♡ 10 6 5
              ♡ 9 8 7
```

After the queen loses to the ace, declarer will later lead the suit from his own hand once again. If West ducks, declarer must reckon with the possibility that he made a *standard* falsecard with an original holding of Q–10–4–2. Notice that the initial play of the king would not create this effect, as West could hardly afford to play the king from K–10–4–2, lest declarer hold the queen in the concealed hand.

In other situations, the defense can play from imaginary equal cards:

```
              ♣ A K 10 9 7 6
♣ J 8                        ♣ Q 2
              ♣ 5 4 3
```

The declarer leads the ♣ 5 and West plays the jack. If the declarer suspects that West has split equals, he may later lose a trick to East's queen.

In choosing a deceptive card to play from equals, the best policy is to make the holding you are representing a believable one.

An opening lead from equal cards is often made in consideration of what dummy is likely to hold in the suit led. On lead against a suit contract with A–K–6–4 of a suit that dummy has bid strongly, the best lead is probably the ace. If the dummy's suit is headed by Q–J without the 10, and the declarer holds a singleton, he may later take a ruffing finesse against third hand's imaginary king instead of choosing a different (possibly successful) line of play.

Another occasion for a deceptive lead from equal cards is when it is desirable to misrepresent the potential entry position. Let us suppose that West is on lead against the auction:

SOUTH	NORTH
1 NT	3 NT

West holds ♠ Q–J–10–8–6–2. The best lead is the deceptive ♠ 10. East's first play will look like a high signal, and declarer may believe that West has hit East's suit. If this plan succeeds, South will probably take losing finesses into the West hand.

Third hand's standard play from equal honors is the lowest of touching cards. Declarer may sometimes be deceived by a change of strategy.

```
              ♠ 4 3
♠ 10 8 6 2              ♠ K Q 7 5
              ♠ A J 9
```

Against South's notrump contract, West leads the

♠ 2. If East believes he will obtain the lead first for the defense, he might well play the king as a deceptive move.

When East later leads the ♠ 5, South may decide his best chance is to hope that East has the 10.

When the declarer must guess which suit to attack, the defense can often mislead him with the play of an apparently unnecessarily high card from *equals*.

♠ A J 9 8 3

♠ 4 2   ♠ K Q 10 5

♠ 7 6

Declarer plays a spade to dummy's 9. If East wins with the 10 (equal with the king and queen on this trick), the declarer may look elsewhere for his tricks. If East wins with a high honor, however, declarer may continue the suit at his next opportunity, thus losing time (and possibly tricks).

The defense often uses a play from equals as a suit preference signal. This frequently occurs when a defender is establishing a suit against a notrump contract, and has a choice of equal cards to use to knock out the declarer's last stopper. The use of a high card shows a possible entry in a high-ranking suit, and the use of a low card shows a possible entry in a low-ranking suit. Another common play from equals involves the play of a high honor from equals to show strength in a high-ranking suit and a low honor from equals to show strengh in a low-ranking suit. See SUIT PREFERENCE SIGNAL.

Declarer's play with equals. The selection of declarer's play with equal cards is designed to misguide the defense as much as possible. The selection of which equal to play depends upon declarer's specific objective.

◊ 2

◊ K Q J 10 9

At a suit contract, declarer (South) must avoid a loser in diamonds (a side suit). If dummy holds a few trump cards, his best chance is to lead the ◊ 9 from his hand. If West holds the ace, he may duck on the assumption that East can win the trick cheaply.

Thus, declarer plays a low equal when he hopes the defense will not use their honor cards. If, in a similar situation, ·the declarer hopes to remove the ace quickly, he should play the king (or queen) on the first round.

At a notrump contract, the declarer is usually interested in concealing strength or feigning strength so that the defenders will not know whether or not they have hit a weak spot in declarer's armor.

♣ 4 3

♣ K Q 10

Against South's notrump contract, West leads the ♣ 5 on which East plays the jack. South should win with the king. By so doing, he may deceive West into believing that East holds the ♣ Q.

♣ 4 3

♣ A K Q

Declarer has a weak spot elsewhere, and hopes the defense will continue clubs. When West leads the ♣ 5 and East plays the jack, declarer should play the king.

Once again this play may lead West to believe that East holds the ♣ Q. If declarer wins with the ace, West will know he has *something* else in clubs unless the unlikely situation of East holding K-Q-J exists. Thus, West may suspect some trickiness. (On the other hand, against an experienced West, the play of the ace may be a good double cross.)

If the declarer is afraid of a continuation of the suit led, he should put on a mock display of power.

♠ 4 3

♠ A K 8 5 2   ♠ 9 7 6

♠ Q J 10

On West's lead of the ♠ 5, East plays the 9. South might well gobble this up with the 10, making sure West knows that he holds the queen and jack as well. If South wins a higher honor, West may tend to place East with more length because of the chance that the declarer lacks the ♠ 10.

When the declarer has a very powerful holding in the suit led, he can often paint a very misleading picture.

♡ Q 6 5

♡ 9 7 3 2   ♡ 10 8

♡ A K J 4

Against South's 3 NT contract, West leads the ♡ 2. Dummy plays low and East plays the 10. To encourage the defense to continue the suit, South's best play is probably the king. In addition to concealing the jack, this play suggests that East may have started with A-J-10. The play of the ace may present the same type of picture, but if holding the ace, declarer might have played dummy's queen on the first trick to gain a tempo by raking in a fast winner.

In general, declarer's best idea is to keep the defense in the dark as much as possible about his holding. However, he sometimes plays with a specific objective in mind.

♠ 8 6 5

♠ A 2   ♠ 7 3

♠ K Q J 10 9 4

Spades are trumps. In drawing trumps, many declarers think it is amusing to lead the 8 from dummy and let it ride. This is a good way to let the dummy know the hand is not violently overbid, but it also gives away a lot of information. West may feel that declarer has taken a successful finesse and he may adopt an active defense in a desperate attempt to defeat the contract. If this is to declarer's benefit, then this method of playing the trump suit is correct. However, if the declarer fears an active defense, he should play a low spade to his king or queen. West may now hope his partner held ♠ J-10-x and that declarer must lose another trick in trump. He may therefore play safe, assuming that if he does not give away a trick with an aggressive lead, the contract will probably be defeated.

(As with all of these deceptive plays which leave possibilities open, how well declarer knows his opponents is an important factor.)

The purpose of declarer's play from equals is often to locate the defensive honors in a suit.

♣ 4 3 2

♣ K Q 10

The declarer is anxious to discover the location of the ♣ A. After he leads the suit from the dummy, his best play against inexperienced players is the king. Against more wary opposition, the queen may be more effective. In the first case, West may fear that the declarer holds the king as his only honor in the suit. However, a more experienced player may decide that the declarer is unlikely to start such a weak suit during the early play.

Declarer is anxious to have West take the ace if he holds it so that he will be able to take informed action on the second round of the suit.

In general, when declarer leads a suit, the play of his highest equal card will conceal his holding in the suit. For example, declarer might lead low to the queen with any of the following holdings:

NORTH	◇ 4 3 2	◇ 4 3 2	◇ 4 3 2
SOUTH	◇ A Q J	◇ Q J 10 6	◇ Q 6

In the last example, of course, the declarer is trying to stop the defense from leading this suit when it gets the lead later in the play.

In a suit contract, the declarer can often conceal a potential ruff from the defense by playing carefully from equal cards.

♡ Q J 10 4 3

♡ 9 8 7 6 5   ♡ 2

♡ A K

West leads the ♡ 9 against a spade contract. By playing low from dummy and winning with the ace, South may lead West to believe that East holds the ♡ K. An alternate form of this deception is to play the queen from the dummy before winning with the ace. This makes it look as if South gave East the opportunity to make a stupid play.

Declarer can often conceal the possibility of taking a deep finesse by leading low from equals.

♠ Q 5

♠ A 10 9 8

By leading the ♠ 8 toward dummy's queen, declarer may induce West to pop in with his king, if he holds it. If the 10 or 9 is led, West may duck smoothly, being more likely to realize the possibility of a finesse against the jack.

♡ Q 3 2

♡ A 9 8 7 6

Declarer has a choice of plays in this situation. By leading the ♡ 6 toward the dummy, he may conceal from West the possibility of an immediate double finesse on the first round. If West ducks smoothly, declarer should probably let the 6 ride and make a good guess on the next round. In this way, he may avoid two losers when West holds J–x or 10–x in hearts (see SUIT COMBINATIONS).

The following situations are similar:

◇ J 5 4

◇ Q 10 2   ◇ K 3

◇ A 9 8 7 6

◇ J 5 4

◇ K 3   ◇ Q 10 2

◇ A 9 8 7 6

The declarer intends to lead toward dummy and play West for 10–x (unless he receives information through action at the table). By leading the 6, he can conceal the possibility of a finesse against the 10, and may find West jumping in with his king or queen (much to his subsequent embarrassment).

Jeff Rubens

PLAY OUT OF TURN. A play is considered to be in turn if it is made after the player to the right has led or played, or if it is a lead by a player who has won the preceding trick. Any other order constitutes a play out of turn, and is covered by the rule for a premature lead or play by a defender, or lead or play from the wrong hand by declarer. See LAWS (Laws 54, 55, 56, and 57).

PLAYED CARD. Each player except dummy plays a card by detaching it from his hand, and facing it on the edge of the table immediately before him. Declarer plays a card from dummy's hand by naming the card he proposes to play; after which dummy picks up the card, and places it face up on his edge of the table. (In playing from dummy's hand, declarer may, if he prefers, pick up the desired card, and place it in such position as to indicate that it has been played.)

In addition, a card must be played if it is a defender's card held so that it is possible for his partner to see its face; or if it is a card from declarer's hand that declarer holds face up in front of him with intent to play, and that is touching or near the table. Declarer must play a card in dummy that he touches for purposes other than arranging or in reaching for the card immediately above or below the card touched. Any player also plays a card by naming or otherwise designating it as the card he proposes to play. Also any penalty card must be played if it can be played legally (without revoking). See LAWS (Law 45).

PLAYER. A participant at a table of bridge, one of an active foursome engaged at bridge; one member of either pair playing against each other.

PLAYER NUMBER. A seven-digit number assigned by the ACBL to a member. The last digit is a self-checking device by which the keypunch machine throws out incorrect numbers. The method by which the checking digit is computed is interesting. Multiply the first six digits by 7, 6, 5, 4, 3, and 2 respectively; then add these products. Divide the total of the products by 11, and note the remainder. This remainder is then subtracted from the divisor, 11, and the resulting difference is the check digit. (If the net result of this work is a remainder of 1, then the number is not used.)

When a player achieves LIFE MASTER status, this is indicated by a change in his player number by the substitution of a letter for the first digit, alphabetically from J for 1 to R for 9.

Player numbers were instituted by the ACBL in July, 1961.

PLAYER OF THE YEAR. The player who, during a given year, earns the greatest number of master points. This award may be made on a national basis (see McKENNEY TROPHY and TOP 500), or on a unit basis for points won in unit sectional (or regional) tournaments, or even on a club basis for points won in unit sectional (or regional) tournaments, or even on a club basis for points won in the individual club's games. In many units a separate award or recognition is given to players who begin the year in a limited category and earn the most points in that category. The categories are ROOKIE (0–5), NON-MASTER (5–20), MASTER (20–50), NATIONAL MASTER (50–100), SENIOR MASTER (100–200) and ADVANCED SENIOR MASTER (200–LIFE MASTER). See also MINI McKENNEY AWARDS.

PLAYING CARDS. The cards, usually pasteboard, used in playing various games. (See also MAGNETIC CARDS, PLASTIC CARDS.) The standard bridge pack (or deck) consists of 52 cards, arranged in four suits of 13 cards each. Among the principal games played in the U.S. are bridge, canasta, casino, chemin-de-fer, cribbage, gin and other rummy games, hearts, piquet, twenty-one (also called blackjack and pontoon), poker, and many varieties of solitaire and patience. Pinochle is played with a special deck, which can be formed from two decks of standard cards. (See PACK for non-standard packs and their makeup, and TAROT for a very special pack.) Each suit is divided into three COURT CARDS and 10 SPOT CARDS. Of the latter, the ACE, or one-spot, ranks highest in bridge (but not necessarily so in other games). Below the ace in rank are the court cards — king, queen, and jack (which has replaced the older term, knave, almost completely) — followed by the spot cards — 10, 9, 8, 7, 6, 5, 4, 3 (or trey), and 2 (or deuce). The suits are identified by the symbols ♠ for spades, ♡ for hearts, ♢ for diamonds, and ♣ for clubs, and rank in that order in bridge games. Today's cards have corner INDICES showing a letter or numeral above a PIP of the suit to which the card belongs, but this is a modern device. Cards lacked such an index as late as 1870.

For other articles in this book referring to playing cards, see COLLECTIONS OF PLAYING CARDS; DEVIL'S PICTURE BOOK; FACE CARDS; FORTUNETELLING; HISTORY OF PLAYING CARDS; MANUFACTURE OF PLAYING CARDS; SUIT; TAXES ON PLAYING CARDS; 10 OR 10 SPOT and other-spot cards; TRANSFORMATION CARDS; and USES OF CARDS.

PLAYING KNOWN CARD. See FALSE-CARDING.

PLAYING TO THE SCORE. A variation in normal play of the cards which is motivated by the scores of the pairs involved in rubber bridge. The net score of each rubber is computed at the end of the rubber, but is carried to the summary sheet in amounts to the nearest hundred. If a certain line of play will produce a trick-score of 150 points if successful, but only 90 points if unsuccessful, while there is a different

line of play that will guarantee 120 points, the declarer should mentally add the scores of each pair and obtain the net score before he determines which line of play to use. If the net score is 220 points, only a score of 150 points on the last deal would make the net score equal some 150 or more and be scored to the higher hundred. If the net score had been 240 points at that time, the need to get the added hundred would only have been 120 points, and the sure line of play should be adopted.

PLAYING TRICKS. Tricks that a hand may be expected to produce if the holder buys the contract; attacking tricks or winners, as distinguished from defensive tricks or winners when the holder must play against an adverse contract. In estimating the playing-trick strength of a hand, the holder assumes that his long suit (or suits) will break evenly and the other three hands, unless the auction has indicated otherwise, and adds the number of tricks his long suit (or suits) is likely to yield to his quick-trick total of the other suits. For example, the following hand

♠ K 5 ♡ A Q J 8 6 2 ♢ A Q 7 ♣ 9 3

contains about seven playing tricks — five in hearts, ½ quick trick in spades, 1½ quick tricks in diamonds.

When the long suit is not solid or semi-solid, estimation of playing tricks becomes more difficult because a second factor must be considered — the position of the missing honor cards. Thus, this suit

♡ K J 8 6 5 3

is worth approximately 3½ playing tricks. With normal distribution, the declarer might make four tricks if he can lead the suit from dummy or find the missing honors well placed, but could be limited to three tricks.

Assessment of playing tricks is particularly important when considering a preemptive bid or an overcall. See RULE OF TWO AND THREE.

PLAYS TO CONCEAL STRENGTH. See DECEPTIVE PLAY.

PLAYS TO CONCEAL WEAKNESS. See DECEPTIVE PLAY.

PLUS VALUE. An added feature of a hand or suit that should be weighed when one is planning a bid or series of bids. There are bidding developments which require evaluation of a hand on a fairly precise basis. Therefore, during a subsequent phase of the auction, if one has been somewhat rigid in describing his holding and does possess plus values such as J–10–9 combinations in suits otherwise protected or strengthened, or a guarded queen, etc., that may be felt to be of help to partner, one is sometimes more liberal in making a final placement of contract than without the aforementioned values.

The term was regularly used in counting HONOR TRICKS, but has little meaning when valuation is by points.

POCKET. One of four rectangular areas in a duplicate board which hold the four hands, designated North, South, East, and West. See LAWS OF DUPLICATE(Law 2).

POINT-COUNT. An almost universally used method of valuation. Many point-counts have become obsolete (see FOUR ACES, REITH, and ROBERTSON). In general use is the high-card valuation introduced by BRYANT McCAMPBELL in 1915 and publicized by MILTON WORK after whom it was named:

Ace	4
King	3
Queen	2
Jack	1

This gives a total of 40 points in the pack, and makes an average hand worth 10 points.

The Work count is slightly less accurate mathematically than the Four Aces count, for example, but its simplicity favored its acceptance. It was regularly used by English experts in the Thirties, but did not find favor with American experts until it was adopted and publicized by FRED KARPIN and CHARLES GOREN in the late Forties. They supplemented the basic high-card count with valuation for distribution (see DISTRIBUTIONAL COUNTS).

All authorities recognize that the 4-3-2-1 count has some weaknesses and recommend certain corrections:

(1) Aces are undervalued, so the presence or absence of aces materially affects the strength of a hand. Two methods are: add ½ point for each ace; or deduct a point for an aceless hand, and add a point for holding four aces.

(2) Tens are valuable cards and are sometimes counted as ½ point or a plus value. One expedient is to consider aces and tens as a group, and to count an extra point if the hand contains three or more such cards.

(3) Unguarded or insufficiently guarded honor cards may not be worth their full point value. An extreme case is a singleton king, which some authorities count as 1 point instead of 3, and a singleton queen, which is sometimes counted as worthless. It is more normal to deduct one point from the value of a singleton king, queen or jack. However, even the singleton ace is not quite as good as it looks because it has little chance of capturing an opposing honor card and is inflexible in the play.

Stayman goes to the extreme of recommending the deduction of a point for each of the following holdings:

K-Q; K-J; Q-J; Q-x; J-x; Q-x-x; J-x-x. It is true that these holdings have a reduced value if the partner has useless small cards in the suit. But if your side is destined to play the hand, there is a good chance that partner will hold a card which will combine effectively with the short honor holding.

(4) Honor combinations are slightly stronger than the same cards would be in different suits. For example, Q-J-x is more effective than Q-x-x in one suit and J-x-x in another. But so much depends on what partner can provide that it is better to make no adjustment in this respect unless there is reason to think that partner's hand will be worthless or nearly worthless; or unless the honor is in a suit bid by part-

ner. For other methods of valuation, see BISSELL SYSTEM; HONOR TRICKS; and LOSING-TRICK COUNT.

POINTED. A term originally coined to describe the combination of the spade and diamond suits (for example a "pointed two-suiter"), since both suits have pips that are pointed at the top. The converse is "rounded," to indicate hearts and clubs.

POINTING CARDS. When four cards have been played to a trick in duplicate, each player turns his own card face down on the edge of the table immediately before him. If his side won the trick, the card is pointed lengthwise toward his partner; if the opponents won the trick, the card is pointed lengthwise toward his opponents. Each player should arrange his own cards in an orderly overlapping row in the sequence played.

At the completion of the play, each player has an accurate count of tricks won and lost; should there be a disagreement, the tricks can be inspected in turn, and the disagreement reconciled. Should any alteration of this order of play of the cards occur, the director must assume the possibility that the player whose cards are disarranged is in error. This order of play should never be disturbed until the director has been summoned in event of disagreement.

POINTS. (1) The score earned by a pair as a result of the play of a hand, including TRICK POINTS, PREMIUM SCORES, and BONUS. (2) A unit by which a hand is evaluated. See POINT-COUNT. (3) The holding of masterpoints that have been credited to a player in the ACBL.

POKER BRIDGE. An epithet attached to a style of bidding that relies heavily on stabbing boldly with bids calculated to produce SWINGS on every hand. Players who can legitimately be accused of using "poker" tactics in bridge are those who constantly overbid or take long chances, and in general try to inculcate many more gambling features into bridge than rightfully belong there.

POLAND. See CONTRACT BRIDGE ASSOCIATION OF POLAND.

POLITICIANS. Many persons occupying high political or military offices have been known also as bridge players. Outstanding among these on a social level was the late President DWIGHT D. EISENHOWER, who made an appearance at the 1961 Summer North American Championships in Washington. He was accompanied by his wartime colleague, General ALFRED GRUENTHER, whose prewar reputation as the leading American tournament director was somewhat eclipsed by his wartime services and his subsequent appointments as Supreme Allied Commander in NATO and president of the American Red Cross. Former Secretary of Agriculture Clinton P. Anderson was a prominent tournament player in the Thirties.

DENG XIAOPING, vice chairman of the People's Republic of China, has revived bridge in his country and plays regularly himself. He fostered team tournaments in his country and was instrumental in having his country join the World Bridge Federation. He played with JAIME ORTIZ-PATIÑO, president of the World Bridge Federation during Patiño's visit there.

The House of Lords and the House of Commons in England have an annual bridge battle that was inaugurated in 1975. After a 1920 total-point victory in 1982, the Lords held a 5-3 match edge.

Former Greek Premier Sophocles Venizelos was a member of the French national team during the Thirties and was European Champion in 1935. In England, WINSTON CHURCHILL was playing bridge when the news of Germany's declaration of war on Russia interrupted his game. IAIN MACLEOD had been a top tournament player and was one of the most influential cabinet ministers as Chancellor of the Exchequer at the time of his death in 1970. In Argentina, Ricardo Argerich was a player of international class until he retired to concentrate upon his diplomatic duties.

POLSKE ZWIAZEK BRYDZA SPORTOWEGO.
See CONTRACT BRIDGE ASSOCIATION OF POLAND.

POOL. The total amount of money that is distributed to winning entries at some duplicate games. To create the pool, the competing pairs may be auctioned off, as in a CALCUTTA, or they may contribute a set amount at the beginning of the game. See GAMBLING AT BRIDGE.

POPULAR BRIDGE. A magazine published bimonthly in the United States. Although articles occasionally deal with happenings in the bridge world, the magazine is dedicated primarily to articles of technical interest and quizzes. The publisher is Robert Wolenik, with MAX HARDY as associate editor. The contributing editors are EDWIN KANTAR, ALFRED SHEINWOLD and FRANK THOMAS.

POPULAR BRIDGE MONTHLY. See INTERNATIONAL POPULAR BRIDGE MONTHLY.

PORTLAND CLUB of London. The principal bridge club of British gentry, nobility, and (at times) royalty; world-famous as promulgator of the laws used in many countries. Founded before 1815 as the Stratford Club, and reorganized 1825, according to tradition, in order to be rid of one objectionable member. Bridge, introduced in 1894 by Lord Brougham, was given a code of laws in 1895, and with subsequent revisions at intervals, gave the Portland Club its reputation as a law-making body (see LAWS). Famous members of the Club in its whist days included JAMES CLAY, William Pole, William Dalton and HENRY JONES (CAVENDISH). GEOFFREY L. BUTLER, former chairman of the BRITISH BRIDGE LEAGUE, has acted as the link between the Portland Club and international bodies such as the EUROPEAN BRIDGE LEAGUE and the WORLD BRIDGE FEDERATION.

PORTLAND RULES. The laws of WHIST according to the English code, named after the PORTLAND CLUB, which officially issued them.

In the early days of CONTRACT BRIDGE and the later days of AUCTION BRIDGE, the use of bidding calls with conventional meaning (such as the Informatory Double of auction or the Vanderbilt Club Bid of contract) were decried by the card committee of the Portland Club, a staid, conservative, British stronghold, and barred in games held in their clubrooms. These rules were called Portland Rules at that time.

PORTUGUESE BRIDGE FEDERATION (FEDERAÇAO PORTUGUESA DI BRIDGE). Founded in 1961 by Conde de Mangualde, in 1982 it had a membership of approximately 450 in three clubs, two in Lisbon and one in Oporto. The Federation is a member of the European Bridge League and participates in European Championships, hosting the 1970 event in Estoril. The main National competitions consist of two Teams-of-Four and two Open Pairs events, one each of Portugal and one each of Lisbon.

Officers, 1982:
President: Manuel Marcal Mendonca Jr.
Secretary: Pedro Matos, Av. Antonio Augusto
   Aguiar, 163-4° Esq.,
   1000 Lisbon, Portugal

POSITION. The place at a table occupied by a player. The various positions are called by the compass points, i.e., North, South, East, and West. Also, the term "position" can correctly be used to describe one's place in the order of bidding during a given auction. "Second" position means that position directly to the left of the dealer. "Fourth" position is the seat to the dealer's right.

POSITIONAL FACTOR. The value of honor cards during the bidding may improve or decline in accordance with the opposing bidding. A king becomes an almost sure trick when the suit is bid by the righthand opponent, but is likely to be worthless if the suit is bid on the left, except as a notrump stopper if the holder of the king is declarer. See RIGHT SIDE.

SIDNEY SILODOR gave the following example:

WEST	NORTH	EAST	SOUTH
—	1♡	Pass	2♡
3◇	3♡	Pass	

South holds:

     ♠ A J 7 3
     ♡ 10 6 3 2
     ◇ K 4 2
     ♣ 10 9

Although South has a relatively strong raise to 2♡, he should pass, because the ◇K has been devalued by the bid on the left. The decision to pass would be even clearer if the minor suits were interchanged and West bid 3♣. In that case North's failure to make the trial bid of 3◇ would imply a lack of interest in game.

POSITIONAL SQUEEZE. A squeeze which is effective against one opponent but not the other. This occurs when the hand opposite the squeeze card has nothing but busy cards; if that hand follows to the squeeze card before the opponent who is menaced, there can be no squeeze.

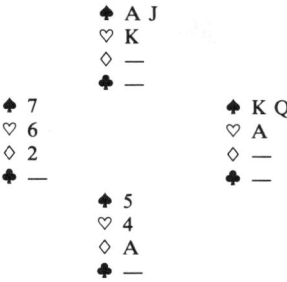

When the ◇ A is led, the North hand is squeezed before East must play, so that the latter is in no difficulty; however, if the East and West hands were reversed, the squeeze would be effective. Positional squeezes are characterized by the fact that the one-card menaces lie to the left of the opponent threatened. See also AUTOMATIC SQUEEZE and SIMPLE SQUEEZE.

Monroe Ingberman

POSITIVE CARDS. See CARDS, NEUTRAL AND POSITIVE.

POSITIVE RESPONSE. A natural constructive response in a forcing situation which provides for an artificial negative response. See FORCING TWO-BID, 2♣ STRONG ARTIFICIAL OPENING.

POSITIVE SLAM DOUBLE. See DOUBLE FOR SACRIFICE.

POST-MORTEM. A term applied to discussion of bridge hands after the conclusion of the play or any time thereafter. Some players aver that they object to constant post-mortems, but it can sometimes be pointed out with a degree of correctness that what they object to is being reminded of their own mistakes. Generally speaking, post-mortems can be of significant value when engaged in by experts, as points of great interest are sometimes highlighted by this type of discussion, and unusual features of a hand brought into better perspective.

In tournament play, long post-mortems should be indulged in only if time permits at the end of a round.

POSTING THE SCORE. Among the duties of the tournament director (and his staff) is the posting of the score as rapidly and conspicuously as possible, for the inspection of the players.

In club games, when TRAVELING SCORE SLIPS are used, matchpoints are awarded on the traveling score slips, and these are posted. Sometimes the matchpoints are posted to a RECAPITULATION SHEET, where they are added and ranked. At no time is the score official until a PROTEST PERIOD has expired.

POWERHOUSE. A descriptive term signifying a really huge (in point value) hand at bridge. A powerhouse could also, but considerably less frequently, be a strong distributional hand with outside

aces or ace combinations, or possibly void features. An alternative term is "rock crusher."

PRECEDENCE IN ENTERING A TABLE. In bridge clubs, precedence is given to that member who first appears in the playing room. The lowest priority belongs to a member leaving an existing table to join the new one. See HOUSE RULES.

PRECISION ASKING BIDS. The PRECISION CLUB system, in its most standard version, allows the 1♣ opener to use asking bids for three purposes: (1) to find out about the length and quality of the trump suit, (2) to find out about responder's control of a particular suit, (3) to find out whether responder can fill in opener's SEMI-SOLID SUIT and what other aces he has.

Trump Asking. The most commonly used is the trump asking bid, which is initiated by the 1♣ opener's single raise of responder's positive suit response. The responses are as follows:

1st step	No top honor
2nd step	Five cards with one top honor
3rd step	Five cards with two top honors
4th step	Six cards with one top honor
5th step	Six cards with two top honors
6th step	Three top honors

Trump asking bids may also be initiated by a simple rebid in responder's suit after responder's initial rebid. These asking bids and responses are used also in the SUPER PRECISION system, which designates them Gamma Trump Asking Bids. For other trump asking devices see TRUMP ASKING BIDS.

Control Asking. After a trump asking bid has been made and responded to, a bid in a new suit by opener asks about responder's controls in a side suit. The controls shown may be either high card or distributional. The responses are:

1st step	No control
2nd step	Third-round control (Q or doubleton)
3rd step	Second-round control (K or singleton)
4th step	First-round control (A or void)
5th step	First- and second-round control (A–K or A–Q)

Opener may ask whether partner's control is a high card or distributional by rebidding the asked suit. Responder shows a high card by bidding the first step (next suit) and the distributional control by bidding the second step.

Ace asking. The third type of asking bid asks whether responder has one of the top three honors in a particular suit. It is initiated by a jump shift rebid by the 1♣ opener after a positive response. The responses give information about another suit as well as about the asked suit. The responses are:

Cheapest notrump	No top honor, no aces
Single raise	Top honor in asked suit, no other aces
New suit	Ace of bid suit, no top honor in asked suit
Jump in new suit	Top honor in asked suit, ace in suit jumped in

Jump in notrump	No top honor in asked suit, but two side aces
Jump raise	Top honor in asked suit with two side aces

See also ASKING BIDS; ROMAN ASKING BIDS: ROMEX TRUMP ASKING BIDS: SUPER PRECISION ASKING BIDS.

PRECISION CLUB. A system developed principally by C. C WEI and used successfully by the Taiwan team in the 1967, 1968, and 1969 Far East Championships. The system attracted international attention during the 1969 BERMUDA BOWL when PATRICK HUANG, M. F. TAI, C. S. SHEN, and FRANK HWANG, all using the Precision Club, spearheaded Taiwan's drive into the final of the tournament. This was the closest a non-European, non-North American team had come to capturing the world team title. The Taiwan team reached the final again in 1970.

In the United States a number of top-level teams were sponsored by Wei to use and popularize the Precision System. One such team won three major ACBL knockout team events within a 19-month period. See PRECISION TEAM.

By 1972, when the Italian BLUE TEAM emerged from retirement to enter the World Team Olympiad, all three of its pairs were using versions of the Precision system. The version currently used by GIORGIO BELLADONNA and BENITO GAROZZO is called SUPER PRECISION.

The chief features of the standard Precision System are as follows:

1 ♣ opening is forcing and artificial, and normally shows a minimum of 16 points. Suit responses other than 1 ◊, which is the conventional negative, are positive, 8 points or more, guarantee at least a five-card suit and, in principle, are forcing to game. With a positive response and 4-4-4-1 distribution, there are two basic methods of responding. The partnership may agree to use the IMPOSSIBLE NEGATIVE: responder bids 1 ◊, then jumps in his singleton, or in notrump if his singleton is in opener's suit. Alternatively an UNUSUAL POSITIVE may be used: responder immediately jumps to 2 ♡, 2 ♠, 3 ♣, or 3 ◊ over 1 ♣ to show a singleton in the suit he jumps in, and four cards in every other suit. As a variation of the unusual positive, the jump can be made in the suit below the singleton, so that opener can economically cuebid the singleton to obtain additional information. Balanced hands are shown by responding either 1 NT (8–10), 2 NT (11–13, or 16 on up), or 3 NT (14–15). After a negative response and a normal rebid, responder will usually bid again with 4–7 points.

If 1 ♣ is overcalled, responder passes with fewer than five points, bids a five-card or longer suit, or makes a CARD-SHOWING DOUBLE with 5–8 points, jumps in notrump with the opponents' suit well stopped and 9–11 points, cuebids with a hand too strong for a negative double, or bids the cheapest notrump with an unbalanced, game-forcing hand. If 1 ♣ is doubled, normal responses are used, except that with a weak hand responder passes with clubs, bids 1 ◊ without clubs or redoubles with both major suits.

After a 1 ◊ negative response, opener rebids 1 NT with 16–18 points, 2 NT with 19–21, or 3 NT with 25–27. A non-jump rebid in a suit is nonforcing: a jump rebid is forcing to game unless opener rebids his suit at the three level.

After a positive response, the auction develops naturally with one exception. A direct raise of responder's suit is an inquiry about the length of responder's suit and the number of top honors he holds, and subsequent suit bids by opener are asking bids. See PRECISION ASKING BIDS. See also SUPER PRECISION ASKING BIDS.

STAYMAN is used after all notrump responses and rebids.

1 ◊, 1 ♡, and 1 ♠ openings are natural and limited to a maximum of 15 points. Major-suit openings promise at least a five-card suit.

1 NT response to a major-suit opening is forcing: 3 NT is a strong balanced raise; double jumps are splinter bids, showing four-card support for opener's major and a singleton or void in the bid suit. Raises are limited and nonforcing, except after 1 ◊, 2 ◊ is forcing and 3 ◊ is pre-emptive. A jump response of 2 NT shows 16 points or more.

1 NT opening is weak, 13–15 points. 2 ♣ and 2 ◊ are nonforcing and forcing Stayman, respectively. However, many Precision experts prefer a stronger range, 14–16 or 15–17. In this case weaker balanced hands must begin with 1 ◊, which becomes a catchall, sometimes made with a doubleton. 2 ◊ opening distributions should include 3-4-1-5 and 4-3-1-5.

2 ♣ is a natural opening, showing a five-card or longer club suit and an unbalanced hand. 2 ◊ is a conventional response: with a minimum, opener bids a four-card major; with a maximum, opener jumps in a four-card major, raises to 3 ◊, or jumps to 3 NT with a solid or semi-solid club suit. A rebid of 2 NT shows two suits outside of clubs stopped. Responder may ask where the stoppers are by bidding 3 ◊; the responses are 3 ♡ to show hearts and diamonds, 3 ♠ to show spades and diamonds, and 3 NT to show both major suits. A rebid of 3 ♣ by opener over the 2 ◊ response suggests a six-card club suit with one side suit stopped; over a 3 ◊ inquiry opener bids hearts or spades if that is where his stopper is, or bids 3 NT if he has diamonds stopped.

2 ◊ is a specialized opening, describing a three-suited hand (4-4-1-4 or 4-4-0-5) with shortage in diamonds and 11-15 points. A 2 NT response requests opener to specify his exact distribution and point range of his opening bid. Other responses are limited and nonforcing.

2 ♡ and 2 ♠ openings are weak two-bids.

2 NT opening is standard (22–24 points).

3 NT opening is gambling, showing a long, solid minor with little side strength.

4 ♣ and 4 ◊ openings are 4 ♡ and 4 ♠ openings, respectively, showing a long, solid suit, with a side ace or king.

See SUPER PRECISION.

PRECISION TEAM. A highly successful team of young experts from the New York City area sponsored by C. C. WEI to use his PRECISION CLUB system between 1970 and 1973. While there have been a number of teams using the Precision system and coached by Wei, the designation *The Precision Team* came to mean the team whose nucleus was STEVEN ALTMAN, THOMAS M. SMITH, JOEL STUART and PETER WEICHSEL, and which won three of the four major ACBL knockout team championships held between August 1970 and March 1972.

With DAVID STRASBERG as a fifth member in 1970, the Precision Team defeated the World champion ACES to win the Spingold. With EUGENE NEIGER replacing Strasberg as the fifth member in 1971, the team successfully defended its Spingold title, becoming only the fifth team to do so since the event began in 1934. Adding ALAN SONTAG as a sixth member, the team won the Vanderbilt in 1972.

In January 1973 four members of the Precision Team entered the LONDON SUNDAY TIMES (since 1981 INVITATIONAL PAIRS) event. Altman–Sontag and Smith–Weichsel finished first and second, respectively, in the select 22-pair field, marking the first time a United States pair had ever finished higher than fourth.

After failing to defend its titles successfully in the 1972 Spingold and 1973 Vanderbilt, the team was disbanded in mid-1973. In the meantime many international stars adopted Precision, including members of the Italian BLUE TEAM, the South American champions from Brazil, and a group of British stars headed by TERENCE REESE.

PRECISION 2 ◇ . See PRECISION CLUB.

PRE-DEALING. A method of (1) producing duplicated boards for play in more than two sections, or (2) producing deals prior to a match so that duplicates of the hand can be published and furnished to spectators or those who prepare slides or frames for exhibition.

Perhaps the first instance of pre-dealing occurred in Johannesburg, South Africa, in December 1962. The hands were pre-dealt and copies made for the spectators for an exhibition match between South African players and a visiting team from England. In modern times, pre-dealing is done by computer. A program is devised so that a random mathematical setup is instilled in the computer, and the computer then distributes the cards to the four compass corners. Printouts then are made of the deals manufactured by the computer. These printouts are packaged and sealed and, in the case of the ACBL, sent to the ACBL Headquarters for storage until they are ready for use. The hand records are sent to the tournament, and kept intact and sealed until it is time for the game in which they will be used. Then, and only then, the tournament director opens the package and distributes the hand records to his fellow directors for distribution among the players. In addition, a special one sheet printout of all the hands is provided to the tournament. If the tournament officials wish, copies may be made of this master sheet for distribution to the players at the end of the session. This has proved very popular at American tournaments.

The same process makes it possible to have ACBL-wide and world-wide games involving the same deals. The hands are packaged and sealed, then mailed to the various areas where games are going to

be held. The games are all held at approximately the same time, so that there is little chance of information being passed from one area to another.

PREEMPTIVE BID or SHUTOUT BID. An opening bid of three or more with a hand containing a long suit and limited high-card strength. The bid is usually defensive in purpose. The preemptive bidder hopes that opponents with strong hands will find it difficult to bid accurately when the auction has started at a high level.

The following considerations may influence the preemptive bidder.

(1) *Length of suit.* An opening three-bid is usually a seven-card suit or a strong six-card suit. An opening four-bid is usually an eight-card suit or a strong seven-card suit. An opening five-bid in a minor is usually a nine-card suit or a strong eight-card suit.

(2) *Vulnerability.* The traditional rule was to take the playing trick strength of the hand and add three tricks when not vulnerable or two tricks when vulnerable. This is an oversimplification, and most experts make preemptive bids more freely than this *two and three* rule would permit.

In the most favorable circumstances, third-hand not vulnerable against vulnerable opponents, some experts would venture 3♠ with a hand as weak as:

♠ K J 10 8 6 4
♡ 4
◇ 3 2
♣ 7 6 5 3

When vulnerable against nonvulnerable, on the other hand, the preemptive bidder should be within two tricks of his bid in his own hand, and even then may lose 500 to save 420.

(3) *Position at the table.* The third player is best placed to preempt, because he knows that he cannot preempt his partner, and the fourth player is almost sure to have the best hand at the table. Preemptive bids by the dealer are also attractive. They run the risk of finding partner with a strong hand, and therefore setting him problems, but there are two opponents who may have strength, and the odds are that the hand *belongs* to them.

Preemptive bids by the second player are less attractive, and should be slightly stronger than preempts by the dealer. Preempts by the fourth player are very rare, and should indicate a solid or near-solid suit if bid at the three-level.

(4) *Strength of suit*, and outside strength. The preemptive bidder prefers to have his honor strength concentrated in the suit bid. This automatically increases his playing strength, decreases the danger of suffering a substantial penalty, and decreases the chance of successful defense against an opposing contract. A doubleton queen in a side-suit is unlikely to play a part in attack, but may be an important factor in defense.

Some players make it a practice not to preempt when holding a four-card major side-suit but this rule is at best doubtful.

(5) *Bidding methods.* Opening three-bids tend to be weaker, and rarer, when using WEAK TWO-BIDS, which are a form of preemptive bid. The weak two is used with many hands which other players would

open with three. The opponents' defensive methods also have to be taken into account. Opening four-bids tend to be weaker when the partnership is using artificial preemptive bids, which tend to be well-defined in strength and suit texture. See 4♣ AND 4◊ OPENING PREEMPT; RUBIN TRANSFERS; 3 NT OPENING. See also TRANSFER OPENING THREE-BIDS. More discretion must be exercised in opening three-bids against players who double for penalties than against players who double for takeout. See DEFENSE TO OPENING THREE-BID.

Responses. Responses to opening three-bids are often of a tactical character, intended to reinforce the preemptive effect of the opening bid. If the dealer opens 3♠, for example, and the third player holds three-card spade support or better, he should rarely pass unless he has sufficient defensive honor strength to defend against 4♡. If the third player has a hand so weak that he fears an adverse slam, he may take more positive action by bidding 5♠, or 6♠, or venturing some psychic maneuver. This would have the character or an ADVANCE SAVE.

The following points relate to normal constructive responses to preemptive bids.

(1) *Raise to game in a major suit* (e.g., 3♠ – 4♠). Responder must take into account the vulnerability and other factors which influenced the opening bid. If vulnerable, he needs three sound playing tricks in the form of trump honors, aces, kings, and more ruffing values. Queens and jacks in side-suits must be discounted. If not vulnerable, he needs at least four playing tricks – more if circumstances favored a light preempt. But this raise is often made on a much weaker hand for the tactical reasons mentioned above.

(2) *3 NT.* A bid which the opener should almost invariably pass. In response to a minor suit, it shows stoppers in at least two of the unbid suits, and probably a fitting honor in the opener's suit. In response to a major suit, it shows a hand capable of making nine tricks without using the opener's suit. Responder is likely to have a solid minor suit, and might be void in opener's suit.

(3) *Three of a higher-ranking suit* (e.g., 3♣ – 3♡). Forcing to game, showing that the preempt has found responder with a strong hand. The responder's suit should be a good five-card suit or better, and the opener should raise with any slight excuse. The opener should bid 3♠ if he has a spade stopper for notrump purposes; a rebid of 3 NT in this situation would show a *diamond* stopper.

(4) *Four of a lower-ranking suit* (e.g., 3♠ – 4♣; but *not* 3♠ – 4♡, which would be natural). A slam try, inviting the opener to cooperate. Spades are provisionally, but not definitively, agreed on as the trump suit. (The same applies to five of a lower-ranking suit after an opening four-bid.) These bids can be used as ASKING BIDS.

(5) *Five of opener's suit* (e.g., 3♠ – 5♠, or 4♠ – 5♠). A natural slam invitation, implying that responder is not worried about two losers in any side suit. The quality of his trumps may decide opener's course of actions.

PREEMPTIVE JUMP OVERCALL. See WEAK

JUMP OVERCALL.

PREEMPTIVE OVERCALL. A defensive overcall, usually a double or triple jump in a suit, aimed at obstructing the bidding by the opener's side. After an opening bid of 1◊, a jump to 3♡, 3♠, or 4♣ would be preemptive. Standards would be slightly higher than for opening preemptive bids at the same level, because the chance of seriously inconveniencing the opponents is reduced. A vulnerable jump to 3♠ suggests a hand with 7–8 playing tricks.

A jump to the game level is ambiguous. The overcaller is likely to have a preemptive hand, but may make the same bid with a strong hand prepared to abandon hopes of slam in view of the opposing opening. See also DOUBLE JUMP OVERCALL and WEAK JUMP OVERCALL.

PREEMPTIVE RE-RAISE. A three-level rebid by opener in his own suit which has been raised by responder, in order to make it more difficult for the opponents to bid rather than to try for game. Responder is expected to pass this rebid.

In order to try for game, partnerships using preemptive re-raises must bid notrump or bid a new suit either naturally or as a SHORT SUIT GAME TRY, a TWO-WAY GAME TRY, or a WEAK SUIT GAME TRY. See also TRIAL BID.

PREEMPTIVE RESPONSE. A new suit response to a suit opening at a higher level than would be required for a jump shift:

SOUTH	NORTH
1♡	3♣ or 4♣ or 4◊ or 4♠

North normally holds a seven-card suit or eight-card suit, but the exact playing strength varies with circumstances. He must take the vulnerability into account, and also the likelihood of the opponents entering the auction. The suit will normally be a broken one; with a solid or near-solid suit a simple response followed by a jump is more appropriate.

As these responses are rarely used, they can be given conventional meanings. See ASKING BID, SPLINTER BIDS, SWISS, and VOID-SHOWING BID.

For other preemptive responses, see INVERTED MINOR SUIT RAISES and WEAK JUMP SHIFT RESPONSES.

PREFERENCE. When a player bids two suits, and his partner returns to the original suit at the lowest possible level, he is giving simple preference. This is in no way strength-showing, and will usually be passed. Preference at an unnecessarily high level is termed jump preference, and is considered under RESPONDER'S REBID.

Simple preference can occur in five common situations:

(1) *After three bids at the one level* (e.g., 1♣-1♡-1♠). With a minimum responding hand (5–7 points) and three cards in clubs and spades, it is usually best to pass. If the opener has to play a 4–3 spade fit instead of a 5–3 club fit at a higher level, it is no great hardship. A preference to 2♣ would be appropriate with 8–9 points if diamond weakness rules out 1 NT, and responder wishes to give the opener another chance in case he has 17–18 points.

If responder gives preference with three clubs, as he usually would with two spades and three clubs, he need not be afraid of a 3-3 fit. The opener will return to diamonds if he has opened with a prepared club.

The most difficult situation arises when the responder has not more than a doubleton in each of the opener's suits, with exactly five cards in his own suit. A preference to 2♣ should never be given with a doubleton, so the choice lies between a pass, leaving the opener to play in a 4-2 fit with the prospect of a club ruff, or 1 NT if the partnership method permits this to be weak.

(2) *When opener bypasses 1 NT* (e.g., 1♡-1♠ -2◊). Automatic preference to 2♡ is called for if the responder has equal red-suit length (3-3 or 2-2). There is a strong probability that the opener has a five-card heart suit (see OPENER'S REBID). Some authorities suggest a timid pass when the response is a minimum instead of giving preference, but this is born of fear that the opener may continue bidding without justification. With 8-10 points, two hearts and three diamonds, false preference to 2♡ may be appropriate in case the opener has a maximum rebid.

(3) *After a two-over-one response* (e.g., 1♠-2♣- 2♡). Preference to 2♠ is likely to be based on a doubleton, because with three-card support a raise might have been made on the first round. False preference with two spades and three hearts is not unlikely, especially if the partnership treats the 2♡ bid as forcing.

(4) *After a 1 NT response* (e.g., 1♠-1 NT-2♡). The responder gives automatic preference, expecting the opener to hold five spades and four or five hearts. In the rare event that the opener has chosen this sequence with four spades and five hearts, the wrong contract is reached.

If the opener's two suits are a major and a minor, false preference with two of the original suit and three of the second suit may be appropriate, especially at matchpoints. This applies particularly after the sequence 1♠-1 NT-2♣, when the opener is virtually certain to have five spades and four clubs.

(5) *After a 1 NT rebid* (e.g., 1♡-1♠-1 NT-2♣). A delicate situation, because the responder may hold a hand with four spades and five or six clubs which was not strong enough for an original response at the two level. The opener should usually refrain from giving preference, even if he holds three spades. (Alternatively, a partnership may agree that with only four spades, responder should pass 1 NT, in which contract the minor suit may prove useful.)

PREMATURE LEAD OR PLAY.

A lead or play made before the proper time, or before the player's turn to do so. This may occur before the auction has closed, or after. There is no penalty for a premature lead or play by a declarer. See LAWS (Law 23 for card led during the auction, or Laws 54, 57).

PREMATURE SAVE. See ADVANCE SAVE.

PREMIUM. A score made above the line. See BONUS.

PREMIUM SCORE. The score ABOVE THE LINE, consisting of extra tricks, making doubled contracts, rubber bonus, slam awards, honors, and premiums for defeating opposition contracts.

PREPARED CLUB. See SHORT CLUB.

PREPARED HANDS. See MACHINE-PREPARED HANDS; PAR CONTESTS; PRE-DEALING; TWINNING.

PREPAREDNESS, PRINCIPLE OF. The idea, originally called "anticipation" of looking forward to the next round of bidding when selecting a bid. It applies regularly to the opening bidder, but may also apply to the responder or to the opponents of the player who opened the bidding. Specific cases are considered under CHOICE OF SUIT.

PRESIDENTS. American Bridge League; American Contract Bridge League; and United States Bridge Association.

ABL
1927	Ralph R. Richards
1928	Henry P. Jaeger
1929	Robert W. Halpin
1930	Clayton W. Aldrich
1931	Capt. Fred G. French
1932	Waldemar K. von Zedtwitz
1933	Sir Derrick J. Wernher
1934	Ray H. Eisenlord
1935	Louis J. Haddad
1936	H. Huber Boscowitz

ACBL
1937	Gordon M. Gibbs
1938	Nate B. Spingold
1939	James H. Lemon
1940	Elmer J. Babin
1941	Robert J. Gill
1942	Morgan Howard
1943	Albert H. Morehead
1944	Richmond H. Skinner
1945	George A. Alderton, II
1946	Benjamin M. Golder
1947	Raymond J. McGrover
1948	Waldemar K. von Zedtwitz
1949	Dr. Louis Mark
1950	Rufus L. Miles, Jr.
1951	Julius L. Rosenblum
1952	Joseph Cohan
1953	Benjamin O. Johnson
1954	Peter A. Leventritt
1955	Jefferson Glick
1956	Rufus L. Miles, Jr.
1957	Joseph G. Ripstra
1958	Charles J. Solomon
1959	Winslow Randall
1960	Frank T. Westcott
1961	James P. Ferguson
1962	Max Manchester
1963	Jerry M. Lewis
1964	Leo Seewald
1965	Robin B. Mac Nab
1966	Eilif Andersen
1967	John W. Norwood
1968	Joseph J. Stedem
1969	Edgar G. Theus
1970	William A. Baldwin
1971	Carl Rubin
1972	Percy X. Bean
1973	Jerome R. Silverman
1974	Ruth (Mrs. L. W.) McConnell
1975	Lewis L. Mathe
1976	Donald Oakie
1977	Louis S. Gurvich
1978	Walter K. O'Loughlin
1979	Leo J. Spivack
1980	Ira G. Corn, Jr.
1981	James E. Zimmerman
1982	Sydney A. Levey, Jr.

USBA
1932-4	Milton C. Work
1935-7	Ely Culbertson

PRESIDENT'S CUP. Awarded to Non-Master Pairs; presented by MORGAN HOWARD in 1942. Restricted to players below the rank of Senior Master. Results are listed under Summer North American Championships.

PRESSURE BID. An overbid made necessary by opposing action. Suppose this bidding:

WEST	NORTH	EAST	SOUTH
1 ♡	3 ♣	?	

North's 3 ♣ is a weak jump overcall, and East holds three-card heart support and 8 points in high cards. Although he could not have bid 3 ♡ in the ordinary way, even using LIMIT JUMP RAISES, he should bid 3 ♡ at this point under the pressure of the opposing bid. A pass would leave West to consider the possibility that East has a worthless hand. 3 ♡ is therefore less of an overbid than a pass would be an underbid.

In such circumstances 3 ♡ shows the upper range of a raise to 2 ♡ without interference. The opener allows for the pressure, and passes unless he would have considered a game after a single raise.

As a corollary, the responder must overbid similarly with a slightly stronger hand. If he would have made a limit jump raise to 3 ♡ in normal circumstances, he must jump to 4 ♡ over the bid of 3 ♣.

PRIMARY HONORS. Top honors, i.e., aces and kings. The king of a suit may instead be considered a SECONDARY HONOR when it is unaccompanied by the ace and when it is in a suit in which partner is known to be short. Primary honors usually carry more weight in suit contracts than in notrump.

PRIMARY TRICKS. A term first use by P. HAL SIMS to describe high cards which will win tricks no matter who eventually plays the hand.

PRISONERS OF WAR. See BRIDGE IN PRISON CAMPS.

PRISONS, PRISONERS. See BRIDGE IN PRISONS.

PRIVATE CONVENTION. A partnership understanding which is not made known to the opponents. The use of such a convention is a violation of the Laws and the Proprieties: "It is improper to convey information to partner by means of a call or play based on special partnership agreement, whether explicit or implicit, unless such information is fully and freely available to the opponents (see Law 40)." LAWS OF DUPLICATE (Proprieties IV). This requirement is not easy to fulfill in tournament play. Many partnerships have elaborate understandings about the precise natural meaning to be allocated to certain bids and sequences. It is difficult to draw a hard-and-fast line to separate *convention* from *style*.

ACBL standards require that the opponents automatically be alerted to any conventional bid embodying an understanding that is not classified as a Class A CONVENTION. See ALERTING. Other explanations should not be volunteered until the end of the auction. See also EXPLANATION OF CONVENTIONAL CALL OR PLAY.

PRIVATE SCORECARD. See CONVENTION CARD.

PRIZES. It is a strict rule of the ACBL that no cash prizes may be awarded at Sectional or higher tournaments, but most tournaments do provide individual prizes for the winners (and sometimes for the runners-up) in each event. These often take the form of engraved trophies, important for their symbolic rather than their monetary value. However, in recent years ACBL scrip often has been used for prizes.

Many established tournaments have permanent floating trophies for each event upon which each year's winner's name is engraved. Often these are held by the winner until a new winner is determined the following year. The ACBL headquarters has on display all of the trophies from the North American Championships and charity events.

It is common for tournaments not under ACBL sponsorship to offer cash prizes. This is true in many tournaments held in Europe.

PRO SYSTEM. A system employed by a number of West Coast pairs. Many relay sequences are used in order to allow the stronger hand to control the auction and inquire about his partner's strength and pattern.

The principal features of PRO (Pattern Relay Organized) are: intermediate (14–16 HCP) notrump opening; forcing 1 ♣ opening promising either a club suit or a balanced hand with 17–20 points; nonforcing two-over-one responses and jump shifts; four-card major suit openings, with a 1 NT response that is virtually game forcing; reverses based on distribution rather than on high-card strength. The principal slam gadget is the CLARAC SLAM TRY.

PROBABILITIES. See HIGH CARD POINT PROBABILITIES.

PROBABILITIES A POSTERIORI. See PERCENTAGE PLAY; PROBABILITY OF SUCCESSIVE EVENTS.

(1)

A Q 10 7 3 2

9 8 5

When dummy's queen is finessed and loses to East's king, there are two events. The first is that East has the K–J, or alternatively, that he has the singleton king. The second is that in both cases, he would play the king. The second is regarded as certain; resultant probabilities are 6.8% and 6.2%. Assumed is that West has the same choice in both cases, to play either the six or the four. On a second lead, with West following with the other of the small cards, percentage play (slightly) favors the play of the ace.

(2)

A J 10 7 3 2

9 8 5

The finesse of the 9 loses to East's king. The a priori probabilities of relevant distributions are:

6 4 opposite K Q   6.8%
Q 6 4 opposite K   6.2%

In the first case there is no certainty that East will win with the king: he can equally well play the queen. If he is a good player the chances are about equal that he will play either honor, as any other method will be likely to help declarer. While the probability of the first event (that East holds K–Q) is 6.8%, the probability that he will play the king is 50%. Applying the rule for successive events, the probability that East will hold the K–Q, and play the king is 6.8% × 50% or 3.4%. The odds in favor of taking a second finesse are therefore 30 to 17.

(3)

A K Q J 4 3 2

void

Assume that on the ace and king, East plays the 7 and 8, and West the 5 and 6. The only possible distributions are:

WEST	EAST	A Priori Probability
5 6 9	7 8 10	1.78%
5 6 10	7 8 9	1.78%
5 6 9 10	7 8	1.61%
5 6	7 8 9 10	1.61%

All the outstanding cards are insignificant (see CARDS, NEUTRAL AND POSITIVE) in that they cannot take a trick. It can be assumed that defenders play insignificant cards at random, avoiding giving declarer information unnecessarily. There are three ways in which each defender can select two cards from both the first two cases. Thus the play of the four cards in question from these cases is 3.56% × $\frac{1}{9}$ = .39%. There are only six ways in which the particular played cards could occur from the last two cases in the table, so the probability of the selected play is 3.56% × $\frac{1}{6}$ = .54%. The a priori probability of a 4–2 against a 3–3 division is exactly the same as the ratio between these a posteriori probabilities, .54 to .39.

(4) But it is not always apparent to a player that his cards are insignificant.

4 3 2
J 10 9   Q 8 7
A K 6 5

West will appreciate that his cards are of equal value, but East will not know that his are. When West plays the 9 on South's ace, East is unlikely to play the queen. The probabilities of the possible distributions can be calculated only on an assessment of how defenders are likely to play from each. Before South attacks the suit (at an early stage, and after a neutral lead) the odds are about 49 to 36 on a 4–2 division as against a 3–3. Declarer's interpretation of the play of the first two rounds may cause him to change his original play. See MATHEMATICAL ASSUMPTIONS.

Alex Traub and Roy Telfer

PROBABILITIES A PRIORI. Basic probabilities of a given distribution of cards is expressed as a fraction where the numerator is the total number of favorable cases, and the denominator the total

number of (equally likely) possible cases. MATHEMATICS OF BRIDGE explains how these can be computed. Thus before the cards are seen (a priori), the probability a particular player will hold a 4–3–3–3 hand pattern is $\frac{66,905,856,160}{635,013,559,600}$. See HAND PATTERNS and NUMBER OF POSSIBLE HANDS.

In bridge, probability is most commonly shown as a percentage (100 times the above fraction). Play based on a priori probabilities is therefore known as PERCENTAGE PLAY.

Probability of any distribution varies at different stages of the game. Before one has seen any cards, there is a probability (see TABLES, MATHEMATICAL, Table 1) of 10.58% that one will hold a 5–4–2–2 hand pattern. There is the same probability that a particular suit will be distributed 5–4–2–2 to the four players. After a player looks at his hand and sees a suit of five cards, the probability that this suit is distributed 5–4–2–2 among the four players is 21.21% (Table 3). Thus 5–4–2–2 is now less than twice as likely as 5–5–2–1 whereas it was more than three times as probable before any cards were seen. (A priori has become a posteriori). The difference is because it is now known that one player does have five of the suit, and concern is only with the distribution of the remaining eight cards.

Subsequently, if partner's hand is seen to contain a doubleton of the five-card suit, the probability of a 5–4–2–2 distribution of the suit rises to 48.45% (Table 4), and 5–4–2–2 is now more probable than 5–3–3–2 although the latter was more probable in the earlier stages. Concern is now with the distribution of the remaining cards of the suit in only the other two hands.

It is apparent that a priori probabilities take no account of INFERENCES In bidding or play. Use should be made of the former only where more accurate probabilities cannot be drawn from such infrences.

When the opening lead has been made, strict a priori probabilities no longer apply; but if the lead gives no material information, they are altered only very slightly or not at all. See CARDS, NEUTRAL AND POSITIVE.

Alex Traub and Roy Telfer

PROBABILITIES OF DISTRIBUTION. See MATHEMATICAL TABLES, Tables 1, 3, 4, and 4A.

PROBABILITY OF SUCCESSIVE EVENTS. The probability that two events will occur is the product of the probability of each, the latter event's probability being calculated on the assumption that the former has taken place. See DECEPTION and PROBABILITIES A POSTERIORI and, for an unscientific, but practical application, the last example under PERCENTAGE PLAY.

PROBABLE TRICK. A playing trick that can be reasonably counted upon when attempting to forecast the play during the bidding. K–x of a suit bid voluntarily on the right is an example.

PROBLEMS. Usually of three types, SINGLE DUMMY PROBLEMS, DOUBLE DUMMY PROBLEMS, and INFEREN-

TIAL PROBLEMS, which are listed in separate articles.

PROFESSIONAL BRIDGE ASSOCIATION (PBA).

An organization of professional bridge players formed in 1981 and recognized as an accredited professional organization by the ACBL in 1981.

PROFESSIONAL PLAYERS.

Bridge professionalism takes several forms. The most common form consists of experts who are retained to play tournaments in partnership or on teams with lesser players. In addition, many experts teach bridge to pupils of all levels, and some give lessons by playing with the pupil in a tournament. Although bridge may be the full-time profession of writers, editors, and lecturers, they are not considered professional players.

Professionalism in the form of a pro playing with a client is a most controversial subject within the ACBL. Large numbers of members believe professionalism is an evil. They believe it is wrong for some players to hire professional partners so that they will have a better chance to win gold points and become Life Masters or so that they can gain prestige by winning events and placing high in the TOP 500 race. These members believe that professionalism should not be allowed, that a player should have to earn his way to the top rather than paying a professional to help him along. On the other side of the coin are those that see positive advantages to professionalism. Playing with a professional partner and learning how an expert thinks can help an average player become a good one, their argument goes. They also believe that most persons who engage a professional do so in an attempt to learn more about the game, not to amass master points.

The ACBL Board of Directors has been addressing the problem of professional players for many years. Several committees have made various suggestions concerning regulating professionalism. The first major attempt to come to grips with professionalism came in 1975 when the Board set up regulations for Registered Players. Under these regulations, any player who accepted money or other remuneration, directly or indirectly, in excess of his actual expenses, as consideration for playing in an ACBL-sanctioned event, had to become a Registered Player. This policy was in effect for a time, but it did not work out to the satisfaction of its sponsors, and it finally was repealed. The professionalism committee then attempted to find some other avenue.

It was proposed in 1981 that the ACBL sanction certain professional organizations provided they met a set of strict requirements set down by the ACBL. These organizations are expected to maintain a high degree of responsibility and ethics among their members. At the same time, the Board passed a regulation that any player who accepted payment for playing professionally at a regional or North American Championship must be affiliated with one of these professional organizations. The first such organization to receive accreditation was the ASSOCIATION OF PROFESSIONAL BRIDGE PLAYERS (APBP), and four other professional organizations

had been accredited by the end of 1982.

These organizations take different views of their role. The APBP conducted a special money-prize tournament opposite the North American Championships in Minneapolis in 1982. However, the APBP event did not conflict with the ACBL Championships inasmuch as all sessions were held in the morning. The PROFESSIONAL BRIDGE ASSOCIATION (PBA), on the other hand, began an intensive campaign to find players with whom their members could play on a professional basis. Their first major promotion along these lines took place in 1983 when the PBA offered a special "Book a Room, Play a Star" program, whereby a player could play four sessions with a PBA professional if he took part in a package deal with a hotel at the Fall North American Championships at Bal Harbour FL. The ACBL Board commissioned itself to adopt a watchdog attitude concerning these organizations, checking at regular intervals to make sure all the conditions for accreditation were being met. As of 1983, the other accredited organizations, in additions to the APBP and the PBA, were ASSOCIATION OF BRIDGE PROFESSIONALS (ABP), BRIDGE PROFESSIONAL REGISTRATION ORGANIZATION (Bridge Pro), and CONCERNED BRIDGE PLAYERS UNION (CBPU).

Bridge has had its share of wealthy patrons who have sponsored expert bridge teams. In 1968, Dallas financier IRA CORN organized the ACES, the world's first full-time professional bridge team. This was an eminently successful venture, inasmuch as the Aces won the BERMUDA BOWL World Championship in 1970 and 1971. Perhaps the most outstanding illustration of a successful sponsor is MALCOLM BRACHMAN, who led his team to victory in the INTERNATIONAL TEAM TRIALS of 1979 and thereby qualified to play in the Bermuda Bowl in Rio de Janeiro that year. Brachman and his team won the World Championship that year, and Brachman played his share of the matches and thereby qualified for full world champion rating. BUD REINHOLD also led his team to victory in the Team Trials of 1981, and his team went on to win the Bermuda Bowl. However, Reinhold did not play the required number of boards in the final, so did not qualify as a world champion. In the Seventies, shipping magnate C. C. WEI sponsored several teams to popularize his PRECISION SYSTEM. (See PRECISION TEAM.)

In addition, some commercial concerns have sponsored teams in order to promote their products. The LANCIA division of Fiat in Italy sponsored a team that made professsional appearances in various cities in North America. Rothman's Cigarettes was the sponsor of the 1982 Canadian Team Championships. Philip Morris sponsors a series of tournaments leading to a grand champion in Europe each year.

Some professional players make their living, in whole or in part, by playing bridge for high stakes. This is usually in the form of rubber bridge at clubs, but occasionally it takes place in Calcuttas or tournaments at which substantial money prizes are at stake. Until the coming of accredited professional organizations, money-prize tournaments were extremely rare in North America. However, money tournament are the rule rather than the exception in Europe.

PROFESSIONAL TOURNAMENT DIRECTORS ASSOCIATION (PTDA). A professional organization of persons who work for the ACBL and its subsidiary sponsoring organizations as tournament directors at the hundreds of tournaments (as distinguished from club and local-rated events) conducted every year in North America. The principal objective of the PTDA is the development and maintenance of the highest possible standards for the conduct and operation of tournament bridge events.

The PTDA was officially organized in August 1968 at the Summer NAC in Minneapolis and has a membership of 170. The ACBL lists 234 national, regional and sectional rated tournament directors as of September 1982, and of these, 161 are PTDA members. The PTDA is governed by an executive committee consisting of seven regional vice presidents (one of who is elected president), an executive secretary and a treasurer.

The PTDA conducts general membership meetings three times each year. The PTDA sends, at its own expense, a representative to each of the three yearly meetings of the ACBL Board of Directors for the purpose of representing the interests and opinions of the PTDA, providing technical advice in the area of Tournament Regulations and Direction and continuing an active liaison with the ACBL Board and Management.

Major activities of the PTDA have included a joint venture with ACBL Management to standardize the interpretation and application of the 1975 Code of the Laws of Duplicate Contract Bridge. The final product (written by a PTDA member) was published by the ACBL as a loose-leaf booklet titled *Ruling the Game — A Director's Guide to the 1975 Duplicate Code.* Other PTDA activity has been concerned with establishing guidelines for rulings involving the Alert procedure and the preparation of the present interpretation and application of Law 75 which deals with score corrections involving the number of tricks won by each side.

The Tom Weeks Memorial Award is presented annually to the PTDA member demonstrating the greatest progress in all facets of professional tournament direction. Weeks was a national tournament director and first treasurer of the PTDA from Detroit who died suddenly in 1971. Past recipients of the Tom Weeks Memorial Award have been: 1972, SOL WEINSTEIN; 1973, ROGER PUTNAM; 1974, BRIAN MORAN; 1975, FRAN MILLER; 1976, Jerry Shakofsky; 1977, ROBERTA SHIPLEY; 1978, GARY BLAISS; 1979, THOMAS QUINLAN; 1980, Robert Kitchel; 1981, Eleanor Kipperman; and 1982, Jeff Alexander.

Past presidents include HARRY GOLDWATER, HENRY FRANCIS, DALE EGHOLM, WILLIAM WEYANT, Roger Putnam, WILLIAM SCHODER and NELSON ROWE.

PROGRESSION. (1) The movement of players in duplicate; (2) the movement of the boards in duplicate; (3) the movement of players in PROGRESSIVE BRIDGE.

PROGRESSIVE BRIDGE. A form of competition at CONTRACT BRIDGE played in the home or among social groups.

PROGRESSIVE SQUEEZE (or Repeated Squeeze or Repeating Triple Squeeze). A sequence of two squeezes which results in a gain of two tricks. In rare instances three tricks may be gained (see [9]). It is initiated by a triple squeeze which is followed by a simple squeeze, both against the same player. As in an ordinary triple squeeze, all but *two* of the remaining tricks must be in hand before pressure can be exerted. There are several types, of which (1) and (2) are most common.

(1) The requirements for a Type 1 progressive squeeze are:
(a) A one-card threat placed to the left of the opponent threatened.
(b) Two two-card menaces, one in each hand, for example:

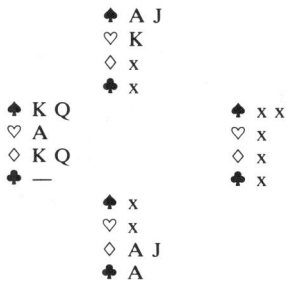

South leads the ♣A, and West is squeezed in three suits. If West discards a spade, South cashes two tricks in that suit which leads to an automatic squeeze against West in hearts and diamonds for the gain of a further trick. If West discards a diamond, South takes two diamonds, which results in a positional squeeze in the majors. Finally, if West discards a heart, South crosses to the ♣A in order to play the ♡K, which results in an automatic squeeze against West in spades and diamonds.

(2) The requirements for a Type 2 progressive squeeze are:
(a) A one-card threat placed to the right of the opponent threatened.
(b) The hand with the one-card threat has an entry in each of the other threat suits.
(c) The hand opposite the one-card threat contains the squeeze card, the remaining threat cards and entries in two of the three threat suits.

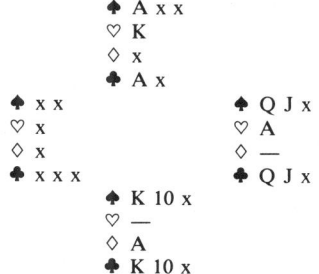

South leads the ◊A, and East is squeezed in three suits. Any discard costs a trick, and leads to a simple squeeze for the loss of another trick by East.

(3) A third form of progressive squeeze may arise, with these requirements:

(a) An extended two-card menace (also called a double threat).

(b) Two one-card menaces opposite the extended threat.

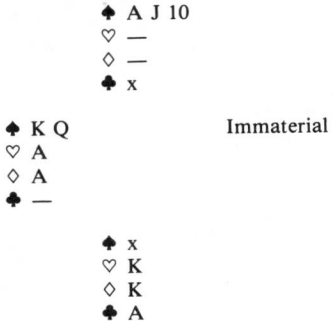

```
        ♠ A J 10
        ♡ —
        ◇ —
        ♣ x

♠ K Q                    Immaterial
♡ A
◇ A
♣ —

        ♠ x
        ♡ K
        ◇ K
        ♣ A
```

South leads the ♣A, and West is squeezed in three suits. If West discards a spade, it is at the cost of two tricks; if West discards a heart or a diamond, South continues with the king of that suit, effecting an automatic squeeze against West.

This squeeze is equally effective if the East and West cards are interchanged, so it is an automatic squeeze.

(4) (Described by Chien-Hwa Wang)

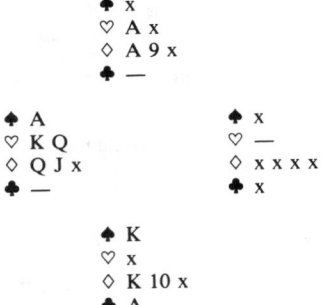

```
        ♠ x
        ♡ A x
        ◇ A 9 x
        ♣ —

♠ A                      ♠ x
♡ K Q                    ♡ —
◇ Q J x                  ◇ x x x x
♣ —                      ♣ x

        ♠ K
        ♡ x
        ◇ K 10 x
        ♣ A
```

South leads the ♣A, and West is squeezed in three suits. If West discards a spade, then South leads the king of that suit, squeezing West in hearts and diamonds: a heart discard permits North to win his hearts, thereby squeezing West in spades and diamonds; if West discards a diamond, South cashes three diamonds, ending in his hand. The last of these squeezes West in the majors.

This is an automatic squeeze, since North's spade is an idle card. The requirements for this squeeze are as follows:

(a) A one-card menace placed to the right of the opponent threatened.

(b) A two-card menace in the hand opposite the one-card threat.

(c) A twin entry menace, with a menace card accompanying each winner.

The squeeze card lies in the same hand as the one-card menace.

(5)

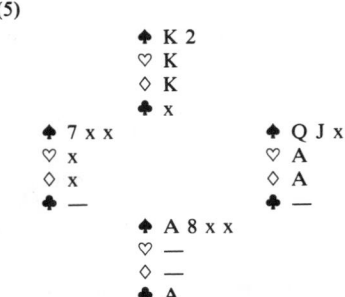

```
        ♠ K 2
        ♡ K
        ◇ K
        ♣ x

♠ 7 x x                  ♠ Q J x
♡ x                      ♡ A
◇ x                      ◇ A
♣ —                      ♣ —

        ♠ A 8 x x
        ♡ —
        ◇ —
        ♣ A
```

The lead of the ♣A squeezes East in three suits, and South eventually wins all the remaining tricks. (Variation of [2])

(6)

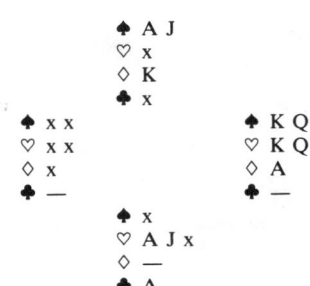

```
        ♠ A J
        ♡ x
        ◇ K
        ♣ x

♠ x x                    ♠ K Q
♡ x x                    ♡ K Q
◇ x                      ◇ A
♣ —                      ♣ —

        ♠ x
        ♡ A J x
        ◇ —
        ♣ A
```

South leads the ♣A, and East is squeezed in three suits. The squeeze gains two tricks for South. (Variation of [2])

(7)

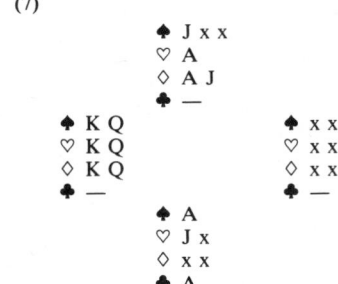

```
        ♠ J x x
        ♡ A
        ◇ A J
        ♣ —

♠ K Q                    ♠ x x
♡ K Q                    ♡ x x
◇ K Q                    ◇ x x
♣ —                      ♣ —

        ♠ A
        ♡ J x
        ◇ x x
        ♣ A
```

South leads the ♣A, and West is squeezed in three suits. A spade discard gives North two spade tricks; a heart discard enables South to take the ♡A, ♠A, and ♡J, squeezing West in spades and diamonds, a diamond discard leads to a crisscross squeeze.

(8)

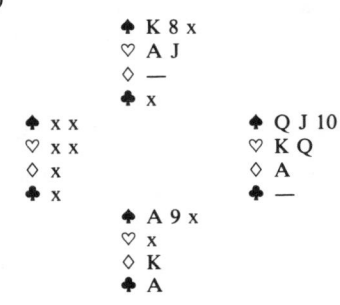

```
        ♠ K 8 x
        ♡ A J
        ◇ —
        ♣ x

♠ x x                    ♠ Q J 10
♡ x x                    ♡ K Q
◇ x                      ◇ A
♣ x                      ♣ —

        ♠ A 9 x
        ♡ x
        ◇ K
        ♣ A
```

South leads the ♣A, and East is squeezed in three suits. If East discards a diamond, South takes two top spades ending in his hand, and plays the ◊K, squeezing East in the majors; a heart discard permits North to win two hearts which squeezes East in spades and diamonds; a spade discard enables South to win three spades ending in his hand, which squeezes East in the red suits.

(9) (Described by CLYDE E. LOVE)

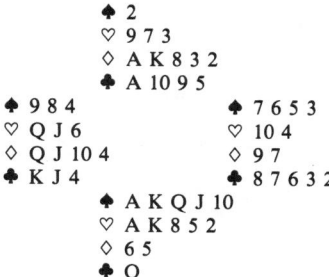

South plays in 7♣ doubled by West. West makes his normal lead of the ◊Q. South starts life with only 10 top tricks, but after he has won the diamond lead and cashed three spades this is the position:

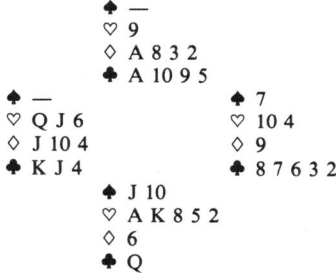

When the fourth spade is led West cannot throw a heart or he will set up three tricks immediately. If West discards a diamond, a low club is discarded from dummy. Declarer then leads a diamond to the ace and ruffs a diamond to establish two tricks, and the cashing of these two new winners squeezes West in clubs and hearts to promote a third trick. The result would be the same if West had discarded a club rather than a diamond.

See also CLASH SQUEEZE; GUARD SQUEEZE: TRIPLE SQUEEZE.

Monroe Ingberman

PROMOTION OF TRUMP HONORS. Revaluation after a trump fit has been found, with trump honors advanced in point value. Players of ability assign a higher value to an honor in a suit bid by partner than to a similar honor in a side suit. For instance, if partner bids hearts and the ♡Q is held, it is almost surely of value, whereas the value of a queen in an unexplored side suit is problematic. Therefore an added value should be assigned when holding an honor in partner's suit. See also GOOD CARDS.

PROPRIETIES. There are three different kinds of improper conduct: breaches of ethics, breaches of good manners, and cheating. Premeditated cheating is unforgivable; it is not dealt with by the Laws at all, for such a highly civilized game as bridge depends upon the assumption that players will not cheat.

Breaches of ETHICS of ETIQUETTE, however, are dealt with by the Laws. The proper code of behavior is set out in the Laws under the title Proprieties. In the tournament world breaches of the Proprieties are punishable by the award of an adjusted score and by disciplinary penalties. In rubber bridge there is no way of adjusting the score except by agreement of the players or as provided in Law 16 (see LAWS).

PROTECT. (1) To guard with a small card, as an honor; (2) to make a bid in order that partner may have another opportunity to bid, thus "protecting" him if he has greater strength than his first call has implied (this usage is obsolescent); (3) in England, to balance; see BALANCING.

PROTECTED SUIT. See GUARD.

PROTECTION. An English term for BALANCING.

PROTEST PERIOD. The time during in which corrections to the score can be filed, whether the error is made by the scorer or by a player at the table. The former are corrected when reported; the latter require proof that an error actually was made. Usually a director will check the scorecards of all players involved before making a decision on whether or not to change a score. When time permits, the protest period for a player correction is usually about 24 hours, and its expiration is clearly indicated on the RECAPITULATION SHEET. When no time is specified, at least 30 minutes after the posting should be allowed. A scorer's error must be corrected if attention is called to it any time during the tournament.

PROTESTS. See APPEAL; COMMITTEE.

PROVEN FINESSE. A finesse whose success is guaranteed. For example:

NORTH
A Q J 7
SOUTH
10 9 5 3

The 10 is led and wins, while right-hand opponent discards. Subsequent finesses in the suit are *proven* or *established*.

PSEUDO ELIMINATION PLAY. See THROW-IN PLAYS.

PSEUDO SQUEEZE. A pseudo squeeze is a play intended to induce a wrong discard by a defender who mistakenly believes that he has been squeezed.

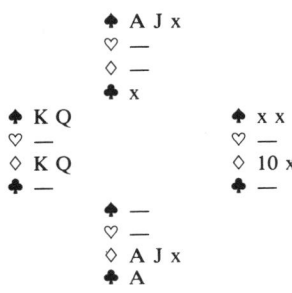

```
          ♠ A J x
          ♡ —
          ◇ —
          ♣ x
♠ K Q                    ♠ x x
♡ —                      ♡ —
◇ K Q                    ◇ 10 x
♣ —                      ♣ —
          ♠ —
          ♡ —
          ◇ A J x
          ♣ A
```

Suppose that West is not aware that South has no spades. South leads the ♣A, and West may discard a diamond hoping that East can protect that suit.

Monroe Ingberman

PSYCHIC BID. Any bid made primarily with the purpose of interfering with the opponent's bidding or play rather than with the idea of aiding the bidding and play of one's own side. See LAWS OF DUPLICATE BRIDGE (Law 40).

PSYCHIC BIDDING. A term coined in 1931 by DOROTHY RICE SIMS, generally meaning bluffing calls to create the illusion of strength or length in a particular suit or to conceal a weakness. From about 1931–34 a wave of blind enthusiasm for psychic bidding swept the country's bridge tables, making it appear that a malignancy was threatening to deform the game that was still in its infancy. Most of these early psychics were hit-or-miss affairs, the bidder never knowing until it was all over whether his ploy had been brilliant or catastrophic.

During this period ELY CULBERTSON, a keen strategist and psychologist who was not above making an occasional psychic himself, was categorically opposed to psychic bidding for the masses. His reasoning was simply that the techniques of the CULBERTSON SYSTEM were designed to create partnership harmony and confidence; any psychic bidding, unquestionably a unilateral and individualistic action, tended to destroy the precision his system was trying to create.

Fortunately the early passion for psychics quickly subsided. Some two decades later, around 1952, psychic openings re-emerged in a more disciplined form as parts of the ROTH-STONE, STAYMAN, KAPLAN-SHEINWOLD, and BULLDOG systems. In the opinions of many experts, however, although the psychic opening had a tendency to force the opponents out of their familiar bidding patterns and into strange and uncomfortable situations, it was never terribly effective against sophisticated opponents, who would act positively when they had good cards in spite of the psychic. By 1964, the Roth-Stone system had eliminated the opening psychic because the complications it created outweighed the benefits it produced.

By and large the most effective psychic bids have been those that misdescribe the bidder's length in a particular suit. Sometimes these psychics promise extreme shortness in the suit; sometimes they promise considerable length in the suit. And when they find gaps in the opponents' defensive bidding con-

ventions, the results can be extremely profitable. The least successful type of psychic bid tends to be one which attempts a bluff as to wholesale strength. The American Contract Bridge League has taken steps to reduce the usage of psychic bids. DON OAKIE was commissioned by the ACBL Board of Directors to state the League's position in an article in the ACBL *Bulletin*. His article appeared in the February 1978 issue. Here are his conclusions:

"It is high time that we call all of our members' and directors' attention, especially at the club level, to the fact that while a psychic bid is legal, it's indiscriminate use is not. People who employ psychic calls against less experienced players may be guilty of unsportsmanlike psyching and thereby be in violation of League regulations. People who psych against their peers may be guilty of frivolous psyching, or of having an unannounced partnership understanding. People who psych against more experienced players will probably get bad boards, and they may lose the few good boards they get by being judged to have indulged in unsportsmanlike psyching, or to have disrupted the game.

"What does this mean to you as a player? If you want to psych any call other than a forcing opening call, go ahead and do it — it's perfectly legal. If you psych on an average of once a month, no player or director is likely to say a word about it. If you can't resist the temptation to do it oftener, sooner or later you're going to run afoul of the Laws or League regulations."

Oakie made these observations about psychic bids in general:

"The excitement of using a psychic bid often exerts an almost irresistible attraction for a new duplicate player. An occasional jaded duplicateer will fall back on psychic bids as a means of having "fun" during a session marked by bad results in the early rounds or where few rating points are at stake. Expert players and the large majority of experienced club and tournament players seldom or never make a psychic bid.

"Psychic bids wear a high price tag. When employed against one's peers their chances of success are at best fifty-fifty. When they fail they can prove to be very costly and when they succeed, in a very short time the cost in loss of partnership confidence can far exceed any momentary advantage gained.

"By its nature, a psychic bid, successful or not, is remembered by the opponents as well as the user's partner. A player who becomes addicted to psychs is soon a marked man. Psychers live in a storm's eye of gloating or infuriated opponents, harried tournament directors and skeptical tournament committees . . . Win or lose, they tend to disrupt the events they enter and thus find the protection extended to them by the Laws is offset by their inability to prove they have not violated the Proprieties.

"An opening psychic bid that carries no conventional forcing meaning or implication is a legal bid. The Laws of Duplicate Contract Bridge state (see LAW 40). 'A player may make any call or play (including an intentionally misleading call — such as a psychic bid — or a call or play that departs from commonly accepted, or previously announced, conventional practice) without prior announcement, provided that such call or play is not based upon a partnership understanding.'

The same Law continues. 'A player may not make a call or play based on a partnership understanding unless an opposing pair may reasonably be expected to understand its meaning or unless his side discloses the use of such call or play in accordance with the regulations of the sponsoring organization.'

"As this Law states, a psychic bid or other call is legal. At the same time nothing in this Law is to be construed as meaning that psychic bids may be used indiscriminately. The Law specifies that a call may *not* be made, if based on a partnership understanding, unless the opposing pair may reasonably be expected to understand its meaning, or unless the opponents have been Alerted.

"A clarification of the term 'partnership understanding' is found in Proprieties, Part IV, section A. 'It is improper to convey information to partner by means of a call or play based on special partnership agreement, whether explicit or implicit, unless such information is fully and freely available to the opponents.'

"The ACBL recognizes that a psychic bid or call is legal. The right to regulate partnership understandings which arise from the usage of calls is specifically authorized by the Laws. Law 40 grants the sponsoring organization the right to regulate explicit partnership understandings (systemic or conventional calls). The Proprieties, Part IV, section A, clarifies that this right to regulate equally applies to implicit partnership understandings (understandings arrived at by usage and experience rather than discussion).

"League regulations do not in any way alter, infringe or nullify any right guaranteed by the Laws. The Laws are in accord with international agreements and cannot be changed unilaterally by the ACBL."

Oakie also stated that the regulations that any partnership understanding not readily available to the opponents must be Alerted neither modifies, contravenes nor supersedes the opposing players' right to inquire as to the partnership understanding of an adverse call. The Alert procedure simply supplements the right to inquire. It provides a mechanism whereby a partnership that has failed to forewarn its opponents about either an explicit or implicit partnership understanding may do so while the auction is actually in progress.

Oakie continued: "Since players rarely think to disclose implicit partnership understandings prior to the situation actually arising during the auction — and for all possible situations it would be impracticle to do so — the protection of the Alert procedure is invaluable where implicit understandings are involved. Where psychic bids are concerned, however, the nature of the bid or call is such that the need to disclose implicit understandings has the effect of practically preventing their use.

"Psychic bids are not soon forgotten by the user's partner. Since such a bid does grossly misstate either the strength or pattern of the hand, or both, the results obtained tend to be memorable where the partner is concerned. In this respect the psychic bid has the same effect as does an extraordinarily good

guess by partner, either as declarer or defender, a particularly spectacular line of play or defense, or a sensationally successful or unsuccessful unilateral save by partner.

"But where the guesses, lines of play and saves are remembered as special cases, the psychic calls tend to become identified with the bidding situation in which they were used. When partner has psyched once, for many sessions to come every time a similar situation arises, his partner will remember and wonder.

"The partner who remembers and wonders is apt to test the water before he takes the plunge of an irreversible action predicated upon his partner's call. A player who thus displays caution may not be deemed to be simply prudent. His caution stems from prior knowledge and experience with *this* partners and thus constitutes prima facie evidence that an implicit partnership understanding exists.

"This caution is never quite as pronounced as it is in the deals that immediately follow the one where partner psyched. Accordingly, while a player's first psychic bid with a new partner is judged to be legal as far as the League regulations are concerned, a second psychic call by the same player during the same event, even in a radically different bidding situation, is judged to establish a pattern of psychic bidding that may well create an implicit partnership understanding.

"Since implicit partnership understandings are available to both members of a partnership, any further psychic bidding by *either* member, in the same event, might be presumed to be a violation of the Proprieties. The director would penalize the partnership accordingly unless the user could prove incontrovertibly that no partnership understanding existed.

Following are some examples of various types of psychic bids:

A psychic that has long been almost so standard a part of the repertoire that it is thought hardly worth using any more is the 1 ♠ butt-in over an opponent's takeout double of partner's 1 ♡ opening. Yet it was used to good effect in the final of the 1966 Bermuda Bowl between Italy and North America.

Dlr: North   ♠ J 10
Vul: None   ♡ A Q 5 4
         ◇ A 8 2
         ♣ 9 8 4 2

♠ K Q 8 6 5   ♠ A 4 2
♡ J 10   ♡ K 9 8
◇ 10 6 4 3   ◇ Q 9
♣ A Q   ♣ K J 10 7 5

         ♠ 9 7 3
         ♡ 7 6 3 2
         ◇ K J 7 5
         ♣ 6 3

WEST	NORTH	EAST	SOUTH
Avarelli	*Mathe*	*Belladonna*	*Hamman*
	1 ♡	Dbl	1 ♠
1 NT	Pass	2 ♣	Pass
2 ◇	Pass	2 NT	All Pass

HAMMAN'S psychic spade response found a flaw in the ROMAN SYSTEM. A double by AVARELLI would have shown spade shortness rather than length. Still, the Italians could have recovered by bidding game in notrump. It was just as well that they did not, however, since after MATHE'S opening ♠J was won by dummy's ace, Avarelli led a spade and covered Hamman's 7 with the 8, playing Hamman for a real suit, and lost a trick to Mathe's 10. Mathe wasted no time in shifting to a diamond to collect five tricks in all. In the replay West made 11 tricks in 4♠.

One of the most spectacularly successful psychics was an opening preemptive psychic by MARTIN COHN of Atlanta, playing with CHARLES MacCRACKEN against PETER LEVENTRITT and HOWARD SCHENKEN in the Vanderbilt Teams at the 1967 North American Championships in Seattle.

Dlr: North
Vul: E–W

```
                    ♠ 10 8 7 6 4 3
                    ♡ A 10 6
                    ◇ K Q 6
                    ♣ 7
    ♠ A                         ♠ K Q 2
    ♡ K J 9 8 7 5 2             ♡ Q 3
    ◇ A J                       ◇ 10 8 7 5 4 3 2
    ♣ A K 4                     ♣ 2
                    ♠ J 9 5
                    ♡ 4
                    ◇ 9
                    ♣ Q J 10 9 8 6 5 3
```

WEST	NORTH	EAST	SOUTH
Leventritt	*MacCracken*	*Schenken*	*Cohn*
	Pass	Pass	3♡

All Pass

Holding a weak hand and a shortage of hearts, Cohn opened the bidding with 3♡ and caught LHO Leventritt with a powerful hand including seven hearts. Leventritt could not double for penalties, so he passed, and 3♡ undoubled became the final contract.

Cohn suffered a six-trick penalty (he could have held it to five), but that still was a huge gain since this was the auction at the other table:

WEST	NORTH	EAST	SOUTH
	Pass	Pass	5♣
5♡	Dbl	All Pass	

North did not lead the ♡A and another, so West made an overtrick for 1050 and a 13–IMP gain.

PSYCHIC CONTROLS.
Devices intended to avert a partnership disaster following a psychic bid.

Controls are usually related to the "disciplined psychic" used in KAPLAN—SHEINWOLD and the original ROTH—STONE. In such cases the opener has 3–6 points, mainly in the suit which he has bid.

Responses of 2 NT and 3 NT can be used to show powerful balanced hands. 2 NT shows a hand with 21–22 points, and therefore interested in game even if the opener is psychic. 3 NT shows a stronger hand that is sure of game even opposite a psychic.

The jump shift remains forcing, and the opener must take care with his rebid. If he has made a psychic opening, he must rebid his suit or rebid in notrump, whichever is the more economical. Conversely, he must avoid these rebids holding a genuine opening. See also SKINNER PSYCHIC CONTROL.

Psychic controls are disallowed in some countries, notably in England, on the theory that the psychic bidder must be prepared to take his chances along with the opponents.

Open to much greater ethical doubt are psychic controls of other actions, such as responses. These are not sanctioned by any leading authority.

PSYCHIC LEAD. See OPENING LEAD.

PSYCHIC PLAY See DECEPTIVE PLAY.

PSYCHOLOGY. See DECEPTIVE PLAY; FALSE-CARDING; PARTNERSHIP PSYCHOLOGY.

PULLING TRUMP. See DRAWING TRUMPS.

PUMP. A colloquialism for FORCE (2). FORCING DECLARER TO RUFF is frequently referred to as pumping the declarer.

PUNCH. Verb: to cause a player (usually dummy or declarer) to use a trump for ruffing; to shorten; noun: the act of shortening in trumps. See FORCING LEADS.

PUPPET STAYMAN. A method of responding to 1 NT devised by KIT WOOLSEY. Responder's 2♣ asks for a *five-card* major. With no five-card major, opener is forced to bid 2◇. Responder now bids the major he doesn't have, or notrump with both majors. Opener is now in a position to select the right denomination without revealing his distribution to the opponents. Puppet Stayman can also be used over 2 NT openers with equal effectiveness.

PUSH. (1) A raise of partner's suit, usually at the partscore level, aimed at pushing the opponents to a level at which they may be defeated. For example:

WEST	NORTH	EAST	SOUTH
1♠	2♡	2♠	

Neither side is vulnerable and South holds:

```
    ♠ 6 5 3
    ♡ K 9
    ◇ A 8 4 2
    ♣ Q 7 3 2
```

It seems likely to South that both sides will make about eight tricks, so he bids 3♡. North is marked with, at worst, a good five-card suit. If East-West continue to 3♠, in which they will have more heart losers than they expect, they may be defeated, and South will have turned a minus score into a plus. The chance of being doubled in 3♡ is slight, and North will be wary of continuing to game.

(2) A board in a team match, in which the result is the same in both rooms (also STAND-OFF).

(3) A rubber in which the net score is zero after ROUNDING OFF.

PUZZLES. In bridge, puzzles are referred to as PROBLEMS, and are usually of three types, DOUBLE DUMMY PROBLEMS, SINGLE DUMMY PROBLEMS, and INFERENTIAL PROBLEMS. Examples of each type appear in this book. Crossword puzzles and acrostics using bridge definitions or texts have been published as bridge magazine features.

Q

QUACK. A term to indicate either the queen or the jack in situations where it is of no consequence which of the two cards is held or played. See RESTRICTED CHOICE.

QUALIFYING. Finishing high enough in a QUALIFYING SESSION to continue competing in the final session(s) of the event. See CONDITIONS OF CONTEST.

QUALIFYING SESSION. In an event of two or more sessions, one or more of them may be designated as qualifying sessions, to select contestants eligible for continued play in the remaining sessions.

QUALITY. See STRENGTH. ELY CULBERTSON stressed "quality" and "quantity" in discussing hand valuation. More modern usage concerns control cards, suit strength or the presence of intermediate cards, etc. See also WORKING CARDS.

QUANTITATIVE. A bid is quantitative if it is natural, limited, and non-forcing. Quantitative is usually used to refer to a 4 NT bid. For situations in which a 4 NT bid is quantitative, see BLACKWOOD.

QUANTITATIVE 4 NT. A term covering a number of situations where 4 NT is a natural bid. See BLACKWOOD.

QUANTITY. See LENGTH.

QUEEN. The third highest card in a suit, and the card most usually finessed for. The expression "dropping the queen" is frequently heard, and refers to situations where a declarer prefers to attempt to capture a queen by playing out higher honors.

QUEEN OF BRIDGE. See KING OR QUEEN OF BRIDGE.

QUEEN OVER JACK. The theory, or speculation, that the queen lies over the jack slightly more often than not is credited to CLAGETT BOWIE.

The assumption is based on the possibility that the queen may have captured the jack in the previous deal with the same deck, and that the cards may not have been separated in the shuffle. This assumption is valid only if declarer's holding in the suit is A–J opposite K–10. With K–J facing A–10, the chances are just as good that the king was used to capture the queen. However, the manner in which the trick is gathered is an important, and uncertain, influence. The theory has meaning only at rubber bridge, if it has any value at all. See TWO-WAY FINESSE.

QUEEN FROM KING-QUEEN. See RUSINOW LEAD.

QUEEN LEAD. Traditionally, the lead of the queen from a long suit promises the jack and usually the 10 or 9 as well. See OPENING LEADS. In alternative methods the lead of the queen promises the king (see RUSINOW LEADS), or the ace and king. The JOURNALIST system of leads against notrump promises either the traditional holding headed by Q–J–10, or a holding of K–Q–10–9. The latter asks the partner of the opening leader to play the jack if he has it, enabling the opening leader to continue without fear of a BATH COUP by declarer.

QUESTIONS. For when to ask questions, see ALERTING: EXPLANATION OF ANY CALL OR PLAY; FACE DOWN LEADS.

QUICK TRICK. A high card holding that in usual circumstances will win a trick by virtue of the rank of the cards in either offensive or defensive play. Of course, in some distributional holdings, or FREAK HANDS, such defensive values evaporate. The accepted table of quick tricks is:

2 quick tricks	A–K of same suit
1½	A–Q of same suit
1	A or K–Q of same suit
½	K–x

QUITTED TRICK. A trick is quitted, in rubber bridge, when the four cards played to it have been gathered together and turned face down in a packet in front of the side which contributed the winning card. Any player has the right to inspect a quitted trick until either he or his partner has led or played to a subsequent trick.

In duplicate, a trick is quitted when all four players have played to it and turned their cards face down. A quitted trick may not be inspected except at the director's specific instruction. If a player wishes to inspect the cards just played to a trick, he may do so only if he has left his own card face up on the table, assuming neither he nor his partner has led or played to the next trick. See LAWS OF DUPLICATE (Law 66).

QUOTIENT. A device used to determine the winner in team competition if a ROUND-ROBIN ends in a tie, either in won and lost matches, or in VICTORY POINTS won and lost. The number of IMPs won by a team is divided by the number lost to determine the quotient. Italy won two European Championships by quotient, over France in 1956 and over Great Britain in 1958.

R

RHO. Right-hand opponent. The oppoent to the right of a player.

RABBI'S RULE. "When the king is singleton, play the ace." A whimsical rule attributed to Milton Shattner, a New York attorney nicknamed "the Rabbi" because of his authoritative pronouncement of this and other convictions governing his play.

RACK. (1) A device used by handicapped players for holding a hand of cards. (2) A device to hold traveling scoreslips for inspection by the players after the game has been scored (see CLOTHESLINE). (3) Colloq., (verb) to ruin opponents by holding exceptionally good cards; (noun) a player who holds such cards; also called a cardrack.

RAGS. A holding of only a few high cards, likely to be insignificant in the bidding or play of a hand.

RAINBOW INDIVIDUAL MOVEMENT. A movement for tournaments between players competing as individuals, in which contestants are divided into groups corresponding to their original starting directions, with separate instructions for progressing to each group. The guide cards are often printed in different colors to make the groups more easily distinguished, and hence the name for the movement. This movement was devised by OSWALD JACOBY and SHEPARD BARCLAY.

In a typical set of guide cards (ACBL 52–player Individual), the North players receive blue cards and sit at the same table throughout. The East players receive yellow guide cards, moving two tables toward the higher number. South players receive white guide cards and move to the next higher numbered table. West players receive pink guide cards and skip a table toward lower numbers, while the boards go to the next lower numbered table. For identification purposes, players take a number: North, the table number; West, the table number plus 13; South, the table number plus 26; and East, the table number plus 39.

The movement in its simple form (as above) will work only when the number of tables is a prime number: 5, 7, 11, 13, 17, 19, or even 23. PAUL MARKS of Chicago devised a variation of this movement for prime number plus one tables (see EIGHT TABLES, TWELVE TABLES, FOURTEEN TABLES), which is based on the Rainbow. MAURY BRAUNSTEIN devised special adaptations of the Rainbow for nine tables and 15 tables. He also devised a stanza movement for 14 tables.

With any prime number of tables, the movement can be carried out in any manner as long as it is remembered that there are five different movements for the four groups of players and the boards. As long as the groups and the boards have different progressions, and continue for succeeding rounds as they moved for the second, no difficulty is encountered. The number of rounds is equal to the number of tables, but can be cut short.

If it is desired to increase the number of partnerships, the South and West players interchange after the first boards in a two-board round, or the West player travels around the table counter-clockwise for three boards to a round; in all cases, the North player remains stationary.

In no case do balanced comparisons result. Session awards are based on results as achieved in each direction.

RAISE. Noun: an increase of the contract in the denomination named by partner; verb: to make a bid increasing the contract in the denomination named by partner. See SINGLE RAISE; DOUBLE RAISE; TRIPLE RAISE.

RAISE IN RESPONDER'S SUIT. See OPENER'S REBID.

RAISER. The player who bids for a greater number of tricks in a suit first bid by his partner.

RANDOM FALSECARDS. See FALSE-CARDING.

RANK. (1) The priority of suits in bidding and cutting. Starting at the bottom, the suits rank in alphabetical order: clubs, diamonds, hearts and spades, with notrump at the top of the list. (2) The trick-taking power of each card within a suit. The ace, king, queen, jack have priority in that order. The lower cards rank numerically.

RANKING BRIDGE PLAYER. See LIFE MASTER, the highest of the categories into which the ACBL ranks players. The ranking of players by means of MASTER POINTS won cannot be construed as definitive as between any two players because of the difference in time during which points were earned, frequency of competition, ability to attend major regional and NORTH AMERICAN CHAMPIONSHIP TOURNAMENTS. Many other national organizations have set up similar systems to identify the more outstanding players.

RANKING OF PLAYERS. A part of the MASTER-POINT PLAN of the AMERICAN CONTRACT BRIDGE LEAGUE. The national offices of the league maintain a record for each player of points won in sanctioned tournaments. Rankings are based on the following table:

Sub-Master	A player who has less than 1 full master point recorded by the league.
Junior Master	A player who has 1 but less than 20 points credited.
Master	A player who has 20 but less than 50 points credited.
National Master	A player who has 50 but less than 100 points credited.
Senior Master	A player with 100 or more points credited.
Advanced Senior Master	A player with 200 or more points credited, including a minimum of 20 RED/GOLD POINTS.
Life Master	A player with 300 or more points credited, including a minimum of 50 RED POINTS. For players beginning to accumulate masterpoints as of January 1, 1969, 25 of these 50 points must be GOLD POINTS. Players with red points already to their credit prior to that date are not subject to this gold point requirement.

For the names of the top-ranking life masters, see LIFE MASTER.

Comparable masterpoint plans are in effect in many other bridge-playing countries, although rankings and requirements differ from country to country. See MASTERPOINT PLAN. In addition, the WORLD BRIDGE FEDERATION has adopted its own masterpoint plan for the ranking of players of international calibre. See WORLD BRIDGE FEDERATION RANKINGS.

RATING POINT CERTIFICATE. See RATING POINTS.

RATING POINTS. Fractional master points awarded in ACBL club duplicate games or championships. Rating points are issued on certificates by the manager of the club in which they are won. Each rating point equals .01 master point, and certificates may be forwarded to the ACBL in blocks of 100 or more rating points within three years of their issuance for crediting to the member's masterpoint total. Slips dated since 1978 may be registered after three years on payment of $1.00 per masterpoint.

REBIDDABLE SUITS. See OPENER'S REBID.

REBIDS IN ORIGINAL SUIT. See OPENER'S REBID.

RECAPITULATION SHEET (RECAP). A large printed form on which the scores on pickup slips are posted at bridge tournaments, and on which matchpoints are assigned to scores, and totals computed. Recapitulation sheets are available in three forms, one for HOWELL MOVEMENT games or team-of-four play, one for MITCHELL MOVEMENT games and a third for SWISS TEAM events. All sheets have a heading where space is provided for names of players and their SEATING ASSIGNMENTS and PLAYER NUMBERS, their overall RANKING, total score (for two or more session events or when FACTORING is involved), CARRYOVER SCORE for two or more session events, and POINTS this session. These headings or copies thereof are the official records from which MASTER POINTS are awarded by the NATIONAL AUTHORITY, and serve as permanent records. To the right of this heading are boxes in which the individual scores on boards 1–36 (subsequent sheets can be appended for more boards) are entered and MATCH POINTS assigned. See also BURNER.

RECIPROCAL SQUEEZE. A variant of the double squeeze. The squeeze card is not an established card in the fourth suit; rather each opponent is squeezed in turn by a winner in the suit guarded by his partner. These are the basic positions:

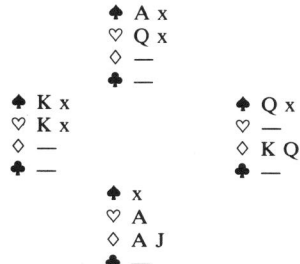

South leads the ♡A, which forces East to discard a spade. Now the lead of the ◇A squeezes West in the majors.

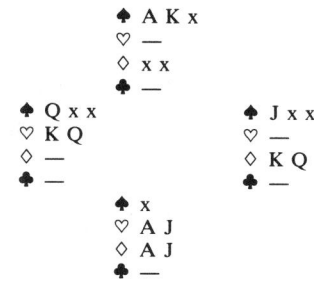

South leads the ♡A, which forces East to discard a spade. Now the lead of the ◇A squeezes West in the majors.

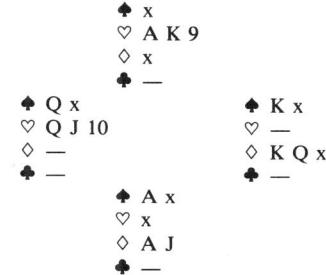

South leads the ◇A, which forces West to unguard spades. Now South leads hearts, and the second winner of that suit squeezes East in spades and diamonds.

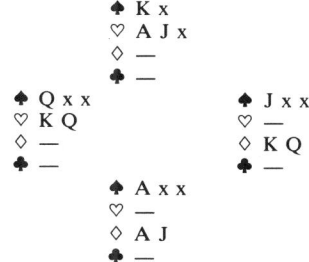

South cashes the ◇A, which forces West to unguard spades. A spade is led to the king followed by the ♡A, which squeezes East in spades and diamonds.

A double squeeze may be played as a reciprocal squeeze by running off all declarer's winners in the fourth suit (which is not guarded by either opponent). This has a dual advantage: it allows more room for defensive error, and it enables declarer to obtain additional information regarding the outstanding cards.

Monroe Ingberman

RECORDING OF MASTER POINTS. The results of each MASTERPOINT event are reported by the tournament director to the ACBL, and points are automatically recorded to the credit of the winners of club games and to those players placing in local, sectional, or higher ranked tournaments provided a player number is given. A postcard announcement is sent to each member whenever new points are recorded for him, stating the amount of the new credit and his total to date in both total points and RED/GOLD POINTS.

Originally all recording was done manually, and the postcard acknowledgments were written out in longhand and mailed to the players. In 1960 it became evident that manual posting would not suffice to maintain individual records for many thousands of members, and a mechanical system of recording was installed.

Fractional master points are issued in the form of unrecorded certificates, to be retained by the player until fractions amounting to one full point or more are accumulated. These certificates may be mailed to the ACBL office where each 100 fractional points is recorded as one full master point.

The ACBL was first to develop a masterpoint plan, but similar plans are now in use by numerous other national bridge governing bodies.

RECORDING OF MATCHES. See BRIDGE-O-RAMA; HAND RECORD; VUGRAPH.

RECTIFICATION. An adjustment made to permit the auction or play to proceed as normally as possible after an irregularity has occurred.

In the bidding stage, irregularities (other than violations of ethical procedure) are covered by specific penalties, as are most of the possible irregularities in the play. However, in the case of a failure to follow suit which is later corrected, it is possible that the offender inadvertently gains information that he is not entitled to under normal play; in this case, rectification is called for.

Occasionally the bidding will have started at a table when it is discovered that the traveling pair has come to the wrong table and should not be playing the board against that opponent. In this case the director may seat the proper pair at the table and have the bidding repeated. If no additional information is gained, the board is permitted to stand; if the bidding progresses differently, then an adjusted score usually is given. See ALCATRAZ COUP and LAWS OF DUPLICATE BRIDGE (Laws 12 and 16).

RECTIFYING THE COUNT. The process of losing a trick or tricks in order to reach a certain number of remaining losers, thus enabling a desired ending to be reached. The most common use of the play is to reduce the number of losers to one, enabling a simple squeeze to be executed.

```
                    ♠ 3 2
                    ♡ A K 6
                    ♢ A Q 7 2
                    ♣ A K Q 5
    ♠ Q J 10 8                    ♠ K 9 7 6
    ♡ 3 2                         ♡ J 10 9 8
    ♢ 6 5                         ♢ J 10 9 8
    ♣ 9 8 7 4 3                   ♣ 2
                    ♠ A 5 4
                    ♡ Q 7 5 4
                    ♢ K 4 3
                    ♣ J 10 6
```

West leads the ♠Q against South's 6 NT contract. South has eleven winners. The contract will succeed if either hearts or diamonds are favorably divided.

Another chance is a squeeze against an opponent holding guards in both red suits. This squeeze will operate only if South has but one loser remaining. If South wins the first trick, he can no longer make his contract. Instead, he should rectify the count by allowing West to hold the first spade. South wins any continuation, and runs his black winners, squeezing East between the red suits. For another example, see LOSER-ON-LOSER.

Monroe Ingberman

RED AND BLACK GERBER. See BLACK AND RED GERBER.

RED DOT. A small circle of red paper with a gummed back that duplicate players may paste on their CONVENTION CARD to indicate that they use nonstandard opening leads. The purpose is to alert the opponents that opening leads may not be what they seem.

RED POINT. Master points won in regional and NORTH AMERICAN CHAMPIONSHIP TOURNAMENTS are required for the advancement of players to ADVANCED SENIOR MASTER and LIFE MASTER status in the ACBL. To distinguish points won at these larger and more important events, the ACBL uses the term "red points". Fifty "colored" (red/gold) points are one of the requirements for promotion to Life Master status. At least 25 of the 50 must be gold. Twenty red points are needed to qualify for Advanced Senior Master. See also GOLD POINT; RANKING OF PLAYERS; REGIONAL AND NATIONAL POINTS.

REDEAL. A second or subsequent deal by the same dealer to replace his first deal. See LAWS OF CONTRACT BRIDGE, Part III Section 10. Hands are never redealt at duplicate except in special cases on the director's instructions.

REDOUBLE. A call that increases the scoring value of odd tricks or undertricks at a bid that an opponent has doubled. It has the effect of multiplying a doubled penalty or premium by two.

When the standard of play is high, redoubled contracts are rare. Ill-judged doubles of game or slam contracts may lead to redoubles. At rubber bridge and IMP play, the mathemathics of the scoring table favor redoubles at high levels.

In a high-level competitive auction, an expert may occasionally redouble when he expects his contract to fail by one trick. He is prepared to sacrifice 100 or 200 points in the hope of driving the opponents into continuing in their own suit and conceding a penalty.

A special situation arises when an artificial bid is doubled and redoubled. At a high level, when a CUEBID or a response to BLACKWOOD has been doubled, the redouble is generally regarded as control-showing. Whether the control shown is first-round or second-round is a matter of partnership agreement. At a low level the situation is different:

WEST	NORTH	EAST	SOUTH
			1 NT
Pass	2 ♣	Dbl	Redbl

The redouble shows a desire to play in clubs: the opening bidder probably has a five-card club suit.

This is the one area where there is likely to be a change in scoring rules. Making a redoubled contract at present is worth 50 points for the insult. But this brings about some strange situations at high levels. Making 5 ◊ redoubled with an overtrick vulnerable is worth 1350, less than the value of 6 ◊ (1370). But making 5 ◊ redoubled with an overtrick not vulnerable (950) is worth *more* than making 6 ◊ (920). Therefore, the LAWS COMMISSION is giving strong consideration to the idea of changing the bonus for making a redoubled contract to 100 points, instead of the present 50.

For other redoubling situations see DOUBLES OF NOTRUMP BIDS; KOCK-WERNER REDOUBLE; RESPONSES OVER OPPONENT'S TAKEOUT DOUBLE; SOS REDOUBLE.

REDOUBLE OUT OF ROTATION. An improper bid when it is partner's or right-hand opponent's turn to call. If it is partner's turn to call, he must pass and continue to pass for the balance of the auction. If the partner of the offender has the opening lead, declarer may require or forbid him to lead a specified suit. Also the offender is not permitted to redouble the same bid which he redoubled out of turn.

If it is the turn of the right-hand opponent to bid, the redouble must be repeated if this opponent passes; if the opponent bids, the offender may make any legal call, but his partner must pass at his next opportunity. See LAWS (Law 32).

RE-ENTRY. A card by which a player who has had the lead (including the opening lead) can regain it.

REFUSE. (1) Deliberate failure to win a trick because of reasons of strategy. (2) Used in the sense of refusing to finesse, i.e., not taking what was previously a winning finesse in order to ensure the contract. (3) An obsolete term formerly used in WHIST and AUCTION BRIDGE, the laws of which define it as "to fail to follow suit", as distinguished from RENOUNCE. See DISCARD. See DANGER HAND; DUCK; HOLD UP.

REGENCY WHIST CLUB (New York City). Formerly Regency Club, founded in 1936 and merged with the WHIST CLUB of New York in 1964. It has remained at 15 East 67th Street since it began its very successful career, with many of the outstanding bridge personalities among its members. These have included: the founder, Mrs. T. Charles Farrelly, a noted New York bridge teacher; B. JAY BECKER; JOHN CRAWFORD; SAM FRY, JR.; CHARLES GOREN; MICHAEL T. GOTTLIEB; EDWARD HYMES, JR.; THEODORE A. LIGHTNER; CHARLES S. LOCHRIDGE; ALBERT MOREHEAD; FLORENCE OSBORN; CURT H. REISINGER; HOWARD SCHENKEN; ALFRED SHEINWOLD; SHERMAN STERNS; ALAN TRUSCOTT; HAROLD S. VANDERBILT; WALDEMAR K. VON ZEDTWITZ. Honorary members include WINGATE BIXBY, GENERAL ALFRED GRUENTHER, WALTER MALOWAN, and HAROLD S. VANDERBILT.
President, 1982: Edgar Nye
Secretary: Cordelia Menges

REGIONAL AND NATIONAL POINTS. Regional points are master points won in championship events at regional tournaments under the earlier MASTERPOINT PLAN of the ACBL. This took cognizance of the larger fields and wider geographical distribution of players at its major tournaments by giving special recognition to winners of points in these tournaments (referred to as "red points", "regional reds", or "pink points"), keeping a record of these points separate from those won in lesser tournaments.

National points were a special award for success in NORTH AMERICAN CHAMPIONSHIPS. Each three National points were the equivalent of five Regional points.

Under the new program all red points are of the same value and the old ratio for conversion of Regional to National point values is eliminated.

REGIONAL TOURNAMENT. Generally, see CHAMPIONSHIP TOURNAMENTS. For results of particular regional tournaments, see Appendix II.

REGISTERED PLAYER. See PROFESSIONAL PLAYERS.

REID CONVENTION. See RESPONSIVE DOUBLE.

REISINGER MEMORIAL TROPHY. Donated by the Greater New York BA in 1965 in memory of CURT H. REISINGER and awarded to the winners of the Fall Open Teams Championships under which heading past results are listed. It replaced the historic CHICAGO TROPHY. The winners of the Reisinger are entitled to compete against the winners of the GRAND NATIONAL CHAMPIONSHIPS (2), SPINGOLD TROPHY, VANDERBILT CUP (1) and in Bermuda Bowl Trials, the CANADIAN NATIONAL TEAMS Championship for the right to represent North America or the United States in the next year's WORLD CHAMPIONSHIPS. See INTERNATIONAL OPEN TEAM SELECTION.

REISINGER TROPHY. Donated by CURT H. REISINGER in 1930, for the Knockout Teams-of-Four contest in the Eastern States Championships, under which heading past results are listed.

REITH ONE OVER ONE. A system of bidding described by GEORGE REITH in a series of five books published 1930-33. Approach bidding was used, and four-card suits were bid freely. Responses and bids were kept to minimum levels, and third-hand openings were somewhat shaded. The essence of the system, a forerunner of methods considered as *Standard* by postwar writers, was the principle of emphasizing distribution in early bidding rounds as opposed to showing strength. The one-over-one response made it incumbent upon opening bidder to bid at least once more.

REITH POINT COUNT. An appraisal by GEORGE REITH of the relative values of high cards, primarily for notrump bidding. The values assigned were ace = 6, king = 4, queen = 3, jack = 2, ten = 1. See REITH ONE OVER ONE.

RELAY. (1) A minimum bid unrelated to the bidder's hand, aimed simply at keeping the bidding open so that the bidder's partner can describe his hand. An example is the LEBENSOLD rebid of 3♣, which is a forced bid. For the full development of this principle, see RELAY SYSTEM. (2) The practice of sharing boards at duplicate bridge, usually necessitated by a six-, eight-, or twelve-table MITCHELL MOVEMENT in which 24 boards are to be played. (3) In England, the equivalent of a BYESTAND.

RELAY STAND. See BYESTAND.

RELAY SYSTEMS. Systems based on the idea that one player should make a series of minimum bids, or relays, until he has acquired sufficient information about his partner's hand to be able to fix the final contract.

The first relay system was developed by PIERRE GHESTEM of France, about 1950, and was used by him very successfully in world championships, mainly with RENÉ BACHERICH. In 1963 he played it with CLAUDE DELMOULY, using the name MONACO. This encouraged other European theorists to develop relay systems, notably DR. BERTRAND ROMANET, with "Alpha", and Pierre Collets, with "Beta". Both these date from 1965.

An important impetus came with work done about 1972 by DAVE CLIFF. He can be considered the Father of modern relay methods, with Ghestem as the Grandfather. Cliff's ideas were adopted and refined by a group of young players including MATT GRANOVETTER, RON RUBIN and MICHAEL BECKER. Their successes with the ULTIMATE CLUB attracted new interest in the relay principle and attracted imitators in many parts of the world who developed a series of relay languages. The most important of these is the SYMMETRIC RELAY SYSTEM.

RELAY TABLE. (1) One of the tables at which the players are sharing boards for that round with an adjacent table. (2) See BYE STAND.

RELAYS OVER WEAK TWO BIDS. A method of responding to weak two bids using the cheapest bid—either notrump if the opening bid was 2♠, or the next higher suit—as a relay bid. The relay asks opener to bid a stopper outside his suit if he has one. If his stopper is in the relay suit, he rebids in notrump. Lacking any stopper, opener rebids his own suit. Using this method, the relay bid is the responder's only forcing bid. See WEAK TWO-BIDS.

REMAINDERS. The remaining cards of a four-card or longer suit, outstanding in the other three hands at the table. Two- and three-card remainders are called balanced remainders. One-card and four-card remainders, however, are called unbalanced remainders.

REMOVE. To bid on when partner has doubled for penalties.

RENEGE. A popular colloquial synonym for REVOKE. However, the term does not appear in the Laws of Bridge and is borrowed from such games as pinochle.

RENOUNCE. A term from AUCTION BRIDGE, meaning to fail to follow suit when able to do so; also (noun), the play involving such failure. The term was dropped from the 1935 LAWS OF CONTRACT BRIDGE, but was earlier used to designate a REVOKE that had not yet become established. See REFUSE.

REOPEN THE BIDDING. See BALANCING.

REPEATED SQUEEZE. See TRIPLE SQUEEZE.

REPEATING TRIPLE SQUEEZE. See PROGRESSIVE SQUEEZE.

REPECHAGE. A second chance after being defeated in a knockout competition. At present it is in effect only in the Rosenblum Cup Teams, which takes place during the World Pairs Championships (played in even-numbered years not divisible by 4). Defeated teams move into a swiss competition. The five top teams in the swiss standings at the time the winners of the three brackets of knockouts are determined join the three losers of the last round of the knockout competition in a mini-knockout. The team winning the mini-knockout moves into the Rosenblum semifinals along with the three winners of the knockout brackets. In 1978, Poland, defeated earlier in the compeition, won the mini-knockout and then went on to win the Rosenblum Cup. See also DOUBLE KNOCKOUT.

REPLAY DUPLICATE. A form of duplicate in which just two pairs play against each other, playing the same boards but first in one position (i.e., North–South and then the other, East–West). Although this form of duplicate attained some currency in the Twenties, it quickly became obsolete simply because a board could so easily be remembered by the players. Even the process of playing the boards one way one week and the other the next was of no avail against pairs who had even the merest semblance of competent memories.

RE-RAISE. A colloquialism for opener's rebid of three of his suit after responder has raised to two:

1♠	2♠
3♠	

RESCUE. To bid another suit, or conceivably notrump, when partner has been doubled for penalties.

The most common rescuing situation arises when an overcall has been doubled. There are three points for the overcaller's partner to consider:

(1) His length in the doubled suit. The more cards he holds, the less desirable, a rescue becomes — it is rarely right with a doubleton, and virtually never right with more than two cards.

(2) The level of the potential rescue. Rescuing is more likely to be effective at the one-level, and may sometimes be attempted when holding a singleton or void in the doubled suit but no suit of more than five cards. See KOCK-WERNER REDOUBLE; SOS REDOUBLE. There is less case for rescuing if it must be done at a higher level.

(3) The quality of the rescuer's suit compared with

the likely quality of the doubled suit. There must be a reasonable expectation that the rescuer's suit is more substantial than the doubled suit. In most circumstances a strong six-card suit or a seven-card suit is necessary.

Another common rescue situation occurs when a 1 NT opening has been doubled. Here it is seldom right for responder to SIT if he has no high-card strength or if he has a long suit. See DEFENSE TO DOUBLE OF 1 NT.

RESCUE BID. A bid, based on a long suit, made with less than normal values because of a misfit with partner's bid suit after it has been doubled.

RESERVE PLAYER. In an event for teams of four or more members, any team member not currently playing. A reserve player is eligible to replace an active member during the current or later sessions, but only under conditions announced by the director or published in advance. In major tournaments reserve players are barred from watching their teammates, and usually they are not permitted to watch play at an adjoining table.

RESOCK, REWIND. To redouble (obsolescent slang).

RESPOND. To answer in the language of bidding. To pass, however, is not to respond.

RESPONDER'S REBID. Many bids on the second round by the responding hand are covered under separate headings: DELAYED GAME RAISE; DOUBLE RAISE, FOURTH SUIT FORCING; GOLDSCHMIDT; JUMP REBIDS BY RESPONDER; 1 NT RESPONSE; PREFERENCE; REVERSE; SINGLE RAISE; STAYMAN ON SECOND ROUND; 3 NT RESPONSE; TRIAL BID; TRIPLE RAISE; 2♣ REBID BY RESPONDER AS ONLY FORCE AFTER 1 NT REBID; 2 NT RESPONSE; UNBID MINOR SUIT FORCE.

Other situations which can arise are discussed below.

(1) *After three suits at the one-level*

(a)

1♣	1♡
1♠	1 NT

An ill-defined sequence in standard methods, but usually regarded as encouraging (8–10). This leaves unsolved problems at both ends of the range.

(a)	(b)
♠ 5	♠ J 7
♡ K 8 7 6 4	♡ A J 6 3 2
◊ Q J 7 4 2	◊ K J 5
♣ 9 3	♣ J 8 4

With hand (a) a pass is unthinkable; 1♠ is probably a 4-1 fit, and could even be a 3-1 fit. 1 NT is the only conceivable action, but is a considerable overbid if 1 NT is viewed as constructive. A plausible solution is to regard the 1 NT rebid as having the same strength as an original 1 NT response to 1♣ 6–9 or possibly 10.

Hand (b) offers an easy 2 NT rebid if that is nonforcing (see Jump Rebids by Responder); but in standard methods, with 2 NT forcing, responder must choose between an overbid of 2 NT, an under-

bid of 1 NT, or a *manufactured* 2 ◊ .

(b)

1♣	1♡
1♠	2♠

Usually indicates four-card trump support and 7–10 in high cards. But occasionally the raise must be given with three-card support, even without a ruffing value:

♠ K 7 2
♡ A K 4 2
◊ 7 3 2
♣ 10 8 6

After

1♣	1♡
1♠	

there is no sensible alternative to 2♠ .

Other sequences are listed under FOURTH SUIT FORCING; PREFERENCE; JUMP REBIDS BY RESPONDER.

(2) *After three suits ending at the two-level*

(c)

1◊	1♠
2♣	2◊

Normally a six-card suit and mildly encouraging; but if 3♣ is regarded as nonforcing, then 2◊ is discouraging.

(d)

1◊	1♠
2♣	2 NT

10–12 points in high cards, with at least a single stopper in the unbid suit. Similarly

1♠	2♣
2♡	2 NT

(e)

1◊	1♠
2♣	3♣

Also encouraging but not forcing, 10–12 points in high cards, and four-card, or conceivably five-card, club support.

Similarly

1♠	2♣
2♡	3♡

Other sequences are listed under Fourth Suit Forcing, Preference, and Jump Rebids by Responder.

(3) *After a 1 NT rebid*

(f)

1◊	1♡
1 NT	2♡

A six-card heart suit, presumably, and highly discouraging. Opener almost invariably passes.

(g)

1◊	1♡
1 NT	2◊

Discouraging, but game might still be possible if opener is able to give delayed preference for hearts.

(h)

1◊	1♡
1 NT	2♣

Nonforcing and neutral. The opener should not rebid 2 NT, but may give preference to 2♡ or raise to 3♣ , either of which might lead to a game. Responder is likely to have five hearts and four or five clubs. With only four clubs he should not retreat from 1 NT automatically: with 3–5–1–4 distribution it may be best to leave 1 NT, especially in a pair contest. This change of suit is forcing in ROTH-STONE.

(i)

1 ◇	1 ♡
1 NT	2 NT

Nonforcing and encouraging. The strength depends on the range of the 1 NT rebid, but responder indicates that the combined hands have a minimum of 23–24 points.

(j)

1 ◇	1 ♡
1 NT	2 ♠

See REVERSE.

(k)

1 ◇	1 ♡
1 NT	3 ♣

A jump shift, forcing to game. An unbalanced distribution, and very likely a weakness in the unbid suit, spades.

(l)

1 ◇	1 ♡
1 NT	3 ◇

Forcing in standard methods, but nonforcing in ACOL and in some expert partnerships.

(m)

1 ◇	1 ♡
1 NT	3 ♡

Forcing in *standard*, but the nonforcing treatment is popular and more logical. A game-going hand with a six-card heart suit can jump to 4 ♡.

(4) *After a minimum rebid in the original suit*

(n)

1 ◇	1 ♠
2 ◇	2 ♠

Encouraging with a six-card suit. With a hand without prospects, responder can pass 2 ◇.

(o)

1 ◇	1 ♠
2 ◇	2 ♡ or
	3 ♣

Forcing, probably with 5–5 or 5–4 distribution. But it may be necessary to make the rebid in a three-card suit:

♠ A Q 5 4 3	♠ A Q 5 4 3
♡ A Q 4	♡ 8 4
◇ J 6 2	◇ J 6 2
♣ 8 4	♣ A Q 4

(p)

1 ◇	1 ♠
2 ◇	2 NT

Encouraging but nonforcing. 10–12 points and presumably guards in both unbid suits.

(q)

1 ◇	1 ♠
2 ◇	3 ◇

Encouraging but not forcing. Probably 10–12 points and weak in the unbid suits.

(5) *After a single raise of responder's suit*

(r)

1 ◇	1 ♠
2 ♠	2 NT

Encouraging and nonforcing. Presumably stoppers in the unbid suits, 10–12 points, a four-card spade

suit.

(s)

1 ◇	1 ♠
2 ♠	3 ◇

Encouraging and nonforcing. 10–12 points. Probably a four-card spade suit with four or five diamonds.

(t)

1 ◇	1 ♠
2 ♠	3 ♣

Forcing, and perhaps only a three-card club suit. Responder may be aiming for 3 NT, or trying to find whether the opener has some reserve strength for a spade game.

(u)

1 ◇	1 ♠
2 ♠	3 ♠

Encouraging but not forcing. Probably a six-card spade suit with no special features in the unbid suits.

RESPONDING HAND. The hand, or player, facing opening bidder; the partner of the initial bidder.

RESPONDING TO OVERCALLS. There are some essential differences between responding to an overcall and responding to an opening bid. In choosing the best action, responder should take into consideration the following facts:

(1) The overcaller need not have as many as 13 high card points.

(2) Unless responder has a good trump fit, there usually will not be a game.

(3) Although the overcaller has announced possession of a strong five-card or longer suit (occasionally a four-card suit headed by top honors at the one level), opener has neither guaranteed nor implied support of any other suit.

(4) It is not necessary to respond to an overcall, even with a fairly good hand, unless responder has trump support.

(5) There are very few forcing responses to an overcall.

Because so many responses to overcalls are not forcing in STANDARD AMERICAN, many players have adopted the cuebid in the opponent's suit as an all-purpose force. The cuebid usually shows a forward-going hand interested in game and asks partner for a further description of his hand. If the overcaller merely rebids the same suit, that indicates a minimum for the overcall, and the cuebidder can pass. If the overcaller bids anything else, however, the bid shows better than a minimum. Game almost always will be reached in these circumstances, and slam is not at all out of the question.

The responder has to be very careful in the choice of responses, other than the cuebid, because any bid may be the final bid for his side.

Left-hand opponent opens 1 ◇ and partner overcalls 1 ♠. You hold:

♠ Q 9 6 5 4
♡ 6 5
◇ 4
♣ A 10 8 4 2

Bid 4 ♠. There are many hands your partner can

hold which will produce game opposite this dummy. And even if 4♠ doesn't make, the contract could easily be a fine save against the opponents' game.

> ♠ Q 6 5
> ♡ K 8 4
> ◇ 5 3
> ♣ A K 8 4 2

Bid 2◇. This is a good offensive hand, but much depends on the strength of partner's overcall. If partner rebids 2♠, chances for game are remote and responder should pass. However, any other bid by opener should be enough incentive to reach at least a game. Slam is not out of the question — partner could hold:

> ♠ A K J 8 4 3
> ♡ A 6
> ◇ 4
> ♣ Q 10 9 5

There are many players who differentiate between a new-suit response at the one level and one at the two level. They consider the one-level responses to be nonforcing. However, they feel a two-level new-suit response should be considered forcing because a two-level overcall usually is equivalent to an opening bid.

A jump cuebid — 1◇–1♠–Pass–3◇ — often is used in modern systems. The most common meaning for this bid is a limit raise in the overcaller's suit, leaving the simple cuebid as a general direction bid seeking further information.

In general, single raises are constructive, but double raises are preemptive in nature.

Responses to notrump overcalls in general are a matter of partnership agreement. Many players agree that all systems (Jacoby Transfers, Stayman, etc.) are off — others agree that all systems are still on, just as if partner had opened 1 NT. The usual method of seeking a major-suit fit, however, is to cuebid the opponent's suit — 1◇–1 NT–Pass–2◇ asks the notrump overcaller to bid a four-card major if he has one, otherwise to bid 2 NT.

RESPONSE. Usually bid by a player whose partner has opened the bidding, but may be used to describe a response to a takeout double, cuebid, conventional bid, etc. For responding to an opening bid of one, see CHOICE OF SUIT; DOUBLE RAISE; JUMP SHIFT; 1 NT RESPONSE; ONE-OVER-ONE RESPONSE; PREEMPTIVE RESPONSE; SINGLE RAISE; SPLINTER BID; 3 NT RESPONSE; TRIPLE RAISE; 2 NT RESPONSE; TWO-OVER-ONE RESPONSE; UP THE LINE.

RESPONSES OVER OPPONENT'S TAKEOUT DOUBLE. The usual treatment is:

(1) A *suit response* is nonforcing and unconstructive, but promises at least a five-card suit. At the two-level (e.g., 1♡—double—2♣ a six-card suit is probable.

(2) *1 NT* is mildly constructive, with about 7–9 points.

(3) A *single raise* is preemptive, and slightly weaker than it would be without the double.

(4) A *double raise* is preemptive, showing a distributional hand which would normally make a single raise.

(5) A *triple raise* is also preemptive, with extra playing-trick strength.

(6) A *redouble*, showing almost any strong hand with a minimum point-count of about 10. Usually the redoubler will have a defensive hand, and the opening bidder will not take a further bid at his next turn unless he has a distributional hand unsuited to defense.

With a four-card or better fit in the opener's suit, a redouble is unattractive because it makes it simple for the opponents to find a fit for a possible save. A direct raise to game in a major may be preferable, and there is a conventional possibility:

(7) *2 NT* and *3 NT* have no natural meaning, because a good hand with balanced distribution would redouble. Some players, following the ACOL SYSTEM, use 2 NT to denote a hand which would have made a LIMIT JUMP RAISE to three of opener's suit if there had been no double. This method is popularly known as JORDAN. By a logical extension, 3 NT can be used to show a strong raise to game when the opening bid was a major suit. For alternative treatments, see 2 NT RESPONSE (Over Opponent's Takeout Double).

(8) *Jump suit responses* (e.g., 1◇—double—2♠). This bid shows at least a six-card suit, but the strength is a matter of partnership agreement. There are four schools of thought: (1) forcing to game; (2) forcing for one round; (3) not forcing and a hand of intermediate strength (about 9 points in high cards); (4) preemptive, say Q–J–x–x–x–x and no other asset.

(9) A *pass* usually shows a weak hand unsuitable for any positive action. But a pass followed by a bid on the following round can be used to show a hand with fair defensive strength. For example:

> ♠ A 5 3
> ♡ Q 6 4
> ◇ K 6 3 2
> ♣ 7 4 3

If partner's 1♠ opening is doubled, a possible tactic is to pass and bid 2♣ on the next round. This must show a stronger hand than an immediate bid of 2♣.

Some players treat a suit response over a double as forcing, and a small minority bid exactly as they would have done without the double.

RESPONSIVE DOUBLE (originated by Dr. F. Fielding-Reid, Dania FL). The use of a double for takeout when there has been an immediate raise to the two- or three-level over partner's TAKEOUT DOUBLE. For example:

WEST	NORTH	EAST	SOUTH
1◇	Dbl	2◇	?

South holds:

> ♠ J 6 5 2
> ♡ Q 10 9 5
> ◇ 3
> ♣ Q 7 6 3

It would be cowardly to pass, and South is not nearly strong enough to make a CUEBID of 3◇. He does not want to guess which suit to bid, so he makes a responsive double. In this situation, it is very seldom that South will wish to make a PENALTY DOUBLE.

The double would also be used if East had raised to 3◇ instead of 2◇.

The doubler may have a balanced hand if his high-card strength is somewhat improved:

♠ 4 3 2
♡ A Q 9
◇ Q 8 5 2
♣ J 8 6

This would be ideal for a responsive double if an opening spade bid were doubled and raised to 2♠, and would be the most convenient action if the opposition had bid clubs, diamonds or hearts.

The minimum strength required for a responsive double varies slightly with the level of the auction. With a balanced hand, a double of 2♠ might be made with 6 points; a double of 3♠ would need at least 9 points.

The convention normally applies to any bid at the two- or three-level, but a few players use a double of 3♡ or 3♠ for penalties.

An extension of the responsive idea can be used in the following situation:

WEST	NORTH	EAST	SOUTH
	1♡	2♣	2♡
Dbl			

A penalty double of a free raise is very seldom required, so by partnership agreement West's double can show length in spades and diamonds.

RESTRICTED CHOICE. The play of a card which may have been selected as a choice of equal plays increases the chance that the player started with a holding in which his choice was restricted.

The Rule of Restricted Choice is a rule of card play which can enable the declarer to take the correct action in situations which used to be thought of as guesswork.

The underlying principles were first discussed by ALAN TRUSCOTT in the *Contract Bridge Journal*. Later, these principles were unified by TERENCE REESE in his book, *Master Play*.

THE BASIC PRINCIPLE

Following is the sort of card combination which can call the Rule of Restricted Choice into operation:

Example 1:

NORTH (dummy)
♠ Q J 9

SOUTH (declarer)
♠ 4 3 2

South has to develop a trick in this suit. He leads low to dummy's queen and East wins with the king. Upon regaining the lead, South again leads toward the North hand. Should South play the jack or 9 from dummy? Is one play superior or is South faced with a guess?

If either East or West now holds both the ace and 10, South's play is immaterial. The jack will score if West holds the ace and East holds the 10. The 9 is winning play if West holds the 10 and East holds the ace. Thus the following summary of the situation can be constructed:

	West originally held:	East originally held:
Jack gains when	A	K 10
9 gains when	10	A K

It is important to notice that this summary is sufficient, for when it comes time for South to make the final decision, he already knows that East held the king. Thus, South can exclude from the reckoning all distributions in which East does not hold the king.

The two possible distributions of the East–West honors given above are equally likely to occur, but the two plays are not of equal merit. To the statement, "the two crucial defensive holdings are equally likely," should be added, "provided there is no information regarding the distribution of honor cards in the suit."

In fact, there is such information. There is a direct inference to be drawn from the fact that East won the first trick with the *king*. Consider the first possible honor holding given above. If this is the actual distribution of East–West honor cards, East was forced to play his ♠ K on the first round; his choice was restricted. This is not true in the second case, where East had the option of winning the first trick with the *ace* instead of the king. His choice was *not* restricted.

It can be presumed that if East started with A–K, he would play the ace some percentage of the time. When East actually plays the king on the first round, the probability that he started with the A–K is diminished because with both honors *he might have played the other one.*

For the sake of argument, assume that East would play his equal honors with equal frequency, winning with the king 50% of the time and winning with the ace 50% of the time. It can be demonstrated that this is, in fact, East's best strategy.

Under this assumption, imagine that declarer is playing the Example 1 combination 200 times. On 100 of these deals, East starts with the ♠K-10. On the other 100 deals, East starts with the ♠A-K. Since, on the second 100 deals, East wins with the king only 50 times, certain things become clear.

East wins the king from an honor holding of K-10 on 100 occasions. But East wins the king from an honor holding of A-K on only 50 occasions. On the other 50 deals on which East hold A-K, he wins with the ace!

From this one may conclude that the jack is the superior play on the second round of spades. In fact, it is exactly twice as good a play as the 9. The position is exactly the same if East wins the first trick with the ace and not the king.

The above conclusions may be checked by examining all possible honor distributions. If either defender holds *all three* honors, declarer will succeed or fail regardless of his plays, so these combinations can be omitted. This leaves the following possibilities, all equally probable before the suit is played for the first time:

	West holds	East holds
(a)	A K	10
(b)	A 10	K

(c)	K 10	A
(d)	A	K 10
(e)	K	A 10
(f)	10	A K

Each of the above situations is equally probable. Assume that each case occurs 100 times in 600 deals in all. Since East will (it is assumed) play equal honors with equal frequency, he wins a high honor on the first round on the following occasions:

	East wins with ♠ A	East wins with ♠ K
(a)	0	0
(b)	0	100
(c)	100	0
(d)	0	100
(e)	100	0
(f)	50	50
TOTAL	250	250

Thus, East will win with a specified honor 250 times. Of these 250 times, declarer triumphs automatically in cases (b) or (c); a total of 100. Of the remaining 150, the jack is the winning play 100 times in case (d) or (e), but the 9 is right only 50 times in case (f).

Thus declarer's play of a card combination such as Example 1, far from being a blind guess, is subject to very definite analysis.

The logic behind the rule is simple. If the player in question had a choice of plays, he might have elected the other option. Therefore, there is a presumption that he did not have the option. Thus, in Example 1, when East wins with the ♠K, the chances favor the play of the jack on the second round. The jack play caters to the situation in which East started with ♠K–10, where he had no choice of plays on the first round, rather than the situation in which East had a choice of plays from A–K.

Other Card Combinations. The Rule of Restricted Choice can be applied to many more combinations:
Example 2:

NORTH (dummy)
J 9 4

SOUTH (declarer)
Q 3 2

South needs one trick, and is forced to attack the suit himself. He leads low to the queen, and West wins with a high honor. Later, South leads again toward the North hand. If West follows low, what should South do?

Applying the Rule of Restricted Choice, South should reason that if West held both high honors, he might have chosen the other one to capture the queen. But if West started with the high honor and the 10, his choice was restricted. The percentage play is the 9.

Example 3:

NORTH (dummy)
K 10 9

SOUTH (declarer)
4 3 2

South leads toward the North hand and finesses the 9, losing to a middle honor. On the next lead, South should finesse the 10.

A Mistake to Avoid. Care must be taken to avoid mistaken applications of the Rule of Restricted Choice.
Example 4:

NORTH (dummy)
K J 9

SOUTH (declarer)
4 3 2

South requires one trick here. He leads up to the North hand, and decides to play the jack. East wins with the queen. Declarer has gained no information whatsoever as to the distribution of the outstanding honors. On the next lead declarer is faced with a guess. *There was no choice of plays involved for East*, who would win the jack with the queen whenever he held that card. The Rule of Restricted Choice does not apply.

Example 5:

NORTH (dummy)
♠ A Q 10 7 6 5

SOUTH (declarer)
♠ 4 3 2

South hopes to take six tricks here, and leads a spade to North's queen, which East wins with the king. Later, South wants to pick up the remainder of the suit. Once again, there is no application of the Rule of Restricted Choice. The percentage play (barring side distributional inferences) is the ace.

Lower Odds. In the above examples of the Rule of Restricted Choice, declarer was faced with a choice of plays, one of which was exactly twice as good as the other. Restricted Choice situations do not always give such good odds as that.

There is a large class of card combinations in which declarer's correct play under the Rule of Restricted Choice gives him less than two-to-one odds.

Example 6:

NORTH (dummy)
K 10 9 8 7 6

SOUTH (declarer)
A 3 2

South leads the ace from his hand, West follows with the 4 and East drops the QUACK.* South leads toward the dummy, and West follows with the 5. Assuming (as always) no important inferences to be drawn from the play of other suits, how should South play?

To answer that question, one starts by reflecting that the following distribution of East–West cards

(a)	WEST	EAST
	5 4	Q J

is *slightly* more probable (before the suit is played) than the following distribution:

(b)	WEST	EAST
	Q 5 4	J

---

*We have already shown that from declarer's point of view it makes no difference whether East plays the queen or jack. Thus, terminology such as *quack* can be used to simplify both the discussion and the thinking.

Also, the chance of East holding Q–J is *slightly* more probable than the following distribution:

(c)	WEST	EAST
	J 5 4	Q

But East is *less* likely to have Q–J doubleton than he is to have a singleton *quack*. In other words, (b) and (c) together are greater than (a).

Thus, the correct play on the second round is to finesse. The odds favoring this play as opposed to the drop are slightly less than two to one.

Example 7:

NORTH (dummy)
A J 10 9 8 7

SOUTH (declarer)
4 3 2

South wishes to take five tricks. The best play is to take two finesses. This fails to bring in the suit (if such was possible) only when East holds K–Q. It is easily seen that all other plays are inferior.

A common argument given about this combination is the following: It is best to take two finesses because it gains against more distributions than any other play. Once you have finessed the first time, you must follow through and finesse the second time.

This is an unfortunate way to get the right answer. According to the first part of this argument, if you finesse the jack and it loses to the king or queen, when you lead up to the dummy the second time, you have two possible combinations of cards:

	West holds	East holds
Case 1	6 5	K Q
Case 2 (a)	K 6 5	Q
(b)	Q 6 5	K

After the first trick, either Case 2 (a) or Case 2 (b) disappears, so only two relevant combinations remain, and the first is (initially) more probable. Therefore, the argument indicates playing for the drop on the second round.

The correct argument for the second finesse is that if East started with a singleton honor, his choice was restricted on the first round. Thus, the odds on the second finesse are *almost* two to one.

Another Mistake to Avoid. Some combinations are superficially similar to those in the last section, but do not admit exact application of the Rule of Restricted Choice.

Example 8:

NORTH (dummy)
A 2

SOUTH (declarer)
K Q 9 8 7 6

Declarer leads the 6 to the ace in dummy, and West plays the 10 or jack. According to the principles developed in the previous section, although an original West holding of doubleton J–10 is more likely than the holding of a particular singleton honor, it is now more likely that West had a singleton honor than two honors doubleton.

That is true so far as it goes, but declarer should *not* finesse on the second round. West may well have J–10–3!

Example 9:

NORTH (dummy)
A 2

SOUTH (declarer)
K 9 8 7 6

South needs three tricks before the defense makes two. He leads the 6 to the ace, and West plays the jack. If West has the singleton jack, South must finesse coming back. Declarer must avoid a mistaken application of the Rule of Restricted Choice. It is true that a singleton jack is more likely than either Q–J or J–10 doubleton. But the king is the right play if West has *either* of the two doubleton honor combinations, and these two together exceed the probability of a singleton jack.

Higher Odds. There are still other types of suit combinations that admit application of the Rule of Restricted Choice. Sometimes the declarer can obtain even higher odds than two-to-one in favor of the correct play. The odds mount appreciably in the following three examples:

Example 10:

NORTH (dummy)
A K Q 10

SOUTH (declarer)
4 3 2

Declarer plays off the A–K, and the jack fails to drop. He later leads toward the tenace in the North hand. If West follows with a small card, the percentage play is the queen. Assuming no relevant information about the side suits, East is a slight favorite to hold the jack.

Example 11:

NORTH (dummy)
A K Q 9

SOUTH (declarer)
4 3 2

Dummy's holding is slightly weaker than in the previous example. Declarer cashes the A–K. West follows with two small cards, but East drops an honor. Best play is to enter the South hand and finesse. If West follows to the third round with a small card, it is slightly less than two to one that he holds the missing honor.

Example 12:

NORTH (dummy)
A K Q 8

SOUTH (declarer)
4 3 2

Dummy's holding has been further debilitated — but the Rule of Restricted Choice is even more rewarding. When the ace and king are cashed, East drops two of the missing honors. Declarer's best play is to enter the South hand and finesse the 8.

The odds in favor of this play can be computed as follows. If East held J–10–9 originally, there were six ways in which he could have played two honors to the first two tricks. Only one of these ways was chosen; therefore the weight of this combination is only one-sixth its original chance. But if East held two blank honors originally, he still had two ways to play them and chose one of them. Therefore this combination carries only half its original weight. J-10-9 is slightly more likely than any particular doubleton (before any cards are played), but the finesse still has odds of almost three to one in its favor.

Following is an example of such a situation from actual play in a pair tournament:

Example 13:

NORTH (dummy)
2

SOUTH (declarer)
Q J 8 7 6 5 4

Declarer entered the North hand, and led the singleton deuce. East followed with the 9. South contributed the jack, and West won with the king. South later regained the lead, and was forced to lead a trump from his own hand. Should he play the queen or the 8?

If the suit originally split 4-1, the card played at this stage is of no significance. Thus a 3-2 division can be assumed. If the doubleton was in the East hand, the 9 could have come from A-9 or 10-9, holdings which initially were equally likely. But if East had 10-9, he would presumably have played the 10 half the time. Furthermore, if East held 10-9, West must have started with A-K-3 and *he* might have won with the ace instead of the king. The Rule of Restricted Choice can be applied against *both* opponents in the same suit! Furthermore, the 9 could have come from 10-9-3.

Since the play of a small card on the second round caters to both applications of the Rule of Restricted Choice *and* guards against the false card, it is clearly the superior play.

The odds in favor of this play as opposed to the play of the queen can be computed as follows: Disregarding the false card, the odds in favor of the play of a small card are four to one. If East held A-9, the play of both opponents was restricted. There was only one way in which they could have played their cards. If East held 10-9, however, each opponent had a choice of two plays, giving them four different ways in which their cards could have been played.

Now consider the case in which East may have falsecarded from 10-9-3. This is another specific distribution of cards divided three and two, so it was originally equally likely as all the others. However, the weight of this double application of the Rule of Restricted Choice still applies. Thus, the correct odds are five to one.

Applications. An application of the Rule of Restricted Choice would have saved the United States team several IMPs on this deal from the 1958 Bermuda Bowl match against Italy.

Example 14:

♠ K 4 2
♡ 8 3
◇ K 9 3 2
♣ A K 8 7

♠ A 5
♡ Q 10 9
◇ A Q J 7 6 5
♣ 10 4

SOUTH	NORTH
1 ◇	2 ♣
2 ◇	2 ♠
2 NT	3 NT
Pass	

West led the ♡ 5 which East won with the king. A low heart was returned and South was faced with a guess. After consideration, he played the queen. This proved to be the wrong move as West had led from A-x-x.

The consensus of expert opinion was that South's play was correct. The *Bridge World* commentator wrote:

"... I think South's play is correct. If the hearts are 4-4, South's play makes relatively little difference; only if the lead was from three is it crucial. And a lead from three to the jack seems a little more attractive than from three to an ace."

This point — and psychological considerations — are important factors in deciding which card to play. But such factors have a lot of ground to make up. On the auction, a heart lead might be expected from *any* holding of three to an honor. And according to the Rule of Restricted Choice, the 10 is a two-to-one percentage favorite, for if East had started with five hearts to the A-K, he might have played the ace on the first round. With five hearts to the K-J, his choice was restricted to the play of the king. Another way of looking at it is that the combination of A-x-x and K-x-x in West's hand are together twice as likely as J-x-x.

Here is another situation in which the Rule of Restricted Choice should be applied when the defenders attack a suit.

Example 15:

♠ A K J 3
♡ Q
◇ 10 8 4
♣ A K J 10 5

♠ Q 10 9 8 6
♡ J 10 5
◇ K 3 2
♣ Q 9

At rubber bridge South is declarer at 4 ♠ with no East-West bidding.

West leads a small heart which East wins with the ace. It is apparent that the contract will be made unless the defense takes three diamond tricks. East shifts to the quack of diamonds.

South knows that East is a good enough player to have shifted to the quack of diamonds from any of these holdings:

(1) ace, quack and small card(s)
(2) queen, jack and small card(s)
(3) quack and small card(s)

Even with restricted choice considerations put aside (which makes (2) less probable), playing low caters only to case (2) so South goes up with the king.

Naturally, West takes the ◇ A and continues with a small diamond. Now the 9 becomes important. The only relevant holdings now are:

(4) East started with Q-J and small card(s) but not the 9. (If East led from Q-J-9, the game is over.)

(5) East started with quack–9 and possibly small card(s).

Q–J and quack–9 seem to be equally likely possibilities but, as usual, the Rule of Restricted Choice tells us that with (4) East might have selected the other honor to lead. And so the correct play is the 10.

Similar considerations can arise when the declarer attacks a suit.

Example 16:

    ♠ Q 10 9 7 6
    ♡ 4 2
    ◇ 5 3
    ♣ K 6 5 4

    ♠ A K J 8
    ♡ A K 3
    ◇ K 4 2
    ♣ 10 9 7

South plays in 4♠ at rubber bridge. West leads the ◇ Q, East takes the ace, and returns the suit. South wins, ruffs his last diamond in dummy (East discarding a heart), plays a trump to the ace, and plays three rounds of hearts. West discards a diamond on the third round of hearts, which is ruffed in dummy. Now a spade to the king extracts both remaining trumps. Since both defenders have shown with two spades and 6–2 in the red suits, it is clear that both have three clubs, and the position is:

Example 17:

    NORTH
    ♠ 10
    ♡ —
    ◇ —
    ♣ K 6 5 4

    SOUTH
    ♠ J 8
    ♡ —
    ◇ —
    ♣ 10 9 7

South needs one club trick (or a ruff and sluff) to make his contract. He leads the 9 (it can be verified that this is a superior play to the 7), and West plays the queen.

This play would be made from any of the holdings of ♣ A–Q–x, ♣ Q–J–x, or ♣ Q–x–x. Even with Restricted Choice set aside, the king is the best play. But East wins and returns a low club.

South must rely on the Rule of Restricted Choice and play the 10.

A little-known safety play shows that the Rule of Restricted Choice can be applied to spot cards as well as honors.

Example 18:

    NORTH (dummy)
    J 7 6 5

    SOUTH (declarer)
    A Q 9 8

South has adequate entries to both hands, and needs three tricks in this suit. The correct play is to lead low from the North hand and finesse the queen. If this loses to the king, South next plays the ace. It is easily verified that this play will fail to produce three

tricks only when West holds the blank king.

Suppose it be asked: why, after West wins the king, should declarer play West for the remaining cards rather than East?

Suppose East played the 3 on the first round of the suit. If East started with 10–4–3–2, he had a choice of three low spots to play on the first round. He might equally well have played any of the low cards, therefore this holding can be counted only with a weight of one-third. On the other hand, if East started with the singleton three, his choice was restricted.

To check this computation, notice that if declarer goes after the suit with the intention of playing the ace on the second round, he loses only when West starts with the singleton king (one distribution) but if he intends to play to the jack on the second round, he loses when East starts with the singleton 4, 3, or 2 (three distributions). As has been seen, the correct odds can always be discovered by returning to the original possibilities before any cards have been played (see Example 1).

The Rule of Restricted Choice may even be applied to the opening lead.

Example 19:

    ♠ A 4 3 2
    ♡ A K 4 3 2
    ◇ J 10
    ♣ J 2

    ♠ K Q J 10 9 8
    ♡ 6 5
    ♣ K Q
    ♣ A Q 10

NORTH	SOUTH
1♡	4 NT
5♡	6♠
Pass	

West leads the ◇ 7, and East wins with the ace. East shifts to a low club. Should South finesse?

There are two plays open to declarer. First, he can duck the club lead, hoping that East has the king. Second, he can rise with the ace, draw trump, and try to ruff out the heart suit. This play depends on a 3–3 heart split.

The chance of an even split in hearts is about 36%. The club finesse appears to offer a 50% chance, and therefore seems the better play. However, South must consider West's choice of opening leads. If East holds the ♣K, West started with a collection of small cards in each minor suit. If this was the case, he would have led a club about half the time. Since West did *not* lead a club, there is some presumption that his club–diamond holdings were not equivalent. If we assume West would lead a club half the time with equal minor suit holdings, the club finesse is only a 33% chance, and should therefore be rejected in favor of the attempt to split the hearts 3–3.

                    Jeff Rubens

RESULT PLAYER. A partner (or kibitzer) who helpfully suggests a line of play that would have been successful after declarer has failed with a different line of play. *Second guesser* is a synonym..

RETAIN THE LEAD. To continue to lead the first card to a trick by virtue of having won the previous trick.

REVALUATION. The reassessment of a hand in the light of the bidding. Certain features of a hand may improve or deteriorate in value in the light of the bidding around the table. See DISTRIBUTIONAL COUNTS.

If partner shows a strong two-suited hand, secondary suit honors are of greater significance in those suits, but are probably useless in the other suits. A shortage in partner's side suit, together with a few trumps, is more valuable than a shortage in another suit which is likely to be duplicated.

Kings and queens in a suit bid by an opponent improve if the bid was on the right, and deteriorate if the bid was on the left (see POSITIONAL FACTOR).

A holding of three small cards in a suit bid by an opponent at a low level is a liability, but improves if the opponents raise the suit strongly to a high level. It is then reasonable to assume that partner has no more than a singleton. In such circumstances a doubleton is less attractive, because there is an increased chance that there will be two losers.

REVERSE. An unforced rebid at the level of two or more in a higher ranking suit than that bid originally — usually a strength-showing bid. The English definition of a reverse by the opener is slightly wider in scope: a bid of a third suit in an uncontested auction which prevents responder from returning to the original suit at the level of two. This allows for the situation described in England as a high reverse. The following are standard reversing sequences:

WEST	EAST	WEST	EAST
1♣	1♠	1♡	2♢
2♡		2♠	

Examples of reverses by responder:

WEST	EAST	WEST	EAST
1♢	1♡	1♠	1♢
2♢	2♠	1♠	2♡

All reverses, by opener or responder, show strong game possibilities — the combined strength is rarely less than 23 points. In most systems, reverses imply that the first-bid suit consists of at least five cards and the second is shorter.

There has been a change of thinking concerning reverses when the Two Over One forcing to game system is used.

WEST	EAST
1♡	2♣
2♠	

Since the two-level response to the opening bid already created a situation that called for reaching game under most circumstances, the reverse by opener does not necessarily show any additional strength beyond the opening bid.

In traditional methods reverses are not forcing after a one-level response. Many experts, particularly those of the scientific school, treat them as forcing. Whether this applies to 1♡–1 NT-2♠ is a doubtful point.

If all four suits are bid, it is doubtful whether the term reverse should be applied, and the inference

that the reverser's orginal suit is at least five cards in length is less strong. See FOURTH SUIT FORCING and LEBENSOLD CONVENTION.

REVERSE COUNT. A method of giving count by playing low-high to indicate an even number of cards and playing high-low to indicate an odd number of cards.

REVERSE DISCARDS. See UPSIDE-DOWN SIGNALS.

REVERSE DRURY. A variation of the DRURY convention in which opener's responses to the 2♣ inquiry are changed. A rebid of opener's suit is the only negative rebid opener has. Other rebids are natural and forward-going. The advantages of this method are (1) by returning to his suit opener is taking up the most space, making it harder for the opponents to enter the auction; and (2) the opponents are deprived of the opportunity to make a lead-directing double of 2♢.

REVERSE FLANNERY. An opening bid of 2♢ to show a minimum opening hand with four hearts and five spades. This convention is used almost solely by pairs that use CANAPÉ styles of bidding, e.g., BLUE TEAM CLUB, in which this distribution is difficult to show. Since such pairs usually use a 2♢ opening for some other purpose, the reverse FLANNERY bid is usually 2♡.

REVERSE SEQUENCE LEAD. See RUSINOW LEAD.

REVERSE SWISS. The use of unusual jump shift rebids by opener to make a game raise of responder's suit, promising a wealth of high cards rather than just suitable distribution. For alternative uses of such jumps see FRAGMENT BIDS and SPLINTER BIDS.

REVERSING DUMMY. See DUMMY REVERSAL.

REVIEWING THE BIDDING. A player who does not hear a call distinctly may forthwith require that it be repeated. Any player may, when it is his turn to call, require that all previous calls be restated unless he is required by law to pass. In rubber bridge, after the auction is closed, any player may require such a review before his side has faced any cards. In duplicate, after the auction is closed, the declarer or either defender may require such a review at his own first turn to play. See LAWS (Law 20); LAWS OF DUPLICATE (Law 20). See also FACE DOWN LEADS; EXPLANATION OF ANY CALL OR PLAY.

REVOKE. The play of a card of another suit by a player who is able to follow suit, or comply with a lead penalty. Any player, including dummy if he has not forfeited his rights, may ask whether a play constitutes a revoke, and demand its correction.

If a revoke by a defender is corrected, the card played in error constitutes a penalty card.

A revoke becomes established after either member of the offending side leads or plays to the next trick, or if the revoking side makes a claim or concession. In rubber bridge there is a two-trick penalty if the revoking side won two or more tricks after the revoke trick, or a one-trick penalty if the revoking side won only one trick after the revoke trick. The trick on which the revoke occurred is counted as having been won after the revoke. In duplicate, if the revoking side won the revoke trick, that trick plus one of any tricks won thereafter by the revoking side are transferred from the revoking side; if the revoking side lost the revoke trick but won one or more tricks thereafter, the penalty is the transfer of one trick.

No player is ethically required to call attention to his own revoke, but a player should not commit a second revoke to conceal the first offense. See LAWS (Laws 61-64).

REVOLVING DISCARDS. A method of discarding which assigns a suit preference meaning to the first discard on any hand. There are two possible procedures which are similar in effect but vary slightly in execution.

(1) A low card calls for the suit below the suit in which the signal is given, and a high card for the suit above. The suits are considered in a circle with spades below clubs. Thus a low club discard on a heart lead would call for a spade, and a high club would call for a diamond. This version was developed in England, primarily for notrump defense, and is credited to J. Attwood.

(2) A low card calls for the lower-ranking of the other two suits, and a high card for the higher-ranking. This was advocated by HY LAVINTHAL, the inventor of suit preference by signaling, who gave this example:

```
              ♠ K 8 5
              ♡ 6
              ◇ K 10 9 8 4
              ♣ Q 7 3 2
   ♠ Q J 4 2              ♠ 10 7 3
   ♡ J 9 7 3 2           ♡ A Q 5
   ◇ A 6 5               ◇ 7 2
   ♣ 9                   ♣ J 10 8 6 4
              ♠ A 9 6
              ♡ K 10 8 4
              ◇ Q J 3
              ♣ A K 5
```

South plays in 3 NT after opening 1 NT. West leads the ♡3, and East correctly plays the queen. (After the play of the ace there would be no way to defeat the contract.) South wins the ♡Q with the king, and leads diamonds. West holds up the ace until the third round in order to get a signal from East. Normal signals would not help, because East cannot spare a heart, and a black-suit discard would be unenlightening. Using the Lavinthal discard signal the ♣4 asks for a heart, and the ♣10 would carry the same message. Using the revolving method given in (1), the ♣3 or the ♣J would be appropriate.

REX BRIDGE. A Swedish variation on contract in which any player may introduce a Rex call at any time, ranking between spades and hearts. It is a notrump contract except that the ace of each suit ranks below the deuce, and the king is the high card in each suit, other cards maintaining their rank with respect to the king.

R/H 4 NT CONVENTION. A nonjump bid of 4 NT after a trump suit has been established to ask about the three top trump honors. Partner responds to 4 NT by bidding five of the trump suit with none of the top three trump honors, 5 NT with all three honors, or a nontrump suit with one or two honors, as follows:

Lowest side suit	= king or queen.
Middle side suit	= ace.
Highest side suit	= any two of the top three honors.

RHYTHM. Bidding and play at a uniform speed. The stress here is on uniformity and not on speed. An expert player attempts to foresee the possible problems that may evolve during the bidding of a hand before choosing his first action so that he may avoid the agony of a later HUDDLE. Since a good player knows that a huddle followed by a pass, or even a double, places the onus on his partner not to be influenced by the fact that he had a problem, he will try to solve his future problems before they occur rather than later.

In the play of the hand, the shrewd declarer will sometimes attempt to cause opponents to be careless in the defense by playing with unusual rapidity, as though the hand was practically a PIANOLA. When confronted by a rapid tempo on declarer's part, a thoughtful defender will deliberately slow his own tempo so that he will have the opportunity to analyze declarer's play to see whether or not he has a problem.

In the play of the hand, too, the necessity for defenders to establish a rhythmic tempo to their play is important. In attempting to locate a particular card, such as an adversely held ace or queen, declarer is frequently put on the right track by applying the old adage "he who hesitates, has it." While a declarer takes advantage of a hesitation at his own risk (see PROPRIETIES), the opponent who hesitates before making a play with intent to deceive the declarer is being downright unethical.

RIDE. (1) To take a finesse with, fail to cover; for example, "dummy's jack was led and declarer let it ride." (2) A large penalty, derived from underworld argot in which a victim is "taken for a ride" by his would-be murders.

RIFFLE. A light shuffle of the deck; a flexing of the deck with the cards bent and held between the fingers so that a rapid motion ensues as the pack is straightened out.

RIGHT-HAND PLAYER. The player who, in rotation, acts before the referencing player. There are distinctions in the rules between irregular acts committed by the right-hand or left-hand player. The term is generally used, however, to refer to the player on declarer's right, after play commences. See RHO for a similar term.

RIGHT SIDE. The hand of the declaring partnership which can more successfully cope with the opening lead against the chosen contract. For example, assuming all other suits are adequately stopped, the hand holding A–Q–x opposite partner's x–x–x is the *right side* from which to play the hand. Sometimes there is no right or wrong side.

The *rightness* of one side and *wrongness* of the other may relate to factors other than the safety of the declarer's holding in the suit led; for example, the inability of one defender to lead the suit profitably (e.g., from K–x–x–x when the declaring side has the ace and queen), or the inability of one defender to diagnose the most effective lead whereas from his partner's hand the right lead would be obvious.

Sometimes it is impossible to know on the basis of the two hands of the declaring partnership which side is the right side. For example, when East and West have the following heart holdings

	WEST	EAST
	♡ Q x	♡ A x

and a heart is led against 3 NT, declarer does not know even upon seeing dummy whether or not the hand is being played from the right side. In this case the *right* side is the side that requires the hand with the ♡K to be on lead.

RIGHTS, PLAYER'S. A player does not forfeit his rights if a director is called when an irregularity occurs. Neither does an opponent of the violator lose any rights if the violator or his partner is the first to call attention to the irregularity.

RIPO. See BLACKWOOD AFTER INTERFERENCE.

RIPSTRA. Over 1 NT, the use of an overcall in a minor to show a three-suited hand, devised by the late J. G. RIPSTRA, Wichita KS. The bid guarantees a shortage in the unbid minor:

(a)	(b)
♠ A Q 4 3	♠ A Q 8 4 3
♡ K J 6 2	♡ K J 6 2
◊ K 10 6 3	◊ 6
♣ 8	♣ Q 6 3

On (a) bid 2◊; on (b) bid 2♣. The strength qualifications for the bid naturally vary according to vulnerability. It can be made freely at favorable vulnerability and should rarely be made at unfavorable vulnerability.

Some players use the convention with greater emphasis on the major suits, employing it with, for example, a 5-5-2-1 distribution.

A disadvantage of the convention is that it has a relatively low frequency. It is more suited to matchpoint events than to rubber bridge or IMP scoring. It is, however, useful in defense against a GAMBLING 3 NT OPENING.

See also ASPRO; ASTRO; BROZEL; EXCLUSION BID; LANDY.

ROBERT COUP. The unnecessary expenditure of a trump in order to preserve a plain suit card to lead later in the play. (Analyzed and named by ROBERT DARVAS of Hungary.) (See hand at the top of right column.)

Spades are trump and East leads the ♡4. If South discards his diamond, his only other trick will be the ♠A. But if South ruffs and *leads* the ◊5, West will

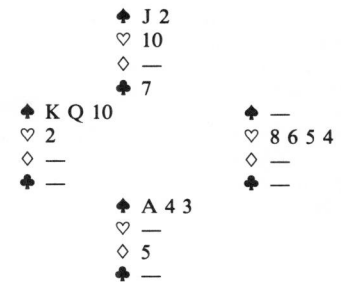

be limited to one trump trick.

The coup may be executed early in the play as in this example given by JEFF RUBENS.

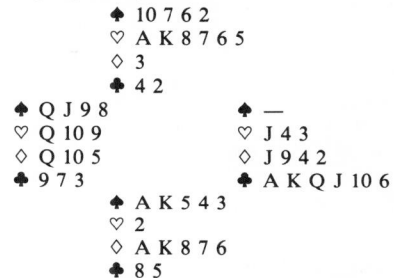

Against South's 4♠ contract, West leads the ♣9. East overtakes with the 10, cashes the ace and, unwisely, continues with a third round of clubs. South ruffs in the closed hand and plays the K♠; when the trump situations revealed, declarer is obliged to play West for completely balanced distribution. The ◊A-K and a diamond ruff, followed by the ♡A-K and a heart ruff, leads to this end position:

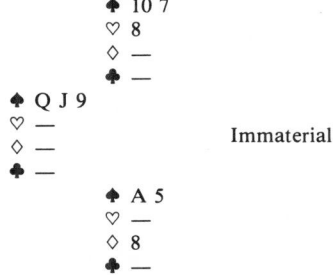

South produces his last diamond and West has no reply. The essential feature of the play was for South to reduce his trump holding by accepting the ruff and sluff in the long hand. The fifth spade could not be of use against any distribution but might get in the way if trumps broke badly. See also UNDERRUFF.

ROBERTSON POINT-COUNT. A point count published by Edmund Robertson in 1904.

Ace counts 7 points
King counts 5 points
Queen counts 3 points
Jack counts 2 points
10 counts 1 point.

A slight variation of this is the Bamberger point count used by the VIENNA SYSTEM, in which the jack counts one point and the 10 is not counted.

With a total of 64 points in the pack, if both hands are balanced, 39 points should produce a game in notrump or a major suit; and 52 points should produce a small slam.

ROBINSON. A defensive bidding system against the FORCING CLUB, devised by KIT WOOLSEY and named after his oft-times partner, STEVE ROBINSON. Double is strong, showing 16+ HCP. A 1 ◇ overcall shows either a black two-suiter or a red two-suiter. A 1 ♡ overcall shows either a major two-suiter or a minor two-suiter. 1 ♠ is natural, but can be very weak. 1 NT shows a club-heart two-suiter or a diamond-spade two-suiter. All bids of two of a suit are natural one-suited overcalls.

ROLLING BOX. A device used in major tournaments in Central and South America in combination with SCREENS. A square tray is mounted on rollers, providing spaces for all players to place their bidding cards (from the BIDDING BOX) in their proper turn. When the two players on one side of the screen have made their bids in this way, the box is rolled underneath the curtain.

This method has two obvious advantages and may be headed for wider use. It reduces the number of officials needed, since MONITORS are not required to repeat the bids in pairs. And there is a reduced chance of misunderstandings, which often occur in international championships with screens and monitors.

ROBOT BRIDGE PLAYER. A Bendix G-15 computer was built in the shape of a bridge robot, into which Prof. R. F. Jackson of The University of Delaware programmed bridge skills. It was displayed at a Western Regional in 1958, in a hand requiring a VIENNA COUP to make a grand slam. Opponents' plays were typed into Sputternik, as the robot was called, by the operator and Sputternik typed out his and the dummy's plays. See AUTOMATON CONTRACT BRIDGE PLAYER.

ROCK-CRUSHER HANDS. Hands of really enormous proportions, laden with points. A forcing two opening bid would usually qualify as a rock-crusher.

ROCKWELL TROPHY. For the North American Mixed Pair Championship, donated by Helen Rockwell in 1946; it replaced the HILLIARD TROPHY contested as a four-session event at the Fall North American Championships under which heading past results are listed.

ROMAN ASKING BIDS. A feature of the ROMAN SYSTEM which, in part, is also included in the 1969 version of the KAPLAN-SHEINWOLD SYSTEM. Both systems limit the use of the asking bids to jump bids that would otherwise be meaningless; so if an opening bid of 1 ♠ is raised to 3 ♠, 4 ♠ would be a cuebid and 5 ♠ would be an asking bid. The Roman responses are:

1st step	No control
2nd step	Singleton
3rd step	King
4th step	Ace
5th step	Void
6th step	A–K or A–Q (rare)

If responder cannot be short in the asked suit, the second and fifth steps are dropped. An older and better known version of Roman asking bids which is a feature of the KAPLAN-SHEINWOLD SYSTEM, restricts the responses to four steps. First step shows no control; second step shows king or singleton; third step shows ace of void; fourth step shows A–K (rarely A–Q) or perhaps singleton ace. These are called ALPHA ASKING BIDS.

Roman asking bids are also used in certain specialized sequences, the most common of which occur after a 1 ♠ opening bid and a jump in a new suit by opener. Responder bids according to his holding in opener's suit as follows:

1st step	Two or three low cards
2nd step	Singleton or void
3rd step	A–K, or Q singleton or doubleton
4th step	A–K or Q third
5th step	Four low cards
6th step	A–K, or Q fourth
7th step	Two of the top three honors
8th step	Two of the top three honors fourth
9th step	Three top honors

These are called BETA ASKING BIDS. See also ASKING BIDS; FULWILER CONVENTION; PRECISION ASKING BIDS; ROMEX TRUMP ASKING BIDS; SUPER PRECISION ASKING BIDS; SPLINTER BIDS; VOID-SHOWING BIDS.

ROMAN BLACKWOOD. A 4 NT convention which can help to determine which ace is missing if the partnership holds three. The responses are:

5 ♣	0-3 aces
5 ◇	1-4 aces
5 ♡	2 aces of the same color or rank
5 ♠	2 aces of unlike color and rank

A variation adopted by some BLUE TEAM CLUB users is to reverse the meanings of the traditional Roman responses of 5 ♣ and 5 ◇; the 5 ♣ response is used to show one or four aces in order to facilitate further non-Blackwood exploration of slam on the hands where slam is a more likely proposition.

A subsequent 5 NT bid asks for kings in the same way.

The 4 NT bidder can easily determine from the previous auction the meaning of a 5 ♣ or 5 ◇ response. 5 ♠ is also unambiguous, but a 5 ♡ response does not pinpoint the aces precisely. If, for example, a player with the ♣ A receives the response of 5 ♡, he knows that his partner holds the ♡ A and another ace.

A British variation is designed to avoid this ambiguity.:

5 ♡	2 aces of the same color
5 ♠	2 aces of the same rank
5 NT	2 aces of unlike color and rank

This may, however, rule out the possibility of asking for kings. The general advantage of the convention is that it may be effective when the 4 NT bidder has a void. If his partner has two aces, it is usually possible to tell whether the void is facing an ace.

When making a decision to go to the six-level, it is usually sufficient to know the number of aces possessed by the partnership. But for grand slam purposes, the identify of a missing king may be vital. For this reason some partnerships abandon the precise identification of the two aces held, and use the 5 ♡ response to show two aces with no extra values, and the 5 ♠ response to show two aces in a hand with extra values. Alternatively, there can be advantages in using these Roman responses in combination with other conventions. See ACE-SHOWING RESPONSES; BYZANTINE BLACKWOOD; ROMAN GERBER; ROMAN KEY CARD BLACKWOOD.

ROMAN GERBER. A modified version of the GERBER 4 ♣ slam convention. A response of 4 ◇ shows three aces or none; 4 ♡ shows four aces or one; 4 ♠ shows two aces. If the 4 ♣ bidder continues with the cheapest bid, he asks for kings and subsequently queens in the same way. The next-cheapest bid asks for clarification of the previous response. With one or three of the specified honor cards, responder bids the control he has or does not have. With two honors to be identified, he makes the minimum bid if they are of the same color; the second possible bid if they are unmatched in color and rank; and the third possible bid if both are majors or minors. See ACE IDENTIFICATION.

ROMAN JUMP OVERCALL. The use of a jump overcall to show a two-suited hand, specifically the suit bid and the next-higher-ranking suit excluding opener's suit. For example, if the opening bid is 1 ◇, an overcall of

2 ♡	shows ♡ and ♠
2 ♠	shows ♠ and ♣
3 ♣	shows ♣ and ♡

The strength shown is about the minimum for an opening bid or slightly more. Very strong two-suiters are shown by a conventional overcall of 2 NT.

ROMAN KEY CARD BLACKWOOD. A form of BLACKWOOD in which the king of trumps is counted as a fifth ace. It has gained in popularity recently among American experts. The responses are similar in nature to ROMAN BLACKWOOD:

5 ♣	0 or 3 aces
5 ◇	1 or 4 aces
5 ♡	2 or 5 aces

In its original version, a response of 5 ♠ was reserved to show two aces with extra values. The modern interpretation uses 5 ♡ to show 2 or 5 aces without the queen of trumps while 5 ♠ shows 2 or 5 aces with the queen of trumps. A minor disadvantage of this method occurs when hearts are the agreed trump suit. If the Blackwood bidder holds only one ace without the queen of trumps he is well advised to not use the convention — a 5 ♠ response would prove most embarrassing.

An extension allows the 4 NT bidder to ask for the queen of trumps after a response of 5 ♣ (if spades or hearts are trumps) or 5 ◇ (if spades are trumps). The bid of the next higher-ranking suit (5 ◇ after 5 ♣) asks for the trump queen. A signoff in the trump suit

denies the queen. A jump to six of the trump suit indicates the queen, while a cuebid shows extra values along with the trump queen.

It is important that the partnership have a firm understanding of which suit is the trump suit before embarking on a Key Card auction. A popular method sets the priorities as follows: (1) opener's suit if he opened with a strong two-bid; (b) the agreed trump suit; (c) responder's suit if he jump shifts and then bids key card; (d) the last bid suit. Again, partnership agreement is most important.

ROMAN LEADS. See RUSINOW LEADS and FOURTH HIGHEST.

ROMAN MUD. A method of leading from four small cards. The opening leader leads the second highest from his four small cards, then he follows with the highest, then with the third highest and finally plays the lowest.

ROMAN SYSTEM. Developed by WALTER AVARELLI and GIORGIO BELLADONNA, and used successfully in many WORLD CHAMPIONSHIPS. The chief features are:

1 ♣ opening is forcing, and may show four distinct types of hands. It usually shows 12–16 points with 4-3-3-3 or 4-4-3-2 distribution. After a negative response of 1 ◇ (usually less than 9 points), the opener bids a major if he can, or 1 NT. After a positive response in a suit (minimum of 8–11 points), the opener shows a minimum by a single raise, a rebid of 1 NT, or a bid of a new suit on the same level.

Other positive responses are: 1 NT, 12–16 points; 2 NT, more than 16 points, over which opener rebids conventionally to show his exact point-count.

1 ♣ may also be bid with (1) 21–22 points and balanced distribution, in which case the rebid will be a jump in notrump; or (2) an unbalanced gamegoing hand, in which case the opener will jump rebid in a suit and responder rebids conventionally by six steps to show his holding in opener's suit; or (3) a two-suited hand with at least a four-card club suit and five cards in another suit and 17–20 points, in which case the opener will rebid in clubs.

If an opponent overcalls a 1 ♣ opening, an immediate cuebid by responder shows 12–16 points without a stopper and suggests a notrump contract.

1 ◇, 1 ♡, and 1 ♠ openings are natural (usually at least a four-card suit) and forcing, and guarantee at least one suit of more than four cards. With two suits, the shorter suit is opened (CANAPÉ principle), unless the shorter suit is clubs. With 5-3-3-2 distribution the opening bid is occasionally in the lower-ranking three-card suit other than clubs. A five-card suit may be opened and rebid with a minimum.

With fewer than 9 points, responder makes a single raise or makes the cheapest possible response, both of which are negative. Rebids are natural except for 1 NT, which shows a minimum opening with five cards in the negatively bid suit. Other suit responses are positive, showing 9 points or more. Notrump responses are as over 1 ♣ (except 1 ♠—1 NT, which is negative).

1 NT opening shows a balanced hand with 17–20 points. Responses of 2♣ and 2◇ are GLADIATOR. Responses of two of a major or three of a minor are forcing to game, and opener rebids by steps to show support and opening-bid strength; the first two steps show minimum openings with poor and good support respectively; the third and fourth steps show maximum openings with poor and good support respectively. Other responses are natural and limited.

2♣ and 2◇ openings show three-suited hands (4-4-4-1 or 5-4-4-0 distributions) with 12–16 and 17–20 points respectively. A response of 2 NT is positive and asks the opener to show his short suit. Minimum suit responses are negative and may sometimes have to be made in a three-card suit. If the suit response strikes opener's shortage, he makes the cheapest possible suit rebid. See also ROMAN 2◇.

2♡ and 2♠ openings show at least a five-card suit, together with four or five clubs. A 2 NT response asks opener to clarify his distribution by bidding a three-card suit with 5-4-3-1 distribution, three clubs with 5-4-2-2, 3 NT with 5-5-2-1, four of a minor with 5-5-3-0, or rebidding a six-card suit.

2 NT opening shows a balanced hand with 23–24 points. Responses are as over 1 NT.

Asking bids are used after a suit has been agreed, usually a jump in a new suit at the level of four or higher. If responder can be short in the asked suit, the responses are by six steps: the first step shows no control, second step shows a singleton, third step shows the king, fourth step shows the ace, fifth step shows a void, and the sixth step shows the ace-king, or occasionally the ace-queen. If responder cannot be short in the asked suit, the second and fifth steps are deleted. Different asking bids are also used in certain special situations. See ROMAN ASKING BIDS.

Overcalls are limited to a maximum of 12 points, and are normally made only on a good suit.

Takeout doubles show 12–16 points. If third hand passes, responder bids his shortest suit if he can do so at the level of one or two. See EXCLUSION BID. Otherwise normal responses are given. If third hand bids, a double is for takeout.

1 NT overcall is equivalent to a 1 NT opening bid, although the distribution might be slightly unbalanced. Responses are as over a 1 NT opening.

Jump overcall shows a two-suiter, the bid suit and the next higher-ranking, excluding the opener's suit. The distribution is usually 5-5 or 5-6 with a five- to six-loser hand.

2 NT jump overcall shows a strong two-suiter, excluding the opener's suit. Responder bids the lower unbid minor and the overcaller bids an unbid suit, holding the bid suit and partner's conventionally named suit, or 3 NT with both unbid suits.

Overcalls in the opponent's suit are natural. A jump cuebid shows a very strong three-suiter with a singleton or void in the opponents' suit and a four-loser hand. See also ROMAN BLACKWOOD.

ROMAN 2◇. A bid showing a strong hand with 5-4-4-0 or 4-4-4-1 distribution. This feature of the ROMAN system can be used with standard methods. The original range of 17–20 is sometimes increased

by one or two points. A 2 NT response is positive, and asks the opener to bid his short suit. Other responses are natural and negative, but may be in an economical three-card suit. If the response is in opener's shortage he makes the minimum possible rebid.

An alternative method of responding, proposed by MARSHALL MILES, is to respond 2♡ on all weak hands. Other responses are natural and forcing to game. In all cases the opener bids his shortage on the second round, except that a notrump rebid shows a shortage in the suit bid by responder, whether naturally or artificially.

A version of the Roman 2◇ is also a part of BLUE TEAM CLUB. See BLUE TEAM 2◇.

ROMEX AWARD. See ROSENKRANZ AWARD.

ROMEX STAYMAN (or ROST for short). After an opening 2 NT, or after second-round 2 NT bids to show similar hands of slightly different strength (see ROMEX SYSTEM), the Stayman inquiry includes a special rebid of 3 NT to show both major suits. 3♠ shows a five-card spade suit, and 3♡ shows four or five hearts. 3◇ denies any of the above, and 3♡ is then an inquiry for spades, seeking a 4-4 fit. Similarly after a 3♡ rebid, 3♠ asks for clarification. Opener bids 3 NT with a four-card heart suit. This arrangement allows the partnership to locate 3-5 fits in the major suits.

ROMEX SYSTEM. A 2♣ system with special bids to show hands of intermediate strength devised by GEORGE ROSENKRANZ of Mexico City. The distinguishing feature of the system is the use of the MEXICAN 2◇ opening (showing a balanced hand with 19–20 HCP) and the DYNAMIC NOTRUMP opening (showing a balanced hand with 21–22 HCP or an unbalanced hand within one or two points of the requirements for a 2♣ opening).

2♣ (artificial, for very strong hands) and one-bids are normal, except that one-bids are limited by the failure to open 2◇ or 1 NT. The lack of a natural notrump opening is balanced by the special one-bid limitation: opener, with a balanced hand, can make a minimum rebid in notrump with 13–16 HCP or jump with 17–18 HCP. An EASTERN SCIENTIFIC structure is used after major-suit openings.

Special methods include: Notrump cuebids to show the ace and king of the trump suit; special asking bids, in preference to cuebidding, after a strength- or weakness-showing opening; the *Romex raise* to show extra values through an otherwise impossible 4 NT bid; step responses to many strong bids and asking bids; emphasis on slam-bidding devices. See ROMEX TRUMP ASKING BIDS.

In the modern version of the system (1982), the balanced structure has been rearranged as follows:

19–20	1 NT followed by 2 NT
21–22	2♣ followed by 2 NT
23–24	2◇ followed by 2 NT
25–26	2 NT

On the next round ROMEX STAYMAN is used, together with transfer bids.

Jeff Rubens

ROMEX TRUMP ASKING BIDS. A series of asking bids designed to learn the strength of responder's holding in a particular suit, that suit being assumed to be trumps unless and until opener makes an asking bid in another suit. The asking bid, used after a game-forcing 2♣ opening in the ROMEX System, is initiated by a jump shift rebid by opener. The responses are in steps:

1st step	void or singleton
2nd step	doubleton
3rd step	three cards
4th step	four or more cards
5th step	singleton ace, king, or queen

If responder shows any holding other than a singleton, opener can ask about responder's honor cards in the suit by making the cheapest notrump bid. The responses are:

1st step	none of top three honors
2nd step	one of top three honors
3rd step	two of top three honors
4th step	all three top honors

If opener bids a new suit, he in effect changes the trump suit and the asking process begins anew. See also ASKING BIDS; PRECISION ASKING BIDS; ROMAN ASKING BIDS; SUPER PRECISION ASKING BIDS.

ROMEX 2◊ OPENING. See MEXICAN 2◊.

RONF. An acronym for *raise only non force*. Used as a response to WEAK TWO-BIDS.

ROPI. See BLACKWOOD AFTER INTERFERENCE.

ROSENBLUM CUP TEAMS. A new event added to the World Pair Championships in 1978 in honor of JULIUS ROSENBLUM, former president of the WORLD BRIDGE FEDERATION. Although the event is primarily a knockout, it has an unusual feature — a defeated team gets a second chance, or REPECHAGE. At the start, the top eight European seeds are placed in one knockout group, the top eight North American in another, and the top eight from the rest of the world in a third. The remaining teams then are distributed among the three sections. Knockouts are conducted within the groups, leading to three winners. Meanwhile, the losers play in a concurrent Swiss Teams with a Victory Point scale that equalizes those who are knocked out early and those that are knocked out late. The three losers from the knockout finals then engage in a mini-knockout with the five leaders in the Swiss Teams. The winner of the mini-knockout then joins the three knockout winners in the semifinals. The seven losers in the mini-knockout then return to the Swiss Teams. The winner of the Swiss is awarded third place behind the two finalists. The semifinalists are considered tied for fourth, and the remaining overall positions are determined by the final Swiss Team standings. For results see WORLD CHAMPIONSHIPS V.

ROSENKRANZ AWARD. Endowed by GEORGE ROSENKRANZ, the "Romex" Award for the Best Bid Hand of the Year is presented annually by the INTERNATIONAL BRIDGE PRESS ASSOCIATION. It is made to the players who, in partnership, have produced the best bidding sequence. The Award is given only in respect of a hand which occured in play, whether in a tournament, match or private play. The Panel takes into account accuracy, originality and psychological factors. The result in play need not be a determining factor. For a list of winners see INTERNATIONAL BRIDGE PRESS ASSOCIATION AWARDS.

ROSENKRANZ DOUBLE. A convention invented by GEORGE ROSENKRANZ of Mexico to help an overcaller more accurately gauge his holding in light of partner's response. If a player overcalls an opening bid and the next player makes a bid, a double by the partner of the overcaller shows a raise in partner's suit that includes the ace, king or queen of that suit. If the partner of the opening bidder makes a negative double over the overcall, then a redouble by the partner of the overcaller shows a raise with one of the top three honors. Conversely, if the partner of the overcaller, in either situation, merely raises the suit bid by the overcaller, this indicates that he does not hold one of the top three honors in partner's suit.

ROSLER MOVEMENT. See TEAM-OF-FOUR MOVEMENT.

ROTATION. The order in which actions take place at the bridge table. In the bidding stage, the dealer has the first action, followed in turn by the player on his left, his partner, and the right-hand opponent. In the play of the cards, the player to declarer's left has the initial lead. The duty of making the initial lead to each subsequent trick falls on the player whose card was the winning card played to the preceding trick. Any deviation from this clockwise rotation in bidding or play constitutes an irregularity; in tournaments, the director should be summoned when such an irregularity occurs.

ROTH CLUB SYSTEM. A 1♣ SYSTEM devised by ALVIN ROTH and based on many facets of the ROTH-STONE SYSTEM, including strong notrump openings and five card majors. The 1♣ opening promises at least 19 points if the hand is balanced, or at least 17 if unbalanced. A 2♣ opening promises a genuine club suit and a five-card spade suit. The 1◊ opening is a catchall bid used for other hands, including hands with long club suits.

ROTH POINT-COUNT. See DISTRIBUTIONAL COUNTS.

ROTH-STONE ASTRO. See ASTRO.

ROTH-STONE SYSTEM. Developed by ALVIN ROTH and TOBIAS STONE. Many of their ideas have been adopted by tournament players using standard methods. Since the publication of the 1953 book on the system, Roth has modified the system considerably, describing his new ideas in a second book published in 1958. Among the features of the revised system are:

(1) Sound opening bids in first and second position. The minimum requirement is 14 points, in-

cluding at least 10 high card points, which is about one point more than in standard methods.

(2) Five-card majors in first and second position.

(3) 1 NT RESPONSE TO A MAJOR, FORCING by an unpassed hand after a major-suit opening.

(4) A single raise in a major suit is constructive. It shows 10–12 points and is never passed by a first- or second-seat opener. With a void or singleton in a side suit and 10–12 points, responder, if he is an unpassed hand, jump raises to show shortness in the other major (e.g., 1 ♡ –3 ♡ shows a singleton or void in spades), or jumps to 4 ♣ or 4 ◇ with shortness in the bid suit. A strong major raise is shown by a conventional jump to 3 ♣, which guarantees a minimum of four trumps and 13 points. Opener usually rebids conventionally to show whether or not he has a singleton, or, if not, the number of high trump honors he holds, but he may jump in a new suit as an asking bid.

(5) Two-over-one response (e.g., 2 ♣ in response to 1 ♠) normally shows at least 11 points. It is forcing for one round and guarantees that responder will bid again.

(6) Opening bids of 1 ♣ and 1 ◇ may be prepared with a three-card suit. After a major-suit response, opener jumps to four of his minor with a strong six-card suit and weak four-card support for responder's major, jumps to four of the major with strong four-card support and a weak minor suit, jumps to four of the other minor (or to 4 ♡ after a 1 ♠ response) with a singleton in the bid suit and a strong raise, or jumps to three of the other major with a strong, balanced hand and four-card support.

(7) Jump shift responses are weak, except by a passed hand in a non-competitive auction.

(8) Over one of a suit, a jump to 2 NT by an unpassed hand is unlimited, at least 13 points, and a jump to 3 NT is BABY BLACKWOOD.

(9) After a third- or fourth-seat major-suit opening, responder jumps to 3 NT to show a strong, distributional raise, jumps to 4 ♣ to show a distributional raise with slightly fewer high cards, or jumps to 4 ◇ to show a strong raise with no singleton or void.

(10) 1 NT opening is standard (16–18). Responses of 2 ♣ and 2 ◇ are forcing and slam-try STAYMAN respectively. 2 NT forces opener to bid a minor; if responder then rebids a major, it shows a singleton. Jump responses to the three-level are weak, but mildly invitational in the major suits. TWO-WAY STAYMAN is also used over 2 NT (21–23), except that 3 ♣ shows slam interest.

(11) TEXAS.

(12) GERBER over notrump openings.

(13) 2 ♣ opening is forcing to game. 2 ♡ is the conventional negative response and 2 ◇ is an artificial positive response, showing the equivalent of an ace and a king. Responses of 2 and 3 NT show balanced hands with 8–9 and 10–12 scattered points respectively.

(14) WEAK TWO-BIDS with 2 NT the only forcing response by an unpassed hand. 2 NT and a raise of opener's major are invitational by a passed hand.

(15) 3 NT opening shows a strong preempt in one of the four suits. If responder bids 4 ♣, he warns opener not to bid game in a minor.

(16) NEGATIVE DOUBLES.

(17) RESPONSIVE DOUBLES only after an overcall (e.g., 1 ♣ –1 ♠ –2 ♣, double is responsive).

(18) WEAK JUMP OVERCALLS.

(19) UNUSUAL NOTRUMP.

(20) Bids in the opponents' suit are sometimes natural. After 1 ♣ –pass–1 ♠, an overcall of 2 ♣ or 2 ♠ would be natural.

(21) A takeout double may be light, 10 high card points with 4-4-4-1- or 4-4-5-0 distribution. An immediate cuebid of opponent's suit is equivalent to a strong takeout double, 18 points or more.

(22) When an opponent overcalls 1 NT, 2 ♣ is a weak takeout and double is a strong takeout, 8 points or more, but may be passed.

(23) When an opponent opens 1 NT, 2 ♣ and 2 ◇ show the bid minor and spades, 3 ♣ and 3 ◇ show the bid minor and hearts, and double shows the major suits unless the notrump opening is weak, in which case it shows at least 15 high card points.

(24) After 1 ♡ or 1 ♠ –pass–1 NT, 2 ♣ and 2 ◇ overcalls show the bid minor and the unbid major.

(25) After 1 ♣ or 1 ◇ –pass–1 NT, 2 ♣ and 2 ◇ overcalls show the unbid minor with spades or hearts respectively, and double shows the major suits.

(26) In a competitive auction where a sacrifice may be considered, a double of a slam contract at equal or favorable vulnerability shows no defensive tricks.

(27) A balancing bid of 2 ♣ is equivalent to a light takeout double.

ROTHSCHILD TROPHY. Donated in 1938 by Mrs. Meyer D. Rothschild for the Sub-Senior Master Teams, a two-session Board-a-Match event restricted to players below the rank of Senior Master. It is contested at the Summer North American Championships, under which heading past results are listed.

ROUND. A part of a session of bridge at a tournament during which the players and the boards remain at a table. When two boards are played during a round, its duration should be about 15 minutes. Three board-rounds require about 20 minutes; four-board rounds 25.

In rubber bridge, a round refers to the three or four rubbers (or double rubbers) during which each of the players plays with each of the other players as partners.

ROUND HAND. A colloquialism for a hand with BALANCED DISTRIBUTION, particularly 4-3-3-3. Flat and square are also used to describe such a hand.

ROUND-ROBIN. A form of competition in which each of the contesting groups (usually teams, though occasionally pairs) plays against each of the other groups entered in head-on competition. "League" is used as an equivalent term in England.

Round-robin team contests are increasing in popularity in individual playing areas, frequently requiring months to complete. KNOCKOUT TOURNAMENTS frequently end up in a round-robin of surviving teams. Round-robins frequently are used to determine semifinalists and finalists in WORLD TEAM

CHAMPIONSHIPS. See CARRYOVER.

When a round-robin fails to establish a winner, some other device must be used, such as QUOTIENT.

ROUNDED. A term used to describe the combination of hearts and clubs, these suits having pips rounded at the tops. The converse is POINTED to indicate spades and diamonds.

ROUNDING OFF. At rubber bridge, it is customary to record the results of a rubber to the nearest 100 points. In America, 50 points are counted as an extra 100, but in Europe it is customary to ignore them. For maintaining a running record of the results of a rubber game, a BACK SCORE sheet is used, showing each player as plus or minus some number of hundreds of points, and this provides the basis of settling the game. Some players use a banker who distributes poker chips at the beginning of a game, and rubbers are settled at the end of each by passing the chips from losers to winners, and they are redeemed by the banker at the end of the session.

ROVER. A method of handling a half table in a MITCHELL MOVEMENT. The Rover is an alternative to the PHANTOM pair and the BUMP MITCHELL. The Rover pair may play in either direction, but North-South is preferable because the movement is easier to administer with a North-South sit-out. The Rover pair is assigned a number one higher than the number of full tables in play. After sitting out the first round the Rover pair enters the game by replacing one of the pairs playing in their direction. After playing the round at that table, the Rover pair moves to another table, usually skipping a table up the line. Meanwhile the pair displaced for the previous round resumes its natural position and progression. This continues for as many rounds as there in the game.

To start the game, boards are distributed only to full tables, as if there were no half table. This means that the boards never sit out, so all boards have the same top and the game can be curtailed at any point without having to factor boards. However, the pairs that sit out must be factored up.

This movement is good for almost all numbers of tables. In a game with an even number of full tables, there is an East-West skip after the halfway round. Although the usual move for the Rover pair is to skip a table up the line, there are exceptions when the number of full tables is not a prime. The Rover movement for 9½ tables is especially unusual. Guide cards for Rover pairs in most sizes of half-table games, including the 9½, are available from the AMERICAN CONTRACT BRIDGE LEAGUE. The Rover movement can cause complications, the same as all half-table movements.

Here are suggested Rover movements for various size games:

10½ — Out, 3, 5, 7, 9, 4, 6, 8, 10
11½ — Out, 3, 5, 7, 9, 11, 2, 4, 6
13½ — Out, 3, 5, 7, 9, 11, 13, 2, 4, 6, 8, 10, 12
14½ — Out, 3, 5, 7, 9, 11, 13, 4, 6, 8, 10, 12, 14
15½ — Out, 2, 4, 6, 8, 10, 13, 15, 3, 5, 7, 9, 11
16½ — Out, 2, 4, 6, 8, 10, 12, 14, 3, 5, 7, 9, 11

The movement for 9½ tables involves use of a set of guide cards with East–West 10 as the Rover. Pairs

1 and 7 both have unusual moves. The movement for the Rover pair —Out, 3, 5, 7, 1, 4, 6, 8, 9. The movement for pair 1: 1, 2, 9, 4, 5, 3, 7, Out, 6. The movement for pair 7: 7, 8, 3, 2, 6, 4, 5, Out. All other pairs move normally, going in at their normal table after their sit-out.

Both 8½ and 12½ tables lend themselves more satisfactorily to a PHANTOM pair. Pair 9 (or pair 13) in either direction is a phantom.

ROYAL SPADES (popularly LILIES). The spade suit when scored at nine points per trick, in an early phase of bridge whist.

RUBBER. A unit of measurement of games at home or club bridge, hence the expression, "rubber bridge." A rubber must consist of at least two games, but not more than three. The first side to win two games wins the rubber, and a premium is earned on the basis of whether the opponents have won any game. If they have not, the winning side's premium is larger (700 as against 500). If a rubber is stopped before either side has actually won two games, it is called an "unfinished rubber," and there is a somewhat smaller bonus (300) to the side having won one game. If no game has been won by either side but a partial does exist, there is a small premium (50) to the side having the partial.

RUBBER BRIDGE. The original and the most popular form of contract. However, DUPLICATE and CHICAGO bridge have increased in popularity. Rubber bridge was the basis for the development of the game that has occurred in the past 35 years, attracting much of the original interest of players all over the world. Rubber bridge is played for points, which sometimes may represent a monetary value per point. Tactics at this type of bridge differ from those used at tournament or duplicate. The premium for winning a rubber of two games where the opponents have not won a game is high, and even in a three-game rubber, that is, one where both sides have scored a game, the premium is substantial. In rubber bridge, therefore, considerable effort is expended toward winning games, and risks in the bidding are taken to secure that end. (But see VALUE OF GAME.) Penalties can be inflicted by the opponents if too little regard for safety has been observed by a side. These penalties become more severe when the incurring side has won a game, that is, when they become vulnerable. The competitive features of rubber bridge are sometimes overlooked by players who manifest their principal bridge endeavors in the tournament field. Many club players deplore the tendency toward Chicago and long for the days when rubber was the only game played. In fact, there are large clubs in the East and elsewhere where rubber bridge has disappeared entirely in favor of Chicago, rubber being a somewhat slower type of action, and Chicago being fast-paced. See PARTNERSHIP RUBBER BRIDGE.

RUBBER BRIDGE TACTICS. Should one be willing to go two down at equal vulnerabilty to save game?

At duplicate this is a matter of simple arithmetic.

Each time the sacrifice will show a profit, for other things being equal, one concedes 300 to 500 against a game that is worth 400 or 600. At rubber bridge other things are rarely equal, and simple arithmetic is a poor guide. The issue is determined by the personal equation. With a good partner and mediocre opponents, there is always the risk of a phantom sacrifice, of going down to prevent them from going down.

Opponents may have a certain game, one that would be made *in the other room.* But there is no other room, and mediocre opponents miss a good many certain games.

Conversely, when partner is the weakest player at the table, the cheapest sacrifice may prove expensive, for what attraction can there be in prolonging a rubber when you start every hand at a disadvantage?

Broadly speaking, there is little future in sacrificing at rubber bridge. The profit margin is too narrow, and it is generally best to leave this dubious pastime to the other side.

When the best slams are not so good. How about slams? At duplicate, the odds are clearly in favor of bidding a slam which depends on one of two finesses. At rubber bridge, the decision never rests with abstract figures, but always with concrete personalities.

Who will be declarer, you or partner? If it is partner and he goes down playing it his way, it will be poor consolation to know that he would have made it had he played it differently. It will be more painful still if on the next hand he concedes a needless penalty and then, through bad defense, allows opponents to bring home an impossible slam.

Of course, when a good partner is in control, and opponents may be expected to slip in defense, you can bid slams with less than an even money chance. Faces alter cases, and it's the people, not the mathematical probabilities, that make the true odds.

Double the player, not the contract. If an overbidder calls 4♠, double him if there seems any reason for doing so. But if the 4♠ call was made by an underbidder, pass. When in doubt, you double the man rather than the contract.

The statistically minded can look at it from another angle. the overbidder's record shows that he often goes down. He is a bad risk actuarially, and in doubling him the odds are favorable.

Not so the underbidder, who seldom gives away penalties. The best tactics against him are to open light, to intervene boldly, and to make a general show of strength. You may put him off, but you are not likely to score much above the line. The underbidder's main contribution to your welfare will come from the games and slams he makes but dares not bid.

Confusion — for confusion's sake. Psychic bids can be most rewarding, yet here again everything depends on the uncertain quality of partner and opponents. Each player must be studied separately and treated strictly on his demerits.

In principle it pays to create confusion for confusion's sake, so long as you remain in control. With little defense against opponent's major, but support for partner's minor, you can bid notrump. With support for partner's major you can bid a nonexistent minor. If you are doubled, you have a ready-made escape, and meanwhile you may throw the other side off balance. Sometimes you will steal a hand that does not belong to you. Sometimes you will mislead an opponent in the play of the hand. But you will draw your biggest dividends on all those occasions, the vast majority, when you bid honestly and are unjustly suspected of bluffing. For it is not psyching but the reputation of psyching which creates confusion in the adversary's mind.

Much the same is true of inhibitory bids. If you have decided to bid 6♦ over partner's 3♦, let us say, you may derive a twofold advantage from a spurious cuebid. Holding a worthless doubleton in clubs, call 4♣ on the way round. It may discourage a club lead, which you do not want. Better still, it may induce the lead you do want next time, when you make your cuebid, deliberately, on A-K-J or A-Q or K-x. Of course, you must be careful to throw the bait to the *same* opponent. First show suspicion, then exploit it. For it is the essence of rubber bridge to play the players, as well as the cards.

Every hand forms part of a pattern. In theory every hand must be treated in isolation, but in practice this is not true at all. At roulette red and black have equal chances every time the wheel spins regardless of how many reds or blacks have come up before. This is because the wheel is a purely mechanical device.

As soon as the human element is introduced, this no longer applies. Every move is influenced by those that have preceded it, and neither emotion nor superstition can be left out of account.

If you have been doubled into game, you may take certain risks in partscore situations for the next half-hour or so — provided that you are up against the same opponents. They will surely hang back, fearful of suffering the same ignominy twice in quick succession.

The partner problem. Handling a weak partner is, perhaps, the most difficult art at rubber bridge. Of course, you want to prevent partner playing the hand, and of course you don't want him to know that you are trying to prevent him. Fortunately, weak players are singularly unobservant and with a little luck you will get away with it again and again.

On a balanced hand, intending to rebid notrump, there is a good case for opening a weak minor in preference to a strong major. That way you are likely to get the notrump bid in first. At the same time, you may discourage an unwelcome lead. Even a 1◊ opening on J-x-x may have something to commend it. It is a prepared bid — prepared to steer the contract into your own hand.

In defense, a little cynicism is seldom out of place. Opponents are in 3 NT. What do you lead from K-7-6 in a suit bid by partner? The 6? Are you sure that he deserves the compliment? Perhaps he was brought up to believe that it is sinful not to lead the highest of partner's suit. Humor him. Never hesitate to do the wrong thing with the right partner.

There are times when you can take advantage of partner's shortcomings, reversing on the sketchiest of values or falsecarding wantonly. Opponents may be misled with impunity when partner is not good enough to be deceived.

When not to concentrate. The key to success at bridge at every level lies in concentration. But whereas at duplicate, and more especially in pairs events, concentration can never be relaxed, since every hand can be a top or bottom, at rubber bridge the good tactician takes an occasional breather, just as champions do at boxing or at tennis. If declarer can fulfill his contract of 2♢ he need not try too hard to make three or four. In terms of money the result will probably be the same, so why waste the effort? An extra ounce of mental energy may be all-important on the next hand or on the one after when the contract is a difficult game or slam.

The winning player has his lapses, but he usually knows when he can afford to have them, and is quick to concentrate and to give of his best when the need arises. That is why when he nods the cards so often forgive him. See also PARTNERSHIP PSYCHOLOGY.

Victor Mollo

RUBBER DUPLICATE. A form of duplicate bridge using rubber bridge scoring. The boards are pre-duplicated by the director in preparation for a straight team-of-four match, and each deal is played simultaneously at the two tables. Play continues exactly as at rubber bridge, ignoring, or course, the vulnerability shown by the boards, until a rubber is scored at either table. The other table is then instructed to add its score as an unfinished rubber, counting the normal 300 for a game and 50 for a partscore. The table at which a rubber was completed is entitled to know whether a rubber was scored in the other room also, but *not* by which side it was scored.

The final score is calculated by adding the precise results of all rubbers i.e., not rounded off to the nearest 100) including the unfinished rubber, if any, when play ends. It is usual to play the match in two equal halves, with a change of opponents at half-time.

The director must move constantly between the two playing tables to observe the possibilities that a rubber will be completed. Table 1, for example, must not be permitted to start Board 8 if there is a chance that Table 2 will complete a rubber on Board 7.

Two matches can be conducted simultaneously using the same boards. In a 16-board half-match, Match A would start with Board 1 while Match B started with Board 9. This introduces the possibility of a fouled board, and the director should have an extra pre-duplicated board available to meet this situation.

Rubber duplicate is rarely played except in England, where the Devonshire Club Cup, a knockout contest between leading London social clubs, is conducted on these lines. It has been won many times by the Royal Automobile Club.

RUBIN TRANSFERS. Devised by IRA RUBIN of Paramus NJ as a method of preventing the opponents from finding a cheap sacrifice against a game or slam, and used in the 1966 BERMUDA BOWL.

4♣ opening describes a hand containing either a long, semi-solid major suit with 3½ to 4 honor tricks, or a long minor suit with 2½ to 3 honor tricks and no voids. Responder will usually bid 4♢ to allow opener to show his suit. Major-suit responses are slam tries, and minor-suit responses show a solid suit missing the king, queen, or jack, which opener may raise to slam with three first-round controls.

4♢ opening shows a strong major suit with 2½ to 3 honor tricks. 4♡ is the normal response, while 4♠ shows active interest in a heart slam, but only mild interest in a spade slam. Responses in the minors are cuebids, agreeing either major as trump, and 4 NT is BLACKWOOD.

4 NT opening shows a strong minor-suit hand with one or more voids. Responder bids 5♣ or 5 NT with three or four aces respectively.

Game openings in any of the four suits are weak preempts, denying much high-card strength. Alternatively, a hand with greater high-card or playing strength can be shown by an opening bid of one followed by a jump to game.

See 4♣ AND 4♢ OPENING TRANSFERS.

RUFF. To trump a lead of a plain suit, other than the trump suit, winning the trick if no higher trump is played.

RUFF AND DISCARD (or Ruff and Sluff). When a defender leds a suit of which both declarer and dummy are void, the declarer gets a ruff and sluff; he can discard a loser from one hand and ruff in the other.

This may be declarer's only way of making a contract when too many losers are present. To compel a defender to give a ruff and sluff, he must be placed in the lead after all his safe exit cards have been removed.

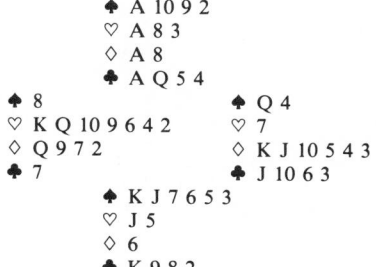

West opens 3♡, North doubles, South jumps to 4♠ and North raises to 6♠. Owing to the unfortunate club break, declarer apparently has a club loser as well as a heart. The two suits are guarded by different opponents, so no squeeze operates, and the only way to make the contract is by compelling as defender to concede a ruff and discard.

The heart lead is won, trumps are drawn and clubs are tested. Finding that he has a club loser, declarer continues by ruffing out diamonds and playing off the remaining clubs, throwing East into the lead. As expected after West's opening three-bid, East has no more hearts, and has to return a diamond. South throws the ♡J from his own hand, and ruffs in dummy.

A defensive weapon

It can be winning defense to present declarer with a ruff and sluff even when the defender has safe exit cards in other suits. The usual occasion is when declarer is short of trumps, and has to lose the lead before he can develop a side suit.

```
              ♠ K 10 9 3
              ♡ A K 7 3
              ◇ K J 7
              ♣ A 9
  ♠ 8 7                        ♠ A Q 6
  ♡ 10 5 2                     ♡ 6 4
  ◇ 8 5 4 3                    ◇ A 10 9
  ♣ J 7 5 3                    ♣ K Q 8 6 2
              ♠ J 5 4 2
              ♡ Q J 9 8
              ◇ Q 6 2
              ♣ 10 4
```

East's 1♣ opening is passed to North, who doubles. South responds 2♡, and passes his partner's raise to three. West has no clue to the killing spade lead, and plays a club, which is won in dummy. After three rounds of trumps, South leads a spade to dummy's 10, and the queen wins, West starting an echo.

East may cash a club, and exit passively with ace and another spade, expecting to beat the hand if West has the ◇ Q, for then the declarer would eventually lose two diamonds. If East follows that reasoning, the contract is made because South has the ◇ Q.

By forcing declarer with repeated club leads, East succeeds no matter who has the ◇ Q and despite giving South a ruff and sluff. After the ♠ Q, East plays a second and third round of clubs. It does not matter in which hand declarer ruffs, for when East comes in with the ♠ A he plays another club, taking declarer's last trump. South has only eight tricks, East has three, and must make the ◇ A and the long club.

The lesser evil

In the above example the defender had no choice but to concede a ruff and sluff. Sometimes he has an option, albeit an unattractive one, such as leading into a tenace. If the situation does not lend itself to complete analysis, the defender should prefer to give a ruff and sluff rather than concede a trick in a side suit. This is particularly so when both declarer and dummy have four cards in the same side suit.

```
              ♠ J 8 2
              ♡ A K 9 5
              ◇ A 10 9 7
              ♣ A 8
  ♠ 9 5                        ♠ A 10 7 6 4
  ♡ 8 6 4                      ♡ 10 2
  ◇ 5 3                        ◇ K Q 6
  ♣ 10 9 7 6 5 4               ♣ K Q 3
              ♠ K Q 3
              ♡ Q J 7 3
              ◇ J 8 4 2
              ♣ J 2
```

East's 1♠ opening is passed to North, who doubles. South lands in 4♡, and the defense starts with two rounds of spades. Fearing a ruff, declarer pulls three rounds of trumps before touching the minor suits. South places East with all the missing high cards,

and takes out the third round of spades before putting East on play with ace and another club. East counts declarer for four diamonds in his own hand as well as in dummy, so he gives him a ruff and sluff instead of leading a diamond. South still has to lose two diamonds, and is defeated, but had East returned a diamond the contract would have been made.

On the relatively few occasions when it is better to lead into a tenace than to concede a ruff and sluff, the usual reason is that a ruff and a sluff would enable declarer to establish a long card in a side suit. This suit will usually be distributed 4–3 between dummy and the declarer.

```
              ♠ Q 10 7 4
              ♡ A K 4
              ◇ Q 10 2
              ♣ K 10 9
  ♠ 9 2                        ♠ A J 3
  ♡ J 10 8 5                   ♡ 7 6 3 2
  ◇ 9 6 5 4                    ◇ A J 7
  ♣ Q 5 4                      ♣ J 7 2
              ♠ K 8 6 5
              ♡ Q 9
              ◇ K 8 3
              ♣ A 8 6 3
```

South opens 1♣ and after a forcing 2 NT response lands in 4♠. West leads the ♡ J, and South seeks to improve his chances by taking three rounds of hearts before leading a trump to the king and a trump back to dummy. East scores two trump tricks, but then has a choice of rotten apples. South had bid clubs, and if East plays the suit, declarer brings it in without loss, and makes his contract, for he has already discarded a diamond on the third round of hearts, and now loses only to the ◇ A. East's choice, therefore, lies between conceding a ruff and discard or playing a diamond.

Declarer had only eight ready tricks, so East willingly gives him a ninth by playing ace and another diamond. South still has to lose a club, and is defeated.

If East concedes a ruff and discard instead, South ruffs in hand, and sluffs a club from dummy. The third round of clubs if ruffed on the board, a diamond led to South's king provides a ninth trick, and the long club is the tenth.

RUFF AND RUFF. A rare endgame situation described by JEAN BESSE, Switzerland, in which the declarer is offered a ruff and discard, and the only winning play is to ruff in *both* declaring hands.

```
              ♠ K J 10 2
              ♡ Q J 8
              ◇ K 10 4 3
              ♣ K 3
  ♠ A Q 8                      ♠ 7 6 5
  ♡ 10 4 2                     ♡ K 7 6 5
  ◇ A J 6                      ◇ 7
  ♣ A 10 7 4                   ♣ Q 9 8 6 5
              ♠ 9 4 3
              ♡ A 9 3
              ◇ Q 9 8 5 2
              ♣ J 2
```

South plays in 3 ◇ after West has opened the bidding

with 1♠, and the opening lead is the ♡2. The ♡8 forces the king, and the ace wins. A diamond is led to dummy's king. West naturally ducking, and dummy's two winning hearts are cashed.

A trump is continued, and West takes two trump tricks. He shifts to a low club, and South guesses right, putting up dummy's king. He returns a club, and West wins with the ace in this position:

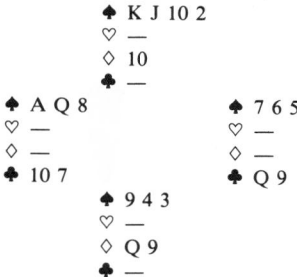

```
                    ♠ K J 10 2
                    ♡ —
                    ◇ 10
                    ♣ —
   ♠ A Q 8                        ♠ 7 6 5
   ♡ —                            ♡ —
   ◇ —                            ◇ —
   ♣ 10 7                         ♣ Q 9
                    ♠ 9 4 3
                    ♡ —
                    ◇ Q 9
                    ♣ —
```

West returns a club, the best defense, and the only winning play for South is to ruff in dummy and overruff with his queen. He continues with the ♠9. If dummy discards any spade on the club lead, West can defend the position.

For a related situation, see ONE-SUIT SQUEEZE.

RUFF AND SLUFF. See RUFF AND DISCARD.

RUFFING FINESSE. A play by which a finesse is successful if the missing honor lies behind the finesse holding. With a singleton opposite a holding of A-Q-J, a simple finesse may be taken by leading the singleton and playing the jack, thus providing immediate discard on the ace if this is needed. The other possibility, granting no problem of entry, is to play for the king to be behind the high card holding. In this case the ace is played at the first trick, and the queen led. If the queen is covered, the trick can be ruffed; if not covered a sluff is taken. The bidding may give some clue to the missing king's location. When the declarer has no information to guide him, he should choose the ruffing finesse in preference to the simple finesse for the reason that the ruffing finesse will lose one less trick when it fails.

If the 10 is missing, the ruffing finesse becomes less attractive:

```
        A Q J 3 2

             4
```

The play of the ace followed by the queen cannot produce more than three tricks in all, with the help of two ruffs. Entries permitting, it is slightly better to ruff a low card on the second round and lead the queen later.

The all-out play of finessing the queen on the first round offers the chance of four tricks, with the help of one ruff, if the left-hand opponent began with K-x-x.

Similarly, with a singleton opposite A-K-J-10-x, a first-round finesse must be taken if it is essential to make five tricks in the suit.

RUFFING SQUEEZE. See TRUMP SQUEEZE.

RUFFING TRICK. A trick won by ruffing; usually

a ruffing trick is a trick won by a trump which would otherwise be of little or no value. See COUP EN PASSANT; ELOPEMENT. Exceptions are the CROSSRUFF, where both hands contribute to the ruffing values, and the DUMMY REVERSAL, where the normal method of play is reversed and the hand containing the long trumps is used for ruffing. In hand evaluation under the POINT-COUNT, system the responding hand, after finding a trump fit with partner, may add substantially for shortness in a side suit. See DISTRIBUTIONAL COUNTS.

RULE OF ELEVEN. A mathematical calculation applicable when the original lead is construed as a FOURTH-HIGHEST ONE. It is sometimes possible to obtain an exact reading of the distribution in all four hands.

The discovery of the rule is generally credited to ROBERT F. FOSTER, and was published by him in his *Whist Manual*. First put in writing in a letter from Foster to a friend in 1890, it is said to have been discovered independently by E.M.F. Benecke of Oxford at about the same time.

The rule states: "Subtract the pips on the card led from 11; the result gives the number of higher cards than the one led in the other three hands." Counting such cards in his own hand and in the dummy, both the leader's partner and the declarer can determine the number of such cards in the concealed hand of the other.

The application of the rule is easier than stating it. For example:

```
                  DUMMY
                  K 5 2
        7 led               A 10 9 3
```

If the lead of the 7-spot is a fourth-best lead, third hand subtracts 7 from 11 and knows that four cards higher than the 7-spot are held in his, dummy's, and declarer's hands. He has three and dummy one, therefore declarer has no card higher than the 7, which can be permitted to ride.

Frequently only the declarer gains from the application of this rule.

```
                  DUMMY
                  A Q 9 5 4
        6 led               3 played
                  10 7 2
```

Since declarer sees in his own hand and the dummy five cards higher than the 6-spot, he can bring in the entire suit by successively finessing against the king, jack and 8-spot.

The Rule of Eleven often spots a singleton lead. For example:

```
                  DUMMY
                  A 10 8 7 4
        5 led               K 9 3 2
                  DECLARER
                  Q J 6
```

If five is subtracted from 11, the third hand knows that this is the number of cards higher than the 5-spot held by himself, dummy and declarer. He sees six of them so declarer holds none if his partner's lead is a fourth best. Declarer ducks, the king is played, and declarer plays a seventh card higher than five. Third hand sees all cards lower than the 5; therefore the lead is not from a doubleton, and can be presumed to be a singleton.

The rule is based on an honest lead of fourth best in a suit. There is a modern tendency to be less revealing on the opening lead, with the lead of a small card indicating a suit whose return is desired and a middle card to indicate a suit to be abandoned. Care must therefore be taken not to apply the rule rigorously when the lead is not certainly a fourth best. See also RULE OF TWELVE, RULE OF FIFTEEN (2).

RULE OF FIFTEEN. (1) A rule of thumb as to whether or not the bidding should be opened in fourth seat. The rule states that fourth hand should open the bidding if the number of high card points and the number of spades totals 15 or more. The theory behind the rule is that if the high cards are likely very evenly divided between the two partnerships, fourth hand should open only with a spade suit that will facilitate his side's competing in the auction.

(2) A generalization of the RULE OF ELEVEN which allows third hand to determine what numerical "rule" to apply in conjunction with various types of spot-card leads other than fourth highest. The type of lead employed and the rule to be applied always total 15. For example, the rule of *eleven* is applicable to *fourth* best leads; the RULE OF TWELVE is used with *third* best leads; a rule of *ten* would be applicable to *fifth* best leads. See RULE OF ELEVEN.

RULE OF N-MINUS-ONE. A rule for squeezes published in the *Red Book on Play* by ELY CULBERTSON. This is his definition:

Count the number of busy cards in plain suits held by one adversary. This number is represented by the symbol N. N-minus-one equals the number of uninterrupted winners the declarer needs for a squeeze.

This rule is applied at a time when the opponent to be squeezed has been stripped of all idle cards. At that point declarer must be capable of taking all but one of the remaining tricks. See RECTIFYING THE COUNT.

There are exceptions to this rule: see SQUEEZE WITHOUT THE COUNT; SECONDARY SQUEEZE; TRIPLE SQUEEZE.

RULE OF SIXTEEN. With borderline hands in fourth position, the number of spades is crucial. The rule suggests that a bid should be made only if the number of points plus the number of cards in the spade suit totals 16 or more. However, this is on the cautious side, and a RULE OF FIFTEEN has merit.

RULE OF TWELVE. A mathematical calculation applicable when the original lead is construed as a THIRD HIGHEST LEAD. The rule states, "Subtract the pips on the card led from 12; the result gives the number of higher cards than the one led in the other three hands." The application of the rule is similar to the application of the RULE OF ELEVEN. Example:

DUMMY

K 10 7

6 led   A J 8 2

If the lead of the six-spot is a third-best lead, third hand subtracts 6 from 12 and knows that six cards higher than the six-spot are held in his hand, dummy's and declarer's hand. He has three and dummy has three, so if the lead was third highest, he will be able to win cheaply by topping whatever card is played from dummy. See RULE OF FIFTEEN (2).

RULE OF TWO AND THREE. A guide to preemptive opening bids and overcalls. The player taking preemptive action cannot afford to be set more than 500 unless he is saving against a slam. He can therefore risk being defeated by two tricks doubled vulnerable or three tricks doubled not vulnerable.

A simple way of considering this matter is to assume that a vulnerable partner can make two tricks, and a nonvulnerable partner three tricks. Therefore, a player who opens 4♠ should have an eight playing trick hand if he is vulnerable, and a seven playing trick hand if he is not vulnerable.

These traditional requirements are often modified by position at the table, methods of scoring, and other circumstances. They have no mathematical validity, though they are sound psychologically. See PREEMPTIVE BID.

RULE OF X-PLUS ONE. A formula conceived by ELY CULBERTSON as an aid to planning the play at notrump. If it is desired to establish long cards in a suit, estimate the number of losing tricks in the suit before it can be established (X) and add one to this number. This is the number of stoppers in opponents' long suit needed to be able to cash the long cards.

RULING. An adjudication by the director after an irregularity has occurred at a bridge tournament; in rubber bridge, an application of an applicable law by agreement among the players.

RULINGS OUT OF THE BOOK. In all tournament play, whether at the club level or at the level of International competition, the director should carry a rule book (LAWS OF DUPLICATE BRIDGE) to the table where an irregularity occurs and quote the rule that applies directly from the book. The familiarity of the director with the provisions of the laws is not in question, but the player is far more apt to accept a ruling against him graciously if the rule is read to him directly. Particularly does this practice avoid the dubious one of a club director giving HOME TOWN RULINGS to his steady customers.

RUN. (1) Bidding: to take partner out in a different suit (or notrump) if he is doubled. (2) Play or run (a suit): to cash all the winning cards of an established or solid suit by playing them one after the other.

RUN OUT OF TRUMPS. To exhaust of trumps, usually by forcing the player to ruff. See CONTROL MAINTENANCE.

RUSH ASKING BID. A method of asking bids devised by COURTLAND RUSH, St. Joseph MO, and incorporated into the BULLDOG SYSTEM. It differs from other asking bid procedures in that it inquires about controls *outside* the asked suit.

The responder counts controls outside the asked suit on the NORMAN principle (each ace, 1 point; each king, ½ point) and responds on the following scale:

Cheapest available bid	0 or ½ or 2½
Next available bid	1 or 3
Third available bid	1½ or 3½
Fourth available bid	2 or 4

This scale is reduced by ½ point if responder is known to be very weak or if opener is known to be enormously strong.

RUSINOW LEADS. The principle of leading the second-ranking of touching honors, devised by SYDNEY RUSINOW and used by him, Philip Abramsohn, and Simon Rossant in the Thirties. These leads were unaccountably barred in ACBL tournaments until 1964.

Ever since WHIST was *the* game, the standard lead from either A–K or K–Q has been the king. This ambiguity often gives third hand an unsolvable problem. Here is only one example of many:

♠ 6 5 2

♠ K   ♠ J 10 4

♠ ?

Against a suit contract by South, West leads the ♠K. If he has K–Q, East wants to play the jack to ncourage him to continue. But if he has A–K, East wants to play low to get him to shift. (If East plays the jack, West may try to give East a ruff, and even if he shifts a trick will be lost if South has ♠ Q-9-x.)

Some players favor the lead of the ace from A–K. Unfortunately this practice substitutes one problem for another. Often an ace should be led against a suit contract *without* the king. But if this lead convention is used, a guessing situation is created — so much so that one is reluctant to lead an unsupported ace even when it might be right to do so.

A sound solution was proposed thirty years ago by Sydney Rusinow — the lead of the second highest from touching honors (king from A–K, queen from K–Q, etc.). Though endorsed by ELY CULBERTSON, these leads soon fell out of favor in America. They were adopted by many Europeans, however, notably the users of the ROMAN CLUB and later the LITTLE MAJOR. The details are:

A denies the king (except with A–K doubleton — see below).

K from A–K. Third hand should signal with the queen or a doubleton.

Q from K–Q. Third hand should signal with the ace or jack, but not with a doubleton if dummy has three or four small. (Declarer may duck, and partner may continue into his A–J.)

J from Q–J; 10 from J–10; 9 from 10–9. Note that this blends nicely into MUD leads of second highest from three spot cards.

With more than two honors in sequence, the second highest is still led (Q from K-Q-J, etc.), followed by a lower one in most cases. The Romans lead second highest from an interior sequence also (10 from K-J-10, 9 from K-10-9 or Q-10-9). This deserves more study; in any case, the problem is not too important, for the K-J-10 is not usually a desirable combination to lead from, and the fourth

highest is perhaps a better choice from the other two holdings.

Rusinow leads are used *only* on the first trick against a suit contract in a suit which partner has not bid. Later in the hand, or in partner's suit, the highest card should be led from touching honors.

If the touching honors to be led are doubleton, the top card should be led. Then when you play the second honor, partner will know you have no more of the suit. On the following hand, this special feature of the Rusinow leads was crucial.

Matchpoints.
Dlr: North
Vul: E–W

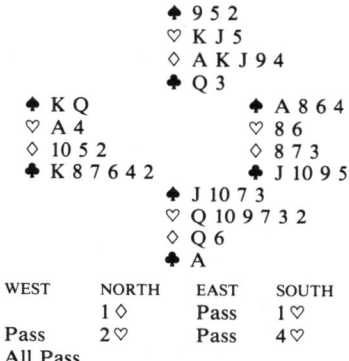

WEST	NORTH	EAST	SOUTH
	1 ◇	Pass	1 ♡
Pass	2 ♡	Pass	4 ♡
All Pass			

Playing Rusinow leads, West opens the ♠K, which East instantly identifies as a doubleton (if it is a singleton, South has a hidden five-card suit). He plays the 8, then overtakes the queen, and returns a spade for West to ruff, setting the contract.

Playing standard leads, East has to guess. He cannot be sure that West would have led low to the second trick holding ♠ K-Q-x, for West might have been afraid East would shift to a club. Nor would it have helped West to have opened the queen, for East would surely have overtaken and tried for a club trick.

Against Notrump Contracts. If Rusinow leads work so well against suit contracts, should they be used against notrump also? Many think not, because the purpose of a lead against notrump is entirely different. Against a suit, third hand has to know what specific honors the leader has, so the A–K ambiguity must be resolved. Against notrump, third hand has to know whether partner has led his side's best suit — that is, whether he has honors in the suit led, not which specific ones they are. See JOURNALIST LEADS.

Lawrence Rosler

RUSSIA. Bridge is little played in Russia, where chess is the dominant game, but the Russian *WHIST* variant Vint may have been a forerunner of bridge (see BIRITCH, or RUSSIAN WHIST and HISTORY OF BRIDGE). Some of the leading chess players, notably Paul Keres, play bridge as a recreation. Some tournament bridge is played in Estonia, especially at the University of Tartu. In the late Sixties Russia became more active in tournament competition and participated in several tournaments in iron curtain countries.

In 1973 the Associated Press reported from Moscow that the *bourgeois game of contract bridge* had been banned from play in clubs because the *passion for bridge* had been found to be *socially harmful* by the State Sports Committee. Bridge is, however, allowed to be played in private by consenting adults.

S

SAC. Colloquialism for SACRIFICE, as in "We took the sac''.

S.A.C.C. A forerunner of PLAFOND, named for its originators and reported by SIR HUGH CLAYTON (probably one of them) in *The Times of India*, July 15, 1914, placing it five or six years earlier than BELLANGER'S dating of the advent of Plafond in Paris. It does not appear to have caught on outside India.

A side received credit toward game only for tricks for which they had bid. Bonuses for slams were of an order that made it worth running the risk of being set: 1,000 for grand slam, 500 for small slam, 250 for five odd. (This idea of a demi-slam bonus, at times suggested for contract bridge, has always been rejected as overrewarding a timid approach to slam bidding.) Tricks not bid for received no score. In addition to scoring game for tricks bid for to a value of 30 points, a game was credited to the side that, since completion of a previous game, scored a total of 500 by honors, penalties and points for slam. The avowed purpose of this rule was to discourage "flag-flying" and allow earlier completion of a rubber. From this distance in time, however, it would seem that the rule exaggerated one of the flaws in the auction scoring base used in S.A.C.C. and in Plafond — the penalties were already severe in ratio to a 250-point rubber bonus.

SACRIFICE (or SAVE). Sacrifice bidding over opponents' game contracts can be much more profitable at duplicate scoring than at rubber bridge. One will never see a successful "money" player chortling with triumph after going down 500 to stop a vulnerable game — one has saved very few points, if any, and would rather have had whatever small chance there was of setting the opponents' contract. However, losing 500 instead of 620 at duplicate can yield a high matchpoint score.

Remember, though, that one will earn a fat score with one's sacrifice only when most of the field is bidding game with his opponents' cards. Suppose that one holds this hand; nonvulnerable against vulnerable: (See hand at top of next column.) Certainly, the opponents will make their game more often than not — one has too good a fit with partner and too little defense to expect a set. Certainly, one will go down 500 or less at 4♠. Should one sacrifice? The auction makes it clear that most of the other pairs who hold the opponents' cards will not be in game. Say that this deal is played in a partscore eight times, in 4♡ twice, in 4♠ doubled twice. Then, if

```
          ♠ J 8 5
          ♡ 8 6 2
          ◇ J 7
          ♣ K 10 7 6 4
```

WEST	NORTH	EAST	SOUTH
		1♡	Pass
2♡	2♠	3♡	Pass
Pass	3♠	Pass	Pass
4♡	Pass	Pass	?

4♡ makes, one will score 1 point for letting it play, or 3 points for saving; if 4♡ goes down, one saving scores 11 points for letting it play or 1 point for saving. So one stands to gain 2 or lose 10 — and the odds are nowhere near 5 to 1 that the game will make.

In contrast, suppose that one holds the same hand on this auction:

WEST	NORTH	EAST	SOUTH
		1♡	Pass
3♡	3♠	4♡	?

Now, the whole field is likely to be in game. Say that six pairs are allowed to play 4♡, while the other six double 4♠. Either for passing or for bidding 4♠ one will score 9 points if he is right, 3 points if he is wrong — it is an even-money bet. At these odds, the price is right for a sacrifice, since 4♡ will make perhaps three-quarters of the time. Remember that the determining factor in matchpoint play is not "how much?" but "how often?" Thus, the most important factor in sacrifice bidding at duplicate is the spirit of the enemy bidding: be reluctant to sacrifice when the opponents stagger into game even if one thinks they are likely to make; be alert to sacrifice against confident auctions when it appears that everyone else will be in game too.

Next in importance is the vulnerability. To be set more than the value of the enemy game is irritating at any scoring, but it is a major disaster at matchpoints. Thus, one never really "sacrifices" when the vulnerability is unfavorable (vulnerable against not vulnerable). If one outbids the opponents, it must be with some notion that the contract might make; that if it goes down, it will be down only one. On equal vulnerability (both vulnerable or nonvulnerable), one can loosen up, outbidding the opponents even when certainly going down. Here, there should be some hope of going down only one; otherwise, there is too much danger of down three for a zero. One cannot be really frisky with one's sacrifice bidding unless the vulnerability is favorable (not vulnerable against vulnerable) so that one can afford down three. For instance, suppose one holds:

```
          ♠ 2
          ♡ A Q J 8 4
          ◇ 8 5 2
          ♣ K Q 9 4
```

Open 1♡; left-hand opponent doubles; partner raises to 2♡; and right-hand opponent jumps to 4♠. It sounds as though the opponents have bid a normal game — should a sacrifice be considered? Obviously, pass if the vulnerability is unfavorable; there is no chance to win ten or eleven tricks. Equally obviously, bid 5♡ if it is favorable; the opponents are more likely than not to make their game, and have little prospect of scoring 700. What about equal vulnerability?

The single most probable result is that the opponents can make their game while the defenders will be down only two. But it is advisable to pass. The combination of two less likely chances — (a) that one might beat 4♠, plus (b) that one might go down three — outweighs the single most likely one. The opponents are merely favorites to make game; they might go down. And the defenders are merely a favorite to win nine tricks; after a single raise, a try for game would not be made, and this means there is no assurance of making even 3♡.

A hidden advantage of sacrifice bidding is the chance that the opponents will be pushed one higher and will go down. This accentuates the vulnerability differences. On unfavorable vulnerability, the opponents are longing to double the defenders; on equal vulnerability, they are willing to double; but on favorable vulnerability, they are reluctant to double and may well be pushed overboard. When the vulnerability is favorable, the odds favoring sacrifice bidding are simply magnificent. One should consider sacrificing against a confidently bid game whenever he and partner have a suit fit plus a little distribution. It is estimated that between one-third and one-half the time there is a paying nonvulnerable sacrifice available against a vulnerable suit game. See also ADVANCE SAVE and PHANTOM SACRIFICE.

SAFETY LEVEL. The maximum bid a partnership is willing to reach, presumably without undue risk, in order to investigate a higher contract or compete against enemy bids.

At times, one partner may wish to suggest a slam. If his hand is not strong enough to guarantee a contract above the level of game, he must make a slam try below game. The game level is then his safety level. If his hand is strong enough to guarantee the safety of an above-game contract (such as 4 NT or five of a major suit), he may, if he wishes, make a slam try above game. In this case, the safety level is 4 NT, 5♠ or whatever.

When the bidding becomes competitive, the previous bids of a partnership often indicate they hold the strength to reach a certain level. This is their safety level and the contract should not be sold (undoubled) to the opponents below this level. See RULE OF TOTAL TRICKS.

For example: South opens with a strong two-bid, forcing to game. If East–West enter the auction, North–South have a safety level at game, implicit in South's bid. North–South will not allow East–West to buy the contract below game unless they feel a satisfactory penalty will be obtained. See also FORCING BID; FORCING SEQUENCES; SLAM BIDDING.

SAFETY PLAY. The safety play appropriate to any particular SUIT COMBINATION is classified under that heading. The following discussion deals with applications of the safe-play idea.

In a broad sense, a "safety play" would be a play in which declarer is attempting to reduce to a minimum the risk of losing his contract. If safety play is defined in this manner, every hand would naturally be reduced to finding the safety play, and applying it.

However, as the term is actually used in bridge, it refers specifically to *the play of a suit*, as contrasted to the play of the entire hand. A safety play is the play of a suit in such a manner as to protect against an abnormal or bad break in that suit, thereby either eliminating or minimizing the danger of losing the contract. Fundamentally, most types of safety plays are used almost exclusively in rubber bridge and team play, although there are many standard safety plays which are applicable equally to both rubber bridge and duplicate bridge. Since in most safety-play situations, declarer sacrifices a possible overtrick to attain his objective, such a play is generally losing tactics at matchpoint duplicate play, where the overtrick can be worth as much as a game itself. See MATCHPOINT PLAY.

Let us examine a few illustrations of the safety play.

```
          ♠ 7 5 4
          ♡ Q 9 6 4
          ◇ A 8 4
          ♣ A K 3

          ♠ A K 3
          ♡ A J 10 3 2
          ◇ K 2
          ♣ 6 5 2
```

Playing rubber bridge, South arrives at a 4♡ contract. West opens the ♣J, dummy's king is put up — and East drops the ♣Q.

In rubber bridge, declarer has no problem as to how to proceed. He has ten sure tricks. So, with the safety of the contract being the sole consideration, a low trump is led, taken with the ace, and a low trump is led back. West wins with the king, and the declarer is home safely. But if the trump finesse had been tried, declarer would not have enjoyed the future of the hand:

```
                    ♠ 7 5 4
                    ♡ Q 9 6 4
                    ◇ A 8 4
                    ♣ A K 3
   ♠ 10 6 2                        ♠ Q J 9 8
   ♡ K 5                           ♡ 8 7
   ◇ 10 7                          ◇ Q J 9 6 5 3
   ♣ J 10 9 8 7 4                  ♣ Q
                    ♠ A K 3
                    ♡ A J 10 3 2
                    ◇ K 2
                    ♣ 6 5 2
```

As is evident, if declarer had taken the trump finesse, it would have lost, and West would have returned a club for East to trump. Declarer would then have gone down a trick.

In duplicate bridge, the proper play of the hand is not as simple, for your objective cannot be defined specifically. Should you play safe, or should you try for the overtrick by taking the heart finesse? Obviously, East's ♣Q is singleton, and the trump finesse, if it loses, will result in declarer's defeat. But can declarer, in a duplicate game, afford a safety play in the trump suit, and give up a fifty-fifty chance for an overtrick (if the trump finesse is successful)? If the trump finesse is taken successfully, declarer will get a top or a tie-for-top on the board. If it loses, he gets a bottom or tie-for-bottom on the board. Another factor which must be considered by declarer at matchpoint play is that at the other tables West might not open a club, in which case the declarers at those tables will all take the trump finesse, since they will have no reason to fear that East will trump a club.

Thus, in duplicate bridge, one can play for a top or a bottom by taking the trump finesse for the king. In rubber bridge, the finesse is not even considered, for the safety of the contract is the sole concern.

Here is another safety-play deal. The game is rubber bridge. South is declarer, playing a 6♠ contract.

♠ A 9 8 2
♡ A 6 5
◇ 8 3
♣ K Q 7 4

♠ K 10 7 6 4
♡ K Q 8 2
◇ A K
♣ A 2

West opens the ◇ Q, declarer winning with the king. It is apparent that if the four outstanding trumps are divided either 2-2 or 3-1, there is no problem, since in these cases South cannot possibly lose more than one spade trick. But if they are divided 4-0, then danger exists.

Proper safety-play technique, to avoid the loss of more than one spade trick, is to lead a low spade at trick two, and when West follows with a low spade, to insert the *8-spot* from dummy. Either the 8 will win, or it will be captured by East's jack (or queen). If East's jack wins, then there will remain but two outstanding spades, and declarer's ace and king will pick them up on the two succeeding rounds of trumps.

But to take this safety play in duplicate bridge would be losing tactics, for if the four outstanding trumps were divided 2-2, declarer would be throwing away an overtrick. And surely the four outstanding trumps are more likely to be divided 2-2 than 4-0.

In rubber bridge, the safety play is insurance against a bad break that would defeat declarer's slam contract. The cost of the insurance is the payment of a possible overtrick, worth 30 points. In duplicate bridge, the overtrick could be worth its weight in gold, and might well mean the difference between winning and losing a tournament, and the rubber bridge safety play becomes a duplicate bridge "unsafety" play. See also EXPECTATION.

Fred Karpin

SAN FRANCISCO CONVENTION. A 4 NT convention, sometimes called the Warren convention, with responses showing aces and kings in one bid. Aces are counted as three points and kings as one point, and the responses are:

5♣	less than 3 points
5◇	3 points
5♡	4 points
5♠	5 points
5 NT	6 points, etc.

By inspecting his own hand, the 4 NT bidder can almost always judge what his partner's response represents in aces and kings. A response of 5♡ must show an ace and a king, or four kings.

The convention results in some disadvantage if the responder's hand is strong. If he has three aces, the response of 6♡ may take his side too high.

SANCTION. The permission given by the ACBL to a club, unit or district to hold a duplicate event within ACBL territory. In general a specific sanction to hold a tournament must be obtained from the League in advance of the date scheduled for the tournament. The League sends the sponsoring organization a form suitable for use in reporting the results of the tournament and this report is used by the ACBL to record MASTER POINTS won by the contestants.

SANCTIONED CLUBS. Groups of players desirous of holding periodic duplicate tournaments. These clubs are either cooperative organizations of players, groups within another organization such as a church, a YMCA, a commercial organization, or a proprietary club run by an individual or small groups to which other players are invited. These clubs award Rating Point Certificates for their regularly scheduled games. For every 12 regularly scheduled games, or once each calendar quarter, a Club Tournament game may be held. All points awards won at the Club Tournament are issued by the club on Blue Ribbon Certificates. Two Charity Club Tournaments, one Olympiad Fund Club Tournament and one Membership Tournament are also allocated to each club annually under regulations of the League.

SANDWICH. A term used in Europe to describe an overcall or bid made in fourth position after both opponents have bid. For example:

WEST	NORTH	EAST	SOUTH
			1◇
Pass	1♠	2♣	

The term emphasizes the danger of bidding in such circumstances.

SANDWICH DEFENSE. A group of defensive suit combination plays calling for the play of the second-highest card from particular broken holdings.

NORTH
J x x

EAST
A Q 10

NORTH
10 x x

EAST
A J 9 or K J 9

NORTH
9 x x

EAST
K 10 8 or Q 10 8

In each case dummy's highest card is "sandwiched" by the second and third cards held by East. East must lead his second card, the top of the sandwich, to neutralize dummy's card. The importance of the play can be seen by putting appropriate combinations in declarer's hand: in (1) K–x–x; in (2) Q–x–x (or A–Q–x); in (3) A–J–x.

The same plays must be made if these positions are turned 180 degrees, with the lead in the West hand and the card to be sandwiched hidden, but the play is less obvious.

For a similar play by the declarer, see BACKWARD FINESSE.

SANS ATOUT. Notrump. The term is French.

SAVE. See SACRIFICE.

SCANDINAVIAN CHAMPIONSHIPS. See NORDIC CHAMPIONSHIPS.

SCHENKEN SYSTEM. An artificial 1♣ system devised by HOWARD SCHENKEN, New York City, and played by him in World Championship competition in partnership with PETER LEVENTRITT.

The main features of the system are:

(1) 1♣ opening. Forcing, and used on almost all strong hands. It shows a minimum of 17 high-card points or the distributional equivalent. There are three types: balanced notrump type with 19–22; slightly unbalanced hand with 17 or more; strong distribution with 14 or more.

1♢ is the conventional negative response, 0–6 points. 2♣ is also artificial, showing a semi-positve response of 7–8 points, including at least one king or ace, and promising a rebid. Other responses are positive, natural, and forcing to game. After an overcall up to 3♢, a double is "positive," for takeout, and shows at least 9 points.

After a 1♢ negative response, showing less than 9 points: a non-jump suit rebid may be passed; a jump suit rebid is forcing for one round; a 1 NT rebid shows 19–20; a 2 NT rebid shows 21–22.

STAYMAN is used after a 1 NT response or rebid.

(2) One bids in other suits are limited, with a maximum of 16 points. Responder normally passes with less than 8 points.

All raises and notrump responses are limited and non-forcing. A jump to game in a major may be based on high-card strength or distribution, because the limited opening has excluded slam chances. 3♣ response to a major is equivalent to a strong raise (16–17 points including distribution) and requests opener to bid a singleton.

(3) 1 NT opening is standard (16–18). 2♣ response is non-forcing STAYMAN. 2♢ shows an unbalanced responding hand (with a singleton or void), no four-card major, is game forcing and requests opener to show major suit stoppers.

(4) 2♣ is a natural opening with at least a good five-card club suit. A response of 2♢ asks opener to show a four-card major.

(5) 2♢. An artificial forcing opening bid used to locate specific honors. A 2♡ response denies an ace; other minimum responses are ace-showing, except that 2 NT shows the heart ace. With two aces,

responder jumps in the higher ranking ace with touching aces, 3 NT with non-touching aces, or 4♣ with the black aces. The opener follows with minimum rebids to locate kings and queens in the same way.

A 2 NT rebid over 2♡ shows 23–25, and may be passed. A 3 NT rebid shows 26–27.

(6) 2♢ and 2♡ are weak two-bids, 8–12 points and a suit of reasonable strength. 2 NT is the only forcing response.

(7) 2 NT. Shows a minimum of five cards in each minor suit with 10–12 high card points not vulnerable, 13–16 high card points vulnerable.

(8) 3 NT opening is based on a solid minor suit with 8½–9 playing tricks and no side suit worse than Q–x.

(9) 3♣. A solid six- or seven-card suit, 10–15 points.

(10) Preemptive jump overcalls depending on the vulnerability.

SCHROEDER SQUEEZE. A triple trump squeeze without the count in a three-card position. This unique ending was executed in play by Dirk Schroeder of Wiesbaden, Germany.

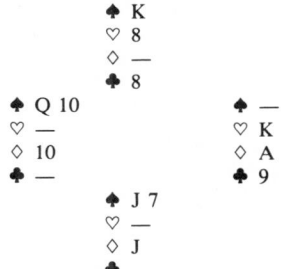

With spades trump, and the lead in North, on the lead of the ♠K East was squeezed. If he threw the winning heart or club South would have a winner to lead from dummy at the twelfth trick. If he threw the ♢A, South would ruff something and score his ♢J at the finish.

The complete deal was:

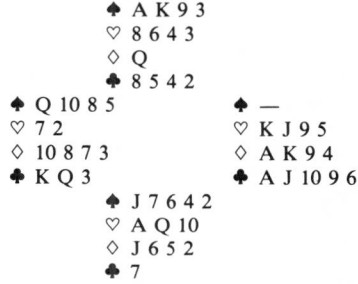

In 3♠ doubled the defense led two rounds of clubs. South ruffed, entered dummy with a high spade, finessed the ♡10, and surrendered a diamond. After a third round of clubs was ruffed in the closed hand South ruffed a diamond, finessed the ♡Q, and led the ♡A. West ruffed and led a diamond and then ruffed in dummy to produce the ending shown.

SCHWAB CUP. For the World Pairs Championship, first contested in Cannes in 1962. Originally presented by Charles M. Schwab in 1933 for contest between the United States and England (see ANGLO-AMERICAN MATCHES). The trophy was redonated to the World Bridge Federation by the heirs of ELY CULBERTSON.

"SCIENTISTS" VS. "TRADITIONALISTS" MATCH. A 180-deal match, held in New York City in mid-January of 1965, sponsored by *The Bridge World* in an attempt to determine the value of highly technical and artificial bidding systems that had come to the fore in the Sixties. The "Scientist" partnerships — AL ROTH-TOBIAS STONE, VICTOR MITCHELL-SAM STAYMAN, ROBERT JORDAN-ARTHUR ROBINSON with non-playing captains JULIUS ROSENBLUM and EDGAR KAPLAN — were allowed to use any artificial convention. Their "Traditionalist" adversaries — B. JAY BECKER-DOROTHY HAYDEN, LEW MATHE-MEYER SCHLEIFER, ERIC MURRAY-SAMMY KEHELA with nonplaying captains CHARLES SOLOMON and BILL ROOT were restricted to standard bidding methods.

In a match that generated considerable public interest, the "Scientists" won by 53 IMPs, 367–314, but the result was generally considered inconclusive since the "Traditionalists" had led at one point by 108 IMPs. The swings were so huge that neither side was willing to concede the superiority of the other's bidding methods.

SCISSORS COUP. A play aimed at cutting the opponents' communications, usually in order to prevent a ruff (sometimes called less descriptively "the coup without a name").

```
              ♠ A 10
              ♡ J 9 7 3
              ◊ J 2
              ♣ K Q 10 7 6
  ♠ 8 7 5 2                    ♠ Q J 4 3
  ♡ 6 5                        ♡ A 8
  ◊ Q 6 3                      ◊ A K 10 8 5 4
  ♣ 9 8 5 2                    ♣ 3
              ♠ K 9 6
              ♡ K Q 10 4 2
              ◊ 9 7
              ♣ A J 4
```

South plays in 4♡ after East has opened the bidding with 1◊. South feels happy when it appears that there are only three losers, but feels much less happy when East wins the opening diamond lead with the king, and shifts to the ♣3. It is obvious that this is a singleton, and that West has a diamond entry to give his partner a ruff.

South must try to cut the diamond communication, so he cashes the ♣A-K and leads the ♣9. Dummy's diamond is discarded, allowing East to win, and the defense can make only one more trick. South's play succeeds whenever East has both missing spade honors, or if East has a trebleton queen and fails to unblock.

SCORE. (1) Noun: the number of game or premium points earned as a result of the bidding and play of a hand, rubber, or session of bridge. (2) Verb: to record the score.

There is slight difference, due to the nature of the games, between the scoring at rubber bridge, CHICAGO, and tournament bridge. The latter, too, has different scoring procedures and values, depending on the type of event. See BOARD-A-MATCH SCORING; CUMULATIVE SCORE; INTERNATIONAL MATCH POINTS; LAWS (Laws 75 to 84); LAWS OF DUPLICATE (Laws 73, 74); MATCHPOINT; MATCHPOINT SCORING.

SCORECARD. See PICK-UP SLIP; SCORE PAD; RECAPITULATION SHEET. A personal (or private) scorecard used in tournaments is called a CONVENTION CARD; when used in PARTY or PROGRESSIVE BRIDGE, it is called a TALLY.

SCORE PAD. A printed tablet of sheets of paper used to keep a record of the numerative functions of a game of rubber or CHICAGO bridge. Score pads come in various shapes and sizes, and some are imprinted with the name of the club at which they are used, but they are all ruled with printed lines, leaving spaces for entering game and partial score results and extra premiums such as undertrick penalties and slam and rubber bonuses and honors.

SCORE SHEET. In club games, the summary sheet on which the MATCHPOINTS won by a pair are entered for ease in totaling; in larger tournaments, the RECAPITULATION SHEET, to which the scores are posted from the PICK-UP SLIPS.

SCORER, OFFICIAL. See TOURNAMENT DIRECTOR.

SCORING. At duplicate, scoring is a fairly complicated operation. At club games, a slip for recording the results on each of the boards in play usually accompanies the board, folded so that it fits into a pocket. Previous results are not immediately apparent until the board has been played. See TRAVELING SCORE SLIP. After the board has been played, all four players are entitled to know the results of previous plays of that board.

In duplicate tournaments, PICK-UP SLIPS are provided at each table for recording the results of each board, round by round. These slips are collected by caddies and brought to the scorer who enters them on a RECAPITULATION SHEET. This sheet provides the information basic to awarding MATCHPOINTS, the total of which is the session or overall total, from which winners and placers are determined.

SCORING ACROSS THE FIELD. A method of scoring a multi-section MATCHPOINT event designed to prevent inequitable score comparisons when the results in one section are at extreme variance with the results in other sections. The score on each board is matchpointed not just against other contestants in the same section but against the contestants in all sections playing in the same direction.

SCORING CORRECTIONS. These are provided for in the regulations covering tournament bridge. The RECAPITULATION SHEET has a space in which the end of the correction period is noted, after which time no more player errors may be corrected. Scorer's errors may be corrected any time through the end of the tournament.

Corrections are made by the scoring staff whenever the score slip is clearly in error — i.e., shows incorrect vulnerability, incorrect addition, etc., or when the slip has been incorrectly transcribed. When the correction involves a question of the results themselves — whether a contract was defeated one or two tricks, or whether extra tricks were scored — the correction may be made, within the limits of the correction period, only if there is reasonable proof that a different score was achieved at the table. Entries on private scorecards of both pairs usually is considered satisfactory proof. See LAWS OF DUPLICATE, Law 75.

At rubber bridge, the rules set a time limit beyond which a correction may not be claimed — in most cases, after the score of the rubber has been determined and agreed upon.

SCORING FORMS. Printed forms on which results of a duplicate board, a session, or an event are entered. Usually the North player enters the score on a TRAVELING SCORE SLIP or a PICK-UP SLIP. If the latter is used, the scorer enters the result on a RECAPITULATION SHEET. Matchpoints are awarded either on the recapitulation sheet if pick-up slips are used, or on the traveling score slips. In team events of head-on competition, each pair keeps a running score of the results on the boards they play, and verification of these slips at each table makes it possible for each team to determine its own score, either in total point or IMP scoring.

SCORING TABLE. The current scoring table is set out in LAWS (Law 84) and LAWS OF DUPLICATE (Law 73). See also FRENCH SCORING and SCORING VARIANTS.

Today's scoring table includes few deviations from the original developed by Vanderbilt in 1925, having survived considerable tinkering, especially in the 1932 code. The 1927 Laws provided that each trick in a notrump contract was worth 35 points; that the premium for making a doubled contract was increased from 50 to 100 if vulnerable (if redoubled, the premiums were 100 and 200); and the penalties for undertricks increased as the tricks won fell farther short of contract, as follows:

PENALTIES

Undertricks (Scored in Adversaries' honor score):

	Points
If Undoubled (When Declarer is Not Vulnerable)	
per trick	50
If Undoubled (When Declarer is Vulnerable)	
for first trick	100
for subsequent tricks	200
If Doubled (When Declarer is Not Vulnerable)	
first two tricks, per trick	100
for third and fourth tricks, per trick	200
for subsequent tricks, per trick	400
If Doubled (When Declarer is Vulnerable)	
for the first trick	200
for subsequent tricks, per trick	400

Redoubling doubles the doubled premiums and penalties.

Partly on the theory that the higher scores were largely responsible for the enormous popularity of contract bridge, the 1932 Laws sharply increased slam bonuses and also increased penalties, with non-vulnerable undertricks as well as vulnerable undertricks punished on a rising scale:

PREMIUMS

	Not Vulnerable			Vulnerable		
Little Slam	500	500	500	750	750	750
Grand Slam	1500	1500	1500	2250	2250	2250

PENALTIES

Undertricks	Not Vulnerable			Vulnerable		
	Not Dbld	Dbld	Re-Dbld	Not Dbld	Dbld	Re-Dbld
First	50	100	200	100	200	400
Inc. ea. add. by	—	50	100	50	100	200
Thus:						
2nd is worth	50	150	300	150	300	600
3rd is worth	50	200	400	200	400	800

Furthermore, the value of tricks made in notrump contracts alternated: first, third, fifth, and seventh trick were worth 30 each; the second, fourth, and sixth, 40 each. Also, the premium for making a doubled contract was dropped.

The distortions imposed by this inflated scoring were corrected within three years — the shortest period ever for the issuance of a new Laws code. In the forty years following issuance of the 1935 code, the only change in scoring was the restoration in the 1943 Laws of a bonus for making a doubled contract, 50 points whether or not vulnerable.

SCORING VARIANTS. Several kinds of scoring variants have been introduced to make tournament bridge or rubber bridge a better competition. Among the more important are: (1) FRENCH SCORING, to make four of a major and 4 NT of equal value. (2) PENALTY LIMITS in TOTAL POINT SCORING and PROGRESSIVE BRIDGE to limit the SWING on one hand. (3) Different TOPS in final competition of multi-session events or all sessions of important tournaments. (4) IMPS FOR PAIR GAMES, to make conditions comparable to INTERNATIONAL MATCH-POINTS. (5) HYBRID SCORING to combine advantages of BOARD-A-MATCH and aggregate scores in team events.

SCOTTISH BRIDGE UNION. This union consists of 249 clubs located in six regional districts, Western, Eastern, Northern, Southern, Central, and Ayrshire, with a membership in 1982 of approximately 10,500. The Union is affiliated with the British Bridge League, and annually competes for the CAMROSE TROPHY, winning the event six times since 1964, two of those being jointly with England. The SBU also operates an independent masterpoint program; its awards are on an identical scale as the awards of the English Bridge Union.

Officers, 1982:
President: George Hay
Secretary: Morag Malcolm, Shawbost, Brookfield,   By Johnstone, Renfrewshire, Scotland

SCRAMBLED MITCHELL MOVEMENT. A modification of the MITCHELL MOVEMENT, used when it is desired to produce one winning pair. Each pair plays approximately one-half the boards North–South and the rest East–West. This is accomplished by switching the arrows designating North so that they point to the original East simultaneously at the end of certain rounds. The original East–West pairs, having adopted a moving pattern, continue to move, and the original North–South pairs remain at their tables, even though the arrows have been switched and they are playing the East–West hands.

Howell or Three-quarter movements are technically preferred. Balanced comparison is never achieved in the Scrambled Mitchell movement. RUSSELL BALDWIN suggested that BALANCED COMPARISONS can be approached by three ARROW SWITCHES so spaced that the rounds are divided into four unequal groups. GEORGE BEYNON and Frank Farrington give the following table for various sized sections to approach balanced comparisons.

Tables		Arrow North	Arrow East
6	Rounds	1,2,5	3,4,6
7	Rounds	1,2,5	3,4,6,7
8	Rounds	1,2,5,6	3,4,7,8
9	Rounds	1,2,3,5,7	4,6,8,9
10	Rounds	1,2,3,6,8	4,5,7,9,10
11	Rounds	1,2,3,5,6,8	4,7,9,10,11
12	Rounds	1,2,3,6,7,9	4,5,8,10,11,12
13	Rounds	1,2,4,5,10,12,13	3,6,7,8,9,11
14	Rounds	1,2,4,5,10,12,13	3,6,7,8,9,11
15	Rounds	1,2,3,4,7,8,9,12	5,6,10,11,13

These were improved by LAWRENCE ROSLER in 1964, as a result of prolonged mathematical calculations. The following tables give as close to a perfect balance of comparisons as can be obtained.

Tables		Arrow North	Arrow East
6	Rounds	1,2	3,4,5
7	Rounds	1,2,3,4,5	6,7
8	Rounds	1,4	2,3,5,6,7
9	Rounds	1,2,4,8,9	3,5,6,7
10	Rounds	1,4,5,7,8,9	2,3,6
11	Rounds	1,2,4,10	3,5,6,7,8,9,11
12	Rounds	1,2,4,6,7,8	3,5,9,10,11
13	Rounds	1,2,3,5,6,9	4,7,8,10,11,12,13
14	Rounds	1,3,9,13	2,4,5,6,7,8,10,11,12

SCRAMBLING. The art of maneuvering into a tolerable contract when the opponents are intent on collecting a low-level penalty. This often calls for the use of an SOS REDOUBLE. One of the commonest situations occur when 1 NT is doubled for penalties. See DEFENSE TO DOUBLE OF 1 NT.

SCRAMBLING PLAYS, SCRAMBLING SIGNALS. See DECEPTIVE PLAY.

SCREEN. An opaque barrier placed diagonally across the bridge table so that no player can see his partner. Perforce each player can see only one opponent. The screen has an opening in the center where the board in play is placed. Directly above the board is some sort of curtain arrangement that can be lifted or pulled aside once the bidding is complete. This permits all players to see the cards being played, but the opening is shallow enough that the players still cannot see their partner's face. The screen extends to the floor, blocking partners' feet from each other, the result of a foot-tapping incident in the 1975 Bermuda Bowl (see BERMUDA INCIDENT). The bidding is done by BIDDING BOX. Bids from one side of the table

are revealed to the players on the opposite side either by MONITORS calling them aloud or by using some sort of ROLLING BOX. Both bids are relayed to the other side of the table simultaneously so that it is more difficult to discern who huddled.

Screens were used for the first time by the ACBL during the Vanderbilt Knockout Teams in 1974. The first appearance of screens at a world championship took place at the 1975 Bermuda Bowl in Bermuda. At first there was a great deal of controversy about the use of screens. Those who opposed their use felt that screens would create the public impression that a lot of cheating takes place in high-level bridge. They also felt that screens would be distracting and dehumanizing. Those in favor felt that screens would forestall charges of cheating (see CHEATING ACCUSATIONS). However, screens received almost unanimous acclaim from the players who used them right from the outset. The players felt it made competing ethically much easier – they no longer had to worry about making facial expressions, they no longer had to bend over backward because of partner's huddle – they no longer knew when partner huddled. Certain rule violations, such as leads out of turn or bids out of turn, became very rare because only one side of the table was involved at a time and such violations could be adjusted without any improper information being transmitted to partner. As a result of these benefits, screens are used in late rounds of almost all major team and some pair championships. See FRANCO BOARDS.

SCRIP. Financial certificates issued by the ACBL for use as prizes at tournaments. The certificates may be used to purchase bridge supplies, pay ACBL dues or pay for tournament entries.

SEAT. The position which a contestant takes at a table; usually designated by one of the four principal points of the compass, North, South, East, or West. The first two and the last two are partners, and each pair is the opponent of the other pair.

SEATING ASSIGNMENTS. At duplicate tournaments, the ENTRIES sold to the players carry a section designation, a table number, and a direction. These are the seating assignments. For subsequent sessions of the same event, players either take their original seating assignments and await DIRECTOR'S INSTRUCTIONS, or pick up a new entry blank or GUIDE CARD for the subsequent session.

SECOND GAME. The second game of a rubber. Two games are required to win a rubber, and at the conclusion of a rubber a side may have won one, two, or no games, during that rubber, but the winning of any second game immediately ends the rubber.

SECOND GUESSER. See RESULT PLAYER.

SECOND HAND PLAY. The old whist rule of "second hand low" is sound enough as a rule of thumb, but there are many possible exceptions. The following are the most important and crucial situations.

(1) In a suit contract, declarer leads low toward a suit headed by K–Q or K–J. The left-hand defender has the ace, and he knows that the lead may be a singleton. Unless there is clear-cut reason for grabbing tricks quickly, the defender should usually duck without hesitation. If he fails to make his ace, it may not matter — declarer would presumably have been able to secure a discard. But if he puts up the ace, declarer is likely to benefit. If dummy has K–Q two tricks are established, and if dummy has K–J declarer avoids a guess.

The prompt duck is usually best in the reverse situation, when a singleton is led from dummy. The reasons are similar.

(2) In a suit contract declarer leads toward his hand in a suit in which dummy holds several small cards. There is a possibility that declarer has a singleton king. In this case the ace should be played if the defender has the queen or jack, because declarer cannot then make a losing guess.

(3) A second hand high play with a king or queen may be aimed at preventing a suit establishment.

```
                 ♣ A J 10 3 2
  ♣ K 5 4                      ♣ Q 7 6
                 ♣ 9 8
```

Dummy has no side entry. When South leads a club, West must play high (and would do the same with the queen instead of the king). South cannot make more than one club trick. If West wrongly played low, East would have to hold up his queen to prevent South's making four tricks in the suit.

Other reasons for playing second hand high include: an urgent need to establish partner's suit before his entry is removed; the need to avoid a throw-in; and the need to prevent declarer's ducking a trick to the other defender in an elimination position.

For other considerations involving second hand play see COVERING HONORS and PLAY FROM EQUALS.

SECOND NEGATIVE RESPONSE AFTER ARTIFICIAL FORCING OPENING. A rebid by a responder who has made a negative response to his partner's strong artificial opening bid, such as 2 ◊ in response to 2 ♣, that shows a hand worth about 0–3 points. Some partnerships use HERBERT NEGATIVE, the cheapest possible suit rebid by responder, as the second negative; others use the cheaper minor suit rebid. See also DOUBLE NEGATIVE; 2 ◊ ARTIFICIAL RESPONSE TO FORCING 2 ♣.

SECONDARY EVENT. An event at a North American Championship held concurrently with a championship event. Such events, which are open to players eliminated from the major events and to new players, are usually two sessions long and carry regional rating. See CHAMPIONSHIP TOURNAMENTS, SIDE GAME.

SECONDARY HONORS. The lower honors, i.e., queens and jacks. The king of a suit may also be considered a secondary honor when it is not accompanied by the ace. Secondary honors generally carry their weight better in notrump than in suit contracts,

especialy when they are not located in partner's long suits. See PRIMARY HONORS.

SECONDARY SQUEEZE. A squeeze in which the squeeze card is followed by the loss of one or more tricks to the opponents.

(1) *Squeeze Establishment* (also called delayed duck squeeze by DR. CLYDE E. LOVE and squeeze suit-out by GEORGE S. COFFIN). A squeeze establishment has these characteristics: one opponent possesses a guard to a long menace and a winner in a suit which declarer seeks to establish. The preliminary squeeze forces him to discard an additional winner or a card which may be led to his partner's winner.

The endings are based on simple squeeze positions except that declarer has two losers with no convenient way to RECTIFY THE COUNT. Thus, in effect, the rectification of the count takes place after the lead of the squeeze card. Some typical positions:

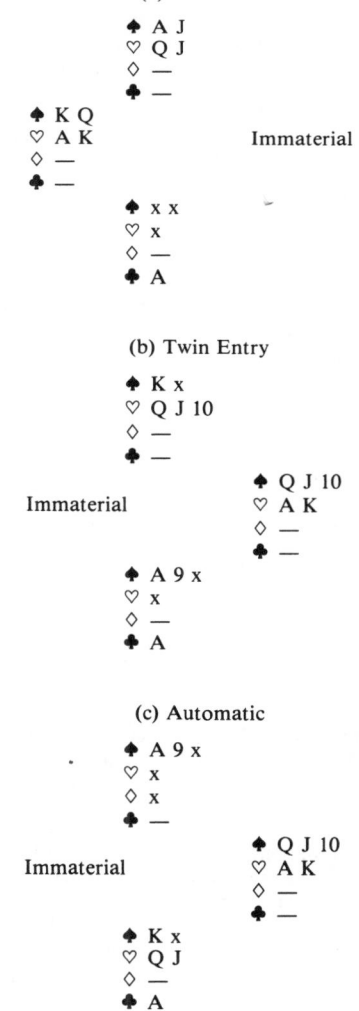

(a) Positional

```
              ♠ A J
              ♡ Q J
              ◊ —
              ♣ —
  ♠ K Q
  ♡ A K                Immaterial
  ◊ —
  ♣ —
              ♠ x x
              ♡ x
              ◊ —
              ♣ A
```

(b) Twin Entry

```
                 ♠ K x
                 ♡ Q J 10
                 ◊ —
                 ♣ —
                             ♠ Q J 10
  Immaterial                 ♡ A K
                             ◊ —
                             ♣ —
                 ♠ A 9 x
                 ♡ x
                 ◊ —
                 ♣ A
```

(c) Automatic

```
                 ♠ A 9 x
                 ♡ x
                 ◊ x
                 ♣ —
                             ♠ Q J 10
  Immaterial                 ♡ A K
                             ◊ —
                             ♣ —
                 ♠ K x
                 ♡ Q J
                 ◊ —
                 ♣ A
```

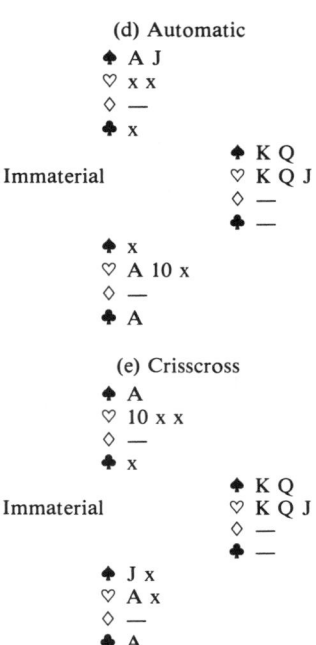

(d) Automatic

♠ A J
♡ x x
◇ —
♣ x

Immaterial

♠ K Q
♡ K Q J
◇ —
♣ —

♠ x
♡ A 10 x
◇ —
♣ A

(e) Crisscross

♠ A
♡ 10 x x
◇ —
♣ x

Immaterial

♠ K Q
♡ K Q J
◇ —
♣ —

♠ J x
♡ A x
◇ —
♣ A

In all the above cases, South leads the ♣A. Defender must discard a heart in order to protect his spade guard. South can then lead a heart in order to establish a trick for himself in that suit.

In (a) through (e) above, a defender was forced to discard a second winner in the suit which declarer sought to establish. In a minor variation (sometimes called a squeeze elimination [ROMANET]), the opponent is squeezed out of a side winner or a card which may be led to partner's winner.

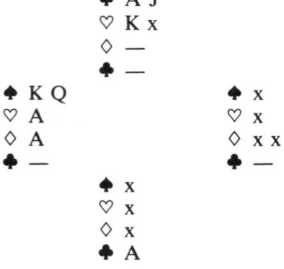

♠ A J
♡ K x
◇ —
♣ —

♠ K Q   ♠ x
♡ A   ♡ x
◇ A   ◇ x x
♣ —   ♣ —

♠ x
♡ x
◇ x
♣ A

South leads his ♣A, and West is squeezed in three suits. He must discard the diamond winner, and North discards a spade. Now South can concede a heart and establish North's king. Had the diamond winner been with East and a small diamond in the West hand, West would have been forced to part with his exit card to his partner's winner.

(2) *Squeeze Throw-In* (also known as squeeze strip). An opponent guards a two-card menace which is in the form of a tenace combination, and he also holds a winner which corresponds to a low card in that suit held by declarer. Declarer intends to lead the low card, throwing the opponent into the lead, to force a play into the tenace.

If the opponent has been stripped of exit cards in all other suits, he still may have too many winners in the throw-in suit. In that case, the preliminary squeeze reduces the number of surplus winners which the defender can hold in the throw-in suit.

A. Declarer has a major tenace, and the throw-in is followed by two tricks for declarer. Declarer may have two or more losers.

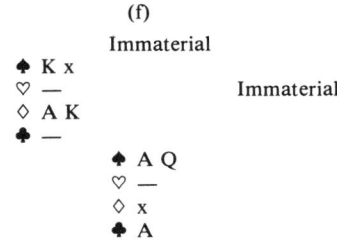

(f)

Immaterial

♠ K x
♡ —
◇ A K
♣ —

Immaterial

♠ A Q
♡ —
◇ x
♣ A

Squeeze card with tenace.

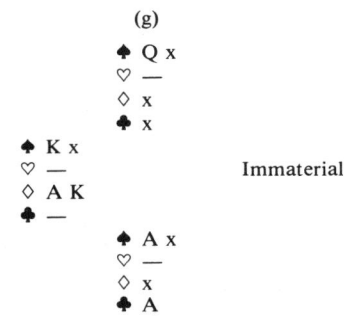

(g)

♠ Q x
♡ —
◇ x
♣ x

♠ K x
♡ —
◇ A K
♣ —

Immaterial

♠ A x
♡ —
◇ x
♣ A

Split tenace.

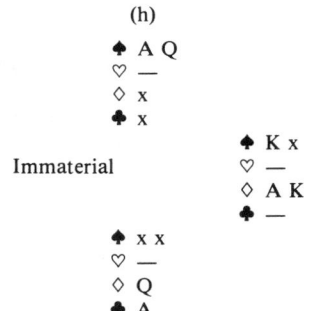

(h)

♠ A Q
♡ —
◇ x
♣ x

Immaterial

♠ K x
♡ —
◇ A K
♣ —

♠ x x
♡ —
◇ Q
♣ A

Squeeze card opposite tenace.

In (f) through (h), the ♣A is led, forcing the defender to part with a diamond winner. Now South leads the diamond, and the defender is thrown in to lead away from his ♠K. Note that the tenace may be with or opposite the squeeze card, or split between declarer and dummy.

B. Opponent has the major tenace, and the throw-in is followed by one trick for the declarer. Declarer has three losers.

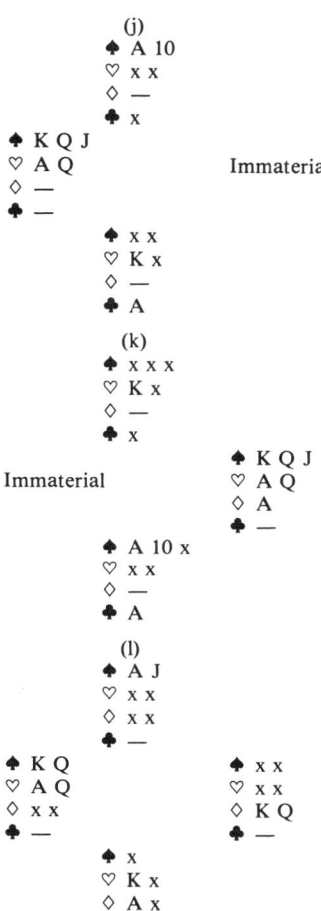

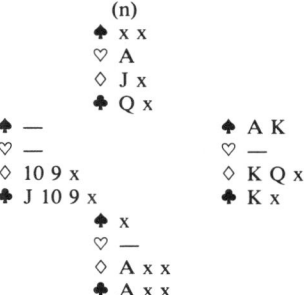

South leads the ♣A, which forces the defender to discard a surplus winner— ♠J in (j), ◇A in (k), or a potential exit card, the diamond, in (l). Now South takes his spade tricks, and exits in spades, so that he ends up by taking a trick with his ♡K.

When declarer has a major tenace, so that the defenders cannot afford to lead away from his stopper (Dr. Love calls this a vulnerable stopper), then the endplay is effective when declarer has two losers, as shown in A. The preliminary squeeze may force the defender to discard a surplus winner (as indicated) or an exit card. In this situation

South leads the ♣A, and West is forced to discard his exit card in hearts. Now he can be thrown in with a diamond, and forced to lead a spade into declarer's tenace.

C. Three-suit variants: in the case where one opponent has guards in three suits, which include at least one vulnerable stopper (i.e., declarer has a major tenace in one of the suits), the squeeze works when declarer has three or more losers. Precisely three losers are required only if the defender has a potential exit card in one of the suits.

South has four losers, and the squeeze must fail since East has a potential exit card in diamonds. North leads the ♡A, and East throws a spade. Now East wins the next spade, and plays a high diamond to the ace. He wins the next diamond, but he can now play a low diamond to West's 10, so that the end play is ineffective.

The squeeze establishment also has a three-suit variant which will gain a trick if declarer has three or more losers. Again, precisely three losers are required only if the defenders can kill one of the menace cards.

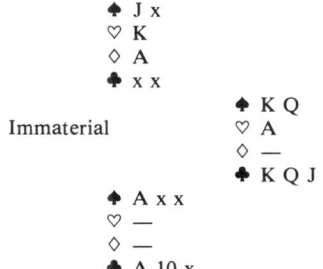

South has three tricks on top. The ◇A is led and East is squeezed in three suits. He must discard a potential club trick. North leads a club, and declarer ducks, in order to establish his 10, which furnishes him with a fourth trick.

In certain squeeze-establishment plays, declarer may duck two or even three times in order to establish a trick for himself; understandably such positions arise rarely in play.

In another rare variant, the secondary squeeze involving three suits may result in the gain of two tricks to declarer: with three losers in hand, a squeeze-establishment play concedes one trick to the opponents, and adds one trick to declarer's stock. As a result, the count has been rectified, and declarer may be able to continue with a simple squeeze for the gain of another trick.

For related squeeze situations, see STEPPINGSTONE SQUEEZE; VICE SQUEEZE; WINKLE SQUEEZE.

Monroe Ingberman

SECTION. A group of contestants who constitute a self-contained unit in the competition in one event for one session of a tournament.

SECTIONAL, SECTIONAL TOURNAMENT. See CHAMPIONSHIP TOURNAMENTS.

SEED, SEEDING. The assignment of certain tables to particularly strong contestants when entries are sold so as to assure that there will be no preponderance of strong pairs in direct competition within any one section. It is desirable to seed weak pairs also to prevent an imbalance of weakness in a particular section. In pair events, tables 3 and 9 are usually reserved for seeded players; at national tournaments, tables 3, 6 and 9 usually are reserved. In board-a-match team competitions, adjacent pairs of tables such as 1 and 2, 9 and 10, 17 and 18, etc., are used for spotting the strongest teams through the field. In individual tournaments, an effort is made to assure that the North players, at least, are able to keep score. In a Swiss Team event, half the field is seeded for the first match, and each seed is paired against an unseeded team. Subsequent pairings are random, subject to the general rules for Swiss Teams.

ACBL North American Championships knockout events (Vanderbilt and Spingold) utilize various formulas for seeding which include not only masterpoint holdings but recent performances by the players.

SEESAW SQUEEZE. See ENTRY-SHIFTING SQUEEZE.

SELECTION OF INTERNATIONAL TEAMS. See INTERNATIONAL OPEN TEAM SELECTION; INTERNATIONAL WOMEN'S TEAM SELECTION.

SEMIFINAL. (1) The round of four or six in a knockout team tournament. (2) In a pair, team or individual tournament, the round immediately following the qualifying round and immediately preceding the final round.

SEMI-PSYCHIC. A departure from normal bidding methods which is not a complete bluff but is still intended to deceive the opponents. The term usually refers to an opening bid well below minimum values, but LEAD-INHIBITING BIDS belong in the same category.

SEMI-SET GAME. A rubber bridge session involving five or more players in which one pair (sometimes two pairs), such as a husband and wife, play as partners except when one of them is cut out.

SEMI-SOLID SUIT. A suit of at least six cards which appears to contain only one loser; a suit that is one high card short of being a SOLID SUIT, for example, AKJ10xx, AQJxxx, AKxxxxx, KQJxxxx.

SEND IT BACK. Redouble (colloquialism).

SENIOR AND ADVANCED SENIOR MASTER PAIR CHAMPIONSHIP, NORTH AMERICAN CHAMPIONSHIP. See MILES TROPHY.

SENIOR MASTER. A high-ranking player in the AMERICAN CONTRACT BRIDGE LEAGUE. See RANKING OF PLAYERS.

SENIOR MASTER INDIVIDUAL CHAMPIONSHIP. See BEYNON TROPHY.

SENIOR TOURNAMENTS. Competitions in which only players older than a specified age — usually 55 — may play. The first such tournament was a sectional staged at Sun City FL in 1977. The reaction from participants was so enthusiastic that regional tournaments for seniors only are now held.

SEQUENCE. Two or more cards in consecutive order of rank, as A–K–Q (three-card sequence) or Q–J–10–9 (four-card sequence). See PLAY FROM EQUALS.

SEQUENCE DISCARDS. The discard of an honor normally shows an honor sequence, of which the discard is the highest. Therefore the discard of a queen denies the king, and guarantees the jack and usually the 10.

The same principle applies in following suit when a top honor has already been played. This follows the more general principle of discarding the highest card which can be spared in transmitting a signal.

SEQUENCE OF ROUNDS. In a session of bridge the sequence of rounds is broken up for a few necessary irregularities. After about half the rounds have been played, the traveling pairs in a section with an even number of tables and no bye stand must skip a table. In board-a-match team events, there is often an irregularity at the halfway point where traveling pairs make an irregular progression as do the boards they have just played. When the number of teams is an even number, there are at least two, and sometimes three, irregularities. See PROGRESSION.

SEQUENCE RE-ENTRY. A type of suit preference signal. After leading a king against notrump from a combination headed by K–Q–J, the defender can follow with the queen or the jack at choice, in order to suggest a re-entry in a high- or low-ranking suit. See SUIT PREFERENCE SIGNAL.

SERES SQUEEZE. A rare triple squeeze in a three-card ending discovered by TIM SERES of Sydney, Australia in 1965. Playing in 6♣, he arrived at the following ending with the lead in dummy:

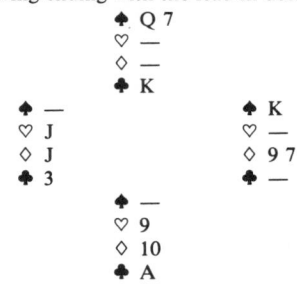

The ♠7 was ruffed, establishing the queen, and West was triple squeezed. An unusual feature is that one of the three cards he is trying to retain is a trump loser. See BACKWASH SQUEEZE.

The complete deal was:

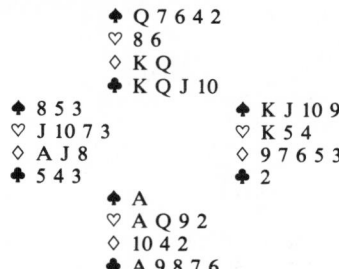

```
              ♠ Q 7 6 4 2
              ♡ 8 6
              ◇ K Q
              ♣ K Q J 10
   ♠ 8 5 3                    ♠ K J 10 9
   ♡ J 10 7 3                 ♡ K 5 4
   ◇ A J 8                    ◇ 9 7 6 5 3
   ♣ 5 4 3                    ♣ 2
              ♠ A
              ♡ A Q 9 2
              ◇ 10 4 2
              ♣ A 9 8 7 6
```

A club was led, and South won in dummy and finessed the ♡Q. He cashed the ♠A and led a diamond. West put up the ◇A and led a second trump. South won in dummy, ruffed a spade, and entered dummy with a diamond for another spade ruff. The ♡A and a heart ruff left the three-card ending shown above.

SERIES GAMES. Formerly duplicate sessions in a club which counted as a unit for points or prizes. As of January 1969, the ACBL no longer sanctioned series games for point awards.

SERPENT'S COUP. When the serpent tempted Eve, she gave in and tried the forbidden fruit and then got Adam to do the same. This coup is similar —it tempts a defender—and the fruit looks very appealing.

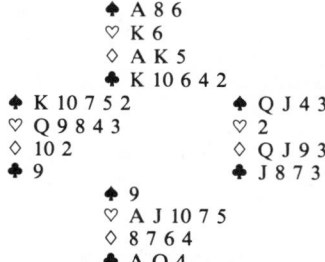

```
              ♠ A 8 6
              ♡ K 6
              ◇ A K 5
              ♣ K 10 6 4 2
   ♠ K 10 7 5 2                ♠ Q J 4 3
   ♡ Q 9 8 4 3                 ♡ 2
   ◇ 10 2                      ◇ Q J 9 3
   ♣ 9                         ♣ J 8 7 3
              ♠ 9
              ♡ A J 10 7 5
              ◇ 8 7 6 4
              ♣ A Q 4
```

West led the ♣9 which was won with the ace. A heart to the king was followed by a second heart. East showed out, playing the ♠3 and the 10 lost to West's queen. West returned the ◇2, this was won with dummy's king.

At this point, declarer does not know whether the diamond suit is divided 5–1, 4–2 or 3–3. A club to the queen will lead to defeat if the diamonds are 3–3 and East has a diamond entry: Ace, king an another diamond will lead to immediate defeat if East has four diamonds. The low diamond play at this point makes the contract legitimately if the diamonds are 3–3 and gives far greater temptation to East to give his partner a diamond ruff if they are 4–2 or 5–1. East would be loathe to give West a club ruff since that play establishes the club suit while there still entries to dummy.

Alternatively, if the diamonds are 4–2, with East

having the four diamonds, declarer has two heart losers and two diamond losers. Declarer can't play the ♠A and trump a spade—West will have more trumps and be able to force declarer.

One play offers a better chance. At trick five declarer led a small diamond from the table. East won the jack and West followed with the 10.

East might hesitate to return a club since that would establish dummy's club suit and leave entries to it as well. But why not return a diamond? The worst that could happen is that West would trump the now bare ◇A.

East bit the apple and returned a diamond and West did trump it. The Serpent's Coup had worked.

West returned a spade, won the ace in dummy. Declarer trumped a spade back to his hand. The ♡A pulled one of West's trumps and the ♡J followed in this position:

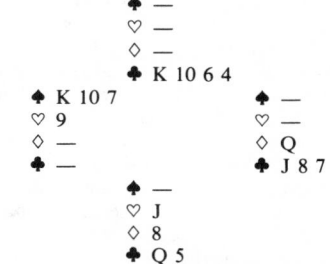

```
              ♠ —
              ♡ —
              ◇ —
              ♣ K 10 6 4
   ♠ K 10 7                   ♠ —
   ♡ 9                        ♡ —
   ◇ —                        ◇ Q
   ♣ —                        ♣ J 8 7
              ♠ —
              ♡ J
              ◇ 8
              ♣ Q 5
```

The Serpent's Coup ended with a two-suit squeeze.

SESSION. A period of play during which each contestant is scheduled to play a designated series of boards against one or more opponents. A session may consist of one or more rounds.

SET. Noun: the failure or defeat of a contract. Verb: to defeat a contract by at least one trick.

SET GAME. A pre-arranged match between two partnerships, with each pair almost always remaining the same for the duration of the contest. There have been set games where one of the players has been spelled for a while by some other player who had been waiting in reserve for such an instance. But generally set games involve four people and last for several rubbers as previously agreed upon.

The CULBERTSON-LENZ MATCH was the most publicized set game in history. However, there was wide interest in the more recent match between the SHARIF BRIDGE CIRCUS (OMAR SHARIF, GIORGIO BELLADONNA, BENITO GAROZZO, and CLAUDE DELMOULY) and English experts JONATHAN CANSINO and JEREMY FLINT (with CLAUDE RODRIGUE spelling FLINT for part of the match), which was held in London in 1970. The stakes were enormous — 1 pound ($2.40) a point. Over the course of 80 rubbers, of which Sharif had agreed to play a minimum of 52, the Circus won by 5,470 points.

SET UP. To establish one or more cards in the hand of the player himself, his partner, or an opponent.

SET UP SUIT. See ESTABLISHED SUIT.

SEVEN or SEVEN-SPOT. The eighth-ranking card in a suit, located between the 8 and the 6.

SEVEN-ODD. Seven tricks over book, or 13 tricks in all.

SEVEN TABLES. At duplicate, seven tables provide for competition among 28 players as individuals, 14 pairs or seven teams-of-four. This is an ideal number of tables — it provides a basic pattern for all numbers of tables up to 13 for pair contests, and is an excellent base for larger individual tournaments.

Since seven is a prime number, the RAINBOW MOVEMENT is suitable for an individual contest. Three boards to a round, with the West players moving counterclockwise around the table at the end of each board of the round, provides each player with 21 different partners. Six is top and 63 is average.

Thirteen rounds of two boards each makes the HOWELL MOVEMENT an ideal competition for pair events, each pair meeting every other pair, with almost perfectly BALANCED COMPARISONS throughout the field and at least 12 and no more than 14 direct comparisons between pairs. The MITCHELL MOVEMENT can also be used when two fields are desirable, six rounds of four boards, or seven rounds of three or four boards being the usual contest.

As a team contest, the regular team-of-four progression, boards going to the next lower and traveling pairs skipping a table to lower numbers, provides six uninterrupted rounds for 24 boards, without any irregularities in the progression. A Swiss Team movement is not recommended. Three-way matches are necessary, and pairings are at best difficult after the second round. For IMP matches, use the team-of-four progression and score each match on IMPs.

For 6½ or 7½ tables, see HALF TABLES.

SEXTET BRIDGE. A seldom played bridge game for six players, playing as two partnerships of three each. Two new suits were introduced, called rackets and wheels. The 50% increase in the number of suits and players in the game results in a total number of legal auctions with all players participating ($(6 \times 66^{49} - 1)/5 = 1.7251787 \times 10^{89}$) that exceeds by a substantial margin the probable total number of atoms in the universe (about 10^{64} as estimated by physicist Sir James Jeans).

Robert True

SHADE, SHADED. A bid made on slightly less than technical minimum requirements.

SHAKE. A colloquialism meaning DISCARD.

SHARIF BRIDGE CIRCUS. A touring professional team of world class players, organized and headed by movie star OMAR SHARIF, to play a series of exhibition matches against leading European and North American teams.

The Circus made its debut late in 1967, when Sharif, GIORGIO BELLADONNA, CLAUDE DELMOULY, BENITO GAROZZO, and Leon Yallouze, all playing the BLUE TEAM CLUB, defeated the Dutch international team in matches sponsored by newspapers and played in three Netherlands cities before enthusiastic

audiences, who viewed the competition on BRIDGE-O-RAMA. Using this format — a match against a highly rated team with the play-by-play displayed to the audience accompanied by expert commentary — the Circus made an extended tour in 1968. It defeated teams in Italy and London, lost its first matches to The Netherlands and Belgium in The Hague, and made a swing through six North American cities — Montreal, Toronto, Los Angeles, Dallas, New Orleans and New York — winning the majority of the matches. (Several of the American matches were three-cornered contests involving the Circus, the local team, and the ACES.)

A second tour in 1970 received a spectacular send-off when JEREMY FLINT and JONATHAN CANSINO challenged Sharif and company to a 100-rubber pair game in London (later reduced by time pressure to 80 rubbers). The stakes were an unprecedented British pound ($2.40) per point, plus an additional bonus of 1,000 on the net result of each four rubbers. The match attracted wide newspaper and magazine coverage in the United States as well as in Europe. Sharif won by a margin of 5,470 points and collected over $18,000 but this was a comparatively small sum against the expenses of staging the match and taping the highlights for a series of television shows planned for later syndication.

This was immediately followed by a tour of seven North American cities — Chicago, Winnipeg, Los Angeles, St. Paul, Dallas, Detroit and Philadelphia. In addition to matches against powerful teams of local stars, the tour included a marathon 840-deal match against the Aces, who accompanied the Circus throughout the tour. The Circus defeated the allstar teams in Chicago, Winnipeg and St. Paul, but lost all its other matches, bowing to the Aces by 101 IMPs (1,793–1,692) after the lead had seesawed excitingly from city to city. PIETRO FORQUET joined the Sharif team in Dallas but could not reverse the effect of the exhausting schedule, which included numerous personal appearances by Sharif.

Despite commercial sponsorship of more than $50,000 in 1970, neither of the American tours proved a financial success, although both resulted in wide publicity for bridge.

SHARK. An expert player, but more particularly one who specializes in playing for money and is adept at this type of competition.

SHARPLES CONVENTION. Devised by JAMES and ROBERT SHARPLES of England — a "natural" extension of the STAYMAN convention.

A responder who sees slam possibilities frequently faces a problem if he uses Stayman, and does not find an immediate fit. If the responder has 4-4-3-2 or 4-4-4-1 distribution, he may wish to explore the possibility of a 4-4 fit in a minor suit.

Opposite a 16- to 18-point notrump, responder holds:

    ♠ K J 7 5
    ♡ 4
    ◇ A Q 5 2
    ♣ A 10 5 3

The Sharples idea is to bid four of a minor suit on

the second round, showing specifically a four-card suit and sufficient strength to play in at least 4 NT:

OPENER	RESPONDER
1 NT	2♣
2♡	4♣

The opener rebids his hand naturally. If he has four-card club support, he raises to 5♣ or 6♣ in accordance with his estimation of slam prospects. If four-card club support is lacking, opener can make a natural suit bid of 4◊ or 4♠ (although in some styles a four-card spade suit may have been excluded by the 2♡ rebid). 4 NT and 5 NT would be natural bids announcing that the opener's distribution was 4-3-3-3.

All notrump bids at any stage should be regarded as natural.

Suppose responder holds:

♠ J 3
♡ K J 7 5
◊ A Q 5 2
♣ A 5 3

The bidding goes:

OPENER	RESPONDER
1 NT	2♣
2♣	4◊

By jumping to 4◊, responder denies a four-card club suit, and keeps open the possibility of playing a slam in a red suit.

SHIFT (or switch). To change suit from one originally led on defense; alternately, a change of suit by declarer in the development of his play. Shift can also be used to describe a bid in a new suit by either the opening bidder, his partner, or an overcaller or his partner, as JUMP SHIFT, ONE-OVER-ONE, etc.

SHOMATE MOVEMENT. For INDIVIDUAL TOURNAMENTS of 8, 9 or 10 tables. These movements are noncyclic and must be conducted with GUIDE CARDS, and, while very difficult to post rapidly, provide excellent comparison among all the players entered in the competition.

SHOOTING. The art of playing deliberately for an abnormal result.

Occasionally near the end of a tournament, a couple of tops are needed in order to have any chance of winning. Two or three average results would be just as fatal to one's chances as bottoms. Under these circumstances, playing for abnormal results is justified. Playing for top or bottom is called shooting.

Many players, quite wrongly, think of shooting as equivalent to overbidding. In fact, good shooting will consist of underbidding as often as overbidding. The aim should be to arrive at a contract which is wrong but only slightly wrong.

To bid a game or a slam which has a 30–40% chance of success is an intelligent "shot"; but it is equally sensible to stop short of game or slam which is a 60–70% chance. In each case the shooter is hoping for the less likely result.

But the best chance to shoot intelligently is in the play of the hand.

NORTH
♠ x x
♡ x x x
◊ x x
♣ A 8 x x x x

SOUTH
♠ A Q x
♡ A K x x
◊ A Q x
♣ K 9 x

West leads a spade against South's 3 NT contract. Declarer wins East's king with the ace, and attacks clubs. Normally he would play the king, and then duck a round. This is the percentage play because the odds are slightly against a 2–2 club break. Obviously if declarer plays the king, then leads the nine to dummy's ace, his contract will be placed in jeopardy. For one who wishes to shoot, this is a wonderful opportunity. By placing the ace on the second round (unless West shows out), he can be almost certain of a top (or bottom).

Marshall Miles

SHORT CLUB. The short *prepared* or *convenient* club is an original opening bid made on a three-card club suit. It was first advocated by the FOUR ACES as a means of providing a comfortable rebid. In principle it requires a minimum of Q-x-x (to support a lead), and failing this, opener may choose instead to open with 1◊. It is most often used by the disciples of systems that require five cards for a major suit opening.

For example:

♠ A 6 5 4
♡ A Q 3 2
◊ A 8
♣ 9 7 6

When playing FIVE-CARD MAJORS the hand is opened with 1♣. When the hand contains two clubs and three diamonds, an opening diamond bid is usually preferred. It is essential in these systems for responder to mention his four-card major holding, if at all feasible, in order to find the all-important major-suit *fit*. All players, even those who initiate weak major-suit bids, will at times resort to the Short Club.

Some specialized bidding systems use an artificial club opening as an introduction to a very strong hand (see BLUE TEAM CLUB, SCHENKEN SYSTEM, VANDERBILT CLUB), but it is to be understood that the short club, per se, is not a system but an opening bid to facilitate future rebids, and may be passed by partner. When otherwise used it is more properly announced as 1♣ ARTIFICIAL AND FORCING, and in such cases it does not promise any particular length or strength in the club suit itself.

Inexperienced players often assume that a 1♣ bid is likely to be short. Using standard methods it is very unlikely: A four-card or five-card suit is far more likely, and even six-card suit is more likely than three. See also CHOICE OF SUIT.

SHORT HAND. A term used to describe the hand

of the partnership that contains the fewer cards in the trump suit, such as in the reference, "declarer (or the defenders) took the ruff in the short hand." Occasionally, the term may be applied to a hand that is short in a non-trump suit and therefore expects to ruff.

SHORT HOWELL MOVEMENTS. Methods of conducting a one-winner duplicate tournament when the object is to complete the game in just under three hours; provision is made for 11 rounds of two boards each. The six-table game is the regular HOWELL game, with APPENDIX TABLES being added for the seven-, eight-, nine-, and ten-table game.

To get BALANCED COMPARISONS, the stationary pairs other than the one with the highest number alternate between North–South and East–West positions, making the switch to and fro at various times. Guide cards are available giving complete information; the following table gives starting assignments, with numbers 12 and higher stationary. Boards are played in order at each table, starting with the set indicated in the table below. Pairs, in moving, replace the pair with the next lower number, number 1 replacing pair 11.

	6 tables		7 tables		8 tables		9tables		10 tables	
#1	12vl	1	14vl	1	16vl	1	18vl	1	18vl	1
#2	6v7	4	4v6	2	4v15	2	5v17	2	5v17	2
#3	11v4	6	9v10	3	11v13	3	11v16	3	11v16	3
#4	3v9	8	7v3	4	14v10	4	2v10	4	10v19	4
#5	2v5	9	12v2	5	9v8	5	15v9	5	20v2	4
#6	10v8	11	11v13	6	5v7	6	7v8	6	15v9	5
#7			5v8	7	3v12	7	14v6	7	7v8	6
#8					2v6	8	4v13	8	14v6	7
#9							3v12	9	4v13	8
#10									3v12	9

(Tables 4 and 5 relay throughout)

SHORT SUIT. In an original hand of 13 cards, a suit containing three or fewer cards. See SINGLETON, DOUBLETON.

SHORT-SUIT GAME TRIES. These were developed as part of the KAPLAN-SHEINWOLD system, but can be used effectively with any standard system.

When the opening major-suit bid has been raised to two, the opener tries for game by bidding his shortest suit. For example:

♠ A K 6 5 3
♡ A 5 2
◇ 8
♣ K J 7 4

The bidding goes:

OPENER	RESPONDER
1 ♠	2 ♠
3 ◇	

This asks responder to go to 4 ♠ if his values are mainly outside diamonds. If responder rebids 3 ♡, that would also be a short-suit try, expressing doubt about game prospects.

This method gives a partnership a chance of judging whether strength is duplicated. A disadvantage is that it may help the opponents to find a cheap save. One defender may double the short-suit try, and en-

courage his partner to take the save. It may also provide a clue to the most effective lead and subsequent defense.

It is best to restrict these bids to the situations when a major has been raised and there has been no interference.

The specific sequence 1 ♡ — 2 ♡ — 2 ♠ may need special consideration. The 2 ♠ rebid may be needed as a natural rebid, especially if the opening bidder has not guaranteed a five-card heart suit.

For alternative methods see TWO-WAY GAME TRIES, WEAK SUIT GAME TRY.

SHORT-SUIT LEADS. An opening lead of a singleton or a doubleton is often indicated when the leader examines his hand in the light of the bidding.

Against either notrump or a trump contract, a short-suit lead is normal when partner has bid the suit. (Partner's bid suit is less automatic as a lead with greater length; against a trump contract it may be necessary to aim quickly for tricks elsewhere.)

The short-suit lead is also indicated when there is a bidding inference that this is partner's suit, and that he will have the entries to make use of it. TERENCE REESE gives this example:

SOUTH
♠ Q 5 3
♡ J 8 6 2
◇ 7 4
♣ Q 7 6 3

After the bidding:

WEST	EAST
1 ♣	1 ♠
2 ♣	2 NT
3 NT	

South should lead a diamond. The hand is too weak to hope to do much with hearts, so a diamond is led in the hope of hitting partner's strength. If South held the ♠ A instead of the ♠ 3, a heart lead would be indicated.

A short-suit lead may be made for passive reasons, usually because other leads seem unattractive. This is most likely to be desirable if the bidding suggests that the declaring side has no long suit, and that therefore there is no urgent need to attack.

In a suit contract a short-suit lead is most desirable if the trump holding suggests that there are real prospects of obtaining a ruff. (A–x, A–x–x, or K–x–x would be ideal.) Conversely a short-suit lead, particularly of a singleton, may be a mistake when there is no ruffing prospect, because it may help declarer to play a suit which would have presented problems. A singleton trump is usually a bad lead (but see TRUMP LEADS).

Against notrump, a short-suit lead is indicated when the opening leader is very weak, and no entries are available to make use of a long weak suit. The leader should try to hit his partner's suit, although this may turn out to declarer's advantage. (For this reason the long weak suit may prove best as a passive lead.) A short-suit lead is required when the leader's partner has doubled notrump, and no suit has been bid:

WEST	NORTH	EAST	SOUTH
			1 NT
Pass	3 NT	Dbl	Pass
Pass	Pass		

SHORTEN. To force; to shorten in trumps by forcing to ruff. See FORCING LEADS.

SHOW OUT. To fail to follow suit for the first time during the play of that suit.

SHOW UP SQUEEZE. A squeeze which permits declarer to avoid a guess between a finesse and a play for a drop.

```
             K J x x x
   ? x x x                  ? x
             A x
```

If South can put pressure on West, forcing two discards in the vital suit, the ace and king can be cashed with confidence, knowing the queen will show up on one side or the other.

SHOWING PREFERENCE. See PREFERENCE.

SHUFFLE. Noun: the mixing together of the pack of cards prior to the next, or first deal. Several thorough mixings, or shuffles, are required as it is important that the deck be mixed completely from deal to deal. Verb: to mix the cards.

SHUT-OUT BID. See PREEMPTIVE BID.

SIDE. A team of two in a rubber game or a CHICAGO game. The term can also describe a pairing in a duplicate contest, or, in team-of-four play, the entire team of whatever number.

SIDE GAME. A one-session event at a CHAMPIONSHIP TOURNAMENT, run concurrently with a championship event, and, at North American Championships, concurrently with SECONDARY EVENTS as well. At North American Championships, morning side games are held daily, and midnight ZIP Swisses are held frequently.

SIDE SUIT. In bidding, a suit of at least four cards held by a player whose first bid is in another suit.

In play, a suit of at least four cards other than trumps held by declarer in his own hand or dummy.

SIGN-OFF BID. A bid which is intended to close the auction. These sometimes occur in partscore situations:

WEST	EAST	WEST	EAST	WEST	EAST
1 ♦	1 ♠	1 NT	2 ♠	1 ♠	1 NT
1 NT	2 ♠				2 ♠

In each case the player bidding notrump has limited his hand, so partner can place the final contract. In each case, partner is saying that the values of the combined hands are not strong enough for game and that the best place to play probably is spades because the spade bidder has a long suit of spades — probably at least six and maybe more.

Other sign-off bids occur at the game level. The most common is the raise to 3 NT by the partner of a player who opened 1 NT.

In general sign-off bids occur when a player names a contract after partner has severely limited his hand both as to point-count and distribution.

SIGNALS, SIGNALING. The language of defensive play, by which defenders can legitimately exchange information about the makeup of their hands. Various methods of signaling are discussed under the following titles: BECHGAARD SIGNALS; BLUE PETER; DISCARDING; HIGH-LOW; KELLY SOLID-SUIT SIGNALS; LENGTH SIGNALS; ODD-EVEN DISCARDS; REVOLVING DISCARDS; SUIT PREFERENCE SIGNAL; TRUMP SIGNAL; UPSIDE-DOWN SIGNALS.

SILENCE. Observed during the play of important matches, by consent of all, especially by the kibitzers. In the playing rooms of the top-level clubs, any noise or disturbance of the games is severely frowned upon, and should a disturbance occur, the officer of the day or other official will usually make the necessary remonstrance.

SILODOR TROPHY. For the Spring North American Open Pairs Championship. Presented in 1963 in memory of SIDNEY SILODOR and made retroactive to include winners of the event since it started in 1958. Past results are listed under Spring North American Championships.

SIMON AWARD. Endowed by JOHN E. SIMON this award for the Bridge Sportsman of the Year is presented annually by the INTERNATIONAL BRIDGE PRESS ASSOCIATION. It is made to the player deemed worthy of special mention for behavior showing a high degree of sportsmanship. The behavior to be considered by the panel is not restricted to the year in question: the actions and general deportment of any nominee during his or her bridge career may be taken into account. For a list of winners see INTERNATIONAL BRIDGE PRESS ASSOCIATION AWARDS.

SIMPLE. (as applied to an overcall or response). Non-jump; merely sufficient to overcall or respond.

SIMPLE FINESSE. A finesse for a single card held by the adversaries.

SIMPLE HONORS. A term used in auction bridge to denote three honors in the trump suit, for which 30 points were scored.

SIMPLE OVERCALL. A minimum overcall.

SIMPLE SQUEEZE. A squeeze which acts against one opponent in two suits. The minimum requirements are: (1) a two-card menace and a one-card menace, both guarded by the same opponent; (2) all the remaining tricks but one.

The card which forces the defender to discard a busy card is called the squeeze card. The squeeze card must be a winner played from the hand opposite the two-card menace, so that the two menaces and the squeeze card cannot all be in the same hand. The two-card menace contains a master card, which provides an entry to one of the menaces.

The following are the basic endings for a simple squeeze:

(1) Positional (or one-way) squeeze:

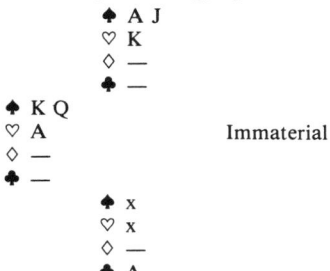

South plays the ♣A, and West is squeezed. When West discards one suit, North discards the other, and so takes the remaining tricks.

In this example, spades are the two-card menace and hearts the one-card menace. The squeeze card is the ♣A. Declarer has on top two of the remaining three tricks.

In this position both West and North have been reduced to busy cards, but West must discard first so that declarer can choose his discard accordingly, resulting in the gain of a trick. If, in this position, the East and West cards are interchanged, then the squeeze is inoperative.

(2) Split two-card menace:

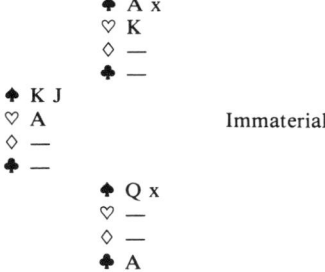

In this variation, the two-card menace is split between North and South. The North hand contains the master card (the ♣A in this example), but the South hand contains the menace (here the ♣Q). The (split) two-card menace is still said to be opposite the squeeze card (here the ♣A) provided that a master card of that menace is properly situated, as here.

(3) AUTOMATIC SQUEEZE:

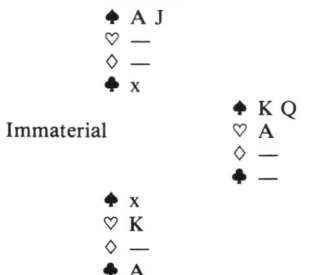

(a) As usual, the two-card menace is opposite the squeeze card, but now the one-card menace accompanies the squeeze card. This means that the North

had has an idle card (see BUSY CARD AND IDLE CARD) which can be played on the ♣A; that is, North's discard does not depend on the opponent's play. As a result, the squeeze is automatic in that it operates against either opponent if the same opponent guards both menace cards.

(b) Twin-entry menace:

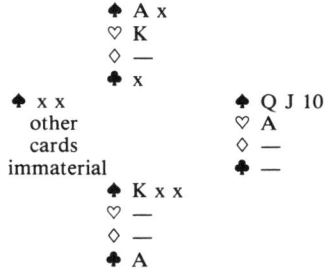

When South plays the ♣A, East is squeezed. The position is automatic; even though the one-card menace is opposite the squeeze card, there is compensation in the form of an extra winner in the long menace, which is now called a twin-entry two-card menace.

(c) Criss-cross squeeze:

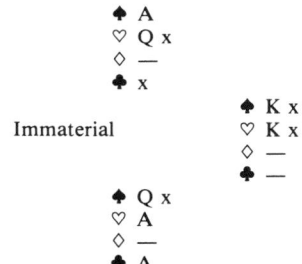

South leads the ♣A, which forces East to unguard one of his major suit kings. If East discards a spade, declarer takes the ace of that suit, dropping East's king, returns to hand with the ♡A to cash the ♠Q. If East can foresee the impending squeeze, he may be able to make a deceptive play, blanking one of his kings early, thereby presenting South with a guess as to what the end position is.

Monroe Ingberman

SIMPLIFIED CLUB SYSTEM. Originated by LARRY WEISS and played by him successfully in North American Championships competition. It combines some of the features of the BLUE TEAM CLUB and the ROMAN SYSTEM:

(1) 1♣ shows 16 points or more, and responses show controls. A 2♣ rebid shows a stronger hand with game values, and the responses again show controls. A 2♢ rebid shows a strong three-suiter.

(2) 1♢, 1♡, and 1♠ guarantee a two-suited hand, at least 5–4, and the shorter suit is bid first unless it is clubs. 1 NT is an artificial positive response showing at least 10 points. The suit immediately above the opener's is an artificial negative, but the responder is not required to use it if he has some fit with the opener.

(3) 1 NT is 12–15 points.

(4) 2♣ is 11–16 and three-suited.

(5) Other two-bids show single-suited hands with 11–16 points. Club hands are shown by 2 NT (14–17) or 3♣ (11–14).

SIMPLIFIED PRECISION.

A version of the PRECISION CLUB system that differs from Standard Precision essentially in that (1) it uses no asking bids, (2) its 2◊ opening shows diamond length rather than diamond shortness, and (3) its four-level minor-suit openings are natural preempts. Compare also SUPER PRECISION.

SINGLE RAISE.

A raise of opener's one-level suit opening to the two-level. The normal range of the bid is 6–9 high-card points; but 10 is possible, and less than 6 is common when there is distributional compensation.

The higher the rank of the opener's suit, the less length is required by responder to raise. 1♠ tends to be a five-card suit, and can be raised freely with three-card support (and the five-card major-suit bidders might raise conceivably with a doubleton). 1♡ is often raised to two with three-card support, but a raise to 2◊ almost invariably indicates four cards or more. This is a possible exception:

♠ 4 3
♡ 5 2
◊ A 5 2
♣ Q 9 7 4 3 2

In reply to 1♣, even four-card support may not be sufficient. With a 3-3-3-4 hand, 1◊ might be preferred to 2♣. (See BIDDABLE SUITS.)

For some special treatments of single raises see SINGLE RAISE IN MAJOR, CONSTRUCTIVE; INVERTED MINOR SUIT RAISES.

Rebids by the opener below the game level are almost always game invitations. (See SHORT-SUIT GAME TRIES; TRIAL BIDS; TWO-WAY GAME TRIES; WEAK SUIT GAME TRY.) But see PREEMPTIVE RERAISE. Many partnerships make an exception if the opener raises again; this can conveniently be regarded as a preemptive measure, especially if the suit is a minor.

A rebid of 2 NT (1♡ — 2♡ — 2 NT) shows 17–18 points, and is not forcing. If responder then rebids a lower-ranking suit, he is showing a long suit and general weakness, and expects to be passed.

SINGLE RAISE IN MAJOR, CONSTRUCTIVE.

In ROTH-STONE, a raise from 1♠ to 2♠ or 1♡ to 2♡ that shows 10–12 points and is very rarely passed.

♠ K 5 4
♡ A 9 6 3
◊ Q J 6
♣ 8 4 3

See 1 NT RESPONSE TO MAJOR, FORCING.

SINGLE RAISE IN RESPONDER'S SUIT.

See OPENER'S REBID.

SINGLETON.

An original holding of exactly one card in a suit (see WORTHLESS SINGLETON/DOUBLETON). Also called a STIFF. For valuation in a suit contract see DISTRIBUTIONAL VALUES.

SINGLETON-SHOWING BID.

See SPLINTER BID.

SINGLETON SWISS.

See SPLINTER BID.

SIT, SIT FOR.

To pass partner's PENALTY DOUBLE or TAKEOUT DOUBLE.

SITTING.

Gerund: a session of bridge. Participle: descriptive term referring to one's position at the table, i.e., North, West, etc.; also used in a sentence to describe possession of a hand or a holding, in which case the exact holdings are always given. See SESSION, SEAT.

SIX or SIX-SPOT.

The ninth highest card in a suit.

6 NT OPENING.

A very rare opening bid showing a balanced hand with 12 sure tricks. Responder should raise if he holds an ace or a king. (To raise with a queen is doubtful.)

SIX OF A SUIT OPENING.

The theoretical meaning of this bid is a 12-trick hand which is missing only the ace or king of trumps. Such a hand has such low frequency that the bid is idle. It is perhaps more sensible to reserve it for a freak hand, possibly a complete two-suiter, which is likely to offer some play for 12 tricks. This has the required preemptive value, and does not encourage the opponents to save, as they would if the opener had guaranteed 12 tricks.

SIX-ODD.

Six tricks over book or 12 tricks in all.

SIX TABLES.

At duplicate, six tables provide for competition among 24 players as individuals, 12 pairs or six teams.

In addition, there is available a 25 player movement, which can be used for a one-session game using 30 boards, or a two-session game using only 25 boards per session.

As a pair contest, either the MITCHELL or HOWELL MOVEMENT can be used. If a Mitchell is used, tables 1 and 2 share boards by relay throughout, with a bye-stand between tables 4 and 5, traveling pairs moving to higher numbered, and boards to lower numbered tables. The full six rounds must be played, usually four boards to the round. Top is 5, average is 72. If Howell movement is used, the full 11-round, 22-board movement is desirable for an early finish. For a longer game, the nine-round, three-boards-to-a-round, THREE-QUARTER MOVEMENT is excellent.

For a team game have the moving pairs skip a table in the lower direction. After the first round have the moving pairs skip an extra table. After the second round the moving pairs move normally. After the third round the East–West pairs skip an extra table and the boards skip a table. The move after the fourth round is normal. For the last round tables 1 and 4, 2 and 5, 3 and 6 shuffle the boards and relay. East–West Pair 1 follows these moves; 5, 2, 6, 3; then to 4 for the relay. A Swiss Team Movement is not practical for so few teams. For IMP matches use movement shown for a team-of-four and score each match on IMPs.

For 5½ tables of 6½ tables, see HALF TABLE.

SIXTEEN, RULE OF. See RULE OF SIXTEEN.

SKINNER PSYCHIC CONTROL (developed by COL. RICHMOND H. SKINNER, Wilmington DE). Use of certain forcing bids to guard against the possibility that the opener has made a disciplined (3- to 6-point) psychic bid. See PSYCHIC CONTROLS.

SKINNER RESPONSES TO A 1 NT OPENING (devised by COL. RICHMOND H. SKINNER, Wilmington DE). After a 1 NT opening bid, 2♣ requests opener to show a four-card major or rebid 2 NT with a maximum or to bid 2♢ with a minimum. If opener rebids 2♢, responder will usually show a major, and opener either raises with four-card support, bids 2♠ over 2♡ or rebids 2 NT with no major. A jump to 3♡ or 3♠ after an initial response of 2♣ shows a four-card suit and is game-forcing. To make a minor-suit slam try, responder jumps to 3♢ (natural), bids 2♣ followed by 3♣ (natural) or bids 2♣ followed by 3♢ (both minors).

SKINNER TWO-BIDS (devised by COL. RICHMOND H. SKINNER, Wilmington DE). A method of responding to a strong two-bid that allows opener to pinpoint certain key cards in responder's hand. 2♣ opening is artificial and forcing to 2 NT or three of a major. 2♢, 2♡, and 2♠ opening bids are natural, game-forcing, and request responder to bid a suit in which he holds an ace, bid 2 NT with no ace or to jump in the suit of the lowest-ranking ace with more than one ace.

SKIP, SKIP MOVEMENT. An irregularity in the progression of the traveling pairs (or the boards) in a MITCHELL MOVEMENT pair game with an even number of tables, where it is not necessary that all contestants play every board in play. Skips also are used in certain forms of team movements, notably board-a-match events with an even number of tables. Skips also are employed in certain individual events, notably the 15-table movement.

SKIP BID. In a wide sense, any bid at a level higher than is required by the previous auction. In practice, a skip bid is used to refer to weak preemptive actions, whether as an opening bid, an overcall or a response. (See PREEMPTIVE BID, WEAK JUMP OVERCALL, and PREEMPTIVE RESPONSE.) To avoid the ethical problems that may arise after preemptive action, the SKIP-BID WARNING is usually used in the United States.

SKIP–BID WARNING. A notice given to the opponent by a player who is about to skip at least one level of the bidding. Such a player announces, "I am about to make a skip bid, please wait." The next player to make a call is expected to hesitate approximately 10 seconds before making his call.

The reason for this warning is that immediate actions by the player on the left of the player who makes a skip bid can give partner information to which he is not entitled. For instance, a quick pass could be construed as showing few if any values. A quick double could mean that the player has a very good hand. Long thought before finally making a call or a bid could easily indicate a hand on which no clear-cut action is called for.

All these actions could be perfectly ethical for the player who makes them. However each one puts a very strong ethical burden on partner. Partner is not supposed to act on the basis that a quick pass shows very little strength, a quick double shows a lot of strength, and a slow pass or bid shows doubt as to whether the pass or the double should have been made. Since the skip-bid warning requires approximately a 10-second hesitation at all times by the next player to call, right-hand opponent should no longer have an ethical problem when left-hand opponent is forced to hesitate under all circumstances.

SAM FRY JR. was the first to propose such a compulsory pause — he suggested it in 1938. The ACBL adopted this procedure in 1957.

When BIDDING BOXES are used in international matches where SCREENS are not in use, the player who is about to make a skip-bid places a sign saying "Stop!" on the table. He then makes his skip bid, and the next opponent to call must refrain from making his call until after the skip bidder has picked up the "Stop" sign. Skip-bid warnings are not necessary when screens are in use because the two calls from the same side of the table are called to the attention of the players on the other side of the screen at the same time.

SLAM. The winning of 12 tricks (SMALL SLAM, previously called little slam) or all 13 tricks (GRAND SLAM). An original object in the earliest forms of WHIST (some of which were called "Slamm"), these results were rewarded by bonuses in BRIDGE-WHIST and auction bridge regardless of the declaration, so much so that in auction bridge a side that bid seven and won 12 tricks still received the 50-point premium for a small slam although the contract was down one. In contract bridge, however, slam bonuses are paid only when the slam is both bid and made.

SIMS–CULBERTSON MATCH. See CULBERTSON-SIMS MATCH.

SIMS SYSTEM. A system of contract bidding originated circa 1930–32 by P. HAL SIMS. The system stressed strong first- and second-hand opening bids (with corresponding "protection" by third or fourth hand); strong four-card biddable suits, with the opening bid made in the lower ranking. All opening bids of two or three in a suit were forcing, both showing hands strong in honor value, but the three-bid showing length as well. Weak defensive bids were not made when vulnerable. The system also employed forcing overcalls and informatory doubles.

SIMULTANEOUS CALLS, LEADS, OR PLAYS. Covered in appropriate sections of LAWS and LAWS OF DUPLICATE. The treatment is that, if one of the simultaneous acts is in legal rotation, that act stands; the other act, which is perforce out of rotation, is treated as a call, lead or play out of rotation and the penalty applicable to such act is invoked.

SINGAPORE CONTRACT BRIDGE ASSOCIA-

TION. Founded in 1965, when Singapore left the Malaysian Federation, the Association is a member of the Far East Bridge Federation and participates in Far East Championships, hosting the event in 1972.

Officers, 1982:
President: S.Y. Kong
Secretary: C.S. Wu, P.O. Box 47, Newton Post
   Office, Singapore, II

SINGLE COUP. A coup in which declarer shortens his hand once in trumps by ruffing a card from dummy, in order to reduce his trump holding to the same number held by his right-hand opponent. See COUP.

SINGLE DUMMY PROBLEMS. A solver is given the two hands of a partnership holding, approximating the conditions facing a declarer at the bridge table. Among the foremost inventors of these problems is PAUL LUKACS of Israel, who presents these.

(a)
        NORTH
        ♠ 6 3 2
        ♡ Q J 4
        ◊ A Q 6 5 4
        ♣ 6 2

        SOUTH
        ♠ A K 8
        ♡ 8
        ◊ K 8 2
        ♣ A K Q J 10 9

South plays 6♣ against the lead of the ♡5. East takes the first trick with the ♡A, and returns a low heart. Assuming that West holds the ♡K, South can claim the contract. Why?

(b)
        NORTH
        ♠ K 8 5
        ♡ 8 4 3 2
        ◊ 6
        ♣ A 10 9 8 7

        SOUTH
        ♠ A Q 7
        ♡ K Q J
        ◊ K 10 9 8 4
        ♣ K 2

Against South's 3 NT contract, West leads the ♣4. East's jack is taken by South's king. Next comes a successful club finesse, East following suit. What is the right continuation?

Solutions. (a) South trumps the heart return; then plays all his trumps (discarding one diamond and two spades from the dummy). The ◊ A–K are cashed in that order. If both opponents follow, there is no problem. If West holds the diamond guard and the ♡K, he is squeezed in the two red suits on the second spade lead. If East holds the diamond guard, after the third lead of diamonds, West has the ♡K and East the diamond guard. Neither, then, has three spades, and declarer can claim the last three tricks in that suit.

(b) The solution hinges on the continuation of the club suit; should declarer play the ace and then the nine, he has an impossible discard to make on the second play; discarding either a second diamond or a heart gives the opponents a chance to establish that suit, while a spade discard costs a trick in the suit.

Therefore, the potential club loser must be lost immediately, by leading the nine at trick three, before leading the ace.

SINGLE GRAND COUP. A GRAND COUP in which the declarer shortens his hand once in trumps, to reduce his holding to the same number as held by his right hand opponent, by ruffing one winner from the dummy.

SLAM BIDDING. The methods by which slam contracts are investigated. Accuracy in this department of the game is vital for the winning player, since successful slams are rewarded with large bonuses, and those that fail are severely penalized (the undertrick penalty *plus* the value of the game contract). Ironically, the history of championship matches is studded with failures in the slam zone.

The two vital ingredients of a successful slam contract are power and controls. Before launching into a slam a partnership must not only determine that it has the general values to take 12 or 13 tricks in its best denomination; it must also be reasonably certain that the defense is unable to defeat the contract at the very start. To that end, a large part of modern slam bidding machinery is geared to the investigation of trump-suit solidity and first- and second-round controls. See SLAM CONVENTIONS.

The creation of a game-forcing situation in the early rounds of the bidding often provides the spark for slam investigation. See FAST ARRIVAL, PRINCIPLE OF. In addition, a variety of conventions have been devised to give slam-related information simultaneously with the announcement of a trump fit. See CONGLOMERATE MAJOR RAISES; JACOBY 2 NT; SPLINTER BID; SUPER SWISS; UNBALANCED SWISS RAISE; VALUE SWISS RAISES.

After a satisfactory trump fit has been established, either player may activate the search if he suspects the possibility of a slam. There are various ways in which the slam may be approached.

Cuebidding of a control, usually an ace, invites partner to cooperate if his hand is suitable.

WEST	EAST
♠ A K J 10 4	♠ 8
♡ K J 9 8	♡ A Q 10 7 3 2
◊ 6 2	◊ Q 5 4
♣ K 9	♣ A J 3

The bidding:

WEST	EAST
1♠	2♡
4♡	5♣
5♡	

In bidding 5♣, East shows the ace of that suit, and asks West how he feels about slam. Having nothing to spare for his bid, West signs off by returning to the agreed trump suit.

Frequently this slam try can be made below the game level:

WEST	EAST
♠ A K J 9 8	♠ Q 10 4 3
♡ 10 6	♡ K Q 9 7
◊ A 10 4	◊ K Q 2
♣ K J 9	♣ Q 2

The bidding:

WEST	EAST
1 ♠	3 ♠
4 ◇	4 ♠

Over East's forcing raise, West shows slam interest by bidding 4 ◇, a convenient try which does not commit the partnership beyond game. Lacking primary controls, East declines.

WEST	EAST
♠ A J 8	♠ K Q 10 6 3
♡ K 10 7 6	♡ A 3
◇ A Q 10 7	◇ 8 3 2
♣ K 9	♣ A 8 6

The bidding:

WEST	EAST
1 NT	3 ♠
4 ◇	4 ♡
4 ♠	5 ♣
6 ♠	

The bid of 4 ◇ by West is not by way of suggesting an alternative trump suit; spades are agreed on by inference, for lacking spade support West would simply bid 3 NT. The 4 ◇ bid is a slam try showing, in addition to the diamonds, a maximum notrump with good spade support. With two primary controls, East accepts the invitation by showing the ♡ A. West has nothing further to say, but when his partner makes a further overture, he bids the slam.

After first-round controls have been cuebid, subsequent cuebids in the same suit indicate second-round control.

WEST	EAST
♠ A 10 3	♠ K J 9
♡ A K 9 8 2	♡ Q J 10 6 5
◇ A 4 3	◇ 8
♣ K 7	♣ A Q 8 6

The bidding:

WEST	EAST
1 ♡	3 ♡
3 ♠	4 ♣
4 ◇	4 ♠
5 ♣	5 ◇
7 ♡	

The hands lend themselves to a smooth sequence where first- and second-round controls are shown in turn, until West, having heard enough, bids the grand slam. See CUEBIDS TO SHOW CONTROLS.

A Voluntary Bid Beyond the Game Level in an uninterrupted sequence is a specialized form of slam try usually inquiring about control of a specific suit.

WEST	EAST
♠ A K J 10 8 7	♠ Q 9
♡ Q 4	♡ 7 6
◇ A 10 7	◇ K Q 9 8 4
♣ K 6	♣ A Q 10 7

The bidding:

WEST	EAST
1 ♠	2 ◇
3 ♠	4 ♣
4 ◇	4 ♠
5 ♠	Pass

Since East did not raise the spades directly, his 4 ♠

bid is interpreted by West as a mild slam try. With the minor suits under control, West's 5 ♠ bid requires his partner to bid the slam if he has as good as second-round control in the unbid suit, hearts, so that East, though holding quite a useful hand, is compelled to pass.

If the opponents have been in the bidding, a bid at the five-level in the agreed trump suit asks partner to bid a slam if he controls the enemy suit, unless one member of the partnership has already cuebid that suit.

(a)

WEST	NORTH	EAST	SOUTH
			1 ♡
2 ♠	3 ♡	Pass	5 ♡

(b)

WEST	NORTH	EAST	SOUTH
			1 ♡
1 ♠	3 ♡	Pass	3 ♠
Pass	4 ♡	Pass	5 ♡

In (a) South has a powerful hand, but one which probably contains losing spades:

♠ 10 9
♡ A Q 10 9 7
◇ A K J 3 2
♣ A

In (b) South has shown control of spades, but he has poor trumps:

♠ —
♡ J x x x x x
◇ A K Q x x
♣ A K

This does not apply to sequences where the opponents' bidding forces the auction to the five-level.

WEST	NORTH	EAST	SOUTH
			1 ♡
1 ♠	3 ♡	4 ♠	5 ♡

South has no slam pretensions; he merely feels that doubling 4 ♠ will not produce a satisfactory penalty, and prefers his chances of making 11 tricks in hearts.

Positional Slams. Occasionally a slam can be made from one side of the table, but may fail if played from the other. Thus a player with a vulnerable tenace holding should endeavor to become declarer to protect his tenuous assets from a possibly damaging opening lead.

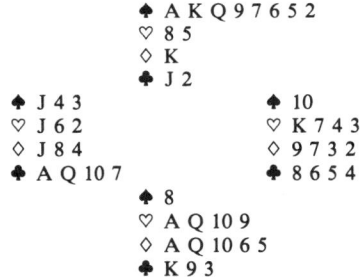

This hand is from the 1962 Bermuda Bowl match between Great Britain and North America. In one room the American North played in 4 ♠, making 11 tricks after a club lead.

The British bidding was:

SOUTH (Priday)	NORTH (Truscott)
1 ◇	2 ♠
3 ♡	4 ♣
4 NT	5 ◇
6 NT	

North's 4 ♣ bid, after his jump shift, showed a solid suit. Ascertaining through BLACKWOOD that the ♣ A was missing, South bid the slam in notrump to protect his ♣ K from a possible fatal lead through.

♠ A J 10 8	EAST
♡ K	♠ K Q 7 3 2
◇ A Q 10	♡ A 10 8 3
♣ K Q J 10 2	◇ J 8 7
	♣ 6

The bidding:

WEST	EAST
1 ♣	1 ♠
4 ♣	5 ♡
6 NT	

West accepts his partner's slam try, but corrects to notrump, realizing that in 6 ♣ a diamond lead might break the contract. See RIGHT SIDE.

Asking About Controls. Since controls are a necessary feature of successful slams, several conventions have been devised to determine the number of aces and kings held by a partnership. The most widely used is the BLACKWOOD convention:

WEST	EAST
♠ A	♠ K 8
♡ K 10 8 7	♡ A Q 9 6 3 2
◇ A 5	◇ K Q 10
♣ A Q 9 8 7 6	♣ 10 3

The bidding:

WEST	EAST
1 ♣	1 ♡
4 ♡	4 NT
5 ♠	5 NT
6 ◇	6 ♡
Pass	

The 4 NT and 5 NT bids are conventional, and West responds by showing his aces and kings (5 ♠ = three aces; 6 ◇ = one king). Though East has a very powerful hand in light of his partner's strong bidding, he cannot venture beyond six, for he knows that one critical king is missing.

Blackwood, valuable in determining the *total number* of aces and kings held by a partnership, should not be used by a player interested in identifying a *specific control*.

West holds:

♠ A K Q 10 8 7 6
♡ 10
◇ 3 2
♣ A Q 3

and the bidding proceeds:

WEST	EAST
1 ♠	2 ♣
3 ♠	4 ♣

At this point West would like to be in a slam if his partner holds the ◇ A, but if East has only one ace and it is the ♡ A there is a strong likelihood that the defense can take the first two diamond tricks before

West gets in. Since a 5 ◇ response to a Blackwood 4 NT will leave him none the wiser, he is better off bidding 5 ♣, inviting his partner to cuebid his ace if he has one. Alternatively, ASKING BIDS have been devised to allow inquiry into the amount and nature of control of a particular suit.

Trump Suit Quality. In investigating the prospects of a grand slam contract, the solidity of the trump suit is a critical factor. When a trump suit has been agreed upon, a 5 NT bid can be used conventionally as the GRAND SLAM FORCE, requiring the responder to bid seven if he holds two of the top three trump honors.

West holds:

♠ Q J 8 7
♡ A K Q J 9
◇ —
♣ A K Q 2

and the bidding proceeds:

WEST	EAST
2 ♡	2 ♠

At this point West's sole concern is the spade suit and a bid of 5 NT, agreeing spades by inference, will permit East to bid seven holding the ace and king, otherwise settling for a small slam.

Blasting. The success of slam contracts often turns on the opening lead. A more adventurous approach to slam bidding is therefore resorted to either when a player despairs of locating a key card in his partner's hand, or when he feels that the opponents are more likely to profit from a scientific investigation.

South holds:

♠ K 7 4 3
♡ A K J 10 6 2
♡ —
♣ 6 5 4

and the bidding proceeds:

NORTH	SOUTH
1 ♠	2 ♡
2 ♠	6 ♠

6 ♠ must have an excellent chance of coming home without a club lead and, rather than tip off the opponents, North prefers to blast. In the same vein, a player may take pains to bid a nonexistent suit enroute to a slam, to ward off a possibly lethal lead.

South holds:

♠ Q J 7 6 2
♡ —
◇ A K 10 8 3 2
♣ 3 2

In response to an opening spade bid by his partner, he may well bid six directly. However, against ingenuous opponents, it may pay to bid a psychic 2 ♣ first in an effort to induce a favorable lead.

The bidding of slams in notrump usually involves a less arduous procedure, especially in sequences that stem from opening bids in notrump. The point-count formula, quite accurate in the evaluation of balanced hands, has reduced these to simple arithmetic: by adding his points to those shown by his partner's bid, the responder is usually in a position to place the final contract.

South holds:

♠ Q J 8
♡ A J
♢ K Q 3
♣ K J 8 4 2

In response to his partner's 1 NT opening showing a minimum of 16 points, South can leap straight to six counting at least 33 points in the combined hands. With an in-between hand, the responder requires his partner's cooperation:

OPENER	RESPONDER
♠ K J 2	♠ Q 9 8 3
♡ A Q	♡ K J 4
♢ A K 8 7 6	♢ Q 10 9
♣ A Q 4	♣ J 10 6

The bidding:

OPENER	RESPONDER
2 NT	4 NT
6 NT	

In bypassing the game level, responder shows an interest in slam, and asks his partner to continue with a maximum holding. See EXPECTED NUMBER OF CONTROLS IN BALANCED HANDS.

Since in notrump sequences, the 4 NT bid has a quantitative meaning, the Blackwood convention is inoperative. A bid of 4♣, the GERBER convention, is used instead to check on aces and kings.

Slams in Duplicate. In general, players tend to be conservative when bidding slams at matchpoint duplicate. This is conditioned by the form of scoring—a minus score usually produces a poor result. Players usually prefer the higher scoring denominations even though a slightly superior contract is available in a minor suit.

At matchpoint play, a 50% chance of success justifies bidding a small slam, and a 67% chance justifies bidding the grand slam. Expert players will frequently take into account intangible factors such as the quality of the competition.

See VALUE OF GAME for the reasoning behind the inclusion of a value of 350 for the first game.

Sammy Kehela

SLAM CONVENTIONS. Specialized methods adopted for slam exploration include the following conventions which are listed separately: ACE IDENTIFICATION; ACE-SHOWING RESPONSES; ACOL DIRECT KING CONVENTION; ACOL 4 NT OPENING; ASKING BIDS; AUSTRALIAN ASKING BIDS; AUTOMATIC ACES; BABY BLACKWOOD; BARON COROLLARY; BARON SLAM TRY; BLACK AND RED GERBER; BLACKWOOD; BOLAND CONVENTION; BOWERS VARIATION; BYZANTINE BLACKWOOD; CLARAC SLAM TRY; CONGLOMERATE MAJOR RAISES; CONTROLS; CUEBIDS TO SHOW CONTROLS; CULBERTSON 4-5 NT; CULWOOD CONVENTION; DECLARATIVE-INTERROGATIVE 4 NT; BLACKWOOD AFTER INTERFERENCE; 4♣ BLACKWOOD; FRAGMENT BID; GERBER; GRAND SLAM FORCE; INTEREST-SHOWING BIDS; KEY-CARD BLACKWOOD; KEY-CARD GERBER; KING CONVENTION; LEBOVIC ASKING BID; MALOWAN 6♣ CONVENTION; MATHE ASKING BID; MINOR SUIT STAYMAN; NORMAN 4 NT; OUT-OF-THE-BLUE CUEBID; ROMAN ASKING BIDS; ROMAN BLACKWOOD; ROMAN GERBER; ROMAN KEY CARD BLACKWOOD; RUSH ASKING BID; SAN

FRANCISCO CONVENTION; SHARPLES CONVENTION, SPLINTER BID; SUPER BLACKWOOD; SUPER GERBER; SUPER SWISS; SUPPRESSING THE BID ACE; TRUMP ASKING BID; TWO-WAY STAYMAN; VOID-SHOWING BIDS. See also topics such as EXPECTED NUMBER OF CONTROLS IN BALANCED HANDS; FAST ARRIVAL, PRINCIPLE OF; RIGHT SIDE; SAFETY LEVEL.

SLAM DOUBLE CONVENTIONS. See DOUBLE FOR SACRIFICE; LIGHTNER DOUBLE.

SLAM LEADS. Opening leads against slam contracts frequently involve some special considerations. The general principle is to make passive leads against grand slams and active leads against small slams, but there are many exceptions to this.

An attacking lead against a small slam is often necessary when the bidding indicates a long, establishable suit in the dummy. It may then be necessary for the defense to lead from a king or a queen, in the hope of establishing a trick in the suit led before dummy's suit can be established for discards.

But if declarer and dummy both seem likely to have balanced hands, whether or not the contract is notrump, a passive lead is indicated. A deceptive lead is often appropriate, such as a third-best, a fifth-best, or the lower of touching honors. Misinforming the leader's partner is usually less important than misleading the declarer. Assessing the safety of a lead depends on the bidding as well as the suit holding. A low trump is safe from three small if the declaring side can be credited with at least nine trumps; but it would be unsafe against a likely eight-card trump fit, because partner may have Q-x.

The lead of an ace is right more often than some authorities indicate. Apart from the obvious advantage at matchpoint of preventing an overtrick, the ace lead is desirable if the opposing bidding has been crowded or rushed in such a way that two top losers are not unlikely. See also LIGHTNER DOUBLE.

SLIDING BOX. A device, first used in Central America–Caribbean Championships, that facilitates the use of BIDDING SCREENS. A square tray, mounted on rollers, slides under the curtain as necessary. Each player has one side of the tray allotted to him. He places bidding cards on it in appropriate rotation. This avoids the need for monitors, and the confusion which often has resulted when players have failed to understand the monitor is eliminated.

SLIVER BID. An extension of the SPLINTER BID principle, devised by GEORGE ROSENKRANZ for use with weaker responding hands. With four- or preferably, five-card trump support for a major suit opening and fewer than 10 HCP, the standard response would be a jump to game. When such a hand includes a singleton or void and a minimum of three controls including at least one king (2 controls — ace or void; 1 control — king or singleton) possession of a "sliver" is indicated by a response of 3 NT. Opener's rebids: Sign off in the major with more than five losers and a hand poor in HCP and controls. With at least six high-card controls, or five controls and a singleton, 15 or more HCP and fewer than six losers, opener explores slam possibilities by bidding the suit where responder's singleton or void will represent duplication and be of least value.

Responder's rebids: Sign off by bidding game in agreed suit if singleton or void is opposite partner's "exclusion" rebid. With shortage elsewhere, rebid by steps: 1st step: Singleton in lower unbid side suit. 2nd step: Singleton in higher suit. 3rd step: Void in lower unbid suit. 4th step: Void in higher unbid suit. In counting steps, game bid in the agreed trump suit — the sign-off — is omitted.

SLOW PASS. A pass at a slow tempo which reveals that the passer was considering an alternative action. This may be quite harmless; if the passer takes the final decision for his side and becomes the declarer or the dummy, no ethical problem can arise.

In other circumstances the slow pass is liable to convey improper information to the partner, who must do his best not to be influenced by that information.

Four particular cases are worth distinguishing:

(1) A player who considers making an opening bid and then passes has implied that he holds close to an opening bid. In such circumstances, after he has hesitated, the player should prefer a subminimum opening to a subethical pass.

(2) A slow pass may reveal ambitions at a higher level. If a player passes slowly when his partner raises 1♠ to 2♠, he has indicated faint game possibilities. Admittedly this information will not be significant unless an opponent indiscreetly balances.

(3) The slow pass is most revealing in competitive auctions. Some of the problems are solved by the SKIP-BID WARNING, but such situations often lead to protests. It is often difficult not to be influenced subconsciously. Some associations, notably the Greater New York BA, on the initiative of EDGAR KAPLAN, believe that adjustments should be made in such cases in the same way as offenses against the normal rules of the game. The slow-passing side is penalized in the same way that they would be for, say, a revoke, and there is no suggestion of unethical conduct. In order to provide standards and to avoid *ad hoc* judgments, some tournament protest committees apply a so-called 80% rule. If the Committee finds that there was in fact a slow pass, it will ordinarily rescind the action taken by the partner of the slow passer if it believes such an action would normally be taken less than 80% of the time.

(4) A slow pass which ends the auction may be revealing when the passer's partner will be on lead. There may be an indication that a LEAD-DIRECTING DOUBLE was contemplated.

In one special case a slow pass is quite harmless. A forcing pass at a high level by the side which is on the offensive does not convey information, because partner does not know whether the alternative contemplated was a bid or a double.

See also HUDDLE.

SLOW PLAY. As opposed to careful or thoughtful play, slow play is discourteous not only to the opponents of the moment, but to all the other competitors in an event as well. In rubber bridge, it decreases the number of hands that can be played in a session; in duplicate tournaments, a consistently slow pair can delay the entire game by many minutes.

Contributing to slow play as defined here are some or all of these violations of the proprieties of duplicate play: (1) delay in coming to the table after the round has been called; (2) discussion of boards previously played; (3) failure to pass at least one completed board promptly, or pass one board if the other has not been completed; (4) inattention during the bidding necessitating frequent reviews of the auction; (5) post-mortems, particularly those involving the player whose duty it is to score the board just played; (6) failure to accept a ruling from the director pleasantly and promptly in the event of an infraction; (7) blaming previous opponents for present tardiness instead of concentrating on finishing the present hand; (8) waiting for a miracle to change opponent's aces to deuces so that a bad contract will not receive its deserved result. The LAWS OF DUPLICATE specifically provide that as a matter of courtesy a player should avoid "Prolonging play unnecessarily for the purpose of disconcerting the other players." (Proprieties III.)

In national and international championships a team which repeatedly exceeds the time limit allowed for play is subject to penalties. The penalty may take the form of a matchpoint or victory-point "fine." It may be as extreme as exclusion of a team from an event. In team events, the penalty sometimes takes the form of barring offending pairs from playing as partners in later rounds.

SLUFF. To discard a worthless card; to dispose of a loser by throwing it off on the lead of a suit not held by the sluffer. The word derives from *slough* — to cast off.

SMALL CARD. A card in a suit lower than the 6, although the 6 itself on occasion might be considered a small card.

SMALL SLAM. The bidding and making of six-odd, or 12 tricks in all, for which the premium, scored above the line in rubber bridge, but in regular fashion in CHICAGO or DUPLICATE, is 500 points when not vulnerable and 750 points when vulnerable. See SLAM BIDDING for a mathematical treatment of percentage expectation of success for the bid. See also MATHEMATICAL VALUE OF GAME.

SMITH CONVENTION. (1) A club takeout as a DEFENSE TO OPENING THREE-BID, devised by CURTIS SMITH, (2) a 4 NT slam convention devised by William S. Smith and Gertrude Smith of Waterbury CT, in 1935 and which was popular for many years. Identical in principle with the NORMAN 4 NT, but different in one detail. A response of 5♠ showed specifically one ace and three kings, while 5 NT was used to show two aces and one king. (3) Also applied to the cheating device said to have been used at rubber bridge: holding a YARBOROUGH, one player announces that he has 14 cards, and his partner, also with a poor hand, announces 12, and rapidly mixed the two hands together. If partner has a good hand, he suggests a recount.

SMITH SIGNAL. An attitude signal given at the first opportunity by the partner of the opening leader against a notrump contract to indicate the degree of enthusiasm for the opening leader's suit. If defender's first spot card is low, this indicates he cannot stand a continuation in the opening leader's suit should opening leader regain the lead. Conversely, following with a high spot card pinpoints the desirability of a second lead in the original suit led. The opening leader can give the same kind of signal — a high spot card indicates a desire to have the opening suit continued should partner gain the lead; a low spot card suggests trying something else. The signal sometimes is attributed to T. R. H. Lyons of Great Britain, but I. G. Smith of Great Britain suggested virtually the same signal as early as the December 1963 issue of *British Bridge World*.

Here is how the signal works:

```
              ♠ 9 7
              ♡ Q 10 2
              ◇ 7 6 5 4
              ♣ A K Q J
♠ A 10 8 4 2                ♠ Q J 5
♡ 9 8 7                     ♡ K J 6 4
◇ K 3                       ◇ 10 9 8
♣ 9 7 3                     ♣ 10 8 2
              ♠ K 6 3
              ♡ A 5 3
              ◇ A Q J 2
              ♣ 6 5 4
```

```
SOUTH          NORTH
1 ◇            2 ♣
2 NT           3 NT
```

West leads the ♣4 against 3 NT. Declarer wins East's jack with the king and leads a club to dummy. East should play the ♣10 on this trick, meaning please continue. (Notice that it would be virtually useless for East to give his partner the count in the club suit here.) Declarer takes the diamond finesse, and when West wins the king he cashes four spade tricks for one down. Now suppose the East and South cards had been slightly different:

```
              ♠ 9 7
              ♡ Q 10 2
              ◇ 7 6 5 4
              ♣ A K Q J
♠ A 10 8 4 2                ♠ J 6 5
♡ 9 8 7                     ♡ A J 6 4
◇ K 3                       ◇ 10 9 8
♣ 9 7 3                     ♣ 10 8 2
              ♠ K Q 3
              ♡ K 5 3
              ◇ A Q J 2
              ♣ 6 5 4
```

The bidding is the same and West, who has the same hand as before, makes the same opening lead and sees the same dummy. Again declarer wins the ♣J with the king and leads a club. This time, however, East cannot stand a spade continuation from partner, so he contributes the ♣2. Declarer takes a diamond finesse, losing to the king. West now knows he can't afford to continue spades from his side of the table, and he exits with the ♡9. East grabs the trick,

returns the ♠6, and the contract fails by two tricks.

SMITH TROPHY. Awarded to the winners of the Life Master Women's Pairs contested at the Fall North American Championships, under which heading past results are listed. Donated by CHARLES H. GOREN in 1969 in memory of his longtime partner HELEN SOBEL SMITH.

SMOLEN TRANSFER BID. An adjunct to STAYMAN and JACOBY TRANSFER BIDS for game-going hands, devised by MIKE SMOLEN of Los Angeles, to allow the notrump opener to become the declarer in responder's long suit after responder has used Stayman with 5-4 or 6-4 in the major suits. Using Smolen Transfers, after the auction has started

```
NORTH          SOUTH
1 ♡            2 ♣
2 ◇
```

South jumps to three of his four-card major suit, showing that he has more than four cards in the other major. If opener has three cards in the unbid major, he bids game in that major. If opener has only a doubleton he bids 3 NT and, if responder has six cards in the unbid major, he continues by bidding four of the suit just below his unbid major, as a transfer bid.

SMOTHER PLAY. A rare end position that permits capture of a defender's virtually certain trump winner.

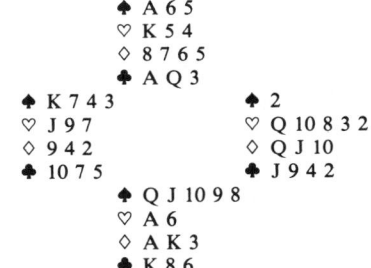

```
              ♠ A 6 5
              ♡ K 5 4
              ◇ 8 7 6 5
              ♣ A Q 3
♠ K 7 4 3                   ♠ 2
♡ J 9 7                     ♡ Q 10 8 3 2
◇ 9 4 2                     ◇ Q J 10
♣ 10 7 5                    ♣ J 9 4 2
              ♠ Q J 10 9 8
              ♡ A 6
              ◇ A K 3
              ♣ K 8 6
```

South plays 6♠. The contract appears doomed, for declarer must lose a diamond trick and West's trump king is sufficiently protected to elude capture by normal finessing. However, the opening lead of a diamond is won, and the ♠10 and 9 are finessed, West declining to cover. South continues with three rounds of clubs, the ace, king, and a heart ruff in his own hand. The ◇A is taken, leaving the following ending:

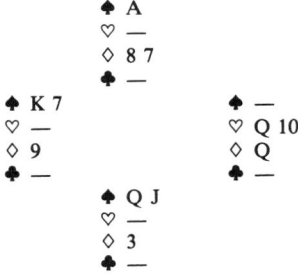

```
              ♠ A
              ♡ —
              ◇ 8 7
              ♣ —
♠ K 7                       ♠ —
♡ —                         ♡ Q 10
◇ 9                         ◇ Q
♣ —                         ♣ —
              ♠ Q J
              ♡ —
              ◇ 3
              ♣ —
```

East is thrown in with a diamond and has nothing

but hearts to return. South ruffs with the queen, and West is helpless. Also known as the "disappearing trump trick." See also DEVIL'S COUP.

SNAP. Abbreviation for STRONG NOTRUMP AFTER PASSING. Frequently the initials are used as a word.

SOCIAL BRIDGE. Played in a home for moderate or no stakes, bridge can still be highly skillful and competitive. For larger gatherings, see PARTY BRIDGE and PROGRESSIVE BRIDGE. In expert circles, social bridge increasingly is taking the form of team-of-four competition.

SOCK, SOCK IT. Slang for "I double." Used at the table, it is difficult to determine whether it is more impolite than unethical or vice versa.

SOLID SUIT. A holding which is expected as a trump or at notrump to win as many tricks as there are cards in the suit. Theoretically it should contain an many high cards as there are outstanding cards in the suit: A-K-Q-x-x-x-x-x-x might lose a trick if all four cards are in the same hand. CULBERTSON gave as his definition of reasonable expectancy of the solidity of a suit the rule of thumb that a suit was solid if half the outstanding cards were in one hand, the entire suit could still be picked up by successive leads.

An alternate definition, similar in effect, is "a suit which can be expected to lose no tricks with a singleton in dummy, and may lose no tricks opposite a void." By this standard, A-K-Q-x-x-x-x, A-K-Q-10-x-x qualify, but A-K-Q-x-x-x does not.

SOLOMON AWARD. Endowed by the late CHARLES J. SOLOMON, this award for the Bridge Hand of the Year is presented annually by the INTERNATIONAL BRIDGE PRESS ASSOCIATION. It is made to the player who has produced the best play of a hand, whether as declarer or defender, during the year in question. There is also a cash award to the person who wrote up the hand if an IBPA member. For a list of winners see INTERNATIONAL BRIDGE PRESS ASSOCIATION AWARDS.

SOLOMON TROPHY. A WBF trophy in honor of CHARLES J. SOLOMON awarded to the nation with the best overall victory-point record in the WORLD PAIR OLYMPIAD. The United States has won the trophy since its inception in 1966.

SOLOWAY JUMP SHIFT. See JUMP SHIFT.

SORTING THE HAND. The act of arranging the cards of a hand into suits and by order within suit after he cards have been dealt. Many fine players, after arranging their hand, then remove a couple of cards from a long suit and put them apart from the rest of the cards in the suit as a protection against an inadvertent glance of an opponent. Among the habits that experienced players develop are the placing of a singleton in the middle, rather than at an end of the hand, and the avoidance of rearranging a hand when a suit has been exhausted therefrom. It is a violation of the proprieties to note from what part of a hand an opponent or partner draws a card in order to get a clue as to his holding or distribution.

SOS REDOUBLE. A redouble calling on partner to select another denomination. It applies whenever there is no possibility of the redouble being applied in a natural sense.

WEST	NORTH	EAST	SOUTH
			1♣
Dbl	Pass	Pass	Redbl

South may have opened on a short club suit. His redouble requests North to bid his best suit outside of clubs as a rescue. However, in a major suit such a redouble would be strength-showing, not an SOS.

A double of an opening weak notrump bid often prompts an SOS redouble. For example:

WEST	NORTH	EAST	SOUTH
			1 NT
Dbl	2♣	Dbl	Pass
Pass	Redbl		

This sequence implies that North is planning to play in some other suit, and does not hold clubs. South should bid his lowest-ranking four-card suit, and if his only suit is clubs he should bid his lowest-ranking three-card suit.

If South retreats into 2◊ and an opponent doubles, North might redouble again to ask South to select a major suit. Similar situations arise when the opening notrump bid is doubled and redoubled. It is the doubling side which is then on the run, perhaps using SOS redoubles in an attempt to find the best part-score fit at the level of two.

In rare circumstances a player may redouble his partner's bid as an SOS instead of his own bid.

WEST	NORTH	EAST	SOUTH
			1♣
Pass	Pass	Dbl	Pass
Pass	Redbl		

If North could not respond to 1♣ he cannot wish to redouble naturally. The redouble therefore shows extreme shortage in clubs and begs South to pick another denomination.

For a specialized SOS redouble, see KOCK-WERNER REDOUBLE.

SOUND BIDDING. A bidding system stressing elevated standards for some opening bids and overcalls. ROTH-STONE opening bids in first or second position are examples of sound bids. A sound bidder refers to one whose bids, rebids and responses are fully justified by his holding, and who, when choices of bids are available, will choose the more conservative action.

SOUTH. One of the compass points used in describing the players at the table. South is partnered by North, and is OVER the East hand but UNDER the West hand. In bridge writing for general reading, South is conventionally the declarer, and this usage is followed in this book. However, in reporting International Matches and other major events, the actual positions at the table are used.

SOUTH AFRICAN TEXAS. A special method of

transfer bids at the level of four. After an opening bid of 1 NT or 2 NT, a jump to 4♣ requires the opener to bid 4♡, and 4◇ asks for 4♠.

This was the original form of DAVID CARTER'S TEXAS convention, and was developed independently in South Africa. It was quickly abandoned in the U.S. in favor of red-suit transfer bids which permit the use of 4♣ as GERBER. The South African version has the psychological advantage that the responses do not sound natural, and the opener is protected from a lapse of memory.

SOUTH AMERICAN BRIDGE CONFEDERATION (CONFEDERACION SUDAMERICANA DE BRIDGE).

Founded in 1948, the confederation consists of the bridge associations of 10 South American countries: Argentina, Bolivia, Brazil, Chile, Colombia, Ecuador, Paraguay, Peru, Uruguay and Venezuela. The South American Confederation runs an annual team championship for its member countries, with the winning country gaining the right to represent South America in the World Championships. (For past results of the South American Championships, see Appendix III.)

Officers, 1982:
President: Gerardo Meyer
Secretary: Ernesto Velarde, Paraguay 1280, Ap. 101
    Montevideo, Uruguay

SOUTHERN AFRICAN BRIDGE FEDERATION.

This federation was formed in 1954, as the South African Bridge Federation, consisting at that time of the Transvaal Contract Bridge League, which represented the European Clubs, and the Transvaal Contract Bridge Board of Control, which represented the non-European Clubs. In 1963, the Central African Bridge Association was incorporated into the Federation, and the name was changed to the present title. With a total membership in 1982 of approximately 5,000, the Federation participates in the Olympiads, finishing second in the 1968 and 1972 World Women's Team Olympiad, and 1974 World Women's Pair Olympiad, and annually sponsors National Open Team and Open Pairs championships.

Officers, 1982:
President: Julius Butkow
Secretary: Joe Goldberg, Box 89347, Lyndhurst
    2106, South Africa

SPADES.

The highest ranking of the four suits at bridge. The 13 cards of the suit are indicated with a black symbol, ♠; the ace of the suit usually carries a special design trademarked by the manufacturer, on its face.

SPANISH BRIDGE FEDERATION (FEDERACIÓN ESPANOLA DE BRIDGE).

Founded in 1941, by 1982 it had a membership of more than 2,000. The Federation is a member of the European Bridge League and regularly sends teams to compete in both Open and Women's series; it also participates in World Olympiads, hosting the 1974 World Pair Olympiad. Tournaments are held on both the regional and national level.

Officers, 1982:

President: Jose Torre Maure
Secretary: Francisco Corbella, Mallorca 290, Entlo.
    2°, Barcelona, 9, Spain

SPECIFIED CARDS, ODDS GOVERNING. See ODDS GOVERNING SPECIFIED CARDS.

SPECIFIED SUIT.

A suit of which the lead may be required or forbidden because of an irregularity earlier in the auction or play.

SPECTATOR.

A person who watches a bridge tournament without actually taking part. This is differentiated from a KIBITZER, whose presence is limited to a particular table. The conduct of spectators is governed by the LAWS (Proprieties V). Misconduct by a kibitzer may result in a penalty against the side responsible for the kibitzer's presence. See LAWS OF DUPLICATE (Law 11).

Some of the larger championship events and all of the international and intercity matches draw large numbers of interested viewers for whom provision is usually made. Such provision is sometimes in the form of small raised grandstands surrounding the table to accommodate more spectators than can be taken care of in chairs, and range up to the BRIDGE-O-RAMA or VUGRAPH facilities which enable hundreds of viewers to watch the play of all four hands simultaneously with the play itself. The hand is shown on the screen and the bidding is added as it takes place. Each card is crossed off as played. Adding to the enjoyment of the spectators is the commentary offered by experts as the hands are bid and played. Of course the greatest number of spectators of a bridge match are the viewers of televised matches. See TELEVISION.

SPIDER MOVEMENT. See WEB MOVEMENT.

SPINGOLD TROPHY.

For the NAC Master Teams Championship, donated by NATHAN SPINGOLD in 1934 for what was then called the World Championship Masters Team-of-Four and played originally as a separate knockout event. In 1938 this event became a part of the Summer NAC (under which results are listed), superseding the CITY OF ASBURY PARK TROPHY event. In the Fifties and Seventies the Spingold helped select a number of U.S. international teams; it ranks with the Vanderbilt as the most highly prized trophy in the ACBL calendar. The winners of the Spingold are entitled to compete against the winners of the GRAND NATIONAL TEAMS, REISINGER MEMORIAL TROPHY and VANDERBILT CUP for the right to represent North America or the United States in World Championship team play. See INTERNATIONAL OPEN TEAM SELECTION.

SPLINTER BID.

A variation of the FRAGMENT BID idea, in which an unusual jump guarantees a fit for partner's last named suit, shows a singleton or void in the suit in which the jump is made, and suggests a slam. Alternatively known as an anti-fragment or singleton-showing bid, and often confused with the fragment bid. In general, any jump during the auction when a nonjump or lower-level jump would be forcing (assuming asking bids are not being used) may be considered a splinter bid. On this basis, the device can be used in a wide variety of situations. For example, the last bid in the following auctions would be a splinter:

(1)	SOUTH	NORTH
	1♠	4♣

(2)	SOUTH	NORTH
	1♡	3♠

(3)	SOUTH	NORTH
	1♠	1♠

(4)	SOUTH	NORTH
	1♠	2♢
	4♣	

(5)	SOUTH	NORTH
	1♠	2♢
	2♡	4♣

(6)	SOUTH	WEST	NORTH	EAST
	1♠	1♡	3♡	

(7)	SOUTH	WEST	NORTH	EAST
	1♡	1♠	2♠	3♡

There are two cases that require partnership agreement:

(8)	SOUTH	NORTH
	1♠	4♡

Most of those players who use splinter bids consider North's 4♡ bid a splinter, but the standard interpretation is also possible.

(9)	SOUTH	NORTH
	1♠	2♣
	3♡ or 4♡	

One of South's bids, but not both, should be a splinter.

For alternative treatments, see ASKING BIDS, CONGLOMERATE MAJOR RAISES, SWISS CONVENTION, VALUE SWISS RAISES, VOID-SHOWING BIDS, MINI-SPLINTER.

SPLIT. See BREAK.

SPLIT EQUALS. See PLAY FROM EQUALS.

SPONSORING ORGANIZATION. The group which sponsors bridge tournaments conducted under the LAWS OF DUPLICATE (Law 76). Generally, this is a club or clubs for tournaments of local rating; a unit of the American Contract Bridge League for sectionally rated tournaments; a conference of units or a very large unit for regionally rated tournaments; and the American Contract Bridge League itself for the national tournaments. See COMMITTEE.

SPONSORS. See PROFESSIONAL PLAYERS.

SPOT CARD LEADS. See JOURNALIST LEADS; OPENING LEADS; THREE SMALL CARDS, LEAD FROM.

SPOT CARDS. Cards ranking below the jack, from the 10 down to the 2.

Of the 13 tricks which are won on each deal, approximately eight are won with aces, kings, queens, and jacks; the remaining five tricks are won with the lower cards — the 10s, 9s, 8s, 7s, etc. Generally speaking, a fraction more than five tricks is won by the lower cards in trump contracts, since the low trumps win tricks which are not available in notrump contracts.

Through the years, all the emphasis on winning tricks has been on aces, kings, queens, and jacks (HONOR TRICKS, POINT-COUNT) and quite naturally so, since these cards are the leaders in the area of winning tricks. However, as can be observed from the above, the lower cards are not merely pawns in the trick-taking field.

SPREAD. (1) Verb: to spread the hand, either as a claim or as a concession of the remaining tricks. See CLAIM OR CONCESSION for the proper method of making such a claim. (2) Noun: the difference between the minimum and maximum values shown by a particular bid; in STANDARD AMERICAN, the range of values for an opening bid of 1 NT is 16 to 18 high-card points, a spread of three, while an opening bid of one in a suit may have a high-card point-count spread of 11 to 24, or 14 points. Prior to 1971, the ACBL limited the spread of notrump openings to 4 points; of weak two-bid openings to 6 to 12 high-card points.

SPRING NORTH AMERICAN CHAMPIONSHIPS. Formerly called the Spring Nationals. This annual tournament of the AMERICAN CONTRACT BRIDGE LEAGUE was first convened in 1958. The most important event is the VANDERBILT CUP contest. In 1968 the tournament attracted a total of 13,535 tables, a record for the series. For past results of Spring North American Championships, see Appendix 1.

SPRING NORTH AMERICAN CHAMPIONSHIPS

Year	Site	Tables	Year	Site	Tables
1958	Atlantic City	3,076	1973	St. Louis	8,418
1959	Seattle	4,124	1974	Vancouver BC	8,329
1960	Jackson MS	3,485	1975	Honolulu	10,234
1961	Denver	4,910	1976	Kansas City	8,790
1962	Lexington KY	4,703	1977	Pasadena	12,713
1963	St. Louis	6,556	1978	Houston	9,388
1964	Portland OR	6,950	1979	Norfolk VA	8,273
1965	Cleveland	8,128	1980	Fresno CA	9,669
1966	Louisville KY	7,929	1981	Detroit	8,221
1967	Seattle	7,098	1982	Niagara Falls	9,020½
1968	New York City	13535	1983	Honolulu	11,697½
1969	Cleveland	8,958	1984	San Antonio	
1970	Portland OR	7,025	1985	Montreal	
1971	Atlanta	9,706	1986	Portland OR	
1972	Cincinnati	9,495	1987	Kansas City	

SPUTNIK. See NEGATIVE DOUBLE.

SQUARE HAND. Bridge geometry is peculiar; square hand, flat hand, and round hand all describe 4-3-3-3 distribution.

SQUEEZE. A play which forces an opponent to discard at a time when he would prefer not to do so. The forced discard will cost the opponent at least one trick, sooner or later.

In most cases, a squeeze compels an opponent to discard a winner, a potential winner, or a guard to a winner. The most familiar squeezes have the following requirements:

a. Two threat (or menace) cards, at least one of which is accompanied by a winner in that suit.

A threat card is any card that will take a trick provided the opponents unguard that suit. (When a threat card is accompanied by a winner in that suit, it is called a two-card threat.)

b. The hand opposite at least one of the two-card threats contains a card in the suit of the threat card.

This card provides a means of reaching the two-card threat in the opposite hand.

c. The opponent to be squeezed holds no idle cards. This usually requires that the squeeze player can win all but one of the remaining tricks. (See RECTIFYING THE COUNT)

When these conditions have been satisfied, the card played to the next trick forces an unwanted discard from at least one opponent.

This card is called the squeeze card. It is usually a winner played from the hand opposite the two-card threat. If both menaces are in the same hand, only the opponent who is to the left of the squeeze card is affected. These are called positional (or one-way) squeezes. In an automatic squeeze, either opponent can be subjected to pressure. This occurs when the squeeze card is accompanied by a menace card, so that the hand opposite has one card which is immaterial and furnishes an automatic discard.

The term "squeeze" was coined by SIDNEY LENZ well after the operation of a squeeze had been recognized and analyzed. Originally a squeeze was simply called a coup. In the heyday of American whist it was known as "putting the opponent to the discard." Circa 1910 J. B. ELWELL called squeeze play "forcing discards," and this term was in general use until Lenz in the middle Twenties, inspired by a squeeze play in a professional baseball game, introduced his new term.

For various types of squeeze and aspects of squeeze play see ALTERNATIVE SQUEEZE; AUTOMATIC SQUEEZE; BACKWASH SQUEEZE; BARCO SQUEEZE; BONNEY'S SQUEEZE; BUSY CARD AND IDLE CARD; CLASH SQUEEZE; COMPOUND SQUEEZE; COMPOUND TRUMP SQUEEZE; COUNT SQUEEZE; CRISSCROSS SQUEEZE; DEFENSE TO A SQUEEZE; DOUBLE SQUEEZE; ENTRY SQUEEZE; ENTRY-SHIFTING SQUEEZE; GUARD SQUEEZE; HEXAGON SQUEEZE; HEXAGON TRUMP SQUEEZE; ISOLATING THE MENACE; JETTISON SQUEEZE; MENACE; ONE-SUIT SQUEEZE; OVERTAKING SQUEEZE; POSITIONAL SQUEEZE; PROGRESSIVE SQUEEZE; PSEUDO SQUEEZE; RECIPROCAL SQUEEZE; RECTIFYING THE COUNT; RULE OF N-MINUS ONE; SCHROEDER SQUEEZE; SECONDARY SQUEEZE; SERES SQUEEZE; SHOW UP SQUEEZE; SIMPLE SQUEEZE; SQUEEZE FINESSE; SQUEEZE WITHOUT THE COUNT; SQUEEZED POSITION; STEPPINGSTONE; SUBMARINE SQUEEZE; SUICIDE SQUEEZE; THREAT CARD; TRANSFER SQUEEZE; TRANSFERRING THE MENACE; TRIPLE SQUEEZE; TRUMP SQUEEZE; UNBLOCKING SQUEEZE; VICE; VIENNA COUP; WINKLE.

Monroe Ingberman

SQUEEZE FINESSE. Closely related to the GUARD SQUEEZE. In each case, declarer threatens to take a successful finesse. In a guard squeeze, the opponents are not equally threatened, whereas the squeeze finesse is characterized by the presence of a symmetric menace which must be guarded with an equal number of cards by both opponents.

(1) Four-card squeeze finesse menaces:

Triple tenaces

```
      K 9                    K 2
Q 8        10 5    or   Q 8        10 5
      J 2                    J 9
```

These positions may lead to a squeeze or throw-in of either opponent.

Quadruple tenaces

```
      K 8                    K 2
Q 7        10 9    or   Q 7        10 9
      J 2                    J 8
```

In these positions, only West can be thrown in successfully.

(2) Six-card squeeze finesse menaces:

Triple tenaces

```
       K 9 x                    K 3 2
Q 8 x        10 5 x   or   Q 8 x        10 5 x
       A J 2                    A J 9
```

Either opponent may be thrown in.

Quadruple tenaces

```
       K 8 x                    K 3 2
Q 7 x        10 9 x   or   Q 7 x        10 9 x
       A J 2                    A J 8
```

Only West can be thrown in.

(3) Squeeze-Finesse positions (at notrump):

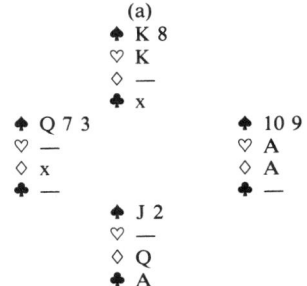

(a)
```
              ♠ K 8
              ♡ K
              ◇ —
              ♣ x
♠ Q 7 3              ♠ 10 9
♡ —                 ♡ A
◇ x                 ◇ A
♣ —                 ♣ —
              ♠ J 2
              ♡ —
              ◇ Q
              ♣ A
```

South has two of the remaining tricks. The ♣A is led and East is squeezed in three suits. He must discard a spade, and now South leads the ♠J to smother the 10. If West's small diamond is exchanged for the king, this merely opens up the possibility of a squeeze throw-in against West.

(b)
```
              ♠ K 3 2
              ♡ 10 2
              ◇ —
              ♣ —
♠ Q 7 x              ♠ 10 9 x
♡ —                  ♡ Q J
◇ x x                ◇ —
♣ —                  ♣ —
              ♠ A J 8
              ♡ K
              ◇ —
              ♣ A
```

South has four of the remaining five tricks. The ♣A squeezes East in two suits. He must discard a spade, but declarer can now pick up three tricks in spades by leading the jack through West.

The squeeze fails if the ♠8 and ♠2 are interchanged.

(c)

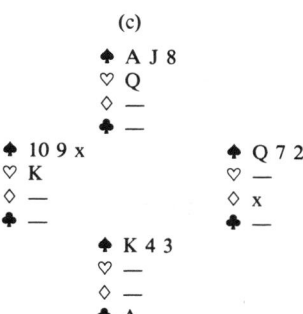

```
              ♠ A J 8
              ♡ Q
              ◇ —
              ♣ —
♠ 10 9 x              ♠ Q 7 2
♡ K                   ♡ —
◇ —                   ◇ x
♣ —                   ♣ —
              ♠ K 4 3
              ♡ —
              ◇ —
              ♣ A
```

The ♣A squeezes West in two suits. West discards a spade, and declarer leads the ♠A, and then runs the jack through East to pick up the suit.

The ♠8 and ♠2 may be interchanged without affecting the squeeze. East's small diamond may be exchanged for the ♡A, but the squeeze still works.

(4) Squeeze Finesse at Trumps (also called simply TRUMP SQUEEZE).

Simple

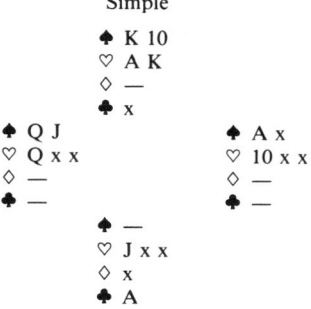

```
              ♠ K 10
              ♡ A K
              ◇ —
              ♣ x
♠ Q J                 ♠ A x
♡ Q x x               ♡ 10 x x
◇ —                   ◇ —
♣ —                   ♣ —
              ♠ —
              ♡ J x x
              ◇ x
              ♣ A
```

Diamonds are trumps. The ♣A is led and West is squeezed. If he discards a heart, declarer cashes the two top hearts, re-enters his hand by ruffing a spade to cash the ♡J. If West discards a spade, the ♠K can be led to ruff out the ace, and smother the queen, establishing North's 10.

Double

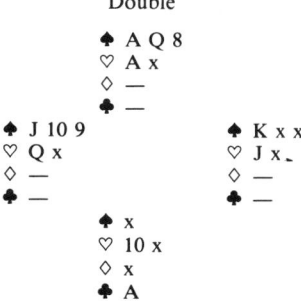

```
              ♠ A Q 8
              ♡ A x
              ◇ —
              ♣ —
♠ J 10 9              ♠ K x x
♡ Q x                 ♡ J x_
◇ —                   ◇ —
♣ —                   ♣ —
              ♠ x
              ♡ 10 x
              ◇ x
              ♣ A
```

Diamonds are trumps. The ♣A is led and West is squeezed. If he discards a spade, the ace and queen of that suit are led, ruffing out the king and smothering West's honors. If West discards a heart,

then North throws a heart and East is caught in a standard trump squeeze.

Monroe Ingberman

SQUEEZE MNEMONICS. An acronym or other set of initials used as a reminder of the ingredients necessary for the operation of a squeeze. Among the more well-known mnemonics are:

(1) Clyde Love's BLUE:
B = Busy (one defender Busy in two suits)
L = Loser (one Loser remaining)
U = Upper (at least one threat in Upper hand)
E = Entry (to the threat card)

(2) George Coffin's EFG (to Enter Freedom, force the Guards):
E = Entry (to the threat card)
F = Forcing card
G = Guards (in one defender's hand)

(3) John Brown's STEM:
S = Share-out or Substance
T = Timing (count has been rectified)
E = Entries (to the threat card)
M = Menaces

Robert True

SQUEEZE SUIT-OUT. A particular form of SECONDARY SQUEEZE.

SQUEEZE WITHOUT THE COUNT. An unusual variation of the squeeze. In order for a squeeze to be effective, declarer ordinarily must have all but one of the remaining tricks (see RULE OF N-MINUS-ONE). However, this is not invariably the case. In certain squeeze positions declarer gives up a trick after the squeeze. This is called a "squeeze without the count" (see SECONDARY SQUEEZE).

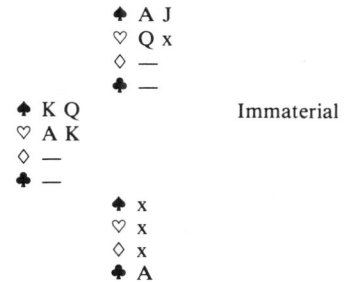

```
              ♠ A J
              ♡ Q x
              ◇ —
              ♣ —
♠ K Q                      Immaterial
♡ A K
◇ —
♣ —
              ♠ x
              ♡ x
              ◇ x
              ♣ A
```

South leads the ♣A which squeezes West, despite the fact that South has only two of the last four tricks. West must discard a heart; now South leads a heart to establish the queen.

SQUEEZED POSITION (PLAYING TO). In the development of the understanding of squeezes, SIDNEY LENZ invented the idea of a squeeze card, and this concept has dominated the analysis of squeeze play ever since. Indeed, some writers have even given special names, for example "reciprocal squeeze," where the actual squeeze card could not be identified.

(1)
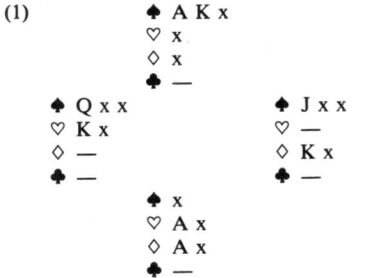

In this double automatic position, for instance, there is no separate and identifiable squeeze card. The two red aces are led, and each opponent is squeezed by the ace of his partner's suit.

As more and more squeeze positions have been identified, the burden of remembering them for use in play has become impossible except for the most expert, and in trying to simplify the rules for the less expert players it has been found that, by abandoning the concept of a squeeze card, the number of end positions can be reduced, and, in particular, the more complex ones can be forgotten. This has probably always been the practice in expert circles, and was almost implied by ELY CULBERTSON in his "Red Book."

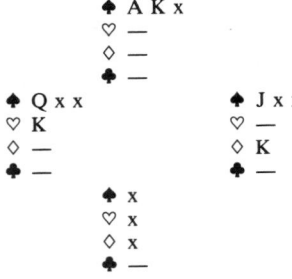

For example, in No. 1 above, if South cashes his red aces, he has achieved the "squeezed position." South is on lead, but both East and West have yet to play. This one position is all automatic double squeezes, and squeeze cards, reciprocal squeezes, simultaneous and interrupted automatic double squeezes, can all be forgotten.

The following are simple automatic squeezes:

(2)
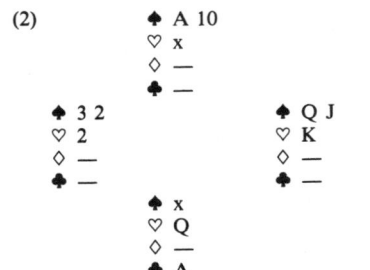

(3)
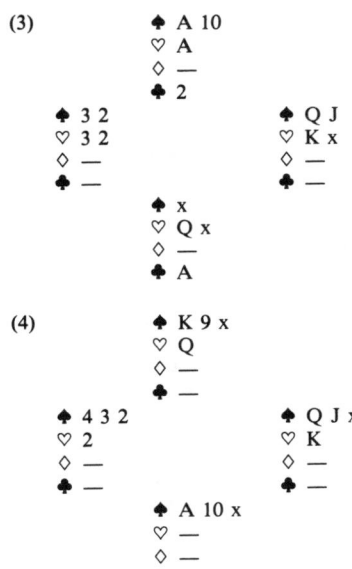

(4)

These three endings, Nos. 2, 3, and 4, can all be represented by one squeezed position, No. 5, with South on lead. North and South have both played, but the opponent with the high cards, either East or West, must now play and is squeezed. In No. 2 the ♣A squeezes either East or West, the ♡x being thrown from North. In No. 3 we first Vienna-Coup with the ♡A, and then the ♣A squeezes whichever opponent holds the high cards.

In No. 4 we have to imagine North as South in No. 5.

(5)
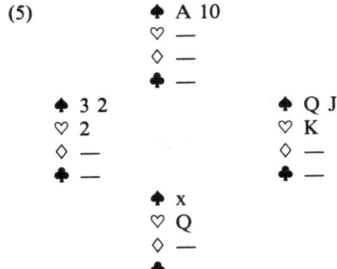

Examples could be given for all varieties of squeezes but this would be tedious, so let the following suffice:

(6)
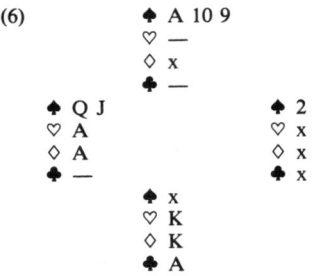

(7)

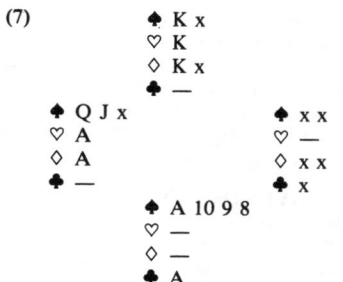

Examples Nos. 6 and 7 are two triple squeeze positions, both automatic, in which the lead of the ♣A squeezes opponent into promoting one of declarer's kings, then squeezing him a second time when that king is played, when the other ace or the guard to declarer's long suit must be given up. Example No. 8 is either of these reduced to the squeezed position, with South on lead. No. 7 has to be turned upside down to get to No. 8, but as the position is automatic, this is of no consequence.

(8)

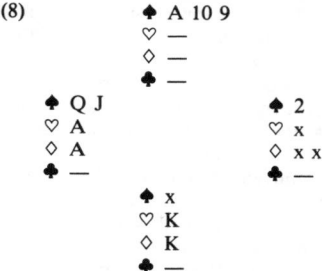

Finally, the simple trump squeeze. Although the three examples, Nos. 9, 10, and 11, all appear to be different, once one plays down to the squeezed position they all become the same.

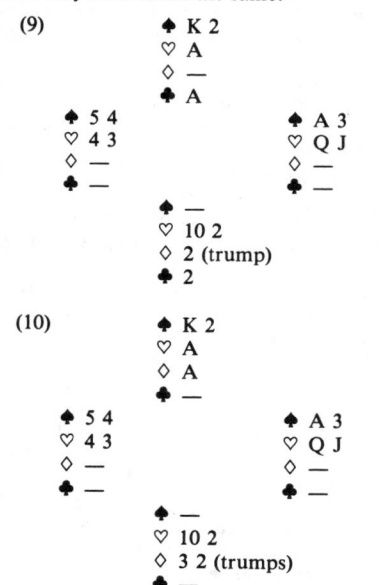

Trump squeezes are always automatic. In No. 9 the lead of the ♣2, or in No. 10 the lead of a trump,

squeezes the opponent (in this case East) who holds the high cards. If he throws a spade the ♣2 is led and trumped, North is re-entered and the ♠K is cashed. If the throws a heart the ♡A is cashed, a spade is ruffed, and the last heart made.

(11)

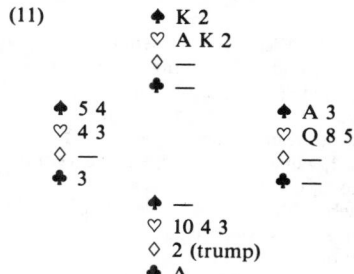

In No. 11 the ♣A is led and North's ♡2 discarded. If East throws a spade North is entered with a heart, the ♣2 is ruffed, and North re-entered to make the ♠K. If East throws a heart, North's ♡A–K are cashed and a spade ruff puts South in again to make the ♡10.

(12)

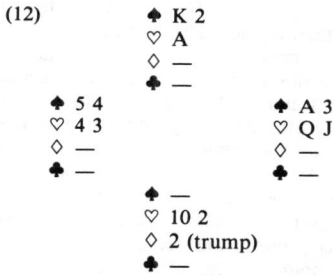

Each of the above three cases reduces to the squeezed position, No. 12, with East to discard and then North to lead. This is a much simpler position to remember—in fact it is all simple trump squeezes, and is one position instead of three.

STACK, STACKED. (1) The cards are said to be stacked against one when a single opponent holds all or nearly all of the cards in a crucial suit. (2) To stack a deck is to arrange cards in an undealt deck in order to put predetermined holdings into one or more hands. See CHEATING.

STAKES. Rubber bridge is frequently played for stakes. Although it is a social game, the addition of stakes does provide an incentive to careful and accurate bidding and play.

In major bridge clubs, where membership and card fees are not inconsiderable, stakes range from one-half cent to three cents per point; in home and social games, stakes are usually much more modest.

STAND, STAND FOR. To pass one's partner's PENALTY DOUBLE or TAKE-OUT DOUBLE.

STAND-OFF. A colloquialism for either a rubber with no net score (after ROUNDING OFF); a hand in which HONOR SCORE balances undertrick penalties: or a deal in a team game (BOARD-A-MATCH, IMP, or TOTAL POINTS) on which neither team gains.

STAND UP. In defensive play, a high card that wins a trick. A suit is said to stand up until it is trumped by the declarer. On the offense or on the defense, too, a high card is said to stand up if it wins the trick, even though a higher card may be outstanding in the suit.

STANDARD AMERICAN. A nebulous term applied to the methods of bidding most commonly used in the United States. It approximates closely the methods advocated by CHARLES GOREN.

Among serious tournament players the WEAK TWO-BID is standard, while rubber bridge players continue to use the FORCING TWO.

Another debatable issue is the idea that jump bids by responder are always forcing. This is implicit in Goren's methods.

In parts of the United States, especially California, expert methods include limit bids, sign-off bids and nonforcing jumps to a much greater extent than in the East, South and Midwest.

STANZA MOVEMENT. A method of conducting a combined-section pairs game whereby the scoring of the first half the game can be completed while the second half is taking place. The method was devised by MAURY BRAUNSTEIN of Schenectady NY. The most common application takes place in twinned sections using a 25-top, usually with 14 tables in each section, although this is not necessary. Boards numbered 1–14 are distributed at tables 1–7 and tables 8–14 in each section. After six rounds, the boards are removed from one section and replaced with boards 15–28. After seven rounds, the boards are removed from the other section and replaced with boards 15–28. At this point, Boards 1–14 have been played the full complement of 26 times and are ready for matchpointing. When using this movement, great care must be taken in the original placement of boards and the switches during the sixth and seventh rounds — otherwise the resultant mixups consume more time than is saved by the early matchpointing.

STARTING TIME. Events at bridge tournaments are announced in the advertising material, and it is a measure of a director's and tournament committee's efficiency to have the games start promptly as scheduled. At or near the end of each session, the director clearly announces the starting time for the next session. If it is a continuation of an event, the director may assess penalties for tardiness.

After the scheduled starting time, late players may be added to the event if the director can do so without restarting it or unduly delaying the game. Such late entries are accepted by the director at his discretion, and no player has an automatic right to be so accepted.

STAYMAN AFTER OVERCALL. When there is an overcall after a 1 NT opening, all minimum minor-suit bids can be used to explore for major-suit contracts. After a 2♣ overcall, 2◇ asks for a major. 3♣ over a 2◇ overcall is similar, and the bidding can stop at four of a minor. After a major-suit overcall, responder bids his longer minor to show length in the unbid major. This plan was devised by

R. Maltais, Kenogami PQ.

Although the above method is espoused by the author of the STAYMAN CONVENTION, the modern treatment is to play that a cuebid is Stayman, asking for both majors over a minor-suit overcall and the other major after a major-suit overcall. See also LEBENSOLD.

STAYMAN CONVENTION. The response of 2♣ to 1 NT or 3♣ to 2 NT asking opener to bid a four-card major suit.

The convention was invented by GEORGE RAPÉE, but the first article on the convention (*The Bridge World*, June 1945) was authored by SAM STAYMAN, and the convention was named for the writer rather than the inventor. The device quickly became standard practice throughout the world, vying with the BLACKWOOD CONVENTION as the most popular. Rapée and Stayman were a strong, established partnership at this time.

The convention was played in the early Thirties by EWART KEMPSON of England and a group of Boston players. J. C. H. MARX of London, England, also had used a similar 2♣ convention prior to 1945, but his first written presentation, in the *Contract Bridge Journal*, did not appear until 1946. According to Marx, he developed his ideas concerning the club response independently and was not aware of the *Bridge World* article when he put his ideas about the convention into printed form.

The original convention provided for opener to rebid 2◇ with a minimum hand and 2 NT with a maximum. S. J. SIMON, England, suggested the simplification which became generally adopted: opener automatically rebids 2◇ if he does not have a major suit.

The use of higher-level rebids by the opener (such as 3♣ to show both major suits) is frowned on by the leading authorities: such bids tend to give excessive information to the opponents and prevent responder's using Stayman with a weak unbalanced hand.

The authorities are divided on the correct rebid for the opener holding both majors. It makes little difference and partnership agreement is not essential. Whether 2♣ or 2♡ is preferred, the opener can bid the other major if responder rebids 2 NT or 3 NT.

Responder has a wide range of possible rebids, many of which are subject to varying interpretations.

(1) *Two of a major suit*. This can be treated in three ways: (a) Forcing (usually described as *forcing Stayman*). The bidding must continue at least as far as 2 NT. This permits a slow approach to the game and slam level with strong hands; but most experts reject this treatment because strong hands can be bid satisfactorily by bidding the suit at the three-level on the first or second round. (b) Encouraging (usually described as *non-forcing Stayman*). This is the standard procedure. Responder indicates game possibilities, together with a five-card suit, or possibly a six-card suit. (c) Weak. This shows an unbalanced hand and no game interest. The suit bid is likely to be four cards only. If the opener has only a doubleton in the suit, he must make a further bid: over 2♡ he bids

2♣ with a three-card suit because responder presumably has spades; over 2♣ he bids 3♣ if he has a club suit, and otherwise 2 NT. (See article by ALAN TRUSCOTT in *Bridge Bridge World,* Feb/March 1959.)

(2) *2 NT.* This is encouraging, showing the same strength as an immediate raise to 2 NT. If the opener showed a major, responder now implies that he holds the other major. If the opener rebid 2◇, responder simply indicates he has one or both majors.

(3) *Three of a minor suit.* The standard treatment is for 3♣ to be weak, with a six-card of seven-card club suit with no game interest. 3◇ remains ambiguous, and can be treated as forcing or encouraging. (But see WEISSBERGER convention.) However, many experts use immediate jumps to 3♣ and 3◇ as preemptive (as in ROTH-STONE and KAPLAN-SHEINWOLD) in which case the delayed bid of 3♣ or 3◇ is clearly forcing to game; responder is exploring the possibility of a minor-suit game or slam.

(4) *Three of an unbid major suit* (always a jump unless opener bid spades). Forcing and shows a five-card suit.

(5) *Raise to three of a major.* A natural invitation to game, showing four-card support for the major suit.

(6) *3 NT.* A natural bid, implying that responder holds an unbid major (or possibly two unbid majors). The opener may continue in the unbid major if he has both.

(7) *Four of a minor suit.* When opener shows a major, 4♣ can be Gerber by partnership agreement. In Acol, 4♣ and 4◇ are used to show a suit or specifically four cards and a hand with slam ambitions (SHARPLES CONVENTION). All subsequent bids by both players are natural.

(8) *4 NT.* An ambiguous bid, but most players who use Gerber would treat it as quantitative. A 4-3-3-3 hand would make an immediate raise to 4 NT. (And a 4-4-3-2 hand could use the Sharples convention above.)

Other rebids by the responder are natural.

The above sequences apply to 1 NT opening bids of any range. However, the employment of a weak notrump strengthens the argument for using nonforcing Stayman. See also GLADIATOR; 1 NT OPENING; TWO-WAY STAYMAN.

The use of a conventional 2 NT response to a 1 NT opening (forcing opener to rebid 3♣) changes the Stayman structure. Now a 2♣ response no longer guarantees that responder has a four-card major, since his only method of showing a notrump raise is to bid 2♣ followed by 2 NT. Therefore the 2♣ response to 1 NT in these circumstances requres an Alert by opener.

STAYMAN ON SECOND ROUND. This is standard in one situation:

SOUTH	NORTH
2♣ (artificial)	2◇
2 NT	3♣

As no suit has been naturally bid, the responder can bid as he would opposite a 2 NT opening, with the knowledge that the opener is slightly stronger.

By partnership agreement this can be extended to other notrump rebids:

SOUTH	NORTH
1♣	1♡
1 NT	2♣ (asking for a spade suit)

This checkback procedure permits the opener to conceal a four-card major suit on the second round if he wishes, but deprives the responder of some natural rebids. If the rebid is 2 NT, 3♣ is not available for players who use it as preparation for a sign-off at the three level (see WOLFF CONVENTION). See CROWHURST CONVENTION, TWO CLUB REBID BY RESPONDER AS ONLY FORCE AFTER 1 NT REBID, UNBID MINOR SUIT FORCE.

STAYMAN FOR STOPPERS.

TWO-WAY STAYMAN may also be used in a way in which only the 2♣ bid searches for a 4-4 major suit fit. The 2◇ bid would then be used to discover whether the partnershp has all suits sufficiently well stopped to play in notrump. Responder normally reserves his 2◇ bid for a hand containing a singleton or a void. The bid asks opener to bid whichever major suit he has guarded. Suits containing four cards headed by the queen, or three headed by the queen and 10, are considered minimum suficient stoppers. With both major suits guarded opener should bid 2 NT. If opener does not have the responder's short suit stoped, responder can explore other game, or slam, possibilities.

STAYMAN SYSTEM.

Specialized methods of bidding advocated by SAMUEL M. STAYMAN, formerly played by him in international competition in partnership with VICTOR MITCHELL.

STAYMAN 2◇.

See ARTIFICIAL 2◇ and 2♣ OPENINGS.

STEINER TROPHY.

For the Individual Master Championship, donated by ALBERT and PHILIP STEINER in 1934. This event was played as an independent tournament. In 1958 it became part of the Fall North American Championships until 1960, when it was withdrawn. Past results are listed under Fall NAC.

STEP RESPONSES TO STRONG ARTIFICIAL TWO–BIDS.

Responses to a 2♣ STRONG ARTIFICIAL OPENING that show, by steps, how many controls responder holds, counting a king as one control and an ace as two. As described in *The Bridge Journal,* a 2◇ response shows 0-1 control, a 2♡ response shows 2 controls, a 2♣ response shows an ace and a king (3 controls), a 2 NT response shows three kings (3 controls), a 3♣ response shows 4 controls and so on. The theory underlying using the 2 NT response to show three kings is that if the hand is to be played in notrump it will more likely be played from the RIGHT SIDE. This method of responding is similar to that used in BLUE TEAM CLUB. See also NORMAN 4 NT.

A modification proposed by EDGAR KAPLAN requires responder to bid 2◇ with 0-6 points and 2♡ shows more than 6 points; both bids, however, show fewer than two controls. Most other responses are amended accordingly: a 2♣ response shows two controls, 2 NT still shows three kings, 3♣ shows one ace and one king, $3\diamond$ shows four controls, and so forth. See ACE-SHOWING RESPONSES.

STEPPINGSTONE SQUEEZE. A secondary squeeze in which the opponents must choose between a throw-in and a suit establishment play, each of which enables declarer to gain a trick. (Analyzed and named by TERENCE REESE).

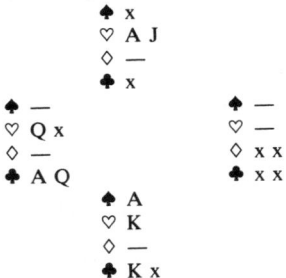

South leads the ♣A, and West is squeezed in two suits. In order to retain his guard in hearts, he must throw a club. If West discards the ♣Q, South takes the ♡K, and exits with a club, forcing West to lead a heart to North's ace; if West discards the ♣A, South's king is established.

The blocked suit must include two winners, one in each hand, but the higher must be in dummy. South must have a one-card menace against the same player who protects the blocked suit. In the diagram position, if the East and West cards were reversed, the squeeze would still be effective. See also ENTRY SQUEEZE and WINKLE SQUEEZE.

Monroe Ingberman

STERN SYSTEM. See VIENNA SYSTEM.

STIFF. (1) Adjective or noun: Colloquialism for SINGLETON, frequently used in reference to a major honor (ace, king, or queen) without guards. (2) Verb: Colloquially, to blank; to discard the guards.

STODDARD TROPHY. The Tom Stoddard Trophy was instituted to honor the founder of duplicate bridge on the West Coast. It is awarded each year to the player winning the most masterpoints during BRIDGE WEEK. The winners:

1970	Ed Davis	1977	Harold Guiver
1971	Roger Bates	1978	Hermine Baron
1972	David Ashley	1979	Ed Davis (tied with)
1973	Bill Sides		Stelios Touchtidis
1974	Jim Robison	1980	Barry Crane
1975	Paul Maier	1981	Stelio Touchtidis
1976	Paul Ivaska	1982	Barry Crane

STONE AGE ACOL WITH PAKISTANI PRE-EMPTS. A system devised by MUNIR ATA-ULLAH of Pakistan. All opening bids from $2\diamond$ through $4\diamond$ have multiple meanings — some have as many as seven possible meanings. Subsequent bids identify the hand type, suit quality, etc. It is difficult to bounce quickly to the best spot because the type of hand opened must be determined first. It is also difficult to bid defensively against this complicated system.

STOP BID. A bid which fixes the final contract and commands partner to pass. Responses of 4♠ or 3 NT to an opening notrump bid are examples. SIGN-OFF BIDS are virtually stop bids, but in some cases the partner may have a reason to violate and continue with the auction. See PREEMPTIVE RERAISE.

STOPPER. A card which may reasonably be expected to or actually does stop the run of a suit. To be counted in the auction as a stopper, a high card, except an ace, must usually be accompanied by lower cards so that it will not have to be played on a higher one if the holder of the higher card decides to play for the drop. The number of low cards, or guards, needed is in inverse proportion to the rank of the honor. Thus, the king must ordinarily be accompanied by at least one guard, and the queen by at least two unless the bidding indicates that a higher ranking card is held by partner. Stoppers are particularly important at notrump contracts. See GUARD; NOTRUMP BIDDING.

STOPPING BELOW GAME. The decision to "stop on a dime" in 2 NT or three of a major may be influenced by a variety of factors: vulnerability, method of scoring and psychological reasons.

It is usually considered advisable to reach for optimistic vulnerable games at rubber bridge and IMP scoring. A look at the mathematics involved (see VALUE OF GAME) indicates that this holds true for IMP scoring but not for rubber bridge. In matchpoint scoring, theory suggests that a game should be bid with a 50% chance, but in practice experts tend to be slightly conservative unless the opposition is weak. In such circumstances 3 NT, down one, is likely to be a worse score than 2 NT, made with an overtrick. It is desirable to make sure of a plus score.

STRAIN. A term encompassing all four suits plus notrump. See DENOMINATION.

STRENGTH. The top-card holding in a suit, either as stoppers in notrump, for drawing adversely held trumps, for trick-taking potential, or to set up LONG CARDS as winners.

STRENGTH-CONCEALING PLAYS. See DECEPTIVE PLAY.

STRENGTH-SHOWING BIDS. In some special situations a suit bid can be used to show strength rather than length or control. This applies particularly when exploring for a 3 NT contract as an alternative to an obvious minor-suit possibility.

The following are typical cases. The suit bid might conceivably be as weak as Q–J–x, but would usually contain at least 4 points.

(a)

WEST	EAST
1 $\diamond$	2 ♣
3 ♣	3 ♡

(b)

WEST	EAST
1 NT	3 $\diamond$
3 ♡	

hands so that a later lead by a defender will permit him to trump in one hand and sluff a loser from the other. Often combined with endplay as in "strip and endplay". See ENDPLAY; SQUEEZE; THROW IN.

STRIPED-TAIL APE DOUBLE. An inhibitory double of an opposing game contract made by a player who feels sure his opponents can make a slam. The doubled contract with overtricks scores less than the score for bidding and making the slam. So named by JOHN LOWENTHAL and SAMUEL SCAFFIDI in a *Bridge Journal* article because the doubler flees like a striped-tail ape in the face of a redouble. The same tactics can be applied at the small slam level if a grand slam can be made.

STRONG ACE ASKING BIDS OTHER THAN 4♣ OR 4 NT. See SUPER GERBER.

STRONG JUMP OVERCALL. See JUMP OVER-CALL.

STRONG MINOR RAISES. See INVERTED MINOR SUIT RAISES.

STRONG NOTRUMP. An opening bid of 1 NT that meets the following requirements: the hand must have a point-count of 16, 17, or 18; must be of balanced distribution, 4-3-3-3, 4-4-3-2, or 5-3-3-2 with the proviso that the doubleton be headed by at least the queen; at least three suits must be protected and the fourth suit at least x–x–x. See 1 NT OPENING.

Some players shade the requirements to 15 points, and some feel that 18 points is too strong for the bid.

Many experts treat the other requirements flexibly. They may open 1 NT with a weak doubleton because they foresee rebid problems after a suit opening; and they may occasionally open 1 NT with a six-card minor and 6-3-2-2 distribution.

Even stronger 1 NT opening bids are advocated in some systems, notably ROMAN, SIMS, and VANDERBILT. For strong notrump openings that are forcing for one round, see DYNAMIC NOTRUMP, LITTLE ROMAN CLUB SYSTEM, ROMEX SYSTEM.

STRONG NOTRUMP AFTER PASSING (abbreviated to SNAP). A response of 1 NT by a passed hand as a strong bid, showing 9–12 points. An idea introduced by JEREMY FLINT and TONY PRIDAY.

This permits the bidding to stay in a comfortable low-level contract when the opener has a minimum or sub-minimum hand. The notrump bidder promises a relatively balanced hand, and denies holding a five-card major suit which could have been bid at the level of one. The idea often gives an advantage in a partscore deal, and is therefore of most value in a matchpoint event.

For a device with similar objectives, see DRURY.

STRONG PASS. Any of several systems used in various parts of the world whereby an opening pass indicates the values for an opening bid, while various opening bids indicate values less than sufficient for an opening bid in most other systems. Partner of the opening passer is usually required to open the bidding, and the process puts strong pressure on the opposition. Since the meaning of many ordinary sequences is reversed, the opposition must work out entirely new defensive bidding systems. Strong pass systems first gained popularity in Poland, but many partnerships throughout the world now employ some version of the strong pass.

STRONG SUIT. A suit of four or more cards containing a minimum of six points.

STRONG TWO-BID. See FORCING TWO-BID.

SUBMARINE SQUEEZE. The concession of a trick by declarer in order to correct the count for a squeeze. If declarer gives up the trick on a lead by the opponents, he is said to be RECTIFYING THE COUNT; however, if the trick is conceded at a time when declarer holds the lead, some writers call this move a submarine squeeze.

SUB-SENIOR MASTER TEAMS. See ROTHSCHILD TROPHY.

SUBSTITUTE. (1) Call. When a player makes an illegal call, he may be required to substitute a legal call, with appropriate penalties against his partner, under provisions of LAWS (Laws 25–27, 30–33, 36–38).

(2) Player. A player who, in rubber bridge, replaces a member of the table who is called away or must leave during or before the finish of a rubber. Such a substitute must be acceptable to all members playing at the table; and he would be assumed to have no financial responsibility unless agreed otherwise.

(3) Player. In duplicate play, a player who is permitted by the director to replace a player who is unable to finish a session or play in a second or later session. Such substitution is at the discretion of the director, guided by the League regulations contained in the ACBL HANDBOOK in the United States, or other regulatory bodies for tournament competition.

(4) Board. In team play, a board is introduced by the director at a table when an irregularity has occurred that makes a normal result impossible. Such a board is withdrawn after play, but reinstated when the teammates of the pairs who played it are scheduled to play that board. If the substitute board is needed on the replay (after the teammates have recorded a result), an offending side causing the substitution may be playing for at best a halved board.

SUCCESSIVE EVENTS, PROBABILITY OF. See PROBABILITY OF SUCCESSIVE EVENT.

SUCKER DOUBLE. A double of a freely bid game or slam contract by a player who is relying solely on defensive high-card strength. Against good opponents such doubles rarely show more than a small profit. They can, however, show a disastrous loss, especially when the double helps declarer to make his contract. The probability is that the declaring side has distributional strength to compensate for the relative lack of high-card strength.

SUFFICIENT BID. A bid of the same number of a higher ranking denomination or of a greater number in a lower ranking suit or the same denomination. If the enforcement of a penalty permits a player to substitute a sufficient bid for an incorrect call, a double of an opponent's bid may not be substituted; even though such double is a legal call. See INSUFFICIENT BID.

SUICIDE SQUEEZE. A squeeze inflicted by a defender on his partner. (But as this name is hardly accurate, it is called by some the Cannibal Squeeze.) Inaccurate defense may lead to this position, but there are times when the opponents have no recourse.

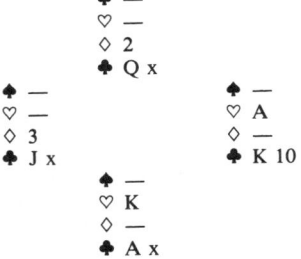

West, on lead, produces a suicide squeeze on his partner if he cashes the high diamond. If East discards the ♡ A, South discards the low club, winning two tricks. If East discards the ♣ 10, South discards the ♡ K. Proper defense calls for a club lead. If North were on lead, the small diamond lead would produce the simple squeeze against East.

This is essentially a simple squeeze position, with North on lead, but the squeeze card is a loser. Thus declarer must have all but two of the remaining tricks. In addition, the player who wins the squeeze card must have no other winner which he can cash. When these additional requirements are met, any simple squeeze ending may lead to a suicide squeeze, as can other squeeze positions.

Monroe Ingberman

SUIT. The group to which each card in a pack belongs. Modern packs have four suits. Until the 16th century, there was no agreement as to number; Hindu cards had 10, and packs of 5–11 suits were used in one country or another. In the Thirties there was a brief flurry of interest in a fifth suit, but it faded.

Three different sets of symbols have been developed which are in use today:

International (British, American, French); spades, hearts, diamonds and clubs.

Trappola (Italy, Spain, Latin countries); cups, coins, swords, and cudgels.

German (Germany, Austria, Bohemia, Poland, Hungary); hearts, leaves, bells and acorns, with the Swiss modification of blossoms and shields for the latter two.

In 1862 an American chauvinist issued a patriotic deck of Union Playing Cards with suits of stars, flags, shields and eagles. Card players were not chauvinistic.

Our club design is the clover-leaf of the French but the name is from the trappola deck; the diamond design is also French, but the name is an English descriptive term; the heart design is from the German pack; the spade design is the French pikehead, but the name is from the trappola deck.

The attribution of the suit names to the four orders of society — hearts for the church, spades for the military, clubs for the peasantry, and diamonds (tiles) for the merchants — was made long after the development of the suit names and symbols. See PLAYING CARDS.

Albert Field

SUIT, NUMBER OF CARDS IN. For notations used, see MATHEMATICS OF BRIDGE.

(1) A player can have x cards of a given suit in $13Cx \times 39C(13-x)$ ways. The percentage probability is found by multiplying this by 100 and dividing by $52C13$. A player can have exactly five spades, then, in $13C5 \times 39C8 = 79,181,063,676$ ways. The percentage is

$$\frac{7,918,106,367,600}{636,013,559,600} = 12.469\%$$

(2) A player can have x cards of one suit and y cards of another suit in $13Cx \times 13Cy \times 26C(13-x-y)$ ways. He can have five spades and four hearts, then, in $13C5 \times 13C4 \times 26C4 = 13,575,064,750$ ways. The percentage is 2.166%.

(3) If 26 cards are known (such as after the dummy is exposed), of which y are the cards of the suit in question, a player can have x cards in that suit in $(13-y)Cx \times (26-13+y)C(13-x)$ ways. If four spades are seen (y), he can have five spades in $9C5 \times 17C8$ ways. This computes to 3,063,060 ways, or a percentage of 29.451%.

SUIT COMBINATIONS. The correct treatment of particular suit combinations by declarer is a highly complex subject. The classified analysis on the following pages is the first attempt in bridge literature at a comprehensive coverage.

To find any particular combination, first count the number of high-card points held by the defense in the crucial suit. Find the appropriate section, which is subdivided according to the number of cards held by the declaring side.

The play of each combination is considered in two ways. First from the angle of safety plays, the number of tricks required is given together with the appropriate play and the percentage prospects. Second, where no particular number of tricks is required, but declarer simply wants to do as well as possible, the indicated maximum play (abbreviated to MAX) is given, with the expectation of tricks if this line is followed.

Whenever the symbol *x* is used, it should be assumed to be a completely insignificant spot card. In many cases the replacement of an x by an 8 or a 7 would affect the play or the percentages.

Dummy is always assumed to have the greater length. When the same holding occurs *the other way up*, with the length in declarer's hand, the analysis and percentages are identical (except in very rare cases when psychological considerations apply).

**Galerie
ST.JAMES**

Auctioneers/Appraisers

727 LAKE ST.
OAK PARK, ILLINOIS 60301
PHONE 386-5319 or 524-8870

ANTIQUE & ESTATE AUCTION

Friday Feb. 5, 6PM   Preview from 3 PM

Ruby Glassware. Cut Glass. Bohemian Decanter &
Glasses. Postcards & Collectible paper items.
Oriental Dolls. 1st Day Covers. Linens.
Foreign Coins. U.S. Pennies inc. mis-strikes.
Trunk. Sterling Silver. Costume & Sterling
Jewelry. Old Wooden Blocks. Dresser & Mirror.
Lg. Drop-leaf Sofa Table. Beautiful Uph. Sofa.
Mirrors. Carved Wood Elephant Figs., Occ. table
Humidifiers. OFFICE FURNITURE: Toshiba BD-7816
Copier, 3 Bookcases. Computer Stand, Office
Credenza, Beautiful Wood Grained Office Desks.
Coat Rack. Portable Elec. Typewriter, Olivetti
Ll Computer, Anti-static Chair Mats, 2 Swivel
chairs, lg. Postal Scale, Lamps & other access.
typewriter tables. Odyssey game. Upright
Freezer. Box lots kitchen items. Garcia elec.
fish finder. Stereo components inc. Pioneer
SX1010 receiver,Dual 1257 turntable & much more.
Brass Plant Stands. Lamps. Bx lots.

Dummy Declarer	Tricks Required		% Chance of Success	Tricks per Deal

I. THE DEFENSE HAS NO POINTS

(a) Declarer Has Six Cards

1. A K Q J 9
   x
       5   Cash top honors in the hope of dropping the ten   72

(b) Declarer Has Seven Cards

2. A K Q J 9 x
   x
       6   Cash top honors   86
       5   Finesse the nine, in case East is void   99

3. A K Q J 9
   x x
       5   Cash top honors in the hope of dropping the ten   87

4. A K Q 9 x
   J x
       5   Cash top honors in the hope of dropping the ten   87

5. A K Q J 8
   x x
       5   Cash top honors*   84
          (*But against defenders who would not false-card from 10 9x or 10 9xx, cash the jack and finesse the eight if the nine or ten appears from East)   85

6. A K Q 8 x
   J x
       5   See (5) above   84

(c) Declarer Has Eight Cards

7. A K Q 8 x
   J x x
       5   Cash the jack first in case East is void   98

II. THE DEFENSE HAS ONE POINT

(a) Declarer Has Five Cards

8. A K Q 10
   x
       4   Finesse the ten   50

(b) Declarer Has Six Cards

9. A K Q 10 9
   x
       5   Play off the top honors. This is fractionally better than the immediate finesse   36

10. A K Q 10 x
    x
        5   Finesse the ten   31
        4   Finesse the ten   81
        Max   Finesse the ten   4.12

11. A K Q 10
    x x
        4   Cash the queen, and then finesse the ten   50

12. A K Q 9
    x x
        4   Finesse the nine; hope that West has both the jack and ten   24

13. A K 10 x
    Q x
        4   Cash the queen, and then finesse the ten   50

14. A K 9 x
    Q x
        4   Play off the queen, king, and ace, hoping that the jack and ten fall in three rounds*   10
           (*But against defenders who would not false-card from J10x, cash the queen and finesse the nine if East drops an honor)   11

(c) Declarer Has Seven Cards

15. A K Q 10 9 x
    x
        6   Cash the top honors   54

Dummy Declarer	Tricks Required		% Chance of Success	Tricks per Deal

II. THE DEFENSE HAS ONE POINT (cont'd)

	Dummy Declarer	Tricks Required		% Chance of Success	Tricks per Deal
16.	A K Q 10 x x x	6 5 4 MAX	Cash the top honors Finesse the ten Finesse the ten, in case East is void Cash the top honors	52 91 99	 5.37
17.	A K Q 10 9 x x	5	Play off the top honors	54	
18.	A K Q 10 x x x	5 4 MAX	Play off the top honors Cash the ace, and finesse the ten Play off the top honors	52 93	 4.39

19.	A K Q 9 x
	x x
		5
		
		4
		
		MAX
			Play off the top honors, hoping that the jack and
			  ten drop in three rounds
			Lead small to the nine, in case East has a void or
			  small singleton
			Play off the top honors*
			  (*But against defenders who would not false-
			  card from J10x, cash the ace and finesse the
			  nine if East drops an honor)
				
				39
				
				90
					
					4.23
					
					4.24

20.	A K 10 9 x Q x	5	Play off the top honors	54	
21.	A K 10 x x Q x	5 4 MAX	Play off the top honors Cash the queen and finesse the ten Play off the top honors	52 93	 4.39
22.	A K 9 x x Q 10	5 4 MAX	Cash the queen, king, and ace Cash the queen, and run the ten Cash the queen, and run the ten	54 100	 4.44
23.	A K x x x Q 10	5 4 MAX	Finesse the ten Finesse the ten Finesse the ten	42 92	 4.34

24.	A K 9 x x
	Q x
		5
		4
		
		MAX
			Play off the top honors
			Cash the queen, and finesse the nine if an honor
			  drops from East
			Play off the top honors*
			  (*But against defenders who would not false-
			  card from J10x, cash the queen, and finesse
			  the nine if an honor drops from East)
				39
				
				86
					
					4.23
					
					4.24

25.	A K Q 10 x x x	4	Cash the king and queen; if both follow, play the ace. This is 2% better than a third-round finesse	61	

26.	A K Q 9
	x x x
		4	Cash the queen and king; if an honor drops from
			  East, finesse the nine next. This is 6% better
			  than cashing the three top honors regardless
				48	

27.	A K 10 x Q x x	4	See (25) above	61	
28.	A K 9 x Q x x	4	See (26) above	48	
29.	A K x x Q 10 x	4	Cash the ace, queen, and king. This is 4% better than a second-round finesse	55	
30.	A 10 x x K Q x	4	See (25) above	61	
31.	A 9 x x K Q x	4	See (26) above	48	
32.	A x x x K Q 10	4	Cash the king, queen, and ace. This is 4% better than a second-round finesse	55	

(d) Declarer Has Eight Cards

33.	A K Q 10 x x x x	7 6 MAX	Play off the top honors Finesse the ten, in case East is void Play off the top honors	73 98	 6.70

Dummy Declarer	Tricks Required		% Chance of Success	Tricks per Deal

II. THE DEFENSE HAS ONE POINT (cont'd)

	Dummy Declarer	Tricks Required		% Chance of Success	Tricks per Deal
34.	A K Q 9 x x x x	6	Play off the top honors* (*But against defenders who would not false-card from J10x, cash the ace and finesse the nine if an honor appears from East)	68 70	
		5	Lead small to the nine, in case East is void	98	
35.	A K Q 8 x x 10 x	6	Play off the top honors	73	
		5	Lead small to the ten	100	
		Max	Play off the top honors		5.70
36.	K Q 9 x x x A x	6	Play off the top honors* (*But against defenders who would not false-card from J10x, cash the ace and finesse the nine if an honor appears from East)	68 70	
37.	A K 9 x x Q 8 x	5	Cash the ace and queen (or the queen and ace), hoping for a 3–2 break or a singleton honor with East* (*But against defenders who would not false-card with J10x, cash the ace, and finesse the eight if West drops an honor)	73 76	
		4	Lead small to the eight or nine	100	
38.	A K 10 x Q 9 x x	4	Cash the ace. If the eight falls, play the next top honor from the hand on the left of the eight. Otherwise guess which honor to play next (*Assuming that the eight is not a false-card from J8xx)	92*	
39.	A K 9 x Q 8 x x	4	Cash the ace. If an honor appears, cash the next top honor from the hand on the left of the J or 10	79	
40.	A K 9 x Q x x x	4	Cash the queen, in case West has J10xxx	75	

(e) Declarer Has Nine Cards

	Dummy Declarer	Tricks Required		% Chance of Success	
41.	A K Q 8 x x x 9 x	7	Lead the nine, and play the ace whatever happens. This saves a trick if West covers with J10xxx	90+	
42.	A K Q 7 x x 8 x x	6	Lead the eight, and play the ace whatever happens. This saves a trick if West is lulled into covering with J109x	90+	
43.	A K 10 x x x Q 9 x	6	Lead the ace first in case either opponent is void	100	
44.	A K 9 x x x Q x x	6	Play the queen first, in case East is void	95	
45.	A K Q 7 x 8 x x x	5	Lead the eight, and play the ace whatever happens. This saves a trick if West is lulled into covering with J109x	90+	
46.	A K 10 x x Q 9 x x	5	Cash the ace first, in case either opponent is void	100	
47.	A K 9 x x Q x x x	5	Cash the queen first, in case East is void	95	

III. THE DEFENSE HAS TWO POINTS

(a) Declarer Has Five Cards

	Dummy Declarer	Tricks Required		% Chance of Success	
48.	A K J 10 x	4	Finesse the jack. This line is 6% better than trying to drop the queen	11	

(b) Declarer Has Six Cards

Dummy Declarer	Tricks Required		% Chance of Success	Tricks per Deal

III. THE DEFENSE HAS TWO POINTS (cont'd)

49. A K J 10 9 x	5	Finesse the jack	18	
50. A K J 9 8 x	5	Lead small to the jack or nine, playing West for Q10x or Q10	5	
	4	Lead small to the jack	58	
	MAX	Lead small to the jack		3.63
51. A K J 9 x x	4	Finesse the nine; if this loses to the ten, finesse the jack	24	
	3	Finesse the jack and then the nine, *or* finesse the nine and then the jack	76	
52. A K 9 8 J x	4	Run the jack; if it is covered, finesse the nine next. West must have Q10, Q10x or Qxxxxx	6	
	3	Lead the jack; if it loses, finesse the nine next	76	
53. A K 9 x J x	3	Lead small to the jack. If this loses, finesse the nine	74	
54. A J 9 8 K x	4	Cash the king and, unless an honor appears from East, finesse the jack	6	
	3	Cash the king and, unless an honor appears from East, finesse the jack or nine*	69	
	MAX	Cash the king and, unless an honor appears from East, finesse the jack or nine* (*This line is only fractionally better than running the nine, which will be superior if West is likely to have fewer cards in the suit than East)		2.75
55. A J x x K 9	3	Finesse the nine; if this loses to the ten, cash the king and ace	68	
56. A K 9 J x x	3	Lead small to the nine, hoping that West has both the queen and ten	24	
57. A K x J 9 8	3	*Either* run the nine *or* run the jack. Guess whether West has the bare queen or East the bare ten* (*But against defenders who can be relied upon to cover the nine with the ten, lead the nine, and play the ace and king if it is not covered; if the nine is covered, run the jack next)	24 29	

(c) Declarer Has Seven Cards

58. A K J 10 9 x x	6	Finesse the jack. This line is 8% better than trying to drop the queen	27	
59. A K J 9 8 7 x	6	Finesse the jack	19	
	5	Finesse the jack. This line is 2% better than cashing the ace and king, and 1% better than finessing the nine	71	
60. A K J 10 9 x x	5	Finesse the jack. Do not cash the ace first: Qxxx with West is more likely than Q with East	43	
61. A K J 9 x x x	5	Finesse the jack, alternatively cashing the ace first	19	
	4	Finesse the nine; if this loses to the ten, cash the ace and king	73	
	3	Finesse the nine, and then the jack *or* finesse the jack and then the nine, *or* cash the ace, and then finesse the jack or nine	94	
	MAX	Finesse the nine; if this loses to the ten, cash the ace and king		3.85
62. A K 9 8 x J x	5	Run the jack *or* lead small to the nine	9	
	4	Cash the ace and then run the jack	73	
	MAX	Run the jack. If it is covered, finesse the nine; if it loses, cash the ace; if it holds, cash the ace		3.79

Dummy Declarer	Tricks Required		% Chance of Success	Tricks per Deal

III. THE DEFENSE HAS TWO POINTS (cont'd)

	Dummy Declarer	Tricks Required		% Chance of Success	Tricks per Deal
63.	A K 9 x x J x	5	Run the jack *or* lead small to the nine. West must hold Q10x	7	
		4	Lead small to the jack; if it loses, cash the ace and king	68	
		3	Lead small to the jack; if it loses, finesse the nine	99	
		MAX	Lead small to the jack; if it loses, cash the ace and king		3.62
64.	A J x x x K 9	5	Cash the king, and then finesse the jack	18	
		4	Lead small to the nine	68	
		3	Cash the king, and then finesse the jack	94	
		MAX	Cash the king, and then finesse the jack		3.74
64A.	K J 9 x x A x	5	Cash the ace and then finesse the jack. (If East plays the ten, play for the queen to drop unless East is capable of a falsecard from 10 x x.)	20.99	
		4	Cash the ace and then finesse the jack or the nine. If East plays the queen, finesse the nine	69.04	
		MAX	Cash the ace and then finesse the jack.		3.84
65.	A K J 10 x x x	4	Cash the ace, and finesse the ten	51	
66.	A K J 9 x x x	4	Cash the ace, and finesse the jack	29	
		3	Cash the ace. Then lead toward dummy, and play the king if the ten fails to appear. Then lead up to the jack	85	
		MAX	Cash the ace, and finesse the jack		3.07
67.	A K J x x x x	4	Cash the ace, and finesse the jack	18	
		3	Play off the ace and king, and then lead up to the jack	77	
		MAX	Cash the ace, and finesse the jack		2.87
68.	A K 10 x J x x	4	Cash the ace, and then lead small to the ten. Don't lead the jack for the finesse; West may have Qx	28	
69.	A K 9 8 J x x	4	Run the jack; if this is covered, finesse the nine	25	
		3	Play the ace, and if no honor appears, run the nine; if it loses, run the jack through next* (*Assuming East would not duck with Qxx, this line only loses when West has 10x. If East is a very good defender, play the king if the nine loses to the ten)	94 84	
		MAX	Run the jack; if this is covered, finesse the nine; if the jack loses, cash the ace and king		3.01
70.	A K 9 x J x x	4	Lead small to the nine, hoping that West has Q10 or Q10x	9	
		3 ⎫ MAX ⎭	Cash the ace and, unless the ten appears, lead small to the jack; if the jack loses, cash the king	84	2.88
71.	A K x x J 10 9	4	Finesse the jack	50	
		3	Finesse the jack *or* play the ace, and then finesse the jack	100	
72.	A K x x J 9 8	4	Run the nine and then the jack *or* run the jack and then the nine, hoping that West has Q10x or either Q or Qxxxx	8	
		3	Play the ace, and lead small to the jack	78	
		MAX	Run the nine; if it loses to the ten, run the jack next		2.85

	Dummy Declarer	Tricks Required		% Chance of Success	Tricks per Deal

III.   THE DEFENSE HAS TWO POINTS (cont'd)

	Dummy Declarer	Tricks Required		% Chance of Success	Tricks per Deal
73.	A K x x J 9 x	4	Play the ace, hoping that West has the singleton queen	1	
		3 } Max }	Play the ace and then lead small to the jack or nine	78	2.79
74.	A K x x J x x	3 } Max }	Play the ace and lead to the jack	69	2.69
75.	A J 9 8 K x x	4	Cash the king, and finesse the jack	29	
		3	Cash the king, and lead toward dummy, playing the ace unless the ten appears	85	
		Max	Cash the king, and finesse the jack		3.07
76.	A J 9 x K x x	4	Cash the king, and finesse the jack	29	
		3	Cash the king and ace; then lead to the jack	85	
		Max	Cash the king, and finesse the jack. If it loses, cash the ace		3.07
77.	A J x x K 9 x	4	Cash the king, and finesse the jack	19	
		3	Cash the king and ace; then lead to the jack	85	
		Max	Cash the king, and finesse the jack		2.98
78.	A J x x K x x	4	Cash the king, and finesse the jack	18	
		3	Cash the king and ace; then lead to the jack	77	
		Max	Cash the king, and finesse the jack		2.87
79.	K 9 x x A J x	4	Finesse the jack; then play the ace and king* (*Against defenders who would not falsecard from Q10x, finesse the nine if East drops the queen under the ace)	21 27	
		3	Lead small from dummy, and play the ace unless the ten appears. Then, unless West drops the ten, lead small to the jack	84	
		Max	Finesse the jack; then play the ace and king		3.03
80.	J 10 x x A K x	4	Cash the ace, and then run the jack. This line is only 1% better than cashing the two top honors	20	
81.	J 9 8 x A K x	4	Cash the ace and king, unless the queen drops from West* (*But if West is good enough to falsecard from Q10, we have to play the king, even if the queen falls under the ace)	12 11	
		3	Cash the ace and king; then lead to the jack	85	
82.	J x x x A K 9	4	Lead small to the nine, hoping that East has Q10 or Q10x	9	
		3 } Max }	Cash the ace and king; then lead to the jack	85	2.90

(d)   Declarer Has Eight Cards

	Dummy Declarer	Tricks Required		% Chance of Success	Tricks per Deal
83.	A K J 10 9 x x x	7	Finesse the jack. This line is 4% better than playing off the ace and king	37	
84.	A K J 9 8 7 x x	7	Finesse the jack	34	
		6	Finesse the nine or, more profitably, finesse the jack	85	
85.	A K J 10 x x x x	6	Finesse the jack. Don't cash the ace first: Qxxx with West is more likely than Q with East	48	
		5	Finesse the jack	98	
		Max	Finesse the jack		5.46

Dummy Declarer	Tricks Required		% Chance of Success	Tricks per Deal

III. THE DEFENSE HAS TWO POINTS (cont'd)

86. A K J 9 x x
     x x

6	Finesse the jack, alternatively cashing the ace first*	37	
	(*Against defenders who would not falsecard from 10x, cash the ace, and play the king if the ten falls from East)	40	
5 } Max }	Cash the ace, and finesse the jack	88	5.22

87. A K J x x x
     x x

6	Finesse the jack, alternatively cashing the ace first	34	
5 } Max }	Cash the ace, and then finesse the jack	85	5.17

88. A K 9 8 7 x
     J x

6	Run the jack. If it is covered, guess whether to finesse for or drop the ten next	16	
5 } Max }	Run the jack. If it loses, cash the ace and king; if it is covered, guess as above	87	5.03

89. A K 9 8 x x
     J x

6	Run the jack. If it is covered, guess whether to finesse or cash the ace next	16	
5	Lead small to the jack, and then cash the ace and king (which will be best if West is likely to be short in the suit) *or*		
	Run the jack, cashing the ace and king if it loses, and guessing if it is covered (which will be best if East is likely to be short in the suit)	85	
Max	Run the jack, guessing what to do next if it is covered		5.01

90. A K 9 x x x
     J x

6	Run the jack. If it is covered, finesse the nine *or* cash the ace	14	
5	Lead small to the jack; then cash the ace and king	85	
4	Lead small to the jack	100	
Max	Lead the jack, if it is covered, finesse the nine next		4.94

91. A J 8 x x x
     K 9

6	Play the king. If the queen drops from East, run the nine; otherwise finesse the jack	37	
5	Cash the king, and then lead the nine, and finesse the jack	88	
4	Lead small to the nine	100	

92. A J x x x x
     K 9

6	Cash the king, and finesse the jack	34	
5	Cash the king, and lead the nine, intending to finesse the jack	88	
4	Lead small to the nine	100	
Max	Cash the king, and finesse the jack		5.20

93. A K 9 8 x
     J x x

5	Play the ace. Then play the king unless the queen has appeared from East	30	
4	Play the ace, and unless an honor appears, lead low to the jack	96	
Max	Lead the jack. If it is covered, finesse the nine; if it loses, cash the ace		4.14

94. A K 9 x x
     J x x

5	Play the ace and king (unless the queen drops from East)	30	
4	Play the ace, and if the ten fails to appear, lead small to the jack	96	
Max	Play the ace and king		4.09

Dummy Declarer	Tricks Required		% Chance of Success	Tricks per Deal

III. THE DEFENSE HAS TWO POINTS (cont'd)

95. A K 7 6 x
J 9 8

- **5** — Lead the nine to the ace. (This makes it harder for West to falsecard with queen from Q10, as it would help a declarer with J9.) If the queen falls, finesse accordingly; if not, cash the king
  Assuming no falsecard: **33**
- **4** — Play the ace, and if no honor appears, lead low to the jack   **98**
- **MAX** — Cash the ace and king*   **4.11**
  (* If West would not falsecard from Q10)   **4.14**

96. A K x x x
J 10 9

- **5** — Finesse the jack. Don't cash the ace first: Qxxx with West is more likely than queen with East   **48**
- **4** — Finesse the jack   **100**

97. A K x x x
J 9 8

- **5** — Cash the ace and king*   **27**
  (*But against defenders who would not falsecard with Q10, finesse the nine if West drops the queen on the first round)   **30**
- **4** — Play the ace, and lead small to the jack   **88**
- **3** — Run the jack *or* lead small to the jack   **100**
- **MAX** — Cash the ace, and unless West is void, lead small to the king*   **4.01**
  (*If West would not falsecard with Q10)   **4.04**

98. A K x x x
J 9 x

- **5** — Play the ace and king*   **27**
  (*But against defenders who would not falsecard with Q10, finesse the nine if West drops the queen on the first round)   **30**
- **4** — Play the ace, and lead small to the jack   **88**
- **MAX** — Play the ace and king   **3.99**

99. A J 9 x x
K x x

- **5** } **MAX** { — Cash the king, and finesse the jack*   **40**   **4.27**
  (*But against defenders who would not falsecard, it is fractionally better to play the ace if East drops the ten on the first round)

100. A J x x x
K 9 x

- **5** — Lead low to the jack*   **34**
  (*Against defenders who would not falsecard from Q10, finesse the nine next if the queen appears from West)   **37**
- **4** — Play the ace, and unless an honor appears from West, lead low to the nine   **96**
- **3** — Play either top honor   **100**
- **MAX** — Play the king, and finesse the jack   **4.22**

101. A 9 x x x
K J x

- **5** — Finesse the jack. Don't cash the ace first, for East may have the singleton queen   **37**
- **4** — Play the king, and unless the ten appears, lead low to the jack   **96**
- **3** — Finesse the jack, and cash the king *or* play the king and lead small to the jack   **100**
- **MAX** — Finesse the jack   **4.30**

102. J 9 8 x x
A K x

- **5** — Play the ace, and unless the queen appears from West, king*   **33**
  (*But if West would falsecard from Q10, cash the king next whatever happens)   **30**
- **4** — Play the ace and king   **88**

103. A K J 10
x x x x

- **4** — Play the ace, and finessee the jack   **53**

104. A K 9 x
J x x x

- **4** — Play the ace and king   **30**
- **3** — Play the ace, and then lead small to the nine or jack   **100**
- **MAX** — Play the ace and king   **3.21**

Dummy Declarer	Tricks Required		% Chance of Success	Tricks per Deal

III. THE DEFENSE HAS TWO POINTS (cont'd)

105. A K 8 x	4	Play the ace and king	27	
J x x x	3	Play the ace; if the ten or nine appears from East, lead small to the jack	92	
	MAX	Play the ace and king		3.14
106. A K x x	4	Play the ace and king	33	
J 9 8 x	3	Play the ace, and unless the ten appears from East, run the nine	100	
	MAX	Play the ace and king		3.24
107. A J x x	4	Finesse the jack	37	
K 9 x x	3	Play the ace, and lead small to the nine	100	
	MAX	Finesse the jack; if it loses, play the ace next		3.34
108. A 10 8 x	4	Lead the jack to the ace *or* the ten to the king, and then take a second-round finesse. This gives the extra chance of a defender covering with Qx or Qxx		
K J 9 x			53+	

(e) Declarer Has Nine Cards

109. A K J x x x x x	8	Play the ace and king. This line is 8% better than a first-round finesse	53	
x	7	Finesse the jack, in case East is void	95	
	MAX	Play the ace and king		7.44
110. A K J x x x x	7	Play the ace and king. This line is 2% better than a second-round finesse	53	
x x				
111. A K 9 x x x x	7	Play the ace and king	53	
J x	6	Lead low to the jack	100	
	MAX	Play the ace and king*		6.44
		(*But against defenders who would always cover the jack, and would not falsecard with Q10, lead the jack, and play the ace whatever happens, finessing the nine next if East plays the queen)		6.48
112. A J x x x x x	7	Play the king and ace	53	
K 9	6	Lead small to the nine, in case West is void	100	
	MAX	Play the king and ace		6.48
113. A K J 10 x x	6	Play the ace and king	58	
x x x				
114. A K 9 x x x	6	Play the ace and king	53	
J x x	5	Play the ace	100	
115. A K 8 x x x	6	Play the ace and king	53	
J x x	5	Lead small toward dummy, and cover whatever West plays	100	
	MAX	Play the ace and king		5.48
116. A K x x x x	6	Lead the jack to the ace; then cash the king	53	
J 10 9				
117. A K x x x x	6	Play the ace and king	53	
J 9 8	5	Lead small to the jack *or* (best) run the nine	100	
	MAX	Play the ace and king		5.48
118. A J x x x x	6	Play the ace and king	53	
K 9 x	5	Play the ace	100	
	MAX	Play the ace and king		5.53
119. A 9 x x x x	6	Play the ace and king	53	
K J x	5	Play the king	100	
	MAX	Play the king and ace		5.53

Dummy Declarer	Tricks Required		% Chance of Success	Tricks per Deal

III. THE DEFENSE HAS TWO POINTS (cont'd)

120. A K 8 x x J x x x	5	Play the ace and king* (*Against defenders who would always cover the jack, lead the jack, and play the ace whatever happens. If West covers and the ten or nine drops from East, finesse the eight next. This line will be better if East is likely to be short in the suit)	53 53	
	4	Lead small to the eight *or* small to the jack	100	
	Max	Play the ace and king		4.48
121. A K x x x J 10 9 x	5	Play the ace and king. This line is 2% better than a second-round finesse	58	
122. A J 9 x x K 10 8 x	5	Lead the jack to the king *or* lead the ten to the ace, and play for the drop on the second round. This gives the extra chance of a defender covering with Qxx	58	
123. A J x x x K 9 8 7	5 4	Play the king and ace, in case East is void Play the ace, in case West is void	58 100	
124. A J x x x K 9 x x	5 4	Cash the ace and king, preferably in that order Play the ace (best) *or* finesse the jack or nine	53 100	
125. A 9 x x x K J x x	5 4	Play the ace and king in either order Play the king (best), *or* finesse the jack	53 100	
126. A x x x x K J 9 8	5 4	Play the ace and king, in case West is void Play the king, in case East is void	58 100	
127. J 10 9 x x A K x x	5	Play the ace and king; this line is 2% better than a second-round finesse	58	
128. J x x x x A K 8 x	5 4 Max	Play the ace and king Lead small to the eight, in case West is void Play the ace and king	53 100	 4.48

(f) Declarer Has Ten Cards

129. A K 9 x x x x x J x	8	Lead the jack, and play the ace whatever happens. This line succeeds against all 2–1 breaks and when West is lulled into covering with Q10x	78+	
130. A K 9 x x x x J x x	7	See (129) above	78+	
131. A J x x x x x K x x	7	Lead the king, in case East is void	89	
132. A K 9 x x x J x x x	6	See (129) above	78+	
133. A J x x x x K x x x	6	See (131) above*	89	
133a. K x x x x x A J 9 8	6	*But if there is no side entry to dummy, play the ace, as the only way to avoid a suit block is to find a singleton queen	26	
134. A K 9 x x J x x x x	5	See (129) above	78+	
135. A J 9 x x K 10 x x x	5	Lead the ten to the ace, *or* lead the jack to the king. Guess who is most likely to be void	89	
136. A J x x x K x x x x	5	See (131) above	89	

Dummy Declarer	Tricks Required		% Chance of Success	Tricks per Deal

IV. THE DEFENSE HAS THREE POINTS
A. THE KING

(a)   Declarer Has Five Cards

137.	A Q J 9	4	The only hope is that West has K10 doubleton	0.3	
	x	3	Lead small to the nine	52	
		MAX	Lead small to the nine		2.53

(b)   Declarer Has Six Cards

138.	A Q J 9 8	5	Finesse the queen. The only hope is that West has K10 doubleton	1	
	x	4	Finesse the nine*	41	
		MAX	Finesse the nine*		3.42

(*The nine finesse is only 0.36% better than the queen finesse)

139.	A Q J 9	4	Finesse the queen, hoping that West has K10 or K10x	5	
	x x	3 }	Finesse the queen. If it holds, finesse the jack; if it loses, cash the ace and jack*	68	2.73
		MAX }			

(*This assumes that East will duck the queen with Kx or Kxx. If not, it is better to finesse the nine if the queen loses)   76

140.	A Q 9 8	4	Run the jack. If it is covered, finesse the nine next	5	
	J x	3 }	Run the jack. If it losses, finesse the nine; if it holds, finesse the queen*	76	2.81
		MAX }			

(*This assumes that West will cover the jack with Kxxxx or Kxxx, and that East will win with Kx or Kxx. If they would withhold the king in such circumstances, it is better to cash the ace and queen if the jack loses)   68

| 141. | A Q 9 x | 3 | Lead small to the jack and finesse the nine next whatever happens | 56 | |
| | J x | | | | |

| 142. | A Q 8 x | 3 | Lead the jack. If it holds, finesse the queen; if it loses, cash the ace; if it is covered, run the nine* | 68 | |
| | J 9 | | | | |

(*The best defense is for East not to win with Kx or Kxx, and for West not to cover with Kxxxx or Kxxx)

| 143. | A Q x x | 3 | Lead small to the nine, hoping that East has the singleton ten or king* | 50 | |
| | J 9 | | | | |

(*Or that he will mistakenly play the king from Kx)   54

| 144. | A Q 9 | 3 | Lead small to the nine *or* (best) run the jack; if it is covered, finesse the nine | 24 | |
| | J x x | MAX | Run the jack; if it is covered, finesse the nine next | | 2.24 |

| 145. | A Q x | 3 | Run the nine *or* (best) run the jack; if it is covered, run the nine next | 24 | |
| | J 9 8 | MAX | Run the jack; if it is covered, run the nine next | | 2.24 |

| 146. | A x x | 3 | Lead the queen. If it is covered, play the jack, if the queen holds, guess* | 5 | |
| | Q J 9 | | | | |

(*But against defenders who might cover unnecessarily—let us assume half the time—finesse the nine if the queen is covered and lead the jack next if the queen holds)   15

Dummy Declarer	Tricks Required		% Chance of Success	Tricks per Deal

IV. THE DEFENSE HAS THREE POINTS (cont'd)
A. THE KING (cont'd)

(c) Declarer Has Seven Cards

147. A Q J 9 8 7 x	6	Finesse the queen. The only hope is that West has K10 doubleton	2	
	5 } Max }	Finesse the queen; then cash the ace	62	4.63
148. A Q J 9 x x x	6	Finesse the queen, hoping that West has K10 doubleton	2	
	5	Finesse the queen; then cash the ace	58	
	4	Finesse the nine; then cash the ace	92	
	3	Finesse the nine; then cash the ace	99	
	Max	Finesse the queen; then cash the ace		4.46
149. A Q J 9 8 x x	5	Finesse the queen; if it loses, cash the ace and jack	19	
	4 } Max }	Finesse the queen; if it loses, cash the ace and jack	71	3.91
150. A Q 9 8 x J x	5	Lead small to the nine *or* (best) run the jack, finessing the nine next if it is covered	9	
	4 } Max }	Run the jack. If it loses, cash the ace; if it is covered, finesse the nine; if it holds, finesse the queen	70	3.79
151. A Q 9 x x J x	5	Lead small to the nine *or* (best) run the jack, finessing the nine next if it is covered	7	
	4	Lead small to the jack. If it holds, play the ace; if it loses, play the ace	58	
	3	Finesse the nine on the first or second round	93	
	Max	Run the jack. If it holds, finesse the nine; if it loses, cash the ace and queen; if it is covered, finesse the nine		3.54
152. A Q x x x J 9	4	Lead small to the nine; if it loses, run the jack next*	49	
	3 } Max }	Lead small to the nine; if it loses, run the jack next*	93	3.42
		(*This line will also produce four tricks if East is tempted to play the king from Kx)	56	
153. A Q x x x J x	4	Lead small to the jack, hoping that the suit divides 3–3 or that East has Kx	44	
	3	Play the ace, and lead small to the jack, in case West has the singleton king	86	
	Max	Lead small to the jack		3.29
154. Q J 9 8 7 A x	5	Run the queen, cashing the jack next if it is covered	2	
	4	Play the ace, and lead to the queen	63	
	Max	Run the queen, cashing the jack next if it is covered* (*Playing the ace and leading to the queen makes only .004 tricks fewer, and will be the best line if West is more likely to be short in the suit)		3.63
155. Q J 9 x x A x	4	Play the ace, and lead to the queen	59	
	3	Play the ace, and lead to the nine	94	
	Max	Play the ace, and lead to queen		3.49
156. Q J x x x A 9	4	Lead small to the nine	50	
	3	Lead small to the nine	93	
	Max	Lead small to the nine		3.43

	Dummy Declarer	Tricks Required		% Chance of Success	Tricks per Deal

IV. THE DEFENSE HAS THREE POINTS (cont'd)

A. THE KING (cont'd)

	Dummy Declarer	Tricks Required		% Chance of Success	Tricks per Deal
157.	A Q J x x x x	4 3 Max	Finesse the queen, hoping that West has Kxx Play the ace, and lead to the queen, in case East has the singleton king Finesse the queen	18 69	 2.86
158.	A Q 10 x J x x	4	Lead small to the ten, and then small to the queen. Do not lead the jack in case West has K or Kx	27	
159.	A Q 9 8 J x x	4 ⎫ Max ⎬ 3	Run the jack. If it is covered, finesse the nine; if it holds, lead to the nine; if it loses, cash the ace and queen Finesse the queen. If it holds, run the jack; if it loses, cash the jack and ace	 25 79	 3.03
160.	A Q 9 x J x x	4 3 Max	Lead low to the nine, hoping that West has K10 or K10x Finesse the queen. If it loses, cash the jack and ace; if it holds, lead low to the nine Run the jack. If it is covered, finesse the nine; if it loses, cash the ace and queen	9 72 2.78	
161.	A Q 8 7 J x x	4 3 ⎫ Max ⎬	Run the jack, hoping that East has the singleton nine or ten Lead the jack. If it loses, cash the ace, and finesse the eight next if the nine or ten drops from East; if it holds, finesse the queen; if it is covered, finesse the eight and then the seven next* (*Assuming that West will not cover with Kxxx, K10xxx, or K9xxx)	2 59	 2.61
162.	A Q 8 x J x x	3	Lead small to the queen. If it holds, lead the jack next unless the nine or ten has appeared from West; if it loses, cash the jack, and finesse the eight next if the ten or nine drops from East* (*This line is only slightly superior to the alternatives of leading small to the jack (56%) and running the jack (53%))	57	
163.	A Q x x J 9 8	4 3 ⎫ Max ⎬	Run the jack, and then the nine (best) *or* run the nine. Hope that West has K10x or either Kxxxx or K Lead the jack. If it loses, cash the ace; if it is covered, run the nine next	8 77	 2.85
164.	A Q x x J 9 x	4 3 ⎫ Max ⎬	Play the ace, hoping that West has the singleton king Play the ace, and lead small to the jack	1 64	 2.65
165.	A 9 8 7 Q J x	4 3 Max	Lead the queen. If it holds or is covered, lead the jack next Lead small to the queen. If it holds, lead small to the jack; if it loses, cash the jack and ace Lead the queen. If it loses, cash the jack and ace; if it holds or is covered, lead the jack next	9 83 2.88	
166.	A 9 x x Q J x	3 ⎫ Max ⎬	Lead small to the queen. If it holds, lead small to the jack; if it loses, cash the jack and ace	83	2.83
167.	Q J 9 x A x x	4 3 ⎫ Max ⎬	Play the ace, hoping East has the singleton king Play the ace and then lead to the queen and jack	1 78	 2.79

Dummy Declarer	Tricks Required		% Chance of Success	Tricks per Deal

IV. THE DEFENSE HAS THREE POINTS (cont'd)
A. THE KING (cont'd)

	Dummy Declarer	Tricks Required		% Chance of Success	Tricks per Deal
168.	Q J x x A x x	3	Play the ace, and lead low to the queen; then lead low to the jack	69	
169.	J 9 8 7 A Q x	4	Run the nine. If it is covered, run the jack	10	
		3	Finesse the queen. If it holds, run the jack; if it loses, cash the ace and jack* (*This line offers extra chances if West is tempted to win the queen with K10xxx)	78 83	
		MAX	Run the jack. If it is covered, run the nine next		2.86
170.	J 9 8 x A Q x	4	Finesse the queen. If it holds, run the nine, hoping that East has K10, Kx, or K	9	
		3	Finesse the queen. If it holds, lead the jack, if it loses, cash the ace and jack* (*This line offers extra chances if West is tempted to win the queen with K10xxx)	78 83	
		MAX	Finesse the queen. If it holds, run the nine; if it loses, cash the ace and jack		2.85
171.	J 9 x x A Q x	4	Finesse the queen, and then cash the ace, hoping that East has K, Kx, or K10	9	
		3	Lead small to the ace, unless the ten appears from East; then lead to the queen and jack	69	
		MAX	Finesse the queen, and then cash the ace		2.77
172.	J x x x A Q 9	4	Lead small to the nine, hoping that East has K10 or K10x	9	
		3	Lead small to the queen. If it holds, finesse the nine; if it loses, cash the ace	71	
		MAX	Lead small to the nine. If it loses, finesse the queen		2.77

(d) Declarer Has Eight Cards

	Dummy Declarer	Tricks Required		% Chance of Success	Tricks per Deal
173.	A Q J 9 x x x x	7	Finesse the queen, hoping that West has Kx or K10	14	
		6	Play the ace, and lead the queen	79	
		5	Finesse the nine, in case East is void	98	
		MAX	Finesse the queen		5.86
174.	A Q J 9 x x x x	6	Finesse the queen	34	
		5	Finesse the queen; if it loses, cash the ace	85	
175.	A Q 9 8 x x J x	6	Finesse the queen, and run the jack if it holds *or* run the jack; if it loses, cash the ace; if it holds, finesse the queen; if it is covered, guess	14	
		5	As above	85	
176.	A Q 9 x x x J x	6	Finesse the nine *or* finesse the queen *or* lead the jack and guess next time	14	
		5	Run the jack. If it is covered, finesse the nine next	82	
		4	Safeguard against East being void by leading the jack, leading to the jack or finessing the nine	98	
		MAX	Run the jack. If it is covered, finesse the nine next		4.94
177.	A Q x x x x J 9	5	Lead small to the jack	76	
		4	Lead small to the nine, in case West is void	98	
		MAX	Lead small to the jack* (*But against defenders who would play the king from Kx as East, lead small to the nine and run the jack next)		4.72 4.73

Dummy Declarer	Tricks Required		% Chance of Success	Tricks per Deal

IV. THE DEFENSE HAS THREE POINTS (cont'd)

A. THE KING (cont'd)

178. A Q x x x x J x	5 ⎱ MAX ⎰	Play the ace. This succeeds if the suit divides 3–2 or there is a singleton king somewhere	73	**4.70**
179. Q J 9 x x x A x	6	Lead the queen. If it is covered, finesse the nine, hoping East has Kx	10	
	5	Play the ace, and lead to queen	79	
	4	Play the ace; fails only if West is void	98	
	MAX	Lead the queen, finessing the nine next if it is covered		**4.83**
180. A Q 10 x x J x x	5 ⎱ MAX ⎰	Finesse the queen. Don't lead the jack in case West has the singleton king	37	**4.33**
181. A Q 9 7 6 J 8 x	5	Run the jack. If it is covered, finesse the nine next	25	
	4	Run the jack *or* finesse the queen	90	
	MAX	Run the jack. If it is covered, finesse the nine next		**4.14**
182. A Q 9 x x J 8 x	5	Finesse the queen. If it holds, guess whether to play the ace or the jack next* (*If West would not falsecard with K10, finesse the eight if the king appears on the first round)	16 19	
	4	Finesse the queen *or* run the jack *or* play the ace and lead small to the jack	88	
	MAX	Finesse the queen, guessing what to do if it holds		**4.04**
183. A Q 9 x x J x x	5	Finesse the queen *or* run the jack. Guess whether West has K10x, Kxx, or Kx	14	
	4	Finesse the queen, and lead to the nine if it holds *or* play the ace, and lead to the jack	88	
	3	Finesse the queen	98	
	MAX	Finesse the queen. If it loses, cash the jack; if it holds, lead to the nine		**3.99**
184. A Q 8 x x J x x	5	Finesse the queen; if it holds, lead small to the eight* (*If East would not falsecard from 109x, lead the jack if the nine or ten appears on the first round)	14 17	
	4	Lead small to the ace, unless the nine or ten appears from West; then lead low to the jack (best) *or* run the jack; if it is covered, lead low to the eight unless the nine or ten has dropped	79	
	3	Run the jack. If it is covered, lead low to the eight unless the nine or ten has dropped from East (best)	98	
	MAX	Finesse the queen. If it holds, lead small to the eight		**3.86**
185. A Q x x x J 9 8	5	Lead the jack. If it holds, finesse the queen; if it is covered, guess whether to run the nine or play the ace next	16	
	4 ⎱ MAX ⎰	Lead the jack. If it loses, cash the ace; if it holds, finesse the queen; if it is covered, run the nine	85	**4.01**
	3	Lead the jack (best) or lead small to the jack	100	
186. A Q x x x J 9 x	5	Finesse the queen. If it holds, guess whether to lead the nine or the jack next* (*If West would not falsecard from K10, finesse the nine if the king appears from West)	14 16	
	4	Play the ace, and lead small to the jack	79	
	3	Play the ace, or finesse the queen	98	
	MAX	Finesse the queen, and cash the ace next		**3.88**

	Dummy Declarer	Tricks Required		% Chance of Success	Tricks per Deal

IV. THE DEFENSE HAS THREE POINTS (cont'd)

A. THE KING (cont'd)

	Dummy Declarer	Tricks Required		% Chance of Success	Tricks per Deal
187.	A Q x x x J x x	5 4 Max	Finesse the queen, and then play the ace Play the ace, and lead toward the jack, in case East has the singleton king Finesse the queen	14 73	 3.80
188.	A 9 x x x Q J x	5 4 3 Max	Lead the queen. If it holds, lead the jack, hoping that West has Kxx or K10 Lead small to the queen. If it holds, lead to the jack Lead small to the queen Run the queen. If it holds, lead the jack	14 93 100	 3.96
189.	A x x x x Q J 9	5 4 3 Max	Lead the queen. If it is covered, play the jack next; if it holds, lead the jack next* (*This assumes that West will cover with Kx about once in four times—best defense) Lead small to the queen, and then small to the jack Lead the queen *or* lead small to the queen Lead the queen. If it is covered, play the jack; if it holds, lead the jack next* (*The best defense is now for West never to cover with Kx)	14 85 98	 3.85
190.	Q J 9 x x A x x	5 4 Max	Lead the Queen. If it holds, lead the jack; if it is covered, finesse the nine* (*This assumes that East will cover with Kx half the time; if he always covers, this line will produce five tricks) Play the ace, and lead toward the queen Lead the queen. If it loses, play the ace; if it holds, play the ace; if it is covered, finesse the nine* (*But if West would not duck the queen with K10xx, lead the jack if the queen holds; and if East would always cover with Kx, lead the jack if the queen holds)	15 20 88	 3.93 3.98 4.03
191.	J 9 8 x x A Q x	5 4 ⎱ Max ⎰	Finesse the queen. If it holds, guess whether East has Kx or Kxx Finesse the queen. If it loses, cash the ace; if it holds, run the nine	16 93	 4.10
192.	J x x x x A Q 9	5 4 ⎱ Max ⎰	Finesse the queen *or* finesse the nine Finesse the queen. If it holds, lead small to the nine; if it loses, cash the ace	14 85	 3.96
193.	A Q J x x x x x	4 3 Max	Finesse the queen Play the ace, and lead to the queen Finesse the queen	34 87	 3.18
194.	A Q 10 x J x x x	4	Finesse the ten. Don't lead the jack in case West has the singleton king	37	
195.	A Q 9 8 J x x x	4 3 Max	Lead the jack. If it is covered, finesse the nine; if it holds, lead small to the nine Lead small to the queen. If it loses, cash the ace; if it holds, lead to the nine Both the above lines produce	27 97	 3.16
196.	A Q 9 x J x x x	4 3 ⎱ Max ⎰	Finesse the queen *or* run the jack, guessing whether West has Kx or K10x Finesse the queen. If it loses, cash the jack; if it holds, finesse the nine	14 90	 3.03

	Dummy Declarer	Tricks Required		% Chance of Success	Tricks per Deal

IV. THE DEFENSE HAS THREE POINTS (cont'd)

A. THE KING (cont'd)

	Dummy Declarer	Tricks Required		% Chance of Success	Tricks per Deal
197.	A Q 8 x J x x x	4	Finesse the queen; if it holds, lead small to the eight* (*If East would not falsecard from 109x, lead the jack next if the nine or ten drops)	14 17	
		3	Lead the jack. If it is covered, lead small to the eight unless the nine or ten has appeared from East	81	
		Max	Finesse the queen; if it holds, lead small to the eight		2.90
198.	A Q x x J 9 8 x	4	Finesse the queen, hoping that West has K, Kxxx, K10, or Kx	19	
		3 } Max }	Finesse the queen. If it loses, play the ace; if it holds, run the nine	97	3.16
199.	A Q x x J 9 x x	4	Finesse the queen. If it holds, guess whether to lead the jack or play the ace	16	
		3	Play the ace, and lead small to the queen	90	
		Max	Finesse the queen; then play the ace		3.03
200.	A Q x x J x x x	4	Finesse the queen; then play the ace, hoping West has Kx	14	
		3	Play the ace, and lead small to either honor	73	
		Max	Finesse the queen; then play ace		2.84
201.	A 9 8 x Q J x x	4	Lead the queen. If it is covered, cash the jack; if it holds, lead the jack. Hope that West has Kxx, K10, or Kxxx* (*It has been assumed that, if the queen is led, West will cover ⅓ of the time with Kx, and East will win ⅓ of the time with K10xx. This is the best defense)	16	
		3	Lead the queen (best). If it loses, cash the ace; if it holds, lead small to the nine *or* lead small to the queen. If it loses, cash the jack; if it holds, lead small to the nine	97	
		Max	Lead the queen. If it loses, cash the ace; if it is covered, run the nine; if it holds, lead small to the nine* (*It has been assumed that, if the queen is led West will cover ⅓ of the time with Kx, and East will win ⅓ of the time with K10xx. This is the best defense)		3.10
202.	A x x x Q J x x	3	Play the ace, and lead to the queen. This fails only if East has a void or a small singleton	87	
203.	Q J 9 x A x x x	4	Lead the queen. If it holds, lead the jack; if is covered, finesse the nine next* (*This assumes that East will cover ½ the time with Kx; if he always covers, this line will produce four tricks)	15 20	
		3	Play the ace and lead to queen	90	
		Max	Lead the queen. If it holds, play the ace; if it is covered, finesse the nine* (*But if West would not duck the queen with K10xx, lead the jack next if the queen holds)		2.97 3.02
204.	Q J x x A 9 x x	4	Lead the queen. If it holds, lead the jack; if it loses or is covered, cash the jack	14	
		3	Lead small to the queen. If it loses, cash the jack; if it holds, lead small to the nine	97	
		Max	Lead the queen, and play the jack next whatever happens		3.00

Dummy Declarer	Tricks Required		% Chance of Success	Tricks per Deal

IV. THE DEFENSE HAS THREE POINTS (cont'd)
A. THE KING (cont'd)

(e) Declarer Has Nine Cards

205.	A Q J 10 x x x x x	8	Finesse the queen; Kx with West is more likely than K with East	27
206.	A Q 9 x x x x J x	7 6 MAX	Finesse the queen Run the jack *or* lead small to the jack Finesse the queen	33 95 6.23
207.	Q J x x x x x A x	7 MAX	Run the queen, hoping West has Kx Run the queen	20 6.11
208.	A Q 9 x x x J x x	6 } MAX }	Finesse the queen, hoping that West has Kxx, K10, Kx, or K	33 5.28
209.	A Q 8 x x x J x x	6 5 MAX	Finesse the queen Lead the jack, in case East is void Finesse the queen	27 95 5.17
210.	A Q 7 x x x J 9 8	6 5 MAX	Finesse the queen Play the ace *or* finesse the queen Finesse the queen	33 100 5.33
211.	A Q x x x x J 9 8	6 5 MAX	Finesse the queen, hoping that West has Kxx, K10, Kx, or K If West is more likely to be void, play the ace or finesse the queen; if East is more likely to be void, run the jack or lead small to the jack Finesse the queen	33 95 5.28
212.	A x x x x x Q J 9	6 5 MAX	Run the queen Run the queen (best) *or* lead small to the queen Run the queen	27 95 5.22
213.	A x x x x x Q J x	6 5 MAX	Run the queen Lead small to the queen, in case West is void Run the queen	20 95 5.11
214.	Q J 9 x x x A x x	6 } MAX }	Lead the queen. If it is covered, cash the Jack	27 5.22
215.	Q J x x x x A x x	6 5 MAX	Run the queen Play the ace, and lead to queen Run the queen	20 95 5.11
216.	J 9 8 x x x A Q x	6 5 MAX	Finesse the queen Finesse the queen *or* play the ace Finesse the queen	33 100 5.33
217.	A Q J x x x x x x	5 MAX	Finesse the queen Finesse the queen	45 4.40
218.	A Q 9 7 x J 8 x x	5 4	Finesse the queen. A singleton king with West is more likely than K10xx Finesse the queen, in case West is void	33 100
219.	A Q 9 x x J x x x	5 MAX	Finesse the queen Finesse the queen	33 4.28
220.	A Q 8 x x J x x x	5 4 MAX	Finesse the queen Run the jack, in case East is void Run the jack. If it is covered, and the nine or ten drops from East, finesse the eight next	27 95 4.21
221.	A 9 8 x x Q J x x	5 4 MAX	Run the queen. If it is covered, cash the jack Run the queen (best) *or* lead small to the queen Run the queen. If it is covered, cash the jack next	27 100 4.27

Dummy Declarer	Tricks Required		% Chance of Success	Tricks per Deal

IV.   THE DEFENSE HAS THREE POINTS (cont'd)
A.   THE KING (cont'd)

222.	A 9 x x x Q J x x	5	Run the queen, hoping that West has Kxx, K10, or Kx	27
		4	Lead small to the queen	100
		MAX	Run the queen		4.22
223.	A x x x x Q J 9 x	5 } MAX }	Run the queen. If it is covered, cash the jack	27	4.22
224.	A x x x x Q J x x	5	Run the queen, hoping that West has Kx	20
		4	Play the ace, and lead to the queen	95
		MAX	Run the queen		4.11
225.	Q J 9 x x A x x x	5 } MAX }	Run the queen. If it is covered, cash the jack	27	4.22
226.	Q J x x x A x x x	5 4 MAX }	See (224) above	⎰20 ⎱95	4.11
227.	J 9 8 x x A Q x x	5	Finesse the queen; then cash the ace. Unless West plays the ten	33
		4	Finesse the queen (best) or cash the ace	100
		MAX	Finesse the queen; then cash the ace		4.33

(f)   Declarer Has Ten Cards

228.	A J 9 x x x x x Q x	8 } MAX }	Run the queen	50	7.50
229.	A Q J x x x x x x x	7 } MAX }	Finesse the queen	50	6.50
230.	A J 9 x x x x Q x x	7 } MAX }	Run the queen. Don't finesse the jack in case East is void	50	6.50
231.	Q J x x x x x A x x	7 } MAX }	Run the queen	39	6.39
232.	A Q J x x x x x x x	6 } MAX }	Finesse the queen	50	5.50
233.	A J 9 x x x Q x x x	6 } MAX }	See (230) above	50	5.50
234.	Q J x x x x A x x x	6 } MAX }	Run the queen	39	5.39
235.	A Q J x x x x x x x	5 } MAX }	Finesse the queen	50	4.50
236.	A J 9 x x Q x x x x	5 } MAX }	See (230) above	50	4.50
237.	A x x x x Q J x x x	5 } MAX }	Run the queen	39	4.39

(g)   Declarer Has Eleven Cards

238.	A Q J x x x x x x x x	6	Play the ace. The singleton king with East is 2% more likely than Kx with West	52

B.   THE QUEEN-JACK
(a)   Declarer Has Six Cards

239.	A K 10 9 8 x	5	Play the ace and king, hoping that the queen- jack are bare	1
		4	Lead small to the ten	45
		MAX	Lead small to the ten		3.46

Dummy Declarer	Tricks Required		% Chance of Success	Tricks per Deal

IV. THE DEFENSE HAS THREE POINTS (cont'd)

B. THE QUEEN-JACK (cont'd)

240.	A K 10 9 x x	4	Lead small to the ten, hoping that West has QJx or QJ	5	
		3 ⎱ Max ⎰	Finesse the ten; if this loses, finesse the nine next	76	2.81
241.	A 9 x x K 10	3	Lead small to the ten; then cash the king and ace	55	

(b) Declarer Has Seven Cards

242.	A K 10 9 x x x	5	Finesse the ten, hoping that West has QJx or QJ	9	
		4	Finesse the ten; then finesse the nine	66	
		3	Play the ace, and then finesse the ten *or* finesse the ten and then the nine	94	
		Max	Finesse the ten; then finesse the nine		3.69
243.	A 10 x x x K 9	4	Lead small to the nine	61	
		3	Lead small to the nine	92	
243A.	A 10 9 x x K x	5	Play the king; then the ace	3	
		4	Play the king, then the ace (unless East shows out)	61	3.54
		Max			
		3	Play the king, then finesse the nine or ten	93	
244.	A K 10 9 x x x	4	Finesse the ten, hoping that West has both the queen and jack	24	
		3	Finesse the ten; if it loses, cash the ace, and finesse the nine (best) *or* play the ace, and then finesse the ten and nine	78	
		Max	Finesse the ten; if it loses, cash the ace, and finesse the nine		3.00
245.	A K 9 x 10 x x	4	Finesse the nine, hoping that West has QJx or QJ	9	
		3	Play the ace. If no honor drops from East, lead small to the nine next	72	
		Max	Finesse the nine		2.78
246.	A 10 9 x K 8 x	4	Play the king. If an honor drops from East, finesse the nine	4	
		3 ⎱ Max ⎰	Lead small to the eight. If it loses, run the ten next* (*This line fails only when West has QJ, QJx, or QJxx. In practical play, however, it might be better to lead small to the king, and then finesse the ten and nine: for East may split his honors with QJx, QJxx, etc.)	82	2.84
247.	A 10 x x K 9 x	4	Play the ace and king, hoping that the queen and jack are doubleton	3	
		3 ⎱ Max ⎰	Lead low to the nine; then cash the king and ace* (*This assumes that East would never split his honors from QJxx and longer; if this is not so, lead low to the king and then finesse the ten)	75	2.77
248.	A 10 x x K x x	3 ⎱ Max ⎰	Play the king, and unless an honor appears from East, lead small to the ten* (*But if West might be tempted to split his honors, it might be better to play the king and ace and lead to the ten)	56	2.56

(c) Declarer Has Eight Cards

249.	A K 10 9 x x x x	6	Finesse the ten, hoping that West has QJ or QJx	14	
		5	Play the ace. If an honor drops from East, play the king; otherwise finesse the ten	88	
		Max	Finesse the ten. If it loses, play the ace and king		4.94

Dummy Declarer	Tricks Required		% Chance of Success	Tricks per Deal

IV. THE DEFENSE HAS THREE POINTS (cont'd)

B. THE QUEEN-JACK (cont'd)

	Dummy Declarer	Tricks Required		% Chance of Success	Tricks per Deal
250.	A 10 9 x x x K x	6	Play the ace and king, hoping that the queen-jack are doubleton	7	
		5 ⎱ Max ⎰	Play the king, and unless an honor drops from East, lead small to the ten	88	4.92
251.	A 10 x x x x K 9	6	Play the king and ace, hoping that the queen-jack are doubleton	7	
		5	Lead small to the nine	82	
		4	Lead small to the nine	98	
		Max	Lead small to the nine		4.83
252.	A K 10 9 x x x x	5	Finesse the ten, hoping that West has QJxx, QJx, or QJ	22	
		4 ⎱ Max ⎰	Finesse the ten. If it loses, cash the ace next	90	4.10
253.	A K 9 x x 10 x x	5	Run the ten, hoping that West has QJ or QJx* (*Or will cover with Qxx or Jxx)	14	
		4	Play the ace. Unless an honor appears, run the ten next	88	
		3	Play the ace	100	
		Max	Lead small to the nine		3.96
254.	A K 8 x x 10 x x	5	Play the ace and king, hoping that the queen-jack are doubleton	7	
		4	Play the ace, and lead small to the ten	82	
		3	Lead small to the ten	100	
		Max	Play the ace, and lead small to the ten		3.78
255.	A 10 9 x x K x x	5	Play the king. If an honor falls from East, finesse the ten	9	
		4	Play the king, and finesse the ten	88	
		3	Play the king, and finesse the ten	98	
		Max	Play the king, and finesse the ten		3.95
256.	A 10 x x x K 9 x	5	Play the king and ace, hoping that the queen-jack are doubleton	7	
		4	Lead low to the nine; then cash the king	90	
		3	Play the king, or lead small to the nine	100	
		Max	Play the king, and unless an honor appears, lead low to the ten		3.94
257.	A 10 x x x K 8 x	5	Play the king and ace, hoping that the queen-jack are doubleton	7	
		4	Play the king, and unless an honor drops from East, lead small to the ten (best), *or* lead small to the ten; if an honor appears from West, lead small to the eight next. The latter method might be better if West is more likely to be short in the suit	82	
		Max	Play the king, and unless an honor appears from East, lead small to the ten		3.87
258.	A 10 x x x K x x	5	Play the king and ace, hoping that the queen-jack are doubleton	7	
		4	Play the king, and unless an honor appears from East, lead small to the ten	82	
		3	Play the king, in case East is void	98	
		Max	Play the king, and unless an honor appears from East, lead small to the ten		3.87
259.	A K 10 9 x x x x	4	Finesse the ten	24	
		3 ⎱ Max ⎰	Finesse the ten; if it loses, cash the ace	90	3.14
260.	A K 8 x 10 x x x	4	Play the ace and king, hoping that the queen-jack are bare	7	
		3	Play the ace. Then either lead small to the		

Dummy Declarer	Tricks Required		% Chance of Success	Tricks per Deal

IV. THE DEFENSE HAS THREE POINTS (cont'd)

B. THE QUEEN-JACK (cont'd)

		eight, *or* if an honor has appeared from West, small to the ten	82	
	MAX	Play the ace. Unless an honor appears from West, lead small to the ten next		2.85
261. A 10 9 8 K x x x	4	Play the ace, and run the ten if an honor appears, *or* cash the king and finesse the ten if an honor appears	9	
	3 ⎱ MAX ⎰	Run the ten. If an honor appears from East, finesse the eight next; if the ten loses, cash the king. Alternatively, if East is more likely to be short in the suit, finesse the ten first and cash the ace if it loses	94	3.00
262. A 10 x x K 9 x x	4	Play the ace and king, hoping that the queen and jack will be doubleton	7	
	3 ⎱ MAX ⎰	Lead small to the ten, and then cash the ace, *or* lead small to the nine, and then cash the king; the latter line will be better if West is likely to be short in the suit	94	2.98
263. A 10 x x K 8 x x	4	Play the ace and king, hoping that the queen-jack will be bare	7	
	3	Lead small to the ten. If it loses, cash the ace; if West plays the jack or queen on the first round, lead small to the eight next	87	
	MAX	Play the king, and unless an honor appears from East, lead small to the ten		2.91
264. A 10 x x K x x x	4	Play the ace and king, hoping that the queen-jack will be bare	7	
	3 ⎱ MAX ⎰	Play the king, and unless an honor appears from East, lead small to the ten	84	2.91

(d) Declarer Has Nine Cards

265. A K 10 9 x x x x x	6 ⎱ MAX ⎰	Play the ace. If an honor drops from East, finesse the ten	46	5.42
266. A K 8 x x x 10 x x	6	Play the ace and king	41	
	5	Lead small to the eight, *or* run the ten, *or* lead small to the ten	95	
	MAX	Lead the ten, and play the ace whatever happens; then play the king		5.36
267. A 10 x x x x K 9 x	6	Play the ace, and finesse the nine if an honor appears from West, *or* play the king, and finesse the ten if an honor appears from East	46	
	5	Lead small to the nine or ten	100	
	MAX	Play the ace, and finesse the nine, *or* play the king and finesse the ten		5.42
268. 9 8 7 6 x x A K 5	6	Play the ace and king	41	
	5	Lead small to the five	95	
	MAX	Play the ace and king		5.31
269. A K 10 9 x x x x x	5 ⎱ MAX ⎰	Play the ace. If an honor drops from East, finesse the ten next; otherwise play the king	46	4.42
270. A K 9 x x 10 x x x	5 ⎱ MAX ⎰	Play the ace. If an honor drops from East, finesse the nine	46	4.42
271. A K 8 x x 10 x x x	5	Play the ace and king	41	
	4	Lead small to the eight, *or* run the ten, *or* lead small to the ten	95	
	MAX	Lead the ten, and play the ace whatever happens; then play the king. This line saves a trick if West is tempted to cover with QJ9x.		4.31+

	Dummy Declarer	Tricks Required		% Chance of Success	Tricks per Deal

IV. THE DEFENSE HAS THREE POINTS (cont'd)
B. THE QUEEN-JACK (cont'd)

	Dummy Declarer	Tricks Req.		% Chance	Tricks/Deal
272.	A 10 x x x K 9 x x	5	Play the ace (or king). If an honor falls, finesse the nine (or ten)	46	
		4	Lead small to the nine or ten	100	
		MAX	Play the ace (or king). If an honor falls, finesse the nine (or ten)		4.42

(e) Declarer Has Ten Cards

273.	A K x x x 10 9 8 x x etc.	5	Lead the ten, and play the ace whatever happens; this saves a trick when West is lulled into covering with QJx	78+	

V. THE DEFENSE HAS FOUR POINTS
A. THE ACE

(a) Declarer Has Five Cards

274.	K Q J 9 x	3	Finesse the nine	50	

(b) Declarer Has Six Cards

275.	K Q J 9 8 x	4	Play the king, queen, and jack	36	
		MAX	Play the king, queen, and jack		3.36
276.	K Q J 9 x x	4	Finesse the nine	31	
		3	Finesse the nine	82	
		MAX	Finesse the nine		3.13
277.	K Q J 9 x x	3 } MAX }	Lead to the king; then finesse the nine	55	2.55
278.	K Q 9 x J 8	3	Lead to the jack, and run the eight next	51	
279.	K Q 9 x J x	3	Lead to the jack; then finesse the nine	51	
280.	K Q x x J 9	3	Finesse the nine	50	

(c) Declarer Has Seven Cards

281.	K Q J 9 x x x	5	Lead to the king; then play the queen and jack	52	
		4	Finesse the nine	92	
		3	Finesse the nine, in case East is void	99	
		MAX	Lead to the king; then play the queen and jack		4.38
282.	K Q J 9 8 x x	4 } MAX }	Lead to the king; then lead to the queen	61	3.61
283.	K Q J 9 x x x	4	Lead to the king; then lead to the queen	58	
		3	Lead to the king; then finesse the nine	94	
		MAX	Lead to the king; then lead to the queen		3.46
284.	K Q J x x 9 x	4	Lead to the king; then lead to the queen	44	
		3	Lead small to the nine, in case West has a void or small singleton	93	
		MAX	Lead to the king; then lead to the queen		3.31
285.	K Q 9 x x J 8	4	Lead to the jack; then play to the king and queen	54	
		3	Lead small to the eight, *or* (best) lead to the jack and then run the eight	100	
		MAX	Lead to the jack; then play the king and queen		3.49
286.	K Q 9 x x J x	4	Lead to the jack, and then lead to the king	52	
		3	Lead to the jack, and then finesse the nine	93	
		MAX	Lead to the jack, and then lead to the king		3.40

	Dummy Declarer	Tricks Required		% Chance of Success	Tricks per Deal

V. THE DEFENSE HAS FOUR POINTS (cont'd)

A. THE ACE (cont'd)

	Dummy Declarer	Tricks Required		% Chance of Success	Tricks per Deal
287.	K Q x x x J 9	4	Finesse the nine. This offers a 5% better chance than hoping for a 3–3 break	42	
		3	Finesse the nine	93	
		Max	Finesse the nine		3.25
288.	K Q J 9 x x x	3	Lead to the king, to the queen, and to the jack. This is fractionally better than the third-round finesse	78	
289.	K Q 9 x J x x	3	Lead to the king, then to the jack, then to the queen. This is 2% better than the third-round finesse of the nine	62	
290.	K Q x x J 9 x	3	Lead to the king; then lead to the jack	56	
291.	K Q x x J x x	3	Lead to the king, and then to the queen. This is 8% better than leading to honors at random and hoping for a 3–3 break	45	
292.	K 9 x x Q J x	3	Lead to the queen and then to the jack; play the king on the third round. This is 1% better than the third-round finesse of the nine	67	
293.	K x x x Q J 9	3	Lead to the queen, and then to the jack	63	

(d) Declarer Has Eight Cards

	Dummy Declarer	Tricks Required		% Chance of Success	Tricks per Deal
294.	K Q J 9 x x x x	6	Lead to the king; then play the queen and jack	76	
		5	Finesse the nine, in case East is void	98	
		Max	Lead to the king; then play the queen and jack		5.72
295.	K Q J x x x 9 x	5	Lead to the king; then play the queen and jack	76	
		4	Lead small to the nine, in case West is void	98	
		Max	Lead to the king, and then play the queen and jack		4.72
296.	K Q x x x x J 9	5	Lead to the jack, and then to the king	76	
		4	Finesse the nine, in case West is void	98	
		Max	Lead to the jack, and then to the king		4.72
297.	K Q 10 7 x J x x	4 } Max }	Lead to the jack first; this fails only if West is void	98	3.98
298.	K Q 9 x x J 8 x	4	Lead to the king, and then to the jack	88	
299.	K Q 9 x x J x x	4 } Max }	Lead to the king, and then to the jack	88	3.86
300.	K Q 8 x x J x x	4	Play to a high honor, and play the jack on the first or second round	76	
		3 } Max }	Lead small to the jack. This fails only when West is void	98	3.74
301.	K Q x x x J 9 x	4 } Max }	Lead to the king, and then to the jack, or lead to the jack and then to the king. The latter line is better if East is likely to be short in the suit	76	3.74
302.	K Q J 9 x x x x	3	Lead to the king first, in case West has the singleton ace	90	
303.	K Q 9 x J 8 x x	3	Lead to the king, and then to the jack. This fails only when West has a small singleton	92	
304.	K Q 9 x J x x x	3	Lead to the king, and then to the jack. This fails only when West has a void or a small singleton	90	

	Dummy Declarer	Tricks Required		% Chance of Success	Tricks per Deal

V. THE DEFENSE HAS FOUR POINTS (cont'd)
A. THE ACE (cont'd)

	Dummy Declarer	Tricks Required		% Chance of Success	Tricks per Deal
305.	K Q 8 x J x x x	3	Lead low to the jack first, in case East is void	78	
306.	K Q 7 x J 9 x x	3	Lead to the king and then to the queen* (*But if East would not falsecard from A108x, lead to the king, and if the eight drops from East, lead to the jack next; otherwise lead to the queen)	87 90	
307.	K Q x x J 9 x x	3	Lead to the king, and then to the queen	87	

(e) Declarer Has Nine Cards

	Dummy Declarer	Tricks Required		% Chance of Success	Tricks per Deal
308.	K Q 9 x x x J 8 x	5	Lead to the king	100	
309.	K Q 8 x x x J x x	5	Lead small to the jack. This fails only when West is void	95	
310.	K Q 9 x x J 8 x x	4	Lead small to the king	100	
311.	K Q 8 x x J x x x	4	Lead small to the jack, in case East is void	95	

B. THE KING-JACK

(a) Declarer Has Five Cards

	Dummy Declarer	Tricks Required		% Chance of Success	Tricks per Deal
312.	A Q 10 9 x	4	Finesse the queen, hoping that West has king-jack only	0.3	
		3 ⎰ Max ⎱	Finesse the ten. If it holds, play the ace and queen	13	2.14
313.	A Q 10 x x	3	Finesse the ten, hoping that West has both the king and jack	24	
		2	Finesse the queen and then the ten, *or* (best) finesse the ten and then the queen	76	
		Max	Finesse the ten; if it loses, finesse the queen		2.00
314.	A Q 9 x x	2	Finesse the nine, and then finesse the queen	63	
315.	A 10 9 Q x	3	Lead the queen, hoping that East has the singleton jack	0.2	
		2 ⎰ Max ⎱	Run the queen, finessing the ten next if it loses	76	1.76
316.	A 10 x Q x	2	Lead small to the queen. If it loses, finesse the ten	74	
317.	Q 10 9 A x	3	Play the ace, hoping that East has the singleton king	0.2	
		2 ⎰ Max ⎱	Play the ace, and guess whether to play the queen or ten next	53	1.53
318.	Q x x A 10	2	Finesse the ten	52	

(b) Declarer Has Six Cards

	Dummy Declarer	Tricks Required		% Chance of Success	Tricks per Deal
319.	A Q 10 9 8 x	5	Finesse the queen, hoping that West has the king-jack only	1	
		4	Finesse the ten. If it holds, play the ace and queen	23	
		Max	Finesse the ten; then play the ace and queen		3.24

	Dummy Declarer	Tricks Required		% Chance of Success	Tricks per Deal

V. THE DEFENSE HAS FOUR POINTS (cont'd)
B. THE KING-JACK (cont'd)

	Dummy Declarer	Tricks Required		% Chance of Success	Tricks per Deal
320.	A Q 10 9 x x	4 3 } Max }	Finesse the ten, hoping that West has KJ or KJx Finesse the ten; if it loses, finesse the nine	5 63	2.68
321.	A Q 10 8 x x	4 3 } Max } 2	Finesse the ten, hoping West has KJ9 only Finesse the eight, and guess whether to finesse the ten or queen next, *or* finesse the ten and guess whether to finesse the queen or eight next Finesse the eight, ten, or queen, and guess which finesse to take next	1 33 86	2.19
322.	A Q 9 8 x x	3 2 } Max }	Finesse the eight, and guess whether to finesse the nine or queen next Finesse the eight; if it loses, finesse the nine	24 86	2.09
323.	A 10 9 x Q x	3 } Max }	Lead small to the queen, and finesse the nine next	24	2.24
324.	Q 10 9 8 A x	3	Run the ten. Then play the ace and queen* (*But if East might be tempted to cover with Kxx, the best practical chance is to lead the queen first)	23 27	
325.	Q 9 x x A 10	3 } Max } 2	Finesse the ten, and then play the ace and queen Finesse the ten, *or* play the ace and run the ten	23 100	2.23
326.	Q x x x A 10	2 } Max }	Finesse the ten. If it loses to the jack, cash the ace, and if the king fails to appear, play small from the queen	68	1.68
327.	A Q 10 x x x	3 2 Max	Finesse the ten Finesse the queen and then the ten, *or* (best) finesse the ten and then the queen Finesse the ten; if it loses, finesse the queen	24 76	2.00
328.	A Q 9 x x x	2 } Max }	Finesse the nine, and then finesse the queen	63	1.63
329.	A Q x 10 x x	3 2 Max	Finesse the queen, hoping that West has king-jack only Play the ace, and lead low to the queen Lead toward the ace-queen, and play the ace unless the jack appears from West; then lead low to the queen	1 55 1.56	
330.	A Q x x x x	2 } Max }	Lead small from the ace-queen in case East has the singleton king; then finesse the queen* (*And if East panics into playing the king from Kx)	50 54	1.50
331.	A 10 9 Q x x	3 2 } Max }	Lead the queen, hoping that East has the singleton jack, *or* play the ace, hoping that West has the singleton king Lead small to the ten; if it loses to the jack, finesse the nine* (*But if East would play the king from Kx, run the ten first; if this loses to the jack, finesse the nine next)	0.5 76 78	1.77
332.	A 10 x Q x x	2	Lead small to the queen; if it loses, finesse the ten next	74	
333.	A x x Q 10 9	3 2 } Max }	Lead the queen, hoping that East has the singleton jack, *or* play the ace, hoping that West has the singleton king Run the ten; if it loses, run the queen* (*But if East would play the king from Kx, lead small to the ten; if this loses to the jack, run the queen next)	0.5 76 78	1.77

Dummy Declarer	Tricks Required		% Chance of Success	Tricks per Deal

V.   THE DEFENSE HAS FOUR POINTS (cont'd)
B.   THE KING-JACK (cont'd)

(c)   **Declarer Has Seven Cards**

334.	A Q 10 9 x x	6	Finesse the queen, hoping that West has king-jack only	2
	x	5	Finesse the queen; then play the ace	40
		4	Lead toward the dummy, and play the ace unless the jack appears from West; then lead the queen	89
		Max	Finesse the queen; then play the ace		4.28
335.	A Q 10 9 x	5	Finesse the ten	9
	x x	4	Finesse the ten; if it loses, finesse the nine next	59
		3	Finesse the queen, and lead to the ten if it holds, *or* (best) finesse the ten	93
		Max	Finesse the ten; if it loses, finesse the nine next		3.61
336.	A Q 9 8 x	4 }	Finesse the nine, and finesse the queen next if it loses	
	x x	Max }		33	3.09
		3	Finesse the nine, and finesse the eight next if it loses	82
337.	A Q x x x	4	Play the ace, and lead to the queen, *or* finesse the queen and then cash the ace, *or* (best) lead small to the ten, and then finesse the queen	18
	10 x	3	Lead small to the ten, and then finesse the queen* (*And there is the additional chance of East playing the king from Kx)	71
				78
		2 }	Lead small to the ten, and then finesse the queen. This fails only when West has the singleton jack	
		Max }		99	2.88
338.	A 10 9 x x	4 }	Run the queen, and finesse the ten next if it loses, *or* lead small to the ten and run the queen next	
	Q x	Max }		36	3.23
		3	Play the ace	89
		Max	Run the queen, and finesse the ten next if it loses, *or* lead small to the ten, and run the queen next		3.23
339.	Q x x x x	4	Play the ace, and lead to the queen, *or* (best) finesse the ten	18
	A 10	3	Lead small to the ten	68
		2	Play the ace, and lead to the queen. This fails only when West has a void or a small singleton	94
		Max	Lead small to the ten		2.86
340.	A Q 10 9	4	Finesse the ten, hoping that West has both the king and jack	24
	x x x	3	Finesse the queen, and then the ten, *or* (best) finesse the ten and then the nine	76
		Max	Finesse the ten and then the nine		3.00
341.	A Q 10 8	4	Finesse the eight	11
	x x x	3	Finesse the queen; then finesse the ten	53
		2	Cash the ace, *or* (best) lead to the ten, and if it loses and the nine fails to appear on the second round, cash the ace next	91
		Max	Finesse the eight. If it loses, finesse the queen. If that loses, cash the ace		2.51
342.	A Q 10 x	4	Finesse the ten, hoping that West has KJx	7
	x x x	3	Finesse the queen, and finesse the ten next	47
		2	Play the ace on the first or second round. The best line is to finesse the ten and cash the ace next if it loses	85
		Max	Finesse the ten, and finesse the queen next if it loses		2.36

	Dummy Declarer	Tricks Required		% Chance of Success	Tricks per Deal

V. THE DEFENSE HAS FOUR POINTS (cont'd)

B. THE KING-JACK (cont'd)

	Dummy Declarer	Tricks Required		% Chance of Success	Tricks per Deal
343.	A Q 9 8 x x x	3	Finesse the eight, and finesse the nine next if it loses	50	
		2	Finesse the eight. If it loses, (best) lead toward dummy and play the ace unless the jack or ten appears from West	91	
		MAX	Finesse the eight. If it loses, finesse the nine. If that loses, cash the ace		2.39
344.	A Q 9 x x x x	3 } MAX } 2	Finesse the nine, and finesse the queen next if it loses	32	2.08
			Play the ace, and lead to the nine, *or* (best) finesse the nine, and play the ace next	79	
345.	A Q x x 10 x x	3	Play the ace, and unless the jack appears from East lead small to the queen* (*And if West would not falsecard from KJ, lead to the ten if the king appears from West on the first round)	21 22	
		2	Play the ace, and then lead low to the ten; then lead to the queen. This fails only when West has Jx	94	
		MAX	Finesse the queen; if it loses, lead small to the ten. If the queen holds, play the ace* (*And if West would not falsecard from KJ, lead to the ten i fthe king appears from West on the first round. But if East would play the king from Kx, the best practical play is to lead low to the ten; if this loses, finesse the queen)		2.05 2.06 2.10
346.	A Q x x x x x	3	Play the ace, and lead to the queen, *or* finesse the queen	18	
		2	Lead low from dummy, then play the ace, and then lead to the queen	77	
		MAX	Play the ace, and lead to the queen		1.87
347.	A 10 9 8 Q x x	4	Run the queen, hoping that East has the singleton jack	1	
		3 } MAX }	Finesse the ten and then the nine, *or* (best) run the queen, and finesse the ten next if it loses	76	2.77
348.	A 10 9 x Q 8 x	4	Run the queen, hoping that East has the singleton jack	1	
		3	Run the eight, and then run the queen, *or* (best) run the queen, and then finesse the ten	76	
		MAX	Run the queen, and finesse the ten next if it loses		2.77
349.	A 10 9 x Q x x	3 } MAX }	Lead small to the ten. If it loses to the jack, lead small to the nine. If the ten loses to the king, cash the queen, and finesse the nine	68	2.68
350.	A 10 x x Q 9 x	3 } MAX }	Lead small to the nine, and finesse the ten next if it loses to the jack. If East plays the king on the first round, finesse the nine next	52	2.52
351.	A 10 x x Q x x	3	Lead small to the queen, and finesse the ten next if it loses. If East plays the king on the first round, cash the queen and ace	28	
		2 } MAX }	Play the ace, and unless the jack appears from West, lead small to the queen	94	2.16
352.	A x x x Q 10 9	3	Finesse the ten. If it loses to the king, finesse the nine. If the ten loses to the jack, run the queen next. If East plays the king on the first round, finesse the ten next* (*And if West omits to falsecard with KJx)	50 57	
353.	Q 10 9 8 A x x	4	Play the ace, hoping that East has the singleton king	1	
		3 } MAX }	Run the ten, and run the nine next if it loses	69	2.69

	Dummy Declarer	Tricks Required		% Chance of Success	Tricks per Deal

V. THE DEFENSE HAS FOUR POINTS (cont'd)

B. THE KING-JACK (cont'd)

	Dummy Declarer	Tricks Required		% Chance of Success	Tricks per Deal
354.	Q x x x A 10 9	3 } Max } 2	Finesse the ten, and finesse the nine next if it loses Finesse the ten and then the nine (best), *or* play the ace and run the ten	68 100	2.68
355.	Q x x x A 10 x	3 } Max } 2	Lead small to the queen, and finesse the ten next if it loses. If West plays the king on the first round, play the ace next Play the ace, and unless the jack appears from West, lead small to the ten. This fails only when West has Jx	26 94	2.12
356.	10 9 8 7 A Q x	4 3 Max	Run the ten, hoping that East has KJ or KJx Finesse the queen. If it loses, run the ten; if the queen holds, run the ten Run the ten, and finesse the queen next	9 62 	2.69
357.	10 9 x x A Q x	4 3 } Max }	Finesse the queen, hoping that East has king-jack only Finesse the queen. If it holds, play the ace; if the queen loses, run the ten next	2 47	2.48

(d) Declarer Has Eight Cards

	Dummy Declarer	Tricks Required		% Chance of Success	Tricks per Deal
358.	A Q 10 9 x x x x	7 6 } Max }	Finesse the queen, hoping that West has king-jack only Finesse the queen, in case East has the singleton jack	3 56	5.55
359.	A Q 10 9 x x x x	6 5 4 Max	Finesse the ten Finesse the queen, and then the ten, *or* (best) finesse the ten and then the queen Finesse the queen, *or* (best) finesse the ten Finesse the ten, and if it loses, finesse the nine	14 71 98 	4.83
360.	A Q x x x x 10 x	5 4 3 Max	Play the ace, and then lead to the queen* (*But if East would play the king from Kx, lead to the ten, and then finesse the queen) Lead small to the ten, and then finesse the queen Lead small to the ten, in case either opponent is void Lead small to the ten, and then finesse the queen	37 44 93 100 	4.27
361.	A 10 9 x x x Q x	5 } Max }	Run the queen. If it loses, finesse the jack next	60	4.53
362.	Q 9 x x x x A 10	5 Max	Play the ace, and then either run the ten or lead the ten to the queen Play the ace, and then either run the ten or lead the ten to the queen* (*The latter line is better against defenders who might cover the ten with Jxx)	59 	4.55
363.	Q x x x x x A 10	5 4 3 Max	Finesse the ten Play the ace, and lead to the queen Finesse the ten Finesse the ten	47 88 100 	4.32
364.	A Q 10 9 x x x x	5 4 } Max }	Finesse the ten and then the nine Finesse the ten and then the nine	22 76	3.96
365.	A Q 10 8 x x x x	5 4 Max	Finesse the ten Finesse the queen; if it loses, finesse the ten Finesse the ten; if it loses, finesse the queen	16 66 	3.70
366.	A Q 10 x x x x x	5 4 Max	Finesse the ten Finesse the queen; if it loses, finesse the ten Finesse the ten and then the queen	14 66 	3.64

	Dummy Declarer	Tricks Required		% Chance of Success	Tricks per Deal

V. THE DEFENSE HAS FOUR POINTS (cont'd)

B. THE KING-JACK (cont'd)

				% Chance	Tricks per Deal
367.	A Q 9 x x 10 x x	5	Lead small to the nine, *or* run the ten	14	
		4	Finesse the queen, in case East has the singleton jack	71	
		Max	Finesse the nine and then the queen, *or* run the ten, and finesse the nine if it loses. The latter line will be better if East is likely to be short in the suit		3.80
368.	A Q 9 x x x x x	4	Finesse the nine and then the queen	50	
		3	Finesse the nine. If it loses, finesse the queen (best), *or* play the ace	87	
		Max	Finesse the nine and then the queen		3.35
369.	A Q x x x 10 x x	5	Finesse the queen, hoping that West has king-jack only	3	
		4	Play the ace, and unless the king appears from West, lead small to the queen	50	
		3	Play the ace, and lead small to the ten; this fails only if either opponent is void	96	
		Max	Lead to the ace, and unless West plays the king, lead small to the queen* (*If West plays the jack on the first round, finesse the queen immediately; good defenders, however, will play the king from king-jack only)		3.41
370.	A Q x x x x x x	4	Finesse the queen, *or* (best) play the ace, and lead small to the queen	34	
		3 } Max }	Play the ace, and lead small to the queen	85	3.17
371.	A 10 9 x x Q x x	4 } Max }	Finesse the ten and then the nine, *or* run the queen, and finesse the ten next if it loses. The latter line is better if East is likely to be short in the suit	71	3.69
372.	A 10 x x x Q x x	4	Play the ace, and lead small to the queen, *or* lead small to the queen, and if it loses, finesse the ten next	50	
		3 } Max }	Play the ace, and lead small to the queen. This fails only if either opponent is void	96	3.46
373.	A 9 7 x x Q 10 8	5	Lead the queen, hoping that East has the singleton jack	3	
		4 } Max }	Lead the queen; if it loses, run the ten next* (*But if East would play the king from Kx, and West would not falsecard with KJ, lead low to the ten; if this loses to the jack, run the queen next)	76 83	3.79 3.83
374.	A 9 x x x Q 10 8	5	Lead the queen, hoping that East has the singleton jack	3	
		4	Lead the queen; if it loses, run the ten next* (*But if East would play the king from Kx and West would not falsecard with KJ, lead low to the ten; if this loses to the jack, run the queen)	74 83	3.77 3.83
		3	Lead the queen, *or* lead small to the ten, in case either opponent is void	100	
375.	A 9 x x x Q 10 x	4 } Max }	Lead small to the ten; if it loses to the jack, run the queen next* (*And there is the extra chance that East will play the king from Kx)	62 72	3.60
		3	Lead small to the ten. This fails only if East is void	98	

Dummy Declarer	Tricks Required		% Chance of Success	Tricks per Deal

V.   THE DEFENSE HAS FOUR POINTS (cont'd)
B.   THE KING-JACK (cont'd)

376. A x x x x Q 10 9	4	Run the queen; if it loses, run the ten* (*But if West would not falsecard with KJ or KJx, lead small to the nine. If this loses to the jack, run the queen; if the nine loses to the king, finesse the ten.	60	
			62	
		And if East would play the king from Kx:)	72	
	3	Lead small to the nine	98	
	Max	Lead small to the nine; if it loses to the jack, run the queen through next* (*And if West would not falsecard with KJ or KJx, finesse the ten if the nine loses to the king)		3.57 3.60
377. A x x x x Q 10 x	4 } Max } 3	Play the ace, and then guess whether to lead to the queen or the ten Lead small to the ten. If it loses or holds, lead small to the queen next	50 90	3.36
378. Q 10 9 x x A 8 x	5	Lead small to the ace, hoping that East has the singleton king	3	
	4 } Max }	Finesse the eight. If it loses to the jack, run the queen next; if the eight loses to the king, run the ten next* (*But if West would play the king from Kx, lead low to the ten; if this loses to the jack, finesse the eight next)	71 72	3.74
379. Q 10 9 x x A x x	5	Play the ace, hoping that East has the singleton king	3	
	4 } Max }	Play the ace and lead small to the ten* (*But if West would play the king from Kx, lead small to the ten; if it loses to the jack, run the queen next)	67 72	3.68 3.70
380. Q x x x x A 10 x	4	Play the ace, and unless the king appears from West, lead small to the queen	50	
	3	Play the ace, and lead small to the ten. This fails only if either opponent is void	96	
	Max	Lead small to the ten, and then cash the ace, *or* lead small to the queen, and finesse the ten next if it loses		3.41
381. 10 x x x x A Q x	5	Finesse the queen, hoping that East has king-jack only	3	
	4	Play the ace, and lead small to the queen, *or* finesse the queen, and then cash the ace	50	
	3	Play the ace, and lead small to the queen. This fails only if either opponent is void	96	
	Max	Finesse the queen, and then cash the ace		3.47
382. A Q 10 9 x x x x	4	Finesse the ten	24	
	3	Either finesse the ten *or* finesse the queen; if it loses, finesse again	76	
	Max	Finesse the ten; if it loses, finesse the nine		3.00
383. A Q 10 8 x x x x	4	Finesse the ten	16	
	3	Finesse the queen; if it loses, finesse the ten	68	
	Max	Finesse the ten; if it loses, finesse the queen		2.73
384. A Q 9 x x x x x	3 } Max }	Finesse the nine, and then finesse the queen	52	2.38

	Dummy Declarer	Tricks Required		% Chance of Success	Tricks per Deal

V. THE DEFENSE HAS FOUR POINTS (cont'd)

B. THE KING-JACK (cont'd)

385.	A Q x x 10 x x x	4	Finesse the queen, hoping that West has king-jack only	3	
		3	Finesse the queen, *or* play the ace, and lead small to the queen	50	
		2	Play the ace, and lead small to the queen	100	
		Max	Lead small from the ten, and unless the jack appears, play the ace; then lead small to the queen		2.54
386.	A Q x x x x x x	3	Finesse the queen, *or* play the ace, and lead small to the queen*	34	
			(*But if East would not falsecard from Jx, play the ace, and duck on the second round if the jack appears from East)	37	
		2 } Max	Play the ace, and lead small to the queen	87	2.21
387.	A 10 9 8 Q x x x	4	Lead the queen, hoping that East has the singleton jack, *or* play the ace, hoping that West has the singleton king	3	
		3 } Max	Finesse the ten; if it loses to the jack, finesse the nine*	78	2.81
			(*But if West would not falsecard with KJxx, and East would play the king from Kx, run the ten. If the ten loses to the jack, finesse the nine; if the king appears on the first round, play the ace next)	84	2.84
388.	A 10 9 x Q 8 x x	4	See 387 above	3	
		3	See 387 above	78	
389.	A 10 9 x Q x x x	3	Finesse the ten, and then finesse the nine, *or* lead the queen, and finesse the ten next if it loses. The latter line is better if East is likely to be short in the suit	73	
390.	A 10 x x Q 9 x x	3 } Max	Play the ace, and lead small to the nine*	69	2.69
			(*But if East would play the king from Kx, lead small to the nine. If this loses to the jack, finesse the ten next; if East plays the king on the first round, play the ace next)	71	2.71
391.	A 10 x x Q x x x	3	Play the ace, and lead small to the queen (best), *or* lead small to the queen, and finesse the ten next if it loses, *or* lead small to the queen, and cash ace next if it loses	50	
		2	Play the ace, and either lead to the queen (best) or to the ten	100	
		Max	Play the ace, and lead small to the queen		2.50
391A.	Q x x x A 10 8 7	4	Lead the queen, hoping that East has the singleton jack	2.83 2.83	
		3 Max	Lead the ace, followed by the seven or eight and guess whether to play the queen or duck in dummy. If East's first play is the nine, jack, or king, lead the ten on the second round intending to play low from dummy	61.62	2.62
		2	Play the ace	100	

	Dummy Declarer	Tricks Required		% Chance of Success	Tricks per Deal

V. THE DEFENSE HAS FOUR POINTS (cont'd)

B. THE KING-JACK (cont'd)

	Dummy / Declarer	Tricks Required		% Chance of Success	Tricks per Deal
392.	A x x x Q 10 9 x	4	Play the ace, hoping that West has the singleton king	3	
		3 } Max }	Play the ace, and lead low to the ten* (*But if East would play the king from Kx, lead small to the ten. If it loses to the jack, run the queen next; if the king appears on the first round, play the ace next)	69 74	2.72 2.74
393.	A x x x Q 10 x x	3 } Max }	Play the ace, and lead small to the ten	64	2.53
		2	Play the ace, and then lead low to the ten (best) or low to the queen	90	
(e)	**Declarer Has Nine Cards**				
394.	A Q 10 9 x x x x x	8	Finesse the queen	20	
		7	Finesse the queen (best), *or* finesse the ten	72	
		Max	Finesse the queen		6.92
395.	A Q 10 x x x x x x	7	Finesse the queen, hoping that West has Kxx, KJ, or Kx	27	
		6	Play the ace, and lead small to the queen	78	
		Max	Finesse the queen; if it loses, cash the ace next		5.94
396.	A Q x x x x x 10 x	7	Finesse the queen	20	
		6	Lead small from the ten, and play the ace unless the jack appears; then lead to the queen	78	
		5	Lead small to the ten	100	
		Max	Finesse the queen		5.87
397.	A 10 9 8 x x x Q x	7	Run the queen, hoping that East has the singleton jack	6	
		6 } Max }	Run the queen; if it loses, play the ace next	77	5.83
398.	A 10 9 x x x x Q x	7	Run the queen, hoping that East has the singleton jack	6	
		6	Run the queen, and play the ace next if it loses, *or* lead small to the queen, and play the ace next if it loses. The latter line is better if West is more likely to be short in the suit	72	
		Max	Run the queen; if it loses, play the ace next		5.78
399.	Q 10 9 x x x x A x	7	Play the ace, hoping that East has the singleton king	6	
		6 } Max }	Play the ace, and lead to the queen	78	5.84
400.	Q x x x x x x A 10	6 } Max }	Play the ace, and lead to the queen	78	5.73
		5	Finesse the ten	100	
401.	A Q 10 x x x x x x	6	Finesse the queen	27	
		5	Play the ace, and lead small to the queen	83	
		Max	Finesse the queen; if it loses, play the ace next		4.98
402.	A Q x x x x x x	6	Finesse the queen	20	
		5	Play the ace, and lead small to the queen	78	
		Max	Finesse the queen		4.92
403.	A Q x x x x x x x	6	Finesse the queen	20	
		5	Play the ace, and lead small to the queen	72	
		Max	Finesse the queen		4.81
404.	A 10 9 x x x Q x x	6	Lead the queen, hoping that East has the singleton jack, *or* play the ace, hoping that West has the singleton king	6	
		5 } Max }	Play the ace, and lead small to the queen	78	4.84

Dummy Declarer	Tricks Required		% Chance of Success	Tricks per Deal

V. THE DEFENSE HAS FOUR POINTS (cont'd)
B. THE KING-JACK (cont'd)

405. A 10 x x x x Q x x	5 } Max }	Play the ace, and lead small to the queen	78	4.78
406. A x x x x x Q 10 9	6	Lead the queen, hoping that East has the singleton jack, *or* play the ace, hoping that West has the singleton king	6	
	5	Play the ace and lead small to the queen* (*But if East would play the king from Kx, lead small to the ten; if it loses to the jack, run the queen next)	78 89	
	4	Run the ten, *or* lead small to the ten, *or* run the queen, and play the ace if it loses	100	
	Max	Play the ace, and lead small to the queen		4.79
407. A x x x x x Q 10 x	6	Play the ace, hoping that West has the singleton king	6	4.79
	5 } Max }	Play the ace, and lead small to the queen	78	
408. Q 10 9 x x x A x x	6	Lead the queen, hoping that West has the singleton jack, *or* play the ace, hoping that East has the singleton king	6	
	5 } Max }	Play the ace, and lead to the queen* (*But if West would play the king from Kx, lead small to the ten; if it loses to the jack, run the queen next)	83 89	4.89
409. Q 8 x x x x A 10 9	6	Play the ace, hoping that East has the singleton King, *or* lead the queen, hoping that West has the singleton jack	6	
	5 } Max }	Play the ace, and lead to the queen	83	4.89
410. Q x x x x x A 10 x	5 } Max }	Play the ace, and lead small to the queen	78	4.78
411. 10 x x x x x A Q x	6	Finesse the queen	20	
	5	Play the ace, and lead small to the queen	78	
	Max	Finesse the queen		4.92
412. A Q 10 x x x x x x	5	Finesse the queen	27	
	4	Play the ace, and lead to the queen	83	
	Max	Finesse the queen; if it loses, play the ace next		3.98
413. A Q x x x 10 x x x	5	Finesse the queen	20	
	4	Play the ace, and lead to the queen	78	
	Max	Finesse the queen		3.92
414. A Q x x x x x x x	5	Finesse the queen	20	
	4	Play the ace, and lead to the queen	72	
	Max	Finesse the queen		3.81
415. A 10 9 x x Q 8 x x	5	Lead the queen, hoping that East has the singleton jack, *or* play the ace, hoping that West has the singleton king	6	
	4 } Max }	Play the ace, and lead small to the queen* (*But if East would play the king from Kx, lead small to the eight; if this loses to the jack, run the queen next)	83 94	3.89
416. A 10 9 x x Q x x x	5	Lead the queen, hoping that East has the singleton jack, *or* play the ace, hoping that West has the singleton king	6	
	4 } Max }	Play the ace and lead small to the queen* (*But if East would play the king from Kx, run the ten; if this loses to the jack, run the queen next)	78 84	3.84

Dummy Declarer	Tricks Required		% Chance of Success	Tricks per Deal

V. THE DEFENSE HAS FOUR POINTS (cont'd)

B. THE KING-JACK (cont'd)

417. A 10 x x x Q 9 x x	5	Lead the queen, hoping that East has the single-ton jack, *or* play the ace, hoping that West has the singleton king	6	
	4 } Max	Play the ace, and lead to the queen* (*But if East would play the king from Kx, lead small to the nine; if this loses to the jack, run the queen next)	83 89	3.89
418. A 10 x x x Q x x x	4	Play the ace, and lead small to the queen	78	
419. A x x x x Q 10 9 8	5	Lead the queen, hoping that East has the single-ton jack, *or* play the ace, hoping that West has the singleton king	6	
	4 } Max	Play the ace, and lead to the queen* (*But if East would play the king from Kx, lead small to the ten, and run the queen next if it loses to the jack)	83 94	3.89
420. A x x x x Q 10 9 x	5	Lead the queen, hoping that East has the single-ton jack, *or* play the ace, hoping that West has the singleton king	6	
	4 } Max	Play the ace, and lead to the queen* (*But if East would play the king from Kx, lead small to the ten, and run the queen next if it loses to the jack)	83 89	3.89

(f) Declarer Has Ten Cards

421. A Q 10 x x x x x x x etc.*	5 Max	Finesse the queen Finesse the queen	39	 4.28
422. A Q x x x 10 9 8 x x etc.*	5 } Max	Lead the ten, and play the queen, giving an extra chance if West is tempted to cover with KJx	39	4.28
423. A 10 9 x x Q x x x x etc.*	5 4 Max	Play the ace, hoping to drop the singleton king Lead small to the queen, *or* (best) lead small to the ten Play the ace	26 100	 4.15

(g) Declarer Has Eleven Cards

424. A Q 10 x x x x x x x x etc.*	6	Play the ace. This line is fractionally better than the queen finesse	52	

*N.B. Similar principles apply if declarer's ten or eleven cards are distributed differently between his hand and dummy

VI. THE DEFENSE HAS FIVE POINTS

A. THE ACE-JACK

(a) Declarer Has Five Cards

425. K Q 10 9 x	3	Finesse the ten	11	
426. K Q 10 x x	2	Lead to the king, and whether it holds or loses, lead to the queen next* (*But this assumes that East will duck the king if he holds Ax(xxx), which is best defense. If he always wins with these holdings, lead to the king; if it holds, lead to the queen; if the king loses, finesse the ten next)	52 76	

	Dummy Declarer	Tricks Required		% Chance of Success	Tricks per Deal

VI. THE DEFENSE HAS FIVE POINTS (cont'd)
A. THE ACE-JACK (cont'd)

	Dummy Declarer	Tricks Required		% Chance of Success	Tricks per Deal
427.	K 10 x Q x	2	Lead to the queen, and then finesse the ten	50	
428.	K x x Q 10	2	Finesse the ten	50	

(b) Declarer Has Six Cards

429.	K Q 10 9 8 x	4	Finesse the ten, hoping that West has AJx, Jxx, AJ, Jx, or J	18	
430.	K Q 10 9 x x	4	Finesse the ten	14	
		3	Lead to the king; then play the queen. This line gains a trick when East has AJ, Jx, or J	72	
		MAX	Finesse the ten		2.82
431.	K Q 10 9 x x	3	Finesse the ten	50	
432.	K Q 9 8 x x	3	Finesse the nine, hoping that West has AJ10, J10x, or J10	5	
		2 ⎱ MAX ⎰	Finesse the nine. If this loses to the jack or ten, finesse the eight next*	79	1.85
			(*But if East would not duck with Ax, Axx, A10xx, or AJxx, lead to the king; if it holds, lead to the queen; if the king loses, finesse the nine)	81	
433.	K Q x x 10 x	2	Lead small to the ten. If the ten loses, play to the king; if the king holds, play small from the queen	56	
434.	K Q 10 x x x	2	Lead to the king and, whether it holds or loses, lead to the queen next*	55	
			(*But if East would not duck the king if he holds the ace, lead to the king: if it loses, finesse the ten; if the king holds, lead to the queen)	76	
435.	K 10 x Q x x	2	Lead small to the queen, and then finesse the ten	51	

(c) Declarer Has Seven Cards

436.	K Q x x x x x	5	Duck one round, and then play the king (best), *or* lead the king	36	
		4	Duck one round; then either duck again or lead the king	86	
		MAX	Duck one round, and then lead the king		4.20
437.	K Q 10 8 x x x	5	Finesse the ten. If the jack appears from West, duck the next round	21	
		4	Finesse the ten or the eight	68	
		3	Finesse the ten or the eight	94	
		2	Finesse the ten or the eight	99	
		MAX	Finesse the ten		3.82
438.	K Q 10 9 x x x	4	Finesse the ten*	42	
			(*But if East would not duck with Axx, lead to the king; if it holds, lead to the queen; if the king loses, finesse the ten)	43	
		3	Finesse the ten	93	
		MAX	Finesse the ten		3.35

	Dummy Declarer	Tricks Required		% Chance of Success	Tricks per Deal

VI. THE DEFENSE HAS FIVE POINTS (cont'd)

A. THE ACE-JACK (cont'd)

	Dummy Declarer	Tricks Required		% Chance of Success	Tricks per Deal
439.	K Q 9 8 x x x	4	Lead to the king; if it holds, lead to the queen	21	
		3	Lead to the king, and whether it holds or loses, lead to the queue next* (*But if East would not duck with Ax, lead to the king; if it holds, lead to the queen; if the king loses, lead to the nine)	74 76	
		2	Lead to the king. If it loses, lead to the nine; if the king holds, lead to the queen or nine; *or* finesse the nine, and if it loses, finesse the eight	96	
		Max	Lead to the king, and whether it holds or loses, lead to the queen next* (*But if East would not duck with Ax, play to the nine if the king loses and to the queen if the king holds)		2.90 2.92
440.	K Q x x x 10 x	4	Lead small to the king; then lead to the queen	18	
		3	Lead small to the ten, and then lead to the king. This saves a trick when East has AJ only	61	
		2	Lead to the king and then to the queen, *or* lead small to the ten and then to the king. The latter line will be better if West is more likely to be short in the suit	93	
		Max	Lead to the king and then to the queen		2.71
441.	K Q 10 9 x x x	3	Lead to the king, and whether it holds or loses, finesse the ten next* (*This assumes that East will duck about half the time with Ax and Axx, which is the best defense. If he always wins with these holdings, play to the queen if the king holds, and finesse the ten if the king loses. Similarly, if East always ducks with Ax and Axx, play the queen if the king loses, and finesse the ten if the king holds)	51 54 52	
442.	K Q 9 8 x x x	3	Finesse the nine	24	
		2	Finesse the nine. If it loses, play to the king; if that loses, finesse the eight (best), *or* play to the king. If it loses, finesse the nine and, if necessary, the eight; if the king holds, play to the queen (best), or finesse the nine	89	
		Max	Finesse the nine. If it loses, lead to the king; if that loses, finesse the eight		2.13
443.	K 10 9 x Q x x	3	Lead small to the queen; then finesse the ten	53	
444.	K 10 x x Q 9 x	3 ⎫ Max ⎬	Lead small to the queen; then finesse the ten. This is better than leading to the king first, for there is time to discover whether the insertion of the ace by East is from AJ doubleton or A singleton	31	2.31
445.	K x x x Q 10 9	3	Finesse the ten	50	
446.	K x x x Q 10 x	3 ⎫ Max ⎬ 2	Lead small to the ten and then small to the queen, hoping that East has AJ, AJx or Jxx Lead small to the queen and then small to the ten	19 77	1.95
447.	10 9 8 7 K Q x	3	Lead to the king. If it holds, lead to the queen; if the king loses, cash the queen* (*This assumes that West will duck with Axx, which is the best defense. If he always wins with this holding, lead to the king: if it holds, lead to the queen; if the king loses, run the ten next)	36 45	

Dummy Declarer	Tricks Required		% Chance of Success	Tricks per Deal

VI. THE DEFENSE HAS FIVE POINTS (cont'd)

A. THE ACE-JACK (cont'd)

(d) Declarer Has Eight Cards

448. K Q x x x x x x   6   ⎱   Duck the first round, in case the ace is singleton;
       —   MAX ⎰   then play the king and queen   73   5.70

449. K Q 10 x x x x   6   Finesse the ten   34
       x   5   Finesse the ten   85
                 4   Finesse the ten   98
              MAX   Finesse the ten   5.17

450. K Q x x x x x   6 ⎱   Lead to the king, hoping that West has the double-
       x   MAX ⎰   ton ace   14   4.80
                5   Play small from both hands, in case the ace is sin-
                    gleton; then play the king and queen   73

451. K Q 10 x x x   5 ⎱   Lead to the king. If it holds, lead to the queen; if
       x x   MAX ⎰   the king loses, cash the queen next*   47   4.30
                    (*But if East would not duck with Ax, finesse
                    the ten if the king loses and lead to the queen
                    if the king holds)   54   4.40
                4   Lead to the king. If it loses, finesse the ten; if the
                    king holds, guess which honor to play next   88

452. K Q x x x x   5 ⎱   Lead to the king and then to the queen   34   4.17
       10 x   MAX ⎰
                4   Lead to the king and then to the queen (best) *or*
                    lead small to the ten   85
                3   Lead to the king *or* lead small to the ten. The latter
                    line will be better if West is more likely to be
                    short in the suit   98

(d) Declarer Has Eight Cards

453. K Q 10 x x   4 ⎱   Lead to the king, and whether it holds or loses,
       x x x   MAX ⎰   finesse the ten next*   55   3.43
                    (*This assumes that East will duck about half
                    the time with Ax. If he always ducks with this
                    holding, finesse the ten if the king holds, and
                    play the queen if the king loses.   59
                    Similarly, if East always wins with Ax, finesse
                    the ten if the king loses, and lead to the queen
                    if the king holds)   57

454. K 9 x x x   4   Lead small to the queen. If it holds, finesse the
       Q 10 x   nine; if the queen loses, either play the king or
                    finesse the nine   46
             MAX   Lead small to the queen, and then finesse the
                    nine   3.42

455. K x x x x   4   Finesse the ten   48
       Q 10 9   3   Finesse the ten   98
              2   Finesse the ten (best), *or* lead to the queen   100
            MAX   Finesse the ten   3.46

456. K x x x x   4 ⎱   Lead small to the king, and then finesse the ten*   37   3.20
       Q 10 x   MAX ⎰   (*The alternative is to lead small to the king or
                    queen, playing the other top honor if it loses
                    and ducking the next round if it holds, but this
                    line is inferior against defenders who would not
                    take the ace immediately)
             3   Lead small to the queen, and then lead small to
                    the ten   88

Dummy Declarer	Tricks Required		% Chance of Success	Tricks per Deal

VI.   THE DEFENSE HAS FIVE POINTS (cont'd)
A.   THE ACE-JACK (cont'd)

457. K Q 10 x / x x x x — 3 } MAX — Lead to the king, and whether it holds or loses, finesse the ten next* — 57 — 2.47
(*This assumes that East will duck about half the time with Ax. If he always ducks with this holding, finesse the ten if the king holds, and play the queen if it loses. — 61
Similarly, if East always wins with Ax, play to the queen if the king holds, and finesse the ten if the king loses) — 59

458. K 10 x x / Q x x x — 3 } MAX — Lead to the queen, and then finesse the ten — 40 — 2.27
2 — Play small from both hands; then lead to the queen — 90

459. K 9 8 7 / Q x x x — 3 } MAX — Lead to the queen, and then finesse the nine, hoping that East has 10, J, Ax, A10, AJ, or Axx; *or* lead to the king, and then run the nine. The latter line will be better if West is more likely to be short in the suit — 23 — 2.12
2 — Finesse the nine. If this loses to the jack or ten, guess which honor to lead to next; if the jack or ten appears from West, run the eight, *or* run the nine. If this loses to the jack or ten, guess which honor to lead to next; if the jack or ten appears from East, finesse the eight — 94

460. K x x x / Q 10 9 8 — 3 — Lead to the queen, and then run the ten, *or* lead to the king, and then finesse the ten — 56

461. K x x x / Q x x x — 3 } MAX — Lead to either honor, and duck on the next round, hoping to find the right opponent with the doubleton ace — 14 — 1.84
2 — Play low from both hands, in case the ace is singleton, and then lead to either honor — 73

(e)   Declarer Has Nine Cards

462. K Q 8 x x x x / 10 x — 6 } MAX — Lead small to the king, and then small to the queen — 72 — 5.67
5 — Lead small to the ten — 100

463. K Q 10 9 x / x x x x / etc.* — 4 — Lead small to the king; if it loses to the ace, lead to the queen next — 77

464. K 9 x x x / Q 10 x x / etc.* — 4 — Lead to the king, and play the queen next if it loses, *or* lead to the queen, and play the king next if it loses — 59

465. K 9 x x x / Q x x x / etc.* — 4 } MAX — Lead small to the queen; if an honor appears from East, finesse the nine next — 53 — 3.48
3 — Lead small to the queen, in case East is void — 95
*N.B. Similar principles apply, if declarer's nine cards are distributed differently between his hand and dummy

(f)   Declarer Has Ten Cards

466. K 8 x x x x / Q 10 x x / etc.* — 5 — Lead small to the king. This fails only if East is void — 89

*N.B. Similar principles apply if declarer's ten cards are distributed differently between his hand and dummy

	Dummy Declarer	Tricks Required		% Chance of Success	Tricks per Deal

B. THE KING-QUEEN

(a) Declarer Has Five Cards

467.	A J 10 9 x	3	Finesse the jack; then play the ace	7	
468.	A J 10 x x	2	Finesse the jack; then finesse the ten	76	
469.	A J 9 x x	2	Finesse the nine; if it loses to an honor, finesse the jack next*	37	
			(*If West inserts a high honor on the first round, still finesse the nine next, for West should falsecard with holdings like K10x, Q10x, etc. If he would not falsecard in this way, and would split high honors on the first round, finesse the jack next if the king or queen appears from West)	50	

(b) Declarer Has Six Cards

470.	A J 10 x x x —	4	Play the ace, and then lead small from the jack-ten, hoping that the king-queen are doubleton or tripleton	10	
		3 } Max }	Play the ace, and then lead small from the jack-ten, in case there is a doubleton honor	78	2.83
471.	A J 10 9 8 x	4	Finesse the jack, and then play the ace, hoping that West has xxxxx, KQx, KQ, Kx Qx, K, or Q	14	
472.	A J 10 9 x x	3	Finesse the jack, and then finesse the ten	50	
473.	A J 9 x x x	3	Finesse the jack, hoping that West has KQ10 only	1	
		2 } Max }	Finesse the nine. If it loses to the ten, play the ace and a small card; if the nine loses to a high honor, finesse the jack next* (*And if East omits to falsecard with KQ10)	41 42	1.42
474.	A J x x 10 x	2	Lead small to the ten; if it loses, play the ace, and lead small from the jack* (*But if East would play an honor from Qx, Kx, or Qxx, lead small to the ten, and finesse the jack next if it loses)	55 65	
475.	A J 10 x x x	2	Finesse the jack, and then finesse the ten	76	
476.	A J 9 x x x	2	Finesse the nine, and then finesse the jack. If West inserts a high honor on the first round, still finesse the nine next; West should falsecard with K10x, etc.* (*But if West would split high honors and would not falsecard, finesse the jack next if West plays the king or queen on the first round)	38 50	
477.	A J 8 10 x x	2	Lead small to the eight. If this loses to a high honor, finesse the jack next* (*And if West is tempted to split his honors from KQ and others)	39 51	
478.	A J x 10 x x	2	Lead small to the jack; then play the ace* (*But if East might be tempted to play an honor from Kx, Qx, or Qxx, lead small to the ten, and then finesse the jack)	33 41	
479.	A x x J 10 9	2	Run the jack, and then run the ten	76	

Dummy Declarer	Tricks Required		% Chance of Success	Tricks per Deal

VI.   THE DEFENSE HAS FIVE POINTS (cont'd)
B.   THE KING-QUEEN (cont'd)

(c)   Declarer Has Seven Cards

480.	J 10 x x x x A	5	Play the ace, and then lead small from the jack-ten, hoping that the king-queen are doubleton	3	
		4	Play the ace, and then lead small from the jack-ten, in case there is a doubleton honor	65	
481.	A J 10 9 x x x	5 ⎫ Max ⎭	Finesse the jack, and then cash the ace	23	4.08
		4	Play the ace, and then lead the jack, in case East has a singleton honor	89	
482.	A J 10 9 x x x	4 ⎫ Max ⎭	Finesse the jack, and then finesse the ten	53	3.45
		3	Finesse the jack	92	
483.	A J 9 x x x x	4 ⎫ Max ⎭	Finesse the nine, and then finesse the jack	12	2.58
		3	Finesse the nine, and the jack	55	
		2	Finesse the nine, and the jack This fails only when West has a void or a singleton, or when East has a singleton ten	91	
484.	A J 10 9 x x x	3	Finesse the jack, and then finesse the ten	76	
485	A J 10 x x x x	3 ⎫ Max ⎭	Finesse the jack, and then finesse the ten	45	2.28
		2	Play the ace, and lead small to the jack, *or* finesse the jack, and then play the ace	85	
486.	A J 9 8 x x x	3	Finesse the eight, and then finesse the nine	37	
		2	Finesse the eight, the nine, and, if necessary, the jack (best), *or* finesse the jack, the eight, and then the nine	89	
		Max	Finesse the eight, the nine, and, if necessary, the jack		2.26
487.	A J 9 x x x x	3 ⎫ Max ⎭	Finesse the nine, and then finesse the jack, hoping that East has x, xx, xxx, Qxx, Kxx, or void	22	1.89
		2	Play the ace, and lead to the nine, *or* finesse the nine and the jack, *or* finesse the jack and the nine	68	
488.	A J 8 x 10 x x	3	Lead small to the eight. If this loses to the king or queen, lead from the ten, and play the ace unless the nine appears from West*	26	
			(*And if West omits to falsecard with 9xxx And if West is tempted to split his honors with KQx)	28 33	
		2	Play the ace, and unless an honor appears from West, lead small to the ten. This fails only when West has Kx or Qx	90	
		Max	Lead small to the eight. If this loses to the king or queen, lead from the ten, and play the ace unless the nine appears from West. If the eight loses to the nine, lead small to the jack next*		2.15
			(*And if West falsecards with 9xxx And if West splits his honors with KQx)		2.16 2.22
489.	A J x x 10 x x	3	Lead small to the jack, hoping that West has KQ or KQx	9	
		2	Lead small to the ace, and unless an honor appears from West, lead small to the ten next. This fails only when West has Kx or Qx	87	

	Dummy Declarer	Tricks Required		% Chance of Success	Tricks per Deal

VI. THE DEFENSE HAS FIVE POINTS (cont'd)

B. THE KING-QUEEN (cont'd)

		Max	Lead small to the ace, and unless an honor appears from West, lead small to the ten*		1.90
			(*But if East would play an honor from Kx or Qx, lead small to the ten, and finesse the jack next if it loses to West)		1.93
490.	A 9 8 7 J x x	3	Run the nine. If this loses to the king or queen from West, run the jack next, hoping that East has 10 or 10x*	6	
			(*But if East would not falsecard with 10x, run the nine; if the ten appears from East, play the ace next; if the king or queen appears from East or the nine loses to the king or queen from West, run the jack next.	8	
			And if East would play a high honor from K10 or Q10, run the nine; if the king or queen appears from East, or the nine loses to the king or queen from West, run the jack next. This succeeds when East has 10, 10x, Q10, or K10)	9	
		2 } Max }	Run the jack. If it loses, finesse the nine next; if that loses, finesse the eight	89	1.90
491.	A x x x J 10 9	3 2	Run the jack and then the ten Run the jack and then the ten	28 100	
492.	J x x x A 10 x	3 } Max }	Lead small to the ten, and then play the ace, hoping that East has KQ or KQx	9	1.93
		2	Play the ace, and unless an honor appears from West, lead small to the ten	87	

(d) Declarer Has Eight Cards

493.	A J 10 9 x x x x	6 } Max }	Finesse the jack, and then play the ace	43	5.39
494.	A J 10 x x x 9 x	5 } Max }	Lead small to the ten; then run the nine. Do not lead the nine for the first finesse: West may have a singleton honor	60	4.56
495.	A J 9 x x x x x	5	Finesse the nine, and then finesse the jack* (*If West would not falsecard with 10xx, play the ace if the nine loses to a high honor, and the ten fails to appear on the second round)	27 31	
		4 } Max }	Finesse the nine, and then finesse the jack	79	4.04
		3	Finesse the jack or the nine in case East is void	98	
496.	A J x x x x 10 x	5	Lead small to the ten, and finesse the jack next, or run the ten and lead up to the jack next	24	
		4 } Max }	Lead small to the ten, and finesse the jack next	90	4.14
		3	Lead small to the ten	100	
497.	A 9 8 x x x J x	5	Lead small to the jack, hoping that East has K10 or Q10	7	
		4	Lead small to the jack and then to the nine, or play the ace, or run the jack, and finesse the nine next, or lead toward the ace, and play small unless an honor appears from West	85	
		3	Lead small to the jack	100	
		Max	Lead small to the jack. If an honor wins from East, run the jack next; if East plays the ten on the first round, cash the ace next		3.92

Dummy Declarer	Tricks Required		% Chance of Success	Tricks per Deal

VI. THE DEFENSE HAS FIVE POINTS (cont'd)
B. THE KING-QUEEN (cont'd)

498. A 9 x x x x
J x

5 — Lead small to the jack, hoping that East has K10 or Q10 — **7**

4 — Lead small to the jack; if the ten appears from East, finesse the nine next — **73**

MAX — Lead small to the jack. If an honor wins from East, run the jack next; if East plays the ten on the first round, finesse the nine — **3.76**

499. A J 10 x x
x x x

4 }
MAX } — Finesse the jack, and then finesse the ten — **63** — **3.50**

3 — Finesse the jack, and then play the ace, *or* finesse the jack and then the ten (best) — **90**

500. A J 9 x x
x x x

4 }
MAX } — Finesse the nine, and then finesse the jack*
(*If West would not falsecard from 10xx, play the ace if the nine loses to a high honor, and the ten fails to appear on the second round) — **33** ... **36** — **3.15**

3 — Finesse the nine, and then finesse the jack — **84**

501. A J 8 7 x
10 x x

4 }
MAX } — Run the ten. If it is covered, lead to the eight next; if the ten loses to East, finesse the jack next*
(*But if West would not falsecard with K9 or Q9, and would not split his honors with KQ9, lead small to the eight. If this loses to the nine, lead to the ten next; if the eight loses to a high honor, finesse the seven next; and if the king or queen appears from West on the first round, run the eight next.
And if West would split his honors with KQx or KQ9) — **42** ... **44** ... **47** — **3.35** ... **3.37** ... **3.40**

3 — Lead small to the jack. If it loses, lead small to the ten next. This fails only if West is void. — **98**

502. A J x x x
10 x x

4 — Lead small to the jack, and then cash the ace — **37**

3 — Play the ace, and lead small to the ten. This fails only to a 5–0 break — **96**

MAX — Lead small to the jack, and then cash the ace*
(*But if East would play an honor from Kx or Qx, lead small to the ten, and then finesse the jack) — **3.19** ... **3.24**

503. A 9 8 7 x
J x x

4 — Run the nine. If it loses to the king or queen from West, run the jack; if the king or queen appears from East, either run the jack or cash the ace*
(*This assumes that East will play an honor from K10 or Q10 about half the time, which is the best defense. If he would always play the high honor from these holdings, run the nine, and run the jack next if it loses to the king or queen on either side) — **13** ... **16**

3 — Run the nine. If this loses to the ten, run the jack next; if the nine loses to the king or queen on either side, lead small to the jack. This fails only when either opponent is void, or West has the singleton ten — **93**

MAX — Run the nine. If this loses to the ten, run the jack next; if the nine loses to the king or queen from West, run the jack next; if the king or queen appears from East on the first round, lead small to the jack next — **2.97**

	Dummy Declarer	Tricks Required		% Chance of Success	Tricks per Deal

VI. THE DEFENSE HAS FIVE POINTS (cont'd)

B. THE KING-QUEEN (cont'd)

	Dummy Declarer	Tricks Required		% Chance of Success	Tricks per Deal
504.	A x x x x J 10 9	4 3 2 MAX	Run the jack and then the ten Run the jack and then the ten Run the jack Run the jack and then the ten	54 96 100	 3.50
505.	J 10 9 x x A x x	4 3 MAX	Run the jack and then the ten Play the ace, *or* lead low to the jack. This fails only if West is void Run the jack and then the ten	60 98	 3.56
506.	A J 10 9 x x x x	3	Finesse the jack and then the ten	76	
507.	A J 10 x x x x x	3 } MAX }	Finesse the jack and then the ten	65	2.54
508.	A J 9 x x x x x	3 } MAX } 2	Lead small to the nine; then finesse the jack* (*And if West would not falsecard with 10xx, play the ace if the nine loses to a high honor, and the ten fails to appear on the second round) Play the ace, *or* take two finesses	35 38 84	2.19
509.	A J 8 x 10 x x x	3 2 MAX	Run the ten. If it loses to East, finesse the jack next; if the ten is covered, finesse the eight next Lead small to the jack, and finesse the eight next if it loses (best), *or* play the ace, and lead small to the ten Finesse the jack; if it loses, finesse the eight next	 44 100	 2.37
510.	A J x x 10 x x x	3 } MAX } 2	Finesse the jack; then cash the ace Play the ace, and lead small to either honor	37 100	2.32
511.	A 9 8 7 J x x x	3 2 MAX	Run the nine. If it loses to the king or queen from West, run the jack; if East plays an honor on the first round, cash the ace next* (*But if East would play an honor from K10 or Q10, run the nine, and run the jack next if it loses to the king or queen on either side) Run the nine. If this loses, lead small to the eight next. This fails only when West has the singleton ten Play the ace, and then run the nine	13 16 97	 2.05

(e) Declarer Has Nine Cards

	Dummy Declarer	Tricks Required		% Chance of Success	Tricks per Deal
512.	A J 10 9 x x x x x	7 } MAX }	Play the ace, *or* finesse the jack, and then play the ace	66	6.66
513.	A J 10 9 x x x x x	6 } MAX }	Finesse the jack and then the ten	76	5.76
514.	A J 9 x x x x x x	6 5 MAX	Play the ace, and lead to the jack, *or* finesse the jack* (*But if West would not falsecard with K10x, Q10x, or 10x, lead toward dummy, and play the ace unless the ten appears from West. And if West splits his honors with KQx) Finesse the jack or the nine, in case East is void Finesse the jack* (*But if West would not falsecard with K10x, Q10x, or 10x, lead toward dummy, and play the ace if the ten fails to appear)	53 59 66 95	 5.48 5.50

Dummy Declarer	Tricks Required		% Chance of Success	Tricks per Deal

VI. THE DEFENSE HAS FIVE POINTS (cont'd)
B. THE KING-QUEEN (cont'd)

515. A 8 7 x x x x J 10	6 ⎱ Max ⎰ 5	Run the jack, and then play the ace; this gains a trick when East has the singleton nine Run the jack, in case East is void	47 95	5.42
516. A J 10 x x x x x x	5 ⎱ Max ⎰	Finesse the jack and then the ten	76	4.71
517. A J 9 x x x x x x	5 ⎱ Max ⎰	Finesse the nine. If this loses to the king or queen, finesse the jack next* (*But if West would not falsecard with K10x, Q10x, or 10x, lead toward dummy, and play the ace if the ten fails to appear. And if West splits his honors with KQx)	57 59 66	4.53 4.55 4.61
518. A J x x x x 10 x x	5 ⎱ Max ⎰	Lead small to the jack, or play the ace, and lead small to either honor	 66	 4.66
519. A 9 x x x x J x x	5	Play the ace, and lead small to the jack	53	
	4 Max	Lead small to the jack Lead toward dummy, and play the nine if West follows small; otherwise play the ace, and lead small to the jack	100	 3.48
520. A x x x x x J 10 9	5 ⎱ Max ⎰	Run the jack and then the ten	71	4.71
	4	Run the jack	100	
521. A J 10 9 x x x x x	4	Finesse the jack and then the ten	76	
522. A J 9 x x x x x x	4 ⎱ Max ⎰	Finesse the nine; if this loses to the king or queen, finesse the jack next* (*But if West would not falsecard with K10x, Q10x, or 10x, lead toward dummy, and play the ace if the ten fails to appear from West. And if West splits his honors with KQx)	57 59 66	3.53 3.55 3.61
523. A J x x x 10 x x x	4 ⎱ Max ⎰	Finesse the jack, or play the ace, and lead small to either honor	 66	 3.66
524. A 9 x x x J x x x	4	Play the ace, and lead small to the jack	53	
	3 Max	Lead small to the jack, or lead small to the n̄ine Lead toward dummy, and play the nine if West follows small; otherwise play the ace, and lead to the jack	100	 3.53
525. A x x x x J 10 9 8	4	Run the jack and then the ten	76	

(f) Declarer Has Ten Cards

526. A J 10 x x
x x x x x
etc.*
	4 ⎱
	Max ⎰
		Lead to the jack, in case East is void
		
		*N.B. Similar principles apply if declarer's ten
		  cards are distributed differently between his
		  hand and dummy.
			89	3.89

VII. THE DEFENSE HAS SIX POINTS
A. THE ACE-QUEEN

(a) Declarer Has Five Cards

527. K J 9 x x	2 ⎱ Max ⎰ 1	Finesse the nine and then the jack, or finesse the jack and then the nine Immaterial: take two finesses	 24 78	1.02

Dummy Declarer	Tricks Required		% Chance of Success	Tricks per Deal

VII. THE DEFENSE HAS SIX POINTS (cont'd)

A. THE ACE-QUEEN (cont'd)

(b) Declarer Has Six Cards

528.	K J 10 9 x x	3	Finesse the jack and then the ten	18
529.	K J 9 8 x x	3	Finesse the eight, hoping that West has AQ10, Q10x, or Q10	5
		2 ⎱ Max ⎰	Finesse the eight; if this loses, finesse the nine next	63	1.68
530.	K x x x J 9	1	Lead small to the nine or jack; if this loses, lead to the king. Finessing the nine first will be better against East, who might be tempted to play an honor from AQ and others	75
531.	K J 9 x x x	2 1 Max	Finesse the jack or the nine Immaterial: take two finesses Finesse the jack, and guess which to play next if the queen wins, *or* finesse the nine, and guess which to play next if the ten wins	25 79	1.04
532.	K J x x x x	2 ⎱ Max ⎰ 1	Lead to the jack, hoping that West has both the ace and queen Lead to the jack and then to the king (best), *or* lead to the king and then to the jack	24 76	1.00
533.	K 9 8 J x x	2 1 ⎱ Max ⎰	Lead small to the king, hoping that West has AQ doubleton or the singleton queen Finesse the eight; if this loses to the ten, guess whether to play to the nine or king next* (*But if East would play a high honor from AQ and others, run the nine first; if this loses to the ten, lead to the king next)	1 80 88	0.81
534.	K x x J 9 x	2 1 Max	Lead small to the king, hoping that West has the ace-queen doubleton or the queen singleton Lead small to the king and then back to the jack or nine (best), *or* lead to the nine and then to the king, *or* lead to the jack and then to the king. The last two lines will be better if East is more likely to be short in the suit Lead small to the king and then back to the jack or nine	1 76	 0.77
535.	K x x J x x	2 1 Max	Lead small to the king, hoping that West has the ace-queen doubleton Lead small to the king and then small to the jack (best), *or* lead small to the jack and then small to the king. The latter line will be better if East is more likely to be short in the suit* (*But if East would play an honor from AQ and others, lead small toward the jack, and duck whatever happens; then lead small to the king) Lead small to the king and then small to the jack	1 74 79	 0.75

(c) Declarer Has Seven Cards

536.	K J 9 8 x x x	3 2 Max	Finesse the eight, hoping that the queen and ten are both with West Finesse the eight; if this loses to the ten, finesse the nine next (best), *or* finesse the jack, and then finesse the eight Finesse the eight and then the nine	24 76	 2.00

Dummy Declarer	Tricks Required		% Chance of Success	Tricks per Deal

VII. THE DEFENSE HAS SIX POINTS (cont'd)
A. THE ACE-QUEEN (cont'd)

537.	K 10 8 x	3	Finesse the eight	20
	J x x	2	Finesse the ten. If it loses to the queen, lead small to the jack and then to the king; if the ten loses to the ace, finesse the eight next	79
		Max	Finesse the eight. If this loses to the nine, finesse the ten next	1.95
538.	K 10 x x	3	Finesse the ten, hoping that West has AQ or AQx	9
	J x x	2	Lead small to the king; then lead small to the ten	69
		Max	Finesse the ten. If this loses to the queen, lead small to the king next	1.76
539.	K 9 8 7	3	Run the jack, hoping that East has the singleton ten	1
	J x x	2	Run the jack, and then finesse the nine. If the ace appears from West on the first round, finesse the nine, and if necessary, the eight (best), *or* finesse the nine. If this loses to the queen, lead to the jack next; if the ace appears from West, finesse the nine next; if the nine loses to the ten, finesse the eight next*	76
			(*But if West would not falsecard with AQ10 or AQ10x, run the nine. If this loses to the ten, finesse the seven next; otherwise run the eight.	77
			And if East is tempted to play an honor from AQxxx)	78
		Max	Run the jack. If it loses to the ace or queen from East, lead small to the nine next; if the ace appears from West on the first round, finesse the nine and, if necessary, the eight	1.77
540.	K x x x	2	Lead small to the jack, and then small to the ten. This fails only when West has AQ doubleton, AQ and at least two others, or the singleton or doubleton queen	75
	J 10 x			
541.	K x x x	2	Lead small to the nine. If the ten or queen appears from East, lead small from the king next; otherwise lead small to the king	47
	J 9 x	1 } Max }	Lead small to the nine, then small to the jack, and then small to the king. This fails only when West has the Q10 doubleton	98	1.36
542.	K x x x	2 } Max }	Lead to the jack, and then, unless the queen appears from East, lead to the king, *or* lead to the king and then to the jack. The latter line will be better if West is more likely to be short in the suit	26	1.12
	J x x	1	Lead small from both hands; then, unless the queen has appeared from West, lead to the jack; then lead to the king. This fails only when West has Qx	94

(d) Declarer Has Eight Cards

543.	K 10 8 x x	4	Run the jack. If this is covered, finesse the eight next	25
	J x x	3	Finesse the ten, and run the jack if it loses to the ace (best), *or* lead small to the king, and then small to the jack	90
		Max	Finesse the ten; if this loses to the ace, run the jack	3.12

Dummy Declarer	Tricks Required		% Chance of Success	Tricks per Deal

VII. THE DEFENSE HAS SIX POINTS (cont'd)
A. THE ACE-QUEEN (cont'd)

544.	K 9 8 x x J x x	4	Lead small to the king, hoping that West has the AQ only	3	
		3	Lead small to the eight. If it loses to the ten, finesse the nine next; if the ace appears from West on the first round, lead small to the jack	84	
		MAX	Finesse the eight. If it loses to the ten, finesse the nine next; if the ace appears from West on the first round, lead small to the king		2.82
545.	K x x x x J 10 x	4	Lead small to the king, hoping that West has the AQ only	3	2.83
		3 } MAX }	Lead small to the jack, and then small to the ten	85	
		2	Lead small to the jack. This fails only when East is void	98	
546.	K x x x x J 9 x	4	Lead small to the king, hoping that West has AQ doubleton	3	2.58
		3 } MAX }	Lead small to the nine and then small to the king	63	
		2	Lead small to the nine, and then small to the jack. This fails only if East is void	98	
547.	K J 9 8 x x x x	3	Finesse the eight	27	
		2	Finesse the eight and then the jack (best), or finesse the jack and then the eight, or lead small to the king	83	
		MAX	Finesse the eight; if it loses to the ten, finesse the jack		2.10
548.	K 10 8 x J x x x	3	Run the jack. If this is covered, finesse the eight next	27	
		2	Finesse the ten. If this loses to the queen, lead small to the jack; if the ten loses to the ace, run the jack (best), or lead small to the king, and then small to the jack	92	
		MAX	Finesse the ten. If this loses to the queen, lead small to the jack; if the ten loses to the ace, run the jack		2.16
549.	K 9 8 7 J x x x	3	Lead small to the king, hoping that West has the ace-queen doubleton or the queen singleton	6	1.94
		2 } MAX }	Finesse the nine. If this loses to the queen, lead small to the jack; if the nine loses to the ten, finesse the eight	88	
550.	K x x x J 10 8 x	3 } MAX }	Run the jack. If the ace appears from West, run the ten next; if the jack loses to the ace from East, guess whether to lead small or run the ten next; if the jack is covered, guess whether to lead to the ten or to the eight next*	14	
			(*This assumes that West will always play the ace from ace-queen doubleton and will cover with Qx about half the time, which is the best defense. If he always covers with Qx, lead to the eight if the jack is covered, lead the ten if the jack loses to the ace from East, and run the ten if the ace appears from West on the first round	17	2.01
			Similarly, if West never covers with Qx, lead small to the king if the jack loses to the ace from East, lead to the ten if the jack is covered, and run the ten if the ace appears from West on the first round)	17	2.01

Dummy Declarer	Tricks Required		% Chance of Success	Tricks per Deal

VII. THE DEFENSE HAS SIX POINTS (cont'd)

A. THE ACE-QUEEN (cont'd)

Dummy Declarer	Tricks Required		% Chance of Success	Tricks per Deal
	2	Lead small to the jack, and then small to the king. This fails only when East has a void or a small singleton	92	
551. K x x x J 10 x x	3	Lead small to the king, hoping that West has AQ doubleton	3	
	2	Lead small to the king and then small to the jack, *or* lead small to the jack. The latter line will be better if East is more likely to be short in the suit	87	
	MAX	Lead small to the king, and then small to the jack		1.90
552. K x x x J 9 x x	3	Lead small to the king, hoping that West has AQ doubleton	3	
	2 ⎱ MAX ⎰	Lead small to the king and then small to the nine	70	1.71
	1	Lead small to the nine (best), *or* lead toward the king, and duck if West fails to play an honor, *or* lead small to the jack	100	
553. K x x x J x x x	3	Lead small to the king, hoping that West has AQ doubleton	3	
	2	Lead toward the king, and duck if the queen fails to appear; then lead to the king (best), *or* lead to the king and then to the jack	50	
	1 ⎱ MAX ⎰	Lead toward the king, and duck if the queen fails to appear; then lead to the king and finally to the jack	100	1.54

(e) Declarer Has Nine Cards

Dummy Declarer	Tricks Required		% Chance of Success	Tricks per Deal
554. K J 9 x x x x x x*	4 MAX	Lead small to the jack Lead small to the jack	33	3.17
555. K J x x x x x x x*	4 MAX	Lead small to the jack Lead small to the jack	33	3.11
556. K 9 8 7 x J x x x*	4 3 MAX	Lead small to the king Lead small to the nine (best), *or* run the nine Lead small to the king	27 94	3.16
557. K x x x x J 10 9 8*	4	Run the jack	50	
558. K x x x x J 10 x x*	4 3 MAX	Lead small to the king Lead small to the king, in case West is void Lead small to the king	33 95	3.28
		*N.B. Similar principles apply if declarer's nine cards are distributed differently between his hand and dummy		

(f) Declarer Has Ten Cards

Dummy Declarer	Tricks Required		% Chance of Success	Tricks per Deal
559. K J x x x x 10 x x x*	5	Finesse the jack	63	
560. K x x x x x J 10 9 x*	5	Run the jack	63	
		*N.B. Similar principles apply if declarer's ten cards are distributed differently between his hand and dummy		

Dummy Declarer	Tricks Required		% Chance of Success	Tricks per Deal

B. THE KING-QUEEN-JACK

(a) Declarer Has Five Cards

561.	A 10 9 8 x	2	Finesse the ten, and then play the ace	25	

(b) Declarer Has Six Cards

562.	A 10 9 8 x x	3 ⎫ MAX ⎬ 2	Finesse the ten, and then play the ace	16	1.99
			Play the ace, and then lead low from the 1098; this gains a trick when East has a singleton or doubleton honor	87	
563.	A 10 9 8 x x	2	Finesse the ten and then the nine	77	

(c) Declarer Has Seven Cards

564.	A 10 9 8 x x x	4 ⎫ MAX ⎬ 3 2	Finesse the ten, and then cash the ace	65	3.55
			Finesse the ten, and then play the ace (best), *or* play the ace	91	
			Finesse the ten, in case East is void	99	
565.	A 10 9 8 x x x	3 ⎫ MAX ⎬ 2	Finesse the ten and then the nine; then play the ace	74	2.70
			Finesse the ten and then the nine (best), *or* play the ace	96	
566.	A 10 9 8 x x x	2	Finesse the eight, nine, and, if necessary, ten	89	
567.	A 10 9 x x x x	2	Finesse the ten and then the nine; then play the ace	68	
568.	A 10 x x 9 x x	2	Lead small to the nine. If this loses to West, finesse the ten next. If an honor appears from East on the first round, lead small to the nine again; if East shows out or plays another honor, finesse the ten next; otherwise play to the ace	51	

(d) Declarer Has Eight Cards

569.	A 10 9 8 x x x x	5 ⎫ MAX ⎬ 4	Play the ace, in case East has a singleton honor	85	4.81
			Finesse the ten, in case East is void	98	
570.	A 10 9 8 x x x x	4 ⎫ MAX ⎬ 3	Finesse the ten and then the nine	90	3.88
			Finesse the ten and then the nine	98	
571.	A 10 9 8 x x x x	3 ⎫ MAX ⎬ 2	Finesse the ten and then the nine	92	2.90
			Finesse the ten and then the nine	98	
572.	A 10 x x x 9 x x	3 2 ⎫ MAX ⎬	Play the ace, and lead small to the nine	85	
			Lead small to the nine and then small to the ten	100	2.82
573.	A 8 7 x x 10 x x	3 ⎫ MAX ⎬ 2	Run the ten, *or* lead small to the ten, in case East has the singleton nine	71	2.69
			Run the ten, *or* lead small to the ten, in case East is void	98	

Dummy Declarer	Tricks Required		% Chance of Success	Tricks per Deal

VII. THE DEFENSE HAS SIX POINTS (cont'd)
B. THE KING-QUEEN-JACK (cont'd)

| 574. | A 10 9 8 | 2 | Finesse the ten and then the nine; this fails only | | |
| | x x x x | | when West has a void or a small singleton | 92 | |

(e) Declarer Has Nine Cards

575.	A 10 9 8 x x x x	7	Play the ace, hoping for a 2–2 division	41	
	x	6 ⎱	Finesse the ten, and then play the ace	95	6.36
		Max ⎰			
576.	A 10 9 x x x x	6	Play the ace, hoping for a 2–2 division	41	
	x x	5 ⎱	Finesse the ten, and then play the ace	95	5.36
		Max ⎰			
577.	A 10 x x x x	5	Play the ace	41	
	9 x x	4	Lead small to the ten, *or* lead small to the nine	95	
		Max	Lead small to the ten or nine; then play the ace		4.36
578.	A 10 x x x	4	Play the ace, hoping for a 2–2 division	41	
	9 x x x	3	Lead small to the ten or nine	95	
		Max	Lead small to the ten or nine; then play the ace		3.36

VIII. THE DEFENSE HAS SEVEN POINTS
A. THE ACE-KING

(a) Declarer Has Five Cards

579.	Q J 9 8	2	Finesse the eight. If it loses to the ace or king		
	x		on either side, lead the queen and jack next	11	
580.	Q J 9	1	Lead to the queen and then to the jack	78	
	x x				
581.	Q 9 x	1	Lead small to the jack. If it loses to West,		
	J x		finesse the nine next	62	
582.	Q x x	1	Finesse the nine	51	
	J 9				

(b) Declarer Has Six Cards

583.	Q J 9 8	2	Finesse the nine	51	
	x x				
584.	Q x x x	1	Finesse the nine. If it loses to the ten, play the		
	J 9		jack and then low from the queen*	56	
			(*This is only fractionally better than leading		
			small to the jack and then ducking two rounds,		
			and the latter line might be better if East is		
			more likely to be short in the suit)		
585.	Q J 9	1	Lead to the queen and then to the jack	79	
	x x x				
586.	Q 9 x	1	Lead small to the jack. If it loses to West, finesse		
	J x x		the nine next	64	
587.	Q x x	1	Lead to either honor and then back to the other	49	
	J x x				

(c) Declarer Has Seven Cards

588.	Q J 9 x x	3 ⎱	Lead to the queen and then to the jack	38	2.12
	x x	Max ⎰			
		2	Finesse the nine, and then lead to the queen	80	
		1	Lead to the queen and then to the nine or jack		
			(best), *or* finesse the nine, and then lead to		
			the queen	96	

Dummy Declarer	Tricks Required		% Chance of Success	Tricks per Deal

VIII. THE DEFENSE HAS SEVEN POINTS (cont'd)
A. THE ACE-KING (cont'd)

589.	Q J x x x 9 x	3 } MAX }	Lead to the queen and then to the jack	30	1.98
		2	Lead to the queen and then to the jack	73	
		1	Lead small to the nine. This fails only when West has the singleton ten	99	
590.	Q J 9 8 x x x	2 } MAX }	Lead small to the queen. If it loses, finesse the nine next	63	1.63
591.	Q J 9 x x x x	2 } MAX }	Lead small to the queen. If it loses, finesse the nine next	55	1.46
592.	Q J x x 9 x x	2 } MAX }	Lead to the queen and then to the jack	49	1.38
		1	Lead small to the queen. If it loses, lead small to the nine and then small to the jack. This fails only when West has the doubleton ten	95	
593.	Q J x x x x x	2 } MAX }	Lead to the queen and then to the jack	45	1.28
		1	Lead to the queen; if it loses, duck one round, and then lead to the jack (best), *or* duck one round, and then lead to the queen and jack	85	
594.	Q 9 8 x J x x	2	Lead small to the jack. If it loses to West, finesse the nine next; if an honor appears from East on the first round, lead to the jack again	56	
595.	Q x x x J 9 x	2 } MAX }	Lead small to the nine. If it loses to a high honor from West, lead small to the queen; otherwise lead small to the jack	33	1.30
		1	Lead small to the nine and then small to the jack. This fails only if West has A10 or K10	97	
596.	Q x x x J x x	2	Lead small to the queen or jack, and then back to the other honor, hoping to find either opponent with AKx or the right opponent with AK doubleton	16	
		1	Lead toward the jack and duck; then lead to the jack and to the queen. This fails only when West has Kx or Ax	87	
		MAX	Lead small to the jack. If it loses, duck the next round, and then lead to the queen		0.93

(d) Declarer Has Eight Cards

597.	Q J 10 6 x x 8 x	4 } MAX }	Lead to the queen and then to the jack	85	3.83
		3	Lead small to the eight, in case West is void	100	
598.	Q J 9 8 7 x x x	3	Lead small to the queen. If it loses, finesse the nine	75	
599.	Q J x x x x x x	3 } MAX }	Lead to the queen and then to the jack	63	2.50
600.	Q 10 9 6 x J x x	3 } MAX }	Lead the jack, in case East is void	98	2.98
601.	Q x x x x J 9 x	3	Lead small to the queen. If it loses to East, finesse the nine next; if an honor appears from West on the first round, lead to the queen again	48	
		2 } MAX }	Lead small to the nine and then small to the jack. This fails only if East is void	98	2.41
602.	Q J 9 8 x x x x	2	Lead small to the queen. If it loses, finesse the nine	77	

Dummy Declarer	Tricks Required		% Chance of Success	Tricks per Deal

VIII. THE DEFENSE HAS SEVEN POINTS (cont'd)
A. THE ACE-KING (cont'd)

603.	Q 9 8 7 J x x	2	Lead small to the jack. If it loses to West, finesse the nine next	66	
604.	Q 9 x x J x x x	2 } Max } 1	Lead small to the jack. If it loses to West, finesse the nine next Finesse the nine (best), *or* lead small to the queen and then small to the jack, in case West has a bare honor	64 100	1.58
605.	Q x x x J x x x	2 } Max } 1	Lead to the queen (or jack); if it loses, duck the next round Duck the first round, and then lead small to either honor	37 100	1.32

(e) Declarer Has Nine Cards

606.	Q J 7 x x x x 9 x	5 } Max } 4	Lead small to the queen and then to the jack Lead small to the nine, in case West is void	84 100	4.79
607.	Q x x x x x J 9 x	4	Finesse the nine. This only fails when West has AK10x, AK10, or 10	83	
608.	Q J 8 x x 10 7 x x	3 } Max }	Lead small to the queen, in case either opponent is void	100	3.00
609.	Q J x x x x x x x	3 } Max }	Lead small to the queen and then small to the jack	83	2.78
610.	Q 9 x x x J x x x	3	Lead small to the jack and then small to the queen, *or* finesse the nine. The latter line will be better if West is more likely to be short in the suit	83	

B. THE ACE-QUEEN-JACK

(a) Declarer Has Five Cards

611.	K 10 9 x x	1	Finesse the ten and then the nine	78	
612.	K 10 x x x	1	Finesse the ten and then lead to the king	63	

(b) Declarer Has Six Cards

613.	K 10 9 8 x x	2	Finesse the ten and then the nine	50	
614.	K 10 9 x x x	1	Finesse the ten and then the nine	79	

(c) Declarer Has Seven Cards

615.	K 10 9 8 x x x	2	Finesse the eight and then the nine	76	
616.	K 10 9 x x x x	2 } Max }	Finesse the nine and then the ten	61	1.51
617.	K 10 x x 9 x x	2 } Max } 1	Lead small to the ten and then small to the king Lead small to the king, and then, unless an honor appears from West, small to the nine (best), *or* lead to the ten and then to the nine	37 90	1.25

Dummy Declarer	Tricks Required		% Chance of Success	Tricks per Deal

VIII. THE DEFENSE HAS SEVEN POINTS (cont'd)
B. THE ACE-QUEEN-JACK (cont'd)

	Dummy Declarer	Tricks Required		% Chance of Success	Tricks per Deal
618.	K 10 x x x x x	2 } Max	Lead small to the ten and then small to the king	32	1.08
		1	Duck one round; then lead finesse the ten, and lead to the king	79	
619.	K 9 8 7 x x x	2	Lead to the nine and then to the king (best), *or* lead to the king, hoping that West has the ace and two other cards	18	
		1 } Max	Finesse the seven and then the eight. This fails only if West has xx, x, or a void	95	1.11
620.	K x x x x x x	2	Duck one round, and then lead to the king (best), *or* lead to the king, hoping that West has the ace and two other cards	18	
		1	Duck two rounds, and then lead to the king	77	
		Max	Duck one round, and then lead to the king		0.87

(d) Declarer Has Eight Cards

621.	K 10 9 x x x x x	3 } Max	Finesse the ten and then the nine	75	2.66
		2	Finesse the ten and nine (best), *or* lead to the king	92	
622.	K 10 x x x 9 x x	3 } Max	Finesse the ten, and then lead small to the king	63	2.56
		2	Finesse the ten. If it loses to the jack or queen, lead small to the nine next. This fails only if West is void	98	
623.	K 10 9 8 x x x x	2	Finesse the eight and then the nine	83	
624.	K 10 x x x x x x	2 } Max	Finesse the ten, and then lead to the king	52	1.38
625.	K x x x x x x x	2	Lead small to the king, preferably ducking one round first	34	
		1	Duck one round. Then either lead small to the king (best), *or* duck a second round	87	
		Max	Duck one round, and then lead small to the king		1.21

(e) Declarer Has Nine Cards

626.	K 10 9 x x x x x x	5	Lead small to the king, hoping that West has the doubleton ace	20	
		4 } Max	Finesse the ten. This gains a trick when East is void or has the singleton ace	89	3.98
627.	K 10 x x x x 9 x x	5	Lead small to the king, hoping that West has the doubleton ace	20	
		4 } Max	Finesse the ten, and then lead small to the king	89	4.03
628.	K 8 x x x x 10 x x	5 } Max	Lead small to the king, hoping that West has the doubleton ace	20	3.94
		4	Lead toward the king, and play the king if the nine fails to appear from West*	84	
			(*But West should falsecard from QJ9)	78	
		3	Lead small to the ten	100	
629.	K x x x x x x x x	5 } Max	Lead small to the king, hoping that West has the doubleton ace	20	3.81
		4	Duck one round, and then lead small to the king	72	

Dummy Declarer	Tricks Required		% Chance of Success	Tricks per Deal

VIII. THE DEFENSE HAS SEVEN POINTS (cont'd)

B. THE ACE-QUEEN-JACK (cont'd)

	Dummy Declarer	Tricks Required		% Chance of Success	Tricks per Deal
630.	K 9 x x x x x x x	4 } Max } 3	Lead small to the king, hoping that West has the doubleton ace Duck one round, and then lead small to the king	20 72	2.81
631.	K 8 x x x 10 x x x	4 } Max } 3	Lead small to the king, hoping West has the doubleton ace Lead toward the king, and play the king if the nine fails to appear from West* (*But West should falsecard from QJ9)	20 84 78	2.98

IX. THE DEFENSE HAS EIGHT POINTS

(a) Declarer Has Five Cards

	Dummy Declarer	Tricks Required		% Chance of Success	Tricks per Deal
632.	Q 10 9 8 x	2	Finesse the ten, hoping that West has J, AJ, KJ, or Jx	2	
633.	Q 10 x x x	1	Finesse the ten, and then lead to the queen	37	

(b) Declarer Has Six Cards

	Dummy Declarer	Tricks Required		% Chance of Success	Tricks per Deal
634.	Q 10 9 8 x x	2	Finesse the ten and then the nine	18	
635.	Q 10 x x x x	2 1 } Max }	Lead to the queen, hoping that West has the AKJ only Lead to the ten and then to the queen	1 41	0.42
636.	Q 10 9 x x x	1	Finesse the ten and then the nine	51	
637.	Q 10 x x x x	1	Finesse the ten, and then lead to the queen	38	

(c) Declarer Has Seven Cards

	Dummy Declarer	Tricks Required		% Chance of Success	Tricks per Deal
638.	Q 10 x x x x x	3 } Max } 2 1	Lead to the ten and then to the queen Lead to the ten and queen Lead to the ten and queen	12 55 91	1.58
639.	Q 10 x x x x x	2 } Max } 1	Lead to the ten and then to the queen Lead to the ten and queen (best), *or* duck one round and then lead to the ten and queen, *or* lead to the queen and then to the ten	22 68	0.89
640.	Q 9 8 7 x x x	2 1 } Max }	Lead small to the queen Finesse the seven and then the eight	7 85	0.88
641.	Q x x x 10 9 x	2 1 } Max }	Lead small to the queen, hoping that West has AKx or AKJ Lead small to the ten and then small to the nine. This fails only when West has AJ or KJ	7 97	0.97
642.	Q x x x 10 x x	2 1 } Max }	Lead small to the queen, hoping that West has AKx or AKJ Lead small to the ten. If an honor appears from East, lead small to the ten again; if the ten loses to West on the first round, duck one round, and then lead to the queen	7 70	0.70

(d) Declarer Has Eight Cards

	Dummy Declarer	Tricks Required		% Chance of Success	Tricks per Deal
643.	Q 10 x x x x x x	3 } Max } 2	Finesse the ten, and then lead to the queen Finesse the ten, and then lead to the queen, in case East is void	33 84	2.15

	Dummy Declarer	Tricks Required		% Chance of Success	Tricks per Deal

IX. THE DEFENSE HAS EIGHT POINTS (cont'd)

644.	Q x x x x 10 x x	3	Lead small to the queen. If the jack appears from West, cover with the queen, and duck the next round; if the ace or king appears on the first round, lead to the queen again	20	
		2 ⎫ MAX ⎬	Lead toward the queen, and duck the trick. If an honor appears on the first round, lead small to the ten next; otherwise lead to the queen	90	1.95
		1	Lead small to the ten, in case West is void	100	
645.	Q x x x x x x x	3 ⎫ MAX ⎬	Lead small to the queen	14	1.88
		2	Duck one round, and then, unless the ace or king appears from East, lead small to the queen	82	
646.	Q 10 x x x x x x	2 ⎫ MAX ⎬	Finesse the ten, and then lead to the queen	35	1.19
647.	Q x x x 10 x x x	2 ⎫ MAX ⎬	Lead small to the queen, and then, unless the jack appears from West, lead small to the ten	20	1.15
		1	Lead small to the queen and then small to the ten, *or* lead from the ten, and duck unless the jack appears from West; then, unless the ace or king appears from East, lead small to the queen. The latter line will be better if East is more likely to be short in the suit	94	
648.	Q x x x x x x x	2	Lead small to the queen	14	
		1	Duck one round, and then lead small to the queen	84	
		MAX	Lead small to the queen		0.92

(e) Declarer Has Nine Cards

649.	Q 10 9 x x x x x x *	3 MAX	Finesse the ten Finesse the ten	70	2.66
650.	Q x x x x x x x x *	3 ⎫ MAX ⎬	Lead small to the queen, *or* duck one round, and then lead small to the queen *N.B. Similar principles apply if declarer's nine cards are distributed differently between his hand and dummy.	53	2.48

X. THE DEFENSE HAS NINE POINTS

(a) Declarer Has Seven Cards

651.	J 10 8 x x x x	1	Lead to the jack, and then either lead to the ten or finesse the eight	73	
652.	J 10 x x x x x	1	Lead to the jack and then to the ten	68	
653.	J x x x 10 x x	1	Lead small to the ten. If it loses to West, duck the next round, and then lead small to the jack	69	

(b) Declarer Has Eight Cards

654.	J x x x x 10 x x	2 ⎫ MAX ⎬	Lead small to the ten. If it loses to West, lead small to the jack	88	1.88
		1	Lead small to the ten	100	
655.	J 10 x x x x x x	1	Lead small to the jack and then small to the ten	84	
656.	J x x x 10 x x x	1	Lead small to the jack (or ten). If it loses, lead small to the other honor	92	

E. C.

SUIT DISTRIBUTION. There are 39 possible suit distributions. For the percentage play in handling any combination, see SUIT COMBINATIONS. For relative frequency of the occurence of each pattern, see MATHEMATICAL TABLES, Table 1.

SUIT OPENING BID. See OPENING SUIT BID.

SUIT PATTERNS. For the 39 suit patterns, ranging from a balanced 4–3–3–3 to an outlandish 13–0–0–0, and the percentage frequency of each, see MATHEMATICAL TABLES, Table 1.

SUIT PLACING. The process of marking during the bidding the suit lengths around the table. See CARD READING; COUNTING THE HAND.

SUIT PREFERENCE SIGNAL. A device in defensive play whereby a player may indicate a desire to have his partner lead one suit rather than another, when his partner has a choice. This method, devised by HY LAVINTHAL in 1934, has had a greater effect on expert play than any other development of the 20th century and ranks with the HIGH-LOW SIGNAL and distributional echo of the 19th century. In various countries the suit preference signal is known by the names of bridge writers, especially WILLIAM E. McKENNEY and B. JAY BECKER, who adopted and publicized it but did not otherwise contribute to it.

The signal never applies to the suit led to the current trick, and seldom to the trump suit, so it is designed to guide partner's choice between the other two suits. The essence of the suit preference signal is this: When partner, having the lead, seems likely to switch suits or when partner may have a choice of suits when next he obtains the lead, the play of a conspicuously high card calls for a lead in the higher-ranking suit in question, the play of a conspicuously low card calls for the lead of the lower-ranking suit.

Properly used, the suit preference signal does not interfere with conventional encouraging and discouraging plays and discards.

In the following example, the suit played is significant, so a suit preference does not apply, and the signal is a standard COME-ON.

```
              ♠ A K Q J 10
              ♡ A K Q J 10
              ◊ 7
              ♣ 8 4
 ♠ 8 6 5                      ♠ 9 4 3
 ♡ 9 6 3 2                    ♡ 8 7
 ◊ A K 10 8 2                 ◊ Q J 6 5 4
 ♣ 6                          ♣ K 5 3
              ♠ 7 2
              ♡ 5 4
              ◊ 9 3
              ♣ A Q J 10 9 7 2
```

Against South's 6♣ contract, West opens the ◊K. Glancing at the dummy, East may feel quite pessimistic, for at first glance, his king of trumps looks as if it will be trapped. But on further examination, East sees that if he can get his partner to continue diamonds, dummy will be reduced to one trump, and the ♣K becomes untrappable. So on the lead of

the ◊K, he plays the unnecessarily high ◊Q, and when West continues the suit, forcing dummy to ruff, declarer can no longer take two finesses through the ♣K.

The suit preference signal, at superficial glance, may appear to be related to East's come-on signal of the ◊Q in the above hand. Actually there is no relationship whatsoever.

```
              ♠ K Q J 2
              ♡ K 6
              ◊ K Q 10 7
              ♣ 8 6 3
 ♠ 3                          ♠ 6
 ♡ A J 8 5 4                  ♡ Q 10 7 3 2
 ◊ 8 5 3 2                    ◊ A 9 6 4
 ♣ 10 5 2                     ♣ 9 7 4
              ♠ A 10 9 8 7 5 4
              ♡ 9
              ◊ J
              ♣ A K Q J
```

How North–South arrived at a 6♠ contract, missing two aces, is irrelevant. Sufficient to say that it probably happens every day in every bridge club in the country. In a fair proportion of these situations, certainly, the defense slips, and declarer "steals" his unmakable contract.

Against the contract, West opened the ♡A, which won the trick. At a loss as to what to play next, West decided to shift to a club, and declarer waltzed home with his contract, discarding his diamond on the ♡K. Had West shifted to a diamond at trick two, East would have cashed his ace. How could the defenders have gotten together to direct their defense? Answer: the suit preference signal.

The purpose of this signal is to eliminate the guesswork as to which of two suits partner should lead in situations like the one above. The reference to "two suits" may appear to be a typographical error, but actually it is not. Of the four suits, the trump suit is automatically eliminated, for when partner gives any signal whatsoever, it is never to direct the lead of the trump suit. Also, the suit being led, on which the suit-preference signal is being given, is excluded. That leaves the leader with a choice to two "obvious" suits. In the deal presented, after West cashed his ♡A, either a heart continuation or a trump lead were "impossible" plays. So it became a choice of clubs or diamonds.

On the lead of the ♡A, had East-West been employing this suit preference signal, East would have played the ♡Q (or the 10) which, on examination of the dummy, should not have been construed as asking for a heart continuation. The ♡Q would have said to West: "Play the higher ranking of the two obvious suits!"

Stating the suit preference signal as a principle, it comes to this: Whenever partner plays an unnecessarily high card which is obviously not a come-on-in-this-suit signal, it commands partner to lead the higher of the other two nontrump suits; whenever partner plays a very low card which is obviously not a no-interest-in-this-suit signal, that low card asks partner to shift to the lower of the two suits. If the partner of the leader has no interest in either of the two obvious suits, he will play some intermediate card in the suit being led.

When correctly applied, the play of either an unnecessarily high card or an obviously low card will be unmistakable. Partner will (almost) invariably make the right shift when he is properly directed.

It was mentioned that this convention is misapplied by a great many bridge players. The reason behind this is that offenders attempt to apply it indiscriminately.

♠ A K 6
♡ K 7 5
◇ J 8 7 3
♣ 9 4 2

♠ 9 5 4 2
♡ Q 6 3
◇ Q 9 6 2
♣ A 6

Against South's 4♠ contract, West elects to open the ♣A, East plays the 10, and South, declarer, the three-spot. West, having discovered only recently the new toy called a suit preference signal, now demonstrates his recently acquired "knowledge" by banging down the ♡Q, saying to himself, "My partner's ♣10 was a command to me to lead the higher of the two obvious suits." Utter nonsense! East wanted clubs continued, and so he, in conventional fashion, played the unnecessarily high ten-spot. The suit preference signal is used only when it *must be obvious* that another suit is wanted.

The actual deal was:

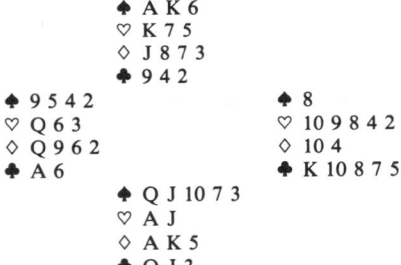

♠ A K 6
♡ K 7 5
◇ J 8 7 3
♣ 9 4 2

♠ 9 5 4 2   ♠ 8
♡ Q 6 3   ♡ 10 9 8 4 2
◇ Q 9 6 2   ◇ 10 4
♣ A 6   ♣ K 10 8 7 5

♠ Q J 10 7 3
♡ A J
◇ A K 5
♣ Q J 3

Probably the most frequent situation in which the suit preference signal is applied is when leading a suit which partner is obviously going to trump. It is necessary to direct him to play back a specific suit so that another ruff can be secured. The RANK of the card led when giving him the first ruff becomes the clear-cut signal; if an unnecessarily high card is led, partner is to return the higher of the two obvious suits (trumps and the suit being led are eliminated); if an obviously low card is led, he is to return the lower-ranking of the two suits. (See hand at top of next column.)

Against South's 4♠ contract, West opens the ♣3, dummy plays the jack, and East's ace captures the trick. It is, of course, perfectly apparent to East that the three-spot is a singleton, for it could not be fourth best, nor could it be the top of a worthless doubleton. So East is going to return a club for West to trump, and employing the suit preference signal, he returns the *10*. When West trumps the trick, he recognizes the ten-spot as being unnecessarily high, and he now plays back a heart (as opposed to a dia-

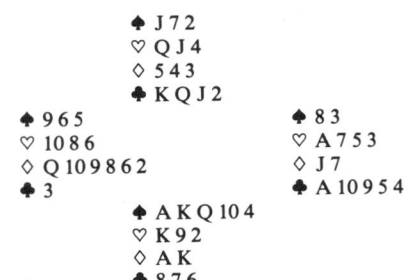

♠ J 7 2
♡ Q J 4
◇ 5 4 3
♣ K Q J 2

♠ 9 6 5   ♠ 8 3
♡ 10 8 6   ♡ A 7 5 3
◇ Q 10 9 8 6 2   ◇ J 7
♣ 3   ♣ A 10 9 5 4

♠ A K Q 10 4
♡ K 9 2
◇ A K
♣ 8 7 6

mond) which East wins, returning another club for West to trump for the setting trick. It is apparent that if West had not played back a heart, declarer would have captured any other return, drawn trumps, and fulfilled his contract.

Suppose this had been the situation:

♠ J 7 2
♡ Q J 4
◇ 5 4 3
♣ K Q J 2

              ♠ 8 3
              ♡ 9 7 5 3
              ◇ A 7
              ♣ A 10 9 5 4

The ♣3 is led, and upon winning the opening lead, East would now lead back the ♣4, an obviously low card, directing West to return the lower of the two nontrump suits (diamonds rather than hearts); and upon this return, East would now give his partner another ruff.

In expert circles, the suit preference convention has been extended to cover situations where the signal is given on the play of some side suit (any suit except the trump suit). The signal is made by high-low discards.

Fred Karpin

SUIT SIGNALS. See LENGTH SIGNALS.

SUIT TAKE-OUT. See RESPONSE.

SUMMARY SHEET. See RECAPITULATION SHEET.

SUMMER NORTH AMERICAN CHAMPION-SHIPS. Formerly called the Summer Nationals. This annual tournament held since 1929 takes place in July or early August. These championships, usually the largest of the three North American Championships, were originally under the auspices of the AMERICAN BRIDGE LEAGUE, and since 1938 have been controlled by the AMERICAN CONTRACT BRIDGE LEAGUE. In the Thirties they were played at Asbury Park NJ and lasted eight days. In postwar years the program was gradually enlarged to nine days, and in 1969 it became a ten-day tournament.

In 1930 the knockout team event attracted an entry of 16 teams, and 22 pairs were entered in the Master Pairs for the von Zedtwitz Gold Cup. In the postwar years the size of the tournaments expanded rapidly, partly as a result of the impetus given by the masterpoint scheme. A peak was reached in 1979 in Las Vegas with 18,517 tables, an all-time world record. For past results of Summer North American

Championships, see Appendix 1.

The selection of cities and hotels for such mammoth tournaments presents great problems. Allocation are usually made five years in advance. See also NORTH AMERICAN CHAMPIONSHIPS.

SUMMER NORTH AMERICAN CHAMPIONSHIPS

Year	Site	Tables	Year	Site	Tables
1929	Chicago		1968	Minneapolis	9,857
1930–41	Asbury Park		1969	Los Angeles	11,470
1942–47	New York City		1970	Boston	12,584
1948–49	Chicago		1971	Chicago	13,566
1950	Columbus		1972	Denver	11,449
1951	Washington		1973	Washington D.C.	16,043
1952	Cincinnati	3,093	1974	New York City	15,310
1953	St. Louis	3,054	1975	Miami Beach	10,368
1954	Washington	4,496	1976	Salt Lake City	10,722
1955	Chicago	4,619	1977	Chicago	13,170
1956	New York City	5,679	1978	Toronto	18,408
1957	Pittsburgh	5,625	1979	Las Vegas	18,517
1958	Miami	4,068	1980	Chicago	11,889
1959	Chicago	6,939	1981	Boston	14,079
1960	Los Angeles	8,462	1982	Albuquerque	9,776
1961	Washington	7,989	1983	New Orleans	
1962	Minneapolis	5,820	1984	Washington	
1963	Los Angeles	12,486	1985	Las Vegas	
1964	Toronto	11,150	1986	Toronto	
1965	Chicago	14,511	1987	Baltimore	
1966	Denver	10,112	1988	Salt Lake City	
1967	Montreal	10,926			

SUOMEN BRIDGELIITTO. See FINNISH BRIDGE LEAGUE.

SUPER BLACKWOOD. A method of asking for aces when 4 NT would be a natural bid.

EASLEY BLACKWOOD lists three situations in which 4 NT woud be natural. (a) when the partnership has not bid a suit; (b) when no suit has been agreed, and the 4 NT bidder has previously bid notrump; (c) when no suit has been agreed, and a notrump bid immediately preceded 4 NT.

In each of these situations Blackwood suggests that a bid of four in the lowest-ranking unbid suit should ask for aces with step responses. A subsequent 5 NT bid asks for kings in the same way.

The Super Blackwood bid will usually be 4♣ which lines it up with the GERBER convention.

SUPER CONVENTION. See EXCLUSION BID.

SUPER GERBER. An ace-asking convention devised by ROBERT GOLDMAN for use when a minor suit fit has been established, or when the last bid was 3 NT, so that a 4 NT call would be natural. The Super Gerber bid is the lowest possible bid in an unbid suit or in a suit that cannot be deemed trumps; if all suits are unavailable or ambiguous, the Super Gerber bid is a jump to 5♣.

Over establishment of a minor suit fit, either expressly or by implication, the Super Gerber bid is a jump to four of the cheapest unbid suit:

(a)		(b)		(c)		(d)	
1♦	3♦	1♣	3♣	1♦	2♦	1♦	1♥
4♥		4♦		4♣		3♦	4♣

The last bid in each auction is Super Gerber. The use of Super Gerber in minor suit auctions is designed to allow 4 NT to be used as a balanced general strength slam try, and to provide an ace-asking bid that does not risk getting the partnership beyond the game level with too few aces.

Responses as used by the ACES TEAM are in steps as follows:

1st step	0 or 3 aces
2nd step	1 or 4 aces
3rd step	2 aces
4th step	2 aces with extra value outside the trump suit
5th step	2 aces and a useful void
higher step	1 ace and a useful void

In showing one ace and a void, the void suit is bid if it ranks lower than the trump suit; the trump suit is bid if the void suit is higher ranking.

SUPER PRECISION. A version of the PRECISION CLUB system used by GEORGIO BELLADONNA and BENITO GARROZO in which there are many specialized bids and asking sequences. It differs from standard Precision in the following essential respects:

Notrump responses to 1♣ are revised: 1 NT is enlarged to encompass hands worth 8–13 points. A 2 NT response shows 14 or more points, with no upper limit. A 3 NT response shows a solid seven-card suit, with or without a side suit stopper. Opener's rebids over 3 NT ask about high card controls, or identification of responder's suit.

Over interference with 1♣, controls are shown (A = 2, K = 1). After a one-level overcall, a double shows 6 or more points with 0–2 controls, 1 NT shows 3 controls and a stopper, 2♣ shows 3 controls without a stopper, 2♦ shows 4 controls, 2 NT shows 5 or more controls; bids of 3♣, 3♦, and one, two, or three of a major are all natural, showing 0–2 controls.

Over a two level overcall the double shows a balanced hand with as many as 3 controls; 2 NT shows 3 or 4 controls with a stopper; a cuebid shows 5 or more controls; suit bids are natural, showing unbalanced hands with 0–3 controls. Over a three level overcall the responses are similar.

2♦ opening may be 4-3-1-5 or 3-4-1-5 as well as 4-4-0-5 and 4-4-1-4. A 2 NT response asks for clarification of distribution and strength. 3♣ and 3♦ rebids show the hands with three spades and three hearts respectively; 3♥ and 3♠ rebids show 4-4-1-4 distribution, of minimum and maximum strength; 4♣ and 4♦ rebids shows 4-4-0-5 distribution of minimum and maximum strength.

Super Unusual Positive is used in responding to 1♣ with 4-4-4-1 hands. An immediate jump to 3♣ shows a singleton in a black suit, a jump to 3♦ shows a singleton in a red suit; both show minimum high card values. Opener's bid of the next suit asks where responder's singleton is: responder bids the first step with the minor suit singleton, or the second step with the major suit singleton. Immediate jump responses of 3♥, 3♠, 4♣, and 4♦ over 1♣ show maximum values and a singleton in the next higher suit. Opener's bid of the next suit (responder's short suit) asks for controls — first step = 4, second step = 5, etc.

Three level minor suit openings are offensive rather than purely preemptive. 3♣ shows a seven-playing-trick hand with a semi-solid club suit and an outside entry. 3♦ shows any solid seven-card suit with an outside entry (devised by OMAR SHARIF). In response to 3♦, 3♥ is a sign-off to play in opener's suit; 3 ♠ is a general constructive bid. Over 3 ♠ opener bids 3 NT if he has a minor suit, 4 ♣ if his suit is hearts and he has a side void or singleton, 4 ◇ if his suit is spades and he has a side void or singleton; 4♡ and 4♠ are natural and deny a side void or singleton. Responder may ask opener where his shortness lies.

3 NT opening shows a preemptive minor suit opening similar to standard openings of 4 ♣ or 4 ◇. Responder retreats with a weak hand by bidding 4 ♣ which opener passes if his suit is clubs, or corrects to 4 ◇.

Asking bids of several kinds are used after a 1 ♣ opening, each with its own series of responses. These include bids designated *Alpha*, in which opener asks about responder's support for opener's suit; *Beta*, in which opener asks about responder's length and strength in a particular suit; *Gamma* which asks about trump honors; *Delta*, which asks about length and strength in a specific suit after a notrump bid or STAYMAN response. See SUPER PRECISION ASKING BIDS.

SUPER PRECISION ASKING BIDS.

Any of a number of types of asking bids in the SUPER PRECISION system as played by GIORGIO BELLADONNA and BENITO GAROZZO, used by the 1 ♣ opener to ask a variety of questions, such as trump suit quality, high card or distributional controls, and responder's support for opener's suit.

Alpha Support Asking Bids. After a positive response in a suit, a new suit bid by opener asks about responder's support for opener's suit and his overall controls. Support is defined as Q–x–x or better. A hand with 0–2 controls is considered minimum, four or more controls is maximum, and three controls can be considered in either category. The responses are in five steps:

1st step	no suppport, minimum
2nd step	no suppport, maximum
3rd step	support, minimum
4th step	support, maximum
5th step	four cards, maximum

Further definition of responder's support may follow.

Beta Suit Asking Bids. After a negative 1 ◇ response to 1 ♣, a jump to 2 ♡ or 2 ♠ by opener is a Roman-style asking bid inquiring about responder's strength and length in that suit. The responses are the first eight steps set out in ROMAN ASKING BIDS. See also Delta Suit Asking Bids below.

Gamma Trump Asking Bids. Initiated by the 1 ♣ opener's single raise of responder's positive suit response, the responses show trump quality and length as set forth in PRECISION ASKING BIDS. Delayed trump asking bids are also available.

Delta Suit Asking Bids. After a positive response in notrump, a jump in a suit by opener is used to determine the number of cards and honors held by responder in that suit. The responses are:

1st step	no honors, doubleton or tripleton
2nd step	doubleton honor
3rd step	tripleton honor
4th step	four headed by an honor
5th step	two honors doubleton or tripleton
6th step	four headed by two honors

Control Asking Bids. After a suit fit has been established, a direct bid of 4 ♣ is control asking. If cuebidding has begun, 4 ♣ is a cuebid. There is one exception: if responder's first bid suit was clubs, then 4 ◇ is the control asking bid. Responses are in steps, with the first step showing none or one. See PRECISION ASKING BIDS. However, it may be agreed to vary the first step according to responder's previously shown strength.

Special Suit Asking Bids. After a Control Asking Bid, a new suit by opener asks responder to show his length and strength in the new suit as follows:

1st step	void or singleton
2nd step	doubleton
3rd step	tripleton
4th step	one of top three honors, any length
5th step	two of top three honors, any length
6th step	three top honors, any length

SUPER SWISS.

An expansion of the SWISS CONVENTION recommended by HUGH W. KELSEY that allows responder to make a forcing raise of opener's major suit while announcing immediately whether he has a singleton, and whether he has a void, and if he has neither, showing whether he has good controls. Responder bids one of four steps, the first step being the bid next above a single jump raise (3 ♠ over 1 ♡, 3 NT over 1 ♠):

1st step	void (unidentified)
2nd step	singleton (unidentified)
3rd step	two or three aces, denies a singleton or void
4th step	fewer than two aces, denies a singleton or void

After responder has shown a singleton or void, opener makes the cheapest bid to ask where responder's shortness lies; after the response, opener will usually be able to use BLACKWOOD to ask about aces.

For alternative methods see CONGLOMERATE MAJOR RAISES, UNBALANCED SWISS RAISE, VALUE SWISS RAISES.

SUPER UNUSUAL POSITIVE.

A set of artificial jump responses to a PRECISION CLUB opening to show 4-4-4-1 distribution and to specify minimum or maximum strength. See SUPER PRECISION.

SUPERSTITIONS.

Common as regards cards ever since games were first played. Some persons have the reputation of being good or bad cardholders. Substance is lent to such superstitions by the fact that a large number of instances is required to demonstrate the so-called law of averages. When tossing coins, it may require 1000 tosses to arrive at a point where there exists even a rough parity in the number of head and tail tosses. It is similar with cards. If one collates records on a series of several hundred hands held, one will find that the point-count holdings over the course will average about 10 points. There are numerous superstitions occurring at or applying to bridge games, such as shuffling the cards in a certain way, or positioning the deck after the cut, or using a certain pencil for scoring but for no other purpose, or getting up from one's seat and walking around one's chair or around the entire table "for luck" after a bad hand or a bad run of cards. A common superstition involves choices of seats or decks of cards after the cut for partners. Other players believe their luck will desert them if attention is drawn to it by calling them "lucky" or "the big winner," and so on, ad infinitum.

SUPPORT. Verb: to raise. Noun: (1) a raise; (2) whatever strength partner has in support of one's bid. See TRUMP SUPPORT.

SUPPRESSING THE BID ACE. Ace-asking conventions such as BLACKWOOD are occasionally used when the responding hand is already known to have a particular ace. The holder may have made a cuebid or shown a solid suit. In such cases the partnership should agree whether the ace already identified should be shown when responding to the conventional bid. Similar questions arise when the partnership has used a VOID-SHOWING BID. It is preferable to agree that the ace of a suit in which partner is known to be void should not be shown. Lacking any agreement, however, the previous bidding should be disregarded and the number of aces shown in the normal way.

SURE TRICK. A trick that a player must win. For example: the ace of trumps, the guarded king of trumps when it is behind the ace, the ace of a suit you intend to lead against notrump.

The lead of an ace against a suit contract, even though it be from a short suit not mentioned in the bidding, is not necessarily a sure trick, as declarer or dummy may be void. See HONOR TRICK, QUICK TRICK.

The term is also used by GEORGE COFFIN to describe single-dummy problems in which correct play will ensure the making of a specific number of tricks.

SURPLUS CARDS. A card in excess of 13 in a bridge hand, before the play begins or a card in excess of the number of tricks remaining to be played after play has commenced. See LAWS (Laws 11, 68), LAWS OF DUPLICATE (Laws 13, 67). See MISSING CARD.

SUSPENSION. See DISCIPLINARY CODE; EXCLUSION.

SVERIGES BRIDGEFORBUND. See SWEDISH BRIDGE LEAGUE.

SWEDISH BRIDGE LEAGUE (SVERIGES BRIDGEFORBUND). Founded in 1933, in 1982 it had approximately 17,500 members. The League participates in all European and Nordic Championships, and World Olympiads. Sweden won the World Women's Teams in 1968, the European Championships in 1939, 1952 and 1977, and the European Women's Championships in 1962 and 1967. Sweden hosted the European Championships in Stockholm in 1936 and 1956 and the Bermuda Bowl and World Pairs Championship in 1970. National events for Open Teams and Open Pairs attract 400 teams and 4,500 pairs, respectively.

Officers, 1982:

President: Nils Jensen
Secretary: Lars Filipsson, Karlaplan 8, Stockholm, 11460, Sweden

SWINDLE, SWINDLING. Legitimate methods of attempting to get better than deserved results are discussed under DECEPTIVE PLAY, FALSE-CARDING, LEAD-INHIBITING BID, and PSYCHIC BIDDING.

SWINE (Sebaski-Woods-I-Notrump-Escape). Developed in Australia. If 1 NT is doubled, pass forces opener to redouble. Then responder may pass for penalties or bid the cheaper of touching suits. With a weak single-suited hand responder redoubles, requiring a 2♣ bid. A direct 2♣ shows clubs and hearts; 2◇ shows diamonds and spades. Direct 2♡ and 2♠ has moderate values; direct 2NT is strong and unbalanced.

SWING. The difference between the actual score made on a deal and "what might have been" were the bidding, play, or defense different. Thus if poor dummy play by declarer results in down one on a vulnerable 6♠ contract, the swing is said to be 1,530 points.

The term is frequently used in team matches to name the actual gain or loss on a single hand. The term may be in total points or in IMPs. If North–South of a team make 3♠ for 140 points and their teammates defeat 4♠ by 50 points, the swing is 190 points or 5 IMPs. See SWING HAND.

SWING HAND. A term used to denote a hand on which successful or unsuccessful result by a partnership produces a very decisive change in overall results of a rubber or a match.

Consider this hand from a recent European championship:

```
Vul: N-S      ♠ Q 5 3
Dlr: South    ♡ A Q J
              ◇ K
              ♣ A Q J 9 4 3
  ♠ A 7 4                    ♠ K 10 9
  ♡ 10 8 5 2                 ♡ K 9 7 6 4 3
  ◇ 10 8 7 3                 ◇ 4
  ♣ 6 5                      ♣ 10 8 2
              ♠ J 8 6 2
              ♡ —
              ◇ A Q J 9 6 5 2
              ♣ K 7
```

WEST	NORTH	EAST	SOUTH
			1◇
Pass	3♣	3♡	4◇
4♡	4 NT	6♡	Pass
Pass	6 NT	Pass	7◇
Dbl	7 NT	Dbl	Pass
Pass	Redbl	All Pass	

On the bidding above, East led a diamond, and North–South were plus 2,930 points. In the other room, North–South reached a contract of 6♣, down one, for a score of −100, a swing of over 3,000 points on a single hand.

SWISS BRIDGE FEDERATION (FÉDÉRATION

SUISSE DE BRIDGE). Founded in 1950 in Geneva, by 1982 it had a membership of approximately 2,300 in 33 affiliated clubs. The Federation annually sponsors teams in the European Championships, and hosted the tournament in Montreaux in 1954 and in Lausanne in 1979. It also participates in World Team Olympiads, finishing fifth in 1964 and sixth in 1968. The Federation holds annual competitions for National Championships in Open Teams, Knockout Teams, Masters Pairs, Mixed Pairs, Open Pairs, a Par Contest and limited Knockout Teams. The Swiss system of masterpoint awards is unique in that master points cannot be carried forward from one year to the next. Players earn a permanent rank by winning a certain number of master points for several consecutive years, but this rank may be lost if a successful record is not maintained. Also, the masterpoint value of a given tournament depends not only on the size and length of the tournament, but also on the number of participating National Series (highest ranking) players.

Officers, 1982:

President: Marc Hodler
Secretary: Wolf Achterberg, 1, rue Contamines, 1208 Geneva, Switzerland

SWISS CONVENTION. A response of four in a minor suit to an opening of one in a major suit shows a standard forcing raise to the three-level. This is a strength-showing substitute used by players employing limit jump raises. (3 NT is sometimes used for the same purpose, for example in KAPLAN-SHEINWOLD).

The usual high-card strength would be 13–15.

> ♠ A Q x x
> ♡ K′ J x x
> ◇ A x x
> ♣ x x

Over 1 ♡ or 1 ♠, the response is 4 ♣ or 4 ◇ to show a hand too strong in high cards to raise directly to game. It also suggests a relatively balanced hand, because responder would bid a side suit and raise to game on the second round with a two-suiter.

The distinction between 4 ♣ and 4 ◇ is a matter of partnership agreement, but the trend is toward using 4 ♣ as the more forward-going bid. When 4 ♣ and 4 ◇ are the only forcing raises employed, one of the following treatments is usual:

(1) Trump quality: 4 ♣ shows (and 4 ◇ denies) four trumps headed by at least two of the top three honors, or five or more trumps headed by at least the ace or king.

(2) Controls: 4 ♣ shows (and 4 ◇ denies) three aces, or two aces and the king of trumps.

(3) Controls or Trumps: 4 ♣ emphasizes good controls, and 4 ◇ emphasizes strong trumps.

Several methods have been developed which combine the jumps to four of a minor with other jump responses in order to allow for a finer distinction among types of strong raises. See CONGLOMERATE MAJOR RAISES, SUPER SWISS, UNBALANCED SWISS RAISE, VALUE SWISS RAISES.

For other conventional uses of four of a minor in response to one of a major, see ASKING BID, SPLINTER BID, and VOID-SHOWING BID.

SWISS MOVEMENT. A partial round-robin movement similar to the method used for many years in major chess tournaments when insufficient time is available for a complete round robin.

The basic feature of a Swiss movement is that after the first round, winning teams or pairs are pitted against each other for the second round, and losers face each other. For each succeeding round, new pairings are made on the basis of the records of the matched teams or pairs with the added proviso that no two teams or pairs may play a second match against each other. Scoring is usually by international match points, although BOARD-A-MATCH and HYBRID SCORING are feasible.

Team events: Although many attempts at adapting the Swiss method to team contests have been made in the past, it was not until 1967 when JOHN HAMILTON and MARC LOW developed the present method, which was first tried and proved successful at a Cincinnati Sectional, that Swiss team contests became popular. The idea caught on quickly throughout the ACBL and resulted in a spectacular increase in team attendance at sectional and regional tournaments, more than doubling the size of the previous board-a-match team events in many cases. The first North American Swiss team was held at the 1970 Spring North American Championships in Portland OR.

The team event is divided into a series of short, IMP-scored matches. The original field is seeded, with seeded teams competing against non-seeded teams during the first round. Pairings for each succeeding round are determined by the won-loss records of the teams. However, within each group of teams that have equal records, pairings from the second round on are random. Since sufficient matches must be scheduled to produce a significant won-loss record, a minimum of two sessions of play usually is required. When possible, more matches are scheduled than needed to reduce the field to one undefeated team, so that a team is not necessarily eliminated from a chance to win the event by a single loss. An odd number of entries creates difficulties, but can be handled in various forms. The most common are short round-robins, lasting as long as one regular match, in which each winning team is given credit for half a match. The other common method is a three-team round-robin playing the full number of boards, so that a round lasts as long as two full matches. In either case, there is no comparison of scores until the round-robin is completed.

An alternate method of scoring Swiss Teams is to convert IMP results into Victory Points. Pairings are then based on Victory-Point totals, not wins and losses. The team with the most Victory Points is declared the winner.

Pair events: The ACBL introduced Swiss pair contests in 1970. As in the team event, the pairs play a series of short matches against each other, with each board IMPed against a computed average for the field. Pairings may be based on wins and losses or on VICTORY POINTS.

Some of the difficulties encountered are: (1) the boards must be duplicated for each round and (2) since pair events attract larger fields than team contests, it may be difficult to determine an overall winner in two sessions.

SWISS POINTS. A method of breaking ties for prize purposes in Swiss Team events. The scores of all the teams that played against each team involved in the tie are added together. The team whose opponents' total is higher is declared the winner for prize purposes. Occasionally there is a refinement of this method — only those matches which take place in the second half of the contest are counted in totaling the Swiss Points.

SWISS TEAMS, NORTH AMERICAN CHAMPIONSHIP. See Appendix I, Fall NAC.

SWITCH. See SHIFT.

SWORDS. One of the suits in early PLAYING CARDS. Still used in the trappola deck (see SUIT).

SYMMETRIC RELAY SYSTEM. A modern relay system developed by a group of New Zealand players. It was first described by ROY KERR and Walt Jones, and played successfully in international championships by Paul Marston and Malcolm Sims.

A major difference between Symmetric and the ULTIMATE CLUB is that almost all Symmetric responses to the strong club opening, other than the 1 ◇ negative, are natural. (This makes the system somewhat more acceptable to tournament committees and directors.) The responder describes his distribution, with sequences which usually end at the three-level. The opener can then relay to find the number of controls and the location of high cards. If the response is a negative 1 ◇ a relay of 1 ♡ asks responder to use the normal descriptive sequences but two steps higher than they would otherwise be.

The general structure is based on five-card major openings (as opposed to Ultimate, which uses four-card majors.) In response to 1 ♡ and 1 ♠, 1 NT is used as a strong relay. See RELAY SYSTEMS.

SYMMETRY. See LAW OF SYMMETRY.

SYNDICATED ARTICLES. See BRIDGE COLUMNS.

SYSTEMS. See BIDDING SYSTEMS.

T

TABLE. Four players, two pairs, or one team, in duplicate play, for individual, pair, and team movements suitable to a particular number to tables, see TWO, THREE, FOUR, etc., to FIFTEEN TABLES.

The table most frequently used for bridge is a folding square table, about 30 inches on a side, and from 26½ to 27½ inches in height. The accouterments should include two score pads, two decks of bridge cards, two sharp pencils, ashtrays, coasters, and four chairs.

TABLE GUIDE CARDS. A large card placed under the boards in the center of a table, containing instructions for the players. See GUIDE CARD.

TABLE MANNERS. Bridge is a social game, and good manners at the bridge table are as necessary for full enjoyment of the game as in any other form of sociability. See ETIQUETTE, PROPRIETIES.

TABLE NUMBERS. Rectangular, large cards in the center of the table, which give the number of the table in the section; sections are distinguished by the color of the table card, on a six-color repeating pattern; white for sections A, G, N, T, and Z; yellow for B, H, O, and U; green for C, J, P, and V; orange for D, K, Q, and W; blue for E, L, R, and X; pink for F, M. S, and Y.

TABLE PRESENCE. One of the features that make a good bridge player into an expert is the undefinable something that is referred to as table presence. It is a combination of INSTINCT, if this quality actually exists; the drawing of correct inferences from any departure from RHYTHM by the opponents; the exercise of DISCIPLINE in bidding; and perhaps the most important, the ability to coax maximum performance from his partner, and the ability to make the opponents feel that they are facing a player of a higher order.

TABLE SPACING. The arrangement of tables in a hall for an event of a duplicate tournament. For comfortable play tables should be spaced with nine-foot centers. When the available space does not permit the ideal arrangement, reduction to eight feet between centers is practicable. The minimum spacing permitting any degree of comfort is a trifle over seven feet between centers in a row. When the rows cannot be spaced at least eight feet apart, staggering of tables in adjoining rows can be resorted to.

The setup of tables within the section should put the last table in the section near the first so that boards and players have a minimum of movement. This can be done with a hairpin arrangement, utilizing two rows of seven, eight or nine tables.

TABLES, MATHEMATICAL. See MATHEMATICAL TABLES.

TACTICS. Various maneuvers in the play of the hand, bidding nuances and choices of action, taking into consideration the methods of scoring, quality of the competition and conditions of contests.

TAIWAN. See CHINESE TAIPEI BRIDGE ASSOCIATION.

TAKEOUT. A bid at a denomination other than one previously named by partner, as distinguished from a raise. See JUMP SHIFT and RESPONSE.

TAKEOUT DOUBLE. The use of a low-level double in certain circumstances as a request to partner to bid an unbid suit. This is a "natural" convention, because a penalty double of an opening suit bid of one can hardly exist; a player with great strength in the opponent's suit prefers to lie in wait (see TRAP

PASS). The idea of doubling for a takeout appears to have been devised independently by MAJOR CHARLES PATTON in New York and BRYANT McCAMPBELL in St. Louis in 1912–13 and probably by others.

For the problems involved in distinguishing a takeout double from a penalty double, see DOUBLE.

By far the most common takeout double occurs when it immediately follows an opening bid of one in a suit. The doubler normally indicates a hand worth an opening bid with at least three-card support for all unbid suits. However, the respective vulnerability and the rank of the opener's suit may play a part in the decision.

♠ A Q x x
♡ x
◇ K x x
♣ J 10 x x x

At favorable vulnerability, a double of 1♡ can be ventured. If the doubler's partner can fit spades, a cheap save in 4♠ over 4♡ is likely to materialize. There would be less reason to double if the opener's suit were a minor, of if the doubler held only three spades. A player who doubles a major-suit opening tends to hold four cards in the unbid major, and this may be a factor in deciding to double.

The high-card strength required for the double increases: (a) as the distribution becomes less suitable; (b) if the doubler is vulnerable; (c) if the opener's suit is spades, which will force a response at the two-level.

The following would be minimum vulnerable doubles of 1♠:

♠ x	♠ x x	♠ x x x
♡ A Q x x	♡ A J x x	♡ A Q x
◇ K J x x	◇ K Q x x	◇ A J x x
♣ K x x x	♣ K J x	♣ K J x

A nonvulnerable double would be justified in each case if a jack were removed.

The distributional requirement, that at least three cards should be held in each unbid suit, should rarely be broken unless the doubler is very strong, with at least 17 high-card points:

♠ x x
♡ A Q x x x
◇ A Q x
♣ K Q x

Over 1♠, 1◇ or 1♣, a double followed by a minimum bid in hearts is appropriate. The hand is clearly too strong for a simple overcall.

A takeout double is normally made with any strong hand unsuitable for other actions such as a 1 NT overcall, a strong jump overcall, or a cuebid. The maximum for a double is a hand just short of the requirements for an immediate cuebid, unless the cuebid is being used as a specialized bid (ASTRO, MICHAELS, etc.) in which case there is no upward limit. Very strong hands are often shown by doubling and following with a cuebid: the idea that such bidding shows a desire to play in the opponent's suit is virtually obsolete.

Subsequent bidding

For action by the opener's partner, see RESPONSES OVER OPPONENT'S TAKEOUT DOUBLE. The following summarizes possible actions by the doubler's partner if the bidding starts:

1◇   Dbl   Pass   ?

(1) *Minimum suit response* (1♡ or 1♠ or 2♣). A forced response which may have no high-card points. The normal maximum is 8 points, but see (3) below. Responder prefers a major suit to a minor, so 2♣ is more likely to be five cards than four. 1♡ is not infrequently bid with a three-card suit because there is no alternative: if responder's only suit is diamonds he has to invent an economical bid. Even 1♠ might be a three-card suit, with 3-2-5-3 distribution for example.

The doubler passes these responses automatically if he has a minimum or near-minimum double. Further action shows that game is still possible in the face of responder's announced weakness. A raise of responder's suit or a bid in a new suit should show at least 17 points in high cards (or perhaps 16 if responder's jump shift would have been forcing). A minimum rebid in notrump is very constructive, suggesting a hand too strong to overcall 1 NT (i.e., 19–20 points).

In one case responder may make an uneconomical response:

♠ A x x x
♡ K x x x
◇ x x x
♣ x x

1♠ is a better response than 1♡, as responder can then continue readily to 2♡ if, as is likely, the opponents contest with 2♣ or 2◇.

(2) *1 NT response*. Indicates a relatively balanced hand with moderate strength and a stopper in the opener's suit. The exact strength is a matter of style, and expert opinions vary. The conservative view is to reserve the bid for hands with 8–10 or perhaps 11 points. But this sets problems when responder has a hand such as:

♠ K J 10 x
♡ x x x
◇ Q x x
♣ x x x

Many authorities, such as EDGAR KAPLAN, therefore recommend a range of 6–9.

(3) *Jump shift* (2♡, 2♠ or 3♣). There are two treatments. The majority of experts, and the majority of authorities, play this jump shift as encouraging but not forcing. The high-card strength is likely to be 9–11, but might be eight with a five-card suit. The jump in a major suit is often a four-card suit: in a minor at least five cards are desirable.

However, some experts treat the jump as forcing. In this case the minimum strength should be 10–11. The disadvantage is that the range of the nonjump response becomes uncomfortably wide.

(4) *Cuebid* (2◇). Shows any hand which can guarantee game but cannot be sure of the final resting place. The bid is totally unrelated to the opener's suit. Some players use the cuebid slightly more freely:

♠ A Q x x
♡ K J x x
◇ J x x
♣ x x

Rather than make a nonforcing jump in one of the major suits, and perhaps pick the wrong suit, a possible treatment is to cuebid 2♢, intending to raise either major to the three-level. The doubler then passes with a minimum, because the responder would have bid game himself if he could.

(5) *2 NT response.* Shows 11–12 points, and at least a single stopper in the opener's suit. The strength will depend slightly on the range adopted for the 1 NT response, in (3) above. If that is 6–9 the 2 NT bid may be made with 10; if 1 NT is 8–11, 2 NT is likely to be 12.

(6) *3 NT response.* Usually a double stopper in the opener's suit and 13–16 points. Alternatively, responder may have a single stopper and a long minor suit which he expects to run with the help of doubler's expected fit. With more than 16 points, responder may suspect that the opener or the doubler has psyched, and proceed more slowly with a cuebid.

(7) *Higher suit responses.* (3♢, 3♠, 4♣, 4♡, 4♠, 5♣). Natural limited bids based on a long suit (usually six cards or longer). Responder expects to make his contract if doubler has a minimum.

(8) *Pass.* Great length and strength in diamonds (see PENALTY PASS).

After action by opener's partner

Action by third hand relieves the doubler's partner of his obligation to bid, but he should still make a "free" response if he has moderate values and can do so at a convenient level.

(9) *After a redouble.* A pass shows weakness. (The idea that responder should ignore the redouble, and therefore pass for penalties is virtually obsolete.) However, the responder is almost certain to have a hand with little strength, very probably less than six points. A suit bid should therefore not be construed as showing any strength: the chance that the doubler's side will wish to bid constructively toward game is negligible. Responder should usually show a four-card suit if he can do so at the level of one, and five-card suit at the level of two. It is especially important for him to bid the cheapest suit, should he hold it and fear that partner may take out in a suit he cannot support.

(10) *After a change of suit by opener's partner.* If responder can bid a suit of his own at the one-level, he should usually do so with five points, and make the normal encouraging jump with nine. Slightly more is needed to bid at the two-level, but the free two-level response (1♢–Dbl–2♣–2♠) should be made more freely, than the jump shift when third hand has passed.

(11) *After a raise by opener's partner.* The opener's partner is trying to shut out the doubler's partner, who must often strain his resources in order to avoid being shut out. For a treatment of hands which do not offer an obvious bid, see RESPONSIVE DOUBLE.

Other takeout doubles

These can usually be identified by the general rule that a double of a suit bid at the level of one or two is for a takeout when partner has not bid. The most important cases are as follows:

(12) *The balancing double.* See BALANCING.

(13) *The double of two suits* (1♣–Pass–1♡–Dbl). In standard practice this may show a relatively weak distributional two-suiter, or a strong relatively balanced hand. However, when both opponents are bidding and partner is silent, there are obvious dangers in entering the auction. ("Bidding in sandwich" is the European phrase.) Many tournament players therefore dispense with a natural 1 NT overcall in this position (or 2 NT if the bidding is at the two-level) and treat a notrump bid as UNUSUAL. This takes care of the distributional two-suited hands, and the double can be reserved for relatively balanced hands, strong in high cards.

(14) *The double of a 1 NT response* (1♡–Pass–1 NT–Dbl). This is the only situation in which a double of a notrump bid is for takeout, but the takeout aspect is not very pronounced; partner will pass more often than he will pass any other takeout double. The double may have to be made with a strong balanced hand which would have overcalled 1 NT if opportunity had offered.

(15) *The double of a raise* (1♡–Pass–2♡–Dbl). Vulnerability and the rank of opener's suit are important considerations here. At favorable vulnerability a double of 2♡ may be made lightly with suitable distribution because a save in 4♠ seems possible. A double of 2♠ commits the doubler's side to the three-level, and does not offer such good prospects of a save, so solid values are needed by the doubler. The double of a minor-suit raise emphasizes the major suits; and may be made freely: the probability that the doubling side has a fit is increased by the opening side's established fit.

(16) *The double of a suit response to a 1 NT opening* (1 NT–Pass–2♡–Dbl). Here again vulnerability and the rank of the suit are important factors. If the suit is red, offering the possibility of play at the two-level, a nonvulnerable player may double with as little as 10 points and favorable distribution. He can rely on strengh in his partner's hand because the opener's side has announced its intention of stopping at the two-level, and is in effect balancing.

(17) *Doubles of weak two-bids and weak three-bids* can be regarded as takeout. See DEFENSE TO OPENING THREE-BIDS.

TALLIES. Prepared cards for the recording of results at the end of each round (four deals) in PROGRESSIVE or PARTY BRIDGE. These can be purchased at most gift and stationery stores.

TAM II 2♣ AND 2♢ OPENINGS. A system of strong artificial opening bids for use with balanced hands of 22–29 high card points or unbalanced game-going hands. The 2♢ opening shows a balanced hand with 22–25 points. Responses include transfers, STAYMAN- type bids, and a 2♡ relay asking opener to specify whether he has a minimum or maximum.

The 2♣ opening may be made with a balanced hand with 26–29 points, which will be revealed by a rebid in notrump. Or it may be made with an unbalanced hand, in which case opener will rebid in a suit. A 2 NT response is negative, denying as much as one QUICK TRICK. A simple suit response promises one or more quick tricks, shows an ace or king in the suit bid, and denies the ace or king of any lower ranking suit. A jump shift response shows at least a six-card suit, headed by two of the top three honors.

TANK. A colloquialism in the phrase "go into the tank" meaning to fall into a protracted HUDDLE.

TAP. A colloquialism for shortening a hand in trumps by forcing it to ruff. See FORCE(2).

TAP THE TABLE. (1) Give an informal ALERT. (2) Make an informal PASS.

TARDINESS. Late arrival at rubber bridge games curtails the length of time available for play, and is inconsiderate of the host or hostess. At duplicate tournaments far more people may be inconvenienced when the start of a second session may be delayed some little time while the director seeks substitutes for non-shows. Purchase of an entry into an event obligates the players to abide by the conditions of play, including reporting on time for all following sessions of the same event. See TIME LIMIT ON RIGHT TO PLAY.

TAROT. The pack of 22 numbered cards without suit signs that were part of the first pack known to be used in Europe; or a pack containing these 22 atouts (atutti, trumps) plus 56 other cards divided into four suits, each with ten SPOT CARDS and four COURT CARDS. Not all packs are alike, but the basic cards were:

 0 The fool (*Il Pazzo or Il Matto*), like a jester (most packs omit the numeral)
 1 The juggler (*Bagatto*), wand or cup in hand, items of legedermain on the table in front of him
 2 The papess (*La Papessa*), double crowned, seated, book in hand
 3 The empress (*L'Imperatrice*), singly crowned, scepter and shield
 4 The emperor (*L'Imperator*), perhaps Charlemagne, scepter in hand
 5 The pope (*Il Papa*), crowned, carrying staff, seated before two columns
 6 Love (*Amore*), Cupid aiming a double arrow at two of three persons
 7 The chariot (*La Carrozza*), shows one driver and two horses
 8 Justice (*La Giustizia*), a woman, sword in one hand, scales in other
 9 The hermit (L'Eremita), an old man, lantern in right hand
10 Wheel of fortune (La Ruota della Fortuna), a crowned figure with sword above a wheel with one figure going up and another down
11 Force (*La Forza*), either a man opening the jaws of a lion, or a woman breaking a pillar
12 The hanged man (*Il Penduto*), suspended upside-down by one foot
13 Untitled, picturing Death, a skeleton wielding a scythe over fragments of people
14 Temperance (*La Temperanza*), an angel pouring water from one jug into another
15 The devil (*Il Diavolo*), winged, with pitchfork and forked tail, threatening one or more figures
16 The tower (*La Torre*) being struck by lightning as two men fall
17 The star (*La Stella*), a nude woman pouring water from two jugs into a stream
18 The moon (La Luna), a profile face, riding over rooftops, with dogs baying below
19 The sun (*Il Sole*), full-face, shining on two boys in breechcloths
20 The angel (*L'Angelo*), blowing a trumpet over people rising from the grave
21 The world (*Il Mondo*), a female in a wreath; an angel, a winged beast, a cow, and a lion are in each corner.

The first tarot cards appeared in Italy, probably in the fourteenth century, and the original suits were

cups, coins, swords and cudgels: the court cards, king, queen, cavalier and knave.

Albert Field

TAXES ON PLAYING CARDS. The first tax on playing cards in the United States was levied in 1862, to raise money for the War Between the States, varying from 1 to 15 cents (or 15% of the cost, whichever was greater), until 1866 when it became 6 cents per pack. This tax was repealed in 1883 and not reinstated until the depression of Cleveland's second administration, when a 2-cents-a-pack tax was imposed under the Act of August 27, 1894. Since that time it has been retained by the Federal Government as a constant source of revenue. The levy remained constant until the necessity of increased revenue following World War I caused an increase in 1920 to 8 cents a pack, increased to 10 cents in 1925, and recently, 1961, to 13 cents. Revenues exceeded $5 million dollars in 1929, and over $8 million in 1962. This tax was lifted on July 1, 1965.

The first tax levied on playing cards, so far as the records show, was imposed in England in the reign of James I (1615).

TEACHING IN BRIDGE. The first teacher of games in the bridge family was also one of the most successful. The ladies of good family to whom EDMUND HOYLE taught WHIST were charged at the rate of one guinea an hour, equivalent to at least $50 an hour in modern terms. His celebrated "Short Treatise," published in 1743, which became a best-seller for more than a century, was intended as a textbook for his students.

The first professional teacher of whist in America was Miss Kate Wheelock, who began teaching in Milwaukee in 1886. She achieved immediate success, touring the continent to lecture in all the principal cities. The whistograph which she invented for use in her classes was the forerunner of the VUGRAPH used by the ACBL in modern times. She was the first woman to be made an associate member of the American Whist League, and CAVENDISH called her "The Whist Queen."

Whist teaching was a highly suitable occupation for ladies of some status and education who needed to supplement their incomes, and many others followed Miss Wheelock's example. The first prominent male teacher was Charles Stuart Street of New York City, who began in 1890.

The most successful teacher of BRIDGE WHIST, and of AUCTION BRIDGE up to the time of his death, was undoubtedly JOSEPH B. ELWELL. Among his most prominent successors was JOSEPHINE CULBERTSON. In the Twenties MILTON WORK and WILBUR WHITEHEAD organized conventions for teachers, issuing certificates to those who had completed courses. A similar procedure was followed later by ELY CULBERTSON, and later still by CHARLES GOREN, who was one of the highest-paid teachers of all time before he decided to concentrate on writing.

Many persons turned to bridge teaching as a temporary occupation during the Depression years, and at its peak the membership of the Culbertson National Studios totaled some 6,000. The number of teachers dwindled markedly when prosperity returned, but increased again in the postwar years, particularly after Goren's point-count methods gained general currency.

In the Sixties and Seventies, the number of teachers has continued to grow. Their ranks include many players of the highest quality, and for students with tournament ambitions the playing lesson has increased in popularity. See AMERICAN BRIDGE TEACHERS' ASSOCIATION, from which information about a wide range of teaching books and materials can be obtained. See also AUTOBRIDGE and LESSON HANDS.

TEAM. Four or more players competing as a unit in bridge tournaments. For one-session events, four players constitute a team; in two-session or longer events, up to six players are permitted.

In mixed team events, no two members of the same sex are permitted to play as partners.

TEAM-OF-EIGHT MATCH. A four-table team contest in which each team has eight active players.

TEAM-OF-FOUR EVENTS. Contests between teams of four, five, and six players are a standard part of duplicate tournaments at the sectional or higher level. These events are usually conducted according to the SWISS MOVEMENT with IMP SCORING. (BOARD-A-MATCH was the most popular form of scoring prior to the late 1960s.) Occasionally the field is divided into two or more flights, divided by masterpoint limits or smoking preferences. At regional tournaments, team contests limited to men, women, or mixed partnerships frequently held in addition to open team events.

Experienced duplicate bridge players generally consider that team-of-four competition is the most challenging and demanding. Most major international matches are at team-of-four competition. Specific conditions of contest vary from tournament to tournament as to type of scoring, number of members on a team (although only four play at any one time), and entry requirements.

Other types of team-of-four contests have increased in popularity, but are not generally suitable for tournament play at sectional level: (1) KNOCKOUT; (2) DOUBLE ELIMINATION; (3) ROUND ROBIN. See also HYBRID SCORING, TOTAL POINT SCORING.

TEAM-OF-FOUR MOVEMENTS. These are based, for small games, on the movement originated by the AMERICAN WHIST LEAGUE in the nineteenth century. With an odd number of teams, the movement is completed in one round less than the number of competing teams, and each progression is the same, the boards moving toward the lower numbered tables, and the traveling pairs skipping a table to the next lower number. By omitting middle rounds, this is adaptable to large games by an irregularity in the movement at the midpoint. After half the boards are played, the traveling pairs return the boards just played to their home table, and get their new table assignment for the next round by adding 12 (if 24 boards constituted a session, 14 in a 28-board session) to their original number, and go-

ing to the resultant sum for the next round. (If the sum is greater than the highest numbered table, subtract the number of tables in play from the sum, and progress to that table.)

With an even number of teams in competition, this movement does not provide competition between all teams. For many years this was compensated for by a phantom table so that one North-South and one East–West pair sat out each round.

To overcome this difficulty, MAJOR CHARLES L. PATTON devised a movement based on the HOWELL schedule, and a relay movement was produced later by SHEPARD BARCLAY. Both had advantages over the American Whist League movement for even-numbered teams. In the early Fifties, at the suggestion of RICHARD FREEMAN, the American Whist League movement was modified by two irregularities. After two (or three) 14-table rounds, traveling pairs skip an extra table, boards progressing normally; after all but two (or three) rounds, both the traveling pairs skip an extra table, and the boards skip a table. All but one match is completed by the end of the movement, and this last match can be played by relaying new boards as in a head-on match.

In 1963, LAWRENCE ROSLER devised a two-section team movement (very reminiscent of the BARCLAY MOVEMENT of the Thirties). One of its salient features is that discussion of the last set or a glimpse of the next round's boards is not a defect of the movement. Sections of equal size are required. East-West pairs in the two sections interchange; after boards are twinned in the home section, a MITCHELL progression is used in both sections, except that in *one* of the sections, the East–West pairs remain stationary, and the North–South pairs move. This allows both pairs of a team to play a given board on the same round. However, it means that both partnerships of half the teams will be moving pairs, while both pairs of the remaining teams will be stationary.

A modification of the Rosler method called the MIRROR MITCHELL, which is used in most NORTH AMERICAN CHAMPIONSHIPS BOARD-A-MATCH events, allows each team to have one stationary pair. A regular MITCHELL MOVEMENT is used in one section. In the other sections the boards progress each round to the next lower numbered table, while the pairs skip one table toward the lower numbered table.

These movements apply to board-a-match and abbreviated IMP events. See SWISS MOVEMENTS.

TEAM OLYMPIAD. See WORLD TEAM OLYMPIAD.

TEAM-OF-TWELVE (or more) MATCH. A team contest in which each team has 12 (or more) active players.

TEAM TRIALS. See INTERNATIONAL OPEN TEAM SELECTION.

TEAMMATES. A term applied to the other members of a team of four (five or six). During the play of an event, the term is usually used to refer to the other pair, rather than including one's partner in the term.

TELEVISION. The importance of bridge players as an audience with high rating has been clearly demonstrated by television. Perhaps the first regular television show featuring bridge by Robert Lee Johnson in Los Angeles. In a later program in Miami, WILLIAM SEAMON presented challenging pairs who played rubber bridge against the previous week's winners. Much the same format was developed nationally by CHARLES GOREN in his nationally distributed, sponsored program, "Championship Bridge." Another important TV show was headed by EASLEY BLACKWOOD in Indianapolis, and the first bridge telecast on pay TV was devised by ALFRED SHEINWOLD in Los Angeles in 1964. Many championship bridge events, including the 1957 and 1962 Bermuda Bowl, have been televised locally, but the first to be shown on a national network was the final of the Open Pairs event telecast from Los Angeles in the 1963 Summer North American Championships.

"Play Bridge with the Experts", created by Ed Allen, was a public TV series that was carried on public TV stations all over the United States starting in 1974. Emceed by NATHAN OSTRICH, each program featured a guest expert and four ACBL members who were called upon to solve bidding, dummy-play and defensive problems. In 1981, the British Broadcasting Corporation televised a series of bridge programs entitled "Grand Slam". The shows featured four American players (JACQUI MITCHELL, GAIL MOSS, MATT GRANOVETTER and NEIL SILVERMAN) in five-board matches against four British players (NICOLA GARDENER, PAT DAVIES, JEREMY FLINT and CLAUDE RODRIGUE). Both series were well received.

Closed-circuit television has been an increasingly popular method of complementing and enhancing BRIDGE-O-RAMA or VUGRAPH presentation of bridge contests. For the first time at a major event, the open room play of the 1967 Bermuda Bowl final in Miami Beach was telecast to the Bridge-O-Rama audience. Closed-circuit television was also used extensively by the SHARIF BRIDGE CIRCUS to present its exhibition matches, and by the Swedish Bridge League for its coverage of the 1970 Bermuda Bowl and World Pair Championship in Stockholm. A new standard was set at the WORLD PAIR CHAMPIONSHIPS at Biarritz, France, in 1982 when a full-size movie screen was set up for the spectators. TV cameras presented all the action at the table being covered in spectacular color and detail. Every grimace, every hitch, every mannerism was visible to the spectators who were able to "live" with their heroes through every agonizing decision and every brilliant play. A secondary screen displaying the hand and showing how the bidding and play progressed was set up next to the movie screen.

TEMPO. (1) The element of timing in card play, with special reference to the use of opportunities to make an attacking lead. (See hand at top of right column.)

West leads two rounds of hearts against South's 4♠ contract. South should avoid losing a tempo by cashing the ♠ A-K immediately, and then starting his diamonds. The defenders can score the two remaining trumps but cannot damage the contract. If

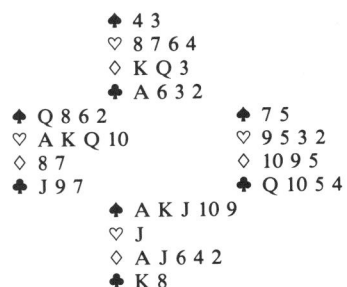

South loses a tempo by taking a spade finesse, the defense will continue hearts, reducing South's trumps to one fewer than West's. Should South allow this to happen, the defense will score a trick with a long heart and defeat the contract.

(2) The speed with which a bid or a play is made. Experienced players attempt to adjust the speed of their own bidding and play so as always to use the same tempo, and thus not convey information to partner or to the opponents.

Players sometimes seek to force a rapid tempo of play, hoping to gain an advantage by encouraging an error by the opponents or by obtaining information from the opponents' pauses to think. The best defense against this somewhat unsporting tactic is to refuse to alter the tempo of one's own play, or even to slow the tempo down so as to protect one's partner. The term tempo, however, does not stretch to include deliberate hesitation when in fact a player has no problem.

TEMPORIZING BID. See WAITING BID.

TEN or TEN-SPOT. The fifth ranking card in each suit; at trump it is the lowest ranking honor card.

TEN TABLES. At duplicate, 10 tables provide for competition among 40 players as individuals, 20 pairs or 10 teams-of-four. Ten tables can be used as a SWISS MOVEMENT, but after the first round one of the winners almost certainly will play a losing team. This will frequently iron itself out after the second round. One way to correct this is to use VICTORY POINT scoring.

As an individual tournament, the SHOMATE MOVEMENT is available, but the entry of scores, matchpointing and movement of the players makes it an extremely difficult game to run. It's much easier to get four more players and use the 11 table, or 44 player, RAINBOW MOVEMENT. The ACBL has available guide cards for 10 tables with irregular moves for the moving players where seven rounds of three boards each are played. This is a much simpler movement, but each player can be partners with only 21 of the other 39 players.

As a pair game the 10-table THREE-QUARTER MOVEMENT is preferable as a one-winner movement. As a MITCHELL game, the most common method is to pass out three boards to a table, have the East-West players skip after the fifth round, and play nine rounds. If it is desired to play all the boards, a relay can be set up between Tables 1 and 10 with the byestand between Tables 5 and 6. For 9½ tables and 10½ tables, see HALF TABLES.

The recommended movement for 10 teams-of-four is the standard team-of-four movement with two modifications. The East–West, or moving, pairs skip a table in the lower direction, while the boards move to the next lower table. After the second round the East–West pairs skip an extra table. After the sixth round the East–West pairs skip an extra table and the boards skip a table. East–West pair 1 moves, 9, 7, 4, 2, 10, 8, 5 and 3. Remember to skip the boards after the sixth round. If it is desirable to play a ninth round, East–West pairs 1 to 5 add five to their number and go to that table. East–West pairs 6 to 10 subtract five from their number and go to that table. 1 and 6, 2 and 7, 3 and 8, 4 and 9, and 5 and 10 relay newly shuffled boards during this final round.

For an interesting variation of the 10-table game see the BLACKPOOL MOVEMENT. This is also adaptable to 9½ tables.

TENACE. Two cards in the same suit of which one ranks two degrees lower than the other; the *major* tenace is A–Q; the *minor* tenace is K–J; more broadly, any holding of cards not in sequence in a suit.

TEXAS CONVENTION. A transfer bid, originated independently by DAVID CARTER of St. Louis MO, and Olle Willner of Stockholm, Sweden. It is used after an opening 1 NT or 2 NT bid to make the strong hand declarer in a high suit contract. With a hand justifying a game contract, the responder jumps to 4♡ holding a six-card or longer spade suit; the opener is required to bid 4♠. Similarly, 4◇ requires the opener to bid 4♡.

The convention is usually limited to those sequences in which the responder has a major suit. But 4♣ can be used in the same way to show diamonds, and 4♠ to show clubs.

A South African variation uses 4♣ to ask for hearts and 4◇ to ask for spades. This has a psychological advantage, alerting an absent-minded partner who might otherwise pass a 4♡ bid that asked for spades, but it has the disadvantage of ruling out the use of the GERBER convention.

As in the case of bidding against JACOBY TRANSFER BIDS, the fourth player can show a two-suited hand by previous partnership agreement. 4 NT would show minor suits; a double would show the suit doubled and the non-touching suit; and a cuebid in responder's genuine suit would show two suits of the same color (COLORFUL CUEBID).

THAILAND. See CONTRACT BRIDGE LEAGUE OF THAILAND.

THIN. An adjective used to describe (1) a hand without BODY; "a thin 15-count" indicates a hand with 15 high card points but lacking intermediates; (2) a makable game with fewer than 26 HCP between the two hands.

THIRD (similarly fourth, fifth, sixth, etc.). An adjective, that when used after naming a specific card, counts the number of cards held in the suit, e.g., ace-third denotes the holding of A–x–x.

THIRD BEST. See THIRD HIGHEST LEAD.

THIRD HAND. In the bidding, the partner of the dealer; in the play, the partner of the leader to a trick. For considerations affecting the third hand in the bidding after two passes, see BORDERLINE OPENING BIDS and PASSED HAND.

THIRD-HAND BIDS. See BORDERLINE OPENING BIDS and PASSED HAND.

THIRD HAND PLAY. Correct play by the partner of the opening leader is often the key to successful defense. The old whist rule of "third hand high" is generally right when a small card is led and dummy has low cards.

If dummy has an honor which the third player can beat, he should play his second-highest card if that is a 9 or better:

```
              Q 7 4
J 10 6 2                  K 9 3
              A 8 5
```

West leads the 2, dummy plays low, and East should play the 9. But if the 9 and 8 were interchanged, East should play high.

Sometimes the third player cannot afford to make any effort to win the trick:

```
              Q 10 2
J 9 7 3                   K 6 4
              A 8 5
```

If West leads the 3, South plays low from dummy, East must play low. If he plays the king, South makes three easy tricks. After the duck, the third trick remains in contention.

The right play for the third player can depend on entry considerations:

```
              Q 7 2
J 9 5 3                   K 8 4
              A 10 6
```

If East has no card of entry he should play the 8-spot. (West can then continue the suit safely.) However, if East has the next entry he must play the king. (East can then continue the suit safely.)

The remainder of this article will deal with third hand play against notrump. Some of the suggested plays won't always work, but at least they are food for thought.

```
              x x
J x x x x                 A Q x
              K 10 x
```

East should play the queen to the first trick to make it difficult for South to make a hold-up play. The stronger East's hand the more important it is to play the queen. With no entry of any sort, the ace and then the queen is probably best. Partner can be misled by the play of the queen if he later regains the lead.

As declarer, you expect that a good defender will presumably play the ace and then queen only if he's entryless or if his original holding is A–Q–J. In the latter case South should win the second trick and block the suit.

A similar situation arises here:

```
              x x
Q x x x x                 A J x
              K 10 x
```

If East has a strong hand and a sure entry, it pays to play the jack rather than the ace and then the jack. Again the jack makes it difficult for declarer to hold up. If East is weak he should play the ace and then the jack. A partner who has led originally from K-10-x-x-x seldom appreciates the fine nuance of the jack to the first trick.

$$x$$
A 9 x x x   K J x
$$Q\ 10\ 8\ x$$

Here again the jack at trick one may be the only card to defeat the contract. If East's hand is entryless he should play the jack.

If East plays the king and then the jack, East-West can never realize their full potential in the suit. If East has a side entry he should still probably play the jack. Playing the king and then the jack might induce West to think that East has the 10. Indeed, with the K-J-10 East would surely play that way.

Here's one where East should purposely fool his partner.

$$x\ x$$
A 9 x x x   Q J 10
$$K\ x\ x$$

East must play the jack to the first trick rather than the 10. If the 10 is played West may think that East has J-10-x, and wait for a lead through. However, when the jack drives out the king, West will know that either declarer has another stopper (K-Q-10) and it won't cost to continue, or that partner has the queen and the rest of the tricks belong to the defense.

If you are fortunate or unfortunate enough to have a partner who leads short suits against no-trump, you might remember these. Assume you are East and have not bid the suit:

$$8\ 5\ 4$$
3 2   A K J 10 9
$$Q\ 7\ 6$$

West leads the 3, and if East-West need five tricks, East should play the ace and then the jack. South will surely duck thinking that East has the doubleton. Also:

$$7\ 6\ 5$$
3 2   A J 10 9 8
$$K\ Q\ 4$$

Assuming you have divined the situation, you should play the 10 to the first trick, and if you regain the lead, try the jack. Again South will probably duck in the hope that the suit is blocked.

When the partner is known to have a four-card suit, and dummy has a doubleton 9, 10 or jack, some unusual positions arise. For instance:

$$10\ 5$$
K 8 3 2   A 9 4
$$Q\ J\ 7\ 6$$

Assuming dummy plays low, East saves a trick by playing the 9. One could interchange dummy's 10 with either the jack or the queen, and the result is the same. It is good to remember this combination because if it comes up and you try the 9, the full position might be:

$$10\ 3$$
K Q 8 2   A 9 4
$$J\ 7\ 6\ 3$$

In cases like this it pays to know when your play might have worked. Again in this position East should play his second best:

$$9\ 2$$
A 7 4 3   J 8 5
$$K\ Q\ 10\ 6$$

Many tricks are given up by the defenders when third hand fails to play middle in these fairly common situations:

$$10\ 2$$
K 8 6 4   Q 7 5
$$A\ J\ 9\ 3$$

Playing the 7 if dummy plays low holds declarer to two tricks: playing the queen gives declarer three. The position would be the same, of course, if North and South exchanged the 9 and the 10.

$$10\ 5$$
A 8 4 2   J 7 6
$$K\ Q\ 9\ 3$$

Playing the 6 to trick one saves a trick.

Let's look at a few cases now where partner is likely to have a five-card suit.

$$10\ 6\ 3$$
A 9 7 5 4   J 8 2
$$K\ Q$$

It should be fairly obvious that if East plays the jack to the first trick, declarer must make two tricks in the suit.

$$10\ 5\ 2$$
Q 9 8 7 3   J 6 4
$$A\ K$$

If West will be the first to regain the lead, it makes things much easier if East plays low to the first trick. If East is the first to regain the lead, it may not matter. However, if East plays low and finds the suit to be:

$$10\ 5\ 2$$
K Q 9 7 3   J 6 4
$$A\ 8$$

the result is disastrous.

Here is a fairly standard position:

$$10\ 2$$
A 9 7 4 3   Q 8 5
$$K\ J\ 6$$

Here East must play the 8 or give North-South a trick they do not deserve.

East also has the RULE OF ELEVEN to help him out. Consider the following layout:

$$\diamond\ 10\ 4\ 3$$
$\diamond$ A K 9 6 2 $\diamond$ J 8 7
$$\diamond\ Q\ 5$$

Using the rule of eleven, East knows that South has but one card above the 6. As it can't be the 9 (West would then have A-K-Q-6), the jack can't possibly be right. In fact, this is the actual hand: (See hand at top of next page.)

South plays in 3 NT and West leads the $\diamond$ 6. Dummy plays low and if East casually plays the jack, there is

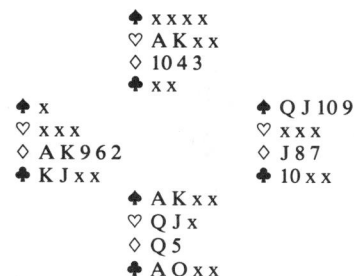

```
             ♠ x x x x
             ♡ A K x x
             ◇ 10 4 3
             ♣ x x
♠ x                        ♠ Q J 10 9
♡ x x x                    ♡ x x x
◇ A K 9 6 2                ◇ J 8 7
♣ K J x x                  ♣ 10 x x
             ♠ A K x x
             ♡ Q J x
             ◇ Q 5
             ♣ A Q x x
```

no further defense.

South plays off his major suit winners ending up in his own hand and eventually exits with a diamond. West is forced to play into South's club tenace.

If East retains the jack, the hand cannot be made.

Any real bridge player would not dream of putting up the jack in the following situation:

```
             10 x x
K Q 9 8                J x x
             A x x
```

If West leads the 8 and dummy goes low the jack just can't be right.

When East has a doubleton picture and dummy the 10, East must ask himself who is more likely to get the next lead. If it is partner, it is usually right to duck if partner leads the 7:

```
             10 x x
Q 9 8 7 x              J x
   or
K 9 8 7 x
             A K x
               or
             A Q x
```

Once again East does not look so good if West was leading from K–Q–9–7–x.

Third hand must also consider the possibility of a suit block.

```
             x x
A J 9 8                Q 7 x x x
             K 10
```

If East plays the queen in the diagram position, he blocks the suit.

Reprinted from an article by Edwin Kantar in the *American Bridge Digest*, August 1963.

THIRD HIGHEST LEAD. The lead of the highest card but two. This is standard when holding three cards headed by an honor. When the suit is longer, the third highest is led as a matter of system by some players. In fact, more and more players are leading third and fifth best, especially against notrump contracts. This type also may be used as a deceptive lead. A player who holds 10–5–4–2 and a weak hand may choose to lead the 4 followed by the 2. His purpose is to suggest a five-card suit, in the hope that declarer will make losing avoidance plays which are unnecessary, and which he would not have made if he had known that the opening leader's suit was a four-carder. For third-hand play when third highest leads are used, see RULE OF TWELVE. See also THREE SMALL CARDS, LEAD FROM; JOURNALIST LEADS.

THIRD SUIT BID. A bid in a new suit by the opener after a ONE-OVER-ONE or TWO-OVER-ONE RESPONSE. Such bids are non-forcing in standard methods, but there are other treatments: (a) Forcing in KAPLAN-SHEINWOLD if opener bids both minor suits; (b) Forcing in ROTH-STONE after a two-over-one response; strong after a one-over-one response and a rebid at the two-level; (c) Forcing in BARON in all situations; (d) Forcing in TWO-OVER-ONE GAME FORCE after a two-over-one response. See OPENER'S REBID.

THIRTEEN TABLES. At duplicate, 13–tables provide competition among 52 players as individuals, 26 pairs, or 13 teams-of-four. In the development of bridge tournament movements, it was early recognized that 13 rounds of two boards each, 3½ hours of play approximately, came close to being the ideal game. For this reason, 13 tables is considered to be the ideal for section size because every player plays each of the boards in play. However, 13 tables is not ideal for a SWISS MOVEMENT because of the odd number of teams. But it is possible to run a Swiss Team by utilizing a three-way match. By doing so you are limited to an even number of rounds — usually six is considered best.

Since 13 is a prime number, the RAINBOW MOVEMENT is practical and is generally used for individual tournaments. This can be cut to 11 or 12 rounds for a shorter game without introducing any complications. To maximize the number of partnerships, South and West can exchange positions after the first board of each round.

For a pair game, the simple MITCHELL MOVEMENT is used, or a SCRAMBLED MITCHELL if one winner is necessary. For two sessions a straight or scrambled Mitchell can be used the first round. For the second session use two-seven table Howell movements with duplicated hands. Put the first-session North–Souths into one section and the first session East–Wests into the other section. Have the players take their second-session seats by using their first-session pair numbers and going to that table. There will be no pair 14 in either section. When the other pairs are assigned to meet pair 14 they will play each other in whatever section is designated. They will play all new opponents except for the pair they meet when they would normally sit out. Twelve is top on a board and 156 is average. No factoring is required.

As a team-of-four game, the regular progression is an excellent movement. East–West players skip a table in the lower direction and the boards move to the lower table. There are no interruptions in the movement, and all other teams are met in the course of the event.

For 12½ and 13½, see HALF TABLES.

THIRTEENER. The card remaining in a suit when all other cards in that suit have been played on the first three tricks of the suit.

THREAT CARD (or menace). A threat card is a potential winner. It will take a trick provided that the opponent's holding in that suit can be weakened sufficiently.

The term "menance" (or "threat card") may be

used in one of the following specialized senses:

(1) Isolated menance: A menace consisting of one card, as the queen in the diagram.

```
          Q
    A        K
       x
```

(2) Two-card menance: A two-card holding, consisting of a winner in the suit accompanied by a **menace, as in the diagram.**

```
        A J
   K Q       x x
       x
```

(3) Split two-card menace: A two-card menace in which the winner and the threat card are in opposite hands, as in this diagram:

```
        A x
   K J       x x
       Q x
```

(4) Double menace: A threat card against both opponents (the diagram for a one-card menace, above, shows a double menace).

(5) Extended two-card menace: A two-card menace accompanied by one or more cards in that suit with the property that if the two-card menace is established, then the whole suit will run, e.g.:

```
        A J 10
   K Q       x x x
       x x
```

In this diagram if West discards the queen (or king) he permits South to cash *two* additional tricks in the suit.

(6) Recesses menace: A menace card is accompanied by two (or more) winners in that suit, e.g.:

```
        A K 9
   Q J 10     x x x
       x
```

North's holding is a recessed menace against West.

(7) Twin entry menace: One hand contains a winner and one (or more) small card(s) while the opposite hands holds a winner, a menace, and one (or more) small card(s) in that suit, e.g.:

```
        K x
   Q J x
       A 10 x
```

This suit is a twin-entry menace against West.

THREE or THREE-SPOT. The second-lowest card in a given suit, ranking between the 2 and the 4, sometimes called "trey."

THREE-BID. See PREEMPTIVE BID.

THREE-CARD SUITS, BIDS IN. In many situations the most convenient bid available may be in a three-card suit. Some of the more common examples are:

(1) In opening the bidding. Most frequent is an opening bid of 1 ♣, to keep the bidding at a low level and avoid an opening in a poor four-card major suit. Less common is an opening of 1 ◇ with a three-card suit, although this is standard practice with 4-4-3-2 distribution using five-card majors or with three small cards in clubs. Semi-psychic opening bids of

1 ♠ with a three-card suit are sometimes made, especially third-hand, nonvulnerable, with a subminimum opening. Opening bids in a three-card suit, of any rank, are often required in the ROMAN SYSTEM.

(2) In responding. A response in the lowest possible suit is sometimes made with a three-card suit, especially if the suit is strong, because no good alternative presents itself:

(a)	(b)
♠ J x x	♠ A K x
♡ x x x	♡ x x
◇ A K x	◇ x x x x
♣ x x x x	♣ x x x x

(a) A response of 1 ◇ to 1 ♠ is slightly preferable to 1 NT or 2 ♣.
(b) Some experts might choose to respond 1 ♠ to 1 ♡, although the orthodox 1 NT is, of course, not wrong.

(3) In rebidding. See OPENER'S REBID.

(4) In responding to a TAKEOUT DOUBLE.

See also FOURTH SUIT FORCING, FRAGMENT BID, INTEREST-SHOWING BID, TRIAL BID.

3 ♣ RESPONSE AS MAJOR RAISE. A convention devised by ALVIN ROTH to make a strong major suit raise while conserving space for exchange of information as to trump suit texture, singletons and controls below the game level. Over the 3 ♣ response, opener rebids 3 ◇ if he has any singleton; without a singleton he rebids 3 ♡, 3 ♠ or 3 NT with two, one, or none of the top three trump honors, respectively. If opener has bid 3 ◇, responder can show his own trump texture in the same way. Four-level bids show high card or distributional controls.

3 ♣ RESPONSE TO 1 NT. This bid is used in various ways, depending on the system. Some play it as a game force with slam interest; some as an invitation, asking partner to go on to 3 NT with a reasonable fit; some play it as a sign-off bid. At one time it was used to seek a major fit — a STAYMAN prototype, but this usage is obsolete.

3 ♣ STAYMAN. See 2 NT OPENING.

THREE-HANDED BRIDGE. Many three-handed versions of bridge have been devised. Apart from TOWIE, described separately, two games deserve consideration.

In the traditional *cutthroat* game, the players bid for a hidden dummy. The bidding continues until a bid, doubled or redoubled, is followed by two passes. The player on declarer's left leads, and the dummy is spread between the two opponents. The scoring is normal, declarer scoring a 700 rubber bonus only if neither defender has a game. Plus scores only are recorded for each player, and settlement is made on the net difference in scores.

An alternative game with a pre-exposed dummy was devised by GEORGE S. COFFIN in 1932. It is sometimes called *triangle contract* or *trio bridge.* The laws are as follows:

(1) The three players are designated as North, South, and East. North and South *bid* as well as play as partners against East and his exposed dummy.

There is no West player. Nor is there a second dummy, because North and South always play with closed hands, even if one or the other is declarer.

(2) To begin a game, the three players draw cards; the two players who draw the highest cards play as partners as North and South against East, who has the dummy for the entire rubber.

(3) For the first deal only, South shuffles either pack. Then East cuts and South deals while North shuffles the still pack. For the next hand, East cuts and North deals while South shuffles the still pack. Thereafter, North and South continue to deal alternately.

(4) East never deals or shuffles, but always cuts.

(5) Dummy is exposed before there is any bidding. Hence, if any dummy card is faced up during the deal, it is not treated as an exposed card. If a card is turned up in any other hand, there must, of course, be a new deal.

(6) South always calls first regardless of who dealt; North bids second. Dummy never bids, for East bids on the combined 26 East-West cards. If any player makes a bid, the auction continues indefinitely until two consecutive passes close it.

(7) As in four-handed bridge, the left-hand opponent (LHO) of declarer makes the opening lead. If South is declarer, dummy leads first; if North is declarer, East leads; or if East is declarer, South leads.

(8) If the revoke is established against East, he cannot be penalized for it unless South or North has called attention to East's failure to follow suit on the revoke trick. This special rule for three-handed bridge is called *the courtesy of the table*, and it is due to the fact that East has no partner to say "having none?" This service is rendered by North and/or South.

(9) Regular contract bridge scoring is used. After the net amount of a finished rubber has been computed, East wins or loses *twice* the net amount because he collects dummy's gain or suffers dummy's loss.

(10) At the end of each rubber, North shifts into the vacant chair on his right and becomes redesignated as South and his former partner as East.

3 NT. The lowest, quantitatively, bid that produces a game from a zero score; nine tricks without benefit of a trump suit.

3 NT OPENING. Traditionally this shows a balanced hand with 25–27 points. But with such hands most experts bid 2 ♣ followed by 3 NT and therefore prefer to use the 3 NT opening for some other purpose, such as:

(1) GAMBLING 3 NT.

(2) Weak minor suit pre-empt, comparable to a standard 4 ♣ or 4 ◇ opening. This method is useful for those who use 4 ♣ AND 4 ◇ OPENING TRANSFERS to show strong major suit hands.

(3) Solid major suit preempt with no side suit aces and at most one side king. This use, suggested by EDWIN KANTAR, is designed to ease responder's task of judging his side's game or slam prospects. The recommended responses are as follows: 4 ♣ asks

opener to bid a side king if he has one; 4 ◇ transfers to opener's suit; 4 ♡ or 4 ♠ indicates that responder wants to be declarer and has tried to guess opener's suit (if he misguesses, opener should correct); 4 NT asks about queens; 5 NT asks opener to bid a GRAND SLAM if he can play opposite a void.

3 NT OVERCALL. An overcall at the game level, usually made on a strong balanced hand or one of a preemptive nature.

NORTH	EAST
3 ♠	3 NT

In the above example East's hand might be:

> ♠ A J 9
> ♡ K 2
> ◇ A J 10 6 4
> ♣ K Q 2

It would be inadvisable for East to double 3 ♠ (OPTIONAL) since he has poor support for the "other major." Normally, the double of one major suit invites partner to bid the other if he can. East therefore "gambles" on 3 NT. In these awkward situations it is generally a good idea arbitrarily to place 8 points in your partner's hand and proceed accordingly. An opponent's double or raise from partner will clarify the situation.

In many situations the 3 NT overcall is gambling and semi-preemptive in nature. For example:

SOUTH	WEST
1 ♡	3 NT

or

NORTH	EAST	SOUTH	WEST
1 ♡	Pass	1 ♠	3 NT

In both examples West is trying to "steal" 3 NT. His holding might be:

> ♠ 6
> ♡ K 5
> ◇ A K Q 7 6 3 2
> ♣ 8 7 6

If an opponent doubles, it usually is incumbent upon partner of overcaller to run out into 4 ♣ if he has nothing of great value. A pass by partner would indicate a desire to play 3 NT. Note that this bid is usually made when not vulnerable, and partner must exercise good judgment in determining his action, lest a catastrophe develop.

3 NT REBID. See OPENER'S REBID.

3 NT RESPONSE to an opening suit bid of one. There are a number of treatments which can be adopted:

(1) *Standard.* Shows 16–18 points and any 4-3-3-3 distribution.

(2) *Limit.* Shows 13–15 points and any 4-3-3-3 distribution (ACOL SYSTEM).

(3) *Conventional.* Used with limit raises to show a standard forcing jump raise of 13–15 points when the opening bid was in a major (invented by MONROE INGBERMAN). For alternative methods of solving this problem see DELAYED GAME RAISE and SWISS CONVENTION.

(4) *Distributional.* Shows a 13–15 point raise with a side suit singleton when the opening bid was in a major (ACES SCIENTIFIC SYSTEM).

(5) *Extra Strong or Distributional.* Shows one of a series of CONGLOMERATE MAJOR RAISES. In response to a 1 ♡ opening, 3 NT would show 17–18 points. In response to a 1 ♠ opening, 3 NT would be as in (4) above.

(6) *Ace-asking.* See BABY BLACKWOOD.

(7) *Psychic control.* Showing 23 points or more, and therefore a hand which offers a play for game opposite a psychic opening bid; this assumes a ROTH-STONE psychic with 3–6 points concentrated mainly in the bid suit. If the opening bidder has a normal opening he proceeds to a slam: the combined strength already suggests a grand slam.

THREE–ODD. Three tricks over book or nine tricks in all.

THREE–QUARTER MOVEMENT. One of a series of pair movements arranged by SAM GOLD for 16 to 24 pairs inclusive. Each of the movements calls for 26 boards to be played against each of 13 opposing pairs. The movement is usually controlled by printed guide cards placed in the center of each table, but may also be controlled by individual guide cards given to each pair. The 12-pair movement is also a three-quarter movement, with each pair meeting nine other pairs in three-board rounds.

The games are completed in one session, and all pairs are ranked as one field. The movements provide an approach to BALANCED COMPARISONS, and are very desirable for clubs wishing to play exactly 26 or 27 boards, and to produce only one winning pair. The table below gives starting assignments for the first round. Pairs 1 through 13 move cyclically, replacing the lower numbered pair, with pair 1 replacing pair 13, while the boards are moved to the next lower numbered table, and from table 1 to the byestand. Pairs 14 and higher remain stationary, but ARROW SWITCHES at these tables should be introduced to secure balanced comparisons among these pairs.

	16 Pairs	18 Pairs	20 Pairs
Table 1	16v1 1–2	18v1 1–2	20v1 1–2
2	4v15 3–4	17v12 3–4	6v19 3–4
3	11v13 5–6	8v5 5–6	18v8 5–6
4	14v7 7–8	2v10 7–8	13v17 7–8
5	10v9 9–10	13v9 9–10	3v7 9–10
6	5v12 11–12	7v16 11–12	12v16 11–12
7	3v8 13–14	15v6 13–14	15v2 13–14
8	2v6 15–16	11v4 15–16	11v5 15–16
9	Boards on	14v3 17–18	14v10 17–18
10	byestand	Boards on	9v4 19–20
11	17–26	byestand	Boards on
12		19–26	byestand
			21–26

	22 Pairs	24 Pairs
Table 1	7v8 1–2	7v8 1–2
2	22v1 3–4	22v1 3–4
3	21v3 5–6	21v3 5–6
4	20v5 7–8	20v5 7–8
5	2v19 9–10	2v19 9–10
6	10v18 11–12	10v18 11–12
7	12v17 13–14	12v17 13–14
8	4v16 15–16	4v16 15–16
9	15v11 17–18	15v11 17–18
10	13v14 19–20	14v13 19–20
11	6v9 21–22	6v23 21–22*
12	Boards on	24v9 21–22*
	byestand	*Constant relay; boards
	23–26	on byestand 23–26

In the 12-pair game the moving pairs are 1 through 9. Pairs 10, 11 and 12 remain at the same table, but not necessarily in the same direction. Arrow switches should be given to make a balanced comparison between the stationary pairs. Pair 12 should remain stationary. Pair 11 should sit North-South rounds 1, 2, 3, 6 and 7, and East-West rounds 4, 5, 8 and 9. Pair 10 should sit North-South rounds 1, 2, 5 and 6, and should follow the next lower number through the game, with pair 1 following 9, 2 following 1, etc.

	12 Pairs
Table 1	12v1 1–3
2	11v4 4–6
3	10v8 7–9
4	2v7 10–12
5	9v6 13–15
6	5v3 16–18
	Boards on
	byestand
	19–27

THREE-QUARTER NOTRUMP. The use of a weak notrump in all situations except vulnerable against non-vulnerable. Players who combine this with a fourth-hand weak notrump at all vulnerabilities (safe because neither opponent can double and dummy must have some values) can be said to play 13/16ths.

THREE SMALL CARDS, LEAD FROM. There are three distinct schools of thought.

(1) *Top of nothing.* The traditional lead of the 8, for example, from 8 5 2, is advocated by most textbooks. This has the advantage of advising partner immediately that no high honor is held, but it has some disadvantages. It clarifies the suit distribution for the declarer also; it leads to ambiguity on the second round because partner cannot be sure whether the lead was from three cards or two; and it may waste a significant card, especially if the lead is an unsupported 9. Partners using this treatment must agree which card should be played on the second round of the suit. Most experts believe in following with the middle card, whether leading or following suit. This identifies a doubleton with certainty if the second card is the lowest possible. There is no technical objection to the alternative of following with the lowest card, in which case a doubleton is identified if the second card played is the highest possible.

Whether there is any partnership agreement, it is important to play quickly. Hesitation clearly shows the three-card holding and is unethical.

(2) *Low Lead.* Some experts, mainly of the ROTH-STONE or JOURNALIST persuasion, lead the lowest of three small cards. (In pursuing this principle to the ultimate, TOBIAS STONE has been known to lead the 8 from 10 9 8.) This avoids the disadvantages of the top of nothing lead, but leaves partner in doubt whether the lead is from an honor. (An obvious exception is the highest card is led in the suit that has been bid by partner and raised by the leader.)

(3) *Mud.* The lead of the middle card, usually to be followed by the top card. The term is derived from the initial letters of middle-up-down, and the lead is used by an increasing minority. It avoids most disadvantages, but may not be as clear to partner as

the other methods. A few expert partnerships have no clear-cut agreement, but use the method which seems best adapted to the particular situation. The top card is led if partner is likely to need to know about honors rather than length. The bottom card is led if length is the vital factor. And the middle card is chosen if it is desired to keep declarer in doubt.

THREE–SUITER. A hand with at least four cards in each of three suits, and therefore distributed 4-4-4-1 or 5-4-4-0. For oepning the bidding with a three-suiter see BIDDABLE SUITS, BORDERLINE OPENING BIDS, and CHOICE OF SUIT. For specialized three-suiter conventions see BLUE TEAM 2♢, BROZEL, EXCLUSION BID, KANTAR CUEBID, PRECISION CLUB (2♢ opening), ROMAN SYSTEM (2♣ opening), ROMAN 2♢. For systems of showing three-suiters in response to an artifical 1♣ opening, see PRECISION CLUB (Impossible Negative; Unusual Positive), SUPER PRECISION (Super Unusual Positive). For a convention allowing the opening bidder to show a strong three-suiter, see ALLEN OVER 2♣.

THREE TABLES. At duplicate, three tables provide for competition among 12 (or 13) players as individuals, five or six pairs, or three teams-of-four.

As an individual tournament, 11 rounds are required for 12 players, 12 for 13 players. Conduct of such a game is described under INDIVIDUAL MOVEMENT for 12 or 13 players.

As a pair contest, the HOWELL MOVEMENT is far superior to the MITCHELL, as it provides that each pair of players will meet with each other pair as opponents. For the three-table Howell setup, see HOWELL MOVEMENT. If there are five pairs, pair 6 should be the phantom, and the other pairs sit out the round corresponding with their number.

As a team event, a three-team round-robin can be successfully conducted in two halves, using three sets of boards. Half of each team remains North–South in both halves. Setup of boards and players is as follows:

1st half	Table 1	NS1 vs. EW2 first set of boards
	2	NS2 vs. EW3 second set of boards
	3	NS3 vs. EW1 third set of boards
2nd half	Table 1	NS1 vs. EW3 third set of boards
	2	NS2 vs. EW1 first set of boards
	3	NS3 vs. EW2 second set of boards

Team 1 has met team 2 on the first set of boards and team 3 on the third set of boards, completing their two matches; and the match between teams 2 and 3 was completed on the second set of boards. Board-a-match scoring is possible, as is total point or IMP scoring. If each team wins and loses one match, a winner can be determined by total boards won in both matches for BOARD-A-MATCH SCORING; total points in aggregate scoring; or ratio of points won to points lost in IMP SCORING. See QUOTIENT.

For 2½ tables or 3½ tables, see HALF TABLES.

THREE–TWO–ONE–ONE-HALF COUNTS. See FOUR ACES SYSTEM.

THROUGH STRENGTH. The old whist idea that one should lead "through strength" is one of the least valuable bridge rules of thumb. The implication is that the player on declarer's left should

generally lead a suit in which dummy is strong.

In many situations it is much safer to lead a suit in which dummy is weak than a suit in which dummy is strong. The defender must consider carefully before leading away from an honor, just as he would in making an opening lead. To lead a suit with no card above the 10 rarely costs a trick, although it may avoid a guess for the declarer.

Some situations need little discussion. If dummy has A-K-x, for example, a lead from a queen is dangerous, and other leads are safe or almost safe. The following examples deal with more difficult cases. In each case dummy is shown with three cards: the danger or lack of it is little affected if dummy has an extra small card.

(1) Dummy has A-x-x. A lead from a jack is relatively safe. A lead from the queen is more dangerous. A lead from the king is worst of all.

(2) Dummy has A-Q-x or A-J-x. A lead from the king is again very dangerous. A lead from the jack (or queen) is less dangerous. From a holding headed by K-J or K-10, the second honor should be led.

(3) Dummy has K-Q-x. A lead from the jack is dangerous. A lead from the ace is relatively safe.

(4) Dummy has K-J-x. A lead from the ace is safe. A lead from the queen is dangerous. However, this consideration may cause declarer to misguess if he holds a doubleton and a lead is made from the queen.

(5) Dummy has K-x-x. All leads from single honors (except the 10) are bad. Worst is from the queen; least bad is from the ace.

(6) Dummy has Q-x-x. The lead from the king is now safest, and the lead from the ace is worst.

(7) Dummy has J-x-x . The lead from the ace is worst. It is better to lead from the queen than from the king.

(8) Dummy has x-x-x. In this case, the lower the honor to be led from, the safer the lead. Leading from the jack is almost completely safe, and leading from the queen costs only if declarer has A-K-J. The lead "through weakness" is usually safer than a lead "through strength."

For the converse situation, see UP TO WEAKNESS, under which heading a general principle covering the above situations is set out.

THROW AWAY. (1) To discard. (2) To defend or play so badly that a very poor score results.

THROW IN. (1) To make a THROW-IN PLAY. (2) In rubber bridge, to toss the cards into the center of the table, after four passes. Used in Great Britain as a synonym for PASS OUT.

THROW-IN PLAYS. The term *endplay* originally referred to techniques applied during the last three or four tricks of a deal. Now an endplay may be said to occur at any stage of the play provided that it involves a squeeze, a trump coup, or a throw-in. Loosely applied, endplay is used incorrectly as a synonym for throw-in. In a throw-in play, an opponent gains the lead, but it costs him a trick (or more) to do so. There are three types of throw-in, according to the means whereby the opponent thrown in loses a trick.

(1) Tenace Throw-in (usually shortened to *throw-in*). An opponent is thrown in and forced to lead from a broken honor holding at the cost of a trick.

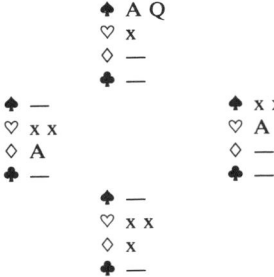

South has placed East with the ♠ K. In order to avoid a losing finesse, a heart is led and East is forced into the lead. He must lead into North's spade tenace.

(2) Trump Throw-in (also known as an *elimination play*). An opponent is thrown in and forced to concede a ruff and discard.

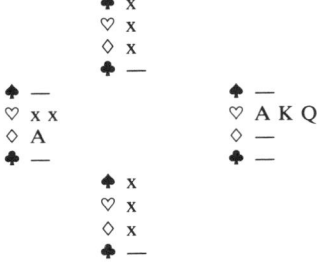

Spades are trumps, and South apparently has two unavoidable losers in hearts and diamonds. However, a heart is led, which forces East into the lead. He must continue a heart, permitting South to discard the losing diamond while ruffing the heart in the dummy.

The distinction between these two types of throw-in does not rest on the contract, trump or notrump, but on the mechanism involved. Both types may occur at a trump contract. At a trump contract, the opponent who is thrown in may be faced with a choice of plays, each of which costs a trick; thus the various categories of throw-in may overlap.

(3) Entry Throw-in. The opponent who gains the lead must play a suit in which declarer has established tricks to which there is no entry.

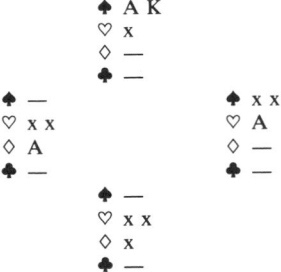

South has the lead in a notrump contract. North's two spade tricks are inaccessible. However, a heart

lead saddles East with the necessity of leading a spade to the next trick, providing the entry to dummy's hand.

Proper execution of a throw-in play requires declarer to consider two questions: (a) the stripping, or elimination, process: this means that declarer must assure himself that, once thrown in, the defender has no safe lead; and (b) the throw-in card: at the judicious moment, declarer must be able to lose the lead to that opponent whose hand has been stripped of safe exit cards.

Declarer may strip an opponent's hand by plain suit leads, by ruffing, or by a preliminary squeeze (see SECONDARY SQUEEZE). Sometimes a perfect elimination is not possible, and declarer must hope for favorable distribution.

```
                ♠ Q x x x
                ♡ K x x
                ◇ A x x
                ♣ K x x
   ♠ K J                      Immaterial
   ♡ x x
   ◇ K J x x x
   ♣ Q J 10 x
                ♠ A 10 x x x x
                ♡ A x x
                ◇ Q x
                ♣ A x
```

South has become declarer at a 5 ♠ contract reached by trying for a slam. A club was led by West, won by the ace. The A ♠ was cashed, followed by a club to the king and ruffing a third club (stripping both hands of clubs). Two top hearts were played, declarer hoping to strip West of exit cards in that suit, followed by a spade, throwing West into the lead. Since West in fact had no more hearts, his choice was between a club or diamond, either of which would forfeit a trick.

Certain suit combinations lend themselves to a throw-in. In the following combinations, the throw-in card is in the critical suit, which the defenders must return at the cost of a trick:

A Q 9	A J 10	K 10 x	Q J x	K 9 x	A 10 x
x x x	x x x	x x x	x x x	J x x	J 9 x

In each case, South leads low, and then simply covers the card played by West. Provided East has been stripped of all other exit cards, he will have to return this suit; in this way declarer can hold his losses in the suit to a minimum.

There are other combinations in which an extra trick is guaranteed, provided the opponents must open up the suit. The throw-in card must be in some other suit.

A 10 x	K x x	K 9 x	Q x x
J x x	J x x	Q 10 x	J x x

Finally, there are certain combinations in which declarer's prospects are improved if the opponents can be forced to lead the suit. Again, the throw-in card must be in some other suit:

A 10 x	A x	A x x
K 9 x	Q x	J 9 x

There are many suit combinations which can provide the means for a throw-in play. The most common is an eight-card holding, missing the king and queen, A–x–x opposite J–x–x–x–x. Declarer leads the ace, and then plays a small card in the suit after the elimination is complete. If either player holds K–Q of that suit, he can be thrown in; even if he holds K–x or Q–x, he may neglect to unblock, or else it may cost him a trick to do so.

Many throw-in plays are named after the means employed to strip the hand or throw-in the opponents. One such would be a crossruff strip, and another a loser-on-loser elimination. The latter is a commonly available maneuver, although is often missed in practice.

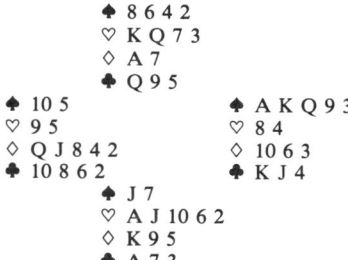

```
              ♠ 8 6 4 2
              ♡ K Q 7 3
              ◇ A 7
              ♣ Q 9 5
  ♠ 10 5                   ♠ A K Q 9 3
  ♡ 9 5                    ♡ 8 4
  ◇ Q J 8 4 2              ◇ 10 6 3
  ♣ 10 8 6 2               ♣ K J 4
              ♠ J 7
              ♡ A J 10 6 2
              ◇ K 9 5
              ♣ A 7 3
```

After East opened the bidding with 1♠, South became the declarer at 4♡. Spades are led and declarer ruffs high on the third round. Placing East with the ♣K for his opening bid, South draws trumps in two rounds, plays the ◇ A–K, followed by a diamond ruff, ending in dummy. So dummy's last spade is led, on which South discards a losing club, throwing East into the lead. East must concede a ruff and sluff, or lead from his club tenace.

The throw-in usually follows the elimination, but this is not invariably the case.

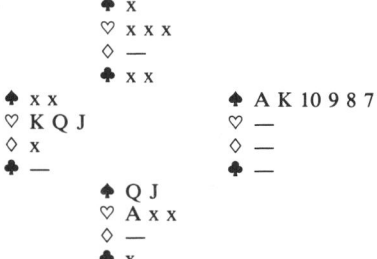

```
              ♠ x
              ♡ x x x
              ◇ —
              ♣ x x
  ♠ x x                    ♠ A K 10 9 8 7
  ♡ K Q J                  ♡ —
  ◇ x                      ◇ —
  ♣ —                      ♣ —
              ♠ Q J
              ♡ A x x
              ◇ —
              ♣ x
```

Clubs are trumps and South requires four of the remaining tricks, with only three in sight. A spade is led, won by East. On the spade continuation, North discards a heart. On the next spade, North discards another heart, while South ruffs. South can now lead the ♡A and win both of dummy's trumps for three more tricks.

In a double elimination, either opponent may win the throw-in card, but the declarer gains a trick in either case.

(4) Double Elimination.

(See hand at top of right column.)

Diamonds are trumps, and South requires four of the remaining tricks. A club is led which may be won by either opponent. If West's queen holds, he must lead into South's spade tenace; if East overtakes with the ♣K, South's jack is established.

There are certain rare positions in which the

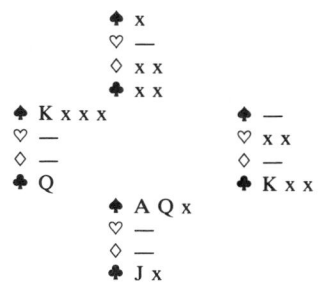

```
              ♠ x
              ♡ —
              ◇ x x
              ♣ x x
  ♠ K x x x                 ♠ —
  ♡ —                       ♡ x x
  ◇ —                       ◇ —
  ♣ Q                       ♣ K x x
              ♠ A Q x
              ♡ —
              ◇ —
              ♣ J x
```

declarer can bring off a repeating elimination, in which the same defender can be thrown in several times to make a losing lead.

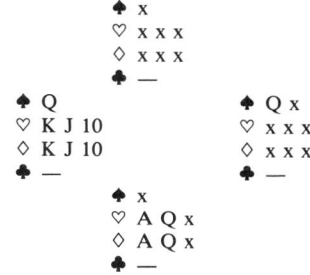

```
              ♠ x
              ♡ x x x
              ◇ x x x
              ♣ —
  ♠ Q                       ♠ Q x
  ♡ K J 10                  ♡ x x x
  ◇ K J 10                  ◇ x x x
  ♣ —                       ♣ —
              ♠ x
              ♡ A Q x
              ◇ A Q x
              ♣ —
```

Spades are trump. South leads a spade and West is thrown in. Whatever card he returns, South wins two tricks in that suit and throws West in again with the third round of the suit. West must now give declarer two tricks in the second suit. South, starting with two tricks, ends up with four.

(5) Pseudo Elimination. A defender may believe that he has been thrown in and must concede a trick, although this may not be the case. Usually this occurs when the defender fears to give declarer a ruff and sluff. This may not benefit declarer for either of two reasons: he may have concealed another card of that suit in his hand, or else the ruff and discard permits declarer to discard a card which was not a loser in any case.

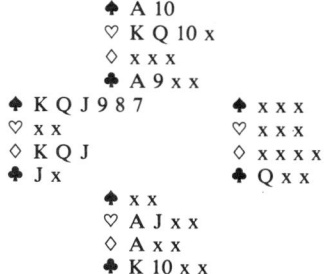

```
              ♠ A 10
              ♡ K Q 10 x
              ◇ x x x
              ♣ A 9 x x
  ♠ K Q J 9 8 7             ♠ x x x
  ♡ x x                     ♡ x x x
  ◇ K Q J                   ◇ x x x x
  ♣ J x                     ♣ Q x x
              ♠ x x
              ♡ A J x x
              ◇ A x x
              ♣ K 10 x x
```

South is declarer at 5♡. A spade is led, won by the ace. Trumps are drawn, the ◇A is taken, and the suit continued. West wins two diamonds and a spade. The only correct defense is a spade continuation, although South can discard a club in one hand while ruffing the spade in the other. South still has a club loser. However, if West is reluctant to give the sluff and ruff, he will lead a club, permitting South to avoid a loser in that suit.

(6) Defense Against a Throw-in. Often the

defenders can foresee an impending throw-in. They have several ways of escaping the endplay.

(a) By retaining an Exit Card.

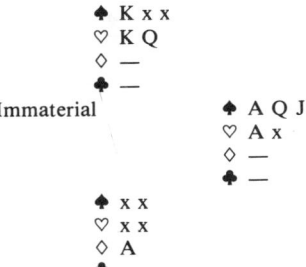

At notrump, South leads the ◊ A, throwing a spade from the North hand, East must discard a spade, not the small heart. If he discards the small heart, South can throw him in the lead with a heart, and East is forced to lead the spade. If he holds the small heart, he can exit with it after winning the ♡ A, forcing the spade lead to come to him from North.

(b) By Unblocking.

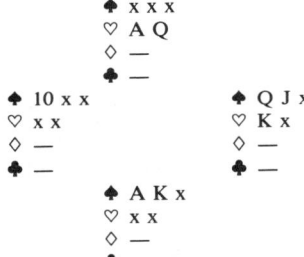

South cashes the ♠A-K on which East must unblock by playing his honors, so that West can win the third round of spades with the 10, returning a heart, to ensure a trick for East's king.

(c) By Playing Second Hand High.

```
        A Q 8
10 x x          K J 9
        x x x
```

South leads small, intending to insert the 8. East can win with the 9, but then must lead into North's tenace. When South plays small, West must rise with the 10 to protect his partner from the endplay.

(d) By Refusing to Assist in the Elimination.

```
              ♠ x x x
              ♡ K J x
              ◊ A x x
              ♣ x x x x
♠ A K x x x              ♠ J x x
♡ x x                   ♡ x
◊ K x x                 ◊ Q J x x x x
♣ K J x                 ♣ 10 x x
              ♠ Q x
              ♡ A Q x x x x x
              ◊ x
              ♣ A Q 9
```

After West opened 1♠, South became the declarer at 4♡. West took two top spades. West must switch to hearts or diamonds. South does not have enough

entries to dummy to ruff out spades and diamonds to strip the West hand before leading a club. See also PARTIAL ELIMINATION.

Monroe Ingberman

THROWING THE LEAD (into a desired defender's hand). See THROW-IN PLAYS.

TICKETS. A colloquialism used in various ways to refer to (1) pick-up slips, (2) private score cards, or (3) the right high cards for a particular action — "He had the tickets."

TIERCE. A term, obsolete in bridge, used to describe a sequence of three cards, one or more of which usually has honor rank.

TIES. The equality of scores in a session or event of bridge competition.

TIGHT. A colloquialism for SINGLETON, particularly in describing a singleton high honor, refers also to doubleton honors as in A–K or K–Q tight. STIFF is also used.

TIME LIMIT ON RIGHT TO PLAY. This is usually at the discretion of the director. In some tournaments the sponsoring organization sets a deadline beyond which purchase of additional entries depends on the need to fill in sections. In second and later sessions of multi-session events, the director must seek substitutes for pairs who are late to report. If the qualified players do not appear within 10 minutes of the scheduled time, their right to play is canceled, although usually they are permitted to enter subsidiary events if they have not gone into their second round. For other time limits, see SLOW PLAY.

TIME VALUATION. See TEMPO.

TIMING. An element in the play of a hand. The order in which trumps are pulled, losers are trumped, and side suits are developed are elements that enter into both declarer's and defenders' play.

TOP. (1) On a board: the best score made in the play of a particular hand in a duplicate tournament; its value in matchpoint play is one less than the number of times the board was in competition. If one pair earns a top, their opponents must score zero points or a bottom. (2) Score: the best score for a session of play among the contestants in direct competition (3) A card: to play a card higher in rank than the ones previously played by the second or third player to play to the trick.

TOP AND BOTTOM CUEBID. An immediate overcall in the opponent's major suit to show the highest and lowest ranking unbid suits. See also MICHAELS CUEBID.

TOP OF INTERIOR SEQUENCE. See INTERIOR SEQUENCE.

TOP OF NOTHING. See THREE SMALL CARDS, LEAD FROM.

TOP SCORE. The highest number of matchpoints available to any contestant in direct competition. See MATCHPOINT; SCORING ACROSS THE FIELD; BAROMETER SCORING. In North America and some other areas of the world, top is one less than the number of times a board is in play. In Europe and some other areas, it is more common to make top two less than double the number of times a board is in play. The second method results in scores exactly twice as large as the first method, the major difference being that halves are eliminated. In American tournaments, fields are divided into sections and tops usually are figured within each section or, in some major events, combinations of sections. It is common in other parts of the world to score across the entire field, making for much larger tops.

TORINO BULL. The trophy for the World Women's Team Olympiad, presented by the City of Turin, Italy, on the occasion of the 1960 Olympiad. See WORLD CHAMPIONSHIPS for winners.

TOTAL POINT SCORING. (British term is aggregate scoring.) Computation of scores based on points earned minus points lost, from the scoring table of contract bridge (see LAWS OF CONTRACT BRIDGE (Law 84), LAWS OF DUPLICATE (Law 73)); the scoring used at rubber bridge or CHICAGO.

As a form of scoring in pair tournaments, total point scoring was complicated by the imposition of PENALTY LIMITS and the resulting EXCESS POINTS. It has been almost wholly eliminated, generally in favor of MATCHPOINT SCORING, but occasionally, in important matches, by IMPS FOR PAIR GAMES or scoring by VICTORY POINTS.

As a form of scoring in team games, it is adaptable particularly for match play in head-on contests. IMP scoring has largely replaced total point scoring. The RESINGER TROPHY knockout teams in the EASTERN STATES REGIONAL was the last important knockout event to replace total point scoring with IMP scoring, doing so in 1965.

TOTAL SCORE. See TOTAL POINT SCORING.

TOTAL TRICKS, LAW OF. See LAW OF TOTAL TRICKS.

TOUCHING CARDS. (1) Cards that are in sequence in the same suit, as the 10 and 9 in a holding of K–10–9–6. See SEQUENCE and PLAY FROM EQUALS. (2) With fingers: in duplicate bridge, it is illegal for any player to touch any cards other than his own, unless he is arranging the dummy's cards and so declares. See LAWS OF CONTRACT BRIDGE (Law 7).

TOUCHING HONORS. A holding of two or more honors that are in sequence. In a holding of Q–J–10–7 of a suit, the first three are touching honors.

TOUCHING SUITS. Suits that, within the order of ranking, are next to each other; spades and hearts, hearts and diamonds, and diamonds and clubs are touching suits. For some purposes, such as selecting

the suit for an opening bid, clubs and spades are regarded as touching, with the clubs the "higher" suit.

TOURNAMENT. In the days of WHIST, gatherings of players for the purpose of competing at the game were termed "congresses." As auction bridge replaced whist, the term "congress" gave way to tournament, as the accent shifted from sociability to competition. Club games among local groups up to competition at national and international level are all so described.

The essentials of a tournament are the planning thereof by a SPONSORING ORGANIZATION, publicity and promotion, the programming of events, the competition itself, the SCORING and determination of winners, and the HOSPITALITY in connection therewith. Various aspects of tournament play and references to the results of important tournaments are treated in special articles in this book. See DUPLICATE BRIDGE and CHAMPIONSHIP TOURNAMENTS.

TOURNAMENT COMMITTEE. See COMMITTEE.

TOURNAMENT DIRECTOR. The official representative of the sponsoring organization, responsible for the technical management of the tournament, subject to the LAWS OF DUPLICATE and to supplementary regulations announced by the sponsor.*

Classification of Directors. Tournaments directors are trained by the ACBL and ranked according to ability and experience, determining the kind of event each is qualified to direct. Exclusive of qualified, certified and local directors authorized to conduct games at affiliated Duplicate CLUBS, in 1982 there were 227 such tournament directors of sectional rank or higher. In the following classifications, the figures in parentheses are the number qualified in that group as of 1982.

National directors (15). Full-time salaried employees of the ACBL, qualified to provide top-flight direction at international, national and regional tournaments. When schedules permit, their services are also available as chief directors of sectional tournaments, ensuring smooth conduct of these events as well as trained supervision of other directors on the staff.

Associate national directors (16). Although not usually full-time salaried ACBL employees, the members of this group are fully qualified to serve as chief directors at regional and sectional events.

Regional directors (102). Ranked at four levels, from R–1 through (highest) R–4 and certified as proficient in all aspects of tournament management. Qualified for assignment as director-in-charge for sectional tournaments, as well as for staff service at regional and national events.

Sectional directors (94). Certified by ACBL as fully qualified to assist a senior director at sectional and higher-rated tournaments. Ranked S–1 through (highest) S–4.

*Note: Throughout this book, "Director," when capitalized, refers to a member of the Board of Directors of a governing body and not to a tournament director.

Local directors. Recognized by the ACBL as qualified to assist higher-rated directors at sectional tournaments in their home areas.

Trainee directors. Sponsoring Units may assign to their tournaments individuals as yet unrated directors/scorers for practice and training by the assigned qualified director(s), who will give such trainees all possible assistance and instruction. Although they may be paid a small session fee, such trainees are not counted as members of the required professional staff. A trainee may work a maximum of eight sessions in that status. Thereafter, unless his work meets standards that would qualify him for rating as a local director, he may not be engaged as a professional assistant for further tournaments.

Scorer. If the director (or any assistant) has more than one score sheet to total at the end of a session, he is authorized to assign one competent scorer to matchpoint and total each extra sheet. This work is usually performed by one or more of the contestants after the game. No certification is required, but the director should select the best qualified individuals available.

Tournament directors listed by the ACBL in 1982 in its two top categories are:

National Tournament Directors

Bill Adams	Jack Hudgins
Gary Blaiss	Karl Johnson
Maury Braunstein	*Jerry Machlin
Harry Clark	Phil Merry
Sid Davidson	Becky Rogers
Bob Dischner	Sol Weinstein
*Harry Goldwater	John Wiser
John Hamilton	Phil Wood
John "Spider" Harris	
*retired	

Associate National Tournament Directors

Esther DeRaad	Bill Schoder
Dale Egholm	Bobbie Shipley
Max Hardy	Buddy Spiegel
Mike Linah	Paul Stehley
Brian Moran	Ken Stone
Roger Putnam	Stan Tench
Tom Quinlan	William Weyant
Nelson Rowe	Walter Wilson

TOWIE. A form of bridge devised for three players but intended to be played usually by four, five or more players, of whom only three play at one time but the others participate in the defenders' score against the declarer. The game was originated in Paris in 1931 by two Americans, J. Leonard Replogle and Paulding Fosdick, who were then living abroad. In 1935 Replogle, with the assistance of WILLIAM HUSKE, sought to make towie a popular game in the United States, with only moderate success, though it is still played. The principal books on the game were written by Huske and by STUYVESANT WAINWRIGHT, JR.

The deal in towie conforms to that of certain earlier three-hand bridge games: After dealing four hands, the dealer turns up six cards of the dummy, after which the auction proceeds as in any three-handed game. Scoring is based on the 1932 INTERNATIONAL CODE, which differs from later codes in undertrick penalties and in the fact that notrump tricks count 35 each.

The three active players bid for the dummy. The high bidder becomes declarer. If he fulfills his contract, he collects from every other player, active or inactive; if he loses, he pays every such player. After each deal, one player is replaced by an inactive player, in order of precedence except that a player who is not vulnerable takes precedence over a vulnerable player.

If a game contract is not reached, the hands are thrown in, and a GOULASH follows. See also THREE-HANDED BRIDGE.

TRAIN BRIDGE. See COMMUTER BRIDGE.

TRANCE. A protracted break in the tempo of the play, in which a player attempts to solve a problem. Trances and huddles are frequent causes of ethical difficulties and disputes. See HUDDLE and SLOW PLAY.

TRANSFER BIDS. Bids aimed principally at making a strong hand declarer. It is often advantageous for the lead to come up to the stronger hand and for it to remain concealed.

Transfer bids were first used in the United States by DAVID CARTER (see TEXAS CONVENTION) and subsequently developed by OSWALD JACOBY (see JACOBY TRANSFER BIDS). These bids were independently devised by Olle Willner of Stockholm, Sweden, who discussed the use of transfers in a series of articles in *Bridge Tidningen* in 1953–54.

The original form of transfer bid was the Texas Convention, and SOUTH AFRICAN TEXAS is a revised form. See also French RELAY SYSTEM, SOUTH AFRICAN TEXAS.

Another purpose of transfer bids is to distinguish between weak and strong opening preempts, to enable responder to judge whether to try for slam. See 4♣ AND 4♦ OPENING TRANSFERS; 4 NT OPENING AS MINOR PREEMPT; RUBIN TRANSFERS.

TRANSFER OPENING PREEMPTS. See 4♣ AND 4♦ OPENING TRANSFERS; 4 NT OPENING PREEMPT; RUBIN TRANSFERS; TRANSFER OPENING THREE-BIDS.

TRANSFER OPENING THREE-BIDS. A development of the TEXAS principle. They have three technical advantages. First, the lead comes up to the hand which is likely to be strong in the side suits. Second, the defense is more difficult because little is known about the declarer's strength and distribution. Third, the opening bidder may be able to show a freak two-suited hand by bidding his second suit on the second round.

A technical disadvantage is that it is easier for the opponents to take action than it would be after a normal three-bid: a double and a cuebid in the opener's genuine suit are available as takeout bids of varying strength. Also, a preemptive bid in clubs cannot be made at the level of three.

A practical disadvantage is that an absentminded partner may forget that the convention is being used. Also, it may gain an unfair advantage against opponents unfamiliar with the convention.

Used in the World Championship by PIERRE GHESTEM and RENE BACHERICH. Not classified by the ACBL for tournament use.

TRANSFERS OVER DOUBLES OF 1 NT. A four-suit escape method. A redouble is a transfer to clubs, 2♣ transfers to diamonds, 2◊ to hearts and 2♡ to spades. If responder redoubles and then bids 2◊ over the forced 2♣, he is asking opener to bid his better major.

TRANSFER SQUEEZE.
A squeeze play which results from TRANSFERRING THE MENACE. The following hand was played by ALAN TRUSCOTT in the 1958 European Championships:

```
              ♠ 7 6 4 3
              ♡ Q 8
              ◊ Q 9 7 2
              ♣ A J 8
♠ K                        ♠ 9 8 4 2
♡ 9 6 5 3                  ♡ K J
◊ J 10 8 5                 ◊ K 6 4 3
♣ K 10 9 4                 ♣ 5 3 2
              ♠ A Q J 10
              ♡ A 10 7 4 2
              ◊ A
              ♣ Q 7 6
```

West led the ◊ J against 4♠, which was ducked around to the ace. A heart to the queen and king brought a spade return, and the finesse of the queen lost to the king. A heart was returned and won by South, who led a second round of trumps, revealing the bad split. A low heart was ruffed and overruffed, and East exited with his last trump. The ♣ J was finessed, and the ◊ Q was led to transfer the diamond menace. East covered, South ruffed, and two winning hearts squeezed West in the minor suits.

TRANSFERRED TRICK.
A trick transferred to the nonoffending side after a revoke has been established. See LAWS OF DUPLICATE (Law 64).

TRANSFERRING THE MENACE.
The process whereby control of a suit is transferred from one opponent to the other.

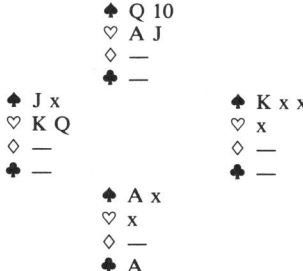

South has menaces in two suits, so that the material for a squeeze is present, but each opponent controls one menace, and neither can be squeezed. If the lead is in the North hand, the ♠ Q is led forcing East to play the king which is taken by the ace. The spade menace is no longer the queen guarded by East's king but the 10 guarded by West's jack, so that West has BUSY CARDS in two suits, and he is squeezed by the lead of the ♣ A. But if the lead had been in the South hand, the lead of the ♣ A would have effected a GUARD SQUEEZE against West.

Monroe Ingberman

TRANSFORMATION CARDS.
These are specially designed packs whose faces include the various pips on the suit cards as part of an overall design.

During the last century, a number of artists tried their hands at creating pictures that would incorporate all of the pips, in their usual locations, into larger designs, generally of human or animal figures.

The first such cards seem to have been made by J. G. Cotta, in Tübingen, Germany, in 1805, with several different packs produced by him in the next few years. English transformation cards appeared first in Ackerman's *Repository* in 1818, and several other packs soon followed.

About 1850, sets of cards appeared in London, New York, Munich, Vienna and Paris, partially duplicates in design, some cards being different while others appear in three or four of the packs. Because of the widespread copying, it is difficult to know which versions were original. Grimaud and Hart put their names on packs, and some artists' initials can be found, but precise dating appears impossible.

Issued in New York were the Eclipse Comic cards, designed by F. H. Lowerre in 1876, Tiffany & Company issued their Harlequin cards three years later; these same designs were used for the first series of Kinney Brothers Cigarette cards. A second Kinney series followed with all new designs. In 1895, the United States Playing Card Company published its own packs, called "Hustling Joe" and "Vanity Fair."

Albert Field

TRAP.
A defensive bidding system against the FORCING CLUB. Double indicates a heart suit and 1◊ shows a spade suit. 1♡ shows either a black two-suiter or a red two-suiter. 1♠ shows either both minors or both majors. 1 NT shows either a club-heart two-suiter or a diamond-spade two-suiter. All bids at the two level show either the suit bid or a three-suiter short in the suit bid. See TRAP WITH TWO-LEVEL TRANSFERS.

TRAP BID
(or trap bidding). An inconsistent sequence of bids which traps partner by showing strength denied by an earlier bid.

For example:

SOUTH	NORTH
1♣	1♠
3♠	4♠
5♡	

South's raise to 3♠ was encouraging but nonforcing. North accepted the invitation to bid game, perhaps straining his values to do so, and is now faced by a slam invitation.

South's bidding cannot be correct. If he is strong enough to bid 5♡, he must have been too strong to make the invitational bid of 3♠. His bidding means that his side must play below game or above game, but cannot stop in 4♠. See also IMPOSSIBLE BID and PRESSURE BID.

TRAP PASS.
A pass by a player holding a strong defensive hand, hoping that the opposition will bid themselves into difficulties. It is usually made by a

player holding length and strength in the suit bid by the opener on his right:

♠ 6
♡ A Q 10 7 4
◇ K J 7
♣ A K 5 3

If the right-hand opponent opens the bidding with 1♡, there is no good alternative to a pass. There is strong evidence that the hand is a misfit, and that it will pay to defend. If 1♡ is passed out, the result should be reasonable.

The same principle applies, only less forcefully, in a balancing position. A player with the above hand may consider passing if an opening bid of 1♡ is followed by two passes. This would certainly be sound tactics at matchpoint scoring against vulnerable opponents, as a score of 200 for the defense would beat all partscore results.

A trap pass becomes a doubtful proposition when holding 18 or 19 high-card points, and is usually unwise with 20 or more. The danger of passing up a game in favor of a small penalty becomes too great.

Passes with strong hands by the player on dealer's right after an opening suit bid and a suit response are similar in principle, although the motive is slightly different: the prospect of a penalty is reduced, but the danger of taking action is greater. With a hand of exceptional strength, the fourth player should not necessarily rely on the fact that responder's bid is technically forcing. It is not at all unlikely that the dealer has made a psychic bid, and if he passes, the other defender cannot be expected to balance with a very weak hand.

An unusual, and experimental, type of trap pass may sometimes be ventured by the partner of the opening bidder:

♠ 6
♡ K 8 5 3
◇ A J 4 2
♣ Q 10 5 4

If partner opens 1♠ and the next player passes, there is something to be said for a prompt pass if not vulnerable against vulnerable opponents. There is no certainty of a game, and if 1♠ is passed out the loss is unlikely to exceed 300. On the other hand, the fourth player may balance, in which case the penalty should not be less than 500 and might be 1,400. Such experiments should not be tried in matchpointed events (except when SHOOTING). See also MARMIC SYSTEM.

TRAP PLAY. See DECEPTIVE PLAY.

TRAP WITH TWO-LEVEL TRANSFERS. A defensive bidding system against the FORCING CLUB. 2♣ shows diamonds or the majors; 2◇ shows hearts or the black suits; 2♡ shows spades or the minors; 2♠ shows clubs or the red suits; 2 NT shows hearts and clubs; 3♣ shows diamonds and spades. See TRAP.

TRAVELING SCORE SLIP. The official score of each deal in a pair duplicate game may be recorded either of two ways: on a traveling score-slip or an individual pick-up card.

A majority of clubs and lesser championship events use the *traveling score-slip*. This slip travels with the board, folded and inserted in a pocket so that the scores for the tables which have played it earlier are not visible until the slip is opened after the board has been replayed. The score at the new table is then entered.

At the end of the session, when the board has been played at each table in the game, all the results will have been entered on the slip. The tournament director will then work out the match points as shown here:

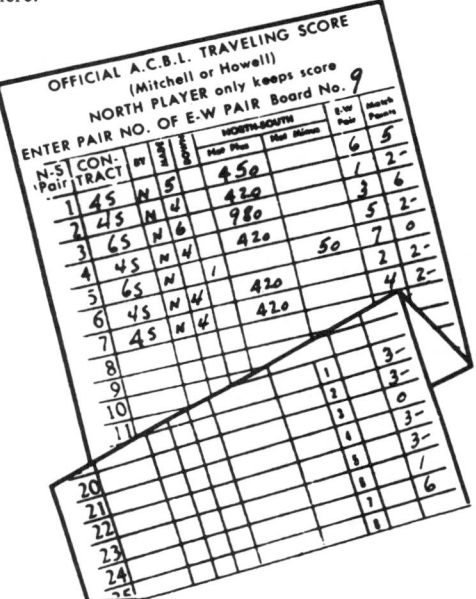

The completed traveling score slip gives you a full picture of how Match Points are awarded. First the North-South scores are figured. Each score is awarded 1 point for every poorer score, ½ point for every exactly equal score. It does not matter how much better one score is than another; the only thing that counts is how many pairs your score beats. Thus, the pair that bid and made 6♠ scored 530 points more than the next higher team, but got only one more Match Point. The pair that scored 450 for making five-odd got only 30 points more than each of the four pairs that bid and made exactly four, but that 30 points turns out to be worth 2½ Match Points more. The four pairs that got equal 420 scores were awarded 2½ Match Points; 1 for the one pair they beat; ½ for each of the three pairs they tied. The pair that was set at 6♠ got a zero.

The East-West pairs might be figured exactly the same way. But the simple way is to give East-West the reciprocal of the North-South score: that is, deduct the N-S score from the possible top score, 6, and give East-West the difference.

After several results have been entered, the contestants have an opportunity to compare their result with others previously recorded, and estimate an approximate final result. See CALIFORNIA SCORING, COMPARING SCORES, ESTIMATION.

TRAY. Whist term (still surviving) for the contraption to hold cards in duplicate competition. See BOARD, DUPLICATE.

TREASURERS. Those who have held this position in the AMERICAN BRIDGE LEAGUE and the AMERICAN CONTRACT BRIDGE LEAGUE are:

1927–28	Clayton W. Aldrich
1929	E. J. Tobin
1930–31	J. J. Lafferty
1932–34	Russell Baldwin
1935	David Burnstine (Burns)
1936	Gordon M. Gibbs
1937	J. N. S. Brewster, Jr.
1938–40	Gordon M. Gibbs
1941–42	J. H. Block
1943–44	Ralph W. Gresham
1945–47	Bertram Lebhar, Jr.
1949–51	Ralph W. Gresham
1952–66	Harry J. Fishbein
1966–69	Samuel Stayman
1969–70	Percy X. Bean
1970–72	Jerome Silverman
1973–74	Walter O'Loughlin
1975–76	Donald A. Moeller
1976–78	Lawrence Jolma
1979–80	Sydney A. Levey
1981	Lawrence Jolma
1982	Donald A. Moeller

TREATMENT. A natural bid that indicates a desire to play in the denomination named (or promises or requests values in that denomination), but that also, by agreement, gives or requests additional information on which further action could be based. A treatment thus differs from a CONVENTION, which is a bid that gives or requests information unrelated to the denomination named. For example, a LIMIT JUMP RAISE is a treatment; but a LIMIT JUMP RAISE TO SHOW A SINGLETON in a side suit is a convention. INVERTED MINOR SUIT RAISES and PREEMPTIVE RE-RAISES are other examples of treatments.

TREFLE SQUEEZE SYSTEM. A 1♣ system widely played in Belgium. 1♣ shows *either* a hand with 17 points or more, regardless of distribution; *or* a normal opening bid (13–16 points) including at least five clubs. Responses are by point-count steps: 1◇, 0–5 points; 1♡, 6–8 points; 1♠, 9–11 points, etc. If there is an immediate overcall, a pass shows 0–5 points, the next higher suit 6–8, etc. The opener rebids clubs at the first opportunity to show the weak variety of club bid.
A 2♣ opening is strong and artificial, also with step responses (2◇, 0–3; 2♡, 4–5, etc.). Other two bids show a strong suit and about 15 points. 1 NT as an opening shows 15–16 points.
This system has more difficulty than most artificial systems in dealing with interference bids. See TWO-SUITER conventions.

TRELDE LEADS (developed by JOHN TRELDE of The Netherlands). A method of leading from honor sequences to distinguish between a genuine sequence of three touching honors and a false sequence of only two touching honors. The principle is that from a genuine sequence the highest card is led and from a false sequence the second highest card is led. Partner should be able to determine which combination the lead is from by his and dummy's holding in the suit.

Leads from A-K doubleton, a suit headed by A-K-Q and internal sequences follow accepted practices.

TREY. The 3 or three-spot of each suit.

TRIAL BID. A game suggestion made by bidding a new suit after a major suit fit has been located:

SOUTH	NORTH
1♡	2♡
3♣	

North-South have provisionally agreed to play a heart contract, although a final contract of 3 NT is not completely excluded. However, it is completely impossible that the right contract could be clubs, so the club bid can only be an exploring maneuver. If North has no interest in game, he signs off with 3♡. If he wants to accept the invitation, he bids 4♡ or 3 NT. As a rare alternative, he may bid an unbid suit in which he has strength, as a move toward 3 NT.

The usual practice is for South to make his trial bid in a suit in which he needs support, so it will generally contain at least three cards and at least two losers. Possible holdings would be: x-x-x, A-x-x, K-10-x-x, J-x-x-x, and many others.

The responder therefore takes his holding in the trial bid suit into account when making the decision whether to bid game. If his holding is neither maximum nor minimum in strength, he allows himself to be encouraged if he has honor strength or a shortage in the trial bid suit. Conversely, he should tend to reject the invitation if he has three or four small cards in the suit; a holding headed by the jack is only a slight improvement.

In one special case, the final contract may be in a suit other than the one originally agreed on:

SOUTH	NORTH
1♠	2♠
3♡	4♡

4♡ may easily prove a superior contract to 4♠. If South holds four hearts, and North holds four, five, or six, spades will be an inferior landing place if the spade fit is 5-3.

There are two other situations in which bids of similar types are made.

SOUTH	NORTH
1♣	1♠
2♠	3♡

North's bid invites 4♠, and suggests some length in hearts, in which he would welcome support.

SOUTH	NORTH
1♣	2♣
2♡	

This is not a trial bid, because no major suit has been agreed on. A heart fit is still possible, but it is very likely that the partnership will head for 3 NT. South will tend to bid a suit in which he is strong, rather than a suit in which he is weak. His heart suit might be A-Q-x, but in no circumstances could it be x-x-x unless he was making a psychic effort to inhibit a lead.

Similarly:

SOUTH	NORTH
1♡	2♡
2♠	3♣

With three hearts and four spades in North, or with five hearts and four spades in South, the spade contract may be superior. However, restraint must be exercised. South's spade bid may be a three-card suit; hence a jump in spades by responder is unwise and unnecessary. See also INTEREST-SHOWING BID; PREEMPTIVE RE-RAISES; SHORT-SUIT GAME TRIES; SINGLE RAISE; TWO-WAY GAME TRIES; WEAK SUIT GAME TRY.

TRIATHLON. A three-event tournament, usually conducted over three days. The first event is a team-of-four. Then the teams break down into pairs for a pairs contest. The final event is an individual. The winner is the player who has the best aggregate score. Since team events are scored differently from pair and individual events, the sponsoring organization has to set up a conversion scale that gives each event a proportional weight in the final standings.

TRICK. Consists of four cards played in rotation after an initial lead of one of the cards by the player whose turn it was to lead or to play first to the trick. A trick of four cards can be won by virtue of the winning card being highest in rank (number) of the four played; or because the card led is "long," that is, a remaining card in one's hand of a suit not held by any other player; or by having a trump card played to it either by declarer or dummy or either defender.

TRICK APPROPRIATED IN ERROR. A packet of the four cards played to a trick that has been gathered in by the pair of which neither contributed the winning card. Such a trick must be restored to the side that contributed the winning card if discovered before the second succeeding deal. See LAWS (Law 69).

TRICK POINTS. Points scored for fulfilled contracts toward the game. See BELOW THE LINE.

TRICK-SCORE. The value of the odd tricks of fulfilled contracts toward the winning of the game; in clubs or diamonds, 20 points each; in hearts or spades, 30 points each; at notrump, 40 points for the first and 30 for each subsequent trick. In French tournament play the fourth trick at notrump has been reduced to 20 points so that 4♡, 4♠, and 4 NT each score 120 points. See FRENCH SCORING. Different trick scores operate in auction bridge and plafond.

TRINIDAD AND TOBAGO CONTRACT BRIDGE LEAGUE. Competes annually with Barbados in an Open and Women's team event.
Officers, 1982:
President: Barbara Johnston
Secretary: Florrie Kelshall, 6 Strathclyde Avenue, Cascade, Trinidad, West Indies

TRIPLE COUP. A series of plays by the declarer in which he trumps three cards from the dummy's hand in order to shorten his own trump suit to the number held by his right-hand opponent. The purpose is to

lead a card from the dummy at the eleventh or twelfth trick which the right-hand opponent must trump (being void of all other suits), and thus permit declarer to win the last two tricks by virtue of his own trumps being over those of his opponent. If the cards deliberately trumped by the delarer are side suit winners in their own right the coup is termed a grand coup. See COUP, TRIPLE GRAND COUP.

TRIPLE GRAND COUP. A grand coup in which the declarer shortens his hand three times in trumps, to reduce his holding to the same number as held by his right-hand opponent, by ruffing three winners from the dummy.

TRIPLE RAISE. A raise of partner's opening suit bid to the four-level. In a major suit the bid indicates that a fine distributional fit has been found, but slam prospects are remote. A typical hand for responder would include an ace, a singleton, five trumps, and 7-10 points in high cards. None of these requirements is essential, but the hand should give promise of nine tricks opposite a minimum opening bid. The opener can assume that responder does not hold two aces, for he would then be likely to bid more slowly in case slam possibilities exist. See FAST ARRIVAL, PRINCIPLE OF.

In a minor suit the bid is rarer, and indicates an even more distributional hand. It is markedly preemptive in character, weaker in high cards than the major suit raise, and a typical distribution would be 6-5-2-0.

The raise of the major-suit opening to game can have a much wider range, up to perhaps 14 points in high cards, if the opening bid is limited as in the PRECISION, SCHENKEN, and BLUE TEAM CLUB systems. See also DOUBLE RAISE and DELAYED GAME RAISE.

TRIPLE SQUEEZE. A squeeze against one opponent in three suits. It is a combination of three simple squeezes against the same opponent, which justifies the term.

The term triple squeeze is often used to encompass squeezes which produce one trick and squeezes which produce two tricks. The latter is described under PROGRESSIVE SQUEEZE. See also BARCO SQUEEZE; CLASH SQUEEZE; COMPOUND SQUEEZE; GUARD SQUEEZE; HEXAGON SQUEEZE.

The minimum requirements for a triple squeeze are two one-card menaces and a two-card menace with an entry opposite the squeeze card.

These are the basic end positions:

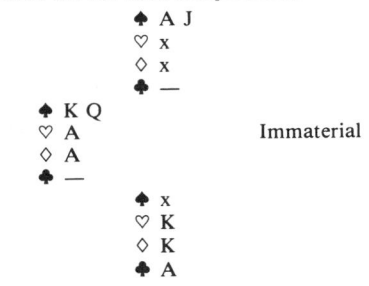

South leads the ♠A, and West must surrender a

spade, establishing a trick for South in that suit. (Any other discard permits South to win all four tricks.)

In this position the hand opposite the squeeze card has one menace. Since North has two idle cards, the position is automatic and either opponent may be squeezed.

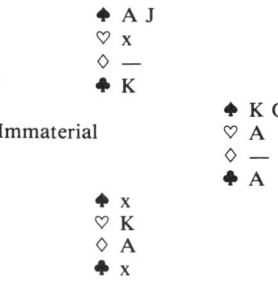

South leads the ◊ A, and East is squeezed in three suits. He must part with a spade or a club to restrict declarer to three of the last four tricks.

In this position the hand opposite the squeeze card has two menaces. The ending shown is automatic and works equally well against either opponent.

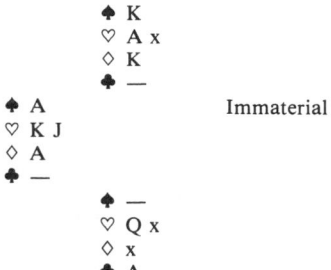

This is a variation of the above position, which is positional. If the East and West cards are transposed, the squeeze is ineffective. South leads the ♣ A, and West is squeezed in three suits.

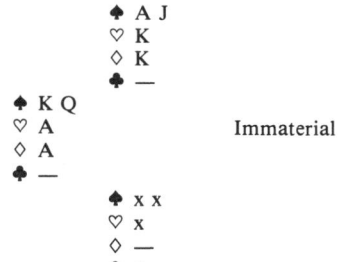

South leads the ♣ A, and West is squeezed, permitting South to win two more tricks.

In all these squeezes South has all but *two* of the remaining tricks. This is a characteristic of triple squeezes.

In rare situations the triple squeeze may win two tricks immediately.

In this position there are three two-trick threats: (See hand at top of right column.)

South has only four tricks on top, but the ♣ A squeezes West in three suits, and any discard costs

him two tricks.

Two two-trick threats (the great VIENNA COUP)

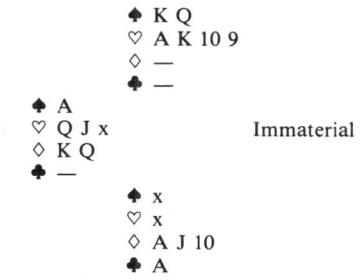

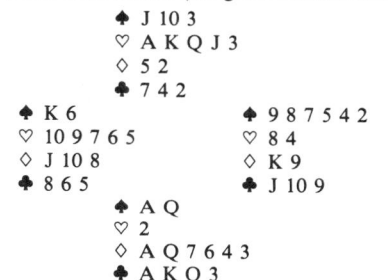

Clubs are led and South must take all the tricks in a notrump contract.

South takes four club tricks, and West is squeezed in three suits. A discard of a spade or diamond costs two tricks, so West must throw a heart. South cashes the ♣ A, and then runs the hearts, squeezing West in spades and diamonds.

See also PROGRESSIVE SQUEEZE. For repeating triple squeezes, see BONNEY'S SQUEEZE; CLASH SQUEEZE; GUARD SQUEEZE; OVERTAKING SQUEEZE.

Monroe Ingberman

TRIPLETON. A holding of three cards in a given suit in a particular hand. The term is usually used to describe an original, or dealt, combination; as, an ace-king tripleton in diamonds. For an opening lead from a small tripleton, see THREE SMALL CARDS, LEAD FROM.

TROPHIES. Those trophies competed for in International events are listed under the following headings: BERMUDA BOWL; CROWNINSHIELD TROPHY; CULBERTSON TROPHY; LENZ TROPHY; SCHWAB CUP; SOLOMON TROPHY; TORINO BULL; VANDERBILT CUP (2); VENICE TROPHY; WORLD BRIDGE FEDERATION TROPHY; ROSENBLUM CUP.

ACBL Trophies are listed separately: ASSOCIATION OF AMERICAN PLAYING CARD MANUFACTURERS TROPHY; BAIRD TROPHY; BALDWIN MEMORIAL TROPHY; BARCLAY TROPHY; BEYNON TROPHY; CAVENDISH TROPHY; CHICAGO TROPHY; COFFIN TROPHY; FABER CUP; FISHBEIN TROPHY; GODDARD TROPHY; GOLDER CUP; GOREN TROPHY; HERMAN TROPHY; HILLIARD TROPHY; KEM CARD TROPHY; KEOHANE TROPHY; LANDY TROPHY; LEBHAR TROPHY; LEVENTRITT TROPHY; LIGHTMAN TROPHY; MACHLIN TROPHY; MC KENNEY TROPHY; MARCUS CUP; MID-ATLANTIC CUP; MILES TROPHY; MOREHEAD TROPHY; MOTT-SMITH TROPHY; MOUSER TROPHY; PRESIDENT'S CUP; REIS-

INGER MEMORIAL TROPHY; ROCKWELL TROPHY; ROTHSCHILD TROPHY; SILODOR TROPHY; SMITH TROPHY; SPINGOLD TROPHY; STEINER TROPHY; VANDERBILT CUP (1); WERNHER TROPHY; WESTCOTT TROPHY; WHITEHEAD TROPHY; VON ZEDTWITZ GOLD CUP.

TRUMP. The suit named in the final bid, other than notrump. Such suit is the TRUMP SUIT, and a card of the trump suit, when played, is a winner over any card of a plain (not trump) suit; if two or more trumps are played on the same trick, the highest trump card played wins the trick.

TRUMP ASKING BID. A convention used to inquire about key cards in the trump suit. As used in conjunction with ASKING BIDS as developed by ELY CULBERTSON, a call of 4 NT asked partner to describe his holding in the trump suit, as follows:

5♣	No ace, king, or queen
5◇	One of three top honors
5♡	Two of three top honors
5♠	All three top honors

If the 4 NT bidder now bids 5 NT, partner must show his trump length by a series of artificial responses. If the response to an asking bid is at the five level, 5 NT can be used as a trump asking bid for honor cards but it is not possible to follow up by asking for trump length. See also BARON SLAM TRY; BYZANTINE BLACKWOOD; GRAND SLAM FORCE; KEY CARD BLACKWOOD; KEY CARD GERBER; MALOWAN 6♣ CONVENTION; PRECISION ASKING BIDS; ROMEX TRUMP ASKING BIDS.

TRUMP CONTROL. See CONTROL MAINTENANCE and TRUMP SUIT MANAGEMENT.

TRUMP COUP. See COUP.

TRUMP ECHO. See TRUMP SIGNAL.

TRUMP KING. See conventions listed under TRUMP ASKING BID.

TRUMP LEADS. The opening lead of a trump is not a first-line lead, and it will turn out to be costly if the particular deal happens to be one where it was necessary for the defenders to cash tricks in a hurry, or not get them. Nevertheless, there are circumstances where an opening trump lead figures to be eminently proper. (Trump leads should *not* be made merely because one does not know what else to lead.)

Here are the major situations: (1) Where the bidding has indicated that dummy will be able to trump some of declarer's losing tricks; (2) Where the leader has reason to fear an aggressive lead in some other suit, lest it be beneficial to declarer; (3) Where there is a desire to mislead declarer as to the true state of affairs in the trump suit, as, for example, talking him out of taking a finesse that he figures to take if left to his own resources.

The following hands illustrate some of the situations in which a trump opening should be made.

Where the bidding has indicated that dummy will

be able to trump some of declarer's losing tricks, a trump should be opened.

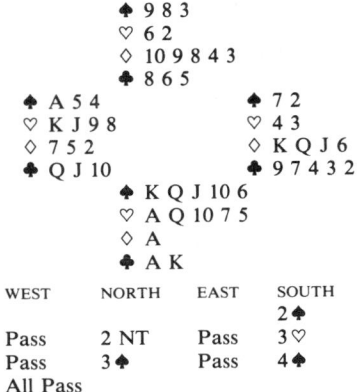

WEST	NORTH	EAST	SOUTH
			2♣
Pass	2 NT	Pass	3♡
Pass	3♠	Pass	4♠
All Pass			

What could be more "normal" than to open the ♣Q? If made, this will be won by declarer and promptly he will bang down the ace and another heart. A belated shift by West to the ace and another trump permits South to trump one of his losing hearts with dummy's last trump; the closed hand entered with the ◇A, picking up the last outstanding trump and conceding a further heart trick. Declarer makes 4♠.

Based on the bidding, West should open the ace and follow with another trump. From the bidding it is apparent that South has a minimum of five spades and five hearts. It is clear that North prefers spades (however mildly) to hearts as the trump suit. West should immediately make every effort to reduce dummy's ruffing power and prevent dummy from ruffing hearts, especially since West has the ♡K–J–9–8 behind South's rebid suit.

With the ace of trumps lead, followed by another trump (and a third trump when West regains the lead in hearts), declarer will be defeated, losing three heart tricks and a trump trick.

Where you want to mislead declarer as to the true state of affairs in the trump suit; as, for example, talking him out of taking a finesse which he figures to take if left to his own resources, a trump lead may turn out to be the winning lead.

The deal which illustrates this point arose in the Men's Pair Championship of 1956. The West defender was DR. RICHARD GREENE.

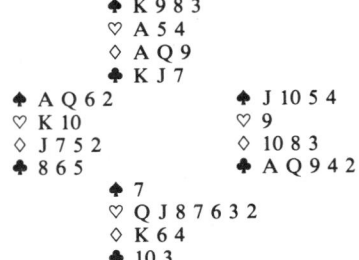

North-South vulnerable, North deals. The bidding:

WEST	NORTH	EAST	SOUTH
	1 NT	Pass	4♡
Pass	Pass	Pass	

West opened the 10 of trumps on the reasoning:

(a) On the bidding, North figured to have the ♡A, and South figured to have a long heart suit.

(b) Even if South had something like an A–Q–J–x–x–x and dummy the x–x–x of hearts, West would still make his king, since declarer couldn't possibly diagnose the situation. (Upon winning the opening lead with the jack, declarer would enter dummy, and lead a low heart, ·finessing East for the king.)

What would you, as declarer, have played to the first trick? Probably the same as our declarer did: he went up with the ace on the hope that West was leading from the doubleton 10–9 and, hence, East had the singleton king.

Had Dr. Greene not opened a trump, declarer, upon obtaining the lead, would probably have made the standard PERCENTAGE PLAY of leading the queen of trumps and finessing. As it was, he was "talked out" of finessing, and thus went down, losing two clubs, one spade, and, of course, the king of trumps.

The following specific situations suggest a trump lead, although circumstances may indicate another selection:

(1) The opponents have bid three suits and ended up in a fourth.

(2) Declarer, raised in his suit, has bid notrump, and been put back to his suit.

(3) The declaring side appears to have a good fit (5–4 or 4–4) in one suit and a misfit in the other suits. For example:

WEST	EAST
1♠	2♢
2♡	4♡

(4) The bidding indicates that dummy has exactly three trumps.

(5) A takeout double has been passed for penalties.

(6) An opening suit bid of one has been passed out, and the opening leader has a weak hand. Partner's failure to balance suggests long, strong trumps.

(7) Your side has been doubled for penalties, and one opponent has removed the double.

(8) Your side has opened the bidding with a notrump bid.

(9) Against a high-level sacrifice bid, when the declaring side appears to have little high-card strength.

Note also that a small trump is usually the desirable lead from holdings which would call for the highest in a plain suit: x–x–x, x–x; or J–10–x. See VINJE SIGNALS.

Fred Karpin

TRUMP PETER. See TRUMP SIGNAL.

TRUMP PICK-UP. A play that reduces trump loss by plain suit leads. It usually involves the lead of a side suit through an opponent in order to pick up his seemingly inviolable trump holding. (See hand at top of right column.)

Against South's 6♢ contract, West leads the ♡A and continues the suit in response to his partner's violent signal. Dummy ruffs and leads the ♢K, revealing the trump break. Declarer would have had

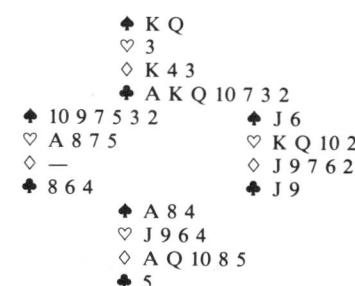

```
              ♠ K Q
              ♡ 3
              ♢ K 4 3
              ♣ A K Q 10 7 3 2
♠ 10 9 7 5 3 2            ♠ J 6
♡ A 8 7 5                ♡ K Q 10 2
♢ —                      ♢ J 9 7 6 2
♣ 8 6 4                  ♣ J 9
              ♠ A 8 4
              ♡ J 9 6 4
              ♢ A Q 10 8 5
              ♣ 5
```

no difficulty in finessing East out of his jack of trumps if dummy had not been forced to ruff; as it is, however, he has to utilize the club suit for that purpose. At trick three declarer leads a diamond to his 8 and then starts the clubs. If East ruffs, declarer overruffs, draws trumps, and enters dummy with a spade to make the good clubs. If East refuses to ruff, South discards his spades and hearts until the following position is reached.

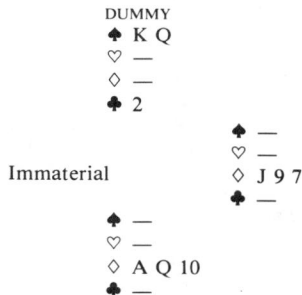

```
        DUMMY
        ♠ K Q
        ♡ —
        ♢ —
        ♣ 2
                      ♠ —
                      ♡ —
Immaterial            ♢ J 9 7
                      ♣ —
        ♠ —
        ♡ —
        ♢ A Q 10
        ♣ —
```

Dummy is on lead, and East is helpless to prevent declarer from taking the balance.

See COUP; DEVIL'S COUP; GRAND COUP; SMOTHER PLAY.

TRUMP PROMOTION. The creation of trump tricks through forcing the premature use of the trump cards of the opposition.

There are several ways in which trump tricks can be promoted: (1) forcing ruffs (see FORCING DECLARER TO RUFF) so as to make trump tricks by length; (2) COUP EN PASSANT so as to make trump tricks by position (see ELOPEMENT); (3) ruffing to force out honors (see UPPERCUT) so as to make trump tricks by force of cards; (4) threatening an overruff to force out honors so as to make trump tricks by force of cards.

In these examples, spades are trump, and East has led a plain suit of which both South and West are void. The best technique to promote trump tricks is to discard behind a player who has wasted a valuable card attempting to stop an overruff.

```
        WEST
        ♠ A J
                SOUTH
                ♠ K Q 10 9 8 7 6 3
```

South must ruff with an honor to shut out West's jack. West discards and now has promoted a second trump trick. Notice that West must not overruff!

WEST
♠ K 10 2

SOUTH
♠ A Q J 9 8 7 3

South must ruff with queen or jack to prevent West's 10 from winning. West discards and now makes two trump tricks.

WEST
♠ J 3 2

SOUTH
♠ A K Q 10 9 8 7

A trick is promoted for West's jack.

Jeff Rubens

TRUMP-REDUCING PLAY. A play designed to reduce the number of trumps in a hand, usually as a preparation for the trump pick-up. The principal trump-reducing plays are the simple and grand coup, the preliminary throw-in to force the lead of a ruffable suit, and the discard of a trump on a trick taken by a higher trump.

TRUMP SIGNAL. A play by defenders to indicate length of trump holding. The play of an intermediate card followed by s subsequent play of a lower card in the trump suit (HIGH-LOW SIGNAL) has the definite meaning that a third trump is held. The use of such a signal is important if the player has a potential RUFFING TRICK to indicate to partner that he still has the ability to trump a suit of which he is void. Note that the high-low trump signal to show a third card in the suit is the reverse of the meaning of an echo in a nontrump suit.

Some players use the trump signal whenever they hold three trumps. But as the defenders can count declarer's trumps from the bidding far more often than vice versa, it is better to confine its use to situations in which there is a real prospect of a ruff. See also VINJE SIGNALS.

TRUMP SUIT. The principles governing the choice of a trump suit are well established. The following are basic rules, subject to certain exceptions.

(1) Eight cards or more between the partnership constitute a satisfactory trump suit.

(2) If the partnership can find an eight-card (or longer) fit in a major suit, the contract should usually be played in that suit.

(3) If the partnership has values for game (i.e., 25–26 points), the contract should be 3 NT if no major-suit is available.

The following discussion centers on some of the exceptions.

When to play with less than eight trumps. Occasionally a trump suit in which the partnership has only seven cards may be the best bet, especially if the suit is strong (at least three of the top four honors) and one of the other suits appears to be weak. This type of hand is not uncommon:

♠ A Q 10 8 4	♠ K 6
♡ 8 7	♡ 9 3
◇ K 6 2	◇ A Q J 10 7
♣ K Q 3	♣ 10 8 6 4

These hands are on the borderline between partscore

and game as far as values go. Clearly the only sound game contract is 4♠, which needs a 3–3 break in spades or the ♠ J falling doubleton. Notice the symptoms which point to this seven-card trump suit: a strong trump suit and a marked weakness in another suit.

When the seven-card trump suit is split 4–3, a strong trump suit and a weak side suit are still the signs to look for, but there is a further and most important complication. For the contract to be a good one, it is usually necessary for the hand which is shorter in the trump suit to be able to ruff the weak suit.

♠ A K J 5	♠ Q 6 2
♡ 9 8 5	♡ 3
◇ K 10 5	◇ A Q J 9 2
♣ A 7 3	♣ 10 8 6 4

4♠ is a lay-down, barring very bad breaks, and on a heart lead West can certainly make 11 tricks and perhaps 12. Although the 5–3 fit in diamonds looks like a better bet than spades, 5◇ has no chance whatever. As the heart ruffs come in the long trump hand, 10 tricks are the limit. The fact that the heart shortage is with the spade shortage is doubly advantageous; there is a positive profit, in that the heart ruffs score extra tricks, and a negative profit in that heart ruffs do not weaken control of the trump suit.

The converse position is much less attractive:

♠ A K J 5	♠ Q 6 2
♡ 3	♡ 9 8 5
◇ K 10 9 5 2	◇ A Q J
♣ A 7 3	♣ 10 8 6 4

If you play this hand in 4♠, and ruff the second heart, you are uncomfortably placed. It looks as though a 4–2 spade break will be fatal, but the play is interesting. West should cash his ♠ K-J, leaving two trumps at large, and then play diamonds. A defender ruffs and plays another heart, and now West can please himself whether he ruffs and continues diamonds, or simply discards a club loser. Is there a simpler way of dealing with West's problems? He should, of course, quietly discard his two club losers on the second and third rounds of hearts, then a fourth heart can be ruffed in dummy.

So in this situation declarer has made 10 tricks by skillful play, and can never make more; while in the previous case, with the heart and spade shortages in the same hand, he makes 10 tricks without effort, and will often make more.

The moral is that a 4–3 fit in a strong suit will be satisfactory if the hand with three trumps has a shortage in the enemy suit. But if the hand with four trumps is going to be forced to ruff, the bidding should be more cautious: there will certainly be problems of control which may be difficult to solve.

Seven trumps divided 6–1 or 7–0, on the other hand, will usually prove adequate, because declarer can accept ruffs without losing control. But here also it is better for the suit to be fairly robust, and if a six-card suit has only one high honor, there may well be a better spot to play the hand.

To play with six trumps is nearly always a mistake. It is true that a strong 6–0 fit will play well, and occasionally a strong 5–1 fit may be the best spot; it is even possible to construct hands on which the only game to be made is in a strong 4–2 fit. But for practical purposes we can rule out any deliberate intention of playing in a trump suit in which the opposition have the majority of cards. If, when dummy goes down, the combined hands prove to have only six trumps, then the bidding has probably failed.

When to reject an eight-card fit. There are three situations in which 3 NT should be preferred to four of a major suit.

Type I:

♠ K J 7	♠ A 4
♡ 9 7 6 3 2	♡ K 8 4
◇ Q 10 7	◇ K J 9
♣ A 3	♣ K Q J 9 6

Although there is a ruff to be had in dummy, both hands are balanced and the heart suit is very feeble. If East opens 1 NT (strong), West should simply raise to 3 NT, and make no effort to play in hearts. If East has good hearts, the suit will pull its weight in notrumps. It is easy to see that 3 NT is a virtual certainty, while 4 ♡ needs a 3–2 heart break with the ace well placed.

Type II:

♠ A 4	♠ 8 6
♡ A K Q J 8 3	♡ 10 6 2
◇ A 5	◇ J 7 4
♣ A 7 6	♣ J 9 8 4 3

Here the possible trump suit, far from being weak, is absolutely solid. But there are nine sure tricks in notrump and little chance of 10 in hearts, because the East hand has no usable ruffing value. This is, of course, easy for West to spot, because he can count nine tricks in his own hand; but the position will be difficult and perhaps impossible to diagnose if some of West's strength is transferred to East. If West has eight tricks in his hand, he can sometimes take the gamble that East will produce the ninth, and that the opponents will not manage to cash five tricks.

To land this sort of contract the tricks have to be quick ones; aces in the side suits are essential, and the presence of minor honors will suggest that the suit contract is preferable. There is a paradoxical element in this: in a general way, the presence of aces normally suggests a suit contract, and the presence of minor honors suggests notrump.

Failure to recognize type III often does not show on the score sheet, so it usually stays unrecognized.

Type III:

♠ J 5 3 2	♠ A Q
♡ K J 7 5	♡ Q 6 3 2
◇ A Q	◇ K J 7 5
♣ Q J 4	♣ K 8 7

Suppose East opens 1 NT (15–17). West should now reason along these lines: our combined count is about 30, so game is very easy, but there is no slam; even if there is a major-suit fit, the suit game may fail through a bad break, while 3 NT is surely ironclad. So West raises to 3 NT, which is impregnable, while 4 ♡ would fail with a little bad luck, a 4–1 trump break, and the ♠K with South. These tactics may cost 20 or 50 points aggregate, but this is a good insurance except at matchpoint pairs.

In the slam zone there are other considerations

which may cause us to reject a combined eight-card major suit holding. The most common symptom is a weak trump suit:

♠ A 8 6 3	♠ J 7 4 2
♡ A Q J 7	♡ K 3
◇ A K 6	◇ 4 2
♣ J 7	♣ A K Q 10 8

Twelve tricks are obviously a lay-down in clubs or notrump, but many players would arrive disastrously in 6 ♠, which needs the 7% miracle of doubleton ♠K–Q. To avoid this type of trap often requires fine bidding judgment. This is another example in which the major suit has one loser only, but that denomination is still wrong:

♠ A 10 8 7 6 3	♠ K 5
♡ K Q 2	♡ 9 7 6
◇ A Q	◇ K 8 4
♣ J 6	♣ A K Q 10 8

6 ♠ again needs a miracle. 6 NT is a good contract, with slightly better than an even chance: as well as the ♡A with South, we can hope for a lucky spade position or a squeeze against North if he holds all the major-suit honors. But far and away the best contract is 6 ♣, in which the twelfth trick may come from hearts, or from ruffing out the spade suit. Again the strength of the trump suit proves more important than the length.

It may sometimes be advisable to reject an eight-card fit headed by the three trump top honors:

♠ A Q 7 5 4	♠ K 8 3
♡ K	♡ Q J 6 5
◇ A Q 9 3	◇ K
♣ K 9 4	♣ A Q 7 5 2

6 ♠ and 6 ♣ are obviously both sound contracts, depending on a 3–2 trump break. But with a lot of general strength about, 6 NT will often offer more chances. Here the notrump slam makes if either black suit breaks, or if a squeeze develops.

When to play in five of a minor. As it is much easier to make nine tricks than 11, contracts of five in a minor suit are rare. It is nearly always possible to play in 3 NT, or in a seven-card major-suit fit.

This is particularly true in matchpoint duplicate events, when a successful contract of 5 ♣ or 5 ◇ usually scores badly: other pairs are likely to score slightly more by making 10 tricks in notrump or a major.

To play in a minor-suit game with a 4–4 or 5–3 fit is very rare indeed. When it does happen, it is usually because *both* minor suits are held, and there is no seven-card fit in a major:

♠ x	♠ x x x x
♡ A x	♡ K x x
◇ A x x x	◇ K x x x
♣ A K x x x x	♣ x x

5 ◇ is the only possible game. It requires 3–2 breaks in both minor suits, representing a 46% chance.

This demonstrates two common symptoms of minor-suit games; a completely exposed suit, and obvious ruffing values (singleton or void) in each hand.

If a solid six-card minor suit is held opposite a balanced hand, 3 NT is usually right. But in some cases it may be possible to diagnose a serious weakness, and play in the minor suit:

WEST	EAST
♠ x x x	♠ A K x
♡ x	♡ x x x
◇ A Q x x x x	◇ K x x x
♣ A K x	♣ Q J x

The bidding may start:

WEST	EAST
1 ◇	2 NT
3 ♣	3 ♠

after which the heart weakness is identified and the diamond game is reached. As is often the case when the choice lies between 3 NT and a minor suit, the players bid suits in which they have strength but not necessarily length (see STRENGTH-SHOWING BIDS).

Interchanging East's rounded suits would produce a different contract:

WEST	EAST
♠ x x x	♠ A K x
♡ x	♡ Q J x
◇ A Q x x x x	◇ K x x x
♣ A K x	♣ x x x

In this case the first three bids would be the same, but East's second bid would be 3 NT, showing stoppers in both major suits, and West would subside. Ten tricks in notrump are certain, and 11 are likely, while 5 ◇ needs a high heart lead or an endplay to succeed.

TRUMP SUIT FALSE-CARDING. See FALSE-CARDING.

TRUMP SQUEEZE. A squeeze in which the ruffing power of the trump suit plays an essential part. Here is an example of the most common form of simple trump squeeze:

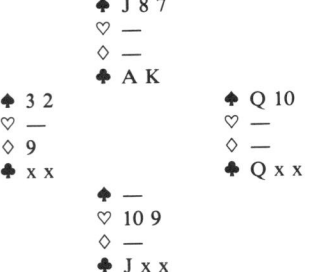

Hearts are trumps, and South leads a trump, discarding a spade from dummy. East is squeezed. If he discards a spade, dummy is entered with a club, and the ♣ Q is ruffed out. If East discards a club, then South cashes his winners in that suit, dropping the queen, and he returns to hand by ruffing a spade in order to cash the established ♣ J. This squeeze is automatic, and it has a distinct resemblance to the CRISSCROSS SQUEEZE with a trump taking the place of an isolated master card in the other position.

These are the characteristic elements of the trump squeeze:

(1) *A split menace*, guarded on the right. But see BACKWASH SQUEEZE.

(2) A ruffing menace, also guarded on the right (a ruffing menace consists of two low cards in dummy,

and a trick can be established by ruffing provided RHO weakens his guard in that suit).

(3) Dummy must have two entries, either in the split menace (as above) or by means of an additional entry in a third suit.

If both menaces are guarded on the left, the trump factor is not essential, and we have an ordinary simple squeeze against LHO.

It is worth noting that the squeeze takes place while declarer retains a trump; in most squeeze positions the last trump must be played before the pressure is felt.

There are two more simple trump squeeze positions:

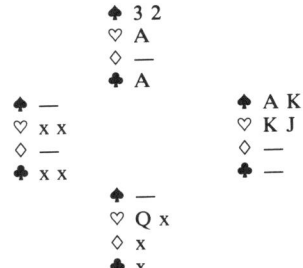

Diamonds are trumps. A club is led to the ace, and East is squeezed. A spade discard enables South to ruff out East's spade guard, and a heart discard permits North to cash the ace of that suit. The South hand is re-entered with a spade ruff, and the ♡ Q is cashed.

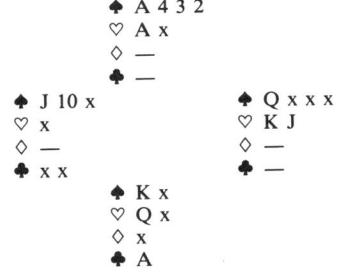

Diamonds are trumps. The ♣ A is led and East is squeezed. A spade discard unguards his stopper, which can be ruffed out; a heart discard establishes the queen once the ace is cashed.

"Squeeze-Finesse at Trumps"

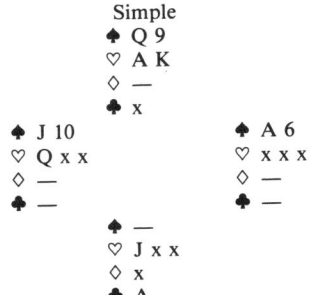

Diamonds are trumps. The ♣ A squeezes West. If a heart is thrown, the ace and king of that suit are cashed, South re-enters his hand by ruffing a spade in order to cash the ♡ J. If a spade is thrown, a heart is led to North, and the ♣Q is led to ruff out the ace and establish the 9.

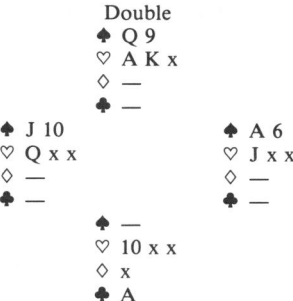

Double
♠ Q 9
♡ A K x
◇ —
♣ —

♠ J 10   ♠ A 6
♡ Q x x   ♡ J x x
◇ —   ◇ —
♣ —   ♣ —

♠ —
♡ 10 x x
◇ x
♣ A

Diamonds are trumps. South leads the ♣A, and West is squeezed. A spade discard enables South to ruff out East's stopper. If a heart is discarded, East is subjected to a simple trump squeeze.

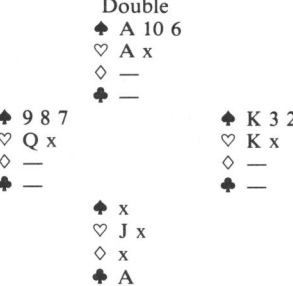

Double
♠ A 10 6
♡ A x
◇ —
♣ —

♠ 9 8 7   ♠ K 3 2
♡ Q x   ♡ K x
◇ —   ◇ —
♣ —   ♣ —

♠ x
♡ J x
◇ x
♣ A

Diamonds are trumps. South leads the ♣A, and West is squeezed. A spade discard enables South to establish a spade by leading to the ace, and returning the 10. A heart discard places East in a simple trump squeeze.

Trump Guard Squeeze

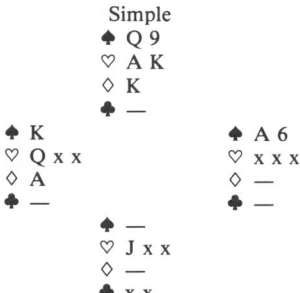

Simple
♠ Q 9
♡ A K
◇ K
♣ —

♠ K   ♠ A 6
♡ Q x x   ♡ x x x
◇ A   ◇ —
♣ —   ♣ —

♠ —
♡ J x x
◇ —
♣ x x

Clubs are trumps. A trump is led, and West is squeezed in three suits. A diamond discard establishes the king; a heart discard permits South to play ace and king of that suit, establishing the jack, with a spade ruff as re-entry; a spade discard allows South to lead a heart to the king, and lead a spade, trump-finessing East's ace.

(See hand at top of right column.)

Clubs are trumps. A trump is led, and West is squeezed in three suits. A diamond discard establishes the king; a heart discard places East in a

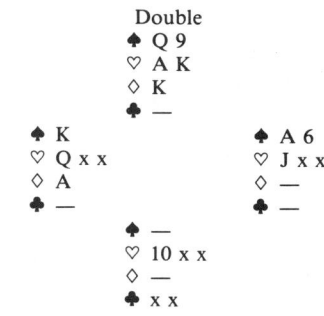

Double
♠ Q 9
♡ A K
◇ K
♣ —

♠ K   ♠ A 6
♡ Q x x   ♡ J x x
◇ A   ◇ —
♣ —   ♣ —

♠ —
♡ 10 x x
◇ —
♣ x x

establishes the king; a heart discard places East in a simple trump squeeze; a spade discard permits South to ruff out East's ace.

Monroe Ingberman

TRUMP SUIT MANAGEMENT. The manner in which declarer utilizes the trump suit in the play of the hand.

The proper technique in handling the trump suit varies, depending first upon the length and the division of the trump suit in the combined hands, i.e., declarer and dummy, and secondly the manner in which the outstanding trumps are distributed in the defenders' hands. Generally speaking, the minimum number of trumps required for a game contract is eight, and the most favorable distribution is four in the dummy and four in the declarer's hand, referred to as:

The 4–4 Fit: The main advantage of this division is that declarer can stand being forced to ruff twice in either hand, reserving the other for purposes of drawing trump. If one opponent holds four trumps, the situation will be much more satisfactory with a 4–4 than a 5–3 distribution; declarer must then take the precaution of looking to his side suits before tackling trumps:

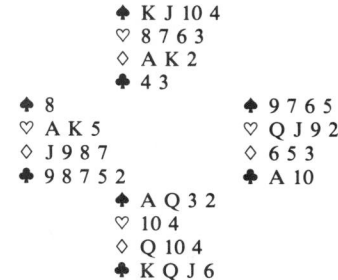

♠ K J 10 4
♡ 8 7 6 3
◇ A K 2
♣ 4 3

♠ 8   ♠ 9 7 6 5
♡ A K 5   ♡ Q J 9 2
◇ J 9 8 7   ◇ 6 5 3
♣ 9 8 7 5 2   ♣ A 10

♠ A Q 3 2
♡ 10 4
◇ Q 10 4
♣ K Q J 6

Against 4♠, West opens with the ♡K. If the defense continues hearts, declarer ruffs the third round and knocks out the ♣A. East leads his last heart and South ruffs with the ace, draws trump, and takes the rest. On any other defense, declarer makes 10 tricks by ruffing his losing club high in the dummy before drawing East's trumps.

The 4–4 distribution lends itself ideally to cross-ruffing; in this type of play the declarer must be careful to cash his side-suit winners before attempting to score his trumps separately.

(See hand at top of next page.)

The contract is 4♡, against which West leads the

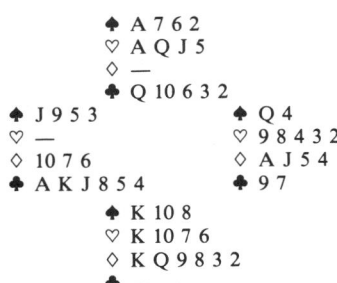

```
              ♠ A 7 6 2
              ♡ A Q J 5
              ◇ —
              ♣ Q 10 6 3 2
♠ J 9 5 3                    ♠ Q 4
♡ —                          ♡ 9 8 4 3 2
◇ 10 7 6                     ◇ A J 5 4
♣ A K J 8 5 4                ♣ 9 7
              ♠ K 10 8
              ♡ K 10 7 6
              ◇ K Q 9 8 3 2
              ♣ —
```

♣K. Declarer ruffs and is in a position to make 10 tricks in spite of the vile distribution, provided he makes the ♠A-K before he ruffs the third club. Failure to do so would give East an opportunity to discard a spade, and declarer would then be unable to enjoy both of his spade winners.

The 4–3 Fit: When the dummy holds only three trumps, facing four in declarer's hand, the play is unlikely to proceed favorably. These hands normally play better in notrump, especially at the higher levels; exceptionally (e.g., when the opponents have an established suit), they are the only ones available. These contracts frequently call for delicate handling.

The problem of control is critical, and declarer must often establish his side-winners before embarking on drawing trumps.

```
              ♠ K 4 3
              ♡ Q 10
              ◇ Q J 9 7 4
              ♣ K 3 2
♠ 6 5 2                      ♠ 10 8 7
♡ A K 7 4 3                  ♡ J 9 8 6 2
◇ A 3                        ◇ 6 2
♣ 10 5 4                     ♣ A 7 6
              ♠ A Q J 9
              ♡ 5
              ◇ K 10 8 5
              ♣ Q J 9 8
```

4♠ is the only possible game contract, and, as the cards lie, cannot be defeated. The defense does best to play hearts at every opportunity, and South ruffs the second round and plays diamonds. West plays a third round of hearts which is ruffed in dummy. Declarer now knocks out the ♣A and ruffs a further heart in dummy. Only now can he afford to draw trumps, and when they break he claims the balance with good diamonds and clubs.

Sometimes declarer can retain control of a shaky trump suit by refusing to ruff.

```
              ♠ K Q 10
              ♡ 4 3 2
              ◇ Q J 9 7
              ♣ A 10 4
♠ 8 7 6 4                    ♠ 9 5
♡ A K Q 8 5                  ♡ J 9 7
◇ 10                         ◇ 8 6 5 2
♣ Q 6 5                      ♣ J 9 8 7
              ♠ A J 3 2
              ♡ 10 6
              ◇ A K 4 3
              ♣ K 3 2
```

Against 4♠, West leads three top hearts. If declarer

ruffs and draws trump, West will be left with a long spade which he will use to interrupt the run of the diamonds, and cash his remaining heart winners. South can ensure the contract against all reasonable distributions by discarding his losing club on the third round of hearts. If the defense persists with a fourth round, he is able to ruff in dummy, preserving his own trump length, and is in a position to draw all West's trumps and take the rest of the tricks with minor-suit winners.

A less obvious example from the same family:

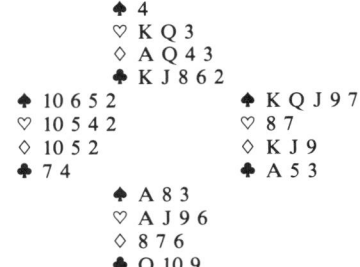

```
              ♠ 4
              ♡ K Q 3
              ◇ A Q 4 3
              ♣ K J 8 6 2
♠ 10 6 5 2                   ♠ K Q J 9 7
♡ 10 5 4 2                   ♡ 8 7
◇ 10 5 2                     ◇ K J 9
♣ 7 4                        ♣ A 5 3
              ♠ A 8 3
              ♡ A J 9 6
              ◇ 8 7 6
              ♣ Q 10 9
```

South plays in ♡4 after East had bid spades, and West leads the ♠2, East playing the jack. Declarer's best play is to let East hold the trick, ruffing in dummy if spades are continued. Declarer is now in a position to draw trumps and give up a club trick while still maintaining control of the enemy suit. Attacking the trump suit by forcing declarer to ruff is by far the most effective form of defense against 4–3 trump contracts. Curiously enough, declarer can often turn this to his advantage and succeed in an otherwise impossible contract.

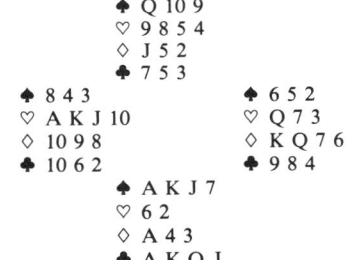

```
              ♠ Q 10 9
              ♡ 9 8 5 4
              ◇ J 5 2
              ♣ 7 5 3
♠ 8 4 3                      ♠ 6 5 2
♡ A K J 10                   ♡ Q 7 3
◇ 10 9 8                     ◇ K Q 7 6
♣ 10 6 2                     ♣ 9 8 4
              ♠ A K J 7
              ♡ 6 2
              ◇ A 4 3
              ♣ A K Q J
```

3 NT is safe as the cards lie but, unsure of the heart suit holding, North-South settled reasonably enough in 4♠, West leading the ♡K. If West shifts at trick two, South has four inescapable losers — two hearts and two diamonds — and must go one down. A heart continuation looks tempting however, and South ruffs the third round with the ace, leads the ♣7 to dummy's nine, and ruffs the fourth round of hearts with the king. He now overtakes the ♣J to draw trump in dummy, discarding his losing diamond. Four club tricks plus the ◇A (in addition to the five trump tricks) round out the contract.

It is sometimes possible for declarer to counter the forcing game, utilizing a strong side-suit for the purpose of weakening the defender's trump holding. (See hand at top of next page.)

Against ♠4, West leads two top hearts, declarer ruffing the second round. If South attempts to draw all

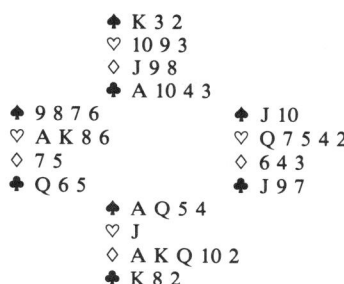

the outstanding trumps, the hand collapses. In order to succeed, he must draw only two rounds of trumps with the ace and queen, and then start the diamonds. If West ruffs the third diamond to lead a heart, South ruffs with his last trump, crosses to dummy's ♣A, and draws West's last trump with the king, making 11 tricks. West does better by refusing to ruff, discarding his clubs instead. After finishing with the diamonds, South perforce leads a club. West ruffs and leads a third heart, and he cannot be prevented from scoring a further trump, but declarer still makes 10 tricks. See also CONTROL MAINTENANCE; DRAWING TRUMPS; ELOPEMENT.

Sammy Kehela

TRUMP SUPPORT. A variable factor, depending on the nature of the bid which is being supported. (See BIDDABLE SUITS.) In general, a player will be very ready to give support if he knows that his side has eight cards in the suit and may give a single raise when a combined seven-card holding is guaranteed and there are reasonable prospects of eight.

In most situations in constructive bidding, a suit bid promises four cards, and therefore four cards are needed for any kind of raise. But many special cases should be noted.

(1) *Five-card support* may be desirable if there is a fair chance that the suit being raised consists of three cards only. This applies particularly to minor-suit raises when the five-card major rule is being used and the incidence of prepared minors is therefore high. KAPLAN-SHEINWOLD, for example, insists on five-card support for a preemptive jump raise of a minor suit; and a single raise in a minor may be avoided with four-card support if there is any convenient alternative. In standard methods, there is a tendency to avoid raising 1♣ with four-card support. With 3-3-3-4 distribution, an expert would often choose a response of 1◊ in preference to a raise to 2♣.

(2) *Three-card support* may be given to any suit which is known or expected to be of at least five cards (e.g., a five-card major opening; a response of 2♡ to 1♠; or an overcall).

Three-card support is normally considered adequate for a single raise of a major suit bid by opener or responder at the first opportunity. Many players prefer the three-card holding to be headed by a high honor, but consider the following cases:

(a) ♠ 4 3 2
♡ 3 2
◊ 4 3 2
♣ A Q 4 3 2

(b) ♠ 4 3 2
♡ 3 2
◊ A Q 2
♣ A Q 4 3 2

In (a) an opening bid of 1♠ should be raised to 2♠. Much more often than not the opener will hold more than four spades. The raise is a lesser evil than 1 NT, because of the weakness in hearts. The responder does not wish to play notrump, nor to allow a heart bid by the opposition at the level of two.

Hand (b) opens the bidding with 1♠ and gets a response of 1♠. A raise to 2♠ is again a lesser evil than a rebid of 1 NT, for similar reasons.

A jump raise or a raise of a secondary suit requires at least four-card support, but there are occasional exceptions on a least-evil basis:

(c) ♠ A Q 3
♡ 10 8 5 4 2
◊ A 5 3 2
♣ 2

(d) ♠ K 6 4
♡ 4 2
◊ A Q 6 4 3
♣ 5 4 2

Hand (c) has to respond to a fourth-hand opening bid of 1♠ and a jump to 3♠ is superior to a non-forcing bid of 2♡.

Hand (d) has responded 1◊ to an opening bid of 1♠ and the opener has rebid 1♠. With the prospect of a ruffing value in hearts, responder is not unwilling to play in a 4-3 fit, and the mildly constructive raise to 2♠ is much better than a completely negative preference bid of 2♣.

(3) *Two-card support* may be given to any suit which is known or expected to be of at least six cards (e.g., any opening preemptive bid; a vulnerable overcall at the level of two; and almost any suit which has been bid twice (see OPENER'S REBID).

In an emergency, a doubleton may be sufficient to raise a suit which is known to be of at least five cards:

(e) ♠ 7 5
♡ 2
◊ A 8 6 5 3
♣ J 7 6 5 2

(f) ♠ K 7 6 5 3
♡ A 4
◊ A Q 4 2
♣ 8 6

Hand (e) should raise 1♠ to 2♠ playing five-card majors, partly for preemptive reasons and partly because there is no good alternative (unless a 1 NT response is forcing). The alternative is a pass.

Hand (f) opens 1♠, and the response is 2♡, showing at least a five-card suit. A raise to 3♡ is superior to a rebid of the anemic spade suit.

(4) *One-card support* is usually adequate only when the suit has been bid so strongly as to indicate that support is not needed. An exceptional case is suggested by TERENCE REESE:

South holds:

♠ Q J 6 2
♡ 8 6 5 4
◊ A K 4 3
♣ Q

Vul: None

WEST	NORTH	EAST	SOUTH
1♡	2♣	2♡	?

Reese's suggestion, endorsed by an expert panel, was to bid 3♣. With bidding all round the table, North's overcall is likely to be a distributional one based on a good six-card suit; 3♣ is likely to be the best contract for North-South; and East-West may be tempted to bid 3♡, which South can double effectively, and be surprised by the club situation. This is one case of a useful general rule: in competitive situations raises should be given more freely.

TRUMP SWISS CONVENTION. See SWISS CONVENTION.

TRUMP TRICK. A playing trick in the trump suit.

TRUNCATED HOWELL MOVEMENT. A shortening of the HOWELL MOVEMENT to terminate at the end of 13 rounds, 26 boards. Since this did not give balanced comparison, it is no longer used but has been replaced by the THREE-QUARTER MOVEMENT.

TRUSCOTT DEFENSE. A system of two-suited takeouts that can be used over strong artificial openings of 1♣, 2♣, 1◇ or 2◇. See DEFENSE TO STRONG ARTIFICIAL OPENINGS.

TRUSCOTT 2◇. See TWO-WAY STAYMAN.

TURKEY (TURKEY GAME, TURKEY SHOOT). A colloquial term used to describe events in a tournament other than major championships, such as secondary events, consolation events and side games.

TURKISH BRIDGE FEDERATION (TÜRKIYE BRIÇ FEDERASYONU). Organized in the Spring of 1965, its membership, which is governed by the Turkish Law of Associations, is limited to clubs, not individuals. As of 1982, there were nine member clubs with approximately 250 tournament players. The Federation became a member of the European Bridge League in 1968; it participated in its first European Championship in 1969, and sent representatives to the 1972 and 1974 World Olympiads. National events contested annually include Annual Pairs, Open Pairs and Annual Teams-of-Four Championships. A masterpoint program was introduced in the fall of 1968.

Officers, 1982:
President: Gunduz Pamuk
Secretary: Dr. Varujan Alyanak, P.K. 280,
  Osmanbey, Istanbul, Turkey

TURN. (1) Noun: the appropriate moment for a player to make a bid or play; (2) verb: to quit a card at duplicate or a trick at rubber bridge after all four players have played.

TWELVE, RULE OF. See RULE OF TWELVE.

TWELVE TABLES. At duplicate, 12 tables provide for competition among 48 players as individuals, 24 pairs or 12 teams-of-four.

There are several movements available for a 48 player individual game, but for a one-session game, the appendix RAINBOW MOVEMENT devised by PAUL MARKS provides the easiest movement and scoring. Four stationary player seats are assigned: 12, North at table 1; 24, East at table 2; 36, South at table 3; and 48, West at table 4. Players numbers 1 to 11 sit North at the corresponding tables; numbers 13 to 23 sit East at tables 1 to 11; numbers 25 to 35 sit South

at tables 1 to 11; and numbers 37 to 47 sit West at tables 1 to 11. (However, four of these players, one from each group, find their new seats occupied by the stationary players, 45 to 48.) These players for the first round and their counterparts at every successive round play boards 23 and 24 at table 12. Otherwise, at the end of each round, North players skip a table to lower numbers, South players skip a table to higher numbers, East players go to the next higher number table, and West players skip two tables to higher numbers, boards going to next lower numbered tables. For purposes of progression and board numbers, table 12 is ignored, and is filled each round with players, finding stationary players in the seats to which they are assigned. Each player thus plays 22 of the 24 boards in the 11 rounds. Ten is top and 110 average.

As a pair game, 22 boards can be played in 11 rounds, traveling players skipping a table after round 6. By inserting a byestand between tables 7 and 8, and relaying boards between 1 and 2, 24 boards can be played. The game may be either straight or SCRAMBLED MITCHELL. The THREE-QUARTER MOVEMENT can be used for 26 boards; or eight or nine rounds of three boards played, utilizing the skip movement at the halfway point for a longer game.

As a team game, there are several choices. As a SWISS TEAM game 12 tables is a good movement. At the end of the second round of play there are probably three teams with two wins and no losses. By a random selection you determine which of the three teams play each other. Then you determine which team with a 1–1 record plays the other team with two wins and no losses. This is, again, by random selection.

For team-of-four play there are options. None of the movements are easy since the even number of tables requires special moves for the moving pairs. You can distribute two boards per table and have the East–West pairs skip a table in the lower direction. After the first round you follow the normal team progression of the moving pairs skipping a table in the lower direction with the boards moving to the next lower table. After the second round the moving pairs skip an extra table. For the next six rounds the moving pairs follow the normal progression of skipping a table in the lower direction. After the eighth round the moving pairs skip an extra table and the boards skip a table. Following the 10th round, East–West pairs 1 through 6 add six to their number and go to that table number, and East–West pairs 7–12 subtract six from their number and go to that table. New boards are given out at tables 1 through 6 and, after being shuffled and dealt, are relayed with the table six numbers higher (1 and 7, 2 and 8, etc.) The problem with this movement is that the teams play only 22 boards. By putting out three boards to a table and eliminating the relay round, 30 boards can be played in a session. The movement can be curtailed to 24 boards by eliminating the first and 10th rounds. At the start of the game East–West pairs 1 through 4 add eight to their number and go to that table; pairs 5–12 subtract four from their number and go to that table. After the first round, the moving pairs skip an extra table. After the seventh round, the moving pairs skip an extra table and the boards skip a table.

For 11½ and 12½ tables, see HALF TABLES.

TWINNING. The process used to produce identical boards to be played in two (or more) sections. To twin the boards in a two-board movement (either for social purposes or for scoring with a multiple top), the odd-numbered boards are passed out, one to a table, in one section and the even-numbered boards are passed out in the other. As the boards are being shuffled and played, a second board of the same number is put on the table. After play is complete and the score is recorded, the twinning is done. There are several methods, but this one works best. The cards in the second board are divided into suits, and each player picks up one suit. Each player faces the hand just played in front of him. Then each player distributes his suit to the four players to match the cards in front of them. Once all the cards from the second board are distributed, each player puts the hand actually played back in its original board, then puts the twinned hand in the second board. The director then picks up the twinned board and brings it to the correct table in the other section, where the board is played "as is", that is without being shuffled.

When boards are being twinned over three sections, one section is given the odd boards and another the even boards. The director then gives each table an additional two boards of the same number to duplicate. Meanwhile, the third section is patiently waiting. However, the first twinned board at each table is brought to the third section, so that the third section finishes first-round play at approximately the same time as the two sections where twinning took place.

Sometimes boards are twinned when three boards are being played per round. This can cause complications for the director, but concentration and care are all that are needed to make the method work.

Experienced directors find that duplicating across two sections requires about 15 minutes and across three, 20 minutes. In multisection events (more than three) other methods are available.

In multi-section events, when it is desirable to have the same hands in play in all sections, ACBL computer-dealt hands usually are used. These are available in groupings of even numbers starting with two sections and going as high as needed. See COMPUTER-DEALT HANDS.

TWO or TWO-SPOT. The lowest-ranking card in any given suit. Sometimes referred to as the deuce, this card is just below the 3 in precedence.

TWO-BID. The bid of two in a suit as an opening bid is used in many different ways by various players. Specialized uses are referred to in the following articles: ACOL TWO-BID; ARTIFICIAL 2◊ AND 2♣ OPENINGS; BENJAMIN; BLUE TEAM 2◊; FLANNERY 2◊; FLANNERY 2♡; MEXICAN 2◊; ROMAN SYSTEM (2♣ Opening); ROMAN 2◊; SKINNER TWO-BIDS; TAM II; 2♣ AND 2◊ OPENINGS; 2♣ STRONG ARTIFICIAL OPENING; WEAK TWO-BIDS.

2♣ ARTIFICIAL BALANCING TAKEOUT. See BALANCING 2♣ FOR TAKEOUT.

2♣ CONVENTIONS. *Openings:* See 2♣ OPENING AS MULTI-SUITER; 2♣ SYSTEMS; 2♣ STRONG ARTIFICIAL OPENING. *Responses:* See DRURY; GLADIATOR; STAYMAN CONVENTION; STAYMAN SECOND ROUND; 2♣ REBID BY RESPONDER AS ONLY FORCE AFTER 1 NT REBID. *Takeouts:* See TWO-SUITER CONVENTIONS.

2♣ OPENING AS MULTI-SUITER. The principal conventions that use a 2♣ opening bid to show a two-suited hand are features of the BIG DIAMOND SYSTEM, ROMAN SYSTEM, and ROTH CLUB SYSTEM.

2♣ FOR MINORS, 2◊ FOR MAJORS. A 2◊ overcall of 1 NT shows both major suits. The 2♣ overcall shows length in both minor suits.

2♣ REBID BY RESPONDER AS ONLY FORCE AFTER 1 NT REBID. A convention devised by EDWIN KANTAR to provide a full range of rebids by responder over a 1 NT rebid by opener. Using 2♣ as the only forcing rebid by responder, all other two-level suit bids are discouraging and jump bids at the three-level invite game. For example:

	(a)			(b)	
1♣		1♡	1♣		1♡
1 NT		3♡	1 NT		3◊

The last bid in each of the above sequences is nonforcing but invitational. See also CROWHURST CONVENTION; STAYMAN ON SECOND ROUND; UNBID MINOR SUIT FORCE.

2♣ RESPONSE TO NOTRUMP. See GLADIATOR; SKINNER RESPONSES TO A 1 NT OPENING; STAYMAN CONVENTION.

2♣ SYSTEMS. Many bidding systems use 2♣ as the opening bid with strong hands, irrespective of the holding in the club suit. Information on such systems is included in the following articles: ACE-SHOWING RESPONSES; ACOL; ARTIFICIAL 2◊ AND 2♣ OPENINGS; BARON; BENJAMIN; BULLDOG; CAB; KAPLAN-SHEINWOLD; OFFICIAL; ROMEX; ROTH-STONE; TAM II.

2♣ STRONG ARTIFICIAL OPENING. An artificial opening bid on powerful hands which is the cornerstone of many systems. A response of 2◊ is usually negative. See 2◊ ARTIFICIAL RESPONSE TO FORCING 2♣ OPENING. See also SECOND NEGATIVE RESPONSE AFTER ARTIFICIAL FORCING OPENING. The first use of the bid of 2♣ in this way is credited to DAVID BURNSTINE at the Raymond Club, New York City, in 1929, but some experts used 2♣ for all strong hands, and this concept gradually superseded the FORCING TWO-BID in serious tournament play. It is usually used in combination with WEAK TWO-BIDS, but may be combined with INTERMEDIATE TWO-BIDS of various types.

Originally the 2♣ bid was forcing to game. In modern practice many experts announce it as forcing to 2 NT (after a 2◊ response), to cover two common exceptions:

SOUTH	NORTH
2♣	2◇
2♡	2 NT
3♡	

North may pass. This widens the use of the 2♣ opening to include a powerful one-suited hand where game may be missed if partner passes with 4–5 points, or slam may be missed because it becomes difficult for opener to show his strength clearly if he commences with a bid of one. The game-forcing nature of the opening two-bid was modified by CULBERTSON to exclude just such a situation after a 2 NT response; opener made a minimum rebid of the same suit, viz.:

SOUTH	NORTH
2♡	2 NT
3♡	

Another exception tightens the gaps in the structure of notrump bids:

SOUTH	NORTH
2♣	2◇
2 NT	

North may pass. Under this method, instead of the book standard of 22–24 (or 21–23), a 2 NT opener shows 21–22 (or 20–22) while 2♣ followed by 2 NT shows 23–24 (or 22–24).

If the opener's suit is·a major, the 2♣ bidder may be better off than the user of the forcing two:

SOUTH	NORTH
2♣	2◇
2♠	

The 2♣ bidder has gained a round of bidding. North has given a negative response already, and can bid his hand naturally on the second round. Similarly playing forcing two:

SOUTH	NORTH
2♣	2 NT
3♣	

or

2♡	2 NT
3♡	

Responder is unable to show lower ranking suit without going past 3 NT, whereas with

SOUTH	NORTH
2♣	2◇
2♠	

responder can show any long suit without bypassing a notrump game. On the other hand, in one situation the forcing-two bidder may have the advantage if his suit is clubs:

SOUTH	NORTH
2♣	3◇

Using the 2♣ bid, and with North holding a positive response in diamonds, the bidding is already at the level of three, and South has not bid clubs. If his opening is a minimum, he may not wish to bid 4♣ and so go beyond 3 NT.

The forcing-two player, however, can bid both suits naturally and remain at the two-level.

In rare situations, preemptive action by the opponents may also put the 2♣ opener at a disadvantage in that he has not yet shown his suit (or one of two suits).

Standard for a positive response to 2♣ varies, but most authorities insist on 1½ quick tricks (an ace and a king, or three kings). Others are satisfied with an ace, or a good suit headed by king and queen with some plus values; these treatments have the advantage that positive responses can be given more frequently. 2 NT can be regarded as an exception. Some players make this response with 8 points or more, irrespective of quick trick strength.

After a positive response, the opener will usually rebid as though the response had been negative. Therefore, 2♣–2♡–2 NT, or 2♣–3♣–3 NT, shows the balanced minimum hand with 23–24 points. Similarly, 2♣–2♡–3 NT would show a balanced hand with 25–27.

In systems employing an artificial strength-showing bid of 1♣, a bid of 2♣ may be the equivalent of a standard 1♣ opening, including a long club suit. See also ACE-SHOWING RESPONSES and FORCING TWO-BID.

TWO-DEMAND BID. See FORCING TWO-BID.

2◇ ARTIFICIAL OPENING. As a strong forcing opening bid, see ARTIFICIAL 2◇ AND 2♣ OPENINGS, BENJAMIN convention, ROMEX SYSTEM, SCHENKEN SYSTEM, TAM II 2♣ AND 2◇ OPENINGS. As a two-suited or three-suited opening bid, see conventions listed in 2◇ OPENING AS MULTI-SUITER.

2◇ AS ONLY POSITIVE RESPONSE. See 2◇ ARTIFICIAL RESPONSE TO FORCING 2♣ OPENER.

2◇ ARTIFICIAL RESPONSE TO FORCING 2♣ OPENING. In response to a 2♣ STRONG ARTIFICIAL OPENING a 2◇ response is usually negative, showing about 0–7 points. Alternatives are to use this response as:

(1) Automatic. The 2◇ bid is nondescriptive, but gives opener room to describe his hand. See ALLEN OVER 2♣.

(2) Positive. Responder's 2◇ shows 8 or more points, but says nothing about his distribution. All other responses are negative, showing 0–7 points with length in the suit bid.

(3) Double Negative. Responder's bid shows 0–3 points. With this treatment it is possible to use a 2♡ response artificially either to show specifically 4–7 points (see STEP RESPONSES TO STRONG ARTIFICIAL TWO-BIDS), or as a neutral bid showing at least 4 high-card points and allowing opener to describe his hand.

(4) ACE-SHOWING RESPONSE.

2◇ ARTIFICIAL RESPONSES TO 1 NT OPENING. Convention used in response to 1 NT opening bids. An artificial convention designed to solve particular notrump bidding problems. In conjunction with the various conventions so used, a substitute sequence may be required to show a weak hand with a long diamond suit: an immediate 3◇; or 2♣ followed by 3◇; or 2◇ followed by 3◇. See FLINT 2◇; GLADIATOR; JACOBY TRANSFER BID; TWO-WAY STAYMAN.

2 ◇ NEGATIVE, 2 ♡ NEUTRAL. See 2 ◇ ARTIFICIAL RESPONSE TO FORCING 2♣ OPENER.

2 ◇ OPENING AS MULTI-SUITER. There are several conventions that use a 2 ◇ opening to show a two-suited or three-suited hand. The principal ones are BLUE TEAM 2 ◇, FLANNERY 2 ◇, ROMAN 2 ◇. In addition, a 2 ◇ opening shows a three-suited hand in the PRECISION CLUB system and a hand with both major suits in the BIG DIAMOND SYSTEM. See also MULTI-2 ◇.

2 ♡ ARTIFICIAL RESPONSE TO 2♣ OPENING. See STEP RESPONSES TO STRONG ARTIFICIAL TWO-BIDS; 2 ◇ ARTIFICIAL RESPONSE TO FORCING 2♣ OPENING.

2 NT FORCING RESPONSE TO WEAK TWO-BIDS. See WEAK TWO-BIDS.

2 NT OPENING. This shows a balanced hand with 21-22 points, and might be made with 20 points. This is the standard expert treatment. The traditional range of 22-24 continues to be used by most players who use FORCING TWO-BIDS. See also 2 NT OPENING FOR MINORS.

Theoretically the distribution should be the same as for an opening notrump bid: 4-3-3-3, 4-4-3-2, or 5-3-3-2 with the five-card suit a minor. However, the 2 NT opening often has to serve as a *least evil* choice with hands too strong to open with one of a suit and not strong enough for a forcing opening. 5-3-3-2 with a major suit is frequently opened with 2 NT, and occasional departures such as 6-3-2-2 or 5-4-2-2 are permissible.

Responses are as follows:

(1) *3♣.* Stayman, asking opener to bid a major suit. With no major he bids 3 ◇, and if responder then bids a major, he shows a five-card suit. Holding both majors, either suit may be bid by partnership agreement, and agreement is not essential. If responder then bids 3 NT, the opener bids his second major.

A rebid of four in a major suit, other than a raise, can be used to show a club/major two-suiter with mild slam ambitions.

A rebid of 3 NT by the opener virtually does not exist in standard methods. It can be used by partnership agreement to show a hand with no interest in a major-suit contract, perhaps a doubleton in each.

A variation normal in England (due to the BARON SYSTEM) is for the opener to bid all his suits up the line. 3 ◇ would show a diamond suit but would not deny a major. 3 NT would show that the opener's only suit was clubs. This method facilitates minor-suit slam bidding but is somewhat inefficient when responder is 5-4 or 4-5 in the major suits.

(2) *3 ◇.* Used by many experts as the FLINT convention. In a natural sense the bid shows at least five diamonds, and is a slam suggestion. Many players play this as a JACOBY TRANSFER BID to hearts.

(3) *3 ♡ or 3♠.* Forcing and shows a five-card suit. The suit may be longer [see (6) below]. The responder is asking the opener to choose between the major-suit game (with three-card support) or 3 NT (with a doubleton in responder's suit). However, the responder may have slam interests, so the opener makes a cuebid (2 NT — 3 ♡ — 4 ◇) if he has good

support and a suitable hand for slam purposes. Many players play 3 ♡ as a JACOBY TRANSFER BID to spades. See also AUTOMATIC ACES; EXPECTED NUMBER OF CONTROLS IN BALANCED HANDS; ROMEX STAYMAN.

(4) *3 NT.* A range of 4-10, although a thin 4-point hand may be passed. An occasional 3-point hand (K-x-x-x-x) may be worth a raise.

(5) *4♣ or 4 ◇.* These bids are usually conventional (GERBER, TEXAS, or SOUTH AFRICAN TEXAS). In a natural sense they would show a strong suit, but are very rare.

(6) *4 ♡ or 4♠.* In standard methods this shows a six-card suit with mild slam ambitions. Holding a weaker hand with a six-card major, responder must bid his suit at the three-level and then rebid it. Many experts, especially in England, use the jump to game as a signoff, in which case three of a major followed by four is a mild slam invitation.

(7) *4 NT.* A natural invitation to 6 NT, holding about 11 points. Responder's distribution is likely to be 4-3-3-3, but might be 4-4-3-2 or 5-3-3-2 if no major suit is held (see MILLER SLAM CONVENTION).

(8) *5♣ or 5 ◇.* A very unbalanced weak hand. A seven-card suit and a void would be typical. The opener is expected to pass, but might bid six with a fine fit and excellent controls.

(9) *5 ♡ or 5♠.* A strong invitation to bid six, based on a six-card suit.

(10) *5 NT.* This has no natural meaning, but is used by some experts as an invitation to 7 NT. With no interest in a grand slam, the opener bids 6 NT.

(11) *6 NT.* A balanced hand, probably 4-3-3-3, with 12-14 points.

For an alternative system of responding, see MILES RESPONSES TO 2 NT OPENINGS.

2 NT OPENING FOR MINORS. A convention using a 2 NT opening bid to show a hand worht 10-13 not vulnerable or 14-16 points vulnerable, and at least five cards in each minor suit. Responses at the three- and four-level are not forcing.

2 NT OVERCALL. Can be used in six different ways:

(1) *Natural.* To show a 2 NT opening bid without about 22 points. This helps to define the range of a 2 NT bid preceded by a takeout double, which would indicate 19-20. These two procedures can be interchanged by partnership agreement. STAYMAN would apply with partnerships that use it after a 1 NT OVERCALL.

(2) *Unusual.* To show a minor two-suiter. The minimum strength would vary according to vulnerability. At favorable vulnerability, a 6-5 distribution with 6 points in the suits would usually be considered adequate. At unfavorable vulnerability both the hand and the suits should be distinctly stronger. The maximum strength would be a hand justifying an immediate CUEBID in the opponent's suit.

Many players play 3 ♡ as a JACOBY TRANSFER BID to spades.

In BLUE TEAM CLUB, 2 NT applies over minor suits also and shows the lowest unbid suits: hearts and diamonds over 1♣, and hearts and clubs over 1 ◇. See DEFENSE TO TWO-SUITED INTERFERENCE.

(3) *Preemptive.* To indicate a long broken suit

lower in rank than the opening bid, justifying a preemptive bid at the level of three. Partner is expected to bid 3♣ if third hand passes, to permit his side to reach the appropriate suit; but third hand seldom passes. This is not needed playing WEAK JUMP OVERCALLS and has dubious value in any event.

(4) *Roman.* To show a strong two-suited hand, in which the suits are not specified. Responder bids the lowest unbid suit, and if the 2 NT bidder shows a suit, he holds that suit and the suit in which responder made his artificial response. 3 NT would show the two unbid suits. (For weaker two-suited hands, see JUMP OVERCALL.)

(5) *Modern.* To show a strong hand with a near-solid minor suit, for example:

♠ A 2
♡ K 5
◇ J 4 2
♣ A Q J 9 6 2

Responder may raise to 3 NT, or bid 3♣ with no interest in game. In the latter case the overcaller passes or converts to 3◇. In borderline cases, responder is guided by possession of a key card in his partner's minor. With a diamond honor he bids 3♣, and converts a 3◇ rebid to 3 NT. With a club honor he responds 3◇, giving the overcaller the choice between 3◇ and 3 NT.

(6) *Artificial.* When an immediate cuebid in the opener's suit is given a specialized meaning (as in MICHAELS CUEBID), 2 NT can be used to show a hand of game-going strength, with 3♣ as a conventional negative response.

2 NT REBID. See OPENER'S REBID.

2 NT RESPONSE (to Opening Suit Bid of One). There are five treatments which can be adopted.

(1) *Standard.* 13–15 points and game forcing. The responder raises with any balanced distribution. If he rebids at the three-level in a suit, it will usually show an aversion to notrump: he is likely to have a singleton or void. The responder must then move cautiously:

♠ Q 3
♡ A 8 6 2
◇ A Q J
♣ J 8 5 3

The bidding:

NORTH	SOUTH
1♠	2 NT
3♣	3◇

The most useful bid South can make is a call at the three-level in a suit in which he holds considerable strength. If this corresponds to North's shortage, he will know that 3 NT will be safe, and that there would be duplicated values in a high suit contract. But if North's shortage is in an unbid suit, he will know that a suit contract will be preferable to notrump. Responder should avoid raising opener's secondary minor suit, although he may do so at a later stage if circumstances warrant it.

A possible additional use for the 2 NT response, suggested by MARSHALL MILES, is for balanced hands with about 19 points. Whatever the opener rebids, the responder then suggests a slam, usually by rebid-

ding 4 NT. This makes it clear that responder cannot have the normal 2 NT response.

(2) *Limit.* 11–12 points, encouraging but not forcing. The bidding can stop short of game in three ways: (a) an immediate pass by the opener, holding a minimum balanced hand; (b) after a rebid of his own suit by opener, showing a subminimum opening and, usually, a six-card suit (a typical ACOL sign-off bid); (c) after a bid of a new suit by the opener and a preference bid at the three level by responder. The responder must give jump preference to 4♡ or 4♠ if his hand is particularly suitable for the suit game.

In choosing a rebid at the three-level, responder should consider the possibility of bidding a strong suit, as in (1) above. The Miles variation for balanced hands with about 19 points is not available since 2 NT is not forcing.

If responder has passed originally, a response of 2 NT is always a limit bid (unless DRURY or SNAP is being used).

(3) *Baron.* 16–18 points and game forcing. In this system the responses of 2 NT and 3 NT are inverted. After 3 NT (12–14) it is usually easy for the opener to select a suitable game; and the 2 NT response leaves more room for exploration on hands on which a slam is likely.

(4) *Psychic Control.* 21–22 points, and therefore offering prospects of game if the opening bidder has a systemic ROTH-STONE psychic.

In all the cases listed, with the possible exception of (4), the 2 NT response normally has a 4-3-3-3 distribution, or 4-4-3-2 with the doubleton in the opener's suit.

(5) *Conventional.* Used with limit raises to show a standard forcing jump raise when the opening bid was in a major (invented by Oswald Jacoby). A rebid of 4♣ shows a minimum opening, and 3 NT and 3♠ show hands of increasing strength. Rebids at three- and four-level in a new suit show singletons and voids respectively.

2 NT (As A Negative Response To Strong Two-Bids). The traditional negative response to a strong opening two-bid, showing fewer than 7 or 8 points, counting high cards plus distribution.

2 NT RESPONSE (As A Relay To 3♣). A convention whereby a response of 2 NT to a 1 NT opening forces the opener to rebid 3♣. If the responder has a weak hand with a long club suit, he passes. If he has instead a weak hand with a long diamond suit, he bids 3◇, which opener is required to pass.

Some partnerships also use the relay when responder has a three-suited game-going hand with a singleton in one of the major suits. The responder shows this type of hand over opener's forced 3♣ bid by bidding the suit of his singleton.

2 NT RESPONSE (Over Opponent's Takeout Double). An artificial response to an opening bid, devised by ALAN TRUSCOTT, which may be used in any of several ways, depending on whether the opening was in a suit or in notrump, and on the partnership's understanding: (1) as a limit raise over opener's suit bid, showing about 9 to 11 points with three or four trumps; (2) as a preemptive raise of opener's minor suit bid, normally promising five or six trumps and unbalanced distribution; this use allows responder to jump to three of opener's minor to show a limit raise, and permits opener to bid game in notrump from what is more likely to be the RIGHT SIDE; (3) when opener's bid was 1 NT, as a relay to 3♣, see LEBENSOLD convention; (4) when opener's bid was 1 NT, as a takeout bid implying that responder has a strong two-suiter, with which he cannot risk redoubling because the double may have been made on a long running suit.

TWO–ODD. Two tricks over book or eight tricks in all.

TWO OVER ONE GAME FORCE. A method of bidding in which a two-level simple new-suit response to an opening suit bid is forcing to game, e.g., 1♠ – 2♣ or 1♡ – 2♢. When using this system, it is customary to use the FORCING 1 NT response to a major to handle certain types of intermediate hands. The method is used primarily in conjunction with FIVE-CARD MAJORS. When using this system, it usually is not wise to open the bidding with a minimum if the hand is flat or if the points are mostly queens and jacks. The two-over-one forcing response allows the partnership to test slam possibilities while the bidding level is still low.

TWO OVER ONE RESPONSE. A minimum response in a lower-ranking suit to an opening suit bid. For example, 1♡ –2♣.

The minimum strength required for this response is 10 points in standard methods. Rather more is required in ROTH-STONE and KAPLAN-SHEINWOLD, when responder guarantees a second bid; rather less in ACOL, when 8 points may be sufficient.

The maximum strength is a hand just short of a JUMP SHIFT, i.e., about 17 points in standard methods or about 15 points in Acol. For players using WEAK JUMP SHIFT RESPONSES, the two over one has no upper limit.

The longest suit is usually chosen for the response, and if two five-card suits are held, the higher-ranking is given preference. If the sequence is specifically 1♠ –2♡, the responder virtually guarantees a five-card suit, and the opener can raise confidently with three-card support or conceivably with a doubleton. Any response in the suit immediately lower in rank is likely to be at least five cards (1♡ –2♢, or 1♢ –2♣).

For other aspects of this response, see CHOICE OF SUIT and UP THE LINE.

TWO–SUITER. A hand with one suit of more than four cards and another suit of more than three cards. The term used to be confined to hands with at least five cards in each of two suits. A 5-4 distribution was called a semi-two-suiter. For opening the bidding with a two-suiter, see BORDERLINE OPENING BIDS and CHOICE OF SUIT.

TWO–SUITER CONVENTIONS. Several defensive two-suiter conventions are listed under the following headings: ASTRO, ASTRO CUE-BIDS, BROZEL, COLORFUL CUE-BIDS, COPENHAGEN, CRASH, DEFENSE TO STRONG ARTIFICIAL OPENINGS, LANDY, LEA SYSTEM, MICHAELS, PANAMA, ROBINSON, ROMAN JUMP OVER-CALLS, TOP AND BOTTOM CUE-BID, TRAP, TRAP WITH TWO-LEVEL TRANSFERS, TRUSCOTT, UNUSUAL NOTRUMP, UPPER SUITS CUE-BID. Offensive-type two-suited conventions include BIG DIAMOND SYSTEM (2♣ and 2♢ openings); FLANNERY 2♢; FLANNERY 2♡; ROMAN SYSTEM (2♡ and 2♠ openings).

TWO TABLES. At duplicate, two tables provide for competition among eight (or nine) players as individuals, four pairs of players, or two teams-of-four.

As an individual tournament among eight players, seven rounds are required so that each player will play with each other player as a partner. Conduct of this game is described under INDIVIDUAL MOVEMENTS for eight or nine players.

As a pair tournament, three rounds are required. In each round the boards are relayed between the two tables, and scores can be determined almost instantly by direct comparison. Pair 4 is North–South at table 1, facing pair 1 as East–West; at table 2, pair 2 is North–South, and pair 3 is East–West. The better score between the North–South pairs is awarded 1 point, the East–West players at the other table (having the better East–West score) also receiving a point.

New boards are brought in (or the same boards are reshuffled) for round 2, pair 3 replacing 2, 2 replacing 1 and 1 replacing 3 for positions. This is repeated for the third round with a third set of boards. Eight boards to a round give about a three-hour game.

As a contest between two teams of four, the game may be divided into halves. if it is desired to have each pair of one team in head-on competition with both pairs of the other team. Otherwise it may be played straight through. In each half, one-quarter of the total number of boards to be played are shuffled at each table and played; the boards are then exchanged between tables. Scoring may be BOARD-A-MATCH, AGGREGATE (or total points), or scored by IMP. The latter is preferred by most top players.

For 2½ tables see HALF TABLES.

TWO-WAY FINESSE. A recurring type of situation in which a FINESSE may be taken through either opponent. For example:

(a)	(b)
NORTH	NORTH
♠ A 10 3 2	♠ K 10 2
SOUTH	SOUTH
♠ K J 5 4	♠ A J 3

The question, of course, is whom to play for the ♠Q. East or West?

In many cases, in the absence of any clues revealed during the bidding or the play, it becomes a pure guess. Quite a few players, in these circumstances, will finese West for the queen, on the theory QUEEN OVER JACK. Of course, this method of taking a two-way finesse is rather on the unscientific side. In the absence of any external clues, a queen can frequently be located without resorting to guesswork. Here is such a case.

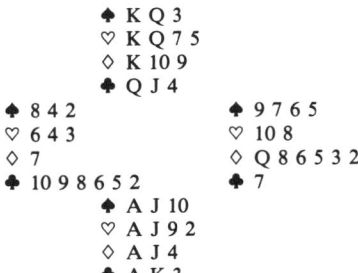

```
                ♠ K Q 3
                ♡ K Q 7 5
                ◇ K 10 9
                ♣ Q J 4
    ♠ 8 4 2                    ♠ 9 7 6 5
    ♡ 6 4 3                    ♡ 10 8
    ◇ 7                        ◇ Q 8 6 5 3 2
    ♣ 10 9 8 6 5 2             ♣ 7
                ♠ A J 10
                ♡ A J 9 2
                ◇ A J 4
                ♣ A K 3
```

South arrived at 7 NT, against which West opened a club, dummy's jack winning. Declarer counted 12 tricks, and perceived that the thirteenth trick would be obtained only in the diamond suit. Whom to finesse for the ◇ Q, East or West?

At trick two South cashed the ♣ K, East discarding a diamond. Three rounds of spades were then taken, everybody following suit. Next, three rounds of hearts were played and declarer paused to take inventory.

West was known to have started with six clubs, three spades and three hearts. Hence he had, at most, one diamond. Dummy's ◇ K was then played, and when West followed suit, all of his thirteen cards were accounted for. A diamond was now led off the board, and the ◇ J was finessed successfully, for declarer's thirteenth trick.

On occasion, when declarer is confronted with a two-way finesse, he can maneuver his play so that an opponent will lead that suit to him, thereby giving declarer a "free finesse." The deal which follows illustrates this point.

```
                ♠ Q J 8 5 2
                ♡ A Q 4
                ◇ A 10 6
                ♣ 7 5
    ♠ 10                       ♠ 7 4
    ♡ J 10 9 7                 ♡ 6 5 3
    ◇ 7 5 3                    ◇ Q 9 8 2
    ♣ K J 9 8 2                ♣ Q 10 4 3
                ♠ A K 9 6 3
                ♡ K 8 2
                ◇ K J 4
                ♣ A 6
```

South arrived at a 6♠ contract. West opened the ♡J, dummy's queen winning. The opponents' trumps were picked up in two rounds, after which the ♡A-K were cashed. Next came the ♣A, followed by another club, and this position was reached:

```
                ♠ Q J 8
                ♡ —
                ◇ A 10 6
                ♣ —
    ♠ —                        ♠ —
    ♡ 10                       ♡ —
    ◇ 7 5 3                    ◇ Q 9 8 2
    ♣ J 9                      ♣ Q 10
                ♠ 9 6 3
                ♡ —
                ◇ K J 4
                ♣ —
```

It mattered not which opponent won the trick. If a heart or a club were returned, declarer would trump it in dummy, while simultaneously discarding the ◇ 4 from his own hand. If the winner of the club lead led a diamond, declarer would surely make three diamond tricks.

In the actual play, West, who had won the club lead, led a diamond, East's queen falling to declarer's king via a free finesse.

The rules of thumb for taking two-way finesses fall under six headings. They all assume that other things are equal, which they very seldom are. In almost all cases, one defender will appear more likely to have missing honor cards, or to have greater length in the crucial suit.

(1) *Technical*. Play the left-hand opponent for the missing honor. Without the honor, he might have selected a passive opening lead in that suit. His selection of another opening lead is a slight indication that he may hold the missing queen.

(2) *Practical*. Declarer can often take advantage of the fact that the defenders are human.

```
        DUMMY
        ♡ A 10 8 4

        DECLARER
        ♡ K J 9 3
```

By leading the jack, South may induce West to cover with the queen (or think revealingly about covering). The cover would be necessary if South started with a doubleton jack (or with a tripleton jack, but in that case he would be unlikely to lead the jack). West has no temptation to cover if South has bid the suit, or if the 9 is visible in dummy as well as the 10. If West plays low without thought, South plans to put up dummy's ace and finesse on the way back. Note that this would be risky technically if dummy did not hold the 8. East would be able to make a trick from an original holding of Q–8–7–x.

(3) *Superstitious*. The QUEEN-OVER-JACK rule is such a slight indication that it virtually ranks with the Belgian rule that the younger player always has the queen. If it has any value, the king-over-queen and ace-over-king must be very slightly superior rules, because more significant cards are involved.

Such rules normally have no applicability at tournament play, where the cards played to a trick are not gathered together. In England, however, it is habitual to sort the hand into suits at the end of each duplicate deal. If two adjacent honor cards were in the same hand on the previous deal and were not separated in the shuffle, the tendency will be for the jack to lie over the queen and the queen to lie over the king.

(4) *Psychological*. P. HAL SIMS claimed that the first defender to speak, light a cigarette, order a drink or react in similar fashion could be expected to hold the queen. This would be an attempt to show nonchalant disinterest, but in fact betray nervousness.

Other two-way finesses.

```
        (a)                        (b)
    DUMMY                      DUMMY
    ♠ Q 10 5                   ♠ J 9 5

    DECLARER                   DECLARER
    ♠ K 9 7                    ♠ Q 8 4
```

(a) is a two-way finesse for the jack. (b) is a two-way finesse for the 10.

For other specific situations, see SUIT COMBINATIONS.

TWO–WAY GAME TRIES. (devised by ROBERT EWEN). A method that combines both long-suit and short-suit game tries after a major-suit raise. If the auction starts 1♡, 2♡, opener bids 2 NT, 3♣ or 3♢ to make a short-suit game try in spades, clubs or diamonds respectively. A 2♠ rebid by opener forces responder to bid 2 NT, after which opener bids 3♣, 3♢ or 3♡ to make a long-suit try in clubs, diamonds or spades respectively. If the auction begins 1♠, 2♠, a new suit by opener on the three-level is a short-suit try in the agreed suit. A 2 NT rebid by opener forces responder to bid 3♣, after which opener bids 3♢, 3♡ or 3♠ to make a long-suit try in diamonds, hearts or clubs respectively. Reraises of the major (1♡, 2♡, 3♡) are general-strength game tries. This method may be expanded to include raises of overcalls, or as a slam try after a forcing double raise.

TWO–WAY NOTRUMP. The use of two different point-count ranges for a 1 NT opening bid. WOODSON TWO–WAY NOTRUMP is one form, as is the use of a WEAK NOTRUMP not vulnerable with a standard notrump vulnerable, and also the THREE-QUARTER NOTRUMP.

TWO–WAY STAYMAN. Any of a variety of conventions that use a 2♣ response to a 1 NT opening as STAYMAN and use a 2♢ response to 1 NT as a supplement to Stayman. The following describe the principal use of the 2♢ responses.

(1) *Double-barreled Stayman.* 2♣ is used for hands which cannot guarantee game, and 2♢ for hands which wish to force to game. After 2♣, the opener's rebids are normal, and the responder's rebids are all nonforcing. As responder's second-round jump to 3♣, for example, would not be forcing, a two-level rebid can be regarded as weak. (See Stayman convention.) The meaning of 2♣ followed by a jump to the four-level is a matter of partnership agreement.

Over 2♢, the opener normally shows a major suit or rebids 2 NT; but he can rebid at the three-level in a suit or in notrump if he wishes, showing a five-card suit, or a maximum 4-3-3-3 hand without a major. When there is a possibility of a minor-suit slam, a fit can be explored at the level of three because a forcing situation exists.

(2) *Stayman 2♢.* A forcing to game response showing an unbalanced minor-suit hand: no four-card major suit, and a singleton or a void is a necessary requirement. The opener rebids in a suit to show concentrated strength (e.g., A, K, J — not necessarily a four-card suit) and 2 NT to show scattered strength. If the concentrated strength proves to be opposite responder's shortage, he will know that 3 NT is playable and that there is duplication of values for a suit contract. The subsequent bidding is also aimed at determining whether there is a serious notrump weakness.

(3) *Roth 2♢.* A response that is forcing to game

and invitation to slam. This convention allows slam exploration without getting past the game level.

Like Doubled-barreled Stayman, the 2♢ response asks opener about his four-card majors; unlike Double-barreled Stayman, the 2♣ response can be followed by rebids that are game-forcing as in simple STAYMAN. Opener's rebids show whether he has one or both four-card majors, of if he has none, whether he has a minimum or maximum notrump.

(4) *Murray 2♢* asks the opener to bid his longer major suit, bidding a three-card suit if necessary. With equal length (4-4 or 3-3) in the majors the opener bids 2♡. One advantage of the convention is that it permits responder to bid weak unbalanced hands with 5-5 or 4-4 in the major suits. The responder does not promise any strength whatever, although he can have a strong hand. A rebid of 2 NT by the responder asks the opener to bid four-card suits up the line.

The opener's rebid must be in a major suit unless he has two major-suit doubletons, in which case he bids a six-card minor suit or 2 NT.

(5) *August 2♢*, developed concurrently with Murray 2♢ and patterned on similar principles, is also a takeout for the majors with the added proviso that any suit rebid by responder is a sign-off. This permits responder to use the convention with a weak 4-5 major-minor two-suiter. If the opener rebids the wrong major, responder retreats to his minor. With a weak minor two-suiter, responder first bids 2♣ (Stayman), then rebids 3♣.

(6) *Truscott 2♢*, devised by ALAN TRUSCOTT of New York and used widely in Israel. After the 2♢ response, opener defines his distribution and responder uses relay bids, as follows: With 4-3-3-3 hands opener rebids 2 NT and shows his suit after a 3♣ relay. with 4-4-3-2 hands, opener bids 3♢ with both minors; with a major and a minor, he bids the suits in that order; with both majors he bids 2♡ and then 2 NT. In all cases after opener's two suits have been identified, the next relay by responder asks for a two-step clarification of opener's distribution; the first step shows that the doubleton ranks below the tripleton. With five hearts, spades, or clubs, opener bids the suit, and after a relay he rebids 3♡, 3♠, or 3 NT to show the lowest, middle, or highest ranking doubleton, respectively. If opener has a five-card diamond suit, he shows it and simultaneously identifies his doubleton by bidding 3♡, 3♠, or 3 NT directly over 2♢. Responder can use a meaningless bid below the 3 NT level to ask whether opener is minimum or maximum.

TWO–WAY TWO–BIDS. A method devised by IRA RUBIN to open the bidding with a two-level bid with a strong, intermediate or weak hand. An opening bid of two in any suit *usually* is weak, showing a weak two-bid type hand in the suit just above the bid suit (2♣ = 2♢, 2♢ = 2♡, 2♡ = 2♠, 2♠ = 3♣). Both partner and the opponents assume at the start that the opening bid is weak, and partner is expected to make responses in line with a weak two-bid opener — opener's suit with a non-game hand, 2 NT asking for a feature, etc. However, opener may have a *strong* hand, in which case his opening bid is either his suit in a one-suiter or one of his suits in a two-suiter. Here are typical rebids after opener bids 2♡ and responder, with a weakish hand, bids 2♠, the suit opener holds if his hand is weak:

OPENER	RESPONDER
2♡	2♠

3♡ — an excellent one-suiter, not enough for game, with values in the side suits; not forcing. A typical hand:

    ♠ K Q x   ♡ A Q J 10 x x   ◇ K Q J   ♣ x

3♣/3◇ — a second suit; a one-round force. A typical hand:

    ♠ x   ♡ A K J 10 x   ◇ K 10   ♣ A Q J 9 x

The hand could be even stronger. One advantage over opening a Standard 2♣ is that you start to get your suits in early, thus making it more difficult for the opponents to preempt you out of your right spot.

4♣/4◇ — highly distributional and fairly powerful hand. A typical holding:

    ♠ x   ♡ A K J 10 x x   ◇ A K Q x x   ♣ x

4♡ — A hand good enough to make game, but not strong enough to open a Standard 2♣, e.g.:

    ♠ A Q   ♡ A K J 9 x x x x   ◇ Q J x   ◇ —

U

USBA. Abbreviation for UNITED STATES BRIDGE ASSOCIATION, one of the predecessor organizations from which AMERICAN CONTRACT BRIDGE LEAGUE emerged.

USBA GRAND NATIONALS. See UNITED STATES BRIDGE ASSOCIATION.

OPEN TEAM

YEAR	WINNERS	RUNNERS-UP
1934	Howard Schenken,	Walter Malowan,
	Michael Gottlieb,	Lee Landon,
	David Burnstine,	Lester Bachner,
	Richard L. Frey	Sydney Rusinow
1935	Howard Schenken,	Walter Beinecke,
	Michael Gottlieb,	Jean (John) Mattheys,
	Oswald Jacoby,	Hugh Jackson,
	Sherman Stearns,	Charles Van Vleck
	Richard L. Frey	
1936	Josephine Culbertson,	Edward Hymes,
	Waldemar von Zedtwitz,	B. Jay Becker,
	Sam Fry,	Merwyn (Jimmy) Maier,
	Mitchell Barnes	Charles Lochridge
1937	David Burnstine,	Edward Burns,
	Merwyn (Jimmy) Maier,	Stanley Sanders,
	Howard Schenken,	Morris Schoenfield
	B. Jay Becker	Len Reiter

MIXED TEAM

YEAR	WINNERS	RUNNERS-UP
1935	John Sherman,	M. Kalman,
	Ruth Sherman,	Richard L. Frey,
	Richard Kahn,	Gussie Planco,
	Mrs. Fred Greenbaum	J. Arnold Farrer
1936	Mrs. George Harris,	Doris Fuller,
	Jean (John) Mattheys,	Mitchell Barnes,
	Mrs. Josiah Thaw,	Barbara Collyer,
	Raymond Balfe	Waldemar von Zedtwitz
1937	Henry Chanin,	Mrs. S. A. Herzog,
	Mary Clement,	Doris Fuller,
	Charles Lochridge,	Robert Appleyard
	Mrs. N. Demarest	Jack Shore

OPEN PAIR

YEAR	WINNERS	RUNNERS-UP
1934	Howard Schenken,	A. Mitchell Barnes,
	Michael Gottlieb	Edward Hymes, Jr.
1935	Merwyn (Jimmy) Maier,	Morrie Elis,
	Sherman Stearns	Fred Kaplan

1936	Oswald Jacoby,	Sherman Stearns,
	David Burnstine	Merwyn (Jimmy) Maier
1937	Oswald Jacoby,	Waldemar von Zedtwitz,
	Lester Bachner	Merwyn (Jimmy) Maier

MIXED PAIR

YEAR	WINNERS	RUNNERS-UP
1936	Waldemar von Zedtwitz,	M. Lovejoy,
	Barbara Collyer	Winfield Liggett
1937	Henry Chanin,	Millie Tansill,
	Mary Clement	Raymond Balfe

ULTIMATE CLUB. The first totally integrated relay system to be substantially successful in tournament play. It is based on ideas propounded by DAVE CLIFF of Basking Ridge NJ, and was developed and refined by MATT GRANOVETTER, RON RUBIN and MIKE BECKER.

The advantage of this system, and of other relay methods, is that it greatly increases the number of meaningful auctions. The relay is a meaningless bid (usually but not invariably a minimum action) that asks partner to describe his hand further.

After a strong 1♣ opening, the responder describes his hand in three stages: the number of aces, kings and queens; and the exact distribution; and the location of the high cards.

In response to 1◇, 1♡ or 1♠, 2♣ by the responder is a relay, an artificial game force requiring a description by the opener. 2◇ in response to one of a major is an artificial invitation.

In response to 1 NT, 2♣ is a relay requiring an exact description. See RELAY SYSTEMS.

UNAUTHORIZED INFORMATION. Information which is given to a partner by means other than a legal call or play. Such information may be conveyed by questions, tone of voice, special emphasis, mannerisms, grimaces, remarks, squirms, or huddles. If such information is received, a player should be governed by Law 16 of either rubber or duplicate bridge. See ALERTING; EXPLANATION OF ANY CALL OR PLAY.

At times in duplicate games a player may inadvertently overhear a remark by a contestant about a particular board which he has not as yet played. Such a fact should be reported to the director who will act in a manner as fair as possible to the player so reporting. See LAWS (Law 16).

UNBALANCED DISTRIBUTION. Referring to either the distribution of the suits in a hand or the distribution of one suit among the four hands, unbalanced is opposed to BALANCED DISTRIBUTION. Among the requirements for unbalanced distribution is the combination of one or more long suits and one or more singletons or voids. A 5–4–2–2 distribution is on the borderline between balanced and unbalanced distribution.

UNBALANCED PATTERN. Hands which are eminently unsuited for notrump play or defensive properties. See MATHEMATICAL TABLES for frequency of occurrence. When a pattern is decidedly unbalanced, FREAK hands and results are to be suspected.

UNBALANCED SWISS RAISE. Part of the ACES SCIENTIFIC SYSTEM, used in combination with VALUE

SWISS RAISES to provide a full range of game-forcing raises in response to a major suit opening. A jump response of three of the other major is used to show 10–12 points with a singleton somewhere in the hand; a jump to 3 NT shows 13–15 points with a singleton.

Opener makes the cheapest bid to locate responder's singleton. Responder answers by bidding one of the next three steps; two of the steps will be natural suits and will show the singleton in the suit bid; the other step will be either 3 NT or four of the trump suit, and will show a singleton in the remaining suit. See also CONGLOMERATE MAJOR RAISES, SUPER SWISS.

UNBEATABLE. See COLD.

UNBID MINOR SUIT FORCE. After opener has made a rebid of 1 NT, it is sometimes useful for responder to have available a low-level forcing bid, either to inquire about opener's support for responder's suit, or to provide flexibility for responder's description of his own hand. Some pairs thus use a 2♦ REBID BY RESPONDER AS ONLY FORCE AFTER 1 NT REBID; some use a 2♣ rebid as STAYMAN ON SECOND ROUND. Both of these conventions can be amended slightly to allow responder to use the unbid minor suit as his forcing call; when the opening bid has been 1♣, this modification has the advantage of permitting responder to sign off in his partner's suit.

UNBID MINOR AS DELAYED STAYMAN. After the opener rebids 1 NT in an uncontested auction, responder bids the unbid minor as a checkback on opener's major suit holdings.

UNBID SUIT. Suit or suits which have not been bid by declarer or his partner during the auction. Frequently, without any attractive opening lead, a player will select a lead on the basis that a suit has been unbid. (This applies frequently to a major suit against a notrump contract.)

At some point in the auction, it may be desirable to make a bid in a previously unbid suit as a WAITING BID. See FOURTH SUIT FORCING AND ARTIFICIAL.

UNBLOCKING. Throwing a high card in play in order to gain some advantage for the hand opposite.

A 10 6 2

J 9 8 3   K 7 5

Q 4

Dummy has no side entry. West leads the 3 won by East's king. South unblocks with his queen, permitting a later finesse of the 10 so that South makes two tricks. Similarly:

A 9 5 3

J 10 8 7   K 6 2

Q 4

Dummy has no side entry. West leads the jack, won by East's king. South unblocks the queen, and makes two tricks by a later finesse of the 9.

Q 10 5 3

K 8 7 2   6 4

A J 9

If South needs an entry to dummy later in spades, he must be careful to win the opening lead with the ace.

A blind spot for many players is the internal block:

A K Q 4 3   A 7 6 4 2

or

10 8 7 6   K Q 9 8

If one defender holds J–x–x, five tricks cannot be run without a side entry to dummy. The perverse arrangement of the spot cards makes it impossible for South to win the fourth round of the suit with a low card in dummy. Declarer can sometimes maneuver to discard one of his spot cards on an opponent's suit.

UNBLOCKING SQUEEZE. A simple positional squeeze characterized by the fact that, although the last three tricks are *on top,* lack of entries prevents declarer from cashing them.

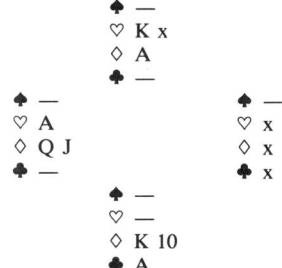

The ♣A squeezes West. If he throws the ♡A dummy's ♡K is established. If he throws a diamond dummy's ◇A is unblocked, allowing South to cash the ◇K and 10.

The following deal, composed by G. A. Dickinson, is an attractive example which may be treated as a double dummy problem:

♠ A K Q
♡ K 10 9 6 3 2
◇ A K
♣ 6 4

♠ 9 7 6 3   ♠ 10 8
♡ Q J   ♡ A 8 7 5 4
◇ 10 7 6 5 4 3 2   ◇ J
♣ —   ♣ 10 8 5 3 2

♠ J 5 4 2
♡ —
◇ Q 9 8
♣ A K Q J 9 7

South plays in 7♣. West leading the ♡Q to the king, ace, and a low ruff by South. There are, in a way, 13 tricks on top, but there are entry problems.

Solution: South leads a diamond to dummy's ace, and cashes the ♠K–Q. A club is then led and finessed and the clubs are run. On the last trump West must discard the ♡J—which it is assumed that he won't do—or reduce his holding to either one spade or one diamond. North's hand is unblocked by the discard of the ace of the suit bared by West, leaving South two tricks to cash in it. The second of these puts pressure on West again, the squeeze in hearts and the remaining suit being repeated. This may be termed a Repeating Jettison Squeeze. See also ENTRY SQUEEZE.

UNCONSTRUCTIVE. A bid which is distinctly discouraging, but does not bar partner from making a further move.

UNDER. To the right of. Thus, South is under West, etc. A king or any other card may be said to be under another card if the positional factor applies as above.

UNDER THE GUN. A term borrowed from poker in which game the phrase refers to the hand betting immediately after the dealer. In bridge there are various meanings, both in bidding and play. The term can be used in bidding situations to cover the position where a hand or player can be said to be "under the gun" if he is bidding directly after a preemptive bidder and before a hand which has not yet been heard from. The term also can describe a position where a player has to meet a bid-or-double situation at the slam level. In play, it is used to describe the hand between dummy and declarer that has a high card or high cards that are finessble and are in a vulnerable position thereby.

UNDERBID. A bid lower than the value of the hand warrants. Although such bids are usually made because of inferior judgment, they may sometimes be made consciously and deliberately. One justification would be a tactical situation in which the opponents seem likely to save if the full value of the hand is bid. If the final contract is reached with, apparently, less assurance, the opponents may be deterred from saving. An underbid may also be made as an upside-down type of SHOOTING.

UNDERBIDDER. A player who regularly bids slightly less than the value of his hand warrants. He is rarer, and easier to play with, than the overbidder. His psychological motivation is usually a reluctance to be set in any contract. His tendencies manifest themselves in the later rounds of bidding, so that he will never push toward a borderline game. His partners therefore tend to overbid slightly in certain situations. After a two-over-one response, responder may choose to jump to 3 NT at his second turn, holding 12 points, a hand on which he would normally be content to bid an invitational 2 NT.

UNDERLEAD. The lead of a low card in a suit in which the master card or cards is held. This is routine in notrump contracts, but is unusual in trump contracts.

```
              K 7 2
    A 10 8 3            Q 9 6 5
              J 4
```

If West gains the lead early in the play, and leads a low card, South should guess right. West would be unlikely to lead from the queen, and give South the chance of a trick he could not otherwise make. As the cards lie, one trick is all the defenders can make if they play passively.

But if West can find the lead of a low club originally, South is almost sure to go wrong and play low from dummy. Underleads of aces as the opening lead are distinctly daring, but may sometimes be

risked if the bidding suggests strongly that dummy will have the king of the suit.

Another motive for an underlead is an urgent desire to get a particular lead from partner, perhaps for a ruff. The following celebrated example occurred in the 1958 Bermuda Bowl.

```
              ♠ A K 8 4
              ♡ A 7 6 3 2
              ◇ 5
              ♣ A J 8
    ♠ 10 6 5 3 2          ♠ Q J 9
    ♡ 9                    ♡ 10 5
    ◇ A J 10 8 7 4 3       ◇ K Q 2
    ♣ —                    ♣ K Q 6 5 4
              ♠ 7
              ♡ K Q J 8 4
              ◇ 9 6
              ♣ 10 9 7 3 2
```

Neither side was vulnerable. The bidding:

WEST	NORTH	EAST	SOUTH
		1 NT	2 ♡
2 ♠	3 ♣	Pass	3 NT
5 ◇	5 ♡	Pass	Pass
Dbl	Pass	Pass	Pass

PIETRO FORQUET, West for Italy, judged that his partner's most likely entry was the ◇ K. He therefore led the ◇ 3, a suit preference signal. East duly won and returned the ♣ K. West ruffed, and East had to make a club trick to defeat the contract.

In the other room the ◇ A was led against 5 ♡. The contract could not then be defeated. South was able to strip the hand and endplay East. See OVERLEAD.

UNDERRUFF. To play a low trump when a trick has already been ruffed with a higher trump. It can be the right play whether the previous ruff was by an opponent or by partner. The undertrump, though unusual, is necessary in many situations.

(1) To avoid a trump surplus (simple trump coup). It is often a disadvantage to hold too many trumps. When reduced to only trump cards you may be forced to ruff a trick belonging to your partner, and then lead away from or into a tenace position.

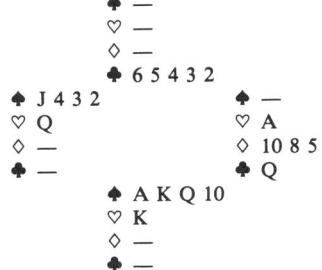

```
              ♠ —
              ♡ —
              ◇ —
              ♣ 6 5 4 3 2
    ♠ J 4 3 2          ♠ —
    ♡ Q                ♡ A
    ◇ —                ◇ 10 8 5
    ♣ —                ♣ Q
              ♠ A K Q 10
              ♡ K
              ◇ —
              ♣ —
```

South is declarer at a spade contract, and needs four tricks to make it. The lead is in North's hand. A club is led which East covers. South, knowing the trump position, realizes his only chance is to ruff high.

West must undertrump to avoid a trump endplay. If West discards, South will lead his losing heart. West must ruff and lead into a spade tenace.

When West undertrumps, declarer is helpless. If he leads a heart, East will win and play a diamond through South's trump holding. (If South ruffs this high, West must undertrump perforce!)

In the following deal an underruff was necessary at the third trick, because East could not spare any cards in the side suits.

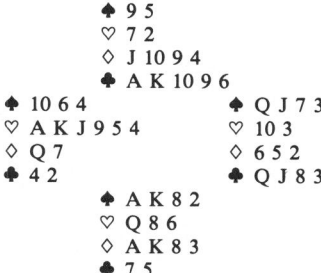

```
              ♠ 9 5
              ♡ 7 2
              ◇ J 10 9 4
              ♣ A K 10 9 6
♠ 10 6 4                    ♠ Q J 7 3
♡ A K J 9 5 4              ♡ 10 3
◇ Q 7                      ◇ 6 5 2
♣ 4 2                      ♣ Q J 8 3
              ♠ A K 8 2
              ♡ Q 8 6
              ◇ A K 8 3
              ♣ 7 5
```

South played in 5 ◇, and West led two high hearts. East played high-low, perhaps wrongly, and when the ◇ J could not be overruffed at the third trick West was marked with the ◇ Q. East had a discard problem which he solved by underruffing with the ◇ 2; any black suit discard would have made the play easy for South.

The contract failed, although South could have succeeded by very accurate play. Two high spades, a spade ruff and four rounds of trumps would have squeezed East in the black suits.

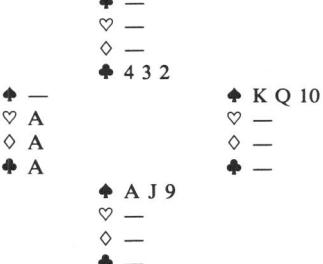

```
              ♠ —
              ♡ —
              ◇ —
              ♣ 4 3 2

♠ —                        ♠ K Q 10
♡ A                        ♡ —
◇ A                        ◇ —
♣ A                        ♣ —
              ♠ A J 9
              ♡ —
              ◇ —
              ♣ —
```

Again North is on lead with South the declarer at a spade contract. South needs two more tricks for the contract. When a club is led from dummy, East must ruff high to prevent South from scoring the ♠ J.

South can now undertrump with the ♠ 9, leaving East to lead into an established tenace. If South overruffs, he must concede two spade tricks to East.

(3) To be able to lead a plain suit card at a later time (ROBERT COUP). In certain positions, it is profitable to be able to lead a plain suit card rather than a trump.

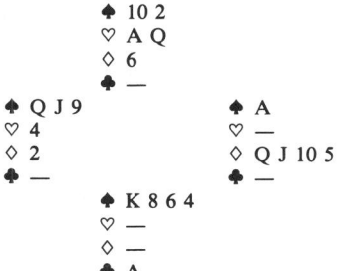

```
              ♠ 10 2
              ♡ A Q
              ◇ 6
              ♣ —

♠ Q J 9                    ♠ A
♡ 4                        ♡ —
◇ 2                        ◇ Q J 10 5
♣ —                        ♣ —
              ♠ K 8 6 4
              ♡ —
              ◇ —
              ♣ A
```

West leads against South's spade contract. South

needs three tricks to produce the contract.

West leads the ♡ 4 which East ruffs with the ♠ A. This appears to give West two natural trump tricks, but South underruffs! East returns a diamond and South ruffs again. South now leads the ♠ A. West must ruff with a high honor to prevent dummy's ♠ 10 from winning this trick. Dummy discards and West must now lead away from his remaining spade honor.

If South does not preserve the ♠ A to lead toward dummy, he will be defeated. When a low trump is led from the South hand, West wins with the jack *and dummy must follow suit.* West can now lead the ♠ Q, smothering North's 10, and setting up the ♠ 9 for the setting trick.

(4) To avoid a premature squeeze (anti-positional squeeze). It is sometimes possible to avoid making a premature discard by undertrumping.

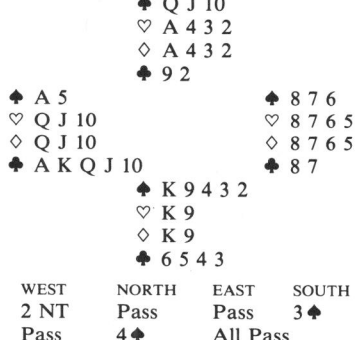

```
              ♠ Q J 10
              ♡ A 4 3 2
              ◇ A 4 3 2
              ♣ 9 2
♠ A 5                      ♠ 8 7 6
♡ Q J 10                  ♡ 8 7 6 5
◇ Q J 10                  ◇ 8 7 6 5
♣ A K Q J 10              ♣ 8 7
              ♠ K 9 4 3 2
              ♡ K 9
              ◇ K 9
              ♣ 6 5 4 3
```

WEST	NORTH	EAST	SOUTH
2 NT	Pass	Pass	3 ♠
Pass	4 ♠	All Pass	

East had a poor hand but he played the star role. West led the ♣ K and promptly shifted to ace and another trump. Dummy won and another club was won by West. West now shifted to the ♡ Q which declarer won with the king.

When declarer ruffed a club in dummy, East had to undertrump to defeat the contract. If he discarded from a red suit, South would have been able to establish a trick in that suit in dummy by ruffing, and the contract would have been made. After East underruffed, declarer was helpless.

Jeff Rubens

UNDERTRICK. Each trick by which declarer's side fails to fulfill its contract. For the penalties for each undertrick, see LAWS (Law 84), LAWS OF DUPLICATE (Law 73).

UNDERTRUMP. See UNDERRUFF.

UNDOUBLE. See DOUBLE FOR SACRIFICE.

UNFACED HAND. During the play, the hands of the declarer and both defenders. After the opening lead, the declarer's partner's hand is faced up on the table so that all players may see the cards (dummy's hand). Prior to the play, none of the hands is faced. A player in claiming or conceding tricks faces his hand in properly presenting his claim. See CLAIM OR CONCESSION; DEFENDING HAND; DUMMY.

UNFINISHED RUBBER. A rubber ended by agreement before either side has won two games. A side which has won one game is credited with a bonus of 300 points; a side which has a partial, if only one side, is credited with a bonus of 50 points.

UNINTENTIONAL. A violation of rules, ethics, or proprieties is assumed in bridge circles to be unintentional, not deliberate. It is the purpose of the LAWS to provide indemnities for the nonoffending side to permit an accurate or fairly accurate result on the board or a hand. Any intentional violation is in contravention of the philosophy of the game, as a contest involving ladies and gentlemen. An assumption that a violation is intentional by an opponent is as much a violation of ethics as would be such an intentional violation itself.

UNIT-WIDE GAME. A game of Unit Championship rating held simultaneously at three or more locations in the Unit. Each Unit is entitled to hold one Unit-wide Championship a year for each full 200 members, up to a maximum of seven such championships. If more than one such game is held in a year, each game must be scheduled for a different day of the week. All masterpoint awards for unit-wide games are issued by the ACBL.

UNITED STATES BRIDGE ASSOCIATION. One of the predecessor organizations which merged to form the AMERICAN CONTRACT BRIDGE LEAGUE. The purpose of this association was to organize a national tournament in which participation would be based on skill alone, and which would be a thorough enough test so that its winners could be clearly recognized as national champions.

The Grand National Plan which this organization evolved was a pyramiding series of qualifying tournaments starting with open local tournaments, city, state, and regional tournaments, and culminating in the GRAND NATIONAL (1).

In addition to the organization of tournaments truly national in scope, the United States Bridge Association was a charter member of the International Contract Bridge Union which was organized in 1934 under the joint sponsorship of the United States Bridge Association, the National Bridge Association of Great Britain, and the French Contract Bridge Association. Both the USBA and the ICBU owed much to ELY CULBERTSON, the first president of the international organization, and a member of the executive committee of the former (MILTON C. WORK, the Grand Old Man of Bridge, was president).

The American Bridge League (organized 1927) and the International Bridge League (headquarters at The Hague, Holland) existed concurrently, and some short-lived rivalry between the two organizations was eliminated in 1937 when the American Contract Bridge League resulted from the amalgamation of the two United States organizations.

Results of national tournaments prior to the merger are included under USBA GRAND NATIONALS.

UNITED STATES INTERNATIONAL REPRE-SENTATIVES. The names of players who have

represented the U. S. or North America in international team events may be found under ANGLO-AMERICAN MATCHES, FRANCO-AMERICAN MATCHES, INTERNATIONAL OPEN TEAM SELECTION, WORLD TEAM OLYMPIAD, INTERNATIONAL WOMEN'S TEAM SELECTION, VENICE TROPHY, ROSENBLUM CUP and WORLD CHAMPIONSHIPS.

UNITED STATES PLAYING CARD TROPHY. Donated by the United States Playing Card Company for the two-session Commercial & Industrial Team Championship held at the Summer North American Championships, under which past results are listed. This event is open only to teams of four, five, or six players, all of whom are full-time or pensioned employees of the same commercial or industrial organization or government bureau. Replaced the ASSOCIATION OF AMERICAN PLAYING CARD MANUFACTURERS TROPHY in 1965.

UNITS OF THE ACBL. Totaling 319 in 1982, units of the ACBL have been formed at different times and under different conditions, and they differ widely among themselves in background, scope, and membership. Some limit their activity to a given town or city, others comprise two or more states.

The jurisdiction of a unit consists of a geographical area, bounded in its application and charter, and each unit has jurisdiction over its own members, while participating in the management of the League.

A new unit may be formed in any area where no unit exists, provided there are 100 or more members in the area to be organized. In the process of formation, a provisional charter may be granted with more than 50 members if a reasonable prospect of reaching the 100-member status exists.

The unit is expected to perform certain functions:

(1) Establish and maintain a membership of at least 100.

(2) Promote and stimulate interest in duplicate bridge among members and prospective members by providing an attractive program of bridge events.

(3) Expand and increase membership by interesting new players.

(4) Conduct or supervise tournaments events at which masterpoints and rating points are awarded under League regulations.

(5) Establish and maintain contact with neighboring units, supporting each other's activities.

(6) Conduct annual election by popular vote for officers and/or Directors.

(7) Elect, in collaboration with other units in the district, a member of the National Board of Directors, a first and a second Alternate Director, and three representatives to the National Board of Governors.

(8) Adopt bylaws consistent with those of the ACBL, which must be filed with the League.

(9) Assume fiscal responsibility for funds collected on behalf of the League, and membership dues from its members, submitting semi-annual financial reports to its officers; maintain accurate records.

UNLAWFUL. An action not in accordance with the

mechanics of the game, as described in Parts I to III of LAWS.

UNLIMITED BID. A bid with wide limits in valuation. The bid with the widest limit of all is a STAYMAN response to a weak notrump, which could range from a worthless hand to a hand worth a forcing opening bid. Other unlimited bids are discussed under ONE OVER ONE, OPENING SUIT BID, and TAKEOUT DOUBLE.

UNMAKABLE. A contract which cannot succeed if the defense does not cooperate with the declarer, i.e., does not do as well as can be done. Frequently an unmakable contract succeeds, however, because the defense is comparatively in the dark about the declarer's holding. Unmakable is the opposite of COLD (Unbeatable), and, like this term, is relative.

UNMIXED PAIRS. An event in which all pairs must consist of either two women or two men.

UNSEEDED KNOCKOUT TEAMS. A method first tried in 1982 for improving the attendance at knockout team events. Random draws determine the pairings for all rounds leading up to the final. It is theoretically possible, but not too likely, that the two best teams in the field would meet each other in the first round.

UNUSUAL JUMP. See ASKING BIDS; FRAGMENT BID; GRAND SLAM FORCE; LEBOVIC ASKING BID; ROMEX TRUMP ASKING BIDS; SPLINTER BID; SUPER GERBER; SUPER SWISS; VOID SHOWING BIDS.

UNUSUAL NOTRUMP. A method of showing two-suited hands in competitive situations. The convention, which normally indicates length in the minor suits, was devised by ALVIN ROTH in 1948 and developed by him with TOBIAS STONE.

An overcall of 2 NT after a major-suit opening is often used to show minor suits (see 2 NT OVERCALL).

In many situations the unusual notrump is a balancing move:

(a)

WEST	NORTH	EAST	SOUTH
			1 ♠
Pass	1 NT	Pass	2 ♣
Pass	Pass	2 NT	

(b)

WEST	NORTH	EAST	SOUTH
			1 ♠
Pass	2 ♣	Pass	Pass
2 NT			

In both cases the unusual notrump bidder wishes to contest the partscore, and invites his partner to pick a minor. Case (b) is slightly safer than (a), because the known fit for North-South in spades increases the chance that East-West have a fit.

The unusual notrump may be used when the auction is still very much alive: (See auction at top of right column.)

In (c) both North and South are limited and are unlikely to go beyond the level of two. West can rely on some strength from East, who should not enter-

(c)

WEST	NORTH	EAST	SOUTH
			1 ♠
Pass	1 NT	Pass	2 ♣ or 2 ♡
2 NT			

(d)

WEST	NORTH	EAST	SOUTH
			1 ♡
Pass	1 ♠	Pass	2 ♠
2 NT			

tain any hopes of game. In (d), North is not limited, but the North-South fit gives West some assurance of an East-West fit. If the vulnerability is favorable for East-West, 5 ♣ or 5 ◇ may prove a cheap save if North-South go to 4 ♠.

An original pass may serve to identify the unusual notrump, as when the dealer overcalls 1 NT after a fourth-hand major-suit opening bid. Many players apply the convention whenever the opponents have bid two suits:

(e)

WEST	NORTH	EAST	SOUTH
			1 ♣
Pass	1 ♡	1 NT	

(f)

WEST	NORTH	EAST	SOUTH
			1 ♠
Pass	2 ◇	2 NT	

It would seldom be right for East to make a notrump bid in a natural sense, because he would be laying himself open to a heavy penalty opposite a probably worthless dummy. With a strong defense hand he would prefer to stay out of the auction, and expect to defeat any game contract.

So in this case East's bid shows great length (at least 5–5) in the unbid suits. This is an extension of the convention (optional by partnership agreement) to situations not limited to minor suits.

The unusual notrump can be used when your side has already bid, and even when your side has opened the bidding:

(g)

WEST	NORTH	EAST	SOUTH
			Pass
3 ♡	Dbl	Pass	4 NT

(h)

WEST	NORTH	EAST	SOUTH
			1 ♣
4 ♠	4 NT		

In (g) South shows a good minor two-suiter, probably not far short of an opening bid. North may be able to jump to 6 ♣ or 6 ◇. In this case the unusual notrump is an attacking weapon.

When the bidding has been seriously crowded by an opponent's preemptive action, 4 NT is usually a takeout bid rather than BLACKWOOD. In (h) SIDNEY SILODOR suggested the 4 NT bid on this hand:

♠ —
♡ K Q 6 5 3
◇ A J 9 8 3
♣ 9 7 2

The bid indicates a desire to play at the five-level, with a free choice left to partner.

The unusual notrump can operate when the user has already bid a minor suit:

(i)

WEST	NORTH	EAST	SOUTH
			1 ♠
2 ♣	2 ♠	Pass	Pass
2 NT			

(j)

WEST	NORTH	EAST	SOUTH
			1 ♠
1 ♡	Pass	4 ♡	4 NT

In (i), West wishes to contest the partscore, and is likely to have five or six clubs and four diamonds. If his second suit was hearts he would double. In (j), South is likely to have five diamonds and six clubs: 4 NT is his only way to indicate this distribution.

The unusual notrump is usually made by the side which did not open the bidding. In (h) and (j) above, its use by the opener's side is shown, and here are two further examples:

(k)

WEST	NORTH	EAST	SOUTH
			1 ♢
1 ♠	Pass	4 ♠	4 NT

(l)

WEST	NORTH	EAST	SOUTH
			1 ♡
1 ♠	Pass	2 ♠	Pass
Pass	2 NT		

In (k), South's second suit must be hearts: with a minor two-suiter he would bid 5 ♣ to offer an easy choice at the level of five. In (l) North cannot wish to play 2 NT when he could not bid over 1 ♠; clearly he has a weak minor two-suiter.

UNUSUAL NOTRUMP AND MINORS. See LEA SYSTEM.

UNUSUAL 1 NT OVERCALL. An overcall of 1 NT as a two-suited takeout rather than as the standard 16–18 point balanced hand. See also 2 NT OVERCALL (2).

UNUSUAL POSITIVE. A set of artificial jump responses to a PRECISION CLUB opening to show 4-4-4-1 distribution.

UNUSUAL OVER UNUSUAL. See DEFENSE TO TWO-SUITED INTERFERENCE.

UP THE LINE. The practice of making the cheapest bid when responding or rebidding with two or three four-card suits, laid down as a principle by the BARON SYSTEM. The idea is employed in many bidding styles, with some reservations.

♠ K 8 4 3
♡ K 8 4 3
♢ A J
♣ K 10 5

A 1 ♡ response to an opening bid in either minor suit gives the opener the opportunity to rebid in spades. If he fails to do so, responder can assume that there is no spade fit, and bid 3 NT.

This idea has validity but there are many cir-

cumstances in which expert players would depart from the principle.

(1) If there is a great disparity in the strength of the suits:

♠ A Q J 3
♡ 8 4 3 2
♢ A J
♣ Q 10 5

The chief arguments in favor of bidding 1 ♠ in response to a minor-suit opening are that a heart response might lead to a notrump contract with an unguarded heart suit, and that a high heart contract might result in a weak trump holding. The opposing view is that 1 ♡ may inhibit a heart lead in notrump, and that a 1 ♠ response may exclude a 4–4 fit in hearts.

(2) With two strong major suits:

♠ K Q J 3
♡ A Q 5 2
♢ 8 3
♣ 9 4 2

Some authorities recommend a response of 1 ♠ to an opening bid in a minor, with the intention of bidding hearts on the next round.

The choice of response is closely connected with the treatment of BIDDABLE SUITS. If the opener is not expected to rebid 1 ♠ with a bad four-card suit, the spade response is necessary to avoid missing a possible fit.

A disadvantage is that 1 ♠ followed by a heart bid tends to suggest a five-card spade suit. The "up the line" response of 1 ♡, used by players who do not impose standards for biddable suits, leads to a problem if the opener rebids his suit. In that case an eccentric reverse bid of 2 ♠ may be tried.

(3) With one major suit and one minor suit:

(a)	(b)
♠ Q J 7 3	♠ 8 2
♡ 8 2	♡ Q J 7 3
♢ Q J 7 3	♢ Q J 7 3
♣ J 7 2	♣ J 7 2

In each of these cases there is a good argument for rejecting the 1 ♢ response to 1 ♠ in favor of the major suit. The danger of 1 ♢ is that opposing intervention may shut out the major suit, which is a serious possibility in case (b). In case (a), 1 ♠ may work well by shutting out an opposing heart contract.

But if the responding hand is stronger, there is less likelihood of intervention, and therefore less reason to prefer the major-suit response.

If the response is at the two-level, the minor-suit response is preferable. The chance of interference is slight, and a response of 2 ♡ to 1 ♠ is generally expected to show a five-card or longer suit.

UP TO. (1) Toward the hand that will play last to a particular trick, as in UP TO WEAKNESS. (2) Toward a vulnerable third-hand holding such as K-x-x or K-Q-x, as opposed to leading away from such a holding.

UP TO WEAKNESS. The old whist maxim recommending a lead "up to weakness" is valid but not very helpful. It is quite true that a lead by declarer's right-hand opponent up to a completely worthless holding in dummy will never give away a trick, although it may help the declarer if he is short of entries to dummy. But it is seldom that dummy is so obliging.

The following discussion will consider defender's problems in this situation on the assumption that the suit in question is distributed evenly around the table. If one player is known to be short or is likely to be short, the prospects are of course altered.

Crucial situations are classified in increasing order of dummy strength.

(1) Dummy has 9-x-x. Almost invariably a safe lead, but the defender should be careful to lead the 10 from holdings headed by K-10 or Q-10.

(2) Dummy has 10-x-x. The defender must lead the jack from holdings headed by A-J or K-J. If leading from a single honor, the higher the honor the safer the lead. A-x-x is completely safe, while J-x-x is the most dangerous.

(3) Dummy has J-x-x. Again, the higher the honor the safer the lead. A-x-x is relatively safe, while Q-x-x is very dangerous.

(4) Dummy has Q-x-x. A lead from the jack is virtually safe. A lead from the ace or king is very dangerous.

(5) Dummy has K-x-x. The lead from the ace is very dangerous. The lead from the jack or queen is almost completely safe.

(6) Dummy has A-x-x. All leads are relatively safe, with J-x-x slightly the safest and Q-x-x the least safe.

The general principle applying in all the above cases is also applicable when leading through dummy. The defender should avoid breaking a suit in which an honor is poised over the honor ranking immediately below it. In other words, one should avoid leading from a jack up to a 10, a queen up to a jack, a king up to a queen, or an ace up to a king. Similarly, one should avoid leading from a jack through a queen, a queen through a king, or a king through an ace.

This applies also if dummy has two honors. It is obviously unwise to lead from a king up to A-Q, or a queen up to A-J or K-J. See also THROUGH STRENGTH.

UPPER SUITS CUEBID.
An immediate overcall in the opponent's suit to show the two highest ranking unbid suits. See also MICHAELS CUEBID.

UPPERCUT.
A ruff, usually by a defender, aimed at promoting a trump trick for partner.

```
              ♠ 4 3 2
   ♠ J 5                ♠ Q 6
              ♠ A K 10 9 8 7
```

In a spade contract, West leads a suit of which East and South are void. East ruffs with his ♠Q, ensuring a trump trick for the defense. If South overruffs, the jack wins a trick.

A defender with a completely useless trump holding should usually ruff with his highest trump if he gets the opportunity. A ruff with a card as low as the six can possibly effect an uppercut and promote a trump trick for the defense.

UPSIDE-DOWN SIGNALS. The use of a low card in defense to encourage a continuation of a suit, or a shift to a suit, and a high card to discourage. The method is credited to KARL SCHNEIDER of Vienna Austria, but seems to have been first published by E. K. O'Brien in a *Bridge World* article in 1937.

The chief theoretical advantage of this procedure is that a player may not be able to spare a high card from a strong holding:

```
              ♠ 10 7 6 3
   ♠ J 5                ♠ K Q 9 2
              ♠ A 8 4
```

West leads the J♠ against 3 NT, because his own suit has been bid by declarer. East has to drop the deuce, because he cannot spare the 9. Using normal methods, it is now difficult for West to continue the suit when he gains the lead. But he continues happily using upside-down signals. Notice that if East had had a weak holding, such as Q-8-4-2, he could have spared the 8 as a discouraging card.

Other advantages claimed for this method are that it is harder for declarer to false-card effectively, and that a one-card discard signal during the defense may be clearer than with normal methods.

URUGUAY BRIDGE ASSOCIATION (ASOCIACIÓN URUGUAYA DE BRIDGE). Formed in 1948, the Association is a member of the South American Confederation and participates in South American Championships, hosting the event in 1950, 1953, 1958, 1964, 1971, and 1977. Uruguay won the Women's Team Championship in 1966, 1967, 1971 and 1974.

Officers, 1982:

President: Jacobo Pineyrua S.

Secretary: Alberto Giambruno, Sarandi 584, Montevideo, Republica, Oriental del Uruguay

USEFUL SPACE PRINCIPLE. When allocating bidding space under partnership agreements, assign it where it is most useful without reference to natural or traditional meanings of calls. This may involve deciding which tasks are most important to accomplish and arranging adequate space to perform those tasks efficiently. Techniques for allocating space include "lumping" (giving over all extra space to one function), "spreading" (giving increments of space to each of several functions, usually by removing most or all space from one task deemed less important), and making compromises (not making use of all available space in order to achieve some or all of a transcending objective). According to JEFF RUBENS in a series of articles in *The Bridge World*, several popular conventions and many standard methods are based on a misguided idea of simplicity. "They are not well designed because they ignore the Useful Space Principle," he wrote. Rubens studied the BLACKWOOD convention, among others, to illustrate the principle. He pointed out that bidding the suit immediately *above* the agreed trump at the four level allows more room for control asking and trump length asking, while 4 NT works perfectly well as the cuebid in the suit that initiates a Blackwood sequence. For example, if the auction has begun 1♡–3♡, then 4♠ would be Blackwood and 4 NT would be a spade cuebid. If the agreed suit is clubs, then 4 ◇ would be Blackwood and 4 NT would be a diamond cuebid. However, if the agreed suit is spades, then 4 NT is Blackwood. Specialized responses allow much more specific exploration of slam possibilities. Rubens also offered new structures for new-suit responses to overcalls and new methods for using the GRAND SLAM FORCE, while pointing out that many other applications also are possible.

USES OF CARDS. Although playing cards are made for the playing of games, individual cards have been used for other purposes. Since the backs were (until about 120 years ago) blank and unmarked, paper was scarce and expensive, and playing cards used the very finest quality paper obtainable, cards were practical to use for purposes where standardization was an asset.

Both handwritten and printed visiting cards were made on card backs, as were tickets and identifying passes. Workmen dismantling the Bastille carried such passes to distinguish them from the crowds of curious visitors who interfered with their work.

In France and in Canada, cards were used in emergencies as money. Several libraries used them for their original index cards. At one time it was fashionable to write social invitations on them. Advertisements were printed and written on them.

Old cards and sheets of cards were used to stiffen the covers of books, and some of our knowledge of early cards comes from discoveries of these fragments. And, of course, they are the building blocks for constructing a house of cards.

UTILITY. A British expression which summarizes the straightforward bidding methods used there in many rubber bridge clubs: strong notrump (16–18); 2♣ as the forcing opening; intermediate two bids; and 3 NT for takeout over opposing three-bids.

UTILITY NOTRUMP RESPONSE. See CHURCHILL STYLE.

V

VALET. One of the court cards in decks of cards used centuries ago, decks that were ancestors of present-day cards. The term survives in French, meaning the equivalent of English jack or knave.

VALIDATION. In duplicate bridge, the certifying by the director of the correctness of an auction or play; the approval of the opponents to a correction of the scoring of the results of a board of duplicate play; the initialing of a pair score in team play by the opponents of this pair on a set of boards.

VALUATION. Valuation of a hand is covered under particular types of valuation in the following articles: ACE VALUES; BISSELL SYSTEM; BODY; DISTRIBUTIONAL COUNTS; DUPLICATION OF DISTRIBU-

TION; DUPLICATION OF VALUES; GOOD CARDS; HONOR TRICK; LOSING TRICK COUNT; PLUS VALUE; POINT COUNT; POSITIONAL FACTOR; PROMOTION OF TRUMP HONORS; REVALUATION; and ROBERTSON POINTCOUNT.

VALUE OF GAME. The calculation of the favorable percentage necessary to justify bidding for game in different situations is complicated by the uncertain value of a PART-SCORE. The arbitrary figure of 50 assigned by the LAWS for the purposes of duplicate bridge and unfinished rubbers is not realistic at rubber bridge. Assigning the more plausible figure of 150 when both sides are vulnerable, and 100 in other situations, the following table can be constructed. It is assumed that the choice lies between 3♠ and 4♠.

First game
    Profit from a successful game bid   200 (300 less 100)
    Loss from failing in game   240 (100 plus 90 plus 50)
    Odds required for bidding game:
    6 to 5 on, or 55%

Second game
    Profit from a successful game bid   300 (400 less 100)
    Loss from failing in game   290 (100 plus 90 plus 100)
    Odds required for bidding game:
    30 to 29 against, or 49%

Game against vulnerable opponents
    Same as for first game

Deciding Game
    Profit from bidding game
    successfully   350 (500 less 150)
    Loss from failing in game   340 (150 plus 90 plus 100)
    Odds required for bidding game:
    35 to 34 against, of 49%

These figures may be regarded as slightly optimistic, in that no weight has been given to the situation where opponents may double, increasing the loss by 50 or 100 points; or to those situations where neither three nor four can be made, but four will be doubled and defeated 300 or 500 to 500 or 800 points. Assuming correct bidding, it also must be assumed that the doubled contract will be set far more often than it will be made.

At any form of duplicate, the calculation is simpler. At matchpoints, any game should be bid with a 50% chance, other things being equal. At IMPs, games should be bid more freely: with a 37% chance when vulnerable, or a 45% chance not vulnerable.

At CHICAGO, assuming a constant value of 100 points for a partscore, a nonvulnerable game should be bid with a 55% chance or better, and a vulnerable game with a 43% chance or better.

Dorothy Hayden Truscott

VALUE OF PARTSCORE. In duplicate, a bonus of 50 points is awarded for successful less-than-game contracts. In CHICAGO, a partscore remaining at the end of four deals is not rewarded; except on the last deal, a partscore earned is worth 100 points. These values are not realistic in rubber bridge. See PARTSCORE BIDDING.

VALUE SWISS RAISES. An expansion of the SWISS CONVENTION used in the ACES SCIENTIFIC SYSTEM to show a range of forcing balanced raises in response to an opening bid of 1♡ or 1♠. The ranges shown are as follows:

VANDERBILT CLUB SYSTEM. HAROLD S. VAN-DERBILT, who invented the game of Contract Bridge in 1925, was the first to advocate use of a 1♣ opening bid as an artificial bid to show a strong hand, and of a 1◇ artificial negative response to show a weak hand. He wrote three books, now long since out of print, on his Club Convention prior to 1934; and his Club Convention was very popular until his books were no longer available.

After a lapse of about thirty years, interest in 1♣ systems revived. The BLUE TEAM CLUB, which helped to win many WORLD CHAMPIONSHIPS for Italy, uses an opening 1♣ convention very like the Vanderbilt Club, and the SCHENKEN SYSTEM, used in two World Championships, is an even closer relation.

In 1964, Vanderbilt wrote a modernized version of his system entitled *The Club Convention Modernized*, which may be summarized as follows:

(1) Opening Bids with Mediocre Suit Types of Hands

Opening bids of 1◇, 1♡, 1♠, and 2♣ have the same minimum high-card point requirement as opening bids of one in a suit in other systems, but the high-card point range is limited to about 6 points, or to one-half that of other systems, because with a good suit type of hand you open 1♣. Consequently, you give partner at the outset a better picture of your high card strength than when you open with one of a suit using other systems. This is the greatest of the many advantages of club systems.

To open 2♣, you should have not less than a five-card club suit including 5 points in high cards. When no other bid is available, open 1◇ on a three-card 5 high-card point suit.

(2) Opening Bids with Good Suit Types of Hands

Open 1♣ (a one-round force) whenever you hold a hand containing about 16 or more high-card points and five or more offensive tricks; except that, for expert use only, a 2◇ (instead of 1♣) forcing to game, specific ace on the first round, and, if desired, king on the second round and queen on the third round asking bid is recommended when holding, say:

♠ A K J 8 7 4 3
♡ A Q 6
◇ —
♣ A K 5

in which case if responder holds:

♠ Q 9
♡ K 7 4
◇ 8 7 6 3
♣ Q 9 6 4

The partnership auction would go: 2◇ (specific aces?), 2♡ (no ace), 2♠ (specific kings?) 3♡ (K♡), 3♠ (specific queens?), 5♣ (two queens of same color, but they must be black since opener holds the Q♡), 7♠, pass.

(3) Response to Any 1♣ Bid

(a) Respond 1◇ (the negative response and a one-round force) unless you hold at least: two aces; or three kings; or one ace, one king, and one queen; or two kings and two queens; or a six-card suit headed by the A–K; in any of which cases, force to game by responding with a natural bid other than 1◇.

(b) A 2♡, 2♠, 3♣, or 3◇ response shows a solid five-card or longer suit.

(c) A 3♡, 3♠, 4♣, or 4◇ response shows a six-card or longer suit requiring only the ace, king, or queen to make it solid, plus sufficient outside high-card strength to qualify for a positive response.

(d) A 1 NT response shows a good hand with at least one high honor (ace, king, or queen) in every suit, and slam possibilities opposite a good 1♣ opening.

(4) Opening Bids with Notrump Types of Hands

Open:

(a) 1 NT with 16, 17, or 18 high-card points (the usual standard requirement).

(b) 1♣ with 19 or 20 high-card points, followed by 1 NT over a 1◇ response.

(c) 1♣ with 23 or 24 high-card points followed by 2 NT over a 1◇ response.

(d) 2 NT with 21 or 22 high-card points.

(e) 1♣ with nine probable tricks and a stopper in every suit followed by 3 NT over a 1◇ response.

(f) 3 NT with about eight or nine probable tricks, most of them in minor suits. This bid is partly preemptive, and is best made third hand after two passes. For example, open 3 NT, third hand holding:

♠ 7 5
♡ K 8
◇ A K Q 10
♣ A K Q J 10

(5) Effect of an Overcall or a Double of a 1♣ Bid

(a) A double of an overcall or a redouble of a double is the equivalent of a positive response. So is a one jump bid in notrump which is also the equivalent of responding 2 NT to 1♣, after an intervening pass.

(b) A minimum notrump response is encouraging but not forcing, and shows a stopper in the suit of the overcall.

(c) A minimum suit response is encouraging but not forcing.

(d) A jump suit response is forcing for one round only. For example, holding:

♠ K Q 10 9 7 5
♡ 8 5
◇ Q 10 5
♣ 9 7

respond 2♠ after your partner's 1♣ opening has been overcalled with 1♡.

(6) Other Opening Bids

(a) 2♡, 2♠, and (except for expert use) 2◇ are defensive shut-out bids as in other systems that employ 2♣ as the only forcing to game opening bid.

(b) 3♣ and 3◇ show solid seven- (exceptionally six-) card suits and invite 3 NT.

(c) 3♡ and 3♠ show seven playing tricks but the suit need not be solid.

(7) Other Conventions

(a) STAYMAN: If the partnership bidding goes 1♣, 1◇, 1 NT, 2♡ or 2♠; or 1 NT, 2♡ or 2♠, opener must pass because of responder's failure to bid 2♣ (Stayman) over 1 NT before showing his major.

(b) The cheapest available of GERBER or BLACK-WOOD. Since a 1♣ opening does not rank as a bona fide club bid, it does not prevent the subsequent use of a Gerber 4♣ jump bid to ask for aces.

Harold S. Vanderbilt

VANDERBILT CUP. (1) For the National Knockout Team Championship, donated by HAROLD S. VANDERBILT in 1928. The organizing body 1928–57 was the Vanderbilt Cup Committee. It was contested annually in New York until 1958 when it became part of the Spring North American Championships, under which heading past results are listed. The Vanderbilt often is used to help select United States and North American international teams. It ranks with the Spingold as the most highly prized trophy in the ACBL calendar. The winners of the Vanderbilt are entitled to complete against the winners of the GRAND NATIONAL CHAMPIONSHIPS (2), REISINGER MEMORIAL TROPHY and SPINGOLD TROPHY, for the right to represent North America or the United States in the next year's Bermuda Bowl. See INTERNATIONAL OPEN TEAM SELECTION. (2) For the World Olympiad Team Championship, presented by Harold S. Vanderbilt on the occasion of the first World Team Olympiad held in Turin, Italy, in 1960. See WORLD CHAMPIONSHIPS for winners. The two events are among the few for which the winners receive individual replicas of the trophy, a practice initiated by the donor from the first running of the events, and perpetuated by a $100,000 trust fund administered by the ACBL under the terms of Vanderbilt's will.

VANIVA PROBLEM. One of the most famous of all DOUBLE-DUMMY PROBLEMS; composed by SIDNEY LENZ in 1928 in a contest promoted by Vaniva Shaving Cream.

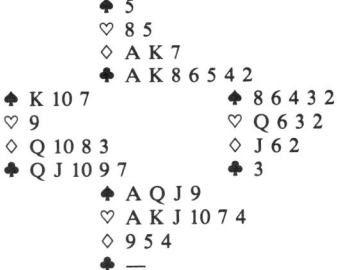

South to make 7♡ after the lead of the ♣Q. Solution: North wins the first trick, South discarding a diamond, North leads the other top club.

If East trumps, South overruffs, North ruffs out West's best spade, and one trump finesse captures East's queen.

If East sheds a spade, South ruffs, North ruffs out West's best spade, and South wins the trump finesse and his remaining spades. North wins a top diamond and coups East's trumps.

If East sheds a diamond, South sheds a spade and finesses trumps. North wins a top diamond and South finesses and runs all his trumps to triple squeeze West.

VENEZUELAN BRIDGE FEDERATION (FEDERACIÓN VENEZOLANA DE BRIDGE. Founded in 1955, by 1982 the federation had more than 1,500 members. The Federation participates in the South American Championships, hosting the 1963, 1970 and 1978 events and winning the Open Teams in 1963, 1965, and 1966, and represented the South

American Confederation in the 1966 and 1967 World Championships. National events held annually are Open Teams and Open Pairs.

Officers, 1982:
President: German Otero
Secretary: Celina Espejo, ⁰/₀ Altamira Tennis Club, 3A, Av. de Altamira, Caracas, Venezuela

VENEZUELAN TRANSFERS. A systemized method of responding and rebidding to strong notrump openings, developed principally by ROBERTO BENAIM, and first used by the Venezuelan Team in the 1966 Bermuda Bowl. The method is now obsolete.

VENICE TROPHY. Since 1978 an official world championship for women's teams representing continental zones of the WBF. The trophy was first awarded in 1974 to the winner of a challenge match between the European Bridge League's women's champions and a women's team representing the ACBL. In a 140-board match played in Venice concurrently with the 1974 BERMUDA BOWL, the United States team defeated by a score of 297–262 the world champion Italian women's team which had theretofore been unbeaten in five years of women's competition.

UNITED STATES	ITALY
Bette Cohn	Marisa Bianchi
Emma Jean Hawes	Luciana Canessa
Betty Ann Kennedy	Rina Jabes
Marietta Passell	Maria Antonietta Robaudo
Carol Sanders	Anna Valenti
Dorothy Truscott	Maria Venturini
Ruth McConnell (npc)	Giovanni Pelucchi (npc)

The trophy, donated by the City of Venice, was again played for in 1976 opposite the Bermuda Bowl. In Monte Carlo the United States team defeated the British, Women's European Champions of 1975, in a match of 140 deals with the final score USA 395, Great Britain 211.

UNITED STATES	GREAT BRITAIN
Emma Jean Hawes	Charlie Esterson
Betty Ann Kennedy	Nicola Gardener
Jacqui Mitchell	Fritzi Gordon
Gail Moss	Sandra Landy
Carol Sanders	Rixi Markus
Dorothy Truscott	Rita Oldroyd
Ruth McConnell (npc)	Graham Cooke (npc)

In 1978 the Venice Trophy was an official event on the WBF calendar. It was held concurrently with the Rosenblum Open Teams championship during the New Orleans World Pair Championships. Women's teams representing five WBF Zones contested the Venice Trophy. Europe was represented by Italy; North America by the United States; South America by Argentina; the Far East by the Philippines and the South Pacific by Australia. Qualifying scores in the five-session round-robin were U.S. 71, Italy 65, Argentina 49, Australia 40, Philippines 35. In the two-session final the U.S. defeated Italy 229½ to 140.

UNITED STATES	ITALY	ARGENTINA
Mary Jane Farell	Marisa Bianchi	Maria de Diaz
Emma Jean Hawes	Luciana Capodanno	Maria Elena Icapraro
Marilyn Johnson	Marisa D'Andrea	Adriana C. de
Jacqui Mitchell	Enrica Gut	Martinez de Hoz
Gail Moss	Andreina Morina	Marta Matienzo
Dorothy Truscott	Anna Valenti	Clara Monsegur
Ruth McConnell (npc)	Guido Barbone (npc)	Mercedes de Schenone
		Adolfo Campos (npc)

AUSTRALIA	PHILIPPINES
Ivy Dahler	Amy Austria
Elizabeth Havas	Winnie Monsod
Fay Landy	Letty de Padua (capt.)
Claire Lester	Helen Small
Barbara McDonald	Helen Tubangui
Cecile Miles	Forence Yap
Ian McCance (npc)	

In 1981 the Venice Trophy was played opposite the Bermuda Bowl in Port Chester NY by women's teams representing five WBF Zones. Europe was represented by Great Britain; North America by the United States; South America by Brazil; Central America–Caribbean by Venezuela; and South Pacific by Australia. Qualifying round-robin scores were U.S. 181½, Great Britain 173, Brazil 170, Australia 144½, Venezuela 100. In the final Great Britain defeated the United States 160⅔ to 122.

GREAT BRITAIN	UNITED STATES	BRAZIL
Pat Davies	Nancy Gruver	Agota Mandelot
Maureen Dennison	Edith Kemp	Sylvia Figueira de
Nicola Gardener	Betty Ann Kennedy	Mello
Sandra Landy	Judi Radin	Maria Elizabeth
Sally Sowter	Carol Sanders	Murtinho
Diana Williams	Kathie Wei	Susy Powidzer
Derek Rimington	C.C. Wei (npc)	Alicia Saade
(npc)		Maria Lena Brito E
		Silva
		Lia Cintra (npc)

AUSTRALIA	VENEZUELA
Felicity Beale	Rosanna Bonanni
Sue Edwards	Fida Hirschaut
Barbara Gill	Morella Pietri
Pauline Gumby	Esther Sasson
Sue Hobley	Ivy Smith
Di Smart	Elisabeth Solar
Cecile Miles (npc)	Agnesa Stern (npc)

The WBF scheduled future Venice Trophy contests for odd-numbered years opposite the Bermuda Bowl. After skipping 1983 the new plan was to take effect beginning in 1985.

VERIFY (a score). In pair play, it is the duty of the North player to fill out the pick-up slip or traveling score and of the traveling pair or one of its members to verify (by initialing in a box provided on pick-up slips) the score as correct; in match play at teams-of-four, both pairs keep a record of their scores at each table, and each pair must verify the score slip of its opponents, from which the results of the match can be determined.

When recapitulation sheets are used for posting the results of play, a scorer noting an unusual score (such as 5 ♡ Dbld for 650 points on a nonvulnerable board, or a set of four tricks undoubled with both sides vulnerable) will indicate with a small check mark that the score has been verified as correct before he has posted it.

VICE SQUEEZE. A secondary squeeze that leads to a suit establishment play. (Analyzed and named by TERENCE REESE; the American spelling would be *vise*.)
(See hand at top of next column.)

South leads the ♣A, and West is squeezed in two suits. If he discards the ♡K, then South's queen will take a trick; if he discards a spade, South can establish a trick in that suit.

The position looks like an automatic squeeze against West which has been modified in a particular way: instead of a two-card menace we have a vice

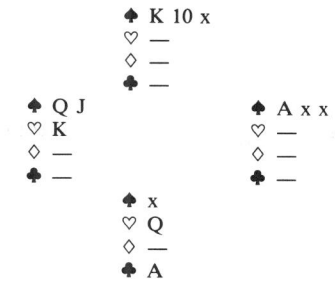

menace consisting of the second best card of the suit accompanied by a card which can be established if West weakens his second-round stopper.

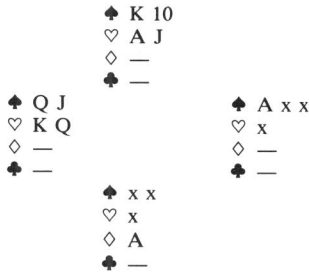

South leads the ♦A, which forces West to unguard hearts or to discard his second-round trick in spades.

This position is a modification of the simple positional squeeze. The vice menace does not provide an entry, so that North's threat must be accompanied by a master card in the suit, which makes it a two-card threat.

In addition to the requirements stated above, East must have no trick to cash besides his stopper in the doubly guarded suit.

South loses a trick after the squeeze, so that he needs all but two of the remaining tricks in the diagram positions.

Monroe Ingberman

VICTORY POINTS. In a contest among a great number of teams with a limited number of sessions, each team plays a relatively small number of deals against each of the other teams, ranging from 32 in the round-robin of the WORLD CHAMPIONSHIPS to as few as two deals in some smaller events. Various methods have been devised to counteract the excessive rewards to a 10- or 20-point swing in BOARD-A-MATCH SCORING, and to the slam contract made at one table and defeated at the other in IMP or TOTAL POINT SCORING.

The scoring method favored by many experts awards the IMP score on each board. The total IMP score on the boards of the match are then converted to victory points in accordance with a predetermined scale. This is the method most used in European Championships and in the round-robin portions of the Bermuda Bowl and World Team Olympiad.

The following scale has been used in recent World Championship team events when 32-board matches are played:

IMP DIFFERENCE	VICTORY POINTS
0 — 3	10 — 10
4 — 10	11 — 9
11 — 16	12 — 8
17 — 22	13 — 7
23 — 28	14 — 6
29 — 34	15 — 5
35 — 40	16 — 4
41 — 46	17 — 3
47 — 52	18 — 2
53 — 58	19 — 1
59 — 64	20 — 0
65 — 73	20 — (− 1)
74 — 82	20 — (− 2)
83 — 91	20 — (− 3)
92 — 100	20 — (− 4)
101 and more	20 — (− 5)

A unique scoring method known as the ZIRINSKY FORMULA is used in Far East Championships. The formula (the maximum VPs available are 8):

$$VP = 4 \ \frac{A + M}{B + M} \ (8 \text{ maximum})$$

A is the IMP score of the winning team, B the IMPs of the losing team. M is the number of flat boards in the match (a new refinement).

The theory is that quotient is more important than margin. Winning 40–20 should be worth more than winning 100–80.

VPs are used frequently in Swiss Team competitions and in round-robins with short matches. Here are the VP scales most often used in such competitions:

IMP DIFFERENCE

Victory Points	6-7-8 Board Match	9-10-11 Bd. Match	12-13-14 Bd. Match
10-10	0	0	0
11-9	1	1	1-2
12-8	2-3	2-3	3-5
13-7	4-5	4-5	6-8
14-6	6-7	6-8	9-12
15-5	8-9	9-11	13-16
16-4	10-12	12-15	17-21
17-3	13-15	16-19	22-26
18-2	16-18	20-24	27-32
19-1	19-21	25-29	33-38
20-0	22-25	30-35	39-45
20 − (− 1)	26-29	36-41	46-53
20 − (− 2)	30-34	42-48	54-63
20 − (− 3)	36 or more	49 or more	64 or more

Even in win-loss type Swiss events, a form of victory points often is used in the ACBL. To receive credit for a full win, a team must win by 3 or more IMPs. A win by 1 or 2 IMPs constitutes a 3/4 win, with the losing team getting the other 1/4 point. However, the team winning the match receives the entire match masterpoint award.

VIENNA COUP. An unblocking play made in preparation for a squeeze. Declarer plays off a master card which establishes a high card for an opponent. This clears the way for an automatic squeeze. Here is an example:
(See hand at top of right column.)

The menaces are correctly positioned for an automatic squeeze against East. Hearts should be a one-card menace, and spades the two-card menace. Therefore the ♡A should be played before the squeeze card, which is the ◇A.

If the ◇A is played prematurely, as in the diagram position, then East can discard a heart with impunity, for declarer can establish the ♡Q by crossing to the ace, but he cannot return to his hand

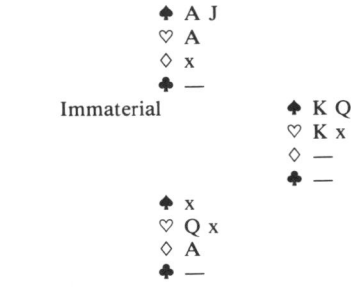

to cash the queen.

Monroe Ingberman

VIENNA SYSTEM. Based on an artificial 1♣ bid for hands of normal strength, and an aritficial 1 NT bid for strong hands. Devised in 1935 by DR. PAUL STERN, this was the first highly conventional system to achieve international success. (See WORLD CHAMPIONSHIPS.) Also known as the Austrian System, it has been played in many countries. In postwar years its main adherents have been in Iceland and Australia.

The Bamberger point count (7-5-3-1) was originally used, but many Vienna players have preferred the standard 4-3-2-1 point-count which is employed in the following system summary. (References are to high-card points.)

(1) *1♣* shows 11–17 points and no suit except clubs longer than four cards. 1◇ is the negative, or HERBERT, response showing 0–7 points. With a six-card or longer suit, an alternative negative response is available: a negative jump to two of a major or three of a minor suit. Over 2◇ the opener rebid at the one level, keeping the bidding as low as possible. (This treatment very closely resembles the ROMAN SYSTEM.)

Responses of one in a major or two in a minor are positive but limited, showing 8–11 points. The opener can pass or make a natural rebid: any jump rebid would be encouraging but not forcing.

The strongest response to 1♣ is 1 NT, showing 12 points or more. This almost always leads to game, but the responder can pass if the opener rebids 2 NT at any stage.

(2) *1◇, 1♡, or 1♠* shows a five-card suit with 11–17 points. Responses are standard except that 2 NT is limit and nonforcing.

(3) *1NT* shows 18 points at least, and is unlimited; any distribution is possible. With 0–7 points, the responder gives a negative response of 2♣ or a negative jump to 3◇, 3♡, or 3♠.

With 8 points or more, responder bids a five-card suit; but the jump to 3♣ is made only if the suit is very strong. With a broken five-card club suit, the response is sometimes 2 NT, which denies a five-card diamond suit and also a total of five cards in the major suit. For other hands containing between five and eight cards in the major suits the response is 2◇, which is therefore a two-way bid.

After a negative response of 2♣, a rebid of 2◇ asks for a major suit.

(4) *Two-bids* should be specialized asking bids,

but most adherents of the system prefer standard methods.

(5) *Three-bids in a minor* are strong, with a powerful suit and an outside trick.

(6) *Other opening bids* are standard.

VINJE SIGNALS. Signals devised by Helge Vinje which pinpoint many distributions and situations that are ambiguous in standard signaling.

Distribution Signals: The length of a suit is shown by leading (counting lead) or by following suit or by discarding (counting signal) in this manner:

2-card suit:	high-low	
4-card suit:	next lowest — lowest	} even number
6-card suit:	third lowest — lowest	
3-card suit:	lowest — next lowest	
5-card suit:	lowest — next lowest	} odd number
7-card suit:	lowest — third lowest	

The New Third-Hand Rule: On a counting lead from a long suit against a notrump contract, third hand should play high except in the following case: If dummy and third hand hold only spot cards in the suit, and the sum of leader's, dummy's and third hand's cards totals 11, third hand should play his lowest card.

The New Trump Signal: The new trump signal indicates the distribution type. High-low shows the hand has the distribution pattern of one suit with an even number of cards, three odd. Low-high shows the hand has the distribution pattern of one suit with an odd number of cards, three even.

Positive and Negative Signals: Positive or negative signals to show strength or weakness should be used generally on ace leads in situations where the defenders are obviously compelled to make their quick tricks immediately.

They should be used particularly on ace leads against slam contracts. The lead denies the king and asks primarily for the king in partner's hand. They should also be used on honor leads, in accordance with the rules for signalling on sequence leads against notrump contracts and against trump contracts. A positive signal is given by playing the *lowest card* in the suit. A negative signal is given by playing the *third lowest* card in the suit but the *next lowest* if the third lowest is an *active card*.

Suit Preference Signal: The suit preference signal should be used in situations where the defender in the lead is *obviously* compelled to switch to a suit other than the one played, and needs guidance from his partner. When partner plays an unusually high card he wants the higher ranking of the possible suits in return. When partner plays a low card he wants the lower ranking of the possible suits in return.

Combined Signalling: The use of a positive or a negative or a suit preference signal should be combined with a delayed distributional signal according to the following rules: The first signalling card indicates a positive or a negative or a suit preference signal, according to the respective rules. The second signalling card in the same suit is a delayed distributional signal indicating the *remaining* length in that suit.

New Table for Opening Sequence Leads Against

Notrump Contracts:

Holding in suit	Lead	Reading
A K x (x-)	Ace	Partial sequence without other honors in the suit.
A K J (x-) K Q 10 (x-)	King	Incomplete sequence lacking the queen or the jack
A K Q (x-) Q J 10 (x-) Q J 9 (x-)	Queen	Two or no higher honors than the queen. Holding A–K–Q the second lead indicates the original suit length: king (13) shows an odd number; ace (14) shows an even number.
A Q J (x-) K Q J (x-) J 10 9 (x-) J 10 8 (x-)	Jack	Two or no higher honors than the jack. Holding K–Q–J the second lead or play indicates the original suit length: queen (12) shows an even number; king (13) shows an odd number.
A Q 10 (9-) A J 10 (x-) K J 10 (x-) 10 9 x	10	Two or no higher honors than the 10. With two higher cards the sequence is an intermediate one.
A 10 9 (x-) K 10 9 (x-) Q 10 9 (x-) 9 8 x	9	Two or no higher cards than the 9. With two higher cards the sequence is an intermediate one.

Appropriate signalling: Unblock with an honor second, unless this is likely to result in the loss of a trick. Use a counting signal when dummy holds at least three cards in the suit. Use any complementing card, followed by the next-lowest card, when the lead shows an incomplete sequence and dummy as well as partner holds exactly three cards in the suit. Use a positive or negative signal to show the existence or non-existence of a card touching the actual sequence, followed by a distributional signal on the next round, when dummy holds at most two cards in the suit.

New Table for Opening Sequence Leads Against Trump Contracts

Holding in suit	Lead	Reading
A K (x-)	Ace	When holding an even number (A = 14).
	King	When holding an odd number (K = 13). Exception: Against slam contracts the lead from A K (x) should always be the king, partner using counting signal.
K Q J (x-) K Q (alone)	King	Ambiguous: partner should read the lead as a counting lead from A–K with an odd number, unless dummy or partner has the ace. The second lead or play indicates the original suit length: queen (12) shows an even number; jack (11) shows

			an odd number.
A K Q (x-)	Queen	Ambiguous: partner	
K Q x (x-)		should read the lead as K–	
		Q–x. Holding A–K–Q the	
		second lead or play in-	
		dicates the original suit	
		length: king (13) shows an	
		odd number; ace (14)	
		shows an even number.	
Q J x (x-)	Jack	Unambiguous.	
J 10 x (x-)	10	Generally unambiguous.	
A J 10 (x-)			
K J 10 (x-)			
10 9 x (x-)	9	Generally unambiguous.	
A 10 9 (x-)			
K 10 9 (x-)			
Q 10 9 (x-)			
9 8 x (x-)	8	Generally unambiguous.	
K 9 8 (x-)			
Q 9 8 (x-)			
J 9 8 (x-)			

Note: The lead from A–K–Q–(x) may alternatively be the ace or the king according to the rules for a counting lead from A–K–(x-).

Appropriate signalling:

1. On a counting lead from A–K–(x-) partner should:

   Use a *counting signal* if dummy has at least three cards, including the queen, in the suit. Use a *trick counting signal* on all other occasions by signalling as follows:

   (a) Playing the *lowest card* (low-high) indicates that the defenders can make *either one or three tricks in relation to declarer's closed hand*. The three tricks may arise from a ruff or from the queen or from J–10–x.

   (b) Playing the *third lowest card*, but the next lowest if the third lowest is an *active card*, means that the defenders can make two tricks in the suit, either because declarer has only two cards in the suit, or because partner cannot assist in making a third trick.

2. On a sequence lead showing K–Q–(J), with dummy or partner holding the ace, partner should use a counting signal if dummy holds the ace; use a counting signal or overtake when he himself holds the ace.

3. On a sequence lead showing K–Q–x or A–K–Q partner should use a positive or negative signal to show whether or not he holds the ace or jack; use a counting signal if dummy holds at least three cards, including the jack, or if dummy holds A–J.

Indicating a Sequence When Following Suit or When Discarding: A sequence is indicated by *playing the lowest card* in the sequence when the card *has a possibility of influencing* the trick; a sequence is indicated by *playing the highest card* in the sequence when the card *will not influence* the trick; a sequence is indicated by *discarding the highest card* in the sequence. When holding a complete sequence, the sequence

as well as the suit length may be indicated.

A K Q (x-)	The queen indicates the complete sequence. The next play may now indicate the length of the suit (original length): The king (13) indicates an odd number; the ace (14) indicates an even number.
K Q J (x-)	The jack indicates the complete sequence. The next play may now indicate the suit length (original length): The queen (12) indicates an even number; the king (13) indicates an odd number.

When holding A–K, the sequence as well as the suit length may be indicated:

A K (x-)	The ace followed by the king indicates an even number in the suit; the king followed by the ace indicates an odd number in the suit.

VIOLATION. (1) The disregard of a law of propriety. It is assumed that any violation that occurs is either through carelessness or ignorance. A PENALTY for a violation is enforced in an attempt to INDEMNIFY the nonoffending side, not to punish the offender. (2) A deliberate breach of a system agreement. Judgment may occasionally lead an expert player to pass a FORCING BID or to continue bidding after a SIGN-OFF BID, but such violations should be very rare if partnership confidence is to be maintained.

VIOLATION OF ETHICAL CONDUCT. An act of a player that deviates from the spirit or the form as described in PROPRIETIES; since there are no direct penalties for such violation, it is perhaps even more reprehensible than a deviation for which penalties are prescribed.

VIOLATION OF SYSTEM. A player is at any time entitled to violate his partnership agreement, and most players do so from time to time in minor ways. Major violations, such as passing a forcing bid, are very rare indeed among good players.

VISE SQUEEZE. See VICE SQUEEZE.

VOID. An original holding with no cards in a suit. CHICANE is a much older term, and BLACK a synonym in current use.

VOID-SHOWING BIDS. The use of a jump bid which has no natural meaning to show a void suit. The idea was revived by E. M. L. Beale, of Cambridge University, England, about 1948, following a prototype idea once adopted by ELY CULBERTSON.

According to this idea, the last bid in each of the following sequences would show specifically a void in the suit bid, and, by inference, a good suit fit with partner.

	WEST	NORTH	EAST	SOUTH
(a)				1♡
	Pass	4♣		
(b)				1♣
	Pass	1♡	Pass	3♣ or 4◊
(c)				1◊
	1♠	3♠		

The following are examples of opportunities for using the bid at later stages in the auction:

Dlr: South
Vul: Both

```
                ♠ 10 6 2
                ♡ Q 8 7 5 4
                ♢ 4
                ♣ K 8 3 2
♠ A K J 9 5 3               ♠ 7
♡ J 2                       ♡ A 6 3
♢ A 10 9 6 5                ♢ K J 8 3 2
♣ —                         ♣ 10 6 5 4
                ♠ Q 8 4
                ♡ K 10 9
                ♢ Q 7
                ♣ A Q J 9 7
```

This deal was reported in *The Bridge World*, August 1951, from the Master Team-of-Four final. Both teams reached 5 ♢ played by East after this bidding:

WEST	NORTH	EAST	SOUTH
			1 ♣
2 ♠	Pass	3 ♢	Pass
5 ♢	Pass	Pass	Pass

If East–West had been using void-showing bids, West could have used one over 3 ♢.

WEST	NORTH	EAST	SOUTH
			1 ♣
2 ♠	Pass	3 ♢	Pass
5 ♣	Pass	5 ♡	Pass
7 ♢	Pass	Pass	Pass

When East shows first-round control of hearts by his cuebid, the grand slam becomes a good proposition. If East's diamonds turn out to be headed by queen-jack instead of the king, the opening bid by South suggests that the finesse will win. If East's diamonds had been still weaker, he would not have made the encouraging grand slam try of 5 ♡. As it was he knew that all his high cards were working, and was able to visualize a crossruff.

Void-showing bids will sometimes make it possible to apply the brakes when duplication of values is present:

Dlr: South
Vul: E–W

```
                ♠ K Q 10 7 4
                ♡ 10 6 5 3
                ♢ —
                ♣ K Q J 2
♠ 9 5                       ♠ A 8 3 2
♡ 8 4 2                     ♡ 9
♢ 8 5 4 2                   ♢ 10 9 7 3
♣ A 9 7 3                   ♣ 10 6 5 4
                ♠ J 6
                ♡ A K Q J 7
                ♢ A K Q J 6
                ♣ 8
```

In the 1953 Bermuda Bowl both the American and Swedish teams bid to 6 ♢ missing two aces. This is a not uncommon disaster when one side holds everything else in the pack except two aces. Ace-showing conventions are of limited value when a void is present, although BLACKWOOD has some void-showing possibilities. (See also SUPPRESSING THE BID ACE.)

Using a void-showing bid, the final contract would be 5 ♡.

(a) Using a strong two-bid

SOUTH	NORTH
2 ♡	4 ♢
4 ♡	5 ♡
Pass	

(b) Using a conventional 2 ♣ bid

SOUTH	NORTH
2 ♣	2 ♠
3 ♡	5 ♢
5 ♡	Pass

For alternative treatments, see conventions listed under UNUSUAL JUMP.

VOLUNTARY BID. See FREE BID.

VON ZEDTWITZ GOLD CUP. For the Life Master Pairs Championship, donated by WALDEMAR VON ZEDTWITZ in 1930; one of the most highly regarded pair events in the ACBL calendar. It is contested at the Summer North American Championships, under which heading past results are listed. Until Life Masters became numerous, the trophy was contested by master players who had qualified by winning a previous national championship. It was then a four-session event, and the field was limited to 64 pairs so that a complete movement could be played.

The trophy was originally presented on the basis that three wins by one player would secure him outright possession of the trophy, and this feat was achieved by HOWARD SCHENKEN in 1934. The cup was subsequently put back into competition by the donor.

The cup was stolen in 1954 while in the possession of John Hubbell, who at that time held the Life Master Pairs title. The theft immediately followed a television appearance during which he had exhibited the trophy and given the address of his bridge club at which the cup was normally displayed. The trophy was not recovered and the present cup is an exact replica.

VUGRAPH. (Often spelled viewgraph outside the United States.) A method of presenting an important match to an audience larger than can be accommodated around a bridge table. In the closed room, the board is dealt, bid, and played, with a recorder at the table noting the bidding, opening lead, and result obtained. The board and record are sent to a copier, who writes the hands, bidding, and play with wax pencil on a framed cellulose sheet, a form of hand record. The board is then sent to the open room where a microphone connected to the exhibition hall is used by a director in charge to relay the calls, leads, plays, and results to an operator in the exhibition hall. The frame is sent to the exhibition hall, where an operator, with a wax pencil, records the bids, plays, and results as announced from the open room on the frame which is put into an overhead projector, remaining visible to the audience in greatly enlarged form on a screen. Bidding is recorded in boxes on the printed frame, cards as played are crossed out form the hands, and results tabulated for further reference on the side of the screen.

Required for Vugraph presentation are a recorder in the closed room, a scribe, a director and commentator in the open room, and an operator at the projector who doubles as or is assisted by a commentator. Equipment needed is a dozen or so prepared frames, an overhead or rearview projector, a screen, and wax pencils. Frames are reusable, easily cleaned with carbon tetrachloride. For more elaborate setup, see BRIDGE-O-RAMA.

VULNERABILITY. The condition of being subject to greater undertrick penalties, and eligible to receive greater premiums as provided by the scoring table. In rubber bridge, vulnerability comes about by having won one game toward rubber. In duplicate bridge, vulnerability is arbitrarily assigned by board numbers.

Vulnerability in duplicate is on a 16-board cycle, repeating for each succeeding 16 boards; boards 1, 8, 11 and 14 have no vulnerability; boards 2, 5, 12, and 15 have North-South vulnerable, East-West not vulnerable; boards 3, 6, 9 and 16 have East-West vulnerable, North-South not vulnerable; boards 4, 7, 10 and 13 have both sides vulnerable. This can be remembered fairly easily by the 16 letters forming this arrangement:

> O N E B
> N E B O
> E B O N
> B O N E

where O stands for no vulnerabilty, N for North-South, E for East-West and B for both.

In CHICAGO, a four-hand variation of rubber bridge, the vulnerability also is arbitrarily assigned in similar fashion; no vulnerability on the first hand; declarer vulnerable on the second and third hands; and everyone vulnerable on the last hand. A variation in a few clubs that is technically perhaps a slight improvement assigns the vulnerability on the second and third hands to the opponents of the dealer.

The feature of vulnerability gives rise to many variations in the strategy of bidding and play; these variations probably are foremost among the reasons for the great interest which contract bridge has stimulated.

VULNERABLE. A term applied to a side which has won a game, and is thus exposed to greater undertrick penalties and entitled to greater premiums for slams and doubled overtricks. The term was suggested to HAROLD VANDERBILT by a fellow passenger on the cruise on which Vanderbilt devised the game of contract bridge.

W

WBF. See WORLD BRIDGE FEDERATION.

WBF MASTERPOINTS. Points won in a tourna-

ment conducted by the WORLD BRIDGE FEDERATION or in WBF-approved ZONAL CHAMPIONSHIPS (1). See WORLD BRIDGE FEDERATION PLAYER RANKINGS.

WBF PLACING POINTS. Points, other than WBF MASTERPOINTS, awarded by the WORLD BRIDGE FEDERATION to winners and very high finishers in WBF tournaments and Zonal team championships. A certain number of placing points are needed to achieve the WBF rankings of Grand Master and World Master. See WORLD BRIDGE FEDERATION PLAYER RANKINGS.

WAITING BID. A temporizing bid by a player who aims to extract information from partner rather than give information about his own holding. This is usually made in a minor suit, perhaps in a three-card suit.

A prepared opening bid of 1♣ with a three-card suit is in a sense a waiting bid. For examples of waiting responses, see THREE-CARD SUITS, BIDS IN. The following is an example of a waiting rebid:

> ♠ A J 5
> ♡ A K 6
> ♢ Q 5 2
> ♣ K Q 7 3

After an opening bid of 1♣ and a jump shift response of 2♢, the best rebid is 2 NT. The opener has no intention of stopping short of a small slam, and has thoughts of a grand slam, but his best move is to proceed cautiously, extracting more information from the responder before heading slamwards.

For another type of waiting bid, see the 2 NT response described under IMPOSSIBLE BIDS.

WAIVE A PENALTY. In rubber bridge, either member of a partnership, without consulting the other member, may waive a penalty (condone an irregularity); if either member so elects, the right to enforce a penalty is forfeited. In duplicate, players do not have the right to waive penalties on their own initiative, and the director may allow or cancel any waiver of penalties made by the players without his instructions. However, the right to penalize an irregularity may be forfeited. See LAWS (Law 15), LAWS OF DUPLICATE (Laws 10, 11).

WALLET. British name for a form of DUPLICATE BOARD in which each pocket is formed in the fold of a wallet-shaped receptacle. The board can be folded into one-half size for ease in carrying. Plastic wallet boards are popular in Europe. They were used in the 1932 World Bridge Olympics.

WALPURGIS DIAMOND. A convention used by JOHN COLLINGS and PAUL HACKETT of Great Britain. As an opening bid, 1♢ shows either 0-8 high card points with any distribution, of 12-20 points with at least four diamonds, or any 4-3-3-3 with 20-22 points. It is used in conjunction with their specialized opening pass, which shows 9-12 points and any distribution.

WALSH SYSTEM. A style of bidding popular in the West, sometimes known as Western Roth-Stone or West Coast Scientific; its chief architect was RICHARD WALSH. The principal features are strong 1 NT openings with nonforcing STAYMAN and JACOBY TRANSFER BIDS, five-card major suit openings with a forcing 1 NT response, and usually some form of SWISS major suit raises. Direct limit raises promise a side-suit singleton; jump shift responses are preemptive. Minor suit raises are INVERTED (see INVERTED MINOR SUIT RAISES), and a 1 ◊ response to 1 ♣ usually denies a four-card major suit.

Two-over-one responses are game forcing. Over a 2 ♣ response to 1 ◊, opener has specialized responses: 2 ♡ or 2 ♠ shows a four-card suit and no extra values; 2 NT shows 4–4–3–2 distribution and no extra values, and 2 ◊ usually shows five or more diamonds, but may be forced with 3–3–4–3 distribution and poor clubs.

Other methods include MATHE ASKING BIDS, COMPETITIVE DOUBLES, rebid of new minor suit by responder forcing after opener's 1 NT rebid, opening 4 ♣ and 4 ◊ bids to transfer to 4 ♡ and 4 ♠, respectively, negative and responsive doubles.

WANG TRUMP ASKING BIDS. Bids at relatively low levels to ask about trump honors. The responses are given in three steps as follows:

First step	= none of the top three honors.
Second step	= one of the top three honors.
Third step	= two of the top three honors

WAR ORPHANS SCHOLARSHIPS, INC. An educational foundation incorporated 1943 in New York State by officers and governors of ACBL; in the eight years of its existence it awarded about $800,000 in scholarship benefits to sons and daughters of members of the U.S. armed services who in World War II suffered service-connected to battle-connected deaths. Tournament winners 1943–46 accepted printed certificates instead of prizes, the cost of trophies going to the scholarship fund, and special tournaments plus individual contributions and income from general solicitations made up the remainder of the fund. The board of WOS was composed of official representatives of the armed services of the U.S. and officers of the ACBL. They were: Gen. Peter C. Harris, former Adjutant General, Chairman American Legion scholarship committee, Chairman; Gen. Frank T. Hines, Veterans Security Administrator, President; WILLIAM E. MCKENNEY, Executive Secretary ACBL, Vice-President; ALBERT H. MOREHEAD, President ACBL, Secretary and Treasurer; Watson B. Miller, Federal Security Administrator, former Executive Secretary American Legion; Gen. James A. Ulio, Adjutant General U.S.A.; Adm. Randall Jacobs, Chief of Naval Personnel; Adm. Raymond Chalker, Commandant U.S. Coast Guard; Gen. G. Peck, Commandant U.S. Marine Corps.

WARNING PARTNER. A privilege of all players (including a dummy who has not intentionally looked at another hand) if the player feels that his partner is about to commit an irregularity. Examples: "It's not your lead, partner." "No hearts, partner?" "The lead is the dummy, partner." It is not permitted during the auction to warn partner about a convention you or an opponent may be us-

ing, or to review the auction to apprise partner of a previous bid you think he may have misunderstood. See ALERTING.

WARREN. See SAN FRANCISCO.

WASHING-LIST. See BACK SCORE.

WEAK JUMP OVERCALL. The use of a jump overcall in a suit as preemptive. A FOUR ACES innovation of the thirties, credited to OSWALD JACOBY, and embodied in ROTH-STONE and later systems.

Over a 1 ◊ opening, 2 ♡, 2 ♠ or 3 ♣ would show the equivalent of a WEAK TWO-BID — 6–12 points, and a six-card or perhaps seven-card suit.

For many years, strong jump overcalls were a basic part of the Goren bidding system, which was the system used by the vast majority of players. However, the double values of the weak jump overcall — telling the whole story about a hand in one bid while throwing up a blockade against the opponents' bidding — caused Goren to incorporate the weak jump overcall into his standard bidding system.

The weak jump overcall must always take the vulnerability situation into account. Not vulnerable against vulnerable, a weak jump to the level of two could be made on a good five-card suit and little else. A vulnerable jump to the three-level against nonvulnerable would almost always be too dangerous with a weak hand. For this reason, SAM STAYMAN advises a strong jump overcall at unfavorable vulnerability.

The opening bidder's partner often faces a bidding problem after a weak jump overcall. If he makes his normal bid, but one level higher, he may easily be giving a wrong impression of the strength of his hand. If he passes, this could mean that the overcaller has achieved his objective — to buy the contract cheaply. Many players use the NEGATIVE DOUBLE against weak jump overcalls. The usual agreement is that the negative double shows a hand that would have responded with a natural bid at a lower level, but is not strong enough to make that natural bid at this higher level. The negative double can also show other types of holdings — the next call by the negative doubler should make clear the type of hand he holds. Another possible solution is for minimum bids in a new suit to be nonforcing (NEGATIVE FREE BID). However, if this method is used, it becomes necessary to use a cuebid in the opponent's suit, a jump in a new suit, possibly 2 NT and pass as forcing calls.

The weak jump overcall would not apply in the pass-out position, for there would be no object in preempting. In that situation a jump would be made with slightly less than the values needed for a strong jump. But if the opponents bid two suits, the jump retains its preemptive character.

Some leading players, notably in Philadelphia, rely considerably on the negative inferences which can be available using the weak jump overcall. They treat simple overcalls as stronger than in standard methods, and respond to them as to an opening one bid. See also DOUBLE JUMP OVERCALL.

WEAK JUMP SHIFT RESPONSES. The use of a

jump response in a new suit as a preemptive bid. After an opening 1♣, a response of 2♦ would be made by a player whose only asset was ♠ K–J–6–5–4–2. This works for the subminimum responding hands with a six-card or seven-card suit, but greatly increases the problem of bidding strong hands which would normally make a jump shift. The simple suit response becomes overloaded, because it may be made with a hand of any strength from 6 points upwards.

Nevertheless, the weak jump shift response has merit in that it enables a player to describe his hand in just one bid while stealing a level of bidding from the opponents. The bid also makes it much easier for the opening bidder to assess his hand. He knows, as a result of a single bid, that his partner has a hand that probably will play best in his suit, and the opener also knows there is little hope for game unless he holds close to an opening force.

Like all preemptive bids, the weak jump shift response exerts pressure on an opponent with a good hand. The fourth player should bid as he would over an opening one-bid: double for a takeout, and bid 2 NT on a hand which would open 1 NT (16–18). See ROTH-STONE SYSTEM and OGUST REBIDS.

WEAK NOTRUMP. An opening 1 NT with a minimum hand is an integral part of many systems. The usual range of the bid is 12–14 points, although the PRECISION SYSTEM uses a range of 13–15 points. The usual corollary is that a rebid of 1 NT shows a hand too strong to open with 1 NT (15–17 in KAPLAN-SHEINWOLD, 15–16 in the English systems).

Each of these systems has some special features in response, but with a suitable adjustment of range any normal principles of responding to a strong notrump can be followed.

A structure developed specifically for responding to a weak notrump opening by Mark Melchiori, Spring Arbor MI, relies extensively on transfer bids. With a weak hand responder may transfer to his longest suit by bidding the next lower-ranking suit, raise to 2 NT as a takeout for the minors, or bid 2♣ (STAYMAN) and over 2♦ by opener, rebid 3♦ as a takeout for the majors. With an invitational hand, responder will usually transfer and raise or rebid another suit; specialized invitations are a jump to 3♦ to invite game in hearts and a raise to 2 NT followed by 3 NT to invite a notrump game if opener has a fit for responder's minors and stoppers in the major suits. With a game-forcing hand, responder can transfer and jump in another suit, transfer to a minor and raise (slam invitational), or raise to 2 NT and rebid a suit on the three-level (distributional game-force that could not be shown by other methods). See also FLINT 2♦.

Some special tactical situations arise when 1 NT by the dealer has been passed and the responder is very weak. The fourth player is almost certain to have a strong hand, and there is a danger of conceding a heavy penalty, so third hand may have to take evasive action:

♠ 6 2
♡ 9 7 4 3
♦ J 10 7 3
♣ 9 5 3

2♦ is the best action because it will not be easy for the opponents to double for penalties. A pass is likely to lead to a contract of 1 NT doubled, down three or four tricks. If the black suits were reversed, a conventional 2♣ response would be possible with the intention of passing any rebid. But see DOUBLE OF 2♣ RESPONSE TO 1 NT.

Competitive bidding is much more common and much more critical when the weak notrump is being used. The opponents frequently need some conventional defensive arrangement such as ASTRO, BROZEL, EXCLUSION BIDS, LANDY, or RIPSTRA. A double of a weak notrump should be for penalties, and partner should rarely remove the double: only a weak hand with a long suit would justify a takeout. The doubler should have a better hand than the notrump bidder, whether the double is made immediately or in the pass-out position.

When a weak notrump is doubled, opener's side will often need a conventional arrangement for escaping to their best suit contract. One method, proposed by Henry Shevitz of Detroit, is that redouble by responder asks opener to bid his better minor, 2♦ is a request for his better major, and 2♣ shows one minor, not necessarily clubs. If 2♣ is doubled, responder corrects to diamonds if that is his suit. See also SWINE.

The action by fourth hand after a two-level response needs consideration. A double of a STAYMAN 2♣ response is usually taken to be an indication of a good club suit for lead-directing purposes. The modern tendency among some experts is to double 2♣ or any suit takeout at the level of two with a hand which would have doubled if responder had passed 1 NT.

For other details about notrump bidding, see JACOBY TRANSFER BIDS; 1 NT OPENING; STAYMAN; TEXAS; etc.

WEAK NOTRUMP OVERCALL. The use of an overcall of 1 NT is the equivalent of a weak notrump opening. This permits a defender to enter the auction on many hands which he would normally pass, but the value is doubtful because the overcaller will often be doubled for penalties with no escape. Sometimes confined to nonvulnerable situations.

The opener's partner follows the procedure for bidding over a normal strong notrump overcall. He usually doubles with 9 points or more, because his side is almost sure to have the balance of strength. With a weaker hand he can bid a five-card or longer suit at the two-level, which is unconstructive. And he can make a CUEBID of 2 NT with a strong unbalanced hand. See also BARON NOTRUMP OVERCALL.

WEAK SUIT. A suit which the opponents are likely to lead, and in which they can probably cash several tricks. Sometimes the term refers to an unstopped suit, but if a notrump contract is being considered it could also apply to a suit in which the opponents hold nine or more cards and in which only one stopper is held.

The weakness of a suit is relative to the auction. A small doubleton is often regarded as a weak suit for the purposes of a 1 NT opening, although there are two schools of thought, and many players would not allow themselves to be deterred.

For the purposes of a notrump rebid, a small

doubleton in an unbid suit is unthinkable, and a small tripleton is highly unattractive. The chance that the opponents will lead the suit is increased, and the chance that partner can guard it is decreased.

If a side has bid three suits, a notrump bid requires at least one positive stopper and preferably two in the fourth suit.

Sometimes anything less than a double stopper would certainly represent a weak suit:

WEST	NORTH	EAST	SOUTH
			1 ◇
Dbl	Pass	3 NT	

As West is likely to have a diamond shortage, the jump to 3 NT shows a double diamond stopper. Anything less would constitute a weak suit, unless perhaps East held a single stopper with a long strong club suit.

WEAK SUIT GAME TRY. A rebid by opener in his weakest suit to try for game after responder has raised the major suit opening bid to two. Sometimes called a "help suit game try." For example if opener holds:

     ♠ A K x x x   ♡ x x x   ◇ x   ♣ A Q J x

the bidding goes

OPENER	RESPONDER
1 ♠	2 ♠
3 ♡	

Opener's 3 ♡ bid asks responder to bid game in spades if he has either strength or shortness in hearts. Responder might hold any of the following hands:

(a)	(b)	(c)
♠ Q x x x	♠ Q x x x	♠ Q x x x
♡ J x x	♡ A x x x x	♡ x
◇ A x x x x	◇ J x x	◇ A J x x x
♣ x	♣ x	♣ x x x

With hand (a) responder would sign off in 3 ♠ since he has no help for opener's anemic hearts. With hand (b) or hand (c), however, responder would bid game in spades since his strength in (b) and his singleton in (c) can take care of the heart situation.

A disadvantage of weak suit game tries is that it usually reveals to the opponents the vulnerable spot of opener's hand, and therefore the defender's most advantageous point of attack.

WEAK TAKEOUT. An English term for a natural unconstructive suit response to 1 NT. See WEAKNESS RESPONSE.

WEAK TWO-BIDS. The use of suit openings of two other than clubs as a preemptive bid. A prototype of the weak two was used in auction bridge, and adopted in the VANDERBILT CLUB SYSTEM. Subsequently CHARLES VAN VLECK, New York, was responsible for an ultra-weak two-bid. HOWARD SCHENKEN developed the modern weak two-bid along lines similar to Vanderbilt's. It was later incorporated into most modern American systems, and into the NEAPOLITAN and BLUE TEAM CLUB systems.

Most authorities require a six-card suit for a weak two-bid, with about 8–11 points in high cards mainly concentrated in the bid suit. But these requirements are commonly relaxed, especially in third seat, and many players simply announce a range of 6–12 high-card points. Vulnerability and position at the table may be a factor in deciding whether to make a weak two-bid.

Responses. There a number of schools of thought, and the responses and rebids need precise partnership agreement.

(1) *Raise to four.* A two-way bid: perhaps a hand which expects to make game, or perhaps a preemptive action of the ADVANCE SAVE variety. The left-hand opponent may have a difficult decision with a strong hand.

(2) *Raise to three.* Originally a constructive invitation to opener to bid game, but many players use the raise preemptively. In the latter case the responder's trick-taking expectation for the combined hands may vary from nine tricks to as few as six tricks at favorable vulnerability.

(3) *Suit takeout.* Normally natural and forcing. Psychic responses are sometimes used, especially at the level of two. An alternative treatment which has increased in popularity is to play suit takeouts as nonforcing and unconstructive, indicating that the responder has a misfit and expects a better result playing in his one long strong suit. Responder must bid 2 NT whenever he wishes to make a forcing bid.

(4) *2 NT.* Usually a one-round force. A rebid by opener in his own suit can be used to show a minimum; some players prefer to show a minimum by a 3 ♣ rebid. Using either agreement, a rebid in another suit shows a high-card FEATURE and better than a minimum hand. If responder then gives a mere preference to opener's original suit on the second round, the defenders should find out whether the opener is encouraged or permitted to continue: if not, a psychic should be suspected. Similarly, it is important for both the opener's side and the defenders to know whether the opener is permitted to rebid above the level of three in his original suit. A raise of 2 NT to 3 NT, if permitted, should show a solid suit.

A 2 NT response is occasionally used as a natural nonforcing invitation to 3 NT; but it can very rarely be right to stop in 2 NT after a weak two-bid.

(5) *Ogust.* A system of rebidding to 2 NT devised by HAROLD OGUST that requires opener to describe the strength of his hand and the quality of his suit by a series of artificial bids. OGUST REBIDS are as follows:

3 ♣	minimum strength, poor suit
3 ◇	maximum strength, poor suit
3 ♡	minimum strength, good suit
3 ♠	maximum strength, good suit

Some partnerships prefer to reverse the meanings of the 3 ◇ and 3 ♡ rebids.

(6) *McCabe Adjunct.* Described by J. I. McCabe, Columbia SC, in *The Bridge World*, January 1955, this is a method of playing at the three-level in a new suit. After the 2 NT response, the opener is required to rebid 3 ♣, irrespective of his holding. The responder can now play in his long suit at the three-level, either by bidding it or by passing 3 ♣. Each partnership must decide the meaning of 2 NT followed by a simple preference bid: this should be treated as constructive if an immediate raise would

have been preemptive.

(7) *Relays.* The cheapest response — either 2 NT if the opening bid was 2 ♠, or the next higher suit. The relay asks opener to bid a stopper outside his suit if he has one. If his stopper is in the relay suit, he rebids in notrump. Lacking any outside stopper, opener rebids his own suit. Using this method, the relay is responder's only forcing bid.

(8) *Two Relays and a Transfer.* A single raise is constructive. 2 NT is natural and not forcing. Almost all other responses are artificial and forcing for at least one round. The bid of the cheapest suit is a relay, forcing to game and asking opener to bid his lowest ranking feature (ace, king, singleton or void). Without a feature, opener rebids his suit. The bid of the second higher ranking suit, i.e., 2 ♠ over 2 ◇ or 3 ♣ over 2 ♡, is forcing and game invitational. This relay asks partner to show his point count. With a minimum (6–9), opener rebids his suit. With a maximum (10–12), opener makes the cheapest suit rebid. Since the direct raise is constructive, a transfer bid is used to make a preemptive raise. The bid of the suit just below the suit of the weak two-bid forces opener to rebid his suit.

Defense. Standard procedure is to bid as over a one-bid: double for takeout, and bid 2 NT on a hand which would qualify for a strong notrump opening bid. But many other defensive arrangements are possible, including all the methods listed under DEFENSE TO OPENING THREE-BIDS.

To combat players addicted to psychic suit responses to a weak two-bid, some players use a double of the response for penalties. But if the suit response is natural and *nonforcing*, the double should be a normal takeout action.

WEAKNESS–CONCEALING PLAYS. See DECEPTIVE PLAY.

WEAKNESS RESPONSE. A natural response which indicates a strong desire to close the auction at that point.

The most common case is the response of 2 ♠, 2 ♡, or 2 ◇ to an opening 2 NT bid. Using standard methods, with the STAYMAN 2 ♣ convention, responder shows at least a five-card suit and no desire to progress toward game.

In very rare circumstances the opener may make one further bid if he has a fine fit with responder, presumably four cards, a maximum notrump opening consisting largely of top honors, usually including two of the three top honors in responder's suit. If opener raises to the three level and the contract fails, it may prove that the raise has forestalled a successful balancing action by the opponents.

If the opener bids a new suit 1 NT—2 ♡—3 ♣, he implies a fit with responder's hearts plus a concentration of strength in clubs. This helps responder to evaluate game chances.

Another example of a weakness response:

WEST	NORTH	EAST	SOUTH
			1 ♣
1 NT	2 ♡		

North's failure to double 1 NT marks him with a weak hand (less than 8 or 9 points) and heart length.

South will rarely be strong enough to attempt a game, and should rarely rescue. A suit bid or a simple raise over a takeout double is similar in principle.

Weakness responses, which are natural, are often confused with negative responses, which are conventional. Examples of these would be a negative 2 ◇ response to a conventional 2 ♣ bid, or a HERBERT NEGATIVE.

WEB MOVEMENT. The Web Movement was devised by National Tournament Director JOHN "SPIDER" HARRIS in 1977 and is described by him as follows:

It is not uncommon to have, at least in small tournaments, sessions of from 16 to 22 tables in which a movement of reasonable technical adequacy is required, such as in a Master Pairs or an Open Pairs Final. In the past the standard procedure has been to use twinned 3/4 movements and combined match-pointing.

These movements are universally disliked by players and are not too popular with directors. They do have the purported advantage provided by rotating comparisons, but this is the subject of some disagreement. In all other respects the web movements are, in my opinion, superior.

In effect, these movements consist of two subsections in which the boards circulate independently, while the moving pairs progress to the other subsection after playing at the highest numbered table in one. In all cases, the traveling pairs move each round to the next higher numbered table, boards move next lower within each sub-section. The 18-table game will be described in detail; the others will be understood by simply glancing at the Master Sheet* and remembering what happened in the 18-table progression.

Basic Distribution of Boards. Tables 1–9 play one set ("A"), tables 10–18 another ("B"). Stationary pairs at 1–9 play the boards in ascending sequence, those at 10–18 in descending. Boards 1–2 start at Table 1, 3–4 at 2, etc. up to 17–18 at 9. The board order is inverted and displaced in the other sub-section: 25–26 start at Table 18, 1–2 at 17, 3–4 at 16, etc. to 15–16 at 10. Note that on round one, Boards 1–16 may be duplicated in the two sub-sections, 17–18 and 25–26 may either be duplicated at tables 9 and 18 respectively, or pre-duplicated (preferred). Boards 19–24 must be duplicated by the staff.

Movement of Boards and Players. Traveling pairs always move to the next higher numbered table. THERE IS NO SKIP. "A" boards move down until they reach Table 1 at which point they go to a bye-stand to re-enter at Table 9. "B" boards move down until they reach Table 10 at which point they go to the other bye-stand to re-enter at Table 18.

Seeded Tables. Assuming that Table 1 is to be seeded, the only suitable tables are:**

Sixteen tables — 1, 5, 9, 13. Eighteen tables — 1, 7,

---

*Master Sheets can be obtained upon request from the Tournament Division, ACBL Headquarters.

**Actually, in some cases other NUMBERS will work, but in 20– and 22–table progressions only two tables will mutually meet in both directions.

13. Twenty tables — 1, 9. Twenty-two tables — 1, 12.

Seating Assignments. In Open Pairs Finals, there is the restriction that no two pairs shall meet who met in the qualifying session. Where there are only two qualifying sections, the A qualifiers are simply made N-S, the B's E-W. For three qualifying sections, a schedule accompanies each Master Sheet for assigning pair numbers. It is assumed that the use of these progressions will never occur where there are more than three qualifying sections.

John "Spider" Harris

WEI AWARD. Endowed by C. C. WEI, the "Precision" Award for the Best Article or Series of Articles on a Bidding System or Convention is presented annually by the INTERNATIONAL BRIDGE PRESS ASSOCIATION. It is made to the originator and/or author of such article or series. The Award is given only in respect of an article or series which appears in a newspaper or other publication which is in general circulation. For a list of winners see INTERNATIONAL BRIDGE PRESS ASSOCIATION AWARDS.

WEISS CONVENTION. See DEFENSE TO OPENING THREE BID.

WEISSBERGER CONVENTION. An extension of the STAYMAN convention to ask for three-card major suits, suggested by JOHN PRESSBURGER and developed by ALAN TRUSCOTT and Maurice Weissberger. It is intended for use with English-style Stayman in which a secondary jump to 3 ♡ or 3 ♠ is invitational and not forcing, and is an optional feature of the ACOL system. Suppose the bidding proceeds:

OPENER	RESPONDER
1 NT	2 ♣
2 ◇	3 ◇

The bid of 3 ◇ has little or no natural meaning in Acol. The Weissberger idea is to use it to inquire for three-card major suits. This helps the responder to solve three types of bidding problems:

(1) A game-going hand with five spades and four hearts.

(2) A game-going hand with five spades and five hearts.

(3) A hand with five spades and five hearts on which game is doubtful.

As the responder is certain to have 5 spades, holding three spades the opener bids 3 ♠ with a minimum hand; 4 ♠ holding a maximum.

With only a doubleton spade, the opener bids 3 ♡ holding a minimum hand and 3 NT holding a maximum.

In all cases the responder has no problem in selecting the best final contract.

Notice that there are two other cases in which the convention is *not* needed:

(4) A game-going hand with four spades and five hearts. In this case the responder bids 3 ♡ immediately over 1 NT, and relies on the opener to show a four-card spade suit if he can.

(5) A hand with four in one major and five in the other on which game is doubtful. In this case the responder bids three of the five-card major suit over the opener's 2 ◇ rebid. This sequence is strictly non-

forcing in Acol.

WELSH BRIDGE UNION. Founded about 1934, it was formed by three areas. North, West, and East. The Union competes nationally for five cups: Open Teams (Welsh Cup) and Women's Teams, both knockout events, International Pairs (restricted to Welsh International players), National Pairs, and a League event. Since 1961 the WBU has operated a master-point program with awards won by members of the English Bridge Union registrable with the EBU.

Officers, 1982:
President: Colin Smith
Secretary: Mrs. Aherne, 19 Penygraig, Rhiwbina
  Cardiff, Glamorgan CF4 6ST

WERNHER TROPHY. For the North American Championship Men's Pairs, donated by SIR DERRICK WERNHER in 1934; contested at the Summer NAC until 1962 and subsequently at the Spring NAC, under which heading results are listed.

WEST. The player who sits at the left of South at a table of bridge. South is to his right and North to his left. He is the partner of East.

WEST COAST SCIENTIFIC. See WALSH SYSTEM.

WESTCOTT TROPHY. Awarded to the winner of the International Fund Pairs at the Summer NAC, donated in memory of FRANK T. WESTCOTT in 1974 by his widow.

WESTERN BRIDGE ASSOCIATION. A short lived Chicago-based membership organization which published *The Contract Bridge Magazine*, 1933–34, edited by EDWARD M. LAGRON.

WESTERN CONFERENCE. Originally PACIFIC BRIDGE LEAGUE, founded by TOM STODDARD, it became known as the Western Division in 1948, and the Western Conference in 1956 when it merged with ACBL. Current member districts are 17, 20, 21 and 22.

Functions of Western Conference. (1) Publishes *The Contract Bridge Forum*, a newspaper distributed to Western Conference members nine times a year. The *Forum* offers the members an opportunity to keep informed of activities throughout the conference and provides the districts a means by which to communicate with their membership about unit and district affairs; (2) Assists member units in promotion of Novice and Junior games at regionals; (3) Schedules regionals, handled by the Conference Coordinator, preventing conflicts with member districts and/or neighboring districts.

The last president of the Western Division, the late WINSLOW RANDALL, was the first president of the Western Conference. Other presidents:

1956	Lewis L. Mathe	1963	Kelsey Petterson
1957	Robin B. Mac Nab	1964	Lewis L. Mathe
1958	Hugh Edwards	1965	Max N. Manchester
1959	C. F. Crossley Jr.	1966	Robin B. Mac Nab
1960	Roy R. Hislop	1967	Eilif B. Andersen
1961	Tom Bussey	1968	Donald Oakie
1962	Lewis L. Mathe	1969	Paul Rhodes

1970	Percy X. Bean	1977	George T. Clemens
1971	Maurice E. Hole	1978	George T. Clemens
1972	Maurice E. Hole	1979	Herbert L. Smith
1973	Alfred B. Gilpin	1980	Herbert L. Smith
1974	Alfred B. Gilpin	1981	Chris Wilson
1975	David R. Tuell	1982	Chris Wilson
1976	David R. Tuell	1983	Robert O. Wingeard

WESTERN CUEBIDS. Generally, a cuebid of a suit bid by an opponent to ask about stoppers for no-trump play, rather than promising such stoppers. See CUEBIDS IN OPPONENT'S SUIT; DIRECTIONAL ASKING BID.

WESTERN ROTH–STONE. See WALSH SYSTEM.

WETZLAR TROPHY. Awarded for distinguished services to bridge, this trophy was presented in memory of Edwin A. Wetzlar in 1935. The first winners were:

1935	H. Huber Boscowitz	1938	Alfred Gruenther
1936	Waldemar von Zedtwitz	1939	Nate B. Spingold
1937	Gordon Gibbs	1940	Harold S. Vanderbilt

After 1940 the Wetzlar was presented to ACBL HONORARY MEMBERS, under which heading the recipients are listed.

WHISK. An alternative name for whist. It was an English lower-class term, according to Dr. Samuel Johnson, used until about the end of the eighteenth century.

WHIST. A game of cards of English origin gradually evolved from several older games such as triumph, trump, ruff and honors, swabbers, and WHISK. Whist is played by four persons, two partners against two partners. A regular pack of 52 cards is dealt, 13 to each player. The last card dealt is turned face up on the table. Its suit becomes the trump suit. This card remains on the table until it is the dealer's turn to play to the first trick, when he may return it to his hand. The player at the left of the dealer makes the first lead, and the play proceeds as in bridge except that all four hands are concealed; there is no DUMMY. Six tricks taken make the BOOK. Each trick won over the book scores one point for the partners winning that trick. The range of possible scores for either set of partners is from one to seven. Any number of deals may be played. Scoring is by games. The English code of laws provides for rubber bonuses and honor bonuses. At the conclusion of play the side having the greatest number of points is the winner. The game of whist has, in general, been superseded in the United States by changing versions of the basic game—by bridge, AUCTION BRIDGE and CONTRACT BRIDGE. It is still played widely in Great Britain and the U.S. See also AMERICAN WHIST LEAGUE; BIBLIOGRAPHY; CONTRACT WHIST.

WHIST CLUB. A club of men interested in whist and later in all successive forms of bridge, founded in New York 1893, merged with the REGENCY CLUB of New York 1964. Because nearly all of its members were men of great wealth and prominence (including bridge prominence, such as HAROLD S. VANDERBILT, J. B. ELWELL, MILTON WORK, ELY CULBERTSON), unquestioned authority in the making of bridge laws for the U.S. was accorded to the Whist Club for

more than 40 years. Two earlier codes of contract bridge laws were voluntarily withdrawn when in 1927 the Whist Club produced a code for contract bridge (formulated by a committee composed of Harold S. Vanderbilt, H. C. Richard, Charles Cadley, Raymond Little, and William Talcott). Later the Whist Club's committees collaborated with the Portland Club of London and French Bridge Federation in producing the first and second international codes (1932, 1935), and Whist Club representatives have served continuously on the NATIONAL LAWS COMMISSION for the laws of 1943, 1948, 1949, and 1963.

WHITEHEAD TROPHY. For the North American Championship Women's Pairs, donated by WILBER C. WHITEHEAD in 1930; contested at the Summer NAC until 1962 and subsequently at the Spring NAC, under which heading results are listed.

WHITFELD SIX. The father of all end-game problems, devised and published on January 31, 1885, by W. H. Whitfeld, mathematical tutor at Cambridge, England, who was Cavendish's successor as Card Editor of the London *Field*. (Known as the "Whitfield Six" through a common mispronunciation of the inventor's name.)

Hearts are trumps. South must lead and make all the tricks.

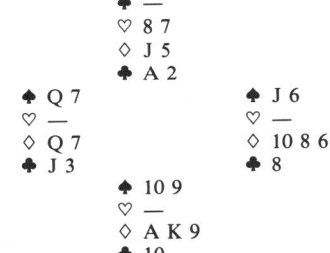

Solution. South cashes the ◇ A, unblocking the jack from dummy to prepare for a possible finesse. A spade is ruffed and the last trump from dummy is cashed, on which South discards the ♣ 10. The only temporary defense is for East to keep diamonds and the high spade, and for West to keep clubs and the ◇ Q. The ♣ A from dummy then squeezes East. The Whitfeld Six is a type of double guard squeeze.

WIDE OPEN. A phrase describing a suit in which declarer has no stopper or is extremely vulnerable to attack. For example, "Declarer was wide open in trumps."

WINKLE SQUEEZE. A secondary squeeze that forces the opponents to choose between a throw-in or an unblock, each of which costs a trick. (Analyzed and named by TERENCE REESE.) Declarer has enough winners for all but one of the remaining tricks, but he cannot take all his tricks because of entry problems.
(See hand at top of next page.)

South leads the A ♡, and East is squeezed in two

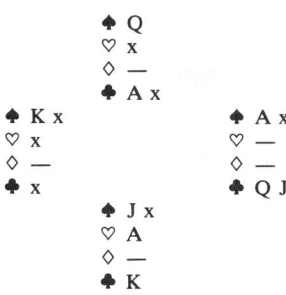

suits. In order to retain his club guard he must discard a spade. If East discards the ♠A, South cashes the ♣K, and exits with a spade, winning the ♠J at the end; if East discards a small spade, the play proceeds the same way, but East wins the spade exit, and he must give North a club for the last trick.

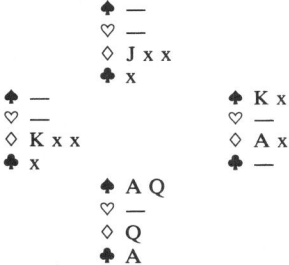

South leads the ♠A, and East is squeezed in two suits. A diamond must be discarded in order to protect the ♠K. If East discards a low diamond he will be thrown in to lead from his ♠K; if he discards the ◇A, South takes the ♠A, and then leads a diamond, eventually winning a trick with the jack. See also ENTRY SQUEEZE and STEPPINGSTONE SQUEEZE.

Monroe Ingberman

WINNER. (1) A card that may reasonably be expected to win a trick in dummy or declarer's hand. On defense, a card that will win a trick during the play of a given hand may be termed a winner as well. (2) The player, the pair or team with the highest score in an event at a duplicate tournament. Winners and runners-up of duplicate games are eligible to compete in special WINNERS' GAMES.

WINNERS' GAMES. Sessions of club play at duplicate in which eligibility to complete was limited to players who had, within a prescribed period (usually one month) won one or placed second in two regularly scheduled sanctioned games, or won at least one full master point in a sectional or regional tournament within that time. This program is no longer is effect.

WINNING CARD. The card that takes the trick. In a notrump declaration this is always the highest card played in the suit that has been led; it may be a LONG CARD, led in a suit to which the other players cannot follow. In suit declarations, the above will apply, except that on a trick where more than one trump is played it is the highest trump that will win the trick.

WINSLOW SYSTEM. See WINSLOW, T. N.

WITHDRAW A CARD. It is not permitted to withdraw a card previously played except to correct a revoke, or a card played by an opponent after such a card was withdrawn. Declarer may insist that a card he had called to be played from dummy be substituted for a card actually put into the playing position by the dummy. In this case, too, the opponent may without penalty withdraw his card and substitute a different proper card. See, however, ALCATRAZ COUP for a possible situation that calls for a redress under the general powers of the director.

WOLFF CONVENTION. Devised by BOBBY WOLFF to allow responder to sign off at the three level after opener has made a jump rebid of 2 NT. Responder's rebid of 3♣ asks opener to bid three of responder's suit if he has three-card support, and otherwise to bid 3◇. Responder can then sign off by passing, by bidding 4♣, or by introducing a new suit of lower rank than his first suit; a rebid of 3 NT by responder would be a mild slam try in clubs.

WOMEN'S INTERNATIONAL TEAM TRIALS. See INTERNATIONAL WOMEN'S TEAM SELECTION.

WOMEN'S KNOCKOUT TEAMS, NORTH AMERICAN CHAMPIONSHIP. See COFFIN TROPHY.

WOMEN'S PAIRS. An event at duplicate competition between pairs of women players. Awards are 20% lower than for events of comparable size and duration open to any players. At most sectional tournaments, the women's pairs event is held on Friday afternoon.

WOMEN'S PAIRS, NORTH AMERICAN CHAMPIONSHIP. See WHITEHEAD TROPHY.

WOMEN'S SWISS TEAMS, NORTH AMERICAN CHAMPIONSHIP. See Appendix I, Summer NAC.

WONDER BIDS. A defensive bidding system against strong artificial club sequences. They are used when vulnerable — IDAK (or IDAC) is used when not vulnerable.

The system works this way. If RHO opens an artificial club or responds artificially to a 1♣ opening:

1. Any non-jump suit bid shows that suit *or* the other three (let partner guess). Responder obviously can't raise blindly, but can: (a) bid 1 NT with four or more cards in the Wonder suit (not forcing if the Wonder bidder has the three-suited hand); (b) bid two of any suit with four or more cards *if* he also has tolerance for the Wonder suit. The overcaller passes or returns to his real Wonder suit. The Wonder bidder redoubles for takeout if doubled in his short suit.

2. Double shows the major suits.

3. Notrump shows the minor suits.

4. A jump in diamonds shows diamonds and hearts, a jump in hearts shows hearts and clubs, a jump in spades shows spades and a minor (notrump asks which minor).

WOODSON TWO-WAY NOTRUMP. This requires an opening notrump bid holding 10-12 points or 16-18 points and a hand with balanced distribution. It was devised in 1952 by WILLIAM B. WOODSON.

This two-way treatment sets problems for both sides, and its supporters believe that the defending side will frequently find its problems insoluble. The opener's partner can usually determine his partner's range without difficulty.

A response of 2♣ to 1 NT asks for clarification, and the rebids are:

2◇ or 2♡	10-12 points
2♠ or	
2 NT	16 points
3♣	17-18 points

Responder can use a bid of 3◇ on the second round to check for four-card major suits.

If 1 NT is doubled, the 1 NT bidder redoubles to show the weak notrump range of 10-12 and demand a rescue. (A reversal of this procedure would seem to have some advantages, with a redouble to show the strong range.)

Responder can sign off with 2♠, 2♡, or 2◇ if he has no prospects of game opposite a strong notrump; and may head directly for game if he wishes to be in game opposite the weak variety.

Until the contrary is proved, the defenders should bid on the assumption that the notrump bid is weak. A double is in order with a full opening bid or better.

WORK POINT-COUNT. A 4-3-2-1 point-count based on the BRYANT McCAMPBELL count of 1915, publicized and advocated by MILTON WORK, circa 1923. See POINT-COUNT.

WORKING CARDS. High cards which, on the basis of the auction, rate to mesh well with partner's hand for suit play. For example, a SECONDARY HONOR or an unsupported king is usually discounted opposite a known singleton, whereas any of the top honors is likely to be "working" if it is in one of partner's suits. See also GOOD CARDS.

WORLD BIDDING CONTEST. See INTERNATIONAL BRIDGE ACADEMY.

WORLD BRIDGE FEDERATION. A successor of the INTERNATIONAL BRIDGE LEAGUE, the WBF was founded in August 1958 at Oslo, Norway, by representatives of the American Contract Bridge League, the European Bridge League, and the Australian Bridge Council.

The WBF aims to provide a central organization to bind together the national controlling bridge organizations of the world. More specifically, its objects are:

(1) To promote, foster, and control the game of contract bridge.

(2) To apply the International Laws of contract bridge.

(3) To promote and conduct quadrennial WORLD CHAMPIONSHIP team tournaments on the basis of one team only for each control (the Olympiad).

(4) To conduct the BERMUDA BOWL contest, in every year in which there is no Team Olympiad.

(5) To promote and conduct quadrennial World Championship pair tournaments.

(6) To conduct World Championship par contests.

(7) To conduct such other contests as from time to time are agreed upon.

Member countries must have a minimum of 250 individual members, and belong to the zonal organization if one exists.

The zones of the WBF are: (1) Europe, (2) North America, including Bermuda, (3) South America, (4) Asia and the Middle East, (5) Central America and the Caribbean, (6) Far East, (7) South Pacific, (8) All countries not affiliated with any of the other zones, namely Egypt, North African and South African NCBOs.

The Federation's Board of Governors consists of one representative of each member country. It meets whenever and wherever a Team or Pair Olympiad is held.

The 1982 officers of the Federation were:

President: Jaime Ortiz-Patiño, 54/56 route de Vandoeuvres, 1253 Geneva, Switzerland

1st Vice-President: Ed Theus, Oklahoma City OK

2nd Vice-President: Nils E. Jensen, Solna, Sweden

3rd Vice-President: Benno Gimkiewicz, Bangkok, Thailand

Secretary: Richard L. Goldberg, Memphis TN

Treasurer: Lewis L. Mathe, Los Angeles

General Counsel: Robert A. Howes, New York City

Honorary Chairman: Geoffrey L. Butler, London, England

Executive Council
Jose Damiani, France
Alberto A. Calvo, Panama
Mazhar Jafri, Pakistan
Rueben Kunin, Switzerland
Ernesto d'Orsi, Brazil
Denis Howard, Australia
Vincent O. Remey, United States

BARON ROBERT DE NEXON became the first President of the WBF in 1958 and was succeeded in 1964 by CHARLES J. SOLOMON, who had been the original Vice-President. In 1968, COUNT CARL BONDE was elected President. He held the post until the election of JULIUS ROSENBLUM in 1970. JAIME ORTIZ-PATINO took over the presidency in 1976. See also BERMUDA BOWL; INTERNATIONAL BRIDGE LEAGUE; WORLD PAR CONTESTS; WORLD CHAMPIONSHIPS.

WORLD BRIDGE FEDERATION LAWS COMMITTEE. In 1983 the Committee consisted of:

Ed Theus, United States, Chairman
Geoffrey L. Butler, Great Britain, President Emeritus
Jean Besse, Switzerland
Carlos Cabanne, Argentina
Santanu Ghose, India
Colin Harding, Great Britain
Denis Howard, Australia
Edgar Kaplan, United States
Jaime Ortiz-Patiño, WBF President
William J. Pencharz, Great Britain

WORLD BRIDGE FEDERATION PLAYER RANKINGS. The ranking of players according to the world masterpoint plan of the World Bridge Federation. The three ranks, in descending order, are Grand Master, World Master, and International Master.

The rank of Grand Master is achieved by accumulating 200 or more WBF PLACING POINTS, and winning at least one major WBF event or four non-major events. The rank of World Master is achieved by accumulating 50 WBF points plus 5 WBF placing points, and winning at least one WBF championship or ZONAL CHAMPIONSHIP (1) or three NATIONAL CONTRACT BRIDGE ORGANIZATION championships. The rank of International Master may be achieved either by accumulating 10 WBF points, or by winning an NCBO championship and being nominated by an NCBO and being recognized by the appropriate WBF committee.

Each NCBO is allowed to nominate a certain number of players who have not won 10 WBF points to be International Masters. The number each NCBO may nominate is based principally on its membership population. In the United States the ACBL nominated as International Masters the top approximately 220 ACBL master point holders who had won a North American Championship and who did not otherwise hold world ranking; the AMERICAN BRIDGE ASSOCIATION nominated several ABA players for such ranking.

Grand Masters, World Masters, and International Masters having 10 or more WBF points hold their ranks for life. International Masters with fewer than 10 WBF points hold their rank for four years and are then subject to review.

As of 1982 the following players held the ranks of Grand Master and World Master:

GRAND MASTERS

1.	Belladonna, Giorgio	(Italy)	1767
2.	Garozzo, Benito	(Italy)	1632
3.	Forquet, Pietro	(Italy)	1475
4.	D'Alelio, Massimo	(Italy)	1260
5.	Avarelli, Walter	(Italy)	1200
6.	Hamman, Robert	(United States)	940
7.	Pabis Ticci, Camille	(Italy)	910
8.	Wolff, Bobby	(United States)	770
9.	Jacoby, James	(United States)	628
10.	Goldman, Bobby	(United States)	582
11.	Eisenberg, Billy	(United States)	535.5
12.	Trézel, Roger	(France)	480
13.	Jaïs, Pierre	(France)	469
14.	Soloway, Paul	(United States)	447
15.	Lawrence, Michael	(United States)	440
16.	Ghestem, Pierre	(France)	383
17.	Cintra, Gabino	(Brazil)	372.5
18.	Castelo Branco, Marcelo	(Brazil)	361
19.	Shapiro, Boris	(Great Britain)	353
20.	Bacherich, René	(France)	350
21.	Rubin, Ira	(United States)	346
22.	Chagas, Gabriel	(Brazil)	341
23.	Assumpção, Pedro Paulo	(Brazil)	336.5
24.	Becker, B. Jay	(United States)	332
25.	Reese, Terence	(Great Britain)	323
26.	Truscott, Dorothy Hayden	(United States)	322
27.	Rapée, George	(United States)	304
28.	Stayman, Samuel M.	(United States)	299
29.	Farell, Mary Jane	(United States)	276
30.	Pittala, Vito	(Italy)	272
31.	Markus, Rixi	(Great Britain)	269
32.	Kreyns, Hans	(The Netherlands)	262
33.	Franco, Arturo	(Italy)	255
34.	Hamilton, Fred	(United States)	242
35.	Mathe, Lewis	(United States)	236
36.	Gordon, Fritzi	(Great Britain)	234
37.	Delmouly, Claude	(France)	233
38.	Siniscalco, Guglielmo	(Italy)	225
39.	Johnson, Marylyn	(United States)	224
40.	Fonseca, Christiano	(Brazil)	218
41.	Kantar, Eddie	(United States)	216
42.	Mitchell, Jacqui	(United States)	204
43.	Valenti, Anna	(Italy)	202

44.	Bourchtoff, Gérard	(France)	200
45.	Hawes, Emma Jean	(United States)	200

WORLD MASTERS

1.	Murray, Eric	(Canada)	440
2.	Kehela, Sammy	(Canada)	395
3.	Kay, Norman	(United States)	295
4–5.	Jordan, Robert	(United States)	291
	Robinson, Arthur	(United States)	291
6.	Flint, Jeremy	(Great Britain)	278
7.	Roth, Alvin	(United States)	270
8.	Svarc, Henri	(France)	260.5
9.	Lebel, Michel	(France)	247
10.	Chemla, Paul	(France)	247
11.	Huang, Patrick	(Taiwan)	237
12.	Boulenger, Jean-Michel	(France)	224
13.	Tai, Min-Fan	(Taiwan)	211
14.	Passell, Michael	(United States)	197
15.	Bianchi, Marisa	(Italy)	190
16.	Moss, Gail	(United States)	185
17.	Kaplan, Edgar	(Untied States)	183
18.	Mari, Christian	(France)	181
19.	Gardener, Nico	(Great Britain)	175
20.	Leventritt, A. Peter	(United States)	172
21.	Root, William	(United States)	170
22.	Wilkosz, Andrzej	(Poland)	167.5
23.	Roudinesco, Jean-Marc	(France)	163
24.	Barbosa, Sergio	(Brazil)	162
25.	Rodrigue, Claude	(Great Britain)	156
26.	Seres, Tim	(Australia)	154
27–28.	Babsch, Fritz	(Austria)	153
	Manhardt, Peter	(Austria)	153
29.	Mayer, Ferry	(Italy)	150
30.	Rose, Albert	(Great Britain)	148
31.	Goren, Charles H.	(United States)	148
32.	Priday, Richard	(Great Britain)	148
33.	Perron, Michel	(France)	146
34.	Vivaldi, Antonio	(Italy)	144
35.	Mitchell, Victor	(United States)	144
36.	Stone, Tobias	(United States)	139
37.	Stoppa, Jean Louis	(France)	138
38–39.	D'Andrea, Marisa	(Italy)	137
	Capodanno, Lucianna	(Italy)	137
40.	Cummings, Richard John	(Australia)	136
41.	Charney, Gerry	(Canada)	135
42.	Swanson, John C.	(United States)	133
43.	Besse, Jean	(Switzerland)	131
44–45.	Gardener, Nicola	(Great Britain)	131
	Landy, Sandra	(Great Britain)	131
46.	Cheng, Conrad K. R.	(Taiwan)	129
47.	Shen, C. S.	(Taiwan)	128
48.	Silborn, Gunborg	(Sweden)	127
49.	Sbarigia, Silvio	(Italy)	124
50.	Nygren, Britt	(Sweden)	124
51.	Paulsen, Erik	(United States)	122.5
52.	Macieszczak, Andrzej	(Poland)	122.5
53.	Ross, Hugh L.	(United States)	120.5
54.	Crissey, William	(Canada)	120
55.	Attaguile, Luis	(Argentina)	118.5
56.	Santamarina, Agustin	(Argentina)	117.5
57.	Mosca, Carlo	(Italy)	115
58.	Fisher, Dr.John	(United States)	113
59.	Lin, Harry S. C.	(Taiwan)	111
60.	Tarlo, Joël	(Great Britain)	110
61.	Zanasi, Italo	(Italy)	110
62.	Krauss, Donald P.	(United States)	110
63.	Robaudo, Maria	(Italy)	109
64.	Smilde, Roelof	(Australia)	108
65.	Castelo Branco, Pedro	(Brazil)	107.5
66.	Cabanne, Carlos	(Argentina)	107.5
67.	Priday, Jane	(Great Britain)	105
68.	Mondolfo, Renato	(Italy)	105
69.	Sowter, Sally	(Great Britain)	104
70.	Jabes, Rina	(Italy)	104
71.	Garabello, Giuseppe	(Italy)	100
72.	Bernasconi, Pietro	(Switzerland)	99
73.	Borin, James	(Australia)	98
74.	Tintner, Léon	(Australia)	97
75–76.	Stetten, Jacques	(France)	95
	Rocchi, Egisto	(Argentina)	95
77.	Howard, Denis	(Australia)	95
78.	Jacobson, Rita	(South Africa)	94
79.	Nail, G. Robert	(United States)	94
80.	Arnold, Russ D.	(United States)	93
81.	Hsiao, Elmer C. H.	(Taiwan)	93
82.	Catzeflis, Georges	(Switzerland)	91
83.	Von Der Porten, Ron	(United States)	90
84.	Ortiz-Patiño, Jaime	(Switzerland)	89
85.	Solodar, John	(United States)	88
86.	Desrousseaux, Gérard	(France)	88
87.	Goslar, Gerda	(South Africa)	85
88–89–90.	Levin, Bobby	(United States)	85

	Meckstroth, Jeff	(United States)	85
	Rodwell, Eric	(United States)	85
91.	Feldesman, Philip	(United States)	84
92.	Lazard, Sidney	(United States)	82
93.	Rosen, William A.	(United States)	79
94.	Berisso, Alberto	(Argentina)	78.5
95.	Gruver, Nancy	(United States)	76
96–97.	Mansell, Petra	(South Africa)	76
	Schnieder, Alma	(South Africa)	76
98–99.	Bishop, Clifford	(United States)	75
	Ellenby, Milton Q.	(United States)	75
100.	Gordon, Lula	(Switzerland)	74
101.	Hwang, Frank K.	(Taiwan)	73
102.	Shen, K. W.	(Thailand)	73
103.	Sucharitakul, Kovit	(Thailand)	71
104.	Hazen, Lee	(United States)	70
105–106.	Elliot C. Bruce	(Canada)	68
	Sheardown, Percy E.	(Canada)	68
107.	Calvente, Ricardo	(Spain)	66
108–109.	Durran, Jane	(Great Britain)	65
	Shanahan, Dorothy	(Great Britain)	65
110.	Beron, Thelma	(South Africa)	60
111.	Fleming, A. Leslie	(Great Britain)	60
112.	Saulino, William	(Italy)	60
113.	Sachs, Sue	(United States)	59
114.	Lerner, Marcelo	(Argentina)	59
115–116.	Morenas, Genevieve	(France)	55
	Serf, Marianne	(France)	55
117.	Pariente, Jacques	(France)	55
118.	Wohlin, Jan	(Sweden)	55
119.	Oakie, Don	(United States)	54
120.	Messina, Giuseppe	(Italy)	53
121–133.	Camara, Helen	(England)	50
	Canessa, Luciana Romanelli	(Italy)	50
	Chanfray, Annie	(France)	50
	Choucry, Aida	(England)	50
	Erikson, Karin	(Sweden)	50
	Martensson, Eva	(Sweden)	50
	Morcos, Josephine	(England)	50
	Moss, Mary	(Great Britain)	50
	Naguib, Suzanne	(England)	50
	Portugal, Helen	(United States)	50
	Segander, Rut	(Sweden)	50
	Venturini, Maria Vittoria	(Italy)	50
	Werner, Britta	(Sweden)	50
134–136.	Lattes, Roger	(Great Britain)	50
	Romanet, Bertrand	(France)	50
	Steen, Douglas	(United States)	50

WORLD BRIDGE FEDERATION POINTS. See
WBF MASTER POINTS; WBF PLACING POINTS; WORLD BRIDGE FEDERATION PLAYER RANKINGS.

WORLD BRIDGE FEDERATION TROPHY. For
the World Women's Pairs Championship. First contested in Cannes, France, in 1962. See WORLD CHAMPIONSHIPS for results.

WORLD BRIDGE OLYMPIC. See WORLD PAR CONTESTS.

WORLD CHAMPIONSHIPS. There have been
four distinct categories of World Championship bridge.

I. Pre-World War II

1935 (the first official meeting between the champions of Europe and the American Bridge League.) New York City United States defeated France by 2,810 points over 300 boards.

UNITED STATES	FRANCE
David Burnstine	Pierre Albarran
Michael Gottlieb	Baron Robert de Nexon
Oswald Jacoby	M. Georges Rousset
Howard Schenken	Emanuel Tulumaris
	Sofocle Venizelos

1937 (under the auspices of the International Bridge League) Budapest, Hungary. Austria defeated United States by 4,740 points.

OPEN WINNERS	OPEN RUNNERS-UP
AUSTRIA	UNITED STATES
Karl von Bluhdorn	Ely Culbertson
Dr. Edward Frischauer	Josephine Culbertson

Walter Herbert	Helen Sobel
Hans Jellinek	Charles C. Vogelhofer
Udo von Meissel	
Karl Schneider	
Dr. Paul Stern (npc)	

WOMEN'S WINNERS
Austria

Mariane Boschan	Lisl Klauber
Gertrude Brunner	Rixi Markus
Ethel Ernst	Ditta Riemer
Gretl Joseffy	Gertrude Schlesinger

II. Bermuda Bowl.

1950 (played in Bermuda). United States defeated Great Britain by 3,360 and Sweden-Iceland by 4,720; Sweden-Iceland defeated Great Britain by 1,940.

UNITED STATES	GREAT BRITAIN
John Crawford	Maurice Harrison-Gray (c)
Charles Goren	Leslie Dodds
George Rapée	Nico Gardener
Howard Schenken	Kenneth Konstam
Sidney Silodor	Joel Tarlo
Samuel Stayman	Louis Tarlo

SWEDEN-ICELAND

Einar Werner (c)	Nils-Olof Lilliehook
Gunnal Gudmundson	Einar Thorfinnson
Rudolph Kock	Jan Wohlin

1951 (played in Naples). United States defeated Italy by 116 IMPs.

UNITED STATES	ITALY
B. Jay Becker	Paoli Baroni
John Crawford	Eugenio Chiaradia
George Rapée	Pietro Forquet
Howard Schenken	Mario Franco
Samuel Stayman	Augusto Ricci
Julius Rosenblum (npc)	Guglielmo Siniscalco
	Carl'Alberto Perroux (npc)

1953 (played in New York). United States defeated Sweden by 8,260 points.

UNITED STATES	SWEDEN
B. Jay Becker	Dr. Einar Werner
John Crawford	Gunnar Anulf
Theodore Lightner	Rudolph Kock
George Rapée	Robert Larsen
Howard Schenken	Nils-Olof Lilliehöök
Samuel Stayman	Jan Wohlin
Joseph Cohan (npc)	

1954 (played in Monte Carlo). United States defeated France by 49 IMPs.

UNITED STATES	FRANCE
Cliff Bishop	Jacques Amouraben
Milton Ellenby	Rene Bacherich
Lewis Mathe	Jean Besse (Switz)
Don Oakie	Pierre Ghestem
William Rosen	Marcel Kornblum
Douglas Steen	Karl Schneider (Austria)
Benjamin Johnson (npc)	

1955 (played in New York). England defeated the United States by 5,420 points.

ENGLAND	UNITED STATES
Leslie Dodds	Cliff Bishop
Kenneth Konstam	Milton Ellenby
Adam Meredith	Lewis Mathe
Jordanis Pavlides	John Moran
Terrence Reese	William Rosen
Boris Schapiro	Alvin Roth
Reginald Corwen (npc)	Peter Leventritt (npc)

1956 (played in Paris). France defeated United States by a score of 342 IMPs to 288 IMPs.

FRANCE	UNITED STATES
René Bacherich	Myron Field
Pierre Ghestem	Charles Goren
Pierre Jaïs	Lee Hazen
Robert Lattès	Richard Kahn
Bertrand Romanet	Charles Solomon
Roger Trézel	Samuel Stayman
Baron Robert de Nexon (npc)	Jeff Glick (npc)

1957 (played in New York). Italy defeated United States by a score of 10,150 points.

ITALY	UNITED STATES
Walter Avarelli	Charles Goren
Giorgio Belladonna	Boris Koytchou
Eugenio Chiaradia	Peter Leventritt
Massimo de'Alelio	Harold Ogust
Pietro Forquet	William Seamon
Guglielmo Siniscalco	Helen Sobel

Carl'Alberto Perroux (npc)	R.L. (Skinny) Miles, Jr. (npc)

1958 (played in Como, Italy). Italy defeated United States 211 to 174 IMPs and Argentina 239 to 167 IMPs. United States defeated Argentina 255 to 193 IMPs.

ITALY	UNITED STATES
Walter Avarelli	B. Jay Becker
Eugenio Chiaradia	George Rapée
Massimo d'Alelio	Alvin Roth
Pietro Forquet	Sidney Silodor
Guglielmo Siniscalco	Tobias Stone
Carl'Alberto Perroux (npc)	Joseph Ripstra (npc)

ARGENTINA	
Carlos Cabanne	Alberto Blousson
Alejandro Castro	Ricardo Calvente
(co-captains)	Marcelo Lerner

1959 (played in New York). Italy defeated United States 233 to 183 IMPs and Argentina 218 to 178 IMPs. United States defeated Argentina 252 to 209 IMPs.

ITALY	UNITED STATES
Walter Avarelli	Harry Fishbein
Giorgio Belladonna	Sam Fry, Jr.
Eugenio Chiaradia	Leonard Harmon
Massimo d'Alelio	Lee Hazen
Pietro Forquet	Sidney Lazard
Guglielmo Siniscalco	Ivar Stakgold
Carl'Alberto Perroux (npc)	Charles Solomon (npc)

ARGENTINA	
Alberto Berisso	Arturo Jaques
Ricardo Calvente	Egisto Rocchi
Alejandro Castro	Dr. Luis Santa Coloma (npc)
Carlos Dibar	

1961 (played in Buenos Aires). Italy defeated Argentina, 422 to 282, defeated France, 371 to 261, defeated North America, 382 to 262. North America defeated Argentina, 411 to 284, defeated France 262 to 236. France defeated Argentina, 339 to 287.

ITALY	NORTH AMERICA
Walter Avarelli	John Gerber
Giorgio Belladonna	Paul Hodge
Eugenio Chiaradia	Norman Kay
Massimo d'Alelio	Peter Leventritt
Pietro Forquet	Sidney Silodor
Benito Garozzo	Howard Schenken
Carl'Alberto Perroux (npc)	Frank Westcott (npc)

FRANCE	ARGENTINA
René Bacherich	Jorje Bosco
Claude Deruy	Ricardo Calvente
Pierre Ghestem	Alejandro Castro
José le Dentu	Hector Cramer
Roger Trézel	Carlos Dibar
Robert de Nexon (npc)	Carlos Cabanne (npc)

1962 (played in New York). Italy defeated Argentina 420 to 328; defeated North America 331 to 305. North America defeated Argentina 400 to 242; defeated Great Britain 345 to 332. Great Britain defeated Argentina 318 to 311.

ITALY	NORTH AMERICA
Walter Avarelli	Charles Coon
Giorgio Belladonna	Mervin Key
Massimo d'Alelio	Lewis Mathe
Eugenio Chiaradia	Eric Murray
Pietro Forquet	George Nail
Benito Garozzo	Ron Von Der Porten
Carl'Alberto Perroux (npc)	John Gerber (npc)

GREAT BRITAIN	ARGENTINA
Nico Gardener	Luis Attaguile
Kenneth Konstam	Alberto Berisso
Anthony Priday	Carlos Cabanne
Claude Rodrigue	Ricardo Calvente
Albert Rose	Arturo Jaques
Alan Truscott	Egisto Rocchi
Louis Tarlo (npc)	Desiderio Blum (npc)

1963 (played in St. Vincent(. Italy defeated United States 313 to 294; defeated France 421 to 236; defeated Argentina 372 to 282. United States defeated France 340 to 251; defeated Argentina 496 to 261. France defeated Argentina 453 to 319. Played in June 1963.

ITALY	NORTH AMERICA
Giorgio Belladonna	Peter Leventritt
Eugenio Chiaradia	George Nail
Massimo de'Alelio	James Jacoby
Pietro Forquet	Robert Jordan
Benito Garozzo	Arthur Robinson
Camillo Pabis-Ticci	Howard Schenken
Carl'Alberto Perroux (npc)	John Gerber (npc)

FRANCE	ARGENTINA
René Bacherich	Luis Attaguile
Gérard Desrousseaux	Ricardo Calvente
Pierre Ghestem	Egisto Rocchi

Jacques Stetten	Marco Santamarina
Dr. Georges Théron	Alfredo Saravia
Léon Tintner	Luis Schenone
Baron Robert de Nexon (npc)	Guillermo Malbran (npc)

1965 (played in Buenos Aires). Italy defeated United States 304–230; defeated Argentina 325–237; defeated Great Britain 354–233. United States defeated Argentina 359–250. Because of charges of irregular procedure against the partnership of Terence Reese and Boris Schapiro, nonplaying captain Ralph Swimer of Great Britain forfeited the match with United States after leading 288–242 with twenty boards to play, and forfeited to Argentina after winning 380–184.

ITALY	UNITED STATES
Walter Avarelli	B. Jay Becker
Giorgio Belladonna	Ivan Erdos
Massimo d'Alelio	Dorothy Hayden
Pietro Forquet	Peter Leventritt
Benito Garozzo	Kelsey Petterson
Camillo Pabis Ticci	Howard Schenken
Sergio Osella (npc)	John Gerber (npc)
Carl'Alberto Perroux (co-captain)	

ARGENTINA	GREAT BRITAIN
Luis Attaguile	Jeremy Flint
Alberto Berisso	Maurice Harrison-Gray
Carlos Cabanne	Kenneth Konstam
Marcelo Lerner	Terence Reese
Egisto Rocchi	Albert Rose
Agustín Santamarina	Boris Schapiro
Eduardo Marquardt (npc)	Ralph Swimer (npc)

1966 (played in St. Vincent). Italy defeated North America 319–262; defeated Venezuela 362–203; defeated The Netherlands 326–198; defeated Thailand 486–143. North America defeated Venezuela 398–260; defeated The Netherlands 477–243; defeated Thailand 359–234. Venezuela defeated The Netherlands 331–247; defeated Thailand 326–290. The Netherlands defeated Thailand 293–230.

ITALY	NORTH AMERICA
Walter Avarelli	Philip Feldesman
Giorgio Belladonna	Robert Hamman
Massimo d'Alelio	Sammy Kehela
Pietro Forquet	Lewis Mathe
Benito Garozzo	Eric Murray
Camillo Pabis Ticci	Ira Rubin
Carl'Alberto Perroux (npc)	Julius Rosenblum (npc)

VENEZUELA	THE NETHERLANDS
Roberto Benaim	Moritz Blitzblum
David Berah	Pieter Boender
Mario Onorati	Hans Kreyns
Roger Rossignol	Leo Oudshoorn
Renato Straziota	R. De Leeuw
Francis Vernon	Bob Slavenburg
Jean Alpert (npc)	Capt. Gut Kramer (npc)

THAILAND
Ananta Boonsupa
Reggie Gaan
Benno Gimkiewicz
Hasan Istenveli
Somboom Nandhabiwat
Thawee Raengkhan (captain)

1967 (played in Miami Beach). Italy defeated North America 338–227 in the final; in the playoff for third place, France defeated Thailand 182–133. In the qualifying round robin, the scores were: Italy 170, North America 161, France 132, Thailand 73, Venezuela 64.

ITALY	NORTH AMERICA
Walter Avarelli	Edgar Kaplan
Giorgio Belladonna	Norman Kay
Massimo d'Alelio	Sammy Kehela
Pietro Forquet	Eric Murray
Benito Garozzo	William Root
Camillo Pabis Ticci	Alvin Roth
Guido Barbone (npc)	Julius Roseblum (npc)

FRANCE	THAILAND
Jean-Michel Boulenger	Ananta Boonsupa
Dr. Jacques Pariente	Reggie Gaan
Jean-Marc Roudinesco	Benno Gimkiewicz
Jacques Stetten	Somboon Nandhabiwat
Henri Svarc	K.W. Shen
Léon Tintner	Cherd Stiajitt
René Huni (npc)	Henrik Lau (npc)

VENEZUELA
Roberto Benaim
David Berah
Edgar Loynaz
M. Romanelli
Roger Rossignol
Francis Vernon
Robert Chapin (npc)

1969 (played in Rio de Janeiro). Italy defeated Taiwan 429–182 in the final; in the playoff for third place. North America defeated France 150–115. In the qualifying round robin, the scores were: Italy 185, Taiwan 166, North America 141, France 126, Brazil 116.

ITALY	TAIWAN
Walter Avarelli	Frank Hwang
Giorgio Belladonna	Patrick Huang
Massimo d'Alelio	Chi-Kuo Shen
Pietro Forquet	K.W. Shen
Benito Garozzo	Kovit Suchartkul
Camillo Pabis Ticci	Miafar Tai
Angelo Tracanella (npc)	Charles Wei (npc)

NORTH AMERICA	FRANCE
Billy Eisenberg	Jean-Michel Boulenger
Bobby Goldman	Gérard Desrousseaux
Robert Hamman	Jacques Stetten
Eddie Kantar	Henri Svarc
Sidney Lazard	Dr. Georges Théron
George Rapée	Léon Tintner
Oswald Jacoby (npc)	René Huni (npc)

BRAZIL
Pedro Paulo Assumpção
Marcelo Castello
Gabriel Chagas
Decio Coutinho
Roberto de Mello
Adelstano Porto D'Ave
Paulo Plinio de Barros (npc)

1970 (played in Stockholm). North America defeated Taiwan 64–14 victory points in the final; in the playoff for the third place. Norway defeated Brazil 24–16 victory points. In the qualifying round robin, the scores were: North America 229, Taiwan 151, Brazil 136, Norway 118, Italy 105.

NORTH AMERICA	TAIWAN
Billy Eisenberg	Conrad Cheng
Bobby Goldman	Elmer Hsiao
Robert Hamman	Patrick Huang
James Jacoby	Harry Lin
Michael Lawrence	Min-Fan Tai
Bobby Wolff	David Mao (npc)
Oswald Jacoby (npc)	

NORWAY	BRAZIL
Erik Höie	Pedro Assumpção
Tore Jensen	Paulo Plinio de Barros
Knut Koppang	Eduardo Bastos
Bjorn Larsen	Octavio Gabizo de Faria
Andre Ström	Sinesiom Ferreira
Willy Varnås	Gabriel Chagas
Baard Baardsen (npc)	Eros Amaral (npc)

ITALY
Giuseppe Barbarisi
Enrico Cesati
Bruno De Ritis
Vittorio La Galla
Armando Morini
Riccardo Tersch
Angelo Tracanella (npc)

1971 (played in Taipei). The United States Aces defeated France 243–182 in the final; in the 64-board playoff for third place Australia defeated Taiwan 174–134; in the 32-board playoff for fifth place. Brazil defeated North America 79–63. In the qualifying round robin, the scores were: Aces 228, France 182, Australia 154, Taiwan 118, Brazil 103, North America 98.

ACES	FRANCE
Billy Eisenberg	Jean-Michel Boulenger
Bobby Goldman	Pierre Jaïs
Bob Hamman	Jean-Marc Roudinesco
James Jacoby	Jean-Louis Stoppa
Michael Lawrence	Henri Svarc
Bobby Wolff	Roger Trézel
Oswald Jacoby (npc)	René Huni (npc)

AUSTRALIA	TAIWAN
Jim Borin	Conrad Cheng
Norma Borin	Stephen Chua
Richard Cummings	Elmer Hsiao
Denis Howard	Patrick Huang
Tim Seres	Vicente Reyes
Roelof Smilde	Min-Fan Tai
Jessel Rothfield (npc)	Charles Wei (npc)

BRAZIL	NORTH AMERICA
Eros Amaral	Edgar Kaplan
Pedro Paulo Assumpção	Norman Kay
Gabriel Chagas	Donald Krauss
Gabino Cintra	Lewis Mathe
Adelstano D'Ave	John Swanson
Tibor Kenedi	Richard Walsh
Alan Truscott (npc)	Lee Hazen (npc)

1973 (played in Guaruja, Brazil). Italy defeated the United States

Aces 330–205 in the final. In the qualifying round-robin, the scores were: Aces 177, Italy 176, Brazil 148, North America 140, Indonesia 101.

ITALY	ACES
Giorgio Belladonna	Mark Blumenthal
Benito Bianchi	Bobby Goldman
Pietro Forquet	Robert Hamman
Benito Garozzo	James Jacoby
Giuseppe Garabello	Michael Lawrence
Vito Pittala	Bobby Wolff
Sandro Salvetti (npc)	Ira G. Corn, Jr. (npc)

1974 (played in Venice) Italy defeated North America 195–166. Brazil defeated Indonesia in the playoff for third place, 182–181. In the qualifying round-robin the final Victory Point standings were: Italy 149; North America 148; Brazil 111; Indonesia 82, France 71; New Zealand 17.

ITALY	NORTH AMERICA
Giorgio Belladonna	Mark Blumenthal
Benito Bianchi	Bobby Goldman
Soldano de Falco	Robert Hamman
Pietro Forquet	Sammy Kehela
Arturo Franco	Eric Murray
Benito Garozzo	Bobby Wolff
Sandro Salvetti (npc)	Ira G. Corn, Jr. (npc)

1975 (played in Bermuda). Italy defeated North America 215–189 in the final. In the semifinals, Italy defeated Indonesia 280–134 and North America defeated France 159–147. In the qualifying round-robin, the scores were: Italy 134, North America 116, France 105, Indonesia 90, Brazil 73.

ITALY	NORTH AMERICA
Giorgio Belladonna	Billy Eisenberg
Gianfranco Facchini	Robert Hamman
Arturo Franco	Eddie Kantar
Benito Garozzo	Paul Soloway
Vito Pittala	John Swanson
Sergio Zucchelli	Bobby Wolff
Sandro Salvetti (npc)	Alfred Sheinwold (npc)

1976 (played in Monte Carlo). North America defeated Italy 232–198 in the final. In the qualifying round-robin, the scores were: North America 131; Italy 119; Israel 114; Brazil 109; Australia 82½; Hong Kong 32½.

NORTH AMERICA	ITALY
Billy Eisenberg	Giorgio Belladonna
Fred Hamilton	Pietro Forquet
Erik Paulsen	Benito Garozzo
Hugh Ross	Arturo Franco
Ira Rubin	Vito Pittala
Paul Soloway	Antonio Vivaldi
Dan Morse (npc)	Sandro Salvetti (npc)

1977 (played in Manila). The North American challengers defeated the North American defenders 245–214.5 in the final. In the qualifying round-robin the final Victory Point standings were: Defending Champions 136.75; North American Challengers 119.75; Sweden 94.75; Argentina 91; Australia 79; Taiwan 68.75.

NORTH AMERICA	DEFENDING CHAMPIONS
Billy Eisenberg	Fred Hamilton
Robert Hamman	Mike Passell
Eddie Kantar	Erik Paulsen
Paul Soloway	Hugh Ross
John Swanson	Ira Rubin
Bobby Wolff	Ron Von der Porten
Roger Stern (npc)	Jerome Silverman (npc)
Steve Altman (coach)	Ed Theus (npc)

1979 (played in Rio de Janeiro). North America defeated Italy 253–248 in the final. In the qualifying round-robin the final Victory Point standings were: Italy 180; North America 176; Australia 166; Taiwan 127½; Central America-Caribbean 123½; Brazil 108.

NORTH AMERICA	ITALY
Malcolm Brachman	Giorgio Belladonna
Billy Eisenberg	Soldano de Falco
Bobby Goldman	Arturo Franco
Eddie Kantar	Benito Garozzo
Mike Passell	Lorenzo Lauria
Paul Soloway	Vito Pittala
Ed Theus (npc)	Guido Barbone (npc)
	Sandro Salvetti (npc)

1981 (played in Port Chester, New York). United States defeated Pakistan 271–182⅓. In the semifinals United States defeated Poland 178–119; Pakistan beat Argentina 174–113⅔. The qualifying round-robin scores were: United States 160½; Pakistan 151; Poland 146; Argentina 145; Great Britain 142½; Australia 131; Indonesia 129.

UNITED STATES	PAKISTAN
Russ Arnold	Nishat Abedi
Robert Levin	Nisar Ahmed
Jeff Meckstroth	Jan-e-Alam Fazli
A. E. (Bud) Reinhold	Munir Ata-Ullah
Eric Rodwell	Zia Mahmood

John Solodar
Tom K. Sanders (npc)

Masoou Salim
Sattar Cochinwala (npc)

III. World Team Olympiad, held quadrennially.

1960 Turin, Italy.

OPEN WINNERS	OPEN RUNNERS-UP
France (16 V.P.)	Great Britain (15 V.P.)
Pierre Jaïs	Terence Reese
Roger Trezél	Boris Schapiro
Gérard Bourchtoff	Albert Rose
Claude Delmouly	Nico Gardener
René Bacherich	Jeremy Flint
Pierre Ghestem	Ralph Swimer
Baron Robert de Nexon (npc)	Louis Tarlo (npc)

WOMEN'S WINNERS
UAR
Helen Camara
Aida Choucry
Samika Fathy
Loula Gordon
Josephine Morcos
Suzanne Naguib
Sergio de Polo (npc)

1964 New York, USA

OPEN WINNERS	OPEN RUNNERS-UP
Italy	United States
Walter Avarelli	Robert Hamman
Giorgio Belladonna	Robert Jordan
Massimo d'Alelio	Donald Krauss
Pietro Forquet	Victor Mitchell
Benito Garozzo	Arthur Robinson
Camillo Pabis Ticci	Samuel Stayman
Sergio Osella (npc)	Frank Westcott (npc)

WOMEN'S WINNERS
Great Britain
Irene (Dimmie) Fleming
Fritzi Gordon
Jane Juan
Rixi Markus
Mary Moss
Dorothy Shanahan
Harold Franklin (npc)

1968 Deauville, France

OPEN WINNERS	OPEN RUNNERS-UP
Italy	United States
Walter Avarelli	Robert Jordan
Giorgio Belladonna	Edgar Kaplan
Massimo d'Alelio	Norman Kay
Pietro Forquet	Arthur Robinson
Benito Garozzo	William Root
Camillo Pabis Ticci	Alvin Roth
Angelo Tracanella (npc)	Julius Rosenblum (npc)

WOMEN'S WINNERS
Sweden
Britt Blom
Karin Eriksson
Eva Martensson
Rut Segander
Gunborg Silborn
Britta Werner
Lotty Saaby (npc)

1972 Miami Beach, Florida, USA

OPEN WINNERS	OPEN RUNNERS-UP
Italy	United States
Walter Avarelli	Bobby Goldman
Pietro Forquet	Jim Jacoby
Mimmo D'Alelio	Robert Hamman
Benito Garozzo	Paul Soloway
Giorgio Belladonna	Mike Lawrence
Camillo Pabis Ticci	Bobby Wolff
Umberto Barsotti (npc)	Lee Hazen (npc)

WOMEN'S WINNERS
Italy
Marisa Bianchi
Anna Valenti
Rina Jabes
Antonietta Robuado
Luciana Romanelli
Maria Venturini
Giovanni Pelucchi (npc)

1976, Monte Carlo

OPEN WINNERS	OPEN RUNNERS-UP
Brazil	Italy
Gabino Cintra	Giorgio Belladonna
Christiano Fonseca	Pietro Forquet

Marcelo Branco
Pedro Paulo Assumpção
Gabriel Chagas
Sergio Barbosa
Serge Apoteker (npc)

Benito Garozzo
Arturo Franco
Carlo Mosca
Silvio Sbarigia
Sandro Salvetti (npc)

WOMEN'S WINNERS
Italy
Anna Valenti
Rina Jabes
Maria Robaudo
Luciana Capodanno
Marisa D'Andrea
Marisa Bianchi
Giovanni Pelucchi (npc)

1980, Valkenburg, The Netherlands

OPEN WINNERS	OPEN RUNNERS-UP
France	United States
Paul Chemla	Paul Soloway
Christian Mari	Ira Rubin
Michel Lebel	Robert Hamman
Michel Perron	Bobby Wolff
Henri Svarc	Fred Hamilton
Philippe Soulet	Mike Passell
	Ira Corn (npc)

WOMEN'S WINNERS
United States
Dorothy Hayden Truscott
Emma Jean Hawes
Gail Moss
Jacqui Mitchell
Mary Jane Farell
Marilyn Johnson
Ruth McConnell (npc)

IV. World Pair Championship.

1962, Cannes, France

OPEN PAIRS WINNERS	OPEN PAIRS RUNNERS-UP
France	Great Britain
Pierre Jaïs	Terence Reese
Roger Trézel	Boris Schapiro

WOMEN'S PAIRS WINNERS	WOMEN'S RUNNERS-UP
Great Britain	France
Rixi Markus	Fanny Pariente
Fritzi Gordon	C. Serf

MIXED TEAMS WINNERS	MIXED TEAMS RUNNERS-UP
Great Britain	The Netherlands
Rixi Markus	Mme. Westerfield
Fritzi Gordon	Mme. Hoogenkamp
Boris Schapiro	Herman Filarski
Nico Gardener	A. Kornlijnslijper

1966, Amsterdam, The Netherlands

OPEN PAIRS WINNERS	OPEN PAIRS RUNNERS-UP
Netherlands	United States
Bob Slavenburg	Dr. John Fisher
Hans Kreyns	James Jacoby

WOMEN'S WINNERS	WOMEN'S RUNNERS-UP
Great Britain	United States
Joan Durran	Sue Sachs
Jane Juan	Nancy Gruver

MIXED PAIRS WINNERS	MIXED PAIRS RUNNERS-UP
United States	Great Britain
Mary Jane Farell	Joan Duran
Ivan Erdos	Maurice Weissberger

1970, Stockholm, Sweden

OPEN PAIRS WINNERS	OPEN PAIRS RUNNERS-UP
Austria	Italy
Fritz Babsch	Benito Garozzo
Peter Manhardt	Federico Mayer

WOMEN'S WINNERS	WOMEN'S RUNNERS-UP
United States	Great Britain
Mary Jane Farell	Rixi Markus
Marilyn Johnson	Fritzi Gordon

MIXED PAIRS WINNERS	MIXED PAIRS RUNNERS-UP
United States	Great Britain
Barbara Brier	Rixi Markus
Waldemar von Zedtwitz	Switzerland
	Georges Catzeflis

1974, Las Palmas, Spain

OPEN PAIRS WINNERS	OPEN PAIRS RUNNERS-UP
United States	Italy
Robert Hamman	Leandro Burgay
Bobby Wolff	Antonio Abato

WOMEN'S WINNERS	WOMEN'S RUNNERS-UP
Great Britain	South Africa
Fritzi Gordon	Gerda Goslar

Rixi Markus   Rita Jacobsen

MIXED PAIRS WINNERS   **MIXED PAIRS RUNNERS-UP**
Switzerland   United States
Loula Gordon   Jacqui Mitchell
Tony Trad   James Cayne

   1978, New Orleans, Louisiana USA

OPEN PAIRS WINNERS   **OPEN PAIRS RUNNERS-UP**
Brazil   Canada
Marcelo Branco   Eric Kokish
Gabino Cintra   Peter Nagy

WOMEN'S WINNERS   **WOMEN'S RUNNERS-UP**
United States   United States
Kathie Wei   Betty Ann Kennedy
Judi Radin   Carol Sanders

MIXED PAIRS WINNERS   **MIXED PAIRS RUNNERS-UP**
United States   United States
Barry Crane   James Jacoby
Kerri Shuman   Heitie Noland

   1982, Biarritz, France

OPEN PAIRS WINNERS   **OPEN PAIRS RUNNERS-UP**
United States   The Netherlands
Chip Martel   Max Rebattu
Lew Stansby   Anton Maas

WOMEN'S WINNERS   **WOMEN'S RUNNERS-UP**
United States   United States
Carol Sanders   Lynn Deas
Betty Ann Kennedy   Beth Palmer

MIXED PAIRS WINNERS   **MIXED PAIRS RUNNERS-UP**
Canada   United States
Dianna Gordon   Peggy Sutherlin
George Mittelman   John Sutherlin

V. Rosenblum Cup Teams.

   1978 (played in New Orleans, Louisiana). Poland defeated Brazil 164–80.

POLAND   BRAZIL
Marian Frenkiel   Gabriel Chagas
Andrzej Macieszczak   Pedro Paulo Assumpção
Andrzej Wilkosz   Gabino Cintra
Janusz Polec   Marcelo Branco
    Roberto Taunay
    Sergio Barbosa

   1982 (played in Biarritz, France) France defeated the United States 178–161.

FRANCE   UNITED STATES
Michel Lebel   Chip Martel
Philippe Soulet   Lew Stansby
Dominique Pilon   Peter Pender
Albert Feigenbaum   Hugh Ross
Pierre Schemeil (npc)   Kit Woolsey
    Ed Manfield

VI. Venice Trophy Teams.

   1974 (played in Venice, Italy). United States defeated Italy 297–262.*

UNITED STATES   ITALY
Betty Cohn   Marisa Bianchi
Emma Jean Hawes   Luciana Canessa
Betty Ann Kennedy   Rina Jabes
Marietta Passell   Antonietta Robaudo
Carol Sanders   Anna Valenti
Dorothy Hayden Truscott   Maria Venturini
Ruth McConnell (npc)   Giovanni Pelucchi (npc)

   1976 (played in Monte Carlo). United States defeated Great Britain 395–211.*

UNITED STATES   GREAT BRITAIN
Emma Jean Hawes   Charley Esterson
Betty Ann Kennedy   Nicola Gardener
Jacqui Mitchell   Fritzi Gordon
Gail Moss   Sandra Landy
Carol Sanders   Rixi Markus
Dorothy Hayden Truscott   Rita Oldroyd
Ruth McConnell (npc)   Graham Cooke (npc)
Peter Pender (coach)

   1978 (played in New Orleans, Louisiana. In the final the United States defeated Italy 229½–140. Qualifying round-robin scores were: United States 71; Italy 65; Argentina 49; Australia 40; Philippines 35.

UNITED STATES   ITALY
Mary Jane Farell   Marisa Bianchi
Emma Jean Hawes   Luciana Capodanno
Marilyn Johnson   Marisa D'Andrea
Jacqui Mitchell   Enrica Gut
Gail Moss   Andreina Morini
Dorothy Hayden Truscott   Anna Valenti

Ruth McConnell (npc)   Guido Barbone (npc)

   1981 (played in Port Chester, New York). In the final Great Britain defeated the United States, 160⅔–122. Qualifying round-robin scores were: United States 181½; Great Britain 173; Brazil 170; Australia 144½; Venezuela 100.

GREAT BRITAIN   UNITED STATES
Pat Davies   Nancy Gruver
Maureen Dennison   Edith Kemp
Nicola Gardener   Betty Ann Kennedy
Sandra Landy   Judi Radin
Sally Sowter   Carol Sanders
Diana Williams   Katherine Wei
Derek Rimington (npc)   C. C. Wei (npc)
    Ron Andersen (coach)

Future Tournaments

1983   Stockholm, Sept. 26 — Oct. 8
1984   Seattle, Oct. 27 — Nov. 10
1985   New Delhi, India
1986   ACBL site to be determined
1987   Jamaica
1988   European site to be determined

WORLD MASTER. See WORLD BRIDGE FEDERATION PLAYER RANKINGS.

WORLD OLYMPICS. See WORLD PAR CONTESTS.

WORLD PAIRS CHAMPIONSHIP. A tournament conducted quadrennially by the WORLD BRIDGE FEDERATION consisting of three pair events — Open Pairs, Ladies Pairs and Mixed Pairs — plus the ROSENBLUM CUP TEAMS. For results see WORLD CHAMPIONSHIPS.

WORLD PAR CONTESTS. International events using prepared deals (see PAR CONTESTS). The idea of a series of par tournaments conducted throughout the world was conceived by ELY CULBERTSON and in 1932 the first World Bridge Olympic, using the parhand format, was held. Culbertson founded the National Bridge Association, a nonprofit corporation, in the same year, to conduct the tournaments. The bridge world's principal experts, regardless of their affiliation in the bridge politics of those times, constructed the prepared deals, and Culbertson's staff did the central management and scoring. Each contestant paid a fee of one dollar, of which half went to the game captain (who pre-arranged the hands and directed his game), and half was retained by the NBA. In 1932 and 1933, both American and World Olympics were conducted: from 1934 on, only the World Olympics. In 1934 self-dealing cards (marked on their backs to show which player should receive each card for the particular deal) and folding duplicate boards (later called bridge WALLETS) were supplied without extra charge by the NBA. The World Bridge Olympic reached its peak in 1934 with 70 countries and nearly 90,000 players entered, but even in that year the NBA lost money. In 1938 the ACBL took over the management, with WILLIAM Mc KENNEY in charge and GEOFFREY MOTT-SMITH constructing the hands, but problems of foreign exchange as well as diminished interest caused the tournament to be abandoned after 1941.

   The Olympic trophies were famous. For the American event, the two largest silver trophies of bridge history were provided. One of them is now

---

*Non-World Championship event.

the MCKENNEY TROPHY; the other was lost in circumstances that had a lasting effect on insurance law. A winner, entitled to one year's possession only, pawned the trophy. A court ruled that since it was his honest intention to redeem it within the year, he was not liable although, he found himself later without funds to redeem it, nor was the pawnbroker responsible for having sold it when the time for redemption had passed. The insurance underwriter paid its value to the NBA. The two World trophies each contained $5,000 worth of pure platinum but Culbertson, who donated them, never relinquished personal title to them and sold them for their value in platinum when the tournament was discontinued. Individual prizes were given to all international and national winners and to state winners in the United States and provincial winners in Canada, both North-South and East-West, so the list of winners for each year was long indeed.

In 1951, the World Par Contest was revived by Australia and won by Dr. J. L. Thwaites and Dr. E. L. Field of Melbourne, Australia, in that year. It was held in 1961 and 1963 under the auspices of the World Bridge Federation. The WBF intended to hold this event biennially, but it has not been held since 1963. The organizers in 1961 and 1963 were MICHAEL J. SULLIVAN and ROBERT E. WILLIAMS (Australia). Winners of these events, which had the status of World Championships, were:

1932	N–S	Byrne Baldwin, Ruth Baldwin, East Orange, NJ
	E–W	Lewis Frank, Robert Mayer, Detroit, MI
1933	N–S	Hilda Slager, Fred Levy, Montgomery, AL
	E–W	Leo Craine, J. Fredrick Benedict, Sherburne, NJ *(tied with)*
		Otto Krefting, Isak Nielson, Oslo, Norway
1934	N–S	Dr. Eugene Hilb, Robert Darvas, Budapest, Hungary
	E–W	Mrs. Gene Hill, Mrs. George Whitaker, Winston-Salem, NC
1935	N–S	Dr. L. L. von Barkow, Mrs. C. von Kamensky, Dresden, Germany
	E–W	Popy Lotou, Stephen Zotos, Athens, Greece
1936	N–S	R. E. Horner, Alfred Harris, Ottawa, Canada, *(tied with)*
		S. Rivlin, Capt. W. H. Ricardo, Cardiff, Wales
	E–W	Dr. Paul Stern, Dr. Paul Kaltenegger, Vienna, Austria
1937	N–S	Dr. O. P. Hampton, Jr., Walter Boeger, University City, MO
	E–W	William Savery, Jr., J. E. Muckley, Seattle, Wash.
1938	N–S	Tore Sandgren, Bertil Fant, Stockholm, Sweden
	E–W	Irwin Fisher, Harold Karp, Baltimore, MD
1940	N–S	J. M. Learmonth, E. Learmonth, Maracaibo, Venezuela
	E–W	Mrs. A. C. Bryant, Mrs. C. H. Drury, Ketchikan, Alaska
1941	N–S	Robert Willson, George Gooden, San Francisco, CA
	E–W	Marjorie Foote, Charles Miller, Jr., Phoenix, AZ
		Terrence Reese, Claude Rodrigue, London, England
		Gerard Desrousseaux, Dr. Bernard Romanet, Paris, France
1961		Terrence Reese, Claude Rodrigue, London, England
1963		Gerard Desrousseaux, Dr. Bernard Romanet, Paris, France

United States winners were:

1932		(International winners: see above.)
1933		(International winners: see above.)
1934	N–S	Elsieh Powell, Robert Powell, Freeport, TX
	E–W	(International winners: see above.)
1935	N–S	Cecile Guthrie, G. A. Smith, Conneaut, OH
	E–W	Mrs. Theodore Ahrenbeck, Jr., M. O. McDonald, Houston, TX
1936	N–S	Arthur Cowperthwait, Tucson, AZ, Ralph Cash, Phoenix, AZ
	E–W	George Sherbaum, Memphis, TN
		Larry Shurlds, Shelby, TN

1937		(International winners: see above.)
1938	N–S	W. H. Gharrity, Mrs. W. H. Gharrity, Chippewa Falls, WI
	E–W	(International winners: see above.)
1939	N–S	Marcella Miller, Dr. Mandel Shimberg, Leavenworth, KS
	E–W	Anton Bugge, Mrs. C. C. Covington, Houston, TX
1940	N–S	G. R. Trimmer, Dell Keating, Glasgow, Mont.
	E–W	Mrs. Galloway Morris, Sylvester Lowery, Philadelphia, PA
1941		(International winners: see above.)
1961		Lawrence Rosler, Murray Hill, NJ
		Roger Stern, New York, NY
1963		Lawrence Rosler, Murray Hill, NJ
		Roger Stern, New York, NY

WORLD TEAM OLYMPIAD. A WBF tournament conducted quadrenially starting in 1960, consisting of an open event and a women's team event. In 1960 NCBOs having a very large number of members were allowed to enter more than one team. On this basis Sweden entered two teams and the United States entered four in the open event. Since 1960 each NCBO has been allowed to enter only one team in each event of the Olympiad. For results see WORLD CHAMPIONSHIPS (III); for method of team selection in the United States see INTERNATIONAL OPEN TEAM SELECTION, INTERNATIONAL WOMEN'S TEAM SELECTION, WORLD TEAM OLYMPIAD WOMEN'S SELECTION.

WORLD TEAM OLYMPIAD WOMEN'S SELEC-TION. The United States has sent women's teams to each of the World Women's Team Olympiads, using various selection methods. For the 1960 event, a committee consisting of the five most recent ACBL presidents attending the 1959 Fall North American Championships selected the team, by choosing three pairs of women who finished first or second in any NAC championship event during 1959.

For 1964, a trial by pairs was held, similar to the trials held during that period for the INTERNATIONAL OPEN TEAM SELECTION. For 1968 a round-robin was held, for which four pairs qualified. Each pair played a 32-board match in partnership with each of the other pairs, and npc MARGARET WAGAR was empowered to select any three of the four pairs.

For 1972, women's teams were to earn points in the major NAC team championships and play off to determine the 1972 U.S. women's team. However, one team amassed so many points that it was designated without a playoff.

For 1976, women were permitted to earn *selection points*, either as a team or as pairs on all-women teams in the Vanderbilt, Spingold, Reisinger and Spring Women's Team events. The available points ranged from 1 point for being runner-up in the Spring Women's Teams to 28 for winning the Vanderbilt of Spingold. To be selected intact, a team must have won more qualification points than any individual pair, except that if there was only one higher pair, a four-person team plus the high-ranking pair would form the six-member team.

For 1980, women earned qualifying points on all-women teams in the Vanderbilt, Spingold, Reisinger, Grand National and Women's Knockout Team events. The Olympiad Qualifying Points Schedule for the 1980 U.S. Ladies team showed a range from .7 of a qualification point for finishing 17–32 in the Women's Knockout to 21 for winning the Vanderbilt, Spingold, Reisinger or Grand National. Rules provided that qualification points be *declared* to the entire team, without specifying partnerships or by pairs, but that should the original team be reduced to three or fewer members, points previously credited to the team were lost.

The following were U.S. women's teams in the first six Olympiads:

1960	1964
Agnes Gordon	Agnes Gordon
Dorothy Hayden	Muriel Kaplan
Malvine Klausner	Alicia Kempner
Helen Portugal	Helen Portugal
Sylvia Schwartz	Stella Rebner
Jo Sharp	Jan Stone
Charles Solomon (npc)	Paul Hodge (npc)
1968	1972
Hermine Baron	Mary Jane Farell
Nancy Gruver	Emma Jean Hawes
Emma Jean Hawes	Marilyn Johnson
Dorothy Hayden	Jacqui Mitchell
Suzanne Sachs	Peggy Solomon
Rhoda Walsh	Dorothy Hayden Truscott
Margaret Wagar (npc)	Margaret Wagar (npc)
1976	1980
Mary Jane Farell	Mary Jane Farell
Emma Jean Hawes	Emma Jean Hawes
Marilyn Johnson	Marilyn Johnson
Jacqui Mitchell	Jacqui Mitchell
Gail Moss	Gail Moss
Dorothy Hayden Truscott	Dorothy Hayden Truscott
Ruth McConnell (npc)	Ruth McConnell (npc)

See also VENICE TROPHY.

WORTHLESS SINGLETON/DOUBLETON. A holding of one or two cards below honor rank in a suit; usually at notrump play such a holding is a detriment to success. In the trump suit, either holding is less than adequate for trump support until the suit has been rebid twice.

WRITTEN BIDDING. A variation in the bidding technique, so that each bidder writes his bid on a sheet (designed to facilitate the placing of each bid in a proper box) which is passed to him as it becomes his turn to bid. The theory is that any extra time a player might take in a huddle can be construed as a review of previous bidding, as shown on the sheet, and no information can be conveyed to the partner by mannerism, gesture, or inflection, and the need for a review of the bidding at any time is removed. The pad passed around is frequently referred to as the DUMB BIDDER. It has also been used in International Matches, because it lends itself to symbolic notation, understood even with a severe language barrier. See BIDDING BOXES, FRANCO BOARD.

WRONG BOARD. Occasionally the play of a wrong board is commenced before it is discovered that it is a wrong board. if this occurs, the director should be summoned and he will act under LAWS OF DUPLICATE, Law 15.

WRONG SIDE. The hand of the declaring partnership which is less well equipped to cope with the opening lead. See RIGHT SIDE.

X

X. (1) A symbol used in lower case in bridge literature to signify an insignificant small card in any suit, a card lower than a 10. Thus, K–x–x, means the king and two low cards in that suit. (2) A capital X indicates a double, and is used in recording bidding by hand in important matches. Similarly, XX means "redouble."

X PLUS ONE, RULE OF. See RULE OF X PLUS ONE.

Y

YARBOROUGH. Any hand at bridge containing no card higher than a nine, named after an English lord who customarily would wager 1,000 pounds to one against the chance of such a hand being held by a player. The odds against holding a Yarborough are 1,827 to one. In post-mortem discussions the term "Yarborough" has gained currency to describe bad hands which do not meet the strict requirements.

YOUNGEST LIFE MASTER. The first player to be recognized as the Youngest Life Master was JOHN R. CRAWFORD who was Life Master #19 in 1939. He was 24 years old, and much the youngest of a select group of players. It was not until 1952 that the 20–year age barrier was broken by "Quiz Kid" RICHARD FREEMAN. DIANE BARTON-PAINE was the first woman to achieve this status and she kept that record until 1973 when CONNIE McGINLEY broke her record by seven months. REGINA BARNES smashed both records in 1976 when she broke the 15–year barrier. In 1982 first Adair Gellman and a short time later Tricia Thomas broke the youngest Woman Life Master record. Gellman was 14 years, 6 months and 4 days. Thomas was 14 years, 26 days. In 1981 DOUGLAS HSIEH became a Life Master at the age of 11 years, 10 months and 4 days. The following players were the Youngest Life Masters at the time they achieved that status:

1952	Richard Freeman	18 yrs. 10 mos. 7 days
1961	Diane Barton-Paine	18 yrs. 12 days
1965	Kyle Larsen	15 yrs. 11 mos.
1968	Joseph Livezey	15 yrs. 5 mos.
1973	Bobby Levin	15 yrs. 4 mos.
1975	Michael Freed	15 yrs. 20 days
1976	Regina Barnes	14 yrs. 11 mos.
1977	Steve Cochran	14 yrs. 5 mos. 20 days
1980	Billy Hsieh	13 yrs. 7 mos. 15 days
1981	Andrew Kaufman	13 yrs. 4 mos. 15 days
1982	Douglas Hsieh	11 yrs. 10 mos. 4 days

See also KING OR QUEEN OF BRIDGE.

YUGOSLAVIA BRIDGE FEDERATION (BRIDGE SAVEZ JUGOSLAVIJE). Reactivated in 1967 in Belgrade, with approximately 250 members, the federation is located principally in Belgrade, Zagreb and Ljubljana. Prior to World War II, the League was an active member of the European Bridge League, tying for second place in the 1935 European Championships in Brussels, and finishing second in 1939 at The Hague. During the years when there was no official organization, Yugoslav players continued to enter international tournaments — World Pairs Championship 1962, European Championships and International Bridge Festivals in Austria, Italy and Yugoslavia — and national events were held for Open Teams and Open Pairs. The Federation is a member of the European Bridge League and has applied for membership in the WBF.

Officers, 1982:

President: Prijezda Popovic

Secretary: Branislav Vasiljevic, Knez Mihajova 24
  11000 Beograd, Yugoslavia

Z

ZERO. The lowest score possible on a duplicate board, hence loosely, a very bad score. It also refers to a lost board in a team-of-four contest. Note that a score on a board of zero points (all four hands pass) may be any matchpoint score from none to top.

ZERO OR TWO HIGHER LEADS. An opening lead convention designed to eliminate the ambiguity of standard honor leads. The lead of the 10 or 9 promises either zero or two higher honors in the suit, while the lead of the jack denies any higher honors. Leads of the ace, king, and queen retain their standard meanings. These leads may be used against any contract or only against notrump, and may also be used throughout the deal. Proponents claim that the opening leader's partner usually has no trouble deducing the true situation, and that it keeps declarer in the dark better than do JOURNALIST LEADS or RUSINOW LEADS.

ZIMBABWE BRIDGE UNION. This union was formed initially as the Rhodesia Bridge Union in 1967, to replace the Central Africa Bridge Union. Membership of the Union for some years included clubs in Mozambique and Malawi, but in 1982 was comprised of six clubs in Zimbabwe with a total of some 600 members. The Union has a program of 10 annual national and provincial tournaments together with an International Congress for players from neighboring countries. Past Chairmen are: AUBREY G. PETERS, 1968–1969, 1976; J. Gordon Heather, 1970–1971; Russell A. Court, 1972–1973; David F. Salomon, 1974–1975; Brian Freeman, 1977–1978, TOM J.E. BOURDILLON, 1979–1981.

Officers, 1982:

Chairman: William Hepburn

Secretary: Mrs. Jane Ivy, P.O. Box 1074, Harare,
  Zimbabwe

ZIP SWISS. A special version of Swiss Teams designed to be finished in a short time, usually as a one-session event at the end of a day's championship play. The usual format is to conduct the game with five-board matches, five minutes per board, and five matches per game.

ZIRINSKY FORMULA. A method of determining victory points long used in Far East Championships. All "push" boards (with zero IMPs) are scored as one to each team. Then the winning score is multiplied by four and divided by the losing score, with a maximum of eight VPs. The losing team received the balance of the eight points at stake. The "push board" provision was introduced by the inventor, Victor Zirinsky of Hong Kong, as a modification to

the original idea which gave inequitable results in low-scoring matches.

LEADING BRIDGE PERSONALTIES

A

AARONS, Stephen H. (b. 1937) of Toronto represented Canada in the World Mixed Pairs, Rosenblum Cup Teams 1978. His regional wins include Can-Am Open Teams 1969, Canadian Nat'l Men's Pairs 1974, District 2 GNT, Zone 1 1979, Gateway City Swiss Teams Flt. A 1981. An alumnus of the University of Toronto, Aarons is a barrister and solicitor and was appointed Queen's Counsel in 1977. He served Ontario Unit as director 1966–1972 and was District 2 director 1972–1975.

ABEDI, Nishat M. H. (b. 1939) of Karachi, Pakistan, born in Allahabad, India, accountant, one of the leading players of Pakistan, placed second in the Bermuda Bowl 1981. He has won numerous national titles and has accumulated more than 50,000 ranking points in Pakistan.

ABELSON, Roger P. (b. 1943) of Berkeley CA won Life Master Men's Pairs 1981. His regional wins include Tri-State BAM Teams and Keystone BAM Teams 1969. Abelson, a graduate of Cornell, is active in community development. During the mid-Sixties he worked with Dr. Martin Luther King Jr. as a community organizer in voter registration drive in the South, was a national organizer against U.S. involvement in the Vietnam War and organized the first International Children's Parade for UNICEF.

ABENTE SAGUIER, Dr. Victor Fernando (Quiqui) (b. 1910) of Asunción, Paraguay represented Paraguay in five South American Championships. Doctor in Law and Social Sciences at the Facultad de Derecho of the Universidad Nacional de Asunción since 1937, he formerly was editor of two newspapers and is a frequent contributor to *Bridge Argentino*. Abente Saguier was the founder and first president of Paraguay Bridge Association in 1953. His non-bridge honors include the "Cruzeiro de Sul" awarded him by Brazil in 1937.

ABRAHAMS, Stanley J. (b. 1940) of Auckland, New Zealand, born in Glasgow, Scotland, a commercial manager, represented New Zealand in the Bermuda Bowl 1974, World Team Olympiad 1972, Far East Championships 1973, 1978, 1981. He has won many major New Zealand tournaments, including Nat'l KO Teams 1972, NZ Open Teams 1978, 1979, 1980.

ABRAMS, Elsie of Pompano Beach FL, registered nurse and bridge club director, won Fall NAC Mixed Pairs 1960 and placed second in Fall NAC Women's Teams 1963. Her regional wins include New England Fall Mixed Teams 1958, KO Teams 1960, Southeastern Women's Teams 1962, 1963, 1964, 1971.

ABRAMS, Marilyn (b. 1922) of Los Angeles won Fall secondary NAC Women's Pairs 1977, Pacific Southwest Women's Pairs 1971, California Capital Women's Pairs 1981, Bridge Week Women's Pairs 1979, 1981, Master Women's Pairs 1981, Mixed Teams 1975, Golden State Women's Pairs 1974, Mixed Pairs 1977. A former bookkeeper, Abrams now teaches bridge.

ACH, Jacques L., Sr. (1903–1971) of Cincinnati, attorney and accountant, co-invented the Ach-Kennedy schedules (1935) which were the first HOWELL MOVEMENTS with perfectly BALANCED COMPARISONS. Ach graduated from Harvard University. He was a contributor to *The Bridge World* in the Thirties.

ACHMATOWICZ, Dr. Selim (b. 1933) of Warsaw, Poland, university chemistry lecturer, was npc of Poland's International Team 1961–1964. He won the Baltic Bowl 1964, Hungarian Open Pairs 1959, Balaton Bowl 1963. His national titles include Open Teams 1962, 1963, 1964, 1968.

ACKERMAN, Gerald W. (Jerry) (b. 1925) of Ramsey NJ won the MARCUS CUP 1954, Pocono Open Teams 1951, Asbury Park Open Pairs 1951. He has served the North Jersey BA as a member of the Board 1958–1964, and as vice president 1960–1961.

ADAMS, Bill R. (Tornado) (b. 1930) of Wichita KS has been a national tournament director since 1970. He is a former supervisor at Boeing Company.

ADAMS, Charles True (1900–1942) of Chicago, utilities attorney, was a valuable contributor to the OFFICIAL SYSTEM. One of the first widely read authors on contract bridge, his *Contract Bridge Standardized* was published in 1928. Adams was co-editor-in-chief (with MILTON C. WORK) of *The Bridge Magazine*, and Director of the AMERICAN AUCTION BRIDGE LEAGUE in 1927. See BIBLIOGRAPHY, C.

ADAMS, Dee (Mrs. W. Harrison) of Memphis, real estate broker, won Mississippi Valley Women's Pairs 1961, Mid-South Spring Open Teams 1971, Women's Pairs 1974.

ADAMS, Maynard D. (Ace) (b. 1912) of Lincolnshire IL, company president, won Fall NAC Men's Teams 1946, FABER CUP 1948, and five Open Teams — All-American, Central States, Midwest, Western States and Great Lakes regionals between 1943 and 1956.

ADAMS, Peggy (d. 1974) of New York City was an ACBL staff member who worked in the masterpoint department from 1948 to 1966 and wrote the feature "Club Corner" for the *Bulletin*. Under the stage name of Peggy Hart she was in vaudeville in her youth, playing the Keith Circuit and picture theaters. In 1950 she became Life Master No. 300 and at that time was the second Life Master in ACBL headquarters, the first being the late ALVIN LANDY. She won the Fall NAC Women's Teams 1955 and was second in the same event 1952.

ADAMS, Robert T. (b. 1923) of Lafayette CA, research chemist, won Fall NAC Mixed Pairs 1957. His numerous regional titles include Fall NAC secondary Mixed Pairs 1968, Bridge Week Mixed Pairs 1957, Open Teams 1964, 1973, All-Western Open Teams 1960, KO Teams 1967, Oregon Trail Open Teams 1965, Pacific Southwest Open Teams 1969. He authored a bridge column for the American Chemical Society magazine, *The Vortex*, 1967–1978.

ADAMS, W. Harrison (b. 1926) of Memphis, attorney, won Southern Conf. Fall Master Pairs, Men's Pairs 1958, Mid-South Spring Open Teams 1971.

ADAMS, William E. (b. 1917) of Hamden CT, retired aeronautical and product engineer, won the Fall NAC Senior Master Individual 1953, secondary Swiss Teams 1972, New England Mixed Teams 1961, 1962, Open Teams 1968, Swiss Teams 1969.

ADELSMAN, Rony M. (b. 1951) of Chicago won several regional events including Central States Swiss Teams 1978, Midwest Spring Master Pairs, Men's Swiss Teams 1981, Midwest Fall Master Pairs 1981. Adelsman, a graduate of M.I.T. and Purdue, is assistant professor of Accounting and Management Science at the University of Chicago.

ADKINS, Miles C. (b. 1928) of Coulee City WA, wheat farmer, won Oregon Trail Master Pairs 1968, Intermountain Men's Pairs 1972, KO Teams 1971, 1981, Open Pairs 1981, Pacific Southwest Men's Pairs 1970, Puget Sound Open Pairs 1974.

ADLER, Betty (Mrs. Julian, formerly Mrs. Raymond Goldberg) (b. 1927) of Baltimore represented the United States in the World Mixed Teams 1972 and won Summer NAC Women's Pairs 1959, Spring NAC Women's KO Teams 1977, 1979, placed second in 1980 and in Summer Master Mixed Teams 1970, 1974, 1978. Adler is the winner of numerous regional events since 1961. She has been an active bridge teacher since 1960 and a qualified director since 1981, directing mainly on bridge cruises.

ADLER, Julian (Buddy) (b. 1917) of Baltimore, company president, represented the United States in the World Mixed Teams 1972 and placed second in Summer NAC Non-Master Pairs 1961, Master Mixed Teams 1970, 1974, 1978. He won several regional events including Keystone Swiss Teams 1971, 1972, 1973, 1974, Pittsburgh Open Pairs 1979, Washington Bridge Week Swiss Teams 1976, District 6 GNT 1975.

ADLER, Patricia. See SHEINWOLD, PATRICIA.

AFDAHL, Darwin F. (b. 1940) of Virginia Beach VA has been a U.S. Navy pilot since 1962. He won Rocky Mountain Open Pairs 1970, British Columbia

KO Teams 1973, Mid-Atlantic Men's Pairs 1976, Open Swiss Teams 1978, Open Pairs 1979, Men's Swiss Teams 1979.

AGRAN, Nat (b. 1908) of Bradenton FL, formerly a Philadelphia lawyer, won the BEYNON TROPHY 1948, Eastern States Mixed Pairs 1951, Mid-Atlantic Fall Open Teams 1955, Sun City Swiss Teams 1981, Gold Coast Swiss Teams 1981.

AGRUSS, Billie (b. 1913) of San Diego won Central States Open Teams 1949, Mixed Pairs 1950, All-American Open Teams 1948, Mississippi Valley Open Teams 1949. Agruss taught bridge and English in Korea and Taiwan, and English in China during temporary residence in those countries.

AGUW, Maximiliaan, (b. 1941) of Manado, Indonesia, police officer, represented Indonesia in the Bermuda Bowl 1973, 1974, 1981, World Team Olympiad 1976, 1980. He was Far East champion 1972, 1973, 1979, 1981, and has won many national pair and team events. Before taking up bridge in 1968, he won several regional chess championships.

AHMED, Nisar (b. 1936) of Karachi, Pakistan, chartered accountant, placed second in the Bermuda Bowl 1981. He was Asian champion 1981, placed second in the Far East Championships 1979 and won many national titles.

AJANIA, Nurdin G. (b. 1934) of Nairobi, Kenya, financial director, represented Kenya in the World Team Olympiad 1968, 1980, World Open Pairs 1978.

AKTURK, Hans (b. 1932) of Ann Arbor MI, born in Kars, Turkey, won Upper New York State Swiss Teams 1973, All-American Swiss Teams 1975, Motor City Master Pairs 1980, Great Lakes Open Pairs 1974, Men's Swiss Teams 1977, 1979, Men's Pairs 1977, Mixed Pairs 1977, Master Swiss Teams 1979, 1980. A company director, Akturk is listed in *Who's Who in Finance and Industry*.

ALBANO, Helen D. of Newark NJ was a charter member of the ABTA and its president in 1967. She was president and founder of "Bridge for the Blind," a non-profit organization of some 118 volunteers who teach bridge to the blind throughout the United States, Canada, South Africa, Iran and Israel. Albano formerly wrote a column titled "Chuckles" for the ABTA *Quarterly* and is the author of the popular textbook, *Analysis and Practical Application of the Goren Method*. Her textbook was translated into Braille, together with her program of necessary lessons and techniques. See BIBLIOGRAPHY, C.

ALBARRAN, Pierre (1894–1960) of Paris, France, born of French parentage in the West Indies, was the leading figure in French bridge until his death. European champion in 1935, he represented France on 32 occasions including the Challenge Match against the FOUR ACES in 1935 and in the European Championships in 1950. Albarran won 19 national championships particularly in the period 1932–1939. His chief contributions to theory were a distributional count, ACE-SHOWING RESPONSES to the 2♣ forcing opening bid, and the development of CANAPÉ, or bidding a short suit before a long one. This principle has been followed by many leading French players, such as PIERRE JAÏS and ROGER TRÉZEL, and has influenced the ROMAN and NEAPOLITAN systems which have won for Italy many Bermuda Bowls. Albarran also was twice member of the French Davis Cup team during the years when France was a tennis power. His many writings include *Canapé* and *Encyclopédie du Bridge Moderne*; with BARON de NEXON *Notre Méthode de Bridge*, and with JOSE le DENTU *Le Memento du Bridge, Souvenirs et Secrets, Le Championnat du Monde de Bridge, Bridge pour tous*, and *Cent Donnes Extraordinaires*. See BIBLIOGRAPHY, E, G.

ALBERSHEIM, Alberta G. (Mrs. Walter J.) (b. 1906) of Waban MA, placed second in Fall NAC Women's Pairs 1958 and won Eastern States Mixed Pairs 1954, Mixed Teams 1967, New England Master Pairs 1972, Fall NAC secondary Women's Pairs 1980, Summer NAC secondary Open Pairs Flt. B 1981. She served as a Board member of Eastern Massachusetts BA for 10 years and was treasurer of the Summer NAC 1970. A graduate of New York University Law School 1929, Albersheim is a former NY attorney. She has 19 grandchildren from her two natural children and six adopted foreign children.

ALBERT, Michael L. (b. 1938) of Omaha NE, formerly of Kingston, Jamaica, food broker, won several regional events including Motor City Men's Swiss Teams 1980, Big Sky Master Pairs 1981, Mississippi Valley Men's Pairs 1981.

ALCONE, Isabelle (Isa) (b. 1920) of New York City, born in China, co-owner of a bridge club, won Spring NAC secondary Individual 1962, Fall NAC secondary Women's Teams 1968, NY-NJ Mixed Pairs 1969.

ALCORN, Margaret. See GAER, MARGARET.

ALDER, Phillip D. (b. 1951) of London, England, editor of *Bridge Magazine*, represented Great Britain in the CAMROSE TROPHY match 1980, Junior Camrose 1971, 1972, Junior European and Junior Common Market 1976. His national wins include Two Stars Pairs Championship in 1973. He is the inventor of Alder Transfer Preempts. An honors graduate of University College, Alder formerly taught computer science and chemistry.

ALDERTON, George A., II (1904–1982) of Detroit was ACBL president in 1945, ACBL vice president, ACBL Honorary Member in 1956 and former president of the Midwest Conference and Michigan BA. Born in Saginaw MI, Alderton was a 1928 graduate of the University of Michigan Law School and had been a probate and tax attorney in private practice until his death. He won Midwest Open Pairs 1949.

ALDRICH, Clarence (Clayton) W. (1871–1961), a Cleveland furniture store owner, was active in form-

ing the AMERICAN BRIDGE LEAGUE in 1927. He was president of the ABL in 1930 and a member of the executive committee in 1933.

d'ALELIO, Massimo (Mimmo) (b. 1916) of Naples, Italy, residing in Rome, lawyer and advertising man, WBF Grand Master #4, one of the world's great players, was Bermuda Bowl champion 1957, 1958, 1959, 1961, 1962, 1963, 1964, 1965, 1966, 1967, 1968, 1969, 1972, European champion 1956, 1957, 1958, and placed second in 1955, 1962, 1963. His national wins include Open Teams 1953, 1956, 1957, 1959, 1963, 1964. See BLUE TEAM.

ALFANDRE, Ellen of New York City won Summer NAC Master Mixed Teams 1973, Eastern States Mixed Teams 1969, New England Fall Mixed Swiss Teams 1970.

ALLAN, Thomas W. (b. 1951) of Houston won the Intercollegiate Championship 1975, District 16 GNP 1978, 1980, Texas Mid-Summer Swiss Teams 1979, Spring NAC secondary Open Pairs Flt. B 1979. A graduate of the University of Missouri, Allan is a mechanical engineer.

ALLEN, Craig R. (b. 1946) of Chicago, stockbroker and options trader, won Central States II Men's Teams 1979, Master Pairs 1980, District 13 GNP 1981. He served the Chicago CBA as a Board member and tournament chairman 1978–1980.

ALLEN, Ellen B. (Lulie) (Mrs. Larry C.) of Summerville SC, secretary/bookkeeper and horse breeder, won 17 Mid-Atlantic regional events including Summer Open Pairs 1967, KO Teams 1977, Women's Pairs 1979, Spring Open Pairs 1969, Women's Pairs 1972, KO Teams 1975, 1979, Fall Swiss Teams 1969, Women's Pairs, Swiss Teams 1971, Winter Women's Pairs 1971, KO Teams 1976, 1981, Master Pairs 1977.

ALLEN, Larry C. (b. 1935) of Summerville SC, construction engineer, company president, won 12 Mid-Atlantic regional events including Spring Open Pairs 1969, Swiss Teams 1971, KO Teams 1975, 1979, Summer KO Teams 1977, Fall Swiss Teams 1969, 1971, Winter KO Teams 1976, 1981, Master Pairs 1977. Allen has served South Carolina Unit 160 for several years as a member of the Board, vice president and president.

ALLEN, Zenobia (formerly Rucker) (d.1975) of Detroit, bridge teacher, was a top woman player in the ABA from 1955. Her record shows over 30 national events including the Mixed Pairs 10 times.

ALLINGER, Paul (b. 1929) of Alameda CA, accountant, represented the United States in the World Team Olympiad 1960. He won Fall NAC Men's Pairs 1956, Men's Teams 1962, Chicago (since 1965 the Reisinger) 1962, Spingold 1958 and placed second in Fall NAC Open Pairs 1957, Men's Teams 1956, Men's Pairs 1961. He has won numerous regional titles and is the co-inventor of ASTRO.

ALLISON, Karen R. of Toronto ON, formerly of New York City, for 20 years a data processing specialist, now owns a small software company. Allison was the first woman ever to represent Canada in the World Team Olympiad 1976. She also represented Canada in World Women's Pairs and Mixed Pairs 1978, World Women's Team Olympiad 1980. She represented the United States in the World Women's Pairs 1970 and 1974. Allison won Fall NAC Women's Teams 1968, Spring NAC Women's Teams 1969, placed second 1981 and in Life Master Women's Pairs 1969. She has numerous regional wins including Can-Am KO Teams 1972, Canadian Nat'l Women's Teams 1981. She was elected to the ACBL Laws Commission in 1982. Allison is active in a group which sponsors refugee Vietnamese families to begin new lives in Canada.

ALOUF, Yehosoua (b. 1900) of Ramat Gan, Israel, born in Russia, retired physical education supervisor, published the Israeli magazine *Bridge* and originated and compiled the Hebrew glossary of bridge terminology.

ALPAUGH, Nancy T. (formerly Mrs. Ray Zoller) of New Orleans, former bridge teacher, won the World Mixed Teams 1972, Summer NAC Master Mixed Teams 1977, 1978, 1979, Spring NAC Women's KO Teams 1978 and many regional titles including Fall NAC secondary Swiss Teams 1981, Summer secondary Women's Pairs 1979, 1981.

ALPERN, Steven R. (b. 1943) of Jasper TN, spice merchant, won Summer NAC secondary Golder Master Pairs 1974, Fall NAC secondary Swiss Teams 1979, Canadian Nat'l KO Teams 1975, Central States Swiss Teams 1979, 1980, BAM Swiss Teams 1978.

ALTAY, Andrew J. (Andy) (b. 1947) of Toronto, born in Budapest, program analyst, won Fleur-de-Lys Swiss Teams 1972, Cambrian Shield Open Pairs 1973, Canadian Nat'l KO Teams 1973, Upper NY State KO Teams 1975, District 2 GNT 1976.

ALTMAN, Marion W. (b. 1929) of Roslyn NY, former rare book librarian and Long Island History archivist, won Keystone Mixed Pairs 1964, Eastern States Women's Pairs 1970, Fun City Women's Pairs 1973, New York Winter Women's Pairs 1974, Puerto Rico Master Pairs 1976. She formerly taught bridge and backgammon at a local high school and was active in the ERA movement.

ALTMAN, Steven B. (b. 1943) of Tenafly NJ, financial planning manager, one of the leading American players, won the Spingold 1970, 1971, Vanderbilt 1972, MOREHEAD CUP 1967, LONDON SUNDAY TIMES PAIRS 1973, and placed second in Reisinger 1967, Spingold 1968, 1978. He has won numerous regionals. Altman was an original member of the PRECISION TEAM and one of the youngest to play in the final of the Spingold. He coached the U.S. team in the 1973 Bermuda Bowl and the winning U.S. team in the 1977 Bermuda Bowl.

ALUJAS, Gustavo of Buenos Aires, Argentina represented Argentina in the Bermuda Bowl 1981. He was South American champion 1981 and has won several national titles including Open Teams 1981, Mixed Teams 1980.

AMANULLAH II (1892–1960), Emir of Afghanistan 1919–1929, abdicated partly because of his obsession with auction bridge. This pastime displeased his Muhammadan subjects, especially because (according to orthodox Muhammadans) it is a sacrilege to depict the human form on cards or in any other way.

AMARAL, Eros (b. 1915) of São Paulo, Brazil, insurance agent and bridge writer, represented Brazil in the World Team Olympiad 1964. He won South American Open Teams 1955, 1962, Brazilian Championships 1955, 1961, 1962, and placed second in the South American Championships 1954, Brazilian Championships 1953, 1954. His writings include *The Limit System* and a newspaper column.

AMSBURY, Joe (b. 1929) of London, England, writer and editor of *Popular Bridge Monthly*, won the GOLD CUP 1970 and many other tournaments.

ANDERSEN, Eilif B. (1907–1977) of Los Angeles was president of the ACBL in 1966. A vital member of the Board of Directors from 1956–1958 and 1961–1967, Andersen chaired the finance, building fund, headquarters site, and other important committees. He sponsored the ACBL's acceptance of the district organization plan. In the early Sixties Andersen founded and presided over the Association of Los Angeles County Bridge Units (ALACBU), and in 1967 he was elected president of the Western Conference. Andersen also founded and edited *Southern California Bridge News*.

ANDERSEN, Ronald E. (b. 1941) of Dallas, formerly of New York City, professional bridge writer, player, and teacher, former stock broker, is one of the most successful American players. Andersen represented the U.S. in World Open Pairs 1974, 1978, Rosenblum Cup Teams 1978. In 1981 Andersen played in the first international bridge tournament ever held in mainland China (Shanghai), and coached the U.S. VENICE TROPHY team. He won Fall NAC Life Master Men's Pairs 1970, Summer NAC Mixed Teams 1971, Spring NAC Men's Teams 1974, Blue Ribbon Pairs 1978, Reisinger 1980, Life Master Pairs 1982. He placed second in the Vanderbilt 1974, 1977, 1979, 1980, Spring NAC Open Pairs 1974, Blue Ribbon Pairs 1975. In 1974 Andersen won the MOTT-SMITH TROPHY with a record 250 masterpoints. Twice McKENNEY TROPHY winner, he was the first to win more than 2000 master points in one year and holds the record for the greatest number ever accumulated (2725 MPs, 1980). Since 1969 he has won more than 150 regional titles.

Andersen is involved in a host of bridge activities. He lectures, hosts panel shows and emcees bridge programs at NACs and regionals all over North America. He delivered a lecture at Chinese University in Shanghai with the aid of KATHERINE WEI as translator. He is the developer of DOOP and contributor to the development of the PRECISION SYSTEM. Andersen is a certified club director, has served the Kansas State BL as a member of the Board, and was entertainment coordinator for the 1980 Fall NAC. Devyn Press editor-in-chief, Andersen authored two pamphlets in the "Championship Bridge Series" titled *"Killing Their Notrump"* and *"Matchpoint Tactics"*, edited four books on Precision, is associate editor of *International Precision Newsletter*, and has written articles for the ACBL *Bulletin* and several other bridge periodicals throughout the world. Andersen is the author of *Where and How High*, and the co-author of five books on Precision, *Matchpoint Precision*, *Making the Most of Your Limited Opening Bids*, *Profits From Preempts*, *Perfect Your Notrump Bidding* and *Action for the Defense*.

ANDERSEN, Susan. See PICUS, SUSAN.

ANDERSON, A. Norman of San Francisco, born in Birkenhead, England, won more than 25 regional titles including Summer NAC secondary Swiss Teams 1972, California Capital Men's Pairs 1976, Open Swiss Teams 1980, Mid-Winter Holiday Open Swiss Teams 1976, All-Western KO Teams 1970.

ANDERSON, Emilie B. (Skip) (b. 1927) of Elmhurst IL, won Wisconsin Women's Pairs 1978, 1980, Champagne Women's Pairs 1980.

ANDERSON, Jean Baird of Seattle, interior designer, won Yakima Valley Swiss Teams 1974, British Columbia Mixed Pairs 1977, Master Pairs 1980, Puget Sound Open Pairs 1973, Women's Pairs 1980.

ANDERSON, John C. (Big John) (b. 1942) of Sixes River OR, formerly of California City CA and Eugene OR, is one of the leading bridge personalities of the Northwest. He won Summer NAC Master Mixed Teams 1971 and more than 40 regional events including Canadian KO Teams, Open Pairs, Swiss Teams, Master Pairs 1971, Bridge Week Men's BAM Teams, Open Swiss Teams 1978, Unmixed Pairs 1980, Big Sky KO Teams, Open Pairs 1981, Missouri Valley KO Teams, Master Pairs, Men's Pairs 1980. Anderson is a regular participant as panelist or commentator on bidding shows. He formerly taught school on both the elementary and college levels.

ANDERSON, Ken S. (b. 1941) of Greensboro NC, vice president and account executive, won Mid-Atlantic Men's Pairs 1968, Swiss Teams 1972, District 7 GNT 1976.

ANDERSON, Madeline L. (1901-1973) of Seattle was a bridge writer, teacher and club owner. She wrote the ACBL *Bulletin* feature "Coastwise" 1949-1960. Anderson founded and served as secretary of the Wisconsin-Michigan BA, was secretary of the Michigan BC, and became secretary of the ACBL in 1957. She was vice president of the ABTA,

co-founder of the Canada-U.S. Bridge matches and a member of the ACBL Goodwill Committee.

ANDERSON, Sharon Roe (b. 1944) of Minneapolis, administrator, won Wisconsin Women's KO Teams 1981, District 14 Swiss Teams 1981, Gopher Women's Pairs 1981.

ANDERSON, William M. (1905-1969) of Toronto, an actuary, authored the most widely used DISTRIBUTIONAL POINT COUNT.

ANDREWS, Jim of Vancouver BC, won British Columbia Open Pairs 1973, Swiss Teams Flt. A 1979, Peach Festival Swiss Teams 1974, Oregon Trail Swiss Teams 1974.

ANSAY, Nadine. See LIECHTENSTEIN, PRINCESS NADINE VON.

ANTHONISEN, Robert C. Jr. (Rob) (b. 1941) of Altadena CA, sales representative, won Pacific Southwest Men's Pairs 1981, Golden Gate Swiss Teams 1977, 1978, Holiday Festival Open Pairs 1979, Raincross Open Pairs 1981.

ANTUNES, Manuel Costa (b. 1930) of Lisbon, Portugal, civil engineer, represented Portugal in the European Championships 1966, 1974. His national wins include Open Teams six times, Open Pairs twice.

APFEL, Dr. Kalman (b. 1907) of West Palm Beach FL, won the Spingold 1956, Vanderbilt 1954, Summer NAC secondary Golder pairs 1952, Non-Master Pairs 1942, Sub-Senior Master Teams 1946, Eastern States KO Teams 1966, New York Winter Swiss Teams 1974.

APFELBAUM, Jay M. (b. 1951) of Pittsburgh won the Blue Ribbon Pairs 1976 and Mid-Atlantic Summer KO Teams 1974. A graduate of Temple University 1980, he is a law student and a sectional director.

APPLETON, John P. Jr. (Jack) (b. 1934) of Roslindale MA, insurance claims supervisor, won New England Fall Swiss Teams 1972, 1976, 1977, Fleur-de-Lys Master Pairs Flt. A 1972.

APPLEYARD, Robert (b. 1909) of New York City, bridge teacher and club director, won the Chicago (since 1965 the Reisinger) 1947, Vanderbilt 1948, Life Master Pairs 1939, 1945, and placed second in Fall Master Individual 1950, 1956, Spring NAC Men's Teams 1950, Life Master Pairs 1936. His many regional successes include Central States Men's Pairs 1949, Florida Men's Teams 1959, 1960, Mid-South Spring Master Pairs 1945.

ARGERSINGER, Amelia S. (b. 1915) of Scottsdale AZ, formerly of Ann Arbor MI, won All-American Women's Pairs 1963, Mixed Pairs 1966, Great Lakes Women's Pairs 1959, Mixed Pairs 1971, District 11 Women's Pairs 1968, Motor City Women's Pairs 1968, Champagne Women's Pairs 1971.

ARMSTRONG, John (b. 1952) of Formby, England, actuary and systems analyst, represented Great Britain in the European Championships 1979, CAMROSE TROPHY matches 1978, 1979, 1980. His national wins include Swiss Teams Congress 1980, 1981, Life Master Pairs 1979, Spring Bank Holiday Foursomes 1979, 1981. He placed second in the Life Master Pairs 1980, Spring Foursomes 1980, 1981, Crockford's 1980, 1981. Armstrong graduated with first class honors in mathematics from Cambridge University. He is an accomplished pianist.

ARNALL, Marie R. (b. 1917) of Orange TX, bridge teacher, won Champagne KO Teams, Swiss Teams 1980, Texas Capital 1980, King Cotton Swiss Teams 1980, Republic of Texas KO Teams 1981.

ARNDT, Ann Z. of Hermosa Beach CA, administrative supervisor, won Golden State Open Pairs 1969, Pacific Southwest Mixed Pairs 1969, Navajo Trail Women's Pairs 1970, Raincross Women's Swiss Teams 1979, Los Angeles Winter Women's KO Teams 1978, Women's Master Pairs 1979.

ARNDT, Martin (b. 1929) of Houston, sales representative, placed second in Spring NAC Open Pairs 1978 and won Spring NAC secondary Open Teams 2nd Flt. 1969, District 5 Master Pairs 1971, Texas Capital Mixed Pairs 1977, Corpus Christi Men's Pairs, Swiss Teams 1978.

ARNOLD, Carrie E. (b. 1896) of Ft. Lauderdale FL, first played bridge in Chicago in 1928 and she still plays every day — sometimes twice a day. She placed second in Fall NAC Life Master Women's Pairs 1963 and won Florida Women's Teams 1962, Southeastern Women's Pairs 1962, Women's Teams 1962, 1963, 1964, 1967.

ARNOLD, RUSSELL D. (b. 1924) of North Miami Beach, born in Winnipeg, Canada, accountant, was Bermuda Bowl champion 1981. He won the Spingold 1963, Grand National Teams 1973, Reisinger 1979, Vanderbilt 1980 and placed second in Vanderbilt 1960, GNT 1980. Arnold has over 20 regional wins including Florida KO Teams 1969, Mid-Atlantic KO Teams 1974, North Florida KO Teams, Men's Pairs, Open Pairs 1980. He is a graduate of the University of Minnesota.

ARNTHORSSON, Hördur (b. 1939) of Kópavogur, Iceland, office manager, represented Iceland in the European Championships 1977, World Open Pairs 1974. His national titles include Icelandic Teams 1976 (second in 1972, 1973), Icelandic Pairs 1977 (second in 1974), Cup Master Teams 1977, 1981. He was Reykjavik team champion 1978, pairs champion 1977, 1979.

ARNTHORSSON, Orn (b. 1945) of Reykjavik, Iceland, office manager, represented Iceland in the European Championships 1974, 1977, 1979, 1981, World Team Olympiad 1980. His national wins include Icelandic Pairs 1976, 1980, Icelandic Teams 1977, 1978, 1980.

ARON, Adrien (b. 1902) of Paris, France, bridge writer, was European champion 1935 and represented France in the Franco-American Plafond Match against the ELY CULBERTSON U.S. team in 1933 (see PLAFOND). He won the French Open Team Championship 1932–1939. He is the author of *L'Art du Bridge*, of many magazine articles and co-author of *Les 102 Donnes d'un Grand Match*. See BIBLIOGRAPHY, G.

ARONSON, Sidney (b. 1911) of Brookline MA, formerly of Arlington VA, attorney and former Deputy Assistant Inspector General, U.S. Department of Agriculture, 1969–1974, won the Chicago (since 1965 the Reisinger) 1949 and placed second in the Life Master Pairs 1959. His regional wins include Summer NAC secondary Swiss Teams 1981, New England Men's Pairs 1938, Open Pairs 1941, Master Pairs 1942, Master Teams 1950, Mid-Atlantic KO Teams Fall 1971, Summer 1972, Open Teams Winter 1966, Open Pairs Winter 1965.

AROSEMENA, Bentzon Leopoldo (Polin) (b. 1922) of Lima, Peru, born in Nice, France, gas station owner, represented Peru in the South American Championships as a member of the Peruvian National Team. He was national all-events champion 1974 through 1980.

ARST, Frieda (Mrs. B. H.) of Chicago, bridge teacher, won Spring NAC Women's Teams 1966, Life Master Women's Pairs 1973 and placed second in Spring NAC Women's Teams 1972. Her regional titles include Summer NAC secondary Golder Master Pairs 1967, Fall Women's Pairs 1973, Spring Women's Swiss Teams 1972, 1973, Central States Women's Pairs 1957, 1961, 1962, 1965, 1967.

ARVEDON, Lloyd B. (b. 1953) of West Roxbury MA, senior sales representative, won several regionals including Fall NAC secondary Open Swiss Teams 1976, Can-At Master Swiss Teams, Open Swiss Teams 1978, Mixed Pairs 1977, Nat'l Capital Men's Swiss Teams 1978, Swiss Teams Flt. A 1980, District 3 Open Swiss Teams 1981, Men's Swiss Teams 1979, New York Winter Open Pairs Flt. A 1979, Fleur-de-Lys KO Teams, Men's Pairs 1979.

ASBER, A. Joseph (b. 1932) of Bethlehem PA, draftsman, won Can-Am Open Pairs 1955, Eastern States Open Pairs 1971, Mid-Atlantic Men's Swiss Teams Fall 1976, District 4 GNT 1979, Zone II GNT 1981.

ASHLEY, David D. (b. 1941) of Las Vegas, expert bridge, backgammon and poker player, won Spring NAC Men's Teams 1976. He has over 20 regional wins including Rocky Mountain KO Teams, Men's Pairs 1971, Bridge Week Mixed Teams 1970, BAM Teams 1972, KO Teams 1978, Pacific Southwest Open Pairs 1969, 1970, Swiss Teams 1976, Midwinter Holiday KO Teams 1974, Open Pairs 1976, Flt. A Swiss Teams 1979, Men's Pairs 1981, Gem State Flt. A Swiss Teams 1980, Open Pairs and Master Pairs 1981. Ashley is also a backgammon champion.

ASHTON, John C. (b. 1948) of Portland OR, regional tournament director, placed second in Spring NAC Open Pairs 1977. His regional wins include Oregon Trail KO Teams 1973, 1976, Swiss Teams 1976, Tri-Cities Swiss Teams 1975, District 20 GNT 1977, Inland Empire Swiss Teams 1980.

ASKEW, Mabs A. (b. 1918) of Downey CA writes a weekly bridge column for *Southeast News* and teaches totally handicapped M.S. patients to play bridge. She has been chairman or co-chairman of BRIDGE WEEK events for many years and of the Spring NAC 1977. She won Golden State Master Pairs 1965.

ASRIEL, Roberto (b. 1905) of Santiago, Chile, born in Vienna, Austria, bridge teacher, represented Chile in the World Team Olympiad 1960,1968, South American Championships 1959, 1961, 1964, 1966, 1970, 1976, 1977. He won Zone ''America'' Commonwealth Jubilee Celebrations 1951.

ASSUMPÇÃO, Pedro Paulo (b. 1935) of São Paulo, Brazil, director of an import-export company, WBF Grand Master, one of the leading players of South America, won the World Team Olympiad 1976 and placed second in the Rosenblum Cup Teams 1978. He was South American champion 1967, 1968, 1969, 1970, 1971, 1972, 1973, 1974, 1975, 1977, 1978. He also represented Brazil in the Bermuda Bowl 1969, 1970, 1971, 1973, 1974, 1975, 1976, 1979, World Team Olympiad 1968, 1972, 1980, World Open Pairs 1974, 1978. He won the Deauville Teams 1970, 1975, 1977, 1978 and many Brazilian championships.

ATA-ULLAH, Munir Ahmed (b. 1940) of Lahore, Pakistan, born in India, placed second in Far East Championships 1978 and was a finalist in the Bermuda Bowl 1981. He won the Spring Foursomes (Great Britain) in 1976. He is a graduate of Punjab University, Pakistan 1960 and of Oxford 1963. A former lawyer, he is presently a managing director of a United Arab Emirates company.

ATUESTA, Jorge (b. 1926) of Bogotá, Colombia, engineer, represented Colombia in the South American Championships 1964, 1966, 1968. His national titles include Open Teams 1965, 1966, 1967, Master Pairs 1967.

AUGUST, William J. (b. 1926) of Springfield MA, bridge teacher, writer, lecturer and certified club director, was affiliated with Goren International 1962–1976 lecturing on cruises and teaching classes for training teachers. His writings include several pamphlets on bidding and directing and he is the author of the August 2 ◇ Convention. See TWO-WAY STAYMAN. Formerly he was president and vice president of the New England BC, regional vice president of the ABTA, and special assistant to EASLEY BLACKWOOD. His regional wins include Long Island Master Pairs 1969, Southeastern Open Teams 1970, New England Master Pairs 1974.

AVARELLI, Walter (b. 1912) of Rome, Italy, lawyer, WBF Grand Master #5, one of the world's great players, was Bermuda Bowl champion 1957, 1958, 1959, 1961, 1962, 1964, 1965, 1966, 1967, 1968, 1969, 1972 and European champion 1956, 1957, 1958, 1959. He also represented Italy in the World Team Olympiad 1960. His national wins include Italian Cup 1954, Italian Open Teams 1954, 1959, 1960, 1963. In 1975 Avarelli was a member of the Italian Lancia Challenge Team. He is the co-inventor of the ROMAN SYSTEM. See also BLUE TEAM and BIBLIOGRAPHY, C.

AWAD George L. (b. 1923) of Forest Hills NY, born in Cairo, Egypt, systems computer analyst and former engineer, represented Egypt in the World Team Olympiad 1964. His regional wins include Long Island KO Teams 1969, Mixed Pairs 1970, Fun City KO Teams 1970, Eastern States KO Teams 1972, All-Western Mixed Pairs 1961, Florida Life Master Pairs 1968.

AWAD, Marie (Mrs. George) of Forest Hills NY, born in Cairo, Egypt, French teacher and tax consultant, represented Egypt in the World Team Olympiad 1964. Her regional wins include Long Island KO Teams 1969, Mixed Pairs 1970, Fun City KO Teams 1970, Eastern States KO Teams 1972, All-Western Mixed Pairs 1961, Florida Life Master Pairs 1968.

AXTELL, Loren R. (b. 1936) of Jacksonville FL, computer programmer, won several regional titles including District 9 GNT 1977, GNP 1979, Mid-Atlantic Open Pairs 1978, 1981, Swiss Teams 1974, North Florida Men's Pairs, Open Pairs Flt. A 1977.

AYERS, Robert W. (b. 1946) of Lafayette LA, won several regional events including District 5 Men's Pairs, Mixed Pairs 1972, Men's Pairs 1974, Houston Mid-Winter Open Pairs Flt. A 1981, Washington Bridge Week KO Teams 1977, Fall NAC secondary Swiss Teams Flt. A 1980. He is a bank vice president in charge of lending.

B

BABIN, Elmer J. (b. 1902) of Shaker Heights OH, attorney, presided over the ACBL in 1940. He graduated from Harvard 1923 and Western Reserve Law School 1926, Babin played his first duplicate bridge in March 1930. The following month he won the Open State Pairs championship and in June the AWL Open Pairs. He also won Western States Open Teams 1934, Open Pairs 1939, before retiring from bridge tournament play in 1951.

BABSCH, Fritz (b. 1933) of Vienna, Austria, civil engineer, won the World Open Pairs 1970. He represented Austria in the World Team Olympiad 1968. He has won numerous European titles.

BACH, Norman (1903–1971) is best remembered for initiating and organizing the first post-World War II World Championships, held in Bermuda in 1950.

These games are now known as the BERMUDA BOWL. An accountant from Paget East, Bermuda, Bach enjoyed several bridge exploits, including capturing the GOLD CUP for Great Britain in 1938 and acting as playing captain of the British team in the European Championships in 1938 and 1939.

BACHER, Paula. See RIBNER, PAULA.

BACHERICH, René (b. 1906) of Lille, France, merchant, WBF Grand Master, won the Bermuda Bowl 1956, World Team Olympiad 1960. He also represented France in the World Team Olympiad 1964, Bermuda Bowl 1954, 1961, 1963. He was European champion 1953, 1955, 1962 and placed second 1956, 1961. His national wins include Open Teams 1962. See RELAY SYSTEM.

BACKMAN, Joseph G. (b. 1901) of Worcester MA, retired lawyer, won USBA New England Open Teams 1936. Backman was the first president of both Central Massacusetts BA 1936 and Worcester County BC 1937.

BACKSTROM, James H. (b. 1949) of San Diego, real estate salesman, won Fall NAC secondary Open Pairs 1981, District 22 GNT 1975, Pacific Southwest KO Teams 1975.

BACON, Francis M. III, (1899–1983) of New York City, stockbroker, in 1975, as the only surviving member of the first game of contract bridge played aboard the S.S.*Finland*, November 1, 1925, he contributed much new information regarding the background of the origin of the game and helped to pinpoint its date.

BAER, Henry (b. 1930) of Dallas, born in Germany, attorney, won International City Open Pairs 1974, Texas Spring Swiss Teams 1976, Mixed Pairs 1970, Acapulco Fiesta Open Pairs Flt. A 1980, Missouri Valley Swiss Teams 1970. He has served District 16 as executive secretary since 1960.

BAFF, Martin A. (b. 1927) of Beachwood OH, founder and president of a wholesale plumbing supply firm, won District 5 GNT 1981, Zone IV 1981, All-American Swiss Teams 1975, Men's Swiss Teams 1979, Canadian Nat'l Men's Pairs 1977.

BAILEY, Doris E. (Mrs. Evan) of San Diego won Pacific Southwest Swiss Teams, Women's Swiss Teams 1977, Open Pairs 1980, Bridge Week Women's Swiss Teams 1978, Puget Sound Mixed Pairs 1980.

BAILEY, Evan (b. 1929) of San Diego, physicist, tied for second in the Reisinger 1981 and won several regional events including Bridge Week BAM Teams 1976, Pacific Southwest Men's Pairs 1978, 1979, Master Pairs 1981.

BAILEY, Maureen (formerly O'Brien) (1899–1963) served as bridge editor of the San Francisco *Chronicle* for some 25 years. She was ACBL Honorary Member in 1946. With Ivy Oeschger she co-authored three bridge books. See BIBLIOGRAPHY, E.

BAINS, Kenneth R. (b. 1944) of Dallas, computer sales representative, won Big D Men's Swiss Teams 1974, Mid-South Master Pairs 1974, Land of Coron-ado Swiss Teams 1976, 1980, Alamo City Swiss Teams 1976, Missouri Valley Swiss Teams 1978, Republic of Texas Men's Pairs 1978, District 15 Swiss Teams 1978, Toast of Tulsa Open Pairs 1981.

BAIRD, Barbara (b. 1934) of Columbia MD won Mid-Atlantic Women's Swiss Teams 1976, 1980, Women's Pairs 1981. An Air Force wife for 20 years, Baird spent much time in Europe and received honors and gifts from Germans for her efforts in promoting participation in bridge between Germans and Americans.

BAIRD, Carol S. See HUTCHINSON, CAROL S.

BAIRD, James C. (1878–1963) a widely traveled bridge player, competed in 40 American states. He lived in a town named after him, Baird MS, formerly Johnsonville. Twice he headed the Mississippi unit, and the ACBL feted him by naming him Honorary Member in 1951. His wife, Mary Elizabeth Baird, was ACBL Honorary Member in 1947, the year she died; in her memory Baird donated the Baird Trophy for the NAC Open Individual.

BALAILA, Jack (b. 1923) of Haifa, Israel, travel agent, represented Israel in the World Team Olympiad 1964, European Championships 1966. Born in Beirut, he played with the Lebanese team before moving to Israel in 1954 where he was a member of the Israeli team in subsequent years. His national successes include Open Pairs 1962.

BALANOW, Richard I. (b. 1932) of Houston, financial consultant, won Summer NAC secondary Leventritt Pairs 1965, Mid-Am-Can Open Pairs 1961, Central States Mixed Pairs 1963.

BALCOMBE, Keith R. (b. 1954) of Oshawa ON, born in London, England, purchasing agent and production control manager, won Nat'l Capital KO Teams 1978, District 4 KO Teams, Swiss Teams 1979, District 5 Men's Swiss, Swiss Teams 1979, Canadian Nat'l Swiss Teams 1980, Can-Am Swiss Teams, Open Pairs 1981, Zone 3 CNT 1981.

BALDON, Suzanne (b. 1920) of Paris, France was European champion 1953, 1954. She also represented France in the World Women's Teams 1964, European Women's Championships 1957, 1967. Her national wins include Women's Teams several times.

BALDWIN, Robert H. (Bobby) (b. 1950) of Tulsa OK, professional card player, won King Cotton KO Teams 1975, Land of Coronado Swiss Teams 1976, Missouri Valley KO Teams 1976, Oklahoma City Men's Swiss Teams 1981. Baldwin has won four world championships in three different forms of poker and has written two books about poker.

BALDWIN, Col. Russell J. (1889–1969) of Norwalk

CT, formerly of Cleveland, was an army officer and expert on tournament procedure. One of the leading American bridge personalities, he was active as an organizer from the earliest days of contract bridge, and became a director of the American Bridge League and its treasurer shortly after its foundation in 1927.

A member of the ACBL Laws Commission (originally Committee) since its foundation in 1933, Baldwin was primarily responsible for the first Duplicate Code issued in 1935 and played a considerable part in formulating subsequent codes.

He was the author of the McKenney–Baldwin schedules for HOWELL MOVEMENTS, and constructed other movements. His many contributions to tournament procedure included the official ACBL method of dealing with fouled boards.

Baldwin was active as a tournament director 1927–41, and after war service became ACBL business manager, 1946–51. He was recalled to military service at the outbreak of the Korean War, and returned to the ACBL in charge of tournament scheduling 1958–63. He was ACBL Honorary Member in 1943.

His writings included many magazine contributions, and he was a contributing editor to the *Bridge Encyclopedia*.

BALDWIN, William A. (1907–1978) of Albuquerque NM, as 1970 ACBL President, was the man most instrumental in relocating national headquarters in Memphis. His interest in this project grew naturally from his career as a building and land developer. Other capacities in which he served bridge were as president of the Western Conference, trustee of the Charity Foundation and chairman of the ACBL Board of Directors (1971). He was ACBL Honorary Member in 1978. On an international level, Baldwin was ACBL representative to the WBF and treasurer of that body.

BALFE, Raymond A. (1895–1969) of New York City enjoyed the distinction of winning national championships in both auction and contract bridge, taking the 1926 All-American Open Pairs (auction) title with WALDEMAR VON ZEDTWITZ as well as the 1936 USBA Grand National Mixed Teams (contract).

BALLANTYNE, Aidan (b. 1951) of Vancouver BC, spectrographer and assayer, won Peach City Master Swiss Teams Flt. A 1978, British Columbia Men's Pairs 1979, Tri-Cities KO Teams 1979. Ballantyne is the editor of *The Matchpointer* and frequent contributor to *The Dino Bridge Buff*.

BALLARD, Jude H. (Mrs. Neil) (b. 1931) of Mercer Island WA placed second in Spring NAC Women's Teams 1967. Her several regional wins include Oregon Trail Master Pairs 1963, Master Women's Pairs 1971, Women's Swiss Teams 1975, Puget Sound Master Swiss Teams Flt. A 1978, Inland Empire Women's Pairs, Swiss Teams 1971.

BALLARD, Neil (b. 1920) of Mercer Island WA won several regional events including Hawaii KO Teams 1970, Inland Empire Swiss Teams 1971,

Puget Sound Master Swiss Teams Flt. A 1978, Pacific Northwest Open Teams 1955, Open Pairs 1960, Oregon Trail Master Pairs 1963, District 19 GNP 1980.

BALLENTINE, Lyle E. (1949–1982) of Charleston SC, director of a manufacturing corporation, won several regional events including Mid-Atlantic Spring KO Teams 1974, 1975, 1981, Master Pairs 1972, Fall Master Pairs 1971.

BALLESTEROS, Carmen Veloso (b. 1922) of Rizal, Philippines, was Far East champion 1957. She also represented the Philippines in the World Women's Pairs 1962, Far East Championships 1960, 1963. Her national titles include Mixed Teams 1965, Mixed Pairs 1956, 1957, Open Pairs 1965, Open Teams 1961, Women's Pairs 1957, 1958, Women's Individual 1956.

BANDONI, Franco (b. 1942) of Toronto, born in Pisa, Italy, represented Canada in the World Team Olympiad 1976. His several regional wins include Canadian Nat'l KO Teams 1971, 1980, Swiss Teams 1971, 1979, Men's Swiss Teams 1978, Open Pairs 1981, Master Pairs 1974, All-American Master Pairs 1976, District 5 Men's Swiss Teams 1980, District 2 GNT 1973, GNP 1979, 1980.

BANK, Julius C. (b. 1913) of Chicago, CPA, won Spring NAC Men's Teams 1946 and placed second in the Spingold 1948. His regional wins include All-American Open Teams 1944, Central States Open Teams 1947, 1956, Atlantic City Open Pairs 1936.

BARAN, Boris (b. 1945) of Montreal, university lecturer in computer science, represented Canada in the Rosenblum Cup Teams 1978. His regional wins include Spring NAC secondary Swiss Teams 1979, Canadian Nat'l Open Pairs 1981, Can-Am Swiss Teams 1974, District 3 Men's Pairs, Swiss Teams 1979, Capital District Fall Master Swiss Teams 1977, Long Island KO Teams 1980, and since its inception, he has been a finalist in the CANADIAN NATIONAL TEAMS competition.

BARBEY, Henry I. (1832–1906) of New York, a cosmopolitan who spent many years in Europe, is credited by JOSEPH B. ELWELL and ROBERT F. FOSTER with introducing bridge to New York in 1893. A yachtsman, banker and company director, the colorful Barbey is best remembered for writing the first code of laws for the new game, dated 1892.

BARBONE, Guido of Italy, columnist and bridge writer, was npc of the Italian Team in the Bermuda Bowl 1967, npc of the winning Women's Team in the European Championships 1977 and of the second place Women's Team in the Venice Trophy 1978. He has served as president of the ITALIAN BRIDGE FEDERATION since 1978 and has been a member of the executive committee of the EBL and vice president of the IBPA since 1981. His writings include *The Complete Book of Bridge*, *Funny Bridge* and *Complete Book of Duplicate Bridge*.

BARBOSA, Sergio Marinho (b. 1942) of Rio de Janeiro, Brazil, engineer and economist, Brazilian government official, won the World Team Olympiad 1976, South American Championships 1971 and placed second in the Rosenblum Cup Teams 1978. He also represented Brazil in the South American Championships 1971, 1979, World Open Pairs 1978. His national wins include Open Teams (four times) and Open Pairs.

BARBOUR, Kenneth R. (b. 1938) of Paradise Valley AZ, represented Great Britain in the European Championships 1963. He won the British Team Trials 1962, GOLD CUP 1963 and placed second in Summer NAC Master Mixed Teams 1970. His regional wins include New England Mixed Teams 1967, Mixed Pairs 1966, 1967. Born in Glasgow, Scotland, educated at Cambridge, England, Barbour is a computer executive. Before his retirement from bridge he contributed to *The Bridge World*, *British Bridge World* and *Bridge Journal*.

BARCLAY, Shepard (1889–1955) was a bridge writer, publisher, lecturer, and club director. Born in St. Louis, he became a resident of New York City in 1927. In that year he bought *Auction Bridge Magazine* from J. T. Smith and sought to make it a mass magazine, featuring the editorship of MILTON C. WORK and WILBUR C. WHITEHEAD, cartoons by such famous illustrators as his brother McClelland Barclay, John Held, Jr., Tony Sarg, Jefferson Machamer, and H. T. WEBSTER, and articles by famous writers including RING LARDNER, Edgar Guest, and Clarence Buddington Kelland. The magazine failed (1929), and its mailing list was used by ELY CULBERTSON to start *The Bridge World*. Barclay conducted a bridge page, with doggerel pertaining to bridge as a regular feature, in the New York *Herald Tribune*, 1929–34, and during those years also ranked the ten best (or most successful) players of each year annually for *Collier's* magazine. He conducted bridge clubs and duplicate games. Barclay wrote many books on bridge (see BIBLIOGRAPHY, E), and from 1932 until his death he wrote a daily newspaper feature on bridge for King Features Syndicate. He was a member of the executive committees of the ABL and ACBL 1936–49, and was named ACBL Honorary Member in 1948.

BARDACH, David (b. 1916) of Tel Aviv, Israel, born in Poland, book publishing executive, represented Israel in the World Open Pairs 1966, European Championships 1967. He won Tel Aviv Teams 1977 and placed second in Israel Nat'l Pairs 1978, Nat'l Teams 1976, 1977, 1979. Since 1979 Bardach has been honorary secretary of the EUROPEAN BRIDGE LEAGUE and a member of its Management Committee, and since 1981 a member of the WORLD BRIDGE FEDERATION Executive Council. He has also served the ISRAEL BRIDGE FEDERATION 1969–1972 in various executive positions.

BARDOLA, Marcel (b. 1925) of Zurich, Switzerland, mathematician, represented Switzerland in the European Championships 1959 through 1963. His national titles include Open Teams five times,

Open Pairs 1953, 1959, 1961, 1962. He is the former secretary-general of the SWISS BRIDGE FEDERATION.

BARE, Dorothy O. (Mrs. Gerald W.) of Pacific Palisades CA, travel agent, won Summer NAC Master Mixed Teams 1970. Her regional wins include Pacific Southwest Open Teams 1966, Disneyland Open Teams 1970, Mid-Winter Holiday Open Swiss Teams Flt. A 1979.

BARE, Gerald W. (b. 1933) of Pacific Palisades CA, civil engineer, won Summer NAC Master Mixed Teams 1970 and placed second in the Reisinger 1966. He is the winner of several regional events including Bridge Week KO Teams 1973, 1977, Open Pairs 1980, Las Vegas Swiss Teams 1971, Palm Springs Swiss Teams 1971, Pacific Southwest Open Pairs 1972, Los Angeles Winter KO Teams, Master Pairs 1979, Oil City Master Pairs 1978, Hawaii Men's Swiss Teams 1980, Oregon Trail Open Teams 1961.

BARLOW, Edward J. (b. 1933) of Sunnyvale CA, computer programmer, placed second in Fall NAC Men's Teams 1965, Spring NAC Men's Teams 1967. He is the winner of several regional events including District 21 GNT 1974, 1975, 1976, All-Western Life Master BAM Teams 1971, 1975, California Capital Swiss Teams 1975, Golden State Open Pairs 1963, Bridge Week Master Pairs 1968.

BARLOW, James F. (b. 1950) of Pittsburgh, audit control clerk, placed second in Spring NAC Men's Pairs 1982 and won District 5 Men's Pairs 1977, KO Teams 1978, Open Pairs 1980, All-American Swiss Teams Flt. A 1981.

BARNES, A. Mitchell (Mitch) (b. 1906) of New York City, former executive vice president of Travel With Goren, was one of the leading East Coast players in the early years of bridge. He won many USBA and AWL titles including USBA Grand National Open Teams 1936, AWL All-American Open Teams 1934, 1935. Life Master No. 14 in 1938, Barnes won Fall NAC Open Pairs 1937, Spingold 1941, Chicago (since 1965 the Reisinger) 1946, and placed second in Vanderbilt 1933, Spingold 1938, Chicago 1938, 1941, Summer NAC Mixed Teams 1934, Spring NAC Men's Teams 1946, USBA Grand National Open Pairs 1934, Mixed Teams 1936. His numerous regional wins include USBA Grand Nat'l Region 2 BAM Teams 1933, Southeastern Mixed Pairs 1939, Eastern States KO Teams (Reisinger) 1935, 1937. In 1953 he reactivated bridge cruises on American Export Lines.

BARNETT, Harry (b. 1914) of Glasgow, Scotland, retired bookkeeper/accountant, represented Scotland in nine international matches and was a member of the victorious CAMROSE TROPHY team twice. His national titles include Open Teams and Open Pairs twice. He reached the Scottish Cup semifinal playing with his brothers Michael, Hymie and Sol.

BARNETT, Lewis B. (b. 1934) of Blacksburg VA, teacher and researcher in biochemistry, won The

Netherlands Open Teams 1962, 1963, Jewish Nat'l Fund Open Pairs (The Netherlands) 1963. His regional wins include Mid-Atlantic Swiss Teams 1973, 1974. He contributed to The Netherlands' monthly bridge magazine, *Bridge*, while a resident of that country, 1961–1963.

BARNETT, Sol (1913–1979) of Glasgow, Scotland, represented Scotland in 19 international matches and was a member of the winning CAMROSE TROPHY team twice. His national titles include Open Teams and Open Pairs. After retiring from the furniture manufacturing business, Barnett became extremely active in SCOTTISH BRIDGE UNION administration, tournament organization and direction.

BARNICLE, John F. (b. 1925) of Lutherville MD, senior management consultant, Mid-Atlantic Open Pairs 1976, 1978, Swiss Teams 1978, 1979, Washington Bridge Week Open Pairs 1975, District 6 GNT 1975. Barnicle has been active in bridge administration for more than 25 years and has served as president of New Jersey BL, Delaware State BA and Maryland BA.

BARON, Arthur (Aaron) (b. 1923) of Los Angeles, journalist, won many regionals including Bridge Week Master Teams 1956, Master Pairs 1957, KO Teams 1961, Pacific Southwest Master Pairs 1955.

BARON, Hermine (Mrs. Arthur) of Los Angeles, one of the leading American women players, represented the United States in the World Women's Teams 1968, World Women's Pairs 1978. Baron won Spring NAC Women's Teams 1964, 1968, Women's Pairs 1968, 1982, Fall NAC Life Master Women's Pairs 1963, Summer NAC Life Master Pairs 1966, and placed second in Spring Women's Teams 1967, 1974, Women's Pairs 1967, 1977, 1975, 1980, Blue Ribbon Pairs 1971. She has won over 100 regional events and has more master points than any other women in this country (see LIFE MASTER). Winner of the McKENNEY TROPHY in 1964 and 1970, her winning total of 1,370 master points in the 1964 competition stood as the all-time record until 1969. See also HANDICAPPED PLAYERS.

BARON, Leo of Salisbury, Zimbabwe, judge, inventor of the BARON SYSTEM, has made many important contributions to bidding theory. His British wins includes the GOLD CUP 1946, 1951. Baron retired from bridge after his emigration to Zimbabwe in 1952. He is the co-author of *The Baron System of Contract Bridge.* See BIBLIOGRAPHY, C.

BARON, Randall S. (Randy) (b. 1949) of Shelbyville KY, writer and publisher, Summer NAC secondary Silver Trophy Pairs Flt. B 1977, District 11 KO Teams 1974, 1977, Midwest Fall Men's Swiss Teams 1979, Central Florida Open Pairs 1980, Florida Men's Pairs 1971, Great Lakes Master Pairs 1981. Owner of a bridge supplies business, Baron is also co-owner of DEVYN PRESS, publisher of bridge books. He has authored four paperback books on bridge, including *Popular Conventions, #1* of *Championship Bridge Series.* See BIBLIOGRAPHY, C.

BARONI, Paolo (b. 1911) of Milan, Italy, technical director in the silk industry and bridge writer, was European champion 1951 and placed second in 1952. His national wins include Italian Open Teams 1937, 1938, Mixed Teams 1947. Baroni helped found the ITALIAN BRIDGE LEAGUE in 1936. He is a frequent contributor to *Bridge d'Italia.*

BARREDO, Manuel (b. 1901) of Manila, Philippines, businessman, won the Far East zone of the second World Par Championships. His national wins include Open Pairs 1954, 1959. He was the first president of the PHILIPPINE CONTRACT BRIDGE LEAGUE.

BARRETT, Annette (b. 1934) of Miami won Southeastern Master Pairs 1966, Women's Pairs 1969, Open Teams 1968, Swiss Teams 1978, Women's Swiss Teams 1981, Mid-Atlantic KO Teams 1973, Florida Mixed Pairs 1972, KO Teams 1981, North Florida Women's Pairs 1980.

BARRETT, William K. (Billy) (1909–1981) of Atlanta became one of the youngest players to win a national championship when he and the late JOHNNY RAU captured the Chicago Trophy (since 1965 the Reisinger) in 1930. The two were credited in *Watson's Play of the Hand* and other sources as being the first to use psychic bids in a national tournament. A lawyer, Barrett served two terms in the Georgia House of Representatives.

BARROW, James M. of Miami Beach won more than 40 regional events and placed second in the McKENNEY TROPHY competition 1980. His regional wins include Mid-South Men's Pairs 1970, 1971, Southeastern Swiss Teams 1980, Men's Swiss Teams 1975, Mississippi Valley Swiss Teams 1978, 1980, North Florida Open Pairs 1969, Men's Pairs 1979, KO Teams 1980, Central Florida Mixed Pairs 1980, Mid-Atlantic Swiss Teams 1978, 1979, Open Pairs 1982.

BARROW, Rhoda. See LEDERER, RHODA.

BARROWS, Ira B. (b. 1945) of Langhorne PA, attorney, won Summer NAC secondary Swiss Teams 1st Flt. 1975, District 4 Men's Swiss Teams 1976, 1978, 1979, 1981, Washington Bridge Week Men's Swiss Teams 1976, 1977, Mid-Atlantic Men's Pairs, Men's Swiss Teams 1979, District 4 GNT 1979, 1981, Zone II 1981.

BARSOTTI, Dott. Umberto of Rome, Italy, was npc of the Italian Teams that won the World Team Olympiad 1972, European Championships 1969, 1971. He is vice president of the ITALIAN BRIDGE FEDERATION.

BART, Leslie C. (b. 1947) of Potomac MD, accountant, won Fall Life Master Men's Pairs 1972. His more than 17 regional titles include Mid-Atlantic Summer Open Pairs 1974. Swiss Teams 1973, KO Teams 1977, 1978, Fall KO Teams 1976, 1977, 1978. See also LANCIA TEAMS.

BARTLETT, Ralph (b. 1940) of Rochester NY, stereo equipment salesman, won Upper New York State Men's Swiss Teams 1973, Swiss Teams 1975, Keystone Spring Swiss Teams 1976, Southeastern Open Pairs, Men's Swiss Teams 1976, Wolverine KO Teams 1980, Nat'l Capital Master Pairs 1977, Mid-Atlantic Open Pairs 1980, Great Lakes Swiss Teams 1980.

BARTON, Lionel O. (b. 1942) of Missouri City TX, born in Buxton, Guyana, geophysicist, won ABA Summer Open Teams 1981, Spring Open Teams 1982, Summer Open Pairs 1980 and more than 15 other national titles. He was Spring Nationals "Player of the Year" 1976, Summer 1981, and won the William A. Friend award 1978. He is a club director and ABA Southwestern section vice president.

BARTONE, Vincent J. (b. 1951) of Centreville VA, communications systems specialist, won District 5 Swiss Teams 1979, District 4 Men's Pairs 1980, Mid-Atlantic Open Pairs 1981. He formerly edited the Stamford DBC *Bulletin*.

BARTON-PAINE, Dianne M. (b. 1943) of San Francisco, electronic banking project manager, became a Life Master in 1961 at the age of 18, the youngest at that time to achieve that status. Publicity of her feat included a story in the *Saturday Evening Post* and a guest appearance on *To Tell The Truth*. Also in 1961 Barton-Paine became one of the ACBL's youngest tournament directors and now holds a Regional 2 rating. She won Golden State Women's Pairs 1976, Mid-Winter Holiday Women's Teams 1977.

BARTUSEK, Mark J. (b. 1955) of Fullerton CA, aerospace computer programmer, won Fall NAC secondary Swiss Teams Flt. B 1978, Bridge Week Men's Pairs 1978, Swiss Teams Flt. B 1980, Raincross Swiss Teams Flt. A 1980. In 1978 he was MINI McKENNEY National Master of the Year.

BASTOS, Eduardo (b. 1930) of Rio de Janeiro, Brazil, insurance company branch manager, represented Brazil in the Bermuda Bowl 1970 and was South American champion 1969.

BATCHELLER, John (b. 1941) of Springfield MA, bridge club owner, director and teacher, won New England KO Swiss Teams Flt. A 1980, New England Summer Swiss Teams 1976, New England Fall Swiss Teams 1978, Nat'l Capital Open Pairs 1977, Tri-State Winter Swiss Teams 1977, Olympic Swiss Teams 1976. He formerly served as editor of Western Massachusetts *Bulletin*, president of Unit 196 and has been a member of its Board since 1966.

BATES, Jean G. (formerly Theus) (b. 1916), real estate investor, won Fall NAC secondary Women's Swiss Teams 1976, Southeastern Women's Teams 1973, Life Master Pairs 1977, Hawaii Women's Swiss Teams 1977, All-American Mixed Pairs 1977.

BATES, Roger W. (b. 1947) of New York City, formerly of Tucson and Las Vegas, options trader, one of the leading American players, won the MOTT-SMITH TROPHY 1975, Vanderbilt 1975, 1976, Spingold, 1976, Blue Ribbon Pairs 1971 (second in 1974), Fall Life Master Men's Pairs 1976 (second in 1977), and second in Spring NAC Men's Teams 1975. He is also the winner of the 1980 Cavendish Club Invitational Pairs and more than 50 regional events including Spring NAC secondary Swiss Teams 1974, Fall Open Pairs 1974.

BAUER, Charles (b. 1924) of Louisville KY, restaurant owner, won Midwest Spring Men's Pairs 1960, Midwest Fall Men's Pairs 1973, District 11 KO Teams 1974, 1977.

BAUSHER, Larry P. (b. 1939) of Wallingford CT won Summer NAC secondary Swiss Teams 1976, Can-At Master Pairs 1973, Long Island Swiss Teams 1973, Tri-State Winter Swiss Teams 1976, New England Summer Swiss Teams 1976, New York Winter Swiss Teams 1976, New England Master Swiss Teams 1980, Fall Swiss Teams 1978, 1979. Bausher, a graduate of UCLA, is engaged in biochemical and pharmacological research at Yale.

BAZE, Diane. See HAYWARD, DIANE.

BAZE, Grant S. (b. 1943) of Woodland Hills CA, one of the leading players of the West Coast, won the Pan-American Invitational Pairs 1974, 1975, Reisinger 1970, Spingold 1975, FISHBEIN TROPHY 1975, and placed second in the Reisinger 1971, Spring NAC Men's Teams 1972. He has won many regional events including Fall NAC secondary Open Pairs 1978, District 21 GNT 1973, 1977, Zone 8 1973, Oregon Trail Open Pairs, Men's Pairs 1976. Baze, a former bridge professional and expert rubber bridge player, is a computer programmer.

BEALE, Felicity of Melbourne, Australia, born in Yugoslavia, was Far East Women's champion 1973. She also represented Australia in the Far East Women's Championships 1978, 1981, World Women's Teams 1980, Venice Trophy Teams 1981. Her national wins include Women's Interstate Teams 1976, 1977, 1981.

BEALL, Ron (b. 1944) of Oakland CA, research scientist, won Fall NAC Swiss Teams 1981. His regional wins include Mid-Atlantic Fall Open Pairs 1971, Pacific Southwest Master Swiss Teams 1979.

BEAN, Anne (Mrs. Percy X.) (b. 1915) of Olympia WA won Fall NAC secondary Women's Swiss Teams, Swiss Teams 1976, Puget Sound Open Pairs Flt. A 1979. She is past president of Unit 441.

BEAN, Percy X. (b. 1916) of Olympia WA was president of the ACBL in 1972 and has been a member of the Board since 1964, chairman of the Board in 1973 and president of the ACBL Charity Foundation 1974-1981. He was one of the principal sponsors of the GRAND NATIONAL CHAMPIONSHIPS (2). A member of IBPA, Bean is editor and publisher of *Mad Mad World of Bridge*, a newsletter strongly championing players of less than expert class. A retired executive, he was given Olympia's first Citizen of the Year award in 1968.

BEARD, Fran (Mrs. Samuel) (b. 1929) of Dallas, travel agent, placed second in Spring NAC Women's Teams 1973. Her regional wins include Summer NAC secondary Women's Pairs 1974, Fall Women's Swiss Teams 1977, 1978, Texas Mid-Winter Women's Pairs 1971, Fall Women's Pairs 1973, Oklahoma City Women's Swiss Teams 1981.

BEARD, Samuel J. (Sam) (b. 1926) of Dallas, business executive, won Summer NAC secondary Men's Pairs 1972, District 15 Mixed Pairs 1969, District 16 GNT 1974. He is a former president of District 16 and the Dallas BA.

BEASLEY, Henry Mountifort (Pops) (1875–1949) of London England, born in India, an army officer and bridge writer, was one of the leading personalities in British bridge. He captained the British team in the SCHWAB CUP 1933 and won the GOLD CUP 1932. Bridge columnist, author of a number of books, and the originator of a 1♣ system called after him, Beasley was co-founder and chairman of two of London's most important card clubs, CROCKFORD'S and the HAMILTON.

BEATTY, R. Stephen (Steve) (b. 1949) of Birmingham AL, staff analyst, won Mid-South Swiss Teams 1976, 1981, Mid-Atlantic Open Pairs 1979. He is former president and treasurer of Birmingham BA. Beatty is a long distance runner.

BEAULIEU, Helene (b. 1932) of Sherbrooke PQ, bridge club owner, won Summer NAC secondary Silver Trophy Pairs Flt. B 1979, Fall NAC secondary Swiss Teams Flt. B 1981, Can-Am Swiss Teams 1979, Women's Swiss Teams 1980, Can-At Swiss Teams Flt. A 1980, New England Summer Mixed Pairs 1975.

BECHELY, Joseph (b. 1928) of Los Angeles, mathematician, Bridge Week KO Teams 1955, 1974, Open Teams 1962, Los Angeles Winter Open Pairs 1974, Orange County Master Pairs 1974.

BECKER, B. Jay (b. 1904) of Flushing NY, attorney, bridge columnist and bridge teacher, born in Philadelphia where he trained as a lawyer at Temple Law School and lived until 1937, is one of the greatest players of all time. Life Master #6, WBF Grand Master, Becker was Bermuda Bowl champion 1951, 1953, and also represented the United States in the Bermuda Bowl 1958, 1965, 1973, World Team Olympiad 1960. He had the rare distinction of winning a North American Championship in his first year of tournament play. His introduction to duplicate play was early in 1932 when he entered and won a special pair contest organized by GEN. ALFRED M. GRUENTHER, using unpublished hands from the just-concluded CULBERTSON-LENZ MATCH. In the Summer NAC of that year he placed second in the Challenge Teams of Four (now the Spingold) and in the Mixed Pairs (HILLIARD TROPHY). At the Fall

NAC he won his first major title, the Chicago Trophy (since 1965 the Reisinger), an event he was to win on seven subsequent occasions, 1939, 1942, 1943, 1950, 1953, 1954, 1956. Becker has had equal success in the other major team championships, winning the Spingold seven times, 1936, 1938, 1944, 1947, 1952, 1957, 1972, and the Vanderbilt eight times, 1944, 1945, 1951, 1955, 1956, 1957, 1959, 1981. His win in 1981 came at the age of 76; no one has ever won a major championship at a greater age. His 22 NAC team victories are also a record, and no player has won a larger total of major NAC events.

Becker had the best record of any player in the Master Individual Championship, winning in 1937 and 1948, and placing second in 1934, 1941, 1949, and 1955. It is curious to note that he has never won an NAC mixed pair or mixed team event, although his chief successes in the early Sixties were with DOROTHY HAYDEN TRUSCOTT. In a two-year period, 1962–1964, they won the three most important NAC pair championships — Fall NAC Open Pairs 1962, the Blue Ribbon Pairs 1963, and the Life Master Pairs 1964.

Becker's other wins include AWL All-American Open Pairs, Open Teams 1935, and the FISHBEIN TROPHY 1972. He was second in 27 NAC events, and his numerous regional wins include Eastern States KO Teams (Reisinger) 1935, 1942, 1971, 1976.

Considered to be perhaps the most conservative of leading experts, Becker adopted very few bidding conventions, declining to play even the almost universally used STAYMAN convention. He was, however, among the first to adopt and recommend SUIT-PREFERENCE SIGNALS.

Becker managed three New York clubs, the CAVENDISH 1942–1947, the New York Bridge WHIST 1948–1950 and the REGENCY 1951–1956. He was associated with the Card School of New York 1952–1957 and became the bridge columnist for King Features Syndicate in 1956. He became a member of the ACBL Laws Commission in 1954. A contributor to *The Bridge World* and ACBL *Bulletin*, Becker is a member of the Editorial Advisory Board of the *Bridge Encyclopedia*. About six months a year he spends as bridge maestro on cruise ships and has gone around the world four times. See also BUENOS AIRES AFFAIR, FAMILY.

BECKER, James W. (Jim) of New York City, bridge teacher, bridge club and travel agency owner and manager, is the winner of more than two dozen regional events including Intercollegiate Par Championship 1959, 1960, Tri-State Men's Pairs 1969, Eastern States Individual, Mixed Teams 1969, Swiss Teams 1970, Puerto Rico Open Pairs 1970, Master Pairs 1978, Men's Pairs, Swiss Teams 1979, 1980, Mexican nationals Men's Pairs, Mixed Pairs 1974, 1975, Open Pairs 1978, 1982, Long Island Men's Pairs 1979, Swiss Teams 1980, Open Pairs 1981, District 3 Men's Pairs 1978, Men's Swiss, Master Pairs 1979, Spring NAC secondary Swiss Teams 1978, Southeastern Men's Pairs 1980, Swiss Teams 1981. Becker translated GIORGIO BELLADONNA and BENITO GAROZZO'S book *Precision and Superprecision*, an adaptation of C. C. WEI'S *Precision Club*, from Italian into English.

BECKER, Michael M. (b. 1943) of New York City, one of the leading American players, represented the United States in the Bermuda Bowl 1973, Rosenblum Cup Teams 1978, 1982. He won the MOREHEAD TROPHY 1967, Spingold 1972, 1980, Vanderbilt 1977, 1981, and placed second in the Reisinger 1967, Spingold 1968, Vanderbilt 1978, Grand National Teams 1981, Spring NAC Men's Teams 1968, Life Master Pairs 1975. His regional wins include Spring NAC secondary Mixed Pairs 1974, Eastern States KO Teams (Reisinger) 1971, 1976, New England Master Teams 1968, New York-New Jersey Swiss Teams 1971, New York Swiss Teams 1972, KO Teams 1980, Zone I GNT 1981. Becker has served on numerous committees of the Greater New York BA 1966–1980, was its president in 1980 and vice president in 1979, 1981. He has also served as treasurer of the CAVENDISH CLUB (New York) 1979. A graduate of Baruch College, he is an options trader. His business partner, RON RUBIN, is also his bridge partner of six years. A member of a famous bridge-playing family which boasts six Life Masters (see FAMILY), Becker was introduced to the game at an early age. At the Summer NAC in 1961 he won the Teenyear Pairs and just two years later became a Life Master at age 19. From 1981–1982 he was a member of the ACES TEAM. He is co-author of *The Ultimate Club*. See BIBLIOGRAPHY, C.

BECKER, R. Jay (Bob) (b. 1944) of Boston, actuary, won Fall NAC Swiss Teams 1979. His regional wins include Long Island Men's Pairs 1969, 1972, New England Winter Swiss Teams 1979, 1981, District 25 GNT 1979, Tri-State Winter Mixed Pairs 1971, Summer NAC secondary Swiss Teams 1971, District 4 Flight A Pairs 1979.

BECKER, Simon (Skippy) (b. 1899) of Philadelphia, born in Zloczow, Poland, retired court stenographer, won the Chicago (since 1965 the Reisinger) 1944 and placed second in Spingold 1944, Chicago 1946, Fall NAC Open Pairs 1949, 1960. His regional wins include Keystone KO Teams 1955, Men's Pairs 1966, Keystone Fall Men's Swiss 1970, Eastern States (Reisinger) KO Teams 1942, Open Pairs 1964, District 4 Men's Swiss Teams 1980. Becker has been a member of the Board of Directors and of the Conduct and Ethics Committee of the Philadelphia CBA for 30 years and was president of the Cavendish Club (Philadelphia) in 1973. He was the non-playing captain of the American team in the 1976 match with England held in Philadelphia. A top checker player, he was 1923 Pennsylvania champion. See FAMILY.

BECKER, Steven (b. 1937) of Cos Cob CT, bridge teacher and writer, won Fall NAC Swiss Teams 1980, New England Winter Open Teams 1968. He is a frequent contributor to ACBL *Bulletin* and formerly was its executive editor 1970–1972 and from 1964–1970 its advertising manager and assistant editor. Becker is a graduate of Queens College. He has ghost written one book and several bridge columns. See FAMILY.

BECKMAN, Terence L. (Terry) (b. 1947) of Minneapolis, printer, won Central States I Swiss Teams 1977, Master Pairs 1974, Iowa Swiss Teams 1974, KO Teams 1981, Gopher Men's Pairs, Swiss Teams 1976, Thunderbird KO Teams, Swiss Teams 1975.

BEECHER, Martha S., of Las Vegas, tax consultant, won Gem State Swiss Teams Flt. A 1980, Open Pairs, Master Pairs Flt. A 1981, Pacific Southwest Swiss Teams 1976, Cotton Boll KO Teams 1977, Los Angeles Winter Master Swiss Teams Flt. A 1977, Raincross Master Pairs Flt. A 1979, Mid-Winter Holiday Swiss Teams Flt A 1979, Navajo Trail Swiss Teams 1981, Wine Country KO Teams 1982, Las Vegas Swiss Teams 1982.

BEERS, Dale G. (b. 1950) of Cromwell CT, actuary, won Summer NAC Senior/Advanced Senior Master Pairs 1974, Fall NAC Swiss Teams 1980. His regional wins include New England Summer KO Teams 1978, Fall KO Teams 1979, KO Swiss Teams 1981. Beers formerly played semi-pro baseball.

BEERY, James L. Jr., of Lauderhill FL, radio engineer, won the Grand National Teams 1973. His regional wins include Southeastern Men's Teams 1974, North Florida Fall Mixed Pairs 1976, Mid-South Swiss Teams 1975.

BEERY, Marietta (Mrs. James L. formerly Mrs. William Passell, nee Bucklin) (b. 1935) of Lauderhill FL, one of the leading American women players, won the Venice Trophy 1974, Spring NAC Women's Teams 1971 (second in 1973), Summer NAC Master Mixed Teams 1972, Fall NAC Life Master Women's Pairs 1970. Her numerous regional titles include Fall NAC secondary Women's Teams 1968, 1969, Spring Women's Swiss Teams 1973, Southeasern Mixed Pairs 1966, 1967, Women's Teams 1974, New York-New Jersey Women's Pairs 1974, 1975.

BEGIN, Jackie (b. 1917) of Montreal represented Canada in the World Women's Teams 1968, 1972, World Women's Pairs 1970. She won Fall NAC Women's Teams 1952 and many regional titles including Canadian Nat'l Open Teams 1963, Can-Am Open Teams 1956, 1957, 1965.

BEGLEY, Francis P. (b. 1906), retired stockbroker, won the Spingold 1956, Vanderbilt 1954 and placed second in the Life Master Pairs 1957. His regional wins include Summer NAC secondary Non-Master Pairs 1942, Eastern States Open Pairs 1948, New York Winter Swiss Teams 1973.

BÉGUIN, Pierre (b. 1911) of Geneva, Switzerland, architect, was playing captain of the Swiss team which competed in the European Championships 1951, 1952, 1953, 1954, 1955, 1956. His national titles include Open Teams 1951, 1953, 1956, 1957, 1958, Open Pairs 1954, 1955, 1956, Swiss Cup 1952, 1955, 1956. He was the founder of the SWISS BRIDGE FEDERATION.

BEINECKE, Walter (1888–1961), a corporation executive in New York City, was a leading figure in bridge administration. He was vice president of the WHIST CLUB in New York and of the USBA. A member of the Laws Commission from its formation in 1933, Beinecke assisted in the preparation of all the codes issued from that time until his death. He came in second in the 1936 Vanderbilt, and in 1942 and 1943 he served as an ACBL Director.

BELL, Alan C. (b. 1925) of Los Angeles, born in Windsor ON, one of the most successful West Coast players, stands No. 51 on the top 100 masterpoint holder list. He has won more than 150 regionals including the MARCUS CUP 1962, Fall NAC secondary Open Pairs Flt. C 1974, Summer Swiss Teams 1976, Pacific Southwest KO Teams 1970, 1971, Mixed Pairs 1969, All-Western Master Pairs 1969, Men's Swiss Teams 1973, Oregon Trail KO Teams 1975, 1977, 1978, Mid-Atlantic KO Teams 1976, 1977, Men's Swiss Teams, Master Pairs, 1979, Men's Pairs 1980, Mississippi Valley KO Teams 1978, 1980, Master Pairs 1980. Bell served as director of the Chicago CBA 1955-1963.

BELL, Bruce C. (b. 1910) of Auckland, New Zealand, chartered accountant, industrialist and bridge writer, was Fourth World Par Olympiad champion 1963. He represented New Zealand in the Far East Championships 1964, 1972, npc 1973, 1974. His national wins include Open Pairs 1950, 1957, 1958, 1966, Open Teams 29 times between 1947 and 1972. His writings include bridge articles for newspapers and magazines in New Zealand, United States, and United Kingdom. He lectures on bridge both on and off television. He is a member of the Most Excellent Order of the British Empire (M.B.E.). This honor was awarded him by Queen Elizabeth in 1979 for his services to the game of bridge, and is the second such award in the Commonwealth, the first being made to RIXI MARKUS of England. A Life Member and past president of the New Zealand CBA, Bell founded the Auckland Bridge Centre which has some 20 affiliated clubs.

BELL, Frank A. (b. 1950) of Birmingham MI, data processing supervisor, won Summer NAC secondary Swiss Teams 1974, Canadian Nat'l KO Teams 1974, Great Lakes Men's Pairs 1973, Master Pairs 1975, All-American Swiss Teams 1974, 1976, Motor City KO Teams 1977, Swiss Teams 1978, District 12 GNT 1976, 1977, 1978, Zone I 1976, 1978. Bell graduated from University of Michigan.

BELL, Valerie of Christchurch, New Zealand represented New Zealand in the Far East Women's Championships 1971, 1976 and won New Zealand Pairs 1962, Canterbury Pairs 1962, Open Teams 1963, Open Pairs 1966, Australia Nat'l Women's Pairs 1976.

BELLADONNA, Giorgio (b.1923) of Rome, Italy, public official, WFB Grand Master #1, for many years the world's greatest player, was Bermuda Bowl champion 1957, 1958, 1959, 1961, 1962, 1963, 1964, 1965, 1966, 1967, 1968, 1969, 1972, 1973, 1974, 1975. Belladonna is the only player who participated in all 16 Italian world victories. He announced his

retirement from the Italian Team in 1979. He was European champion in 1956, 1957, 1958, 1959, 1965, 1967, 1969, 1971, 1973, 1979. His national wins include the Italian Cup 1954, Open Teams 1954, 1959, 1960, 1963, 1966, 1970, 1972, 1974, 1975, 1977, 1978. He also won ACBL Spring NAC Men's Pairs 1971. Columnist for the newsweekly *L'Espresso*, Belladonna is the co-inventor of the ROMAN SYSTEM. See BIBLIOGRAPHY, C.

BELLANGER, Pierre (1877-deceased) of Paris, France, was captain of the first French team to play an international match against an American team (1933; see FRANCO-AMERICAN MATCHES). He was ahead of his time as a theorist in card play, and his book on finesses, *Les Impasses au Bridge* was a notable work. He formulated the doctrine, which only received general endorsement after many years of debate, that PROBABILITIES A PRIORI are a reliable guide to the play after some cards have appeared. If declarer discovers, for example, that West started with five clubs and East with two clubs, the odds of 5-2 in favor of West's holding the missing ♣Q are not affected by the fact that West has discarded three clubs. Bellanger also analyzed correctly a number of situations which were not generally understood until the principle of RESTRICTED CHOICE was formulated 20 years later.

He was secretary general of the Commission Française de Bridge in the Thirties, and took an active part in formulating the 1935 Laws. Other writings included *Les 102 Donnes d'un Grand Match* as well as many magazine articles. See BIBLIOGRAPHY, D, G.

BENAIM, Roberto (b. 1924) of Caracas, Venezuela, publicity executive, officially ranked #2 player in Venezuela, was South American champion 1965, 1966. He also represented Venezuela in the World Team Olympiad 1968, Bermuda Bowl 1966, 1967, South American Championships seven times. His national wins include Open Teams 11 times.

BENDERSKY, Marion F. (Mrs. Louis) of Memphis is ACBL Director of Board Communications, ACBL Director of Elections, ACBL District Supervisor. Formerly she was ACBL Club Department Supervisor and wrote the feature *Club Corner* for the ACBL *Bulletin* from 1974-1977. Bendersky is a former bridge teacher, director and club owner.

BENEDICT, J. Frederic (Fred) (b. 1910) of West Des Moines IA, real estate broker, won World Olympic 1933, USBA Open Teams 1933, Gopher Open Teams 1972, Great Plains Men's Swiss Teams 1979. Benedict has served as an ACBL Director and member of the Board of Governors, and as president and director of the Central New York BA and the Hawkeye Bridge Unit. He has held several civic positions including mayor of Norwich NY 1948-1952.

BENJAMIN, Albert L. (b. 1909) of Glasgow, Scotland, company director, former bridge writer and club owner, won Scottish Open Teams six times and represented Scotland 17 times in CAMROSE TROPHY matches, winning in 1964. He is the co-author of *Tournament Bridge for Everyone*. Other writings include regular contributions to *Bridge Magazine* and a daily bridge column 1937–1976. See BIBLIOGRAPHY, F.

BENNETT, James E. Jr. (b. 1936) of Hartford CT, insurance company supervisor, won Spring NAC Amateur Swiss Teams 1976 and placed second in Blue Ribbon Pairs 1979. His numerous regional wins include Spring NAC secondary Men's Pairs 1979, District 3 Swiss Teams 1977, Men's Swiss Teams 1979, Open Pairs Flt. A 1980, New England Individual KO Teams 1974, New England Masters Master Swiss Teams 1975, Swiss Teams 1976, Swiss Teams Flt. A 1979, New England Knockout Swiss Teams 1982, Eastern States KO Teams (Reisinger) 1965, District 25 GNT, Zone I 1980.

BENNETT, John G. See BENNETT MURDER.

BENONYSSON, Eggert (b. 1908) of Reykajavik, Iceland, radio technician, represented Iceland in the European Championships 1958, 1961. His national titles include Open Teams six times from 1951 to 1963, Open Pairs 1959, 1962.

BENSON, Kirk W. (b. 1949) of Atlanta, computer programming manager, won Spring NAC secondary Swiss Teams 1979, Men's Pairs 1980, Nat'l Capital KO Teams, Men's Swiss Teams 1978, Open Pairs 1980, Mid-Atlantic Open Pairs 1977, KO Teams Flt. A 1981, Florida Men's Pairs 1975, District 5 KO Teams 1980. He has written articles for the Toronto Unit magazine *The Kibitzer* and the District 7 magazine *Pips and Tips*.

BENSON, Leo O. (1907–1979) of Chicago, bridge columnist, teacher and ACBL regional tournament director, was the first person to become both an ABA Life Master and an ACBL Life Master (No. 3572 in 1962). He won the Gopher Open Pairs 1958.

BENTINCK, Lord Henry William (1804–1870) of England, fourth son on the 4th Duke of Portland, a well-known whist player, originated the BLUE PETER, probably the first defensive signal in any card game of the whist family.

BERAH, David A. (b. 1921) of Caracas, Venezuela, born in Yugoslavia, industrialist and bridge writer, officially ranked #3 player in Venezuela, was South American champion 1963, 1965, 1966. He also represented Venezuela in the World Team Olympiad 1960, 1964, 1968, World Open Pairs 1966, Bermuda Bowl 1966, 1967, South American Championships 12 times. He has won every Venezuelan national title on multiple occasions, including Open Teams 11 times. Berah has contributed to the ACBL *Bulletin*, *The Bridge World*, and many other periodicals. He has been Sunday bridge columnist for *The Daily Journal* since 1968. Berah was president of the VENEZUELAN BRIDGE FEDERATION 1977–1981 and is currently president of the CENTRAL AMERICAN AND CARIBBEAN FEDERATION executive committee. A former British Royal Air Force pilot, Berah learned how to play bridge in the desert prior to Montgom-ery's push against Rommel's Panzer divisions.

BERGER, Mark A. (b. 1927) of Fort Lee NJ, sales representative, placed second in Summer NAC Master Mixed Teams 1974. His regional wins include Tri-State Men's Pairs 1968, 1970. Long Island Men's Pairs 1970, New York-New Jersey Men's Pairs 1975. Berger owns his own small plane which he often flies to tournaments. He is an oboist with the Queens Symphony Orchestra.

BERCUSON, Kenneth B. (b. 1950) of Washington, DC, assistant professor of economics, won District 3 Men's Swiss Teams 1979, New York Winter Open Pairs Flt. A 1979, Mid-Atlantic Open Pairs 1981.

BERENBAUM, Carl (b. 1946) of Philadelphia, mathematics teacher, won Long Island Swiss Teams 1976, District 4 Master Pairs, GNP 1981, New York Swiss Teams Flt. A 1980. He also teaches bridge at a Senior Adult center and is a member of the ABTA.

BERG, Mary Lee of Clearwater FL, bridge teacher and director, won Midwest Women's Pairs 1961, 1962, Mixed Pairs 1963, Southeastern Women's Teams 1973, Florida Life Master Pairs 1970.

BERGEN, Marty A. (b. 1948) of White Plains NY, bridge professional, former math teacher and computer programmer, won Spring NAC Men's Teams 1981 and placed second in the Grand National Teams 1979, Vanderbilt 1982. His many regional wins include Summer NAC Sub-Senior Master Teams 1967, Upper New York State Open Pairs 1970, Swiss Teams 1974, New England Summer KO Teams 1979, Swiss Teams 1980, Tri-State Men's Pairs 1977, Men's Swiss Teams 1981, Mixed pairs 1982, Keystone Master Pairs 1972, Men's Pairs 1973, District 3 Men's Swiss Teams 1980, Men's Pairs 1981. Bergen has a regular article in the Master Pointers section of the ACBL *Bulletin*.

BERGLUND, Sven Erik (b. 1936) of Stockholm, Sweden, auditor, represented Sweden in World Team Olympiad 1964, European Championships 1965, 1971, and as npc in the Bermuda Bowl 1977, World Team Olympiad 1976, 1980, European Championships 1977, 1979. His national wins include Swedish Mixed Pairs.

BERGOVOY, Bernie (b. 1930) of Oakland CA, president of a data processing company in partnership with HUGH ROSS, won Spring NAC Men's Teams 1970. His regional wins include the MARCUS CUP 1972, All-Western KO Teams 1969, 1975, Golden Gate Master Pairs 1973, KO Teams 1978, California Capital KO Teams 1977, Mid-Winter Holiday Open Pairs 1978, District 21 GNT 1978.

BERISSO, Alberto (b. 1922) of Buenos Aires, Argentina, Doctor of Economics, was South American champion 1958, 1959, 1961, 1962. He also represented Argentina in the Bermuda Bowl 1959, 1962 1965, World Team Olympiad 1972. His national wins include Master Pairs 1960, 1968, 1971,

Master Individual 1958, 1969, Mixed Pairs 1968, 1969, 1971, 1974, Open Teams 1953, 1956, 1958, 1960, 1961, 1963, 1967, Open Pairs 1958, 1962, Interclubs 1962, 1968, 1969, 1970, 1971, 1973, 1974, 1975, 1977, GABARRET CUP four times.

BERKOWITZ, David L. (b. 1949) of Harmon Cove NJ, certified public accountant, one of the leading American players since 1976, won the Blue Ribbon Pairs 1978, Spring NAC Men's Teams, Men's Pairs, MOTT-SMITH TROPHY 1982 and placed second in the Spingold 1976, Blue Ribbon Pairs 1977, Vanderbilt 1980. His more than 50 regional titles include Fall NAC secondary Swiss Teams Flt. A 1979, Summer Open Pairs, Swiss Teams 1975, Mixed Pairs Flt. A 1980, Men's Pairs Flt. A 1981, District 24 GNT 1979, GNP 1980. Berkowitz is president of the Greater New York BA and has been a member of its Board since 1976.

BERKOWITZ, Lisa W. (Mrs. David L., nee Halpern) (b. 1952) of Harmon Cove NJ, certified public accountant, won Fall NAC secondary Swiss Teams Flt. A 1980, District 4 Women's Pairs, Open Pairs 1981, District 3 KO Teams 1980, Canadian Nat'l Open Pairs 1980, Southeastern Open Pairs Flt. A 1981, Autumn Leaf Open Pairs Flt. A 1981, Tri-State Women's Swiss Teams 1982.

BERKSON, Irving A. (b. 1915) of Skokie IL, company president, won Summer NAC secondary Goddard Pairs 1959, Mid-Am-Can Open Teams, Open Pairs 1956, Midwest Spring Open Teams 1960. Berkson now plays only rubber bridge.

BERLIN, Norman (b. 1907) of Scottsdale AZ, formerly of Norfolk, real estate investor, won Mid-Atlantic Men's Teams 1956, Men's Pairs 1957, Open Teams 1964, 1965, Master Pairs 1971.

BERNARD, Joan E. (b. 1925) of Bradenton FL won the MARCUS CUP 1971, Southeastern Women's Teams 1973, 1976, Mid-Atlantic KO Teams 1975, 1976, Open Teams 1965, Mid-South Master Pairs 1974, Puerto Rico Women's Pairs 1980.

BERNASCONI, Pietro (b. 1932) of Geneva, Switzerland, bridge teacher and club manager, represented Switzerland in the World Team Olympiad 1960, 1964, World Open Pairs 1962, European Championships 1958, 1959, 1961, 1962, 1963, 1965, 1967. His national successes include Open Teams five times and Open Pairs twice.

BERNING, Dorothy E. of Lake Worth FL, retired advertising traffic manager, placed second in Summer NAC Senior and Advanced Senior Master Pairs 1950 and won the MARCUS CUP 1951, Eastern States Women's Pairs 1960.

BERNSTEIN, Andrew J. (b. 1942) of Atlanta, formerly of New York City, one of the leading American players, represented the United States in the Bermuda Bowl 1973, and won the Spingold 1972. His numerous regional wins include Spring NAC secondary Swiss Teams 1981, Summer NAC

secondary BAM Teams 1976, Swiss Teams 2nd Flt. 1975, Mid-Atlantic Fall Swiss Teams 1970, 1975, Winter KO Teams 1977, Open Pairs 1982, Spring Men's Pairs 1975, Swiss Teams 1977, 1980, Eastern States Open Pairs (Goldman) 1969, KO Teams (Reisinger) 1971 among many others. He is the developer of the two-way EXCLUSION BID overcall convention. Bernstein served as chairman of District 7 Judiciary Committee 1981–1982. By profession a clinical psychologist, he is now co-owner of DEVYN PRESS. He co-authored *Do You Know Your Partner*.

BERNSTEIN, Moshe J. (b. 1946) of Teaneck NJ, formerly of Chicago, college professor, won Spring NAC secondary Open Pairs, Swiss Teams 1973, Mississippi Valley Swiss Teams 1974, District 4 Men's Swiss Teams 1977, Men's Pairs 1978, Mid-Atlantic Swiss Teams 1977, Washington Bridge Week Men's Swiss Teams 1977.

BESSE, Jean (b. 1914) of Geneva, Switzerland program director and bridge writer, one of the outstanding bridge players of Europe, represented Switzerland in the World Team Olympiad 1960, 1964, 1968, European Championships 12 times and represented Europe in the Bermuda Bowl 1954. His national titles include French Open Teams, Swiss Open Teams. Besse won the BOLS BRIDGE TIPS competition in 1976. He is the originator of Swiss Acol and is a contributing editor, *Bridge Encyclopedia*.

BETHE, Henry (b. 1944) of Port Washington NY, banker, won Fall NAC Life Master Men's Pairs 1968, HERMAN TROPHY 1968. His many regional wins include Summer NAC secondary Open Pairs Flt. A 1981, Fall Men's Swiss Teams 1978, New York-New Jersey Swiss Teams 1970, Men's Pairs 1971, Mixed Pairs 1976, Fun City Men's Pairs 1971, KO Teams 1975, Canadian Nat'l KO Teams 1977, Can-At Open Pairs 1977, Bermuda Swiss Teams 1982. He is also the winner of the New York TRIATHLON championship 1979, 1980. Bethe wrote a computer program for scoring IMP pairs. He was associate editor of *Post Mortem* 1973–1978. He is a contributing editor, *Bridge Encyclopedia*.

BETHE, Kitty (Mrs. Henry, nee Munson) (b. 1950) of New York City, computer systems executive, won Summer NAC Senior and Advanced Senior Master Pairs 1975. Her regional wins include Fall NAC secondary Women's Swiss Teams 1976, New York Winter Women's Pairs 1978, Mixed Pairs 1979, District 3 Women's Swiss Teams 1979, Can-At Open Pairs 1977, NY-NJ Mixed Pairs 1976.

BETTS, Laurence (b. 1950) of Vancouver BC, lawyer, won District 19 GNT 1978, Puget Sound Master Pairs Flt. A 1979, Swiss Teams Flt. A 1981, Peach Festival Swiss Teams 1974, KO Teams 1978, White Hat KO Teams 1977, Emerald Empire KO Teams 1979, Oregon Trail KO Teams 1982. He served as manager of Unit 430 1973–1975 and contributes to its publication, *The Matchpointer*.

BEYNON, George W. (1864–1965) an authority on tournament direction, was born in Portage La

Prairie MB and lived in St. Petersburg FL. One of the leading personalities in the world of bridge, Beynon studied at Wesley University, Winnipeg, and his first career was that of a professional hockey player in Hamilton ON. He made music his major occupation, studying at La Scala in Milan and later directing orchestras in Europe and America. After becoming an American citizen in 1904, Beynon developed a successful plan for synchronizing music with silent films. He was the musical director of *Birth of a Nation* (1915) and other early sucesses, and retired to East Orange NJ in 1917.

Forced out of retirement by the 1929 crash, Beynon made a new career in bridge. After directing games in New Jersey and writing a Newark bridge column, he joined the Culbertson organization in 1935 as office manager and became secretary general for the USBA. He rapidly became an authority on MOVEMENTS and continued to report tournaments.

After the USBA amalgamated with the ABL in 1937, Beynon served the ACBL as field tournament director 1937–55 and as ACBL *Bulletin* editor 1939–52. After his second retirement in 1955 he was made consultant on matters of tournament direction and named ACBL Honorary Member.

After moving from New York to St. Petersburg in 1955, Beynon founded a successful correspondence school for directors and began writing a weekly bridge column for the St. Petersburg *Times*. When he celebrated his 100th birthday in September, 1964, he was probably the oldest working newspaperman in America.

His writings include *Bridge Directors's Manual*, the standard work on duplicate organization (see BIBLIOGRAPHY, F), as well as many magazine articles. He was a contributing editor of the *Bridge Encyclopedia*.

BHARGAVA, Divakar (b.1945) of Gibbsboro NJ, born in Sadabad, India, won Fall NAC secondary Open Pairs 1972, New England Men's Pairs 1974, District 25 GNT 1974, California Capital Master Pairs 1971.

BHATIA, Gena G. (Mrs. Kumar) of Euclid OH, sales representative, won District 5 Women's Swiss Teams 1980, Labor Day Women's Swiss Teams 1980, 1981, Wolverine Master Pairs 1978.

BHATIA, Kumar N. (b. 1942) of Euclid OH, born in India, sales representative, won All-American Men's Pairs 1977, Open Pairs Flt. A, Swiss Teams 1979, Wolverine Master Pairs 1978. He is a past president of Unit 125 and District 5.

BHAVNANI, Krishin H. (b. 1930) of Carlisle MA, born in Sind, India, won District 5 Open Pairs 1960, Master Pairs 1963, New England KO Teams 1967, California Capital Master Pairs 1971, District 25 GNP 1981, New England KO Swiss Teams 1982. Bhavnani is the co-inventor of American Relay and Super-Canapé systems. A graduate of M.I.T., he is involved in software-based ionospheric research.

BIANCHI, Benito (1924–1979) of Leghorn, Italy,

furrier, WBF Grand Master, one of Europe's outstanding players, was Bermuda Bowl champion 1973, 1974, European champion 1965, 1967, 1969, 1971 (played on five other teams representing Italy in the European Championships), won the Italian Cup (four times), the Italian Mixed Teams (twice), and the Italian Open Teams 1961. He was co-developer of the LEGHORN DIAMOND (LIVORNO) SYSTEM.

BIANCHI, Marisa (Mrs. Benito) (b. 1928) of Leghorn, Italy, one of the world's great women players, won the World Women's Teams 1972, 1976, and represented Italy in seven European Women's Championships, winning in 1970, 1971, 1973, 1974, 1977. She also won European Common Market Women's Teams 1971, 1973, Italian Mixed Teams twice and British Women's Teams 1973.

BICIOCCHI, Stephen A. (b. 1947) of Fairport NY, senior industrial engineer, won District 4 KO Teams 1977, Nat'l Capital KO Teams 1977, New England Individual KO Teams 1979, New England Masters Master Swiss Teams 1977, District 25 GNP 1980, District 4 GNP 1981.

BIDDLE, John R. (b. 1928) Canal Winchester OH, won Spring NAC Open Pairs 1965. His regional wins include Great Lakes Open Teams 1962, Midwest Spring Life Master Pairs 1972, Wolverine Swiss Teams 1978, District 11 Open Pairs 1971, Swiss Teams 1972, GNT 1974.

BIRMAN, David of Tel Aviv, Israel, born in Wroclaw, Poland, represented Israel in the European Junior Championships 1970, World Team Olympiad 1980, European Championships 1981. Birman won the 1977 MACCABIAH GAMES, Israeli Pairs 1980 (second in 1976), Israeli Teams 1977, 1978, 1979 and placed second in 1980, 1981. Other wins include Tel Aviv Open Teams 1977, 1980, 1982, Open Pairs 1976. He was captain of the Israeli Junior Team 1980 and coach 1979–1982. Birman, an industrial engineer, teaches bridge and directs tournaments at the Disabled Soldiers Recreational Center and co-edits the *Israeli Bridge Bulletin*.

BIRNBACH, Ethel J. (b. 1927) of Portland OR, private investor, won Oregon Trail Women's Pairs 1974, Puget Sound Women's Swiss Teams 1977, Mid-Winter Holiday Open Pairs Flt. A 1981.

BISHOP, Clifford W. (b. 1921) of Detroit, advertising executive, one of the leading players of the Middle West, was Bermuda Bowl champion 1954. He also represented the United States in the Bermuda Bowl 1955. He won the Spingold 1953, 1954 and placed second in Spring NAC Men's Pairs 1951, Men's Teams 1953. His numerous regional titles include Spring NAC secondary Swiss Teams 1975, All-American Open Teams 1948, 1955, Southeastern Open Teams, Men's Teams, Men's Pairs 1974, Cambrian Shield KO Teams 1974, 1976, Southeastern Swiss Teams, Men's Pairs, 1974, Men's Swiss Teams 1974, 1976, 1977, Motor City Men's Pairs 1974, Master Pairs 1975, Men's Swiss Teams 1976.

BITMAN, Jack (b. 1922) of Denver won the Grand National Teams 1980. His regional titles include Rocky Mountain KO Teams 1972, Open Pairs 1974, 1976, Swiss Teams 1975, Swiss Teams Flt. A 1980.

BITNER, Stanislaw (b. 1922) of Warsaw, Poland, economist and bridge writer, represented Poland in many international matches including European Championships 1962, 1963, 1966, 1967. He won Yugoslav Open Pairs 1965 and placed second in Open Teams 1964. Polish Player of the Year 1962, his national successes include Open Teams 1957. He is a frequent contributor to *Brydz*.

BIXBY, Wingate (1900-1979) of New York City, investment banker and stock broker, won Fall NAC Mixed Pairs 1936 and placed second in the Vanderbilt 1939. Bixby led the unofficial United States teams which won the Pan-American Championships in 1938, 1955 and 1958. He served as president of the Regency Club 1950–1963 and of Crockford's Club of Chicago 1938.

BJERKAN, Cheri (Mrs. James) of Elmhurst IL, pension consultant, placed second in Spring NAC Women's KO Teams 1978, 1979, 1981. Her 14 regional wins include Spring NAC secondary Swiss Teams 1973, Central States II Women's Pairs 1978, Women's Swiss Teams 1979, Swiss Teams, Open Pairs 1980, Champagne Master Pairs 1975, Swiss Teams 1978, Women's Swiss Teams 1979, District 13 GNT 1976.

BJERKAN, James R. (Jim) (b. 1947) of Elmhurst IL, estimator and contract project manager, won several regional events including Central States II Swiss Teams Flt. A 1979, Open Pairs, Swiss Teams 1980, Central States Open Pairs 1980, Champagne Swiss Teams 1978, Tri-Unit Mixed Pairs 1975, Southeastern Open Pairs Flt. A 1980, District 13 GNT 1976. He has served on the Chicago CBA Grand National Committee since 1976 and was CCBA player of the year 1980.

BLACK, Ethelyn F. (b. 1916) of Modesto CA, attorney, won Intermountain Swiss Teams, Open Pairs 1977, Mount Shasta Master Swiss Teams 1978, Big Sky KO Teams 1979, White Hat KO Teams 1979, Hawaii KO Teams, Women's Swiss Teams 1979, Mid-Winter Holiday Swiss Teams 1979.

BLACKERBY, Kirk A. (b. 1941) of San Jose CA, professor of economics, won numerous regional events including Oregon Trail KO Teams 1970, Men's Pairs 1972, California Capital KO Teams 1972, Swiss Teams 1976, All-Western KO Teams 1971, Golden Gate Swiss Teams 1974, KO Teams 1977, Golden State Men's Pairs 1975, Swiss Teams 1976, Intermountain KO Teams 1973, Tri-Cities KO Teams 1975, Rogue River Valley Master Pairs, Swiss Teams 1973, District 21 GNT 1980.

BLACKWOOD, Easley R. (b. 1903) of Indianapolis is one of the famous bridge personalities in the world. He is perhaps most notable for his invention of the BLACKWOOD 4 NT convention. A former insurance manager, since 1964 he has presided over Blackwood Bridge Enterprises and has directed bridge activities on 32 luxury ship cruises. He served as ACBL Executive Secretary 1968–1971, president of both the Mid-West Conference and Central Indiana Unit. He is a history buff, enjoys chess and music. Formerly he was a singer and string player. A bridge teacher and former bridge club owner, Blackwood was awarded Honorary Membership in the AMERICAN BRIDGE TEACHERS' ASSOCIATION in 1978. He was honored by the mayor of his city who proclaimed October 28, 1977 "Easley Blackwood Day". The ACBL named him Honorary Member in 1980. He won Mid-West Fall Men's pairs 1944, Southern Conference Open Teams 1962. His writings include *Bridge Humanics*, *Blackwood on Bidding*, *Blackwood on Slams*, *Winning Bridge with Blackwood*, *Play of the Hand with Blackwood*, articles for many magazines including the ACBL *Bulletin*, and a syndicated newspaper column. See BIBLIOGRAPHY, C, D, E.

BLAIR, Jack (b. 1933) of Tulsa OK, oil executive, one of the leading Southwest players, represented the United States in the World Open Pairs 1962. He won Fall NAC Men's Pairs 1960, Spring NAC Men's Teams 1972, Life Master Pairs 1973, MOTT-SMITH TROPHY 1972 and placed second in Fall NAC Open Pairs 1961, 1964, Reisinger 1973, Vanderbilt 1972. His numerous regional wins include Summer NAC secondary Swiss Teams 1973, Missouri Valley Open Teams 1965, KO Teams, Swiss Teams 1971, Open Pairs 1975, District 15 Open Pairs Flt. A 1980. See FORTUNE.

BLAISS, Gary (b. 1934) of Austin TX, national tournament director since 1979, won Mexican Nationals KO Teams Flt. B 1982.

BLAKEY, Helen M. (Mrs. Robert) (b. 1945) of Columbia MD, software configuration manager, won the Grand National Pairs 1981, Fall NAC secondary Women's Swiss Teams 1976, Summer Mixed Pairs 1975, Mid-Atlantic Master Swiss Teams, Women's Swiss Teams 1980, Open Pairs Flt. A 1981, Swiss Teams 1975, District 4 Master Pairs 1978, Canadian Nat'l KO Teams 1976, Washington Bridge Week Swiss Teams 1976.

BLAKEY, Robert C. (b. 1946) of Columbia MD, senior software engineer, won the Grand National Pairs 1981, Summer NAC secondary Mixed Pairs 1975, Mid-Atlantic Swiss Teams 1975, Men's Swiss Teams 1978, Master Swiss Teams 1980, Open Pairs Flt. A 1981, Canadian Nat'l KO Teams, Men's Swiss Teams 1976, Washington Bridge Week Swiss Teams 1976, District 4 Master Pairs 1978.

BLANCHARD, Katherine A. (b. 1889) of El Toro CA, retired school teacher, placed second in Fall NAC Life Master Women's Pairs 1968 and won Pacific Southwest Women's Pairs 1960, Rocky Mountain KO Teams 1969, Bridge Week Women's Pairs 1969, All-Western Mixed Pairs 1962.

BLASBAND, Gertrude of Philadelphia won Fall

NAC Women's Teams 1963 and placed second in Fall NAC Mixed Pairs 1966. Her regional wins include Texas Open Pairs 1962, Keystone Mixed Pairs 1959, Southeastern Women's Swiss Teams 1978, District 4 Women's Pairs 1979.

BLOM, Britt. See NYGREN, BRITT.

BLOOM, Betty (Mrs. Steven H., formerly Crowther) of Duanesburg NY won Summer NAC Master Mixed Teams 1979. Her regional titles include New England Summer KO Teams 1978, Fall KO Teams 1981, Mississippi Valley Open Pairs 1978, 1980, Midwest Fall KO Teams 1978, Autumn Leaf Swiss Teams Flt. A 1981, District 8 GNT 1980.

BLOOM, Steven H. of Duanesburg NY, assistant professor of math, won Summer NAC Master Mixed Teams 1979. His regional wins include Summer NAC secondary President's Pairs 1973, Mississippi Valley Men's Pairs, Swiss Teams 1975, Open Pairs 1978, 1980, New England Summer KO Teams 1978, Fall KO Teams 1981, Iowa Master Pairs 1976, District 15 Summer Swiss Teams 1977, All-American Swiss Teams 1977, Midwest Fall KO Teams 1978, Great Lakes Men's Swiss Teams 1979, Autumn Leaf Swiss Teams Flt. A 1981, District 3 Men's Swiss Teams 1981, District 8 GNT 1980.

BLOOMFIELD, Ruth E. (b. 1925) of Chicago won Fall NAC Life Master Women's Pairs 1971, Bermuda Women's Pairs 1976.

BLOUSSON, Alberto (1908-1967) of Buenos Aires, Argentina, was South American champion 1948, 1957, 1958. He also represented Argentina in the Bermuda Bowl 1958. His national wins included Open Teams 1938, 1942, 1949, 1955, Open Pairs 1942, 1943, 1947 and he was top record holder in the Master Individual Championship.

BLUHM, Louis E. (Lou) (b. 1940) of Atlanta, bridge professional, one of the leading American players, placed third in the World Mixed Pairs 1978. He won the Reisinger 1972, Spingold 1974, 1977, Vanderbilt 1979 (second in 1978), Fall NAC Blue Ribbon Pairs 1977, Men's Teams 1977 (second in 1973). He also won the Cavendish Invitational 1981 and more than 50 regional events including Summer NAC secondary Swiss Teams 1979, Fall Swiss Teams 2nd Flt., Open Swiss Teams 1975, District 7 GNT 1974, 1979, 1980, 1981, Zone III 1981, GNP 1979, 1981 and many Mid-Atlantic regionals.

BLUM, Desiderio (1906-1966) of Buenos Aires, Argentina, businessman, was npc of the Argentine team in the 1962 Bermuda Bowl. He was South American champion 1959, 1962, 1964 and won Argentine Open Teams 1958, Open Pairs 1950, 1958. He served as president of the ARGENTINE BRIDGE ASSOCIATION 1957-1959.

BLUM, Shirley R. (b. 1930) of Fresno CA, small business owner, won Golden State KO Teams 1968, Swiss Teams 1978, Swiss Teams Flt. A 1981.

BLUMENTHAL, Brenda J. (b. 1946) of Castro Valley CA, bridge professional, won Southeastern Women's Swiss Teams 1975, Capital District Fall Women's Swiss Teams 1977, Golden State KO Teams 1978, All-Western Swiss Teams 1978, All-Southern Mixed Pairs 1979, Oregon Trail Open Pairs Flt. A 1979, Mississippi Valley KO Teams 1979, Rocky Mountain Swiss Teams 1980, Bridge Week Women's Pairs 1980, North Florida Swiss Teams 1980, Mount Shasta Swiss Teams 1981.

BLUMENTHAL, Mark E. (b. 1942) of Chicago, one of the leading American players until 1977 when complications arising from open heart surgery caused his retirement from active participation in tournament bridge, was a member of the ACES TEAM 1972-1974. He placed second in the Bermuda Bowl 1973, 1974, won the Vanderbilt 1973, 1977, MOTT-SMITH TROPHY 1977, and placed second in the Spingold 1976. His numerous regional titles include Spring NAC secondary Open Swiss Teams 1977, Summer Swiss Teams Second Flt. 1975, Swiss Teams Flt. A 1980, MARCUS CUP 1968 and the following KO Teams: Eastern States 1965, District 11 1971, Fun City 1971, New England 1971, Indy 500 1973, Keystone 1974, 1975, Mid-Atlantic 1974, Midwest Spring 1975, Washington Bridge Week 1975.

BLUMENTHAL, Maxine of Bellevue WA, department store executive, won All-Western Master Pairs 1974, Gem State Swiss Teams 1974, Puget Sound Mixed Pairs 1972, 1977, Open Pairs 1978, British Columbia Swiss Teams Flt. A 1981.

BLUSTEIN, Mary Ruth (Mrs. Maurice) of Mercer Island WA, assistant buyer, won Oregon Trail Mixed Pairs 1969, KO Teams 1972, Yakima Valley Women's Pairs 1974, Puget Sound Women's Pairs 1977, Can-Am Open Pairs Flt. A 1979, British Columbia Open Pairs Flt. A 1980, Indian Summer Swiss Teams Flt. A 1981.

BLUSTEIN, Maurice J. of Mercer Island WA, born in Malines, Belgium, won Oregon Trail KO Teams 1972, Can-Am Open Pairs Flt. A 1979, British Columbia Open Pairs Flt. A 1980, Indian Summer Swiss Teams Flt. A 1981.

BOARDMAN, Kathrin M. (Mrs. Peter R.) (b. 1949) of Auckland, New Zealand, university lecturer and school teacher, was Far East Women's champion 1981. She also represented New Zealand in the World Women's Teams 1980. Her national wins include Interprovincial Teams 1978, 1979, 1980, 1981.

BOECK, Jens (b. 1916) of Copenhagen, Denmark, bridge writer and editor, has been the bridge editor of *Jyllands-Posten* since 1981. Formerly he was the editor of the Danish magazine *Dansk Bridge* and a contributing editor, First Edition, *Bridge Encyclopedia*. He has written several books on bridge including *The Small Bridge Dictionary*, *Bid Modern*, *Play Modern Bridge*.

BOEDER, John (b. 1943) of Roseville MN, computer systems designer, won All-American Swiss Teams 1975, Canadian Nat'l Swiss Teams 1975, District 5 Swiss Teams 1976, Roughrider Swiss Teams 1979, District 14 GNP 1981. He writes a column for the District 5 publication.

BOEHM, George A. W. (b. 1922) of New York City, writer, editor, mathematician, won Eastern States KO Teams (Reisinger) 1955. He served two terms as vice president of Greater New York BA and was editor of its publication, *Post-Mortem*, in the early Sixties. He has contributed several articles to *The Bridge World* including a two-part exposition of LEBENSOLD which he popularized.

BOEKHORST, André of Utrecht, The Netherlands, chemistry teacher, represented The Netherlands in the European Championships 1969 and won National Pairs 1969. He has served as secretary of NETHERLANDS BRIDGE LEAGUE and as executive committee member of the EUROPEAN BRIDGE LEAGUE. Boekhorst has written a weekly column for *De Volkskrant* since 1974 and has been the chief editor of *Bridge* since 1970.

BOENDER, Pieter (1919–1974) formerly of The Hague, The Netherlands, was a city official and bridge columnist. Boender represented The Netherlands in the World Team Olympiad 1964, European Championships 1956, 1959, 1961, 1963, 1965. He won National Open Teams 1950, 1959, 1960, 1961, 1964, Master Pairs 1961. He co-authored *Zakencyclopedie voor Bridgers*.

BOESGAARD, Knud-Aage, (b. 1950) of Copenhagen, Denmark, accountant, represented Denmark in the European Open Teams 1975 and won European Junior Open Teams 1970, Nordic Junior Open Teams 1971, 1973, and all three major Danish national titles 1975. See IBPA AWARDS.

BOGAERTS, Louis (b. 1907) of Antwerp, Belgium, business manager, represented Belgium in the World Open Pairs 1962, European Championships 1954, 1955, 1957. His national titles include Belgian Open Teams 1956, 1959. He served as president of the BELGIUM ROYAL BRIDGE FEDERATION 1960–1966.

BOGAIR, Dr. Nahum (b. 1912) of Tel Aviv, Israel, pediatrician and lecturer, represented Israel in the European Championships 1965 and won Tel Aviv Open Teams 1964. He is a former president of ISRAEL BRIDGE FEDERATION.

BOGUCH, Gaye (b. 1950) of Bellevue WA, former clinician, won Rogue River Valley Women's Swiss Teams 1976, Puget Sound Women's Swiss Teams 1977, Indian Summer Women's Pairs 1977, Oregon Trail Swiss Teams 1981, District 20 GNT, Zone VIII 1980.

BOLLS, Lt. Col. Larry R. (b. 1939) of Mather AFB, CA, Air Force officer, won Spring NAC Amateur Swiss Teams 1977, California Capital Open Pairs Flt. A, Swiss Teams 1981. Bolls wrote a bridge column for both the NATO publication and an Italian

newspaper for three years while stationed in Naples. He is nationally-ranked at table tennis .

BONANNI, Rosanna of Caracas, Venezuela, represented Venezuela in the Venice Trophy teams 1981. She was Central American and Caribbean Women's Teams champion 1980, 1981, 1982 and placed second in the South American Championships 1972. Her national titles include women's and open events.

BONDE, Count Carl (b. 1897) of Moerkoe, Sweden, landed estates owner, was npc of the Swedish Open Team and Women's Team on many occasions. He served as president of the SWEDISH BRIDGE LEAGUE 1960–1965, president of the EUROPEAN BRIDGE LEAGUE 1965–1969, president of the WORLD BRIDGE FEDERATION 1968–1970. Bonde is an Honorary Member of the WBF, the EBL and the Swedish Bridge Federation.

BONNEY, C. Jack (1904–1982) of Ozona FL, formerly of Armonk NY, accountant and bridge teacher, won Spring NAC secondary Non-Master Pairs 1945, Mid-Atlantic Fall Open Teams 1953, Upper New York State Men's Pairs 1961. He organized the Westchester Contract BA and was its first president and also served as president of the Miami Bridge Club in the late Thirties. A bridge teacher and director in Westchester County NY from the Forties until 1975, he wrote several bridge teaching handbooks including *Master Bridge Teaching Guide*. See BIBLIOGRAPHY, E.

BONNEY, Mildred C. (Mrs. C. Jack, formerly Betzler) (b. 1917) of Ozona FL, bridge teacher and accountant, placed second in Spring NAC Women's Pairs 1952 and won Mid-Atlantic Fall Open Teams 1953, Eastern States Women's Pairs 1959, New England KO Open Pairs 1973. Bonney served as secretary-treasurer of Westchester CBA 1949–1952.

BONOMI, Robert F. (b. 1918) of Memphis, has been ACBL Public Relations Director since 1973. A graduate of University of Idaho 1942, Bonomi has had long experience in public relations and news organizations, including editor, Associated Press, 1947–1948. He is a member of Public Relations Society of America. Bonomi produces several publications for the ACBL including *Club Managers' Digest*, *Unit Officers' Newsletter*, *Duplicate Insight*, *Unit Awards Program* and *Lunch-time Team Leagues*. He first played duplicate in a P. O. W. camp in Poland 1944.

BOOKSTAVER, John D. (b. 1942), marketing manager, won New England KO Teams 1972, Mid-Atlantic Summer Open Pairs 1971, Keystone Swiss Teams 1969, Golden Gate Master Pairs, Swiss Teams 1976.

BOONSUPA, Ananta (b. 1934) of Bangkok, Thailand, marketing manager, was Far East champion 1965. He also represented Thailand in the Bermuda Bowl 1966, 1967, World Team Olympiad 1968, Far East Championships 1962, 1965, 1966, 1969, 1970.

His national wins include Thailand Master Individual 1960, Open Pairs 1961, Open Teams 1963, 1964, 1965, Mixed Pairs 1964.

BORAK, Bernard (b. 1910) of Fort Lauderdale FL, born in Leipzig, Germany, retired insurance broker, represented Czechoslovakia in prewar European Championships and in the first world championship 1937 in Budapest. He won Eastern States Open Pairs (Goldman) 1962.

BORBELY, Linda. See PETERSON, LINDA.

BORIN, Jim (b. 1935) of Melbourne, Australia, bridge club owner, teacher and writer, born in London, England, represented Australia in the Bermuda Bowl 1971, 1977, 1979, World Team Olympiad 1972. He is the winner of Zone 7 Championships 1970, 1971, Australia Nat'l Individual 1974, 1976, 1977, Mixed Pairs 1977, 1979, Open Pairs 1980, McCutcheon Trophy (Australian McKenney) 1972, Interstate Teams 1962, 1968. He contributes to *Australian Bridge* and is co-author of *Our Precision Style.* See BIBLIOGRAPHY, C.

BORIN, Norma of Melbourne, Australia, bridge club owner, teacher and writer, represented Australia in the Bermuda Bowl 1971, 1977, 1979, World Team Olympiad 1972. She won Zone 7 Championships 1970, 1971, Australian Interstate Teams 1968, Open Pairs 1980, Mixed Pairs 1977, 1979, Women's Individual 1981, McCutcheon Trophy (Australian McKenney) 1981. She is co-author of *Our Precision Style.* See BIBLIOGRAPHY, C.

BORK, Harry (b. 1909) of Hamilton ON, business manager, represented Canada in the World Team Olympiad 1960. He placed second in Fall NAC Senior Master Individual 1951 and won Canadian Nat'l Mixed Pairs 1960, KO Teams 1968.

BOSCO, Jorge (b. 1920) of Buenos Aires, Argentina, lawyer, represented Argentina in the Bermuda Bowl 1961. His national wins include Open Teams 1951, 1953, 1966, Master Individual 1965, Master Pairs 1967, 1976, Interclubs 1961, 1963, 1964, 1979.

BOSCOWITZ, Herbert H. (Hubie) (b. 1902) of New York City won AWL All-American Open Teams 1933, Summer NAC Master Mixed Teams 1932 and placed second in the Vanderbilt 1934. The first recipient of the WETZLAR TROPHY, Boscowitz was president of the AMERICAN BRIDGE LEAGUE in 1935 and was responsible for introducing the MASTERPOINT PLAN, which became the basis of the ACBL's subsequent prosperity.

BOSE MULLICK, S. G. of India, president of the BRIDGE FEDERATION OF INDIA 1982, captained the Indian Women's Team to victory in the Far East Championships 1978.

BOULENGER, Jean-Michel (b. 1934) of Paris, France, one of the leading French players, represented France in the World Team Olympiad 1964, 1976, Bermuda Bowl 1967, 1969, European Championships 1963, 1965. He was European champion 1966, 1970, 1974, runner-up in 1967 and has won many French national titles.

BOURCHTOFF, Andrée (Mrs. Gérard) (b. 1923) of Paris, France, was European Women's champion 1953, 1954 and also represented France 1957, 1958. Her national wins include Women's Teams.

BOURCHTOFF, Gérard (b. 1923) of Paris, France, company director, WBF Grand Master, won the World Team Olympiad 1960 and also represented France in the World Team Olympiad 1968, 1972, European Championships 1952, 1956, 1959, placing second in 1956, 1959. He won many national titles including Open Teams many times, Open Pairs 1959 and English Master Pairs 1960.

BOURDILLON, Tom J. E. (b. 1938) of Harare, Zimbabwe, university lecturer, represented Zimbabwe in international matches 1976, 1977, 1980, 1982. His national titles include Matabeleland Open Teams 1975, 1976, 1979, Open Pairs 1977, 1978, Mashonaland Open Teams 1975, 1978, Open Pairs 1981, Midlands Open Teams 1976, 1980. He served as chairman of ZIMBABWE BRIDGE UNION 1979–1980.

BOWIE, Clagett (Clag) (b. 1907) of Falls Church VA, mathematician, won Fall NAC secondary Senior Master Individual 1949, Keystone Open Pairs 1955, Eastern States Open Pairs (Goldman) 1970, Mid-Atlantic Spring KO Teams 1973. Bowie was educated at Princeton and Harvard Law School. From 1942 until his retirement in 1972 he worked for industry as a mathematician. In 1971 he discovered and published a theorem in matrix algebra. He is credited with the queen-over-jack rubber bridge theory (see QUEEN OVER JACK and TWO-WAY FINESSE).

BOWMAN, John T. (b. 1947) of Ottawa ON, computer operator, won Can-At Swiss Teams 1975, 1977, BAM Teams 1977, Fleur-de-Lys Open Pairs 1973, Swiss Teams 1979, Can-Am Open Pairs 1980, Cambrian Shield KO Teams 1973, Upper New York State Swiss Teams 1972, Bluenose Mixed Pairs 1981. His frequent bridge partner is his twin brother, Bill.

BOYCE, Mildred L. (b. 1947) of Austin TX, purchasing agent, won Spring NAC Women's Pairs 1980 and placed second in Spring NAC Women's Teams 1975.

BOYD, Peter A. (b. 1950) of Falls Church VA, computer programmer, won more than 25 regionals since 1973 including Fall NAC secondary Swiss Teams 2nd Flt. 1976, Swiss Teams Flt. B 1980, Spring NAC secondary Silver Trophy Pairs Flt. A 1981, Upper New York State KO Teams, Men's Pairs 1974, Swiss Teams 1975, Keystone Open Pairs 1973, 1975, Washington Bridge Week KO Teams 1977, District 4 KO Teams 1981, District 5 Master Pairs 1975. He is a graduate of Harvard University.

BRACERAS, Jaime of Buenos Aires, Argentina was South American champion 1976. His national wins include Open Teams 1968, Open Pairs 1969,

Master Individual 1971, 1972, Interclubs 1968, 1969, 1970, 1971, 1973, 1974, 1975.

BRACHMAN, Malcolm K. (b. 1926) of Dallas, independent oil operator, former physicist and life insurance executive, one of the leading American personalities, was Bermuda Bowl champion 1979. He also represented the United States in the Rosenblum Cup Teams 1978. He won the Reisinger 1976, 1980, Vanderbilt 1978, Spingold 1978 and placed second in the Spingold 1973, Vanderbilt 1976, Spring NAC Men's Teams 1970. His more than 50 regional wins include Fall NAC secondary Silver Trophy Pairs Flt. A 1981, Men's Swiss Teams 1976, Central States II Men's KO Teams, Swiss Teams, Men's Swiss Teams 1981. Brachman was educated at Harvard University and Yale University.

BRACHMAN, Minda (Mrs. Malcolm K.) (b. 1931) of Dallas won Summer NAC Master Mixed Teams 1968 and placed second in Summer NAC Life Master Pairs 1971. Her more than 40 regional wins include 29 Knockout Team titles and Pacific Southwest Mixed Pairs 1977, King Cotton Master Pairs 1980, Mount Shasta Open Pairs 1981.

BRADLEY, Kenn (b. 1933) of Tulsa OK, attorney, won many regional titles including Missouri Valley Swiss Teams 1971, Master Pairs 1973, KO Teams 1975, Mid-South Swiss Teams 1972, 1974, Oklahoma City Men's Swiss Teams, Open Pairs Flt. A 1981, Mid-Winter Holiday KO Teams 1975, Oil City KO Teams 1978, District 15 KO Teams 1978. He is a former president of Unit 158.

BRADY, Phil (b. 1947) of Philadelphia, computer professional, won more than two dozen regional events including Spring NAC secondary Swiss Teams 1981, Fall NAC secondary Silver Trophy Pairs Flt. A 1980, Zone II GNT 1981, District 5 Men's Pairs 1979, 1981, Men's Swiss Teams 1980, District 4 Swiss Teams 1977, KO Teams 1978, Men's Pairs 1979, All-American Swiss Teams 1978, Open Pairs 1980 and many others including seven Mid-Atlantic regional titles.

BRALL, Carlyn (Mrs. Ira) (b. 1911) of New York City, editorial consultant, won Spring NAC Women's Teams 1955, 1958. Her regional wins include Keystone Mixed Pairs 1957, New York-New Jersey Women's Pairs 1959, Eastern States Mixed Teams 1955, 1968. Former editor of Greater New York BA's *Post-Mortem* and editorial assistant to WALDEMAR VON ZEDTWITZ and ALBERT MOREHEAD, Brall has edited several bridge books including *Goren Answers the Bridge Problems.*

BRAMLEY, Bart (b. 1948) of Avon CT, consulting computer programmer, won Spring NAC Men's Teams 1980, placed second in 1976 and in the Spingold 1981, Fall NAC Mixed Pairs 1981. His many regional wins include Summer NAC secondary Open Pairs 1974, Spring Men's Swiss Teams 1973, Open Swiss Teams 2nd Flt. 1976, Fall Swiss Teams Flt. A 1979, District 25 GNT 1976, GNP 1981, Zone I 1980, New England Summer Swiss Teams 1975,

1978, KO Teams 1976, Upper New York State KO Teams 1976, Fun City KO Teams 1975, New England Knockout and Individual KO Teams 1977.

BRANCO, Marcelo Castelo (b. 1945) of Rio de Janeiro, Brazil, construction engineer and government official, WBF Grand Master, one of the world's leading players, was South American champion 1968, 1971, 1972, 1973, 1975, 1977, 1978. He and GABINO CINTRA share with Jaïs-Trézel the distinction of having won both the World Team Olympiad (1976) and the World Open Pairs (1978). He placed second in the Rosenblum Cup Teams 1978 and also represented Brazil in the Bermuda Bowl 1969, 1973, 1974, 1979, World Team Olympiad 1980, World Open Pairs 1974. His national wins include Brazilian Open Teams 1967, 1968, 1969, 1973, 1974, 1978, 1979, Open Pairs 1972.

BRANCO, Pedro Paulo C. (P. P.) (b. 1940) of Rio de Janeiro, Brazil, insurance technician, one of the leading South American players, was South American champion 1969, 1972, 1973, 1978, 1979, 1981, Open Pairs 1969. He also represented Brazil in the Bermuda Bowl 1973, 1974, 1976, World Team Olympiad 1972, 1980, World Open Pairs 1974.

BRANNON, Robert Means (1882–1944) of New York City, born in Columbus GA, businessman, bridge studio owner and bridge writer, authored many early books on contract including *The Incomparable Club Convention,* a book on the Vanderbilt System, and *Foolproof Contract.* See BIBLIOGRAPHY, C, E.

BRASHLER, Ted of Lockport IL, real estate investor, won several regional events including Spring NAC secondary Swiss Teams 1972, Summer NAC secondary Silver Trophy Pairs Flt. A 1978, Tri-Unit KO Teams 1971, Central States Swiss Teams 1973, Men's Pairs 1977, Missouri Valley Swiss Teams 1975, Wisconsin Oktoberfest Men's Swiss Teams 1976, Open Pairs Flt. A 1978, Gopher Open Pairs Flt. A 1981.

BRATCHER, Robert L. (b. 1930) of Oceanside CA, regional tournament director, won Fall NAC secondary Commercial and Industrial Pairs 1962, Midwest Open Teams 1963, Mid-Atlantic Mixed Pairs 1963, ABA National Open Teams 1962.

BRAUNSTEIN, Marion (Mrs. Maurice) (b. 1917) of Schenectady NY, auditor, won Summer NAC secondary Sub-Senior Master Teams 1956. She is a regional tournament director.

BRAUNSTEIN, Maurice F. (Maury) (b. 1914) of Schenectady NY, national tournament director, won Can-Am Open Teams 1955, New England Open Teams 1955, and other regionals. Braunstein, a graduate of Columbia, formerly was a computer processing director for the State of New York. He began his career as a tournament director in 1954 and soon found directing more of a challenge than playing. He became a national tournament director in 1968 when he retired from his New York work.

He is in charge of all nationally-rated events at North American Championships. He made his debut as a World Bridge Federation director in 1972 and was the in-charge director at the 1973 Bermuda Bowl in Guaruja, Brazil. He now is assistant chief director at all world championships. He is the originator of several duplicate movements, including the STANZA MOVEMENT. Braunstein is known worldwide for his bow ties which have become his trademark at tournaments everywhere.

BRAUSS, Stephen P. (b. 1943) of Creve Coeur MO, teacher, won District 8 Swiss Teams 1979, GNT 1979, GNP 1981, Champagne Men's Pairs 1980.

BRECHNER, Dora of New London CT won Summer NAC secondary Mixed Pairs 1965, New York-New Jersey Women's Pairs 1966, Keystone Women's Pairs 1968. Brechner lives in Israel for most of each year and since 1974 has represented Israel in the European Championships, World Women's Teams and World Women's Pairs.

BRENNER, James J. of Las Vegas, formerly of Ft. Lauderdale FL, accountant, won Florida Life Master Pairs 1969, Swiss Teams 1971, Mid-Atlantic Swiss Teams 1969, Southeastern Men's Teams 1971.

BRICKLIN, Albert R. (b. 1913) of Scottsdale AZ, automobile manufacturer, won Fall NAC secondary Men's Swiss Teams 1972, Motor City Men's Pairs 1974, Mid-Atlantic Swiss Teams 1969, Desert Empire Open Pairs Flt. A 1979, Puerto Rico Mixed Pairs 1972.

BRIDSON, Edward W. (b. 1951) of Toronto, born in Douglas, Isle of Man, high school math teacher, won Upper New York State KO Teams 1975, Motor City Open Pairs 1976, Master Pairs 1981, Mid-Atlantic Mixed Pairs 1978, District 5 Men's Swiss Teams 1980, Swiss Teams 1978, Can-Am Swiss Teams 1980, Gateway City Swiss Teams Flt. A, KO Teams, Swiss Teams 1981.

BRIDSON, Pamela (b. 1951) of Montreal, computer analyst, bridge teacher and writer, represented Canada in the Rosenblum Cup Teams, World Women's Teams 1980. Her regional wins include Nat'l Capital Women's Swiss Teams 1980, Open Pairs Flt. A 1981, Mid-Atlantic Mixed Pairs 1978, Can-Am Open Pairs 1981, Canadian Nat'l KO Teams 1981, Mixed Pairs 1980, Tri-State Women's Swiss Teams 1982, District 4 Fall Women's Swiss Teams 1981.

BRIER, Barbara S. (b. 1923) of North Miami, bridge teacher, one of the leading American women players, won the World Mixed Pairs 1970, Summer NAC Master Mixed Teams 1965, and placed second in the Mixed Teams 1956, Fall NAC Open Pairs 1955, Mixed Pairs 1963, Spring NAC Women's Pairs 1971. Her regional wins include the MARCUS CUP 1958, Fall NAC secondary Women's Swiss Teams 1972, Open Pairs Flt. B 1977, Southeastern Women's Teams 1971, 1974, Eastern States KO Teams (Reisinger) 1973, 1974.

BRIGHT, Mary A. of Cambridge MA, editor and writer, won Can-At Open Pairs 1973, Mixed Pairs 1974, KO Teams 1975, Master Swiss Teams, Open Swiss Teams 1978. She is the former editor of *New England Bridge Bulletin*.

BRIGHTLING, Richard J. (b. 1949) of Neutral Bay, Australia, formerly of New Zealand, bridge teacher and bridge supply company manager, represented New Zealand in the Bermuda Bowl 1974, Far East Championships 1973. He won New Zealand Open Teams 1972 and placed second in 1981 and in Open Pairs 1975, 1977.

BRISSMAN, Jon C. (b. 1944) of Fountain Valley CA, bridge professional, won Bridge Week Swiss Teams 1978, Pacific Southwest Mixed Pairs 1978, Mid-Winter Holiday Open Pairs 1979, Golden State Swiss Teams Flt. A 1980, Men's Pairs 1982, Raincross Swiss Teams 1980.

BRITTON, Sonya (Mrs. John) of Dublin, Ireland, represented Ireland in the European Championships 1962, World Women's Teams 1972, 1976, World Women's Pairs 1978, and was npc in the World Women's Teams 1980. Her national titles include Mixed Pairs (twice), Women's Teams (four times), and National Team-of-Four. She has served as president of Contract BA of Ireland, as vice president of the IRISH BRIDGE UNION 1981-1982, and as a IBU delegate to the EUROPEAN BRIDGE LEAGUE.

BROCH, José (b. 1913) of Argentina, born in Austria, leather goods manufacturer, won Argentine Open Teams 1959, 1962, Open Pairs 1966, 1971, Master Individual 1977, Interclubs 1954, 1972.

BROD, Geoffrey A. (b. 1942) of Manchester CT, data processing manager, won New England Labor Day Swiss Teams 1979, New England Knockout Swiss Teams Flt. A 1981, District 3 Open Pairs Flt. A 1980.

BRODY, Harvey D. (b. 1939) of San Francisco, controller, won All-Western Open Pairs 1972, Men's Pairs 1978, Master Teams 1974, Mid-Winter Holiday Master Pairs 1975, Men's Pairs 1978, Golden Gate Open Pairs Flt. A, Master Pairs 1977, Wine Country Master Pairs, Swiss Teams Flt. A 1982, District 21 GNT 1978, GNP 1979.

BROER, Lawrence B. (Bertie) (b. 1923) of Johannesburg, South Africa, chartered accountant and auditor, represented South Africa in the World Team Olympiad 1968, 1972, 1980, MACCABIAH GAMES 1977, 1981, placing second in 1977. His national wins include National Teams 1979, 1981, Pioneer Teams 1964, 1971, 1981, Interprovincial Teams 1965, 1970, 1974. Broer served as Transvaal Bridge Union chairman 1967 and Hillbrow Duplicate BC chairman since 1967.

BROGI, Giovan Battista (b. 1920) of Livorno, Italy, wholesale drug company manager, won Belgian Open Teams 1961, and represented Italy in the European Championships 1961, 1962, placing second in

1962. His national wins include the Italian Cup 1955, 1957, 1961, Italian Open Teams 1961. He has been a tournament director since 1961.

BROOKS, Dorsey W. (b. 1926) of Warren MI, financial administrator, placed second in Summer NAC Master Mixed Teams 1971. He was Intercollegiate champion 1949 and won Fall NAC secondary Mixed Pairs 2nd Flt. 1963, BAM Swiss Teams 1979, Summer Leventritt Pairs 1970, Great Lakes Open Pairs 1965, Motor City Swiss Teams 1970, Men's Swiss Teams 1977, Bermuda Men's Pairs 1974, Swiss Teams 1979, Mexican Nat'l Swiss Teams Flt. A 1981.

BROOKS, Zerrene (Mrs. Dorsey) of Warren MI, bridge teacher and recreational consultant, placed second in Summer NAC Master Mixed Teams 1971. She won Fall NAC secondary Mixed Pairs 2nd Flt. 1963, Motor City Swiss Teams 1970, Bermuda Swiss Teams 1979, Great Lakes Women's Pairs 1979, Mexican Nat'l Swiss Teams Flt. A 1981.

BROTMAN, Oscar J. (b. 1904) of Flushing NY, controller, won the Spingold 1940 and Eastern States KO Teams (Reisinger) 1946. As a partner of ALVIN ROTH, he contributed to the early development of the ROTH-STONE SYSTEM.

BROWN, Claude R. (b. 1930) of Malaysia, company director, represented Malaysia in the Far East Championships 1966, 1968, 1970.

BROWN, Dudley B. (b. 1935) of Grandview WA, Army Reserve technician, won Oregon Trail Men's Paris 1966, Intermountain Swiss Teams 1972, Inland Empire Swiss Teams 1973. He has served District 19 as president, Board member and as chairman of various committees. Brown is executive editor of *The Dino Bridge Buff.*

BROWN, H. Sanborn (b. 1906) of Grosse Pointe Farms MI, architect, won Summer NAC Life Master Pairs 1957, and placed second in the De La Rue International Pair Championship, London, England 1957. He also won the MARCUS CUP 1949, Midwest Spring Open Pairs 1956. He served as ACBL Board of Governors member 1944–1958 and as Michigan BA president 1964–1966.

BROWN, John (1887–deceased) of Grimsby, England, director of a Kenyan coffee plantation was author of *Winning Tricks, Bidding Craft,* and the classic *Winning Defence* as well as many magazine articles. See BIBLIOGRAPHY, C, D.

BROWN, Phyllis (Mrs. Hugh) (b. 1926) of Brisbane, Australia, was Far East champion 1974 and won Australian Women's Pairs 1973, Interstate Women's Teams 1973.

BROWN, Stephen C. (b. 1946) of Mount Royal PQ, data administrator, won Summer NAC secondary Men's Pairs Flt. A 1978, Nat'l Capital Men's Swiss Teams 1978, Swiss Teams Flt. A 1980, Can-Am KO Teams 1978, Fleur-de-Lys KO Teams 1979, District

1 GNP 1981.

BRUCE, Arthur Loring. See CROWINSHIELD, FRANK.

BRUCE, David (formerly Burnstine) (1900–1965) of Los Angeles was Life Master #1. A tremendously successful player in the early Thirties, he headed a group that made the Contract Bridge Club in New York the center of the most expert game of the times. Burnstine, the name by which he went during his bridge career, introduced the artificial 2♣ opening bid to show a strong hand (including A-K, A-K, A), with other two bids not gameforcing, a method which became the most widely used among experts of the day and later developed into the cornerstone of ACOL.

Known as a soothing partner but an unsettling opponent, Burnstine played with OSWALD JACOBY and with HOWARD SCHENKEN on the first of the outstanding teams, the FOUR HORSEMEN, captained by P. HAL SIMS, and authored the first book on that team's system (*Four Horsemen's One Over One,* 1932). In 1933, with Schenken, Jacoby, and RICHARD L. FREY, joined shortly afterward by MICHAEL T. GOTTLIEB, he organized the FOUR ACES, the team that took the leadership in the field and held it, with several amendments in personnel, for the next decade. With his teammates he wrote *Four Aces System of Contract Bridge,* 1935 (See BIBLIOGRAPHY, C). In the brief interlude between the reins of the Four Horsemen and the Four Aces, Burnstine helped to organize and played on the BID-RITE TEAM.

An all-around star, Burnstine was rated by many of his teammates as the best bidder in the game. Brashly self-confident, Burnstine frequently locked horns with CULBERTSON and rarely came out second best. His impressive tournament record includes a victory in the first official World Championship in 1935 and many national championships including AWL All-American Open Teams (Contract) 1932, (Auction) 1931, 1932, 1933, USBA Open Teams 1934, 1937, Open Pairs 1936, ABL Challenge Teams 1931, 1933, 1937, Spingold 1934, 1936, 1938, Vanderbilt 1931, 1934, 1935, 1937, 1938, Summer NAC Master Mixed Teams 1931, 1933, Life Master Pairs 1931, 1933, 1936, Fall Men's Pairs 1934, Master Individual 1933. He also won the prestigious Eastern States Open Teams (Reisinger) 1931–1934.

BRUELHEIDE, Frank E. (1885–1943) of Minneapolis was a bridge book publisher, writer and lecturer. After graduating from Chicago Institute of Arts he entered the field of bridge and became an associate of ELY CULBERTSON. Later he became a Director of the ACBL and organized the Bridge League of the Northwest. A prolific lecturer, Bruelheide traveled throughout the U.S. lecturing, teaching and broadcasting over radio in the interests of bridge promotion. He published and edited his own magazine, *Bridge Digest,* 1936–1939. His writings include several articles for *The Bridge World* and other publications, pamphlets on bridge such as *Duplicate Bridge Guide* and the book *Party Bridge.* See BIBLIOGRAPHY, A, F.

BRUN, Johannes (1891–deceased) of Oslo, Norway,

army officer and bridge writer, was a founding member of the NORWEGIAN BRIDGE ASSOCIATION in 1932 and president in 1934. In 1937 he became president of the INTERNATIONAL BRIDGE LEAGUE, a forerunner of the WORLD BRIDGE FEDERATION. Brun was also a founding member of the EUROPEAN BRIDGE LEAGUE (1947) and was elected an honorary member in 1957. He represented Norway in the European Championships for six consecutive years and placed second in both the pair and team championship in 1933. He was awarded the IBL prize for the most distinguished player in 1934. Brun was the bridge editor of *Aftenposten*, and a contributor to several bridge publications.

BRUNZELL, Anders (b. 1938) of Gothenburg, Sweden, mathematics and physics teacher, was European champion 1977. He also represented Sweden in the Bermuda Bowl 1977, World Team Olympiad 1968, 1972, World Open Pairs 1970, 1974, European Championships 1967, 1969, 1973, 1974, 1975, 1979. He was Nordic champion 1968.

BRYANT, Jack N. (b. 1934) of St. Louis, data processing manager, won District 8 Swiss Teams 1979, GNT 1979, GNP 1981.

BUCHANAN, Dorothy (Mrs. Robert, formerly Kantor) of Minneapolis, bookkeeper, won Fall NAC Life Master Women's Pairs 1982 and several regional titles including Pheasant KO Teams 1970, 1972, Gopher Women's Pairs, KO Teams 1971, Master Pairs 1973, Canadian Prairie Master Pairs 1970, KO Teams 1972, Tri-Unit Mixed Pairs 1971, Iowa KO Teams 1972. Buchanan has served as Unit 103 president, vice president, chairman of state and regional tournaments, District 14 Board member, member of the ACBL Board of Governors and ACBL Board of Directors.

BUCHMEIER, Horst (b. 1942) of Vienna, Austria, Public relations manager, represented Austria in the World Team Olympiad 1972, World Pair Olympiad 1970, 1974. His tournament successes include many Austrian titles.

BUCKMAN, Kate of Downsview ON, ACBL Honorary Member 1973, introduced duplicate to Vancouver in 1951 and subsequently has operated a duplicate and rubber bridge club in Toronto which teaches 300 to 350 students a year.

BUDIN, Barnett (d. 1964) of Philadelphia, printer, was ACBL Director 1963–1964 and past president of the Keystone Conference and Philadelphia Unit. He co-authored *Bridge Players Digest of Conventions*. See BIBLIOGRAPHY, C.

BUFILL, Rafael (b. 1926) of Barcelona, Spain, engineer, represented Spain in the World Team Olympiad 1964, European Championships 1967, was npc of the European Women's Team 1965 and member of the National Spanish Team. His national wins include open team and pair events.

BULLER, Lt. Col. Walter (1887–1938) of London,

England, author and leading personality in British bridge in the Thirties, won the first English National Pairs 1932, organized the first ANGLO-AMERICAN MATCH, 1930, and captained the English team. Buller was the leading protagonist of *British Bridge* or direct methods of bidding without conventional forcing bids. He was a bridge columnist and wrote several books including *Reflections of a Bridge Player, From Auction to Contract* and *How to Play Contract Bridge*. See BIBLIOGRAPHY, E, G.

BURGER, Charles F. (Chuck) (b. 1936) of Bloomfield MI, attorney, one of the leading American players, represented the United States in the World Open Pairs 1970. He won the Blue Ribbon Pairs 1970, Life Master Men's Pairs 1969, Spring NAC Master Men's Teams 1969 and placed second in the Reisinger 1981, Summer NAC Master Pairs 1969, 1973. He was co-winner of the HERMAN TROPHY 1970. His numerous regional titles include Fall NAC secondary Swiss Teams 1981, Central States KO Teams 1971, Master Pairs 1976, Motor City Men's Swiss Teams 1981.

BURKA, Paul J. (b. 1942) of Austin TX, senior editor of *Texas Monthly*, former attorney, won Fall NAC secondary Open Pairs 1970, Texas Fall Master Pairs, Men's Pairs 1973. He is editor of *Scorecard*, the District 16 publication.

BURKE, John M. (b. 1923) of Kansas City MO, mechanical contractor, won District 15 KO Teams 1977, 1978, Missouri Valley Men's Pairs 1978, Mid-South Master Pairs Flt. A 1978, Indian Summer KO Teams 1979. He is past president of Missouri Valley Conference and a former member of the ACBL Board of Governors 1957–1958.

BURNHAM, Dr. Charles J. (b. 1919) of Birmingham AL, ophthalmologist, won Spring NAC Open Teams 1960. His regional wins include Southern Conference Fall Open Pairs, Men's Pairs 1962, Open Teams 1963, Mid-South Fall Open Pairs, Swiss Teams 1974, Mid-Atlantic Winter Open Pairs Flt. A 1978.

BURNSTEIN, Anne (Mrs. Robert) of Las Vegas, one of the leading players of the Western States, won Life Master Women's Pairs 1963, Spring NAC Women's Teams 1951, 1962, 1979, Women's Pairs 1979, Summer NAC Mixed Teams 1952, 1953, Mixed Pairs 1946, 1952, and placed second in Life Master Women's Pairs 1962, Fall NAC Women's Teams 1955. Her numerous regional titles include Fall NAC secondary Women's Swiss Teams 1977, Southeastern Women's Teams 1953, 1955, 1956, Women's Pairs 1951, Desert Empire Open Teams 1963. Burnstein is the sister of EDITH KEMP and WILLIAM SEAMON. See FAMILY.

BURNSTINE, David. See BRUCE, DAVID.

BURSTEIN, Franklin D. (b. 1933) of Springfield NJ, real estate investor and manager, won Fall NAC secondary Men's Swiss Teams 1975, Tri-State Open Teams 1967, Keystone Open Teams 1968.

BURRÓ, Juan Pascual (b. 1938) of Asunción, Paraguay, represented Paraguay in the South American Championships 1965, 1969, 1971. His national wins include Open Teams 1964, 1966, 1970.

BUSH, Gary (b. 1952) of Indianapolis, sales engineer, won Fall NAC secondary Swiss Teams Flt. A 1980, Midwest Fall KO Teams 1978, Men's Swiss Teams 1981, Wisconsin Swiss Teams Flt. A 1981.

BUSSEY, Thomas E. (b. 1918) of Vancouver WA, retired personnel director, won Spring NAC Men's Teams 1967, Intermountain Open Pairs 1962. He is past president of the WESTERN CONFERENCE and Vancouver and Portland Units.

BUSTROS, Fady (b. 1905) of Beirut, Lebanon, newspaper manager and bridge columnist, represented Lebanon in the World Team Olympiad 1960, 1964, European Championships 1954, 1956, 1957, 1961, 1962. His national successes include Open Teams and Open Pairs, each six times.

BUTCHER, Thomas D. (b. 1932) of Tokyo, Japan, born in Defiance OH, English teacher and translator, represented Japan in the Far East Championships 1962, 1963, 1965, 1966, 1969, 1971, 1975 and won Far East Open Pairs 1964. He has won all of Japan's major championships (except the Mixed Pairs and Mixed Teams) and most of the team championships many times. Butcher is the former editor of Japan CBL *Bulletin* and bridge columnist of *Mainichi Daily News*.

BUTCHER, William J. (b. 1918) of Hartford CT, business owner, won New England KO Teams 1960, Master Teams 1967, Southeastern Swiss Teams, Life Master Pairs 1974, Olympic Men's Swiss Teams 1978, Upper New York State Master Swiss Teams 1976. He is past president of the Connecticut BA.

BUTKOW, Hyman (b. 1927) of Johannesburg, South Africa, accountant, represented South Africa in the World Team Olympiad 1968, 1972, 1976. His national wins include Open Pairs 1965, 1967, 1978, 1979, Open Teams 1970, 1971, 1976, 1978, 1980, 1981, Interprovincial Teams 1963, 1965, Pioneer Teams 1964, 1968, 1977, 1978, 1979, 1981.

BUTKOW, Julius (Big Julie) (b. 1933) of Johannesburg, South Africa, chartered accountant and auditor, represented South Africa in the World Team Olympiad 1968 and captained the SA team in 1976. His national wins include South Africa Open Teams 1970, 1971, Open Pairs 1965, Pioneer Teams 1964, 1968, Interprovincial Teams 1965. Butkow is the chief tournament director and organizer in South Africa. He has served as president of the SOUTH AFRICA BRIDGE FEDERATION since 1969, chairman of the Johannesburg BC since 1965, and was a member of the World Bridge Federation Executive Council 1976. A member of the editorial staff of the South African *Bridge Bulletin* since 1960, Butkow is noted

for his "Big Julie" articles.

BUTLER, David C. (b. 1949) of Keswick VA, won Mid-Atlantic Swiss Teams 1977, 1978, Open Pairs 1979, Open Pairs Flt. A 1978.

BUTLER, Evelyn M. (b. 1920) of Rancho La Costa CA, won Hawaii Women's Swiss Teams 1977, 1980, California Capital Open Pairs Flt. A 1978. Butler organized the Bishop CA Unit in 1958.

BUTLER, Geoffrey L. (b. 1898) of London, England, journalist, is one of the leading personalities in the bridge world. He has served world bridge as an executive member of the WORLD BRIDGE FEDERATION and the EUROPEAN BRIDGE LEAGUE, chairman of the BRITISH BRIDGE LEAGUE, vice president of the ENGLISH BRIDGE UNION, and as chairman of several of their committees. He represented EBL and the PORTLAND CLUB in preparation of the 1963 Code of Laws. Through the years he has won many pair and team events in England. Butler is the co-author of *Two Clubs System of Bidding* and is a contributing editor, *Bridge Encyclopedia*. See BIBLIOGRAPHY, C and BUENOS AIRES AFFAIR.

BUTLER, Dr. John (b. 1921) of Cardiff, Wales, physician, won Welsh Open Teams six times, Swiss Teams three times, Master Pairs four times, National Pairs twice. He represented Wales in international competitions 58 times between 1955 and 1982. He has served as president of the WELSH BRIDGE UNION and as vice chairman of the BRITISH BRIDGE LEAGUE. He has been a member of the Card Committee, PORTLAND CLUB, since 1968.

C

CABANNE, Carlos (b. 1917) of Buenos Aires, Argentina, dentist, a leading South American player, represented Argentina in the Bermuda Bowl 1958, 1962, 1965, 1977, World Team Olympiad 1964, 1968, 1972, 1976, 1980. He was South American champion 23 times and his national wins include Argentine Open Teams 1945, 1946, 1949, 1961, 1963, 1965, 1967, 1971, 1972, 1976, 1979, Open Pairs 1948, 1955, 1956, 1977, Mixed Teams 1950, 1954, 1960, 1965, 1966, 1967, 1972, 1973, 1974, 1975, 1976, 1979, 1981, Mixed Pairs 1958, 1973, Master Pairs 1959, 1978, Interclubs 1944, 1946, 1955, 1957, 1960, 1965, 1978, 1980 and the GABARRET CUP 1972. Named Honorary Member of the SOUTH AMERICAN BRIDGE CONFEDERATION in 1980, he served as its secretary and president. He was director and president of the ARGENTINE BRIDGE ASSOCIATION, a member of the WORLD BRIDGE FEDERATION executive committee 1961, 1962, 1964 and 1969–1977, and has been a member of its laws commission since 1970. Cabanne is a frequent contributor to bridge publications, the author of seven books including *Bridge Razonado de A hasta Q*, *Bridge Razonada para Principiantes* and a member of the Editorial Advisory Board, *Bridge Encyclopedia*.

CABOT, Antonio (b. 1933) of Barcelona, Spain, industrialist, represented Spain in the World Team Olympiad 1960, 1964, World Open Pairs 1962, European Championships 1959, 1963.

CABRAL, Francisco Costa, (b. 1943) of Lisbon, Portugal, technician, represented Portugal in the European Championships 1971. His national wins include Open Teams twice.

CACHO, José Antonio (b. 1923) of Mandaluyong, Philippines, company president, represented the Philippines in the World Team Olympiad 1964, Far East Championships 1960. He was Director of the PHILIPPINES CONTRACT BRIDGE LEAGUE 1950–1967.

CACHO, Maxine Carmelo (Mrs. José A.) (b. 1922) of Mandaluyong, Philippines, was Far East Women's champion 1967 and won the Hong Kong-Manila Interport Tournament 1960. She served as secretary of the PHILIPPINES CONTRACT BRIDGE LEAGUE 1961–1964.

CAFFERATA, Mike P. (b. 1948) of Toronto, born in England, computer science and math teacher, won Can-At Swiss Teams 1975, 1980, Open Pairs 1980, Canadian Nat'l Mixed Pairs 1978, Nickel City KO Teams, Swiss Teams, Open Pairs 1978, Gateway City Swiss Teams, KO Teams 1981.

CAHN, Nell B. (b. 1935) of Shreveport LA won Texas Spring Women's Pairs 1967, Mid-South Open Pairs, Swiss Teams 1976. Cahn has served as president and vice president of Unit 170.

CAHN-SPEYER, Anton (b. 1918) of Bogotá, Colombia, born in Vienna, Austria, public accountant, represented Colombia in the South American Championships 1963, 1964, 1966, 1968, Caribbean Championships 1964, 1966 and was Caribbean champion 1968. His national wins include Open Teams 1962, 1964, 1965, 1966, 1967, Master Pairs 1967, 1968, Open Pairs 1964.

CALDWELL, George A. of Fredericton NB, bridge teacher and club operator, won Can-At Open Pairs 1969, 1974, KO Teams 1971.

CALE, Helen (b. 1912) of Glendale CA, bridge teacher and writer, won the BARCLAY TROPHY 1949, 1950 and placed second in Fall NAC Mixed Pairs 1957. Her regional wins include Bridge Week Open Teams 1948, Women's Pairs 1954, Master Women's Pairs 1971. She served as president of the ABTA 1969–1970, president of the ACBL Western Division 1950, and as chairman of the Los Angeles Unit.

CALEY, Martin J. (Marty) (b. 1947) of Ottawa, sales representative, won Cambrian Shield KO Teams 1973, Can-At Open Pairs 1975, Fleur-de-Lys Swiss Teams 1979, Can-Am Open Pairs 1980, Nat'l Capital KO Teams, Men's Swiss Teams, Open Pairs 1981.

CALHEIROS, Francisco (b. 1929) of Lisbon, Portugal, economist, represented Portugal in the European Championships 1967, 1971. His national wins include Open Teams three times, Open Pairs twice. He is a former president of the PORTUGUESE BRIDGE FEDERATION.

CALLAHAM, Thomas M. (b. 1934) of Covington VA, pharmacist, won Spring NAC BAM Teams Flt. A 1981, Rocky Mountain Open Teams 1969, Mid-Atlantic Fall Master Pairs 1970, Swiss Teams 1972, Spring Open Pairs 1977, Master Pairs 1976, District 11 Men's Pairs 1978, Men's Swiss Teams 1979.

CALVENTE, Ricardo (1918) of Madrid, Spain, formerly of Buenos Aires, Argentina, industrialist, represented Argentina in the Bermuda Bowl 1958, 1959, 1961, 1962, 1963. He was South American champion 1959, 1961, won Spanish national Open Teams 1979, Mixed Pairs 1975, French international Open Pairs 1974, Argentine Mixed Teams 1950, 1963, Master Individual 1960, Master Pairs 1963, national Interclubs 1966, 1967.

CAMARA, Helen (Ninny) (b. 1907) formerly of Cairo, Egypt, born in Greece, was World Women's Team champion 1960 and also represented Egypt in the World Women's Teams 1964, Women's European Women's Teams 1949, 1961, Open Teams 1956. Her national successes include Open Teams 1937, 1946, 1950, 1953, 1959, Interclubs 1931, 1934, 1947, Mixed Teams 1959, 1960, 1961. She has contributed to various bridge periodicals.

CAMBEROS, Héctor R. (b. 1948) of Capital Federal, Argentina, chemical engineer, represented Argentina in the Bermuda Bowl 1977, 1981, World Team Olympiad 1980. He was South American champion 1979, 1980, 1981 and won the Rio Open Pairs 1977, BSAS Open Pairs 1980. His national wins include Argentine Open Teams 1981, Mixed Pairs 1979, Interclubs 1979, GABARRET CUP 1979. He is former editor of Bridge Para Todos.

CAMPBELL, Clifford V. (C.C.) (b. 1949) of Thunder Bay ON, life insurance underwriter, won Buffalo Mixed Pairs 1977, Swiss Teams Flt. B 1980, Thunder Bay Swiss Teams 1981, Canadian Nat'l Teams Zone 4 1982. He has won many trophies and awards for excellence in curling.

CAMPBELL, L. Andrew (b. 1942) of Los Angeles, mathematician, won Pacific Southwest Men's Swiss Teams 1977, Master Pairs Flt. A 1981, District 10 GNT, Zone VII 1981.

CANESSA, Luciana R. of Rome, Italy, won the World Women's Teams 1972, European Women's Teams 1970, 1971, 1973.

CANNELL, P. Drew (Panama) (b. 1952) of Toronto, computer programmer, represented Canada in the World Open Pairs 1974, and Panama in the World Open Pairs 1978, World Team Olympiad 1980, and was a member of the Panamanian team which won the Central American and Caribbean Zonal Team Championships 1978. His ACBL regional wins include Thunder Bay Swiss Teams

1973, District 2 GNT 1974, Gopher KO Teams 1975, Buffalo Men's Swiss Teams 1976, Canadian Nat'l Men's Swiss Teams 1982.

CANSINO, Jonathan, (b. 1939) of London, England, stockbroker, one of Europe's foremost players, represented Great Britain in the European Championships 1965, 1970, England in the CAMROSE TROPHY matches 1964, 1965. He won the GOLD CUP 1965, National Pairs 1964, Crockford's Cup 1964, 1966, 1968, 1972, Life Master Pairs 1966, 1971.

CANTOR, Augusta (Gussie) (1909–1982) of New York City, bookkeeper, won several regionals including Summer NAC secondary Sub-Senior Master Teams 1947, Fall Women's Pairs 1980, Eastern States Master Pairs 1963, Tri-State Master Pairs 1972, New England Mixed Pairs 1964, Keystone Conference Women's Pairs 1968, Southeastern Mixed Pairs 1975.

CAPODANNO, Luciana of Naples, Italy, won the World Women's Teams 1976 and placed second in the Venice Trophy Teams 1978. She was European Women's champion 1974, 1977.

CAPPELLETTI, A. Michael (b. 1942) of Alexandria VA, lawyer, one of the leading players of the East Coast, placed third in the World Mixed Teams 1974 and also represented the United States in the World Open Pairs 1974, 1978. He won Summer NAC Master Mixed Teams 1967 and placed second in Fall NAC Mixed Pairs 1967, Blue Ribbon Pairs 1973, 1977, Spring Men's Teams 1979. His more than 30 regional wins include Fall NAC secondary Open Teams 2nd Flt. 1970, New England KO Teams 1965, 1972, 1975, 1981 and numerous Mid-Atlantic regional titles. He authored two conventions: CAPPELLETTI OVER NOTRUMP and CAPPELLETTI TWO-SUITED CUEBIDS. He has served as president and vice president of the Mid-Atlantic Conference, president of the Washington BL, and has been a member of ACBL Board of Governors for more than 10 years.

CAPPELLETTI, Katherine H. See WALVICK, KATHERINE H.

CAPPS, Richard A. (b. 1944), of Baton Rouge LA, school principal and teacher, won Mid-South Swiss Teams 1980, 1981, Crescent City Open Pairs 1981, Big D Winter Master Pairs 1982.

CARANSA, Maurits of Amsterdam, The Netherlands, entrepreneur, was named IBPA "Bridge Personality of the Year" in 1978 for his fortitude in continuing the 1977 CARANSA TOURNAMENT just days after he was released by kidnappers who demanded a ranson of $4 million. Caransa and his sister were the only two members of their immediate family to survive the Nazi holocaust.

CARAVELLI, Gerald A. (b. 1943) of Des Plaines IL, one of the leading players of the Middle West, won Fall NAC Mixed Pairs 1974, Summer NAC Master Mixed Teams 1975, Spring NAC Men's Pairs 1976, Open Pairs 1982, Grand National Teams 1978,

and placed second in Spring NAC Men's Teams 1971, Vanderbilt 1977, Summer NAC Senior and Advanced Master Pairs 1964, Master Mixed Teams 1980, Fall NAC Swiss Teams 1979. He has won more than 80 regional events including Spring NAC secondary Swiss Teams 1974, 1977, Master Pairs 1975, Open Pairs A-D 1978, District 13 GNT 1975, 1977, 1978, 1981, Zone VI 1977, 1978, 1981, Central States KO Teams 1969, 1972, 1973, Life Master KO Teams 1979, Men's Swiss Teams 1977, BAM Teams 1981. Caravelli served as tournament chairman, president and vice president of the Chicago CBA. A graduate of University of Illinois 1963, he is a staff accountant with a Chicago insurance firm.

CARINI-MAZZACCARA, Marchese Silvio (b. 1907) of Florence, Italy, wine industry executive, is a former member of the executive committees of the EUROPEAN BRIDGE LEAGUE, WORLD BRIDGE FEDERATION, ITALIAN BRIDGE FEDERATION, and of the Editorial Advisory Board, *Bridge Encyclopedia.*

CARLAFTIS, George (b. 1937) of Athens, Greece, consulting engineer, WBF Grand Master, officially ranked #1 player of Greece, represented Greece in the World Team Olympiad 1976, 1980, European Championships 1967, 1969, 1970, 1971, Balkan Championships 1978. His national successes include the Kyriakos Trophy (Greek McKenney) 1977, Team Trials 1966, 1968–1976, 1978–1981, Open Pairs 1965–1971, 1979–1981, Swiss Teams 1981, Mixed Teams 1976, 1977, 1979, Mixed Pairs 1967, 1973, 1975, 1977, 1978, 1981, Master Pairs 1978, 1979, Interclubs 1972, 1973, 1974, 1976, 1981, He served as executive treasurer of the HELLENIC BRIDGE FEDERATION 1974–1975, as npc of the Greek Ladies Team at the European Championships 1975 and was a regular contributor to *Greek Bridge Review* 1967–1968.

CARLIER, Paul H. (b. 1931) of Brussels, Belgium, secretary general of European committee of consulting firms, former barrister, won Belgian Mixed Teams 1974, Division III and IV Teams. He is president of BELGIAN BRIDGE FEDERATION and chairman of Brussels' Committee and French Speaking League. Carlier is director of the Brussels Chamber of Commerce.

CARLSON, Isabella S. (Mrs. E. N.) of Webster Groves MO, former bridge teacher, cruise conductor, club director, one of the early pioneers of bridge in the St. Louis area, helped organize the St. Louis Unit in the Thirties and the St. Louis Women's Bridge League, of which she was president for many years. She is past president of the St. Louis Unit and former member of ACBL Board of Directors and ACBL Charity Committee. Her regional wins include Mississippi Valley Master Pairs 1958, Women's Pairs 1962.

CARNEY Jean (b. 1924) of Scottsdale AZ, bridge professional, won Fall NAC secondary Swiss Teams 1970, Desert Empire Open Teams 1968, Women's Pairs 1972, Rocky Mountain Open Teams 1969, Oregon Trail Mixed Pairs 1976, Golden Gate Swiss Teams 1976.

CARPENTER, Curtis M. (b. 1947) of Folsom LA, bank branch manager, won Mid-South Swiss Teams 1971, Crescent City Open Pairs 1977, Men's Pairs 1981.

CARPENTER, Frederic Ives (Fred) (b. 1903) of Walnut Creek CA, writer and educator, won Inter-Mountain Master Pairs 1957, Open Pairs 1958, All-Western Open Teams 1956, New England Master Pairs 1946. Carpenter taught at Harvard from 1929 to 1933 and at the University of California at Berkeley from 1946 to 1950. He resigned from Berkeley in 1950 in protest to the Regents' firing of teachers who refused to sign loyalty oaths. The open letter he wrote at that time is cited in university classrooms today for its eloquence and clarity of statement on freedom.

CARROAD, Michael R. (b. 1940) of Cheverly MD, operations research analyst, won Mexican Nat'l Master Pairs 1976, District 4 Men's Pairs 1976, Bermuda Swiss Teams 1981, Mid-Atlantic Master Pairs, 1973, Master Swiss Teams 1980, Swiss Teams Flt. A 1981. He is a graduate of New York University.

CARROLL, Charles B. (Chuck) (b. 1956) of Minneapolis, computer programmer and systems analyst, placed second in Spring NAC Men's Pairs 1982. His regional wins include All-American Open Pairs 1978, KO Teams 1979, District 5 KO Teams 1978, Open Pairs 1980, GNP 1981.

CARROLL, Judith. See MOSKOWITZ, JUDITH.

CARRUTHERS, John G. (b. 1947) of Toronto, systems analyst, represented Canada in the Rosenblum Cup Teams 1978. He won Summer NAC secondary Silver Trophy Pairs Flt. A 1981, Motor City Open Pairs 1972, Swiss Teams 1975, Canadian Nat'l Swiss Teams 1973, KO Teams 1976, 1979, Men's Swiss Teams 1978, 1979, 1980, Buffalo Centennial Open Pairs 1974, Bermuda Men's Pairs 1978, District 5 Open pairs 1979, Great Lakes Swiss Teams 1979 and is the first winner of the RICHMOND TROPHY (Canadian McKenney) 1974.

CARSCADDEN, Lorne R. (b. 1942) of Winnipeg MB, manager of computer systems design and development, won Canadian Prairie Swiss Teams 1971, District 2 Swiss Teams 1973, Buffalo KO Teams 1980.

CARSON, Mike of Fort Lauderdale FL, won Southeastern Men's Teams 1974, Life Master Pairs 1971, 1972.

CARSTENSEN, Svend (1899-1977) of Copenhagen, Denmark, bridge writer and editor, pioneered electronic computer scoring system and founded one of the biggest pair tournaments in the world. Co-founder of the IBPA, he was bridge editor of *Berlingske Tidende* 1946-1969.

CARTER, David C. (b. 1906) of St. Louis MO, building and loan executive, one of the leading players of the Middle West, was alternate for the 1963 North American Bermuda Bowl team. He won the McKENNEY TROPHY 1954, Life Master Pairs 1954, Fall NAC Men's Teams 1950, Men's Pairs 1957 and placed second in the Spingold 1953, 1962, Fall NAC Open Pairs 1946, 1953, 1954, Men's Pairs 1960. His many regional wins include All-American Open Pairs 1945, 1956, Men's Pairs 1954, Mississippi Valley Open Teams 1955, 1963, Open Pairs 1952, 1953, Men's Pairs 1958, 1967, 1973, Mixed Pairs 1963, Master Pairs 1967, Missouri Valley Open Teams 1954, 1955, Open Pairs 1965, Men's Pairs 1959, Mid-South Mixed Pairs 1976. He is past president of the Missouri Valley Conference and former vice president of the Midwest Conference. Carter is the originator of transer bids in the form now known as SOUTH AFRICAN TEXAS (see also TEXAS.) He also originated the double-barreled variety of TWO-WAY STAYMAN, in which 2♣ is a one-round force and 2♢ is forcing to game.

CARTER, Frances (Mrs. David C.) (b. 1910) of St. Louis MO, placed second in Fall NAC Open Pairs 1946, Mixed Pairs 1957. Her regional wins include Mississippi Valley Women's Pairs 1954, 1960, Missouri Valley Open Teams 1954, 1955, Mid-South Spring Open Teams 1959.

CARTER, Jack (b. 1904) of Cardiff, Wales, local government official, represented Wales on many occasions and won six Welsh Open Teams and three Mixed Teams events. He helped found the Welsh BA (later Union) in 1933 and acted as its Honorary Secretary and tournament manager 1944-1948.

CARTER, Kay (b. 1921) of Seminole FL, insurance agency secretary/treasurer, placed second in Summer NAC Women's Pairs 1962, Spring NAC Mixed Pairs 1965 and won Keystone Mixed Pairs 1963, Mid-Atlantic Fall Open Pairs 1968, Great Lakes Open Pairs 1961, Mixed Pairs 1962.

CARTER, Richard M. (b. 1909) of Port Charlotte FL, retired insurance executive and actuary, won All-American Open Teams 1946, Midwest Spring Open Teams, Open Pairs 1954, Open Teams, Men's Pairs 1964, Swiss Teams, BAM Teams 1971, Southern Conference Open Teams 1955.

CARTWRIGHT, George H. (Duke) (b. 1906) of Toronto, teacher of commercial subjects, is a retired ACBL associate national tournament director.

CASABAL, Leon (1892-1965) of Buenos Aires, Argentina was a pioneer of Argentine bridge. He was a bridge columnist for *La Nación* in the early Thirties and participated in a radio match against ELY CULBERTSON'S team in 1936. Casabal authored *Bridge de Hoy*, 1930.

CASEMENT, Robert of Chicago, won Central States Life and Senior Master Teams 1961, Midwest Fall Open Teams 1959. He is the former editor of *The Kibitzer*, published by the Chicago Unit.

CASEN, Drew A. (b. 1950) of New York City, accountant, placed second in Spring NAC Men's

Teams 1982 and won District 4 Master Pairs 1977, Tri-State Mixed Pairs 1980, District 3 Swiss Teams Flt. A 1980, Big Apple Swiss Teams Flt. A 1981.

CASH, Ralph A. (b. 1904) of Phoenix, insurance agent, one of the leading players of the Southwest for over three decades, was the U.S. winner of the World Olympic 1936. His many regional wins include Desert Empire Open Teams 1959, 1962, 1966, KO Teams 1967, Men's Pairs 1956, 1958. He has held many executive positions including president of the Western Division 1954, member of the WESTERN CONFERENCE and ACBL executive committees, chairman of the Phoenix Unit and general chairman of the Fall NAC in Phoenix 1962.

CASLAN, David F. (b. 1948) of Indianapolis, attorney, won District 5 Open Pairs 1972, District 11 KO Teams 1974, 1977, Great Lakes Men's Pairs 1977, Central States Master Pairs 1980, Midwest Fall Men's Swiss Teams 1981.

CASTRO, Alejandro (b. 1916) of Lima, Peru, formerly of Buenos Aires, Argentina, business manager, represented Argentina in the Bermuda Bowl 1958 and was many times winner in all Argentine events. He was also a member of the Peru National Team which competed in the South American Championships 1976, 1978, 1980. 1981. In 1957 he authored the book *Rebland System.*

CATON, Don J. (b. 1941) of Pensacola FL, city attorney, placed second in the Life Master Pairs 1980 and won Spring NAC secondary Swiss Teams 2nd Flt. 1971, Mid-South Open Pairs 1970, 1973, Men's Pairs 1970, 1971, Azalea City Master Pairs 1980. He was Florida junior tennis champion and ranked fifth in the U.S. in singles and second in doubles in the mid-Fifties. Caton also was a table tennis champion.

CATZEFLIS, Georges (b. 1931) of Lausanne, Switzerland, engineer, represented Switzerland in the World Team Olympiad 1964, 1968, World Open Pairs 1962, 1966, European Championships 1965. He won Swiss Master Pairs 1963, 1964, 1965.

CAVENDISH, pseudonym of Henry Jones (1831–1899), a famous London whist authority. Cavendish was the name of the club to which Jones belonged, and the name he chose under which to publish his first book on whist in 1863. This book, *The Laws and Principles of Whist Stated and Explained, and Its Practice Illustrated on an Original System, by Means of Hands Played Completely Through,* became the most popular guide to the game of whist since Hoyle's *Short Treatise. Cavendish on Whist* (book spine title) went through many editions and revisions, incorporating Jones's latest and best theories. He was the author of a number of other books on whist, among them *Whist Developments, American Leads,* and *The Plain-Suit Echo,* 1885, *Card Essays, Clay's Decisions* and *Card Table Talk,* 1890, and *American Leads Simplified,* 1891. With Nicholas Browse Trist he developed the system of whist play named by him the "American Leads,"

which encountered rather violent opposition in some quarters, but nevertheless enjoyed great popularity in England, and even greater in America. Jones made a tour of America in 1893 during which he attended the third Annual Congress of the AMERICAN WHIST LEAGUE, of which he was an honorary member. See BIBLIOGRAPHY, A.

CAYLEY, Henry Francis (Frank) (1910–1981) of Sydney, Australia, broadcaster, historian, bridge writer and teacher, won the Australian Par Championships 1940, 1948, Australasian Par Point Championships 1953, 1958, and placed fourth in the World Par Contest 1951. He was npc of the Australian team in the World Team Olympiad 1968. One of Australia's few Grand Masters, his national victories included Open Teams 1964, 1965, 1967, Open Pairs 1959, 1967, Individual 1971. He was a bridge correspondent for the *Sydney Morning Herald,* vice president of the IBPA, president of New South Wales BA, and chairman AUSTRALIAN BRIDGE FEDERATION. Cayley conducted bridge cruises to the U.S. and Europe. He authored *Modern Contract Bridge* and *Contract Bridge-Play* and *Contract Bridge-Bidding.* See BIBLIOGRAPHY, C, D.

CAYNE, James (b. 1934) of New York City, investment banker, represented the United States in the World Open Pairs 1970, 1974 and placed second in the World Mixed Pairs and World Mixed Teams 1974. He won Summer NAC Master Mixed Teams 1966, Fall NAC Life Master Men's Pairs 1969, Reisinger 1977, Spring NAC Men's 1969, and placed second in the Life Master Pairs 1969, 1973, Reisinger 1981. He won many regionals including Fall NAC secondary Swiss Teams 1981, Central States Life Master Pairs 1963, Master Pairs 1976, Eastern States Open Pairs (Goldman) 1968, KO Teams (Reisinger) 1977, Long Island KO Teams 1976, Swiss Teams 1978, New York Winter Swiss Teams Flt. A 1978, KO Teams 1981. Cayne was playing captain of the gold medalist team in the 1981 MACCABIAH GAMES.

CEARLEY, Boyce L. (1941–1982) of Fort Smith AR, a dentist, was a tremendous asset to Arkansas bridge. Through his own personal efforts, duplicate games were organized in Fort Smith and Fayetteville. He trained directors and instituted a novice program, and organized the first sectional in western Arkansas and was tournament chairman all nine times the tournament was held. Boyce, a cancer victim, died in Niagara Falls after competing in the GNP finals. His many regional wins include Missouri Valley Men's Swiss, Master Pairs, 1978, Open Pairs, 1977 and Mid-South KO Teams and Open Pairs, 1978.

CEDERBORG, Warren J. (b. 1945) of Pleasanton CA, realtor and developer, won Golden State KO Teams 1970, Men's Pairs 1971, Palm Springs Men's Pairs, KO Teams, 1971, Golden State KO Teams 1973, Open Pairs, Men's Pairs 1976, All-Western Men's Swiss Teams 1973, Master Swiss Teams Flt. A 1978, Mid-Winter Holiday Open Pairs 1972. A graduate of California State University at Hayward, Cederborg is a published poet. He was a frequent contributor to *Contract Bridge Forum* and authored *Coffee with Mary Jane Farell*.

CHAGAS, Gabriel P. (b. 1944) of Rio de Janeiro, Brazil, commodity trading executive, one of the world's leading players, WBF Grand Master, was South American champion 1967, 1968, 1969, 1970, 1972, 1973, 1974, 1975, 1977, 1978, won the World Team Olympiad 1976 and placed second in the Rosenblum Cup Teams 1978. He also represented Brazil in the Bermuda Bowl 1969, 1970, 1971, 1973, 1974, 1975, 1976, 1979, World Team Olympiad 1972, 1976, 1980, World Open Pairs 1974, 1978. He has won many Brazilian titles. Chagas is a regular contributor to Brazilian and foreign bridge publications.

CHAIT, Gene (b. 1943) of Chicago won Fall NAC secondary Open Pairs 1981, Summer President's Cup 1965, Gopher Swiss Teams 1973, 1978, Open Pairs 1973, 1976, Master Pairs 1974, Central States I Open Pairs 1976, 1977, Swiss Teams, KO Teams 1977, II Swiss Teams 1980, District 13 GNP 1980.

CHAMBERS, Neil J. (b. 1946) of North Hollywood CA represented Canada in the Rosenblum Cup Teams 1978 and was coach for the Canadian team during the World Team Olympiad 1980. He won Spring NAC Men's Teams 1978, 1981, Fall NAC Swiss Teams 1977. His more than 30 regional wins include Inland Empire KO Teams 1970, Swiss Teams Flt. A 1980, Oregon Trail Swiss Teams 1970, 1975, Open Pairs 1978, British Columbia KO Teams 1972, 1978, Open Pairs 1978, Swiss Teams Flt. A 1980, 1981, Hawaii KO Teams, Men's Swiss Teams, Swiss Teams 1978, Indian Summer Swiss Teams 1972, 1981. He created the Chico 2 ◇ bid.

CHAN, Hin Cheung (b. 1918) of Malaysia, company director, represented Malaysia in the Far East Championships 1963, 1965, 1966, 1970, 1973, 1974.

CHANDLER, Mitchell G. (b. 1949) of Birmingham MI, financial systems consultant, won Summer NAC secondary Silver Trophy Pairs Flt. A 1980, Motor City Mixed Pairs 1977, Great Lakes KO Teams 1979, Veterans Day Swiss Teams, Men's Pairs 1981, District 12 GNP 1979.

CHANDROSS, Howard (b. 1946) of Long Beach NY, tax accountant, won more than 25 regionals including Summer NAC secondary Men's Pairs Flt. A 1977, Fall Swiss Teams 1st Flt. 1974, District 3 Men's Swiss Teams 1979, Master Pairs, Swiss Teams Flt. A 1980, Can-Am Men's Pairs, Swiss Teams Flt. A 1979, Puerto Rico Men's Pairs 1980, Swiss Teams 1981, Long Island Swiss Teams Flt. A 1980, Open Pairs 1981, District 4 Men's Swiss Teams 1976, 1978, Men's Pairs 1981, Capital District Fall Men's Pairs, Open Pairs Flt. A 1977.

CHANG, Godfrey (b. 1937) of Honolulu, supervisory computer specialist, won Hawaii Men's Pairs 1969, Mixed Pairs 1972, Master Pairs 1973, 1981, KO Teams 1976. He has served the Honolulu Unit as

treasurer, vice president and tournament chairman.

CHANG, Hsi-tzun (b. 1939) of Taipei, Taiwan, represented Taipei in the World Team Olympiad 1980, Far East Championships 1977, 1981. He was Far East pair champion 1977 and both pair and team champion in 1981. He has won more than 10 national championships.

CHANG, Morris (b. 1931) of Dallas, senior vice president of Texas Instruments, won Big D Swiss Teams 1974, Master Pairs 1972, Open Pairs 1978, 1980, Rocky Mountain Swiss Teams Flt. A 1977, Master Pairs 1979, Mid-South Spring KO Teams 1973. He is graduate of M.I.T. and Stanford.

CHANG, Yin-tsun of Taipei, Taiwan, represented Taipei in the World Team Olympiad 1980, Far East Championships 1977, 1981. He was Far East pair champion 1977, pair and team champion in 1981. He has won more than 10 national championships.

CHAPMAN, Richard H. (b. 1931) of Los Angeles, electrical and building contractor, owner of a counseling center, won Hawaii Swiss Teams 1976, Cotton Boll Men's Swiss Teams 1977, Pacific Southwest Mixed Pairs 1979.

CHARNEY, Gerald (Gerry) (b. 1933) of Toronto, barrister and solicitor, represented Canada in the World Team Olympiad 1968, 1972, Rosenblum Cup Teams 1978 and captained the Canadian team in the World Team Olympiad 1980. His regional wins include Summer NAC secondary Swiss Teams Flt. A 1978, Canadian Nat'l Men's Swiss Teams 1977, Swiss Teams Flt. A 1979, KO Teams 1980, District 2 GNT 1975.

CHATZINOFF, Kenneth (Ken) (b. 1945) of Maple Shade NJ, won Fall NAC Amateur Men's Pairs 1976, Fall NAC secondary Open Pairs 1979, Mid-Atlantic Open Pairs 1977.

CHAZEN, Bernard L. (Bernie) (b. 1942) of Tamarac FL, former teacher and systems analyst, won Spring NAC Men's Teams 1971, Fall NAC Mixed Pairs 1973. His numerous regional titles include Fall NAC secondary Mixed Pairs 1974, Golden Gate Master Pairs Flt. A 1976, 1980, Swiss Teams 1976, New York-New Jersey Conference Men's Pairs 1973, Swiss Teams 1975, Oregon Trail Men's Pairs, Mixed Pairs 1976, All-Western Master Pairs Flt, A 1977, District 21 GNT, Zone VII 1979.

CHEATWOOD, Ferman D. (b. 1913) of Oklahoma City OK, retired traffic manager, was one of the pioneers of bridge in Oklahoma. He has held various positions at the District and national level for the past 30 years including president of District 15. He won Rocky Mountain Master Pairs 1952, Texas Fall Mixed Pairs 1956, Tulsa Open Pairs Flt. A 1981.

CHEMLA, Paul (b. 1944) of France, one of the leading European players, won the World Team Olympiad 1980, Common Market Open Teams 1972, European Open Pairs Championship 1976 and represented France on many other occasions. Because of his turbulent disposition, he is known as "l'enfant terrible du bridge".

CHEN, Chi Ping (b. 1924) of Taipei, Taiwan, corporation vice president, was Far East champion 1967, 1970.

CHEN, Kuo Yong (b. 1944) of Taipei, Taiwan, insurance administrator, represented Taiwan in the Far East Championships 1977, 1981, Bermuda Bowl 1979, World Team Olympiad 1980. He won the China Cup 1977, 1980, 1981, Taiwan Governor's Cup 1977, Taipei Mayor's Cup 1975, 1978, 1980.

CHENG, Kai Kwong, (b. 1945) of Winnipeg MB, born in China, electrical engineer, won Saskatchewan KO Teams, Master Swiss Teams Flt. A 1979, Swiss Teams 1980, Gopher Open Pairs Flt. A 1980, KO Teams 1981, Buffalo Swiss Teams 1978.

CHENG, Kuen-Ren (Conrad) (b. 1934) of Taipei, Taiwan, trader, bridge writer and teacher, won the Far East Open Pairs 1963, 1969, Open Teams 1969, 1971, 1976, 1978 and placed second in the Bermuda Bowl 1970. He also represented Taiwan in the Bermuda Bowl 1970, 1971, 1977 and in the Far East Championships 14 times. Cheng is the author of *Modern Systems and Theory of Bidding* in Chinese.

CHERNOFF, Victor B. (b. 1937) of Los Angeles, consulting actuary, won numerous regional events including Eastern States Open Pairs (Goldman) 1970, Keystone Open Pairs 1971, Mid-Atlantic Swiss Teams 1973, Golden State KO Teams, Men's Pairs, Open Pairs 1980, Master Pairs Flt. A 1982, Raincross KO Teams 1980, Swiss Teams 1981, Bridge Week KO Teams 1976, Master Men's Pairs, Swiss Teams Flt. A 1981, Mid-Winter Holiday Swiss Teams 1981, Copper State Master Pairs Flt. A 1977, Cotton Boll Men's Pairs 1977, Los Angeles Winter Swiss Teams 1975, Wine Country Swiss Teams Flt. A 1982, District 23 GNT 1980.

CHEW, James H. (b. 1944) of Tulsa OK, oil company owner, won Mid-Atlantic Swiss Teams 1978, Gem State Swiss Teams, Master Swiss Teams 1978, Texas Mid-Summer KO Teams 1979, Toast of Tulsa KO Teams 1981. Chew is a top ranked golfer.

CHIARADIA, Eugenio (The Professor) (1917–1977) of Naples, Italy, formerly of São Paulo, Brazil, Professor of Philosophy, was one of the world's great players. Chiaradia invented the NEAPOLITAN CLUB, the first conventional bidding system that became the killing arm of the BLUE TEAM, the famous Italian team of which he was, at the start, the undisputed leader. Winner of Bermuda Bowls 1957, 1958, 1959, 1961, 1962, 1963, and European Championships 1951, 1956, 1957, 1958, and 1959, his favorite partner was MIMMO D'ALELIO, but he played often with PIETRO FORQUET, his personal pupil. National successes included Italian Open Team 1951, 1956, 1957, 1959, and 1963. During his residence in Brazil, he coached the Brazilian national team. Until his retirement from active bridge competitions, due to health conditions, he lived completely for bridge, studying technique, perfecting his system. Chiaradia co-authored *Fiori Napolitano*. See BIBLIOGRAPHY, C.

CHILCOTE, Mary J. (Mrs. William) (b. 1926) of Cleveland, placed second in Fall NAC Mixed Pairs 1970 and won Fall NAC secondary Swiss Teams 1970, Spring NAC secondary Mixed Pairs 1973, Las Vegas KO Teams 1971, Navajo Trail Swiss Teams 1973, Motor City KO Teams 1975, All-American Women's Swiss Teams 1981, Desert Empire Women's Pairs 1972.

CHILDS, Derrell W. (b. 1934) of Garland TX, CPA, won Texas Mid-summer Master Pairs 1979, International City Mixed Pairs 1974, Republic of Texas Men's Pairs 1981. He served the Dallas BA as president, treasurer and Board member.

CHILDS, O. Allen Jr. (Al) (b. 1934) of Little Rock AR, bridge teacher and professional bridge player, won numerous regional events including Mid-South KO Teams 1976, 1978, Swiss Teams 1979, Open Pairs Flt. A 1979, Missouri Valley Open Pairs 1977, Oklahoma City Open Pairs Flt. A 1981, District 10 GNT 1977, 1979, Zone IV 1977, 1979. He has served Unit 161 and District 10 in various executive positions and is a member of the ACBL Board of Governors. Childs is editor of the *Mid–South Bridge Forum*. He was educated at Oklahoma State University and University of Arkansas.

CHODOROW, Claire (b. 1924) of Kenmore NY, bridge teacher and club director, won District 5 Women's Pairs 1978, 1979, Canadian Nat'l Women's Swiss Teams 1980.

CHONG, Antonio T. (Tony) (b. 1927) of Taipei, Taiwan, born in Panama, corporation chairman and vice president, captained the Taiwan team which won the Far East Championships 1976, 1978, 1981 and represented Taiwan in the World Team Olympiad 1980. He also captained the Far East team in 1977 and the Bermuda Bowl team in 1979. He placed second in the Far East team trials 1977 and won two national open team events plus numerous regional events. Chong has served as vice president of the FAR EAST BRIDGE FEDERATION and executive director of the CHINESE TAIPEI BRIDGE ASSOCIATION.

CHOUCRY, Aida (b. 1922) of Cairo, Egypt, was World Women's Team champion 1960 and also represented Egypt in the World Women's Teams 1964. Her national wins include Egyptian Open Pairs, 1972, Open Teams 1974, Mixed Pairs 1965, 1968, 1975, 1976, Mixed Teams 1968, 1969, 1973, 1976, 1981, Marathon Pairs 1965, 1971, 1973, Interclub Teams 1969, 1970, 1972.

CHRISTENSON, Sharon L. (b. 1938) of Edina MN, advertising salesperson, former school and piano teacher, won Gopher Women's Pairs 1973, Open Pairs 1977, Pheasant Open Pairs 1972, District 14 GNT 1974, Northwest Iowa Swiss Teams 1978.

CHRISTIAN, Col. William F. (b. 1914) of Chipley FL, retired Army officer, won the Spingold 1946, Spring NAC Men's Pairs 1960 and placed second in Fall NAC Life Master Men's Pairs 1964. His many regional wins include Washington Bridge Week KO Teams 1974, New England Master Teams 1965, Mid-South Spring Open Teams 1968, Missouri Valley Swiss Teams 1971, Master Pairs 1973, District 15 KO Teams 1969. Christian served in World War II and the police actions in South Korea and Vietnam for a total of 13 years overseas service. He was awarded the Bronze Star, Silver Star 1944, French Croix de Guerre 1945, 1st OLC Bronze Star 1951, Legion of Merit 1967, Air Medal 1967. With the Spingold win in 1946 he shares the distinction with his teammate, Capt. MARK HODGES, of being the first members of the military service on active duty to win a North American Championship.

CHRISTIANSEN, Leif (b. 1914) of Nordstrad-shogda, Norway, actuary and bridge columnist, represented Norway in the European Championships 1938, 1939, 1948, 1951, 1952, 1955, 1956. He was Nordic champion 1946, 1949 and his national successes include Open Teams 1938, 1942, 1947, 1949, 1951, 1952, Open Pairs 1946, 1956.

CHRISTIE, Agatha (1890–1976), pre-eminent British writer, wrote more than 100 works, among them 60 detective novels and 19 volumes of short mystery stories. One of these, *Cards on the Table*, concerns a murder committed during a bridge game. Poirot solves the mystery by ascertaining the abilities and bidding styles of each player, and the contracts they reached.

CHRISTOPHER, Jean (Mrs. Frank) of Darian IL placed second in Spring NAC Women's Teams 1973 and won Fall NAC secondary Women's Pairs 1973, Central States Open Teams 1969.

CHU, Y. M. (b. 1922) of Hong Kong, businessman, was Far East champion 1959, placed second 1963, 1965, 1969 and represented Hong Kong in Far East Championships on other occasions. His national wins include Master Teams 1960, 1963, 1968, Open Teams 1958, 1962, 1969, 1970, Master Pairs 1959, Open Individual 1958.

CHUA, Stephen (b. 1919) of Parañaque, Philippines, businessman, one of the leading players of the Philippines, was Far East champion 1957, 1958, 1970. He also represented the Philippines in the World Team Olympiad 1960, 1964, 1972 and in the Far East Championships since 1958. The leading masterpoint holder since 1955, he has won every national championship many times including Philippines Open Teams six times, Open Pairs 10 times, KO Teams 13 times, Master Pairs 11 times, Intercommerical Teams 1976, 1979, 1980, Tuason Cup 1971, 1975, 1976, 1979, 1972 (twice), PCBL Challenge Cup 1976, 1980.

CHURCHILL, S. Garton (Church) (b. May 13, 1900) of Great Neck NY, retired attorney, one of the great American bridge players and personalities, won the Life Master Pairs 1937, 1948, setting two records on the second occasion in partnership with CECIL HEAD. They scored 65½% as an average of four sessions, and 77.4% in a single session. Churchill won the Chicago (since 1965 the Reisinger) 1932, placed second in 1933, 1939, 1941, 1942, and in Summer NAC Master Mixed Teams 1937, Asbury Challenge Teams 1931. His regional wins include Eastern States KO Teams (Reisinger) 1937, 1938, 1939, New Jersey State Master Pairs 1947, 1959, Summer NAC secondary Senior Pairs 1959.

Churchill graduated from Ohio Wesleyan University in 1922 and Harvard Law School 1926. His bridge-playing activities were somewhat curtailed after 1944 due to his law practice and his desire to spend time with his family, but his interest in bridge never diminished. The originator of the CHURCHILL SYSTEM, he advocated ideas that were often scoffed at in the early Thirties but were generally adopted some 20 years later. These original theoretical ideas were set out in *Contract Bidding Tactics at Match-Point Play* and articles in *The Bridge World*. See BIBLIOGRAPHY, C.

CHURCHILL, Sir Winston (1874-1965). The great British war leader and historian played bridge in his younger days although it is doubtful whether he ever played contract. According to historian A. J. P. Taylor's biography of Lord Beaverbrook, "Aitken (Max Aitken, later Lord Beaverbrook) . . . went to Admiralty House with Smith (F. E. Smith, later Lord Birkenhead). There they found Churchill with two Liberal friends. While waiting for news and for the Liberals to go away, four of them played bridge—seemingly a universal habit among politicians at this time. Aitken, as usual, was the odd man out. A dispatch box was brought in. It contained the news that Germany had declared war on Russia. Churchill . . . went off to mobilize the fleet. Aitken took over Churchill's partly played hand, finding himself 'in an extremely unfavorable tactical position.' Smith and Aitken remained at Admiralty House until it was almost morning, but Churchill did not return."

This was perhaps comparable to an episode in English history several centuries earlier, although Churchill did not follow the example of Sir Francis Drake in 1588: On hearing of the approach of the Spanish Armada, Drake, in no rush to interrupt his game, announced, "We can finish the rubber and beat the Spaniards too." However, the rubber that Drake was playing was not bridge but bowls.

Lady Violet Bonham Carter reported that "Winston was even more dangerous [than her father, British Prime Minister Herbert Asquith] for he played a romantic game untrammeled by conventions, codes or rules. To cut with Winston was to both his private secretaries a severe ordeal . . . Winston declared, doubled and redoubled with wild recklessness." When one of his discards had proved misleading: "The cards I throw away are not worthy of observation, or I should not discard them. It is the cards I *play* on which you should concentrate your attention." When he had pained his partner by squandering a king: "The king cannot fall unworthily if it falls to the sword of the ace."

CIMON, Francine (b. 1950) of Montreal, physics teacher, represented Canada in the World Women's Teams 1976, 1980, World Women's Pairs 1978. She won Summer NAC secondary Silver Trophy Pairs Flt. A 1977, 1981, District 3 Open Pairs Flt. A 1981, Can-Am KO Teams 1978, Canadian Nat'l Teams Zone 2 1981, 1982, District 1 GNP 1982.

CINTRA, Gabino (b. 1942) of Rio de Janeiro, Brazil, IBM executive, WBF Grand Master, one of the world's leading players, won the World Team Olympiad 1976, World Open Pairs 1978 and placed second in the Rosenblum Cup Teams 1978. He was South American champion 1970, 1972, 1973, 1975, 1977, 1978. He also represented Brazil in the Bermuda Bowl 1971, 1973, 1974, 1976, 1977, 1979, World Team Olympiad 1980, World Open Pairs 1974. He was Brazilian champion 1970, 1972, 1973, 1974. Cintra contributes to Brazilian bridge publications.

CINTRA, Lia B. (Mrs. Gabino, formerly Penna) of Rio de Janeiro, Brazil, was South American Women's champion 1971, 1972, 1973. She served as npc of the Brazilian Women's Team in the South American Championships 1980, 1981 and in the Venice Trophy Teams 1981.

CIVETTA, Germano A. (Jerry) of Los Angeles, accountant, won Bridge Week Men's Pairs 1969, Desert Empire Open Pairs 1969, Pacific Southwest Men's Pairs 1976.

CLARK, Douglas H. (b. 1930) of Kingston ON, football team manager, won Can-Am Men's Pairs 1970, KO Teams 1973, Swiss Teams 1974, Canadian Nat'l Swiss Teams 1973. A 1952 graduate of Queen's University, Clark now manages its football team which has been conference champion four times and Canadian champion 1978.

CLARK, Harry (b. 1932) of Boles AR, has been an ACBL national tournament director since 1978.

CLARK, Phil (b. 1953) of Potomac MD, economist, won Summer NAC Swiss Teams 1973, Upper New York State Men's Swiss Teams 1974, Swiss Teams 1975, Canadian Nat'l Swiss Teams 1976, Keystone Spring Men's Pairs 1976, Mid-Atlantic Men's Swiss Teams 1979, 1980, Swiss Teams 1981, District 6 GNT, Zone I 1981.

CLARK, Ralph D. (b. 1938) of Costa Mesa CA, computer programmer, won Fall NAC Commerical & Industrial Pairs 1959, Mid-Atlantic Summer Open Teams 1966, Pacific Southwest Master Pairs 1968.

CLARK, Stephen R. (b. 1941) of San Ramon CA, retired lawyer, won California Capital Swiss Teams 1975, Men's Pairs 1975, Golden Gate Open Pairs 1973, All-Western Master Teams Flt. A 1975, Mount Shasta Open Pairs Flt. A 1981, District 21

GNT 1975, 1976.

CLARKE, Gale M. (Mrs. Harry J.) of McLean Va, bridge teacher, won Spring NAC Women's Pairs 1969 and represented the United States in the World Women's Pairs 1970.

CLARKE, Tom (b. 1946) of Lake Charles LA, insurance agency owner, won several regionals including Mid-South Unmixed Pairs 1978, KO Teams 1979, 1980, Master Pairs 1979, Master Swiss Teams 1980, Saskatchewan KO Teams 1980, Puerto Rico Men's Pairs 1981, Toast of Tulsa Unmixed Pairs 1981. He served Unit 221 and District 10 in various executive positions.

CLARKE, Truesdale (b. 1905) of Rochester NY, attorney, won Can-Am Open Pairs 1953, Open Teams 1958, Men's Pairs 1953, Upper New York State Men's Pairs 1973.

CLARREN, David B. (b. 1918) of Minneapolis, insurance agent, won the Vanderbilt 1947 and placed second in the Spingold 1949, 1953. Formerly one of the leading players in Minnesota, Clarren won numerous regional titles including Central States Open Teams 1944, Open Pairs 1946, Gopher KO Teams 1967, 1971, Open Teams 1958, 1963, 1967, Master Pairs 1960, Men Pairs 1959, 1960, 1969, 1970, Mid-Am-Can Open Teams 1961, 1962, 1963, Master Pairs 1958, Men's Pairs 1958, 1960. A pioneer of bridge development in Minnesota, he taught bridge for many years and lectured on TV for 52 weeks in 1960.

CLAY, James (1805–1873) of London, England, was the leading British WHIST authority between HOYLE and CAVENDISH. His chief work was *Treatise on the Game of Whist* (1864).

CLAYTON, Sir Hugh Byard (1877–1947) of India, born in Queensland, was one of the inventors of S.A.C.C., the initials of the four players living in India who developed this earlier prototype of PLAFOND about 1912. During World War I he served in the Intelligence Department, was Commissioner of Bombay (1919–1928), and was knighted in 1938.

CLERKIN, Dennis E. (b. 1950) of Bloomington IN, professional bridge player and instructor, placed second in Fall NAC Swiss Teams 1977 and won Spring NAC secondary Swiss Teams 1981, Summer Open Pairs Flt. A 1979, All-American Open Pairs 1977, Champagne Master Pairs 1978, Great Plains Open Pairs, Master Pairs, Swiss Teams 1979, Mid-South KO Teams 1979, Central Florida Swiss Teams 1980, Azalea City Open Pairs Flt. A 1980.

CLERKIN, Gerald P. (Jerry) (b. 1952) of North Vernon IN, professional bridge teacher and player, placed second in Fall NAC Swiss Teams 1977 and won Spring NAC secondary Swiss Teams 1981, All-American Open Pairs 1977, District 5 Open Pairs 1978, Distict 8 Men's Pairs 1979, Space City Men's Swiss Teams 1980, Azalea City Open Pairs Flt. A 1980.

CLEVELAND, Charles R. (Chip) (b. 1942) of Bend OR, controller, won Oregon Trail Swiss Teams 1972, British Columbia Master Pairs 1972, Redwood Empire Swiss Teams 1975, District 20 GNT 1973, 1974, 1975, Zone VII 1974. He has been president of Unit 476 since 1975.

CLEVELAND, John W. (b. 1947) of London, England, formerly of Bend OR, systems analyst, won Oregon Trail Men's Pairs 1970, Swiss Teams 1972, KO Teams, Master Pairs 1975, Redwood Empire Swiss Teams 1975, District 20 GNT 1973, 1975.

CLIFF, David L. (b. 1932) of Basking Ridge NJ, school teacher and principal, won New England Master Teams 1956, 1976, Open 1960, KO Teams 1961. He was one of the earliest theorists in the modern trend toward RELAY SYSTEMS and was a co-originator of the SPLINTER BID.

CLINKINBEARD, Helen A. (Mrs. J. E.) (b. 1919) of Knoxville TN, club director, won Mid-Atlantic Fall Open Pairs, Master Pairs 1960, Spring Women's Pairs 1981, Summer Swiss Teams 1971, District 11 Swiss Teams 1971.

COCHINWALA, A. Sattar of Karachi, Pakistan, businessman, placed second in the Far East Championships 1978 and won many Pakistan tournaments including Open Teams 1971, 1972. He was npc of the Pakistan team in the Bermuda Bowl 1981.

CODY, Judi L. (b. 1945) of Rye Beach NH won Fall NAC secondary Swiss Teams 1979, Upper New York State Women's Swiss Teams 1976, Tri-State Women's Pairs 1980, New England Fall Open Pairs Flt. A 1981.

COFFIN, George S. (b. 1903) of Waltham MA, author, publisher and distributor of bridge books and supplies, won *The Bridge World* international problem-solving contest 1930. His principal bridge work is *Bridge Play Four Classics*, a 960-page compilation of his earlier works *Endplays, Bridge Play from A to Z, Double Dummy Bridge* and *Bridge Perfect Plays and Match Point Ways* appended by *The Bridge Writer's Manual*. Coffin also wrote many volumes on games other than bridge (poker, pinochle, cribbage, etc.) and is now revising his publication on wild mushrooms. Coffin's other roles include co-founder of ABTA and first editor of its quarterly magazine; developer of THREE-HANDED BRIDGE; creator of many items of bridge equipment; publisher of many bridge books, including Beynon's *Bridge Director's Manual*, his own *Bridge Director's Logistics*, books by British writers; author of magazine and newspaper articles and of *Instant Bridge Bidding*; contributing editor, *Bridge Encyclopedia*. See BIBLIOGRAPHY, C, D, E.

COHAN, Joseph (1899–1958), a businessman of Wooster OH, born in Canada, presided over the ACBL in 1952. He placed second in Fall NAC Men's Teams 1947, 1949 and won All-American Men's Pairs 1953, Mid-West Spring Mixed Pairs 1949, Mississippi Valley Open Team 1953.

COHEN, Allan R. (b. 1934) of Wauconda IL, chemical engineer, placed second in Summer NAC Senior and Advanced Senior Master Pairs 1958 and won Fall NAC secondary Men's Teams 1963, Wisconsin Open Pairs 1978, Central States II Men's Swiss Teams 1979, Men's Pairs 1981.

COHEN, Barry. See CRANE, BARRY.

COHEN, Ben (1907–1971) of Hove, Sussex, England was an author, publisher and distributor of bridge books and stationery supplies. A pioneer of duplicate bridge in the early Thirties, Cohen was one of the originators of the ACOL system and author of many books on Acol, bridge quizzes, and other card games. Articles under his by-line appeared in many magazines including the South African *Bridge Bulletin*, the Indian *Onlooker*, and the *Japanese Bulletin*. He was a former editor of *Bridge Magazine*, and with RHODA BARROW LEDERER co-edited the European edition of *The Official Encyclopedia of Bridge*. See BIBLIOGRAPHY, C, D, E, J.

COHEN, Beverly M. of Buffalo NY, former ski instructor, won District 5 Women's Pairs 1979, 1980, Canadian Nat'l Women's Swiss Teams 1980.

COHEN, David (1897–1982) of Belfast, Ireland, represented Ireland in the European Championships 1956, and Northern Ireland in more than 70 CAMROSE TROPHY matches, a record. He achieved a remarkable record in the 1969–1970 season by winning 11 out of 15 major Irish tournaments at the age of 72, perhaps the best performance ever by a veteran player. He served as president of the IRISH BRIDGE UNION 1962–1963 and as chairman of NORTH OF IRELAND BRIDGE UNION 1956.

COHEN, Gerald S. (b. 1943) of Albany NY, transportation planner and mathematician, was Intercollegiate champion 1967. He won Upper New York State Swiss Teams 1974, Capital District Fall Men's Swiss Teams 1977, District 3 Men's Swiss Teams 1980, GNT 1975.

COHEN, Gilbert A. (Gil) (b. 1950) of Arlington VA, account manager, won several regional events including Upper New York State Swiss Teams 1975, District 4 Men's Swiss Teams 1976, Central States II Swiss Teams 1975, Mid-Atlantic Open Pairs 1980, Swiss Teams Flt. A 1981. He is a graduate of M.I.T.

COHEN, Harvey C. (b. 1935) of Encino CA, attorney, won Spring NAC Open Pairs 1967. His regional wins include Bridge Week KO Teams, Open Teams 1964, MARCUS CUP 1966. He was a member of the Los Angeles team which defeated the SHARIF BRIDGE CIRCUS 1970.

COHEN, Israel (b. 1913) of Washington, merchant, won Fall NAC Open Pairs 1952 and placed second in the Chicago (since 1965 the Reisinger), Summer NAC Master Mixed Teams 1963, Open Individual 1956. He won Eastern States Men's Pairs 1957, Keystone Conf. Open Teams 1959, Men's Pairs 1957, New York-New Jersey Open Teams 1960.

COHEN, Jan of Los Angeles, accountant, won Fall NAC secondary Women's Pairs 1977, Bridge Week Mixed Teams 1975, Master Swiss Teams Flt. A 1979, Master Women's Pairs Flt. A 1971, 1981, Women's Pairs 1981, California Capital Women's Pairs 1981.

COHEN, Jay (b. 1927) of Alexandria VA, traffic engineer, won Mid-Atlantic Spring Master Pairs 1967, Summer Master Pairs, Swiss Teams 1972, Keystone Men's Swiss Teams 1971, 1972, KO Teams 1975, Washington Bridge Week KO Teams 1975, 1976, Long Island Open Pairs 1976, District 4 Men's Swiss Teams, Swiss Teams 1976. He is past president of Washington BL.

COHEN, Jay R. (b. 1941) of Springfield VA, mortgage banker, won Keystone Men's Swiss Teams 1971, 1972, KO Teams 1975, Long Island Open Pairs 1976, District 4 Men's Swiss Teams, Swiss Teams 1976, Washington Bridge Week KO Teams 1975, 1976.

COHEN, Kenneth L. (b. 1948) of Philadelphia PA, bridge and backgammon teacher, placed second in Fall NAC Mixed Pairs 1973, Spingold and Life Master Pairs 1977. He won Spring NAC secondary Master Pairs 1972, Summer Open Pairs 1975, Open Pairs Flt. A 1981, Washington Bridge Week Men's Pairs 1974, KO Teams 1975, 1976, Florida Life Master Pairs 1972, District 4 Men's Swiss Teams 1976, 1980, GNT 1974, Eastern States Men's Pairs 1976, Mid-Atlantic Fall Men's Pairs 1976, Indy 500 KO Teams 1973, Keystone KO Teams 1973, Fun City KO Teams 1976.

COHEN, Larry N. (b. 1959) of Mount Vernon NY, marketing and purchasing agent, represented the United States in the World Open Pairs, Rosenblum Cup Teams 1982. He won the Spingold 1981, Blue Ribbon Pairs 1981 and placed second in Grand National Pairs 1980, Spring NAC Open Pairs 1979. His regional wins include Summer NAC secondary Commercial Teams 1978, 1979, 1980, 1981, Fall Swiss Teams Flt. A 1979, New England Summer KO Teams 1981, District 4 Swiss Teams Flt. A 1980, District 3 Men's Swiss Teams 1978, Swiss Teams 1979, GNT Zone II 1980.

COHEN, Lawrence (Larry) (b. 1943) of Los Angeles, pharmacist, won the Spingold 1973, 1976, Reisinger 1973, Grand National Teams 1974, Vanderbilt 1975, 1976, Blue Ribbon Pairs 1968, HERMAN TROPHY 1973, MOTT-SMITH TROPHY 1976, Spring NAC Men's Pairs 1976, and placed second in the Blue Ribbon Pairs 1968, Spring NAC Men's Teams 1971, Vanderbilt 1973. His numerous regional titles include Spring NAC secondary Swiss Teams 1974, Fall Swiss Teams 1975, Central States KO Teams 1965, 1972, 1973, Open Pairs 1973, Champagne Open Teams 1969, 1971, 1974, Swiss Teams 1974. Bridge Week Men's Pairs 1973, Swiss Teams 1976, Golden Gate KO Teams, Swiss Teams 1975. Cohen is a graduate of University of Wisconsin where he was Intercollegiate champion in 1966. He is the co-author of *Breakthrough in Bridge*. See BIBILIOGRAPHY, C, HOUSTON AFFAIR and LANCIA TEAMS.

COHEN, Mark D. (b. 1951) of Rego Park NY, investment manager, won Summer NAC Master Mixed Teams 1979 and placed second in Fall NAC Swiss Teams 1979, Vanderbilt 1982. His more than 20 regional titles include Big Apple Open Pairs Flt. A 1978, KO Teams 1981, Champagne KO Teams 1976, 1977, Swiss Teams 1977, Central States II Master Pairs 1977, Cambrian Shield Open Pairs 1976, New England Knockout Swiss Teams 1980, Open Pairs 1981, Fall Open Pairs 1979, Summer Open Pairs 1980.

COHEN, Nathan (Mr. Money Bags) (b. 1915) of Memphis, ACBL assistant treasurer and finance officer at North American Championships since 1948, worked with ELY CULBERTSON as production manager of Autobridge sets 1936–1946. In 1931 Cohen won 56 medals in various track events.

COHEN, Rafael (b. 1893) of Budapest, Hungary, retired merchant, was World champion 1934, European champion 1934 and placed second 1935–1937. He was Hungarian champion 1939–1935,1960 and was npc of Hungary's national team 1963–1968.

COHEN, Ralph (b. 1926) of Memphis, formerly of Montreal, assistant executive secretary of the ACBL since 1971, represented Canada in the World Team Olympiad 1964. He placed second in Spring NAC Amateur Swiss Teams 1977 and won numerous regionals including Can-Am Open Teams 1952, 1954, 1957, Men's Pairs 1957, New England Open Pairs 1965, 1969, Open Teams 1969, Indian Summer Master Pairs Flt. A 1979. He was a member of Montreal's victorious Intercity Team 1967, 1968. Cohen is a former president of Montreal BL and served as co-chairman of the Summer NAC 1967. An occasional contributor to the ACBL *Bulletin*, he contributed to the Fourth Edition, *Bridge Encyclopedia*. See FAMILY.

COHEN, Robert of Merrimack NH, formerly of Acton MA, won Fleur-de-Lys Open Pairs 1974, Can-Am KO Teams 1974, Tri-State Master Pairs 1974, Keohane Individual KO Teams 1975.

COHEN, Ruth M. (1915–1966) of New York City, business executive, bridge teacher and director, was a charter member of AMERICAN BRIDGE TEACHERS' ASSOCIATION (ABTA). She authored many booklets, among them *How to Make Teaching a Paying Proposition, Elements of Play, At-a-Glance Duplicate Scoring*, and *How to Match Point*. See BIBLIOGRAPHY, D.

COHEN, Stasha (Mrs. Mark D., formerly Wroblewski) (b. 1954) of Rego Park NY, computer analyst, won Spring NAC Women's KO Teams 1982, Summer NAC Women's Swiss Teams 1982. Her numerous regional wins include Fun City Swiss Teams 1975, District 4 Women's Swiss Teams 1977, Washington Bridge Week Swiss Teams 1977, New England Knockout Open Pairs 1981, Summer Open Pairs 1980, Tri-State Swiss Teams 1979, Big Apple KO Teams 1981. Cohen was National Master of the Year 1976. She is a graduate of Barnard College.

COHEN, William E. (Billy) (b. 1958) of Memphis, born in Montreal, won Fall NAC Swiss Teams 1978 and placed second in the Spingold 1982. His numerous regional wins include Mississippi Valley KO Teams 1979, 1981, Swiss Teams 1979, 1980, Open Pairs Flt. A 1979, Open Pairs 1981, Holiday Festival Men's Pairs, Swiss Teams 1979, Mid-South Master Pairs 1978, Open Pairs 1979, White Hat Master Pairs Flt. A 1979, Bridge Week Master Pairs Flt. A 1980, District 10 GNT, Zone IV 1979. See FAMILY.

COHLER, Dean A. (b. 1927) of Northbrook IL, CPA and financial officer and consultant, won Summer NAC secondary Swiss Teams 1971, Central States I Open Pairs 1978, Mid-Atlantic Swiss Teams Flt. A 1981. He served in various executive positions in the Chicago CBL including president.

COHN, Bette L. of Sarasota FL, formerly of Atlanta, won the VENICE TROPHY 1974, Summer NAC Mixed Pairs 1966, Fall NAC Women's Teams 1967, Life Master Women's Pairs 1970. Her regional titles include New England Master Pairs 1965, District 11 KO Teams 1969, Mid-Atlantic Open Teams 1970, Thanksgiving Women's Pairs 1972, Mid-South Women's Pairs 1974, Southeastern Women's Swiss Teams 1976, Texas Labor Day Mixed Pairs 1979, Puerto Rico Women's Pairs 1980.

COHN, Janice. See HORWITZ, JANICE.

COHN, Martin J. (Marty) (b. 1923) of Atlanta, retired business executive, placed second in the De La Rue International Pair Championship in London 1957. He won the Life Master Pairs 1957, Summer NAC Mixed Pairs 1966 and placed second in Fall NAC Men's Pairs 1961, Summer NAC Master Mixed Teams 1964, Spring NAC Men's Teams 1969. His many regional wins include District 11 KO Teams 1969, Southern Conference Fall Open Teams 1962, Great Lakes Open Teams 1961, 1968, Thanksgiving KO Teams 1973, Texas Fall KO Teams 1964, Mid-Atlantic Spring Swiss Teams, Men's Pairs 1970, Summer Men's Pairs 1977, Mexican Nat'l Swiss Teams 1972, Mississippi Valley Open Teams 1969, Senior Citizens Men's Pairs 1981.

COHN, Steven (b. 1942) of Cincinnati, computer operations supervisor, won District 5 Open Pairs 1969, District 11 Men's Pairs 1970, Open Teams 1974. Cohn is past president of Cincinnati BA.

COLBERT, David R. (b, 1952) of Toronto, math and physics teacher, won Canadian Nat'l Swiss Teams 1975, Nickel City KO Teams, Swiss Teams, Open Pairs 1978, Can-At Swiss Teams, Open Pairs 1980, Gateway City Swiss Teams, KO Teams 1981. A graduate of University of Toronto where he was a track and field champion, Colbert is now coaching track and field events and is the present Canadian record-holder in indoor 800m relay.

COLE, William P. (Bill) (b. 1950) of Silver Spring MD, engineer and professional bridge teacher, placed second in Summer NAC Master Mixed Teams 1981 and won Mid-Atlantic Open Pairs Flt. B

1979, Open Pairs 1980.

COLEMAN, Charles N. (b. 1896) of Corpus Christi TX, estate trustee, former army officer, teacher, won Mid-South Spring Men's Pairs 1949, Texas Fall Men's Pairs 1962, Open Pairs 1971. He organized the South Texas Unit in 1951 and served as president. He is a graduate of Baylor University.

COLKER, Richard E. (b. 1946) of Rockville MD, psychologist, won Summer NAC secondary Individual 1980, District 4 Men's Pairs 1981, Fall Men's Swiss Teams 1981, Mid-Atlantic Swiss Teams Flt A 1979, Men's Swiss Teams 1981.

COLLIER, Gladys W. (b. 1922) of East Hampton NY, mathematician, represented the United States in the World Women's Pairs 1970. She placed second in Fall NAC Life Master Women's Pairs 1969 and won Keystone Mixed Pairs 1967, Southeastern Open Pairs 1968, Fun City Mixed Pairs 1971.

COLLINGS, John D. R. (b. 1933) of London, England, retired London and Swiss bank officer, one of Europe's leading players, represented Switzerland in the World Open Pairs 1970, European Championships 1970, Great Britain in the Bermuda Bowl 1981, European Championships 1965, and England in CAMROSE TROPHY matches four years, winning each year. He also won the GOLD CUP 1965, Daily Telegraph Cup 1959, 1965, Crockford's Cup 1964, 1966, Life Master Pairs 1966, LONDON SUNDAY TIMES PAIRS (since 1981 INVITATIONAL PAIRS CHAMPIONSHIP) 1969. With JACK NUNES, Collings won both pair and team championships at the 1965 international tournament at Juan-les-Pins, a record.

COLLYER, Barbara. See KACHMAR, BARBARA.

COLSON, Sharon M. (b. 1946) of Kirkland WA, CPA, won Oregon Trail Amateur Open Pairs 1976, Open Pairs A–D 1981, Indian Summer Open Pairs Flt. A 1981.

CONLIN, David A. (b. 1923) of Phoenix, semi-retired real estate broker and developer, won Bridge Week Master Pairs 1960, Desert Empire Open Teams 1959, KO Teams 1967.

CONWAY, John T. (b. 1938) of Lockport NY, company vice president, won Spring NAC secondary Swiss Teams 1981, Upper New York State Men's Swiss Teams 1974, District 5 Master Pairs 1976, Golden State Swiss Teams Flt. A 1980, Pacific Southwest Swiss Teams 1981.

COOK, Dean (b. 1915) of Oakland CA, retired bridge teacher and director, won All-Western Open Teams 1957, 1963, Bridge Week Open Teams 1957, Crater Lake Open Teams 1970.

COOK, Dorothy Jane (D. J.) of Vero Beach FL, bridge teacher and writer, won All-American Mixed Pairs 1945, Central States Mixed Pairs, Women's Teams 1947, Women's Pairs 1948, Life Master Teams 1961. She is a former president and executive vice president of the ABTA. Cook, the daughter of famed Chicago Tribune political cartoonist, Casey Orr, authored *Learn to Play Winning Bridge* and *Cook and Deal*. See BIBLIOGRAPHY, E.

COOK, Edward M. II (b. 1901) of Palo Alto CA, commercial real estate developer, won Spring NAC Men's Pairs 1935, 1937, Bridge Week Men's Pairs 1958, Pacific Southwest Men's Pairs 1967.

COOK, Mary of Idaho Falls ID is a frequent contributor to the ACBL *Bulletin* and the author of *Confession of a Bridge Addict*.

COOK, Michael L. (Mike) (b. 1946) of Fayetteville AR, professional bridge player, placed second in the Grand National Teams 1975 and won Headquarters KO Teams 1978, Mid-South Swiss Teams 1979, Men's Pairs 1975, District 10 GNT 1978.

COOLIK, J. Samuel (b. 1943) of Atlanta, stockbroker, won Fall NAC secondary Men's Teams 1972, Mid-South Summer Men's Pairs 1971, 1975, Spring Men's Pairs 1972, Swiss Teams 1973, Mid-Atlantic Fall Swiss Teams 1976, KO Teams 1978, Summer KO Teams 1975, Thanksgiving Open Pairs, KO Teams 1972, District 7 GNT 1979.

COOMBS, Norman D. (b. 1934) of Harrison OH, consultant and stock options trader, won Fall NAC Life Master Men's Pairs 1978. His regional wins include Midwest Spring Men's Pairs 1970, Swiss Teams Flt. A 1982, Fall Men's Swiss Teams 1977, District 11 KO Teams 1977, Master Pairs 1976, GNP 1981. Coombs is a graduate of Ohio State.

COOMBS, William V. (Bill) (b. 1943) of Hamilton OH, corporate tax auditor, won Midwest Winter Swiss Teams 1974, Fall Master Pairs 1974, Swiss Teams 1978, 1980, District 11 Swiss Teams 1974, KO Teams 1977, Winter Open Pairs 1976, GNT 1979.

COON, Charles A. (b. 1931) of Gloucester MA, real estate broker and bridge teacher, one of the leading American players, represented North America in the Bermuda Bowl 1962. He won the Team Trials 1961, Vanderbilt 1961, Summer NAC Master Mixed Teams 1962, Fall NAC Life Master Men's Pairs 1964, Blue Ribbon Pairs 1966 and placed second in Spring NAC Men's Teams 1964, 1968, Reisinger 1961. He has won a great many regional tiltes.

COOPER, Martin J. (b. 1923) of Northbrook IL, pharmacist, won Southeastern Mixed Pairs 1960, Open Pairs 1961, Midwest Mixed Pairs 1961, Bermuda Master Pairs 1978.

COOPER, Roslyn (Mrs. Martin J.) (b. 1926) of Northbrook IL won Southeastern Mixed Pairs 1960, Open Pairs 1961, Midwest Mixed Pairs 1961, Bermuda Master Pairs 1978.

CORBIN, Jeff (b. 1948) of Wichita KS, stockbroker, won Missouri Valley KO Teams, Swiss Teams 1977, Toast of Tulsa Men's Pairs 1977, Mid-

Atlantic KO Teams 1978, Mid-South Spring Swiss Teams 1978, Summer Master Swiss Teams 1978, Fall KO Teams 1978, District 15 GNT 1977.

CORDES, Craig M. (b. 1944) of Baton Rouge LA, mathematics professor, won Mid-South Swiss Teams 1971, 1980, Holiday Swiss Teams Flt. A 1979, Crescent City Open Pairs 1981, District 10 GNP 1981.

CORDOEIRO, José Antonio (b. 1946) of Lisbon, Portugal, represented Portugal in the European Championships 1967, 1970, 1974. His national wins include Open Pairs.

COREN, Richard A. (b. 1954) of Lauderhill FL, law student, won Southeastern Master Pairs, Men's Swiss Teams 1974, Space City Men's Swiss Teams 1980, Gold Coast Men's Swiss Teams 1981.

CORMACK, Janas C. (Jan) (b. 1941) of Auckland, New Zealand, legal executive and journalist, was Far East Women's champion 1981 and placed second in 1978. She also represented New Zealand in the Far East Championships 1977, 1978, 1979, 1981, World Women's Teams 1980. She won Auckland Provincial Pairs 1976, 1978, 1980. Cormack writes a weekly column for *New Zealand Woman's Weekly*.

CORN, Ira G. Jr. (1921–1982) of Dallas, cofounder, executive and director of Michigan General Corp., former Assistant Professor SMU, was one of the leading bridge personalities in the Southwest area as organizer, financier, and captain of the Aces (the world's first professional bridge team), administrator for the Dallas BA, and successful tournament player. President of the Dallas BA 1968, tournament chairman 1966–1967, Board member since 1965, Corn was also ACBL president 1980. His wins include Spring NAC Mixed Pairs 1963, Men's Teams 1968, and Vanderbilt 1973, in addition to several regional titles. Corn, listed in *Who's Who In America* since 1971, wrote *The Story of The Declaration of Independence* 1977. See also ACES TEAM.

CORNELL, Michael L. (b. 1947) of Auckland, New Zealand, accountant, represented New Zealand in the Bermuda Bowl 1974, World Team Olympiad 1972, 1980, Far East Championships 1973, 1978, 1979, 1981. His national wins include New Zealand Teams 1972, 1973, 1977, 1978, Open Pairs 1981. Other wins include North Island Pairs 1971, Teams 1978, 1980.

CORWEN, Reginald F. of Leeds, England, clock importer, one of the leading European bridge personalities, was npc of Great Britain's Team in the Bermuda Bowl 1955 and in many European Championships. He served as a member of the European BL tournament committee and as chairman of the English Bridge Union.

COSTELLO, James D. (b. 1926) of Seattle, born in Calgary AB, engineer, won Puget Sound Mixed Pairs 1970, District 19 GNT, Zone VII 1973. He has been a tournament director since 1968 and has a Regional 2 rating.

COTTON, Cameron R. (b. 1956) of Sacramento CA, clerk, was Rookie of the Year 1979 (see MINI McKENNEY). He won California Capital Swiss Teams Flt. B 1979, 1981, Golden Gate Swiss Teams Flt. B 1980, Golden State Swiss Teams Flt. B 1980, Mount Shasta Master Pairs Flt. A 1981.

COURTENAY, F. Dudley (1892-deceased) of South Dennis MA, manufacturer of the first metal duplicate boards, was a major figure in the bridge battles of the early Thirties. He founded BRIDGE HEADQUARTERS, and was a member of the group which produced the OFFICIAL SYSTEM in opposition to ELY CULBERTSON. Courtenay's chief contribution to theory was the development of the LOSING TRICK COUNT, an unusual and important method of hand valuation, which he described in his book *The System the Experts Play*. His other writings include *Standardized Code of Contract Bridge Bidding, The Losing Trick Count, The Standard Manual on Play,* and *Standardized Contract Bridge Complete.* See BIBLIOGRAPHY, C, D, E.

COWAN, Donald S. (b. 1931) of Toronto, accountant turned booking agent, represented Canada in the World Team Olympiad 1976, Rosenblum Cup Teams 1978. His regional wins include Canadian Nat'l Open Teams 1962, 1971, 1979, Men's Swiss Teams 1978, 1980, All-American Open Teams 1960, Mixed Pairs 1961, Can-Am Open Teams 1961, Great Lakes Swiss Teams 1970, District 2 GNT 1973.

COWAN, Philip M. (Flip) (b. 1943) of New York City, attorney, won Fall NAC Swiss Teams 1980. His regional titles include Fun City Men's Pairs 1970, New York-New Jersey Open Pairs 1973, Capital District Fall Men's Swiss Teams 1977, Mid-Atlantic Open Pairs 1980.

COWGER, Dorothy J. of Canoga Park CA placed second in Spring Women's Teams 1970 and won Oregon Trail Women's Pairs 1970.

COX, Karl C. (b. 1936) of Medfield MA, accountant, won Can-At KO Teams, Open Teams 1974, Eastern States Men's Pairs 1971, Olympic Open Pairs 1976.

COX, Margaret C. (Marge) (b. 1954) of Mentor OH, real estate company owner, won District 5 Women's Swiss Teams, Mixed Pairs 1977, All-American Swiss Teams 1976, Women's Swiss Teams 1981.

COX, Stephen P. (Reno) (b. 1946) of Novato CA won Summer NAC secondary Swiss Teams 2nd Flt. 1973, Midwest Fall KO Teams 1973, 1975, Mid-Atlantic Spring Open Teams 1972.

COYLE, William (Willie) (b. 1937) of Renfrew, Scotland, science and mathematics teacher, represented Scotland in 11 international matches and was a member of the victorious CAMROSE

TROPHY team once. He represented Great Britain in the Bermuda Bowl 1976 and placed third. His national titles include Open Teams twice. He is one of four Scottish players to compete in the *London Sunday Times Pairs* (since 1981 Invitational Pairs Championship) and the British Trials. He won the GOLD CUP 1969, 1973.

CRAMER, Héctor (1901-1974) of Buenos Aires, Argentina, represented Argentina in the Bermuda Bowl 1961. He was South American champion 1954, 1957. His national wins include Argentine Open Teams 1935, 1938, 1940-1943, 1949, 1952, 1954, 1964, Open Pairs 1935, 1942, 1943, 1955. Cramer was one of the world's great rubber bridge players.

CRANE, Barry of Studio City CA, formerly of Detroit, television producer and director, one of the leading American players, the ACBL's top masterpoint holder (see LIFE MASTER), is considered by many to be the top matchpoint player of all time. He won the World Mixed Pairs 1978, Summer NAC Mixed Teams 1953, 1954, 1980, Spring NAC Open Pairs 1964, 1970, 1971, 1972, 1974, 1977, Men's Pairs 1966, Fall NAC Mixed Pairs 1975, 1977, Open Swiss Teams 1978 and placed second in Summer NAC Master Mixed Teams 1969, Fall NAC Mixed Pairs 1971, 1974, Spring NAC Men's Teams 1971, Open Pairs 1976. He won the McKENNEY TROPHY 1952, 1967, 1971, 1973, 1975, 1978 and placed second in 1961, 1962, 1963, 1964, 1981. He is the winner of the MOTT-SMITH TROPHY 1971, 1974, the Oeschger Trophy (West Coast McKenney) 1961, 1962, 1963, 1967, the STODDARD MEMORIAL TROPHY 1980. Crane has won hundreds of regional events; more than 130 since 1974. In October 1968 he became the ACBL's leading masterpoint holder, replacing OSWALD JACOBY who had held the top spot since 1962.

CRANE, Joshua (1869-1964) of Lantana FL, was a sportsman, bridge writer; an American long a resident of England who was prominent in polo, football, golf and yacht racing as well as in bridge. In the mid-Thirties he sponsored the visit of a New England team to London, where matches were played against leading English teams. His own system of bidding, the Crane System, was set out in *Common Sense in Contract Bidding.* See BIBLIOGRAPHY, C.

CRANE, Lois (formerly Oke) (b. 1922) of Marysville WA, bookkeeper, won Northwest Open Teams 1958, Master Pairs 1960, Women's Pairs 1959.

CRAPKO, Boris D. (Buddy) (b. 1937) of Richmond BC, land developer, won several regional titles including Pacific Northwest KO Teams 1969, 1970, Master Pairs 1966, Oregon Trail Men's Pairs 1973, Puget Sound Open Teams 1972, Klondike Swiss Teams 1974, District 19 GNT 1974, 1975.

CRAWFORD, Carol (Mrs. John, formerly Stalkin and Ross) (1934-1982) of New York City, won Fall NAC Mixed Pairs 1958, Spring NAC Women's Teams 1966. She placed second in the Women's Teams 1972, Summer NAC Master Mixed Teams

1974, 1975, Fall Life Master Women's Pairs 1976. World backgammon champion in 1973, she was one of only three women ever to win the title.

CRAWFORD, John R. (1915–1976) of New York City, bridge teacher and writer, was acknowledged as one of the world's great players. His total of 37 ACBL national titles up to 1964 exceeded any other player's record at that time. By winning three consecutive Bermuda Bowls 1950, 1951, 1953, and by other performances abroad, he established a solid international reputation. He also represented the United States in the Bermuda Bowl 1958, World Team Olympiad 1960.

His 10 wins in the Chicago Trophy (since 1965 the Reisinger), 1937, 1938, 1939, 1942, 1946, 1947, 1953, 1954, 1956 and 1961, set a record. The first of these wins, at the age of 22, gave him his first national title at a younger age than any of the other great American players. Two years later he became Life Master #19, at that time much the youngest of a select band.

His other national wins include Spingold 1943, 1948, 1950, 1952, 1957; Vanderbilt 1941, 1946, 1950, 1951, 1955, 1956, 1957, 1959, 1960; Fall NAC Men's Teams 1956, 1961; Mixed Teams 1942, 1945, 1948, 1957; Life Master Pairs 1943; Summer NAC Men's Pairs 1939; Fall NAC Mixed Pairs 1945, 1948, 1949, 1959; Master Individual 1956. His 23 seconds in national events include five in the Life Master Pairs. In 1957 he achieved a unique grand slam of national team titles by holding simultaneously the Vanderbilt, Spingold, Chicago, Men's and Mixed Team Championships. He demonstrated his adaptability by achieving national successes with many different partners and earned a reputation for competitive repartee, table presence and psychological awareness.

An expert on many card games and forms of gambling, Crawford lectured extensively during his wartime army service in an attempt to help servicemen avoid being cheated. He helped to found the New York Card School in 1950, and moved to New York City from Philadelphia in 1959.

His writings include *Crawford's Contract Bridge, How to Be a Consistent Winner in the Most Popular Card Games*, books on canasta, samba, and a column for *The Elks Magazine*. See BIBLIOGRAPHY, E.

CREED, Harold (Bud) (b. 1921) of Garland TX, bridge club owner and teacher, former engineer, placed second in Spring NAC Men's Pairs 1960 and won All-American Open Teams 1952, Open Pairs 1957, 1958, Mixed Pairs 1953, Texas Fall Open Teams 1964, 1970, International City KO Teams 1974, Missouri Valley Swiss Teams 1971, Master Pairs 1979, Midwest Fall Open Teams 1960, Spring Open Teams 1962.

CREED, Harold N. (Harry) (b. 1909) of Toronto, retired businessman, won several regional events including Canadian Nat'l Open Pairs 1961, Mixed Pairs 1967, Men's Pairs 1969, Keystone Conference Open Teams 1958, District 5 Swiss Teams 1970, Fleur-de-Lys Master Pairs Flt. A 1974.

CROCKER, Anthony F. (b. 1952) of South Pasadena CA, assistant actuary, won Spring NAC Amateur Swiss Teams 1977.

CROOKER, Jerry (b. 1947) of San Antonio, bank lending and operations officer, won Capital City KO Teams 1977, Corpus Christi Swiss Teams 1978, Big D Winter Men's Pairs 1980. A Vietnam veteran, he won eight separate outstanding service medals and ribbons.

CROOKS, William L. (Bill) of Macon MO won Missouri Valley KO Teams 1972, 1973, District 15 KO Teams 1977, Men's Pairs 1980, GNP 1981, Indian Summer KO Teams 1979, Springfield KO Teams, Open Pairs Flt. A 1980.

CROSBY, Robert F. (b. 1947) of Edmonton AB, public administrator, won several regional events including Spring NAC secondary Swiss Teams 2nd Flt. 1974, Klondike Swiss Teams, Swiss Teams Flt. A 1980, District 18 GNT 1974, 1976, 1977, 1978, 1979, Zone VII 1976, 1977, 1978, 1979, Canadian National Teams Zone 5 1980, 1981.

CROSSLEY, Dr. C(larence) F. Jr. (Cap) (b. 1924) of Las Vegas, physician and anesthesiologist, won numerous regional events including All-Western KO Teams 1955, Desert Empire Open Teams 1962, 1963, Rocky Mountain Men's Pairs 1963, Big D Bridge Week Swiss Teams 1974, Oil City KO Teams, Master Swiss Teams 1978, Desert Empire Master Swiss Teams 1978, Pacific Southwest Swiss Teams 1976, Mid-Winter Holiday KO Teams 1975, Pikes Peak Swiss Teams Flt. A, Master Pairs 1980. He is a former president of District 17, the WESTERN CONFERENCE, Marin County CA and Nevada Units. See FAMILY.

CROSSLEY, Dr. David M. (b. 1948) of Las Vegas, anesthesiologist, won the Vanderbilt 1974. His numerous regional wins include Golden Gate KO Teams 1974, Mid-Winter Holiday KO Teams 1974, 1975, Rogue River Valley KO Teams 1973, Golden Gate KO Teams 1974, Bridge Week Mixed Pairs 1976, Cotton Boll Swiss Teams 1977, District 17 GNT 1975, 1976. See FAMILY.

CROSSLEY, Robert F. (Bob) (b. 1951) of Mill Valley CA, professional bridge player and teacher, independent film maker, won the Vanderbilt 1974. His more than 20 regional titles include Mid-Winter Holiday Open Pairs 1968, KO Teams 1974, All-Western Master Pairs Flt. A 1978, KO Teams, Swiss Teams Flt. A 1981, Bridge Week KO Teams 1979, British Columbia KO Teams 1979, California Capital KO Teams 1979, Golden Gate KO Teams 1974, District 17 GNT 1976. See FAMILY.

CROUNSE, Eleanor B. of Paducah KY, won Spring NAC Women's Teams 1962, Summer NAC Mixed Pairs 1964, District 11 Women's Pairs 1970, Champagne Open Pairs 1970.

CROWHURST, Eric (b. 1935) of Reading, England, accountant, is a contributor to *British Bridge*

World, ACBL *Bulletin*, and other periodicals. He also contributed the unique SUIT COMBINATIONS section of the *Bridge Encyclopedia*. He is the inventor of the CROWHURST CONVENTION, which is widely used by British tournament players. Crowhurst is the author of *Acol in Competition* and other books on British bidding.

CROWN, Ronald (b. 1927) of South Palm Beach FL, formerly of London, England, bridge teacher, represented England in the CAMROSE TROPHY match 1961, won the Tollemache Cup three times and the Richard Lederer Cup twice. His regional wins include New England Winter Open Teams 1968, Eastern States KO Teams (Reisinger) 1969. His bridge teaching career began in England and from 1965-1970 he was a partner in the Card School of New York. Presently he teaches approximately 500 students per week. He has contributed articles to *The British Bridge World* and ACBL *Bulletin*.

CROWNINSHIELD, Frank (1872-1947) wrote *The Bridge Fiend* and other books under the pseudonym of Arthur Loring Bruce. He was president of the Cavendish Club in New York from 1935 to 1946 and donor of the Crowninshield Trophy. Crowninshield served as editor of *Vanity Fair* from 1914 to 1935, and subsequently as associate editor of *Vogue* and director of *Condé Nast*.

CRUZ, Joao Nuño Moreira (b. 1936) of Lisbon, Portugal, lawyer, represented Portugal in the European Championships 1965, 1966, 1967, 1970, 1971. His national wins include Open Teams four times, Open Pairs three times.

CUKOFF, Henry (b. 1949) of Montreal, tournament director, won New England Spring Open Pairs 1972, Canadian Nat'l Open Pairs 1973, Can-Am Swiss Teams 1973. Cukoff has been directing since 1974 and attained the rating of Regional 4 in 1981.

CULBERTSON, Ely (July 22, 1891–December 27, 1955) stood for many years as America's foremost authority on contract bridge. Generally credited with making the game an internationally popular pastime, Culbertson was also an author and lecturer on mass psychology and political science. He was born in Romania but was an American citizen from birth by registration with the U.S. consul, being the son of Almon Culbertson, an American mining engineer who had been retained by the Russian government to develop the Caucasian oilfields and who had married a Russian woman, Xenia Rogoznaya, daughter of a Cossack *atamon* or chief. Culbertson belonged to a pioneer American family settled about Titusville and Oil City, PA, and later joined the Sons of the American Revolution to refute rumors that he had changed his name or falsified his ancestry. He attended *gymnasia* in Russia and matriculated at Yale (1908) and Cornell (1910), but in each case remained only a few months. Later (1913-14) he studied political science at l'École des Sciences Économiques et Politiques at the University of Paris (Sorbonne) and in 1915 at the University of Geneva in Switzerland, but he was largely self-educated, and the erudition for which he was admired can principally be attributed to a self-imposed and invariable regimen of reading a book designed to improve his knowledge at least one hour before going to sleep each night. In this he was aided by an aptitude for languages. He conversed fluently in Russian, English, French, German, Czech, Spanish, and Italian, had a reading knowledge of Slavonic, Polish, Swedish, and Danish–Norwegian, and a knowledge of classical Latin and Greek.

In 1907 Culbertson participated as a student in one of the abortive Russian revolutions. He pursued his revolutionary ideas in labor disputes in the American Northwest and in Mexico and Spain (1911-1912), serving as an agitator for the union and syndicalist sides.

[The foregoing biographical data, all of which is a matter of official record, is here given in detail because it has been disputed in various writings about Culbertson.]

After the Russian Revolution of 1917 wiped out his family's large fortune there, Culbertson lived for four years in Paris and other European cities by exploiting his skill as a card player. In 1921 he returned to the U.S., almost penniless, and continued to derive his chief living from winnings in card games. In 1923, having acquired some reputation as a bridge player, he married Mrs. Josephine Murphy Dillon (see CULBERTSON, JOSEPHINE), one of the highly reputed bridge teachers in New York City. Together they became a successful pair as tournament players and bridge authorites.

Between 1926 and 1929, the then new game of contract bridge began to replace auction bridge, and Culbertson saw in this development an opportunity to overtake the firmly entrenched authorities on auction bridge. Culbertson planned a long-range campaign that included the construction of a dogmatic system; publication of a magazine to appeal to group leaders in bridge; authorship of a bridge textbook to serve as a "bible"; organization of professional bridge teachers; dramatization of himself and his wife as largely fictitious personalities; and expansion of the appeal of bridge by breaking down religious opposition to card playing.

The plan proved conspicuously successful. Culbertson founded his magazine, *The Bridge World*, in 1929, and through the same corporation published his earliest bridge books, all of which were best sellers; manufactured and sold bridge players' supplies including the introduction of Kem playing cards; maintained an organization of bridge teachers (Culbertson National Studios) which at its peak had 6000 members; and conducted bridge competitions through the United States Bridge Association and the World Bridge Olympics and American Bridge Olympics. In its best year, 1937, The Bridge World, Inc., grossed more than $1,000,000, of which $220,000 were royalties payable to Culbertson before profits were calculated.

As a regular tournament competitor Culbertson had the best record in the earliest years of contract bridge. In 1930 he won the Vanderbilt and American Bridge League Knockout Team events, also the ABL Board-a-Match Team event, and finished second in the Master Pairs. That year he led a team that played the first international match, in England, and defeated several teams there. In 1933 and 1934 his teams won the SCHWAB CUP. After 1934 Culbertson seldom played tournament bridge, but he was second in the ABL's 1935 matchpoint team contest and in the International Bridge League's first intercontinental tournament in 1937. Culbertson continued to play high-stake rubber bridge until about two years before his death.

The success of Culbertson's *Blue Book* in 1930 caused the established auction bridge authorities to join forces to combat his threatened domination of contract bridge. (See BRIDGE HEADQUARTERS and OFFICIAL SYSTEM.) Culbertson countered by challenging the leading player among his opposition, SIDNEY LENZ, to a test match, offering five-to-one odds. Culbertson's victory in this match, played in the winter of 1931–32, fortified his leading position (see CULBERTSON-LENZ MATCH). The great publicity accorded the match enriched Culbertson: he and his wife both acquired contracts for widely syndicated newspaper articles, he made a series of movie shorts for $360,000, and he received $10,000 a week for network radio broadcasts. In 1935 Culbertson tried to recapture the magic of his match against Lenz by playing a similar match against P. HAL and DOROTHY SIMS (see CULBERTSON-SIMS MATCH), but although the Culbertsons won this match also, there was no such publicity advantage as accrued from the Lenz match.

The publicity accorded Culbertson throughout his professional career can be attributed equally to his unquestioned abilities, his colorful personality and his flamboyant way of life. Culbertson lived in the grand manner, with total disregard of expense whether at the moment he happened to be rich or penniless. Once he strolled into Sulka's (then) on Fifth Avenue in New York and bought $5,000 worth of shirts. He smoked a private blend of cigarettes that cost him $7 a day. When he decided to buy a Duesenberg automobile in 1934 he did not sell his Rolls Royce but gave it away. His home for years was an estate in Ridgefield CT, with a 45-room house, several miles of paved and lighted roads, greenhouses, cottages, lakes, and an enclosed swimming pool with orchids growing along its periphery. He always had caviar with his tea and made special trips to Italy to buy his neckties. When he died in 1955, he owned five houses for his own use, four of them with swimming pools. But Culbertson rationalized these extravagances as publicity devices. He actually lived in one small room with a cot and a table, and he spent most of his time pacing the floor and thinking. In 1933, when a newspaper reporter asked him, "Mr. Culbertson, how did you get ahead of those other bridge authorities?" he answered, "I got up in the morning and went to work."

Culbertson's contributions to the science of contract bridge, both practical and theoretical, were basic and timeless. He devised the markings on duplicate boards for vulnerability and the bonuses for games and partscores. He was the first authority to treat distribution as equal or superior to high cards in formulating the requirements for bids. Forcing bids, including the one-over-one, were original Culbertson concepts, as were four-card suit

bids, limited notrump bids, the strong two-bid, and wholesale ace-showing including the 4 NT slam try.

These were presented in the historic *Lesson Sheets on the Approach-Forcing System* (1927) and in numerous magazine articles written by Culbertson in the Twenties and early Thirties. Specific bridge principles attributable to Culbertson, separately described, include among others ASKING BIDS, the GRAND SLAM FORCE, JUMP BIDS, and the NEW-SUIT FORCING principle, which Culbertson first introduced and later repudiated.

In 1938, with war imminent in Europe, Culbertson lost interest in bridge and thereafter devoted his time to seeking some grand achievement in political science. To effect world peace he proposed international control of decisive weapons and a quota for each major nation in tactical forces. After formation of the United Nations, to which Culbertson's ideas made a discernible contribution, he persisted in a campaign to give it adequate police power. At one time 17 U.S. Senators and 42 U.S. Congressmen subscribed to a proposed joint resolution of Congress advocating Culbertson's proposals. But in the course of these activities Culbertson lost his position as the leading bridge authority; by 1950 or earlier, CHARLES GOREN had surpassed him in the sale of books and other bridge writings and in the adherence of bridge teachers and players. However, when a bridge HALL OF FAME was inaugurated in 1964, nine years after his death, Culbertson was the first person elected. Though never an ACBL Life Master, he was named Honorary Member in 1938.

Ely and Josephine Culbertson were divorced in 1938 and in 1947 Culbertson married Dorothy Renata Baehne, who was 35 years younger than he. There were two children by each of his marriages.

Culbertson suffered in late years from a lung congestion (emphysema) and died at his last home, in Brattleboro VT, of a common cold that proved fatal because of the lung condition.

BIBLIOGRAPHY. Minor works by Ely Culbertson, such as paperbound books and pamphlets, are literally too numerous to mention, and all or nearly all were written by members of Culbertson's staff, as also were most of the newspaper and magazine articles published under Culbertson's name from 1932 on. Earlier articles in bridge periodicals were written by Culbertson, as were the following of his major books, each of which was published in many editions: *Contract Bridge Blue Book*, 1930; *Culbertson's Self-Teacher*, 1933; *Red Book on Play*, 1934; *The Gold Book*, or, *Contract Bridge Complete, 1936*; and *Point-Count Bidding*, 1952.

Culbertson's autobiography, *The Strange Lives of One Man*, was published in 1940. His principal works on political science were *Total Peace*, 1943, and *Must We Fight Russia?*, 1947. See BIBLIOGRAPHY, C, D, E, G, K.

CULBERTSON, Josephine (Mrs. Ely) (February 2, 1898–March 23, 1956) stood in her own right as a renowned bridge teacher, player and writer. She was born Josephine Murphy in Bayside NY (now part of New York City). In 1919 she married James Dillon, and was widowed by his suicide shortly thereafter. Her interest in bridge commenced when she became secretary to WILBER C. WHITEHEAD. On June 11, 1923 she married ELY CULBERTSON and collaborated with him in the development and teaching of the Culbertson or Approach-Forcing systems of auction and contract bridge. During her teaching career, 1922–1930, she was reputedly the highest-paid bridge teacher. Through the Twenties and into the Thirties, Culbertson was known as "the modern miracle — the woman who can play on even terms with the best men." She was the first woman to achieve highest championship caliber, and as such was unique in her times, before the advent of HELEN SOBEL and others. As a member of the Bridge World team, with WALDEMAR VON ZEDTWITZ as her partner and later MICHAEL GOTTLIEB and ALBERT MOREHEAD, Culbertson won several national and international championships including the SCHWAB CUP 1933, 1934. Paired with her husband, she played many high-stake set games, won international matches in England and France, and achieved national fame in the CULBERTSON-LENZ MATCH, 1931–1932, and CULBERTSON-SIMS MATCH, 1935. Culbertson was co-founder of The Bridge World magazine, 1929, and inaugurated its "Pro et Contra" department, which appeared under her name until her death. She was often on radio bridge shows, including two long series with her husband. She participated briefly in motion pictures made by her husband.

Jo, as she insisted she be called by her close friends, was red-haired, blue-eyed, slender and tall, "a lovely thing". She attracted people to her because of her sweet nature, her gentle ways and her gaiety. Charming to everyone, Culbertson was as glamorous as a movie star — the world of bridge was at her feet as was the world of fashion. Every paper, every smart magazine sang her praises and quoted not only her success at the bridge table, but also her beautiful clothes and the chic with which she wore them. Yet she remained the same modest, charming woman.

Josephine and Ely Culbertson were divorced in an uncontested action brought by Culbertson in Reno NV in 1938, though they continued as business partners and co-editors. She died March 23, 1956, of a cerebral stroke, 87 days after Ely's death.

Culbertson won ABL Open Challenge Team 1930, Vanderbilt 1930, and placed second in the Life Master Pairs 1930, Open Pairs 1928 (both of these events played for the first time on these dates), Chicago 1935, NAC Women's Pairs 1930.

At all times, Culbertson was an active editor of all books on the CULBERTSON SYSTEM. She was co-author of the historic Lesson Sheets on the Approach System (1927) and made the first arrangement of material for Culbertson's Summary (1932), the largest-selling bridge book. However, her widely syndicated newspaper column, 1931–56, her department in The Bridge World, and the several books published under her name were largely prepared by The Bridge World technical staff; the best-known of these is Contract Bridge for Beginners, 1937. See BIBLIOGRAPHY, E.

CULBERTSON, Thomas N. of Edinburgh, Scotland, lawyer, former teacher of classics, the first Scottish Grand Master and leading Scottish master-

point holder since 1974, represented Great Britain in the World Open Pairs 1970, 1982, Common Market Mixed Teams 1981 (placed third) and represented Scotland in 17 CAMROSE TROPHY matches. He has won every Scottish national competition, in most cases on several occasions. He was a member of the first Scottish team to win the GOLD CUP. His British Bridge League wins include a second Gold Cup win and three team events. He also won several European Bridge League team and pair events.

CULLINAN, John E. Jr. (b. 1919) of Oswego NY, attorney, won Can-Am Open Pairs 1966, 1979, Upper New York State Men's Pairs 1973, Olympic Open Pairs, Open Pairs Flt. A 1978. Cullinan served on many committees and held many executive positions on the local and national levels including ACBL Board member.

CUMMINGS, Michael (b. 1944) of Willowdale ON, computer programming consultant, won several regional events including Great Lakes Open Teams 1970, Can-Am KO Teams 1974, 1977, Canadian Nat'l Swiss Teams 1972, Men's Swiss Teams 1977, 1978, 1980, KO Teams 1979, District 2 GNT 1975.

CUMMINGS, Richard John (b. 1932) of Sydney, Australia, bridge teacher, one of the leading Australian players, represented Australia in the Bermuda Bowl 1971, 1976, 1977, 1979, 1981, World Team Olympiad 1960, 1964, 1968, 1980. His national titles include Open Team 1959, 1962, 1963, 1974, Open Pairs 1957, Individual 1962, Par 1960, 1962, 1963. Cummings was delegate to the AUSTRALIAN BRIDGE FEDERATION and a member of New South Wales Bridge Council. He is a contributor to international bridge magazines.

CUNNEEN, Kathryn M. (Katie) (b. 1931) of Portland OR, won Oregon Trail Mixed Swiss Teams 1975, Women's Swiss Teams 1977, Women's Pairs 1978, Puget Sound Women's Pairs 1974. Cunneen is an administrative secretary, bridge club owner and director, bridge columnist and special feature writer for the Oregonian. Her special features for this statewide newspaper earned her a certificate of commendation from the ACBL 1982. She also contributes to the ACBL Bulletin and the Contract Bridge Forum. A club and local director, she directs and teaches aboard cruise ships several times a year.

CUNNINGHAM, Mildred E. (1898–1983) of San Clemente CA, retired bridge teacher, placed second in Summer NAC Women's Pairs 1948, 1949, and won Central States Mixed Pairs 1944, Master Individual 1946, Open Pairs 1956, Southeastern Women's Teams 1967.

CUNNINGHAM, Rosalie R. of Auckland, New Zealand, real estate agent, was Far East champion 1981 and also represented New Zealand in the Far East Championships 1977.

CURRENT, Dr. A. C. Jr. (b. 1928) of Gastonia NC, dentist, won Mid-Atlantic Spring Open Teams 1959, Men's Pairs 1967, Fall Open Teams 1961.

CURRY, David E. L. (b. 1943) of Ottawa, taxi cab driver, won Nat'l Capital Men's Swiss Teams 1978, 1980, Fleur-de-Lys Swiss Teams 1979, Can-Am Swiss Teams 1980.

CUSHNER, Mary Lou (Cush) (b. 1936) of Brookline MA, court reporter, placed second in Spring NAC Women's Teams 1977 and won Spring NAC secondary Swiss Teams 1979, District 3 Women's Swiss Teams 1980, 1981, New England Knockout Master Pairs 1976, Can-At KO Teams 1977, Southeastern Women's Swiss Teams 1980.

CZEKAŃSKA, Irena of Warsaw, Poland, represented Poland in the World Mixed Pairs 1966, European Championships 1965. Her national wins include Mixed Teams 1964.

D

DA COSTA, Donald (b. 1927) of Toronto, formerly of New Kingston, Jamiaca, bridge club manager, won Canadian Nat'l Open Teams 1961, Mixed Pairs 1965, Can-Am Mixed Pairs 1962, Open Teams 1959.

DAHL, Carl B. Jr. (b. 1943) of Rockford IL, research engineer, won Spring NAC secondary Open Pairs Flt. A 1976, All-American Swiss Teams 1975, Great Lakes KO Teams 1978, Midwest Fall Swiss Teams 1978.

DAIGNEAULT, Pierre (b. 1947) of Laval PQ, sociologist, director of research, won several regionals including Summer NAC secondary Men's Pairs Flt. A 1978, Can-Am Open Pairs 1975, KO Teams 1978, Fleur-de-Lys KO Teams 1979, National Capital Swiss Teams Flt. A 1980, District 5 KO Teams 1980, District 1 GNP 1981. Daigneault has served as vice president of the Montreal BL since 1979. He is a graduate of McGill University.

DALATI, Henri of Beirut, Lebanon, represented Lebanon in the World Team Olympiad 1960, 1964, European Championships 1954, 1956, 1957, 1961, 1962, 1963 and won many national titles. He is a former secretary of the LEBANESE BRIDGE FEDERATION.

DALLAS, Richard N. (b. 1916) of North Hollywood CA, born in London, England, organic chemist, won Fall NAC Open Pairs 1968. His regional wins include Mexican Nat'l Master Pairs 1968, Orange County Open Teams 1972, Raincross KO Teams 1980, Master Pairs 2nd Flt. 1981, Palm Springs Swiss Teams 1975, District 23 GNT 1980.

DALTON, Roy S. (b. 1955) of Mississauga ON, bridge teacher, represented Canada in the Rosenblum Cup Teams 1978. Dalton became the youngest-ever Life Master in Canada 1974. His regional wins include Canadian Nat'l Swiss Teams 1975, KO Teams Flt. A 1981, Nickel City KO Teams, Swiss Teams 1978, District 2 GNT 1977, 1978.

DALY, Victor R. (b. 1895) of Washington DC, retired government deputy director and travel consultant, was one of the 36 founders of the AMERICAN BRIDGE ASSOCIATION at Hampton VA in 1932. For many years he was a prominent figure in the ABA, serving as its president from 1950–1965, vice president 1941–1949, and he has been President Emeritus since 1965. He was a member of the ACBL Goodwill Committee and a contributing editor, *Bridge Encyclopedia*. A graduate of Cornell, Daly received The Distinguished Service Award from the U.S. Dept. of Labor 1955, had two articles on labor problems entered into the Congressional Record and was listed in *Who's Who in America* 1976 edition.

DAM, Else (b. 1915) of Copenhagen, Denmark, bridge teacher, was European Women's champion 1948, 1949 and placed second in 1950. She won 11 Danish national titles.

DAMIANI, José. (b. 1939) of Paris, France, industrialist, has won many national titles. He is vice president of the EUROPEAN BRIDGE LEAGUE and president of the FRENCH BRIDGE FEDERATION. Damiani is a member of the Executive Committee of the WORLD BRIDGE FEDERATION.

DAMM, Mrs. Otti (b. 1918) of Copenhagen, Denmark, bridge teacher, was European Women's champion 1949, 1955, 1957, 1958 and placed second twice. Her many national successes include Open Teams twice and many Women's Teams titles.

D'ANDREA, Baffi Marisa of Naples, Italy, won World Women's Teams 1976, placed second in 1978, and won European Women's Teams 1976, 1977.

DANIELS, Alan J. (b. 1943) of Los Angeles, staff accountant and portfolio manager, won Fall NAC secondary Swiss Teams 1981, Inland Empire Swiss Teams 1973, District 23 GNP 1981.

DANILENKO, Alex (b. 1924) of Philadelphia, accountant and photographer, won Spring NAC secondary Mixed Pairs 1969, 1970, Mid-Atlantic Open Teams 1952, District 4 Fall Open Pairs 1977.

DARLING, Dean A. of Harwood MD won several regional titles including Mid-Atlantic Summer Men's Pairs 1971, Swiss Teams 1975, Fall Men's Pairs 1971, Master Pairs 1974, District 6 GNT 1976.

DARVAS, Robert (1903–1957) of Budapest, Hungary was an active composer of bridge problems, interesting deals and bridge articles. The foremost bridge journalist of Hungary, Darvas contributed to many magazines including *European Bridge Review* and the *Bridge Magazine*. He co-authored *Right Through the Pack* and *Spotlight on Cardplay*. See BIBLIOGRAPHY, H.

DAUTELL, Eugene G. (Duke) (b. 1921) of Los Angeles, bridge teacher and former insurance agent, won Fall NAC Men's Teams 1951, Summer NAC secondary MARCUS CUP 1952, Spring Men's Pairs 1977, Bridge Week Swiss Teams 1974, Midwest Open Teams 1957.

D'AVE, Adelstano P. (b. 1928) of Brazil, insurance broker, was South American champion 1967, 1968, 1971. He also represented Brazil in the World Team Olympiad 1964, 1968, Bermuda Bowl 1969, 1971, and as npc of the South American champions 1972, World Team Olympiad champions 1976 and the Bermuda Bowl teams 1973, 1974. He has won 13 national titles in Open Pairs and Open Teams.

DAVIDSON, Sidney L. (b. 1918) of San Francisco, ACBL national tournament director, began his career in 1956 and achieved his present rating in 1972. He is the tournament coordinator of District 20, 21, and regional tournament manager for District 20. He contributed to the simplification of fouled board calculations, carryover computations and evolved and modified various movements including the MIRROR MITCHELL TEAM MOVEMENT. A graduate of Medical College of Virginia, he is a former dentist.

DAVIS, Anita (Pigeon) (b. 1924) of Beaumont TX placed second in Spring NAC Women's Teams 1975. Her regional titles include Fall NAC secondary Women's Swiss Teams 1968, 1972, Mexican Nat'l Mixed Pairs 1971, Big D Mixed Pairs 1972, Texas Master Pairs 1957, Women's Pairs 1958, 1968, Open Pairs 1961, Capital City Women's Pairs 1972, Mid-South Swiss Teams 1973, Women's Pairs 1975, Women's Master Swiss Teams 1976. Davis has served on various committies in Unit 201 and was a bridge columnist for *Beaumont Enterprise* and *Beaumont Journal* for 25 years.

DAVIS, Chester P. Jr. (Chet) (b. 1922) of Arlington MA, company president, former lawyer, placed second in the Blue Ribbon Pairs 1979 and won many regionals including Fall NAC secondary Master Pairs 1973, Spring Men's Pairs 1979, New England KO Teams 1963, 1969, 1973, Swiss Teams 1971, 1978, Swiss Teams Flt. A 1980, Southeastern Men's Pairs 1967, Swiss Teams 1974, Life Master Pairs 1974, District 25 GNT 1973, 1975, 1980, Zonal 1973, 1980. Davis is a past president of the Eastern Massachusetts BA.

DAVIS, Lt. Col. Dougall M. (b. 1921) of Oklahoma City OK, Air Force officer, represented Japan in Far East Championships 1961 and won four Japanese team championships 1961–1963.

DAVIS Edgar F. Jr. (Ed) (b. 1942) of Los Angeles, system analyst, won more than 25 regionals including Fall NAC secondary Men's Teams 1971, Spring Swiss Teams 1975, Summer Open Pairs 1976, Bridge Week Swiss Teams 1968, 1970, 1979, 1981, Mixed Pairs 1970, Open Pairs 1975, Master Men's Pairs Flt. A 1979, Master Swiss Teams Flt. A 1981, Los Angeles Winter Swiss Teams 1976, Master Pairs Flt. A 1979, Open Pairs Flt. A 1981, Pacific Southwest Swiss Teams 1975, Master Pairs Flt. A 1978, Golden State Open Pairs, Master Swiss Teams Flt. A 1978, All-Western Swiss Teams Flt. A 1979, Orange County KO Teams 1974, District GNT 1977, 1979, Zone VIII 1977. He is a graduate of UCLA.

DAVIS, Kerri. See SHUMAN, KERRI.

DAVIS, Vickie (b. 1922) of Dallas, construction company president, won Mississippi Valley Master Pairs 1968, Texas Swiss Teams 1970, Int'l City KO Teams 1974, Mexican Nat'l Master Pairs 1973, Republic of Texas Woman's Pairs 1973. She was elected Woman Builder of the Year in Dallas 1979.

DAVIS, Wilfred M. (b. 1920) of Atlanta, sales manager, won Mid-Atlantic Fall Men's Pairs 1956, 1958, Mixed Pairs 1961.

DAWKINS, George S. (b. 1931) of Austin TX, professor of business, won Fall NAC Mixed Pairs 1970. His regional wins include Fall NAC secondary Men's Swiss Teams 1977, Mid-South Spring Master Pairs 1963, Summer Open Teams 1967, Big D KO Teams 1970, Republic of Texas KO Teams 1970, Open Pairs 1978, Texas Capital KO Teams 1975, Texas Labor Day Master Swiss Teams 1979, Corpus Christi KO Teams 1978, Acapulco Fiesta Swiss Teams 1980, District 16 GNT, Zone VI 1976.

DAWSON, Dennis L. (b. 1946) of Woburn MA, bridge club owner, director and teacher, won Spring NAC secondary Men's Swiss Teams 1973, Olympic Master Pairs Flt. A, Swiss Teams 1975, Can-At KO Teams 1975, Master Swiss Teams 1978, New England Knockout Swiss Teams Flt. A 1980, Masters Swiss Teams Flt A 1981, Individual KO Teams 1974. Dawson is the editor of *Northeast Bridge.*

DAWSON, Jacqueline M. (Jackie) (Mrs. Dennis) (b. 1945) of Woburn MA, bridge club owner, director and teacher, won New England Individual KO Teams 1974, Knockout Swiss Teams Flt. A 1980, Can-At KO Teams 1975, Olympic Master Pairs Flt. A, Swiss Teams 1976.

DAYBOCH, Ethel F. of St. Paul MN placed second in Summer Master Mixed Teams 1977 and won Gopher Master Pairs 1958, Swiss Teams 1965, 1967, 1974, KO Teams 1968, 1969, Women's Swiss Teams 1976, Canadian Prairie Open Pairs 1967, 1968, District 14 GNT 1976, 1979, GNP 1980.

de. For names beginning with **de**, see main element of the name.

DEAN, Charles Y. (b. 1918) of Taichung, Taiwan, aeronautical researcher, represented Taiwan in the Far East Championships 1958, 1959. His national wins include Open Teams 1957, 1958, 1959, 1963, Open Pairs 1960. He is the author of *Dean's Diamond System.*

DEAS, Lynn (b. 1953) of Schenectady NY, bridge teacher, research consultant, won Summer NAC Master Mixed Teams 1982, placed second in 1981 and in Spring NAC Women's Knockout Teams 1981. Her numerous regional wins include Mid-Atlantic Fall Swiss Teams 1978, Women's Swiss Teams 1980, Spring Master Swiss Teams 1978, Women's Swiss Teams 1980, 1981, Open Pairs Flt.

A 1981, Summer KO Teams 1980, Canadian Nat'l KO Teams Flt. A 1981, District 4 Fall Women's Swiss Teams 1981. She graduated from Catawba College *magna cum laude*.

DEATON, Linda. See PERLMAN, LINDA.

DEBONNAIRE, Carlos Augusto (b. 1940) of Lisbon, Portugal, commerical director, represented Portugal in the European Championships 1965, 1966, 1970, 1974. His national wins include Open Teams four times, Open Pairs once.

DEBONNAIRE, Jose Antonio (b. 1943) of Lisbon, Portugal, technician, represented Portugal in the European Championships 1965, 1966, 1974. His national wins include Open Teams and Open Pairs, three times each.

DÉCSI, Gábor (b. 1919) of Budapest, Hungary, retired accountant, was a member of the winning Hungarian team in matches against Austria, Germany and Brussels 1964. His national wins include Hungarian Open Teams 1963, 1966, 1968, 1972, Open Pairs 1964, 1966, 1967, 1969. He won the Danube Cup 1966, defeated the Italian "Team B" 1968, and won Venice Open Pairs 1970. He represented Hungary 40 times in international competitions including European Championships 1969.

DÉCSI, Leslie (Lásló) (1909–1969) of São Paulo, Brazil, born in Budapest, was European champion 1934, second in 1935, 1936. After 1946 he lived in Brazil and was South American champion 1955 and represented Brazil in the World Team Olympiad 1964. He co-authored *The Limit System*, and was a contributor to *European Bridge Review*.

DEDICHEN, Herman (d. 1958) of Denmark was honorary secretary of the EUROPEAN BRIDGE LEAGUE from 1947 until his death. After World War II he invited the European countries to participate once again in the European Championships, and succeeded in reactivating these events in 1948. A member of the governing board of the DANMARKS BRIDGE FORBUND, he was considered one of the influential figures of the international scene.

DEERY, Desmond (b. 1939) of Belfast, Northern Ireland, solicitor and bridge columnist, represented Ireland in the World Team Olympiad 1964, European Championships 1962, 1966, npc 1967. His national wins include Open Teams 1962, Open Pairs 1959, 1961, 1963. His ACBL titles include Bridge Week Open Teams, Master Pairs 1964. Deery was honorary secretary of NORTH OF IRELAND BRIDGE UNION and IRISH BRIDGE UNION. He was the leading masterpoint holder in Ireland 1963–1964.

DE FALCO, Dano of Padua, Italy, won the World Team Olympiad 1974, European Championships 1973, 1979, Common Market Teams Championships 1977, 1979.

DeHARPPORTE, Ronald E. (b. 1938) of Edina MN, company owner and president, won Gopher Master Teams 1968, 1969, 1971, Men's Pairs 1978, 1979. He is University of Minnesota graduate.

DEIK, Adriana (b. 1941) of Santiago, Chile, English teacher, was South American champion 1978. She also represented Chile in the South American Championships 1979, 1980, 1981.

DEJARDIN, Florent (b. 1937) of Brussels, Belgium, represented Belgium in the European Championships five times and in other international competitions. His national wins include Belgium Open Teams 1967, 1968, 1969, 1970, 1971, 1980, 1981, Mixed Pairs and Mixed Teams twice each, Belgium Cup three times. He is a frequent contributor to various international bridge magazines.

DEL GALLEGO, Tina (b. 1949) of Makati, Philippines, secretary, was Far East Women's Teams champion 1978, 1979, 1982, and represented the Philippines in Far East Championships 1981, World Women's Teams 1980 and in other international competition. Her national titles include Open Teams 1979, 1981, Master Pairs 1979, 1980, Intercommercial Teams 1981, Tuason Cup 1980, PCBL Challenge Cup 1981. She is treasurer of the PHILIPPINE CONTRACT BRIDGE LEAGUE.

DELMOULY, Claude (b. 1927) of Paris, France, bridge teacher and writer, WBF Grand Master, won the World Team Olympiad 1960 and represented France in the World Team Olympiad 1968, 1972, European Championships 1957, 1959, 1965. His national wins include French Open Pairs 1959, Open Teams 1960, 1962, English Master Pairs 1960 and many other successes. Delmouly is a contributor to various bridge periodicals and the author of *Tous les Secrets de Bridge* and *Le Bridge d'aujourd'hur* with Pariente.

DELOGU, Richard F. (Rick) (b. 1954) of St. Catharines ON, researcher, won Gateway City Swiss Teams 1981, Can-Am Swiss Teams Flt. A, KO Teams 1980, Zone 3 CNT 1981.

DELOUCA, Sophia (1916–1982) of Athens, Greece, lawyer, was the third-ranking woman player of her country at the time of her death. She represented Greece in the European Championships 1970, World Women's Teams 1976, World Women's Pairs 1966, European Women's Championships 1967, 1969, 1971, 1973, 1974, 1975, 1977 and 1979. Her national titles include Open Teams 1966, Mixed Pairs 1967, 1973, 1977, 1978, 1981. Delouca translated the International Duplicate Code into Greek 1967 and was Greek delegate to the EBL Congress 1979.

DE MARTINO, Richard A. (Rich) (b. 1939) of Riverside CT, insurance executive, won Fall NAC Swiss Teams 1980. His regional titles include Eastern States Men's Pairs 1967, 1968, Men's Teams 1969, New England Knockout Open Pairs 1971.

DENBY, Charles W. D. (b. 1930) of Huntington NY, accountant, won Spring NAC Men's Teams 1960. He teaches adult education bridge courses.

DENNARD, Robert W. (Bob) (b. 1944) of Ormond Beach FL, college administrator, won Southeastern Open Pairs 1971, Florida Open Teams 1974, 1981, North Florida Fall Swiss Teams 1976, Open Pairs Flt. A 1979, Mid-Atlantic Swiss Teams 1974, District 9 GNT 1977.

DENNINGER, Tracy, Jr. (b. 1924) of Altamonte Springs FL, formerly of Bermuda, condominium association manager, former resort hotel manager, represented Bermuda in the World Team Olympiad 1968, 1972, 1976, Pan American Invitational Pairs 1974. His regional titles include Spring NAC secondary Individual 1951, Bermuda Men's Pairs 1972, Swiss Teams 1977.

DENNISON, Maureen of Middlesex, England, sales representative, won the Venice Cup 1981, Common Market Championships 1979, 1981, European Women's Championships 1981.

DENNY, Jack (b. 1911) of Bradenton FL, formerly of Akron OH, sales representative and bridge club owner, formerly one of the leading players of the Middle West, represented the United States in the World Open Pairs 1962. He won Fall NAC Men's Teams 1951 and placed second in Spring NAC Men's Pairs 1951, 1958, Open Pairs 1961. His numerous regional titles include Fall NAC Swiss Teams 2nd Flt. 1969, All-American Open Teams 1967, Mixed Pairs 1969, Florida KO Teams 1970, Southeastern Men's Swiss Teams 1974, 1977, Men's Pairs 1977, Florida BAM Teams, Master Pairs 1976, Central Florida KO Teams 1980, Mid-Atlantic KO Teams 1981, Midwest Fall Men's Swiss Teams 1978, District 5 Men's Swiss Teams 1981.

DENNY, Jill (Mrs. Jack) (b. 1916) of Bradenton FL, formerly of Akron OH, bridge club owner, won several regional events including Fall NAC Swiss Teams 2nd Flt. 1969, Midwest Fall Open Teams 1960, District 11 Open Teams 1962, All-American Open Teams 1967, 1969, Southeastern Women's Swiss Teams 1975, North Florida Women's Pairs, Swiss Teams 1977, Florida BAM Teams, Master Pairs 1976, Senior Citizens Open Pairs Flt. A 1981.

D'ENTREMONT, Arthur L. (Art) (b. 1932), civil aviation inspector, former RCAF pilot, won Canadian Thanksgiving Men's Pairs 1970, Canadian Swiss Teams 1971, Buffalo Swiss Teams 1975, KO Teams 1980.

DE RAAD, Esther of Fairfax VA, has been an ACBL associate national director since 1974. She became a club director in 1955 and a tournament director in 1963. She has been secretary of the Mid-Atlantic Bridge Conference since 1968.

DERBY, Allan W. (b. 1924) of Montreal, cost accountant, bridge teacher and director, won Bermuda Master Pairs, Open Pairs 1972, Can-Am Mixed Pairs 1956, Open Pairs 1960.

DERMER, Dale M. (b. 1935) of Monroeville PA, foundation membership secretary, won District 4

Women's Pairs 1976, District 5 Women's Swiss Teams 1979, 1981, All-American Swiss Teams Flt. A 1981.

DERUY, Claude (b. 1927) of Vimy, Pas de Calais, France, bailiff and tournament director, represented France in the World Par Contest 1963, Bermuda Bowl 1961, World Team Olympiad 1964. He placed second in the European Championships 1961 and won French Open Teams 1962. He is the author of *Bien jouer au Bridge.*

DESCHAPELLES, Alexandre Louis Honoré Lebreton, sometimes referred to as Guillaume le Breton (1780–1847), a Frenchman of good family, was described by his contemporary, JAMES CLAY, English whist authority, as the finest whist player, "beyond any comparison, the world has ever seen." Deschapelles excelled at other games among them billiards, Polish draughts, and chess. Fighting in one of the many wars of his time, he lost his right hand, but continued to play whist, and, more remarkably, billiards. He invented the coup which bears his name (see DESCHAPELLES COUP) and a number of other coups. He published only fragments of a projected extensive work on whist. See BIBLIOGRAPHY, A.

DESPAIN, D. Genevieve (Genne, formerly Winter), bridge teacher, placed second in Spring NAC Women's Pairs 1978 and won Spring NAC secondary Swiss Teams 1978, Mid-Atlantic Women's Pairs 1978, Women's Swiss Teams 1979, Crescent City Master Pairs 1977.

DESROUSSEAUX, GÉRARD, (b. 1927) of Paris, France, bridge teacher and writer, won the World Par Contest 1963, was European champion 1962, and represented France in the Bermuda Bowl 1963, 1969, World Team Olympiad 1964, 1968, European Championships 1965, 1967, 1979. His national wins include Open Teams 1955, Open Pairs 1956, 1962, Mixed Teams 1960 and other successes. He is a contributor to French periodicals and the co-author of *Le Bridge d'Ecole Française* with IRÉNÉE BAJOS De HÉRÉDIA.

DEUTSCH, June A. of Chicago won Spring NAC Women's Teams 1966, 1981, placed second in 1972, 1979, won Fall NAC Life Master Women's Pairs 1973, placed second in 1979. Her numerous regional wins include Spring NAC secondary Women's Swiss Teams 1972, 1973, Summer Open Pairs Flt. B 1975, Fall Women's Swiss Teams 1977, Central States Women's Pairs 1961, 1962, 1965, 1967, Mixed Pairs 1967, 1970, Central States II Master Pairs 1975, Women's Swiss Teams 1977, 1979, Tri-Unit Women's Pairs 1970, 1973, Wisconsin Women's Swiss Teams 1976, 1978, Women's Pairs 1976, District 8 Summer Women's Swiss Teams 1981.

DEUTSCH, Tobi of Evanston IL, marketing director, won Copper State Women's Pairs 1977, Southeastern Mixed Pairs 1980, Wisconsin Women's Pairs 1980, Central States Open Pairs 1981, Central States II Women's KO Teams 1981, Motor City Women's Swiss Teams 1981.

DE WITT, Joan M. of Chicago, account executive and mathematics consultant, won Summer NAC Master Mixed Teams 1977, 1978, 1979, 1982. Her many regional wins include Motor City Swiss Teams 1972, Women's Swiss Teams 1978, Central States Women's Pairs 1980, 1981, Mississippi Valley Women's Pairs 1977, Springfield 1980, Tri-State Women's Swiss Teams 1981. She is a trustee of the ACBL Charity Foundation and member of the ACBL Goodwill Committee. De Witt is a graduate of Vanderbilt University.

DEWITZ, Egmont von (b. 1907) of Cologne, Germany, represented Germany in the World Team Olympiad 1960, 1964 and in almost every European Championships since 1938. His national titles include Open Teams 15 times.

DHERS, Alberto J. (b. 1932) of Caracas, Venezuela, university professor, represented Central American-Caribbean in the Bermuda Bowl 1979 and in many South American Championships. Dhers has won 20 Venezuelan national championships in the past 10 years. He was the founder and first president of the only bridge club in Caracas and president of the organizing committee of International Bridge Tournaments in Caracas 1976, 1978. Dhers is a graduate of University of Buenos Aires. He teaches high–level bridge.

DÍAZ, Eduardo (b. 1933) of Buenos Aires, Argentina, bank official, won Argentine Open Teams 1966, 1973, 1974, Mixed Teams 1961, 1970, Interclubs 1963, 1964, 1979, GABARRET CUP 1966.

DIBAR, Carlos F. (1911–1965) of Buenos Aires, Argentine, judge, was South American champion 1954, 1957. He also represented Argentina in the Bermuda Bowl 1959, 1961. His national wins include Open Teams 1937, 1938, 1956, Open Pairs 1947, Master Pairs 1962. Dibar served as secretary, Argentine Bridge Commission 1936, 1938, and director, ARGENTINE BRIDGE ASSOCIATION 1962, 1963. He coauthored the Dibar system.

DICKENS, Charles (1812–1870), famed English novelist, describes Mr. Pickwick's discomfort after being inveigled into a WHIST game with three imposing women in Chapter 35 of *The Pickwick Papers*.

DI FELICE, Dominic A. (Dom) (b. 1949) of Toronto, born in Gagliano, Italy, mathematics teacher, won Canadian Nat'l Master Pairs 1971, Mixed Pairs 1973, Can-Am Open Pairs 1974.

DIONISI, Antonio H. (Tony) (b. 1934) of New York City, formerly of Tokyo, Japan, banker, won the Reisinger 1970 and placed second in 1971 and in Spring NAC Men's Teams 1966. His regional wins include Eastern States KO Teams 1965, Open Pairs 1971, Mixed Pairs 1970, Keystone Open Teams 1965, Tri-State Swiss Teams 1980.

DISBROW, Bennett L. of Wallingford PA, insurance broker, bridge teacher and columnist, co-authored with CHARLES J. SOLOMON *Slam Bidding and Point-Count* and *How to Bid and What to Lead*. See BIBLIOGRAPHY, C.

DISCHNER, Robert J. (Dish) (b. 1920) of Santa Ana CA, ACBL national tournament director since 1972, began his directing career in 1950 while employed by the U.S. Postal Service.

DIVIS, Henry C. Jr. (b. 1947) of Richardson TX, won Big D Unmixed Pairs 1974, Land Of Coronado KO Teams 1974, Swiss Teams 1976, Silver Anniversary KO Teams 1974, Missouri Valley Open Pairs 1975, Men's Swiss Teams 1978, King Cotton Swiss Teams 1975.

DIXON, Christopher P. (b. 1944) of London, England, bridge club proprietor, placed second in the European Championships 1971 and represented Great Britain in the World Team Olympiad 1972, England in the CAMROSE TROPHY matches 1972, 1973, 1974, 1975. He won the GOLD CUP 1972, 1974. Dixon is a regular contributor to *Bridge Magazine*.

DIXON, Maria L. (Mrs. Christopher P.) of London, England, represented Great Britain in the European Women's Championships 1974. She won the Whitelaw Cup 1974, Lady Milne Cup 1974.

DOANE, Alan H. (b. 1937) of Halifax NS, professional gambler, former accountant and realtor, won Can-At KO Teams 1971, 1980, Swiss Teams 1973, 1976, Unmixed Pairs 1978, Bluenose BAM Teams Flt. A 1981, District 1 GNT 1978. Doane is past president of the Eastern Canada BC, District 1, and former member of the ACBL Board of Governors.

DOCKMAN, Newton (b. 1915) of Minneapolis, won several regional titles including Gopher Open Teams 1958, 1960, Open Pairs 1959, KO Teams 1967, Mid-Am-Can Open Teams 1961–1962, Intercity champion 1962.

DODDS, Leslie W(illiam) (1903–1975) of London, England, import/export merchant, was one of the leading players in England until a stroke in 1961 ended his bridge career. One of the originators of the CAB SYSTEM, which was employed by a number of British experts, Dodds was Bermuda Bowl champion 1955, European champion 1948, 1949, 1950, 1954. He represented Great Britain in the European Championships 1952, 1953, 1955 and his many national wins include the GOLD CUP 1938, 1949, 1956, 1960, Master Pairs 1955.

DOHL, Dennis P. (b. 1949) of Vancouver BC, government employee, won Peach City Swiss Teams, Master Swiss Teams Flt. A 1978, District 19 GNT 1976, GNP 1981.

DONAGHY, Ernest C. (b. 1897) of Mexico Beach FL, retired statistician, won Western States Open Teams 1938. Donaghy was one of the first six to be named ACBL associate national director when that rating was created in 1963.

DONAGHY, George F. (b. 1928) of Memphis,

ACBL Service Division Manager since 1968, is in charge of supplies and playing arrangements at North American Championships. Before joining the ACBL staff he was a regional tournament director. He is a contributing editor, *Bridge Encyclopedia*.

DONALDSON, R. J. (Jim) (1937–1982) of South Squamish BC was a brilliant bridge technician and theoretician. He won Inland Empire KO Teams 1970; British Columbia Master Pairs 1971, Men's Pairs, Master Pairs 1977, Flt. A Open Pairs 1978, KO Teams 1980; Fall NAC Open Swiss Teams 1977; Can-At Individual 1977.

DONNELLY, John L. (1905–1981) of Bellevue WA, industrial engineer, won Pacific Northwest Open Team 1955, Inter-Mountain Open Pairs 1958, Oregon Trail Men's Pairs 1966. He authored *Happiness Is a Squeeze*. See BIBLIOGRAPHY, D.

DONNELLY, Thomas C. (b. 1952) of Buffalo, graphic designer, won Upper New York State Master Swiss Teams 1976, All-American Master Pairs 1977, Presque Isle KO Teams, Swiss Teams 1977, District 5 Men's Swiss Teams 1979.

DORFAN, Jacob G. (b. 1938) of Pretoria, South Africa, accountant, represented South Africa in World Team Olympiad 1976, Maccabiah Games 1981. His national titles include South African Open Pairs, Open Teams 1974, Interprovincial Teams 1976, 1978, 1980.

DORMER, Albert G. (b. 1925) of London, England, bridge writer, won the GOLD CUP 1958, 1963. He was the editor of *British Bridge World* 1962–1964, former associate editor of the ACBL *Bulletin* 1964–1965, and contributing editor to the *Bridge Encyclopedia*. In 1982 he resigned the post of editor of the INTERNATIONAL BRIDGE PRESS ASSOCIATION *Bulletin*, a position he had held for 10 years, in order to devote more time to the editorship of *World Bridge News* and to accept a position as executive assistant to the president of the WORLD BRIDGE FEDERATION. Dormer was named "Bridge Personality of the Year" for 1981 (see IBPA AWARDS). His writings include articles for many international bridge magazines; his ACBL *Bulletin* series, *Dormer on Deception*, was a classic. He is the co-author of *The Acol System Today*, *The Bridge Player's Dictionary*, *The Bridge Player's Alphabetical Handbook*, *The Complete Book of Bridge*, *The Play of the Cards*, *How to Play a Better Game of Bridge*, *Bridge for Tournament Players*, *Blueprint for Bidding*; *The Acol System Applied to American Bridge*, *The Acol System of Bidding*, and the author of *Powerhouse Hands*. See BIBLIOGRAPHY, C, D, E, F.

DORN, H. Charlie (b. 1919) of San Jose CA, bridge teacher, retired naval aviator, placed second in Fall NAC Mixed Pairs 1981. His many regional titles including All-Western KO Teams 1968, 1971, Open Teams 1968, Intermountain KO Teams 1972.

D'ORSI, Ernesto (b. 1936) of São Paulo, Brazil, financial director, represented Brazil in the World Open Pairs 1974, 1978, Rosenblum Cup Teams 1978. He was captain of the Brazilian teams that were South American champions in 1970, 1977 and runners-up in 1976, and of the Women's teams 1970, 1973, 1974, 1975, 1976, 1977 which won in 1973, 1975 and were runners-up in 1977. He won Brazilian Open Teams 1978, was runner-up in 1967, 1973, 1975, 1981, and won numerous São Paulo State Regional Championships. D'Orsi is a member of the Executive Council of the WORLD BRIDGE FEDERATION, member of the Zoning, Pan American and Rules and Regulation Committee of the WBF, member of the Executive Council of the SOUTH AMERICAN BRIDGE CONFEDERATION, and regional vice president of the IBPA. From 1970 to 1978 he was Executive Council member of the BRAZILIAN BRIDGE FEDERATION and served as a member of the Organizing Committee for the 1973 and 1979 Bermuda Bowl, vice chairman and general coordinator in 1979. He authored the Complete Specification for the Bermuda Bowl and Venice Trophy for the WBF. D'Orsi has a weekly newspaper column in *O Estado de São Paulo*, is a regular contributor to *Revista Brasileira de Bridge*, and the author of *Leilão Defensivo*.

DOUGHTY, Richard E. (b. 1943) of Baton Rouge LA, business co-owner, won Spring NAC Men's Teams 1977 and placed second in the Reisinger 1975. His regional titles include Summer NAC secondary Mixed Pairs 1973, Fall 1973, Mid-South Swiss Teams 1969, 1980, Open Pairs 1971, Master Pairs 1969.

DOW, Stephen J. Jr. (b. 1943) of Fremont CA, tile contractor, won California Capital Mixed Pairs 1977, Men's Pairs 1978, Golden State Men's Pairs 1975. He is a graduate of Syracuse University.

DOWNES, E(dwin) Hall (1897–1976) of Dover DE was a bridge teacher, writer and educator. A graduate of the Naval Academy, 1920, Downes remained at Annapolis for three years as instructor to midshipmen. He later received a Master's degree in Education from Columbia University and served in that field for the rest of his life, not only in the public schools of Delaware but also in the Navy and with American industry abroad.

In the early Thirties Downes promoted bridge through his books, radio, and lectures; he was called "ace of Contract teachers". His writings included self-teachers and he was *"Town and Country"* editor for *The Bridge Magazine* (1931–1933). A book by him on the Culbertson system provoked a lawsuit by ELY CULBERTSON who claimed that his name could not be used by other writers. He counterclaimed against Culbertson, who had warned booksellers not to sell Downes' books on pain of legal action. Downes won both suits, the courts holding that the name of a system was public property. The case had permanent importance in legal history, both in respect of plagiarism and of unfair practices.

DOWNING, Frances B. (Fran) of Memphis, ACBL *Bulletin* advertising manager, won Navajo Trail Swiss Teams 1971. Downing is a graduate of University of Texas at El Paso.

DREW, Douglas A. (b. 1930) of Toronto, company vice president, member of the ACBL Board of Directors, served as president of the Ontario Unit 166 from 1964–1967 and 1975, and of District 2 from 1971–1974. He has continuously served the interest of tournament bridge since 1958 at all levels and served on the Ontario Unit Board 1958-1983 and as co-chairman the 1986 Summer North American Championships. He is a graduate of University of Saskatchewan.

DREYFUS, Jack (b. 1913) of New York City, formerly a leading bridge player, is reputed also to be the best American player of gin rummy. He won AWL Southern New England Open Teams 1937. Founder of the Dreyfus Fund, and "wizard of Wall Street", he is the author of *A Remarkable Medicine Has Been Overlooked*, a book about the drug Dilantin.

DRIVER, Gordon P. (b. 1947) of Sandown, South Africa, data processing manager, represented South Africa in the World Team Olympiad 1972, 1976, 1980. His national wins include South Africa Teams 1979, Interprovincial Teams 1975, 1979, Pioneer Teams 1971.

DRUCKER, Ned (b. 1916) of New York City, salesman, won the Vanderbilt 1952, 1954 and placed second in the Life Master Pairs 1951, Fall NAC Open Pairs 1943. His regional titles include Eastern States Open Pairs 1945, Master Pairs 1968, New England Fall Mixed Teams 1970.

DRURY, Douglas A. (1914–1967) of Sebastopol CA, stockbroker, bridge teacher and club owner, was best known for his invention of the DRURY CONVENTION. He early made his mark as a tournament player while living in Toronto. He won Summer NAC Men's Pairs 1954, 1955, Master Mixed Teams 1956. A capable and popular bridge administrator, he served as a member of the ACBL Board of Governors, Systems and Conventions Committee, and ACBL Goodwill Committee.

DRURY, Peggy (Mrs. Douglas) of Vallejo CA, won several regionals including Navajo Trail KO Teams 1969, Golden Gate Mixed Pairs 1971, Capital City Women's Pairs 1972, Hawaii Open Teams 1968, Oregon Trail KO Teams 1967, Open Teams 1968.

DUCHOVNI, Zeev (b. 1912) of Tel Aviv, Israel, export manager, represented Israel in the World Team Olympiad 1964, European Championships 1965. He has won several national titles.

DUDKA, Bette C. of Alexandria VA, executive secretary and administrative assistant, won Summer NAC secondary Women's Pairs 1975, Mid-Atlantic Spring Women's Pairs 1979, Summer Open Pairs 1979. She has served in various executive postions on the local and national level including secretary of District 6 Board of Governors, president of the Mid-Atlantic Conference and co-chairman of the 1984 Summer North American Championships.

DUDLEY, Winifred M. (Mrs. Paul) of Honolulu, formerly of Yokohama, Japan, won Japanese Prince Takamatsu Open Teams 1955, 1956, Princess Takamatsu Mixed Pairs 1958.

DUFFY, Dr. Charles (b. 1905) of New Bern NC, physician, won Mid-Atlantic Fall Open Teams 1960, Winter Master Pairs 1965, Southern Conference Master Pairs 1964.

DUFOUR, R(ichard) W. Jr. (R. W.) (b. 1940) of Edina MN, attorney, won numerous regional events including Canadian Nat'l KO Teams, Open Pairs, Master Pairs, Open Teams 1971, Big Sky KO Teams, Swiss Teams 1971, Pheasant KO Teams 1970, Iowa Swiss Teams 1971, Men's Pairs 1973, KO Teams 1976, Roughrider Swiss Teams 1975, Open Pairs 1977, Gopher Men's Swiss Teams 1976, KO Teams 1977, District 14 GNT 1976.

DUMBOVICH, Miklos (b. 1949) of Budapest, Hungary, mechanical engineer, represented Hungary in the European Championships 1973, 1975, 1977, 1979, 1981, World Team Olympiad 1976, 1980. His national titles include Hungarian Open Teams 1974, 1978, 1979, 1981, Open Pairs 1978, 1979, 1980, Hungary Cup 1974, 1976, 1981. He is the leading masterpoint holder in Hungary.

DUNCAN, Alexander H. (Sandy) of Dunfermline, Scotland, computer manager, represented Great Britain in the Common Market Championships, World Open Pairs 1978, 1982, represented Scotland in CAMROSE TROPHY matches 16 times. His national titles include Scottish Cup twice, National Pairs and Multiple Teams three times each, Men's Teams four times, Master Pairs and Individual once each. He is Scotland's youngest Grand Master, a ranking he achieved at age 32.

DUNNE, J. Patrick of Miami was one of the best known blind bridge players. Dunne gave a demonstration of his skill in 1940 when he and partner, WALDEMAR VON ZEDTWITZ won a duplicate game at the *Cavendish Club* (New York). He co-authored *Championship Bridge*. See BIBLIOGRAPHY, K.

DUNPHY, Alwina M. formerly Mrs. R. E. Duncan) (b. 1906) of St. Petersburg FL won Summer NAC Women's Pairs 1951, Western States Mixed Pairs 1944, Midwest Women's Pairs 1944.

DU PONT, Lea C. (b. 1939) of Wilmington DE and Rome, Italy, placed second in Fall NAC Swiss Teams 1981 and won Fall NAC secondary Swiss Teams Flt. A 1980, Mid-Atlantic Women's Pairs 1970. She spends 10 months a year in Europe and plays regularly in major European championships. Her European wins include Coppa Italia 1977, Venice Open Pairs 1978, Deauville Open Pairs 1980.

DURAND, Charles A. (b. 1904) of Montreal, bridge teacher, retired dentist, wrote *Améliorons notre bridge* and *Le jeu de la carte et ses techniques*. He has introduced bridge to a number of Golden Age Clubs and to groups of handicapped people.

DURHAM, Louise (Honeychile) of Durant MS, first Life Master in Mississippi, won Central States Women's Pairs 1951, Mid-South Open Teams 1957, Missouri Valley Women's Pairs 1954. She served as ACBL director and secretary, co-chairman of the Goodwill Committee and the World Bridge Federation Friendship Committee, and is past president of the Mississippi BA. Durham was named ACBL Honorary Member 1974.

DURRAN, Joan of Welwyn Garden City, England, one of the world's leading women players, won the World Women's Pairs 1966, European Women's Teams 1961, 1966 and placed second in the World Mixed Pairs 1966. She represented Great Britain in the World Women's Teams 1960, Women's Pairs 1970, European Women's Championships 1962, 1965, 1969. Her national successes include Hubert Phillips Bowl, Lady Milne Cup, and several victories in the Whitelaw Cup competition, and with JANE PRIDAY she was runner-up in the Life Master Pairs, the highest placing ever by a women's pair.

DYE, Dr. Arthur M. (1896–1980) of Charlotte NC was the first blind bridge player to become an ACBL Life Master. A perfect sportsman, Dye never took advantage of his affliction; when he pulled wrong cards, he refused to allow opponents to let him retract his plays. When Dye made Life Master at the New Orleans Winter Nationals in 1956, he received a standing ovation. A charter member and long-time president of the Charlotte BA, he served as president of the Mid-Atlantic Bridge Conference. He shared with CHARLES GOREN in 1959 the ACBL Honorary Member award. See HANDICAPPED PLAYERS.

E

EARL, Christopher W. (Chris) (b. 1951) of Portland OR, won Oregon Trail Swiss Teams 1972, KO Teams 1975, 1977, Peach Festival KO Teams 1974, Mount Shasta Swiss Teams 1974, Puget Sound Swiss Teams 1974, District 20 GNT 1973, 1974, Zone VII 1974.

EARL, Stephen R. (b. 1947) of Rocky Hill CT, personnel manager, won Long Island Swiss Teams 1973, Tri-State Swiss Teams 1976, Nassau-Suffolk Open Pairs Flt. A 1980, New England Knockout Swiss Teams Flt. A 1981. He is president of the Connecticut BA and a member of the District 25 Board.

EATON, Ruth (died 1981) of Sydney, Australia, saleswoman, was Far East Women's champion 1973, 1974, and also represented Australia in the World Women's Teams 1968. She won National Women's Pairs 1969, 1972, and Interstate Women's Teams 10 times between 1951 and 1972.

EBER, Marilyn L. of Englewood CO won Fall NAC secondary Swiss Teams 1978, Pikes Peak KO Teams 1980, Rocky Mountain KO Teams 1981. She is a Denver art museum docent.

EBER, Neville (Noodles) (b. 1944) of Johannesburg, South Africa, bridge teacher and writer, represented South Africa in the World Team Olympiad 1972, 1976, MACCABIAH GAMES 1977. The leading masterpoint holder in South Africa, he won Pioneer Teams 1967, 1977, 1978, 1979, South African Open Pairs and Open Teams. A member of the IBPA, he writes a bridge column for the *Star* and has authored *You Too Can Play Bridge Well*. Eber is a graduate of Witwatersrand University. He is a South African backgammon champion.

EBERSON, Gertrude L. of St. Petersburg FL, won Spring NAC Women's Teams 1949 and placed second in Spring NAC Women's Pairs 1960, Summer NAC Master Mixed Teams 1954.

ECKER, Wynne (Mrs. Richard H.) of New York City won Fall NAC Women's Teams 1954 and was second in Spring NAC Women's Pairs 1956. She won Eastern States Women's Pairs 1955, 1958, New York-New Jersey Mixed Pairs 1967.

ECONOMIDY, Ann (Mrs. Byron) of La Habra Heights CA won Spring NAC Women's Pairs 1973 with her mother VIVIAN WILLIAMSON and placed second in Fall NAC Life Master Women's Pairs 1978. Her regional wins include District 11 Women's Swiss Teams 1978, Mid-Winter Holiday Open Pairs–A 1980.

ECONOMIDY, Byron of La Habra Heights CA placed second in the Grand National Teams 1973. His regional wins include Fall NAC secondary Life Master Men's Pairs 2nd Flt. 1970, South Texas Mixed Pairs 1971, Mid-Winter Holiday Open Pairs–A 1980, Raincross Swiss Teams Flt. A 1981.

EDWARDS, John M. (Mike) (b. 1940) of Rock Island IL, accountant, won Upper New York State Swiss Teams 1969, Tri-State Swiss Teams 1969, Can-Am Open Pairs 1972, Great Plains Men's Swiss Teams 1979.

EDWARDS, Mary (b. 1907) of Esher, Surrey, England, was European Women's champion 1959 and the first winner of *The Sunday Telegraph* competition for 1963–1964, a win she repeated the following year. She won *The Daily Telegraph* Cup in 1963 and many events in Surrey. See FORTUNE.

EGHOLM, Dale (b. 1928) of St. Paul, ACBL associate national tournament director, has been in the field of tournament direction since 1968.

EHLER, David F. (b. 1943) of Rocky Hill CT, analytical chemist, won New England Fall KO Teams 1977, Swiss Teams 1978, 1981, Summer Open Pairs 1978, 1981, Knockout Swiss Teams Flt. A 1979.

EHRLENBACH, Julius (Jack) (1894–1979) of Los Angeles was Life Master #56, a designation he earned in 1946 to become the first Life Master on the West Coast and the first one west of Chicago. A well-known teacher and a bridge player with very few peers, he taught the game to hundreds of players. He won the BARCLAY TROPHY 1949 and 1950 and scores of regional championships. He had a lifetime total of 5753 master points and was on the list of the "Top 100" masterpoint holders from its inception through November 1977.

EISENBERG, William P. (Billy) (b. 1937) of Los Angeles, financial manager, former professional backgammon and bridge player, WBF Grand Master, one of the world's leading players, was Bermuda Bowl champion 1970, 1971, 1976, 1977, 1979 and also represented North America in the Bermuda Bowl 1969, 1973, 1975. The only American to win five Bermuda Bowls, Eisenberg accomplished this feat with four different partners. He won the Spingold 1969, 1973, Vanderbilt 1971, 1978, Reisinger 1970, 1974, 1976, Grand National Teams 1974, 1976, Life Master Pairs 1968, Spring NAC Men's Teams 1968. He placed second in the Spingold 1970, Vanderbilt 1966, 1970, 1973, 1976, Reisinger 1968, 1981, Spring NAC Men's Teams 1969, Men's Pairs 1981. His numerous regional titles include the MARCUS CUP 1961, Bridge Week Open Pairs 1968, Swiss Teams 1969, 1971, KO Teams 1972, Mexican Nat'l Swiss Teams 1973, Master Pairs 1974. Eisenberg won the World Backgammon Championship in 1974. See ACES TEAM.

EISENHOWER, Dwight D. (1890–1969) never relinquished a keen interest in bridge from the time he was a captain in the U.S. Army through his presidency of the United States (1953–1961), and even after retirement. In Gibraltar on Nov. 7, 1942, the day of the landing at Casablanca which constituted the first Allied invasion after the fall of France, during the nerve-racking period when the landing had begun and the first news had not yet come back to his headquarters, he relaxed in a celebrated bridge game with Mark Clark, ALFRED M. GRUENTHER and Harry C. Butcher. Similarly, he used bridge as a regular recreation while Supreme Allied Commander before the invasion in Normandy, while NATO chief in Paris, and while in the White House; and after his retirement from the presidency he was host at occasional games at his houses at Gettysburg PA and Palm Springs CA. His skill has been characterized by OSWALD JACOBY as "superior—capable of holding his own in the best club games below the most expert." When asked who he would choose as his NATO deputy in 1950 he said, "Al Gruenther — he's the best bridge player" (among the generals). When Gruenther called him from Chicago at 7 A.M. one day in 1960 to tell him to read *The New York Times* bridge column of that morning because it reported one of his hands, Eisenhower replied, "I've already read it."

EISENLORD, Ray H. (1884–1965), an accountant from Erie PA, was ABL President in 1934 and one of the originators of the MASTER-POINT PLAN.

EISENSTEIN, Lilyan P. (Mrs. Robert A.) (b. 1940) of Beverly Hills CA, bank founder, real estate and travel agent, won Rogue River Valley Open Pairs 1976, Pacific Southwest Women's Pairs 1976, Gem State Swiss Teams 1976. She is a member of the ACBL Goodwill Committee.

EISENSTEIN, Robert A. (b. 1933) of Beverly Hills CA, film producer, attorney, president of property management company, won Rogue River Valley Men's Pairs 1976, Gem State Swiss Teams 1976. Eisenstein was elected District 23 representative to the ACBL Board of Directors in 1982. He is past president of District 23, the Westwood Unit, and is a member of the ACBL Goodwill Committee. Eisentein is a graduate of New York University and Harvard Law School.

EKEBLAD, Russell A. (1946) of Providence RI, marketing and sales vice president, won Upper New York State Men's Swiss Teams 1972, Fun City Life Master Pairs 1972, New England Masters Master Pairs Flt. A 1973, Bermuda Swiss Teams 1979, District 25 GNT 1975, GNP 1981.

ELIAS, Enrique L. (Quique) (b. 1937) of Lima, Peru, university law professor, represented Peru in the World Team Olympiad 1972, in South American Championships and was a member of the Peruvian National Team for 13 years. He was first National player all events 1974, 1975, 1976, 1978. He is past president of the PERUVIAN BRIDGE ASSOCIATION.

ELIASSON, Hjalti (b. 1929) of Kópavogi, Iceland, electrician, represented Iceland in the World Team Olympiad 1960, 1968, 1976, World Open Pairs 1974, European Championships 1963, 1969, 1970, 1971, 1973, 1974, 1977, 1979, Nordic Championships 1964, 1966. His national wins include Icelandic Cup Teams 1964, 1980, Open Teams 1962, 1965, 1969, 1971, 1972, 1977, 1978, 1980, Open Pairs 1963, 1966, 1968, 1970, 1971, 1973, 1974. He built a large electric bridge-o-rama in 1961 which has been used to display all major bridge events in Iceland.

ELIS, Estelle (Mrs. Morrie, formerly Mrs. Drescher) of Lauderhill FL, won Summer NAC Master Mixed Teams 1937, placed second in 1945 and in Spring NAC Women's Pairs 1940.

ELIS, Morrie (b. 1907) of Lauderhill FL, retired company president, for many years was one of the leading American players. In 1934 he represented the United States in a match against the Bermuda team which the U.S. won. He won the McKENNEY TROPHY 1938, 1940, Vanderbilt 1949, Summer NAC Master Mixed Teams 1937, Life Master Pairs 1938, 1940, Fall Master Individual 1940, 1950, and placed second in Asbury Challenge Teams 1937, Spingold 1937, 1938, Vanderbilt 1943, 1954, Fall NAC Open Pairs 1939, Master Individual 1946, Men's Pairs 1934, 1937, 1938, 1939, 1940, 1947. His numerous regional titles include Eastern States KO Teams (Reisinger) 1936, 1940, Southeastern Swiss Teams 1980, Gold Coast Men's Swiss Teams 1981. A 1928 graduate of New York University, Elis assisted WILLIAM E. McKENNEY in formulating and establishing the ACBL Charity Foundation from 1933 to 1937. He constructed hands for Autobridge and wrote a column for *Bridge World* from 1936 to 1940. Elis was the 1932 New York City Table Tennis champion and semi-finalist in the National Table Tennis Championship.

ELLENBY, Milton Q. (b. 1923) of Skokie IL, actuary and physicist, one of the outstanding American players of the postwar period, was Bermuda Bowl champion 1954 and also represented the United States in the Bermuda Bowl 1955. He won Spingold 1953, 1954, Spring NAC Men's Pairs 1951 (second in 1954), Summer NAC Master Mixed Teams 1957, Life Master Pairs 1953, Fall NAC Open Pairs 1955, FISHBEIN TROPHY 1953. His numerous regional wins include Central States Master Pairs 1956, KO Teams 1966, 1969, Mississippi Valley Open Teams 1951, Open Pairs 1954, District 13 GNT 1975. Ellenby was a physicist on the Manhattan Project for three years. In the mid-Forties he was a state and regional chess champion.

ELLIOTT, C. Bruce (b. 1922) of Weston ON, estimator, formerly one of the outstanding Canadian players, represented Canada in the World Team Olympiad 1960, 1968. He won the Spingold 1964, 1965 and placed second in Summer NAC Life Master Pairs 1964. His numerous regional wins include Spring NAC Mixed Swiss Teams 1975, Can-Am Open Teams 1963, 1965, Open Pais 1965, Canadian Nat'l Open Teams 1951, 1959, 1961, 1965, 1967, 1972, Open Pairs 1955, 1958, 1962, 1969, 1976, Men's Pairs 1960, Mixed Pairs 1952, 1977, 1979, Southeastern Swiss Teams 1980.

EL SHAFEI, Abdel Aziz (b. 1931) of Cairo, Egypt, general manager of Nova Park, Cairo, former minister of sports and general secretary of Egyptian cabinet, represented Egypt in the World Team Olympiad 1968, European Championships 1963. He is past president of the EGYPTIAN BRIDGE FEDERATION. An Olympic athlete, he represented Egypt in the 1952 and 1960 Olympics in both swimming and water polo. President of the Swimming Federation 1971–1977 and secretary of the Olympic Committee 1969–1977, he took a major part in the negotiations to free the Israeli athletes during the Munich Olympic Games in 1972. He graduated from Cairo University.

ELWELL, Joseph Bowne (1873–1920) was the principal American authority on the original game of bridge (bridge-whist) and on the early form of auction bridge. However, he is remembered chiefly as the victim of one of the most celebrated murders of the century.

Born February 23, 1873 in Cranford NJ, Elwell began his bridge career about 1900 as a bridge teacher, and quickly became a favorite of high society in New York City and Newport RI. He was a regular high-stake player at the Whist Club of New York and other clubs, and he and his regular partner, HAROLD S. VANDERBILT, were considered the strongest American pair from about 1910 to 1920. Elwell amassed a considerable fortune, chiefly through speculation in Wall Street, and at the time of his death owned more than 20 race horses. His books, most of which went through several editions and sold in large quantities, included *Elwell on Bridge*, 1902; *Advanced Bridge*, 1904; *Practical Bridge*, 1906; *Bridge Axioms and Laws*, 1907; *Elwell on Auction Bridge*, 1910; *Elwell's New Auction*

Bridge, 1920. His annotations of the hands played in a 1903 par-hand tournament (*Bridge Tournament hands,* 1904) show great skill at analysis.

On the morning of June 11, 1920, Elwell's housekeeper found him fatally shot in the private house that he occupied alone on West 70th Street. He had been shot only about an hour earlier, and the motive was not robbery because none of the considerable amount of money and jewelry in the house was touched. Several women had keys to the house; he was separated from his wife. The case received wide publicity, and has been the subject of several books and hundreds of articles. Officially the murder was never solved, though it is generally believed that the police knew the murderer but had insufficient evidence. Several novelists used the setting of the case for mystery novels in which they supplied their own solutions.

Mrs. J. B. Elwell remained active as a bridge teacher into the Thirties. See BIBLIOGRAPHY, A.

ELZANOWSKI, Jerzy (b. 1918) of Warsaw, Poland, managing director, represented Poland in the European Championships 1962, 1966, was npc of Poland's International Team and won Beirut Festival Open Teams 1968. His national wins include Polish Open Teams 1960, 1961, 1965, Individual 1960 (second in 1964), Mixed Teams 1964, Open Pairs 1965 (second in 1959).

EMERY, Sue (b. 1920) of Memphis, formerly of Wichita Falls TX, has been editor of the ACBL *Bulletin* since 1972 and co-editor of the ACBL *Daily Bulletin* at North American Championships for 65 consecutive tournaments, more than 21 years, and co-editor of the World Championships Daily Bulletin 1972, 1975, 1978. A graduate of Harding College, she formerly taught school, was a newspaper reporter, owned and operated a bridge club and taught bridge. She has been a tournament director since the early-Sixties and directed in many Texas tournaments with her husband, John W. "Big John" Emery (1926–1972), a well-known ACBL associate national tournament director. She won Texas Mixed Pairs 1963, Open Teams 1965. Former associate editor of *Texas Bridge*, she is the author of the ACBL publication *No Passing Fancy* and a contributing editor, *Bridge Encyclopedia*.

ENGEL, Michael (b. 1935) of New York City, born in Berlin, Germany, stockbroker, placed second in the Chicago (now the Reisinger) 1965, and won New England Master Teams 1961, Open Teams 1964, Eastern States Men's Teams 1967.

EPPERSON, William E. (b. 1931) of Ridgefield NJ, commercial airline pilot, former USAF officer, won Fall NAC Swiss Teams 1980. His regional wins include Fall NAC secondary Swiss Teams 1979, Southeastern Mixed Pairs 1975, District 4 Open Pairs Flt. A 1978, District 3 Mixed Pairs 1980.

EPSTEIN, Mrs. Bert of Los Angeles, bridge teacher, won Spring NAC Women's Pairs 1959, Summer NAC secondary Women's Pairs 1969, Hawaii Women's Pairs 1957, Golden State

Women's Pairs 1965.

EPSTEIN, Isadore (Eppy or Iz) (b. 1908) of Tacoma WA, born in Grodno, Russia, retired teacher, won Pacific Northwest Men's Pairs 1949, Open Teams 1956, Master Pairs 1957, Rocky Mountain Open Pairs 1952, Inter-Mountain Open Teams 1958, Master Pairs, Open Pairs 1960.

EPSTEIN, Mark D. (b. 1937) of South Orange NJ, computer programming and systems manager, won New York-New Jersey Mixed Pairs 1971, Fun City Men's Pairs 1972, Big Apple Open Pairs 1979, Keystone Master Pairs 1973, District 3 GNP 1979. Epstein has served the New York-New Jersey BL as vice president, tournament chairman and member of the Board. He is a graduate of M.I.T.

EPSTEIN, Roberta E. (Mrs. Mark D., nee Erde) (b. 1936) of South Orange NJ, computer science teacher, won Fall NAC Women's Teams 1960, 1961, placed second in 1971 and in Spring NAC Women's Pairs 1981. Her regional titles include Summer NAC secondary Women's Pairs 1971, Spring Swiss Teams Flt. A 1981, New York-New Jersey Mixed Pairs 1971, Tri-State Women's Pairs 1973, All-Western Women's Swiss Teams 1973, Big Apple Open Pairs 1978, District 4 Fall Open Pairs 1979, District 3 GNP 1979. She was educated at Cornell University and Columbia University.

ERDENBAUM, Israel (b. 1920) of Tel Aviv, Israel, born in Krakow, Poland, engraver and tournament director, represented Israel in the European Championships 1972, was npc of the Israeli Women's Teams 1973, 1981, and captain of Israeli Open Team 1970. He won Israeli Teams 1971. Israel's chief tournament director, he also directs at World Olympiads and European Championships. Erdenbaum is editor of the Israeli *Bridge Magazine* and ISRAEL BRIDGE FEDERATION National Sports Captain.

ERDOS, Ivan (1924-1967) edited the popular "Dupliquiz" column for the ACBL *Bulletin*. A leading player, teacher, and writer, Erdos also contributed to *American Bridge Digest* and wrote *Bridge A La Carte*. He was bridge editor of *San Diego* magazine and several Southern California newspapers. Born in Budapest, Erdos lived in England from 1939 to 1951 before moving to Los Angeles, where he worked as a travel agent. He won the World Mixed Pairs 1966 and represented North America in the Bermuda Bowl 1965. He won Spring NAC Men's Teams 1959, Men's Pairs 1962.

ERGÜDEN, Garland I. (b. 1951) of Atlanta, advertising agency art director, won Spring NAC secondary Swiss Teams Flt. A 1979, Mid-Atlantic Swiss Teams 1977, KO Teams 1977, Open Pairs 1979, Bicentennial KO Teams, Swiss Teams 1976, Mid-South Holiday KO Teams 1979, North Florida Women's Pairs 1978, Space City Women's Swiss Teams 1980, Azalea City KO Teams 1980, Florida Swiss Teams 1981. She is secretary of District 7.

ERICKSON, Gail A. (b. 1938) of San Diego, ac-

countant, bridge teacher and club director, won Pacific Southwest Women's Pairs 1976, Los Angeles Winter Women's Swiss Teams 1976, Bridge Week Master Women's Pairs Flt. A 1980, District 22 GNT 1975.

ERICKSON, Nels of San Diego, bridge teacher, won several regional events including Summer NAC secondary Leventritt Pairs 1969, All-Western KO Teams 1972, Hawaii Men's Pairs 1973, Swiss Teams 1974, 1975, Bridge Week Open BAM Teams 1977, Men's Pairs 1979, Pacific Southwest KO Teams, Men's Pairs 1977, Golden State KO Teams 1977.

ERIKSSON, Karin (b. 1914) of Stockholm, Sweden, won the World Women's Teams 1968, Nordic Women's Teams 1957, 1966, 1968. Her national titles include Women's Pairs and Mixed Pairs.

ETTER, Bob G. (b. 1945) of Stockton CA, formerly of Memphis, assistant math professor, won Fall NAC Swiss Teams 1981. His regional titles include Spring NAC secondary Swiss Teams 1980, District 15 Men's Pairs 1976, Pacific Southwest Master Swiss Teams 1979, Bridge Week KO Teams 1979. Etter was educated at University of Georgia and Rice University. He was placekicker for the Atlanta Falcons 1968-1969 and All SEC football and baseball 1964-1967.

ETTLINGER, Douglas M. (Duggie) of Johannesburg, South Africa, trial lawyer, represented South Africa in the World Team Olympiad 1980, MACCABIAH GAMES 1977. His national titles include South African Open Teams 1968, 1979, 1981, Open Pairs 1977, Pioneer Teams 1964, 1968, 1970, 1981, Interprovincial Teams 1963, 1970, 1974, 1979. He served as Southern Africa representative to the WORLD BRIDGE FEDERADION Executive Council 1970, 1974 and as chairman of Transvaal Bridge Union 1975-1976 and 1981. Ettlinger is a graduate of Witwatersrand University. He writes a weekly bridge column for the *Rand Daily Mail*.

EVANS, Allan E. (b. 1929) of Manhattan Beach CA, stockbroker, won Las Vegas KO Teams 1971, Desert Empire Swiss Teams 1972, District 22 Men's Swiss Teams 1976. He is past president of District 23 and Westwood Unit. Evans is a graduate of UCLA.

EVANS, Donald S. (b. 1933) of Sydney, Australia, bridge teacher, represented Australia in the World Team Olympiad 1964 and won Australian Open Teams five times and the Individual 1963.

EVANS, Mrs. Ralph (Penguin) (1906-1977), hotelier in Bournemouth, England, began her 40-year bridge career at the Wessex Club in Bournemouth in 1936 where she won the Hardwicke Trophy with partner VICTOR MOLLO and teammates IAIN MacLEOD and TERENCE REESE. She was European Women's Teams champion 1950, 1951, 1952 and was second in 1939 as well as second in the GOLD CUP 1950. In 1953 she toured the U.S. as a member of the British Women's Team.

EVANS, Rex (b. 1918) of Auckland, New Zealand, chartered accountant, represented New Zealand in the World Team Olympiad, De La Rue World Pair Championship 1957, World Bridge Federation Par Point Contest 1961, 1963 in which he placed first each time in the South Pacific Zone, Far East Championships 1964, 1971. His national wins include New Zealand Open Teams 12 times, Open Pairs three times, winner in New Zealand section in Australasian Olympiads many times. He is a former president of the New Zealand Bridge Council, Auckland Bridge Council and Northern Contract Bridge Club. His writings include magazine articles and a newspaper column for the *New Zealand Herald*.

EVANS, Stephen P. (Swiz) (b. 1952) of North Hollywood CA, computer program analyst, won Spring NAC secondary Swiss Teams 2nd Flt. 1975, Mixed Teams 1977, Los Angeles Winter KO Teams 1974, Bridge Week KO Teams 1981, District 23 GNT, Zone VIII 1975, District 22 GNT 1980.

EVANS, Tom H. (b. 1949) of San Diego, program administrator, won All-American KO Teams 1976, 1977, Upper New York State Open Pairs 1976, Pacific Southwest KO Teams 1979, Golden State Swiss Teams Flt. A 1980.

EVITT, David John (b. 1946) of Auckland, New Zealand, sales director, represented New Zealand in the Far East Championships 1975, 1978, World Team Olympiad 1976. His national titles include New Zealand KO Teams 1972, Open Teams 1977, 1978, Interprovincial Teams 1978. His regional titles include Provincial Teams 12 times and Provincial Pairs 9 times between 1970 and 1981. He has served as president, chairman, executive committee member of Auckland CBC and committee member of NEW ZEALAND BRIDGE ASSOCIATION.

EVITT, Jane O. (b. 1949) of Christchurch, New Zealand, science and mathematics teacher, represented New Zealand in World Women's Team Olympiad 1980. She was Far East Women's champion 1981, placed second in 1978, was the top female masterpoint winner in New Zealand 1978. Evitt, a member of the IBPA, writes a weekly bridge column for *Christchurch Star* and teaches bridge in clubs, high school and in the community center.

EWEN, Ira (b. 1931) of Jamaica NY, high school principal, placed second in Summer NAC Senior and Advanced Senior Master Pairs 1959 and won New England Master Teams 1963, Long Island KO Teams 1970. Ewen is a graduate of Harvard.

EWEN, Robert B. (b. 1940) of Miami, psychology professor, author, won Eastern States KO Teams (Reisinger) 1972, Mid-Atlantic KO Teams 1973, Fun City Swiss Teams 1973. Intercollegiate champion 1958, 1963, he was educated at Cornell and University of Illinois. Ewen has written one book on psychology for the general public and two college psychology textbooks. He is the creator of TWO-WAY GAME TRIES, author of articles for *Bridge World*, including the popular bridge word puzzles, the ACBL

Bulletin, former associate editor of *Bridge Journal*, a contributing editor, *Bridge Encyclopedia*, and the author of six books including *Opening Leads, Doubles for Takeout, Penalties and Profit, Preemptive Bidding, Contract Bridge: A Concise Guide, The Teenager's Guide to Bridge* and *The Defensive Bidding Quiz Book*. See BIBLIOGRAPHY, C, D, J.

EWINGTON, Frances (b. 1917) of Hawera, New Zealand, won several national championships including New Zealand Pairs, Dunhill Teams, Allard Cup.

F

FABER, Eberhard (1859–1946), pencil manufacturer from New York City, gained fame as a player of both whist and bridge. As a whist player he presided over the AMERICAN WHIST LEAGUEand belonged to the Knickerbocker Whist Club. As a bridge player he was named Honorary Member of the ABL in 1930, and he presented the Faber Challenge Trophy for the National Open Team auction bridge championship.

FACCHINI, Gianfranco (b. 1937) of Bologna, Italy, lawyer, was Bermuda Bowl champion 1975. He won Italy Cup 1970, 1974, London *Sunday Times* Pairs (since 1981 Invitational Pair Championship) 1974, Monte Carlo Pairs 1974. During the 1975 Bermuda Bowl he was accused of illicit communications through foot signals. See BERMUDA INCIDENT.

FALENDER, Mrs. Arch, of Indianapolis won Midwest Women's Pairs 1971, Spring Women's Pairs 1970, Indy 500 Women's Pairs 1973.

FALK, Allan (b. 1947) of Lansing MI, attorney and Commissioner of Michigan Court of Appeals, won Summer NAC secondary Silver Trophy Pairs Flt. A 1980, Great Lakes Swiss Teams 1977, KO Teams 1979, Central States Open Pairs 1979, Midwest Swiss Teams 1973 and was runner-up in the World Bidding Contest 1980.He is president of Unit 195 and a Board member of District 12. A member of the IBPA, Falk has contributed articles to *Bridge World*, and is the writer and publisher of a bridge newsletter since 1975. He is the co-inventor of the Supersplinter convention. A graduate of Michigan State University and Yale University Law School, Falk was named to Outstanding Young Men of America 1975.

FALK, Charlotte F. (b. 1934) of Atlanta, won Fall NAC secondary Swiss Teams 1972, Spring Master Pairs 1976, Southeastern Women's Swiss Teams 1973, 1976, 1979, Celebrity Master Pairs 1977, North Florida Mixed Pairs 1977.

FANG, Hien-Chee (b. 1912) of Taipei, Taiwan, research institute president and vice chairman, one of the leading players and bridge promoters of the Far East, was captain of the Taiwan open team in the Bermuda Bowl 1971, Far East Championships 1973, and was the advisor of the Taiwan women's team in the Far East Championships 1982. He served as executive director of CHINESE TAIPEI CONTRACT BRIDGE ASSOCIATION for eight terms. Co-founder of Lightning Bridge Club, he developed Precision Bidding and Training System.

FARELL, Jules of Beverly Hills CA, retired computer programmer, placed second in Summer NAC Master Mixed Teams 1969. His numerous regional wins include Palm Springs Open Pairs, KO Teams 1971, Hawaii Swiss Teams 1972, Pikes Peak KO Teams 1972, Pacific Southwest Swiss Teams 1973, Mid-winter Holiday Open Pairs 1972, Golden Gate KO Teams 1973, Los Angeles Winter Swiss Teams Flt. A 1979.

FARELL, Mary Jane (Mrs. Jules, formerly Mrs. Arnold Kauder) of Beverly Hills CA, bridge teacher, one of the world's leading women players, WBF Grand Master, won the World Mixed Pairs 1966, World Women's Pairs 1970, World Women's Teams 1980, Venice Trophy 1978. She won Spring NAC Women's Teams 1968, 1970, 1972, 1974, 1975, 1976 (second in 1967, 1973), Summer NAC Women's Pairs 1960, Master Mixed Teams 1949, 1950, 1955 (second in 1969), Life Master Pairs 1978 and placed second in Fall NAC Life Master Women's Pairs 1965, 1966, 1967, 1968. Her more than 100 regional wins include Fall NAC secondary Swiss Teams 1973, Spring Mixed Pairs 1949, 1959. In the summer of 1964 she was named *Los Angeles Times* "Woman of the Year" in recognition of gaining first place among women in the masterpoint rankings of the ACBL, displacing HELEN SOBEL SMITH. In October of 1981 she held fourth place in the all-time rankings, behind BARRY CRANE, HERMINE BARON and PAUL SOLOWAY.

FARIA, Octavio G. de (b. 1920) of Brazil, company director, was South American champion 1971 and also represented Brazil in the Bermuda Bowl 1970. His national titles include Brazilian Open Teams 1969, 1973, 1974.

FARLEY, Joe R. (b. 1935) of Sacramento CA, insurance sales manager, won several regional events including Rocky Mountain Mixed Pairs 1969, Oregon Trail KO Teams 1968, Open Teams 1969, California Capital KO Teams 1976, Men's Pairs 1978, Swiss Teams Flt. A 1980, Golden Gate Mixed Pairs 1978, Mount Shasta Master Swiss Teams 1978.

FARMER, John D. (b. 1952) of Independence MO, loss prevention engineer, won Summer NAC secondary President's Pairs 1973, District 8 GNP 1979, 1980, GNT 1980.

FARNSWORTH, Harold Y. (Hy) (b. 1940) of Murray UT, won Summer NAC secondary Open Pairs 1976, Bridge Week Men's Pairs 1974, Golden State Master Swiss Teams Flt. A 1978.

FARQUHARSON, Donald G. (b. 1906) of St. Helier, Channel Islands, born in Jamaica, formerly of Toronto, retired barrister and company vice president, rose to the rank of Brigadier General in the Canadian Army during World War II. He won the

Chicago (since 1965 the Reisinger) 1936 and placed second in Fall NAC Mixed Pairs 1956.

FARRINGTON, Frank (1908–1980) of Bolton, Lancaster, England, textile consultant, represented England in Camrose match vs. Wales, England vs. France 1952, and London vs. Paris 1965. He won the GOLD CUP 1959, CROCKFORD'S CUP 1958, 1961. Farrington is the author of *Duplicate Bridge Movements*. See BIBLIOGRAPHY, F.

FASKOW, Donald R. (b. 1934) of Pittsburgh, pension and financial consultant, placed second in the Chicago (since 1965 the Reisinger) 1963, Life Master Men's Pairs 1967. His numerous regional wins include Spring NAC secondary Open Pairs 1970, Mid-Atlantic Fall Master Pairs 1967, Open Teams 1970, Independence Day Open Teams 1969, 1970, Great Lakes Open Pairs 1973, Spring Men's Pairs 1972, Keystone Fall Swiss Teams 1973, All-American Swiss Teams 1977, District 5 GNT 1973.

FATHY, Mrs. Samika (1923–1975) of Cairo, Egypt was World Women's Team champion 1960 and also represented Egypt in World Women's Teams 1964. Her national wins include Mixed Teams 1959, Interclubs 1962.

FAZLI, Jan-e-Alam (Jani) (b. 1939) of Karachi, Pakistan, lawyer, tax consultant, placed second in the Bermuda Bowl 1981. He also represented Pakistan in the World Team Olympiad 1980, Far East Championships 1973, 1976, 1977. He has won more than 10 major tournaments in Pakistan. He contributes bridge articles in Karachi *Evening Star* and is a former secretary of the Pakistan BA. Fazli writes poetry in Urdu language.

FEAGIN, John E. Jr. (Jack) (b. 1948) of Atlanta, attorney, won Summer NAC secondary Men's Pairs Flt. A 1980, Celebrity Men's Swiss Teams 1977, North Florida Swiss Teams 1977, Mid-Atlantic Men's Pairs 1979. Feagin has served as president, vice president and member of the Board of both Unit 114 and District 7, GNT coordinator and Atlanta tournament chairman.

FEDDER, Blair Y. (b. 1948) of Parker CO, commercial leasing agent, won Summer NAC Amateur Pairs 1976, Southeastern Open Pairs 1976, Rocky Mountain Swiss Teams 1981.

FEIGUS, Jay T. (b. 1892), retired labor relations mediator, won the Vanderbilt 1948 and placed second in the Spingold 1942. His regional wins include MARCUS CUP 1951, Eastern States KO Teams (Reisinger) 1947, 1949.

FEILER, Kent G. (b. 1942) of Chicago, consulting firm owner, won Central States I KO Teams 1975, 1981, II Swiss Teams 1976, Champagne Swiss Teams 1976, Mississippi Valley Open Pairs 1977, Gopher Swiss Teams 1978, Wisconsin Swiss Teams Flt. A 1981. Feiler served as Board member of the Chicago CBA 1978–1980.

FEIN, Hal (b. 1913) of Miami Beach, music

publisher, won Spring NAC secondary Men's Pairs 1971, Men's Teams 1972, Eastern States KO Teams (Reisinger) 1971, Tri-State Open Teams 1968, Men's Pairs 1971, 1975. He is a graduate of Columbia University. Fein was vice president of Columbia Pictures 1969–1972. He is credited with discovering many now famous recording artists.

FEINGOLD, Adolph (b. 1920) of Ottawa, design engineering division manager, former professor of engineering, won Summer NAC secondary Open Pairs 1973, Canadian Nat's Swiss Teams 1973, Cambrian Shield KO Teams 1973, Fleur-de-Lys Swiss Teams 1974. A graduate of University of Genoa, Italy, Feingold was founding chairman of the Department of Mechanical Engineering at University of Ottawa and a member of the University Board 1976–1979.

FELDESMAN, Philip (b. 1919) of New York City, diamond merchant, one of the leading American players, represented the United States in the World Open Pairs 1962, Bermuda Bowl 1966. He won the HERMAN TROPHY 1962, MOTT-SMITH TROPHY 1965, 1966, Reisinger 1969, Vanderbilt 1965, 1966, Summer NAC Life Master Pairs 1961, 1962, 1967, Master Mixed Teams 1973, Fall NAC Senior/Advanced Senior Master Individual 1957, Open Pairs 1961, Spring NAC Men's Pairs 1961, 1962, Men's Teams 1962, 1963, 1966 and placed second in the Spingold 1969, Vanderbilt 1969, Spring NAC Men's Teams 1965, Open Pairs 1967, Blue Ribbon Pairs 1967, Chicago (now the Reisinger) 1965. His numerous regional titles include Eastern States KO Teams (Reisinger) 1962, 1963, 1964, 1973, 1974, Master Pairs 1961, Southeastern Men's Teams 1959, Open Pairs 1969, KO Teams 1969.

FELDHEIM, Harold (b. 1936) of Hamden CT, computer programmer, bridge writer and editor, won New York-New Jersey Men's Pairs 1973, New England Summer Mixed Pairs 1976, Open Pairs 1977, Knockouts Swiss Teams Flt. A 1979, Fall Swiss Teams 1979. He is the owner and editor of *New Haven Bridge Forum*, has contributed to the ACBL *Bulletin* and authored *The Weak Two-Bid in Bridge*, *Winning Swiss Team Tactics in Bridge*, *Negative and Responsive Doubles in Bridge* and *100 Famous Bridge Hands*. See BIBLIOGRAPHY, C, F.

FELDMAN, Lynne (Mrs. Mark, formerly Rogers) of Goleta CA, deputy county council, former assistant city attorney, won Summer NAC Master Mixed Teams 1979, Fall NAC secondary Swiss Teams Flt. A 1980, All-Western Mixed Pairs 1977, Open Pairs Flt. A 1979, Women's Pairs 1980, Golden Gate Open Pairs 1974, Mixed Pairs 1977, Mid-Winter Holiday Women's Swiss Teams 1974, Wine Country Women's Pairs 1981.

FELDMAN, Mark D. (1951) of Goleta CA, economics professor, won Spring NAC Men's Teams 1974, Summer Master Mixed Teams 1979 and placed second in the Vanderbilt 1974, 1980, Grand National Pairs 1981. His more than 30 regional titles include Can-Am Open Pairs 1971, Master Pairs Flt. A 1975,

New England Spring Open Pairs 1971, Summer KO Teams 1975, 1976, Fall Swiss Teams 1975, Keohane Individual KO Teams 1976, 1980, Knockouts KO Teams 1974, All-Western Master Teams 1976, Mixed Pairs, 1977, KO Teams 1978, Wine Country Swiss Teams Flt. A 1981. He is a graduate of M.I.T.

FELDMAN, Ron (b. 1950) of Berkeley CA, professional bridge player, placed second in the Life Master Pairs 1978, Spring NAC Men's Teams 1979. His more than 30 regional titles include Spring NAC secondary Swiss Teams 1979, British Columbia KO Teams 1978, 1980, Swiss Teams Flt. A 1980, Oregon Trail KO Teams 1978, Open Pairs Flt. A 1980, Klondike Men's Pairs 1976, 1978, Puget Sound KO Teams 1976, Open Pairs 1981, California Capital Swiss Teams 1976, 1980. A graduate of California State University at Hayward, Feldman, a former elementary school counselor, received congressional recognition for his work with children. He has directed more than 35 performances of his popular "Bidding Contest", a vugraph show sponsored by entertainment committees of regionals and North American Championships. Feldman is chief executive officer of ASSOCIATION OF PROFESSIONAL BRIDGE PLAYERS (APBP Inc.) 1981.

FELDMAN, Ronald W. (Ron) (b. 1948) of Los Angeles, accountant, won Summer NAC secondary Open Pairs Flt. B 1977, Toast of Tulsa Swiss Teams 1977, Bridge Week Master Swiss Teams Flt. A 1979, Los Angeles Winter KO Teams 1978.

FELDSTEIN, Gretchen S. (Mrs. Harold) of Melbourne FL won Spring Women's Teams 1953, Women's Pairs 1960 and placed second in Summer NAC Women's Pairs 1953. Her regional titles include Fall NAC secondary Open Pairs 1965, MARCUS CUP 1950, Southeastern Women's Teams 1970, All-Southern Open Pairs 1979, Sun City Seniors Open Pairs 1980.

FELDSTEIN, Harold F. (1919) of Melbourne FL, retired computer systems analyst and ACBL national tournament director, placed second in Spring NAC Men's Pairs 1948. His regional titles include MARCUS CUP 1950, Fall NAC secondary Open Pairs 1965, All-Southern Open Pairs 1979, Sun City Seniors Open Pairs 1980.

FELLER, Robert H. (Bob) (b. 1952) of Albany NY, attorney, won the Grand National Pairs 1980. His regional titles include New England Summer Open Pairs 1976, Fall KO Teams 1981, Individual KO Teams 1980, Autumn Leaf Swiss Teams Flt. A 1981, District 3 Men's Swiss Teams 1980, Capital District Fall Men's Swiss Teams 1977.

FELLOWS, Barbara A. (Mrs. James E., formerly Staton) (b. 1938) of Omaha won Spring NAC Women's Pairs 1976. Her regional titles include Great Lakes Women's Swiss Teams 1979, Cornhusker Master Pairs 1977, Northwest Iowa Women's Swiss Teams 1978, Pheasant Swiss Teams 1978, Iowa Swiss Teams 1972, 1981.

FELLOWS, James E. (Jim) (b. 1932) of Omaha, deputy city attorney, won Missouri Valley Open Teams 1967, Western Iowa Swiss Teams 1975, Men's Swiss Teams 1980, District 15 Spring KO Teams, Master Pairs 1981. He is the editor of *Big Club* and the former publisher of *Declarer*.

FELTS, James M. (Jim) (b. 1947) of Nashville, general manager, placed second in the Grand National Teams 1975 and won Mid-Atlantic Men's Pairs 1973, 1980, Open Pairs 1980, Opryland KO Teams 1981, Mid-South KO Teams 1981, District 10 GNT 1975, 1978, 1981, Zonal 1975, 1981, GNP 1981. Felts is a graduate of Vanderbilt.

FENKEL, Stanley O. (b. 1902) of Deerfield Beach FL, formerly of Elkins Park PA, company vice president, former plastics manufacturer, Life Master #43, placed second in the Spingold 1944, Chicago (since 1965 the Reisinger) 1946, Vanderbilt 1954. Fenkel was founder and former secretary and treasurer of the Cavendish Club of Philadelphia.

FENWICK, Thomas (b. 1928) of Geneva, Switzerland, director, represented Switzerland in the World Team Olympiad 1960, 1968, European Championships 1965. His national titles include Master Pairs 1963, 1964, 1965. He is a contributor to *The Bridge World*.

FERENCZY, György, (b. 1902) of Budapest, Hungary, pianist, was European champion in 1938 and Hungarian champion 1938.

FERER, Leland E. (b. 1927) of Miami Beach, import manager and bridge writer, won Summer NAC Master Mixed Teams 1958, placed second in 1967 and in Fall NAC Mixed Pairs 1972, Blue Ribbon Pairs 1966. His many regional wins include Central States Mixed Pairs 1951, KO Teams 1967, Florida Men's Teams 1961, Mixed Pairs 1967, Southeastern Open Teams 1966. He is a former vice president of the Florida Unit and editor of its *Bridge News*.

FERGUSON, James P. (1907–1981) of North Palm Beach FL, was President of the ACBL in 1961 when the League was busy converting to a data processing system for master points and memberships. As president, Ferguson worked on establishing bridge as a spectator sport, promoting such bridge exhibitions as vugraph and Bridge-O-Rama. Previous to his tenure as president, Ferguson, a candy manufacturer, served three terms on the ACBL Board of Directors.

FERNANDO, William (b. 1917) of Malaysia, organization director, represented Malaysia in the Far East Championships 1963, 1965, 1966, 1972, 1973, 1974.

FIELD, Albert (b. 1916) of Astoria NY, teacher, contributing editor, *Bridge Encyclopedia*, is a collector of playing cards with the largest collection in the world. Field is also the official cataloguer for Salvador Dali.

FIELD, Myron (formerly Fuchs) (1912–1974), New York stockbroker, garnered four major national titles and placed second some 11 times. Field represented the U.S. in the 1956 Bermuda Bowl.

FIGUEIREDO, Gustavo J. (b. 1921) of Rizal, Philippines, pharmaceutical executive, placed second in the Far East Championships 1967 and also represented Philippines in the World Team Olympiad 1968. His national successes include Philippines Open Teams twice. He is a former director of PHILIPPINES CONTRACT BRIDGE LEAGUE.

FILARSKI, Herman W. (1913–1982) of Deil, The Netherlands, wine merchant, bridge teacher and journalist, was one of the leading European bridge personalities. Filarski, who learned how to play bridge while in a German prison camp during World War II, placed second in the World Mixed Teams 1962 and also represented The Netherlands in the World Open Pairs 1962, in many European Championships and other events 1947 to 1962. His many national successes included Open Pairs and Open Teams. He served several terms as executive vice-president of the INTERNATIONAL BRIDGE PRESS ASSOCIATION. He originated the idea of a *Daily Bulletin* for major championships in 1955, and he also was the author of the BOLS TIP and the BOLS BRILLIANCY competitions. The articles generated in these contests received coverage in almost every bridge-playing country in the world, and eventually the Tips were gathered in a book. Contributor to many bridge magazines and to 15 Dutch periodicals, Filarski was the author of several books and an editor of *Nederlandse Bridge Bond*. He was named IBPA "Man of the Year" in 1977.

FINCH, Charles L. (Tuna) (b. 1946) of Lancaster CA, won Pacific Southwest KO Teams 1975, 1977, Men's Pairs 1977, Bridge Week Open Teams 1977, Swiss Teams 1978, Open Pairs Flt. A 1979, Golden State KO Teams 1977, Gem State Open Pairs 1976, District 17 Fall KO Teams 1976, Hawaii Swiss Teams 1977, Los Angeles Winter Swiss Teams 1977. A communications and computer technician, Finch received special recognition for contributions to the successful space shuttle landing at Edwards AFB on November 14, 1981.

FINCKELSTEIN, Abe (b. 1908) of Brussels, Belgium, bridge teacher and writer, represented Belgium in the World Team Olympiad 1964 and in many European Championships. He placed third in the De La Rue International Pairs Championship 1957 and won many national titles. He is a frequent contributor to and technical director of the Belgian magazine *Bridge*.

FINKEL, Lewis M. (Lew) (b. 1946) of Providence RI, attorney and CPA, won New England Knockouts Swiss Teams 1979, 1981, District 25 GNT 1975, 1979.

FISHBEIN, Harry J. (1898–1976) of New York City, president of the famous Mayfair Club, authored the FISHBEIN CONVENTION. An outstanding player who wore a beret as his trademark, Fishbein netted an outstanding total of 17 national firsts and 19 seconds. He represented the United States in the Bermuda Bowl 1959 and served as npc of the 1960 U.S. World Olympiad Team. His service to bridge undisputed, Fishbein held the office of Treasurer of the ACBL for 14 years (1952–1966), and was named Honorary Member in 1966.

FISCHER, Gary (b. 1942) of Miami, bridge club owner, director and teacher, former computer programmer, won Florida Open Teams 1971, Southeastern Men's Teams 1971, Open Teams 1972. Fischer was a Russian linguist while in the Army. In 1980 he was Miami singles bowling champion.

FISCHER, Norman H. (b. 1941) of Columbus OH, research mathematician, placed second in the Life Master Men's Pairs 1969, Spring NAC Men's Teams 1969. His numerous regional titles include Summer NAC secondary Open Pairs A–D 1979, Motor City Open Pairs 1971, Swiss Teams Flt. A 1981, Mid-Atlantic Summer Master Pairs 1971, Men's Swiss Teams 1979, District 11 Winter Life Master Pairs 1971, Open Pairs Flt. A 1981, Great Lakes Swiss Teams 1980, Men's Pairs 1981, All-American Master Pairs Flt. A 1979, KO Teams 1980, Midwest Fall Master Pairs 1980, Spring Swiss Teams Flt. A 1981, Opryland Open Pairs Flt. A, Swiss Teams Flt. A 1981, District 11 GNT 1974, 1976, 1977, Zone III 1976, GNP 1980, 1981. Fischer served as vice president and president of District 11 and is a member of its Board. He was educated at Case Institute of Technology and Ohio State University.

FISHER, Arnold H. (Arnie) (b. 1938) of Cherry Hill NJ, won Mid-Atlantic KO Teams 1974, Men's Pairs 1977, Men's Swiss Teams 1978, 1981, Swiss Teams Flt. A 1979, District 4 Swiss Teams 1977, 1978, Men's Pairs 1981, Fall Men's Swiss Teams 1981, GNT 1978, GNP 1981. A graduate of University of Pennsylvania, Fisher is a university instructor of German and Russian language.

FISHER, Cecille of Toronto represented Canada in the World Women's Teams 1964. Her regional titles include Canadian Nat'l Mixed Pairs 1959, 1962, Women's Pairs 1976, 1981. She was the 5th ranked tennis player in Ontario for ten years.

FISHER, David C. (b. 1944) of Houston, formerly of Columbia SC, computer programmer, won Mid-South Open Pairs 1969, Mid-Atlantic Winter KO Teams 1972, 1973, Swiss Teams 1973, Open Pairs 1974, Spring KO Teams 1975, District 7 GNT 1973.

FISHER, Dr. John W. (b. 1925) of Dallas, physician, one of the leading American players, placed second in the World Open Pairs 1966. He won the McKENNEY TROPHY 1972, Vanderbilt 1965, Grand National Teams 1975, Spring NAC Open Pairs 1970, 1971, 1972, 1974, Fall Open Pairs 1958, Summer NAC Master Mixed Teams 1964, placed second in 1961, 1967, 1972 and in Spring NAC Men's Teams 1954, 1956, 1971, Open Pairs 1976. His more than

100 regional titles include Fall NAC secondary Swiss Teams Flt. A 1978, Summer Master Mixed Teams 2nd Flt. 1971, Texas Fall Open Teams 1959, 1960, Open Pairs 1952, 1957, Men's Pairs 1953, 1957, Mixed Pairs 1960, Big D KO Teams 1976, Master Swiss Teams, Swiss Teams, Master Pairs 1980, California Capital Master Pairs Flt. A, Open Pairs Flt. A, Swiss Teams Flt. A 1979, Missouri Valley Swiss Teams 1960, 1970, 1973, 1974, 1975, 1978, Open Pairs 1974, 1978. He served as president of the Dallas BA 1960–1961 and is the inventor of the FISHER DOUBLE.

FISHER, Margaret L. (b. 1912) of Washington DC, technical writer, won Senior/Advanced Senior Master Pairs 1953. Her regional titles include Mid-Atlantic Fall Open Teams 1954, 1960, Spring Open Pairs 1960. Fisher was a bridge columnist for Washington *Evening Star* 1948–1960. She was the founder and secretary of Northern Virginia BA.

FISHER, Richard C. (Dick) (b. 1921) of Tokyo, Japan, born in Elizabeth NJ, manager, bridge columnist, won Northeastern Open Teams 1943. A resident of Japan since 1945, he represented Japan in the Far East Championships several times and has won every national and regional event in Japan except Women's and Mixed Pairs. Fisher founded and directed two clubs which sponsored a team-of-four event, the forerunner of the Prince Takamatsu Cup. This led to the organization of the JAPAN CONTRACT BRIDGE LEAGUE. The author of a weekly bridge column in Japan Times, Fisher is one of the few remaining foreigners still playing high-level tournament bridge in Japan. He is a Harvard graduate.

FISKE, Robert S. (b. 1943) of River Vale NJ, computer consultant, won New England Masters Swiss Teams Flt. A 1979, Master Swiss Teams 1978, Knockouts Swiss Teams 1978, Mid-South Master Swiss Teams 1975, All-American Swiss Teams 1978, Can-At Swiss Teams 1978, Bermuda Swiss Teams 1979. Fiske is a graduate of M.I.T.

FITZGIBBON, Nicholas (Nick) (b. 1948) of Dunlaoire, Ireland, telecommunications engineer, represented Ireland in the World Team Olympiad 1972, 1976, 1980, World Open Pairs 1978, 1982, European Championships 1975, 1977, 1979, Common Market Championships 1975 (placing second), 1981. His national wins include CBAI Open Pairs 1971, 1976, 1978, 1982, Men's Pairs 1973, 1975, Open Teams 1976-1981, Men's Teams 1971, 1972, 1976, 1977, 1980, 1981, IBU Open Teams 1971, 1972, 1974, 1975, 1981, 1982, Open Pairs 1979. He is a graduate of Trinity College, Dublin.

FLADER, Michael F. (b. 1947) of Minneapolis, bridge club manager, won Iowa Men's Pairs 1977, Gopher Men's Pairs 1977, Master Pairs 1978. Flader is a Board member of Unit 103 and the editor of *Gopher Bridge News*.

FLANAGAN, Barbara J. (Mrs. Michael) (b. 1933) of Westlake Village CA, won Spring NAC secondary Women's Pairs 1980, Bridge Week Mixed Pairs

1975, All-Western Open Pairs Flt. A 1978, California Capital Swiss Teams 1981, Los Angeles Winter Mixed Pairs 1979.

FLANAGAN, Michael L. (b. 1939) of Westlake Village CA, supervisory survey statistician, won Bridge Week Mixed Pairs 1975, Open Pairs 1979, All-Western Open Pairs Flt. A 1978, Los Angeles Winter Mixed Pairs 1979, California Capital Swiss Teams 1981, District 22 GNT 1978, GNP 1979. A graduate of University of Washington, Flanagan was U.S. Intercollegiate Bowling Champion 1961.

FLANNERY, William L. (b. 1932) of Pittsburgh, formerly of McKees Rocks PA, placed second in the Chicago (since 1965 the Reisinger) 1963, Fall NAC Life Master Men's Pairs 1967, Summer Mixed Pairs 1968. His regional titles include Upper New York State Open Teams 1963, 1965, Mid-Atlantic Fall Master Pairs 1967, Winter Open Pairs 1968. He is the originator of the FLANNERY 2♢ convention.

FLEISCHMAN, Richard K. (b. 1941) of Hilo HI and Buffalo NY won Spring NAC secondary Mixed Swiss Teams 1975, District 11 KO Teams 1969, Can-Am KO Teams 1972, Peach Festival KO Teams 1974, All-American KO Teams 1976, 1977, Hawaii Master Pairs, Swiss Teams 1976, Presque Isle KO Teams 1977. Educated at Harvard and State University of New York at Buffalo, Fleischman, a professor of history at University of Hawaii, is currently on exchange at Buffalo.

FLEISHER, Martin E. (b. 1958) of Teaneck NJ, law student, placed second in the Grand National Teams 1976 thus giving him the distinction of being the youngest (17 years, 10 months) ever to compete in the finals of a NAC knockout championship. His regional titles include District 3 Men's Swiss Teams 1978, Autumn Leaf Swiss Teams Flt. A 1981. A graduate of Swarthmore College, Phi Beta Kappa, Fleisher was Intercollegiate champion in 1977.

FLEMING, Ian (1908–1964), famous British novelist and creator of James Bond, pits 007 against the diabolical Drax in a high-stake bridge game in his short story, *Bridge at Blades* which has been anthologized in *Grand Slam*. Bridge plays an important part in the plot of *Moonraker*, a 007 novel. See DISTRIBUTIONAL VALUES.

FLEMING, Irene (Mrs. A. Leslie) (Dimmie) (b. 1911) of Tunbridge Wells, England, board manufacturer and distributor of bridge supplies, formerly one of the leading European women players, won the World Women's Teams 1964 and was European Women's champion 1951, 1952, 1959, 1963. She placed second in the European Open Championship 1953 (the only woman ever to represent Great Britain in the Open series). She also represented Great Britain in the World Women's Teams 1960, World Women's Pairs 1962, 1970, 1974 and toured the United States in 1953 as a member of the British Women's Team. Her national titles include the GOLD CUP 1950, British Women's Teams 1945, 1951, 1958, 1959, English Women's Teams 1947, 1951, 1953,

1958, 1959, 1980. Secretary of the ENGLISH BRIDGE UNION 1956–1975, she is now vice president and Honorary Life Member. A regular contributor to *Bridge Magazine* and news reporter for London *Times*, she is a contributing editor, *Bridge Encyclopedia*.

FLINT, Honor (Mrs. Jeremy) of London, England, represented Great Britain in the World Women's Pairs 1970, 1973, 1974, European Women's Teams 1970, 1971. Her national titles include English Women's Teams 1970, 1972, Spring Foursomes 1971, 1972, 1973. Her ACBL regional titles include Rocky Mountain Open Teams, Midwest Fall Open Teams, Inter-Mountain Women's Pairs, all 1966.

FLINT, Jeremy M. (b. 1928) of London, England, one of the most successful players on both sides of the Atlantic was European champion 1963, placed second in 1971 and in the World Team Olympiad 1960. He also represented Great Britain in the World Open Pairs 1962, 1970, World Team Olympiad 1964, 1972, 1976, 1980, Bermuda Bowl 1965, European Championships 1962, 1970, 1974, 1975, 1977. He won the Far East Open Pairs 1973 and his national titles include British Master Pairs 1963, 1964, GOLD CUP 1964, 1976, Spring Foursomes 1971, 1972, 1973, 1977, Life Master Pairs 1964, 1973. During his 1966 year's tour of the United States he won Mid-Atlantic Winter Open Teams, Men's Pairs, All-American Open Teams, Bridge Week Open Pairs, Inter-Mountain Men's Pairs, Open Teams, New England Master Pairs, Pacific Northwest Fall Open Teams, Midwest Fall Open Teams, Open Pairs, District 4 Open Teams, Men's Pairs, Southern Conference Spring Master Pairs and placed second in the McKENNEY competition. Flint achieved the unique distinction of making Life Master of the ACBL within 11 weeks. He is the originator of FLINT 3♣, FLINT 3♢, and FLINT 2♢ and co-originator of MULTICOLORED 2♢, LITTLE MAJOR SYSTEM and the Flint–Pender System. He has authored *Tiger Bridge*, *Bridge in the Looking Glass*, *Trick 13*, *Competitive Bidding* and *Instruction for the Defense*. He also wrote a book about horse racing, his favorite sport.

FLODQVIST, Sven–Olov (Tjolpe) (b. 1940) of Farsta, Sweden, computer analyst and bridge editor, was European champion 1977. He also represented Sweden in the Bermuda Bowl 1977, World Team Olympiad 1976, 1980, European Championships 1971, 1974, 1975, 1977, 1979, 1981. His national successes include Swedish Open Teams 1971, 1972, 1978, 1979. He is bridge editor of *Dagens Nyheter*, editor of *Bridgetidningen* since 1979, and the author of a book about the Carrot Club system.

FLOREA, Harold R. (Happy) (b. 1914) of Winter Park FL, retired engineering manager, won Fall NAC secondary Master Individual Flt. C 1960, Florida Mixed Pairs 1969. He introduced Swiss movement to bridge team play when a director of a 27-team Long Island Industrial BL in 1962.

FLOURNOY, Carolyn C. of Shreveport, food columnist and restaurant critic, cooking teacher, won

Fall NAC Mixed Pairs 1970. Her regional titles include Texas Fall Open Teams 1957, 1971, KO Teams 1971. A graduate of Centenary College and Northwestern University, she writes continuing bridge stories for *Shreveport Times* and has served as publicity chariman for tournaments for more than 25 years.

FLOYD, Jason H. (b. 1908) of Gulfport MS, lawyer, won Mid-South Open Pairs, Mixed Pairs 1942, Open Teams 1962, Gulf Coast Open Teams 1972.

FOLLINE, Emily (b. 1907) of Columbia SC, bridge studio owner, won the Chicago (since 1965 the Reisinger) 1949, Spring Women's Teams 1943, 1944, 1945, 1946, placed second in 1942, and in Summer NAC Mixed Teams 1946, 1947. Her numerous regional titles include Spring NAC secondary Open Individual 1950, Mid-Atlantic Fall Open Teams 1956, 1964.

FONG, Y. T. of Hong Kong, businessman, represented Hong Kong in the Far East Championships eight times. His national wins include Open Teams, Master Teams, Open Pairs, Master Pairs.

FONSECA, Christiano G. (b. 1940) of Brazil, banker, WBF Grand Master, was World Team Olympiad champion 1976, South American champion 1970, 1971, 1972, 1973. He also represented Brazil in the Bermuda Bowl 1973, 1974, World Open Pairs 1974. His national titles include Brazilian Open Teams 1970, 1972, 1973, 1974.

FORBES, Dr. Robert Y. (b. 1924) of London, England, medical administrator, won Scottish national Pairs 1956, 1957, English Master Individual 1959. He represented Scotland 17 times and England once in CAMROSE TROPHY matches.

FORBES, Sheila A. of Toronto, born in Scotland, law clerk, won Canadian Nat'l Mixed Pairs 1968, Women's Pairs 1969, Swiss Teams 1972, KO Teams 1979, Women's Swiss Teams 1981, Can-Am KO Teams 1972, Cambrian Shield Swiss Teams 1972. Great Lakes Swiss Teams 1979.

FORQUET, Pietro (b. 1925) of Naples, Italy, banker, WBF Grand Master #3, one of the greatest players of all time, formerly was considered by many to be the best player in the world. He won the World Team Olympiad 1964, 1968, 1972, Bermuda Bowl 1957, 1958, 1959, 1961, 1962, 1963, 1965, 1967, 1969, 1973, 1974. Perhaps the greatest of the Italian players during the BLUE TEAM's remarkable string of 10 consecutive World Championships from 1957–1969, Forquet established a reputation for calm, unruffled performances, apparently immune from the nervous tension which often afflicted his opponents. Using the NEAPOLITAN SYSTEM, he played equally well with three different partners, GUGLIELMO SINISCALCO, EUGENIO CHIARADIA, and BENITO GAROZZO. In 1972 he adopted the PRECISION SYSTEM which he used with Garozzo in the Olympiad, and then in partnership with BENITO BIANCHI in

the 1973 and 1974 Bermuda Bowls. Forquet won the European title in 1951 when making his first appearance in the event at the age of 26, and won the title again in 1956, 1957, 1958, 1959. His many national titles include Italian Open Teams 1951, 1956, 1957, 1959, 1963, 1967, 1968. He is the author of *Play with the Blue Team* and bridge columnist for *Panorama*. See BLUE TEAM.

FORRESTER, Anthony R. (b. 1953) of Ossett, England, chartered accountant, former banker, was Common Market champion 1981, Junior European champion 1978, and also represented Great Britain in the World Team Olympiad 1980, Junior European Championships 1976, Junior Common Market 1979 (placing second) and in 12 CAMROSE TROPHY matches. His numerous national titles include Crockford's Cup 1980, 1981, Hubert Phillips' Cup 1977, GOLD CUP 1981, Life Master Pairs 1978, Swiss Teams Congress 1978, 1979, 1980, 1981, Spring Bank Foursomes 1979, 1981, Spring Foursomes 1979, 1980, 1981, Swiss Teams 1980, 1981. He is a graduate of Manchester University. Forrester is a frequent contributor to *International Popular Bridge Monthly* and *Bridge Magazine*.

FORSTER, Dale E. (1942) of Eugene OR, real estate broker, won the Intercollegiate Championship 1964, Pacific Northwest Fall Open Pairs 1964, Rocky Mountain Open Pairs 1969, Mid-Winter Holiday KO Teams 1971, Oregon Trail KO Teams 1975, Open Teams 1969, Canadian Mixed Pairs 1970, District 20 GNT 1974, 1975, Zone VII 1974.

FORTIN, Dr. Raymond G. (b. 1945) of Montmagny PQ, physician, former math teacher, won Spring NAC secondary Open Pairs Flt. A 1975, Fleur-de-Lys Swiss Teams 1975, Can-Am Swiss Teams 1981, Zone 2 Canadian Nat'l Teams 1981.

FOSTER, Robert Frederick (1853–1945), world-famous authority on card games, invented the RULE OF ELEVEN. Born in Scotland, Foster was a surveyor and prospector for gold, and in this capacity traveled the globe. After making and losing two fortunes, he established himself as the world's leading authority on cards by writing *Foster's Complete Hoyle* (1897), a copy of which was inserted into the time capsule at the 1939 New York World's Fair. Although the Rule of Eleven is his chief theoretical contribution, he promoted numerous ideas in his *Vanity Fair* magazine column and in the New York *Sun*. His various writings traced the successive developments of bridge — auction and contract. Foster was an AWL Director, and he later wrote the first set of laws for contract bridge. Up to age 85 he continued to lecture on games throughout the world, and to teach and conduct duplicate games in New York. In addition to writing on various subjects, he wrote at least 50 books on card games. See BIBLIOGRAPHY A, E, J.

FOX, Betty (Mrs. G. C. H., formerly Mrs. Trevor Harris), (b. 1903) of London, England, bridge teacher and bridge studio co-owner, was European

Women's champion 1966 and also represented Great Britain in the European Women's Teams 1965, 1967. In 1964 she won English Bridge Union Women's Teams, County Teams-of-Four, British Women's Teams-of-Four, Women's Individual and London's Women's Pairs, a complete sweep of all the major women's events. She served as the official training officer of the English Bridge Union Teacher's Training Association.

FOX, G. C. H. (Foxy) (b. 1914) of London, England, bridge teacher and bridge studio co-owner, journalist and author, represented Great Britain in a CAMROSE TROPHY match and won the Daily Telegraph Cup, Pachabo Cup, Tollemache Cup, Portland Pairs and British Mixed Pairs. A frequent contributor to *British Bridge World*, *Bridge Magazine*, and bridge correspondent of the *Daily Telegraph*, he is the author of *Sound Bidding at Contract, Duplicate Bridge, Its Procedures and Tactics, Master Play, the Best of International Bridge, Modern Bidding Systems in Bridge, Bridge, the Elements of Play, The Daily Telegraph Bridge Quiz* among others. See BIBLIOGRAPHY, C, F, H, J.

FOX, John H. (b. 1932) of Seal Beach CA, consulting physicist, won Mid-Am-Can Men's Pairs 1963, Florida Men's Pairs 1966, Desert Empire Master Pairs 1975, Los Angeles Winter Swiss Teams 1975, Golden State KO Teams, Open Pairs, Men's Pairs, Swiss Teams Flt. A 1980, Pacific Southwest Men's Pairs 1981, District 23 GNT 1980. Fox is a graduate of University of Rochester and UCLA. He has written several books on poker, a satire on attending college and numerous technical articles, and is president of Bacchus Press, publishers of books on varied subjects.

FOX, Joseph L. (b. 1937) of Ridgewood NJ, reinsurance company executive, won Spring NAC Men's Pairs 1977.

FOX, Robert S. (b. 1919) of Boynton Beach FL, cardboard products manufacturer, won New England KO Teams 1953, 1956, 1959, 1962, 1963, Open Teams 1952, 1954, 1958, 1962, Bermuda Open Teams 1970, 1972.

FOX, Siddy S. (b. 1940) of Hoffman Estates IL, computer programmer, won Mid-Atlantic Women's Pairs 1969, Keystone Women's Pairs 1970, District 5 Women's Pairs 1970.

FRAENCKEL, Mrs. Rigmor (b. 1909) of Copenhagen, Denmark, bridge teacher, was European Women's champion 1948, 1949, 1955, 1957, 1958. She also represented Denmark in the World Women's Teams 1960,1964. She was Nordic Women's Teams champion four times and she won Danish Open Teams, Mixed Teams.

FRANCIS, Dorthy A. (Mrs. Henry G.) (b. 1940) of Memphis, bridge writer, won Can-At Swiss Teams 1981. She is co-editor of World Championship *Daily Bulletins* since 1979 and a contributor to the ACBL *Bulletin* and ACBL North American Cham-

pionship *Daily Bulletins*. She won the BOLS prize for the best article on the 1978 World Championships and several other IBPA bridge writing awards.

FRANCIS, Henry G. (b. 1926) of Memphis, formerly of Nahant MA, editor, bridge columnist and ACBL associate national tournament director, has been Executive Editor of ACBL publications since 1973. These publications include ACBL *Contract Bridge Bulletin* and the annual *World Championship Book* (since 1973), Daily Bulletins at World Championships (since 1977) and co-editor of Daily Bulletins at all North American Championships since 1972. Francis is editor-in-chief of this edition of *The Official Encyclopedia of Bridge*. Regional vice president of the INTERNATIONAL BRIDGE PRESS ASSOCIATION, he is a weekly bridge columnist for the *Boston Herald-American*. A graduate of Boston College, Francis began his journalistic career in 1947 as a sportswriter for the *Boston Traveler*, and later served as copy, layout, sports and news editor for both the *Boston Traveler* and the *Boston Herald* until those papers closed shop in 1972. Starting in 1958 Francis also served as a tournament director, assisting at and running tournaments mostly in the Northeast and the Maritime provinces of Canada. In 1972 he became associate editor of the ACBL *Bulletin* and took over as Executive Editor the following year. He got his start in bridge writing and editing in 1955 when he founded and became the first editor of the *New England Bridge Bulletin*, a post he held from 1955–1964 and from 1967–1972. Francis has won several bridge-writing prizes for articles in the ACBL *Bulletin* and the World Championships *Daily Bulletins*. He was president of the PROFESSIONAL TOURNAMENT DIRECTORS ASSOCIATION from 1968–1972. His regional titles include New England Open Pairs 1958, Can-At KO Team 1968, 1969, 1970, Can-At Swiss Teams 1981.

FRANCO, Arturo (b. 1946) of Milan, Italy, insurance agent, WBF Grand Master, was Bermuda Bowl champion 1974, 1975, European champion 1973, 1975, 1979. His national wins include the Italy Cup 1972, 1973, Mixed Teams 1967, 1970.

FRANCO, Mario of Milan, Italy, was European champion 1951 and runner-up 1952, 1955. He also represented Italy in the Bermuda Bowl 1951. His national successes include Italian KO Teams, Open Teams 1955 and many others. He is co-originator of the MARMIC SYSTEM.

FRANKEL, Arnie (b. 1931) of Laurel MD, retired CPA, won Fall NAC secondary Swiss Teams 1980, Washington Bridge Week Master Pairs 1974, Mid-Atlantic Swiss Teams 1979, District 4 Men's Pairs 1979, Men's Swiss Teams 1981.

FRANKEL, Jean (b. 1926) of New Orleans, bridge teacher, placed second in Summer NAC Master Mixed Teams 1961, Women's Pairs 1965, Spring NAC Women's Teams 1968 and won Mid-South Summer Mixed Pairs 1962, 1966, 1970, Swiss Teams 1970, Women's Pairs 1975, Winter KO Teams,

Swiss Teams 1973, Florida Women's Pairs, Mixed Pairs 1977, Celebrity Women's Pairs, Women's Swiss Teams 1977.

FRANKLIN, Harold (b. 1915) of Leeds, England, tournament director and bridge writer, represented Great Britain in the European Championships 1952, 1956 and was npc of the World Women's Teams champions 1964, European Women's Teams 1965, 1967. He won the GOLD CUP 1954, 1960, Master Pairs 1952 and other national titles. He is the chief tournament director of the WORLD BRIDGE FEDERATION and the ENGLISH BRIDGE UNION. He is a member of the Laws Commission of the EUROPEAN BRIDGE LEAGUE and the WBF Tournament Planning Committee. Franklin is a regular broadcaster, bridge columnist of the *Yorkshire Post* and co-author of *World Bridge Championship 1955*. See BIBLIOGRAPHY, G.

FRANKLIN, Marc S. (b. 1959) of Palo Alto CA, banking strategic planner, was KING OF BRIDGE 1977. He won Mid-Winter Holiday Master Pairs Flt. A 1976, Master Swiss Teams 1977, Open Pairs A–D 1981, all in partnership with his brother MATT K. FRANKLIN. He was a National Merit Scholar, and in 1979 won $12,000 on the *Wheel of Fortune* show.

FRANKLIN, Matthew K. (Matt) (b. 1961) of Palo Alto CA, college student, was KING OF BRIDGE in 1978. He won Mid-Winter Holiday Master Pairs Flt. A 1976, Master Swiss Teams 1977, Open Pairs A–D 1981, all in partnership with his brother MARC S. FRANKLIN.

FRASER, A. A. Douglas (b. 1940) of Mount Royal, Quebec, insurance company treasurer, represented Canada in the Rosenblum Cup Teams 1978. He won Summer NAC Master Mixed Teams 1981 and placed second in 1974. His regional titles include Canadian Nat'l Open Teams 1973, Nat'l Capital Swiss Teams 1975, Men's Swiss Teams 1978, Open Pairs 1980, KO Teams 1981, Fleur-de-Lys KO Teams, Men's Pairs 1979, Can-Am Swiss Teams Flt. A 1981, District 1 GNT 1976, Zone 2 CNT 1981. Fraser is a contributor to *Melange*.

FRASER, Sandra E. (Mrs. Douglas) (b. 1944) of Mount Royal PQ, born in Palmerston North, New Zealand, import manager, won Summer NAC Master Mixed Teams 1981 and placed second in 1974. Her regional titles include National Capital Swiss Teams 1975, Women's Swiss Teams, Open Pairs 1980, KO Teams 1981, Can-Am Swiss Teams Flt. A 1981, Fleur-de-Lys KO Teams, Women's Pairs 1979. She is vice chairman for Eastern Canada of the ACBL Goodwill Committee.

FRED, James D. (Dave) (b. 1947) of South Bend IN, assistant professor of accounting, won Spring NAC secondary Swiss Teams 1981, Midwest Spring Master Pairs, Men's Swiss Teams 1981, Fall Men's Swiss Teams 1977, KO Teams 1978, Wolverine Master Swiss Teams 1979, Open Pairs Flt. A 1980, All-American Men's Pairs 1975, Mad City Open Pairs, Men's Swiss Teams 1979, District 11 Open Pairs Flt. A 1979, Cambrian Shield Open Pairs 1980, Thunder Bay Swiss Teams 1981.

FREDD, Claudius G. (b. 1921) of College Park GA, retail liquor distributor, won more than 300 AMERICAN BRIDGE ASSOCIATION tournaments over four decades including ABA National Open Teams 1974. He is a former member of the ABA Board, editor of the ABA *Bulletin*, and chairman of ABA Tournament Authority. He graduated from Tuskeegee Institute, Phi Beta Kappa. Fredd is a former chess master.

FREED, Dr. Eugene H. (Gene) (b. 1930) of Brentwood CA, plastic surgeon, won Summer NAC secondary Mixed Pairs Flt. A 1977, Summer Swiss Teams 1979, Raincross KO Teams 1979, Men's Pairs 1981, All-Western Men's Pairs 1977, Cotton Boll Men's Pairs 1977, District 17 Master Swiss Teams 1978, California Capital Master Pairs 1981, Golden State Swiss Teams 1981. Freed was educated at San Diego State University and University of Southern California.

FREEDMAN, Richard N. (b. 1945) of Medfield MA, senior software architect, won New England Master Pairs 1971, Eastern States Open Pairs (Goldman) 1972, Motor City Open Teams 1973. Freedman programmed a computer scoring system for the first officially computer-scored sectional (Lexington MA 1977). This program was later used for North American Championships, Grand National Pairs finals and for the World Olympiad in 1978. He was educated at M.I.T. and University of Western Ontario.

FREEDMAN, Robert P. (b. 1926) of Buffalo NY, attorney, won Spring NAC Open Pairs 1969, Summer NAC Master Mixed Teams 1956, placed second in 1955 and in the Life Master Pairs 1970. His numerous regional titles include Upper New York State Open Pairs 1957, 1972, Open Teams 1960, 1970, 1971, KO Teams 1980, Master Pairs 1965, Presque Isle KO Teams 1977, District 5 Men's Swiss Teams 1976, GNT 1973, 1976, 1977, 1978, 1979, Zone III 1979. He was a member of the ACBL Board 1956–1957.

FREEMAN, Louise K. (Mrs. Richard, formerly Mrs. W. C. Robinson) of Atlanta won Summer NAC Master Mixed Teams 1961, Mid-Atlantic Fall Open Teams 1962, 1964, Spring Open Teams 1961, 1962, 1965, Summer Open Teams 1967.

FREEMAN, Richard A. (b. 1933) of Atlanta, won Fall NAC Men's Teams 1955, 1962, 1966 (second in 1958, 1977), Summer NAC Master Mixed Teams 1961, Vanderbilt 1979 (second in 1975), and placed second in the Spingold 1959, Reisinger 1965, Blue Ribbon Pairs 1970. His numerous regional titles include Summer NAC secondary Swiss Teams 1979, Mid-Atlantic Fall Open Teams 1951, 1956, 1962, 1964, KO Teams 1976, 1978, Master Pairs 1975, Open Pairs 1981, Winter Open Teams 1958, 1965, Eastern States KO Teams (Reisinger) 1960, 1961. A graduate of University of Chicago and George Washington University, Freeman was a "Quiz Kid" of radio fame 1941, 1944, 1945 and became ACBL's YOUNGEST LIFE MASTER in 1952 at the age of 18.

FREIER, Morris H. (Morrie) (b. 1926) of Minneapolis, transportation planner, placed second in the Life Master Pairs 1966, Summer Master Mixed Teams 1977. His regional titles include Gopher Open Teams 1958, 1965, 1967, 1974 Men's Pairs 1964, 1974, KO Teams 1968, 1979, Open Pairs Flt. A 1981, Buffalo Men's Swiss Teams, Swiss Teams 1978, District 14 GNT 1976, 1979, GNP 1980.

FRENCH, Capt. Fred G. (1893–1937) of Philadelphia, an army officer, bridge teacher and writer, was 1931 President of the ABL and a member of the Advisory Council which drafted and approved the OFFICIAL SYSTEM.

FRENCH, Thomas C. (b. 1941) of Wichita KS, professor of mathematics, won Missouri Valley Men's Pairs 1967, KO Teams, Swiss Teams 1977, Toast of Tulsa Men's Pairs 1977, District 15 Open Teams 1967, GNT 1977.

FRENDO, Paul (b. 1923) of Udine, Italy, public relations executive, was European champion 1969. He also represented Italy in the World Open Pairs 1970, 1978 and played with the BLUE TEAM in several international matches on the European circuit. His national titles include Italian Cup 1969, Open Teams 1969, 1970. A member of the IBPA, Frendo contributes articles to *Bridge d'Italia, Tutto Bridge, Le Bridgeur,* and *The Bridge World.*

FRENKIEL, Marian (b. 1919) of Warsaw, Poland, journalist for Polish Radio, won the Rosenblum Cup Teams 1978 and also represented Poland in the World Mixed Pairs 1966, and was npc of the Polish team in the World Team Olympiad 1980. He won the Baltic Bowl 1966 and his national wins include Polish Open Teams 1960, 1961, 1965, Open Pairs 1965, Mixed Pairs 1965.

FREY, Mabel A. (Mrs. Richard L.) (b. 1905) of New York City, recorder at many international championships, won two consecutive Women's Pairs at the Eastern States Regional in partnership with her mother, Gussie Planco in 1935–1936. She also won New England KO Teams 1936.

FREY, Richard L(incoln) (b. February 12, 1905) of New York City, writer, editor and champion player, was editor of the ACBL *Bulletin* 1958–1970, editor-in-chief of the first three editions of the *Bridge Encyclopedia* and editor emeritus of this edition. His first major tournament victory was the Eastern States Open Pairs (Goldman) 1930. He recorded high finishes in the earliest Master Individual contests. As an original member of the BID-RITE TEAM (1931–1932) and of the FOUR ACES (1933–1935), he won most of the highest-ranked North American Championships. He had the best tournament record in 1934. He was No. 8 in the first group of players to be designated Life Masters when that designation was created. He won the Vanderbilt, Spingold and Eastern States Open Pairs (Goldman) in 1942. For more than 20 years he had the highest percentage of North American Championship victories won out of events entered.

Other successes include Asbury Park Challenge Teams 1933, Vanderbilt, Spingold, Master Pairs, Grand National Teams, all 1934, and Grand National Teams 1935. He was second in seven other North American Championships and won five other regional championships.

In 1935 Frey resigned from the Four Aces to join the Culbertson organization as sales manager for KEM CARDS. He was an editor of *The Bridge World* magazine, technical consultant on the CULBERTSON SYSTEM and a player on Culbertson teams, often as Culbertson's partner. After the sale of Kem in 1937, Frey returned to the advertising business. He had begun a daily newspaper bridge column in 1937, took over writing the Four Aces column in 1944, and in 1954 merged the two in collaboration with HOWARD SCHENKEN. In 1970, when he turned the column over to Schenken, his was the longest continuously published syndicated bridge feature in the United States. His books on canasta (1950–1951) sold more than a million copies, and his *According to Hoyle* (1956) nearly three million. He is the author of *How to Win at Contract Bridge in Ten Easy Lessons* (1958) and several other books.

From the mid-Forties until he joined the ACBL in 1958, Frey was a free-lance writer on diverse non-fiction subjects for some of the major magazines. Following his retirement from the ACBL in 1970, he became chairman of the Goren Editorial Board, editor of the *Precision Club Newsletter* and a consultant on a variety of bridge projects. Elected president of the INTERNATIONAL BRIDGE PRESS ASSOCIATION in 1970, he resigned in 1981 to become president emeritus.

Frey pioneered in bridge exhibitions and TV shows, initiated the Intercity Challenge Matches (1960) and the North American Rubber Bridge Championship (1962); served as chief commentator at BRIDGE-O-RAMA exhibitions of North American Championships and World Championships; edited 12 World Championship and World Olympiad Hand Books and the records of four International Team Trials. See BIBLIOGRAPHY, E. G.

FRIEDBERG, Joel M. (b. 1954) of New York City, real estate broker, attorney, bridge professional and Regional 1 tournament director, won Summer NAC Senior/Advanced Senior Master Pairs 1973, Fall NAC Mixed Pairs 1977. His more than two dozen regional titles include Spring NAC secondary Men's Pairs 1976, Summer Swiss Teams 1975, District 4 Open Pairs, Men's Swiss Teams 1981, Fall Men's Swiss Teams 1979, District 3 Men's Swiss Teams, Swiss Teams Flt. A 1980, Can-At KO Teams, Master Pairs 1979, Capital District Fall Men's Pairs, Open Pairs Flt. A 1977, North Florida KO Teams 1980, Southeastern KO Teams 1980, Mid-Atlantic Master Pairs 1978.

FRIEDENBERG, Judi. See RADIN, JUDI.

FRIEDLAND, Peter E. (b. 1952) of Palo Alto CA, computer scientist, won Golden State Master Pairs 1975, Mid-Winter Holiday Master Swiss Teams 1977, Golden Gate KO Teams 1978, Holiday Festival Swiss Teams 1979. A graduate of Princeton and

Stanford, Friedland was captain of National Champion College Bowl Team, Stanford 1977, University Scholar at Princeton 1970–1974, and Westinghouse Science Talent Search winner 1970.

FRIEDLANDER, Jerome M. (Jerry) (b. 1906) of Jupiter FL, ACBL regional tournament director, won Eastern States Open Pairs (Goldman) 1945, KO Teams (Reisinger) 1947, Can-Am Open Teams 1953, Canadian Nat'l Open Teams 1957, Upper New York State Open Teams 1960. A tournament director since 1950, he attained his Regional 4 rating in 1979.

FRIEDMAN, Howard (b. 1924) of Monroeville PA, commercial photographer, won District 5 Swiss Teams 1977, Labor Day Men's Pairs, Fall Men's Pairs 1978. Friedman is a former president and Board member of the Pittsburgh BA, photo reporter and contributor to District 5 *Bridgeview*.

FRIEDMAN, Jan. See MARTEL, JAN.

FRIEDMAN, Maurice (b. 1939) of New York City, estate consultant, professional bridge player and teacher. Regional wins include Spring NAC secondary Swiss Teams 1982, Summer NAC secondary Board-A-Match Teams 1981, Fall NAC secondary Board-A-Match Teams 1980.

FRIEDMANN, Marcel (b. 1924) of New York City, born in Antwerp, Belgium, bridge teacher, former diamond dealer, won Eastern States Men's Teams 1967, Long Island Open Teams 1972, Men's Pairs 1978, Sun City Seniors Mixed Pairs 1980, Wisconsin KO Teams 1980. He is a former Board member of the Greater New York BA, chairman of its Seeding Committee, and U.S. representative to the PARAGUAYAN BRIDGE ASSOCIATION since 1982.

FRIESNER, Richard A. (Rich) (b. 1952) of Cambridge MA placed second in the Spingold 1980, 1981 and won Central States Swiss Teams 1973, California Capital KO Teams 1975, District 21 GNT, Zone VII 1979. A graduate of University of Chicago and University of California at Berkeley, Friesner is a postdoctoral research fellow at M.I.T.

FRISCHAUER, Edward (1895–1964) of Hollywood CA, criminal lawyer and real estate broker, was one of the greatest dummy-players of all time. Born in Vienna, he served in the Austro-Hungarian army during World War I, then emigrated to the U.S. in 1938, after Austria was annexed by Germany. He was World Champion 1937 as a member of the Austrian Team which played in Budapest. He won the BARCLAY TROPHY and placed second in Spingold 1953. A host of regional wins include Bridge Week KO Team 1952, Master Team 1951, Mixed Team 1953, Master Pairs 1954, Open Pairs 1944, Mixed Pairs 1954, Men's Pairs 1955, Pacific Southwest Open Team 1946, 1957, 1958, Open Pairs 1948, Men's Pairs 1950, Mixed Pairs 1950, All-Western Open Team 1957.

FRY, Sam, Jr. (b. 1909) of New York City, secretary of the REGENCY WHIST CLUB (New York City), one of the outstanding American Bridge players and personalities, represented North America in the Bermuda Bowl 1959. He won AWL Open Teams, Open Pairs 1933, 1934, USBA Open Teams 1936, ABL Asbury Challenge Teams 1933, Men's Pairs 1934, Spingold 1937, 1941, 1945, Vanderbilt 1958. He placed second in the Vanderbilt 1933, 1935, 1942, Summer NAC Master Mixed Teams 1957, Life Master Pairs 1940, Fall NAC Open Pairs 1933, 1947. His numerous regional titles include Eastern States KO Teams (Reisinger) 1935, 1938, 1939, Mixed Teams 1949, Master Pairs 1951, 1958. Fry was LIFE MASTER No. 10 when that category was created in 1936; he was 26 years old, the youngest of the 10. His writings on bridge and other games include How to Win at Bridge with Any Partner and a modern edition of Watson's *Play of the Hand at Bridge*. He was a contributing editor of *The Bridge World* (1932–1966), and of the *Bridge Encyclopedia*. See BIBLIOGRAPHY, E.

FRYDRICH, Julian (b. 1937) of Tel Aviv, Israel, journalist, born in Poland, was European champion 1975 and also represented Israel in the World Team Olympiad 1980, European Championships 1966, 1967, 1969, 1970, 1971, 1973, 1974. He is the former sports captain of the ISRAEL BRIDGE FEDERATION.

FUA, Constant (Cota) (b. 1909) of Cuernavaca, Mexico, retired business executive, bridge writer and tournament director, represented Mexico in the World Team Olympiad 1964, World Open Pairs 1962, Rosenblum Cup Teams 1978. His regional titles include Mexican Nat'l KO Teams 1951–1958 inclusive, Open Pairs 1962, Men's Pairs 1955, 1962, Mixed Pairs 1960. Fua served as tournament chairman of the Mexican Nationals for more than 12 years and as secretary of the Mexican Unit for many years. Former bridge correspondent of *The Excelsior*, he is editor of *Bridge en Mexico* and the author of *Mexico Juega Bridge* and *Bridge International*.

FUKUSHIMA, Everett A. (b. 1944) of Aiea HI, attorney, won Fall NAC secondary Open Teams 2nd Flt. 1971, Desert Empire Men's Pairs 1972, Open Pairs 1975, Mount Shasta Open Teams 1974, Hawaii KO Teams 1976. Educated at University of Hawaii and Golden Gate University, he has been Hawaii State Senate Republican attorney since 1976.

FULLER, Haskell E. (Hack) (b. 1940) of Riverside CT, formerly of Portland OR, company president, won Spring NAC secondary Swiss Teams 1970, Oregon Trail Open Teams 1970, KO Teams 1971, Tri-Cities Swiss Teams 1975, District 20 GNT 1973. Fuller obtained a degree in chemical engineering from Stanford University 1962. His extensive travel abroad allows him to play bridge in many foreign countries.

FULWILER, C. H. (1886–1980) of Albuquerque, investment and finance counselor, was the inventor of the FULWILER CONVENTION. He was President of the Western Division ACBL in 1940, served on the

ACBL Board of Directors, and as a player had many regional wins.

FURBECK, Barbara W. (b. 1924) of Wilmington DE won Fall NAC Life Master Women's Pairs 1976. She formerly was a research chemist and has one patent. Furbeck is a graduate of Salem College.

FURMAN, David B. (b. 1941) of Lansdowne PA, financial analyst and collection specialist, won Fall NAC Swiss Teams 1980, Fall NAC secondary Swiss Teams 1980, Texas Mid-Winter Swiss Teams 1971.

FURNISH, Bradley J. (b. 1951) of Kansas City MO, graduate teaching assistant, won Beef State Open Pairs 1971, Northwest Iowa KO Teams, Master Pairs 1978, District 15 GNT 1975.

G

GABARRET, Adolfo (1890-1956) of Buenos Aires, Argentina, writer and journalist, was a pioneer of bridge in Argentina. He was a long time participant in the Argentine BA and its tournaments affairs. The GABARRET CUP was donated in honor of his memory. He was South American champion in 1954 and won Argentine Open Teams 1940, 1941, 1943. Gararret participated in a radio match against Culbertson's team in 1936. Bridge columnist for both domestic and foreign magazines, he authored several books and translations.

GABBEY, Hugh M. (b. 1907) of Helen's Bay, Northern Ireland, banker, represented Ireland in the European Championships 1958. His national wins include Open Teams three times, Northern Ireland Open Pairs four times and Mixed Pairs seven times.

GABRIEL, Charles P. (Charlie) (b. 1933) of Dallas, corporate executive, won the Grand National Teams 1975. His numerous regional titles include Fall NAC secondary Swiss Teams Flt. A 1978, Texas Spring and Fall Open Teams 1961, Big D Winter Swiss Teams 1974, 1980, Master Swiss Teams, Master Pairs 1980, Mid-South Swiss Teams 1978, Missouri Valley Open Pairs 1979, Indian Summer Swiss Teams Flt. A 1979, Rocky Mountain Master Pairs 1980. A graduate of East Texas State University and Texas Christian University, Gabriel was a nuclear scientist 1962-1970.

GABRILOVITCH, Andrew E. (Andy) (b. 1925) of Stamford CT, staff executive, won the Spingold 1961 and placed second 1959. His regional titles include Eastern States KO Teams (Reisinger) 1960, 1961, Keystone Conference Open Pairs 1958, Fall Men's Pairs 1971, Men's Teams 1970, 1971, 1973, KO Teams 1974, Bermuda Swiss Teams 1978. He is past president of the Washington BL.

GAER, Gerald W. (Jerry) (b. 1934) of Scottsdale AZ, sales manager, won several regional titles including Fall NAC secondary Men's Pairs 1971, Mid-Winter Holiday KO Teams 1970, California Capital KO Teams 1970, 1971, Copper State Master Swiss Teams 1977, Desert Empire KO Teams 1974, 1981.

GAER, Margaret E. (Maggie) (Mrs. Gerald W., formerly Alcorn) of Scottsdale AZ, bridge teacher and professional player, won Summer NAC Women's Pairs 1954, Fall NAC Women's Teams 1959, Life Master Women's Pairs 1964, Spring NAC Women's Pairs 1954, 1964 and placed second in Fall NAC Mixed Pairs 1964. Her numerous regional titles include Mid-Atlantic Women's Pairs 1953, Missouri Valley Mixed Pairs 1959, Open Teams 1961, All-Western Open Pairs 1962, Mixed Pairs 1963, Women's Pairs 1971, Mid-Winter Holiday KO Teams 1970, California Capital KO Teams, Open Pairs 1971, Desert Empire Open Teams 1974, Copper State Master Swiss Teams 1977.

GAINES, Joel. See KANSIL, PRINCE JOLI.

GALE, Bee. See SCHENKEN, BEE.

GALLAGHER, Jacqui. See MITCHELL, JACQUI.

GALLEY, Dwight (Bubbie) (b. 1949) of Houston, engineer, won nine ABA national titles and more than 50 ABA regional titles. He was Life Master Player of the Summer Nationals 1973, Spring Nationals 1982. He won the William A. Friend award 1980. Galley is a contributor to the ABA *Newsletter*.

GANDHI, Mohandas Karamchand (1869–1948), world-renowned Indian spiritual leader and advocate of the philosophy of active non-violence, not only indulged in occasional games of bridge but even used bridge as a metaphor to illustrate a basic Hindu belief.

Gandhi was trained as an attorney in England. During his years as a student, he emulated the British gentleman, taking dancing lessons, learning to play the violin, and enjoying sessions of bridge. In fact, "Mahatma" (or "Great Soul," as he came to be called) insists that the very first occasion on which he felt the influence of God in his life came during a bridge game at an English resort. According to Gandhi, a female member of his foursome began making lascivious advances toward him. The lonely Gandhi, having left his bride at home in India, was about to succumb to temptation. Then the hand of God stopped him.

As he advanced spiritually, Gandhi never denigrated his bridge playing or other youthful experiences, looking upon them as formative. In fact, when he later developed firm theological beliefs, mostly based upon orthodox Hinduism, he used bridge to discuss the relationship between *kharma/* (predetermined fate) and *dharma/* (Man's action).

Kharma is analogous to the hand dealt at bridge; *Dharma* is how man plays the hand. Man is not bound to a predetermined destiny because he may play his hand well or poorly, and it is ultimately up to him whether he wins or loses. The final result of a man's life develops from his learning, striving, and skill — not just from the hand he is dealt.

GANLEY, Susan (b. 1948) of Ann Arbor MI, bridge

teacher, won several regionals including District 4 Open Pairs 1978, Canadian Nat'l Women's Pairs 1979, Great Lakes Master Swiss Teams 1980, District 8 Swiss Teams 1980, Midwest Fall Women's Swiss Teams 1981, Spring Women's Swiss Teams 1981, All-American Swiss Teams 1981, Veterans Day Swiss Teams 1981.

GARABELLO, Giuseppe of Albenga, Italy, won the Bermuda Bowl 1973.

GARBER, Keith E. (b. 1945) of Woodside NY, options broker, won Keystone Swiss Teams 1969, Fun City Men's Pairs 1972, Eastern States Open Pairs (Goldman) 1976, 1980. He was one of the members of the original C. C. WEI Precision Team.

GARBER, Ronald A. (Ron) (b. 1937) of Los Angeles, chemistry professor, won Spring NAC secondary Swiss Teams 2nd Flt. 1975, Los Angeles Winter KO Teams 1974, Bridge Week Master Pairs 1979, Swiss Teams 1980, KO Teams 1981, District 23 GNT, Zone VIII 1975. Garber is a contributing editor of *Southern California Bridge News* and a contributor to *The Bridge World*. A graduate of University of Illinois and UCLA, he is doing research into new methods for blood test genetics to determine parentage.

GARDENER, James L. (b. 1946) of Lansing MI placed second in Spring NAC Men's Teams 1981. His regional titles include Midwest Spring Swiss Teams 1973, District 5 Swiss Teams 1973, Great Lakes KO Teams 1979, Canadian Nat'l Open Pairs 1981, Wolverine Open Pairs 1981, Thunder Bay Swiss Teams 1981, Motor City Open Pairs Flt. A 1981.

GARDENER, Nico (formerly Goldinger) (b. 1908) of London, England, born in Riga, Latvia, one of the leading European players, won the World Mixed Teams 1962 and placed second in the World Team Olympiad 1960. He also represented Great Britain in the Bermuda Bowl 1950, 1962, and in five European Championships, winning in 1950, 1961 and placing second in 1953. His national wins include the GOLD CUP 1946, 1951, 1954, 1958, 1967, 1968, 1970, Master Pairs 1953, London *Sunday Times* Pairs (now Invitational Pairs) 1970. A bridge teacher and writer, Gardener is the director of London School of Bridge and its founder. His interest include chess, ballet, languages (he speakes four fluently), and ballroom dancing for which he has many medals. He is the inventor of GARDENER NOTRUMP OVERCALL CONVENTION and the co-author of *Bridge for Beginners* and *Card Play Technique*. See FAMILY and BIBLIOGRAPHY, D, E.

GARDENER, Nicola P. (b. 1949) of London, England, one of the world's leading women players, won the Venice Trophy 1981, European Women's Championships 1975, 1979, 1981 and also represented Great Britain in the Venice Trophy 1976, World Women's Teams 1980, EWC 1970, 1973, 1974. Her national successes include British Women's Teams 1971, GOLD CUP 1975, Crockford's Cup 1976, Pachabo Cup 1967, 1979, Lederer Cup

1969, Hubert Phillips' Cup 1980, CAMROSE TROPHY 1981, Spring Foursomes 1980, 1981. She has been a director of the London School of Bridge since 1977. Her interests include painting and art, antiques, stamp collecting, dancing, beekeeping, films and theatre. See FAMILY.

GARDENER, Patricia (formerly Mrs. Nico) of Canford Cliffs, England, represented Great Britain in the European Women's Championships 1938, 1953, 1955, 1957. Her national successes include British Women's Teams 1970, 1972 and other titles. She is a former director of the London School of Bridge. See FAMILY.

GARDENER, Robert R. (b. 1946) of Glen Ellyn IL, company vice president and controller, won Spring NAC secondary Swiss Teams 1973, Gopher Men's Pairs 1972, Tri-Unit Men's Pairs 1970, Mixed Pairs 1973, Central States Swiss Teams 1978, BAM Swiss Teams 1978, Master Pairs 1979, Wisconsin KO Teams 1978.

GARDINER, Dr. Henry G. (b. 1918) of Fort Worth TX, psychiatrist, won Republic of Texas Men's Pairs 1964, 1970, Captial City Swiss Teams 1977.

GARDINER, Jerre J. (Mrs. Henry G.) (b. 1927) of Fort Worth TX, bridge teacher, won Fall NAC secondary Women's Swiss Teams 1978, Big D Open Pairs 1976, Capital City Swiss Teams 1977, Republic of Texas Women's Pairs 1981, Oklahoma City Women's Swiss Teams 1981.

GARDNER, Thomas W. (Tom) (b. 1921) of Troy MI, company vice president, won Florida Swiss Teams, Life Master Pairs 1975, Veterans Day Swiss Teams 1981.

GARFIELD, Evelyn D. of Marblehead MA, accountant, won New England KO Teams 1960, Master Women's Pairs 1968, Women's Pairs 1970, Swiss Teams 1971, Upper New York State Mixed Pairs 1970.

GARGRAVE, Jeffrey J. (Jeff) (b. 1949) of San Jose CA, lawyer, won Great Lakes Swiss Teams 1973, Men's Pairs 1977, Motor City Master Pairs, Swiss Teams, Music City Swiss Teams 1973, Midwest Spring Open Pairs 1975, District 11 Swiss Teams 1974, GNT 1973, 1976, Zone III 1976.

GARNER, Michael of Ventnor NJ, formerly of Chicago, option trader, won Keystone Men's Pairs 1970, Master Pairs 1973, Puerto Rico Men's Pairs 1971, Open Pairs 1971, Swiss Teams 1971, Central States I KO Teams 1974.

GARNER, Stephen C. (b. 1955) of Minneapolis, college student, placed second in Spring NAC Men's Teams 1978. His more than 20 regional titles include Summer NAC secondary Men's Pairs 1976, Roughrider KO Teams 1977, 1981, Master Pairs 1979, Wisconsin KO Teams 1976, 1981, Master Pairs 1981, Thunder Bay Master Pairs, Swiss Teams 1977, District 14 GNT 1977, 1980, 1981, Zone VI 1981,

GNP 1978, 1980.

GAROZZO, Benito (b. 1927) of Rome, Italy, jewelry-store owner, considered by many experts as the world's best player during his World Championship years, won the World Team Olympiad 1964, 1968, 1972, Bermuda Bowl 1961, 1962, 1963, 1965, 1966, 1967, 1969, 1973, 1974, 1975 and placed second in the World Open Pairs 1970, Bermuda Bowl 1976, 1979. He was European champion 1969, 1971, 1973, 1975, 1979. Until 1976 he was never on a losing team in international competition. Garozzo and PIETRO FORQUET formed one of the great partnerships of the world through 1972. From 1972 to 1976 he had paired with GEORGIO BELLADONNA in what many considered to be the best partnership in the world. A GRAND MASTER, Garozzo ranks second behind Belladonna in the WBF standings. He was a member of the LANCIA TEAM that toured the United States in 1975. His national wins include Italian Open Teams 1958, 1963, 1967, 1968 among many others. He won Fall NAC secondary Swiss Teams 1980. Garozzo is co-creator (with Belladonna) of SUPER PRECISION, and the co-author of *Precision and Superprecision Bidding*, *The Blue Club*, and *The Italian Blue Team Bridge Book*. See also BLUE TEAM.

GARRELL, Shirley A. (Lucy) (Mrs. Burton, formerly Neilson) (b. 1925) of Agincourt ON is a Regional 4 tournament director. She won All-American Mixed Pairs 1961, Canadian Nat'l Women's Pairs 1961, Upper New York State Swiss Teams 1971.

GARRISON, John R. (b. 1947) of Seattle, data processing consulting firm manager, won British Columbia Swiss Teams 1973, 1976, District 19 GNT 1979, 1981.

GARYN, Stephen (b. 1936) of Woodbury NY, tax accountant, won Tri-State Men's Swiss Teams 1980, Long Island Swiss Teams 1981, District 24 GNP 1981.

GATES, Georgiana C. (b. 1945) of Houston, consultant programmer, won All-Western Women's Swiss Teams 1973, Mixed Pairs 1974, Mount Shasta Master Pairs 1974, Mid-Winter Holiday Women's Teams 1974, District 15 Women's Swiss Teams 1977.

GAULT, Gregory F. (b. 1941) of Raleigh NC, educator, won International City Men's Pairs 1971, District 7 GNT 1975, Washington Bridge Week Mixed Pairs 1977.

GELEERD, William L. Jr. (1930) of Highland Park IL, wine importer, won Summer NAC Senior and Advanced Senior Master Pairs 1971.

GENUD, Maury (b. 1940) of Tarzana CA, child psychologist and teacher, won Spring NAC Open Pairs 1967. His regional titles include Mid-South Fall Open Teams 1967, Rocky Mountain Men's Pairs 1968, 1969, KO Teams 1969. Genud was ACBL analyst of the 1965 Team Trials report,

former contributor to *Bridge World* and columnist for *Los Angeles Bridge News*.

GEORGE, Jan V. (b. 1942) of Pittsburgh, former school teacher, won Motor City Open Pairs 1979, District 5 Women's Swiss Teams 1979, Women's Pairs 1980, District 11 Women's Swiss Teams 1980, Canadian Nat'l Swiss Teams 1981. She is the editor of the Unit 142 monthly newsletter, *Post Mortem*.

GERARD, Alice S. of Orlando FL, accountant and tax consultant, won the MARCUS CUP 1971, Florida Mixed Pairs, Swiss Teams 1972, Open Pairs 1976, Mid-Winter Holiday Women's Pairs 1979, Mid-Atlantic Swiss Teams 1969, 1981.

GERARD, Ronald (Ron) (b. 1944) of White Plains NY, attorney, won the Spingold, Blue Ribbon Pairs 1981, and placed second in the Grand National Teams 1976, Grand National Pairs 1980. His numerous regional titles include New York-New Jersey Open Pairs 1973, 1976, Keystone Master Pairs 1974, District 3 Men's Swiss Teams 1978, 1979, Tri-State Men's Pairs, Men's Swiss Teams 1979, District 4 Swiss Teams 1980, District 3 GNT 1975, 1978, Zone II 1976, 1978, 1980. He is a member of the NAC Appeals Commitee, and is chairman of District 3 and Unit 188 Conduct and Ethics Committee. Gerard is a graduate of Harvard and University of Michigan Law School.

GERBER, John (May 18, 1906–January 28, 1981) of Houston, famous as the inventor of the Gerber 4♣ ace-asking bid, was one of the leading players and personalities in bridge.

Gerber served for two years on the ACBL Board of Directors and he was a highly important and influential power in bridge politics. At North American Championships, this early riser, knowledgeable and inquisitive, could usually be found in a comfortable chair in the hotel lobby, collecting and dispensing information.

Gerber was non-playing captain of North American Teams in the Bermuda Bowl competitions of 1962, 1963 and 1965.

He was in the eye of a storm on more than one occasion. In 1962 in New York he split the partnerships of BOBBY NAIL–MERVIN KEY and LEW MATHE–RON VON DER PORTEN, putting Mathe and Nail together in an unusual move that worked well and almost took the title from Italy.

The next year in St. Vincent, Italy, he again broke up long established partnerships, pairing Nail with HOWARD SCHENKEN and benching PETER LEVENTRITT and JIM JACOBY. This move was *not* a success and may have cost the Americans the championship. It followed a little known incident that occurred at the time Gerber arrived at the Grand Hotel Bilia. An anonymous letter written in Italian was delivered to him. He secured a translator, but after the first paragraph was read to him, he asked the translator to stop; to deliver the letter to Italy's captain, CARL' ALBERTO PERROUX, and to explain that Gerber had listened only to the first paragraph. The writer had accused the BLUE TEAM of cheating.

Perroux, after reading the letter to his team, suggested that the match be played with screens running across the tables (this was 12 years before present-day screens were employed — but Gerber would have none of it. The goodwill engendered by this exchange inspired Perroux and his team to present their championship trophies to Gerber and the American team in what was described as the greatest act of sportsmanship in bridge history.

When Gerber's daring move to pair Schenken with Nail backfired, he faced a lot of flak, but the Board nevertheless appointed him captain of the next Bermuda Bowl team in 1965. That was the time when two members of his team brought cheating charges against a British partnership. (See BUENOS AIRES AFFAIR.) Gerber spent 10 minutes in the grandstand watching the famous British pair who were accused of using finger signals to tell each other how many hearts were held. The 10 minutes were enough to convince him, and he became one of the strongest witnesses against the pair when the World Bridge Federation suspended them.

A very strong captain, Gerber was a great player in his own right, winning the Chicago (since 1965 the Reisinger) 1964, Summer NAC Master Mixed Teams 1964, Spring NAC Men's Pairs 1959, Men's Pairs 1953 and placed second in the Spingold 1954, 1967, Chicago 1957, 1959, Spring NAC Men's Pairs 1957, Summer NAC Master Mixed Teams 1967, Fall NAC Mixed Pairs 1953, 1968, Life Master Men's Pairs 1974. He won many, many regional titles including Spring NAC secondary Mixed Pairs 1958, Summer NAC secondary Mixed Pairs 1976, Fall NAC secondary Men's Teams 1965, 1968, and represented North America in the 1961 Bermuda Bowl in Buenos Aires. See BIBLIOGRAPHY, C.

GERONTOPOULOS, Panos (b. 1949) of Athens, Greece, university professor, land surveyor, tournament director and bridge writer, is the author in Greek of *Parabolic Victory Points' Scales* and *On the Comparability of Pairs' Movements*. He has been the bridge correspondent of the national daily *Messimvrini* since 1980, and was a regular contributor to *Greek Bridge* magazine 1976–1977. He has been an IBPA member since 1975, a member of the EUROPEAN BRIDGE LEAGUE Youth Committee since 1978, and the Greek Delegate to the EBL Congress since 1981. He is a graduate of University of Thessaloniki, Greece, Oxford University, England, and University of Graz, Austria.

GERSTMAN, Daniel M. (b. 1948) of Buffalo NY, insurance salesman, won Spring NAC Open Pairs 1981. His regional titles include Summer NAC secondary Swiss Teams 2nd Flt. 1972, Fall Open Pairs 1972, Upper New York State Men's Pairs 1972, All-American KO Teams 1976, 1977, District 4 KO Teams 1978, District 5 Master Pairs, Men's Swiss Teams 1980, Labor Day Men's Swiss Teams 1980, Canadian Nat'l Men's Swiss Teams 1981, Veterans Day Open Pairs Flt. A 1981. Gerstman is the editor of *Bridge Buff*, newsletter of Unit 116.

GERSTMAN, Nat of Buffalo NY, is a weekly columnist for the *Buffalo Courier-Express*. A leading player in his area, his regional titles include New England Open Teams 1965, 1966, 1969, Master Pairs 1976, Canadian Nat'l Swiss Teams 1975, Tri-State Open Pairs, Men's Pairs 1967.

GHESTEM, Pierre (b. 1929) of Lille, France, merchant, WBF GRAND MASTER and one of the leading players of the world, was Bermuda Bowl champion 1956, World Team Olympiad champion 1960, European champion 1953, 1955, 1962 (second in 1956, 1961). He also represented France in the Bermuda Bowl 1954, 1961, 1963, European Championships 1965. His national wins include French Open Teams 1962, 1964. He is the inventor of the complex MONACO SYSTEM with which he had many major successes in partnership with RENÉ BACHERICH.

GIBBS, Gordon M. (1898–1968) of Rochester NY had the unique distinction of serving as the last president of the ABL and the first president of the ACBL (1937). He also served as treasurer of the League for seven years. His massive figure — he was a member of the New York Giants football team — was a familiar sight at early tournaments. He was the occasional partner and teammate of such luminaries as CHARLES GOREN, HARRY FISHBEIN, HELEN SOBEL and SIDNEY SILODOR, and his bridge victories included several regional titles.

GIBSON, Terry (b. 1947) of McKinney TX, professional poker player, won Missouri Valley Master Pairs 1973, Open Pairs 1975, Land of Coronado Swiss Teams 1976, 1980, Big D Unmixed Pairs 1974, Mid-South Master Swiss Teams 1978, King Cotton Men's Pairs 1980, Oklahoma City Men's Swiss Teams 1981. He played in the 1979 and 1980 World Series of Poker at Benny Binion's Horseshoe in Las Vegas.

GIDDINGS, Ruth of Dublin, Ireland, represented Ireland in the World Women's Teams 1960, 1964 and in many European Women's Championships, placing second in 1954. Her national wins include four Irish Open Pairs and five Mixed Pairs.

GILL, Brigadier General Robert J. (1889–1983) of Baltimore, retired attorney, presided over the ACBL in 1941, was chairman of the ACBL Committee on Membership Eligibility 1952 and was named 1945 Honorary Member in recognition of his contributions to the League. Gill served in both World Wars and received many military decorations. In 1945 he was appointed chief military counsel to Supreme Court Justice Robert Jackson at the War Trials in Nurenburg.

GILLESPIE, Luke (b. 1949) of Wayland MA, computer programmer, won New England Swiss Teams 1974, Masters Swiss Teams 1974, Fall KO Teams 1979, Swiss Teams 1981, Can-Am KO Teams 1975, District 25 GNT, Zone I 1980.

GILPIN, Alfred B. (Big Al) (b. 1915) of Riverside CA, bridge teacher and club director, won Fall NAC secondary Swiss Teams 1976. Gilpin has been an active member of the ACBL Board of Governors since 1964, its vice chairman 1980–1982, and a member of the Board of Directors 1969–1975. He also served two terms as president of the Western Conference and was a member of its assembly for nine years. He retired from the U.S. Civil Service Commission where he had been Project Head for the Navy Air-Launched Missile program.

GIMKIEWICZ, Benno (b. 1922) of Bangkok, Thailand, born in Hamburg, West Germany, merchant, was Far East champion 1963, 1966 and also represented Thailand in the World Team Olympiad 1964, 1976, 1980, World Open Pairs 1966, 1970, 1974, Bermuda Bowl 1966, 1967. His national successes include Master Teams 1963, Open Teams 1964, 1980, Master Individual 1959, Interclub Open Teams 1963. Gimkiewicz has been FAR EAST BRIDGE FEDERATION Honorary Secretary since 1976, member of the WORLD BRIDGE FEDERATION Executive Council since 1975, and third vice president of the WBF since 1978. In 1975 he served as chief tournament director of the Far East Championships in Bangkok. He writes a weekly column in Bangkok *Nation Review*.

GINSBERG, Martin (b. 1935) of New York City, options trader, former manufacturer, won the MARCUS CUP 1961, New York-New Jersey Open Pairs 1960, Men's Pairs 1961, Open Teams 1966, Bermuda Open Pairs 1968, Long Island KO Teams 1975, Eastern States KO Teams (Reisinger) 1978.

GIOVINE, Michele (b. 1922) of Milan, Italy, car agent and bridge writer, placed second in the European Championships 1952, 1955. His national wins include the Italian Cup 1955, 1958, Italian Open Teams 1955. He is the author of a book in Italian on the MARMIC SYSTEM which he co-invented.

GIRAGOSIAN, Robert P. (Bob) (b. 1950) of Bakersfield CA, operations manager, won All-Western Life Master Pairs 1973, District 22 GNT 1974, Raincross KO Teams 1978, Golden State Swiss Teams Flt. A 1981.

GIROU, Mike (b. 1947) of Columbia MO, computer scientist, won Thunder Bay KO Teams, Open Pairs 1981, Iowa KO Teams 1981. Girou is president of his own computer programming firm and is involved in real estate development. He is listed in *Who's Who in the Midwest*.

GIVAN, Paula K. (b. 1945) of Los Gatos CA, programming writer, won All-Western Swiss Teams 1978, Mid-Winter Holiday Master Swiss Teams 1978, Golden Gate Mixed Pairs 1980. She is a regular contributor to *The Contract Bridge Forum* and her Unit newsletter, *Di-Rek'Tor*, which she edited 1975–1976.

GLASER, Leo (b. 1946) of Willowdale ON, company manager, won Can-Am KO Teams 1978, 1980, Swiss Teams Flt. A 1980, Nat'l Capital Open Pairs 1975, Men's Swiss Teams 1980, Gateway City Swiss Teams 1981, District 1 GNP 1981, GNT Zone III 1981.

GLATT, Arthur (1909–1975), a financial consultant

from Lincolnwood IL, was technical advisor to the TV program "Championship Bridge." As a player, he won three national titles and finished second six times.

GLENN, Richard M. C. (b. 1917) of Sarasota FL, formerly of Richmond VA, retired stockbroker, won Mid-Atlantic Spring Men's Pairs 1956, 1971, Mid-South Master Pairs 1974, Men's Pairs 1974, Summer NAC secondary Commercial and Industrial Teams 1961.

GLENN, Robert L. (Bob) (b. 1948) of Chicago Ridge IL, company vice president, won Summer NAC secondary Silver Trophy Pairs Flt. A 1978, Canadian Nat'l Men's Pairs 1981, Great Lakes Master Swiss Teams 1978, Central States II Master Pairs 1978, Midwest Spring Open Pairs 1981.

GLICK, Jefferson (Jeff) (b. 1906) of North Miami Beach, born in Cleveland, bridge administrator, one of the leading American bridge personalities, was npc of the United States team which placed second in the Bermuda Bowl 1956. He won the Spingold 1949, Chicago (since 1965 the Reisinger) 1949, Fall NAC Men's Teams 1947, 1948, 1954, 1958, Mixed Pairs 1941, Asbury Challenge Teams 1934, and placed second in the Spingold 1934, 1952, Chicago 1952. His numerous regional titles include Southeastern Open Teams 1953, 1954, Men's Teams, Men's Pairs 1952, Mixed Pairs 1944, Southern Conference Open Teams 1956, Open Pairs 1953, 1957, Mid-South Spring Open Teams, Open Pairs 1956. In 1945 he was instrumental in organizing the Florida Unit, subsequently the largest unit of the ACBL. He was its president 1949–1965 and was executive manager from 1965–1979. He served as chairman of two international tournaments and four North American Championships, all held in Miami. Glick was ACBL president in 1955 and was named HONORARY MEMBER in 1964.

GLICK, Vera (Mrs. Jefferson) of Miami Beach won Fall NAC Women's Teams 1953, Mixed Pairs 1941. She won several regional titles including Fall NAC secondary Goddard Pairs 1946, Southeastern Open Teams 1953, 1954, Mixed Pairs 1944, Mid-South Open Teams, Women's Pairs 1956, Southern Conference Fall Open Pairs 1953. She served as co-chairman of the 1975 Summer North American Championships held in Miami.

GLUBOK, Brian (b. 1959) of New York City, placed second in the Spingold 1980, Grand National Teams 1981 and won District 3 Open Pairs 1977, All-Western Mixed Pairs 1979, New England Summer Swiss Teams 1980, Nassau-Suffolk Swiss Teams Flt. A 1980, Wisconsin KO Teams 1980, Eastern States KO Teams (Reisinger) 1980. He was the youngest to ever win the Eastern States Reisinger KO Teams, an event that had status as a national championship in the early days and which to this day retains great prestige. He was 20 years old, breaking the record of KYLE LARSEN who first won it in 1973 at the age of 23. Glubok is a 1982 graduate of Amherst College.

He has contributed bridge articles to various publications and also writes on non-bridge subjects.

GLYKIS, Evangelos (b. 1920) of Athens, Greece, importer/exporter and industrialist, represented Greece in the World Team Olympiad 1968. His national titles include Mixed Pairs 1968, Open Teams 1976, 1977, Mixed Teams 1978, Swiss Teams 1981. He also won Egyptian Open Teams 1967. President of the HELLENIC BRIDGE FEDERATION since 1975, he is a former member of its executive council and its former secretary general. He is also a member of the EUROPEAN BRIDGE LEAGUE Masterpoints Committee and Rules and Ethics Committee and has served as npc of Greek teams. He is the author of *Tournament Directors' Guide* in Greek.

GLYNNE, Anthony C. (Tony) (b. 1947) of Beaverton OR, formerly of Birmingham, England, professional bridge player, bridge teacher and director, represented England in the 1975 CAMROSE TROPHY match versus Wales. He has won more than 15 regional titles since 1976 including Summer NAC secondary Swiss Teams Flt. A 1981, Oregon Trail Swiss Teams Flt. A 1980, 1981, Men's Swiss Teams 1976, Master Pairs 1977, Puget Sound Swiss Teams Flt. A 1980, KO Teams, Swiss Teams 1981, Inland Empire Swiss Teams, Master Pairs 1980, Gem State KO Teams 1980. After graduating from Birmingham University in 1963, he became the education producer of Uganda TV in East Africa. While in Africa he climbed Mt. Kilimanjaro. From 1967 to 1975 he was the senior producer for BBC radio in Birmingham and interviewed a variety of entertainment stars.

GODFREY, Kerr M. (Deputy Dog) (b. 1951) of Austin TX, cable TV installer, won Puerto Rico Master Pairs 1980, Crescent City KO Teams 1981, Toast of Tulsa Men's Swiss Teams 1981.

GODFREY, Lucile (b. 1897) of Colorado Springs CO, bridge teacher, won Rocky Mountain Women's Pairs 1957, 1970, Desert Empire Master Pairs 1957, New England Fall Women's Pairs 1961.

GOENKA, P. C. of India, is president of the BRIDGE FEDERATION OF ASIA AND THE MIDDLE EAST and president emeritus of the BRIDGE FEDERATION OF INDIA. He captained the Indian women's team at the World Olympiad in 1980.

GOETZEE, Wouter, (b. 1921) of Curaçao, Netherlands Antilles, accountant, won National Open Teams 1961. He is a former president of the Dutch BL, Curaçao District, and one of the pioneers of the Netherlands Antilles BA of which he is an Honorary Member.

GOLD, Don (b. 1919) of San Jose CA, is the author of *Intermediate Two-Bids in Bridge*. Born in London, England, Gold served with the British Royal Air Force during WW II. A computer programmer, he has been a member of the Stanford Systems Programming Group since 1963. See BIBLIOGRAPHY, C.

GOLD, Richard K. (b. 1951) of Norwalk CA, mechanical enginer, won Spring NAC secondary Swiss Teams 1980, Cotton Boll Master Pairs 1977, District 23 GNP 1981, GNT, Zone VII 1981.

GOLD, Sam (1908–1982) of Montreal, a retailer, tournament director and a member of the National Laws Commission, was one of the leading Canadian players. In 1948 he became Life Master No. 132, the second Canadian to achieve that rank. Gold represented Canada in the 1964 Olympiad Open Teams, won Canadian-American Open Teams 1952, 1954, 1966, 1967, Men's Pairs 1956, 1957 and was a member of the Montreal Intercity Team which won the Congress Trophy in Montreal 1967 and in New York 1968. He was a charter member of the Montreal Bridge League in the early Thirties and was instrumental in having the MBL affiliate with the ACBL in 1946. Gold contributed many new tournament movements to the ACBL, the most notable being the THREE-QUARTER MOVEMENT now universally used for one-winner duplicate games.

GOLDBERG, Freddie (Mrs. Richard L.) of Memphis, earlier of Nashville and Stamford CT, former bridge teacher, won Tri-State Women's Pairs 1968. Her active bridge career proved a valuable background for her role as wife of the ACBL Executive Secretary. She is a member of the NAC Goodwill Committee.

GOLDBERG, Richard L. (b. 1922) of Memphis, earlier of Nashville and Stamford CT, has been ACBL Executive Secretary and General Manager since 1971. His first official connection with the ACBL was as a regional tournament director in 1959 and a national tournament director in 1961. He was brought to ACBL National Headquarters in New York to take over tournament scheduling in 1963 and was groomed for ACBL's top job by serving as assistant to the Executive Secretary 1965–1971, when he succeeded EASLEY BLACKWOOD. The smooth transition of ACBL Headquarters from Greenwich to Memphis was achieved under his aegis. Goldberg is active in WORLD BRIDGE FEDERATION affairs. Zone II representative in 1972, he was elected secretary of the WBF in 1981 and also serves as assistant treasurer. He is a member of the ACBL Laws Commission, the ACBL Goodwill Committee, and the editorial board of the *Bridge Encyclopedia*.

GOLDBERG, Steve of Miami, won the Reisinger 1972, Spingold 1974 and placed second in Spring NAC Men's Teams 1973. His regional titles include Mid-Atlantic Spring Men's Pairs 1970, Summer KO Teams, Master Pairs 1972.

GOLDBERG, Victor (b. 1923) of Glasgow, Scotland, company director, represented Great Britain in the World Open Pairs 1962, 1966, European Championships 1969, 1980, Common Market 1979, and represented Scotland in CAMROSE TROPHY matches more than 50 times. He was a member of the first Scottish team to win the Camrose Trophy in 1964, a win he repeated the following year. He won the GOLD CUP 1969, 1973, 1976, the Scottish Cup eight times, Scottish National Pairs three times and the *Sunday Times* Pairs 1980.

GOLDBERG, Victor J. (b. 1954) of Halifax NS, lawyer, won Summer NAC secondary Mixed Pairs Flt. A 1978, Fall Swiss Teams-A 1979, Can-At KO Teams 1980. He served as District 1 representative to the ACBL Board of Governors and was founding president of *Halifax Bridge World* 1981.

GOLDBLATT, Eric (b. 1900) of Helen's Bay, Northern Ireland, wholesale merchant and bridge writer, represented Ireland in the World Team Olympiad 1964 and represented Northern Ireland on more than 80 occasions. His national successes include Irish Open Pairs and every major NORTH OF IRELAND BRIDGE UNION title at least three times.

GOLDER, Colonel Benjamin M. (1894-1946) died the day before the close of his term as 1946 President of the ACBL. A graduate of the University of Pennsylvania Law School, Golder was a member of the Pennsylvania State Legislature from 1916 to 1924. He also served in World War I. He was later elected to the U.S. House of Representatives, where he served from 1924 to 1933. Colonel Golder was proclaimed ACBL Honorary Member in 1947. A trophy in his memory, the GOLDER CUP, was put into play 1947.

GOLDFEIN, Jerome R. (Jerry) (b. 1956) of Chicago, options trader, won the Grand National Teams 1979. His more than 20 regional titles include Champagne KO Teams 1976, 1977, Swiss Teams 1977, Open Pairs 1978, Wisconsin Swiss Teams 1976, KO Teams 1978, Master Pairs 1980, Canadian Nat'l KO Teams 1975, Men's Swiss Teams, Central States II Master Pairs 1977, BAM Swiss Teams 1978. Goldfein is a graduate of Northern Illinois University. He is a tournament table tennis player.

GOLDING, Wendy M. of Perth, Western Australia, financier, represented Australia in the World Women's Teams 1972, World Women's Pairs 1974.

GOLDMAN, Bernard (b. 1912) of Needham MA, retired color research engineer, won New England KO Teams 1955, Fall Men's Pairs 1952, Mixed Pairs 1944, Open Pairs 1945.

GOLDMAN, Robert (Bobby) (b. 1938) of Dallas, financial analyst, professional bridge player and teacher, WBF Grand Master #10, one of the world's leading players, was Bermuda Bowl champion 1970, 1971, 1979, World Mixed Teams champion 1972. He also represented the United States in the Bermuda Bowl 1969, 1973, 1974, World Team Olympiad 1972, World Mixed Pairs, World Open Pairs, Rosenblum Cup Teams 1978. In 1977 he won both the pair and team event at the PAN-AMERICAN INVITATIONAL CHAMPIONSHIPS. He won the Spingold 1969, 1978, Reisinger 1970, 1976 1980, Vanderbilt 1971, 1973, 1978, Fall NAC Life Master Men's Pairs 1964, Men's Teams 1969, Life Master Pairs 1968, Spring NAC Men's Teams 1968. He placed second in the

Vanderbilt 1966, 1970, 1976, Spingold 1970, Fall NAC Men's Teams 1966, 1967, Blue Ribbon Pairs 1968, Reisinger 1968, 1977, Spring NAC Men's Teams 1969. Goldman had won three world championships, two NAC pair events and many NAC team events before ever winning his first *regional* pair event in 1974.

In the early Seventies Goldman taught bridge classes, as many as 17 per week. He wrote lesson plans, computer bridge practice hands, a computer program to evaluate bidding probabilities, and TV scripts for *Play Bridge With the Experts*. Goldman is the originator of SUPER GERBER and other elements of ACES SCIENTIFIC SYSTEM. He is the author of *Aces Scientific* and *Winners and Losers at the Bridge Table*. His interests include current events, U.S. government and tennis. See ACES TEAMS and BIBLIOGRAPHY C, L.

GOLDSCHMIDT, David (1905-1955), a Hartford CT machinery manufacturer, won several regional tournaments and originated the GOLDSCHMIDT NO-TRUMP BIDDING FEATURES, which are still popular in the Hartford area. He was the first Life Master in Connecticut (1950).

GOLDSMITH, Arthur S. (b. 1909) of Shaker Heights OH, attorney, Life Master #42, won the Spingold 1949, Chicago (since 1965 the Reisinger) 1949, Fall NAC Men's Teams 1947, 1954, 1958 and placed second in the Spingold 1946, 1952, Chicago 1952. His regional titles include All-American Open Teams 1953, Men's Pairs 1978, Open Pairs Flt. A 1979. Goldsmith is a graduate of Yale, Phi Beta Kappa, and Western Reserve University Law School where he received the *Order of Coif*.

GOLDSTEIN, Abraham M. (Abe) (1902-1982) of Flushing NY won Fall NAC secondary Senior Master Individual 1950, Eastern States Master Pairs 1943, 1949, KO Teams (Reisinger) 1949. A bridge teacher and director for more than 25 years, club owner for 10 years, Goldstein was the mentor of many young players who became successful, notably BOBBY LEVIN. He authored *Common-Sense Bridge for the Intermediate Player*. See BIBLIOGRAPHY, E.

GOLDSTEIN, Gratian (Mrs. L. J.) (b. 1919) of Coral Gables FL, one of the leading women players of the Southeast, represented the United States in the World Women's Pairs 1962, 1970. She won Fall NAC Women's Teams 1948, 1953, Life Master Women's Pairs 1969, Summer NAC Women's Pairs 1947, 1948, Master Mixed Teams 1955, 1958 and placed second in the Blue Ribbon Pairs 1966, Spring NAC Women's Teams 1971, Fall NAC Mixed Pairs 1972, Summer NAC Mixed Teams 1967. Her numerous regional titles include Fall NAC secondary Silver Trophy Pairs Flt. A 1978, Summer Women's Pairs Flt. A 1978, Midwest Spring Open Pairs 1945, Florida Open Pairs 1961, Mixed Pairs 1967, Southeastern Open Teams 1966, Women's Teams 1970, Women's Pairs 1970, 1978, Mexican Nat'l KO Teams 1978.

GOLDSTEIN, Lin (b. 1962) of Berkeley CA, college

student, won the first Fall NAC Non-Life Master Pairs event 1981.

GOLDSTEIN, Stephen of New York City, won Spring NAC Men's Teams 1974 and placed second in the Vanderbilt and Reisinger 1974 and won Fun City KO Teams 1972, New England KO Teams 1974.

GOLDWATER, Bob (b. 1924) of Hartsdale NY, is the Sunday bridge columnist for eight newspapers in Westchester NY and contributes a monthy column to a magazine.

GOLDWATER, Henry A. (Harry) (b. 1901) of Yonkers NY, has been an ACBL national tournament director since 1957. Since 1962 he has served as an advisor to the ACBL Laws Commission and is a contributing editor to the *Bridge Encyclopedia*. See also GOLDWATER RULE.

GOODEN, George S. (1904–1981) of Carmel CA was a bridge writer, lecturer, tour conductor, member of the ACBL Board of Directors 1959, and President of the ABTA 1962–63. In 1941 he won the World Olympic par contest in addition to several Pacific Coast regional events in the Thirties. Gooden taught more than 250,000 pupils, lectured on radio and in department stores and authored many books and booklets for teaching purposes. These include *Contract Bridge Bidding and Play: Self-Teaching Lesson Course for Beginning Players* (1964), the first programed bridge instruction book for beginners. He also co-authored *Sherlock Holmes, Bridge Detective*. See BIBLIOGRAPHY, E, H.

GOODMAN, Aaron (b. 1901) of Montreal, born in Bristol, England, export/import businessman, won Spring NAC Men's Pairs 1942. His regional titles include Can-Am Open Teams 1952, 1954, 1966, 1967, Men's Pairs 1956. He has served as treasurer and director of the CANADIAN BRIDGE FEDERATION and director and president of the Montreal BL.

GOODWIN, Jude (b. 1953) of Rossland BC, freelance artist, is the author of *Table Talk*, a book of cartoons based on her monthly cartoon strip which appears in the ACBL *Bulletin*. Active in promoting bridge, she edits and publishes her Unit newsletter, chairs tournaments and serves as Unit governor.

GOODWIN, Thomas L. (b. 1941) of Portland ME, attorney, won Can-At Open Pairs 1979, New England Summer Swiss Teams, Fall KO Teams 1980. He has edited *Daily Bulletins* for New England regionals since 1978 and is co-editor of *Northeast Bridge*.

GOOKIN, Robert W. (Bobby) (b. 1945) of Annandale VA, law student, won Summer NAC secondary Mixed Pairs Flt. A 1979, Mid-Atlantic Swiss Teams 1978, KO Teams 1981, District 4 Open Pairs Flt. A 1981.

GONZALEZ–VALE, Manuel (b. 1923) of Caracas, Venezuela, engineer, was South American champion 1963, 1966. He also represented Venezuela in the World Team Olympiad 1964, Bermuda Bowl 1967.

GOPPERT, Clarence H. (1908) of Phoenix, formerly of Prairie Village KS, won the McKENNEY TROPHY in 1979 and placed second in 1976. His more than 90 regional titles include Fall NAC secondary Swiss Teams 1974, 1977, Summer Swiss Teams 1977, 1979 and many, many Swiss and knockout team events. Goppert is a retired banker who has had control of or substantial interests in 20 banks, up to 17 at one time. He is chairman of the Goppert Foundation which he established in 1962.

GORDEN, William S. (b. 1949) of Mansfield CT won New England Summer Swiss Teams 1979, Fall KO Teams 1977, Swiss Teams 1979.

GORDON, Agnes L. (1906–1967) was a renowned American bridge player. Born in Ontario, she moved to Buffalo NY but remained a Canadian citizen for life. In world competition, she placed second in the World Women's Teams 1964 and also represented the United States in the World Women's Teams 1960, World Open Pairs 1962. To her credit stand 10 national titles, six seconds, and many regional victories. Gordon was noted for her grace and courtesy at the bridge table as well as her effervescence away from it. Her score of 506½ on a 325 average with ERIC MURRAY is one of the highest single-session scores ever recorded at a NAC.

GORDON, Clarice (b. 1915) of Livonia MI, bridge club director, former bridge teacher, won Motor City Women's Pairs 1967, District 11 Master Pairs 1970, Wolverine Women's Pairs 1977.

GORDON, Dianna M. (b. 1944) of Toronto, travel agent, won the World Mixed Pairs 1982 and also represented Canada in the World Women's Teams 1976, 1980, World Mixed Pairs, World Women's Pairs, Rosenblum Cup Teams 1978. She placed second in Spring NAC Women's Teams 1981 and won several regional titles including Canadian Nat'l KO Teams 1973, New England Spring Swiss Teams 1973, Fleur-de-Lys KO Teams 1973, Can-Am Master Swiss 1977, Swiss Teams Flt. A 1978, District 5 KO Teams 1979. She is a graduate of Toronto University.

GORDON, Fritzi (Mrs. Paul) (b. 1916) of London, England, WBF Grand Master, formerly one of the great women players of the world, won the World Women's Teams 1964, World Mixed Teams 1962, World Women's Pairs 1962, 1974 (placed second in 1970), European Women's Championships 1950, 1951, 1952, 1959, 1961, 1963, 1975. She represented Great Britain on eight other occasions and toured the United States in 1953 as a member of the British Women's Team. Her national successes include the GOLD CUP 1957, 1961, Lady Milne Cup, Phillip Morris championship and numerous other titles in Europe. Her partnership with RIXI MARKUS was once the strongest women's partnership in the bridge world.

GORDON, Loula (b. 1918) of Switzerland, formerly of Alexandria, Egypt, was World Women's Teams champion 1960. She was Lebanon Pairs champion

1954 and has several national championship wins in Open Teams and Open Pairs.

GORDON, Robb (b. 1956) of Livonia MI won District 11 Men's Pairs 1979, Thunder Bay Swiss Teams 1981, Great Lakes Men's Swiss Teams 1981. Gordon is a technical consultant in the field of nuclear medicine.

GORDON, Sam (1875–1968) of Portland OR, as "The Kibitzer" wrote one of the longest-established bridge columns in the world, which appeared in Portland OR and Seattle WA. Gordon was also a noted composer of bridge verse.

GORDY, Edward L. (d.1979) of West Palm Beach FL was long a driving force in the AMERICAN BRIDGE TEACHERS ASSOCIATION, which he served as president in 1975 and as director-at-large in 1979. Gordy and his wife, Laura Jane, devised valuable flash cards for teaching the play of the hand, and a game kit to improve one's bridge playing ability, *Easy Bridge*. They were master-rated ABTA teachers who also served as club directors and cruise directors. He produced the ABTA's *Standard American Report* for bridge teachers. Gordy was a member of the IBPA and contributed many articles to various bridge publications.

GORDY, Laura Jane (b. 1912) of West Palm Beach FL, bridge teacher and writer, with her late husband Edward devised flash cards, the *Easy Bridge* game, and covered the Bermuda Bowl for the ABTA *Quarterly* in 1973. She is regional vice president of the ABTA and a member of the IBPA.

GOREN, Charles H(enry) (b. March 4, 1901) of Miami Beach, born in Philadelphia and a long resident also in New York, became the successor to ELY CULBERTSON as the world's foremost contract bridge authority. Author, lecturer, teacher, TV personality and star player, he was known to millions as "Mr. Bridge." Goren learned to play bridge in a casual game with coeds at McGill University where he studied law, earning a LLB in 1922 and a Masters degree in 1923. He was admitted to the Pennsylvania Bar in 1923 and practiced law in Philadelphia for 13 years until the publication of his first book, *Winning Bridge Made Easy*, 1936, when he turned "temporarily" to bridge as a business career. In the meantime he retained his membership in the bar, but he never practiced law again.

A late starter in the tournament world (1931), he won his first major events in 1933 (USBA and ABL Open Teams). He worked for a while with MILTON WORK, and compared to names like Culbertson, LENZ, and SIMS, was almost an unknown when the Chicago *Tribune* and the New York *Daily News* chose to syndicate his daily newspaper articles as a replacement for Culbertson, who had moved to another syndicate. A fine writer and analyst, an excellent speaker, and an indefatigable worker, Goren soon knocked out Culbertson "on points." His remarkable string of tournament victories put him at the very top of the masterpoint winners list — a place he held uninterruptedly from 1944 to 1962.

And his introduction of point-count valuation, adding points for distribution to the high-card values of 4, 3, 2, 1 for ace, king, queen, jack, swept all other systems into the discard, and made his methods into what came to be called STANDARD AMERICAN. More important, because this valuation method proved much easier to learn, it helped make millions of new bridge players, giving the game a lift it had not enjoyed since the first boom of the early Culbertson years.

The name of Goren became synonymous with bridge to the millions; his importance as a world figure was recognized when he was front-covered by *Time* magazine. He made the first successful series of bridge shows on television, "Championship Bridge with Charles Goren," produced by Walter Schwimmer, continuing to run through 1964. In 1963, it was estimated that he had sold more than 8 million books. In addition to his daily newspaper column (with a readership of over 34 million), he was writing a weekly column for *Sports Illustrated* and a monthly article for *McCall's Magazine*, not to mention regular contributions to *Bridge World* and to bridge magazines throughout the world, as well as sporadic appearances in more general publications. It was estimated that his annual income and his total earnings from bridge had far surpassed those of Culbertson.

He was named ACBL Honorary Member in 1959 and was one of the first three players elected to the HALL OF FAME in 1963. He has been a member of the ACBL Laws Commission since 1956, is a former contributing editor of *Bridge World* and a former member of the Editorial Advisory Board of the *Bridge Encyclopedia*. His writings on the game far outnumber those of anyone before him, with major works translated into a dozen different languages. His books include: *Better Bridge for Better Players*; *Standard Book of Bidding*; *Contract Bridge Made Easy: A Self-Teacher*; *Point-Count Bidding in Contract Bridge*; *Goren Presents the Italian Bridge System*; *New Contract Bridge in a Nutshell*; *Sports Illustrated Book of Bridge*; *Goren's Winning Partnership Bridge*; *Charles Goren's Bridge Complete*; and *Goren on Play and Defense*.

A lifelong bachelor, Goren may genuinely be said to have been married to the game. In spite of his work as writer, lecturer, promoter, TV personality (unlike Culbertson, who grew bored with the game when he had become successful), Goren has always been devoted to tournament play. (He seldom played rubber bridge, and never for high stakes; he considered his playing status amateur and once turned over to the Damon Runyon Cancer Fund the full amount of a $1,500 purse which he won in a charity tournament played in Las Vegas.) Before his retirement from active competition in 1966, he had captured virtually every major bridge trophy in U.S. tournament play, the McKENNEY TROPHY a record eight times. His tournament record includes: won the Asbury Challenge Teams 1937; Spingold 1943, 1947, 1960; Chicago (since 1965 the Reisinger) 1937, 1938, 1939, 1942, 1943, 1950, 1957, 1963; Vanderbilt 1944, 1945; Fall NAC Men's Teams 1952, 1965; Mixed Teams 1938, 1941, 1943, 1944, 1948, 1954; Life Master Pairs 1942, 1958; Fall NAC Open Pairs

1940; Men's Pairs 1938, 1943, 1949; Mixed Pairs 1943; Master Individual 1945; USBA and ABL Open Teams 1933; placed second in the Spingold 1939, 1950; Chicago 1944, 1951; Vanderbilt 1934, 1936, 1949, 1950, 1953, 1955, 1959, 1962; Fall NAC Men's Teams 1946, 1955; Mixed Teams 1946, 1949, 1950, 1951; Life Master Pairs 1953; Fall NAC Men's Pairs 1935; Mixed Pairs 1934. Because of his many contributions to bridge, the ACBL Board of Directors, at its fall meeting in 1969, honored Goren by conferring on him the title "Mr. Bridge," and he was awarded the honorary degree of Doctor of Laws by McGill University in 1973. See BIBLIOGRAPHY, B, C, D, E, H, J.

GORFKLE, Kenneth of Sausalito CA won more than 20 regional titles including All-Western KO Teams 1972, 1975, Master Teams 1973, 1976, Golden Gate KO Teams 1971, Open Pairs 1974, Swiss Teams 1975.

GORGIAS, George (b. 1935) of Athens, Greece, mechanical engineer, ranked #6 among Greek players, represented Greece in the European Championships 1970, World Open Pairs 1966, Balkan Championships 1978. His national wins include Greek Open Teams 1968, 1970-1976, 1978, 1979, 1980, Open Pairs 1965, 1967, 1968, 1969, 1970, 1971, 1972, 1974, 1975, 1978, Interclubs 1974, 1976, Philip Morris Cup 1975. He was an executive member of the HELLENIC BRIDGE FEDERATION 1974–1975, npc of the Greek team in the European Championships 1971 and was a contributor to *Greek Bridge Review* 1967–1968. Gorgias is a 1956 graduate of M.I.T. and participated in U.S. Intercollegiate Ski Championships in 1955.

GOSLAR, Gerda of Johannesburg, South Africa, born in Germany, bridge teacher, placed second in the World Women's Teams 1968, 1972, Women's Pairs 1974 and also represented South Africa in the World Team Olympiad 1960, World Open Pairs 1966, World Women's Pairs 1970. Her national titles include South African Individual 1957, Open Teams 1961, 1973, Open Pairs 1958, 1964. She is the co-founder of the first Women's Bridge Association in South Africa in 1961 and was its chairman until 1964.

GÓTH, Gábor (b. 1911) of Budapest, Hungary, lawyer, won Hungarian Open Teams 1961, 1962, 1964, 1965, 1967, Open Pairs 1962 and was a member of the victorious Hungarian team against Czechoslovakia 1963, Germany 1964, Brussels 1964 and Austria 1965.

GÖTHE, Hans G. (b. 1937) of Spanga, Sweden, computer expert, was European champion 1977 and also represented Sweden in World Team Olympiad 1964, 1968, 1972, 1976, 1980, World Open Pairs 1970, 1974, Bermuda Bowl 1977, European Championships 1973, 1979, 1981, Caransa Teams 1977, 1978. His national titles include Swedish Open Teams 1967, 1969, 1970, 1972, 1978, 1979, Mixed Teams 1980.

GOTTLIEB, Michael T. (1902–1980) of Hillsborough CA held the distinction of playing on both the Culbertson team and the FOUR ACES, and won deserved recognition when the ACBL designated him Life Master #9. Born in New York City, Gottlieb early established a reputation as a champion, netting some 13 USBA titles in the years 1929–1935, along with three second place finishes. One of Ely Culbertson's partners in the famous CULBERTSON-LENZ match, Gottlieb played on Culbertson's team against England and France in 1933. Soon he proved a key member of the Four Aces team that dominated the bridge scene in the mid-Thirties. In 1935, with HOWARD SCHENKEN, Gottlieb launched forth on a successful bridge tour of Europe, taking on all comers. On their return to America, Gottlieb and Schenken rejoined their teammates to defeat the champions of Europe, France, in the first world championship match. Retiring from tournament play in 1936, Gottlieb devoted his energies to his hotel in Millbrae CA and to Gottlieb Enterprises, which specialized in the development of gas wells. He owned shopping centers and hotels in Phoenix, and for 10 years held a seat on the New York Stock Exchange. Near the end of his life Gottlieb made a pleasant return to the bridge world, winning several sectionals and regionals. See BIBLIOGRAPHY, C.

GOUDSMIT, F. W. (1899–1971) of Amsterdam, The Netherlands, lawyer and bridge columnist, was second in the European Championships 1932, 1933, 1934, and represented The Netherlands on many other occasions. His many national wins included Open Teams 11 times between 1933 and 1956. He authored several books on bidding and play and translated several books from English into Dutch, including works by ELY CULBERTSON and S. J. SIMON.

GOUGH, William L. (Billy) (b. 1951) of Oreland PA, bridge teacher, won Summer NAC secondary Mixed Swiss Teams, Swiss Teams 1st Flt. 1975, Fall Swiss Teams 1980, Keystone Open Pairs 1966, Swiss Teams 1970, 1974, 1975, Mid-Atlantic Men's Swiss Teams 1979, 1980, Swiss Teams 1975, Washington Bridge Week Men's Swiss Teams 1976, 1977, New York-New Jersey Open Pairs 1974, Mixed Pairs 1975, Missouri Valley Master Pairs 1975, Tri-State Winter Mixed Pairs, Men's Pairs 1976, District 4 Men's Swiss Teams 1977, 1978, 1979, 1981, Men's Pairs 1977, 1978, GNT 1974, 1979, 1981, Zone II 1981. Gough has been a Board member of Unit 141 since 1975. He won his first regional and played in the Blue Ribbon Pairs in 1966 at age 15.

GOULD, Edward A., Jr. (b. 1928) of Manchester NH, sales representative, former president of District 25, has been a member of the ACBL Board of Directors since 1973.

GOULD, Lawrence E. (Larry) (b. 1942) of Decatur GA, financial officer, won the Spingold 1974, placed second in 1977 and in Spring NAC Men's Teams 1973. His numerous regional titles include Summer NAC secondary Swiss Teams 1973, Mid-Atlantic Fall Open Pairs 1970, 1973, KO Teams 1975, 1978, Swiss Teams 1976, Summer KO Teams

1971, 1975, Open Pairs 1980, District 7 GNT 1980, 1981, Zone III 1981, GNP 1979, 1981.

GOWDY, Bruce D. (b. 1930) of Willowdale ON, senior controller, one of the leading players of Canada, became an ACBL Life Master at the age of 20 after 16 months of tournament play. He represented Canada in the World Team Olympiad 1960, 1972, 1976, World Open Pairs 1978. He won the Spingold 1949 and placed second in 1964. Gowdy holds the record for being the youngest player ever to win a major knockout event when he won the Spingold at the age of 19. His regional titles include Canadian Nat'l Open Teams 1949, 1950, 1951, 1952, 1953, Mens's Swiss Teams 1980, KO Teams 1979, District 2 GNT 1977, 1978. He is a graduate of University of Western Ontario.

GOWDY, John R. (b. 1948) of Toronto, courier service owner, won Great Lakes Swiss Teams 1979, London Swiss Teams 1979, Canadian Nat'l Men's Swiss Teams 1980, Motor City Master Pairs 1981, Gateway City Swiss Teams Flt. A 1981.

GRABEL, Julia W. (Julie) (Mrs. Ross) (b. 1948) of Huntington Beach CA won Tri-State Women's Pairs 1980, Raincross Swiss Teams Flt. A 1981, Bridge Week Mixed Pairs 1981, Los Angeles Winter Mixed Pairs 1981.

GRABEL, Ross D. (b. 1950) of Huntington Beach CA, company owner, won Spring NAC Men's Teams 1980, Summer NAC Men's Swiss Teams 1982. His numerous regional titles include Spring NAC secondary Non-Mixed Pairs 1972, Summer Swiss Teams 1978, Golder Master Pairs 1978, New York Winter Open Pairs 1974, 1978, Swiss Teams 1976, Upper New York State KO Teams 1974, 1977, New England Individual KO Teams 1976, Summer Open Pairs 1979, Fall Open Pairs 1977, KO Teams, Swiss Teams 1978, Long Island Open Pairs 1978, District 3 KO Teams 1979, Bridge Week Mixed Pairs 1981, Los Angeles Winter Mixed Pairs 1981, District 25, Zone II 1977.

GRACE, Brian G. (1942) of Wichita KS, trial attorney, won Fall NAC secondary Commercial and Industrial Pairs 1963, Non-Life Master Men's Pairs 1964, Missouri Valley Open Teams 1964, Master Pairs 1973. He is a graduate of University of Kansas.

GRAFT, Larry W. (b. 1934) of Sacramento CA, ACBL tournament director, began directing in 1963 and in 1979 advanced to a Regional 4 rating. He served as president of the Sacramento Unit 1963–1965 and as a Board member of District 21 1964–1981. Graft is a former sales executive, rocket engine test cooordinator, and navigator in the U.S. Air Force. He is a 2-handicap golfer.

GRANOVETTER, Matthew (b. 1950) of New York City, bridge professional, pianist and composer, placed second in the World Mixed Teams 1974. He won Spring NAC Men's Teams 1975, 1982, Open Pairs 1972, and placed second in the Reisinger 1976, 1977. He played in the INVITATIONAL PAIR CHAMPION-

SHIP (formerly London *Sunday Times* Pairs) 1977, 1978, 1980, 1981, and was a member of the New York team that defeated the Lancia Team in 1975 (see LANCIA TOURNAMENTS). His regional titles number more than 35 including Summer NAC secondary Swiss Teams Flt. A 1977, Eastern States KO Teams (Reisinger) 1975, 1977, Puerto Rico Men's Pairs 1972, Swiss Teams 1972, 1974, 1977, 1978, Open Pairs, Master Pairs 1977, New York Winter Swiss Teams Flt. A 1978, 1981, District 4 Fall Open Pairs Flt. A 1981, Nat'l Capital Open Pairs Flt. A 1981. His first bridge article was printed in *The Declarer* and extensively quoted in the New York *Sunday Herald Tribune* in 1964; others have appeared in *The Bridge World* and *Popular Bridge*. One of the originators of the RELAY SYSTEM, he is the co-author of *The Ultimate Club*. In 1981 he appeared in 13 episodes of *Grand Slam* TV challenge match made for the BBC. Granovetter is a graduate of Hunter College. His interests include acting, theater, writing, directing, classics and cooking. See IBPA AWARDS, BIBLIOGRAPHY C.

GRANT, Richard G. (Dick) (b. 1942) of Zeballos BC, personnel supervisor, won Spring NAC secondary Swiss Teams 2nd Flt. 1974, Pacific Northwest Men's Pairs 1969, District 18 Open Pairs 1975, District 18 GNT 1974, 1976, Zone VII 1976. He is a former vice president and president of Unit 391.

GRANTHAM, John M. (b. 1944) of Amarillo TX, retail store owner, former commodity broker and professional bridge player, won the Blue Ribbon Pairs and the HERMAN TROPHY 1971. His more than 25 regional titles include Summer NAC secondary Swiss Teams 1974, Fall Swiss Teams 1974, Mount Shasta KO Teams, Swiss Teams 1972, Desert Empire Master Pairs 1972, Men's Pairs 1974, All-Western Men's Pairs 1972, Life Master Pairs 1973, Master Teams Flt. A 1975, Land of Coronado KO Teams 1974, 1976, Swiss Teams 1974, Gem State Mixed Pairs, Men's Pairs 1976, Bermuda Master Pairs 1981. Grantham was educated at Kansas University and West Texas State. He is the brother of BECKY ROGERS, national tournament director.

GRANTHAM, Robin. See LENT, ROBIN.

GRAVES, J(ames) Allan (b. 1949) of Vancouver BC, family counsellor, former educator, represented Canada in the World Team Olympiad 1980, World Open Pairs 1974, 1978. He placed second in the Reisinger 1978 and won Canadian National Teams 1980, 1981. His more than 30 regional wins include Summer NAC secondary Swiss Teams Flt. A 1978, Oregon Trail Swiss Teams 1975, KO Teams 1971, 1981, All-Western KO Teams, 1972, Master Teams 1973, British Columbia Men's Pairs, Open Pairs 1972, 1981, KO Teams 1977, Swiss Teams 1981.

GRAVES, S. Susan (b. 1942) of Indianapolis, biology teacher, won Mississippi Valley Open Pairs 1973, District 11 Master Pairs 1977, GNT 1978. She was the receipient of the Easley Blackwood Trophy (awarded to the Indiana player acquiring the most master points during a calendar year) in 1970.

GRAY, Charles (b. 1930) of Philadelphia, professional engineer and building contractor, won Keystone Master Pairs 1973, Mid-Atlantic Swiss Teams 1981, District 4 Open Pairs 1976, Men's Swiss Teams 1980, Swiss Teams Flt. A 1981. Gray has served in various executive positions in Philadelphia Unit 141 and District 4, and was co-chairman of the 1972 Fall NORTH AMERICAN CHAMPIONSHIPS. He is a charter member of the PROFESSIONAL TOURNAMENT DIRECTORS ASSOCIATION and has been directing since 1960. He was tournament director for the first OMAR SHARIF BRIDGE CIRCUS visit to Philadelphia in 1968 and organized the first knockout team event in Philadelphia bridge history, including a vugraph exhibition. He is a graduate of Drexel University.

GRAY, Maurice Harrison-. See HARRISON-GRAY, MAURICE.

GREEN, Farrell B. (1937) of Coon Rapids MN, comptroller, won Gopher Open Teams 1959, 1961, 1974, Open Pairs 1960, 1962, 1967, 1981, Mid-Am-Can Open Teams 1963.

GREENBERG, Byron L. (b. 1927) of Houston, restaurant club consultant, won Fall NAC Open Pairs 1953 and placed second in the Spingold 1972, Reisinger 1973. His many regional titles include Missouri Valley KO Teams 1971, 1974, 1975, 1976, Master Pairs 1976, Open Teams 1972, 1973, 1979, Houston Mid-Winter Master Swiss Teams Flt. A, Swiss Teams 1981, Toast of Tulsa KO Teams 1977, Swiss Teams 1979, District 15 KO Teams, Swiss Teams Flt. A 1980, Men's Pairs 1978, GNT 1974, 1978, Zone VI 1974.

GREENBERG, Julie T. (Bug) (Mrs. Steve) (b. 1938) of Memphis, ACBL Tournament Coordinator since 1978, is a former ACBL tournament director (1956–1978). She is the author of *Duplicate Decisions* and the monthly ACBL *Bulletin* feature "Ruling the Game." She was educated at Newcomb College and Tulane University.

GREENBERG, Nate (b. 1910) of Scottsdale AZ won Rocky Mountain KO Teams 1973, Navajo Trail KO Teams 1969, Men's Swiss Teams 1977, Open Pairs 1981.

GREENBERG, Steve N. (b. 1931) of Memphis, lease broker, won numerous regional titles including Fall NAC secondary Non-Master Pairs 1953, Mixed Pairs 1970, Missouri Valley KO Teams 1971, 1974, Open Teams 1972, Mid-South KO Teams 1974, 1975, 1978, Master Pairs 1974, Toast of Tulsa Swiss Teams 1979, Crescent City Mixed Pairs 1981, District 10 GNT, Zone IV 1979.

GREENE, Richard P. (b. 1910) of New Orleans, dentist, won Mid-South Open Teams 1944, 1948, 1960, 1963, Master Pairs 1963, 1964, Missouri Valley Master Pairs 1973. Greene was a charter member and second president of the Mid-South Conference and a past president of the Louisiana BA. He has served as chairman or co-chairman of many regionals and of five North American Championships held in New Orleans.

GREENHUT, Carol A. See SIMON, CAROL A..

GREER, Nancy J. (Mrs. James) (b. 1943) of Brewer ME, bookkeeper, won New England Masters Master Swiss Teams 1978, Can-At Mixed Pairs, Master Pairs 1978.

GREGORY, Stephen C. (b. 1947) of Sterling VA, attorney, won Mid-Atlantic Spring Open Pairs, Fall KO Teams 1972, 1973. He served as editor of the NVBA newsletter in 1979 and has been a contributing columnist since 1976, resuming as editor in 1982.

GRESHAM, Ralph W. (d. 1966) of East Orange NJ, Treasurer of AT&T, likewise served five years as treasurer of the ACBL and as a member of its Steering Committee during the crucial reorganization period of 1948–49.

GRESHAM, William Lindsay (1909–1962) of New Rochelle NY, noted American novelist, used the tarot pack as background material in his macabre story about carnival life, *Nightmare Alley*, from which an excerpt appears in *The Fireside Book of Cards*.

GRIEVE, William P. (Billy) (b. 1929) of White Plains NY, mathematician, one of the leading American players, represented the United States in the World Team Olympiad 1960. He won the Spingold 1959 (second in 1960, 1969), Reisinger 1969, 1970, 1971 (second in 1972), Summer NAC Mixed Teams 1960, Fall NAC Men's Pairs 1958, Spring NAC Men's Teams 1975. His numerous regional titles include Eastern States KO Teams (Reisinger) 1960, Mississippi Valley Open Teams 1951, New England KO Teams, Open Teams 1957, Mid-South Spring Open Teams 1960.

GRIFFEY, Larry R. (b. 1944) of Jacksonville FL, statistics professor, won Southeastern Open Pairs 1971, Florida Swiss Teams 1974, 1976, 1981, Mixed Pairs 1974, Mid-Atlantic Summer Swiss Teams 1974, Fall Swiss Teams 1974, District 9 GNT 1977, 1979.

GRIFFIN, Edward F. (b. 1947) of Sydney, Australia, solicitor, was Far East Pairs champion 1972 and also represented Australia in the Far East Championships 1972, 1973, 1974. His national successes include the McCutcheon Trophy in 1973, awarded for the highest number of master points earned in a calendar year.

GRIFFIN, Estee (b. 1931) of New York City, system manager, won Eastern States Mixed Teams 1961, Fun City KO Teams 1971, Long Island KO Teams 1968, New York Winter Life Master Pairs 1975, Tri-State Swiss Teams 1980. She has served as tournament chairman, vice president and president of the Greater New York BA and is the former assistant editor of *The Bridge World*, associate editor of *Post*

Mortem, and promotion director of *The Bridge Journal*.

GRIFFIN, Thomas C. (b. 1936) of New York City, social worker, placed second in Summer NAC Senior and Advanced Senior Master Pairs 1959. His regional titles include Fun City KO Teams 1971, New York-New Jersey Open Pairs 1967, Open Teams 1970, New England Winter Open Teams 1968, Long Island KO Teams 1968. He has served the Greater New York BA in various executive positions. Griffin is a former associate editor of *The Contract Bridge Bulletin* and *The Bridge Journal*.

GRIGG, Claire. See LESTER, CLAIRE.

GRIGGS, Eloene T. of Washington DC, bridge teacher, former club owner and director, is general secretary of the IBPA and has served in many executive positions in the ABTA, including president, and is on the editorial staff of the *ABTA Quarterly*. She organized many service-connected women's clubs and has been a member of the National Council of Women since 1954. She is listed in *Who's Who of American Women*, *World's Who's Who of Women* and several other biographical dictionaries.

GRISCOM, Dr. John H. (b. 1929) of Nashville, physician, won Mid-Atlantic Open Pairs 1976, Men's Pairs 1980, 1981, Midwest Fall Open Pairs Flt. A 1978, Opryland KO Teams 1981, District 10 GNT, Zone III 1981.

GRONER, Alexander (Alex) (b. 1914) of Poway CA, president of a corporate journalism company, was a former editorial writer for the *Cleveland Press*, correspondent for *Time*, *Life*, and *Fortune*. He is the creator of duplicate movements for Swiss pairs and Multiple teams of multiple pairs which are described in his book *Duplicate Bridge Direction*. See BIBLIOGRAPHY, F.

GRONER, Edward L. (Ed) (b. 1929) of Duncan OK, product manager, won Big D Men's Swiss Teams 1974, Toast of Tulsa Master Pairs 1977, Missouri Valley Swiss Teams 1979.

GROSS, Saul K. (b. 1954) of New York City, attorney, won Upper New York State Swiss Teams 1975, Keystone Spring Master Pairs 1976, Nassau-Suffolk Open Pairs 1977, Intercollegiate Championship 1979, District 4 Fall Swiss Teams 1979.

GROSS, William M. (Bill) (b. 1930) of Harrisburg PA, attorney, ACBL president in 1983, has served as ACBL Board member from District 4 since 1972 and is a former member of the ACBL Board of Governors. He is past president of District 4, Central Penn Unit and the Harrisburg Bridge Club. Gross was co-chairman of the Fall North American Championships in Lancaster PA in 1972 and 1980. A former bridge columnist, he wrote regularly for the Harrisburg *Sunday Patriot-News*. Gross is a graduate of University of Pennsylvania and Harvard Law School. Past president of the American Lung Association, he currently is a member of its National Board of Directors. His interests include college football, white-water rafting, and computers.

GRUENTHER, General Alfred M. (1899–1983) of Washington DC, a recognized authority on duplicate contract bridge and the outstanding director of bridge tournaments in America in the Thirties, acted as chief referee in the CULBERTSON-LENZ MATCH 1931–1932. He authored *Duplicate Bridge Simplified*, *Duplicate Bridge Guide*, and *Duplicate Contract Complete*, and was one of the authors of *Famous Hands of the Culbertson–Lenz Match*. He was Honorary president of the WORLD BRIDGE FEDERATION since its inception in 1958 until he resigned from all bridge activities in 1978. Gruenther was awarded the WETZLAR TROPHY 1938, 1944 and was named ACBL Honorary Member in 1944. He was a charter member of the ACBL Laws Commission and its Honorary Member 1948–1978, chairman of the ACBL Charity Foundation 1964–1965 and a former member of the Editorial Advisory Board of *Bridge Encyclopedia*.

Gruenther served 38 years in the U.S. Army; his final military assignment was Supreme Commander, Allied Powers, Europe, 1953–1956. He retired December 31, 1956, and from 1957 to 1964 was president of the American Red Cross, serving with particular devotion and special interest in its youth program. Besides awards from other countries for International Red Cross league activities (nine Red Cross Societies), he had been decorated by fourteen governments other than the United States. He was the recipient of the Distinguished Service Medal with two Oak Leaf cluster, and the Legion of Merit from this country. He had honorary degrees from 31 American colleges and universities. See EISENHOWER, DWIGHT D. and BIBLIOGRAPHY, F.

GRUVER, Nancy G. (b. 1931) of Ellicott City MD, one of the leading American women players, placed second in the World Women's Pairs 1966, Venice Trophy 1981. She also represented the United States in the World Women's Teams 1968, 1978, 1982. She won Spring NAC Women's Pairs 1965, Women's Teams 1966, 1973, 1978, 1980, Summer NAC Master Mixed Teams 1975, (second in 1969), Fall NAC Mixed Pairs 1977, (second in 1976), Life Master Women's Pairs 1967, 1979, 1981 (second in 1980). Her numerous regional titles include Spring NAC secondary Swiss Teams 2nd Flt. 1976, District 4 Fall Women's Pairs 1965, 1978, Women's Swiss Teams 1979, Keystone Women's Pairs 1966, 1973, Women's Teams 1971, 1973, Mid-Atlantic Master Pairs 1975, Women's Swiss Teams 1980. She is a graduate of University of Maryland and a former elementary school teacher. A past president of the Women's BL of Maryland and Board member of the Maryland BL, she has served as co-chairman of the NAC Appeals Committee since 1975 and was elected to the ACBL Laws Commission 1982.

GUAGLIARDO, Matthew T. (Matt) (b. 1945) of Fresno, financial management advisor and portfolio manager, won California Capital Swiss Teams 1971. He was chairman of the 1980 Spring NORTH AMERI-

CAN CHAMPIONSHIPS held in Fresno and the driving force behind its success. He has also served as chairman and hospitality chairman of several regionals. He is the creator and co-producer of many novel bridge hospitality functions including *The Bridge Gong Show, Bridge Anagram-Antics, Dr. N. T. Lausuun* (comic strip), *Bridge All-Star Challenge, ACBL Celebrity Squares,* and *Vugraph Individual.* Guagliardo is a member of the ACBL Charity Committee and the ACBL Goodwill Committee. He has served in various executive positions in his Unit and in District 22, including president of District 22 1980, 1981. He has edited many regional *Daily Bulletins* on the West Coast, edited the Fresno Unit publication and District 22 news for the *Contract Bridge Forum,* and has contributed to the ACBL *Bulletin.* He is the founder and executive director of the PROFESSIONAL BRIDGE ASSOCIATION. In 1976 he was honored by the City of Fresno and named to the "Ambassadors Club" for "contribution of time and self" in promoting Fresno as a convention site.

GUDJOHNSEN, Stefán (b. 1931) of Gardabae, Iceland, managing director, represented Iceland in the World Team Olympiad 1968, 1976, European Championships 1958, 1961, 1963, 1967, 1969, 1971, 1973, 1977. His national titles include Iceland Open Teams 1956, 1958, 1959, 1960, 1961, 1963, 1964, 1966, 1967, 1969, 1974, 1981, Open Pairs 1959. He served as chairman and treasurer of Bridgefélag Reykjavikur for many years and has written bridge columns in *Vísir* for 25 years.

GUDMUNDSSON, Gunnar (b. 1920) of Reykjavik, Iceland, banker, represented Europe in the Bermuda Bowl 1950 and represented Iceland in the World Team Olympiad 1960, European Championships 1950, 1951, 1956, 1961. His national titles include Icelandic Open Teams 1953, 1954, 1957, 1962, 1965, 1973, Open Pairs 1955.

GUERIN, Donald H. (b. 1942) of Sacramento CA, real estate appraiser, placed second in Summer NAC Senior and Advanced Senior Master Pairs 1965 and won District 11 Men's Pairs 1966, Las Vegas Swiss Teams 1974, California Capital KO Teams 1976, Golden State Master Pairs 1973, Los Angeles Winter Swiss Teams 1974, District 22 KO Teams 1972, Master Pairs 1974, All-Western Master Pairs 1980.

GUIVER, Harold B. (Squeezer) (b. 1925) of Long Beach CA, formerly of New Orleans, mortgage company co-owner, one of the leading players of the West Coast, won the Chicago (now the Reisinger) 1962, Spring NAC Men's Teams 1962, Fall NAC Men's Teams 1962, and placed second in the Chicago 1961, Vanderbilt 1961, 1963, Spring NAC Men's Teams 1974, Spingold 1975. His numerous regional titles include Fall NAC secondary Men's Teams 1972, Swiss Teams 1979, 1981, All-Western Open Teams 1959, 1964, Master Pairs 1971, Bridge Week Master Pairs 1962, 1977, KO Teams 1967, 1977, Men's Pairs 1972, Los Angeles Winter KO Teams 1974, 1977, Southeastern Swiss Teams 1981. Guiver is a graduate of University of Southern California and was a member of its NCAA tennis

championship team. His special outside interest is football. Formerly he was vice president of the Los Angeles Rams and assistant general manager of the New Orleans Saints. He was named Contract Negotiator of the Year in 1980 by Sports Illustrated for his role as an agent representing professional football players.

GULLBERG, Tommy S. (b. 1943) of Solna, Sweden, bridge teacher, was European Junior team champion 1968. He also represented Sweden in the World Team Olympiad 1972, 1975, 1980, World Open Pairs 1974, European Championships 1981. He served as chairman of the Swedish Tournament Committee 1971–1973 and was a member of the Youth Committee 1973–1976. He is the author of a teaching book for the SWEDISH BRIDGE LEAGUE, and is a contributor and former editor of the SWL publication.

GUMBY, Pauline (b. 1949) of Mosman, Australia, computer programmer, former mathematics teacher, represented Australia in the Far East Women's Championships 1979, World Women's Teams 1980, Venice Trophy 1981.

GUNATILAKA, Pitswong (b. 1911) of Bangkok, Thailand, tournament director and bridge teacher, represented Thailand in the World Team Olympiad 1972, Far East Championships 1969, 1970, 1971, 1974. His national successes include all major tournament titles. He directs tournaments held in Bangkok including the 1966 Far East Championships. Gunatilaka is the first and only professional bridge instructor in Thailand. Author of *New Bangkok System,* he is the former advisor to Thammasart University bridge magazine.

GUOBA, John M. (b. 1949) of Toronto, attorney, won Canadian Nat'l Open Pairs 1972, KO Teams 1976, Men's Swiss Teams 1978, Motor City Swiss Teams 1975, District 2 GNT 1979, Zonal 1979, 1981.

GUPTA, Subhash (b. 1947) of Calgary AB, born in India, mechanical engineer, won Klondike Swiss Teams Flt. A 1978, Swiss Teams 1980, Buffalo Swiss Teams, Master Pairs 1980, District 18 GNT 1979, Zone VII 1979, Canadian National Team Zone 5 1981.

GURVICH, Louis S. (b. 1921) of Metairie LA, was president of the ACBL in 1977. He was chairman of the Board in 1978, chairman of the Board of Governors 1967–1971 and served on many committees prior to his presidency, including the committee that approved and defined the present day convention chart and convention card. He was general chairman of the 1978 World Olympiad in New Orleans, a member of the WBF executive committee 1977, and chairman of the rules committee 1977, 1979, co-chairman in 1978. Gurvich is a former president of the Mid-South Conference and the Louisiana BA. He represented the United States in the World Mixed Teams 1974. He placed second in Summer NAC Mixed Teams 1961 and won Mid-South Spring Open Pairs 1958, Open Teams 1962, 1965, 1967, 1973, KO

Teams 1973, Mid-South Summer Men's Pairs 1962, Mixed Pairs 1962, 1965, Bermuda Swiss Teams 1977. Gurvich is a graduate of Louisiana State University. He is president of a guard and detective agency employing 300 men both nationally and internationally. His interests include numismatics, philately, travel and tennis.

GURWITZ, Michael L. (b. 1947) of San Francisco, tax attorney, won New England KO Teams 1972, New York-New Jersey Swiss Teams 1973, Bridge Week KO Teams 1974, Puget Sound KO Teams 1974 Mount Shasta KO Teams 1974, Gem State Swiss Teams 1974, All-Western KO Teams 1975, Life Master BAM Teams 1976, California Capital Master Swiss Teams 1977.

GUTOWSKY, Ace Jr. (1909–1976) of Oklahoma City won acclaim both as a bridge player and as a football star. On the gridiron Gutowsky played professionally from 1931 to 1938, and was fullback for the Detroit Lions when they won the world championship in 1935. After his retirement from football he worked as an aircraft sales representative. His bridge victories came in the Fifties and included Spring NAC Men's Teams in 1951. Ace was his given name.

GWOZDZINSKY, Margie (The Countess) of New York City, born in Gliwice, Poland, systems analyst, won Fall NAC secondary Women's Pairs 1971, Long Island Women's Pairs 1972, Washington Bridge Week Women's Pairs 1976, Eastern States Women's Pairs 1976, District 4 Fall Open Pairs 1981. She is a graduate of City College of New York.

H

HAAS, Bunny of Atlanta, attorney and real estate broker, won 10 regionals including Golden State Mixed Pairs 1976, Mid-Winter Holiday Women's Pairs 1976, Emerald Empire Mixed Pairs 1977, Raincross Women's Pairs 1978, Swiss Teams 1980, Hawaii KO Teams 1980, Mid-Atlantic KO Teams 1981.

HABERMAN, Barbara (Bari) (Mrs. Sigmund, formerly Rappaport) (b. 1935) of New York City, options trader, former English teacher, one of the leading American women players, won the FISHBEIN TROPHY 1971, Life Master Pairs 1971, 1972, Fall NAC Life Master Women's Pairs 1977, and placed second in Spring NAC Women's Teams 1969, 1971, Women's Pairs 1978, Summer Master Mixed Teams 1966, 1974, 1975, Fall Life Master Women's Pairs 1974. Her numerous regional titles include Spring NAC secondary Open Pairs 1971, Swiss Teams 1978, Swiss Teams 2nd Flt. 1976, Summer Women's Pairs 1971, Fall Mixed Pairs 1972, Eastern States KO Teams (Reisinger) 1966, 1968, 1975, Open Pairs (Goldman) 1977, 1978, 1979, Women's Pairs 1979, Tri-State Winter Swiss Teams 1971, Women's Pairs 1973, Open Pairs 1974, Women's Swiss Teams 1979. After sweeping the pairs events in a sectional tournament, she was named honorary Men's Pairs cham-

pion, so that her record would not be flawed.

HABICHT, Velma J. (Val) of Fort Lauderdale FL, formerly of Wakefield MA, won Summer NAC secondary Swiss Teams 1981, Tri-State Women's Pairs, Mixed Pairs 1971, New England Individual 1972.

HACKETT, Paul D. (b. 1941) of Manchester, England, bridge club co-owner, former bridge professional, represented Great Britain in the World Team Olympiad 1976, Bermuda Bowl 1981. He placed second in the Common Market Pairs 1981. He won the National Masters and has won or been second in every major British event. He is the author of *Bridge for Beginners and Intermediate Players* and contributes articles to *Popular Bridge Monthly*.

HADDAD, Betty (formerly Windley) (b. 1924) of Arlington VA, painter, represented the United States in the World Women's Pairs 1962. She won Fall NAC Mixed Pairs 1954, Summer NAC Women's Pairs 1961, Keystone Conference Mixed Pairs 1963, Open Teams 1956, 1961, Southeastern Open Teams 1965.

HADDAD, Louis J. (b. 1900) presided over the ACBL in 1935. A Chicago insurance counselor, born in Iowa, he won many auction bridge events 1928–1932 and the HILLIARD TROPHY in 1935.

HADDAD, Said (b. 1916) of Bal Harbour FL, contractor, won Fall NAC Mixed Pairs 1954, Spring NAC secondary Individual 1956, Eastern States Men's Pairs 1960, Keystone Conference Open Teams 1951, 1956, Mixed Pairs 1963, Southeastern Open Pairs 1962, Open Teams 1965. He is a former director and treasurer of the Washington BL.

HADDEN, Lt. Col. David A. (b. 1944) of Waldorf MD, bioenvironmental engineer, won Spring NAC Men's Pairs 1973, Mid-South Master Swiss Teams 1975.

HAFFNER, Judy (b. 1940) of Pittsburgh won District 5 KO Teams 1978, Women's Swiss Teams 1981, All-American Swiss Teams Flt. A 1981.

HAGEDORN, Barry H. (b. 1935) of Houston, business executive, won Fall NAC secondary Open Pairs 1974, Men's Swiss Teams 1977, Summer Commercial and Industrial Teams 1978, 1979, 1980, 1981, Republic of Texas KO Teams 1970, Open Pairs 1978, Texas Fall Master Pairs, Men's Pairs 1969, KO Teams 1971, Master Swiss Teams 1979, Summer Open Pairs 1971, KO Teams 1978, Big D Swiss Teams 1972. Hagedorn served as entertainment chairman of the 1970 Houston Fall NAC and as co-chairman of the 1978 Houston Spring NAC, as well as various executive positions in Unit 174 and District 16. He has contributed a series to the Texas bridge publication *Scorecard*.

HAGEDORN, Mimi S. (Mrs. Barry H.) (b. 1935) of Houston, bridge cruise director, won Summer NAC secondary Commercial and Industrial Teams 1978, 1979, 1980, 1981, Texas Fall Mixed Pairs 1971.

HAGEN, Fred J. (b. 1914) of Seattle, company president, won Pacific Northwest KO Teams 1969, Peach Festival Men's Pairs 1974, Puget Sound Men's Swiss Teams, Swiss Teams 1977, Oregon Trail Swiss Teams 1978.

HAGEN, Paul W. of Vancouver BC, consulting programmer, won Klondike Swiss Teams 1974, District 17 Fall KO Teams 1976, British Columbia Swiss Teams Flt. A 1979, District 19 GNT 1974, 1975, Canadian National Teams Zone 6 1981.

HAHN, Charlotte K. (b. 1935) of Riviera Beach MD, bridge club manager and director, won Summer NAC secondary Women's Pairs 1975, Mid-Winter Holiday Women's Pairs 1976, Canadian Nat'l Women's Pairs 1977, District 5 Women's Pairs 1977, Mid-Atlantic Swiss Teams 1978.

HALE, William J. (Bill) (b. 1946) of Haskins OH, school principal, club owner and director, won several regional titles including Midwest Fall Swiss Teams 1974, Great Lakes Open Pairs 1978, Champagne Master Pairs 1979, Southeastern Individual 1975, District 5 Open Pairs Flt. A, Swiss Teams Flt. A 1981, Motor City Swiss Teams Flt. A 1981, Veterans Day Swiss Teams Flt. A 1981, Wolverine Master Swiss Teams 1981, District 12 GNT 1980, 1981, Zone IV 1980, 1981.

HALL, James M. (Jim) (b. 1940) of Minneapolis, insurance salesman, won numerous regional titles including Gopher KO Teams, Swiss Teams 1969, Men's Pairs 1973, 1981, Iowa Swiss Teams, 1973, 1974 1979, Men's Pairs 1974, KO Teams 1975, 1979, Roughrider KO Teams 1977, 1981, Swiss Teams 1981, Pheasant Open Pairs 1972, 1978, Mad City Open Pairs Flt. A 1979, Wisconsin Men's KO Teams, Open Pairs Flt. A 1981, Thunder Bay KO Teams 1981, District 14 GNT 1975, 1980.

HALL, Jeffrey M. (Jeff) (b. 1951) of Schenectady NY, computer programmer, won the Grand National Pairs 1980 and placed second in Summer NAC Senior and Advanced Senior Master Pairs 1972. His regional titles include District 4 Swiss Teams 1977, William Keohane Individual KO Teams 1981, District 3 Men's Swiss Teams 1981, Autumn Leaf Swiss Teams Flt. A 1981, District 3 GNP 1981.

HALLE, Diana K. (b. 1924) of Boca Raton FL, lawyer, won Fall NAC Amateur Women's Pairs 1976. She is a graduate of Cornell University.

HALLE, Ranik (b. 1905) of Oslo, Norway, editor and bridge columnist, represented Norway in the European Championships 10 times, placing second in 1938. He won 12 national championships. He was president of the INTERNATIONAL BRIDGE PRESS ASSOCIATION 1960-1964, and honorary member and former president of the NORWEGIAN BRIDGE ASSOCIATION. Halle is a former member of the Editorial Advisory Board, *Bridge Encyclopedia*.

HALLEE, Gerald F. (Jerry) of Bothell WA, computer systems analyst, designer and programmer,

won the Vanderbilt 1969, Senior/Advanced Senior Master Pairs 1963 and placed second in Spring NAC Men's Pairs 1969. His regional titles include Rocky Mountain Master Pairs 1964, Bridge Week Master Men's Pairs 1967, KO Teams 1969, 1970, Golden State Open Pairs 1968.

HALLÈN, Hans-Olof (b. 1929) of Malmö, Sweden, bridge consultant, was Swedish team champion and Nordic champion in 1964. Senior director of the EUROPEAN BRIDGE LEAGUE, Hallen began directing in 1950 and has directed at international championships since 1970. He has contributed articles to *Sydsvenska Dagbladet* and *Modern Bridge*. He was awarded the EBL Honor Medal in 1981.

HALLER, Gert F. of Boise ID, formerly of Baker OR, retired rancher, won Fall NAC secondary Swiss Teams 1971, Oregon Trail Master Pairs 1970, Klondike Mixed Pairs 1972.

HALLER, Robert H. (Bob) (b. 1909) of Baker OR, retired mining engineer and cattle rancher, won Fall NAC secondary Swiss Teams 1971, Oregon Trail Master Pairs 1970, Klondike Mixed Pairs 1972.

HALLORAN, Julia S. (b. 1928) of Wooster OH, writer, won Midwest Women's Pairs 1957, Motor City Women's Pairs 1970, 1971, District 5 Women's Swiss Teams 1978, All-American Women's Swiss Teams 1981.

HALPERIN, Richard M. (b. 1940) of Skokie IL, real estate broker, won Summer NAC secondary Swiss Teams 1980, Great Lakes Open Pairs 1972, Men's Pairs 1963, Florida KO Teams 1970, Champagne Open Pairs 1975, KO Teams 1976, Southeastern Men's Swiss Teams 1976, Mississippi Valley Open Pairs 1976, Midwest Fall Swiss Teams 1977. He is a former editor of *The Kibitzer*. He is known as the "Wizard of Odds" for his facility to calculate odds instantaneously on almost any event.

HALPERIN, Sue A. (Mrs. Richard) (b. 1938) of Skokie IL placed second in Spring NAC Women's Teams 1978, 1979, 1981. Her numerous regional titles include Summer NAC secondary Swiss Teams 1979, Florida KO Teams 1970, Central States I Master Pairs 1970, Women's Pairs 1974, II Women's Swiss Teams 1977, 1979, Women's Pairs 1978, Swiss Teams 1977, Open Pairs 1980, Wisconsin Women's Swiss Teams 1976, 1978, Women's Pairs 1980, Champagne Women's Swiss Teams 1979, Motor City Women's Swiss Teams 1981, Wolverine Swiss Teams 1981, District 8 Summer Women's Swiss Teams 1981. She is the secretary of the Chicago CBA. A graduate of Michigan State University, she is a former teacher of the blind.

HALPIN, Robert (1896-1972) of Chicago, a printing company president, was one of the founding fathers of the ABL and presided over that body in 1929. That same year he won the Chicago Trophy (since 1965 the Reisinger).

HAMAOUI, Steve (b. 1954) of Caracas, Venezuela,

born in Cairo, Egypt, manager, represented Venezuela and Central America–Caribbean in the World Open Pairs 1978, 1983, Bermuda Bowl 1979, South American Championships 1976, 1978. He won the CAC Championships 1977 and placed second in the South American Championships 1978. His national titles include Open Pairs, Mixed Pairs, Open Teams, Mixed Teams.

HAMILTON, Frederick (Fred) (b. 1936) of North Lauderdale FL, professional bridge player and teacher, one of the world's leading players, was Bermuda Bowl champion 1976 and placed second in 1977, and in the World Team Olympiad 1980. He also represented the United States in the World Team Olympiad 1976, World Open Pairs 1977, 1982, Rosenblum Cup Teams 1978, 1982. He won the HERMAN TROPHY 1974, Reisinger 1974, 1975, 1978, 1979, Vanderbilt 1977, Spingold 1979, Summer NAC Master Mixed Teams 1976, Team Trials 1975, 1979. He placed second in the Vanderbilt 1972, 1981, Spingold 1981, Reisinger 1981, Spring NAC Men's Teams 1980, Grand National Teams 1974. His scores of regional titles include Spring NAC secondary Master Pairs 1974, Open BAM Swiss Teams 1978, Fall Men's Swiss Teams 1980, Master Pairs 1972. In 1982 he won the Cavendish Club Invitational Pair Championship. Hamilton passed the 10,000 masterpoint mark in 1978 and became a WBF Grand Master in 1981.

HAMILTON, James J. (Jim) (1937) of Wallingford CT, travel representative, won several regional titles including Spring NAC secondary Swiss Teams 1978, District 3 Men's Pairs 1978, Men's Swiss Teams 1979, 1980, Master Pairs 1979, Puerto Rico Master Pairs 1978, Men's Pairs 1979, Southeastern Men's Pairs 1980, Open Pairs 1981, Long Island Men's Pairs 1979, Swiss Teams Flt. A 1980, Thunder Bay Swiss Teams Flt. A 1981.

HAMILTON, John T. (Buckeye) (b. 1933) of Columbus OH, ACBL national tournament director, has been director-in-charge at NORTH AMERICAN CHAMPIONSHIPS since 1976. He began directing full-time in 1965 and three years later was elevated to the rating of national director. He won Mid-Atlantic Men's Pairs 1975, Spring NAC secondary Swiss Teams 2nd Flt. 1965. Treasurer of PROFESSIONAL TOURNAMENT DIRECTORS ASSOCIATION since 1970, Hamilton has also served as director of the Miami Valley BA 1960–1966, treasurer of the Central Ohio BA 1966–1969, and vice president of the Midwest Conference 1967–1968. With MARC LOW he contributed to the SWISS TEAM MOVEMENT. A Rhodes Scholar, Hamilton was educated at the U.S. Military Academy at West Point (where he stood second in his class), Balliol College, Oxford, England and Ohio State University.

HAMILTON, Margie A. (Mrs. Fred) (b. 1954) of North Lauderdale FL, won California Capital Master Pairs 1977, Los Angeles Winter Master Swiss Teams 1977, Raincross Mixed Pairs 1978.

HAMMAN, Barbara R. (b. 1937) of Los Angeles,

medical lab technician, won Spring NAC secondary Mixed Pairs Flt. A 1980, Republic of Texas Swiss Teams 1973, Palm Springs KO Teams 1973, Big D Women's Swiss Teams 1974, Navajo Trail Swiss Teams 1975.

HAMMAN, Robert D. (Bob) (b. 1938) of Dallas, insurance agent and professional bridge player, WBF Grand Master #6 (the top American), one of the world's great players, won the World Open Pairs 1974, Pan American Invitational Pairs 1974, 1976, 1977, Bermuda Bowl 1970, 1971, 1977, placed second in 1966, 1973, 1974, 1975, and in the World Team Olympiad 1964, 1972, 1980. He also represented North America in the Bermuda Bowl 1966, 1969, World Open Pairs 1970, 1978, Rosenblum Cup Teams 1978, and won the Teams Trials 1969, 1971, 1973, 1977, 1979. He won the Vanderbilt 1964, 1966, 1971, 1973 (second in 1968, 1970, 1981), Spingold 1969, 1979, 1982 (second in 1970), Reisinger 1962, 1970, 1978, 1979, (second in 1968), Grand National Teams 1975, 1977, Blue Ribbon Pairs 1964, Life Master Pairs 1980, Spring NAC Men's Teams 1969 (second in 1980), FISHBEIN TROPHY 1969, HERMAN TROPHY 1978, and placed second in Fall NAC Life Master Men's Pairs 1980, 1981. Hamman has won scores of regional titles which include Summer NAC secondary Men's Pairs 1975, Spring Mixed Pairs Flt. A 1980, Fall Commercial and Industrial Pairs 1959. His interests include backgammon and sports. See ACES TEAM and GRAND MASTER.

HAMMEL, Alma. See SPRECKELS, ALMA.

HAMMERICH, Johannes J. J. (b. 1919) of Caracas, Venezuela, born in Denmark, lawyer and business executive, represented Venezuela in the World Team Olympiad 1960, World Open Pairs 1966, 1974, South American Championships 1971, Central American–Caribbean Zonal Championships 1970, 1971, and was npc of the Venezuelan National Team 1957-1962, Olympiad Team 1964. His national wins include Open Teams four times, Open Pairs three Times and Mixed Teams twice. Hammerich is co-founder of the VENEZUELAN BRIDGE FEDERATION and its vice president 1960–1978. He also served as secretary-general of the SOUTH AMERICAN BRIDGE CONFEDERATION 1962–1969, as a member of the Executive Council of the WORLD BRIDGE FEDERATION 1962–1978, its assistant secretary 1964–1968, and 1st vice president 1968–1978. He is honorary member of several bridge associations and societies.

HAMMOND, Thomas E. (b. 1933) of Redmond WA, consulting structural engineer, won Puget Sound KO Teams 1969, Men's Swiss Teams 1976, Yakima Valley Open Pairs 1972, Klondike Swiss Teams 1976, District 19 GNT 1977, 1979. He served the Seattle Unit as a Board member, vice president, and editor of its publication.

HAMUI, Jose J. (Johnny) (b. 1935) of Mexico City, company president and director, represented Mexico in the World Team Olympiad 1976, 1978, MAC-

CABIAH GAMES 1977. He won Summer NAC Master Mixed Teams 1980, Spring NAC secondary Swiss Teams Flt. A 1980, District 16 KO Teams 1981, Mexican Nat'l Swiss Teams 1978. Hamui is president of the Mexican Bridge Unit and treasurer of the MEXICAN BRIDGE FEDERATION. He was Jai-Alai champion 1955, 1958, 1962, 1966 and a member of the Mexican Jai-Alai Olympic Team 1968.

HANCOCK, John H. (Jack) (b. 1923) of Deming NM, formerly of San Francisco, mathematician, won Spring NAC Mixed Teams and placed second in the Vanderbilt 1951. His regional wins include Spring NAC secondary Mixed Pairs 1956, Bridge Week Mixed Pairs 1956, Open Teams 1961, Pacific Southwest Men's Pairs, Open Pairs 1947, Palm Springs KO Teams 1967, Golden Gate Master Pairs 1967, 1968, Open Pairs 1967, Open Teams 1968.

HANDELSMAN, Lewis N. (Lew) (b. 1948) of Malverne NY, management consultant, won more than 10 regionals including Summer NAC secondary Men's Pairs Flt. A 1977, Tri-State Men's Swiss Teams 1978, Swiss Teams 1979, Washington Bridge Week Swiss Teams 1977, Acapulco Fiesta Open Pairs 1980, Mexican Nat'l Swiss Teams 1981, Long Island Open Pairs 1981.

HANN, Gary S. of Ann Arbor MI, formerly of New York City, real estate investment counselor, placed second in Spring NAC Men's Teams 1979 and won Great Lakes Swiss Teams 1971, Open Pairs 1974, Master Pairs 1975, Men's Swiss Teams 1979, Mid-Atlantic KO Teams, Men's Swiss Teams, Men's Pairs, Swiss Teams 1977, Master Pairs, Swiss Teams 1978, District 5 KO Teams 1977, 1979, Wolverine Men's Swiss Teams 1977, KO Teams 1978, Midwest Spring Non-Mixed Pairs, Swiss Teams 1978, Champagne KO Teams 1979. He served as a Board member of the Michigan BA 1979–1980 and was a contributing editor to its publication, *Table Talk* 1971–1975, was a member of the ACBL Board of Governors 1978–1981, and was ACBL 2nd Alternate Director from District 12 in 1981.

HANNA, William J. (Bill) (b. 1931) of Bethesda MD, one of the leading players on the West Coast until he retired from active play in 1961, represented the United States in the World Team Olympiad 1960. He won the Spingold 1958, Chicago (since 1965 the Reisinger) 1960. His numerous regional titles include Mississippi Valley Open Teams 1956, Rocky Mountain Open Pairs 1953, Men's Pairs 1953, 1954, Pacific Southwest Master Pairs 1955, Open Teams 1951, 1954, Men's Pairs 1954, 1956. Hanna contributed many bridge articles to various publications including *Bridge World*, and wrote the monthly column *Western Dateline* for the ACBL *Bulletin*. He co-authored *Precision Power Bidding* and the BULLDOG SYSTEM (see BIBLIOGRAPHY, C). A graduate of UCLA, Hanna formerly taught at University of Texas, City University of New York, Michigan State University, and The American University. He is currently professor of Community Development and Co-Director of the Center for Family, Housing, and the Community at University

of Maryland, College Park, and editor of the international journal, *Comparative Urban Research*.

HANSEN, Carl S. (b. 1928) of Burlington WA, storage and moving company owner, won Puget Sound KO Teams 1968, 1969, Inter-Mountain Open Pairs 1967, Tri-Cities Open Pairs 1975, Klondike Swiss Teams 1976, Emerald Empire Open Pairs 1977, District 19 GNT 1977.

HANSON, Keith V. of Edina MN, physical education teacher, won Summer NAC secondary Swiss Teams 1971, Central States I Men's Pairs 1972, Champagne Men's Pairs 1971, Iowa Open Pairs, Swiss Teams 1979, Non-Mixed Pairs 1976, Gopher Master Pairs 1972, KO Teams 1979, 1980, Open Pairs Flt. A 1980, District 14 GNT 1973. Hanson teaches bridge and directs club games and formerly taught college bridge classes for credit.

HARARI, Victor (b. 1914) of Buenos Aires, Argentina, born in Argentina, textile representative, won Argentine Open Teams 1939, Open Pairs 1970, Mixed Teams 1962, Interclubs 1940, 1981.

HARBIN, Rodger V. (b. 1942) of Culver City CA, won Fall NAC secondary Swiss Teams 1981, Mid-Winter Holiday Men's Pairs 1976, Swiss Teams 1978, District 23 GNP 1979.

HARDY, Mary E. (Mrs. Max, formerly Senti) of Hawthorne CA won Spring NAC secondary Open Pairs Flt A 1977, Rocky Mountain Women's Pairs 1969, Open Teams 1971, Desert Empire Unmixed Pairs 1981, Hawaii Mixed Pairs 1981.

HARDY, Max L. (1932) of Hawthorne CA, ACBL associate national tournament director, bridge teacher, writer and publisher, won more than 25 regional events including Fall NAC secondary Swiss Teams Flt. B 1980, Summer Swiss Teams 2nd Flt. 1976, Intermountain Men's Pairs, Open Pairs, Swiss Teams 1977, Hawaii Men's Swiss Teams 1977, Men's Pairs 1978, KO Teams 1979, 1980, Mixed Pairs 1981, Mid-Winter Holiday Swiss Teams 1979, Swiss Teams Flt. A 1980, Mexican Nat'l Swiss Teams 1977, 1981, Mount Shasta Master Swiss Teams 1978, Swiss Teams 1981, and seven additional knockout events. Hardy has been a tournament director since 1961 and was assigned the rating of associate national in 1973. The author of *Five Card Majors— Western Style*, which went through four printings, he has now released a follow-up book *Two over One Game Force*. Co-author of *Play My Card*, Hardy has contributed articles to every U.S. bridge publication, is an associate editor of *Popular Bridge*, and was the founding editor of *Southern California Bridge News*. One of the leading publishers of bridge books, he currently has 15 books in print and another 10 awaiting publication. He has served as vice president of Inglewood Unit, editor of its publication, and as 1st vice president of District 23. Hardy is a graduate of Chicago Musical College of Roosevelt University and a former composer, conductor, singer and music teacher. His interests include word games and sports. See BIBLI-OGRAPHY, C.

HARGROVE, R. Clyde (b. 1918) of Shreveport LA, lawyer, won Texas Mid-Winter Men's Pairs 1973, Mid-South KO Teams, Master Swiss Teams 1980.

HARKAVY, Harold (1915–1965), Miami Beach bridge club manager, gained national renown as a player. Harkavy, a native New Yorker, was one of the world's greatest at declarer play, and a brilliant though unorthodox bidder. He won Summer NAC Master Mixed Teams 1952, 1953, 1955, 1957, (second in 1947, 1964), Chicago (since 1965 the Reisinger) 1952, Vanderbilt, Spingold 1963, and placed second in the Chicago 1945, Spingold 1953, Blue Ribbon Pairs 1963.

HARKER, William C. (Bill) (b. 1942) of Sunol CA, computer programmer, won California Capital Swiss Teams 1975, All-Western Master Teams 1975, Mount Shasta Open Pairs Flt. A 1981, District 21 GNT 1975, 1976.

HARMON, Leonard B. (b. 1919) of New York City, insurance company president, formerly one of the most successful American players, represented North America in the Bermuda Bowl 1959 and the United States in the World Team Olympiad 1960. He won the McKENNEY TROPHY 1958, Spingold, Chicago (since 1965 the Reisinger) 1958, Vanderbilt 1958, Spring NAC Open Pairs 1958 and placed second in the Spingold 1958, Chicago 1959, Vanderbilt 1966, Summer NAC Master Mixed Teams 1959. His many regional titles include Leventritt Pairs 1964, Eastern States KO Teams (Reisinger) 1959, 1970, Master Pairs 1958, Mixed Teams 1968, Keystone Open Teams 1962, Upper New York State Open Teams 1958. He is a former president and treasurer of Greater New York BA and chairman of the Judiciary Committee in District 24. Harmon is a graduate of New York University.

HARPER, Gary M. of Delta BC, game store owner, won Peach Festival Swiss Teams 1974, Yakima Valley Men's Pairs 1974, White Hat KO Teams 1977, District 19 GNT 1978. He is vice president of Unit 430 and editor of its newsletter *Matchpointer* and the originator of the column *It's Your Bid*.

HARRIS, John T. (Spider) (b. 1930) of Houston, ACBL national tournament director, began his career in 1961. He was educated at Rice University and University of Houston. Harris was Intercollegiate champion 1952. See WEB MOVEMENT.

HARRIS, Joseph F. (Joe) (b. 1940) of Albuquerque, computer programmer, won Rocky Mountain Swiss Teams 1976, Navajo Trail KO Teams 1977, Desert Empire Open Pairs 1981, District 17 GNT 1974.

HARRIS, Marguerite (Tommy) (b. 1896) of New York City, won Fall NAC Women's Teams 1954 and placed second in 1952. Her regional titles include Eastern States Mixed Teams 1961, Women's Pairs 1951, 1957, New England Mixed Teams 1947, New York-New Jersy Women's Pairs 1959. From 1946 to

1969 she was an ACBL staff member in charge of the Club Department and writer of the ACBL *Bulletin* feature *Club Corner*.

HARRIS, Shirlee (b. 1934) of Houston, former teacher, represented the United States in the World Open Pairs 1962. She won Spring NAC Mixed Pairs 1960, 1962, Central States Life and Senior Master Teams 1960, Rocky Mountain Mixed Pairs 1959, 1961, Midwest Fall Open Teams 1960, All-Western Women's Pairs 1965, Tri-Unit Mixed Pairs 1968.

HARRISON, Broma Lou. See REED, BROMA LOU.

HARRISON, Payne of Dallas, retired accountant and business executive, won Mid-South Spring Open Teams, Men's Pairs 1946, Rocky Mountain Open Pairs 1963, Texas Fall Regional Men's Pairs 1963, 1967, Open Pairs 1967, Mixed Pairs 1975, Texas Spring Regional Men's Pairs 1965, 1968, KO Teams, Master Pairs 1969, Missouri Valley KO Teams 1967, Lone Star Mixed Pairs 1975.

HARRISON-GRAY, Maurice (Gray) (1900–1968) of London, England, was one of the world's leading player-writers. Gray was European champion 1948, 1949, 1950 and 1963 (acting as playing captain except in 1963), and represented Great Britain in the Bermuda Bowl 1950, World Open Pairs 1962, World Team Olympiad 1964, European Championships 1958. He won the coveted GOLD CUP seven times, won many other national championships, was a member of the group which developed the ACOL SYSTEM in the Thirties, and a leading exponent of the LOSING-TRICK COUNT. Bridge editor of London *Evening Standard*, *Country Life*, and many other newspapers and periodicals, Gray authored *Country Life Book of Bridge,* co-authored *Winning Points at Match-Point Bridge* and was a contributing editor, *Bridge Encyclopedia*. See BIBLIOGRAPHY, F, H.

HART, Norman de Villiers (1888–1976) of London, England won English Inter-County Championship. He authored *Daily Telegraph Book of Contract Bridge*, *Bridge Player's Bedside Book*, and co-authored *Right Through the Pack*, *Vienna System of Contract Bridge*, and *Quintessence of CAB*. See BIBLIOGRAPHY, C, H.

HARTWICH, Hans (b. 1923) of Vienna, Austria, placed second in the European Championships 1957 and also represented Austria in the European Championships 1950, 1956. He was playing captain of the Austrian team in the World Team Olympiad 1960. His national wins include Austrian Open Teams several times.

HATFIELD, Glynn P. (b. 1946) of Barrington Passage NS, tax accountant, won Can-At Open Pairs 1969, KO Teams 1971, Master Pairs 1977. He is the founder and first editor of the Maritime Unit publication *The Bridgeline*.

HATHORN, John B. (1925–1964) of Houston, though stricken by polio in 1954, still achieved Life Master status in 1956. He went on to become a bridge writer and leading bridge personality in the Southwest. In 1959 Hathorn founded *Texas Bridge* which he published and edited until his death. Among his writings are several booklets on bidding and play, most written in collaboration with G. ROBERT NAIL. See BIBLIOGRAPHY, D, E, F.

HAUGHIE, William J. (Bill) (b. 1942) of Hamilton, New Zealand, computer service bureau general manager, represented New Zealand in the World Team Olympiad 1976, Far East Championships 1971, 1975. His national titles include New Zealand Teams 1973, 1974, 1979, 1980, Open Pairs 1975, 1979. He contributes articles to *New Zealand Bridge*.

HAUSE, Terry E. (b. 1947) of San Jose CA, mathematics teacher, won Spring NAC Open Pairs 1976, Spring NAC secondary Swiss Teams 1980, District 21 GNP 1981.

HAVAS, George (b. 1947) of Canberra, Australia, computer scientist, theoretical mathematician, represented Australia in the Bermuda Bowl 1977, World Team Olympiad 1978, 1982, Far East Championships 1971, 1974, 1976. He won Far East Open Pairs 1971 and placed second in both Open Pairs and Open Teams in 1976. His national titles include Victor Champion Cup, Australian Open Pairs, Open Teams. He is the author of *The Australian Book of Bridge* and a weekly newspaper column in *The Australian*. Havas is a former councillor of the AUSTRALIAN BRIDGE FEDERATION and the Australian Capital Territory BA.

HAWES, EMMA JEAN (Mrs. David B.) of Fort Worth TX, one of the leading American women players, is one of only eight women WBF Grand Masters in the world. She won the Venice Trophy 1974, 1976, 1978, World Women's Teams 1980. She also represented the United States in the World Women's Pairs 1974, World Women's Teams 1968, 1972, 1976. She won Fall NAC Open Pairs 1958, Life Master Women's Pairs 1966, 1978 (second in 1972), Spring NAC Women's Teams 1967, 1970, 1972, 1974, 1975, 1976, Women's Pairs 1981 (second in 1968, 1976), Summer NAC Master Mixed Teams 1964 (second in 1952, 1967, 1972). Her numerous regional titles include Texas Open Teams, Women's Pairs, Mixed Pairs 1960, Mid-South Spring Mixed Pairs 1949, 1965, Missouri Valley Master Pairs 1961, North Texas KO Teams 1961, Open Teams 1963, Harvest Festival Open Pairs 1977, Oklahoma City Women's Swiss Teams 1981, Republic of Texas Women's Pairs 1981. A former president of the Fort Worth Unit, she is a member of the ACBL Goodwill Committee and ACBL Board of Governors. She is a graduate of Cornell University.

HAWKINS, Allen W. Jr. (b. 1949) of Birmingham AL, bank examiner, won Azalea City Swiss Teams 1980, Mid–South KO Teams 1981, District GNT, Zone III 1981.

HAWKINS, Proctor (b. 1937) of Las Vegas, placed second in Summer NAC Senior/ Advanced Senior Master Pairs 1969. His numerous regional titles include Summer NAC secondary Individual 1971, Fall Tournament of Champions 1973, Navajo Trail KO Teams 1973, Bridge Week Master Pairs 1973, Men's Master Pairs 1976, District 15 Master Pairs 1974, KO Teams 1978, Swiss Teams Flt. A 1980, Texas Mid-Winter Master Swiss Teams, Swiss Teams 1981, Pikes Peak Swiss Teams Flt. A, Master Pairs 1980, Desert Empire Open Pairs 1973, Open Pairs 1974, Master Swiss Teams 1978, District 17 GNT 1975, 1976, 1977, 1979, Zone VI 1979.

HAYASHI, James J. (Jim) (b. 1943) of San Jose CA, engineer, won Summer NAC secondary Commercial and Industrial Teams 1969, Golden Gate Men's Pairs 1973, Swiss Teams 1974, Open Pairs 1976, KO Teams 1977, Central California KO Teams 1973, Redwood Empire Swiss Teams 1975, California Capital Swiss Teams 1976, Golden State Swiss Teams 1976, Holiday Festival Master Pairs 1979, District 21 GNT 1980.

HAYDEN, Dorothy. See TRUSCOTT, DOROTHY HAYDEN.

HAYDEN, Garey (b. 1944) of Tucson, professional bridge instructor and co-owner of a travel agency, one of the leading players of the Southwest, won Spring NAC Men's Teams 1973, Open Pairs 1975, Men's Pairs 1977 and placed second in the Blue Ribbon Pairs 1972, Life Master Pairs 1976. His more than 80 regional titles include Summer NAC secondary Swiss Teams 1977, Fall Open Pairs Flt. A, Swiss Teams 1974, Land of Coronado Men's Pairs 1972, KO Teams 1972, 1978, Swiss Teams 1972, 1974, Hawaii Swiss Teams 1974, 1975, 1977, 1978, KO Teams, Men's Swiss Teams 1978, Desert Empire KO Teams 1972, 1973, 1981, Southeastern KO Teams 1973, Men's Swiss Teams, Swiss Teams 1979, Rocky Mountain KO Teams 1976, 1977, Swiss Teams 1981, Puget Sound KO Teams, Open Pairs 1975, Swiss Teams Flt. A 1981. Hayden has been a certified director since 1980 and directs on bridge cruises.

HAYS, G. Gard (b. 1933) of Verndale WA, engineer, won Fall NAC Men's Pairs 1961, Spring NAC Men's Pairs 1964, Golden State Open Teams 1963, Oregon Trail Open Teams 1966, Pacific Northwest KO Teams 1969.

HAYWARD, Diane (b. 1936) of San Francisco edited the 4th edition, *Bridge Encyclopedia*. Formerly assistant editor of the *Contract Bridge Forum*, she is the editor of *Daily Bulletins* at many West Coast regionals, *Daily Bulletin* assistant at North American Championships, and contributor to the ACBL *Bulletin*. She is a graduate of California State University at Hayward. Genealogy is her avocation.

HAZEN, Lee (b. 1905) of New York City, attorney, for many years one of the leading American bridge players and personalities, represented the United States in the Bermuda Bowl 1956, 1959 and was designated npc of the North American team in the 1971 Bermuda Bowl. He won the Spingold 1942, 1947, 1955, (second in 1945, 1958), Chicago (since

1965 the Reisinger) 1945, 1949, (second in 1941, 1942), Vanderbilt 1939, 1942, 1949, 1958, (second in 1944, 1947), Summer NAC Men's Pairs 1945, Master Individual 1941 (second in 1940), and placed second in the Life Master Pairs 1946. His regional titles include Eastern States KO Teams (Reisinger) 1944. ACBL attorney since 1942, Hazen was a driving force in the modernization of the ACBL in the late Forties. He was ACBL Director in 1940, ACBL vice president 1945–1947, named ACBL Honorary Member in 1958, and was a member of the ACBL Laws Commission from 1942 until 1973 when he resigned and was named member emeritus. Currently he is trustee and treasurer of the ACBL Charity Foundation. He was the founder and former vice president of Greater New York BA. He is a contributing editor, *Bridge Encyclopedia*. Prior to his graduation from Columbia University in 1926 and New York University Law School 1930, he played professional baseball.

HEAD, Cecil L. (b. 1910) of Hendersonville NC, formerly New York City, retired attorney, won Summer NAC Life Master Pairs 1948. His regional titles include New England KO Teams 1933, 1934, 1939, 1941 (twice), 1945, 1946 (twice), 1947, 1951, 1954, Mid-Atlantic Open Pairs 1980. (See S. GARTON CHURCHILL for records set by Head and Churchill when winning the Life Master Pairs in 1948.) Head was educated at Harvard and Yale.

HEARD, Helen M. (Suzie) (formerly Townsend and Moore) of Altadena CA, won Hawaii Open Pairs 1964, Rocky Mountain Open Pairs 1968, KO Teams 1967, Master Pairs 1965, All-Western Mixed Pairs 1969, ALACBU Winter Open Pairs 1969, Oregon Trail Mixed Pairs 1966, Swiss Teams 1978, Klondike Open Pairs 1974, Swiss Teams 1976, Inter–Mountain Master Pairs 1974, Evergreen Master Pairs 1976, Pacific Northwest Spring Open Teams 1967.

HECKEL, Virginia of Miami Beach won Spring NAC Women's Teams 1969, Spring NAC secondary Swiss Teams 1970, Central States Women's Pairs 1969, 1971.

HEDDEN, Wendell W. of Wichita KS, retired sales manager, won District 15 Swiss Teams 1975, GNT, Zone VI 1973. Hedden has been a certified director since 1968 and chairman of Wichita bridge tournaments since 1965.

HEINE, Charles H. (Chuck) (b. 1930) of Ellicott City MD, CPA, won Florida Open Pairs 1975, Fall NAC secondary Swiss Teams 1980, District 4 Men's Swiss Teams 1981.

HEITNER, Abigail (Abby) (Mrs. Paul) (b. 1946) of Bramalea ON won Can-At KO Teams 1970, 1973, Open Teams 1970, 1975, New England Knockout Swiss Teams 1977, Nat'l Capital KO Teams 1978, District 5 Open Pairs Flt. A 1980, Bluenose Swiss Teams 1981. She also won South Africa Transvaal Women's Teams 1974.

HEITNER, Paul L. (the Whale) (b. 1939) of Bramalea ON, computer systems consultant, won

Life Master Pairs 1970, Men's Teams 1976 and placed second in Spring NAC Men's Pairs 1972. His numerous regional titles include Spring NAC secondary Swiss Teams 2nd Flt. 1976, Swiss Teams Flt A 1981, Can-At KO Teams 1970, 1973, Open Teams 1969, 1970, 1975, Canadian Nat'l KO Teams 1977, National Capital KO Teams 1978, Open Pairs 1980, District 5 Open Pairs Flt. A 1980, District 3 GNT 1977, 1978, Zone I 1979, GNP 1980, Canadian National Teams 1980. He also won events in South Africa in 1974. A leading bridge theorist, he is the co-developer with JOHN LOWENTHAL of the CANARY CLUB SYSTEM. He was the co-founder and managing editor of *Bridge Journal*, now out of print.

HELDRING, Ernst (1904–1971) of Amsterdam, The Netherlands, attorney, was active in the EUROPEAN BRIDGE LEAGUE, serving as a Director 1952–1971, and as Secretary 1958–1971. He also served as president of NETHERLANDS BRIDGE LEAGUE 1949–1959 and was a member of the Editorial Advisory Board, *Bridge Encyclopedia*.

HELLER, Max (b. 1916) of St. Louis, public relations consultant, won Midwest Fall Men's Pairs 1962, Mississippi Valley Men's Pairs 1961, 1967, 1970, Mixed Pairs 1960, District 8 GNT, Zone V 1975.

HELLER, Phyllis (Phyll) (b. 1934) of Pittsburgh, sectional tournament director, won All-American Swiss Teams 1975, 1979, District 5 Women's Pairs 1968, Women's Swiss Teams 1977, 1981, GNT 1974.

HEMRICOURT, Count Claude de (b. 1913) of Brussels, Belgium, company director, represented Belgium in the World Mixed Teams 1962, in many European Championships and was captain of the Belgian team several times. His national titles include Open Teams 1948, 1949, 1951, 1952, 1955, 1956, 1959, Open Pairs 1949, Mixed Teams 1960, 1961, 1962. He has served as a member of the Belgian Bridge Commission and was vice president of the EUROPEAN BRIDGE LEAGUE 1969–1973.

HENDERSHOTT, Robert (b. 1925) of Seattle, fruit grower and tournament director, won Pacific Northwest Men's Pairs 1958, 1962, Master Pairs 1964, Oregon Trail Open Teams 1966, 1978, All-Western Men's Pairs 1963, Peach Festival Men's Pairs 1974, Puget Sound Men's Swiss Teams, Swiss Teams 1977, Men's Pairs 1979.

HENDERSON, Richard B. (Rick) (b. 1933) of Los Angeles, accountant, won numerous regional titles including Inter–Mountain Open Teams, Master Pairs 1970, KO Teams 1972, Mid-Atlantic Open Pairs 1974, 1980, Washington Bridge Week KO Teams 1974, All-Western Master Pairs 1978.

HENKE, Charles (Chuck) (b. 1934) of Aurora CO, won the Blue Ribbon Pairs 1965. His regional titles include Pacific Northwest Master Pairs 1962, Rocky Mountain Men's Pairs 1962, Inter-Mountain Open Teams 1965, Open Pairs 1966, Oil City Master Swiss Teams 1978, Desert Empire Master Pairs 1978. A former bridge lecturer and director, Henke directed on cruises 1964–1966. Currently he is safety coordinator with the National Child Safety Council, working with law enforcement agencies to promote child safety in the community.

HENKE, Ron S. (b. 1943) of Oklahoma City, research chemist, won District 15 Master Pairs 1976, Open Pairs 1980, Land of Coronado Swiss Teams 1976, Toast of Tulsa Master Pairs 1979.

HENRY, Dr. Joseph L. (b. 1924) of Newton Centre MA, was the top ranking player of the ABA for 12 years until his retirement from competition. He became an ABA Life Master in nine months and won more than 20 ABA National Championships. He also won ACBL Mid-Atlantic Summer KO Teams 1962. Educated at Howard University, Xavier University, University of Illinois and Harvard University, Henry is associate dean, professor and department chairman of the Harvard School of Dental Medicine, and chairman of the Board of Trustees, Illinois College of Optometry (the first non-optometrist to be named to this position). He is listed in *Who's Who in the World*.

HENRY, Renee B. (b. 1928) of Ellicott City MD, won Fall NAC secondary Swiss Teams Flt. B 1980, Mid-Atlantic Women's Pairs 1980, Women's Swiss Teams 1976, 1980.

HERBERT, Edmund J. (Ed) (b. 1935) of Phoenix, retired from the U.S. Army, won Inter-Mountain Mixed Pairs 1964, Pacific Southwest Men's Pairs 1964, Bridge Week Open Teams 1971, Desert Empire Mixed Pairs 1963, Master Pairs 1973.

HERBERT, Walter (1902–1975) of San Diego, conductor of the San Diego Opera, formerly general director of the Houston Opera Company, was the originator of the HERBERT CONVENTION. Advocated by Herbert when he was a member of the 1937 Austrian Team that defeated ELY and JOSEPHINE CULBERTSON, HELEN SOBEL and Charles Vogelhofer representing the U.S. to win the World Bridge Team championship, the convention was applied in many ways in the VIENNA SYSTEM.

HÉRÉDIA, Irénée Bajos de (b. 1918) of Paris, France, chief tournament director of the FRENCH BRIDGE FEDERATION, directed many international tournaments including the World Pair Championships in Cannes 1962. He is the co-author with Desrousseaux of *Le Bridge d'Ecole Française* and the originator and adviser of OMNIUM.

HERMAN, Ira (b. 1943) of New York City, export manager, won District 3 Swiss Teams Flt. A 1980, Big Apple Swiss Teams Flt. A 1981, New York Winter Open Pairs Flt. A 1981.

HERMAN, Lou (1908–1950) a Houston jeweler formerly of New York, won the Mid-South Open Teams in 1949. The LOU HERMAN TROPHY was given in his memory by his widow, Sally Lipton.

HERR, Barbara C. (b. 1920) of Wilmington DE, won Fall Life Master Women's Pairs 1976. Since 1977 she has been chairman of the Governor's Commission on the Status of Women (DE).

HERRINGTON, Gaye W. (b. 1938) of Culver City Ca, municipal court judge, won Bridge Week Mixed Pairs 1970, All-Western Mixed Pairs 1971, Los Angeles Winter Women's Swiss Teams 1976, Raincross Open Pairs 1979, Mid-Winter Holiday Swiss Teams Flt. A 1979.

HERRMANN, John P. (b. 1945) of Franklin TN, professional bridge player, former mathematics teacher, placed second in Fall NAC Swiss Teams 1977 and won Champagne Men's Pairs 1972, Mid-Atlantic Men's Pairs 1975, KO Teams 1981, District 11 Open Pairs 1976, Mid-South Master Pairs 1976.

HERTZBERG, Dr. Howard (b. 1936) of Alpine NJ, orthopedic surgeon, won Fall NAC secondary Men's Swiss Teams 1975, 1980, Open Pairs 1976, Southern Conference Fall Open Pairs 1964.

HERTZBERG, Robert K. (Hertz) (b. 1949) of Fair Lawn NJ, company vice president, won District 3 Open Pairs Flt. A, Master Pairs 1981, Mid-Atlantic Open Pairs Flt. A 1980.

HERVEY, George F. (George John Frangopulo Hervey) (1897–1981) was a noted free-lance British journalist and author. Card correspondent of *The Field* (1940), bridge correspondent of *The Western Morning News* (Plymouth 1953), and contributor to *Bridge Magazine*, he published six books on bridge, including *The Bridge Player's Bedside Book*, as well as other publications on card games and books on other subjects. See BIBLIOGRAPHY, B.

HESSEL, Paul A. (b. 1940) of Buffalo Grove IL, won Summer NAC secondary Swiss Teams 1980, Central States KO Teams 1976, 1981, Tri-Unit Swiss Teams 1975, District 11 Open Pairs Flt. A 1980, Wisconsin Swiss Teams Flt. A 1980, District 13 GNT 1979. He owns a pension consultant firm.

HESTHAVEN, Dennis G. (b. 1946) of Racine WI, account executive, won All-American Master Pairs 1978, District 11 Men's Swiss Teams 1979, Master Pairs 1981, Midwest Fall Swiss Teams 1980.

HETZER, Lloyd R. (b. 1946) of Van Nuys CA won Fall NAC secondary Blue Ribbon Pairs 1970, Mid-Atlantic Open Pairs 1970, Mid-South Swiss Teams 1972, District 10 GNT 1973, 1974.

HEWITT, Richard G. (Dick) (b. 1927) of Irvington NY, attorney, has been a member of the ACBL Board of Directors since 1975. He formerly served as president of Westchester CBA 1960–1961, president of District 3 Coordinating Committee 1965–1975, as a member of ACBL Executive Committee 1977–1980, as treasurer of the 1968 Spring and 1974 Summer North American Championships, as chairman of the 1981 Bermuda Bowl Committee, and as chairman of various other committees. He won New England Open Teams 1974. Hewitt was educated at

Williams College and Columbia University.

HEWITT, Shirley A. (Mrs. Richard G.) (b. 1926) of Irvington NY, won Upper New York Women's Pairs 1961, New England Knockouts Swiss Teams 1974, Fall NAC secondary Women's Swiss Teams 1976.

HICKS, Arthur A. (Adrian) (b. 1907) of Vancouver BC, semi-retired bridge teacher and director, won several regional titles including Pacific Northwest Master Pairs 1957, 1960, Open Teams 1956, Oregon Trail Men's Pairs 1958, KO Teams 1973, Inter-Mountain Open Teams 1958, 1963, Evergreen Mixed Pairs 1976, British Columbia Swiss Teams 1971, Open Pairs 1980.

HIGASHIUCHI, Kazuo (Jake) (b. 1912) of Park Forest IL, research chemist, won Central States Mixed Pairs 1955, Life and Senior Master Teams 1960, KO Teams 1963.

HILL, Marion H. (b. 1913) of Hawera, New Zealand, retired accountant, was Far East Women's champion 1976. Her national titles include New Zealand Women's Pairs.

HILLIARD, Olga (1891–1979) of New York City donated the ABL trophy for Mixed Pairs, which is still given at the ACBL Spring North American Championships for a two-session event. She was victor of two national events and finished second twice.

HILTON, James R. (Jim) (b. 1946) of Summit NJ, attorney, won Summer NAC secondary Open Pairs, Swiss Teams 1974, Fall Swiss Teams Flt. B 1980, Long Island KO Teams 1978, Eastern States KO Teams (Reisinger) 1978, New York Winter Swiss Teams Flt. A 1979.

HIRON, Alan M. (Al) (b. 1933) of London, England, computer and games consultant, represented Great Britain in the European Championships 1967 and was npc of Great Britain's Women's Team in the European Championships 1969, 1974. His national wins include the GOLD CUP 1963, Crockford's Cup 1964, 1966, Spring Foursomes 1966, 1974. He has held positions in both the London County CBA 1975–1979 and ENGLISH BRIDGE UNION 1976–1977.

HIRSCH, Ernest (Ernie) (b. 1932) of Orinda CA, born in Mannheim, Germany, operations research analyst, former research chemist, won All-Western Open Teams 1965, Men's Swiss Teams 1973, Golden Gate Master Teams 1973, Golden State Master Pairs 1975, Mid-Winter Holiday KO Teams 1976.

HIRSCH, Harriette (b. 1935) of Lincolnwood IL, language arts and social studies teacher, won Central States Open Teams 1969, Women's Pairs 1970, Summer NAC secondary Women's Pairs Flt. A 1980. She is a certified director and teaches bridge.

HIRSCH, Tannah (b. 1933) of New York City, formerly of Johannesburg, South Africa and Jerusa-lem, Israel, president of Goren International since 1978, bridge writer and editor, won South Africa Congress Teams 1957, Natal Teams 1958, Jerusalem Pairs 1962, 1963, 1964, ACBL Mid-Atlantic Summer Men's Pairs 1968, Tri-State Swiss Teams 1970, 1980, Bermuda Swiss Teams 1977, 1978. He is the co-author of *Tournament Book of the 2nd World Olympiad Pairs.* He edited the *Daily Bulletin* at the European Championships 1965, 1974, and was associate editor and editor of the ACBL *Bulletin* 1967-1972. Hirsch has contributed articles to *Bridge World, Nederlands Bridge, South African Bridge Bulletin,* and *Popular Bridge.* See BIBLIOGRAPHY, G.

HIRSCHBERG, Ralph (1906–1962) set a record by capturing the Reisinger Trophy six times, including four consecutive wins, 1956–1959. Victor in numerous other events, Hirschberg was a New York city insurance broker.

HIRSCHHAUT, Fida (b. 1937) of Caracas, Venezuela, born in Dorohoi, Roumania, boutique owner, represented Central America-Caribbean in the Venice Trophy Teams 1981, Venezuela in the South American Women's Championship 1972, 1976, World Women's Teams champion 1980 and placed second in 1972. She won the Team Trials, National Open Teams, Women's Pairs, Mixed Pairs, Mixed Teams, Open Pairs.

HIRSCHEY, Charles S. (b. 1912) of Carthage NY, company executive, won Can-Am Open Teams 1958, Men's Pairs 1953, 1964, Open Pairs 1967, Upper New York State Men's Pairs, Mixed Pairs 1956, Can-At KO Teams 1969.

HIRSTY, Helen R. (b. 1927) of Wilmington DE, fingernail sculptress, won Mid-Atlantic Women's Pairs 1970, 1981, District 4 Fall Women's Swiss Teams 1978.

HITCHENS, Robert M. (Bob) (b. 1937) of Seattle, associate broker, won Spring NAC secondary Open Pairs 2nd Flt. 1964, Oregon Trail Open Pairs 1971, Inland Empire Open Pairs 1971, Puget Sound Open Teams 1968, Men's Pairs 1973, Klondike Swiss Teams 1976, District 19 GNT 1977.

HOADLEY, Frank M. (Professor) (b. 1923) of New Orleans, professor of English, won Spring NAC Men's Pairs 1960 and placed second in the Spingold 1959, Reisinger 1975. His numerous regional titles include Keystone Open Teams 1959, Mid-South KO Teams 1970, Men's Pairs, Master Pairs, Open Pairs 1973, Swiss Teams 1975, 1976, Missouri Valley KO Teams 1975, 1976, Mixed Pairs, Master Pairs 1976, Crescent City KO Teams, Men's Pairs 1977, District 10 GNT 1976, GNP 1979, 1981.

HOBLEY, Susan C. (b. 1952) of New South Wales, Australia, represented Australia in the Far East Championships 1972, 1973, 1979, 1981, World Women's Teams 1980, Venice Trophy Teams 1981.

HOBLIT, Charles S. (Sid) (b. 1901) of Pompano Beach FL, former cab company owner, won All-

American Men's Pairs 1946, 1948, 1949, Midwest Spring Men's Pairs 1949. Hoblit devised a system of ACE-SHOWING RESPONSES to forcing two-bids. He is a former member of the Board of Directors and past president of the Michigan BA,

HOBSON, Brian H. (b. 1915) of Nairobi, Kenya, born in Watford, England, company chairman, represented Kenya in the World Team Olympiad 1968, 1980, World Open Pairs 1978.

HOCEVAR, Don of Southfield MI, won the MARCUS CUP 1970, Canadian Nat'l KO Teams 1971, Cambrian Shield KO Teams 1974, Presque Isle Swiss Teams 1977, District 12 GNT, Zone I 1973.

HOCHFELD, Emanual (Manny) (1930–1972), a Chicago stockbroker, was one of the leading players of the Midwest. His record includes four national wins, five national seconds and numerous Central States regional wins.

HOCHZEIT, Michael of Israel, building contractor, was European champion 1975. He also represented Israel in the World Team Olympiad 1972, World Open Pairs 1974, World Mixed Pairs 1970.

HODAPP, Thomas (b. 1942) of Cincinnati, advertising executive, won the Life Master Men's Pairs 1978 and placed second in the Blue Ribbon Pairs 1969. His more than 25 regional titles include Opryland Swiss Teams Flt. A 1981, Midwest Spring Swiss Teams Flt. A 1981, Harvest Festival Swiss Teams 1981, District 11 Life Master Pairs 1972, Men's Pairs 1970, Master Pairs 1976, KO Teams 1977, Men's Swiss Teams, Open Pairs Flt. A 1981, GNT 1974, 1976, 1977, Zone III 1976, GNP 1980, 1981.

HODGE, Paul (1910–1976) was known as an expert player and bridge commentator. Representing North America in the 1961 Bermuda Bowl, the Houston bridge teacher finished second. Hodge also acted as non-playing captain of the U.S. Women's team in the 1964 World Team Olympiad. Soft spoken but articulate, he added polish to many ACBL vugraph presentations and panel shows. In 1955 Hodge captured both the FISHBEIN and the HERMAN trophies for outstanding performances at national tournaments. He won nine national events, came in second in eight national events, and had numerous regional wins.

HOERSCH, Joel J. (b. 1937) of Carlsbad CA, newspaper composition programmer, placed second in the Reisinger 1981. His several regional titles include Bridge Week Open Pairs 1972, BAM Teams 1976, Pacific Southwest Master Pairs 1969, Men's Swiss Teams 1976, 1977, KO Teams 1975, Swiss Teams Flt. A 1981, Holiday Festival KO Teams, Swiss Teams 1979, Pikes Peak Swiss Teams 1980.

HOFFER, Fred (b. 1937) of Montreal, merchandiser, placed second in the Spingold 1964 and won Canadian Nat'l Open Pairs 1959, Open Teams 1960, Master Pairs 1966, 1978, Can-Am Open Pairs 1968, KO Teams 1976, Master Swiss Teams 1977, Swiss Teams Flt. A 1981, Olympic Men's Swiss Teams 1978, District 1 GNT 1975, 1977, 1979, Zone I 1977, Canadian National Teams Zone 2 1981.

HOFFMAN, Arthur H. (b. 1935) of Maplewood NJ, insurance consultant, won Summer NAC secondary Commercial and Industrial Teams 1974, 1975, 1976.

HOFFMAN, David L. (b. 1945) of Canberra, Australia, university lecturer, represented Australia in the World Team Olympiad 1972, Far East Championships 1971. He placed second in Australian Open Teams 1971, 1981, Open Pairs 1969, Open Individual 1980 and won several regional titles including ACT Open Pairs 1972, 973, Open Teams 1973, 1979, Mixed Pairs 1973, 1977, 1980. He is ACT tournament secretary, former masterpoint secretary 1971-1981 and AUSTRALIAN BRIDGE FEDERATION masterpoint secretary 1973-1975.

HOFFMAN, Martin of London, England, bridge writer, winner of many European tournaments, is one of the fastest analysts in the game. He is the author of *Hoffman on Pairs Play* and a frequent contributor to the IBPA *Bulletin*. Hoffman is a survivor of Auschwitz.

HOFFMANN, Michael of St. Paul MN won Spring NAC Open Pairs 1973, Gopher Men's Pairs, Master Pairs 1977, Swiss Teams 1979, 1980, Northwest Iowa Swiss Teams 1978, Pheasant Men's Pairs 1978.

HÖIE, Erik (b. 1928) of Stavanger, Norway, tailor, represented Norway in the Bermuda Bowl 1970, European Championships 1959, 1961, 1965, 1969. He authored *Stavanger-grangen*, a work on 1 NT opening bids and responses.

HOLLAND, George T. (b. 1947) of Dartmouth NS, leasing manager, won Fleur de Lys Swiss Teams 1974, Nat'l Capital Swiss Teams 1975, Bluenose Open Pairs Flt. A 1981. Holland served as Unit 166 tournament chairman 1973–1975.

HOLLINGSWORTH, S. Wayne (b. 1940) of Dayton OH, computer analyst, won Fall NAC secondary Open Pairs A–D 1979, Music City Swiss Teams 1973, Midwest Men's Swiss Teams 1980, Fall Swiss Teams 1978, District 11 GNT, Zone IV 1981.

HOLLIS, Ailsa R. (b. 1910) of Auckland, New Zealand, bridge teacher, represented New Zealand in the Far East Championships 1971. Her national titles include Australian Women's Teams 1968, Women's Pairs 1968, New Zealand Teams 1971. She was the New Zealand representative to the Asian Pacific Chess Championships 1975 and the World Chess Olympiad 1976.

HOLT, Clarice K. (b. 1911) of Fort Worth TX, oil executive, won Summer NAC Women's Pairs 1962, Fall Mixed Pairs 1962, and placed second in Fall NAC Women's Teams 1964. Her numerous regional titles include Mid-South Spring Open Pairs, Women's Pairs 1955, Summer Open Teams 1967, Texas Fall KO Teams 1971, Land of Coronado Women's

Swiss Teams 1978.

HOOD, Pat L. (b. 1936) of Austin TX, secretary, won several regional titles including Fall NAC secondary Master Pairs 1974, Mid-South Summer Open Pairs 1968, Capital City KO Teams 1972, Republic of Texas Mixed Pairs 1973, Int'l City Swiss Teams 1974, Copper State Master Swiss Teams Flt. A 1977, Corpus Christi Swiss Teams 1978.

HOOKER, Jim L. (b. 1937) of Los Angeles, formerly of Dallas, independent oil operator, won the Grand National Teams 1975. His numerous regional titles include Fall NAC secondary Swiss Teams 1973, Texas Fall Swiss Teams 1973, Master Pairs 1974, Hawaii Swiss Teams 1976, 1979, Rocky Mountain Open Pairs 1975, Mid-South Men's Master Swiss Teams 1976, Big D KO Teams 1976, Mexican Nat'l Open Pairs 1976. Hooker is a graduate of Southern Methodist University.

HORN, James D. (Stormy) (b. 1929) of El Paso TX, satellite meteorologist, won several regional titles including Spring NAC secondary Men's Pairs 1973, Rocky Mountain Men's Pairs 1970, KO Teams 1975, Open Pairs Flt. A 1979, Swiss Teams Flt. A 1981, International City Swiss Teams 1974, Master Pairs 1979, Pikes Peak Master Pairs 1976, Open Pairs Flt. A 1978. He is the co-author of *The System*.

HORNER, David L. (b. 1937) of Oklahoma City, tax accountant, won Mid-South BAM Teams 1968, Texas Fall Swiss Teams 1971, Republic of Texas Open Pairs 1976, Toast of Tulsa Master Pairs 1979, Missouri Valley Men's Swiss Teams 1979.

HORNING, Edmund M. (Ted) (b. 1940) of Thornhill ON, synicated bridge columnist, bridge studio and travel agency owner, professional bridge teacher and player, represented Canada in the World Open Pairs 1970, 1978, Rosenblum Cup Teams 1978. He placed second in the Blue Ribbon Pairs 1978 and won Can-Am KO Teams 1977, Swiss Teams, Open Pairs Flt. A 1981, KO Teams 1982, District 5 KO Teams 1980, Labor Day Open Pairs Flt. A 1980, Gateway City Master Pairs 1981, Motor City Men's Swiss Teams 1981, Canadian National Teams Zone 3 1981. He served as vice chairman of the CANADIAN BRIDGE FEDERATION National Championship Committee in 1977. Horning writes a syndicated daily column, *Canadian Bridge*, which is published in 26 Canadian newspapers. In addition to his many activities, he is also a sectional tournament director.

HOROBETZ, Helen C. (b. 1915) of Chula Vista CA, bridge cruise director and lecturer, ACBL NAC Press Room staff member, bridge writer, has been involved in bridge organization in District 22 for many years. She has served as hospitality chairman, tournament chairman and she instituted the District's regional *Daily Bulletin* which she edits. She is a contributor to the ACBL *Bulletin*, *Southern California Bridge News*, *Contract Bridge Forum*, and the ABTA *Quarterly*. She has been a member of the AMERICAN BRIDGE TEACHERS ASSOCIATION since 1973, served as its regional vice president 1974–1978

and is currently Director at Large and a member of the committee that edits the *Report of ABTA Committee on Standard American*. Horobetz has held various executive positions in Unit 519 and in District 22. She also was second alternate to the ACBL Board of Directors, a member of the Board of Governors, and is a member of the ACBL Goodwill Committee and ACBL Charity Committee.

HOROBETZ, Lynn K. of San Diego, travel agent, bridge teacher and writer, former college teacher, won Pacific Southwest Swiss Teams Flt. A 1981. She has contributed articles to the ACBL *Bulletin*, the *Contract Bridge Forum*. She has edited many Western regional *Daily Bulletins*, and written and directed regional bridge shows.

HOROWITZ, Jeffrey (b. 1943) of Cheshire CT, financial executive, won New England Summer Swiss Teams 1976, Fall Swiss Teams 1978, 1979, Swiss Teams Flt. A 1980, New York Winter Swiss Teams 1977, Tri-State Winter Swiss Teams 1976.

HORTON, Sally (Mrs. Mark, formerly Sowter) (b. 1953) of Nottingham, England, typesetter, won the Venice Trophy 1981, European Women's champion 1979, 1981, Common Market Women's champion 1979, 1981. Her national titles include British Women's Teams 1979. She placed second in the GOLD CUP 1979, 1980. She is executive editor of *International Popular Bridge Monthly*.

HORWITZ, Donald G. (Don) (b. 1925) of Edina MN, real estate agent, placed second in the U.S. Zone World Pair Olympiad 1963. His regional titles include Summer NAC secondary Leventritt Pairs 1962, Gopher Open Teams 1960, 1966, 1969, 1970, Men's Pairs 1960, KO Teams 1968, Midwest Fall Men's Pairs 1959, Mid-American-Canadian Men's Pairs 1965, Canadian Prairie Swiss Teams 1969. He is a contributing editor to the *Bridge Encyclopedia*.

HORWITZ, Janice (formerly Cohn) (b. 1924) of Butler PA, bridge teacher and club director, won Summer NAC Master Mixed Teams 1969, Fall NAC secondary Women's Teams 1975, Midwest Fall Women's Pairs 1967, Gopher Open Teams 1973. She was the recipient of the Harmon Wilkes Sportsmanship award in Chicago 1976.

HOWARD, Denis W. (b. 1932) of Sydney, Australia, solicitor, one of the leading Australian players, represented Australia in the Bermuda Bowl 1971, 1976 , World Team Olympiad 1964, 1968, and was npc in 1981. His national titles include Australian Open Teams 1958, 1959, 1961, 1962, 1963, 1964, 1965, 1967, Open Pairs 1957, 1961, 1962, 1964, 1965, 1971. President of the AUSTRALIAN BRIDGE FEDERATION, Howard formerly served as ABF councillor 1960-1974, New South Wales BA councillor 1972-1974, and as editor of *Australian Bridge*. He is Australia's representative on the WORLD BRIDGE FEDERATION Executive Council.

HOWARD, Laurence B. Jr. (Larry) (b. 1927) of Nashville, corporation chairman of the Board, won

Mid-South Master Pairs 1971, Big D Mixed Pairs 1972, District 11 Open Pairs 1977, Mid-Atlantic Swiss Teams 1975, Music City Master Pairs 1977.

HOWARD, Laurence B. III (Bryan) (b. 1958) of Nashville, lawclerk, won Music City Master Pairs 1977, Mid-Atlantic Open Pairs Flt. B 1979, Space City Open Pairs Flt. B, Crescent City Master Pairs 1981.

HOWARD, Morgan H. (1893–1965) of North Hollywood CA, born in Pennsylvania, for many years a top executive of the Hearst publishing enterprise in Pittsburgh and New York, was President of the ACBL in 1942. The trophy which bears his name is awarded to the winners of the President's Pair event held at the Summer NAC.

HOWARD, Randy L. (b. 1950) of Mar Vista CA, former cameraman, placed second in Spring NAC Amateur Swiss Teams 1977 and won Redwood Empire KO Teams 1975, Pacific Southwest KO Teams 1974.

HOWARD, Sarah B. (b. 1919) of Newport News VA, won Mid-Atlantic Fall Women's Pairs 1953, 1955, Spring Mixed Pairs 1957. She has held many offices and chairmanships in Unit 110 including vice president. Legally blind since 1957, she is the statewide representative for Leader Dogs for the Blind, attending Lions Club functions to explain services of the Leader Dog program.

HOWELL, Edwin Cull (April 21, 1860–December 16, 1907) is credited with the invention of the HOWELL MOVEMENT in 1897.

Born in Nantucket MA to clergyman George Howell and his wife Frances Sarah Cull, Howell attended prep school Charlier Institute in New York City prior to entering Harvard in July 1877. He left Harvard in March 1881 before completing his degree and taught in a private school in Asbury Park NJ for a year. Returning to Harvard in 1883 he graduated eleventh in his class and took honors in math. Howell taught math at John Hopkins University, 1884–1885, and in two private schools.

Leaving the teaching field in 1887, Howell joined the staff of the *Daily News* in Baltimore, and for 14 years beginning 1889 worked for the *Boston Herald* becoming assistant city editor in 1896 and assistant news editor in 1898. In July 1903 he became assistant in the National Almanac Office of the U.S. Navy in Washington DC, a position he held until his death.

Howell learned whist at Harvard, becoming its best player. He took a prominent part in the activities of the American Whist League, and in 1896 published *Howell's Whist Openings: a systematic treatment of the short-suit game*, and in 1897 the *Howell Method of Duplicate Whist for Pairs*. See BIBLIOGRAPHY, A.

HOYLE, Edmond (1679–1769), a London, England barrister, was the first authority on whist and other games, and the first professional teacher of whist. His famous work was perhaps the best seller of the eighteenth century, and had the longest title of any book ever written on cards: *A Short Treatise on the Game of Whist, Containing the Laws of the Game, and also Some Rules Whereby a Beginner May, with Due Attention to Them, Attain to the Playing It Well*. It was published in 1742, and quickly went through several editions as well as being pirated extensively.

Hoyle's technique was surprisingly modern. He introduced the idea of inferring the nature of unseen hands from the fall of the cards, and discussed matters of probability. He also included a Code of Ethics and Fair Play, which was embodied almost without change in the LAWS OF AUCTION nearly two centuries later.

He was the first person to establish a tradition of law and order in card games, whence the phrase, now used to describe correct procedure in anything, "according to Hoyle." The book of laws by Hoyle was reprinted verbatim through the years. The prominent London Clubs eventually did make certain changes as to style and working from time to time, especially in the nineteenth century, but Hoyle's imprimatur remained on most editions. He achieved considerable fame during his lifetime, and his name has since become a household word. Any collection of rules of card, table, or board games is still termed a Hoyle. See BIBLIOGRAPHY, A.

HSIEH, Douglas H. L. (Dougie) (b. 1969) of New York City, won Polar Men's Pairs, Swiss Teams 1980 at the age of 10. He became ACBL YOUNGEST LIFE MASTER in 1981. See FAMILY.

HSIEH, William C. (Billy) (b. 1966) of New York City, high school student, was YOUNGEST LIFE MASTER in 1980. His regional titles include Space City KO Teams 1980, Southeastern Men's Swiss Teams 1980, Polar KO Teams, Master Swiss Teams 1980, Klondike KO Teams 1980. See FAMILY.

HSU, J. Y. (b. 1916) of Taipei, Taiwan, born in Kiangsu, China, textile merchant and bridge writer, was Far East Open Pairs champion 1959, 1969. He also represented Taiwan in international events in 1960, 1962, 1966, 1967, 1972, 1973. He is the author of *Contract Bridge for Beginners* and *Conventions*, and translator of 30 bridge books into Chinese. Hsu is the former chief editor of *Chinese Bridge Magazine*.

HUANG, Patrick K. (b. 1943) of Taipei, Taiwan, born in Shanghai, China, export sales manager, one of the leading players of the Far East, represented Taiwan in the Bermuda Bowl 1969, 1970, 1971, 1977, 1979 (second in 1969, 1970), World Team Olympiad 1964, 1972, 1976, 1980. He is the youngest player ever to represent his country in a major international championship when he participated in the Far East Championships in 1958 at the age of 15. In all he played in 14 FEC, winning the Open Teams 1967, 1969, 1976, 1978, 1981, Open Pairs 1963, 1967, 1976, the best record achieved by any Far East bridge player. He has been closely associated with C. C. WEI in the developing of the PRECISION CLUB system 1964-1969, and in the developing of Bionic Bridge since 1978.

HUGGARD, Richard T. (Dick) (b. 1936) of Ypsilanti MI, personnel manager, won Cambrian Shield KO Team, Open Teams 1974, Motor City Mixed Pairs 1973, Men's Swiss Teams 1976, 1979, Great Lakes Men's Swiss Teams 1979, Master Swiss Teams 1980, All-American Men's Swiss Teams 1980.

HUDECEK, Carl J. (b. 1934) of Toledo OH, physicist, won Fall NAC Life Master Men's Pairs 1966. His regional titles include Midwest 1 Open Teams 1957, 1960, 1974, Motor City Men's Swiss Teams 1976, Wolverine Swiss Teams 1978, District 12 GNT, Zone IV 1980, 1981. He is past president of Unit 105 and District 12, and is a member of the ACBL Goodwill Committee.

HUDGINS, John L. (Jack) (b. 1929) of Nashua NH, ACBL national tournament director, won Summer NAC secondary Sub-Senior Master Teams 1961, Mid-Atlantic Summer KO Teams 1962. A tournament director since 1960, Hudgins achieved the rating of national director in 1968.

HUDGINS, William D. Jr. (Doug) (b. 1947) of Richmond VA, bank assistant vice president, won Mid-Atlantic Spring Men's Pairs 1971, 1979, 1981, Master Pairs, Men's Swiss Teams 1979. Hudgins served as a member of the Board of the Richmond BA 1976-1977.

HUDSON, Robert R. (b. 1921) of Dunedin, New Zealand, company director and investment consultant, won New Zealand Open Teams 1966. He is past president of New Zealand CBA and former associate editor of *New Zealand Bridge*, a publication to which he still contributes articles.

HUGHES, Robert V. of Manchester CT, systems analyst and consultant, won New England Individual KO Teams 1974, Knockout Swiss Teams 1974, 1978. Hughes is a graduate of Columbia University.

HUGHES, Roy D. (b. 1954) of Willowdale ON, senior systems analyst, represented Canada in the Rosenblum Cup Teams 1978. His regional wins include Canadian Nat'l Swiss Teams 1975, Men's Swiss Teams 1977, Cambrian Shield Swiss Teams 1975, Nat'l Capital Open Pairs 1978, District 2 GNT 1977, 1978, Canadian National Teams Zone 3 1981.

HUGHES, T. Robert of Fort Collins CO, attorney, won Inter-Mountain Master Swiss Teams 1977, Desert Empire KO Teams 1978, Navajo Trail KO Teams 1979, Big Sky KO Teams 1979, Golden Gate Open Pairs Flt. A 1979, Rocky Mountain KO Teams 1979, White Hat KO Teams 1979.

HUGSTAD, James A. (Jim) (b. 1939) of Rochester MN, information developer, won Gopher Open Pairs 1969, KO Teams 1977, Swiss Teams 1979, 1980, Buffalo Centennial Swiss Teams 1974, District 14 GNT 1978. Hugstad has served in various executive positions for both Unit 103 and District 14, including president, and is member of the ACBL Goodwill Committee.

HULGAARD, Dr. Johannes (b. 1932) of Aarhus, Denmark, orthopedic surgeon, represented Denmark in the World Team Olympiad 1960, European Championships 1956, 1957, 1965, 1967, 1974, 1975. He won Nordic Open Teams 1973. His national titles include Danish Open Teams 1956, 1957, 1960, 1961, 1963, 1964, 1965, 1966, 1973, 1974, Open Pairs 1969, 1970. He is the co-author of *Modern Acol*.

HULGAARD, Lida (b. 1939) of Aarhus, Denmark, lawyer, represented Denmark in the World Team Olympiad 1964, Open Teams 1974, 1975, European Women's Championships 1963, 1967. She won Nordic Open Teams 1973. Her national titles include Danish Open Teams 1966, 1973, 1974, Open Pairs 1968, 1969.

HUME, L. HAMPTON (1924-1969) of Atlanta represented the United States in the World Open Pairs 1962. He won Spring NAC Open Pairs 1961 and placed second in Summer NAC Master Mixed Teams 1964. He has many regional wins to his credit. In 1964 Hume published a magazine, *Modern Bridge*.

HUMER, Norman D. (Fish) (b. 1940) of Boston, taxi driver, former computer programmer, won several regional titles including Spring NAC secondary Men's Swiss Teams 1973, Summer Open Pairs Flt. A 1975, Can-At Mixed Pairs 1974, KO Teams 1975, Master Swiss Teams, Swiss Teams 1978, Tri-State Winter Open Pairs 1973, Men's Pairs 1974, New England Knockouts KO Teams 1973, Can-Am KO Teams 1974, District 25 GNT, Zone II 1973, GNP 1981.

HUNT, John J. (b. 1910) of Trumbull CT, attorney, won New England Spring Individual 1961, 1965, Open Teams 1968. He is a past president of New England Conference and the Connecticut BA.

HUNT, Michael E. of Slidell LA, real estate broker, won Gulf Coast Mid-South Open Pairs, Swiss Teams 1972, Mid-South Swiss Teams 1976.

HUNT, Richard W. (b. 1931) of Jakarta, Indonesia, born in Brockton MA, controller, won Los Angeles Winter Swiss Teams 1975, Bridge Week Swiss Teams Flt. B 1980, Missouri Valley KO Teams 1979. He also won Jakarta Fall Teams 1978, Malaysia Summer Open Pairs 1972, Singapore Fall Swiss Teams 1973.

HUNTE, August J. (Augie) (b. 1928) of San Leandro CA, general manager, won Winter Holiday KO Teams 1970, California Capital Master Pairs, Swiss Teams 1972, Central California Swiss Teams 1973, Golden Gate Master Pairs 1977, Great Plains Men's Swiss Teams 1979.

HURDLE, John D. (b. 1946) of Vancouver BC, postal clerk, won Evergreen Men's Pairs 1976, Peach City KO Teams 1978, District 19 GNT 1976.

HUSKE, William H. (1879-1945), of New York City, a native of Ulverton, Quebec, spent 30 years in the newspaper business. He was associated with International News Service as a reporter and later became district manager in Marion OH. From 1927 to 1929 he was associated with the Cleveland *Plain Dealer* as its bridge editor. He covered the first famous "grudge" bridge match between ELY CULBERTSON and GEORGE REITH who came from New York to play Carl Robertson, an editorial writer for the *Plain Dealer*, and RALPH R. RICHARDS of Detroit. As a result of his coverage he became the associate editor of *Bridge World*, and in 1932 was made editor of this magazine. He was editor of the ACBL *Bulletin* 1937–1939, and wrote many articles on bridge and towie, the three-handed game he helped sponsor.

HUSSEIN, Ahmed D. (b. 1941) of New York City, born in Cairo, Egypt, stockbroker, represented Egypt in the World Open Pairs 1978. He won Fall NAC Mixed Pairs 1978 and placed second in the Life Master Pairs 1975. His regional wins include Summer NAC Swiss Teams 2nd Flt. 1973, Spring Open Pairs Flt. B 1979, New York–New Jersey Men's Pairs 1974, Puerto Rico Swiss Teams 1977, District 3 Swiss Teams Flt. A 1979, District 4 Fall Men's Swiss Teams 1979, Nassau-Suffolk Swiss Teams Flt A 1980.

HUSTON, Craig L. (b. 1945) of Portland OR, computer programmer, bridge teacher, won Oregon Trail KO Teams 1977, 1978, 1980, Open Pairs Flt. A 1981, Puget Sound Open Pairs Flt. A 1977, 1980, Swiss Teams Flt. A 1980, Indian Summer Open Pairs Flt. A 1977, District 20 GNP 1979, GNT, Zone VIII 1981.

HUTCHINSON, Carol (formerly Baird) of Seattle, travel agent, won Puget Sound Open Pairs 1973, Master Pairs 1975, Women's Pairs 1980, Yakima Valley Swiss Teams 1974, British Columbia Master Pairs 1980.

HUTCHINSON, Mary L. (Mrs. Robert D.) (b. 1916) of Lethbridge AB, won Hawaii Open Teams 1955, Pacific Northwest Master Pairs 1959, 1962, Mixed Pairs 1959, Inter-Mountain Master Pairs 1959.

HUTCHINSON, Robert D. (b. 1905) of Lethbridge AB, retired farmer, won Hawaii Men's Pairs, Open Teams 1955, Rocky Mountain Men's Pairs 1960, Canadian Men's Pairs 1968.

HWANG, Frank K. (b. 1940) of Warren NJ, born in Shanghai, China, research mathematician, placed second in the Bermuda Bowl 1969. He also represented Taiwan in the World Team Olympiad 1964, 1972, Far East Championships 1958, 1959, and was coach of the Far East champion Taiwan team 1981. He first represented Taiwan in 1958 when he was 18 along with his brother PATRICK K. HUANG who was 15. He has published numerous articles in mathematical magazines concerning the mathematics of constructing Howell rotations.

HYATT, M. Irene (b. 1929) of Boulder CO, bridge

club owner, won Spring secondary Women's Pairs 1976, Inter-Mountain Women's Pairs 1971, Navajo Trail Swiss Teams 1977, Oil City Women's Pairs 1978. A certified director, a member of the ABTA and IBPA, she has served as president and Board member of Unit 359 and has contributed articles to *The Contract Bridge Forum*.

HYMES, Edward, Jr. (1908–1962), a New York attorney, was a colorful figure in the early days of contract bridge. Life Master No. 23, Hymes was one of the leaders among the "Young Turks" who gained their seasoning as members of the Deal Cub group closely associated with P. HAL SIMS at his summer home in Deal NJ. He won his first major national championship, the 1935 Fall Open Pairs, with fellow Columbia alumnus OSWALD JACOBY, then added one Vanderbilt and four Spingold wins. Hymes was a lifetime member and a former president of the CAVENDISH CLUB in New York.

HYLAND, Daniel A. (b, 1929) of Arlington Heights IL, bank brokerage firm president, won Spring NAC Open Pairs 1975.

I

IN DER MAUR, Gangolf (b. 1931) of Klagenfurt, Austria, represented Austria in the World Team Olympiad 1968 and in several World Open Pairs and European Championships.

INGBERMAN, Monroe J. (b. 1935) of White Plains NY, college professor, won several regional titles including Summer NAC secondary Men's Pairs 1969, Southeastern KO Teams, Open Pairs 1969, Great Lakes Open Pairs 1963, Central States KO Teams 1962, 1966, Life and Senior Master Pairs 1962, Men's Pairs 1963, Eastern States KO Teams (Reisinger) 1970, 1976, 1982, District 3 GNT 1977, 1978, Zone 2 1978. He is the inventor of the FRAGMENT BID, 3 NT RESPONSE as a forcing major raise, and for many years has been a frequent contributor to bidding structure including SPLINTER BID, UNUSUAL OVER UNUSUAL, method for Inverted Minors, Structured Reverses, 3 NT to ask for a singleton after a jump major raise (Mathe Asking Bid), modified Roman Keycard Blackwood. Ingberman is a contributing editor, *Bridge Encyclopedia*. He was educated at University of Chicago and Northwestern University.

INGRAM, Henry St. John (1888–1974) of Farnborough, Kent, England, printer, bridge writer and editor, represented England in the SCHWAB CUP 1936, was captain of the British team in some prewar championships, and won the GOLD CUP 1936 in addition to other national successes. Ingram was editor of *Contract Bridge Journal* 1950–1955, contributing editor for *Britannica* and *Chambers* encyclopedias, and authored *How to Win at Bridge*. See BIBLIOGRAPHY, C, E.

INOUE, Shiro (b. 1915) of Tokyo, Japan, securities

company senior advisor, former bank president, won several national titles including Princess Takamatsu Cup 1968, 1972, Prince Takamatsu Cup 1970, Fujiyama Cup 1970, Yamada Cup 1965, 1971, 1977. He is a Life Master in both the United States and Japan. Inoue served as president of JAPAN CONTRACT BRIDGE LEAGUE 1969–1972.

INOUE, Utako (Mrs. Shiro) (b. 1914) of Tokyo, Japan, former secretary, represented Japan in the Far East Championships 1964, 1969 and the Philippines in 1974. Her national titles include Yamada Cup 1971, Princess Takamatsu Cup 1968, 1972, Fujiyama Cup 1968. She holds Life Master status in the United States, Japan, and the Philippines.

IRWIN, Florence (1865–1956), a well-known New York City novelist, bridge teacher and expert on auction bridge, wrote one of the first books on contract bridge in 1927. In the early 1900's she was bridge editor of the *New York Times*. See BIBLIOGRAPHY, A, C.

ISAACS, E. Sydney (Syd) of London ON, university associate registrar, represented Canada in the World Women's Teams 1976. She won Spring NAC Master Mixed Teams 1975, Canadian Nat'l Master Teams 1969, Mixed Pairs 1977, 1979, Women's Pairs 1973, Motor City Swiss Teams 1973, Southeastern Swiss Teams 1980.

ISRAEL, Dr. Robert H. (b. 1900) of Key Colony Beach FL, psychiatrist, won Keystone Fall Men's Pairs 1960, Mixed Pairs 1958, Open Teams 1959, Upper New York State Open Pairs 1959, Men's Pairs 1960.

ITABASHI, Mark M. (b. 1954) of Rancho Palos Verdes CA, computer analyst, independent commodities trader, won several regional titles including Fall NAC secondary Swiss Teams 1981, Raincross Swiss Teams 1979, 1980, Swiss Teams Flt. A 1980, Navajo Trail KO Teams 1977, Pacific Southwest Open Pairs Flt. A 1979, California Swiss Teams 1980, Bridge Week Swiss Teams 1981, Desert Empire Swiss Teams 1981, District 23 GNT 1980.

IVASKA, J. Paul Jr. (b. 1941) of Las Vegas, office manager, bridge professional, won Spring NAC Amateur Swiss Teams 1976, Fall Swiss Teams 2nd Flt. 1968, Swiss Teams 1979. His numerous regional titles include Spring NAC secondary Swiss Teams 1975, Fall Swiss Teams 1977, Mixed Pairs Flt. A 1981, Bridge Week Men's Pairs 1971, KO Teams 1973, Open Pairs 1975, Open Pairs Flt. A 1978, Master Swiss Teams 1981, Pacific Southwest KO Teams 1973, Orange County KO Teams 1974, Hawaii Men's Swiss Teams 1977, Bakersfield Swiss Teams 1974, Los Angeles Winter Swiss Teams 1977, Raincross Open Pairs Flt. A 1980, District 23 GNT, Zone VIII 1977.

IVEY, Ernest M. (Ernie) of Milpitas CA, systems engineer, won Spring NAC Open Pairs 1976, Summer NAC secondary Swiss Teams 1976, All-Western Mixed Pairs 1981.

J

JABBOUR, Zeke (Xique) of Ann Arbor MI, bridge professional, placed second in Spring NAC Men's Teams 1979, Fall Life Master Men's Pairs 1979. His numerous regional titles include All-American KO Teams 1978, Men's Swiss Teams 1980, Swiss Teams Flt. A 1981, Wolverine KO Teams 1978, Master Swiss Teams 1979, Midwest Fall Master Pairs, Swiss Teams 1978, District 5 Men's Swiss Teams 1978, KO Teams 1979, Men's Pairs, Swiss Teams Flt. A 1981, Great Lakes Men's Swiss Teams 1979, Master Swiss Teams 1980, Champagne KO Teams 1979, London Open Pairs 1979, District 8 Swiss Teams 1980, Motor City Men's Swiss Teams 1981, Veterans Day Swiss Teams, Swiss Teams Flt. A, Men's Pairs 1981. Formerly associated with all aspects of the theatre, Jabbour has lent his expertise to variety shows at North American Championships.

JABES, Rina of Milan, Italy, won the World Women's Teams 1972, 1976, European Women's Teams 1970, 1971, 1973, 1974.

JABON, Joseph A. (b. 1925) of Seattle, was born in New Orleans, where he was one of the "Whiz Kids" team that included SIDNEY LAZARD, Ron Dreyfus and Noel Duvic. Jabon placed second in Fall NAC Open Pairs 1965 and won several regional titles including Spring NAC secondary Individual 1959, Oregon Trail Open Teams 1963, 1966, 1968, Master Pairs 1962, 1977, KO Teams 1972, Open Pairs 1974, Pacific Northwest Master Pairs 1961, Open Pairs 1965, Mid-South Spring Mixed Pairs 1950, Inland Empire KO Teams 1971, Puget Sound Master Pairs 1969, British Columbia Master Pairs 1973, Evergreen Open Pairs 1975, District 19 GNT 1979.

JACKSON, Clement T. (b. 1944) of Albuquerque, systems analyst, won Navajo Trail KO Teams, Swiss Teams 1977, International City Open Pairs 1974, District 17 GNT 1974.

JACKSON, Connie H. (b. 1935) of Nashville, won District 15 Women's Pairs 1976, North Florida Women's Pairs 1978, Space City Women's Swiss Teams 1980.

JACKSON, Frank L. (b. 1919) of San Francisco, bridge club owner, teacher, columnist, placed second in Fall NAC Master Individual 1959 and won Bridge Week Open Pairs 1957, All-Western Open Pairs 1957, Open Teams 1960, Master Pairs 1961. He is a former member of the WESTERN CONFERENCE executive committee.

JACKSON, Joan S. (b. 1947) of Dallas placed second in Summer NAC Amateur Pairs 1976 and won Mid-South Open Pairs 1980, Missouri Valley Mixed Pairs 1976, Republic of Texas Open Pairs 1981.

JACOB, Dan R. (b. 1951) of Vancouver BC, born in Bucharest, Romania, fire protection engineer, was National Master of the Year (see MINI MCKENNEY) 1979. His regional titles include Emerald Empire KO

Teams 1979, British Columbia Men's Pairs 1981, Nat'l Capital KO Teams 1981, Canadian National Teams Zone 6 1981. He also won the Romanian Junior Championship 1975.

JACOBI, Ernst (b. 1914) of Zurich, Switzerland, chemical engineer, represented Switzerland in the World Team Olympiad 1960 and in many European Championships. His national successes include Open Teams seven times, Open Pairs 1957, 1961, 1962, Mixed Pairs 1963.

JACOBS, Walter L. (Wally) (b. 1896) of Bay Harbor Island FL, won Fall NAC Open Pairs 1936, 1939. His regional titles include All-American Open Teams 1938, Open Pairs 1939, Central States Open Teams 1938. Jacobs was the founder, president and chief executive officer of Hertz Rent-a-Car Corporation 1918 through 1960. He is the recipient of the Horatio Alger award.

JACOBSON, Ann (b. 1940) of Stockton CA, staff accountant, won Fall NAC Swiss Teams 1981. Her regional titles include Spring NAC secondary Swiss Teams 1980, Cotton Boll Women's Swiss Teams 1977, Pacific Southwest Master Swiss Teams 1979, Rogue River Valley Women's Swiss Teams 1976, Hawaii Mixed Pairs 1976, Golden State Women's Pairs 1976, Deseret Classic Mixed Pairs 1977, Bridge Week KO Teams 1979.

JACOBSON, Gerald N. (Jerry) (b. 1945) of Fullerton CA, systems and programming manager, won Pacific Southwest Swiss Teams Flt. A 1980, Raincross Swiss Teams Flt. A 1980, Swiss Teams 1979, Bridge Week Open Pairs 1981, District 22 GNT 1977, 1979. He is a graduate of University of Pittsburgh. He won three NASA Group Achievement Awards; Pioneer 10 (1974), new tracking station software (1978), Voyager (1981).

JACOBSON, Rita (b. 1911) of Johannesburg, South Africa, placed second in the World Women's Teams 1968, 1972, World Women's Pairs 1974. She also represented South Africa in the World Women's Teams 1964, 1976, 1980, World Women's Pairs 1962, 1966, 1970, MACCABIAH GAMES 1977. Her national wins include South Africa Open Teams 1970, 1971, 1973, 2975, Open Pairs 1959, Pioneer Teams 1968, Interprovincial Teams 1963, 1964, 1974. She has served the SOUTH AFRICAN BRIDGE FEDERATION as honorary treasurer since 1974 and as masterpoint secretary since 1958. Jacobson contributes bridge articles to *The Citizen* and *The Star*, daily newspapers in South Africa.

JACOBUS, Marc S. (b. 1951) of Castro Valley CA, bridge professional, won Fall NAC Life Master Men's Pairs 1972 and placed second in the Reisinger 1974. His more than 60 regional titles include All-Western KO Teams, Swiss Teams Flt. A 1981, BAM Teams 1980, Golden State Swiss Teams 1980, 1981, KO teams, Master Pairs 1978, Golden Gate Mixed Pairs 1979, KO Teams 1980, Mississippi Valley KO Teams, Master Pairs, Swiss Teams 1979, Rogue

River Valley KO Teams, Swiss Teams 1980, Oregon Trail KO Teams, Open Pairs Flt. A 1979, Swiss Teams Flt. A 1981, Bridge Week KO Teams 1980, Puget Sound Swiss Teams, KO Teams 1981, Men's Pairs 1980, Men's Swiss Teams 1979, District 25 GNT 1974, 1977, Zone II 1977.

JACOBY, James O. (b. 1933) of Richardson TX, stockbroker, WFB Grand Master #9, one of the world's leading players, won the Bermuda Bowl 1970, 1971, World Mixed Teams 1972, and placed second in the Bermuda Bowl 1963, 1973, World Team Olympiad 1972, World Open Pairs 1966, World Mixed Pairs 1978. He won the Spingold 1969, Chicago (since 1965 the Reisinger) 1955, Reisinger 1970, 1977, Vanderbilt 1965, 1967, 1971, 1981, Fall NAC Men's Pairs 1956, Spring NAC Men's Teams 1968, 1972, 1973, Summer NAC Master Mixed Teams 1968, Grand National Teams 198. He placed second in the Spingold 1957, 1962, 1970, 1973, 1976, Vanderbilt 1970, Fall NAC Men's Teams 1954, 1968, Mixed Pairs 1963, Blue Ribbon Pairs 1976, Summer NAC Life Master Pairs 1968, 1971, Spring NAC Men's Teams 1969. He is the winner of scores of regional titles. He is the co-author with his father, OSWALD JACOBY, of JACOBY TRANSFER BID and JACOBY 2 NT, and a syndicated bridge column. Jacoby has frequently served as a member of the Board of Governors and is past president of the Dallas BA. He is a graduate of Notre Dame. His interests include backgammon, sports and opera. See ACES TEAM and FAMILY.

JACOBY, Mary Zita (Mrs. Oswald) (b. 1909) of Dallas placed second in Summer NAC Master Mixed Teams 1935 and won Mid-South Summer Open Teams 1961, Texas Fall Open Teams 1960, Texas Spring Mixed Teams 1966. She is a former tennis champion. She is the only woman whose husband and son have won world titles. See FAMILY.

JACOBY, Oswald (Ozzie, Jake) of Dallas, bridge columnist, is one of the great players of all time. He first achieved international preeminence as a bridge player as partner of SIDNEY LENZ in the CULBERTSON-LENZ MATCH, but he had already established himself as a champion at auction and contract. He next became a member of the famed FOUR HORSEMEN and FOUR ACES teams. His selection by Lenz over players of greater experience and with whom Lenz had practiced partnerships was early recognition of the brilliance and skill that were later to bring Jacoby to the top of the ACBL's list of all-time masterpoint winners.

Jacoby, born in Brooklyn on Dec. 8, 1902, left Columbia in his junior year to become an actuary, completing the examination of the Society of Actuaries in 1924 to become, at age 21, the youngest person ever to do so. After four years with Metropolitan Life, he went into business for himself, but his success was cut short by the 1929 stockmarket crash.

Jacoby's victory-studded career includes many oddities. He played in (and won) his first auction tournament in July, 1929 — the National Team

Championship of the AMERICAN WHIST LEAGUE. But he had already won the first big contract pair tournament ever played, the Goldman Pairs event in the Eastern States Championships held in February of that year. Later on, he set a record by winning the GOLDMAN TROPHY three times in 20 years, the only occasions on which he entered. Afterward, he became a national champion, winning two AWL pair and team events.

After the Culbertson–Lenz match, Jacoby was for nearly two years secretary of the UNITED STATES BRIDGE ASSOCIATION, thus being associated with ELY CULBERTSON. Late in 1933, however, he helped to form the original Four Aces team, which dominated the bridge world for the next several years. In this period, in addition to AMERICAN BRIDGE LEAGUE triumphs, he won two pair championships and four team championships of the USBA. As of December 7, 1941 Jacoby held first place in the ACBL masterpoint ranking.

Jacoby had two months of Army service in World War I, when he was 15, and was awarded the victory medal. On Dec. 7, 1941 he was playing in the Fall NAC Open Pairs in Richmond VA when the Pearl Harbor attack was announced. He immediately left the tournament and did not play again for four years. During most of that time he served as a specialist in the Navy, from which he eventually was separated with the rank of lieutenant commander. Returning to competition in 1945, he found CHARLES GOREN far ahead in the masterpoint rankings. He had done very little about returning to the top when he again returned to duty in 1950 for service in the Korean war. He served as a commander in Intelligence and was a member of the original staff at the Panmunjom armistice conference. This return to service cost him his place on the American team in the first Bermuda Bowl matches. However, he had represented the ABL in international competition as far back as 1935 when the Four Aces team defeated the French, champions of Europe, in the first official World Championship encounter. (See WORLD CHAMPIONSHIPS.)

Returning from two years of Korean service, Jacoby found he dropped out of the first 10. By 1958 he had managed to move back into sixth place, still far behind Goren. At that time he decided to make a determined effort to regain the #1 position. By 1962, he had done so. Between 1959 and 1963, he won the McKENNEY TROPHY four times in five years; the only player at that time older than 50 to win the trophy, Jacoby won it at ages 57, 59, 60 and 61. In 1963 he became the first player to acquire more than 1,000 points in a single year. His winning total that year was 1,034. In 1967, he surpassed the 10,000-point mark, at which time he retired from active competition for the McKenney Trophy. Almost exactly one year later he relinquished his position as top masterpoint holder to BARRY CRANE.

In 1950, Jacoby became the daily bridge columnist for Newspaper Enterprise Association, serving several hundred newspapers. He established a record on April 22, 1982 when his 10,000th article was printed. (Goren's name has appeared on more than this number, but he has not written any columns for many years.) Jacoby wrote books on poker, canasta,

gin rummy and mathematical odds. Jacoby also continuously maintained a practice as a consulting actuary, served for six years as a member of the Board of Visitors of Harvard Observatory (for the last three, under the chairmanship of then Senator John F. Kennedy), became an expert on computers, and was frequently consulted on question of tournament movements, elimination schedules and scoring.

He won a North American Championship (the Chicago in 1955) with his son, JAMES JACOBY, and scored many victories with his wife for 50 years, MARY ZITA JACOBY, hoping to add to his titles the missing one — most master points owned by any husband and wife, regardless of when acquired.

Jacoby was elected to the bridge HALL OF FAME in 1965 and was named ACBL Honorary Member in 1967. As npc of the North American teams for 1969, 1970, and 1971, Jacoby captained the first North American Bermuda Bowl champion teams (1970, 1971) in more than a decade.

His North American Championship titles are as follows: Spingold 1934, 1936, 1938, 1939, 1945, 1950, 1959; Vanderbilt 1931, 1934, 1935, 1937, 1938, 1946, 1965; Chicago (since 1965 the Reisinger) 1955; Master Individual 1935; Master Mixed Teams 1968; Life Master Pairs 1936; Men's Teams 1952, 1959; Open Pairs 1935, 1960, 1964; Men's Pairs 1934, 1939, 1949. He also won USBA Grand National Open Teams 1934, 1935, 1937, Open Pairs 1936, 1937 and ABL Men's Teams 1931, 1932, AWL Team-of-Four 1929, 1931, 1933, Open Pairs 1933, HERMAN TROPHY 1960. He placed second in many NAC events and won countless regional titles including the MARCUS CUP 1955. In 1973 he won the World Championship of Backgammon.

Jacoby pioneered many bidding ideas, including FORCING 2 NT, JACOBY TRANSFER BIDS, and WEAK JUMP OVERCALLS. More recently his innovations have included developments of GERBER and BLACKWOOD, and a specialized use of TWO NOTRUMP and THREE NOTRUMP RESPONSES. His most recent innovations are the use of TWO-WAY STAYMAN in connection with Jacoby Transfer Bids after 2 NT opening and after 2♣-anything-2 NT, and he invented the use of 2♡ as a double negative response to 2♣ with 2 NT a positive heart response and 2♢ the usual waiting bid. Among his writings are *The Four Aces System, What's New in Bridge, Win at Bridge with Oswald Jacoby, Win at Bridge with Jacoby Modern, The Backgammon Book* (with JOHN CRAWFORD), and many books on mathematics, gambling, poker, and other card games, including canasta, in which he had the two best-selling books. See BIBLIOGRAPHY, B, C, E, M, and FAMILY.

JAEGER, Henry P. (1888–1971) of Cleveland Heights OH won trophies in whist, auction, and contract. He was President of the ABL in 1928 and Honorary Member of the ACBL in 1939. A bridge writer and lecturer, Jaeger was a member of the group which promoted the OFFICIAL SYSTEM.

JAEGER, Jane (Mrs. Lewis M.) (b. 1914) of Miami, formerly of New York City, won the Chicago (since 1965 the Reisinger) 1947, Fall NAC Open Pairs

1945, Summer NAC Master Mixed Teams 1951, Grand National Teams 1973, and placed second in the Vanderbilt 1956. Her regional titles include Fall NAC secondary Women's Swiss Teams 1977, Eastern States KO Teams (Reisinger) 1945, Mixed Teams 1946, Mixed Pairs 1949, Women's Pairs 1966, Southeastern Women's Pairs 1966, KO Teams 1968. She and her late husband were the first married couple to attain Life Master ranking, #74 and #94 respectively, in 1947.

JAFRI, Mazhar of Pakistan is representative to the WBF Executive Council from Zone 4 and secretary of the BRIDGE FEDERATION OF ASIA AND THE MIDDLE EAST. Jafri was primarily responsible for the creation of the new WBF zone that produced Pakistan as a Bermuda Bowl finalist in 1981, the first year the new zone was eligible to send a team.

JAFRI, Syed Saeed (b. 1916) of Pakistan, is president of PAKISTAN BRIDGE ASSOCIATION and vice president of BRIDGE FEDERATION OF ASIA THE THE MIDDLE EAST. He was educated at Allahabad, India and School of Oriental Studies, London, England. Formerly with the Indian Civil Service, Jafri migrated to Pakistan and joined the Civil Service of Pakistan in 1947. He retired from Civil Service and presently is chairman and president of various businesses and agencies. He has attended or presided over a large number of international conferences including ECOSOC, ECAFE, Asian Productivity Organizaton Preparatory Conference, and APO Africa Conference.

JAÏS, Pierre (b. 1913) of Paris, France, physician, WBF Grand Master, is one of the great players of the world. His partnership with ROGER TRÉZEL, one of the strongest in the world from 1950 to 1970, demonstrated the efficiency of the *tendance canapé* (or modified canapé), and set a unique record by winning all three major world titles: Bermuda Bowl 1956, World Team Olympiad 1960, World Open Pairs 1962. He was European champion in 1955, 1970 and placed second in 1954, 1956, 1959. Jaïs won the London *Sunday Times Pairs* (since 1981 INVITATIONAL PAIRS CHAMPIONSHIP) 1963, and many French national titles. His writings include *How to Win at Rubber Bridge, Apprenez á mieux jouer au bridge, Bridge simple et moderne, La majeure cinquième,* and *Jeu de la carte contre le declarant,* and many contributions to French periodicals. See BIBLIOGRAPHY, E.

JALAVA, Matti (b. 1926) of Helsinki, Finland, salesman, represented Finland in the European Championships 1956, 1963, Nordic Championships 1962. His national successes include Open Teams 1949, 1958, 1960, 1962, 1963.

JALBUENA, Lydia (b. 1923) of Manila, Philippines, retired secretary, represented the Philippines in the World Team Olympiad 1964, World Women's Pairs, World Mixed Teams 1962, World Women's Teams 1972, 1980, Far East Championships 1962, 1965, 1966, 1968, 1970, 1975, 1976, 1977, 1978, 1979, 1981. Her national wins include PCBL Challenge Cup 1981, Open Pairs 1962, 1968, 1969, 1978, 1979, Open Teams 1971, 1972, 1975, 1979, 1981, Tuason Cup 1972, 1973, 1974, 1980. She served as a member of the PCBL Board 1978–1980 and as chairman of the tournament committee 1978, 1980.

JANITSCHKE, Jan P. (b. 1947) of Denver, professional bridge player and teacher, won the Life Master Men's Pairs, Grand National Teams 1980, Summer NAC Men's Swiss Teams 1982. His more than 60 regional titles include Summer NAC secondary Swiss Teams 1976, Swiss Teams Flt. A 1979, Fall Swiss Teams Flt. A, Swiss Teams 1978, Mid-Winter Holiday KO Teams 1973, Missouri Valley Swiss Teams 1974, KO Teams, Open Pairs Flt. A 1978, Rocky Mountain Swiss Teams 1977, 1980, Men's Pairs 1977, 1979, KO Teams 1981, California Capital KO Teams, Swiss Teams Flt. A 1980, Acapulco Master Pairs, Open Pairs 1981, Wine Country KO Teams 1981, Pacific Southwest Men's Swiss Teams, Swiss Teams Flt. A 1982. He plays most frequently with his brother Craig. Janitschke is a graduate of Colorado State College. He is an excellent pianist and violinist and has performed as a soloist twice with local symphony orchestras as a teenager.

JANITSCHKE, V. Craig (b. 1951) of Lacey WA, real estate agent, won the Life Master Men's Pairs, Grand National Teams 1980, Spring NAC Open Pairs 1982. His more than 75 regional titles include Summer NAC secondary Swiss Teams Flt. A 1979, Fall Swiss Teams Flt. A, Swiss Teams 1978, Spring Open Pairs 1980, California Capital KO Teams, Men's Pairs, Swiss Teams Flt. A 1980, Oregon Trail Men's Pairs, Master Pairs 1982, Pacific Southwest Master Pairs, Men's Swiss Teams, Swiss Teams Flt. A 1982, Mid-Winter Holiday Master Pairs, Open Pairs Flt. A 1981, Los Angeles Winter Swiss Teams, Master Pairs 1981, Veterans Day Master Pairs, Swiss Teams Flt. A 1981, Champagne KO teams, Men's Swiss Teams 1981, Indian Summer Swiss Teams, Master Pairs 1981, Hawaii Open Pairs, Swiss Teams 1981, Desert Empire Open Pairs Flt. A, Swiss Teams Flt. A 1981, Master Pairs 1980. His most frequent partners are his brother, Jan, and BARRY CRANE. He has served the Denver Unit in various capacities. Janitschke is a graduate of University of Colorado. Formerly a pianist for a ballet company, he was State of Colorado champion pianist (junior high division) in 1966.

JANNERSTEN, Eric (1912–1982) of Stockholm Sweden, editor and publisher, was one of the leading bridge personalities of Europe. He represented Sweden on several occasions including European Championship 1951, and won many national titles. He was a founder of the INTERNATIONAL BRIDGE PRESS ASSOCIATION and as its executive secretary-treasurer until his retirement in 1975 was a power in the promotion of bridge on the international level. Jannersten founded, in 1939, *Bridgetidningen* Sweden's internationally acclaimed bridge magazine. Bridge columnist since 1940, Jannersten was editor and publisher of *European Bridge Review* 1949-1951, authored best-selling books on bridge, and published about 40 bridge books. He headed a bridge school from 1938, with an estimated 150,000 pupils. Other activities included a radio program, "Bridge on the Air," directing World Team Olympiad 1960 and 1964, European Championship 1962, and other national tournaments, and acting as BRIDGE-O-RAMA commentator. He invented the BIDDING BOX, which is now used in all major national and international events.

JAQUES, Arturo F. (b. 1923) of Buenos Aires, Argentina, travel agent and bridge writer, represented Argentina in the World Team Olympiad 1964, 1972, Bermuda Bowl 1959, 1962. He was South American champion 1958, 1959, 1961, and placed second in 1955, 1956 and 1970. His national titles include Argentine Open Teams 1950, 1954, 1958, 1960, 1961, 1963, 1965, 1967, 1969, 1971, 1972, 1976, 1980, Master Pairs 1963, 1965, 1966, 1974, 1975, Open Pairs 1951, 1959, 1960, 1964, 1965, 1974, 1979, 1980, Individual 1955, Mixed Pairs 1956, 1962, 1970, 1972, Mixed Teams 1956, 1959, 1965, 1966, 1967, 1972, 1973, 1974, 1975, 1976, 1979, 1981. He won the GABARRET CUP 1959, 1960 and was the top Argentine masterpoint holder 1960 through 1975. He is a former vice president of the IBPA and former editor of *Bridge Argentino*. He contributes to many bridge periodicals and is a contributing editor, *Bridge Encyclopedia*.

JAWORSKI, Antoni (b. 1930) of Warsaw, Poland, sanitation engineer, represented Poland in the European Championships 1965, 1967. He won Hungarian Balaton Bowl 1963, Belgian Open Pairs 1964, Baltic Bowl 1964, Polish Open Teams 1962, 1963, 1964, 1966.

JAYE, Eli (b. 1910) of New York City, company president, won Eastern States KO Teams (Reisinger) 1954, Mixed Teams 1955, Open Pairs (Goldman) 1964, Keystone Conference Open Teams 1952, 1955, Florida Men's Pairs 1970. Jaye is past president of the Greater New York BA and a former member of the ACBL Charity Committee.

JEANS, Christopher G. (b. 1944) of Doylestown PA, computer programmer, placed second in Fall NAC Life Master Men's Pairs 1969 and won Pittsburgh Mixed Pairs 1969, Mid-Atlantic Swiss Teams 1970, Keystone KO Teams 1973, District 4 GNT 1973.

JEDRZEJOWSKI, Kyzysztof (b. 1941) of Warsaw, Poland, electronics engineer, represented Poland in the European Championships 1967, European Junior Championships 1968. He placed third in the World Par Contest 1963 and won Polish Open Teams 1966, 1968, Mixed Teams 1966.

JEFFERSON, Leonard A. Jr., (Len) (b. 1922) of Arlington TX, bridge writer, retired federal employee, represented the United States in the World Pairs 1974, 1978. He won ABA National Open Teams 1969, 1976, 1977, 1979, 1980, numerous regional titles, and the Friend Award

1979, 1980. Jefferson is bridge writer for the *Arlington Daily News*. He has served bridge for many years in various capacities including organizer of bridge clubs and Units, tournament chairman, ABA/ACBL liaison (1976-1982).

JELLINEK, Hans, born in Vienna, Austria, was deported by the Germans from Norway in 1940 and died in a concentration camp. He was World Champion 1937 and European Champion 1936. His partnership with KARL SCHNEIDER was considered the strongest in Europe in the mid-Thirties.

JENSEN, Nils E. (b. 1920) of Stockholm, Sweden, president and owner of an electric company, represented Sweden in the World Mixed Teams 1962, World Mixed Pairs 1966, 1974, World Open Pairs 1978 and placed second in the Far East Championships 1977. He served as npc for Sweden's European and Nordic Championships teams. Jensen organized the Bermuda Bowl and Olympiad held in Stockholm 1970, the World Pairs Olympiad in Las Palmas 1974, and the Bermuda Bowl in Stockholm 1983. He served as president of the SWEDISH BRIDGE LEAGUE 1965-1970, and held many executive positions in the EUROPEAN BRIDGE LEAGUE since 1969 including vice president 1973-1980, and president since 1980. Jensen has represented Zone 1 in the WORLD BRIDGE FEDERATION since 1971, and has been 2nd vice president since 1978.

JESNER, George D. (b. 1925) of Canberra, Australia, formerly of Glasgow, Scotland, master draper, bridge teacher and writer, was a member of the victorious Scottish Team in the CAMROSE TROPHY series 1964. He won Scottish Open Teams twice and Open Pairs.

JOHNSON, Benjamin O. (1906-1976), counsel and member of the Executive Committee of the WBF, presided over the ACBL in 1953. An attorney from Spartanburg SC, Johnson served as npc of the U.S. Bermuda Bowl Team in 1954 and as chairman of the ACBL Charity Foundation. Johnson won the CHICAGO TROPHY (since 1965 the Reisinger) in 1949.

JOHNSON, Chester (Chet) (b. 1940) of Chicago, stock chaser, one of the leading ABA players, ranked 7th in master points with over 6100, won ABA National Open Teams 1977, KO Teams 1982, ACBL Central States I Men's Pairs 1982.

JOHNSON, George W. (b. 1923) of Charlotte NC, U.S. Postal Service director of finance, won several AMERICAN BRIDGE ASSOCIATION regional and national titles. He has been active in ABA bridge administration since 1968 and will serve as its president in 1984. He was elected to the ACBL Goodwill Committee in 1979. Johnson is an executive board member of Goodwill Industries. He was Elk of the Year 1969 and Potentate, NABBAR Shrine Temple 1971-1972.

JOHNSON, Jared A. (b. 1948) of Golden CO, bridge writer, former lawyer, has been bridge editor for the *Denver Post* since 1977. He has also contributed articles to *Popular Bridge*.

JOHNSON, Karl (b. 1924) of Moline IL has been an ACBL national tournament director since 1967. His directing career began in 1960.

JOHNSON, Marilyn K. (b. 1928) of Houston, WBF GRAND MASTER, one of the world's leading women players, won the World Women's Pairs 1970, Venice Trophy 1978, World Women's Teams 1980, and also represented the United States in the World Women's Pairs 1974, 1978, World Women's Teams 1972, 1976. She won Fall NAC Mixed Pairs 1968, 1973, Spring NAC Women's Teams 1974, 1975, 1976, (second in 1973), Life Master Pairs 1978 (she and her partner MARY JANE FARELL were the first women pair ever to win this event). She placed second in Spring NAC Women's Pairs 1967, Mixed Pairs 1969, Summer Master Mixed Teams 1969. Her numerous regional titles include All-Western Open Teams 1960, KO Teams 1967, Open Pairs 1970, Bridge Week Open Teams 1964, 1965, Golden Gate KO Teams, Open Pairs 1969, Open Teams 1971. Johnson is a graduate of Wellesley College. She is manager of Information Services for a major oil company and is very active in information professional societies, in which she has held several national offices.

JOHNSON, Perry L. (b. 1948) of Southfield MI, management consultant, placed second in Spring NAC Men's Pairs 1979 and won Wolverine Non-Master Pairs 1978, Great Lakes Open Pairs Flt. A 1980, Motor City Men's Pairs 1980.

JOHNSON, Peter (b. 1912) of Chestnut Hill MA, bridge teacher, placed second in Fall NAC Mixed Pairs 1960 and won New England KO Teams 1943, Spring Open Teams 1953, 1955, Master Pairs 1948, Mixed Teams 1957, Men's Pairs 1955, 1956.

JOHNSON, Ralph E. (b. 1932) of Reno NV, formerly of Eugene OR, investor, former real estate broker, won Calgary Open Pairs 1973, Inland Empire Swiss Teams 1976, Oregon Trail Master Swiss Teams 1978. Johnson has served as president and vice president of District 20 and as chairman of its Conduct and Ethics Committee.

JOHNSON, Robert Lee of Los Angeles, bridge lecturer and broadcaster, was a prominent pioneer in the teaching of bridge on radio and TV.

JOHNSON, Sallie B. of New York City, bridge teacher, formerly one of the leading American women players, represented the United States in the World Women's Pairs 1970 and won the Deauville Individual 1970. She won Spring NAC Women's Teams 1955, 1958, 1960, 1961, 1968, and placed second in Spring NAC Women's Pairs 1969, Summer NAC Master Mixed Teams 1957, 1974. Her many regional wins include Fall NAC secondary Women's Teams 1968, 1969, Eastern States Women's Pairs 1962, 1968, New England Fall Women's Pairs 1955, New York–New Jersey Open Teams 1963.

JOLMA, Lawrence N. (Larry) of Portland OR, business broker, won Spring NAC Men's Teams 1967, secondary Men's Pairs 1975, Rogue River Valley Men's Teams 1976, Oregon Trail KO Teams 1974. Jolma has been a member of the Board of Directors since 1966. He has also served as ACBL treasurer, District 20 Board member, Western Conference Board member, and is a past president of Unit 487.

JOLMA, Marjorie L. (Mrs. Lawrence) of Portland OR, won Oregon Trail KO Teams 1974, Women's Pairs 1961, 1974, Women's Swiss Teams 1977.

JONES, Alan K. (Kent) (b. 1937) of Huntsville TX, university professor, won Lone Star Open Pairs 1969, South Texas Master Pairs 1974, District 16 GNT 1974.

JONES, Dr. Arnold P. (Doc) (b. 1932) of Chicago, psychologist, served as president of the ABA 1972–1974, 1977–1981. He was the first ABA president to be ranked in the top 25 list of ABA masterpoint holders. Jones was educated at Western Michigan University, De Paul University and University of Illinois. Formerly associate professor of educational psychology at Northeastern Illinois University, Jones is currently vice chancellor for personnel at City College of Chicago.

JONES, Henry. See CAVENDISH.

JONES, Markland G. (Mark) (b. 1944) of Mesa AZ, engineer, won North Florida Swiss Teams 1977, Mid-Winter Holiday KO Teams 1977, Summer NAC secondary Golder Master Pairs 1979.

JONES, Michael D. of San Francisco, bridge professional, won Golden State Open Pairs 1970, Texas Capital Swiss Teams 1975, Navajo Trail Open Pairs 1971, Men's Pairs 1975, Mid-Winter Holiday Swiss Teams 1976, Hawaii Men's Pairs 1976, California Capital Men's Pairs 1976, Swiss Teams, Mixed Pairs 1980.

JONES, Richard L. (Dick) (b. 1935) of Sacramento CA, real estate broker, won Oregon Trail Open Teams 1967, KO Teams 1968, 1973, Tri-Cities Swiss Teams 1975, California Capital KO Teams 1976, Mount Shasta Swiss Teams, Men's Pairs, Master Swiss Teams 1978.

JONES, Wendy E. (b. 1942) of Thunder Bay ON, receptionist, won Gopher Women's Pairs 1979, Thunder Bay Women's Pairs 1979, Nat'l Capital Women's Pairs 1981.

JORDAN, John S. III (Big John) (b. 1939) of Washington DC, economist, former math teacher, won several ABA national titles including ABA Summer KO Teams Flt. A 1975, KO Teams Flt. B 1969, Spring Open Pairs 1982, Men's Teams 1976, Swiss Teams 1980 and placed second in ABA Spring Mixed Pairs 1982, KO Teams Flt. A 1978, Summer Mixed Teams 1970. He has also won many ABA sectional (equivalent to ACBL regional) titles. Jordan is president of Banneker BC and an ABA tournament director. He is a graduate of Queens College.

JORDAN, Robert F. (b. 1927) of Cincinnati, businessman, formerly one of the outstanding American bridge players, placed second in the World Team Olympiad 1964, 1968 and also represented the United States in the World Open Pairs 1962 and North American in the Bermuda Bowl 1963. He won the McKENNEY TROPHY 1960, MOTT-SMITH TROPHY 1961, 1962, Vanderbilt 1961, 1968, Reisinger 1966, 1967, Summer NAC Master Mixed Teams 1959, Spring NAC Open Pairs 1960, 1962, and placed second in the Vanderbilt 1965, Chicago (since 1965 the Reisinger) 1961, Spring NAC Mixed Pairs 1961, Fall NAC Men's Pairs 1956. His numerous regional titles include Eastern States KO Teams (Reisinger) 1960, 1961, Mixed Teams 1958, Keystone Open Pairs 1958, Mid-Atlantic Summer Open Teams 1960, All-American Men's Pairs 1960, District 4 Open Pairs 1964, 1965, Open Teams 1965. Jordan and ARTHUR ROBINSON, thought by many to be the best American partnership in the 1960's came, out of retirement to play in the *Bicentennial Bridge Match* against Great Britain in 1976.

JOTCHAM, Ray (b. 1941) of Scarborough ON, mathematics and computer science teacher, placed second in the Spingold 1964 and won Eastern States Open Pairs (Goldman) 1963, Can-Am Open Teams 1964, 1967, 1969, Master Pairs 1974, Pittsburgh Labor Day KO Teams 1980. Jotcham is a sectional tournament director in the eastern Ontario area.

JOURDAIN, Patrick D. (b. 1942) of Cardiff, Wales, bridge club manager, first Grand Master in Wales, represented Wales in the World Open Pairs 1970, 1974, and Wales and Scotland in CAMROSE TROPHY matches. He won the Camrose Trophy for Scotland 1976, 1977, BBL GOLD CUP 1976, and all major team titles in Scotland and Wales. Jourdain is the editor of the INTERNATIONAL BRIDGE PRESS ASSOCIATION *Bulletin*, and the co-author (with TERENCE REESE) of *Squeeze Play is Easy*.

JOURDAN, Edwin Rogers (Roger) (b. 1950) of Del Ray Beach FL, professional bridge player and teacher, won more than 30 regional titles including Spring NAC secondary Swiss Teams 1978, Mexican Nat'l KO Teams 1978, District 8 KO Teams 1979, Master Swiss Teams, Master Pairs 1980, Pikes Peak Swiss Teams Flt. A, Swiss Teams 1980, Saskatchewan KO Teams, Men's Pairs 1980, Black Hills Rodeo KO Teams, Swiss Teams 1980, Inland Empire Swiss Teams, Men's Pairs 1980, Wisconsin Open Pairs, Men's Swiss Teams 1980. Jourdan has served Unit 128 as a member of the Board, as tournament chairman and is a former member of ACBL Board of Governers.

JOYCE, David J. (b. 1942) of Chicago, commodity futures broker, attorney, won Fall NAC Open Pairs 1966, Bridge Week Master Pairs 1970, 1974, Summer NAC secondary Commerical Teams 1977.

JOYCE, Randolph (Randy) (b. 1947) of Raleigh NC, office manager, won Fall NAC secondary Men's Pairs 1977, Washington Bridge Week Open Pairs, Swiss Teams 1974, Mid-Atlantic Winter Swiss Teams 1981, Open Pairs 1979, 1980, Men's Pairs 1969, Spring Swiss Teams 1972, Fall Swiss Teams 1968, 1971, 1973, 1974, District 7 GNT 1977, 1978, GNP 1981. Joyce has served as president of Unit 119 (1979–1981) and as a member of the ACBL Board of Governors (1977–1981).

JUAN, Jane. See PRIDAY, JANE.

JUSTAN, Sheldon (b. 1949) of Scranton PA, self-employed, placed second in Fall NAC Amateur Men's Pairs 1976 and won Summer NAC secondary Swiss Teams 1980, Spring Open Pairs 1978, District 4 Men's Pairs, Open Pairs 1977, Open Pairs Flt. A 1979, Fall Men's Swiss Teams 1979. He has served as vice president and president of Unit 120 and is District 4 Board member and a member of the ACBL Board of Governors.

JUSTL, Thomas M. (b. 1949) of Maple Shade NJ, accounting manager, won Fall NAC secondary Swiss Teams 1980, District 4 Men's Swiss Teams, Fall Men's Swiss Teams 1977, Tri-State Swiss Teams 1975, Mid-Atlantic Swiss Teams 1978, Big Apple Open Pairs Flt. A 1978.

K

KACHMAR, Barbara (formerly Collyer) (1911–1982) of Beverly Hills CA, formerly of New York City, won USBA Mixed Pairs 1936, Spring NAC Women's Teams 1960, 1961 (second in 1963), Fall NAC Women's Pairs 1962, and placed second in Summer NAC Master Mixed Teams 1934. Her writings included many entertaining contributions to *Bridge World*, *Modern Bridge* and other periodicals.

KAHN, Richard F. (b. 1911) of New York City, retired motion picture sales executive, formerly one of the leading American players, placed second in the Bermuda Bowl 1956. He won the Chicago (since 1965 the Reisinger) 1949, Vanderbilt 1953, Spingold 1955, Life Master Pairs 1951, Summer NAC Master Mixed Teams 1951, Fall NAC Mixed Pairs 1939, Grand National Mixed Teams 1933, and placed second in Fall NAC Open Pairs 1951. His numerous regional titles include Eastern States KO Teams (Reisinger) 1956, 1957, 1958, 1959, 1969, Open Pairs 1947, Master Pairs 1960. He was co-founder of the Card School of New York in 1950 and served both the CAVENDISH CLUB and the Greater New York BA for 10 years. Kahn is a graduate of Columbia.

KALES, Eugene L. (b. 1943) of Arlington VA, accountant, won Mid-Atlantic KO Teams 1975, District 6 GNT, Zone III 1973.

KALMIN, Lester R. (b. 1938) of Pretoria, South Africa, chartered accountant, represented South Africa in the World Team Olympiad 1976, MACCABIAH GAMES 1981. His national titles include South African Open Teams 1974, Open Pairs 1974, Interprovincial Teams 1976, 1978, 1980.

KAMALAKARA RAO, Y. of Hyderabad, India, captained the Indian Open Team in the World Team Olympiad in 1980 and in the Far East Championships in 1972. He is secretary of the BRIDGE FEDERATION OF INDIA and editor of the Indian *Bridge World*. A national director, he was chief tournament director for the BFAME Championships held in 1981 and the first Indian to be appointed as tournament director for the World Championships (1982).

KAMB, Judge John G. (b. 1929) of Mount Vernon WA, district court judge, won Puget Sound KO Teams 1968, 1969, British Columbia Men's Pairs 1970, Tri-Cities Open Pairs 1975, Emerald Empire Open Pairs 1977. He has served as District 19 representative to the ACBL Board of Governors, and as president of Unit 439.

KAMIL, Michael S. (b. 1960) of Fort Lee NJ, won several regionals including Bluenose KO Teams 1981, Autumn Leaf Men's Swiss Teams 1981, Southeastern Swiss Teams 1982, London Bridge KO Teams 1982, William Keohane Individual KO Teams 1982, Tri-State Mixed Pairs, Open Pairs Flt. A 1981, District 3 Men's Pairs 1981, GNT Zone II 1981.

KAMINSKI, Amos (b. 1929) of New York City, born in Tel-Aviv, Israel, investment manager, former physicist, placed second in Summer NAC Master Mixed Teams 1974 and won New York Winter Open Pairs 1972, Rocky Mountain KO Teams 1973, Fun City KO Teams 1973, 1976.

KANSIL, Prince Joli (formerly Joel D. Gaines) (b. 1943) of Honolulu, born in New York City, is the inventor of BRIDGETTE and many other card games, word games and board games that have been marketed nationally. He is the author of the *Backgammon Quiz Book* and is backgammon columnist for *Games* magazine. He was co-founder of the Eastern Collegiate Bridge League and personal assistant to the late ALBERT H. MOREHEAD.

KANTAR, Edwin B. (Eddie) (b. 1932) of Los Angeles, professional bridge player, teacher and writer, one of the outstanding world player–writers, WBF GRAND MASTER, was Bermuda Bowl champion 1977, 1978 and runner-up in 1975. He also represented North America in the Bermuda Bowl 1969, the United States in the World Open Pairs 1970, 1982, MACCABIAH GAMES, placing third in 1977 and first in 1981, and in the 1977 Pan-American Invitational Championships, winning Open Teams. He won the Spingold 1961, 1962, 1974, Chicago (since 1965 the Reisinger) 1962, 1965, Reisinger 1977, 1981, Vanderbilt 1964, Grand National Teams 1974, 1976 and placed second in the Vanderbilt 1961, 1968, 1973, 1976, 1978, Reisinger 1968, Fall NAC Open Pairs 1962, Men's Pairs 1962, Spring NAC Men's Pairs 1967. Kantar has won numerous regional titles including MARCUS CUP 1960, Bridge Week KO Teams 1958, 1959, 1972, Open Teams 1961, 1962, Open Pairs 1958, Los Angeles Winter Swiss Teams 1978, Central States II Men's KO Teams, Men's Swiss Teams, Swiss Teams 1981. His frequent contributions to *Bridge World* and other periodicals include many "Test Your Play" features. He also contributes frequently to ACBL *Bulletin*, *Popular Bridge*, *Tuttobridge*, *Bridge D'Italia*, *Le Bridgeur*, *Revista Brasileira de Bridge*, *International Popular Bridge Monthly*, and *Bridge Magazine* and is a contributing editor, *Bridge Encyclopedia*. He has authored 11 books; *Introduction to Declarer's Play*, *Introduction to Defender's Play*, *Bridge Bidding Made Easy*, *Bridge Conventions*, *Bridge Humor*, *Test your Bridge Play* (Vol. I and II), *Gamesman Bridge*, *Improving Your Bidding Skills*, and *Defend With Your Life*. Kantar is a graduate of University of Minnesota. He played in the 1957 World Table Tennis Championships and is currently a California ranked paddle tennis player. He also enjoys racquetball and tennis. See LANCIA TEAMS and BIBLIOGRAPHY, C, D, E , L.

KANTAR, Phyllis of Los Angeles, senior programmer/analyst, won MARCUS CUP 1966, Bridge Week Mixed Pairs 1971, Master Swiss Teams 1979, Disneyland Open Pairs 1970. Since 1967 she has been assistant editor of *Popular Bridge*.

KANTOR, Dorothy. See BUCHANAN, DOROTHY.

KANTOR, Simon W. (b. 1925) of Ridgewood NJ, born in Brussels, Belgium, research company vice president, won New England Fall Mixed Teams 1959, Men's Pairs 1960, Long Island Men's Pairs 1972, Upper New York State Open Teams, Open Pairs 1968, Eastern States Master Pairs 1969.

KANZEE, Stephen (b. 1948) of Berkeley CA, real estate investor, won California Capital Unmixed Pairs 1976, Golden State Swiss Teams 1978, Mid-Winter Holiday Swiss Teams 1981, Golden State Swiss Teams 1981.

KAPLAN, Arthur (b. 1941) of Merrick NY, plant manager, former teacher, is the inventor of DUOBRIDGE.

KAPLAN, Betty (Mrs. Edgar, formerly Mrs. Alfred Sheinwold) of New York City, former director of a music school, won Summer NAC Master Mixed Teams 1963, Spring NAC Women's Teams 1965, Fall NAC Life Master Women's Pairs 1964, Mixed Pairs 1965, and placed second in Summer NAC Master Mixed Teams 1959, Spring NAC Women's Pairs 1962. Her regional successes include Spring NAC secondary Mixed Swiss Teams 1976, Eastern States Mixed Pairs 1962, Mixed Teams 1957, Bermuda Open Teams 1972, 1974, 1975, 1979, Open Pairs 1974, Long Island Swiss Teams 1975. She is circulation manager of *The Bridge World*.

KAPLAN, Edgar (b. 1925) of New York City, bridge writer and teacher, has been editor and publisher of *The Bridge World* since 1967. One of the world's leading players and expert analyst, he placed second in the World Team Olympiad 1968, in the International Team Trials 1966, and also represented North America in the Bermuda Bowl 1967, 1971, World Open Pairs 1978, 1982. Kaplan was assistant captain of the U.S. team in 1964, and many times coach to North American teams, which benefited from his detailed knowledge of European systems. He won the McKENNEY TROPHY 1957, Vanderbilt 1953, 1968, 1970, 1981, Spingold 1967, 1968, Chicago (since 1965 the Reisinger) 1958, Reisinger 1966, 1967, 1971, Spring NAC Men's Teams, Open Pairs 1966, Summer NAC Master Mixed Teams 1963, Fall NAC Men's Teams 1955, 1966, Blue Ribbon Pairs 1974, Life Master Men's Pairs 1973, Mixed Pairs 1965, Master Individual 1957. He placed second in the Reisinger 1969, Spingold 1965, 1971, 1978, Vanderbilt 1958, 1965, Fall NAC Men's Teams 1958, 1961, Life Master Men's Pairs 1965, Summer NAC Master Mixed Teams 1959, 1968, Spring NAC Men's Pairs 1970, Men's Teams 1975. He won numerous regional titles including the MARCUS CUP 1949, Summer NAC secondary Golder Master Pairs 1953, Mixed Pairs 1967, Spring Mixed Swiss Teams 1976, Eastern States KO Teams (Reisinger) 1954, 1956, 1957, 1958, 1959, 1970, Open Teams 1957, Open Pairs 1951, Mixed Pairs 1962. In 1979 Kaplan was named "Bridge Personality of the Year" by the IBPA. Appointed co-chairman of the ACBL Laws Commission in 1978, Kaplan is a former ACBL Board member and former partner in the Card School of New York. He is the co-inventor of the KAPLAN-SHEINWOLD system and the author of several books including *How to Play Winning Bridge* (co-author), *The Complete Italian System of Winning Bridge*, *Winning Contract Bridge Complete*, *Competitive Bidding in Modern Bridge*, *Duplicate Bridge: How to Play, How to Win*. Kaplan is a contributing editor to the *Bridge Encyclopedia*. See BIBLIOGRAPHY, C, E.

KAPLAN, Leonard S. of Atlanta, certified public accountant, won Tri-State Open Pairs 1975, Fun City Open Pairs 1975, Celebrity Master Pairs 1977, North Florida Swiss Teams 1977.

KAPLAN, Michael D. (b. 1943) of Marina Del Rey CA, vending company owner, won several regional titles including Desert Empire KO Teams 1974, Mid-Winter Holiday KO Teams 1972, Navajo Trail Open Pairs 1975, Rocky Mountain Master Pairs 1973, Palm Springs Master Pairs 1975, Pacific Southwest Open Pairs Flt. A 1978.

KAPLAN, Muriel (1920–1970) of New York City won the Women's Team Trials in 1963 and placed second in the World Women's Teams 1964.

KARAMOY, Walter D. (b. 1940) of Jakarta, Indonesia, company manager, represented Indonesia in the World Team Olympiad 1976, Bermuda Bowl 1974, 1981, Far East Championships 1977, 1978, 1981. His national titles include Open Teams 1973, Mixed Teams 1975, Intercity Teams 1975, 1976, 1980.

KARIM, Aminul (b. 1941) of Glen Ellyn IL, college dean, won Tri-Unit Master Pairs 1975, Central States I Swiss Teams 1978, II BAM Swiss Teams 1978, Wisconsin KO Teams 1978, District 13 GNP 1981.

KARN, WILLARD S. (1898–1950), a member of the FOUR HORSEMEN, wrote *Karn's Bridge Service* as well as articles for *The Bridge World*. A New York executive, Karn won more than five national championships. See BIBLIOGRAPHY, E.

KARP, Leonard (b. 1920) of Hillsdale NJ, former bridge club owner and cruise director, won several regional titles including the MARCUS CUP 1954, District 3 Men's Swiss Teams 1977, Bermuda Men's Pairs 1979, Bluenose KO Teams 1981, District 3 GNT, Zone II 1981.

KARPIN, Fred (b. 1913) of Silver Spring MD, bridge teacher, lecturer and writer, one of the leading personalities of the East Coast, placed second in Fall NAC Open Teams 1946. Karpin is one of the orginators of the POINT-COUNT method of distributional hand valuation. He was bridge editor for the *Washington Post* 1965-1981. He is the author of *Contract Bridge: the Play of the Cards*, *Psychological Strategy in Contract Bridge*, *How to Play (and Misplay) Slam Contracts*, and *Winning Play in Contract Bridge: Strategy at Trick One*, *The Finesse*, *The Art of Card Reading*, *Winning Play in Tournament and Duplicate Bridge: How the Experts Triumph*. He is the co-author of *The Complete Book of Duplicate Bridge* and a contributing editor to the *Bridge Encyclopedia*. See BIBLIOGRAPHY, C, D, E.

KASDAY, Tony (b. 1936) of Las Vegas, businessman, former bridge club owner and director, won Spring NAC Amateur Swiss Teams 1976. His regional titles include Bridge Week Master Pairs 1967, Can-At KO Teams 1974, 1977, Swiss Teams 1974, Master Pairs Flt. A 1976, Mid-Atlantic Men's Swiss Teams, Open Pairs 1977, Swiss Teams 1976, Tri-State Winter Open Pairs, Swiss Teams 1977, Wolverine KO Teams 1977, District 4 KO Teams 1977, Nat'l Capital KO Teams 1977.

KASLE, Gaylor L. (b. 1941) of Tucson AZ, professional bridge player, travel agency president, won Spring NAC Men's Teams 1973 and placed second in the Reisinger 1978. Kasle has won scores of regionals including Spring NAC secondary Swiss Teams 1974, Open Pairs 1976, Summer Mixed Pairs 1976, Fall Swiss Teams 1974, Swiss Teams 2nd Flt. 1975, Mixed Pairs 1976, Southeastern KO Teams 1973, Men's Teams 1970, 1971, Open Pairs 1972, Swiss Teams 1976, Open Pairs Flt. A 1978, Desert Empire KO Teams 1973, 1979, 1981, Swiss Teams, Swiss Teams Flt. A 1979, Master Swiss Teams 1978, Hawaii Swiss Teams 1974, 1975, Men's Swiss Teams 1979, 1981, KO Teams 1981. See FAMILY.

KASLE, Lee (Mrs. Sidney) of Tucson AZ, mother of GAYLOR KASLE, won Spring NAC Women's Teams 1959 a few months after becoming a Life Master. She had a number of wins with her husband Sidney Kasle who died in 1960 and in 1973 she won District 17 Women's Pairs. See FAMILY.

KASLE, Sharon (Mrs. Gaylor) (b. 1937) of Tucson AZ, figure salon manager, won Spring NAC secondary Mixed Pairs 1971, Texas Fall Mixed Pairs 1970, Desert Empire Women's Pairs 1973, Swiss Teams 1972, Mexican Nat'l KO Teams 1977.

KASPRZAK, Marek (b. 1936) of Warsaw, Poland, forestry engineer, represented Poland in the European Championships 1965, 1967, and won the Hungarian Balaton Bowl 1963, Belgian Open Pairs 1964, Baltic Bowl 1964, Beirut Festival Open Teams 1968. His national successes include Open Teams 1961, 1963, 1964, 1966.

KASS, Irving (b. 1915) of Hollywood FL, retired insurance agent, won the Vanderbilt 1952. His regional titles include Eastern States KO Teams (Reisinger) 1950, All-Southern Open Pairs Flt. A 1979, Southeastern Life Master Pairs 1976.

KASS, William J. (Bill) (b. 1942) of Albuquerque, won Navajo Trail KO Teams, Unmixed Pairs 1981, Desert Empire Open Pairs 1981.

KASSAY, Michael B. (b. 1926) of Huntington NY, born in Budapest, Hungary, engineer, was a member of the Hungarian national team in 1956 and the winner of five Hungarian national titles. He won Eastern States Mixed Teams 1962, New England Open Teams 1965, 1966.

KATZ, Emanuel (b. 1915) of North Miami Beach, realtor and private investor, won several regional titles including Canadian Nat'l Open Teams 1957, Can-Am Open Teams 1953, Upper New York State Open Pairs 1958, Mixed Pairs 1958, 1959, 1961, 1963, 1965, Southeastern Open Pairs 1979, All-Southern Open Pairs Flt. A, Men's Pairs 1979.

KATZ, Harold (b. 1935) of Memphis, ACBL staff member since 1973, sectional director, won Mid-South Spring Swiss Teams 1971. Katz is proofreader and assistant editor for the ACBL *Bulletin*. A former civil engineer, he graduated from University of Pennsylvania.

KATZ, Moshe (b. 1920) of Tel Aviv, Israel, born in Suwalki, Poland, sales manager, bridge teacher, represented Israel in the World Team Olympiad 1964, 1972, 1978, European Championships 1965, 1966, 1967, MACCABIAH GAMES 1981. His national successes include Tel Aviv Open Teams 1965, 1966, 1977, 1979, 1980. Katz is the author in Hebrew of *Acol for Beginners and Advanced Students*.

KATZ, Dr. Richard H. (b. 1942) of Beverly Hills CA, physician, won the Spingold 1973, 1976, Reisinger 1973, Grand National Teams 1974, Vanderbilt 1975, 1976, FISHBEIN TROPHY 1973, 1976, Blue Ribbon Pairs 1968, Fall NAC Open Pairs 1967, Summer NAC Master Mixed Teams 1976, and placed second in the Vanderbilt 1973, Blue Ribbon Pairs 1969. His numerous regional titles include Spring NAC secondary Swiss Teams 1974, Bridge Week Swiss Teams 1974, 1976, KO Teams 1974, Men's Pairs 1973, Mid-Atlantic KO Teams 1974, Missouri Valley KO Teams 1973, Rocky Mountain KO Teams 1974.

A graduate of the University of Wisconsin, Katz was Intercollegiate champion in 1966. He is the co-author of *Breakthrough in Bridge*. See BIBLIOGRAPHY, C, HOUSTON AFFAIR and LANCIA TEAMS.

KATZ, Stanley B. (b. 1949) of Glenview IL, office manager, won Summer NAC secondary Swiss Teams Flt. B 1977, Champagne Open Pairs 1977, Midwest Spring Open Pairs 1979.

KATZ, Steve (b. 1950) of Memphis, college English instructor, is a contributing editor to this edition of the *Bridge Encyclopedia*, and a book reviewer for the ACBL *Bulletin*. He won Spring NAC secondary Open Pairs 1982, Crescent City Swiss Teams Flt. A 1981.

KAUDER, Arnold J. (Arnie) (b. 1908) of Los Angeles, retired electronics engineer, won Summer NAC Master Mixed Teams 1949, 1950, 1955. His regional titles include All-Western Master Pairs 1946, Bridge Week Open Teams 1951, Open Pairs 1949, Men's Pairs 1950, Mixed Pairs 1949, Pacific Southwest Open Pairs 1957, New England Open Pairs 1944. Kauder is a graduate of UCLA.

KAUDER, James S. (b. 1943) of Los Angeles, attorney, bridge writer, won Eastern States Open Pairs (Goldman) 1966, Golden State Swiss Teams 1971, Master Pairs 1977, Bridge Week Men's Pairs 1972, Unmixed Pairs 1978, California Capital Open Pairs 1972, Los Angeles Winter Swiss Teams Flt. A, 1979, Pikes Peak Open Pairs Flt. A 1980. He is the author of *The Bridge Philosopher* and formerly contributed to the ACBL *Bulletin* and *The Bridge World*. He is the son of MARY JANE FARELL and ARNOLD KAUDER.

KAUDER, Mary Jane. See FARELL, MARY JANE.

KAUFMAN, George S. (1889–1961), famous New York dramatist, was a prominent rubber bridge player. Kaufman was honorary member of the CAVENDISH CLUB and a member of CROCKFORD'S CLUB and REGENCY CLUB. Many of his humorous writings about bridge appeared in *The New Yorker*, and have often been reprinted. They include "Kibitzers' Revolt," and the ingenious suggestion that bridge clubs should post on the bulletin board the information that North–South (or East–West) are holding good cards.

KAUFMAN, István (b. 1922) of Budapest, Hungary, company manager, represented Hungary 150 times in international competitions, including the European Championships 1969, 1970, 1971, 1973, 1975, World Team Olympiad 1980 and he was npc of the Hungarian Junior Team 1968. He was a member of the victorious Hungarian team in matches against Czechoslovakia 1963, Germany 1964, Belgium 1964 and Austria 1965. His national titles include Open Teams 1954, 1955, 1956, 1961, 1962, 1963, 1964, 1965, 1967, 1969, 1971, 1979, Open Pairs 1959, 1960, 1961, 1968, 1972, 1974, 1975, Mixed Pairs 1963, 1964. He served as secretary general of HUNGARIAN BRIDGE ASSOCIATION in 1972.

KAUFMAN, Warren G. (b. 1929) of Bowie MD, won Mid-Atlantic Men's Swiss Teams 1978, Swiss Teams 1981, Bermuda Men's Pairs 1981. He is the father of Andrew (youngest new Life Master and National Master of the Year 1981) and Chris (Senior Master of the Year 1980).

KAY, Judy (Mrs. Norman) (b. 1934) of Narberth PA, bridge teacher, former legal secretary, won Summer NAC secondary Mixed Pairs 1967, Keystone Conference Women's Teams 1972, Southeastern Women's Swiss Teams 1978.

KAY, Norman (b. 1927) of Narberth PA, investment executive, one of the world's leading players, represented the U.S. in the World Team Olympiad 1960, 1968, World Open Pairs 1978, 1982, North America in the Bermuda Bowl 1961, 1967, 1971. He won the MCKENNEY TROPHY 1955, Chicago (since 1965 the Reisinger) 1961, Vanderbilt 1959, 1960, 1968, 1970, 1981, Fall NAC Men's Teams 1955, 1961, 1966, Men's Pairs 1962, Life Master Men's Pairs 1973, Blue Ribbon Pairs 1974, Spring NAC Open Pairs 1963, 1966, Men's Teams 1966, Men's Pairs 1958, Spingold 1967, 1968, Reisinger 1966, 1967, 1971, Master Individual 1955. He placed second in the Reisinger 1969, Spingold 1960, 1961, 1965, 1971, 1978, Chicago 1960, Vanderbilt 1958, 1965, Spring NAC Men's Teams 1963, 1975, Men's Pairs 1962, 1965, 1970, Summer NAC Men's Teams 1967, Fall Men's Teams, Men's Pairs 1958. ACBL *Bulletin* (Oct. 1977) named him the top performance player for the double decade 1957-1977. Kay is the co-author of *The Complete Book of Duplicate Bridge.* He is a former Philadelphia CBA board member. Kay is a graduate of Philadelphia College of Pharmacy. He owns harness horses and collects baseball cards. See BIBLIOGRAPHY, F.

KAYE, Dorothy R. (Mrs. Richard, formerly Talmage) (b. 1923) of Denver, won Fall NAC Life Master Women's Pairs 1968, Spring NAC secondary Open Pairs Flt. A 1977. She is a licensed helicopter pilot.

KAYE, Richard I. (b. 1923) of Denver, business executive, won Spring NAC Men's Pairs 1970, Rocky Mountain KO Teams 1973, Men's Pairs 1974, Swiss Teams 1977, 1981, Oregon Trail KO Teams 1969, Big Sky Master Pairs 1971, Iowa Men's Pairs 1971, All-Western Men's Pairs 1977.

KEARSE, Judge Amalya L. (b. 1937) of New York City, formerly one of the leading American women players, won Spring NAC Women's Pairs 1971, Fall NAC Life Master Women's Pairs 1972 and seven ABA national championships 1972-1973. Her regional titles include Spring NAC secondary Women's Swiss teams 1973, Mixed Pairs 1974, Fall Swiss Teams-A 1979, Fun City KO Teams 1973, Keystone Open Pair 1974, All-Western Women's Pairs 1972. The IBPA honored her as the "Bridge Personality of the Year" in 1980. She has served the Greater New York BA as counsel to the Board 1970-1979, Board member 1966-1975, Conduct and Ethics Committee counsel 1970-1973, chairman

1973-1979 and various other committees. She served as a member of the ACBL Board of Governors 1970-1976, member of the NAC Appeals Committee, 1971-1975, and as a member of the ACBL Laws Commission since 1975. Kearse is a member of the Charles Goren Editorial Board and was the editor of the 3rd edition, *Bridge Encyclopedia.* She authored *Bridge Conventions Complete*, *Bridge at Your Fingertips*, was co-translator of *Championship Bridge* (JOSE LE DENTU, *Bridge a la une*), and translator and editor of *Bridge Analysis*) (Le Dentu). Her non-bridge writings include several legal publications. A graduate of Wellesley College and University of Michigan Law School, she is a United States Court of Appeals circuit judge. Kearse is listed in *Who's Who of American Women.* See BIBLIOGRAPHY B, E.

KEEL, Darrell E. (b. 1940) of Aberdeen WA, senior account insurance agent, won Spring NAC secondary Men's Pairs 2nd Flt. 1970, Tri-Cities Atomic Swiss Teams Flt. A 1979, British Columbia KO Teams 1979. Keel, a certified director, is co-founder of Tri-Cities BC.

KEHELA, Sami R. (Sammy) (b. 1934) of Toronto, born in Baghdad, Iraq, professional bridge player, one of the world's great players, represented Canada in the World Team Olympiad 1960, 1964, 1968, 1972, 1976, 1980 (with ERIC MURRAY, the only *pair* in the world to represent their country in *every* World Team Olympiad since its inception), Rosenblum Cup Teams 1978, 1982 (placed third), World Open Pairs 1966, 1970, 1974, 1978, 1982, North America in the Bermuda Bowl 1966, 1967, 1974, and was coach for the North American team in the Bermuda Bowl 1962, 1963, 1965. He won the Team Trials 1966, 1973, Vanderbilt 1966, 1970, Spingold 1964, 1965, 1968, Blue Ribbon Pairs 1967, Fall NAC Life Master Men's Pairs 1963, Life Master Pairs 1969 and placed second in the Spingold 1963, Blue Ribbon Pairs 1969, Reisinger 1969, 1972. His numerous regional titles include Summer NAC secondary Swiss Teams Flt. A 1978, Canadian Nat'l Open Teams 1959, 1961, 1965, 1967, 1979, KO Teams 1980, Mixed Pairs 1959, 1962, Can-Am Men's Pairs 1960, Canadian Prairie Master Pairs 1967, Upper New State Men's Pairs 1965, 1967, Open Pairs 1963, Open Teams 1965, Canadian National Teams 1980, 1981. He was formerly editor of Ontario *Kibitzer,* bridge columnist for *Toronto Life,* contributor to the ACBL *Bulletin,* contributing editor, *Bridge Encyclopedia.*

KEHOE, Robert A. (Bob) (b. 1946) of San Bernardino CA, contact representative, bridge professional, won Fall NAC Swiss Teams 1978. His regional titles include Spring NAC secondary Swiss Teams 1st Flt. 1974, Swiss Teams Flt. A 1980, Can-Am KO Teams 1974, Keohane Individual KO Teams 1975, Tri-State Master Pairs 1974, Canadian Nat'l Swiss Teams 1974, Los Angeles Winter KO Teams 1978, California Capital Swiss Teams Flt. A 1979, Mid-Winter Holiday Swiss Teams 1981.

KEIDAN, Bruce of Monroeville PA, bridge columnist, won District 4 Men's Swiss teams 1977, GNT 1976. Keidan was the first to notice unusual foot movements by one Italian pair during the 1975 Bermuda Bowl. See BERMUDA INCIDENT.

KEITH, Dorothy (Dottie) (b. 1926) of Coral Gables FL, former interior designer, placed second in Spring NAC Women's Pairs 1961 and won Southeastern Master Pairs 1961, Women's Pairs 1960, 1963.

KELETI, Andor (b. 1901) of Budapest, Hungary, retired hotel keeper, was World champion and European champion in 1934. He placed second in the European Championships 1935, 1936, 1937. He was Hungarian champion 1929-1935, and Budapest champion 1931.

KELLER, Brenda J. (b. 1943) of Boise ID, former Dept. of Health anti-smoking coordinator, won more than 15 regional titles since 1978 including Cincinnati NAC secondary Swiss Teams-A 1979, Klondike Oil City Swiss Teams, Women's Pairs 1978, Mid-Winter Holiday KO Teams 1979, California Capital KO Teams, Swiss Teams Flt. A 1980, British Columbia KO Teams 1980, Gem State Open Pairs 1980, Inland Empire Open Pairs 1980.

KELLER, Karl V. (b. 1932) of Norman OK, company president, won Toast of Tulsa Swiss Teams 1979, Rocky Mountain KO Teams 1979, Missouri Valley Swiss Teams 1979, Mid-Winter Holiday Master Pairs 1979, District 15 Open Pairs 1978, Land of Coronado KO Teams, Master Pairs, Swiss Teams 1980. Keller played football for his alma mater, University of Oklahoma. During the Sixties he was the chief engineering test pilot for Rockwell International. In 1966 he flew Arthur Godfrey on the *Around the World Flight* setting 22 world records.

KELLEY, John J. (Jack) (b. 1929) of Germantown TN, is ACBL Director of Administration. Kelley is a graduate of University of Bridgeport.

KELLY, Jack (1916-1970) of Sutton, Ireland was a government accountant, bridge writer, and one of Ireland's greatest players. He represented Ireland in the World Team Olympiad 1960, 1964, World Open Pairs 1962, European Championship 1954, 1959, 1965. His national wins include every major event on the Irish calendar. Bridge correspondent to the *Irish Times* and a regular contributor to many international bridge magazines, including *Bridge Magazine*, a contributing editor, *Bridge Encyclopedia*, Kelly was IBPA president 1964-1970.

KELLY, Myldred of Atlanta, formerly of Clark NJ, won Spring NAC secondary Amateur Swiss Teams 2nd Flt. 1976, Fun City Open Pairs 1975, Keystone Women's Swiss Teams 1974, Tri-State Winter Open Pairs 1976, North Florida Swiss Teams 1977.

KELLY, Nathan (1876-1959), prominent player of whist, auction, and contract, invented KELLY SOLID SUIT SIGNALS. A lawyer and bridge teacher from Boston, Kelly won many AWL national titles, and several regional championships at contract.

KELNER, Louis (b. 1907) of Forest Hills NY, accountant, stockbroker, and ACBL regional tournament director, won the Spingold 1956 and placed second in the Life Master Pairs 1956. His regional titles include Summer NAC secondary Golder Master Pairs 1952, Eastern States Individual 1952, Upper New York State Men's Pairs 1957.

KELSEY, Hugh Walter (b. 1926) of Edinburgh, Scotland, novelist, one of the world's greatest bridge writers and journalists, represented Scotland many times in matches against England, Wales and Northern Ireland. His national titles include the GOLD CUP twice, Open Teams, Open Pairs, Master Pairs, Master Individual (five times). Kelsey is the originator of Tartan Two Bids, SUPER SWISS and other conventions. His books include *Killing Defense, Advanced Play, The Tricky Game, Test Your Trump Control, The Mind of the Expert, A Tough Game, How to Improve Your Bridge, Matchpoint Bridge, Logical Bridge Play, Slam Bidding, Winning Card Play, Test Your Communications, Test Your Card Reading* and *Test Your Finessing.* Perhaps his most outstanding work is *Adventures in Card Play*, which he co-authored with GEZA OTTLIK. See BIBLIOGRAPHY, D, E.

KEMP-FREILICH, Edith J. (Mrs. Julian, formerly Seligman, nee Seamon) of Miami Beach, bridge teacher, one of the great American women players of all time, placed second in the VENICE TROPHY 1981. She won the Vanderbilt 1963, Spingold 1963, Chicago (since 1965 the Reisinger) 1946, 1952, Spring NAC Women's Teams 1962, 1979, 1980, Women's Pairs 1941, 1942, 1943, 1946, 1979, Summer Master Mixed Teams 1947, 1952, 1953, 1957, 1974, Fall NAC Open Pairs 1943, Life Master Women's Pairs 1977, 1979, 1981. She placed second in the Spingold 1953, 1972, Reisinger 1964, Summer Life Master Pairs 1962, Master Mixed Teams 1942, 1945, 1948, Grand National Teams 1980, Fall Life Master Women's Pairs 1973, 1974, 1980, Spring NAC Women's Teams 1971, Women's Pairs 1957, 1978. She has won scores of regional titles including Summer NAC secondary Mixed Pairs 1968, Spring Swiss Teams 2nd Flt. 1976, Swiss Teams 1978. See FAMILY.

KEMPNER, Alicia (Mrs. Ralph) of Los Angeles, formerly one of the leading women players of the West Coast, placed second in the World Women's Teams 1964. She won Summer NAC Master Mixed Teams 1946, 1954, 1960, Spring NAC Women's Teams 1962, 1969 and placed second in Fall NAC Mixed Pairs 1955, Spring NAC Women's Pairs 1965. Her numerous regional titles include Spring NAC secondary Swiss Teams 1970, Bridge Week Master Teams 1954, Open Pairs 1950, 1954, Mixed Pairs 1951, Master Women's Pairs 1967, 1968, Southeastern Women's Teams 1965, Palm Springs Women's Pairs 1971.

KEMPNER, Ralph of Los Angeles, stockbroker, formerly one of the leading players of the West Coast, won Fall NAC Open Pairs 1936 and placed second in the Spingold 1948. His regional titles include All-American Open Teams 1939, Open Pairs 1939, All-Western Master Teams 1954, Men's Pairs 1952, Open Pairs 1950, Bridge Week Mixed Teams 1954, Master Teams 1952, 1954, Men's Pairs 1965, Central States Open Teams 1938, Los Angeles Winter Men's Pairs 1977.

KEMPSON, Captain Ewart (1895–1966) of Gainford, England, army officer and bridge writer, was one of the leading European bridge personalities. In the Thirties he was the staunchest supporter of the WALTER BULLER method called "British Bridge," or direct bidding without the use of forcing bids. His many tournament successes include English National Pairs, and he was npc of British Women's Team which won the European title in 1952 and toured the United States in 1953. A prolific writer, Kempson authored 21 books on bridge including *Kempson on Contract*, *How to Win at Contract Bridge*, *More Bridge Quizzes*, *First Book of Bridge Problems*, *Second Book of Bridge Problems* (with PAUL LUKACS), *Tournament Bridge for Everyone*; and co-authored *Quintessence of CAB: the CAB System of Bridge* and *Bridge Quiz*. He was editor and director of *Bridge* magazine from 1949 and a contributing editor, *Bridge Encyclopedia*. See BIBLIOGRAPHY, C, E, F, G, H, J.

KENDRICK, Boots K. (Mrs. J. O.) (b. 1925) of Anchorage placed second in Summer NAC Master Mixed Teams 1961 and won Mexican Nat'l Open Teams 1960, Polar Mixed Pairs 1974, Midnight Sun Mixed Pairs, Master Pairs, Open Pairs 1977.

KENEDI, Tibor (b. 1915) of São Paulo, Brazil, industrialist, represented Brazil in the World Olympiad 1964, South American Championships four times. His national successes include Open Teams six times.

KENNEDY, Betty Ann (Mrs. J. E., formerly Mrs. J. F. Welch) of Shreveport LA, one of the leading women players of the world, won the VENICE TROPHY 1974, 1976, (second in 1981) and the World Women's Pairs 1982, (second in 1978). She also represented the United States in the World Women's Pairs 1974. She won Summer NAC Master Mixed Teams 1960, Spring NAC Women's Teams 1978, 1980 and placed second in Fall NAC Life Master Women's Pairs 1971, 1981. Her numerous regional titles include Summer NAC secondary Women's Pairs 1972, 1973, Spring Swiss Teams 2nd Flt. 1976, Mid-South KO Teams 1972, 1978, Master Pairs 1958, 1973, Open Pairs 1970, 1971, 1972, Women's Pairs 1969, 1974, 1976, 1978, Swiss Teams 1973, 1978, Master Swiss Teams 1978. She has served as vice president of Unit 170, as a member of the NAC Appeals Committee, as chairman of Unit 170 Appeals Committee and as member of District 10 Judiciary Committee.

KENNEDY, Charles T. (deceased) of Cincinnati was one of the leading Midwest tournament directors in the Thirties, and co-inventor of the Ach-Kennedy schedules (1935) which provided the first HOWELL MOVEMENTS with perfectly BALANCED COMPARISONS.

KENNEDY, George J. (b. 1901) of New York City, bridge teacher and writer, placed second in Fall NAC Men's Pairs 1940 and won Eastern States Mixed Teams 1940. He is the originator of a bidding style which provides for control-showing bids in many situations and author of *The Kennedy System of Bridge*. See BIBLIOGRAPHY, C.

KENNEDY, John E. (Jack) (b. 1920) of Shreveport LA, industrialist, won Spring NAC Men's Pairs 1973 and placed second in 1976. His numerous regional titles include Fall NAC secondary Men's Swiss Teams 1977, Mid-South KO Teams 1972, Master Pairs 1971, Open Pairs 1970, 1975, Swiss Teams 1978, Hawaii Men's Pairs, Swiss Teams 1979, Big D Winter Master Swiss Teams, Swiss Teams 1980. He has served on the ACBL Board of Governors, as president of Unit 170, and as vice president of District 10.

KENT, Donald S. (b. 1908) of Asunción, Paraguay, born in Chicago, manufacturers' representative, won Paraguayan Open Teams, Open Pairs, Individual. Kent was several times president of the PARAGUAY BRIDGE FEDERATION.

KEOHANE, Ethel (Mrs. William H.) (b. 1901) of Wellesley Hills MA, retired administrative secretary, one of the most successful players in the New England area, placed second in Spring NAC Women's Teams 1952, 1977. She won numerous regional titles including Fall NAC secondary Swiss Teams 1976, Spring Swiss Teams 1979, New England Mixed Pairs 1948, 1951, 1959, Open Teams 1951, 1967, 1968, 1974, Mixed Teams 1942, 1946, 1948, 1949, 1950, 1956, KO Teams 1949, Master Teams 1949, Women's Pairs 1942, 1948, 1950, Open Pairs 1970, Fall Swiss Teams 1974, Can-Am Swiss Teams 1979, Women's Swiss Teams 1980, Eastern States Women's Pairs 1978, Mid-Atlantic Swiss Teams 1980, Can-At Open Pairs 1970, Swiss Teams Flt. A 1980, District 3 Women's Pairs, Women's Swiss Teams 1980, District 8 Women's Pairs 1980. She served as secretary of the Eastern Massachusetts BA for 18 years. She was named ACBL HONORARY MEMBER for 1982.

KEOSATIT, Somsak (1940) of Bangkok, Thailand, represented Thailand in the World Team Olympiad 1964, 1972, 1976, Far East Championships four times. He won the Asian Mixed Teams 1982 and has won all national major events between 1968–1982 including Open Teams 12 times.

KERGER, Joe (b. 1948) of Calgary AB, born in Germany, won Saskatchewan KO Teams 1975, Swiss Teams 1978, Klondike Swiss Teams Flt. A 1978, 1982, Master Pairs 1974, White Hat KO Teams 1977, Indian Summer Men's Pairs 1981. A former construction estimator, Kerger currently is in the tournament bridge supply business.

KERR, Robert A. (Bob) (b. 1935) of Maywood CA, transportation analyst, placed second in Spring NAC Men's Pairs 1971 and won Bridge Week Open Pairs 1967, Mixed Pairs 1980, Pacific Southwest Swiss Teams 1975, Emerald Empire Swiss Teams 1977, Los Angeles Winter Swiss Teams 1974, Mixed Pairs 1980, Golden State Master Pairs 1973.

KERR, Roy P. (b. 1934) of Christchurch, New Zealand, professor of mathematics, represented New Zealand in the Bermuda Bowl 1974. His national successes include Open Teams 1971, Open Pairs 1973. He is a pioneer of relay methods, described by him in *The Symmetric Relay.*

KERWICK, Paul A. (b. 1912) of Cranston RI, state administration adviser, former federal administration supervisor, won Fall NAC secondary Swiss Teams 2nd Flt. 1953, New England Spring Open Pairs 1961, Fall Master Teams 1951. He has served as president of Unit 145 and the New England Bridge Conference.

KERWIN, Madeleine (1882–1965), who introduced bridge in the CAVENDISH CLUB in 1926, was a bitter antagonist of ELY CULBERTSON. In 1931 she became second president of the ABL and helped codify the OFFICIAL SYSTEM, designed to replace Culbertson's as the public favorite. More succesful than this effort was her theoretical work as one of the originators of the FORCING TWO-BID. Her writings include the first book on the Sims System (*The One Over One for Everyone*) as well as some five other books and numerous bridge articles. See BIBLIOGRAPHY, C.

KESSLER, Gary D. (b. 1953) of Springfield IL, won Mid-South Holiday Swiss Teams 1979, Midwest Fall Men's Swiss Teams 1979, District 8 Summer Swiss Teams Flt. A 1981, Champagne KO Teams 1982. He is the brother of MARK KESSLER.

KESSLER, Mark N. (b. 1947) of Springfield IL won Fall NAC secondary Swiss Teams-A 1979, Central States I Swiss Teams 1979, 1980, Open Pairs 1975, II Open Pairs 1975. He is the brother of GARY KESSLER.

KESZYCKI, Marian (b. 1927) of Colchester CT, born in Poland, land developer, won New England Masters Swiss Teams 1970, 1976, Master Swiss Teams 1975, Summer Swiss Teams 1976, Individual KO Teams 1974. Keszycki was a Polish commando during WWII.

KEY, Mervin (b. 1929) of Belize, British Honduras, formerly of Houston, attorney, formerly one of the leading players of the Southwest, represented North America in the Bermuda Bowl 1962. He won the Chicago (since 1965 the Reisinger) 1964 and placed second in the Chicago 1960, Fall NAC Men's Teams 1961, Life Master Men's Pairs 1964. His regional titles include Texas Spring Open Pairs 1959, Lone Star Mid-Winter KO Teams 1977.

KHAUTIN, Richard L. (b. 1940) of New York City, accountant, won the Blue Ribbon Pairs 1972, Eastern States Men's Pairs 1972, Tri-State Open Pairs 1970.

KIMBALL, Anita (Mrs. Frank) of Los Angeles, corporation officer, won Great Lakes Swiss Teams 1976, 1977, Golden State Swiss Teams 1977, Puget Sound KO Teams 1977, Midnight Sun KO Teams 1977, Raincross Swiss Teams 1978.

KIMBALL, Frank of Los Angeles, corporation president, international gem consultant, won Great Lakes Swiss Teams 1976, 1977, British Columbia KO Teams 1977, Golden State Swiss Teams 1977, Oregon Trail Men's Swiss Teams 1977, Puget Sound KO Teams 1977, Midnight Sun KO Teams 1977, Raincross Swiss Teams 1978.

KIMELMAN, Neil D. (b. 1954) of Winnipeg MB, public relations officer, won Buffalo KO Teams 1977, Open Pairs 1977, 1978, Peach City KO Teams 1978, Pheasant KO Teams 1978.

KIMURA, Rokuro (b. 1908) of Ashiya-shi, Japan, placed second in the Prince Takamatsu Cup 1950. Kimura was one of the original members of the JAPAN CONTRACT BRIDGE LEAGUE when it was founded in 1958. He was vice president 1972–1981 and was named Honorary Life Member in 1981.

KINCAID, Arthur R. (b. 1911) of Liberty MO, attorney, placed second in the Spingold 1953. His regional titles include Mississippi Valley Open Teams 1952, Open Pairs 1951, Missouri Valley Open Teams 1959, Open Pairs 1961, Men's Pairs 1961, 1965, Springfield KO Teams 1980, District 15 Open Teams 1968, Open Pairs 1968, GNP 1981. He served two terms as president of Missouri Valley Bridge Conference. Kincaid was a member of the Missouri Legislature 1937–1943 and city attorney 1945-1951.

KING, David W. (b. 1951) of Omaha NE, information systems director, won Gopher Men's Swiss Teams 1976, KO Teams 1977, Men's Pairs 1982, Northwest Iowa Men's Swiss Teams 1978. King contributes to the Unit 241 newsletter, *The Big Club.*

KING, Frank P. Jr., (b. 1933) of Alexandria VA, U.S. Air Force non-commissioned officer, won Oregon Trail Men's Pairs 1971, Keystone Master Pairs, Open Pairs 1973, Mid-Atlantic Master Pairs 1974, Open Pairs 1977, Swiss Teams 1978, Wine Country Swiss Teams 1981. King currently is the leading masterpoint holder among members of the Armed Forces on active duty.

KING, Georgette (Mrs. J. David) of Miami Beach FL, part-time bookkeeper, won All-American KO Teams 1975, All-Southern Women's Pairs 1979, District 9 GNP 1981. She was Florida State Rookie of the Year in 1975. A certified director, she directs on bridge cruises.

KING, J. David (b. 1923) of Miami Beach, professional bridge player, won numerous regional titles including Central States Life and Senior Master Pairs 1960, Inter–Mountain Open Teams 1970, KO Teams 1973, Land of Coronado KO Teams 1974, Desert Empire Men's Pairs, Swiss Teams 1973, District 9 GNP 1981. King is a graduate of U.S. Naval Academy.

KING, Mary T. See WILLIAMS, MARY T.

KINSELLA, Jocelyn Y. (Mrs. A. E., formerly Hutchinson) of Wellington, New Zealand, property consultant, was Far East champion 1981 and placed second in 1971. She also represented New Zealand in the Far East Championships 1972, 1977, World Women's Teams 1980. She won Australian Individual, Women's Pairs, Women's Teams 1968, New Zealand Teams 1969, North Island Pairs 1970. She is columnist for *New Zealand Times* and is a contributor to *New Zealand Bridge*.

KIRBY, Graham T. (b. 1955) of Orford, Warrington, England, researcher, represented Great Britain in the Junior European Championships, European Championships, CAMROSE TROPHY matches and Junior Camrose Trophy matches. His national titles include Spring Foursomes, Swiss Teams Congress, and placed second in Crockford's Cup 1980, 1981.

KIRKHAM, Jim (b. 1936) of Carlsbad CA, won Summer NAC secondary Open Pairs 1979, Pacific Southwest Swiss Teams 1978, 1979, Desert Empire Open Pairs 1979, Golden State Swiss Teams 1980, District 15 Men's Swiss Teams 1982.

KIRNER, Maria (b. 1944) of Vienna, Austria, manager, represented Austria in the European Women's Championships 1973, 1975, World Women's Teams 1978. She won Venice Open Pairs 1981, and has won Austrian Teams several times.

KIRTLAND, Edith M. (Mrs. Sidney) (b. 1905) of Miami, certified bridge teacher and club director, won Southeastern Women's Teams 1957, Open Teams 1961, Florida Master Pairs 1961. She served as manager of Greater Miami CBL for many years.

KIRTLAND, Cmdr. Sidney W. (b. 1894) of Miami, retired naval officer, won Southeastern Open Teams 1950, 1961, Open Pairs 1946, Men's Pairs 1971. Kirtland graduated from the U.S. Naval Academy. Life Master #462 (1952), he was the first to achieve this status while on active duty in the Navy.

KITCHEL, Robert H. (b. 1931) of Union Grove AL, is a regional 4 tournament director. A former stockbroker, he began directing in 1968. He has served as PTDA representative to the ACBL Board of Directors.

KITZES, Dr. David L. (b. 1938) of Providence RI, cardiologist, won New England Master Teams 1962, District 11 Open Teams 1967. A bridge theorist, he helped formulate the principles of the American Design system.

KIVEL, Joseph (Joe) (b. 1934) of Costa Mesa CA, account executive, won several regional titles including Mid-Atlantic Open Teams 1970, 1973, 1975, 1978, Master Pairs 1968, 1973, Men's Pairs 1978, Keystone Fall Master Pairs, Open Pairs 1973, Desert Empire Master Pairs 1975, District 4 Swiss Teams 1977, Golden State Swiss Teams Flt. A 1980, District 6 GNT 1976.

KIVEL, Mickie of Potomac MD, technical writer, won several regional titles including Mid-Atlantic Swiss Teams 1973, 1975, 1978, Women's Swiss Teams 1981, 1982, Golden Gate Swiss Teams 1980, District 4 Swiss Teams 1977, District 6 GNT 1976.

KLAR, Carol of Houston, retired jewelry designer, placed second in Summer NAC Master Mixed Teams 1967, Fall Mixed Pairs 1968, Spring Women's Teams 1975 and won several regionals including Spring NAC secondary Mixed Pairs 1967, Summer Mixed Pairs 1976, Fall Women's Teams 1968, 1972, Texas Fall Mixed Pairs 1967, Mexican Nat'l Open Pairs 1968, Swiss Teams 1975, Florida Swiss Teams 1975. Republic of Texas Open Pairs 1970.

KLAR, Robin. See LENT, ROBIN.

KLAS, Leo (b. 1921) of Chicago, formerly of Prague, Czechoslovakia, technician, represented Czechoslovakia in the European Championships 1966, 1967, against Poland 1961, 1962, Hungary 1963. He won Czechoslovakia Open Teams 1962, 1963, 1964.

KLAUSNER, Malvine (Mrs. Siegfried) (b. 1902) of Beverly Hills CA, formerly one of the leading women players of the West Coast, represented the United States in the World Women's Teams 1960. She won Summer NAC Master Mixed Teams 1953 and placed second in Fall NAC Mixed Pairs 1965. Her regional titles include Pacific Southwest Women's Pairs 1967, Bridge Week Master Pairs 1951, 1959, Mixed Teams 1961, 1967, Open Teams 1957, Women's Pairs 1956, Desert Empire Open Teams 1957, 1958.

KLAUSNER, Siegfried (1898–1949) of Beverly Hills CA, born in Vienna, was a leading Austrian player in the Thirties. In 1932 he invented plastic playing cards, those now manufactured in the United States under the name "Kem Cards".

KLEIN, Alejandro (1913–1979) of Buenos Aires, Argentina, plastics manufacturer, won Argentine Open Teams 1959, 1962, Open Pairs 1954, 1971. He was a contributor to *Bridge Argentino*.

KLEIN, Melvin A. (Mel) (b. 1940) of Parsippany NJ, computer systems analyst, won Summer NAC secondary Commercial and Industrial Teams 1974, 1975, 1976. Klein was president of the Commerical Bridge League of Northern New Jersey in 1974.

KLEINMAN, Danny (b. 1937) of Los Angeles, writer, former computer programmer, won Bridge Week KO Teams 1976, Non-Mixed Pairs 1974, Individual 1979, Los Angeles Winter Individual 1979. Kleinman designed and programmed the first backgammon computer — Jack Gammon. This led to teaching backgammon, ultimately to writing about backgammon and other writing. He is the author of *Bridge Scandal in Houston, Understanding Bidding: Foundations, Understanding Bidding: Ramifications, Advice to the Bridgelorn,* and *The Bridge Weird Anthology.* (See BIBLIOGRAPHY, B, C.) Kleinman is also the author of several conventions, and of several books on other games.

KLINGER, Ronald D. (Ron) (b. 1941) of New South Wales, Australia, born in Shanghai, China, bridge writer, teacher, editor and publisher, was Far East champion 1970. He also represented Australia in the Bermuda Bowl 1976, World Team Olympiad 1976, 1980, World Open Pairs 1978. His national successes include Interstate Teams 1969, 1977, 1980, Australian Open Teams 1975, Open Pairs 1977, 1979 Mixed Pairs 1977. He won the Bols Brilliancy Prize 1976, 1978, 1980. Klinger is the editor of *Australian Bridge* and the author of several books including *Bridge Basics, Basic Bridge, Fingertip Bridge Finder, Playing to Win at Bridge, Winning Bridge, Trick by Trick, Bridge Without Error, How to Play Contract Bridge,* and a number of monographs. He is the author of *Unusual 2 NT Opening, K-Splinters* and *Extended Ogust Conventions.* A graduate of University of Sydney, he was awarded the Medal in Law by that university. He is a former solicitor and university lecturer.

KLUEWER, Ann (b. 1924) of Reseda CA, legal transcriber, won several regional titles including Fall NAC secondary Open Pairs 1968, Orange County Open Teams 1972, Palm Springs Swiss Teams 1975, Navajo Trail Women's Pairs 1977, Emerald Empire Swiss Teams, Women's Pairs 1977, Bridge Week Master Swiss Teams Flt. A 1978, Raincross Swiss Teams 1980, Mid-Winter Holiday Women's Pairs 1980, District 23 GNT, Zone VII 1981.

KLUKOWSKI, Julian (b. 1939) of Warsaw, Poland, mathematician, represented Poland in the World Team Olympiad 1964, European Championships 1963, 1965, 1967, and placed second in the World Par contest 1963. He won the Hungarian Balaton Bowl 1963, Baltic Bowl 1964. His national successes include Open Teams 1962, 1963, 1964, 1966, 1967, Mixed Teams 1965, 1966, Mixed Pairs 1966.

KNIEST, Thomas W. (b. 1945) of Clayton MO, certified public accountant, won Mississippi Valley KO Teams 1978, 1980, Men's Pairs 1980, District 8 Swiss Teams 1979, GNT, Zone V 1974.

KNOWLES, Donna X. of Sepulveda CA, won Las Vegas Women's Pairs 1971, Bridge Week Women's Pairs 1977, 1979, Raincross Women's Swiss Teams 1979, Los Angeles Winter Women's KO Teams 1978, 1981, Women's Pairs 1978.

KOHN, Walter Steiner (1908–1969) of Santiago, Chile, attorney and merchant, represented Chile in South American Championships. He won National Open Teams, Individual 1958, 1961, National Mixed Pairs 1963, and many more successes. In addition, he had many tournament wins in Czechoslovakian events prior to 1938, when he moved to Chile.

KOKISH, Eric O. (b. 1947) of Montreal, bridge journalist, teacher, professional player, one of the outstanding Canadian players, placed second in the World Open Pairs 1978 and also represented Canada in the World Open Pairs 1974, 1976, 1982, Rosenblum Cup Teams 1978, 1982 (placing third), World Team Olympiad 1980, MACCABIAH GAMES 1981. He won the Vanderbilt 1974, Spring NAC Men's Teams 1978, and placed second in the Vanderbilt 1980, Spring Men's Teams 1974, Amateur Swiss Teams 1977. He won the Canadian Grand National Team championship 1980, 1981 and numerous regional titles including Spring NAC Swiss Teams, Swiss Teams Flt. A 1978, Kokish has written large portions of the ACBL World Championship books since 1980, is editor of *Melange de Bridge,* on the staff of *Bridge World,* and contributes frequently to *International Popular Bridge Monthly, Australian Bridge, Canadian Bridge Digest,* the ACBL *Bulletin,* and many foreign journals. He has served as Unit 151 Conduct and Ethics chairman for many years, was president of Unit 151, was District 1 GNT coordinator twice and Judiciary Committee chairman, Canadian Bridge Federation Zone Director, and a member of the ACBL Goodwill Committee. Kokish is a graduate of McGill University. His interests include collecting bridge literature, professional sports, the stock market, fine dining and travel. See IBPA AWARDS.

KOKISH, Sharyn (nee Linkovsky) (b. 1950) of Montreal, bookkeeper, one of the leading Canadian women players, represented Canada in the World Women's Teams 1972, 1976, 1980, World Women's Pairs, Mixed Pairs, Rosenblum Teams 1978, World Open Pairs 1982. She placed second in Spring NAC Women's Teams 1981, Amateur Swiss Teams 1977 and won numerous regional titles including Summer NAC secondary Golder Pairs 1971, Spring Swiss Teams Flt. A 1978, Mixed Swiss Teams 1975, Can-Am Master Swiss Teams 1977, Swiss Teams Flt. A 1978, Canadian Nat'l KO Teams 1973, Nat'l Capital Women's Swiss Teams 1978, 1980, New England Fall Mixed Pairs, Mixed Swiss Teams 1972, Spring Swiss Teams 1973, Capital District Fall Women's Swiss Teams 1977, Mexican Nat'l KO Teams 1978, Olympic Swiss Teams 1978, Southeastern Women's Pairs 1980, Fleur-de-Lys KO Teams 1973, District 1 GNT 1974, 1975. Kokish was the youngest woman Life Master in Canada and the youngest woman to represent her country in international competition (1972). She is associate editor of *Melange de Bridge,* the Unit 151 publication.

KOKKES, Jacobus C. (Jaap) (b. 1923) of Amsterdam, The Netherlands, mathematics teacher, placed second in the European Championships 1966 and also represented The Netherlands in the World Open Pairs 1962, World Team Olympiad 1960, 1964, European Championships 1957. His national titles include Open Teams 1962, Open Pairs 1963, 1964.

KOLKER, Larry M. (b. 1928) of St. Louis, rubber bridge club owner, professional bridge teacher and player, won the Vanderbilt 1962. His numerous regional titles include Mississippi Valley Open Teams 1962, Men's Pairs 1962, 1963, Missouri Valley KO Teams 1978, Mid-South Swiss Teams 1974, Lone Star Mid-Winter Swiss Teams 1977, Iowa KO Teams 1977, Deseret Classic KO Teams 1977, Republic of Texas KO Teams 1978, District 8 GNT, Zone 5 1974, 1976.

KONSTAM, Kenneth W. (1906–1968) of London, England, journalist and one of Europe's leading players, was Bermuda Bowl champion 1955. He also represented Great Britain in the Bermuda Bowl 1950, 1962, 1965, World Team Olympiad 1964, World Championships 1937, European Championship 12 times (a record), winning in 1948, 1949, 1950, 1954, 1961, 1963. He won the GOLD CUP 1949, 1956, 1960, 1964 as well as other successes. One of the leading exponents of the CAB system, Konstam was bridge editor of London *Sunday Times*.

KONSTANTINOVSKY, Elias (Lucho) (b. 1934) of Mexico DF, bridge club owner and teacher, represented Mexico in the World Open Pairs 1974, 1978, World Team Olympiad 1980, MACCABIAH GAMES 1981. He won Summer NAC Master Mixed Teams 1980. His regional titles include Spring NAC secondary Swiss Teams Flt. A 1980, Fall Swiss Teams 1975, Pacific Southwest KO Teams 1981. He contributes articles to Mexican bridge publications, and has served as chairman of the 1982 Mexican Nationals and as a Board member of the MEXICAN BRIDGE FEDERATION.

KOOPMAN, Richard D. (b. 1942) of Dayton OH, won All-American Open Teams 1972, Motor City Swiss Teams 1974, Great Lakes Swiss Teams 1973, District 11 Swiss Teams, GNT 1973.

KORNFELD, Warren (b. 1939) of Jericho NY, data processing firm executive, won the Blue Ribbon Pairs 1972. His regional titles include Fall NAC scondary Men's Pairs 1980, Tri-State Open Pairs 1970, Eastern States Men's Pairs 1972.

KOSTAL, Irwin J. (Irv) (b. 1935) of Simi Valley CA, computer programmer, won Fall NAC secondary Open Pairs 1971, Bridge Week Swiss Teams 1968, Palm Springs Swiss Teams 1975.

KOSTAL, James J. (b. 1941) of San Diego, bridge club owner, former owner of interior design firm, won Spring NAC secondary Silver Trophy Pairs Flt. B 1980, Mexican Nat'l Men's Pairs 1980, Desert Empire Open Pairs Flt. A 1980. He served as president of the La Jolla Unit 1980–1981.

KOUTSOUKOS, Spiros (b. 1935) of Athens, Greece, represented Greece in the World Team

Olympiad 1976, European Championships 1975, Balkan Championships 1978. Officially ranked #8 player in Greece, his national titles include Greek Team Trials 1972, 1974, 1975, 1976, Open Teams 1969, 1974, 1975, 1976, 1977, 1978, 1979, 1980, Open Pairs 1973, 1976, 1978, Mixed Teams 1976, 1977, 1979, Mixed Pairs 1974, Interclubs 1972, 1973, 1976, 1981. Koutsoukos is technical staff member of the Greek Atomic Energy Committee.

KOVÁCS, László, (b. 1910) of Budapest, Hungary, technician, was the winner of the International Open Pair event in Budapest 1937 and the Hungarian winner of the World Par Contest 1937. He represented Hungary in the European Championships 1969, 1970, 1971, and was npc of the Hungarian Women's Team. His national titles include Hungarian Open Teams 1960, Open Pairs 1959, 1960. He was a member of the winning Hungarian team against Poland 1963, Czechoslovakia 1963, Germany 1964, Brussels 1964, Austria 1965.

KOVÁCS, Zoltán (b. 1943) of Budapest, Hungary, physicist, bridge teacher and author, represented Hungary in the European Championships 1973, 1975, 1977, 1979, 1981, World Team Olympiad 1976, 1980, in other international competitions, and was npc of the Hungarian Juniors Team 1982. He had multiple wins in the Hungarian Open Teams, Open Pairs and Hungary Cup, and won the Socialist Cup. He is the author of a textbook for beginners and advanced players and is a contributor to the Hungarian monthly *Bridzsélet*.

KÖVER, Helen of Brussels, Belgium, placed third in the World Mixed Teams 1962 and represented Belgium in many European Women's Championships, placing second in 1950, 1955, 1956, 1959. She won the Common Market Mixed Teams 1967, 1969, Women's Pairs 1969. Her national wins include Mixed Teams 1953, 1954, 1959, 1960, 1961, 1969, Mixed Pairs 1951, 1952, 1960, 1964, 1966, 1967.

KOYTCHOU, Boris (b. 1919) of New York City, born in France, semi-retired bridge teacher and lecturer, one of the outstanding players in France, and later in the U.S., represented France in the European Championships 1948, 1949, 1950, North America in the Bermuda Bowl 1957. He won three French national team championships. Koytchou won the Spingold 1956, 1960, Chicago (since 1965 the Reisinger) 1963, and placed second in the Vanderbilt 1955, 1962, 1965. His regional titles include Eastern States KO Teams (Reisinger) 1954. He has served as chairman of the Card Committee and Board member of the Regency Whist Club (NYC).

KOYTCHOU, Noreen (Mrs. Boris, formerly Mrs. Richard Walsh) of New York City won Bridge Week Open Teams 1963, Mixed Teams 1962, All-Western Master Pairs 1963, Pacific Southwest Open Teams 1964.

KOZLOVE, Lawrence M. (Larry) (b. 1945) of Louisville KY, bank vice president, won Spring

NAC Men's Pairs 1978 and placed second in 1975 and in the Spingold 1977. His numerous regional titles include Spring NAC secondary Swiss Teams 1978, Fall Mixed Pairs Flt. A 1977, All-American Open Pairs 1972, 1973, Men's Pairs 1974, Swiss Teams 1976, Mid-Atlantic Open Pairs 1973, 1980, Swiss Teams 1973, District 5 Master Pairs, Swiss Teams 1974, Open Pairs 1976, District 11 Open Pairs 1974, Men's Swiss Teams 1981, Spring Swiss Teams 1974, Winter Swiss Teams 1976, GNT 1974, 1976, Zone III 1976, GNP 1979. Kozlove is a graduate of University of Louisville.

KRANSBERG, Gladys (b. 1910) of North Miami Beach FL, placed second in Fall NAC Mixed Pairs 1960 and won New England Mixed Teams 1966, Women's Pairs 1968, Southeastern Women's Swiss Teams 1977.

KRAUSS, Donald P. (b. 1937) of Los Angeles, stockbroker, one of the leading American players, placed second in the World Team Olympiad 1964 and represented North American in the Bermuda Bowl 1971, the United States in the World Open Pairs, Rosenblum Cup Teams 1978. He won the Team Trials 1963, International Playoff matches 1970, MACCABIAH GAMES 1981, Vanderbilt 1964, Chicago (since 1965 the Reisinger) 1962, Reisinger 1971, Spring NAC Men's Teams 1970 and placed second in the Springold 1971, Spring NAC Men's Teams 1972, Fall NAC Life Master Men's Pairs 1981. His numerous regional wins include Oregon Trail Open Teams 1961, Inter–Mountain Master Pairs 1961, All-Western Master Pairs 1962, KO Teams, Master Teams Flt. A 1974, Bridge Week KO Teams 1966, Motor City KO Teams 1976. Krauss is a graduate of Stanford University.

KREHBIEL, Carol B. (b. 1930) of Ireland IN, restaurant owner, won Spring NAC secondary Open Pairs 1976, Fall Mixed Pairs 1976, Rocky Mountain Mixed Pairs 1976, District 11 Master Pairs 1976, Central Florida Swiss Teams 1980, Midwest Women's Swiss Teams 1980, Mississippi Valley Women's Pairs 1981.

KREIJNS, Hans. See KREYNS, J. T. M. (HANS).

KREKORIAN, James E. (b. 1952) of Charlotte NC, bridge teacher and club director, won Summer NAC secondary Non-Master Pairs 1975, Fall Open Pairs 1980, Mid-Atlantic Open Pairs 1981, District 7 GNP 1981. He is a graduate of Duke University.

KREMER, Norbert (b. 1941) of Alexandria VA, professional backgammon player, won Summer NAC Master Mixed Teams 1982, placed second in 1981 and in the Grand National Teams 1973. His regional titles include Missouri Valley Open Teams 1968, Mid-Atlantic Men's Pairs 1980, Canadian Nat'l KO Teams 1981, District 3 Men's Swiss Teams 1981, District 8 GNT 1973, Zone V 1973, 1976.

KREPS, William G. T. III (Bill) of Lake Katrine NY, computer programmer, won New England Summer Swiss Teams 1981, Autumn Leaf Men's Pairs 1981, District 3 GNT, Zone II 1980.

KREYNS, J. T. M. (Hans) (b. 1925) of Rotterdam, The Netherlands, painting contractor, WBF Grand Master, one of the world's great players, won the World Open Pairs 1966 and placed second in the European Championships 1965, 1966. He also represented The Netherlands in the World Open Pairs 1970, World Team Olympiad 1980, European Championships 1967. He has won numerous national titles.

KROESEN, Willem Egbert (1872–1946) of The Hague, The Netherlands, an official of the Dutch East Indies government, born in Batavia, was co-founder of the INTERNATIONAL BRIDGE LEAGUE and its Honorary Secretary from 1936 until the IBL was ended by World War II. He also served as secretary of the NETHERLANDS BRIDGE LEAGUE.

KROGULSKA, Jolanta (b. 1940) of Warsaw, Poland, mathematician, represented Poland in the European Women's Championships 1965, 1966, 1967. Her national titles include Mixed Teams 1965, Open Teams 1967, 1968.

KROGULSKI, Zbigniew (b. 1935) of Warsaw, Poland, building engineer, won Baltic Bowl 1964, Polish Open Teams 1962, 1963, 1964, 1966, 1968, Mixed Teams 1965.

KUAI, Henry of Hong Kong, engineer, represented Hong Kong in the Far East Championships five times. His national titles include Open Teams, Master Teams, Open Pairs.

KUAI, S. Y. (b. 1912) of Hong Kong, engineer, was Far East champion in 1959, 1960, and placed second in 1963. He also represented Hong Kong in the FEC 1962. His national titles include Open Teams, Open Pairs.

KUBISTA, Dr. Josef (b. 1931) of Sweden, formerly of Prague, Czechoslovakia, pediatrician, represented Czechoslovakia on many occasions, and won the Baltic Cup 1963. His national titles include Open Teams four times, Open Pairs twice during the Sixties. He migrated to Sweden in 1968.

KUEHL, Florine W. (formerly Walters) (b. 1939) of St. Louis, placed second in Spring Women's Teams 1978, 1979 and won numerous regional titles including Southeastern Swiss Teams 1973, Tri-Unit Swiss Teams 1975, Central States I Women's Pairs 1976, II Women's Swiss Teams 1977, 1979, Wisconsin Women's Swiss Teams 1976, 1978, Champagne Open Pairs 1972, Swiss Teams 1978, Mad City Women's Swiss Teams 1979, Springfield Women's Swiss Teams 1980, District 11 Women's Pairs 1981.

KUKLEWICZ, Czeslaw (b. 1926) of Cracow, Poland, accountant, represented Poland in the World Team Olympiad 1964, World Open Pairs 1962, European Championships 1963, 1965. He won Belgian Open Teams 1964.

KUO, Che-Hung (b. 1952) of Taipei, Taiwan, engineer, won the Far East Open Teams Championship 1976, 1978, 1981, Open Pairs 1976. He also represented Taiwan in the FEC 1973, 1974, 1979, Bermuda Bowl 1977, 1979, World Team Olympiad 1976, 1980, World Open Pairs 1978. His national titles include the China Cup 1976, 1978, 1979, 1980, 1981, Governor's Cup 1974, 1977, 1978, 1980, 1982. He is the author of *Chinese Precision* and contributor to *China Bridge Magazine*.

KURLANDER, Norman A. (b. 1938) of Flushing NY, options trader, placed second in Spring NAC Men's Teams 1973 and won Long Island Men's Pairs 1975, Swiss Teams Flt. A 1982, New York–New Jersey Swiss Teams 1975, Eastern States Men's Pairs 1977, Big Apple Swiss Teams 1978.

KUROKAWA, Akio (b. 1937) of Tokyo, Japan, bridge teacher and club operator, represented Japan in the Far East Championships 1966, 1967. His national titles include KO Teams three times and Open Teams twice, Prince Takamatsu Cup more than 10 times. He is the author of *Introduction to Bridge Play*. Kurokawa is a graduate of Keio University.

KUSHNER, Jack B. (1903–1963) of Longmeadow MA, bridge teacher and writer, won Fall NAC Open Pairs 1950, and All-American Men's Pairs 1950. President of the New England Bridge Conference 1962, Kushner was co-inventor of TNT system and author of *The Kushner System* and many booklets. See BIBLIOGRAPHY, C.

KUZ, Robert P. (b. 1953) of Selkirk MB, highway construction inspector, won Buffalo KO Teams 1977, Open Pairs 1977, 1978, Unmixed Pairs, Master Pairs 1978, Peach City KO Teams 1978, Pheasant KO Teams 1978, Gopher KO Teams 1981.

KYRIAKAIDES, Sosso (b. 1915) of Athens, Greece, outstanding woman player and official, represented Egypt in the World Women's Teams 1937, placing third, represented Greece in the World Team Olympiad 1968 and was npc of the Greek Women's Team in the European Championships 1971. Kyriakaides had many successes in Egypt 1936–1961. Her national successes in Greece include Open Team Trials 1968, Open Teams 1966, 1967, Mixed Pairs 1968, 1969, 1970, 1975, 1976, Mixed Teams 1977, 1978, 1979, Interclubs 1972. Co-founder of HELLENIC BRIDGE FEDERATION in 1965, she has served as its vice president 1965–1968, 1971–1973, and was named honorary vice president in 1980.

KYRIAKOS, Costas G. (b. 1928) of Athens, Greece, bridge writer and executive assistant, is bridge columnist for the national daily *Vradini* and the weekly *Epikaira*. He authored three books in Greek and is co-translator of *Bridge Course Complete* by VICTOR MOLLO. Kyriakos was npc of the Greek junior team in the Junior European Championships 1974 and established the Kyriakos Trophy (Greek equivalent of the MCKENNEY TROPHY) 1977. He served as executive member of the HELLENIC BRIDGE FEDERATION 1971–1973. His interests include philately.

KYRIAZIS, Agamemnon G. (b. 1917) of Athens, Greece, tourist agent, represented Greece in the European Championships 1970. His national successes include Open Teams Trials 1967, 1970, 1975, Open Teams 1966, 1968, 1970, 1971, 1972, 1973, 1974, 1975, 1976, Open Pairs 1967, 1969, 1971, 1974, 1975, Mixed Pairs 1971, Interclubs 1974, 1976, Greek segment, Philip Morris Cup 1975.

L

LAAKSO, Bjarne (b. 1923) of Helsinki, Finland, salesman, represented Finland in many European and Nordic Championships. His national titles include Open Teams (eight times) and Open Pairs (twice). He is a former director of the FINNISH BRIDGE LEAGUE.

LABINS, Stephen H. (b. 1933) of West Hartford CT, manufacturer's representative, won numerous regional titles including New England Masters Swiss Teams 1970, 1974, Master Men's Pairs 1971, Knockout KO Teams 1970, 1975, Swiss Teams 1977, Fall Mixed Swiss Teams 1972, Open Pairs 1976, Swiss Teams 1973, Summer KO Teams 1979, New York Winter Men's Pairs 1971, Tri-State Winter Swiss Teams 1974, New York–New Jersey Swiss Teams 1974, District 25 GNT, Zone II 1973.

LABOUGLE, Alfredo M. (b. 1931) of Buenos Aires, Argentina, attorney and ranch owner, represented Argentina in the World Open Pairs 1974. His national titles include Interclubs 1968, 1969, 1970, 1971, 1973, 1974, 1975, 1977, Campeonato de la Republica, Condordia 1961, and placed second in Argentine Open Pairs 1967, Mixed Pairs 1976. He was a delegate to the WORLD BRIDGE FEDERATION 1965-1974 and an executive committee member of the ARGENTINE BRIDGE ASSOCIATION 1962-1970.

LACKMAN, Helen F. (Mrs. Herman) (b. 1910) of Cincinnati, bridge teacher and club director, former librarian, won the MARCUS CUP 1950, Midwest Spring Women's Pairs 1951.

LA COUR, Patricia of Baton Rouge LA, won Summer NAC secondary Mixed Pairs 1973, Fall Mixed Pairs 1973, Mid–South Women's Pairs 1973.

LACOUR, Ronald T. (Ron) of Baton Rouge LA, insurance and real estate broker, former bridge professional, won more than 60 regional titles including Evergreen Men's Pairs 1975, KO Teams 1976, Golden State Open Pairs 1972, KO Teams 1977, Klondike KO Teams, Men's Pairs 1974, 1976, Swiss Teams 1976, Mid–Winter Holiday Men's Swiss Teams 1974, Swiss Teams, Open Pairs 1976, Big D Winter Men's Pairs 1974, Master Pairs 1982. He also won Japan Men's Pairs 1965, 1966. In the early Sixties he was a pitcher for the San Francisco Giants farm club.

LAFLEUR, Diane (formerly Mraz, nee Wasserman)

(b. 1927) of La Jolla CA, bridge club owner, won more than 25 regional titles including Summer NAC secondary Swiss Teams 1972, Hawaii Swiss Teams 1976, KO Teams 1977, Women's Pairs, Mixed Pairs 1979, Pacific Southwest Open Pairs 1973, KO Teams 1976, 1978, Klondike KO Teams 1978.

LAGRON, Edward N. a Chicago bridge teacher and lecturer, was president of the Western Bridge Association 1933-1934 and editor-in-chief of its *Contract Bridge Magazine*. He emceed the ''Bridge Club of the Air,'' a twice-weekly Chicago radio show of the early Thirties, and in 1933 authored *Defensive Bridge*, the first book to cover thoroughly the subject of defense. See BIBLIOGRAPHY, E.

LAI, Jennifer (b. 1960) of Taiwan, university student, is the youngest member of the Taiwan Women's Team. She was on the winning team of the Intercollegiate Bridge Tournament in 1980.

LAIR, Mark (b. 1947) of Canyon TX, bridge professional, one of the leading American players, won the Vanderbilt 1979, Summer Master Mixed Teams 1977, 1978, 1979, and placed second in the Reisinger 1978, 1980, Blue Ribbon Pairs 1972. He has won more than 130 regional titles including Spring NAC secondary Master Pairs 1971, Swiss Teams 1976, Summer Swiss Teams 1977, Fall Swiss Teams 1974, Hawaii KO Teams 1981, Mexican Nat'l KO Teams 1980, 1981, Open Pairs 1981, Mid-Winter Holiday KO Teams 1973, 1979, Master Pairs 1973, Thunder Bay KO Teams, Open Pairs 1981.

LALL, Hemant (b. 1951) of Houston, born in Lucknow, India, systems analyst, placed second in Fall NAC Mixed Pairs 1980 and won Corpus Christi Men's Pairs 1978, Toast of Tulsa Swiss Teams 1979, Big D Winter Mixed Pairs 1980, Mid-South Master Pairs 1980. He represented Uttar Pradesh in the National Bridge Team Championships of India in 1971 at the age of 19.

LAMB, Charles (1775-1834). See BATTLE, SARAH in General Information section.

LAMBARDI, Pablo of Buenos Aires, Argentina was South American champion 1979, 1980. His national titles include Open Teams, Master Pairs, GABARRET CUP 1980, Mixed Teams 1978.

LAMBRINOS, Alecos (b. 1950) of Athens, Greece, bridge teacher, is the officially ranked No. 4 player of Greece. He represented Greece in the Junior European Championships 1974, European Championships 1977, Balkan Championships 1978. His national titles include Team Trials 1979, 1982, Open Teams 1978, 1979, 1981, Open Pairs 1975, 1978, Swiss Teams 1981, Mixed Teams 1977, 1978, Mixed Pairs 1975, 1976, Interclubs 1974, 1977, 1980, Master Pairs 1978, Junior Pairs 1974, Greek segment, Philip Morris European Cup 1975.

LAMPREY, Charles V. (b. 1938) of White Plains NY, one of the leading players of the East Coast,

placed second in the Grand National Teams 1979, Spring NAC Men's Teams 1982. He has won many regional titles including Summer NAC secondary Golder Pairs, Men's Pairs 1971, Fall Men's Swiss Teams 1978, New England Masters Swiss Teams 1966, 1970, 1973, Men's Pairs 1971, Knockouts Swiss Teams 1977, KO Teams 1970, 1975, 1980, Fall Swiss Teams 1973, Open Pairs 1976, Summer KO Teams 1979, Can-Am Master Swiss Teams 1977, Swiss Teams Flt. A 1978, Eastern States KO Teams (Reisinger) 1981, Big Apple KO Teams 1981, Southeastern KO Teams 1981.

LANDA, Sallie M. (b. 1925) of Boca Raton FL, formerly of Fargo ND, won Rough Rider Women's Pairs 1977, Gopher Women's Swiss Teams 1976, Buffalo Women's Swiss Teams 1978, Southeastern Women's Swiss Teams 1981. She is past manager and originator of two duplicate clubs in Fargo and past president of the Fargo CBL.

LANDAU, Charles S. (1898-1981) of Mount Lebanon PA was a former member of the Board of Directors and longtime bridge administrator in the Pittsburgh area. He was ACBL Honorary Member 1976.

LANDAU, Eric (b. 1945) of Rockville MD, software development manager, won Canadian Nat'l Swiss Teams 1976, KO Teams 1981, Upper New York State Swiss Teams 1975, District 4 Swiss Teams 1978, District 5 Master Pairs 1978, Men's Pairs 1979. Landau is past president of the Rochester Area BA. He codified and popularized the EHAA system, a highly natural style that included an opening notrump range below the range of an opening bid (9-12 originally, but now 10-12 because the ACBL bans sub-minimum notrump bids).

LANDAU, Judith (Judy) (b. 1947) of Dunedin FL, sales representative, won Summer NAC secondary Swiss Teams 1973, Upper New York State Swiss Teams 1975, Canadian Nat'l Swiss Teams 1976, District 4 Women's Swiss Teams, Swiss Teams 1978, Mid-Winter Holiday Swiss Teams 1978. She is a past president of the Rochester Area BA.

LANDEN, Stephen W. (b. 1952) of Bloomfield Hills MI, computer programmer and analyst, placed second in the Grand National Pairs 1979, Grand National Teams 1982. His more than 30 regional titles include Spring NAC secondary Non-Mixed Pairs 1972, Summer Board-A-Match Teams 1976, Swiss Teams 1974, All-American Swiss Teams 1974, 1976, Open Pairs Flt. A 1981, Wolverine KO Teams 1980, Master Pairs 1981, Motor City KO Teams 1977, Swiss Teams 1978, Men's Pairs, Master Pairs 1980. In 1980 he was named ''Sportsman of the Year'' (see IBPA AWARDS).

LANDER, Rhoda. See WALSH, RHODA.

LANDLEY, Wilson W. (b. 1917) of Orlando FL, retired U.S. Civil Service employee, won Summer NAC Life Master Pairs 1958. His regional titles include Florida Men's Pairs 1969, Southeastern Mixed Pairs 1950. Landley is a graduate of Rollins College.

LANDO, Albert M. (1931) of Toronto, accountant, was npc of the Canadian Team in the World Teams Olympiad 1964, 1968. He won Can-Am Open Teams, Open Pairs 1962, Upper New York State Master Pairs 1967.

LANDON, John T. Jr. (b. 1944) of Rochester NY, engineer, won Summer Senior and Advanced Senior Master Pairs 1968, Spring NAC secondary Men's Pairs 1969, Upper New York State Open Teams 1969, Mid-Atlantic Summer Open Pairs 1968.

LANDOW, William (Billy) (b. 1940) of Cherry Hill NJ, marketing and sales executive, won District 4 Open Pairs 1963, Open Teams 1969, Men's Swiss Teams 1976, 1980, New York–New Jersey Open Pairs 1966, Open Teams 1967, Keystone Open Teams 1968, 1973, KO Teams 1975, Long Island Open Pairs 1978, Central States II Swiss Teams Flt. A 1979. Landow is a graduate of Temple University.

LANDRETH, George H. (b. 1927) of San Antonio, consulting petroleum engineer and wild rice farmer, was Non-Master of the Year 1981 (see MINI McKENNEY). He won Navajo Trail Swiss Teams, Swiss Teams Flt. A 1981, Puget Sound Swiss Teams Flt. A 1981, Los Angeles Winter Swiss Teams Flt. A 1981, Las Vegas Swiss Teams 1982, British Columbia Swiss Teams 1982. Landreth, a big game hunter, won the Weatherby Big Game Trophy in 1970. He was National Horse Polo champion in 1968.

LANDY, Alvin (1905–1967) was the top executive of the ACBL from 1950 until his sudden death. Born in Cleveland, Landy graduated from Western Reserve University in 1925 and received his law degree from that school in 1927. After serving in World War II, Landy joined the ACBL as tournament director and shortly thereafter became the League's business manager (1948). In his capacity as executive secretary, Landy was known for his temperance and wisdom. He was named Honorary Member of the ACBL in 1957.

Landy's service to bridge took many forms. He was secretary of the ACBL Charity Foundation from the time of its inception, playing a key role in its creation and helping to build it into a quarter-million dollar annual project at the time of his death. Also a member of the ACBL Laws Commission, Landy acted as secretary of that body from 1956. He helped found and served as one of the original officers of the WBF. From 1958 to 1966 he was secretary-treasurer. Landy originated the convention bearing his name — 2♣ over the opponents' 1 NT requesting partner to bid one of the majors. As a player he won several major titles, including the Spingold in 1949 and four victories in the Fall NAC Men's Teams. Landy was Life Master #24.

LANDY, Fay D. (b. 1925) of Brisbane, Australia represented Australia in the World Women's Teams 1972, Venice Trophy 1978, Far East Women's Teams 1971.

LANDY, Sandra (b. 1938) of Hove, Sussex, England, university lecturer, has been a member of the British Women's Team since 1967. She won the Venice Trophy 1981 and was European Women's champion 1975, 1979, 1981, and Common Market champion twice. She also represented Great Britain in the Venice Trophy Teams 1976, World Women's Teams 1980. Her national titles include several Women's Teams championships, and Crockford's Cup. She placed second in the GOLD CUP. Landy was educated at Oxford and Cambridge.

LA NOUE, Jack of New Orleans placed second in the Reisinger 1975. He won several regional titles including Spring NAC secondary Swiss Teams 2nd Flt. 1972, Fall Open Pairs 1971, Mid-South KO Teams 1970, Master Pairs 1969, Swiss Teams 1976, Lone Star Mid-Winter BAM Teams 1977.

LAPIDES, Patricia A. (Pat) (b. 1938) of San Diego, formerly of Baltimore, bridge professional, won Spring NAC Women's Teams 1981 and placed second in 1980. Her regional titles include Spring NAC secondary Swiss Teams Flt. A 1979, 1982, Mid-Atlantic Women's Pairs 1973, Master Pairs 1977, Keystone Fall Women's Swiss Teams 1973, District 4 Fall Master Pairs 1976, Women's Swiss Teams 1979, Upper New York State Spring Open Pairs Flt. A 1980, Bridge Week Women's Swiss Teams 1982.

LAPIDES, Steven R. (b. 1943) of Baltimore, data processing engineer, won Fall NAC Life Master Men's Pairs 1975. His regional titles include Mid-Atlantic Swiss Teams 1969, 1972, Open Pairs 1972, 1978, KO Teams 1976, Washington Bridge Week Swiss Teams 1975.

LARDNER, Ring(old) Wilmer (1885–1933), famous American author, wrote two short stories on bridge, both of which appear in anthologies: "Contract" in *Treasury of Gambling Stories*, and "Who Dealt" in *Grand Slam*.

LARSEN, Bjorn (b. 1921) of Bryn, Norway, inspector and bridge columnist, represented Norway in the European Championships 1948, 1965, npc 1966. He was Nordic champion three times and Norwegian champion five times. He served as secretary of the NORWEGIAN BRIDGE FEDERATION 1954–1962.

LARSEN, John L. of Minneapolis won Gopher Open Pairs 1968, Iowa Swiss Teams 1971, Buffalo Centennial Swiss Teams 1974. See HANDICAPPED PLAYERS.

LARSEN, Kyle A. (b. 1950) of Walnut Creek CA was the youngest player ever to win a major North American Championship team title when he won the Reisinger in 1968 at the age of 18. He became a Life Master at age 15, the youngest player to do so at the time (see YOUNGEST LIFE MASTER). Larsen also won Spring NAC Men's Pairs 1968, Reisinger 1977, Spingold 1980, Grand National Teams 1982, and placed second in the Vanderbilt 1971, Spring NAC Men's Teams 1970. His numerous regional titles include All-Western KO Teams 1969, Master Teams 1972.

Open Pairs Flt. A 1980, Golden Gate Swiss Teams Flt. A 1969, Bridge Week KO Teams 1971, Southeastern KO Teams 1970, Eastern States KO Teams (Reisinger) 1973, 1974, California Capital KO Teams 1977, 1978, Open Pairs Flt. A 1977, Hawaii Men's Pairs 1980. See also IBPA AWARDS.

LARSON, Bernice E. (b. 1911) of Greenfield WI, retired nursing administrator, won Fall NAC Life Master Women's Pairs 1974, Gopher Women's Pairs 1972, Mississippi Valley Master Pairs 1974, Midwest Fall Swiss Teams 1978. She is a former president of Wisconsin-Upper Michigan BA and Greater Milwaukee BA and District 13 1st alternate to the ACBL Board of Directors.

LARSSON, Odd (b. 1924) of Oslo, Norway, represented Norway in the European Championships several times. His national titles include Open Teams 1950, 1953, 1954, 1957, 1958, 1960, 1963, Open Pairs 1957, 1961.

LASUT, Hengky (b. 1947) of Manado, Indonesia, government official, was Far East champion 1972, 1973, 1974, 1979, 1982. He also represented Indonesia in the Bermuda Bowl 1973, 1974, 1975, 1981, World Team Olympiad 1976, 1980. His national titles include Open Teams 1972, 1973, 1977, 1981, Intercity Teams 1976, 1978, Open Pairs 1980.

LATTÉS, Robert (b. 1924) of Paris, France, mathematician, was Bermuda Bowl champion 1956, European champion 1955. He won numerous national titles before his retirement from tournament play in 1961. He is a former contributor to the British *Bridge Magazine* and other periodicals.

LAURIA, Lorenzo (b. 1946) of Rome, Italy, insurance broker, one of Europe's outstanding players, was European champion 1979, placed second in 1977 and in the Bermuda Bowl 1979. His national titles include Italian KO Cup 1980, Open Teams 1982.

LAVALLEE, Paul E. (b. 1940) of Providence RI, insurance representative, won New England Fall Swiss Teams 1976, 1977, Summer Swiss Teams 1979, Masters Swiss Teams Flt. A 1979, Can-At Swiss Teams 1976, Capital District Fall KO Teams 1977, Bermuda Men's Pairs 1980.

LAVERY, Vivian. See WHALEN, VIVIAN.

LAVINGS, Paul W. (b. 1945) of Sydney, Australia, bridge club manager, represented Australia in the Bermuda Bowl 1981. His national titles include Australian Team Trials 1973, 1974, 1978, 1980, 1981, Open Pairs 1978, Blue Ribbon Pairs 1980, 1981, Open Teams 1975, 1976, 1981. He was ABF Zone 7 champion in 1974. He placed second in ACBL Life Master Pairs 1981. Lavings is councillor for youth bridge, New South Wales Bridge Federation.

LAVINTHAL, Hy (1894-1972) invented the suit preference signal in 1933-34. A retail store manager and innovative bridge teacher from Trenton NJ,

Lavinthal also served as associate editor of *The Bridge World*. In 1963 his book *Defense Tricks* explained all the stipulations of his theory of defense. See BIBLIOGRAPHY, D.

LAWRENCE, Michael S. (b. 1940) of Kensington CA, one of the world's leading player-authors, won the Bermuda Bowl 1970, 1971, placed second in 1973 and in the World Team Olympiad 1972. He won the International Playoff Match 1969, HERMAN TROPHY 1965, Vanderbilt 1967, 1971, 1973, 1977, (second in 1970), Spingold 1969 (second in 1970, 1976, 1980), Reisinger 1965, 1970, 1977, 1980, Grand National Teams 1978, 1979, Spring NAC Men's Teams 1964, 1968 (second in 1969), and placed second in the Blue Ribbon Pairs 1965, 1968, 1971, Life Master Men's Pairs 1978. Lawrence has won scores of regional titles including Fall NAC secondary Men's Teams 1969, Summer Master Mixed Teams 1970, MARCUS CUP 1972, Mixed Pairs 1972, Spring Swiss Teams Flt. A 1978. He passed the 10,000 masterpoint mark in 1978 and is a WBF GRAND MASTER. A notable author, Lawrence has written six bridge books and one book on backgammon. Two of his books, *How to Read Your Opponents' Cards* and *The Complete Book on Overcalls in Contract Bridge* were named "book of the year" by ALFRED SHEINWOLD and are generally considered to be classics. His other titles include *Judgment at Bridge*, *The Complete Book on Balancing in Contract Bridge*, and *Play a Swiss Teams of Four with Mike Lawrence*. See ACES TEAM and BIBLIOGRAPHY, C, E.

LAWRENCE, Stephen J. (b. 1924) of El Paso TX, mathematician, won Republic of Texas Mixed Pairs 1972, International City KO Teams 1974, Unmixed Pairs 1979, Los Angeles Winter Men's Pairs 1978, Land of Coronado Master Pairs, Open Pairs Flt. A 1982. Lawrence has served Unit 159 and District 16 in various executive positions including president.

LAY, James E. Jr. (b. 1944) of Chattanooga TN, certified public accountant, won Mid-Atlantic Swiss Teams 1973, 1977, 1980, Fall Open Pairs 1969, District 11 Swiss Teams 1971.

LAZARD, Sidney H. (b. 1930) of New Orleans, oil investor, one of the most successful American players, represented North American in the Bermuda Bowl 1959, 1969, the United States in the World Team Olympiad 1960. He won the Team Trials 1968, Vanderbilt 1970, Spingold 1958, 1968, Chicago (since 1965 the Reisinger) 1960, Summer NAC Master Mixed Teams 1963, 1977, 1978, 1979, 1982. He placed second in the Spingold 1954, 1966, 1973, Vanderbilt 1967, Reisinger 1968, 1969, 1975, Spring NAC Men's Teams 1954, 1956, 1961, 1965, Men's Pairs 1967, Summer NAC Master Mixed Teams 1961, Fall NAC Mixed Pairs 1959. Lazard won numerous regionals including Mid-South KO Teams 1974, Swiss Teams 1975, Men's Pairs 1976, Crescent City KO Teams, Men's Pairs 1977, Missouri Valley KO Teams 1975, 1976, Big D Winter Open Pairs Flt. A 1982.

LAZARUS, Edmond P. (b. 1937) of Baltimore won

Spring NAC Men's Pairs 1968. His numerous regional wins include Summer NAC secondary Men's Pairs 1963, Upper New York Master Pairs 1964, Mid-Atlantic Summer Open Teams 1965, Spring Open Teams 1969, Independence Day Open Teams 1968, District 4 Open Teams 1968, Keystone Fall Men's Swiss Teams 1970, Open Teams 1968.

LAZARUS, Joseph (1909–1981) of Salford, Lancaster, England, company director, represented Great Britain in the European Championships 1959, England in CAMROSE TROPHY matches 1953, 1958, 1960. He won the GOLD CUP 1959, National Pairs 1958, EBU Mixed Teams 1938, Crockford's Cup 1959. He established a record with three consecutive wins in Northern Pairs 1956–1968.

LAZARUS, Shirlee (b. 1932) of Encino CA, photofinishing company owner and executive, placed second in Summer NAC Master Mixed Teams 1975 and won numerous regional titles including Mid-South Open Teams 1964, 1965, 1968, 1971, 1973, Women's Pairs 1975, 1976, Missouri Valley Women's Pairs 1970, 1971, Republic of Texas Master Pairs 1970, Celebrity Women's Pairs, Women's Swiss Teams 1977, Motor City Women's Swiss Teams 1976, Florida Women's Pairs 1977.

LEARY, James B. (Jim) (b. 1938) of Minneapolis, stockbroker and attorney, won Summer NAC secondary Swiss Teams 1971, Mid–Am–Can Open Pairs 1966, Central States I Men's Pairs 1972, Gopher Men's Swiss Teams 1976, Roughrider Swiss Teams 1975, Buffalo Centennial Swiss Teams 1974, Black Hills Rodeo Swiss Teams 1976.

LEARY, James M. (Jim) of Livermore CA, scientific programming specialist, won Western Celebrity Mixed Pairs 1976, Puget Sound KO Teams 1976, Pacific Southwest Men's Swiss Teams 1976, California Capital Mixed Pairs 1976, All-Western Master Pairs 1976, Golden State Swiss Teams 1978, Golden Gate Swiss Teams 1980.

LEARY, Patricia L. (Mrs. James) of Livermore CA, scientific programmer, won Spring NAC Women's Pairs 1974 and placed second in Spring NAC Women's Teams 1980. Her regional titles include Orange County Women's Pairs 1972, California Capital Mixed Pairs 1976, Women's Pairs, Mixed Pairs 1977, Golden Gate Swiss Teams 1977, 1978, 1980, All-Western Women's Pairs 1977, 1980, Western Celebrity Mixed Pairs 1976, Mount Shasta Women's Pairs 1978, Wine Country Women's Pairs 1981. Leary is a graduate of New York University.

LEAVITT, Arnold K. (Arny) (b. 1932) of Lincolnwood IL won the Grand National Teams 1979 and placed second in Fall NAC Open Pairs 1964. His numerous regional wins include Summer NAC secondary Open Pairs Flt. B 1980, Midwest Open Teams 1961, 1962, Central States KO Teams 1962, Master Pairs 1969, 1972, 1974, Open Pairs 1978, District 8 Master Pairs, Swiss Teams 1975, Southeastern Mixed Pairs, Men's Swiss Teams 1976, Champaign Master Pairs 1976, Midwest Fall Master

Pairs 1977, Tri-Unit Swiss Teams 1974. He won the Chicago CBA Harmon Wilkes Trophy in 1980 and was CCBA Player of the Year in 1979.

LEAVITT, Carol (Toddy, formerly Mrs. J. J. Ruther) (b. 1936) of Chicago, bridge teacher, placed second in Spring NAC Women's Teams 1965. She won Central States Life and Senior Master Pairs 1960, All-American Women's Pairs 1961, Midwest Open Pairs 1963.

LEAVITT, Sandi (Mrs. Arnold) (b. 1933) of Lincolnwood IL won Spring NAC Women's Teams 1981 and placed second in 1979 and in Fall NAC Mixed Pairs 1975, Life Master Women's Pairs 1979. Her numerous regional titles include Summer NAC secondary Open Pairs Flt. B, Swiss Teams Flt. A 1980, Fall Women's Swiss Teams 1977, Central States I Women's Pairs 1976, KO Teams 1980, II Swiss Teams 1971, Master Pairs 1980, Women's Swiss Teams 1977, 1979, Open Pairs, Swiss Teams 1977, District 8 Swiss Teams 1975, Summer Women's Swiss Teams 1981.

LEBEL, Michel (b. 1944) of Paris, France, bridge writer, one of the world's leading players, won the World Team Olympiad 1980, Rosenblum Cup 1982. He was European champion 1974 and placed second in the Common Market Junior Teams 1969, Open Teams 1975, European Championships 1973, 1976. He also represented France in the Bermuda Bowl 1974, World Team Olympiad 1976, European Championships 1975, 1979. Lebel has won more than 10 national titles. He is the co-author of seven books including *Tout le Monde Peut Jouer au Bridge, Même Les Enfants.*

LE BENDIG, Alan P. (b. 1948) of Shreveport LA, business owner, former salesman, won several regional titles including Big D Men's Swiss Teams 1974, Mid-South Swiss Teams 1976, KO Teams 1979, 1980, Master Pairs 1979, Master Swiss Teams 1980, Texas Mid-Summer Swiss Teams 1979, Saskatchewan KO Teams 1980, Puerto Rico Men's Pairs 1981, Mid-Winter Holiday Swiss Teams Flt. A 1981. He actively encourages novice players to participate in duplicate games and was co-chairman of the first ex-quota novice sectional in the country.

LEBENSOLD, Kenneth W. (b. 1947) of New York City, mathematics professor, won Fall NAC secondary Men's Teams 1969, Can-At Swiss Teams 1969, Fun City KO Teams 1972, 1975, New England Knockouts KO Teams 1974. He frequently is credited with inventing the LEBENSOLD CONVENTION, but disclaims any connection with the convention. See IBPA AWARDS.

LEBHAR, Bretram, Jr. (1907–1972), under the name of Bert Lee, had a national reputation as a sportscaster and later as a bridge player and administrator. In his private life Lee owned radio and television stations in Florida. He won the Spingold 1940, Summer NAC Master Mixed Teams 1946, and placed second in the Chicago (since 1965 the Reisinger), Vanderbilt 1946, 1947, Spingold 1953, Life Master Pairs 1945, Spring NAC Men's Pairs 1936. But perhaps his greatest achievements arose from his work as treasurer of the ACBL from 1945 to 1947 and as a member of the Steering Committee. In the late Forties Lebhar was instrumental in the modernization of the ACBL.He was perhaps the first man to visualize the ACBL's vast potentiality for expansion, and his farsighted efforts were recognized when he was made ACBL Honorary Member in 1963. Also one of the founders of the Greater New York BA, and its first President in 1948, Lebhar donated the LEBHAR TROPHY to the ACBL.

LEBIODA, Lukasz (b. 1943) of Cracow, Poland, university chemist, represented Poland in the World Open Pairs 1966. He won the Juan-les-Pins Festival Individual 1965, Baltic Bowl 1965 and placed second in Polish Open Teams 1967, 1968.

LEBOVIC, Wolf (Willy) (b. 1931) of Toronto, born in Brustura, Czechoslovakia, builder and developer, was npc of the Canadian Women's Team in the World Team Olympiad 1964. He won Spring NAC Men's Pairs 1963, Fall NAC Blue Ribbon Pairs 1967. His regional titles include Spring NAC secondary Individual 1965, Upper New York State Men's Pairs 1965, Canadian Nat'l Master Pairs Flt. A 1974. He is the originator of the LEBOVIC ASKING BID convention.

LECKIE, Samuel (b. 1930) of Glasgow, Scotland, accountant, represented Great Britain in the World Open Pairs 1962, European Championships 1968, and represented Scotland in 17 CAMROSE TROPHY matches. He was a member of the victorious Scottish Teams in the Camrose Trophy matches 1964, 1965. His national titles include Open Teams twice, Scottish Cup three times, GOLD CUP twice. Leckie was one of four Scottish players to compete in the INVITATIONAL PAIRS CHAMPIONSHIPS (formerly London *Sunday Times* Pairs) and the British Teams Trials.

LE DENTU, José (b. 1917) of Paris, France, born in Madagascar, bridge journalist and TV commentator, won five French Open Team Championship titles before retiring from tournament play in 1957. He was npc of the French women's team at the World Women's Teams 1964. Le Dentu authored *Bridge à la Une*, *120 Donnes et Problémes du Bridge*, and co-authored *Bridge pour tous*, *Memento du bridge*, *Le Championnat du monde*, *Cent donnes extraordinaires*, *Souvenirs et secrets*, *L'Aristocratie du Bridge*, and *100 Questions — 100 Réponses*, *Le Bridge*. He is the author of many newspaper columns and magazine articles. Le Dentu is an Honorary Member of the IBPA. He is competition editor of *Revue Française de Bridge et le Bridgeur* and a contributing editor to the *Bridge Encyclopedia*. See BIBLIOGRAPHY, B, E, H.

LEDERER, Anthony Richard (Tony) (1919–1976) of England, bridge player and administrator, won his first trophy when he was 14 and played in most of the winning teams captained by his father, RICHARD LEDERER. For several years he served as a

delegate to the council of the EUROPEAN BRIDGE UNION and as one of its directors, and served as chairman of the London CCBA. He instituted the Richard Lederer Memorial Trophy in memory of his father, and with Jill Gatti founded the Charity Challenge Cup Simultaneous Pairs. With his wife RHODA BARROW LEDERER, he was a prime mover in the formation of the EBU Teachers' Association. He was co-editor of *Daily Bulletins* at the 1974 World Open Pairs and Bermuda Bowl. He co-authored *Learn Bridge with the Lederers*. See BIBLIOGRAPHY, E.

LEDERER, Rhoda (Mrs. Anthony, formerly Barrow) of Chalfont St. Peter, England, bridge writer, columnist and teacher, was co-editor of *The Bridge Players' Encyclopedia* (British edition of The Official Encyclopedia of Bridge). She is the co-author or author of many books including *Precision Bridge*, (English version of the ERIC JANNERSTEN book), *Basic ACOL*, *ACOL-ite's Quiz*, *Conventions Made Clear*, *Opening Leads to Better Bridge*, and *The ABC of Contract Bridge*. Lederer was the editor of the IBPA *Bulletin* 1967–1971 and co-editor (with Eric Jannersten) of two IBPA books. She is secretary of the English Bridge Union Teachers' Association, and Honorary Life Master teacher of the American Bridge Teachers' Association. She co-edited *Daily Bulletins* at the 1974 World Open Pairs and Bermuda Bowl. See BIBLIOGRAPHY, C, D, E.

LEDERER, Richard (1894–1941) of London, England, club owner and writer, was the first great figure in British bridge. He represented Britain in the 1934 SCHWAB CUP match and won the GOLD CUP 1933, 1934, and 1939. At the end of the Thirties, Lederer's Club was the training ground for a group of players including MAURICE HARRISON-GRAY, KENNETH KONSTAM, ADAM MEREDITH, and TERENCE REESE, subsequently dominant in the British tournament game. Lederer's writings included *Lederer Bids Two Clubs*. See BIBLIOGRAPHY, C.

LEE, Jerome of Minneapolis won Gopher Open teams 1969, 1970, KO Teams 1979, 1980, Master Pairs 1980, Canadian Prairie Open Teams 1969, Roughrider Swiss Teams 1979, Oktoberfest Open Pairs, Swiss Teams 1977.

LEE, Dr. Sidney (b. 1911) of London, England, physician and surgeon, was npc of the winning British Women's Team in the European Championships 1951 and of Great Britain's team in the World Team Olympiad 1964. His national successes include GOLD CUP 1948, 1950, 1952, 1953, 1957, and multiple wins in CAMROSE TROPHY matches, Mixed Teams, Individual, Daily Telegraph Cup, Pachabo Cup.

LEFEBVRE, Daniel H. (b. 1920) of Studio City CA, purchasing agent, won Pacific Northwest Mixed Pairs 1960, Fall Open Pairs, Men's Pairs 1963.

LEIBENDERFER, Ralph J. (1882–deceased), a New York City attorney, was one of the great players of auction bridge. he won the Eastern Auction Open Teams 1927, 1928, and was a regular member of the famous Knickerbocker Whist Club team which included SIDNEY LENZ, WINFIELD LIG-GETT, GEORGE RIETH, and P. HAL SIMS. He was associated with ELY and JOSEPHINE CULBERTSON in the foundation of *The Bridge World* magazine, acting as its counsel, and was official referee for Culbertson in the CULBERTSON-LENZ MATCH. Leibenderfer wrote articles for *The Bridge World, Vanity Fair, Auction Bridge Magazine,* as well as book reviews and introductions to many books.

LEIBOWITZ, Seymour H. (b. 1918) of Miami Beach, formerly of Lebanon PA, retired clothing manufacturer, won several regional titles including Summer NAC secondary MARCUS CUP 1968, Swiss Teams 2nd Flt. 1975, Keystone Open Teams 1971, 1973, 1974, Master Pairs 1969, 1974, KO Teams 1974, 1975, Mid-Atlantic KO Teams 1974, Southeastern Open Pairs Flt. A 1978.

LEITE-RIBEIRO, Dr. Samuel (b. 1902) of São Paulo, Brazil, physician, was South American champion 1949 and placed second in 1950. He won Brazilian Open Teams 1950, 1962.

LEMAÎTRE, André (1911–1980) of Antwerp, Belgium, business executive, bridge organizer and writer, was one of the greatest contributors to the cause of world bridge. He captained the Belgian Team 1959–1963, npc 1966, 1969–1973, and won German Open Teams 1956, 1968, 1961, 1962, 1965, Mixed Pairs 1968, Open Pairs 1955, 1956, Belgian Teams II 1966, KO Teams 1961. Lemaître was president of the EUROPEAN BRIDGE LEAGUE and secretary of the WORLD BRIDGE FEDERATION. He was an outstanding organizer and administrator for three decades, first for Germany, then for Belgium, then for Europe and finally for the world. Lemaître translated rules and established various tournament regulations for the GERMAN BRIDGE FEDERATION. Newspaper columnist and contributor to various bridge periodicals, Lemaître was a founder member of the INTERNATIONAL BRIDGE PRESS ASSOCIATION and in 1973 was chosen IBPA "Man of the Year". He was a contributing editor, *Bridge Encyclopedia.*

LEMON, James H. (1903–1977) was ACBL president in 1939. He was a frequent golf partner of President Dwight Eisenhower, who honored Lemon by appointing him special ambassador for ceremonies celebrating the independence of the Republic of Ghana. As a bridge player, Lemon was Director of the Washington Bridge League and served for many years as a member of the ABL and ACBL Executive Committees.

LENNON, Aidan (b. 1926) of Belfast, Ireland, executive officer, represented Ireland in the European Championships 1961. His national successes include Northern Ireland Open Teams.

LENT, Robin (formerly Grantham, nee Klar) (b. 1952) of Tempe AZ, bridge teacher, was youngest woman ever to win a major championship when she won Spring NAC Women's Pairs 1970. Regional titles include Champagne Open Teams 1973, Land of Coronado KO Teams, Open Teams 1972.

LENZ, Sidney S(imon) (July 12, 1873–April 12, 1960) was an author and champion player at whist and all forms of bridge and expert in many other games and sports. A series of coups in the lumber business had made him prosperous, and by age 30 he was rich. He promptly retired and devoted the rest of his life to competition, writing, reading and travel. First he took up bowling, and one of his records, an average of 240 over 20 consecutive games (1909), stood up for nearly 20 years. In 1909 he became engrossed in whist, and in 1910 he won the AMERICAN WHIST LEAGUE's principal national team championship (Minneapolis Trophy). Altogether he won more than 600 whist and bridge competitions, ranging from club duplicate games to his 14 national championships. His Knickerbocker Whist Club auction bridge team (Lenz, WINFIELD LIGGETT, P. H. SIMS, GEORGE REITH and RALPH J. LEIBENDERFER) was considered the strongest in the country. He won the last tournament he played in, the GOLDMAN CUP pairs at the Eastern Championships of 1932, then ranked as a national event.

Lenz had remarkable versatility in intellectual, coordinative, and athletic competitions. He played chess against José Capablanca and tennis against "Little Bill" Johnston with small odds. He was scratch at golf and "shot his age" at 69. At table tennis he was of championship caliber. Professional magicians considered him the best amateur ever elected honorary member of the American Society of Magicians. His special skill at dealing seconds impelled him to refuse to play card games for stakes. However, whist and bridge were his greatest loves, and he thought of himself primarily as a bridge player.

Lenz wrote several books on auction and contract bridge; and the first of them, *Lenz on Bridge* (1926), is ranked as a classic. He wrote many short stories with bridge settings. As a part owner and associate editor of the former humorous magazine *Judge,* Lenz conducted double-dummy problem contests that served greatly to publicize bridge. He contributed articles on bridge to many other magazines including the bridge magazines, and occasionally wrote bridge columns for newspapers, including *The New York Times.*

In 1931 Lenz joined the advisory council of BRIDGE HEADQUARTERS, and contributed to the OFFICIAL SYSTEM. He represented this group in the CULBERTSON-LENZ MATCH, from which he acquired lasting fame despite his loss. In his later years Lenz appeared frequently at major tournaments as an honorary referee.

At whist he won the American Whist League Open Pairs Championship 1910, 1918, 1919, 1920, representing the Knickerbocker Whist Club, and the Men's Pairs 1914, 1916, 1930, 1933, Open Teams 1929 and combination Open Teams and Pairs 1931; in auction in the American Whist League Championships he won Open Teams 1924, Open Pairs 1927, 1928, representing the Knickerbocker Whist Club; in contract he won the Eastern States Open Pairs 1932.

The technical contributions of Sidney Lenz to contract bridge are hard to define. His effort to introduce a new call, the "challenge," to replace the takeout double, was unsuccessful. His bidding system at contract bridge, the one-two-three, gave way to the artificial 2♣ bid with intermediate (strong) two-bids in other suits. The Lenz echo, a distribution-showing high-low from a four-card holding, remains standard among experts, but Lenz disclaimed credit for it, saying that it was standard among whist experts, and he merely taught auction players to use it. In 1965 he was elected to the Hall of Fame. See VANIVA PROBLEM and BIBLIOGRAPHY, A, E.

LEON, Philip H. (b. 1927) of Grosse Pointe Farms MI, private investor, won many regionals including Summer NAC secondary MARCUS CUP 1970, Swiss Teams Flt. B 1974, Cambrian Shield KO Teams 1972, 1974, 1980, Swiss Teams Flt. A 1980, District 5 Open Teams 1968, Canadian Nat'l KO Teams 1971, Great Lakes Mixed Pairs 1971, Swiss Teams Flt. A 1981, Indy 500 KO Teams 1973, District 11 KO Teams 1969, Open Pairs Flt. A 1979, Motor City Open Teams 1968, Master Pairs 1973, Wolverine Master Swiss Teams 1981, Presque Isle Swiss Teams 1977, District 12 GNT, Zone I 1973. Past president of the Michigan BA, Leon has been an MBA Board member since 1966, vice-chairman of the NAC Appeals Committee since 1970 and for many years was a member of the ACBL Board of Governors.

LERENA, Raul (b. 1916) of Buenos Aires, Argentina, bank official, bridge columnist and writer, won Argentine Open Teams 1950, 1957, Master Individual 1952. He was Bermuda Bowl tournament director 1961, 1965. Lerena has edited *Bridge Argentino* since 1966.

LERNER, Fred M. (b. 1943) of Markham ON, restaurant general manager, won Can-Am Master Pairs 1972, Motor City Swiss Teams 1975, District 2 GNT, Zone I 1979. He served as Metropolitan Toronto BA ethics and deportment officer 1972-1973.

LERNER, Dr. Marcelo H. (b. 1923) of Buenos Aires, Argentina, physician and surgeon, represented Argentina in the Bermuda Bowl 1958, 1962, 1965, World Team Olympiad 1964, 1972. He was South American champion 1957 and placed second in 1967, 1970, 1977. He won Argentine Open Teams 1955, 1963, 1965, 1967, 1969, Open Pairs 1964, 1965, Master Pairs 1961, 1965, 1966, 1969, Mixed Teams 1955, Mixed Pairs 1966, Master Individual 1960, Interclubs 1956, 1959, GABARRET CUP 1964, 1965.

LE SAVOY, Sylvia (b. 1920) of Providence RI, bridge teacher and certified director, won New England Master Women's Pairs 1967, Tri-State Winter Women's Pairs 1974, District 4 Fall Women's Swiss Teams 1976, 1977.

LESSER, Richard C. (b. 1924) of Glenmont NY, mathematician, computer scientist, educator, won New England KO Teams 1952, Master Teams 1958, Master Pairs 1959, Upper New York State Open Teams 1956, Intercollegiate Championship 1950.

LESSER, Thomas M. (b. 1943) of Chatsworth CA,

attorney, won Fall NAC secondary Men's Swiss Teams 1971, All-Western Open Pairs 1968, Pacific Southwest Open Pairs 1964, Disneyland Open Teams 1970, Orange County KO Teams 1974, Bridge Week Swiss Teams 1970, Master Men's Pairs 1979, Master Swiss Teams 1981.

LESTER, Claire (formerly Grigg) of Perth, Western Australia was Far East Women's champion 1977. She also represented Australia in the World Women's Teams 1972, World Women's Pairs 1974, Venice Trophy Teams 1978.

LEVAN, Betty M. (b. 1918) of Bakersfield CA, won several regional titles including Golden State Mixed Pairs 1963, 1964, 1965, Hawaii Open Pairs 1974, Mixed Pairs 1974, Women's Swiss Teams 1977, 1979, Master Pairs 1978, California Capital Open Pairs Flt. A 1978, Oil City Open Pairs 1978, Pacific Southwest Women's Pairs 1981.

LEVENTRITT, Peter A. (b. 1916) of New York City, formerly one of the outstanding American players, teachers and lecturers, represented North American in the Bermuda Bowl 1955 (npc), 1957, 1961, 1963, 1965, and was coach of the South African Women's Team in the World Team Olympiad 1968. He won the Spingold 1956, 1960, Chicago (since 1965 the Reisinger) 1941, 1949, Vanderbilt 1953, 1964, Life Master Pairs 1944, 1951, Summer NAC Master Mixed Teams 1949, 1950, 1959, Fall NAC Mixed Pairs 1950, Men's Teams 1966, and placed second in the Chicago 1943, 1953, Vanderbilt 1947, 1948, 1955, 1959, 1962, 1967, Fall NAC Men's Teams 1955, Open Pairs 1948, 1951, Mixed Pairs 1949, Summer NAC Master Mixed Teams 1947, Master Individual 1952. His many regional successes include events in Eastern States, Mid-South, New York-New Jersey and others. Leventritt was president of the ACBL 1954 and assistant treasurer 1945–1946. He is a past president of the Greater New York BA and the Card School of New York, which he co-founded. Leventritt pioneered the use of the SCHENKEN SYSTEM in partnership with its inventor.

LEVERONE, Anne M. (b. 1947) of St. Louis, business manager, teacher, placed second in Fall NAC Life Master Women's Pairs 1978 and won District 11 Women's Swiss Teams 1978, District 8 Women's Pairs 1979, Springfield Women's Swiss Teams 1980.

LEVEY, Sydney A. Jr. (b. 1927) of Fresno CA, controller, CPA, was ACBL president 1982, ACBL Treasurer 1979, 1980, and has been District 22 representative to the ACBL Board of Directors since 1975. He served as chairman of the ACBL Systems and Convention Committee 1976–1980. His numerous regional titles include Fall NAC secondary Men's Swiss Teams 1980, Bridge Week Open Teams 1960, 1961, Golden State KO Teams 1968, 1978, Men's Pairs 1978, Open Pairs, Swiss Teams Flt. A 1981, California Capital Master Pairs 1974, All–Western Life Master Pairs 1973, Mid–winter Holiday Men's Pairs 1980, District 22 GNT 1974. Levey is a graduate of University of San Francisco.

LEVIN, Irving (b. 1925) of St. Louis Park MN, salesman, won several regional titles including Gopher Men's Pairs 1958, Open Teams 1959, 1961, Mid-American-Canadian Open Pairs 1962. He was Intercity champion 1962.

LEVIN, Muriel (Mutzie) (b. 1922) of Chicago, retired office manager, won Summer NAC Senior and Advanced Senior Master Pairs 1965.

LEVIN, Paula. See RIBNER, PAULA.

LEVIN, Robert J. (Bobby) (b. 1957) of Miami Beach, one of the outstanding young American players, was Bermuda Bowl champion in 1981, the youngest player ever to win a world championship. He achieved Life Master status in 1973, the youngest ever to do so at that time (see YOUNGEST LIFE MASTER), and was KING OF BRIDGE in 1975. In 1971 at age 13 he won his first tournament, a sectional Men's Pairs event with his bridge teacher, the late ABE GOLDSTEIN. Levin won the Vanderbilt 1980, Reisinger, Blue Ribbon Pairs, LOU HERMAN TROPHY 1979, Spring NAC Open Pairs 1978, and placed second in the Grand National Teams 1978. He has won more than 35 regional titles including Summer NAC secondary Open Board-A-Match Teams 1976, Fall Swiss Teams 2nd Flt. 1975, Open Pairs 1978.

LEVIN, William K. (b. 1925) of Brookline MA, attorney, bridge club director, won numerous regional titles including New England Spring Open teams 1957, 1959, 1960, 1961, Fall KO Teams 1961, Open Pairs 1960.

LEVINREW, George E. (b. 1905) of Jerusalem, Israel, bridge columnist for *Jerusalem Post*, formulated the LEVINREW system. He is the author of *Points and Patterns* and coordinator of the Hebrew University *Forum*. Born in Newark NJ, Levinrew immigrated to Israel in 1965. He is a graduate of Harvard University.

LEVINSON, Delle (b. 1920) of Skokie IL, artisan and artist, won Summer NAC Senior and Advanced Senior Master Pairs 1965, Fall NAC Life Master Women's Pairs 1971.

LEVINSON, Michael A. (b. 1952) of Daly City CA, computer programmer, won Fall NAC Life Master Men's Pairs 1981. His regional titles include District 4 Men's Swiss Teams 1976, Upper New York State Men's Swiss Teams 1976, Tri-State Winter Men's Swiss Teams 1977, Pacific Southwest Swiss Teams 1979. Levinson is a graduate of Union College. He is a former tournament chess player.

LEVITT, Evelyn (Mrs. Harold) (b. 1919) of Wilmington DE, bridge teacher, lecturer and director, won Spring NAC Women's Teams 1978, 1981 and placed second in 1976 and in Fall NAC Mixed Pairs 1969. Her numerous regional titles include Fall NAC secondary Women's Teams 1968, 1977, Summer Swiss Teams Flt. B 1974, Eastern States Mixed Pairs 1959, 1960, Keystone KO Teams 1973, Mid-Atlantic

Wom's Swiss Teams 1981, Rochester Spring Women's Swiss Teams, Open Pairs 1980, District 4 GNT 1973, 1978, Swiss Teams 1978, Swiss Teams Flt. A 1981, Spring Open Pairs 1979. She is past president of Unit 190 and of District 4 and a former member of the NAC Appeals Committee. Levitt is a graduate of Temple University.

LEVITT, Jerry (b. 1918) of Clayton MO, bridge teacher and columnist, won Vanderbilt 1962 and placed second in the Grand National Teams 1973. His regional titles include Mississippi Valley Open Pairs 1953, 1961, Men's Pairs 1962, 1979, Mixed Pairs 1974, Swiss Teams 1977, Missouri Valley Mixed Pairs 1968.

LEVITT, Paul A. (b. 1939) of Azle TX, life insurance management consultant, formerly one of the leading players of the Southwest, won Fall NAC Mixed Pairs 1962, and placed second in the Spingold 1966, Vanderbilt 1967. His numerous regional titles include Mid-American-Canadian Master Pairs 1959, 1960, Mid-South Spring Open Pairs 1963, Open Teams 1965, 1968, Summer Open Pairs 1965, 1966, Open Teams 1966, Texas Spring KO Teams 1968, Summer KO Teams 1967, Republic of Texas Master Pairs 1970, Open Teams 1973, District 14 KO Teams 1973, Big D Swiss Teams 1976.

LEVY, Louis (b. 1921) of Los Angeles, formerly of Fort Lee NJ, retired businessman, won Summer NAC Life Master Pairs 1958, New York-New Jersey Men's Pairs 1968. He was National Open chess co-champion in 1972.

LEVY, Lt. Col. Michael D. (b. 1941) of Anchorage AK, born in Kobe, Japan, won Spring NAC Amateur Swiss Teams 1977, California Capital Swiss Teams, Open Pairs Flt. A 1981.

LEVY, William N. (b. 1941) of Medford NJ, attorney, won Fall NAC secondary Men's Pairs 1975, Mid-Atlantic Swiss Teams 1975, Men's Swiss Teams 1979, 1980, Washington Bridge Week Men's Swiss Teams 1976, Tri-State Winter Men's Pairs 1976, District 4 Men's Swiss Teams 1979.

LEWIS, Catherine M. (Cay) of Richland WA, accountant, bridge teacher, won Pacific Northwest Women's Pairs 1957, Open Teams 1959, 1961, Inland Empire Women's Pairs 1980, Oregon Trail Open Pairs-A-D 1980.

LEWIS, Lt. Col. Edwin R. (b. 1931) of Falls Church VA, computer science teacher, bridge club owner teacher and director, won seven Japanese Team Championships 1961–1963 and represented Japan in the Far East Championships 1961. He won Southern Conference Spring Open Teams 1966, Mid-Atlantic Independence Day Master Pairs 1968, Mid-Atlantic Swiss Teams 1978, 1979, District 5 Swiss Teams 1977, District 4 Open Pairs Flt. A 1978. He is the author of *Extended Jacoby Transfer* convention.

LEWIS, Harlow S. (b. 1932) of Wynnewood PA, investment advisor, won the Reisinger 1970, Spring

NAC Men's Pairs 1975, Fall NAC Life Master Men's Pairs 1967 and placed second in the Spingold 1974, Reisinger 1971, Men's Teams 1967. He won several regional titles including Intercollegiate Championship 1953, Eastern States KO Teams (Reisinger) 1965, District 4 Open Teams 1966, Keystone Open Teams 1965, New York–New Jersey Open Pairs 1971, Fun City KO Teams 1971. He is past president of the Philadelphia BA.

LEWIS, Jerry M. (1895–1965) was President of the ACBL in 1963 and chairman of the Board of Directors in 1962 and 1964. He served under General John Pershing in both the Mexican War and World War I and was decorated with a Distinguished Service citation. A Dallas sales executive, Lewis won several regional titles.

LEWIS, Nancy of Boca Raton FL, formerly of Warren OH, won Summer NAC secondary Mixed Pairs 1970, Southeastern Women's Teams 1971, 1974.

LEWIS, Paul J. (b. 1952) of Berkeley CA, professional bridge player, private investor, former attorney, one of the outstanding players of the West Coast, won Spring NAC Open Pairs 1980, Summer NAC Master Mixed Teams 1981. His more than 40 regional titles include Fall NAC secondary Silver Trophy Pairs Flt. B 1978, Mississippi Valley KO Teams, Swiss Teams 1979, Master Pairs 1979, 1981, Black Hills Rodeo KO Teams, Open Pairs 1980, All-Western KO Teams, Swiss Teams Flt. A 1981, Mexican Nat'l Master Pairs 1979, 1980, British Columbia KO Teams, Swiss Teams 1981.

LEWIS, Robert N. (b. 1937) of McLean VA, computer specialist, placed third in the World Mixed Teams 1974 and won Can-At KO Teams 1974, Mid-Atlantic Summer Open Teams 1971, Keystone Fall Men's Swiss Teams 1970.

LEWIS, Walter E. (b. 1940) of Pascagoula MS, bridge teacher, Gulf Coast Mid-South Swiss Teams 1972, won Crescent City Swiss Teams Flt. A 1981. He has served as president of Pas-Point DBC since 1961 and has been a Board member of Unit 180 since 1964. See HANDICAPPED PLAYERS.

LICHTENBERG, Jose (Pepe) (b. 1927) of Naucalpan, Mexico, born in Warsaw, Poland, industrialist, represented Mexico in the World Open Pairs 1978. He won Bridge Week Master Swiss Teams Flt. A 1977, Pacific Southwest Open Pairs Flt. A 1980, KO Teams 1981, Gold Coast Open Pairs Flt. A, Master Pairs 1981, District 16 Unmixed Pairs 1981.

LICHTMAN, Edward L. (b. 1949) of Winnipeg MB, accountant, placed second in Spring NAC Amateur Swiss Teams 1976 and won Saskatchewan Master Pairs 1975, Roughrider KO Teams 1979, Thunder Bay KO Teams, Master Pairs 1979.

LIECHTENSTEIN, Princes Nadine von (formerly Nadine Ansay) of Paris, France, placed second in the World Women's Teams 1960 and represented

France in several European Women's Championships. Her national titles include French Mixed Teams and several Women's Teams. She is the organizer of annual international festivals at Deauville and Cannes.

LIGAS, Stephan L. (Walrus) of San Diego, formerly of Wollaston MA, senior systems programmer, New England Masters Swiss Teams 1974, Fall Swiss Teams 1974, 1981, KO Teams 1979, District 25 GNT, Zone I 1980.

LIGGETT, Cmdr. Winfield S., Jr. (1881–1937), executive officer of the U.S.S. *Montana* in World War I, retired from the Navy and became a bridge writer, teacher, and lecturer. One of the leading pre-war American bridge personalities, Liggett partnered SIDNEY LENZ during the last part of the CULBERTSON-LENZ MATCH and won numerous national championships at whist, auction and contract. He was a member of the Advisory Council on the Official System and authored *Contract Bridge Summary* and co-authored *Winning Leads at Contract Bridge*. See BIBLIOGRAPHY, E.

LIGHTMAN, M(alcolm) A. (1892–1958) of Memphis TN was associated with the motion picture business. He won the Life Master Pairs 1945 and the Chicago (since 1965 the Reisinger) 1947.

LIGHTNER, Theodore A. (September, 1893–November 22, 1981) of New York City was one of the great players of the world and a leading figure in bridge from the earliest days of contract. He was named LIFE MASTER #7 when the category was created by the AMERICAN BRIDGE LEAGUE in 1936. Born in Grosse Pointe MI, later a resident of Chicago and New York City, Lightner was a graduate of Yale in 1915 and of Harvard Law School in 1918, and had a seat on the New York Stock Exchange.

He partnered ELY CULBERTSON during a part of the CULBERTSON-LENZ MATCH and was a member of the Culbertson team which won victories over British teams in 1930, 1933, 1934 (see ANGLO-AMERICAN MATCHES). Lightner was Bermuda Bowl champion 1953 and won the Spingold 1937, 1939, 1945, Chicago (since 1965 the Reisinger) 1947, Vanderbilt 1930, Life Master Pairs 1932, 1935, Fall NAC Open Pairs 1928. He placed second in the Spingold 1941, Chicago 1932, 1934, Vanderbilt 1937, 1938, 1939, 1941, 1945, Life Master Pairs 1931, 1947 and won numerous regional titles. A contributor to the development of the CULBERTSON SYSTEM, he was also the inventor of the LIGHTNER DOUBLE of slam contracts. His writings include *High Lights of the Culbertson System*, 1933, *Famous Hands of the Culbertson–Lenz Match* (co-author), 1932, and frequent contributions to *The Bridge World*.

LILIE, Harold J. of Woodmere NY, insurance agent, won Spring NAC Men's Teams, Men's Pairs, MOTT-SMITH TROPHY 1982. His more than 35 regional titles include Summer NAC secondary Open Pairs-A 1978, Men's Pairs Flt. A 1981, New York-New Jersey Swiss Teams 1973, 1976, Mixed Pairs 1972,

1973, Tri-State Men's Pairs 1973, 1980, Eastern States Men's Teams 1969, KO Teams (Reisinger) 1979, District 4 Open Pairs 1976, Fall Master Pairs 1977, Men's Swiss Teams 1979, Summer KO Teams 1981, District 3 Swiss Teams 1978, KO Teams 1980, Long Island KO Teams 1977, 1981.

LILIE, Joyce (Mrs. Harold) of New York City, school teacher, won Summer NAC secondary Open Pair-A 1978, New York-New Jersey Conference Swiss Teams 1976, Can-At KO Teams 1977, District 3 Mixed Pairs 1977, Swiss Teams 1978, KO Teams 1980, District 4 Women's Pairs 1981.

LIM, Dr. Teong Wah (b. 1932) of Malaysia, virologist, represented Malaysia in the Far East Championships 1962, 1965, 1966, 1968, 1970, 1972, 1973.

LIN, Harry S. C. (b. 1939) of Taipei, Taiwan, bank employee, placed second in the Bermuda Bowl 1970 and was Far East champion 1967, 1971, 1976, 1978. He also represented Taiwan in the Bermuda Bowl 1979, World Team Olympiad 1972. His national titles include the Governor's Cup 1967.

LIN, Joan (b. 1946) of Taiwan, bank employee, represented Taiwan in the Far East Championships six times and placed second twice.

LINAH, Mike (b. 1942) of Covina CA, formerly of New York City, has been an ACBL associate national tournament director since 1975. In 1978 he was a member of the directing staff at the World Pair Olympiad in New Orleans.

LINCZMAYER, Lajos (b. 1942) of Budapest, Hungary, mechanical engineer, bridge writer, represented Hungary in the European Championships 1973, 1975, 1977, 1979, 1981, World Team Olympiad 1976, 1980. He won several international teams and pairs titles in Austria and Yugoslavia and the Venice Bridge Festival team event twice. His national titles include Hungarian Open Teams and Open Pairs. Linczmayer is a contributor to the Hungarian monthly *Bridzsélet* and is the author in Hungarian of *Defensive Bidding*. He won the 1981 SOLOMON AWARD (see IBPA AWARDS).

LINDOP, David R. (b. 1946) of Toronto, born in England, business systems analyst, represented Canada in the Rosenblum Cup Teams 1978. He won several regional titles including Canadian Nat'l KO Teams 1973, 1979, Open Pairs 1976, Men's Swiss Teams 1980, Can-Am Master Pairs 1972, KO Teams 1977, Cambrian Shield Open Pairs 1973, Master Pairs 1976, Upper New York State KO Teams 1975, Fleur-de-lys Swiss Teams 1972, District 5 Open Pairs 1979. He is a graduate of University of Toronto.

LINDQVIST, Jörgen (b. 1945) of Stockholm, Sweden, bridge editor of *Expressen*, was European champion in 1977. He also represented Sweden in the Bermuda Bowl 1977, World Team Olympiad 1972, European Championships 1970, 1974, 1975,

1979, 1981. He won Swedish Open Teams 1971, 1972, 1977, Open Pairs 1977, 1978.

LINDSAY, Cameron A. (b. 1940) of Vancouver BC, stockbroker, won several regional titles including Can-Am Open Teams 1968, 1972, Canadian Nat'l Master Teams 1969, Mixed Pairs 1970, Master Pairs 1975, Peach City Swiss Teams 1978.

LINDSEY, John H. II (b. 1942) of DeKalb IL, associate math professor, won Bridge Week Open Pairs 1971, Champagne Open Pairs 1978, Central States Swiss Teams 1979, 1980, Mad City KO Teams 1979. Lindsey is a graduate of Harvard University.

LING, Robert F. (b. 1939) of Clemson SC, born in Hong Kong, professor of statistics, won Summer NAC secondary Commerical and Industrial Teams 1971, Mid-Atlantic Open Pairs Flt. A 1979, Fall Open Pairs 1964.

LINHART, William James (Jim) (b. 1936) of Ridgefield NJ, associate staff analyst, professional bridge player, won Summer NAC Master Mixed Teams 1975. His numerous regional titles include Summer NAC secondary Men's Pairs 1974, Swiss Teams 1975, Fall Swiss Teams 2nd Flt. 1975, Bridge Week Open Teams 1963, All-Western Open Teams 1965, District 15 KO Teams 1969, Upper New York State Swiss Teams 1976, Canadian Nat'l Men's Pairs 1975, Mid-Winter Holiday Swiss Teams 1976, Puerto Rico Swiss Teams 1977, Mid-Atlantic Swiss Teams, Men's Pairs 1978, Polar KO Teams, Master Swiss Teams 1980, Mid-Atlantic KO Teams 1980, Gem State Open Pairs Flt. A 1981.

LIPIN, Max (b. 1908) of West Bloomfield MI, company president, won Southeastern Men's Teams, 1962, 1969, Open Teams 1962, District 5 Open Teams 1964.

LIPSCHUTZ, Salomon (b. 1905) of Antwerp, Belgium, diamond merchant, won Belgian Invididual 1952, Open Teams 1957, 1958, 1961, 1962.

LIPSCOMB, Winsom Mary of Sydney, Australia was Far East Women's champion 1973, 1974. She also represented Australia in the World Women's Teams 1960, 1968. Her national titles include Interstate Women's Teams 1961, 1967, 1969, 1972, 1974, National Women's Pairs 1959, 1961.

LIPSITZ, Peggy. See REICH, PEGGY.

LIPSITZ, Robert H. (b. 1942) of Annandale VA, computer analyst, won the World Mixed Teams 1974. He won Summer NAC Life Master Pairs 1976 and placed second in Summer NAC Master Mixed Teams 1973, Vanderbilt 1978, Reisinger 1976, 1977, Life Master Pairs 1977. He won numerous regional titles including Fall NAC secondary Swiss Teams 2nd Flt. 1976, District 4 KO Teams 1981, Swiss Teams 1976, 1977, 1978, Open Pairs 1978, Mid-Atlantic Swiss Teams 1973, 1976, 1980.

LIPTON, Dr. William V. (1901–1977) of New York City, dentist, won the Vanderbilt 1953, Fall NAC Men's Pairs 1942 and placed second in the Chicago (since 1965 the Reisinger) 1955. He introduced the magazine *Post Mortem* and was widely thought to be the original author of its famous "Cynical Observer" column. He served as ACBL Board member 1956-1959, as well as presiding over the Greater New York and the New York–New Jersey Bridge Associations.

LITVACK, Irving A. (b. 1937) of Willowdale ON, bridge club owner, represented Canada in the Rosenblum Teams 1978, MACCABIAH GAMES 1977, 1981. He won Can-Am Men's Swiss Teams 1980, 1981, KO Teams 1981, District 2 GNT 1977, 1978, Canadian National Teams Zone 3 1981.

LIVEZEY, Joseph C. (Joey) (b. 1953) of Springfield PA, professional bridge player and teacher, club owner, was the YOUNGEST LIFE MASTER in 1968, breaking by six months the record formerly held by KYLE LARSEN. His more than 30 regional titles include Spring NAC secondary Swiss Teams Flt. A 1979, Summer Swiss Teams Flt. A 1975, Open Pairs 1979, New England Mixed Teams 1968, Keystone Master Pairs 1969, Swiss Teams 1975, Mid-Atlantic Swiss Teams 1974, 1981, Men's Swiss Teams 1980, 1981, Open Pairs 1975, Summer Master Pairs 1974, Washington Bridge Week Men's Swiss Teams 1976, 1977, Mixed Pairs 1976, Open Pairs 1977.

LIVINGSTON, Alene F. (Mrs. Milton M.) (b. 1908) of Paducah KY, won Spring NAC Women's Teams 1962. She was the first certified director in Paducah.

LOBBEN, Mickey H. (formerly Rosenthal) (b. 1933) of Encino CA, psychologist, placed second in Summer NAC Master Mixed Teams 1970 and won Fall NAC secondary Women's Teams 1967, New England Mixed Teams 1967, Mixed Pairs 1966, 1967. She is a graduate of Skidmore College.

LOCHRIDGE, Charles (1905–1970), noted for the brilliance of his dummy play, was a member of the BID-RITE TEAM. President of a New York retailing company and a bridge teacher as well, Lochridge won some five NAC championships and gained second place several times.

LOCKWOOD, Robert K. (Bob) (b. 1922) of Farmington MI won Japan Nat'l Mixed Pairs 1955, Open Pairs 1954 and placed second in the Philippine Nat'l Individual 1957.

LOEW, Lawrence (Larry) (b. 1925) of Memphis, accountant, has served as ACBL Comptroller since 1967. He is a graduate of New York University.

LOEWENTHAL, Edward (b. 1907) of New York City, stockbroker, placed third in the World's Fair Open Pairs 1933. His regional titles include Eastern States Men's Pairs 1954, KO Teams (Reisinger) 1955, New York-New Jersey Open Pairs 1958, Southeastern Men's Teams 1959. He is a past president of the Greater New York BA.

LONG, Effie. See WHITE, EFFIE.

LONG, Larry A. (b. 1942) of Russell KY, senior research chemist, won Spring NAC secondary Open Teams Flt. A 1981, Mid-Atlantic Master Pairs 1976, District 11 Men's Pairs 1978, Men's Swiss Teams 1979, Canadian Nat'l Men's Pairs Flt. A 1981, Midwest Spring Open Pairs Flt. A 1981, District 5 Labor Day Master Pairs 1981.

LONG, May Belle (b. 1901) of El Paso TX, former physical education teacher and tennis coach, won Spring NAC Women's Pairs 1961, Navajo Trail Swiss Teams 1971.

LOOBY, James V. (Jim) (b. 1947) of Burbank CA, communications consultant, won Mid-Atlantic KO Teams 1973, 1974, Keystone Men's Pairs 1974, Eastern States Men's Pairs 1973, Puerto Rico Swiss Teams 1974, Midwest Spring KO Teams 1975, Los Angeles Winter Swiss Teams 1975, Bridge Week KO Teams 1976, Raincross KO Teams 1980.

LOOKS, Harry A. (b. 1952) of St. Louis, merchandise controller, won Summer NAC Senior and Advanced Senior Master Pairs 1973. His regional titles include New England Summer Swiss Teams 1975, Long Island Swiss Teams 1977, KO Teams 1979.

LOPATA, Monte L. (b. 1919) of St. Louis, senior partner in accounting firm, won Mississippi Valley Men's Pairs 1961, 1970, Midwest Fall Men's Pairs 1962, District 8 GNT, Zone V 1975.

LOPUSHINSKY, Patricia F. (b. 1944) of Edmonton AB, born in London, England, registered nurse, won Saskatchewan Swiss Teams 1975, Calgary Swiss Teams 1973, White Hat Women's Pairs 1979.

LORBER, Michel B. (b. 1958) of Hampstead PQ, computer systems designer, won Fall NAC secondary Swiss Teams Flt. B 1981, Olympic Master Swiss Teams 1978, Can-At Swiss Teams 1980, Can-Am Swiss Teams 1981. He was Canadian Senior Master of the Year in 1977.

LORD, Roger E. III (b. 1941) of St. Louis, advertising executive, placed second in the Grand National Teams 1973. His regional titles include Fall NAC secondary Swiss Teams 1970, Missouri Valley Open Teams 1967, Open Pairs 1972, Mississippi Valley Men's Pairs 1973, District 8 Summer Men's Swiss Teams 1981, District 15 Spring KO Teams 1981.

LORENTZ, Gabriel M. (Gaby) (b. 1937) of Sydney, Australia, born in Budapest, Hungary, solicitor and company director, represented Australia in the Far East Championships 1978, 1981, Bermuda Bowl 1981. His national titles include Australian Open Pairs 1973, Open Teams 1973, 1981.

LORTZ, Henry A. (b. 1950) of Seattle, computer consultant, won several regional titles including Inland Empire Open Teams, Master Pairs 1973, Puget Sound Swiss Teams 1976, Mixed Pairs 1980, Men's

Swiss Teams 1979, British Columbia Swiss Teams 1973, Open Pairs Flt. A 1978, 1979, Oregon Trail Master Pairs 1977, Evergreen Swiss Teams 1976, District 19 GNT, Zone VII 1973.

LOVE, Clyde E. (d. 1960) of Ann Arbor MI, professor of mathematics, was a specialist on squeeze play. His writings included *Squeeze Play in Bridge*, *Bridge Squeezes Complete*, and many magazine articles. See BIBLIOGRAPHY, D.

LOUVEAUX, Dr. J. T. C. (b. 1911) of Elizabethville, Zaire, physician, won Central Africa Open Teams 1962, Katanga Open Teams 1959, 1960, Zambia Open Teams 1956, 1957, 1959, 1960, 1963, 1965.

LOW, Marc E. (b. 1935) of Dayton OH, mathematician, won several regional titles including Summer secondary MARCUS CUP 1962, Missouri Valley Master Pairs 1957, Central States Open Pairs 1962, Senior and Life Master Teams 1964, All–American Open teams 1968, Open Pairs 1971. With JOHN HAMILTON he adapted chess pairings to create the SWISS MOVEMENT in 1967.

LOWE, Leon H. (b. 1947) of Pinckney MI, government auditor, Great Lakes Master Pairs 1979, Motor City Swiss Teams 1980, Men's Pairs 1981.

LOWENTHAL, John (b. 1938) of New York City, computer systems consultant, former professional bridge player and teacher, won Spring NAC Men's Teams 1976 and placed second in the Grand National Teams 1981. His regional titles include Spring NAC secondary Swiss Teams 2nd Flt. 1976, New England KO Teams 1966, Open Teams 1968, Fall Swiss Teams 1980, Eastern States KO Teams (Reisinger) 1981. He is the co-author of the CANARY CLUB system. He created the computer system which reports U.S. national election returns (1970).

LOWERY, Sylvester (b. 1914) of Longport NJ, builder and developer, won U.S. Zone World Bridge Olympics 1940. He placed second in Fall NAC Mixed Pairs 1966 and won Keystone Conference Mixed Pairs 1959, Texas Fall Open Pairs 1962. Lowery is a past president of the Philadelphia CBA, Philadelphia Whist Association, Cavendish Club of Philadelphia, the Keystone Conference, and former chairman of the ACBL Conduct and Ethics Committee. He served as referee in the first Bermuda Bowl in 1950 and was npc of the Philadelphia women's team which played against the visiting British women's team in 1953.

LOWINSKI, Stefan (1908-1965) of Warsaw, Poland, teacher, represented Poland in the World Open Pairs 1962. He won Polish Open Teams 1957, 1958, 1960, 1961, Open Pairs 1965, Individual 1958.

LOYNAZ, Edgar (b. 1908) of Caracas, Venezuela, engineer, represented Venezuela in the World Team Olympiad 1964, Bermuda Bowl 1967, South American Championships five times, including 1963 and 1966, the years he was champion. His national titles

include National Open Teams twice, Open Pairs three times.

LU, Frank P. S. (b. 1925) of Christchurch, New Zealand, born in Tinghai, China, professor of industrial administration, represented New Zealand in the World Team Olympiad 1972 and was npc of the New Zealand team in the Bermuda Bowl 1974. His national wins include five pair championships and two team titles. He served as president of the New Zealand BA 1974–1975.

LUBLIN, Glenn A. (b. 1951) of Silver Spring MD, professional bridge player, placed second in Fall NAC Swiss Teams 1981. His more than 20 regional titles include Fall NAC secondary Swiss Teams 2nd Flt. 1976, Open Pairs 1979, Summer BAM Teams 1981, Canadian Nat'l KO Teams 1975, Swiss Teams 1976, Upper New York State Men's Swiss Teams 1974, Swiss Teams 1975, Mid-Atlantic Swiss Teams 1976, 1977, 1979, 1981, KO Teams 1978, 1979, Men's Swiss Teams 1979, 1980.

LUDWIG, R. J. (b. 1918) of Schenectady NY, modern languages teacher, placed second in Fall Senior Master Individual 1954, and won New England Master Pairs 1954, Men's Pairs 1955, 1956.

LUEBKEMAN, Bob (b. 1940) of Walnut Creek CA, real estate broker, won Navajo Trail KO Teams 1969, Inland Empire Swiss Teams 1971, Golden State Unmixed Swiss Teams 1976.

LUKACS, Paul (1915–1982) of Tel Aviv, Israel, actuary, represented Israel in the European Championships 1965 and placed fourth in the World Par Championship 1961. He won Tel Aviv Open Teams several times. His writings included articles for the Hungarian *Bridge Life*, columns in the *European Bridge Review* and *Bridge Magazine*. Lukacs was a contributor to *The Bridge World*, ACBL *Bulletin* and the *Bridge Encyclopedia*. He co-authored *Spotlight on Cardplay*, *Second Book of Bridge Problems*, and *Bridge Hands for the Connisseur*. See BIBLIOGRAPHY, H, J,

LURIE, Myrna J. (b. 1940) of Wallingford CT, executive assistant, won Fall NAC secondary Women's Swiss Teams 1980, District 3 Women's Swiss Teams 1977, Tri-State Women's Pairs 1978.

LUSKY, John A. (b. 1951) of Portland OR, attorney, won Oregon Trail Master Swiss Teams Flt. A 1979, Swiss Teams Flt. A 1981, Emerald Empire Men's Pairs, KO Teams 1979, Tri-Cities Swiss Teams Flt. A 1979, District 20 GNT 1979, 1980.

LUX, Thompson G. (Tom) of Kansas City MO won Cornhusker Open Pairs 1975, Missouri Valley KO Teams 1977, District 15 KO Teams 1970, GNT 1978.

LUYTEN, Louis (b. 1911) of Antwerp, Belgium, represented Belgium in the European Championships 1953. His national titles include Belgian Open Teams 1962, 1963.

LYON, Thomas (b. 1936) of Washington, bridge club manager, District 5 Open Teams 1966, Mid-Atlantic Open Pairs, Open Pairs Flt. A 1981, Spring Men's Pairs 1969, Independence Day Men's Pairs 1970. He is a graduate of Lycoming College.

LYONS, Torrence B. (Ted) (b. 1901) of Pittsburgh, bridge teacher, certified director, lecturer and writer, served the ABTA in various executive positions, including president 1980-1981. Since 1974 he has written the column *Lyons Den* for the *ABTA Quarterly*. He is a member of the IBPA. He is one of the 122 to be awarded a Master Bridge Teachers Certificate by the ABTA. Lyons is a graduate of University of Pittsburgh.

M

MacASLAN, David F. See ASLAN, DAVID F.

MacCRACKEN, Charles M. (Cricket) (b. 1941) of Memphis, ACBL Tournament Coordinator, began his directing career in 1963 and had achieved Regional 3 rating when he joined the ACBL staff at headquarters in 1972. He placed second in Spring NAC Men's Teams 1969 and won numerous regional titles including Golden State Open Teams 1968, Golden Gate KO Teams, Open Teams Flt. A 1969, Hawaii Open Teams 1968, 1969, Inter–Mountain KO Teams 1968, 1969, Open Pairs 1971, Oregon Trail Open Teams 1967, 1968. He has been secretary of the ACBL Laws Commission since 1978. His interests include collecting limited edition plates and antiques.

MacDUFF, R. C. of Maple Ridge BC won Inter-Mountain KO Teams 1971, Oregon Trail Open Pairs 1973, Puget Sound Open Pairs 1972, Klondike Open Pairs 1972.

MacHALE, J. P. (Joe) (b. 1922) of Dublin, Ireland, university secretary, represented Ireland in the World Open Pairs 1962, World Team Olympiad 1972, European Championships regularly since 1952. He has won every major Irish title.

MACHLIN, Gertrude (Trudy) (Mrs. Jerome) (b. 1918) of Silver Spring MD, bridge teacher and sectional director, won Fall NAC Mixed Pairs 1967.

MACHLIN, Jerome S. (Jerry) (b. 1913) of Silver Spring MD, retired ACBL national tournament director, began his career in the early Forties when his famous uncle, AL SOBEL asked him to assist at tournaments. Machlin became a full-time director in 1950 and retired in 1979. He served as Mid-Atlantic treasurer for many years, Unit secretary 1955-1956, and acted as ACBL Tournament Coordinator for Districts 6 and 7 for more than 12 years. He is well-known as author of the Washington BL *Bulletin* column *The Poor Man's 30 (& 60) Days* and the book *Tournament Bridge: An Uncensored Memoir*. See BIBLIOGRAPHY, L.

MacLAREN, John M. (b. 1926) of Edinburgh, Scotland, actuary, represented Scotland more than 30 times in CAMROSE TROPHY matches and was a member of the winning team in 1964, 1965. He was captain of the British Open Team in the Common Market Championships 1980. His national titles include Scottish Open Teams 1961, National Pairs 1956, 1957. He served as president of SCOTTISH BRIDGE UNION 1967.

MacLEAN, Carole J. (Mrs. Hugh, formerly Jerpbak) (b. 1942) of Minneapolis, bridge teacher, won Wisconsin Women's KO Teams 1981, District 14 Summer Swiss Teams Flt. A 1981, Women's Pairs 1981. She is a graduate of University of Minnesota

MacLEAN, Hugh C. (b. 1938) of Bloomington MN, backgammon and bridge club owner, represented the United States in the World Open Pairs 1974. He won Fall NAC Life Master Men's Pairs 1970, Spring NAC Men's Teams 1974, and placed second in the Vanderbilt 1977, Spring NAC Open Pairs 1974, Blue Ribbon Pairs 1975. His more than 50 regional titles include Summer NAC secondary Golder Master Pairs 1975, Canadian Prairie Master Pairs 1970, KO Teams 1972, Pheasant KO Teams 1970, 1972, Champagne Open Pairs Flt. A 1979, Gopher Men's Pairs, KO Teams 1971, Master Pairs 1973, Swiss Teams 1976, Tri-Unit KO Teams 1974, Iowa KO Teams 1972, Swiss Teams 1976, Thunderbird KO Teams, Master Pairs, Swiss Teams 1975.

MacLEOD, Iain (1913–1970) of London, England, cabinet minister and journalist, was one of the great British players. One of the originators of the ACOL SYSTEM, he began his bridge career while a student at Cambridge University where he captained his team in the first Inter-Varsity Bridge Match. By 1936 he was an international player and won the GOLD CUP the following year as a member of the famous Acol team (MAURICE HARRISON-GRAY, JACK MARX, and S. J. SIMON). Former bridge editor of the London *Sunday Times*, MacLeod authored *Bridge Is an Easy Game*. See BIBLIOGRAPHY, E.

Mac NAB, Robin B. (b. 1915) of Bozeman MT, hotel owner, cattle rancher, won Inter-Mountain Master Pairs 1957, Mid-Atlantic Fall Open Teams 1965. Mac Nab was president of the ACBL in 1965, a member of the ACBL Board of Directors 1956–1981, a former member of the ACBL LAWS COMMISSION, and past president of the WESTERN CONFERENCE. He also served on the executive council of the WORLD BRIDGE FEDERATION 1965–1973. Mac Nab writes a monthly column for the District 18 *Bulletin* insert. He is a graduate of Cornell University. His interests include writing, trout fishing and model railroading. He was a member of the U.S. Olympic track and field squad in 1936.

MADDOCKS, Judith (b. 1923) of Dearborn MI, teacher, won Motor City Women's Pairs, Mixed Pairs 1967. She is a contributing editor of Michigan BA publication, *Table Talk*, and was its editor 1960-1974.

MADDOX, Marilyn A. (Mrs. Myles) (b. 1929) of Pleasant Ridge MI, bridge teacher, won Great Lakes Mixed Pairs 1967, 1968, Open Teams 1974, Master Swiss Teams 1978, Women's Pairs, Swiss Teams Flt. A 1981, London Women's Swiss Teams 1979, Wolverine Master Swiss Teams 1981.

MADDOX, Myles V. of Pleasant Ridge MI, teacher, won Spring NAC secondary Open Pairs 1981, Great Lakes Mixed Pairs 1967, 1968, Open Teams 1971, 1974, Swiss Teams Flt. A 1981, Master Swiss Teams 1978. Maddox is a former Board member and president of Michigan BA.

MAGEE, Lee T. (b. 1928) of Prairie Village KS, attorney, won Missouri Valley KO Teams 1973, Open Teams 1968, District 15 Open Teams 1968, Master Pairs 1981, Mid–Am–Can Men's Pairs 1967, Iowa Master Pairs 1977. He is a master chess player.

MAHMOOD, Zia (b. 1946) of London, England, born in Karachi, Pakistan, chartered accountant and company executive, represented Pakistan in the 1981 Bermuda Bowl and placed second.

MAHONEY, Mabel of El Dorado AR won Canadian KO Teams 1970, Women's Pairs 1969, Klondike KO Teams 1972, Inter-Mountain KO Teams 1972, Hawaii Open Teams 1969, 1972, Master Pairs 1970.

MAIER, Merwyn D. (Jimmy) (1909–1942) of New York City, a member of the FOUR ACES from 1937 to 1942, was a leading player of the pre-World War II era. He won the Spingold 1938, 1939, Vanderbilt 1937, 1938, Fall NAC Men's Pairs 1940, Life Master Pairs 1941, Master Individual 1939 and placed second in the Spingold 1936, 1941, Chicago (since 1965 the Reisinger) 1934, Vanderbilt 1935, 1941, Master Individual 1936.

MAIER, Paul R. (b. 1949) of Encino CA, salesman, won the STODDARD TROPHY 1975, Bridge Week Swiss Teams 1975, Master Men's Pairs 1977, Los Angeles Winter Swiss Teams 1974, Spring NAC secondary Open Pairs 1977, Desert Empire KO Teams, Men's Pairs 1975, Pacific Southwest Swiss Teams 1975, All-Western Open Pairs Flt. A 1977, Mount Shasta Open Pairs Flt. A, Master Swiss Teams 1978, Golden Gate Master Pairs 1972, Men's Pairs 1980.

MALEC, David R. (Dave) (b. 1942) of Davenport Iowa, district sales manager, placed second in Fall NAC Amateur Men's Pairs 1975 and won Mid-South Swiss Teams 1974, Wisconsin Men's Swiss Teams 1978.

MALLANDER, Antha L. (b. 1917) of Houston, bridge teacher, held various executive positions in the ABTA including president 1976–1978. A member of the IBPA, she contributes articles to the *ABTA Quarterly* and formerly for newspapers in Colorado and Texas. Mallander, a Master Goren Teacher, is the author of *Goren-Standard American Point Count Bidding System Student Manual* and is active in promoting bridge as a college credit course.

MALLETT, Joseph L. (J.L.) (b. 1930) of Baton Rouge LA, businessman, won Corpus Christi Master Pairs, Swiss Teams 1978, Mid-South Men's Pairs 1978, Mississippi Valley Swiss Teams 1978.

MALOWAN, Walter (1882–1966), originator of the MALOWAN 6♦ CONVENTION, was one of the leading players of the pre-World War II period. Born in Austria, Malowan moved to New York City where he was an exporter. He was secretary and honorary member of the REGENCY CLUB, and secretary of CROCKFORD'S CLUB. Author of many articles, Malowan collaborated with SIDNEY LENZ on newspaper articles. Malowan won the AWL Open Teams in 1933.

MANCHESTER, Max M. (1914–1969) of Portland OR was executive secretary of the Oregon Public Employees Retirement System; was ACBL chairman of the Board 1960, 1961, president 1962, and named Honorary Member in 1963. Manchester won the FAll NAC Men's Pairs 1961.

MANDALA, Adolfo of Buenos Aires, Argentina, won Argentine Master Pairs 1976, 1981, Open Pairs 1973, 1981, Mixed Teams 1979, 1981, Interclubs 1980.

MANDEL, Larry A. (b. 1947) of Van Nuys CA, won the 1974 Team Trials, Spring NAC secondary Swiss Teams 2nd Flt. 1975, Desert Empire Open Teams 1974, Stockton Master Pairs 1973, District 22 Swiss Teams 1974, Los Angeles Winter KO Teams 1976.

MANDELL, Jeffrey T. (Jeff) (b. 1943) of Chicago, attorney, won Central States Open Teams 1972, 1974, Champagne Open Pairs 1973, Mississippi Valley Open Pairs 1972, Swiss Teams 1972, 1976, District 13 GNT, Zone V 1977, 1978.

MANDELL, Sidney (b. 1907) of Miami Beach, retired attorney, won the Vanderbilt 1952, 1954, Florida Men's Pairs 1972.

MANDELOT, Agota (b. 1941) of São Paulo, Brazil, born in Budapest, Hungary, was South American Women's champion 1975, 1980, 1981, and also represented Brazil in the World Women's Teams 1976, 1980, World Women's Pairs 1978, Venice Trophy 1981. She was Brazilian champion three times and São Paulo State champion six times.

MANFIELD, Edward A. (b. 1943) of Arlington VA, economist, placed second in the Rosenblum Cup Teams 1982, Spingold 1979, 1981, Reisinger 1980, Spring NAC Open Pairs 1981. He won the 1979 Cavendish Invitational and numerous regionals including Mid-Atlantic Fall KO Teams 1971, 1976, Open Pairs 1977, 1981, Spring Men's Swiss Teams 1978, KO Teams 1980, District 4 Swiss Teams 1976, 1977, 1978, District 6 GNT 1974, 1978, 1979, Zone III 1974, 1978, GNP 1979, 1981. See also IBPA AWARDS.

MANGAN, Betty of San Antonio, bridge club

operator, placed second in Fall NAC Life Master Women's Pairs 1970 and won South Texas Open Pairs 1968.

MANHARDT, Peter (b. 1936) of Vienna, Austria, director of Austrian Road safety board, won the World Open Pairs 1970 and numerous national and international titles.

MANIAS, Panos (b. 1932) of Athen, Greece, trader, represented Greece in the World Team Olympiad 1976, 1980, World Open Pairs 1978, European Championships 1969. He is the officially ranked #5 player in Greece. His national titles include Team Trials 1969, 1976, 1980, Open Teams 1969, 1971, 1974, 1975, 1977, 1980, 1981, Mixed Teams 1979, Interclubs 1973, 1976, 1980. Manias was npc of the Greek National Team in the Junior European Championships 1978. He is a former champion basketball player.

MANN, Timothy (Tim) (b. 1949) of Yuma AZ, archaeologist, won Summer NAC secondary Swiss Teams 1979, Desert Empire Swiss Teams 1980, District 17 GNP 1981.

MANNING-FOSTER, A(lfred) E(dye) (1874–1939) of London, England was one of the leading pre-war bridge players. Founder of *Bridge Magazine* and its editor until 1939, he was foreign contributing editor of *The Bridge World*, and bridge correspondent of the *Times* (London) for many years. A leading figure in the European Bridge League, he was the founder and first president of the BRITISH BRIDGE LEAGUE (1931), and was named ABL Honorary Member 1933. His writings include *Auction Bridge for All*, *Contract Bridge for All*, and *Baby Contract Book*. See BIBLIOGRAPHY, A, C.

MANOS, Dr. John T. (b. 1924) of East Norwich CT, physician, won Eastern States Mixed Teams 1961, Bermuda Open Teams 1962, 1970, 1972.

MANOUSSAKIS, Emmanuel M. (b. 1926) of Athens, Greece, industrialist, was European Open Pairs champion 1976. His national titles include Greek Open Teams 1969, Open Pairs 1966, Interclubs 1973. He is vice president of the HELLENIC BRIDGE FEDERATION and former executive member, treasurer and secretary general.

MANRIQUE, Hector of Caracas, Venezuela, engineer, was CAC champion 1973, 1977. He also represented Venezuela in several Central American–Caribbean and South American Championships. He has won several national titles.

MANSELL, Petra (b. 1923) of Durban, South Africa, bridge teacher, placed second in the World Women's Teams 1968, 1972. She also represented South Africa in the World Women's Teams 1960, 1976, World Team Olympiad 1964. Her national titles include South African Teams 1965, 1967, 1972, 1976, 1977, 1978, 1980, Open Pairs 1960, 1975, 1980, Pioneer Teams 1975, 1976, Interprovincial Teams 1973, 1977.

MANSFIELD, Steve A. (b. 1943) of Seattle, IRS agent, won Puget Sound Men's Pairs 1976, Master Swiss Teams Flt. A 1978, Oregon Trail Open Pairs 1977, Emerald Empire Master Pairs 1977, Indian Summer Swiss Teams 1977.

MANTAIGU, Marie de (1901–1977) of Paris, France was European Women's Teams champion 1939, 1953, 1954 (captain in 1953), European Women's Pairs champion 1935, and represented France on other occasions. Before her retirement from tournament bridge in 1956, she won many national championships.

MAO, Ying Pa (David) (b. 1919) of Taipei, Taiwan, born in Kiangsu, China, corporation president, was npc of the Taiwan team in the Bermuda Bowl 1970 and represented Taiwan in the World Team Olympiad 1964, Far East Championships 1962, 1965, 1966, 1968. He has won numerous national titles. Mao is a former executive secretary of the CHINESE TAIPEI CONTRACT BRIDGE ASSOCIATION.

MARCUS, Edward N. (1895–1952), for whom the MARCUS CUP is named, was a clothing manufacturer from Boston. He served as ACBL Board member and President of the New England BA. Marcus won the Chicago (since 1965 the Reisinger) in 1949.

MARCUS, Frank W. (b. 1914) of Hartsdale NY, born in Berlin, Germany, company president, won Summer NAC secondary Commercial and Industrial Teams 1978, 1979, 1980, 1981.

MARCUS, Harriet (Mrs. Frank) (b. 1917) of Hartsdale NY, company executive, won Summer NAC secondary Commercial and Industrial Teams 1978, 1979, 1980. She is a graduate of Barnard College.

MARI, Christian (b. 1945) of Paris, France, one of the leading European players, won the World Team Olympiad 1980. A member of the French team since 1973, Mari won the Common Market Open Teams 1973, European Championships 1974, and also represented France in the Bermuda Bowl 1974, European Championships 1973, 1979, 1980.

MARISCAL, Laura (Mrs. Elias Konstantinovsky) (b. 1939) of Mexico D.F., bridge club owner and teacher, won Summer NAC Master Mixed Teams 1980, Fall NAC secondary Swiss Teams 1975, Mexican Nat'l Women's Pairs 1976, Land of Coronado Mixed Pairs 1978, Pacific Southwest KO Teams 1981.

MARK, Dr. Louis (1893–1954), in whose honor the MARK MEMORIAL TROPHY was donated, was an international authority on chest ailments. The first Life Master in Columbus OH, Mark was ACBL president in 1949 and Honorary Member in 1950.

MARK, Louise Fu-Ming (Lulu) (b. 1934) of North York ON, born in Shanghai, China, senior systems analyst, represented Canada in the World Women's Teams 1964, 1968. She won Summer NAC Women's Pairs 1965.

MARKOTICH, Frank (b. 1949) of Scarborough ON, chartered accountant, won Canadian Nat'l Swiss Teams Flt. A 1980, Motor city Open Pairs 1978, District 4 Spring KO Teams, Swiss Teams 1979, District 5 Swiss Teams 1979, Wolverine Swiss Teams 1980, District 2 GNP 1982.

MARKOVICS, Andrew M. (Marko) (b. 1947) of Sydney, Australia, born in Hungary, bridge club owner, was WBF Zone 7 champion 1974, won the National Team Trials 1974, Australian Open Teams 1982.

MARKS, Arthur (1908–1965) of New York City, a mathematics teacher and tournament director, was a contributing editor to the *Bridge Encyclopedia*. He won the Western States Open Pairs in 1943.

MARKS, John G. (b. 1937) of Philadelphia, mechanical engineer, club director, won Spring NAC secondary Open Pairs 1982, Keystone Fall Men's Swiss Teams 1975, District 4 Men's Swiss Teams 1978, Master Pairs 1979. Marks served as president of Unit 141 1981–1982.

MARKS, Paul N. (1908–1968), ACBL national tournament director from 1957, devised APPENDIX MOVEMENTS for 7-, 11-, and 13-table RAINBOW INDIVIDUAL MOVEMENTS. Marks, of Maywood IL, was an accountant as well as a teacher of mathematics and bridge.

MARKUS, Rika (Rixi) (b. 1910) of London, England, born in Austria, one of the greatest woman players of all time and one of the fastest analysts, was the first woman to become a WBF GRAND MASTER. She is the winner of 12 international championships, more than any other woman player, and was a key member of the Austrian Women's Team which, under the captaincy of DR. PAUL STERN, won the first two European Women's Championships, 1935 and 1936, and the World Women's Championship 1937. She fled to England when Hitler's forces marched into Austria in the Spring of 1938. Until she was naturalized in 1950, she could not play internationally for Britain. Her first and most accomplished partner for many years was LADY DORIS RHODES. They won many titles together including the Two Stars event, a very prestigious pairs event in Britain, the Lady Milne and Whitelaw Cups several times, and toured the United States in 1953 as members of the British Women's Team. Subsequently Markus formed a partnership with FRITZI GORDON, which formerly was the strongest woman's pair in the world. Together they won the World Women's Pairs 1962, 1974, World Mixed Teams 1962, World Women's Teams 1964. Markus represented Great Britain in many European Women's Championships, winning in 1951, 1952, 1959, 1961, 1963, 1966, 1975, and in many Olympiad events, finishing second in the World Mixed Pairs, World Women's Pairs 1970. Her national titles include the GOLD CUP 1961, Master Pairs 1957 and many others. Markus was named Bridge Personality of the Year in 1974 (see IBPA AWARDS). The following year she received the M.B.E. from Her Majesty for her con-

tributions to bridge. She has been bridge editor of the *Guardian* since 1955 and from 1975 to 1980 wrote a daily column in the *Evening Standard*. A contributor to many periodicals including *The Bridge World* and *Bridge Magazine*, she is the author of seven books including *Bid Boldly, Play Safe, Common Sense Bridge, Aces and Places, Bridge Around the World* and *Bridge Table Tales*. See BIBLIOGRAPHY, H, and BUENOS AIRES AFFAIR.

MARSCH, John E. (b. 1938) of Winnipeg MB, businessman, won Calgary KO Teams, Men's Pairs 1973, British Columbia KO Teams 1970, 1977.

MARSH, Edward (Bud) (b. 1927) of Phoenix, formerly of Montreal, realtor, bridge teacher, won Spring NAC Amateur Swiss Teams 1977. His numerous regional titles include Canadian Nat'l Mixed Pairs 1949, Open Pairs 1951, 1952, Can-Am Men's Pairs 1949, 1975, Mixed Pairs 1951, Open Teams 1949, 1952, 1954, New England Open Pairs, Open Teams 1969.

MARSH, Dr. Samuel (b. 1912) of Forest Hills NY, physician, won Gold Coast Men's Swiss Teams, Men's Pairs 1981, Tri-State Men's Pairs 1981.

MARSHALL, Cynthia B. (Cindy) (b. 1947) of Oak Ridge TN, accountant, Fall NAC secondary Swiss Teams 1979, Mid-Atlantic Women's Pairs, Open Pairs 1981.

MARTEL, Charles U. (Chip) (b. 1953) of Davis CA, professor of computer science, won the World Open Pairs and placed second in the Rosenblum Cup Teams 1982. He won the Reisinger 1981, HERMAN TROPHY 1981, Grand National Teams 1982 and placed second in the Grand National Pairs, Blue Ribbon Pairs 1981. He won the ROSENKRANZ AWARD 1979. His numerous regional titles include Upper New York State KO Teams 1974, All-Western Master Teams 1976, Master Pairs 1977, KO Teams 1978. Martel was educated at M.I.T. and University of California at Berkeley.

MARTEL, Jan (Mrs. Chip, formerly Mrs. Lew Stansby, nee Friedman) (b. 1943) of Davis CA, lawyer, won Spring NAC Women's Pairs 1974 and placed second in Spring NAC Women's Teams 1980. Her regional titles include Golden Gate Master Pairs 1971, California Capital Women's Pairs 1977, All-Western Women's Pairs 1977, Master Swiss Teams Flt. A 1978. A graduate of University of California at Berkeley, she was a visiting associate professor of law, teaching in areas of tax and estate planning. She received the Order of Coif 1968, was clerk to a California Supreme Court Justice 1969, became a certified tax specialist 1981, served as vice president of American Jewish Congress of Northern California 1980–1981 and is a member of the Board of Directors of San Francisco Estate Planning Council.

MARTENSSON, Eva (b. 1924) of Stockholm, Sweden, won the World Women's Teams 1968. She was Nordic Women's champion 1957, 1966, 1968.

MARTIN, Bruce of El Paso TX won Navajo Trail Open Teams 1969, 1977, Master Pairs 1977, Texas Mid-Winter Open Pairs 1971, Land of Coronado Open Pairs 1972, Master Pairs 1974.

MARTIN, Christianne (b. 1914) of Paris, France, was European Women's champion 1939, 1954, 1956. She also represented France in the European Women's Championships 1936, 1948, 1949, 1950, 1951, 1955, 1965. Martin won the International Mixed Pairs twice and had many national successes in Open and Mixed Teams.

MARTIN, Ira (b. 1897) of Fort Myers FL, bridge teacher, is the author of *The Ins and Outs and Wins of Contract Bridge.*

MARTIN, Phillip (b. 1953) of Brooklyn Heights NY, data processing consultant, placed second in the Grand National Teams 1981. He won Fun City Swiss Teams 1975, Washington Bridge Week Swiss Teams 1977, District 3 Men's Swiss Teams 1979, New England Fall Swiss Teams 1980, Eastern States KO Teams (Reisinger) 1981.

MARTINEAU, Joel B. (b. 1948) of Vancouver BC, health food store owner, won Oregon Trail Men's Pairs 1972, KO Teams 1981, Canadian Prairie KO Teams 1971, British Columbia KO Teams 1973, White Hat Men's Pairs 1981, Indian Summer Men's Pairs 1981, Peach City Swiss Teams Flt. A 1982, District 19 GNP 1982.

MARTINO, Michael J. (Mike) (b. 1936) of Hamilton ON, lawyer, executive, won Spring NAC Men's Pairs 1969. His regional titles include Canadian Nat'l KO Teams 1968, Men's Pairs 1968, 1971, Mixed Pairs 1971.

MARTINS FERREIRA, Nelson (b. 1921) of São Paulo, Brazil, businessman, was South American champion 1956, 1974. He also represented Brazil in the World Team Olympiad 1960.

MARTINS FERREIRA, Synesio (b. 1922) of São Paulo, Brazil, businessman, was South American champion 1969, 1974. He also represented Brazil in the World Team Olympiad 1960, 1968, 1972.

MARX, John C. H. (Jack) (b. 1907) of London, England, bridge journalist, was European champion 1950 and selected to represent Britain (did not play due to ill health) in the Bermuda Bowl 1950. His national titles include the GOLD CUP 1937, 1947, 1971. He served the BRITISH BRIDGE LEAGUE and ENGLISH BRIDGE UNION in various capacities for many years, and was president of the Middlesex County BA 1982. Marx was a regular contributor to *Contract Bridge Journal* 1946–1948, *British Bridge World* 1950–1956, and presently contributes regularly to *Illustrated News.* He is one of the originators of the ACOL SYSTEM, and is the originator of the BYZANTINE convention. Marx also developed the club major-asking response to an opening notrump independently of GEORGE RAPÉE, inventor of the STAYMAN CONVENTION, but his first published work did not ap-

pear until after SAM STAYMAN's *Bridge World* presentation.

MASON, Jane (b. 1933) of Maplewood NJ won Fun City KO Teams 1970, Eastern States KO Teams (Reisinger) 1972, District 3 Swiss Teams 1977.

MASOOD, Salim. See SALIM, MASOOD.

MASTERSON, Marcia W. of Pacific Palisades CA, stockbroker, won Spring NAC Amateur Swiss Teams 1977. Her regional titles include Los Angeles Winter Master Pairs 1974, Pacific Southwest Women's Swiss Teams 1976, Swiss Teams Flt. A 1981, Golden Gate Women's Pairs 1977, Emerald Empire Swiss Teams, Women's Pairs 1977.

MASTRON, Dr. Victor (b. 1920) of Yorba Linda CA, physician and surgeon, won Inter-Mountain Men's Pairs 1969, Canadian KO Teams 1970, District 18 KO Teams, Open Pairs 1970, Mid-Winter Holiday Open Teams 1970, Golden Gate KO Teams 1971. A navigator in World War II, he received the *Distinguished Flying Cross* and the *Air Medal* (8 oak leaf clusters).

MATHE, Eugenie M. (Mrs. Lewis) (b. 1925) of Canoga Park CA, U.S. Census Bureau survey clerk, won the European Open Teams at Lake Balaton, Hungary, 1975. She won Summer NAC Master Mixed Teams 1970 (second in 1975), Fall NAC Mixed Pairs 1971. Her regional titles include Fall NAC secondary Women's Swiss Teams 1976, Bridge Week Mixed Teams 1963, Mixed Pairs 1960, All-Western Open Teams 1966. Mathe has been chairman of the Publishing Committee of ALACBU since 1979. She edited *Southern California Bridge News* 1979–1982 and authored the monthly column *The L.O.L.* from 1966. She was awarded the annual Harry Emrich Memorial Trophy in 1981 for outstanding contributions to bridge.

MATHE, Lewis L. (Lew) (b. 1915) of Canoga Park CA, real estate appraiser and broker, WBF Grand Master, one of the great bridge players of the world, noted for his adaptability and table presence, was the leading exponent of the direct method of bidding favored on the West Coast. He was Bermuda Bowl champion in 1954 and also represented North American in the Bermuda Bowl 1955, 1962, 1966, 1971, and the United States in the World Team Olympiad 1960. He won the International Playoff Match 1970, MOTT-SMITH TROPHY 1959, 1964, 1967, HERMAN TROPHY 1957, Spingold 1954, Vanderbilt 1964, 1966, 1967, Chicago (since 1965 the Reisinger) 1959, 1960, 1962, Reisinger 1971, Blue Ribbon Pairs 1964, Fall NAC Men's Teams 1957, 1962, Open Pairs 1957, Mixed Pairs 1971, Spring NAC Open Pairs 1959, Men's Teams 1970, Summer NAC Life Master Pairs 1963, 1967, Master Mixed Teams 1970. He placed second in the Team Trials 1965, Spingold 1953, 1971, 1974, Reisinger 1966, Blue Ribbon Pairs 1967, Summer NAC Master Mixed Teams 1953, Men's Pairs 1961, Spring NAC Open Pairs 1964, 1967, Men's Teams 1972, Mixed Pairs 1959. He won the 1975 European Open Teams at Lake Balaton, Hungary, and a host of West Coast regional titles. He is the originator of the MATHE ASKING BID. Mathe was ACBL president in 1975, chairman of the ACBL Board in 1976, chairman of the ACBL Board of Governors 1968, WBF representative from the ACBL and WBF treasurer since 1977. He was three-time president of the WESTERN CONFERENCE and ACBL Board member from District 23 1958–1961 and 1970–1982.

MATHEWS, David J. (b. 1969) of Auckland, New Zealand, systems analyst, represented New Zealand in the World Team Olympiad 1980, Far East Championships 1975, Team Trials 1981. His national titles include New Zealand KO Teams 1973, 1976.

MATHEWS, Luise. See EMBRY, LUISE.

MATHIS, James L. (b. 1927) of Williamsville NY, bank executive, represented the United States in the World Open Pairs 1970. He won Spring NAC Open Pairs 1969 and placed second in the Life Master Pairs 1970. His regional titles include Upper New York State Open Teams 1964, 1970, 1971, Master Pairs 1965, Open Pairs 1972, Presque Isle KO Teams 1977, District 4 Spring KO Teams 1980, District 5 Men's Swiss Teams 1976, GNT 1973, 1976, 1977, 1978, 1979, Zone III 1979, GNP 1982.

MATTHESS, Bob of Incline Village NV won Spring NAC secondary Swiss Teams 1970, All-Western KO Teams 1973, Navajo Trail Open Pairs 1970.

MATTHEWS, Judge Ben G. (b. 1926) of Shelbyville KY, attorney and bank executive, won several regional events including Fall NAC secondary Swiss Teams 2nd Flt. 1961, Texas Spring Master Pairs 1962, Midwest Men's Pairs 1955, Open Teams 1971, Mississippi Valley Men's Pairs 1965, Blue Grass Swiss Teams 1975, District 11 Open Pairs 1978.

MATTHEWS, Jackie A. (b. 1936) of Medford OR, teacher, won Oregon Trail Women's Pairs 1979, British Columbia Women's Pairs 1979, Puget Sound Open Pairs Flt. A 1979, Gem State Women's Pairs 1981, Wine Country Swiss Teams 1982.

MATZ, Norma (b. 1916) of Miami Beach, won Spring NAC Women's Teams 1952, 1954 and many regional titles.

MAUGHAM, (William) Somerset (1874–1965), famous novelist and short story writer, once called bridge "the most entertaining and intelligent card game the wit of man has so far devised." He often used card playing in his settings. In *Three Fat Women of Antibes* three middle-age women are looking for a congenial fourth, a story anthologized in *Grand Slam*. In *Ashenden*, his slightly fictionalized memoirs, he records playing contract bridge "with which I was not very familiar" during World War I – one of earliest references to the modern game in print. Maugham wrote the introduction to Charles H. Goren's book *The Standard Book of Bidding*. See CONTRACT BRIDGE.

MAUPIN, Evelyn of San Antonio, teacher, placed second in Spring NAC Women's Teams 1962 and won Southeastern Women's Teams 1961, Florida Women's Pairs 1974, Individual 1960.

MAURER, Marguerite (b. 1921) of Skaneateles NY, small business owner, won Can-Am Women's Pairs 1960, 1963, 1964, Upper New York State Women's Pairs 1960.

MAY, Albert E. (b. 1909) of Ft. Lauderdale FL, former professor of mathematics, won Central States Open Teams 1964, 1968, Can-At Mixed Pairs 1973, Mid-Atlantic Open Pairs 1978.

MAY, Helene F. (Mrs. Albert) (b. 1909) of Ft. Lauderdale FL, former model and secretary, won Central States Open Teams 1964, 1968, Can-At Mixed Pairs 1973, Mid-Atlantic Open Pairs 1977.

MAY, Walter R. (b. 1930) of Endicott NY, university official, won Upper New York State Open Teams 1956, 1975, New England Fall Open Teams 1958, Master Pairs 1959, Tri-State Men's Swiss Teams 1977, Keystone Swiss Teams 1974, 1975, Autumn Leaf Men's Swiss Teams 1981, District 4 Swiss Teams 1977, 1978, GNT 1975, 1978, Zone III 1975, GNP 1982.

MAYBIN, Laura of Columbia SC won Mid-Atlantic Women's Pairs 1972, 1974, Open Teams 1973.

MAYER, Edward (1901–1980) of London, England, lawyer, represented Great Britain in SCHWAB CUP match 1933 and won unofficial matches against American teams 1954 and 1956. He won the GOLD CUP 1932, and English Open Teams 1948. Mayer served as Council Member of British Bridge League. Bridge correspondent of London *Times* for more than 20 years, he was the author of *Money Bridge*. See BIBLIOGRAPHY, E.

MAYER, Ferdinando (Ferry) (b. 1912) of Trieste, Italy, advertising executive, was European champion 1971 and placed second in the World Open Pairs 1970. His national titles include Italian Open Teams 1965, 1970, KO Teams 1969.

McALEAR, Allen L. (b. 1928) of Bozeman MT, attorney, won Inter-Mountain Swiss Teams 1971, Puget Sound Open Pairs 1969, District 18 KO Teams, Open Teams 1971, Calgary Master Pairs 1973. He is a former WESTERN CONFERENCE Board member and past president of District 18.

McAVOY, James M. (b. 1950) of Victoria BC, accountant, won Evergreen KO Teams 1975, British Columbia Swiss Teams 1977, Swiss Teams Flt. A 1981, District 19 GNT 1978, Canadian Nat'l Teams Zone 6 1981.

McBRIDE, Fred H. (b. 1917) of Greensboro NC won Spring NAC secondary Golder Master Pairs 1976, Florida Men's Pairs 1975, Mid-Atlantic KO Teams, Open Pairs 1974, Swiss Teams 1975, Men's Swiss Teams 1979, 1982.

McCALLON, Dr. William R. (Bill) (b. 1930) of Hyattsville MD, veterinarian, won Midwest Spring Swiss Teams 1976, Mid-Atlantic KO Teams 1972, 1975.

McCALLUM, Karen T. (b. 1946) of New York City, graphics designer, professional bridge player and teacher, won Spring NAC secondary Open Pairs 1981, Central States Master Pairs 1981, New York Winter Women's Pairs 1978, District 4 Fall Women's Swiss Teams 1981, Southeastern Women's Swiss Teams 1981, Canadian Nat'l Mixed Pairs 1981.

McCAMPBELL, Bryant (d. ca 1930) of St. Louis claimed invention of the TAKEOUT DOUBLE as well as the 4–3–2–1 POINT-COUNT. There is no reason to doubt that he arrived at both ideas independently, though perhaps not first. McCampbell was one of the most successful players of auction bridge and author of perhaps the first book (*Auction Tactics*, 1915) to describe the strategy of the successful rubber-bridge player.

McCAMPBELL, Leavelle (1880–1946) of New York City was chairman of the Whist Club committee which produced the first generally accepted *Laws of Contract Bridge*, 1927; he assisted in many later revisions of the Laws.

McCANCE, Ian (b. 1927) of Mount Waverley, Australia, senior lecturer in physiology, represented Australia in the World Team Olympiad 1968 and as npc of the Venice Trophy Team 1978 and Open Team in the World Team Olympiad 1980. His national titles include Interstate Teams 1966, 1968, 1972, Australian Open Pairs 1967. McCance writes a bridge column for *Toorak Times*. He has served as vice president and councillor to the Victorian BA.

McCANDLESS, Dianne M. (b. 1942) of Thunder Bay ON, former teacher, won Gopher Women's Pairs 1979, Thunder Bay Women's Pairs 1979, Nat'l Capital Women's Pairs 1981.

McCOMAS, M. Stanley (Stan) (b. 1908) of Indianapolis, bridge writer and teacher, former insurance executive, is associated with EASLEY BLACKWOOD in his bridge writings. McComas won Midwest Fall Open teams 1960, Mixed Pairs 1946.

McCONNELL, Ruth (Mrs. Lee W.) of Columbia City IN, was ACBL president in 1974, the first woman to hold that office. She was chairman of the ACBL Board of Directors in 1975 and a Board member from 1965. McConnell served as npc of the United States Women's Olympiad team in 1976, 1980, VENICE TROPHY team 1974, 1976, 1978, and was instrumental in upgrading the Venice Trophy to a WBF Championship. She won District 11 Mixed Pairs 1968, Mississippi Valley Women's Pairs 1970, 1981. Creator of the *Midwest Monitor*, she was its editor 1963-1967.

McCRACKIN, Nancy P. (b. 1922) of Albuquerque, artist, won Spring NAC secondary Individual 1953,

Desert Empire Open Teams 1965, Women's Pairs 1969, 1971.

McCRARY, Marilyn of Des Moines IA won Summer NAC Master Mixed Teams 1971.

McCRAY, Royce W. (b. 1941) of Cedar Rapids IA, refractionist, won Spring NAC secondary Swiss Teams 2nd Flt. 1973, Gopher Master Teams 1972, Iowa Swiss Teams 1979, KO Teams, Men's Swiss Teams 1980, District 14 GNT 1973.

McCRORY, Mary R. of San Diego won Palm Springs KO Teams 1971, Rocky Mountain Open Pairs 1971, Navajo Trail Master Pairs 1969.

McDANIEL, Garner N. of Houston, realtor, one of the most succesful women players of the Southwest, won Spring NAC Women's Teams 1963, 1966, Women's Pairs 1967, and placed second in the Women's Teams 1962, Women's Pairs 1963, 1966, Summer NAC Master Mixed Teams 1963. Her regional titles include Fall NAC secondary Women's Pairs 1975, Texas Fall KO Teams 1970, Spring Mixed Pairs 1964, Missouri Valley Open Pairs 1973, Mid-South Swiss Teams 1973, Women's Master Swiss Teams 1976, Southeastern Women's Swiss Teams 1976.

McDONALD, Allen (Al) of Ottawa ON won Fleur-de-Lys KO Teams 1974, Open Teams, Open Pairs 1973, Upper New York State Swiss Teams 1972.

McELWAIN, Constance (Mrs. John Alden) (b. 1931) of Burlington MA, programmer, won New England Fall Women's Pairs 1959, Mixed Teams 1963, Upper New York State Open Pairs 1962.

McGARRY, Dennis J. (b. 1947) of Shaker Heights OH, computer programmer, placed second in Summer NAC Senior and Advanced Senior Master Pairs 1970, Master Mixed Teams 1980, Fall Life Master Men's Pairs 1979. His more than 30 regional titles include Spring NAC secondary Men's Pairs 1972, Swiss Teams Flt. A 1982, All-American Mixed Pairs 1971, Men's Pairs 1972, KO Teams 1976, 1977, 1978, Swiss Teams Flt. A 1982, Midwest Fall Men's Swiss Teams 1977, 1978, Master Pairs, Swiss Teams 1978, Spring Master Pairs 1975, 1976, Great Lakes Swiss Teams 1975, Master Swiss Teams 1978, Open Pairs 1976, Men's Pairs 1979, KO Teams 1982.

McGERVEY, John D. (b. 1931) of Cleveland Heights OH, physics professor, won Keystone Conference Open Teams 1955, Central States Master Pairs 1955, District 5 Open Teams 1960.

McGINLEY, Constance S. (Connie) (b. 1956) of Philadelphia, business owner, won Summer NAC secondary Mixed Swiss Teams, Swiss Teams 1976, BAM Teams 1981, Mid-Atlantic Swiss Teams 1975, Keystone Swiss Teams 1974. McGinley became the youngest woman Life Master in 1973 at the age of 17. See YOUNGEST LIFE MASTER.

McGROVER, Raymond J. (1905–1974), 1947

ACBL president, played a major role in the 1948 reorganization of the League and later assisted in the formation of the 1963 Laws. A New York City attorney, McGrover was president of the Long Island BL for seven years.

McKEE, Jay T. (b. 1948) of Clinton MS, contractor, placed second in Spring NAC Men's Pairs 1971 and won Fall NAC secondary Open Pairs 2nd Flt. 1971, Fall Men's Swiss Teams 1978, Golden Gate KO Teams 1971, Beef State KO Teams 1971, District 17 Master Pairs 1973, Lone Star Mid-Winter KO Teams 1977.

McKENNEY, William E. (November, 1891–March 26, 1950) whose memory the McKENNEY TROPHY perpetuates, gained fame as a bridge columnist, philanthropist and administrator.

McKenney contributed daily bridge columns to Scripps–Howard newspapers from 1929 to 1950. So widely read was his work that in Europe the SUIT-PREFERENCE SIGNAL became known as the "McKenney Convention" instead of being attributed to its inventor, HY LAVINTHAL.

McKenney's dedication to bridge and to its organizations extended well beyond the written word. In 1927 he helped found the American Auction Bridge League. He became chairman of its committee on laws and then executive secretary in 1928, and continued as secretary of both the ABL and ACBL until 1948. Having founded the National Laws Commission in 1932, McKenney chaired it from 1935 through 1948.

Several times McKenney contributed his privately earned income to the ABL and ACBL. For example, in 1929 he founded Bridge Supplies, Inc., which sold trophies, scoring supplies, and other merchandise. In 1936 he donated this corporation to the ABL. He devoted nearly all his time to the interests of the successive bridge leagues.

To a degree McKenney acquired a spirit of proprietary control which became increasingly inconsistent with the interests of the ACBL, as it became larger and more financially stable. The year 1948 found McKenney deposed in favor of democratic control of the ACBL.

McKenney founded both the ABL and the ACBL charity programs. Through these channels he led the League to endow the Children's Cancer Ward at Memorial Hospital in New York City, and to establish WAR ORPHANS SCHOLARSHIPS.

He won ABL Fall National Open Pairs 1929.

McKINNEY, Richard L. (Dick) (b. 1928) of Edmonton AB, professor of mathematics, won Inland Empire Swiss Teams 1971, White Hat Swiss Teams 1977, Big Sky Open Pairs Flt. A 1979, Inter-Mountain Swiss Teams 1975.

McMAHAN, Mike (b. 1935) of Huntington Beach CA, office furniture store manager, placed second in the Reisinger 1966. His numerous regional titles include Fall NAC secondary Mixed Pairs 1971, Summer Golder Master Pairs 1969, Desert Empire Open Teams 1959, All-Western Open Pairs 1963, Open

Teams 1964, Pacific Southwest Master Pairs 1963, Bridge Week Open Pairs 1965, Master Men's Pairs 1968, 1975, Golden State Open Teams 1966, Master Pairs 1975, Los Angeles Winter Master Pairs 1977.

McMAHAN, Robert F. (Bob) (b. 1930) of Florence SC, commodity and stockbroker, won Mid-Atlantic Summer Open Teams 1961, Spring Open Pairs, KO Teams 1973, Men's Pairs 1963, Swiss Teams 1980, Fall Swiss Teams 1977.

McMAHON, Mary M. of Sydney, Australia, investor, was Far East Open Teams champion 1970, Women's Team champion 1973, 1974. She also represented Australia in World Women's Teams 1960, 1968. Her national titles include Interstate Women's Teams 1951, 1954, 1962, 1963, 1964, 1965, 1969, 1970, 1972, Women's Pairs 1969, 1972, Women's Individual 1962, 1970.

McNEELY, Brooks N. (b. 1946) of Knoxville TN, computer programmer, won Fall NAC secondary Swiss Teams 1979, Mid-Atlantic Swiss Teams 1972, Open Pairs 1981. McNeely is a former chess and tennis champion.

McORMOND, R. Gordon (Gord) (b. 1952) of Vancouver BC, financial analyst, former mathematics teacher, won British Columbia Swiss Teams 1977, White Hat KO Teams 1977, Men's Pairs 1981, Klondike Open Pairs Flt. A 1978, Puget Sound Men's Pairs 1978, Emerald Empire KO Teams 1979, Nat'l Capital KO Teams 1981, Peach City Swiss Teams Flt. A 1982, Canadian Nat'l Teams Zone 6 1981, District 19 GNT 1978, GNP 1982.

McPHERRAN, Robert A. (b. 1915) of New York City, formerly one of the leading American players, won the Spingold 1939, Vanderbilt 1940, 1941, Summer NAC Master Mixed Teams 1936, Fall Master Individual 1946 and placed second in the Vanderbilt 1939, Fall NAC Mixed Pairs 1940. His numerous regional titles include Summer NAC secondary MARCUS CUP 1940.

McWILLIAMS, William R. (Bill) (b. 1928) of North Hollywood CA, computer engineer, won Bridge Week Master Pairs 1958, KO Teams 1962, Mixed Teams 1966, Pacific Southwest Open Pairs 1958, Rocky Mountain Open Pairs 1958, All-Western KO Teams 1973.

MECKSTROTH, Jeffrey J. (Jeff) (b. 1956) of Columbus OH, professional bridge player, one of the leading American players, rose rapidly from KING OF BRIDGE in 1974 to Bermuda Bowl champion in 1981. He represented the United States in the World Open Pairs 1982 and won the HERMAN TROPHY 1980, MOTT-SMITH TROPHY 1979, 1980, Vanderbilt 1980, 1982, Reisinger 1979, Life Master Men's Pairs 1979, Spring NAC Open Pairs 1979, Fall NAC Mixed Pairs 1980. He placed second in the Reisinger 1980, Vanderbilt 1979. His more than 75 regional titles include 19 Knockout Teams and 22 Swiss Teams events. Meckstroth wrote the introduction to *The*

Mexican Contract and is a frequent contributor to the *Precision Newsletter*. A former high school golf champion, he remains an active player.

MECKSTROTH, Patricia S. (Patty) (Mrs. Jeffrey, née Adamle) (b. 1951), mathematics teacher, won Fall NAC Mixed Pairs 1980. Her regional titles include Central States II Mixed Pairs 1979, Women's KO Teams, Master Pairs 1981, All-American Mixed Pairs 1981, KO Teams, Swiss Teams 1982, Mid-Atlantic 4th of July KO Teams, Open Pairs Flt. A 1980, Midwest Spring Women's Swiss Teams 1981, KO Teams 1982, Fall Women's Swiss Teams 1981. Her father, Tony, and brother, Mike, were former professional football players.

MEINL, Wolfgang (b. 1947) of Vienna, Austria, export sales manager, represented Austria in the European Championships twice and was npc of the winning team in the European Junior Championship 1976. His national titles include Austrian Teams 11 times and Open Pairs twice.

MELCHIOR, Edward F. (b. 1909) of St. Louis, comptroller, won Mississippi Valley Open Teams 1957, 1960, Mixed Pairs 1967, Open Teams 1969, Central States Men's Pairs 1953.

MELLO, Roberto Figueira de (b. 1950) of Rio de Janeiro, Brazil, engineer, was South American champion 1968, 1978, 1979 and runner-up in 1981. He also represented Brazil in the Bermuda Bowl 1969, 1979. His national wins include three Open Team titles.

MELLO, Sylvia de Almeida Rego Figueira de (Tubiska) (b. 1958) of Rio de Janeiro, Brazil, economist, was South American Women's champion 1975, 1980, 1981. She also represented Brazil in the World Women's Teams 1980, Venice Trophy 1981. She was Brazilian champion 1977, 1981.

MELMAN, Fredric L. (Fred) (b. 1935) of Agoura CA, bridge teacher and director, won Fall NAC Amateur Men's Pairs 1976, Summer NAC secondary Commerical and Industrial Teams 1974, 1975, 1976, Tri-State Swiss Teams 1973, Bridge Week Unmixed Pairs 1977. He is a former Board member of New Jersey BL and former Board member and president of Unit 532.

MELO, Manuel Fontes Pereira de (b. 1921) of Estoril, Portugal, represented Portugal in the European Championships 1966, 1967, 1974. His national titles include Open Teams six times and Open Pairs five times.

MELSON, Richard T. (Dick) (b. 1946) of Bloomington MN, computer systems analyst, placed second in Spring NAC Men's Pairs 1977, Men's Teams 1978. His more than 25 regional titles include Summer NAC secondary Men's Pairs 1976, Roughrider KO Teams 1977, 1981, Master Pairs 1977, Open Pairs 1981, Swiss Teams 1975, 1981, Iowa Open Pairs 1977, Swiss Teams 1979, 1980, Master Pairs 1980.

MELTON, Dr. Robert A. (b. 1930) of Wilmington NC, pediatrician, won Mid-Atlantic Open Teams 1962, 1971, Mixed Pairs 1966.

MENG, Gloria (b. 1944) of Taipei, Taiwan, bank employee, represented Taiwan in the Far East Championships since 1969, placing second twice.

MERBLUM, Franklin P. (Frank) (b. 1949) of Bloomfield CT, actuary, won Fall NAC secondary Swiss Teams 1972, New England Men's Pairs, Master Teams 1968, Fall Mixed Pairs 1977, 1978, Knockouts Swiss Teams Flt. A 1981.

MEREDITH, Adam (1913–1976) of New York City, formerly of London, was one of the brilliant players of the world; noted for his skill in dummy play, especially in making "unmakable" contracts, and for unconventional bidding maneuvers. Meredith was semi-retired in 1957 when he moved to New York from London. He was Bermuda Bowl champion in 1955, European champion 1949, 1954 and also represented Great Britain in the European Championship 1955, 1957, 1959. His British wins include the GOLD CUP five times and the Master Pairs 1960. Meredith co-authored (with LEO BARON) *Baron System of Contract Bridge*. See BIBLIOGRAPHY, C.

MERIWETHER, Virginia (b. 1917) of Laguna Hills CA, formerly of Des Moines IA, won Spring NAC secondary Women's Pairs 1973, Mid-Am-Can Open Pairs 1958, District 15 Master Pairs 1967.

MERRILL, Glenn E. (b. 1917) of Biloxi MS, business owner, won Florida Open Pairs 1972, Mid-South Swiss Teams 1976, Holiday Swiss Teams 1979, Crescent City Master Pairs 1977, Opryland Men's Swiss Teams 1981. His special interest is collecting bridge memorabilia; he has accumulated four scrapbooks and hundreds of books and monthly publications from all over the world.

MERRILL, Jay (b. 1955) of Gaithersburg MD was the first ever KING OF BRIDGE (1973). He placed second in the Reisinger 1974 and won NAC secondary Swiss Teams 1978, Fall Open Pairs Flt. A 1976, Upper New York State KO Teams 1974, Men's Swiss Teams 1973, Men's Pairs 1974, Canadian Nat'l Open Pairs 1974, KO Teams 1978, New England Knockout Swiss Teams 1975, KO Teams 1977.

MERRIMAN, Mary A. (b. 1913) of Camillus NY won Can-Am Open Pairs 1953, Upper New York State Master Pairs 1970, Women's Swiss Teams 1972, 1974. She is a past president of Unit 112 and Upper New York State Conference.

MERRY, Philip H. (b. 1924) of Tulsa OK, ACBL national tournament director since 1963, won Mid-South Spring Open Teams 1957. He served as chairman of the Conduct, Deportment and Ethics Committee of the PROFESSIONAL TOURNAMENT DIRECTORS ASSOCIATION. Merry is a contributing editor, *Bridge Encyclopedia*.

MERSKY, Essie (b. 1919) of St. Paul MN won

Gopher Master Teams 1968, Master Pairs 1968, 1970, Women's Swiss Teams 1976, Oktoberfest Women's Swiss Teams, Master Pairs 1977, Wisconsin Women's KO Teams, Women's Swiss Teams 1981, Roughrider Women's Pairs 1981.

MESSER, Alan W. (b. 1934) of Upper Montclair NJ, data processing consultant, former actuary, won Fall NAC Men's Teams 1960. His regional wins include Eastern States KO Teams (Reisinger) 1967, Long Island KO Teams 1968. Messer pioneered the recorder system in the Greater New York BA. He is a tennis umpire at major professional tournaments and a marathon runner.

METCALF, Dennis E. (b. 1948) of Portland OR, economist, won Oregon Trail KO Teams 1973, 1976, Mixed Pairs 1977, Swiss Teams, Swiss Teams Flt. A 1980, Open Pairs Flt. A 1981, Puget Sound Open Pairs Flt. A 1977, Swiss Teams Flt. A 1980, District 20 GNT 1977, 1981, Zone VIII 1981.

MEYER, Babe (Mrs. Frank H.) (b. 1908) of Virginia Beach VA, placed second in Fall NAC Mixed Pairs 1948 and won Mid-Atlantic Spring Women's Pairs 1964.

MEYER, Florence (Mrs. Bert W.) (b. 1915) of La Canada CA, won Spring NAC Amateur Swiss Teams 1977. Her several regional titles include Golden State Mixed Pairs 1969, Bridge Week Mixed Teams 1960, 1963, Master Pairs 1962, Women's Pairs 1971, Los Angeles Winter Women's Pairs 1974, Pacific Southwest Women's Swiss Teams 1976, Golden Gate Women's Pairs 1977.

MEYER, Jean-Paul (b. 1936) of Paris, France, engineer, represented France in the European Championships 1963, 1975. He has won several national titles. Meyer is the co-author of *Du non classé à l'Expert* and editor of the official magazine of the French League, *Revue Française de Bridge-le Bridgeur*.

MEYER, Kenneth C. (Ken) (b. 1947) of Lebanon PA, project manager, District 4 GNP 1979, GNT 1977, 1981, Zone II 1981.

MEYER, Robert J. (b. 1951) of Maryland Heights MO, accountant, won North Florida Swiss Teams 1977, Springfield Open Pairs 1980, Mississippi Valley Swiss Teams Flt. A 1982, District 8 GNP 1979, 1980, GNT 1980.

MICHAELS, Charles (1884–1962) of New York City was active in promoting bridge among the younger group. He introduced contract as a course of study at Queens College while a teacher there, and later taught in the Manhasset and Great Neck high schools, stimulating the juvenile interest in an unusual scientific manner. Founder of Barclay Bridge Supplies, Inc., Michaels co-authored *Ideal Student Textbook*. See BIBLIOGRAPHY, E.

MICHAELS, Michael N. (1924–1966) of Miami Beach, bridge writer and lecturer, one of the leading players of the Southeast, placed second in the Spingold 1959, Spring NAC Open Pairs 1962. His many regional successes included the MARCUS CUP 1953. He is best known as the inventor of the MICHAELS CUE-BID, and for his long-time association with CHARLES GOREN in various journalistic enterprises.

MICHAELS, Terry (b. 1927) of Prairie Village KS, formerly of Washington, secretary, bridge teacher and director, won Summer NAC Master Mixed Teams 1955 (second in 1963), Spring NAC Women's Teams 1963, 1966, 1973, 1979 (second in 1961, 1962, 1963, 1980), Women's Pairs 1967 (second in 1957, 1963, 1966). Her numerous regional titles include Fall NAC secondary Women's Swiss Teams 1972, Summer Mixed Pairs Flt. A 1977, Mexican Nat'l Women's Pairs 1973, Southeastern Women's Pairs, Mixed Pairs 1973, Women's Swiss Teams 1979, Keystone Women's Pairs 1973, Music City Women's Swiss Teams 1973, Washington Bridge Week KO Teams 1974, Women's Swiss Teams 1977, Mid-Atlantic Women's Swiss Teams 1978. Michaels established the Bridge Center of Washington and operated it for 10 years.

MICHAUD, Gerald L. (b. 1929) of Wichita KS, attorney, represented the United States in the Rosemblum Cup Teams 1978, and was International Team alternate 1963. He won Summer NAC Life Master Pairs 1974, Fall NAC Life Master Men's Pairs 1974, and placed second in the Spingold 1962, Spring NAC Men's Teams 1962. His numerous regional titles include Rocky Mountain Open Teams 1953, Mid-Am-Can Open Teams 1959, Open Pairs 1964, Missouri Valley KO Teams 1971, Open Teams 1973, District 15 KO Teams 1974, Master Pairs 1975. He was Intercollegiate champion 1951 representing Washburn University where he earned his A.B., L.L.B. and J.D. Michaud is past president of Kansas State BA and former District 15 alternate to the ACBL Board of Governors.

MICHELL, Jean E. (b. 1925) of Orinda CA, bridge teacher, won more than 15 regional titles including Golden Gate Women's Pairs 1972, Swiss Teams 1977, 1978, 1980, Mixed Pairs 1978, 1979, All-Western Women's Pairs 1981, Emerald Empire Open Pairs, Swiss Teams 1982. Michell is a former president and vice president of Unit 499 and Unit representative to District 21.

MIGNOCCHI, Mirette (b. 1926) of New York City, born in Vienna, Austria, real estate manager, former bridge club owner and teacher, won Mexican Nat'l Mixed Pairs 1974, 1975, Open Pairs 1978. In 1980 she was awarded a certificate of appreciation for outstanding services to the Greater New York BA.

MILES, Marshall L. (b. 1926) of San Bernardino CA, lawyer and bridge writer, represented the United States in the World Open Pairs 1962. He won the FISHBEIN TROPHY 1961, Spingold 1961, 1962, Chicago (since 1965 the Reisinger) 1962, Reisinger 1965, Life Master Pairs 1961, and placed second in the Vanderbilt 1961, Fall NAC Open Pairs 1962, Spring NAC Men's Pairs 1962, 1972. His numerous regional titles include MARCUS CUP 1960, Bridge Week KO Teams 1958, 1959, 1972, 1974, 1976, Open Teams 1957, 1961, Open Pairs 1953, 1958, Raincross Master Pairs 1978, Swiss Teams Flt. A 1980, KO Teams 1981, Los Angeles Winter Open Pairs 1974, KO Teams 1978. Miles was educated at Claremont Men's College and University of California at Los Angeles. His writings include *How to Win at Duplicate*, *All 52 Cards*, *Marshall Miles Teaches Logical Bridge*, and many articles for *The Bridge World*, *American Bridge Digest*, and the ACBL *Bulletin*. He is a contributing editor, *Bridge Encyclopedia*. See BIBLIOGRAPHY, D, E, F.

MILES, R(ufus) L. Jr. (Skinny) (b. 1907) of Virginia Beach VA, investment executive, formerly one of the leading American bridge personalities, was president of the ACBL 1950, 1956, and a member of many of its administrative committees for nearly two decades. He was named HONORARY MEMBER in 1952. Miles is a past president of the Mid-Atlantic Confernece. He was npc of the North American Bermuda Bowl team in 1957 and of the United States team in the World Team Olympiad 1960. He won Mid-Atlantic Fall Open Teams 1956, 1964, Spring Men's Teams 1956, Winter Open Teams 1965. See also MILES TROPHY.

MILES, Sidsel K. (Cecile) (b. 1937) of Adelaide, South Australia, born in Oslo, Norway, former secretary, was Far East champion 1975, 1977 and also represented Australia in the Far East Championships 1979, World Women's Teams 1976, Venice Trophy 1978. In 1981 she was npc of the Women's Team which competed for the Venice Trophy; the first female captain of an Australian international team. Her national titles include Interstate Teams 1967, 1980.

MILLER, Arthur M. (b. 1924) of Beverly Hills CA, manufacturer and importer, placed second in the Vanderbilt 1956, Chicago (since 1965 the Reisinger) 1958 and won Southern Conference Fall Master Pairs 1957, Southeastern Men's Pairs 1955.

MILLER, Bernard A. (Bernie) (b. 1940) of Framingham MA, attorney, won Spring NAC secondary Men's Swiss Teams 1973, Tri-State Open Pairs 1973, Men's Pairs 1974, New England Knockouts KO Teams 1973, Individual KO Teams 1978, 1978, Masters Master Swiss Teams 1977, Fall Master Pairs 1974, Summer KO Teams 1982. Miller is past president and former Board member of Unit 108, and a former member of the ACBL Board of Governors and ACBL Rules and Protest Committee.

MILLER, Charles of Houston, investment analyst, won Fall NAC Men's Teams 1964, Texas Spring Men's Pairs 1959, 1967, Mid-South Summer Mixed Pairs 1965, Southern Conference Spring Men's Pairs 1965.

MILLER, Frances J. (Irma) (b. 1921) of Florissant MO, tournament director, former bridge club owner and teacher, began her directing career in 1962. She

achieved the rating of Regional 4 in 1976. Miller is a former PTDA secretary and representative to the Board of Directors meetings.

MILLER, Harvey H. (b. 1929) of Chicago, real estate broker and investor, won Fall NAC Amateur Men's Pairs 1975 and placed second in North American Swiss Teams 1979. His more than 20 regional titles include Fall NAC secondary Swiss Teams 1979, Summer Swiss Teams 1980, Midwest Fall Open Pairs 1964, Central States I KO Teams 1974, 1980, 1982, Men's Pairs 1976, Open Pairs 1977, II Swiss Teams 1977, Men's Pairs 1978.

MILLER, Jim (b. 1940) of Dallas won Mid-South Men's Pairs 1973, Swiss Teams 1981, Capital City Master Pairs 1972, King Cotton Master Pairs 1975, Lone Star Life Master Pairs 1975, Missouri Valley Open Pairs 1975, Mexican Nat'l Mixed Pairs 1977, Harvest Festival Swiss Teams 1977.

MILLER, Joseph P. of Tulsa OK won Rocky Mountain KO Teams 1969, Open Teams 1971, Toast of Tulsa KO Teams 1977, Open Pairs Flt. A 1979, Missouri Valley Master Pairs 1977, District 10 Men's Pairs 1978.

MILLER, Joyce (formerly Dodson) (b. 1946) of Bettendorf IA won Roughrider Open Pairs 1975, Gopher Swiss Teams, Women's Pairs 1980.

MILLER, Lauren A. (b. 1943) of Vancouver BC, postman, former French teacher and social worker, won British Columbia Swiss Teams 1977, Swiss Teams Flt. A 1981, District 19 GNT 1978, Canadian National Teams Zone 6 1981.

MILLER, Martin E. (Marty) (b. 1937) of Campbell CA, rubber bridge and backgammon club owner, former social worker, won several regional titles including California Capital KO Teams 1972, Oregon Trail KO Teams 1970, Stockton KO Teams 1972, 1973, District 18 KO Teams 1975, British Columbia Open Pairs 1970, Golden Gate Master Pairs 1969, Mid-Winter Holiday Master Pairs 1968, Swiss Teams Flt. A 1981, Golden State Swiss Teams Flt. A 1981. He served as president of Unit 507 in 1978.

MILLER, Portia of Pittsburgh won Midwest Spring Open Teams 1962, All-American Mixed Pairs 1963, 1973, Women's Swiss Teams 1981, District 5 Women's Swiss Teams 1978, 1980.

MILLER, Richard A. (Dick) (1911–1983) of York PA, account executive, bridge writer, won Mid-Atlantic Open Pairs 1950, Bermuda Open Teams 1972. One of the founders of the Keystone Conference (now District 4), he was a member of its Board from 1951 and was president in 1960–61. He was also one of the founders of Unit 168 and served as its president in 1963, and was a member of the ACBL Board of Governors. Miller wrote a weekly column for *The National Observer* 1962–1977, *York Gazette and Daily* 1945–1965, and prior to his death a monthly column for *The American Way*, American Airlines' inflight magazine. One of the early exponents of the point-count method of evaluation, he wrote *Point Count Bidding* in 1947, the first application of point-count to suit bidding. Other works by Miller are *It's a Bidder's Game, Bridge Brilliance and Blunders*, and *More Bridge Brilliance and Blunders*. See BIBLIOGRAPHY, C, H.

MILLER, Walter G. II (b. 1938) of Mountain View CA, personal investor, won Golden Gate Swiss Teams 1972, All-Western Swiss Teams 1978, Mid-Winter Holiday Master Swiss Teams 1978. Miller is a contributor to the *Contract Bridge Forum* and former editor of the Palo Alto Unit newsletter.

MILLERD, James A. (Jim) (b. 1927) of Dana Point CA, company vice president, won Summer NAC secondary Leventritt Pairs 1955, Bridge Week Open Teams 1957, Mid-Am-Can Open Pairs 1955, Pacific Southwest Master Pairs 1970.

MILLION, Ruth of Union City CA won Summer NAC Master Mixed Teams 1951. Her regional titles include Spring NAC secondary Mixed Pairs 1956, Hawaii Master Pairs 1955.

MILLWARD, C. J. (b. 1925) of Kitwe, Zambia, solicitor, formerly a leading player in Central Africa, won Zambia Open Pairs 1959, 1962, 1963, Open Teams 1961, 1962, 1964, Southern Rhodesia Open Pairs 1963, 1964, Open Teams 1964, Central Africa Open Teams 1960, 1962 and placed second in seven other major events. He is former vice chairman of the CENTRAL AFRICA BRIDGE ASSOCIATION.

MILNES, Eric Charles (b. 1912) of Bradford, Yorks, England, customs and excise officer, won the English Bridge Union Mixed Teams twice, Northern Pairs twice. He is the former editor of *Bridge Magazine*. Milnes is the co-author of *Improve Your Dummy Play*, and *Bridge Hands for the Connoisseur*. See BIBLIOGRAPHY, H.

MINER, Carole A. (b. 1941) of Rochester MN, programming development manager, won Gopher Swiss Teams 1979, 1980, KO Teams 1977, Oktoberfest Women's Swiss Teams 1977, Iowa Open Pairs Flt. A 1981, Wisconsin Women's Swiss Teams 1981, District 14 GNT 1978.

MINKEN, Joanne (b. 1928) of Northridge CA won Cotton Boll Swiss Teams 1977, Orange County Swiss Teams 1974, Los Angeles Winter Open Pairs Flt. A 1980.

MITCHELL, George (b. 1928) of Bellaire OH, accountant, won All-American Open Pairs 1960, Great Lakes Open Teams 1962, District 5 Open Teams 1970, Florida Open Pairs 1974, Mid-Atlantic Swiss Teams 1980, KO Teams 1982.

MITCHELL, Jacquelyn M. (Jacqui) (Mrs. Victor, nee Balos) (b. 1936) of New York City, bridge teacher, one of the outstanding women players of the world, WBF GRAND MASTER, won the VENICE TROPHY 1976, 1978, World Women's Teams 1980 and placed second in the World Mixed Teams, World Mixed Pairs 1974. She also represented the United States in the World Women's Teams 1972, 1976, World Women's Pairs 1974, 1978, 1982, World Mixed Pairs 1978, 1982, Rosenblum Cup Teams 1982. She won Spring NAC Women's Teams 1965, 1970, 1974, 1975, 1976, Women's Pairs 1971, 1975, 1977, and placed second in the Women's Teams 1973, 1982, Women's Pairs 1962, 1970, 1974. Her numerous regional titles include Fall NAC secondary Swiss Teams 1973, Spring Swiss Teams 2nd Flt. 1977, Eastern States KO Teams (Reisinger) 1962, 1963, 1964. She won New York Blue Ribbon Individual 1977 and was New York Player of the Year in 1958, her second year of tournament play. She is a long-distance runner.

MITCHELL, John Templeton (April 3, 1854–November 7, 1914) of Chicago is known as the "Father of Duplicate Whist" because of the movements of boards and players he designed for tournaments. The most notable is the MITCHELL MOVEMENT. See also HISTORY OF BRIDGE.

Born in Glasgow, Scotland, Mitchell was a lineal descendant of Sir Roger Kirkpatrick, a famous highland chieftain who supported Wallace and Bruce in the struggle for Scottish independence *circa* 1350. In 1875 Mitchell immigrated to the United States and became a naturalized citizen. In 1888 he took up whist and saw a cutting from the London *Field* regarding a duplicate whist match between two clubs in his native Glasgow, using James Allison's AUTOMATIC HAND REGISTERS.

This enthused Mitchell on duplicate whist and he formed the Chicago Duplicate Whist Club. He wrote the world's first book on duplicate whist, 1891, revised in 1896. He joined the Hyde Park team-of-four in 1895 that won the fifth American Whist League Congress (national championship).

Mitchell, a director in the American Whist League, favored the long-suit game and his modified American leads were published in *Whist* of September 1896. See BIBLIOGRAPHY, A.

MITCHELL, Victor (b. 1923) of New York City, bridge teacher, one of the outstanding American players, placed second in the World Team Olympiad 1964, Mixed Teams 1974 and also represented the United States in the World Team Olympiad 1960. He won the Spingold 1956, 1959, Fall NAC Life Master Men's Pairs 1962, Spring NAC Men's Teams 1962, 1963. He placed second in the Chicago (since 1965 the Reisinger) 1955, Vanderbilt 1969, Spingold 1969, Life Master Pairs 1954, 1955, Spring NAC Men's Pairs 1955, Men's Teams 1965, Fall Life Master Men's Pairs 1965. His numerous regional titles include Spring NAC secondary Swiss Teams 2nd Flt. 1977, Summer Swiss Teams Flt. A 1977, Eastern States KO Teams (Reisinger) 1955, 1962, 1963, 1964, Open Pairs 1958, Master Pairs 1966.

MITTELMAN, George of Toronto won the World Mixed Pairs 1982 and also represented Canada in the Rosenblum Cup Teams 1978, 1982 (placing third), World Team Olympiad 1980, World Open Pairs 1982. He placed second in the Reisinger 1978. His more than 25 regional titles include Canadian Nat'l Swiss Teams 1970, Swiss Teams Flt. A 1982, KO Teams 1973, Master Pairs 1979, Men's Swiss Teams 1977, 1982, Can-Am Swiss Teams 1973, Swiss Teams Flt. A 1978, KO Teams 1977, 1981, Master Swiss Teams 1977, London KO Teams, Swiss Teams, Men's Swiss Teams 1979, Canadian National Teams 1980, 1981.

MIZELL, Patrick M. (b. 1944) of Shreveport LA, owner of computer brokerage firm, won Mid-South Open Pairs, Swiss Teams 1976, Men's Pairs 1975, KO Teams 1978, Master Swiss Teams 1982, Champagne KO Teams 1982, Land of Coronado Men's Swiss Teams, Swiss Teams 1982. Mizell is a past president of District 10.

MIZUTANI, Eizo (b. 1933) of Tokyo, Japan, bridge teacher and writer, national tournament director, represented Japan in the Far East Championships 1962, 1965, 1968, 1969, 1972. His national titles include KO Teams five times, Round Robin Teams three times, Teams-of-Four twice. He is an officer of the JAPAN CONTRACT BRIDGE LEAGUE. Mizutani is the co-author of *Contract Bridge Nyumon* and *Contract Bridge no Subete*.

MODLIN, Merle A. (Cuckoo) (b. 1940) of Johannesburg, South Africa, bridge teacher, represented South Africa in the World Women's Teams 1976. She won South Africa Pioneer Teams 1978.

MOELLER, Donald A. (b. 1925) of Dayton OH, banking executive, former CPA, has been District 11 representative to the ACBL Board of Directors from 1973 and was ACBL treasurer in 1975. Moeller was first president of District 11 1970-1972, and president of the Miami Valley BA 1968-1970. He is a graduate of Northwestern University.

MOFFAT, John R. (b. 1949) of Mt. Vernon WA, attorney, won Tri-Cities Master Pairs 1975, Mid-Winter Holiday Men's Swiss Teams 1976, Peach City Master Pairs 1978, Oregon Trail Master Pairs 1979. He is District 19 representative to the ACBL Board of Governors.

MOGAL, Sol (b. 1911) of Croton on Hudson NY, import company president, won the Chicago (since 1965 the Reisinger) 1949, Spingold 1946, 1949 (second in 1952), Fall NAC Men's Pairs 1947, Men's Teams 1947, 1948, 1954. His regional titles include Summer NAC secondary MARCUS CUP 1951, Eastern States KO Teams (Reisinger) 1952.

MOHAN, John A. (b. 1939) of Tiburon CA, investment consultant, professional bridge player, one of the leading American players, represented the United States in the World Open Pairs, Mixed Pairs, Rosenblum Cup Teams 1978. He won the Vanderbilt 1975, 1976, Spingold 1976, Fall NAC Mixed Pairs 1972, Life Master Men's Pairs 1976 (second in 1977). His more than 60 regional titles include Summer NAC secondary Men's Pairs, Swiss Teams 1972, Fall Swiss Teams 1977. Mohan is a graduate of

University of Chicago. See also LANCIA TEAMS.

MOHR, Mark D. (b. 1939) of Maplewood NJ, options trader, former attorney and school teacher, won Summer NAC Senior/Advanced Senior Master Pairs 1961. His regional titles include Fun City KO Teams 1970, Tri-State Open teams 1967, Keystone Open Teams 1968. Mohr is a past president of the New Jersey BL and former editor the *The Declarer*.

MOLLEMET, Peter D. (b. 1943) of Williamsville NY, tournament director, won Canadian Nat'l Swiss Teams 1975, District 4 Swiss Teams 1977. A tournament director since 1975, he achieved the rating of Regional 3 in 1981. He is editor of the District 5 monthly publication *Bridgeview*.

MÖLLER, Jakob R. (b. 1940) of Reykjavík, Iceland, industrial relations executive, represented Iceland in the Nordic Championships 1973, 1975, European Championships 1975, World Team Olympiad 1978. He won Icelandic Open Teams 1973, 1979. He is vice president of the ICELANDIC BRIDGE UNION.

MØLLER, Steffen Steen (b. 1939) of Copenhagen, Denmark, represented Denmark in the World Team Olympiad 1968, 1972, European Championships 1966, 1969, 1970, 1971, 1974, 1975. His national titles include Danish Open Pairs 1974, Open Teams 1970, 1971, 1975. He is a contributor to the official magazine of the DANISH BRIDGE LEAGUE, *Dansk Bridge*, bridge columnist of *Berlingske Tidende*, and the author of three books.

MOLLO, Victor (b. 1909) of London, England, born in St. Petersburg, Russia, bridge writer, former bridge columnist of the London *Evening Standard*, is one of the leading personalities of the world among bridge writers. Mollo was educated at Brighton College and London University. During World War II he worked as editor in the European services of the British Broadcasting Corporation; he worked for the BBC for 30 years, retiring in 1969. His interests include wine, gourmet food, politics and conversation. Though primarily a rubber bridge player, Mollo has won many national events including the Portland Pairs twice, the Melville Smith Trophy, Crockford's Cup, and the Devonshire Cup 13 times. He is perhaps best known as the author of *Bridge in the Menagerie*. His characters appear in print in five bridge publications; *Bridge Magazine*, *Bridge Tidnigen*, *Bridge i Norge*, *Bridge d'Italia*, and the ACBL *Bulletin*. He is the author or co-author of more than 20 bridge books including *Card Play Technique, Streamlined Bridge: or Bidding Without Tears, Bridge with a Master, Bridge in the Fourth Dimension, Streamline Your Bidding, Bridge à la Carte,* and *Confessions of an Addict,* his autobiography. He is a contributing editor, *Bridge Encyclopedia.* See BIBLIOGRAPHY, B, C, D, E, K, L.

MONDOLFO, Renato (b. 1916) of Trieste, Italy, stamp collector and merchant, was European champion 1965, 1967, 1969, 1971. His national titles include Italian Open Teams 1965, 1970, Knockout Cup 1969.

MONK, Charles (b. 1926) of Brussels, Belgium, association manager and bridge columnist, represented Belgium in the World Team Olympiad 1960, 1964, 1968, World Open Pairs 1962, 1968, European Championships 1961, 1965. His national wins include Open Teams (three times), Mixed Teams, Open Pairs, Master Pairs, Mixed Pairs. His writings include *Système Complet des Enchères Modernes*. See BIBLIOGRAPHY, C.

MONSEGUR, Martin S. (b. 1941) of Buenos Aires, Argentina, lawyer, represented Argentina in the South American Championships 1975, Bermuda Bowl 1977, World Team Olympiad 1980. His national titles include Master Individual 1981, Open Teams 1975, Mixed Pairs 1981, Interclubs 1979, 1980, and the GABARRET CUP 1975.

MONTGOMERY, DeWitt Hall (Hal) (b. 1952) of Portland OR, commercial real estate manager and broker, won Oregon Trail Men's Pairs 1975, Men's Swiss Teams 1976, Master Swiss Teams 1978, KO Teams 1980, Emerald Empire KO Teams 1982, District 20 GNP 1981.

MONZINGO, Ken (b. 1939) of San Diego, theater press agent/promotions director, publisher/editor, won Fall NAC secondary Open Pairs 1981, Hawaii Men's Swiss Teams 1977, Bridge Week Master Swiss Teams, Unmixed Pairs 1979, Raincross Open Pairs 1979, Mid-Winter Holiday Swiss Teams Flt. A 1979, Pacific Southwest KO Teams 1980, Oregon Trail Swiss Teams Flt. A 1982. He is the editor and publisher of *Contract Bridge Forum*, the WESTERN CONFERENCE publication. He has served as Pacific Southwest regional manager and photographer for many West Coast regionals. Monzingo is a graduate of North Texas State University.

MOORE, Dorothy H. (b. 1928) of Dallas, corporation executive, won Fall NAC Life Master Women's Pairs 1975. Her regional titles include Spring NAC secondary Mixed Pairs 1963, Big D Mixed Pairs 1976, Bermuda Women's Pairs 1975. She was deputy captain of the U.S. Women's Team at the World Team Olympiad 1980. She edited books published by the ACES TEAM and the bridge column of the late IRA G. CORN, JR.. Moore was listed in the July 1978 issue of *Fortune Magazine* as one of the top 10 women in big business.

MORAN, Brian, J. (b. 1938) of Ellicott City MD, associate national tournament director, won Mid-Atlantic KO Teams 1973, 1974, 1976. He served as president of Virginia State BA 1972-1977. Moran is a graduate of Notre Dame.

MORAN, John H. (b. 1909) of Camarillo CA, club director, former bridge instructor and cruise director, represented North America in the Bermuda Bowl 1955. He won the Spingold 1954, Blue Ribbon Pairs 1965, and placed second in the Chicago (since 1965 the Reisinger) 1958, Fall NAC Men's Teams

1953, Mixed Pairs 1954. He won numerous regional titles between 1950-1970 including MARCUS CUP 1957, Bridge Week KO Teams 1954, Open Teams 1947, Rocky Mountain Master Pairs, Open Pairs 1951, Men's Pairs 1962, Mixed Pairs 1956, Texas Fall Open Teams, Open Pairs 1953, Inter-Mountain Open Teams 1961, 1965, 1967, Open Pairs 1966, Oregon Trail KO Teams 1967.

MORAN, Vance I. (b. 1925) of Agoura CA, businessman, won District 17 Fall Swiss Teams 1976, Bridge Week Men's Master Pairs 1980, Navajo Trail Open Pairs Flt. A 1979.

MORATH, Anders (Carrot) (b. 1944) of Järfälla, Sweden, computer services manager, was European Junior champion 1968 and European champion 1977. He also represented Sweden in the European Championships 1971, 1979, 1981, Bermuda Bowl 1977, World Team Olympiad 1976, 1980, World Open Pairs 1970, 1974, 1978. He is ranked #7 among Swedish masterpoint holders. Morath is the co-author of the CARROT CLUB convention.

MORCOS, Josephine (b. 1923) of Cairo, Egypt, was World Women's Teams champion 1960. She also represented Egypt in the World Women's Teams 1964, 1968, 1978. Her national titles include Egyptian Open Pairs 1971, 1975, Open Teams 1974. She was chairman of the Heliopolis Bridge Committee 1972-1982 and has been an active in Egyptian bridge organization from 1958.

MORDECAI, Daniel (Dan) (b. 1932) of Denver, business consultant, won numerous regional titles including Fall NAC Swiss Teams 1977, Rocky Mountain KO Teams 1968, 1972, Open Teams 1961, 1969, 1972, Master Pairs 1966, Men's Pairs 1957, 1964, Mixed Pairs 1970, Open Pairs 1974, 1976, Open Pairs FLt. A 1979, Swiss Teams Flt. A 1980, 1982, Bridge Week Open Pairs 1970. He also won Cavendish Club Invitational Pairs 1980.

MOREHEAD, Albert Hodges (August 7, 1909–October 5, 1966) of New York City was a League official, bridge author, writer and editor in general fields.

Morehead was an officer and Director of the United States Bridge Association when that organization amalgamated with the American Bridge League in 1937. A Governor of the ACBL 1937, President 1943, Chairman of the Board 1943-1945 and Honorary Member in 1946, Morehead was also a member of the ACBL Laws Commission and in charge of production of the International Laws of Contract Bridge in 1943 and subsequent years.

Born in Flintstone GA and educated at Baylor and Harvard, Morehead was only 25 when he played on the Culbertson team that defeated the British in 1934 in the second international match for the SCHWAB CUP. He won or placed high in several national and regional tournaments.

Ely Culbertson hired him in 1932 because of his outstanding ability as a player and analyst and made him technical editor of *The Bridge World* in 1933, but Morehead proved so invaluable that in 1934 he was made general manager of all Culbertson enterprises. Morehead relinquished tournament play in order to handle, in addition to publication of the magazine, the editing (and in the case of the *Red Book on Play*, much of the writing) of Culbertson books, the *Bridge Encyclopedia*, 1935, of endorsements, the management details of Crockford's Clubs both in New York and Chicago, and the executive direction of KEM Playing Cards, Inc., which he sold within four years for a profit of more than half a million dollars.

Morehead was the first bridge editor of *The New York Times*, writing a Sunday column from 1935 and a daily column from 1959. He resigned from the *Times* late in 1963 to devote full time to the writing, editing and publishing of the dictionaries, encyclopedias and thesauruses that made him one of the foremost American lexicographers. His works also include many "Hoyle" books giving the rules of card games, on which he was the leading modern American authority.

In 1946 Morehead retired from *The Bridge World* except in an advisory capacity and as director of the Master Solvers' Club and devoted his time to other pursuits. He authored many bridge books, including *Bridge the Expert Way, Contract Bridge Summary*, and *Morehead on Bidding* which won the IBPA *"Bridge Book of the Year"* award in 1966. See BIBLIOGRAPHY, C, E.

MORENAS, Geneviève (b. 1926) of Lyon, France, bridge teacher, won European Mixed Pairs Championship 1976 and placed second in the World Women's Teams 1960, European Women's Teams 1966, 1981. She has won many national titles.

MORI, Lawrence K. (Larry) (b. 1948) of Southfield MI, psychotherapist, placed second in the Grand National Pairs 1979. He was Intercollegiate champion 1976 and won more than 20 regional titles including Summer NAC secondary Open Pairs 1976, Spring Men's Swiss Teams 1982, Midwest Spring Open Pairs 1978, KO Teams 1982, Fall Swiss Teams 1978, All-American Master Pairs 1976, KO Teams, Swiss Teams, Open Pairs Flt. A 1982.

MORRELL, Clinton D. (Clint) (b. 1945) of Marlborough MA, economist, won Spring NAC secondary Swiss Teams 1982, New England Masters Swiss Teams 1972, Master Swiss Teams 1977, Knockouts Open Swiss 1979, Individual KO Teams 1978, Individual 1980, Tri-State Open Pairs Flt. A 1979. He is a graduate of Boston College.

MORRIS, Robert F. (Tiger) (b. 1922) of Cincinnati, advertising agency field representative, placed second in the Blue Ribbon Pairs 1969. He won Midwest Spring Mixed Pairs 1956, All-American Open Teams 1968, District 5 Swiss Teams 1977, Blue Grass KO Teams 1975, Midwest Men's Swiss Teams 1980, Spring Swiss Teams Flt. A 1982.

MORRIS, Zelda M. (b. 1915) of Hawkes Bay, New Zealand, was Far East champion 1976. She also represented New Zealand in the Far East Championships 1968, 1970, 1971, 1972, 1974, 1975, WBF Zone 7 Women's Teams six times. She won the Australian Congress 1968.

MORSE, Dan (b, 1938) of Houston, pharmacist, one of the leading playing of the Southwest, won Fall NAC Mixed Pairs 1964, Grand National Teams 1977, Spingold 1977, and placed second in the Spingold 1967, Life Master Pairs 1979, Blue Ribbon Pairs 1980. He was npc of the Reisinger team winners in the Teams Trials 1974, 1975, Spingold team 1976 and of the winning Bermuda Bowl team 1976. His numerous regional titles include Spring NAC secondary Men's Pairs 1971, Men's Swiss Teams 1972, Swiss Teams 1975.

MORSE, Jo (b. 1932) of Silver Spring MD, one of the leading North American women players, won the World Mixed Teams 1974 and also represented the United States in the World Women's Pairs 1974. She won Spring NAC Women's Teams 1973, 1977, 1979, 1981 and placed second in 1980 and in Summer NAC Master Mixed Teams 1973. Her more than 40 regional titles include Spring NAC secondary Women's Swiss Teams 1982, Open Pairs Flt. A, Mixed Pairs, Summer Swiss Teams 1971, Fall Open Pairs 1981, Mid-Atlantic KO Teams 1973, Keystone Master Pairs 1971, Women's Pairs 1975, Fall Master Pairs 1970, 1971, Mid-Atlantic Women's Pairs 1971, 1978, Open Pairs 1972, Swiss Teams 1972, 1978, Women's Swiss Teams 1978, 1979, 1980, 1981, KO Teams 1973, 1980, Master Swiss Teams 1978. She has served the Washington BL as Board member, secretary, and treasurer.

MOSES, Tod M. (b. 1955) of St. Louis, accountant, won Mid-Winter Holiday Men's Swiss Teams 1976, Champagne Swiss Teams 1978, 1981, Springfield Open Pairs 1980.

MOSHER, Robert E. (Bob) (b. 1937) of San Miguel Allende, Mexico, retired professor of mathematics, won New England Master Teams, Master Pairs 1962, Open Pairs 1964, Midwest Fall Open Teams 1965.

MOSKOWITZ, Judith (Judy) (formerly Carroll) (b. 1941) of Livingston NJ, supermarket consultant, won Mid-Atlantic Summer Women's Pairs 1964, New York-New Jersey Women's Pairs 1970, Keystone Women's Teams 1974.

MOSS, Gail H. (b. 1938) of New York City, bridge teacher, one of the leading women players of the world, won the VENICE TROPHY 1976, 1978, World Women's Teams 1980 and placed second in the World Mixed Teams 1972, Venice Trophy Teams 1980. She also represented the United States in the World Women's Pairs 1974, 1978, 1982, World Mixed Pairs 1974, 1978, 1982, Rosenblum Cup Teams 1982. She won Summer NAC Master Mixed Teams 1967, 1972, Spring NAC Women's Teams 1971, 1974, 1975, 1976 (second in 1973, 1982), Women's Pairs 1975, 1977 (second in 1970, 1972, 1974), Fall NAC Mixed Pairs 1978. Her numerous regional titles include Fall NAC secondary Women's Teams 1968, 1969, Summer Master Mixed Teams

2nd Flt. 1970, Spring Swiss Teams Flt. A 1981, Open Pairs Flt. B 1979. Moss is active in bridge administration; she is a past president of the Greater New York BA and District 24, and a former member of the ACBL Board of Governors.

MOSS, Mary (Mrs. John) (1920–1981) of London, England won the World Women's Teams 1964 and European Women's Championships 1963. She also represented Great Britain in the World Women's Pairs 1962. Her national titles include Mixed Pairs.

MOSS, Michael E. (b. 1935) of New York City, stockbroker, placed second in the World Mixed Teams 1972 and also represented the United States in the World Open Pairs 1974. He won Summer NAC Life Master Pairs 1970, Master Mixed Teams 1967, 1972 and placed second in Spring NAC Men's Pairs 1966. His numerous regional titles include Summer NAC secondary Master Mixed Teams 2nd Flt. 1970, Summer Mixed Pairs 1965, Eastern States KO Teams 1965, Southeastern KO Teams 1970, Men's Pairs 1965, 1972, Mexican Nat'l Men's Pairs, Mixed Pairs 1970.

MOTT-SMITH, Geoffrey (1902–1960) of New York City, born in Honolulu, was co-chairman of the ACBL Laws Commission, editor of the ACBL *Bulletin* 1935–1936, contributor to *The Bridge World*, writer and cryptographer.

Mott-Smith was one of the first to operate a bridge club and to direct bridge tournaments, and was director of the annual Intercollegiate Tournaments and other "par" bridge events. He worked with ELY CULBERTSON in the organization of the United States Bridge Association and with WILLIAM E. McKENNEY in the early years of the ACBL. During World War II, he served as chief instructor for the OSS in the training of cryptographers and cryptanalysts.

He authored or co-authored more than 29 books on games and served as games consultant for the Association of American Playing Card Manufacturers. Mott-Smith was a great player, brilliant theorist and one of the soundest and most lucid of the early writers on contract bridge. See BIBLIOGRAPHY, C, and MOTT-SMITH TROPHY.

MOUAT, Andrew J. (1870–1956) of Evanston IL was the leading personality in whist organization during the lifetime of the AMERICAN WHIST LEAGUE. He was its chief tournament director for more than 40 years, serving as its president, secretary, and tournament committee chairman. He was editor of *Whist Review* 1915–1919 and ACBL Honorary Member 1948.

MOULIA, Simone (1913–1970) of Brussels, Belgium, typewriter saleswoman, was one of the leading European women players. She represented Belgium in the World Women's Teams 1964, placed second in the European Women's Championships 1950, 1955, 1956, 1959, and represented Belgium on several other occasions. She placed third in the Mixed Team event at Cannes 1962 and won 15 national titles in open, mixed, and women's events.

MOUSER, Hal of Chicago won several regional titles including Midwest KO Teams 1972, Oktoberfest Swiss Teams 1976, Canadian Nat'l Men's Swiss Teams 1978, Gopher KO Teams 1978, Mad City KO Teams 1979, Central States I BAM Teams 1982, II Open Pairs Flt. A, Swiss Teams 1978, District 13 GNT, Zone VI 1980.

MOUSER, William S. (1912–1963) of Detroit, presumed dead when his private plane was lost over Lake Erie. He was a speech therapist and for 10 years Sunday bridge columnist for the *Detroit News*. Mouser served both as president and treasurer of the Michigan BA and was a member of the ACBL Board 1963. His wins include the All-American Open Team 1959. See MOUSER TROPHY.

MOWRY, Oris (b. 1936) of Longview WA, school counselor, won Klondike Open Pairs 1972, Puget Sound Open Teams 1972, Oregon Trail Swiss Teams Flt. A 1979, 1981, 1982, Rogue River Valley Master Pairs 1973, Bridge Week Non-Mixed Pairs 1973, Emerald Empire KO Teams 1979, Tri-Cities Swiss Teams Flt. A 1979, District 20 GNT 1979.

MOYSE, Alphonse, Jr. (Sonny) (1898–1973) was the publisher and editor of *The Bridge World* from 1956 to 1966, a bridge author and champion player. Born in Summit MS, Moyse spent most of his boyhood in Cincinnati and then settled in New York City. When the crash of 1929 ended his career as a stockbroker, he adopted bridge as a profession. In 1934 he joined the organization of ELY CULBERTSON, partly as an associate editor of *The Bridge World* but chiefly as writer of syndicated newspaper articles that were published under the names of Ely and JOSEPHINE CULBERTSON. From that time until 1956 he wrote two bridge columns each day, a total of more than 20,000, in addition to many magazine articles and editorial work on Culbertson books. Moyse was managing editor of *The Bridge World* 1939–43, and was publisher and chief editor 1946–56. On the death of Culbertson in 1955 he bought the Bridge World, Inc., from the Culbertson estate, and was president and general manager of it until 1963 when he sold it to McCall Corp., remaining as publisher and editor of the magazine until his retirement in 1966. Perhaps Moyse's most admired writings are humorous articles about the bridge exploits of his wife, Jackie Moyse, whom he depicts as the typical member of ladies' luncheon-club bridge games. Though a comparatively infrequent contestant in tournaments, he won Fall NAC Men's Team 1949, Spring NAC Men's Pairs 1963, and several regional events. Moyse was an original member of the Editorial Advisory Board, *Bridge Encyclopedia*. In 1973, a few weeks before his death, Moyse was selected as the first American to be named an IBPA Honorary Member. See BIBLIOGRAPHY, G.

MUELLER, Jane (Mrs. A. H, formerly Mrs. Charles Hall) of Cincinnati, former retirement consultant, represented the United States in the World Women's Pairs 1962. She won Spring NAC Women's Pairs 1960, Midwest Spring Open Teams 1948, 1949, Mixed Pairs 1957, Southeastern Open Teams 1966, Women's Teams 1970.

MUHSAM, Gertrude (Mrs. Rudolf, formerly Brunner) (1909–1979) of New York City, born in Vienna, Austria, was assistant manager of the CAVENDISH CLUB (New York) and an outstanding player. She was European Women's Teams champion 1935, 1936, 1937, and captain 1935–1937.

MUIR, William A. (Bill) (b. 1950) of Kansas City MO, insurance underwriter, won Beef State Open Pairs 1971, Mississippi Valley Men's Pairs 1974, Mid-South Men's Pairs 1976. He is the former editor of *The Declarer*, the Unit 131 newsletter.

MULFORD, Kay (formerly Kirkpatrick) (b. 1945) of Cincinnati, bridge teacher and director, won Midwest Spring Women's Swiss Teams 1980, 1981, Women's Pairs 1981.

MUNAFO, Paul M. (b. 1939) of Huntsville AL, engineer, won Mid-South Master Pairs 1966, 1969, Men's Pairs 1973, 1979, Swiss Teams 1973, 1976, 1979, Mixed Pairs 1976, District 11 Swiss Teams 1977, Central Florida Swiss Teams 1980, Mid-Atlantic Swiss Teams Flt. A 1981, District 10 GNT 1982. (See also MOREHEAD TROPHY.) He is past president of District 10. Munafo was educated at M.I.T. and Tulane University. His field is the prevention of premature structural failure in space vehicles; he is chief of metallurgical and failure analysis branch at NASA, designers of the space shuttle.

MUNIR, Ata-Ullah. See ATA-ULLAH, MUNIR AHMED.

MUNN, Dorothy (Mrs. Charles, née Spreckels) (b. 1913) of San Francisco, won Southeastern Mixed Pairs, Master Pairs 1963, Bridge Week Mixed Teams 1965, Pacific Southwest Mixed Pairs 1966.

MURDOCH, Elinor (b. 1901) of Birmingham AL, bridge teacher, won Fall NAC Master Individual 1934 (second in 1933), Women's Pairs 1931 (second in 1930), Mixed Pairs 1931, Summer NAC Master Mixed Teams 1933. Her regional titles include Summer NAC secondary Golder Master Pairs 1958, Southeastern Fall Women's Pairs 1964, Mexican Nat'l Master Pairs 1965, Mid-South Open Pairs, Swiss Teams 1974, Mid-Atlantic Open Pairs Flt. A 1978. She is a past president of the Alabama BA.

MURPHY, James A. (b. 1942) of Chesapeake VA, computer programmer, private investor, won Fall NAC secondary Master Pairs 1972, Mid-Atlantic KO Teams 1972, 1980, Swiss Teams 1973, Men's Swiss Teams 1980.

MURPHY, John T. (Jack) (b. 1920) of Calgary AB, locomotive engineer, won Canadian Prairie Open Teams 1965. He served as president of Unit 390 1964–1965 and of the CANADIAN BRIDGE FEDERATION 1975, 1976, 1977. In 1972 he became the first Canadian to be appointed assistant chairman of the ACBL Goodwill Committee, a position he held for eight years. He was the Canadian delegate to the Board of Governors meeting of the World Bridge Federation 1976, 1980.

MURRAY, David S. (b. 1921) of Alexandria VA placed second in Summer NAC Master Mixed Teams 1954 and won Mid-Atlantic Fall Men's Pairs 1953, 1959, Summer Men's Pairs 1963, Keystone Conference Open Teams 1956.

MURRAY, Eric R. (b. 1928) of Toronto, barrister and solicitor, one of the world's outstanding bridge players and personalities, represented North America in the Bermuda Bowl 1962, 1966, 1967, 1974, and Canada in the World Team Olympiad 1960, 1964, 1968, 1972, 1976, 1980, Rosenblum Cup Teams 1978, 1982 (placing third), World Open Pairs 1970, 1974, 1982. He won the Team Trials 1966, HERMAN TROPHY 1963, Vanderbilt 1961, 1970, Spingold 1964, 1965, 1968, Fall NAC Life Master Men's Pairs 1963, Men's Teams 1962, Mixed Pairs 1963, Summer NAC Life Master Pairs 1969, Master Mixed Teams 1956, 1962, Men's Pairs 1954, 1955, and placed second in the Blue Ribbon Pairs 1969, Reisinger 1969, 1972, Chicago (since 1965 the Reisinger) 1961, Spring NAC Men's Pairs 1965, Summer NAC Master Mixed Teams 1954. His numerous regional titles include Summer NAC secondary MARCUS CUP 1959, Swiss Teams Flt. A 1978, Open Pairs Flt. A 1981. He won the Canadian National Teams 1980, 1981. Murray was the organizing chairman of the Summer North American Championships 1964, past president of Eastern Canadian Bridge Conference and Ontario Unit, and former director of District 2. He devised the MURRAY 2◊ convention and co-authored the DRURY convention. Murray is a contributing editor to the *Bridge Encyclopedia*.

MURRAY, James Laidlaw (b. 1893) of Mayals, Swansea, Wales, former administrative manager, private secretary, was one of the founders and past presidents of the WELSH BRIDGE UNION and a member of the BRITISH BRIDGE LEAGUE council 1964-1968. He represented Wales in many international competitions and won numerous Congresses in England.

MURRAY, Ken (b. 1941) of Willowdale ON, sales representative, represented Canada in the World Open Pairs 1982. He won Summer NAC secondary Open Pairs 1978, Motor City Open Pairs 1978, District 4 Spring KO Teams, Swiss Teams 1979, Wolverine Swiss Teams 1980, District 2 GNP 1982.

MURTINHO, Joâo of Rio de Janeiro, Brazil, was South American champion 1955 and 1956. He was the chief organizer of the 1969 Bermuda Bowl, the first world championship held in Brazil.

MURTINHO, Maria Elizabeth Braga (Lizzie) (b. 1946) of Rio de Janeiro, Brazil, clinical psychologist, was South American Women's champion 1972, 1973, 1975, 1980, 1981. She also represented Brazil in the World Women's Teams 1968, 1980, Venice Trophy Teams 1981, South American Championships, 1970, 1971, 1974, 1976. She is a former contributor to *Jornal do Brazil*.

MUSUMECI, Lt. Col. Joseph (b. 1921) of Richardson TX, bridge columnist, won Texas Conference Open Teams 1955, 1961, Big D Swiss Teams 1976,

Men's Pairs 1982, Alamo City Unmixed Pairs 1976, Republic of Texas Master Swiss Teams 1981. He is past president of the San Antonio BL and the former coach of the ACES TEAM. He was associated with the late IRA CORN in the bridge column *Aces on Bridge*. A member of the IBPA, Musumeci was appointed to the panel of judges for the BOLS BRILLIANCY AWARDS 1978, 1980. He served in the U.S. Air Force for 21 years.

MYERS, Anne. See PRESSMAN, ANNE.

MYRANS, Colette (b. 1915) of Deurle, Belgium, saleswoman, represented Belgium in the World Women's Teams 1964 and on several other occasions. She placed second in the European Women's Championships 1955, 1956, 1959. Her national titles include Mixed Teams 1955, 1956, 1961, Women's Pairs 1954, 1955, 1960, 1963, Mixed Pairs 1958.

N

NAGUIB, Suzanne (Suzy) (b. 1921) of Cairo, Egypt won the World Women's Team 1960. She also represented Egypt in the World Women's Teams 1964 and in several European Championships. Her national titles include Mixed Pairs 1953, Interclubs 1963. Naguib is a former Board member of the EGYPTIAN BRIDGE FEDERATION.

NAGY, Edward A. (Ed) (b. 1946) of Oakland CA, attorney, won Summer NAC Master Mixed Teams 1979. His numerous regional titles include Fall NAC secondary Open Pairs Flt. A 1981, California Capital KO Teams 1971, Master Pairs, Swiss Teams 1972, Open Pairs 1976, Swiss Teams Flt. A 1981, Mid-Winter Holiday KO Teams 1970, Master Pairs 1975, Stockton Swiss Teams 1973, Golden Gate Open Pairs Flt. A 1977, Bridge Week Swiss Teams Flt. A 1980.

NAGY, Peter I. (b. 1942) of Chicago, formerly of Montreal, professional bridge player, one of the leading players of Canada, represented Canada in the World Open Pairs 1978 (placing second), 1982, Rosenblum Cup Teams 1978, 1982, World Team Olympiad 1980. He won Spring NAC Amateur Swiss Teams 1977, Men's Teams 1978, and placed second in the Vanderbilt 1980, Blue Ribbon Pairs 1978, Spingold 1982, Canadian National Teams 1980, 1981. He won more than 20 regional titles inlcuding Spring NAC secondary Swiss Teams, Swiss Teams Flt. A 1978. Nagy has been District 1 representative to the ACBL Board of Governors from 1979. Born in Budapest, Hungary, he was forced to flee his country in 1957 and migrated to Canada. He spoke neither English nor French but by 1958 had become proficient enough to be at the top of his class. In 1961 he was valedictorian of his high school class. After Nagy graduated from Princeton University in 1967 he worked in the computer field until 1974. See also IBPA AWARDS.

NAGY, Zoltan of Canberra, Australia, public servant, was WBF Zone 7 champion 1974. His national titles include Interstate Teams 1970, 1974.

NAIL, Betty (Mrs. G. Robert, formerly Harding) (b. 1923) of Houston won Spring NAC Women's Pairs 1958. Her regional titles include Mississippi Valley Open Teams 1958, Mixed Pairs 1962, Missouri Valley Women's Pairs 1957, South Texas Mixed Pairs 1974, Lone Star Mid-Winter Swiss Teams 1977.

NAIL, G. Robert (b. 1925) of Houston, bridge teacher and writer, one of the most successful American players of the postwar period, represented North America in the Bermuda Bowl 1962, 1963. He won the Team Trials 1962, Fall NAC Men's Teams 1965, Vanderbilt 1967, Summer NAC Life Master Pairs 1974, Fall NAC Life Master Men's Pairs 1974 and placed second in the Chicago (since 1965 the Reisinger) 1960, Spingold 1953, 1962, Fall NAC Men's Teams 1961, Men's Pairs 1949, Blue Ribbon Pairs 1980, Spring NAC Men's Teams 1964, Summer NAC Life Master Pairs 1979. He is the originator of the BIG DIAMOND SYSTEM and the co-author of *Winning Duplicate, How to Play the Hand,* and *Revolution in Bridge.* See BIBLIOGRAPHY, C, D, and NUISANCE BID.

NAKAMURA, Yoshiyuki (b. 1944) of Tokyo, Japan, bridge instructor, represented Japan in the Far East Championships 1968, 1969, 1972, 1978, 1979. His national titles include the Prince Takamatsu Cup 10 times. Nakamura is a regular contributor to JCBL *Bulletin.*

NANDHABIWAT, Somboon (b. 1923) of Bangkok, Thailand, bank managing director, was Far East champion 1961, 1963, 1966. He also represented Thailand in the Bermuda Bowl 1966, 1967, 1968, was captain of the Thailand team in the World Team Olympiad 1964, 1972, 1976, 1980, and captain and/or player in the Far East Championships 1972–1981. The #1 ranked Life Master of Thailand, he has won every major national event 1951–1981 including Open Teams 10 times. He is president of the BRIDGE ASSOCIATION OF THAILAND and the FAR EAST BRIDGE FEDERATION. Nandhabiwat originated the BANGKOK CLUB system. He is president of Thai Bankers Association and chairman of Foremost Dairies.

NASH, Garrett G. (b. 1919) of University City MO won the Vanderbilt 1962. His regional titles include New England Fall Master Pairs 1969, Midwest Spring Swiss Teams 1979, Champagne Open Pairs Flt. A 1980. Nash is a graduate of University of Chicago. A former member of the U.S. International Table Tennis Team, he was ranked #1 in the U.S. in 1939, and third in the world in 1948. He is a former professional baseball player and U.S. Army officer.

NASH, James L. (Jim) (b. 1946) of Omaha NE, insurance company training supervisor, won Summer NAC secondary Men's Pairs 1968, Nebraska KO

Teams 1973, Northwest Iowa Men's Swiss teams 1978, District 14 GNP 1982. Nash is a staff writer for the Unit 241 bridge publication.

NATHAN, Marc W. (b. 1953) of Miami, personnel manager, won Spring NAC Open Pairs 1981 and placed second in 1982. His numerous regional titles include District 5 KO Teams 1974, 1975, All-American Swiss Teams 1975, KO Teams 1979, District 4 KO Teams 1978, Labor Day Men's Swiss Teams 1980, New England Spring KO Teams 1978, Veterans Day Open Pairs Flt. A 1981.

NATHANAEL, Dimitri (b. 1934) of Athens, Greece, born in Zurich, Switzerland, textile trader, the officially ranked #10 player in Greece, represented Greece in the European Championships 1971, 1977. His national titles include Team Trials 1971, Open Teams 1969, 1972, 1973, 1976, 1978, 1980, 1981, Open Pairs 1976, Master Pairs 1979, Mixed Teams 1976, Interclubs 1972, 1981. He is the originator of the Apollo bidding system and bridge correspondent of the national daily *Kathimerini*. Nathanael is an executive member of the HELLENIC BRIDGE FEDERATION.

NATHANSON, Neil L. (b. 1941) of Little Ferry NJ, office manager, placed second in the Grand National Teams 1976 and won Tri-State Winter Swiss Teams 1974.

NATHER, Nola M. (b. 1919) of Christchurch, New Zealand, was Far East Women's Team champion 1976 and also represented New Zealand in the Far East Women's Championships 1973, 1979. She won Australian Women's Pairs 1976 and placed second in New Zealand Open Teams 1976. She is a former president of Crockford's Club.

NEEDHAM, Richard E. (1887–1956) of Greenville PA, bridge writer, tournament organizer and ABL tournament director, was one of the most active tournament promoters for many years in western Pennsylvania, Ohio, West Virginia and upstate New York. His writings included *Auction Bridge Sidelights*, 1927, *Contract Bridge Condensed*, 1930, and *Tournament Tactics at Contract Bridge*, 1934. See BIBLIOGRAPHY, F.

NEEDHAM, Shirley M. of Orinda CA, community college instructor, won Golden Gate Women's Pairs 1972, Master Teams 1973, Mid-Winter Holiday Swiss Teams 1973, Women's Swiss Teams 1976, Emerald Empire Swiss Teams 1982.

NEIGER, Eugene J. (Gene) (b. 1936) of New York City, stockbroker, one of the leading East Coast players, won the Spingold 1971, Vanderbilt 1972. His numerous regional titles include Long Island KO Teams 1971, 1972, California Capital KO Teams 1974, Eastern States Men's Pairs 1977, KO Teams (Reisinger) 1980. He also won the New York Blue Ribbon Individual 1979. See PRECISION TEAM.

NEIKIRK, E. Bruce (b. 1944) of Prospect KY, attorney, won District 11 KO Teams 1974, 1977, GNP 1982, Midwest Fall Men's Swiss Teams 1979.

NEILL, Bruce G. of Sydney, New South Wales, Australia, computer systems consultant, represented Australia in the Far East Championships 1979. His national titles include Australian Open Pairs 1976, Interstate Teams 1979.

NEILSON, Shirley. See GARRELL, SHIRLEY.

NELSEN, Timothy A. (Tim) (b. 1947) of New York City, attorney, won Summer NAC secondary Swiss Teams 1981, Puerto Rico Swiss Teams 1980, 1981, Open Pairs 1981, New York Winter Swiss Teams Flt. A 1980.

NELSON, Beverly Jean (BJ) (b. 1939) of Indianapolis, business owner, former bridge club owner and teacher, placed second in Spring NAC Women's KO Teams 1978, 1979 and won Summer NAC secondary Open Pairs 1971, Champagne Women's Pairs 1976, 1977, Central States II Mixed Pairs 1976, Great Lakes Open Pairs 1977.

NELSON, Martin E. (b. 1944) of Annapolis MD, nuclear engineer, associate professor, won Mid-Atlantic Open Pairs 1973, 1980, Men's Pairs 1982, Swiss Teams Flt. A 1981, 4th of July Master Swiss Teams Flt. A 1980, New England Spring Swiss Teams 1977.

NELSON, Warren G. (b. 1940) of Carmichael CA, retail manager, won Golden Gate Unmixed Pairs 1976, Mount Shasta Open Pairs 1978, Holiday Festival Swiss Teams 1979.

NEUBURGER, Frederic (Fred) (b. 1944) of Liverpool NY, controller, won numerous regional titles including Upper New York State Open Pairs 1973, Swiss Teams 1975, Men's Pairs 1980, National Capital Master Pairs 1977, District 4 Spring Men's Swiss Teams 1982, Summer Men's Swiss Teams 1981, District 5 Master Pairs 1979. Neuburger is columnist and former co-editor of the CNYBA Unit newsletter

NEUFFER, Henry H. (Hap) (b. 1950) of Columbia SC, restaurateur, won Spring NAC secondary Silver Trophy Pairs Flt. A 1979, Florida Open Pairs 1974, Bicentennial Swiss Teams 1976, Mid-Atlantic Men's Pairs 1977.

NEUMAN, Cyrus (b. 1921) of Miami, attorney, won the Spingold 1958 and placed second in 1954. He won Southeastern Open Pairs 1956, 1957, Men's Pairs 1961, Men's Teams 1956, Open Teams 1959.

NEVINS, Emilie of Ft. Lauderdale FL won Summer NAC Senior and Advanced Senior Master Pairs 1956 and placed second in Spring NAC Women's Pairs 1955. Her regional wins include secondary Swiss Teams Flt. A 1974, Upper New York State Women's Pairs 1956, 1958, Puerto Rico Master Pairs 1973, Southeastern Women's Swiss Teams 1975. Nevins is a graduate of Syracuse University.

NEWBILL, Martha (b. 1908) of New Port Richey FL, former school teacher and bridge teacher, won Mississippi Valley Women's Pairs 1952, 1953, Mid-South Women's Pairs 1958, Rocky Mountain Open Teams 1956, North Florida Open Pairs 1978, Sun City Seniors Swiss Teams 1980.

NEWMAN, Bert A. of Dearborn Heights MI placed second in Summer NAC Senior and Advanced Senior Master Pairs 1971, Spring NAC Men's Teams 1981. He won more than 15 regional titles including Spring NAC secondary Open Pairs A-D 1981, Canadian Nat'l KO Teams 1974, Men's Swiss Teams 1978, 1979, All-American KO Teams 1978, Men's Swiss Teams 1979, Wolverine Men's Pairs 1978, KO Teams 1980.

NEWMAN, Lois (b. 1907) of Beverly Hills CA won Bridge Week Mixed Teams 1962, Open Pairs 1961, Master Pairs 1954, Women's Swiss Teams 1974, All-Western Women's Pairs 1966, Golden State Mixed Pairs 1967, 1968.

NEWTON, Jessie (b. 1922) of Wrexham, Wales, teacher, represented Wales in nine CAMROSE TROPHY matches and 15 Lady Milne Trophy matches. She won Welsh Open Teams three times and Welsh Ladies Teams nine times. Newton served as chairman of the BRITISH BRIDGE LEAGUE 1980–1982, as secretary 1966–1978, and as president of the WELSH BRIDGE UNION 1974–1975, 1977–1978.

NEXON, Baron Rebert de (1892–1967) of Paris, France, perfume company president, racer and breeder of horses, was one of the great figures in the world of international bridge. He was European champion 1935 and represented France in the 1935 World Championships against the FOUR ACES. He was npc of the French Team in the World Team Olympiad 1960, 1964 and in several European Championships. His many national wins include French Open Teams and Pairs. With HERMAN DEDICHEN and others, de Nexon was instrumental in recreating the EUROPEAN BRIDGE LEAGUE. He was president of the WORLD BRIDGE FEDERATION 1958–1964, and was President Emeritus of the WBF 1964–1967 and of the EBL 1965–1967. He was president of the FRENCH BRIDGE FEDERATION 1941–1965 and the EBL 1950–1965. He was co-author, with PIERRE ALBARRAN, in 1935, of *Notre Méthode de Bridge*, basis of the point-count system of today, *Le Bridge pour tous*, *Le Memento de bridge*, and *Souvenirs et secrets*. See BIBLIOGRAPHY, E.

NICHOLS, Joyce H. (formerly Simmons) (b. 1931) of Charleston SC, medical department supervisor, won Florida Open Pairs 1960, Mid-Atlantic Open Pairs 1972.

NICKELL, Frank T. (Nick) of Raleigh NC, accountant, won more than 15 regional titles including Fall NAC secondary Swiss Teams 2nd Flt. 1975, Mid-Atlantic KO Teams 1973, 1974, 1975, 1976, Open Teams 1968, Open Pairs 1980, 1981.

NICKLASSON, David A. (Batman) (b. 1943) of Minneapolis, bridge club director and teacher, won Summer NAC secondary Swiss Teams 1971, Fall Open Pairs-A 1977, Mid-Am-Can Open Teams 1965, Iowa Open Teams, Open Pairs 1971, Tri-Unit Men's Pairs 1971, Cambrian Shield Master Pairs 1972, District 14 Men's Pairs 1970, Master Pairs 1971, Champagne Master Pairs 1971, Gopher Open Pairs 1968, Men's Pairs 1980, Black Hills Rodeo Swiss Teams 1976.

NIEBERDING, Joseph H. (b. 1908) of St. Louis, retired executive, won Midwest Fall Master Individual 1954, Mississippi Valley Men's Pairs 1968, Central States Men's Pairs 1974.

NIELSEN, Aksel J. (1900–1981) of Copenhagen, Denmark, "the Nestor of the Danish bridge press," edited *Dansk Bridge* 1941–1946 and contributed to *Berlingske Tidende* and *Weekend-Avisen*. He authored three books in English including *Bridge with the Three Musketeers*.

NISAR, Ahmed. See AHMED, NISAR.

NISHAT, Abedi M. H. See ABEDI, NISHAT M. H.

NOLAND, Helen (Heitie) (b. 1920) of Lake Charles LA won the World Mixed Teams 1972 and placed second in the World Mixed Pairs 1978, Spring NAC Women's Teams 1973. Her numerous regional titles include King Cotton KO Teams 1972, Lone Star Master Pairs 1969, Int'l City Women's Pairs 1974, Mexican Nat'l Mixed Pairs 1978, KO Teams 1979, Houston Mid-Winter Master Swiss Teams 1981.

NORMAN, Barbara (Mrs. John) of La Jolla CA won Pacific Southwest Women's Swiss Teams 1977, Mexican Nat'l Swiss Teams 1977, Desert Empire Open Pairs 1978, California Capital KO Teams 1979.

NORMAN, John H. (b. 1929) of La Jolla CA, research chemist, Mexican Nat'l Swiss Teams 1977, Desert Empire Open Pairs 1978, California Capital KO Teams 1979. He is past president of La Jolla and Beach Unit and District 22.

NORTH, Frederick L. of Hove, Sussex, England, bridge writer and teacher, former British Army officer, represented England in CAMROSE TROPHY matches, World Open Pairs 1962, 1966. His national titles include the GOLD CUP 1962, Devonshire Cup six times, Telegraph Cup three times. In 1957 he swept the Torquay Congress by winning the Pre-Congress Pairs, Mixed Pairs, Master Pairs, Open Pairs, Men's Teams. North has been president of Sussex County CBA from 1971. His writings include contributions to *Bridge Magazine* and several books co-authored with JEREMY FLINT; *Tiger Bridge*, *Bridge in the Looking Glass*, *The Golden Principles of Dummy Play*, and *The First Principles of Dummy Play*. See BIBLIOGRAPHY, E.

NORTON, Dorothea (b. 1925) of Bothell WA won Pacific Northwest Open Teams 1964, 1965, Women's Pairs 1964, 1966.

NORWOOD, Barbara B. (Mrs. Robert) (b. 1938) of Austin TX won Spring NAC Women's Pairs 1980, Texas Capital Mixed Pairs 1975, Acapulco Fiesta Swiss Teams 1980, Republic of Texas Open Pairs Flt. A 1981, District 16 GNP 1981.

NORWOOD, John W. Jr. (b. 1908) of Greenville SC, insurance agent, was ACBL president 1967 and a member of the Board of Directors 1961-1967. He won Mid-Atlantic Summer Men's Pairs 1960, 1961, 1966, Open Teams 1961, Open Pairs 1964, Fall Master Pairs 1962, Open Teams 1965.

NORWOOD, Robert E. (Bob) (b. 1935) of Austin TX, senior research associate, won Texas Master Pairs 1970, Republic of Texas Open Pairs Flt. A 1981, Acapulco Fiesta Swiss Teams 1980. Norwood was Unit 107 Board president in 1982, District 16 Board vice president, co-chairman District 16 Regional Committee.

NOSZKA, Gloria E. (1923-1983) of Pittsburgh, real estate agent, represented the United States in the World Women's Pairs 1970, 1974. She won Spring NAC Women's Pairs 1969, Spring NAC secondary Mixed Pairs 1970, Canadian Nat'l Open Teams 1971, All-American Open Pairs 1967, Swiss Teams 1975, District 5 Swiss Teams 1977. She was a former swimming champion.

NOVAK, Phyllis (b. 1927) of Seattle, geological assistant, won Spring NAC Women's Pairs, Mixed Pairs 1958, Women's Teams 1962. Her regional titles include Pacific Northwest KO Teams 1969, Open Teams 1964, 1965, Puget Sound Swiss Teams 1972, Indian Summer Women's Pairs 1977, British Columbia Swiss Teams Flt. A 1979, District 19 GNT 1974, 1975.

NOVAK, Ruth M. (b. 1909) of Salem IL won Spring NAC Women's Teams 1962. Her regional titles include Champagne Open Pairs 1970, Mississippi Valley Women's Pairs 1970.

NOVRUP, Svend (b. 1945) of Kerteminde, Denmark, journalist and author in the fields of bridge, chess, games, literature and opera, is active in international bridge as a player, several times tournament director, or editor of daily championship bulletins. He is member of the executive committee of the IB-PA and president of AIPE, the chess equivalent of IBPA. Novrup is the author of several bridge books including *Bogen om Bridge*, and contributor to magazines in nine languages.

NOWAK, Janusz (b. 1928) of Warsaw, Poland, represented Poland in the European Championships 1966. He won the Polish Individual 1968.

NUGIT, Trudi (b. 1929) of Northridge CA, born in Czechoslovakia, interpreter, insurance underwriter, placed second in Spring NAC Women's Teams 1974, Fall Life Master Women's Pairs 1975 and won Mexican Nat'l Open Teams 1973, District 17 Fall Swiss Teams 1976, Bridge Week Women's Pairs 1971, Master Swiss Teams 1979. Nugit served in the Israeli Army 1948-1950.

NUNES, Jack (b. 1912) of London, England, company director, one of the leading British players, first represented England in 1950 and has done so on many occasions since. His national titles include the GOLD CUP, 1955, 1958, 1963, 1977, Crockford's Cup several times, Portland Cup three times, Tollemache Cup, *Daily Telegraph* Cup, Southern Counties Pairs. In 1965 with John Collings he created a record at Juan-les-Pins, winning the pairs and teams championships. He is the author of Nunes Grand Slam Force and Nunes 2 NT conventions, and the book *Improve Your Bridge*. This book led to the only two instructional television bridge series shown on British television, *Bridge for Beginners*, and *Improve your Bridge*.

NUPPONEN, Paavo (b. 1928) of Helsinki, Finland, bank accountant, represented Finland in six European Championships and six Nordic Championships. He won five national championships.

NUTTING, Willard H. III (Bill) (b. 1945) of Kensington CA, controller, won the Grand National Pairs 1982. His regional titles include Intercollegiate Championship 1963, Golden Gate Master Pairs 1974, All-Western Open Pairs 1971, Mixed Pairs 1975. He is past president of Unit 497 and former treasurer of District 21.

NYGREN, Britt (formerly Blom) (b. 1925) of Norrköping, Sweden, won the World Women's Teams 1968, European Women's Championships 1967, Nordic Women's Championships 1964, 1966, 1978, 1980. Her national titles include Mixed Pairs and 10 women's titles.

O

OAKEY, Lawrence B. (Larry) (b. 1937) of Minneapolis, accountant, placed second in Spring NAC Men's Teams 1978 and won more than 40 regionals including Summer NAC secondary Leventritt Pairs 1966, Canadian Prairie Men's Pairs 1970, Open Pairs 1971, Swiss Teams 1972, Calgary KO Teams 1973, Mixed Pairs, Master Pairs 1975, Iowa Swiss Teams 1970, 1979, 1980, KO Teams 1979, Gopher Swiss Teams 1977, KO Teams 1980, Roughrider KO Teams 1977, 1981, Men's Pairs 1981.

OAKIE, Donald A. (Don) (formerly Donald Akira Aoki) (1914-1983) of San Jose CA, one of the leading American bridge personalities, was the first of Japanese descent to win the Bermuda Bowl (1954) and the first ACBL member to become a Life Master with 300 red points. He represented the United States in the World Team Olympiad 1960. He won the Spingold 1953, Chicago (since 1965 the Reisinger) 1958, and placed second in Spring NAC Men's Pairs 1959. He also won numerous regionals. For many years Oakie was involved with bridge administration; ACBL president 1976, chairman of the

ACBl Board of Directors 1977 and a Board member 1967–1981, co-chairman of the ACBL Laws Commission since 1975, WBF Laws Commission 1974, president of the WESTERN CONFERENCE 1966. Oakie was the principal draftsman of the revised American format of the 1974 Laws of Duplicate and he revised and rewrote the *ACBL Handbook* 1973, 1974, 1975. He authored *Simplified Standard American Bridge Bidding* (see BIBLIOGRAPHY, C). Oakie was named "Sportsman of the Year" by the IBPA in 1976 (see IBPA AWARDS).

OAKS, Alan W. (b. 1938) of Memphis, executive secretary of the ACBL Charity Foundation and ACBL Operations Manager, won Fall NAC secondary Swiss Teams 1979, Men's Swiss Teams 1980, Oregon Trail Open Teams 1967, Pacific Northwest Open Pairs 1967. He is a frequent contributor to the ACBL *Bulletin*. Oaks is a graduate of University of Oregon.

O'BRIEN, Patrick L. (P.L.) of Dobbins CA, professional bridge teacher, computer programmer, won Pacific Northwest Spring Open Teams 1967, Palm Springs KO Teams 1971, Oregon Trail Master Pairs 1974, Open Teams 1973, Mount Shasta Open Pairs, Swiss Teams 1974. O'Brien, a hemophiliac, is a member of the National Hemophilia Society, honorary member of Royal Hemophilia Society and a member of Yuba College Disabled Students Committee. See HANDICAPPED PLAYERS.

ODDIE, Thomas H. (b. 1911) of Palos Verdes Estates CA, born in Ballarat, Australia, physicist, represented Australia in the World Team Olympiad 1960 and won numerous titles in Australia 1933–1960. He is a graduate of University of Melbourne.

ODOHERTY, Eileen of Dublin, Ireland, civil servant, represented Ireland in the World Women's Pairs 1978 and in many European and Common Market Championships. She won Common Market Women's Teams 1980. Her national titles include Women's Pairs, Mixed Pairs, Women's Teams, Open Pairs, Open Teams.

O'DONNELL, Marilyn E. (b. 1939) of Columbia MD, travel agency representative, won Mid-Atlantic Women's Swiss Teams 1976, 1978, 1979, Women's Pairs 1978, 1980, 1981.

O'DOWD, John L. (b. 1929) of Hamilton ON, former bridge club owner, won Canadian Nat'l Open Teams 1958, KO Teams 1968. He is founder and first president of Hamilton and District BA.

OEST, John N. (Jack) (b. 1952) of Chicago, attorney, won Champagne Master Pairs 1977, Wisconsin KO Teams 1978, District 13 GNT, Zone VI 1981. He is a graduate of Denison University.

O'GRADY, Angeline (Andy) (b. 1935) of Miami, professional bridge teacher and player, won Southeastern Swiss Teams 1972, Mixed Pairs 1977, Florida Life Master Pairs 1973.

OGUST, Harold A. (1916–1978) of New York City was the president and founder of Goren International, Inc., a plastics manufacturer, travel agent, originator of OGUST REBIDS after WEAK TWO-BIDS, and an outstanding player. He represented the United States in the Bermuda Bowl 1957, World Team Olympiad in 1960. He won the Spingold 1956, 1960, Reisinger 1957, 1963.

OHMANN, Carol R. (b. 1934) of Ormond Beach FL, bridge club manager, director and teacher, won North Florida Swiss Teams 1978, Fall Swiss Teams 1976, Open Pairs Flt. A, Master Pairs 1977, Southeastern Women's Pairs 1977. She won the Mary B. Hughes Trophy 1977.

OKEN, Daniel (b. 1917) of Miami, real estate and land developer, won Keystone Fall Master Pairs 1968, North Florida Fall Swiss Teams 1977, Open Pairs 1976, Headquarters Open Pairs 1978, Southeastern Men's Swiss Teams 1980, Gold Coast Men's Swiss Teams 1981.

OKEN, Louise (Mrs. Daniel, formerly Sharp and Mowbray) (1937–1983) of Miami, real estate developer, won Fall NAC Mixed Pairs 1966. Her regional titles included Florida Life Master Pairs 1971, Mexican Nat'l Master Pairs 1970, North Florida Fall Open Pairs 1976, Swiss Teams 1977, Headquarters Open Pairs 1978.

OLIVER, Vincent A. (b. 1959) of Newport Beach CA, marketing consultant, won Summer NAC secondary Silver Trophy Pairs Flt. B 1977, Central States II Swiss Teams 1978, All-Western Swiss Teams 1978, Raincross Swiss Teams Flt. A 1980.

OLMEDO ZUMARÁN, Alejandro (b. 1902) of Buenos Aires, Argentina, solicitor, was South American champion 1950, 1953, 1957. His national titles include Argentine Open Teams 1935, 1952, Open Pairs 1953, 1956, Interclubs 1947, 1951, 1952, 1957.

O'LOUGHLIN, Walter K. (b. 1910) of Towson MD, retired executive, won Mid-Atlantic Men's Pairs 1978, Summer Mixed Pairs 1968, Mexican Nat'l Unmixed Pairs 1978, Fall NAC secondary Men's Swiss Teams 1980. He was ACBL president 1978, ACBL Director 1962–1965, 1971–1980, ACBL treasurer 1973–1975, president Maryland BA 1956, president Mid-Atlantic Conference 1970–1972. O'Loughlin is a graduate of Catholic University of America.

OLSEN, Arne (b. 1939) of Oslo, Norway, represented Norway in the European Championships 1965, Nordic Championships 1964. He won Nordic Open Teams 1965.

OLSEN, Jack (b. 1925) of Rollinsville CO, journalist and author, formerly wrote for *Sports Illustrated*. He is the author of *The Mad World of Bridge* and co-author of *A New Approach to Bridge*. See BIBLIOGRAPHY, B.

OLSEN, Per (b. 1941) of Oslo, Norway, represented Norway in the European Championships 1965, Nordic Championships 1964. He won Norwegian Open Pairs 1965.

OLSZEWSKI, Andrzej (b. 1918) of Warsaw, Poland, represented Poland in the European Championships 1962, 1966. He won Polish Open Pairs 1963, Open Teams 1965.

O'MALIA, Bernard E. (Barney) (b. 1904) of Hawthorne NV, casino owner, placed second in the Reisinger 1978 and won numerous regional titles including Inter-Mountain KO Teams 1969, Men's Pairs 1971, Pacific Southwest KO Teams 1969, 1979, 1980, Master Pairs 1973, Open Pairs Flt. A 1975, Desert Empire Master Swiss Teams 1978, KO Teams 1981.

ONORATI, Mario (b. 1928) of Caracas, Venezuela, business executive, the leading player in Venezuela, was South American champion 1963, 1965. He also represented Venezuela in the World Team Olympiad 1960, 1964, 1968, Bermuda Bowl 1966, 1967. His national titles include Open Teams five times, Open Pairs, Mixed Teams.

ONSTOTT, John H. (b. 1944) of New Orleans, finance company president, won Golden Gate Swiss Teams 1974, District 22 Men's Pairs 1974, Mid-South Swiss Teams 1976, Holiday Swiss Teams Flt. A 1979, Mid-Atlantic Open Pairs 1976, Wisconsin Men's Pairs, Men's Swiss Teams 1980.

OREFFICE, Paul F. (b. 1927) of Midland MI, company president, won Spanish Open Pairs 1964. His regional titles inlcude Southeastern KO Teams 1968, Florida Men's Pairs 1968, Great Lakes Swiss Teams 1979. Oreffice is a graduate of Purdue University.

O'REILLEY, Edward C. (b. 1936) of Kingston ON, business administrator, won Can-At KO Teams 1969, 1970, Swiss Teams 1970. He founded the Brockville DBC and assisted in founding three other clubs. O'Reilley is a former treasurer of Eastern Canada Bridge Conference

ORLETT, Paul V. (b. 1934) of Kansas City MO, bridge club owner, won Missouri Valley KO Teams 1972, District 14 Master Pairs 1969, Mid-Winter Holiday Swiss Teams 1974, Northwest Iowa KO Teams 1978, Indian Summer KO Teams 1979, District 15 GNT 1979, 1981, Zone V 1981.

OROCK, Lt. Col. Mary J. (b. 1939) of Abilene TX, Air Force officer, registered nurse, won Western Iowa Open Pairs 1975, Rocky Mountain Swiss Teams 1977, Mid-Winter Holiday Open Pairs Flt. A 1977, Big Apple Women's Pairs 1979.

ORTIZ-PATIÑO, Jaime (b. 1928) of Geneva, Switzerland, has business interests throughout the world. Elected president of the WORLD BRIDGE FEDERATION in 1976, re-elected in 1978 and again in 1982, he was WBF vice president 1974-1975 and treasurer of the EUROPEAN BRIDGE LEAGUE 1974–1975. As WBF

president he has been instrumental in forming two new zones — CENTRAL AMERICAN-CARIBBEAN and ASIA AND THE MIDDLE EAST — and in adding many new countries to the WBF roster, including the People's Republic of China. He also has carried through many ideas — bidding screens, bidding boxes, ban on wandering — to protect world bridge contests from the slighest hint of misconduct. Ortiz-Patino represented Switzerland in the World Team Olympiad 1964, 1968, World Open Pairs 1962, Rosenblum Cup Teams 1982, European Championships 1955, 1956, 1959, 1961, 1962, 1963, 1965, 1967. He placed fifth in the World Par Point Contest 1961. His national titles include Open Teams 1953, 1956, 1959, 1961, KO Teams 1955, 1956, 1960, 1962, 1963.

OSBORN, Florence of Mount Carmel CT, bridge columnist and lecturer in the humanities, was bridge editor of the New York *Herald Tribune* from 1936 until the newspaper was discontinued in 1966, and of the New York *American.* Her writings include *How's Your Bridge Game?* and many magazine articles. Osborn formerly conducted a bridge interview radio program, and has made many television appearances. She is a contributing editor, *Bridge Encyclopedia.* See BIBLIOGRAPHY, J.

OSELLA, Sergio of Milan, Italy was npc of the Italian champions in the World Team Olympiad 1964, Bermuda Bowl 1965, European Championships 1963, 1966.

OSHLAG, Richard J. (b. 1945) of Memphis, business manager for the *ACBL Bulletin,* won several regional titles including New York Winter Life Master Pairs 1971, Mid-Atlantic KO Teams 1973, Mid-South Swiss Teams 1974, Men's Pairs 1975, Headquarters KO Teams 1979, Space City Open Pairs Flt. A 1980, District 10 GNT 1978. Oshlag was Unit 188 Master Player of the Year 1972. He is a contributing editor, *Bridge Encyclopedia.*

OSIE, Judith (b. 1936) of Johannesburg, South Africa, represented South Africa in the World Women's Teams 1976, 1980, MACCABIAH GAMES 1977. Her national titles include South African National Teams 1970, 1971, 1973, 1981, National Pairs 1973.

OSOFSKY, Aileen (b. 1926) of New York City, won District 3 Women's Swiss Teams 1979, District 4 Women's Pairs 1980, Mexican Nat'l Women's Pairs 1981.

OSTFIELD, Roni J. of Pittsburgh won District 5 KO Teams 1974, 1975, Canadian Nat'l Mixed Pairs 1976, All-American KO Teams 1979, Labor Day Women's Swiss Teams 1980.

OSTRICH, Dr. Nathan (b. 1928) of Lafayette LA, optometrist, won Mexican Nat'l Open teams 1970, Men's Pairs 1969, Mixed Pairs 1971, Mid-South Swiss Teams 1973, Open Pairs 1976. He is the founder of the S.W. Louisiana Unit. He produced the TV series "Play Bridge with the Experts."

OSTROW, Albert A. (1910–1961) of Malverne NY was an authority on card games, and the author of numerous books, among them, *The Complete Card Player* and *The Bridge Player's Bedside Companion*. He was a consultant on card games to the Association of American Playing Card Manufacturers 1960–1961. See BIBLIOGRAPHY, B, K.

OTSTOTT, Herminia (b. 1926) of Rizal, Philippines, represented the Philippines in the Far East Women's Championships 1966, Hong Kong-Manila Interport tournament 1963. Her national titles include Women's Pairs 1957, 1958, Open Teams 1961, Mixed Teams 1967.

OTTLIK, Géza (b. 1912) of Budapest, Hungary, writer, novelist, essayist, translator, editor, represented Hungary 1936–1938 in international competitions against Austria, Czechoslovakia, Germany, Poland, and 1971–1972 against Sweden and Yugoslavia. He was International Par Contest champion 1936 and World Olympic Central European winner 1938. His national titles include Open Teams, Master Pairs, National Cup. Ottlik is the editor of the Hungarian *Bridge Review* and co-author of *Adventures in Card Play*. He contributes to *Bridge World*, *Australian Bridge*, *Bridge Tidningen*. He authored and introduced new concepts, categories, general principles and devices in card-play technique, coining notions such as ENTRY SQUEEZE, BACKWASH SQUEEZE, ELOPEMENT, Elbow-Room, ENTRY-SHIFTING SQUEEZE, Non-Material Plays, Rio Finesse, and KO Squeeze. Ottlik won the International Bridge Academy's first "Article of the Year" award 1968.

OUDSHOORN, Nicolaus D. (Nico) (b. 1906) of Ryswijk, The Netherlands, importer, is chief of Dutch Bridge-Rama, a member of the national technical staff for European Championshps, tournament manager of European Championships 1963, 1965, 1966 and World Team Olympiad 1968, World Pair Olympiad 1974. He is Honorary EBL Tournament Director.

OUIMET, Jean G. (b. 1934) of Tacoma WA, born in Montreal, retired from the USAF, won Puget Sound Men's Swiss Teams 1977, California Capital KO Teams 1979, Missouri Valley KO Teams 1979.

OVALLE, Jorge C. of Santiago, Chile, civil engineer, was South American champion 1951 and placed second in 1955, 1957 1961. His national titles include Open Teams 1955, 1956, 1957, 1958, 1961, 1963.

OVERBY, J. Jefferson (Jeff) (b. 1953) of Coconut Grove FL, attorney, won Mid-South Mixed Pairs 1976, Mid-Atlantic Men's Pairs 1976, Puerto Rico Men's Pairs 1977, Midwest Fall Men's Swiss Teams, Men's Pairs 1977, North Florida Open Pairs 1979. He was Master of the Year 1975 (see MINI McKENNEY).

O'YANG, Helen (b. 1955) of Taiwan, accountant, won the Mayor's Cup 1979, Governor's Cup 1978.

OZORIO, L. A. (b. 1911) of Hong Kong, businessman, was Far East champion 1959, 1960. His national titles include Open Teams, Master Teams, Open Pairs, Master Pairs, Mixed Pairs.

P

PABIS TICCI, Camillo (b. 1920) of Florence, Italy, engineer, WBF Grand Master #7, one of the world's great players, was Bermuda Bowl champion 1963, 1965, 1966, 1967, 1969, World Team Olympiad champion 1964, 1968, 1972. His national titles include Italian Cup 1961, Open Teams 1964. He is past president of Florence BA. He is columnist for the newsweekly *L'Europeo*, frequent contributor to *Bridge d'Italia*, and the co-author of *Smazzate in Evidenza* and *Ricordi in Vetrina*.

PADEREWSKI, Ignace Jan (1860–1941), Polish pianist, composer, statesman, developed a passion for bridge in the last ten years of his life, playing morning, noon and quite often all night. Questioned about his ability at the bridge table he replied that his game was in the same class with his piano playing but added in modesty that that was only moderately good. A successful endplay or making a vulnerable slam gave him more satisfaction than the homage of his audiences after a brilliant concert.

PADGET, John E. (b. 1945) of Seattle, restaurant manager and bridge teacher, won Mid–Winter Holiday Swiss Teams 1971, Puget Sound Open Pairs, Master Pairs 1971, All-Western Swiss Teams 1970, KO Teams 1972, Open Teams 1970, Bridge Week Master Pairs 1971, Rogue River KO Teams 1973, Hawaii Mixed Pairs 1974.

PADUA, Leticia de (Letty) (b. 1930) of Rizal, Philippines, represented the Philippines in the World Women's Pairs 1962, Venice Trophy Teams 1978, Far East Championships 1963 and won the Far East Zone World Par contest 1963. She served as PCBL president 1977.

PAES de BARROS, Paulo P. (b. 1941) of São Paulo, Brazil, assessor, was South American champion 1966, 1969, 1974. He also represented Brazil in the Bermuda Bowl 1970, 1975, World Team Olympiad 1968, 1972, World Open Pairs 1970, Bermuda Bowl 1970, 1975.

PAI, Ton Seek (b. 1921) of Honolulu, attorney, won Hawaii Men's Pairs 1956, Master Pairs 1968, 1976, Swiss Teams 1980.

PALMER, Beth (b. 1952) of Silver Spring MD, lawyer, placed second in the World Women's Pairs 1982, Summer NAC Master Mixed Teams 1981 and won Spring NAC secondary Women's Pairs 1979, Mid-Atlantic Spring and Fall Women's Swiss Teams 1980.

PALOCZ, Eugenio (b. 1906) of Santiago, Chile,

born in Budapest, Hungary, businessman, represented Chile in the World Team Olympiad 1964, South American Championships 1956, npc of the Chilean Teams in the SAC 1979, World Team Olympiad 1972. He won Chilean International Team Trials 1959, Open Pairs many times, and numerous other titles. Palocz was national boxing champion of Hungary 1922-1923.

PALOCZ, Matilde S. (Mrs. Eugenio) (b. 1910) of Santiago, Chile, born in Budapest, Hungary, represented Chile in the World Women's Teams 1964. She is a former swimming and tennis champion.

PALSSON, Asmundur (b. 1928) of Reykjavik, Iceland, represented Iceland in the World Team Olympiad 1960, 1968, 1976, European Championships 1963, 1969, 1970, 1971, 1973, 1974, 1977, 1979, npc in 1981. His national titles include Iceland Open Teams 1962, 1965, 1969, 1971, 1972, 1977, 1978, 1980, Open Pairs 1963, 1966, 1968, 1970, 1971, 1973, 1974.

PANCOE, Frank (b. 1950) of Chicago, bank commercial lending officer, won Central States I KO Teams 1975, 1981, 1982, District 13 GNP 1981.

PANG, Vern H. (b. 1950) of Hacienda Heights CA, born in Honolulu, computer systems consultant, won Rogue River Valley KO Teams 1973, Hawaii KO Teams 1976, Swiss Teams 1981, All-Western Open Pairs Flt. A 1981.

PAPASTAVROU, Dimitri of Athens, Greece, lawyer, represented Greece in the European Championships 1971. His national titles include Team Trials 1971, 1972, Open Pairs 1973, 1976, Open Teams 1969, 1973, 1974, 1980, Interclubs 1972. He served as secretary general of the HELLENIC BRIDGE FEDERATION 1971-1973, 1974 and was bridge columnist of the national daily *Kathimerini* 1974-1981.

PARENT, Henri F. (b. 1925) Montreal, company president, won Canadian Nat'l Open Teams 1960, Can-Am Men's Pairs, Open Teams 1967. He is past president of the Montreal BL, District 1, served as an ACBL Director 1967-1979 and is a former representative to the executive council of the WBF. Parent contributed to the organizing and sanctioning of a bridge club in a terminal patient hospital.

PARETI, Robert E. (Bob) (b. 1929) of Des Plaines IL, company owner, won Fall NAC Amateur Men's Pairs 1975, Central States Open Pairs, Swiss Teams 1976, KO Teams 1980.

PARIENTE, Dr. Jacques (b. 1929) of Paris, France, physician, was European champion 1966 and also represented France in the World Open Pairs 1962, European Championships 1958, 1959, 1967 and served as captain of the French Women's Team. His national titles include French Open Teams 1956. He is the co-author of *Le Bridge d'aujourd'hui*.

PARKER, Abner (Ab) (b. 1902) of Los Angeles, born in Russia, management consultant, is a former

director of the ACBL Charity Foundation and organized the first District-wide Charity game.

PARKER, Joshua B. (Josh) (b. 1956) of New York City, lawyer, won Summer NAC secondary Swiss Teams, Golder Master Pairs 1978, Keohane Individual 1975, New England Knockout KO Teams 1978, Swiss Teams 1980, Fall KO Teams, Swiss Teams 1978, Summer Open Pairs 1979, Tri-State Swiss Teams 1977, Wolverine KO Teams 1977, Long Island Open Pairs 1978, District 3 KO Teams 1979.

PARKER, Judy of Greenwich CT won Summer NAC secondary Women's Pairs 1970, New York Winter Mixed Teams 1971, Tri-State Winter Open Teams 1974.

PARKER, George W. (b. 1933) of Millbrae CA, accountant and attorney, won Oregon Trail KO Teams 1970, Golden State KO Teams 1970, 1972, Polar KO Teams, Men's Pairs 1974.

PARKER, Steven J. (b. 1945) of Brookeville MD, personnel counselor, one of the leading East Coast players, won the World Mixed Teams 1974, Reisinger 1972, Fall NAC Mixed Pairs 1969, 1976, and placed second in the Reisinger 1976, Summer NAC Master Mixed Teams 1973, Grand National Teams 1977. His numerous regional titles include Spring NAC secondary Master Pairs 1973, Mid-Atlantic KO Teams 1974, Master Pairs 1970, 1971, 1976, Mixed Pairs 1976, Open Pairs 1973, Swiss Teams 1973, 1976.

PARKS, William (Bill) (b. 1949) of Butte MT, student, won Deseret Classic Unmixed Swiss Teams 1977, Mid-Winter Holiday Swiss Teams Flt. A 1980, District 18 GNT, Zone VI 1981.

PARR, Siddy S. See FOX, SIDDY S.

PARTOS, George (b. 1907) of Miami Beach, retired bookkeeper, formerly owned one of the largest private collections of bridge books and periodicals. He is a contributing editor, *Bridge Encyclopedia*.

PASKIN, Stephen R. (Steve) (b. 1942) of Albany NY won Tri-State Swiss Teams 1973, Upper New York State Master Pairs 1974, 1976, Capital District Fall Master Swiss Teams 1977.

PASQUINI, Paolo (b. 1944) of Caracas, Venezuela, born in Rome, Italy, insurance broker, was Central American-Caribbean champion 1977, placed second in 1981, and in the South American Championships 1975, 1978. His national titles include Venezuela Open Pairs 1974, 1975, 1977, 1982, Open Teams 1974, 1975, 1976, 1977, 1979, 1981, Mixed Teams 1976, 1978, 1979, 1980, 1982. Pasquini was a Board member of the VENEZUELAN BRIDGE FEDERATION 1979 and member of the honor committee 1977-1978.

PASSELL, MARIETTA. See BEERY, MARIETTA.

PASSELL, Michael J. (b. 1947) of Garland TX, bridge professional, one of the leading American players, won the Bermuda Bowl 1979, placed second in 1977 and in the World Team Olympiad 1980. He also represented the United States in the World Open Pairs, Rosenblum Cup Teams 1978, 1982. He won the MOTT-SMITH TROPHY, FISHBEIN TROPHY 1978, McKENNEY TROPHY 1976, Vanderbilt 1978, 1982, Spingold 1978, Reisinger 1976, Grand National Teams 1981, Spring NAC Open Pairs 1978 and placed second in Vanderbilt 1976, Reisinger 1980, Summer NAC Life Master Pairs 1976. His more than 150 regional titles include Spring NAC secondary Swiss Teams 2nd Flt. 1972, Open Pairs 1974, Swiss Teams Flt. A 1980, Fall Open Pairs 1978. He learned to play bridge during high school vacations by watching his brother WILLIAM PASSELL teach bridge classes. Passell is among the top 10 all-time masterpoint holders (see LIFE MASTER).

PASSELL, Nancy L. (Mrs. Michael) (b. 1949) of Garland TX, former teacher, won Land of Coronado KO Teams 1980, Desert Empire Open Pairs Flt. A 1980, Mexican Nat'l Swiss Teams Flt. A 1981, Republic of Texas Open Pairs 1981, Mid-Atlantic Open Pairs Flt. A 1981, Oklahoma City Women's Swiss Teams 1981.

PASSELL, William L. (Bill) (b. 1930) of Fort Lauderdale FL, bridge teacher, one of the leading players of the South, won Summer NAC Master Mixed Teams 1972, Fall NAC Mixed Pairs 1960, and placed second in the Grand National Teams 1980. His numerous regional titles include Fall NAC secondary Men's Teams 1968, Spring Swiss Teams 1978, Eastern States KO Teams (Reisinger) 1969, 1978. He won the New York Blue Ribbon Invitational Individual 1978.

PATRIAS, Christopher P. (Chris) of Minneapolis, accountant, regional tournament director, won Summer NAC Senior and Advanced Senior Master Pairs 1972, Gopher Men's Swiss Teams 1976, Black Hills Rodeo Swiss Teams 1976, District 14 GNT 1979.

PATTERSON, Lucille E. (Lucy) of Sacramento CA won Spring NAC Women's Pairs 1964, Spring NAC secondary Amateur Swiss Teams 2nd Flt. 1977, Pacific Northwest Mixed Pairs 1955, Desert Empire Open Teams 1956, Inter-Mountain Open Teams 1958, Golden State Women's Pairs 1967, All-Western Women's Pairs 1968, Bridge Week Women's Pairs 1972, California Capital Swiss Teams 1979, Rogue River Valley Mixed Pairs 1976, Mount Shasta Women's Pairs 1981.

PATTON, Major Charles Lee (1851–1941) was a pioneer of bridge organization from 1906. Born in Mississippi, resident of New York City after 1888, Patton was the originator of the Patton movement (see TEAM-OF-FOUR MOVEMENT), and one of those who claimed invention of the TAKEOUT DOUBLE.

PAUL, Abe (b. 1943) of Roswell GA, born in Gunzenhausen, West Germany, associate actuary, won Bermuda Men's Pairs 1978, Nat'l Capital KO Teams 1978, Can-Am Open Pairs Flt. A 1980.

PAUL, Mariana (Mary) (Mrs. Maurice) of Montreal, born in Bucharest, Romania, accountant, represented Canada in the World Women's Teams 1968, 1972 1980, Rosenblum Cup Teams 1978. She won Can-Am Mixed Pairs 1971, Wolverine Swiss Teams 1980, District GNT 1973. She is a former president of Montreal Team-of-Four BL.

PAUL, Maurice (Moose) (b. 1923) of Toronto, born in Belgium, sales representative, won Summer NAC secondary MARCUS CUP 1958, Can-Am Open Teams 1957, Mixed Pairs 1971, Canadian Nat'l Men's Swiss Teams 1980, District 2 GNT 1973. He also won the Intercity Championship (Montreal vs Chicago) 1967. Paul created the first Team-of-Four Bridge League on the North American continent in 1956 in Montreal. He is a member of the ACBL Charity Committee, the ACBL Goodwill Committee and the NAC Appeals Committee.

PAULS, Brian (b. 1940) of Winnipeg MB, barrister, solicitor, bridge writer, won Summer NAC secondary Leventritt Pairs 1966, 1968, President's Cup Pairs 1962, Mid-Am-Can Master Pairs 1963, Gopher Men's Pairs 1966, Open Pairs 1970, Buffalo Men's Swiss Teams 1976, District 2 GNT 1974.

PAULSEN, Erik (b. 1926) of Culver City CA, born in Oslo, Norway, design engineer, one of the leading American players, won the Bermuda Bowl 1976 and placed second in 1977. He also represented the United States in the World Team Olympiad 1976, World Open Pairs 1970. He won the Chicago (since 1965 the Reisinger) 1962, Reisinger 1968, 1974, 1975, Blue Ribbon Pairs 1969, placed second in the Vanderbilt 1963, Reisinger 1966, Spring NAC Men's Pairs 1959, and won numerous regional titles.

PAVLICEK, Richard F. (b. 1945) of Ft. Lauderdale FL, bridge teacher and writer, one of the leading players of the South, won the Grand National Teams 1973, Reisinger 1982, and placed second in the Spingold 1978, Grand National Pairs 1982. His numerous regional titles include Summer NAC secondary Swiss Teams 1982, Southeastern Men's Teams 1970, 1974, Life Master Pairs 1971, 1977, North Florida Open Pairs Flt. A 1978, KO Teams 1979, Puerto Rico Men's Pairs, Open Pairs 1976. He is editor of *Gold Coast Bridge News*, a contibutor to *Florida Bridge News*, *The Bridge World*, and co-author of *Modern Bridge Conventions*. See BIBLIOGRAPHY, D.

PAVLIDES, Jordanis T. (b. 1903) of London, England, company director, was Bermuda Bowl champion 1955, European champion 1954. He also represented Great Britain in the European Championships 1955. He won the GOLD CUP 1949, Master Pairs 1948 and other national events. Pavlides is the author of *One Page Guide to Bidding*.

PAYNE, Dorothy of Memphis placed second in Fall NAC Women's Teams 1954 and won Southern Conference Open Pairs 1962, Puerto Rico Open Teams 1973. She is a former Director of the Memphis Unit.

PEAKE, Lyle R. (b. 1944) of Hollywood CA, professional bridge player, won Western Celebrity Men's Swiss Teams 1976, Bridge Week Master Swiss Teams 1979, Raincross KO Teams 1979.

PEARSON, Don B. of Boston won Spring NAC Men's Teams 1970 and placed second in Fall NAC Life Master Men's Pairs 1968. He won ALACBU Open Teams 1969.

PEDERSEN, Darryl (Pete) (b. 1936) of Bellevue WA, cost accountant, placed second in Spring NAC Men's Pairs 1964. His regional titles include Fall NAC secondary Swiss Teams Flt. A 1981, Puget Sound KO Teams 1970, 1971, 1972, Swiss Teams Flt. A 1978, Tri-Cities Swiss Teams 1975, Oregon Trail Men's Pairs 1978, British Columbia Men's Pairs 1978, District 19 GNT Zone VIII 1981.

PELKA, David G. (b. 1943) of Los Angeles, company executive, won Pacific Southwest KO Teams 1974, Mid-Winter Holiday Men's Pairs 1979, Master Pairs 1980, Bridge Week Unmixed Pairs 1981.

PELL, Margaret (b. 1926) of Norfolk, realtor, won Fall NAC secondary Senior Master Individual 1960, Mid-Atlantic Women's Pairs 1976, Women's Swiss Teams 1980, Fall Women's Pairs 1959.

PELUCCHI, Giovanni (b. 1907) of Milan, Italy, industrialist, was npc of the Italian Team in the European Championships 1962, 1966, 1967. He was the organizer of the 1958 Bermuda Bowl and author of several articles in *Bridge d'Italia*.

PENCHARZ, William J. (b. 1945) of London, England, solicitor, captained the British Open Team in the European Championships 1979, World Team Olympiad 1980, Common Market Championships 1981. He won the GOLD CUP 1979, Crockford's Cup 1978, Spring Foursomes 1971, 1972, British Team Trials 1981. He is a contributor to *Bridge Magazine* and *International Popular Bridge*. Pencharz is vice chairman of the ENGLISH BRIDGE UNION, committee member of the EUROPEAN BRIDGE LEAGUE, member of the WBF Laws Committee, chairman of the EBL League Laws Committee and of the Middlesex CBA. He is a graduate of Cambridge University.

PENDER, Peter A. (b. 1936) of Forestville CA, resort owner and executive director, one of the leading American players, won the Pan-American Invitational Pairs 1974, 1975, and placed second in the Rosenblum Cup Teams 1982. He won the McKENNEY TROPHY 1966, Reisinger 1968, 1970, 1981, Fall NAC Life Master Men's Pairs 1967, Grand National Teams 1982, and placed second in the Reisinger 1971, Spingold 1974, Fall NAC Mixed Pairs 1964. His numerous regional titles include MARCUS CUP 1958, Fall NAC secondary Open Pairs 1978. Pender was coach of the United States World Women's Team 1972, 1976 and the Venice Trophy Team 1976 and represented the United States in the World Mixed Teams 1974, World Open Pairs 1982. He has served as commentator at numerous Team Trials and World Championships, and as a member of

numerous Appeals Committees including the WBF. Pender is a United States Figure Skating Association and Canadian Figure Skating Association gold medalist and former figure skating coach. He was director of Human Rights Foundation 1977 and president of Russian River Business Association 1980. He is an accomplished pianist.

PENNINGTON, Lee H. (b. 1926) of Yonkers NY, math teacher, won several ABA National championships including KO Teams 1979, Open Pairs Spring and Summer 1977 and several sectional (equivalent to ACBL regional) titles. An ABA tournament director since 1979, he has served as NYC tournament committee chairman and as national coordinator of ABA "point races".

PEREIRA de SOUSA, Caio Luis (b. 1905) of São Paulo, Brazil, civil engineer, was South American champion 1956, 1962. He won Brazilian Open Teams 1958, 1959, 1961.

PERES, Charles (b. 1930) of Chicago, options and futures trader, won the MOREHEAD TROPHY 1967, Summer NAC Master Mixed Teams, Men's Pairs 1969, Grand National Teams 1978, and placed second in the Reisinger 1967, Spring NAC Open Pairs 1973. His regional titles include District 11 Men's Pairs 1962, Central States Life and Senior Master Teams 1962, KO Teams 1966, 1969, 1970, Motor City Swiss Teams 1972.

PERKINS, Frank K. (1891–1971) of Newton MA, was a civil engineer and a bridge writer. For about 30 years he wrote daily bridge columns for the *Boston Herald*. He won wide acclaim for his chess and bridge-playing skills and writings as well as his expertise as a fly fisherman. He wrote numerous instructional texts on bridge, including *Vital Tricks at Contract Bridge*, *Modern Contract Standards*, many articles for *The Bridge World*, and served as bridge consultant to *Grolier's Encyclopedia* and the *American Heritage Dictionary*. An outstanding player, Perkins was second in the Reisinger 1931, and won New England Knockout Teams seven times. Founder of New England BL, he acted as its secretary, treasurer, and tournament director until 1946. See BIBLIOGRAPHY, C, D.

PERLMAN, Howard M. (b. 1943) of Southfield MI, bridge and backgammon club owner, placed second in the Vanderbilt 1972 and in the Grand National Teams 1974. His regional titles include Summer NAC secondary Leventritt Pairs 1971, Fall Open Pairs 1974, Central States KO Teams 1971, Open Pairs 1972, 1973, All-American KO Teams 1974, Motor City KO Teams 1973, Las Vegas Open Pairs 1974, District 5 Open Pairs 1975, Southeastern Swiss Teams 1976.

PERLMAN, Linda M. (formerly Deaton) (b. 1945) of Southfield MI, land developer consultant, won Southeastern Women's Swiss Teams 1972, 1981, Motor City Women's Swiss Teams 1979, 1980, Open Pairs Flt. A 1980, Central States I Women's Pairs

1975, District 5 Women's Pairs, Open Pairs 1975, Midwest Spring Women's Swiss Teams 1981.

PERLMUTTER, Mark J. (b. 1960) of La Jolla CA, university student, won Spring NAC secondary BAM Teams Flt. A 1981, Mid-South Holiday Swiss Teams 1979, Toast of Tulsa Master Pairs 1981, Mid-Winter Holiday Swiss Teams 1981.

PERLSTEIN, Lila E. (b. 1925) of Roslyn Heights NY placed second in Spring NAC Women's Teams 1976 and won Spring NAC secondary Amateur Swiss Teams 2nd Flt. 1976, Keystone Women's Swiss Teams 1974, District 3 Women's Swiss Teams 1979, New York Winter Women's Pairs 1981, District 4 Women's Swiss Teams 1981, Autumn Leaf Women's Swiss Teams 1981.

PERRON, Michel (b. 1951) of Paris, France, one of the outstanding players of France, won the World Team Olympiad 1980. He also represented France in the Junior European Championships 1971, European Championships 1979, 1981.

PERROUX, Carl Alberto (1905–1977) of Modena, Italy, a trial lawyer, was one of the leading personalities of world bridge. He was npc of the winning Italian team in Bermuda Bowl 1957, 1958, 1959, 1961, 1962, 1963, 1965, 1966; European Championship 1951, 1956, 1957, 1958, 1959. A former president of the ITALIAN BRIDGE FEDERATION, Perroux was technical advisor to the Italian National Team. He authored *The Blue Team — Our Story of Bridge*.

PERTIERRA, Jose Luis M. (b. 1941) of Manilla, Philippines, senior supervisor, represented the Philippines in the Far East Championships 1974, 1975, ASEAN Championships 1980, 1981. His national titles include Open Pairs 1978, 1979, 1980, Open Teams 1971, 1972, 1975, 1979, 1981, KO Teams 1972, 1975, Tuason Cup 1972, 1973, 1974, Marlboro Cup 1979, Intercommercial Teams 1981. He is a former secretary and member of PCBL Board of Directors.

PERUTZ, Sidney (b. 1933) of Dallas won Mid-South Summer Women's Pairs 1966, Texas Fall Mixed Pairs 1968, Capital City Mixed Pairs 1969, King Cotton Swiss Teams 1969.

PESTANER, James F. (Jim) (b. 1923) of Potomac MD, radiation chemist, won Spring NAC Men's Pairs 1959, Bridge Week Open Pairs 1960, Inter-Mountain Men's Pairs 1965.

PETERS, Aubrey G. (b. 1917) of Gweru, Zimbabwe, electrical engineer, won Zimbabwe Open Teams 1969, Open Pairs 1969, 1976, Master Pairs 1975, Mashonaland Open Teams 1975, 1977, Open Teams 1975, Midlands Open Teams 1976. Peters was chairman of the sub-committee of the CENTRAL AFRICAN BRIDGE ASSOCIATION which formed the ZIMBABWE (initally Rhodesia) BRIDGE UNION in 1967. He was chairman of the ZBU 1968, 1969, 1976.

PETERS, Herbert G. (b. 1930) of Bristol TN, attorney, won Mid-Atlantic Open Teams 1968, 1971, 1972, Open Pairs Flt. A 1980, Blue Grass Master Pairs 1975.

PETERS, Thomas J. (Tom) (b. 1943) of Houston, geophysicist, placed second in Spring NAC Open Pairs 1978, Fall NAC Swiss Teams 1978. He won Midwest Men's Pairs 1968, 1970, South Texas Swiss Teams 1974, Corpus Christi Swiss Teams 1978, District 16 GNT 1978.

PETERSEN, Vibeke (b. 1924) of Copenhagen, Denmark, bridge teacher, was European Women's Teams champion 1955, 1957 and also represented Denmark in the World Women's Teams 1964. Her national titles include Women's Teams 1950, 1955, Open Teams 1958, 1959, Open Pairs 1962, Mixed Pairs 1958, 1960, 1961.

PETERSON, Harrison V. (b. 1914) of Los Angeles, credit union manager/treasurer, won Pacific Southwest Men's Pairs 1960, Open Teams 1966, Disneyland Open Teams 1970. He is a co-founder of ALACBU. He was the first chairman of ALACBU Ethics Committee and set up a question and answer column in the *Southern California Bridge News*. He was president of the Los Angeles Unit 1959, 1960, 1961, 1972, 1973.

PETERSON, Linda M. (formerly Borbely) (b. 1952) of Berkeley CA, professional bridge player, won Summer NAC Master Mixed Teams 1981. Her regional titles include Fall NAC Silver Trophy Pairs Flt. B 1978, Pacific Southwest Women's Pairs 1975, District 17 Fall Women's Pairs 1976, Golden Gate Women's Pairs 1976, Navajo Trail KO Teams 1977, All-Western Mixed Pairs 1979, Mount Shasta Swiss Teams 1981.

PETERSON, Muriel (b. 1919) of Griffith IN, real estate broker, placed second in Spring NAC Women's Teams 1973 and won District 8 GNT 1977, GNP 1981.

PETERSON, Olive A. (1894–1965) of St. Davids PA, was a great player and teacher whose career spanned from auction to contract bridge. She was closely associated with MILTON C. WORK with whom she won many auction and contract championships. Subsequently she was associated with CHARLES GOREN. Her National Auction Bridge titles include the Women's Pairs 1931 and Women's Team 1932. In contract she won the NAC Women's Team title twice, the Women's Pairs three times, the Mixed Team four times, including three successive victories 1942, 1943, 1944. Her writings include *Work-Peterson Accurate Valuation System*, *101 Celebrated Hands*, *Simplified Digest of Culbertson System*, and *Common-Sense Contract*. See BIBLIOGRAPHY, C, H.

PETTERSON, Kelsey (b. 1911) of Las Vegas, retired attorney, represented North America in the Bermuda Bowl 1965. He won Spring NAC Men's

Teams 1962 and placed second in the Vanderbilt 1964. His numerous regional titles include Bridge Week Mixed Teams 1967, Open Pairs 1961, 1962, Master Pairs 1973, All-Western Open Teams 1959, District 5 Open Teams 1965, Pacific Southwest Open Teams, Open Pairs 1966, Men's Pairs 1973. He was a member of the ACBL Board of Directors 1967–1970 and is a former president and attorney of the WESTERN CONFERENCE. Petterson was npc of the Los Angeles team in *Sports Illustrated* Trophy matches.

PETTIJOHN, Fran of Indianapolis IN placed second in Fall NAC Women's Teams 1966 and won Midwest Fall Open Teams 1960, Women's Pairs 1960, 1978, Women's Swiss Teams 1978, Champagne Women's Pairs 1979, Florida Swiss Teams 1981, District 11 Women's Pairs 1976, Master Pairs 1980.

PETTIS, William C. (Bill) (b. 1948) of Washington DC won Mid-Atlantic KO Teams 1973, 1974, 1977, 1978, Open Teams 1973, 1974, 1976, Open Pairs Flt. A 1977, 4th of July Men's Swiss Teams 1980.

PETTIT, Randall S. (Randy) (b. 1943) of Atlanta, insurance company assistant manager, won Celebrity Men's Swiss Teams 1977, Mid-Atlantic Swiss Teams 1978, Men's Pairs 1979, Opryland Men's Swiss Teams 1981.

PEYSER, Kenneth (b. 1937) of Chicago won District 15 KO Teams 1974, 1975, District 5 Swiss Teams 1973.

PHILIPPAS, Michael (b. 1938) of Montreal, born in Greece, college professor, won Oregon Trail KO Teams 1971, Men's Pairs 1970, District 1 GNT 1976.

PHILLEY, Mary. See WILLIAMS, MARY.

PHILLIPS, Duncan R. (b. 1930) of Toronto, lawyer, represented Canada in the World Team Olympiad 1972, World Open Pairs 1962, 1966. He won Summer NAC secondary Leventritt Pairs 1970, Canadian Nat'l KO Teams 1972, Open Teams 1958. Phillips was founder and first president of the Metropolitan Toronto BA.

PHILLIPS, Hubert (1891–1964) of London, England was editor of *British Bridge World* 1936–1939, and one of the pioneers of bridge organization in England. For many years he was internationally the most eminent author of intellectual and mathematical puzzles under the names "Caliban" and "Dogberry," and of cryptic crosswords. He authored some 70 books on various subjects including general knowledge quiz books and dectective stories, and was the resident expert on Britain's most famous radio quiz program. Essayist and leader-writer for the London *News Chronicle*, Phillips' many bridge writings included *Brush Up Your Bridge*, *The Elements of Contract*, *Bridge at Ruff's Club*, and *Bridge with Goren*. See BIBLIOGRAPHY, E, H, L.

PHILLIPS, Joyce (Mrs. Duncan) of Toronto represented Canada in the World Women's Teams 1964, World Mixed Pairs 1966. She won Canadian Nat'l Mixed Pairs 1971, Canadian Swiss Teams 1971.

PHILLIPS, L. James (b. 1935) of Chicago, buyer, won Fall NAC secondary Open Pairs 1966, Spring Swiss Teams 1972, Motor City Open Teams 1971, Pheasant Swiss Teams 1972, Central States I Master Pairs 1973, Life Master KO Teams 1978, BAM Teams Flt. A 1981, Tri-Unit Men's Pairs 1974, Wisconsin Open Pairs Flt. A 1980. Phillips is a former president of the Chicago CBC.

PHILLIPS, Martin (b. 1916) of Chattanooga TN, company president, won Southern Conference Open Pairs 1959, North American Rubber Bridge Championship 1963.

PHILLIPS, Nancy C. (b. 1928) of Tulsa OK, won District 15 BAM Teams 1969, Big D IMP Pairs 1976, Missouri Valley Women's Pairs 1976.

PIASKI, E. John (b. 1945) of Raleigh NC, accountant, won Mid-Atlantic Summer KO Teams 1973, Men's Swiss Teams, Open Pairs Flt. A 1979, Swiss Teams 1975, Fall KO Teams 1973, Swiss Teams 1973, 1975, Spring KO Teams 1975.

PICKETT, James R. (Randy) (b. 1946) of Tigard OR, attorney, won Oregon Trail Master Swiss Teams 1979, Swiss Teams 1980, Swiss Teams Flt. A 1981, 1982, KO Teams 1982, District 20 GNT 1977, 1979, GNP 1981.

PICUS, Susan J. (Sue) (formerly Andersen) (b. 1948) of Wheaton IL, computer scientist, won Summer NAC Master Mixed Teams 1971, Spring NAC Women's Teams 1972. Her regional titles inlcude Spring NAC secondary Women's Swiss Teams 1973, Summer Mixed Pairs Flt. A 1980, Keystone Open Pairs 1973, Roughrider KO Teams 1975, Gopher Swiss Teams 1976, District 15 Swiss Teams 1975, Mad City Women's Swiss Teams 1979, Puerto Rico Swiss Teams 1978.

PIETRI, Luis (b. 1931) of Philadelphia, insurance salesman, one of the top-ranking players in the AMERICAN BRIDGE ASSOCIATION, won ABA Open Teams 1968, 1970, 1972, 1978, Open Pairs 1963, 1966, 1968, 1972, 1973 and all other major titles at least once. ACBL regional wins include Keystone Men's Swiss Teams 1971 (twice), 1972 (twice), Puerto Rico Open Teams, Open Pairs, Men's Pairs 1971, Rochester Men's Swiss Teams 1980, District 4 GNT 1974, 1976.

PIETRI, Morella of Caracas, Venezuela, business executive, represented Central American–Caribbean in the Venice Trophy Teams 1981, World Women's Teams 1980. She won CAC Women's Teams 1980, 1981. She has won several national titles.

PIGOT, David R. (1900–1965) of Dublin, Ireland, solicitor, was CBAI champion between 1936 and

1949, and represented Ireland in international events both as player and npc. He served as president CBAI 1946, vice president 1955–1965; member of WBF Executive Committee; member of EBL Executive Committee 1952–1965 and chairman of EBL Tournament Committee 1957–1965. He contributed to the revision of the IMP scale and to the preparation of 1964 Olympiad regulations. He was a member of the Editorial Advisory Board, *Bridge Encyclopedia*.

PIGOT, Peter (b. 1932) of Dublin, Ireland, economist, represented Ireland in the World Open Pairs 1962, 1966, European Championships 1965, 1967, 1969, 1970, 1971, 1973, 1974, 1975. His national wins include all major championships. He is bridge columnist for the *Irish Independent* and contributor to *Irish Bridge Journal*.

PILTCH, Howard J. (b. 1948) of Brookline MA, real estate broker, placed second in Spring NAC Men's Teams 1976 and won Tri-State Swiss Teams 1975, Mid-Atlantic Swiss Teams 1976.

PINTO, Rui (b. 1941) of Oporto, Portugal, represented Portugal in the European Championships 1969, 1970, 1971. His national wins include Open Teams.

PIRO, Evelyn of Federal Way WA, apartment house owner and manager, was one of the pioneers of bridge organization in the Northwest. She is responsible for the foundation of several tournaments including the PACIFIC NORTHWEST and various units and clubs. She was chairman of the Seattle Unit 1949, 1950, Portland Unit 1950, 1951, co-chairman ACBL Goodwill Committee 1962, ACBL Director 1958–1961, 1964.

PISK, George M. (b. 1932) of Austin TX, born in Vienna, Austria, former English professor, won more than 20 regional titles including Fall NAC secondary Men's Teams 1964, 1977, Master Pairs 1974, Texas KO Teams 1970, Labor Day Mixed Pairs, Master Swiss Teams 1979, Capital City KO Teams 1972, Mexican Nat'l Non-Mixed Pairs 1979, Acapulco Fiesta Swiss Teams 1980, Mount Shasta Swiss Teams, Men's Pairs 1981, Toast of Tulsa Men's Swiss Teams 1981. Pisk is co-founder and co-owner of Bridge Studio of Austin.

PITTALA, Vito (b. 1927) of Turin, Italy, professor of mechanical engineering, WBF Grand Master, was Bermuda Bowl champion 1973, 1975, European champion 1979, and runner-up in the Bermuda Bowl 1976, 1979. His national successes include Open Teams 1971, 1972, 1974, 1975, 1976, 1977.

PLATE, August (Gus) of Houston won Texas Mid-Winter KO Teams 1973, Open Teams 1971, Texas Fall Swiss Teams 1971.

PLAUT, John R. (b. 1945) of Santiago, Chile, systems engineer, represented Chile in the World Team Olympiad 1972, South American Championships 1979, 1980. His national titles include Golden Cup five times, and three open championships.

Plaut made a Spanish translation of the ROMAN SYSTEM.

POE, Edgar Allan (1809–1849), American poet and critic, wrote a number of stories of mystery and occultism. He was interested in detection, cryptology, and whist. In his famous detective story, *The Purloined Letter*, he embodied a fine analysis of the mental aspects of whist in the plot. He also discussed whist at some length in *The Murders in the Rue Morgue*.

POLAK, Ebi J. (b. 1912) of Antwerp, Belgium, diamond dealer and bridge columnist, represented Belgium in the World Team Olympiad 1964, 1968, 1972, and in many European Championships. His national titles include Open Teams eight times, Mixed Teams twice, Open Pairs three times and Master Individual five times. He is the first Life Master and top masterpoint–holder in Belgium. Polak is a former editor of the Belgian magazine *Bridge*.

POLAK, Gunther (b. 1933) of Chicago, insurance investigator, placed second in the Blue Ribbon Pairs 1964, and won Summer NAC Golder Pairs 1961, Central States Life and Senior Master Teams 1961, 1978, Mixed Pairs 1965, 1969, Master Pairs 1973, 1974, Men's Pairs 1969, 1971, KO Teams, Open Pairs 1967, BAM Teams Flt. A 1981.

POLÁK, Milos (b. 1932) of Waterloo ON, born in Prague, Czechoslovakia, accountant, bridge club manager and teacher, represented Czechoslovakia in several international contests. His national titles include Czechoslovakian Open Teams 1960, 1961, 1962, 1963, 1964, 1965, 1967, Open Pairs 1961, 1963, Mixed Pairs 1962. Polák was the co-founder of the CZECHOSLOVAK BRIDGE ASSOCIATION in 1961, its vice president and secretary general 1961–1968, and co-founder of the European Junior Championship 1968. He is the former editor of the Czechoslovak bridge magazine.

POLET, Guy (b. 1949) of Waterloo, Belgium, civil engineer, represented Belgium in the European Championships 1977, 1979, 1980, 1981, Common Market Championships 1975, 1977, 1981. His national titles include Belgian Open Pairs 1979, Open Teams 1980, 1981.

POLISNER, Jeffrey D. (Jeff) (b. 1939) of Walnut Creek CA, attorney, won several regional titles including Fall NAC secondary Open Pairs Flt. A 1981, Midwest Fall Open Teams 1963, District 5 Mixed Pairs 1964, Golden Gate Master Pairs 1973, All-Western KO Teams 1975, Midwinter Holiday Open Pairs 1978, Master Pairs 1981, Bridge Week Swiss Teams Flt. A 1980, California Capital Swiss Teams Flt. A 1981. Polisner was president of Unit 499 1980, 1981, vice president of District 21 1981, chairman of District 21 Judiciary and Conduct and Ethics Committee 1981. He was appointed to the NAC Appeals Committee 1979 and the ACBL Laws Commission 1982.

POLLACK, Rozanne (Mrs. William, formerly Marel) (b. 1948) of New York City, placed second in Spring NAC Women's Pairs 1981 and won Washington Bridge Week Swiss Teams 1977, District 3 Swiss Teams Flt. A 1980, Women's Swiss Teams 1979, District 4 Fall Open Pairs 1°79, Long Island Women's Pairs, Open Pairs 1979, Southeastern Swiss Teams 1981, Puerto Rico Open Pairs, Swiss Teams 1981, New England Summer KO Teams 1981.

POLLACK, William (b. 1951) of New York City, computer system designer, won more than 20 regional titles including Summer NAC secondary Men's Pairs 1974, Summer Swiss Teams 1979, New York Winter Swiss Teams 1975, 1980, Upper New York State KO Teams 1976, Washington Bridge Week Swiss Teams 1977, Tri-State Men's Swiss Teams 1979, Southeastern Open Pairs 1980, Swiss Teams 1981, New England Summer KO Teams 1981, Puerto Rico Men's Pairs 1980, Swiss Teams 1981, District 3 KO Teams 1979, Swiss Teams Flt. A 1980, GNT, Zone II 1978. He is a member of the NAC Appeals Committee and Board member of the Greater New York BA. Pollack was the youngest ACBL tournament director ever in 1967 at the age of 16. He is a graduate of Columbia University.

POLLENZ, Lynne J. (b. 1955) of Mountain View CA, senior decision analyst, won Upper New York State Swiss Teams 1975, Keystone Spring Master Pairs 1976, Bridge Week Women's Pairs 1980.

POLUNSKY, Harry (1895–1972) of San Angelo TX was a food merchant who owned one of the largest private collections of books on playing cards and games played with them. He was a contributor to various magazines and a contributing editor, *Bridge Encyclopedia.*

PONTIOUS, Frances (Bitsy) of Beaumont TX, former medical secretary, won Fall NAC Mixed Pairs 1962, Texas Master Pairs 1957, Open Pairs 1961. She was the first president of Unit 201 in 1957 and its executive secretary 1966–1980.

POOL, W. Gerald (b. 1908) of Honolulu, bank comptroller, won Hawaii Master Pairs, Mixed Pairs 1961, Men's Swiss Teams 1975. He is a former chairman of Honolulu and Spokane Units.

POPE, Benjamin A. III (Ben) (b. 1946) of Virginia Beach VA, controller, won Mid-Atlantic Spring Open Pairs 1971, KO Teams 1973, Summer KO Teams, Men's Swiss Teams 1980.

POPPER, Leslie A. (b. 1937) of Peabody MA, born in Budapest, Hungary, computer scientist, won New England KO Teams 1965, 1969, Master Pairs 1974, Master Swiss Teams 1977, Keystone Open Teams 1966, Fall Men's Pairs 1969, Mid-Atlantic Spring Open Pairs 1967, Canadian Nat'l Master Pairs 1969, Fun City KO Teams 1972, Keohane KO Teams 1978, 1979. Popper is past president of District 25 and Eastern Massachusetts BA.

PORTUGAL, Helen (Mrs. Morris) of Los Angeles, one of the leading American woman players, placed second in the World Women's Teams 1964 and also represented the United States in the World Women's Teams 1960, World Women's Pairs 1962. She won Life Master Pairs 1960, Fall NAC Life Master Women's Pairs 1961, Mixed Pairs 1951, 1953, Summer NAC Master Mixed Teams 1962, Spring NAC Women's Teams 1969, and placed second in the Vanderbilt 1964, Spring NAC Women's Teams 1959, 1963, 1964, Spring NAC Women's Pairs 1961. She has won numerous regional titles. See also LIFE MASTER.

PORTUGAL, Morris (b. 1916) of Los Angeles, bridge teacher, one of the leading players of the West Coast, won Life Master Pairs 1960, Fall NAC Mixed Pairs 1953 (second in 1965), and placed second in the Vanderbilt 1964. His numerous regional titles include All-Western Open teams 1958, Bridge Week KO Teams 1956, 1961, Master Teams 1951, Open Teams 1947, 1960, 1961, Master Pairs 1957, Open Pairs 1946, Mixed Pairs 1951, 1953, Oregon Trail Mixed Pairs 1966, Open Teams 1973, 1978, Golden Gate KO Teams 1971, Los Angeles Winter Open Pairs Flt. A 1980. See also LIFE MASTER.

POTTER, Maj. John R. (b. 1936) of Millersville MD, USAF officer, school teacher, won Spring NAC secondary Swiss Teams 1971, 1972, Music City Open Teams 1973, King Cotton KO Teams 1975, District 15 Men's Pairs 1976, Mid-Atlantic Swiss Teams 1979, District 17 GNT, Zone VI 1978.

POTTS, Virginia P. (Ginna) (b. 1912) of Midland TX won North Texas Open Teams 1959, Women's Pairs 1961, District 15 Women's Pairs 1969.

POULDJIAN, Esmerian (b. 1901) of Paris, France, was European Women's Teams champion 1939, 1956, 1965 and placed second in World Women's Teams 1960. She has many international and national successes.

POULSEN, Elaine (b. 1929) of Brisbane, Australia, physiotherapist, was Far East Women's Teams champion 1974. Her national wins include Women's Interstate Teams 1973, Women's Pairs 1973.

POWELL, Richard P. (Dick) (b. 1908) of Fort Myers FL, novelist, is the author of *Tickets to the Devil,* a bridge novel published in 1968; foreign editions have been published in England, Scandinavia, Germany and Italy. Powell, a certified director from 1970, is manager of the Coconut DBC of which he is past president. A writer since 1930, he is the author of 19 published novels, four of which have been made into movies: *The Philadelphian,* filmed as *The Young Philadelphians; Pioneer, Go Home!,* filmed as *Follow That Dream; Don Quixote, U.S.A.,* filmed as *Bananas;* and *The Build-Up Boys* (published under the pen name Jeremy Kirk), filmed as *Madison Avenue.* See BIBLIOGRAPHY I.

PRAHL, Patricia A. (Patty) (b. 1916) of Seattle

won Spring NAC secondary Swiss Teams 1975, Oregon Trail Women's Pairs 1973, 1976, Indian Summer Unmixed Swiss Teams 1977, Gem State Women's Pairs 1978, Peach City Women's Pairs 1982.

PRALL, Jack W. (b. 1914) of Toledo OH, retired postal clerk, one of the founders of District 12, is a former president and vice president of District 12 and of the Northern Ohio BA. He was District 12 representative to the ACBL Board of Directors 1963–1965.

PRATT, John M. (b. 1904) of Flint MI, scholar, retired teacher and General Motors executive, was named chairman of the ACBL Goodwill Committee 1979. He is a former president of Unit 200, Heart of America BC, and former vice president of Hartford BC. Pratt organized other bridge clubs and was chairman of sectional and regional tournaments. He taught bridge to more than 2000 individuals in the Flint area. In 1973 he did a series of 10 contract bridge lessons on TV.

PRESSBURGER, John (b. 1913) of Munich, Germany, British national born in Czechoslovakia, represented Prague in matches against London and Leeds 1946, 1947, represented Germany in the World Team Olympiad 1968, World Open Pairs 1966, 1970, European Championships 1971, 1974. His national successes include Czech Open Teams 1938 and 15 German titles. He is a contributor to *Deutsches Bridge Verbands-Blatt* and is bridge columnist of *Suddeutscher Zeitung*. Pressburger was instrumental in the development of the WEISSBERGER CONVENTION.

PRESTON, Richard (b. 1907) of London, England, certified accountant, represented England on many occasions in CAMROSE TROPHY matches and in the 1962 World Open Pairs. His national titles include the GOLD CUP 1955, Crockford's Cup twice, Life Master Pairs four times.

PRICE, Steven T. (b. 1951) of Napa CA, controller, former USAF officer, won All-Western KO Teams, Master Teams 1977, Mid-Winter Holiday KO Teams 1977, Open Pairs Flt. A 1980, District 21 GNT 1980, GNP 1982.

PRIDAY, Angela Jane (Jane) (Mrs. Richard A., formerly Mrs. Pedro Juan) (b. 1936) of London, England, one of the leading women players in the world, won the World Women's Pairs 1966, World Women's Teams 1964, European Women's Teams 1961, 1963, 1966, and also represented Great Britain in the European Women's Championships 1962, 1965, 1969, 1971, World Women's Pairs 1970. She won CAMROSE TROPHY matches vs Scotland twice, GOLD CUP 1972, Crockford's Cup 1981, Whitlaw Cup 1966, 1968, English Mixed Teams 1970, EBU Two Stars Pairs 1968, Spring Foursomes 1976, and was runner-up in partnership with JOAN DURRAN in the Life Master Pairs 1966, the highest position ever gained by a women's pair in that event.

PRIDAY, Richard Anthony (Tony) (b. 1922) of London, England, chairman of hardwood importer/merchant firm, one of the leading British players, was European champion 1961. He also represented Great Britain in the Bermuda Bowl 1962, World Team Olympiad 1972, 1976, 1980, European Championships 1966, 1971, 1973, 1974, 1975, 1977, 1979, in 28 CAMROSE TROPHY matches, and was npc of the British Women's Team in the World Women's Teams 1960. He won the GOLD CUP 1964, 1967, 1968, 1970, 1972, 1974, 1976, Crockford's Cup 1981, English Mixed Teams 1961, 1964, 1970, Sunday Times Trophy 1970, EBU Two Stars Pairs 1968, Spring Foursomes 1967, 1977. Priday has held various executive positions in the BRITISH BRIDGE LEAGUE and ENGLISH BRIDGE UNION from 1966. He is bridge columnist for London *Sunday Telegraph* from 1961, and a contributing editor, *Bridge Encyclopedia*. See also BUENOS AIRES AFFAIR.

PRIEST, David A. (b. 1940) of North Hollywood CA, professional bridge player, won several regional titles including Las Vegas KO Teams 1971, Master Swiss Teams 1978, Golden State KO Teams 1973, Pacific Southwest Open Pairs Flt. A 1977, Men's Pairs 1975, Mid-Winter Holiday KO Teams 1973, Palm Springs Open Pairs 1975.

PRIMMER, Terre (b. 1944) of Culver City CA, electrical engineer, won Las Vegas Master Pairs 1971, Open Pairs Flt. A 1978, Bridge Week Master Swiss Teams 1978.

PRISYON, Jerome B. (Jerry) (b. 1927) of Valley Stream NY, sales manager, is a leading bridge figure in the New York area as a bridge cruise lecturer, administrator, Board member, and former president of the Greater New York BA. He originated a novice program for the GNYBA, which included printed hand analyses. It was later adopted and expanded by the ACBL. Prisyon is a former regional tournament director.

PRITCHARD, J. Barry (b. 1942) of Edmonton AB, mathematics teacher, won Klondike Master Pairs 1978, Swiss Teams 1980, District 18 GNT, Zone VII 1976, 1978, 1979.

PROBST, Donald E. (b. 1942) of Endicott NY, programmer/accountant, won Summer NAC secondary Swiss Teams 1978, New England Men's Pairs 1974, KO Teams 1978, Keystone Spring Swiss Teams 1976, Tri-State Winter Men's Swiss Teams 1977, Presque Isle Swiss Teams 1977, Capital District Fall Swiss Teams 1977, New York Winter Open Pairs Flt. A 1978, District 4 KO Teams 1978, GNT, Zone III 1975.

PROMBOIN, Ronald L. (Ron) (b. 1945) of Chicago, economist, won All-Western Men's Swiss Teams 1973, Open Pairs Flt. A 1979, Hawaii Men's Pairs, Swiss Teams 1973, District 21 GNT 1974. He is a former contributor to Palo Alto *Kibitzer*.

PROMISLOW, Helen T. (Teeni) of Winnipeg MB,

city councillor, won Summer NAC secondary MAR-CUS CUP 1964, Canadian Open Pairs 1970, Buffalo Master Pairs 1972, Roughrider Open Pairs 1979.

PRONIEWICZ, Ferenc (b. 1919) of Budapest, Hungary, won Hungarian Open teams 1955, 1957, 1969, 1978 and was a member of the victorious Hungarian team against Czechoslovakia 1963, Germany 1964, Belgium 1964, Austria 1965. He was first in six-nations team contest 1976, 1980 and won the Danubius Cup 1980. He has been npc of Hungary's national team from 1976.

PROSNITZ, Eugene (Gene) (b. 1932) of Brooklyn NY, attorney, won Fall NAC secondary Men's Teams 1969, Silver Trophy Pairs 1979, Spring Swiss Teams 1979, Long Island Open Teams 1972, Men's Pairs 1974, New England Fall Open Pairs 1978, Nassau-Suffolk KO Teams 1980, District 3 Swiss Teams Flt. A 1980.

PROTHRO, James T. (Tommy) (b. 1920) of Lakewood OH, football coach, won Rocky Mountain KO Teams 1969, Mexican Nat'l Swiss Teams 1972, Golden Gate Men's Pairs 1972. Prothro is a graduate of Duke University. He was a blocking back for the Duke team and went on to coach football at Oregon State University, UCLA, and subsequently for the Los Angeles Rams and the San Diego Chargers. He retired as executive vice president of the Cleveland Browns in 1982.

PSAROUDAKIS, Nicolas (b. 1936) of Athens, Greece, lawyer, officially ranked #9 player in Greece, represented Greece in the World Team Olympiad 1976, European Championships 1969, 1971. His national titles include Team Trials 1969, 1971, 1972, 1976, Open Teams 1969, 1973, 1974, 1975, 1977, 1980, 1981, Open Pairs 1973, Interclub 1972. He is a graduate of Athens University.

PUTNAM, Roger (Wyatt) (b. 1942) of Redmond WA, associate national tournament director since 1977, began his directing career in 1967.

PUTTAERT, Louis (b. 1914) of Brussels, Belgium, bridge teacher, represented Belgium in the World Team Olympiad 1964, 1972, World Open Pairs 1962, European Championships 1962, 1963, 1965, 1967, 1973, 1974. He has won many national championships.

PYK, Einar (b. 1935) of Saltsjöbaden, Sweden, radiologist, represented Sweden in the World Team Olympiad 1976, 1980, World Open Pairs 1970, 1974, European Championships 1966, 1970, 1973. His national titles include Swedish Teams 1966, 1969, 1970, 1978, 1979, 1980.

Q

QUINLAN, Thomas J. (T.Q.) (b. 1942) of Richmond CA, tournament director, editor, won Gem State Men's Pairs 1972. ACBL associate national tournament director from 1981, he began his directing career in 1964. Quinlan is president of the PTDA and has served as District 21 Grand National Pairs and Teams Coordinator from 1974. Quinlan was editor of *Contract Bridge Forum* 1970–1981 and has been District 21 editor for the CBF from 1967.

QUINN, Anne of Dublin, Ireland, civil servant, has represented Ireland as a player and captain of the women's team from 1959. She won EEC Women's Pairs 1981. Her national titles include Women's Teams 11 times, Mixed Pairs, Women's Pairs, Open Pairs, Open Teams several times.

QUINN, Terry (b. 1945) of Washington, novelist, former editor and ghostwriter, authored *The Great Bridge Conspiracy*. See BIBLIOGRAPHY, I.

QUIOGUE, Alberto R. (Albert) (b. 1956) of Parañaque, Philippines, senior project analyst, represented the Philippines in the World Team Olympiad 1980, Far East Championships 1978, 1979, 1981, ASEAN Championships 1979, 1980, 1981. His national titles include Open Pairs, KO Teams 1981. A director since 1969, he was assistant tournament director at Far East Women's Championships 1977, ASEAN Championships 1980.

QUIOQUE, Thomas Jr. (b. 1954) of Philippines, export manager/life insurance sales manager, represented the Philippines in the Far East Championships 1981, ASEAN Championships 1980.

R

RABINOWITZ, Marc A. (b. 1949) of Copley OH, para-actuary, won Spring NAC secondary Swiss Teams 1981, District 11 Swiss Teams 1977, All-American KO Teams 1981.

RADIN, Judi (Mrs. Michael, formerly Solodar, nee Friedenberg) (b. 1955) of New York City, bridge teacher and writer, one of the leading American women players, was World Women's Pairs champion 1978 and placed second in the Venice Trophy Teams 1981. She won Spring Women's KO Teams 1977, 1980, Women's BAM Teams 1971, Summer NAC Women's Pairs 1978, and placed second in Spring Women's KO Teams 1982, Reisinger 1974, Vanderbilt 1979. Her more than 100 regional titles include Spring NAC secondary Swiss Teams 1978, Summer Silver Trophy Pairs Flt. A 1979, Fall Swiss Teams Flt. A 1979. Radin is a contributing editor to the *Precision Newsletter* and the co-author of *Precision 1♣ Complete*. She is a graduate of Columbia University.

RADJEF, Terry L. (b. 1937) of Carrollton TX, born in Paris, France, auditor, former electrical engineer, won Mid-South Men's Pairs 1969, Open Pairs 1973, Swiss Teams 1978, Lone Star Mid-Winter Men's

Pairs 1977, Motor City Swiss Teams 1977, Harvest Festival KO Teams 1977, Texas Labor Day Master Pairs 1979.

RADWAN, Sadek (b. 1942) of Cairo, Egypt, company director, represented Egypt in the World Open Pairs 1978 and was npc of the Egyptian Team in the World Team Olympiad 1980. His national titles include Egyptian Open Teams 1976, 1978, Open Pairs 1974, 1976. Radwan is vice president of the EGYPTIAN BRIDGE FEDERATION.

RADWIN, Robert S. (b. 1950) of Culver City CA, professional bridge player, research and development technical consultant, won Fall NAC secondary Swiss Teams 1981, Pacific Southwest KO Teams, Master Pairs 1974, Swiss Teams 1979, California Capital Men's Pairs 1977, Mixed Pairs 1978, Mid-Winter Holiday Men's Pairs 1979, Master Pairs 1980. He is a Class A chess player.

RAENKHAM, Thawee (b. 1907) of Bangkok, Thailand, retired professor, represented Thailand in the Far East Championships six times between 1967–1979, Asian Championships 1981, 1982 and was npc of the Thailand Team that won the Far East Championships 1963, 1965. He is the officially ranked #3 player in Thailand. His national titles include all major events between 1951–1981. Raenkham was president of the CONTRACT BRIDGE LEAGUE OF THAILAND 1951–1966 and has been its honorary president since 1975. He is a graduate of John Hopkins University. Raenkham was Thailand's Deputy Minister of the Interior 1958–1967.

RAGAZZO, Vincent L (b. 1938) of Kent OH, retired computer analyst, won Canadian Nat'l Swiss Teams 1972, 1981, Can-Am Men's Pairs 1976, Midwest Spring Men's Pairs 1981.

RAGLAND, William H. Jr. (Bill) (b. 1943) of Boulder CO, company owner, won Navajo Trail Swiss Teams 1971, Oil City Master Swiss Teams 1978, Rocky Mountain Men's Pairs 1981, Swiss Teams 1982. Ragland is a former president of the Boulder Unit.

RAINWATER, Ross (b. 1948) of Beaverton OR, professional bridge player, won more than 35 regional titles including Fall NAC secondary Master Pairs 1978, Swiss Teams 1981, Oregon Trail KO Teams 1977, 1978, 1980, Open Pairs 1978, Big Sky Swiss Teams 1979, KO Teams 1981, Puget Sound Swiss Teams, KO Teams 1981.

RALPH, Mark P. (b. 1946) of Richmond CA, insurance salesman, won District 22 Master Pairs 1974, GNT 1973, 1979, Las Vegas Swiss Teams 1974, California Capital Swiss Teams Flt. A 1980, All-Western Master Pairs 1980.

RAMSEY, Guy (d. 1959) of London, England was a journalist and author. His writings include *Aces All* and many magazine articles. Bridge editor for London *Daily Telegraph*, Ramsey was the first president of European (now International) Bridge Press

Association (1958–1959). See BIBLIOGRAPHY, K.

RAND, Alfred (b. 1907) of New York City, investment manager, won Spring NAC Men's Teams 1982, Southeastern Swiss Teams 1972,New York Winter Swiss Teams Flt. A 1981, Fun City Men's Pairs 1975, Tri-State Men's Pairs 1980, District 4 Fall Men's Swiss Teams 1979, Men's Pairs 1978.

RAND, Nissan (b. 1930) of Tel Aviv, Israel, born in Kosice, Czechoslovakia, executive scientist, nutritionist, represented Israel in the European Championships 1965, 1966, 1967, was captain of the team 1966, 1967. His national titles include Israel Open Pairs 1965, Tel Aviv Open Pairs 1964, 1965, Open Teams 1964, 1967. He is bridge columnist for *Ha-Aretz*, a leading Israeli newspaper.

RAND, Rita L. (Mrs. Alfred) of New York City, investor, won Southeastern Swiss Teams 1972, New York Winter Swiss Teams 1981, Canadian Nat'l Women's Swiss Teams 1981, District 4 Fall Open Pairs Flt. A.

RANDALL, Winslow H. (1897–1983) of Redlands CA was ACBL president in 1959. An ACBL Director for many years, Randall was president of the WESTERN CONFERENCE in 1955.

RANK, Peter C. (b. 1938) of Los Angeles, attorney, formerly one of the leading players of the West Coast, won the McKENNEY TROPHY 1965, Spring NAC Men's Pairs 1966, Open Pairs 1977, Fall NAC Mixed Pairs 1968, and placed second in Summer NAC Master Mixed Teams 1969. He has won many regional titles including Bridge Week Open Teams 1965, Master Men's Pairs 1971, Open Pairs 1974, Golden Gate Mixed Pairs 1966, 1968, Open Pairs 1968, 1969, 1975, KO Teams 1969, 1970, Open Teams 1971, Pacific Southwest Master Pairs 1977, Raincross Men's Swiss Teams 1978. He is a former president of District 21 and was a commentator at NAC and international tournaments 1968–1980. Rank is the developer of bridge musicals as entertainment at North American Championships. He has written, scored and produced four productions based on Broadway musicals: *My Fair Little Old Lady*; *The Lesser Vice* (*Guys and Dolls*); *Partnership! Partnership!* (*Kiss Me Kate*); and *Annie Bid Your Slam*. Rank is a graduate of Stanford University and University of California School of Law at Berkeley.

RAPÉE, George (b. 1915) of New York City, attorney and real estate investor, WBF Grand Master, one of the great players of the world, was Bermuda Bowl champion 1950, 1951, 1953. He also represented North America in the Bermuda Bowl 1958, 1959, and the United States in the World Team Olympiad 1960. He won the Team Trials 1968, FISHBEIN TROPHY 1968. Rapée has the best record of success in the three major NAC team championships, winning 21 and finishing second in 18 during the years 1942 to 1980: Spingold 1944, 1948, 1950, 1952, 1957, 1968, Chicago (since 1965 the Reisinger) 1945,

1947, 1953, 1954, 1956, Reisinger 1970, 1971, Vanderbilt 1946, 1950, 1951, 1955, 1956, 1957, 1959, 1970; second in Spingold 1943, 1947, 1955, 1960, 1961, 1966, 1976, 1980, Chicago 1948, 1950, Reisinger 1968, 1969, 1972, Vanderbilt 1942, 1944, 1952, 1965, 1967. He also won Spring NAC Men's Teams 1975, Summer NAC Master Mixed Teams 1960, Fall NAC Men's Pairs 1950, Master Individual 1944, 1949, and placed second in Fall NAC Men's Teams 1946, 1948, Mixed Pairs 1955, Spring NAC Men's Teams 1972, Summer NAC Master Mixed Teams 1952, 1968. Rapée is the inventor of the STAYMAN convention, which shares with BLACKWOOD the distinction of being the most widely played convention throughout the world.

RAPPAPORT, Barbara. See HABERMAN, BARBARA.

RAPPLEYEA, Fred A. (b. 1918) of Houston, retired company executive, won All-American Open Teams 1954, 1957, Central States Open Teams 1956, Great Lakes Open Pairs 1959, Rocky Mountain Open Pairs 1965.

RASKIN, Raymond L. (b. 1943) of Gulph Mills PA, chemist, won Fall NAC secondary Swiss Teams 1980, Keystone KO Teams 1973, District 4 Men's Swiss Teams, Men's Pairs 1978, GNT 1973, 1979, Spring Men's Swiss Teams 1980, 1982, Fall Swiss Teams 1979, Men's Swiss Teams 1981. Raskin is president of District 4 and past president of the Philadelphia CBA.

RASMIDATTA, Vibul (b. 1928) of Bangkok, Thailand, banker, was Far East champion 1965. He also represented Thailand in the Far East Championships seven times between 1965–1975, Asian Bridge Championships 1982, World Team Oylmpiad 1972. His national titles include all major events between 1961–1981. He is a committee member of the CONTRACT BRIDGE LEAGUE OF THAILAND.

RAU, John (1908–1981) of Walnut Creek CA was one of the leading figures in the early days of contract bridge. In 1930 Rau and WILLIAM K. BARRETT caused a sensation at their first national tournament by extensive use of psychic bids and by winning the Open Team championship (now the Reisinger) as a pickup team with ELY CULBERTSON and W. James Carpenter. Rau won the National Open Pairs Championship in 1934 and was second in the Vanderbilt (twice) and the Spingold as well as other major victories in important Eastern tournaments. He was protege and special assistant to P. HAL SIMS in the early Thirties when the Sims mansion in Deal NJ was summer headquarters for all the principal bridge experts. When the category of Life Master was created by the American Bridge League in 1936, Rau was not included on the original list, having quit bridge to seek his fortune in the business world. Through the vagaries of the bridge league's bookkeeping system in those days, Rau's early exploits were never recognized with master points, so when he moved to California and resumed playing bridge, he started a second bridge career and became a Life Master in three years. He was almost surely the only new Life

Master in history to have finished first or second in such events as the National Open Pairs, the Reisinger, the Vanderbilt and the Spingold.

RAUTENBERG, Lee H. (b. 1951) of Commack NY, microcomputer systems programmer/designer, placed second in Fall NAC Mixed Pairs 1976. He won Fall NAC secondary Swiss Teams 1974, Keystone Fall Swiss Teams 1975, Canadian Nat'l Men's Swiss Teams 1976, District 4 Men's Swiss Teams 1976, Master Pairs 1977, Fall Open Pairs 1979.

REBNER, Stella (b. 1910) of Los Angeles, born in Vienna, Austria, formerly one of the leading American women players, placed second in the World Women's Teams 1964 and won the Women's Teams Trials 1963, Summer NAC Master Mixed Teams 1952, 1953, Fall NAC Women's Teams 1957, 1962, and placed second in Fall NAC Mixed Pairs 1959. Her numerous regional titles include All-Western Open Pairs 1958, 1959, Mixed Pairs 1958, Bridge Week KO Teams 1953, Open Pairs 1959, Women's Pairs 1948, Master Women's Pairs 1967, Mixed Teams 1966, Desert Empire Open Pairs 1958.

REED, Broma Lou (Mrs. Richard, formerly Harrison) (b. 1932) of Boulder CO, teacher, won Rocky Mountain Open Pairs 1961, Women's Pairs 1969, KO Teams 1975, Swiss Teams Flt. A 1981, Canadian Open Pairs 1969, Master Pairs 1977, Missouri Valley Swiss Teams 1974, Navajo Trail Open Pairs 1969, Desert Empire Swiss Teams 1980.

REED, Richard P. (Dick) (b. 1934) of Boulder CO, scientist, won more than 25 regional titles including Spring NAC secondary Men's Pairs 1973, Fall Men's Swiss Teams 1977, Missouri Valley Open Teams 1974, Open Pairs 1973, Canadian Open Pairs 1969, Navajo Trail Open Pairs 1969, Master Men's Pairs, Swiss Teams 1971, Master Pairs 1977, Pikes Peak KO Teams 1972, Open Pairs, Master Pairs 1976, Rocky Mountain Men's Pairs 1970, KO Teams 1975, Swiss Teams Flt. A 1981, Oil City Open Pairs Flt. A 1978.

REESE, Ann H. (b. 1938) of Smyrna GA, educator, former model, won Mid-Atlantic Women's Pairs, Swiss Teams 1978, Women's Swiss Teams 1979. Reese formerly hosted a bi-weekly TV show.

REESE, Terence (b. 1913) of London, England, formerly one of the world's greatest players and a preeminent bridge author and journalist, learned bridge at the age of six and played in tournaments at the age of 14. His numerous successes and infrequent failures in championships of every kind led him to be considered by many authorities the top-ranking player in the world. A WBF Grand Master, he was Bermuda Bowl champion 1955 and placed second in the World Team Olympiad 1960, World Open Pairs 1962. He was World Par champion 1961, European champion 1948, 1949, 1954, 1963 and also represented Great Britain in the World Team Olympiad 1964, Bermuda Bowl 1965, and European Championships on five other occasions. He has also won many British championships, including the GOLD CUP eight times and the Master Pairs seven times.

In the 1965 Bermuda Bowl, Reese and his partner BORIS SCHAPIRO were accused of conveying information about the heart suit through finger signals. Both were convicted by the WORLD BRIDGE FEDERATION, but were acquitted after a more exhaustive investigation by a special inquiry set up by the BRITISH BRIDGE LEAGUE. (See BUENOS AIRES AFFAIR). In his defense, Reese wrote *Story of an Accusation*.

Reese was one of the originators of the ACOL system in the Thirties, and of the LITTLE MAJOR. His many important contributions to the game include: the conduct of regular bridge radio programs; acting as Bridge-O-Rama commentator; bridge correspondent of the London *Observer* and *Evening News*, as well as other periodicals; editor of the British *Bridge World* 1955-1962. From 1955 he has been one of the most prolific authors of bridge books. His titles include: *Reese on Play*; *The Expert Game*; *The Bridge Player's Dictionary*; *The ACOL System Today*; *Play Bridge with Reese*; *Develop Your Bidding Judgment*; *Bridge for Tournament Players*; *Precision Bidding and Precision Play*; *Bridge at the Top*. He is the co-author of *The Complete Book of Bridge, Backgammon — The Modern Game*; *The Art of Defense in Bridge*; *Squeeze Play Made Easy* and many others in the Master Bridge Series. See BIBLIOGRAPHY, C, D, E, F, G.

REICH, Louis I. (b. 1949) of Potomac MD, computer programmer, placed second in Spring NAC BAM Teams 1976 and won Spring NAC secondary Swiss Teams 2nd Flt. 1976, Summer Swiss Teams 1978, Fall Open Pairs Flt. A 1976, New England Summer Open Teams 1973, 1975, Fall Open Teams 1973, Master Pairs Flt. A 1976, Individual KO Teams 1977, Knockout KO Teams 1977, Can-Am KO Teams 1974, Canadian Nat'l Swiss Teams 1974, KO Teams 1978, New York-New Jersey Swiss Teams 1974, Fun City KO Teams 1975.

REICH, Peggy (Mrs. Louis, formerly Lipsitz, Parker) (b. 1941) of Potomac MD, bridge teacher, won the World Mixed Teams 1974, Fall NAC Mixed Pairs 1969, 1976, and placed second in Summer NAC Master Mixed Teams 1973. Her regional titles include Mid-Atlantic Master Pairs, Mixed Pairs 1976, Summer Master Pairs, Open Pairs 1970, Swiss Teams 1973.

REICHMUTH, Eleanor A. of Billings MT, bridge teacher and club director, won Rocky Mountain Women's Pairs 1949, Inter-Mountain Mixed Pairs 1959. A pioneer of bridge in Montana, she began directing in 1934 and has been instrumental in starting many duplicate clubs. She received an ACBL Service Award for having directed a club continuously for 25 or more years (actually about 35).

REID, Thomas F. (Tom) (b. 1940) of St. Louis, computer scientist, won Republic of Texas Swiss Teams 1973, Southeastern Swiss Teams 1973, Mid-South Men's Pairs 1978, Wolverine Open Pairs Flt. A 1979, District 8 GNT, Zone V 1981.

REINHOLD, Arthur E. (Bud) (b. 1913) of Highland Park IL, furniture industry consultant, was Bermuda Bowl champion 1981. He won the Spingold 1973, Reisinger 1973, 1979, Vanderbilt 1980 and placed second in the Vanderbilt 1973, Grand National Teams 1978. His more than 25 regional wins include Summer NAC secondary BAM Teams 1976, Swiss Teams 1982, Champagne KO Teams, Swiss Teams 1974, Mid-Atlantic KO Teams 1974, 1978, 1979. Reinhold, a graduate University of Chicago Business School, is a former naval officer.

REISINGER, Curt H. (1891-1964) of New York City was a principal patron of contract bridge and the AMERICAN CONTRACT BRIDGE LEAGUE in the early years of both. Reisinger was a great-grandson of Anheuser and a grandson of Busch, the co-founders of the brewery from which he inherited the great wealth that enabled him to become a stalwart financial supporter of the game, as well as a noted philanthropist on a far larger scale. Among the positions in which he served were Director of the UNITED STATES BRIDGE ASSOCIATION, president of the Greater New York BA, and chairman of the ACBL. In 1953 Reisinger was ACBL Honorary Member. See REISINGER TROPHY.

REITH, George (1876-1939) of Yonkers NY, bridge expert and writer, was one of the leading American bridge personalities. Reith took up bridge in 1927 after he retired from the brokerage business. In 1929 he won the first Eastern States Pairs championship with OSWALD JACOBY. He won many titles including the CHICAGO TROPHY (now the Reisinger) 1932. Reith authored four books on bridge — *The Art of Successful Bidding*, *Contract*, *Accurate Contract*, and *Reith's One-Over-One*. He was at one time chief exponent of the one-over-one system of bidding. Reith was chairman of the Knickerbocker Whist Club Card Committee for 15 years, president of Crockford's Club, executive vice-president of the USBA and ACBL Board member. He created, and acted as chairman of, the Eastern States Championships, which for many years was one of the largest regionals in the United States. See BIBLIOGRAPHY, A, C.

REITMAN, Dr. Nelson R. (b. 1911) of New Milford NJ, dentist, won Eastern States Mixed Pairs 1958, Mixed Teams 1960, Men's Pairs 1961. He is a regional tournament director.

REMEY, Joan F. of Southfield MI, budget analyst, won Spring NAC Open Pairs 1971 and placed second in Summer NAC Master Mixed Teams 1971, 1975, 1980, Fall NAC Life Master Women's Pairs 1976, 1977, Women's Teams 1960, Spring NAC Women's Teams 1965. Her more than 30 regional titles include MARCUS CUP 1970, Spring NAC secondary Open Pairs Flt. A 1980, All-American Women's Pairs 1958, 1974, Open Teams 1959, 1973, Mixed Pairs 1959, Open Pairs 1976.

REMEY, Vincent O. of Southfield MI, retired company executive, won Spring NAC Open Pairs 1971 and placed second in Summer NAC Master Mixed Teams 1971, 1975, 1980, Life Master Pairs 1948,

Spring Open Pairs Flt. A 1980,. His numerous regional titles include MARCUS CUP 1970, Spring NAC secondary Open Pairs 1981, Fall Swiss Teams 1980, All-American Open Teams 1959, 1973, Mixed Teams 1959, Men's Pairs 1965, 1978, Mixed Pairs 1959, Wolverine Swiss Teams 1977, 1979, Men's Pairs 1980, Men's Swiss Teams 1977, Master Swiss Teams 1981. Remey has been a member of the ACBL Board of Directors from 1974. In 1981 he was elected to serve as the ACBL representative to the WORLD BRIDGE FEDERATION. He is editor of the Unit 137 publication, *Table Talk* and a contributor to *The Bridge World*.

RENNELS, Audrey (b. 1940) of Pleasanton CA, bridge teacher, computer programmer, won Summer NAC secondary Commercial and Industrial Teams 1972, All-Western Women's Pairs 1970, Mid-Winter Holiday Women's Swiss Teams 1974.

REQUARD, Daniel C. (b. 1945) of Naperville IL, fund raiser, won Mid-South Fall Open Pairs 1969, Midwest Spring Open Pairs 1970, Swiss Teams 1972, Tri-Unit Open Pairs 1972, Wisconsin Open Pairs, Open Pairs Flt. A 1978, Champagne KO Teams 1982, Central States I Swiss Teams 1982.

RETEK, George (b. 1936) of Montreal, born in Budapest, Hungary, chartered accountant, won Can-Am Swiss Teams 1976. A member of the ACBL Board representing District 1 since 1979, he is a member of several of its committees including Canadian Affairs. He is a former treasurer and tournament chairman of the Montreal BL. Retek is a graduate of Sir George Williams University.

REUSCHLEIN, Steven E. (b. 1947) of Middleton WI, accountant, won Mississippi Valley Swiss Teams 1975, Wisconsin Mixed Pairs 1976, Swiss Teams Flt. A 1978, Central States Swiss Teams 1982.

REVELL, A. Richard (b. 1913) of Prospect Heights IL, retired accountant, won Fall NAC Men's Pairs, Men's Teams 1950. His regional wins include Summer NAC secondary Golder Pairs 1949, 1955, All-American Open Teams 1948, Central States Open Teams 1949, Midwest Spring Open Teams 1959. He was Director of the Chicago CBA 1961–1965 and received its Sportsmanship Award.

REX-TAYLOR, David (b. 1947) of Hounslow, England, book publisher, editor and bridge organizer, is the editor of the INTERNATIONAL BRIDGE PRESS ASSOCIATION *Bulletin* and director of Bibliagora, book publishers. He founded the British Rubber Bridge Championship and the *Evening Standard* Congress.

REYES, José J. (1910–1980) of Pasay City, Philippines was an attorney, real estate broker, planter and bridge columnist. He was formerly president of the FAR EAST BRIDGE FEDERATION 1957–1963, and had played an important role in its formation in Manila in 1957. Reyes was Far East delegate to the WORLD BRIDGE FEDERATION EXECUTIVE COUNCIL and presi-

dent of PHILIPPINE CONTRACT BRIDGE LEAGUE 1956–1963. Reyes was Far East champion 1958 and captain of the Philippine team in the World Team Olympiad 1960. His national titles include Open Teams 1959, 1960, 1961, Open Pairs 1955, and Individual 1957.

REYES, Vicente (b. 1937) of San Bruno CA and Pasay City, Philippines, mechanical engineer and bridge columnist, was Far East Open Pairs champion 1974. He also represented the Philippines in the World Team Olympiad 1960, 1964, Far East Championships 1962–1967, 1970–1973, 1975. His national titles include Philippines Open Teams 1958, 1959, 1960, 1962, 1971, 1975, Open Pairs 1961, 1964, 1970, 1971, KO Teams 1971, 1974, Master Pairs 1964, 1974, 1975, Tuason Cup 1971, 1972, 1974, Intercommercial Teams 1976.

REYNOLDS, Robert (b. 1925) of Coral Gables FL, bridge teacher, represented the United States in the World Open Pairs 1962. He won Fall NAC Master Individual 1960 and placed second in the Vanderbilt 1960, Life Master Pairs 1961. His numerous regional titles include Florida KO Teams 1969, Men's Teams 1961, Men's Pairs 1959, Open Pairs 1964, Southeastern Men's Teams 1951, 1963, 1965, 1972, KO Teams 1968, Men's Pairs 1961, Open Teams 1951, 1959, Open Pairs 1960, Senior Citizens Swiss Teams 1982.

REYSA, Gloria (formerly Turner) (b. 1925) of Dallas, secretary, one of the leading Midwest women players, won Fall NAC Master Mixed Teams 1957, 1961 (second in 1953), and placed second in the Vanderbilt 1951. Her more than 20 regional wins include Central States Open Teams 1954, Open Pairs 1960, 1961, Big D Women's Teams 1974, Missouri Valley Open Pairs 1975, King Cotton Master Pairs 1975, Mexican Nat'l Mixed Pairs 1977.

RHATIGAN, Jack K. (b. 1931) of Cottage Grove MN, pharmacist, won Spring NAC Open Pairs 1973. His regional wins include Gopher Master Pairs 1977, Swiss Teams 1979, 1980, Iowa Men's Pairs 1977, Swiss Teams 1978, Buffalo Swiss Teams 1974, Pheasant Men's Pairs 1978.

RHODE, George L. (b. 1949) of Norcross GA, rehabilitation specialist, won Fall NAC secondary Swiss Teams 1979, Mid-South KO Teams 1979, Opryland Men's Swiss Teams 1981, Florida KO Teams 1981. He served as chairman of the District 8 college bridge program and Unit 179 bridge school. He is a feature writer for *Pips and Tips* and the District 10 *Bulletin*.

RHODES, Kathryn M. (Kay) (b. 1910) of Rohnert Park CA, formerly of New York City, an outstanding woman player with two unusual records — four consecutive wins in Spring NAC Women's Pairs 1955, 1956, 1957, 1958, and seven consecutive seconds in Fall NAC Women's Teams 1952–1958, won the Chicago (since 1965 the Reisinger), Spring NAC Women's Pairs 1949, and placed second in

Summer Master Mixed Teams 1942, Spring Women's Pairs 1944. Her numerous regional titles inlcude Mid-Atlantic Fall Women's Pairs 1952, Midwest Spring Open Pairs 1955, Eastern States Mixed Teams 1949.

RHODES, Lady Doris (1898–1982) of London, England, was European Women's champion 1951, 1952. She also represented Great Britain in the European Women's Championships on four other occasions and England in the SCHWAB CUP 1933, World Women's Teams 1960. Lady Rhodes was the "first and most accomplished partner for many years" of RIXI MARKUS. Together they won the prestigious Two Star event and toured the U.S. in 1953 as members of the British women's team.

RIBNER, Paula (formerly Bacher, Levin) (b. 1908) of New York City, for many years one of the leading women players of the East Coast, won the Chicago (since 1965 the Reisinger) 1947, Spring NAC Women's Teams 1951, Fall NAC Mixed Pairs 1946 and placed second in Spring NAC Women's Teams 1946, Fall NAC Open Pairs 1952, Mixed Pairs 1949, Summer NAC Women's Pairs 1944. Her numerous regional titles include Eastern States Mixed Teams 1943, 1947, Women's Pairs 1947, Southeastern Women's Pairs 1953, 1954, 1966, Mixed Pairs 1952, Women's Teams 1965, KO Teams 1968.

RICE, Robert M. (b. 1925) of Copenhagen, Denmark, managing director, represented Norway in the Nordic Championships 1962. He won Norwegian National Teams 1962, East Danish Open Teams 1959, ACBL MARCUS CUP 1954.

RICH, Pauline S. (Polly) of Chattanooga TN, company executive, won Inter-Mountain KO Teams 1977, Music City Swiss Teams 1977, Big Sky Swiss Teams Flt. A 1979, Mid-Atlantic KO Teams 1980, 1981, 1982, Open Pairs 1980, Mexican Nat'l KO Teams 1977, Gem State Swiss Teams 1981, Los Angeles Winter Swiss Teams Flt. A 1981.

RICHARDS, Ralph R. (1876–1943) of Detroit, founder and first president of the American Bridge League, was an accountant, bridge teacher, writer, lecturer and leading tournament player. Born in Chicago, Richards played bridge at the old Chicago Whist Club and won many honors at whist and auction bridge. He was an active member of the American Whist League and while attending the Congress at Hanover NH in the Summer of 1927, he proposed an organization to sponsor, promote and develop the game of bridge. The American Auction Bridge League (subsequently American Bridge League) was the first national organization devoted entirely to bridge. At its initial tournament at Chicago in December of 1927, Richards and teammates THEODORE A. LIGHTNER, WALDEMAR VON ZEDTWITZ and ELY CULBERTSON won the team-of-four championship. The second meeting of the League was held in Cleveland in 1928, at which time contract bridge was introduced for tournament play. In 1929 the tournament went back to Chicago and Richards and his partner, WILLIAM E. McKENNEY, tied for first in the Open Pairs. Richards authored *Championship Bridge*, and co-authored *Common Sense Contract*. See BIBLIOGRAPHY, C, G.

RICHARDSON, Larry (b. 1941) of Kansas City MO, systems engineer, won Fall NAC secondary Men's Pairs 1973, Missouri Valley KO Teams 1971, 1974, 1977, Springfield Swiss Teams 1980, District 15 KO Teams 1974, 1975, GNT 1974, 1979, Zone VI 1974.

RICHMOND, David G. (1906–1980) of Winnipeg MB, pharmacist, represented Canada in the World Open Pairs 1962. He was active in promoting bridge in Canada and in 1974 donated the Richmond Trophy, the Canadian equivalent of the McKENNEY TROPHY.

RIEGLE, Jim E. (b. 1950) of Ottawa ON, statistician, won Nat'l Capital Open Pairs 1975, Men's Swiss Teams 1980, Can-Am KO Teams 1978, 1980, Swiss Teams Flt. A 1980, District 1 GNP 1981, GNT Zone III 1981.

RIELY, Terry (b. 1943) of Houston, sales representative, won Texas Mid-Winter KO Teams, Master Pairs 1973, Big D Open Pairs 1974, Navajo Trail Open Pairs 1979, District 16 GNT 1978.

RIGMAIDEN, Roscoe N. (b. 1918) of Philadelphia, retired U.S. Postal superintendent, is first in the AMERICAN BRIDGE ASSOCIATION masterpoint rankings, and first winner of the William A. Friend award for most master points won in a year. He was the top-ranked ABA player 1969–1970, 1974–1977 and won the leading player award in the ABA Summer Nationals 1966 and 1968, Spring Nationals 1969. He has won all major ABA titles including Open Pairs six times and Open Teams four times. Rigmaiden in the founder and only president of a local ABA club, "The I.M.P.'s" from 1969. He is a former member of the ABA Executive Board, chairman of the National Ethics Committee, and contributor to the ABA *Bulletin*. Rigmaiden is a graduate of Prairie View College.

RIMINGTON, Derek C. of Beckenham, Kent, England, bridge journalist, author and editor, computer manager, was npc of the British Women's Team Common Market and Venice Trophy champions 1981. His numerous national titles include the GOLD CUP 1956, Crockford's Cup 1976, Hubert Philips Cup 1980, Madeira Mixed Pairs 1981, English Spring Foursomes twice, Life Master Pairs, Life Master Individual, Pachabo Cup, Tollemache Cup. Rimington is columnist for *The Field* magazine, syndicated columnist for *Jersey Evening Post*, *Western Morning News*, *Kentish Times*, *Country Gentleman's* magazine, and a regular contributor to *Bridge Magazine*, *International Popular Bridge Monthly*, *South African Bridge Magazine*, and *Tuttobridge*. He is the author of *Learn Bridge from the Experts*, and co-author of *Bridge Quiz from a New Angle*. Rimington was *Daily Bulletin* editor at the European Championships 1961, 1979, and the editor of several bridge books.

RIND, Michael D. (Mike) (b. 1944) of Glen Burnie MD, attorney, won Fall NAC secondary Swiss Teams 1980, Mid-Atlantic Men's Pairs 1973, Master Pairs 1981.

RIORDAN, Beverly (b. 1928) of Ypsilanti MI, chemistry and biology teacher, won Motor City Mixed Pairs 1971, 1973, All-American Women's Pairs 1974, Cambrian Shield Swiss Teams 1974. She was the first woman president of the Michigan BA and is a member of the ACBL Rules and Ethics Committee.

RIPSTRA, Joseph G. (Rip) (1900–1982) of Wichita KS, investor, mechanical contractor, was npc of the United States team in the Bermuda Bowl 1958. He placed second in the Chicago (since 1965 the Reisinger) 1955, Fall NAC Men's Pairs 1949 and won numerous regional titles. Ripstra helped develop the Kansas State BA and was active on the national scene for many years. A member of the ACBL Board of Directors 1945–1958, he was instrumental in increasing the number of members on the ACBL Board from 8 to 23 when the ACBL merged with the WESTERN CONFERENCE. Ripstra was president of the ACBL 1957. He is the inventor of the RIPSTRA convention.

RIVAS, Alvaro (b. 1921) of Bogotá, Colombia, lawyer, represented Colombia in the South American Championships 1963, 1966, 1968, Caribbean Championships 1965. His national titles include Open Teams 1963, Open Pairs 1965, 1966.

RIVAS, Bernardo (b. 1923) of Bogotá, Colombia, economist, represented Colombia in the South American Championships 1963, 1966, 1968. His national titles include Open Teams 1961, 1963, Master Pairs 1965.

RIVAS, Maria Christina de (b. 1927) of Bogotá, Colombia was South American Women's champion 1968, 1970. She also represented Colombia in the South American Championships 1963, South American Women's Championships 1964, 1965, 1966, 1967. Her national titles include Open Teams 1961, 1963, Master Pairs 1965.

RIVERS, Loretta R. (b. 1938) of Monroe LA, won Fall NAC secondary Women's Swiss Teams 1974, Mid-South Women's Pairs, Swiss Teams 1976, Bermuda Swiss Teams 1977. Rivers is a former president of Unit 211.

ROBAUDO, Maria Antonietta of Genoa, Italy was World Women's Teams champion 1972, 1976, European Women's Teams champion 1970, 1971, 1973, 1974.

ROBB, Paul H. (b. 1923) of Casselberry FL, bridge professional, won Fall NAC secondary Mixed Pairs 1975, District 4 Men's Swiss Teams 1981, Gateway to Space Swiss Teams Flt. A 1982.

ROBBINS, Glenn L. (b. 1949) of Miami, attorney, won Fall NAC secondary Swiss Teams 1980, Mid-Atlantic Swiss Teams 1979, Men's Swiss Teams 1978.

ROBBINS, Dr. Larry D. (b. 1954) of Chicago, physician, won the Grand National Teams 1979. His regional titles include Intercollegiate Championship 1976, Summer NAC secondary Open Pairs 1976, Great Lakes KO Teams 1976, Champagne Swiss Teams 1976, All-American Master Pairs 1976.

ROBERTS, Gregory D. (Greg) (b. 1943) of Roswell GA, regional insurance marketing director, won Mid-Atlantic Men's Pairs, Open Pairs 1970, Swiss Teams 1975.

ROBINSON, Arthur Guy (b. 1936) of Villanova PA, bridge teacher, one of the outstanding American players, placed second in the World Team Olympiad 1964, 1968, Bermuda Bowl 1963 and also represented the United States in the World Open Pairs 1962, 1966. He won the Team Trials 1967 (second in 1962), Vanderbilt 1961, 1968, Reisinger 1966, 1967, Spring NAC Open Pairs 1962, and placed second in the Vanderbilt 1965, Chicago (since 1965 the Reisinger) 1961, Fall NAC Master Individual 1960. He won numerous regional titles.

ROBINSON, Dr. Charles (b. 1922) of Fort Worth TX, gastroenterologist, won Missouri Valley Open Teams 1954, 1971, Republic of Texas KO Teams 1973, Texas Fall Open Pairs 1973, Big D Open Pairs 1976, Rocky Mountain Open Pairs Flt. A, Swiss Teams Flt. A 1977, Capital City Swiss Teams 1977, Harvest Festival Master Pairs 1977. Robinson has written and directed several skits presented at Fort Worth tournaments.

ROBINSON, Eric S. (b. 1956) of New Haven CT, university student, won the Grand National Pairs 1979, New England Summer Swiss Teams 1975, Long Island Swiss Teams 1977, Swiss Teams Flt. A 1981.

ROBINSON, Frances E. (b. 1908) of Philadelphia, former teacher, won Fall NAC Women's Teams 1947, 1949. Her regional wins include Spring NAC Individual 1958, Keystone Women's Pairs 1961, District 4 Women's Pairs 1960. In 1953 she was a member of one of the U.S. teams that played against the visiting British women's team (which included RIXI MARCUS and LADY DORIS RHODES). She is the mother of ARTHUR GUY ROBINSON.

ROBINSON, Maurice (b. 1918) of New York City, attorney and social worker, was president of the AMERICAN BRIDGE ASSOCIATION 1964–1969 and one of its national tournament directors.

ROBINSON, Stephen W. (b. 1941) of Arlington VA, supervisor computer specialist, one of the leading American players, won the World Mixed Teams 1974 and also represented the United States in the World Open Pairs 1974, 1978. He won the HERMAN TROPHY 1972, Reisinger 1972, Blue Ribbon Pairs 1973, 1975, Spring NAC Men's Pairs 1972, Men's Teams 1978, and placed second in the Spingold 1979, Fall NAC Life Master Men's Pairs 1971, 1972, Spring NAC Men's Teams 1973, 1974, Men's Pairs 1973, 1974, Summer NAC Master Mixed Teams 1973, Grand National Teams 1977. He is the winner of more than 40 regional titles which include Spring NAC secondaryMaster Pairs 1973, Swiss Teams 1978, Summer Mixed Swiss Teams 1975, Open Pairs Flt. A 1982. He is the co-inventor of the CRASH convention. Robinson served the Washington BL as a Board member 1972–1981 and as president 1979 and was District 6 representative to the Board of Governors 1975–1981. He is a graduate of University of Maryland.

ROBISON, James R. (b. 1942) of Los Angeles, professional bridge teacher and player, won Fall NAC Swiss Teams 1979 and placed second in Spring NAC Open Pairs 1980, Summer NAC Men's Swiss Teams 1982. He has won more than 20 regional events including Spring NAC secondary Open Pairs 1980, Bridge Week Men's Pairs 1974, Men's BAM Teams 1978, Unmixed Pairs 1979, Swiss Teams Flt. A 1981.

ROCCHI, Egisto (b. 1922) of Buenos Aires, Argentina, wholesale furrier, was South American champion 1959, 1961, 1964, 1976, 1979, 1980 and also represented Argentina in the Bermuda Bowl 1959, 1961, 1962, 1963, 1965, World Team Olympiad 1964, 1968, 1976. His national titles include Argentine Open Teams 1950, 1953, 1958, 1960, 1961, 1964, 1969, 1977, 1978, 1979, Open Pairs 1951, 1961, 1963, 1967, 1976, 1978, Mixed Teams 1956, 1963, 1968, 1969, Master Individual 1976, Interclubs 1958, 1959, 1962, 1966, 1967, 1969, 1970, 1971, 1973, 1974, 1975, 1977, GABARRET CUP 1963, 1969, 1971, 1978. Rocchi is a Director of the ARGENTINE BRIDGE ASSOCIATION.

ROCK, Lawrence J. (b. 1945) of University Heights OH, pension consultant, won District 5 Mixed Pairs 1977, GNP 1980, All-American KO Teams 1979. Rock is president of Unit 125 and a contributor to District 5 and Unit 125 bridge publications.

ROCKAWAY, Dr. Harold (Rocky) (b. 1926) of Houston, psychiatrist, won the HERMAN TROPHY 1964, Fall NAC Open Pairs, Men's Teams 1953, Chicago (since 1965 the Reisinger) 1964, and placed second in Fall NAC Men's Teams 1956, Life Master Men's Pairs 1964. His regional titles include Texas Fall KO Teams 1969, Open Teams, Open Pairs 1954, Labor Day Open Pairs A-D 1979, Lone Star Mid-Winter KO Teams 1977, Houston Mid-Winter KO Teams 1981.

RODRIGUE, Claude (b. 1930) of London, England, stockbroker, one of the leading British players, was World Par champion 1961, European champion 1961 and also represented Great Britain in the Bermuda Bowl 1962, World Team Olympiad 1972, 1976, 1980, World Open Pairs 1970, 1974, 1982, European Championships 1966, 1967, 1969, 1971, 1973, 1974, 1975, 1977, 1979, and Egypt in the European Championships 1956. He won the GOLD CUP 1957, 1964, 1974, Crockford's Cup, Richard Lederer Cup, CAMROSE TROPHY, Master Individual, Master Pairs, Mixed Pairs, London *Sunday Times* Pairs (since 1981 INVITATIONAL PAIRS CHAMPION-

SHIP). Rodrigue is the only player to compete in *all* London *Sunday Times* Pairs. His writings include contributions to *Bridge Magazine*, *British Bridge World* and other periodicals.

RODRIGUÉ, Maria Elena Cucullu de of Buenos Aires, Argentina was South American Women's champion 1957, 1961, 1962 and also represented Argentina in the World Women's Teams 1968, 1972. Her national titles include Open Teams 1976, Open Pairs 1970, Mixed Teams 1960, 1965–67, 1972–76, 1979, 1981, Master Pairs 1972, Master Individual 1967, Mixed Pairs 1968, 1969, 1971.

RODWELL, Eric V. (b. 1957) of West Lafayette IN, professional bridge player, one of the leading American players, was Bermuda Bowl champion 1981. He won the Reisinger 1979, Vanderbilt 1980, 1982, MOTT-SMITH TROPHY 1980, Fall NAC Life Master Men's Pairs 1979, Spring NAC Open Pairs 1979, Summer NAC Life Master Pairs 1980, and placed second in the Reisinger 1980, Spingold 1979. He has won close to 60 regional titles, more than 40 of which have been in partnership with JEFF MECK-STROTH; District 16 Swiss Teams Flt. A, Swiss Teams, Open Pairs Flt. A, Master Pairs 1981, White Hat Swiss Teams Flt. A, Swiss Teams, KO Teams, Open Pairs 1981, Mad City Open Pairs, Men's Swiss Teams, KO Teams 1979. He is an accomplished pianist.

ROET, Leo (b. 1903) of Hallandale FL, won Fall NAC Men's Teams 1949, Summer NAC Master Mixed Teams 1951, Life Master Pairs 1949 and placed second in Fall NAC Open Pairs 1945, 1950, 1952.

ROGASNER, Ruth W. (b. 1919) of Baltimore, tennis club assistant manager, won Mid-Atlantic Summer Women's Pairs 1962, District 4 Master Pairs 1966. She is the co-creator of the Unmixed Pairs event which was first implemented at Maryland BA games in 1967.

ROGERS, John R. (b. 1929) of Tucson AZ, regional-3 tournament director, won Rogue River Valley Open Pairs 1973, Golden State Men's Pairs 1975, Unmixed Swiss Teams 1976, Puget Sound KO Teams 1976, Pacific Southwest Men's Swiss Teams 1976, Los Angeles Winter Open Pairs 1980, District 17 GNP 1981. Rogers is a retired USAF Lt. Col.

ROGERS, Martha C. (Marty) (b. 1929) of Rancho Cordova CA, executive secretary, won Golden State Women's Pairs 1968, All-Western Women's Pairs 1969, Rogue River Valley Open Pairs 1973. She has served Unit 505 as president, secretary and Board member.

ROGERS, Rebecca (Becky) (Mrs. John R., nee Grantham, formerly Schmieder) (b. 1939) of Tucson AZ, ACBL national tournament director, former school teacher, won Navajo Trail Women's Pairs, Open Pairs 1973, Golden State Swiss Teams 1980, Los Angeles Winter Open Pairs 1980. An ACBL national tournament director since 1979, she is currently the only woman with this rating and the second woman ever to achieve this rating (see WEISBACH, DEAN). Rogers is an accomplished pianist.

ROGERS, Reece D. (b. 1951) of Memphis, financial planner, placed second in the Grand National Teams 1974. He won Mid-South Open Pairs 1976, Master Pairs 1979, KO Teams 1981, Headquarters KO Teams 1978, Opryland KO Teams 1981.

ROHAN, Karl (b. 1934) of Salzburg, Austria, managing director, represented Austria in the European Championships three times and in the World Team Olympiad 1980. His national titles include national Team championship 1978, 1979, 1980, Austria Open Pairs 1976, 1978. Rohan has served as vice president and president of the AUSTRIAN BRIDGE FEDERATION. He was awarded the Golden Medal of Honor for services to the Republic of Austria.

ROMANET, Dr. Bertrand (b. 1921) of Paris, France, physician and bridge writer, was Bermuda Bowl champion 1956, World Par champion 1963, European champion 1955. He won many international and national titles including French Open Teams 1950, 1951, 1954, 1962. Romanet served as president of the Bridge Club of Physicians, and as director of the FRENCH BRIDGE FEDERATION. He is the inventor of the Alpha System. His writings include *Le Squeeze au Bridge*, 1954, *Les Bases du Bridge Moderne*, 1957, *Bridge Total*, 1966, and *Bridge Gagnant*, 1968. He is a contributor to the *Bridge Encyclopedia* and many bridge periodicals. See BIBLIOGRAPHY, D, E.

RONCARELLI, Mimi (1908–1980) of Montreal was a bridge club owner and outstanding player. Her wins included Fall NAC Women's Team 1947, Can-Am Open Team 1960, Canadian Nat'l Open Teams 1963, New England Women's Pairs 1966. She represented Canada in the World Women's Teams 1964.

ROOSEN, Russell W. (b. 1908) of Southfield MI, bridge club manager, was one of Detroit's most prominent bridge figures in the early days of contract as a teacher, lecturer, instructor via radio, and problem composer. At exhibitions he demonstrated a remarkable memory by playing 10 separate hands simultaneously while blindfolded. Director of the Knickerbocker Bridge Club (Detroit) 1952–1967, he currently manages the Metro Bridge Club (Berkley MI). He authored *When to Play Bridge and How (1933)*, and was bridge columnist for the Detroit *Free Press*. Roosen has been a member of *The Bridge World* panel since 1956. His regional titles include All-American Open Teams 1955, Motor City Mixed Pairs 1969, KO Teams 1974, Swiss Teams 1979, District 12 GNT, Zone I, 1973. He won the Michigan BA "Player of the Year" award five times.

ROOT, William S. (Bill) (b. 1923) of Boca Raton FL and New York City, bridge teacher, lecturer and writer, one of the world's outstanding bridge teachers and players, placed second in the World Team Olympiad 1968 and also represented North America in the Bermuda Bowl 1967. He won the

Chicago (since 1965 the Reisinger) 1957, Spingold 1961, 1966, 1967, Vanderbilt 1968, Reisinger 1967, 1982, Summer NAC Men's Pairs 1953. He placed second in the Reisinger 1966, Spingold 1963, 1974, 1978, Spring NAC Men's Teams 1963. His numerous regional titles include Eastern States KO Teams (Reisinger) 1960, 1961, 1966, 1968. He served as national tournament director for the Intercollegiate Par-Hand Bridge Tournament 1959–1965. Also from 1959–1965 he represented the Association of American Playing Card Manufacturers as its authority on card games. Root has taught tens of thousands the game of bridge in the past 25 years, and organized many duplicate bridge clubs in the Greater New York area. Annually he conducts a bridge cruise with as many as 200 in his group. He is a contributing editor to the *Cromwell-Collier Encyclopedia* and the *Bridge Encyclopedia*. Root is the author of several books including *Introduction to Bidding, Contract Bridge Outlines, Standard Bidding*, and the co-author of *Modern Bridge Conventions*. See BIBLIOGRAPHY, C, D.

ROSA, Federico (1910–1972) of Milan, Italy, bridge writer and tournament director, was co-founder of the ITALIAN BRIDGE FEDERATION in 1936. He was organizer and director of national and international bridge events and served as its Secretary General. Director of *Bridge d'Italia*, editor of a bridge column, Rosa authored *L'A B C del Bridge*. He was also a contributing editor, *Bridge Encyclopedia*.

ROSE, Albert (1908–1970) of London, England, textile converter, was a leading European player. He was second in World Team Olympiad 1960 and also represented Great Britain in the Bermuda Bowl and World Pair Olympiad 1962, European Championships 1957. He was European champion 1961 and placed second 1953. His national titles include the GOLD CUP 1951, 1954, 1958, 1963.

ROSE, Irving N. (Ox) (b. 1938) of London, England, born in Glasgow, Scotland, insurance associate, former bridge club manager, one of the leading British players, represented Great Britain in the World Open Pairs 1974, World Team Olympiad 1976, Bermuda Bowl 1981, European Championships 1967, 1973, 1974, 1975, 1977, 1981. He won the CAMROSE TROPHY eight times, Crockford's Cup twice, Lederer Cup four times, Two Stars event twice, Spring Foursomes six times, and Master Pairs.

ROSE, Steven M. (b. 1949) of Mount Prospect IL, computer programmer, won Great Lakes Swiss Teams 1974, Mississippi Valley Swiss Teams 1974, Champagne Open Pairs 1977, District 8 Swiss Teams Flt. A 1981.

ROSEN, Edward L. (Eddie) (b. 1929) of Los Angeles, formerly of Chicago, controller, won Summer NAC Life Master Pairs 1959, Spring NAC Mixed Pairs 1960, 1962. His numerous regional titles include Central States Men's Pairs 1956, Open Teams 1958, Open Pairs 1965, 1969, KO Teams 1965, Life and Senior Master Teams 1960, Master Pairs 1954.

He served as Board member of the Chicago CBA 1960–1968.

ROSEN, Eunice M. (Mrs. William) (b. 1930) of Highland Park IL, freelance editor, won Summer NAC Master Mixed Teams 1958, 1966, and placed second in Spring NAC Women's Teams 1972. Her numerous regional titles include Central States Swiss Teams 1976, Life and Senior Master Teams 1959, Women's Pairs 1963, Women's KO Teams 1981, KO Teams 1967, 1977, Midwest Open Teams 1959, 1967, Open Pairs 1959, Great Lakes Master Pairs 1980, Wolverine Swiss Teams 1981, Champagne KO Teams 1981.

ROSEN, Norman B. (Norm) (b. 1928) of Narberth PA, salesman, won Summer NAC secondary Mixed Pairs Flt. A 1974, Keystone Swiss Teams 1973, District 4 Master Pairs 1979, Swiss Teams Flt. A 1981. An ABTA member since 1968, Rosen is a bridge teacher and director.

ROSEN, William A. (Billy) (b. 1928) of Highland Park IL, options trader, one of the outstanding American players of the postwar period, was Bermuda Bowl champion 1954 and placed second in 1955. He won the Bermuda Bowl at age 25, the youngest player ever to win that title until 1981 when the record was broken by BOBBY LEVIN. Rosen won the McKENNEY TROPHY 1953, Spingold 1953, 1954, Life Master Pairs 1953, Fall NAC Men's Pairs 1952, Spring Men's Teams 1980, Summer NAC Master Mixed Teams 1958, 1966 (second in 1965), Grand National Teams 1978. His numerous regional titles include Central States Open Teams 1962, Life and Senior Master Teams 1959, Master Pairs 1957, 1962, 1969, 1975, Open Pairs 1963, Men's Swiss Teams 1977, 1980, Life Master KO Teams 1979, BAM Teams 1981

ROSENBERG, Beverly of Sherman Oaks CA, won Spring NAC Women's Pairs 1982, placed second in 1977, 1980, and in the Women's Teams 1973. Her numerous regional titles include Spring NAC secondary Women's Swiss Teams 1982, Summer Master Women's Pairs 1972, Bridge Week Women's Swiss Teams, Mixed Pairs 1978, Women's Pairs, Master Women's Pairs Flt. A 1982, Los Angeles Winter Master Swiss Teams Flt. A 1978, Women's KO Teams 1979, Women's Master Pairs Flt. A 1980.

ROSENBERG, Michael (b. 1954) of New York City, formerly of Glasgow, Scotland, options trader, won the CAMROSE TROPHY 1974, 1976, 1977, three Junior Camrose Trophies, Junior European Championships 1978, London *Sunday Times* Pairs (since 1981 INVITATIONAL PAIRS CHAMPIONSHIP) 1976, and placed second in the Cavendish Invitational 1978. He also represented Great Britain in the Common Market Championships 1975 and is the youngest person ever to represent Scotland and Britain in the Camrose Trophy and European Championships, respectively. He won the GOLD CUP 1976, Scottish Rayne Trophy 1972, and placed second in the British Team Trials 1976, Scottish Teams Trials 1973. He placed second in the Spingold 1980, Grand National Teams 1981.

He represented Scotland in the World Student Chess Olympiad 1969, 1980, 1971, 1972.

ROSENBERG, Milton (b. 1944) of Evanston IL, precious metals broker, one of the leading players of the Middle West, won Spring NAC Men's Teams 1980, Grand National Teams 1978, and placed second in the Vanderbilt 1977. His more than 50 regional titles include Summer NAC secondary Swiss Teams 2nd Flt. 1975, Spring Swiss Teams 1977, Fall Silver Trophy Pairs 1977, Central States KO Teams 1969, 1972, 1973, Open Pairs 1973, Men's Swiss Teams 1977, 1978, 1980, Life Master KO Teams 1979, BAM Teams 1981.

ROSENBERG, Ronald (b. 1921) of Bronx NY, accountant and purchasing agent, won the Spingold 1956 and placed second in Fall NAC Men's Teams 1951. His regional wins include Eastern States Open Pairs 1965, Keystone Conference Open Pairs 1954, 1962, Men's Pairs 1952, 1953, 1954.

ROSENBLATT, Marvin (b. 1929) of Hartford CT, realtor, won numerous regional titles including Fall NAC secondary Swiss Teams 2nd Flt. 1975, Spring Swiss Teams 2nd Flt., Mixed Pairs 1976, New England Fall Master Teams 1958, 1969, 1969, Open Pairs 1963, 1967, Open Teams 1970, Men's Pairs 1971, Summer KO Teams 1977, Keystone Fall Swiss Teams 1973, Can-Am Men's Pairs 1976, Southeastern KO Teams 1980, Mid-Atlantic Swiss Teams Flt. A 1980.

ROSENBLOOM, Edith L. (b. 1903) of Miami Beach, former high school teacher, won Spring NAC Mixed Pairs 1951, New York–New Jersey Women's Pairs 1961, Keystone Women's Pairs 1957. She is a graduate of Temple University.

ROSENBLOOM, James (Jimmy) (b. 1954) of New York City, investment advisor, won Upper New York State KO Teams 1974, Open Teams, Men's Teams 1973, New England Open Pairs 1974, Mixed Pairs 1981, Metropolitan KO Teams 1974, District 3 Open Pairs Flt. A 1977, Big Apple Swiss Teams 1978, New York Winter KO Teams 1981.

ROSENBLUM, Julius (1906–1978) of New Orleans was president of the ACBL 1951, president of the WORLD BRIDGE FEDERATION 1970–1976, and one of the leading American bridge personalities. A native of Memphis, Rosenblum moved to New Orleans in 1935. He began playing duplicate bridge in 1943 and won his first major bridge championship, the Mid-South Open Teams in 1944. He won many regionals after that and won the Spring NAC Men's Pairs in 1960. He led the U.S. team that defeated Italy in the 1951 Bermuda Bowl, and played briefly in that event — thus becoming the only person to have captained and played on a team that defeated the Italians. He also captained U.S. international teams in 1963, 1966, 1967 and 1968. Rosenblum became secretary-treasurer of the WBF in 1966, and became a voting member of the WBF Executive Committee in 1968 when he was appointed to replace WALDEMAR VON ZEDTWITZ, who retired. In 1974 Rosenblum was elected to an unprecedented third term as president of the WBF, and was elected to the WBF Committee of Honor. The INTERNATIONAL BRIDGE PRESS ASSOCIATION voted the Charles Goren award for "Man of the Year" to Rosenblum in 1975. In 1977 the AUSTRALIAN BRIDGE FEDERATION named him to Life Membership, the first non-Australian to be so honored. He was ACBL Honorary Member in 1970.

ROSENBLUM, Natalie (Mrs. Julius) of New Orleans was official hostess for her late husband and a familiar figure at numerous world and international events. She won Southeastern Mixed Pairs 1953, Women's Teams 1958, Mexican Nat'l Women's Pairs 1962, Bermuda Mixed Pairs 1962.

ROSENBLUM, Robert D. (b. 1927) of San Diego, travel agent, bridge studio owner, won Pacific Southwest Master Pairs 1967, District 22 GNT 1975, GNP 1979. He is a past president of Unit 539 and District 22 Board of Directors. Rosenblum has been bridge columnist for the San Diego *Union* since 1968.

ROSENDORFF, Hans-Gunther (b. 1910) of Subiaco, Western Australia, born in Berlin, Germany, bridge journalist, retired librarian, was npc of the Australian women's team in the Far East Championships 1973–1977, World Women's Teams 1976. His national titles include Individual 1965, 1966, Men's Pairs 1975. Rosendorff has held various executive positions including president of West Australia BA and Councillor for the AUSTRALIAN BRIDGE FEDERATION. He has authored a weekly column in *The West Australian* since 1956 and in *Weekend News* (Perth) since 1978.

ROSENDORFF, Nigel K. (b. 1952) of Subiaco, Western Australia, bridge club owner and teacher, won Australian Under 30 Pairs and Teams 1982 and placed second in Australian Victor Champion Cup 1981, Blue Ribbon Pairs 1976. Rosendorff is the only bridge professional in Western Australia. He is bridge columnist for the Australian *Sunday Times*.

ROSENFELD, Louis M. (1907–1980) of Baltimore was a bridge teacher, writer and tournament director. Former president of the Mid-Atlantic Bridge Conference and the Maryland BA, Rosenfeld authored two books on opening bids and opening leads. His wins include the Keystone Open Teams 1955.

ROSENKRANZ, Edith (Mrs. Jorge, nee Stein) of Mexico DF, represented Mexico in the World Mixed Pairs 1966, 1970, 1974, 1978, 1982, World Open Pairs 1966, 1974, 1982, World Women's Pairs 1962, 1970, World Women's Teams 1964, 1976, 1980. She placed second in Summer NAC Mixed Teams 1967 and won Mexican Nat'l Swiss Teams 1974, 1976, 1982, Master Pairs 1960, Mixed Pairs 1955, Bridge Week Open Pairs 1957, District 16 Swiss Teams Flt. A 1981. She is Mexico's leading woman masterpoint holder and the winner of the John Pike Memorial Trophy for best overall performance at the Mexican Nationals 1970, 1975, 1976.

ROSENKRANZ, Jorge (George) (b. 1916) of Mexico DF, the leading Mexican player and theorist, represented Mexico in the World Open Pairs 1962, 1966, 1970, 1974, 1978, 1982, World Team Olympiad 1972, 1980, npc of both Mexican teams in the World Team Olympiad 1964. He won the Grand National Teams 1981, Spingold 1976, Vanderbilt 1975, 1976 and placed second in the Teams Trials 1982, Vanderbilt 1978, Reisinger 1980, Blue Ribbon Pairs 1974, Spring NAC Men's Teams 1975. The first Life Master in Mexico, Rosenkranz has won numerous regional titles and the John Pike Memorial Trophy for best overall performance at the Mexican Nationals 1969, 1974, 1980, 1981, 1982. He established the ROSENKRANZ AWARD in 1975 and won the PRECISION AWARD in 1976 (see IBPA AWARDS). His writing includes contributions to the ACBL *Bulletin* and other bridge periodicals, and he is the author of *The Romex System of Bidding*, *Win With Romex*, and *Bid Your Way to the Top* (see BIBLIOGRAPHY, C.). Rosenkranz is the inventor of DYNAMIC NOTRUMP, MEXICAN TWO DIAMONDS, ROSENKRANZ DOUBLES and author of the ROMEX SYSTEM. He is the president of Mexican National Federation of Bridge. A chemist and founding chairman of Syntex Corporation, he made scientific contributions in the field of steroid hormones, namely cortisone and birth control pills.

ROSLER, Lawrence (Larry) (b. 1934) of Murray Hill NJ, computer program development manager, former physicist, placed second in the World Par Championship 1961. He won North American Zone World Par Championship 1963, Spring NAC Men's Pairs 1965, Eastern States KO Teams (Reisinger) 1967, Open Pairs 1960. He is the former chairman of the Intercollegiate Par Tournament Advisory Committee; he collaborated with BILL ROOT and JEFF RUBENS in creating and judging par hands. He also served as vice president and president of the New Jersey BL 1967–1970. Rosler developed some TEAM-OF-FOUR MOVEMENTS and helped introduce and popularize Swiss teams competition. He assisted in the writing of *Bridge is a Partnership Game* and *Better Bidding in 15 Minutes*. Rosler was editor of the now defunct *The Bridge Journal*. He contributes articles to *The Bridge World* and is a contributing editor to the *Bridge Encyclopedia*. Rosler is co-inventor of ASTRO and ASTRO CUE-BID.

ROSMARIN, Michael G. (b. 1948) of Jamaica NY, computer programmer, bridge club co-owner, won New England Summer Open Pairs 1975, KO Teams 1980, Keystone Fall Men's Swiss Teams 1975, Tri-State Men's Swiss Teams 1977, 1978, Men's Pairs, Mixed Pairs 1979, Nassau-Suffolk KO Teams 1980, New York Winter Open Pairs Flt. A 1981.

ROSNER, Warren M. (b. 1944) of Nanuet NY, systems analyst, won the Spingold 1981, Blue Ribbon Pairs 1980, Spring NAC Men's Pairs 1980, 1981, and placed second in the Grand National Teams 1979, Vanderbilt 1982. His regional titles include Fall NAC secondary Men's Pairs 1972, Tri-State Men's Swiss Teams 1980, 1981, District 3 Swiss Teams 1979. He posted an 84.7% game in the GNP qualifying game 1981.

ROSS, Harry (b. 1928) of Des Moines IA, born in Vienna, Austria, public relations officer, won Nebraska KO Teams 1973, Iowa Swiss Teams 1973, Gopher Swiss Teams 1980.

ROSS, Hugh L. (b. 1937) of Oakland CA, born in Montreal, one of the outstanding American players, was Bermuda Bowl champion 1976. He also represented the United States in the Bermuda Bowl 1977 and the World Team Olympiad 1976. He won the Teams Trials 1975, Reisinger 1968, 1974, 1975, 1981 (second in 1966), Grand National Teams 1982. His numerous regional titles include the MARCUS CUP 1963. He is a graduate of McGill University. Ross, a systems analyst, is co-owner of a data processing service bureau.

ROSS, John (b. 1948) of Flin Flon MB, project superintendent, won Buffalo Master Pairs 1976, Swiss Teams Flt. A 1979, Klondike Open Pairs 1978, Saskatchewan Master Pairs 1978. He is the founder of the Flin Flon DBC and co-founder of the Northern Manitoba Unit. He is president of Unit 245.

ROSSIGNOL, Roger (1928–1976) of Caracas, Venezuela, was South American champion 1963, 1965, 1966. He also represented Venezuela in the World Team Olympiad 1960, 1964, 1968, World Open Pairs 1966, Bermuda Bowl 1966, 1967, South American Championships 11 times. His national titles include Open Teams nine times, Open Pairs, Mixed Teams.

ROSSMAN, Betty (Mrs. Walter) (b. 1917) of Portland OR won Oregon Trail KO Teams 1974, Women's Swiss Teams 1977, British Columbia Women's Pairs 1981.

ROTH, Alvin L. (Al) (b. 1914) of New York City, president, owner and manager of The Mayfair Club, one of the great players of all time, is generally considered the most original bidding theorist of his bridge generation. He placed second in the World Team Olympiad 1968 and also represented North American in the Bermuda Bowl 1955, 1958, 1967. He won the HERMAN TROPHY 1952, FISHBEIN TROPHY 1963, 1965, 1966, Spingold 1940, 1956, 1957, 1963, 1967, Chicago (since 1965 the Reisinger) 1946, 1952, Reisinger 1967, Vanderbilt 1943, 1963, 1968, Life Master Pairs 1956, 1971, 1972, Fall NAC Men's Teams 1955, 1961, Summer NAC Master Mixed Teams 1952, 1953, 1955, 1965, Fall NAC Open Pairs 1942, Mixed Pairs 1952, Master Individual 1943, Spring NAC Open Pairs 1960, Men's Teams 1969, 1971. He placed second in the Team Trials 1967, Spingold 1943, 1945, 1953, 1961, Chicago 1937, 1954, Reisinger 1966, Vanderbilt 1975, Life Master Pairs 1965, Fall NAC Open Pairs 1958, Men's Teams 1957, Summer NAC Master Mixed Teams 1945, 1963, 1974, 1975, Spring NAC Men's Teams 1973, 1977. His numerous regional titles include Spring NAC secondary Mixed Pairs 1959, Fall Mixed Pairs 1972, Eastern States KO Teams (Reisinger) 1946, 1960, 1961, 1966, 1968, Open Pairs (Goldman) 1961, 1977, 1978, 1979. He is the co-inventor of the ROTH-STONE SYSTEM; his many contributions to bid-

ding theory include the UNUSUAL NOTRUMP and the NEGATIVE DOUBLE. Roth is the author of *The Roth-Stone System: Al Roth on Bridge*, and co-author of *The Roth-Stone System*, *Bridge is a Partnership Game*, *Modern Bridge Complete*, and *Bridge for Beginners*. See BIBLIOGRAPHY, C, E.

ROTHFIELD, Jessel M. (b. 1917) of Melbourne, Australia, born in Dundee, Scotland, company director, was Far East champion 1968, 1970 and also represented Australia in the Ear East Championships 1967, 1969 and as npc of the Australian team in the Bermuda Bowl 1971. He won Australian National Pairs 1970, ACBL Fall NAC secondary Men's Teams 1969. He was president of the AUSTRALIAN BRIDGE FEDERATION 1967–1971, and organized the 15th Far East Championships 1971. Rothfield is a former member of the WORLD BRIDGE FEDERATION Executive Council. He is a marathon runner.

ROTHLEIN, Robert R. (b. 1922) of Orlando FL, general contractor, won the Spingold 1958 and placed second in 1954. His regional titles include Southeastern Open teams 1959, Men's Teams 1954, 1956, 1966, 1968, Open Pairs 1956, 1957, Men's Pairs 1953, 1959, Mixed Pairs 1958. Rothlein is a former governor of the Florida Unit and president and founder of the Central Florida Unit.

ROTMAN, Daniel (Danny) (b. 1932) of Skokie IL, one of the leading players of the Midwest, won the Life Master Pairs 1959, MOREHEAD TROPHY 1967, Summer NAC Master Mixed Teams 1969, Grand National Teams 1978, and placed second in the Spring NAC Open Pairs 1963, 1973, Men's Teams 1965, Reisinger 1967. His numerous regional titles include Central Staes KO Teams 1966, 1969, 1980, Open Pairs 1960, 1969, Midwest Open Teams 1959, 1965, Mixed Pairs 1965.

ROTMAN, Florence (Mrs. Daniel) of Skokie IL, stock options trader, former backgammon teacher, won Summer NAC Mixed Teams 1969, Spring NAC Women's Pairs 1978, Motor City Open Teams 1972, Midwest Fall Women's Pairs 1977.

ROTZELL, Peggy (1929–1969) was of one the leading bridge teachers of Philadelphia. Her many victories included NAC Women's Teams 1956, 1958. Rotzell edited the ACBL *Bulletin* feature "Hand o' the Month" in the early Sixties and authored two books, *Bridge Play and Defense* and *Bridge Bidding Complete*. See BIBLIOGRAPHY C, D.

ROUDINESCO, Jean-Marc (b. 1932) of Paris, France, was European champion 1966, 1970 and also represented France in the Bermuda Bowl 1967, European Championships 1967. His national titles include Open Teams 1963, 1965. He is the author of *L'intelligence du Bridge*, and *La Majeure par 5*. He is a contributor to *Revue Française de Bridge*, *Bridgeur*.

ROUSSIN, Denise of Ottawa ON, computer programmer, represented Canada in the World Women's Teams 1975. She was the top Canadian woman masterpoint winner for 1977. Her regional titles include Can-At Swiss Teams 1975, BAM Teams, Swiss Teams 1977, Open Pairs Flt. A 1980, Capital District Fall Women's Swiss Teams 1977, Bluenose BAM Teams 1981, District 4 Summer Swiss Teams 1981.

ROUSSOS, George P. (b. 1931) of Athens, Greece, consulting soil engineer, officially ranked #7 player in Greece, represented Greece in the European Championships 1967, 1975, 1977, World Open Pairs 1966, and was npc of the Greek women's team at the World Women's Teams 1976. His national successes include Team Trials 1974, 1975, 1977, Open Teams 1967, 1973, 1975, 1977, Mixed Teams 1976, 1977, 1980, 1981, Mixed Pairs 1968, 1977, 1978, 1979, Interclub 1974. He was a member of the HELLENIC BRIDGE FEDERATION executive council 1974–1975.

ROUSSOU, Anna (Mrs. George Roussos) (b. 1938) of Athens, Greece, social worker, officially ranked #2 woman player, won the Kyriakos Trophy (Greek McKenney) for women 1977, 1978. She represented Greece in the World Women's Teams 1976, European Women's Championships 1974, 1975, 1977. Her national titles include Women's Team Trials 1975, 1976, Women's Pairs 1976, 1978, Mixed Teams 1976, 1977, 1980, 1981, Mixed Pairs 1968, 1977, 1978, 1979. Roussou is a former HELLENIC BRIDGE FEDERATION executive member and Council of Discipline member.

ROVERE, Ernest of San Francisco, journalist, author, director of Contract Bridge Cruises, one of the leading bridge personalities, won Summer NAC Master Mixed Teams 1955. His numerous regional titles include All-Western Open Pairs 1945, 1951, Men's Pairs 1948, 1957, 1958, Mixed Pairs 1955, Bridge Week KO Teams 1958, Mixed Teams 1942, Master Pairs 1938, 1940, 1947, Men's Pairs 1948, Mixed Pairs 1939, Individual 1946, Rocky Mountain Open Pairs 1955. Rovere is bridge editor for the San Francisco *Chronicle*. He was bridge columnist at the San Francisco *Call Bulletin* for 23 years and a commentator on radio and TV bridge programs in that city. He served as a member of the ACBL Board of Directors 1957–1960. Rovere is a contributing editor to the *Bridge Encyclopedia* and the author of *Leads, Signals and Discards*, *Modern Point-Count Contract Bridge*, and *Contract Bridge Complete*. See BIBLIOGRAPHY, D, E.

ROWE, Nelson G. (b. 1913) of Smyrna GA, ACBL associate national tournament director, began his directing career in 1946. He served as president of the Georgia Unit for four terms and was an ACBL Board member 1956–1957.

ROWLANDS, Robert J. (Bob) (b. 1942) of London, England, government officer, represented Great Britain in the World Open Pairs 1970, England in various CAMROSE TROPHY matches, European Championships 1966. He has won all major national titles except the Two Stars event and the GOLD CUP in which he placed second. Rowlands is a contributor to *Bridge Magazine*.

ROY, Patrice (Pat) (b. 1927) of Sherbrooke PQ, company owner, won Summer NAC secondary Silver Trophy Pairs Flt. A 1979, New England Summer Mixed Pairs 1975, Can-Am Swiss Teams 1979, Can-At Swiss Teams Flt. A 1980.

ROYER, Barth E. (b. 1947) of Bexley OH, attorney, won Midwest Fall Men's Swiss Teams 1980, 1981, District 11 GNT 1980, GNP 1981. Royer is bridge columnist for the *Columbus Dispatch*.

ROZECKI, Aleksander (b. 1912) of Warsaw, Poland, bridge writer and editor, represented Poland in the World Team Olympiad 1964, European Championships 1957. His national titles include Open Teams 1957, 1958, Individual 1961. He co-authored two bridge books for the less experienced player. Rozecki is the former executive editor of *Brydz*.

RUBBRA, Fredrick C. (Fred) of Nassau, Bahamas, born in Canada, retired stockbroker, represented Bahamas in the World Team Olympiad 1972, 1976, 1980, World Open Pairs 1970. His numerous regional titles include Spring NAC secondary Swiss Teams 1974, 1975, 1979, 1981, Puget Sound KO Teams 1973, Canadian Nat'l Open Teams 1974, Mid-Atlantic Swiss Teams 1977, Gem State Open Pairs Flt. A 1981, District 15 Spring Swiss Teams Flt. A 1981. Rubbra is the founder, honorary president, and representative to the WORLD BRIDGE FEDERATION of the BAHAMAS CONTRACT BRIDGE CLUB.

RUBENS, Gayle (b. 1939) of Miami Beach won Keystone Women's Pairs 1973, Fall Women's Swiss Teams 1971, 1972, 1973.

RUBENS, Jeff (b. 1941) of Scarsdale NY, co-editor of *The Bridge World* since 1967, mathematician, computer scientist, educator, bridge writer and editor, represented North American in the Bermuda Bowl 1973. He won the Team Trials 1972, Spingold 1972, Spring NAC Men's Teams, Men's Pairs 1965. His regional titles include Intercollegiate Championship 1958, Summer NAC secondary Swiss Teams 1973, Eastern States KO Teams (Reisinger) 1970, 1976, New England Open Pairs 1964, Master Pairs, Master Teams 1962, New York Winter Swiss Teams 1973. Rubens collaborated with BILL ROOT and LARRY ROSLER in creating and judging par hands for the Intercollegiate Par Hand Tournament. He edited *The Bridge Journal* (now defunct) 1963–1966. Rubens was the BOLS TIP competition winner 1977, and Precision Award winner twice (see IBPA AWARDS). He is the author of *Secrets of Winning Bridge*, co-author of *Test your Play as Declarer*, *Modern Bridge Bidding Complete* and *Bridge for Beginners*. He is a contributing editor to the *Bridge Encyclopedia*. See BIBLIOGRAPHY, C, E.

RUBIN, Judge Carl B. (b. 1920) of Cincinnati, attorney, and since 1979 Chief Judge United States District Court for the Southern District of Ohio, was ACBL president 1971. He was a member of the ACBL Board of Directors 1966–1973 and was named

ACBL Honorary Member in 1981. Rubin is a graduate of University of Cincinnati. He was a member of the Cincinnati Civil Service Commission 1960–1966 (chairman 1964–1966), and president of the Southwest Ohio Regional Transit Authority 1970–1971.

RUBIN, Ira S. (b. 1930) of Paramus NJ, retired mathematician, computer analyst consultant and instructor, one of the world's great players, WBF GRAND MASTER, won the Bermuda Bowl 1976, placed second in 1966, 1977, and in the World Team Olympiad 1980. He also represented the United States in the World Team Olympiad 1960, 1976, World Open Pairs 1966, 1970. He won the Team Trials 1965, 1975, 1980, FISHBEIN TROPHY 1959, 1962, HERMAN TROPHY 1970, Reisinger 1969, 1974, 1975, 1976, 1978, 1980, Vanderbilt 1965, 1966, Spingold 1956, 1959, 1966, 1979, Life Master Pairs 1962, Blue Ribbon Pairs 1970, Spring NAC Men's Pairs 1958, 1961, 1962, Open Pairs 1961. He placed second in the Reisinger 1965, Vanderbilt 1968, 1969, 1971, 1980, 1981, Spingold 1957, 1969, Life Master Pairs 1954, 1955, 1963, Summer NAC Master Mixed Teams 1957, Fall NAC Men's Pairs 1955, Spring Men's Teams 1976, 1980. His regional titles include Eastern States KO Teams (Reisinger) 1973, 1974. He is the inventor of RUBIN TRANSFERS and TWO-WAY TWO-BIDS. Rubin has college degrees in mathematics and communications. He is the author of a digital computer textbook.

RUBIN, Ronald R. (Ron) (b. 1948) of Livingston NJ, options trader, former regional tournament director, represented the United States in the Rosenblum Cup Teams 1978, 1982. He won the Vanderbilt 1977, 1981, Spring NAC Men's Teams 1975, Spingold 1980, 1982, and placed second in Vanderbilt 1978, Team Trials 1980, Grand National Teams 1980. His regional titles include Fall NAC secondary Swiss Teams 1974, Eastern States KO Teams (Reisinger) 1975, 1976, New York Winter KO Teams 1980. He won *The Bridge World* "Challenge the Champs" competition 10 months is a row and the ROSENKRANZ AWARD in 1976. In 1978 he finished second in the amateur backgammon tournament in Las Vegas. Rubin is a co-author of *The Ultimate Club*. See BIBLIOGRAPHY, C, IBPA AWARDS and LANCIA TEAMS.

RUBINOW, Morton L. (1927–1962) of New York City was a bridge teacher and one of the leading American players. A faculty member at The Card School, he pioneered in giving bridge lessons through phonograph records, *Play Bridge with Morton Rubinow* and *Advanced Bridge Conventions*. Rubinow represented the United States in the World Team Olympiad 1960, won the HERMAN TROPHY 1959, Spingold 1959, Fall NAC Open Pairs, 1959, Spring NAC Men's Pairs 1961, as well as many regional events.

RUDMAN, William K. Jr. (Bill) (b. 1948) of Castro Valley CA, mechanical engineer, won California Capital KO Teams 1975, Mid-Winter Holiday KO Teams 1977, Golden State Open Pairs Flt. A 1981.

RUDOLPH, Richard P. (b. 1938) of Pickerington OH, planning engineer, won Summer NAC secondary Open Pairs Flt. A 1977, Midwest Spring Men's Pairs 1972, 1979, Open Pairs 1975, Fall Men's Swiss Teams 1977, 1980, 1981, Blue Grass Open Pairs 1975, District 11 Non-Mixed Pairs 1977.

RUIA, Ramniwas R. (1900–1979) of Bombay, India was captain of the Indian Team in the World Team Olympiad 1960. His national titles include Open Teams 1959, Master Pairs 1960, 1961. He was president of the BRIDGE FEDERATION OF INDIA and president of the Bombay CBA. Ruia was a WBF executive committee member. He donated the Ruia Gold Trophy in 1960.

RUNEBERG, Lorenzo (b. 1916) of Helsinki, Finland, doctor of forestry, represented Finland in the European Championships 1938, 1940, 1950, 1951, 1953, 1955, 1957, 1962. He won Finnish Open Teams 1948, 1950, 1951, 1952, Open Pairs 1938, 1946, 1947, 1955, 1957, Mixed Pairs 1960, 1961. Runeberg is a former vice president of the FINNISH BRIDGE LEAGUE.

RUNEBERG, Ulla (Mrs. Lorenzo) (b. 1916) of Helsinki, Finland, represented Finland in the European Championships 1962, European Women's Teams Championship 1950, 1951, 1953, 1955, 1956, 1961. She won Finnish Open Teams 1948, 1950, 1951, 1952, Open Pairs 1946, 1947, Mixed Pairs 1960, 1961.

RUPP, Henriette (Henree) (b. 1906) of Indianapolis placed second in Fall NAC Women's Teams 1966, Western States Mixed Pairs 1941, Open Teams 1942.

RUSH, Courtland (Court) (b. 1917) of St. Joseph MO, district sales manager, won Pacific Northwest Master Pairs 1964, Inter-Mountain Master Pairs 1960, Oregon Trail Open Teams 1963, 1966, Master Pairs 1960, 1961. He is the inventor of RUSH ASKING BID.

RUSH, Doris (Mrs. G. Rufus) (b. 1927) of Lubbock TX won Texas Spring Open Teams 1962, Women's Pairs 1970, District 15 KO Teams 1968, Land of Coronado Women's Swiss Teams 1978, Master Pairs 1982.

RUSH, G. Rufus (b. 1923) of Lubbock TX, real estate developer, won Texas Spring Open Teams 1962, District 15 KO Teams 1968.

RUSINOW, Sydney (1907–1953) of Newark NJ, businessman, silver mine owner, designed a system of opening leads that bears his name (see RUSINOW LEADS). In 1933 he won the Vanderbilt and throughout the Thirties was the winner of several prestigious Eastern States and New England titles.

RUSKIN, Stanley C. (b. 1935) of Pittsburgh, company president, won Fall NAC secondary BAM

Swiss Teams 1979, District 5 Swiss Teams 1969, Men's Swiss Teams 1978, GNT, Zone I 1975, Motor City Swiss Teams 1970.

RUSSELL, Clifford (b. 1919) of Miami FL, banker, builder and developer, one of the leading American players, represented the United States in the Rosenblum Cup Teams 1978. He won the Spingold 1963, 1977, Vanderbilt 1963, 1975, 1979, Grand National Teams 1977, and placed second in the Spingold 1954, 1972, Vanderbilt 1975, Reisinger 1964, Summer NAC Master Mixed Teams 1964, Spring NAC Men's Teams 1973, 1977, Blue Ribbon Pairs 1963, 1970, Grand National Teams 1980, Grand National Pairs 1982. His more than 60 regional titles include Spring NAC secondary Men's Pairs 1980, Summer Swiss Teams 1979. Russell is a graduate of University of Arizona. He is past chairman of Metropolitan Museum of Art (Coral Gables) and of 1st National Bank of Hialeah.

RUST, Gail H. of Philadelphia, bridge club co-owner, won Mid-Atlantic Women's Swiss Teams 1978, 1979, District 4 Women's Swiss Teams 1980.

RUTLEDGE, W. Thomas Jr. (Tom) (b. 1939) of Charleston SC, bank executive, attorney, won Fall NAC secondary Swiss Teams 1972, Mid-Atlantic Swiss Teams 1965, KO Teams 1975, 1976, 1979, 1981, Open Pairs 1981, 1982. He is past president and vice president of the Mid-Atlantic Conference and past president of the South Carolina Unit.

RUTSTEIN, Donald I. (b. 1927) of Evanston IL, salesman, won ABA Summer Nat'l KO Teams 1978. His ACBL regional titles include Fall NAC secondary Senior Master Individual 1954, Central States Open Teams 1954, 1972, KO Teams 1962, 1977, Champagne Open Teams 1967, Tri-Unit Open Teams 1972, Great Lakes Open Teams 1965, Mississippi Valley Open Teams, Open Pairs 1972.

RYAN, Marion of Indianapolis IN placed second in Summer NAC Women's Pairs 1950, Fall NAC Women's Teams 1966. She won All-American Open Pairs 1944, Central States Open Pairs 1949.

RYDER, Robert W. (b. 1935) of Caldwell NJ, consulting actuary, won Fall NAC secondary Open Pairs 1969, Men's Swiss Teams 1980, Summer Golder Master Pairs 1980, Tri-State Open Teams 1967, Keystone Open Teams 1968, Men's Pairs 1974, Eastern States Men's Pairs 1973.

S

SABURI, Ken (b. 1901) of Tokyo, Japan, retired managing director, is a former president, advisor, and honorary president of the JAPAN CONTRACT BRIDGE LEAGUE. He presided over the Far East

Championships when they were held in Tokyo 1964, 1979. Saburi is a contributor to the JCBL *Bulletin*.

SACHEN, William F. (Bill) of Waukegan IL, lawyer, editor and publisher of *Bridge Buff's Bulletin*, is the owner of one of the largest private bridge libraries in the world. Sachen is 2nd vice president of the ABTA and chairman of its committee to chose "Bridge Teacher's Book of the Year". He is a contributing editor to the *Bridge Encyclopedia*. Sachen is a graduate of Millikin University and Northwestern University. He is a collector of playing cards and anything associated with playing cards and card games.

SACKS, David L. (b. 1948) of Los Angeles, clothing store owner, placed second in Spring NAC Men's BAM Teams 1979, Summer NAC Life Master Pairs 1978, and won Summer NAC secondary Men's Pairs 1982, Bridge Week Swiss Teams 1976, Master Pairs 1979, KO Teams 1981, Las Vegas Master Swiss Teams 1978.

SACHS, David S. (Dave) of Baltimore, actuary, represented the United States in the World Open Pairs 1970. He placed second in Spring NAC Open Pairs 1969, Summer NAC Master Mixed Teams 1970, 1974, 1978 and won Keystone Conference Swiss Teams 1971, 1972, 1973, 1974, Keystone Fall Swiss Teams Flt. A 1981, Washington Bridge Week Swiss Teams 1976, Mid–Atlantic Swiss Teams 1976, 1981, Master Pairs 1976, Open Pairs 1976, 1979, 4th of July Master Swiss Teams Flt. A 1980. He is a former president of the Maryland BA.

SACHS, Edith of New York City, real estate broker, won Summer NAC Master Mixed Teams 1973, Eastern States Women's Pairs 1969.

SACHS, Herbert (Herb) of Pittsburgh won Fall NAC secondary BAM Swiss Teams 1979, All-American Men's Pairs 1969, Motor City Open Teams 1970, Mid-Atlantic Open Teams 1970, Keystone Fall Open Teams 1973, District 5 Men's Pairs 1969, Men's Swiss Teams 1978, GNT, Zone I 1975, Bermuda Men's Pairs, Swiss Teams 1972, Midwest Spring Swiss Teams 1969.

SACHS, Suzanne H. (Sue) (Mrs. David S.) of Baltimore, travel agency owner, one of the leading American women players, placed second in the World Women's Pairs 1966 and also represented the United States in the Olympiad Women's Teams 1968, World Open Pairs 1970. She won the MOTT-SMITH TROPHY 1969, Spring NAC Women's Pairs 1965, Women's Teams 1966, 1977, 1979, Fall NAC Life Master Women's Pairs 1967 and placed second in Spring NAC Women's Teams, Open Pairs 1969, Summer NAC Master Mixed Teams 1970, 1974, 1978. She has won numerous regional titles.

SACUL, Denny J. (b. 1948) of Jakarta, Indonesia, businessman, was Far East champion 1974, 1979, and placed second in 1981. He also represented Indonesia in the Far East Championships 1971, 1975, 1976, 1977, 1978, Bermuda Bowl 1973, 1981, World

Team Olympiad 1980. His national titles include Intercity Teams 1972, 1978, 1979, Mixed Teams 1980, Open Teams 1977.

SAID, Chuck (b. 1937) of Nashville, professional bridge player and teacher, won Spring NAC secondary Open Pairs 1969, Mixed Pairs 1972, Cambrian Shield KO Teams, Open Teams 1972, Mid–Atlantic Master Pairs 1974, Open Pairs Flt. A 1981, All–American Men's Pairs 1973, District 11 Master Pairs 1974, Southeastern Men's Pairs, Men's Swiss Teams 1977, Midwest Fall Men's Pairs, Men's Swiss Teams 1977, Puerto Rico Men's Pairs 1977, Indian Summer Open Pairs 1979, Space City Open Pairs 1980. Born in Baghdad, Iraq, he formerly worked as an editor, writer, and was active in radio programming and theater.

ST. LUCE, Dr. Ralph (b. 1934) of Miami, formerly of Jamaica, represented Jamaica in the World Team Olympiad 1968, Central American-Caribbean Championships 1971, 1972, 1973, 1974, winning three times and placing second once. He has won every major Jamaican title.

SAITO, Morse (Lucky) (b. 1926) of Kobe, Japan, educator and newspaper columnist, won several national titles including East–West Japan championships. For the past 24 years he has been bridge columnist for *Mainichi Daily News*. Born in Hoquiam WA, Saito learned to play bridge in a relocation camp during World War II.

SAKS, Jay E. (b. 1955) of Cote St. Luc QB, company executive, won Can-Am Master Pairs 1977, Men's Swiss Teams 1980, 1981.

SALGO, Gábor (b. 1917) of Budapest, Hungary, retired journalist, edited the Hungarian monthly *Bridzsélet* 1973–1981. He is bridge columnist for the *Daily News* and a contributor to the IBPA *Bulletin*. Salgo is international contacts secretary, BUDAPEST BRIDGE ASSOCIATION, and a member of the EUROPEAN BRIDGE LEAGUE executive committee in charge of East European bridge affairs.

SALIM, Masood (Soodi) (b. 1940) of Karachi, Pakistan, businessman, won BFAME Championship 1981, placed second in the Bermuda Bowl 1981, in the Far East Championships twice, and won several Pakistan national championships.

SALTSMAN, A. David (b. 1936) of Montreal, stockbroker, placed second in Spring NAC Open Pairs 1975 and won Can-Am Open Teams 1961.

SALTSMAN, Barbara J. (Mrs. David, formerly Siblin) (b. 1936) of Montreal, bridge teacher, represented Canada in the World Women's Teams 1972. She placed second in Summer NAC Master Mixed Teams 1974 and won Can–Am Women's Pairs 1969, 1970, 1976, Southeastern Women's Swiss Teams 1979.

SALTZ, Jack B. of New York City, brokerage firm executive, placed second in Summer NAC Master

Mixed Teams 1974 and won Fun City KO Teams 1973, Puerto Rico Men's Pairs 1973.

SALVETTI, Sandro of Milan, Italy, npc of Italy's Bermuda Bowl champions in 1973, 1974, 1975, npc of Italy's European champions in 1973, 1975, 1979, chose to continue to use SERGIO ZUCHELLI and GIANFRANCO FACCHINI after the 1975 BERMUDA BOWL INCIDENT when the pair were reprimanded for foottapping.

SANBORN, Stephen E. (b. 1954) of Poughkeepsie NY, computer marketing analyst/consultant, won Spring NAC Men's Pairs 1980 and several regionals including District 3 Swiss Teams 1979, Men's Swiss Teams 1980, GNT, Zone II 1980, District 4 Fall Open Pairs 1977, Eastern States Men's Pairs 1979, New England Summer Swiss Teams 1981.

SANCHEZ–FOGARTY, Magda C. (b. 1909) of Mexico DF, landscaper and orchard owner, represented Mexico in the World Women's Teams 1972, 1980, World Women's Pairs 1966, 1970, 1974, and won Mexican Nat'l Mixed Pairs 1961, Women's Pairs, Master Pairs 1971. She authored *Sistema Moderno de Bridge Contrato*.

SANDERS, Carol L. (Mrs. Thomas K.) (b. 1932) of Nashville, one of the world's leading women players, won the World Women's Pairs 1982, Venice Trophy 1974, 1976, placed second in 1981 and in World Women's Pairs 1978. She also represented the United States in World Women's Pairs, Mixed Pairs 1962, 1974, Mixed Teams 1974. She won Spring NAC Women's Pairs 1962, Women's Teams 1963, 1978, 1980, Summer NAC Master Mixed Teams 1976, 1982, Fall NAC Open Pairs 1964. She placed second in the Chicago (since 1965 the Reisinger) 1961, Spring NAC Open Pairs 1960, Women's Teams 1982, Fall Life Master Women's Pairs 1971, 1981, Mixed Pairs 1979. She has won numerous regional titles including Spring NAC Mixed Pairs 1961. Sanders has been a *Bridge World* panelist and Nashville Unit Board member for more than 20 years. She also served as president of Unit 179, vice president of District 10 and representative to the ACBL Charity Committee.

SANDERS, Thomas K. (Tom) (b. 1932) of Nashville, warehouse developer and lessor, one of the leading American players, represented the United States in the World Open Pairs 1962, 1974, 1978, World Team Olympiad 1972, Rosenblum Cup Teams 1978, and as npc of the 1981 Bermuda Bowl champions. He won the Spingold 1977, Blue Ribbon Pairs 1977, Vanderbilt 1979, Summer NAC Master Mixed Teams, Life Master Pairs 1982. He placed second in the Spingold 1963, Chicago (since 1965 the Reisinger) 1961, Reisinger 1973, Vanderbilt 1978, Spring NAC Open Pairs 1960, Men's Pairs 1963, Fall NAC Mixed Pairs 1979. His numerous regional titles include Spring NAC secondary Mixed Pairs 1961, Fall Men's Teams 1962, 1972, Swiss Teams A–D 1979. He won the Cavendish Club Invitational Individual 1979, Open Pairs 1981, and competed in the International Invitation Matches in Deauville

1979. Sanders is a member of the ACBL Board of Directors, a past president of the Mid–State BA, chairman of the 1977 and 1981 Opryland Regionals, Unit 179 delegate to District 10, Grand National Teams coordinator for District 10 1979, a member of the ACBL Board of Governors, a member of the NAC Appeals Committee and a member of the ACBL Goodwill Committee. He is the only graduate of Vanderbilt University to win the Vanderbilt Trophy.

SANTA COLOMA, Luis de (1908–1981) of Buenos Aires, Argentina, lawyer and landholder, was president of the ARGENTINE BRIDGE ASSOCIATION 1967–1981 and for more than 20 years played a leading role in Argentine bridge. He was npc Argentine team in the Bermuda Bowl 1959, South American Championships 1967, 1971, 1975.

SANTAMARINA, Agustín (b. 1934) of Buenos Aires, Argentina, landholder, represented Argentina in the World Team Olympiad 1964, 1968, 1972, 1976, 1980, Bermuda Bowl 1965, 1977, 1981. He was South American champion 1962, 1964, 1976, 1979, 1980, 1981. His national titles include Argentine Open Teams 1956, 1965, 1967, 1970, 1973, 1974, 1977, 1981, Open Pairs 1959, 1960, Master Pairs 1981, Mixed Pairs 1967, Interclubs 1962, 1965, 1969, 1970, 1971, 1973, 1974, 1975, 1977, GABARRET CUP 1973, 1974, 1977, 1981.

SANTAMARINA, Marcos (b. 1931) of Buenos Aires, Argentina, landholder, represented Argentina in the Bermuda Bowl 1963. He was South American champion 1962 and won Argentine Open Teams 1956, 1968, Master Individual 1963, 1973, Interclubs 1962, 1968, 1969, 1970, 1971, 1973, 1974, 1975.

SANTIAGO, Rudisinda L. (Rudy) (Mrs. Victorino P.) of Manila, Philippines was Far East Women's champion 1979. She also represented the Philippines in the Far East Women's Championships 1978.

SANTIAGO, Victorino P. (Vic) (b. 1924) of Manila, Philippines, civil engineer, represented Philippines in the Far East Championships 1974, 1978 and was npc of the Women's Team 1979, Open Team 1981. He is past president of the Philippines CBL.

SANTOS, Jorge Monteiro Dos (b. 1941) of Lisbon, Portugal, lawyer, represented Portugal in the European Championships 1969, 1970. His national wins include Open Teams four times, Open Pairs once.

SANTOS, Rui Silva (b. 1944) of Lisbon, Portugal, electrical engineer, represented Portugal in the European Championships 1969, 1971. His national wins include Open Teams twice.

SAPIRE, Leon (b. 1910) of Johannesburg, South Africa, attorney and bridge writer, was npc of the South African Open Teams and Women's Team in the World Team Olympiad 1960. He won South African Open Pairs 1955, placed second in 1956 and in Open Teams 1958. He is the founder and editor of

Bridge Bulletin. Sapire is a former IBPA vice president, former executive member of the WORLD BRIDGE FEDERATION, founder and honorary life vice president of the Contract Bridge Council of South Africa.

SAPIRE, Max (b. 1912) of East London, South Africa, managing director, represented South Africa in the World Team Olympiad 1960. He won South African Pairs Par Contest 1954 (second in 1962), national Open Pairs three times, Interprovincial Teams four times. He has been active in bridge administration at the local, district and national levels. Sapire contributes to *British Bridge World*, *South African Bridge Bulletin*, *New Zealand Bridge* and is the author of a book on Culbertson asking bids. He is the inventor of several bidding ideas including SOUTH AFRICAN TEXAS.

SARAVIA, Alfredo (b. 1908) of Buenos Aires, Argentina, real estate official, represented Argentina in the Bermuda Bowl 1963. He was South American champion 1964 and won Argentine Open Teams 1940, 1941, 1947, 1954, Open Pairs 1944, 1959, Mixed Teams 1955, 1957, 1959, 1962, Interclubs 1939, 1941, 1945, 1950, 1961, 1966. He is a former president of the Argentine BA.

SARON, Robert (b. 1923) of St. Petersburg FL, stockbroker, former company executive, won Fall NAC secondary Commercial and Industrial Pairs 1961, Swiss Teams 1979, Southeastern Open Teams 1962, Men's Swiss Teams 1976, Florida Men's Pairs 1974, Senior Citizens Swiss Teams 1981, 1982. Saron has been District 9 representative to the Board of Directors since 1977. He was four times president of Unit 128, served more than 30 years as a member of its Board, and formerly was a president of District 9. He was bridge editor of St. Petersburg *Times* and authored *Medical Directory of Good Bridge*.

SARON, Sally (Mrs. Robert) (b. 1931) of St. Petersburg FL, company executive, registered nurse, won Fall NAC secondary Commercial and Industrial Pairs 1961, Swiss Teams 1979, Florida Women's Teams 1961, Mixed Pairs 1963, Southeastern Mixed Pairs 1963.

SASSON, Esther of Caracas, Venezuela, born in Manchester, England, artist, represented Venezuela in the World Women's Teams 1960, 1964, 1968, 1972, 1976, 1980, represented Central American-Caribbean for the Venice Trophy 1981. She has multiple wins in all national pair and team championships.

SATHER, J. Stanley (Stan) (b. 1940) of Portland OR, jail guard, won Oregon Trail Swiss Teams 1981, KO Teams 1982, Puget Sound KO Teams 1976, District 20 GNT, Zone VIII 1980, GNP 1982.

SAVDIE, Raymond (b. 1936) of Bogotá, Colombia, born in Cairo, Egypt, was Caribbean champion 1968 and also represented Colombia in the South American Championships 1964, 1967, Caribbean Championships 1965. His national titles include Open

Teams 1967, Master Pairs 1966, 1968.

SAVOSTIN, Nicolas (b. 1906) of Brussels, Belgium, sales manager, represented Belgium in the World Team Olympiad 1960, 1964 and in many European Championships. His national wins include Open Teams, Mixed Teams, Open Pairs, Mixed Pairs. He has contributed to Belgian and Italian magazines.

SAWIRUDIN, Munawar (b. 1948) of Jakarta, Indonesia, secretary to chamber of commerce, was Far East champion 1979. His national titles include Intercity Teams 1979, 1980.

SAYED, Floyd E. (b. 1925) of Detroit, insurance agent, won Motor City KO Teams 1974, Open Teams 1968, 1979, Open Pairs 1968, Men's Pairs 1975, 1981, Mixed Pairs 1976, District 12 GNT, Zone I 1973. He is past president of Michigan BA.

SBARIGIA, Silvio (b. 1944) of Rome, Italy, pharmaceutical chemist, placed second in the World Team Olympiad 1976, was European champion 1975 and runner-up 1974. His national titles include Mixed Teams 1972.

SCAFFIDI, Sam (b. 1935) of Mingo Junction OH, social worker, won Midwest Fall Open Teams 1960, Great Lakes Open Teams 1962, District 5 Swiss Teams 1970, All-American KO Teams 1978. See STRIPED-TAIL APE DOUBLE.

SCANAVINO, Eduardo (b. 1941) of Buenos Aires, Argentina, bridge club manager and teacher, was South American champion 1976, 1979, 1980, 1981 and placed second in 1968, 1969, 1971, 1972, 1977. He also represented Argentina in the Bermuda Bowl 1977, 1981, World Team Olympiad 1976, 1980. His national titles include Master Individual 1980, Open Teams 1966, 1973, 1974, 1977, 1981, Interclubs 1979, 1980. Scanavino is a former junior division chess champion.

SCATASSA, Eva M. (b. 1943) of West Nyack NY, secretary, won Capital District Fall Women's Pairs 1977, Can-Am Open Swiss Teams, Open Pairs Flt. A 1978, District 4 Women's Swiss Teams 1981.

SCHAAB, Gail K. (b. 1941) of Hickam AFB HI won Spring NAC Women's Pairs 1976, Cornhusker Master Pairs 1977, Northwest Iowa Women's Swiss Teams 1978, Pheasant Swiss Teams 1978.

SCHALTZ, Peter (b. 1950) of Graasten, Denmark, wholesaler, won European Junior Open Teams 1970, Nordic Junior Open Teams 1971, 1973. He also represented Denmark in the European Championships 1975. He won all three major national titles, Danish Cup, Open Teams, Open Pairs, in 1975.

SCHAPIRO, Boris (b. 1909) of London, England, WBF Grand Master, was Bermuda Bowl champion 1955 and won the World Mixed Teams 1962. He placed second in the World Team Olympiad 1960, World Open Pairs 1962. He also represented Great Britain in the World Team Olympiad 1964, Bermuda Bowl 1965 and in 10 European Championships winning in 1948, 1949, 1954, 1963. He won the GOLD CUP 1946, 1947, 1948, 1950, 1952, 1953, 1956, 1960, 1964, 1965, Crowinshield Trophy 1948, Master Pairs 1947, 1954, 1956, 1959, 1962, and many other national championships. He is the author of *Bridge Card by Card* and *Bridge Analysis* (*Boris Schapiro on Bridge*) and bridge editor of London *Sunday Times*.

In the 1965 Bermuda Bowl Schapiro and his partner TERENCE REESE were accused of conveying information about the heart suit through finger signals. Both were found guilty by the WORLD BRIDGE FEDERATION. However, an exhaustive investigation set up by the BRITISH BRIDGE LEAGUE concluded that there was insufficient evidence. See BUENOS AIRES AFFAIR.

SCHAUFFELBERGER, W. K. A. (1902–1972) of Sydney, Australia, chief director of the New South Wales BA, captained the first Australian team to compete in an international contest, the World Team Olympiad at Turin, 1960. He also was the playing captain of 11 N.S.W. teams and one Australian team. He was the winner of 12 national titles, including Open Pairs 1954, 1959, and N.S.W. Open Teams, 1968. He served as treasurer of the AUSTRAILIAN BRIDGE FEDERATION, and vice-president of New South Wales BA.

SCHEINBERG, Martin R. (b. 1930) of New York City, systems engineer, won Fall NAC Men's Teams 1960, Summer NAC secondary President's Pairs 1956, New England Fall Mixed Teams 1960. He was a pioneer in scoring tournament results and predealing hands by electronic data processing equipment. See COMPUTERS.

SCHEMEIL, Pierre (b. 1921) of Paris, France, born in Egypt, former lawyer and finance counsel, bridge writer, represented Switzerland in the World Open Pairs 1962, represented Lebanon in the European Championships 1952, represented Egypt in the European Championships 1953, 1954, 1958, 1959, 1961, represented France in the World Open Pairs 1970, 1974, 1978 and was npc of the French teams that won the World Team Olympiad 1980 and ROSENBLUM CUP 1982. He won French Open Teams three times, Open Pairs 1963, Lebanese Open Teams, Open Pairs, Egyptian Open Teams, Open Pairs, Mixed Pairs.

SCHENKEN, Bee (Mrs. Howard, formerly Bee Gale of New York City) (b. 1916) of Rancho Mirage CA, one of the world's most successful women rubber bridge players, won Fall NAC Mixed Pairs 1957, Women's Teams 1958, 1960, 1961, 1969, Spring NAC Women's Teams 1964, 1968, placed second in 1963, 1967, and in the Reisinger 1966, Summer NAC Master Mixed Teams 1958, Spring NAC Women's Pairs 1969. She has won numerous regional titles and several international titles including Deauville Open Pairs eight times. She is an active fund raiser for various charities.

SCHENKEN, Howard (September 28, 1905–February 20, 1979) of New York City, real estate investor, bridge author and columnist, was one of the great players of the world, by the majority of U.S. experts (as indicated by several polls) considered the best player of all time. He is credited with introduction of several aspects of playing technique and deceptive play now standard, plus the WEAK TWO-BID, the forcing TWO-OVER-ONE, the prepared opening bid ("anticipation"), and other bidding devices. Schenken's Raymond Club team, 1927–1929, first successfully broke the reign of the established men's clubs in tournament competition. After occasional appearances with the FOUR HORSEMEN and BID-RITE teams, Schenken was a founder of the FOUR ACES and participated in their long series of victories including victory over the French European champions in 1935 in the first official World Championship (see WORLD CHAMPIONSHIPS) and a winning tour of Europe in pair matches with MICHAEL T. GOTTLIEB, the next year. World Champion 1950, 1951, 1953; represented U.S. World Olympiad 1960, and North American World Championships 1961, 1963, 1965. His five wins in the Life Master Pairs 1931, 1933, 1934, 1941, 1943, and his ten wins in the Spingold 1934, 1936, 1938, 1939, 1943, 1945, 1948, 1950, 1952, 1960, the Vanderbilt won ten times, 1934, 1935, 1937, 1938, 1946, 1950, 1955, 1956 1957, 1964, each constitutes a record. Other national wins include Reisinger 1968, Chicago 1957, 1963, Fall Nat'l Men's Team 1949, Mixed Team 1935, Mixed Pairs 1957, Master Individual 1932. He was second in national events 19 times (See also USBA Championship.) Schenken was an ACBL Board member, and IBPA honorary member in 1973. His writings included *Four Aces System of Contract Bridge*, 1935; *Better Bidding in Fifteen Minutes* and *Howard Schenken's Big Club* (see SCHENKEN SYSTEM), and *Education of a Bridge Player*. He took over the Four Aces syndicated bridge column in 1943, in 1957 merged it with RICHARD L. FREY'S to become co-author of longest continuously published nationally syndicated bridge feature. In 1970, he became the sole author of the column. He was a contributing editor, *Bridge Encyclopedia*. See BIBLIOGRAPHY, C, K.

SCHENONE, Mercedes Guerrico de of Buenos Aires, Argentina, was South American Women's champion 1948, 1949, 1950, 1951, 1953, 1961, 1962, 1977, 1979. She also represented Argentina in the World Women's Teams 1972, Venice Trophy Teams 1978. Her national titles include Open Teams 1951, 1965, 1971, Open Pairs 1957, Mixed Teams 1959, 1963, 1965, 1966, 1967, 1972, 1973, 1974, 1975, 1976, 1979, 1981, Mixed Pairs 1949, 1954, 1962, 1965, 1970, 1972, Interclubs 1955, 1957, 1965.

SCHERMER, John (b. 1948) of Seattle, painting contractor, won Fall NAC Swiss Teams 1977, Spring NAC Men's BAM Teams 1978. He won more than 25 regional titles including Summer NAC secondary Open Pairs 1974, Fall Master Pairs 1975, Hawaii KO Teams, Men's Swiss Teams, Swiss Teams 1978, British Columbia KO Teams, Open Pairs 1978, Inter-Mountain Swiss Teams 1974, KO Teams 1977, Indian Summer Swiss Teams 1981.

SCHEUER, Jerome (1889–1979) of Brookline MA was an insurance broker, prominent lawn tennis official at the national and international levels, and a bridge writer. He won the New England Knockout Teams 12 times between the years 1938–1954. His writing included contributions to *Bridge Magazine* and *The Bridge World*. He was a contributing editor *Bridge Encyclopedia*.

SCHICK, Dorothy E. of Shaker Heights OH won All-American Mixed Pairs 1967, Women's Swiss Teams 1981, Women's Pairs 1982, Great Lakes Women's Swiss Teams 1981, Canadian Nat'l Women's Pairs 1964.

SCHILLER, Rona G. (b. 1940) of Huntington NY, bridge club director, won Long Island Women's Pairs 1978, District 3 Women's Pairs 1979, Mexican Nat'l Swiss Teams 1981, District 24 GNT 1980, GNP 1981.

SCHIPPERHEYN, Ton (b. 1938) of Amstelveen, The Netherlands, bridge journalist and author, is bridge columnist for *Het Parool* and provincial syndicated newspapers, editor and contributor to *Bridge* and co-author (with CORNELIS (CEES) SINT) of 18 books including *From Start to Finish*, *Modern Acol Book* and *Test Your Bridge*. Schipperheyn is assistant director of NETHERLANDS BRIDGE LEAGUE.

SCHIPPERS, Elly (b. 1943) of Amstelveen, The Netherlands, systems analyst, represented The Netherlands in the World Women's Teams 1980, European Women's Championships 1979, 1981. She won the EC Women's Pairs 1980 and placed second in the Common Market Women's Pairs 1981. Her national titles include Women's Pairs, Mixed Teams 1979, 1981, Mixed Pairs 1982.

SCHLEIFER, Meyer (b. 1908) of Los Angeles, bridge teacher, one of the leading American players, represented the United States in the World Team Olympiad 1960. He won Summer NAC Life Master Pairs 1966, BARCLAY TROPHY 1947, and scores of regional titles including All-Western KO Teams 1974, Master Teams 1972, 1974, Master Pairs 1943, Open Pairs 1942, 1943, 1947, Mixed Pairs 1965, Bridge Week KO Teams 1951, 1954, 1957, 1960, 1965, 1970, 1971, Master Teams 1947, 1956, Mixed Teams 1956, 1961, 1967, Open Teams 1939, 1940, 1941, 1945, 1946, 1949, 1958, 1959, Master Pairs 1943, 1963, Open Pairs 1942, 1943, 1947, 1948, Men's Pairs 1956, 1963.

SCHLEPPEGRELL, Thorald W. (Terry) (b. 1953) of Anchorage, retail clerk, won Polar Swiss Teams 1974, Open Pairs 1977, 1980.

SCHMIEDER, REBECCA. See ROGERS, REBECCA.

SCHNEIDEMAN, Leslie M. (1910–1978) of Wellington, New Zealand, company director, was a notable New Zealand bridge leader. Under his management New Zealand experienced a phenomenal expansion of clubs and playing strength. He became an international figure in 1970 when he became Zone 7 Delegate to the WORLD BRIDGE FEDERATION, and two years later was appointed to the WBF Executive Council. He was president of NEW ZEALAND BRIDGE ASSOCIATION 1959–1963, 1964–1969, 1970–1977. A national master in New Zealand ranking, Schneideman was frequently npc of New Zealand open and women's teams.

SCHNEIDER, Gerald C. (Jerry) (b. 1932) of Chesterfield MO, sales representative, won Mississippi Valley Swiss Teams 1973, KO Teams 1978, Men's Pairs 1979, District 8 Men's Swiss Teams 1981, GNT 1978.

SCHNEIDER, Karl (1904–1977) of Vienna, Austria, an engineer, was one of the great players of the world. World champion 1937, European Champion 1936, Schneider represented France in the Bermuda Bowl 1954, represented Austria five times in the European Championships, placing second 1951, 1957. Schneider, who retired from international play in 1957, was captain of the Austrian national team for five years.

SCHODER, William J. (Kojak) (b. 1932) of Boca Raton FL, ACBL associate national tournament director, began his directing career in 1959 on a part-time basis. In 1966 he achieved a Regional rating and in 1980 an associate national rating. He is a contributor to *Florida Bridge News, Gold Coast Bridge News* and *Trumpet*. Schoder is past president of the PTDA. He serves as chief director for the South American Bridge Federation and the Central American and Caribbean Bridge Federation. Schoder has been a World Bridge Federation director since 1972. A retired USAF pilot, he was awarded many decorations including the Distinguished Service Medal, Distinguished Flying Cross, Bronze Star and 10 Air Medals. Schoder is a graduate of Queens College of the University of City of New York. A linguist, he is fluent in Spanish, German and French.

SCHOENBORN, Michael (The Shoe) (b. 1943) of Toronto, born in Dessau, Germany, lawyer, won Olympic KO Teams 1976, Motor City Swiss Teams 1975, Canadian Nat'l Open Pairs 1977, Men's Swiss Teams 1980. He is a contributor to *The Kibitzer* and *Canadian Bridge Digest.*

SCHOENFELD, Brian L. (b. 1946) of Hillsborough NC, accountant, won Mid-Atlantic KO Teams 1972, 1973, 1980, Swiss Teams 1974, District 5 Master Pairs 1975, District 6 GNT 1976. Schoenfeld is a past president of Unit 146.

SCHOLIN, Rainer (b. 1930) of Helsinki, Finland, economist, represented Finland in the European Championships 1956, 1959, Nordic Championships 1955, 1962. His national wins include Finnish Open Teams 1958, 1960, 1962, 1963.

SCHOPFLOCHER, Donald P. (b. 1952) research scientist, won Saskatchewan Swiss Teams 1973, 1975, Men's Pairs 1973. He is a former bridge club owner, director and teacher.

SCHOR, David M. (b. 1950) of San Diego, psychotherapist, won District 5 KO Teams, District 11 Swiss Teams 1977, Los Angeles Winter Swiss Teams Flt. A 1980.

SCHOUCAIR, Henri A. (b. 1920) of Beirut, Lebanon, engineer, represented Lebanon in the European Championships 1954, 1956, 1957, 1959, 1962 and as npc of the Lebanese Team in the World Team Olympiad 1960. His national wins include Open Teams, Open Pairs several times each. He is a former chairman of the LEBANESE BRIDGE FEDERATION.

SCHREIBER, Michael J. (b. 1952) of Hawthorne CA, two-way radio communications agent, won Spring NAC Open Pairs 1980. His more than 30 regional titles include Summer NAC secondary Open Pairs Flt. B, Bridge Week Master Men's Pairs Flt. A 1980, Men's Pairs, Master Pairs 1981, Pacific Southwest KO Teams 1977, Swiss Teams 1979, Master Pairs, Men's Pairs 1980, Mid–Winter Holiday Open Pairs, Men's Pairs 1977, Swiss Teams 1979. He won the Intercollegiate Championship in 1973 with his brother WILLIAM SCHREIBER. Using the pseudonym Sol I. Taryman, he was the original moderator for the ''Problem Solvers Panel'' in the *Southern California Bridge News.*

SCHREIBER, William L. (Bill) (b. 1947) of Sepulveda CA, accountant, won Desert Empire Open Teams 1972, Open Pairs 1970, Las Vegas Swiss Teams 1973, Palm Springs Swiss Teams 1973, Los Angeles Winter KO Teams 1975. He was Intercollegiate champion 1973.

SCHROEDER, David A. (b. 1950) of Las Vegas, baseball handicapper, won Life Master Men's Pairs 1977 and several regionals including Mid-Atlantic Swiss Teams 1975, 1979, KO Teams 1977, Washington Bridge Week Men's Pairs 1976, Bicentennial KO Teams, Swiss Teams 1976, Toast of Tulsa Open Pairs 1979, North Florida Swiss Teams 1979. He is also a backgammon champion.

SCHULD, Diana K. (Mrs. Frank) (b. 1938) of Glen Head NY, music teacher, placed second in the Life Master Pairs 1967 and won Summer NAC secondary Open Pairs 1973, New England Open Teams 1971, Fun City Women's Pairs 1973, Puerto Rico Women's Pairs 1979, 1981.

SCHULD, Frank P. Jr. (b. 1927) of Glen Head NY, bridge club owner and teacher, placed second in the Life Master Pairs 1967 and won Summer NAC secondary Open Pairs 1973, New England Open Teams 1971. Schuld was a member of the committee that established District 24 and he was instrumental in bringing about separate unit status for Nassau–Suffolk BA. He is the author of *The Simple Squeeze in Bridge* (see BIBLIOGRAPHY, D).

SCHULLE-MOHAN, Kay (Mrs. John Mohan) of Tiburon CA, professional bridge player, won more than 25 regional titles including Hawaii Swiss Teams 1976, KO Teams 1977, 1978, Women's Swiss Teams

1978, Puget Sound Swiss Teams Flt. A 1981, Gem State Open Pairs Flt. A 1980, Pacific Southwest KO Teams 1978, Klondike KO Teams 1978, Los Angeles Winter Mixed Pairs 1976, 1977, Women's Swiss Teams 1977. With her husband she conducted weekend bridge seminars in resort areas.

SCHULTE, Edward G. (b. 1946) of Miami, salesman, won Florida Life Master Pairs 1974, Mid-Atlantic Open Pairs 1978, 1979, Mississippi Valley Men's Pairs 1978, KO Teams 1980, Mid–South Men's Pairs 1979, Space City Men's Pairs 1976, District 8 KO Teams 1979, Southeastern Swiss Teams 1980.

SCHUTZE, Kenneth R. (b. 1949) of Austin TX, research assistant, won the Life Master Pairs 1979 and placed second in Fall NAC Swiss Teams 1977, 1979. His regional titles include Fall NAC secondary Swiss Teams 1979, Texas Fall Master Pairs 1973, Harvest Festival KO Teams 1977, Houston Mid–Winter Open Pairs Flt. A 1981, Big D KO Teams 1978.

SCHWAB, Charles M. (1862–1939) of New York City was a noted financier, steel magnate and patron of bridge. He was president of the Whist Club of New York, played on its teams, and was *ex officio* member of the committee that participated in the first International Code of Contract Bridge Laws, 1932. See SCHWAB CUP.

SCHWAB, Clara (Mrs. Irving W., formerly Dwyer) (b. 1908) of Springfield MO won Missouri Valley Women's Pairs 1954, Mixed Pairs 1961, Mississippi Valley Mixed Pairs 1955. She is a past president of Southwest Missouri Unit which she founded.

SCHWAB, Irving W. (b. 1900) of Springfield MO, attorney, won Mississippi Valley Mixed Pairs 1955, Men's Pairs 1956, Missouri Valley Mixed Pairs 1961. Schwab was instrumental in the formation of the ACBL Goodwill Committee.

SCHWARTZ, Adrian (b. 1944) of Kiriat Ono, Israel, engineer, represented Israel in the World Teams Olympiad 1968, 1972, 1980, European Championships 1970, 1971, 1973, 1974, 1977, 1979, 1981. His national wins include Open Pairs 1968, 1969, 1971.

SCHWARTZ, Elmer I. (b. 1903) of Shaker Heights OH, attorney, won the Chicago (since 1965 the Reisinger) 1949, Fall NAC Men's Teams 1958 and placed second in the Spingold 1946, Chicago 1952. His regional titles include Keystone Mixed Pairs 1953, All-American Men's Pairs, Mixed Pairs 1965, Open Pairs 1964. He is past president of District 5.

SCHWARTZ, Eugene (b. 1916) of Mercer Island WA, retired airline captain, won Pacific Northwest Open Teams 1959, Master Pairs 1960, 1961, Puget Sound Open Pairs 1982.

SCHWARTZ, Judy A. (b. 1933) of Roslyn NY, bridge teacher, won Tri-State Women's Pairs 1972, Long Island Women's Pairs 1975, Fun City Women's Pairs 1975.

SCHWARTZ, Norman A. of Phoenix won Mid-Atlantic Open Teams 1971 (twice), Men's Pairs 1971.

SCHWARTZ, Peter L. (b. 1934) of Hampstead QB, railway marketing director, won Can-Am Open Pairs 1957, Open Teams 1956, 1957, Men's Pairs 1975, 1977. A bridge teacher, he instructs at junior colleges and aboard cruise ships.

SCHWARTZ, Richard C. (b. 1943) of Brooklyn NY, program analyst, won Summer NAC secondary Commercial and Industrial Teams 1967, Tri-State Open Teams 1968, Great Lakes Men's Pairs 1965.

SCHWARTZ, Sybila G. (Billie) (b. 1903) of Sun City AZ, formerly of Anaconda MT, retired executive, won Inter-Mountain Women's Pairs 1958, 1960, Open Teams 1959. She is past president of the Anaconda Unit.

SCHWARTZ, Sylvia (Mrs. Elmer I.) (1907–1978) of Shaker Heights OH represented the U.S. in the World Women's Team Olympiad 1960. Other bridge accomplishments include second place Summer NAC Women's Pairs 1959, and regional wins Keystone Mixed Pairs 1953, All-American Open and Mixed Pairs 1964.

SCHWENCKE, John A. (Jack) (b. 1916) of North Palm Beach FL, real estate developer, won Spring NAC Swiss Teams 1978, Southeastern KO Teams 1973, Men's Swiss Teams, Swiss Teams 1979, Desert Empire KO Teams 1973, Hawaii KO Teams, Men's Swiss Teams, Swiss Teams 1978, All-Southern Swiss Teams 1979, Eastern States KO Teams (Reisinger) 1979, Gold Coast Men's Swiss Teams 1981, Mexican Nat'l Men's Pairs, Open Pairs Flt. A 1982.

SCOPE, Ivan H. (b. 1934) of San Francisco, worker's compensation consultant, won the Grand National Pairs 1982. His regional titles include All-Western Master Pairs, Mixed Pairs 1970, Master Teams 1975, California Capital KO Teams 1972, Swiss Teams 1975, Golden State Swiss Teams 1978, District 21 GNT 1974, 1975, 1976.

SCOTT, Gratz M. (1882–1935) of New York City, bridge teacher and president of the CAVENDISH CLUB of New York, was an outstanding figure in whist and bridge for 25 years. Scott and teammates, WILBUR C. WHITEHEAD, EDWIN A. WETZLAR, and RALPH R. RICHARDS, were co-winners of the first national contract bridge tournament ever held, the 1928 Board-a-Match competition for the HAROLD S. VANDERBILT TROPHY. The following year he placed second.

SCOTT, Joe V. (b. 1947) of Rogers AR, quality control engineer, former mathematics teacher, won Missouri Valley Men's Swiss Teams, Master Pairs 1978, Mid-South Open Pairs 1978, Toast of Tulsa Swiss Teams 1979, Oklahoma City Open Pairs Flt. A 1981, District 10 GNT, Zone IV 1977, 1979, GNP 1981.

SCOTT, Ronald J. (b. 1930) of Hamilton, New Zealand, dairy farmer, represented New Zealand in the Far East Championships 1971. He won New Zealand Open Teams 1973, 1974.

SEALY, Donald L. (Larry) (b. 1955) of Huntsville AL, systems analyst, won several regionals including Music City KO Teams 1977, Mid–South KO Teams 1979, Space City Men's Swiss Teams, Swiss Teams Flt. A 1980, Mid–Atlantic KO Teams 1980, Swiss Teams 1980, 1981, Midwest Swiss Teams 1980, Mid–South Men's Pairs 1981.

SEAMON, Michael E. (b. 1960) of North Miami Beach won Florida Open Pairs Flt. A 1981, Southeastern Master Pairs 1977, Gateway to Space Men's Pairs 1982.

SEAMON, Rita (Mrs. William E.) of Miami Beach, bridge teacher, won Summer NAC Master Mixed Teams 1974 and placed second in Spring NAC Women's Pairs 1961. She won Southeastern Mixed Pairs 1959, 1968, Central Florida Mixed Pairs 1978, Puerto Rico Open Pairs 1978, Gateway to Space Open Pairs 1982, District 9 GNP 1980, GNT 1982.

SEAMON, William E. (Billy) (b. 1917) of Miami Beach, retired banking executive, one of the leading American players, represented North American in the Bermuda Bowl 1957. He won the Spingold 1956, 1963, Vanderbilt 1963, Grand National Teams 1973, Summer NAC Master Mixed Teams 1974, and placed second in the Chicago (since 1965 the Reisinger) 1954, Vanderbilt 1960, Fall NAC Men's Teams 1952, Spring NAC Men's Teams 1973, Grand National Teams 1978, 1980. He has won numerous regional titles including Summer NAC secondary Mixed Pairs 1968. Seamon is a contributing editor to the *Bridge Encyclopedia* and a former syndicated bridge columnist. He is the brother of EDITH KEMP-FREILICH and ANNE BURNSTEIN. See FAMILY.

SEARS, Richard C. (Dick) (b. 1936) of Palisades NY, employee benefits consultant, won New England Spring Open Teams 1959, KO Teams 1958, 1961, 1964, New England Fall Mixed Teams 1957.

SEBASTIAN, Jonas (b. 1945) of Manila, Philippines, mathematics teacher, theater director, represented Philippines in the Far East Championships 1981.

SECKER, Stella (b. 1936) of Lower Hutt, New Zealand, salaries officer, was Far East Women's champion 1981. She also represented New Zealand in the Far East Championships 1977, World Women's Teams 1980.

SEEWALD, Leo J. (b. 1908) of South St. Paul MN, retired teacher, was ACBL president in 1964, a member of the ACBL Board of Directors, Board of Governors, and chairman of the ACBL Masterpoint Plan Committee. He also served as president of the Minnesota Unit and as director of the Mid-American-Canadian Conference.

SEEWALD, Reine (Mrs. Leo J.) (b. 1899) of South St. Paul MN won Mid-Am-Can Women's Pairs 1957. She was ACBL secretary in 1963.

SEGANDER, Rut (b. 1917) of Karlsborg, Sweden, won the World Women's Teams 1968, European Women's Championships 1962, 1967, Nordic Women's Championships. Her national titles include Women's Pairs.

SEIDMAN, Solomon (Sol) (b. 1909) of Brooklyn NY, retired social studies teacher and bridge lecturer, won several regional titles including Spring NAC secondary Individual 1949, Fall Swiss Teams 1979, Keystone Open Teams 1962, Fun City KO Teams 1970, Eastern States KO Teams (Reisinger) 1972, District 3 Swiss Teams 1977, Bermuda Swiss Teams 1979. He has been co-chairman of the NAC Appeals Committee for many years and has served on the Board of Directors since 1974. A former president of District 24, he was also chairman of the Board of the Greater New York BA. Seidman was vice chairman of the Protest and Appeals Committee at the World Pair Championships 1982. He was eduated at New York University and City College of New York.

SELIGMAN, Barbara of Dublin, Ireland, company director, represented Ireland in the World Women's Pairs 1970, 1974, European Championships 1962, 1963, 1965, 1967, 1969, 1971, 1973, 1974, 1975. Her national wins include all major Irish titles.

SELIGMAN, Edith. See KEMP-FREILICH, EDITH.

SELYMES, Emery of Seattle won Puget Sound KO Teams 1970, 1971, 1972, Master Pairs 1975, Inland Empire Open Pairs 1976.

SENDER, Elfreda E. (b. 1931) of Johannesburg, South Africa, born in Bamerg, Germany, former secretary, placed second in the World Women's Teams 1968 and also represented South Africa in the World Women's Teams 1964, 1980, MACCABIAH GAMES 1977. Her national titles include New Zealand Women's Teams 1970, 1971, Women's Pairs 1973.

SERES, Thomas P. (Tim) (b. 1925) of Randwick, NSW, Australia, born in Vienna, Austria, of Hungarian parentage, sales representative, one of the world's great players, was Far East champion 1968, 1970 and also represented Australia in the World Team Olympiad 1960, 1964, 1968, 1972, 1976, 1980, Bermuda Bowl 1971, 1976, 1977, 1979, 1981, Far East Championships 1971, 1972, 1973, 1975, 1976, 1977, 1978, 1979. His national titles include Open Teams 1948, 1949, 1950, 1952, 1954, 1955, 1957, 1959, 1961, 1962, 1963, 1964, 1965, 1967, 1970, 1974, 1975, 1976, 1978, 1979, 1980, Sitmar Cup 1976, 1977, 1981, Open Pairs 1954, 1961, 1962, 1964, 1965, 1967, 1974, 1978, Mixed Pairs 1975, 1980, Par Point 1952, 1962, 1963, WBF Zone 7 champion 1970, 1971, 1974. He won the McCutcheon Trophy for the most masterpoints scored in 1974. Seres, a member of the IBPA, contributes to several international bridge publications and is a contributing columnist for *The Sun Herald*. He discovered the SERES SQUEEZE. The Australian Bridge Association named him an Honorary Life Member.

SERF, Marianne (b. 1931) of Paris, France, bridge teacher, one of the leading French players, was European Women's champion 1969 and placed second in the World Women's Pairs 1962. She also represented France in the World Women's Teams 1964, 1968, European Women's Championships 1963, 1967, 1981. Serf has won many national titles.

SERVER, Lenore (Len) (b. 1937) of River Vale NJ, business exective, won Puerto Rico Women's Pairs 1977, District 4 Women's Swiss Teams 1981, Bluenose KO Teams 1981. A certified director since 1971, she directs bridge games on cruise ships.

SESTITO, Bruno S. (b. 1950) of Sharon MA, mathematics teacher, bridge teacher, won Wolverine Open Pairs 1977, District 11 Non-Mixed Pairs 1977, Canadian Nat'l Swiss Teams 1977, Motor City Open Pairs 1977, Midwest Fall Swiss Teams 1980, District 11 GNT 1980. From 1976 to 1981 he was weekly bridge columnist for the *Columbus Dispatch*.

SEXTON, F. Holton (b. 1926) of Greens Fork IN, real estate broker and dairy farm manager, won Summer NAC secondary Mixed Pairs 1971, Southern Conference Open Pairs 1954, Midwest Open Pairs 1960, Open Teams 1971, Florida Mixed Pairs 1973.

SHAH, Ramniklal K. (R.K.D.) (b. 1929) of Nairobi, Kenya, company director, insurance consultant, represented Kenya in the World Team Olympiad 1980. His national titles include Steel Africa Pairs 1978, Brighton Gold Cup 1975, 1980. He has served as committee member of Kenya BA since 1969 and as chairman 1975-1976.

SHALLON, Marty (b. 1952) of Van Nuys CA, accountant, placed second in the Spingold 1975, Spring NAC Men's Teams 1974. He won Pacific Southwest Master Pairs 1976, Bridge Week KO Teams 1977, Los Angeles Winter KO Teams 1974 (twice), 1977. Shallon is a graduate of UCLA.

SHALOM, Felix (b. 1917) of Kingston, Jamaica, textile executive, won many national titles including Open Teams 15 times. He is past president of the Jamaica BA.

SHANAHAN, Dorothy of London, England, statistician, won the World Women's Teams 1964, and was European Women's champion 1961, 1966. Her national titles include English Women's Teams, Mixed Teams twice each, National Pairs 1956.

SHANBROM, Helen (b. 1919) of Tamarac FL, retired teacher, placed second in Fall NAC Women's Teams 1960 and won All-American Open Teams 1962, 1965, Great Lakes Open Teams 1963, Midwest Spring Mixed Pairs 1959.

SHARIF, Omar (b. 1932) of Paris, France, formerly of Egypt, motion picture star, represented the UAR in the World Team Olympiad 1964 and was playing captain of the Egyptian Team in the World Team Olympiad 1968. His national wins include Interclubs 1960, 1962, 1963, 1964. Sharif won the 1963 Golden Globe award and also was nominated for an Academy Award in 1963 as best supporting actor for his performance in *Lawrence of Arabia*. One of the most active promoters of bridge, he makes many public appearances on syndicated TV shows as a proponent of the game. He organized the SHARIF BRIDGE CIRCUS and participated in one of the highest stake set games in history (see SET GAMES). Sharif was a member, with many former members of the BLUE TEAM, of the Lancia Bridge Team in 1975 (see LANCIA TOURNAMENTS). He won the SIMON AWARD in 1974 (see IBPA AWARDS). Sharif is the author of *Ma vie au bridge* and since 1975 the co-author of the Goren newspaper bridge column.

SHARP, Robert G. (b. 1910) of Miami Beach, retired real estate broker, formerly one of the leading players of the South, won the Grand National Teams 1973, Fall NAC Men's Teams 1959, Mixed Pairs 1966, and placed second in the Blue Ribbon Pairs 1964. His numerous regional titles include Mississippi Valley Master Pairs 1959, Open Pairs 1960, 1962, 1965, Open Teams 1965, Southeastern KO Teams 1967, Open Teams 1972, Men's Teams 1968, Senior Citizens Swiss Teams 1981. He is a former president of the Midwest Conference, the Cincinnati BA and the Florida BA.

SHARPLES, James (b. 1908) of Caterham, Surrey, England, retired bank officer, placed second in the European Championships 1958 and also represented Great Britain in the European Championships 1956. He represented England in more than 20 CAMROSE TROPHY matches between 1950-1977. Sharples won the GOLD CUP 1962, 1967, 1968, 1969, 1971, 1979 (placed second five times), Life Master Pairs 1950, Crockford's Cup 1948, 1963, 1978, Hubert Philips Cup four times, Two Stars event five times, National Open Pairs 1955, Melville Smith Cup 1955. He is the twin brother of Robert. Together they were the first players to reach EBU Life Master and Grand Master ranks. Currently they are the two leading EBU masterpoint holders. Sharples is a bidding competition panelist for *Bridge Magazine* and *International Popular Bridge Monthly*.

SHARPLES, Robert (b. 1908) of Caterham, Surrey, England, retired bank official, placed second in the European Championships 1958 and also represented Great Britain in the European Championships 1956. He represented England in more than 20 CAMROSE TROPHY matches between 1950-1977. Sharples won the GOLD CUP 1962, 1967, 1968, 1969, 1971, 1979 (second five times), Crockford's Cup 1948, 1963, 1978, Hubert Philip's Cup four times, Two Stars event five times, Life Master Pairs 1950, National Open Pairs 1955, Melville Smith Cup 1955. He is the twin brother of James. Together they were the first two players to achieve EBU Life Master and Grand Master ranks. Currently they are the two leading masterpoint holders. Sharples is a bidding competition panelist for *Bridge Magazine* and *International Popular Bridge Monthly*.

SHAUFEL, Elyakim (b. 1945) of Tel Aviv, Israel, born in Poland, was European champion 1975. He also represented Israel in the World Team Olympiad, World Open Pairs 1972, European Championships 1966, 1967, 1969, 1971, 1973, 1974. His national titles include Open Pairs 1966, 1967, 1972, 1973, 1974.

SHAW, Mark P. (b. 1949) of Greenbelt MD, law librarian, won Canadian Nat'l KO Teams 1975, Mid-Atlantic Open Pairs 1974, Washington Bridge Week Men's Pairs 1975.

SHAW, Shirlee R. (b. 1924) of Concord CA, medical assistant, won Fall NAC Non-Life Master Pairs 1981.

SHEARDOWN, Percival E. (Shorty) (b. 1911) of Toronto, bridge club manager, one of the most consistent tournament winners before the inauguration of tournament and masterpoint ratings, started playing tournament bridge in 1933 and was Canada's first Life Master (1948). Sheardown represented Canada in the World Team Olympiad 1960, 1968. He won the Spingold 1964, 1965, FISHBEIN TROPHY 1964 and placed second in the Life Master Pairs 1964. His numerous regional titles include Canadian Nat'l Open Teams 1951, 1953, 1961, 1965, 1967, Master Pairs 1971, Open Pairs 1969, District 2 GNT 1973.

SHEEHAN, Robert M. (b. 1939) of London, England, animal physiologist, computer systems analyst, commodity broker, one of the leading British players, represented Great Britain in the World Team Olympiad 1972, 1976, 1980, World Open Pairs 1974, European Championships 1971 (runner-up), 1973, 1974, 1975, 1981, Bermuda Bowl 1981. He won the GOLD CUP 1972, Life Master Pairs 1982, Crockford's Cup.

SHEFCHIK, C. Milton (b. 1939) of Hopkins MN, professional bridge player, won numerous regional titles including Mid-Am-Can Open Teams 1965, Canadian Prairie Open Teams 1968, Gopher Master Pairs 1969, KO Teams 1979, Men's Pairs 1980, Iowa KO Teams, Swiss Teams 1979, Buffalo Open Pairs 1980, Wisconsin Men's KO Teams 1981.

SHEINWOLD, Alfred (Freddy) (b. 1912) of Los Angeles, formerly of New York City, born in London, England, bridge author and columnist, is one of the most successful player-writer personalities. During World War II he was the chief code and cipher expert of the OSS. He graduated from City College of New York in 1933. From 1945-1955 he sang with the Cantata Singers.

Sheinwold was npc of the North American Team in the 1975 Bermuda Bowl (see CAPTAIN). He won the Chicago (since 1965 the Reisinger) 1958, Spring NAC Men's Teams 1964, and placed second in the Chicago 1959, Vanderbilt 1958. His regional titles are numerous.

Sheinwold was editor of *The Bridge World*

1934-1963, successively as technical editor, managing editor and senior editor, and editor of the ACBL *Bulletin* 1952-1958. He has been editor-in-chief of *Autobridge* since 1938. For years he was bridge editor of the Los Angeles *Times*; currently he is syndicated bridge and backgammon columnist for Los Angeles *Times* Syndicate, a contributing editor of *Popular Bridge*, and games editor for *Argosy*. He pioneered bridge lesson on Pay TV 1963-1964.

Sheinwold served as chairman of the LAWS COMMISSION OF THE ACBL 1964-1975, as chairman of the Appeals Committee at North American Championships, as chairman of the ACBL Board of Governors 1970-1973, and as a member of the Editorial Advisory Board, *Bridge Encyclopedia*. He was named ACBL Honorary Member for 1983.

Co-inventor of the KAPLAN-SHEINWOLD system, he has authored 13 bridge books, notably *Five Weeks to Winning Bridge*, which has sold more than 1,000,000 copies, and a series of *Pocket Books of Bridge Quizzes*. See BIBLIOGRAPHY, C, D, E, F.

SHEINWOLD, Betty. See KAPLAN, BETTY.

SHEINWOLD, Patricia Fox (formerly Mrs. Alfred, previously Mrs. Julian Adler) (b. 1934) of New York City, author and bridge teacher, won Spring NAC Women's Teams 1963, Keystone Conference Open Teams 1955. Sheinwold teaches bridge to the blind; one of her most noted students is jazz pianist George Shearing. She is the author of *Husbands and Other Men I've Played With*, and several books on other subjects.

SHELNUTT, John L. of Atlanta won Motor City Mixed Pairs 1970, All-American Mixed Pairs 1970, Mid-Atlantic Fall Swiss Teams 1969.

SHELTON, Montie of Dallas, secretary, won Fall NAC secondary Women's Swiss Teams 1978, Republic of Texas Women's Pairs 1976, Lone Star Mid-Winter Women's Pairs 1977, Toast of Tulsa Women's Pairs 1977, Oklahoma City Women's Swiss Teams 1981.

SHEN, Chun Shan (C.S.) (b.1933) of Hsin Chun, Taiwan, formerly of Lafayette IN, born in Nanking, China, professor of physics and astrophysics, one of the leading Far East players, placed second in the Bermuda Bowl 1969 and was Far East champion 1976. He also represented Taiwan in the World Team Olympiad 1964, 1972, Far East Championships 1962, 1963, 1966. His national wins include Taiwan Open Teams 1955, 1956, 1967, 1976, 1979, 1980, Open Pairs 1955, 1972. Shen, a world-class Go player, was one of the original Precision players who helped C.C. WEI develop the PRECISION CLUB system.

SHEN, K. W. (b. 1911) of Bangkok, Thailand, merchant, placed second in the Bermuda Bowl 1969 as a member of the Taiwan Team and was Far East champion 1961, 1966 as a member of the Thailand Team. He also represented Thailand in the Bermuda Bowl 1967, World Team Olympiad 1964, Far East Championships 1960.

SHENKIN, Barnet J. (b. 1950) of Glasgow, Scotland, carpet importer, represented Scotland 16 times between 1974–1981 and represented Great Britain in the World Open Pairs 1972, Common Market Championships 1975, 1977, 1979, European Championships 1977, 1979. He won the LONDON SUNDAY TIMES PAIRS (since 1981 INVITATIONAL PAIRS) 1976, 1980, GOLD CUP 1973, 1977, Lederer Cup 1977, 1979, Woolwich Foursomes 1979, Portland Mixed Pairs 1978, BBL Swiss Teams 1975.

SHEPARD, Edward V. (1869–1937) of New York City, civil engineer, born in Massachusetts, was one of America's leading authorities on the mathematics of bridge, having devoted many years to studying card probabilities. Called by ELY CULBERTSON, "a giant of the Old Guard," Shepard was a pioneer in many areas of bridge. He was the first to establish a college for the teaching of bridge and the qualifying of bridge teachers, the first to teach bridge over the radio in 1923, and one of the first to teach and write on contract bridge in 1924 and 1925. A member of the advisory council of the ABL, he assisted in drafting and approving the OFFICIAL SYSTEM. He contributed articles to numerous magazines, had a syndicated newspaper column, and authored several books including, *Scientific Auction Bridge*, *Win at Bridge*, *Contract Bridge Standardized*, and *Correct Contract Bridge*. See BIBLIOGRAHY, A, C, E.

SHEPHERD, Richard of Atlanta won the FISHBEIN TROPHY 1974, Spingold 1974. His numerous regional wins include Summer NAC secondary Swiss Teams 1973, Mid-South KO Teams 1974, 1976, Open Teams 1970, Men's Pairs 1976, Mid-Atlantic KO Teams 1974, 1975, 1976, 1977, 1978, Swiss Teams 1975, 1976, 1977, Open Pairs 1976, District 7 GNT 1974, 1979, 1980, 1981, Zone III 1981.

SHERBURN, Robert L. (b. 1943) of Ada MI, part owner of a steel brokerage firm, won Motor City Master Pairs 1973, Open Pairs 1970, Mixed Pairs 1971, KO Teams 1976, Great Lakes Men's Pairs 1965, Open Pairs 1975, Swiss Teams Flt. A 1981, Midwest Swiss Teams 1975, Cambrian Shield Swiss Teams Flt. A, KO Teams 1980, Wolverine Master Swiss Teams 1981.

SHERIDAN, John K. (b. 1948) of Indianapolis IN, attorney, won Spring NAC Men's Pairs 1978, placed second in 1975 and in the Spingold 1977, 1979. His more than 25 regional wins include Spring NAC secondary Swiss Teams 1978, District 11 Open Pairs 1972, 1974, Swiss Teams 1974, Men's Swiss Teams, Men's Pairs 1980, District 5 Master Pairs, Swiss Teams 1974, Open Pairs 1976, All-American Open Pairs 1972, 1973, Swiss Teams 1976.

SHERMAN, Ruth T. (1903–1965) of New York City was one of the leading players of the East Coast for 30 years. She won Summer NAC Mixed Teams 1935, a victory she repeated in 1945. She won a total of 10 major titles including the Chicago (now the Reisinger) 1944, the Vanderbilt 1953, and the Master Pairs 1946.

SHEVITZ, Dr. Henry A. (b. 1942) of Orchard Lake MI, physician, won District 5 Open Pairs 1965, Motor City Open Teams 1967, Great Lakes Swiss Teams 1971, Open Pairs 1979. He plays flute and piano with a symphony orchestra and a chamber music group.

SHIPLEY, Roberta D. (Bobbie) (b. 1933) of Mundelein IL, ACBL associate national tournament director, won Iowa Master Pairs 1969, Mid–Winter Holiday Women's Pairs 1978, Great Lakes Women's Swiss Teams 1979, 1981, Midwest Spring Women's Swiss Teams 1981. She is a contributor to the Chicago *Kibitzer*. Shipley, a director since 1965, received the associate national rating in 1981.

SHMUKLER, Pauline (Mrs. Albert) (b. 1913) of Miami Beach, formerly of Philadelphia, bridge teacher, placed second in Fall NAC Women's Teams 1946, 1954. Her numerous regional titles include Mid-Atlantic Fall Mixed Pairs 1952, Keystone Conference Open Teams 1952, 1955, Open Pairs 1959, Southeastern Women's Swiss Teams 1978. She was forced to curtail her bridge playing activities in 1954 due to an automobile accident.

SHNEIDER, Alma H. (b. 1928) of Durban, South Africa, bridge teacher, placed second in the World Women's Teams 1968, 1972, and also represented South Africa in the World Women's Pairs 1972. Her national titles include South Africa Open Teams 1965, 1967, 1972, 1976, 1977, Open Pairs 1971, 1975, Pioneer Teams 1975, 1976, Interprovincial Teams 1973, 1977. She is past president of the SOUTHERN AFRICAN BRIDGE FEDERATION and a former secretary and chairman of the Durban BC.

SHOOP, Homer (b. 1912) of North Webster IN, retired banker, placed second in the Life Master Pairs 1980 and won numerous regionals including Desert Empire Men's Pairs 1959, Midwest Fall Men's Pairs 1960, Upper New York State Men's Pairs 1959, Pacific Southwest Men's Pairs 1964, Polar Master Pairs 1965, Central States II Swiss Teams 1979, Cambrian Shield Open Pairs 1980, Gold Coast Swiss Teams 1981. He is the founder of the International Palace of Sports youth foundation which annually awards the KING OR QUEEN OF BRIDGE title. Shoop is a former tennis tournament player.

SHORT, Brian D. (b. 1944) of Edinburgh, Scotland, data processing manager, represented Scotland in 16 CAMROSE TROPHY matches, and represented Great Britain in the Common Market Championships 1977, World Open Pairs 1978, 1982. His national titles include Scottish Cup twice, National Pairs three times, Men's Team's four times, and many others. Short is a graduate of Edinburgh University.

SHORT, Karol K. (b. 1934) of Miami, tennis pro, won Southeastern Women's Pairs 1969, Mixed Pairs, Swiss Teams 1972. Nicknamed "Golden Goddess of Tennis" she was ranked the #5 woman player in the United States and #6 in the world in the Fifties. She was banned from playing at Wimbledon until she covered her gold lamé panties with white lace. Short turned pro in 1959 and toured with the

Harlem Globetrotters and Althea Gibson. She is special events chairman of the American Cancer Society.

SHOUP, Russell O. (b. 1947) of Dayton OH placed second in Fall NAC Swiss Teams 1979. He won numerous regional titles including Motor City Master Pairs 1974, Men's Pairs 1971, Midwest Spring Swiss Teams 1981, Open Pairs 1978, Fall Master Pairs 1974, Canadian Nat'l Swiss Teams 1977, Master Pairs 1976.

SHRAGE, Dr. Marcus (b. 1919) of Dublin, Ireland, physician, represented Ireland in the European Championships 1951, 1954, 1955, 1957, 1958, 1963, 1966, 1967. His national titles include IBU Open Teams, Mixed Pairs, CBA of Ireland Open Teams, Men's Teams.

SHUMAN, Kerri (Mrs. Michael) of Los Angeles, professional bridge player, one of the leading American women players, won the World Mixed Pairs 1978, the McKENNEY TROPHY 1974, Fall NAC Mixed Pairs 1975, 1977 (second in 1971, 1974), Spring NAC Women's Pairs 1972, Summer Master Mixed Teams 1980, Spring NAC Women's Teams 1978 (second in 1974), and placed second in Fall NAC Life Master Women's Pairs 1975. Her more than 80 regional titles include Spring NAC secondary Swiss Teams 1974, 1975, Open Pairs 1975, Mixed Swiss Teams 1976, Summer Swiss Teams Flt. A 1979, Women's Pairs Flt. A 1981, Hawaii Master Pairs, Mixed Pairs, Open Pairs, Women's Swiss Teams, Swiss Teams Flt. A 1982. She owns and races thoroughbred horses.

SHUMAN, MICHAEL (b. 1931) of Los Angeles, professional bridge player, one of the leading West Coast players, won Spring NAC Men's Teams 1962, placed second in 1974 and in the Chicago (since 1965 the Reisinger) 1961, Fall NAC Men's Pairs 1959, Spring NAC Open Pairs 1962. His more than 50 regional titles include Summer NAC secondary Swiss Teams 1972, Spring Mixed Swiss Teams, Men's Pairs 1976. Shuman is a former managing editor of *Contract Bridge Forum*. His writings include the column "Dummy Play Technique" in the *Forum* and contributions to *The Bridge World* and other magazines and tabloids. He owns and races thoroughbred horses.

SIDELL, Steven (b. 1947) of Seattle, investor, travel consultant, won Oregon trail KO Teams 1970, Open Pairs 1972, Klondike Swiss Teams 1974, Canadian Men's Pairs 1970, Inland Empire Master Pairs, Swiss Teams 1973, Peach City Men's Pairs 1978, Puget Sound Swiss Teams 1976, Men's Pairs, Swiss Teams Flt. A 1981. Sidell is a former president of the Seattle Unit and of District 19.

SIDES, William C. of Arcadia CA, bank executive, placed second in the Spingold 1975, Spring NAC Men's teams 1974. He won numerous regional titles including Spring NAC secondary Swiss Teams 2nd Flt., Swiss Teams 1975, Bridge Week KO Teams 1973, 1977, Master Swiss Teams Flt. A 1979, 1981,

Los Angeles Winter Open Pairs Flt. A 1976, Master Pairs 1980. One of the top-ranking players of the AMERICAN BRIDGE ASSOCIATION, he set a record at the 1969 ABA Summer Nationals by winning five major events and finishing second in another.

SIEBERT, Allan P. (b. 1942) of Little Rock AR, company president, won several regionals including Fall NAC secondary Men's Teams 1967, Open Pairs 1973, Big D Master Pairs 1974, Mid-South KO Teams 1976, Open Pairs 1980, District 15 Master Pairs 1977, Swiss Teams Flt. A 1980, Mississippi Valley Master Pairs 1977, Music City Open Pairs Flt. A 1977, Missouri Valley Swiss Teams 1971.

SIEBERT, David A. (b. 1940) of Little Rock AR, company executive, won more than 25 regional titles including Fall NAC secondary Men's Teams 1967, Open Pairs 1973, Mid-South Master Pairs 1972, 1975, 1978, Open Pairs 1970, KO Teams 1975, Men's Pairs, Open Pairs Flt. A 1979, Wisconsin Men's Pairs, Men's Swiss Teams 1980.

SIEGEL, George I. (b. 1940) of Los Angeles, engineer, won Pacific Southwest Open Pairs Flt. A 1978, Raincross Swiss Teams 1979, Golden State Swiss Teams Flt. A 1980, Los Angeles Winter KO Teams 1980.

SIEGELMAN, Harold L. (b. 1951) of Alexandria VA, federal employee, won Fall NAC secondary Silver Trophy Pairs Flt. B 1980, Silver Anniversary Swiss Teams 1974, Buffalo Centennial Master Pairs 1974, Mid-Atlantic Men's Swiss Teams 1978, Open Pairs 1980.

SIEGRIST, John Mark (b. 1941) of Nepean ON, government employee, placed second in the Canadian Nat'l Teams and won Summer NAC secondary Open Pairs 1973, District 1 GNP 1980. He is vice president of Eastern Ontario BA and editor of its publication *The Recap*.

SIGTHORSSON, Thorarinn (b. 1939) of Reykjavik, Iceland, dentist, represented Iceland in the World Open Pairs 1974, 1978, European championships 1977. His national titles include Icelandic Cup 1979, 1981, Teams 1976, 1981, Pairs 1977, 1979.

SIGURHJARTARSON, Karl (b. 1941) of Reykjavik, Iceland, manager, represented Iceland in the World Open Pairs 1974, European Championships 1970, 1973, 1974. His national titles include Open Teams 1970, 1971.

SIGURSDDON, Torin (b. 1931) of Reykjavik, Iceland, meteorologist, represented Iceland in the European Championships 1967 and won Icelandic Open teams 1963, Open Pairs 1962, Reykjavik Open Teams 1963.

SIGUROSSON, Thorgeir (1934–1971) of Reykjavik, Iceland, accountant, won Icelandic Open Teams 1958, 1960, 1963, Open Pairs 1959, 1960. He represented Iceland in the European Championships 1967.

SILBER, Albert J. (b. 1912) of Birmingham MI, attorney, won All-American Open Teams 1959, Men's Pairs 1965, Great Lakes Open Pairs 1966, Open Teams 1968, Motor City Men's Swiss Teams 1976, Senior Citizens Men's Pairs 1981. Silber was captain of the team which defeated the SHARIF BRIDGE CIRCUS in 1970. He is past president of the Michigan BA.

SILBERSTEIN, David S. (b. 1951) of North Bergen NJ, research assistant, won Summer NAC Senior and Advanced Senior Master Pairs 1974, New England Individual 1973.

SILBERWASSER, Roger (b. 1923) of Brussels, Belgium, born in Austria, bridge club manager, represented Belgium in the World Team Olympiad 1960, World Open Pairs 1962, European Championships 1961, 1966, 1967. His national titles include Open Teams 1960, 1961, 1962, Open Pairs 1961, Master Pairs 1961, 1963.

SILBORN, Mrs. Gunborg (b. 1924) of Norrköping, Sweden, won the World Women's Teams 1968, European Women's Championships 1967, Nordic Women's Championships 1964, 1966, 1978, 1980 and nine national women's titles.

SILBY, Frances (formerly Singer) (b. 1916) of Ft. Lauderdale FL, formerly of Overland Park KS, retired psychiatric social worker, won Spring NAC secondary Swiss Teams 1973, Summer Swiss Teams Flt. A 1974, Bermuda Women's Pairs 1974. Puerto Rico Master Pairs 1973.

SILODOR, Sidney (1906–1963) of Havertown PA, lawyer, bridge lecturer, writer, and instructor, was one of the world's top players. He was on the North American team that won the World Championship in the first Bermuda Bowl matches in 1950 and also represented North America in that event in 1958 and 1961, as well as playing for the U.S. in the World Olympiad of 1960. Silodor won the McKENNEY TROPHY in 1946, and set a record when he won the NAC Mixed Pairs five times. He won more than 30 North American Championships, including the Vanderbilt eight times, the Spingold and the Mixed Teams three times each. At his death he was a member of the ACBL Board and holder of the Open Pairs Championship, a title which he had first won in 1941 and again in 1945. He was the third highest on the list of all-time masterpoint winners, with a total of 6,450 — a figure great enough to hold that place until a year after his death when his total was surpassed by NORMAN KAY, who had been his regular partner. Silodor authored many articles for *The Bridge World* and a newspaper column. His books included *Silodor Says*, *Contract Bridge According to Silodor and Tierney*, and *The Complete Book of Duplicate Bridge*. See BIBLIOGRAPHY, C, E, F.

SILVA, Lionel D. da (b. 1911) of Manila, Philippines, insurance underwriter, represented Philippines in the World Team Olympiad 1960, 1964, Far East Championships 1959–1963, winning in 1957, 1958. His national titles include Open Teams 1956, Master Pairs 1958, Open Pairs 1961.

SILVER, Joseph (b. 1941) of Montreal, trial lawyer, one of the leading Canadian players, represented Canada in the World Open Pairs 1974, 1978, Rosenblum Cup Teams 1978. He won the Vanderbilt 1974, Spring NAC Men's Teams 1981, placed second in 1973 and in Summer NAC Master Mixed Teams 1974. His numerous regional titles include New England KO Teams 1971, 1972, Open Teams 1969, Can-Am Open Teams 1969, 1973, 1979, Open Pairs 1970, Men's Swiss Teams 1980, Master Swiss Teams 1977, KO Teams 1976, Canadian Nat'l KO Teams 1978, Master Pairs 1979. He contributes to *Melange de Bridge* and is a panelist for *The Bridge World*.

SILVERMAN, Jerome R. (Jerry) (b. 1912) of Mill Valley CA, retired attorney and account executive, won New York–New Jersey Men's Pairs 1959. Active in bridge administration for many years, Silverman was ACBL president in 1973, ACBL treasurer 1970–1972, chairman of the ACBL Goodwill Committee 1975, ACBL representative to the WBF 1973–1976, trustee of the ACBL Charity Foundation 1974, president of the ACBL Charity Foundation 1980–1982, vice president of the WBF 1976–1978, a member of the ACBL Board of Directors 1966–1975 and a member of the Laws Commission of the ACBL. He is a former president of the New Jersey BL, New York–New Jersey Bridge Conference and District 21. He served as npc of the North American Team in the 1977 Bermuda Bowl. Silverman is a graduate of Rutgers University School of Law. Leisure activities include directing on bridge cruises. He is the father of NEIL M. SILVERMAN.

SILVERMAN, Neil M. (b. 1949) of New York City, options trader, former genealogical researcher, represented the United States in the World Open Pairs, Rosenblum Cup Teams 1978. He won the Life Master Pairs 1976, Spring Men's Pairs 1980, placed second in 1981 and in the Reisinger 1977. His more than 20 regional wins include Fall NAC secondary Swiss Teams 2nd Flt., Men's Pairs 1974, Summer Swiss Teams 1978. Silverman played in the INVITATIONAL PAIRS CHAMPIONSHIP, placing third, won the gold medal at the MACCABIAH GAMES and made a 13 segment TV show on bridge for the British Broadcasting Corp., all in 1981.

SILVERMAN, Shirley (Mrs. Harry J.) (b. 1928) of White Plains NY, bridge writer and editor, won District 4 Women's Swiss Teams 1977, Tri-State Women's Swiss Teams 1980, Long Island Open Pairs Flt. A 1981. She served as chairman of the ACBL Board of Governors 1975–1978 and as president of Unit 188. She is a co-owner of BARCLAY BRIDGE SUPPLIES. A member of the ABTA and IBPA, she has written several teacher's manuals and edited *Expert Bridge*.

SILVERSTEIN, Dr. Bruce M. (b. 1951) of Lancaster PA, physician, won Mid-Atlantic Open Pairs 1975, 1979, Swiss Teams 1981, Nassau-Suffolk Swiss Teams 1977, District 4 Fall Men's Swiss Teams, GNT 1977.

SILVERSTEIN, Nate (b. 1909) of Memphis, born in Poland, bridge club manager, won dozens of regional titles including Mid-South Spring Open Teams 1964, Open Pairs 1959, Master Pairs 1973, Summer Open Pairs 1962, Open Teams 1965, Fall Master Pairs 1967, 1970, Southern Conference Fall Open Teams 1952, 1956, 1958, Master Pairs 1965, Open Pairs 1958, Men's Pairs 1952, Mississippi Valley Open Teams 1965, Men's Pairs 1964. For more than 30 years a devoted promoter of bridge, he was a member of the ACBL Board of Directors 1968–1971 and was largely responsible for the move of ACBL Headquarters to Memphis. He has been president of Unit 144 many times and serves as vice president of the ACBL Charity Foundation.

SILVERSTONE, Victor (b. 1940) of Glasgow, Scotland, chartered accountant, represented Scotland in 10 international matches and was a member of the victorious CAMROSE TROPHY team once. His national titles include Open Teams twice. He is one of four Scottish players to compete in the INVITATIONAL PAIRS and the British Trials.

SIMITZ, Robert J. (b. 1924) of Bolingbrook IL, insurance supervisor, won Central States Open Pairs 1955, Master Pairs 1954.

SIMMONS, Joyce H. of Charleston SC, manager, won Florida Open Pairs 1960, Mid-Atlantic Winter Open Pairs 1972, Thanksgiving Swiss Teams 1972.

SIMON, Adaline (Mrs. John E.) (b. 1901) of St. Louis won Fall NAC Women's Teams 1959 and numerous regional titles including Midwest Spring Mixed Pairs 1956, Fall Open Teams 1960, Mixed Pairs 1960, Mid-South Open Pairs 1957, Women's Pairs 1958, Mississippi Valley Master Pairs 1959, 1963, Missouri Valley Mixed Pairs 1957, Rocky Mountain Open Teams 1956.

SIMON, Andrzej (b. 1934) of Krakow, Poland, chemical engineer, bridge journalist, represented Poland in the World Pairs 1966. He was overall winner at the Beirut Festival 1968 and won Beirut Festival Open Teams 1968, Juan-les-Pins Festival Open Teams 1965. He is a former secretary of the European Bridge League Junior Division and assistant secretary of the IBPA. He edited the IBPA *Bulletin* 1966–1967.

SIMON, Edith of Memphis, ACBL librarian 1972–1983, served as administrative secretary for the Chicago CBA 1964–1972. She is a member of the ACBL Goodwill and Charity Committees. Simon is a contributing editor, *Bridge Encyclopedia.*

SIMON, Harold (b. 1931) of Reseda CA, pharmacist, won Desert Empire Open Teams 1960, Bridge Week Open Teams 1961, 1962.

SIMON, John E. (b. 1897) of St. Louis, limited partner in brokerage firm, represented the United States in the World Open Pairs 1962. He won Spring NAC Men's Teams 1972, 1973 and placed second in Spring NAC Open Pairs 1961. He won numerous regional titles including Fall NAC secondary Men's

Teams 1965, Open Teams 1969, Midwest Open Teams 1954, 1956, 1958, Mississippi Valley Open Teams 1953, 1958, Missouri Valley Open Teams 1955, 1961. Simon was named ACBL Honorary Member in 1962. He was chairman of the ACBL Goodwill and Membership Committees, trustee of the ACBL Charity Foundation, president of the Midwest Conference and of the St. Louis Unit. He is the donor of the SIMON AWARD (see IBPA AWARDS).

SIMON, S. J. (Simon Skidelsky or Skid) (1904–1948), novelist and bridge writer, was one of the best-loved British bridge personalities. One of the originators of the ACOL SYSTEM, he was European champion 1948 and also represented Great Britain in the European Championships 1939. His many national wins include the GOLD CUP 1937, 1947. His many successful humorous novels in collaboration with ballet expert Carol Brahms include *Bullet in the Ballet, No Bed for Bacon,* and *Trottie True.* A contributor to *The Bridge World,* Simon wrote the classic *Why You Lose at Bridge, Design for Bidding,* and *Cut for Partners.* See BIBLIOGRAPHY, C, E, H.

SÍMONARSON, Símon (b. 1933) of Reykjavik, Iceland, contractor, represented Iceland in the European Championships 1963, 1967, 1970, 1975, 1979, World Team Olympiad 1968, 1976, 1980. His national titles include Icelandic Open Teams 1958, 1960, 1964, 1966, 1967, 1974, 1979, Open Pairs 1959, 1960, 1969. From 1975 to 1981 he was bridge columnist for *Dagbladid.*

SIMONARSSON, Hallur of Reykjavik, Iceland, journalist, represented Iceland in the European Championships 1967, 1969. His national titles include Open Teams 1964, 1966, 1967, 1969, 1974.

SIMONS, Edgar (b. 1928) of San Jose CA, professor of mathematics, won All-American Men's Pairs 1960, District 5 Open Teams 1963, Mid-Winter Holiday Master Swiss Teams 1977, All-Western Swiss Teams 1980.

SIMPSON, Carreen S. (b. 1944) of Fountain Valley CA, school teacher, won Mid-Winter Holiday Mixed Pairs 1976, Los Angeles Winter Mixed Pairs 1978, Raincross Swiss Teams Flt. A 1981.

SIMPSON, Gene (b. 1942) of Fountain Valley CA, advertising salesman, won Fall NAC secondary Men's Swiss Teams 1976, Mid-Winter Holiday Mixed Pairs 1976, Los Angeles Winter Mixed Pairs 1978, Raincross KO Teams 1979, Swiss Teams 1980, Swiss Teams Flt. A 1981, Desert Empire Open Pairs 1979, Pacific Southwest Men's Pairs 1980, Bridge Week Swiss Teams, KO Teams 1981.

SIMS, Dorothy Rice (1889–1960) of Deal NJ was one of the leading personalities of the early days of bridge. Born June 24, 1889 at Asbury Park NJ, she was the daughter of Isaac L. Rice, first manufacturer of the submarine and patron of chess and other recreational activities. From her teens she was active in competition, holding the U.S. motorcycle speed championship for women (1911) and becoming one of the first U.S. aviatrixes, in which capacity she met and married P. HAL SIMS. She was a noted sculptress and designed the CITY OF ASBURY PARK TROPHY. Her writings included several bridge books as well as works in fields other than bridge. Acquiring an interest in bridge through her husband, she became a sucessful player. Her wins include ABL Auction Women's Pairs 1929, AWL Open Team 1929, Open Pairs 1930 and NAC Mixed Team 1930. In 1935 she was her husband's principal partner in a 150-rubber match against ELY and JOSEPHINE CULBERTSON (see CULBERTSON-SIMS MATCH). She is widely credited with "inventing" the psychic bid, but probably initiated only the popular name for it; however, she wrote the first book on the subject, *Psychic Bidding*, 1932. After her husband's death, she toured the world several times as a political correspondent for various newspapers. See BIBLIOGRAPHY, C, K.

SIMS P(hilip) Hal (1886–1949) of Deal NJ was one of the greatest American players, and his system had the largest expert following. Born in Selma AL, Sims represented U.S. banks in foreign countries from 1906–1916. As a member of the U.S. Army Air Corps in 1917 he met Dorothy Rice, a U.S. aviatrix in transport service, whom he married. After World War I Sims devoted himself chiefly to competitive sports, in which he excelled, and to bridge. He held a national trapshooting record and won the Artists' and Writers' Golf Tournament in 1937. In auction bridge he was a member of the highest-ranked team, the Knickerbocker Whist Club team, which included SYDNEY S. LENZ, WINFIELD S. LIGGETT, GEORGE REITH, and RALPH J. LEIBENDERFER. He was captain of the contract bridge team called the FOUR HORSEMEN, whose other members were WILLARD S. KARN, OSWALD JACOBY and DAVID BURNSTINE. This team won most of the principal American tournaments 1931–1933.

The SIMS SYSTEM, a subjective approach based on Sims' desire to dominate every pair and team of which he was a member, left little impression on contract bridge methods used by experts from 1935 on; first- and second-hand opening one-bids were stronger than third- and fourth-hand bids; notrump bids were always strong but had wide limits; psychic bids were used freely; high preemptive bids were eschewed. In 1935 Hal and Dorothy Sims tested this system in a 150–rubber match against ELY and JOSEPHINE CULBERTSON, and were defeated (see CULBERTSON-SIMS MATCH). Sims' books include *Money Contract*, *Master Contract* (his definitive work, largely by SIR DERRICK WERNHER) and several lesser works.

Sims was one of the most colorful characters in bridge history. Called "the shaggy giant", Sims' commanding presence (6′4″ in height, more than 300 lbs, in weight, big-boned and muscular) augmented his claim to authority. For more than five years his mansion in Deal NJ was summer headquarters for the principal experts and the promising new players. He controlled the ABL for several years without holding formal office. He founded the Deal Club, a bridge club at which the principal U.S. and international experts played from 1930–1935. His skill as a raconteur and his personal charm were proverbial. He died of a heart attack while bidding a hand in a game at the Havana Country Club, where he and his wife spent their winters after 1946. See BIBLIOGRAPHY, C.

SINISCALCO, Guglielmo (b. 1921) of Naples, Italy, professor of civil engineering, WBF Grand Master, one of the world's great players, was Bermuda Bowl champion 1957, 1958, 1959, European champion 1951, 1956, 1957, 1958 and second in 1952. His national titles include Italian Open Teams 1949, 1951, 1956, 1957, 1959.

SINT, Cornelis J. (Cees) (b. 1940) of Broek in Waterland, The Netherlands, mathematics teacher, bridge writer and journalist, represented The Netherlands in the European Championships 1970, 1971, 1973, 1975, 1977, 1981, World Open Pairs 1970, 1978, World Team Olympiad 1972. His national titles include Open Pairs 1970, 1978, Open Teams 1971–1975, 1977–1979. He is an editorial staff member of *Bridge*, the publication of the Nederlandse Bridge Bond. Sint is the co-author (with TON SCHIPPERHEYN) of 18 bridge books including *From Start to Finish*, *Modern Acol Book* and *Test Your Bridge*.

SITHISARIPUTRA, Boonita (b. 1946) of Bangkok, Thailand, company executive and director, represented Thailand in the Far East Championships 1967, 1968, 1969, 1971, 1973, 1975, 1976, 1977, 1978, 1979, 1981, World Women's Teams 1980. She won ASEAN Women's Teams 1980, Mixed Teams 1982 and was runner-up in the Far East Women's Teams 1979, ASEAN Women's Teams 1981. Her national successes include all major titles. She is the youngest winner ever of a major event (Mixed Pairs) in Thai bridge history in 1961 at the age of 17.

SIU, M. C. of Hong Kong, businessman, represented Hong Kong in the Far East Championships three times. His national victories include Open Teams, Master Teams, Open Pairs, Master Pairs, Mixed Pairs, Individual.

SKELTON, Juanita M. (b. 1956) of Dallas, bridge teacher, won Fall NAC Mixed Pairs 1979. Her regional titles include Golden Gate Swiss Teams Flt. A 1979, Women's Pairs 1980, Los Angeles Winter Women's KO Teams 1979, Hawaii Women's Swiss Teams 1980, Oklahoma City Women's Swiss Teams 1981. Skelton was 1979 Senior Master of the Year (see MINI McKENNEY).

SKINNER, Lt. Col. Richmond H. (Dick) (b. 1898) of Dallas, one of the leading American bridge personalities, won Eastern States KO Teams (Reisinger) 1940, New England Fall Mixed Teams 1947, 1952, KO Teams, Master Teams 1948, Men's Pairs 1946, Mixed Pairs 1947, 1948. He invented SKINNER PSYCHIC CONTROLS, SKINNER RESPONSES TO A 1 NT OPENING, and SKINNER TWO-BIDS and originated a point-count method in 1932 in which an ace was assigned 5 points, king 3 points, queen 2 points, and jack 1 point. He was ACBL president 1944 and a member of the ACBL Executive Committee from formation through 1944. Skinner also served as president of the Mid-Atlantic BA, Keystone Conference and New England BA. He was educated at M.I.T. and California Institute of Technology. A civil engineer by training, he had a varied career; U.S. Army officer, pipe organ builder and installer, pilot and flying instructor, top flight tennis player and referee (awarded the McGovern Cup for national tennis umpire of the year 1972), and longtime member of the New Hampshire Legislature.

SKOLNIK, Mel D. (b. 1942) of Newport Beach CA, investor, won the McKENNEY TROPHY 1981. Since 1975 he has won more than 45 regional titles including Summer NAC secondary Swiss Teams Flt. A 1981, Fall BAM Teams Flt. A 1981, White Hat Swiss Teams, Swiss Teams Flt. A, KO Teams, Open Pairs 1981, Hawaii KO Teams, Men's Swiss Teams 1981, Wisconsin Open Pairs, Men's Swiss Teams 1981.

SKOROUPO, Roman (1900–1971) of Helsingfors, Finland, businessman and bridge writer, was prominent in the administration of bridge. He was for many years a member of the Executive Committee of both the EUROPEAN BRIDGE FEDERATION and the WORLD BRIDGE FEDERATION, and was a familiar figure at World Team Olympiads, where he served on the Appeals Committee. He also served as secretary general of the FINNISH BRIDGE LEAGUE. An active bridge writer, Skoroupo was also a contributing editor, *Bridge Encyclopedia*.

SKOTTE, Gulle (b. 1917) of Copenhagen, Denmark, was European Women's champion 1948, 1955, 1957 (second in 1951), Nordic Women's Team champion 1947, 1951, 1955, 1961, 1962. Her national wins include Open Teams 1951, 1953, Open Pairs 1953, and the Women's Teams six times between 1945 and 1952.

SLAGER, Hilda K. (Mrs. Julian H.) (b. 1908) of Montgomery AL won the international North–South Pairs Championship in the 1933 World Bridge Olympic, the United States North–South Pair Championship in th 1932 World Bridge Olympic, Mid-South Spring Open Teams 1958, Mid-Atlantic Fall Women's Pairs 1981, District 10 GNP 1981.

SLAVENBURG, Cornelis (Bob) (1917–1981) of Rotterdam, The Netherlands, merchant, won the World Open Pairs 1966 and also represented The Netherlands in Bermuda Bowl 1966, World Open Pairs 1970, European Championships 1951, 1959, 1965, 1966, 1967. His national titles include Open Teams four times and Open Pairs three times.

SLEMMONS, George W. of Bellevue WA won Spring NAC Men's Pairs 1974, Fall NAC secondary Swiss Teams Flt. A 1981, Oregon Trail Men's Swiss Teams, Swiss Teams 1971, Yakima Valley Swiss Teams 1974, Puget Sound KO Teams 1970, 1971, 1972, Swiss Teams Flt. A 1978, District 19 GNT, Zone VIII 1981.

SLINGER, James W. (b. 1938) of Fresno CA, philosophy professor, won Golden State KO Teams 1978, District 22 GNT 1974, 1981, Zone VII 1981, GNP 1980. He is a past president of Unit 522.

SLOAN, Jesse (b. 1913) of Van Nuys CA, real estate loan broker, former bridge club owner, won the Vanderbilt 1952, Summer NAC secondary Mixed Pairs 1963, Southeastern Open Teams 1940, Bridge Week KO Teams 1962.

SMART, Diana F. of Doncaster East, Victoria, Australia, former psychology lecturer, represented Australia in the Far East Women's Championships 1978, 1981, World Women's Teams 1980, Venice Trophy Teams 1981. Her national titles include Open Interstate Teams 1973, Women's Interstate Teams 1976, 1977, 1981, Women's Pairs 1975.

SMILDE, Roelof A. (b. 1930) of Sydney, Australia, bridge teacher, one of the leading Australian players, was Far East champion 1968, 1970 and also represented Australia in the World Team Olympiad 1964, 1968, 1972, Bermuda Bowl 1976. His national titles include Open Teams 1958, 1961, 1962, 1963, 1965, 1974, Open Pairs 1974.

SMITH, Beverly G. (formerly King) (b. 1948) of Redondo Beach CA, commercial artist, won Navajo Trail Mixed Pairs, Master Pairs 1970, Los Angeles Winter Women's Swiss Teams 1976.

SMITH, Curtis (b. 1925) of Conroe TX, engineer, one of the leading players of the Southwest, won the Spingold 1966, 1977, Fall NAC Open Pairs 1960, Grand National Teams 1977, and placed second in the Spingold 1972, Chicago (since 1965 the Reisinger) 1960, 1964, Fall NAC Open Pairs 1953, Life Master Men's Pairs 1970, Life Master Pairs 1963. Smith also won numerous regional titles. He is a contributor to the ACBL *Bulletin*, the author of *Bidding Through Logic*, and the inventor of the SMITH CONVENTION. See DEFENSE TO OPENING THREE-BID; BIBLIOGRAPHY, C.

SMITH, David B. (b. 1951) of Lafayette CA, project manager, won Golden Gate Open Pairs Flt. A 1978, KO Teams 1974, Swiss Teams 1975, All-Western KO Teams 1975, 1978, Master Teams 1976, California Capital Master Swiss Teams 1977. Smith was narrator for the MIKE LAWRENCE bridge tapes.

SMITH, David L. (b. 1949) of South Yarra, Victoria, Australia, scientist, represented Australia in the Bermuda Bowl, Far East Championships 1981. He won the Team Trials 1981, Victor Champion Cup 1980, 1981, National Open Teams 1981.

SMITH, David W. (b. 1944) of Butner NC, behavior modification specialist, represented Korea in the Far East Championships 1969. He placed second in the Grand National Teams 1973 and won numerous regionals including Fall NAC secondary BAM Swiss Teams 1979, Champagne Master Pairs 1972, Men's Pairs 1973, Tri-Unit Open Pairs, Swiss Teams 1972, Mid-Atlantic KO Teams 1976, 1977, Open Pairs

1980, Men's Pairs 1980, Men's Swiss Teams 1977, 1979, Master Pairs 1979. Smith contributes articles to the ABTA *Quarterly* and local newspapers.

SMITH, Duncan H. (b. 1948) of Victoria BC, nursing orderly, won British Columbia Men's Pairs 1970, Swiss Teams 1977, 1981, District 6 GNT 1978, Canadian Nat'l Teams Zone 6 1981.

SMITH, Hazel (Mrs. Fred R.) (b. 1914) of St. Petersburg FL, retired teacher, won Canadian Prairie Women's Pairs 1965, Navajo Trail Open Teams 1966, Can-At Mixed Teams 1968.

SMITH, Helen of Philadelphia, insurance broker, placed second in Fall NAC Mixed Pairs 1973, Spring Women's KO Teams 1976 and won Spring NAC secondary Master Pairs 1972, Fall Women's Swiss Teams 1976, Mixed Pairs Flt. A 1977, Summer Golder Master Pairs 1973, Keystone KO Teams 1973, Women's Teams 1972, Washington Bridge Week KO Teams 1976.

SMITH, Helen Martin (Mrs. Stanley, formerly Mrs. Al Sobel and Mrs. Jack White) (1910–1969) of Detroit was universally ranked as probably the greatest woman bridge player of all time. Born in Philadelphia, she enjoyed a brief stage career as a chorus girl and appeared in several stage shows including "Animal Crackers" with the Marx Brothers. Another chorus girl taught her how to play bridge and she rocketed to stardom at the card table. In 1934, as Mrs. Jack White, she won the Women's Pairs Championship, the first of her many titles. Shortly after her second marriage (to AL SOBEL, 1937–1945, ending in divorce), she was invited by ELY CULBERTSON to represent the United States, playing with JOSEPHINE CULBERTSON and Charles Vogelhofer in a World Championship conducted by the INTERNATIONAL BRIDGE LEAGUE in 1937 in Budapest, won by Austria. This was tacit recognition that Culbertson, like many other experts, considered her the equal of any male player, a view which became that of CHARLES GOREN in 1940 when they won the NAC Open Pair title, their first of many championships, playing in what was to become one of the most enduring and successful partnerships in bridge history. Together they won the De La Rue International Invitation Pairs Tournament in London in 1957, represented North America in the Bermuda Bowl 1957 and the United States in the World Team Olympiad of 1960, and won many of the 33 national championships credited to Smith, including the Life Master Pairs twice. In 1963, after a long residence in New York City, Smith moved to Miami Beach.

Her 33 titles included the Spingold five times, the Chicago (now the Reisinger) four times, and the Vanderbilt twice. In addition to her many national and regional titles, Smith won the McKENNEY TROPHY 1944, and the FISHBEIN TROPHY 1958. By 1948 she had amassed the greatest number of master points of any woman, taking over the top spot from SALLY YOUNG, and holding it uninterruptedly until 1964. She was the author of *All the Tricks* and several magazine articles. See BIBLIOGRAPHY, E.

SMITH, Herbert L. (b. 1932) of Burlingame CA, born in Vienna, Austria, accountant, won Fall NAC secondary Open Pairs 1978, All-Western KO Teams, Master Pairs 1970, Men's Pairs 1974, California Capital Open Pairs 1975, Swiss Teams 1976, Golden Gate KO Teams 1977, Golden State Men's Pairs 1975, Swiss Teams 1976, Tri-Cities KO Teams 1975, District 20 GNT 1980. District 21 representative to the ACBL Board of Directors, Smith is past president of District 21 and the WESTERN CONFERENCE.

SMITH, Leon E. (b. 1944) of Jacksonville FL, computer programmer, won Florida Swiss Teams 1974, 1981, Mixed Pairs 1970, Men's Pairs 1977, Mid-Atlantic Swiss Teams 1974, Open Pairs 1981.

SMITH, Paul C. (b. 1914) of Pacific Palisades CA, retired business executive, won Bridge Week Master Pairs 1955, Central States Open Pairs, Open Teams 1940.

SMITH, Ronald (Ron) (b. 1950) of North Miami Beach, formerly of St. Louis, professional bridge player, one of the leading American players, won the Blue Ribbon Pairs 1979 and placed second in the Grand National Teams 1973, Reisinger 1978. He won more than 70 regional titles including Summer NAC secondary Swiss Teams Flt. A 1981, Fall BAM Teams Flt. A 1981, Mid-South Open Teams 1972, 1974, Men's Pairs 1981, Open Pairs 1978, 1979, Master Pairs 1978, Black Hills Rodeo KO Teams, Open Pairs, Swiss Teams 1980, Mississippi Valley Open Pairs Flt. A, KO Teams, Swiss Teams 1979, Central Florida KO Teams, Men's Pairs, Open Pairs Flt. A 1980. Smith has performed as a concert pianist.

SMITH, Ronald L. (Ron) (b. 1947) of Chattanooga TN, formerly of Opelika AL, Flagstaff AZ and Los Angeles, professor of mathematics, won Spring NAC Men's Teams 1977 and placed second in the Grand National Teams 1975. He won more than 30 regional titles including Golden Gate Open Teams 1974, Palm Springs Open Pairs 1973, Raincross Open Pairs Flt. A, KO Teams 1978, Klondike Men's Pairs, Swiss Teams Flt. A 1980, Gem State Swiss Teams Flt. A 1980, District 11 Men's Swiss Teams 1981. He is past president of Unit 352.

SMITH, Terry (b. 1936) of Manhattan Beach CA, general administrator, former regional tournament director, was ACBL tournament coordinator 1968–1970, ACBL executive assistant 1970–1974, member of the drafting committee of the 1975 Laws of Duplicate, and ACBL organizer for the 1972 World Olympiad. While at headquarters, Smith contributed to the *Bulletin* and the *Bridge Encyclopedia*. He is a graduate of University of Chicago.

SMITH, Thomas M. (b. 1938) of Greenwich CT, bridge editor and writer, one of the leading American players, was an original member of the PRECISION TEAM which won the Spingold 1970, 1971, Vanderbilt 1972. His numerous regional wins include New England KO Teams 1968, Long Island KO Teams 1971, 1972. He was Intercollegiate champion 1965. Smith is a contributor to the ACBL *Bulletin* and *Bridge Journal*. He served as editorial manager of the second edition of the *Bridge Encyclopedia*, World Championship handbooks 1966–1972, as editorial assistant and business manager of the ACBL *Bulletin* 1966–1973, and as editor of *Post-Mortem*, the Greater New York BA publication. Smith currently is director of activities for the Cavendish Club.

SMITH, Verna M. (b. 1911) of Goleta CA, won Bridge Week Women's Pairs 1953, All-Western Women's Pairs 1956. Smith is a charter member of the ACBL Goodwill Committee.

SMITH, William H. (Bill) (b. 1909) of Fort Myers Beach FL, formerly of Tarrytown NY, retired teacher, was associate editor of the ACBL *Bulletin* 1958–1964. He became a tournament director in 1944 and directed bridge games on many cruises.

SMYTH, Dale (Niki) of Huntington Beach CA, bridge teacher, won Southern Conference Fall Open Pairs 1954, Midwest Spring Open Pairs 1959, Blue Grass Women's Pairs 1968.

SMOLEN, Michael (Mike) (b. 1940) of Marina Del Rey CA, attorney and commodity trader, one of the leading American players, won Spring NAC Men's Teams 1976 (second in 1974), Summer Men's Swiss Teams 1982, Fall NAC Swiss Teams 1978, Mixed Pairs 1979, FISHBEIN TROPHY 1982. His more than 50 regional titles include Fall NAC secondary Men's Swiss Teams 1971, Open Pairs 1980, Spring Swiss Teams 2nd Flt. 1975, Summer Open Pairs 1976, Men's Pairs Flt. A 1979. He devised the SMOLEN TRANSFER BID.

SMOLEN, Steven F. (Steve) (b. 1946) of Manhattan Beach CA, computer consultant, won Spring NAC Amateur Swiss Teams 1977. He regional wins include Summer NAC secondary Swiss Teams Flt. B 1974, Oregon Trail Open Teams 1973, All-Western Master Teams 1973, Yakima Valley Open Pairs 1974, Mount Shasta Swiss Teams 1974, Golden State Mixed Pairs 1977, Bridge Week Mixed Teams 1975.

SMOLENSKY, Pat (b. 1924) of Calgary AB, bridge teacher, represented Canada in the World Women's Pairs 1966, 1978. She won Inter-Mountain Women's Pairs 1959, Canadian Prairie Women's Pairs 1965, Saskatchewan Open Pairs 1975, South Saskatchewan Women's Pairs 1973. She is the editor of Calgary *Kibitzer*.

SNIDER, Wayne B. (b. 1947) of Mt. Prospect IL, assistant traffic manager, won Summer NAC secondary Swiss Teams 1971, Indy 500 Open Teams 1973, Mississippi Valley Open Teams 1974, Central States I Swiss Teams 1978, Men's Pairs 1973, Great Lakes Swiss Teams 1978, Champagne Open Pairs Flt. A 1981.

SNITE, Fred Jr. (d. 1955) of Miami Beach, lived for the last 19 years of his life in an iron lung. He was a regular competitor in ACBL tournaments and was

named ACBL Honorary Member in 1954. See HANDICAPPED PLAYERS.

SNOVEL, E. X. (b. 1933) of San Antonio, retired Air Force officer, won Capital City KO Teams 1977, Corpus Christi Swiss Teams 1978, Big D Winter Men's Pairs 1980, Master Swiss Teams 1982, Harvest Festival Unmixed Pairs 1981.

SNYDER, Ada-Claire (A.C.) (b. 1921) of Warrenton VA, freelance writer, former school teacher, won Mid-Atlantic Open Pairs 1974, Women's Pairs 1975, Women's Swiss Teams 1977.

SOBEL, Alexander M. (Al) (March 28, 1901–May 18, 1972) of New York City was one of the leading bridge personalities. Sobel won his greatest fame as a director of bridge tournaments, but he was also noted as a writer, a quizmaster and a wit. He was the third person to be the North American Championships Tournament Manager for the ACBL, following ALFRED M. GRUENTHER and RUSSELL BALDWIN, holding that position from 1942 until his retirement in 1969. Sobel, a graduate engineer of Massachusetts Institute of Technology, turned to bridge during the depression "rather than sell apples." He directed tournaments from September 1934 in the U.S., Canada, Mexico, Argentina, France, Italy, England, and Brazil with guest appearances in Hong Kong, Tokyo, and the Philippines. His debut as manager of a major tournament was in 1935 when he substituted for Gruenther at the Eastern States Championships, then a national tournament. He became the unofficial quiz master of the bridge players when the craze for quizzes about the time of "Ask Me Another" resulted in the bridge experts playing a similar game late at night after almost every tournament session. For three years, 1948–1951, he wrote the questions for the Bob Hawk *Lemac* radio quiz. His commanding voice created a tournament directorial style; until the great crowds of the Fifties Sobel seldom needed a microphone. In 1937 he married HELEN MARTIN WHITE; they divorced in 1945. He became a member of the ACBL Laws Commission 1943, was the first Honorary Member of the JAPAN CONTRACT BRIDGE LEAGUE, and was ACBL Honorary Member in 1949. Sobel was one of a group of four talented writers who worked for ELY CULBERTSON in the early Thirties. Culbertson's summonses to "Al" regularly created confusion, since, in addition to Sobel, the others were ALBERT MOREHEAD, ALFRED SHEINWOLD and ALPHONSE MOYSE JR. A former associate editor of the ACBL *Bulletin*, Sobel authored "30 Days," a popular monthly diary column for that publication from 1944 until his retirement in 1969, when it became a bi-monthly column entitled "60 Days." He was also a former editor of the West Coast publication, *Contract Bridge Forum* and contributing editor, *Bridge Encyclopedia*.

SOBEL, Helen Martin. See SMITH, HELEN MARTIN.

SOKOLOW, David I. (b. 1950) of Winnipeg MB, comptroller, won Roughrider Men's Pairs 1977, Saskatchewan KO Teams, Master Swiss Teams Flt. A, Men's Pairs 1978, Swiss Teams, Master Pairs

1980, Buffalo KO Teams, Men's Swiss Teams, Swiss Teams 1978, Gopher KO Teams 1981.

SOKOLOWER, Lester (b. 1931) of Nutley NJ, merchandiser, won Keystone Mixed Pairs 1961, Bermuda Open Pairs 1968, New England KO Teams 1966, NY-NJ Open Teams 1966.

SOLAR, Elizabeth (b. 1935) of Caracas, Venezuela, administrator, represented Venezuela in the World Women's Teams 1974, 1980, World Women's Pairs 1978, and represented Central American-Caribbean in the Venice Trophy Teams 1981. She was CAC champion 1979, 1980, 1981 and placed second in the South American Championships 1972.

SOLAR, Rosa Maria Pascual Lacrest de of Barcelona, Spain represented Spain in the World Women's Pairs 1974, World Women's Teams 1980, European Championships 1974. She has won many national titles.

SOLODAR, John (Hopper) (b. 1940) of New York City, director of systems and programming, was Bermuda Bowl champion 1981 and also represented the United States in the Rosenblum Cup Teams 1978. He won Fall NAC Life Master Men's Pairs 1968, Vanderbilt 1980 and placed second in the Spingold 1976, 1980. His numerous regional titles include Southeastern KO Teams 1969, 1970, Eastern States KO Teams (Reisinger) 1968, Fun City KO Teams 1975, Long Island KO Teams 1978, District 14 Summer KO Teams 1981. Solodar was New York manager for the SHARIF BRIDGE CIRCUS 1968.

SOLODAR, Judi. See RADIN, JUDI.

SOLOMON, Charles J. (1906–1975) of Philadelphia, attorney, bridge administrator, teacher and author, was one of the leading figures in the world of contract bridge. Life Master #16 in 1939, he amassed a lifetime total of 6594 master points and won 12 national titles, including the Chicago (now the Reisinger) 1937, 1938, 1939, 1944; Spingold 1955; Men's Teams, 1952, 1965; Mixed Teams 1949, 1950, 1959; and others, in addition to 16 second places and numerous regional wins. In 1956 he was a member of the U.S. International team, and he served as non-playing captain of the open team in 1959 and the U.S. women's team in 1960. He donated the CHARLES J. SOLOMON TROPHY to the WORLD BRIDGE FEDERATION in 1966, given to the country with the best record in pair events at World Pair Championship. Solomon was ACBL president in 1958 and chairman of the Board in 1944, 1955 and 1957, ACBL Honorary Member 1961. On the international level, he was on the organizing committee and helped to found the World Bridge Federation. He served as WBF vice president 1958-1964, as president 1964-1968, as chairman of the Board 1968-1972, and as honorary chairman from 1972 until his death. He also served with distinction on the ACBL Laws Commission from 1940 to 1960 and was on the Editorial Advisory Board *Bridge Encyclopedia*. Solomon was the author of *Slam Bidding and Point Count* and *No Trump Bidding*, and

was bridge editor of the *Philadelphia Inquirer* for 30 years. He sponsored the Solomon Award of the INTERNATIONAL BRIDGE PRESS ASSOCIATION, given annually for the best description of a bridge deal in the world press. See BUENOS AIRES AFFAIR.

SOLOMON, Eliezer N. (Ely) (b. 1944) of Riviera Beach MD, born in Bombay, India, software engineer, placed second in Fall NAC Swiss Teams 1978 and won Mid-Atlantic Open Pairs 1973, New England Knockout Swiss Teams 1977, District 4 Open Pairs 1977.

SOLOMON, Peggy (Mrs. Charles J., formerly Mrs. Benjamin Golder) (b. 1910) of Philadelphia, one of the leading American women players for three decades, represented the United States in the World Women's Pairs 1966. She won the Chicago (since 1965 the Reisinger) 1944, Summer NAC Master Mixed Teams 1949, 1950, 1959 (second in 1939, 1940), Spring NAC Women's Teams 1957, 1964, 1968, 1970 (second in 1948, 1953, 1954, 1961, 1967), Spring NAC Women's Pairs 1960, and placed second in the Spingold 1944, Vanderbilt 1954, Chicago 1953, Fall NAC Mixed Pairs 1961, Life Master Women's Pairs 1965, 1966, 1967. Her numerous regional titles include Fall NAC secondary Women's Teams 1963, 1964, 1965, Summer Women's Pairs 1964, District 5 Women's Swiss Teams 1978, 1980, District 4 Women's Pairs 1979.

SOLOMONS, Patricia B. (Pat) of Honolulu, real estate firm vice president, won Summer NAC secondary Commercial and Industrial Teams 1970, Hawaii Open Teams 1973, Women's Pairs 1974.

SOLOWAY, Paul (b. 1941) of Bothell WA, professional player, WBF Grand Master, one of the great players of the world, was Bermuda Bowl champion 1976, 1977, 1979 and placed second in the World Team Olympiad 1980. He also represented the United States in the World Team Oympiad 1972, and North America in the Bermuda Bowl 1973, 1975. He won the Team Trials 1975, 1977, HERMAN TROPHY 1976, McKENNEY TROPHY 1968, 1969, Fall NAC Life Master Men's Pairs 1965, Summer NAC Master Mixed Teams 1966, Vanderbilt 1969, 1978, Spingold 1978, Reisinger 1976, 1980, Grand National Teams 1974, 1976, and placed second in the Vanderbilt 1971, 1976, Spingold 1973, Spring NAC Men's Teams 1970, Men's Pairs 1969. Soloway won the Pan-American Invitational Championship 1977. His regional titles number more than 250.

SONTAG, Alan (b. 1946) of New York City, professional player, one of the leading American players, represented the United States in the World Open Pairs 1974, 1978, Rosenblum Cup Teams 1978. He won the INVITATIONAL PAIRS CHAMPIONSHIP 1972, 1975, Vanderbilt 1972, Reisinger 1973, Spingold 1980, 1982, Life Master Pairs 1977, Spring NAC Men's Teams 1971, 1979, Fall NAC Life Master Men's Pairs 1971, and placed second in the Vanderbilt 1975, 1981, Reisinger 1977, Life Master Pairs 1972. He also won the INVITATIONAL PAIRS CHAMPIONSHIP 1973, 1975, the Cavendish Club Invitational 1976, 1977 and numerous regional titles. Son-tag was named "Sportsman of the Year" 1975 (see IBPA AWARDS). A syndicated bridge columnist, he is the author of *The Bridge Bum, Power Precision*, and the co-author of *Improve Your Bridge Fast*. See BIBLIOGRAPHY C, K, PRECISION TEAM and LANCIA TEAMS.

SORENSEN, Dennis E. (b. 1946) of Portland OR, mathematics teacher, won numerous regional titles including Oregon Trail Swiss Teams 1981, Puget Sound Swiss Teams, Master Pairs, KO Teams 1981, Republic of Texas Swiss Teams 1976, 1981, District 20 GNT, Zone VIII 1980. He was Intercollegiate champion 1978.

SORRI, Kalevi (b. 1924) of Helsinki, Finland represented Finland in the European Championships 1953, 1954, 1957, 1965. His national titles include Open Teams (eight times), Open Pairs 1951.

SORRI, Keijo (b. 1926) of Helsinki, Finland represented Finland in the European Championships 1953, 1954, 1957, 1962, 1965. His national titles include Open Teams (eight times), Open Pairs 1951.

SOTO, Ana de of Bogotá, Colombia, born in Reus, Spain, was South American Women's champion 1968. She also represented Colombia in the South American Championships 1963, South American Women's Championships 1964, 1965, 1966, 1967. Her national titles include Open Teams 1961, 1963.

SOULES, Gary E. (b. 1950) of San Francisco, part owner of a para-legal firm, won Summer NAC secondary Swiss Teams 1976, California Capital KO Teams 1977, Golden Gate KO Teams 1978, Men's Pairs 1979, All-Western KO Teams 1979, 1980, Open Pairs Flt. A 1981.

SOULET, Philippe (b. 1954) of Paris, France, bridge teacher, one of the leading players of France, won the World Team Olympiad 1980. He also represented France in the European Championships 1970, 1981 and won numerous national and international tournaments.

SOUTHWELL, Mary Virginia of Memphis won Music City Open Pairs 1977, Headquarters Swiss Teams 1978, Space City Women's Pairs 1980, Mid-South Women's Pairs 1981, Gold Coast Swiss Teams 1981.

SOWTER, Anthony P. (Tony) (b. 1946) of Nottingham, England, won seven CAMROSE TROPHY matches and placed second in the Common Market Teams 1979, European Championships 1981. He also represented Great Britain in the Bermuda Bowl 1981. His national titles include the GOLD CUP, National Pairs, National Mixed Pairs. Sowter is the managing editor of *International Popular Bridge Monthly*. He contributes regularly to the magazine and is the author of two books.

SPACK, Bension (Busi) (b. 1930) of Lima, Peru, company executive, represented Peru in the South

American Championships 1979, 1980, 1981. He served the Peruvian Bridge Commision as director and president.

SPAIN, Elizabeth Patricia (Pat) of Los Angeles won Summer NAC secondary Sub-Senior Master Teams, President's Pairs 1963, Fall Women's Pairs Flt. B 1965. Winner of many ABA national events, Spain is a former Western vice president of the ABA.

SPARKS, Jeffrey M. (b. 1948) of Greensboro NC, senior claims representative, won Mid-Atlantic KO Teams, Men's Pairs 1975, Master Pairs 1977, Swiss Teams 1978, 1980, 1981, Open Pairs 1978, 1979. He served as president of Unit 169 for three terms.

SPICKETT, Peggy of Newport Wales represented Great Britain in the World Women's Pairs 1962 and Wales in numerous CAMROSE TROPHY and Lady Milne matches. Her national titles include National Open Teams 1957, Women's Teams 1953, 1955, 1960, 1964, 1965.

SPIEGEL, Bernard M. (Buddy) (b. 1947) of Bethel CT, computer programming manager, associate national tournament director, formerly was ACBL Tournament Coordinator and Tournament Division Manager, and secretary to the ACBL Laws Commission. While he was at headquarters Spiegel authored the ACBL *Bulletin* feature "Ruling the Game". He is a graduate of State Technical Institute of Memphis and State University of New York.

SPIEWAK, Walter of Sudbury MA won Can-At KO Teams 1969, 1973, Open Teams 1969, Open Pairs 1974.

SPILIOPOULOS, Nicolas B. (b. 1913) of Athens, Greece, retired lawyer, was npc of the Greek Team at the European Championships 1969. He won Greek Open Pairs 1966, Open Teams 1969. Spiliopoulos co-founded the HELLENIC BRIDGE FEDERATION 1965, served as its vice president 1965–1971, 1973–1975 and since 1980, and edited its official publication *Greek Bridge Review* 1967–1968.

SPILIOPOULOU, Anna of Athens, Greece, represented Greece in the World Women's Teams 1976, European Championships 1971, 1973, 1974, 1975, 1977. She won Open Team Trials 1979, Women's Team Trials 1971, 1975, 1976, Open Teams 1971, 1979, Master Pairs 1980, Women's Pairs 1976, 1978, Mixed Teams 1976, 1980, 1981, Mixed Pairs 1981. Officially ranked #1 woman player, she won the Kyriakos Trophy (Greek McKenney) for women 1979, 1980, 1981.

SPINGOLD, Nathan B. (Nate) (1886–1958) of New York City, publicist, motion picture executive, patron of the arts, was the most influential man in bridge administration 1937–1943. Born in Chicago, he became a reporter on *The Chicago Examiner, The Chicago Record Herald* and *The Chicago Tribune*. Spingold's interest in show business brought him to New York City. In 1932 he joined Columbia Pictures in a public relations capacity and continued his association with the company until his death. In 1940 he was named to the board of directors, and three years later was appointed vice president in charge of advertising, publicity and development. In 1954 he became vice president of the company. As leading art collectors, Nate and Frances Spingold owned an outstanding gallery of French impressionist paintings and contemporary American art. Active in bridge from its earliest days, Spingold donated the prestigious trophy which bears his name and in 1936 he was named ABL Honorary Member. Spingold was influential in effecting a peaceful merger between the AMERICAN BRIDGE LEAGUE and the UNITED STATES BRIDGE ASSOCIATION in 1937 and became president of the newly formed AMERICAN CONTRACT BRIDGE LEAGUE the following year. He served for many years on the League's Board of Governors and Board of Directors. Spingold was also president of the CAVENDISH CLUB in New York.

SPITALNICK, Richard L. (b. 1947) of Mountain View CA, accountant, placed second in Spring NAC Amateur Swiss Teams 1977 and won Rogue River Valley Master Pairs 1976, Mid-Winter Holiday Men's Pairs 1976, Men's Pairs 1977, California Capital Men's Pairs 1977, All-Western Men's Pairs 1978, 1979, District 21 GNT 1980.

SPITZ, Marshall R. (b. 1943) of Swampscott MA, real estate manager, won Golder Master Pairs 1973, New England Master Teams 1966, KO Teams 1967.

SPIVACK, Leo J. (b. 1926) of Chicago, investment banker, former lawyer, won Central States KO Teams 1971, District 11 Open Teams 1967. ACBL president in 1979, Spivack has been a member of the Board of Directors since 1970 and chairman of the ACBL Appeals and Charges Committee, 1974, 1975, 1977, 1978, 1982. He was chairman of the Board 1980, chairman of the WBF Appeals Committee 1980–1981. A Board member of Chicago CBA since 1965, he served as its president 1968–1970. Spivack was educated at University of Chicago and Northwestern University.

SPOTTS, Robert L. (b. 1937) of El Sobrante CA, project manager, placed second in Spring NAC Men's Teams 1967, won Bridge Week KO Teams, Mixed Teams 1968, Golden Gate Master Pairs 1966, KO Teams 1972, Master Teams 1973.

SPRECKELS, Alma E. (formerly Rosekrans, Coleman, Hammel), won several regional titles including Bridge Week KO Teams 1971, Master Pairs 1963, Mixed Teams 1948, All–Western Life Master Teams 1972, 1974, KO Teams 1974, 1976, California Capital Master Pairs 1976, Pacific Southwest Swiss Teams 1971, 1972,

SPURWAY, Paul F. (b. 1926) of Melton Mowbray, England, accountant, represented Great Britain in the World Open Pairs 1962. He won English Open Teams 1959, 1977, Welsh Cup 1958, 1962, National Pairs 1959, 1962, 1964, Master Pairs 1959, 1960, 1961, 1965 and placed second in several national events including the GOLD CUP 1962. He served as vice chairman of the ENGLISH BRIDGE UNION 1968–1973.

SQUIRE, Norman (b. 1907) of London, England, bridge writer, won De La Rue Int'l Par Tournament 1957, GOLD CUP 1946, 1954, 1958 and other national titles. Competition editor of *Bridge Magazine* for many years, Squire is the author of more than a dozen books including *The Theory of Bidding*, *Guide to Bridge Conventions*, *Bidding at Bridge*, *Squeeze Play Simplified*, and the co-author of *Winning Points at Match-Point Bridge*. He has made many contributions to bidding theory: OUT-OF-THE-BLUE CUE-BID; development of the principle of FOURTH SUIT FORCING. Squire is a contributing editor, *Bridge Encyclopedia*. See BIBLIOGRAPHY C, F.

STACHOWICZ, Dr. Jerzy (b. 1926) of Katowice, Poland, physician, represented Poland in the European Championships 1962, 1966. He won Hungarian Open Pairs 1959, Polish Open Teams 1959, Open Pairs 1960.

STACK, Donald L. (b. 1939) of Roeland Park KS, analytical chemist, won Cornhusker Master Pairs 1975, Indian Summer Mixed Pairs, Open Pairs Flt. A 1979, Iowa Open Pairs Flt. A 1979, District 14 Summer Open Pairs Flt. A 1981, District 15 Master Pairs 1980, GNT 1979, 1981, Zone V 1981, GNP 1981, Spring Open Pairs Flt. A 1981.

STACK, Donna J. (b. 1943) of Roeland Park KS, sales representative, won Missouri Valley Women's Pairs 1977, Indian Summer Open Pairs Flt. A, Mixed Pairs 1979, Iowa Open Pairs Flt. A 1979, District 14 Summer Open Pairs Flt. A 1981, District 15 Master Pairs, Swiss Teams 1980, GNT 1979, 1981, Zone V 1981, GNT 1981, Spring Open Pairs Flt. A 1981.

STAFFORD, Jeff (b. 1939) of Pearisburg VA, attorney, won Summer NAC secondary Open Pairs A-D 1979, Swiss Teams 1980, Mid-Atlantic KO Teams 1973 (twice), 1979, Open Teams 1973, 1974, Master Pairs 1975, Open Pairs 1981 (twice), Bicentennial Men's Pairs, Open Pairs 1975. He is a member of the Virginia House of Delegates.

STAKGOLD, Alice (Mrs. Ivar) of Newark DE won Summer NAC Master Mixed Teams 1969.

STAKGOLD, Ivar (b. 1925) of Newark DE, born in Oslo, Norway, mathematics professor, placed second in the Bermuda Bowl 1959 and also represented the United States in the World Team Olympiad 1960. He won the MOTT-SMITH TROPHY 1958, Spingold 1962, Chicago (since 1965 the Reisinger) 1958, Vanderbilt 1958, Spring NAC Open Pairs 1958, Summer NAC Master Mixed Teams 1969, and placed second in the Spingold 1958, Fall NAC Men's Teams 1957, Spring NAC Open Pairs 1963. He won numerous regionals including Summer NAC secondary President's Pairs 1964. He also won English Melville Smith Teams 1968 and placed second in Crockford's Cup 1968.

STALLARD, M. Berl (b. 1913) of Miles City MT, accountant, is the creator of "First-Up", a method of bidding which uses no conventions, and the author of several books on this subject. He and his wife Helen also introduced Instant Bridge, a bridge-like game that requires no bidding. Stallard is treasurer and business manager of IBPA and a former treasurer for ABTA.

STAMPF, Abraham (Mori) (b. 1937) of Tel Aviv, Israel, merchant, represented Israel in the World Team Olympiad 1968, 1972, 1980, European Championships 1970, 1971, 1973, 1975, 1977, 1979. His national wins include Open Pairs 1969, 1969, 1971. Stampf won the 1977 MACCABIAH GAMES.

STANGE, Sharron A. (b. 1942) of Evanston IL won Summer NAC secondary Swiss Teams 1979, Spring Master Pairs 1980, Hawaii Open Pairs Flt. A 1979.

STANLEY, Mrs. Emory D., Jr. of Seattle won Fall NAC secondary Swiss Teams 1976, Spring Swiss Teams 1975, Inter–Mountain KO Teams 1970, Desert Empire KO Teams 1972, Yakima Valley Master Pairs 1974, Polar Open Pairs 1974, Klondike Master Pairs 1976.

STANSBY, Jan. See MARTEL, JAN.

STANSBY, Lew (b. 1940) of Oakland CA, one of the leading American players, won the World Open Pairs and placed second in the Rosenblum Cup Teams 1982. He also represented the United States in the Rosenblum Cup Teams 1978. He won the Reisinger 1965, 1981, Vanderbilt 1967, Spingold 1975, Grand National Teams 1982, and placed second in the Blue Ribbon Pairs 1981. Stansby won the ROSENKRANZ ROMEX AWARD in 1979 (see IBPA AWARDS).

STAPPENBECK, Harry A. (b. 1939) of Uniondale NY, bridge lecturer, teacher and director, placed second in the Spingold 1974 and won Fall NAC secondary Swiss Teams Flt. B 1980, New York-New Jersey Open Pairs 1970, Nassau-Suffolk Open Pairs 1977, Long Island KO Teams 1978, Eastern States KO Teams (Reisinger) 1978, New York Winter Swiss Teams Flt. A 1979. At 6 ft. 11 in. he is the world's tallest expert.

STARK, Eric of Vancouver BC, retired realtor, won Pacific Northwest Open Teams 1956, Men's Pairs 1957, Open Pairs 1955, British Columbia Mixed Pairs 1981.

STARK, Dr. Gary (b. 1931) of Portland OR, dentist, won Spring NAC Men's Teams 1967, Oregon Trail KO Teams 1974, Master Pairs 1967.

STARR, Jeffrey C. (b. 1949) of Southfield MI placed second in the Grand National Teams 1974 and won more than 35 regional titles including Spring NAC secondary Men's Pairs, Open Pairs 1973, All-American KO Teams 1974, 1975, Open Teams 1974, 1976, Master Pairs, Open Pairs 1974, Motor City Open Pairs 1969, KO Teams 1975, 1977,

Swiss Teams 1978, Men's Swiss Teams 1981. He was lead singer in the revue staged at 1981 Spring NAC. Other interests include stock options, backgammon, reading, sports and movies.

STARR, Robert E. (Bob) (b. 1919) of Centerville MA, retired bridge club owner, teacher and director, won numerous regional titles including Summer NAC secondary Non-Master Pairs 1947, New England KO Teams 1956, 1959, 1962, 1963, Open Teams 1952, 1954, 1958, 1962. A bridge columnist, Starr writes for several newspapers and magazines. He is a graduate of Brown University. His interests include the stockmarket, Rotary Club and antiques.

STARTZEL, John T. (b. 1934) of Arlington Heights Il, profit planning manager, won Tri-Unit Men's Pairs 1970, Central States Master Pairs 1979, Men's Pairs 1981.

STAUBER, Allan G. (Al) (b. 1944) of Poughkeepsie NY, coin and bullion broker, represented the United States in the World Open Pairs and Rosenblum Cup Teams 1982. He won the MOTT-SMITH TROPHY 1981, Spingold 1981, Blue Ribbon Pairs 1980, Spring NAC Men's Teams, Men's Pairs 1981, and placed second in the Grand National Teams 1979.

STAYMAN, Josephine L. (Tubby) (Mrs. Samuel) (b. 1924) of New York City and Palm Beach FL, former gift shop owner, placed second in the World Mixed Teams 1974 and won Southeastern Open Teams 1972, Florida Swiss Teams 1977.

STAYMAN, Samuel M. (b. 1909) of New York City and Palm Beach FL, one of world's greatest players, portfolio manager, investor and bridge author, WBF Grand Master, was Bermuda Bowl champion 1950, 1951, 1953 and placed second in the World Team Olympiad 1964. He also represented North American in the Bermuda Bowl 1956 and the United States in the World Team Olympiad 1960. He won the Spingold 1942, 1944, 1948, 1950, 1952, 1955, 1959, Chicago (since 1965 the Reisinger) 1945, 1947, Vanderbilt 1942, 1946, 1950, 1951, Summer NAC Life Master Pairs 1965, Fall NAC Men's Teams 1952, 1962, Open Pairs 1959, Spring NAC Men's Teams 1963, 1980. He placed second in the Spingold 1947, 1969, Chicago 1950, Reisinger 1976, 1977, Vanderbilt 1944, 1945, 1952, 1969, Fall NAC Men's Teams 1948, 1955, Men's Pairs 1945, Life Master Pairs 1950, Spring NAC Men's Teams 1965 and won numerous regional titles including Eastern States KO Teams (Reisinger) 1939, 1940, 1951, 1963. In the June 1945 issue of *The Bridge World* he described a convention, invented by his then partner GEORGE RAPÉE, which subsequently became known as STAYMAN. President of the Cavendish Club (New York), he has served as ACBL Treasurer 1966–1969 and as trustee of the ACBL Charity Foundation. Stayman was named ACBL Honorary Member in 1969 and ABTA Honorary Member in 1979. He is the author of *Expert Bidding*, *The Complete Stayman System of Contract Bidding*, and *Do You Play Stayman?* He is a contributing editor, *Bridge Encyclopedia*. See BIBLIOGRAPHY, C.

STEARNS, Sherman (1900–1965) of New York City, real estate broker, was one of the leading American players of the Thirties, and a member of the FOUR ACES TEAM during its later years. Among his national championships were USBA Open Team and Open Pairs, 1935; Vanderbilt 1938, 1941; Life Master Pairs, 1938. He placed second in five national events and had numerous regional successes.

STEDEM, Joseph J. (b. 1899) of Palm Springs CA, retired executive vice president of the Hertz Corporation, placed second in the NAC Senior Master Individual 1952 and won Midwest Spring Open Pairs 1949, Central States Mixed Pairs 1950. He was ACBL president 1968, a member of the Board of Directors 1949–1950 and 1964–1969, president of the ACBL Charity Foundation 1973–1974, trustee 1972–1975 and was named ACBL Honorary Member 1971. He is a former president of the Midwest Bridge Conference and of the Chicago CBA. Stedem helped initiate the ACBL policy, begun in 1949, of holding North American Championships in many centers. Previously all such tournaments had been held in the Greater New York area, but the experiment of attempting a NAC in Chicago in 1949 proved most successful. As a result, players in all sections of the ACBL have had the opportunity to play in NAC at not too great a distance from their homes. Stedem also was instrumental in the reorganization of the ACBL, working with WALDEMAR VON ZEDTWITZ.

STEEN, Douglas (b. 1927) of Los Angeles, physicist and economist, one of the leading West Coast players until his retirement in 1956, was Bermuda Bowl champion 1953. He won the Spingold 1953, Summer NAC Master Mixed Teams 1952, and placed second in Fall NAC Men's Teams 1953, Men's Pairs 1954. Steen is co-inventor of the BULLDOG SYSTEM and co-author of *Precision Power Bidding*. See BIBLIOGRAPHY, C.

STEEN, Harry S. (b. 1922) of Beverly Hills CA, stockbroker, won Pacific Southwest Open Teams 1957, 1958, Bridge Week Men's Pairs 1969.

STEGEMAN, Dr. Charles A. (Chuck) (b. 1945) of Eagan MN, physician, won Summer NAC secondary Swiss Teams 1971, Iowa Open Teams 1971, 1979, 1980, Open Pairs 1971, KO Teams 1979, Gopher Master Pairs 1979, Roughrider Master Pairs 1979, KO Teams, Men's Pairs, Open Pairs, Swiss Teams 1981. He is a contributor to *Gopher Bridge News*.

STEHLY, Paul E. (Fred) (b. 1925) of Minneapolis, associate national tournament director since 1968, formerly represented the tournament directors at the ACBL Board of Directors meetings.

STEIL, Leo F. (b. 1925) of Pt. Coquitlan BC, seaman, won Pacific Northwest Open Teams 1962, Men's Pairs 1966, Master Pairs 1967, Saskatchewan Open Pairs 1975, District 19 GNT 1976.

STEIN, James D., Jr. (b. 1941) of Marina Del Rey CA, mathematician, won the MARCUS CUP 1972, Bridge Week Master Pairs 1969, 1974, Life Master Pairs 1970, District 23 GNT, Zone VIII 1975.

STEIN, Joan S. (b. 1934) of River Hills WI, former festival ticket director, won Fall NAC Life Master Women's Pairs 1974. Her more than 20 regional wins include Tri-Unit Women's Pairs 1971, Gopher Open Pairs, Swiss Teams 1975, Motor City Women's Pairs 1977, Women's Swiss Teams 1979, 1980, Swiss Teams Flt. A 1981.

STEIN, Ethan (b. 1946) of Jamaica NY, attorney, bridge teacher, placed second in Summer NAC Senior and Advanced Senior Master Pairs 1974 and won more than 20 regional titles including Long Island Swiss Teams 1977, KO Teams 1979, District 3 Open Pairs Flt. A 1979, Men's Swiss Teams 1979, 1980, 1981, Master Pairs 1980.

STEIN, Sylvia (b. 1921) of Southfield MI, one of the leading Midwest women players, represented the United States in the World Women's Pairs 1962, 1970. She won the HERMAN TROPHY 1969, Life Master Individual 1958, Spring NAC Women's Pairs 1962, Women's Teams 1965, 1968, Life Master Women's Pairs 1969 and placed second in Summer NAC Master Mixed Teams 1965, 1967, Fall NAC Mixed Pairs 1958, Women's Teams 1960, Master Mixed Teams 1960, 1962, Life Master Women's Pairs 1964, Spring NAC Women's Teams 1965, 1971. She has won numerous regional titles.

STEINBERG, Philip (b. 1904) of Pompano Beach FL, born in Russia, company president, won numerous regionals including Central States Men's Pairs 1953, Mississippi Valley Mixed Pairs 1961, Missouri Valley Men's Pairs 1963.

STEINBERG, Ruth (Mrs. Philip) (b. 1909) of Pompano Beach FL won numerous regionals including Central States Open Pairs 1953, Women's Pairs 1951, Mixed Pairs 1954, Mississippi Valley Open Teams 1953, Women's Pairs 1963, 1969, 1972, Mixed Pairs 1965.

STEINER, Albert (1901–1977) of Cincinnati, president of a toy manufacturing company, won the Chicago (now the Reisinger) in 1933, and Western States Mixed Pairs 1935. He was co-donor of the STEINER TROPHY.

STEINER, George M. (b. 1945) of Seattle, investment broker, one of the leading Northwest players, won Spring NAC Men's Pairs 1974. His more than 25 regional titles include Fall NAC secondary Swiss Teams Flt. A 1981, Puget Sound KO Teams 1970, 1971, 1972, Mixed Pairs 1977, Open Pairs, Swiss Teams Flt. A 1978, All-Western Master Pairs 1974, Men's Pairs 1980.

STEINER, Philip (b. 1901) of Cincinnati, retired company executive, won the Chicago (since 1965 the Reisinger) 1933, Western States Mixed Pairs 1935. He was ABL vice president 1936, a member of the Board 1930–1938, committee chairman 1934, and ACBL Honorary Member 1937. He is the co-donor of the STEINER TROPHY.

STEINFELDT, Sherman Irving (Irv) (b. 1918) of Minneapolis, company president, won Pheasant KO Teams 1972, Gopher Open Teams 1972, Iowa Open Pairs 1972, Tri-Unit Men's Pairs 1973, Midwest Spring Men's Pairs 1975. His avocation is directing bridge on cruises.

STENGEL, Harold J. (b. 1947) of Allston MA, mathematics teacher, won New England Master Swiss Teams 1977, 1978, KO Teams 1978, 1979, District 3 KO Teams 1981, District 25 GNP 1979, 1980.

STENGER, Dr. Charles A. (b. 1922) of Bethesda MD, clinical psychologist, won Mid-Atlantic Swiss Teams 1980. A member of the ACBL Board of Directors since 1980, he is chairman of the ACBL Committee on Higher-than-LM-Status and president of District 6. He previously was president of the Mid-Atlantic Conference and the Washington BL and chairman of the District 6 Judiciary Committee. Stenger retired after a long career in the Veterans Administration which included serving as national director of a staff of 1400 psychologists. He was educated at Western Reserve University, Akron University and Vanderbilt University.

STENGER, E. Jeanne (Mrs. Charles A.) (b. 1924) of Bethesda MD won Mid-Atlantic Women's Swiss Teams 1978, 1979, 1980, Swiss Teams 1980.

STEPHENS, Daisy W. (b. 1907) of Shreveport LA won Fall NAC Amateur Women's Pairs 1975, Bermuda Women's Pairs 1972, Mexican Nat'l Women's Pairs 1967.

STERN, Gerda (b. 1925) of Sydney, Australia, born in Poland, government interpreter and translator, was Far East Women's champion 1973, 1974, and also represented Australia in the Far East Women's Championships 1977, World Women's Teams 1968. Her national titles include Interstate Women's Teams 1964, 1967, 1972, 1974, Women's Trials 1971, 1973, 1974, Women's Individual 1973, Women's Pairs 1981.

STERN, Dr. Paul (1892–1948) of Vienna, Austria, lawyer, bridge writer and teacher, escaped to London and became a naturalized British subject. A founder of the AUSTRIAN BRIDGE FEDERATION 1928, he was its first president 1929. He was npc of the Austrian World champion teams 1937 and Austrian European Women's champion team 1935, 1936. He was World Par champion 1936, European champion 1932, 1933. Stern is the inventor of VIENNA (AUSTRIAN) SYSTEM, author of *Stern Austrian System*, co-author of *Two-club System of Bidding*, *Beating the Culbertsons*, and others. Number 11 on the Nazi list for extermination, he returned his World War I Iron Cross to the Nazi High Command with an insulting letter.

STERN, Paul S. (b. 1942) of Southfield MI, brokerage company branch manager, won Motor City Open Pairs 1974, Men's Swiss Teams 1976, District 12 GNT 1975.

STERN, Richard I., Jr. (b. 1945) of North Hollywood CA, data processing manager, won Spring NAC secondary Open Pairs 1973, Central States Open Teams 1974, Gopher Open Pairs, Swiss Teams 1973.

STERN, Roger D. (b. 1934) of New York City, financial corporation president, attorney, was npc of the Bermuda Bowl champion team 1977 and of the North American Team in the 1973 Bermuda Bowl. He placed second in the World Par Contest 1961 and won the U.S. Zone World Par Contest 1963, Spring NAC Men's Teams 1965, Summer NAC Mixed Pairs 1969, Eastern States Open Pairs 1960, District 5 Open Pairs 1964, Rocky Mountain Men's Pairs 1967, Eastern States KO Teams (Reisinger) 1976. He was the first president of District 24 and served as president of the Greater New York BA. He has been a member of the ACBL Board of Governors since 1972, a member of the LAWS COMMISSION OF THE ACBL since 1978, and serves as vice chairman of the NAC Appeals Committee. Stern is the co-inventor of ASTRO and ASTRO CUEBID and co-author of several *Bridge World* articles, including a series outlining a modern style of defensive bidding. He is a graduate of Columbia College and Columbia University Law School.

STERNBERG, Dr. James H. (Dr. J) (b. 1937) of Ft. Lauderdale FL, physician, radiologist, won Spring NAC Men's Teams 1979. Rookie of the Year in 1977 (see MINI-McKENNEY), he has won numerous regional including Can-Am Swiss Teams 1978, KO Teams, Swiss Teams 1979, New England KO Teams 1979, Long Island KO Teams 1980.

STETTEN, Jacques (b. 1926) of Paris, France, builder, was European champion 1962 and placed second in 1961. He also represented France in the Bermuda Bowl 1963, 1967, 1969, European Championships 1966. His national titles include Open Teams 1961, 1963.

STEUER, Joseph B. of Memphis placed second in Fall NAC Amateur Men's Pairs 1975 and won Spring NAC secondary Open Pairs 1978, Celebrity Swiss Teams 1977, Headquarters Swiss Teams 1978, Mid-South Men's Pairs, Unmixed Pairs 1978, Gold Coast Swiss Teams 1981.

STEUER, Marie Louise (b. 1927) of Memphis won Spring NAC secondary Open Pairs 1978, Celebrity Swiss Teams 1977, Headquarters Swiss Teams 1978, Space City Women's Pairs 1980, Mid-South Women's Pairs 1981, Gold Coast Swiss Teams 1981.

STEVENS, John R. (b. 1941) of Toronto, technical director of chemical lab, former chemistry university lecturer, represented Canada in the World Open Pairs, Rosenblum Cup Teams 1978. He won Upper New York State Master Pairs 1975, Canadian Nat'l Master Pairs 1975, Gateway City Open Pairs Flt. A 1981.

STEWART, Frank R. (b. 1946) of Birmingham AL, professional bridge player, teacher and writer, represented Korea in the Far East Championships 1968. He won Space City Master Pairs 1976, Mid-South Men's Pairs 1974, Mid-Atlantic Men's Swiss Teams 1980, Opryland KO Teams 1981. Stewart is a contributor to the ACBL *Bulletin*, *The Bridge World* and *Popular Bridge*. He graduated from University of Alabama where he sang with the symphony, chorus and opera.

STEWART, Frederick M. (Fred) (b. 1948) of Accord NY, stockbroker, won Summer NAC Life Master Pairs 1981, New England Summer Swiss Teams 1981, Eastern States Open Pairs (Goldman) 1982.

STEWART, John G. (b. 1951) of Halifax NS, lawyer, won Spring NAC secondary Open Pairs Flt. A 1974, Can-At KO Teams 1980, District 1 GNT 1978. He is a founding member of *Halifax Bridge World* and one of its contributors.

STEWART, Lilly (b. 1910) of Laguna Hills CA won Pacific Northwest Open Teams 1954, 1958, Master Pairs 1960, Women's Pairs 1960, 1962, Inter–Mountain Open Teams 1957.

STICKNEY, Jane K. of McComb MS, won Summer NAC secondary Mixed Pairs 1976, Mid-South Swiss Teams 1973, Mixed Pairs 1976, Gem State Women's Pairs 1976.

STICKNEY, William L. (b. 1913) of Boynton Beach FL, retired company executive, won All-American Open Pairs 1942 when playing duplicate for the first time, Central States Life and Senior Master Teams 1962, Florida KO Teams 1967. He is a former director and president of Chicago CBA and a contributor to its publication *Kibitzer*.

STIEFEL, John D. (Jay) (b. 1944) of Wethersfield CT, actuary, won Spring NAC Amateur Swiss Teams 1976. He won several regionals including Fall NAC secondary Open Pairs 1979, New England KO Teams 1974, Summer Swiss Teams 1976, Fall Swiss Teams 1976, 1978, KO Teams 1979, District 3 KO Teams 1981. He writes the Sunday bridge column for the *Hartford Courant*.

STODDARD, Peggy (Mrs. Thomas W.) of Laguna Hills CA, retired real estate broker, won Pacific Southwest Mixed Pairs 1953, All-Western Women's Pairs 1966. She assisted her husband in many PACIFIC BRIDGE LEAGUE and ACBL Western Division activities. She was secretary of the PBL 1936–1937 and a contributor to *The Contract Bridge Forum*. A member of the ACBL Goodwill Committee since 1952, she was awarded a silver card for "Outstanding Services to Bridge" by the ACBL in 1969.

STODDARD, Tom (1896–1976) of Laguna Hills CA, "Father of Bridge on the West Coast," was one of the outstanding personalities of American bridge, a pioneer in bridge teaching and bridge-club management, founder of the PACIFIC BRIDGE LEAGUE, and former ACBL executive. In 1931 Stoddard owned a Los Angeles hotel, at a time when most hotels were going bankrupt. He conceived the idea of making his hostelry a center for bridge lessons and duplicate games. The project was a sensational success, at its peak employing 11 teachers and conducting games daily from 9:20 a.m. to midnight. Stoddard founded the PBL in 1933 and was responsible for the wildfire growth of bridge on the West Coast. The PBL included the 11 Far Western states, the territories of Hawaii and Alaska and the Canadian provinces of British Columbia and Alberta, and rapidly reached a membership in the thousands, promoting two major tournaments (the All-Western and Bridge Week) and many minor ones. Stoddard also founded the *Contract Bridge Forum* in the early Thirties and during its nearly 50 years of publication it has been the voice of the PBL, the Western Division of the ACBL, and the WESTERN CONFERENCE. Collaboration between the ACBL and the PBL began in 1940 when they agreed on a uniform masterpoint system. In 1946 Stoddard turned over his bridge business to his associates, and in 1948 he agreed to amalgamation of the PBL and national organizations, an arrangement consummated in 1956. At this time he was elected President Emeritus of ACBL, Western Division and ACBL Board member. Named ACBL Honorary Member in 1960, he was also a member of the Goodwill Committee. In May of 1976 he was awarded the rare "Certificate of Service" citation by the ACBL Board of Directors for his long and devoted service to bridge and to the League. Stoddard was a regional correspondent for the ACBL *Bulletin*.

STOLKIN, Carol. See CRAWFORD, CAROL.

STONE, A. Kenneth (Sky King) (b. 1910) of Fort Worth TX, associate national tournament director since 1965, began directing in 1950. He owns and manages an air and cruise travel agency.

STONE, Janice G. (Jan) (Mrs. David H. Fulton) of Miami Beach, formerly of New York City, placed second in the World Women's Teams 1964 and won Women's Teams Trials 1963, Spring NAC Women's Teams 1956, 1969, Fall NAC Life Master Women's Pairs 1965, Summer NAC Master Mixed Teams 1965. She placed second in the Spingold 1959, Master Mixed Teams 1956, Women's Teams 1961, 1962 and won numerous regional titles including Fall NAC secondary Women's Teams 1968, 1972, Summer Mixed Pairs 1963, Swiss Teams 2nd Flt. 1973. Stone became a Life Master in seven months, the first to attain that status in such a short time. She is also a backgammon champion. A radio and TV actress from childhood, she starred on many nationally prominent TV dramatic and variety shows. Between 1974–1978 she was an executive in a family owned mining operation.

STONE, Robert F. (b. 1946) of Concord NH, private economic consultant, won Summer NAC secondary Swiss Teams 2nd Flt. 1971, Golder Master Pairs 1972, New England Master Pairs 1973, Upper New York State Men's Swiss Teams 1972.

STONE, Tobias (Stoney) (b. 1921) of New York City, bridge author, one of America's leading bridge players, represented North America in the Bermuda Bowl 1958 and the United States in the World Team Olympiad 1960, World Open Pairs, Mixed Pairs 1966. He won the FISHBEIN TROPHY 1956, McKENNEY TROPHY 1956, Spingold 1956, 1957, Chicago (since 1965 the Reisinger) 1952, 1961, Vanderbilt 1949, 1959, 1960, Life Master Pairs 1956, Spring NAC Men's Teams 1961, 1963, Men's Pairs 1961, Summer NAC Master Mixed Teams 1965, Fall NAC Open Pairs 1942, Master Individual 1953. He placed second in the Spingold 1953, 1961, 1963, Vanderbilt 1969, Spring NAC Men's Teams 1959, Open Pairs 1958, 1965, Summer NAC Master Mixed Teams 1956, Life Master Pairs 1942, 1965, Fall NAC Open Pairs 1958, Men's Pairs 1952. Stone won dozens of regional titles including the MARCUS CUP 1960, Eastern States KO Teams (Reisinger) 1942, 1944, 1961, 1963, 1967, 1973, 1974, Open Pairs (Goldman) 1957, 1961. Stone and partner AL ROTH were the first Americans to win the Deauville invitation pair event; they scored a record-breaking 82% game. He also is an international backgammon champion. Co-inventor of the ROTH-STONE SYSTEM, he has made many contributions to bidding theory. He is the co-author of *Bridge is a Partnership Game* and *The Bridge World* department "What Do You Play and Why?" See BIBLIOGRAPHY, C.

STOTHART, C. David (b. 1924) of Ottawa ON, director, senior management staffing, placed second in Canadian Nat'l Teams 1981 and won Can-At KO Teams, Open Teams 1968, Fleur-de-Lys Open Pairs 1974, Can-Am Swiss Teams 1979, District 1 GNP 1980.

STOUT, Alan F. (Herman) (b. 1949) of Cedar Rapids IA, field auditor, won Spring NAC secondary Swiss Teams 1972, Pheasant KO Teams 1973, Tri-Unit Master Pairs 1974, Gopher KO Teams 1977, District 14 GNP 1981.

STRASBERG, David I. (b. 1928) of Cooper City FL, personnel agency owner, won the Spingold 1970, FISHBEIN TROPHY 1970, and placed second in the Chicago (since 1965 the Reisinger) 1958, Spring NAC Men's Pairs 1968, Summer NAC Master Mixed Teams 1970, Grand National Teams 1980. His numerous regional wins include Spring NAC secondary Men's Pairs 1980, Eastern States KO Teams (Reisinger) 1969, Master Pairs 1956, Men's Pairs 1970, Florida Unmixed Pairs 1976, Mixed Pairs 1977, Mid-Atlantic Open Pairs 1977. See also PRECISION TEAM.

STRAUCH, Kathleen P. (Cathy) (b. 1940) of San Diego, realtor, won Fall NAC secondary Women's Teams 1971, Pacific Southwest Swiss Teams, Women's Swiss Teams 1977, Bridge Week Women's Swiss Teams 1978.

STREET, Robert P. (b. 1913) of Gresham OR, auditor, won Spring NAC secondary Mixed Pairs 1950, Southeastern Men's Teams 1962, Pacific Northwest Open Pairs 1956, 1960, Men's Pairs 1950, 1956, Master Pairs 1952, 1954, 1955.

STREET, Venita (formerly Summers) (b. 1917) of Honolulu won Spring NAC secondary Mixed Pairs 1950, Pacific Northwest Master Pairs 1952, 1954, 1955, Open Pairs 1950.

STREISAND, James B. (b. 1955) of Buffalo, surgical resident, won District 5 Men's Swiss Teams 1979, GNT 1980, 1982.

STRICKLAND, Fred E. III (b. 1945) of Atlanta, bridge teacher, former attorney, won Fall NAC secondary Swiss Teams 1972, Open Pairs 1974, Spring Master Pairs 1976, Summer Men's Pairs Flt. A 1980, Mid-Atlantic Men's Pairs 1970, Open Pairs 1977, Celebrity Master Pairs, Men's Swiss Teams 1977, North Florida Mixed Pairs 1977. He served as president of Unit 114 in 1982.

STROM, Louis André (b. 1927) of Stavanger, Norway, meteorologist, represented Norway in the Bermuda Bowl 1970, European Championships 1960, 1961, 1965, Nordic Championships 1964. He has won numerous national titles. Strom is bridge columnist for a local newspaper.

STUART, Joel H. (b. 1939) of Forest Hills NY, options trader, won the Spingold 1970, 1971, Vanderbilt 1972, and placed second in Spring NAC Men's Teams 1968. His regional titles include Long Island KO Teams 1971, 1972, Metropolitan Swiss Teams 1974, District 24 GNT, Zone II 1974. See PRECISION TEAM.

STUCKER, Robert (b. 1930) of Athens, Greece, formerly of Houston, represented the United States in the World Open Pairs 1962, represented Greece in the European Championships as playing captain 1970, World Open Pairs 1978. He placed second in Fall NAC Open Pairs 1961, Spring NAC Men's Teams 1964 (see FORTUNE). Greek national wins include Open Teams 1967, 1968, 1974, 1977, 1981, Interclubs 1973, 1976. Stucker is co-inventor of the BIG DIAMOND SYSTEM.

STURM, Charlotte G. (b. 1927) of Los Angeles, secretary, placed second in Summer NAC Senior and Advanced Senior Master Pairs 1965 and won Los Angeles Winter Swiss Teams 1974, Wine Country Open Pairs Flt. A 1982.

SUCHARTKUL, Kovit of Bangkok, Thailand, tin miner, was Far East champion 1961, 1963 and placed second in the Bermuda Bowl 1969.

SUGAR, Paul (b. 1928) of Chicago, company vice president, placed second in Fall NAC Mixed Pairs 1975 and won numerous regionals including Summer NAC secondary Swiss Teams Flt. A 1980, Sub-Senior Master Teams 1948, Central States KO Teams 1964, 1979, Open Teams 1971, 1977, Open Pairs 1981, Tri-Unit Open Pairs 1973, Swiss Teams 1974. Sugar is a former director, treasurer and legal counsel of the Chicago CBA.

SUKONECK, Ronald M. (b. 1949) of Falls Church VA, legal administrator, won numerous regional titles including Mid-Atlantic KO Teams 1975, Swiss Teams 1977, Men's Pairs 1978, Men's Swiss Teams 1980, Master Pairs 1981, District 4 KO Teams 1981, Open Pairs 1977, 1979.

SULLIVAN, Michael J. (Mick) (1894–1974) of Brisbane, Australia, accountant, did much to promote contract bridge in Australia, particularly in Brisbane, when it came on the scene in 1932. He was co-founder of the WORLD BRIDGE FEDERATION in 1958, chairman of its Constitution Committee, and a member of WBF Executive Board. Sullivan organized 1951 Jubilee Year World Olympic, 1954 Bidding Championship, 1961 and 1963 WBF Global Par Championships, and was joint formulator of Laws of Par Point Contract Bridge 1963 (International Code). World Par Zonal winner 1939, 1940, 1941, his national titles include Par wins 1937, 1939, 1943, 1950, 1957. In 1974 he was made the first Honorary Life Member of the AUSTRALIAN BRIDGE FEDERATION. He contributed many double-dummy problems to the British *Bridge Magazine*.

SUNDBY, Robert D. (b. 1925) of Monona WI, lawyer, won Central States I Open Teams 1971, Champagne Master Pairs 1977, Wisconsin Open Pairs 1980, District 13 GNT 1981. Sundby is the author of *Breakthrough in Bridge*.

SUNDELIN, Per Olof (Peo) (b. 1937) of Stockholm, Sweden, computer analyst and consultant, one of the leading players of Sweden, was European champion 1977. He also represented Sweden in the Bermuda Bowl 1977, World Team Olympiad 1976, 1980, World Open Pairs 1970, 1974, 1978, European Championships 1963, 1965, 1970, 1974, 1975, 1979, 1981. He won the INVITATIONAL PAIRS CHAMPIONSHIP 1981. His national titles include Open Teams 1971, 1972, 1978, 1979, 1980. An IBPA member, he occasionally contributes to international bridge magazines.

SUNDSTROM, Patty of Indianapolis IN, won Midwest Women's Pairs 1970, 1971, 1978, Women's Swiss Teams 1978, Indy 500 Women's Pairs 1973, Champagne Women's Pairs 1979, District 11 Women's Pairs 1976, Florida Swiss Teams 1981.

SUNG, Leslie L. of Hong Kong, former newspaper editor, was Far East champion 1975. His national wins include Open Teams, Master Teams, Open Pairs, Mixed Pairs, Individual. He is former chairman of Hong Kong BA.

SUOZZO, John P. (b. 1950) of Teaneck NJ, area supervisor, won Bluenose KO Teams, Open Pairs 1981, District 3 GNT 1981.

SUSSEL, Andrée (b. 1914) of Paris, France, antique dealer, was European Women's Team champion 1956, 1965, 1969 and also represented France in the European Women's Championships 1958, 1959, 1962, 1966, 1975. Her national titles include French Mixed Teams 1962.

SUSSKIND, Alan L. (b. 1952) of Oak Park IL, securities margin specialist, won Spring NAC secondary Swiss Teams 1973, Fall Swiss Teams, Swiss Teams-A 1979, Mississippi Valley Open Teams 1974, Missouri Valley Swiss Teams 1975, Keystone KO Teams 1975, Fall Swiss Teams 1975, Can-Am KO Teams 1975, Great Lakes Swiss Teams 1978, Champagne Swiss Teams 1978.

SUTHERLIN, John C. (b. 1936) of San Francisco, portfolio manager, one of the leading players of the West Coast, placed second in the World Mixed Pairs 1982 and also represented the United States in the Rosenblum Cup Teams 1982. He won Summer NAC Master Mixed Teams 1976, Spingold 1981 and placed second in Fall NAC Mixed Pairs 1962, Swiss Teams 1982, Spring NAC Men's Teams 1967. His numerous regional titles include Golden Gate Master Pairs 1966, Swiss Teams Flt. A 1979, 1980, Golden State Master Pairs 1978, All-Western Master Teams 1971, Hawaii Master Pairs 1973, 1981, Swiss Teams 1981, Mid-Winter Holiday Swiss Teams 1980.

SUTHERLIN, Peggy (Mrs. John C., nee Berry) (b. 1937) of San Francisco, airline stewardess, one of the outstanding women players of the West Coast, placed second in World Mixed Pairs 1982. She won Fall NAC Mixed Pairs 1972 (second in 1962), Summer Master Mixed Teams 1976. Her numerous regional wins include Golden Gate Open Teams 1963, Mixed Pairs 1969, All-Western Women's Pairs 1965, California Capital Mixed Pairs 1974, Bridge Week Women's Swiss Teams 1978, Hawaii Women's Pairs 1970, 1980. A Mayflower descendant, she is an amateur genealogist; it is in this capacity that she is a contributing editor to the *Bridge Encyclopedia*.

SUTTON, Iona N. (b. 1911) of Wichita Falls TX, former bridge teacher, won Texas Fall Women's Pairs 1959, Spring Women's Pairs 1958, Open Teams 1968.

SVARC, Henri (b. 1928) of Paris, France, textile factory director, one of the leading French players, was World Team Olympiad champion 1980, European champion 1966, 1970, 1974 and placed second in 1967. He also represented France in the World Team Olympiad 1964, 1976, World Open Pairs 1962, Bermuda Bowl 1967, 1969, 1974, European Championships 1954, 1956, 1958, 1959, 1965, 1969, 1973. In 1966 he and partner JEAN MICHEL BOULENGER were named Europe's outstanding pair. National titles include Open Teams (many times), Open Pairs.

SWAN, Mary Margaret of Houston, publisher, won Fall NAC Mixed Pairs 1964, Texas Spring Master Pairs 1961.

SWANDER, Shirley A. (b. 1930) of Mission KS, artist, won Fall NAC Women's Teams 1955, Summer NAC secondary Women's Pairs 1968, Southern Conference Fall Open Teams, Women's Pairs 1955, Missouri Valley KO Teams, Women's Pairs 1973, GNT, Zone VI 1973.

SWANSON, John C. Jr. (b. 1937) of Mission Viejo CA, one of America's leading players, computer programmer, represented North America in the Bermuda Bowl 1971, 1973, 1975, 1977. He won Spring NAC Men's Teams 1970, Men's Pairs 1959, Vanderbilt 1969, 1977, Grand National Teams 1974, 1976, and placed second in Life Master Men's Pairs 1968, Spingold 1973. His numerous regional titles include Pacific Southwest Open Teams, Master Pairs 1964, Bridge Week Master Pairs 1965, 1966, Open Teams 1973. Swanson is a contributor to *Southern California Bridge News*, *The Bridge World*, and the ACBL *Bulletin*. He co-authored ''Recap Bridge'', computer dealt hands with analysis, and co-developed the WALSH SYSTEM.

SWANSON, Paul (b. 1932) of Morgantown WV, company president, an outstanding player, represented the United States in the World Open Pairs 1974. He won the MOTT-SMITH TROPHY 1972, Summer NAC Master Mixed Teams 1976, Life Master Pairs 1973, Spring NAC Men's Teams 1972, Men's Pairs 1979, placed second in 1978 and in the Chicago (since 1965 the Reisinger) 1963, Reisinger 1973, 1980, Vanderbilt 1972, Life Master Men's Pairs. He won numerous regional titles including Summer NAC secondary Swiss Teams 1973, Mid-Atlantic Open Teams 1970 (twice), Master Pairs 1972, District 11 KO Teams, Master Pairs 1971, Rocky Mountain Swiss Teams Flt. A, Open Pairs Flt. A 1980.

SWARTHOUT, David M. (b. 1942) of Detroit, test research analyst, won Motor City Men's Pairs 1969, Midwest Swiss Teams 1973, Great Lakes KO Teams 1979, Open Pairs 1981.

SWEARINGEN, Gladys (b. 1913) of St. Louis, retired secretary, won Summer NAC Women's Pairs 1953.

SWEARINGEN, Stephen R. (b. 1943) of Arlington VA, computer programmer, won numerous regional titles including Fall NAC secondary Silver Trophy Pairs Flt. A 1980, Mid-Atlantic KO Teams 1974, 1976, Open Teams 1968, 1971, 1972, 1976, 1981, Open Pairs 1973, 1980, 1981, Master Pairs 1977.

SWIMER, Ralph (b. 1914) of London, England, company director, placed second in the World Team Olympiad 1960 and also represented Great Britain in the European Championships 1962, 1967, World Open Pairs 1962. His national titles include the GOLD CUP 1955, Life Master Pairs 1949, 1951, 1958, 1961. He was npc of the British Teams in the Bermuda Bowl 1965. See BUENOS AIRES AFFAIR.

SYDNOR, Caroline R. (b. 1913) of Alexandria VA, journalist and bridge writer, is the author of *Bridge Made Easy*, three volumes each with its special deck of cards coded to deal 40 lesson hands.

SZURIG, Zbigniew (b. 1938) of Warsaw, Poland represented Poland in the World Team Olympiad 1964, European Championships 1963, 1965, npc of the Women's Team 1966. He placed second in the World Par contest 1963 and won Hungarian Open Pairs 1959, Balaton Bowl 1963, Baltic Bowl 1964. His national titles include Open Teams 1962, 1963, 1964, 1966, 1968, Individual 1959. Szurig is one of the leading Polish bridge theorists. He is the co-author of *Modern Bridge*.

T

TABAK, Gabi (b. 1915) of Melbourne, Australia, born in Germany, was Far East Women's champion 1973.

TAGGART, Linda (b. 1942) of San Francisco, systems project manager, won All-Western Open Pairs 1974, Golden State Women's Pairs 1975, Mid-Winter Holiday Women's Swiss Teams 1976.

TAI, Min Fan (b. 1938) of Taipei, Taiwan, importer, one of the leading Far East players, placed second in the Bermuda Bowl 1969, 1970. He also represented Taiwan in the World Team Olympiad 1964 and several Far East Championships. His national titles include Open Pairs 1963.

TAKAHASHI, Satoru (b. 1913) of Tokyo, Japan, diplomat, former ambassador to Spain, represented Japan in the Far East Championships and won the the Takamatsu Cup in 1958. Takahashi is a former president of JAPAN CONTRACT BRIDGE LEAGUE.

TALMADGE, Dorothy R. See KAYE, DOROTHY R.

TAMRES, Margery (b. 1925) of Pittsburgh, bookkeeper, represented the United States in the World Women's Pairs 1974. She won District 5 Women's Pairs 1969, Women's Pairs 1980, Women's Swiss Teams 1981, Keystone Fall Women's Pairs 1971, All-American Swiss Teams 1975, 1979.

TANNEN, Harold (b. 1911) of Memphis, retired insurance executive, won Music City Open Pairs 1977, Headquarters Swiss Teams 1978, Gold Coast Swiss Teams 1981.

TARLO, Joel (b. 1905) of London, England, lawyer, was European champion 1963. He also represented Great Britain in the Bermuda Bowl 1950, World Team Olympiad 1964, European Championships 1955, 1956, 1962, 1965, npc 1959. His national wins include the GOLD CUP 1939, 1961.

TARLO, Louis (b. 1911) of London, England, solicitor, was European champion 1950. He also represented Great Britain in the Bermuda Bowl 1950, European Championships 1951, 1952, 1956, 1958, 1965, 1966, 1967, 1969. He was npc of the Great Britain team in the Bermuda Bowl 1962, World Teams Olympiad 1960, 1972, European Championships 1961, 1963, 1970, 1971, 1973, 1974, 1975. Tarlo has served the ENGLISH BRIDGE UNION in various executive positions including chairman.

TAUBE, Richard (Dick) (b. 1938) of Columbia MD, attorney, won numerous regionals including Fall NAC secondary Open Pairs 1976, Men's Pairs 1980, Mid-Atlantic Swiss Teams 1974, Open Pairs 1973, KO Teams 1975, Golden State Swiss Teams 1980, New England Swiss Teams 1981. He served as chairman of the 1973 Summer NAC and has been active in bridge administration since 1965.

TAYLOR, Edward O. (b. 1912) of Glendale CA, marketing director, formerly one of the leading West Coast players, won the Chicago (since 1965 the Reisinger) 1959, 1962, Fall NAC Men's Teams 1959, 1962, Open Pairs 1957, Life Master Pairs 1963, Spring NAC Open Pairs 1959, and placed second in the Vanderbilt 1963.

TAYLOR, Eileen (b. 1907) of Auckland, New Zealand, was Far East Women's champion 1976. She also represented New Zealand in the Far East Championships 1971, 1972, 1973, 1977. Her national titles include New Zealand Open Teams 1957, 1959, 1960, 1961, 1962, 1963. Taylor was New Zealand's second Life Master in 1964.

TAYLOR, Jeffrey F. (b. 1941) of Kwajalein, Marshall Islands, teacher, was Intercollegiate champion 1964. He won Pacific Northwest Open Pairs 1964, 1967, Oregon Trail Open Teams 1969, Men's Pairs 1970, Master Pairs 1971, Canadian Master Pairs 1969, 1970, Rocky Mountain Open Pairs 1969, District 20, Zone VII 1974.

TAYLOR, Pauline J. of Detroit, retired decorative arts curator, was the first woman president of the AMERICAN BRIDGE ASSOCIATION (1969–1973). An active promoter of bridge since 1949, she was also president of the Detroit Unit 1956–1961 and founder of the first women's duplicate club there. Her ABA national titles include Mixed Teams 1952, Women's Pairs 1957, Individual 1974.

TAYLOR, Ross M. F. (b. 1954) of Waterloo ON, born in Glasgow, Scotland, won Canadian Nat'l Swiss Teams Flt. A 1980, Can-Am Swiss Teams 1981, Nat'l Capital KO Teams 1978, District 5 Swiss Teams 1979, Gateway City KO Teams 1981, District 2 GNP 1981, CNT Zone 3 1981.

TEAGUE, Harriet G. (Mrs. Terry) (b. 1916) of Birmingham AL, won Southern Conference Fall Open Teams 1963, Women's Pairs 1964, Florida Open Pairs 1973, Bermuda Master Pairs 1974.

TEAGUE, Terry (b. 1904) of Birmingham AL, insurance agent, won Southern Conference Fall Open Teams 1963, Men's Pairs 1962, Mid-South Open Teams 1974, Florida Open Pairs 1973, Bermuda Master Pairs 1974. Teague was an ACBL Director 1957–1960.

TEEL, Jane H. (Mrs. Robert J.) (b. 1942) of Rockford AL, former editor and teacher, won North Florida Open Pairs 1977, Central Florida Swiss Teams 1978, Space City Open Pairs 1976, Mid-Atlantic Open Pairs 1975, 1978, District 10 GNP 1981, 1982.

TEEL, Judge Robert J. (b. 1946) of Rockford AL, district judge, won Mid-South Men's Pairs 1974, Mid-Atlantic Open Pairs 1975, 1978, Space City Open Pairs 1976, Master Pairs 1980, North Florida Open Pairs 1977, Central Florida Swiss Teams 1978, District 10 GNP 1981, 1982.

TEIXEIRA, Carlos Spinola (b. 1939) of Lisbon, Portugal, company director, represented Portugal in the European Championships 1966, 1967, 1970, 1974. His national titles include Open Teams four times, Open Pairs twice.

TEJPAR, Abdul (b. 1921) of Nairobi, Kenya, company director, represented Kenya in the World Open Pairs 1978 and has won every major title in Kenya. Tejpar is a former chairman of KENYA BRIDGE ASSOCIATION.

TELFER, Roy L. (b. 1898) of Plymouth, England, army officer, made many contributions to the field of bridge mathematics including *Practical Odds at Bridge* and *Probabilities in Contract Bridge*. He served as a tournament director at the 1961 European Championships. Contributor of many magazine articles, Telfer also was contributing editor, *Bridge Encyclopedia*. See BIBLIOGRAPHY, M.

TEMMERMANN, Simone de (b. 1917) of Paris, France, musician, was European Women's Teams champion 1956, 1965, 1969. She also represented France in the European Championships 1955, 1959, 1961, 1965, 1974. She won French Mixed Teams 1960, Women's Teams 1955, 1960, Pairs Mixed Teams 1960, Women's Pairs 1952, 1954, 1955, 1956, 1960, 1961.

TENCH, Stanley (b. 1929) of Ottawa ON, director of government computer centre, won Can-At KO Teams 1968, 1969, 1970. An ACBL associate national tournament director, he developed the Tench movement.

TEPPER, Barbara (b. 1930) of Verona NJ, medical group administrator, won Spring NAC Women's Teams 1969. Her regional titles include the MARCUS CUP 1961, Summer NAC secondary Women's Pairs 1967, Fall Women's Teams 1967, Keystone Open Teams 1968. She is a graduate of Syracuse University.

TESSMER, Maxine F. (b. 1912) of Belton TX, was Far East Pairs champion 1961, representing Japan.

TEXTOR, Karel (b. 1926) of Prague, Czechoslovakia, technician, represented Czechoslovakia in the European Championships 1966, 1967, against Poland 1961, 1962, and Hungary 1963. His national titles include Open Teams 1962, 1963, 1964.

THEIMER, Ernst T. (b. 1910) of Rumson NJ won Summer NAC secondary Sub-Senior Master Teams 1945, New York-New Jersey Conference Mixed Pairs 1967. A former chess champion turned bridge enthusiast, Theimer served as president and tournament chairman of the New Jersey BL and for five years wrote a weekly bridge column for *Newark News*. He is the author of *The Bridge Adventures of Androcles MacThick* and has contributed to *The Bridge World*. Theimer, a retired chemical industry executive, now presides over a fast food processing firm.

THÉRON, Dr. Georges (1922–1970) of Paris, France, physician and bridge writer, was one of the leading players of France. He was European champion 1962, second in 1967. He also represented France in World Open Pairs 1962, Bermuda Bowl 1963, 1969, World Team Olympiad 1964, European Championships 1965. His national successes include French Open Teams 1952, Open Pairs 1962. His writings include contributions to PIERRE ALBARRAN's *Encyclopedie*, and articles for French and foreign magazines. He translated into French JACK OLSEN's *The Mad World of Bridge*.

THEUS, Edgar G. of Oklahoma City OK, attorney, placed second in Fall NAC Life Master Men's Pairs 1966 and won Mid-South Spring Open Teams 1955, Open Pairs 1957, Texas Spring Master Pairs 1965, Missouri Valley Open Teams 1961, Men's Pairs 1968. Theus, a member of the Board of Directors since 1961, was president of the ACBL in 1969 and chairman of the Board in 1970. He has served on the executive committee, the appeals and charges committee, the finance and tournament committees. He has served on the ACBL Laws Commission, chaired the International Laws Commission, is 1st vice president of the WORLD BRIDGE FEDERATION, was co-captain of the defending Bermuda Bowl team in 1977 and was captain of the North American Bermuda Bowl team in 1979.

THOMAS, D. Michael (b. 1938) of Pittsburgh, company president, won All-American Men's Pairs 1962, Mixed Pairs 1963, Mississippi Valley Open Teams 1968, Mid-Am-Can Open Pairs 1967, Central States Men's Pairs 1964, 1965, 1966, Texas Fall KO Teams 1964, Mid-South Spring Open Pairs 1964. Thomas was a member of the Chicago team which challenged the SHARIF BRIDGE CIRCUS.

THOMAS, Frank of Los Angeles, syndicated bridge columnist, former leading boy actor of stage and screen, playwright, scriptwriter, actor for radio and TV, retired from the theatrical side of the entertainment field in 1962 to begin bridge teaching in association with GEORGE GOODEN, reaching as many as 18,000 students a year in department stores. Editor and publisher of the ABTA *Quarterly* since 1969, he was elected ABTA president in 1981. He writes a syndicated bridge column and is the author of several books including *Sherlock Holmes, Bridge Detective* (in collaboration with Gooden) and *Sherlock Holmes, Bridge Detective, Returns*. Thomas is a member of the IBPA.

THOMAS, Fred R. (b. 1925) of Downey CA, bridge teacher, authored *Universal ♣, "The" System for Everyone*.

THOMAS, James O. (Jim) (b. 1938) of Olympia WA, won Mid-Winter Holiday Master Pairs 1971, Puget Sound Men's Pairs 1972, Oregon Trail Men's Swiss Teams 1976. He is past president of Unit 441.

TOMCHIN, Stanley of New York City won Summer NAC Master Mixed Teams 1973 and placed second in the Vanderbilt 1975.

THOMSON, Douglas A. (Doug) (b. 1937) of Winnipeg MB, systems engineer, won British Columbia KO Teams 1970, Men's Pairs 1972, Calgary KO Teams 1973, District 18 Master Pairs 1975, Roughrider Open Pairs 1979, Thunder Bay Master Pairs 1979, MARCUS CUP 1964.

THOMSON, J. Douglas (Doug) (b. 1914) of Christchurch, New Zealand, medical practitioner, represented New Zealand in matches against Australia 1968, 1969, 1970, 1971. His national titles include Open Pairs 1968, 1969, 1972, Interprovincial Teams 1967, 1969, 1971.

THOMSON, Robert D. (Bob) (b. 1957) of Emeryville CA, computer programmer, won Fall NAC Swiss Teams 1981, Pacific Southwest Master Swiss Teams 1979.

THORFINNSSON, Einar (1906–1980) of Reykjavik, Iceland, banker, was one of Iceland's leading players. He represented Iceland in the World Team Olympiad 1960, European Championships 1950, 1951, 1958, 1971, Europe in the Bermuda Bowl 1950. His national titles include Open Teams 1953, 1954, 1957, 1962, 1965, 1970, 1971, 1972, and Open Pairs, 1956.

THORNTON, Susan M. (b. 1932) of Dayton OH placed second in Summer NAC Master Mixed Teams 1977 and won New England Fall Women's Pairs 1966.

THUMIM, Eugene (b. 1912) of Shaker Heights OH, retired bridge writer and consumer affairs specialist, won Eastern States Open Pairs (Goldman) 1956, All-American Open Teams 1958, Men's Pairs 1972, Can-Am Open Teams 1966.

THUMIM, Rose (Mrs. Eugene) (b. 1912) of Shaker Heights OH, bridge teacher, former bridge club manager, won Can-Am Open Teams 1966, District 5 Open Teams 1967.

THURRELL, Robert F. (b. 1920) of Wellesley Hills MA, insurance executive, won Rocky Mountain Men's Pairs 1948, New England Open Teams 1967, Open Pairs, KO Teams 1970.

TIERNAN, Agatha D. (1884–1981) of Brandon VT was a bridge teacher, writer and lecturer. As a director at the CAVENDISH CLUB (New York) she was granted the first club sanction for a monthly masterpoint game. She was named ACBL Honorary Secretary in 1960. Her playing achievements include second place in Spring NAC Women's Teams 1951.

TIERNAN, Mary Elizabeth (b. 1907) of Brandon VT won Fall NAC Women's Teams 1956 and placed second in 1951. Her regional titles include Keystone Open Teams 1958, Women's Pairs 1954.

TIERNEY, John A. (b. 1917) of Ft. Lauderdale FL, retired USNA mathematics professor, contributed to *The Bridge World* and co-authored *Contract Bridge: According to Silodor and Tierney*. See BIBLIOGRAPHY, E.

TILLES, Jules (1907–1976), of New York City, bridge teacher, club owner and tournament director, was business manager of the Greater New York BA 1957–1972. He placed second in NAC Mixed pairs 1952 and won Eastern States Open Pairs 1943, 1950 and 1954.

TIMMERMAN, Steve (b. 1942) of Wichita KS, chimney sweep, won District 15 Swiss Teams 1975, KO Teams, Open Pairs Flt. A 1978, Springfield KO Teams, Open Pairs Flt. A 1980.

TINTNER, Léon, (b. 1910) of Paris, France, born in Austria, publisher, was European champion 1962, 1966. He also represented France in the Bermuda Bowl 1963, 1967, 1969. His many national championships include Open Teams twice, Interclubs twice.

TISH, Morris (b. 1918) of Skokie IL, professor of English, won Central States KO Teams 1963, Men's Pairs 1952, Master Teams 1958.

TOBIN, E. J. (Ned) (1868–1953) of Miami and Chicago was one of the founders of the AMERICAN BRIDGE LEAGUE. He served as its first secretary in 1927 and 1928, became treasurer in 1929, and was made an Honorary Member in 1932. Tobin, a contributor to the Chicago *Record Herald* and the *Daily Journal*, was the holder of many whist championships. He authored *Sound Principles of Auction Bridge*.

TODD, Robert J. (b. 1950) of Winnipeg MB, computer programmer analyst, won Buffalo Individual 1976, KO Teams 1977, Unmixed Pairs 1978, Swiss Teams Flt. A 1980, Peach City KO Teams 1978, Saskatchewan Men's Pairs 1978.

TOIBIN, Niall J. (b. 1959) of Dublin, Ireland, university student, represented Ireland in the World Team Olympiad 1980, World Open Pairs 1982. He won Common Market Open Pairs and Junior Teams. His Irish titles include Master Pairs 1981, 1982, Nat'l Pairs 1981, 1982, Nat'l Teams twice.

TOLEDANO, John H. (Buster) (b. 1907) of New Orleans, bridge teacher, placed second in Fall NAC Men's Teams 1956 and won Mid-South Open Teams 1944, 1961, 1962, Men's Pairs 1944, Southern Conference Fall Open Teams 1960.

TOLSTOI, Count Lev Nikolaevich (1828–1910) famous Russian novelist, used the Russian game VINT, a form of bridge whist, as background for his long short story "The Death of Ivan Illych". See HISTORY OF BRIDGE and LITERATURE AND BRIDGE.

TOLSTOY, Leo. See TOLSTOI, COUNT LEV NIKOLAEVICH.

TOM, Merle H. (b. 1935) of Cos Cob CT, attorney, represented the United States in the World Open Pairs 1974. He won Spring NAC Open Pairs 1972, Men's Teams 1974 and placed second in the Vanderbilt 1974, Men's Teams 1977. He has won numerous regionals including Spring NAC secondary Men's Swiss Teams 1982, Summer Swiss Teams 1975, 1978, Eastern States KO Teams (Reisinger) 1978, Open Pairs (Goldman) 1975.

TONKIN, Joel Larry (b. 1938) of Leawood KS, attorney, won District 15 Summer KO Teams 1977, Indian Summer KO Teams 1979, Springfield Swiss Teams 1980.

TOONE, George L. (b. 1935) of Napa CA, manufacturing engineer, won All-Western Men's Pairs 1968, Master Teams 1977, Mid-Winter Holiday Open Pairs Flt. A 1980, District 21 GNP 1981, 1982.

TORNAY, Claire J. (Mrs. George) (b. 1940) of New York City, teacher, won Life Master Women's Pairs 1980 and placed second in Fall NAC Swiss Teams 1981. Her regional wins include Eastern States Master Pairs 1970, Long Island Women's Pairs 1979, District 3 Women's Swiss Teams 1979.

TORNAY, George F. Jr. (b. 1936) of New York City, consulting actuary, won Spring NAC Men's Teams 1980. His regional wins include Nassau-Suffolk KO Teams 1980, Fun City KO Teams 1972.

TORRENCE, Anita C. (b. 1942) of Columbus OH, bridge teacher, won All-American Mixed Pairs 1976, Women's Swiss Teams 1980, Midwest Fall Women's Pairs 1980.

TOWNSEND, Mary Beth of Baton Rouge LA, backgammon and bridge teacher, placed second in Spring NAC Women's Teams 1968 and won Fall NAC secondary Women's Pairs 1975, Missouri Valley Women's Pairs 1958, South Texas KO Teams 1971, Mid-South Women's Pairs 1973, Open Pairs 1976, Music City Women's Swiss Teams 1973, Lone Star Swiss Teams 1977, Mississippi Valley Master Pairs 1978.

TRAANE, Nils (1925-1980) of New York City, engineer, composed many double-dummy problems published in *The Bridge World* and the British *Bridge Magazine*.

TRACANELLA, Angelo of Milan, Italy was npc of the Italian teams that won the Bermuda Bowl 1969, World Team Olympiad 1968, European Championships 1965, 1967.

TRAD, Antoine (Tony) (b. 1928) of Geneva, Switzerland, formerly of Cairo, Egypt, one of the leading Swiss players, represented Egypt in the European Championships 1954, 1956, 1961, 1962, represented Switzerland in the European Championships 1967. His Egyptian national successes include Open Teams 1953, 1954, 1955, 1956, 1957, 1958, 1960, 1961, 1962, 1963, Open Pairs 1953, 1961, and many other titles in Egypt and Switzerland. He is a former technical advisor to the EGYPTIAN BRIDGE FEDERATION.

TRAUB, Alexander A. (Alec) (b. 1911) of Cape Town, South Africa, wool merchant and bridge writer, won South African Par event 1953, Open Teams 1955, 1962 and placed second in 1956, 1957. He served as IBPA awards secretary 1975–1982. His writings include contributions to *Le Bridgeur*, a translation of *Mathematical Theory of Bridge*, authorship of *Point-Count Expectancy Tables*, *Trump Technique*, and co-authorship of *Probabilities Contract Bridge*. He is editor of *Practical Odds at Bridge* and a contributing editor to the *Bridge Encyclopedia*. See BIBLIOGRAPHY, D, M.

TRAVIS, Barbara (née Gill) (b. 1959) of Adelaide, Australia, clerk, represented Australia in the Venice Trophy Teams 1981. She won Australian Interstate Teams 1979, 1980, and placed second in Mixed Pairs 1979, Women's Pairs 1980. Travis was the youngest winner, first and only female, of the McCutcheon Trophy (Australian McKenney) 1979.

TREITEL, David H. (b. 1954) of Stamford CT, management and economic consultant, won Fall NAC Swiss Teams 1980.

TRELDE, John (b. 1921) of Copenhagen, Denmark, dentist, represented Denmark in the European Championships 1958, 1959, 1969, 1970, 1971 and won Danish Open Teams 1970, 1971. He invented many systems and conventions including COPENHAGEN CONVENTION, TRELDE LEADS and Trelde asking bids.

TRENT, Paul (b. 1936) of New York City, attorney, won Spring NAC Men's Teams 1969, 1971. He was Intercollegiate Par champion 1957 and won several regional events including Eastern States Open Pairs (Goldman) 1973, New England Master Teams 1961, Master Pairs 1970, Long Island KO Teams 1976, District 24 GNT 1978.

TRENT, Sandra (Mrs. Paul, formerly Roark) of New York City won Summer NAC secondary Mixed Teams 1970, Mixed Pairs 1969, New England Master Pairs 1968, Keystone Women's Pairs 1972, New York Winter Life Master Pairs 1975, Long Island KO Teams 1976.

TRÉZEL, Roger (b. 1918) of Paris, France, journalist, WBF Grand Master, one of the great players of the world. His partnership with PIERRE JAÏS has been outstanding in international events. Bermuda Bowl champion in 1956, he won the World Team Olympiad 1960, World Open Pairs 1962, and was European champion 1955, 1970 (second in 1956, 1959). He also represented France in the Bermuda

Bowl 1961. His national titles include Open Teams and Open Pairs. Trézel is the author of *La Clé du bridge*, *Cartes sur table*, a series of booklets (*Cahiers du bridge* I-VIII), and co-author (with TERENCE REESE) of *Elimination Play in Bridge*, *Snares and Swindles in Bridge*, and *The Art of Defense in Bridge*. See BIBLIOGRAPHY, D.

TRITT, James F. (Jim) (b. 1946) of Fresno CA, attorney, won Golden State Men's Pairs 1978, Swiss Teams Flt. A 1981, Mid-Winter Holiday Men's Pairs 1980.

TRITTER, Lorand R. (b. 1929) of Houston, company regional director, won more than 40 regional titles including Texas Fall KO Teams 1970, Mid-Winter KO Teams 1971, Mid-Am-Can Open Teams 1956, 1958, Master Pairs 1965, South Texas Open Pairs 1974, Texas Capital Master Pairs 1980, Wisconsin Open Pairs, KO Teams 1978. Tritter is a former president and vice president of District 16.

TRUE, Robert H. (b. 1944) of Tucson AZ, systems analyst, mathematician, bibliographer, is a contributing editor to the *Bridge Encyclopedia*. His research (1974–1975) contributed greatly to clarifying the early HISTORY OF BRIDGE, the probable origin of the name of the game, and the acquisition from Cambridge University Library of a copy of the 1886 pamphlet on BIRITCH, first recorded publication of rules of the game. He won Mid-Atlantic Open Pairs 1978.

TRUSCOTT, ALAN F. of New York City, born April 16, 1925 in England, is a leading international player-writer. He has been bridge editor for *The New York Times* since 1964 and he is president of the INTERNATIONAL BRIDGE PRESS ASSOCIATION. A frequent contributor to British *Bridge World*, *The Bridge World*, ACBL *Bulletin* and other magazines throughout the world, Truscott also was executive editor of the three previous editions of the *Bridge Encyclopedia* and served as an editor on this edition as well. After serving as secretary of the BRITISH BRIDGE LEAGUE 1957–1962, Truscott worked as associate editor of the ACBL *Bulletin* 1963 to 1964. He was European champion 1961 and represented Great Britain in the European Championships in 1951 and 1958. He represented Great Britain in the 1962 Bermuda Bowl, where he finished third. He has represented the United States in world competition in Mixed Teams 1972 and 1974, Mixed Pairs, 1970, 1974, 1978 and 1982, and the Rosenblum Cup Teams 1982. He invented the Truscott Card, now widely used to prevent seating errors in team play. He has authored several conventions, including TRUSCOTT DEFENSE TO STRONG CLUB, TRUSCOTT 2◇ (Relay Two-Way Stayman) and 2 NT OVER A TAKEOUT DOUBLE of partner's opening bid to show a limit raise. Contributions to theory include RESTRICTED CHOICE. His writings include *Contract Bridge*, *The Great Bridge Scandal*, *Practical Bridge*, and *Master Bridge By Question and Answer*. He was the co-translator of *Championship Bridge* (le DENTU, *Bridge a la une*). He was non-playing captain of the Bermuda team in the 1964 World Olympiad. National successes include Master Individual 1953, 1958; and Fall NAC Men's Team 1968. He also has won several secondary North American Championships as well as a large number of regional titles. Truscott served as president of the International Bridge Academy and the Greater New York BA from 1977-1979. At present he is serving as president of District 24. Outside interests include tennis, running and world politics. It is not uncommon to see him run three to four miles during a lull in the action at a tournament. He is a former chess champion (Oxford University). See also BUENOS AIRES AFFAIR and BIBLIOGRAPHY, B, C, E, H.

TRUSCOTT, Dorothy Hayden (Mrs. Alan) of New York City, bridge teacher, author, mathematician, WBF Grand Master, one of the great women bridge players of all time, overtook RIXI MARKUS in 1980 to become the number one woman player in world rankings. She has been selected 13 times to represent the United States in international competition. Truscott and HELEN SOBEL SMITH are the only two women ever to have played on the North American team for the Bermuda Bowl. She won four world titles: the Venice Trophy in 1974, 1976 and 1978 and the World Women's Teams in 1980. She was second in the Bermuda Bowl in 1965 and placed third in the World Women's Teams 1968, 1972, 1976, World Women's Pairs 1962, 1974 and World Open Pairs 1966 (the only woman ever to finish in the top 10 in this event).

She has won 17 North American Championship titles including four playing with partners with whom she had never played a session of bridge before: Blue Ribbon Pairs 1963, Life Master Pairs 1964, Fall NAC Mixed Pairs 1959, Open Pairs 1962, Spring NAC Women's Teams 1967, 1970, 1972, 1974, 1975, 1976, 1982, Women's Pairs 1959, 1961, 1966, 1978, 1981, Summer NAC Women's Swiss Teams 1982. She placed second in the Vanderbilt 1964, Spingold 1965, 1968, Summer NAC Master Mixed Teams 1957, 1960, 1967, 1972, Spring NAC Women's Pairs 1961, 1968, 1972, 1976, Women's Teams 1963, 1964 and won numerous regional titles.

Among her contributions to bridge theory are the UNUSUAL JUMP to show a singleton now called the SPLINTER BID, and the responses to BLACKWOOD AFTER INTERFERENCE now called DOPI.

Truscott is the author of *Bid Better, Play Better*, *Winning Declarer Play*, and the co-author with ALAN TRUSCOTT of *Teach Yourself Basic Bidding*. She is bridge columnist for *Pan Am Clipper*, contributes to various magazines and is a contributing editor to the *Bridge Encyclopedia*. She is engaged in writing a historical novel about New Amsterdam. See BUENOS AIRES AFFAIR.

TSACNARIS, Francine J. (Fran) (b. 1923) of Los Angeles, bridge teacher, won Spring NAC secondary Women's Pairs 1977, Bridge Week Women's Pairs 1973, 1976, Master Women's Pairs Flt. A 1977, 1980, Mixed Teams 1966, 1970, Los Angeles Winter Open Pairs Flt. A 1976, Master Swiss Teams Flt. A 1978. She formerly wrote a bridge column for *Southern California Bridge News* using the pseudonymn I. Noalle.

TSAI, Paul Chung-tseng (b. 1931) of Taipei, Taiwan, born in Shanghai, China, attorney, represented Taiwan as npc of the Taiwan team that competed in the Rosenblum Cup Teams 1978, Far East Championships 1979, 1980. He won the Taipei Mayor's Cup 1981 and many national events. Tsai served as managing director of the CHINESE TAIPEI BRIDGE ASSOCIATION and as director of the International Bridge Foundation.

TSCHEKALOFF, Alex (b. 1927) of Westlake Village CA, computer programmer, represented the United States in the World Open Pairs 1970. He won Fall NAC Life Master Men's Pairs 1965, Blue Ribbon Pairs 1969 and placed second in Spring NAC Men's Pairs 1961. His numerous regional wins include Bridge Week Mixed Teams 1963, 1968, Open Teams 1967, Desert Empire Open Teams, Open Pairs 1960, Pacific Northwest Open Pairs 1962, Master Pairs 1965, Open Teams 1961, 1966, Mid-Winter Holiday Swiss Teams 1972, Los Angeles Winter KO Teams 1980.

TSIANG, George Y. C. (b. 1919) of Hong Kong, business executive, was Far East champion 1959 and placed second in 1963. His national titles include many team and pair events. He served as vice chairman of Hong Kong CBA for two years and was active in the promotion of the FAR EAST BRIDGE FEDERATION.

TSOU, Leslie K. (Buddha) (1919-1983) of Eugene OR, born in Shanghai, retired restaurateur, won more than 50 regional titles including Oregon Trail Open Pairs 1969, Master Pairs 1975, KO Teams 1970, 1975, 1977, 1978, All-Western KO Teams 1971, Master Pairs 1976, Navajo Trail KO Teams, Master Pairs, Swiss Teams 1979, Hawaii Swiss Teams 1977, 1980, Men's Swiss Teams 1977. He served as Unit president many times.

TU, Ya Pin (b. 1952) of Taipei, Taiwan, systems engineer, was Far East champion 1978. He also represented Taiwan in the Bermuda Bowl 1979. Tu won the Argentine Pro-Amateur Pairs 1979.

TUASON, Severo S. (1909-1973) of Manila, Philippines, civil engineer, was a distinguished bridge administrator, both in the FAR EAST BRIDGE FEDERATION and in the WORLD BRIDGE FEDERATION where he served as a member of the Executive Council. Far East Champion 1959, Tuason represented Philippines in the World Team Olympiad 1960.

TUBBS, Lewis G. (1902-1971) of Arlington VA, bridge instructor and club director, was an ACBL Board member 1965-1968, and former president of Washington BA. Tubbs placed second in Summer NAC Master Mixed Teams 1954. He is the author of *How We Teach and Play Contract Bridge*.

TUCKER, Dr. James L. of Abilene TX, eye surgeon, won Fall NAC secondary Swiss Teams 2nd Flt. 1975, Big D KO Teams 1972, Republic of Texas KO Teams 1973, King Cotton Swiss Teams 1975, Land of Coronado KO Teams 1978. Tucker was promoted to Brigadier General in the Air Force Reserves Medical Corps 1980.

TUELL, David R. Jr. (b. 1936) of Tacoma WA, attorney, won Puget Sound Men's Pairs 1969, Southeastern Mixed Pairs 1969, Las Vegas Men's Pairs 1973, Oregon Trail Open Pairs Flt. A 1980, Indian Summer Swiss Teams Flt. A 1981. Tuell is a former president of the WESTERN CONFERENCE.

TURECKI, Dr. Stanley K. (b. 1938) of New York City, born in Vilna, Poland, child psychiatrist, former resident of Sweden and South Africa, won Eastern States Men's Pairs 1970, Long Island Life Master Pairs 1970, South African Open Teams 1965, 1967, 1968.

TURNER, Gloria. See REYSA, GLORIA.

TYLER, Frances (1897–1978) of Cincinnati was one of the senior bridge columnists in the world. She began her long career in bridge as an instructor for the Culbertson studios in 1930. In 1933 she became a bridge columnist for *The Enquirer* and retained this position until six months before her death.

U

UNSON, Rosemarie A. (Rose) (b. 1934) of Manila, Philippines, pension house manager and owner, was Far East Women's Teams champion 1979. She also represented the Philippines in the Far East Women's Teams 1973, 1974, 1976, 1977, 1978, 1980, 1981 and was npc of the Philippines Open Team in the FEBF 1975.

URBANIAK, Roger L. (b. 1943) of Mercer Island WA, realtor, won Indian Summer Swiss Teams Flt. A 1981, Mid-Winter Holiday Open Pairs Flt. A 1979, Men's Pairs 1981, Oregon Trail KO Teams 1972, Open Pairs Flt. A 1982.

URBANIAK, Susan J. (Mrs. Roger) of Mercer Island WA won Oregon Trail KO Teams 1972, Open Pairs 1974, Yakima Valley Women's Pairs 1974, Puget Sound Women's Pairs 1973, 1977, Indian Summer Women's Pairs 1981.

URE, Carol (b. 1946) of Seattle, research supervisor, won Summer NAC secondary Women's Pairs 1976, Oregon Trail Women's Swiss Teams 1975, Puget Sound Master Swiss Teams 1978.

UTEGAARD, Helen S. of Carmichael CA, born in Peking, China, a leading American women player, won Spring NAC Women's Teams 1973, 1981, Summer NAC Master Mixed Teams 1975 (second in 1980), Fall NAC Mixed Pairs 1974. Her regional titles include Eastern States Mixed Pairs, Women's Teams 1968, Mid-Atlantic KO Teams 1973, Open Pairs 1972, Women's Pairs 1970, Mid-South Women's Pairs, Open Pairs 1975.

V

VAHALA, Vera (b. 1917) of Perth, Western Australia, born in Czechoslovakia, represented Australia in the World Women's Teams 1972, Far East Women's Championships 1971.

VALENTI, Anna (Mrs. Paolo) (b. 1917) of Leghorn, Italy, WBF Grand Master, one of the world's greatest women players, sister-in-law and customary partner of MARISA BIANCHI, won the World Women's Teams 1972 (second in 1980) and placed second in the Venice Trophy Teams 1974, 1978. She was European Women's champion 1970, 1971, 1973, 1974, and also represented Italy in many other European Women's Championships. She won European Common Market Women's Teams 1971, 1973, British Women's Teams 1973, Italian Cup twice, Italian Mixed Teams four times, Open Teams twice. See FAMILY.

VAKIL, Piyush (b. 1941) of Camp Hill PA, born in Ahmedabad, India, chemical engineer, won the Spingold 1975, Fall NAC secondary Swiss Teams A-D 1979, Palm Springs KO Teams 1967, All-Western Life Master Teams 1971, Mixed Pairs 1973, District 21 GNT 1974, District 5 GNT 1978, 1979, Zone 3 1979.

VAN COURT, Wendell A. (Woody) (b. 1926) of Youngstown OH, English teacher, won Canadian Nat'l Swiss Teams 1972, 1981, Men's Pairs 1979, Mixed Pairs 1981, District 11 Swiss Teams 1979.

VAN DEN BORRE, Joseph (Jo) (b. 1917) of Ghent, Belgium, public relations executive, tournament director, and columnist, was npc of the Belgian Women's Teams in the World Women's Teams 1964 and European Women's Championships 1963. He is the chief tournament director of Belgium and has been International Tournament Director of the World Bridge Federation since 1970. He is the author of bridge columns in many newspapers and a contributor to many periodicals.

VANDERBILT, Harold Stirling (July 6, 1884–July 4, 1970) of Newport RI was a bridge authority whose revisions of auction bridge scoring principles created modern contract bridge, a system-maker and a champion player. He was born at Oakdale NY into the richest and most famous American family of that time. His father, William Kissam Vanderbilt, died in 1920 leaving an estate of some 54½ million dollars. Vanderbilt graduated from Harvard Law School in 1910, then entered his family's railroad business, New York Central, founded by his great-grandfather, Commodore Cornelius Vanderbilt. For many years he was a successful business executive. His greatest fame in competitive fields is as a yachtsman — and his revision of right-of-way rules, followed for all sailing vessels, are still known as the Vanderbilt Rules. Nevertheless, his lasting fame is more likely to come from his contributions to bridge.

Vanderbilt took up bridge seriously in 1906, and

his partnership with J. B. ELWELL was considered the strongest in the U.S. from 1910 to 1920. During that period the contract bridge principle — counting only bid tricks toward game — was often proposed and as often rejected, except for the limited success of PLAFOND (see HISTORY OF BRIDGE). Experimenting with the proposed new game while on a cruise late in 1925, Vanderbilt originated the factors of vulnerability and inflated slam bonuses; and, a more decisive contribution, he produced a scoring table so balanced as to make nearly every aggressive or sacrifice bid an approximately even bet, allowing just enough differential to permit the exercise of nice judgment.

The rapid spread of contract bridge from 1926 to 1929 is largely attributable to Vanderbilt's espousal of it; his social standing made the game fashionable. Vanderbilt's technical contribution was even greater. He devised the first unified system of bidding, being solely responsible for the artificial 1♣ bid to show a strong hand, the negative 1◊ response, the *strong* (16- to 18-point) notrump on balanced hands only, and the weak two-bid opening. These and his other principles were presented in his books, *Contract Bridge Bidding and the Club Convention*, 1929; *The New Contract Bridge*, 1930; *Contract by Hand Analysis*, 1933; and *The Club Convention Modernized*, 1964.

Vanderbilt was a member of the Laws Committee of the Whist Club of New York that made the American laws of contract bridge (1927, 1931) and the first international code (1932). Then he became chairman of that committee, and largely drafted the international code of 1935, the American code of 1943, and the international codes of 1948 and 1949. He remained Co-chairman of the National Laws Commission of the ACBL for the 1963 laws.

In 1928 Vanderbilt presented the Harold S. Vanderbilt Cup for a national team-of-four championship. This became and remained for many years the most coveted American team trophy, not least because of the replicas donated personally by Vanderbilt to the winners. In 1960 Vanderbilt supplied the permanent trophy for the World Bridge Federation's Olympiad Team tournaments, again adopting the policy of giving replicas to the winners.

As a player, Vanderbilt always ranked high. In 1932 and 1940 he won his own Vanderbilt Cup. He played by choice only in the strongest money games, and was a consistent winner. His regular partnership with WALDEMAR VON ZEDTWITZ was among the strongest and most successful in the U.S. In 1941 he retired from tournament bridge, but he continued to play in the most expert rubber bridge games, in clubs and at home.

In 1968, Vanderbilt spent more than $50,000 to recreate the lost molds for the replicas of the American trophy and to provide a quantity of replicas of both trophies sufficient to last from 20 to 40 years. To perpetuate this practice of awarding individual replicas, Vanderbilt further bequeathed to the ACBL a trust fund of $100,000 — a gift that wisely foresaw the possibility of inflation, but provided that excess funds, if any, can be donated in Vanderbilt's name to a charity of ACBL's choice. When last purchased, replicas of the American trophy cost

$600; of the Olympiad trophy, $500.

In 1969, the World Bridge Federation made Vanderbilt its first honorary member. When a BRIDGE HALL OF FAME was inaugurated in 1964, Vanderbilt was one of the first three persons elected. Member Advisory Board *Bridge Encyclopedia*. See BIBLIOGRAPHY, C, E.

VANDER LAAN, Isabel B. (b. 1916) of Cuyahoga Falls OH, YWCA executive, won Pittsburgh Women's Swiss Teams 1980, Midwest Fall Women's Swiss Teams 1980, Upper New York State Women's Pairs 1971.

VAN DER PAS, Maria (Marÿke) (b. 1949) of Utrecht, The Netherlands, chemistry student, represented The Netherlands in the European Women's Championships 1979, World Women's Teams 1980, World Women's Pairs 1982. She won European Women's Pairs and The Netherlands Women's Pairs.

VANDERPORTEN, William S. (Bill) (b. 1910) of Sunrise FL, retired Job Corps coordinator, won Summer NAC secondary President's Pairs 1940, Eastern States Men's Pairs 1958. He was associated in the founding of Long Island BL in the Thirties.

VAN GELDER, Jacq (b. 1902) of Fort Lauderdale FL, retired accountant, won Southeastern Swiss Teams 1982. He is the author of the ACBL *Bulletin* feature *Mixed Masters* and a contributor to other bridge publications. Van Gelder has directed bridge activities on more than 100 cruises since 1972. He is a former billiard champion.

VAN HOOSE, Alfred H. III (Alf) of Seattle won Mid-South Open Teams 1973, Open Pairs 1971, Mid-Atlantic Men's Pairs 1969.

VAN NESS, John P. (b. 1940) of Aspen CO, attorney, won Summer NAC Amateur Pairs 1976, Oil City KO Teams, Master Swiss Teams 1978, Desert Empire KO Teams 1978.

VAN OPPEN, Carol G. J. (b. 1935) of Amsterdam, The Netherlands, bridge columnist and teacher, represented The Netherlands in the World Team Olympiad 1972, 1976, 1980, World Open Pairs 1968, 1978, European Championships 1971, 1979. His national titles include Open Teams nine times, Mixed Pairs 1967, 1969, Open Pairs 1981. A bridge theorist, he is the developer of AMSTERDAM CLUB SYSTEM and modified various existing conventions. Van Oppen is bridge columnist of *Algemeen Dagblad* and contributor to *Bridge*.

VAN OSSEL, Lucienne of Antwerp, Belgium represented Belgium in the World Team Olympiad 1972, World Women's Teams 1960, 1964, 1968, World Women's Pairs 1966, 1970, European Women's Teams 1961, 1963, 1965, 1966, 1970, 1974. Her national wins include Women's Pairs five times, Mixed Pairs twice. She is the top Belgian woman masterpoint holder.

VAN VLECK, Charles Edward (1886–1950) of New York City, was a pioneer of new bidding methods in the Thirties. He originated the WEAK JUMP SHIFT RESPONSES subsequently adopted by the ROTH-STONE SYSTEM, and advocated ultra weak WEAK TWO-BIDS. His system, which was based on the VANDERBILT CLUB SYSTEM, was probably the first to use the THREE-QUARTER NOTRUMP. Van Vleck placed second in the Vanderbilt 1943.

VAN ZANDT, Esta V. of Houston, born in Calcutta, India, bridge teacher, placed second in the Far East Women's Championships (represented Okinawa) 1966. She won Summer NAC Master Mixed Teams 1981, Fall NAC Mixed Pairs 1981 and placed second in Spring NAC Women's Teams 1973. Her numerous regional titles include Spring NAC secondary Swiss Teams 1978, Summer Women's Pairs Flt. A 1979, Southeastern KO Teams 1981, Mississippi Valley Open Pairs Flt. A, Swiss Teams Flt. A 1981.

VÉG, Dr. Tibor (b. 1926) of Budapest, Hungary, lawyer, represented Hungary 15 times in international competitions. He won Hungarian Open Teams 1963, 1966, 1968, 1972, Open Pairs 1964, 1966, 1967, 1969, Venice Open Pairs 1970, and was a member of the victorious Hungarian team in matches against Poland 1973, Austria 1964, Germany 1964 and Brussels 1964. Vég served as vice president of BUDAPEST BRIDGE ASSOCIATION 1965–1970. He devised the Vég bidding system, as played in Hungary and Italy. Vég is a contributor to *Bridzsélet* and *Bridge d'Italia*.

VELASCO ORDÓÑEZ, Eduardo M. (b. 1923) of Buenos Aires, Argentina, government officer, bridge teacher and writer, won National Open Teams 1955, 1957, 1966, 1969, Master Pairs 1973, Master Individual 1967, Interclubs 1956, 1961, 1963, 1964. He is the author of several books including *Bridge Razonado* and *Apuntes Sobre Remates Avanza Dos*.

VELILLA-LACONICH, Emilio L. (b. 1940) of Asunción, Paraguay, lawyer, represented Paraguay in the South American Championships four times and won several national tournaments. He has been a Board member of the PARAGUAY BRIDGE ASSOCIATION since 1960.

VENTURINI, Maria V. of Rome, Italy won the World Women's Teams 1972, European Women's Teams 1970, 1971, 1973.

VERGARA, Etelvina S. de (b. 1904) of Buenos Aires, Argentina, formerly one of the leading woman players of Argentina, was South American Women's champion nine times. She also represented Argentina in the World Women's Teams 1964, 1972. Her national titles include Open Teams, Open Pairs 1937, Master Pairs 1957, 1959, Mixed Teams 1958, 1970, Master Individual 1957, 1961. Vergara is a founder and life member of the Buenos Aires BA.

VERGARA, Osualdo (b. 1946) of Santiago, Chile,

civil engineer, represented Chile in the South American Championships 1978, 1979, 1980, 1981.

VERGOED, Floris J. (Hans) (b. 1948) of Delft, The Netherlands, pharmacist, represented The Netherlands in the World Team Olympiad 1976, 1980, World Open Pairs 1974, 1978. His national titles include Open Teams 1976, 1981, Open Pairs 1976, Mixed Pairs 1981. He is a contributor to *Haagsche Courant* and *Bridge*.

VERNAY, Colby K. (b. 1942) of Lacon IL, basketball coach, won more than 20 regional titles including Fall NAC secondary Men's Pairs 1971, Summer Open Pairs 1972, Texas Fall Open Teams 1966, Central States I Open Pairs 1975, Swiss Teams 1979, II Swiss Teams 1972, 1980, Open Pairs 1975, Mississippi Valley KO Teams, Men's Pairs, Master Pairs 1980.

VERNE, Jules (1828-1905), famous French author of *Voyages Extraordinaires*, his 43-year output of 60-odd volumes, is called "The Father of modern science fiction". In his most successful "voyage" novel, *Around the World in Eighty Days*, his hero, Phileas Fogg, makes his extraordinary wager over the whist table at the Reform Club with his whist partners. Throughout the course of the voyage, Phileas Fogg plays whist with fellow travelers.

VERNOFF, Lee (Mrs. Milton) of Los Angeles won Southeastern Women's Teams 1948, 1948, 1950, 1951, Women's Pairs 1944, 1945.

VERNOFF, Milton (b. 1905) of Los Angeles, retired attorney, won Summer NAC Master Mixed Teams 1938. His numerous regional titles include Bridge Week KO Teams 1971, Master Pairs 1953, Pacific Southwest Men's Pairs 1953, 1955, 1957, 1958, 1966, Swiss Teams 1971, 1972, All-Western KO Teams 1974, 1976. Vernoff pioneered bridge on television in Florida and served as president of the Florida Unit.

VERNON, Francis W. (b. 1934) of Caracas, Venezuela, civil engineer, was South American champion 1965, 1966. He also represented Venezuela in the World Team Olympiad 1968, Bermuda Bowl 1966, 1967, South American Championships 1968. His national titles include Open Teams 1965, 1967, 1968. He was Central American-Caribbean Open Pairs champion 1973, 1977 and represented CAC in the Bermuda Bowl 1979.

VINE, Frank (b. 1927) of Hamilton ON, attorney, won Spring NAC Men's Pairs 1969, Can-Nat KO Teams, Men's Pairs 1968, Swiss Teams 1975, London Bridge Open Pairs Flt. A 1982. He is a contributor to *The Bridge World*, ACBL *Bulletin* and other publications.

VIOLIN, Roxy R. (b. 1929) of Tarzana CA, contractor and consultant, won Spring NAC Mixed Pairs 1970 and placed second in FAll NAC Life

Master Men's Pairs 1973. His regional wins include All-Western Master Pairs 1964, Navajo Trail Mixed Pairs 1970, El Paso Unmixed Pairs 1979.

VISWANATHAN, Srinivasan (Vish) (b. 1948) of Calgary AB, born in Madras, India, engineer, won more than 15 regionals including Calgary Swiss Teams 1973, Open Pairs 1975, Klondike Open Pairs 1976, Swiss Teams, Swiss Teams Flt. A 1980, White Hat Master Pairs Flt. A 1981, Canadian Nat'l Teams Zone 5 1981. He is a contributor to *Canadian Bridge Digest*.

VOGEL, Claude F. (b. 1942) of Chicago, mathematics teacher, won the Grand National Teams 1979 and more than 20 regionals including Summer NAC Swiss Teams Flt. A 1980, Tri-Unit KO Teams 1971, Open Teams 1970, Champagne KO Teams 1976, 1977, Central States II Master Pairs 1976, Open Pairs 1978, Wisconsin Open Pairs Flt. A, Swiss Teams Flt. A 1980.

VOIGHT, Axel (b. 1908) of Risskov, Denmark, chemistry professor and bridge columnist, represented Denmark in the World Team Olympiad 1960, European Championships 1952, 1953, 1956, 1957, 1965, 1967. His national titles include Open Teams 1941, 1952, 1956, 1957, 1960, 1961, 1963, 1964, 1965, 1966, 1973, 1974.

VON DER PORTEN, Ron (b. 1936) of San Francisco, bridge professional, one of the leading American players, placed second in the Bermuda Bowl 1977 and represented North America in the Bermuda Bowl 1962. He won the Chicago (since 1965 the Reisinger) 1962, Vanderbilt 1967, Spingold 1975, 1980 and placed second in the Vanderbilt 1961, 1963, 1971, Blue Ribbon Pairs 1965, Spring NAC Men's Teams 1970. In addition, he has won numerous regional titles. Von der Porten has been commentator for some of world's biggest bridge matches, including CBS-TV match between ACES TEAM and Goren All-Stars, and he frequently directs bridge games on cruises. He is the author of *Introduction to Defensive Bidding*. See BIBLIOGRAPHY, C.

VON ELSNER, Don B. (b. 1909) of Hilo, HI, novelist and bridge writer, won Hawaii Open Teams 1952, Men's Pairs 1962, 1968, Open Pairs 1970. He is the author of many mystery novels; in several of these bridge is featured, notably *The Jake of Diamonds* (originally titled *How to Succeed at Murder Without Really Trying*) in which the setting is a Hawaii Regional, and several leading real-life experts play a part–the first book of the series featuring bridge pro Jake Winkman as the hero. He has been a member of *The Bridge World* Master Solvers' Panel for 30 years and is a frequent contributor to *Popular Bridge*. See BIBLIOGRAPHY, I.

VON ZEDTWITZ, Waldemar K., linguist and lexicographer, president emeritus of the ACBL, is one of the great players of all time. He was born May 8, 1896 in Berlin, son of a German (Saxon) baron, to whose title he succeeded when his father died a few months after his birth, and of an American mother. Thereby he acquired dual citizenship, and after World War I he adopted United States citizenship, relinquishing his title.

Von Zedtwitz has been noted for versatility in playing with exponents of different systems. He was an early contributor to the CULBERTSON SYSTEM, a contributor and consultant in connection with the FOUR ACES SYSTEM, a member of the BRIDGE WORLD TEAM that won the first international matches (1930) in England and France, a member of one of the most successful all-time partnerships with HAROLD S. VANDERBILT playing the club convention, and a regular partner of P. HAL SIMS, S. GARTON CHURCHILL, the FOUR ACES, CHARLES E. VAN VLECK and many others. Later his regular partners included HAROLD HARKAVY, EDITH KEMP and BARBARA BRIER. He was one of the first ten to be named Life Master (No. 4) when that category was created by the ABL in 1936.

Beginning his tournament bridge career in 1923, von Zedtwitz won many national auction bridge championships and has won nearly all contract bridge championships. In 1930 he gave the GOLD CUP for Master Pairs (now Life Master Pairs) and won it the first year. His other tournament successes are: World Mixed Pairs 1970, USBA Grand National Teams, Mixed Pairs 1936, Spingold 1937, 1941, 1947, Chicago (since 1965 the Reisinger) 1932, 1945, Vanderbilt 1930, 1932, 1940, Master Mixed Teams 1940, 1942, 1945, 1965, Life Master Pairs 1930, Open Pairs 1928, 1937, Men's Pairs 1946, Master Individual 1936. He placed second in USBA Mixed Teams 1936, Spingold 1936, 1940, 1949, 1953, 1963, Chicago 1930, 1933, 1936, 1941, 1942, Vanderbilt 1937, 1938, 1943, 1945, 1960, Reisinger 1964, Mixed Teams 1933, 1935, 1956, Life Master Pairs 1933, 1939, Open Pairs 1935, Men's Pairs 1938, 1953. His numerous regional titles include Eastern States KO Teams (Reisinger) 1937, 1944, 1973, 1974.

Von Zedtwitz was ABL Honorary Member in 1931, ABL president in 1932, and was awarded the WETZLAR TROPHY in 1936. When dissension threatened to break up the ACBL in 1948, the contesting factions agreed on von Zedtwitz as president and chairman with carte blanche; and in these positions he is credited with saving the League. Immediately upon rehabilitation of the League at the end of 1949, he returned this power to the ACBL Board of Directors. He was a charter member of the ACBL LAWS COMMISSION, and as co-chairman, played the most active role in preparation of the international code of 1963. A member of the GNYBA Board, he was elected to the ACBL Board in 1962. As such he organized the ACBL Charity Foundation. (See CHARITY PROGRAM OF THE ACBL.) He was a director of the WBF and chairman of its committee on INTERNATIONAL MATCH POINTS, being largely responsible for the schedule adopted in 1961, and also chairman of its Rules Committee for the 1964 World Olympiad.

Von Zedtwitz won a major backgammon tournament in Hawaii at age 82. His other interests include Bridgette, travel, tennis and golf.

W

WACHSMAN, David P. (b. 1942) of New City, NY, data processing executive, won Summer NAC secondary Men's Pairs Flt. B 1977, District 3 Swiss Teams Flt. A 1979, Men's Pairs 1980. He is past president of North Jersey BA.

WACHTER, John E. (b. 1919) of Wauwatosa WI, company president, won Fall NAC secondary Life Master Men's Pairs 1969, Gopher KO Teams 1971, Men's Teams 1969, 1970, Tri-Unit Men's Pairs 1972, Master Pairs 1975, Cornhusker KO Teams 1975, Mad City Swiss Teams Flt. A 1979. He is past president of the Milwaukee Unit.

WADAS, Judith L. (Judy) (b. 1936) of Avon CT, insurance company executive, placed second in Fall NAC Mixed Pairs 1981 and won Summer NAC secondary Swiss Teams 1978, Spring Swiss Teams 1979, Eastern States Women's Pairs 1981, District 3 Swiss Teams Flt. A 1981.

WADE, Barry (b. 1939) of Johannesburg, South Africa, managing director, represented South Africa in the World Team Olympiad 1980. He won South Africa Open Teams 1979, Open Pairs 1966, Pioneer Teams 1967, 1969, 1972, 1973, Interprovincial Teams 1979.

WAGAR, Margaret (Mrs. Wilkinson) of Atlanta, bridge teacher and writer, one of the great American woman players of all time, npc of the United States World Women's Team 1968 and 1972, shares with KAY RHODES a record number of wins in Spring NAC Women's Pairs 1944, 1955, 1956, 1957, 1958. She won the Spingold 1946, 1948, Chicago (since 1965 the Reisinger) 1941, Spring NAC Women's Teams 1940, 1943, 1944, 1945, 1946, 1964, 1965, Summer NAC Master Mixed Teams 1942, 1945, 1948, 1954, 1964, Fall NAC Open Pairs 1947, 1948, Mixed Pairs 1948, 1949, Life Master Women's Pairs 1962. She placed second in Spring Women's Teams 1952, 1953, 1954, 1955, 1956, 1957, 1958, 1964, Summer NAC Life Master Pairs 1943, Master Mixed Teams 1933, 1949, 1950, 1962, 1967. Her NAC secondary wins are the MARCUS CUP 1958, HILLIARD TROPHY 1933, 1945. She served on the ACBL Board of Directors 1960-1972. Wagar was named ACBL Honorary Member in 1979.

WAGNER, Willem M. (b. 1926) of Amsterdam, The Netherlands, tournament director since 1962, was appointed assistant chief tournament director of the EUROPEAN BRIDGE LEAGUE in 1982. He was organizing chief for the 1980 World Team Olympiad and assistant chief organizer for the 1982 World Championships. Wagner heads an organic chemistry research laboratory. He also is an expert in marine biology.

WAGRODZKI, Krzysztof (b. 1941) of Warsaw, Poland, lawyer, represented Poland in the European Championships 1967, Junior Championships 1968. He won Polish Open Teams 1967.

WAINWRIGHT, Louise (Mrs. Stuyvesant) (b. 1902) of Southampton NY, former antique shop owner, placed second in Summer NAC Master Mixed Teams 1941, HILLIARD TROPHY 1939 and won Eastern States KO Teams (Reisinger) 1941 (the first woman ever to win this prestigious event), Mixed Teams 1940, 1941, 1944. In 1935 she donated a trophy in her name for the winners of the Eastern States Women's Pairs.

WAINWRIGHT, Stuyvesant (1891-1975) of New York City and Naples FL was a stockbroker, avid sportsman, and a descendant of Peter Stuyvesant. He was a member of the Vanderbilt Cup Tournament Committee 1928-1957, member of the Whist Club Committee on laws for international codes of 1932 and 1935, and vice president of the Regency Club, New York. Wainwright placed second in Summer NAC Mixed Teams 1943. A promoter of the game TOWIE, he authored *Towie Tactics* in 1946.

WAKEMAN, Robert P. (1913-1981) of Upper Montclair NJ, a systems engineer, was a director of the New Jersey BL and its former bridge editor as well as bridge editor of *Newark Evening News*. He was a contributing editor, *Bridge Encyclopedia*. In 1960 Wakeman won Fall NAC Men's Teams and New England Fall Mixed Teams.

WALKER, Judith E. (Judy) of Oklahoma City OK, accounting clerk, won Missouri Valley Swiss Teams 1976, Women's Swiss Teams 1979, Toast of Tulsa Swiss Teams Flt. A 1981.

WALDMANN, Arthur J. (b. 1933) of Rocky Hill CT, sales manager, won Spring NAC Men's Pairs 1975 and placed second in the Spingold 1974, Spring NAC Men's Teams 1977. His more than 20 regional wins include Spring NAC secondary Open Pairs 1970, Swiss Teams 1977, Summer Men's Pairs 1971, Upper New York State Open Pairs 1975, KO Teams 1976, New England Knockout KO Teams 1977, 1982, Swiss Teams 1975, Summer KO Teams 1977, Individual KO Teams 1975, 1977.

WALLACE, Charlton (1904-1979) of Cincinnati, bridge writer, was a founder-member of the INTERNATIONAL BRIDGE PRESS ASSOCIATION and in 1978 was elected an honorary member of the IBPA. He was a bridge associate of ELY CULBERTSON, P. HAL SIMS and other greats. A director of the AWL, and Midwest president of the USBA in 1936, Wakeman was bridge editor of the *Cincinnati Post-Times-Star* from 1933 until his death. He was a contributing editor, *Bridge Encyclopedia*.

WALLACE, Jane V. (Mrs. Charlton) of Cincinnati won Fall NAC Women's Teams 1947, All-American Open Pairs 1946, Midwest Spring Open Teams 1949, 1980, District 11 Women's Pairs 1964.

WALLACE, Wilfred N. W. (b. 1908) of Summer Hill, NSW, Australia, chemist, was World Par champion 1937 with a 100% score. His national titles include Interstate Open teams 1948, 1964,

1965, 1967, Open Pairs 1940, 1944, 1948, 1953, 1958, 1966.

WALSH, Alan D. (b. 1945) of Sydney, Australia, systems analyst, was Far East Open Pairs champion 1972. He also represented Australia in the Far East Championships 1972, 1973, 1974. He won Australian Interstate Teams 1973.

WALSH, Rhoda (nee Lander) of Woodland Hills CA, bridge professional and attorney, one of the leading American women players, placed third in the World Women's Teams 1968 and won Spring NAC Women's Teams 1968, Women's Pairs 1968, 1972, Summer NAC Master Mixed Teams 1976, Fall NAC Life Master Women's Pairs 1968, 1972. Her numerous regional titles include Spring NAC secondary Swiss Teams 1970, Fall Swiss Teams 1981, Bridge Week Mixed Teams 1965, 1969, 1970, Mixed Pairs 1966, 1974, Women's Pairs 1967, Open Teams 1972, 1973, Los Angeles Winter Women's KO Teams 1981. She is the co-author of *Recap Bridge*.

WALSH, Richard R. (b. 1936) of Zurich, Switzerland, commodities and currencies analyst, formerly one of the leading American players, represented North America in the Bermuda Bowl 1971. He won the Team Trials 1970, Vanderbilt 1969, Spring NAC Men's Teams 1970, Men's Pairs 1970 and placed second in the Spingold 1959. His more than 50 regional wins include Bridge Week Mixed Teams 1962, 1969, Mixed Pairs 1966, Master Pairs 1965, 1966, Open Pairs 1965, Master Men's Pairs 1967, Men's Pairs 1966, 1967.

WALSHE, Col. George Gordon J. (1873–1959) of London, England represented his country in the ANGLO-AMERICAN MATCH 1934, and was one of the referees in the CULBERTSON-LENZ MATCH in 1932. He was co-inventor of the CAB SYSTEM. Walshe wrote under the pseudonym of "Yarborough" for the *Sunday Times*, and authored *Count to Win at Bridge*, *Let's Play CAB*, and *Slams Made Simple*. With F. DUDLEY COURTENAY he wrote *The Losing Trick Count*, *Standard Manual of Play*, and *Standardized Code of Contract Bridge*. See BIBLIOGRAPHY, C.

WALSHE, Patrick G. (b. 1954) of Dublin, Ireland, computer programmer/analyst, won the European Common Market Open Championship 1981 and also represented Ireland in European Junior Championships 1978, 1980, European Championships 1981, World Team Olympiad 1980, World Open Pairs 1982. His national titles include Men's Pairs 1980, 1981, 1982, Master Pairs 1981, 1982, Mixed Pairs 1980, CBAI Teams five times, All-IRL Teams three times. He is an executive of the CONTRACT BRIDGE ASSOCIATION OF IRELAND.

WALUYAN, Ferdinand R. (Felix) (b. 1942) of Jakarta, Indonesia, management consultant, one of the leading Far East players, won the Far East Championships 1979, 1982 and placed second in 1981. He also represented Indonesia in the Far East

Championships 1975, 1976, 1977, Bermuda Bowl 1973, 1981, World Team Olympiad 1980. His national titles include Intercity Teams 1971, 1974, 1979, 1980, Open Teams 1977, 1980, Mixed Teams 1979.

WALVICK, Katharine H. (Kathie) (Mrs. Walter J., formerly Mrs. Mike Cappelletti)** (b. 1942) of McLean VA, legal assistant, one of the leading women players of the East Coast, won Summer NAC Master Mixed Teams 1967, Fall NAC Life Master Women's Pairs 1980, and placed second in the Blue Ribbon Pairs 1973, 1977, Fall NAC Mixed Pairs 1967. Her numerous regional wins include Mid-Atlantic Open Teams 1967, 1970, 1979, KO Teams 1972, 1979.

WALVICK, Walter J. (b. 1942) of McLean VA, attorney, won the HERMAN TROPHY 1975, Fall NAC Life Master Men's Pairs 1975 and placed second in the Life Master Pairs 1974. His regional wins include Mid-Atlantic KO Teams 1971, 1972, 1976, Open Teams 1969, Open Pairs 1978. He is a former director and vice president of the Washington BL.

WARDEN, Phillip J. (b. 1947) of Madison WI, painting contractor, won Tri-Unit Open Pairs 1969, Mississippi Valley Swiss Teams 1975, Wisconsin Swiss Teams Flt. A 1978, Open Pairs 1980.

WARNER, David (b. 1911) of Bala-Cynwyd PA, stockbroker, placed second in Summer NAC Master Mixed Teams 1947, Fall NAC Mixed Pairs 1957 and won District 4 Men's Pairs 1962, Eastern States Mixed Teams 1958, Keystone Open Teams 1960, Men's Pairs 1965. Warner is a member emeritus and former president of Philadelphia CBA and former ACBL vice president.

WARNER, Janet M. (b. 1907) of Pampa TX, retired secretary, won Summer NAC Women's Pairs 1962, Desert Empire Open Pairs 1961.

WARREN, Emily (Mrs. Prescott) (1876-deceased) of Newton MA, daughter of Francis Edgar Stanley, inventor of the Stanley steam car, was a prominent New England bridge teacher and radio lecturer in the Twenties and Thirties, and bridge writer. She was a columnist for the *Boston Transcript* and authored several books on games including *Auction and Contract Bridge Condensed*, and co-authored *Contract Bridge of 1930*. See BIBLIOGRAPHY, A, C.

WARSHAUER, Judge Bernard J. (b. 1920) of Sumter SC, won Spring NAC secondary Open Pairs 1971, Mid-Atlantic Spring KO Teams 1973, 1979, Men's Pairs 1977, Master Pairs 1975, 1976, Winter KO Teams 1972, Fall Master Pairs 1962. He has been District 7 representative to the ACBL Board of Directors since 1979, and is past president of Unit 160. Warshauer is a contributor to the District 7 publication and former editor of the Unit 160 publication. He was educated at The Citadel and University of North Carolina Law School.

WARSHAUER, Genie (Mrs. Bernard, formerly

Means) (b. 1938) of Sumter SC, bridge teacher, won Mid-Atlantic Master Pairs 1975, 1976, KO Teams, Women's Swiss Teams 1979, Swiss Teams 1980, Fall NAC secondary Open Teams 1981.

WARZEK, Frank G. of San Jose CA, physicist, won Summer NAC Commercial and Industrial Teams 1969, Golden Gate Men's Pairs 1973, Mid-Winter Holiday Master Pairs 1974, California Capital Open Pairs 1975, All-Western Swiss Teams 1978, Holiday Festival Master Pairs 1979.

WATANABE, Clara (b. 1919) of Honolulu, accountant, won Hawaii Open Teams 1960, Open Pairs 1958, Women's Pairs 1959, 1969, 1972, 1974, 1976, 1977, Mixed Pairs 1960, 1970, 1972. She is a former president and secretary of Unit 470.

WATSON, Louis H. (1907–1936) of New York City was a leading player of the Thirties. *Collier's* magazine of March 24, 1934, ranked Watson as the fourth greatest player in the world on the basis of his tournament record. He won the AWL Open Teams and Open Pairs, 1933 and 1934, Asbury Challenge Teams 1932, Cavendish Club Individual in 1933, and placed second in four major events including the Vanderbilt 1933. Watson was a widely followed analyst, acting as daily columnist for the New York *Post*, and as Technical Editor for *The Bridge World*. His writings included the classic *Watson on the Play of the Hand*, and *Contract Bridge*. See BIBLIOGRAPHY, D. E.

WEBBER, Robert F. (b. 1946) of Clawson MI, certified public accountant, financial reporting manager, won Spring NAC secondary Swiss Teams 1973, 1981, Summer Open Pairs 1978, Motor City Open Pairs 1974, KO Teams 1978, Great Lakes Master Pairs 1977, All-American Master Pairs 1981. He served as president and tournament chairman for Michigan BA, executive secretary, treasurer and tournament coordinator for District 12. See also HIGHEST SCORE.

WEBSTER, Harold Tucker (1885–1952), noted syndicated cartoonist, was best known for the character "The Timid Soul," which he created. He used bridge as the topic of many of his humorous pictures. Born in West Virginia, he lived most of his adult life in New York City. He co-authored cartoon books on bridge with ELY CULBERTSON (1932), Caswell Adams (1948), Philo Clark Calhoun (1948, 1949), William Johnston (1924) and authored *Grand Slams*, 1938. See BIBLIOGRAPHY, L.

WEED, Charles E. (b. 1931) of Dallas, corporate vice president, won the Grand National Teams 1975, Fall NAC Swiss Teams 1978. His more than 40 regional wins include Navajo Trail Master Pairs, Swiss Teams 1975, Houston Mid-Winter Swiss Teams 1973, Master Swiss Teams 1981, Mid-South KO Teams 1972, Swiss Teams 1973, 1978, Rocky Mountain KO Teams 1981, Republic of Texas Master Swiss Teams 1981.

WEED, Marion D. of Lake Kiowa TX, interior decorator, represented the United States in the World Women's Pairs 1978. She won Fall NAC Life Master Women's Pairs 1975, Summer NAC Master Mixed Teams 1976. Her regional wins include Summer NAC secondary Women's Pairs 1974, Navajo Trail Swiss Teams 1975, Bermuda Master Pairs, Women's Pairs 1975, Big D Swiss Teams 1976, Alamo City Swiss Teams 1976.

WEGLARSKI, Peter Z. (b. 1948) of West Chester PA, computer project leader, won numerous regionals including Summer NAC secondary Open Pairs 1977, Fall Open Pairs 1979, Long Island Open Pairs 1976, Mid-Atlantic Men's Pairs, Swiss Teams 1977, Men's Swiss Teams 1979, All-American Swiss Teams 1978, Open Pairs 1980, Big Apple Men's Pairs 1979, Nassau-Suffolk Swiss Teams 1977, District 4 Men's Swiss Teams 1979, GNT 1977.

WEI, Charles C. (C.C.) (b. 1914) of New York City, born in Shanghai, China, shipbuilding magnate, was npc of the Taiwan Team in the World Team Olympiad 1964, Bermuda Bowl 1969, and npc of the North American Venice Trophy Team 1981. Wei devised the PRECISION bidding system which was used successfully by the Taiwan Team in the 1969 and 1970 Bermuda Bowl, by the PRECISION TEAM in winning the 1970 and 1971 Spingold and 1972 Vanderbilt, and by the Italian Team in winning the 1972 World Team Olympiad and the 1973 and 1974 Bermuda Bowl. See SPONSORS. Wei is a former trustee of the ACBL Charity Foundation. He won Puerto Rico Open Pairs 1970, Swiss Teams 1972, Mid-Atlantic Summer Swiss Teams 1972, Metropolitan Open Pairs 1974. See HIGHEST SCORE. Wei is the author of many books and articles on Precision and Super Precision. See BIBLIOGRAPHY, C.

WEI, Katherine (Kathie) (Mrs. Charles C.) (b. 1930) of New York City, born in Peking, China, writer and lecturer on the PRECISION CLUB system, one of the leading American women players, won the World Women's Pairs 1978 and placed second in the Venice Trophy Teams 1981. She won Spring NAC Women's Teams 1971, 1980 (second in 1973, 1982), and placed second in the Vanderbilt 1974, 1977, 1979. Her more than 100 regional wins include Spring NAC secondary Women's Swiss Teams 1973, Summer Golder Master Pairs 1977, Silver Trophy Pairs Flt. A 1979, Fall Swiss Teams 1973, 1979, Silver Trophy Pairs Flt. A 1977. Wei was appointed advisor to the Shanghai Bridge League while attending the first international bridge tournament ever held in China (March 1981). She was co-captain and manager of the Taiwan team that finished second in the 1969 Bermuda Bowl, non-playing captain of the Taiwan team in the 1971 Bermuda Bowl and the 1972 World Team Olympiad. She is a Board member of the Greater New York BA, a member of the ACBL Goodwill Committee and a trustee of the ACBL Charity Foundation. Wei, a graduate of Shanghai University School of Nursing, was a medical facility administrator for 15 years, retiring in 1972. She is a contributor to various national and international bridge publications, author of her biography, and co-author of *Action For the Defense* and *One Club Complete*. See BIBLIOGRAPHY, C.

WEI, Stella (b. 1946) of China, bank employee, represented the Republic of China in the Far East Women's Championships five times, placing second twice.

WEICHSEL, Nancy E. (Mrs. Arthur Blaustein) (b. 1945) of Walnut Creek CA, former backgammon and bridge professional, won Summer NAC Master Mixed Teams 1976. Her regional wins include Tri-State Winter Swiss Teams 1971, Southeastern Life Master Pairs 1973, Puerto Rico Swiss Teams 1973, Metropolitan KO Teams 1974, Upper New York State KO Teams 1975.

WEICHSEL, Peter M. (b. 1943) of Flushing NY, bridge professional, one of the leading American players, won the FISHBEIN TROPHY 1980, International Team Trials 1982, Spingold 1970, 1971, 1980, 1982, Vanderbilt 1972 (second in 1975, 1981), Reisinger 1973, Spring NAC Men's Teams 1979 (second in 1968), Men's Pairs 1980, Summer NAC Master Mixed Teams 1976, Fall NAC Life Master Men's Pairs 1971, Life Master Pairs 1977 (second in 1972). He won the Cavendish Club Invitational 1976, 1977, London *Sunday Times* Pairs 1975 (second in 1973) and numerous regional titles including Eastern States KO Teams (Reisinger) 1977, 1979. See also LANCIA TEAMS and PRECISION TEAM.

WEIK, Thomas W. (b. 1942) of Womelsdorf PA, stockbroker, placed second in Summer NAC Life Master Pairs 1974 and won Mid-Atlantic Fall KO Teams 1971, District 4 GNT 1973.

WEIL, Elina A. (b. 1921) of Sacramento CA, bridge cruise director, won All-Western Women's Pairs 1968, California Capital Women's Pairs 1977, Hawaii Swiss Teams 1980.

WEILAND, Alexander (b. 1947) of Des Plaines IL, accountant, won Central States I Swiss Teams 1972, KO Teams 1975, 1979, II Mixed Pairs 1977, Tri-Unit Swiss Teams 1972, Champagne Swiss Teams 1976.

WEINBERG, Manuel M. (b. 1907) of Frederick MD, lawyer and company director, won Mid-Atlantic Spring Open Pairs 1961, Summer Master Pairs 1962, Fall Open Teams 1966.

WEINER, Mrs. George S. (b. 1905) of Joplin MO, won Missouri Valley Women's Pairs 1958, 1965, Keystone Mixed Pairs 1958.

WEINER, Howard N. (b. 1944) of Southfield MI, attorney, won Spring NAC secondary Open Pairs 1981, Motor City Open Pairs 1981, Great Lakes Men's Swiss Teams 1981.

WEINER, Leo B. (b. 1906) of Chicago, club director and manager, won several regionals including Summer NAC secondary Golder Master Pairs 1966, Central States Life and Senior Master Teams 1957, Open Pairs 1943, 1953, Mississippi Valley Open Teams 1962, Men's Pairs 1951, 1953, 1956, Mixed

Pairs 1957, Champagne Men's Pairs 1977, Springfield Master Pairs 1980.

WEINSTEIN, Howard M. (b. 1953) of Chicago, won more than 20 regional titles including Spring NAC secondary Non-Master Pairs 1972, Iowa Open Teams, Men's Pairs 1974, KO Teams 1975, Open Pairs 1977, Roughrider KO Teams, Open Pairs 1977, Gopher Master Pairs 1979.

WEINSTEIN, Jerry J. (b. 1936) of Northbrook IL, certified public accountant, won Summer NAC secondary Swiss Teams 1971, 1980, Central States I KO Teams 1976.

WEINSTEIN, Sol (b. 1949) of Yonkers NY, ACBL national tournament director, began his career in 1969 and achieved his current rating in 1979.

WEINSTEIN, Steven M. (b. 1964) of Accord NY, student, won Summer NAC Life Master Pairs 1981, New England Summer Swiss Teams 1981. He was the youngest player ever to win a North American Championship. See also KING OR QUEEN OF BRIDGE.

WEISBACH, Dean (Mrs. Frank) (b. 1911) of Cincinnati, ACBL Operations Division Manager 1970–1976, was an ACBL national tournament director 1956–1970, the first woman to achieve this rating.

WEISBACH, Frank (1905–1981) of Cincinnati was a leading Midwest player and expert analyst. Life Master #80 in 1947, he was an active player for three decades. He won the Life Master Pairs in 1947, was second in the Spingold 1951 and won numerous regional events.

WEISS, Albert (Dingy) (b. 1900) of Miami Beach, formerly one of the leading American players, won the Vanderbilt 1963, 1965, Fall NAC Open Pairs 1939, 1951, Spring NAC Men's Teams 1946 and placed second in the Spingold 1953, 1972, Life Master Pairs 1949, 1962, Master Individual 1945, Men's Teams 1952. His numerous regional titles include All-American Open Teams 1938, 1939, Open Pairs 1938, Master Individual 1938, 1939, Southeastern Men's Teams, Open Pairs 1960, Open Teams, KO Teams 1968, Desert Empire Open Teams 1968.

WEISS, David J. (b. 1944) of Pasadena CA, psychology professor, placed second in the Reisinger 1981 and won Pacific Southwest Master Pairs, Men's Pairs 1969, Bridge Week Open Pairs 1972, BAM Teams 1976, Swiss Teams 1975, Palm Springs Swiss Teams 1973, Los Angeles Winter KO Teams 1975, Holiday Festival KO Teams, Swiss Teams 1979. Weiss is a contributor to *The Bridge World* and *Southern California Bridge News*.

WEISS, Larry of Encinitas CA, photographer, represented the United States in the World Open Pairs 1974. He placed second in Fall NAC Mixed Pairs 1970 and won numerous regionals including Fall NAC secondary Swiss Teams 1970, Open Pairs

A-D, Open Pairs 1978, Spring Swiss Teams 1979, Summer Goddard Pairs 1966, All-Western Men's Pairs 1975, Bridge Week KO Teams 1963, 1965, Master Men's Pairs 1975. He is the author of several *Bridge World* articles and is the originator of the WEISS CONVENTION and SIMPLIFIED CLUB SYSTEM.

WEISS, Lawrence (1905–1979) of Brookline MA, attorney, was one of the leading players of New England, and has numerous regional wins to his credit including Open Teams 1957, 1960, 1961, 1963 and Knockout Teams 1938, 1939, 1941 (twice), 1942, 1945, 1957, 1961, and 1964. Weiss was chairman of the committe to revise ACBL bylaws in 1949 and is credited with devising administrative methods used by the ACBL since then. A former ACBL vice president and president of the New England Bridge Conference, Weiss authored *Contract Bridge: The Bidding Structure*. See BIBLIOGRAPHY, C.

WEISS, Richard S. (b. 1946) of Medford MA, attorney, won New England Masters Swiss Teams 1974, Summer Swiss Teams 1974, Can-Am KO Teams 1975. He is a graduate of University of Massachusetts at Amherst and Suffolk University. He has authored a dog racing handicapping book which is currently being serialized in *Gambling Times*.

WEITZNER, Jerome B. (Jerry) (b. 1941) of Danville CA, hospital forms designer, won Summer NAC secondary Commercial and Industrial Teams 1972, All-Western Men's Teams 1973, Hawaii Open Teams 1968, 1973, District 21 GNT 1974. Weitzner is past president of Unit 499.

WELCH, Lawrence J. (Larry) (b. 1895) of Indianapolis, retired realtor and appraiser, won the Chicago (since 1965 the Reisinger) 1935, Central States Open Teams 1939, 1943, All-American Open Teams 1941, 1942, 1945, Master Individual 1946.

WELLS, Nell (formerly Childs) of San Francisco, bridge teacher, first woman Life Master on the Pacific Coast, won the BARCLAY TROPHY 1946, 1951, 1955, and numerous regionals including All-Western Open Teams 1957, Bridge Week Open Teams 1948, 1957, Master Pairs 1954, Open Pairs 1951, Women's Pairs 1942, 1961, Golden Gate Women's Pairs 1973.

WELTMAN, Dr. Harold (b. 1931) of Kingston PA, dentist, placed second in Fall Amateur Men's Pairs 1976 and won Spring NAC secondary Open Pairs 1978, Summer Swiss Teams 1980, District 4 Men's Pairs, Open Pairs 1977, Spring Open Pairs Flt. A 1979, Fall Men's Swiss Teams 1979, Puerto Rico Master Pairs 1976. He is past president of Unit 120 and former vice president of District 4.

WENDT, Edward G. Jr. (Jay) (b. 1928) of New York City, insurance company executive, placed second in the Chicago (since 1965 the Reisinger) 1961 and won Spring NAC secondary Commerical and Industrial Teams 1958, Golder Master Pairs 1961, Eastern States Master Pairs 1959, Men's Pairs 1974,

New England Mixed Teams 1958, New York-New Jersey Open Pairs 1965.

WENNBERG, Tom (b. 1908) of Gothenburg, Sweden, bridge columnist and teacher, represented Sweden in the European Championships 1934, 1935, 1948, placing second in 1948. He was Nordic champion 1948 and won Swedish Open Pairs 1961.

WERDELIN, Dr. Ole (b. 1933) of Copenhagen, Denmark, physician, represented Denmark in the European Championships 1961, 1965, 1973, 1974 and won Danish Open Teams 1963, 1974.

WERDELIN, Stig (b. 1937) of Copenhagen, Denmark, lawyer, represented Denmark in the World Team Olympiad 1972, European Championships 1961, 1970, 1971, 1973, 1974, 1975. He won Danish Open Teams six times, Open Pairs 1972, 1973, 1974.

WERNHER, Sir Derrick J. (1889–1947) of London, England and New Deal NJ was one of the originators of the masterpoint system. Wernher presided over the ABL in 1933 and was chairman of its Master Plan Committee, was a member of the Board of Directors of the AWL, and donor of the WERNHER TROPHY. He placed second in the Asbury Challenge Teams 1936 and won the Reisinger 1930.

WEST, Leslie (b. 1944) of Walnut Creek CA, computer services director, won numerous regionals including Golden Gate KO Teams 1969, 1970, 1974, Golden State KO Teams 1970, Open Teams 1968, Bridge Week Master Men's Pairs 1967, Canadian Open Teams 1968, Desert Empire KO Teams 1969, Mid-Winter Holiday KO Teams 1976.

WESTCOTT, Frank T. (1901–1974) of North Attleboro MA, engineer and contractor, was one of the outstanding American bridge personalities. He was non-playing captain of the North American Team World Championship 1961 and U.S. World Team Olympiad 1964. Westcott won numerous regional titles including New England Knockout Teams and Mixed Teams five times each, and was second in Spring NAC Men's Team 1964. He presided over the ACBL 1960, was Honorary Member 1968, a former member of the ACBL Board, president of the New England Bridge Conference and of the Eastern Massachusetts BA. See WESTCOTT TROPHY.

WESTFALL, David L. (b. 1950) of Spokane WA, antique dealer, won Oregon Trail Men's Swiss Teams 1976, Master Pairs 1979, Mid-Winter Holiday Men's Swiss Teams 1976, Peach City Master Pairs 1978, Big Sky Master Pairs 1979, District 19 GNP 1981.

WESTHEIMER, Gerald J. (Jeff) (b. 1934) of New York City, commodity specialist, represented the United States in the World Open Pairs 1970. He won the Reisinger 1969, and placed second in the Vanderbilt 1968, 1969, Spingold 1969.

WETZLAR, Edwin A. (d. 1934) of New York City was a leading personality in the early years of whist and bridge. He won the Vanderbilt 1928, Summer Master Mixed Teams, 1933, second in the Vanderbilt 1929 and won AWL Open Pairs 1931 and 1933. Wetzlar was a Board member of the AMERICAN WHIST LEAGUE. See WETZLAR TROPHY.

WEYANT, Janet A. (Mrs. William S.) (b. 1931) of Cincinnati won Champagne Women's Pairs 1976, 1977, District 15 Summer Women's Swiss Teams 1977, District 5 Women's Pairs 1977, Mid-Atlantic Women's Pairs 1978, Swiss Teams 1980, Great Lakes KO Teams 1978, Midwest Fall Swiss Teams 1978, Spring Women's Pairs, Women's Swiss Teams 1981, Motor City Open Pairs 1979.

WEYANT, William S. (Bill) (b. 1920) of Cincinnati, ACBL associate national tournament director, began directing in 1962 and achieved his current rating in 1972. A former scientist in charge of Antarctic atmospheric research, he was awarded a Congressional medal in 1960. Mount Weyant, Antarctica, was named for him.

WHALEN, Vivian (formerly Lavery) of Sea Cliff NY, bridge club owner, placed second in Spring NAC Women's Teams 1976 and won Summer NAC secondary Mixed Pairs Flt. B 1974, Fall Swiss Teams 1st Flt. 1974, Eastern States Mixed Teams 1961, Mixed Pairs 1966, New York Winter Open Teams 1974, Tri-State Winter Women's Swiss Teams, Women's Pairs 1977, District 4 Women's Swiss Teams 1977, Long Island Women's Pairs 1977, Mexican Nat'l Swiss Teams 1981.

WHITE, Barry A. (b. 1945) of Gresham OR, tax consultant, won Oregon Trail Open Teams 1972, Men's Pairs 1970, KO Teams 1975, Peach Festival KO Teams 1974, District 20 GNT 1973, 1974, 1975, 1981, Zone VII 1974, 1981.

WHITE, Dorothy Collins (b. 1904) of Racine WI, former tournament director and bridge teacher, was known as "Mrs. Bridge" in Racine. She was an ACBL Board member 1964 and executive secretary of the Wisconsin-Upper Michigan BA for more than 15 years.

WHITE, Effie L. (formerly Long) (b. 1918) of Mason TX, tournament director and Goren bridge teacher, won Eastern States Mixed Teams 1963. Associated with CHARLES H. GOREN for many years, she conducted the Goren national forums in New York 1968–1970 and numerous cruises 1965–1977, was selected as coordinator of the Goren Teacher Society in 1965, co-authored with Goren *Introduction to Bridge* and was associate editor of *Goren Teacher Manual*. She is past president of the ABTA. She has written articles for the ABTA *Quarterly*, *Popular Bridge*, and was columnist for local newspapers.

WHITEBROOK, Charles H. (b. 1908) of Ft. Lauderdale FL, retired advertising agency executive, won Fall NAC Open Pairs 1949, Eastern States Open Pairs 1947, Florida Master Pairs 1960, Southeastern Open Teams 1955, 1956, 1972. He served as an ACBL Board member 1951–1977 and as president of Florida Unit 1961, 1963. Sunday columnist of *Ft. Lauderdale News* since 1977, he formerly edited and published *Florida Bridge News*.

WHITELEY, Frank R. (b. 1918) of Tampa FL, cigar manufacturer, won Spring NAC secondary Mixed Pairs 1966, Mid-South Open Teams 1969, Southeastern Men's Teams 1974, Central Florida Men's Pairs 1978.

WHITEHEAD, Wilbur C(herier) (1866–1931) of New York City was one of the world's greatest bridge authorities. He was president of the Simplex Automobile Company, but bridge held such a fascination for him that he retired from business to devote his whole life to bridge in 1910. At that time he was living in France and wrote his first publication, *Royal Spades*. A second book was published in London in 1913. His first book appearing in America was *Whitehead's Convention of Auction Bridge* in 1914. He was the inventor of many of the outstanding conventions of bidding and play, the quick trick table of card values, the Whitehead system of requirements for original bids and responses, and the Whitehead table of preferential leads. He was instrumental in standardizing procedures in auction bridge and later in contract bridge. Whitehead was a member of the team which won the Vanderbilt in 1928, the first year it was put into play, and was second the following year. He was a contributing editor of *The Bridge World* and published several books, including *Auction Bridge Standards* which explained the Whitehead system. See BIBLIOGRAPHY, A, E, H.

WHITESEL, William F. Sr. (b. 1940) of Coeur d'Alene ID, farming operation manager, bridge teacher, won more than 20 regionals including Oregon Trail KO Teams 1971, 1973, 1977, British Columbia KO Teams 1971, Open Pairs 1970, Men's Pairs 1973, Gem State KO Teams 1976, Puget Sound Men's Pairs 1977, Big Sky Swiss Teams 1979.

WHITWORTH, George F. (Rick) (b. 1949) of Concord CA, systems programmer, won Summer NAC secondary Golder Master Pairs 1979, California Capital Master Pairs 1980, Golden State Open Pairs Flt. A 1981.

WIDDER, Dr. Lajos (1893–1979) of Budapest, Hungary, lawyer and author, was European champion 1938, Hungarian champion 1937, 1938, 1939, 1955, 1957, Hungarian winner of the World Par Contest 1937. His writings include *Tournament Bridge* and *The Technique and Tactics of Bridge Playing*.

WIGNALL, John R. (b. 1932) of Christchurch, New Zealand, stockbroker, represented New Zealand in the Bermuda Bowl 1974, World Team Olympiad 1972, 1976, Far East Championships 1964, 1971, 1973, 1975, 1976, 1977. His national wins include Open Pairs 1964, 1965, 1970, 1971, 1973, 1974, 1976, Open Teams 1972, 1981. He is bridge columnist for two newspapers.

WIJAYA, Jasin (b. 1940) of Jakarta, Indonesia, billiard center manager, was Far East champion 1972, 1979. He also represented Indonesia in the World Team Olympiad 1980, Bermuda Bowl 1981, Far East Championships 1967, 1969, 1970, 1972, 1976, 1977, 1981. His national titles include Intercity Teams 1965, 1968, 1970, 1972, Open Pairs 1965, Open Teams 1968, 1972, 1977, 1980.

WILDY, Marion Edwin (1910–1978) of Aiea HI, born in Arkansas, former naval supplies supervisor, bridge teacher and tournament director, won Hawaii Open Teams 1956, Mixed Pairs 1957. He was the first black ACBL Life Master (#1225, 1956). Wildy was president of Honolulu Unit in 1964.

WILEY, Kent (b. 1937) of Oak Park IL, government administrator, won Fall NAC secondary Mixed Pairs 1969, Spring Swiss Teams 1972, Summer Open Pairs 1980, Tri-Unit Open Pairs 1971, Men's Pairs 1972, 1974, Mixed Pairs 1969, Iowa Open Pairs 1974, Florida Swiss Teams 1972.

WILEY, Lois (Mrs. Kent) of Oak Park IL, chiropractic physician, won Fall NAC secondary Mixed Pairs 1969, Spring Swiss Teams 1972, 1973, Summer Open Pairs 1980, Central States Open Teams 1969, 1974, Tri-Unit Open Pairs 1971, Mixed Pairs 1969, Iowa Open Pairs 1974, Southeastern Mixed Pairs 1974, Women's Swiss Teams 1975. The most successful blind player, she is a familiar sight at tournaments with her seeing-eye dog. See HANDI-CAPPED PLAYERS.

WILKINS, Robert H. (Bob) (b. 1911) of Memphis, retired ACBL executive, served bridge in various capacities for many years. He became a tournament director in 1952 and held the rating of national tournament director in 1965 when he was appointed ACBL tournament coordinator. From 1968 to 1978 he was director of ACBL elections and director of communications for the ACBL Board of Directors. He also served as executive secretary of the ACBL Charity Foundation 1969–1973. Wilkins has contributed to many bridge publications including the Chicago CBA *Kibitzer*. He is past president of the CCBA. By profession a librarian, Wilkins was educated at Oberlin College and Western Reserve University.

WILKOSZ, Andrzej (b. 1935) of Krakow, Poland, metallurgist, won the Rosenblum Cup Teams 1978. He also represented Poland in the World Team Olympiad 1964, 1972, 1976, European Championships 1963, 1965. He won the LONDON SUNDAY TIMES PAIRS (since 1981 INVITATIONAL PAIRS) 1972, Belgian Open Teams 1964, Beirut Festival Open Teams 1968, Polish Mixed Teams 1968, Open Pairs 1962.

WILKS, Betty N. (b. 1918) of Pittsburg KS, former bridge teacher, won Mississippi Valley Women's Pairs 1956, Missouri Valley Mixed Pairs 1955, Women's Pairs 1957, 1977, Mexican Nat'l Master Pairs 1978.

WILL, Mary Ann (formerly Miller) (b. 1937) of Dearborn MI, supervisor, former research chemist, won District 5 Master Pairs 1970, Champagne Women's Pairs 1972, Motor City Women's Pairs 1975, Wolverine Women's Swiss Teams 1977, Great Lakes Women's Swiss Teams 1979, 1981.

WILLIAMS, Diana P. (b. 1950) of Epsom, Surrey, England, civil servant, won the Venice Trophy 1981, European Women's Championships 1981, Common Market Championships 1979, 1981. She is a contributor to *International Popular Bridge Monthly* and *Bridge Magazine*.

WILLIAMS, Don R. (b. 1931) of Kansas City MO, economist, placed second in Spring NAC Men's Teams 1962 and won District 15 Open Teams 1967, 1969, KO Teams 1969, 1970, 1977, Indian Summer KO Teams 1979, Midwest Open Pairs Flt. A 1980, Springfield Swiss Teams 1980.

WILLIAMS, Mary C. (formerly Philley) (b. 1927) of Houston, attorney, placed second in Summer NAC Master Mixed Teams 1964 and won Texas KO Teams 1970, Mexican Nat'l Women's Pairs 1973. She is a former secretary and vice president of District 16 and was the first editor of its publication, *Scorecard*.

WILLIAMS, Phyllis L. (b. 1907) of London, England, was European Women's champion 1950, 1951, 1952, and also represented Great Britain 1949, 1953, 1955, 1956, 1965, 1967. She toured the United States in 1953 as a member of the British Women's Team. Her national titles include Women's Teams 1952, 1956, 1964.

WILLIAMS, Robert Edward (1917–1974) of Sydney, Australia, represented Australia World Team Olympiad 1960. His national successes include Open Team 1947, 1948, 1949, 1950, 1952, 1959. He was handsetter and organizer for Par Point Global Championships 1961, 1963, joint formulator of the Laws of Par Point Contract Bridge 1963, and vice president of the Australian Bridge Council.

WILLIAMS, Robert T. (Bob) (b. 1926) of Alamogordo NM, electronic technician, won Mexican Nat'l Open Pairs 1969, 1970, District 17 GNP 1981. He served as president of Unit 388.

WILLIAMS, Dr. Sam of Spring Valley CA, won Pacific Southwest Open Pairs 1971, Men's Pairs 1969, District 17 Master Pairs 1973, Palm Springs Swiss Teams 1973.

WILLIAMS, William W. Jr. (Billy) (b. 1920) of Raleigh NC, insurance agency owner and manager, won Fall NAC secondary Senior Master Individual 1955, Mid-Atlantic Open Teams 1961, 1962, 1971, 1972, Woodson Open Pairs 1980.

WILLIAMSON, Vivian (b. 1912) of Roswell NM, bridge teacher, won Spring NAC Women's Pairs 1973. She is a Board member of Unit 382.

WILLIS, Col. J. Tim (b. 1913) of Houston, retired bridge club owner, former school teacher, won Japanese Open Teams 1952, Spring NAC secondary Open Pairs-A 1978, Texas Fall Open Teams 1962, Open Pairs Flt. A 1979. A graduate of West Point, Willis is a retired Army officer.

WILMOT, Quentin S. (b. 1947) of Reno NV, computer operator, casino employee, won District 11 Open Pairs 1977, Great Lakes Open Pairs 1977, Rocky Mountain Men's Pairs 1980, Mid-Winter Holiday Swiss Teams 1981. Wilmot is a former city chess champion.

WILSON, B. J. (b. 1922) of San Antonio, rancher, won Spring NAC secondary Women's Pairs 1978, Texas Summer Open Teams 1968, Mid-South Fall Open Teams 1968.

WILSON, Bert S. (b. 1915) of Ventnor NJ, freelance writer, bridge columnist and lecturer, won Mid-Atlantic Mixed Pairs 1963. He has been a Board member of Philadelphia CBA since 1963. Wilson is the co-author of *Hold Our Bridge Hands*.

WILSON, Chris H. (Mrs. Courtland Adams) (b. 1920) of Phoenix, has been a member of the ACBL Board of Directors since 1977 and president of the WESTERN CONFERENCE since 1981. She was president of the Phoenix Unit for four years. One of the founders of District 17, she is a member of its Board and has served on its executive committee. She is a former member of the ACBL Board of Governors and the Western Conference Board. Wilson is a member of the ACBL Goodwill Committee and ACBL Charity Committee and was chairperson of the 1971 Fall North American Championships.

WILSON, Louise C. (b. 1914) of Greenville MS, won Mexican Nat'l Women's Pairs 1960, Mississippi Valley Open Teams 1960, Women's Pairs 1957, Southern Conference Women's Pairs 1957, Golden Gate Individual 1968.

WILSON, Mike A. (b. 1950) of Vancouver BC, stockbroker, won Puget Sound KO Teams 1976, Master Pairs 1979, Mid-Winter Holiday Swiss Teams 1975, British Columbia Mixed Pairs 1977. See HANDICAPPED PLAYERS.

WILSON, Robert W. (1909-1965) of New Kensington PA, aluminum company employee, organized and was active in the Pittsburgh Industrial League for 19 years. An authority on double-dummy problems, he was a frequent contributor to many bridge magazines including the ACBL *Bulletin* and was a contributing editor, *Bridge Encyclopedia*.

WILSON, Walter T. (b. 1910) of Auburndale FL, bridge teacher and writer, has been an ACBL associate national tournament director since the mid-Fifties.

WILTON, Herbert C. of Cincinnati, real estate salesman, placed second in Summer NAC Master Mixed Teams 1958 and won Great Lakes Open Teams 1962, Midwest Open Pairs 1968. He is a former president and secretary of Cincinnati BA.

WINGES, Bert (b. 1942) of Ottawa ON, administration officer, won Can-Am Open Pairs 1969, Men's Pairs 1970, Can-At Swiss Teams 1975, 1977, BAM Teams 1977, Fleur-de-lys Swiss Teams 1973, KO Teams 1974, Bluenose BAM Teams 1981, District 4 Summer Swiss Teams 1981, District 1 GNT 1973.

WINKLER, Peter of Atlanta, assistant professor of Mathematics at Emory University, is the discover of ENCRYPTED SIGNALS. He graduated from Harvard University, *summa cum laude*, holds a Ph.D in mathematics from Yale, and is a former Navy cryptologic officer.

WINSLOW, Thomas Newby (1861-1942), bridge author and system-maker, was born in North Carolina and later resided in East Orange NJ. His system, introduced in a series of booklets beginning in 1930 and in the book *Win with Winslow* (1933), anticipated the FOUR ACES SYSTEM in its 1½-1-½ point-count and CANAPÉ in showing the lowest four-card suit first, regardless of the strength of that suit. See BIBLIOGRAPHY, C.

WISDOM, William E. (Ned) (b. 1949) of Spencer NC, federal employee, won Fall NAC secondary Men's Pairs 1977, Mid-Atlantic Open Pairs Flt. A 1978, 1981, Swiss Teams 1981, Labor Day Open Pairs Flt. A 1981, District 7 GNT 1977, 1978, GNP 1981. He is past president of Unit 169.

WISEMILLER, James P. (b. 1943) of Powell OH, systems consultant, won Spring NAC Open Pairs 1965, Midwest Fall Open Teams 1963, Men's Swiss Teams 1980, All-American Men's Pairs 1970.

WISER, John (b. 1926) of Beaconsfield PQ, ACBL national tournament director since 1970, won Can-Am Men's Pairs 1954. From 1961-1963 he was director of a bridge TV show. Wiser, who began his bridge career in 1950, has been an accredited WBF tournament director since 1972.

WISNIEWSKI, Jerzy (b. 1928) of Warsaw, Poland, jeweler, represented Poland in the World Team Olympiad 1964. He won Polish Open Pairs 1959 and placed second in 1958, 1966.

WITTES, Jon (b. 1942) of Los Alamitos CA, school psychologist, placed second in Summer NAC Men's Swiss Teams 1982 and won numerous regionals including Fall NAC secondary Swiss Teams 1968, Golder Master Pairs 1969, Bridge Week KO Teams 1973, Men's Pairs 1971, Mixed Pairs 1980, Swiss Teams 1981, All-Western KO Teams 1972, Los Angeles Winter KO Teams 1974, Master Pairs 1979, Open Pairs Flt. A 1981, Pacific Southwest KO Teams 1973, Master Pairs 1976, 1978, Swiss Teams Flt. A 1980.

WITTES, Pamela S. (Pam) (Mrs. Jon) (b. 1944) of Los Alamitos, clothing store owner, won Spring

NAC secondary Women's Pairs 1977, Bridge Week Women's Pairs 1970, 1973, 1976, Mixed Pairs 1980, District 17 Fall Swiss Teams 1976, Mid-Winter Holiday KO Teams 1978, Pacific Southwest Swiss Teams Flt. A 1980.

WOHLIN, Jan (b. 1924) of Stockholm, Sweden, bridge teacher, one of the great players of Europe, represented Sweden-Iceland in the Bermuda Bowl 1950, Sweden in 1953. He was European champion 1952 and placed second in 1948, 1949, 1950. Wohlin won many Scandinavian championships and 15 national titles. He is the co-inventor of EFOS SYSTEM and co-author of *Winning Pairs Technique* and *Play Safe — and Win.*

WOLD, Edward M. Jr. (Eddie) (b. 1951) of Houston, bridge professional, one of the leading American players, represented the United States in the Rosenblum Cup Teams 1978, 1982. He won the McKENNEY TROPHY 1982, International Team Trials 1982, Grand National Teams 1977, 1981, Spingold 1977, Vanderbilt 1979, 1982 and placed second in the Reisinger 1980. He has won more than 150 regionals since 1976 including Spring NAC secondary Swiss Teams 1976, Men's Pairs 1980, Master Pairs 1981, Summer Swiss Teams 1979. Wold is a graduate of Rice University.

WOLF, Jack (b. 1934) of Stafford TX, sales manager, won Missouri Valley Open Teams 1961, 1962, Open Pairs 1962, Mixed Pairs 1971, Texas Fall Unmixed Pairs 1974, 1979, KO Teams 1979.

WOLF, Mary of Philadelphia, semi-retired clinical psychologist and family therapist, won two different categories of the MINI McKENNEY in successive years — Non-Master in 1980 and Senior Master in 1981. She won Mid-Atlantic Swiss Teams 1981, Women's Swiss Teams 1981, 1982, Big Apple Mixed Pairs 1982.

WOLFE, Edward C. (1883–1972) of Cleveland OH was a bridge expert writer, whose success at whist and auction bridge helped make him one of the earliest of the recognized authorities on contract bridge. A member of the Advisory Council of Bridge Headquarters, he helped draft the OFFICIAL SYSTEM. After Culbertson's defeat of Lenz, he joined the Culbertson staff, organizing teachers' conventions and lecturing. A former Contributing editor of *The Bridge World* and *British Bridge Magazine,* Wolfe authored *The Play of the Cards at Contract Bridge.* See BIBLIOGRAPHY, D.

WOLFF, Elizabeth (Betsey) (b. 1937) of Dallas, administrative assistant, won the World Mixed Teams 1972 and placed second in Spring NAC Women's Pairs 1971, 1982, Women's Teams 1973. Her regional wins include Texas Fall Master Pairs 1968, KO Teams 1971, Missouri Valley KO Teams 1974.

WOLFF, Robert S. (Bobby) (b. 1932) of Dallas, business consultant, WFB Grand Master #8, one of the world's great players. He won Bermuda Bowl 1970, 1971, 1977, World Open Pairs 1974, World

Mixed Teams 1972. He placed second in the World Team Olympiad 1972, 1980, Bermuda Bowl 1973, 1974, 1975, and also represented the United States in the World Open Pairs 1978, 1982, Rosenblum Cup Teams 1978, 1982. He won the Pan American Invitational 1974, 1976, 1977, Spingold 1969, 1979, 1982, Vanderbilt 1971, 1973, Reisinger 1970, 1978, 1979, Grand National Teams 1975, 1977, Spring NAC Men's Teams 1972, 1973, MOTT-SMITH TROPHY 1973, FISHBEIN TROPHY 1979. He placed second in the Spingold 1967, 1970, Reisinger 1964, Vanderbilt 1981, Spring NAC Men's Teams 1969, 1980, Life Master Pairs 1960, 1968. Wolff won numerous regionals including Fall NAC secondary Swiss Teams 2nd Flt. 1973, Men's Swiss Teams 1977, Open Pairs 1981, Summer Open Pairs Flt. C 1981. In 1981 Wolff was elected to the ACBL Board of Directors. He is a graduate of Trinity University.

Wolff wrote, programmed and developed *Bridge Bidding* programs for use on home computers, and developed the WOLFF CONVENTION. Since 1982 the "Aces" syndicated bridge column appears under his byline. He contributed to *Play Bridge With the Aces* and *Winning Bridge.* Wolff has been on three TV bridge programs: *What's Your Bid?*, 1957–1958; *Play Bridge With the Experts*, 1974; and *The Aces vs Goren*, 1971. See ACES TEAM.

WOLKIN, Philip (b. 1948) of Shaker Heights OH, house renovator, won Canadian Nat'l Men's Pairs 1977, District 5 KO Teams 1978, All-American Men's Swiss Teams 1979, Great Lakes Swiss Teams 1980, Labor Day Swiss Teams Flt. A 1980.

WONG, John (b. 1928) of Hacienda Heights CA, formerly of Japan and Taiwan, computer specialist, was the first Life Master in Japan. He represented Taiwan in the World Team Olympiad 1964 and represented Japan in Far East Championships from 1958, winning the Far East Open Pairs 1961 and placing second in the Open Teams 1958, 1964. He won Takamatsu Open Teams 1955, 1956, 1962, *Japan Times* Cup 1959, 1960, 1961, 1963, Mixed Pairs 1960, Master Individual 1961, Trial Pairs 1962, ACBL Pacific Southwest Open Pairs 1966, Bridge Week Open Pairs 1976, Los Angeles Winter Men's Swiss Teams 1976. He is a former director and secretary of JAPAN CONTRACT BRIDGE LEAGUE and former editor of its publication.

WONG, Kok Leong (b. 1925) of Malaysia, oil executive, represented Malyasia in the Far East Championships 1965, 1966, 1968, 1970, 1973, 1974.

WONG, Larry (b. 1929) of Portland, Jamaica, company director, won Central American and Caribbean Championships 1971, 1972, 1974. He served as a Jamaica BA executive committee member.

WOOD, Jim (b. 1938) of Takoma Park MD, bridge writer and editor, won Fall NAC secondary Men's Swiss Teams 1980, Mid-Atlantic Open Pairs 1975, Open Pairs Flt. A 1981. Wood served three terms as Washington BL president and is the editor of the WBL publication and daily bulletins for all WBL tournaments.

WOOD, Nadine K. (b. 1935) of Silver Spring MD, bridge club director, placed second in Summer NAC Women's Swiss Teams 1982 and won Mid-Atlantic Summer Women's Swiss Teams 1980, Fall Swiss Teams Flt. A 1980, Bermuda Women's Pairs, Swiss Teams 1981.

WOOD, Philip A. (b. 1921) of Richmond BC, ACBL national tournament director, won Inter-Mountain Mixed Pairs 1966. A former baseball writer and statistician, Wood began his directing career in 1954. In 1968 he became the first Canadian to achieve the rating of national tournament director. He has served as tournament manager for District 18 since 1971. Wood also manages country club bridge activity in greater Vancouver, averaging more than 400 tables per month. A former member of the RCAF, he was awarded the Distinguished Flying Cross in 1944.

WOODARD, William F. (b. 1947) of Matthews NC, computer systems consultant, won Upper New York State Swiss Teams 1974, Open Pairs 1970, New England Fall Open Pairs 1974, Mid-Atlantic KO Teams 1973, Keystone Men's Pairs 1973, Canadian Nat'l Open Pairs 1974, Fleur-de-lys Master Pairs 1975, Capital District Fall Men's Swiss Teams 1977. He is a past president of Unit 115.

WOODRUFF, Fred M. of Metairie LA won Mid-South Swiss Teams, Open Pairs 1972, Men's Pairs 1973, Azalea City KO Teams 1980.

WOODS, Jo (1899–1977) of Little Rock AR, bridge teacher and writer, was the first president of the AMERICAN BRIDGE TEACHERS'ASSOCIATION. She wrote many books and booklets for bridge teachers and students including *At the Bridge Table* and *Little Green Book*.

WOODSON, William B. (b. 1921) of Charlotte NC, computer consultant, won Fall NAC secondary Swiss Teams Flt. A 1977, Southeastern Individual 1950, Mid-Atlantic Fall Open Pairs 1954, Open Teams 1965, Master Pairs 1961. Woodson served as a member of the ACBL Board of Directors 1973–1979, president of the Mid-Atlantic BA for two terms and as president and treasurer of Unit 153. He was a special consultant to the ACBL in 1967, was awarded a Certificate of Service by the Board in 1968 and was elected to the South Carolina Bridge Hall of Fame. He is the inventor of WOODSON TWO-WAY NOTRUMP and the author of *Woodson Two-Way Notrump* and *Woodson Electronic Bidding System*. See BIBLIOGRAPHY, C.

WOODWORTH, Robert M. (Woody) (b. 1911) of St. Petersburg FL, bridge lecturer, teacher and writer, won Florida Mixed Pairs 1960, 1963, 1972, KO Teams 1967, Life Master Pairs 1974, Mexican Nat'l KO Teams 1978, Sun City Swiss Teams 1980, 1981, Open Pairs Flt. A 1982. He is past president of the Florida Unit. Woodworth was awarded a prize for bridge articles by the IBPA of which he is a member. He is bridge columnist for *St. Petersburg Times* and a contributor to bridge publications.

WOOLES, Krishna G. (b. 1950) of Christchurch, New Zealand, solicitor, represented New Zealand in the Far East Championships 1979. He won New Zealand Open Teams 1981, KO Teams 1979, 1981, Interprovincial Teams 1975, 1978, 1981.

WOOLSEY, Christopher R. (Kit) (b. 1943) of Arlington VA, systems analyst, one of the leading American players, placed second in the Rosenblum Cup Teams 1982 and also represented the United States in the World Open Pairs 1974, 1978, 1982. He won the Blue Ribbon Pairs 1973, 1975, Spring NAC Men's Teams 1978 and placed second in the Spingold 1979, 1981, Grand National Teams 1977, Reisinger 1980, Fall NAC Life Master Men's Pairs 1971, 1972, Spring NAC Men's Pairs 1973, 1974, Open Pairs 1981. His numerous regional wins include Fall NAC secondary Swiss Teams-A 1979, Spring Swiss Teams 1978, Open Pairs 1981, Eastern States KO Teams (Reisinger) 1981. He also won the Cavendish Invitational Pairs 1979. Woolsey is the author of *Modern Defensive Signals, Partnership Defense in Bridge, Matchpoints* and co-author of *Clobber Their Artificial Club*. See BIBLIOGRAPHY, C and IBPA AWARDS.

WOOLWORTH, W. Howard (1889–deceased) of Hialeah FL, formerly of Niagara Falls, wrote a bridge column for the Buffalo Courier-Express for 22 years. His bridge section occupied more space than any other U.S. bridge column, often a full newspaper page. He served as contributor and editor of *Florida Bridge News*.

WORK, Milton C. (September 15, 1864–June 27, 1934) was the outstanding American authority on auction bridge, and a noted player and authority in whist and in contract bridge. He was born in Philadelphia and took three degrees at the University of Pennsylvania.

From 1887 to 1917 Work practiced law in Philadelphia. In 1917 he took a leave of absence to tour the U.S. with WILBUR C. WHITEHEAD, organizing bridge competitions and lecturing on bridge, to promote the sale of Liberty bonds. The success of the tour, coupled with the fact that his bridge books were already selling in large quantities, induced him to quit the practice of law and adopt bridge as a career.

Work's whist career began as president of the U. of P.'s whist club where he organized and played in the first duplicate whist team-of-four match ever held between clubs (1881). He helped found the American Whist League (1893), and was captain of the Hamilton Club team of Philadelphia, which won several whist tournaments. Work's first book, *Whist of Today* (1895) was published at his own expense for a gift to friends, but it demonstrated the clarity of style for which his later books were so admired. He turned to bridge and then to auction bridge as those games became preeminent. His first book on auction bridge (1913) began a series that outsold all other bridge books by a wide margin until the appearance of ELY CULBERTSON'S *Blue Book* in 1930. From 1917 through 1931 Work was acknowledged the greatest BRIDGE AUTHORITY, with stature equivalent to that of Cavendish in whist before him and Culbertson and CHARLES H. GOREN in contract bridge after him. In 1965, he was elected to the Bridge Hall of Fame.

Work became a member of the laws committee of the Whist Club (New York) in 1909. He largely wrote and controlled the 1915 auction bridge laws, which revolutionized the scoring, and the 1917 laws, for which the contract bridge principle was first considered and rejected. He was 1927 Honorary Member of the American Bridge League and Honorary Chairman of its Laws Committee. He was president of the UNITED STATES BRIDGE ASSOCIATION (1933–1934).

Work became a founder and chief editor of the earliest auction bridge magazines, the *Work–Whitehead Auction Bridge Bulletin* (1924–26) and its successor, the *Auction Bridge Magazine* (1927–29). Assisted by Whitehead, he served as chief authority on the first series of bridge games broadcast on radio (1926–29). In 1928 his fame was so great that he was paid $7,000 per week to give brief lectures on bridge in the course of vaudeville presentations.

Work's considerable fortune was substantially lost in the stockmarket crashes of 1929–1930, and he resumed some bridge activities from which he had retired. In 1931 he participated in the founding of BRIDGE HEADQUARTERS and the promulgation of the OFFICIAL SYSTEM, being chief architect of the system and principal author of its official books. As a player he was not highly rated by his peers, but in 1933–34 he resumed tournament play in contract bridge and won five consecutive sectional tournaments as a member of a team that included Goren, OLIVE PETERSON, and Fred French. See BIBLIOGRAPHY, A, C, E, H.

WORTHINGTON, Richard P. (b. 1948) of South Bend IN, company executive, won Great Lakes KO Teams 1978, Wolverine Master Swiss Teams 1979, Open Pairs Flt. A 1980.

WRIGHT, Lionel R. (b. 1953 in England) of Auckland, New Zealand, bank manager, represented New Zealand in the World Team Olympiad 1980, Far East Championships 1976, 1977, 1978. He won New Zealand Open Pairs 1978 and placed second in Open Teams 1978, 1979, 1980, KO 1978, Dunhill 1979, 1980.

WYATT, E. Jade (b. 1945) of Charleston WV, state employee, won Midwest Fall Women's Pairs 1980, District 11 Spring Open Pairs 1974, District 5 Mixed Pairs 1972, Fall Master Pairs 1981.

X

XIAOPING, DENG is Vice Chairman of the People's Republic of China. He was honored by the INTERNATIONAL BRIDGE PRESS ASSOCIATION as the 1980 Bridge Personality of the Year. According to the citation, he "set an example to the Chinese people, who are finding that bridge playing can lead to international friendship through membership in the World Bridge Federation." The game of bridge was not recognized by the People's Republic of China for many years. Xiaoping revived the game in China and has made it into a respectable sport. He has fostered bridge competition on an international level, and the People's Republic of China now is a member of the World Bridge Federation.

Y

YALIRAKIS, Dimitri (Jimmy) (b. 1931) of Athens, Greece, civil engineer, the officially ranked #2 Greek player, represented Greece in the World Team Olympiad 1976, 1980, World Open Pairs 1966, European Championships 1967, 1969, 1970, 1971. His national titles include Open Teams 1966, 1968, 1969, 1970, 1971, 1972, 1973, 1974, 1975, 1976, 1978, 1980, 1981, Open Pairs 1965, 1966, 1967, 1968, 1969, 1970, 1971, 1979, 1980, 1981, Master Pairs 1978, 1979, Interclubs 1972, 1973, 1974, 1976, 1981, Kyriakos Trophy (Greek McKenney) 1979, 1980, 1981. A former contributor to bridge magazines, he authored *Natural Bidding in Bridge* (in Greek) 1967.

YANG, Chodchoy S. (Esther) (b. 1944) of Bangkok, Thailand, company executive and exporter, placed second in the Far East Women's Teams 1979. She also represented Thailand in the Far East Women's Championships 1975, 1976, 1977, 1978, 1981, World Women's Teams 1980. Her national titles include Women's Teams 1975, 1976, 1977, 1978, 1979, 1980, 1981, 1982, Women's Pairs 1975, 1977, 1978, 1980, 1981, Mixed Teams 1980, 1981, 1982. She is vice president of CONTRACT BRIDGE LEAGUE OF THAILAND.

YANG, K. T. (b. 1933) of Manila, Philippines, was Far East Open Pairs champion 1974. He also represented the Philippines in the Far East Championships 1967, 1975, 1976, 1977, 1978, 1979. His national titles include Open Pairs 1964, 1971, 1975, 1976, Open Teams 1971, 1978, 1981, Master Pairs 1963, 1969, 1971, KO Teams 1970, 1971, 1972, 1975, 1977, 1978, Tuason Cup 1975, 1977, 1978, Intercommercial Teams 1976, 1979, 1980, 1981.

YANKO, Richard F. (b. 1939) of Southfield MI, attorney, placed second in the Grand National Teams 1974 and won Central States II Swiss Teams 1974, Motor City KO Teams 1973, Open Pairs 1969, Men's Pairs 1970, 1979, Men's Swiss Teams 1977, Master Pairs 1975, Swiss Teams 1979.

YAP, Florence (Mrs. Robert, formerly Leung) of Manila, Philippines, interpreter, was Far East Open Teams champion 1957 (second in 1962), Far East Women's Teams champion 1979. She also represented the Philippines in the Far East Open Teams

1966, 1968, 1977, 1978, Far East Women's Teams 1976, 1981, World Women's Teams 1968, Venice Trophy Teams 1978.

YAP, Robert (b. 1919) of Manila, Philippines, manufacturer, was Far East champion 1957 and placed second 1962. He also represented the Philippines in the World Team Olympiad 1964, 1968, 1972. His national titles include Open Teams 1960, 1978, 1979, 1980, KO Teams 1957, 1958, 1960, 1961, 1963, 1978, 1979, 1980, Mixed Teams 1957, 1958, Master Pairs 1957, Open Pairs 1955, Mixed Pairs 1956, 1957, 1958, 1959.

YARINGTON, Richard B. (Dick) (b. 1952) of Seattle, realtor, won Oregon Trail Mixed Pairs 1975, KO Teams 1981, Peach City Men's Pairs 1978, Klondike Open Pairs Flt. A 1978, Tri-Cities Open Pairs 1979.

YAVITZ, Jerome A. of Miami Beach, real estate developer, won Summer NAC Mixed Teams 1974 and placed second 1964.

YELLIS, Robert (b. 1952) of Great Neck NY, bridge club owner, won Keystone Men's Pairs 1974, Woodson KO Teams 1980, New England Individual KO Teams 1981, District 24 GNP 1979, GNT 1980.

YELTON, Carey M., Jr. (b. 1934) of Glencoe IL, financial consultant and restaurateur, Intercollegiate champion 1953, 1954, won Central States I Swiss Teams 1972, KO Teams 1977, Southern Conference Open Teams 1961, Mississippi Valley Swiss Teams 1972.

YODER, Frank E. III (b. 1944) of Fort Wayne IN, realtor, won Champagne Master Pairs 1980, All-American Men's Pairs 1981, Midwest Spring Men's Swiss Teams 1981.

YOMTOV, Bernard D. (Bernie) (b. 1946) of Nashville, company executive, placed second in the Grand National Teams 1975 and won Fall NAC secondary Non-Life Master Men's Pairs 1969, Music City KO Teams 1977, Mid-Atlantic Open Pairs Flt. A 1979, Space City Swiss Teams Flt. A 1980. Yomtov edited *Partnership Defense* and assisted in the editing of the 1980 *World Championship Book*.

YOST, E. Lowell (b. 1922) of Wichita KS, retired company president, placed second in Fall NAC Life Master Men's Pairs 1970 and won Republic of Texas Open Teams 1970.

YOUNG, Sally (Mrs. R. C.) (1906–1970) of Narberth PA was one of the great woman players of all time. She was Life Master #17, the first woman player ever to earn Life Master status. Between 1937 and 1958, she set a record by winning the Spring NAC Women's Teams seven times and finishing second three times. Among her other successes were four wins for the Chicago Trophy (since 1965 the Reisinger); four wins in the Women's Pairs; five wins in the Mixed Teams, and one each in the Fall Open and Mixed Pairs. During the late Thirties she was among the favorite partners of CHARLES GOREN.

YUDIN, Mark E. (b. 1947) of Montreal, tournament director, won Can-Am Open Pairs 1975, Men's Pairs 1977, Nat'l Capital Swiss Teams 1975.

YU KHE SIONG, Margaret (b. 1908) of Manila, Philippines, was Far East Women's champion 1967.

YUE, Dr. Wen Y. (b. 1918) of Excelsior MN, born in Fujian, China, anesthesiologist, won Summer NAC Senior/Advanced Senior Master Pairs 1972.

Z

ZABEL, Gunar of Copenhagen, Denmark, civil engineer, while president of the DANISH BRIDGE LEAGUE (1969–1975) increased its membership by 50%. He initiated master points, adult education in bridge and other innovations. Zabel served as a member of the Executive Committee of the EUROPEAN BRIDGE LEAGUE from 1973.

ZAKIN, Sandy (b. 1940) of Chicago, media advertising specialist, won Spring NAC secondary Master Pairs 1980, Summer Swiss Teams 1979, Hawaii Mixed Pairs 1971, Open Pairs Flt. A 1979, Gopher Open Teams 1973, Central States Women's Pairs 1974, Open Pairs 1976.

ZAMZAMI, Amran (b. 1930) of Jakarta, Indonesia, company executive, was npc of the Indonesian Team in the World Team Olympiad 1980, Bermuda Bowl 1981, Far East Championships 1970, 1979, 1981. He won Singapore Open Teams 1977, 1978, Malaysia Open Teams 1977, Indonesia Open Teams 1970.

ZANALDA, David E. (b. 1932) of Buenos Aires, Argentina, court official, was South American champion 1981 and placed second in 1965, 1970. He also represented Argentina in the World Team Olympiad 1968, 1972, 1976, Bermuda Bowl 1981. His national wins include Open Teams 1966, 1970, 1977, 1978, 1979, 1981, Open Pairs 1968, 1976, Master Pairs 1973, Master Individual 1967, 1968, GABARRET CUP 1970. He is bridge correspondent for the newspaper *La Nación*.

ZANALDA, Jorge of Buenos Aires, Argentina won Argentine Open Teams 1978, 1979, Mixed Teams 1970, Master Individual 1975.

ZANANIRI, Marcel (b. 1915) of Kuwait, formerly of Cairo, Egypt, chemist, represented Egypt in the World Team Olympiad 1964, Deauville Olympiad 1968. As Egypt's top ranked player in the 1960s and early 1970s, he won all major events on many occasions. He is a contributor to many international bridge periodicals.

ZÁNKAY, Péter (b. 1919) of Budapest, Hungary, retired catering manager, bridge theoretician and organizer, is the editor-in-chief of *Bridzsélet*, author of *Bridge* (in Hungarian), and bridge columnist for *Free Time Magazine*. Zankay is regional IBPA organizer for East Europe and chairman of the Rules and Ethics Committee and of Tournament Directors Examination Committee, BUDAPEST BRIDGE ASSOCIATION. He has won many local competitions.

ZANOTTI-CAVAZZONI, Ulrico (b. 1905) of Asunción, Paraguay, company president, represented Paraguay in the South American Championships 1953, 1954, 1956, 1962, 1964. He founded PARAGUAY BRIDGE ASSOCIATION and is presently its captain general.

ZAWISZA, Jerzy (b. 1908) of Wilmington DE, retired bridge club manager, placed second in Fall NAC Men's Teams 1960.

ZECKHAUSER, Richard J. (b. 1940) of Cambridge MA, professor of political economy, won the Blue Ribbon Pairs 1966 and placed second in Spring NAC Men's Teams 1968. He was Intercollegiate champion 1961 and won the MARCUS CUP 1963, New England KO Teams 1964, 1975, New York–New Jersey Men's Pairs 1962, Upper New York State Open Teams 1966.

ZELLER, John Nigel (Nigel) (b. 1951) of Wembley, Australia, formerly of Mississauga ON, computer programmer, won District 4 Spring KO Teams, Swiss Teams 1979, District 5 Swiss Teams 1979 and placed second in the Canadian Team Trials 1980.

ZEVE, Vic D. (b. 1899) of Wilton Manors FL, retired mortgage broker, won Summer NAC Open Pairs 1952, Fall NAC Men's Teams 1958. He served as president of District 9 1975–1975. Zeve is the author of *Method Bidding*.

ZIA, Mahmood. See MAHMOOD, ZIA.

ZILIC, John P. (b. 1939) of Houston, insurance underwriter, won Fall NAC Open Pairs 1966 and placed second in Swiss Teams 1978. His more than 20 regional wins include Fall NAC secondary Open Pairs 1975, All-American Open Teams 1961, Texas Fall Swiss Teams 1974, Texas Mid-Winter KO Teams 1973, Master Pairs 1977, Corpus Christi Swiss Teams, Men's Pairs 1978.

ZILIC, Virginia A. (Mrs. John P.) (b. 1939) of Houston placed second in Fall NAC Swiss Teams 1978 and won Missouri Valley Mixed Pairs 1971, Texas Fall Women's Pairs 1971, Swiss Teams 1974, Texas Mid-Winter KO Teams 1973, Corpus Christi Swiss Teams 1978.

ZIMMERMAN, James E. (Jim) (b. 1942) of Shaker Heights OH, attorney and account executive, represented the United States in the World Open Pairs 1978, 1982. He won Fall NAC Mixed Pairs 1981 and placed second in Summer NAC Master Mixed Teams 1975. His more than 60 regional titles include District 5 Labor Day KO Teams, Open Pairs Flt. A, Swiss Teams Flt. A 1981, Cambrian Shield

Open Pairs Flt. A, Swiss Teams Flt. A, KO Teams, Master Pairs 1980. District 5 representative to the ACBL Board of Directors since 1973, Zimmerman was ACBL president in 1981 and chairman of the Board in 1982. As president he led a group of 30 ACBL members to the first major bridge tournament on Chinese soil in Shanghai, China. He is a graduate of Denison University and Case Western Reserve Law School.

ZOLLER, Nancy. See ALPAUGH, NANCY.

ZOLLER, Raymond G. (Ray) (b. 1934) of Calabasas CA, sales manager, won Fall NAC Life Master Men's Pairs 1966. His numerous regional wins include District 5 Open Teams 1971, Master Pairs 1964, Mixed Pairs 1971, Great Lakes Open Teams 1968, 1972, Mid-South Swiss Teams 1975, Golden State Swiss Teams 1977. He has been a panelist for *The Bridge World* feature Master Solvers' Club and You Be the Judge since 1964.

ZOTOS, Loucas (b. 1951) of Athens, Greece, officially ranked #3 player, represented Greece in the European Championships 1977, Junior European Championships 1974, Balkan Championship 1978. He won Team Trials 1979, 1982, Open Teams 1978, 1979, 1981, Open Pairs 1975, 1978, Swiss Teams 1981, Master Pairs 1978, Junior Pairs 1974, Mixed Teams 1977, 1978, 1979, Interclubs 1974, 1977, 1980, Philip Morris Cup 1975, Kyriakos Trophy (Greek McKenney) 1978.

ZUCCHELLI, Sergio (b. 1934) of Bologna, Italy, pharmaceutical representative, represented Italy in the Bermuda Bowl 1975. He won the LONDON SUNDAY TIMES PAIRS (since 1981 INVITATIONAL PAIRS) 1974, Common Market Junior Teams 1967. His national titles include the Italian Cup 1967, 1970, 1974, Open Teams 1967, 1970, 1971. See also BERMUDA INCIDENT.

ZUMARÁN, Ricardo (b. 1930) of Montevideo, Uruguay, farmer, represented Uruguay in all South American Championships since 1959, and tied for first place in 1962. His national titles include Team Trials 1957, 1959, 1960, 1961, 1962, Open Teams 1958, 1960, 1961, 1963, Open Pairs 1957, 1958, Individual 1956.

ZWAAN, Reinder René (René) (b. 1946) of Amsterdam, The Netherlands, bridge teacher and journalist, represented The Netherlands in the World Team Olympiad 1980, European Championships 1980, Common Market Championships 1981. His titles include National Teams 1980, Open Teams 1977, 1979, Open Pairs 1970, Caransa Open Teams 1979, Rome Open Teams 1980. Zwaan contributes to *Bridge* and other bridge publications.

ZWERLING, Marc (b. 1949) of Portland OR, attorney, won more than 25 regional titles including Spring NAC secondary Mixed Pairs 1979, Mid-Winter Holiday Men's Swiss Teams 1974, Open Pairs Flt. A 1975, Men's Pairs 1978, Oregon Trail KO Teams 1978, Swiss Teams 1981.

APPENDIX I
North American Championships

AMERICAN BRIDGE ASSOCIATION NATIONAL CHAMPIONSHIPS.

OPEN TEAMS

1934 — Egbert Clarke, J. C. Graham, Dr. Louis P. Rolerfort, D. Edward Smith

1935 — Dr. E. Brandon, Lawrence Grant, Bernard Gray, George Gilmer, Dr. B. Withers

1936 — Gilhooly F. Benoit, William A. Friend, Clyde L. Long, Allan L. Parkinson, Percy E. Thomas

1937 }
1938 } James P. Holt, Othello A. Moore
1939 — Lawrence Buser, Oliver Landry

1939 — Gilhooly F. Benoit, William A. Friend, Albert E. Hawkins, Joseph Niles

1940 — Larence Buser, James P. Holt, Oliver Landry, Othello A. Moore

1941 — Roscoe Alexander, Caesar E. Barron, Leon A. Jones, Kermit D. Ross

1942 — Caesar E. Barron, Dewey M. Carr, Kermit D. Ross, Allan L. Woolridge

1943 — Robert Banks, Dr. William Richie, Glenn Stewart, Alvin Wilkes

1944 — Zach H. Brooks, Kelly C. Brown, Louis Clay, Othello A. Moore, Lola Scales

1946 — Kenneth F. Cox, Richard Cunningham, Charles Hanson, Samuel White

1947 — Zach H. Brooks, Kelly C. Brown, Louis Clay, Othello A. Moore, Lola Scales

1948 — Dewey M. Carr, Victor R. Daly, Kermit D. Ross, Allan L. Woolridge, Mrs. Clyde Woolridge

1949 }
1950 } Dorothy Alexander, Roscoe Alexander, Leon A. Jones

1952 — Caesar E. Barron, Morris Garrett

1952 — Alfred A. Bishop, Kenneth F. Cox, James H. Smith, Samuel White

1953 — William Chapman, Lyda Goggins, George Hall, Allan L. Woolridge, Mrs. Clyde Woolridge

1954 — Howard M. Bowman, Martin Gertler, Kai Larson, Ruth Million

1955 }
1956 } Roscoe Alexander, Robert Friend
1957 } William A. Friend, Dr. Joseph Henry
       Leon A. Jones

1958 — Alfred A. Bishop, Kenneth F. Cox, James Garcia, Samuel White

1959 — Caesar E. Barron, Oliver Cassell, Frederick O. Petite, Allan L. Woolridge, Mrs. Clyde Woolridge

1960 — Caesar E. Barron, Oliver Cassell, Walter Mann, Frederick O. Petite

1961 — Jim Becheley, Robert D. Hamman, William Hanna, Stella Rebner

1962 — Robert Bratcher, Mary Cocherell, Dr. Guy Ginn, Robert Landry *(tied with)* Doris Brooks, Dr. Joseph Henry, Stanley Jarrett, Ronald Searcy

1963 — Jean Haley, Andrew Mells, Charles Pyant, Janice Wilkins

1964 — Roscoe Alexander, Dr. Joseph Henry, Leon A. Jones, Mrs. Clyde Woolridge

1965 }
1966 } Zenobia Allen, Andrew Mells, Samuel White
       Bertram Hudson, Daniel Scrivens

1967 — Dr. Arthur R. Flowers, Glenn Fowlkes, George Hall, J. Herbert Kerr, Charles Pyant, Arthur Wills

1968 — James Garcia, Dr. Guy A. Ginn, Luis Pietri, Roscoe Rigmaiden, Ronald Smith, Hollis Steed

1969 — Doris Brooks, Leonard Jefferson, Dr. William Lipton, J. Prisyon, Murray Schnee, Sol Seidman

1970 — Dr. Arthur R. Flowers, Douglas Fullwood, Andrew Mells, Luis Pietri, Roscoe Rigmaiden, William Sides

1971 — Robert Becker, Mark Blumenthal, Oscar Cohen, William Landow, Harlow Lewis, Alan Sontag

1972 — Dr. Arthur R. Flowers, Douglas Fullwood, Amalya Kearse, Andrew Mells, Luis Pietri, William Sides

1973 — Zenobia Allen, Richard Halperin, Harvey Miller, Robert Price, Roscoe Rigmaiden, Joyce Williams

1974 — Zenobia Allen, Claudius G. Fredd, Robert Landry, Beverly Lucas, Samuel Lucas

1975 — *Herbert Bryan, Orlando Croft, John S. Jordan III, Robert Seymour

1976 — *Douglas Fullwood, Beverly Lucas, Samuel Lucas, Louis Sutherland

1977 — Reginald Chapman, Leonard Jefferson, Chester Johnson, Arnold Jones (Spring)
       Marv Dauer, Ed Davis, Al Okuneff, David Sachs, George Siegel, Perry Van Hook (Summer)

———
*Knockout Team Summer

1978 — Alfred Bishop, Douglas Fullwood, Samuel & Beverly Lucas, Luis Pietri, Louis Sutherland (Spring)
       Richard Halperin, Harvey Miller, Paul Sugar, Don Rutstein, Claude Vogel, Carey Yelton (Summer)

1979 — Dr. Arthur R. Flowers, Chester Johnson Andrew Mells, Herbert Taylor, Arthur Wills (Spring)
       Lawrence Berkley, Lee Pennington, Jeffrey Stroud, John Washington, William E. Williams (Summer)

1980 — Kenneth Cox, Clinton Elmore, Charles Hanson, Leonard Jefferson, Robert Seymour (Spring)
       Robert Canty, Theodore Griffith, Sandra Stevenson, Norman Sweeting (Summer)

1981 — Paul Ivaska, Tony Kasday, William Sides, Eddie Thomas (Spring)
       Lionel Barton, Dwight Galley, Samuel Lucas, Beverly Lucas, Robert Price, Joyce Williams (Summer)

1982 — Lionel Barton, Dwight Galley, Samuel Lucas, Beverly Lucas, Robert Price, Joyce Williams (Spring)

OPEN PAIRS

1934 — Louis Collins, Mrs. Louis Collins
1935 — Dr. A. Maurice Curtis, Dr. W. Wethers
1936 — Lyda Goggins, Horace R. Miller
1937 — James P. Holt, Othello A. Moore
1938 — Gilhooly Benoit, William A. Friend
1939 — Leon A. Jones, James McDougald
1940 — Hazel Facey, Lucius Fields
1941 — Dr. A. Maurice Curtis, Allan L. Parkinson
1942 — William A. Friend, Lyda Goggins
1943 — Courtland Booker, Lewis White
1944 — Eloise Landry, Elvert Marsh
1946 — Roscoe Alexander, Leon A. Jones
1947 — Kelly C. Brown, Louis Clay
1948 — Elvert Marsh, Rexcell Watkins
1949 — William A. Friend, Dr. Fred Slaughter
1950 — Richard Cunningham, Zenobia Rucker
1951 — Alexander Herndon, Evelyn Herndon
1952 — William A. Friend, Dr. Fred Slaughter
1953 — Louis Clay, Zenobia Rucker
1954 — Willliam A. Friend, Hollis Steed
1955 — Robert Friend, William J. Friend
1956 — James Garcia, Elvert Marsh
1957 — Sandy Gholston, Marion Griffis
1958 — Alfred A. Bishop, Dr. Joseph Henry
1959 — Roscoe Alexander, Zenobia Hall
1960 — James Lee, Carlisle Pratt
1961 — Kenneth F. Cox, Samuel White
1962 — Walter Hampton, Frank Tucker
1963 — Luis Pietri, Roscoe Rigmaiden
1964 — Alfred A. Bishop, Dr. Joseph Henry
1965 — Bertram Hudson, Andrew Mells
1966 — Luis Pietri, Roscoe Rigmaiden
1967 — Robert Price, William Sides
1968 — Luis Pietri, Roscoe Rigmaiden
1969 — Lawrence Berkley, Arthur Wills (Spring)
       Dr. Milton Haley, Arthur Reid (Summer)
1970 — Robert Canty, Sylvester Lee (Spring) *(tied with)* Theodore Griffith, Ben Siegel
       William Sides, Douglas Fullwood (Summer)
1971 — F. Maxie Davis, James Dozier (Spring)
       Robert Price, Joyce Williams (Summer)
1972 — Amalya Kearse, Luis Pietri (Spring)
       Dr. Guy A. Ginn, Theodore Griffith (Summer)
1973 — Amalya Kearse, Luis Pietri (Spring)
       Dr. Felix Dunn, Sarah Dunn (Summer)
1974 — Dr. Arthur F. Flowers, Andrew Mells (Spring)
       Vivian Banks, Franklyn Taylor (Summer)
1975 — Reginald Chapman, Roscoe Rigmaiden (Spring)
       Dr. Arthur R. Flowers, Andrew Mells (Summer)
1976 — Douglas Fullwood, Louis Sutherland (Spring)
       Bobbye Caldwell, Robert Landry (Summer)
1977 — Lee Pennington, William E. Williams (Spring)
       Lee Pennington, William E. Williams (Summer)
1978 — James Garcia, Dr. Milton Haley (Spring)
       Taylor Cox, Vernette Wills (Summer)
1979 — Reginald Chapman, Roscoe Rigmaiden (Spring)
       Reginald Chapman, Roscoe Rigmaiden (Summer)
1980 — Douglas Fullwood, Louis Sutherland (Spring)
       Dwight Galley, Lionel Barton (Summer)
1981 — Paul Ivaska, William Sides (Spring)
       Douglas Fullwood, Louis Sutherland (Summer)
1982 — Mildred Anderson, John S. Jordan III (Spring)

ACBL CHAMPIONSHIPS

FALL NORTH AMERICAN CHAMPIONSHIPS

OPEN TEAMS. This event is contested for the REIS-INGER TROPHY (originally the CHICAGO TROPHY until 1965). It is a six-session Open Team-of-Four event scored by Board-a-Match. It was contested as a four-session championship until 1966.

WINNERS

1929 1. Max M. Cohen, Louis J. Haddad,
Robert W. Halpin, Nils M. Wester
2. Carlton R. Drake, James Kelly,
Paul D. Parcells, Charles Rilling

1930 1. William K. Barrett, W. James Carpenter,
Ely Culbertson, Johnny Rau
2. Mary Clement, Dorothy Rice Sims,
P. Hal Sims, Waldemar K. von Zedtwitz

1931 1. Elizabeth Banfield, Cmdr. Winfield S. Liggett, Jr.,
Frances Newman, George Unger
2. David Burnstine, Oswald Jacoby,
Willard S. Karn, P. Hal Sims

1932 1. B. Jay Becker, S. Garton Churchill,
George Reith, Waldemar K. von Zedtwitz
2. Ely Culbertson, Michael T. Gottlieb,
Oswald Jacoby, Theodore A. Lightner

1933 1. Charles A. Hall, Albert Steiner,
Philip Steiner, Richard M. Wildberg
2. B. Jay Becker, S. Garton Churchill,
P. Hal Sims, Waldemar K. von Zedtwitz

1934 1. Henry S. Dinkelspiel, Jr., Lewis Jaeger,
Bernard Rabinowitz, Maurice Seiler
2. Theodore A. Lightner, Merwyn D. Maier,
John P. Mattheys, Sherman Stearns

1935 1. F. Roland Buck, Joseph E. Cain,
Lawrence J. Welch, Edson T. Wood
2. Ely Culbertson, Josephine Culbertson,
Richard L. Frey, Albert H. Morehead

1936 1. Marge Anderson, Donald G. Farquharson,
Mrs. J. A. Faulkner, Percy E. Sheardown
2. Arthur Glatt, Laura Heiner,
John R. Smith, Albert Weiss

1937 1. John R. Crawford, Charles H. Goren,
Charles J. Solomon, Sally Young
2. Oscar J. Brotman, William Perry,
Alvin Roth, S. S. Vorzimer

1938 1. John R. Crawford, Charles H. Goren,
Charles J. Solomon, Sally Young
2. A. Mitchell Barnes, Mary Clement,
Benedict Jarmel, Waldemar K. von Zedtwitz

1939 1. B. Jay Becker, John R. Crawford,
Charles H. Goren, Charles J. Solomon,
Sally Young
2-4. Jack Cushing, Seymour Kaplan,
Al Leibowitz, Edward N. Marcus,
2-4. Oswald Jacoby, Merwyn D. Maier,
Robert A. McPherran, Waldemar K. von Zedtwitz
2-4. Henry Auslander, Joseph Davis,
Jacob D. Lindy, Catherine W. Samberg

1940 1. Harry Feinberg, Jeff Glick,
Maury J. Glick, Louis Newman
2. Alfred R. Dick, C. William Potts,
James Sheern, Edward R. Thomas

1941 1. Peter A. Leventritt, Simon Rossant,
Helen Sobel, Margaret Wagar
2. A. Mitchel Barnes, S. Garton Churchill,
Lee Hazen, Charles S. Lochridge,
Waldemar K. von Zedtwitz

1942 1. B. Jay Becker, John R. Crawford,
Charles H. Goren, Sidney Silodor
2. S. Garton Churchill, Harry J. Fishbein,
Lee Hazen, Waldemar K. von Zedtwitz

1943 1. B. Jay Becker, Charles H. Goren,
Sidney Silodor, Helen Sobel
2. Samuel Katz, Bertram Lebhar, Jr.,
Peter A. Leventritt, Simon Rossant

1944 1. Simon Becker, Peggy Golder,
Ruth Sherman, Charles J. Solomon
2. B. Jay Becker, Charles H. Goren,
Sidney Silodor, Helen Sobel

1945 1. Lee Hazen, George Rapee,
Samuel M. Stayman, Waldemar K. von Zedtwitz

2. Ambrose Casner, Harold J. Harkavy,
Ralph Hirschberg, Harold A. Ogust, Jack Shore

1946 1. A. Mitchel Barnes, John R. Crawford,
Alvin Roth, Edith Seligman
2. Simon Becker, Stanley O. Fenkel,
Fred D. Karpin, Louis Newman

1947 1. Paula Bacher, Jane Jaeger,
Kay Rhodes, Sally Young
2-3. John R. Crawford, Theodore A. Lightner,
George Rapee, Samuel M. Stayman
2-3. Robert Appleyard, Morris Berliant,
Malcolm A. Lightman, Simon Rossant

1948 1. George Boeckh, C. Bruce Elliott,
Agnes Gordon, Charlotte Sidway
2. John R. Crawford, George Rapee,
Sidney Silodor, Samuel M. Stayman

1949 1. Lee Hazen, Larry Hirsch, Richard Kahn,
Peter A. Leventritt, Jack Shore
2-3. Sidney Aronson, Emily Folline,
Benjamin O. Johnson, Ludwig J. Kabakjian,
Edward N. Marcus
2-3. Jeff Glick, Arthur S. Goldsmith,
Alvin Landy, Sol Mogal, Elmer I. Schwartz

1950 1. B. Jay Becker, Myron F. Field,
Charles H. Goren, Sidney Silodor,
Helen Sobel
2. John R. Crawford, George Rapee,
Edward N. Marcus, Howard Schenken,
Samuel M. Stayman

1951 1. Corti Boland, C. Bruce Elliot,
Micky M. Miller, Percy E. Sheardown
2. B. Jay Becker, Charles H. Goren, Myron F. Field,
Sidney Silodor, Helen Sobel

1952 1. Harold Harkavy, Edith Kemp,
Alvin Roth, Tobias Stone
Edward H. Cohen, Jeff Glick,
2. Arthur S. Goldsmith, Elmer I. Schwartz

1953 1. B. Jay Becker, John R. Crawford,
George Rapee, Samuel M. Stayman
2. Harry J. Fishbein, Peter A. Leventritt,
Ruth Sherman, Charles J. Solomon, Peggy Solomon

1954 1. B. Jay Becker, John R. Crawford,
George Rapee, Sidney Silodor
2. Israel Cohen, Paul Kibler,
Alvin Roth, William Seamon

1955 1. Ben Fain, George Heath, Paul Hodge,
James Jacoby, Oswald Jacoby
2. William V. Lipton, Victor Mitchell,
W. Miller Nelson, Joseph G. Ripstra

1956 1. B. Jay Becker, John R. Crawford,
George Rapee, Sidney Silodor
2. Ben Fain, Paul Hodge,
Oswald Jacoby, Dick Sutton

1957 1. Charles H. Goren, Harold A. Ogust,
William S. Root, Howard Schenken, Helen Sobel
2. Robert Y. Barrett, Ben Fain, Harry J. Fishbein,
John Gerber, Paul Hodge

1958 1. Leonard B. Harmon, Ralph Hirschberg,
Edgar Kaplan, Alfred Sheinwold, Ivar Stakgold
2. Arthur M. Miller, John H. Moran,
David Strasberg, Jay Wendt

1959 1. Lewis L. Mathe, Donald A. Oakie,
Meyer Schleifer, Edward O. Taylor
2. Harry J. Fishbein, John Gerber,
Paul Hodge, Charles J. Solomon

1960 1. Ollie Adams, William Hann,
Sidney H. Lazard, Lewis L. Mathe
2. Oswald Jacoby, Mervin Key,
G. Robert Nail, Curtis Smith

1961 1. John R. Crawford, Norman Kay,
Alvin Roth, Sidney Silodor, Tobias Stone
2-3. Charles Coon, Robert F. Jordan,
Eric R. Murray, Arthur G. Robinson
2-3. Harold B. Guiver, Carol Sanders,
Thomas K. Sanders, Michael Shuman

1962 1-2. Paul Allinger, Harold B. Guiver,
Lewis L. Mathe, Ron Von der Porten,
Erik Paulsen, Edward O. Taylor
1-2. Robert D. Hamman, Eddie Kantar,
Donald P. Krauss, Marshall Miles

1963 1. Charles H. Goren, Peter A. Leventritt,
Harold A. Ogust, Howard Schenken
2. Donald R. Faskow, William L. Flannery,
Herbert Sachs, Paul Swanson

1964 1. John Gerber, Paul Hodge,

     Mervin Key, Harold Rockaway
2. Harold Harkavy, Edith Kemp,
     Cliff Russell, Curtis K. Smith,
     Bobby Wolff, Waldemar K. von Zedtwitz

1965 1. Eddie Kantar, Michael S. Lawrence,
        Marshall Miles, Lew Stansby
     2. Michael Engel, Paul Feldesman,
        Richard Freeman, Ira S. Rubin

1966 1. Robert F. Jordan, Edgar Kaplan,
        Norman Kay, Arthur G. Robinson
     2-3. Gerald W. Bare, Harold B. Guiver,
         Lewis L. Mathe, Mike McMahan,
         Erik Paulsen, Hugh Ross
     2-3. William S. Root, Alvin Roth,
         Bee Schenken, Howard Schenken

1967 1. Robert F. Jordan, Edgar Kaplan, Norman Kay,
        Arthur G. Robinson, William S. Root, Alvin Roth
     2. Steve Altman, Michael M. Becker,
        Charles Peres, Daniel Rotman

1968 1. Kyle Larsen, Erik Paulsen,
        Peter A. Pender, Hugh Ross, Howard Schenken
     2. Billy Eisenberg, Bobby Goldman, Robert D. Hamman,
        Eddie Kantar, Sidney Lazard, George Rapee

1969 1. Philip Feldesman, William Grieve,
        Ira Rubin, Gerald Westheimer
     2. Edgar Kaplan, Norman Kay, Sammy R. Kehela,
        Sidney Lazard, Eric R. Murray, George Rapee

1970 1-2. Billy Eisenberg, Bobby Goldman, Robert D. Hamman,
         James Jacoby, Michael S. Lawrence, Bobby Wolff
     1-2. Grant S. Baze, Anthony H. Dionisi, William P. Grieve,
         Harlow S. Lewis, Peter A. Pender, George Rapee

1971 1. William Grieve, Edgar Kaplan,
        Norman Kay, Donald P. Krauss,
        Lewis L. Mathe, George Rapee
     2. Grant S. Baze, Anthony H. Dionisi,
        Harlow S. Lewis, Peter A. Pender

1972 1. Lou Bluhm, Steve Goldberg,
        Steven J. Parker, Stephen W. Robinson
     2. William Grieve, Sammy R. Kehela,
        Eric R. Murray, George Rapee

1973 1. Larry Cohen, Dr. Richard H. Katz,
        Bud Reinhold, Alan Sontag, Peter Weichsel
     2. Jack Blair, Byron L. Greenberg,
        Thomas K. Sanders, Paul Swanson

1974 1. Fred Hamilton, Erik Paulsen,
        Hugh Ross, Ira S. Rubin
     2. Stephen Goldstein, Marc S. Jacobus,
        Jay Merrill, Steve Sion, John Solodar

1975 1. Fred Hamilton, Erik Paulsen,
        Hugh Ross, Ira S. Rubin
     2. Richard E. Doughty, Frank. M. Hoadley,
        Jack LaNoue, Sidney H. Lazard

1976 1. Malcolm K. Brachman, Billy Eisenberg,
        Bobby Goldman, Eddie Kantar,
        Mike Passell, Paul Soloway
     2. Matt Granovetter, Robert H. Lipsitz,
        Steven J. Parker, Samuel M. Stayman

1977 1. Jim Cayne, Alan Greenberg,
        James Jacoby, Kyle Larsen, Michael S. Lawrence
     2. Matt Granovetter, Robert H. Lipsitz,
        Neil Silverman, Samuel M. Stayman

1978 1. Ira. G. Corn, Jr., Fred Hamilton, Robert D. Hamman,
        Ira S. Rubin, Bobby Wolff
     2. Allan Graves, Gaylor Kasle, Mark Lair,
        George Mittleman, Barney O'Malia, Ron Smith

1979 1-2. Russ Arnold, Bobby Levin, Jeff Meckstroth,
         Bud Reinhold, Eric Rodwell
     1-2. Ira. G. Corn, Jr., Fred Hamilton, Robert D. Hamman,
         Ira S. Rubin, Bobby Wolff

1980 1. Ron E. Andersen, Malcolm K. Brachman,
        Bobby Goldman, Eddie Kantar,
        Michael S. Lawrence, Paul Soloway
     2-3. Mark Lair, Jeff Meckstroth,
         Mike Passell, Eric Rodwell,
         George Rosenkranz, Eddie Wold
     2-3. Roy Fox, Ed Manfield, Paul Swanson, Kit Woolsey

1981 1. Chip Martel, Peter A. Pender,
        Hugh Ross, Lew Stansby
     2-3. Roger Bates, Chuck F. Burger, Jim Cayne,
         Billy Eisenberg, Alan Greenberg
     2-3. Evan Bailey, L. Andrew Campbell,
         Joel Hoersch, David J. Weiss

BLUE RIBBON PAIRS. This event is contested for the CAVENDISH TROPHY. It is a six-session pair event

with two qualifying sessions, two semifinal sessions, and two final sessions. Entry is restricted to winners and runners-up in Regional Championships and high finishers in North American Championships during the previous three years, members of current Grand National District Championship teams, members of current official teams representing the ACBL or member countries of the ACBL, together with the top 100 masterpoint holders.

WINNERS

1963 1. B. Jay Becker, Dorothy Hayden
      2. Harold Harkavy, Cliff Russell

1964 1. Robert D. Hamman, Lewis L. Mathe
      2. Gunther Polak, Robert G. Sharp

1965 1. Chuck Henke, John H. Moran
      2. Michael S. Lawrence, Ron Von der Porten

1966 1. Charles Coon, Richard Zeckhauser
      2. Leland Ferer, Gratian Goldstein

1967 1. Sammy R. Kehela, Baron Wolf Lebovic
      2. Phil Feldesman, Lewis L. Mathe

1968 1. Larry Cohen, Dr. Richard H. Katz
      2. Bobby Goldman, Michael S. Lawrence

1969 1. Erik Paulsen, Alex Tschekaloff
      2-4. Sammy R. Kehela, Eric R. Murray
      2-4. Tom Hodapp, Robert F. Morris
      2-4. Larry Cohen, Dr. Richard H. Katz

1970 1. Chuck F. Burger, Ira S. Rubin
      2. Richard Freeman, Cliff Russell

1971 1. Roger Bates, John M. Grantham
      2. Hermine Baron, Michael S. Lawrence

1972 1. Richard Khautin, Warren Kornfeld
      2. Garey Hayden, Mark Lair

1973 1. Steve Robinson, Kit Woolsey
      2. Kathie Cappelletti, Mike Cappelletti

1974 1. Edgar Kaplan, Norman Kay
      2. Roger Bates, George Rosenkranz

1975 1. Steve Robinson, Kit Woolsey
      2. Ron E. Andersen, Hugh C. MacLean

1976 1. Jay Apfelbaum, Bill Edelstein
      2. James Jacoby, David Berkowitz

1977 1. Lou Bluhm, Thomas K. Sanders
      2. Kathie Cappelletti, Mike Cappelletti

1978 1. Ron E. Andersen, David Berkowitz
      2. Ted Horning, Peter Nagy

1979 1. Bobby Levin, Ron Smith
      2. James Bennett, Chester Davis

1980 1. Warren Rosner, Allan Stauber
      2. Dan Morse, G. Robert Nail

1981 1. Larry N. Cohen, Ron Gerard
      2. Chip Martel, Lew Stansby

OPEN PAIRS. This event was contested for the CAVENDISH TROPHY until 1963, when the Open Pairs became a secondary event with the introduction of the BLUE RIBBON PAIRS. It was a four-session event with two qualifying and two final sessions.

WINNERS

1928 1. Theodore A. Lightner, Waldemar K. von Zedtwitz
      2. Ely Culbertson, Josephine Culbertson

1929 1-2. William E. McKenney, Ralph R. Richards
      1-2. Hortense Evans, Mrs. Sidney Lovell

1930 1. Louise W. Bright, P. S. Germain
      2. B. Foster, Ann W. Loftus

1931 1. Willard S. Karn, P. Hal Sims
      2. Olga Hilliard, Louis H. Watson

1932 1. Willard S. Karn, P. Hal Sims
      2. Oswald Jacoby, Louis H. Watson

1933 1. Charles A. Hall, Richard M. Wildberg
      2. Sam Fry, Jr., Waldemar K. von Zedtwitz

1934 1. Charles S. Lochridge, Johnny Rau
      2. Harry J. Fishbein, Herman Goldberg

1935 1. Edward Hymes, Jr., Oswald Jacoby
      2. Paul D. Parcells, Charles W. Rilling

1936 1. Walter Jacobs, Ralph Kempner
      2. Allyne Paris, John R. Smith

1937	1.	A. Mitchell Barnes, Waldemar K. von Zedtwitz
	2.	Philip Abramsohn, Harry J. Fishbein
1938	1.	Frank E. Bubna, Mollie Funk
	2.	Alphonse J. Moyse, Jr., Helen Sobel
1939	1.	Walter L. Jacobs, Albert Weiss
	2.	Philip Abramsohn, Morrie Elis
1940	1.	Charles H. Goren, Helen Sobel
	2.	Henry Chanin, Harry J. Fishbein
1941	1.	Sidney Silodor, Sally Young
	2.	Philip Abramsohn, Harry J. Fishbein
1942	1.	Alvin Roth, Tobias Stone
	2.	Harry J. Fishbein, Waldemar K. von Zedtwitz
1943	1.	Ruth Chase Goldberg, Edith Seligman
	2.	Ned Drucker, Milton Moss
1944	1.	Ambrose Casner, Ralph Hirschberg
	2.	Aaron J. Frank, Arthur S. Goldsmith
1945	1.	Jane Jaeger, Lewis M. Jaeger
	2.	William D. Levin, Leo Roet
1946	1.	B. Jay Becker, Sidney Silodor
	2.	David C. Carter, Frances Carter
1947	1.	Helen Sobel, Margaret Wagar
	2.	Sam Fry, Jr., Ruth Sherman
1948	1.	Helen Sobel, Margaret Wagar
	2.	Peter A. Leventritt, Edson T. Wood
1949	1.	Gardner E. Goldsmith, Charles H. Whitebrook
	2.	B. Jay Becker, Simon Becker
1950	1.	Mark Kelliher, Jack B. Kushner
	2.	Leo Roet, Edson T. Wood
1951	1.	Arthur Glatt, Albert Weiss
	2.	Richard Kahn, Peter A. Leventritt
1952	1.	Israel Cohen, Vic D. Zeve
	2.	Paula Bacher, Leo Roet
1953	1.	Byron L. Greenberg, Harold Rockaway
	2.	David C. Carter, Curtis K. Smith
1954	1.	George Heath, Paul Hodge
	2.	F. Ayres Bombeck, David C. Carter
1955	1.	Milton Q. Ellenby, Emanuel Hochfeld
	2.	Barbara Brier, Waldemar K. von Zedtwitz
1956	1.	Ben Fain, Paul Hodge
	2.	Norman Kay, Charles J. Solomon
1957	1.	Lewis L. Mathe, Edward O. Taylor
	2.	Paul Allinger, Sidney H. Lazard
1958	1.	Dr. John W. Fisher, Emma Jean Hawes
	2.	Alvin Roth, Tobias Stone
1959	1.	Morton L. Rubinow, Samuel M. Stayman
	2.	William P. Grieve, Emanuel Hochfeld
1960	1.	Oswald Jacoby, Curtis K. Smith
	2.	Simon Becker, Eugene Davidson
1961	1.	Philip Feldesman, Ira S. Rubin
	2.	Jack Blair, Robert Stucker
1962	1.	B. Jay Becker, Dorothy Hayden
	2.	Eddie Kantar, Marshall Miles

LIFE MASTER MEN'S PAIRS.

This event is contested for the MOUSER TROPHY. It is a four-session event with two qualifying sessions and two final sessions, restricted to Life Masters. Before 1963 it was restricted to National Masters and players of higher rank.

WINNERS

1961	1.	G. Gard Hays, Max Manchester
	2.	Martin J. Cohn, Hampton Hume
1962	1.	Sam Fuoto, Victor Mitchell
	2.	Hal Kandler, Kelsey Petterson
1963	1.	Sammy R. Kehela, Eric R. Murray
	2.	Harry J. Fishbein, Charles J. Solomon
1964	1.	Charles Coon, Bobby Goldman
	2-3.	Mervin Key, Harold Rockaway
	2-3.	Jack Blair, Col. William Christian
1965	1.	Paul Soloway, Alex Tschekaloff
	2.	Edgar Kaplan, Victor Mitchell
1966	1.	Carl J. Hudecz, Ray Zoller
	2.	Gaylor Kasle, Ed Theus
1967	1.	Harlow S. Lewis, Peter A. Pender
	2.	Donald R. Faskow, William L. Flannery
1968	1.	Henry Bethe, John Solodar
	2.	Don Pearson, John Swanson

1969	1.	Chuck F. Burger, James Cayne
	2.	Norman H. Fischer, Christopher G. Jeans
1970	1.	Ron E. Andersen, Hugh C. MacLean
	2.	Curtis K. Smith, E. Lowell Yost
1971	1.	Alan Sontag, Peter Weichsel
	2.	Stephen W. Robinson, Kit Woolsey
1972	1.	Leslie C. Bart, Marc S. Jacobus
	2.	Stephen W. Robinson, Kit Woolsey
1973	1.	Edgar Kaplan, Norman Kay
	2.	Roxy Violin, Ed Weiner
1974	1.	Gerald L. Michaud, G. Robert Nail
	2.	John Gerber, Daniel Kaim
1975	1.	Steve Lapides, Walt Walvick
	2.	Marc Culberson, Robert Visokey
1976	1.	Roger Bates, John Mohan
	2.	Steve Altman, Thomas M. Smith
1977	1.	David Hoffner, David Schroeder
	2.	Roger Bates, John Mohan
1978	1.	Norm Coombs, Tom Hodapp
	2.	Kevin Castner, Michael S. Lawrence
1979	1.	Jeff Meckstroth, Eric Rodwell
	2.	Zeke Jabbour, Dennis McGarry
1980	1.	V. Craig Janitschke, Jan Janitschke
	2.	Robert D. Hamman, Paul Swanson
1981	1.	Roger Abelson, Mike Levinson
	2.	Robert D. Hamman, Donald P. Krauss

LIFE MASTER WOMEN'S PAIRS

This event is contested for the HELEN SOBEL SMITH TROPHY. It is a four-session event with two qualifying sessions and two final sessions, restricted to Life Masters. Prior to 1963 it was restricted to National Masters and players of higher rank.

WINNERS

1961	1.	Dorothy Hayden, Helen Portugal
	2.	Gratian Goldstein, Jane Mueller
1962	1.	Barbara Kachmar, Margaret Wagar
	2.	Anne Burnstein, Edith Kemp
1963	1.	Anne Burnstein, Hermine Baron
	2.	Carrie Arnold, Neva L. Gray
1964	1.	Margaret Alcorn, Betty Kaplan
	2.	Agnes Gordon, Sylvia Stein
1965	1.	Ann Sheaber, Jan Stone
	2.	Mary Jane Farell, Peggy Solomon
1966	1.	Emma Jean Hawes, Dorothy Hayden
	2.	Mary Jane Farell, Peggy Solomon
1967	1.	Nancy Gruver, Edith Sachs
	2.	Mary Jane Farell, Peggy Solomon
1968	1.	Dorothy Talmage, Rhoda Walsh
	2.	Katherine Blanchard, Mary Jane Farell
1969	1.	Gratian Goldstein, Sylvia Stein
	2.	Karen Allison, Gladys W. Collier
1970	1.	Bette L. Cohn, Marietta Passell
	2.	Louise Krauss, Betty Mangan
1971	1.	Ruth Bloomfield, Della Levinson
	2.	Betty Ann Kennedy, Carol Sanders
1972	1.	Amalya Kearse, Rhoda Walsh
	2.	Emma Jean Hawes, Dorothy Hayden Truscott
1973	1.	Frieda Arst, June Deutsch
	2.	Edith Kemp, Barbara Rappaport
1974	1.	Bernice Larson, Joan Stein
	2.	Edith Kemp, Barbara Rappaport
1975	1.	Dorothy Moore, Marion Weed
	2.	Nancy Gruver, Helen Utegaard
1976	1.	Barbara Furbeck, Barbara Herr
	2.	Carol Crawford, Joan Remey
1977	1.	Edith Kemp, Barbara Rappaport
	2.	Bernadine Jenkins, Joan Remey
1978	1.	Emma Jean Hawes, Dorothy Hayden Truscott
	2.	Ann Economidy, Anne Leverone
1979	1.	Nancy Gruver, Edith Kemp
	2.	June Deutsch, Sandi Leavitt
1980	1.	Kathie Cappelletti, Claire Tornay
	2.	Nancy Gruver, Edith Kemp
1981	1.	Nancy Gruver, Edith Kemp
	2.	Betty Ann Kennedy, Carol Sanders

MIXED PAIRS. This event is contested for the ROCKWELL TROPHY. It is a four-session Mixed Pairs event with two qualifying sessions and two final sessions.

WINNERS

1946	1.	Anne Burnstein, Alvin Roth
	2.	David C. Carter, Frances Carter
1947	1.	Evelyn Ansin, Charles H. Goren
	2.	John R. Crawford, Margaret Wagar
1948	1.	John R. Crawford, Margaret Wagar
	2.	Charles C. Johnson, Mrs. Frank Myer
1949	1.	John R. Crawford, Margaret Wagar
	2.	Paula Bacher, Peter A. Leventritt
1950	1.	Peter A. Leventritt, Ruth Sherman
	2.	William Thiemann, Mrs. William Thiemann
1951	1.	Edith Rosenbloom, Sidney Silodor
	2.	Edward Burns, Shirley Fairchild
1952	1.	Anne Burnstein, Alvin Roth
	2.	Ella Tilles, Jules Tilles
1953	1.	Jewel Hodge, Paul H. Hodge
	2.	John Gerber, Celeste Mounce
1954	1.	Said Haddad, Betty Windley
	2.	Zenobia Allen, John H. Moran
1955	1.	Sidney Silodor, Helen Sobel
	2.	Alicia Kempner, George Rapee
1956	1.	Sidney Silodor, Helen Sobel
	2.	Donald G. Farquaharson, Agnes Gordon
1957	1.	Bee Gale, Howard Schenken
	2.	Frances Carter, David Warner
1958	1.	Carol Ross, Edwin J. Smith
	2.	Louis J. Cohen, Sylvia Stein
1959	1.	John R. Crawford, Dorothy Hayden
	2.	Sidney H. Lazard, Stella Rebner
1960	1.	Elsie Abrams, William L. Passell
	2.	Peter Johnson, Gladys Kransberg
1961	1.	Art Comstock, Margaret Muirhead
	2.	Charles J. Solomon, Peggy Solomon
1962	1.	Clarice K. Holt, Paul Levitt
	2.	Peggy Jean Berry, John C. Sutherlin
1963	1.	Agnes Gordon, Eric R. Murray
	2.	Barbara Brier, Jerry Brier
1964	1.	Dan Morse, Mary Margaret Swan
	2.	Margaret Alcorn, Peter A. Pender
1965	1.	Betty Kaplan, Edgar Kaplan
	2.	Malvine Klausner, Morris Portugal
1966	1.	Robert G. Sharp, Louise Sharp
	2.	Gertrude Blasband, Sylvester Lowery
1967	1.	Gertrude Machlin, Kit Woolsey
	2.	Kathie Cappelletti, Mike Cappelletti
1968	1.	Marilyn Johnson, Peter C. Rank
	2.	John Gerber, Carol Klar
1969	1.	Peggy Parker, Steve Parker
	2.	Evelyn Levitt, David R. Treadwell
1970	1.	George S. Dawkins, Carolyn C. Flournoy
	2.	Mary Chilcote, Larry Weiss
1971	1.	Eugenie Mathe, Lewis L. Mathe
	2.	Barry Crane, Kerri Davis
1972	1.	John A. Mohan, Peggy Sutherlin
	2.	Leland Ferer, Gratian Goldstein
1973	1.	Bernie Chazen, Marilyn Johnson
	2.	Kenneth L. Cohen, Helen Smith
1974	1.	Gerald A. Caravelli, Helen Utegaard
	2.	Barry Crane, Kerri Shuman
1975	1.	Barry Crane, Kerri Shuman
	2.	Sandi Leavitt, Paul Sugar
1976	1.	Peggy Lipsitz, Steve Parker
	2.	Nancy Gruver, Lee Rautenberg
1977	1.	Joel Friedberg, Nancy Gruver
	2.	Barry Crane, Kerri Shuman
1978	1.	Ahmed Hussein, Gail Moss
	2.	Dave McClintock, Janet McClintock
1979	1.	Juanita Skelton, Mike Smolen
	2.	Carol Sanders, Thomas K. Sanders
1980	1.	Jeff Meckstroth, Patty Meckstroth
	2.	Hemant Lall, Jan Lall
1981	1.	Esta Van Zandt, James E. Zimmerman
	2-3.	Charlie Dorn, Bonnie LaRochelle
	2-3.	Bart Bramley, Judy Wadas

MASTER INDIVIDUAL. This event was contested for the KARN TROPHY (1931–1933) and the STEINER TROPHY from 1934.

WINNERS

1931	1.	Willard S. Karn
	2.	Richard L. Frey
1932	1.	Howard Schenken
	2.	David Burnstine
1933	1.	David Burnstine
	2.	Elinor Murdoch
1934	1.	Elinor Murdoch
	2.	B. Jay Becker
1935	1.	Oswald Jacoby
	2.	David Burnstine
1936	1.	Waldemar K. von Zedtwitz
	2.	Merwyn D. Mayer
1937	1.	B. Jay Becker
	2.	George Unger
1938	1.	Richard Ecker, Jr.
	2.	Harry Fishbein
1939	1.	Merwyn D. Maier
	2.	Alvin Landy
1940	1.	Morrie Elis
	2.	Lee Hazen
1941	1.	Lee Hazen
	2.	B. Jay Becker
1942	1.	Harry J. Fishbein
	2.	Olive Peterson
1943	1.	Alvin Roth
	2.	Charles Solomon
1944	1.	George Rapee
	2.	Robert T. Chatkin
1945	1.	Charles H. Goren
	2.	Albert Weiss
1946	1.	Robert A. McPherran
	2.	Morrie Elis
1947	1.	Charles J. Solomon
	2.	Jack Cushing
1948	1.	B. Jay Becker
	2.	Myron Field
1949	1.	George Rapee
	2.	B. Jay Becker
1950	1.	Morrie Elis
	2.	Robert Appleyard
1951	1.	Sidney Silodor
	2.	John Crawford
1952	1.	Harry J. Fishbein
	2.	Peter Leventritt
1953	1.	Tobias Stone
	2.	Larry Hirsch
1954	1.	Edward Burns
	2.	F. Ayres Bombeck
1955	1.	Norman Kay
	2-3.	Alvin Roth, B. Jay Becker
1956	1.	John R. Crawford
	2.	Robert Appleyard
1957	1.	Edgar Kaplan
	2.	Dr. Ernest E. Karshmer
1958	1.	Sylvia Stein
	2.	John Crawford
1959	1.	Leo Pressburg
	2.	Frank L. Jackson
1960	1.	Robert Reynolds
	2.	Arthur Robinson

GRAND NATIONAL ROOKIE PAIRS. This Grand National contest was designed exclusively for new recruits. To be eligible each player must have fewer than 20 master points. The winning pair from each of the 25 ACBL Districts and one pair at large compete for the title at the Fall North American Championships.

WINNERS

1979	1.	David Chen, Paul Chen
	2.	Walter Bell, David Kresge
1980	1.	Peter Ngan, Sunny Ngan

2. Thomas Sproule, Thomas Suman
1981 1. George Berfield, Pat Chatta
2. John Kissell, John Levengood

NORTH AMERICAN SWISS TEAMS.

This six-session Open Swiss Team event has two qualifying sessions, two semifinal sessions and a two-session final with Victory Point scoring.

WINNERS
1977 1. Neil Chambers, Jim Donaldson, Bruce Ferguson, Clarence Goppert, John Schermer
2. Dennis Clerkin, Jerry Clerkin, John Herrmann, Kenneth Schutze
1978 1. Barry Crane, Bob Kehoe, Mike Smolen, Charles Weed
2. Ira Chorush, Thomas Peters, Ely Solomon, John Zilic, Virginia Zilic
1979 1. Hermine Baron, R. Jay Becker, Paul Ivaska, Jim Robison
2. Gerald Caravelli, Mark Cohen, Ralph Katz, Harvey Miller, Ken Schutze, Russell Shoup
1980 1-2. Steve Becker, Philip Cowan, Rich DeMartino, Judy Rich
1-2. Dale Beers, William Epperson, Dave Furman, Dave Treitel
1981 1. Ron Beall, Bob Etter, Ann Jacobson, Bob Thomson
2. Lea duPont, Benito Garozzo, Glenn Lublin, Claire Tornay

AMATEUR WOMEN'S PAIRS.

A four-session event with two qualifying rounds and two final rounds open to all players except ACBL members who are *Registered Players*.

WINNERS
1975 1. Mrs. George L. Brown, Daisy Stephens,
2. Ann Roberts, Pauline Tindal
1976 1. Diana Halle, Joyce Wise
2. Sheila Latus, Mary Rachels

AMATEUR MEN'S PAIRS.

A four-session event with two qualifying rounds and two final rounds open to all players except ACBL members who are *Registered Players*.

WINNERS
1975 1. Harvey Miller, Jr., Bob Pareti
2. Dave Malec, Joe Steuer
1976 1. Ken Chatzinoff, Fred Melman
2. Sheldon Justan, Dr. Harold Weltman

SECONDARY CHAMPIONSHIPS

OPEN PAIRS.

This four-session event with two qualifying sessions and two final sessions became a secondary event with the introduction of the BLUE RIBBON PAIRS.

WINNERS
1963 Armand Barfus, Ronald Schonan
1964 Sammy R. Kehela, Carol Sanders
1965 Harold Feldstein, Gretchen Feldstein
1966 John P. Zilic, David J. Joyce
1967 John E. Wachter, Dr. Richard H. Katz
1968 Ann Kluewer, Richard N. Dallas
1969 Robert W. Ryder, Barbara Birnholz
1970 William B. Johnson, Paul J. Burka
1971 Joe Titone, Irv J. Kostal

NON–LIFE MASTER MEN'S PAIRS.

This event is restricted to non-Life Masters. It was contested as a three-session event with two qualifying rounds and one final round in 1963; a four-session event with two qualifying sessions and two final sessions from 1964 through 1969; and a two-session playthrough event thereafter.

WINNERS
1963 Mike Cappelletti, Jonathan Snelling
1964 Brian Grace, Mike Harlow
1965 Richard Eichler, Kyle Larsen
1966 Jerry Locks, Sam Schultz
1967 Jerry Kuchler, Jr., Jim McMullin
1968 Arthur Granville, Paul Greenberg
1969 Jim Foster, Bernie Yomtov
1970 R. L. Dombos, Jack Longman
1971 Mark Bischoff, Ed Neff
1972 Ronald Fischer, Kit Wong
1973 Jeff Bayonne, Stan Strachan

NON–LIFE MASTER WOMEN'S PAIRS.

This event was restricted to non–Life Masters. It was contested as a three-session event with two qualifying rounds and one final round in 1963; a four-session event with two qualfying sessions and two final sessions from 1964 through 1969; and a two-session playthrough event thereafter.

WINNERS
1963 Mrs. Ray Lewis, Genevieve Roehr
1964 Mrs. Herman Straheim, Mrs. Julius Truelson
1965 Edna Ferber, Elizabeth Spain
1966 Gerry Cooper, Flo Orner
1967 Diane Harmon, Lois Jimerson
1968 Pat Bergin, Cheryl A. Shepard
1969 Dorothy Caldwell, Peggy McCleskey
1970 Ola Davison, Edith Rosenberg
1971 June Berken, Barbara Brasted
1972 Helen Cheng, Elaine Jacobson
1973 Donna Hill, Ruth Mercer

MEN'S TEAMS.

This is a two-session event held in the Spring North American Championships in 1962 and subsequently in the Fall NAC, scored by Board-a-Match prior to 1971, when scoring was changed to international matchpoints with Swiss pairing.

WINNERS
1962 Harold B. Guiver, Alphonse Moyse, Jr. Kelsey Pettersen, Thomas K. Sanders, Mike Shuman
1963 James Alexander, Phil Carson Allan R. Cohen, Kurt Forsythe
1964 William Granberry, Clay McFarland Charles Miller, George Pisk
1965 John Gerber, Charles H. Goren Paul Hodge, G. Robert Nail, John E. Simon
1966 Philip Feldesman, Edgar Kaplan, Norman Kay Peter A. Leventritt, Victor Mitchell
1967 William Cook, Jr., Allan Siebert David Siebert, Jack Walton
1968 John Gerber, Paul Hodge, William Passell George Rosenkranz, Allan Truscott
1969 Bobby Goldman, Gaylor Kasle Mike King, Michael S. Lawrence *(tied with)* Gene Prosnitz, Kenneth Lebensold Jessel Rothfield, Wally Scott
1971 Ed Davis, Paul Ivaska Thomas M. Lesser, Mike Smolen *(tied with)* Bruce Evans, Norman Levin W. T. Nakamura, Sidney Willner
1972 Albert R. Bricklin, Samuel Coolik, Jr. Harold B. Guiver, Thomas K. Sanders
1974 Richard Degen, Michael Griffith Jerry Pietscher, A. B. Thomas
1975 Frank Burstein, Howard Hertzberg Julius K. Rosenblum, Nate Silverstein
1976 Malcolm Brachman, Bobby Goldman Paul Soloway, Leonard Wisbey
1977 George Dawkins, Barry Hagedorn, Jack Kennedy George Pisk, Dick Reed, Bobby Wolff
1978 Dennis Cohen, John Coufal John Jeffrey, Jay T. McKee *(tied with)* Y. M. Chu, Bob McClendon

Joe Payne, Gene Simpson *(and)*
Henry Bethe, Edgar Kaplan
Norman Kay, Chuck Lamprey
1980 Syd Levey, Alan Oaks, Walter O'Loughlin
Vince Remey, Jim Wood *(tied with)*
Fred Hamilton, Edgar Kaplan, Norman Kay
Roger Stern, Per Olof Sundelin *(and)*
Bert Chansky, George Groves
Arthur Kong, Don Williams *(and)*
Ron E. Andersen, Bobby Goldman, Paul Soloway
George Rosenkranz, Eddie Wold *(and)*
Richard Celler, Howard Hertzberg
Nathan Ostrich, Bob Ryder

WOMEN'S TEAMS.

This is a two-session event held in the Spring North American Championships in 1962 and subsequently in the Fall NAC, scored by Board-a-Match prior to 1971, when scoring was changed to international matchpoints with Swiss pairing.

WINNERS
1962 Mildred Bright, Mrs. Melvin Cornillaud,
Eleanor Crounse, Arlene Livingston, Ruth Novak
1963 Gertrude Blasband, Olive Peterson
Peggy Rotzell, Peggy Solomon
1964 Mary Jane Farell, Agnes Gordon
Peggy Solomon, Margaret Wagar
1965 Agnes Gordon, Peggy Solomon
Sylvia Stein, Margaret Wagar
1966 Anna Conroy, Marian Erickson
Edna Lee, Frances Thompson
1967 Bette L. Cohn, Carol Krupp
Mickey Rosenthal, Barbara Tepper
1968 Isa Alcone, Karen R. Allison
Evelyn Levitt, Jan Stone *(tied with)*
Betty Berkitz, Anita Davis
Carol Klar, Sylvia Stein *(and)*
Sallie Johnson, Gail Moss
Marietta Passell, Bee Schenken
1969 Sallie Johnson, Gail Moss
Marietta Passell, Bee Schenken
1971 Virginia Burke, Judy Casalena
Cathy Jones, Marion Merryweather
1972 Bonnie Brier, Anita Davis, Carol Klar
Terry Michaels, Jan Stone
1974 Sylvia Chavers, Loretta Rivers
Judy Ruch, Ann Westrom
1975 Janice Cohn, Gloria Harris
Barbara Nudelman, Sylvia Simon
1976 Anne Bean, Shirley Hewitt
Eugenie Mathe, Jean Theus *(tied with)*
Kitty Bethe, Susan Mamelok
Sally Sipherd, Lillian Vine *(and)*
Fran Beard, Helen Blakely
Evelyn Levitt, Helen Smith
1977 Anne Burnstein, June Deutsch
Jane Jaeger, Sandi Leavitt
1978 Fran Beard, Jerre Gardiner
Montie Shelton, Jeanne Titus
1980 Louise Cavallero, Fran Esposito, Myrna Lurie
Grace Postman, Kate Weil

OPEN PAIRS.

A two-session event.

WINNERS
1969 Don B. Grove, Harold J. Peck
1970 Charles Baron, Meyer Schleifer
1971 Jack La Noue, Chuck Pitard
1972 Divakar Bhargava, Daniel M. Gerstman
1973 Allan Siebert, David Siebert
1974 Gerald Lipsig, Robert McGaffey
1975 Ira Chorush, John Zilic
1976 Dr. Howard Hertzberg, Richard Taube
1977 Steve Sion, Jim Sternberg
1978 Herb Smith, Larry Weiss
1979 John Berry, Lou Katz
1980 Flight A: Corinne Gellman, Carl Nelson
        Flight B: Andy Boyer, Brad Theurer
1981 Flight A: Chris Compton, Rick Price
        Flight B: Paul Boudreau, Don Gallaher

SUB-NATIONAL MASTER TEAMS.

This is a two-session Board-a-Match event restricted to players below the rank of National Master.

WINNERS
1958 G. E. Clark, Albert W. James
D. N. MacKellar, W. R. Shaw
1959 Mrs. Orville Bert, Mrs. J. W. Fleming
Leon Katz, Sandy Kessler
1960 Warren Colbert, Seymour Ehrlich
George Klorman, Elliott Schulman
1961 Ann Hardwicke, Mrs. C. P. Hardwicke
W. R. Long, Dan Moody
1962 D. A. Drake, Mrs. D. A. Drake
Folger Johnson, Mrs. Folger Johnson *(tied with)*
E. B. Maxwell, Mrs. E. C. Maxwell
D. K. McElfresh, Mrs. W. V. Nold
1963 Melvin N. Greenberg, R. P. Hodges
Herbert D. Katz, James Titzel
1964 Haskell Edmonds, Shirl Edmonds
Harry Janssen, Robert E. Mangney
1965 J. Starr Farish, Tim Smith
Thelma J. Taft, William R. Taft
1966 Edward Banks, Wilson Heard
Clarence L. Shelton, Marion Tiemeier
1967 Billy M. Perry, Lorraine Perry
Barbara Barton, Wesley Barton
1968 Douglas Blagdon, Richard Jacobs
Allen Kandell, John Kasdan

COMMERCIAL AND INDUSTRIAL PAIRS.

This is a two-session pair event limited to pairs that are full-time or pensioned employees of the same commercial or industrial firm, educational or nonprofit organization or government bureau.

WINNERS
1958 Wyandotte Chemicals
William F. Pesold, Eugene Weipert
1959 Douglas Aircraft
Ralph D. Clark, Robert D. Hamman
1960 Halle & Stieglitz
Robert Levy, Marvin Sirot
1961 Saron Pharmacal Company
Robert Saron, Sally Saron
1962 Montrose Bridge Studio
Mary Cocherell, Robert Bratcher
1963 Campus Hideway
Les Gerig, Brian Grace
1964 Saron Chemical Company
Robert Saron, Sally Saron
1965 Bank of America
Dave Geary, George Strohl
1966 Ford Motor Company
Roger Richman, Bernard Weinstock
1967 McDonnell Douglas
Donald C. Geers, Brooks Sharp
1968 General Dynamics Convair
Wayne B. Evans, Thomas G. Ludwig
1969 Oldsmobile
Robert W. Bacon, Robert J. Mosher
1970 First Business Computing
Lee M. Green, Lorand Tritter

SWISS TEAMS.

A four-session team event scored by international matchpoints, with two qualifying sessions and two final sessions.

WINNERS
1970 Jean Carney, Mary Chilcote, Carl F. Cronemiller
Roger E. Lord, Alan Truscott, Larry Weiss
1971 James Darling, Phyllis Darling
Gert Haller, Robert H. Haller
1972 Helen Buechler, Bertha Hutcheon
Jerry Rowley, Lonnie Rowley *(tied with)*
Charlotte Falk, Franklin Merblum
W. T. Rutledge, Jr., Fred E. Strickland
1973 Mark Bischoff, Ed Neff
Char Potysman, Vic Potysman
1974 Howard Chandross, Lee Rautenberg
Francis Whalen, Vivian Whalen

1975　Gonzalo Herrera, Elias Konstantinovsky
　　　Laura Mariscal, Miguel Reygadas
1976　Anne Bean, Alfred Gilpin
　　　Donald A. Oakie, Mrs. Emory Stanley
1977　Hermine Baron, Paul Ivaska
　　　John Mohan, Daniel Mordecai
1978　Marilyn Eber, V. Craig Janitschke
　　　Jan Janitschke, Stephen Strauss

SILVER TROPHY PAIRS This two-session flighted Open Pairs event was first contested at the Summer North American Championships in 1976 and is held at each of the three NAC. Flight A is unlimited, Flight B requirements are 0–1500 and Flight C requirements are 0–300. A Revere bowl trophy on a base is given to each winner.

WINNERS
1976	Flight A:	Jay Merrill, Lou Reich
	Flight B:	Kim Gilbert, Dale Sims
	Flight C:	Eric Holder, Edward Klein
1977	Flight A:	Milt Rosenberg, Kathie Wei
	Flight B:	Charlotte Oesterle, Les Senour
	Flight C:	C. N. Bradford, Jr., Evelyn Bradford
1978	Flight A:	Gratian Goldstein, Sylvia Stein
	Flight B:	Paul J. Lewis, Linda Peterson
	Flight C:	Paul Richards, Bob Sloane
1979	Flight A:	Gene Prosnitz, Dan Zirker
	Flight B:	Dick Early, Sherry Early
	Flight C:	Susan Green, Christopher Hough
1980	Flight A:	Phil Brady, Stephen Swearingen
	Flight B:	Glenn Robbins, Harold Siegelman
	Flight C:	Jonann Brown, Bonnie Shortall
1981	Flight A:	Malcolm Brachman, Paul Soloway
	Flight B:	Jimmy Horn, Rita Shugart
	Flight C:	Peter Colagrosso, Larry Kolton

SENIOR MASTER INDIVIDUAL. This event was contested for the BEYNON TROPHY.

WINNERS
1947　Albert Weiss
1948　Nat Agran
1949　Clagett Bowie
1950　Abe Goldstein
1951　James Epstein
1952　Harvey Cohen
1953　William E. Adams
1954　Donald Rustein
1955　W.W. Williams, Jr.
1956　Marjorie Salisbury
1957　Philip Feldesman
1958　R. Norman Miller
1959　Thomas B. Commander
1960　Margaret Pell

INDIVIDUAL. Revived in 1966, this two-session Open event replaced the two Individual championships that were discontinued in 1960.

WINNERS
1966　Dr. Irvin J. Littman
1967　Bernard L. Tighe, Jr.
1968　Patrick Mahoney
1969　Dr. Edward F. Gudgel
1970　Jonnie Nix
1971　Jane Thomas
1972　Emanuel Hochberg
1973　Robert Bishop
1974　Irving Rasmussen
1975　Michael Zerbini
1976　William Cook
1977　Barbara Johnson
1978　Paul Boudreau

SWISS TEAMS SECOND FLIGHT. This two-

session event is scored by International Match-points, restricted to non-qualifiers from the four-session secondary Swiss Team event.

WINNERS
1970　Freida B. Alderman, Mrs. Walter E. Eubank,
　　　James Martin, Andrew Meyer
1971　Marcia Hearst, Goldie Leeper,
　　　Nanette Posner, Betty Posner
1972　William Adams, Robert F. Bassell,
　　　George H. Effros, Neal Felsinger
1973　Jim Hooker, James Jacoby,
　　　Clarence Strouse, Charles Weed, Bobby Wolff
1974　William Root, Marvin Rosenblatt,
　　　Ron Rubin, Neil Silverman
1975　Lou Bluhm, Gaylor Kasle, Bobby Levin,
　　　Jim Linhart, Nick Nickell, James Tucker
1976　Peter Boyd, Robert Lipsitz,
　　　Glenn Lublin, Eugene O'Neill

MEN'S PAIRS. A two-session event.

WINNERS
1971　Jerry Gaer, Colby K. Vernay
1972　Warren Rosner, Paul Sidikman
1973　Don Kerr, Larry Richardson
1974　Patrick J. Brennan, Jr., Neil Silverman
1975　Charles Fleisher, William Levy
1977　Randy Joyce, Bill Wisdom
1978　Michael Murphy, Michael Schira
1980　Warren Kornfeld, Richard Taube
1981　Bob Burton, Louis Castanier

WOMEN'S PAIRS. A two-session event.

WINNERS
1971　Myrna Bergman, Margie Gwozdzinsky
1972　Barbara Bellino, Barbara Bentley *(tied with)*
　　　Elyse Katz, Polly Riggs
1973　Frieda Arst, Jean Christopher
1974　Starla Burns, Doris Romm
1975　Garner McDaniel, Mary Beth Townsend
1977　Marilyn Abrams, Jan Cohen
1978　Ella Auch, Marianne Brogan
1980　Alberta Albersheim, Augusta Cantor
1981　Marilyn Christy, Sylvia Doryland

MIXED PAIRS. A two-session event.

WINNERS
1970		Anne Trenholm, Steve Greenberg
1971		Mike McMahan, Shirley McMahan
1972		Barbara Rappaport, Alvin Roth
1973		Richard Doughty, Patricia LaCour
1974		Bernie Chazen, Carol Greenhut
1975		Freda Engle, Paul Robb
1976		Gaylor Kasle, Carol Krehbiel
1977	Flight A:	Larry Kozlove, Helen Smith
	Flight B:	Jerry Jackson, Lorraine Seward
1978	Flight A:	Stephen Donahue, Patricia Sanders
	Flight B:	Ann Farek, Stephen Robinson
1981	Flight A:	Hermine Baron, Paul Ivaska
	Flight B:	Ed Piken, Eva Piken

OTHER SECONDARY EVENTS
(All two-session regionally-rated events)

WINNERS
1970
Open Teams Second Flight:
　　　Kathie Cappelletti, Mike Cappelletti,
　　　Eric Kokish, Don Piafsky
Blue Ribbon Pairs Second Flight:
　　　Steven M. Cohn, Lloyd Hetzer
Life Master Men's Pairs Second Flight:
　　　William B. Acker, Byron Economidy
Life Master Women's Pairs Second Flight:
　　　Pat Terk, B. J. Wilson

Open Pairs Second Flight:
Don R. Laird, Charlie Tupper
Mixed Pairs Second Flight:
Pat Gowdey, Mike Shira
1971
Open Teams Second Flight:
Karen Allison, Everett Fukushima, Steve Lent,
Vern Pang, Gary Soules
Blue Ribbon Pairs Second Flight:
Bette Scope, Ivan Scope
Open Pairs Second Flight:
Jay T. McKee, Keiji Taira
1972
Swiss Teams:
Art Cohn, Trudy Cohn,
James Gobert, Dave Richardmeyer
Master Pairs:
Fred Hamilton, Jim Murphy
1973
Swiss Teams:
Mary Jane Farell, Marilyn Johnson,
Jacqui Mitchell, Kathie Wei
Master Pairs:
Chester Davis, Dr. Robert B. Tator
Open Pairs:
Virginia Burke, Gary Crain
Tournament of Champions:
Proctor Hawkins, Kelsey Petterson
1974
Master Pairs:
Pat Hood, George Pisk
Open Pairs:
Flight A: Roger Bates, Garey Hayden
Flight B: Barry Hagedorn, Patsy New
Flight C: Alan Bell, Kirk Benson
Swiss Teams:
Clarence Goppert, John Grantham,
Garey Hayden, Gaylor Kasle, Mark Lair
Women's Pairs:
Mrs. D. Buckshorn, Mrs. F. Clifford Wright
Non-Mixed Pairs:
Ross Grabel, Steve Landen
1975
Swiss Teams:
Lou Bluhm, Larry Cohen,
Dan Morse, George Rosenkranz
1976
Master Pairs:
Flight A: Mark Blumenthal, Mark Klugman
Flight B: Donna Lloyd, Thomas Lloyd
Swiss Teams:
Alberta Albersheim, Lloyd Arvedon,
Ethel Keohane, Joe Quinn
1977
Master Pairs:
Flight A: David Leonard, Eleanor Turoff
Flight B: Glenn Selby, Mrs. Glenn Selby
Open Pairs:
A — Class A: Terry Borne, David Nicklasson
B — Class A-D: Barbara Brier, Darryle Forrest
Swiss Teams
Flight A: Jerry Helms, Bill Seddon,
Alston Woodson, William Woodson
Flight B: Bill Holliday, Tim Kowarsky,
William Pollans, Michal Wolf
1978
Open Pairs:
A — Class A: Margot Bunday, Stuart Bunday
B — Class A-D: Alan Truscott, Larry Weiss
Open Pairs:
Smoking: Bobby Levin, Mike Passell
Non-Smoking: Grant S. Baze, Peter A. Pender
Master Pairs:
Flight A: Hank Mullaney, Ross Rainwater
Flight B: Dan Boulay, Marilyn Boulay
Swiss Teams:
Flight A: Dr. John Fisher, Charles Gabriel,
Jan Janitschke, V. Craig Janitschke
Flight B: Mark Bartusek, Gary Kessler,
Sidney Levin, Steve Weinstein
1979
Open Pairs:
A — Class A: Lawrence Hayes, Geoffrey Hintze

B — Class A-D: Wayne Hollingsworth, Robert Sulgrove
Seven Hills Swiss Teams:
Alan Oaks, Sol Seidman, Bob Saron,
Sally Saron, James E. Zimmerman
Eden Park Swiss Teams:
Foxy Hall, Joan Hall,
Cindy Marshall, Brooks McNeely
Swiss Teams:
A — Class A: Amalya Kearse, Mark Kessler,
Al Susskind, Kit Woolsey *(tied with)*
Bruce Ferguson, Victor Goldberg,
Brenda Keller, Don Presse, Milton Stern
B — Class A-D: Gerald Bare, Harold Guiver,
Carol Sanders, Thomas Sanders,
Piyush Vakil, James E. Zimmerman
Swiss Teams:
Steve Alpern, Judi Cody,
William Epperson, Harvey Miller
Kenneth Schutze, Al Susskind
Delta Queen Pairs:
Glenn Lublin, John Stiefel
Tri-State Open Pairs:
Ken Chatzinoff, Pete Weglarski
Swiss Teams:
Flight A: Ron E. Andersen, Dave Berkowitz, Bart Bramley,
Larry N. Cohen, Judi Radin, Kathie Wei
Flight B: Joanne Coyle, Pat Mowbray,
Nancy Palcic, Richard Palcic
1980
Open Pairs:
Smoking: Juanita Skelton, Mike Smolen
Non-Smoking: Helene Bauman, John Shannonhouse
Swiss Teams:
Smoking: Bob Bauer, Arnie Frankel,
Charles Heine, Glenn Robbins *(tied with)*
Jeffrey Dunn, Lynn Jones,
Michael Rind, Joseph Trapani *(and)*
Martin Eddert, Dave Furman,
William Gough, Tom Justl
Non-Smoking: Linda Germain, Linda Joseph,
Dick Leonard, Marty Robins
Swiss Teams:
A — Class A: Jim Ayres, Roger Diederich,
Tom Laishley, John Welch
B — Class A-D: Peter Boyd, Max Hardy,
Jim Hilton, Harry Stappenbeck
Susquehanna River:
BAM Teams: Lea duPont, Mickey Friedman, Benito Garozzo,
Billy Landau, Frank Mastrola
Swiss Teams: Rene Henry, Chuck Heine,
Gen Heine, Glenn Robbins
Swiss Teams:
Flight A: Gary Bush, Lynne Feldman,
Bruce Ferguson, Lisa Halpern
Flight B: Donald Bridges, Phillip Feuerwerger,
David Rosenberg, Robert Silverman
Keystone Pairs:
Tom Horan, Jim Krekorian
1981
Open Pairs:
Smoking: James Backstrom, Ken Monzingo
Non-Smoking: Gene Chait, Peggy Hitt
Swiss Teams:
Smoking: Alan Daniels, Rodger Harbin, Robert Radwin,
Ross Rainwater, Terry West
Non-Smoking: Nancy Alpaugh, Chuck Burger, James Cayne,
Harold B. Guiver, Mark Itabashi, Rhoda Walsh
Open Pairs:
Flight A: Ed Nagy, Jeff Polisner
Flight B: Marilyn Enke, Anthony Franzese
Open Teams:
Flight A: Ron E. Andersen, Roger Bates, Benito Garozzo,
Mel Skolnik, Ron Smith *(tied with)*
Douglas Doub, Faith Fieldman,
Bernard Warshauer, Genie Warshauer
Flight B: Paul Boudreau, Don Gallaher,
Ed Piken, Eva Piken *(tied with)*
Gen Geiger, Don Von Elsner,
K. D. Von Elsner, M. G. Von Elsner *(and)*
Helene Beaulieu, Michel Lorber,
Patrice Roy, Ernie Szavay
Flight C: Rob Miller, Rai Osborne,
Gary Robinson, Ron Siegrist
Swiss Teams:
Flight A: Richard Lang, Darryl Pedersen,

Flight B: George Slemmons, George Steiner
Patty Bowman, Lin Goldstein,
John Theye, Bill Williges

Open Pairs:
Bobby Wolff, Deborah Wolff

For the award to the player gaining the greatest number of master points during the Fall NAC, see HERMAN TROPHY.

SPRING NORTH AMERICAN CHAMPIONSHIPS

VANDERBILT TROPHY. This originally was a DOUBLE ELIMINATION Open Team event scored by international matchpoints; usually nine or ten sessions. In 1966 the double elimination method was replaced by three qualifying sessions (subsequently reduced to two), followed by single elimination knockout matches. The preliminary qualifying sessions were dropped in 1970. In 1928 it was scored by Board-a-Match, hence the tie.

WINNERS

1928   1-2.   Ralph R. Richards, Gratz M. Scott,
Edwin A. Wetzlar, Wilbur C. Whitehead
    1-2.   Abraham Brown, Mrs. Sidney Lovell,
Caroline Taylor, Nils M. Wester
1929   1.   Michael T. Gottlieb, Lee Langdon,
John P. Mattheys, Harry B. Raffel
    2.   Ralph J. Leibenderfer, Gratz M. Scott,
Edwin A. Wetzlar, Wilbur C. Whitehead

1930   1.   Ely Culbertson, Josephine Culbertson,
Theodore A. Lightner, Waldemar K. von Zedtwitz
    2-3.   Winfield S. Liggett, Walter Malowan,
George Reith, Howard Schenken
    2-3.   H. Huber Boscowitz, Oswald Jacoby,
Willard S. Karn, P. Hal Sims
1931   1.   David Burnstine, Oswald Jacoby,
Willard S. Karn, P. Hal Sims
    2.   Walter Malowan, John P. Mattheys,
Howard Schenken, Sherman Stearns
1932   1.   Willard S. Karn, P. Hal Sims,
Harold S. Vanderbilt, Waldemar K. von Zedtwitz
    2.   David Burnstine, Richard L. Frey,
Charles S. Lochridge, Howard Schenken
1933   1.   Phil Abramsohn, Benjamin Feuer,
Francis A. Rendon, Sydney Rusinow
    2.   A. Mitchell Barnes, Richard L. Frey,
Sam Fry, Jr., Louis H. Watson
1934   1.   David Burnstine, Richard L. Frey, Michael Gottlieb,
Oswald Jacoby, Howard Schenken
    2.   H. Huber Boscowitz, Charles H. Goren,
Charles S. Lochridge, Johnny Rau
1935   1.   David Burnstine, Michael T. Gottlieb, Oswald Jacoby,
Howard Schenken, Sherman Stearns
    2.   Sam Fry, Jr., Edward Hymes, Jr.,
Merwyn D. Maier, Louis H. Watson
1936   1.   Phil Abramsohn, Irving Epstein,
Harry J. Fishbein, Fred D. Kaplan
    2.   Walter Beinicke, Charles H. Goren,
Lee Langdon, John P. Mattheys
1937   1.   David Burnstine, Oswald Jacoby, Merwyn D. Maier,
Howard Schenken, Sherman Stearns
    2.   B. Jay Becker, Theodore A. Lightner,
Charles S. Lochridge, Harold S. Vanderbilt,
Waldemar K. von Zedtwitz
1938   1.   David Burnstine, Oswald Jacoby, Merwyn D. Maier,
Howard Schenken, Sherman Stearns
    2.   B. Jay Becker, Edward Hymes, Jr.,
Theodore A. Lightner, Charles S. Lochridge,
Waldemar K. von Zedtwitz
1939   1.   Melville Alexander, Sigmund Dornbusch,
Syl Gintell, Lee Hazen, Harry B. Raffel
    2.   Wingate Bixby, Theodore A. Lightner,
Robert A. McPherran, Mrs. S. W. Peck
1940   1.   Edward Hymes, Jr., Charles S. Lochridge,
Robert A. McPherran, Harold S. Vanderbilt,
Waldemar von K. Zedtwitz
    2.   Al Brodsky, Louis Lipschitz,
Herbert Rosenzweig, Alexander Schultz

1941   1.   John R. Crawford, Myron Fuchs,
Robert A. McPherran, Sherman Stearns
    2.   B. Jay Becker, Oswald Jacoby, Theodore A. Lightner,
Merwyn D. Maier, Howard Schenken
1942   1.   Lester R. Bachner, Sigmund Dornbusch, Richard L. Frey,
Lee Hazen, Samuel M. Stayman
    2.   Sam Fry, Jr., Benedict Jarmel,
George Rapee, Helen Sobel
1943   1.   Harry Fagin, Harry J. Fishbein, Fred D. Kaplan,
Alvin Roth, Tobias Stone
    2.   Phil Abramsohn, Morrie Elis, E. O. Keller,
Charles E. Van Vleck, Waldemar K. Von Zedtwitz
1944   1.   B. Jay Becker, Charles H. Goren,
Sidney Silodor, Helen Sobel
    2.   Richard L. Frey, Lee Hazen, Charles S. Lochridge,
George Rapee, Samuel M. Stayman
1945   1.   B. Jay Becker, Charles H. Goren,
Sidney Silodor, Helen Sobel
    2.   Edward Hymes, Jr., Theodore A. Lightner,
Howard Schenken, Samuel M. Stayman,
Waldemar K. von Zedtwitz
1946   1.   John R. Crawford, Oswald Jacoby, George Rapee,
Howard Schenken, Samuel M. Stayman
    2.   Samuel Katz, Bertram Lebhar, Jr., Peter A. Leventritt,
Simon Rossant, Waldemar K. von Zedtwitz
1947   1.   David B. Clarren, Harry Feinberg, Harry J. Fishbein,
Larry Hirsch, Joseph Low
    2.   Lee Hazen, Samuel Katz,
Bertram Lebhar, Jr., Peter Leventritt
1948   1.   Robert Appleyard, Jay T. Feigus,
William M. Lichtenstein, Henry Sonnenblick,
Albert Weiss
    2.   Ambrose Casner, Herman H. Goldberg,
Fred Hirsch, Mrs. Ira Strasser, Albert Wolfe
1949   1.   Morrie Elis, Harry J. Fishbein, Lee Hazen,
Larry Hirsch, Charles S. Lochridge
    2.   B. Jay Becker, Myron Field, Charles H. Goren,
Oswald Jacoby, Helen Sobel
1950   1.   John R. Crawford, George Rapee, Howard Schenken,
Sidney Silodor, Samuel M. Stayman
    2.   B. Jay Becker, Myron Field,
Charles H. Goren, Helen Sobel
1951   1.   B. Jay Becker, John R. Crawford,
George Rapee, Samuel M. Stayman
    2.   Barry Crane, Jack Hancock, Emanuel Hochfield,
Gloria Turner, Hortense Evans
1952   1.   Ned Drucker, Irvin Kass, Sidney Mandell,
Milton Moss, Jesse Sloan
    2.   B. Jay Becker, John R. Crawford, George Rapee,
Howard Schenken, Samuel M. Stayman
1953   1.   Richard Kahn, Edgar Kaplan, Peter A. Leventritt,
William V. Lipton, Ruth Sherman
    2.   Myron Field, Charles H. Goren, Alvin Roth,
Sidney Silodor, Helen Sobel
1954   1.   Dr. Kalman Apfel, Francis P. Begley, Ned Drucker,
Sidney Mandell, Milton Moss
    2.   Morrie Elis, Stanley Fenkel, Simon Rossant,
Peggy Solomon, Charles S. Solomon
1955   1.   B. Jay Becker, John R. Crawford, George Rapee,
Howard Schenken, Sidney Silodor
    2.   Charles H. Goren, Boris Koytchou, Peter A. Leventritt,
Harold A. Ogust, Helen Sobel
1956   1.   B. Jay Becker, John R. Crawford, George Rapee,
Howard Schenken, Sidney Silodor
    2.   Leonard Hess, Jane Jaeger, Lewis M. Jaeger,
William Mason Lichtenstein, Joseph E. Low
1957   1.   B. Jay Becker, John R. Crawford, George Rapee,
Howard Schenken, Sidney Silodor
    2.   Rudolf Bortstiber, Raoul Lichtenstein,
Ozzie J. Ray, Moe Rubenfeld
1958   1.   Harry J. Fishbein, Sam Fry, Jr. Leonard B. Harmon,
Lee Hazen, Ivar Stakgold
    2.   Ralph Hirschberg, Richard Kahn, Edgar Kaplan,
Norman Kay, Alfred Sheinwold, Charles J. Solomon
1959   1.   B. Jay Becker, John R. Crawford, Norman Kay,
George Rapee, Sidney Silodor, Tobias Stone
    2.   Charles H. Goren, Paul Hodge, Peter A. Leventritt,
Harold A. Ogust, Howard Schenken, Helen Sobel
1960   1.   John R. Crawford, Norman Kay,
Sidney Silodor, Tobias Stone
    2.   Russell Arnold, Edith Kemp, Robert Reynolds,
William Seamon, Albert Weiss,
Waldemar K. von Zedtwitz
1961   1.   Charles Coon, Robert F. Jordan,

Eric R. Murray, Arthur G. Robinson
2. Ollie Adams, Harold B. Guiver, Eddie Kantar,
Marshall Miles, Ron Von der Porten
1962 1. Larry Kolker, Carolyn Levitt, Jerry Levitt,
Garrett Nash, George deRuntz
2. Charles H. Goren, Boris Koytchou, Peter A. Leventritt,
Harold A. Ogust, Howard Schenken, Helen Sobel
1963 1. Harold Harkavy, Edith Kemp, Alvin Roth,
Clifford Russell, William Seamon, Albert Weiss
2. Harold B. Guiver, Lewis L. Mathe, Erik Paulsen,
Ron Von der Porten, Edward O. Taylor
1964 1. Robert D. Hamman, Eddie Kantar, Donald P. Krauss,
Peter A. Leventritt, Lewis L. Mathe, Howard Schenken
2. B. Jay Becker, Ivan Erdos, Dorothy Hayden,
Kelsey Petterson, Helen Portugal, Morris Portugal
1965 1. Philip Feldesman, John Fisher, James Jacoby,
Oswald Jacoby, Ira S. Rubin, Albert Weiss
2 Robert F. Jordan, Edgar Kaplan, Norman Kay,
Boris Koytchou, George Rapee, Arthur G. Robinson
1966 1. Philip Feldesman, Robert D. Hamman,
Sammy R. Kehela Lewis L. Mathe, Ira S. Rubin
2. Billy Eisenberg, Ivan Erdos, Bobby Goldman,
Leonard B. Harmon, Tobias Stone
1967 1. James Jacoby, Michael S. Lawrence, Lewis L. Mathe,
G. Robert Nail, Ron Von der Porten, Lew Stansby
2. Sidney H. Lazard, Peter, A. Leventritt, Paul Levitt,
George Rapee, Howard Schenken
1968 1. Robert F. Jordan, Edgar Kaplan, Norman Kay,
Arthur G. Robinson, William S. Root, Alvin Roth
2. Robert D. Hamman, Eddie Kantar,
Ira S. Rubin, Gerald J. Westheimer
1969 1. Gerald F. Hallee, Paul Soloway,
John Swanson, Richard Walsh
2. Philip Feldesman, Victor Mitchell, Ira S. Rubin,
Samuel M. Stayman, Tobias Stone,
Gerald J. Westheimer
1970 1. Edgar Kaplan, Norman Kay, Sammy R. Kehela,
Sidney H. Lazard, Eric R. Murray, George Rapee
2. Billy Eisenberg, Bobby Goldman, Robert D. Hamman,
James Jacoby, Michael S. Lawrence, Bobby Wolff
1971 1. Billy Eisenberg, Bobby Goldman, Robert D. Hamman,
James Jacoby, Michael S. Lawrence, Bobby Wolff
2. Chuck F. Burger, Eddie Kantar, Kyle Larsen,
Ron Von der Porten, Ira S. Rubin, Paul Soloway
1972 1. Steven Altman, Eugene Neiger, Thomas M. Smith,
Alan Sontag, Joel H. Stuart, Peter Weichsel
2. Jack Blair, Fred Hamilton,
Howard M. Perlman, Paul Soloway
1973 1. Mark E. Blumenthal, Bobby Goldman,
Robert D. Hamman, Michael S. Lawrence, Bobby Wolff
2. Larry Cohen, Billy Eisenberg, Eddie Kantar,
Dr. Richard H. Katz, Bud Reinhold
1974 1. David M. Crossley, Robert E. Crossley,
Eric Kokish, Joseph Silver
2. Ron E. Andersen, Mark D. Feldman, Stephen Goldstein,
Merle Tom, Kathie Wei
1975 1. Roger Bates, Larry Cohen, Dr. Richard H. Katz,
John Mohan, George Rosenkranz
2. Richard Freeman, Alvin Roth, Clifford Russell,
Alan Sontag, Stan Tomchin, Peter Weichsel
1976 1. Roger Bates, Larry Cohen, Dr. Richard H. Katz,
John Mohan, George Rosenkranz
2. Malcolm Brachman, Billy Eisenberg, Bobby Goldman,
Eddie Kantar, Mike Passell, Paul Soloway
1977 1. Mike Becker, Mark E. Blumenthal, Fred Hamilton,
Michael S. Lawrence, Ron Rubin, John Swanson
2. Ron E. Andersen, Gerald Caravelli, Hugh C. MacLean,
Milt Rosenberg, Kathie Wei
1978 1. Malcolm Brachman, Bobby Goldman, Eddie Kantar,
Billy Eisenberg, Mike Passell, Paul Soloway
2. Mike Becker, Lou Bluhm, George Rosenkranz,
Ron Rubin, Thomas K. Sanders
1979 1. Lou Bluhm, Richard Freeman, Mark Lair,
Clifford Russell, Thomas K. Sanders, Eddie Wold
2. Ron E. Andersen, Dave Berkowitz,
Jeff Meckstroth, Judi Radin, Kathie Wei
1980 1. Russ Arnold, Bobby Levin, Jeff Meckstroth,
Bud Reinhold, Eric Rodwell
2. Ron E. Andersen, Mark Feldman,
Eric Kokish, Peter Nagy
1981 1. B. Jay Becker, Michael Becker, Edgar Kaplan,
Norman Kay, Ron Rubin
2. Ira Corn, Robert D. Hamman, Fred Hamilton,
Ira Rubin, Alan Sontag, Peter Weichsel, Bobby Wolff

1982 1. James Jacoby, Jeff Meckstroth, Mike Passell,
Eric Rodwell, George Rosenkranz, Eddie Wold
2. Marty Bergen, Mark Cohen, Jerry Goldfein,
Warren Rosner, Luella Slaner

MEN'S TEAMS.

MEN'S TEAMS. This event is contested for the GOREN TROPHY. It is a four-session Board-a-Match event with two qualifying rounds and two final rounds. It was contested as a three-session championship until 1972 and in 1975, held at the Fall North American Championships until 1963.

WINNERS

1946 1. Maynard Adams, Julius Bank, Arthur Glatt,
William McGhee, Albert Weiss
2. A. Mitchell Barnes, John R. Crawford,
Charles H. Goren, George Rapee, Sidney Silodor
1947 1. Jeff Glick, Arthur S. Goldsmith, Jack Kravatz,
Alvin Landy, Sol Mogal
2. Joseph Cohan, Dr. Louis Mark,
Dr. H. Russ Storr, George Unger
1948 1. Jack L. Ankus, Jeff Glick, Alvin Landy,
John H. Law, Sol Mogal
2. John R. Crawford, Edward N. Marcus,
George Rapee, Samuel M. Stayman
1949 1. Muriel Levin, Alphonse Moyse, Jr.,
Leo Roet, Howard Schenken
2. Joseph Cohan, Herbert J. Gerst, Jack L. Ankus,
William Joseph, Dr. H. Russ Storr
1950 1. Edward Burns, John F. Carlin,
David C. Carter, A. Richard Revell
2. Robert Appleyard, Ned Drucker, Fred Hirsch ,
Milton Moss, Milton Vernoff
1951 1. J. Van Brooks, Eugene Dautell, Jack Denny,
Ace Gutowsky, Edwin J. Smith
2. Fred L. Bickel, Joseph J. Foreacre,
Robert Lattomus, Ronald Rosenberg
1952 1. Charles H. Goren, Oswald Jacoby,
Sidney Silodor, Charles Solomon, Samuel M. Stayman
2-3. Samuel Katz, Charles Kuhn,
William Seamon Albert Weiss
2-3. Harry J. Fishbein, Harold Harkavy, Alvin Roth,
Tobias Stone, Waldemar K. von Zedtwitz
1953 1. Ben Fain, John Gerber, George Heath,
Paul H. Hodge, Harold Rockaway
2. Clifford W. Bishop, Harry J. Fishbein,
Arnold Kauder, John H. Moran, Douglas Steen
1954 1. Aaron J. Frank, Jeff Glick, Arthur S. Goldsmith,
Alvin Landy, Sol Mogal
2. Henry Chanin, Dr. John W. Fisher, James Jacoby,
Oswald Jacoby, Sidney H. Lazard
1955 1. Richard Freeman, Edgar Kaplan, Ralph Hirschberg,
Norman Kay, Alvin Roth
2. Charles H. Goren, Peter A. Leventritt,
Charles J. Solomon, Samuel M. Stayman
1956 1. John R. Crawford, Ben Fain,
Paul H. Hodge, Sidney Silodor
2-3. Paul Allinger, Dr. John W. Fisher, Emanuel Hochfeld,
Oswald Jacoby, Sidney H. Lazard
2-3. Barry Crane, Harold Rockaway,
Clarence A. Strouse, John H. Toledano
1957 1. Lewis L. Mathe, Donald A. Oakie,
Meyer Schleifer, Edward O. Taylor
2. Israel Cohen, Richard Freeman, John C. Kunkel,
Alvin Roth, Ivar Stakgold
1958 1. Jeff Glick, Arthur S. Goldsmith, Alvin Landy,
Elmer I. Schwartz, Vic D. Zeve
2. Richard Freeman, Edgar Kaplan,
Norman Kay, Ralph Hirschberg
1959 1. Ollie Adams, Ivan Erdos
Oswald Jacoby, Robert G. Sharp
2. B. Jay Becker, John R. Crawford
Sidney Silodor, Tobias Stone
1960 1. Charles Denby, Burrell I. Humphreys
Alan W. Messer, Marty Scheinberg,
Robert P. Wakeman
2-4. Harry J. Fishbein, John Gerber,
Paul H. Hodge, Charles J. Solomon
2-4. Wilfred Dumas, Donald McGee,
John Siverts, Jerzy Zawisza
2-4. James R. Hughes, Marvin Paulshock
Eli Reich, David R. Treadwell
1961 1. John R. Crawford, Norman Kay, Alvin Roth
Sidney Silodor, Tobias Stone

2. Edgar Kaplan, Mervin Key
Sidney H. Lazard, G. Robert Nail

1962 1-2. Philip Feldesman, Richard Freeman, Victor Mitchell,
Eric R. Murray, Samuel M. Stayman

1-2. Paul Allinger, Harold G. Guiver,
Lewis L. Mathe, Edward O. Taylor

1963 1. Philip Feldesman, Victor Mitchell
Samuel M. Stayman, Tobias Stone

2. B. Jay Becker, Norman Kay, William Root
Sol Rubinow, Sidney Silodor

1964 1. Ivan Erdos, Harold B. Guiver
Michael S. Lawrence, Alfred Sheinwold

2. Charles Coon, G. Robert Nail
Robert Stucker, Frank T. Westcott

1965 1. Harry J. Fishbein, Jeff Rubens
Charles J. Solomon, Roger D. Stern

2. Philip Feldesman, Sidney H. Lazard, Victor Mitchell,
Daniel Rotman, Samuel M. Stayman

1966 1. Philip Feldesman, Richard Freeman,
Edgar Kaplan, Norman Kay

2. Anthony Dionisi, Jeremy Flint,
Harlow S. Lewis, Peter A. Pender

1967 1. Thomas E. Bussey, Jim R. Dunlap,
Lawrence Jolma, Robert P. Patterson, Gary Stark

2. Edward J. Barlow, Phil Read,
Robert Spots, John C. Sutherlin

1968 1. Ira G. Corn, Jr., Billy Eisenberg, Bobby Goldman,
James Jacoby, Michael S. Lawrence, Bobby Wolff

2. Michael M. Becker, Charles Coon, Joel H. Stuart,
Peter Weichsel, Richard J. Zeckhauser

1969 1. Chuck F. Burger, James Cayne,
Alvin Roth, Paul Trent

2-3. Billy Eisenberg, Bobby Goldman, Robert D. Hamman,
James Jacoby, Michael S. Lawrence, Bobby Wolff

2-3. Martin J. Cohn, Norman H. Fischer,
Charles M. MacCracken, Bill Reister

1970 1. Bernie Bergovoy, Donald P. Krauss, Lewis L. Mathe,
Don Pearson, John Swanson, Richard Walsh

2. Eddie Kantar, Kyle Larson,
Paul Soloway, Ron Von der Porten

1971 1. Bernie Chazen, Alvin Roth,
Alan Sontag, Paul Trent

2. Gerald Caravelli, Larry Cohen,
Barry Crane, Dr. John Fisher

1972 1. Jack Blair, James Jacoby, John Simon,
Paul Swanson, Bobby Wolff

2. Grant S. Baze, William Grieve, Donald P. Krauss,
Lewis L. Mathe, Peter A. Pender, George Rapee

1973 1. Garey Hayden, James Jacoby, Gaylor Kasle,
John Simon, Bobby Wolff

2-3. Lou Bluhm, Steve Goldberg,
Lawrence Gould, Stephen Robinson

2-3. John R. Crawford, Norm Kurlanders, Alvin Roth,
Clifford Russell, William Seamon

1974 1. Ron E. Andersen, Mark Feldman, Stephen Goldstein,
Hugh C. MacLean, Merle Tom

2-3. Eric Kokish, Stephen Robinson,
Mike Shuman, Joseph Silver

2-3. Harold B. Guiver, Marty Shallon,
William Sides, Mike Smolen

1975 1. Matt Granovetter, William Grieve,
George Rapee, Ronald Rubin

2. Roger Bates, Edgar Kaplan,
Norman Kay, George Rosenkranz

1976 1. David Ashley, Paul Heitner,
John Lowenthal, Mike Smolen

2. Bart Bramley, Marvin Herbert,
Howard Piltch, Lou Reich, Ira S. Rubin

1977 1. Lou Bluhm, Richard Doughty, Bruce Ferguson,
Irv Kostal, Sidney H. Lazard, Ron Smith, Leslie West

2. Richard Freeman, Alvin Roth, Clifford Russell,
Curtis K. Smith, Merle Tom, Art Waldmann

1978 1. Neil Chambers, Eric Kokisk, Peter Nagy,
Stephen Robinson, John Schermer, Kit Woolsey

2. Steve Garner, Dave Lehman,
Dick Melson, Larry Oakey

1979 1. Allan Cokin, Steve Sion, Alan Sontag,
Jim Sternberg, Peter Weichsel

2. Mike Cappelletti, Ron Feldman, Gary Hann,
David Hoffner, Zeke Jabbour, David Sacks

1980 1. Bart Bramley, Ross Grabel, William Rosen,
Milton Rosenberg, Samuel Stayman, George Tornay

2. Ira Corn, Fred Hamilton,
Robert D. Hamman, Ira Rubin, Bobby Wolff

1981 1. Marty Bergen, Neil Chambers,
Joseph Silver, Allan Stauber

2. Michael Aliotta, Marc Culbertson,
Jim Gardner, Bert Newman

1982 1. Dave Berkowitz, Matt Granovetter,
Harold Lilie, Al Rand

2. Robert Blanchard, Drew Casen,
Chuck Lamprey, Thomas M. Smith

WOMEN'S TEAMS. This event is contested for the COFFIN TROPHY. Until 1976 it was a four-session event scored by Board-a-Match; contested as a three-session championship until 1972 and in 1975; held at the Fall North American Championships until 1963. In 1976 the event became a North American Championship Women's Knockout with Swiss qualifying.

WINNERS

1933 1. Mrs. Greene Fenley, Jr., Mrs. Richard Field,
Mrs. John W. Friedlander, Jane Wallace

2. Mollie Funk, Ethel Gardner,
Marguerite Hoffmeier, Marie White

1934 1. Gail Hamilton, Marguerite Hoffmeier,
Helen Pendelton Rockwell, Anne Rosenfeld

2. Elizabeth Banfield, Phyllis Gardner,
Eva Gross, Dorothy Roberts

1935 1. Doris Fuller, Angela Quigley,
Florence Stratford, Helen White

2. Gail Hamilton, Marguerite Hoffmeier,
Helen Pendelton Rockwell, Anne Rosenfeld

1936 1. Doris Fuller, Angela Quigley,
Florence Stratford, Helen White

2. Marge Anderson, Mrs. J. A. Faulkner,
Marjorie Haldeman, Mrs. G. Keedick

1937 1. Martha Lemon, Mrs. A. Philip Stockvis,
Mrs. Martin West, Sally Young

2. Doris Fuller, Angela Quigley,
Helen Sobel, Florence Stratford

1938 1. Mrs. Galloway Morris, Lillian Peck,
Olive Peterson, Mrs. Donald B. Tansill

2. Mariquita Fullerton, Mollie Funk,
Ann Rosenfeld, Lucille Schwarz

1939 1. Mabel Ervin, Doris Fuller,
Helen Mitchell, Helen Sobel,
Sally Young

2. Sylvia DeYoung, Margaret Katzen,
Catherine W. Samberg, Florence Stratford

1940 1. Helen Levy, Adelaide Neuwirth,
Margaret Wagar, Lottie Zetosch

2. Ruth Horn, Olga Hilliard,
Marguerite McKenney, Gussie Planco

1941 1. Inez Buchannan, Mae Dickens,
Mabel Scott, Linda Terry

2. Doris Fuller, Mrs. Joseph M. Rothschild,
Helen Sobel, Sally Young

1942 1. Peggy Golder, Olga Hilliard,
Olive Peterson, Ruth Sherman

2. Emily Folline, Doris Fuller,
Ethel Gardner, Helen Sobel

1943 1. Emily Folline, Helen Sobel,
Margaret Wagar, Sally Young

2. Eleanor Hirsch, Evelyn Lebhar,
Marguerite McKenney, Florence Stratford

1944 1. Emily Folline, Helen Sobel,
Margaret Wagar, Sally Young

2. Mrs. Mark Godfrey, Mrs. C. W. Neeld,
Dorothy Sullivan, Anne H. Todd

1945 1. Emily Folline, Helen Sobel,
Margaret Wagar, Sally Young

2. Josephine Gutman, Gratian Goldstein,
Marjorie Perlmutter, Gretchen Schildmiller

1946 1. Emily Folline, Helen Sobel,
Margaret Wagar, Sally Young

2. Paula Bacher, Marie Basher,
Jane Jaeger, Pauline Shmukler

1947 1-2. Marge Anderson, Ruby Lyons,
Mimi Roncarelli, Jane Wallace

1-2. Cass Illig, Frances Robinson,
Alma Stewart, Carolyn Sondheim

1948 1. Ruth Gordon, Gratian Goldstein,
Josephine Gutman, Charlotte Sidway

2. Ruth Gilbert, Olive Peterson,
   Edith Seligman, Ruth Sherman,
   Peggy Solomon
1949 1-2. Hortense Evans, Frances Robinson,
   Mrs. Henry Sabatt, Carolyn Sondheim
   1-2. Marianne Boschan, Catherine Cotter,
   Gertrude Eberson, Katherine McNutt
1950 1. Marge Anderson, Mary Bowden,
   Ruth Gordon, G. Eloise Neil
   2-5. Olive Peterson, Ruth Sherman,
   Helen Sobel, Margaret Wagar
   2-5. Shirley Fairchild, Mrs. Ezra Feldman,
   Rose Groves, Luise Mathews,
   Claire Meyer
   2-5. Margaret Byrd, Isabelle Garn,
   Virginia Ploehn, Billy Traveletti
   2-5. Inez Buchanan, Zodie Glover,
   Sally Herman, Mabel Scott
1951 1. Paula Bacher, Anne Burnstein,
   Dolly Rosenfeld, Edith Seligman,
   Sally Young
   2. Thelma Hathorn, Mollie Steiner,
   Agatha Tiernan, Clara Tiernan,
   Mary Elizabeth Tiernan
1952 1. Jackie Begin, Sally Herman,
   Jessie S. Moore, Norma Matz
   2-3. Peggy Adams, Helen Baker,
   Marguerite Harris, Ethel Keohane
   2-3. Kay Rhodes, Ruth Sherman,
   Helen Sobel, Margaret Wagar
1953 1. Gretchen Feldstein, Vera Glick,
   Gratian Goldstein, Lucille Schwarz
   2-3. Mary Jane Kauder, Kay Rhodes,
   Ruth Sherman, Margaret Wagar
   2-3. Elaine Lee, Olive Peterson,
   Roberta Sheronas, Peggy Solomon
1954 1. Wynne Ecker, Doris Fuller,
   Marguerite Harris, Norma Matz
   2-5. Marguerite Bouldin, Lillian Hassler,
   Ann Jervis, Dorothy Payne
   2-5. Marie Cohn, Olive Peterson,
   Pauline Shmukler, Peggy Solomon
   2-5. Kay Rhodes, Ruth Sherman,
   Helen Sobel, Margaret Wagar
   2-5. Margaret Alcorn, Louise Eisenman,
   Emily Folline, Sue Reith
1955 1. Peggy Adams, Carolyn Brall,
   Louise Eisenman, Shirley Johnson,
   Juanita Strich
   2-4. Kay Rhodes, Ruth Sherman,
   Helen Sobel, Margaret Wagar
   2-4. Ann Burnstein, Edith Kemp,
   Paula Levin, Ruth Steinberg,
   Sally Young
   2-4. Ruth Gordon, Josephine Gutman,
   Evelyn Engleman, Margaret Katzen,
   G. Eloise Neil
1956 1. Peggy Rotzell, Jan Stone,
   Charlotte Sidway, Mary Elizabeth Tiernan
   2. Kay Rhodes, Helen Sobel,
   Margaret Wagar, Sally Young
1957 1. Marie Cohn, Mary Jane Kauder,
   Stella Rebner, Peggy Solomon
   2. Agnes Gordon, Kay Rhodes,
   Helen Sobel, Margaret Wagar
1958 1. Carolyn Brall, Bee Gale,
   Sally Johnson, Peggy Rotzell
   2. Kay Rhodes, Helen Sobel,
   Margaret Wagar, Sally Young
1959 1. Margaret Alcorn, Lee Kasle,
   Josephine Sharp, Adelaide Simon,
   Garner McDaniel
   2. Kay Dunn, Jane Herb, Malvine Klausner,
   Helen Portugal, Rose Reif
1960 1. Roberta Erde, Sally Johnson,
   Barbara Kachmar, Bee Schenken
   2. Joan Remey, Helen Shanbrom,
   Sylvia Stein, Marge Stone
1961 1. Roberta Erde, Sally Johnson,
   Barbara Kachmar, Bee Schenken
   2. Mary Jane Farell, Terry Michaels,
   Peggy Solomon, Jan Stone
1962 1. Anne Burnstein, Edith Kemp, Alicia Kempner,
   Stella Rebner, Teddie Warner
   2. Muriel Kaplan, Terry Michaels,
   Garner McDaniel, Jan Stone

1963 1. Pat Adler, Terry Michaels,
   Garner McDaniel, Cora Sanders, Sylvia Stein
   2. Dorothy Hayden, Barbara Kachmar,
   Agnes Gordon, Helen Portugal, Margaret Wagar
1964 1. Hermine Baron, Mary Jane Farell,
   Peggy Solomon, Bee Schenken
   2. Agnes Gordon, Dorothy Hayden,
   Helen Portugal, Margaret Wagar
1965 1. Virginia Heckel, Betty Kaplan,
   Edith Kemp, Jacqui Mitchell
   2. Debbie Polak, Joan Remey,
   Carol Ruther, Sylvia Stein
1966 1-2. Frieda Arst, June Deutsch,
   Sylvia Stein, Carol Stolkin
   1-2. Nancy Gruver, Garner McDaniel,
   Terry Michaels, Sue Sachs
1967 1. Dorothy Hayden, Emma Jean Hawes,
   Agnes Gordon, Margaret Wagar
   2-3. Hermine Baron, Mary Jane Farell,
   Bee Schenken, Peggy Solomon
   2-3. Dolores Bick, Jude Ballard,
   Ruth Needham, Viola Kirkwood
1968 1. Hermine Baron, Mary Jane Farell, Sally Johnson,
   Bee Schenken, Peggy Solomon, Rhoda Walsh
   2. Jane Frankel, Teddy O'Brien,
   Mary Beth Townsend, Esta Van Zandt
1969 1. Karen Allison, Virginia Heckel, Edith Kemp,
   Alicia Kempner, Helen Portugal, Jan Stone
   2. Nancy Gruver, Barbara Rappaport,
   Sue Sachs, Barbara Tepper
1970 1. Mary Jane Farell, Emma Jean Hawes, Dorothy Hayden,
   Marilyn Johnson, Jacqui Mitchell, Peggy Solomon
   2. Dorothy Cowger, Diane Hawes,
   Florence Van Winkle, Freda Van Cleve
1971 1. Judi Friedenberg, Gail Moss, Marietta Passell,
   Helen Utegaard, Kathie Wei
   2. Roberta Epstein, Gretchen Goldstein, Edith Kemp,
   Barbara Rappaport, Sylvia Stein
   Sylvia Stein
1972 1. Mary Jane Farell, Emma Jean Hawes,
   Dorothy Hayden, Sue Picus
   2. Frieda Arst, June Deutsch,
   Eunice Rosen, Carol Stolkin
1973 1. Nancy Gruver, Terry Michaels,
   Jo Morse, Helen Utegaard
   2-4. Nancy Alpaugh, Fran Beard,
   Heitie Noland, Betsey Wolff,
   Esta Van Zandt
   2-4. Mary Jane Farell, Marilyn Johnson, Jacqui Mitchell,
   Gail Moss, Marietta Passell, Kathie Wei
   2-4. Jean Christopher, Muriel Peterson,
   Beverly Rosenberg, Elaine Sternberg
1974 1. Mary Jane Farell, Emma Jean Hawes, Marilyn Johnson,
   Jacqui Mitchell, Gail Moss, Dorothy Hayden Truscott
   2. Hermine Baron, Carol Greenhut,
   Trudi Nugit, Kerri Shuman
1975 1. Mary Jane Farell, Emma Jean Hawes, Marilyn Johnson,
   Jacqui Mitchell, Gail Moss, Dorothy Hayden Truscott
   2. Anita Davis, Mildred Freedman,
   Robin Grantham, Carol Klar
1976 1. Mary Jane Farell, Emma Jean Hawes, Marilyn Johnson,
   Jacqui Mitchell, Gail Moss, Dorothy Hayden Truscott
   2. Evelyn Levitt, Lila Perlstein,
   Helen Smith, Vivian Whalen
1977 1. Betty Adler, Jo Morse,
   Judi Radin, Sue Sachs
   2. Ida Bennett, Mary Lou Cushner,
   Carole Felczer, Ethel Keohane
1978 1. Nancy Alpaugh, Nancy Gruver, Betty Ann Kennedy,
   Evelyn Levitt, Carol Sanders, Kerri Shuman
   2. Cheri Bjerkan, Sue Halperin,
   Beverly Nelson, Florine Waters
1979 1. Betty Adler, Anne Burnstein, Edith Kemp,
   Terry Michaels, Jo Morse, Sue Sachs
   2. Cheri Bjerkan, June Deutsch, Sue Halperin,
   Sandi Levitt, Beverly Nelson, Florine Walters
1980 1. Nancy Gruver, Edith Kemp, Betty Ann Kennedy,
   Judi Radin, Carol Sanders, Kathie Wei
   2. Betty Adler, Pat Lapides, Pat Leary, Terry Michaels,
   Jo Morse, Jan Stansby
1981 1. June Deutsch, Pat Lapides, Sandi Leavitt,
   Evelyn Levitt, Jo Morse, Helen Utegaard
   2. Karen Allison, Cheri Bjerkan, Lynn Deas,
   Dianna Gordon, Sue Halperin, Sharyn Kokish
1982 1. Stasha Cohen, Mary Jane Farell, Nancy Gruver,

　　　　Edith Kemp, Randi Montin, Dorothy Hayden Truscott
2.　Betty Ann Kennedy, Jacqui Mitchell, Gail Moss,
　　Judi Radin, Carol Sanders, Kathie Wei

OPEN PAIRS.

OPEN PAIRS. This four-session event consisting of two qualifying sessions and two final sessions is contested for the SILODOR TROPHY.

WINNERS

1958	1.	Leonard B. Harmon, Ivar Stakgold
	2.	Alvin Roth, Tobias Stone
1959	1.	Lewis L. Mathe, Edward O. Taylor
	2.	Harry J. Fishbein, Charles J. Solomon
1960	1.	Robert F. Jordan, Alvin Roth
	2.	Carol Sanders, Thomas K. Sanders
1961	1.	Mark Hodges, Hampton Hume
	2.	Jack Denny, John E. Simon
1962	1.	Robert F. Jordan, Arthur G. Robinson
	2.	Michael N. Michaels, Mike Shuman
1963	1.	Norman Kay, Sidney Silodor
	2.	Daniel Rotman, Ivar Stakgold
1964	1.	Barry Crane, Oswald Jacoby
	2.	Ivan Erdos, Lewis L. Mathe
1965	1.	John Biddle, James P. Wisemiller
	2.	Ivan Erdos, Tobias Stone
1966	1.	Edgar Kaplan, Norman Kay
	2.	Alvin Roth, William Root
1967	1.	Harvey Cohen, Maury Genud
	2.	Philip Feldesman, Lewis L. Mathe
1968	1.	Ronald Blau, Richard Spero
	2.	Harry J. Fishbein, Charles J. Solomon
1969	1.	Richard Freedman, James L. Mathis
	2.	David Sachs, Sue Sachs
1970	1.	Barry Crane, Dr. John Fisher
	2.	Gerald L. Michaud, G. Robert Nail
1971	1-2.	Barry Crane, Dr. John Fisher
	1-2.	Joan Remey, Vincent Remey
1972	1-2.	Barry Crane, Dr. John Fisher
	1-2.	Matt Granovetter, Merle Tom
1973	1.	Michael Hoffman, Jack Rhatigan
	2.	Charlie Peres, Daniel Rotman
1974	1.	Barry Crane, Dr. John Fisher
	2.	Ron E. Andersen, Hugh C. MacLean
1975	1.	Garey Hayden, Daniel Hyland
	2.	Don Piafsky, Dave Saltsman
1976	1.	Terry Hause, Ernest Ivey
	2.	Barry Crane, Dr. John Fisher
1977	1.	Barry Crane, Peter Rank
	2.	John Ashton, Troy Horton
1978	1.	Bobby Levin, Mike Passell
	2.	Marty Arndt, Thomas Peters
1979	1.	Jeff Meckstroth, Eric Rodwell
	2.	Larry N. Cohen, Dan Zirker
1980	1.	Paul J. Lewis, Michael Schreiber
	2.	Jim Robison, Stelios Touchtidis
1981	1.	Dan Gerstman, Marc Nathan
	2.	Ed Manfield, Kit Woolsey
1982	1.	Gerald Caravelli, V. Craig Janitschke
	2.	Dan Gertsman, Marc Nathan

MEN'S PAIRS.

MEN'S PAIRS. This four-session event consisting of two qualifying rounds and two final rounds is contested for the WERNHER TROPHY. From 1969 through 1971 it was contested as a three-session championship.

WINNERS

1934	1.	David Burnstine, Oswald Jacoby
	2.	Morrie Elis, George Kennedy
1935	1.	Edward M. Cook, Jr., Fred French
	2.	Charles H. Goren, Louis H. Watson
1936	1.	Dr. Richard H. Ecker, Fred D. Kaplan
	2.	Bertram Lebhar, Jr., Samuel Katz
1937	1.	Edward M. Cook, Jr., John C. Kunkle
	2.	Philip Abramsohn, Morrie Elis
1938	1.	B. Jay Becker, Charles H. Goren
	2.	Morrie Elis, Waldemar K. von Zedtwitz

1939	1.	John R. Crawford, Oswald Jacoby
	2.	Henry Chanin, Morrie Elis
1940	1.	Merwyn D. Maier, Robert A. McPherran
	2.	Morrie Elis, Harry J. Fishbein
1941	1.	Joseph E. Low, Simon Rossant
	2.	Joseph Davis, Sidney Silodor
1942	1.	Robert von Engel, Aaron Goodman
	2.	Murray Gross, Dr. William Lipton
1943	1.	Charles H. Goren, Charles J. Solomon
	2.	Dr. Richard H. Ecker, Jr., Fred D. Kaplan
1944	1.	Sigmund Dornbusch, Herman Goldberg
	2.	Ambrose Casner, Ralph Hirschberg
1945	1.	Sylvester Gintell, Lee Hazen
	2.	George Rapee, Samuel M. Stayman
1946	1.	A. Mitchell Barnes, Waldemar K. von Zedtwitz
	2.	Lewis A. Bernard, Jr., Frank Weisbach
1947	1.	Sol Mogal, Tobias Stone
	2.	Morrie Elis, Morris Portugal
1948	1.	Fred Hirsch, Samuel Katz
	2.	Lewis A. Bernard, Jr., Harold Feldstein
1947	1.	Charles H. Goren, Oswald Jacoby
	2.	G. Robert Nail, J. P. Ripstra
1950	1.	Phillip A. Briggs, A. Richard Revell
	2.	George Rapee, Sidney Silodor
1951	1.	Milton Q. Ellenby, Emanuel Hochfield
	2.	Clifford Bishop, Alexander Nusinoff
1952	1.	Arthur C. Grau, William A. Rosen
	2.	Harold Harkavy, Tobias Stone
1953	1.	Harold Harkavy, William Root
	2.	John R. Crawford, Waldemar K. von Zedtwitz
1954	1.	Douglas Drury, Eric R. Murray
	2.	Milton Q. Ellenby, Douglas Steen
1955	1.	Douglas Drury, Eric R. Murray
	2.	Ira S. Rubin, Victor Mitchell
1956	1.	Paul Allinger, James Jacoby
	2.	Robert F. Jordan, Robert Sitnek
1957	1.	David C. Carter, John W. Hubbell
	2.	John Gerber, Paul H. Hodge
1958	1.	William Grieve, Ira S. Rubin
	2.	Norman Kay, Sidney Silodor
1959	1.	Harry J. Fishbein, John Gerber
	2.	Erik Paulsen, Mike Shuman
1960	1.	Jack Blair, William Christian
	2.	David C. Carter, Paul H. Hodge
1961	1.	Philip Feldesman, Ira S. Rubin
	2.	Paul Allinger, Lewis L. Mathe
1962	1.	Philip Feldesman, Ira S. Rubin
	2.	Eddie Kantar, Marshall Miles
1963	1.	Sammy R. Kehela, B. Wolf Lebovic
	2.	Alphonse Moyse, Jr., Thomas K. Sanders
1964	1.	Ed Don Weiner, G. Gard Hays
	2.	Darryl Pederson, Don Nemiro
1965	1.	Lawrence Rosler, Jeff Rubens
	2.	Eric R. Murray, Norman Kay
1966	1.	Barry Crane, Peter C. Rank
	2.	Mark Blumenthal, Michael Moss
1967	1.	Richard Lawrence, Art Price
	2.	Eddie Kantar, Sidney Lazard
1968	1.	Kyle Larsen, Edmond Lazarus
	2.	William Passell, David Strasberg
1969	1.	Michael J. Martino, Frank Vine
	2.	Gerald Hallee, Paul Soloway
1970	1.	Richard Kaye, Richard Walsh
	2.	Edgar Kaplan, Norman Kay
1971	1.	Giorgio Belladonna, Benito Garozzo
	2.	Robert Kerr, Jay T. McKee
1972	1.	Stephen W. Robinson, Kit Woolsey
	2.	Paul Heitner, Marshall Miles
1973	1.	Jack E. Kennedy, David Hadden
	2.	Stephen W. Robinson, Kit Woolsey
1974	1.	George Slemmons, George Steiner
	2.	Stephen W. Robinson, Kit Woolsey
1975	1.	Harlow Lewis, Art Waldemann
	2.	Larry Kozlove, John Sheridan
1976	1.	Gerald Caravelli, Larry Cohen
	2.	Jack E. Kennedy, Bobby Wolff
1977	1.	Joseph Fox, Garey Hayden
	2.	David Lehman, Dick Melson
1978	1.	Larry Kozlove, John Sheridan

    2.   Roy Fox, Paul Swanson
1979 1.   Roy Fox, Paul Swanson
    2.   Perry Johnson, Michael Zerbini
1980 1.   Neil Silverman, Peter Weichsel
    2.   Warren Rosner, Stephen Sanborn
1981 1.   Warren Rosner, Allan Stauber
    2.   Billy Eisenberg, Neil Silverman
1982 1.   David Berkowitz, Harold Lilie
    2.   James Barlow, Chuck Carroll

This event was held in the Summer North American Championships until 1963. A similar event was held at the Spring NACs 1958–1962 with the following results:

WINNERS

1958 1.   Norman Kay, Sidney Silodor
    2.   Jack Denny, Richard Harrison
1959 1.   James Pestaner, John Swanson
    2.   Donald A. Oakie, Meyer Schleifer
1960 1.   Frank Hoadley, Julius L. Rosenblum
    2.   Harold Creed, S. Samuel Gould, Jr.
1961 1.   Morton Rubinow, Tobias Stone
    2.   Erik Paulsen, Alex Tschekaloff
1962 1.   Ivan Erdos, Philip Feldesman
    2.   Norman Kay, Sidney Silodor

WOMEN'S PAIRS. This four-session event consisting of two qualifying rounds and two final rounds is contested for the WHITEHEAD TROPHY. From 1969 through 1971 it was contested as a three-session championship.

WINNERS

1930 1.   Olive Peterson, Maud S. Zontlein
    2.   Josephine Culbertson, Elinor Murdoch
1931 1.   Vivi Hanson, Elinor Murdoch
    2.   Mary Clement, Olga Hilliard
1932 1.   Mrs. Jay S. Jones, Olive Peterson
    2.   Florence Fitch, Maud S. Zontlein
1933 1.   Doris Fuller, Mrs. Courtand Smith
    2.   Marie Black, Mary Clement
1934 1.   Helen Bonwit, Matie White
    2.   Ruth Sherman, Mrs. Thomas Stern
1935 1.   Bertine Teichman, Mable Ulbrich
    2.   Doris Fuller, Olive Peterson
1936 1.   Mrs. Jay S. Jones, Sally Young
    2.   Mable Ervin, Doris Fuller
1937 1.   Mable Ervin, Doris Fuller
    2.   Martha Lemon, Mrs. Martin R. West
1938 1.   Helen Sobel, Sally Young
    2.   Phyllis Gardner, Dorothy Roberts
1939 1.   Helen Sobel, Sally Young
    2.   Doris Fuller, Millicent Tansill
1940 1.   Edith Atkinson, Mrs. John Waidlich
    2.   Estelle Drescher, Gussie Planco
1941 1.   Mae P. Rosen, Edith Seligman
    2.   Ruth Horn, Gussie Planco
1942 1.   Mae P. Rosen, Edith Seligman
    2.   Helen Bonwit, Mrs. D. P. Hanson
1943 1.   Mae P. Rosen, Edith Seligman
    2.   Olga Hilliard, Evelyn Lebhar
1944 1.   Ruth Sherman, Margaret Wagar
    2.   Paula Bacher, Kay Rhodes
1945 1.   Peggy Golder, Olive Peterson
    2.   Ruth Sherman, Margaret Wagar
1946 1.   Edith Seligman, Sally Young
    2.   Anne Bernstein, Mrs. G. Rosenbaum
1947 1.   Gratian Goldstein, Josephine Gutman
    2.   Ruth Sherman, Helen Sobel
1948 1.   Gratian Goldstein, Josephine Gutman
    2.   Mildred Cunningham, Mrs. Harry Mason Smith
1949 1.   Kay Rhodes, Ruth Sherman
    2.   Mildred Cunningham, Mrs. Harry Mason Smith
1950 1.   Mrs. John Kelly, Dorothy Thompson
    2.   Reba Buck, Mrs. George P. Ryan
1951 1.   Alwina M. Dunphy, Mrs. Edward Minear
    2.   Mrs. Frank Fooshe, Mrs. Henry C. Wolfe
1952 1.   Shirley Fairchild, Elaine Lee

    2.   Mildred Betzler, Mrs. Michael Hoffman
1953 1.   Mrs. Harold P. Swearingen, Barbara Weiner
    2.   Gretchen Feldstein, Gratian Goldstein
1954 1.   Margaret Alcorn, Sally Neely
    2.   Paula Levin, Mrs. Max Ritter
1955 1.   Kay Rhodes, Margaret Wagar
    2.   Mrs. Carl I. Conklin, Paula Nevins
1956 1.   Kay Rhodes, Margaret Wagar
    2.   Wynne Ecker, Mrs P. Halbestadt
1957 1.   Kay Rhodes, Margaret Wagar
    2.   Edith Kemp, Terry Michaels
1958 1.   Betty Nail, Phyllis Novak
    2.   Alberta Albersheim, Mrs. M. J. Root
1959 1.   Betty Adler, Dorothy Hayden
    2.   Agnes Gordon, Sylvia Schwartz
1960 1.   Mary Jane Farell, Peggy Solomon
    2.   Mabel Mahoney, Mrs. James Welch
1961 1.   Ruth Gordon, Betty Haddad
    2.   Mrs. Seymour Keith, Rita Seamon
1962 1.   Carol Sanders, Sylvia Stein
    2.   Betty Kaplan, Jacqui Mitchell
1963 1.   Mrs. K. L. Sargent, Mrs. Ray Tobin
    2.   Garner McDaniel, Terry Michaels
1964 1.   Margaret Alcorn, Lucille Patterson
    2.   Ruth Ballantyne, Mrs. Lloyd Scott
1965 1.   Nancy Gruver, Sue Sachs
    2.   Alicia Kempner, Helen Sobel
1966 1.   Virginia Heckel, Edith Kemp
    2.   Garner McDaniel, Terry Michaels
1967 1.   Garner McDaniel, Terry Michaels
    2.   Hermine Baron, Marilyn Johnson
1968 1.   Hermine Baron, Rhoda Walsh
  2-3.   Emma Jean Hawes, Dorothy Hayden
  2-3.   Gloria Cohen, Belle Kauffman
1969 1.   Gale Clarke, Gloria Noszka
    2.   Sallie Johnson, Bee Schenken
1970 1.   Robin Klar, Tina Rockaway
    2.   Jacqui Mitchell, Gail Moss
1971 1.   Amalya L. Kearse, Jacqui Mitchell
    2.   Barbara Brier, Betsey Wolff
1972 1.   Kerri Davis, Rhoda Walsh
    2.   Gail Moss, Judi Solodar
1973 1.   Ann Economidy, Vivian Williamson
    2.   Mary Anderson, Pamela Eckard
1974 1.   Pat Leary, Jan Stansby
    2.   Jacqui Mitchell, Gail Moss
1975 1.   Jacqui Mitchell, Gail Moss
    2.   Hermine Baron, Carol Greenhut
1976 1.   Gail Schaab, Barbara Staton
    2.   Emma Jean Hawes, Dorothy Hayden Truscott
1977 1.   Jacqui Mitchell, Gail Moss
    2.   Hermine Baron, Beverly Rosenberg
1978 1.   Babs Charney, Flo Rotman
    2.   Edith Kemp, Barbara Rappaport
1979 1.   Anne Burnstein, Edith Kemp
    2.   Ann Roberts, Genne Winter
1980 1.   Mildred Boyce, Barbara Norwood
    2.   Hermine Baron, Beverly Rosenberg
1981 1.   Emma Jean Hawes, Dorothy Hayden Truscott
    2.   Roberta Epstein, Rozanne Marel
1982 1.   Hermine Baron, Beverly Rosenberg
    2.   Nancy Alpaugh, Betsey Wolff

This event was held at the Summer North American Championships until 1962. A similar event was held at the Spring NAC 1958–1962 with the following results:

WINNERS

1958 1.   Kay Rhodes, Margaret Wagar
    2.   Mrs. N. L. Cassibry, Ann Smith
1959 1.   Bert Epstein, Blossom Grossblatt
    2.   Betty Coombs, Malvine Klausner
1960 1.   Gretchen Feldstein, Jane Mueller
    2.   Gertrude Eberson, Mrs. M. Jones
1961 1.   May Belle Long, Effie Woods
    2.   Dorothy Hayden, Helen Portugal
1962 1.   Clarice Holt, Mrs. Greeley Warner
    2.   Kay Carter, Mrs. G. M. Sharum

GRAND NATIONAL PAIRS. This is a grassroots event, with the first stage conducted strictly at the club level. Qualifiers then advance to the Unit competition, and the qualifiers there advance to the District finals. A number of pairs (usually three) are qualified at the District level for the North American final, which is held just prior to the Spring North American Championships..

WINNERS
1979 1. Arthur Moore, Eric Robinson
2. Steve Landen, Larry Mori
1980 1. Bob Feller, Jeffrey Hall
2. Larry N. Cohen, Ron Gerard
1981 1. Helen Blakey, Robert Blakey
2. Mark Feldman, Chip Martel
1982 1. Bill Nuttig, Ivan Scope
2. Richard Pavlicek, Cliff Russell

AMATEUR SWISS TEAMS. This team event is open only to those players who are not *Registered Players*. It consists of two qualifying sessions and two final sessions.

WINNERS
1976 1. James Bennett, Paul Ivaska,
Tony Kasday, John Stiefel
2. Ed Lichtman, G. Sekhar,
Bill McTavish, B.M. Maksymetz
1977 1. Larry Bolls, Anthony Crocker, Michael Levy,
Marcia Masterson, Florence Meyer, Steve Smolen
2-3. David Besenfelder, Pete Franks,
Richard Spitalnick, Randy Howard
2-3. Nancy Browne, Peter Nagy, Sharyn Kokish,
Eric Kokish, Bud Marsh, Ralph Cohen

SECONDARY CHAMPIONSHIPS

MIXED PAIRS. A two-sessions event for the HILLIARD TROPHY.

WINNERS
1931 Lewis R. Ayres, Mrs. Richard Jones, Jr.
1932 Charles S. Lochridge, Frances Newman
1933 Fred Levy, Margaret Wagar
1934 Mrs. Theodore Greenbaum, Richard Kahn
1935 Hortense Evans, Louis J. Haddad
1936 Wingate Bixby, Dorothy M. Healy
1937 Harry J. Fishbein, Mrs. Sam Rush
1938 Fred D. Kaplan, Mrs. Sam Rush
1939 Lewis H. Fremont, Florence Stratford
1940 Sidney Silodor, Sally Young
1941 Jeff Glick, Vera Glick
1942 Harry J. Fishbein, Ruth Sherman
1943 Charles H. Goren, Olive Peterson
1944 Sidney Silodor, Helen Sobel
1945 John R. Crawford, Margaret Wagar
1946 Harry J. Fishbein, Paula Bacher
1947 Rose Eidem, Meyer Schleifer
1948 Verna Leonard, Elbert Miller
1949 Arnold Kauder, Mary Jane Kauder
1950 Robert Street, Venita Street
1951 Helen Portugal, Morris Portugal
1952 James Dunn, Kay Dunn
1953 Helen Portugal, Morris Portugal
1954 James Dunn, Kay Dunn
1955 James Dunn, Kay Dunn
1956 Jack Hancock, Ruth Million
1957 Bob Adams, Marilyn Johnson
1958 John Gerber, Phyllis Novak
1959 Mary Jane Farell, Alvin Roth
1960 Shirlee Harris, Edward Rosen
1961 Carol Sanders, Thomas K. Sanders
1962 Jessie Cook, Grant Marsee *(tied with)*

Shirlee Harris, Edward Rosen
1963 Ira G. Corn, Jr., Dorothy Moore
1964 Otto Leesment, Viola Whitney
1965 Herbert A. Beyer, Patricia Beyer
1966 Jerry Stinnett, Frank Whiteley
1967 Harry J. Fishbein, Carol Klar
1968 Dr. Jack J. Louis, Matilda Plaskow
1969 Alex Danilenko, Charlotte Dobin
1970 Alex Danilenko, Gloria Noszka
1971 Sharon Kasle, John Schwencke
1972 Helen Armstrong, Chuck Said
1973 Mary Chilcote, Wellington Lee
1974 Michael Becker, Amalya Kearse
1975 Ruth Gittelman, Anatole Kondratieff
1976 Jo Morse, Marvin Rosenblatt
1977 Alan Truscott, Dorothy Hayden Truscott
1978 Marc Poe, Mary Margaret Swan
1979 Gail Lowy, Marc Zwerling
1980 Barbara Hamman, Robert D. Hamman

NON-MASTER PAIRS. This event is contested for the KEM CARD TROPHY. It is a two-session pair event limited to players with 0 to 49 master points, held at the Fall North American Championships until 1966.

WINNERS
1937 Lt. R. A. Cook, Lt. C. W. Humphreys
1938 Edward W. Perry, Mrs. Edward W. Perry
1939 Mrs. E. Q. Crane, Mrs. R. H. Rishell
1940 Sara Gross, Polly Campbell
1941 Raymond Farber, Hal L. Oliver
1942 Ken Cadwallader, Arthur Waterbury
1943 Dr. Max Mitchell, Herbert Stein
1944 J. O. Gaynor, Marie A. Gaynor
1945 C. Jack Bonney, Bernard P. Lampert
1946 Fletcher Henderson, Barton Bonds
1947 Mrs. M. D. Abuhove, Mrs. Richard Miller
1948 Horace E. Loomis, J. G. McKay
1949 Stan Anderson, Don Kenner
1950 Mrs. J. E. Morris, Mrs. W. Simpson
1951 Mrs. William D. Selikoff, Henry J. Blumenschine
1953 Roger J. Sarfaty, Steve Greenberg
1952 Jessie S. Moore, Leonard C. Hawkins
1954 E. J. Early, Dr. Stephen S. Gernazian
1955 Elzworth L. Esh, Mrs. A. E. Esh
1956 Mrs. Melvin Cohen, Mrs. Milton Sharfstein
1957 Capt. William Ginn, Richard Mayer
1958 Dr. Norman Bolton, Dr. Richard Menczer
1959 Donald Harris, Hubert Royal
1960 Bernard Stephens, Mrs. Bernard Stephens
1961 Joseph Russell, Mrs. Joseph Russell
1962 Carl Berggren, Roger Putnam, Jr.
1963 R. P. Hodges, James Titzel
1964 Evelyn Shagman, Jack Shagman
1965 Gary Robinson, Jeff Reynolds
1966 A. J. Iwasko, Ed Rodgers
1967 Steve Lull, Jim Sherman
1968 Sharon Rushing, Robert Stampf
1969 Robert D. Cooper, Kirk Ritchie
1970 Syd Minkoff, Pearl Minkoff
1971 James Collins, Jerry Jiles
1972 Rick Evarts, Howard Weinstein
1973 Ronald Morgan, Vernon Morgan
1974 Carole Remlinger, Brenda Sandé
1975 Muriel Altus, Philip Altus
1976 Bruce Gilligan, Jane Moore
1977 Larry Goldstein, Judy Pede
1978 Annell Oatley, Dave Oatley
1979 Dale Harrison, Cissy Whitehouse
1980 James Bragg, Ronald Ferrell
1981 Sam Manzo, Sandra Manzo

1982 Rica Soetens, Walter Soetens

MASTER PAIRS. This two-session event is limited to players with 50 or more master points (100+ beginning in 1976). Contested as a three-session event in 1970 and 1971.

WINNERS
1970 Barbara Davis, Dr. Carl Pollock
1971 Mark Lair, Marian Taylor
1972 Kenneth Cohen, Helen Smith
1973 Stephen W. Robinson, Steve Parker
1974 Fred Hamilton, Ira S. Rubin
1975 Gerald Caravelli, Barry Crane
1976 Charlotte Falk, Fred Strickland
1977 Betty Floyd, Robert Futoran
1978 Suzanne Gill, Marc Freedman
1979 Michael Lipson, Don Moen
1980 Sharron Stange, Sandy Zakin
1981 George Rosenkranz, Eddie Wold
1982 Celia Mayers, Bob Rosen

INDIVIDUAL. This two-session open event is contested for the BAIRD TROPHY.

WINNERS
1945 Ted Samuels
1946 Mrs. A. Schlorel Smith
1947 Emily Folline *(tied with)*
      Ludwig Kabakjian
1948 Otto Matthes
1949 Solomon Seidman
1950 Earline Foley
1951 Tracy Denniger
1952 Fred L. Blackmon *(tied with)*
      Nathan W. White
1953 Nancy McCrackin
1954 Dr. Kermit Chadwick
1955 Morton Rubinow
1956 Said Haddad
1957 Walter Wallace
1958 Frances Robinson
1959 Joseph Jabon
1960 Don Wolfson
1961 Carman Woolsey
1962 Isabelle Alcone
1963 Donald Greers
1964 Viola Kushner
1965 Baron Wolf
1966 James L. Miller
1967 Carl F. Cronemiller, Jr.
1968 Solveig Parkas
1969 Richard Fortune
1970 Alice Wick
1971 Phyllis E. Clark
1972 Lilo Grubner
1973 Eleanor Dalton
1974 Norman F. Brooks
1976 John Pranter
1977 J.M. Ferguson
1978 Marc Poe

OPEN PAIRS. A two-session Open Pair event.

WINNERS
1969 Barry Crane, Marilyn Johnson
1970 Donald Faskow, Arthur Waldemann
1971 Barbara Rappaport, Alvin Roth
1972 H. G. Eikleberry, Sara L. Eikleberry
1973 Moshe Bernstein, Greg DeFotis
1974 Barry Crane, Mike Passell
1975 Barry Crane, Kerri Shuman

1976 Gaylor Kasle, Carol Krehbiel
1977 Molly Groger, Paul Maier
1978 Sheldon Justan, Harold Weltman
1979 Jim Bowman, Jim Steehler
1980 V. Craig Janitschke, Vivian Kilstrup
1981 Myles Maddox, Vincent Remey
1982 Clay Hall, Steve Katz

SILVER TROPHY PAIRS. This two-session flighted Open Pairs event was first contested at the Summer North American Championships in 1976 and is held at each of the three NAC. Flight A is unlimited, Flight B requirements are 0–1500 and Flight C requirements are 0–300. A Revere bowl trophy on a base is given to each winner.

WINNERS
1977 Flight A: Dorothy Kaye, Mary Senti
      Flight B: Clifford Morris, Rodger Patterson
      Flight C: S. J. Block, Lou Cooper
1978 Flight A: Mike Murphy, Mike Schira
      Flight B: Ken Bains, Judith McNeff
      Flight C: Lorene Wait, Mary Williams
1979 Flight A: Bob McMahan, Hap Neuffer
      Flight B: Tom Allan, John Royce
      Flight C: Ted Sanders, Steve Shapiro
1980 Flight A: Michael Nash, Dean Weiner
      Flight B: James Kostal, Nick Moss
      Flight C: John Matselboba, Steve Saltsman
1981 Flight A: Peter Boyd, Stephen W. Robinson
      Flight B: Jim Burt, Rich Gabriel
      Flight C: Joe Merdler, Fred Rosenberry
1982 Flight A: Malcolm Brachman, Paul Soloway
      Flight B: Billy Handy, Jr., Ron Vickery
      Flight C: John Mulder, Leonard Smith

SWISS TEAMS. This four-session team event with two qualifying sessions and two final sessions is scored by international match points.

WINNERS
1971 Eileen Cason, William Cason,
      Myrtle Sheets, William Sheets
1972 Mrs. John C. Allen, Louise Hays,
      Harold Rasmussen, Linda Rasmussen *(tied with)*
      Ted Brashler, L. James Phillips, Kent Wiley, Lois Wiley
1973 William Burger, Jeff Isackson,
      Bob Webber, Franklin Yang *(tied with)*
      Ron E. Andersen, Moshe Bernstein,
      Greg DeFotis, Alan Suskind *(and)*
      Beverly Brick, Cecilia Jacob, Jean Joseph,
      Sally Lapin, Frances Singer
1974 Barry Crane, Bob Kehoe, Fred Rubbra, Kerri Shuman
1975 Donald A. Oakie, Patty Prahl,
      Terry Randles, Mrs. Emory Stanley

SWISS TEAMS, Second Flight. This two-session team event for non-qualifiers from the four-session secondary Swiss Team event is scored by international matchpoints. The event was first contested in 1959.

WINNERS
1959 Ed Cahill, Lu Cahill, Bob Street, Lucille Wheeler
1960 Dr. Charles Burnham, Elinor Murdoch,
      S. D. Murphy, Mrs. S. D. Murphy
1961 William Mann, Mrs. William Mann,
      Jack Rothstein, Don Williams
1962 Alan C. Bell, Robert Cruise, Richard Vission, John Zilic
1963 Alice Cohn, Jack Ehrlenbach,
      Ernest Gruenfield, George Willet
1964 Margaret Alcorn, Jane Herb,
      Elizabeth Kaplan, Patricia Sheinwold
1965 Lucy Faris, William Gardner,
      John Hamilton, Marion Hamilton
1966 Hermine Baron, Pidgeon Davis,
      Virginia Heckel, Bee Schenken, Jerome Yavitz *(tied with)*
      Chester Davis, L. James Phillips,
      Dr. Robert Tator, Alan Truscott

1967   Paul Heitner, John Lowenthal,
       Dick Walsh, Rhoda Walsh
1968   Howard Abrams, Edmond Lazarus,
       Vivian Levin, E. R. McKinney, Tom Weik
1969   Robert Alexander, Marty Arndt,
       Bobb Hardies, Marc Low
1970   H. E. Fuller, Robert Lyski,
       Dr. Michael A. Philippas, Tom Weeg
1971   Ruby Allen, Mrs. Robert Clift,
       Joanne Mackintosh, Betty Wiglesworth *(tied with)*
       Lorraine Bailey, Doris Gesell,
       J. B. Hayden, Mrs. A. R. Singleton *(and)*
       Don Caton, Leonard Karp,
       George Kramer, John Potter, Homer Shoop
1972   Richard Doughty, Jack LaNoue,
       Mike Passell, John Potter
1973   Dr. Beth Hatch, Dr. Clifford Hendricks,
       Nancy McCray, Royce McCray
1974   Bob Crosby, Dick Grant, Paul Prince, Bob Teshima
1975   Ira Cohen, Steve Evans, Ron Garber,
       Larry Mandel, Mike Smolen, Bill Sides

AMATEUR SWISS TEAMS, Second Flight. This is a two-session event open only to those players who failed to qualify for the Amateur Swiss Teams final.

WINNERS

1976   Larry Edward, Lois Goren, Myldred Kelly,
       Peter Kurtz, Lila Perlstein, Eric Schwartz
1977   Linda Mitchel, S. Palmer,
       Cedric Pang, Dora Shimada *(tied with)*
       George Lim, Mike Morimoto, Lucille Patterson,
       Estelle Saltzman, Mort Saltzman *(and)*
       Maria Cespedes, Magda Sanchez Fogarty,
       Stefan Reich, Bella Weissmann

OTHER SECONDARY EVENTS

(All two-session regionally-rated events)

WINNERS

1971

Open Pairs Second Flight:
    Mrs. William B. Carlen, Mrs. D. James Foutch
Men's Pairs Second Flight:
    Hal Fein, Dan Morse
Women's Pairs Second Flight:
    Pat Terk, B. J. Wilson

1972

Men's Swiss Teams:
    Hal Fein, Robert D. Hamman, Eddie Kantar, Dan Morse
Women's Swiss Teams:
    Frieda Arst, June Deutsch, Sylvia Stein, Carol Stolkin
Men's Pairs:
    Charles Braman, Dennis J. McGarry
Women's Pairs:
    Mrs. D. Buckshorn, Mrs. F. Clifford Wright
Non-Mixed Pairs:
    Ross Grabel, Steve Landen

1973

Swiss Teams:
    Cheri Bjerkan, Bob Gardner,
    Larry McCaffery, Lois Wiley
Men's Swiss Teams:
    Bart Bramley, Dennis Dawson,
    Norman Humer, Bernie Miller
Women's Swiss Teams:
    Sue Andersen, Roberta Epstein,
    Amalya Kearse, Gail Moss,
    Marietta Passell, Kathie Wei *(tied with)*
    Frieda Arst, Carol Crawford, June Deutsch, Sylvia Stein
Open Pairs:
    Carol Ann Mahaffey, Richard Stern, Jr.
Men's Pairs:
    Stormy Horn, Dick Reed
Women's Pairs:
    Dee Henderson, Virginia Meriwether

1974

Swiss Teams:
    Roger Bates, Gerald Caravelli, Larry Cohen,
    Gaylor Kasle, Dr. Richard H. Katz, John Simon

Mixed Swiss Teams:
    Charles Jaskela, Elizabeth Lee,
    Doreen Maurer, Charles Swanson
Open Pairs:
    Flight A: John Beasy, John Stewart
    Flight B: Janet Corwin, Mrs. Louis Hoyer
    Flight C: Jim McAvoy, Duncan Smith
Men's Pairs:
    Norman Featherston, Mike Kreutzer
Women's Pairs:
    Beverly Ginsberg, Irene Pingree

1975

Swiss Teams:
    Cliff Bishop, Barry Crane,
    Kerri Shuman, Fred Rubbra *(tied with)*
    Gerald Bare, Ed Davis, Paul Ivaska, Bill Sides
Mixed Swiss Teams:
    Bruce Elliott, Dr. Richard K. Fleishman,
    Sydney Isaacs, Sharyn Kokish
Open Pairs:
    Flight A: Raymond Fortin, Denis Lesage
    Flight B: S. C. Kan, Patsy Lum
Men's Pairs:
    Donald Grubb, Lawrence Jolma
Women's Pairs:
    Lurlin Hall, Mary Katherine Herron

1976

Swiss Teams:
    Lou Bluhm, Clarence Goppert, Ron LaCour,
    Mark Lair, Eddie Wold
Swiss Teams Second Flight:
    Nancy Gruver, Edith Kemp, Betty Ann Kennedy,
    Barbara Rappaport, Carol Sanders,
    Helen Utegaard *(tied with)*
    Bart Bramley, John Lowenthal, Lou Reich, Ira S. Rubin
Mixed Swiss Teams:
    Betty Kaplan, Edgar Kaplan, Kerri Shuman, Mike Shuman
Open Pairs:
    Flight A: Carl Dahl, Jr., Ralph Katz
    Flight B: Mike Hogan, John Jay Mills
    Flight C: Gene Archer, Maurice Attias
Men's Pairs:
    Joel Friedberg, Mike Shuman
Women's Pairs:
    Irene Hyatt, Jane Mehegan

1977

Swiss Teams:
    Mark E. Blumenthal, Gerald Caravelli, Milton Rosenberg,
    Arthur Waldemann, Peter Weichsel
Swiss Teams Second Flight:
    Jacqui Mitchell, Victor Mitchell, Bill Roberts,
    Jill Roberts, John Roberts
Mixed Teams:
    Jennifer Evans, Stephen Evans
    Estelle Gregory, Ben Tucker
Men's Pairs:
    Duke Dautell, George Zahler
Women's Pairs:
    Fran Tsacnaris, Pamela Wittes

1978

Swiss Teams:
    Edith Kemp, William Passell, Judi Radin,
    Barbara Rappaport, Esta Van Zandt
Swiss Teams
    Smoking: Jim Becker, Jim Hamilton,
                     Roger Jourdan, Jack Schwencke
    Non-Smoking: Eric Kokish, Larry Kozlove,
                     Peter Nagy, Stephen W. Robinson,
                     John Sheridan, Kit Woolsey
Swiss Teams:
    Flight A: Eric Kokish, Sharyn Kokish, Michael S. Lawrence,
                Peter Nagy, Peter Weichsel
    Flight B: Sam Carver, Clinard Hanby, Bob Labry, Sally Wheeler
    Flight C: Ralph Hollingshead, Sam Nigh,
                Naomi O'Hara, B. R. Pitney
Open Pairs:
    A — Class A: David Hinz, Tim Willis
    B — Class A-D: Gerald Caravelli, Barry Crane
Open Pairs::
    Joe Steuer, Marie Louise Steuer
Men's Pairs:
    Guy Howard, G. Robert Nail

Women's Pairs:
    Pat Terk, B. J. Wilson

1979

Swiss Teams:
    Jerry Jackson, George Rhode,
    Ann Roberts, Genne Winter

Swiss Teams:
Smoking:	James David, Richard Ellis,
	Ledon Hitch, Stephen Morton
Non-Smoking:	Tom Abbott, Bob Gwirtzman, Gene Prosnitz,
	Ethan Stein, Alan Truscott, Larry Weiss *(tied with)*
	Boris Baron, Kirk Benson, Ron Feldman,
	Mark Molson, Bill Pollack, Mark Rosenbloom
	(and) Ida Bennett, Mary Lou Cushner,
	Ethel Keohane, Judy Wadas

Swiss Teams:
Flight A:	Garland Ergüden, Pat Lapides, Joe Livezey,
	DeAne Phillips, Fred Rubbra
Flight B:	Eric Anderson, P. Feuerwerger,
	Mike Kovacich, Elizabeth Nelson

Open Pair:
    Raymond Garea, Robert Hopkins, Jr.

Open Pairs:
Flight A:	Jo Morse, Stephen W. Robinson
Flight B:	Ahmed Hussein, Gail Moss

Mixed Pairs:
    Flight B: Paula Dyba, Malcolm Williamson

Men's Pairs:
    Jim Bennett, Chester Davis

Women's Pairs:
    Beth Palmer, Robin Taylor

1980

Swiss Teams:
    Lucy Gellner, Ed Piken, Eva Piken, Vic Touriel

Swiss Teams:
Smoking:	Richard Gold, Terry Hause,
	Rob Stevens, Ben Tucker
Non-Smoking:	Lorna Crooks, Bob Etter,
	Ann Jacobson, Randi Montin

Swiss Teams:
Flight A:	Jose Hamui, Elias Konstantinovsky,
	Mike Passell, Miguel Reygadas
Flight B:	Wanda Cardella, Don Donohue,
	Norman Woo, Henderson Yeung

Open Pairs:
A — Class A:	Joan Remey, Vincent Remey
B — Class A-D:	Barbara Norman, John Norman

Open Pairs:
    Stan Cabay, George Kelly

Mixed Pairs:
    Flight B: Bea Bahr, Chester Bahr

Men's Pairs:
    Kirk Benson, David Strasberg *(tied with)*
    Clifford Russell, Eddie Wold

Women's Pairs:
    Barbara Flanagan, Mary Karlan

1981

Renaissance:
BAM Teams:	Tom Callaham, Larry Long,
	Lester Perlmutter, Mark Perlmutter
Swiss Teams:	Masood Khan, Nick Markakis,
	Gary Randall, James Sutherland

Grosse Pointe Swiss Teams:
Flight A:	Roberta Epstein, Ron Haack, Paul Heitner, Gail Moss
Flight B	Jack Smith, Marlene Smith,
	Bill Woodcock, Valerie Woodcock

Indian Village Swiss Teams:
    Phil Brady, John Conway, Marc Rabinowitz, John Toy

Mackinac Swiss Teams:
    Andy Bernstein, Dennis Clerkin,
    Jerry Clerkin, Fred Rubbra

Corktown Swiss Teams:
    Bob Crafton, Dave Fred, Gary Hann, Bob Webber

Open Pairs:
A — Class A:	Paul Huxley, Marge Lewan
B — Class A-D:	Marc Culberson, Bert Newman *(tied with)*
	Jeffrey Starr, Dick Yanko

Open Pairs:
Smoking:	Bob Crafton, Howard Weiner
Non-Smoking:	Karen McCallum, Kit Woolsey

Men's Pairs:
    Jim Anderson, Harold Dobson

Women's Pairs:
    Miriam Rycus, Dorothy Schiff

1982

Table Rock Swiss Teams:
    Bob Barr, Arnold Fisher, Bob Gwirtzman, Clint Morrell

Swiss Teams:
Smoking:	Rajat Basu, Don Gray,
	Dan Hyland, Jared Lillenstein
Non-Smoking:	Don Dalpe, Judy Flack,
	David Gordon, Michael Ranis

Swiss Teams:
Flight A:	June Deutsch, Tobi Deutsch, Susan Handelman,
	Pat Lapides, Dennis McGarry
Flight B:	Diana Blithe, Rae Dethlefsen,
	Barbara Doran, Andrew Kaufman

Men's Swiss Teams:
    Ralph Bartlett, Stephen Cooper, Maurice Friedman,
    Leon Lowe, Larry Mori, Merle Tom

Women's Swiss Teams:
    Hermine Baron, Lynn Deas, Evelyn Levitt, Jo Morse,
    Eunice Rosen, Beverly Rosenberg

Open Pairs:
Flight A:	Marla Chaikin, Ron Haack
Flight B:	Adrienne Levy, Kathryn Upp *(tied with)*
	Robert Lewek, Williams Young, Jr.

Open Pairs:
A — Class A:	Petra Bender, Ron Von der Porten
B — Class A-D:	Daniel Marcus, Jacqueline Oman

Goat Island Open Pairs:
    John Marks, Peter Weglarski

Devil's Hole Open Pairs:
    Emanuel Katz, Mary McKenna

For the award to the player gaining the greatest number of Master Points at the Spring North American Championships see MOTT-SMITH TROPHY.

SUMMER NORTH AMERICAN CHAMPIONSHIPS

CHALLENGE TEAMS OF FOUR. The event was contested for the ASBURY PARK TROPHY. The runner-up team in the regularly-scheduled portion of the event had the right to challenge the winners to a play-off. This right was never utilized. In the 1938 North American Championships this event was replaced by the Spingold Master Teams of Four.

WINNERS

1930	1.	Ely Culbertson, Josephine Culbertson,
		Theodore A. Lightner, Waldemar K. von Zedtwitz
	2.	Michael T. Gottlieb, Willard S. Karn,
		Lee Langdon, P. Hal Sims
1931	1.	David Burnstine, Oswald Jacoby,
		Willard S. Karn, P. Hal Sims
	2.	S. Garton Churchill, Travers J. LeGros,
		Dorothy Roberts, A. Phillip Stockvis
1932	1.	Michael T. Gottlieb, Oswald Jacoby,
		Theodore A. Lightner, Louis H. Watson
	2.	B. Jay Becker, Herbert D. Lent,
		George Reith, Anne Rosenfield
1933	1.	David Burnstine, Oswald Jacoby,
		Richard L. Frey, Howard Schenken
	2.	Sam Fry, Jr., Edward Hymes,
		Louis H. Watson, Waldemar K. von Zedtwitz
1934	1.	Aaron Frank, Jeff Glick,
		William Hopkins, Charles H. Porter
	2.	Josephine Culbertson, Theodore A. Lightner,
		Alphonse Moyse, Jr., Sherman Stearns
1935	1.	Sam Fry, Jr., Edward Hymes, Jr., Theodore A. Lightner,
		Merwyn D. Maier, Louis H. Watson,
	2.	A. Mitchell Barnes, H. Huber Boscowitz,
		Charles S. Lochridge, Johnny Rau
1936	1.	Lewis A. Bernard, Louis J. Haddad, Alvin Landy,
		Matthew S. Reilly, Philip Steiner
	2.	E. Melvin Goddard, Sidney Silodor,
		Dr. Henry J. Vogel, Sir Derrick Wernher
1937	1.	David Burnstine, Charles H. Goren, Oswald Jacoby,
		Merwyn D. Maier, Howard Schenken
	2.	Phil Abramsohn, A. Mitchell Barnes, Henry H. Chanin,
		Morrie Elis, Fred D. Kaplan

MASTER TEAMS-OF-FOUR. This event is contested for the SPINGOLD TROPHY. From 1934 through

1937, the Spingold was not part of a North American Championship. In 1938, it replaced the CITY OF ASBURY PARK TROPHY Challenge Teams as an event at the Summer North American Championships. At one time the Spingold was a DOUBLE ELIMINATION event scored by international matchpoints, usually lasting nine or ten sessions, restricted to players of Senior Master rank and higher. In 1965, the Double Elimination method was replaced by three qualifying sessions (subsequently reduced to two), followed by Single Elimination knockout matches. The preliminary qualifying sessions were dropped in 1970.

WINNERS

1934 1. David Burnstine, Richard L. Frey, Michael T. Gottlieb, Oswald Jacoby, Howard Schenken
2. Aaron Frank, Jeff Glick, Louis J. Haddad, Charles A. Hall

1936 1. B. Jay Becker, David Burnstine, Oswald Jacoby, Howard Schenken
2. Sam Fry, Jr., Edward Hymes, Jr., Merwyn D. Maier, Waldemar K. von Zedtwitz

1937 1. Sam Fry, Jr., Edward Hymes, Jr., Theodore A. Lightner, Waldemar K. von Zedtwitz
2. Phil Abramsohn, Lewis Bernard, Morrie Elis, Harry Fishbein, Herbert Goldberg

1938 1. B. Jay Becker, David Burnstine, Oswald Jacoby, Merwyn D. Maier, Howard Schenken
2. A. Mitchell Barnes, Morrie Elis, Fred D. Kaplan, Charles S. Lochridge

1939 1. Oswald Jacoby, Theodore A. Lightner, Merwyn D. Maier, Robert A. McPherran, Howard Schenken
2. John R. Crawford, Myron Fuchs, Charles H. Goren, Charles J. Solomon, Sally Young

1940 1. Oscar J. Brotman, Bertram Lebhar, Samuel Katz, Alvin Roth
2. Sam Fry, Jr., Myron Fuchs, Edward Hymes, Jr., Charles S. Lochridge, Waldemar K. von Zedtwitz

1941 1. A. Mitchell Barnes, Sam Fry, Jr., Edward Hymes, Jr., Waldemar K. von Zedtwitz
2. B. Jay Becker, Oswald Jacoby, Theodore A. Lightner, Merwyn D. Maier, Howard Schenken

1942 1. Sigmund Dornbusch, Richard L. Frey, Lee Hazen, Samuel M. Stayman
2. Jay T. Feigus, Charles Harvey, Samuel Katz, Edward Marcus

1943 1. John R. Crawford, Charles H. Goren, Edward Hymes, Jr., Howard Schenken, Sidney Silodor
2. B. Jay Becker, Harry J. Fishbein, George Rapee, Alvin Roth, Helen Sobel

1944 1. B. Jay Becker, George Rapee, Helen Sobel, Samuel M. Stayman
2. Simon Becker, Edward G. Ellenbogen, Stanley Frenkel, Peggy Golder

1945 1. Sam Fry, Jr., Edward Hymes, Jr., Oswald Jacoby, Theodore A. Lightner, Howard Schenken
2. Harry Fishbein, Lee Hazen, Alvin Roth, Waldemar K. von Zedtwitz

1946 1. William Christian, Mark Hodges, Sol Mogal, Margaret Wagar
2. Jeff Glick, Arthur S. Goldsmith, Alvin Landy, Elmer I. Schwartz

1947 1. B. Jay Becker, Charles H. Goren, Lee Hazen, Helen Sobel, Waldemar K. von Zedtwitz
2. John R. Crawford, George Rapee, Howard Schenken, Sidney Silodor, Samuel M. Stayman

1948 1. John R. Crawford, George Rapee, Howard Schenken, Samuel M. Stayman, Margaret Wagar
2. Julius Bank, Arthur Glatt, Robert W. Halpin, Oswald Jacoby, Ralph Kempner

1949 1. Jeff Glick, Arthur S. Goldsmith, Bruce Gowdy, Alvin Landy, Sol Mogal
2. Henry H. Chanin, David Clarren, Oswald Jacoby, Jack Krause, Waldemar K. von Zedtwitz

1950 1. John R. Crawford, Oswald Jacoby, George Rapee, Howard Schenken, Samuel M. Stayman
2. B. Jay Becker, Charles H. Goren, Sidney Silodor, Helen Sobel, Waldemar K. von Zedtwitz

1951 1. Myron Field, Charles H. Goren,

Sidney Silodor, Helen Sobel
2. Ambrose Casner, Charles A. Hall, Allen P. Harvey, Frank Weisbach

1952 1. B. Jay Becker, John R. Crawford, George Rapee, Howard Schenken, Samuel M. Stayman
2. Jeff Glick, Arthur S. Goldsmith, Alvin Landy, Sol Mogal, Edwin J. Smith, Jr.

1953 1. Clifford Bishop, Milton Q. Ellenby, Donald A. Oakie, William Rosen, Doug Steen
2-5 Ed Burns, David Clarren, Bertram Lebhar, Sam Katz, Albert Weiss
2-5 F. Ayers Bombeck, David C. Carter, John W. Hubbell, Arthur Kincaid, G. Robert Nail
2-5 Harold Harkavy, Edith Kemp, Alvin Roth, Tobias Stone, Waldemar K. von Zedtwitz
2-5 Ivan E. Erdos, Dr. Edward Fischauer, Lewis L. Mathe, Meyer Schleifer

1954 1. Clifford Bishop, Milton Q. Ellenby, Lewis L. Mathe, John Moran, William Rosen
2-4. F. Ayers Bombeck, David C. Carter, John Gerber, John W. Hubbell, Harold Rockaway
2-4. Eddie Burns, Ambrose Casner, Allen P. Harvey, Cliff Russell
2-4 Sidney Lazard, Cyrus Neuman, Lewis Rosen, Julius L. Rosenblum, Robert Rothlein

1955 1. Myron Field, Lee Hazen, Richard Kahn, Charles J. Solomon, Samuel M. Stayman
2. B. Jay Becker, John R. Crawford, George Rapee, Howard Schenken, Sidney Silodor

1956 1-3. Charles H. Goren, Peter A. Leventritt, Boris Koytchou, Harold Ogust, William Seamon, Helen Sobel
1-3. Harold Harkavy, Victor Mitchell, Alvin Roth, Ira S. Rubin, Tobias Stone
1-3. Robert Abeles, Dr. Kalman Apfel, Francis P. Begley, Louis Kelner, Ronald Rosenberg

1957 1. B. Jay Becker, John R. Crawford, George Rapee, Alvin Roth, Sidney Silodor, Tobias Stone
2. Milton Q. Ellenby, Ivan E. Erdos, Emanuel Hochfeld, James Jacoby, Oswald Jacoby, Ira S. Rubin

1958 1. Paul Allinger, William Hanna, Sidney Lazard, Cyrus Neuman, Robert Rothlein
2. Harry Fishbein, Sam Fry, Jr., Leonard B. Harmon, Lee Hazen, Ivan Stakgold

1959 1. William Grieve, Oswald Jacoby, Victor Mitchell, Ira S. Rubin, Morton Rubinow, Samuel M. Stayman
2. Richard Freeman, Andy Gabrilovitch, Frank Hoadley, Mike Michaels, Jan Stone, Richard Walsh

1960 1. Charles H. Goren, Peter A. Leventritt, Boris Koytchou, Harold Ogust, Howard Schenken, Helen Sobel
2. B. Jay Becker, William Grieve, Ralph Hirschberg, Norman Kay, George Rapee, Sidney Silodor

1961 1. Andy Gabrilovitch, Eddie Kantar, Marshall Miles, William Root
2. John R. Crawford, Norman Kay, Alvin Roth, George Rapee, Sidney Silodor, Tobias Stone

1962 1. Leonard B. Harmon, Eddie Kantar, Marshall Miles, Ivan Stakgold
2. David C. Carter, John W. Hubbell, James Jacoby, Gerald Michaud, G. Robert Nail

1963 1. Russell Arnold, Harold Harkavy, Edith Kemp, Alvin Roth, Cliff Russell, William Seamon
2. Sammy R. Kehela, Richard Kahn, William Root, Thomas K. Sanders, Tobias Stone, Waldemar K. von Zedtwitz

1964 1. Bruce Elliott, Sammy R. Kehela, Eric R. Murray, Percy F. Sheardown
2. Marvin Altman, Bruce Gowdy, Fred Hoffer, Ray Jotcham

1965 1. Bruce Elliott, Sammy R. Kehela, Eric R. Murray, Percy Sheardown
2. B. Jay Becker, Dorothy Hayden, Norman Kay, Edgar Kaplan

1966 1. William Root, Alvin Roth, Ira S. Rubin, Curtis K. Smith
2. William Grieve, Sidney Lazard, Paul Levitt, Harold Ogust, George Rapee

1967 1. Edgar Kaplan, Norman Kay, William Root, Alvin Roth
2. John Gerber, Paul H. Hodge, Dan Morse, George Rosenkranz, Bobby Wolff

1968 1. Sammy R. Kehela, Edgar Kaplan, Norman Kay, Sidney Lazard, Eric R. Murray, George Rapee
2. Steve Altman, B. Jay Becker, Michael Becker, Dorothy Hayden

1969 1. Billy Eisenberg, Bobby Goldman, Robert D. Hamman,

    Michael S. Lawrence, James Jacoby, Bobby Wolff
2. Phil Feldesman, William Grieve, Victor Mitchell,
    Ira S. Rubin, Samuel M. Stayman, Jeff Westheimer

1970 1. Steve Altman, Thomas M. Smith, Dave Strasberg,
    Joel Stuart, Peter Weichsel
2. Billy Eisenberg, Bobby Goldman, Robert D. Hamman,
    James Jacoby, Michael S. Lawrence, Bobby Wolff

1971 1. Steve Altman, Eugene Neiger, Thomas M. Smith,
    Joel Stuart, Peter Weichsel
2. Edgar Kaplan, Norman Kay,
    Donald P. Krauss, Lewis L. Mathe

1972 1. B. Jay Becker, Michael Becker,
    Andy Bernstein, Jeff Rubens,
2. Pat Brennan, Byron Greenberg, Edith Kemp,
    Cliff Russell, Curtis K. Smith, Allan Weiss

1973 1. Larry Cohen, Billy Eisenberg, Eddie Kantar,
    Dr. Richard H. Katz, Bud Reinhold
2. Minda Brachman, Sidney Lazard, James Jacoby,
    Paul Soloway, John Swanson

1974 1. Lou Bluhm, Larry Gould,
    Steve Goldberg, Richard Shepherd
2. Harlow Lewis, Lewis L. Mathe, Peter A. Pender,
    William Root, Harry Stappenbeck, Arthur Waldman

1975 1. Grant S. Baze, John Fejervary, Lew Stansby,
    Piyush Vakil, Ron Von der Porten
2. Ira Cohen, Harold Guiver, Marty Shallon, Bill Sides

1976 1. Roger Bates, Larry Cohen, Dr. Richard H. Katz,
    John Mohan, George Rosenkranz
2. Dave Berkowitz, Mark E. Blumenthal, James Jacoby,
    Michael S. Lawrence, George Rapee, John Solodar

1977 1. Lou Bluhm, Dan Morse, Cliff Russell, Curtis K. Smith
    Thomas K. Sanders, Eddie Wold
2. Ken Cohen, Larry Gould, Larry Kozlove, John Sheridan

1978 1. Malcolm Brachman, Bobby Goldman, Eddie Kantar,
    Mike Passell, Paul Soloway
2. Steve Altman, Edgar Kaplan, Norman Kay,
    Richard Pavlicek, William Root, Thomas M. Smith

1979 1. Fred Hamilton, Robert D. Hamman,
    Ira S. Rubin, Bobby Wolff
2. Ed Manfield, Stephen W. Robinson, Eric Rodwell,
    John Sheridan, Kit Woolsey

1980 1. Mike Becker, Kyle Larsen, Ron Rubin,
    Alan Sontag, Ron Von der Porten, Peter Weichsel
2. Rich Freisner, Brian Glubok, Michael S. Lawrence,
    George Rapee, Michael Rosenberg, John Solodar

1981 1. Larry N. Cohen, Ron Gerard, Ralph Katz,
    Warren Rosner, Allan Stauber, John Sutherlin
2. Bart Bramley, Rich Freisner,
    Ed Manfield, Kit Woolsey

LIFE MASTER PAIRS.

This six-session event with two qualifying, two semifinal and two final rounds, restricted to Life Masters, is contested for the VON ZEDTWITZ GOLD CUP.

WINNERS

1930 1. P. Hal Sims, Waldemar K. von Zedtwitz
2. Ely Culbertson, Josephine Culbertson

1931 1. David Burnstine, Howard Schenken
2. Michael T. Gottlieb, Theodore A. Lightner

1932 1. Michael T. Gottlieb, Theodore A. Lightner
2. David Burnstine, Howard Schenken

1933 1. David Burnstine, Howard Schenken
2. P. Hal Sims, Waldemar K. von Zedtwitz

1934 1. Richard L. Frey, Howard Schenken
2. Walter Malowan, Sydney Rusinow

1935 1. B. Jay Becker, Theodore A. Lightner
2. Louis J. Haddad, Charles A. Hall

1936 1. David Burnstine, Oswald Jacoby
2. Robert Appleyard, Isadore Epstein

1937 1. S. Garton Churchill, Charles S. Lochridge
2. Doris Fuller, Dr. Henry J. Vogel

1938 1. Morrie Elis, Sherman Stearns
2. John R. Crawford, Charles J. Solomon

1939 1. Robert Appleyard, Harry J. Fishbein
2. Oswald Jacoby, Waldemar K. von Zedtwitz

1940 1. Harry J. Fishbein, Morrie Elis
2. Sam Fry, Jr., Myron Fuchs

1941 1. Merwyn D. Maier, Howard Schenken
2. John R. Crawford, Oswald Jacoby

1942 1. Charles H. Goren, Helen Sobel
2. Philip Abramsohn, Tobias Stone

1943 1. John R. Crawford, Howard Schenken
2. Sidney Silodor, Magaret Wagar

1944 1. Samuel Katz, Peter A. Leventritt
2. Ambrose Casner, Ralph Hirschberg

1945 1. Robert Appleyard, Malcolm A. Lightman
2. Bertram Lebhar, Jr., Simon Rossant

1946 1. Sidney Silodor, Charles J. Solomon
2. Lee Hazen, Ruth Sherman

1947 1. Allen P. Harvey, Frank Weisbach
2. John R. Crawford, Theodore A. Lightner

1948 1. S. Garton Churchill, Cecil Head
2. Erik Coon, Vincent Remey

1949 1. Ruth Gilbert, Leo Roet
2. Arthur Glatt, Albert Weiss

1950 1. Manuel Sherwin, Dr. C. W. Yorke
2. Edward N. Marcus, Samuel M. Stayman

1951 1. Richard Kahn, Peter A. Leventritt
2. Ned Drucker, Edgar Kaplan

1952 1. William W. Jackson, William Joseph
2-3. Arthur Glatt, Albert Weiss
2-3. John R. Crawford, Howard Schenken

1953 1. Milton Q. Ellenby, William A. Rosen
2. Charles H. Goren, Helen Sobel

1954 1. David C. Carter, John W. Hubbell
2. Victor Mitchell, Ira S. Rubin

1955 1. Ben Fain, Paul H. Hodge
2. Victor Mitchell, Ira S. Rubin

1956 1. Alvin Roth, Tobias Stone
2. John R. Crawford, Sidney Silodor

1957 1. H. Sanborn Brown, Martin Cohn
2. Francis P. Begley, Louis Kelner

1958 1-2. Charles H. Goren, Helen Sobel
1-2. Wilson Landley, Louis Levy

1959 1. Ed Rosen, Dan Rotman
2. Sidney Aronson, Larry Weiss

1960 1. Helen Portugal, Morris Portugal
2. Curtis K. Smith, Bobby Wolff

1961 1. Philip Feldesman, Marshall Miles
2. Paul Kibler, Robert Reynolds

1962 1. Philip Feldesman, Ira S. Rubin
2. Edith Kemp, Albert Weiss

1963 1. Lewis L. Mathe, Edward O. Taylor
2. Ira S. Rubin, Curtis K. Smith

1964 1. B. Jay Becker, Dorothy Hayden
2. Bruce Elliott, Percy E. Sheardown

1965 1. Victor Mitchell, Samuel M. Stayman
2. Alvin Roth, Tobias Stone

1966 1. Hermine Baron, Meyer Schleifer
2. Morrie Freier, Robert Reynolds

1967 1. Philip Feldesman, Lewis L. Mathe
2. Diana Schuld, Frank Schuld

1968 1. Billy Eisenberg, Bobby Goldman
2. James Jacoby, Bobby Wolff

1969 1. Sammy R. Kehela, Eric R. Murray
2. Chuck F. Burger, James Cayne

1970 1. Paul Heitner, Michael Moss
2. Robert Freedman, James Mathis

1971 1. Alvin Roth, Barbara Rappaport
2. James Jacoby, Minda Brachman

1972 1. Alvin Roth, Barbara Rappaport
2. Alan Sontag, Peter Weichsel

1973 1. Jack Blair, Paul Swanson
2. Chuck F. Burger, James Cayne

1974 1. Gerald Michaud, G. Robert Nail
2. Walter Walvick, Thomas Weik

1975 1. Roy Fox, Eugene O'Neill
2. Michael Becker, Ahmed Hussein

1976 1. Robert Lipsitz, Neil Silverman
2. Garey Hayden, Mike Passell

1977 1. Alan Sontag, Peter Weichsel
2. Ken Cohen, Robert Lipsitz

1978 1. Mary Jane Farell, Marilyn Johnson
2. Ron Feldman, David Sacks

1979 1. Ralph Katz, Kenneth Schultze
2. Dan Morse, G. Robert Nail

1980 1. Robert D. Hamman, Eric Rodwell
2. Don Caton, Homer Shoop

1981 1. Fred Stewart, Steve Weinstein
2. Paul Lavings, Bob Richman

SENIOR AND ADVANCED SENIOR MASTER PAIRS.

This four-session event with two qualifying sessions and two final sessions was contested for the R. L. MILES TROPHY through 1975.

WINNERS

1950 1. John Winsten, Mrs. John Winsten
2-3. Dorothy E. Berning, Sims Gaynor
2-3. Dorsey W. Brooks, Fred Gregorich
1951 1. Ben Fain, Julius L. Rosenblum
2. Dorothy Glick, Aaron Ritter
1952 1. Elaine Lee, Hary Feinburg
2. Betty Harding, Mrs. Allan E. van Ness
1953 1-2. Dr. Robert M. Lloyd, Elfric H. Martin
1-2. Margaret L. Fisher, Kiffin Rockwell
1954 1. Armand Fahrer, Richard B. Troxel
2. Richard G. Lesko, Paul A. Schwarz
1955 1. Stanley Rappaport, Herschel Wolpert
2. Robert Sitnek, Betty Windley
1956 1. Nat Gerstman, Mrs. Marshall Nevins
2. George Ateljevich, Robert E. Herb
1957 1-2. Arnold Levine, Harold Solof
1-2. Daniel J. Conroy, William T. Dean
1958 1. Fritz J. Hopf, Mrs. Fritz J. Hopf
2. Allan R. Cohen, Herbert C. Wilton
1959 1. Victor Lohmann, Robert L. Muyres
2. Ira Ewen, Thomas C. Griffin
1960 1. Lillian Hilbert, Forest Lowe
2. Ruth Roe, Stephens Roe
1961 1. Amos Brown, Mark D. Mohr
2. Dr. Ronald Forbes, Jack Howell
1962 1. Leon Shore, George Tornay
2. Richard Dufour, Hugh C. MacLean
1963 1. Gerald Hallee, Paul Soloway
2. Frank Adams, Max Neiman
1964 1. Mrs. R. Gust, Jr., Mrs. Leslie Wilcox
2. Gerald A. Caravelli, Alan Levine
1965 1. Muriel Levin, Delle Levinson
2. Don Guerin, Charlotte Sturm
1966 1. Carla Gross, H. E. Pries
2. Steve Goldstein, Ron Rubin
1967 1. Alvin Levy, Harold Thaw
2. Maryanne Drury, Kenneth Kadis
1968 1. Henry Greenberg, John Landon
2. Howard Abrams, Jim Crumpacker
1969 1. Col. William B. Foster, Bobbie Foster
2. Judy Carmena, Proctor Hawkins
1970 1. Michael Krevor, James Lewis
2. Dennis McGarry, Louis Reich
1971 1. William L. Geleerd, Jr., Marc S. Passman
2. Bert Newman, Dave Turner
1972 1. Chris Patrias, Dr. Wen Y. Yue
2. Robert Bell, Jeff Hall
1973 1. Joel Friedberg, Harry Looks
2. William Post, Alvin Swonger
1974 1. Dale Beers, Dave Silberstein
2. Ethan Stein, Karen Swenson
1975 1. Kitty Munson, Robert Schachter
2. John Brady, Patricia Murphy

MASTER MIXED TEAMS.

This event is contested for the LEBHAR TROPHY (originally for the BARCLAY TROPHY until 1945). A four-session Board-a-Match event, with two qualifying rounds and two final rounds, is restricted to Senior Masters and players of higher rank. In 1969 this event was played in three sessions.

BARCLAY TROPHY

WINNERS

1929 1. Max M. Cohen, Mrs. M. K. Alexander,
Rose Fleischer, R. Frankenstein
1930 1. Cmdr. Winfield W. Liggett, Jr., Dorothy Rice Sims,
P. Hal Sims, Sir Derrick J. Wernher
2. W. Cleveland Cogswell, J. Arnold Farrar,
Doris Fuller, George Reith
1931 1. Mrs. G. A. Bennett, Doris Fuller,
Charles S. Lochridge, George Reith

2. E. M. Baker, Margaret Beech,
William E. McKenney, Mrs. H. D. Stahl
1932 1. Marie Black, H. Huber Boscowitz,
Sam Fry, Jr., Olga Hilliard
2. Mrs. L. Bloomberg, Bernard Cone,
A. Louis Gotthelf, Mrs. Thomas Stern
1933 1. David Burnstine, Elinor Murdoch,
Mrs. Ivan Stengel, Edwin A. Wetzler
2. Dorothy Rice Sims, P. Hal Sims,
Margaret Wagar, Waldemar K. von Zedtwitz
1934 1. Lester R. Bachner, Mrs. Lester R. Bachner,
James H. Lemon, Martha Lemon
2. A. Mitchell Barnes, Barbara Collyer,
Doris Fuller, Dr. Henry J. Vogel
1935 1. Helen Bonwit, Howard Schenken,
Ruth Sherman, Louis H. Watson
2. Mary Clement, Mary Zita Jacoby,
Oswald Jacoby, Waldemar K. von Zedtwitz
1936 1. Hortense Evans, Louis J. Haddad,
Robert McPherran, Elizabeth Whitney
2. B. Jay Becker, Helen Bonwit,
Howard Schenken, Sally Young
1937 1. Philip Abramsohn, Estelle Drescher,
Morrie Elis, Ann Naiman
2. S. Garton Churchill, Phyllis Gardner,
Travers LeGros, Dorothy Roberts
1938 1. Doris Fuller, Charles H. Goren,
Dr. Henry J. Vogel, Sally Young
2. Eleanor Hirsch, John C. Kunkel,
Helen Pendelton Rockwell, Milton Vernoff
1939 1. Robert Chatkin, Valerie Klein,
Alvin Landy, Florence Stratford
2. Edward G. Ellenbogen, Peggy Golder,
Helen Mitchell, Charles J. Solomon
1940 1. Marie Black, Henry H. Chanin,
Olive Peterson, Waldemar K. von Zedtwitz
2. Edward G. Ellenbogen, Peggy Golder,
Helen Mitchell, Charles J. Solomon
1941 1. Charles H. Goren, Sidney Silodor,
Helen Sobel, Sally Young
2. Oswald Jacoby, Louise Wainwright,
Sherman Stearns, Mrs. William A. Tucker
1942 1. John R. Crawford, Olive Peterson,
Margaret Wagar, Waldemar K. von Zedtwitz
2. Philip Abramson, Kay Rhodes,
Edith Seligman, Tobias Stone
1943 1. Charles H. Goren, Olive Peterson,
Sidney Silodor, Helen Sobel
2. Edith Hammond, Pat Lightner,
Walter Malowan, Stuyvesant Wainwright
1944 1. Charles H. Goren, Olive Peterson,
Sidney Silodor, Helen Sobel
2. Marie Basher, Edward Cohn,
John R. Crawford, Margaret Wagar
1945 1. John R. Crawford, Ruth Sherman,
Margaret Wagar, Waldemar K. von Zedtwitz
2. Morrie Elis, Harry J. Fishbein,
Alvin Roth, Edith Seligman

Contested 1946–1955 as a separate National event held on the West Coast)

1946 1. Nell Wells, George Wells,
Kay Dunn, James Dunn
1947 1. Rose Eidem, Meyer Scheifer,
Betty Bysshe, Detmar Walther
1948 1. Alma Rosekrans, Waldemar von Zedtwitz,
Maurice Seiler, Mrs. Maurice Seiler
1949 1. Arnold Kauder, Mary Jane Kauder,
Helen Cale, Jack Ehrlenbach
1950 1. Arnold Kauder, Mary Jane Kauder,
Helen Cale, Jack Ehrlenbach
1951 1. Ruth Smith, Casey Million,
Nell Wells, John Hancock
1952 1. Don Oakie, Mrs. James Moffatt,
Stella Rebner, Doug Steen
1953 1. Barry Cohen, Stella Rebner,
Malvine Klausner, Dr. Eddie Frischauer
1954 1. Harriet Rethers, Clarence Strouse,
Alicia Kempner, Barry Crane
1955 1. Arnold Kauder, Mary Jane Kauder,
Nell Wells, Ernest Rovere

LEBHAR TROPHY

WINNERS

1946 1. Samuel Katz, Alicia Kempner,
Evelyn Lebhar, Bertram Lebhar, Jr.
2. Charles H. Goren, Emily Folline,
Sidney Silodor, Helen Sobel

1947 1. Harry J. Fishbein, Ruth Goldberg,
Ludwig Kabakjian, Edith Seligman
2-3. Emily Folline, Peter A. Leventritt,
David Warner, Sally Young
2-3. Harold Harkavy, Jane Jaeger,
Lewis M. Jaeger, Mrs. G. Strasser

1948 1. John R. Crawford, Charles H. Goren,
Helen Sobel, Margaret Wagar
2. Harry J. Fishbein, Ruth Goldberg,
Ludwig Kabakjian, Edith Seligman

1949 1. Peter A. Leventritt, Charles J.Solomon,
Peggy Solomon, Sally Young
2. John R. Crawford, Charles H. Goren,
Helen Sobel, Margaret Wagar

1950 1. Peter A. Leventritt, Charles J. Solomon,
Peggy Solomon, Sally Young
2. John R. Crawford, Charles H. Goren,
Helen Sobel, Margaret Wagar

1951 1. Jane Jaeger, Ruth Kahn, Leo Roet, Ruth Sherman
2. Myron Field, Ruth Gordon,
Charles H. Goren, Helen Sobel

1952 1. Anne Burnstein, Harold Harkavy,
Alvin Roth, Edith Seligman
2. John R. Crawford, Emma Jean Hawes, George Rapee,
Olive Peterson, Sidney Silodor

1953 1. Anne Burnstein, Harold Harkavy, Edith Kemp,
Alvin Roth, Gloria Turner
2. Emanuel Hochfeld, Mary Jane Kauder,
Lewis L. Mathe, Gloria Turner

1954 1. Charles H. Goren, Sidney Silodor,
Helen Sobel, Margaret Wagar
2. Marianne Boschan, Gertrude Eberson,
David Murray, Lewis Tubbs

1955 1. Gratian Goldstein, Harold Harkavy,
Terry Michaels, Alvin Roth
2. Mary Bowden, Douglas Drury, Richard Freedman
Agnes Gordon, Eric R. Murray

1956 1. Mary Bowden, Douglas Drury, Robert Freeman,
Agnes Gordon, Eric R. Murray
2. Barbara Brier, Jan Stone,
Tobias Stone, Waldemar K. von Zedtwitz

1957 1. John R. Crawford, Milton Q. Ellenby, Harold Harkavy,
Edith Kemp, Gloria Turner
2. Sam Fry, Jr., Dorothy Hayden,
Sally Johnson, Ira S. Rubin

1958 1. Leland Ferer, Gratian Goldstein,
Eunice Rosen, William Rosen
2. B. Jay Becker, Bee Gale,
Betty Goldberg, Howard Schenken

1959 1. Peter A. Leventritt, Robert F. Jordan,
Charles J. Solomon, Peggy Solomon, Sally Young
2. Leonard B. Harmon, Edgar Kaplan, Peggy Rotzell,
Alfred Sheinwold, Betty Sheinwold

1960 1. William Grieve, Alicia Kempner,
George Rapee, Betty Ann Welch
2. B. Jay Becker, Dorothy Hayden,
Norman Kay, Sidney Silodor

1961 1. Richard Freeman, Emanuel Hochfield,
Louise Robinson, Gloria Turner
2. Dr. John Fisher, Jean Frankel, Lou Gurvich,
Boots Kendrick, Sidney Lazard

1962 1. Charles Coon, Agnes Gordon,
Eric R. Murray, Helen Portugal
2. Norman Kay, Sydney Silodor,
Sylvia Stein, Margaret Wagar

1963 1. Sidney Lazard, Betty Kaplan,
Edgar Kaplan, Stella Rebner
2. Israel Cohen, Garner McDaniel,
Terry Michaels, Alvin Roth

1964 1. Dr. John Fisher, John Gerber,
Emma Jean Hawes, Margaret Wagar
2-3. Martin J. Cohen, Hampton Hume,
Bernadine Jenkins, Mary Philley
2-3. Harold Harkavy, Virginia Heckel,
Edith Kemp, Clifford Russell, Jerome Yavitz, Jr.

1965 1. Barbara Brier, Alvin Roth, Jan Stone,
Tobias Stone, Waldemar K. von Zedtwitz
2. Burt Norton, Carol Norton, Alan Press,

William Rosen, Sylvia Stein, Carol Stolkin

1966 1. James Cayne, Judy Dryer, Paul Soloway,
Eunice Rosen, William Rosen
2. Barbara Rappaport, Alvin Roth,
Bee Schenken, Howard Schenken

1967 1. Mike Cappelletti, Kathie Cappelletti,
Michael Moss, Gail Shane
2-4. John Gerber, Norman Kay, Carol Klar,
George Rosenkranz, Edith Rosenkranz
2-4. B. Jay Becker, Dr. John Fisher,
Dorothy Hayden, Emma Jean Hawes
2-4. Leland Ferer, Gratian Goldstein,
Fred Hamilton, Sylvia Stein

1968 1. Minda Brachman, James Jacoby,
Oswald Jacoby, Helen, Sobel Smith
2. Betty Kaplan, Edgar Kaplan,
George Rapee, Carol Stolkin

1969 1. Janice Cohn, Flo Orner, Charles Peres,
Dan Rotman, Ivar Stakgold, Alice Stakgold
2. Barry Crane, Jules Farell, Mary Jane Farell,
Marilyn Johnson, Peter Rank

1970 1. Dorothy Bare, Gerald Bare,
Eugenie Mathe, Lewis L. Mathe
2-3. Ken Barbour, William Daly, Mickey Rosenthal,
Helen Strasberg, Dave Straberg
2-3. Betty Adler, Julian Adler, Dave Sachs, Sue Sachs

1971 1. John Anderson, Ron E. Andersen,
Marilyn McCrary, Sue Picus
2. Dorsey Brooks, Zerrene Brooks,
Joan Remey, Vincent Remey

1972 1. Gail Moss, Michael Moss,
Marietta Passell, William Passell
2. B. Jay Becker, Dr. John Fisher, Emma Jean Hawes,
Alan Truscott, Dorothy Hayden Truscott

1973 1. Ellen Alfandre, Philip Feldesman,
Edith Sacks, Stanley Tomchin
2-5. Robert Lipsitz, Jo Morse, Peggy Parker,
Steve Parker, Stephen W. Robinson
2-5. Doug Fraser, Sandra Fraser,
Barbara Saltsman, Joe Silver
2-5. Mark Berger, Sallie Johnson, Amos Kaminsky,
Jack Saltz, Mona Stocknoff
2-5. Carol Crawford, John R. Crawford,
Barbara Rappaport, Alvin Roth

1975 1. Gerald Caravelli, Nancy Gruver,
Jim Linhart, Helen Utegaard
2-3. Shirlee Lazarus, Eugenie Mathe, Lewis L. Mathe,
Joan Remey, Vincent Remey, James E. Zimmerman
2-3. Carol Crawford, John R. Crawford,
Barbara Rappaport, Alvin Roth

1976 1-2. Dr. Richard H. Katz, Carol Sanders,
Paul Swanson, Marion Weed
1-2. Fred Hamilton, John C. Sutherlin, Peggy Sutherlin,
Rhoda Walsh, Nancy Weichsel, Peter Weichsel

1977 1. Nancy Alpaugh, Joan DeWitt, Mark Lair, Sidney Lazard
2. Ethel Dayboch, Morrie Freier,
Richard Paulsen, Sue Thornton

1978 1. Nancy Alpaugh, Joan DeWitt, Mark Lair, Sidney Lazard
2. Betty Adler, Julian Adler, David Sachs, Sue Sachs

1979 1-3. Betty Bloom, Steven Bloom,
Mark Cohen, Edith Sacks
1-3. Nancy Alpaugh, Joan DeWitt, Mark Lair, Sidney Lazard
1-3. Lynne Feldman, Mark Feldman, Ed Nagy, Sharon Smith

1980 1. Barry Crane, Jose John Hamui, Elias Konstantinovsky,
Laura Mariscal, Kerri Shuman
2. Gerald Caravelli, Dennis McGarry, Joan Remey,
Vincent Remey, Helen Utegaard

1981 1. Doug Fraser, Sandra Fraser, Ralph Katz,
Paul Lewis, Linda Peterson, Esta van Zandt
2. Bill Cole, Lynn Deas, Norb Kremer, Beth Palmer

GRAND NATIONAL TEAMS. The competition is contested for the MOREHEAD TROPHY. The initial stages are contested over the course of several months in the 25 ACBL Districts. By the final stages, held at the Summer North American Championships, the field has been reduced to the eight Zonal Championship Teams.

WINNERS

1973 1. Russell Arnold, James Beery, Jane Jaeger,
Richard Pavlicek, William Seamon, Robert G. Sharp
2. Brian Economidy, Jerry Levitt, Roger Lord,

           Norb Kremer, Dave Smith, Ron Smith

1974 1.   Larry Cohen, Billy Eisenberg, Eddie Kantar,
       Dr. Richard H. Katz, Paul Soloway, John Swanson
     2.   Chuck F. Burger, Fred Hamilton, Howard Perlman,
       Stanley Smith, Jeffrey Starr, Dick Yanko

1975 1.   Dr. John Fisher, Charles Gabriel, Robert D. Hamman,
       Jim Hooker, Charles Weed, Bobby Wolff
     2.   Mike Cook, Jim Felts, Doug Hill, Reece Rogers,
       Ronald L. Smith, Bernie Yomtov

1976 1.   Billy Eisenberg, Eddie Kantar,
       Paul Soloway, John Swanson
     2.   Marty Fleisher, Charlie Friedman,
       Ron Gerard, Halina Jamner,
       Archie McKellar, Neil Nathanson

1977 1.   Robert D. Hamman, Dan Morse, Curtis K. Smith,
       Eddie Wold, Bobby Wolff
     2.   Bobby Lipsitz, Steve Parker,
       Stephen W. Robinson, Kit Woolsey

1978 1.   Gerald Caravelli, Charles Peres, William Rosen,
       Milton Rosenberg, Dan Rotman
     2.   Allan Cokin, Bobby Levin, Bud Reinhold,
       William Seamon, Steve Sion

1979 1.   Greg DeFotis, Jerry Goldfein, Arnold Leavitt,
       Larry Robbins, Claude Vogel
     2.   Marty Bergen, Chuck Lamprey,
       Warren Rosner, Allan Stauber

1980 1.   Jack Bitman, Jan Janitschke,
       V. Craig Janitschke, Dick Lesko
     2.   Russell Arnold, Edith Kemp, William Passell,
       Cliff Russell, William Seamon, Dave Strasberg

1981 1.   Ira Chorush, James Jacoby, Mike Passell,
       George Rosenkranz, Eddie Wold
     2.   Mike Becker, Brian Glubok, John Lowenthal,
       Phillip Martin, Michael Rosenberg, Ron Rubin

SECONDARY CHAMPIONSHIPS

MASTER TEAMS. This two-session team event restricted to players of Senior Master rank and higher was contested for the MARCUS CUP (FABER CUP 1946–1952). It was scored by Board-a-Match until 1972 when scoring was changed to international matchpoints with Swiss pairings. The event was discontinued after the 1978 contest.

WINNERS

1946   Charles B. Groden, Harold Harkavy,
      Elinor Murdoch, Jack Shore
1947   Jack Cushing, Charles H. Saunders,
      Howard Zacks, Helen Zacks
1948   Maynard Adams, F. Ayres Bombeck,
      G. Robert Nail, Edson Wood
1949   H. Sanborn Brown, John F. Carlin,
      Sam Delott, Irving Deuter
1950   Gretchen Feldstein, Gratian Goldstein,
      Helen Lackman, Herman Lackman
1951   Dorothy E. Berning, Jack Cushing,
      Jay T. Feigus, Sims Gaynor *(tied with)*
      Jeff Glick, Arthur S. Goldsmith, Alvin Landy, Sol Mogal
1952   Warren Blank, J. George Boeckh, Jack Denny,
      Duke Dautell, Jerome Jacobs
1953   Lee Hazen, Richard Kahn, Edgar Kaplan,
      Dr. William Lipton, Ruth Sherman *(tied with)*
      Israel Cohen, Richard Freeman,
      Fred Karpin, Michael Michaels
1954   Gerald Ackerman, Leonard Karp,
      Gwen Montgomery, Robert Rice
1955   John Gerber, James Jacoby, Oswald Jacoby,
      Paul Hodge, Walter Wolff, Jr.
1956   A.H. Brown, Mrs. A.H. Brown,
      Richard Hart, F. Bert Powley
1957   John Moran, William Root, Peggy Rotzell, Robert Sitnek
1958   Jackie Begin, Barbara Brier,
      Maurice Paul, Peter A. Pender *(tied with)*
      Fred Berger, Dr. John Fisher,
      Emma Jean Hawes, Margaret Wagar *(and)*
      Mrs. J. Theron Brown, Nathan Gerstman,
      Dr. Richard Greene, Frank Nichols, Charles Whitehead
1959   Nathan Gerstman, Mrs. Thomas McKenna, Eric R. Murray,
      Mrs. William Selikoff, Paul Trent

1960   E.G. Burke, Eddie Kantar, Marshall Miles,
      William Root, Tobias Stone
1961   Armand Barfus, Billy Eisenberg,
      Marty Ginsburg, Jeff Westheimer
1962   Alan Bell, Leona Low, Marc Low,
      Roger Sarfaty, Richard Vission
1963   Hal Kandler, Jim Linhart, Hugh Ross, Richard Zeckhauser
1964   Jack Marsch, Hank Promislow, Helen Promislow,
      Howard Rubin, Douglas Thomson
1965   Ron E. Andersen, Robert Hathaway,
      Darrell Penrod, Charles Shannon
1966   Harvey Cohen, Eddie Kantar,
      Phyllis Kantar, Marshall Miles
1967   Harry J. Fishbein, Julius L. Rosenblum,
      Charles J. Solomon, Peggy Solomon, Sylvia Stein
1968   Howard Abrams, Mark Blumenthal,
      Seymour Leibowitz, Kit Woolsey
1969   Midge Cutler, Jeanne Davison,
      Jack Titus III, Walter A. Willson
1970   Don Hocevar, Philip Leon, Joan Remey, Vincent Remey
1971   Joan Bernard, William Davis, Alice Gerard, William Rowe
1972   Hermine Baron, Bernie Bergovoy,
      Michael S. Lawrence, Jim Stein
1973   Jack Blair, Larry Gould, Richard Shepherd, Paul Swanson
1974   Frank Bell, Jim Hilton, Michael Karson, Steve Landen
1975   Dave Berkowitz, Joel Friedberg, Eddie Kantar,
      Jim Linhart, Merle Tom
1976   Alan Bell, Lex Degroot, Jan Janitschke, Leslie Tsou
1977   Flight A: Barbara Balas, George Balas, Matt Granovetter,
              Jim Roberts, Victor Mitchell
1978   Flight A: Gerry Charney, Allan Graves,
              Sammy R. Kehela, Eric R. Murray
1979   Flight A: Barry Crane, Clarence Goppert, Jan Janitschke,
              V. Craig Janitschke, Kerri Shuman
1980   Flight A: Mark Blumenthal, Sandi Leavitt,
              Paul Sugar, Claude Vogel
1981   Flight A: Elisabeth Brenhouse, Tony Glynne,
              Mel Skonik, Ron Smith

SUB–SENIOR MASTER TEAMS. This two-session Board-a-Match event restricted to players below the rank of Senior Master is contested for the ROTHSCHILD TROPHY.

WINNERS

1938   Mrs. E. Melvin Goodard, Mrs. B.D. Lavine,
      Anne Rosenfeld, Mrs. H.A. Steiner
1939   Mabel Ervin, Ruth Horn, Valerie Klein, Gussie Planco
1940   A.R. Dick, C. William Potts,
      James T. Sheern, Jr., Edward R. Thomas
1941   William Cheeks, Mrs. William Cheeks,
      J.J. Wallendorf, Mrs. J.J. Wallendorf
1942   Mrs. Julius Daub, Arthur Jarmel,
      Morris Strauss, Mrs. C. Van Slochem
1943   Harold Frankenheimer, Mrs. A.P. Hess,
      Ruth Rice Fred Slater
1944   Richard Adams, Mrs. Richard Adams,
      Sigmund Freisinger, E.L. Saqui
1945   Lester A. Doyle, David Goertner, Lee Sager, Ernest Theimer
1946   Dr. Kalman Apfel, Lawrence Blum,
      Charles Lembeck, Oscar Yablon
1947   Augusta Cantor, Andrew Gabrilovitch,
      Victor Mitchell, Henry Mullaney
1948   Melvin Dagovitz, Robert Jonesi, N. Kaufman,
      Paul Sugar, Joseph Weiner *(tied with)*
      Ethel Daybach, H.N. Daybach,
      Dr. A.G. Engel, D.G. Horwitz
1949   M.H. Daskais, B. Gumbin, Jack Gumbin, Bud Randall
1950   Leslie Craig, I.E. Davis, Dr. Henry Goldman, Louis McLean
1951   Clifton Lovenberg, Mrs. Clifton Lovenberg
      Dr. Seward Transue, Mrs. Seward Transue
1952   Paul E. Gable, Sr., Dr. Milton Levitan
      Stanley Schwartz, Jr., Frank Westreich
1953   Jerome Ember, Wayne B. Gidcumb
      Mrs. Wayne B. Gidcumb, L. McCord, Monty McCord
1954   Kent Boyle, Tom Burris, Mr. Don Currie, Louis Sopkin
      (tied with) R.G. Clarkson, Ralph C. Schreyer,
      A.G. Sparks, Edward C. Worden II

1955	Mitchell Edelson, Stanley Lefler, Bryce McAdam, Ross M. Sherrill
1956	Marion Braunstein, Bernard Jereski, Robert Lipton, Winnie Slutsky
1957	Lewis Kaplan, Arnold Levy, Joan Levy, Ronald Walaitis
1958	Dr. Edward Galler, Les Klein, Jim Taylor, Allen Weisbord
1959	Costas Kouskolekas, Elizabeth Swanson, Richard Swanson Robert Whitcomb
1960	Jerome Esterkin, Barbara Feldman, Eugene Grossblatt Jerome Micklin
1961	Jack Hudgins, Jules Jacobson, Renold Lambert, Stan Lipnick, Margaret Panella
1962	Mrs. G. Anderson, Dr. Paul Leck, Mrs. J. McGuiness, Joe Schneider
1963	Clifford Clarke, Guy Dobbs, Dr. Keneshaw Mannings, Elizabeth Spain
1964	Malcolm Coutts, Jane Pollock, Dr. Gordon Shorting, Gordon Turner
1965	Burton Ascheim, John Black. Richard Holver, Edwin Strossberger
1966	Jerry Farrell, Russell Maik, Harold McConnell, Jim Wallen
1967	Marty Bergen, Richard Betz, Kevin Comins, Richard Elder
1968	G.R. Brings, R.A. Engen, Jerry McAllister, P.D. Schwarz
1969	Douglas Blagdon, Howard Einberg, Lawrence Finkelman, Scott Kurman
1970	Stewart Blickman, Tim Lundeen, David N. Olson, Mike Throckmorton
1971	Bobby Adelman, John Carlson, Bernard Reddy, Steven Yellen

MIXED PAIRS. This two-session Mixed Pairs event is restricted to players of Senior Master rank and higher.

WINNERS

1963	Jesse Sloan, Jan Stone
1964	Eleanor Crounse, Richard Lawrence
1965	Dora Brechner, Michael Moss
1966	Bettie Cohn, Martin Cohn
1967	Edgar Kaplan, Judy Kay
1968	Edith Kemp, William Seamon
1969	Sandra Roark, Roger Stern
1970	Gaylor Kasle, Nancy Lewis
1971	Nancy Richardson, F. Holton Sexton
1972	Hermine Baron, Michael S. Lawrence
1973	Richard Doughty, Pat LaCour
1974	Flight A: Bernice Goldstein, Norm Rosen
1975	Helen Blakey, Robert Blakey
1976	John Gerber, Carol Klar *(tied with)* Gaylor Kasle, Jane Stickney
1977	Flight A: Gene Freed, Terry Michaels
1978	Flight A: Beryl Callaghan, Victor Goldberg
1979	Flight A: Janet Gookin, Robert Gookin
1980	Flight A: Dave Berkowitz, Sue Picus

INDIVIDUAL. This two-session open event is contested for the KEOHANE TROPHY (since 1973, but not in play 1978 and 1979).

WINNERS

1971	Proctor Hawkins
1972	Gerald Oehm
1973	Robert A. Hume
1974	Robert Orne
1975	Gary Fischer
1976	Rose Ritter
1977	Charles Deible
1980	Richard Colker
1981	David Ezekiel

OPEN PAIRS. This is a two-session pair event.

WINNERS

1971	Beverly Nelson, Brian Nelson

1972	Colby Vernay, Paul Womack
1973	Diana Schuld, Frank Schuld
1974	Bart Bramley, John Schermer
1975	Dave Berkowitz, Ken Cohen
1976	Larry Mori, Larry Robbins
1977	Sheldon Kirsch, Robert Tracy *(tied with)* Robert Rosenberg, Pete Weglarski
1978	Morris Aboody, Ken Murray
1979	Jim Kirkham, Kitty Podolsky
1980	Jim Siebel, Mark Starr
1981	Sally DeForest, Larry Rabideau

LEVENTRITT PAIRS. This two-session event restricted to non-qualifiers of the Life Master Pairs championship was contested for the LEVENTRITT TROPHY through 1971.

WINNERS

1950	Mrs. W.H. Lehman, Mrs. J.H. McCarthy
1951	Emily Folline, Stella Landauer
1952	Harry Feinberg, Sidney A. Fink
1953	Joe Skinner, Mary Skinner
1954	Fred Berger, Sidney Lazard
1955	Jim Millerd, John Millerd
1956	Murray Gross, Adelaide Neuwirth
1957	James Jacoby, Oswald Jacoby
1958	William Rosen, Pete Szecsi
1959	Jeff Glick, Julius L. Rosenblum
1960	Emma Jean Hawes, Margaret Wagar
1961	David Cox, Mrs. Leonard Robinson
1962	Donald Horwitz, Julien Phillippy
1963	Robert D. Hamman, Donald P. Krauss
1964	Leonard D. Harmon, Ivar Stakgold
1965	Richard Balanow, Steve Honet
1966	Larry Oakey, Brian Pauls
1967	James Jacoby, Adaline Simon
1968	Brian Pauls, Hersh Wolch
1969	Nels Erickson, Jim Miller
1970	Dorsey Brooks, Duncan Phillips
1971	Fred Hamilton, Howard Perlman

MASTER PAIRS. This two-session pair event limited to players of Senior Master rank and higher is contested for the GOLDER CUP.

WINNERS

1947	M. Hamilton, Arthur Schlesinger
1948	Doris Fuller, Mrs. L.G. Weldon
1949	Ivan Half, A. Richard Revell
1950	Frieda Arst, Emanuel Hochfeld
1951	Mrs. J.Y. Bailey, Mrs. E.P. Turnbull
1952	Dr. Kalman Apfel, Louis Kelner
1953	Edgar Kaplan, Dr. Wiliam Lipton
1954	Kenneth S. Donovan, Marvin Paulshock
1955	Herbert Resnick, A. Richard Revell
1956	C. Robert Clements, William W. Shirk
1957	Maury Boehm, Armand Jacoby
1958	Elinor Murdoch, George Rosenkranz
1959	Alvin Goodman, Mrs. David Hollaner
1960	Grant Marsee, Edgar Simons
1961	Gunther Polak, Jay Wendt *(tied with)* J.L. Cabe, Mrs. William C. Miller
1962	Mrs. R.E. Cudahy, Mrs. Wallace Veurink
1963	Beth Crabbs, Terry Crabbs
1964	Richard Barbaris, Mrs. Richard Barbaris
1965	Daniel Marcus, Elizabeth Marcus
1966	Anita Davis, Mary Beth Townsend
1967	Frieda Arst, Leo B. Weiner
1968	Mrs. Harold Friedman, Shirley Snyder
1969	Mike McMahan, Jon Wittes
1970	Alan Dworetzky, Ralph Wesselman

1971	Chuck Lamprey, Sharyn Linkovsky
1972	Russ Ekeblad, Robert Stone
1973	Helen Smith, Marshall Spitz
1974	Steve Alpern, Dr. Norman Williams
1975	Ron E. Andersen, Hugh C. MacLean
1976	Bill Erickson, Fred McBride
1977	Ron E. Andersen, Kathie Wei
1978	Ross Grabel, Josh Parker
1979	Mark Jones, Rich Whitworth
1980	Bob Ryder, Barbara Valvo
1981	Ed Quinlan, Sarah Quinlan

NON–MASTER PAIRS.

This two-session event is restricted to players below the rank of Senior Master.

WINNERS

1971	Betty Leonard, William Leonard
1972	Bruce Boje, R.G. Burton
1973	Peter B. Bloch, Dr. Alfred D. Steinberg Candyce Clayton, David Leibowicz
1974	Bart Bloom, Mike Markovitz
1975	Kurt Lee Gandenberger, James Krekorian

COMMERCIAL AND INDUSTRIAL TEAMS.

This two-session Board-a-Match event is contested for the UNITED STATES PLAYING CARD TROPHY (originally for the ASSOCIATION OF AMERICAN PLAYING CARD MANUFACTURERS TROPHY until 1966).

1956	Eastern Air Lines Jim Day, Max Glasgow, C. Lewis, Margaret Wagar
1957	Equitable Life Arthur Auer, James Kappos, Joseph Plaxico, Albert Snyder
1958	New York Life Lee Haskell, Dorothy Hayden, David Strasberg, E. Wendt, Jr., Nicholas Zampino
1959	Western Electric Mrs. Frank Chemlick, M.F. Fleig, Dolores Keeling, John Nelson, Richard Johnson
1960	Rocketdyne Bernie Botfield, Robert King, W.A. Moser, John Porcella
1961	Reynolds Metals Rudolph Ashton, Harold Franklin, Richard Glenn, James Pecsok
1962	National Security Agency Richard Crump, Ray Fetzner, Ted Leahy, William J. Nucker
1963	Prudential Insurance Kenneth MacKinnon, William Mauskopf, Robert L. Patrick, Fred Rathgeber *(tied with)* Richard Bloch, Irwin Boris, Owen Rye, Roger Young
1964	Prudential Insurance Kenneth MacKinnon, William Mauskopf, Robert L. Patrick, Fred Rathgeber
1965	McDonnell Aircraft J.A. Davis, John Freeman, Don Geers, R.H. Hamilton
1966	Martin Company Glenn E. Kirk, Robert H. Lea, Paul Morehead, Tom Schmied
1967	Sperry Rand Corporation Morris Ashinsky, Richard Cobin, Abe Schoenfeld, Richard Schwartz
1968	Honeywell, Inc. A. Bezat, R. Blazei, W. Chamberlain, Mrs. W. Chamberlain, Jack Mourning, Richard Pidcock
1969	General Electric Norman F. Friedman, Ron A. Hamilton, Jim Hayashi, Frank C. Warzek
1970	Travelers Insurance James Cleary, William Cook, Robert Lipsitz, Robert Meredith, George Perry *(tied with)* Sperry Systems Morris Ashinsky, Richard Cobin, Robert Reiss, Abe Schoenfeld

1971	University of Chicago, Graduate School of Business Robert Ling, Arthur Ramer, George Sorter, Roman Weil
1972	Hospital Association Service Inc. Lee A. Hofacre, Audrey Rennels, Pat Solomons, Jerry Weitzner
1973	IBM Corp., Endicott NY Robert Cofer, Ben Ku, Stan Poplawski, Robert Spitzner
1974	Prudential Insurance Co. Arthur Hoffman, Melvin Klein, Fred Melman, Bart Yohn
1975	Prudential Insurance Co. Arthur Hoffman, Melvin Klein, Fred Melman, Bart Yohn
1976	Prudential Insurance Co. Arthur Hoffman, Melvin Klein, Fred Melman, Bart Yohn
1977	Chicago Mercantile Exchange James Cordas, David Youce, Randy McKay, Leonard Melamed, Brian Monieson, Bert Norton
1978	Harold Leonard & Co., Inc. Larry N. Cohen, Barry Hagedorn, Mimi Hagedorn, Frank Marcus, Harriet Marcus
1979	Harold Leonard & Co., Inc. Larry N. Cohen, Barry Hagedorn, Mimi Hagedorn, Frank Marcus, Harriet Marcus
1980	Harold Leonard & Co., Inc. Larry N. Cohen, Barry Hagedorn, Mimi Hagedorn, Frank Marcus, Harriet Marcus
1981	Harold Leonard & Co., Inc. Larry N. Cohen, Barry Hagedorn, Mimi Hagedorn, Frank Marcus

GODDARD PAIRS.

These are two-session, separate flight events for Men's and Women's Pairs, restricted to Senior Masters and players of higher rank. It was contested as a second flight for non-qualifiers of the NAC Men's and Women's Pairs until those events were moved to the Spring North American Championships in 1963.

WINNERS

1941	Sam Kaufer, Max N. Schwartz
1942	William V. Kirk, Faye Lasarow
1943	Arthur Jarmel, Edward Lembek
1944	Ruth Gordon, Florence Stratford
1945	Nathan Hyman, Leandel C. Levy
1946	Vera Glick, Vera Vaughan
1947	Sidney Aronson, Lawrence Weiss
1948	Mrs. W.J. Donaldson, Ivan Half
1949	James Geilfuss, Martin Lederer
1950	Jack Denny, Edwin J. Smith
1951	James L. Holton, Harry Lees
1952	Ethel Keohane, Frank Westcott
1953	Milton Q. Ellenby, Paul Sugar
1954	F. Ayres Bombeck, Harold Harkavy
1955	George Droder, William A. Rohr
1956	Jim Leonard, Alex Tschekaloff
1957	Mrs. William Keller, Mrs. Vernon Schick
1958	Arthur Robinson, Robert Sitnek
1959	Irving Berkson, Leonard Lehman
1960	Jules Farell, Milton Vernoff
1961	*Men's* Irving Guttman, Robert G. Sharp *Women's* Lois Albright, Mae Posluszny
1962	*Men's* Gordon Anderson, R. Norman Miller *Women's* Mrs. Edward Hartwell, Lois Jacobs
1963	*Men's* George Hershman, Edmon Lazarus *Women's* Mary Bowden, Mrs. Norman Rippon
1964	*Men's* Carl Hudecek, Robert G. Sharp *Women's* Gertrude Blasband, Peggy Solomon
1965	*Men's* David Cox, Jack Mathis *Women's* Louise Mark, Helen Utegaard
1966	*Men's* Kyle Larsen, Larry Weiss *Women's* Judy Dryer, Rhoda Walsh
1967	*Men's* Roy Perry, Olin Sweet *Women's* Barbara Birnholz, Barbara Tepper
1968	*Men's* T.J. Parris, James Nash *Women's* Doris Orlett, Shirley Swander
1969	*Men's* Monroe Ingberman, Charles Peres *Women's* Muriel Donnerstag, Bert Epstein

1970 *Men's* Melvin Klein, Robert A. Zeckhauser
     Women's Shirlee Harris, Judy Parker
1971 *Men's* Chuck Lamprey, Arthur Waldmann
     Women's Roberta Epstein, Barbara Rappaport
1972 *Men's* Loren Elliott, Don Paulsen
     Women's Beverly Rosenberg, Elaine Steinberg

SILVER TROPHY PAIRS This two-session flighted Open Pairs event was first contested at the Summer North American Championships in 1976 and is held at each of the three NAC. Flight A is unlimited, Flight B requirements are 0–1500 and Flight C requirements are 0–300. A Revere bowl trophy on a base is given to each winner.

WINNERS

1976	Flight A:	Ed Davis, Mike Smolen
	Flight B:	H.Y. Farnsworth, Henry Montoya
	Flight C:	George Bennett, Bill Creech
1977	Flight A:	Francine Cimon, François Gauthier
	Flight B:	Randy Baron, Vince Oliver
	Flight C:	George Friedman, Don Scholz
1978	Flight A:	Ted Brashler, Bob Glenn
	Flight B:	Bill Milgram, Leah Milgram
	Flight C:	Mitch Dunitz, Chris Hough
1979	Flight A:	Judi Radin, Kathie Wei
	Flight B:	Helen Beaulieu, Pat Roy
	Flight C:	Ed Bradac, Sharon Koidin
1980	Flight A:	Mitch Chandler, Alan Falk
	Flight B:	Rudi Cataldi, Byron Stefferud
	Flight C:	Andrew Wang, Daniel Windsor
1981	Flight A:	Francine Cimon, John Carruthers
	Flight B:	Adis Dombu, Si Dombu
	Flight C:	Irene Musinsky, Judith Ogan *(tied with)*
		George Kay, Benet Zupan

PRESIDENT'S PAIRS. This two-session event for players below the rank of Senior Master is contested for the MORGAN HOWARD TROPHY (PRESIDENT'S CUP). Until 1972 it was a three-session event, with two qualifying sessions and one final session.

WINNERS

1933 Samuel Katz, Ernest H. Siebert
1934 Cecile Guthrie, Morrie Elis
1935 Herbert Goldsmith, Jack Weisman
1936 Curtis Jacobson, George Rapee
1937 Richard E. Henry, Graham Miller
1938 Morris Crystal, Sam Naiman
1939 Herbert D. Lent, Mrs. Herbert D. Lent
1940 A.B. Stark, William Vanderporten
1941 Judge A.D. Delmar, David Horan
1942 Dr. Kalman Apfel, Francis P. Begley
1943 A. James Mills, Robert Tyson
1944 Luther Hamilton, Fred W. Hawke
1945 Mrs. Richard Adams, Sigmund Freisinger
1946 Nathan Hyman, Leander C. Levy
1947 Robert S. Fox, Robert Starr
1948 Thomas Fenwick, Paul G. Hopkins
1949 Eric R. Murray, John J. Scanlon
1950 Sol Babich, Laura Hardy
1951 Kenneth K. Donovan, Robert E. Newell
1952 James J. Klink, Richard G. Schreitmueller
1953 Joseph Chasson, Leo Weil
1954 T.D. O'Keefe, R.W. Tarares
1955 D.J. McDonald, Irvin Rooks
1956 Richard Hecht, Martin Scheinberg *(tied with)* Nathan Appel, Seymour Cohen
1957 Steve Berg, Sherry Polsky
1958 Cory Walker, Marie Walker
1959 Mrs. Gerald Bass, Tom Leverenz
1960 Lt. Frank Murphy, Earl Hayes
1961 Lt. Col. Arthur Hurow, Mrs. Arthur Hurow
1962 Brian Pauls, Douglas Thompson
1963 Guy H. Dobbs, Elizabeth Spain

1964 Gordon Robertson, Lois Robertson
1965 Gene Chait, Fred Slate
1966 Gus Afendoulis, Johnny Theodore
1967 Keith Beckett, H. Alan Sutton
1968 Walter S. Grey, Lester Cadwell
1969 Marshall Schwartz, R. Joe Wiley
1970 Lin Chui, Patrick Chye
1971 Robert Hupf, Daniel White
1972 Pamela Michael, Stanley Michael
1973 Steven Bloom, John Farmer
1974 Bert Hoffman, Bill Logan
1975 Joel London, Stephen Shepard
1976 James O'Hara, Helen Russell
1977 P.B. Andre, Larry Bass
1978 Toni Elaine Bales, Kenneth Cook
1979 Terry Arsenian, Larry Kolton
1980 Maribeth Miller, Bruce Schutz
1981 Susan Pearson, Laurie Robbins

BEYNON PAIRS. This two-session pair event restricted to non-qualifiers of the Senior/Advanced Senior Master Pair championship was contested for the BEYNON TROPHY. The George W. Beynon Trophy was first awarded in 1966, although the non-Life Master eliminees had competed as a separate flight since 1964. The Beynon Trophy was taken out of play in 1971.

WINNERS

1964 Harry Bloom, Mrs. Harry Bloom
1965 Aladar Fonyo, Joan Fonyo
1966 Ann Efnor, Mrs. Leighton Volker
1967 Dr. Allan Rosen, Mrs. Allan Rosen
1968 David Smith, Dr. John Wotiz
1969 Neil H. Wills, Mrs. Neil H. Wills
1970 John Klayman, Lawrence Lau
1971 Andy Guschwan, Ollie Mullenbach

SWISS TEAMS. This four-session team event, scored by international matchpoints, with two qualifying sessions and two final sessions was contested for the BALDWIN TROPHY. The event was discontinued afer 1976.

WINNERS

1970 Carl Winter, Richard Brian Bojar, Bernie Jaffe, Steve Paul
1971 Jay Albright, Phillip Becker, William Hale, Bob Moyers *(tied with)* R. Jay Becker, Lewis Finkel, Jo Morse, Mark Thompson *(and)* Dean Cohler, Jerry Premo, Wayne Snider, Jerry Weinstein *(and)* Keith Hanson, James Leary, Dave Nicklasson, Chuck Stegeman
1972 Norman Anderson, John Grantham, John A. Mohan, Diane W. Mraz, Mike Shuman
1973 Phil Clark, Judy Landau, Jim Loiselle, Andy Reiver, Jeff Ruben, Jim Walters
1974 Joe Adlersberg, Emilie Nevins, Betty Parker, Frances Singer
1975 Ira G. Barrows, William Gough, Joseph Livezey, Connie McGinley
1976 Ernest Ivey, Barbara Landauer, David Landauer, Bob Lundblad, Gary Soules, Helen Studabaker

SWISS TEAMS, Second Flight. This two-session team event scored by international matchpoints is restricted to non-qualifiers from the four-session secondary Swiss Team event. The event was discontinued after 1976.

WINNERS

1970 Philip Leon, Don Hocevar, Vincent Remey, Joan Remey
1971 Allan J. Cokin, W.D. Dechert, Robert Stone, C.W. Yost

1972   Dan Gerstman, Susan Hudgens, Peter Mollemet, John Toy

1973   Bonnie Brier, Steve Cox, Ahmed Hussein, Jan Stone

1974   Phil Leon, Evelyn Levitt, Steve Smolen, Dan Treadwell

1975   Andy Bernstein, Mark Blumenthal,
Seymour Leibowitz, Milt Rosenberg

1976   Larry Bausher, Max Hardy, Richard Lesko, Paul Ossip

OTHER SECONDARY EVENTS

(All two-session regionally-rated events)

1971

WINNERS
Master Mixed Teams, Second Flight:
B. Jay Becker, Dr. John Fisher, Emma Jean Hawes,
Alan Truscott, Dorothy Hayden Truscott

1972

Men's Pairs:
Sam Beard, John A. Mohan
Women's Pairs:
Betty Ann Kennedy, Carol Sanders

1973

Open Pairs:
Dr. Adolph Feingold, Mark Siegrist
Men's Pairs:
Tim Hollcroft, Bob O'Neill
Women's Pairs:
Mary A. Dyer, Nita Holland

1974

Open Pairs:
Jim Hilton, John Scibelli
Men's Pairs:
Bill Pollack, Jim Linhart
Women's Pairs:
Fran Beard, Marion Weed

1975

Open Pairs:
Flight A: Tom Belle, Zachary Walston
Flight B: Frieda Arst, June Deutsch
Men's Pairs:
Cy Dennen, Robert D. Hamman
Women's Pairs:
Bette Dudka, Charlotte Hahn
Mixed Swiss Teams:
Katherine Evans, William Gough,
Connie McGinley, Stephen W. Robinson
Open Pairs:
Flight A: Mary Bright, Norman Humer
Flight B: Allan Feineman, Pat Samuels
Flight C: Kay Chen, Leighton Chen

1976

Men's Pairs:
Steve Garner, Dick Melson
Women's Pairs:
Janet Daling, Carole Ure

1977

Men's Pairs:
Flight A: Howard Chandross, Lew Handelsman
Flight B: Harry Lampert, Dave Wachsman
Women's Pairs:
Flight A: Mary King, Bernie Petersen
Flight B: Janet Johnson, Valerie Kotulski
Open Pairs:
A — Class A: Paddi Cline, Richard Rudolph
B — Class A-D: Ron Feldman, Michael Schreiber
Open Swiss Teams:
Nancy Alpaugh, Bobby Goldman, Clarence Goppert,
Garey Hayden, Mark Lair
Unmixed Pair Mixed Swiss Teams:
Amelia Hose, Joel London, Rick North, Lucy Shostak

1978

Men's Pairs:
Flight A: Stephen Brown, Pierre Daigneault
Flight B: Arthur Cushman, Paul Ludwig
Women's Pairs:
Flight A: Gratian Goldstein, Sylvia Stein
Flight B: Frances Breakwell, Marlys Buczynski
Open Pairs:
Roland Laframboise, Dave McLellan

Open Pairs:
A — Class A: Harold Lilie, Joyce Lilie
B — Class A-D: Simmy Berish, Vivian Berish
Swiss Teams:
Smoking: Robert Lebi, Jay Merrill,
Renee Molson, Judy Wadas
Non-Smoking: Ross Grabel, Josh Parker,
Don Probst, Alan Schwartz
Swiss Teams:
Michael S. Lawrence, Lou Reich, Merle Tom,
Neil Silverman, Peter Weichsel

1979

Men's Pairs:
Flight A: Tom Hodapp, Mike Smolen
Flight B: Roger Johnson, Ron Schick
Women's Pairs:
Flight A: Nancy Alpaugh, Esta Van Zandt
Flight B: Risa Goldstein, Roz Hirsch
Open Pairs:
Barbara Hill, Joe Livezey
Open Pairs:
A — Class A: Robert Emke, Arline Olesak *(tied with)*
Dennis Clerkin, Chuck Eagle
B — Class A-D: Norman Fischer, Jeff Stafford
Swiss Teams:
Smoking: J.L. Cornelius, Mariano Garcia,
Tim Mann, Doi Nelli
Non-Smoking: Lou Bluhm, Richard Freeman,
Clifford Russell, Eddie Wold
Swiss Teams:
Mark Estes, Roy Hoppe,
Ron Karr, Elaine Rettus *(tied with)*
Gene Freed, Sue Halperin, Judi Smith,
Sharron Stange, Sandy Zakin

1980

Men's Pairs:
Flight A: Jack Feagin, Fred Strickland
Flight B: David Bailey, Steve Johnson
Women's Pairs:
Flight A: Harriette Hirsch, Mimi Metz
Flight B: Jackie Jarigese, Elaine Ryan
Open Pairs:
A — Class A: Britain Beezley, Nancy Beezley
B — Class A-D: Arny Leavitt, Sandi Leavitt
Swiss Teams:
Smoking: Alan Cordell, Leo Melamed,
Brian Moniesen, Jerry Weinstein
Non-Smoking: Henry Greenwald, Richard Halperin, Paul Hessel,
Harvey Miller, Norman Schultz
Swiss Teams:
Sheldon Justan, Art Korth,
Jeff Stafford, Harold Weltman

1981

Men's Pairs:
Flight A: Dave Berkowitz, Harold Lilie
Flight B: Robert Raitman, Al Selling
Women's Pairs:
Flight A: Nancy Alpaugh, Kerri Shuman
Flight B: Pat Kolebas, Evelyn Ogden
Open Pairs:
A — Class A: Alberta Albersheim, Charles Coon
B — Class A-D: Kenneth Cohen, Steve Zuckerman
Swiss Teams:
Smoking: Glenn Eisenstein, Alan Kudisch, Donna Kudisch,
Tim Nelsen, Michael Polowan, Mike Radin
Non-Smoking: Sidney Aronson, Mel Creem,
Val Habicht, Shome Mukherjee
Swiss Teams:
Dave Cantor, Dennis Newman,
Bob Sherman, Pat Sherman
Open Pairs:
Flight A: Henry Bethe, Eric R. Murray
Flight B: Jan Cresto, Morris Feinson

ACBL–WIDE GAMES

		WINNERS	SCORE%
1962	(Summer)	Gertrude Wallendorf, J. Wallendorf	74.81
1963	(Spring)	Ruth Mellett, Mrs. E. G. Obie	75.56
	(Summer)	Reva M. Ford, Doris Klein	74.4
	(Fall)	Walter Kopacz, Witold Stauffer	79.5
1964	(Spring)	Leonard D. Hine, Frances Hull	74.2
	(Summer)	James J. Boudreaux, Alma Inklebarger	78.5
	(Fall)	Ken R. Barbour, Mickey Rosenthal	74.4

1965	(Spring)	Robert Bratcher, Russell Wall	75.6
	(Summer)	Conrad O. Orr, Hannah Scholer	75.6
	(Fall)	Katherine Cowing,	
		Mildred Cunningham	79.5
1966	(Spring)	C. A. Duchene, Peter A. Marson	75.6
	(Summer)	Carol Sanders, Thomas K. Sanders	76.19
	(Fall)	Jack Meyer, Joan Meyer	72.9
1967	(Winter)	Mrs. Sam Cohen, Sam Cohen	75.
	(Spring)	Dr. Lowell Grant, Ruth McConnell	76.3
	(Summer)	Mrs. S. B. Fishburne, S. B. Fishburne	75.8
	(Fall)	Dennis Caro, Al Romm	75.3
1968	(Winter)	Mrs. Elmer Dwyer, Dr. John Sheridan	73.8
	(Spring)	Charles Bensinger, Julius Kozlove	76.1
	(Summer)	Pauline Buechler, Lorayne Lang	75.9
	(Fall)	Jerry Locks, William Odierna	79.9
1969	(Winter)	Joseph Panepinto, James Singmaster	73.8
	(Spring)	Maurice A. Londry, Stewart Loyst	77.3
	(Summer)	Terry Riely, Leon St. Jean	74.4
	(Fall)	Bonnie Lowe, Dean Lowe	76.5
1970	(Winter)	Mrs. A. L. Graham,	
		Mrs. M. E. St. John	78.6
	(Spring)	L. D. Hansen, Gary Polonsky	73.2
	(Summer)	Howard Rosenkranz, Glenn Wiswell	78.3
	(Fall)	Lucille B. Kessler, Raleigh K. Mayfield	75.
1971	(Winter)	Joe Imholte, Stan Zabaglo	73.2
	(Spring)	Mrs. Neal Moore, Neal Moore	82.95
	(Summer)	Gus S. Afendoulis, Johnny Theodore	77.7
	(Fall)	Hal Kandler, Bette Stutzer	77.5
1972	(Winter)	Sammy R. Kehela, Eric R. Murray	80.0
	(Spring)	Diana Scheinman, Marcie Wheatley	79.8
	(Summer)	Dolly Caballero, Josefina De Costas	78.6
	(Fall)	Tena Boutilier, Dolores MacNeil	81.4
1973	(Winter)	Michael Roberts, Jim Wood	77.98
	(Spring)	Subhash C. Gupta, Hari Jagasia	73.51
	(Summer)	Chris Nelson, Denis A. Sakoski	78.
	(Fall)	Joe Kivel, Richard Taube	77.4
1974	(Winter)	Michael Gore, Richard Wagner	75.9
	(Spring)	Carrie Burge, Mary Shipton	77.7
	(Summer)	Corrine Sturm, Walter Sturm	77.
	(Fall)	Mark Conn, Andy Wolf	79.8
1975	(Winter)	Kirk Benson, Angeline O'Grady	75.9
	(Spring)	Ira Chorush, Tony Rosenstein	79.9
	(Summer)	B. C. Williams, Grace Williams	
		tied with Bernie Coleman, Jim McGrath	73.8
	(Fall)	George Siegel, Pauline Tessier	78.98
1976	(Winter)	Edard Bibb, Jim Powell	75.
	(Spring)	Dr. Habib Bazyari, Duane Johnson	78.57
	(Summer)	Bill Doherty, Robert Porteus	75.3
	(Fall)	John Batcheller, Bill Henry	77.65
1977	(Winter)	Richard K. Fleischman, Linda Gorski	
		tied with Don Booker, Lea McDonald	75.
	(Spring)	Libby Fernandez, Leonard Spillman	81.25
	(Summer)	Marie Filandre, Peter Filandre	75.
	(Fall)	France Allard, Michel Allard	78.6
1978	(Winter)	Bill Anderson, Eric Hautala	76.2
	(Spring)	Keith Garber, Carl Lindenman	76.7
	(Summer)	S. Chandra Mohan, Attilio Spaccarelli	74.7
	(Fall)	Robert Gieselman, David Goblirsch	76.8
1979	(Winter)	Betty Caisse, Jeannette Kowalewski	77.4
	(Spring)	Fannie Lee, Mary Melillo	74.4
	(Summer)	Bill Doherty, Paul Walorz	81.9
	(Fall)	Al McDonald, David Stothart	73.9
1980	(Winter)	Jan Briggs Yaple, Chuck Yaple	74.4
	(Spring)	Roger Doughman, Lena Jelusich	75.6
	(Summer)	Faye Harker, Berta Krop	75.
	(Fall)	Bob Schives, Karen Schives	77.
1981	(Winter)	Norma Matthews, Roger Matthews	78.8
	(Spring)	Ken Lowe, John Roblee	75.6
	(Summer)	Frank Guzel, Parks King	73.5
	(Fall)	David Gilbert, John Hazell	76.6

INTERCOLLEGIATE CHAMPIONSHIPS

WINNERS

1940   Radcliffe College

1941   Harvard University

1942   Princeton University

1943–45 (cancelled due to World War II)

1946   Cornell University

1947   University of California (first time on national basis)
     Charles W. Drake, Philip J. Smith

1948   Capital University, Columbus, Ohio
     Charles Krueger, Luther Schleisser, Jr.

1949   Wayne University, Detroit
     Clifford Bishop, Dorsey Brooks

1950   Massachusetts Institute of Technology
     Martin Cornish, Jr., Richard Lesser

1951   Washburn University, Topeka, Kansas
     Gerald Michaud, Bradley Post

1952   Rice Institute, Houston, Texas
     John "Spider" Harris, Richard Sutton

1953   Purdue University (N–S)
     Frank McClure, Carey Yelton, Jr.
   Princeton University (E–W)
     David Bradley, Harlow Lewis

1954   Purdue University (N–S)
     Herman Rose, Carey Yelton, Jr.
   Dartmouth College (E–W)
     Harry Connaro, Robert Sokolsky

1955   Whitman College (N–S)
     William Click, Robert Luther
   University of Texas (E–W)
     Charles Callery, Charles Miller

1956   Harvard University (N–S)
     Franklin Bunn, Boyd Everett, Jr.
   Dartmouth College (E–W)
     Frank Barteaux, Jr., John Strong, Jr.

1957   Cornell University (N–S)
     Frank Goldring, Paul Trent
   Oberlin College (E–W)
     Danny Kleinman, Dick Recht

1958   University of Iowa (N–S)
     Terry Campbell, Peter Kemble
   Cornell University (E–W)
     Robert Ewen, Jeff Rubens

1959   Columbia University (N–S)
     James Becker, Sanford Reder
   Princeton University (E–W)
     John O'Neil, Willard Speakman

1960   Columbia University (N–S)
     James Becker, Sanford Reder
   North Carolina State College (E–W)
     Robert Smith, Richard Stanton

1961   Harvard University (N–S)
     Roman Weil, Richard Zeckhauser
   Stanford University (E–W)
     Mort Goerman, Roger Tippy

1962   University of Iowa (N–S)
     Larry Friedman, Robert Pugh
   Lake Forest College, Illinois (E–W)
     Richard Berger, James Bert

1963   Lake Forest College, Illinois (N–S)
     Richard Berger, James Bert
   University of Illinois (E–W)
     Robert Ewen, Darrell Penrod *(tied with)*
   University of California at Berkeley
     Bill Nutting, Hugh Ross

1964   University of Texas (N–S)
     George Kirkwood, Dan Leightman
   University of Oregon (E–W)
     Dale Foster, Jeff Taylor *(tied with)*
   State University of Buffalo
     Richard Fleischman, Robert Lipsitz

1965   *1st* Cornell University
     Thomas M. Smith, Emil Tobenfeld
   2nd University of Wisconsin
     Larry Cohen, Richard H. Katz

1966   *1st* University of Wisconsin
     Larry Cohen, Richard H. Katz
   2nd University of Minnesota
     Richard Dufour, Morrie Freier

1967   *1st* Rensselaer Polytechnic Institute
     Gerald Cohen, Tony Rosenstein
   2nd University of Colorado
     Michael Copeland, Robert Wherry

1968   *1st* University of Maryland
     Jeff Hand, John Richards II
   2nd University of Michigan
     Ron Gerard, Daniel Suty *(tied with)*
     Rensselaer Polytechnic Institute
     Frank Hacker, Gary Weldin

1969   *1st* Rice University
     Michael Finch, Delmas Parker
   2nd University of Utah
     Reed Coray, Ron Rosenthal

1970   *1st* University of Virginia
     E. Craig Kennedy, Jr., Bruce Platt

      2nd University of Florida
        Markland Jones, Patricia Sprague

1971 *1st* Louisiana State University
        Dennis Conlon, Charles Crosby
      2nd University of North Carolina
        Douglas Stewart, William Wisdom

1972 *1st* State University of New York at Stony Brook
        Raghunath Khetan, Sheo Khetan
      2nd University of Washington
        Neil Chambers, John Schermer

1973 *1st* Loyola University of Los Angeles
        Bill Schreiber, Mike Schreiber
      2nd University of Alabama
        Bob Dennard, Ann Hubmaier

1974 *1st* University of California at San Diego
        Douglas DePoister, Barry Rothstein
      2nd University of Pennsylvania
        Max Bazerman, Marc Nathan

1975 *1st* University of Missouri
        Thomas Allan, Lee Goodman
      2nd Yale University
        Jeff Juster, Andrew Markowitz

1976 *1st* University of Michigan
        Larry Mori, Larry Robbins
      2nd University of Colorado
        Stephen Strauss, Michael Zeitlin

1977 *1st* Swarthmore College in Pennsylvania
        Marty Fleisher, Alan Heubert
      2nd Washington University in St. Louis
        William Doroshow, Robert Alan Portnoy

1978 *1st* University of Texas
        Charles Sterling Darrin, Dennis Sorensen
      2nd Swarthmore College in Pennsylvania
        Marty Fleisher, Alan Heubert

1979 *1st* University of Pennsylvania
        Saul Gross, Howard Lebow
      2nd University of Wisconsin
        Jim Elliott, Mark Kinzer

APPENDIX II
ACBL Regional Championships

Regional Tournaments are listed alphabetically in the Index below, showing the District in which the results of each tournament are reported.

INDEX TO REGIONALS

NAME OF TOURNAMENT	DISTRICT	TOURNAMENT SITES
ALACBU	23	Los Angeles CA
All-American	5	Cleveland, Akron, Toledo OH, Detroit MI
All-Western	21	San Francisco, Palo Alto, Oakland CA
Beef State: see District 14	14	
Bermuda	7	Hamilton, Southhampton
Big D: see Texas Spring – Texas Midwinter	16	
Big D Bridge Week: see Texas Midwinter	16	
Big Sky: see District 18	18	
Bridge Week	23	Pasadena, Los Angeles CA
British Columbia: see Pacific Northwest	19	
Buffalo: see Canadian Prairie	2	
Buffalo Centennial: see Canadian Prairie	2	
Calgary: see District 18	18	
California Capital	21	Sacramento CA
Cambrian Shield	2	Winnipeg MB, Thunder Bay, North Bay, Sault Ste. Marie, Sudbury ON
Canadian	18	Saskatoon SK, Edmonton, Calgary AB
Canadian American (Can-Am)	1	Montreal PQ, Ottawa, Kingston ON
Canadian Atlantic (Can-At)	1	Fredericton, Moncton, St. John NB, Halifax NS
Canadian Nationals	2	Toronto ON
Canadian Prairie	2	Winnipeg MB, Sault Ste Marie, Thunder Bay, Sudbury, London ON
Canadian Prairie	14	Fargo ND
Canadian Thanksgiving: see District 18	18	
Capital City: see Texas Fall – Texas Midwinter	16	
Central California	21	Stockton, Sacramento CA
Central Florida	9	St. Petersburg, Lake Buena Vista, Orlando FL
Central States	13	Lake Geneva, Madison WI, Chicago IL
Champagne	8	Belleville, Springfield, DeKalb IL, South Bend IN
Charlotte: see Mid-Atlantic Fall	7	
Cheyene Frontier: see District 17	17	
Crater Lake: see District 20	20	
Desert Empire	17	Las Vegas NV, Phoenix, Tucson AZ
Disneyland: see Southern California	22	
District 2: see Canadian Prairie	2	
District 4: see Keystone Fall	4	
District 5	5	Pittsburgh PA
District 8	8	Rockford, Decatur, Springfield, Belleville IL
District 11	11	Columbus, Cincinnati OH, Indianapolis IN, Lexington KY
District 14	14	Fargo ND, Sioux Falls SD, Omaha, Lincoln NE
District 14 Summer	14	Lincoln, Omaha NE, Waterloo IA
District 15	15	Kansas City, Wichita KS, Oklahoma City, Tulsa OK
District 17	17	Cheyenne WY, Las Vegas NV
District 18	18	Billings MT, Saskatoon, Regina SK
District 20	20	Medford, Eugene OR, Redding, Eureka CA
District 22	22	Bakersfield, San Bernardino CA
Eastern States	24	New York City
Fall Mid-West: see Mid-West Fall	11	
Fleur-de-Lys	1	Montreal, Quebec City PQ, Kingston, Ottawa ON
Florida	9	Jacksonville, Daytona Beach, Hollywood FL
Fun City	24	New York City
Gem State: see District 18		
Golden Gate	21	Oakland, Santa Rosa, San Jose CA
Golden State	22	San Diego, Fresno, Monterey, Palm Springs CA
Gopher	14	Minneapolis, St. Paul MN
Great Lakes	12	Lansing, Grand Rapids, Kalamazoo MI, Toledo OH
Gulf Coast Mid South	10	Mobile AL
Hawaii	20	Honolulu HI

Southeastern	9	Miami Beach FL
Southern California	22	Anaheim, Palm Springs CA
Southern Conference Fall	10	Western Tennessee, Alabama, Georgia
Southern Conference Spring	10	Western Tennessee, Alabama, Georgia
South Saskatchewan: see District 18	18	
South Texas: see Texas Fall	16	
Sun City	9	Sun City FL
Texas Fall	16	Abilene, Corpus Christi, Dallas, San Antonio TX
Texas Mid-Winter	16	Houston, Dallas
Texas Spring	16	Lubbock, Dallas TX
Texas Summer	16	Fort Worth, Austin, San Antonio, El Paso TX
Thanksgiving: see Mid-Atlantic Thanksgiving	7	
Tri-State	3	Rye, Port Chester, Grossinger NY
Tri-Unit	13	Eau Claire, Milwaukee, Madison, Green Bay WI
Upper New York State	3	Albany, Syracuse NY
Upper New York State	4	Syracuse, Rochester NY
Upper New York State	5	Cleveland OH, Buffalo NY
Washington Bridge Week	6	Arlington VA, Washingon DC
Western States	11	Columbus, Cleveland, Cincinnati OH, Indianapolis IN, Pittsburgh PA, St. Louis MO, Detroit MI
Winter: see New York Winter	24	
Wolverine	12	Kalamazoo, Southfield MI, Bowling Green, Maumee OH
Yakima Valley: see Inland Empire	19	

DISTRICT 1 (Quebec, eastern Ontario, Nova Scotia, New Brunswick, Newfoundland, Prince Edward Island)

CANADIAN-AMERICAN

KNOCKOUT TEAMS

1972   Richard Fleischman, Karen Allison, Shelia Forbes, John Laskin, Robin Wigdor,
1973   Doug Clark, Noreen Sugarman, Jerry Springer, Jack Shinehoft, David Bryce
1974   Mary Bright, Michael Cummings, Robert Cohen, Robert Kehoe, Norman Humer, Lou Reich
1975   Richard Weiss, Ben Goldsmith, Luke Gillespie, Alan Susskind
1976   Joseph Silver, Mark Stein, Fred Hoffer, Marty Sklar
1977   Ted Horning, George Mittelman, David Lindop, Mike Cummings, Eric Kokish, Peter Nagy
1978   Francine Cimon, Francois Gauthier, Stephen Brown, Pierre Daigneault, Leo Glaser, Jim Riegle
1979   Jim Sternberg, Alan Sontag, Peter Weichsel, Harold Lilie, Mark Molson
1980   Leo Glaser, Jim Riegle, Mark Rosenbloom, Rick Delogu
1981   Joseph Silver, Eric Kokish, Peter Nagy, George Mittelman, Irving Livack, Mark Stein

WOMEN'S PAIRS

1951   O. V. Giddings, W. O. Lewis
1952   Mary Edna Maloney, Juliet Hazel
1953   Ruby McKaig, Mrs. C. W. Kenney
1954   Marjorie Anderson, Mrs. J. G. Boeckh
1955   Mrs. Charles Mercer, Mrs. Henry Dutcher *(tied with)* Mrs. C. W. Kenney, Ruby McKaig
1956   A. Maheu, Juliet Hazel
1957   Mrs. R. Fitts, Mrs. F. Drummond
1958   Mrs. Earl Ackerman, Mrs. Francis Harding
1959   Mrs. E. E. Taylor, Agnes Gordon
1960   Marge Maurer, Ruby McKaig
1961   Agnes Gordon, Nell Complin
1962   Mona Spurlock, Mrs. C. W. Fite
1963   Agnes Gordon, Marge Maurer
1964   Agnes Gordon, Marge Maurer
1965   Jackie Begin, Irene Reingold
1966   Jackie Begin, Irene Reingold
1967   Kay Blakeney, Carolyn MacDonald
1968   Irene Reingold, Mrs. Peter Bandler
1969   Barbara Siblin, Ellie Nagy
1970   Barbara Saltsman, Ellie Nagy
1971   Mrs. L. Arseneault, Mrs. L. DuFour
1975   Joan Lupovich, Manya Kugler
1976   Barbara Saltsman, Julie Goldstein
1977   Kati Gottlieb, Heddy Friedman
1978   Katie Belkin, R. Wolfson
1979   Helene Rosenbloom, Helen Keri
1980   Mrs. M. Schecter, Eve Saxe
1981   Lillian Selick, Bella Shier

MASTER PAIRS

1968   Manya Kugler, Leon Berman
1969   Sam Gold, Peter Nagy

1970   Mark Blumenthal, John Solodar
1971   Evelyn Levitt, Dave Treadwell
1972   Fred Lerner, David Lindop
1973   R. Ian McKinnon, Hugh Currie
1974   Ray Jotcham, Gail Jotcham
1975   Mark Feldman, Dave Loomis
1976   Larry Edwards, John Brinley
1977   Jay Saks, Danny Rosenberg

MIXED PAIRS

1951   Jackie Begin, Buddy Marsh
1952   Mignonne Perrault, C. Antoine Geoffrion
1953   Mrs. N.J. Spieckhoff, William Joseph
1954   Nell Complin, Rev. L.A. Tobin
1955   Mrs. J.H. Smith, Vincent Dirvin
1956   Florence LeClaire, Alan Derby
1957   Mrs. P. Brochu, P.E. Laguex
1958   Helen Harrow, Norman Burns
1959   Agnes Gordon, Eric Murray
1960   Richard Edney, M. Edney
1961   Agnes Gordon, Eric Murray
1962   Irene Reingold, Don DaCosta
1963   Phyllis Barrington, Sam Gold
1964   Mimi Roncarelli, William Solomon
1965   Peter Pender, Agnes Gordon
1966   Bernie Stone, Mrs. Bernie Stone
1967   Rose Milgram, Irving Burke
1968   Joe Cohen, Gert Cohen
1969   Rosemary Foland, Jonathan Robinson
1970   Joyce Hall, Fred Sontag
1971   Mary Paul, Maurice Paul

OPEN PAIRS

1951   Emile Beausoleil, George L'Espérance
1952   Jackie Begin, Barry Cohen
1953   Mrs. William Merriman, Howard Foering, Jr.
1954   Edgar Hamel, Paul Charette
1955   Jacqueline Fetsko, Joseph Asber
1956   Tobias Stone, Jan Stone
1957   Jackie Begin, Peter Schwartz
1958   David Thurber, Frank Palen
1959   Rose Carrière, Evaline Prevost
1960   Frances Thurner, Allan Derby
1961   Frank Goldring, Charles Coon
1962   Eric Murray, Al Lando
1963   Jackie Begin, Dan Tait
1964   Eric Viires, John Raynault
1965   Bruce Elliott, Percy Sheardown
1966   John Cullinan, Jr., Ruby McKaig
1967   Charles Hirschey, Bernie Sanders
1968   Marvin Altman, Fred Hoffer
1969   Bob Provencher, Bert Winges
1970   Joseph Silver, Eric Kokish
1971   Mark Feldman, Mark Blumenthal
1972   Dr. Ganti Rao, John Edwards
1973   Louise Ruderman, Joanne Burtin
1974   Dominic DiFelice, Santosh Gangwal
1975   Leon Arnold, Mark Yudin
1976   Larry Edwards, John Brinley

1977 Dave Berkowitz, Steve Sion
1978 Eva Scatassa, Steve Sion
1979 Mary Ruth Blustein, Maurice Blustein
Dave Willis, John Valliant *(Smoking)*
Charles Hirschey, John Cullinan *(Non-Smoking)*
1980 Sue Graham, Abe Paul
John Bowman, Martin Caley *(Smoking)*
1981 Keith Balcombe, Ted Horning
A. Boivin, Jean Castonguay *(Smoking)*
Pam Bridson, Jim Zimmerman *(Non-Smoking)*

OPEN TEAMS

1951 Mrs. D. Prevost, Cecile Mignault,
Florence LeClaire, Rose Carrière
1952 C. Antoine Geoffrion, Aaron Goodman, Buddy Marsh,
Sam Gold, Ralph Cohen
1953 Jerome Friedlander, Murray DeLeeuw,
Emanuel Katz, Agnes Gordon
1954 Howard Foering, Jr., Aaron Goodman,
Ralph Cohen, Sam Gold (*tied with*)
Nell Complin, Gaston Hebert,
Doug Andress, Mary Edna Maloney
1955 Maurice Braunstein, Robert Ludwig,
Paul Zweifel, Raymond Brown
1956 Jackie Begin, Peter Schwartz,
Buddy Marsh, Don Piefsky
1957 Jackie Begin, Maurice Paul,
Ralph Cohen, Peter Schwartz
1958 Charles Hirschey, W. Truesdale Clarke,
John Barrington, Michael Raikes
1959 Don DaCosta, Dr. George Sereny
Mickey Miller, Corti Boland
1960 Mimi Roncarelli, William Solomon,
Jim Ross, Hugh Ross
1961 Dr. Eric Jones, Don Cowan,
Dave Saltsman, Fred Hoffer
1962 Nat Gerstman, Al Lando,
Bill Crissey, Irving Goodman
1963 Agnes Gordon, Eric Murray, Bruce Elliott,
Percy Sheardown, Sammy Kehela
1964 Charles Coon, Marvin Altman,
Fred Hoffer, Ray Jotcham
1965 Jackie Begin, David Silver,
B. Droyon, Hartley Maldaver
1966 Sam Gold, Aaron Goodman, Peter Nagy,
Gene Thumin, Rose Thumin
1967 Alan Doane, Bryson Croswell,
Saul Blum, Ray Jotcham *(tied with)*
Henri Parent, John Findley,
Sam Gold, Aaron Goodman
1968 John Laskin, T.R. Gree, Cameron Lindsay,
J. Brian Johnston, A.N. Stevens
1969 Fred Hoffer, Joseph Silver, Marvin Altman,
Steve Aarons, Ray Jotcham
1970 John Solodar, Mark Blumenthal,
Robert Lipsitz, Arthur Waldmann
1971 David Bryce, Dr. D. Snikeris,
Sylvia Chernin, Mrs. R. Stephens
1972 John Norton, Cameron Lindsay,
John Lloyd, John Stevens
1973 Henry Cukoff, Eric Kokish,
Joseph Silver, George Mittelman
1974 Grant Ardern, Doug Clark,
Stan Lezwoff, Boris Baran
1975 Jacques Meeroff, Robert Lebi,
Jean-Paul Gosselin, Marty Sklar
1976 Bob Hirsch, Ethel Major,
George Retek, Brian Foster
1977 John Rosenfeld, Georges Falardeau,
Joe Seigel, Dr. Rene Gascon
1978 Eva Scatassa, Gladys Collier, Alan Sontag,
Allan Cokin, Steve Sion, Jim Sternberg
1979 Doug Heron, David Stothart,
Robert Kemp, Vincent Dohaney, *(tied with)*
Mark Stein, Joseph Silver,
Mark Rosenbloom, John Sutherlin *(and)*
Jim Sternberg, Mark Molson, Harold Lilie,
Alan Sontag, Peter Weichsel *(and)*
Helene Beaulieu, Pat Roy,
Alberta Albersheim, Ethel Keohane *(and)*
Kathie Wei, Maimie Lee,
Dave Berkowitz, Jeff Meckstroth
1980 Ed Bridson, David Currey,
Michel Lamothe, Jim Zimmerman
1981 Ted Horning, Keith Balcombe,
Robert Lebi, Ross Taylor *(Smoking)*
Raymond Fortin, Kamel Fergani,
Richard Wildi, Michel Lorber *(Non-Smoking)*

MASTER SWISS TEAMS

1977 Joseph Silver, Sharyn Kokish, Fred Hoffer,
Dianna Gordon, George Mittelman, Chuck Lamprey

1978 Allan Graves, Dianna Gordon, George Mittelman,
Chuck Lamprey, Sharyn Kokish
1979 Kathie Wei, Maimie Lee, Judy Tucker,
Jeff Meckstroth, Howard Chandross
1981 Jim Zimmerman, Doug Fraser,
Sandra Fraser, Fred Hoffer

MEN'S PAIRS

1951 C. Antoine Geoffrion, John Raynault
1952 Gesa Klein, Buddy Marsh
1953 Charles Hirschey, W. Truesdale Clarke
1954 John Wiser, George L'Espérance
1955 Fred Root, Francis Janik
1956 Sam Gold, Aaron Goodman
1957 Ralph Cohen, Sam Gold
1958 Noel Duchesne, Reál Olivier
1959 Lou Woodcock, Bert Powley
1960 Eric Murray, Sammy Kehela
1961 Reál Olivier, H. Laliberte
1962 Cass Olson, Dr. Ron Forbes
1963 Dr. William Hutchins, Ed Stanton, Jr.
1964 Charles Hirschey, Bernard Sanders
1965 John Benoit, Mike Cappelletti *(tied with)*
Dr. William Hutchins, M. Melton
1966 Nicholas Kuttis, Eric Viires
1967 Henri Parent, Robert Binsky
1968 Sam Baker, Gustave Dahan
1969 Leon Rosenbaum, Cello Saragea
1970 Doug Clark, Bert Winges *(tied with)*
Mark Rosenbloom, Francois Gauthier
1971 Max Blond, George Benesh
1975 Peter Schwartz, Buddy Marsh
1976 Bruce Dwyer, Vince Ragazzo
1977 Mark Yudin, Peter Schwartz
1978 Charles Hirschey, Crampton Carrick
1979 Howard Chandross, Jim Becker
1980 Bruce Dwyer, Jean Castonguay
1981 Charlie Mulcahy, Charles Coon

MEN'S SWISS TEAMS

1980 Joseph Silver, Irving Litvack, Harold Goldstein, Jay Saks
1981 Joseph Silver, Irving Litvack, Harold Goldstein, Jay Saks

WOMEN'S SWISS TEAMS

1980 D. Thivierge, Helene Beaulieu,
Ethel Keohane, Alberta Alberheim
1981 Rita Redlich, Marilyn Beames,
Dr. Nele Rzad, Gail Anderson

CANADIAN-ATLANTIC

KNOCKOUT TEAMS

1968 Frank Westcott, Charles Coon, Robert Bambrick,
David Stothart, Henry Francis, Stan Tench
1969 Charles Hirschey, Ed O'Reilly, Stan Tench,
Henry Francis, Walter Spiewak
1970 Henry Francis, Ed O'Reilly, Stan Tench,
Paul Heitner, Abby Lifschitz
1971 Alan Doane, Dave Oulton,
George Caldwell, Glyn Hatfield
1972 N. Ferguson, T. Clark, Mrs. T. Clark,
D. Gamble, Mrs. D. Gamble
1973 Paul Heitner, Abby Heitner, Walter Spiewak,
Dave Beer, Merle Tom
1974 Karl Cox, Tony Kasday, Ed Spear,
Joe Giard, Rick Bojar, B. Lewis
1975 Dennis Dawson, Jackie Dawson,
Norman Humer, Mary Bright
1976 Sharron Lewis, Richard Brown,
James Kirby, Gordon Maser
1977 Tony Kasday, Harold Lilie, Joyce Lilie,
Steve Sion, Mary Lou Cushner, Dave Berkowitz
1978 Virginia Giza, Ted Withers,
Babe Stewart, Bill Davis
1979 Joel Friedberg, Ethan Stein,
Jerry Shakofsky, Bob Gwirtzman
1980 Alan Doane, Victor Goldberg, John Stewart,
Don Presse, Roger Jourdan
1981 Leonard Karp, John Suozzo,
Lenore Server, Michael Kamil

OPEN TEAMS

1968 Robert Bambrick, Charles Coon,
Dave Stothart, Frank Westcott *(tied with)*
Mrs. M. Fraser, Mrs. D. MacDonald,
R. Smith, D. Davis
1969 Paul Heitner, Ken Lebensold,
Dave Beer, Walter Spiewak
1970 Mrs. Ed O'Reilly, Ed O'Reilly,
Paul Heitner, Abby Lifschitz
1971 Eric Murray, Arno Hobart,
B. Black, Rod McKenzie

1972   Paul Lavalle, Barbara Lavalle,
       Fred Suzman, John Malley
1973   Arno Hobart, Richard Brown,
       Sharron Lewis, Alan Doane
1974   Karl Cox, Tony Kasday,
       Ed Spear, Joe Giard
1975   Joanne Carlisle, Steven Unger,
       Mike Cafferata, Andy Altay *(tied with)*
       Abby Heitner, Paul Heitner,
       Richard Bojar, George Caldwell *(and)*
       Bert Winges, Denise Roussin,
       John Bowman, Peter Bambrick
1976   Alan Doane, Paul Lavalle, George Caldwell,
       Eric Balkam, Bill Campbell
1977   Bert Winges, M. Denise Roussin,
       John Bowman, Bill Bowman
1978   Jim Middleton, Gil Baldursson,
       Dave Jackson, Frank Jackson *(tied with)*
       Norman Humer, Bob Fiske,
       Mary Bright, Lloyd Arvedon *(and)*
       Glenn Rodger, Barbara Wallace,
       George Mac Lennan, Bill Presse
1979   Clarence Goppert, Mark Lair, Mike Passell,
       Eric Kokish, George Mittelman
1980   Michael Kenny, David Colbert,
       Mike Cafferata, Michel Lorber
1981   Henry Francis, Dorthy Francis,
       Sharron Lewis, Richard Brown *(tied with)*
       Dave Beer, Alice Lanke,
       Abby Heitner, Paul Heitner

MASTER SWISS
1978   Dennis Dawson, Lloyd Arvedon,
       Norman Humer, Mary Bright

BOARD-A-MATCH
1977   Bert Winges, M. Denise Roussin,
       John Bowman, Bill Bowman
1979   Jim Priebe, Joan Priebe,
       Richard Edney, M. Edney
1981   M. Denise Roussin, Bert Winges,
       Bill Bowman, Alan Doane

SWISS TEAMS
Flight A:
1980   Patrice Roy, Helene Beaulieu,
       Ethel Keohane, Ida Bennett

MIXED PAIRS
1968   Mrs. F. Smith, F. Smith
1969   Elaine Kays, Robert Hambly
1970   Mrs. William Jamison, William Jamison
1971   G. Julien, Mrs. M. Bilodeau
1972   Mrs. F. Eichman, F. Eichman
1973   Ruth Mingo, Ian Spencer *(tied with)*
       Mrs. A. May, A. May
1974   Mary Bright, Norman Humer
1977   Sharron Paul, Eric Balkan *(tied with)*
       Alberta Albersheim, Lloyd Arvedon
1978   Nancy Greer, Steve Dunham
1979   Philip Baer, Ann Mendelsohn
1981   John Bowman, Laurie McIntyre

UNMIXED PAIRS
1978   Alan Doane, Don Presse

OPEN PAIRS
1968   Charles Coon, Frank Westcott
1969   George Caldwell, Glyn Hatfield
1970   Ethel Keohane, Frank Westcott
1971   Mrs. E. Mills, E. Mills
1972   Matthew Granovetter, Merle Tom
1973   Mark Feldman, Mary Bright
1974   George Caldwell, Walter Spiewak
1975   Martin Caley, Mark Rosenbloom
1976   Richard Brown, Sharron Lewis
1977   Kitty Bethe, Henry Bethe
1978   Eric Balkam, Sharron Josey
1979   Thomas Goodwin, Edward Spear
1980   David Colbert, Mike Cafferata
1981   Michael Kamil, John Suozzo

OPEN PAIRS
Flight A:
1980   M. Denise Roussin, William Bowman
1981   George Holland, Gerry Callaghan

MASTER PAIRS
1971   Harry Keffer, Tom Lagan
1972   George Effros, Larry Bauscher
1975   Clarence Goppert, Garey Hayden
1976   Tony Kasday, Ed Spear
1977   Dave Oulton, Glyn Hatfield
1978   Nancy Greer, F. Wardwell
1979   Joel Friedberg, Jerry Shakofsky

INDIVIDUAL
1977   Jim Donaldson
1978   Irene Plouffe

MEN'S PAIRS
1980   John McDermott, Rick Binder

WOMEN'S PAIRS
1980   Linda Darter, Roz Spear

FLEUR-DE-LYS

KNOCKOUT TEAMS
1972   André Laliberté, Jacques Patry,
       Joe Bernier, G. Bilodeau
1973   Joseph Silver, George Mittelman, Eric Kokish,
       Sharyn Kokish, Dianna Gordon, Chuck Lamprey
1974   Bert Winges, Al McDonald,
       Bob Provencher, P. Schmaltz
1975   Jacques Laliberté, André Laliberté,
       Jean Bernier, Maurice Larochelle
1976   Richard Hart, Michael Schoenborn,
       Bruce Dwyer, Mac King
1979   Doug Fraser, Sandra Fraser, Stephen Brown,
       Pierre Daigneault, Robert Lebi, Lloyd Arvedon
1980   Peter Nagy, Eric Kokish,
       Allan Graves, George Mittelman

WOMEN'S SWISS TEAMS
1980   Sandra Fraser, Renee Mancuso,
       Sharyn Kokish, Pam Bridson

MEN'S SWISS TEAMS
1980   Leo Glasser, Jim Reigle,
       Michel Lamothe, David Curry

OPEN PAIRS
1972   Paul Hollander, Robert Lebi
1973   Al McDonald, John Bowman
1974   Barry Cohen, David Stothart
1975   Nancy Koffler, Ady Koffler
1976   Karl Cox, Stephen Linehan
1979   Alan DuFour, Denis LaFrance
1980   Paul Heitner, Kirk Benson *(tied with)*
       Berry Callaghan, Gerry Callaghan *(Smoking)*
       Sandra Fraser, Doug Fraser *(tied with)*
       Dr. C.K. Hargrove, Michael Instance *(Non-Smoking)*

OPEN PAIRS
Flight A:
1979   Joe Adlersberg, Peter Nagy
1980   Brian Johnston, John Melvin

OPEN TEAMS
1972   Andy Altay, Dave Lindop,
       J. Sabino, H. Abel
1973   Bert Winges, Bill Bowman,
       Al McDonald, M. Delaney
1974   Dr. Abe Feingold, G. Holland,
       John Bowman, Bill Bowman
1975   Guy Bilodeau, Jacques Patry,
       Jean Lamontagne, Raymond Fortin
1976   Dennis Dawson, Jackie Dawson,
       Chuck Lamprey, John Batcheller
1979   John Bowman, Brian MacKenzie,
       Martin Caley, David Curry
1980   Pierre Daigneault, Stephen Brown,
       Lloyd Arvedon, Robert Lebi

MASTER PAIRS
1972   H. Banks, John Appleton, Jr
1973   Robin Wigdor, Mark Rosenbloom
1974   Harry Creed, T. Margollan
1975   Bill Woodard, Joe Skype
1977   Jackie Dawson, Dennis Dawson

MEN'S PAIRS
1979   Doug Fraser, Lloyd Arvedon
1980   Robert Lebi, Sol Weinstein

WOMEN'S PAIRS
1979   Sandra Fraser, Evelyn Kirsh
1980   Sylvia Fish, Bessie Morris

DISTRICT 2   (Manitoba, central and western Ontario)

CAMBRIAN SHIELD

KNOCKOUT TEAMS
1972   Gary Hann, Chuck Said,
       Phil Leon, Fred Hamilton
1973   Dr. Adolph Feingold, Martin Caley,
       John Bowman, Timothy Edwards-Davies
1974   Phil Leon, Don Hocevar, Cliff Bishop,

Richard Huggard, Fred Will, John Buchheister
1975 Clarence Goppert, Mike Passell, Ron LaCour,
Garey Hayden, Bruce Dwyer
1976 Alan Bell, Alex DeGroot, G. Sekhar,
Bryan Makysmetz, Cliff Bishop
1977 Kathie Wei, Ron Andersen, Gerald Caravelli,
Milt Rosenberg, Hugh MacLean
1978 Roy Dalton, Mike Cafferata,
Dave Colbert, Steve Cooper
1979 Clarence Goppert, Mike Passell, Mark Lair,
George Mittelman, Allan Graves
1980 Phil Leon, James Zimmerman,
Robert Sherburn, Ralph Katz
1981 Jim Hall, Dave Lehman, Mike Girou,
Mark Lair, Eddie Wold

OPEN TEAMS
1972 Eric Murray, Shelia Forbes,
Fred Hamilton, Chuck Said
1973 Serge Chevalier, Francois Gauthier,
Francine Asselin, Jean-Paul Gosselin
1974 Gary Polonsky, John Arblaster,
Beverly Riordan, Richard Huggard
1975 Mac King, John Cunningham,
Roy Hughes, Michael Cummings
1976 Ron Andersen, Hugh MacLean, Gerald Caravelli,
Clarence Goppert, Mark Lair
1977 Dave Lehman, Dick Melson,
Howard Weinstein, Steve Garner
1978 Roy Dalton, Mike Cafferata,
Dave Colbert, Steve Cooper
1979 John Gowdy, Allan Graves, George Mittelman,
Pratap Rajadhyaksha, Steve Cooper, Larry Mori
1980 A. Remikis, Jerry J. Aceti,
Colin J. Van Wallegham, M. Kevin Conway
1981 Wayne Hascall, Dave Fred,
Jim Gardner, Robb Gordon *(tied with)*
Cliff Campbell, Ross Cody,
Mel Johnsen, Roland Laframboise

SWISS TEAMS
Flight A:
1980 James Zimmerman, Robert Sherburn,
Phil Leon, Ralph Katz *(tied with)*
Randy Bellerose, Betty Anne Bellerose, Stephen O'Conner,
Jennine O'Connor, Susan Sanders
1981 James Zimmerman, William Esberg, Jim Becker,
Joan Remey, Jim Hamilton

OPEN PAIRS
1972 J. David King, Mike Passell
1973 David Lindop, Andy Altay
1974 J. Peterson, Jon Wier
1975 Carl Chadwick, Bill Wallace
1976 Claude Vogel, Mark Cohen
1977 Michael Davey, Vicki Anderson
1978 Michael Davey, Vicki Anderson
1979 Gary Hann, Zeke Jabbour
1980 Homer Shoop, Dave Fred
1981 Mark Lair, Mike Girou
Flight A:
1978 Bert Eccles, Philip Baer
1980 James Zimmerman, Ralph Katz

MASTER PAIRS
1972 Ron Kruse, Dave Nicklasson
1973 Karen Allison, Tom Greer
1974 Jerry Aceti, Jack Ross
1975 Mark Feldman, Gerald Caravelli
1976 David Lindop, Andy Altay
1977 Steve Garner, Dave Lehman
1979 Neil Hendry, Paul Holtham
1980 Ralph Katz, James Zimmerman
1981 Ron Morlock, Randy Mertens

MIXED PAIRS
1979 Nancy Cohn, Jerry Cohn

MEN'S PAIRS
1977 Gerald Caravelli, Milt Rosenberg
1978 Gerrard Vogl, D. Hart
1979 Jerry Aceti, Kevin Conway
1981 Dave Skillingstad, Randy Mertens

WOMEN'S PAIRS
1977 Marge Enstrom, Louise Judge
1978 G. Bright, H.M. Nicholson
1979 Judy Overland, Barbara Wood
1981 Carol Anderson, Sherril Craig

INDIVIDUAL
1977 Millie Climie
1979 David Hutchinson

MEN'S SWISS TEAMS
1978 Lloyd Harris, Herve Tremblay,

D. Martin, Dale Freeman
1979 William Rood, Gerald Braz,
Kevin Conway, Jerry Aceti *(tied with)*
Clarence Goppert, Mike Passell, Mark Lair,
George Mittelman, Allan Graves

WOMEN'S SWISS TEAMS
1978 Anne Harris, Dollie Shoveller,
Maria Weber, R. McVittie *(tied with)*
Valerie Sauntry, Gwen Halperin,
J. Deacon, B. McGarry
1979 Clerely Chaney, Marilyn Maddox,
Ruth Dillon, Joan Remey

CANADIAN NATIONAL

KNOCKOUT TEAMS
1968 Frank Vine, Harry Bork,
J. O'Dowd, Michael Martino
1969 William Eisenberg, Robert Goldman, Michael Lawrence,
Robert Hamman, James Jacoby, Robert Wolff
1971 Don Cowan, Franco Bandoni, Cliff Bishop,
Don Hocevar, Phil Leon, Gary Hann
1972 Eric Murray, Sammy Kehela, Duncan Phillips,
Gerry Charney, William Crissey, Bruce Gowdy
1973 George Mittelman, Eric Kokish, Sharyn Kokish,
Dianna Gordon, David Lindop, Andy Altay
1974 Jeffery Starr, Bert Newman, Fred Hamilton,
Steve Landen, Frank Bell
1975 Glenn Lublin, Mark Shaw,
Jerry Goldfein, Steve Alpern
1976 John Carruthers, John Guoba,
Helen Blakey, Bob Blakey
1977 Eric Murray, Paul Heitner,
Henry Bethe, Chuck Lamprey
1978 Joseph Silver, Fred Hoffer, Merle Tom,
Jay Merrill, Lou Reich
1979 Don Cowan, Sheila Forbes, Mike Cummings,
Bruce Gowdy, John Carruthers, David Lindop
1980 Eric Murray, Sammy Kehela,
Gerry Charney, Franco Bandoni
1981 Norbert Kremer, Pam Bridson, Steve Cooper,
Roy Dalton, Lynn Deas, Eric Landau

OPEN TEAMS
1951 Bruce Elliott, Roy Funston,
Bruce Gowdy, Percy Sheardown
1952 Percy Sheardown, Bruce Gowdy,
Bruce Elliott, Roy Funston
1953 Percy Sheardown, Bruce Elliott,
Roy Funston, Bruce Gowdy
1954 Mary Edna Maloney, Doug Andress,
Nell Complin, Gaston Hebert
1955 William Anderson, Marjorie Anderson,
Mickey Miller, Corti Boland
1956 Percy Sheardown, Bruce Elliott,
Doug Drury, Eric Murray
1957 Agnes Gordon, Emanuel Katz,
Robert Freedman, Jerome Friedlander
1958 Duncan Phillips, M. T. King, Lou Woodcock
Dick Hart, J. O'Dowd,
1959 Eric Murray, Bruce Elliott,
Gerry Charney, Sammy Kehela
1960 Gerry Boyd, Henri Parent,
Fred Hoffer, Marvin Altman
1961 Eric Murray, Percy Sheardown, Bruce Elliott
Sammy Kehela, Don DaCosta
1962 Don Cowan, Dr. Eric Jones,
Bruce Mathers, R. Gray
1963 Jackie Begin, Mimi Roncarelli,
Maurice Paul, William Solomon
1964 June Honigman, Chuck Burger,
Dorsey Brooks, Grant Marsee
1965 Eric Murray, Sammy Kehela,
Percy Sheardown, Bruce Elliott
1966 Jack Howell, Dr. Ronald Forbes,
Robert Gray, Milton Miller
1967 Eric Murray, Sammy Kehela,
Percy Sheardown, Bruce Elliott
1970 Joseph Silver, Eric Kokish, Jacques Meerof,
Robert Binsky, George Mittelman
1971 Dr. Adolph Feingold, B. Lagowski,
Gloria Noszka, Franco Bandoni
1972 Woody Van Court, Carol Van Court,
Victor Ragazzo, Steve Haver *(tied with)*
Bruce Elliott, Michael Cummings,
John Laskin, Shelia Forbes
1973 Bert Winges, Ralph Bartlett, Doug Clark,
Leo Takefman, Robert Chow *(tied with)*
Dr. Adolph Feingold, B. Lagowski,
Doug Fraser, Sandra Schamroth *(and)*

John Carruthers, John Cunningham,
A. Lalonde, Lillian Vine
1974 Fred Rubbra, Rhoda Walsh,
Lou Reich, Bob Kehoe
1975 John Toy, Mary McKenna,
Peter Mollemet, Nat Gerstman *(tied with)*
Roy Hughes, David Colbert,
John Rayner, Roy Dalton *(and)*
Hal Mouser, Dennis McGarry,
Bob Richman, John Boeder *(and)*
Bill Pollack, Frank Vine,
John Howlett, Clifford O'Reilly
1976 Glenn Lubin, Phil Clark,
Eric Landau, Judy Landau
1977 Larry Mori, Bruno Sestito,
Jeff Meckstroth, Russell Shoup
1978 Robin Mercer, Steve Unger,
Mark Dunsiger, Abe Greenspan
1979 Eric Murray, Franco Bandoni,
Sammy Kehela, Gerry Charney
1980 Ross Taylor, Keith Balcombe,
Wayne Timms, Frank Markotitch
1981 Woody Van Court, Jan George,
Bernard Olmstead, Vincent Ragazzo

MASTER TEAMS
1965 Eric Murray, Sammy Kehela,
Percy Sheardown, Bruce Elliott
1968 Leo Takefman, Rose Milgram,
Curly Dyson, Simon Bramson
1969 John Stevens, Mrs. Sydney Isaacs,
Cameron Lindsay, John Norton *(tied with)*
Richard Fleischman, Robert Lipsitz, Don Faskow,
Bernie Chazen, Mark Blumenthal

MASTER PAIRS
1967 Fred Will, Richard Levick
1969 Leslie Popper, Norman Humer
1970 Rodney Wilton, Gordon Chapman
1971 Ted Horning, Percy Sheardown
1972 Bernard Weinstock, Ronald Rogalski
1973 Jeffrey Starr, Fred Hamilton
1974 Baron Wolfe Lebovic, Franco Bandoni
1975 John Stevens, Cam Lindsay
1976 Jeff Meckstroth, Russell Shoup
1977 Terrence Kinsella, John Howes
1978 William Purvis, William Boston
1979 Joseph Silver, George Mittelman

MEN'S SWISS TEAMS
1976 Joel Friedberg, Howard Chandross, Lee Rautenberg,
Lew Handelsman, Bob Blakey, Ron Andersen
1977 George Mittelman, Michael Cummings, Gerry Charney,
Peter Nagy, Ted Horning
1978 Don Cowan, John Guoba,
John Carruthers, Mike Cummings *(tied with)*
Franco Bandoni, Cliff Bishop,
Richard Huggard, Douglas Ross *(and)*
Hal Mouser, Jerry Goldfein,
Bert Newman, Greg DeFotis
1979 John Carruthers, Bert Newman,
Bob Crafton, Mark Molson
1980 Michael Schoenborn, Maurice Paul, Steve Cooper,
Peter Bambrick, John Cunningham *(tied with)*
Don Cowan, David Lindop, John Carruthers,
Michael Cummings, Bruce Gowdy, John Gowdy *(and)*
B. MacFarlane, Rob Sewell,
M. Bilon, P. Mathewson
1981 Peter Bambrick, Phil Brady,
Martin Kirr, Dan Gerstman

WOMEN'S SWISS TEAMS
1976 Gwen Cole, Ella O'Marra,
Jeanine Follows, Judy Overland
1977 Jan Miller, Gwenfil Woods, Marie Cole,
Ruth Browning, Kathy Rawlinson
1978 Marion Wright, Isabelle Bennett,
Aileen Wakeford, Audrey McHoul
1979 Bernie Lacy, JoAnn Steigmeyer,
Sandy Pennington, Beverly Onisko
1980 Jessie Rundle, Evelyn Black,
A. Silgailis, Vera Creelman *(tied with)*
Dorothy Freedman, Beverly Cohen,
Claire Chodorow, Shirley Griffith
1981 Shelia Forbes, Karen Allison,
Rita Rand, Gail Moss

MEN'S PAIRS
1959 J. B. Robinson, L. Woodcock
1960 Bruce Elliott, Bruce Gowdy
1961 R. J. Hart, Albert James
1962 Percy Sheardown, Bruce Dwyer
1963 Alvin Landy, Eric Murray
1964 Leonard Cheney, William Lande

1965 Maurice Wallace, William Allison
1966 Robert Lipsitz, Dick Fleischman
1967 William Pollack, Harry Allen
1968 Michael Martino, Frank Vine
1969 Harry Creed, Aaron Goodman
1970 Eric Murray, Duncan Phillips
1971 Bill Pollack, Mike Martino
1972 S. McCallum, Howard Jacobs
1973 Robert Pugh, W. Conkie
1974 Steve Aarons, Alex Kisin
1975 Jim Linhart, Mark Blumenthal
1976 Alan Greer, Fred Bellinger
1977 Martin Baff, Philip Wolkin
1978 Gordon Walker, Sheldon Frommer
1979 Bob Craig, Woody Van Court
1980 Ralph Katz, James Zimmerman
1981 Robert Glenn, Larry Long

MIXED PAIRS
1952 Bruce Elliott, Margaret Bell
1953 Bruce Gowdy, Dorothea Cunningham
1954 Mrs. J. A. Regan, Norm Burns
1955 Michael Raikes, Dorothea Cunningham
1956 Bonamy Sheriff, Mrs. H. A. Russell
1957 Alan Ross, Mrs. Hudson Johnston
1958 Norm Burns, Helen Harrow
1959 Sammy Kehela, Cecille Fisher
1960 Harry Bork, Rita Poder
1961 Richard Freeman, Mrs. W. C. Robinson
1962 Sammy Kehela, Cecille Fisher
1963 Jim Ross, Jackie Begin
1964 Bruce Elliott, Agnes Gordon
1965 Jackie Begin, Don DaCosta
1966 Mrs. R. T. Broad, John Stevens
1967 Mary Bowden, Harry Creed
1968 Shelia Forbes, Curly Dyson
1970 Mrs. R. Brenan, C. Lindsay
1971 Joyce Phillips, Mike Martino
1972 Dr. S. Marinker, Mrs. S. Marinker
1973 Dom DiFelice, Margaret Lerner
1975 Astrid Berg, Ingemann Berg
1976 Roni Ostfield, Marc Nathan
1977 Sydney Issacs, Bruce Elliott
1978 Rosemary Clark, Mike Cafferata
1979 Bruce Elliott, Sydney Issacs
1980 Pam Bridson, Mark Molson
1981 Karen McCallum, Woody Van Court

WOMEN'S PAIRS
1959 Phyllis Barrington, Kay Buckman
1960 H. Toffee, C. McGill
1961 Shirley Reynolds, Kay Boeckh
1962 Agnes Gordon, Jackie Begin
1963 Peggy Simmons, Ida Hall
1964 Dorothy Schick, Lorna Davidson
1965 Mrs. A MacTavish, Mrs. W. E. Weber
1966 Agnes Gordon, Dorothea M. Cunningham
1967 Claire Levin, Mrs. Peter Bandles
1968 Mrs. R. Appleby, Mrs. M. Boyd-Bowman
1969 Kay Alexander, Shelia Forbes
1970 Bernice Peterson, Lorraine Brown
1971 Irene Hodgson, Linda Waldman
1972 Mrs. M. Wagner, Mildred Morgan
1973 Mrs. F. Isaac, Mrs. R. Pearce
1974 Sybil Robinson, Roma Frankel
1975 Margaret Gupta, Janet Halliwell
1976 Cecille Fisher, Amy Biggar
1976 Michi Sakamonto, Charlotte Hahn
1978 Bina Adams, Jane Nelson
1979 Susan Ganley, Mary McKenna
1980 Kathie Wei, Judi Radin *(tied with)*
Eileen MacDiarmid, Mrs. W. Hogg
1981 Cecille Fisher, Amy Biggar

OPEN PAIRS
1952 Barry Cohen, Buddy Marsh
1953 John Swenholt, Truesdale Clarke
1954 Helen Harrow, Hazel Roberts
1955 Bruce Elliott, Percy Sheardown
1956 Alan Ross, J. W. McDonald
1957 Eric Murray, Douglas Drury
1958 Eric Murray, Bruce Elliott
1959 Marvin Altman, Freddie Hoffer
1960 Ben Stone, Hartley Maldaver
1961 Paul Trent, Harry Creed
1962 Eric Murray, Bruce Eliott
1963 Graham Cooke, Hugh Stephenson
1964 C. G. Jeans, Ed Bissel
1965 Henry Bethe, Thomas Smith
1966 Fred Hoffer, Marvin Altman
1967 Hannan Bott, Mrs. Charles Urban
1968 Jimmy Cayne, Chuck Burger
1969 Bruce Elliott, Percy Sherdown

1970	Richard Edney, Mrs. Richard Edney
1971	Nathan Unger, Roselle Selioff
1972	John Guoba, Abe Greenspan
1973	Merle Tom, Henry Cukoff
1974	Jay Merrill, William Woodard
1975	Francis Baragar, Dave Cummings
1976	Brian Hitchcock, Bob Kelly
1977	John Toy, Michael Schoenborn
1978	Michael Aliotta, Richard Huggard
1979	Robert Lebi, Mark Molson
1980	Frank Trieber, III, Joseph Ernsthausen
	Lisa Halpern, Dave Berkowitz *(Smoking)*
	Kathie Wei, Ron Andersen *(Non-Smoking)*
1981	Franco Bandoni, Eric Murray
	James Gardner, Wayne Hascall *(Smoking)*
	Boris Baran, Mark Molson *(Non-Smoking)*

OPEN INDIVIDUAL

1955	Ross Holliday
1957	Morris Timanoff
1958	Don DaCosta
1975	Bruce Dwyer
1976	Robert Cove
1977	Mrs. M. R. Vila
1978	James McBean
1979	Jack Klein
1980	Gerald Leckie
1981	J. Garland

CANADIAN PRAIRIE

KNOCKOUT TEAMS

1972	Doug Thomson, Brian Pauls, H. Wolch,
	Russ Weikle, Larry Oakey
1973	George Watkinson, Pat Scollie,
	Bernie Weiler, Marcella Weiler
1974	Clarence Goppert, Garey Hayden, Gaylor Kasle,
	Mike Passell, Mark Lair
1975	Clarence Goppert, Garey Hayden, Ron Andersen,
	Hugh MacLean, Gerald Caravelli, Terry Beckman
1976	Ron Andersen, Clarence Goppert, Bruce Ferguson,
	Mark Lair, Hugh MacLean
1977	Neil Kimelman, Barry Senensky,
	Bob Todd, Bob Kuz
1978	Doug Fisher, David Sokolow,
	Bryan Maksymetz, G. Sekar
1979	Alan Bell, Ed Lichtman,
	Alex DeGroot, Bryan Maksymetz
1980	Art d'Entremont, B. McTavish, Tom Butterworth,
	Bill Gray, Lorne Carscadden, Mike Rahtjen
1981	Ed Bridson, David Colbert, Mike Cafferata,
	Douglas Fox, Ross Taylor

OPEN TEAMS

1965	Otto Leesment, Karel van Renesse,
	Jack Murphy, Dr. Fred Patterson
1973	Alex DeGroot, W. McTavish,
	Lorne Carscadden, Drew Cannell
1974	Dr. D. Schmeiser, Geraldine Sugarman,
	T. Braun, Art d'Entremont *(tied with)*
	James Leary, John Larsen,
	Jack Rhatigan, James Hugstad
1975	Clarence Goppert, Garey Hayden, Ron Andersen,
	Hugh MacLean, Gerald Caravelli, Terry Beckman
1976	Ron Andersen, Hugh MacLean, Clarence Goppert,
	Mark Lair, Bruce Ferguson
1977	Bernie Melman, Mandel Grower,
	Naomi Silver, Ruth Copp
1978	Kai Cheng, G. Sekhar,
	Doug Fisher, David Sokolow *(tied with)*
	Alex DeGroot, Larry Oakey,
	Alan Bell, Morrie Freier
1979	Alan Morin, Shaune Karen Bratsbert,
	Kenneth Nelson, Bill Treble
1980	Ken MacNeal, Subhash Gupta,
	Ron Smith, Mike Lawrence
1981	Paul Thurston, Rick Delogu,
	Jim Riegle, Leo Glaser *(tied with)*
	Ed Bridson, Douglas Fox,
	David Colbert, Mike Cafferata

Flight A:

1980	John Taillon, Dan Mathieson, Bob Todd,
	David Sired, John Ross
1981	Ed Bridson, Steve Aarons,
	John Gowdy, Arno Hobart

OPEN PAIRS

1965	Sherry Brooks, Gary Mitchell
1972	Ron Andersen, Bernie Coleman
1973	Russ Weikle, Ron Kruse
1974	John Carruthers, Alex Kisin

1975	Gerald Caravelli, Ron Andersen
1976	Clarence Goppert, Mark Lair
1977	Bob Kuz, Neil Kimelman
1978	Bob Kuz, Neil Kimelman
1979	Tom Fox, Phyllis Sornsin
1980	Jane Kunzer, C. Milton Shefchik
1981	Don Domansky, Dave McLellan

Flight A:

1980	M. Walder, Larry Oakey
1981	John Stevens, J. Brian Johnston

MASTER PAIRS

1972	Helen Promislow, Norm Promislow
1974	Harold Siegelman, James Brothers
1975	Ron Andersen, Hugh MacLean
1976	John Munson, J. Ross
1977	Steve Sion, Ron Andersen
1978	Bob Kuz, Barry Senesky
1979	Doug Thomson, Ed Lichtman
1980	Ron Smith, Subhash Gupta
1981	Samuel Aaron, Ted Horning

MIXED PAIRS

1976	C.V. Cambell, Dr. S.M. Bloom
1979	Tom Fox, Phyllis Sornsin

UNMIXED PAIRS

1977	Dave Lehman, Dick Melson
1978	Bob Kuz, Neil Kimelman

MEN'S PAIRS

1965	Doug Thomson, Larry Oakey
1972	Ron Andersen, Hugh MacLean
1979	Alan Bell, Alex DeGroot

INDIVIDUAL

1976	Bob Todd
1979	Rose Orenstein

WOMEN'S SWISS TEAMS

1976	Mrs. J. Forsberg, Nelsine Stuhlman,
	Mrs. T.F. Hassett, Mrs. R.B. Brink
1977	Etta Greenburg, Leona Rose Smithen,
	Jackie Baizley, Dena Grower *(tied with)*
	Evelyn Blankstein, Anne Smithen,
	I. McGlynn, Annabel Walterson
1978	Sallie Landa, C. Wichman,
	Elizabeth Clark, Phyllis Sornsin

MEN'S SWISS TEAMS

1976	Drew Cannell, Alex DeGroot,
	Brian Pauls, Alan Bell *(tied with)*
	Ron Andersen, Hugh MacLean, Clarence Goppert,
	Mark Lair, Bruce Ferguson
1977	Steve Garner, Howard Weinstein,
	Dave Lehman, Dick Melson
1978	Larry Oakey, Morrie Freier,
	Doug Fisher, David Sokolow

WOMEN'S PAIRS

1965	Hazel Smith, Pat Smolensky
1972	Molly Shaffer, Irene Udow
1979	Wendy Jones, Dianne McCandless

DISTRICT 3 (Northern and central New Jersey, eastern New York State)

NEW YORK–NEW JERSEY CONFERENCE

OPEN TEAMS

1958	Jacqui Gallaher, Victor Mitchell,
	Morton Rubinow, David Strasberg
1959	Norman Kay, Tobias Stone,
	John R. Crawford, Sidney Silodor
1960	Terry Michaels, Israel Cohen,
	Peggy Rotzell, Robert Sitnek
1961	Samuel Stayman, Philip Feldesman, Jacqui Mitchell,
	Victor Mitchell, David Strasberg
1962	Dr. Stephen Warner, Teddie Warner,
	John Solodar, Richard Reisig
1963	Sally Johnson, Lt. Col. William Christian,
	Robert Sitnek, Peter Pender
1964	Robert Sitnek, Boris Raymond,
	Lt. Col. William Christian, Sally Johnson
1965	Lt. Col. Murray Schnee, Dr. Kalman Apfel,
	Victor Shen, Alan Rich
1966	Richard Budd, Marty Ginsberg,
	Lester Sokolower, Harry Stappenbeck
1967	Helen Smith, Mike Carson,
	William Landow, Robert Alexander
1968	John Solodar, Peter Weichsel,
	Charles Coon, Marvin Rosenblatt

1969   Mike Cappelletti, Kathie Cappelletti,
      Steve Parker, Peggy Parker
1970   Paul Heitner, Henry Bethe,
      Tom Griffin, Karen Allison
1971   Paula Levin, Lloyd Ribner, Mike Becker,
      Mark Blumenthal, Seymour Leibowitz
1972   Mirette Mignocchi, Michael Mignocchi,
      Jim Becker, Earl Becker
1973   Harold Lilie, Bob Sartorius,
      David Berkowitz, Mike Gurwitz
1974   Bart Bramley, Lou Reich,
      Stephen Labins, Chuck Lamprey
1975   Neil Silverman, Merle Tom, Barbara Rappaport,
      Bernard Chazen, Norman Kurlander
1976   Peter Weichsel, Alan Sontag, Steve Sion,
      Dave Berkowitz, Harold Lilie, Joyce Lilie
1977   James Mason, Dave Mason, Sol Seidman, James Bennett Jr.
1978   Kathie Wei, Ron Andersen, Dave Berkowitz,
      Joyce Lilie, Harold Lilie
1979   Alan Stauber, Ron Gerard, Larry Cohen, Warren Rosner

OPEN PAIRS

1958   Edward Lowenthal, Dillard Bird *(tied with)*
      Phyllis Schofield, Clinton Schofield
1959   Miriam Lees, Robert Racier
1960   Joe Siegelman, Marty Ginsberg
1961   Philip Feldesman, David Strasberg
1962   Amy Bronstein, Dr. Ben Bronstein
1963   Boris Raymond, Fred Dossenbach
1964   Charles Coon, Marvin Rosenblatt
1965   Fred Dossenbach, Jay Wendt
1966   Mike Carson, Bill Landow
1967   David Mason, Tom Griffin
1968   Leonard Cohen, Armand Jacoby
1969   Dave Sachs, Sue Sachs
1970   Paul Heitner, Harry Stappenbeck
1971   Harlow Lewis, Tony Dionisi
1972   Joel Stuart, Gene Neiger
1973   Ronald Gerard, Phil Cowan
1974   William Gough, Phil Brady
1975   Neil Silverman, Merle Tom
1976   Don Oakie, Ron Gerard
Flight A:
1977   James Rosenbloom, Brian Glubok
1978   Robert Serenyi, Jerry Kuklinski
1979   Ron Andersen, Dave Berkowitz
1980   Jim Bennett, Geof Brod
1981   Lisa Berkowitz, Dave Berkowitz

MEN'S PAIRS

1958   Edgar Kaplan, Morton Rubinow
1959   Cecil Friedman, Jerry Silverman
1960   Edgar Bitz, Walter Bitz
1961   Jeff Westheimer, Marty Ginsberg
1962   Dick Zeckhauser, Paul Spiegelman
1963   Arnold Malasky, Gene Prosnitz
1964   Dave Mason, William Passell
1965   Dr. Norman Buch, Dr. Morris Halper
1966   Lewis H. Fattel, Dr. Allen Spiegel
1967   Al Norton, Bernard Nathanson
1968   Lou Levy, David Mason
1969   Leslie Popper, Chester Davis
1970   Art Weinstein, Fred Stewart
1971   Mike Moss, Henry Bethe
1972   Russ Didowski, John H. Wayne
1973   Bernie Chazen, Harold Feldheim
1974   Alvin Roth, Ahmed Hussein
1975   Mark Berger, Ed Andreasian
1976   Robert Quinn, Ronald Fisher
1977   Harold Lilie, Dave Berkowitz
1978   Jim Becker, Jim Hamilton
1979   Bruce Gardner, Tom Menges
1980   Walter Schenker, Norm Rubin
1981   Allan Stauber, William Kreps

WOMEN'S PAIRS

1958   Mrs. Otto Neustadt, Mary Dee
1959   Carolyn Brail, Marguerite Harris
1960   Peggy Rotzell, Mollie Gordon
1961   Edith Rosenbloom, Dorothy Voorhees
1962   Reba Cohen, Jean Kolsby
1963   Mae Bloch, Helen Smith
1964   Lucille Brown, Mrs. Leo Klein
1965   Adele Kotzen, Belle Kauffman
1966   Dora Brechner, Muriel Kaplan
1967   Adele Kotzen, Belle Kauffman
1968   Carol Cohen, Edith Schwartz
1969   Barbara Tepper, Barbara Rappaport
1970   Myldred Kelly, Judy Carroll
1971   Gail Moss, Judi Solodar
1972   Marge Sweet, Mrs. Bert Alperin
1973   Dorothy Hughes, Mabel Mannes
1974   Marietta Passell, Dorothy Hayden Truscott

1975   Marietta Passell, Dorothy Hayden Truscott
1976   Jacqui Mitchell, Jill Roberts
1977   Judi Radin, Lynn Tranopol
1978   Shirley Ordos, Shirley Lemick
1979   Linda Sartorius, Esther Roth
1980   Honey Ellis, Shirley Sperber
1981   Honey Ellis, Shirley Sperber

MIXED PAIRS

1958   Mrs. John James, Benjamin Hirschberg
1959   Jan Stone, Andy Gabrilovitch
1960   Lenore Allen, Dr. Stephen Warner
1961   Dorothy Silverman, Cecil Friedman
1962   Ann Sheaber, David Mason
1963   Marthe Charles, Emanuel Bernstein
1964   Barbara Rappaport, Alvin Roth
1965   Barbara Rappaport, Alvin Roth
1966   Norma Cook, Bruce Longton
1967   Wynne Ecker, Dr. Ernst Theimer
1968   John Solodar, Ellen Alfandre
1969   Charles Coon, Isa Alcone
1970   Patricia Nixon, Bernard Miller
1971   Mark Epstein, Roberta Epstein
1972   Harold Lilie, Joyce Furman
1973   Harold Lilie, Judi Solodar
1974   Al Romm, Rigmor Nilsen
1975   Pam Goldsmith, William Gough
1976   Kitty Bethe, Henry Bethe
1977   Joyce Lilie, Steve Sion
1978   Alan Kudisch, Donna Stoddard
1979   May Giantz, Albert Ross
1980   Halina Jamner, William Epperson

INDIVIDUAL

1958   Joe Siegelman
1975   Sydell Berkowsky
1976   Martin Goldman
1977   Shirley Kip
1978   John Freeman
1979   Helen Armstrong
1980   Jeffery Goldsmith

WOMEN'S SWISS TEAMS

1977   Lisa Mann Burke, Myrna Lurie,
      Julie James, Frances Esposito
1978   Nancy Molesworth, Marcia Warner,
      Charlotte Davidson, Joyce Landau
1979   Judi Radin, Kitty Bethe, Kathie Wei,
      Aileen Osofsky, Ellee Lewis
1980   Marilyn Goldberg, Hannah Russ,
      Charlotte Brasel, Gertrude Goldstein
1981   Lila Perlstein, Nancy Molesworth,
      Halina Jamner, Marlene Zenker

MEN'S SWISS TEAMS

1977   Leonard Karp, Andy Ramsperger,
      Robert Garofalo, Jim Hom
1978   Bob Panek, Larry Cohen, Ron Gerard, Marty Fleisher
1979   Jim Hamilton, Phillip Martin, Ethan Stein, Tom Zeyer
1980   Stephen Sanborn, Allan Stauber, Ethan Stein,
      Joel Friedberg, Marty Bergen
1981   Michael Kamil, Ed Schuster, Walter May, Marty Bergen

MASTER PAIRS

1981   Eileen Brenner, Michael Pickert

SWISS TEAMS

Flight A
1979   Victor Mitchell, Jacqui Mitchell,
      Bill Roberts, Jill Roberts *(tied with)*
      Gail Moss, Ahmed Hussein,
      Ron Gerard, Gene O'Neil *(and)*
      Jack Lacy, David Wachsman, Joan Levy,
      Ralph Wesselmann, Alan Dworetzky, Jim Dederick
1980   Ira Herman, Drew Casen, Bob Gwirtzman, Gene Prosnitz
1981   Steve Bloom, Betty Bloom, Jeff Hall,
      Jeff Juster, Bob Feller, Marty Fleisher

TRI-STATE

OPEN TEAMS

1967   John Barnicle, Mark Mohr
      Frank Burstein, Robert Ryder, Richard Celler
1968   B. Jay Becker, Dorothy Hayden, Hal Fein,
      Richard Schwarts, Alan Truscott
1969   Roger Abelson, Carl Winters,
      Steve Dow, Jr., Mike Edwards
1970   Murray Schnee, Tannah Hirsch, Sol Seidman,
      Jim Becker, Jim Bennett
1971   Al Roth, Alan Sontag, Barbara Rappaport, Bernie Chazen
1972   Steve Altman, Eugene Neiger, Alan Sontag,
      Joel Stuart, Peter Weichsel, Thomas Smith
1973   Steve Paskin, Thomas Trifon, Fred Melman, Ralph Wahl
1974   Charles Friedman, Neil Nathanson,

Ken Parker, Judy Parker *(tied with)*
Steve Altman, Tom Smith, Steve Labins, Chuck Lamprey
1975 Howard Piltch, Thomas Justl,
Jeffery Juster, Andrew Markowitz
1976 Larry Bausher, Jeffery Horowitz, Leon St. Jean, Steve Earl
1977 Tony Kasday, Steve Sion, John Batcheller, Joshua Parker
1978 Fred Klat, Verna Leone, Walt Konstanty, Marge Patri
1979 Mike Radin, Stasha Wroblewski,
Lew Handelsman, Emmett Pollenz
1980 Estee Griffin, Tony Dionisi, Bob Sartorius, Linda Sartorius
Flight A:
1981 Lloyd Arvedon, Arthur Moore,
Eric Robinson, Martin Fleisher

MASTER PAIRS
1972 Augusta Cantor, Robert Bowers
1973 Matt Granovetter, Mark Blumenthal
1974 Bob Cohen, Bob Kehoe

OPEN PAIRS
1967 Nat Gerstman, Judy Slater
1968 William Herrmann, Hazel Smith
1969 Joseph S. Goldberg, Irwin Boris
1970 Warren Kornfield, Richard Khautin
1971 Nancy Weichsel, Peter Weichsel
1972 Dorothy Hayden, Alan Truscott
1973 Norman Humer, Bernard Miller
1974 Alvin Roth, Barbara Rappaport
1975 Les Bart, Leonard Kaplan
1976 Bill Dimler, Myldred Kelly
1977 Tony Kasday, Steve Sion
Flight A:
1978 Bob Quinn, Phyllis Quinn
1979 Robert Barr, Clint Morrell
1980 Victor Mitchell, Bill Roberts
1981 Michael Kamil, Robert Hertzberg

MEN'S PAIRS
1967 Nat Gerstman, Hubert A. Gerstman
1968 Mark A. Berger, Ed Andreasian
1969 James Becker, Shelly de Satnick
1970 J. David King, Mark Berger
1971 Hal Fein, David Strasberg
1972 B. Jay Becker, Alan Truscott
1973 Harold Lilie, Gary Hampar
1974 Norman Humer, Bernard Miller
1975 Jerry Shakofsky, Hal Fein
1976 William Gough, William Levy
1977 Marty Bergen, Alan Schwartz
1978 Bill Roberts, Victor Mitchell
1979 Ron Gerard, Mike Rosmarin
1980 Al Rand, Harold Lilie
1981 Jerome Weissman, Samuel Marsh

WOMEN'S PAIRS
1967 Anita Davis, Helen Strasberg
1968 Freddie Goldberg, Martha Fingerle
1969 Sandy Spero, Suzanne Palmer
1970 Mrs. William Wolfe, Mrs. Phillip Mahrer
1971 Val Habicht, Shirley Petty
1972 Judy Schwartz, Priscilla Rutkin
1973 Roberta Epstein, Barbara Rappaport
1974 Edith Sudikoff, Sylvia LeSavoy
1975 Natalie Flaton, Edda Spangelet
1976 Mrs. W. Hoover, Anne Livezey
1977 Judy Tucker, Vivian Whalen
1978 Myrna Lurie, Nancy Barbato
1979 Judi Radin, Lynne Tarnapol
1980 Judy Cody, Julie Grabel
1981 Wanda Gabrilovitch, Martha Fingerle

MIXED PAIRS
1967 Richard G. Hewitt, Amy Bronstein
1968 Doris Brown, Gil Brown
1969 Bea Strauss, Larry Strauss
1970 Virginia Penick, Murray Cohen
1971 Val Habicht, R. Jay Becker
1975 Judi Solodar, Arthur Waldmann
1976 Justine Perry, William Gough
1977 Arleen Wellman, Steven Slott
1978 Norma Gross, John Schmidt
1979 Marion Rosmarin, Mike Rosmarin
1980 Drew Casen, Janet DeGrazia
1981 Shirley Kamil, Michael Kamil

INDIVIDUAL
1975 Joseph Garlic
1976 Joan Howlson
1977 Alfred Klein *(tied with)*
Paul Seidman
1978 J. Lilienstein
1979 A. J. Gaska
1980 Dr. Lawrence Loewinthan
1981 Tim Sutton

MEN'S SWISS TEAMS
1977 Mike Rosmarin, Alan Schwartz,
Michael Levinson, Don Probst, Walter May
1978 Mike Rosmarin, Alan Schwartz,
Howard Chandross, Lew Handelsman
1979 Ron Gerard, Merle Tom, Gene O'Neil,
Bart Bramley, Bill Pollack
1980 Norm Rubin, Tex Cates, Andy Lohan, Walter Schenker
(tied with) Peter Loeb, Don McSherry, Stanley Groskin,
Al Fisher, Ron VandeBunte *(and)*
Andy Gabrilovitch, Tannah Hirsch,
Phil Cowan, Mark Cohen, Tom Smith *(and)*
Allan Stauber, Steve Sanborn,
Peter Relson, Warren Rosner *(and)*
Rob Gordon, Steve Garyn, Art Brodsky, Don Theodore
1981 Allan Stauber, Warren Rosner, Ethan Stein, Marty Bergen

WOMEN'S SWISS TEAMS
1977 Judy Tucker, Vivian Whalen, Judi Radin, Lynne Tarnapol
1978 Liane Pruzan, Joy Berdon, Eleanor Stillman, Rhoda Levine
1979 Sandy Stern, Barbara Rappaport,
Dorothy Hayden Truscott, Edith Sachs
1980 Rhoda Spencer, Fran Weston,
Selma Schlechter, Molla Munroe *(tied with)*
Marge Ives, Doris Staubi,
Shirley Silverman, Bonnie Dropkin
1981 Kathie Wei, Judi Radin, Joan DeWitt, Esta Van Zandt

UPPER NEW YORK STATE
(See also Districts 4 and 5)

MASTERS PAIRS
1970 Mary Merriman, Everett Hatch
1972 Eric Kokish, Mark Blumenthal
1974 Stephen Paskin, Miles Storfer
1976 Stephen Paskin, Miles Storfer
1979 Jim Becker, Jim Hamilton
1980 Ethan Stein, Howard Chandross
1981 Robert Hertzberg, Andy Ramsperger

MEN'S SWISS TEAMS
1972 Herb Resnick, Henry Penner
Robert Stone, Russ Ekeblad
1974 Phil Clark, Glenn Lublin,
John Conway, Paul DePorte
1976 Mike Levinson, Alan Schwartz,
Allan Stauber, Stephen Bandes
1979 Jim Becker, Jim Hamilton,
Lew Handelsman, Howard Chandross *(tied with)*
Lloyd Arvedon, Ken Bercuson,
James Bennett, Chester Davis
1980 Ron Harvey, Gerald Cohen, Marty Bergen,
Bob Feller, Allan Stauber
1981 George Tourajian, Jeffery Hall, Steve Bloom,
Anthony Prindle, William Nelson, Norm Kremer

WOMEN'S SWISS TEAMS
1972 Jo Morse, Helen Utegaard,
Shirley Neilson, Sharyn Linkovsky *(tied with)*
Anne O'Brien, Mary Merriman,
Mrs. Henry Penner, Joan Noll
1974 Jacqueline Karlen, Joan Noll,
Mary Merriman, Judith Flack
1976 Shirley Weinstein, Judy Cody,
Rusty Rappaport, Cynthia Colin
1979 Evelyn Jacobs, Beatrice Shary,
Irene Wilder, Ann Turai *(tied with)*
Lila Perlstein, Claire Tornay,
Gail Moss, Rozanne Marel
1980 Ethel Keohane, Barbara Ashore,
Martha Marcus, Carolyn Sessler,
Ida Bennett, Mary Lou Cushner
1981 Vicki Loring, Mary Lou Cushner,
Carolyn Sessler, Barbara Ashore

MASTER SWISS TEAMS
1976 Bill Butcher, Tom Donnelly, Don Faix, Leon St. Jean

KNOCKOUT TEAMS
1974 Jay Merrill, Peter Boyd, Charles Martel,
Steve Sion, Ross Grabel, James Rosenbloom
1976 Bart Bramley, Bill Pollack, Peter Weichsel,
Alan Sontag, Ross Grabel, Arthur Waldman
1979 Ross Grabel, Josh Parker,
Bill Pollack, Les Bart
1980 Dave Berkowitz, Lisa Halpern,
Joyce Lilie, Harold Lilie

OPEN TEAMS
1970 Robert Freedman, James Mathis,
Bernard Miller, Mark Feldman
1972 Bill Bowman, John Bowman, Bert Curry, Al McDonald
1974 William Woodard, Gerald Cohen,

Marty Bergen, Ron Harvey
1976   Ron Feldman, Jerry Shakofsky, Jim Linhart,
     David McClintock, Kenneth Schultze
1979   Alan Schwartz, Boris Baran, Mark Molson,
     Robert Lebi, Steve Sanborn, Allan Stauber
Flight A:
1980   Joel Friedberg, Rozanne Marel,
     Bill Pollack, Howard Chandross
1981   Bart Bramley, Judy Wadas,
     Mark Lair, Ron Smith

OPEN PAIRS
1970   William Woodard, Marty Bergen
1972   Robert Freedman, James Mathis
1974   Robert Miller, John Saxe
1976   Jim Davis, Tom Evans
Flight A:
1979   Ethan Stein, Mark Cohen
1980   Ann Reynolds, Jan Mosher
1981   Francine Cimon, Beverly Kraft

MEN'S PAIRS
1970   R. Jack Walford, George Ainslie
1972   Herbert Resnick, Daniel Gertsman
1974   Peter Boyd, Jay Merrill
1976   Ron Andersen, Alan Schwartz
1979   Boris Baran, Mark Molson
1980   Dave Wachsman, Steve Surasky
1981   Marty Bergen, Michael Kamil

WOMEN'S PAIRS
1970   Eva Scatassa, Judy Portale
1972   Jo Morse, Helen Utegaard
1974   Roberta MacLeod, Paula Mann
1976   Florence Rand, Shirley Nelick
1979   Rona Schiller, Selma Silverman
1980   Ida Bennett, Ethel Keohane
1981   M. Bogue, Anne Adams

MIXED PAIRS
1970   Evelyn Garfield, Chester Davis

DISTRICT 4

KEYSTONE CONFERENCE

KNOCKOUT TEAMS
1973   David Treadwell, Evelyn Levitt, Ray Raskin,
     Chris Jeans, Helen Smith, Ken Cohen
1975   Mark Blumenthal, Seymour Leibowitz, Merle Moskowitz,
     Jay Cohen, Bill Landow, Alan Susskind
1981   Kit Woolsey, Peter Boyd,
     Ron Sukoneck, Bob Lipsitz

OPEN PAIRS
Flight A:
1978   Ed Lewis, William Epperson
1979   Ethan Stein, R. Jay Becker
1981   Calvin Janov, Helaine Berger

OPEN TEAMS
1952   Eli Jaye, Albert Shmukler,
     Norman Kay, Edgar Kaplan
1953   Henry Knopf, Fred Bellinger,
     Stuart O'Hagen, Richard Rovner
1954   Ruth Sherman, Edgar Kaplan, John Moran,
     Richard Kahn, Ralph Hirschberg *(tied with)*
     David Bayless, R. Wayne,
     M.J. Root, M. Feldman
1955   Betty Adler, Julian Adler,
     Edward Behrend, Louis Rosenfeld *(tied with)*
     Pauline Shmukler, Simon Becker,
     John McGervey, Eli Jaye
1956   Don Wolfson, Charles Braman,
     William Hall, Mrs. H.M. Steiger *(tied with)*
     David Murray, Alvin Roth,
     Betty Haddad, Said Haddad
1957   Norman Kay, Edgar Kaplan,
     Ralph Hirschberg, Alfred Sheinwold
1958   Reuben Alexander, Charles Coon, David Strasberg,
     Eric Murray, Harry Creed
1959   Terry Michaels, Israel Cohen,
     Bill Christian, Frank Hoadley
1960   Peggy Rotzell, Robert Sitnek, Arthur Robinson,
     Peter Pender, Leonard Harmon
1961   Betty Haddad, Said Haddad,
     Peggy Rotzell, Sidney Aronson
1962   Edgar Kaplan, Elizabeth Sheinwold, Norman Kay,
     Robert Jordan, Andy Gabrilovitch
1963   Sally Johnson, Oswald Jacoby,
     Paul Trent, Lt. Col. William Christian
1964   William Flannery, Herb Sachs,
     Don Faskow, Paul Swanson

1965   Harlow Lewis, Mark Blumenthal, Helen Smith,
     Joseph Asber, Anthony Dionisi
1966   Kathie Cappelletti, Mike Cappelletti,
     Leslie Popper, John Benoit
1967   Andrew Bernstein, Stan Tomchin, Ed Manfield,
     Bernard Chazen, Tom Smith
1968   William Landow, Mike Carson,
     Jim Cayne, Barbara Tepper *(tied with)*
     Robert Ryder, Frank Burstein,
     Richard Celler, Mark Mohr
1969   Alan Sontag, Keith Garber,
     John Bookstaver, Roger Abelson *(tied with)*
     Kathie Cappelletti, Mike Cappelletti,
     Steve Parker, Peggy Parker
1970   William Gough, Ray Raskin,
     Jerry Locks, Libby Silberman
1971   Betty Adler, Julian Adler,
     Sue Sachs, David Sachs
1972   Betty Adler, Julian Adler,
     Sue Sachs, David Sachs
1973   Betty Adler, Julian Adler,
     Sue Sachs, David Sachs
1974   Betty Adler, Julian Adler,
     Sue Sachs, David Sachs
1975   Walter May, Ron Blau,
     Joseph Livezey, William Gough
1976   Ralph Bartlett, Jay Merrill,
     Alan Schwartz, Don Probst
1977   Eugene O'Neill, Phil Brady, Joe Kivel
     Dave Treadwell, Mickie Kivel
1978   Dave Treadwell, Evelyn Levitt,
     Arnold Fisher, Walter May

WOMEN'S TEAMS
1971   Adele Kotzen, Gayle Rubens,
     Nancy Gruver, Betty Adler *(tied with)*
     Irma Slabey, Ethel Silver,
     Ann Gittleman, Marie Gaynor
1972   Judy Kay, Helen Smith,
     Evelyn Levitt, Ruth Blumenthal *(tied with)*
     Betty Adler, Gayle Rubens,
     Judi Solodar, Gloria Rabinowitz
1974   Lila Perstein, Judy Tucker,
     Myldred Kelly, Judy Carrol *(tied with)*
     Lida Rothman, Beatrice Weeks,
     Madeline Knox, Shirley Wigner
1976   Mrs. M.J. Baum, Helene Grove,
     Mrs. M.C. Luteran, Carole Neuberger
1977   Vivian Whalen, Stasha Wroblewski,
     Judy Tucker, Dorothy Posner
1978   Pearl Tyson, Marilyn Reedinger,
     Frances Basenberg, Betty Crosson
1979   Felice Schwartz, Sarah Korbin,
     Nancy Rubin, Evelyn Zamboni *(tied with)*
     Adele Orloff, Barbara Satinsky,
     Pauline Karp, Iris Pollow *(and)*
     Gail Bell, Ferne Kleban,
     Doris Lawrence, Nancy Pecarsky
1980   Gail Rust, Belle Kaufman,
     Joan Crowder, Jeanne Stenger
1981   Barbara Doran, Rae Dethlefsen,
     Gloria Brown, Harriet Goldberg

MEN'S TEAMS
1971   Mark Blumenthal, Luis Pietri,
     Jay Cohen, Art Coren
1972   Mark Blumenthal, Jay Cohen,
     Luis Pietri, Eddie Shapiro
1974   John Killaly, Ralph McGiboney,
     Frank Corredine, Allen Anderson
1976   Paul Cherin, Marshall Blu, Robert W. Brown,
     Edward Helpert, Stuart Sather
1977   Gene Gardner, Bruce Keidan,
     Bill Miller, Moshe Bernstein
1978   Tom Justl, Charles Fleisher, John Marks,
     Fred Ruttenberg, Betty Crosson
1979   Bill Levy, William Gough, Ira Barrows,
     Frank Mastrola, Peter Weglarski
1980   Charles Gray, Merle Moskowitz, Ken Cohen,
     Simon Becker, Bill Landow
1981   George Bloomer, Arnie Frankel,
     Paul Robb, Chuck Heine

OPEN PAIRS
1952   John Crawford, Sidney Silodor
1953   Paul Lisse, Jack Mylott
1954   R. Rosenberg, Fred Bickel
1955   Mary Ann Tergis, Claggett Bowie
1956   Cliff Bishop, Blanche Williams
1957   Peggy Rotzell, Robert Sitnek
1958   Robert Jordan, Andy Gabrilovitch
1959   Mrs. A. Shmukler, Muriel Kaplan

1960	Dave Treadwell, Marvin Paulshook
1961	Betty Adler, Julian Adler
1962	Ronald Rosenberg, Fred Bickel
1963	Dr. W.H. Rogers, Eugene Gardner
1964	Dean Darling, Tommy Ekel
1965	Belle Kauffman, Adele Kotzen
1966	Steve Parker, James Hand
1967	Eugene O'Neill, David Kaufman
1968	Robert Lattomus, Mrs. Robert Lattomus
1969	Kenny Rhodes, Henry Itkin
1970	Steve Parker, Peggy Parker
1971	Vic Chernoff, Jim Bennett
1972	Steve Parker, Stephen Robinson
1973	Peter Boyd, Bill Pettis
1974	Jerry Locks, Fred Klat
1975	Neil Silverman, Merle Tom
1976	Phil Horton, Eph Karch
1977	Ronald Sukoneck, Ely Solomon
1978	Jane Bronstein, Saul Bronstein
1979	Art Korth, Barry Falgout
1980	Barry Crane, Ron Andersen

OPEN PAIRS

1981	Joel Freidberg, Ethan Stein *(Smoking)*
1981	Al Wright, Don Radisill *(Non-Smoking)*

MEN'S PAIRS

1952	Ronald Rosenberg, Fred Bickel
1953	Ronald Rosenberg, Fred Bickel
1954	Ronald Rosenberg, Alvin Goodman
1955	William Warren, H. E. Potts
1956	Aaron Ritter, Joseph Donaldson
1957	Richard Freeman, Israel Cohen
1958	David Warner, Frances O'Keefe
1959	Joe Grinsfelder, J. Fish
1960	Edward Gerard, Leonard Lipstein
1961	Holton Confer, B. L. Graham
1962	Oswald Jacoby, Charles Coon
1963	Jonathan Rintels, Arthur Fribourg
1964	William Flannery, Herb Sachs
1965	David Warner, Art Cohen
1966	Simon Becker, Robert Becker
1967	William Butcher, James Bennett
1968	Mark Blumenthal, Seymour Leibowitz
1969	Charles Friedman, Dave Kaufman
1970	Michael Garner, Lynn Kesselman
1971	James Lipman, Fred Balas
1972	James Becker, William Esberg
1973	Marty Bergen, Bill Woodard
1974	Jim Looby, Bob Ryder
1975	William McCorquodale, A. J. Regenbogen
1976	Glenn Lublin, Phil Clark
1977	Joe Barone, David Lee Warner
1978	Moshe Bernstein, Paul Thomas
1979	Arnie Frankel, Bill Wilson
1980	Vin Bartone, Bill Ehlers
1981	Richard Colker, Arnold Fisher

WOMEN'S PAIRS

1952	W. W. Sketchley, L. M. Baker
1953	H. R. Hathorn, Mrs. Ben Katzen
1954	Mary Elizabeth Tiernan, Claire Tiernan
1955	Mrs. Raymond Goldberg, S. Scheiner
1956	J. R. Younkin, Rosalyn Metzler
1957	Teddy Sabott, Edith Rosenbloom
1958	Marie Gaynor, E. Mitchell
1959	R. Feldman, Ruby Jandorf
1960	Lucille Brown, Lee Amade
1961	Frances Robinson, E. Berkovits
1962	Roberta Erde, Iris Silbertstein
1963	Olive Peterson, Peggy Rotzell
1964	Jean Kolsby, May Rosen
1965	Fay Felman, Hilda Weiner
1966	Nancy Gruver, Sue Sachs
1967	Adele Kotzen, Belle Kauffman
1968	Augusta Cantor, Dora Brechner
1969	Joan Weinrott, Jane Segal
1970	Mrs. E. Wilson, Mrs. William Lewis
1971	Mrs. M. Byrne, Mrs. J. Embury
1972	Gail Moss, Sandra Roark
1973	Terry Michaels, Nancy Gruver
1974	Elsie Lefkowitz, Sylvia Hyman
1975	Betty Adler, Jo Morse
1976	Sunny Hall, Rhoda Jacobs
1977	Faye Roseman, Rhoda Kauffman
1978	Nancy Starr, Harriet Robbins
1979	Gert Blasband, Peggy Solomon
1980	Judy Tucker, Aileen Osofsky
1981	Lisa Halpern, Joyce Lilie

MASTER PAIRS

1968	Eugene O'Neill, Les Roth
1969	Mark Blumenthal, Seymour Leibowitz
1970	Henry Bethe, Richard Fleischman

1971	Jo Morse, Steve Robinson
1972	Marty Bergen, Richard Oshlag
1973	Charles Gray, Michael Garner
1974	Mark Blumenthal, Seymour Leibowitz
1975	Neil Silverman, Merle Tom
1976	Lynne Pollenz, Saul Gross
1977	Lee Rautenberg, Drew Casen
1978	Robert Blakey, Helen Blakey
1979	Norm Rosen, John Marks
1980	Ron Andersen, Kathie Wei

MIXED PAIRS

1952	H. Nolan, J. C. Dougherty
1953	Sylvia Schwartz, Elmer Schwartz
1954	Alvin Goodman, Mrs. Alvin Goodman
1955	R. Goldberg, Jules Chodak
1956	Peggy Solomon, Charles Solomon
1957	Carlyn Brall, Ralph Hirschberg
1958	Norma Weiner, George Weiner
1959	Mrs. Alfred Blasband, Sylvester Lowery
1960	Mrs. M. J. Root, Clyde Dewey
1961	Vivian Lavery, Lester Sokolower
1962	Louis Levy, Ann-Marie Sporing
1963	Betty Haddad, Said Haddad
1964	Marion Altman, Dimitri Pavlista
1965	Norman Kay, Peggy Rotzell
1966	Mrs. H. L. Cromer, John Coppie
1967	Peter Weichsel, Gladys Collier
1977	Linda Hutchinson, Art Weiss

INDIVIDUAL

1953	M.H. Sapira
1977	Frances Sharpe

SWISS TEAMS

Flight A:

1979	Bobby Goldman, Alan Kudisch, Donna Stoddard, Ruth Stober, Lyn Tamres
1980	Larry Cohen, Ron Gerard, Jim Barrow, Roger Jourdan
1981	Dave Treadwell, Evelyn Levitt, Sue Sachs, David Sachs

KEYSTONE FALL

KNOCKOUT TEAMS

1974	Seymour Leibowitz, Mark Blumenthal, William Passell, Andy Gabrilovitch
1981	Kathie Wei, Judi Radin, Ron Andersen, Dave Berkowitz, Harold Lilie

OPEN TEAMS

1958	Harry Glick, Mrs. Harry Glick, Mary Tiernan, Claire Tiernan, Ham Fuss
1960	Richard Lesko, Mrs. Richard Lesko, Eugene Klawier, Gerry Clossen, John McGervey
1961	Ed Worden, Dexter Pattison, Ralph Schreyer, John Siverts *(tied with)* Lester Feirman, Mrs. Lester Feirman, Dr. Theo Ginsburg, Mrs. Theo Ginsburg
1962	Peggy Rotzell, Leonard Harmon, David Mason, Sol Seidman
1963	Doug Flynn, Joe Polchinski, Ida Bennett, James Bennett
1964	Norman Kay, Edgar Kaplan, Robert Jordan, Arthur Robinson
1965	Norman Kay, Edgar Kaplan, Robert Jordan, Arthur Robinson
1966	Peter Pender, Jeremy Flint, Harlow Lewis, Antonio Dionisi
1967	C. L. Antrobus, T. D. Vinson, Mrs. G. C. Braham, W. R. Williams
1968	Ed Lazarus, David Sachs, Phil Feldesman, John Solodar
1969	Mark Blumenthal, William Landow, Sue Sachs, David Sachs
1970	Milton Silver, Martin Rabinowitz, Suzanne Raffel, Gloria Cohen
1971	Robert Lipsitz, Peggy Parker, Steve Parker, Marvin Rosenblatt
1973	Norm Rosen, Bernice Goldstein, Emily Economidis, T. Craig Robinson *(Spring)* Fred Hamilton, Marvin Rosenblatt, Don Faskow, Herb Sachs *(Fall)*
1974	Ron Blau, Connie McGinley, William Gough, Walter May
1975	Alan Susskind, David Temkin, Lee Rautenberg, Robert Rich
1976	Robert Lipsitz, Roger Pics, Steve Parker, Ed Manfield
1977	Robert Lipsitz, Ed Manfield, Paul Swanson, Roy Fox
1978	Paul Swanson, Robert Lipsitz, Roy Fox, Ed Manfield

1979 Jo Morse, Ray Raskin,
      Frank Mastrola, Saul Gross
1981 Bert Winges, Robert Lebi, George Mittelman,
      Bill Bowman, J. Siu, Denise Roussin *(Summer)*

MASTER PAIRS

1966 Mrs. Richard Rogasner, Edward Pierson
1967 Michael Garner, Charles Gray
1968 Daniel Oken, Ruth Oken
1969 Mrs. Joseph Livezey, Jr., Joseph Livezey III
1970 Jo Morse, Stephen Robinson
1971 Steve Robinson, Jo Morse
1973 Ron Andersen, Mark Epstein *(Spring)*
      Frank King, Joseph Kivel *(Fall)*
1974 Joan Levy, Ron Gerard
1975 Kathie Wei, Ron Andersen
1976 Betty Adler, Pat Lapides
1977 Dave Berkowitz, Harold Lilie

MIXED PAIRS

1958 Claire Tiernan, Robert Israel
1960 Jack Denny, Jill Denny
1963 A. Alexander, Belle Kauffman
1964 Norman Kay, Peggy Rotzel
1965 Mrs. D. A. Mott, Earl Douglas

OPEN PAIRS

1958 Dr. Paul Castle, Abe Feigus
1960 Krishin Bhavnani, John P. Burg
1961 Bill Eisenberg, Marty Ginsberg
1962 Sidney Silodor, Norman Kay
1963 Robert Jordan, Arthur Robinson *(tied with)*
      Mike Carson, William Landow
1964 Norman Kay, Edgar Kaplan
1965 Arthur Robinson, Robert Jordan
1966 Mrs. Kenneth Fillingham, William Gough
1967 James Eatherly, Marc Aronson
1968 Marcy West, Joel Schiff
1969 Mrs. Pete Miller, G. Robbins
1970 Dr. Roger Saylor, Dr. Spencer Lebengood
1971 Matt Granovetter, Merle Tom
1973 Reuben Alexander, Harvey Cohen *(tied with)*
      Ron Andersen, Susan Andersen *(Spring)*
      Joseph Kivel, Frank King, *(Fall)*
1974 Chuck Lamprey, Amalya Kearse
1975 Peter Boyd, Bill Pettis
1976 T. Craig Robinson, Charles Gray
1981 Barry Crane, Ron Andersen
Flight A:
1978 Jeff Meckstroth, Judi Radin
1979 Dorothy Goldsmith, Jerry Rowley
1981 Ed Bissell, John Ellis *(Summer)*
      Rita Rand, Matt Granovetter *(Fall)*
Super Flight A:
1978 Jess Stuart, Fred Schmitt
1979 Ronald Sukoneck, Lee Rautenberg
1981 David Berkowitz, Lisa Berkowitz *(Fall)*
Smoking:
1977 Alex Reitarowski, Alex Danilenko
1978 Parke Woodworth, Kenneth Meyer
1979 Elaine Landow, Irv Blank
1981 Glenn Eisenstein, Margie Gwozdzinsky *(Fall)*
Non-Smoking:
1977 Stephen Sanborn, Warren Rosner
1978 David Hoffner, Robert Lipsitz
1979 Roberta Epstein, Rozanne Marel
1981 Jo Morse, Steve Robinson *(Fall)*

MEN'S PAIRS

1958 Henry Auslander, Jerry Gelman
1960 Dr. Robert Israel, John R. Israel
1961 Roger Milio, Edward Van Cott
1962 Dave Warner, Art Cohen
1963 Oswald Jacoby, Chuck Henke
1964 Arthur Grant, Israel Nelson
1965 Leo Klein, Mannie Nagel
1966 Peter Pender, Jeremy Flint
1967 William Flannery, Herb Sachs
1968 Richard Wegman, Ralph Spritzer
1969 Russell Peterson, Daniel Per-Lee
1970 Phil Brady, Frank Brown
1971 Mark Blumenthal, Andy Gabrilovitch
1973 Austin Rich, Galen Graham *(Spring)*
      Ed Junkur, Fred Gillespie *(Fall)*
1974 Howard Chandross, Bob Yellis
1975 Lew Mathe, Gunther Polak
1976 Mark Klugman, William Gough
1977 Robert Ross, George Scharff
1978 Alfred Rand, Jim Becker
1979 Marc Jacobus, Phil Brady
1981 James Wait, Herman Noll *(Summer)*
      William Passell, E. Robert Thomas *(Fall)*

WOMEN'S PAIRS

1958 Mrs. Morris Gladstein, Mrs. Gene Sander

1960 Mrs. Samuel Harrold, Mrs. H. B. Hall
1961 Mrs. Louis Robinson, Mrs. Edward Berkovitz
1962 Evelyn Levitt, M. H. Welch
1963 Ruth Bronne, Mae Chernoff
1964 Dorothy Byrne, Margaret Forker
1965 Sue Sachs, Nancy Gruver
1966 Mrs. W. W. Vosburgh, Mrs. C. Felton
1967 Adele Kotzen, Gayle Rubens
1968 Mrs. D. Solomon, Mrs. L. J. Muskin
1969 Elaine Dumas, Mrs. W. F. Sheldon
1970 Roslyn Sachs, Siddy Parr
1971 Marg Tamres, Grace Moore
1973 Adele Kotzen, Gayle Rubens *(Spring)*
      Janet Tiderman, Jean Vineyard *(Fall)*
1974 Aileen Lane, Rhona Tabor
1975 Eleanor Alboum, Dorothy Silverman
1976 Dolores Ikach, Dale Dermer
1977 Marsha Contrucci, Dot Wilson
1978 Evelyn Levitt, Nancy Gruver
1979 Judi Radin, Frances Platzer
1981 Judith Flack, Leah Gabelman *(Summer)*
      Harriet Robbins, Lorraine Rappaport *(Fall)*

MEN'S TEAMS

1970 Simon Becker, R. Jay Becker,
      J. Resnick, Eugene Davidson *(tied with)*
      David Treadwell, Stephen Robinson,
      Edmond Lazarus, Bob Lewis *(and)*
      Mark Blumenthal, Paul Swanson,
      Don Faskow, Andy Gabrilovitch
1971 Seymour Leibowitz, Luis Pietri,
      Mark Blumenthal, Andy Gabrilovitch
1973 Seymour Leibowitz, Mark Blumenthal,
      Luis Pietri, Andy Gabrilovitch
1975 Michael Rosmarin, Howard Chandross,
      William Holland, Joel Friedburg *(tied with)*
      John Marks, Henry Greer,
      Harvey Cohen, Charles Fleisher
1976 Ira Barrows, William Gough, Giles Belski,
      Joseph Livezey, Ron Andersen
1977 Joseph Livezey, Jim Daniel, Tom Justi,
      Robert Thomas, Bruce Silverstein
1978 Norman Neiger, Paul Chook,
      Jerry Rowley, Louis Krieger
1979 Sheldon Justan, Steve Dunko,
      Al Shrive, Harold Weltman *(tied with)*
      Harold Lilie, Ahmed Hussein,
      Al Rand, Joel Friedberg
1981 Dan Boye, Bernie Gorkin, Fred Neuburger,
      Henry Zee, Mike Edwards *(Summer)*
      Dave Treadwell, Richard Colker,
      Ray Raskin, Arnold Fisher *(Fall)*

WOMEN'S TEAMS

1970 Portia Miller, Fran Egger,
      Mrs. R. Wade, Ann Lytle
1971 Mrs. L. Van Antwerp, Mrs. H. West,
      Mrs. B. Molovinsky, Ella Auch
1973 Pat Lapides, Adele Kotzen,
      Betty Adler, Gayle Rubens
1975 Ramona Karlson, Rena Eiffe,
      Jean Stouffer, Brenda Coffman
1976 Sylvia Le Savoy, Phyllis Chase,
      Lola Jaffe, Sylvia Zalkind
1977 Sylvia Le Savoy, Lola Jaffe,
      Phyllis Chase, Sylvia Zalkind
1978 Helen Hirsty, Antoinette Lutz,
      Jeanne Elkner, Pat Close
1979 Nancy Gruver, Pat Lapides,
      Betty Adler, Evelyn Levitt
1981 Gertrude Snyder, Ruth Cummins,
      Ruth Wineburg, Rosemary Mancuso *(Summer)*
      Pamela Bridson, Karen McCallum,
      Marie Ray, Lynn Deas *(Fall)*

UPPER NEW YORK STATE

(See also Districts 3 and 5)

KNOCKOUT TEAMS

1975 Andy Altay, David Lindop,
      Martin Kirr, Ed Bridson
1977 Tony Kasday, Marvin Herbert, Marc Jacobus,
      Steve Biciocchi, Steve Sion
1978 Don Probst, Dan Gerstman,
      Marc Nathan, Phil Brady
1979 Ken Murray, Wayne Timms, Bryan Culham,
      Frank Markotich, Keith Balcombe, John Zeller
1980 Kathie Wei, Ron Anderson, David Berkowitz,
      Robert Freedman, James Mathis

OPEN TEAMS

1969 Ruby McKaig, John Cullinan, Jr.,
John T. Landon, John M. Edwards
1972 Bill Bowman, Bert Curry,
Al McDonald, John T. Bowman
1973 Steve Sun, James Rosenbloom,
Douglas Ross, Samaresh Maitra *(tied with)*
James Zimmerman, Dennis McGarry,
Hans Akturk, Philip Leon
1975 Gil Cohen, Saul Gross,
Lynne Pollenz, Len Epstein *(tied with)*
James McBean, Mike Cafferata,
Eric Landau, Judy Landau *(and)*
Marissa Wolthausen, Jane Wolfe,
Dr. John Mahrer, Elly Mahrer *(and)*
Walter May, Phil Brady,
William Gough, Fred Neuberger
1977 Walter May, Arnie Fisher,
Robert Freedman, James Mathis *(tied with)*
William Dubay, Jeff Hall,
Joan Harvey, Jay Samuel *(and)*
Bill Bickford, Richard Fink,
Joanne Guoba, Peter Mollomet
1978 Margaret Robertson, Judy Butcher,
Mildred Jones-Bateman, Lorraine Desruisseaux *(tied with)*
Judy Landau, Eric Landau,
Chuck Lamprey, Henry Bethe
1979 Ken Murray, Wayne Timms, Bryan Culham,
Frank Markotich, Keith Balcombe, John Zeller
1980 Kathie Wei, Ron Andersen, Barry Crane,
David Berkowitz, Gerald Caravello
Flight A:
1981 Charles Gray, Jerry Resnick,
Norm Rosen, T. Craig Robinson

MASTER PAIRS

1969 Douglas Andrews, Gordon Chapman
1972 Eric Kokish, Mark Blumenthal
1973 James Zimmerman, Dennis McGarry
1977 Al Lindmark, Robin Spital
1981 Carl Berenbaum, Jeff Ruben

OPEN PAIRS

1969 Paul Heitner, Bernard Chazen
1972 Robert Freedman, James Mathis
1973 Ev Hatch, Fred Neuberger
1975 Bob Miller, John Saxe
1977 Sheldon Justan, Harold Weltman
1978 Susan Ganley, Mickey Lenzner
1979 Evelyn Levitt, Dave Treadwell
1980 Evelyn Levitt, Dave Treadwell
1981 Lisa Halpern, Dave Berkowitz
Flight A:
1978 Suru Subbaro, G. V. Rao
1979 Sheldon Justan, Harold Weltman
1980 Pat Lapides, Joseph Livezey
1981 Glenn Lublin, Robert Gookin

MIXED PAIRS

1969 Mrs. Ben Ku, Dr. Donald Sun

MEN'S PAIRS

1969 Fred Root, Marvin Morris
1972 Herbert Resnick, Daniel Gerstman
1973 Truesdale Clarke, John Cullinan, Jr.
1977 Sheldon Justan, Harold Weltman
1978 Billy Gough, Ray Raskin
1979 Clarence Goppert, Mark Lair
1980 Fred Neuburger, Mike Edwards
1981 Jim Becker, Howard Chandross

WOMEN'S PAIRS

1969 Aileen Lisowski, Ruth Instance
1972 Jo Morse, Helen Utegaard
1973 Mrs. Allen Goldman, Doris Lawrence
1977 Mary McKenna, Ellie Horton
1978 Dorothy Joiner, Mrs. A. T. Scharmach
1979 Marjorie Hardy, Sue Turner
1980 Kathie Wei, Judi Radin
1981 Pam Bastian, Peggy Duffey

MEN'S TEAMS

1972 Herbert Resnick, Henry Penner,
Robert Stone, Russ Ekeblad
1973 Les Bart, Jay Merrill,
James Rosenbloom, Ralph Bartlett
1977 Doug McCorkell, Dick Edney, Rick Olanoff,
Bernie Gorkin, Dan Boye, Peter Katz
1978 Ray Raskin, Billy Gough,
Ira Barrow, Howard Chandross
1979 Clarence Goppert, Mark Lair, Gaylor Kasle,
Jan Janitschke, Craig Janitschke
1980 Luis Pietri, Ray Raskin,
Arnold Fisher, Dave Treadwell

1981 Jack Perlman, Ira Barrows, Joseph Livezey,
Joel Friedberg, Bob Thomas, Billy Gough

WOMEN'S TEAMS

1972 Jo Morse, Shirley Neilson,
Helen Utegaard, Sharyn Linkovsky *(tied with)*
Anne O'Brien, Mary Merriman,
Mrs. Henry Penner, Joan Noll
1973 Mrs. W. Harper, Winnifred Binning,
Mrs. D. Myer, Mary Lou Ruta
1977 Betty Krakeur, Marge Krause,
Shirley Silverman, Martha Grouix
1978 Kathie Wei, Judy Tucker,
Linda Hutchinson, Judy Landau
1979 Audrey Johnson, Mrs. Joseph Amedio,
Anne O'Brien, Marguerite Maurer
1980 Kathie Wei, Judi Radin,
Jo Morse, Evelyn Levitt
1981 Lila Perlstein, Lenore Server,
Eva Scatassa, Gail Moss

DISTRICT 5 (Western Pennsylvania, northeastern Ohio, northern West Virginia, western Maryland, western New York)

ALL-AMERICAN

KNOCKOUT TEAMS

1974 Stanley Smith, William Rosen, Jeffrey Starr,
Howard Perlman, Fred Hamilton
1975 Georgette King, Hal Mouser,
Jeffrey Starr, Fred Hamilton
1976 Jim Zimmerman, Dennis McGarry, Tom Evans,
Dick Fleischman, Dan Gertsman
1977 Jim Zimmerman, Dennis McGarry, Tom Evans,
Dan Gerstman, Richard Fleischman
1978 Dennis McGarry, Bert Newman,
Sam Scaffidi, Zeke Jabbour
1979 Chuck Carroll, Marc Nathan, Roni Ostfield,
Larry Rock, Jeff Darrow.
1980 James Zimmerman, Ralph Katz,
Norman Fischer, Gerald Caravelli
1980 Marc Rabinowitz, Niel Waletzky,
Jeff Darrow, Warren Oberfield.

OPEN TEAMS

1938 Arthur Glatt, Albert Weiss,
Ralph Kempner, Walter Jacobs
1939 Arthur Glatt, Albert Weiss,
Ralph Kempner, Walter Jacobs
1940 Dr. Harry Bernstein, John Carlin, Sam Delott,
Al Stracke, Neil Kent
1941 Reba Buck, Lawrence Welch,
Joseph Cain, Edson Wood
1942 Richard Lee, Lawrence Welch,
Joseph Cain, Edson Wood
1943 Sid Heinrick, David Clarren,
W. Zeigler, Eloise Neil
1944 Albert Weiss, Robert Halpin, Jules Bank,
Dave Clarren, Maynard Adams
1945 Reba Buck, Lawrence Welch,
Edson Wood, J. Van Brooks
1946 Mary O'Brien, Jack Kaplan,
Leonard Goren, Richard Carter
1948 Billie Agruss, J.R. Krause,
Cliff Bishop, Richard Revell
1952 Matie White, Harold (Bud) Creed,
Thelma Hathhorn, Jack Mylett
1953 Charles Goren, Arthur Goldsmith,
Mrs. Harry Emrich, Sidney Fink
1954 Fred Rappleyea, Earl Hyers,
Raymond Healy, Isabelle Garner
1955 Cliff Bishop, Jack Denny,
Russell Roosen, E. Samuel
1956 Tobias Stone, Jan Stone,
Victor Mitchell, Robert Mnuchin
1957 Louis Rosenthal, Gloria Turner,
Emanuel Hochfeld, Fred Rappleyea
1958 Alan Bell, John R. Biddle,
Robert Sharp, Eugene Thumin
1959 Joan Remey, Vincent O. Remey,
William Mouser, Albert Silber

1960 Percy Sheardown, Duncan Phillips, R. Bruce Dwyer, Don Cowan, Dr. Eric Johns
1961 Richard Paulson, Dr. Richard Rovner, Fred Bollinger, Alan Bell
1962 Sylvia Stein, Helen Shanbrom, Julius Young, Jerry Dillon
1963 Irvin Deuter, Edwin Smith, Jr., Oswald Jacoby, Paul Levitt
1964 Grant Marsee, William Reister, Ray Zoller, F. Holton Sexton
1965 Dr. Barry Breakey, Joseph Gittleman, Helen Shanbrom, Al Shanbrom
1966 Jeremy Flint, Peter Pender, Helen Smith, Edwin Smith, Jr.
1967 Jill Denny, Jack Denny, Ralph Vichill, Sid Stacey
1968 Jeff Alexander, Mark Low, Leone Low, Robert Morris, Thomas Hodapp *(tied with)* Martin Cohn, Louis Cohen, Dorsey Brooks, Barnard Werbe, William Panzer
1969 Elmer De Witt, Harry Keirns, Richard Sacks, Mike Trikilis
1970 Martin Kane, Dr. George Chappell, Harry Kohn, Fred Root
1971 Ann McGilvrey, Naomi Phelps, Maureen Irwin, Fran Egger
1972 Hal Mouser, Milton Neher, Rick Koopman, Karen Koopman
1973 James Zimerman, Bob Hardies, Joan Remey, Vincent Remey
1974 Fred Hamilton, Jeffrey Starr, Frank Bell, Steve Landen
1975 Mark Wolfinger, Phyllis Heller, Marge Tamres, Marc Nathan *(tied with)* Bill Hale, David Bondy, Hans Akturk, Carl Hudecek *(and)* Carl Dahl, Tom Young, Dennis Thompson, Gloria Noszka *(and)* Marty Baff, Bill Babb, Marty Arndt, John Boeder
1976 Lloyd Loux, Erma Donahue, Marge Cox, Jim Reiman *(tied with)* Larry Kozlove, John Sheridan, Steve Landen, Jeffrey Starr, Frank Bell, Linda Perlman
1977 Art Waldmann, Don Faskow, Steven Bloom, Mark Lair.
1978 Paul Vickers, Bob Fiske, Phil Brady, Pete Weglarski
1979 Phyllis Heller, Marge Tamres, Yik Young, Kumar Bhatia
1980 Jeff Meckstroth, Eric Rodwell, Marilyn Miller, Robert Levin, Russell Arnold

SWISS TEAMS
Flight A:
1981 James Barlow, Harold Haffner, Judy Haffner, Dale Dermer *(tied with)* Jeff Meckstroth, Zeke Jabbour, Susan Ganley, Vickie Neiberg, Eric Rodwell

MASTER PAIRS
1974 Fred Hamilton, Jeffrey Starr
1975 Fred Hamilton, Hal Mouser
1976 Larry Robbins, Larry Mori
1977 Ralph Katz, Tom Donnelly
1978 Dennis Hesthaven, Randolph Beckham
1980 Shirley Rice, Jim Masters
1981 Carol Alleman, Bob Webber
Flight A:
1979 Norm Fischer, Tom Hodapp

OPEN PAIRS
1938 Arthur Glatt, Albert Weiss
1939 Walter Jacobs, Ralph Kempner
1940 Arthur Glatt, Milton Kirshbaum
1941 Dr. E. J. Hunt, Mrs. W. E. J. Hunt
1942 L. C. Quigley, William Stickney, Jr.
1943 Arthur Glatt, Albert Weiss
1944 George Ryan, Mrs. George Ryan
1945 Frances Carter, David Carter
1946 Edith Smith, Jane Wallace
1947 Dr. R. Staff, Mary O'Bryan
1948 Harold Feinberg, Edson Wood
1949 Charles Sidney Hoblit, Herbert Beyer
1952 Ralph Ittenbach, Syd Kasle
1953 Hazel Foulke, Mrs. J. T. Tobin
1954 Russell Arnold, Morris Freier
1955 Myron Jacobs, Dr. W. Greenburg
1956 David Carter, J.G. Ripstra
1957 Harold (Bud) Creed, William Howe
1958 Harold (Bud) Creed, William Howe
1959 Dan Rotman, Edward Rosen

1960 George Mitchell, John Biddle
1961 Robert Sharp, Gunther Polak
1962 Mrs. Herbert Goetz, Herbert Goetz
1963 Martin Arndt, Dr. L. W. Melander
1964 Elmer Schwartz, Alvin Landy
1965 Frances White, Mrs. Frank Morrison
1966 Bernard Ceifetz, Henry Shevitz
1967 Gloria Noszka, Dr. Norman Williams
1968 Martin Arndt, Bob Hardies
1969 Steve Cohn, Jeff Hohenstein
1970 Lee Houk, Richard Weston
1971 Armand Fahrer, Marc Low
1972 Larry Kozlove, John Sheridan
1973 John Sheridan, Larry Kozlove
1974 Jeff Starr, Fred Hamilton
1975 Stephen Stone, Bob Crafton
1976 Vince Remey, Joan Remey
1977 Jerry Clerkin, Dennis Clerkin
1978 Bernard Fudor, Chuck Carroll
1980 Pete Weglarski, Phil Brady
Flight A:
1979 Arthur Goldsmith, Kumar Bhatia
1981 Steve Landen, Pratap Radjadhyaksha

MEN'S PAIRS
1946 Charles Sidney Hoblit, John Carlin
1947 Irving Deuter, J.G. Ripstra
1948 Herbert Byer, Charles Sidney Hoblit
1949 Charles Sidney Hoblit, John Carlin
1952 Abe Greenspun, Dr. M. Isvitin
1953 Joe Cohan, Harry Emrich
1954 David Carter, Sidney Lazard
1955 Jim Bishop, Edwin Smith, Jr. *(tied with)* J. A. Klar, Myron Jacobs
1956 Tobias Stone, Arthur Cohn
1957 William Jones, J. Lennart Johnson
1958 Charles Braman, Ray Partenfelder
1959 Irving Deuter, Clifford P. Weil
1960 Robert Jordan, Edgar Simons
1961 Terry Bladen, Dr. L.W. Melander
1962 Michael Thomas, Charles Klayer
1963 Jack Hartford, G. Shaffer
1964 William Reister, Grant Marsee
1965 Vincent Remey, Albert Silber
1966 Erwin Berman, Dan Kelston
1967 Martin Arndt, Sam Friedlander
1968 George Lamproplos, Sam Friedlander
1969 Paul Swanson, Herb Sachs
1970 James Wisemiller, Gregg Potts
1971 Jack Adams, Dick Barbaris
1972 Eugene Thumim, Dennis McGarry
1973 Fred Hamilton, Chuck Said
1974 John Sheridan, Larry Kozlove
1975 Eric Rodwell, Dave Fred
1976 Sid Stacey, Lorand Tritter
1977 Kumar Bhatia, Bill Babb
1978 Vincent Remey, Arthur Goldsmith
1979 Frank Treiber III, Frank Treiber
1980 Harry Stratton, Yul Inn
1981 Kurt Mundinger, Frank Yoder

WOMEN'S PAIRS
1937 Mrs. E. W. Atkinson, Mrs. J. E. Waidlich
1939 Mrs. Harold Smith, Jeanette Lefler
1940 Angela Quigley, Florence Meyer
1941 Lillian Mackie, Bedford Fritz
1942 Aubrey MacMillan, B. A. Meixner
1943 Mrs. Harry Mason, Jo Gutman
1944 Ruth Steinberg, Mrs. Harry Lees
1945 Ruth Steinberg, Mrs. Harry Lees
1946 Miriam McKinley, Alberta Briggs
1948 C. G. Taylor, Helene May
1952 Evelyn Engelman, M. C. Monett
1953 E. J. Jungerford, M. Scalabrino
1954 E. A. Styne, Mrs. George Majek
1955 Sadie Kaplan, Shirley Rollins
1956 Dorothy Schick, Mrs. R. C. Dabney
1957 Julia Halloran, Mrs. Calvin Weston
1958 Phyllis Cohn, Joan Remey
1959 Sylvia Stein, Carol Ross
1960 Sylvia Stein, Marie Ver Linden
1961 Jean Carney, Carol Ruther
1962 Julia Halloran, Becky Jones
1963 Amelia Argersinger, Agnes Gordon
1964 Portia Miller, Roz Soldinger
1965 Jeannete Collier, Betti van Kainen
1966 Hezzar Hendee, Louise Porter
1967 Jill Denny, Mrs. J. Russell
1968 Clerely Chaney, Zenobia Allen
1969 Mrs. J. Rosenthal, Marcia Schlessinger
1970 Joyce Wade, Ann Lyle
1971 Eileen Welsby, Rose Kline

1972	Mrs. E. Marquard, Betty Peters *(tied with)*
	Amy Kelley, Mildred Taylor
1973	Carol Schoenberger, Marilyn Ballon
1974	Joan Remey, Beverly Riordan
1975	Sherilyn Larson, June Smith
1976	Yolanda Besser, Julie Serkey
1977	Ann MacAslan, Lyn Semler
1978	Irma Hewlett, Bernice Borg
1979	Sharon Deering, Ivadell Buchko
1980	Cathryne Havrilla, Marilyn Leddy
1981	Beverly Duboc, Lila Smith

MIXED PAIRS

1938	Ottilie Reilly, Jack Kravatz
1939	Mrs. J. J. Jacobs, K. R. Gallagher
1940	Florence Meyer, George Neeves
1941	Frances Nelson, Leo Weiner
1942	Mrs. R. B. Johnstone, Martin Rothman
1943	Mr. S. W. O. Bennett, Dr. S. Manheimer
1944	Elizabeth Johnstone, David Clarren
1945	Dorothy Jane Cook, Milton Fleig
1946	Lois Albright, Frank Marsh
1948	Matie White, W. M. Fulton
1952	Arthur Baum, Mrs. Arthur Baum
1953	Harold (Bud) Creed, Thelma Hathhorn
1954	Rosalie Kaimann, Louis Berg
1955	Lucille Harvie, Grant Marsee
1956	Jo Gutman, Robert Sharp
1957	June Rodkin, Carl Petersen
1958	Bernice Way, Eunice Rosen *(tied with)*
	Jo Sharp, Robert Sharp
1959	Vincent Remey, Joan Remey
1960	Mae Hammerstein, Fred Morganroth
1961	Don Cowan, Shirley Reynolds
1962	Chuck Berger, June Honigman
1963	Michael Thomas, Portia Miller
1964	Elmer Schwartz, Sylvia Schwartz
1965	Cliff Bishop, Agnes Gordon
1966	Amelia Argersinger, Art Price
1967	Mrs. M. D. Allison, William Smith *(tied with)*
	Dorothy Schick, W. F. Fees, Jr.
1968	Judi Friedenberg, Philip Leon
1969	Jill Denny, Jack Denny
1970	Dorothy West, John Shelnutt
1971	Portia Miller, Dennis McGarry
1972	Marcia Richling, James Richling
1973	Ruth Brubaker, Marvin Melamed
1977	Jean Theus, Richard Pavlicek
1978	Evie Williamson, Bob Moyers
1981	Patty Meckstroth, Jeff Meckstroth

MASTER INDIVIDUAL

1938	Albert Weiss
1939	Albert Weiss
1940	George Neeves
1941	Peter Leventritt
1942	Robert Cunningham
1943	David Clarren
1944	Ben Fain
1945	George Carlton
1946	Charlton Wallace

INDIVIDUAL

1976	Mrs. M. D. Johnson
1977	R. Vance
1978	Mrs. Ben Arnoff
1981	Ben Storer

WOMEN'S SWISS TEAMS

1979	Lucy Faris, Mrs. Elmer Stephan,
	Eilee Lewis, Lois Hirshberg
1980	Diane Zucker, Anita Torrence, Doris Dean,
	Audrey Stephan, Steve Terry
1981	Marilyn Finberg, Arlene Port,
	Connie Hoechstetter, Fran Flint *(tied with)*
	Portia Miller, Julia Halloran,
	Mary Chilcote, Dorothy Schick *(and)*
	Gay Hardesty, Kaye Lux,
	Pat Cummings, Marge Cox

MEN'S SWISS TEAMS

1979	Martin Baff, Philip Wolkin,
	Bert Newman, Phil Becker *(tied with)*
	Dick Van Bergen, Paul Rander,
	William Cook, Jr., Joseph Harbert
1980	Mike Aliotta, Richard Huggard,
	Zeke Jabbour, Robert Levi
1981	Doug Synder, Phil Becker,
	Jack Creasey, Howard Le Bow

DISTRICT 5 PITTSBURGH

KNOCKOUT TEAMS

1974	Frank Cymerman, Roni Ostfield,
	Marc Nathan, Max Bazerman
1975	Frank Cymerman, Roni Ostfield,
	Marc Nathan, Max Bazerman
1976	Ron Andersen, Mark Lair, Hugh MacLean,
	Clarence Goppert, Gerald Caravelli
1977	Kathie Wei, Gary Hann, Ron Andersen,
	Gerald Caravelli, Milt Roseberg
1978	Judy Haffner, Harold Haffner,
	James Barlow, Craig Biddle
1979	Gary Hann, Zeke Jabbour,
	Ralph Katz, James Zimmerman
1980	Ray Jotcham, Gail Jotcham,
	Sylvia Cann, David Cummings
1981	Mel Skolnik, Ron Andersen, Eric Rodwell,
	Jeff Meckstroth, Jim Zimmerman

OPEN TEAMS

1958	Dorothy Glick, Harry L. Glick, Mary Elizabeth Tiernan,
	Claire Tiernan, Hamilton Fuss
1960	Carol Lesko, Richard Lesko, Eugene Klawier,
	Jerry Closson, John McGervey
1961	Sidney Silodor, Norman Kay,
	Robert Jordan, Arthur Robinson
1962	Sidney Silodor, Norman Kay, Robert Jordan,
	Arthur Robinson, Oswald Jacoby
1963	Oswald Jacoby, John Lowenthal,
	Peggy Solomon, Charles Solomon *(tied with)*
	Edgar Simons, Zeke Jabbour
	Carl Hudeck, Martin Cohn *(and)*
	Cliff Bishop, Manuel (Sarge) Talbot
	Dr. Joseph Henry, Alfred Bishop, James Hinton *(and)*
	Percy Sheardown, Mrs. Paul Howell
	Robert Robinson, Mort Abrams
1964	Ed Simmons, Chuck Burger,
	Max Lipin, Zeke Jabbour
1965	Dorothy Hayden, B. Jay Becker,
	Kelsey Petterson, Ivan Erdos
1966	Mike Carson, Walt Walvick,
	Tom Lyon, Mike Garner
1967	Eugene Thumin, Rose Thumin,
	Ralph Vichill, Dr. William Babb
1968	Joan Remey, Vincent Remey,
	Phillip Leon, Don Hocevar
1969	Sheldon Margulis, Howard Perlman,
	Judi Friedenberg, Stan Ruskin
1970	George Mitchell, Harold (Bud) Creed,
	Gary Robbins, Sam Scaffidi
1971	Ray Zoller, Howard Perlman,
	Fred Hamilton, Henry Bethe
1972	Jim Zimmerman, Robert Hardies,
	Joan Remey, Vincent Remey
1973	Les Bart, Ken Peyser,
	Jay Merrill, James Gardner
1974	Larry Kozlove, John Sheridan
	Fred Hamilton, Jeffrey Starr
1975	James Zimmerman, Dennis McGarry, Helen Utegaard,
	Nancy Gruver, Vince Remey, Joan Remey
1976	John Boeder, Bill Babb,
	Marvin Melamed, Wellington Lee *(tied with)*
	Ron Andersen, Hugh MacLean, Gerald Caravelli,
	Mark Lair, Clarence Goppert
1977	Gloria Noszka, Howard Friedman,
	Ed Lewis, Robert Morris *(tied with)*
	Jo Morse, Steve Robinson,
	Ron Sukoneck, Dave Treadwell
1978	John Lehmiller, Norma Lehmiller,
	Merceda Carswell, Marian Hough
1979	Vincent Bartone, Jeff Roman,
	Richard Pepper, Barry Falgout
Flight A:	
1980	Larry Mori, Frank Bell,
	Ralph Bartlett, Phil Wolkin
1981	Ralph Katz, Jim Zimmerman
	Zeke Jabbour, Bill Hale

MASTER PAIRS

1961	Harry Fishbein, Robert Sharp
1962	Oswald Jacoby, John Lowenthal
1963	Krishin Bhavnani, John Burg
1964	Ray Zoller, Mike Moss
1965	Joan Hovandec, Jeff Hohenstein
1966	Alan Knaus, Ed Moorehead
1967	Gary Robbins, Mary Louise Reich
1968	Fred Hamilton, Chuck Burger
1969	Fred Hamilton, Chuck Burger
1970	Mary Miller, Robert Stevens
1971	Marty Arndt, Robert Hardies
1972	Eli Reich, Mary Louise Reich
1973	George Hershman, L. Jerome Lee
1974	John Sheridan, Larry Kozlove
1975	Brian Schoenfeld, Peter Boyd
1976	John Conway, Dan Gerstman

1977	Dennis McGarry, Les Bart
1978	Bob Visokey, Marc Culberson
1981	Larry Long, Jade Wyatt
Flight A:
1980	Marshane Russell, Earl Crooks

OPEN PAIRS

1958	Abe Feigus, Dr. Paul Castelle
1960	Krishin Bhavnani, John P. Burg
1961	Sidney Silodor, Norman Kay
1962	Sidney Silodor, Norman Kay
1963	Edward Rosen, S. J. Wright
1964	John Lowenthal, Roger Stern
1965	Bernard Ceifetz, Harry Shevitz
1966	Frank Weisbach, Clifford P. Weil
1967	Frank Mikitaw, Robert LaFleur
1968	Richard Sacks, Bettie Garson
1969	Kenny Rhodes, Henry Itkin
1970	W. L. Scott, Wayne Lewis
1971	Eli Reich, Charles Midelburg
1972	Ann MacAslan, Dave MacAslan
1973	Bob Visokey, Roy Fox
1974	Bob Visokey, Roy Fox
1975	Howard Perlman, Linda Perlman
1976	Larry Kozlove, John Sheridan
1977	Steve Goldberg, Russell Greist
1978	Jerry Clerkin, Mark Sander
1979	Betty Adler, Julian Adler
Flight A:
1979	Richard Finberg, James Klein
1980	Ted Horning, Norm Coombs
1981	Bill Hale, Jim Zimmerman

MEN'S PAIRS

1958	Harry Auslander, Jerry Gelman
1960	Dr. Robert R. Israel, John Israel
1961	Fred Kilchenstein, Martin Cohn
1962	Norman Kay, Alvin Landy
1963	Herman Feldman, Ben Baldwin
1964	Irving Deuter, Grant Marsee
1965	Jack Watson, Gil Brown
1966	Herb Sachs, Stan Ruskin
1967	Charles Solomon, Martin Cohn
1968	William Flannery, Herb Sachs
1969	Charles Solomon, Robert Sharp
1970	Don Faskow, Paul Swanson
1971	Steve Parker, Mark Blumenthal
1972	Robert Ayers, Paul Hall
1973	Jeff Starr, Bert Newman
1974	Roy Fox, Robert Ayers
1975	Marc Culberson, Bob Visokey
1976	Dennis McGarry, Jim Zimmerman
1977	James Barlow, James Bossert *(tied with)*
	John Powers, Joe Manhart *(and)*
	Gil Cohen, Clay Cuthbertson
1978	Howard Friedman, Asim Ulke
1979	Jeff Meckstroth, Gerald Caravelli
1980	Ralph Katz, James Zimmerman
1981	Jim Becker, Howard Chandross *(tied with)*
	Zeke Jabbour, Phil Brady

WOMEN'S PAIRS

1958	Mrs. Morris Gladstein, Glenna Sander
1960	Mrs. Samuel Harrold, Mrs. Paul Hall
1961	Mrs. Paul McGuigan, Mrs. J. R. John
1962	B. Halpern, Selma Bloch
1963	Mrs. Harry Siegel, G. Hertz
1964	Mrs. W. Moldovan, Mrs. John Ratesie
1965	Audrey Melander, Julia Halloran
1966	Terry Michaels, Garner McDaniel
1967	Naomi Phelps, Mrs. Robert Getty
1968	Phyllis Heller, Grace Moore
1969	Mildred Wise, Margie Tamres
1970	Lyn Semler, Siddy Parr
1971	Mrs. P. Corell, Louise Parks
1972	Barbara Letzer, Sandra Schubiner
1973	Kathy Cummings, Pat Cummings
1974	Evelyn Pierce, Mrs. W. Steffee
1975	Andrea Burger, Linda Perlman
1976	Margaret Stehle, Dorothy Greshok
1977	Janet Weyant, Charlotte Hahn
1978	Goldie Frank, Jane McIntyre
1979	Barbara Klein, Sue Lordi
1980	Bernadine Ratesic, Marge Spontak
1981	Naomi Connell, Betty Tatum

MIXED PAIRS

1958	Claire Tiernan, Dr. Robert Israel
1960	Jack Denny, Jill Denny
1961	Morris Silverman, Mrs. Jack Wise
1962	Peggy Solomon, Charles Solomon
1963	Kay Carter, Fred Hamilton
1964	Julie Halloran, Jeff Polisner
1965	Mary Joyce Wade, John Lopeman

1966	Mrs. Robert Fields, Ben Sokol
1967	Trudy Cohn, Arthur Cohn
1968	Peggy Solomon, Charles Solomon
1969	Lois Stusser, Chris Jeans
1970	Joan Remey, Vincent Remey
1971	Linda Deaton, Ray Zoller
1972	Jade Wyatt, Robert Ayers
1973	Ruth Hoffman, Howard LeBow
1974	W. Timothy Walter, Alice Fiscus
1975	Jack Goodykoontz, Vickie Goodykoontz
1976	Kathy Meyer, Henry Zee
1977	Marge Cox, Larry Rock
1979	Goldie Frank, Allen Tan
1980	Jeanne Elkner, Arnold Fisher
1981	Donna Pearson, Ken Bergman

INDIVIDUAL

1975	Roy Latimer
1976	Mrs. R. G. Smiley
1977	Mrs. P. P. Munster
1979	J. S. Rossi
1980	Allan Lazar
1981	L. Bloomberg

MEN'S SWISS TEAMS

1978	Herb Sachs, Stanley Ruskin,
	Steve Goldberg, Russell Griest
1980	Ralph Katz, James Zimmerman, Franco Bandoni,
	Dan Gerstman, Marc Nathan
1981	Tom Mahaffey, Jack Denny, Ralph Katz,
	Joel Friedberg, Ethan Stein

WOMEN'S SWISS TEAMS

1978	Kay Clinton, Jean Evans,
	Betty Pope, Sue Dunn *(tied with)*
	Judy Bernhardt, Regina O'Brien,
	Shirley Irish, Marion Plette
1980	Charlotte Cotton, Mrs. R. H. VanderLaan,
	Mrs. Robert Taylor, Amy Kelly *(tied with)*
	Grace Moore, Sherry Early,
	Gena Bhatia, Roni Ostfield
1981	Phyllis Heller, Judy Haffner, Marge Tamres,
	Dale Dermer, Joan Stein *(tied with)*
	Shirley Early, Gena Bhatia,
	Grace Moore, Marjorie Miller

UPPER NEW YORK STATE
(*See also* Districts 3 and 4)

KNOCKOUT TEAMS

1975	Peter Weichsel, Nancy Weichsel, Alan Sontag,
	Allan Cokin, Steve Sion
1976	Arthur E. (Bud) Reinhold, Robert Levin,
	Frank Bell, Steve Landen
1977	James Zimmerman, Tom Donnelly, John Toy,
	Robert Feldman, Richard Fleischman, James Mathis
1978	Bernice Fudor, David Schorr,
	Chuck Carroll, Phil Wolkin
1979	Dianna Gordon, Mark Molson, Robert Lebi,
	George Mittelman, Dennis McGarry
1980	Ted Horning, Robert Lebi,
	Kirk Benson, Pierre Daigneault

INDIVIDUAL

1978	Mrs. Earl Merrick

OPEN TEAMS

1956	Sidney Lorvan, Richard Lesser
	Walter May, Dr. Paul Zweifel
1957	Alfred Sheinwold, Edgar Kaplan,
	Norman Kay, Ivar Stakgold
1958	Richard Freeman, Leonard Harmon, Mrs. E. P. Cotter,
	Norman Kay, Richard Walsh
1959	Eric Murray, C. Bruce Elliott, Richard Freeman,
	Richard Walsh, Alfred Sheinwold
1960	Agnes Gordon, Jerome Friedlander,
	Richard Freedman, Alvin Landy
1961	Marvin Rosenblatt, Charles Coon
	Chester Davis, Frank Westcott
1962	Charles Coon, Chester Davis,
	Frank Westcott, Marion Rosenblatt
1963	William Flannery, Paul Swanson, Donald Faskow,
	Richard Lesko, Herbert Sachs
1964	Alvin Landy, Emanuel Katz,
	James Mathis, Robert Freedman
1965	Barry Crane, Grant Marsee,
	Eric Murray, Sammy R. Kehela
1966	Chester P. Davis, Jr., Charles Coon, Dick Zeckhauser,
	Marvin Rosenblatt, Frank Westcott

1967 Fred Bellinger, Ray Meyer,
Mrs. Gerald Fried, Gerald Fried
1968 Dr. William Werner, D. Alan Collins,
Simon Kantor, Murray Melton
1969 Ruby McKaig, John Cullinan, Jr.
John Landon, J.M. Edwards
1971 Robert Freedman, James Mathis,
Michael Martino, Frank Vine (tied with)
James Zimmerman, Bob Hardies,
Robert Alexander, E. Jones (and)
Joseph Silver, Eric Kokish,
Robert Lipsitz, Mark Blumenthal
1975 Phil Clark, Peter Boyd,
Ralph Bartlett, Glenn Lublin
1976 Charence Goppert, Mark Lair, Ron LaCour,
Bruce Ferguson, Jim Donaldson
1977 Tom Donnelly, Phil Leon, Don Hocevar,
Ralph Katz, Don Probst
1978 Michael Roche, Ed Bridson,
Eric Shepherd, Marty Kirr
1979 Frank Markotich, John Zeller, Ross Taylor,
Keith Balcombe, Wayne Timms
1980 Kathie Wei, Judi Radin, Michael Radin,
Ron Andersen, Dave Berkowitz, Judy Tucker

MASTER PAIRS
1964 Edmond Lazarus, Dr. Harold McDonald
1965 Robert Freedman, James Mathis
1966 Norman Hall, Fred Sontag (tied with)
John Cullinan, Jr., Jack Burgess
1967 Al Lando, W. J. Crissey
1968 Harry Nuckols, Marty Bergen
1969 Douglas Andrews, Gordon Chapman
1971 Robert Cofer, Robert Spitzner
1976 Evelyn Parker, Franco Bandoni
1977 Ron Andersen, David Berkowitz
1978 Eric Landau, Eric Shepherd
1979 Fred Neuburger, Rich Olanoff
1980 Paul Thurston, Stan Dillabough
Flight A:
1975 Ruth Stevens, John Stevens

OPEN PAIRS
1956 Mrs. Charles Mercer, Charles Mercer
1957 Emanuel B. Katz, Robert Freedman
1958 Charles Coon, Frank T. Westcott
1959 Dr. Robert Israel, Ed Majeroni
1960 Aaron Aroneck, Eugene Smith
1961 Maria Torok, Fred Hess
1962 Constance McElwain, John McElwain
1963 Eric Murray, Sammy Kehela
1964 Mildred Rheault, Jack Goda
1965 Barry Crane, Grant Marsee
1966 Carol Bunnecke, Murray Melton
1967 Marty Arndt, Bob Hugo Hardies
1968 Simon Kantor, Murray Melton
1969 Paul Heitner, Bernard Chazen
1971 Gerald Fried, Mrs. Gerald Fried
1975 Mark Blumentahl, Arthur Waldmann
1976 M. S. Bentley, Barbara Bentley
1977 Joan Remey, Zeke Jabbour
1978 Chuck Carroll, Warren Oberfield
1979 David Lindop, John Carruthers
1980 Chuck Carroll, James Barlow
Flight A:
1980 Abby Heitner, Paul Heitner

MEN'S PAIRS
1956 Charles Hirschey, Charles W. Spencer
1957 Phil Feldesman, Louis Kelner
1958 H. J. Behm, Trusedale Clarke
1959 Homer Shoop, Mike Shuman
1960 Dr. Robert Israel, Ed Majeroni
1961 C. Jack Bonney, Donald L. Stanton
1962 Malcolm McMartin, James Becker
1963 Lt. Col. Charles Hartnoll, Victor Dimarco
1964 Steve Berg, Manuel Goodman
1965 Baron Wolf Lebovic, Sammy Kehela
1966 Stanley Poskanzer, Murray Melton
1967 Sammy Kehela, Steve Aarons
1968 William Merriman, Everett Hatch
1969 Fred Root, Marvin Morris
1971 John Smith, Lyman Spalding
1978 Howard Friedman, Raymond Blake
1979 Eric Landau, Phil Brady
1980 Jack Dalton, Steve Barcus

WOMEN'S PAIRS
1956 Mrs. M. Nevins, Agnes Gordon
1957 C. Gillette, H. Penner
1958 Mrs. M. Nevins, Agnes Gordon
1959 C. N. Frank, C. J. Dennis

1960 Ruby McKaig, Marguerite Maurer
1961 Ann Sheabor, Shirley Hewitt
1962 E. H. Hunt, J. D. Reardon
1963 Mrs. A. N. McTavish, Mrs. W. E. Weber
1964 Agnes Gordon, A. Wright
1965 Mrs. Gerald Fried, Mary McKenna
1966 Ruby McKaig, Mrs. T. J. Peterson, Jr.
1967 Mrs. G. R. Johnson, Mrs. S. B. Rose
1968 Mrs. R. Appleby, Mrs. F. F. Gudgel
1969 Mrs. F. S. Lisowski, Ruth Instance
1971 Mrs. G. Morgan, Mrs. R. Vander Laan
1978 Claire Chodrow, Beverly Cohen
1979 Claire Chodrow, Beverly Cohen
1980 Margie Tamres, Jan George

MIXED PAIRS
1956 Ruby McKaig, Charles Hirschey
1957 Agnes Gordon, Emanuel Katz
1958 Agnes Gordon, Emanuel Katz
1959 Mrs. N. Freedman, K. A. P. Stepanian
1960 Agnes Gordon, Emanuel Katz
1961 Alma Godfrey, Dr. Milton Sandler
1962 Vivian Lavery, Dr. John Manos
1963 Mary McKenna, Emanuel Katz
1964 Mrs. C. Letcher, Fred C. Root
1965 Mary McKenna, Emanuel Katz
1966 Alberta Albersheim, Charles Coon
1967 Joyce Phillips, Don Cowan
1968 Mrs. H. Hobbs, Rev. L. A. Tobin
1969 Mrs. B. Ku, Dr. Donald Sun
1971 Rev. Thomas Kemp, Mrs. J. Schlaerth
1978 Jannette Michienzi, Robert Spero

MEN'S SWISS TEAMS
1976 Robert Freedman, James Mathis,
Jim Zimmerman, Wellington Lee
1977 Joe Cotellessa, Rick Benstock,
Fred Bellinger, Norman O'Brien
1978 Jeff Meckstroth, Ron Andersen,
Dennis McGarry, Zeke Jabbour
1979 David Turner, Bryan Culham,
Wayne Timms, Keith Balcombe (tied with)
John Toy, Mike Donnelly, Buddy Seidenberg,
Tom Donnelly, Jim Streisand
1980 Ed Bridson, Dan Gertsman, Mark Molson,
Phil Brady, Dennis McGarry

WOMEN'S SWISS TEAMS
1976 Kay Lux, Marge Cox, Mildred Sable,
Phyllis Heller, Mary Frazier
1977 Maureen Irwin, Anne Mae Hlebak,
June Gerdes, Edna Alexander
1978 Portia Miller, Julia Halloran,
Peggy Solomon, Joyce Wade
1979 Caroline Pascoe, Laurie Kranyak, Jan George,
Sharon Cleary, Dale Dermer
1980 Portia Miller, Peggy Solomon,
Gena Bhatia, Joyce Wade

DISTRICT 6 (Virginia, Washington, D.C., most of Maryland)

MID-ATLANTIC FALL

KNOCKOUT TEAMS
1971 Walt Walvick, Steve Robinson, Tom Weik,
Ed Manfield, Sidney Aronson
1972 Brian Schoenfeld, James Murphy,
Steve Goldberg, Lou Bluhm
1976 Steve Robinson, Roy Fox, Walt Walvick,
Ed Manfield, Steve Lapides, Paul Swanson
1977 Les Bart, Bill Pettis,
Peter Boyd, Lou Bluhm
1978 Les Bart, Susan Singerbart, Peter Boyd,
Bill Pettis, David Hoffner

MASTER PAIRS
1971 Lou Bluhm, Lyle Ballentine
1972 Lou Bluhm, Steve Goldberg
1976 Dave Sachs, Sue Sachs
1977 Steve Swearingen, Pat Lapides
1980 Robert Priest, Burrill Porter

OPEN TEAMS
1971 Ellen Allen, Larry Allen,
Steve Swearingen, Randy Joyce
1972 Kathie Wei, Charles Wei, Victor Mitchell,
Jacqui Mitchell, Bill Passell, Marietta Passell
1976 Kit Woolsey, Steve Parker,
Richard Shepherd, Bob Lipsitz
1977 Gary Hahn, Mike Cappelletti,

Glenn Lubiin, Ron Sukoneck
1978 Paul DePorte, Gisele Caviness, John Rieser,
Robert Gookin, Pam Koester
1979 Dave Treadwell, John Barnicle, Richard Colker,
Howard Cohen, Arnie Fisher
1980 Nadine Wood, A. Michael Lipson,
Mel Welles, Randy Thompson (tied with)
Steve Robinson, Peter Boyd, Ron Sukoneck,
Robert Lipsitz, Marvin Rosenblatt
1981 George Bloomer, Judith Bloomer,
Bob Klein, David Ruderman

OPEN PAIRS
1971 Ron Beall, Ed Simmons
1972 Alan Kravetz, H. Ketchum
1976 Sue Sachs, Dave Sachs
Smoking:
1977 Roy Fox, Ed Manfield
1978 Steve Lapides, Walt Walwick
1979 Sue Sachs, David Sachs
1980 Gil Cohen, Martin Nelson
1981 Jack Diskin, Gayle Merritt
Non-Smoking:
1977 Joel Weintraub, Shirley Presberg
1978 Rosemary Shaw, Roy Tibery
1979 Audrey Marbach, Kenneth Randall
1980 Ralph Bartlett, Phil Brady
1981 Ken Bercuson, Ed Manfield
Flight A:
1978 Paul DePorte, John Rieser
1979 Richard Taylor, Ralph Turner
1980 Eugene O'Neill, Rick Henderson
1981 Bob Blakey, Helen Blakey

MEN'S PAIRS
1971 Joe Kivel, Dean Darling
1976 Ken Cohen, Mike Moss
1977 Dr. John Fisher, Gary Hahn
1978 Paul Swanson, Roy Fox
1979 Frank Mastrola, Ira Barrows
1980 Steve Carton, Norb Kremer
1981 Phil Shepp, John Chronister

WOMEN'S PAIRS
1971 Ellen Allen, Clara Harlston
1976 Aileen Lane, Rhona Tabor
1977 Mrs. Richard Brubaker, Louise Parks
1978 Sue Reeve, Kay Smith
1979 Ann Sanders, Margaret Dixon
1980 Nancy Tinkley, Connie Kafka
1981 Antoinette Lutz, Helen Hirsty

MEN'S SWISS TEAMS
1976 Mark Dahl, Frank Mastrola, Joey Asber,
Bill Gamble, Mike Rahtjen
1977 Gary Hahn, Bill Blade,
Dave Smith, Mike Cappelletti
1978 Harry Siegelman, Glen Robbins,
Walter Willson, Warren Kaufman
1979 William Levy, Phil Brady, Peter Weglarski,
William Gough, Ira Barrows, Frank Mastrola (tied with)
David Hoffner, Glenn Lublin,
Phil Clark, Mike Cappelletti
1980 William Levy, Frank Mastrola, William Gough,
E. Robert Thoms, Joseph Livezey
1981 David Hoffner, John Rieser, Peter Boyd,
Paul DePorte, Mike Cappelletti

WOMEN'S SWISS TEAMS
1976 Barbara Baird, Marilyn O'Donell,
Rene Henry, Evelyn Fitzgerald (tied with)
Helen Katzen, Edith Rosen,
Alice Adler, Sally Lehrman
1977 Ramona Karlson, Brenda Coffman,
Eleanor Jackson, Martha Sutherland
1978 Terry Michaels, Jo Morse,
Ellasue Chaitt, Lois Anne Lewis
1979 Marilyn O'Donnell, Jeanne Stenger,
Gail Rust, Margie McDevitt
1980 Helen Blakey, Judi Cody,
Beth Palmer, Lynn Deas (tied with)
Kathie Wei, Judi Radin, Nancy Gruver,
Ellasue Chaitt, Jo Morse (and)
Ruth Blumenthal, Barbara Baird,
Renee Henry, Genevieve Heine.
1981 Kathie Wei, Judi Radin, Evelyn Levitt,
Sue Sachs, Jo Morse, Ellasue Chaitt

MIXED PAIRS
1978 Pamela Bridson, Ed Bridson

INDIVIDUAL
1978 Anne Mace

MID-ATLANTIC INDEPENDENCE DAY

KNOCKOUT TEAMS
1972 Walt Walvick, Sidney Aronson,
Michael Cappelletti, Kathie Cappelletti
1973 Robert Ewen, Richard Oshlag, Barry Bragin,
Dr. Frank Mastrola, Marty Bergen, William Woodard
1974 Jay Apfelbaum, Arnold Fisher,
Jim Lambert, Larry Edwards
1975 Jeff Sparks, Archie Sparks,
Bill Cason, Eileen Cason
1979 David Hoffner, Glen Lublin,
Kathie Cappelletti, Mike Cappelletti
1980 Jeff Meckstroth, Patty Meckstroth,
Eric Rodwell, Lynn Deas
1981 Ken Kranyak, Robert Gookin,
Mark Cohen, Paul DePorte

OPEN TEAMS
1966 Robert Nail, John Gerber,
J.G. Ripstra, Mabel Mahoney
1967 Donald Hocevar, Phillip Leon,
Herbert Sachs, Paul Swanson (tied with)
Edward Manfield, Richard Fleischman,
Richard Schwartz, Stephen Goldstein
1968 Julian Adler, Betty Adler,
Edmond Lazarus, Thomas Weik
1969 Mark Blumenthal, Steven Lapides,
Don Faskow, Kit Woolsey
1970 Don Faskow, Herb Sachs,
Paul Swanson, Chris Jeans
1971 Bob Lewis, Norman Schwartz,
Kit Woolsey, Steve Robinson
1972 Vivian Davis, Frances Hultman,
William Williams, Charles Fulton
1973 Robert Lipsitz, Peggy Parker,
Kit Woolsey, Steve Parker (tied with)
Roger Pies, Sheila Pies,
Mickie Kivel, Joe Kivel
1974 Joel Banks, Bob Lindsay,
John Robert, Al Duncker
1975 Robert Blakey, Helen Blakey, Joe Kivel,
Mickie Kivel, Dean Darling
1978 Mark Dahl, David Butler,
Ellasue Chaitt, Tom Justl
1979 Glenn Robbins, Walter Wilson,
Arnie Frankel, Freda Engle
1981 Mary Wolf, Brian Gubok, Glenn Lubin,
Joseph Livezey, Phil Clark (tied with)
T. Craig Robinson, Charles Gray,
Jerry Resnick, Gene Davidson (and)
Bruce Silverstein, Sue Sachs,
David Sachs, Dave Treadwell
Flight A:
1981 Michael Carroad, Martin Nelson,
Gil Cohen, Ellasue Chaitt

MASTER SWISS TEAMS
1980 Helen Blakey, Bob Blakey,
Richard Colker, Dave Treadwell (tied with)
Michael Carroad, Martin Nelson,
Gil Cohen, Ellasue Chaitt (and)
Dave Sachs, Sue Sachs,
Betty Adler, Julian Adler

MASTER PAIRS
1966 Don Bier, M.J. Daniels
1967 Mrs. John Vastine, James Lipman
1968 Edwin Lewis, Joe Kivel
1969 Betty Greenberg, Marjorie Glass
1970 Mike Moss, Gail Moss
1971 Steve Parker, Mike Garner
1972 Jay Cohen, Dean Darling (tied with)
Gary Hann, John Brinley
1973 Alan Wilhide, Michael Carroad
1974 Joseph Livezey, Phil Brady
1975 Peggy McLean, Joe McLean, Jr.
1978 Joel Friedberg, Dave Berkovitz
1979 Alan Bell, Dave Smith
1981 Chuck Malcolm, Mike Rind

MIXED PAIRS
1967 Tom Ekel, Peggy Ekel
1968 Helen Utegaard, Mark Blumenthal
1969 Evelyn Wolf, Kurt Zendig
1971 Sue Sachs, David Sachs
1980 Julian Heicklen, Susan Heicklen

INDIVIDUAL
1980 Robert Hume

OPEN PAIRS
1966 Margaret Wagar, Barry Crane
1967 Edith Sachs, David Sachs
1968 Dale Freese, Earl Bowen

1969   Dianne Lazarus, Kit Woolsey
1970   Henry Bethe, Bernie Chazen
1971   John Bookstaver, Eugene Neiger
1972   Jo Morse, Helen Utegaard
1973   Richard Taube, Kit Woolsey
1974   William Synder, Mrs. William Synder
1975   Bruce Silverstein, Joseph Livezey
Flight A:
1978   Mark Dahl, David Butler
1979   Bruce Silverstein, John Piaski
1980   Patty Meckstroth, Robert Levin
1981   Jim Wood, Tom Lyon
Smoking:
1978   Mike Forman, Don Juran
1979   Jimmy Lipman, Bette Dudka
1980   Eugene Saxe, Philip Cowan
1981   Marge Vonesh, Jim Vonesh
Non-Smoking:
1978   David Hoffner, Mark Rosenbloom
1979   David Butler, Brick Houck
1980   Vin Bartone, Bill Ehlers
1981   Raphael Kahn, Tom Lyon

MEN'S PAIRS

1966   William Woodsen, John Norwood, Jr.
1967   Herbert Sachs, Paul Swanson
1968   Tommy Ekel, Jerry Deutschberger *(tied with)*
      Jeff Stafford, Lewis Barnett
1969   Nick Nickell, Frank Garson II
1970   Tom Lyon, Mike Cappelletti *(tied with)*
      Ronald Perry, H. Philip Monyer
1971   Dean Darling, Joe Kivel
1972   Herb Peters, Warren Roberts
1973   William Vinson, Terry Patton
1975   John Hamilton, John Herrmann
1978   Bob Klein, Emerson Beauchamp
1979   Jack Feagin, Randy Pettit
1980   Alan Bell, Dave Smith
1981   Mike Cappelletti, Jr., Mike Cappelletti

WOMEN'S PAIRS

1966   Jane Clayton, Mrs. L.F. Buschbaum
1967   Mrs. Jules Miller, Muriel Wasserman
1968   Edna Henson, Mildred Anderson
1969   Siddy Parr, Shirley Heinsohn
1970   Lea DuPont, Helen Hirsty
1971   Jo Morse, Jeanne Stenger
1972   Jackie Wilcox, Beverly Sikora
1973   Ellen Berman, Gertrude Berns
1975   Ann Synder, Susan Walbert
1978   Marilyn O'Donnell, Jackie McCallon
1979   Janet McRorie, Jean Metelli
1980   Marilyn O'Donnell, Renee Henry
1981   Barbara Baird, Marilyn O'Donnell

MEN'S SWISS TEAMS

1978   Bob Blakey, Dave Treadwell,
      Arnold Fischer, Ed Manfield
1979   Tom Sikora, Norman Fischer,
      Stan Given, John Piaski *(tied with)*
      Dave Smith, Darwin Afdahl,
      Alan Bell, Fred McBride
1980   Glenn Lublin, Doug Levene,
      Frank Stewart, William Pettis

WOMEN'S SWISS TEAMS

1978   Marilyn O'Donnell, Marjorie McDevitt,
      Jeanne Stenger, Gail Rust
1979   Mary Williams, Genie Warshauer,
      Mary Stewart Hood, Ellasue Chaitt
1980   Jo Morse, Sylvia Levy,
      Nadine Wood, Jeanne Stenger

MID–ATLANTIC SPRING

KNOCKOUT TEAMS

1973   Ben Pope, Brian Schoenfeld, Pete Boyd,
      Dick Taube, Brian Moran, Peter Lesnik
1975   Ronald Sukoneck, Richard Taube, Tom Ekel,
      Bill McCallon, Eugene Kales, Larry Rosenblum

OPEN TEAMS

1973   Victor Chernoff, Les Bart,
      Clagett Bowie, John Rengstorff
1975   Connie McGinley, William Gough,
      Ira Barrows, William Levy

OPEN PAIRS

1973   Lou Bluhm, Steve Swearingen
1975   Jim Wood, Jim Eatherly

MEN'S PAIRS

1973   Lyle Poe, Mike Rind

WOMEN'S PAIRS

1973   Betty Adler, Pat Lapides

MASTER PAIRS

1975   Nancy Gruver, Helen Utegaard

MID–ATLANTIC SUMMER

KNOCKOUT TEAMS

1962   Dr. Joseph Henry, Jack Hudgins, Dr. Mortimer Lipsett,
      Tommy Ekel, Dean Darling
1970   William Eisenberg, Robert Goldman, Robert Wolff,
      Robert Hamman, Michael Lawrence, James Jacoby
1972   Steve Catlett, Richard Hamilton,
      Bill Wick, Bill McCallon
1973   Jeff Stafford, Jo Morse,
      Edmond Piaski, Helen Utegaard
1974   Nick Nickell, Stephen Swearingen, William Pettis,
      Warren Roberts, Lyle Ballentine
1976   Paul Swanson, Richard Shepherd,
      Lou Bluhm, Nick Nickell
1977   Lou Bluhm, Richard Shepherd,
      Peter Rand, Les Bart
1978   A.E. (Bud) Reinhold, Bill Seamon, Steve Sion,
      Robert Levin, Allan Cokin
1980   Jo Morse, Brian Schoenfeld, Steve Robinson,
      Linda Robinson, Ben Polk, Jim Murphy

INDIVIDUAL

1976   Ellie Huddleston
1977   Elwood Spickard

OPEN TEAMS

1960   Margaret Fisher, Edward Allen,
      Robert Shankie, Charles Duffy
1961   Lib Simpson, Anne Yates,
      Bobby McMaham, William Williams *(tied with)*
      Dr. A.C. Current, Jr., John Warlick,
      Bruce Beghardt, James Mitchell
1962   Jim Keating, Marcil Keating,
      Eunice Pratt, Jack Armstrong
1963   Lt. Col. William Christian, Sidney Aronson,
      Robert Sitnek, Andrew Gabrilovitch
1964   Howard Schenken, Bee Schenken,
      Andrew Gabrilovitch, Ivar Stakgold
1965   Edward Harlow, Peggy Harlow,
      Wallace Jones, Daniel Harris *(tied with)*
      Joseph Kivel, Mickey Kivel
      Edmund Lazarus, Dean Darling
1966   Harold Hess, John Coppie, Charles Crum,
      Ray Clark, Manuel Weinberg
1967   Margaret Wagar, Louise Freeman, Richard Freeman,
      Foxy Hall, Richard Shepherd
1968   Mike Cappelletti, Kathie Cappelletti,
      Mark Blumenthal, Steve Lapides
1969   Herbert Swisher, Dee Swisher, Alice Gerard,
      Jim Brenner, Al Bricklin
1970   Mike Cappelletti, Kathie Cappelletti,
      Eric Kokish, Joe Silver
1972   Dr. Mortimer Lipsett, Jo Morse,
      Tommy Ekel, Dean Darling, *tied with*
      Steve Lapides, Richard Taube,
      Kit Woolsey, Jay Cohen
1974   Ellasue Marrs, Richard Taube, Phil Brady,
      Joseph Livezey, Brian Schoenfeld
1976   Tony Kasday, Eric Schwartz,
      Glenn Lublin, Howard Piltch *(tied with)*
      John Barnicle, Dave Treadwell,
      David Sachs, Sue Sachs
1977   Bill Miller, Moshe Bernstein,
      Pete Weglarski, Ted Stryker
1978   Mickie Kivel, Joe Kivel, Kay Afdahl,
      Darwin Afdahl, Frank King, Ed Lewis
1979   Mike Cappelletti, Kathie Cappelletti,
      Dave Hoffner, Glenn Lublin
1980   Bob McMahan, Jim Harris,
      Archie Sparks, Jeff Sparks
1981   Chris Kaufman, Andrew Kaufman,
      Marliese Kaufman, Warren Kaufman

OPEN PAIRS

1960   Peggy Rotzell, Robert Sitnek
1961   Phil Sowers, Charles Wallace
1962   Richard Baum, Mark Borindky
1963   Billy Rainier, Ruth Rainier
1964   John Norwood, William Woodson
1965   Oswald Jacoby, James Jacoby
1966   Steve Swearingen, Herb Peters
1967   Larry Allen, Ellen Allen
1968   Michael Edwards, John Landen
1969   Charles Fulton, Howard Petrea
1970   Steve Parker, Peggy Parker
1972   Steve Lapides, Richard Taube
1973   Ely Solomon, Martin Nelson
1974   Steve Robinson, Richard Henderson

1976   John Barnicle, Dave Treadwell
1977   Tony Kasday, Steve Sion
Flight A:
1979   Tom Lavender, Terry Roman
1980   Ellasue Chaitt, Herb Peters
1981   Norb Kremer, Lynn Deas
Smoking:
1978   John Barnicle, Dave Treadwell
1979   Randy Beckham, Ellasue Chaitt
1980   Nick Nickell, Steve Swearingen
1981   Tom Rutledge, Jeff Stafford
Non-Smoking
1978   Albert May, Helene May *(tied with)*
      Peter Boyd, Les Bart
1979   Melissa Dadant, Ruth Goldman
1980   Harold Siegelman, Bill Cole
1981   David Hoffner, Mike Cappelletti

MASTER PAIRS

1960   Jake Clinkinbeard, Helen Clinkinbeard
1961   Sol Lourie, Albert Brewington
1962   John Coppie, Manuel Weinberg
1963   Mortimer Lipsett, Dr. Richard Rovner
1964   Mrs. Duane Evans, Lewis Tubbs
1966   Peggy Harrison, Tommy Ekel
1967   Lucille Williams, Esther Addlestone
1969   Margaret Shouse, Jane Clayton
1970   Steve Parker, Peggy Parker
1972   Mike Cappelletti, Kathie Cappelletti
1973   Norm Holthouse, W.F. Glover
1974   Robert Leonard, Richard Burton
1976   Steve Parker, Peggy Lipsitz
1977   Jeff Sparks, Archie Sparks
1978   Ray Wilhide, Henry Itkin
1979   Steve Catlett, W. Doug Hudgins, Jr.
1981   Ron Sukoneck, Peter Boyd

MIXED PAIRS

1960   Louise Eisenman, Richard Harrison
1961   Margaret Wagar, Will Davis
1962   Betty Adler, Alan Goldberg
1963   Henrietta Nathan, Bert Wilson
1964   Betty Adler, Alan Goldberg
1965   Mrs. Edward Wilson, Jr., Richard Taube
1968   Walter O'Loughlin, June O'Loughlin
1970   John Tierney, Marian Tierney
1976   Steve Parker, Peggy Lipsitz

MEN'S PAIRS

1960   Andy Gabrilovitch, Robert Jordan
1961   Don Caton, Dave Caton
1962   Edmond Fleischer, Lionel Friedberg
1963   David Murray, John Chappell, Jr
1964   Thomas A. Throop, D. Meade Peebles, Jr
1965   Charles Price, Charles Crum
1966   B. Jay Becker, Elwood Spickard
1967   Richard Freeman, Foxy Hall
1968   Mike Cappelletti, Tannah Hirsch
1969   Howard Abrams, Alf Van Hoose
1970   Stephen Swearingen, Herbert Peters
1976   Bill Blade, Jr, Darwin Afdahl
1977   Peter Weglarski, Arnold Fisher
1978   Walter O'Loughlin, Bill Wolverton
1979   Steve Catlett, W. Doug Hudgins, Jr.
1980   Ann Roubik, Nancy Fijak
1981   Steve Catlett, William D. Hudgins

WOMEN'S PAIRS

1960   Inez Lusby, R. Roberts
1961   Mrs. King Fortson, H.K. Smith
1962   Ruth Rogasner, June O'Loughlin *(tied with)*
      Florence Roberts, Mildred Phillips
1963   Gloria Wilson, Anne Buist
1964   Mrs. A. West, Mrs. G. Carroll
1965   Adele Kotzen, Merle Rubens
1966   Lillian Dillon, Lola Wolford
1967   Dottie Toledano, Earline Foley
1968   Mrs. C. Blumenthal, Betty Adler
1969   Betty Cohn, Joan Remey
1970   Helen Utegaard, Andres Burger
1976   Connie Moerschell, Margaret Pell
1977   Esther Miller, Patty Pearcy
1978   Jo Morse, Kathy Fox
1979   Bette Dudka, Timi Caldwell
1980   Mark Rosenbloom, Steve Shapiro
1981   Ann Roubik, Sherry Spalding

MEN'S SWISS TEAMS

1977   Tony Kasday, Marc Jacobus, Jim Sternberg,
      Marvin Herbert, Steve Sion, Allan Cokin
1979   Steve Catlett, W. Doug Hudgins, Jr.,
      R. H. Hamilton, James Morris
1980   Ron Sukoneck, Phil Clark, Bill Passell,
      Joseph Livezey, Ben Pope, Jim Murphy

1981   Richard Colker, Joseph Livezey,
      Arnold Fisher, Dave Treadwell

WOMEN'S SWISS TEAMS

1977   Pearl Schechter, Mrs. Lamar Jones,
      Mrs. Max Chused, Mrs. Dan Gintis *(tied with)*
      Diane Lending, Sue Walbert,
      Ada Clair Synder, Nancy Wilborg Ryan
1979   Jo Morse, Ellasue Chaitt, Genne Winter,
      Jeanne Stenger, Ann Pettit
1980   Eve Pace, Connie Moerschell,
      Kaye Krebs, Shirley Presberg *(tied with)*
      Lynn Deas, Flo Ham, Kay Afdahl,
      Pat Rhodes, Margaret Pell, Beth Palmer
1981   Mary Wolf, Lynn Deas,
      Beth Palmer, Mickie Kivel

MASTER SWISS TEAMS

1978   J. Richard Burton, Bill Betz,
      Lynn Deas, Harold Triplett *(tied with)*
      Jo Morse, Steve Robinson, Henry Itkin,
      Ray Wilhide, Paul Swanson

WASHINGTON BRIDGE WEEK

KNOCKOUT TEAMS

1974   Terry Michaels, Richard Henderson, Mary Philley,
      William Christian, Jo Morse, Helen Utegaard
1975   Jay Cohen, Roy Fox, Steve Swearingen,
      Mark Blumenthal, Eugene O'Neil, Ken Cohen
1976   Mike Moss, Gail Moss, Ken Cohen,
      Helen Smith, Jay Cohen
1981   Les Bart, Lou Bluhm, Peter Boyd,
      Robert Ayers, Kit Woolsey

OPEN TEAMS

1974   Steve Swearingen, Randy Joyce,
      Nick Nickell, Bill Pettis

SWISS TEAMS

1975   Walt Walvick, Steve Lapides,
      Kathie Cappelletti, Mike Cappelletti
1976   Bob Blakey, Helen Blakey, Dave Sachs,
      Sue Sachs, Betty Adler, Buddy Adler
1981   Lew Handelsman, Phillip Martin, Stasha Wroblewski,
      Howard Chandross, Bill Pollack, Rozanne Marel

MASTER PAIRS

1974   Arnie Frankel, Peter McManus
1975   Mette Smith, David Smith
1976   Larry Gould, Lou Bluhm
1981   Ruth H. Potter, Stephen Potter

OPEN PAIRS

1974   Randy Joyce, Steve Swearingen
1975   John Barnicle, Alan Goldberg
1976   Steve Parker, Roy Fox
1981   Gary Hann, Joseph Livezey

MEN'S PAIRS

1974   Dave Treadwell, Ken Cohen
1975   Mark Shaw, Dale Johannesen
1981   Paul Swanson, Roy Fox

WOMEN'S PAIRS

1974   Betty Adler, Aileen Lane
1975   Marjorie Glass, Natalie Barnicle
1981   Ann Moulden, Flo Roberts

MEN'S SWISS TEAMS

1976   William Levy, Joseph Livezey, William Gough,
      Giles Belsk, Ira Barrows
1981   Ira Barrows, William Gough, Russell Griest,
      Joseph Livezey, Moshe Bernstein

WOMEN'S SWISS TEAMS

1976   Dixie Doggett, Dawn McGrudder, Gertrude Weber,
      Vi Goode, Joan White
1981   Jo Morse, Mary Williams, Betty Adler,
      Sue Sachs, Terry Michaels

MIXED PAIRS

1976   Joseph Livezey, Carole Gould
1981   Greg Gault, Annalee Gault

INDIVIDUAL

1976   Earl Engelman
1981   William Hoffman

District 7   (North Carolina, South Carolina, Georgia, Bermuda, eastern Tennessee)

BERMUDA

OPEN TEAMS

1962   Frank T. Westcott, Dr. John Manos,
      Robert Fox, Chester Davis, Dr. Robert Tator
1966   Mildred Siebert, Sig Siebert
      Betty Reid, Donald Reid

1968   Dr. William Melander, Mrs. William Melander
       Joan Remey, Vincent Remey
1970   Frank T. Westcott, Dr. Robert Tator,
       Dr. John T. Manos, Roy S. Fox, Robert W. McVay
1972   Roy Fox, Frank Westcott, Chester Davis,
       Dr. John Manos, Dr. Robert Tator *(tied with)*
       Richard Miller, Allen Spielholz,
       Herman Horowitz, Ted Gray *(and)*
       Herb Sachs, Roslyn Sachs,
       Alberta Albersheim, Mrs. M. Root *(and)*
       Edgar Kaplan, Betty Kaplan
       Julius Rosenblum, Nate Silverstein
1974   Tony Saunders, Florence Freda,
       Alan Truscott, Dorothy Hayden Truscott
1975   Edgar Kaplan, Betty Kaplan, Alan Truscott,
       Dorothy Hayden Truscott, Julius Rosenblum
1977   Tannah Hirsch, Loretta Rivers, Lou Gurvich,
       Sol Seidman, Tracy Denninger, Mal Martin
1978   Tannah Hirsch, Andy Gabrilovitch, Malcolm Lewis,
       Colin Millington, Ernie Owen, Joe Wakefield
1979   Alberta Albersheim, Ethel Keohane, Judi Cody, Bob Fiske
       (tied with) Mike Passell, Clarence Goppert, Russ Ekeblad,
       Sheila Ekeblad, Dorsey Brooks, Zerrene Brooks
       (and) Mary Hartley, Esther Michelman,
       Sybil Michelman, Frieda Alpert *(and)*
       Edgar Kaplan, Betty Kaplan, Sol Seidman, Dick Hart
1980   Colin Millington, Ernie Owen, Alan Douglas,
       Charles Vaucrosson, David Ezekiel
1981   Martin Chaitt, Ellasue Chaitt,
       Michael Carroad, Nadine Wood

MASTER PAIRS
1968   Dorothy Apple, Catherine Samberg
1970   Irving Gershkoff, Mrs. Irving Gershkoff
1972   Allan Derby, Mrs. Allan Derby
1974   Terry Teague, Mrs. Terry Teague
1975   Charles Weed, Marion Weed
1977   Michael Instance, Ruth Instance
1978   Roslyn Cooper, Martin Cooper
1979   Anne O'Brien, Aaron Aroneck
1980   Virginia Mattocks, Evelyn Tounsley
1981   John Grantham, Joann Grantham

OPEN PAIRS
1962   Richard Frey, Howard Schenken
1966   Carol Krupp, Paul Trent
1968   Marty Ginsberg, Les Sokolower
1970   Pat Beyer, Betty Pope
1972   Jan Barna, Allan Derby
1974   Betty Kaplan, Edgar Kaplan
1975   Bertrand Romanet, Jacqueline Romanet
1977   Richard Frey, Eric Murray
1978   John McDermott, Steve Linehan
1979   Clarence Goppert, Mike Passell
1980   Jim O'Neil, Mary O'Neil
1981   Mollie Ruben, Gloria Brown

MEN'S PAIRS
1962   Dr. Robert Tator, Chester Davis
1966   Chester Davis, Dr. Robert Tator
1968   Maj. Fitz O'Neill, Peter Willcocks
1970   Al Oszy, Ted Clarke
1972   Tracy Denninger, Herb Sachs
1974   Dorsey Brooks, Dr. William Melander
1975   David Buskirk, Paul Van Roekel
1977   John Klayman, Dr. R. B. Roberts
1978   John Carruthers, Abe Paul
1979   Leonard Karp, Jules Pearlman
1980   John McDermott, Paul Lavallee
1981   Ray Wilhide, Warren Kaufman

WOMEN'S PAIRS
1962   Mrs. C. Foster, Ada Wilmot
1966   Eva Leahy, Mary Hartley
1968   Gertrude Galespie, Mrs. H. Wolf
1970   Mrs. Henry Katzen, Mrs. W. L. Lewis
1972   Mrs. G. Nelson, Mrs. W. Stephens
1974   Elsie Abrams, Mrs. L. Singer
1975   Marion Weed, Dorothy Moore
1977   Mrs. M. D. Berman, Dinah Schulman
1978   Anita Kurti, Ruth Bloomfield
1979   Kitty Kac, Mary Bragg
1980   Mrs. Nathan Jacobi, Mrs. J. E. Sternberger
1981   Nadine Wood, Ellasue Chaitt

MIXED PAIRS
1962   Julius Rosenblum, Natalie Rosenblum
1966   Elmer Hoffman, Mrs. Elmer Hoffman

MID–ATLANTIC FALL
KNOCKOUT TEAMS
1972   Brian Moran, Stephen Gregory,
       James Murphy, Ellasue Marrs

1973   Brian Schoenfeld, Jim Looby,
       Steve Gregory, Mike Tierney
1974   Seymour Leibowitz, Mark Blumenthal, Steve Parker,
       Steve Robinson, Kit Woolsey, Lou Bluhm
1975   Lou Bluhm, Richard Shepherd,
       Larry Gould, Les Bart
1976   Andy Bernstein, Garland Ergüden, David Schroeder,
       David Smith, David Hoffner
1977   Gary Hann, Ron Sukoneck, Mike Cappelletti,
       Glenn Lublin, Dave Treadwell
1978   Eddie Wold, Dan Morse,
       Curtis Smith, Cliff Russell
1979   Mike Passell, Clarence Goppert, Eddie Wold,
       Gaylor Kasle, Lou Bluhm
1980   Bob Yellis, Leigh Steinberg,
       Pauline Harrison, Michael Polowan
1981   Tom Mahaffey, Jeff Meckstroth,
       Jack Denny, Robert Levin

OPEN TEAMS
1952   W. B. Joachim, Alex Tschekaloff,
       Stan Judd, Alex Danilenko
1953   Jack Bonney, Mildred Bonney, George Wolf,
       Dr. Fumio Yagi, Mildred Betzler
1954   D. J. Harris, Catherine McGhee,
       Janice Stone, Margaret Fisher
1955   Charles Solomon, Peggy Solomon,
       Nathan Agran, Violet Agran
1956   Emily Folline, R. L. Miles, Jr.
       Louise Eisenman, Richard Freeman
1957   Tobias Stone, Janice Stone,
       John Crawford, Sidney Silodor
1958   Joe McCabe, Robert Lovill, Jr., Joan Remey,
       Irving Deuter, C. P. Weil
1959   Billy Rainier, Ruth Rainier,
       Hyman Silverman, Zelda Silverman
1960   Robert Jordan, Norman Kay, Thomas Sanders,
       Carol Sanders, Margaret Wagar
1961   John Norwood, Jr., Margaret Norwood,
       Foxy Hall, Fred Blackman
1962   Louise Robinson, Eric Murray, Boyd Hughes,
       Richard Freeman, Hampton Hume
1963   Gene Davidson, Hampton Hume, Boyd Hughes,
       Martin Cohn, Foxy Hall
1964   Emily Folline, Richard Freeman, Louise Freeman,
       Norman Berlin, R. L. (Skinny) Miles, Jr.
1965   Robin Mac Nab, John Norwood, Margaret Norwood,
       Marian Powell, William Woodsen
1966   Margaret Wagar, Barry Crane, R. H. Govan,
       Richard Shepherd, Mrs. Richard Shepherd
1967   Jerry Earley, Bernadine Jenkins, John Dodd,
       Foxy Hall, Joan Hall
1968   Herbert Peters, John Sheridan, Nick Nickell,
       Steve Swearingen, Randy Joyce
1969   Nichol Eskridge, Joanne Mackintosh,
       J. J. Gottlet, John Shelnutt *(tied with)*
       William Williams, Jr., Charles Fulton,
       Ellen Allen, Larry Allen
1970   Andy Bernstein, Mark Blumenthal,
       Don Faskow, Paul Swanson
1972   Seymour Leibowitz, Mark Blumenthal, Frank Nickell,
       Thomas Callaham, Herbert Peters
1973   John Piaski, Randy Joyce, Lewis Barnett,
       Bill Pettis, Jeff Stafford
1974   Jeff Stafford, Bill Pettis, Lewis Barnett,
       Randy Joyce, John Piaski
1975   David Schroeder, Frank Zachman,
       Andy Bernstein, Garland Ergüden
1976   David Smith, David Schroeder,
       Garland Ergüden, Happholdt Neuffer
1977   Mark Dahl, Charlotte Hahn,
       David Butler, Kay Afdahl *(tied with)*
       Jeff Sparks, Lynn Deas,
       Dave Smith, Bob McMahan
1978   Randy Pettit, Ann Pettit,
       Ron Cadora, Bob Bisplinghoff
1979   Mike Passell, Clarence Goppert, Gaylor Kasle,
       Lou Bluhm, Dave Schroeder
1980   Robert White, William High,
       George Mitchell, Bill Brunk
1981   Jim Bowman, Alice Gerard,
       Dean Cohler, Pat Cohler

MASTER PAIRS
1959   Abe Vatz, George Wolfe
1960   Jake Clinkinbeard, Helen Clinkinbeard
1961   Marvin Cowell, William Woodson
1962   John Norwood, Bernard Warshauer
1964   Roberta Spikes, Ervin Chauncey
1965   Richard Freeman, Louise Freeman
1966   Mark Blumenthal, Walter Walvick
1967   Don Faskow, Bill Flannery

1968	Curtis Smith, Helen Corbin
1969	Jeff Hand, Barry Bragin
1970	Tom Callaham, Pete McManus
1973	Garey Hayden, Mike Passell
1974	Dean Darling, Frank King *(tied with)*
	Roy Mourer, L. Horton
1975	Jeffrey Zionts, Jeff Stafford
1976	Richard Shepherd, Nick Nickell

MIXED PAIRS

1952	Mrs. Albert Shmukler, Norman Kay
1953	Kathleen McNutt, Rau Henry
1954	Ann Zachary, Mrs. Arthur Dye
1955	Mrs. John Kunkel, Richard Freeman
1956	Emily Folline, Herbert Gerst

OPEN PAIRS

1952	Sidney Silodor, John Crawford
1953	John Parish, Ben Johnson
1954	William Woodson, Bob Lovill, Jr.
1955	Robert Jordan, Bob Sitnek
1956	Robert Olson, Everett Gambill
1957	Al Roth, Betty Haddad
1958	Charlie Swaringen, Anita Swaringen
1959	Virginia Dye, Gene Whitehead
1960	Helen Clinkinbeard, Mrs. A. H. Fay
1961	Sidney Aronson, Marty Chaitt
1962	Algot Shrop, Mrs. Algot Shrop
1963	W. L. Williams, P. H. Wuille
1964	Robert Ling, Harold Dillenbeck
1965	Jamie Cobb, Boyce Robbins
1966	Margaret Wagar, Barry Crane
1967	Foxy Hall, Jerry Earley
1968	George Carter, Kay Carter
1969	James Lay, Jr., Fred Marshall
1970	Gregg Roberts, Larry Gould
1972	Steve Goldberg, Stephen Robinson
1973	Steve Parker, Lou Bluhm
1974	David Hoffner, Mark Shaw
1975	Mark Blumenthal, Garey Hayden
1976	Tom Rutledge, Jeff Stafford
1980	Dick Crump, William Williams, Jr.

Flight A:

1977	David Hoffner, Bill Pettis
1978	Elinor Murdoch, Dr. Charles Burnham
1979	Joe Auer, Mary Ann Comas
1980	Mrs. Louis G. Sullivan, Ron Cadora
1981	Fred Hamilton, Nancy Passell

Smoking:

1977	J. Richard Burton, Fred Strickland
1978	Robert Boyer, Robert Darling
1979	Joe McCabe, Randall Terry
1981	Leon Smith, Loren Axtell

Non-Smoking:

1977	Kal Weiss, Robert True
1978	David McClintock, Janet McClintock
1979	John Kimel, Sue Cooper
1981	Tom Rutledge, Jim Krekorian

MEN'S PAIRS

1952	R. L. Nelson, S. M. Epstein
1953	David Murray, Si Katz
1954	Herbert Gerst, Raymond Farber
1955	Alvin Roth, Said Haddad
1956	Wilfred Davis, Henry Deal
1957	Norman Berlin, Herbert Gerst
1958	Parks King, Jr., Wilfred Davis
1959	David Murray, Roy Banner
1960	Bryan Broadfoot, John Norwood
1961	John Norwood, Bryan Broadfoot
1962	Edmond Fleischer, Lionel Friedberg
1963	Walter Ridenour, J. C. Barefoot
1964	George Smith, Julian Slager
1965	Charlie Swaringen, Lee Thomas
1966	Peter Pender, Robert Sitnek
1967	James Masson, Ed Mendell
1968	Robert Lovill, Jr., Kenneth Anderson, Jr.
1969	Peter Lesnik, Dwight File
1970	Gregg Roberts, Fred Strickland
1972	C. Thomas, Henry Deal
1974	Gaylor Kasle, Garey Hayden
1976	Tom Rutledge, Jeff Stafford

WOMEN'S PAIRS

1952	Kay Rhodes, Louise Eisenman
1953	Margaret Alcorn, W. Howard
1954	Mannie Bayliss, Rena Rosenbloom
1955	Ruth Meyer, Sara Howard
1956	Frances Sydnor, Mrs. Joe Jackson, Jr.
1957	Mrs. Donald Epstein, Mrs. Harold Bernstein
1958	Connie Mitchell, Eleanor David
1959	Zelda Silverman, Margaret Pell
1960	Mrs. E. W. Cummings, Anita Swaringen

1961	H. E. Wagnon, J. Boone
1962	Ruth Rogasner, June O'Loughlin *(tied with)*
	Florence Roberts, Helen Philips
1963	Jane Carter, Pearle Schechter
1964	Mrs. M. B. Mowry, Lena Bailey
1965	Mrs. Edward Davis, Mrs. Baxter Haynes
1966	Mrs. Sol Mirsky, Lynn Pories
1967	Helen Clinkinbeard, Mrs. I. B. Cohen
1968	Maxine Lundin, Mannie Holmes
1969	Mrs. L. W. McIlhany, Polly Phetteplace
1970	Mrs. W. Hoffman, Mrs. R. Broughton
1972	Velma Lamp, Laura Maybin
1974	Nona Walker, Ruth Myers
1976	Sue Reeve, Mette Smith

MID-ATLANTIC SPRING

KNOCKOUT TEAMS

1973	Mary King, David Fisher,
	Bernard Warshauer, Bobby McMahan
1974	Clarence Goppert, Fred McBride, Gaylor Kasle,
	Garey Hayden, Mike Passell
1975	John Piaski, Nick Nickell,
	Mike Tierney, Lyle Ballentine
1976	Randy Joyce, David Smith,
	Alan Bell, Steve Swearingen
1977	Dave Smith, Richard Burton,
	Alan Bell, Phil Brady
1978	Les Bart, Lou Bluhm,
	Peter Boyd, Carol Sanders
1979	Tom Rutledge, Jeff Stafford,
	Ellen Allen, Larry Allen
1980	Jeff Meckstroth, Larry Sealy, Marilyn Miller,
	Kit Woolsey, Ed Manfield
1981	Curtis Smith, Bunny Haas,
	Don Baxter, John Herrmann

OPEN TEAMS

1957	Herah Coplon, Peggy Coplon,
	Ethel Marks, C. Johnson
1959	B. C. Morrow, Ike Wilson,
	Alan Current, Jr., John Warlick
1960	Rone Nordinger, Herbert Gerst,
	Hyman Silverman, Zelda Silverman
1961	Alfred Sheinwold, Ivar Stakgold, Louise Robinson,
	Richard Freeman, Andrew Gabrilovitch
1962	Louise Robinson, Sammy Kehela, Richard Freeman,
	William Williams, Dr. Robert Melton *(tied with)*
	Mrs. R. Richardson, William Woodson,
	Dr. Harold McDonald, Marvin Cowell
1963	Dr. Charles Hall, Jr., Mrs. Charles Hall, Foxy Hall,
	Reuben Smith, Col. James Day
1964	David Carter, Mabel Mahoney,
	Lyle Starr, John Griscom
1965	Leo Silverfield, Joan Bernard,
	Thomas Rutledge, Jr., Robert Fechter
1966	Charles Fulton, William Williams, Jr.
	R. Ashton, R. Glenn
1967	Mark Blumenthal, Walt Walvick, Leslie Popper,
	Mike Cappelletti, Kathie Cappelletti
1968	B. Jay Becker, Dorothy Hayden,
	Margaret Wagar, Barry Crane
1969	Ed Lazarus, Mark Blumenthal,
	Dave Treadwell, Walt Walvick
1970	Thomas Sanders, Carol Sanders,
	Martin Cohn, Betty Cohn
1971	Ellen Allen, Larry Allen,
	Charles Fulton, William Williams
1972	Mrs. L. Perdue, Amalee Grady,
	Mrs. Herbert Long, Mrs. T. Maurer *(tied with)*
	Wes Knight, Mike Hogan,
	George Fraction, Steve Cox *(and)*
	John Sheridan, Larry Kozlove,
	Norman Fischer, Tom Hodapp *(and)*
	Matt Granovetter, Ed Rogers,
	Richard Pavlicek, Fred Rubbra *(and)*
	Stephen Swearingen, Lou Bluhm,
	Tom Callaham, Randy Joyce
1973	Steve Goldberg, Jim Murphy,
	Lou Bluhm, Steve Robinson
1974	Kathy Reitz, Mrs. J. Ingram,
	Carroll Eckles, Mrs. F. Fister *(tied with)*
	Loren Axtell, Larry Griffey,
	Leon Smith, Bob Dennard *(and)*
	Cordette Wall, Mrs. J. Chapman,
	Mimi Little, Sidney Locke
1975	J. G. Biggers, D. Conner Collins,
	Morrill Hall, Charles Hubert
1976	Barry Crane, Dr. John Fisher, Thomas Sanders,
	Carol Sanders, Ron Smith

1977   Andy Bernstein, James Lay,
      Karen Thomas, Fred Rubbra
1979   E. L. Sutton, Connie Kafka,
      Pamela Powell, Jim Barrow
1981   David Hoffner, Larry Sealy,
      Paul Munafo, Mike Cappelletti

Smoking:
1978   Oswald Jacoby, Jim Jacoby, Del Parker,
      Dr. John Fisher, Jim Chew
1980   Bernard Warshauer, Genie Warshauer,
      Jeanne Stenger, Charles Stenger *(tied with)*
      Steve Smid, Thomas W. Daniel,
      Carolyn Watson, Suresh Mahajan *(and)*
      John Tate, Don Hammer,
      Jean Metelli, Janet McRorie *(and)*
      Andy Bernstein, Lynn Ware,
      James Lay, Paula Lay

Non-Smoking:
1978   Curtis Smith, Esta Van Zandt,
      Eddie Wold, Heitie Noland
1980   Bruce Parent, Janet Weyant,
      Ida Bennett, Ethel Keohane

OPEN PAIRS
1957   William Bell, William McCaskill
1959   George Cox, Sam Robinson, Jr.
1960   Margaret Fisher, Edward Allen
1961   Agnes Fischer, Manuel Weinberg
1962   Emanuel Kulbersh, Sophie Kulbersh
1963   Juanita Sauls, Isik Barin
1964   Joseph McCabe, Sr., Joseph McCabe, Jr.
1965   Lou Bluhm, Nancy Smith
1966   Ernest Reinstein, Rudy Rosenberger
1967   M. J. Welles, Jerry Deutschberger
1968   Bill McCallon, Bill Wick, Jr.
1969   Ellen Allen, Larry Allen
1970   Dr. Robert Melton, Lloyd Hetzer
1971   Ben Pope, Steve Gregory
1972   Ron Steele, Mrs. M. Mashburn
1973   Bobby McMahan, James Harris
1974   Dave Landers, John Fitzgerald
1975   Bobby Ledyard, Ron Smith
1976   John Griscom, Joe Kirkpatrick
1977   Tom Callaham, Frank King

Flight A:
1978   Robert Teel, Jane Teel
1979   Ron Perry, Robert Ling
1980   David Hoffner, Mike Cappelletti
1981   Chuck Said, Barbara Zander

Smoking:
1978   Brian Lipscomb, Jere Lipscomb
1979   Ed Schulte, Garland Ergüden
1980   Jim Felts, Keith Woolf
1981   Brooks McNeely, Cindy Marshall

Non-Smoking:
1978   Ed Schulte, Steve Robinson
1979   Roger Roemmich, Bob Bisplinghoff
1980   Doddie Harper, David Birnbaum
1981   Steve Swearingen, Doug Levene

MEN'S PAIRS
1959   W. Kilby Brown, Richard Glenn
1960   Hyman Silverman, Norman Berlin
1961   David Rosenbloom, Herman Kritzik
1963   Bobby Fechter, Bobby McMahan *(tied with)*
      Edwin Travis, T. M. Byar
1964   Frank Weisbach, Fred McBride
1965   Mike Michaels, Sidney Aronson
1966   Richard Glenn, Al Kenton
1967   Mark Blumenthal, Ed Lazarus *(tied with)*
      Dr. A. C. Current, C. D. Thomas, Jr.
1968   W. Edward Thomas, Jesse Hudson
1969   Steve Robinson, Tom Lyon
1970   Ray Kaiser, Jr., Steve Goldberg
1971   Douglas Hudgins, Richard Glenn
1972   Mike Moss, Don Faskow
1974   J. Andersen, John Thames
1975   Thomas Sanders, Barry Crane
1977   Hap Neuffer, Bernard Warshauer
1978   Joe Kivel, Ron Sukoneck
1980   Steve Robinson, Glenn Lublin
1981   John Griscom, David Strayhorn

WOMEN'S PAIRS
1957   Mrs. Neil Rodenberg, Helene Phillips
1959   Mrs. Darrell Sechrest, D. C. Wright
1960   Mrs. Frank Sims, Mrs. Jonathan Stott
1961   Margaret Wagar, Emily Folline
1963   Mrs. David Brown, Mrs. Julian Rountree
1964   Jo Reidelbach, Babe Meyer
1965   Mrs. D. C. Wright, Mrs. D. R. Dunlop
1966   Mrs. Frank Huffman, Marbeth DuBose
1967   Mrs. E. W. Cummings, Mrs. W. D. Fobert

1968   Ellen Barry, Ellen Allen
1969   Mrs. R. A. Small, June Berg
1970   Helen Peek, Mrs. Whitney Milner
1971   Mrs. J. Rhodes, Mrs. R. Critcher
1972   Mrs. L. Harleston, Ellen Allen
1974   Genevieve Long, Julie King
1976   Jane Clayton, Mrs. Byrl C. Logan
1977   Jane Clayton, Mrs. Byrl C. Logan
1978   Mrs. D. F. Crickmer, Mrs. J. E. McGee *(tied with)*
      Janet Weyant, Doris Fiorella *(and)*
      Judith Powers, Mrs. W. C. Lawrence
1980   Jane McCloin, Mrs. Byrl Logan
1981   Helen Clinkinbeard, Cindy Marshall

MASTER PAIRS
1956   Terry Michaels, Charles Lovenberg
1961   Alfred Sheinwold, Ivar Stakgold
1962   Boyd Hughes, Siddy Parr
1963   Rudolph Ashton, Richmond Hamilton
1964   Robert Sharp, Jo Sharp
1965   William Williams, Jr., Rudolph Ashton
1966   Larry Allen, Ellen Allen
1967   Steve Robinson, Jay Cohen
1968   Margaret Wagar, Barry Crane
1969   Earl Ryan, George Smith
1970   Bernadine Jenkins, Mrs. Hampton Hume
1971   Mrs. W. Latzell, Eric Norberg
1972   Paul Swanson, Gail Moss
1973   C. Thomas, Tom Van Zandt
1974   Mrs. H. Knight, Chuck Said
1975   Fred Hamilton, Alan Cohn
1976   Tom Callaham, Larry Long
1977   James Wall, Hugh C. Brown, Jr.

MIXED PAIRS
1956   J. R. Chappell, Jr., Mrs. J. R. Chappell
1957   Sara Howard, Herbert Gerst
1959   Alfred Stidham, Mrs. Alfred Stidham
1960   Beverly Torrey, S. W. Bliley
1961   Edward Harlow, Peggy Harlow
1963   Bob Bratcher, Mary Cocherell

MEN'S TEAMS
1956   Norman Berlin, Dr. Rudy Berlin, Ed Harlow,
      R. L. Miles, Jr., Wallace Jones
1957   Fred McBride, Charles Swaringen,
      Thomas Sanders, Hampton Hume

WOMEN'S TEAMS
1956   Lucy Rogers, Harriet Cole,
      Mrs. James Dearing, Mary Fairley

MID–ATLANTIC SUMMER

KNOCKOUT TEAMS
1971   Steve Goldberg, Richard Shepherd,
      Lou Bluhm, Larry Gould
1973   Jeff Stafford, Bill Pettis, Brian Moran,
      John Piaski, Nick Nickell
1974   A. E. (Bud) Reinhold, Larry Cohen,
      Dr. Richard Katz, Kerri Shuman
1975   Richard Freeman, Richard Shepherd, Gerald Popkin,
      Sammy Coolik, Clifford Russell, Larry Gould
1976   Mike Tierney, Richard Shepherd,
      Lou Bluhm, Steve Goldberg
1977   Ellen Allen, Larry Allen,
      Eleanor Turoff, David Leonard
1978   Cliff Russell, Sam Coolik, Richard Shepherd,
      Richard Freeman, Robert Hamman, Larry Gould
1979   A. E. (Bud) Reinhold, Robert Levin,
      Paul Lewis, Steve Goldberg
1980   Eddie Wold, Kit Woolsey, Jim Linhart,
      Polly Rich, Joe Davidson
1981   Eddie Wold, Peter Boyd, Polly Rich,
      Kit Woolsey, Kirk Benson

OPEN TEAMS
1971   Helen Clinkinbeard, Jake Clinkinbeard, Warren Roberts,
      Herbert Peters, Betty Peters
1973   Mary King, David Fisher,
      Richard Maybin, Laura Maybin *(tied with)*
      Albert Cox, Reid Jones,
      James Lay, Brooks McNeely
1974   Clarence Goppert, Gaylor Kasle, Garey Hayden,
      Mike Passell, Ron LaCour
1975   Larry Gould, Thomas Sanders,
      Carol Sanders, Lou Bluhm *(tied with)*
      Charles Smith, Larry Howard, Jr., Myra Howard,
      Bernadine Jenkins, Nancy Shackelford *(and)*
      John Piaski, Lyle Ballentine,
      Greg Roberts, Mike Tierney
1976   Richard Shepherd, Sam Coolik,
      Larry Gould, Dr. John Fisher *(tied with)*

Joe Adlersberg, Steve Goldberg, Joe Davidson,
Olin Hubert, Lucy Tillman
1977   Richard Guarneri, Edwin Wilson, Gloria Wilson,
J. M. Zucker, Mike McKee
1978   Lou Bluhm, Jim Linhart, Jim Barrow,
Carol Sanders, Bobby Levin
1979   David Hoffner, David Fenster,
Mike Cappelletti, Steve Goldberg
1980   Steve Goldberg, Mike Cappelletti,
Larry Sealy, David Fenster
1981   Grace Gabbai, Julian Gabbai,
Bill Passell, Richard Pavlicek

OPEN PAIRS
1971   Gerald Michaud, Lowell Yost
1973   Larry Kozlove, John Sheridan
1974   Fred McBride, Leo Bart
1975   Robert Teel, Jane Teel
1976   John Onstott, Judy Richardson
Flight A:
1978   Steve Swearingen, Bill Wisdom
1979   Bernie Yomtov, Jim Foster
1980   Larry Gould, Larry Kozlove
1981   Bill Wisdom, Steve Swearingen
Smoking:
1977   Ken Chatzinoff, Jack McArthur
1978   Gary Tinkley, Loren Axtell
1979   Richard Burton, Darwin Afdahl
1980   Cecil Head, Warren Roberts
1981   Richard Freeman, Clifford Russell
Non-Smoking:
1977   David Strasberg, Kirk Benson
1978   Curtis Cheek, Jeff Johnson
1979   Salil Das, Steve Beatty
1980   Eddie Wold, Polly Rich
1981   Nick Nickell, Peter Boyd

MASTER PAIRS
1971   Tom Hodapp, Norman Fischer
1973   James Jacoby, Heitie Noland
1974   Barry Crane, Dr. John Fisher
1975   Richard Freeman, Clifford Russell
1976   Russ Arnold, Robert Levin
1977   James Downs, Eddie Wold

MASTER/NATIONAL MASTER PAIRS
1979   Sue Wood, Josephine Foster *(tied with)*
Paul H. Betts, Knox Wood

SENIOR MASTER PLUS PAIRS
1979   Emory Whitaker, Aubrey Garrison

WOMEN'S PAIRS
1971   Carol Sanders, Bette Cohn
1973   Phyllis Novak, Mrs. P. Ambery
1975   Ann Shauer, Ann Badgett
1976   Margaret Peabody, Jean Kerr *(tied with)*
Ann Roberts, Louise McNider
1977   Janet O'Neal, Jan Steen
1978   Ann Pettit, Genne Winter
1979   Ellen Allen, Eleanor Turoff
1980   Marinesa Letizia, Shirley Hill
1981   Hilda Slager, Madonna Wolke

MEN'S PAIRS
1971   Jerry Earley, John Dodd
1973   Jim Felts, Leonard Spilman
1975   Jeffrey Sparks, Tom Youngblood
1976   Jeff Overby, David Hoffner *(tied with)*
Milton Stern, Mike Passell
1977   Thomas Sanders, Marty Cohn
1978   Lou Bluhm, Jim Linhart
1979   Dr. Saeed Maghsoodloo, Darrell Penrod
1980   Jim Felts, John Griscom
1981   Ronald Babcock, Rod Colville

MID-ATLANTIC THANKSGIVING

KNOCKOUT TEAMS
1972   Martin Cohn, Sam Coolik, Nick Nickell,
Steve Swearingen, Warren Roberts

OPEN TEAMS
1972   Jerry Popkin, Frank Garson, Tom Rutledge,
Joyce Simmons, Steve Swearingen *(tied with)*
Larry Gould, Steve Goldberg, Lou Bluhm,
Richard Shepherd, Steve Robinson

OPEN PAIRS
1972   Carol Sanders, Sam Coolik

MEN'S PAIRS
1972   Dr. John Fisher, Gunther Polak

WOMEN'S PAIRS
1972   Carol Sanders, Bette Cohn

MID-ATLANTIC WINTER

KNOCKOUT TEAMS
1972   Mary King, David Fisher,
Bernard Warshauer, Genie Means
1973   Annette Barrett, Julie Murphy, Walter Murphy,
Russ Arnold, George Mahaffee, Ron LaCour
1974   Ed Collins, Lou Bluhm, Richard Shepherd,
Brian Moran, Jim Looby
1975   Larry Allen, Ellen Allen, Mary King,
David Fisher, Tom Rutledge, Joan Bernard
1976   Tom Rutledge, Larry Allen,
Ellen Allen, Joan Bernard
1977   David Hoffner, David Schroeder,
Andy Bernstein, Garland Ergüden
1978   Peter Boyd, Lou Bluhm, Les Bart,
Thomas Sanders, Carol Sanders, Jeff Corbin
1979   Tom Rutledge, Richard Guarneri,
Genie Warshauer, Bernard Warshauer
1980   Fred White, Mark McLaughlin,
John Cotty, Charles Davis
1981   Larry Allen, Ellen Allen,
Lyle Ballentine, Tom Rutledge

OPEN TEAMS
1965   R. L. (Skinny) Miles, Norman Berlin, Jack Hudgins,
Richard Freeman, Louise Freeman
1966   Jeremy Flint, Peter Pender,
Sidney Aronson, Mark Blumenthal
1967   Steve Catlett, Dick Hamilton,
Bill Wick, Jr., Bill McCullom
1968   Roy Govan, Dennis Heller,
Day Pruitt, Lou Bluhm
1969   Walt Walvick, Dave Treadwell,
Mark Blumenthal, Steve Lapides
1970   Elise Pinckney, Charles Brown,
Hudson Edwards, Tony Devereau
1971   Charles Swaringen, Anita Swaringen,
Patty Randall, Arthur Foreman *(tied with)*
Mrs. Blaine Miller, Jane Felton,
Lillie Copses, Morty Garber
1972   Edward Gay, William Howe,
Evelyn Mason, Dick Wittrup *(tied with)*
Ken Anderson, Lyle Ballentine,
Joe McCabe, Lou Bluhm *(and)*
Art Raeuber, Mrs. L. Galloway, Fred Harb,
Mrs. W. Bomar, James Ferguson
1973   Larry Kozlove, John Sheridan,
Mark Blumenthal, Mark Lair
1974   Leon Smith, Larry Griffey,
Loren Axtell, Bob Dennard
1975   Jack Blair, Paul Swanson,
Fred McBride, Richard Shepherd
1976   Bob Flechter, Denise Murphy,
Seavy O'Neal, Jr., Ivan Aralica *(tied with)*
David Hoffner, Bill Pettis,
Peter Boyd, Steve Swearingen *(and)*
W. F. Howard, Jr., John Kennedy, Jr.,
Dorothy Weigland, M. J. Johnson, Jr.
1977   Richard Shepherd, Sam Coolik,
Lou Bluhm, Larry Gould
1978   Steve Goldberg, Jo Morse, Steve Robinson,
John Fisher, Gary Hann
1979   Steve Goldberg, Ed Lewis, Olin Hubert,
John Potter, Russell Griest
1980   Fred White, David Hall,
Mark McLaughlin, Charles Davis
1981   Randy Joyce, Steve Swearingen, Bill Wisdom,
Jeff Sparks, Phil Brady

OPEN PAIRS
1965   Mark Blumenthal, Sidney Aronson
1966   Ray Wilhide, Charles Boteler
1967   Julian Adler, Jr., Betty Adler
1968   Bill Flannery, Paul Swanson
1969   William Williams, Jr., Joseph Greiner
1970   Ed Mendell, James Masson
1971   Margaret Wagar, Roy Govan
1972   Steve Swearingen, Joyce Simmons
1973   Larry Gould, Lou Bluhm
1974   David Fisher, Bob Fechter
1975   Gloria Wilson, J. M. Zucker
1976   Les Bart, Richard Shepherd
1977   Peggy McLean, A. F. McLean
1978   Jeff Sparks, Randy Joyce
1979   Jeff Sparks, Randy Joyce
Flight A:
1979   Phil Brady, Olin Hubert
1980   Robert Hertzberg, Gary Gordon
1981   Bill Wisdom, Sue Cooper
Smoking:
1980   J. Richard Burton, David Smith

1981   Tom Rutledge, Jeff Stafford *(tied with)*
      Walter Reeves, Chuck Whidden
Non-Smoking:
1980   David Kogut, Rhett Inabinet
1981   Steve Robinson, Peter Boyd

MEN'S PAIRS
1966   Jeremy Flint, Peter Pender
1967   Ronald Schreiber, George Kaufman
1968   Lou Bluhm, Roy Govan
1969   Randy Joyce, Steve Swearingen
1970   Steve Goldberg, Martin Cohn
1971   Fred Rubbra, Jim Linhart *(tied with)*
      Norman Schwartz, Stephen Robinson
1973   Barry Crane, John Fisher
1975   Israel Rubin, Andy Bernstein

WOMEN'S PAIRS
1966   Adele Kotzen, Belle Kaufman
1967   Nancy Gruver, Edith Sachs
1968   Mrs. E. C. McMahan, Mrs. B. M. Lanford
1969   Mrs. E. W. Cummings, Mrs. W. D. Fobert
1970   Mrs. G. Murray, Mrs. G. McKneely
1971   Ellen Barry, Ellen Allen *(tied with)*
      Mrs. W. Thompson, Lucille Ingram
1973   Laura Maybin, Mary King
1975   Mrs. D. Ruben, Merian Meekins

MASTER PAIRS
1965   Dr. Charles Duffy, William Williams, Jr.
1966   Henry Gould, Mrs. Henry Gould
1968   Richard Freeman, Louise Freeman
1969   Dell Thompson, Kal Grunwald
1970   Fran James, Dottie Turner
1971   Norman Berlin, Steve Catlett
1972   Robert Loville, Lyle Ballentine
1973   Barry Crane, Thomas Sanders
1974   N. Crawford, Patty Randall
1975   Genie Means, Bernard Warshauer
1976   Genie Means, Bernard Warshauer
1977   Larry Allen, Ellen Allen
1978   John Fisher, Gary Hann

MIXED PAIRS
1967   Ronald Schreiber, Anne Wilhide

DISTRICT 8   (Illinois except Chicago area, eastern Missouri, western Kentucky, northern Indiana)

CHAMPAGNE

OPEN PAIRS
1967   Eunice Rosen, Paul Sugar
1968   Gerald Caravelli, Milt Rosenberg
1969   John Wachter, Gunther Polak
1970   Eleanor Crounse, Mrs. Elmer Novak
1971   Michael Mueller, Alex Cieslak
1972   Florine Walters, Henry Rabin
1973   Gerald Caravelli, Jeffrey Mandell
1974   Gilbert Morell, Stanley Collier
1975   Richard Halperin, Sheldon Kahn
1976   Ed Rees, Steve Crutcher
1977   Steve Rose, Stan Katz
1978   Jerry Goldfein, John Lindsey *(tied with)*
      Eric Rodwell, Jeff Meckstroth
1980   Leo Rodenborn, Buz Zeman
1981   Jack Stein, Joan Stein
Flight A:
1979   Hugh MacLean, Jerry Welander
1980   Dr. Andrea Rothbart, Garrett Nash
1981   Wayne Snider, Jerry Goldfein

MASTER PAIRS
Flight A:
1970   Jack LaNoue, Robert Pitard
1971   Dave Nicklasson, Larry Oakey
1972   Norman Ehrlich, David Smith
1973   Milt Rosenberg, Gerald Caravelli
1974   Gerald Caravelli, Dr. John Fisher
1975   Gunther Polak, Cheri Bjerkan
1976   Dr. John Fisher, Arnold Leavitt
1977   Jack Oest, Robert Sundby
1978   Don Steinke, Dennis Clerkin
1979   Bill Hale, Dave Bondy
1980   Kurt Mundinger, Frank Yoder
1981   Claire Anderson, Craig Gardner

OPEN TEAMS
1967   Bob Cruise, Gerald Caravelli,

      Milt Rosenberg, Donald Rutstein
1968   Sandi Leavitt, Paul Sugar,
      Anthony Astrologes, Henry Rabin
1969   Dr. Richard Katz, Larry Cohen,
      Andy Schmidt, Joyce Schmidt
1970   Charles Tidball, Murray Sorg,
      Mrs. Richard Moore, Larry Wieser
1971   Barry Crane, Gerald Caravelli,
      Larry Cohen, Milt Rosenberg
1972   Edgar Singleton, Jr., Donald Jordan,
      Philip Slatt, Fred Binder, Jr.
1973   Robin Grantham, John Grantham,
      Clarence Goppert, Garey Hayden
1974   Bud Reinhold, Dr. Richard Katz, Larry Cohen,
      Kerri Shuman, Barry Crane, Bobby Wolff

SWISS TEAMS
1975   Dr. John Fisher, Gerald Caravelli, Milton Rosenberg,
      Larry Kozlove, John Sheridan
1976   Larry Robbins, Kent Feiler,
      Marge Vonesh, Alex Weiland
1977   Dr. John Fisher, Jerry Goldfein, Gerald Caravelli,
      Milton Rosenberg, Mark Cohen
1978   Alan Susskind, Sheldon Kahn, Jim Bjerkan, Flo Walters,
      Cheri Bjerkan, Larry Gould *(tied with)*
      Bill Doroshow, Tony Astrologes,
      Marvin Shapiro, Tod Moses
1979   Tom Webb, Robert Coyne,
      Peter Elliott, Edgar Gentry
1980   Eric Rodwell, Marc Jacobus, Jeff Meckstroth,
      Gaylor Kasle, Marie Arnall
Flight A:
1981   Bill Doroshow, Ed Schultz,
      Bob Meyer, Tod Moses

KNOCKOUT TEAMS
1974   Bud Reinhold, Dr. Richard Katz,
      Larry Cohen, Bobby Wolff
1976   Eric Rodwell, Jerry Goldfein, Claude Vogel,
      Mark Cohen, Harvey Miller Jr., Richard Halperin
1977   Claude Vogel, Jeff Meckstroth, Mark Cohen,
      Larry Mori, Jerry Goldfein
1979   Gary Hann, Zeke Jabbour,
      Alan Bell, Colby Vernay
1980   Gaylor Kasle, Marc Jacobus, Jeff Meckstroth,
      Marie Arnall, Eric Rodwell
1981   Barry Crane, Craig Janitschke,
      Billy Rosen, Eunice Rosen

WOMEN'S PAIRS
1967   Frieda Arst, June Deutsch
1968   Frieda Arst, June Deutsch
1969   Virginia Heckel, Joan DeWitt
1970   Mrs. M. Soffer, Lois Epstein
1971   Amelia Argersinger, Margaret Wagar
1972   Mary Ann Miller, Petra Doran
1973   Bev Merida, Carla Heimer
1974   Grace Grant, Marguerite Stracke
1976   Beverly Nelson, Janet Weyant
1977   Janet Weyant, Beverly Nelson
1979   Fran Pettijohn, Patti Sundstrom
1980   Claire Calahan, Emilie Anderson

MEN'S PAIRS
1967   Herman Bud, John Chmielowiec
1968   Dick Lawrence, Robert Esch
1969   Berman Coleman, Larry Oakey
1970   Hugh MacLean, Ron Andersen
1971   Marshall Spitz, Keith Hanson
1972   John Hermann, Steve Goldberg
1973   David Smith, Bob Jackson
1974   Cy Dennen, James Jacoby
1976   Claude Vogel, Hal Mouser
1977   Leo Weiner, David Adams
1979   Eric Rodwell, Jeff Meckstroth
1980   Glenn Smith, Stephen Brauss

MIXED PAIRS
1967   Mrs. William Stein, David Cook
1968   John Zilic, Delores Witte
1969   Frieda Arst, Jack Wachter
1978   Paula Butler, Charles Eisenberg

INDIVIDUAL
1978   Kathryn Maloney

MEN'S SWISS TEAMS
1979   Mike Williams, Glenn Fidler,
      Alan Gregory Travel, Jack Fife
1981   Barry Crane, Craig Janitschke,
      Billy Rosen, Milt Rosenberg

WOMEN'S SWISS TEAMS
1979   Jil Emerson, Charlotte Miller,,
      Helen Otti, Jean Evans *(tied with)*
      June Deutsch, Frieda Arst,

Sue Halperin, Cheri Bjerkan
1981   Doreen Adelmann, Helen Haeckel,
      Lil Lintzenich, Sylvia Abramson

DISTRICT 8

SWISS TEAMS
1975   Paul Sugar, Gunther Polak,
      Sandi Leavitt, Arnold Leavitt
1977   Jim Letts, Bob Evans,
      C. Holcomb, Yvonne Ellison
1978   Jeff Meckstroth, Eric Rodwell,
      Rony Adelsman, Hal Mouser
1979   Jack Bryant, Tom Kniest, Patrick Arnall,
      Steve Brauss, Colby Vernay
1980   Vicki Neiberg, Zeke Jabbour, Susan Ganley,
      Jeff Meckstroth, Eric Rodwell
1981   Kimmel Jones, David Heimer,
      Steven Rose, Gary Kessler

OPEN PAIRS
1975   Mark Blumenthal, Larry Kozlove
1977   Ron Andersen, Hugh MacLean
1978   Hal Mouser, Jeff Meckstroth
1979   Terry James, Ed Schultz
1980   Ida Bennett, David Gadd
1981   Bill Rosen, Milt Rosenberg

MASTER PAIRS
1975   Ron Smith, Tony Astrologes *(tied with)*
      Gunther Polak, Arnold Leavitt
1977   Hugh MacLean, Tony Astrologes
1978   Bob Glenn, Robert Hayes
1979   Carol Schaffer, Patrick Arnall
1980   Roger Jourdan, Jim Barrow
1981   Bob Evans, Carolyn Holcomb

WOMEN'S PAIRS
1978   Sue Halperin, Cheri Bjerkan
1979   Anne Leverone, Carol Schaffer
1980   Ida Bennett, Ethel Keohane

WOMEN'S SWISS TEAMS
1981   Sandi Leavitt, Cheri Bjerkan,
      June Deutsch, Sue Halperin

MEN'S PAIRS
1978   Gordon Sparks, Harvey Miller
1979   Jerry Clerkin, Dennis Clerkin
1980   Dennis McGarry, Richard Huggard

MEN'S SWISS TEAMS
1981   Roger Lord, Robert Cooper,
      Jerry Schneider, Alan Bell

BOARD-A-MATCH SWISS TEAMS
1978   Bob Gardner, Steve Alpern,
      Jerry Goldfein, Amin Karim

KNOCKOUT TEAMS
1979   Roger Jourdan, Ed Schulte,
      Jim Barrow, Madelynn Carmichael

MASTER SWISS TEAMS
1980   Roger Jourdan, Jim Barrow,
      Norm Combs, Tom Hodapp

MISSISSIPPI VALLEY

WOMEN'S PAIRS
1952   Mildred Cytron, Martha Newbill
1953   Mildred Cytron, Martha Newbill
1954   Frances Carter, R.A. Jervis
1955   Sarah Amster, JoAnn Brumfiel
1956   L.W. Rigney, Mrs. A.H. Wilks, Jr.
1957   Dot Scoggin, Mrs. Jerome Wilson
1958   C.G. Cody, Liz Gerbig
1959   Gertrude Wolfe, Jean Gray
1960   Julia Halloran, Frances Carter
1961   Carol Sanders, Dee Adams
1962   Mrs. H. Leo Levin, Isabelle Carlson
1963   Ruth Steinberg, Carolyn Levitt
1964   Ruth Steinberg, Carolyn Levitt
1965   Carol Sanders, Jane Rosenschein
1966   Eunice Bloom, Aralyn Rosenberg
1967   Mrs. H. Leo Levin, Lillian Goodman
1968   Elaine Gordon, Mrs. Charles Buckner
1969   Mildred Bright, Ruth Steinberg
1970   Ruth McConnell, Mrs. Elmer Novak
1971   Liz Stelzer, Sandy Roberts
1972   Mildred Bright, Ruth Steinberg
1973   Jacqueline Sincoff, Rose Kramer
1974   Mrs. R. Loewenstein, Phillis Brown Collins

1975   Pauline Dombrausky, Ethel Kaufman
1976   Mildred Bright, Ruth Steinberg
1977   Eunice Rosen, Joan DeWitt
1978   Eunice Rosen, Aralyn Rosenberg
1979   June Singer, Sally Greenblatt
1980   Mary Rackers, Darlyne Grannemann
1981   Carol Krehbiel, Ruth McConnell

MEN'S PAIRS
1951   George Rosenschein, Leo Weiner
1952   Milton Ellenby, Bart Kaufman
1953   Dave Goldberg, Leo Weiner
1954   Milton Bierbaum, Barrett Stephenson
1955   Alan Harvey, Jr., J.G. Ripstra
1956   I. Schwab, Leo Weiner
1957   Oswald Jacoby, Alan Bell
1958   Philip Feldacker, David Carter
1959   Barry Crane, James Epstein
1960   James Epstein, Thomas Sanders
1961   Monte Lopata, Max Heller
1962   Larry Kolker, Jerry Levitt
1963   Larry Kolker, Jerry Levitt
1964   Curtis Smith, Nate Silverstein
1965   Fred Ensminger, Ben Matthews
1966   James Epstein, Gunther Polak
1967   Max Heller, David Carter
1968   Joseph Nieberding, Frank Weisbach
1969   Dr. G.H. Berndsen, Dean Williams
1970   Monte Lopata, Max Heller
1971   Chuck Said, Dr. Peter Volpe
1972   Garey Hayden, Roger Bates
1973   David Carter, Roger Lord
1974   John Rosenschein, Bill Muir
1975   Clyde Hassebrock, Steve Bloom
1976   David Carter, Roger Lord
1977   Ira Barrows, Joseph Livezey
1978   Ed Schulte, Ron Smith
1979   Jerry Levitt, Jerry Schneider
1980   Colby Vernay, Tom Kniest
1981   Paul Soloway, Mike Albert

OPEN PAIRS
1951   Arthur Kincaid, Isadore Rosenberg
1952   Margaret Wagar, David Carter
1953   David Carter, Jerry Levitt
1954   Milton Ellenby, Gloria Turner
1955   Alan Harvey, Jr., Frank Weisbach
1956   John Hubbell, Walter Gilbert
1957   Alan Mariam, Carolyn Levitt
1958   Curtis Smith, James Epstein
1959   Gloria Turner, Emanuel Hochfeld
1960   Robert Sharp, Barry Crane
1961   Garrett Nash, Jerry Levitt
1962   Robert Sharp, Barry Crane
1963   Eunice Rosen, Adelaide Simon
1964   Barry Crane, James Epstein
1965   Robert Sharp, Louise Clark
1966   Ross Amann, Kit Woolsey
1967   Barry Crane, Grant Marsee
1968   Henry Rabin, Sandra Rabin
1969   Patrick Arnall, Thomas Kniest
1970   Don Faskow, Paul Swanson
1971   Barry Crane, Gerald Caravelli
1972   Donald Rutstein, Jeffrey Mandell
1973   Susan Graves, Tom Hodapp
1974   Barry Crane, Gerald Caravelli
1975   Barry Crane, Gerald Caravelli
1976   Richard Halperin, Sheldon Kahn
1977   Sandi Leavitt, Kent Feiler
1978   Betty Bloom, Steve Bloom
1979   Ron Wolf, Earl Bennett
1980   Betty Bloom, Steve Bloom
1981   Gerald Caravelli, Billy Cohen
Flight A:
1978   Jeff Meckstroth, Eric Rodwell
1979   Ron Smith, Billy Cohen
1981   Esta Van Zandt, James Zimmerman

MASTER PAIRS
1959   Adelaide Simon, Robert Sharp
1966   James Jacoby, Bud Trenholm
1967   Larry Kolker, David Carter
1968   Bud Creed, Vicki Davis
1969   Richard Christensen, Mrs. Richard Christensen
1970   Donald Cammarata, Robert McClintock
1971   Chuck Said, Dr. Peter Volpe
1972   Ed Schulte, Jr., Jack Spear
1973   Harvey Miller, Jr., Joe Weiner
1974   Elizabeth Lester, Berniece Larson
1975   Babs Charney, Joan Stein
1977   David Siebert, Allan Siebert
1979   Marc Jacobus, Paul Lewis
1980   Colby Vernay, Alan Bell

1981   Paul Lewis, Ron Smith
Flight A:
1976   Grace Grant, Catherine Roebuck
1978   Carol Sanders, Mary Beth Townsend
       SWISS TEAMS
1975   Phil Warden, Steve Bloom,
       Steve Reuschlein, Betty Crowther
1976   Greg DeFotis, Jeff Mandell, Larry Kozlove,
       Kathy Blumenthal, Mark Blumenthal
1977   Jerry Levitt, Lionel Kalish,
       Ernest Stein, Alvin Novack
1978   Mike Passell, Jim Barrow, J.L. Mallett
       Jeff Meckstroth, Robert Levin
1979   Ron Smith, Paul Lewis,
       Billy Cohen, Marc Jacobus
1980   Ron Smith, Billy Cohen, Roger Jourdan,
       Jim Barrow, Jeff Meckstroth, Eric Rodwell
Flight A:
1980   Jeff Meckstroth, Eric Rodwell, Eddie Wold,
       Gaylor Kasle, Marilyn Miller
1981   Barry Crane, Gerald Caravelli, Esta Van Zandt,
       James Zimmerman, Craig Janitschke
       KNOCKOUT TEAMS
1978   Alan Bell, Tom Kniest, Bryan Maksymetz,
       Colby Vernay, Jerry Schneider
1979   Ron Smith, Billy Cohen, Paul Lewis,
       Marc Jacobus, Brenda Blumenthal
1980   Tom Kniest, Ed Schulte,
       Colby Vernay, Alan Bell
1981   Mel Skolnik, Eric Rodwell, Billy Cohen,
       Ron Smith, Jeff Meckstroth
       OPEN TEAMS
1951   Gloria Turner, Milton Ellenby,
       Emanual Hochfeld, William Grieve
1952   J.G. Ripstra, Isadore Rosenberg,
       John Hubbell, Arthur Kincaid
1953   Carolyn Benjamin, Ruth Steinberg
       Alan Marian, Curtis Smith *(tied with)*
       Oswald Jacoby, James Jacoby, Albert Weiss,
       Joe Cohan, John Simon
1954   Pat Ochs, Charles Wiley,
       James Epstein, Robert Woodworth
1955   James Epstein, David Carter,
       Pat Ochs, Charles Wiley *(tied with)*
       George Rosenschein, Jane Rosenschein,
       Mrs. Joseph Johnson, Joseph Johnson
1956   Sidney Lazard, Bill Hanna, Frank Bombeck,
       James Jacoby, Oswald Jacoby
1957   Eddie Melchior, Lillian Tiller,
       Rose Groves, Curtis Finch
1958   Robert Nail, Betty Nail,
       Thomas Sanders, Carol Sanders
1959   Pat Ochs, Bob McClintock, George Runtz,
       Mrs. Jerry Levitt, Jerry Levitt
1960   Mrs. Richard Braznell, Richard Braznell
       Ann Smith, Jerome Wilson
1961   Manny Hochfeld, Ivor Stakgold,
       Gloria Turner, Monroe Ingberman
1962   Leo Weiner, Garret Nash, Pat Ochs,
       Larry Kolker, Charles Wiley
1963   David Carter, Gerald Michaud, Oswald Jacoby,
       Mary Zita Jacoby, Paul Levitt
1964   Fred Rubbra, Homer Shoop, Msgr. Walter Leach,
       John Moran, Chuck Henke
1965   Robert Sharp, Nate Silverstein, George Treadwell,
       Mildred Bright, Mike Thomas
1966   Gaylor Kasle, Curtis Smith,
       Charles Kittle, Rae Kittle
1967   Barry Crane, Grant Marsee,
       William Rosen, Gunther Polak
1968   Dr. Michael Thomas, Gunther Polak,
       Jack Blair, Don Williams
1969   Philip Sincoff, Ed Melchior,
       Marty Cohn, Andy McNeiley
1970   Michael Ledeen, Henry Bethe,
       Don Faskow, Paul Swanson
1971   Barry Crane, Gerald Caravelli,
       Milt Rosenberg, Howard Perlman
1972   Donald Rutstein, Jeff Mandell,
       Alex Weiland, Carey Yelton
1973   Jerry Schneider, Nell Schneider,
       Charles Wiley, Ethel Wiley
1974   Alan Susskind, Moshe Bernstein,
       Wayne Snider, Steve Rose

DISTRICT 9   (Florida, Puerto Rico)

CENTRAL FLORIDA

       SWISS TEAMS
1976   Leon Smith, Larry Griffey,
       Bob Dennard, Steve Hayskar
1977   Tubby Stayman, Sam Stayman, Matt Granovetter,
       Victor Mitchell, Jacqui Mitchell
1978   Robert Teel, Jane Teel,
       Barbara Whalen, Patricia Murphy
1979   Jack Schwencke, Allan Cokin,
       Neil Chambers, John Schermer
1980   Carol Krehbiel, Dennis Clerkin,
       Paul Munafo, Andy Bernstein
Smoking:
1981   Nat Agran, Art Samuels,
       Pat Samuels, Stanley Fenkel *(tied with)*
       George Drake, Helen Drake,
       Helen Welti, Homer Shoop
Non-Smoking:
1981   Cliff Russell, Jim Becker,
       Joel Friedberg, Howard Chandross *(tied with)*
       Milton Lunden, Sidney Reider,
       Muriel Lunden, T. Lindenberg *(and)*
       Joe Steuer, Marie Louise Steuer,
       Harold Tannen, Mary Virginia Southwell
       BOARD-A-MATCH TEAMS
1976   Leon Smith, Larry Griffey,
       Bob Dennard, Steve Hayskar
       OPEN PAIRS
1976   Alice Gerard, Jeff Stafford
1977   Mark Cohen, Bette Grandoff
1978   Sam Stayman, Richard Reiseg
1979   Harold Feldstein, Gretchen Feldstein
1980   Randy Baron, Mark Yeager
Flight A:
1979   Irving Kass, Emanuel Katz,
1980   Ron Smith, Julie Cook
1981   Paul Soloway, Jose Lichtenberg
Smoking:
1981   Duke Edwards, Mike Tierney
Non-Smoking:
1981   Earl Becker, Jay Cohodes
       MASTER PAIRS
1976   Jill Denny, Jack Denny
1977   Carol Ohmann, Michael Grunstein
1978   Shirlee Lazarus, William Passell *(tied with)*
       Curtis Smith, Cliff Russell
1981   Jose Lichtenberg, Mike Passell
       UNMIXED PAIRS
1976   Kirk Benson, David Strasberg
       MIXED PAIRS
1977   David Strasberg, Jean Frankel
1978   Rita Seamon, William Seamon
1979   Paul Lewis, Brenda Blumenthal
1980   Edith Kemp, Jim Barrow
       INDIVIDUAL
1977   H. Feingold
1978   Velma Kinchley
1979   Cassius Peacock, Jr.
1980   Iva Warner
       MEN'S PAIRS
1977   R. L. Piper, H. N. Moore
1978   Frank Whiteley, William McCorquodale
1979   Emanuel Katz, Robert Abeles
1980   Tom Mahaffey, Ron Smith
1981   Sam Marsh, Larry Blum
       WOMEN'S PAIRS
1977   Jean Frankel, Shirlee Lazarus
1978   Edith Kemp, Ardis Heiman
1979   Madelynn Carmichael, Georgette King
1980   Jo Baker, Janet Moore
1981   Muffie Thyrre, Carol Cushing
       KNOCKOUT TEAMS
1980   Tom Mahaffey, Jack Denny,
       Ron Smith, Robert Levin
       MEN'S SWISS TEAMS
1981   Morrie Elis, Richard Coren, Art Coren,
       Irving Guttman, Jack Schwencke *(tied with)*
       Larry Blum, Daniel Oken,
       Robert Abeles, Sam Marsh
       WOMEN'S SWISS TEAMS
1981   Ruth Weinstein, Adele Seidman,
       Gladys Newman, Charlotte Grant *(tied with)*
       Sylvia Grossman, Jacqueline Smith,
       Beverly Luedecke, Susan Cashin

FLORIDA

KNOCKOUT TEAMS
1967 Robert Woodworth, William Stickney,
  Alice Gerard, Al Bricklin
1968 Harry Fishbein, Phil Feldesman, Sam Katz,
  Robert Sharp, Fred Hirsch, Hal Fein
1969 Cliff Russell, Russ Arnold,
  Curtis Smith, Robert Reynolds
1970 Richard Halperin, Sue Halperin, Jack Denny,
  Anthony Astrologes, Tom Mahaffey
1972 Alice Gerard, Jayne Thomas,
  Lois Wiley, Kent Wiley
1973 Mrs. William Loudermilk, Carolyn Lea,
  Dennis Hogan, Myra Hogan
1974 Leon Smith, Larry Griffey,
  Armand Barfus, Bob Dennard
1979 Bud Reinhold, Richard Pavlicek,
  Russ Arnold, Steve Goldberg
1980 Eddie Wold, Cliff Russell, Roger Jourdan,
  Jim Barrow, Joel Friedberg, Bill Passell
1981 Marcia Greenstein, Mrs. B. DeYoung, Annette Barrett,
  Bob Reynolds, George Rhode

MEN'S TEAMS
1959 Sam Katz, John Kunkel,
  Robert Appleyard, Fred Blackmon
1960 John Kunkel, Sam Katz, Fred Hirsch,
  Fred Blackmon, Robert Appleyard
1961 Harry Braverman, Leland Ferer,
  Robert Reynolds, William Seamon
1962 Harold Harkavy, Cliff Russell, Dave Warner,
  Charles Kuhn, Russ Arnold

WOMEN'S TEAMS
1959 V. L. Carlson, Mrs. Dwight Freeman,
  Phyllis Spitz, Lois McCord
1960 Ruby Slentz, Mrs. Sam Royal,
  Louise Hillegass, Mrs. Milton Hudson
1961 Virginia Alderman, Alice Gerard,
  Mrs. A. B. White, Sally Saron
1962 Carrie Arnold, Neva Gray,
  Betty Champion, Elsie Abrams

LIFE MASTER PAIRS
1967 Cliff Russell, Edith Kemp
1968 George Awad, Marie Awad
1969 James Brenner, Ron Schoenau
1970 Hal Raymond, Mary Lee Berg
1971 Louise Mowbry Sharp, Bob Sharp
1972 Ken Cohen, Helen Smith
1973 Angeline O'Grady, Betty Moore
1974 Ed Schulte, Robert Woodworth
1975 Fred Hamilton, Tom Gardner

MASTER PAIRS
1959 John Kunkel, William Seamon
1960 Chester Whitebrook, Howard Rosene
1961 Mrs. Abner Barr, Mrs. Sidney Kirtland
1962 Edith Kemp, Cliff Russell
1963 Jack Schwenke, John Donnell Bacon
1964 Art Lefkowitz, Ronald Schoenau
1965 Mrs. I. Rayburn, Tom Dean
1966 Mrs. C. Flattery, Blanche Englander
1967 Oliver Goddard, Nettie Lazarus
1968 George Barrs, Richard Pavlicek
1969 Frank Babiarz, John Saville
1970 Frank Babiarz, Jo Schachtman
1971 Paul Bernstein, Kent Boyle
1972 William Murphy, Mrs. William Murphy
1973 Paul Graegin, Barbara Graegin
1974 Mrs. W. P. McDonald, Mrs. W. N. Robinson
1975 A. D. Holness, S. N. Mahfood

OPEN PAIRS
1960 Joyce Simmons, Gloria Wilson
1961 Leland Ferer, Gratian Goldstein
1962 Mike Michaels, Russ Arnold
1963 John Schwenke, John Donnell Bacon
1964 Edith Kemp, Robert Reynolds
1965 Robert Rothlein, Mrs. Robert Rothlein
1966 Ruth Mitchell, Phil Carson
1967 Ted Horning, Frieda Horning,
1968 Art Lefkowitz, Armand Barfus
1969 Mike Passell, Jim Barrow
1970 Armand Barfus, Richard Schwartz
1971 Mrs. J. F. Law, Jr., Leon Auerbach
1972 Glenn Merrill, Genne Winter
1973 Terry Teague, Mrs. Terry Teague
1974 George Mitchell, Happoldt Neuffer
1975 Charles Heine, Genevieve Heine
1976 Daniel Oken, Louise Sharp
1977 Robert Teel, Jane Teel
1978 Martha Newbill, Dr. John Fisher
1979 Larry Auerbach, Jeff Overby

Flight A:
1977 Carol Ohmann, Loren Axtell
1978 George Drake, Richard Pavlicek
1979 Roy Green, Bob Dennard
1980 Robert Levin, Russ Arnold
1981 Patricia Gist, Michael Seamon
Smoking:
1980 Paul Soloway, Ron Andersen
1981 Kathleen Rogers, Marie Leaphart
Non-Smoking:
1980 John Brady, Dennis Sharpe
1981 Jack Bonney, Dianne Bonney

MEN'S PAIRS
1959 Robert Reynolds, John Kunkel
1965 C. E. LePaige, William Mussallem
1966 John Fox, Albert Bricklin
1967 Paul Piedmont, J. Davd King
1968 Edward Austin Jones, Paul Oreffice
1969 Harrell Darden, Wilson Landlel
1970 Eli Jaye, Clifford Weil
1971 Randy Baron, Tom Lavender
1972 William Seamon, Sidney Mandell
1973 Allan Cokin, Jim Mahaffey *(tied with)*
  Richard Sugg, Rick Norton
1974 Robert Saron, Richard Glenn
1975 Fred McBride, Kirk Benson
1976 Larry Auerbach, Jim Chappell
1977 Loren Axtell, Leon Smith
1978 A. Seigenfeld, Alan Sontag
1979 R. Stultz, Jim Barrow
1980 Robert Levin, Russ Arnold
1981 O. H. Reissen, R. J. Schaefer

WOMEN'S PAIRS
1959 Patricia Miller, Mervin Ray
1965 Jane Clark, Mrs. William Stem
1966 Edna Lewis, Edin Andrews
1967 Helene Colby, Mellie Loudermilk
1968 Mrs. John Young, Mrs. James Oxford
1969 Evelyn Palmer, Margaret Hall Pate
1970 Arzell McDonald, Jane Ecklund
1971 Helen Barlow, Mrs. L. R. Moscardini
1972 Mrs. James Oxford, Sue Young
1973 Mrs. J. W. McCorquodale, Jane Young
1974 Jane Kelley, Evelyn Maupin
1975 Myrna Saffel, Betty Sue Grandoff
1976 Carol Ann Reynolds, Muffie Thyrre
1977 Helen Shanbrom, Jill Denny
1978 Connie Jackson, Garland Ergüden
1979 Mary Green, Pat Murphy
1980 Barbara Wallace, Annette Barrett
1981 Adeline Ruppert, Hazel Anderson

MIXED PAIRS
1963 Sally Saron, Robert Woodworth
1964 Mrs. Herbert Ameisen, George Davis
1965 Jayne Thomas, Frank Carrieri
1966 Mark Noble, Elizabeth Noble
1967 Leland Ferer, Gratian Goldstein
1968 Myra Holley, Dennis Hogan
1969 Betty Koorey, Harold Florea
1970 Leon Smith, Mrs. Dennis Neville
1971 Joan Bernard, Joe Godefrin *(tied with)*
  Robert Stanfill, Mrs. Robert Stanfill
1972 Robert Woodworth, Annette Barrett
1973 Nancy Richardson, F. Holton Sexton
1974 Larry Griffey, Mrs. Milton Hudson
1975 Maxine Kramer, Robert Levin
1976 Jim Beery, Lyn Beery
1977 David Strasberg, Jean Frankel
1977 Charlotte Falk, Fred Strickland
1978 Dennis Sharpe, Patricia Murphy
1979 Ba'Lint Papp, Margie Dreayer
1980 Carol Sanders, Thomas Sanders

INDIVIDUAL
1960 Evelyn Maupin
1961 Dr. Leonard Manson *(tied with)*
  Arthur Nielsen
1963 Martin Waldron
1964 H. G. Aaron
1965 True Gemzell
1966 Mrs. Allan Johnson
1967 Faye Zearfoss
1968 Gabriel Powers
1969 Herb Lent, Jr.
1970 Ouida J. Wetherington
1974 Frank Redman
1975 Rosemary Mulligan
1976 Myrthel Fly
1977 M. Marxsen
1978 L. Briggs
1979 Naomi Jackson

1980 Mrs. Lee Tombs

SWISS TEAMS

1971 Jack Schwencke, Gaylor Kasle,
      Jim Brenner, Gary Fischer
1975 Tom Mahaffey, Jr., Tom Gardner, Fred Hamilton,
      Carol Klar, Cliff Bishop
1976 Carol Ohmann, Bruce Ohmann,
      Bob Dennard, Jim Titzel
1977 Randy Baron, Bob Meyer, Bill Doroshow,
      Lee Bukstel, Mark Yeager *(tied with)*
      Daniel Oken, Louise Sharp,
      Art Samuels, Mark Jones *(and)*
      Michael Seamon, Rita Seamon, Janice Seamon,
      Bill Seamon, Edith Kemp *(and)*
      Jim Mahaffey, Tracy Denninger,
      Jack Denny, Jill Denny *(and)*
      Claudia Feagin, Jack Feagin,
      Myldred Kelly, Leonard Kaplan *(and)*
      Phil Altus, Muriel Altus,
      Bud Cooper, Vonnie Lavender
1978 Carol Ohmann, George Acker, Elaine Acker,
      Dick Belcher, Flo Friedlander
1979 Eddie Wold, Paul Lewis, Marc Jacobus,
      Cliff Russell, Clarence Goppert, David Schroeder
Flight A:
1981 Garland Ergüden, Andy Bernstein,
      Byron Greenberg, Harry Tudor
Smoking:
1980 Brenda Blumenthal, A. Neill, Paul Soloway,
      Bobby Goldman, Ron Andersen
1981 Jack Mauney, Patricia West,
      Clarda Pribble, Carolyn Lea *(tied with)*
      Fran Pettijohn, Patty Sundstrom,
      Gretchen Funk, Marianne Timmons *(and)*
      Betty Bayard, Bruce Logan,
      Vel Beck, Norma Lenz
Non-Smoking:
1980 T. R. Clay, Michael Grunstein,
      A. W. Pearsall, Polly Mullin
1981 Leon Smith, Larry Griffey,
      Bob Dennard, Bruce Ohmann

PUERTO RICO

WOMEN'S PAIRS

1967 Rose Zellinger, Pearl Halberstadt
1968 Paula Levin, Jane Mason
1969 Mrs. Richard Rosenthal, Grace Simon
1970 Jane Mason, Barbara Birnholz
1971 Barbara Eboli, Josefina Costas
1972 Mrs. J. Sykes, Fran Willis
1973 Jacqui Mitchell, Gail Moss
1974 M. Cooke, C. Grossman
1975 Mrs. T. H. Barnes, Mrs. O. Lott
1976 Mrs. K. E. Davis, Mrs. S. W. Johnson
1977 Lenore Server, Barbara Eboli
1978 Edith Kemp, Ruth Isaacs
1979 Diana Schuld, B. De Lieto
1980 Bette Cohn, Joan Bernard
1981 Diana Schuld, Ruth Stober

MEN'S PAIRS

1967 Robert Reynods, Robert Sitnek
1968 Julius Rosenblum, Nate Silverstein
1969 Joe Weintraub, William Seamon
1970 Thomas Smith, Frank Higginbotham
1971 Luis Pietri, Michael Garner
1972 Matt Granovetter, Zachary Granovetter
1973 Mike Moss, Jack Saltz
1974 Danilo Eboli, Richard Cappalli
1975 Danilo Eboli, Richard Cappalli
1976 Richard Pavlicek, Moe Rubenfeld
1977 Chuck Said, Jeff Overby
1978 Ron Andersen, Dave Berkowitz
1979 Jim Becker, Jim Hamilton
1980 Bill Pollack, Howard Chandross
1981 Tom Clarke, Alan LeBendig

OPEN PAIRS

1967 Vincent Remey, Joan Remey
1968 Frank Higginbotham, Karl Kristiansen
1969 Richard Rosenthal, Mrs. Richard Rosenthal
1970 Charles Wei, Jim Becker
1971 Luis Pietri, Michael Garner
1972 Karl Kristiansen, Frank Higginbotham
1973 Larry Edwards, John Brinley
1974 Cynthia Hinckley, Barbara Eboli
1975 H. Horowitz, Allen Spielholz
1976 Richard Pavlicek, Sylvia Grossman
1977 Matt Granovetter, Neil Silverman
1978 Roger Duret, Daniel Sendral *(tied with)*
      Rita Seamon, Burt Haff

1979 Kathie Wei, Dave Berkowitz
1980 Danilo Eboli, Frank Higginbotham
1981 Tim Nelsen, Rozanne Pollack

MASTER PAIRS

1967 William Seamon, Cliff Russell
1968 Robert Sharp, Jo Sharp
1973 Emile Nevins, Frances Singer
1974 Kathie Wei, Ron Andersen
1975 Neil Silverman, Fred Paul
1976 Marion Altman, Dr. Harold Weltman
1977 Matt Granovetter, Neil Silverman *(tied with)*
      Dave Berkowitz, Jerry Shakofsky
1978 Jim Becker, Jim Hamilton
1979 Bill Roberts, Victor Mitchell
1980 Kerr Godfrey, Dan Morgan
1981 Jerry Shakofsky, Dave Berkowitz

OPEN SWISS TEAMS

1975 Danilo Eboli, Dave Hinckley, Cynthia Hinckley,
      Richard Cappalli, Harry McGuire
1976 Kathie Wei, Jo Morse,
      Dave Berkowitz, Jerry Shakofsky
1977 Matt Granovetter, Ahmed Hussein, Gail Moss,
      Jim Linhart, Mrs. R. Cohen
1978 Kathie Wei, Ron Andersen,
      David Berkowitz, Sue Picus *(tied with)*
      Victor Mitchell, Jacqui Mitchell, Bill Roberts,
      Jill Roberts, Matt Granovetter
1979 Kathie Wei, Jim Becker, Tim Nelsen,
      Judy Tucker, Dave Berkowitz
1980 Kathie Wei, Judi Radin, Jim Becker,
      Dave Berkowitz, Judy Tucker
1981 Jerry Shakofsky, Rozanne Pollack, Bill Pollack,
      Tim Nelsen, Howard Chandross

OPEN TEAMS

1969 Rachel Nachman, Harvey Nachman,
      Hella Solomon, Rick Solomon
1970 Jeff Glick, Vera Glick, George Rosenschein,
      Jane Rosenschein, Stanley Alpert
1971 Larry Pietri, Michael Garner,
      Neil Silverman, Ron Rubin
1972 Danilo Eboli, Richard Cappalli, Karl Kristansen,
      Frank Higginbotham, Mrs. C. Lee *(tied with)*
      Kathie Wei, Jacqui Mitchell, Charles Wei,
      Matt Granovetter, Vic Mitchell
1973 Dr. Rex Goodman, Rena Hetzer,
      Dorothy Payne, Richard Carvel *(tied with)*
      Bud Reinhold, Peter Weichsel, Nancy Weichsel,
      Kyle Larsen, Billy Eisenberg, Marta Dornfeld
1974 Zachary Granovetter, Matt Granovetter,
      Jim Looby, Neil Silverman

MIXED PAIRS

1967 Dr. Harvey Nachman, Mrs. Harvey Nachman
1968 Paula Levin, Lloyd Ribner
1969 Daniel Sendral, Mary Paris
1970 Ruth Russo, Abe Russo
1971 Howard Schenken, Bee Schenken
1972 Alice Gerard, Albert Bricklin

SOUTHEASTERN

KNOCKOUT TEAMS

1967 Nate Silverstein, Jerome Jacobs, Robert Rothlein,
      Robert Sharp, Armand Barfus
1968 Paul Oreffice, Jane Jaeger, Paula Levin,
      John Scanlan, Albert Weiss, Robert Reynolds
1969 Phil Feldesman, John Solodar, Ray Zoller,
      Charles Burger, Monroe Ingberman
1970 Alan Sontag, Mike Moss, John Solodar,
      William Passell, Kyle Larsen, Ray Zoller
1973 Bob Hamman, Jack Schwencke, James Jacoby,
      Garey Hayden, Gaylor Kasle
1979 Mike Passell, Mark Lair, Clarence Goppert,
      Craig Janitschke, Jan Janitschke
1980 Cliff Russell, Eddie Wold, Al Roth, Joel Friedberg,
      Marvin Rosenblatt, Bob Hamman
1981 Ron Andersen, Chuck Lamprey, Judi Radin,
      Carol Sanders, Kathie Wei, Esta VanZandt

OPEN TEAMS

1931 Samuel Rockwell, Thomas Barrett,
      Louis Watson, William Barrett
1933 Edward Barco, W.A. Clark,
      William Cheney Moore, Charles Groene
1934 Whitney Cary, John Tyner,
      John Hardesty, Al Walton
1936 Mrs. Albert Terry, Herman Homa,
      Edward Cohen, Max Goldstein
1937 Baden Parks, David Carter,
      Ed Cohen, Al Terry
1938 Leroy Thurtell, Walter McIntyre,

Lee Morris, John Kunkel
1939 Arthur Goldsmith, Harry Feinberg.
S.L. Guggenheim, Sidney Fink
1940 Phil Abramsohn, Jesse Slutt, C.W. Hutzler,
Henry Chanin, Margaret Wagar
1941 Helen Sobel, Charles Goren,
Peggy Golder, Charles Solomon
1942 Helen Sobel, Charles Goren,
Peggy Golder, Charles Solomon
1943 Mrs. J.J. Wallendorf, J.J. Wallendorf
Dr. W.V. Kirk, Faye Lasarow
1944 Ann Tarr, William McKenney, William Seamon,
Lawrence Weiss, Irving Epstein
1945 William Brown, William Seamon, George Rapee,
Irving Epstein, Milton Vernoff
1946 Marie Basher, Edward Cohn,
Charles Goren, Don Farquharson,
1947 Mrs. Randolph Scott, Randolph Scott
Robert Burleigh, Mrs. Robert Burleigh
1951 Mel Bender, Jack Ankus,
Alan Eber, Robert Reynolds *(tied with)*
Tobias Stone, Edith Kemp,
Waldermar von Zedtwitz, Harry Harkavy
1952 Henry Kemp, Alvin Roth,
Mike Michaels, Robert Sitnek
1953 Jeff Glick, Vera Glick, Bill Root,
Max Turk, Eddie Cohen *(tied with)*
John Kunkel, Robert Racier, Fred Bickel,
Ronald Rosenberg, Alvin Goodman
1954 Jeff Glick, Vera Glick, Max Turk,
William Root, Eddie Cohen
1955 Charles Solomon, Peggy Solomon,
Charles Whitebrook, Julius Rosenblum
1956 Charles Solomon, Peggy Solomon,
Charles Whitebrook, Julius Rosenblum
1957 Amy Cavanaugh, Mrs. Paul Remlinger,
Mabel Niver, Mrs. Thomas McKenna
1958 Barbara Brier, Bee Gale,
Alan Eber, Cliff Russell *(tied with)*
Virginia Alderman, Mrs. Rolf Werdling, Rolf Werdling,
Eddie Cohen, Lucy Hoffman
1959 Bob Reynolds, Bill Seamon
Bob Rothlein, Cy Neyman
1960 Alan Eber, Jack Kravatz,
Harry Harkavy, Cliff Russell
1961 Mrs. Julian Barth, Julian Barth,
Mrs. Sidney Kirtland, Sidney Kirtland
1962 Bob Sharp, Irving Guttman, Max Lipin,
Bob Saron, Art Lefkowitz *(tied with)*
Edith Kemp, Cliff Russell,
Al Eber, Robert Sitnek
1963 Edith Kemp, Cliff Russell,
Alan Eber, Oswald Jacoby
1964 Edith Kemp, Al Eber,
Cliff Russell, Robert Reynolds
1965 Betty Haddad, Said Haddad,
Peter Pender, Bob Sitnek
1966 Mike Michaels, Gratian Goldstein, Leland Ferer,
Alfred Mueller, Jane Mueller
1967 Alex Steinberg, John Schwencke,
Karl Kristiansen, John Swanson
1968 Albert Weiss, Annette Barrett, John Levinson,
Russ Arnold, Sherman Irving (Irv) Steinfeldt
1969 B. Jay Becker, Dorothy Hayden,
Dan Morse, Hal Fein
1970 Dorothy Hayden, Dan Morse,
Hal Fein, William August
1971 Howard Schenken, Bee Schenken, William Seamon,
Joseph Weintraub, Sam Katz *(tied with)*
Hal Fein, Dan Morse,
Ronald Crown, G. Robert Nail *(and)*
Arthur (Bud) Reinhold, Emanuel Hochfeld,
Kyle Larsen, Albert Weiss *(and)*
Harry Fishebein, Fred Hirsch,
Dr. Robert Tator, Robert Fox,
Fred Dossenbach *(and)*
Paula Levin, J. Lowe,
Lorraine Heinrich, Lloyd Ribner *(and)*
Kent Wiley, Lois Wiley,
Bruce Ohmann, Carol Ohmann (and)
Stephen Jaeger, J. Kinard,
Stella Perry, Barbara Shaw
1972 Sam Stayman, Josephine Stayman, Alfred Rand,
Rita Rand, Victor Mitchell, Peter Parella *(tied with)*
William Passell, Fred Rubbra,
Matt Granovetter, Zach Granovetter *(and)*
Mrs. Thomas Lagan, Harry Keffer, Thomas Lagan,
Florence Keffer, Alan Doane *(and)*
Robert Sharp, Ruth Sharp, Gary Fischer,
Arlene Fischer, Andy O'Grady *(and)*
Jacqui Mitchell, Marietta Passell,
Michael Moss, Gail Moss *(and)*

Mrs. Ed Lowenthal, Ed Lowenthal,
Mrs. Joseph Low, Charles Whitebrook,
Joseph Low, Irwin Fischer *(and)*
Eugene Short, Karol Short,
Mrs. Richard Sugg, Richard Sugg
1973 Tom Reid, Henry Rabin,
Florine Walters, Art Samuels
1974 Cliff Bishop, Dr. L. Weisman, Richard Schwartz,
Chester Davis, Bill Butcher

SWISS TEAMS
1975 Bill Roberts, Mrs. Bill Roberts,
Victor Mitchell, Jacqui Mitchell
1976 Sylvia Smith, Gaylor Kasle, Jeffery Starr,
Howard Pearlman, Richard Shepherd
1977 Alfred Roberts, Jill Roberts, Victor Mitchell,
Jacqui Mitchell, Gail Moss
1978 Russ Arnold, Robert Levin, Annette Barrett,
Joel Harwood, Steve Goldberg, Ron Smith
1979 Jack Schwencke, Steve Sion,
Allan Cokin, Garey Hayden
Smoking:
1980 Morrie Elis, Irv Gottman,
Bruce Elliott, Sydney Isaacs
Non-Smoking:
1980 Diana Holt, Roger Jourdan, Jim Barrow,
Ed Schulte, Marty Bergen

MEN'S TEAMS
1951 Waldemar von Zedtwitz, William Seamon, Jack Ankus,
Alan Eber, Robert Reynolds
1952 Louis Levy, Jeff Glick, Alvin Landy,
Julius Rosenblum, Nate Silverstein
1953 Fred Bickel, Lewis Jaeger,
Ronald Rosenberg, Murray Seiler
1954 Leland Ferer, William Seamon, Robert Rothlein,
Frank Nickols, Alvin Roth
1955 Israel Cohen, John Kunkel, Alvin Roth,
Norman Kay, Mike Michaels
1956 Charles Solomon, Robert Sitnek,
Cyrus Neuman, Robert Rothlein *(tied with)*
Murry Gross, Dr. Arthur Salasky,
Ronald Rosenberg, Charles Woldenberg
1957 William Seamon, Cliff Russell, Al Eber,
Harry Harkavy, Tobias Stone
1958 William Seamon, Cliff Russell, Al Eber
Harry Harkavy, Russ Arnold
1959 Dr. Arthur Salasky, Murray Gross,
Phil Feldesman, Edwin Lowenthal
1962 Irving Guttman, Lt. Col. William Christian, Bob Sharp,
Max Lipin, Robert Sitnek
1963 William Seamon, Fred Hirsch, Paul Kibler,
Peter Pender, Robert Reynolds
1964 William Seamon, Robert Reynolds,
Sam Katz, Joseph Weintraub
1965 William Seamon, Sam Katz,
Joseph Weintraub, Robert Reynolds
1966 Jerry Brier, Jerome Jacobs,
Robert Rothlein, Irving Kass
1967 Gaylor Kasle, Robert Wolff
Ivan Erdos, Fred De Marigny
1968 Irving Guttman, Robert Rothlein,
Armand Barfus, Robert Sharp
1969 George Treadwell, Charles Kittle, Max Lipin,
Paul Stern, S.W. Weingarden
1970 Gaylor Kasle, Mike Carson,
Richard Pavlicek, Mike King
1971 John Schwencke, Gary Fischer,
Gaylor Kasle, Jim Brenner
1972 Joseph Weintraub, Bob Reynolds, Sam Katz,
Bill Seamon, Howard Schenken
1973 Lloyd Ribner, Jerry Shakofsky, Michael Moss,
Steve Altman, Victor Mitchell
1974 Richard Huggard, Cliff Bishop,
Joel Harwood, Jack Denney *(tied with)*
Fred McBride, Bernard Moss,
Richard Coren, Art Coren *(and)*
Frank Whiteley, Dan Curtis,
James Epstein, Joseph Ripstra *(and)*
Tom Mahaffey, Richard Pavlicek,
James Berry, Pete Richmond

MEN'S SWISS TEAMS
1975 Jim Jacoby, John Simon, Nate Silverstein,
Jim Barrow, David Strasberg
1976 Cliff Bishop, Bob Saron, Richard Halperin,
Ralph Bartlett, Bill Butcher, Arnold Leavitt
1977 Howard Schenken, Cliff Bishop, Chuck Said,
Tom Mahaffey, Jack Denny
1978 Barry Crane, Cliff Russell, Thomas Sanders,
Curtis Smith, Peter Weichsel
1979 Jack Schwencke, Steve Sion,
Allan Cokin, Garey Hayden

1980 Lee Thomas, J. B. Clifford, Bob Sitnek,
      Daniel Oken, Art Samuels *(tied with)*
      George Hsieh, David Hsieh,
      Billy Hsieh, Ron Andersen
1981 Robert Hamman, Cliff Russell, Russ Arnold, Robert Levin

WOMEN'S TEAMS
1951 Lee Vernoff, Lil Lyell,
      Eva Gross, Mabel Niver
1952 Helen Sobel, Paula Bacher,
      Edith Seligman, Mrs. Joseph Rosenfield
1953 Paula Bacher, Anne Burstein, Jane Jaeger
      Elizabeth Neuman, Helen Sobel
1954 Marie Cohn, Olive Peterson,
      Mrs. John Kunkel, Muriel Kaplan
1955 Ruth Gilbert, Edith Kemp, Paula Levin,
      Liz Eber, Anne Burnstein *(tied with)*
      Barbara Brier, Mildred Cytron,
      Jo Gutman, Gratian Goldstein
1956 Edith Kemp, Liz Eber,
      Paula Levin, Ann Burnstein
1957 Gertrude Wallendorf, Wilma Childress, Lil Lyell,
      Mrs. Bernard Windt, Edith Kirtland
1958 Paula Levin, Natalie Rosenblum, Bee Gale,
      Phyllis Gardner, Jane Jaeger
1959 Violet Agran, Rose Goldman,
      Mrs. Samuel Myers, Ruth Gittelman
1962 Carrie Arnold, Neva Gray,
      Betty Champion, Elsie Abrams
1963 Elsie Abrams, Carrie Arnold,
      Neva Gray, Betty Champion
1964 Elsie Abrams, Carrie Arnold,
      Betty Champion, Neva Gray
1965 Alicia Kempner, Helen Sobel, Paula Levin,
      Bettye Hermanson, Ethel Keohane
1966 Edna Kennedy, Lillian Rudnick,
      Ari Weiss, Susan Shapira
1967 Mildred Cunningham, Carrie Arnold,
      Neva Gray, Carolyn Whitehead
1968 Elinor Evans, Gretchen Roberts,
      Lillian Perlow, Mable Beaver *(tied with)*
      Lil Lyell, Dulcie Grdy,
      Liz Barth, Wilma Childress
1969 Lil Lyell, Liz Barth,
      Wilma Childress, Dulcie Grady
1970 Gratian Goldstein, Adrienne Schwartz,
      Gretchen Feldstein, Jane Mueller
1971 Nancy Lewis, Barbara Brier,
      Mrs. Manuel Clark, Elsie Abrams
1972 Wendy Sameroff, Judi Solodar,
      Linda Deaton, Esta VanZandt
1973 Jean Theus, Joan Bernard, Charlotte Falk
      Mary Lee Berg, Elinor Evans *(tied with)*
      Kathie Wei, Betty Ann Kennedy,
      Gail Moss, Jacqui Mitchell
1974 Barbara Brier, Ann Marie Sporing, Phyllis Smith,
      Nancy Lewis, Marietta Passell

WOMEN'S SWISS TEAMS
1975 Brenda Blumenthal, Lois Wiley,
      Jill Denny, Emilie Nevins
1976 Joan Bernard, Charlotte Falk, Bette Cohn,
      Esta VanZandt, Garner McDaniel, Joan DeWitt
1977 Temi Linzner, Glorie Gottesfeld,
      Gladys Kransberg, Mrs. Julius Shivers
1978 Gertrude Blasband, Sadie Elkins, Esther Hirsch,
      Judy Kay, Pauline Shmukler
1979 Terry Michaels, Charlotte Falk,
      Eleanor Turoff, Carol Ann Reynolds *(tied with)*
      Eleanor Hanlon, Lee Slaughter,
      Shelly Salvi, Dorothy Hobbs *(and)*
      Barbara Saltsman, Gloria Joffe,
      Eva Marcovici, Rachel Levy *(and)*
      Judi Radin, Jacqui Mitchell,
      Lynne Tarnapol, Jill Roberts
1980 Susan Kennedy, Pat Samuels, Barbara Ashare,
      V.J. Sokolov, Mary Lou Cushner
1981 Grace Gabbai, Garland Ergüden,
      Annette Barrett, Marietta Beery *(tied with*
      Bunny Haas, Sheila Ekeblad,
      Shaleen Notaro, Joan Sherman *(and)*
      Linda Perlman, Wendy Sameroff, Joan Stein,
      Liz Sorgi, Jo Morse, Karen McCallum *(and)*
      Mrs. Leonard Hymerling, Betty Pappas,
      Sallie Landa, Mrs. P. Cibotti

SUN CITY

SWISS TEAMS
Smoking:
1980 Lee Bruns, Tom Jones,
      Robert Fulton, Martha Newbill *(tied with)*

      C. H. Sedgewick, Rose Sedgewick,
      Marjorie Wellman, Wayne Wellman *(and)*
      Tex Hooks, Mae Hooks,
      David Hauseman, R. W. Mitchell
1981 C. H. Sedgewick, Rose Sedgewick,
      Wayne Wellman, Marjorie Wellman *(tied with)*
      Cliff Bishop, Robert Sharp,
      Ruth Sharp, William Wise
Non-Smoking:
1980 Tom Mahaffey, Jack Denny,
      James Nichols, Robert Woodworth *(tied with)*
      Margaret Anderson, Mrs. L. S. Martin,
      Virginia McBane, Mrs. W. L. Sheets
1981 Nat Agran, John Scanlon,
      Bob Saron, Bob Reyonds *(tied with)*
      Jack Denny, James Nichols,
      Robert Woodworth, Tom Mahaffey

OPEN PAIRS
1980 Harold Feldstein, Gretchen Feldstein
1981 Louise Koones, Bronnie Wiegman
Flight A:
1981 Jill Denny, Jack Denny

MIXED PAIRS
1980 Pauline Schinman, Marcel Friedmann

INDIVIDUAL
1980 Nell Russell

MEN'S PAIRS
1980 Ralph Fensterwald, Walter Dzik
1981 Martin Cohn, Albert Silber

WOMEN'S PAIRS
1980 Evelyn Palmer, Mrs. M. Hood
1981 Nell Russell, Ruth Holladay

DISTRICT 10   (Arkansas, Louisiana, Mississippi, Alabama, western Tennessee)

GULF COAST MID-SOUTH

OPEN TEAMS
1972 George Daniels, Francis Connor,
      Carolyn Watson, Hans Kaufmann *(tied with)*
      Bart Craig, Bea Crockett,
      Harley McCabe, Lois Beveridge *(and)*
      Fred Hamilton, Norman Schwartz,
      Michael Hunt, Byron Greenberg *(and)*
      Walter Lewis, John Arledge III,
      Cary Pierce, Jason Floyd *(and)*
      Richard Logan, Jamie Bush,
      Guss Ginsburg, Ken Fonte *(and)*
      Mrs. A. Fell, Mrs. William Barber,
      Patsy Warner, Mrs. Richard Miller
1973 Jim Foster, Al Van Hoose III,
      Jim Rainey, Walter Jones
1974 Tim Frick, J. L. Foote,
      Ken Bradley, Betty Foote
1975 Sidney Lazard, Frank Hoadley, James Beery, Jr.,
      Sidney Lazard, Jr., Nancy Zoller, Ray Zoller
1976 Frank Hoadley, Carol Jean Kuhn, Loretta Rivers,
      Betty Alford, Dave Landers
1977 Lil Greenburg, Mary Jane Farell,
      Hugh MacLean, Ron Andersen
1978 Betty Ann Kennedy, Jack Kennedy,
      Dr. John Fisher, Charles Goldner
1979 Mark Perlmutter, Lester Perlmutter,
      Gordon Maroney, Harold Rist *(tied with)*
      Ed Schulte, Jeff Zionts,
      Marvin Shapiro, Larry Kolker *(and)*
      Paul Munafo, Genne Winter, Glenn Merrill,
      Gary Kessler, Sammie Tallent
1980 Allen Hawkins, Mimi Little,
      Carolyn Neyman, Jim Foster

SWISS TEAMS
Flight A:
1979 Craig Cordes, Terry Spector,
      Richard Capps, John Onstott
1980 James Zimmerman, Proctor Hawkins,
      Esta Van Zandt, Byron Greenberg *(tied with)*
      Walter Lewis, Clay Hall,
      John Arledge, Steve Katz

OPEN PAIRS
1972 Fred Hamilton, Michael Hunt
1973 Terry Radjef, Douglas Hill
1974 David Foote, DeAne Phillips
1975 Barry Crane, Helen Utegaard
1976 Mike Cook, Reece Rogers

1977	Russ Mitchell, Curtis Carpenter
1978	Barry Crane, Thomas Sanders
1979	Ron Smith, Bill Cohen
1980	Barbara Slaughter, Cecil King
1981	Craig Cordes, Richard Capps

Flight A:

1979	David Siebert, Al Childs
1980	Tom Snow, Steve Levine

MEN'S PAIRS

1972	George Randall, Dr. Richard Green
1973	Frank Hoadley, Paul Munafo
1974	Paul Soloway, Malcolm Brachman
1975	Bill Drewett, Pat Mizell *(tied with)*
	Richard Oshlag, Mike Cooke
1976	Ron LaCour, Richard Shepherd
1977	Sidney Lazard, Frank Hoadley
1978	Eddie Wold, John Mallet
1979	David Siebert, Paul Munafo
1980	Robert Levin, Mark Lair
1981	Francis Conner, Curtis Carpenter

WOMEN'S PAIRS

1972	Mrs. J. Scott, Mrs. J. Ramsey
1973	Nancy Alpaugh, Esta Van Zandt
1974	Dee Adams, Lillian Goodman
1975	Anita Davis, Helen Utegaard
1976	Carol Sanders, Betty Ann Kennedy
1977	Janice Berenson, Mrs. Bernard Jacobs
1978	Betty Ann Kennedy, Carol Sanders
1979	Linda Hanson, Stella Rainey
1980	Carol Slaughter, Mrs. Joseph Lee
1981	Nancy Schwantes, Jane Eason

MASTER PAIRS

1972	Nancy Alpaugh, Byron Greenberg
1973	Betty Ann Kennedy, Carol Sanders
1974	Wes Irby, Ken Bains
1975	Ann Westrom, Maxine Plummer
1976	Howard Abrahms, Jr., John Herrmann
1977	Glenn Merrill, Genne Winter
1978	David Siebert, James Jacoby
1979	Peggy Jett, Martha Harris
1980	Don Caton, Joe Gottler
1981	Bryan Howard, Olin Hubert

KNOCKOUT TEAMS

1974	Minda Brachman, James Jacoby, Sidney Lazard, Paul Soloway, Mike Passell
1976	Clarence Goppert, Richard Shepherd, Bruce Ferguson, Mark Lair, Al Childs
1977	Frank Hoadley, Sidney Lazard, Carol Sanders, Thomas Sanders, Lou Bluhm
1979	Andy Bernstein, Garland Ergüden, Ron Andersen, Larry Sealy, Milton Stern
1980	Sidney Lazard, Sidney Lazard, Jr., Andy Bernstein, Garland Ergüden, Si Frome, Fred Woodruff
1981	Billy Tate, Kerr Godfrey, Eddie Wold, Dennis Sorensen

MASTER SWISS TEAMS

1975	Bob Fiske, Mariann Miller, Donald Olson, David Hadden
1978	Eddie Wold, Lita Farrar, Terry Gibson, Jim Tigrett, Jeff Corbin

MIXED PAIRS

1976	Jeff Overby, Geraldine Anderson
1977	Jamie Bush, Gerri Hughes
1981	Lorraine Kustin, Steve Greenberg

INDIVIDUAL

1976	Edna Anderson
1977	Kenneth Lindsay
1981	Bill Weakley

MID–SOUTH FALL

KNOCKOUT TEAMS

1974	Lou Bluhm, Richard Shepherd, John Gibbons, Mrs. John Gibbons, Carol Sanders, James Rainey
1975	Curtis Smith, Mark Lair, Steve Greenberg, Joe Elsburg, Esta Van Zandt
1976	Oswald Jacoby, James Jacoby, Sieg Siebert, David Siebert, Allan Seibert
1977	Eddie Wold, Ron Smith, Mark Friedman, Lou Bluhm, Richard Shepherd
1978	Al Childs, Boyce Cearley, Steve Greenberg, Jeff Corbin, Pat Mizell
1979	George Rhode, Sammie Tallent, Dennis Clerkin, Alan LeBendig, Tom Clarke
1980	Alan LeBendig, James Jacoby, Bobby Wolff, Tom Clarke, R. Clyde Hargrove

MEN'S TEAMS

1973	Thomas Sanders, Mark Lair, Mike Passell, Byron Greenberg, James Jacoby, Nate Silverstein
1977	Jack Feagin, Fred Strickland, Randy Pettit, Roger Roemmich

MASTER SWISS TEAMS

1980	R. Clyde Hargrove, Alan LeBendig, James Jacoby, Bobby Wolff, Tom Clarke

OPEN TEAMS

1967	Paul Deal, Paul Munafo, Gerald Kendall, Noel Duvic *(tied with)* J. A. Rockhold, Helen Rockhold, Maury Genud, Mary Beth Townsend, Paul Soloway
1968	August Plate, Dave Horner, B.J. Wilson, Curtis Downs
1969	William Brown, Dr. John Griscom Joe Kirkpatrick, Curtis Smith
1970	Larry Gould, Steve Goldberg, Lou Bluhm, Richard Shepherd
1971	Dennis Conlon, Craig Cordes, Curtis Carpenter, Ernest Gordon, Jr.
1973	Wayne Hollingsworth, Richard Potter, Capt. John Potter, Jeffery Gargrave
1974	Terry Teague, Elinor Murdoch, Dr. Charles Burnham, J.G. Ripstra
1975	Barry Crane, Kerri Shuman, Carol Sanders, Thomas Sanders
1976	Curtis Smith, Buddy Majors, Helen Jessup, Esta Van Zandt
1977	Joe Steuer, Marie Louise Steuer, Beverly Cunningham, Bill Cunningham
1978	Charles Weed, Dr. John Fisher, Bobby Wolff, Del Parker, Jack Kennedy, Betty Ann Kennedy
1979	Barry Crane, Carol Sanders, Thomas Sanders, Lou Bluhm
1980	Richard Doughty, Thomas Daniel, Craig Cordes, Richard Capps

MIXED PAIRS

1967	Frank Hoadley, Nancy Alpaugh
1968	Jerri Gardiner, Dr. Charles Robinson
1971	Mike Passell, Carolyn Watson
1974	Martin Cohn, Bette Cohn
1975	Vincent Remey, Joan Remey
1976	Paul Munafo, Jane Stickney

WOMEN'S TEAMS

1973	Helen Utegaard, Nancy Gruver, Mary Beth Townsend, Terry Michaels *(tied with)* Emy Lynch, Janie Judy, Ruth Francis, Kay Shropshire
1977	Jean Frankel, Nancy Alpaugh, Shirlee Lazarus, Betty Ann Kennedy, Carol Sanders, Esta Van Zandt

OPEN PAIRS

1967	James Jacoby, Charles Kittle
1968	Vaughan Ellzey, Kenneth Robertson
1969	Dan Requard, David Fisher
1970	Mike Passell, Don Caton
1971	Betty Ann Kennedy, Carol Sanders
1973	Barry Crane, Gerald Caravelli
1974	Eleanor Murdoch, Dr. Charles Burnham
1975	Bobby Wolfe, Jack Kennedy
1976	Bobby Wolfe, Jack Kennedy
1977	Tina McKee, Mike Passell
1978	Boyce Cearley, Joe Scott
1979	Don Baxter, Curtis Smith
1980	Allan Siebert, Joan Jackson

Flight A:

1979	George Kendal, Charles McHale
1980	Peggy Jett, Martha Harris

MEN'S PAIRS

1967	Oswald Jacoby, Fred Berger,
1968	Pat Connelly, Julius Rosenblum
1969	Curtis Smith, Dr. John Griscom
1970	Jim Barrow, Dan Daton
1971	Frances Conner, Hans Herbst
1973	Mark Lair, Mike Passell
1974	Frank Stewart, Thomas Sanders
1975	Sam Coolik, Ed Jordan, Jr.
1976	Bill Muir, Jesse Stuart Jr.
1977	Curtis Cheek, Michael Davis
1979	Barry Crane, Thomas Sanders
1980	Don Baxter, Curtis Smith

WOMEN'S PAIRS

1967	Genne Winter, Bettye Floyd
1968	Mrs. B. D. Looney, Mrs. J. A. Brill
1969	Marsha Hulan, Alice Dunhill
1970	Geneva Sangaree, Mrs. L. Hanahan
1971	Annette McHann, Shirley Harrison
1973	Beverly Fleck, Barbara Austin
1974	Betty Ann Kennedy, Carol Sanders

1975 Jean Frankel, Shirlee Lazarus
1976 Shirlee Lazarus, Jean Frankel
1977 Jean Frankel, Shirlee Lazarus
1979 Pat Schwartz, Carol Jane Hoadley
1980 Zee Cunningham, Carol Festervand

MASTER PAIRS
1967 Julius Rosenblum, Nate Silverstein
1969 Richard Doughty, Jack LaNoue
1970 Nancy Alpaugh, Nate Silverstein
1971 Jack Kennedy, Larry Howard
1973 Fred McBride, Richard Shepherd
1974 Joan Bernard, Richard Glenn
1975 Bernard Tighe, Gaylor Kasle
1976 David Siebert, Allan Siebert
1977 Charlotte Falk, Fred Strickland *(tied with)*
      Leonard Kaplan, Richard Shepherd
1978 Jack Burke, Proctor Hawkins
1979 E. M. Zalta, Hemant Lall

LIFE MASTER PAIRS
1968 Charlene Duvic, Carol Jean Kuhn

UNMIXED PAIRS
1978 Joe Steuer, Curtis Downs *(tied with)*
      Tom Clarke, Alan LeBendig

INDIVIDUAL
1975 Mrs. Ernest Norman, Jr.

DISTRICT 10

MID-SOUTH SPRING

KNOCKOUT TEAMS
1965 Paula Levin, Albert Weiss,
      George Willett, J. G. Ripstra
1970 Frank Hoadley, Jack LaNoue,
      Col. William Christian, Jim Linhart
1971 Gaylor Kasle, Paul Soloway, Charlie Kittle,
      Curtis Smith, Rae Kittle
1973 James Jacoby, Morris Chang, Ronny Dreyfus,
      Louis Gurvich, Jean Frankel, Bobby Nail
1974 Minda Brachman, James Jacoby, Sidney Lazard,
      Paul Soloway, Mike Passell
1978 Barry Crane, Betty Ann Kennedy,
      Carol Sanders, Thomas Sanders
1980 Ron Andersen, Billy Hsieh, Paul Soloway,
      Eddie Wold, Mark Lair
1981 Clay Hall, Jim Foster, Allen Hawkins,
      Jim Felts, Thomas Sanders, Reece Rogers

MASTER PAIRS
1957 Lyle Stan, Reba Hunter
1958 Betty Ann Welch, Kenneth Robertson
1959 Bernice Burns, Mrs. J. N. Morrell
1960 Amy Harrison, Theron Brown
1961 Claire Meyer, Theodore Hirsch
1962 Pat Connelly, Oswald Jacoby
1963 Dan Morse, George Dawkins
1964 Thomas Sanders, Carol Sanders
1965 Julius Rosenblum, James Jacoby
1966 Dane Clay, Ann Clay
1967 Barry Crane, Grant Marsee
1968 Jack Walton, Louise Sharp
1969 Fred Berger, Bernard Tighe
1970 Michael Passell, John Potter
1971 Dr. Richard Greene, Ace Gutowsky
1972 Carol Sanders, Esta Van Zandt *(tied with)*
      Bernadette Theobald, Louise Wilson
1973 Nate Silverstein, Frank Hoadley
1974 Wes Irby, Ken Bains
1977 Larry Howard, Bryan Howard
1978 Robert Hamman, David Siebert
1979 Thomas Sanders, Reece Rogers
1980 Mike Davis, Bob Teel
1981 Mel Skolnik, Jeff Meckstroth

OPEN TEAMS
1941 C. P. Williams, John Gerber,
      Ben Fain, Paul Hodge
1942 Ben Fain, John Gerber,
      Mrs. F. H. Gerson, Paul Hodge
1943 Inez Buchanan, Mrs. Randolph Scott,
      Caroline McGarity, L. D. Boone
1944 Lucien Zilberman, Julius Rosenblum, Dr. Richard Greene,
      Jake Toledano, Dottie Toledano
1945 Allyn McKeen, Larry Shurlds,
      Linda Terry, Mrs. John Ogden
1946 Payne Harrison, Capt. Mark Hodges,
      Capt. William Christian, Elinor Murdoch
1947 Garner Green, Jr., Mrs. Garner Green,
      John McCormick, Mrs. John McCormick
1948 Julius Rosenblum, Louis Rosen, Dr. Richard Greene,

      Robert Pitard, Walter Herbert
1949 Elinor Murdoch, Lou Herman,
      Oswald Jacoby, Julius Rosenblum
1950 Harriet Feldman, Mitty Parsons,
      Harry Teles, Rose Groves
1951 Harry Teles, Rose Groves,
      Harriet Feldman, Mitty Parsons
1952 Robert Barrett, Charles Woldenberg,
      John Gerber, Robert Sharp
1953 Thelma Potts, Ann Brandon, Mrs. Curtis Finch,
      Lillian Tiller, Curtis Finch
1954 Oswald Jacoby, James Jacoby,
      Henry Chanin, Dan Westerfield
1955 Shirley Fairchild, Brad Gentry,
      Ed Theus, John Torbett
1956 Charles Goren, David Carter, Nate Silverstein,
      Jeff Glick, Vera Glick
1957 J. G. Ripstra, Jean Krebs, Louise Durham,
      Phil Merry, Mary Lou Merry
1958 Allyn McKeen, Raymond Michaelson,
      Julian Slager, Hilda Slager
1959 David Carter, Frances Carter, Ben Fain,
      George Rosenkranz, Bill Cook, Jr.
1960 William Grieve, George Rapee,
      Curtis Smith, J. A. Rockhold
1961 J. A. Rockhold, Raymond Rockhold, Edward Robertson,
      Curtis Smith, Lucy Alverson
1962 Fred Berger, Louis Gurvich,
      Jean Frankel, Robert Pitard
1963 Joe Skinner, Mary Frances Skinner,
      Fred Hughes, Mrs. W. W. Corn
1964 Oswald Jacoby, Mary Zita Jacoby, Nate Silverstein,
      Paul Levitt, Shirlee Lazarus
1965 Shirlee Lazarus, Jean Frankel, Paul Levitt,
      Lou Gurvich, Robert Pitard
1966 Dane Clay, Ann Clay,
      Mrs. K. S. Reinhardt, Rena Riley
1967 Jean Frankel, Lou Gurvich,
      Barry Crane, Grant Marsee
1968 Paul Levitt, Shirlee Lazarus, James Tallant,
      Chandler Duncan, Col. William Christian
1969 Richard Doughty, Gary Tilly,
      Frank Whitely, David Landers
1970 Jesse Tallman, Joyce Simmons,
      Mrs. F. Likins, Mrs. E. Thompson *(tied with)*
      Morton Nelson, Frank Hoadley,
      Jack LaNoue, J. G. Ripstra
1971 Harrison Adams, Dee Adams, Harold Katz,
      Jack Hudgins, Bill Durbin
1972 Fred Woodruff, Ron Smith,
      Lloyd Hetzer, Marvin Shapiro
1973 Dr. John Fisher, Charles Weed, Jack Kennedy,
      Betty Ann Kennedy, Fred Berger, Sam Coolik *(tied with)*
      Lou Gurvich, Jean Frankel, Shirlee Lazarus,
      Anita Davis, Garner McDaniel, Dr. Nathan Ostrich *(and)*
      Paul Munafo, Jane Stickney,
      Fred Hughes, Margaret Byrd
1974 T. Frick, J. Foote,
      Ben Foote, Kenn Bradley
1975 Jane Stickney, Paul Munafo,
      Jack LaNoue, Donald Oakie *(tied with)*
      Sidney Lazard, Frank Hoadley, Thomas Sanders,
      Carol Sanders, Ron Smith *(and)*
      Pat Mizell, Nell Cahn, Michael Hunt,
      Dale Pierce, Glenn Merrill, Genne Winter *(and)*
      Steve Beatty, John Onstott,
      Judy Richardson, Alan LeBendig *(and)*
      Jamie Bush, Robert Pitard,
      Jimmie Pitard, Jim McMullin
1977 Eddie Wold, Neil Chambers, John Schermer,
      Cardinal Woolsey, Polly Rich
1978 Jamie Bush, Jeff Corbin,
      Bryan Storey, Terry Radjef
1979 James Jacoby, Heitie Noland, Nate Silverstein,
      Al Childs, Mike Cook
1980 Thomas Sanders, Carol Sanders, Bernie Yomotov,
      Larry Sealy, Jim Barrow, Roger Jourdan
1981 Steve Beatty, Jim Miller,
      Ron LaCour, Richard Capps

MIXED PAIRS
1941 Maxcyne Windsor, C. P. Williams
1942 Mrs. J. J. Ogden, Jason Floyd
1943 Mrs. Ed Campbell, John McCormick
1944 Earline Foley, Leo Kershenbaum
1945 Louise Robbins, Lt. H. R. Regelin
1946 Herbert Rice, Grace Coffin
1947 Claire Meyer, Louis Levy
1948 Fred Berger, Mrs. Marshall
1949 Emma Jean Hawes, Ben Fain
1950 H. Moore, J. Jabon
1951 Robert Pitard, Jimmie Pitard

1952	Ted Drake, Mrs. Ted Drake
1953	Mrs. L. Tiller, John Simon
1954	Paula Levin, Peter Leventritt
1955	Shirley Fairchild, J. David King
1956	Charles Goren, Linda Terry
1957	Anita Davis, Fred Berger
1958	Theron Brown, Freddie Berger
1959	Betty Lou Hickman, Jack Blair
1960	Gertrude Eberson, Bob Barrett
1961	Betty Ann Welch, John Kennedy
1963	Mrs. Thomas Youngblood, Hamilton Cage
1964	Thomas Sanders, Carol Sanders
1965	Emma Jean Hawes, Peter Rank
1966	Jackie Smith, John Hyland
1968	Chafford Brown, Mrs. Chafford Brown
1969	Emma Jean Hawes, John Bromberg
1970	Col. J. Stephenson, Vera Stephenson
1971	Esta Van Zandt, Bud Reinhold
1972	Diane Siebert, Dane Clay
1973	George Elzen, Mrs. A. Schexnayder
1976	Mrs. Guy Dunning, David Carter

OPEN PAIRS

1941	Andrew McNeile, Robert Woodworth
1942	Mrs. J. J. Ogden, Jason Floyd
1943	Larry Shurlds, Elinor Murdoch
1944	Dr. R. D. Furlong, Mrs. R. D. Furlong
1945	Sgt. Robert Appleyard, M. A. Lightman
1946	Louise Krause, Joe Rosenfield, Jr.
1947	Mrs. Joe Rosenfield, Jr., Elinor Murdoch
1948	Earline Foley, Jimmie Pitard
1949	John Gerber, Paul Hodge
1950	N. Wallfisch, C. Woldenberg
1951	Ben Fain, John Toledano
1952	Elinor Murdoch, Mrs. Newton Howell
1953	Claire Meyer, Lucien Zilbermann
1954	Maurice Levin, Peter Leventritt
1955	Theron Brown, Clarice Holt
1956	Jeff Glick, Jerry Lewis
1957	Addie Simon, Jr., Edgar Theus
1958	Louis Gurvich, Sidney Lazard
1959	Dr. John Fisher, Nate Silverstein
1960	Jimmy Heymann, Robert Craig
1961	Julius Rosenblum, Frank Hoadley
1962	John Gerber, Edwin Smith, Jr.
1963	Oswald Jacoby, Paul Levitt
1964	Oswald Jacoby, Mike Thomas
1965	Norbert Kramer, John Murphy
1966	Hallie Tighe, Norma Arnold
1967	Mrs. E. L. Goodman, Paul Weiss
1968	Curtis Smith, Charles Kittle
1969	Al Childs, Larry Lockwood
1970	John Kennedy, Betty Ann Kennedy
1971	Howard Abrams, Alf VanHoose
1972	Fred Woodruff, Richard Capps
1973	Frank Hoadley, Don Caton
1974	David Foote, DeAne Phillips
1976	Nell Cahn, Pat Mizell *(tied with)*
	Dr. Nathan Ostrich, Mary Beth Townsend
1977	Mary Virginia Southwell, Harold Tannen
1978	Dr. John Fisher, Del Parker
1979	Nancy Alpaugh, Sylvia Chavers *(tied with)*
	Esta Schwartz, Louise Wilson
1980	Chuck Said, Charlotte Strauss
1981	Barry Crane, Thomas Sanders
Flight A:	
1977	Jack Walton, Allan Siebert
1979	Marc Jacobus, Paul Lewis
1980	Mary Oshlag, Richard Oshlag
1981	Jim Black, Jack Walton

WOMEN'S PAIRS

1941	Cleo Young, Mrs. L. R. Swisher
1942	M. L. Murphy, Mildred Ratliff
1943	Rhea Bonck, Mrs. Tom Casey
1944	Claire Meyer, Dottie Toledano
1945	R. Scott, Mrs. Robert Burleigh
1946	Mary Lou Oldham, Mary Davis
1947	A. H. Hodgson, G. McGhee
1948	Luie Rosen, Elinor Murdoch
1949	Natalie Rosenblum, Elinor Murdoch
1950	Mrs. R. Tete, Mrs. L. Galatoire
1952	L. C. Barrow, C. Shepherd
1953	Jimmie Pitard, Earline Foley
1954	Dolly Rosenfeld, Maurine Parsons
1955	Theron Brown, Clarice Holt
1956	Vera Glick, Mrs. Paul Remlinger
1957	Julia Lucas, Clarice Bonnell
1958	Adaline Simon, Martha Newbill
1959	Jimmie Pitard, Theron Brown
1960	Mabel Rackle, Audrey Evans
1961	Mrs. Charles Thompson, Nancy Jost
1962	Marguerite Wagnon, Mrs. Jack Boone

1963	Natalie Rosenblum, Elinor Murdoch
1964	Ruth Steinberg, Jane Rosenschein
1965	Mrs. Fred Miers, Kay Thalheimer
1966	Anita Villavaso, Genevieve Aillet
1967	Mrs. P. V. Hitt, Mrs. J. T. Martin
1968	Dell Ault, Jo Sharp
1969	Mrs. Bryan Chancey, Mrs. J. Brazille
1970	Eleanor Bransford, Carol Sanders
1971	Dianne Kaiser, Gerri Goff
1972	Peggy Leonard, Gene Roberts
1973	Mary Beth Townsend, Pat LaCour
1974	Dee Adams, Lillian Goodman
1975	Loretta Rivers, Sylvia Chavers
1977	Carol Sanders, Betty Ann Kennedy
1978	Lillian Parker, Angela Carlisi
1979	Virginia Penick, Esta Van Zandt
1980	Mary Virginia Southwell, Marie Louise Steuer
1981	Mary Virginia Southwell, Marie Louise Steuer

WOMEN'S MASTER SWISS TEAMS

1976	Phyllis Smith, Anita Davis, Garner McDaniel,
	Madelyn Carmichael, Sheila Collins

WOMEN'S SWISS TEAMS

1980	Bernadine Jenkins, Connie Jackson, Carol Sanders,
	Nancy Alpaugh, Garland Ergüden

MEN'S PAIRS

1941	Robert Burleigh, L.D. Boone
1942	Ben Fain, Paul Hodge
1943	J. Russell Bailey, J. P. Risics
1944	Ben Fain, Lt. Chester Husted
1945	Lt. Al Harris, L. D. Boone
1946	C. N. Coleman, Payne Harrison
1947	Ed Jordan, William Nelson
1948	Ben Fain, Paul Hodge
1949	Charles Coleman, Joe Farrar
1950	H. Early, M. Soniat
1951	Ben Fain, Jerry Lewis
1952	Allyn McKeen, Pat Connelly
1953	Robert Sharpe, Robbie Robertson
1954	Dan Westerfield, James Jacoby
1956	James Jacoby, Oswald Jacoby
1957	Gerald Michaud, David Carter
1958	Steve Greenberg, Jack Blair, Jr.
1959	Dr. Richard Greene, Byron Greenberg
1960	Martin Cohn, Thomas Sanders
1961	James Jacoby, Dr. John Fisher
1962	Roy Sheffield, J. G. Ripstra
1963	Ronald Dreyfus, Sidney Lazard
1964	James Jacoby, Dr. John Fisher
1965	Charles Coon, Peter Pender
1966	John Gerber, Dan Morse
1967	David Siebert, Jack Walton
1968	John Potter, Richard Potter
1969	Thomas Golding, Charles Roesch
1970	Dr. John Fisher, Fred Berger
1971	Jim Barrow, Don Caton
1972	Sam Coolik, Emery Oxford
1973	Jim Miller, Fred Woodruff
1974	Paul Soloway, Malcolm Brachman
1976	Sidney Lazard, Frank Hoadley
1977	Steve Goldberg, Allan Cokin
1978	Joe Steuer, Thomas Reid
1979	Ed Schulte, Walter Malloy
1980	Barry Crane, Thomas Sanders
1981	Larry Sealy, Ron Smith

MEN'S MASTER SWISS TEAMS

1976	Daniel Kaim, John Gerber,
	Jim Hooker, Fred Berger

MEN'S SWISS TEAMS

1980	Barry Crane, Jerry Clerkin, Dennis Clerkin,
	Thomas Sanders, Larry Sealy *(tied with)*
	Richard Coren, Gaylor Kasle,
	Cy Dennen, Jeff Meckstroth

MASTER SWISS TEAMS

1978	Barry Crane, Thomas Sanders,
	Carol Sanders, Betty Ann Kennedy

MASTER INDIVIDUAL

1942	Peggy Mooney
1943	Clare Levy
1944	Linda Terry
1947	Mrs. John Ogden
1948	Mark Hodges
1950	Mrs. L. Galatoire
1951	Louis L. Rosen
1952	Lillian Tiller
1953	Walter Wilson, Jr.
1954	Esther Woldenberg
1955	James Baird
1957	Mona Spurlock

1958   Mrs. N. Burgner
1976   Dick Claussen

UNMIXED PAIRS
1974   Paul Soloway, Mike Passell

MID-SOUTH SUMMER

KNOCKOUT TEAMS
1968   James Jacoby, Robert Wolff, Michael Lawrence,
     William Eisenberg, Robert Goldman
1972   Jack Kennedy, Betty Kennedy, Carol Sanders,
     Jack Blair, Byron Greenberg, Charles Weed
1974   Carol Sanders, Thomas Sanders, Jack Blair,
     Byron Greenberg, Steve Greenberg
1976   Lou Bluhm, Richard Shepherd, Thomas Sanders,
     Carol Sanders, Larry Gould, Ron Smith
1978   Tom Sanders, Lou Bluhm, Reece Rogers,
     Mike Cook, Richard Oshlag
1981   John Griscom, Jim Felts, Reece Rogers,
     Frank Stewart, Jim Foster

LIFE MASTER PAIRS
1968   Jim Jacoby, Robert Wolff

MEN'S SWISS TEAMS
1981   Glenn Merrill, Jack Despain,
     Randy Pettit, George Rhode

WOMEN'S SWISS TEAMS
1981   Carol Harvey, Janie Judy,
     Ruth Francis, Kathleen Ramsey

OPEN TEAMS
1960   Fred Berger, Dr. Richard Greene,
     Mary Zita Jacoby, Oswald Jacoby
1961   Jim Jacoby, Judy Jacoby, Oswald Jacoby,
     Curtis Finch, Steve Greenberg
1962   John Toledano, Fred Hughes, Margaret Byrd,
     Jason Floyd, Bernard Tighe
1963   Ace Gutowsky, Steve Greenberg,
     Nancy Alpaugh, Dr. Richard Greene
1964   Don Reid, Ira Corn,
     Dorothy Moore, Mark Hodges
1965   Julius Rosenblum, Nate Silverstein, Sidney Lazard,
     Frank Hoadley, Robert Pitard
1966   Oswald Jacoby, Dan Morse,
     Paul Levitt, Shirlee Lazarus
1967   Clarice Holt, Mary Beth Townsend,
     Mickey Finch, George Dawkins
1968   Curtis Smith, Steve Lawrence,
     Esta Van Zandt, Heitie Noland
1969   Hermine Baron, Paul Soloway, Adeline Simon,
     Gaylor Kasle, Norman Anderson
1970   Oswald Jacoby, Lou Gurvich, Jean Frankel,
     Jim Linhart, James Jacoby
1971   John Zilic, Virginia Zilic,
     Esta Van Zandt, Shirlee Lazarus
1972   Kelsey Petterson, Proctor Hawkins,
     Ken Bradley, Oren Moore
1973   Jim Foster, Al Van Hoose,
     Jim Rainey, Walker Jones
1974   Marvin Shapiro, Larry Kolker, Ron Smith,
     Dave Malec, Richard Oshlag
1976   Manya Ogle, Hugh Ogle,
     William McDaniel, Howard Abrams
1978   Barry Crane, Jack Blair,
     Steve Goldberg, Ron Andersen *(Smoking)*
     Joe Steuer, Marie Louise Steuer,
     Mary Virginia Southwell, Harold Tannen *(Non-Smoking)*
1981   Joan Stein, Norman Fischer,
     Bruce Parent, Tom Hodapp *(tied with)*
     Lois Muir, Dick Keith,
     Ellen Anker, Mike Sheldon

OPEN PAIRS
1960   Vera Stephenson, Lt. Jack Payton
1961   Oswald Jacoby, James Jacoby
1962   Jeff Glick, Nate Silverstein
1963   Frank Hoadley, Ronald Dreyfus
1964   George Pisk, Harvey Cohen
1965   Sidney Lazarus, Paul Levitt
1966   Sidney Lazarus, Paul Levitt
1967   Jerry Duval, William Riddle
1968   Pat Hood, George Pisk
1969   Joseph Ripstra, Mort Nelson
1970   Clarice Holt, Charles Robinson *(tied with)*
     David Siebert, Allan Siebert
1971   Richard Doughty, Dr. Richard Greene
1972   Diane Kaiser, Ray Kaiser
1973   Terry Radjef, Douglas Hill
1974   Mark Blumenthal, Seymour Leibowitz
1976   Bob Teel, Jane Teel
1978   Louise Sharp, Daniel Oken

Flight A:
1978   Ron Smith, Robert Levin
1981   Joan Stein, Norman Fischer

WOMEN'S PAIRS
1960   Miarion Coleman, Trudie Caspary
1961   Thelma Potts, Daisy Stephens
1962   Mrs. George Van Geffen, C. Van Geffen
1963   Claire Nelson, Lillian Morais
1964   Kay Chilleteau, Amelia Hurd
1965   Dottie Toledano, Amy Harrison *(tied with)*
     Mrs. R. Gaston, Mrs. C. Kantrow
1966   Fran Beard, Sidney Perutz
1967   Carolyn Hurd, Rose Groves
1968   Mindy Brachman, Shirlee Lazarus *(tied with)*
     Natalie Rosenblum, Paula Levin
1969   Betty Ann Kennedy, Emma Jean Dawes
1970   Jeanne Littrell, Mary Bennett
1971   Toby Bassett, Diane Kaiser
1972   Mrs. Charles McInnis, Mrs. H. Werner
1973   Nancy Alpaugh, Esta Van Zandt
1974   Gloria Colley, Rae Horwitz
1976   Carol Sanders, Betty Ann Kennedy
1978   Kathryn Smith, Tina McKee
1981   Doris Whitlock, Robbie Payne

MEN'S PAIRS
1960   James Jacoby, John Spessard
1961   Lee Brown, Dane Clay
1962   Frank Hoadley, Louis Gurvich
1963   Sidney Lazard, Ronald Dreyfus
1964   Frank Condon, Joel Colglazier
1965   George Dawkins, Brad Gentry
1966   Tom Wood, Dr. Carl Merlin
1967   Dr. Hal Oddie, Dudley Ball
1968   Fred Hamilton, Cliff Bishop
1969   Terry Radjef, Jack Walton
1970   Gerald Michaud, Larry Richardson
1971   Sam Coolik, Emry Oxford
1972   Mike Passell, Julius Rosenblum
1973   Frank Hoadley, Paul Munafo
1974   Robert Teel, Mike Davis
1976   Ed Schulte, Wayne Whalen
1978   Mike Passell, Joseph Miller
1981   Quentin Ball, Andy Bernstein

MIXED PAIRS
1960   Jerri Smith, David Carter
1961   Helen Sobel, Roy Golden
1962   Jean Frankel, Louis Gurvich
1963   Ace Gutowsky, Nancy Alpaugh
1964   Cy Strouse, Luise Mathews
1965   Betsey Wolff, Charles Miller
1966   Lou Gurvich, Jean Frankel
1967   Mary Beth Townsend, G. Robert Nail
1968   Nancy Alpaugh, Paul Munafo
1969   Dr. Martin Anderson, Vadis Hall
1970   Lou Gurvich, Jean Frankel
1971   Carolyn Schoenau, Adrian Dovell
1972   Jerri Gardner, Dr. Charles Robinson

MASTER PAIRS
1960   Wally Wallington, Vaughn Ellzey
1961   Lee Green, Jack Driscoll
1962   Bob Lazard, Sidney Lazard *(tied with)*
     James Jacoby, Robert Nail
1963   Sidney Lazard, Dr. Richard Greene
1964   Sidney Lazard, Dr. Richard Greene
1965   Ruby Stoll, John Gerber
1966   Jack LaNoue, Paul Munafo
1967   Bitsy Pontius, Dr. Ed Dillion
1968   Mrs. E. Balding, Mrs. H. Bell
1969   Nancy Alpaugh, Paul Munafo
1970   Teddy O'Brien, Carol Sanders
1971   Nate Silverstein, Joel Colglazier
1972   Jack Blair, David Siebert
1973   Betty Ann Kennedy, Carol Sanders
1974   Steve Greenberg, Mark Lair
1976   Frank Stewart, Lou Bluhm
1978   Bill Cohen, Ron Smith
1981   Nash Ball, Andy Bernstein

SOUTHERN CONFERENCE FALL*

OPEN TEAMS
1952   M.A. Lightman, Zodie Glover,
     Nate Silverstein, Louis Levy
1953   Charles Goren, Margaret Wagar, Al Walton,
     Henry Chanin, Mark Godges
1954   Eugene Roy, Gertrude Eberson,
     Irving Spiewack, John Moore

*This tournament was discontinued in 1966.

1955 Sidney Smith, Mel Anderson,
Shirley Johnson, Richard Carter
1956 Jeff Glick, Max Turk,
Nate Silverstein, Ray Michelson
1957 Mrs. A. D. White, James West, Andrew Massie,
Mrs. Walter LeSeuer, Rosalie Ronn
1958 Fred Berger, Lou Gurvich, Sidney Lazard,
Nate Silverstein, Dr. John Fisher
1959 Robert Sharp, Josephine Sharp,
Sidney Kasle, Lee Kasle
1961 Joe George, David Hart, James Day, Jr.,
Lewis Loeb, Carey Yelton
1962 Easley Blackwood, Dr. Douglas Trapp,
Sory Davis, Sterling Lanier *(tied with)*
Thomas Sanders, Carol Sanders, Martin Cohn,
Margaret Wagar, Hampton Hume
1963 Elinor Murdoch, Dr. Charles Burnham,
Terry Teague, Mrs. Terry Teague
1964 Richard Freeman, Louise Freeman, Louise Clark,
Robert Sharp, Josephine Sharp
1965 Paul Weiss, Robert Sharp,
Bud Creed, Louise Clark

MASTER PAIRS
1957 Margaret Wagar, Arthur Miller
1958 Harrison Adams, Thomas Sanders
1959 Thomas Sanders, Carol Sanders
1961 William Woodson, Jake McDonald
1962 Diane Siebert, Allen Siebert
1963 Foxy Hall, Vivian Davis
1964 John Armstrong, Dr. Charles Duffy
1965 Jim Jacoby, Nate Silverstein

OPEN PAIRS
1952 Lee Campbell, F. H. Richmond
1953 Vera Glick, Jeff Glick
1954 F. Holton Sexton, Mrs. Dale Smyth
1955 Mrs. P. Semonin, Charles Klayer
1956 Lorraine Zollinger, Cecil Inman, Jr.
1957 Max Turk, Jeff Glick
1958 Nate Silverstein, M.A. Lightman
1959 James McKenzie, Martin Phillips
1961 Martin Cohn, Hamilton Hume
1962 Eleanor Murdoch, Dr. Charles Burham *(tied with)*
Dorothy Payne, Lois Shuptrine
1963 Grace Spencer, Renna Mourer
1964 Capt. Howard Hertzberg, Mrs. Mason Yates
1965 Curtis Smith, Charles Kittle

MEN'S PAIRS
1952 M. A. Lightman, Stanley Maxwell
1953 Jack Feagin, Paul Herndon *(tied with)*
William Downs, Joe Caller
1954 Arthur Kincaid, F. Ayres Bombeck
1955 Richard Goldberg, William Peale
1956 Jeff Glick, Max Turk
1957 Dave Carter, J. Don Daniel
1958 Harrison Adams, Thomas Sander
1959 Thomas Sanders, Hampton Hume
1961 George Harris, Dan Krakowski
1962 Dr. Charles Burhnam, Terry Teague
1963 S. A. Baker, Dr. D. P. Edmundson
1964 Sam Neely, Maurice (Red) Bell
1965 Leon Levinson, Russell Read

MIXED PAIRS
1952 Mrs. E. L. Crew, C. E. Wilson
1953 Mrs. E. L. Crew, C. E. Wilson *(tied with)*
Mrs. J. B. McConnel, Jack Walton
1954 Gertrude Ittenback, Irving Spiewack
1955 Gertrude Smith, Charles Hall
1956 J. Theron Brown, Fred Berger
1957 Mildred Cytron, Dave Carter
1958 Molly Roleson, Max Turk

WOMEN'S PAIRS
1952 Lou Lusky, Reba Hunter
1953 Min Campbell, Gladys Barrett
1954 J. Bailey, Helen Clinkinbeard
1955 Dolly Rosenfield, Shirley Johnson
1956 Mrs. Milton Hudson, E. L. Crew
1957 V. C. Scoggin, Louise Wilson
1958 Shirlee Lazarus, Jean Frankel
1959 Mrs. James Pearson, Mrs. Carl Peterson
1961 Mrs. Ralph Thompson, S. W. Seagull
1962 Lynn Haynes, Jane Clayton
1963 Mrs. Robert Ruppel, Ruby Burton
1964 Elinor Murdoch, Mrs. Terry Teague
1965 Mrs. Mark Porter, Mrs. Jack Spence

INDIVIDUAL
1952 Mrs. Karl Hinig
1953 Clayton Hudson
1956 Luther Hamilton

SOUTHERN CONFERENCE SPRING*

OPEN TEAMS
1963 James McKenzie, Sr., Mrs. James McKenzie,
Jean Hemphill, Phyllis Attaway
1964 Rose Lerman, Edward Sharp,
Robert Sharp, Josephine Sharp *(tied with)*
John Moran, Chuck Henke, J. David King,
Walter Leach, Fredrick Rubbra
1965 Foxy Hall, Hampton Hume, Gloria Cronin,
Jack Blair, Bernadine Jenkins
1966 Robert Morris, John Bowman,
Capt. Ed Lewis, Dorothy Lewis

MASTER PAIRS
1963 Robert Sharp, Josephine Sharp
1965 Foxy Hall, Margaret Wagar
1966 Peter Pender, Jeremy Flint

OPEN PAIRS
1963 Robert Sharp, Josephine Sharp
1964 Hermine Baron, Barry Crane
1965 John Meyers, Guy Elder
1966 Curtis Smith, Dr. Robert Farris

MEN'S PAIRS
1963 Thomas Sanders, Howard Behm
1964 Richard Carter, Lloyd Roberts
1965 Charles Miller, Dan Morse
1966 Barry Crane, Thomas Sanders

WOMEN'S PAIRS
1963 Mrs. Walter Thompson, G. A. Davis
1964 Mrs. Joseph Morris, Cecilia Mahan
1965 Claire Fox, Frances Hultman
1966 Betty Peters, Helen Clinkinbeard

MIXED PAIRS
1964 Margaret Shouse, Arthur Marler

DISTRICT 11 (Central and southern Indiana, central and southern Ohio, most of Kentucky, southern West Virginia)

DISTRICT 11

KNOCKOUT TEAMS
1969 Martin Cohn, Betty Cohn,
Phil Leon, Richard Fleischman
1971 Jack Blair, Mark Blumenthal,
Paul Swanson, Don Faskow
1973 Fred Hamilton, Kenneth Cohen, Phil Leon,
Marc Blumenthal, John Sheridan, Larry Kozlove
1974 Charles Bauer, Bruce Neikirk,
Randy Baron, David MacAslan
1975 Tom Hodapp, Steve Hauer, Russell Shoup,
Capt. Tom Miller, Robert Morris
1977 Bill Coombs, Norm Coombs,
F. Holton Sexton, Tom Hodapp
1981 Seymon Deutsch, Gaylor Kasle,
Garey Hayden, Bobby Wolff

OPEN PAIRS
1962 Shirlee Harris, Ed Rosen
1963 Martin Cohn, Peter Scezci
1964 Charlie Coon, Mike Moss
1965 Jack Blair, Paul Swanson
1966 Bill Flannery, Paul Swanson
1967 Martin Angell, Kimmer Smith
1968 Fred Hamilton, Howard Perlman
1969 Turner Clarke, J. David King
1970 Kenneth Rhodes, Henry Itkin
1971 John Biddle, Jim Wisemiller
1972 Steve Sherman, David Boughman
1973 Mark Blumenthal, Seymour Leibowitz
1974 John Sheridan, Larry Kozlove
1975 Richard Rudolph, Norman Frank
1976 Bill Coombs, John Hermann
1977 Larry Howard, Myra Howard
1978 Ben Mathews, Donald McMullen *(tied with)*
Joe Davis, Ken Goland
1979 Dave Fred, Phil Leon
1980 Paul Hessel, Jerry Goldfein
1981 Tom Hodapp, Norman Fisher

LIFE MASTER PAIRS
1972 Norman Fisher, Tom Hodapp

WOMEN'S SWISS TEAMS
1978 Ann Economidy, Anne Leverone,
Carol Crump, Marilyn Kolker
1979 Janet Rose, Louise Bender,
Dorothy Tennenbaum, Roslyn Brant

*This tournament was discontinued in 1967.

1980	Cheryl Trauber, Jan George, Caroline Pascoe, Roberta Sue Fost
1981	Lynn Ware, Connie Jackson, Bernadine Jenkins, Carol Sanders

MEN'S SWISS TEAMS

1978	Bob Sampson, Arthur Moore, W. Page Morris, Randolph Beckham
1979	Roland Case, Dennis Hesthaven, Larry Long, Tom Callaham
1980	Eric Rodwell, John Sheridan, Jeff Meckstroth, Roger Jourdan, Dick Rudolph, Jim Barrow
1981	Larry Kozlove, Marc Jacobus, Tom Hodapp, Ron Smith

WOMEN'S PAIRS

1962	Mrs. William Eckhart, Mrs. Charles Maudlin
1963	Dalla Pacella, Marie Baum
1964	D. Johnson, Mrs. Charlton Wallace
1965	Mrs. Irving Rosenbaum, Margaret Thompson
1966	Betty Hartley, Agnes Baughn
1967	Margaret Thompson, Agnes Gordon
1968	Amelia Argersinger, Jane Rosenschein
1969	Mary Louise Reich, Eloise Neil
1970	Eleanor Crounse, Mrs. Fredrick Eberson
1971	Carol Sanders, Linda Hanson
1973	Mrs. Arch Falender, Patricia Sundstrom
1977	Barbara Pfeifer, Lillia Leibig
1979	Joan Stein, Sandra Frisch
1980	Linda Highland, Nancy Taylor
1981	Florine Kuehl, Madelynn Carmichael

MEN'S PAIRS

1962	Jerome Yavitz, Charles Peres
1963	Norm Coombs, Ray Zoller
1964	Charlie Coon, Mike Moss
1965	Nate Silverstein, George Treadwell
1966	Edson McKinney, Jr., Don Guerin
1967	Joe Beard, Thomas Johnson
1968	James Finegan, Mel Keisler
1969	Thomas Peters, Ronald Brown
1970	Tom Hodapp, Steve Cohn
1971	Arthur Kaseman, Dr. Charles Bishop
1973	W. MacDonald, Robert Calhoun
1977	William Jimison, Dr. Charles Bishop
1978	Larry Long, Tom Callaham
1979	Robb Gordon, Gabi Ideh
1981	Mel Skolnik, Jeff Meckstroth

MIXED PAIRS

1963	Eloise Neil, Trent Sines
1964	Josephine Sharp, Fred Ensminger
1967	Frank Weisbach, Marion Hamilton
1968	Ruth McConnell, Tom Ezzell

OPEN TEAMS

1962	Jack Denny, Jill Denny, Sylvia Stein, Julie Halloran, Grant Marsee
1963	Joe Beebe, William Riester, Mrs. William O'Hara, William O'Hara
1964	John Simon, Jack Denny, Paul Matthews, William Long
1965	Ayres Bombeck, Mike Thomas, Jack Blair, Paul Swanson
1966	Kit Woolsey, John Hrones, Jr., John Levinson, Jeff Passel
1967	John Levinson, Dan Rotman, Dr. David Kitzes, Leo Spivack *(tied with)* Karl Austin, Jerry Angel, Harrison Marsh, Stephen Zimmerman
1968	John Groben, David Kahane, Wayne Morris, Jack Winkler
1969	John Feld, Thomas Todd, Stephen Zimmerman, Marvin Ferguson
1970	Mrs. Eugene Cain, Eugene Cain Duane Morrow, James Mathews
1971	Helen Clinkinbeard, James Lay, Robert Stone, Allen Cokin
1972	Greg Potts, James Wisemiller, John Biddle, Charles Kopp
1973	Wayne Snider, Ralph Katz, Henry Rabin, Gene Chait
1974	Bill Coombs, Rick Koopman, Steve Cohn, Jeffrey Gargrave *(Winter)* Fred Hamilton, John Sheridan, Jeff Starr, Cliff Bishop, Larry Kozlove *(Spring)*
1975	Ben Matthews, Charles Klayer, Don McMullin, Paul Godfrey
1976	Milt Rosenberg, Mark Blumenthal, Dr. John Fisher, Gerald Caravelli, Larry Kozlove
1977	Marc Rabinowitz, Dave Schor, Bernard Fudor, Marc Nathan
1978	Barry Crane, Jack Blair, Thomas Sanders, Carol Sanders

1979	Richard Finberg, Marilyn Finberg, Wendell Van Court, Douglas Coppock
1980	Eric Rodwell, Larry Mori, Pratap Rajadhyaksha, Jeff Meckstroth, Marilyn Miller
1981	Mel Skolnick, Peter Weichsel, Ron Smith, Jeff Meckstroth

MASTER PAIRS

1964	Hermine Baron, Barry Crane
1965	Robert Sharp, Louise Clark
1966	Raymond Zoller, Philip Leon
1969	Norm Coombs, Gerald Steuernagel
1970	Mrs. John Gordon, John Gordon
1971	Paul Swanson, Jack Blair
1972	Mary Lipp, John Dink, Jr.
1974	Chuck Said, Sammie Tallent *(Winter)* Rhoda Walsh, Kerri Shuman *(Spring)*
1975	Mrs. G.F. Malling, Herbert Peters
1976	Norm Coombs, Tom Hodapp
1977	George Fraction, Pat Thornell
1978	Mike Levine, Vic Rigotti
1979	Sue Stevenson, Liz Sorgi
1980	Fran Pettijohn, Joe Beard
1981	Dennis Hesthaven, Jack Ambach

MIDWEST FALL

KNOCKOUT TEAMS

1973	Morgan Hunter, Dean Carmeris, Steve Cox, Charles Ferry
1975	Cliff Bishop, Hal Mouser, Gabel Ideh, Fred Hamilton, Stephen Cox, Marshall Lewis
1977	Dave Fred, Gary Bush, Steve Bloom, Betty Bloom
1978	Kathie Wei, Ron Andersen, Allan Cokin, Steve Sion
1979	Clarence Goppert, Mike Passell, Paul Soloway, Mark Lair, Eddie Wold
1980	Malcolm Brachman, Bobby Goldman, Mike Lawrence, Eddie Kantar, Ron Andersen, Paul Soloway

MIXED PAIRS

1959	Arlene Klein, Fred Ensminger
1960	Adelaide Simon, Jack Denny
1961	Roslyn Cooper, Martin Cooper
1962	Mrs. John French, Charles O'Rourke
1963	John Bowman, Kay O'Keeffe
1964	Carol Ruther, Steve Honet
1965	Flo Orner, Dan Rotman
1966	Agnes Gordon, Peter Pender
1967	Bernice Larson, Howard Pickett

WOMEN'S SWISS TEAM

1976	Gladys Hildebrand, Renna Mourer, Nita Kemp, Carlene Nielsen
1977	Sandra Frisch, Joan Stein, Patty Lundstrom, Fran Pettijohn
1978	Helen Pieper, Ann Garrison, Susan Jordan, Mary Brower
1979	Julia Bomalaski, Betty Birk, Beth Rogers, Norma Brown *(tied with)* Virginia Flint, Pat Roberts, Pat Slonaker, Nan Novotny
1980	Joan DeWitt, Mrs. R.H. VanderLaan, Shirley Svenson, Mina Ronen
1981	Penny Sommers, Patty Meckstroth, Marinesa Letizia, Susan Ganley

MEN'S SWISS TEAMS

1976	James Reel, Robert Blue, Dick Paulson, Tom Coyle
1977	Dennis McGarry, Jack Denny, Tom Mahaffey, Ron Smith
1978	Chuck Said, Thomas Sanders, Jeff Overby Dennis McGarry, Norm Coombs, Tom Hodapp *(tied with)* Dave Fred, John Bodish, Richard Rudolph, Phil Leon
1979	Randy Baron, Bruce Neikirk, Ralph Letizia, Dennis Clerkin, Gary Kessler
1980	Barth Royer, Charles Kopp, Dave Spitler, Jim Wisemiller, Carl Edwards
1981	David Caslan, Gary Bush, Barth Royer, Dick Rudolph

OPEN PAIRS

1959	Jack Wachter, Jim Hanley
1960	F. Holton Sexton, Paul Mathews
1961	Barry Crane, Robert Sharp
1962	Emanuel Hochfeld, William Rosen
1963	Gunther Polack, Carol Ruther
1964	Harvey Miller, Joe Weiner
1965	Mrs. William Mann, William Mann
1966	Jeremy Flint, Peter Pender
1967	Bill Zurfluh, George Durgin
1972	Harry Gordon, Don Walker

1973 Zue Johantgen, Mrs. W. Crawford
1974 George Hartleben, Kathryn Hartleben
1975 James Walters, Mark Wolfinger
1976 Kathie Wei, Ron Andersen
1977 Jim Foster, John Griscom
1978 Barry Crane, Thomas Sanders
1979 Carol Hammer, Howard Hammer
1980 Pratap Rajadhyaksha, Marilyn Miller *(tied with)*
    Yul Inn, Harry Stratton
1981 Steve Landen, Jeff Meckstroth

MEN'S PAIRS

1959 Jim Felfuss, Al Lindberg
1960 Homer Shoop, Cornelius Kauff
1961 John Wachter, Robert Shepard
1962 Max Heller, Monte Lopata
1963 Oswald Jacoby, Paul Levitt
1964 Howard Schenken, Ivar Stakgold
1965 Francis Carlson, Sambasirerao Koritala *(tied with)*
    Alan Bell, Ross Amann
1966 William Brown, Sam Follmer
1967 Jack Kamin, Larry Mines
1973 Charles Bauer, David Boxley
1976 Jay Wein, John Yuan
1977 Jimmy Miller, Steve Zimmerman
1978 Chuck Said, Jeff Overby
1979 Paul Soloway, Larry Kozlove
1980 Paul Soloway, Malcolm Brachman
1981 Alan Tavel, Gaylor Kasle

WOMEN'S PAIRS

1959 Ethel Benjamin, Dorothy Bramhall
1960 Sally MacLeod, Esther Watson
1961 Sandi Leavitt, Carol Stolkin
1962 Jean Piowaty, E.H. Charlton
1963 Mrs. Phil Paris, Portia Miller
1964 Frieda Arst, Hermine Baron
1965 Laura Herzberg, Elizabeth Hyre
1966 Mrs. Ralph Decker, Mrs. Denver Fuller
1967 Jan Cohn, Joey Sage
1963 Gretchen Funk, Mrs. K. Nielsen
1976 Patty Sundstrom, Fran Pettijohn
1977 Patty Sundstrom, Fran Pettijohn
1978 Eileen Perkins, Flo Rotman
1979 Zoe Hutchins, Joyce Fetterer
1980 Anita Torrence, Jade Wyatt
1981 Zoe Hutchins, Joyce Fetterer

OPEN TEAMS

1959 Eunice Rosen, William Rosen,
    Bob Casement, Al Habel
1960 Adelaide Simon, John Simon,
    Jill Denny, Jack Denny *(tied with)*
    Shirlee Harris, Eunice Rosen,
    Fran Pettijohn, Stan McComas *(and)*
    Bud Creed, Sam Scaffidi,
    John Biddle, Carl Hudecek
1961 William Rosen, Arny Leavitt,
    Ed Rosen, Barry Crane
1962 Barry Crane, Robert Sharp, William Rosen,
    Ed Rosen, Arny Leavitt
1963 John Biddle, Jeff Polsner,
    Bill Riestner, John Wisemiller
1964 Ed Rosen, Allan Zeh, Beverly Farber,
    Worth Vaughan, John Wachter
1965 Marvin Altman, Gloria Turner,
    Dan Rotman, Bob Mosher
1966 Jeremy Flint, Peter Pender,
    Honor Flint, Jack Denny
1967 Eunice Rosen, William Rosen,
    Gunther Polak, Barry Crane
1972 Wayne Snider, Larry Gould,
    Lou Bluhm, John Piaski
1973 Barry Crane, Kerri Shuman,
    Gerald Caravelli, Dr. John Fisher
1974 Carl Hudecek, Frank McClure, Larrie Willinger,
    Dave Bondy, Bill Hale
1975 Malcolm Brachman, Bobby Goldman,
    Robert Sherburn, F. Holton Sexton
1976 Harold McConnell, Bob Sulgrove,
    Jeff Meckstroth, Eric Rodwell
1977 Larri Mori, Zeke Jabbour,
    Dennis McGarry, Pratap Rajadhyaksha *(Smoking)*
    Bill Coombs, Wayne Hollingsworth,
    Greg Potts, F. Holton Sexton *(tied with)*
    Jay Wein, Janet Weyant,
    Bernice Larson, Carol Dahl *(Non-Smoking)*
1978 Gene Chait, Jerry Goldfein,
    Richard Halperin, Mark Cohen
1979 Clarence Goppert, Mike Passell,
    Mark Lair, Eddie Wold
1980 Bruno Sestito, Linda Sestito,
    Bill Coombs, Dennis Hesthaven

1981 Mel Skolnik, Jeff Meckstroth,
    Eddie Wold, Eric Rodwell

MASTER PAIRS

1972 James Zimmerman, Bob Hardies
1974 Russell Shoup, Bill Coombs
1975 Mark Blumenthal, Katherine Evans
1976 Carol Krehbiel, Gaylor Kasle
1977 Zeke Jabbour, Dennis McGarry
1978 June Deutsch, Arnold Leavitt
1979 Roland Case, Sammie Tallent
1980 Michael Smith, John Masters
1981 Eric Rodwell, Rony Adelsman

MIDWEST SPRING

KNOCKOUT TEAMS

1972 Harold Mouser, Noll Butcher,
    Lee Secrist, Lou Vild
1973 Garey Hayden, Barney O'Malia,
    Gaylor Kasle, Roger Bates
1974 Dr. Hans Stocker, Sue Murstein,
    Peter Palm, Beirn Staples
1975 Mark Blumenthal, Andrew Bernstein,
    Lou Bluhm, Jim Looby
1977 Charles Bauer, Bruce Neikirk,
    Randy Baron, Dave MacAslan
1979 Mike Passell, Clarence Goppert,
    Jan Janitschke, Mark Lair
1981 Barry Crane, Carol Sanders, Thomas Sanders,
    James Zimmerman, Ralph Katz

MASTER PAIRS

1968 James Reel, Norm Coombs
1969 William Epperson, Lloyd Roberts
1970 Joan Danner, Richard Laughner
1971 Julius Kozlove, Larry Kozlove
1972 William Riester, John Biddle
1973 Joe Davis, Ev Hatch
1974 Rhoda Walsh, Kerri Shuman
1975 Dennis McGarry, Jim Zimmerman
1976 Dennis McGarry, Jim Zimmerman
1977 Ralph McNeal, Susan Graves
1978 Jan Katz, Cliff Bishop
1979 Barry Crane, Dr. John Fisher
1980 Jim Zimmerman, Bill Jacobson
1981 Dave Fred, Ron Adelsman

MIXED PAIRS

1944 Mrs. M. Gutman, Roland Buck
1945 Mrs. John Kelly, O. K. Fraunstein
1946 Florence Stratford, Stanley McComas
1947 Mrs. H. A. Bridges, Lou Herman
1948 Frances Tyler, Waldemar von Zedtwitz
1949 Marie Flasher, Joe Cohan
1950 Mrs. C. C. Caldwell, Art Grau
1951 Mrs. J. Y. Brown, N. W. Jordan
1952 Howard Heberlein, Mrs. Howard Heberlein
1953 Jo Gelman, Joseph Gelman
1954 Mary Malchie, Dr. Edward Hochman
1955 Mildred Cytron, Garrett Nash
1956 Mrs. I. W. Campbell, Robert Morris *(tied with)*
    Adelaide Simon, Robert Sharp
1957 Charles Hall, Jane Halenkamp
1958 Carol Sanders, Thomas Sanders
1959 Helen Shambron, Dr. William Barron
1960 Mabel Mahoney, Dave Carter
1961 Verna Sanford, Oswald Jacoby
1962 Jim Hughes, Mrs. Jim Hughes
1963 Jack Berg, Mary Lee Berg
1965 Gaylor Kasle, Elaine Zeve
1966 Gloria Cooper, Gunther Polak
1967 Louise Sharp, Robert Sharp
1978 Kerri Shuman, Barry Crane

UNMIXED PAIRS

1977 Bruno Sestito, Richard Rudolph
1978 Barry Crane, Gary Hann

MEN'S SWISS TEAMS

1979 Don Schauwecker, Alan Tavel,
    Gaylor Kasle, Garey Hayden
1980 Wayne Hollingsworth, Bill Wright,
    Robert Morris, Mike Oeschsler
1981 Dave Fred, Ron Adelsman,
    Kurt Mundinger, Frank Yoder

WOMEN'S SWISS TEAMS

1979 Joan Lenze, Everyl Kilsheimer,
    Ann Swain, Shirley Alexander
1980 Carol Krehbiel, Frankie Graves,
    Joan Stein, Kay Kirkpatrick *(tied with)*
    Patti Pearcy, Ruth Lemon,
    Donna Patchell, Frances Van Cleve
1981 Audrey Stephan, Mrs. H. F. Terry,

Lucy Faris, Paddi Cline *(tied with)*
Linda Perlman, Patty Meckstroth,
Susan Ganley, Vickie Neilberg *(and)*
Caroline Pascoe, Jan Weyant, Kay Mulford,
Jean Joseph, Bobbie Shipley

MEN'S PAIRS

1944	Easley Blackwood, Walter Pray
1945	Joseph Cain, Ralph Kempner
1946	Oswald Jacoby, Ace Gutowsky
1947	H. W. Clow, E. R. Page
1948	Jack Kravatz, Maynard Adams
1949	Waldemar von Zedtwitz, Sid Hoblitt
1950	J. Winston, Charles Berman
1951	Julius Kozlove, Leonard Goren
1952	James Millerd, Alan Bell
1953	Edwin Berman, Paul Utz
1954	Earl Crooks, Dr. Peter Bernstein
1955	Howard Logan, Judge Ben Mathews
1956	Cliff Bishop, Louis Cohen
1957	Barney Camin, Robert Toffler
1958	Lennart Johnson, William Jones
1959	John Simon, Jack Denny
1960	Jack Schwartz, Charles Bauer
1961	Paul Mathews, Sexton Holton
1962	Frank Weisbach, Nat Marx
1963	Robert Sharp, Barry Crane
1964	Mel Anderson, Lewis Loeb
1965	Hampton Hume, Jack Blair
1966	Joseph Levinson, Ervin Schless
1967	Mark Low, Alan Bell
1968	Michael Hargrove, Thomas Peters
1970	Norm Coombs, Thomas Peters
1971	Bill Penton, James Johnson
1972	Richard Rudolph, Norman Frank
1973	Larry Robinson, Bernard Precker
1974	Michael Aliotta, Richard Huggard
1975	Hank Moss, Irv Steinfeldt
1977	Russell Shoup, Jeff Meckstroth
1979	Ron Andersen, Richard Rudolph
1980	Gaylor Kasle, Tom Miller
1981	William Jacoby, Vince Ragazzo

WOMEN'S PAIRS

1944	Mrs. Ralph Ittenbach, Mrs. Ralph Duncan
1945	Jo Gutman, Helen Martin Smith
1946	Mary Bowden, Marge Anderson
1947	Ruth Steinberg, Mildred Cytron
1948	Gratian Goldstein, Gretchen Feldstein
1949	Mrs. John Kelley, Dorothy Thompson
1950	Mrs. A. E. Fey, Evelyn Anderson
1951	Kay Wood, Helen Lackman
1952	Jane Mohl, Marion Leonard
1953	Mrs. John Sanford, T. F. Barnes
1954	Dorothy Thompson, S. A. Brower
1955	Mildred Cytron, Ruth Steinberg
1956	Mary Hardy, J. Y. Brown
1957	Jill Gill, Julie Halloran
1958	Nova Morris, Isabel Simpson
1959	Jo Sharp, Jane Rosenschein
1960	Lee Kasle, Mrs. Kenneth Pettijohn
1961	Karol Baum, Mary Lee Berg
1962	Karol Baum, Mary Lee Berg
1963	Mrs. George Kerr, Mrs. Roy Troxel
1964	Betty Cready, Olive Wood
1965	Eloise Neil, Mary Louise Reich
1966	Dell Levinson, Nahoma Rohr
1967	Mrs. Edward Romminger, Merle Priem
1968	Mrs. Doyle Smyth, Mrs. Ross McNutt
1970	Lil Falender, Patricia Sundstrom
1971	Lil Falender, Patricia Sundstrom
1972	Mable Barthel, Marge Smith
1973	Gladys Hilderbrand, Mary Frees
1974	Lillian Kleve, Mrs.John Pattison
1975	Mrs. Kenneth Bruce, Mrs. James Morris
1977	Babs Charney, Joan Stein
1979	Liz Sorgi, Joan Stein
1980	Dorothy Weiss, Phyllis Goldstein
1981	Jan Weyant, Kay Mulford

OPEN PAIRS

1944	Reba Buck, Tom Mahaffey
1945	Gratian Goldstein, Gretchin Schildmiller
1946	Syd Fink, Arthur Goldsmith
1947	Allan Harvey, Frank Weisbach
1948	Elmer Babin, Arthur Goldsmith
1949	Joseph Stedem, George Alderton
1950	Morris Goldman, Eddie Burns
1951	Jack Hancock, Emanuel Hochfeld
1952	Jack Wachter, Howard Heberlein
1953	Gloria Turner, Victor Bennahum
1954	Alan Harvey, Richard Carter
1955	Alan Harvey, Kay Rhodes

1956	Sanford Brown, Vincent Remey
1957	Charles Hall, Charlton Wallace
1958	Robert Sharp, Jo Sharp
1959	Mrs. D. Smyth, Emanuel Isralsky
1960	Thomas Sanders, Carol Sanders
1961	James Cayne, Gunther Polak
1962	Barry Crane, Jim Epstein
1963	George Mitchell, William Riester
1964	Hermine Baron, Barry Crane
1965	Barry Crane, Margaret Wagar
1966	Kimmer Smith, O. M. Angell
1967	Burton Ascheim, Linda Deaton
1968	Herb Wilton, Mrs. Herb Wilton
1969	Henry Bethe, Arthur Waldmann
1970	Lloyd Hetzer, Dan Requard
1971	Marc Low, Leone Low
1972	Howard Perlman, Fred Hamilton
1973	Jeff Starr, Fred Hamilton
1974	Jim Morrison, Jade Wyatt
1975	Richard Rudolph, Jeffery Gargrave
1976	Opal Towler, Mrs. Paul Kouns
1977	Quentin Wilmot, Harvey Miller, Jr.
1978	Russell Shoup, Larry Mori
1979	Dick Bruno, Stan Katz
1980	Robert Hamman, Don Williams
1981	Bob Glenn, Larry Long

OPEN TEAMS

1944	J. Van Brooks, Ray Malchie, Harry Feinberg, Arthur Levy
1945	Edson Wood, Cleon Nafe, William Zeller, Walter Pray
1946	Maynard Adams, Jules Banks, Oswald Jacoby, Jack Kravatz
1947	A. S. Novak, A. E. Stein, James Epstein, Pat Ochs, Robert Woodworth
1948	Jane Halenkamp, Charles Hall, Harold Feldstein, Gretchen Feldstein
1949	Jane Wallace, Charlton Wallace, Charles Hall, Jane Halenkamp, Scott Sublette
1950	G. Robert Nail, Ed Wolter, Isadore Rosenberg, F. Ayres Bombeck
1951	Helen Doern, Sam Delott, John Carlin, Dr. H. McDaniels
1952	William Rosen, Bert Kaufman, Milt Ellenby, Emanuel Hochfeld
1953	Jay Lennon, Sid Hoblitt, J.Van Brooks Fred Ensminger, Mary Van Pelt
1954	Dave Carter, Joseph Ripstra, John Simon, Allen Harvey, Richard Carter
1955	Charles Bensinger, Sam Katz, Jeff Glick, Max Turk
1956	Ruth Steinberg, John Simon, Mildred Cytron, John Parish
1957	Jerome Jacobs, Charles Stimming, Eugene Dautell, Carl Hudecek
1958	Robert Sharp, Jo Sharp, John Simon, Leo Weiner, Louis Rosenthal
1959	June Rodkin, Richard Revell, Danny Rotman, Edward Rosen
1960	Ivan Stakgold, Irv Berkson, William Rosen, Alfred Sheinwold, Art Glatt
1961	Alan Bell, Gunther Polak, Robert Cruise, Jack Blair, Richard Vission
1962	Robert Sharp, Jo Sharp, Portia Miller, Bud Creed, Thomas Mahaffey, Jr.
1963	Mary Cocherell, Bob Bratcher, Robert Jerles, George St. Pierre
1964	Beverly Bechtold, Cecil Inman, Mrs. A. F. Pogue, Fred Blackman, Charlene Buford
1965	Hampton Hume, Jack Blair, Paul Swanson, Marc Low, Carol Sanders
1966	Anthony Astrologes, John Levinson, Richard Halperin, Gerald Caravelli
1967	Barry Crane, Grant Marsee, Gunther Polak, Ray Zoller
1968	Mrs. W. H. Dillingham, W. H. Dillingham, Mrs. Henry Baird, Jane Hall
1969	Don Faskow, Herb Sachs, Paul Swanson, Mark Blumenthal, Dick Fleischman
1970	Ronald Bland, Mrs. Ronald Bland, Jenny Davis, James Gormong *(tied with)* L. James Phillips, John Zilic, Gerald Caravelli, Marvin Altman
1971	Dorothy Thompson, Ben Matthews, Dick Carter, Bill Phillips (Swiss) Dorothy Thompson, Ben Matthews, Dick Carter, Herman Lackman *(tied with)* Holton Sexton, Nancy Richardson, Chuck Stemming, Jerry Epstein (Board-a-Match)
1972	Fred Hamilton, Howard Perlman,

Linda Deaton, Paul Swanson *(tied with)*
John Sheridan, Larry Kozlove,
David Smith, Dan Requard
1973 James Gardner, Allan Falk,
David Swarthout, Jim Fatka
1974 Fred Hamilton, John Sheridan, Jeffrey Starr,
Cliff Bishop, Larry Kozlove
1975 Barry Crane, Gerald Caravelli,
Dr. John Fisher, Milton Rosenberg
1976 Bill Wick, Jr., Stan Given, Bill McCallon,
Rick Henderson, Eugene O'Neill
1977 Paul Munafo, Sammie Tallent,
Eleanor Bransford, Lorand Tritter
1978 Barry Crane, Larry Kozlove,
John Sheridan, Gary Hann
1979 Garrett Nash, Guy Symonds,
Sandy Friedman, Debby Stahl
1980 Eric Rodwell, Larry Sealy, Marilyn Miller,
Jeff Meckstroth, Gaylor Kasle *(tied with)*
Suzanne Cassady, Betty Cassady,
Harold Cassady, Jane Wallace *(Smoking)*
Clare McGillem, Ann McGillem,
Rosanna Lukenbill, Elsa Meeks *(Non-Smoking)*
1981 Ralph McNeal, Noel Clark,
Scott Gates, Russell Shoup
Flight A:
1981 Joan Stein, Norm Fischer,
Tom Sikora, Tom Hodapp
INDIVIDUAL
1956 Louis Jaffe

WESTERN STATES

TEAM OF FOUR
1934 Sidney Fink, Ollie Emrich,
Elmer Babin, A. L. Siegel
1935 Charles Hall, R. M. Wildberg,
Charles Porter, William Hopkins
1936 Alvin Landy, Jeff Glick,
Maury Glick, James Higgins
1937 C. N. Bensinger, Walter Lapp,
Turner Clarke, D. L. Street
1938 Ray Henderson, Henry Auslander,
Harry Quinlivan, Ernest Donaghy
1939 John Simon, A. E. Stein, Gordon Scherck,
C. C. Lockett, Ted Faulkner
1940 Frances Carter, David Carter,
Arthur Kincaid, F. Ayres Bombach
1941 Fritz DuRelle, J. Frank Taylor,
D. L. Street, J. Cleve Iler, Jr
1942 Mrs. A. Coffin, Mrs. E. J. Ittenbach,
Mrs. V. R. Rupp, V. R. Rupp
1943 Maynard Adams, Maude Whitehead,
H. C. Keubler, Jill Denny
1944 Joseph Cain, Leo Roet,
Mrs. Lester Rhodes, Harold Ogust

OPEN PAIRS
1934 Sidney Fink, Ollie Emrich
1935 Charles Porter, William Hopkins
1936 Robert Halpin, Bud Reilly
1937 Art Goldsmith, M. J. Nagusky
1938 Alvin Landy, Jeff Glick
1939 Elmer Babin, Sidney Fink
1940 Jane Wallace, Charlton Wallace
1941 Frances Carter, David Carter
1942 Eula Hill, Millard Kaiser
1943 Frank Nelson, Arthur Marks
1944 Kay Oberrecht, F. Schneider

MIXED PAIRS
1935 Mrs. J. Friedlander, Philip Steiner
1936 Mrs. E. J. Ittenbach, Walter Pray
1937 Matie White, W. M. Fulton
1938 Mrs. C. M. Whitehead, C. M. Whitehead
1939 Mrs M. A. Clark, Ted Faulkner
1940 Mrs. Dewey Miller, Dewey Miller
1941 Mrs. V. R. Rupp, V. R. Rupp
1942 Mrs. Oscar Frisch, M. Hennrich
1943 Fred Ensminger, Jo Gutman
1944 Mrs. R. E. Duncan, T. Colin Alexander

WOMEN'S PAIRS
1937 Matie White, Frances Klein
1938 Stella Culp, Grace Lear
1939 Mrs. Lister Tuholske, Mrs. Harry Tenebaum
1940 Linda Terry, Mrs. W. L. Dickens
1941 Mrs. W. L. Dickens, Inez Buchanan
1942 Jerry Dunlap, Mrs. George Atkins
1943 Mrs. B. T. Lawrence, Mrs. A. W. McNeiley
1944 Mrs. C. J. Sweeney, Mrs. Alfred Bridges

MASTERS INDIVIDUAL
1941 Ernest Stein
1942 Lottie Hagemeyer

DISTRICT 12 (Northwestern Ohio, most of Michigan)

GREAT LAKES

OPEN TEAMS
1959 Paul Kraut, G.R. Targett,
Joe Harrison, Karl Austin
1960 Sid Fink, Lois Fribourg,
Charley Braman, Alex Szabo *(tied with)*
Thelma Hathorn, John Nischwitz,
Dennis Meehan, Bill Gubbins
1961 Marty Cohn, Grant Marsee,
Julius Young, Floyd Sayed
1962 Herbert Wilton, Holton Sexton, John Biddle,
Sam Scaffidi, George Mitchell
1963 Fred Ensminger, Cliff Bishop,
J. Van Brooks, Louis Cohen, *tied with*
Julius Young, Gerald Dillon,
Sylvia Stein, Helen Shanbrom, *tied with*
Don Smith, Arthur Price,
Dr. Harold McDonald, Martin Arndt
1964 Irving Farber, Sidney Lawrence,
Dr. Don Grove, William Rife
1965 Agnes Gordon, Nat Gerstman,
Marvin Altman, Don Rutstein
1966 William Flannery, Donald Faskow,
Stanley Ruskin, Paul Swanson
1967 John Levinson, William Rosen,
Eunice Rosen, Gunther Polak
1968 Martin Cohn, Al Silber,
Ray Zoller, James Rosentiel
1969 Howard Perlman, Sheldon Margulis,
Gary Hann, Chuck Said
1970 Don Cowan, Mike Cummings,
Duncan Phillips, Bruce Elliot
1971 Dick Yanko, Myles Maddox,
Henry Shevitz, Gary Hann
1972 Howard Perlman, Fred Hamilton,
Chuck Burger, Ray Zoller
1973 Russell Shoup, Richard Koopman,
David Linton, Jeff Gargrave
1974 Bob Stuart, Paul Fodor,
A. Korde, Ray Kuusik *(tied with)*
Howard Perlman, Jeffrey Starr,
Fred Hamilton, Bill Rosen *(and)*
William Buhl, James DeSerio,
Robert Pearl, Nick Markakis *(and)*
Dan Suty, Gene Owens,
Marilyn Maddox, Myles Maddox *(and)*
Edward Rosen, Joan Rosen,
Allen Susskind, Steve Rose
1975 James Zimmerman, Dennis McGarry,
Vincent Remey, Joan Remey
1976 Mike Passell, Anita Kimball, Frank Kimball,
Meyer Schleifer, Gaylor Kasle *(tied with)*
Paul Howley, Dorothy Howley,
Arline Olesak, Robert Emke *(and)*
Jack Creasey, Marcia Abramson,
Martin Hirschman, J.M. Keenan
1977 Robert Bridge, Paul Oreffice,
Dr. Charles Roberts, Margaret Roberts *(tied with)*
Wayne Hascall, Bob Crofton,
Allan Falk, Bob Kelly *(and)*
Mary Jane Magerman, Greg Magerman,
Kevin Comins, Gordon Parnes *(and)*
Anita Kimball, Frank Kimball, Fred Hamilton,
Jeffrey Starr, Howard Perlman
1978 Wayne Snider, Sue Coonfield, Mike Polowan,
Alan Bell, Alan Susskind
1979 Katie Thorpe, John Carruthers,
Sheila Forbes, John Gowdy
1980 Ralph Bartlett, Joan Stein,
Philip Wolkin, Norman Fischer
1981 Doug Ogozaly, Stanley Hench,
James Overman, Charlotte Overman
Flight A:
1981 Phil Leon, Myles Maddox
Marilyn Maddox, Robert Sherburn

MEN'S PAIRS
1959 Floyd Sayed, Harry Philip
1960 Lewis Rosenthal, Howard Behm
1961 Barry Crane, Edwin Smith
1962 Barry Crane, Edwin Smith
1963 Brooks Hughes, Richard Halperin

1964 Frank Weisbach, James Weismiller
1965 Richard Schwartz, Robert Sherburn
1966 Cliff Bishop, James Hinton
1967 Grant Marsee, Edwin Smith, Jr.
1968 Bud Smith, Fred Hamilton
1969 B. Jay Becker, Chuck Burger
1970 Myles Maddox, Vincent Remey
1971 Jeff Alexander, James Zimmerman
1972 Larry Cohen, Sheldon Kahn
1973 Frank Bell, Steve Landen
1974 Ron LaCour, Mike Passell
1975 Greg DeFotis, Jerry Goldfein
1976 Bob Visokey, Marc Culberson
1977 David MacAslan, Jeff Gargrave
1979 Vincent Remey, Dennis McGarry
1981 Norman Fischer, Jim Zimmerman

WOMEN'S PAIRS
1959 Amelia Argersinger, Helen McLean
1960 Roberta French, Shurl Glass
1961 Elsie Epstein, Ruth Leland
1962 Kay Barbaris, Linda Deaton
1963 Dorothy Johnson, Maryon Schneider
1964 Mrs. Richard Jones, Louise Goldsmith
1965 Fran Miller, Marge Bellson
1966 Betty Garson, Angie Bianco
1967 Mrs. R. W. Prange, Helen Sherwin
1968 Sylvia Stein, Judi Friedenberg
1969 Sylvia Stein, Judi Friedenberg
1970 Ann Gust, Lynne Goldsmith
1971 Rita Kaplan, Virginia Melkovlan
1972 Joan Remey, Ruth Dillon
1973 Sally Waterstone, Ruth Brownstein
1974 Liz Menthen, Arlene Dickinson
1975 Pauline Stewart, Esther Knight
1976 Nancy Int-Hout, Alice Kerckhoff
1977 Kay Schulz, Carol Findley
1979 Clerely Chaney, Zerrene Brooks
1981 L. Deane, Marilyn Maddox

MASTER SWISS TEAMS
1978 Dennis McGarry, Miles Maddox,
Marilyn Maddox, Joan Remey *(tied with)*
Dave Caprera, Michael Ranis,
Robert Hayes, Bob Glenn
1980 Richard Huggard, Zeke Jabbour,
Susan Ganley, Hans Akturk

MEN'S SWISS TEAMS
1979 Zeke Jabbour, Gary Hann, Hans Akturk,
Steven Bloom, Richard Huggard
1981 Norman Bolton, Robb Gordon, Jim Zimmerman,
Howard Weiner, Martin Hirschman

WOMEN'S SWISS TEAMS
1979 Janet Mahood, Barbara Fellows,
Charlotte Overman, Eileen Sugar *(tied with)*
Lee Alpern, Mary Ann Will, Clerely Chaney,
Carol Crafton, Bobbie Shipley
1981 Bobbie Shipley, Caroline Pascoe,
Mary Ann Will, Dorothy Schick

OPEN PAIRS
1959 Fred Rappleyea, Mel Pike
1960 Bill Gardiner, Ira Zucker
1961 Sylvia Stein, Grant Marsee
1962 Myron Charfoos, Bruce Perkers
1963 Agnes Gordon, Nat Gerstman, *tied with*
Charles Burger, Monroe Ingberman
1964 Lucille Price, Gladys Brownlee
1965 Dorsey Brooks, Jim White
1966 Martin Cohn, Alan Silber
1967 Fred Hamilton, Elwyn Banghart
1968 Gerald Caravelli, Milt Rosenberg
1969 Howard Perlman, Sheldon Margulis
1970 John Gowdy, Des Vincze
1971 Marc Low, Gerald Caravelli
1972 Richard Halperin, Harvey Miller, Jr.
1973 Don Faskow, Paul Swanson
1974 Gary Hann, Hans Akturk
1975 Al Banghart, Robert Sherburn
1976 Dennis McGarry, Helen Utegaard
1977 Beverly Nelson, Quentin Wilmot
1978 Bill Hale, Dave Bondy
1979 Henry Shevitz, Rick Roeder
1980 Perry Johnson, Michael Zerbini

MASTER PAIRS
1974 Ron LaCour, Mike Passell
1975 Frank Bell, Gary Hann
1976 Ron Andersen, Hugh MacLean
1977 David Doran, Bob Webber
1978 Bob Crafton, Dave Doran
1979 Leon Lowe, Raymond Garea
1980 Claude Vogel, Eunice Rosen

1981 Randy Baron, Lee Bukstel
MIXED PAIRS
1962 Rose Abrams, William Flannery
1963 Janet Stewart, Graham Stewart
1964 Sally Kane, Marvin Kane
1965 Lynn Goldsmith, Sid Heinrich
1966 Sally Kane, Marvin Kane
1967 Myles Maddox, Marilyn Maddox
1968 Myles Maddox, Marilyn Maddox
1969 Vincent Remey, Joan Remey
1970 Eddie Brown, Leah Jay
1971 Amelia Argersinger, Philip Leon
1972 Mrs. John Nangle, David Pratt
1973 David Doran, Mary Smith
1979 Vincent Remey, Joan Remey

UNMIXED PAIRS
1978 Dennis Carman, Al Simpson

KNOCKOUT TEAMS
1976 Eric Rodwell, Larry Mori,
Jeff Meckstroth, Larry Robbins
1978 Carl Dahl, Janet Weyant,
Phil Slatt, Richard Worthington
1979 Dave Swarthout, Mitch Chandler, Allan Falk,
Jim Gardner, Craig Mertz

MOTOR CITY

KNOCKOUT TEAMS
1973 Stanley Smith, Richard Yanko, Fred Hamilton,
Jeff Starr, Howard Perlman
1974 Russell Roosen, Vincent Remey, Floyd Sayed,
Dennis McGarry, James Zimmerman
1975 Fred Hamilton, Jeff Starr, Billy Eisenberg,
Hal Mouser, Mary Chilcote
1976 Robert Hamman, Cy Dennen, Don Krauss,
Bob Sherburn, Bob Kelly
1977 Steve Sion, Jeff Starr, Alan Cokin,
Marc Jacobus, Frank Bell, Steve Landen
1978 Marc Culberson, Bert Newman,
Bob Webber, David Doran

OPEN TEAMS
1967 Sanford Fenkel, Robert Peters,
Henry Shevitz, Dick Yanko
1968 Sylvia Stein, Judi Friedenberg,
Floyd Sayed, Phil Leon
1969 Howard Perlman, Sheldon Margulis,
Dick Katz, Larry Cohen
1970 Zoreen Brooks, Dorsey Brooks,
Herb Sachs, Stanley Ruskin
1971 Marc Low, Gunther Polak,
L. James Phillips, Gerald Caravelli
1972 Dan Rotman, Florence Rotman,
Joan DeWitt, Charles Peres
1973 Michael Cummings, Bruce Elliott,
Richard Freedman, Sydney Isaacs
1974 Hal Mouser, Jeff Isralsky,
Rick Koopman, Jeffrey Gargrave
1975 John Carruthers, John Guoba,
Michael Schoenborn, Fred Lerner
1976 Dr. John P. Cannon, Dr. Gary Ault,
Dr. Stuart Starkweather, Patricia Starkweather
1977 Kathie Wei, Ron Andersen, Terry Radjef,
David Siebert, Jo Morse, Gerald Caravelli
1978 Frank Bell, Steve Landen,
Jeff Starr, George Mittelman
1979 Russell Roosen, Floyd Sayed,
Richard Yanko, John Buchheister
1980 Jo Morse, Frank Buchanan,
Leon Lowe, Mike Graham
1981 Joan Stein, Bill Hale,
Norman Fischer, Dave Bondy

OPEN PAIRS
1967 Chuck Burger, Fred Hamilton
1968 Sylvia Stein, Floyd Sayed
1969 Dick Yanko, Jeff Starr
1970 Bob Sherburn, Al Banghart
1971 Linda Deaton, Norman Fischer
1972 Bruce Ferguson, John Carruthers
1973 Eric Shepherd, George Vella
1974 Bob Webber, Paul Stern
1975 Gerald Caravelli, Mark Feldman *(tied with)*
Larry Kozlove, Mark Blumenthal
1976 Eric Shepherd, Ed Bridson
1977 Vince Remey, Bruno Sestito
1978 Ken Murray, Frank Markotich
1979 Janet Weyant, Jan George
1980 Richard Mydloski, Charles Miner
1981 Bob Crafton, Howard Weiner

Flight A:
1979   Larry Mori, Jeff Meckstroth
1980   Linda Perlman, Robert Lebi
1981   Jim Gardner, Dave Swarthout

MASTER PAIRS
1973   Phil Leon, Robert Sherburn
1974   Jeffrey Gargrave, Russell Shoup
1975   Dick Yanko, Cliff Bishop
1976   Ron Andersen, Hugh MacLean
1977   Steve Sion, Marc Jacobus
1978   Ron Smith, Robert Levin
1979   Brooke Nelles, Terry Lesperance
1980   Steve Lander, Hans Akturk
1981   John Gowdy, Ed Bridson

MEN'S PAIRS
1967   Harry Kreitzburg, Ed Moorehead
1968   Steve Berg, Ray Zoller
1969   Dwight Searcy, Dave Swarthout
1970   Cliff Bishop, Dick Yanko
1971   Dr. Hans Stocker, Dr. Russell Shoup
1972   Dr. John Fisher, Barry Crane
1974   Cliff Bishop, Albert Bricklin
1975   Gary Hann, Floyd Sayed
1976   Alan Bell, Harvey Miller, Jr.
1977   Martin Hirschman, Steve Hollingsworth
1978   Fred Duffy, Burt Stern
1979   John Buchheister, Terry Lesperance
1980   Richard Mydloski, Charles Miner
1981   Leon Lowe, Floyd Sayed

WOMEN'S PAIRS
1967   Clarice Gordon, Judy Maddocks
1968   Amelia Argersinger, Margaret Wagar
1969   Sylvia Stein, Judi Friedenberg
1970   Julia Halloran, Portia Miller
1971   Portia Miller, Julia Halloran
1972   Gargi French, Lou Porter
1974   Flora Schwartz, Marilyn Feldman
1975   Clerely Chaney, Mary Ann Will
1976   Lill Wine, Dottie Morochnick
1977   Liz Sorgi, Joan Stein
1978   Bonnie Ward, Lynne Ziegler
1979   Mary Smith, Petra Bender
1980   Joan Remey, Jo Morse
1981   Lynne Schaeffer, Sondra Schubiner

MIXED PAIRS
1967   Cletus Denninger, Judy Maddocks
1968   Ron Andersen, Lynn Andersen
1969   Joan Remey, Russell Roosen
1970   Dorothy West, John Shelnut
1971   Beverly Riordan, Robert Sherburn
1972   Donna House, Dr. Robert House
1973   Beverly Riordan, Richard Huggard
1976   Sylvia Stein, Floyd Sayed
1977   Mitchell Chandler, Anita Schuster
1978   Jack Jessop, Diane Goldhawk

WOMEN'S SWISS TEAMS
1976   Joan Remey, Shirlee Lazarus,
      Jean Frankel, Helen Utegaard
1977   Ann Pavur, Margaret Warfield,
      Diane Goldhawk, Beth Cordial
1978   Kathie Wei, Judi Radin,
      Joan DeWitt, Carol Sanders
1979   Joan Stein, Sandy Frisch,
      Wendy Sameroff, Linda Perlman
1980   Linda Perlman, Wendy Sameroff, Liz Sorgi,
      Joan Stein, Sandy Frisch
1981   Jo Morse, Tobi Deutsch, Susie Handelman,
      Joan Remey, Sue Halperin

MEN'S SWISS TEAMS
1976   Cliff Bishop, Albert Silber, Paul Stern,
      Richard Huggard, Mike Aliotta, Carl Hudecek
1977   Dorsey Brooks, Dr. John Buchheister,
      David Doran, Richard Yanko
1978   Ron Andersen, Jeff Meckstroth,
      Mark Cohen, Bill Doroshow
1979   Mike Aliotta, Dick Huggard,
      Dick Mydloski, Mike Dalton
1980   James Overman, James Fellows,
      Mike Albert, Eric Lyben
1981   Jeff Starr, Ralph Katz, Zeke Jabbour,
      Ted Horning, Mike Shuman, Chuck Burger

WOLVERINE

KNOCKOUT TEAMS
1977   Tony Kasday, Steve Sion, Marc Jacobus,
      Allan Cokin, Josh Parker
1978   Gary Hann, Zeke Jabbour, Dennis McGarry,

      Jeff Meckstroth, Lorand Tritter
1980   Bert Newman, Phil Brady, Ralph Bartlett,
      Steve Landen, Pratap Rajadhyaksha, Marc Culberson

OPEN SWISS TEAMS
1977   Jim Zimmerman, Dennis McGarry,
      Joan Remey, Vincent Remey
1978   Carl Hudecek, Frank McClure,
      John Biddle, George St. Pierre
1979   Dave Doran, Bob Crafton, Vincent Remey,
      Joan Remey, Ralph Katz
1980   Lou Woodcock, Frank Markotich,
      Ken Murray, Mary Paul
1981   Bill Rosen, Eunice Rosen, Sue Halperin,
      Colby Vernay, Alan Bell

OPEN PAIRS
1977   Bruno Sestito, Russell Shoup
1978   Perry Johnson, Joel Dreyer
1980   Ed Turner, Jack Rowicki, *(tied with)*
      Gary Brinker, Joe Ernsthausen
1981   Jim Gardner, Wayne Hascall
Flight A:
1979   Michael Huston, Tom Reid
1980   Dave Fred, Richard Worthington
1981   Bill Rosen, Milt Rosenberg

MASTER PAIRS
1977   Bob Visokey, Marc Culberson
1978   Gena Bhatia, Kumar Bhatia
1979   Charlotte Unger, Mort Unger
1980   James Zimmerman, Ralph Katz
1981   Steve Landen, Pratap Rajadhyaksha

MEN'S PAIRS
1977   Gary Hann, Hans Akturk
1978   Marc Culberson, Bert Newman
1979   Arthur Moore, Alain Moreau
1980   Vincent Remey, Richard Becher

WOMEN'S PAIRS
1977   Clarice Gordon, Jean Sherman
1978   Ann Hamparian, Mary Kelly
1979   Mrs. E. J. DeWitt, Charlotte Cotton
1980   Betty Story, Katie Walters

MIXED PAIRS
1977   Sherilyn Larson, Hans Akturk

MEN'S SWISS TEAMS
1977   Gary Hann, Hans Akturk,
      Phil Leon, Vincent Remey

WOMEN'S SWISS TEAMS
1977   Lee Alpern, Mary Ann Will,
      Suzy Burger, Clerely Chaney

MASTER SWISS TEAMS
1979   Dave Fred, Richard Worthington,
      Zeke Jabbour, Hans Akturk
1981   Jim Zimmerman, Jeffrey Starr, Vincent Remey,
      Joan Remey, Bill Hale *(tied with)*
      Phil Leon, Marilyn Maddox,
      Myles Maddox, Robert Sherburn

DISTRICT 13   (Most of Wisconsin, Chicago area, Upper Michigan Peninsula)

CENTRAL STATES

KNOCKOUT TEAMS
1962   Arnold Leavitt, Monroe Ingberman, Billy Rosen,
      Arthur Glatt, Don Rutstein, Al Press
1963   Merrill Ely, Morris Tish, Kazuo Higashiuchi,
      William Hiura, John Ditto
1964   Eunice Rosen, Sandi Leavitt, Paul Sugar,
      Carol Norton, Bert Norton
1965   Eunice Rosen, Louis Cohen, Richard Katz,
      John Wachter, Worth Vaughn
1966   Charles Peres, Monroe Ingberman, Dan Rotman,
      Ivar Stakgold, Milton Q. Ellenby
1967   Billy Rosen, Eunice Rosen, Gunther Polak,
      Bert Norton, Leland Ferer
1968   Oswald Jacoby, Minda Brachman, Malcolm Brachman,
      Paul Levitt, Paul Soloway, Emanuel Hochfeld
1969   Milton Rosenberg, Gerald Caravelli, Dan Rotman,
      Charles Peres, Milton Q. Ellenby, Bert Norton
1970   Emanuel Hochfeld, Ross Amann,
      Charles Peres, Ivar Stakgold
1971   Dr. Richard Katz, Leo Spivack, John Levinson,
      Fred Hamilton, Charles Burger, Howard Perlman
1972   Gerald Caravelli, Louis Cohen,
      Milton Rosenberg, Ron Andersen
1973   Gerald Caravelli, Louis Cohen, Dr. Richard Katz,
      Milton Rosenberg, Ron Andersen

1974	Michael Garner, Joe Weiner,
	Charles Urban, Harvey Miller, Jr.
1975	Terry Spector, Alex Weiland,
	Kent Feiler, Frank Pancoe
1976	Jerry Weinstein, Al Cordell,
	Paul Hessel, Brian Monieson
1977	Don Rutstein, Gene Chait,
	Eunice Rosen, Carey Yelton
1978	L. James Phillips, Jimmy Cordas,
	Lorand Tritter, Gunther Polak
1979	Gerald Caravelli, Milton Rosenberg,
	Jeff Meckstroth, Billy Rosen
1980	Dan Rotman, Alex Weiland, Bob Pareti,
	Sandi Leavitt, Paul Sugar, Harvey Miller

OPEN PAIRS

1936	E. Hart, Jr., J. K. Howe
1937	H. Besser, Arthur Glatt
1938	Matthew Reilly, Richard Halpin
1939	Ralph Kempner, Walter Jacobs
1940	Julius Bank, Paul Smith
1941	Dr. A. W. Maier, C. H. Brecher
1942	Albert Weiss, Ace Gutowsky
1943	Leo B. Weiner, Richard Revell
1944	Edson Wood, J. Van Brooks
1945	Jack Kravatz, Ann Bryant
1946	Harry Feinberg, David Clarren
1947	Charles Woldenberg, S. N. Ruttenberg
1949	George Ryan, Mrs. George Ryan
1951	Jerome Jacobs, Edson Wood
1952	Hortense Evans, Barry Cohen
1953	Ruth Steinberg, Leo Weiner
1954	Arlene Klein, Jim Martin
1955	Robert Denner, Robert Simitz
1956	Mildred Cunningham, Louis Rosenthal
1957	Melvin Lawhorn, Bob Chandler
1960	Gloria Turner, Emanuel Hochfeld
1961	Gloria Turner, Emanuel Hochfeld (tied with)
	Mabel Mahoney, David Carter
1962	Marc Low, Jack Blair
1963	Emanuel Hochfeld, Billy Rosen
1964	Arthur Kincaid, Dr. Marcel Mooney
1965	John Wachter, Edward Rosen
1966	Richard Katz, Larry Cohen
1967	Barry Crane, Gunther Polak
1968	Sandi Leavitt, Paul Sugar
1969	Dan Rotman, Edward Rosen
1970	Richard Huggard, Michael Aliotta
1971	Dr. F. Griffin, Mrs. F. Griffin
1972	Howard Perlman, Fred Hamilton (Winter)
	Gerald Caravelli, Louis Cohen (Spring)
1973	Louis Cohen, Dr. Richard Katz (Winter)
	Howard Perlman, Milton Rosenberg (Spring)
1974	Gerald Welander, Don Sershon (Winter)
	Kent Wiley, Lois Wiley (tied with)
	Barry Crane, Kerri Shuman (Spring)
1975	Mark Kessler, Colby Vernay (Winter)
	Mark Kessler, Colby Vernay (Spring)
1976	Gene Chait, Sandy Zakin (Winter)
	Jerome Feldman, Bob Pareti (Spring)
1977	Harvey Miller, Charles Urban (Winter)
	Gene Chait, Sandi Leavitt (Spring)
1978	Patricia Schiff, Dean Cohler (Winter)
1978	Arnold Leavitt, Claude Vogel (Spring)
1979	George Sourlis, Elaine Hresta
1980	Cheri Bjerkan, James Bjerkan (Spring)
	Jan Janitschke, Craig Janitschke (Winter)
1981	Tobi Deutsch, Paul Sugar (tied with)
	Hal Mouser, Howard Weinstein

MIXED PAIRS

1939	Mrs. Lesley Cook, Ralph Kempner
1940	Peggy Akin, Elmer Grage
1941	W. H. Tallman, Mrs. W. H. Tallman
1942	Mrs. Phil Spink, Ace Gutowsky
1943	Florence Meyer, William McGhee
1944	Mildred Cunningham, Leo Weiner
1945	Mrs. Mort Ray, Carroll Chase
1946	Miriam McKinley, Leo Weiner
1947	Dorothy Jane Cook, Jack Kravatz
1949	Mrs. Phil Spink, Jean Kempner
1950	Violet Agran, Joseph Stedem
1951	Ellie Marks, Leland Ferer
1952	Billie Travelletti, Robert McKearnan
1953	Joan Fox, Victor Bennehum
1954	Ruth Steinberg, Andy McNeily
1955	Elizabeth Count, Kazuo Higashiuchi
1956	Martha Beasley, Chester Rumpf
1957	Tom Wilder, Ann Conroy
1958	Alberta Briggs, Alan Bell
1959	Rosemary Dowd, Peter Szcesci
1960	Gloria Harris, Dan Rotman
1961	Esther Hubbard, Warren Kriebel

1962	Signe Nelson, Martin Nelson
1963	Mary Bridegroom, Richard Balanow
1964	Debbie Polak, Billy Rosen
1965	Gloria Turner, Gunther Polak
1966	Marion Erickson, Irving Guttman
1967	Morton Deutsch, June Deutsch
1968	Babs Charney, Gerald Hartman
1969	Carol Leavitt, Gunther Polak
1970	June Deutsch, Gene Chait
1971	Robert Price, Joyce Williams
1972	R. Tonn, Mrs. R. Tonn
1973	Warren Tatting, Mrs. Warren Tatting
1976	Beverly Nelson, Mick Dobratz
1977	Alex Weiland, Marge Vonesh
1978	Terry Borne, Valerie Piper
1979	Patty Adamle, Jeff Meckstroth

LIFE AND SENIOR MASTER TEAMS

1957	Leo Weiner, Milton Ellenby, Emanuel Hochfeld,
	Gloria Turner, Thomas Fenwick
1958	Warren Blank, Sidney Kasle,
	Jo Sharp, Robert Sharp
1959	Eunice Rosen, Billy Rosen,
	Leland Ferer, Gratian Goldstein
1960	Eunice Rosen, William Hiura,
	Kazuo Higashiuchi, Shirlee Harris
1961	Emanuel Hochfeld, Ivar Stakgold, Gunther Polak,
	Gloria Turner, Richard Freeman (tied with)
	Grant Marsee, Dorothy Jane Cook,
	Robert Casement, William Stickney
1962	Matthew Reilly, Virginia Heckel,
	Jerry Yavitz, Charles Peres
1964	Sandi Leavitt, Arnold Leavitt,
	Marc Low, Jack Blair

MASTER PAIRS

1952	Frieda Arst, Milton Fleig
1953	Helen Doern, Sam Delott
1954	Edward Rosen, Robert Simitz
1955	Tom Fenwick, John McGervey
1956	Emanuel Hochfeld, Milton Ellenby
1957	Billy Rosen, Tom Fenwick
1958	Frieda Arst, Louis Rosenthal
1959	Ron Wolf, Leo Weiner
1960	J. David King, Carol Ruther
1961	Mabel Mahoney, David Carter
1962	Billy Rosen, Monroe Ingberman
1963	Sandi Leavitt, James Cayne
1964	Sandi Leavitt, Paul Sugar
1965	Matthew Reilly, Virginia Heckel
1966	Melvin Lawhorn, William Sides
1967	Robert Hemmings, Henry Rabin
1968	Anita Kurti, Jack Martin
1969	Arnold Leavitt, Billy Rosen
1970	Sue Halperin, Anthony Astrologes
1971	Max Madsen, Joseph White
1972	Vivian Levin, Phillip Schiffert
1973	Gunther Polak, L. James Phillips
1974	Richard Melson, Terrence Beckman (Winter)
	Arnold Leavitt, Gunther Polak (Spring)
1975	Billy Rosen, Fred Hamilton (Winter)
	Freida Arst, June Deutsch (Spring)
1976	Jim Cayne, Chuck Burger (Winter)
	Claude Vogel, Mark Case (Spring)
1977	Ralph Matlow, Len Ernst
1978	Nancy Browne, Allan Browne (Winter)
	Pratap Rajadhyasksha, Jeff Meckstroth (Spring)
1979	Eric Rodwell, Venkatro Konery (Spring)
	John Startzel, Bob Gardner (Winter)
1980	Dave Caslan, Nick Poulos (Spring)
	Craig Allen, Sandi Leavitt (Winter)
1981	Karen McCallum, Kit Woolsey

MEN'S SWISS TEAMS

1976	Jeff Meckstroth, Bert Newman,
	Eric Rodwell, Larry Mori
1977	Billy Rosen, Milt Rosenberg, Bert Norton,
	Sidney Lazard, Gerald Caravelli
1978	Billy Rosen, Milt Rosenberg,
	Hugh MacLean, Ron Andersen
1979	Bob Price, Craig Allen,
	Bill Wickham, Allan Cohen
1980	Arthur Reinhold, Milt Rosenberg,
	Ron Smith, Billy Rosen

WOMEN'S OPEN TEAMS

1939	Beryle Lundien, Mignon Foley,
	Ruth White, Pearl Ford
1946	Mrs. R. M. Seward, Margaret Akin,
	Eleanor Marks, Susan Harrington
1947	Mrs. P. N. Marks, Mrs. D. J. Cook,
	Gratian Goldstein, Mrs. C. Daw
1976	Terry James, Karen Walker,
	Mrs. L. J. Weinbeck, Norinne Anderson

1977 June Deutsch, Frieda Arst, Sandi Leavitt,
Florine Walters, Sue Halperin
1978 Jan Ivory, Chris Manis,
Joan Williams, Elaine Hrestu
1979 Gloria White, Jen De Reus,
Janette Howard, Mary Greig *(tied with)*
June Deutsch, Frieda Arst, Florine Walters,
Sandi Leavitt, Sue Halperin, Cheri Bjerkan
1980 Betty King, Sally Flaxman,
Kay Hathaway, Susan Agramonte

OPEN TEAMS

1935 Ralph Kempner, Charles Rilling,
M. H. Besser, Arthur Glatt
1936 Ely Culbertson, Louis Haddad,
Robert Halpin, Walter Jacobs
1937 Mrs. Paul Parcells, Jack Howe,
Hortense Evans, Wingate Bixby
1938 Walter Jacobs, Arthur Glatt,
Ralph Kempner, Albert Weiss
1939 Edson Wood, Dr. Cleon Nafe,
Lawrence Welch, F. Roland Buck
1940 A. O. Stracke, Neil Kent,
John Carlin, Sam Delott
1941 Mrs. R. B. Johnstone, Matthew Reilly, Paul Smith,
George Carlton, Jack Howe
1942 Neil Kent, Sam Delott,
Milton Fleig, John Carlin
1943 Joseph Cain, F. Roland Buck,
Edson Wood, Lawrence Welch
1944 Ann Bryant, Harry Feinberg,
Joe Matthews, David Clarren
1945 Edson Wood, J. Van Brooks,
Joseph Cain, Ralph Kempner
1946 Sam Delott, John Carlin,
Mrs. Billie Agruss, Dr. Louis Mark
1949 Mrs. Billie Agruss, John Carlin,
Richard Revell, Sam Delott
1951 Helen Doern, Holis McDaniel,
Sam Delott, M. H. Daskais
1952 Warren Blank, Jerome Jacobs, Maynard Adams,
Jack Kravatz, Edson Wood
1953 Mildred Cytron, J.G. Ripstra,
David Carter, Isadore Rosenberg
1954 Gloria Turner, Emanuel Hochfeld, Paul Sugar,
Don Rutstein, Thomas Thomas
1955 W.L. Bland, Sidney Kasle,
Jerome Jacobs, James Epstein
1956 Frieda Arst, Milton Fleig,
Julius Bank, Maynard Adams *(tied with)*
Isabelle Garn, Raymond Healy,
Fred Rappleyea, Robert Hemmings
1964 Albert May, Helene May,
John Fourness, Theo Fourness
1968 Albert May, Helene May,
Theo Fourness, John Fourness
1969 Robert Solomon, Shirley Solomon, Irwin Kipnis,
Robert Hirsch, Harriet Hirsch *(tied with)*
George Sourlis, Lois Wiley, Kent Wiley,
Muriel Peterson, Jean Christopher
1970 Signe Nelson, Martin Nelson,
Larry Mines, Jack Kamin
1971 Robert Hemmings, Sally Simitz,
Robert Sundby, David Uphoff *(Winter)*
Sandi Leavitt, John Wachter,
Paul Sugar, Charles Urban *(Spring)*
1972 Donald Rutstein, Jeff Mandell,
Carey Yelton, Alex Weiland *(Winter)*
William Orton, Colby Vernay,
Dennis Botch, Dr. B. E. Hoenk *(Spring)*
1973 Ted Brashler, Marilyn Snodell,
Joseph Sturgis, Ken Dubrau *(Winter)*
Claude Weil, Don Florida,
Rich Friesner, John M. Kulig, Jr. *(Spring)*
1974 Richard Stern, Jeff Mandell,
Steve Robinson, Richard Henderson *(Winter)*
Dick Yanko, L. Coggan,
Stephen Landen, Frank Bell *(Spring)*
1975 Bill Brander, Lee Abrams,
Mark Weisman, Howard Engle *(Winter)*
George Sourlis, Chuck Hubecek, Sylvia Van Blarcom,
George Kugar, Sam Van Blarcom, John Mier *(tied with)*
Gil Cohen, Jeff Juster,
John Carlson, Richard Strauss *(Spring)*
1976 Eunice Rosen, Clarence Goppert, Jim Hooker,
Bobby Wolff, Mike Passell, Hermine Baron *(Winter)*
Bob Pareti, Marge Vonesh,
Kent Feiler, Jack Martin *(Spring)*
1977 Hugh MacLean, Terry Beckman,
Steve Garner, Gerald Welander *(Winter)*
1977 Gene Chait, Paul Sugar, Harvey Miller,
Sue Halperin, Sandi Leavitt *(Spring)*

1978 Bob Gardner, Mike Slaven,
Wayne Snider, Aminul Karim *(Winter)*
1978 Ron Smith, Paul Jay Lewis,
Bill Doroshow, Vincent Oliver *(Spring)*
1979 Ronald Henbest, Homer Shoop,
Irving Rosenbaum, Dr. D.S. Schauwecker *(Spring)*
1979 Mark Kessler, Steve Alpern,
Colby Vernay, John Lindsey *(Winter)*
1980 Steve Alpern, John Lindsey,
Colby Vernay, Mark Kessler
1981 J. Williams, B. Laster,
Anthony Gillan, Carl John Yaskowich,
Flight A:
1979 Bill Landow, Mark Blumenthal,
Kit Woolsey, Jim Bjerkan
1980 Don Kerr, Mike Slaven, Lou Ann Slaven,
U. K. Peyser, I. Leonard

WOMEN'S PAIRS

1940 L. G. Quigley, Carolyn Whitehead
1941 Elizabeth Johnstone, Mrs. Harold Sax
1942 H. L. Dick, Mildred Cunningham
1943 Mrs. John R. Kelley, Dorothy Thompson
1944 Ruth Steinberg, Mrs. Harry Lees
1945 Dorothy Thompson, Mrs. John R. Kelley
1946 Mary G. Kearns, Mrs. Ward Burton
1947 Ellie Marks, R. Swindell
1949 Mrs. Harold Rohner, Billie Travelletti
1951 Louise Durham, Ruth Steinberg
1952 Peggy Akin, Jane Mohl
1953 Sari Sumner, Pearl Ford
1954 Alicia DeAlarco, R. W. Reagan
1955 Grace LaBounty, Mrs. J. C. Peebles
1956 Helen O'Brien, Marie Gould
1957 Frieda Arst, Isabelle Garn
1960 Fannie Bloomfield, Jane Bauer
1961 Frieda Arst, June Rodkin
1962 Frieda Arst, June Rodkin
1963 Sandi Leavitt, Eunice Rosen
1964 Mildred Bloom, Mrs. Milfred Soffer
1965 Frieda Arst, June Deutsch
1966 Mrs. George Faris, Agnes Gordon
1967 Frieda Arst, June Deutsch
1968 Mrs. Neal Welch, Carolyn Ludwig *(tied with)*
Florence Heifner, Patricia Yedor
1969 Edith Kemp, Virginia Heckel
1970 Harriet Hirsh, Mimi Metz
1971 Florence Rotman, Virginia Heckel
1972 Nahoma Rohr, Anita Kurti
1973 Sally Flaxman, Betty King
1974 Sue Halperin, Sandy Zakin
1975 Suzanne Burger, Linda Perlman
1976 Sandi Leavitt, Florine Walters
1977 Wendy Hoffman, Betty Gordon
1978 Shirley Seneff, Eileen Perkins
1979 Marjorie Silverman, Marcia Silverman
1980 Joan DeWitt, Delores Witte
1981 Joan DeWitt, Delores Witte

MEN'S PAIRS

1946 James Eskin, Joseph Cannon, Jr.
1947 Milton Fleig, Frank Chemelick
1949 Barry Cohen, Robert Appleyard
1951 Robert Halpin, James Chestnut
1952 Arthur Glatt, Duke Dakais
1953 Edward Melchior, Philip Steinberg
1954 Sam Delott, Robert Mendel
1955 Milton Fleig, Earl Hyers
1956 Edward Rosen, Joseph Miller
1957 Louis Rosenthal, Robert Scollay
1960 Emanuel Hochfeld, Dan Rotman
1961 Ronald Schulman, Jack Foster
1962 Robert Gottlieb, William Katz
1963 Alfred Sheinwold, Monroe Ingberman
1964 Alan Bell, Michael Thomas
1965 Robert Kay, Anthony Astrologes
1966 John Levinson, Anthony Astrologes
1967 Gerald Caravelli, Richard Halperin
1968 Moshe Bernstein, Michael Wolock
1969 Paul Swanson, Gunther Polak
1970 Elliot Post, Anthony Franzese
1971 Gunther Polak, Arnold Leavitt
1971 James Leary, Keith Hanson
1973 Wayne Snider, Henry Rabin
1974 Joseph Nieberding, George Kugar
1975 Ron Murray, Ned Irving
1976 Harvey Miller, Jr., Arnold Leavitt
1977 Ted Brashler, Chuck Shannon
1978 Robert Parks, Nick Suciu
1979 Ronald Rogers, Gordon Sparks
1980 Cy Dennen, Mark Lair
1981 Allen Cohen, John Startzel

MASTER INDIVIDUAL
1951 Mrs. Russell Dailey

INDIVIDUAL
1944 William McGhee *(tied with)*
      Mrs. R. B. Johnstone *(and)*
      Jules Bank
1945 Harry Lees
1946 Mildred Cunningham
1947 Alberta Briggs
1949 A. Nusinoff
1951 Gloria Turner
1952 Marian Schreyer
1953 Mrs. Harmon Wilkes
1954 Robert Chapman
1955 Robert Terp
1960 Jerome Yavitz
1964 Milton Ozaki
1965 Robert Price
1966 Joyce Stade
1967 Clara Blackwell
1968 Ralph Brody
1969 David Corbin
1970 Charles Said

UNMIXED PAIRS
1977 Eric Rodwell, Jeff Meckstroth

BOARD-A-MATCH TEAMS
1968 Albert May, Helene May,
      Theo Fourness, John Fourness
1981 Gunther Polak, L. James Phillips, Milt Rosenberg,
      Billy Rosen, Gerald Caravelli

TRI-UNIT

KNOCKOUT TEAMS
1969 Emanuel Hochfeld, Dan Rotman,
      Charles Peres, Ross Amann
1971 Mark Case, Ted Brashler,
      Mike Marmer, Claude Vogel
1974 Ron Andersen, Jeff Starr, Fred Hamilton,
      Hugh MacLean, Gerald Caravelli
1976 Harold Weinstein, David Lehman, Larry Oakey,
      Steve Garner, Alan Bell
1978 Bob Gardner, Aminul Karim, Lorand Tritter,
      Jerry Goldfein, John Oest
1979 Jerry Goldfein, Claude Vogel, Hal Mouser,
      Eric Rodwell, John H. Lindsey, II
1980 Marc Jacobus, Philippe de Bourbon,
      Marcel Friedman, Brian Glubok
Women's:
1981 Sharon Anderson, Carole Jerpbak,
      Essie Mersky, Arlene Hill
Men's:
1981 Dick Melson, Larry Oakey, Jim Hall,
      David Lehman, C. Milton Shefchik, Steve Garner

OPEN TEAMS
1968 Jack Wachter, Dr. Richard Katz, Larry Cohen,
      Henry Bethe, Worth Vaughan
1969 Mike Polonsky, Herb Deyne,
      Mrs. Frank Golec, Frank Golec
1970 Claude Vogel, Carl Stringer,
      Arthur Ramer, Mark Case
1971 John Tani, Richard Tani,
      Julie Gerken, Marge Vonesh
1972 ·D. Smith, Larry McCaffrey,
      Wayne Snider, Bob Gardner *(tied with)*
      Don Rutstein, Jeff Mandell,
      Alex Weiland, C. Yelton
1973 Robert Rich, Ralph Hoffman,
      Bob Mammoser, Joseph Stokes
1974 Arnold Leavitt, Sandi Leavitt,
      Paul Sugar, Gunther Polak
1975 Gene Chait, Florine Walters,
      Paul Hessel, Henry Rabin
1976 Hal Mouser, Greg DeFotis,
      Mark Cohen, Jerry Goldfein
1977 Ben Blacik, Jerry Lee,
      Essie Mersky, Pat Hassett
1978 Steven Reuschlein, Phil Warden,
      Worth Vaughn, Jeff Miller
1979 Willie Zurfluh, Babs Charney,
      Colby Vernay, John Wachter
1980 Kent Feiler, Claude Vogel, Paul Hessel
      Gary Bush, Barry Schaffer,
1981 Tom Fox, Jim Brothers,
      Ron Morlock, Terry Borne

MEN'S SWISS TEAMS
1976 Lee Esworthy, Robert Hayes,
      Ted Brashler, Charles Shannon

1977 Ron Andersen, Hugh MacLean,
      Russ Weikle, Ron Kruse
1978 Arthur Flashinski, John Fourness,
      Dave Malec, Bhola Singh
1979 Dick Claussen, Dennis Clerkin,
      Eric Rodwell, Dave Fred
1980 David Siebert, Roger Jourdan, Tom Clarke,
      Jim Barrow, John Onstott
1981 Mel Skolnik, Peter Weichsel,
      Eddie Wold, Ron Smith

WOMEN'S SWISS TEAMS
1976 June Deutsch, Sandi Leavitt,
      Sue Halperin, Florine Walters
1977 Essie Mersky, Arlene Hill,
      Joyce DeHarpporte, Carole Miner
1978 June Deutsch, Sue Halperin, Florine Walters,
      Cheri Bjerkan, Sandi Leavitt
1979 Cheri Bjerkan, Eunice Rosen,
      Florine Walters, Sue Picus
1980 Sharon Koldin, D. Woodruff, Emilie Anderson,
      Claire Calahan, Adrienne Volpe, Jean Barry
1981 Arlene Hill, Pat Hassett,
      Essie Mersky, Carole Miner

MASTER PAIRS
1969 Leo Spivack, Charles Burger
1971 Joseph Stokes, James Kaplan
1972 Matt Granovetter, Donald Massey
1974 Colby Vernay, Alan Stout
1975 Aminul Karim, John Wachter
1976 Paul Sugar, Harvey Miller, Jr.
1977 Ben Blacik, Essie Mersky
1978 Terry Beckman, Jane Kunzer
1979 Paul Soloway, Eddie Wold
1980 Gerald Caravelli, Jerry Goldfein
1981 David Lehman, Steve Garner

LIFE MASTER PAIRS
1971 Essie Mersky, Larry Oakey

OPEN PAIRS
1968 William Rosen, Joseph Levinson
1969 Neil Knutsen, Philip Warden
1970 Dr. Richard Katz, Larry Cohen
1971 Lois Wiley, Kent Wiley
1972 Dave Smith, Dan Requard
1973 Sandi Leavitt, Paul Sugar
1974 Fred Hamilton, Jeff Starr
1975 Carl Davis, Jr., Ruth Nathan
1976 Alan Cokin, Mike Passell
1977 Jerry Lee, Pat Hassett
1979 Eric Rodwell, Dave Fred
1981 Mel Skolnik, Eddie Wold
Flight A:
1978 Dan Requard, Ted Brasher
1979 Jim Hall, Howard Weinstein
1980 Claude Vogel, L. James Phillips
1981 Dave Lehman, Jim Hall
Non-Smoking:
1978 Allan Cohen, Dan Requard
1980 Robert Sundby, Phil Warden
Smoking:
1978 James Cordas, Lorand Tritter
1980 Roger Jourdan, Jim Barrow

MEN'S PAIRS
1968 Stan Adamowski, Frank Weisbach
1969 Norman Fink, Robert Jarrett
1970 John Startzel, Bob Gardner
1971 Larry Oakey, David Nicklasson
1972 Jack Wachter, Kent Wiley
1973 Irving Steinfeldt, Lorand Tritter
1974 L. James Phillips, Kent Wiley
1976 Mike Passell, Alan Bell
1978 S.C. Becker, K. Smith
1980 David Siebert, John Onstott

WOMEN'S PAIRS
1968 Mrs. Homer Denison, Mrs. Carl Pohland
1969 Mrs. Edwin Wier, Mrs. Robert Risch
1970 June Deutsch, Freida Arst
1971 Janet Wilkinson, Joan Stein
1972 June Deutsch, Gloria Harris
1973 Dorothy Coakley, Harriet Schnarsky
1974 Sylvia Simon, Gloria Weber
1976 June Deutsch, Freida Arst
1978 Shirley Seneff, Emilie Anderson
1980 Sue Halperin, Tobi Deutsch

MIXED PAIRS
1968 Shirley Harris, John Zilic
1969 Lois Wiley, Kent Wiley
1970 Kent Feiler, Doranne Polcrack
1971 Dorothy Kantor, Hugh MacLean

1973	Bob Gardner, Delores Witte
1975	Cheri Bjerkan, Jim Bjerkan
1976	Steven Reuschlein, Diana Reuschlein

DISTRICT 14 (North Dakota, South Dakota, Minnesota, Iowa, Nebraska, one county of northwestern Wisconsin)

CANADIAN PRAIRIE

KNOCKOUT TEAMS
1972 Hugh MacLean, Dorothy Kantor
Bernie Coleman, Alan Stout

OPEN TEAMS
1967 Jack Marsch, Brian Pauls,
Hersh Wolch, Doug Thomson
1968 Chuck Shefchik, Joyce Schoenecker,
Dale Egholm, Ron DeHarpporte
1969 Jim Hall, Don Horowitz,
Jerry Lee, Ed Langer
1970 Mrs. Edgar Marquart, G. Sekar,
Bruce Pippy, Anne Smithen
1971 Lex DeGroot, N.N. Levi,
Richard Seabrook, L.R. Carscadden
1972 Larry Oakey, Kay Klimmek,
Tim Wernz, Susan Bender *(tied with)*
Paul Lewis, Gene Mogen,
Marg Lightle, Carl Lowless

OPEN PAIRS
1967 Ethel Daybock, Morrie Freier
1969 Doris Rossen, Emma Chernick
1970 Ron Andersen, Arthur Selzer
1971 Essie Mersky, Larry Oakey
1972 Mrs. L. Udow, L. Udow

MEN'S PAIRS
1967 Russell Weike, Larry Oakey
1968 Doug Thompson, Joe Halper
1969 Keith Sandiford, Barry Wolk
1970 Brian Falls, Larry Oakey
1971 Gerry Polonsky, Larry Hansen
1972 Terry Beckman, Howard Weinstein

WOMEN'S PAIRS
1967 Mrs. W. Williams, Margaret Phillips
1968 Ethel Dayboch, Joyce Schoenecker
1969 Jean Gustafson, Charlene Nicholson *(tied with)*
Sally Landa, Phyllis Sornsin
1970 Essie Mersky, Joyce Schoenecker
1971 Mrs. W.F. Acheson, Alice Cullum
1972 Celeste Engebretson, Mrs. E. Nelson

MASTER PAIRS
1967 Sammy Kehela, Baron Wolf Lebovic

MIXED PAIRS
1967 Rose Smithen, Jay Chasenoff

DISTRICT 14

KNOCKOUT TEAMS
1970 Richard Du Four, Hugh MacLean,
Dorothy Kantor, Fred Hamilton
1971 Ron LaCour, Herb Tepperman,
Jay McKee, Mike Passell
1972 Valerie Kotulski, Dorothy Kantor, S. Irving Steinfeldt,
Lorand Tritter, Hugh MacLean, Alan Stout
1973 Jim Jacoby, Jim Nash, Paul Levitt,
Paul Galter, Harry Ross
1974 Clarence Goppert, Mike Passell, Mark Lair,
John Grantham, Henry Divis
1975 Sue Andersen, Ron Andersen,
Hugh MacLean, Terry Beckman
1976 Alan Bell, Lex De Groot,
Bryan Maksymetz, G. Sekhar
1977 Howard Weinstein, Dick Melson, Larry Oakey,
Jim Hall, David Lehman, Steve Garner
1978 Alan Bell, Bob Kuz, Leslie Tsou,
Jan Janitschke, Neil Kimelman, Ron Feldman
1979 Bryan Maksymetz, Ed Lichtman, Lex De Groot,
Milton Schefchik, Alan Bell
1980 Roger Jourdan, Paul Lewis,
Ron Smith, Jim Barrow
1981 Jim Hall, Larry Oakey, Dave Lehman,
Steve Garner, Dick Melson, Chuck Stegeman

OPEN TEAMS
1968 Mrs. A.L. Bauer, Mrs. Rollie Bauer,

Vivian Christensen, Mrs. J.P. Holland
1969 Libby Hoberman, Carrie Watters,
Sue Greenberg, Richard Hoberman
1971 Essie Mersky, Morrie Freier,
Ethel Daybock, Larry Oakey
1972 L. James Phillips, Gunther Polak, Jack Blair,
Dr. John Fisher, Ronald Andersen, Gerald Caravelli
1973 Robert Wolff, Jim Jacoby, Jane King,
Gaylor Kasle, Proctor Hawkins
1974 Tom Fox, Robert Leonard,
Harold Siegelman, Jim Brothers
1975 Jim Leary, David Lehman,
Richard Melson, Richard Du Four
1976 Jim Leary, David Nicklasson,
Terry Borne, Chris Patrias
1977 Clarence Rudy, Mrs. R. Oster,
Mrs. D. Lindberg, Mrs. E.L. Mitchell
1978 Michael Melia, Barbara Staton,
Gail Schaab, Ross Gormon
1979 Pat Hassett, John Boeder,
Jerome Lee, Timothy Wernz
1980 Leslie Tsou, Jim Barrow, Ron Smith,
Rita Alkonis, Roger Jourdan
1981 Chuck Stegeman, Jim Hall,
Dave Lehman, Dick Melson

MEN'S PAIRS
1968 Hoyt Nicholas, Dean Robinson
1970 David Nicklasson, Chuck Stegeman
1975 Hugh MacLean, Ron Andersen
1976 David Lehman, Steve Garner
1977 Allan Mowatt, David Sokolow
1978 Jack Rhatigan, Mike Hoffman
1981 Chuck Stegeman, Larry Oakey

WOMEN'S PAIRS
1968 Mrs. Travis Bunn, Altha Lampert
1970 Mrs. C. Hamilton, Edith Benton
1975 Donna Youngberg, Marge Mott
1976 Marie McDowell, Addie Olson
1977 Sallie Landa, Elizabeth Clark
1978 Hermene Zweiback, Bonnie Wilke
1981 Essie Mersky, Arlene Hill

MASTER PAIRS
1968 Carole Cramer, Maurine Moore
1969 Paul Orlett, Regis Robertson
1970 Wayne Pinsonneault, Paul Winter
1971 David Nicklasson, Chuck Stegeman
1972 Dr. John Fisher, Gunther Polak
1973 Jim Jacoby, Gerald Caravelli *(tied with)*
Ron LaCour, Proctor Hawkins
1974 Richard Du Four, Fred Hamilton
1976 David Lehman, Howard Weinstein
1977 David Lehman, Dick Melson
1978 Marc Jacobus, Tony Morris
1979 Chuck Stegeman, Steve Garner
1980 Hoyt Nickolas, Bruce Wick
1981 G. Sekhar, Bill Gray

OPEN PAIRS
1968 Dale Egholm, Larry Oakey
1969 Larry Tonkin, Bill Crooks
1970 William Erickson, Peder Langsetmo
1971 Brad Furnish, Bill Muir
1972 James Hall, Sharon Moss
1973 Barry Crane, Dr. John Fisher
1974 Arch Bangs, Michael Howland
1975 Scott Nobles, Joyce Dodson
1976 David Lehman, Larry Oakey
1977 Richard Du Four, Howard Weinstein
1978 Jim Hall, Larry Oakey
1979 Helen Promislow, Doug Thomson
1980 Paul Lewis, Ron Smith
1981 Dick Melson, Chuck Stegeman

UNMIXED PAIRS
1980 Tom Fox, W.J. Bradshaw

GOPHER

KNOCKOUT TEAMS
1967 David Clarren, Newton Dockman,
Hugh MacLean, Ron Anderson
1968 Don Horwitz, Morris Freier, Ethel Dayboch,
Jack Wachter, Jim Hall
1969 Morris Freier, Ethel Dayboch,
Don Horwitz, Jim Hall
1971 David Clarren, Dorothy Kantor, Hugh MacLean,
John Wachter, Larry Cohen, Gerald Caravelli
1975 Drew Cannell, Bill McTavish,
G. Sekhar, Norman Levi
1977 Richard DuFour, David King, Alan Stout,
Carole Miner, Jim Hugstad

1978   Bob Anderson, Hal Mouser,
      Greg De Fotis, Jerry Goldfein
1979   Morris Freier, Tom Jensen, Pat Hassett,
      Milton Shefchik, Jerome Lee, Keith Hanson
1980   Keith Hanson, Jerome Lee,
      Larry Oakey, Pat Hassett
1981   David Sokolow, Kai Cheng, G. Sekhar,
      Ron Morlock, Bob Kuz

MIXED PAIRS
1977   Tom Fox, Phyllis Sornsin

MASTER TEAMS
1968   Essie Mersky, Larry Oakey,
      Joyce Schoenecker, Ron DeHarpporte

INDIVIDUAL
1977   Mrs. A. C. Shrafel

OPEN TEAMS
1958   Newton Dockman, Norman Justice,
      David Clarren, Morris Freier
1959   Julien Phillippy, Wes Scheuneman,
      Farrell Green, Irving Levin
1960   Newton Dockman, Paul Levitt,
      Mrs. Saul Shapiro, Don Horwitz
1961   Farrell Green, Irving Levin,
      Julien Phillippy, Herschel Wolpert
1962   Alan Bell, John Zilic,
      Gunther Polak, John Wachter
1963   David Clarren, Newton Dockman,
      Edward Langer, Jerome Lee
1964   Allan Zeh, Edward Rosen, Worth Vaughan,
      Ken Christiansen, John Wachter
1965   Morris Freier, Ethel Daybock, Norman Justice,
      Richard Troxel, Don Horwitz
1966   Don Horwitz, Jim Hall,
      Jerome Lee, Edward Langer
1967   David Clarren, Ethel Dayboch, Morris Freier,
      John Wachter, Grant Marsee
1969   Jim Hall, Jerome Lee,
      Edward Langer, Don Horwitz
1970   Jim Hall, Jerome Lee,
      Edward Langer, Don Horwitz
1972   Fredrick Benedict, Hank Moss
      Sherman (Irv) Steinfeldt, Harry Ross
1973   Janice Cohn, Sandy Zakin,
      Richard Stern, Gene Chait
1974   Morris Freier, Ethel Dayboch,
      Lorand Tritter, Farrell Green
1975   Sheldon Margulis, Floyd Schwade, Joan Stein,
      Martha Francis, David Olson
1976   Sue Andersen, Russ Weikle, Mark Cohen,
      Terry Beckman, Hugh MacLean
1977   Newton Bowers, Jim Swanson,
      David Bowers, Mike Pomper *(tied with)*
      Kit Woolsey, Joyce DeHarpporte,
      Larry Oakley, Arlene Hill *(and)*
      Brian Crossley, D. R. Yarian,
      Jess Cohen, Dr. M. Mosharrafa
1978   Barry Crane, Gerald Caravelli, Gene Chait,
      Harvey Miller, Jr., Kent Feiler
1979   Jim Hugstad, Caroline Miner,
      Mike Hoffman, Jack Rhatigan
1980   Dave McGee, Harry Ross,
      Valerie Ross, Joyce Miller *(tied with)*
      Jim Hugstad, Carole Miner,
      Michael Hoffmann, Jack Rhatigan *(and)*
      Carol Hammer, Howard Hammer,
      Dorothy Rasmussen, Betty Pappas
1981   Mike Premo, Larry Anderson,
      Rod Paxton, Gary Mehlin

MASTER PAIRS
1958   Morris Freier, Ethel Dayboch *(tied with)*
      Lee Magee, Mrs. M. S. Levitt
1959   Edwin Langer, Paul Pink
1960   David Clarren, Allen Bell *(tied with)*
      A. Simmons, R. LaDue
1961   Dee Kennedy, Lucille Thornburg
1962   Mrs. Henry Mott, Harry Platt
1963   Art Weiner, Beverly Torrey
1964   Fred Rubbra, John Moran
1965   Mrs. J. Peilan, Willard Wheeler
1966   Jerome Lee, Edward Langer
1967   Don Faskow, Grant Marsee
1968   Isadore Rosen, Essie Mersky
1969   C. Milton Shefchik, Dorene King
1970   Essie Mersky, Doug Thomson
1971   John Mitchell, Norman Justice
1972   Royce McCray, Keith Hanson
1973   Dorothy Kantor, Hugh MacLean
1974   Gene Chait, Harvey Miller, Jr.
1975   Bob Korte, Kay Korte

1976   Gerald Caravelli, Larry Cohen
1977   Mike Hoffman, Jack Rhatigan
1978   Mike Flader, Patricia Welander
1979   Chuck Stegeman, Howard Weinstein
1980   Jerome Lee, Pat Hassett
1981   Margaret Roberts, Josephine Joseph

OPEN PAIRS
1958   Tom Wilder, Leo Benson
1959   Paul Levitt, Newton Dockman
1960   Herschel Wolpert, Farrell Green
1961   Mel Pike, Fred Rappleyea
1962   Herschel Wolper, Farrell Green
1963   William Campbell, John Tidball
1964   John Cummings, Mrs. John Cummings
1965   D. L. Williams, George Schnurr
1966   Jerome Lee, Edward Langer
1967   Julien Phillippy, Farrell Green
1968   John Larsen, David Nicklasson
1969   Mrs. H. M. Macken, Jim Hugstad
1970   Doug Thomson, Brian Pauls
1971   Isadore Rosen, Mrs. Isadore Rosen
1972   Gene Chait, Gunther Polak
1973   Richard Stern, Gene Chait
1974   Agnes Christo, Ruth Countryman
1975   Sheldon Margulis, Joan Stein
1976   Gene Chait, Harvey Miller, Jr.
1977   Sharon Christenson, Van Christenson
1978   B. W. Berglund, Brian Berglund
1979   David Loken, Anita Loken
1980   Kai Cheng, Keith Hanson
1981   Morris Frier, Farrell Green *(tied with)*
      Jeff Miller, Ted Brashler

MEN'S PAIRS
1958   Herschel Wolpert, Irv Levin
1959   David Clarren, Edward Rosen
1960   David Clarren, Don Horwitz *(tied with)*
      Jerome Lee, J. Gustafson
1961   John Roddewig, Ronald Shulman
1962   Alan Bell, John Zilic
1963   Dr. Glen Dalbey, Ronald Anderson
1964   John Wachter, Morris Freier
1965   John de Blois Wack, Eddie Kantar
1966   Hugh MacLean, Donald Rockstad
1967   Brian Pauls, Morris Kaplan
1968   Robert Gasway, Al Malmon
1969   John Wachter, David Clarren
1970   John Wachter, David Clarren
1971   Gerald Caravelli, Hugh MacLean
1972   Wayne Snider, Bob Gardiner
1973   Jim Hall, Marshall Schneider
1974   Morris Freier, Lorand Tritter
1976   Terry Beckman, Steve Garner
1977   Mike Flader, Mike Hoffman
1978   Ron DeHarpporte, Russ Weikle
1979   Ron DeHarpporte, Russ Weikle
1980   David Nicklasson, C. Milton Shefchik
1981   Jim Hall, Tom Fox

WOMEN'S PAIRS
1958   Ruth Peilen, Rosalyn Litman
1959   M. S. Levitt, Betty Jane Galter
1960   M. Meyer, E. E. Green
1961   Pat Hassett, Marguerite Grue
1962   L. M. Cubbison, B. T. Anderson
1963   Mrs. Edgar Marquart, Mrs. Saul Shapiro
1964   Anne Strom, Mrs. George Fismen
1965   Dorene King, Nelsine Stuhlman
1966   Essie Mersky, Marguerite Grue
1967   Mrs. A. Whittle, Mrs. L. Udow
1968   Tessie Oxman, Dorothea Norman
1969   Mrs. C. P. Doll, Dorothy Rasmussen
1970   Marguerite Grue, Mrs. Myron Hill
1971   Barbara Morris, Dorothy Kantor
1972   Marge Annis, Bernice Larson
1973   Beulah Schochet, Sharon Moss
1974   Marcia Cravaack, Dani Young
1976   Connie Seacord, Karen Faust
1977   Bea Anderson, Pam Weimar
1978   Jean Forsberg, Mrs. Robert Brink
1979   Wendy Jones, Mrs. D. McChandless
1980   Joyce Miller, Terri Melson
1981   Sharon Anderson, Carole Jerpbak

MEN'S SWISS TEAMS
1976   Richard DuFour, David King,
      Christopher Patrias, James Leary

WOMEN'S SWISS TEAMS
1976   Essie Mersky, Pat Hassett,
      Ethel Dayboch, Sallie Landa *(tied with)*
      Maxine Holm, Charleen Mracek,
      Elaine Guldberg, Lyn Arms

IOWA

KNOCKOUT TEAMS
1972 Tom French, Ron Andersen,
　　　Hugh MacLean, Dorothy Kantor
1975 Jim Hall, Howard Weinstein,
　　　Russ Weikle, Terry Beckman
1976 Gaylor Kasle, Mike Passell, Garey Hayden,
　　　Richard DuFour, Shirley Boice
1977 Lil Greenberg, Mary Jane Farell,
　　　Larry Kolker, Charles Wiley
1978 Brad Furnish, Paul Orlett,
　　　John Rosenchein, Marilyn Rosenchein
1979 C. Milton Shefchik, Tom Fox, Chuck Stegeman,
　　　Larry Oakey, David Lehman, Jim Hall
1980 Mike Cannon, Jay Baum, Kathy Baum,
　　　Dennis Cordle, Royce McCray, Lyle Petersen
1981 Bobby Goldman, Jim Jacoby, Dave Lehman,
　　　Terry Beckman, Greg Vasterling, Mike Girou

OPEN TEAMS
1970 Essie Mersky, Ethel Daybock,
　　　Morrie Freier, Larry Oakey
1971 Chuck Stegeman, David Nicklasson,
　　　John Larsen, Richard DuFour, Jr.
1972 Barbara Staton, Chuck Allen,
　　　James Casper, Jim Thurtell
1973 Chuck Cummins, John Oxley,
　　　Harry Ross, Valerie Anderson *(tied with)*
　　　Hal Everley, Barbara Byrne,
　　　Jerry Matulef, Jim Hall
1974 Russell Weikle, Jim Hall,
　　　Howard Weinstein, Terry Beckman
1975 Jim Fellows, Clark Betcke,
　　　Gary Kotulski, Valerie Kotulski
1976 Barry Crane, Gerald Caravelli,
　　　Ron Andersen, Hugh MacLean
1977 Lil Greenberg, Mary Jane Farell,
　　　Larry Kolker, Charles Wiley
1978 Van Christenson, Sharon Christenson,
　　　Mike Hoffmann, Jack Rhatigan
1979 Royce McCray, Mike Edwards,
　　　Jay Baum, Kathie Baum *(tied with)*
　　　Pat Hassett, Morrie Freier,
　　　Jerome Lee, Keith Hanson *(and)*
　　　C. Milton Shefchik, Chuck Stegeman, David Lehman,
　　　Dick Melson, Jim Hall, Larry Oakey
1980 Chuck Stegeman, Dave Lehman,
　　　Larry Oakey, Dick Melson
1981 M. Ali Dogruyusever, Jerry Matulef,
　　　Marilyn Hemenway, Barbara Fellows

MEN'S SWISS TEAMS
1978 Alan Bell, David King,
　　　Jim Nash, Colby Vernay
1980 Barry Crane, Ron Andersen, Owen Miller
　　　Royce McCray, Mike Edwards

WOMEN'S SWISS TEAMS
1978 Tupper Cunningham, Liane Slack,
　　　Barbara Staton, Gail Schaab
1980 Betty O'Donnell, Flores Bonitz,
　　　Leah Nelson, Sue Greenberg *(tied with)*
　　　Eileen Swearingen, Sherry Dogruyusever,
　　　Myrna Rockey, Elaine Graham

MASTER PAIRS
1968 Gerald Caravelli, Milton Rosenberg
1969 Bobbie Shipley, Donald Rockstad
1971 Barry Crane, Gerald Caravelli
1972 Ron Andersen, Tom French
1973 Stan Schiller, Jean Lanteri
1974 Edward Rosen, Joan Rosen
1975 Hugh MacLean, Mark Feldman
1976 Eunice Bloom, Steve Bloom
1977 Lee Magee, LaVerne Magee
1978 Brad Furnish, Marilyn Rosenchein
1979 Bruce Cuthbertson, Ken Hixon
1980 Dave Lehman, Dick Melson
1981 John Koch, Tony Ames

OPEN PAIRS
1968 Essie Mersky, Larry Oakey
1969 Jon Wexler, Gerald Caravelli
1970 Louis Herbester, Phyllis Herbester
1971 Chuck Stegeman, David Nicklasson
1972 Dr. John Gustafson, S. Irving Steinfeldt
1973 Dr. John Fisher, Gunther Polak
1974 Kent Wiley, Lois Wiley
1975 Michael Howland, Capt. Mary Orock
1976 Barry Crane, Gerald Caravelli
1977 Dick Melson, Howard Weinstein
1978 Neville Hochoy, Gary Roberts
1979 Morrie Freier, Keith Hanson
1980 Lyle Kraus, Jerry Ballinger

1981 Jim Milne, Terry Crabbs
Flight A:
1979 Don Stack, Donna Stack
1981 David McGee, Carole Miner

MEN'S PAIRS
1968 Stanley Adamowski, Frank Weisbach
1969 Jon Wexler, Gerald Caravelli
1970 Gunther Polak, Claude Vogel
1971 Barry Crane, Richard Kaye
1973 Hugh MacLean, Richard DuFour
1974 James Hall, Howard Weinstein
1977 Mike Flader, Jack Rhatigan

WOMEN'S PAIRS
1968 Barbara Morris, Mrs. Jarvis Tew
1969 Marilyn Oliver, Virginia Goodall
1970 Frieda Arst, June Deutsch
1971 Johanna Beers, Mrs. William Cushing
1973 Katherine Kenna, Mabel Long
1974 Joan DeWitt, Esta Van Zandt *(tied with)*
　　　Ethel Kaufman, Martha Markley
1977 LaVerne Magee, Jane Senger

MID-AMERICAN-CANADIAN

OPEN TEAMS
1955 Russell Arnold, Harold Harvey, Robert Bullock,
　　　Len Lazarus, Ed Langer *(tied with)*
　　　Joseph Cohen, G. Richard Wilson,
　　　Mrs. John Millunchick, John Millunchick
1956 Mrs. Saul Shapiro, Irving Berkson,
　　　Lorand Tritter, Claude Wetmore
1957 W.A. Schueneman, Harold Harvey,
　　　Maurice Reuben, Edward Langer
1958 Milton Goldberg, Mrs. Jack Bowers, Jack Bowers
　　　Lorand Tritter, Ethel Daybock
1959 Oswald Jacoby, Gerald Michael,
　　　Walter Gilbert, John Hubbell
1960 Ethel Daybock, Morrie Freier,
　　　Bob Casement, Alfred Habel, Jr.
1961 David Clarren, Jerome Lee,
　　　Edward Langer, Newton Dockman
1962 David Clarren, Jerome Lee,
　　　Edward Langer, Newton Dockman *(tied with)*
　　　Robert Bullock, Dick DuFour,
　　　Hugh MacLean, Russ Weikle
1963 David Clarren, John Mitchell, Farrell Green,
　　　Irv Steinfeldt, Miles Fiterman
1964 Dorothy Kantor, Hugh MacLean,
　　　Essie Mersky, Ron Andersen
1965 Gary Krook, John Larsen,
　　　Larry Oakey, Dave Nicklasson *(tied with)*
　　　Hugh MacLean, Dorothy Kantor,
　　　Barbara Morris, C. Milton Shefchik
1966 Jack Wachter, Gerry Hartsman,
　　　Larry Cohen, Mike Ledeen
1967 Alice Mitchell, William Schleusener,
　　　John Nelson, James Smith

MEN'S PAIRS
1955 Harold Harvey, Robert Bullock
1956 H.E. Churchill, Harold Klein
1957 Dr. W. Wayne Sands, Edward Rosen
1958 Alan Bell, David Clarren
1959 Dr. W. Wayne Sands, Edward Rosen
1960 David Clarren, Don Horwitz
1961 Cheng-Ting Hsu, Clifford Colvin
1962 Russ Weikle, Ronald DeHarpporte
1963 John Fox, Hugh MacLean
1964 Phil Sokolof, Lorand Tritter
1965 Jim Hall, Don Horwitz
1966 Russ Weikle, Larry Oakey
1967 Lee Magee, Roger Lord

WOMEN'S PAIRS
1955 Mabel Mulford, Clara Charlet
1956 Beulah Schochet, B.A. Marvy
1957 Marguerite Grue, Reine Seewald
1958 Ethel Daybock, Louis Jacobs
1959 Mrs. Gene Rosenberg, Mrs. Stanley Browne
1960 Carrie Watters, Mrs. William Brennan
1961 Nicky Oram, Lambie Bishop
1962 Madeline Soloman, Anne Meyers
1963 Pat Hassett, Mrs. Robert Brink
1964 Coutzie Taber, Delores Wilson
1965 Mrs. O. F. Meredith, Anne Duvall Kuhns
1966 Nina Farha, Clara Reed
1967 Mrs. W.F. Adams, Marilyn Stewart

MASTER PAIRS
1956 Joyce Terry, Earle Hyers
1957 Mrs. T. A. Krikac, T. A. Krikac
1958 Alan Bell, Dave Clarren

1959	Paul Galter, Paul Levitt
1960	Alan Bell, Paul Levitt
1961	Helene Meyers, Betty King
1962	Anne Myers, Jack Klein
1963	Douglas Thomson, Brian Pauls
1964	John Nelson, Alice Mitchell
1965	Charles Betcke, Lorand Tritter
1966	Hugh MacLean, Dorothy Kantor
1967	Norman Abrahamson, William Schleusener

OPEN PAIRS

1955	Jim Millerd, Alan Bell
1956	Irving Berkson, Frank Schneller
1957	Doug Cannell, H.C. MacFarlane
1958	Virginia Meriwether, Dr. Dan Danes
1959	Ed Wolter, Don Saale
1960	Jim Corisis, Gene Banck
1961	Richard Balanow, Bob Cruise
1962	Irving Levin, John Mitchell
1963	Irv Steinfeldt, Maurice Galvin
1964	David Carter, Gerald Michaud
1965	Mrs. Henry Mott, Mary Specker
1966	Jim Leary, Sean Nisam
1967	D. Michael Thomas, Jack Blair

MIXED PAIRS

1965	Dorothy Kantor, Hugh MacLean
1966	Bee Schenken, Howard Schenken
1967	Roslyn Steinfeldt, Irv Steinfeldt

OPEN INDIVIDUAL

1955	Mrs. Charles Hoyt *(tied with)*
	Jewell Bockwitz
1959	Gregory Judge
1960	Vivian Christensen

SUMMER

KNOCKOUT TEAMS

1975	Ethel Dayboch, Morrie Freier,
	Larry Oakey, Jack Wachter
1977	Malcolm Brachman, Minda Brachman, Bobby Goldman,
	Mike Passell, Paul Soloway
1979	Clarence Goppert, Mark Lair, Mike Passell,
	Ron Smith, Paul Soloway
1981	Bud Reinhold, John Solodar,
	Robert Levin, Russ Arnold

OPEN TEAMS

1975	Kathie Wei, Gerald Caravelli, Hugh MacLean,
	Mark Feldman, Ron Andersen
1977	Clarence Goppert, Mark Lair,
	Rod MacKenzie, Bruce Ferguson
1979	Marilyn Bost, Bruce Ferguson, Dennis Clerkin,
	Tom Clark, Noël Clark

SWISS TEAMS

Flight A:
| 1981 | Jim Hugstad, Arlene Hill, |
| | Sharon Anderson, Carole Jerpbak |

OPEN PAIRS

1975	Tom Lux, Bill Shutts
1977	Paul Soloway, Malcolm Brachman
1979	Dennis Clerkin, Ron Smith
1981	Lyle Petersen, Dianne Warren

Flight A:
| 1981 | Don Stack, Donna Stack |

MASTER PAIRS

1975	Don Stack, Don Brooker
1977	Gail Schaab, Barbara Staton
1979	Dennis Clerkin, Bruce Ferguson
1981	Mike Ness, Paul Winter

UNMIXED PAIRS

| 1977 | Clarence Goppert, Mark Lair |

MEN'S SWISS TEAMS

1979	J. Fredrick Benedict, Dave Camp,
	Ralph Kaufman, John Michael Edwards *(tied with)*
	Jim Gavin, Brian Delaney,
	James Jacobson, August Hunte

WOMEN'S SWISS TEAMS

| 1979 | T. Cunningham, L. Slack, |
| | LaVerne Magee, Jo Beth Threlkeld |

DISTRICT 15   (Kansas, western Missouri, Oklahoma, northwestern Texas)

DISTRICT 15

KNOCKOUT TEAMS

1967	Mike Lawrence, Hugh Ross, James Jacoby,
	Bobby Wolff, Billy Eisenberg, Ira Corn Jr.
1968	Art Kincaid, Richard Ayres, John Hubbell,
	Cortland Rush, Gerald Michaud, Larry Richardson

1969	John Hubbell, Don Williams,
	Gerald Michaud, Larry Richardson
1970	James Russell, Regis Robertson,
	Don Williams, Tom Lux, Paul Orlett
1973	Bud Reinhold, Dr. Richard Katz,
	Larry Cohen, Kyle Larsen
1974	Gerald Michaud, G. Robert Nail, Alan Bell,
	Ken Peyser, Larry Richardson, Don Kerr
1975	Larry Richardson, Jim Russell, Don Kerr,
	Orval Swander, Ken Peyser
1976	Clarence Goppert, Ron LaCour, Mark Lair,
	Bruce Ferguson, Lou Bluhm
1977	Don Williams, Jack Burke, Paul Orlett,
	William Crooks, Larry Tonkin
1978	Kelsey Petterson, Kenn Bradley, Proctor Hawkins,
	Jack Burke, Steve Timmerman
1979	Clarence Goppert, Mark Lair, Kerri Shuman,
	Barry Crane, Mike Passell
1980	Madelynn Carmichael, Gerald Michaud, LaVerne Magee,
	Byron Greenberg, Roger Jourdan, Jim Barrow
1981	Colby Vernay, Jim Fellows,
	Alan Bell, Roger Lord

OPEN TEAMS

1967	Jack Wolf, Dan Keleher,
	Larry Richardson, Don Williams *(tied with)*
	Barry Crane, Tom French, Gunther Polak,
	Milt Rosenberg, Gerald Caravelli
1968	Art Kincaid, Richard Ayres, Ayres Bombeck,
	Lee Magee, Laverne Magee
1969	John Hubbell, Don Williams, Bill Crooks,
	Regis Robertson, Hugh Cassidy
1970	Ed Banks, Jack Blair,
	Steve Greenberg, Henry Bethe
1973	Byron Greenberg, Pam Fields,
	Oswald Jacoby, Gerald Michaud
1974	Malcolm Brachman, James Jacoby,
	Paul Soloway, Mike Passell
1975	Sue Renfro, Nina Farha,
	Rosanna Teichgraeber, Clara Reed *(tied with)*
	Ron Andersen, Susan Andersen, Hugh MacLean,
	Steve Timmerman, Wendell Hedden
1976	Clarence Goppert, Mark Lair, Ron LaCour,
	Bruce Ferguson, Lou Bluhm *(tied with)*
	Howard Weinstein, David Lehman,
	Dick Melson, Steve Garner *(and)*
	Britain Beezley, Nancy Beezley,
	David Hampton, Don Searcy
1977	Steve Bloom, Betty Crowther,
	Paul Portnoy, Robert Portnoy
1978	Mike Passell, Ken Bains, Gaylor Kasle,
	Mrs. Valton Cox, Garey Hayden
1979	Karl Keller, Bob Gow,
	Charles Mote, Byron Greenberg *(tied with)*
	Al Childs, David Siebert, Joe Scott,
	Boyce Cearley, Hermant Lall, Steve Greenberg

SWISS TEAMS

Flight A:
1980	Allan Siebert, David Siebert,
	Byron Greenberg, Proctor Hawkins *(tied with)*
	Milton Stern, Al Childs, Jan Janitschke,
	Boyce Cearley, Craig Janitschke
1981	Fred Rubbra, Kerri Shuman,
	Barry Crane, Andy Bernstein

MEN'S PAIRS

1967	Mike Lawrence, Hugh Ross
1968	Deane Shapiro, Paul Orlett
1969	Gerald Michaud, Larry Richardson
1970	John Gerber, Danny Kaim
1976	Paul Soloway, Garey Hayden *(tied with)*
	Bob Etter, John Potter
1977	Gary Roberts, David Landauer
1978	G. Robert Nail, Byron Greenberg
1980	William Crooks, Jim Crowley
1981	Mel Skolnik, Jeff Meckstroth

WOMEN'S PAIRS

1967	Mrs. Ed Clark, Ruth Mills
1968	Vivian Watkins, Frances Walters
1969	Odell Stewart, Gina Potts
1970	Helen Wilson, Bonnie Roye
1976	Carol Sanders, Connie Jackson
1977	Cubs Conklin, Linda Galloway
1978	Allene Melton, Nadine Milam
1980	Jerie C. Kittell, Trauda Shaw
1981	Ella Wortham, Marie Clark

MIXED PAIRS

1967	Rosalie Sweet, Regis Robertson
1968	Gordon Anderson, Loretta Bunn
1969	Fran Beard, Sam Beard
1976	Barry Crane, Carol Sanders
1977	Joyce Schlozman, Dick Arnett

MASTER PAIRS
1967 Virginia Meriwether, Dr. David Ginns
1968 Alice Peterson, Mary Holloway
1969 Jack Shaw, John Knudsen
1970 Jim Rusell, Paul Orlett
1973 Dr. Richard Greene, Col. William Christian
1974 John Jeffrey, Proctor Hawkins
1975 G. Robert Nail, Gerald Michaud
Flight A:
1976 G. Robert Nail, E. Lowell Yost *(tied with)*
     Ron Henke, Jo Callahan
1977 David Siebert, Allan Siebert
1978 Marc Jacobus, Paul Lewis
1979 Ron Henke, Dave Horner
1980 Don Stack, Donna Stack
1981 Lee Magee, Jim Fellows

OPEN PAIRS
1967 Gerald Caravelli, Milt Rosenberg
1968 Art Kincaid, Richard Ayres
1969 John C. Anderson, Hal C. Halsted
1970 John Hancock, William Gibbs
1974 Barry Crane, Gerald Caravelli
1975 Ron Smith, Tony Astrologes
1976 Clarence Goppert, Mark Lair
1977 Irvin Z. Bremler, Clay Sundermeyer
1978 Curtis Smith, Karl Keller
1979 David Schroeder, Sim Therrell
1980 Ron Henke, Boyce Cearley
1981 Barry Crane, Kerri Shuman
Flight A:
1978 Steve Timmerman, Esta Van Zandt
1979 Billy Marshall, Joe Miller
1980 Jack Blair, John Jelsma
1981 Don Stack, Donna Stack *(tied with)*
     Barry Crane, Kerri Shuman

INDIVIDUAL
1976 Helen Shapley

MASTER SWISS TEAMS
1981 Larry Shapiro, Ed Allen, Julie Green,
     Alan Burcham, Bob Pilshaw *(tied with)*
     Ray Clark, Bob Sloane,
     Mike McGhehey, David Young

UNMIXED PAIRS
1979 Jan Janitschke, Craig Janitschke

MEN'S SWISS TEAMS
1977 Clarence Goppert, Mark Lair, Charles Wiley,
     Larry Kolker, Neil Chambers
1979 Clarence Goppert, Mark Lair, Barry Crane,
     Garey Hayden, Mike Passell

WOMEN'S SWISS TEAMS
1977 JoAnn Kimball, Jo James,
     Margaret Ewing, Helen Jane Henley *(tied with)*
     Carmen Federico, Madelynn Carmichael,
     Janet Weyant, Georgiana Gates
1979 Kerri Shuman, Anne Hambric,
     Linda Hager, Patty Holmes

CHARITY SWISS TEAMS
1980 Donna Stack, Gary Roberts,
     Sally Lapin, Craig Ewing

LAND OF CORONADO

KNOCKOUT TEAMS
1972 Gaylor Kasle, Garey Hayden, Roger Bates,
     Robin Grantham, Jane King
1973 Orval Swander, Shirley Swander,
     Lee Magee, W. Crooks
1974 Moe Rubenfeld, Henry Divis, J. David King,
     John Grantham, Mark Lair
1976 Dianne LaFleur, John Mohan, John Grantham,
     Mike Lawrence, Roger Bates
1978 Garey Hayden, Gaylor Kasle,
     Ron Smith, Dr. Jim Tucker
1980 Karl Keller, Eddie Wold, Lester Dewey,
     Nancy Passell, Bob Stewart
1981 Malcolm Brachman, Minda Brachman, Bobby Goldman,
     Paul Soloway, Mike Lawrence

OPEN TEAMS
1972 Gaylor Kasle, Roger Bates, Garey Hayden,
     Robin Grantham, Jane King
1973 Mark Blumenthal, Dr. John Fisher,
     Gerald Caravelli, Milton Rosenberg
1974 Clarence Goppert, Gaylor Kasle, Garey Hayden,
     John Grantham, Ron LaCour
1976 Henry Divis, Bob Baldwin, Ron Henke,
     Terry Gibson, Wes Irby, Ken Baines
1978 Jan Janitschke, Craig Janitschke, Mark Lair,

Joe Miller, Mike Passell
1980 Terry Gibson, Tom Edwards, Wes Irby,
     Morris Chang, Ken Baines, Bobby Wolff *(tied with)*
     Clayton Ijams, Barbara Ijams,
     Tom McClure, Hal Halsted *(and)*
     Eddie Wold, Karl Keller, Mark Lair, Patricia Vick
1981 Malcolm Brachman, Mike Lawrence,
     Paul Soloway, Bobby Goldman

BOARD-A-MATCH MASTER TEAMS
1976 Malcolm Brachman, Minda Brachman, Bobby Goldman,
     Paul Soloway, Mike Passell

MEN'S SWISS TEAMS
1978 Lee Bauer, Harry Patton, J. C. Paul,
     John Paul, Wayne Smith
1980 Bill Thomas, Frank Fisher, Charlie Wolpert,
     Allan Jacobson, Bill Cook, Hal Task
1981 Terry Gibson, Kenn Bradley,
     J. L. Foote, Bobby Baldwin

WOMEN'S SWISS TEAMS
1978 Clarice Holt, Pauline Love,
     Mildred Kielpinski, Doris Rush
1980 Helen McCrary, Mary Arnold Hefley,
     Anna Marie Fish, Fern Ellington
1981 Jerre Gardiner, Emma Jean Hawes,
     Fran Beard, Montie Shelton *(tied with)*
     Lita Gibson, Hermine Baron, Juanita Skelton,
     Nancy Passell, Linda Spangler

OPEN PAIRS
1972 Bruce Martin, Earle Rudes
1973 Garner McDaniel, Tom Hoddap
1974 Jan Janitschke, Craig Janitschke
1976 Barry Crane, Dr. John Fisher
1978 William Gibbs, John Hancock
1980 Charles Wolpert, Hal Trask
1981 David Foote, Patty Holmes
Flight A:
1981 Al Childs, Joe Scott *(tied with)*
     LaVerne Magee, Kenn Bradley

MASTER PAIRS
1972 Jan Janitschke, Craig Janitschke
1973 Kenn Bradley, Brian Grace
1974 John Griffin, III, Bruce Martin
1976 Mark Lair, Mike Passell
1978 Mark Lair, Mike Passell
1980 Karl Keller, Eddie Wold
1981 Paul Soloway, Malcolm Brachman

MEN'S PAIRS
1972 Roger Bates, Garey Hayden
1973 Mike Harlow, Bill Shutts
1980 Gordon Craig, Jerry Mark
1981 Gaylor Kasle, James Downs

WOMEN'S PAIRS
1972 Jennie Park, Clarice Walker
1973 Shirley Swander, LaVerne Magee
1980 Wanda Streu, Ginger Sweney
1981 Ellen Adams, Dori Smith

NON-MIXED PAIRS
1974 Mike Kaplan, Neil Haflich

MIXED PAIRS
1978 Laura Mariscal, Miguel Reygadas

INDIVIDUAL
1980 Margo Rosser

MISSOURI VALLEY

KNOCKOUT TEAMS
1969 J. G. Ripstra, Morty Nelson
     Bill Christian, Jim Linhart
1970 Malcolm Brachman, Paul Soloway, John Mohan,
     Richard Henderson, Bill Shutts
1971 Jack Blair, Byron Greenberg, Jim Jacoby,
     Minda Brachman, Steve Greenberg, Paul Swanson *(Spring)*
     G. Robert Nail, John Hubbell,
     Larry Richardson, Gerald Michaud *(Fall)*
1972 Don Williams, Paul Orlett,
     Bill Crooks, Regis Robertson
1973 Paul Soloway, Minda Brachman,
     Mike Passell, Mark Lair *(Winter)*
     Orval Swander, Shirley Swander, Lee Magee,
     John Hubbell, William Crooks *(Summer)*
     A.E. (Bud) Reinhold, Dr. Richard Katz,
     Larry Cohen, Kyle Larsen *(Fall)*
1974 Byron Greenberg, Jim Jacoby
     Minda Brachman, Betsy Wolff,
     Bobby Goldman, Steve Greenberg
1975 Byron Greenberg, Thomas Sanders, Carol Sanders,
     Sidney Lazard, Frank Hoadley *(Summer)*

Kenn Bradley, Kelsey Petterson, Joseph Bramer,
Jim McKinney, Proctor Hawkins *(Fall)*
1976 Byron Greenberg, Sidney Lazard,
Frank Hoadley, Robert Baldwin
1977 Tom French, Jeff Corbin,
Tom Lux, Larry Richardson
1978 Mark Lair, Larry Kolker,
Jan Janitschke, Craig Janitschke
1979 Richard Hunt, Dan Windsor,
Jean Ouimet, Fran Dolmage
1980 John Anderson, William Crooks, Bob Stewart,
Steve Timmerman, Arthur Kincaid
1981 Oswald Jacoby, Bob Hamman, Jim Chew,
Peter Weichsel, Alan Sontag

MASTER PAIRS
1957 Marc Low, Ken Bullock
1958 Carolyn Levitt, Jerry Levitt
1959 Patrick Brennan, Jr., Mrs. Patrick Brennan, Jr.
1961 Emma Jean Hawes, Oswald Jacoby
1962 George Cubbon, Claude Simon
1963 Ann Jervis, Betty Coffey
1964 Carol Beegle, Morris Beegle
1965 Hampton Hume, Jim Jacoby
1966 John Anderson, Lloyd McKinley, Jr.
1967 Joan Rosen, Lois Knight
1968 G. Robert Nail, William Brown
1969 Doris Orlett, Wilma Hill
1970 Larry Richardson, Gerald Michaud
1971 Betty Ann Kennedy, Mrs. Al Hagert *(Spring)*
G. Robert Nail, Larry Richardson *(tied with)*
Carl Hipsh, Muriel Hipsh *(Fall)*
1972 Jean Fitzgerrell, Roger Bates
1973 Gaylor Kasle, Roger Bates *(tied with)*
Terry Gibson, Lucian McLaughlin *(Winter)*
Kenn Bradley, Brian Grace *(Summer)*
Dr. Richard Greene, Col. William Christian *(Fall)*
1974 Barry Crane, Dr. John Fisher
1975 Kelsey Petterson, Lloyd McKinley, Jr. *(Summer)*
1976 Byron Greenberg, Frank Hoadley
1977 Mark Lair, Joseph Miller
1978 Joe Scott, Boyce Cearley
1979 Bud Creed, Catherine Fikes
1980 John Anderson, Leo Weiner
1981 Mark Perlmutter, Lester Perlmutter
Flight A:
1975 William Gough, Joseph Livezey

OPEN PAIRS
1952 Shirley Fairchild, William Curtis
1953 Thelma Bailey, J. G. Ripstra
1954 John Gerber, Oswald Jacoby
1955 Ivan Erdos, Lionel Wolfers
1957 F. Ayres Bombeck, Richard Ayres
1958 Oswald Jacoby, Alan Bell
1959 Lucian McLaughlin, Ed J. Rogers, Jr.
1961 Arthur Kincaid, Richard Ayres
1962 William Crooks, Jack Wolf *(tied with)*
Ace Gutowsky, Tom Brown
1963 Edward Monroe, Keith Stenger *(tied with)*
Peggy Cundiff, Richard Cundiff
1964 Forrest Lowe, Mrs. C. O. Hackley
1965 David Carter, John Hubbell
1966 Jim Jacoby, Minda Brachman
1967 Myrt Cheever, Bill Springall
1968 John Cronin, Rosalie Sweet
1969 Regis Robertson, Don Williams
1970 G. Robert Nail, David Lair
1971 Carolyn Frandsen, Mildred White *(Spring)*
Barry Crane, Gerald Caravelli *(Fall)*
1972 Ron Smith, Roger Lord
1973 Dan Mordecai, Dick Reed *(Winter)*
Garner McDaniel, Tom Hodapp *(Summer)*
Barry Crane, Kerri Shuman *(Fall)*
1974 Barry Crane, Dr. John Fisher
1975 Jack Blair, Fran Beard *(tied with)*
Jim Miller, Gloria Reysa *(Summer)*
Henry Divis, Terry Gibson *(Fall)*
1976 Jim Wart, Bill Karnaze
1977 Al Childs, Boyce Cearley
1978 Dr. John Fisher, Del Parker
1979 Charles Gabriel, Charles Weed
1980 Tod Moses, Bob Meyer
1981 Ken Bains, Charlie Weed
Flight A:
1978 Jan Janitschke, Craig Janitschke
1979 Lamar Hallman, Jack Harback
1980 William Crooks, Steve Timmerman
1981 Mike Murphy, Lezlie Anne Dreyfus *(tied with)*
Pat Walker, Ferman Cheatwood

OPEN TEAMS
1952 Arthur Kincaid, F. Ayres Bombeck

John W. Hubbell, Byron L. Greenberg
1953 Dan Westerfield, Mrs. Eugene Miller,
J. G. Ripstra, Thelma Bailey
1954 Charles Robinson, Isadore Rosenberg,
Garrett Nash, David Carter, Frances Carter
1955 Frances Carter, David Carter, John Simon,
Isadore Rosenberg, Charles Rosenberg
1958 Oswald Jacoby, Mrs. William Johnson,
Alan Bell, Mrs. George Sheehan
1959 Arthur Kincaid, Walter Gilbert, John W. Hubbell,
J. G. Ripstra, George Willett
1961 Ed Theus, Jack Wolf,
Margaret Alcorn, Adaline Simon
1962 Paul Levitt, F. Ayres Bombeck, Richard Ayers,
Jack Wolf, Iz Rosenberg
1963 Ace Gutowsky, Marlene Moore,
Myrt Cheever, Jody Inman
1964 J. G. Ripstra, John W. Hubbell
Richard Ayers, Bryan Grace
1965 Mike Thomas, Paul Swanson, Jack Blair,
Bernadine Jenkins, Hampton Hume
1966 Oswald Jacoby, Jim Jacoby, Minda Brachman,
Malcolm Brachman, Michael Thomas
1967 Roger Lord, James Showalter,
Arthur Seltzer, Jim Fellows
1968 Lee Magee, Laverne Magee,
Norb Kremer, Roger Lord
1969 Betty Coffey, Nancy Phillips,
Jackie Meyer, Bobbie Grisham
1970 Dr. John Fisher, Henry Baer,
Charles Weed, Emma Jean Hawes
1971 Dr. Charles Robinson, John Swindle,
John Spessard, Suell Turner *(tied with)*
Kenn Bradley, Mary Lou Merry
LaVerne Magee, Lee Magee *(tied with)*
Bud Creed, Vickie Davis,
Dr. Ted Teel, John Torbett III *(tied with)*
Pat Weddle, Joe Weddle,
Bob Layton, Bob Weingrad *(Spring)*
Jack Blair, Col. William Christian,
Allan Siebert, David Siebert *(Fall)*
1972 Esta Van Zandt, Curtis Smith, Jim Barrow,
Byron Greenberg, Steve Greenberg
1973 Paul Soloway, Minda Brachman, Heitie Noland,
Dr. John Fisher, Jim Jacoby, Barry Crane *(Winter)*
Mark Blumenthal, Dr. John Fisher,
Gerald Caravelli, Milton Rosenberg *(Summer)*
Byron Greenberg, Pam Fields,
Oswald Jacoby, Gerald Michaud *(Fall)*
1974 Jan Janitschke, Mike Kaplan,
Dick Reed, Broma Lou Harrison
1975 Dr. John Fisher, Mark Feldman, Gerald Caravelli,
Alan Susskind, Hugh MacLean, Larry Kozlove *(Summer)*
Gary Schroeder, Tony Astrologes,
Ron Smith, Mark Lair, Ted Brashler *(Fall)*
1976 Pat Walker, Judy Walker,
Mary Blount, Neva Jeske *(tied with)*
D. W. Crisjohn, Louise Dickerson,
C. T. Watkins, Jo Ann Guest
1977 Tom French, David Erickson,
Jeff Corbin, Kim Corbin
1978 Del Parker, Dr. John Fisher,
Ken Bains, Tom Edwards *(tied with)*
Bill Springall, Myrt Cheever,
Gloria Cronin, John Cronin
1979 Ed Groner, Charles Scallon, Karl Keller,
Byron Greenberg, Eddie Wold
1980 Roy Fox, Joel Tonkin,
Don Williams, Larry Richardson

SWISS TEAMS
Flight A:
1981 Marc Jacobus, Polly Rich,
Terry Brown, Tim R. Frick *(tied with)*
Philip Pratt, Daisy Pratt,
Judy Walker, Winston Munn *(tied with)*
Mel Skolnik, Paul Soloway,
Ron Andersen, Jeff Meckstroth

MEN'S PAIRS
1952 W. H. James, J. H. Cullinan
1953 H. E. Woods, Walt H. Theiman
1954 Charles Robinson, Isadore Rosenberg
1955 Prentice Barnes, J. P. Hoover
1957 F. Ayres Bombeck, Richard Ayres
1958 George Cubbon, W. C. Hainline
1959 David Carter, Larry Kolker
1961 G. Robert Nail, Arthur Kincaid
1962 William Bunyan, Morris Beegle
1963 George Rosenstein, Philip Steinberg
1964 Richard D. Hall, John T. Chaney
1965 Dr. Marcel M. Mooney, Arthur Kincaid

1966   Byron L. Gariepy, J. L. Foote
1967   Thomas C. French, Dan Keheler
1968   Ed G. Theus, Dr. James E. Kraft
1969   Bill Crooks, Don Williams
1970   Phil O'Konski, John Oxley
1971   Jim Jacoby, Sam Beard *(tied with)*
       Mike Passell, John Zilic *(Spring)*
       Lloyd McKinney, Jr., Proctor Hawkins *(Fall)*
1972   Dick Holmes, Wendell Hedden
1973   Mike Harlow, Bill Shutts
1975   G. Robert Nail, E. Lowell Yost *(Summer)*
1976   Tim Frick, Don Searcy
1977   Britain Beezley, Jack Harback
1978   Jack Burke, Everett Rees
1979   Marc Jacobus, Paul Lewis
1980   John Anderson, Sheldon Stern
       WOMEN'S PAIRS
1952   Shirley Fairchild, Elaine Lee
1953   Mrs. Clarence Neff, Mary Jo Theiman
1954   Mrs. Dunlap Dwyer, Louise Durham
1955   Marguerite Lagle, Mrs. Marcel L. Mooney
1957   Betty Harding, Betty Wilks
1958   Mary Beth Townsend, Leafy Harrington
1959   Mrs. George Weiner, Barbara Weiner
1961   Nicky Cram, Lambie Bishop
1962   Thelma Bailey, Ann Newland
1963   Ruth Steinberg, Jane Rosenschein
1964   Dorothy Broyles, Marguerite Lagle
1965   Mrs. George Weiner, Barbara Weiner
1966   Annette Broyles, Stephanie Martin
1967   Jo James, Mrs. Garnett Reintjes
1968   Carolyn Frandsen, Mrs. Dallas Davis
1969   Mrs. Paul Jensen, Frances Thompson
1970   Shirlee Lazarus, Esta Van Zandt
1971   Shirlee Lazarus, Esta Van Zandt *(Spring)*
       Gloria Cronin, Myrt Cheever *(Fall)*
1972   Jan Steele, Esta Van Zandt
1973   Shirley Swander, Laverne Magee
1975   Mary Pat Frick, Jackie Meyer *(Summer)*
1976   Nancy Phillips, Mary Pat Frick
1977   Betty Wilks, Donna Stack
1978   Myrt Cheever, Gloria Cronin
1979   Mary Anne Moncier, Linda McRay
1980   Sherrill Burnell, Sharon Ogren
       MIXED PAIRS
1952   Burt Salmon, Hazel Greenberg
1953   Dee Bombeck, Frank Hoadley
1954   Ruth Steinberg, John Simon
1955   E. H. Scurlock, Betty Wilks
1957   Adaline Simon, Jim Jacoby
1958   Oswald Jacoby, Mrs. William Johnson
1959   Margaret Alcorn, Mike Michaels
1962   Joe Taylor, Erline Friedman
1963   Virgil Anderson, Jr., Barbara Weiner
1964   F. Ayres Bombeck, Rosalie Sweet
1965   Carol Sanders, Thomas K. Sanders
1966   Lucian McLaughlin, Pauline French
1967   Dr. W. A. Grosjean, Mrs. Phil Wilcox
1968   Mrs. G. Reardon, A. Ray Phillips
1969   P. J. O'Connell, Mrs. A. Vogt
1970   William Mann, Liane Mann
1971   Jack Wolf, Marlene Wolf *(Spring)*
       John Zilic, Virginia Zilic *(Fall)*
1972   Marcy Conway, George Conway
1976   Joan Jackson, Frank Hoadley
       INDIVIDUAL
1952   Robert T. Brennan
1953   J. C. Rutherford
1954   William L. Haffamier
1955   Mrs. Lewis Cameron
1957   Elizabeth Eastman
1958   Frank E. Adams
1959   Mrs. W. H. Bridges
1976   Mrs. A. L. Egnew
       UNMIXED PAIRS
1981   Tom Clarke, David Siebert
       WOMEN'S SWISS TEAMS
1978   Suzy Livesay, Jean Jones,
       Mary Lou Jackson, Kathy Benson.
1979   Pat Dalziel, Neva Jeske,
       Judy Walker, Mary Blount
1980   Joan De Witt, Florine Kuehl,
       Wendy Hoffman, Anne Leverone
1981   Billie Mitchell, Betty Dickerson, Bonnie Roye,
       Sue Norman, Mayme Parker
       MEN'S SWISS TEAMS
1978   Ned Hager, Jack Harback, Henry Divis,
       Boyce Cearley, Joe Scott
1979   Dave Horner, Lucian McLaughlin, Pat Walker,

       Bill Springall, Sam C. High, Dave Henke
1980   Ken Meistad, Dr. A.J. Fritsch,
       Dale Burns, Ed Monroe.
1981   Dennis Sorensen, Kerr Godfrey,
       George Pisk, Rick Price

DISTRICT 16   (Most of Texas, Mexico)

MEXICAN FIESTA

       KNOCKOUT TEAMS
1980   Eddie Wold, George Rosenkranz, Mark Lair,
       Jeff Meckstroth, Eric Rodwell
1981   Mike Passell, Miguel Reygadas,
       Jose Hamui, Marc Jacobus
       OPEN TEAMS
1980   Bob Norwood, Barbara Norwood,
       George Dawkins, George Pisk
1981   Eddie Wold, Jeff Meckstroth, Mark Lair,
       George Rosenkranz, Eric Rodwell, Barry Crane
       SWISS TEAMS
Flight A:
1981   Eddie Wold, Jeff Meckstroth, Mark Lair,
       Edith Rosenkranz, Eric Rodwell, Barry Crane
       OPEN PAIRS
1980   Howard Chandross, Lew Handelsman
1981   Barry Crane, Jan Janitschke
Flight A:
1980   Bob Hamman, Henry Baer
1981   Jeff Meckstroth, Eric Rodwell
       MASTER PAIRS
1980   Bob Hamman, Seymon Deutsch
1981   Eric Rodwell, Jan Janitschke
       MEN'S PAIRS
1980   Tom Clarke, Alan LeBendig
       WOMEN'S PAIRS
1980   Joy Grief, Thelma Johns
       UNMIXED PAIRS
1981   Jose Lichtenberg, Mike Passell

MEXICAN NATIONALS

       KNOCKOUT TEAMS
1977   Gaylor Kasle, Sharon Kasle, Garey Hayden,
       Polly Rich, Miguel Reygadas
1978   Roger Jourdan, Bob Woodworth, Gratian Goldstein,
       Sharyn Kokish, Eric Kokish, George Keri
1979   Minda Brachman, Malcolm Brachman, Jim Jacoby,
       Paul Soloway, Heitie Noland
1980   Eddie Wold, George Rosenkranz, Sol Dubson,
       Mark Lair, Fred Hamilton
1981   Eddie Wold, Jeff Meckstroth, Mark Lair,
       George Rosenkranz, Eric Rodwell
       OPEN TEAMS
1955   Bob Barrett, John Mothershed,
       Henry Lesky, Robert Friedberg *(tied with)*
       George Rosenkranz, Dr. L. Nagy Leishman,
       V. E. Laska, George Mandoki
1960   Julian Barth, Cy Strouse,
       Dr. John Fisher, Boots Kendrick
1961   Mrs. L. F. Storr, F. Herring,
       Mrs. C. Smith, J. C. Tucker
1962   Lucille Goble, Dr. John Fisher,
       Henry Lesky, Bob Friedberg
1964   Alicia Kempner, Jane Herb, Clarence Strouse,
       Maurice Weil, Russell Fischer *(tied with)*
       Julius Rosenblum, Paul Levitt,
       Nate Silverstein, Dr. John Fisher
1965   Jim Jacoby, Rae Kittle, Charles Kittle,
       Elaine Lee, George Treadwell
1966   G. Robert Nail, Gaylor Kasle, Betsey Wolff,
       Robert Wolff, Alfred de Marigny
1967   Alfred de Marigny, Jim Jacoby, Robert Wolff,
       G. Robert Nail, Marty Cohn
1968   Robert Wolff, Mike Lawrence, Jim Jacoby,
       Bill Eisenberg, Bob Goldman
1969   George Rosenkranz, Dan Morse, John Gerber,
       Margaret Wagar, Dorothy Hayden
1970   Dr. Nathan Ostrich, A. D. Ostrick,
       Steve Greenberg, Milton Stine
1971   George Rosenkranz, Miguel Reygadas, Dan Morse,
       G. Robert Nail, John Gerber
1972   Thomas Sanders, Carol Sanders, Martin Cohn,
       Betty Cohn, Harold Guiver, Tommy Prothro
1973   Bud Reinhold, Bill Eisenberg,
       Rhoda Walsh, Trudi Nugit

1974 George Rosenkranz, Edith Rosenkranz, Roger Bates,
      Sol Dubson, John Grantham *(tied with)*
      Lowell Andrews, Jim Steehler,
      Larry Mills, Jean Mitchell *(and)*
      Malcolm Brachman, Paul Soloway,
      Mike Passell, Jim Jacoby
1975 Barry Crane, Kerri Shuman, Dr. John Fisher,
      Jim Jacoby, Carol Klar
1976 Cecilia Rosenberg, Reiko O'Hara,
      Edith Rosenkranz, Lucrecia Williams *(tied with)*
      Clarence Goppert, Mike Passell, Garey Hayden,
      Gonzalo Herrera, Miguel Reygadas
1977 Max Hardy, Lucille Mitchell,
      John Norman, Barbara Norman
1978 Johnny Hamui, Robert Martel,
      Jean Ehrenberg, Raul Bouffier *(tied with)*
      William Nicodemus, Carol Didier,
      Robert Boyer, Rosalind Josephson *(and)*
      Jacobo Podbilevich, Luis Kaufer,
      Robert Pesaro, Fablo Pisinger
1979 Boyce Holleman, Robert Prevost, Rae Dean Prevost,
      James Graham, Barbara Graham
1980 Kathie Wei, Ron Andersen, Esta Van Zandt,
      Don Baxter, Curtis Smith
1981 Vivian Whalen, Bud Whalen,
      Lew Handelsman, Rona Schiller
Flight A:
1981 Dorsey Brooks, Zerene Brooks,
      Max Hardy, Marc Leventhal *(tied with)*
      William Passell, Hermine Baron,
      Nancy Passell, Ed Banks

MASTER PAIRS
1960 Edith Rosenkranz, Cy Strouse
1961 Mrs. M. F. Ruffner, Walter Leipen
1964 Julius Rosenblum, Paul Levitt
1965 Dr. Charles Burnham, Elinor Murdoch
1966 Curtis Smith, Heitie Noland
1967 Paquita Litwinczak, Mrs. L. Mana
1968 Ann Kluewer, Richard Dallas
1969 Dan Morse, George Rosenkranz
1970 J. David King, Louise Sharp
1971 Magda Fogarty, Maria Teresa Diaz Covarrubias
1972 Mike Passell, Thomas Sanders
1973 Vickie Davis, Bud Creed
1974 Bud Reinhold, Bill Eisenberg
1975 Dane Clay, Ann Clay
1976 Alan Wilhide, Michael Carroad
1977 Michael Lawrence, George Rosenkranz
1978 Betty Wilks, Dr. W. T. Braun
1979 Marc Jacobus, Paul Lewis
1980 Paul Lewis, Paul Swanson
1981 William Passell, Hermine Baron

OPEN PAIRS
1955 Barry Crane, Bella Weissman
1960 Dr. L. Nagy Leishman, Julius Rosenblum
1961 Dan Morse, George Dawkins
1962 Constant Fua, Walter Leipen
1964 Julius Rosenblum, Nate Silverstein
1965 Jo Murphy, Mrs. Chandler Duncan
1966 Betsey Wolff, Robert Wolff
1967 Harvey Cohen, Mrs. Harvey Cohen
1968 Carol Klar, Clarence Strouse
1969 Alex Harrison, Robert Williams
1970 Alex Harrison, Robert Williams
1971 Gaylor Kasle, Dr. James Tucker
1972 Fred Atiyeh, George Malhame
1973 Hermine Baron, Mike Passell
1974 George Rosenkranz, Roger Bates
1975 Peter Gelfand, Eldon Thompson
1976 Robert Wolff, Jim Hooker
1977 Tom Lum, Patsy Lum
1978 Jim Becker, Mirette Mignocchi *(tied with)*
      Chad Woolsey, John Schermer
1979 Steve Sion, James Mahaffey
1980 Don Baxter, Curtis Smith
1981 Anamaria Behrens, Mark Lair
Flight A:
1981 Fred Hamilton, Beatriz Lichtenberg

MIXED PAIRS
1955 George Rosenkranz, Edith Rosenkranz
1960 Mrs. Jack Timon, Alex Harrison *(tied with)*
      Bella Weissman, Constant Fua
1961 Magda Sanchez Fogarty, Walter Leipen
1962 Willa Mae Clymore, Jerry Ferguson
1964 Anita Davis, Jim Hooker
1965 Jim Jacoby, Elaine Lee
1966 Janine Gerard, Joel Menkes
1967 Phyllis Cohn, Martin Cohn
1968 Jim Vaughan, Lorraine Killian

1969 William Muthard, Edith English
1970 Mike Moss, Gail Moss
1971 Anita Davis, Dr. Nathan Ostrich
1972 Mrs. W. Lewis, Harold Guiver
1973 Frankie Taylor, Robert Taylor
1974 Mirette Mignocchi, Jim Becker
1975 Mirette Mignocchi, Jim Becker
1976 Jo Morse, Michael Carroad
1977 Gloria Reysa, Jim Miller
1978 Jim Jacoby, Heitie Noland
1979 Madelynn Carmichael, Ron Smith
1980 Alicia Duran, Luis Sneider

UNMIXED PAIRS
1978 Walter O'Loughlin, Russell Fischer
1979 Russ Mitchell, George Pisk

MEN'S PAIRS
1955 Constant Fua, Roela Resiere
1960 G. Robert Nail, Guy Howard
1961 J. Pike, M. Block
1962 Constant Fua, Julius Rosenblum
1964 Julius Rosenblum, Constant Fua
1965 David Carter, Nate Silverstein
1966 Jim Jacoby, Robert Wolff
1967 Robert Wolff, Alfred de Marigny
1968 Bob Pike, Odon Duran
1969 Dr. Nathan Ostrich, Milton Stine
1970 Dan Morse, Mike Moss
1971 Walter Leipen, Miguel Reygadas
1972 Curtis Smith, Clark Phippin
1973 John Grantham, Mark Lair
1974 Ralph Fensterwald, Jim Becker
1975 George Rosenkranz, Roger Bates
1976 Paul Soloway, Eddie Kantar
1977 Roy Dalziel, Stan Goldstein
1980 Allan DeSerpa, James Kostal
1981 Eric Rodwell, Mark Lair

WOMEN'S PAIRS
1955 E. Casoman, Lois Smith
1960 Mrs. Thomas Golding, Louise Wilson
1961 A. Duran, J. Richmond
1962 Natalie Rosenblum, Jean Frankel
1964 C. Buchman, C. McIntyre
1965 Mrs. Chandler Duncan, Jo Murphy
1966 Anita Davis, Hermine Baron
1967 Daisy Stephens, Mrs. Emmett Strother
1968 Betty Hester, Billie Hester
1969 Mrs. George Kaercher, Madlyn Fleming
1970 Ellie Abrams, Helen Owens
1971 Magda Sanchez Fogarty, Maruca Cespedes
1972 Carol Sanders, Bette Cohn
1973 Terry Michaels, Mary Philley
1974 Nancy Gruver, Helen Utegaard
1975 Sue Garcia, Maria Angeles Ybarra
1976 Laura Mariscal, Bella Weissman
1977 Elena Castellanos, Mrs. J. M. Escobar
1980 Cecilia Rosenberg, Magda Sanchez Fogarty
1981 Judy Tucker, Aileen Osofsky

OPEN INDIVIDUAL
1955 Stephen Goldring
1960 L. B. de Celis
1961 F. K. Thompson
1976 Walter Weber
1977 Lucy Hisel
1978 Rachel Carder
1979 Irina Russek
1980 Zada Tull

TEXAS FALL

KNOCKOUT TEAMS
1968 Ira Corn, Jim Jacoby, Robert Wolff,
      Willian Eisenberg, Robert Goldman, Mike Lawrence
1969 George Rosenkranz, John Gerber, Paul Hodge,
      G. Robert Nail, Dan Morse, Harold Rockaway
1970 Lorand Tritter, Mary Philley, Garner McDaniel,
      Steve Honet, George Pisk
1971 George Dawkins, Barry Hagedorn, Clarice Holt,
      Mary Beth Townsend, Carolyn Flournoy, Betsey Wolff
1975 Jim Jacoby, Heitie Noland, Curtis Smith,
      Esta Van Zandt, Eddie Wold
1976 Malcolm Brachman, Minda Brachman, Bobby Goldman,
      Paul Soloway, Curtis Smith
1977 Jack Walton, Terry Radjef,
      Doris Orlett, Kenneth Schutze
1978 Milton Stern, Gaylor Kasle, Mark Lair,
      David Siebert, Larry Kolker
1979 Don Baxter, Curtis Smith,
      Jack Wolf, Ron LaCour
1981 Malcolm Brachman, Minda Brachman, Bobby Goldman,
      Mike Lawrence, Paul Soloway

MIXED TEAMS

1965 David Carter, Mary Beth Townsend,
     Gloria Cronin, Jack Blair

OPEN TEAMS

1952 Luise Mathews, Robert Sharpe,
     Fred Stilwell, L. R. Robertson
1953 Earl McKale, Louis Longfeld,
     Ed Sandstrom, John Moran
1954 Ben Fain, George Heath, Paul Hodge,
     Harold Rockaway, Oswald Jacoby
1955 Walter Wolff, Robert Wolff, Ben Fain,
     Joe Musumeci, Perry Zeller
1956 Alan Jacobson, Calvert Curry,
     George Rosenschein, David Dye
1957 Carolyn Flournoy, Betty Lou Kickman,
     Ace Gutowsky, Curtis Smith
1959 Emma Jean Hawes, Dr. John Fisher,
     Oswald Jacoby, Jim Jacoby
1960 Emma Jean Hawes, Dr. John Fisher, Jim Jacoby,
     Mary Zita Jacoby, Oswald Jacoby
1961 Emma Jean Hawes, Charles Gabriel, Robert Wolff,
     Walter Wolff, Joe Musumeci
1962 Ben Fain, Victor Emanuel, Jerome Levy,
     Col. Tim Willis, Walter Herbert
1963 John Gerber, Paul Hodge,
     Edwin Smith, Jr., Ace Gutowsky
1964 Bud Creed, Mike Thomas,
     Martin Cohn, Joe Taylor
1965 Lorand Tritter, Sue Emery, Ethel Dayboch,
     Morrie Frier, Mary Philley
1966 Louise Krauss, Jim Vaughan, Colby Vernay,
     Byron Economidy, Mildred Graham
1967 G. Robert Nail, Jim Jacoby,
     Robert Wolff, Alfred de Marigny
1968 Ira Corn, Jim Jacoby, Robert Wolff,
     William Eisenberg, Robert Goldman, Mike Lawrence
1969 Esta Van Zandt, Curtis Smith,
     Jim Jacoby, Heitie Noland *(tied with)*
     Al Childs, Boyce Cearley,
     Gary Tilly, Fred Woodruff
1970 Bud Creed, Vickie Davis, Ed Cohen,
     Jane Cosentino, J. David King
1971 George Dawkins, Dave Horner, August Plate,
     Linda Plate, Carolyn Flournoy
1973 Bob Hamman, Bob Wolff,
     Charles Weed, Jim Hooker
1974 Virginia Zilic, John Zilic, Tom Peters,
     Bob Fiske, Ronald Beall
1975 Del Olds, Marian Olds,
     Marc Freeman, Tina Freeman
1976 Jim Jacoby, Heitie Noland, Charles Weed,
     Marion Weed, Ken Bains, Tom Edwards
1977 Jim Miller, Mike Bukala,
     John Swindle, Jerry Murray
1978 Barry Crane, Esta VanZandt,
     Carol Sanders, Thomas Sanders
1981 Cheryl Traber, Tom Hodapp,
     Mark Kelleher, Stan Kohan

MEN'S PAIRS

1952 John Moran, J. B. Kennedy
1953 Dr. John Fisher, Ronald Dreyfus
1954 Charles Woldenberg, William McGhee
1955 George Heath, Bob Barrett
1956 Alvin Roth, Russell Smith
1957 Sidney Lazard, Dr. John Fisher
1959 Oswald Jacoby, Morris Gouger
1960 R. W. Mitchell, Ed Meyers
1961 Curtis Smith, George Treadwell
1962 Robert McAlpin, Charles Coleman
1963 Dan Morse, Payne Harrison
1964 Brad Gentry, Mickey Finch
1965 Jim Jacoby, Ed Burke
1966 Bill Johnson, John Bromberg
1967 Curtis Smith, G. Robert Nail
1968 Bud Creed, Barry Hagedorn
1969 Bill Kuenstler, Don Fizer
1970 Gaylor Kasle, Dr. Nathan Ostrich
1971 Lorand Tritter, Charles Weed
1973 Lynn Dreyfus, Paul Burka
1975 Barry Hagedorn, Eric Hilton
1976 Curtis Smith, Jackson Bradley
1978 Ken Bains, Wes Irby

WOMEN'S PAIRS

1952 Mrs. Edward Ellis, W. A. Stephens
1953 Mary Hedrick, Pearl Carruth
1954 Julia Lucas, Martha Newbill
1955 J. R. King, Mrs. Joe Davis
1956 Rose Groves, Lillian Tiller
1957 Amye Basil, Mrs. R. M. Tompkins
1959 Iona Barnard, Marguerite Wagnon

1960 Emma Jean Hawes, Betty Ann Welch
1961 Arretta Harper, W. M. Remich
1962 Mrs. Fred Mathews, Pauline Gentry
1963 Fran Beard, June Patterson
1964 Fern Seikel, Ann Jones *(tied with)*
     Flo Peery, Iona Sutton
1965 Mrs. J. M. Curran, Jr., Mrs. R. W. McCullough
1966 Garner McDaniel, Mary Philley
1967 Julia Mason, Mrs. M. B. Killian
1968 Mrs. Harry Reid, Gerry Veselka
1969 Carrie Winfield, Margaret Hastings
1970 Mary Francis Westbrook, Mrs. Robert White
1971 Suzanne Lillienstern, Virginia Zilic
1973 Jeanne Titus, Fran Beard
1975 Mary Van Dewalli, Helen Peterson
1976 Sue Clendenin, Betty Boren
1978 Joyce Clark, Patsy Arndt

MASTER PAIRS

1954 Ace Gutowsky, Edwin Smith, Jr.
1956 Percy Fewell, Alvin Roth
1957 Bitsy Pontious, Anita Davis
1959 Ellen Pryor, Boots Kendrick
1960 Amye Basil, Mrs. R. M. Tompkins
1961 Bill Acker, Morris Gouger
1962 Sue Barnard, Jerry Mark
1963 John Gerber, Paul Hodge
1964 Count Wright, James Clinton
1965 Paul Hodge, Dan Morse
1966 Morrie Frier, Bill Acker
1967 Col. Jerry Stutton, Barnard Brown
1968 Betsey Wolff, Barry Hagedorn
1969 Heitie Noland, Jim Jacoby
1970 Robert Norwood, Barbara Norwood
1971 John Sullivan, Murray Reid
1973 Paul Burka, Kenneth Schutze
1974 Jim Hooker, Kent Jones
1975 Alice Gowdey, Ida Morrow
1976 Paul Soloway, Minda Brachman
1977 Cliff Gillespie, Dr. Charles Robinson
1978 Robert Levin, Ron Smith
1979 Terry Radjef, Richard Love
1981 Seymon Deutsch, Bob Hamman

OPEN PAIRS

1952 Ronny Dreyfus, Dr. John Fisher
1953 Earl McKale, John Moran
1954 Harold Rockaway, Oswald Jacoby
1955 David Carter, Curtis Smith
1956 Oswald Jacoby, Curtis Smith *(tied with)*
     George Heath, Paul Hodge
1957 Sidney Lazard, Dr. John Fisher
1959 Alan Jacobson, Oswald Jacoby
1960 Curtis Smith, Dr. Bob Farris
1961 Bitsy Pontious, Anita Davis *(tied with)*
     Ken Parker, Judy Parker
1962 Edith Balsband, Sylvester Lowery
1963 Beth Roddy, Lennox Roddy
1964 John Gerber, John Yates
1965 Barry Crane, Curtis Smith
1966 Barry Crane, Gunther Polak
1967 Payne Harrison, Butch Adams
1968 Mickey Mangan, Betty Jo Wagner
1969 Dan Keleher, Kent Jones
1970 Art Palmer, William Burbridge
1971 Jim Adams, Charles Coleman
1973 Bob Hamman, Dr. Charles Robinson
1974 George Pisk, Lorand Tritter
1975 Bobby Wolff, Jack Kennedy
1976 Mike Lawrence, Mark Blumenthal
1977 Emma Jean Hawes, Jack Kennedy
1978 Barry Hagedorn, George Dawkins
1979 Oswald Jacoby, Harold Rockaway *(Class A-D)*
     Vi Markle, Gaylor Kasle *(Class A)*
Flight A:
1979 Tim Willis, David Hinz
1981 Jim Jacoby, Gerry Veselka

MIXED PAIRS

1952 Adrienne Crank, Lt. Col. C. C. Merrifield
1953 Effie Woods, Stanley Shuford
1954 Juanita Strich, George Rosenkranz
1955 Shirley Fairchild, Clifford Russell
1956 Lydia Bashara, Ferman Cheatwood
1957 Flo Pieratt, A. Fishl
1959 Effie Woods, Duke Calisch
1960 Emma Jean Hawes, Dr. John Fisher
1961 Jerry Ferguson, Louise LeLaurin
1962 Marian Weed, James Cayne
1963 Sue Camp, Dan Morse
1964 Bernadine Jenkins, David Carter
1965 Frances Lawrence, Steve Lawrence
1966 Anne Trenholm, Henry Baer
1967 John Gerber, Carol Klar

1968   Jim Jacoby, Sidney Perutz
1969   Jim Vaughan, Simone Gibson
1970   Jack Mathis, Sharon Kasle
1971   Byron Economidy, Mimi Hagedorn
1973   Dottie Ann Goodloe, Ron LaCour
1974   G. Robert Nail, Betty Nail
1975   Marlene Wolf, Payne Harrison
1979   George Pisk, Betty Cohn

OPEN INDIVIDUAL
1953   Tom King
1954   Don Hooper
1955   Milton Freedman
1957   Sibyl McCalla
1959   Mrs. W. H. Fair, Jr.

SENIOR MASTER INDVIDUAL
1952   Mrs. L. Nagy Laishman

UNMIXED PAIRS
1974   Ace Gutowsky, Jack Wolf
1976   Jim Jacoby, Jim Hooker *(tied with)*
     Joe Musumeci, Henry Baer
1977   Billie Wilson, Doretha Wiley
1981   Jerry Crooker, Ed Snovel

BOARD-A-MATCH-TEAM
1975   John Gerber, Paul Hodge,. Steve Honet,
     Dan Morse, G. Robert Nail

MASTER SWISS TEAMS
1978   Clarence Goppert, Mark Lair, Jan Janitschke,
     Craig Janitschke, Garey Hayden
1979   George Pisk, George Dawkins,
     Lorand Tritter, Barry Hagedorn

TEXAS MID–WINTER

KNOCKOUT TEAMS
1971   John Crawford, Oswald Jacoby,
     Lorand Tritter, Curtis Smith
1972   Bob Hamman, Clay McFarland, Gaylor Kasle,
     Dr. Jim Tucker, Barbara Hamman
1973   John Zilic, Virginia Zilic, Terry Riely,
     August Plate, Eddie Wold
1974   Malcolm Brachman, Minda Brachman, Jim Jacoby,
     Paul Soloway, Mike Passell
1977   Curtis Smith, Mervin Key, Harold Rockaway,
     Boyce Holleman, Jay McKee
1980   Malcolm Brachman, Minda Brachman, Bobby Goldman,
     Paul Soloway, Eddie Wold
1981   Curtis Smith, Brad Gibbs, Harold Rockaway,
     Don Baxter, Ron LaCour

MEN'S TEAMS
1974   Ken Bains, Tom Edwards,
     Wes Irby, Sherrod Williams *(tied with)*
     Bud Trenholm, Ed Groner,
     Charles Scallon, Alan LeBendig

OPEN TEAMS
1971   Fred Berger, Dr. John Fisher, Alfred de Marigny,
     Bobby Wolff, Charles Weed *(tied with)*
     August Plate, Mrs. August Plate,
     Dave Horner, Evalie Hawes *(and)*
     J. Elwood, Bob Frohman,
     David Furman, Larry Laird *(and)*
     Paul Soloway, Jim Jacoby,
     Charles Kittle, Rae Kittle *(and)*
     Jim Barrow, Lloyd Hetzer,
     John Zilic, Bob Cruise
1972   George Dawkins, Barry Hagedorn,
     Carolyn Flournoy, George Pisk
1973   Jim Jacoby, Bobby Wolff,
     Dr. John Fisher, Charles Weed
1974   Charles Gabriel, Morris Chang,
     Bobby Wolff, Cap Crossley
1977   G. Robert Nail, Betty Nail, Mary Beth Townsend,
     Larry Kolker, Bill Brown
1980   Barry Crane, Dr. John Fisher, Charles Gabriel,
     Carol Sanders, Jack Kennedy, Betty Ann Kennedy
1981   Byron Greenberg, Esta Van Zandt,
     James Zimmerman, Proctor Hawkins

WOMEN'S TEAMS
1974   Minda Brachman, Barbara Hamman,
     Gloria Reysa, Jeanne Titus *(tied with)*
     Beverly Bowling, Elaine Piwetz,
     Elizabeth McGee, Mrs. F. Fredrickson

WOMEN'S PAIRS
1971   Fran Beard, Betsey Wolff
1972   Rose Fox, Mary Cheney
1973   Doris Jean Sanders, Mary Ann Duttenhofer
1974   Mary Jane Farell, Elsa Ganz
1977   Montie Shelton, Fran Beard

1980   Clarabel Wilkins, Helen Voris
1981   Betty Ann Kennedy, Carol Sanders

MIXED PAIRS
1971   June Broussard, C. Borden
1972   Anita Davis, Larry Howard
1973   Mike Passell, Hermine Baron
1977   Eddie Wold, Carol Sanders
1980   Hemant Lall, Jan Elkins

UNMIXED PAIRS
1974   Terry Gibson, Henry Divis

MASTER PAIRS
1971   Paul Hodge, Steve Honet
1972   Morris Chang, Jim Jacoby
1973   Mike Passell, Terry Riely
1974   David Siebert, Allen Siebert
1977   John Zilic, Don Olson
1980   John Fisher, Charles Gabriel
1981   Steve Honet, Gary Oleson

OPEN PAIRS
1971   Frank Smith, Bruce Martin
1972   Juanita McLean, Mabel Robinson
1973   Bobby Goldman, Mark Blumenthal
1974   Terry Riely, Eddie Wold
1977   Bobby Wolff, Jack Kennedy
1980   Bob Hamman, Susie Kennedy *(tied with)*
     Bobby Wolff, Morris Chang
Flight A:
1981   Kenneth Schutze, Bob Ayres

MEN'S PAIRS
1971   Ken Perry, Charles Claflin
1972   Jim Vaughn, Steve Toplansky
1973   R. Clyde Hargrove, J. Hargrove
1974   Ron LaCour, Mark Lair
1977   Terry Radjef, Dan Keleher
1980   Ed Snovel, Charles Gabriel
1981   Mike Lawrence, Eddie Kantar

BOARD-A-MATCH-TEAMS
1977   Phyllis Early, Hunter Early, Jack LaNoue,
     Sidney Lazard, Nancy Alpaugh

MASTER SWISS TEAMS
1980   Barry Crane, John Fisher, Charles Gabriel,
     Carol Sanders, Jack Kennedy, Betty Ann Kennedy
1981   Byron Greenberg, Jim Jacoby, Charlie Weed,
     Heitie Noland, Proctor Hawkins

TEXAS SPRING

KNOCKOUT TEAMS
1968   Alfred de Marigny, Robert Wolff, Curtis Smith,
     Paul Levitt, Dan Morse
1969   Payne Harrison, Butch Adams,
     Ace Gutowsky, Lucian McLaughlin
1970   Malcolm Brachman, Minda Brachman, Paul Soloway,
     George Dawkins, Gail Moss, Mike Moss
1972   James Jacoby, Gene Ricci,
     Heitie Noland, Lorand Tritter
1975   Mark Lair, Robert Baldwin, Ron LaCour,
     John Potter, Lester Dewey
1976   Jim Hooker, James Jacoby, Oswald Jacoby,
     Dr. John Fisher, Robert Wolff
1978   Milton Stern, Gaylor Kasle, Eddie Wold,
     Steve Toplansky, Ken Schutze
1979   Barry Crane, Thomas Sanders,
     Carol Sanders, Ron Feldman
1980   Malcolm Brachman, Minda Brachman, Paul Soloway,
     Barry Crane, Eddie Wold
1981   Mike Passell, Miguel Reygadas,
     Jose Hamui, Marc Jacobus

OPEN TEAMS
1958   Hortense Evans, Barry Crane, Clarence Strouse, Jr.,
     Byron Greenberg, Albert Blair, Jr.
1959   Gina Potts, Jan Hubbard,
     Dorothy Moore, John Torbett
1960   Sidney Lazard, John Gerber,
     Ayres Bombeck, Paul Hodge
1961   Emma Jean Hawes, Sidney Lazard, Charles Gabriel,
     Dr. John Fisher, Robert Wolff
1962   Rufus Rush, Doris Rush,
     Jerry Lewis, Bobby Robertson
1963   Emma Jean Hawes, Sidney Lazard,
     Dr. John Fisher, Robert Wolff
1964   Curtis Smith, Ruth Lee,
     James Jacoby, Heitie Noland
1965   Mrs. E. L. Powell, Mrs. Ty Allen,
     Mrs. C. E. Bast, Mrs. C. B. Bryant
1966   John Gerber, G. Robert Nail,
     Mabel Mahoney, Paul Hodge
1967   Gaylor Kasle, Byron Economidy, Aileen Mundy,

Murray Reid, Billye Baker *(tied with)*
Nancy Alpaugh, Dr. Richard Greene,
Mary Beth Townsend, Betty Ann Kennedy
1968 Bob Davison, Neil Chambers,
Helen Simmons, Iona Sutton
1969 Charles Weed, Sidney Perutz,
Betsey Wolff, Robert Wolff
1970 Mrs. Kurt Hartman, Mrs. Carl Hellums,
Billie Strickland, Nancy Bee Vaughan
1972 Pat Brennan, Kay Brennan, Jim Tucker,
Gaylor Kasle, Roger Bates, Garey Hayden
1975 Dr. James Tucker, Gaylor Kasle, Ron LaCour,
Henry Divis, David Siebert
1976 Henry Baer, Marion Weed, Joe Musumeci,
Esta Van Zandt, Paul Levitt
1978 Eddie Wold, James Downs, Steve Toplansky,
Tony Rosenstein, Ira Chorush
1979 Clarence Goppert, Mark Lair, Mike Passell,
Jan Janitschke, Craig Janitschke
1980 Gaylor Kasle, Garey Hayden, Marie Arnall,
Phyllis McCasland, Mike Passell
1981 Eddie Wold, Jeff Meckstroth, Mark Lair,
George Rosenkranz, Eric Rodwell, Barry Crane

SWISS TEAMS
1978 Mark Dahl, Charlotte Hahn,
David Butler, Kay Afdahl *(tied with)*
Jeff Sparks, Lynn Deas,
Dave Smith, Bob McMahan
Flight A:
1981 Eddie Wold, Jeff Meckstroth, Mark Lair,
Edith Rosenkranz, Eric Rodwell, Barry Crane

OPEN PAIRS
1958 George Heath, Paul Hodge
1959 Marvin Key, G. Robert Nail
1960 Earl Jennings, Buford Slay
1961 Oswald Jacoby, Robert Wolff
1962 Sue Barber, Mrs. Roy Jackson
1963 Barry Crane, Byron Greenberg
1964 Gaylor Kasle, Butch Adams
1965 Myrtle Bledsoe, Truby Bunch
1966 Howard Siefen, Jesse Stuart
1967 Mrs. Fred Matthews, Mrs. Dan Garrett
1968 James Jacoby, Minda Brachman
1969 Mrs. Louis Harris, Florine Shank
1970 June Patterson, Jeanne Littrell
1972 James Jacoby, Morris Chang
1975 Craig Janitschke, Jan Janitschke
1976 Dr. Charles Robinson, Jerre Gardiner
1978 Morris Chang, Robert Wolff
J. Richard Burton, Fred Strickland *(Smoking)*
Kal Weiss, Robert True *(Non-Smoking)*
1981 Barry Crane, Jan Janitschke
Flight A:
1979 Allen Bowman, Bill Barkley
1980 Barry Crane, Dr. John Fisher
1981 Jeff Meckstroth, Eric Rodwell

MEN'S PAIRS
1958 Curtis Smith, J.G. Ripstra
1959 Charles Miller, Tom Higgins
1960 David Carter, J. A. Rockhold
1961 Steve Greenberg, Joseph Taylor
1962 John Yates, Doug Fryman
1963 John Yates, Doug Fryman
1964 Oswald Jacoby, Morris Gouger
1965 Butch Adams, Payne Harrison
1966 Butch Adams, Grady Smith
1967 Dan Morse, Charles Miller
1968 Payne Harrison, Butch Adams
1969 Michael Bruce, Rosy Rosenwald, Jr.
1970 Russell Smith, J. David King
1972 Jerry Roberts, Lloyd Roberts
1975 Craig Janitschke, Jan Janitschke
1976 Fred Fredrickson, C. P. Borden
1978 Barry Crane, Thomas Sanders
1980 James Jacoby, Terry Gibson

WOMEN'S PAIRS
1958 Iona Barnard, Marjorie Lichtenstein
1959 Mrs. Milton Sharfstein, Mrs. Max Lipoff
1960 Lorraine Killiam, Mrs. G. W. Thornton
1961 Helen Allison, Gina Potts
1962 Lou Meadows, Eleanor Neissl
1963 Bitsy Pontious, Beth Stuart
1964 Miriam Weller, Tina Klaus
1965 Betty Boren, Eunice Shannon
1966 Mrs. Frank Hare, Mrs. Frank Welch
1967 Nell Cahn, Mrs. Richard Schultz
1968 Louise Marx, Zula Morphew
1969 Mrs. W. W. Carter, Kay Donaldson
1970 Doris Rush, Mary Dusek
1972 Billie Mitchell, Beverly Mead

1975 Kerri Shuman, Betty Ann Kennedy
1976 Pat Weddle, Pat Crough
1978 Vi Novak, Joanne Fincher
1980 Rosemary Brooks, Betsy Platon

MIXED PAIRS
1959 Jerome Levy, Mrs. Jerome Levy
1960 Myrna Vernor, Paul Hodge
1961 Oleta Yost, Gerald Michaud
1962 Gay Wolfforth, William Wolfforth
1963 Russell Smith, Lucy Hisel
1964 John Gerber, Garner McDaniel
1965 Polly Pandres, Dr. Robert Day
1966 Peggy Boone, Jack Boone
1967 Terry Michaels, Dr. Arthur Salasky
1968 Virginia Miller, Robert Layton
1969 Paul Soloway, Minda Brachman
1970 Henry Baer, Betsey Wolff
1976 Jack Titus, Dorothy Moore

UNMIXED PAIRS
1979 Roxy Violin, Steve Lawrence
1981 Jose Lichtenberg, Mike Passell

MASTER PAIRS
1960 Jack Titus, Don Reid
1961 Mary Margaret Swan, Mrs. W. K. Wood
1962 Jean Horner, Ben Matthews
1963 Oswald Jacoby, Barry Crane
1964 Dottie Duncan, Juanita Weaver
1965 Gaylor Kasle, Ed Theus
1966 Suell Turner, Mrs. Charles Word
1967 Roxibeth Patton, Clay McFarland
1968 Bob Davison, Neil Chambers
1969 Ace Gutowsky, Payne Harrison
1970 Nina Jensen, Frank Jensen
1972 William Copson, Robert Holmes
1975 Gloria Reysa, Jim Miller
1976 Jeffrey Butz, J. Patrick Lang
1979 Stormy Horn, Lorand Tritter
1980 Minda Brachmman, Eddie Wold
1981 Eric Rodwell, Jan Janitschke
Flight A:
1978 Clarence Goppert, Mark Lair

LIFE MASTER PAIRS
1966 Dr. Robert Farris, Curtis Smith

DALLAS IMP PAIRS
1976 Catherine Craig, Kathryn Cralle, *N–S*
Rosalie Sweet, Nancy Phillips, *E–W*

MIXED TEAMS
1966 Mary Zita Jacoby, Oswald Jacoby,
Russell Smith, Midge Cutler

MASTER SWISS TEAMS
1978 Barry Crane, Ron Andersen,
Thomas Sanders, Carol Sanders
1979 Clarence Goppert, Mark Lair, Mike Passell,
Jan Janitschke, Craig Janitschke

TEXAS SUMMER
KNOCKOUT TEAMS
1967 Oswald Jacoby, Malcolm Brachman, Minda Brachman,
Sidney Lazard, Paul Levitt
1970 Dr. John Fisher, Charles Weed, Emma Jean Hawes,
Jack Blair, George Dawkins, Barry Hagedorn
1971 Bobby Goldman, Bob Hamman,
Mike Lawrence, Robert Wolff
1972 Robert Wolff, George Pisk, Pat Hood,
Lorand Tritter, Clarence Strouse
1973 Dr. James Tucker, Dr. Charles Robinson, Garey Hayden,
Gaylor Kasle, Bob Hamman
1974 Bud Creed, Vicki Davis, Judy Brownlee,
John Griffin, Steve Lawrence, Frances Lawrence
1975 Carolyn Flournoy, George Dawkins, Jim Vaughan,
Barry Hagedorn, John Sullivan
1976 Malcolm Brachman, Bobby Goldman,
Paul Soloway, Mike Passell
1977 George Gray, Grady Watkins,
Ed Snovel, Jerry Crooker
1978 George Dawkins, Barry Hagedorn,
Lorand Tritter, George Pisk
1979 Malcolm Brachman, Minda Brachman, Bobby Goldman,
Bob Hamman, Paul Soloway, Jim Chew
1980 Gaylor Kasle, Garey Hayden, Jim Barrow,
Marie Arnall, Mark Lair
1981 Gaylor Kasle, Bob Hamman, Jim Jacoby,
Charles Robinson, Marie Arnall

OPEN TEAMS
1967 Dr. John Fisher, Emma Jean Hawes,
Barry Crane, Gunther Polak

1968 George Gray, B. J. Wilson,
      Walter Desmuke, Betty Witt
1969 Paul Soloway, George Dawkins, Malcolm Brachman,
      Minda Brachman, Barry Hagedorn
1970 Curtis Smith, David Siebert, Jack Blair,
      Jack Ritter, Lowell Yost
1971 Bob Goldman, Robert Wolff,
      E. Burke, Mrs. E. Burke
1972 Curtis Smith, Charles Weed, Jack Blair,
      Byron Greenberg, Paul Swanson
1973 Oswald Jacoby, Tom Reid,
      Barbara Hamman, Paul Levitt
1974 George Pisk, Pat Hood, Stormy Horn,
      Peggy Horn, Mike Kaplan
1975 Joe Conforte, Michael Jones,
      Norman Anderson, Kay Schulle
1976 Dave Hinz, Bob Matcha,
      Jamie Bush, Dennis Sorensen
1977 Dr. Charles Robinson, Jerre Gardiner, Henry Gardiner,
      Jeanne Titus, Jack Titus
1978 Virginia Zilic, John Zilic,
      Marty Arndt, Tom Peters *(tied with)*
      Jerry Crooker, Ed Snovel,
      Grady Watkins, Ed Rawlinson *(and)*
      Mike Passell, John Mallet, George Pisk,
      Pat Hood, Lorand Tritter
1979 Alan LeBendig, Tom Allan,
      Jim Griffin, Tom Clarke
1980 Malcolm Brachman, Eddie Wold,
      Steve Toplansky, Paul Soloway
1981 Malcolm Brachman, Bobby Goldman,
      Paul Soloway, Ron Andersen

MASTER PAIRS
1967 Wilbur McGrew, Celeste Mott *(tied with)*
      R. E. Rinkus, Gene Morrow
1968 Bill Fannin, John Puscas
1969 Ray Carmichael, Madelynn Carmichael
1970 Paul Levitt, Shirlee Lazarus
1971 Richard Schmieder, Garey Hayden
1972 Paul Swanson, Jim Miller
1973 Minda Brachman, Paul Soloway
1974 Jan Janitschke, Craig Janitschke
1975 Lorand Tritter, G. Robert Nail
1976 Ron LaCour, Bruce Ferguson
1977 Esta Van Zandt, Barry Hagedorn
1978 Mike Passell, John Mallett
1979 Derrell Childs, Louise Childs
1980 Lorand Tritter, George Pisk

OPEN PAIRS
1967 Robert Wolff, Lorraine Killian
1968 J. David King, Helen Corbin
1969 Jim Jacoby, Minda Brachman
1970 John Gerber Carol Klar
1971 Betsey Wolff, Barry Hagedorn
1972 Richard Capps, Fred Woodruff
1973 Minda Brachman, Jim Jacoby
1974 Henry Baer, Clement Jackson
1975 Tom Hughes, Jerry Murray
1976 John Sullivan, David Horner
1977 Joe Choate, Elaine Piwetz
1978 Steve Honet, Chris Compton
1979 Charlyne McMullin, Safwat Mishriky
1980 Joe Vanham, Jerry Mark
1981 Joan Jackson, Nancy Passell
Flight A:
1979 Robert Wolff, Morris Chang
1981 Barbara Norwood, Bob Norwood

MEN'S PAIRS
1967 Paul Levitt, Sidney Lazard
1968 Mack Carroll, Alex Harrison
1969 Sam Coolik, George Treadwell
1970 Dr. Charles Robinson, Dr. Henry Gardiner *(tied with)*
      Ace Gutowsky, John Jelsma
1971 Greg Gault, George Good
1972 Robert Hamman, Dr. Charles Robinson
1973 Bill Acker, Barry Hagedorn
1974 John Puscas, Bill Fannin
1975 G. Robert Nail, John Gerber
1976 Scotty Reis, Russ Mitchell
1977 Russ Mitchell, Jim Boyce
1978 Rick Price, Hemant Lall *(tied with)*
      Marty Arndt, John Zilic
1979 Ira Hessel, Dennis Sorensen
1980 Curtis Smith, Don Baxter
1981 Jim Jacoby, Derrell Childs

WOMEN'S PAIRS
1967 Mrs. William Dale, Penny MacLean
1968 Anita Davis, Mrs. Waller Rodes
1969 Lib French, Mrs. Jack Hopper
1970 Carol Sanders, Betty Ann Kennedy

1971 Fran Beard, Betsey Wolff
1972 Anita Davis, Peggy Drury
1973 Polly Pandres, Vicki Davis
1974 Esta Van Zandt, Heitie Noland
1975 Phyllis Early, Joan Dewitt
1976 Montie Shelton, Fran Beard
1977 Janet Parker, Mary Young
1978 Jerry Booth, Inez Beckley
1979 Jimmy Harper, Mary Gordon
1980 Glee Son, Betty Daniel
1981 Jerre Gardiner, Emma Jean Hawkes

MIXED PAIRS
1967 Charles Weed, Marian Weed
1969 Jim Jacoby, Sidney Perutz
1970 Steve Lawrence, Dottie Goodloe
1972 Louise Oliver, Roy Walker
1973 George Pisk, Pat Hood
1974 Louise Childs, Derrell Childs
1975 Barbara Norwood, Earl Jennings
1976 Charles Adler, Elinor Susman
1977 Marty Arndt, Patsy New
1980 Sally Wheeler, Buddy Hanby

INDIVIDUAL
1976 Alline Huff
1977 Jessie Heim

UNMIXED PAIRS
1978 Chris Cunningham, Paul Kelley

MASTER SWISS TEAMS
1981 Charlie Weed, Joe Musumeci,
      Dennis Sorensen, Ross Rainwater

DISTRICT 17 (Arizona, New Mexico, Colorado, southern and eastern Wyoming, southern and eastern Nevada, one county of Utah)

DESERT EMPIRE

KNOCKOUT TEAMS
1967 David Conlin, Ralph Cash, Howard Segal,
      Norman Schwartz, Leonard Marks, Pat Marks
1969 Paul Soloway, Hermine Baron, Gaylor Kasle,
      Leslie West, Barney O'Malia
1970 Norman Anderson, John Mohan, Paul Soloway,
      Hermine Baron, Richard Henderson, Thompson Lux
1971 Mary Chilcote, Allan Evans,
      Dave Priest, Larry Weiss
1972 Sylvia Sadowsky, Gaylor Kasle, Garey Hayden,
      Don Oakie, Mrs. Emory Stanley, Bill Truman
1973 Jack Schwenke, Gaylor Kasle,
      Garey Hayden, Jim Jacoby
1974 Max Hardy, Pat Marks, Margaret Gaer,
      Jerry Gaer, Bill Truman, Mike Kaplan
1975 Paul Maier, Rhoda Walsh,
      Paul Soloway, Bobby Goldman
1976 Jan Janitschke, Craig Janitschke, Romy Gerould,
      Jim Miller, Alan Bell, Allen Kane
1977 Max Hardy, Michael Schreiber,
      Alan Bell, Jan Janitschke
1978 Paul Soloway, Ross Dorfman,
      T. Robert Hughes, John Van Ness
1979 Mark Lair, Eddie Wold, Gaylor Kasle,
      Roger Bates, Clarence Goppert
1980 Peter Weichsel, Fred Hamilton, Marc Jacobus,
      Elizabeth Brenhouse, Mel Skolnik
1981 Barney O'Malia, John Jeffrey, Jerry Gaer,
      Gaylor Kasle, Garey Hayden

OPEN TEAMS
1956 Charles Bull, Mrs. Charles Bull,
      Gerald Patterson, Lucille Patterson
1957 Malvine Klausner, Meyer Schleifer,
      Dan Westerfield, Bruce Isaacs
1958 Malvine Klausner, Meyer Schleifer,
      Dan Westerfield, Bruce Isaacs
1959 Frank Flanagan, Ralph Cash, Gar Farley,
      David Conlin, Leonard Goren
1960 Mary Jane Farell, Jules Farell,
      Alex Tschekaloff, Harold Simon
1961 Richard Walsh, Harold Guiver,
      Don Oakie, Edward Burns
1962 Roy Hislop, Clarence (Cap) Crossley, Sr.,
      Ralph Cash, Dr. Clarence (Cap) Crossley, Jr.
1963 Ralph Cash, Clarence (Cap) Crossley, Sr.
      Anne Burnstein, Dr. Clarence (Cap) Crossley, Jr.
1964 Gerry Bare, Gerald Hallee,
      Richard Henderson, Paul Soloway
1965 Robert Tripp, Charles Payne,
      Dr. John Griffin, Nancy McCrackin

1966	Mary Jane Farell, Lois Newman, Dan Westerfield,
	Ralph Cash, Barry Crane
1968	Matt Bartosik, Henry Kutzman,
	Jean Carney, Albert Weiss
1971	Harold Guiver, Gerald Bare,
	Mike McMahon, Erik Paulsen
1972	John Swanson, Paul Soloway, Charles Phillips,
	Allan Evans, David Priest *(tied with)*
	Cynthia Dunn, Kitty Downs,
	Sharon Kasle, Irving Sadowsky *(and)*
	Hermine Baron, Mike Shuman,
	Richard Henderson, John Mohan *(and)*
	Barry Crane, Dr. John Fisher,
	Bill Schreiber, Michael Schreiber
1973	J. David King, Ron LaCour, Nels Erickson,
	Joan Howard, Elsie Pace
1974	Malcolm Brachman, Paul Soloway,
	Larry Mandel, Ira Cohen
1975	John Casalena, Judy Casalena,
	Hank Wicks, Howard Segel
1976	John Mohan, Mike Lawrence, Roger Bates,
	Mike Passell, Garey Hayden
1977	Pat Resnick, Victor Resnick,
	Florence Greene, Charles Greene
1978	Faye Apt, Mark Bregman,
	Charles High, Marty Aronou
1979	Mark Lair, Eddie Wold, Gaylor Kasle,
	Roger Bates, Clarence Goppert
1980	Tim Mann, Joe Brooks,
	Ted Kissell, George Morton *(tied with)*
	Jim Barrow, Mike Shuman,
	Hermine Baron, Roger Jourdan *(and)*
	Mark Lair, Broma Lou Harrison,
	Pat Dalziel, Pat Norman
1981	Mark Itabashi, Kerri Shuman,
	Jim Robinson, Marc Jacobus

Flight A:

1979	Mark Lair, Eddie Wold, Gaylor Kasle,
	Roger Bates, Clarence Goppert *(tied with)*
	Paul Lewis, Bunny Haas, Jim Robison,
	Ron Andersen, Ross Rainwater
1980	Peter Weichsel, Fred Hamilton, Marc Jacobus,
	Elizabeth Brenhouse, Mel Skolnik
1981	Barry Crane, Mike Shuman,
	Kerri Shuman, Craig Janitschke

MASTER SWISS TEAMS

Flight A:

1977	Jerry Gaer, Margaret Gaer,
	James Hughes, Bruce Ruskin *(tied with)*
	Edith Kemp, Kelsey Petterson,
	Dr. Clarence (Cap) Crossley, Jr., Janet Crossley *(tied with)*
	George Pisk, Pat Hood, Jan Janitschke,
	Ron Feldman, Larry Johnson, Stormy Horn
1978	Barney O'Malia, Gaylor Kasle,
	Proctor Hawkins, Dr. Clarence (Cap) Crossley, Jr.

UNMIXED PAIRS

1980	Barry Crane, Ron Andersen
1981	Mary Senti, Patty Norman

MIXED PAIRS

1956	Dr. William Guenther, Minna Hertel
1957	Malvine Klausner, Meyer Schleifer
1958	Malvine Klausner, Meyer Schleifer
1959	Lois Smith, Dr. Curtis Swartz
1960	Malvine Klausner, Meyer Schleifer
1961	Rose Groves, Bob Seelman
1962	Charlcie Garrett, Donald Holt
1963	Marion Barrett, Edmond Herbert
1964	Carol Dibblee, Orris Mowry
1965	Lois Peterson, Lester Dewey
1967	C. J. Brong, Mitsuko Rustad *(tied with)*
	Rhoda Walsh, Richard Walsh
1970	Hermine Baron, John Mohan
1971	Jim Stein, Hermine Baron

MEN'S PAIRS

1956	Ralph Cash, Don Oakie
1957	E. H. Scurlock, Arthur Schribner
1958	Ralph Cash, Meyer Schleifer
1959	Mike Shuman, Homer Shoop
1960	Joffre Kiamy, Bruce Isaacs
1961	Frank Flanagan, Dwight Neal
1962	Morris Portugal, Richard Walsh
1963	Morris Ribyat, Ted Christianson
1964	Bert Naness, John McEntree
1965	Lester Dewey, Bill Anderson
1966	Leonard Marks, Tony Adler
1967	Paul Soloway, Richard Walsh
1968	Steve Lawrence, Robert Spotts
1969	Ted Mayr, Morris Portugal
1970	Harold Friedman, Paul Robbins

1971	Bud Reinhold, Eddie Kantar
1972	Pete Benjamin, Everett Fukushima
1973	Moe Rubenfeld, J. David King
1974	John Grantham, Jim Jacoby
1975	Mike Schreiber, Paul Maier
1976	Jan Janitschke, Craig Janitschke
1977	Ron Andersen, Hugh MacLean

WOMEN'S PAIRS

1956	Marjorie Foote, Katherine Hobbs
1957	Carolyn Baldwin, Corale Briggs
1958	Margaret Anderson, Myrle McComber
1959	Mary Jane Farell, Pauline Heidelberger
1960	Beverly Attwood, Lois Hesler
1961	Dorothea Blakemore, Clarissa Howard
1962	Marian Brown, Florence Greene
1963	Lidi Skinner, Marian Clark
1964	Peggy Drury, Hermine Baron
1965	Catherine Morriss, Faye Blackwell
1966	Mrs. J. C. Butler, Adele Sidles
1967	Heitie Noland, Esta Van Zandt
1968	Sheila Fahrendorf, Louise Harmonson
1969	Nancy McCrackin, Patricia Waggoner
1970	Judy Stuart, Mrs. L. Anderson
1971	Mrs. Harold Knowles, Hermine Baron
1972	Jean Carney, Mary Chilcote
1973	Diane Jonas, Kerri Shuman *(tied with)*
	Robin Grantham, Sharon Kasle
1974	Barbara Downey, Fran Reiner *(tied with)*
	Kerri Shuman, Carol Greenhut
1975	Zita Bruflat, Edie Huson
1976	Gwenn Gravitt, Marian Schlessman
1977	Tobi Deutsch, Margaret Gaer

MASTER PAIRS

1956	Lionel Wolfers, Grace Thieman
1957	Mrs. William Godfrey, Bob Groetziner
1958	Tom Foster, Conrad Potvin
1959	Ivan Erdos, H. Herbert Law
1960	Malvine Klausner, Meyer Schleifer
1961	Ed Burns, Harold Guiver
1962	Faye Apt, Gary Wilson
1963	Susan Azar, Mrs. D. B. Fisher
1964	Peggy Drury, Doug Drury
1965	Robert Wolff, Marie Grissom
1966	Mrs. Robert Kohler, Ivan Erdos
1967	Richard Walsh, Rhoda Walsh
1968	Jerry Leenerts, Gretchen Leenerts
1969	Doris Heywood, Brooks Ziegler
1970	Florence Herzberg, Arthur Herzberg
1971	Terre Primmer, Steven Turner
1972	John Mohan, John Grantham
1973	Mark Blumenthal, Norman Anderson *(tied with)*
	Helen Portugal, Ed Herbert
1974	Theresa Thompson, Herbert Arnstein
1975	John Fox, Joe Kivel
1976	Dick Reed, Stormy Horn
1977	Joe Payne, Vic Chernoff
1978	Chuck Henke, Laurie Hyder
1979	Barry Crane, Kerri Shuman
1980	Jan Janitschke, Craig Janitschke
1981	Steve Goldberg, Rick Price

OPEN PAIRS

1956	Conrad Potvin, Dr. Arthur Olsen
1957	Mabel Hopps, Jack Ehrlenbach
1958	Stella Rebner, Barry Crane
1959	Oswald Jacoby, Clifford Russell
1960	Eric Paulsen, Alex Tschekaloff
1961	Mrs. Frank Roach, Mrs. Greeley Warner
1962	Oswald Jacoby, Mike Shuman
1963	Richard Walsh, Harold Handler
1964	Barry Crane, Peter Rank
1965	Barry Crane, Peter Rank
1966	Barry Crane, Peter Rank
1967	Heitie Noland, Esta Van Zandt
1968	Norman Schwartz, Leonard Marks
1969	Harry Steen, Germano Civetta
1970	Bill Schreiber, Michael Schreiber
1971	Bill Schreiber, Steve Smolen
1972	Paul Soloway, Malcolm Brachman
1973	Proctor Hawkins, Kelsey Petterson
1974	John Jeffrey, Proctor Hawkins *(tied with)*
	Florance Aspell, Gideon May
1975	Ron LaCour, Everett Fukushima
1976	Dick Reed, Daniel Mordecai
1977	Paul Soloway, Malcolm Brachman
1978	John Norman, Barbara Norman
1979	Gene Simpson, Jim Kirkham
1980	Barry Crane, Ron Andersen
1981	Joe Harris, William Kass

Flight A:

1978	Dr. John Fisher, Del Parker

1979 Albert Bricklin, Ed Lucas
1980 James Kostal, Nancy Passell
1981 Barry Crane, Craig Janitschke

DISTRICT 17

KNOCKOUT TEAMS
1972 Hermine Baron, Mike Shuman,
      Ken Gorfkle, Mike Passell
1976 Brian May, Bob Connop,
      Paul Hagen, Charles Finch
1978 John Mohan, Kay Schulle-Mohan, Diane LaFleur,
      Roger Bates, Mike Passell

MASTER SWISS TEAMS
1978 Jim Robison, David Sacks,
      David Priest, Gene Freed

OPEN TEAMS
1972 Barry Crane, Dr. John Fisher,
      Jim Jacoby, Charles Weed
1973 Paul Soloway, Bill Schreiber,
      Michael Schreiber, Hermine Baron
1974 Don Guerin, Mark Ralph,
      Robert Lipton, Larry Kassis
1976 Trudi Nugit, Pam Wittes,
      Jon Wittes, Vance Moran
1978 Jeff Neal, Charles Berman,
      Harry Basler, Dorothe Koren

MASTER PAIRS
1972 Hermine Baron, Mike Shuman
1973 Sam Williams, Jay McKee
1974 Jim Jacoby, Cy Dennen
1978 Mary Jane Farell, Lil Greenberg
Flight A:
1976 Michael Riesner, Fredric Adler

OPEN PAIRS
1972 Jim Jacoby, Charles Weed
1973 Ken Gorfkle, Barbara Whitesel
1974 Howard Perlman, Jeffrey Starr
1976 Milo Wesley, Rand Pinsky
1978 Jim Robison, Fred Hamilton
Flight A:
1978 Terre Primmer, Maureen O'Rourke

MEN'S PAIRS
1972 Roger Bates, Gaylor Kasle
1973 David Tuell, George Steiner
1974 Ron LaCour, Kelsey Petterson
1976 Si Frome, George Ateljevitch

WOMEN'S PAIRS
1972 Marilyn Edwards Webster, Lucille Virginia Gunter
1973 Pamela Eckard, Lee Kasle
1974 Kerri Shuman, Rhoda Walsh
1976 Linda Borbely, Irene Fredrick

NAVAJO TRAIL

KNOCKOUT TEAMS
1967 Grace Lowden, Jack Ehrlenbach, Gaylor Kasle,
      Leonard Marks, Pat Marks
1968 Matt Bartosik, Richard Grime,
      J. Dan Duke, Allen McAlear
1969 Nate Greenberg, Lee Bushnell,
      Peggy Drury, Robert Luebkeman
1970 Anne Burnstein, Paul Kaye, Jack Perry,
      Milton Agay, Milton Vernoff, Gilbert Kaye
1971 John Mohan, John Padget, J. David King,
      Hermine Baron, Richard Henderson
1973 Kelsey Peterson, Proctor Hawkins, Frank Smith,
      John Erickson, Ron LaCour
1977 Clem Jackson, Laurie Hyder, William Kass,
      Joe Harris, Linda Borbely, Mark Itabashi
1979 Max Hardy, T. Robert Hughes,
      Leslie Tsou, Ron Feldman
1980 Jan Janitschke, Jack Allen, Craig Janitschke,
      Marilyn Eber, Ron Feldman
1981 Mel Skolnik, Elisabeth Brenhouse, Paul Soloway,
      Marc Jacobus, Ron Andersen

MASTER SWISS TEAMS
1979 Del Parker, Dr. John Fisher,
      Craig Janitschke, Jan Janitschke

OPEN TEAMS
1966 Veda Rowley, Howard Coray,
      Jack McEntree, Hazel Smith
1967 Lyn Achning, Bobby Wolff, Gunther Polak,
      Jim Jacoby, Barry Crane
1968 Terry Cochran, Maxine Giffen,
      Pauline McClanahan, Steve Benzon

1969 Jay Woods, Mary Lou Woods,
      Bruce Martin, Earl Rudes
1971 Effie Woods, May Belle Long,
      Fran Downing, Ruth Osthues *(tied with)*
      James Kahan, Daniel Mordecai, Lila Kahan,
      Stormy Horn, Dick Reed *(and)*
      Forrest Clark, Korene Geffen,
      Marian Stone, William Ragland *(and)*
      Pat Brennan, Kay Brennan,
      Lester Dewey, Mark Lair
1973 Jim Jacoby, James McIlroy, Virginia McIlroy,
      Larry Weiss, Mary Chilcote
1975 Barbara Hamman, Bobby Wolff,
      Charles Weed, Marion Weed
1977 Clem Jackson, Hal St. John,
      Bruce Martin, Dick Reed *(tied with)*
      John Tippet, Irene Hyatt, J. G. Van Stee,
      Jo Anne DeBenedittis, Kenneth Brooks, Alan Wood
1979 Jim Bradley, John Neff, Nandkumar Bakshani,
      Tom Richard, Leslie Tsou, Alan Bell
1980 Alan Bell, Roger Jourdan,
      Jim Barrow, Joel Hoersch
1981 Mark Lair, Eddie Wold, Frank Fisher,
      George Landreth, David Siebert *(tied with)*
      Martha Beecher, David Ashley, Craig Janitschke,
      Jan Janitschke, Garey Hayden
Flight A:
1980 Oswald Jacoby, Jim Jacoby, Jim Chew,
      Roger Jourdan, Jim Barrow, Heitie Noland *(tied with)*
      Laura Wyman, Bob Gilroy, Dr. Clarence (Cap) Crossley, Jr,
      Proctor Hawkins, Leslie Tsou, Alice Kinningham
1981 Chris Compton, Morris Chang,
      Bobby Wolff, Gary King *(tied with)*
      Mel Skolnik, Elisabeth Brenhouse, Ron Andersen,
      Paul Soloway, Mark Jacobus *(and)*
      Mark Lair, Eddie Wold, David Siebert,
      George Landreth, John Onstott

MASTER PAIRS
1966 Dr. G. R. Lee, Veda Rowley
1967 Mrs. R. L. Wood, Mrs. H. H. Conger
1968 Max Blustein, Maurice Blustein
1969 J. David King, Mary McCrory
1970 Elaine King, Beverly King
1971 Eugene Sussex, Reina Sussex
1973 Barry Crane, Kerri Shuman
1975 Charles Weed, Dr. John Fisher
1977 Dick Reed, Bruce Martin
1979 John Fisher, Leslie Tsou
1980 Proctor Hawkins, Dr. Clarence (Cap) Crossley, Jr.
1981 Leslie Tsou, Paul Lewis

OPEN PAIRS
1966 Barry Crane, Marilyn Anticouni
1967 Hal St. John, Tom Callaham
1968 Kumico Huston, John Cramer
1969 Broma Lou Harrison, Dick Reed
1970 Robert Matthess, Rhoda Walsh *(tied with)*
      Barry Crane, Dr. John Fisher
1971 Barry Crane, Michael Jones
1973 Becky Schmieder, John Grantham
1975 Michael Jones, Norman Anderson
1977 Al Gardner, Weldon Wells
1979 Terry Riely, Robert Preston
1980 Larry Bertholf, Rich Schmidt
1981 Ruth Greenberg, Nate Greenberg
Flight A:
1979 Mike Shuman, Vance Moran
1980 James Kauder, Sue Coonfield
1981 Phil Guptill, Bob Levey

MEN'S PAIRS
1966 Allen McAlear, Fredrick Walker
1967 Barry Crane, Gunther Polak
1968 Roger Plowman, Russ Summerhayes
1969 Robert Tripp, John Griffin
1970 Dan Mordecai, Dan Salkoff
1971 John Mohan, Richard Henderson
1973 William Vail, Robert Esch
1975 Michael Jones, Norman Anderson
1977 Mike Passell, Ron Feldman

WOMEN'S PAIRS
1966 Hazel Sykes, Mrs. E. M. Gabriel
1967 Mary Frampton, Mrs. John Vickers
1968 Althea Cook, Mrs. Juel Wertz
1969 Selma Berryhill, Margaret Jones
1970 Hermine Baron, Ann Arndt
1971 Mrs. John Marks, Mildred Hobson
1973 Becky Schmieder, Hermine Baron
1975 Ginger Hayes, Valerie Gibbs *(tied with)*
      Peggy Fleming, Peggy Neubeek
1977 Beverly Rosenberg, Ann Kluewer

MASTER MEN'S PAIRS
1971 Dick Reed, Stormy Horn
MASTER WOMEN'S PAIRS
1971 Judy Brownlee, Laurie Hyder
MIXED PAIRS
1970 Beverly King, Roxy Violin
1977 George Pisk, Linda Spangler
UNMIXED PAIRS
1979 Don Maher, J. D. Wiltey
1980 Laurie Hyder, Suzanne Jones *(tied with)*
        Forest Clark, Laurence Goodfellow
1981 William Kass, Jon Munford
INDIVIDUAL
1969 Zelda Colby
1977 Jean Moran
MEN'S SWISS TEAMS
1977 Sylvester Birginal, Charles High,
        Nate Greenberg, John Kiernan
WOMEN'S SWISS TEAMS
1977 Renee Friedman, Phyllis Robbins,
        Claire Whitman, Joan Madrid

ROCKY MOUNTAIN

KNOCKOUT TEAMS
1967 Kelsey Petterson, Helen Moore, Leslie West,
        Jackie Spadero, Morris Portugal, Meyer Schleifer
1968 James Kahan, Lila Kahan,
        Dan Mordecai, Mary Senti
1969 Mary Jane Farell, Kate Blanchard, Joe Miller
        Maury Genud, Tommy Prothro, Harold Guiver
1970 Hermine Baron, Paul Soloway
        Richard Henderson, John Anderson
1971 Hermine Baron, Norman Anderson
        John Mohan, David Ashley
1972 Henry Bethe, Jules Farell, Jack Bitman,
        Mary Jane Farell, Dick Reed, Dan Mordecai
1973 Richard Kaye, Garey Hayden, Amos Kaminski,
        Capt. Jim LaForce, Nate Greenberg
1974 Bud Reinhold, Kerri Shuman, Larry Cohen,
        Dr. Richard Katz, Eddie Kantar
1975 Dick Reed, Broma Lou Harrison,
        Stormy Horn, Bruce Hutcheson
1976 Shirley Boice, Gaylor Kasle, Garey Hayden,
        Meyer Schleifer, Roger Bates
1977 Bud Reinhold, Meyer Schleifer,
        Robert Levin, Garey Hayden
1978 Proctor Hawkins, John Van Ness, Kenn Bradley,
        Dr. Clarence (Cap) Crossley, Jr., Steve Skinner, Ron Smith
1979 Eddie Wold, Karl Keller,
        Neil Chambers, T. Robert Hughes
1980 Barry Crane, Mike Shuman, Kerri Shuman,
        Paul Lewis, Michael Schreiber, Ron Andersen
1981 Jim Jacoby, Charles Weed, Vivian Kilstrup,
        Jan Janitschke, Marilyn Eber
OPEN TEAMS
1948 Eugene Herz, Dr. Arthur Wolf,
        Elizabeth Zent, Lila Kahan *(tied with)*
        Godfrey Stone, Mrs. Godfrey Stone,
        Mrs. F. J. Terhune, Pauline Turner
1949 Merle Parker, Thelma Bailey,
        J. G. Ripsta, James Hopkins
1950 Godfrey Stone, Mrs. Godfrey Stone,
        W. W. Sanders, Mrs. W. W. Sanders
1951 Grace Thieman, Jack Bitman,
        Jerry Gelman, Mary Jo Thieman
1952 H. Leroy Thurtell, James Kahan,
        Shirley Fairchild, John Simon
1953 G. Robert Nail, J. G. Ripstra, Myles Thomas,
        Gerald Michaud, J. Hopkins
1954 Mary Jane Kauder, Douglas Steen,
        Ivan Erdos, William Hanna
1955 Kelsey Petterson, Mrs. Elling Thygeson,
        Betty Coombs, Anne Jones
1956 Martha Newbill, Ruth Steinberg, John Simon
        Adaline Simon, Leo Weiner
1957 Lila Kahan, James Kahan,
        H. Leroy Thurtell, Jack Bitman
1958 Lila Kahan, James Kahan,
        Roy Thurtell, June McClure
1959 Roy Thurtell, James Kahan,
        Lila Kahan, Jack Bitman
1960 Alex Mayer, Ben Aisenberg,
        Ken Doanne, Robert Baptist *(tied with)*
        Clair Morgan, Lucille Godfrey,
        Mrs. A. R. Falb, Mrs. Monte Alderson
1961 Pat Brennan, Jr., Daniel Mordecai,
        Ivor Stakgold, Peter Pender

1962 Lila Kahan, Jack Bitman, James Kahan,
        H. Leroy Thurtell, June McClure
1963 Don Oakie, Alma Coleman,
        Malvine Klausner, Meyer Schleifer
1964 Lila Kahan, James Kahan, H. Leroy Thurtell,
        Jack Bitman, June McClure
1965 Dr. John Cline, Mrs. John Cline,
        Mrs. Phil Clarke, Kay Yingling
1966 Hermine Baron, Peter Pender,
        Honor Flint, Jeremy Flint *(tied with)*
        Bob Bratcher, Mary Cocherell,
        Peggy Yates, Jane Kelly
1967 Rhoda Walsh, Richard Walsh,
        Mary Jane Farell, Jules Farell
1968 Robert Rowley, Gard Hays,
        Lee Voigt, Carol Dibblee
1969 Jean Carney, Florance Aspell, Dan Mordecai,
        Tom Callaham, William Baldwin, Ed Theus
1970 Seth Crain, John Padget, John Herriot, Darwin Afdahl
1971 Gaylor Kasle, Mrs. Foy Proctor,
        Robert Cobb, Nancy Cobb (Swiss)
1971 Joe Miller, Mary Senti, Mike Kaplan, Jack Blair
1972 Dan Mordecai, Evie Mordecai, Jack Bitman,
        June McClure, Henry Bethe, Eddie Bronson *(tied with)*
        Dick Arlen, Jean Bleakley,
        John Cramer, Margaret Scott *(and)*
        Virginia McIlroy, James McIlroy, Jim Jacoby,
        Mary Chilcote, Larry Weiss *(and)*
        Mrs. Steve Sweeney, Kay Leiker,
        George Mason, Gertrude Mason
1973 George Vince, Elaine Walker,
        Neal Walker, Bill Puryear
1974 Mary Jo Thieman, Nancy Dwight,
        Darce Myers, Dot Mohler
1975 Dick Lesko, Carol Lesko,
        June McClure, Jack Bitman
1976 Joe Harris, Jerry Shinkle, Harley Walker,
        Hal St. John, Laurie Hyder, Bill Kass
1977 Jan Janitschke, Craig Janitschke, Robert Hamman,
        Richard Kaye, Alan Bell *(tied with)*
        James Chalfant, Marge Smith,
        Steve Marx, Mary Marx *(and)*
        Michael Howland, Dr. Bruce Wick,
        Mary Jane Orock, Lorene Mitchell
1978 Annice Somers, Bruce Ferguson, Gaylor Kasle,
        Brenda Keller, Garey Hayden
1979 Milton Stern, Mike Lawrence,
        Marc Jacobus, Ron Smith
1980 Brenda Blumenthal, Roger Bates, Algie Neill,
        Craig Janitschke, Jan Janitschke,
1981 Mel Skolnik, Mark Lair,
        Barry Crane, Eddie Wold *(tied with)*
        Dick Kaye, Seymon Deutsch, Gaylor Kasle,
        Bob Hammon, Bobby Wolff *(tied with)*
        Herb Kassner, Blair Fedder,
        Jim Jacoby, Garey Hayden
Flight A:
1977 Dr. Charles Robinson, Robert Hamman, Morris Chang,
        Jim Jacoby, George Pisk
1980 Dan Mordecai, Jack Bitman, Richard Lesko,
        Roy Fox, Paul Swanson
1981 Mel Skolnik, Eddie Wold,
        Barry Crane, Mark Lair *(tied with)*
        Stormy Horn, Broma Lou Reed,
        Dick Reed, Romy Gerould

MASTER PAIRS
1950 William Crooks, G. Robert Nail
1951 Stella Rebner, John Moran
1952 Ferman Cheatwood, Adaline Simon
1953 Shirley Fairchild, John Winston
1954 Mary Jane Kauder, Bobbi Thompson
1955 Ralph Cash, Roy Hislop
1956 Harold Reid, Kay McKenna
1957 Mary Jo Thieman, Robert Groetzinger
1958 Frances Budlong, Jack Ehrlenbach
1959 Richard Reed, Ross Robbins
1960 Alice Sweet, Richard Allen
1961 Keith Stenger, Edward Monroe
1962 Ivan Erdos, Max Turk
1963 Jules Farell, Mary Jane Farell
1964 Gerard Halle, Paul Soloway
1965 Marge Carwin, Betty Jeffrey-Smith *(tied with)*
        Helen Moore, Morris Portugal
1966 Daniel Mordecai, James Kahan
1967 Leslie West, Richard Henderson
1968 Jules Farell, Mary Jane Farell
1969 Robert Baptist, Joe Miller
1970 Barry Crane, Dr. John Fisher
1971 Mark Lair, Lester Dewey
1972 Jan Janitschke, Craig Janitschke

1973	Craig Janitschke, Mike Kaplan
1974	Kerri Shuman, John Grantham
1975	Jim Jacoby, Heitie Noland
1976	Barry Crane, Dr. John Fisher
1977	James Chalfant, Marge Smith
1978	Gerald Bare, Richard Ryder
1979	Bobby Wolff, Morris Chang
1980	Dr. John Fisher, Charlie Gabriel
1981	Merrell Anderson, Jack Larkin

OPEN PAIRS

1948	R. P. Bean, Mrs. R. P. Bean
1949	Thelma Bailey, J. G. Ripsta
1950	Harriet Rethers, Elbert Miller
1951	Stella Rebner, John Moran
1952	Isadore Epstein, Charles Hart
1953	Betty Berkitz, William Hanna
1954	Irving Levine, Owen Rye
1955	Ernest Rovere, Jack Bitman
1956	Mary Jane Kauder, Jules Farell
1957	Charles Woldenberg, Esther Woldenberg
1958	William McWilliams, Jane Wright
1959	Mike Shuman, Alan Bell
1960	Malvine Klausner, Meyer Schleifer
1961	Broma Lou Harrison, Kay LaVelle
1962	Mabel Mahoney, David Carter
1963	Oswald Jacoby, Payne Harrison
1964	Richard Walsh, Gerald Bare
1965	Fred Rappleyea, John Zilic
1966	Jim Linhart, Robert Baptist
1967	Richard Walsh, Rhoda Walsh
1968	Helen Moore, Morris Portugal
1969	Dale Forster, Jeff Taylor
1970	Barry Crane, Dr. John Fisher
1971	Mary Ruth McCrory, Gaylor Kasle *(tied with)* Clyde Graham, David Jordan
1972	Marian Stone, Emma Lankton
1973	Barry Crane, Dr. John Fisher
1974	Jack Bitman, Dan Mordecai
1975	Bobby Goldman, Jim Hooker
1976	Jack Bitman, Dan Mordecai
1978	Mary Jane Farell, Betty Levan
1980	Jim Barrow, Roger Jourdan
1981	Barry Crane, Craig Janitschke

Flight A:

1977	Robert Hamman, Dr. Charles Robinson
1978	Stormy Horn, Dick Reed
1979	Dan Mordecai, Roger Bates *(tied with)* Stormy Horn, Larry Johnson
1980	Paul Swanson, Roy Fox
1981	Bonnie Smith, Hachy Pennell

MEN'S PAIRS

1948	H. Leroy Thurtell, Leonard Wolfe
1949	George Ford, L. Goldstein
1950	M. Coff, Leonard Horwitz
1951	Howard Coray, Don Buie
1952	Myles Thomas, Morton Nelson
1953	William Hanna, Douglas Steen
1954	William Hanna, Douglas Steen
1955	Lew Mathe, Milton Vernoff
1956	Milton Bierbaum, Paul H. Katt
1957	Eugene Herz, Dan Mordecai
1958	Robert Galena, George Ford, Jr. *(tied with)* Walter Thieman, John Haley
1959	Robert Sharp, Sidney Kasle
1960	R. D. Hutchinson, Jack Ehrlenbach
1961	Ed Bookins, Marshall Derby
1962	Chuck Henke, John Moran
1963	Robert Baptist, Dr. Clarence (Cap) Crossley, Jr.
1964	Pat Brennan, Dan Mordecai
1965	Capt. Ron Kibler, John Yates
1966	Neil Haflich, Michael Copeland
1967	Richard Stern, John Cramer
1968	Maury Genud, Leslie West
1969	George Graham, Maury Genud
1970	Stormy Horn, Dick Reed
1971	Paul Soloway, David Ashley
1972	Jay McKee, Del Parker
1973	Mark Lair, Richard Henderson
1974	Richard Kaye, Mike Shuman
1975	Ronald Moore, John Hendrikson
1976	Kal Grunwald, Mel Levine
1977	Jan Janitschke, Craig Janitschke
1978	Jan Janitschke, Craig Janitschke
1979	Jan Janitschke, Craig Janitschke
1980	Mike McKee, Quentin Wilmot
1981	Bill Ragland, J. Booth Myers

WOMEN'S PAIRS

1948	D. C. DeWitt, Elizabeth Zent
1949	Eleanor Reichmuth, J. L. McClellan
1950	Mrs. T. R. Burnett, Corinne Berry

1951	Mrs. Clarence Neff, Kay McKenna
1952	Dorothy Lee, Mrs. Clarence Neff
1953	Eleanor Neal, Dorothy Lee
1954	Malvine Klausner, Carolyn Whitehead
1955	A. F. Moline, Claire Morgan
1956	Julie Allen, Virginia Roberts
1957	Lucille Godfrey, Claire Morgan
1958	Verna Leonard, Natalie Dukes
1959	Miriam Mottelson, Effie Woods
1960	Mrs. Dudley Walker, Mrs. William Swart
1961	Connie English, Susan Bishop
1962	W. J. Byrd, L. J. Ward
1963	Kay McKenna, Mrs. Clarence Neff
1964	Alene Durbin, G. P. Ruppert
1965	Frieda Leventhal, Florence Reed
1966	Edwina Still, June Holbrook
1967	Mrs. R. H. Pyle, Catherine Pratt
1968	Jane Anderson, Mary Mier
1969	Mary Senti, Broma Lou Harrison
1970	Lucille Godfrey, Sally Hollingsworth
1971	Barbara Glenn, Audie Fearheiley
1972	Leeli Occhipiniti, Mrs. Dan Rees
1973	Norma Austermann, Sarah Cohen
1974	Jeanne Kelly, Joyce Sloop
1975	Mrs. Earl Fauver, Jr., Mrs. George McLean
1976	Marie Berckefeldt, Barbara Glenn
1977	Cynthia Smith, Mary Skaats
1978	Lil Smith, Irene Hyatt
1979	Tina Luterman, Linda Jenkins
1980	Flo Newlin, Hachy Pennell
1981	Marcia Ashcraft, M. Bierma

MIXED PAIRS

1950	Mrs. S. Emerson, Joseph Miller
1951	Mrs. R. S. Parker, Harold Love
1952	S. Hanna, William Hanna
1953	Stella Rebner, Clarence Strouse
1954	Mrs. J. Barth, Julian Barth
1955	Morgan Howard, Mrs. Morgan Howard
1956	Malvine Klausner, John Moran
1957	Malvine Klausner, Meyer Schleifer
1958	Mrs. Clarence Neff, James Kahan
1959	Shirlee Harris, Edward Rosen
1960	Mary Jane Farell, Barry Crane
1961	Shirlee Harris, Edward Rosen
1962	Lidi Skinner, Richard Allen
1963	Mrs. J. B. Wilson, H. W. Christ
1964	Monte Alderson, Harold Holtzclaw
1965	Hermine Baron, Peter Rank
1966	Mrs. E. B. Still, William Mullen
1967	Dick Kaye, Virginia Baptist
1968	Stormy Horn, Peggy Horn
1969	Joe Farley, Bunny Schmidt
1970	Hermine Baron, Dan Mordecai
1971	Jim Trussell, Roger Neumann
1976	Carol Krehbiel, Mike Shuman
1977	K. L. Kotten, John Mohan
1979	Linda Rinker, Elliott Gray *(tied with)* Jane Ryan, Lee Ryan

INDIVIDUAL

1948	Eleanor Reichmuth
1969	Joan Irish
1976	Judith Pendery
1977	Mrs. V. F. Mendicino
1979	Leta Mae Watts

MASTER SWISS TEAMS

1978	Paul James, Ruth Hansen, Bobbie Scott, Bill Scott *(tied with)* Ron Smith, Marv Thomsic, Dr. Clarence (Cap) Crossley, Jr. John Van Ness, Steve Skinner, Proctor Hawkins, *(and)* William Ragland, Kathleen Ragland, Pat Henke, Chuck Henke
1979	Robert Baptist, Mary Ramey Baptist, Gerald Oehm, Geir Hauge

DISTRICT 18 (Northwestern Wyoming, Alberta, Saskatchewan, most of Utah, Montana, most of Idaho)

CANADIAN

KNOCKOUT TEAMS

1970	Paul Soloway, Meyer Schleifer, Mabel Mahoney, Mary Jane Farell, Dr. Victor Mastron
1971	John Anderson, Richard DuFour, Allan Graves, Joel Martineau, Ken Gorfkle
1972	Mary Jane Farell, Mabel Mahoney, Norman Anderson, Robert Teshima, Barry Pritchard, Paul Prince
1973	Doug Thomson, Jack Marsch, Allan Graves, Larry Oakey

1974 Clarence Goppert, Mike Passell, Hermine Baron,
Garey Hayden, Ron LaCour
1975 Dale Mehaffey, Ken Scholes,
Neil Chambers, Martin Miller
1976 Clarence Goppert, Mark Lair, Jim Donaldson,
Mike Passell, Ron LaCour, Bruce Ferguson
1977 Joe Kerger, Gary Harper,
Gordon McOrmond, Laurence Betts
1978 John Mohan, Kay Schulle-Mohan, Diane LaFleur,
Mike Passell, Mike Shuman
1979 Max Hardy, Ethelyn Black, John Schermer,
Neil Chambers, T. Robert Hughes
1980 Ron Andersen, Billy Hsieh, Mark Lair,
Paul Soloway, Barry Crane, Eddie Wold
1981 Mel Skolnik, Jeff Meckstroth,
Eric Rodwell, Paul Soloway

UNMIXED SWISS TEAMS
1977 Victor Yip, Gerry Beck,
Ken Dang, Larry Goodfellow

MIXED SWISS TEAMS
1976 Marilyn Chappel, Loreta Burden, Helen Mitchell,
Bruce Ferguson, Jim Donaldson

OPEN TEAMS
1968 Hermine Baron, Morris Portugal,
Leslie West, Norman Anderson
1969 Alan Hampson, Ronald Phelps,
C. W. Wilkinson, William Hepperle
1970 John Anderson, Kenneth Gorfkle,
Norman Anderson, Larry Weiss
1971 John Anderson, Richard DuFour,
Ken Gorfkle, Allan Graves *(tied with)*
Mrs. D. Mitchell, Gary Mitchell, Barry Stewart,
Art d'Entremont, Joyce Phillips *(tied with)*
Miron Balych, Ed Dressler,
Ko-Shing Chao, Oliver Soice
1972 Carl Wilson, John Whillis,
Clive Ashman, Catherine Fergie *(tied with)*
Myrna Thomas, Jean Kittlitz,
Ray Kitlitz, Frank Ratai *(tied with)*
Gladys Sagen, Frances Waters,
Paul Betz, Zola Betz
1973 Terry Gould, Len Racette,
Pat Lopushinsky, S. Viswanathan
1974 Buddy Crapko, Jim Donaldson, Bob Connop,
Steve Sidell, Paul Hagen
1975 Clarence Goppert, Mike Passell,
Garey Hayden, Terry Wilkerson *(tied with)*
Mark Yoshihara, Richard Spackman,
Bjorg Jurkovich, Nick Jurkovich
1976 Clarence Goppert, Mark Lair, Jim Donaldson,
Mike Passell, Ron LaCour, Bruce Ferguson *(tied with)*
Mike Chomyn, Jean Erikson, Lisa Lister,
Helen Heard, Morris Portugal *(and)*
Howard Epley, Bob Hitchens,
Tom Hammond, Carl Hansen
1977 Lisa Lister, Stan Cabay,
Richard McKinney, Christine McKinney
1978 Clarence Goppert, John Schermer, Neil Chambers,
Bruce Ferguson, Brenda Keller
1979 Clarence Goppert, Mike Passell, Mark Lair,
Paul Soloway, Ron Andersen
1980 Karen Kilworth, Robert Crosby,
S. Viswanathan, Subhash Gupta *(tied with)*
Lucille Ellestad, Peter Jones,
Faith Pritchard, J. Barry Pritchard
1981 Mel Skolnik, Jeff Meckstroth,
Eric Rodwell, Paul Soloway
Flight A:
1978 Jill Newbold, Joe Kerger,
Doran Flock, Subhash Gupta
1979 Clarence Goppert, Mark Lair, Mike Passell,
Paul Soloway, Ron Andersen
1980 S. Viswanathan, Robert Crosby,
Ron Smith, Steve Skinner
1981 Mel Skolnik, Jeff Meckstroth,
Eric Rodwell, Paul Soloway

MEN'S PAIRS
1968 Orville Nelson, R. D. Hutchinson
1969 Robert Wobick, Kenneth Waters
1970 Kenneth Gorfkle, Steve Sidell
1971 Dr. J. Averback, G. Sekhar
1973 Jack Marsch, Bill Smith
1974 Garey Hayden, Ron LaCour
1975 Dev Prekhya, Len Racette
1976 Ron LaCour, Ron Feldman
1977 Ron MacCallum, William Humphrey
1978 Dave McClintock, Ron Feldman
1979 Doug Deschner, Ron Bass
1980 Steve Skinner, Ron Smith
1981 Gordon McOrmond, Joel Martineau

INDIVIDUAL
1975 R. P. Clemons
1976 Otto Leesment
1977 Christine MacNeill

WOMEN'S PAIRS
1968 Mary Jane Farell, Mabel Mahoney
1969 Mary Jane Farell, Mabel Mahoney
1970 Hazel Larson, Bess Rutledge
1971 Mrs. J. Byorth, Mrs. J. Biggle
1973 Lois Solinger, Ruthanne Price
1974 Rae Bateman, Mave Treadway
1975 Susan Harris, Peggy Kennedy
1976 Vi Hazlett, Virginia Roberts
1977 Joy Berry, Gerry Sugarman *(tied with)*
Jean Erikson, Karen Kilworth
1978 Brenda Keller, Shelley Nerman
1979 Pat Lopushinsky, Jill Savage
1980 Mona Scott, Inez Svare
1981 Doreen Jaskela, Lea McDonald

MIXED PAIRS
1968 G. E. Joneson, Marguerite Hall
1969 Mary Jane Farell, Robert Spotts
1970 Hermine Baron, Dale Forster
1972 Bob Haller, Gert Haller
1973 Lee Barton, Lucille Ellestad
1975 Maureen Kaufman, Larry Oakey
1976 Eleanor Warawa, Gord Tokarchak
1977 Bill Scott, Bobbie Scott

MASTER PAIRS
1968 Mrs. M. R. Mrazek, John Landeryou
1969 John Anderson, Jeff Taylor
1970 John Anderson, Jeff Taylor
1971 Richard DuFour, John Anderson
1972 Allan Graves, Neil Chambers
1973 Allen McAlear, Diana McAlear
1974 Laurence Betts, Joe Kerger
1975 Doug Thompson, Larry Oakey
1976 Don Oakie, Mrs. Emory Stanley
1977 Dick Reed, Broma Lou Harrison
1978 Mike Chomyn, Barry Pritchard
1979 Billy Cohen, Ron Smith
1980 Bruce Broadfoot, David Lim
1981 Dave Kilworth, S. Viswanathan

OPEN PAIRS
1968 Hermine Baron, Morris Portugal
1969 Broma Lou Harrison, Dick Reed
1970 Doug Thomson, Helen Promislow
1971 Richard DuFour, John Anderson
1972 R. MacDuff, Oris Mowry
1973 Ralph Johnson, Donelia Wilkeson
1974 Helen Heard, Morris Portugal
1975 S. Viswanathan, Dick Grant
1976 S. Viswanathan, Harold Brend
1977 Don Gladman, Helen Roche
1978 John Munson, John Ross
Flight A:
1978 Dick Yarington, Jim McCully *(tied with)*
Ron Smith, Gord McOrmond
1979 Ron Smith, Paul Lewis
1980 Steve Dunn, John Lang
1981 Tony Orlandini, Allan Graves

DISTRICT 18

KNOCKOUT TEAMS
1970 Dr. Victor Mastron, Mary Jane Farell, Mabel Mahoney,
Morris Portugal, Paul Soloway
1971 Ken Gorfkle, Richard DuFour, Allen McAlear,
Vonda White, Miles Adkins, Dr. Bruce Bryson
1973 Diane La Fleur, John Grantham, Mike Shuman,
Hermine Baron, Roger Bates, John Mohan
1974 Mike Passell, Hermine Baron, Paul Soloway,
Minda Brachman, Mark Lair
1975 C. F. Macurdy, Bruce Ferguson, Joe Kerger,
Laurence Betts, Neil Chambers
1977 Lil Greenberg, Mary Jane Farell,
Larry Kolker, Charles Wiley
1978 Douglas Fisher, G. Sekar,
David Sokolow, Kai Cheng
1979 Clarence Goppert, Mike Passell, Paul Soloway,
Mark Lair, John Mohan
1980 Roger Jourdan, Jim Barrow,
Tom Clarke, Alan LeBendig
1981 John Anderson, Ross Rainwater, Miles Adkin,
Ron Feldman, Mike Lippit

OPEN TEAMS
1971 Betty Jurovitch, S. Roan, R. Castle, Lou Poppler,
George Williamson, Shirley Thomas *(tied with)*
James Elliott, C. Crawford,
Paul Betz, Zola Betz *(and)*
Allen McAlear, Robert Rolfson,

Lee Torgrimson, Richard DuFour
1973 Doug Thomson, H. Smithen,
     David Levin, Ron Kurse *(tied with)*
     Dr. Ken Paine, Dr. Mike Tyrrell,
     Doug Schmeiser, Jim Howard *(and)*
     John Padget, Roy Bolton, Kay Schulle
     Don Carson, Don Schopflocher
1974 Philip Steiner, John Schermer,
     Mark Blumenthal, Michael Gurwitz
1975 Doug Rosser, Pat Lopushinsky,
     Don Schopflocher, Richard Ewen
1977 Milton Stern, Barry Crane,
     Kerri Shuman, Mike Lawrence
1978 Clarence Goppert, Mark Lair, Garey Hayden,
     Jim Donaldson, Joe Kerger
1979 Milton Stern, Gaylor Kasle,
     Ross Rainwater, Eddie Wold
1980 David Sokolow, Kai Cheng,
     G. Sekhar, Alan Bell
1981 Mel Skolnik, Paul Soloway,
     Peter Weichsel, Eddie Wold

MASTER SWISS TEAMS
Flight A:
1978 G. Sekar, Douglas Fisher,
     David Sokolow, Kai Cheng
1979 Mike Passell, Mark Lair, Clarence Goppert,
     Paul Soloway, John Mohan
1980 Doug Baldwin, Gerry McCully,
     Vic Hetman, Diane Kinakin
1981 Steve Bates, Vaughn Johnson,
     Pam Forsyth, Brenda Murchison

UNMIXED SWISS TEAMS
1977 William Parks, Ron Rosenthal,
     Don Smith, Dr. G. Richard Lee

MEN'S PAIRS
1970 Gary Mitchell, Art d'Entremont
1971 Ken Gorfkle, John Padget
1973 Don Schopflocher, Don Carson
1974 Paul Soloway, Mike Passell
1975 Ron LaCour, Garey Hayden
1977 Mike Shuman, Mike Passell
1978 David Sokolow, Bob Todd
1980 Roger Jourdan, Jim Barrow
1981 Court Smith, Pat Foley

WOMEN'S PAIRS
1970 Susan Harris, Marie Sollod
1971 Sheila Helmer, Mrs. C. Hestekin
1973 Linda Thierman, Pat Smolensky
1974 P. Angle, Kay Schulle
1975 Lobie Mitchell, Nancy Prince
1977 Pattie Kline, Revah Carlyle
1978 E. Haggart, Carolyn Miller
1980 Lura Head, Jean Armstrong
1981 Joyce Backman, Darby Holmes

MASTER PAIRS
1970 Dr. A. Cook, J. Balfour
1971 Barry Crane, Richard Kaye
1973 Melvin Johnson, Kay Johnson
1974 Paul Soloway, Minda Brachman
1975 Ed Lichtman, Don Mills
1977 Barry Crane, Kerri Shuman
1978 Dr. William Lukas, John Ross
1979 W. J. Bradshaw, William Pellett
1980 David Sokolow, G. Sekhar
1981 Mike Albert, Peter Weichsel

OPEN PAIRS
1970 Dr. Vic Mastron, Morris Portugal
1971 William Whitesel, Leslie Tsou
1973 Mike Shuman, Hermine Baron
1974 Barry Crane, Dr. John Fisher
1975 Leo Steil, Pat Smolensky
1977 Mike Shuman, Hermine Baron
1978 Alan Bell, Lex DeGroot
1979 Bob Paasch, Dixon Schively
1980 Roy Veness, Garey Hayden
1981 John Anderson, Miles Adkins
Flight A:
1978 John Schermer, Neil Chambers
1979 Lynn Johnson, Bill Braun
1980 Ron Andersen, David Hsieh
1981 Bill Booty, Lila Cochran

INDIVIDUAL
1975 Jerry Brundige

INTER-MOUNTAIN

KNOCKOUT TEAMS
1968 Hermine Baron, Paul Soloway, Morris Portugal,
     Betty Levan, Les West, Charles MacCracken

1969 Barney O'Malia, Gaylor Kasle, Charles MacCracken,
     Hermine Baron, Paul Soloway
1970 Donald Oakie, Marguerite Stanley,
     Rosalee Williams, Karen Allison
1971 David Adams, Don Buie,
     Richard Carone, R. MacDuff
1972 Mary Jane Farell, Mabel Mahoney, Charlie Dorn,
     Kirk Blackerby, Leslie Tsou, Richard Henderson
1973 Morris Portugal, Hermine Baron, Mike Passell,
     Moe Rubenfeld, J. David King
1974 Mike Passell, Hermine Baron, Ron LaCour,
     Gaylor Kasle, Garey Hayden
1975 Mike Passell, Gaylor Kasle,
     Garey Hayden, Roger Bates
1976 Alan Bell, Laurence Betts,
     Leslie Tsou, William Whitsel
1977 Gaylor Kasle, Polly Rich, Jeff Meckstroth,
     Neil Chambers, John Schermer
1979 Max Hardy, John Schermer, Neil Chambers,
     Ethelyn Black, T. Robert Hughes
1980 Jan Janitschke, Craig Janitschke, Jim Barrow,
     Ross Rainwater, Tony Glynne, Roger Jourdan
1981 Mel Skolnik, Paul Soloway, Jeff Meckstroth,
     Ron Andersen, Mike Smolen

OPEN TEAMS
1956 James Jackson, Lillian Thompson, Helen Edwards,
     Mrs. E. C. Goblirsch, Dr. E. C. Goblirsch
1957 Lilly Stewart, Doris Hopkins,
     Willow Nepple, Lois Oke
1958 Lucille Patterson, Gerald Patterson,
     Isadore Epstein, Adrian Hicks
1959 Melvin Singleton, Mrs. Ben Goodman,
     Mrs. Amos Felt, Mrs. Joseph Schwarts
1960 Mrs. John Hickes, Dr. John Hickes
     Mrs. George Nilson, Beatrice O'Mahoney *(tied with)*
     Erik Paulsen, Mike Shuman, Alan Bell,
     Mary Jane Farell, Ilya Zorn
1961 John Moran, Don Oakie,
     Helen Haugsten, Grace Meier
1962 Peter Pender, Michael Lawrence,
     Hermine Baron, Peter Rank
1963 June Budd, Adrian Hicks,
     Mrs. M. S. Nemer, Mrs. L. S. Gordon
1964 Dick Speicher, Betty Dougherty,
     Harry Doughty, Louise Doughty
1965 Hermine Baron, Peter Rank, John Moran,
     Michael Lawrence, Chuck Henke
1966 Hermine Baron, Meyer Schleifer,
     Peter Pender, Jeremy Flint *(tied with)*
     Frank Cady, Ken Gorfkle,
     George Steiner, Norm Featherston
1967 Charlotte Kramer, Roberta Hicks,
     Billie McLaughlin, Robert McLaughlin *(tied with)*
     Don Schulte, Hermine Baron, John Moran,
     Peter Rank, Marilyn Johnson
1968 Mrs. A. S. Brown, Mrs. S. Barbo,
     Mrs. R. Faus, Mrs. B. DeTour
1970 Hermine Baron, Richard Henderson, Tom Lux,
     Norman Anderson, J. David King
1971 Norman Berken, June Berken,
     Paul Eagan, Peggy Eagan *(tied with)*
     Allen McAlear, Diana McAlear,
     F. Walker, Mary Walker
1972 Carl Wilson, Dudley Brown,
     Jean Erickson, Mike Chomyn
1973 Gaylor Kasle, Roger Bates, Garey Hayden,
     John Mohan, Jane King
1974 Jim Hooker, Dr. John Fisher, Kerri Shuman,
     John Grantham, Kay Schulle, John Schermer
1975 Paul Prince, Dick McKinney,
     Steve Willard, Bob Teshima
1976 Gaylor Kasle, Mike Passell, Shirley Boice,
     Hermine Baron, Garey Hayden *(tied with)*
     Lilyan Eisenstein, Bob Eisenstein, Barry Crane,
     Kerri Shuman, Mike Shuman
1977 Ethelyn Black, Michael Schreiber, Max Hardy,
     Jeff Meckstroth, Marc Jacobus
1978 Jim Chew, Kerri Shuman, Barry Crane,
     Carol Sanders, Thomas Sanders
1979 William Whitsel, Leslie Tsou,
     Ross Rainwater, Alan Bell
1980 Kay Reese, Rae Bateman, Marshall Decker,
     Elizabeth Jameson, Bonnie Lantz *(tied with)*
     Barney O'Malia, Gaylor Kasle,
     John Mohan, Ron Andersen *(and)*
     Mike Schreiber, Jan Janitschke,
     Craig Janitschke, Paul Lewis
1981 Eddie Wold, Terry Brown,
     Marc Jacobus, Polly Rich

OPEN PAIRS

1956 Marge Harkleroad, Arthur Hill
1957 Robert Hendershott, John Donelly
1958 Fred Carpenter, John Donelly
1959 Mrs. Otto Heidelberger, Jack Ehrlenbach
1960 Isadore Epstein, Adrian Hicks
1961 Harold Guiver, Alex Tschekaloff
1962 Thomas Bussey, Dorothy Bussey
1963 Oswald Jacoby, Paul Levitt
1964 Hermine Baron, Homer Shoop
1965 Lee Jordan, Marshall Siemer
1966 Chuck Henke, John Moran
1967 John Kamb, Carl Hansen
1968 Shirley Thomas, Ken Hummel
1969 Paul Soloway, Hermine Baron
1970 Richard Henderson, Hermine Baron
1971 Steve Smolen, Charles MacCracken
1972 Mike Shuman, Hermine Baron
1973 Barry Crane, Dr. John Fisher
1974 Ron LaCour, Hermine Baron
1975 Robert Crosby, S. Viswanathan
1976 Ron LaCour, Charles Finch
1977 Lil Greenberg, Mary Jane Farell *(tied with)*
     Ethelyn Black, Max Hardy
1978 Mike Passell, Hermine Baron
1979 Eric Rodwell, Jeff Meckstroth
1980 Brenda Keller, Bruce Ferguson
1981 Martha Beecher, David Ashley
Flight A:
1977 Ron Andersen, Hugh MacLean
1978 David McClintock, Janet McClintock
1979 Christie McKinney, Dick McKinney
1980 John Mohan, Kay Schulle-Mohan
1981 Fred Rubbra, Jim Linhart

MEN'S PAIRS

1956 Donald Oakie, George Shaw
1957 Bennie Ignatz, George Welch
1958 George McCann, Jack Ehrlenbach
1959 Marshall Siemer, Lawrence Shadoan
1960 Ivan Erdos, Dr. W. Won Sik You
1961 Don Oakie, Mark Hodges
1962 Ron Borg, William Weinstein
1963 Peter Larson, W.C. Peterson
1964 Melvin Singleton, Dr. Robert Thometz
1965 Jim Pestaner, Jim Linhart
1966 Peter Pender, Jeremy Flint
1967 Otto Leesment, Karel Van Renesse
1968 Brian May, Buddy Crapko
1969 Morris Portugal, Vic Mastron
1970 Otto Leesment, Michael Squier
1971 Barney O'Malia, Gaylor Kasle
1972 Tom Quinlan, Miles Adkins
1974 Gaylor Kasle, John Grantham
1976 John Mohan, John Grantham
1977 Max Hardy, Michael Schreiber
1978 Barney O'Malia, Gaylor Kasle
1979 Marvin Rauch, Bill Flaherty
1980 Rudi Cataldi, Robert Radwin
1981 Mike Smolen, Jeff Meckstroth

INDIVIDUAL

1968 Vonda White
1975 Mrs. Howard Tabor
1976 Walt Holden, Jr.

MASTER PAIRS

1956 Mrs. Richard Bartholomew, Mrs. John Parker
1957 Fredric Carpenter, Neil Ballard *(tied with)*
     Robin Mac Nab, Max Manchester
1958 George McCann, J. Carlton Ehrlenbach
1959 Mary Hutchinson, Donald Oakie
1960 Courtland Rush, Isadore Epstein
1961 Peter Rank, Donald Krauss
1962 Bob Bratcher, Mary Cocherell
1963 Mabel Mahoney, David Carter *(tied with)*
     Mrs. C. J. Stormwind, Paul Carlin
1964 Walter Ensminger, J. D. Shortridge
1965 Madeline McGill, Doug Oram
1966 Don Oakie, Barney O'Malia
1967 Marilyn Johnson, Peter Rank
1968 Hermine Baron, Paul Soloway
1969 Mrs. D. R. Houston, N. L. Moise
1970 Norman Anderson, Richard Henderson
1971 Barry Crane, Dr. John Fisher
1972 Diane Mraz, John Mohan
1973 Mike Passell, Hermine Baron
1974 Helen Heard, Morris Portugal
1975 Barry Crane, Kerri Shuman
1976 Chet Pulcinski, Jim Young
1977 William Bradshaw, William Pellett
1978 George Hardy, William Koski
1979 Dave Westfall, Lila Cochran

1980 Barry Crane, Ron Andersen
1981 David Ashley, Martha Beecher

WOMEN'S PAIRS

1956 J. E. Harris, Lucille Parker
1957 Mrs. Carl Mozzone, Gladys Lantry
1958 Mrs. Amos Felt, Mrs. Joseph Schwartz
1959 Hattie Joffe, Pat Smolensky
1960 Mrs. Amos Felt, Mrs. Joseph Schwartz
1961 June Budd Ruhle, Mrs. Ben Goodman
1962 Virginia Galena, Eleatha Vincent
1963 Margaret Bybee, Aileen Skinner
1964 Aileen Skinner, Eleanor Erlandson
1965 Mrs. L. Jay Egan, Mrs. J. E. Rodgers
1966 Hermine Baron, Honor Flint
1967 Maddie McGill, Joyce Millward *(tied with)*
     Mary Jane Farell, Mabel Mahoney
1968 Mary Jane Farell, Mabel Mahoney
1969 Mrs. John Hewitt, Mrs. E. E. LaFrance
1970 Mrs. David Stratton, Gert Haller
1971 Suzanne Jones, Irene Hyatt
1972 Caroline Smith, Helen Gregory
1974 Lucile Gunther, Joan Madrid
1976 Jane Stickney, Hermine Baron
1977 Kathy Kotlen, Linda Jenkins
1978 Elaine Brockman, Patty Prahl
1979 Kerri Shuman, Helen Cataldi
1980 Carol Dibblee, Lee Payne
1981 Helen Corbin, Jackie Matthews

UNMIXED PAIRS

1975 Roger Bates, Gaylor Kasle

MIXED PAIRS

1956 Roba Leber, Fredrick Morrison
1957 Mrs. S. de Mers, Lee Jordan
1958 Olive Griffith, Marshal Siemer
1959 Arthur Scribner, Helen Scribner *(tied with)*
     Eleanor Reichmuth, Aaron Lipsker
1960 Addie Lee You, Ivan Erdos
1961 Mary Jane Farell, Peter Rank
1962 Mrs. Harry McGlynn, Harry McGlynn
1963 Lilly Stewart, Bill Roberts
1964 Ed Herbert, Bertha Wills
1965 Mrs. Stephen Ondeck, Henry McLane
1966 Phil Wood, Bobbiee Coerner
1967 Dr. William Lukas, Sissy Hartley
1968 Don Morris, Beth Patrick
1969 Matt Bartosik, Marge Triplitt
1974 Charles Roberts, Mrs. John Hickes
1975 Barry Crane, Kerri Shuman
1976 John Grantham, Jo Ann Grantham

MASTER SWISS TEAMS

1977 Dr. Darwin Fielder, Robert Hughes,
     Dick Reed, Garey Hayden
1978 Barry Crane, Jim Chew, Jim Jacoby,
     Thomas Sanders, Carol Sanders, Kerri Shuman
1979 Eddie Wold, Polly Rich, Jeff Meckstroth,
     Eric Rodwell, Gaylor Kasle

UNMIXED SWISS TEAMS

1976 Dale Hutchinson, Dr. Bob Arthur,
     Hadi Allahverdian, Jack Buck
1980 Steve Skinner, Martha Beecher
     Ron Smith, David Ashley
1981 Mel Skolnik, Paul Soloway, Jeff Meckstroth,
     Ron Andersen, Mike Smolen

DISTRICT 19 (British Columbia, Alaska, Washington)

INLAND EMPIRE

KNOCKOUT TEAMS

1970 George Steiner, Jim Donaldson,
     Allan Graves, Neil Chambers
1971 Donald Oakie, Marguerite Stanley,
     Joe Jabon, Dr. E. Christopherson
1972 Hermine Baron, Richard Henderson, John Padget,
     Leslie Tsou, John Mohan
1973 John Mohan, Diane LaFleur, John Grantham,
     Roger Bates, Mike Passell, Garey Hayden
1974 Clarence Goppert, Ron LaCour, Paul Soloway,
     Garey Hayden, Mike Passell
1975 Leslie Tsou, Alan Bell,
     Herbert Smith, Kirk Blackerby
1976 Shirley Boice, Gaylor Kasle, John Mohan,
     Mike Passell, Garey Hayden
1977 Barney O'Malia, Gaylor Kasle,
     Jeff Meckstroth, Michael Schreiber
1979 Leslie Tsou, Ron Feldman, Ross Rainwater,
     Neil Chambers, Aidan Ballantyne

1980	Paul Soloway, Ron Andersen, Peter Weichsel, Elisabeth Brenhouse, Mel Skolnik
1981	Mel Skolnik, Elisabeth Brenhouse, Ron Smith, Eddie Wold, Peter Weichsel

OPEN TEAMS

1971	Neil Ballard, Jude Ballard, Carol Baird, Bob Luebkeman *(tied with)* J. Person, Beverly Person, Mervin Curtis, Mrs. L. Hopkins *(tied with)* Neil Sutherland, Dick McKinney, Jean Erickson, Mike Chomyn *(tied with)* George Slemmons, Dave Sletterholm, Patricia Goodin, Darryl Pederson
1972	John Schermer, Neil Chambers, Ken Gorfkle, Allan Graves
1973	Ken Scholes, Steve Sidell, Henry Lortz, Dudley Brown
1974	George Steiner, George Slemmons, Carol Baird, Jean Anderson
1975	William Whitesel, Dick Jones, Darryl Pedersen, John Ashton, Hack Fuller
1976	Leslie Tsou, Ralph Johnson,, Donella Johnson, Alan Bell, William Whitesel *(tied with)* Milton Stern, Larry Cohen, Mike Lawrence, Lou Bluhm, Mark Blumenthal, Lew Stansby
1977	Frank Burke, Janet Booth, Steve Mansfield, Jim Aitken
1979	Mark Lair, Clarence Goppert, John Mohan, Eddie Wold, Michael Schreiber
1980	Jim Barrow, Roger Jourdan, Leslie Tsou, Ron Feldman, Tony Glynne, John Ashton
1981	Jan Janitschke, Craig Janitschke, John Schermer, Neil Chambers

Flight A:

1979	Tony Glynne, John Lusky, Ross Rainwater, Oris Mowry *(tied with)* Mark Neils, Mark Hanft, Dave Corn, Darrell Keel
1980	Neil Chambers, Sandra Herman, John Anderson, Ross Rainwater
1981	Dave Tuell, Jr., Bunny Tuell, Dick White, Tony Orlandini, Alex Orlandini *(tied with)* Mary Ruth Blustein, Maurice Blustein, Roger Urbaniak, Susan Urbaniak

MASTER PAIRS

1971	John Anderson, Jim Sullivan
1972	William Whitesel, Richard Henderson
1973	Henry Lortz, Steve Sidell
1974	Don Oakie, Marguerite Stanley
1975	John Moffat, John McKnight
1977	Barney O'Malia, Gaylor Kasle

Flight A:

1976	Mike Passell, Fred Hamilton
1979	Eddie Wold, George Rosenkranz
1980	Tony Glynne, Ron Andersen
1981	Barry Crane, Craig Janitschke

OPEN PAIRS

1970	Paul Soloway, Hermine Baron
1971	Bob Hitchens, Dr. Ron Tracy
1972	Tom Hammond, Mark Bailey
1973	Mike Passell, Hermine Baron
1974	Steve Smolen, Peter Rank
1975	John Kamb, Carl Hansen
1976	George Steiner, Emery Selymes
1979	Dick Yarington, Barbara McHarg
1980	Bruce Ferguson, Brenda Keller
1981	Leslie Tsou, Max Hardy

Flight A:

1977	Ross Rainwater, Craig Huston
1979	Michael Schreiber, Neil Chambers
1980	Elisabeth Brenhouse, Peter Weichsel
1981	Jeanette Featherstone, Sharon Colson

MEN'S PAIRS

1970	William Whitesel, Dick Jones
1971	John Padget, Norman Anderson
1974	Laurence Betts, Gary Harper
1979	Greg Holt, Jim Hamil
1980	Roger Jourdan, Jim Barrow
1981	Joe Kerger, Joel Martineau

WOMEN'S PAIRS

1970	Lenora Austin, Betty Kershaw
1971	Jude Ballard, Carol Baird
1974	Mary Ruth Blustein, Susan Urbaniak
1979	Martha Swanson, Bedette Harmon
1980	Donna Bailey, Catherine Lewis
1981	Susan Urbaniak, Carlyn Steiner

UNMIXED PAIRS

1976	Fred Hamilton, Ron LaCour

MIXED PAIRS

1977	George Steiner, Carlyn Rottsolk

INDIVIDUAL

1977	Julie Hendrix

UNMIXED SWISS TEAMS

1977	Barbara Shields, Cecile Richards, Bill Cotton, Goldie Morris *(tied with)* Elaine Brockman, Mickey Condrin, Vi Gilbert, Patty Prahl

PACIFIC NORTHWEST

KNOCKOUT TEAMS

1969	Fred Hagan, Phyllis Novak, Bob Hendershott, Gard Hays, Buddy Crapko
1970	Buddy Crapko, Phyllis Novak, Doug Thomson, Jack Marsch, Dolly Shapiro
1971	Leslie Tsou, John Anderson, William Whitesel, Michael Phillippas
1972	Neil Chambers, Dale Mehaffey, Bill Eisenberg, Kemp Hiatt, John Schermer
1973	Joel Martineau, Darwin Afdahl, Richard Christie, Sandy Gammie
1974	Barry White, Chris Earl, Richard Fleischman, Alan Bell, Leslie Tsou
1975	Jim McAvoy, Ron Smith, Mike Blades, Derek Ward
1976	Clarence Goppert, Fred Hamilton, Mike Passell, Ron LaCour, Bruce Ferguson, Jim Donaldson
1977	Frank Kimball, Ron Andersen, Hugh MacLean, Allan Graves, Jack Marsch
1978	Max Hardy, Neil Chambers, John Schermer, Ron Feldman *(Spring)* Neil Kimelman, Bob Todd, Bob Kuz, John Hurdle, Don Brazeau, Laurence Betts *(Summer)*
1979	John Lanier, Bob Crossley, Darrell Keel, Wayne Fedynak
1980	Jim Donaldson, Brenda Keller, Bruce Ferguson, Craig Janitschke, Paul Lewis, Ron Feldman
1981	Mel Skolnik, Elisabeth Brenhouse, Paul Lewis, Ron Andersen, Paul Soloway

OPEN TEAMS

1949	S. Meyer, Mrs. S. Meyer, Sam Gordon, M. Perlman
1950	Harrison Holmes, Stephan Ungar, C. Holbrook, Marshall Shaw
1951	Wilma Mozzone, Gladys Currie, Fumio Yagi, Takeo Yagi
1952	A. C. Duby, W. Russman, David Harkleroad, G. V. Voight
1953	Marge Harkleroad, David Harkleroad, Earl McKale, John Moran
1954	Betty Amos, Lily Stewart, Andy Wright, Jr., Art Doran
1955	Neil Ballard, John Donnelly, Robert Street, Max Manchester
1956	Eric Stark, Adrian Hicks, Isadore Epstein, Alexander Davidson
1957	Maitland McKenzie, Ed Cahill, Wally Rossman, Horace Dear
1958	Ben Lapidus, Norman Turnbull, George Yoxall, Earle Adams
1959	Dr. Eugene Schwartz, Cap Crossley, Jr., Catherine Lewis, Ruth Beste
1960	Abe Zelikowsky, William Schmidt, Jim Costello, Robert Melosh
1961	Mervin Curtis, Lester Fox, Ruth Beste, Catherine Lewis
1962	Delores Bick, Abe Zelikowsky, Jim Donaldson, Leo Steil, Ron Berg
1963	Pat Crowder, Emery Selymes, Darryl Pederson, Dr. Harold McDonald
1964	Dolores Bick, Max Vernon, Max Stacklies, Buddy Crapko *(Spring)* Andy Wright, Phyllis Novak, Dorothea Norton, John Norton *(Fall)*
1965	Andy Wright, Phyllis Novak, Dorothea Norton, John Norton
1966	Byron Nilsson, Lee Frandsen, Frank Baldwin, Lou Belzberg *(Spring)* Peter Pender, Jeremy Flint, Alex Tschekaloff, Richard Henderson *(Fall)*
1967	Mike Lawrence, Leslie West, Helen Moore, Pat O'Brien, Morris Portugal *(Spring)* Richard Walsh, Rhoda Walsh, Leslie West, Mike Lawrence *(Fall)*
1971	Adrian Hicks, Murdock Smith, Jim Dickie, Mike Strebinger
1972	Garry Rath, D. Birnie, Giles Mackenzie, Brian Johnston, Ed Bishop

1973 John Anthony, Ron Öhmart,
    Harold McAllister, Steve Metzger *(tied with)*
    John Garrison, Pat Dunn,
    Henry Lortz, Ken Scholes
1974 Peter Nixon, Jim Andrews,
    Gary Harper, Laurence Betts
1975 Richard Carter, Kevin McWeeney,
    Andrew Mar, Gerson Miller
1976 John Garrison, Henry Lortz,
    Ken Scholes, Pat Dunn
1977 Lauren Miller, Gordie McOrmond,
    Duncan Smith, Jim McAvoy
1978 Andy Nagy, Anne Nagy,
    Ron Borg, Sandra Borg *(Spring)*
    Dennis Dohl, Marcia Kostynyk,
    Bob Connop, Cam Lindsay *(Summer)*
1979 Mike Passell, Mark Lair, Gaylor Kasle,
    Clarence Goppert, Eddie Wold
1980 Mary Fines, Rose Wrean,
    Donna Morrison, Don Sache
1981 Mel Skolnik, Paul Lewis,
    Paul Soloway, Ron Andersen

OPEN PAIRS
1949 W. Powell, Arthur Vosburg
1950 Max Manchester, Venita Summers
1951 Maynard Orme, Robert Street
1952 G. New, N. P. Monson
1953 John Moran, Joe Hennecke
1954 Robert Street, Lloyd Graham
1955 E. Bunnell, Eric Stark
1956 Robert Street, Lloyd Graham
1957 Carl Koch, Mrs. Carl Koch
1958 Tom Myers, Ralph Kirkwood
1959 Malvine Klausner, Meyer Schleifer
1960 Neil Ballard, Robert Street
1961 Maynard Orme, J. Robert Patterson
1962 Eric Paulsen, Alex Tschekaloff
1963 Dan Lefebvre, Loren Hawkins *(Fall)*
1964 Erik Paulsen, Richard Walsh *(Spring)*
    Jeff Taylor, Dale Forster *(Fall)*
1965 Joe Jabon, Darryl Pedersen
1966 Max Sacklies, Karel van Renesse *(Spring)*
    Barry Crane, Peter Rank *(Fall)*
1967 Frank Schaefers, Jeff Taylor *(Spring)*
    Bill Silver, Alan Oaks *(Fall)*
1969 Hermine Baron, Paul Soloway
1970 William Whitesel, Marty Miller
1971 Robert Wakeman, Ruth Wakeman
1972 Nathan Divinsky, Allan Graves
1973 John Anthony, Jim Andrews
1974 Kyle Larsen, Mike Lawrence
1975 Joe Jabon, Bob Palmer
1976 Dean Ellis, Kit Young
1977 Ron Gardiner, Wayne Fedynak
1978 John Schermer, Neil Chambers *(Spring)*
    Bill Wade, Peggy Coupez *(tied with)*
    Fred Sontag, Selene Jacobson *(Summer)*
1980 Wally Rossman, Adrian Hicks
Flight A:
1978 Jim Donaldson, Henry Lortz *(Spring)*
    Lea McDonald, Don Booker *(Summer)*
1979 Chris Laskowski, Henry Lortz
1980 Mary Ruth Blustein, Maurice Blustein
1981 George Mittelman, Allan Graves

MASTER PAIRS
1952 Robert Street, Venita Street
1953 Ben Johnson, Alvin Landy
1954 Robert Street, Venita Street
1955 Robert Street, Venita Street
1956 Andrew Wright, Jr., Carl Koch
1957 Adrian Hicks, Isadore Epstein
1958 Helen Haugsten, Don Oakie
1959 Grace Meier, Don Oakie
1960 Lily Stewart, Lois Oke
1961 Lois Barde, Joe Jabon
1962 Mary Hutchinson, Chuck Henke
1963 Michael Bruce, Buddy Crapko
1964 Courtland Rush, Bob Hendershott *(Fall)*
1965 Richard Henderson, Alex Tschekaloff *(Fall)*
1966 Karel van Renesse, Buddy Crapko *(Spring)*
    Jim Donaldson, Paul Hagan *(Fall)*
1967 Leo Steil, Phyllis Novak *(Spring)*
    John Kamb, Leo Steil *(Fall)*
1969 John Anderson, Don Nemiro
1970 Paul Soloway, Hermine Baron
1971 Don Brander, Jim Donaldson
1972 Barry White, Chip Cleveland
1973 Bob Palmer, Joe Jabon
1975 Betty Michno, Jim Dickie

Flight A:
1976 Helen Heard, Morris Portugal
1977 Ron Borg, Jim Donaldson
1978 Leslie Tsou, Marc Zwerling
1978 John Moffat, Dave Westfall
1979 Barry Crane, Kerri Shuman
1980 Carol Hutchinson, Jean Anderson
1981 Jim Dickie, Peter Herold

MEN'S PAIRS
1949 Isadore Epstein, Harrison Holmes
1950 Ed Cahill, Robert Street
1951 Jack Ehrlenbach, Hugh Edwards
1952 Carl Wyman, C. Holbrook
1953 William Hanna, Doug Steen
1954 Tommy Myers, Neil Ballard
1955 Otto Leesment, Michael Bruce
1956 Ed Cahill, Robert Street
1957 Max Stackles, Eric Stark
1958 Earle Adams, Max Stackles
1959 Carl Wyman, Henry Craig
1960 Robert Patterson, Adrian Hicks
1961 Jack Goldie, Simon Marinker
1962 Bert Naness, John McEntee *(tied with)*
    Darryl Pedersen, Bob Hendershott
1963 Dan Lefebvre, Emery Selymes *(Fall)*
1964 Eric Stark, Max Stackles *(Spring)*
    Peter Pender, Doug Drury *(Fall)*
1965 Peter Lit, Hugh Ross *(Fall)*
1966 Byron Nilsson, Lee Frandsen *(Spring)*
    Leo Steil, Gard Hays *(Fall)*
1967 Eric Stark, Jacques Ribeyre *(Spring)*
    Gard Hays, Chuck Berry *(Fall)*
1969 Dick Grant, Lee Barton
1970 John Kamb, Duncan Smith
1972 Allan Graves, Doug Thomson
1973 William Whitesel, Alan Bell
1974 Fred Hagen, Bob Hendershott
1975 Ron LaCour, Mark Lair
1976 Laurence Bettes, John Hurdle
1977 Mike Strebinger, Jim Donaldson
1978 George Steiner, Darryl Pedersen *(Spring)*
    Dick Yarington, Steve Sidell *(Summer)*
1979 Andy Nagy, Aidan Ballantyne
1980 Tony Glynne, Craig Janitschke
1981 Dan Jacob, Dennis Dohl

WOMEN'S PAIRS
1949 R. W. Nelson, R. Kelley
1950 Alma Rosenkrans, Hazel Brunn
1951 Veva Duncan, Glow Elmes
1952 Libbie Green, Mrs. K. Leaverton
1953 Lucille Wheeler, Gladys Wilson
1954 Lois Barde, June Koch
1955 Willow Nepple, Lois Oke
1956 Lily Hills, Helen Edwards
1957 Doris Hopkins, Catherine Lewis
1958 Madeline Flaherty, Gladyce Lantry
1959 Willow Nepple, Lois Oke
1960 Louise Stewart, Jean Kennedy
1961 Elizabeth Warren, Ethel Cleworth
1962 Mrs. E. G. Kauffman, Leeta Creary
1963 Hilda Price, Ethel Cleworth *(Fall)*
1964 Delores Bick, Ruth Needham *(Spring)*
    Mrs. Louis Arnold, Dorothea Norton *(Fall)*
1965 Mrs. C. R. Gilman, Thelma Pinkerton *(Fall)*
1966 Marjorie Stone, Virginia Roberts *(Spring)*
    Dorothea Norton, Mrs. Louis Arnold *(Fall)*
1967 Mrs. Phil Hagel, Velma Acres *(Spring)*
    Mary Mansfield, Florence Westwood *(Fall)*
1969 Thelma Kersey, Hilda Reid
1970 Helen O'Rourke, Marion Marlow
1972 Della Allen, Marie Scott
1973 Jennie Redcliffe, Cori Van Viegen
1974 Diane Campbell, Irene Waters
1975 Donna Morrison, Evelyn Hodge
1976 Irene Brown, Helen Hafer
1977 Dorothy Donaldson, Grace Amyes
1978 Nancy Folkins, Alice Ford *(Spring)*
    Mary Thomspon, Virginia Schaefer *(Summer)*
1979 Donna Bartholomew, Jackie Matthews
1980 Mary Arneson, Dorothy MacDonald
1981 Sue Lyski, Betty Rossman

MIXED PAIRS
1949 D. Breher, W. Leary, Sr.
1950 C. B. Manke, Mrs. C. B. Manke
1951 Harriet Rethers, Eddie Styer
1952 Mrs. S. Wilson, Henry Craig
1953 Dr. Harry Basford, Mrs. Harry Basford
1954 Marguerite Hall, Tom Burns
1955 Gerald Patterson, Lucille Patterson

1956 Milton Agay, Carolyn Fantone
1957 Maynard Orme, Lois Oke
1958 Grace Meier, J. Carton Ehrlenbach
1959 Mary Hutchinson, L. Baker
1960 Loretta Arnold, Dan Lefebvre
1961 Eleanor Gordon, Philip Burke
1962 Willow Nepple, Ralph Kirkwood
1963 Marian Grinstein, Michael Bruce
1964 Mary Adams, Tony Marsh *(Spring)*
     David Tuell, Bunny Tuell *(Fall)*
1965 Patty Prahl, Ed Potts
1966 Eleanor Gordon, Leo Steil *(Spring)*
     Gard Hays, Janet Daling *(Fall)*
1967 Marianne Powell, Oswald Jacoby *(Spring)*
     Mary Jane Farell, Charles MacCracken *(Fall)*
1968 Madeline McGill, Dave Folinsbee
1975 Don Campbell, Jean Brach
1976 Marguerite Hall, Adrian Hicks
1977 Mike Wilson, Jean Anderson
1979 Brenda Blumenthal, Marc Jacobus
1981 Eric Stark, Jean Turnbull

LIFE MASTER INDIVIDUALS
1957 Eric Stark

INDIVIDUAL
1976 Ida Taylor
1977 Jeanne Bentley

SENIOR MASTER INDIVIDUAL
1957 Charles Payne

UNMIXED SWISS TEAMS
1976 David Lim, Hugh Hanrieder,
     Al Chapelle, Bruce Broadfoot
1977 Joan Tweter, Harriet Burdick,
     Barbara Wise, Joan Lucas

MASTER SWISS TEAMS
Flight A:
1978 John Mohan, Kay Schulle-Mohan, Mike Passell,
     Diane LaFleur, Roger Bates *(Spring)*
     Doug Andrews, Dennis Dohl,
     Bob Connop, Aidan Ballantyne *(Summer)*
1979 Jim Andrews, Bob Connop, Paul Hagen,
     Phyllis Novak, Ron Borg
1980 Ken MacNeal, Neil Chambers,
     Ron Feldman, Ross Rainwater
1981 Tony Orlandini, George Mittelman,
     Allan Graves, Marty Johnson *(tied with)*
     Neil Chambers, Lynn Blumenthal,
     Maxine Blumenthal, Paul Soloway *(and)*
     Peter Herold, Lauren Miller,
     Jim McAvoy, Duncan Smith

POLAR

KNOCKOUT TEAMS
1971 Maj. Richard Towne, Eunice Towne,
     Maj. Howard Enbysk, Darlyne Enbysk
1974 David Landauer, Barbara Landauer,
     George Parker, Lois Parker
1977 Frank Kimball, Anita Kimball, Ron Andersen,
     Hugh MacLean, Mark Lair
1980 Ron Andersen, Bill Hsieh, Jim Linhart,
     Paul Lewis, Paul Soloway

OPEN TEAMS
1963 Anne Brown, Peg Holland,
     Lillie Hills, Betty Young
1965 Robert Waite, Daniel Moore,
     Mrs. F. B. Sole, Mrs. M. D. Boyer
1968 Kay Moody, Jack Powell,
     Linda Mason, Henry Fisher
1971 Mrs. George Middleton, Mrs. Kenneth McCasky,
     Mrs. Don Anderson, Mrs. Noah Gregg
1974 Peter Jones, Terry Schleppegrell,
     Capt. Dennis Day, Muriel Richens *(tied with)*
     Ruth Wendte, Amy Marek,
     Howard Enbysk, Darlyne Enbysk
1977 Harold Caldwell, Gail Putzel,
     Frank Putzel, Dick Plov
1980 Bunny Haas, Pam Pruitt, Doug Hsieh,
     Bruce Ferguson, Brenda Keller, George Hsieh *(tied with)*
     Ernie Young, Dan Moore,
     Mary Ondeck, Nancy Grant

MASTER PAIRS
1963 Adrian Hicks, Joe Jacobs
1965 Peter Lit, Homer Shoop
1968 Thora Hanson, Patricia Krause
1971 Ernie Young, Dan Moore
1974 Mary Ondeck, Darce Myers
1977 Charles Bennett, Boots Kendrick
1980 Bruce Ferguson, Clarence Goppert

OPEN PAIRS
1963 Lillie Hills, Otto Leesment
1965 Lenore Kramer, Don Oakie
1968 Dan Moore, Lloyd Patrick
1971 Boots Kendrick, Dr. John Fisher *(tied with)*
     Jack Kendrick, Robert Sparks
1974 Don Oakie, Marguerite Stanley
1977 Terry Schleppegrell, Boots Kendrick
1980 Terry Schleppegrell, Bob Barth

MEN'S PAIRS
1963 Otto Leesment, Jack Beeson
1965 Lt. Col. Manus Murtha, Raymond Volkine
1968 Dr. Ron Tracy, Bob Hitchens
1971 Henry Fisher, Jack Beeson
1974 David Landauer, George Parker
1980 Paul Soloway, Doug Hsieh

WOMEN'S PAIRS
1963 Mrs. Bjorg Jurovich, D. K. Ribar
1965 Mary Hutchinson, Mrs. M. E. Berg
1968 Martha Parker, Billie Walker
1971 Mary Jane Farell, Mrs. John McLucus
1974 Laura Farell, Beatrice Aharrah
1980 Maureen Wood, Kay Snow

MIXED PAIRS
1963 Anne Brown, R. C. Werner
1971 Mrs. Don Anderson, Dan Moore
1974 Jack Kendrick, Boots Kendrick
1977 Bob Barth, Boots Kendrick
1980 Ernie Young, Debby Young

UNMIXED PAIRS
1977 Daniel Moore, Henry Fisher

MASTER SWISS TEAMS
1980 Ron Andersen, Billy Hsieh, Jim Linhart,
     Paul Lewis, Paul Soloway

PUGET SOUND

KNOCKOUT TEAMS
1968 John Kamb, Carl Hansen,
     Mark Bailey, Tom Hammond
1969 John Kamb, Carl Hansen,
     Mark Bailey, Tom Hammond
1970 George Steiner, George Slemmons,
     Darryl Pedersen, Emery Selymes
1971 George Steiner, George Slemmons,
     Darryl Pedersen, Emery Selymes
1972 George Steiner, George Slemmons,
     Darryl Pedersen, Emery Selymes
1973 Fred Rubbra, Rhoda Walsh,
     Michael Lawrence, Norman Anderson
1974 Kemp Hiatt, Kerri Shuman,
     Mike Gurwitz, Ron LaCour
1975 Clarence Goppert, Mike Passell, Garey Hayden,
     Gaylor Kasle, Michael Bruce
1976 Stan Sather, John Rogers, Mike Wilson,
     Ron Feldman, Jim Leary
1977 Frank Kimball, Anita Kimball, Ron Andersen,
     Hugh MacLean, Mark Lair
1979 Mike Passell, Mark Lair, Paul Soloway,
     Clarence Goppert, Eddie Wold
1981 Marc Jacobus, Tony Glynne, Ross Rainwater,
     Dennis Sorensen, Nadine Deutsch

OPEN TEAMS
1968 Bob Hitchens, Frank Cady, Ron Tracy,
     Dave Setterholm, Don Glad
1971 Mike Farman, Carla Farman,
     Dr. Jeff Farman, Georgia Farman
1972 William Whitesel, Stan Sather, Oris Mowry,
     Phyllis Novak, Buddy Crapko
1973 Barry Crane, Dr. John Fisher,
     Rick Henderson, Allan Graves
1974 Chris Earl, Dr. E. Christopherson,
     Tom Kinakin, Larry Pfefer
1975 Dr. R. Craig Powers, Peter Nordman, Bob Gunter,
     Dave Whitcher, Robin Whitcher
1976 Dick Barnes, Henry Lortz,
     Ray Loftis, Steve Sidell
1977 Dave Setterholm, Bill Hagen,
     Fred Hagen, Bob Hendershott
1981 John Ashton, Dennis Sorensen, Tony Glynne,
     Marc Jacobus, Ross Rainwater
Flight A:
1978 George Steiner, Richard Lang,
     Darryl Pedersen, George Slemmons
1979 Clarence Goppert, Mike Passell, Mark Lair,
     Eddie Wold, Paul Soloway

1980   Dennis Metcalf, Craig Huston, Ross Rainwater,
Roger McNay, Tony Glynne
1981   George Landreth, Mark Lair, Laurence Betts,
Mike Passell, Craig Janitschke *(tied with)*
Garey Hayden, Kay Schulle-Mohan, John Mohan,
Steve Sidell, William Troupe

MASTER PAIRS
1968   Ed Murray, Viston Smith
1969   Joe Jabon, Thelma Taft
1970   William Whitesel, Dick Jones
1971   Ken Gorfkle, John Padget
1972   Robert Norberg, Dennis Metcalf
1973   Barry Crane, Dr. John Fisher
1974   Barry Crane, Kerri Shuman
1975   Emery Selymes, Carol Baird
Flight A:
1976   Barry Crane, Kerri Shuman
1977   Irene Day, Dianne Hoff *(tied with)*
Patsy Esfeld, Bob Palmer
1978   Lynda Cole, Larry Barton
1979   Laurence Betts, Mike Wilson
1980   Dennis Heller, Cam Trenor
1981   Sue Lyski, Dennis Sorensen

OPEN PAIRS
1968   Barry Crane, Peter Rank
1969   Allen McAlear, G. Gard Hays
1970   John Anderson, Richard Henderson
1971   John Padget, Norman Anderson
1972   Robert MacDuff, Tom Suchanis
1973   Carol Baird, Jean Anderson
1974   Don Nudelman, Miles Adkins
1975   Garey Hayden, Mike Passell
1978   George Steiner, Maxine Blumenthal
1979   Craig Harrison, Janice Randles
1981   Ron Feldman, Mike Passell
Flight A:
1976   John Schermer, Neil Chambers
1977   Craig Huston, Dennis Metcalf
1978   Mark Neils, Frank Burke
1979   Anne Bean, Jackie Matthews
1980   Craig Huston, Elaine Huston
1981   John Anderson, Marc Zwerling

MEN'S PAIRS
1968   Don Bennett, Steve Sidell
1969   David Tuell, Jr., E. L. McNeal
1970   Ken Gorfkle, Richard Henderson
1971   John Anderson, Leslie Tsou
1972   Ed Chow, Jim Thomas
1973   Bob Hitchens, Erich Giese
1974   Richard Feist, Robert Johansen
1975   Jim Young, Rod Caldwell
1976   Cam Trenor, Steve Mansfield
1977   Michael Schreiber, William Whitesel
1978   Fred Sontag, Gordon McOrmond
1979   Bob Hendershott, Joseph Muckley
1980   Marc Jacobus, Craig Janitschke
1981   John Mohan, Steve Sidell

WOMEN'S PAIRS
1968   Anne Bean, Bernice Akin
1969   Mrs. Eugene Tennyson, Mrs. F. Pigato
1970   Lenore Dudley, Eva Cole
1971   Mrs. Fred Peters, Mrs. Lester Seinfeld
1972   Roberta Bratcher, Frances O'Malia
1973   Susan Urbaniak, Olga Andrews
1974   Katie Cunneen, Mary Jane Otness
1975   Elaine Brockman, Helen Abbott
1976   Lois Mason, Virginia Brink
1977   Mary Ruth Blustein, Susan Urbaniak
1978   Beryl Hiatt, Carlyn Steiner
1979   Verna Burns, Irene Day
1980   Carol Hutchinson, Jean Anderson
1981   Jessie Wesselius, Sharon Davidson

MIXED PAIRS
1968   Willow Nepple, Bert Naness
1969   Dennis Busch, Betty Gilman
1970   Mrs. Richard Douglas, Jim Costello
1971   Barbara Bedayan, Viesturs Seglins
1972   George Steiner, Maxine Blumenthal *(tied with)*
Merna Jackson, Bill Hagen
1973   Stephen Bruno, Lynn Blumenthal
1974   Ralph Purves, Elizabeth Lee
1975   Edward West, Mamie Price
1976   Betty Michno, Peter Herold
1977   George Steiner, Maxine Blumenthal
1980   Henry Lortz, Doris Bailey

INDIVIDUAL
1968   James Banks
1974   Kay Powers
1975   Irene Hatherly

1976   Fran Ogino
1977   Mrs. W. Gerrard

MEN'S SWISS TEAMS
1976   Mark Neils, Mark Bailey,
Bob Burton, Tom Hammond
1977   Paul McGough, Bob Hendershott, Fred Hagen,
Bill Hagen, Mike Perrault *(tied with)*
John Anderson, Leslie Tsou, Marc Zwerling,
Mike Rhatjen, Jean Ouimet, Richard DuFour
1979   Chris Laskowski, Henry Lortz,
Bill Hagen, Dave Setterholm *(tied with)*
John Jones, Paul Lewis,
Marc Jacobus, Harold Antonson.

WOMEN'S SWISS TEAMS
1976   Barbara Bedayan, Loretta Arnold,
Glad Currie, Willow Nepple
1977   Gaye Boguch, Donna Christensen,
Ethel Birnbach, Sharon Lee Bruneau
1979   Verna Burns, Irene Day,
Mary Thompson, V. M. Schaefer

MASTER SWISS TEAMS
Flight A:
1978   Carol Ure, Janet Daling, Steve Mansfield,
Neil Ballard, Jude Ballard

DISTRICT 20   (Oregon, northern California, northern Nevada, Guam, Wake, Hawaii, portion of western Idaho)

DISTRICT 20

KNOCKOUT TEAMS
1972   Richard Henderson, Leslie Tsou,
John Grantham, Roger Bates
1973   Bob Crossley, Dave Crossley, Richard Henderson,
Vern Pang, John Padget, Ken Gorfkle
1974   Michael Gurwitz, Bob Crossley, Kay Schulle,
John Schermer, Mike Lawrence
1975   Hermine Baron, Mike Shuman, Ron LaCour,
Randy Howard, Steve Cohen
1976   Gaylor Kasle, Meyer Schleifer, Shirley Boice,
Garey Hayden, John Mohan
1977   Ron Andersen, Clarence Goppert, John Schermer,
Hugh MacLean, Neil Chambers
1979   Gord McOrmond, Laurence Betts, Rhonda Betts,
Dan Jacob, Oris Mowry, John Lusky
1980   Barry Crane, Kerri Shuman, Marc Jacobus,
Ron Andersen, Mike Smolen
1981   Malcolm Brachman, Minda Brachman, Paul Soloway,
Ron Andersen, Eddie Wold

OPEN TEAMS
1970   Dean Cook, Lee Baumann,
Casey Million, Ruth Million
1972   Roger Bates, Garey Hayden,
Peter Rank, John Grantham
1973   Mary Jane Farell, Elsa Ganz,
Leslie Tsou, Kirk Blackerby
1974   William Whitesel, Chris Earl,
Ron LaCour, Pat O'Brien *(tied with)*
Steve Smolen, Peter Rank,
Nick Moss, Everett Fukushima
1975   Leslie Tsou, Alan Bell, Chip Cleveland,
John Cleveland, Kirk Blackerby, Jim Hayashi
1976   Ron LaCour, Clarence Goppert, Dick Schively,
Bruce Ferguson, Dale Mehaffey
1977   Marcia Masterson, Bob Kerr,
Ann Kluewer, Ted Alexander
1978   Dick Jones, Joe Farley,
Leslie Tsou, Marc Zwerling
1979   Miles Adkins, Patsy Esfeld,
Julie Linde, Susan Urbaniak *(tied with)*
Mike Passell, Bruce Ferguson, John Mohan,
Clarence Goppert, Paul Soloway *(and)*
Pam Stratton, Eleanor Rice,
Paul Crariotto, James Rice
1980   Barry Crane, Marc Jacobus,
Kerri Shuman, Ron Andersen
1981   Max Hardy, Linda Peterson, John Anderson,
Ross Rainwater, George Pisk *(tied with)*
Jan Janitschke, Nadene Deutsch,
Bruce Ferguson, Brenda Blumenthal
Flight A:
1979   Mike Passell, Clarence Goppert, Paul Soloway,
John Mohan, Fred Hamilton
1980   Jim Barrow, Roger Jourdan,
Michael Schreiber, Jan Janitschke
1981   Jack Thoresen, Bill Holt,

Betty Dougherty, Patty Below

INDIVIDUAL
1976 Pete Ruganis
1977 Ardis Hunt

MASTER PAIRS
1972 Barry Crane, Dr. John Fisher
1973 Oris Mowry, Robert Norberg *(tied with)*
     Kirk Blackerby, Leslie Tsou
1974 Georgiana Gates, Leslie West
1975 Ron LaCour, Ron Feldman
1977 George Steiner, Carolyn Rottsolk *(tied with)*
     Cam Trenor, Steve Mansfield
1978 Barry Crane, Kerri Shuman
1979 Bruce Ferguson, Brenda Keller
1980 John Anderson, Mike McFaddin
1981 Veronica McMurdie, Cameron Cotton
Flight A:
1976 Richard Spitalnick, Roger Olson

OPEN PAIRS
1970 Hermine Baron, Richard Henderson
1972 Mary Jane Farell, Elsa Ganz
1973 John Rogers, Marty Rogers
1974 Pat O'Brien, Stephen Dow
1975 Mike Shuman, Hermine Baron
1976 Lilyan Eisenstein, Kerri Shuman
1977 Carl Hanson, John Kamb
1978 Mort Saltzman, Warren Nelson
1979 Perry Van Hook, Ross Rainwater
1980 Lee Nee, Paul Morgan
1981 Paul Soloway, Minda Brachman
Flight A:
1978 Paul Maier, Mike Smolen
1979 Fred Hamilton, Hermine Baron
1980 Lee Nee, Paul Morgan
1981 Bill Harker, Steve Clark

MEN'S PAIRS
1970 Stephen Clarke, Ray MacWilliamson
1976 Mike Passell, Robert Eisenstein
1977 Paul Soloway, Leslie Tsou
1978 Dick Jones, George Mattos
1979 Tony Glynne, John Lusky *(tied with)*
     Clarence Goppert, Mike Passell
1980 Barry Crane, Ron Andersen
1981 Ross Rainwater, George Pisk

WOMEN'S PAIRS
1970 Mrs. E. Wilson, Dale Parker
1976 Mary Jane Laylor, Marian Lewis
1977 Ann Kluewer, Marcia Masterson
1978 Jean Michell, Pat Leary
1979 Mary Tungate, June Duhaime
1980 Mabel Urano, Nadine Berwanger
1981 Lucille Patterson, Veronica McMurdie

MASTER SWISS TEAMS
1977 Clarence Goppert, Neil Chambers, Troy Horton,
     Jim Donaldson, John Schermer
1978 Max Hardy, Ethelyn Black,
     Marc Jacobus, Mark Feldman *(tied with)*
     Barry Crane, Kerri Shuman,
     Mike Smolen, Paul Maier *(and)*
     Joe Farley, Dick Jones,
     Leslie Tsou, Marc Zwerling

WOMEN'S TEAMS
1976 Ann Jacobson, Rhonda Foster,
     Connie Delisle, Gayle Boguch

MEN'S TEAMS
1976 David Starratt, Robert Hosford,
     Jack Buck, Lawrence Jolma

HAWAII

KNOCKOUT TEAMS
1970 Neil Ballard, Frank Cady,
     Fred Hagen, Don Glad
1976 Everett Fukushima, Godfrey Chang, Vern Pang,
     Steve Lent, Alfred Levy, Francis Wong
1977 Diane LaFleur, John Mohan, Kay Schulle-Mohan,
     Roger Bates, Mike Passell
1978 Jack Schwencke, Neil Chambers,
     John Schermer, Garey Hayden
1979 Max Hardy, Mike Shuman, John Mohan,
     Kay Schulle-Mohan, Ethelyn Black
1980 Ron Andersen, Bunny Haas, Max Hardy,
     Don Nemiro, Paul Lewis
1981 Mel Skolnik, Ron Smith,
     Mark Lair, Gaylor Kasle

OPEN TEAMS
1952 Marj Harvey, Clarence Garvey,
     Frances von Elsner, Don von Elsner
1953 Mrs. Walter Edwards, Walter Edwards
     Marian Hoffman, Madeline Anderson
1955 Don Oakie, Charles Davidson,
     Mrs. R.D. Hutchinson, R.D. Hutchinson
1956 Val Anastasopulos, Harry Fishel,
     Fitz Donnell, Marian Wildy
1957 Dr. Erwin Cheim, Ton Seek Pai,
     Harry Fishel, Fitz Donnell
1958 Betty Coombs, Fitz Donnell,
     Ton Seek Pai, Harry Fishel
1959 Dr. Erwin Cheim, Fitz Donnell,
     Harry Fishel, Ton Seek Pai
1960 Don Oakie, Clara Watanabe,
     Val Anastasopulos, Gerald Pool
1961 Mark Hodges, Rose Groves,
     Violet Agran, Nat Agran
1962 Frances Wong, Warren Ishii,
     Walter Kau, Wilfred Motokane *(tied with)*
     Burton Marliave, Ted Hervey,
     Bedson Juett, Armin Hurlimann
1963 Ivan Erdos, Ton Seek Pai,
     Howard Settle, Dr. E. Won Sik You
1964 Meyer Schleifer, Jules Farell, Mary Jane Farell,
     Barry Crane, Mabel Mahoney
1965 Henry Baer, Oswald Jacoby,
     Jim Jacoby, Albert Weiss
1966 Jules Farell, Mary Jane Farell, Peter Rank,
     Don Oakie, Mabel Mahoney
1968 Lee Hofacre, Peggy Drury, Charles MacCracken,
     Lt. Col. Walter Escue, Jerry Weitzner
1969 Peter Rank, Dr. John Fisher, Mabel Mahoney,
     Mary Jane Farell, Charles MacCracken
1971 Col. John Kiernan, Shirley Kiernan,
     Michael O'Bradovitch, Irving Berns
1972 Barry Crane, Dr. John Fisher, Mary Jane Farell,
     Jules Farell, Mabel Mahoney, Norman Anderson
1973 Pat Solomons, Jerry Weitzner,
     Ronald Promboin, Lee Hofacre
1974 Mary Louise Carlos, Gaylor Kasle, Garey Hayden,
     Roger Bates, Nels Erickson
1975 Mary Louise Carlos, Gaylor Kasle, Garey Hayden,
     Roger Bates, Nels Erickson
1976 Richard Chapman, Gerri O'Leary,
     Marg Neate, Mary Sheridan *(tied with)*
     Bruce Ferguson, Clarence Goppert, Mark Lair,
     Kerri Shuman, Richard Fleischman *(and)*
     John Mohan, Diane LaFleur, Kay Schulle,
     Michael Shuman, Roger Bates *(and)*
     Nick Moss, Peter Pender,
     Peter Rank, Jim Hooker
1977 Charles Finch, Fara Finch,
     Leslie Tsou, Garey Hayden
1978 Jack Schwencke, Neil Chambers,
     John Schermer, Garey Hayden
1979 Betty Ann Kennedy, Jack Kennedy, John Fisher,
     Jim Jacoby, Jim Hooker, Jim Chew
1980 Barton King, Marion King,
     Elina Weil, Frank Weil *(tied with)*
     Eunice Towne, Margaret Cooling,
     Sandra Dee Martin, Ton Seek Pai
1981 John Sutherlin, Vern Pang, Leslie Tsou
     Craig Janitschke, Jim Zimmerman

MIXED PAIRS
1952 Val Anastasopulos, Harry Fishel
1953 Mrs. Ben Johnson, Ben Johnson
1955 Adm. Joseph Herlihy, Mary Herlihy
1956 H.J. White, Harry Fishel
1957 Val Anastasopulos, Marion Wildy
1958 Marg Harvey, Herb Yokoyama
1959 Ivan Erdos, Addie Lee You
1960 Charles Goren, Clara Watanabe
1961 Sarah Amster, Gerald Pool
1962 Beverly Char, Charles Goren
1963 Addie Lee You, Ivan Erdos
1964 Addie Lee You, Ivan Erdos
1965 James Up de Graff, Lynn Dashiell *(tied with)*
     Mary Jane Farell, Jules Farell
1966 Hermine Baron, Peter Rank
1968 Sally Cady, Frank Cady
1969 Marian Stone, Marvin Stone
1970 Warren Ishii, Clara Watanabe
1971 Sandy Zakin, L. James Phillips
1972 Clara Watanabe, Godfrey Chang
1973 Phyllis Smith, James Zimmerman
1974 Betty Levan, John Padget
1976 Ann Jacobson, Mike Passell
1977 Kay Schulle-Mohan, Jeff Meckstroth
1978 Sally Trask, Marc Zwerling

1979 Roger Bates, Diane LeFleur
1980 Warren Ishii, Maizie Ho
1981 Mary Senti, Max Hardy

INDIVIDUAL
1953 Kurt Geisler
1976 Mrs. Charles Hanson
1977 Jack Koster
1978 Joyce McCarthy
1979 K. T. Pregitzer
1980 Mrs. S. Zucker
1981 J. L. Muchemore

UNMIXED PAIRS
1975 George Lazarnick, Roger Bates

OPEN PAIRS
1952 F. Kirwin, Dr. Erwin Cheim
1953 Val Anastasopulos, Harry Fishel
1955 Betty Coombs, Julian Bomash
1956 Elizabeth Nicholson, Sam Ingraham, Jr.
1957 H. Allen Graham, Al Stacy
1958 Don Oakie, Clara Watanabe
1959 Addie Lee You, Ivan Erdos
1960 Mrs. E. F. Hobart, Lt. Col. Manus Murtha
1961 Jules Farell, Mary Jane Farell
1962 Robert Kimura, Akito Iwahara
1963 Hermine Baron, Barry Crane
1964 Helen Moore, Morris Portugal
1965 Mrs. Steve Schloss, Steve Schloss
1966 Gaylor Kasle, Lucia Lanning
1968 Peter Rank, Jules Farell
1969 Hermine Baron, Paul Soloway
1970 Howard Settle, Don Von Elsner *(tied with)*
     Barry Crane, Peter Rank
1971 Barry Crane, Peter Rank
1972 Barry Crane, Dr. John Fisher
1973 Kerri Shuman, Dr. John Fisher
1974 Betty Levan, Norman Anderson
1975 Jerry Weitzner, Charlton Buckley
1976 Robert Lyski, Susan Lyski
1977 Barry Crane, Kerri Shuman
1978 Jen-Hu Chang, Walter Kau
Flight A:
1979 Sharon Stange, Sandy Zakin
1980 Margaret Eiser, Kerri Shuman
1981 Barry Crane, Craig Janitschke

MASTER PAIRS
1952 J. M. Mardick, Carl Powell
1953 Ben Johnson, John Kunkel
1955 Casey Million, Ruth Million
1956 Grace Meier, Don Oakie
1957 Bruce Howell, Cliff Johnson
1958 D. E. Davis, Dr. J. N. Konde
1959 Sally Heinz, George Gooden
1960 Jen Hu Chang, Alan Sakuma
1961 Jen Hu Chang, W. Gerald Pool
1962 Lloyd Graham, Guy Ginn
1963 Dr. E. Won Sik You, Ivan Erdos
1964 Mabel Mahoney, Meyer Schleifer
1965 Dr. E. Won Sik You, Ivan Erdos
1966 Hermine Baron, Kelsey Petterson
1968 Ton Seek Pai, Howard Settle
1969 Dr. John Fisher, Peter Rank
1970 Mary Jane Farell, Mabel Mahoney
1971 Marilyn Johnson, Mary Louise Carlos
1972 Mrs. Eugene Low, Dr. Eugene Low
1973 John Sutherlin, Godfrey Chang
1974 Gertrude Ebesu, Donald Coleman
1975 Hideko Kanda, Ruby Choy
1976 Richard Fleischman, Ton Seek Pai
1977 Barry Crane, Kerri Shuman
1978 Mary Jane Farell, Betty Levan
1979 Betty Ann Kennedy, Dr. John Fisher
1980 Kerri Shuman, Mike Smolen
1981 John Sutherlin, Godfrey Chang

MEN'S PAIRS
1952 Wilford Dumas, J. D. Clarke
1953 Ben Johnson, John Kunkel
1955 R.D. Hutchinson, Don Oakie
1956 Ton Seek Pai, Harry Fishel
1957 George Gooden, Harry Fishel
1958 Robert Beausoleil, Gaetano Andreozzi
1959 Walter Stein, L. H. Canfield
1960 George Gooden, Harry Fishel
1961 Fitz Donnell, Harry Fishel
1962 Howard Settle, Don von Elsner
1963 Lorin Cox, Martin Kivel
1964 Meyer Schleifer, Max Hodder
1965 Jules Farell, Peter Rank
1966 Kelsey Petterson, Gerald Bare
1968 Fitz Donnell, Don Von Elsner *(tied with)*

Eilif Anderson, Maurice Hole
1969 Alfred Levy, Godfrey Chang
1970 Paul Soloway, Irving Berns
1971 Richard Odlin, Edward Wright
1972 Norman Levi, H. Friesen
1973 Nels Erickson, Ronald Promboin
1974 John Grantham, Norman Anderson
1976 Joe Conforte, Michael Jones
1977 Barry Crane, Mike Passell
1978 Paul Lewis, Max Hardy
1979 Robert Hamman, Jack Kennedy
1980 Kyle Larsen, Ron Von der Porten
1981 Thomas Ryan, S. C. Kan

WOMEN'S PAIRS
1952 F. Kirwin, Jackie Wilcox
1953 Juanita Strich, Viva Lewis
1955 A. Pratt, K. Abbott
1956 H. J. White, M. L. Cleaton
1957 Bert Epstein, Betty Coombs
1958 Clair Morgan, A.R. Falb
1959 Val Anastasopulos, Clara Watanabe
1960 Barbara Ingham, Joan White
1961 Mary Jane Farell, Mabel Mahoney
1962 Mary Bonner, Edna Oakley
1963 Katherine Mullins, Mary Ann Facer
1964 Mrs. Edwin Clark, Louise Durham
1965 Mary Jane Farell, Mabel Mahoney
1966 Julie Cahill, Margaret Cooling
1968 Madlyn Fleming, Martha Kroney
1969 Clara Watanabe, Val Anastasopulos
1970 Patricia Wagner, Peggy Sutherlin
1971 Janet Schroeder, Aline Greenberg
1972 Clara Watanabe, Beverly Char
1973 Mrs. Kenneth Mills, Mrs. Ralph Elliott
1974 Pat Solomons, Clara Watanabe
1976 Julie Cahill, Margaret Cooling
1977 Clara Watanabe, Pat Solomons
1978 Clara Watanabe, Pat Solomons
1979 Diane LaFleur, Kerri Shuman
1980 Val Anastasopulos, Peggy Sutherlin
1981 Vivienne Cooke, Betty Midkiff

HICKAM A.F.B. PAIRS
1958 Mrs. George S. Gooden, George S. Gooden

WESTERN CONFERENCE PAIRS
1960 Mrs. Oron Davis, Mrs. A. D. Persson

WOMEN'S SWISS TEAMS
1975 Edith Neff, Betty Lou Ritch,
     Judy Kiely, Linda Mitchell
1977 Betty Levan, Evelyn Butler,
     Jean Theus, Mary Jane Farell
1978 Mace Greene, Jane Bankhardt,
     Elsie Morris, Lee Hopson
1979 Ethelyn Black, Kerri Shuman, Kay Schulle-Mohan,
     Renee Friedman, Phyllis Robbins
1980 Juanita Skelton, Linda Polisner,
     Barbara Sue Seal, Brenda Keller *(tied with)*
     Shirley Edelson, Jamie Steen,
     Betty Levan, Evelyn Butler
1981 Carole Pajari, Ruth Petrowski, Penny Speese
     Judy Rosen, Hana Cochrane *(tied with)*
     Mickey Heath Latimer, Patricia Chandler,
     Veronica Carroll, Martie von Elsner

MEN'S SWISS TEAMS
1975 W. Gerald Pool, Jean Hu Chang,
     Marshall Goldman, Milton Moss
1977 Max Hardy, Jeff Meckstroth,
     Michael Schreiber, Leslie Tsou *(tied with)*
     Paul Ivaska, Chris Larsen,
     Ken Monzingo, J. Bender Moore
1978 Jack Schwencke, Neil Chambers,
     John Schermer, Garey Hayden
1979 Clarence Goppert, Mark Lair, Gaylor Kasle,
     Eddie Wold, Bruce Ferguson *(tied with)*
     Milton Stern, Fred Hamilton,
     Paul Lewis, Marc Jacobus
1981 Mel Skolnik, Mark Lair,
     Gaylor Kasle, Ron Smith

MID-WINTER HOLIDAY

KNOCKOUT TEAMS
1970 Augie Hunte, Edward Nagy,
     Jerry Gaer, Margaret Gaer
1971 Neal Chambers, Ken Gorfkle,
     Allan Graves, Dale Forster
1972 Jan Janitschke, Craig Janitschke,
     Jim Miller, Mike Kaplan
1973 Mike Passell, Morris Portugal, Helen Portugal,
     Hermine Baron, Mark Lair, Dave Priest

1974 Kerri Shuman, Mike Shuman, Erik Paulsen,
      Bob Crossley, Dave Crossley
1975 Kenn Bradley, Kelsey Petterson, Proctor Hawkins,
      Clarence (Cap) Crossley, David Ashley, Dave Crossley
1976 Leslie West, Ernie Hirsch,
      Troy Horton, William Whitesel
1977 Richard Spitalnick, Bill Rudman, Steve Price,
      Mark Jones, Doug Dang
1978 Hermine Baron, Stelios Touchtidis,
      Pamela Wittes, Jon Wittes
1979 Clarence Goppert, Brenda Keller, Mark Lair,
      Bruce Ferguson, Mike Passell
1980 Mel Skolnik, Elisabeth Brenhouse, Ron Andersen,
      Eric Rodwell, Jeff Meckstroth
1981 Mel Skolnik, Ron Andersen, Ron Smith,
      Robert Levin, Paul Soloway

OPEN TEAMS
1970 Vic Mastron, Morris Portugal,
      Helen Portugal, Norman Anderson
1971 Jim Dunlap, Hank Gagnon, Tom Weeg,
      Jack Marsh, Dorothy Bussey
1972 Alex Tschekaloff, John Padget,
      John Mohan, Bob Henderson
1973 Hugh Ross, Min Ross,
      Shirley Nedham, Joe Nedham
1974 Barney O'Malia, Marc Jacobus,
      Gaylor Kasle, Paul Orlett
1975 Mike Wilson, John Anthony, Dale Mehaffey,
      Ken Scholes, Peter Herold
1976 Joe Conforte, Norman Anderson, Michael Jones,
      Ron LaCour, Jim Linhart, Bernie Chazen
1977 Norm Featherston, Jeannette Featherston,
      Terry Randles, Janice Randles
1978 Rodger Harbin, Dale Gilbert,
      Judy Landau, Sam Wilson
1979 Max Hardy, Ethelyn Black, Michael Schreiber,
      Ron Von der Porten, Bob Hamman
1980 Jim Zimmerman, Ralph Katz,
      John Sutherlin, Gerald Caravelli
1981 Stephen Kanzee, Quentin Wilmot,
      Nick Wiebe, Mark Perlmutter *(Non-Smoking)*
      Vic Chernoff, Bob Kehoe,
      David Siebert, Claude Vogel *(Smoking)*
Flight A:
1979 Chris Larsen, Kay Larsen,
      Gaye Herrington, Ken Monzingo *(tied with)*
      Gerald Bare, Dorothy Bare, David Ashley,
      Martha Beecher, Mike McMahan
1980 Max Hardy, Bruce Fink,
      Ross Rainwater, Bill Parks
1981 D. Benjamin, Alan LeBendig, Chris Compton,
      Jim Barrow, Dennis Clerkin *(tied with)*
      Marty Miller, Faye Parsons, Guy Green,
      Rich Parsons, Toby Green

MEN'S PAIRS
1968 Jerry Lebbert, Sol Rubin
1969 Paul Soloway, Jon Wittes
1970 Robin Booth, David Sweet
1971 William Whitesel, Michael Philippas *(tied with)*
      Joel Martineau, Paul Hagen
1976 Richard Spitalnick, Rodger Harbin
1977 Michael Schreiber, Jeff Meckstroth
1978 Harvey Brody, Marc Zwerling
1979 Robert Radwin, David Pelka
1980 Syd Levey, Jim Tritt
1981 George Steiner, Roger Urbaniak *(Non-Smoking)*
      Alan Bell, David Ashley *(Smoking)*

WOMEN'S PAIRS
1968 Mrs. J. B. York, Miniko Reiter
1969 Betty Selby, Eloise Siepler
1970 Hermine Baron, Mrs. Herb Swisher
1971 Mrs. B. Cotton, Bunny Lewis
1976 Bunny Haas, Charlotte Hahn
1977 Donella Johnson, Donna Christensen
1978 Bobbie Shipley, Jane Kitchel
1979 Helen Gerard, Alice Gerard
1980 Beverly Rosenberg, Ann Kluewer
1981 Carolyn Seuser, Loretta Bromberg *(tied with)*
      Marjorie Blunt, Connie Ham, *(Non-Smoking)*
      Mary Walker, Mrs. F. S. Bills, *(Smoking)*

OPEN PAIRS
1968 Dave Crossley, Bob Crossley
1969 Jon Wittes, Paul Ivaska
1970 Malcolm Brachman, Paul Soloway
1972 Warren Cederborg, Jules Farell
1973 Peter Rank, Peter Pender
1974 Mark Blumenthal, Garey Hayden
1976 Ron LaCour, David Ashley
1977 Michael Schreiber, Jeff Meckstroth

1978 Jeff Polisner, Bernie Bergovoy
1979 John Anderson, Jon Brissman
1980 Kevin Castner, William Doroshow *(A-D)*
      Byron Economidy, Ann Economidy *(A only)*
1981 Rosalind Quiggle, Louis Quiggle, *(A-D Non-Smoking)*
      Matthew Franklin, Marc Franklin *(A-D Smoking)*
      Hank Mullaney, Ethel Birnbach *(A only Non-Smoking)*
      Duane Smith, Ann Smith *(A only Smoking)*
Flight A:
1975 Marc Zwerling, Steve Larson
1977 Mary Jane Orock, Lorene Mitchell
1978 Ron Smith, Mike Smolen
1979 O. A. Godefroy, Roger Urbaniak
1980 George Toone, Steve Price
1981 Bruce Cutherbertson, Elaine Huston, *(Non-Smoking)*
      Barry Crane, Craig Janitschke, *(Smoking)*

MASTER PAIRS
1968 Sam Haber, Martin Miller
1969 Grant Baze, Kirk Jensen
1970 Howard Raymond, James Chrysler
1971 Jim Thomas, Harold Dean Ellis
1972 Erik Paulsen, Hugh Ross
1973 Mark Lair, Mike Passell
1974 Sachi Miki, Frank Warzek
1977 Dave Berkowitz, Gerald Caravelli
1978 Paul Lewis, Ron Smith
1979 Karl Keller, Eddie Wold
1980 Tony Glynne, Chris Larsen *(tied with)*
      Robert Radwin, Dave Pelka
1981 Robert Hamman, Jeff Polisner *(Non-Smoking)*
      Barry Crane, Craig Janitschke *(Smoking)*
Flight A:
1975 Edward Nagy, Harvey Brody
1976 Marc Franklin, Matt Franklin

MEN'S TEAMS
1974 Stephen Skinner, Ron LaCour,
      Marc Zwerling, Ron Smith
1976 John Moffat, Dave Westfall, Dave Whitcher,
      Tod Moses, Al Hollander, William Doroshow

WOMEN'S TEAMS
1974 Georgiana Gates, Lynne Rogers,
      Audrey Rennels, Mary Bright
1976 Shirley Nedham, Jean Michell,
      Linda Taggart, Dianne Barton

MIXED PAIRS
1976 Gene Simpson, Carreen Simpson

INDIVIDUAL
1976 James Holland

MASTER SWISS TEAMS
1977 Marc Franklin, Matt Franklin,
      Edgar Simons, Peter Friedland
1978 Paula Givan, Robert Martin,
      Mary Martin, Walter Miller

OREGON TRAIL

KNOCKOUT TEAMS
1967 Doug Drury, Peggy Drury, John Moran,
      Hermine Baron, Meyer Schleifer
1968 Max Manchester, Dale Forster, Joe Farley,
      William Silver, Dick Jones, Gaylor Kasle
1969 Richard Kaye, Dick Walsh, Rhoda Walsh,
      Paul Ivaska, Leslie West
1970 Leslie Tsou, George Parker, Steve Sidell,
      Marty Miller, Kirk Blackerby
1971 Allan Graves, Bill Whitesel, Haskell Fuller,
      Harold Antonson, Michael Philippas
1972 Mary Blustein, Maurice Blustein, Roger Urbaniak,
      Susan Urbaniak, Joe Jabon
1973 John Ashton, Bill Whitesel, Dennis Metcalf,
      Wally Rossman, Adrian Hicks, Dick Jones
1974 Lawrence Jolma, Marjorie Jolma, Gary Stark,
      Barbara Whitesel, Betty Rossmann, Marietta Larson
1975 Leslie Tsou, Dale Forster, Barry White,
      Chris Earl, John Cleveland, Alan Bell
1976 Troy Horton, Dennis Metcalf, Bob Norberg,
      John Ashton, Richard Cave
1977 Bill Whitesel, Ross Rainwater, Craig Huston,
      Chris Earl, Leslie Tsou, Alan Bell
1978 Leslie Tsou, Ross Rainwater, Marc Zwerling,
      Craig Huston, Ron Feldman, Alan Bell
1979 Clarence Goppert, Mark Lair, Mike Passell,
      Paul Soloway, Ron Andersen, Marc Jacobus
1980 Ross Rainwater, Craig Huston, Hal Montgomery,
      Peter Rapaport, Frank Burke
1981 Tony Orlandini, Joel Martineau,
      Allan Graves, Dick Yarington

OPEN TEAMS
1958 Lily Stewart, Robert Hopkins,

Lois Oke, Willow Nepple
1960   Malvine Klausner, Meyer Schleifer, Milton Agay,
      David Harkleroad, Maynard Orme
1961   Don Krauss, Gerald Bare,
      Harold Guiver, Richard Walsh
1962   Mary Jane Farell, Alice Cohn,
      Peter Rank, Maynard Orme
1963   Don Lefebvre, Joe Jabon,
      Jack Ehrlenbach, Courtland Rush
1965   Marilyn Johnson, Peter Rank,
      Barry Crane, Robert Adams
1966   Joe Jabon, Robert Hendershott,
      Courtland Rush, G. Gard Hays
1967   William Silver, Michael Lawrence, Alan Oaks
      Dick Jones, Charles MacCracken
1968   Barry Crane, Joe Jabon, Peggy Drury,
      Charles MacCracken, Marilyn Johnson
1969   John Anderson, Dale Forster,
      Jeff Taylor, Joe Farley
1970   Harold Antonson, Haskell Fuller, Bill Whitesel,
      Neil Chambers, Dale Mehaffey
1971   George Slemmons, George Steiner,
      Darryl Pedersen, Emery Selymes
1972   Chip Cleveland, John Cleveland, Kathryn Gisler,
      Barry White, Chris Earl
1973   Barney O'Malia, Nick Moss, Pat O'Brien
      Steve Smolen, Morris Portugal
1974   Jim Andrews, Jerry Andrews,
      Mary Alice Hunt, Duane Meador
1975   Bruce Ferguson, Neil Chambers,
      Dale Mehaffey, Allan Graves
1976   Troy Horton, John Ashton, Bob Norberg,
      Dennis Metcalf, Richard Cave
1977   Rex Barber, Mrs. Rex Barber,
      Les Robbins, Ruth Robbins
1978   Morris Portugal, Helen Heard,
      Robert Hendershott, Fred Hagen
1979   Duane Meador, Harry E. Mason,
      Mary Alice Hunt, Barbara Thatcher *(tied with)*
      Clarence Goppert, Mark Lair, Ron Andersen
      Paul Soloway, Mike Passell
1980   Bob Norberg, Dennis Metcalf,
      Randy Pickett, Troy Horton
1981   John Anderson, Gaye Boguch, Dennis Sorenson,
      Stan Sather, Marc Zwerling, Hank Mullaney
Flight A:
1980   Robert Norberg, Roger McNay,
      Dennis Metcalf, Tony Glynne
1981   Mel Skolnik, Ron Andersen,
      Paul Soloway, Tony Glynne *(tied with)*
      Joanne Greene, Marc Jacobus, Eddie Wold,
      Bob Crossley, Paul Lewis *(and)*
      Troy Horton, Oris Mowry,
      John Lusky, Randy Pickett

MEN'S TEAMS

1971   Emery Selymes, George Steiner,
      George Slemmons, Darryl Pedersen
1975   Donald Morey, Ken Bruneau, Jim Thielen,
      Ben Winkelman, Alan Kelly
1976   Dean Ellis, Stephen Hosch,
      Hal Montgomery, Jim Thomas *(tied with)*
      Chris Cunneen, Herbert Park,
      Tony Glynne, Roger McNay *(and)*
      Ed Ulman, Dave Westfall,
      Marvin Rauch, Jim Green
1977   Frank Kimball, Fred Hamilton, Mike Shuman,
      Conrad Evans, Robert Radwin

WOMEN'S TEAMS

1971   Willow Nepple, Judith Sharp,
      Patty Prahl, Elaine Brockman
1975   Shirley Edelson, Jude Ballard, Carol Ure,
      Mary Jane Farell, Lil Greenberg
1976   Dorothy Reddaway, Gayle Cameron,
      Lynn Arms, Freda Whitesel
1977   Katie Cunneen, Betty Rossman,
      Marie Lampi, Marjorie Jolma

MASTER PAIRS

1958   Joffre Kiamy, Bruce Isaacs
1960   Eugene Schwartz, Courtland Rush
1961   Eugene Schwartz, Courtland Rush
1962   Jim Littrell, Joe Jabon
1963   Jude Ballard, Neil Ballard
1965   Dr. Colin Cruikshank, Ronald Tracy
1966   Mrs. Russell Diehl, Mrs. R. W. Carrico
1967   Garry Stark, Jacqueline Stark
1968   Miles Adkins, G. Gard Hays
1969   Henry Craig, Betty Rossman
1970   Robert Haller, Gert Haller
1971   Jeff Taylor, Richard DuFour
1972   Paul Burns, Rex Mudd

1973   David Perkins, Bert Naness
1974   Ron LaCour, Pat O'Brien
1975   Leslie Tsou, John Cleveland
1977   Joe Jabon, Henry Lortz *(tied with)*
      Tony Glynne, Roger McNay
1978   Bruce Ferguson, Jim Donaldson
1979   John Moffat, Dave Westfall
1980   Roger Jourdan, Jim Barrow
1981   Paul Soloway, Ken MacNeal
Flight A:
1976   Troy Horton, Bob Norberg

MASTER MEN'S PAIRS

1971   Fred Squire, John Squire

MASTER WOMEN'S PAIRS

1971   Jude Ballard, Carol Baird

OPEN PAIRS

1958   Ben Lapidus, Norman Turnbull
1960   Barry Crane, Peter Rank
1961   Barry Crane, Peter Rank
1962   Maynard Orme, J. Robert Patterson
1963   Elsa Ganz, Donald Oakie
1964   Peter Rank, Barry Crane
1966   Peter Lit, Michael Lawrence
1967   Ken Christiansen, Dave Setterbolm
1968   Arthur Wright, C. G. Robson
1969   Betty Willing, Leslie Tsou
1970   Barry Crane, Peter Rank
1971   Bob Hitchens, Ron Tracy
1972   Steve Sidell, Dick Lewis
1973   David Gold, R. C. MacDuff
1974   Joe Jabon, Susan Urbaniak
1975   Barney O'Malia, Gaylor Kasle
1976   Gaylor Kasle, Grant Baze
1977   Cam Trenor, Steve Mansfield
1978   Ross Rainwater, Neil Chambers
1979   Jim Green, John Remington
Flight A:
1978   Clarence Goppert, Mark Lair
1979   Marc Jacobus, Brenda Blumenthal
1980   Ron Feldman, Dave Tuell
1981   Craig Huston, Dennis Metcalf
Class A Only:
1980   Florence Parker, Gaylor Kasle
1981   Ron Andersen, Mel Skolnik
Classes A–D:
1980   Joe Diven, Bunny Lewis
1981   M. Don Nudelman, Sharon Colson

MEN'S PAIRS

1958   Adrian Hicks, Robert Hendershott
1960   Alex Allison, Jack Ehrlenbach
1961   Milton Agay, Mike Shuman
1962   Lewis Fox, Forrest Beirne
1963   Ivan Erdos, Joe Brown
1965   Doug Oram, Don Kennard
1966   Dudley Brown, Loren Hawkins *(tied with)*
      John Donnelly, George Gruger
1967   Gaylor Kasle, George Morton
1968   Barry Crane, G. Gard Hays
1969   Walt Schmitz, Jerry McVay
1970   Michael Philippas, Jeff Taylor *(tied with)*
      John Cleveland, Barry White
1971   Alex McBeth, Frank King
1972   Charlie Dorn, Kirk Blackerby
1973   John Strauch, Buddy Crapko
1974   Bob Berger, Hadi Allahverdian
1975   Terry Gould, Hal Montgomery
1976   Grant Baze, Bernie Chazen
1977   Paul Soloway, Mike Passell
1978   George Steiner, Darryl Pedersen
1979   Eugene Fomin, Stephen Plunkett
1980   Roger Bates, Gaylor Kasle
1981   Ken MacNeal, Paul Soloway

WOMEN'S PAIRS

1958   Lucille Patterson, Lucille Wheeler
1960   Mrs. Harry Herron, Mrs. Charles Slick
1961   Marjorie Jolma, Margaret Robson
1962   Lily Stewart, Margaret Kahmann *(tied with)*
      Mrs. Paul Hutchinson, Mrs. Frank Aydelotte
1963   Florence Van Winkle, Maybelle Young
1965   Mrs. J. M. Willis, Mrs. J. M. Weaver
1966   Mrs. Frank Baker, Cathy Jones
1967   Helen Eckersley, Maybelle Young
1968   Ruth Vaughn, Mrs. Elmer Berg
1969   Marybelle Rash, Eunice Ritchie
1970   Florence Van Winkle, Dorothy Cowger
1971   Mary Jane Farell, Elsa Ganz
1972   Marietta Larson, Dee Berry
1973   Elaine Brockman, Patty Prahl
1974   Marjorie Jolma, Ethel Birnbach
1975   Kathy Canoy, Joan Green *(tied with)*

Roberta Hicks, Nancie Jefferis
1976 Elaine Brockman, Patty Prahl
1977 Jean Michell, Vera Jaffe
1978 Katie Cunneen, Marie Lampi
1979 Jackie Matthews, Mary Lou Reinsinger
1980 Dianne Murray, Karen Singer
1981 Jeanne Laing, Isabelle Turner

MIXED PAIRS
1958 Malvine Klausner, Meyer Schleifer
1960 Malvine Klausner, Meyer Schleifer
1961 Max Manchester, Lisa Strebinger
1962 Lucille Wheeler, Maynard Orme
1963 Helen Haugsten, Jack Ehrlenbach
1965 Helen Haugsten, Dick Jones
1966 Helen Moore, Morris Portugal
1967 Bob Norberg, Freda VanCleve
1968 Janie Pearcy, Martin Laylor
1969 Mary Blustein, Darryl Pedersen
1971 Valerie McVay, Jerry McVay
1972 John Anderson, Cheryl Davis
1973 Mike Passell, Hermine Baron
1974 Maurie Kinney, Hermoine Kinney
1975 Dick Yarington, Jacqueline Lyski
1976 Jean Carney, Bernie Chazen
1977 Freda Whitesel, Dennis Metcalf

INDIVIDUAL
1968 Thelma Taft
1969 Mrs. J. W. Kruse
1975 James O'Brien
1976 Michael Eyer
1977 Mrs. Dewey Lundy

MIXED SWISS TEAMS
1975 Troy Horton, Katie Cunneen,
      David McClintock, Janet McClintock

MASTER SWISS TEAMS
1978 Dean Ellis, Steve Clough, Ralph Johnson,
      Hattie Hamlin, Hal Montgomery
Flight A:
1979 Troy Horton, Randy Pickett,
      John Luskey, Oris Mowry

DISTRICT 21   (North central California)

ALL-WESTERN

KNOCKOUT TEAMS
1967 Peter Rank, Robert Adams, Peter Pender,
      Marilyn Johnson, John Swanson, Paul Soloway
1968 Kai Larsen, Grant Baze,
      Augie Hunte, Charlie Dorn
1969 Michael Lawrence, Robert Hamman, Kyle Larsen,
      John Swanson, Bernie Bergovoy
1970 Hermine Baron, Mel Dagovitz,
      Herb Smith, Norman Anderson
1971 John Fejervary, Charlie Dorn, Kirk Blackerby,
      John Swanson, Leslie Tsou, Michael Lawrence
1972 John Padget, Richard Henderson, Jon Wittes,
      Nels Erickson, Allan Graves, Ken Gorfkle
1973 Bob Matthes, Bill McWilliams,
      Jim Robison, Jack Roth
1974 Meyer Schleifer, Don Krauss, Milton Vernoff,
      Alma Spreckles, Ron Von der Porten
1976 Alma Spreckles, Ron Von der Porten, Grant Baze,
      Meyer Schleifer, Milton Vernoff
1977 Steve Price, Bob Bakalish,
      Ray MacWilliamson, Nancy McCullogh
1978 Hugh Ross, Lew Stansby, David Smith,
      Chip Martel, Mark Feldman
1979 Keija Taira, Gary Soules,
      Billy Miller, Hammish Bennett
1980 Gary Soules, Billy Miller,
      Keiji Taira, Alamgir Saeed
1981 Joanne Greene, Bob Crossley, Paul Lewis,
      Marc Jacobus, John Mohan

OPEN TEAMS
1956 Lucille Patterson, Fred Carpenter,
      Benny Ignatz, Rose Ignatz
1957 Nell Wells, Dean Cook,
      Malvine Klausner, Dr.Ed Frischauer
1958 Jules Farell, Mary Jane Farell,
      Morris Portugal, Helen Portugal
1959 Mike Shuman, Eddie Kantar, Harold Guiver,
      Kelsey Petterson, Alex Tschekaloff
1960 Marilyn Johnson, Robert Adams,
      Frank Jackson, Ivan Scope
1961 Paul Allinger, Lewis Mathe,
      Marc Guy Kamens, Bill Tierney
1962 Louis Mathe, Paul Allinger,
      Marc Guy Kamens, Bill Tierney

1963 Virginia Hull, Dean Cook,
      David Ashley, Dan Kleinman
1964 Richard Walsh, Harold Guiver,
      Mike McMahan, Mike Gilbert *(tied with)*
      Melvin Dagovitz, Frank Lee,
      Bernie Bergovoy, Richard Henderson
1965 Rhoda Lander, Jim Linhart,
      Ernie Hirsch, Jim Stein *(tied with)*
      Meyer Schleifer, Dave Drury,
      Alma Coleman, Donald Oakie
1966 Eugenie Mathe, Lewis Mathe,
      Alfred Sheinwold, Leo Pressburg
1967 Hermine Baron, Dan Romm, Leslie West,
      Jon Wittes, Paul Ivaska
1968 Charlie Dorn, Ward Corbin, Walter Gilbert,
      Ivan Scope, Charlton Buckley
1969 Paul Soloway, Malcolm Brachman,
      Ron Von der Porten, John Fejervary
1970 Ron McConnell, Michael Savage, Richard Henderson,
      John Padget, Milon Edwards
1976 Jim Figenshaw, Shirley Frisby, Zakir Mohammed,
      Nell Wells, Dee Saur
1977 Victor Tan, Don Klang,
      Thomas Hanford, Marva Notestine
1978 Frank Warzek, Sachi Miki, Eric Hansen,
      Marian Gaylord, Tina Pearson *(tied with)*
      Bill Langlois, Robert G. Martin,
      Paula Givan, Walter Miller *(and)*
      Vince Oliver, David Mahler,
      Brenda Blumenthal, John Jones
1979 Bob Bakalish, Carol Baxter,
      Ben Gay, Nancy McCullough
1980 Ron Powell, Cliff Hollander,
      Bob Enenstein, Edgar Simons
1981 Carole Dietz, Jan Bulger,
      Alan Becker, Judy Fisher
Flight A:
1979 Barry Crane, Kerri Shuman,
      Ed Davis, Mike Smolen
1980 Elisabeth Brenhouse, Mel Skolnik, Alan Sontag,
      Peter Weichsel, Marc Jacobus (Board-a-Match)
1981 Joanne Greene, Bob Crossley, Paul Lewis,
      Marc Jacobus, John Mohan

MEN'S TEAMS
1973 Warren Cederborg, Tom Tracy, Jerry Weitzner,
      Alan Bell, Ron Promboin, Ernie Hirsch
WOMEN'S TEAMS
1973 Elaine Jaccard, Mildred Mazza, Susy Cole,
      Vi Bigelow, Jeannine Omo *(tied with)*
      Roberta Epstein, Hermine Baron, Kerri Shuman,
      Georgianna Gates, Carol Greenhut

MASTER PAIRS
1939 John Sherman, Clarence Strouse
1940 Walter Herbert, Ernest Rovere
1941 Maureen Bailey, Wilbur Hayhurst
1942 Frank Fee, David Davis
1943 Meyer Schleifer, Norman Perlstein
1944 Malvine Klausner, Dr. Edward Frischauer
1945 Clarence Strouse, Norman Perlstein
1946 Arnold Kauder, Mary Jane Kauder
1947 Dan Westerfield, Ernest Rovere
1956 Frank Fee, George Dunn
1957 Harvey Schmidt, Bernice Krems
1958 Hal Kandler, Erik Paulsen
1959 G. H. Buckley, Elsa Ganz
1960 Jules Farell, Mary Jane Farell
1961 Ivan Scope, Frank Jackson
1962 Don Krauss, Ron Von der Porten
1963 Noreen Walsh, Hugh Ross
1964 Bruce King, Roxy Violin
1965 John Lyon, Paul Allinger
1966 Kay Dunn, Dean Cook
1967 Hal Kandler, Evan Bailey
1968 Helen Moore, Morris Portugal
1969 Alan Bell, Claude Vogel
1970 Ivan Scope, Herb Smith
1971 Kerri Davis, Harold Guiver
1972 Peter Pender, Peter Rank
1973 Sydney Levey, Bob Giragosian *(tied with)*
      John Grantham, Mike Shuman
1974 George Steiner, Maxine Blumenthal
Flight A:
1976 Robert Hamman, John Fejervary
1977 Chip Martel, Bernie Chazen
1978 Bob Crossley, Richard Henderson
1979 Juan Adrover, Grace Noda
1980 Mark Ralph, Don Guerin
1981 JoAnna Lawrence, Sally Nutting

OPEN PAIRS

1935 Hal Pemberton, Roscoe Puffer
1936 John Meyer, Harry Merkle
1937 Jack Ehrlenbach, Edward Taylor
1938 William Savery, Jo Muckey
1939 Jack Ehrlenbach, Edward Taylor
1940 Maureen Bailey, Hal Pemberton
1941 Donald Oakie, Walter Turner
1942 Meyer Schleifer, Lewis Mathe
1943 Meyer Schleifer, Morris Mendelsohn
1944 Malvine Klausner, Dr. Ed Frischauer
1945 Ernest Rovere, Dan Westerfield
1946 Herbert Friedrich, Morris Portugal
1947 Lewis Mathe, Meyer Schleifer
1956 James Dunn, Richard Blenck
1957 Jerry Prager, Frank Jackson
1958 Stella Rebner, Ron Von der Porten *(tied with)*
     Ray Walker, John Blattner
1959 Stella Rebner, Ron Von der Porten
1960 Bennie Ignatz, George Eveleth
1961 Lois Newman, Dean Cook
1962 Margaret Alcorn, Peter Pender
1963 Larry Weiss, Mike McMahan *(tied with)*
     Robert Hamman, Donald Krauss
1964 Ivan Erdos, Max Turk
1965 Rhoda Lander, Michael Lawrence
1966 Malvine Klausner, Conrad Potvin
1967 Jules Farell, Mary Jane Farell
1968 Tom Lesser, Dan Romm
1969 Richard Henderson, Milon Edwards
1970 Peter Rank, Marilyn Johnson
1971 Bill Nutting, Lew Stansby
1972 Harvey Brody, Ken Peyser
1973 Barry Crane, Dr. John Fisher
1974 Linda Taggart, Joan Lenze
Flight A:
1976 Barry Crane, Kerri Shuman
1977 Paul Maier, Mike Smolen
1978 Michael Flanagan, Barbara Flanagan
1979 Ron Prombolin, Lynne Feldman
1980 Michael Lawrence, Kyle Larsen
1981 Vern Pang, Gary Soules

MEN'S PAIRS

1945 Charles Harvey, William Jones
1946 Edward Sandstrom, Edward Taylor
1947 Leo Pressburg, Jack Ehrlenbach
1956 Ernest Noffsinger, Andy Kridl
1957 Milton Vernoff, Ernest Rovere
1958 Casey Million, Ernest Rovere
1959 Ron Von der Porten, George Eveleth
1960 Dr. Henry Tsang, Frank Savstrom
1961 Bedson Juett, Burton Marliave
1962 Robert Sitnek, Peter Pender
1963 William Lang, Jack Ehrlenbach
1964 Peter Pender, Mike Shuman
1965 Jim Gladfelter, Bob Hendershott
1966 George Morton, Ray Walker
1967 Paul Soloway, Richard Walsh
1968 George Mattos, George Toone
1969 Dave Roberts, Jess Bjorklund
1970 Peter Pender, Grant Baze
1971 Alex Haas, George Solberg
1972 John Grantham, John Mohan
1973 Mel Dagovitz, George Strohl
1974 Ron LaCour, Herb Smith
1976 Fred Hamilton, Larry Cohen
1977 Gene Freed, Richard Kaye
1978 Richard Spitalnick, Harvey Brody
1979 George Mattos, Richard Spitalnick
1980 Michael Lawrence, George Steiner
1981 Barry Crane, Craig Janitschke

WOMEN'S PAIRS

1936 Claire Dickson, Harriett Watson
1937 Verna Leonard, Marjorie Mortimore
1938 Bonnie Bates, Jean de Costa
1939 Sally Hutten, Mildred Gillingham
1940 Hazel Brunn, M. H. Jordon
1941 Ann Wesson, Mary Criswell
1942 Ivy Oeschger, Nell Childs
1943 Emily Gibbons, Helen Kirkman
1944 Ivy Oeschger, Nell Wells
1945 Hazel Brunn, Mrs. James Dunn
1946 Mrs. Curtis Smith, Mrs. James Dunn
1947 Verna Leonard, Marjorie Mortimore
1956 Mrs. Carl Smith, Mrs. J. Garrigan
1957 Betty Coombs, Carolyn Fantone
1958 Viola Bennayan, Sylvia Clark
1959 Julia Heimburger, Jay Shaw
1960 Goldie Davis, Mrs. Roger Gaumer
1961 Pat Long, Kathleen Mausser
1962 Mrs. G. E. Frioux, Mrs. A. R. Chapman

1963 Mrs. William Herman, Mary Puncochar
1964 Maxine McElfish, Betty Coombs
1965 Shirlee Harris, Peggy Jean Berry
1966 Peggy Stoddard, Lois Newman
1967 June McDonald, Bessie Borquin
1968 Lucille Patterson, Elina Weil
1969 Sylvia Clark, Marty Rogers
1970 Miriam Roberts, Audrey Rennels
1971 Margaret Gaer, Lee Baumann
1972 Amalya Kearse, Karen Singer
1973 Diane Rushing, Helen Miller
1974 Josephine Draga, Madeliene Murnig
1976 Jacquelin Fox, Arlene Slomka
1977 Jan Stansby, Pat Leary
1978 Marianne Miller, Anna Mae Dana
1979 Carol Simon, Hermine Baron
1980 Pat Leary, Lynne Feldman
1981 Jean Michell, Barbara Murrin

MIXED PAIRS

1956 Verna Leonard, Harry Feinberg
1957 Verna Leonard, Martin Gerther
1958 Stella Rebner, William Hanna
1959 John Brinley, Mrs. A. H. Schreek
1960 Patti Medford, Erik Paulson
1961 Marie Awad, George Awad
1962 Conrad Potvin, Katherine Blanchard
1963 Margaret Alcorn, Peter Pender
1964 Noreen Walsh, Richard Walsh
1965 Mabel Mahoney, Meyer Schleifer
1966 Herb Smith, LaVern Smith
1967 Keiji Taira, Ellen Shampanier
1968 Ward Corbin, Dee Corbin
1969 Helen Moore, Morris Portugal
1970 Ivan Scope, Bette Scope
1971 Ed Davis, Gaye Herrington
1972 Herb Smith, LaVern Smith
1973 Piyush Vakil, Margaret Vakil
1974 Georgianna Gates, Leslie West
1976 Keiji Taira, Nina Hopkins
1977 Mark Feldman, Lynne Rogers
1978 Dave McClintock, Jan McClintock
1979 Linda Peterson, Brian Glubok
1980 Terry Wilkerson, Dale Holden
1981 Joan Ivey, Ernie Ivey

INDIVIDUAL

1968 Anne Grisham
1976 Ed Kennedy
1977 Justin Beck
1978 Paul Kushner
1979 Jack Gonzales
1980 Jackie Devine
1981 Mort Weislow

MASTERS TEAMS

1971 Bob Spotts, John Sutherlin,
     Piyush Vakil, Edward Barlow
1972 Meyer Schleifer, Ron Von der Porten,
     Alma Hammel, Kyle Larsen
1973 Ken Gorfkle, Steve Smolen, Carol Greenhut,
     Allan Graves, David Ashley
1974 Meyer Schleifer, Don Krauss,
     Ron Von der Porten, Alma Spreckles *(tied with)*
     Bill Staats, Mark Singer,
     Harry Brody, Frank Lee
1976 Mike Gurwitz, Mark Feldman, David Smith,
     Ken Gorfkle, Chip Martel
1977 John Mohan, Kay Schulle-Mohan, Diane LaFleur,
     Roger Bates, Mike Shuman *(tied with)*
     Sigrid Price, Steve Price,
     George Toone, George Mattos
1978 Jan Stansby, Bob McLaughlin,
     Mike Lawrence, Warren Cederborg

CALIFORNIA CAPITAL

KNOCKOUT TEAMS

1971 Margaret Gaer, Jerry Gaer,
     Ed Nagy, Milt Levison
1972 Kirk Blackerby, Charlie Dorn, Marty Miller,
     Herb Smith, Ivan Scope, Leslie Tsou
1973 Kirk Blackerby, Charlie Dorn, Marty Miller,
     Helen Rhodes, Jim Hayashi
1974 Eugene Neiger, Diane LaFleur, John Grantham,
     John Mohan, Michael Lawrence
1975 Richard Friesner, Tim Lundeen, William Chiang,
     Bill Rudman, Lew Stansby, Hank Davis
1976 Dick Jones, Joe Farley, Don Guerin,
     Tom Stern, William Whitesel, Bill Sanford
1977 Kay Schulle, Kyle Larsen,
     Gary Soules, Bernie Bergovoy
1978 Piero Arganini, Grant Baze, Chip Martel,

Mike Lawrence, Lew Stansby, Kyle Larsen
1979 John Lanier, Bob Crossley, Jean Ouimet,
John Norman, Barbara Norman
1980 Bruce Ferguson, Brenda Keller, Clarence Goppert,
Jan Janitschke, Craig Janitschke
1981 Mel Skolnik, Ron Andersen, Mike Smolen,
Paul Soloway, Eddie Wold

OPEN TEAMS
1971 James Singer, Matt Guagliardo,
Gail Nicholas, Terry Ansnes
1972 Augie Hunte, Larry Maes,
Ed Nagy, Harvey Brody
1973 Ed Nagy, Augie Hunte,
Bob Spotts, Lew Stansy
1974 Mrs. C. Gilkeson, Mike Shuman, Paul Soloway,
John Swanson, Fred Hamilton
1975 Bill Harker, Steve Clark,
Ed Barlow, Ivan Scope
1976 Kirk Blackerby, Jim Hayashi,
Ron Feldman, Herb Smith
1977 Mary Fast, Harold Clark,
Jerry Underwood, Donna Sutton
1978 Alan Gailfus, Betty Gailfus,
Donna Lee Sutton, Gene Hunsaker
1979 John McMurdie, Ronnie McMurdie, Jim Codron
Willie Lee, Lucille Patterson
1980 Barry Crane, Michael Jones, Norman Anderson,
Mike Smolen, Mark Itabashi, Ron Feldman
1981 Ken Sien, Bob McLaughlin,
George Lim, Dee Sauer *(tied with)*
Mike Flanagan, Barbara Flanagan,
Jack Yeasley, Michael Pearson *(and)*
Reynold Wong, Larry Bolls,
Mike Levy, Gary Robinson
Flight A:
1979 Barry Crane, Dr. John Fisher, Mike Smolen
Bob Kehoe, Ira Cohen,
1980 Bruce Ferguson, Brenda Keller, Clarence Goppert,
Jan Janistschke, Craig Janitschke *(tied with)*
Joe Farley, Bob Burgdorf, Dave Sweet,
Mark Ralph, Bob Kerr
1981 Jeff Polisner, Peter Pender,
Ed Nagy, Hugh Ross

MASTER PAIRS
1971 Diva Kar Bhargava, Joe Houde
1972 Augie Hunte, Ed Nagy
1973 Larry Mandel, Ira Cohen
1974 Sydney Levey, Shirley Levey
1975 Mike Lawrence, Kevin Castner
1976 Alma Spreckels, Ron Von der Porten
1977 Fred Hamilton, Margie Shima Hamilton
1978 Barry Crane, Mike Passell
1979 Barry Crane, Dr. John Fisher
1980 Alan Bell, Rick Whitworth
1981 Jim Robison, Gene Freed

OPEN PAIRS
1971 Robert Borden, Lew Wasselle *(tied with)*
Margaret Gaer, Norman Anderson
1972 James Kauder, Arnold Kauder
1974 Barry Crane, Peter Rank
1975 Frank Warzek, Herb Smith
1976 Sharon Smith, Ed Nagy
1977 Paul Soloway, Kyle Larsen
1978 Evelyn Butler, Betty Levan
1979 Barry Crane, Dr. John Fisher
1980 Barry Crane, Kerri Shuman
1981 Mike Levy, Larry Bolls

MEN'S PAIRS
1971 Ron McConnell, Richard Henderson
1972 Ron McConnell, John Sutherlin
1974 Ron Smith, John Onstott
1976 Michael Jones, Norman Anderson
1977 Richard Spitalnick, Robert Radwin
1978 Stephen Dow, Joe Farley
1979 Robert Boggs, Charles Goosmann
1980 Barry Crane, Craig Janitschke
1981 Ron Powell, Steve Clark

WOMEN'S PAIRS
1971 Mrs. B. Zahlos, Mrs. C. Crawford
1972 Lucille Patterson, Elina Weil
1974 Jan Cohen, Marilyn Adams
1976 Lucille Patterson, Elina Weil
1977 Arlene Slomka, Janet Fitzgerald *(tied with)*
Jan Stansby, Pat Leary
1978 Mary Ann Rapp, Rose Conway
1979 Bonnie Beardsley, Harriet Ohme
1980 Lorna Crooks, Randi Montin
1981 Jan Cohen, Marilyn Abrams

MIXED PAIRS
1974 Peggy Sutherlin, John Sutherlin

1976 Jim Leary, Pat Leary
1977 Stephen Dow, Pat Leary
1978 Robert Radin, Ellamae Coelho
1979 Hamish Bennett, Muriel Richens
1980 Michael Jones, Dolores Sauer
1981 Terry Wilkerson, Dale Holden

MASTER SWISS TEAMS
1977 Peter Pender, Mark Feldman
Michael Gurwitz, David Smith
1978 Debbie Ong, Miriam Salkou,
Evan Nossoff, Dan Dagovitz

INDIVIDUAL
1976 Dorothy Carter
1977 Erma MacLean
1978 James Burg
1979 Dorothy Hill *(tied with)*
Nancy Brill
1980 A. R. Poliak
1981 Nancy Dickason *(tied with)*
Lee Henderson

UNMIXED PAIRS
1976 Jim Skulstad, Stephen Kanzee

GOLDEN GATE

KNOCKOUT TEAMS
1967 Milton Moss, Paul Soloway,
Hermine Baron, Rhoda Walsh
1968 Ira Corn, Jr., Bobby Wolff, James Jacoby,
Michael Lawrence, Bobby Goldman, Billy Eisenberg
1969 Leslie West, Marilyn Johnson, Peter Pender,
Peter Rank, Charles MacCracken
1970 Peter Pender, Hugh Ross, Grant Baze,
Leslie West, Peter Rank
1971 Jay McKee, Paul Soloway, Morris Portugal,
Dr. Vic Mastron, Ken Gorfkle
1972 Mike Shuman, Hermine Baron, John Padget,
John Mohan, Bob Spotts
1973 Jules Farell, Mary Jane Farell,
Dennis Williams, Warren Cederborg
1974 Peter Pender, Leslie West, Dave Crossley,
Bob Crossley, David Smith, Michael Lawrence
1975 Barney O'Malia, Gaylor Kasle,
Lou Bluhm, Larry Cohen
1976 Ladd Vincent, Ben Hulsman III,
John Antoun, Thayer White
1977 Kirk Blackerby, Jim Hayashi,
Herb Smith, Leslie Tsou
1978 Gary Soules, Bernie Bergovoy,
Steve Levy, Peter Friedland
1979 Mike Passell, Mark Lair, Fred Hamilton,
Eddie Wold, Clarence Goppert
1980 Paul Soloway, Peter Weichsel, Marc Jacobus,
Mel Skolnik, Elisabeth Brenhouse
1981 John Anderson, Perry Van Hook, Craig Janitschke,
Jan Janitschke, Ross Rainwater, Ron Feldman

MASTER PAIRS
1962 Mary Jane Farell, Mabel Mahony
1964 Stanley Schloss, Ed Weiner
1966 John Sutherlin, Bob Spotts
1967 Kyle Larsen, Jack Hancock
1968 Jack Hancock, Gaylor Kasle
1969 Ittah Han, Martin Miller
1970 Bob Bratcher, Mark Bartosik
1971 Jan Stansby, Lew Stansby
1972 Rhoda Walsh, Paul Maier
1973 Bernie Bergovoy, Jeff Polisner
1974 Bill Nutting, Lew Stansby
1975 Barry Crane, Mike McMahan
1976 John Bookstaver, Bernie Chazen
1977 Harvey Brody, Augie Hunte
1978 Jack Lacy, Dan Lacy
1979 Helen Jean Fong, Donald Oakie
1981 John Mureness, Calvin Harper
Barometer:
1980 George Mattos, Bernie Chazen

OPEN PAIRS
1962 Doug Drury, Peter Pender
1964 Michael Lawrence, Peggy Berry
1966 Bernie Bergovoy, Helen Portugal
1967 Kyle Larsen, Jack Hancock
1968 Barry Crane, Peter Rank
1969 Peter Rank, Marilyn Johnson
1970 William Slife, Anne Slife
1972 Richard Henderson, Jan Wittes
1973 Joan Weisberg, Sylvia Clark
1974 Lynne Rogers, Lew Stansby
1975 Barry Crane, Peter Rank
1976 Jim Hayashi, Warren Cederborg
1977 Harvey Brody, Ed Nagy

1978 Hugh Ross, Dave Ross
1979 T. Robert Hughes, Neil Chambers
1980 Barry Crane, Ron Andersen
1981 Richard Meffley, Anne Kuenstler
MEN'S PAIRS
1962 Richard Walsh, Evan Bailey
1964 Doug Drury, Dean Cook
1966 Gaylor Kasle, Milton Levison
1967 Chris Barrere, Michael Lawrence
1968 Bernie Ignatz, Norman Anderson
1969 Phil Read, Bob Spotts
1970 Robert Sanner, Robin Booth
1972 Tommy Prothro, Nels Erickson
1973 Frank Warzek, Jim Hayashi
1976 Leslie Tsou, Warren Cederborg
1977 Ben Tucker, Bob Bell
1978 Paul Soloway, Malcolm Brachman
1979 George Mattos, Gary Soules
1980 Paul Maier, Mike Smolen
1981 Jim Lord, William Laubenheimer *(tied with)*
Tom Holdiman, Chuck Burton
WOMEN'S PAIRS
1962 Edwina West, Mrs. Richard Ryder
1964 Florence Shields, Mrs. Harold Middleton
1966 Margaret Costello, Ruth Schneider
1967 Mrs. C. B. Schmidt, Robi Gohn
1968 Mary Jane Farell, Katherine Blanchard
1969 Mrs. W. S. Johnson, Mrs. S. Rice
1970 Beverlee Walker, Lucille Patterson
1972 Jean Michell, Shirley Nedham
1973 Maye Soules, Nell Wells
1976 Renee Friedman, Phyllis Robbins
1977 Florence Meyer, Marcia Masterson
1978 Muriel Richens, Lorraine Foss
1979 Agnes Bennett, Lorraine Foss
1980 Juanita Skelton, Hermine Baron
1981 Pat Leary, Lynne Feldman
MIXED PAIRS
1962 Malvine Klausner, Milton Vernoff
1964 Morris Portugal, Betty Levan
1966 Peter Rank, Ellie Schulte
1967 Barry Crane, Mary Jane Farell
1968 Peter Rank, Rhoda Walsh
1969 Peggy Sutherlin, Richard Henderson
1970 John Anderson, Marianne Churchill
1971 Peggy Drury, Ron LaCour
1976 Roger Beiles, Arline Fulton
1977 Mark Feldman, Lynne Rogers
1978 Jean Michell, Joe Farley
1979 Jean Michell, Marc Jacobus
1980 Paula Gavin, Badar Baqai
1981 John Anderson, Alice Hopkins
UNMIXED PAIRS
1976 Warren Nelson, Cole A. Powell
INDIVIDUAL
1968 James Wilson
1969 Mrs. Robert J. Purcott
1970 Virginia Roberts
1976 Christy Hartsell
1977 Larry North
1978 Don Hayden
1979 Jack Gonzales
1980 Yvonne Slee
1981 Lucille Johnson
MASTER SWISS TEAMS
1973 Ernie Hirsch, Bob Spotts,
Shirley Nedham, Joe Nedham
1977 Bruce Noda, Juan Adrover,
Roy Hoppe, James Kenyon
1978 Malcolm Brachman, Paul Soloway,
John Swanson, Fred Hamilton
OPEN TEAMS
1964 Frank Lee, Mel Dagovitz,
Bernie Bergovoy, Naim Turk
1966 Richard Walsh, John Swanson,
Michael Lawrence, Harold Guiver
1967 Barry Crane, Jules Farell, Mary Jane Farell,
Mabel Mahoney, Hal Kandler
1968 Paul Soloway, Hugh Ross,
Bernie Bergovoy, Jack Hancock
1969 Peter Pender, Grant Baze, Charles MacCracken,
Kyle Larsen, Charlie Dorn
1971 Peter Pender, Peter Rank, Marilyn Johnson,
Grant Baze, Bob Sanner
1972 Walter Miller, George Sturges,
Gary Griffith, J. Peter Franks
1974 Kirk Blackerby, Jim Hayashi,
Ron Smith, John Onstott
1975 Barney O'Malia, Lou Bluhm, Larry Cohen,

Gaylor Kasle, David Smith, Ken Gorfkle
1976 Bernie Chazen, John Bookstaver,
Carol Simon, Jean Carney
1977 Rob Anthonisen, Jean Michell, Pat Leary,
Dennis Williams, Kevin Castner
1978 Rob Anthonisen, Pat Leary, Jean Michell,
Dennis Williams, Jim Skulstad
1979 Clarence Goppert, Mike Passell, Mark Lair,
Fred Hamilton, Eddie Wold *(tied with)*
Bob Bakalish, Carol Baxter,
George Mattos, Linda Peterson
1980 Jean Michell, Mickie Kivel,
Pat Leary, Jim Leary
1981 Sarah Anne Cressy, Lois Parker,
Lenore Karp, Frank King
Flight A:
1979 Bill Cohen, Kay Schulle-Mohan,
Juanita Skelton, John Sutherlin
1980 Malcolm Brachman, Paul Soloway, Ron Andersen,
John Sutherlin, Barry Crane
1981 Joanne Greene, Mark Feldman, Paul Lewis,
Chip Martel, Bob Crossley

DISTRICT 22 (Central and southern California, excluding Los Angeles area)

DISTRICT 22

KNOCKOUT TEAMS
1973 Barney O'Malia, Gaylor Kasle
Garey Hayden, Roger Bates
1974 Eugene Neiger, Roger Bates, JoAnn Grantham,
Diane LaFleur, John Mohan
OPEN TEAMS
1973 David McClintock, Jan McClintock, Alan Daniels,
David Spahlinger, Gary Frankson
1974 Ira Cohen, Paul Ivaska,
Larry Mandel, Jon Wittes
MASTER PAIRS
1973 Gideon May, David Greenwald
1974 Mark Ralph, Don Guerin
OPEN PAIRS
1973 Hal Kandler, Warren Moore
1974 Ron LaCour, Carol Greenhut
MEN'S PAIRS
1974 Ron Smith, John Onstott
WOMEN'S PAIRS
1974 Jan Cohen, Marilyn Abrams

GOLDEN STATE

KNOCKOUT TEAMS
1968 Shirley Blum, Ann Wood, Jean Levey,
Sydney Levey Jr., Carmen Wood, Mary Lou Bert
1969 Paul Soloway, Meyer Schleifer, Charles Baron,
Mrs. Charles Baron, Charles Phillips
1970 George Parker, Ivan Scope, Leslie West,
Kirk Jensen, Warren Cederborg
1971 Hermine Baron, Norman Anderson,
John Anderson, Mike Shuman
1972 Barney O'Malia, George Parker,
Gaylor Kasle, Garey Hayden
1973 Mike Passell, Hermine Baron, Jim Robison, Dave Priest
1974 Eugene Neiger, Roger Bates, Diane LaFleur,
John Mohan, John Grantham
1975 Barry Crane, Kerri Shuman, Rhoda Walsh, Paul Soloway
1976 John Mohan, Diane LaFleur, Roger Bates,
Mike Shuman, Fred Hamilton
1977 Ron LaCour, Michael Schreiber,
Nels Erickson, Charles Finch
1978 Sydney Levey, John Schnell, Jim Slinger,
Ken Matthys, Gene Deetz *(tied with)*
Brenda Blumenthal, Marc Jacobus,
Tony Morris, Paul Jay Lewis
1979 Steve Skinner, Ron Smith, Roger Bates,
David Weiss, Joel Hoersch
1980 Vic Chernoff, Jim Robison, John Jeffrey, John Fox
1981 Mel Skolnik, Elisabeth Brenhouse, Ron Andersen,
Eddie Wold, Paul Soloway
OPEN TEAMS
1963 Stanley E. Schloss, Mrs. Stanley E. Schoss,
Mrs. N. D. Chasnoff, William S. Ashton *(tied with)*
Helen Utegaard, Peggy J. Berry, Paul Lynch,
Robert Spotts, G. Gard Hays
1964 Martin Dagovitz, Bernard Bergovoy,
Naim C. Turk, Frank Lee
1965 Kelsey Petterson, Bea Petterson, Max Turk, Ivan Erdos

1966 Lewis Mathe, Mike McMahan, Gerald Bare,
      Hugh Ross, Erik Paulsen
1967 Jim Ross, Hugh Ross, Kyle Larsen, Bernard Bergovoy
1968 Charles MacCracken, Mike Smolen,
      Rhoda Walsh, Leslie West
1969 Paul Soloway, Malcolm Brachman,
      Hermine Baron, Jon Wittes
1970 Not available
1971 James Kauder, Ann Kauder, Larry Weiss, Charles Kalme
1972 Hermine Baron, Mike Passell,
      Peter Pender, Peter Rank *(tied with)*
      Arthur LaFleur, Diane LaFleur, Norman Anderson,
      Mike Shuman, Kerri Shuman, John Mohan
1973 John Mohan, Diane LaFleur, John Grantham,
      Michael Lawrence, Eugene Neiger
1974 Ira Cohen, Paul Ivaska, Larry Mandel, Jon Wittes
1975 William Kuenstler, Pierre Flatowicz,
      Richard Dinkel, Anne Kuenstler
1976 Jim Hayashi, Kirk Blackerby,
      Larry Weiss, Herb Smith *(tied with)*
      John Mohan, Diane LaFleur, Roger Bates,
      Mike Shuman, Fred Hamilton
1977 Frank Kimball, Anita Kimball, Ray Zoller,
      Eddie Wold, Jim Rosenstiel
1978 Don Donohue, Mary Lou Bert,
      Nancy Tan, Henderson Young *(tied with)*
      Jean Mitchell, Pat Leary, Jim Leary, Ivan Scope *(and)*
      Stephen Kanzee, Dave Yamauchi,
      Shirley Blum, Steve McConnell
1979 Mike Smolen, Ira Cohen,
      Kerri Shuman, Billy Cohen *(tied with)*
      August Ginocchio, Julie Ginocchio,
      Warren Nelson, Jean Michell *(and)*
      Steve Skinner, Ron Smith, Joel Hoersch, David Weiss *(and)*
      Steve Levy, Ed Barlow, Peter Friedland, Bill Langlois
1980 Kitty Podolsky, Jim Kirkham,
      Joe Girdwood, Becky Schmieder *(tied with)*
      Barry Crane, Ron Andersen,
      Ross Grabel, Mike Smolen *(and)*
      Joel Hoersch, Richard Taube, Alan Bell, David Hankin
1981 Joanne Greene, Bob Crossley, Paul Lewis,
      Marc Jacobus, John Mohan *(tied with)*
      Stephen Kanzee, Rick Voss, Nick Wiebe, Gene Freed

MASTER SWISS TEAMS
Flight A:
1978 H. Y. Farnsworth, Greg Champion,
      Ron Rosenthal, Stephen Booth *(tied with)*
      Barry Crane, Kerri Shuman
      Ed Davis, Mike Smolen

MASTER PAIRS
1963 Michael Lawrence, Robert Spotts
1964 Stephen Schloss, Ed Weiner
1965 Dwayne James, Mabs Askew
1966 Lalage Pfahler, Ramona Conway
1967 Ted Richmond, John Rogers
1968 Ed Weiner, Hermine Baron
1969 Hermine Baron, Richard Henderson
1970 Tony Kasday, Paul Ivaska
1971 Alex Tschekaloff, Ed Davis
1972 Barry Crane, Dr. John Fisher
1973 Bob Kerr, Don Guerin
1974 Mark Ralph Don Guerin
1975 Ernie Hirsch, Peter Friedland
Flight A:
1976 Chip Martel, Bernie Chazen
1977 James Kauder, Diane Jonas
1978 Marc Jacobus, John Sutherlin
1979 Frank Warzek, Jim Hayashi
1980 Barry Crane, Ron Andersen
1981 Craig Janitschke, Barry Crane

OPEN PAIRS
1963 Edward Barlow, Evan Bailey
1964 Michael Lawrence, Peggy Jean Berry
1965 Paul Kayfetz, Bill Nutting
1966 Michael Lawrence, Marshall Miles
1967 Barry Crane, Peter Rank
1968 Jerry Hallee, Paul Soloway
1969 Barbara Waite, Ann Arndt
1970 Barry Crane, Michael Jones
1971 John Anderson, Steve Goldberg
1972 Ron LaCour, Garey Hayden
1973 Milton Levison, Robert Hamman
1974 Ron LaCour, Carol Greenhut
1975 Roger Bates, Bruce Maclin
1976 Clarence Goppert, Mark Lair
1977 Jim Robison, Dale Gilbert
1978 Bill Sides, Ed Davis
1980 John Fox, Vic Chernoff
1981 Sydney Levey, Lowell Gist
Flight A:
1979 Rob Anthonisen, Jim Skulstad

1980 Roger Jourdan, Jim Barrow
1981 William Rudman, Rick Whitworth

MEN'S PAIRS
1963 Kelsey Petterson, Eilif Andersen
1964 Doug Drury, Dean B. Cook
1965 Eddie Kantar, John de Blois Wack
1966 Michael Lawrence, Paul Soloway
1967 Bill Tivol, Ralph Anziani
1968 Tony Kasday, Paul Ivaska
1969 Sam Coolik, George Treadwell
1970 Gaylor Kasle, David Carter
1971 Ken Gorfkle, Warren Cederborg
1972 Mike Passell, John Mohan
1974 Ron Smith, John Onstott
1975 Steve Dow, John Rogers *(tied with)*
      Kirk Blackerby, Herb Smith
1976 Fred Hamilton, Mike Passell
1977 Irving Auerbach, John Jeffrey
1978 Sydney Levey, Jim Tritt
1979 Bill Cohen, Ron Smith
1980 Vic Chernoff, John Fox
1981 Mel Skolnik, Ron Andersen

WOMEN'S PAIRS
1963 Lois Newman, Nell Wells
1964 Florence Shields, Mrs. Harold Middleton
1965 Bert Epstein, Muriel Donnerstag
1966 Maria Manslla, Mrs. Charles Herbert Van Pelt
1967 Ruby Hawks, Lucille Patterson
1968 Anne Grisham, Marty Rogers
1969 Mickee Heumann, Alicia Kempner
1970 Marta Kovac, Hermine Baron
1971 D. Koren, Barbara Hays
1972 Mary Jane Farell, Elsa Ganz
1974 Jan Cohen, Marilyn Abram
1975 Linda Taggert, Dianne Paine
1976 Ann Jacobson, Linda Borbely
1977 Barbara Hayes, Adis Dombu
1978 Tommie Smith, Patricia Lee
1979 Marianne Miller, Anna Mae Dana
1980 Beverly Rosenberg, Carole Pincus
1981 Sherry Arnold, Marjorie Robertson

MIXED PAIRS
1963 Morris Portugal, Betty Levan
1964 Betty Levan, Morris Portugal
1965 Morris Portugal, Betty Levan
1966 Barry Crane, Marilyn Anticouni
1967 Paul Soloway, Lois Newman
1968 Charles Harding, Jr., Mary Jane Farell
1969 Florence Meyer, Paul Soloway
1976 Ron Andersen, Bunny Haas
1977 Steve Smolen, Marilyn Abrams
1979 Darlene Kraemer, George Burlison

INDIVIDUAL
1968 Marie Ragle
1977 Hank Parker
1979 Ed Rose

UNMIXED SWISS TEAMS
1976 John Rogers, Albert Chow,
      Biu Wong, Bob Luebkeman
1977 Michael Cumby, Wayne Rudd,
      Jerry Jackson, Keith Bach

UNMIXED PAIRS
1976 Mike Mezin, Leonard Messersmith
1977 Gloria Reiss, Mrs. Richard Zauner

PACIFIC SOUTHWEST

KNOCKOUT TEAMS
1967 Hal Kandler, Hermine Baron,
      David Ashley, Leslie West
1968 Erik Paulsen, Gerald Barr
      Mike McMahan, Harold Guiver
1969 Barney O'Malia, Matt Bartosik,
      Robert Geller, Ron McDonnell
1970 Alan Bell, Hal Kandler,
      Brian Amer, Ed Davis
1971 Hal Kandler, Alan Bell, Paul Heitner,
      Norman Anderson, Hermine Baron
1972 Hermine Baron, Richard Henderson, John Mohan,
      Paul Soloway, Mike Shuman
1973 Richard Henderson, Mike Passell,
      Paul Ivaska, John Wittes
1974 Dave Pelka, Tom Reynolds,
      Randy Howard, Robert Radwin
1975 James Backstrom, Paul Flashenburg, Charles Finch,
      Joel Hoersch, Donna Bartholomew
1976 Diane LaFleur, John Mohan, John Grantham,
      Mike Lawrence, Mike Passell, Roger Bates
1977 Michael Schreiber, Nels Erickson, Charles Finch,
      John Coufal, Max Hardy

1978 John Mohan, Kay Schulle-Mohan, Diane LaFleur,
     Roger Bates, Mike Passell
1979 Barney O'Malia, Gaylor Kasle, John Coufal,
     Tom Evans, John Mohan
1980 Barney O'Malia, John Coufal, Ken Monzingo,
     John Mohan, Paul Soloway, Gaylor Kasle
1981 Jose Lichtenberg, Elias Konstantinovsky, Laura Mariscal,
     Mike Passell, Paul Soloway
     OPEN TEAMS
1946 Seigfried Klausner, Malvine Klausner,
     Rose Reif, Dr. Ed Frischauer
1949 James Dunn, Lewis Mathe,
     Morris Portugal, W. Waterman
1950 Meyer Schleifer, Hugh Edwards,
     Helen Cale, Jack Ehrlenbach *(tied with)*
     Malvine Klausner, Rose Reif
     Dr. Ed Frischauer, W. Kivi
1951 Margery Foote, Ralph Cash
     Allyn Whitehead, Dan Westerfield *(tied with)*
     Rose Reif, William Hanna
     Malvine Klausner, Dr. Ed Frischauer
1952 Detmar Walther, Meyer Schleifer,
     James Dunn, Kay Dunn
1953 Ivan Erdos, Harold Murphy
     Lewis Mathe, Doug Steen
1954 Harry Feinberg, Doug Steen,
     Norbert Kaufman, William Hanna
1955 Joseph Cantor, Siegmond W. Smith,
     Albert Silverman, Benton Dayton
1956 Robert Evans, Gideon May,
     Mrs. Robert J. Marks, Robert J. Marks
1957 Malvine Klausner, Helen Portugal, Harry Steen,
     Dr. Ed Frischauer, James Herd
1958 Malvine Klausner, Helen Portugal, Harry Steen,
     Dr. Ed Frischauer, James Herd
1960 Malvine Klausner, Meyer Schliefer,
     James Dunn, Kay Dunn
1961 Malvine Klausner, Meyer Schliefer,
     James Dunn, Kay Dunn
1963 Mike Shuman, Kathie Ashe,
     J. W. Murphy, David Ashley
1964 John Swanson, Noreen Walsh,
     Hugh Ross, Robert Spotts
1965 Larry Israel, Ivan Erdos, Frank Silver,
     Mike Cappelletti, Lilo DeBurger
1966 Kelsey Petterson, Bea Petterson, Gerald Bare,
     Dorothy Bare, Harrison Peterson
1967 Hal Kandler, Jules Farell, Mary Jane Farell,
     Richard Henderson, Barry Crane
1968 Florence Meyer, Joan Dryer, Judy Dryer,
     Harold Guiver, Harry Tippins
1969 John Swanson, Pat Bradford,
     Robert Adams, Tom Tracy
1971 Meyer Schleifer, Milton Vernoff,
     Ron Von der Porten, Alma Hammel
1972 Alma Hammel, Ron Von der Porten, Milton Vernoff,
     Meyer Schleifer, Dan Mordecai
1973 Mary Jane Farell, Jules Farell,
     Norman Anderson, Elsa Ganz
1974 Roger Doughman, Lena Jelusich,
     Roger Zellmer, Conrad Evans
1975 Ira Cohen, Bill Sides, Ed Davis, Paul Maier *(tied with)*
     Art Mortensen, Richard Degen, John Schuler, Bob Kerr
1976 Martha Beecher, Clarence (Cap) Crossley,
     Proctor Hawkins, David Ashley
1977 John Strauch, Cathy Strauch, Doris Neff, Evan Bailey
1978 Michael Falcon, Carolyn Falcon, D. U. Filman,
     Jim Kirkman, Ken Schumate
1979 Kitty Podolsky, Jim Kirkham,
     Ken Shumate, Mike Levinson *(tied with)*
     Annice Somers, Bruce Ferguson,
     Brenda Keller, Dick Kangas *(and)*
     Iftikhar Baqai, Mike Schreiber,
     Robert Radwin, Mike Smolen
1980 Kay Larsen, Chris Larsen, Beverly Rosenberg, Joe Payne
1981 Phyllis Yates, Kirk Kuhlmann, John Toy, John Conway
Flight A:
1980 Bettye Haugen, Elma Buchanan,
     Bea Murray, Mrs. J. R. Fortner *(tied with)*
     Page Rank, Jerry Jacobson,
     Pamela Wittes, Jon Wittes
1981 Joel Hoersch, Conrad Evans, Lynn Horobetz,
     Roger Zellmer, Marcia Masterson
     MASTER PAIRS
1946 Mabel Ackerman, Earl Ackerman
1947 Ralph Cash, John H. Norman
1948 Malvine Klausner, Rose Reif
1949 Doug Steen, Courtland Rush
1950 Lewis Mathe, Arnold Kauder
1951 Helen Portugal, Morris Portugal

1952 Phil Wood, Sidney Lazard
1953 Barry Cohen, Clarence Strouse
1954 Vinton Hammels, Roy Hislop
1955 Aaron Baron, Lewis Mathe
1956 Mary Jane Kauder, Jules Farell
1957 Stella Rebner, Juanita Strich
1958 Eddie Kantar, Dr. Jay Etkin
1960 Mrs. Harold Hope, Mrs. William S. McDuffee
1961 George Eveleth, Don Cutler
1963 Mike McMahan, Gerald Bare
1964 Richard Walsh, John Swanson
1965 Paul Soloway, Richard Henderson
1966 Jackie Spadero, Larry Weiss
1967 Dr. Lawrence Laughlin, Robert Roseblum
1968 Ralph Clark, Larry Weiss
1969 Joel Hoersch, David Weiss
1970 Jim Millerd, Leo Pressburg
1971 Barry Crane, Bette Messer
1972 Paul Soloway, Malcolm Brachman
1973 Barney O'Malia, Gaylor Kasle
1974 Robert Radwin, Chuck Williams
1975 Ron LaCour, Ron Feldman
1976 Marty Shallon, Jon Wittes
1977 Kerri Shuman, Peter Rank
1978 Ed Davis, Jon Wittes
1979 Hermine Baron, Fred Hamilton
1980 Michael Schreiber, Paul Lewis
1981 L. Andrew Campbell, Evan Bailey
     OPEN PAIRS
1946 William McKenney, Clarence Strouse
1947 Dan Westerfield, Jack Hancock
1948 Malvine Klausner, Dr. Ed Frischauer
1949 Rose Reif, Malvine Klausner
1950 Malvine Klausner, Arnold Kauder
1951 Jane Wright, Stella Rebner
1952 Donald Oakie, Doug Steen
1953 Lewis Mathe, Doug Steen
1954 Malvine Klausner, Meyer Schleifer
1955 Malvine Klausner, Meyer Schleifer
1956 Benton Dayton, Russell Fischer
1957 Arnold Kauder, Mary Jane Kauder
1958 Bill McWilliams, Jane Wright
1960 Richard Cheng, Arthur Fletcher
1961 Al Blinder, Joe Nedham
1963 Helen Portugal, Harry Steen
1964 Tom Lesser, Dan Romm
1965 Jules Farell, Mary Jane Farell
1966 John Wong, Kelsey Petterson *(tied with)*
     Barry Crane, Peter Rank
1967 Kyle Larsen, Michael Lawrence
1968 Hal Kandler, David Ashley
1969 Hal Kandler, David Ashley
1970 Alex Tschekaloff, David Ashley
1971 Dr. Sam Williams, Richard Henderson
1972 Gerald Bare, Harold Guiver
1973 Diane LaFleur, John Mohan
1974 Mike McFaddin, Jim George
1976 John Strauch, Evan Bailey
1980 Evan Bailey, Doris Bailey
Flight A:
1975 Barney O'Malia, Gaylor Kasle
1977 Mary Anne Conway, Dave Priest
1978 George Siegel, Mike Kaplan
1979 Mark Itabashi, Gary Ullman
1980 Jose Lichtenberg, Paul Soloway
1981 Pat Ottman, Paul Mote
     MEN'S PAIRS
1947 Dan Westerfield, Jack Hancock
1948 John H. Norman, Ralph Cash
1949 Hugh Smith, G. Troutt
1950 Dr. Ed. Frischauer, Joe Hennicke
1951 C. P. Williams, James Dunn
1952 Max Manchaster, Robert Marks
1953 Milton Vernoff, Joseph Cantor
1954 William Hanna, Casey Million
1955 Milton Vernoff, Joseph Cantor
1956 William Hanna, Sidney Lazard
1957 Harold Guiver, Milton Vernoff
1958 Dean Cook, Chuck Lane
1960 George Callegher, Harrison Peterson
1961 James Dunn, Erik Paulsen
1963 Richard Walsh, Alfred Sheinwold
1964 Homer Shoop, Ed Herbert
1965 Matt Bartosik, Peter Lit
1966 Andy Pounds, Milton Vernoff
1967 Edward Cook, Adm. W. H. Ginn
1968 Arthur De Voss, Edward Belasco
1969 David Weiss, Sam Williams
1970 Miles Adkins, Jay T. McKee
1971 Richard O'Leary, Dave Pelka *(tied with)*

Gordon Shephard, Warren Moore
1972 John Buchheister, Ed Davis
1973 Kelsey Petterson, Proctor Hawkins
1974 Mike Passell, Mark Lair
1975 Robert Kellermeyer, Dave Priest
1976 Meyer Schleifer, Jerry Civetta
1977 Nels Erickson, Charles Finch
1978 John Strauch, Evan Bailey
1979 John Strauch, Evan Bailey
1980 Michael Schreiber, Gene Simpson
1981 John Fox, Rob Anthonisen

WOMEN'S PAIRS
1947 Mrs. James Rae, Mrs. Frank Newcomb
1948 Mrs. B. B. Morris, Mary Jane Kauder
1949 Ann Goldfine, Emma Goldfine
1950 Malvine Klausner, Mary Jane Kauder
1951 Myrtle Owens, Josephine Hovis
1952 Harriet Feldman, Mrs. Hamilton Moody
1953 Helen Portugal, Kathleen Mausser
1954 E. Caseman, B. Kelly
1955 Betty Berkitz, Marion Moran
1956 Ruth Bay, Betty Allen
1957 Mrs. J. S. Sharpe, Margery Foote
1958 Malvine Klausner, Rose Reif
1960 Mary Jane Farell, Katherine Blanchard
1961 Judith Sharp, Katharine Best
1963 Roberta Heim, Dorothy Van Slyke
1964 Laverne Morrison, Patricia Ann Harnage
1965 Rose Reif, Bonnie Sakamoto
1966 Judy Dryer, Rhoda Walsh
1967 Malvine Klausner, Mrs. Charles Baron
1968 Shirlee Shannon, Gloria Seacat
1969 Georgia Borthwick, Gwen De Jonge
1970 May Soules, Virginia Brown
1971 Marilyn Abrams, Dethe Acre
1972 Robin Grantham, Tina Heath
1973 Mary Jane Farell, Elsa Ganz
1974 Kerri Shuman, Hermine Baron
1975 Linda Borbley, Kerri Shuman
1976 Lilyan Eisenstein, Rhoda Walsh *(tied with)*
      Gail Erickson, Sue France
1977 Bette Messer, Judy McAbee
1978 Lorraine Hathaway, Roberta Grubb
1979 Virginia Rashmir, Ruth DeMore
1980 Margaret Zealear, Jeanne Cook
1981 Mary Jane Farell, Betty Levan

MIXED PAIRS
1946 Mrs. Henry Gross, H. Mendelsohn
1947 Helen Cale, Jack Ehrlenbach
1948 Helen Portugal, Morris Portugal
1949 Edith Rosenkranz, John Moran
1950 Malvine Klausner, Dr. Ed Frischauer
1951 Helen Portugal, Morris Portugal
1952 Ivan Erdos, Rose Reif
1953 Peggy Stoddard, David Davis
1954 Allyn G. Whitehead, Doug Steen
1955 Penelope Ullrich, Fred M. Ullrich
1956 Malvine Klausner, Meyer Schleifer
1957 Mary Jane Kauder, Jules Farell
1958 Malvine Klausner, Meyer Schleifer
1960 Mabel Mahoney, David Carter
1961 Barry Crane, Hermine Baron
1963 Ivan Erdos, Mrs. Robert Kohler
1964 Hermine Baron, Meyer Schleifer
1965 Gail Angel, Alvers Lapins
1966 Dorothy Munn, Don Krauss
1967 Jeannette Gertmenian, Alan Ramo
1968 Mike McMahan, Shirley McMahan
1969 Ann Arndt, Alan Bell
1976 Cheryl Wengrow, Marshall Wengrow
1977 Minda Brachman, Paul Soloway
1978 Faith Feldman, John Brissman
1979 Mary Jane Farrell, Richard Chapman
1981 Kerri Shuman, German Castaneda

INDIVIDUAL
1965 Frank Dilley
1968 Ken Daane
1976 Mrs. S.N. Perkins
1977 Dan Dayan
1978 N.L. Boyer
1979 Veva Duncan

WOMEN'S SWISS TEAMS
1976 Mary Jane Farell, Elsa Ganz,
      Marcia Masterson, Mrs. Bert Meyer
1977 Cathy Strauch, Doris Neef,
      Barbara Norman, Donna Bartholomew

MEN'S SWISS TEAMS
1976 Joel Hoersch, Evan Bailey,
      John Rogers, Jim Leary
1977 Joel Hoersch, John Strauch,

L. Andrew Campbell, Evan Bailey

MASTER SWISS TEAMS
1978 Frieda Kenigson, Norm Levin,
      Bette Willner, Syd Willner
1979 Bob Thomson, Ann Jacobson,
      Bob Etter, Ron Beall

RAINCROSS

KNOCKOUT TEAMS
1978 Marshall Miles, Patty Harnage,
      Ron Smith, Bob Giragosian
1979 Joseph Payne, Gene Freed,
      Lyle Peake, Gene Simpson
1980 Vic Chernoff, Richard Dallas,
      Mike Tierney, Jim Looby
1981 Betty Miles, Marshall Miles,
      Leon Schwartz, Neil Stern

MEN'S PAIRS
1978 Mike Shuman,, Fred Hamilton
1979 Arthur Zail, Leslie Tsou
1980 Mike Tierney, Jim Looby
1981 John Jones, Gene Freed

WOMEN'S PAIRS
1978 Kathie Wei, Bunny Haas
1979 Cordell Goode, Sylvia Matisoff
1980 Shirley Mayr, Barbara Roberts
1981 Shirley Renneisen, Rita Patton

OPEN PAIRS
1979 Ken Monzingo, Gaye Herrington
1980 Ron Vicery, Ron Davis
1981 Michael Schreiber, Jeff Meckstroth
Flight A:
1978 Steve Skinner, Ron Smith
1979 Ira Cohen, Barry Crane
1980 Paul Ivaska, Hermine Baron
1981 Rob Anthonisen, Laurie Anthonisen

OPEN SWISS TEAMS
1978 Frank Kimball, Anita Kimball, Jim Rosenstiel,
      Fred Hamilton, Mark Lair
1979 Mark Itabashi, Gerald Jacobson, Steve Cohen,
      Page Rank, George Siegel
1980 Ron Andersen, Jon Brissman, Paul Lewis,
      Bunny Haas, Mike Sokol *(tied with)*
      Mark Itabashi, Robert Radwin, Ann Kluewer,
      Randi Montin, Gene Simpson
1981 Vic Chernoff, Perry Van Hook,
      Jim Robison, Stelios Touchtidis
Flight A:
1980 Ross Rainwater, Tom Oakley,
      Vince Oliver, Mark Bartusek *(tied with)*
      Mark Itabashi, Marshall Miles,
      Jerry Jacobson, Page Rank
1981 Byron Economidy, Gene Simpson,
      Carreen Simpson, Julie Gravel

MEN'S SWISS TEAMS
1978 Barry Crane, Peter Rank, Nick Moss,
      Mike Smolen, Paul Maier
1979 Harv Waken, Bill Sides,
      John Swanson, Fred Hamilton *(tied with)*
      Leslie Tsou, Ron Feldman,
      Ross Rainwater, David Ashley

WOMEN'S SWISS TEAMS
1978 Nancy Lynge, Eleanor Kipperman, Gwen Womack,
      Betsy Straub, Lois Cogan
1979 Natalie Kaplan, Ann Arndt,
      Donna Knowles, Willo Jean Phillips

MIXED PAIRS
1978 Fred Hamilton, Margie Hamilton

INDIVIDUAL
1978 Ann Donham
1979 Richard Chan

MASTER PAIRS
Flight A:
1978 Marshall Miles, Ira Cohen
1979 Martha Beecher, David Ashley
1980 Paul Soloway, Ron Andersen
1981 Kay Larsen, Chris Larsen

SOUTHERN CALIFORNIA

KNOCKOUT TEAMS
1967 Jack Hancock, Piyush Vakil,
      Mike Lawrence, Robert Spotts
1971 Mary Jane Farell, Jules Farell, Mary McCrory,
      John Padget, Warren Cederborg, Pat O'Brien
1972 Alan Bell, David Weiss, Don Guerin,
      Brian Amer, John Strauch, Joel Hoersch

1973 Barbara Hamman, Robert Hamman, John Fejervary,
     Grant Baze, Ward Corbin
1974 Mike Smolen, Bill Sides, Jon Wittes,
     Tom Lesser, Paul Ivaska, Ed Davis
1975 Kathie Wei, Chester Hirsch, Jacqui Mitchell,
     Victor Mitchell, Ron Andersen
1976 Ron Andersen, Hugh MacLean, Fred Hamilton,
     Mark Lair, Clarence Goppert
1977 Fred Hamilton, Mike Passell, Mike Shuman,
     Kerri Shuman, David Ashley, Martha Beecher

OPEN TEAMS
1967 Rhoda Walsh, Richard Walsh,
     Paul Soloway, John Swanson
1970 Harrison Peterson, Dr. Edward Fradkin, Tom Lesser,
     Dorothy Bare, Perry Van Hook
1971 Barry Crane, Dr. John Fisher,
     Gerald Bare, Erik Paulsen
1972 Irv Kostal, Allen Paul,
     Richard Dallas, Ann Kluewer
1973 David Weiss, Jim Rosenstiel,
     Bill Schreiber, Dr. Sam Williams
1974 Morris Minken, Joanne Minken, Kelsey Petterson,
     Proctor Hawkins, Morris Portugal, Helen Portugal
1975 Gary Ullman, Richard Dallas,
     Ann Kluewer, Irv Kostal
1976 Ralph Kalbus, Dave Priest, Bill McWilliams,
     Roberta Housel, Gay Barber, Mary Anne Conway *(tied with)*
     Ron LaCour, Charles Finch,
     Ray Zoller, Jim Rosenstiel *(and)*
     Barry Crane, Peter Rank,
     Ed Davis, Paul Ivaska
1977 Morris Minken, Joanne Minken,
     Helen Portugal, Morris Portugal *(tied with)*
     Dave Crossley, Bob Crossley,
     John Schermer, Neil Chambers

MASTER PAIRS
1967 Paul Soloway, Richard Walsh
1970 Tom Lolli, Stanley Dollar
1971 Mike Smolen, Alex Tschekaloff
1972 Kerri Davis, Peter Rank
1973 Kelsey Petterson, Proctor Hawkins
1974 Jim Bechely, Marshall Miles
1975 Sam Wilson, Mike Kaplan
1976 N. Jay Brown, Tom Rickard
1977 Ben Tucker, Richard Gold

OPEN PAIRS
1967 Willard Nutting, Larry Weiss
1970 Phyllis Kantar, Agnes Gordon
1971 Barry Crane, Jules Farell
1972 Barry Crane, Dr. John Fisher
1973 Ron Smith, Richard Logan
1974 Ron LaCour, Carol Greenhut
1975 Robert Kellermeyer, Dave Priest
1976 Jim Robison, Mike Smolen
1977 Mike Schreiber, Jeff Meckstroth

MEN'S PAIRS
1967 Mike Lawrence, Paul Soloway
1970 J. David King, Norman Anderson
1971 Leslie West, Warren Cederborg
1972 Ward Corbin, Grant Baze
1975 Paul Soloway, Ron Andersen
1976 Mike Schreiber, Hal Kandler
1977 Gene Freed, Vic Chernoff

WOMEN'S PAIRS
1967 Glayda Lowre, Mrs. S. F. Cyborowski
1970 Shirley Nolan, Margo Hurley
1971 Alicia Kempner, Bee Schenken
1972 Jean Michel, Pat Leary
1975 Dorothy Van Slyke, Roberta Helm
1976 Lil Greenberg, Mary Jane Farell
1977 Beverly Rosenberg, Hermine Baron

MIXED PAIRS
1976 Pat Leary, Jim Leary
1977 Ray Banks, Susan Fisher

INDIVIDUAL
1976 Bill Meierstein

WOMEN'S SWISS TEAMS
1976 Marty Zive, Ann Harmon,
     Caron Mitchell, Ann Withers
1977 Julie Linde, Tanya Alonzo,
     Ann Jacobson, Pat Ferguson

MEN'S SWISS TEAMS
1976 Lyle Peake, Mark Brownstein,
     Allan Evans, James Prentice
1977 Richard Chapman, Tom Oakley,
     Arthur Zail, Robert Riedel

DISTRICT 23 (Los Angeles area)

ALACBU WINTER*

SWISS TEAMS
1969 Don Pearson, Nels Erickson, John Swanson,
     Richard Walsh, Jerry Weitzner
OPEN PAIRS
1969 Helen Heard, Norman Anderson

BRIDGE WEEK

KNOCKOUT TEAMS
1951 Arnold Kauder, Lewis Mathe,
     Meyer Schleifer, Ed Taylor
1952 Malvine Klausner, Dr. Ed Frischauer
     Carolyn Whitehead, Dan Westerfield
1953 Stella Rebner, Harry Feinberg,
     Leo Pressburg, Arthur Strich
1954 Arnold Kauder, Meyer Schleifer,
     Ed Taylor, Lewis Mathe
1955 Eddie Kantar, Jim Bechely, Al Okuneff
     Bobby Wolff, Marshall Miles
1956 Arthur Strich, John Moran,
     Roy Hislop, Conrad Potvin
1957 Lewis Mathe, Ed Taylor,
     Meyer Schleifer, Donald Oakie
1958 Eddie Kantar, Marshall Miles,
     Ivan Erdos, Ernest Rovere
1959 Ivan Erdos, Ira Rubin, Oliver Adams,
     Eddie Kantar, Ernest Rovere, Marshall Miles
1960 Paul Allinger, Donald Oakie,
     Meyer Schleifer, Lewis Mathe
1961 Erik Paulsen, Helen Portugal, Morris Portugal,
     Mike Shuman, Arthur Baron, Jerry Werner
1962 Larry Weiss, Bill McWilliams, Mike Moss,
     Jesse Sloan, Richard Ryder, Warren Blank
1963 John Swanson, Hugh Ross,
     Michael Lawrence, Harold Guiver
1964 Robert Hamman, Don Krauss, Eddie Kantar,
     Marshall Miles, Harvey Cohen
1965 Alma Coleman, Donald Oakie,
     Meyer Schleifer, Doug Drury
1966 Robert Hamman, Don Krauss,
     Lewis Mathe, Ron Von der Porten
1967 Harold Guiver, Michael Lawrence, Helen Portugal,
     Morris Portugal, Barry Crane
1968 Mike Shuman, Robert Spotts, Richard Henderson,
     Hugh Ross, Alex Tschekaloff, Erik Paulsen
1969 Paul Soloway, Hermine Baron, Jerry Hallee,
     Malcolm Brachman, Minda Brachman, Mary Jane Farell
1970 Minda Brachman, Malcolm Brachman, Hermine Baron,
     Paul Soloway, Meyer Schleifer, Gerry Hallee
1971 Alma Hammel, Kyle Larsen, Ron Von der Porten,
     Meyer Schleifer, Milton Vernoff
1972 Bud Reinhold, Billy Eisenberg, Eddie Kantar,
     Jonathan Cansino, Robert Sheehan, Marshall Miles
1973 Mike Smolen, Erik Paulsen, Bill Sides,
     Paul Ivaska, Jon Wittes, Gerald Bare
1974 Marshall Miles, Joe Bechely,
     John Schermer, Mike Gurwitz
1975 Malcolm Brachman, Bobby Goldman, Paul Soloway,
     Michael Lawrence, Mike Passell
1976 Vic Chernoff, Jim Looby,
     Danny Kleinman, Marshall Miles
1977 Gerald Bare, Erik Paulsen, Bill Sides,
     Ira Cohen, Harold Guiver, Marty Shallon
1978 Fred Hamilton, Ross Dorfman,
     David Ashley, Paul Soloway
1979 John Lanier, Bob Crossley,
     Ann Jacobson, Bob Etter
1980 Alan Sontag, Peter Weichsel, Marc Jacobus,
     Mel Skolnik, Elisabeth Brenhouse
1981 David Sacks, Steve Evans, Gene Simpson,
     Ron Garber, Bill Schreiber

MASTER TEAMS
1947 Rose Eidem, Meyer Schleifer,
     Betty Bysshe, Detmar Walther
1952 M. Breslauer, Lewis Mathe,
     Leo Pressburg, Arthur Strich
1953 Arnold Kauder, Mary Jane Kauder,
     Harold Murphy, Ivan Erdos
1954 Shirlee Fairchild, Alicia Kempner,
     Mrs. Leo Kramer, Ralph Kempner
1955 Mrs. B. B. Alston, Don Weld,
     Betty Coombs, Paul Allinger

*A special four-session red-point tournament awarded for 1969 only.

1956   Arthur Baron, Meyer Schleifer,
Ivan Erdos, Lewis Mathe
Flight A:
1977   Miguel Reygadas, Jose Lichtevberg,
Garey Hayden, Gaylor Kaske
1978   Gary Ullman, Ann Kluewer,
Maureen O'Rourke, Terri Primmer
1979   Ken Monzingo, Vic Avery,
Peter Knee, Lyle Peake *(tied with)*
Bill Sides, Randi Martin,
Mark Singer, Ron Feldman *(and)*
Jan Cohen, Marilyn Abrams,
Dennis Cohen, William Hall *(and)*
Barbara Hamman, Phyllis Kantar, Dick Ryder,
Kai Robinson, Art Fletcher *(and)*
Larry Brasler, George Staffmacher,
Al Okuneff, Trudi Nugit
1980   Don Metzger, Jim MacDonald,
Brad Ward, Howard Simpson
1981   Paul Ivaska, Bill Sides,
Ed Davis, Thomas Lesser

OPEN TEAMS

1936   C. Schwartz, W. Graff,
John Meyer, T. Harry Merkle
1937   George Gooden, Dr. Ben Strauss,
William Turner, Donald Oakie
1938   George Gooden, Dr. Ben Strauss,
William Turner, Donald Oakie
1939   Jack Ehrlenbach, Ed Taylor,
Meyer Schleifer, Lewis Mathe
1940   Lewis Mathe, Meyer Schleifer,
Jack Ehrlenbach, Ed Sandstrom
1941   David Burnstine, Lewis Mathe,
Roscoe Puffer, Jr., Meyer Schleifer
1942   Mort Lipsett, F. Thompson,
M. Merkle, Earl Ackerman
1945   Jack Ehrlenbach, Ed Taylor,
Norman Perlstein, Meyer Schleifer
1946   Lewis Mathe, Meyer Schleifer,
Ed Taylor, Jack Ehrlenbach
1947   David Bruce, John Moran, Clarence Strouse, Jr.
Morris Portugal, Herbert Frederick
1949   Meyer Schleifer, Roscoe Puffer, Jr.,
Ed Taylor, Lewis Mathe
1957   John Millerd, James Millerd,
Alan Bell, Marshall Miles
1958   Lewis Mathe, Donald Oakie,
Meyer Schleifer, Ed Taylor
1959   Ed Taylor, Lewis Mathe,
Meyer Schleifer, Donald Oakie
1960   Helen Portugal, Morris Portugal,
Hal Kandler, Sydney Levey
1961   Helen Portugal, Morris Portugal,
Hal Kandler, Sydney Levey *(tied with)*
Marshall Miles, Harold Simon,
Eddie Kantar, Jack Hancock
1962   Harold Simon, Eddie Kantar,
Jim Bechely, Robert Hamman
1963   Noreen Walsh, John Swanson,
Jim Linhart, Bill McWilliams
1964   Derrick Deery, Harvey Cohen,
Marilyn Johnson, Robert Adams
1965   Hermine Baron, Mike Shuman, Arnold Kauder,
Marilyn Johnson, Peter Rank
1966   Harry Tippins, C. N. Tsu,
Judy Dryer, Jean Dryer
1967   Richard Henderson, David Ashley,
Alex Tschekaloff, Al Okuneff
1968   Jack Roth, R. L. Balisok,
Ed Davis, Irv Kostal
1969   James Jacoby, Bobby Wolff, Bobby Goldman,
Billy Eisenberg, Michael Lawrence
1970   Hal Kandler, Alan Bell, Michael Savage,
Tom Lesser, Brian Amer, Ed Davis
1971   Roger Bates, Ed Herbert,
Hank Wick, Harold Segal (Board-a-Match)
John Fejervary, Lee Genud,
Billy Eisenberg, Valerie Calamaro (Swiss)
1972   David Ashley, Mike Smolen, Richard Henderson,
Rhoda Walsh, Grant Baze
1973   Dr. Peter Forbes, Robert Adams,
John Swanson, Paul Soloway (Board-a-Match)
Marta Kovac, Norman Anderson,
Rhoda Walsh, Michael Lawrence (Swiss)
1974   Duke Dautell, Hutch Stern,
Jim Rosenstiel, Caron Mitchell
1975   Paul Maier, Jim Rosenstiel,
David Weiss, Lance Kerr
1976   Perry Van Hook, David Sacks, Patricia Katz,
Dr. Richard Katz, Katherine Cohen, Larry Cohen (Swiss)
Joel Hoersch, Evan Bailey,

Lance Kerry, David Weiss (Board-a-Match)
1977   Barry Crane, Mike Shuman,
Kerri Shuman, Bernie Chazen (Swiss)
Kay Schulle-Mohan, Nels Erickson,
Dave Gilbert, Charles Finch (Board-a-Match)
1978   John Anderson, Greg Nichols, Ross Rainwater,
Charles Finch, Jon Brissman
1979   Barry Crane, Ed Davis,
Kerri Shuman, Mike Smolen
1981   Mark Itabashi, Jon Wittes, Gene Simpson, Ed Davis
Flight A:
1980   Ed Nagy, Bob Kehoe,
Jeff Polisner, Ron Garber
1981   Vic Chernoff, Jim Robison,
Stelios Touchtidis, Ira Cohen

MEN'S TEAMS

1974   Robert Jenson, Clay Conan,
Donald Cooksey, Frank Prior
1978   John Anderson, Dale Gilbert, Jim Robison
Jim George, Mike McFaddin

WOMEN'S TEAMS

1974   Ethel Young, Marvis Jean Hurd,
Shirley Pond, Cynthia Gnam *(tied with)*
Ethel McDermott, Virginia Carrera,
Phyllis Hinkle, Dorothy Barron *(and)*
Barbara Pritchard, Marie Emrich,
Marie Newman, Elizabeth Montwill
1978   Vicci Steinbauer, Cathy Strauch,
Doris Bailey, Donna Bartholomew *(tied with)*
Sally Murphy, Betty Straub,
Grace Bixby, Guin Womack *(and)*
Beverly Rosenberg, Hermine Baron,
Peggy Sutherlin, Pat Leary

MIXED TEAMS

1937   H. Watson, Ray Oakley,
R. Baehr, C. Arnoldy
1938   R. O'Brien, B. Dethridge,
Hal Pemberton, Jack Ehrlenbach *()tied with)*
Maureen O'Brien, Ivy Oeschger,
C. Schwartz, Joe Meyer
1939   Claire Kapp, Spencer Kapp,
Mrs. G. Troutt, G. Troutt
1940   L. Senderman, Harry Merkle,
Mrs. C. Johanson, Ed Sandstrom
1941   Marge Kaiser, Lewis Mathe,
C. Arden, Jack Ehrlenbach
1942   L. Senderman, Dan Westerfield,
B. Stilwell, Ernest Rovere
1943   Mrs. H. Vandersluis, Lt. Col. H. Vandersluis
Mrs. Howard Bowman, Howard Bowman
1944   Ann Goldfine, H. Burnstein,
Emma Goldfine, Rose Reif
1945   F. Cohn, C. Schwartz,
Juanietta Cummings, George Bergmans
1960   Mary Jane Farell, Jules Farell,
Jane Herb, Barry Crane *(tied with)*
Rose Eidem, John Atchley,
Leo Pressburg, Florence Meyers
1961   Kay Dunn, James Dunn,
Malvine Klausner, Meyer Schleifer
1962   Noreen Walsh, Richard Walsh, Dean Cook,
Lois Newman, Hal Kandler
1963   Eugenie Mathe, Lewis Mathe, Alex Tschekaloff,
Florence Meyer, Harold Guiver
1964   Hermine Baron, Helen Portugal,
Barry Crane, Erik Paulsen
1965   Rhoda Lander, Larry Weiss,
Leo Pressburg, Eleanor Landow *(tied with)*
Dorothy Munn, Alma Coleman,
Doug Drury, Ron Von der Porten
1966   Stella Rebner, Fran Tsacnaris,
Paul Soloway, Bill McWilliams
1967   Bea Petterson, Kelsey Petterson,
Malvine Klausner, Meyer Schleifer
1968   Dorinda Lawrence, Robert Spotts,
Peggy Sutherlin, Hugh Ross
1969   Rhoda Walsh, Richard Walsh, Mary Jane Farell
Hal Kander, Barry Crane
1970   Rhoda Walsh, Warren Blank,
Fran Tsacnaris, David Ashley
1975   Gary Ullman, Marilyn Abrams,
Steve Smolen, Jan Cohen
1976   Bruce Fields, Susan Fields,
Allan McDonald, Shawn McDonald

MASTER PAIRS

1938   Dan Westerfield, Ernest Rovere
1939   John Sherman, Clarence Strouse, Jr.
1940   Ernest Rovere, Walter Herbert
1941   Maureen O'Brien, Wilbur Hayhurst
1942   Frank Fee, David Davis

1943 Meyer Schleifer, Norman Perlstein
1944 Malvine Klausner, Dr. Ed Frischauer
1945 Norman Perlstein, Clarence Strouse, Jr.
1946 Arnold Kauder, Mary Jane Kauder
1947 Dan Westerfield, Ernest Rovere
1949 Lewis Mathe, Ed Taylor
1951 Malvine Klausner, Arnold Kauder
1952 Jack Ehrlenbach, H. Edwards
1953 Milton Vernoff, Harry Bierman
1954 Lois Newman, Lewis Newman
1955 Paul Smith, Florence Meyers
1956 John Atchley, Elizabeth Sullivan
1957 Morris Portugal, Arthur Baron
1958 Bill McWilliams, Jane Wright
1959 Malvine Klausner, Jack Ehrlenbach
1960 Charles Harvey, David Conlin
1961 Bill Tierney, Marc Guy Kamens
1962 Florence Meyer, Harold Guiver
1963 Alma Coleman, Meyer Schleifer
1964 Harold Guiver, Derrick Deery
1965 Richard Walsh, John Swanson
1966 Richard Walsh, John Swanson
1967 Tony Kasday, Paul Ivaska
1968 Ed Barlow, Evan Bailey
1969 Al Okuneff, Jim Stein
1970 David Joyce, Jim Stein
1971 Ron McConnell, John Padget
1972 Jean Druer, John Sharron
1973 Kelsey Petterson, Proctor Hawkins
1974 Jim Stein, David Joyce
1975 Jeffrey Morris, Joe Tomasulo
1976 Jackie Gross, Steve Gross
1977 Harold Guiver, Allan Paul
Flight A:
1978 Ron Davis, Kim Bryan
1979 Ron Garber, David Sacks
1980 Barry Crane, Billy Cohen
1981 Michael Schreiber, Barry Crane

OPEN PAIRS
1935 Hal Pemberton, Roscoe Puffer
1936 Joe Meyer, Harry Merkle
1937 Jack Ehrlenbach, Ed Taylor
1938 William Savery, Jo Muckley
1939 Jack Ehrlenbach, Ed Taylor
1940 Maureen O'Brien, Hal Pemberton
1941 Donald Oakie, Bill Turner
1942 Lewis Mathe, Meyer Schleifer
1943 Meyer Schleifer, Morris Mendelsohn
1944 Malvine Klausner, Dr. Ed Frischauer
1946 H. Frederick, Morris Portugal
1947 Lewis Mathe, Meyer Schleifer
1948 Lewis Mathe, Meyer Schleifer
1949 Mary Jane Kauder, Arnold Kauder
1950 George Rapee, Ralph Kempner
1951 Ed Taylor, Lewis Mathe
1952 W. Jones, A. S. Montgomery
1953 Mrs. J. Moffat, Marshall Miles
1954 Mary Jane Kauder, Arnold Kauder
1955 Mary Jane Kauder, Arnold Kauder
1956 Sidney Lazard, Paul Allinger
1957 Ed Taylor, Lewis Mathe
1958 Eddie Kantar, Marshall Miles
1959 Stella Rebner, Barry Crane
1960 Paul Allinger, Jim Pestaner
1961 Kelsey Petterson, Erik Paulsen
1962 Kelsey Petterson, Erik Paulsen
1963 Mary Jane Farell, Jules Farell
1964 Barry Crane, Hermine Baron
1965 Richard Walsh, Mike McMahan
1966 Jeremy Flint, Peter Pender
1967 Sally Murphy, Bob Kerr
1968 Billy Eisenberg, Bobby Wolff
1969 Paul Soloway, Malcolm Brachman
1970 Dan Mordecai, Norman Schwartz
1971 Emmett Keeler, John Lindsay
1972 David Weiss, Joel Hoersch
1973 Barry Crane, Dr. John Fischer
1974 Barry Crane, Peter Rank
1975 Paul Ivaska, Ed Davis
1976 John Wong, Y. M. Chu
1978 Thomas Lebherz, Robert Riedel
1979 Mike Flanagan, Billy Karth
1980 Gerald Bare, Mike McMahan
1981 Jerry Jacobson, Jean Jacobson
Flight A:
1977 Barry Crane, Kerri Shuman
1978 Paul Ivaska, Hermine Baron
1979 Charles Finch, Stelios Touchtidis
1980 Barry Crane, Bruce Ferguson
1981 Steven Cohen, Stelios Touchtidis

MASTER MEN'S PAIRS
1965 Kai Larsen, Hugh Ross
1966 Bill Tierney, Bob Wurdeman
1967 Richard Walsh, Gerald Hallee *(tied with)*
     Leslie West, Don Pearson
1968 Barry Crane, Mike McMahan
1970 Robert McKnight, Stan Crandon
1971 Barry Crane, Peter Rank
1975 Mike McMahan, Larry Weiss
Flight A:
1976 Kelsey Petterson, Proctor Hawkins
1977 Paul Maier, Mike Smolen
1979 Thomas Lesser, Ed Davis
1980 Michael Schreiber, Vance Moran
1981 Stelios Touchtidis, Vic Chernoff

MEN'S PAIRS
1945 Charles Harvey, W. L. Jones
1946 Ed Sandstrom, Ed Taylor
1947 Leo Pressburg, Jack Ehrlenbach
1948 Ernest Rovere, Waldemar von Zedtwitz
1950 Dr. Ed Frischauer, Lewis Mathe
1951 Ralph Sharp, Don Ingham
1952 Ralph Kempner, Albert Kramer
1953 E. S. Quade, Eilif Andersen
1954 Barrett Stephenson, M. Nelson
1955 I. Marker, Melvin Breslauer
1956 James Dunn, Meyer Schleifer
1957 Sidney Lazard, Paul Allinger
1958 Milton Vernoff, Edward Cook, Jr.
1959 Dennis Sullivan, Walter Keller
1960 James Dunn, Paul Allinger
1961 Tony Adler, Leonard Marks
1962 Ed Taylor, Harold Guiver
1963 Max Hodder, Meyer Schleifer
1964 Richard Walsh, Evan Bailey
1965 Roy Hislop, Ralph Kempner
1966 Paul Soloway, Richard Walsh
1967 Paul Soloway, Richard Walsh
1968 Mike Smolen, Brian Amer
1969 Harry Steen, Gerry Civetta
1970 Leonard Kaye, John Rygh
1971 Jon Wittes, Paul Ivaska
1972 James Kauder, Harold Guiver
1973 Larry Cohen, Dr. Richard Katz
1974 Hy Farnsworth, Jim Robison
1975 Doyle Gilbert, Ken Wudrick
1976 Marv Thomsic, John Jeffrey
1977 Mitchell Cooper, Ben Tucker
1978 Mark Bartusek, Jim MacDonald
1979 Morris Schwartz, Nels Erickson
1980 Fred Clauda, Joe Nielson
1981 Paul Lewis, Michael Schreiber

MASTER WOMEN'S PAIRS
1965 Marilyn Johnson, Hermine Baron
1966 Marilyn Anticouni, Barbara Feldman
1967 Stella Rebner, Alicia Kempner
1968 Ellie Schulte, Marilyn Johnson
1970 Marlene Futterman, Marcia Graham
1971 Jan Cohen, Helen Cale
1975 Linda Mandel, Caroline Shallon
Flight A;
1976 Gene Wilson, Virginia Rashmir
1977 Fran Tsacnaris, Jill Meyers
1979 Marcia Graham, Carolyn Cohen
1980 Fran Tsacnaris, Gail Erickson
1981 Jan Cohen, Marilyn Abrams

WOMEN'S PAIRS
1936 Harriet Watson, Claire Dickson
1937 Verna Leonard, Marjorie Mortimore
1938 Bonnie Bates, Jean De Costa
1939 Mildred Gillingham, Sally Hutton
1940 Hazel Brunn, M.H. Jordan
1941 Ann Wesson, Mary Criswell
1942 Ivy Oeschger, Nell Childs
1943 Eunice Gibbons, Helen Kirkman
1944 Ivy Oeschger, Nell Wells
1945 Hazel Brunn, Kay Dunn
1946 Kay Dunn, Mrs. Curtis Smith
1947 Verna Leonard, Marjorie Mortimore
1948 Dorothy Clarke, Stella Rebner
1950 J. Duprau, Helen Portugal
1951 Gertrude Wallach, Betty Allen
1952 Doris Rickards, Katharine Hobbs
1953 C. Smith, Mrs. James Garrigan
1954 Helen Cale, Betty Bysshe
1955 Mary Cartwright, H. P. Cavanaugh
1956 D. Lorber, Malvine Klausner
1957 LaVonne Morrison, Mrs. Harold Hope
1958 Jane Wright, Kay Dunn

1959 Kay Dunn, Jane Herb
1960 Hermine Baron, Patti Medford
1961 Mrs. Henry Gross, Nell Wells
1962 Eugenia O'Hara, Sally Kelsey
1963 Frances Dollar, Mrs. Walter Kent
1964 Edith Bishop, Ethel Hirschfeld
1965 Ramona Gale, Lou Ryel
1966 Marta Kovac, Ann Scharfe
1967 Hermine Baron, Rhoda Walsh
1968 Alicia Kempner, Puff Laverty
1969 Mary Jane Farell, Kate Blanchard
1970 Karen Van Hook, Pamela Wittes
1971 Florence Meyer, Trudi Nugit
1972 Dene Ferris, Barbara Norbury
1973 Fran Tsacnaris, Pamela Wittes
1974 Susan Hinman, Patricia Callahan
1975 Carol Greenhut, Hermine Baron
1976 Fran Tsacnaris, Pamela Wittes
1977 Donna Knowles, Willo Jean Phillips
1978 Mary Nash, Randi Montin
1979 Marilyn Abrams, Donna Knowles
1980 Lynn Pollenz, Brenda Blumenthal
1981 Marilyn Abrams, Jan Cohen

MIXED PAIRS

1936 Shirley Moscovitz, G. Wooten
1937 Eunice Cooney, W. Schroeder
1938 M. Kaiser, Lewis Mathe
1939 Nell Childs, Ernest Rovere
1940 M. Glazer, Mrs. Henry Gross
1941 C. Arden, Jack Ehrlenbach
1942 Conrad Potvin, Helen Remley
1943 Mrs. H. Vandersluis, Lt. Col. H. Vandersluis
1944 Mrs. James Rae, William Wolf
1945 Hazel Brunn, Dan Westerfield
1946 Paula Bacher, Harry Fishbein
1947 Rose Eidem, Meyer Schleifer
1949 Mary Jane Kauder, Arnold Kauder
1951 Helen Portugal, Morris Portugal
1952 Kay Dunn, James Dunn
1953 Helen Portugal, Morris Portugal
1954 Kay Dunn, James Dunn
1955 Kay Dunn, James Dunn
1956 Jack Hancock, Ruth Million
1957 Marilyn Johnson, Robert Adams
1958 Ralph Kempner, Florence Meyer
1959 Eugenia Mathe, Lewis Mathe
1960 Arthur Jones, Anita Jones
1961 Helen Portugal, Erik Paulsen
1962 Mrs. Harry Bierman, Harry Bierman
1963 Bea Petterson, Kelsey Petterson
1964 Dorinda Wheelock, Larry Weiss
1965 Caroline Tucker, Jack Ehrlenbach
1966 Rhoda Walsh, Richard Walsh
1967 Ethel Hirschfeld, Hal Kleigman
1968 Betty Levan, Pete Benjamin
1969 Andy Pounds, Lucille Patterson
1970 Gaye Herrington, Ed Davis
1971 Phyllis Kantar, Paul Soloway
1972 Hermine Baron, John Mohan
1973 Sharon Kehoe, Ron Von der Porten
1974 Robert Chapin, Rhoda Walsh
1975 Mike Flanagan, Barbara Flanagan
1977 Jack Spear, Nancy Spear
1978 Steve Cohen, Beverly Rosenberg
1979 Hermine Baron, Stelios Touchtidis
1980 Pamela Wittes, Jon Wittes
1981 Julia Grabel, Ross Grabel

UNMIXED PAIRS

1972 Barry Crane, Dr. John Fisher
1973 Leslie Tsou, Oris Mowry
1974 Dan Kleinman, Sam Wilson
1976 Louis Altman, Jerome Blumenthal
1977 John Kissenger, Fred Melman
1978 James Edwards, James Kauder
1979 Ronald Wolfson, Tarig Latif *(tied with)*
      Jim Robison, Ken Monzingo
1980 John Anderson, Mike Smolen
1981 Dave Pelka, Robert Radwin

INDIVIDUAL

1936 John Sherman
1937 George Sherman
1938 George Sherman
1939 John Moran
1940 C. L. Taylor
1941 Jo Muckey
1946 Ernest Rovere
1947 Steve Bonner
1948 Mrs. G. C. Reinkins
1949 Allan Green
1950 Elling Thygeson

1951 Nicholas Karoly
1957 Frances Harris
1958 Mrs. Cyril George
1959 Dr. J. H. Wells
1960 John Atchley
1967 Herbert C. Royal
1968 Marie Ryan *(tied with)*
      Melvin Prichard
1969 Richard Edwards
1975 Joseph Childs
1976 Martin Barnett
1977 Eugene Enrione
1978 Richard Neilson
1979 Danny Kleinman
1980 John Melis
1981 Koya Inwanoto

LOS ANGELES WINTER

KNOCKOUT TEAMS

1972 Roger Bates, John Grantham, Margaret Skinner,
      Steve Skinner, Bill Whitesell
1974 Steve Evans, Ron Garber, Harold Guiver,
      Marty Shallon, Jon Wittes
1975 Bill Schreiber, Mike Schreiber,
      Karen Van Hook, David Weiss
1976 Steve Cohen, Ron LaCour,
      Larry Mandell, Jim Rosensteil
1977 Gerald Bare, Harold Guiver, Lew Mathe,
      Erik Paulsen, Marty Shallon, Ed Taylor
1978 Ira Cohen, Marv Dauer, Ron Feldman,
      Bob Kehoe, Marshall Miles
1979 John Anderson, Elisabeth Brenhouse, Mel Skolnik,
      Alan Sontag, Peter Weischel
1980 Sam Cohen, Jim Robison,
      George Siegel, Alex Tschekaloff

SWISS TEAMS

1969 Nels Erickson, Don Pearson, John Swanson,
      Richard Walsh, Jerry Weitzner
1974 Garey Hayden, Lucy Mitchell, Jane Ryan, Lee Ryan
1975 Vic Chernoff, John Fox, Richard Hunt, Jim Looby
1976 Barry Crane, Ed Davis, Nick Moss, Mike Smolen
1977 Hermine Baron, Charles Finch, Paul Ivaska, Jim Robison
1978 Eddie Kantar, Gladys Collier, Paul Soloway, Alan Sontag
Flight A
1980 Doug DePoister, Tom Evans, Marc Rothblatt, David Schor

MEN'S PAIRS

1976 Marshall Rose, Arthur Zail
1977 Ralph Kempner, Ed Malmuth
1978 Lowell Andrews, Steve Lawrence

WOMEN'S PAIRS

1976 Esther Adams, Helen Kaswen
1977 Juanita Schoppa, Sybil Weldon
1978 Donna Knowles, Willo Jean Phillips

MIXED PAIRS

1976 John Mohan, Kay Schulle
1977 Kay Schulle, Mike Shuman
1978 Careen Simpson, Gene Simpson
1979 Barry Crane, Kerri Shuman *(tied with)*
      Barbara Flanagan, Mike Flanagan
1980 Bob Kerr, Elizabeth Lebherz *(tied with)*
      Kerri Shuman, Mike Shuman

INDIVIDUAL

1976 Joe Wiley
1977 Alvin Young
1978 Jean Glenn
1979 Danny Kleinman
1980 Paul Mostman

OPEN PAIRS

1969 Norman Anderson, Helen Heard
1972 John Anderson, Nels Erickson
1979 Steve Cohen, Gary Ullman
1980 Becky Schmieder, John Rogers
Flight A
1976 Ira Cohen, Bill Sides *(tied with)*
      Fran Tsacnaris, Gary Ullman
1977 Joel Levinson, Stelios Touchtidis
1978 Dave McClintock, Janet McClintock
1979 Elisabeth Brenhouse, Peter Weichsel
1980 Joanne Minken, Morris Portugal

MASTER PAIRS

1972 Barry Crane, Dr. John Fisher
1974 Marcia Masterson, Florence Meyer *(tied with)*
      Ronnie Felton, Jeanne Little
1975 Gerald Caravelli, Barry Crane

Flight A
1976 Jim Jacoby, Pat Tierney
1977 Gerald Bare, Mike McMahan
1978 Ed Lovell, Paul Soloway
1979 Ed Davis, Jon Wittes
1980 Randi Montin, Bill Sides

WOMEN'S SWISS TEAMS
1976 Gail Erickson, Gaye Herrington,
Beverly King, Kay Larsen *(tied with)*
Eleanor Coelho, Eleanor Ferguson,
Jill Meyers, Kay Schulle

MEN'S SWISS TEAMS
1976 Lew Gilliam, Dennis Semain, Bill Semain, John Wong

MEN'S MASTER PAIRS
Flight A
1979 Marc Jacobus, Paul Lewis
1980 Bob Crossley, Paul Lewis

WOMEN'S MASTER PAIRS
Flight A
1979 Ann Arndt, Natalie Kaplan
1980 Hermine Baron, Beverly Rosenberg

MASTER SWISS TEAMS
Flight A
1977 David Ashley, Martha Beecher, Dale Gilbert,
Fred Hamilton, Margie Hamilton
1978 Steve Cohen, Jim Robison,
Beverly Rosenberg, Fran Tsacnaris
1980 Jules Farell, Mary Jane Farell, Lil Greenberg,
Diane Jonas, James Kauder

WOMEN'S KO TEAMS
1978 Ann Arndt, Donna Knowles,
Willo Jean Phillips, Barbara White
1979 Hermine Baron, Carol Pincus,
Beverly Rosenberg, Juanita Skelton

DISTRICT 24 (New York City and Long Island)

EASTERN STATES

KNOCKOUT TEAMS (REISINGER)
1930 George Reith, Sir Derrick Wernher,
Winfield Liggett, Jr., P. Hal Sims
1931 Julian Barth, Frank Rendon,
Howard Schenken, David Burnstine
1932 Willard Karn, P. Hal Sims
Oswald Jacoby, David Burnstine
1933 Howard Schenken, David Burnstine,
Richard Frey, Charles Lochridge
1934 Oswald Jacoby, David Burnstine,
Howard Schenken, Michael Gottlieb
1935 A. Mitchell Barnes, B. Jay Becker,
Sam Fry, Jr., Sydney Rusinow
1936 Fred Kaplan, Charles Vogelhofer,
Morrie Elis, Irving Epstein
1937 Charles Lochridge, Waldemar von Zedtwitz,
A. Mitchell Barnes, S. Garton Churchill
1938 Sam Fry, Jr., John Rau, Travers Le Gros,
S. Garton Churchill, Charles Lochridge
1939 Sam Fry, Jr., John Rau, Travers Le Gros,
S. Garton Churchill, Charles Lochridge
1940 Morrie Elis, Sam Stayman, Richmond Skinner,
Myron Fuchs, Maurice Seiler
1941 Louise Wainwright, Oswald Jacoby, John Crawford,
Charles Lochridge, Sherman Stearns
1942 B. Jay Becker, Simon Becker, George Rapee,
Harry Fishbein, Tobias Stone
1943 Helen Sobel, Charles Goren,
Peter Leventritt, Howard Schenken
1944 Harry Fishbein, Waldemar von Zedtwitz, Tobias Stone,
Charles Lochridge, Lee Hazen
1945 Lewis Jaeger, Jane Jaeger, Joseph Low,
William Lichtenstein, Henry Sonenblick
1946 Harry Fishbein, Alvin Roth, Larry Hirsch,
Ralph Hirschberg, Oscar Brotman
1947 Dr. William Lipton, Charles Groden,
Jay Feigus, Jerry Friedlander
1948 Charles Sanders, Jack Cushing,
Howard Zacks, Helen Zacks
1949 Charles Groden, Jack Shore, Abe Goldstein,
Jay Feigus, Dr. William Lipton
1950 Laurence Axmann, Lili Klehmet, Larry Blum,
Abe Rosen, Irving Kass
1951 George Rapee, John Crawford, Simon Rossant,
Sam Stayman, Bertram Lebhar, Jr.
1952 Ralph Hirschberg, Ambrose Casner,
Larry Hirsch, Sol Mogal
1953 Lester Glucksman, William Yablon, Norman Neiger,

Oscar Yablon, Milton Roth
1954 Edgar Kaplan, Ruth Sherman, Eli Jaye,
Norman Kay, Boris Koytchou
1955 George Boehm, Dr. William Lipton,
Edward Loewenthal, Victor Mitchell
1956 Edgar Kaplan, Richard Kahn, Norman Kay,
Ralph Hirschberg, Alfred Sheinwold
1957 Edgar Kaplan, Richard Kahn, Norman Kay
Ralph Hirschberg, Alfred Sheinwold
1958 Edgar Kaplan, Alfred Sheinwold, Norman Kay,
Ralph Hirschberg, Richard Kahn
1959 Edgar Kaplan, Ralph Hirschberg, Richard Kahn,
Alfred Sheinwold, Leonard Harmon, Norman Kay
1960 Alvin Roth, William Grieve, William Root,
Andy Gabrilovitch, Robert Jordan, Richard Freeman
1961 Alvin Roth, Tobias Stone, William Root,
Richard Freeman, Andy Gabrilovitch, Robert Jordan
1962 Phil Feldesman, Sol Rubinow, Jacqui Mitchell,
Victor Mitchell, Morton Rubinow, Sam Stayman
1963 Sol Rubinow, Sam Stayman, Jacqui Mitchell,
Victor Mitchell, Tobias Stone, Phil Feldesman
1964 Victor Mitchell, Jacqui Mitchell, Sam Stayman,
Phil Feldesman, Robert Mnuchin
1965 Mike Moss, John Bennett, Mark Blumenthal,
Harlow Lewis, Anthony Dionisi
1966 Alvin Roth, Murray Schnee, Dr. Kalman Apfel,
William Root, Boris Raymond, Barbara Rappaport
1967 Tobias Stone, John Crawford, Oswald Jacoby,
Alan Messer, Lawrence Rosler
1968 Alvin Roth, William Root, Ralph Chafetz,
John Solodar, Ross Dorfman, Barbara Rappaport
1969 Howard Schenken, Dave Strasberg, Peter Leventritt,
Ronald Crown, Dick Kahn, William Passell
1970 Edgar Kaplan, Leonard Harmon, Jeff Rubens,
Alfred Scheinwold, Norman Kay, Monroe Ingberman
1971 Hal Fein, B. Jay Becker, Mike Becker,
Ralph Chafetz, Andy Bernstein
1972 Dave Mason, Jane Mason, Sol Seidman,
George Awad, Marie Awad
1973 Waldemar von Zedtwitz, Phil Feldesman, Tobias Stone,
Ira Rubin, Kyle Larsen, Barbara Brier
1974 Waldemar von Zedtwitz, Tobias Stone, Kyle Larsen,
Phil Feldesman, Barbara Brier, Ira Rubin
1975 John Crawford, Alvin Roth, Ron Rubin,
Matt Granovetter, Barbara Rappaport
1976 Mike Becker, B. Jay Becker, Ron Rubin,
Roger Stern, Monroe Ingberman, Jeff Rubens
1977 Alan Greenberg, Jim Cayne, Matt Granovetter,
Peter Weichsel, Alan Sontag
1978 Ronald Blau, Martin Ginsberg, Jim Hilton,
Bill Passell, Harry Stappenbeck, Merle Tom
1979 Jack Schwencke, Allan Cokin, Steve Sion,
Peter Weichsel, Harold Lilie
1980 Brian Glubok, Alan Truscott,
Dorothy Hayden Truscott, Gene Neiger
1981 Phillip Martin, Kit Woolsey,
John Lowenthal, Chuck Lamprey

OPEN PAIRS (GOLDMAN)
1929 Oswald Jacoby, George Reith
1930 Geoffrey Mott-Smith, Richard Frey
1931 W. Cleveland Cogswell, Norman Bonney
1932 Winfield Liggett, Jr., Sidney Lenz
1933 Grace Perpall, F. E. Bailey
1934 Oswald Jacoby, David Burnstine
1935 Harry Raffel, Mel Alexander
1936 Jules Wetzlar, Sterns Cunningham
1937 Harry Fishbein, Lewis Bernard
1938 Robert Chatkin, Myron Fuchs
1939 Fred Kaplan, Harold Ziman
1940 Charles Lochridge, Merwyn Maier
1941 Helen Sobel, Charles Goren
1942 Alphonse Moyse, Richard Frey
1943 Abraham Goldstein, Jules Tilles
1944 Mrs. Kenneth Beghold, Eugene Smith
1945 Jerry Friedlander, Ned Drucker
1946 Harry Harkavy, Ambrose Casner
1947 Richard Kahn, Charles Whitebrook
1948 Dr. Kalman Apfel, Frances Begley
1949 Abe Goldstein, Boris Raymond
1950 Jules Tilles, E. I. Phillips
1951 Edgar Kaplan, Boris Raymond
1952 Bertram Lebhar, Simon Rossant
1953 Oswald Jacoby, Harry Fishbein
1954 Jules Tilles, Boris Raymond
1955 Oswald Jacoby, Alfred Sheinwold
1956 Alan Leeds, Eugene Thumim
1957 Tobias Stone, Janice Stone
1958 Jacqui Gallaher, Victor Mitchell
1959 Howard Berger, Dr. George Rothenberg
1960 Lawrence Rosler, Roger Stern
1961 Tobias Stone, Alvin Roth *(tied with)*

Sol Seidman, Norman Neiger
1962 Victor Shen, Bernard Borak
1963 Ray Jotcham, Jacques Guertin
1964 Eli Jaye, Simon Becker
1965 Fred Bickel, Ronny Rosenberg
1966 James Kauder, Ann Nichols
1967 Boris Raymond, Steve Altman
1968 Chuck Burger, James Cayne
1969 Andy Bernstein, Ralph Chafetz
1970 Vic Chernoff, Clagget Bowie
1971 Joe Asber, Anthony Dionisi
1972 Richard Freedman, David Loomis
1973 Carol Krupp, Paul Trent
1974 Paul Berger, Sam Hanna
1975 Neil Silverman, Merle Tom
1976 Carl Lindenman, Keith Garber
1977 Alvin Roth, Barbara Rappaport
1978 Alvin Roth, Barbara Rappaport
1979 Alvin Roth, Barbara Rappaport
1980 Carl Lindenman, Keith Garber
1981 Bob Jones, Dan Zirker

WOMEN'S PAIRS
1935 Mabel Kalman, Gussie Planco
1936 Mabel Frey, Gussie Planco
1937 Ruth Sherman, Margaret Wagar
1938 S. Dykman, N. Noel
1939 M. D. Rothschild, Viola Fuller
1940 Marguerite McKenney, Minnie Hirsch
1941 Barbara Cook, Edith Seligman
1942 Barbara Cook, Edith Seligman
1943 Helen Sobel, Ruth Sherman
1944 Helen Sobel, Ruth Sherman
1945 Helen Sobel, Ruth Sherman
1946 Peggy Adams, Marian Hochheimer
1947 Jane Jaeger, Paula Bacher
1948 Clementine Van Slochem, Henrietta Hess
1950 Geraldine Bison, Doris Brooks
1951 Peggy Adams, Marguerite Harris
1952 Alberta Albersheim, B. C. Martin
1953 Mrs. Chauncey Gibson, Mrs. Byron Brooks
1954 Mary Mitchell, Ottilie Reilly
1955 Wynne Ecker, Ida Goldman
1956 Claire Gilbert, Elsie Mallinson
1957 Marguerite Harris, Peggy Adams
1958 Mae Rosen, Wynne Ecker
1959 Mildred Betzler, Betty Simon
1960 Renee Rosenfield, Dorothy Berning
1961 Ethel Silver, Annie Gittleman
1962 Sylvia Gaines, Mary De Carlo
1963 Mae Rosen, Wynne Ecker
1964 Barbara Rappaport, Enid Asherman
1965 Margaret Wagar, Carol Sanders
1966 Jane Jaeger, Adele Grinberg
1967 Jacqui Mitchell, Ursula Blanton
1968 Bee Schenken, Sally Johnson
1969 Gussie Ritter, Edith Sacks
1970 Marian Altman, Diana Schuld
1971 Frances Fear, Hilda Tax
1972 Abby Heitner, Susan Levenson
1973 Betty Loop, Paula Frenkel
1974 Natalie Goldfarb, Audrey Kurland
1975 Edith Sacks, Enid Asherman
1976 Claire Zuckerberg, Margie Gwozdzinsky
1977 Bea Waldman, Doris Brown
1978 Ida Bennett, Ethel Keohane
1979 Dorothy Hayden Truscott, Barbara Rappaport
1980 Ann Astrachan, Elizabeth Gross
1981 Stasha Cohen, Judy Wadas

MEN'S PAIRS
1951 Sims Gaynor, Oswald Ray
1952 Dr. Raymond Michelson, George Kennedy
1954 Dr. William Lipton, Edward Loewenthal
1955 Dr. Kalman Apfel, Martin Rubinow
1956 Frank Westcott, Bert Koffman
1957 Israel Cohen, Richard Freeman
1958 Bernard Strauss, William Vanderporten
1959 Harry Fishbein, Herman Goldberg
1960 Alvin Roth, Said Haddad
1961 Dr. Nelson Reitman, Dr. William Lipton
1962 Gus Zipser, Richard Wegman
1963 Vic Bennahum, David Halper
1964 Bill Eisenberg, Stan Palmer
1965 Dr. William Lipton, Rudolf Bortstiber
1966 Irving Kass, Martin Cohn
1967 Richard DeMartino, Harry Woodman
1969 Eddie Manfield, Alan Sontag
1970 Dr. Stan Turecki, David Strasberg
1971 Karl Cox, Frank Westcott
1972 Richard Khautin, Warren Kornfeld
9713 Bob Ryder, Jim Looby

1974 Jay Wendt, Richard Lanke
1975 Jay Merrill, Andy Markowitz
1976 Ken Cohen, Mike Moss
1977 Eugene Neiger, Norman Kurlander
1978 John Brinley, Larry Edwards
1979 Steve Sanborn, Allan Stauber
1980 Arthur Bressler, Bernard Bench
1981 Joel Friedberg, Howard Chandross

OPEN TEAMS
1957 Leonard Harmon, Alfred Sheinwold,
Edgar Kaplan, Ivar Stakgold
1978 Bob Gwirtzman, Gregory Habeeb,
Michael Kopera, Nick Rabchenok
1979 Greg Habeeb, Joe Donath,
Dave Daly, Nick Rabchenok

MANHATTAN PAIRS
1959 Howard Robinson, Frances Werthman
1960 Jean Greenfield, Harold Geller

SENIOR MASTER PAIRS
1964 Richard Spero, Joel Stuart
1965 James Mines, Dr. Morley Welles
1966 Martin Bock, Karen Allison

MIXED PAIRS
1941 Phyllis Gardner, Hal Halsted
1942 Helen Sobel, Edward Hymes, Jr.
1943 Helen Sobel, Edward Hymes, Jr.
1944 Peggy Golder, Charles Solomon
1945 Barbara Cook, Ambrose Casner
1946 Helen Levy, Max Schwartz
1947 Mae Solomon, Jack Shore
1948 Helen Levy, Max Schwartz
1949 Lewis Jaeger, Jane Jaeger
1950 Peggy Adams, A. Lewis Gotthelf
1951 Nathan Agran, Violet Agran
1952 Sandra Fox, Kenneth Garlinger
1953 Henrietta Hess, Eugene Bauer
1954 Alberta Albersheim, Joseph Foreacre
1955 Betty Pearly, Benjamin Mitchell
1956 Claire Gilbert, Dr. Kalman Apfel
1957 Harry Fishbein, Ruth Fishbein
1958 Gwen Montgomery, Dr. Nelson Reitman
1959 Harold Levitt, Evelyn Levitt
1960 Harold Levitt, Evelyn Levitt
1961 Edith Kemp, Erwin Seligman
1962 Betty Sheinwold, Edgar Kaplan
1963 James Greenwood, Mrs. James Greenwood
1964 Gladys Kransberg, Chester Davis
1965 Marshall Feld, Rena Feld
1966 Vivian Lavery, Andy Bernstein
1967 Betty Cagan, Tom Smith
1968 Helen Utegaard, Mark Blumenthal
1969 Victor Mitchell, Muriel Ribner
1970 Helen Smith, Anthony Dionisi

INDIVIDUAL
1951 Sidney N. Morse
1952 Louis Kelner
1953 Alexander Steinberg
1954 Joseph Arbee
1955 John McCormick
1956 Edward Panossian
1957 Erwin Seligman
1959 Mrs. Joseph Epstein
1960 Jack Aldridge
1967 James Melrose
1968 John Grassi
1969 Jim Becker

MASTER PAIRS
1951 Sam Fry, Jr. Peter Leventritt
1952 Dr. William Lipton, Ira Rubin
1953 Fred Atiyeh, George Malhame
1954 Ira Rubin, Irving Martin
1955 Lester Glucksman, Monroe Newman
1956 David Strasberg, Ira Rubin
1957 Norman Kay, Ralph Hirschberg
1958 Sam Fry, Jr., Len Harmon
1959 Jay Wendt, Herb Lavine
1960 Richard Kahn, Adam Meredith
1961 Phil Feldesman, Boris Raymond
1962 Herbert Brandon, Frank Carroll
1963 Augusta Cantor, Lorand Tritter
1964 Richard Kahn, Ed Loewenthal
1965 John Benoit, Mike Cappelletti
1966 Victor Mitchell, Jacqui Mitchell
1967 Ronnie Rosenberg, Robert Lattomus
1968 Dr. Kalman Apfel, Ned Drucker
1969 Murray Melton, Simon Kantor
1970 Claire Tornay, Steve Goldstein

MIXED TEAMS
1933 Oswald Jacoby, Geraldine Furlow,

Theodore Lightner, Lillian Peck
1934 Waldemar von Zedtwitz, Geraldine Furlow,
     Oswald Jacoby, Mary Zita Jacoby
1935 Helen Sobel, Howard Schenken,
     Helen Bonwit, Louis Watson
1936 Irving Epstein, Estelle Drescher,
     Barbara Collyer, Al Leibowitz
1937 Howard Schenken, Henry Chanin,
     Helen Bonwit, Margaret Wagar
1938 Howard Schenken, Helen Bonwit,
     Morrie Elis, Mrs. E. Drescher
1939 James Lemon, Mrs. James Lemon,
     Dr. Llewellyn Lord, Mrs. Llewellyn Lord
1940 George Kennedy, Edna Kennedy,
     Louise Wainwright, Walter Malowan
1941 Louise Wainwright, Walter Malowan,
     Mrs. William Tucker, Sherman Stearns
1942 Sally Young, Peggy Golder,
     Charles Goren, Charles Solomon
1943 Mrs. L. W. Noel, Fred Kaplan,
     Paula Bacher, William Levin
1944 Louise Wainwright, Walter Malowan,
     Mrs. William Tucker, Wingate Bixby
1945 Stanley Kreps, Mrs. Stanley Kreps,
     Constance Little, Lee Sager
1946 Pete Leventritt, Samuel Katz,
     Sally Young, Jane Jaeger
1947 Paula Bacher, Phyllis Gardner,
     Lewis Jaeger, Maurice Levin
1949 Helen Sobel, Kay Rhodes,
     Richard Kahn, Sam Fry, Jr.
1955 Ira Brall, Carlyn Brall, Eli Jaye,
     Dorothea Woodington, Edgar Kaplan
1956 Charles Goren, Edith Kemp, Sam Stayman,
     Ruth Sherman, Richard Kahn *(tied with)*
     Jane Jaeger, Lewis Jaeger,
     Phyllis Gardner, Warren Slattery *(and)*
     Claire Gilbert, Valerie Klein, Aaron Green,
     Dr. Kalman Apfel, Louis Kelner
1957 Alfred Sheinwold, Patricia Sheinwold,
     Betty Pearly, Leonard Harmon
1958 Tobias Stone, Janice Stone, Dave Warner,
     Sally Young, Robert Jordan
1959 Phyllis Gardner, Helen Benjamin, Dorothy Tourance,
     Irving Rosenberg, Aaron Ritter
1960 Frances Eichmann, Gwen Montgomery,
     Dr. William Lipton, Dr. Nelson Reitman
1961 Marguerite Harris, Vivian Lavery,
     Dr. Robert Tator, Dr. John Manos *(tied with)*
     Ethel Keohane, Estee Griffin,
     Frank Westcott, Raymond Brown
1962 Dorothy Robinson, Mrs. Sidney Baderson,
     Michael Kassay, Gene Hochman
1963 Frank Carroll, Effie Long,
     Gordon Gibson, Ruth Gibson
1964 Dr. Steve Warner, Teddie Warner,
     Alan Messer, Barbara Tepper
1965 Evelyn Schwartz, John Bennett,
     Ida Bennett, Mike Moss
1966 Marshall Feld, Rena Feld,
     Ed Lazarus, Diane Aiken
1967 Charles Coon, James Bennett, Jr.,
     Alberta Albersheim, Ida Bennett
1968 Leonard Harmon, Marian Harmon,
     Carlyn Brall, Peter Pender
1969 Jane Mason, David Mason,
     Jim Becker, Ellen Alfandre

MEN'S TEAMS

1967 Howard Robinson, Alfred Ruttenberg, Michael Engel,
     Jay Mechutan, Marcel Friedman
1968 Paul Heitner, Larry Orange,
     Steve Altman, Richard Spero
1969 Michael Gurwitz, Donald Bloch, Harold Lilie,
     George Awad, Gene Prosnitz *(tied with)*
     Arnie Neidle, John Hester, Harry Woodman,
     Richard DeMartino, William Johnson *(and)*
     Ishmael Sklarew, Manuel Goodman,
     Richard Billig, Reginald Back

WOMEN'S TEAMS

1967 Barbara Birnholtz, Judith Carroll, Dorothy Silverman,
     Shirley Bederson, Ann-Marie Sporing
1968 Helen Smith, Adele Kotzen,
     Helen Utegaard, Evelyn Levitt
1969 Helen Smith, Mrs. R. P. Kinder, Deborah Cohen,
     Virginia Penick, Marjorie West

FUN CITY

KNOCKOUT TEAMS
1970 Dave Mason, Jane Mason, Mark Mohr,

George Awad, Marie Awad, Sol Seidman
1971 Tom Griffin, Estee Griffin, Anthony Dionisi,
     Chuck Lamprey, Mark Blumenthal, Harlow Lewis
1972 Ken Lebensold, Steve Goldstein, George Tornay,
     Lou Levy, Leslie Popper, Mark Feldman
1973 Jack Saltz, Amos Kaminski,
     Mike Lawrence, Amalya Kearse
1974 Jim Cayne, Peter Weichsel, Nancy Weichsel,
     Steve Sion, Jim Rosenbloom, Carl Lindenman
1975 Lou Reich, Bart Bramley, Steve Goldstein,
     Ken Lebensold, John Solodar, Henry Bethe
1976 Mike Moss, Amos Kaminski,
     Ken Cohen, Tom Smith
1978 Kathie Wei, Ron Andersen, Dave Berkowitz,
     Gerald Caravelli, Harold Lilie
1979 Alan Greenberg, Jimmy Cayne, Matt Granovetter,
     Neil Silverman, Robert Lipsitz
1980 Sam Stayman, George Tornay, Saul Bronstein,
     Peter Czerniewski, Gene Prosnitz, Michael Rosmarin
1981 Henry Bethe, Mark Cohen,
     Stasha Cohen, Chuck Lamprey

OPEN TEAMS

1973 Robert Lipsitz, Bob Ewen, Sam Stayman,
     Tom Merle, Ronnie Rubin, Matt Granovetter
1974 Cliff Russell, Alan Sontag, Peter Weichsel,
     Al Roth, Barbara Rappaport, Joel Stuart
1975 Mark Oshin, Philip Martin,
     Stewart Blickman, Stasha Wroblewski
1976 Dick Kahn, Marty Scheinberg,
     Jim Gobert, Dave Richheimer
1977 Ira Barrows, Bill Miller, Bruce Silverstein,
     Peter Weglarski, Joseph Livezey
1978 Norman Kurlander, Alan Sontag,
     Peter Weichsel, James Rosenbloom
1979 Mel Colchamiro, Alan Tucker,
     Alex Pollenz, Mitchell Pollenz
1980 Brian Glubok, Neil Silverman, Ahmed Hussein,
     Samuel Lev, Martin Hoffman
1981 Ira Herman, Gregory Woods, Rick Zucker,
     John Rengstorff, Drew Casen, Bob Blanchard

MASTER PAIRS
1972 Russ Ekeblad, Gary Hahn
1977 Kevin Hart, Paul Donahue
1978 Tom Justl, Mark Cohen

OPEN PAIRS
1970 Phil Feldesman, Bill Grieve
1971 Jay Feigus, Aaron Greene
1972 Al Roth, Barbara Rappaport
1973 Roger Stern, Sandra Stern
1974 Charles Wei, Merle Tom
1975 Myldred Kelly, Leonard Kaplan
1976 Ira Barrows, Joseph Livezey
1977 David Berkowitz, Harry Stappenback *(Smoking)*
     Joel Friedberg, Saul Gross *(Non-Smoking)*
1978 Roberta Epstein, Mark Epstein
1979 Einar Gudjohnsen, George Venkatesh
1980 Stephen Earl, Judy Merrill
     Alan Sontag, Erik Berger *(Smoking)*
     Jerrold Ginsparg, Jeff Aker *(tied with)*
     Steve Rotman, Monroe Magnus *(Non-Smoking)*
1981 Tom Abbott, Barry Goren

WOMEN'S PAIRS
1970 Edith Sudikoff, Ruth Grossman
1971 Cora Furman, Shirley Krellenstein
1972 Barbara Brier, Carol Lomaskin
1973 Diana Schuld, Marion Altman
1975 Judy Schwartz, Priscilla Rutkin
1976 Bertha Berman, Wendy Berman
1979 Mary Orock, Pat Zieger

MEN'S PAIRS
1970 Paul Kramer, Phil Cowan
1971 Henry Bethe, Steve Goldberg
1972 Keith Garber, Mark Epstein
1973 Nick Phillips, Doug Stewart
1975 Alfred Rand, Harold Lilie
1976 Joel Friedberg, Ron Blau
1979 Peter Weglarski, Bill Coren

MIXED PAIRS
1970 Ethel Keohane, Frank Westcott
1971 Gladys Collier, Alan Sontag
1974 Bill Braucher, Ann Roy
1981 Rosemarie Whitmore, Ike Goodfriend

INDIVIDUAL
1974 John Saxe
1981 Robert Sulman

LONG ISLAND

KNOCKOUT TEAMS
1968 Tom Griffin, Estee Griffin, Ray Brown,

Antony Dionisi, Robert Ewen, Alan Messer
1969   Stan Palmer, Sue Palmer, Marie Awad,
       George Awad, Dave Mason
1970   Ira Ewen, Linda Ewen,
       Robert Bowers, Saralee Bowers
1971   Joel Stuart, Eugene Neiger, Peter Weichsel,
       Steve Altman, Tom Smith
1972   Tom Smith, Peter Weichsel, Gene Neiger,
       Steve Altman, Alan Sontag, Joel Stuart
1975   Henry Bethe, Marty Ginsberg, Ron Blau,
       Alan Truscott, Dorothy Hayden Truscott
1976   Peter Weichsel, Alan Sontag, Paul Trent,
       Sandy Trent, Jim Cayne, Alan Greenberg
1977   Dave Berkowitz, Harold Lilie,
       Allan Cokin, Steve Sion
1978   Jim Hilton, Marty Scheinberg,
       John Solodar, Harry Stappenbeck
1979   Bob Gwirtzman, Harry Looks, Doug·Herron,
       Ethan Stein, Marc Zwerling
1980   Jim Sternberg, Peter Weichsel, Alan Sontag,
       Mark Molson, Boris Baran
1981   Kathie Wei, David Berkowitz,
       Ron Andersen, Harold Lilie
       OPEN TEAMS
1967   Jim Bennett, William Butcher,
       Marv Rosenblatt, Art Waldmann
1972   Judy Tucker, Alan Tucker, Pat Ross,
       Eugene Prosnitz, Marcel Friedman
1973   Dr. Edward Etkind, Steven Earl,
       James Strauss, Larry Bausher
1974   William Natbony, Michael Radin,
       Marc Jacobus, Steve Sion
1975   Betty Kaplan, Richard Kahn,
       Eddie Pinner, Edgar Kaplan
1976   Kerry Lloyd, Tom Maloney,
       Carl Berenbaum, Will Rogers
1977   Ethan Stein, Harry Looks,
       Eric Robinson, Bob Gwirtzman
1978   Jim Cayne, Matt Granovetter, Alan Greenberg,
       Alan Sontag, Peter Weichsel
1979   Nancy Bufano, David Kruter, Norman Buch,
       John Gaidukowski, Herman Horowitz
1980   Jim Becker, Rick Zucker, Jim Hamilton,
       Howard Chandross, Judy Tucker
1981   Don Theodore, Steve Garyn,
       Al Levy, Roger Elston
       MASTER PAIRS
1968   Phil Atiyeh, Chet McLaughlin
1969   William August, Dorothy Hayden
1970   Andy Bernstein, Dr. Stan Turecki
       OPEN PAIRS
1967   Gail Moss, Marshall Spitz
1968   Robert Ryder, Gene Hochman
1969   Henry Itkin, Kenny Rhodes
1970   Rena Feld, Marshall Feld
1971   Mike Moss, Gail Moss
1972   Leon St. Jean, Mark Rosenberg
1973   Audrey Kurland, Terry Riely
1974   Merle Tom, Matt Granovetter
1975   Marshall Schwartz, David Kaufman
1976   Jay Cohen, Peter Weglarski
1977   Harry Bregman, Otto Feuer
1980   Paul Morris, Joe Donath
1981   Cynthia Colin, Shirley Silverman
Smoking:
1978   Bill Landow, Mike Moss
1979   Gaile Goetsch, Cliff Goetsch
1981   Judy Tucker, Jim Becker
Non-Smoking:
1978   Ross Grabel, Josh Parker
1979   Tim Nelsen, Rozanne Marel
1981   Ann Rosner, Roger Nortman *(tied with)*
       Howard Chandross, Lew Handelsman
       MEN'S PAIRS
1967   Charles Brenner, Charles MacCracken
1968   Milton Steinfeld, William Meltzer
1969   R. Jay Becker, Lewis Finkel
1970   Ed Andresian, Mark Berger
1971   Frank Mela, Matt Granovetter
1972   Dr. Simon Kantor, R. Jay Becker
1973   Benson Yadgaroff, Morris Mirzoeff
1974   Robert Taylor, Gene Prosnitz
1975   Norman Kurlander, William Passell
1976   Gary Hann, Bill Erickson
1977   Don Barnett, Robert Gordon
1978   Marcel Friedmann, Alan Kudisch
1979   Jim Becker, Jim Hamilton
1980   Frank Neff, Francis Neff
       WOMEN'S PAIRS
1967   Judy Orange, Claire Tornay

1968   Edith Sacks, Gussie Ritter
1969   Edith Sacks, Gussie Ritter
1970   Natalie Half, Margaret Suran
1971   Ida Bennett, Ethel Keohane
1972   Lila Perlstein, Margie Gwozdzinsky
1973   Barbara Powsner, Marilyn Silverman
1974   Jacqui Mitchell, Jill Roberts
1975   Judy Schwartz, Priscilla Rutkin
1976   Sarah Korbin, Gertrude Goldstein
1977   Stasha Wroblewski, Vivian Whalen
1978   Jane Leigh, Rona Schiller
1979   Rozanne Marel, Claire Tornay
1980   Tina Kraus, Judy Lasker
       MIXED PAIRS
1967   Joan Oates, Herb Sachs
1968   Ann Goldberg, Joe Goldberg
1969   Kathie Cappelletti, Mike Cappelletti
1970   George Awad, Marie Awad
1971   Ellie Miller, Dave Berkowitz

NEW YORK WINTER

       KNOCKOUT TEAMS
1977   Kathie Wei, Ron Andersen, Dave Berkowitz,
       Harold Lilie, Steve Sion, Allan Cokin
1980   Kathie Wei, Ron Andersen, Dave Berkowitz,
       Mike Becker, Ron Rubin, Harold Lilie
1981   Alan Greenberg, Alan Sontag, Sam Lev,
       Jim Cayne, Jim Rosenbloom
       OPEN TEAMS
1972   B. Jay Becker, Jeff Rubens, Mike Becker,
       Roger Stern, Andy Bernstein *(tied with)*
       Al Roth, Barbara Rappaport,
       Neil Silverman, Ron Rubin
1973   Abe Schoenfeld, Francis Begley, Dave Halper,
       Dr. Kalman Apfel, Phil Goodman
1974   John Rengstorff, E. Kayser,
       Nancy Schwantes, Bill Erickson
1975   Bill Pollack, Merle Tom,
       Frank Mirchin, Les Bart
1976   Ross Grabel, Jeff Horowitz,
       Larry Bausher, Steve Sion
1977   William Passell, Marietta Passell,
       Alan Truscott, Dorothy Hayden Truscott
1978   Al Greenberg, Matt Granovetter, Jim Cayne,
       Alan Sontag, Peter Weichsel
1979   Jim Hilton, Bill Pollack, Harry Stappenbeck,
       Tim Nelsen, Frank Mirchin
1980   Mel Colchamiro, Carl Berenbaum,
       Bob Jones, Bob Gwirtzman
1981   Matt Granovetter, Al Rand, Rita Rand,
       Harold Lilie, Dave Berkowitz
       MIXED TEAMS
1971   Paul Heitner, Abby Heitner,
       Ken Parker, Judy Parker
       INDIVIDUAL
1976   Walter Schenker
1979   V. W. Pathare
       OPEN PAIRS
1972   Amos Kaminski, Chuck Papazian
1973   Gail Moss, Mike Moss
1974   Ross Grabel, Mark Rosenberg
1975   Ethel Silver, Emily Economidis
1976   William Rife, Tom Feuer
1977   Robert Lipsitz, Les Bart
1978   Ross Grabel, Don Probst
1979   Lloyd Arvedon, Ken Bercuson
1980   Vic King, Douglas Doub
1981   Ira Herman, Michael Rosmarin
       LIFE MASTER PAIRS
1971   Marty Bergen, Richard Oshlag
1975   Sandy Trent, Estee Griffin
       MEN'S PAIRS
1971   Chuck Lamprey, Stephen Labins
1974   Dr. Gerald Elkind, Dr. Dan Reider *(tied with)*
       William Gough, Phil Brady
1977   Jack Bonney, Arthur Kong
1978   Dave Richheimer, Dr. Edward Etkind
1980   Victor Melman, Simon Erlich
1981   Carl Michelet, Warren Singer
       WOMEN'S PAIRS
1971   Paula Jenshel, Renee Rosenfeld
1974   Marion Altman, Vivian Whalen
1977   Debbie Cohen, Harriet Polonsky
1978   Kitty Bethe, Karen McCallum
1980   Leslie Paryzer, Nancy Widman
1981   Gail Moss, Lila Perlstein

MIXED PAIRS
1972 John Solodar, Judi Solodar
1973 Robert Marshall, Dorothy Goldsmith
1976 Al Roth, Barbara Rappaport
1979 Kitty Bethe, Mark Cohen

DISTRICT 25 (Connecticut, Maine, Massachusetts, New Hampshire, Rhode Island, Vermont)

NEW ENGLAND FALL

MIXED TEAMS
1935 Mrs. Charles Harvey, Charles Harvey, Mrs. Arthur Howard, Arthur Howard
1936 Rosamond Vahey, John Liston, Dorothy Robinson, A. N. Guimerais
1937 Rosamond Vahey, John Liston, Dorothy Robinson, A. N. Guimerais
1938 Mrs. Charles Harvey, Charles Harvey, Minna Levine, Edward Marcus
1940 Mrs. W.B. Bacon, Sidney Wirt, Mrs. Carl Barnet, Carl Barnet
1941 Mrs. Carl Barnet, Carl Barnet, Mrs. W.B. Bacon, Sidney Wirt
1942 Mrs. Raymond Olsen, Raymond Olsen, Ethel Keohane, Orrin Hart
1943 Mrs. Herbert Ansin, Edward Marcus, Florence Hootstein, Everett Clarke,
1944 Betty Hermanson, W. Mark Noble, Dana Wilber, Fredrick Carpenter
1945 Mrs. Milton Casson, Milton Casson, Mrs. Fred Solomon, John O'Donnell
1946 Ethel Keohane, Kenneth Hill, Aileen Skinner, Frank Westcott
1947 Earl Ackerman, Mabel Ackerman, Marguerite Harris, Richmond Skinner
1948 Ethel Keohane, Kenneth Hill, Carolyn Whitehead, Frank Westcott
1949 Ethel Keohane, Kenneth Hill, Selma Raphael, Frank Westcott
1950 Ethel Keohane, Kenneth Hill, Selma Raphael, Frank Westcott
1951 Peggy Solomon, John O'Donnell, Frances Harding, Lawrence Weiss
1952 Mrs. C.N. Lovenberg, Harold Creedon, Florence Johnson, Meredith Jones *(tied with)* Mrs. John Kunkel, John Kunkel, Col. Richmond Skinner, Eve Skinner *(and)* Florence Hootstein, Clayton Clancey, Jr. Dr. C. G. Barrett, Noelle Hartigan
1953 Betty Vail, Warren Mansfield, Helen Sweeny, Robert Starr
1954 Doris Bailey, James Lee, Frances Rosen, Dr. J. F. Roberts
1955 H. Dean Baker, Helen Baker, Edward Noyes, Bee Noyes
1956 Ethel Keohane, Frank Westcott, Constance Kemball, George Durgin
1957 Phyllis Feldman, Peter Johnson, Frances Harding, Richard Sears
1958 William Passell, Elsie Abrams, Edward Wendt, Dorothy Hayden, David Strasberg
1959 Nolan Curry, Carolyn Curry, Grace Coutant, Simon Kantor
1960 Mrs. Martin Scheinberg, Martin Scheinberg, Robert Wakeman, Ruth Wakeman
1961 Ruth Sugenheimer, William Adams, Warren Mansfield, Betty Vail
1962 Ruth Sugenheimer, William Adams, Warren Mansfield, Betty Vail
1963 John McElwain, Constance McElwain, Alberta Albersheim, Charles Coon *(tied with)* Harvey Poock, Aileen Poock, Mrs. S. Kransberg, William Butcher
1964 Vivian Lavery, Dr. John Manos, Marguerite Harris, Dr. Robert Tabor
1965 Marshall Feld, Rena Feld, Alberta Albersheim, Charles Coon
1966 Gladys Kransberg, Chester Davis, Mike Moss, Gail Shane
1967 Mickey Rosenthal, Kenneth Barbour, Mike Cappelletti, Kathie Cappelletti
1968 Morris Schneider, Ann Schneider, Joseph Livezey, Catherine Vosburgh
1969 Don Faskow, Mark Blumenthal, Gloria Cohen, Helen Smith *(tied with)* Nat Gerstman, Pat Elms, David Scheffer, Millie Rheault *(and)* William Adams, Mrs. Manuel Clark,

Warren Mansfield, Betty Vail *(and)* Mrs. Phillip Finkle, Dr. Robert Farelly, Robert Starr, Mrs. Elliott Slack, Etta Stone
1970 Arthur Waldmann, Ellen Alfandre, Ned Drucker, Carol Graham
1971 Chet Davis, Evelyn Garfield, Diana Schuld, Frank Schuld
1972 Sharyn Linkovsky, Eric Kokish, Lois Labins, Steve Labins

MEN'S PAIRS
1935 Edward Marcus, Sidney Green
1936 Sidney Wirt, H. White
1937 H. Keller, Luke Goff
1938 Edward Marcus, Sidney Aronson
1939 Frank Edlin, Norman Bonney
1940 Mark Noble, George Hatch
1941 Lawrence Weiss, Edward Marcus
1942 Mark Noble, Byron Ruiter
1943 Frank Perkins, Edward Marcus
1944 Nathan Kelly, Kenneth Hill
1945 John O'Donnell, Arthur Bell
1946 Sidney Wirt, Richmond Skinner
1947 Lawrence Weiss, Sidney Aronson
1948 David Goldschmidt, George Linde
1949 James Albert, Milton Wayner
1950 Wilbur Johnson, Royal Baker
1951 Frank Westcott, Robert Starr
1952 Bernard Goldman, Milton Casson
1953 Chester Clancy, Gerry Closson
1954 Robert Arthur, Donald Gaudette
1955 Robert Ludwig, Peter Johnson
1956 Robert Ludwig, Peter Johnson
1957 Fred Hess, Thomas Mooney
1958 Donald Gaudette, Chris Ruggiero
1959 Harry Bernstrom, Dean Baker
1960 Simon Kantos, C. R. Greenhow
1961 Myrton Harris, Lee Berrouard
1962 Stephen Labins, Robert Hoffman
1963 Frank Westcott, Robert Starr
1964 David Mason, William Passell
1965 Dr. Edward Etkind, Dr. H. Franklin Bunn
1966 Marshal Feld, William Levin
1967 Robert Lipsitz, Steve Labins
1968 Frank Merblum, Howard Merblum
1969 Harvey Cohen, Richard Borod
1970 Robert Kehoe, Bernard Miller
1971 Marvin Rosenblatt, Art Waldmann
1972 Marshall Feld, James Bennett

KNOCKOUT TEAMS
1977 Richard Hecht, William Gorden, Mark Rosenberg, David Ehler
1978 Josh Parker, Don Probst, Ross Grabel, Alan Schwartz
1979 Luke Gillespie, Steve Ligas, John Stiefel, Dale Beers
1980 Tom Goodwin, Ethan Stein, Allan Stauber, Marty Bergen
1981 Bob Feller, Jerry Cohen, Steve Bloom, Betty Bloom

WOMEN'S PAIRS
1931 Eleanor Bancroft, Mrs. Prescott Warren
1932 Mrs. Robert Kimball, Clare Smith
1933 Eleanor Bancroft, Mrs. Prescott Warren
1934 Dorothy Robinson, Rosamond Vahey
1935 P. H. Blanding, S. B. Levy
1936 T. L. Haugen, J. F. Kutz
1937 W. B. Bacon, Eleanor Bancroft
1938 Minna Levine, Mrs. Milton Casson
1939 Maude Flanders, W.S. David
1940 Dorothy Robinson, Faith Ziegler
1941 Mrs. William Lyons, Mrs. David Golden
1942 Ethel Keohane, Mrs. Raymond Olsen
1943 Mrs. Herbert Ansin, Florence Hootstein
1944 Mrs. William Davis, Maude Flanders
1945 Frances Harding, Mae Solomon
1946 Frances Harding, Mae Solomon
1948 Ethel Keohane, Eve Skinner
1949 Selma Raphael, Lena Ramer
1950 Ethel Keohane, Minna Levine
1951 L. H. Rogers, Hedda Stieglandt
1952 Frances Harding, Mae Solomon
1953 Mae McCarthy, Mary Hartley
1954 Selma Raphael, Florence Hoostein
1955 Sally Johnson, Rhoda Krupa
1956 Mrs. William Hanlon, Alberta Albersheim
1957 Edythe Silverton, Lilian Hummel
1958 Hedda Steiglandt, Frances Rosen
1959 Constance McElwain, Frances Harding
1960 Diane Goldman, Anne Welansky
1961 Winnie Slutsky, Alma Godfrey

1962	Kitty Creedon, Helen Walcott
1963	Diane Goldman, Geraldine Gottlieb
1964	Lucy Sagalyn, Mary Hartley
1965	Patricia Dye, Dorothy Joiner
1966	Sue Thornton, Mimi Roncarelli
1967	Phyllis Prager, Ruth Grossman
1968	Mrs. Earl Dunham, Mildred Prouty
1969	Eleanor Wynn, Etta Stone
1970	Evelyn Garfield, Mary Bright
1971	Jean Cunningham, Ceil Weiss
1972	Dorothy Smith, Sally Smith

INDIVIDUAL

1977	Gary Schwartz
1978	Don Levy
1979	Neva Kaufman

MIXED PAIRS

1930	Arthur Holt, Rosamond Vahey
1931	K. Tufts, J. Arnold Farrer
1932	Mrs. John Rock, J. Arnold Farrer
1933	Helen Lyons, Elliott Brown III
1934	Mrs. Charles Smith, John Barry
1935	Mrs. Charles Harvey, Charles Harvey
1936	Mrs. V.A. Hicks, J. Holden
1937	Mrs. Robert Kimball, Robert Kimball
1937	Mrs. W. M. Hurd, Stephen Weiss
1938	Minna Levine, Edward Marcus
1938	Marie Cohn, Paul McNulty
1939	Frances Harding, Dr. F. Fouillard
1939	Bert Levin, Claire Levin *(tied with)*
	Frances Harding, Dr. F. Fouillard
1940	Dorothy Harvey, Robert Elzholz
1940	Mrs. Milton Casson, Milton Casson
1941	Frances Harding, Lawrence Weiss
1942	Arthur Bell, Mrs. W. J. Lyons
1942	Frances Harding, Byron Ruiter
1943	Mrs. W. M. Hurd, Warren Hopkins
1943	Mrs. Nathan Kelly, Nathan Kelly
1944	Mrs. D. Golden, Bernard Goldman
1944	Madeline Rooney, Oliver Westbury
1945	Frances Harding, Lawrence Weiss
1945	Mrs. Milton Casson, Milton Casson
1946	Edward Marcus, Mrs. Herbert Ansin
1946	Mrs. Herbert Ansin, Charles Goren
1947	Marie Cohn, R. Wechsler
1948	Ethel Keohane, Frank Westcott
1949	Florence Hoostein, Sidney Aronson
1950	Mrs. L. H. Rogers, Ralph Breitstein
1951	Ethel Keohane, Frank Westcott
1952	Betty Vail, David Goldschmidt
1953	Betty Vail, Warren Mansfield
1954	Doris Bailey, James Lee
1955	Ida Finlay, Chester Davis, Jr.
1956	Pedro Cabral, Evelyn Garfield
1957	Carol Graham, Robert Easterbrook
1958	Frances Harding, Charles Coon
1959	Ethel Keohane, Frank Westcott
1960	Rosa Ryans, David Wynne
1961	Helen Walcott, Robert Fox
1962	Alberta Albersheim, Charles Coon
1963	Florence Johnson, Robert McVey
1964	Augusta Cantor, Alan Rich
1965	Alberta Albersheim, Charles Coon
1966	Mickey Rosenthal, Ken Barbour
1967	Mickey Rosenthal, Ken Barbour
1968	Col. A. Abbott, Mary Hartley
1969	Evelyn Schwartz, William Butcher
1970	Polly Riggs, David Rosen
1971	Gail Moss, Mike Moss
1972	Sharyn Linkovsky, Eric Kokish
1977	Rosemarie Merblum, Frank Merblum
1978	Rosemarie Merblum, Frank Merblum
1979	Michael Moss, Gail Moss

OPEN PAIRS

1973	Mort Backer, Lucy Backer
1974	William Woodard, Jay Merrill
1975	Charles Coon, Steve Sion
1976	Steve Labins, Chuck Lamprey
1977	Ross Grabel, John Malley
1978	Gene Proshitz, Ethan Stein
1979	Dave Berkowitz, Mark Cohen

Flight A:

1981	Ron Sukoneck, Judi Cody

Smoking:

1980	Joseph Broderick, Jay Scavone
1981	Ron Haack, Gail Moss

Non-Smoking:

1980	Tony Petronella, Fredric Suzman
1981	Albert Ross, May Glantz

MASTER PAIRS

1974	Bernard Miller, Leslie Popper

1975	William August, Robert Lavin
1976	Steve Sion, Allan Cokin

SWISS TEAMS

1973	Bart Bramley, Chuck Lamprey,
	Lou Reich, Steve Labins
1974	Alberta Albersheim, Ethel Keohane,
	Ken Kadis, Ulhas Nayak
1975	Steve Sion, Marc Jacobus, Allan Cokin,
	Mark Feldman, Gerald Caravelli
1976	Jack Appleton, Rick Binder, Harry Banks,
	Henry DuLaurence, Paul Lavallee, George Caldwell
1977	Rick Binder, Henry DuLaurence, Harry Banks,
	Jack Appleton, George Caldwell, Paul Lavallee
1978	Jeff Horowitz, Larry Bausher, Chester Davis,
	James Bennett, John Batcheller, John Stiefel *(tied with)*
	Ross Grabel, David Ehler, Josh Parker, Dick Hecht
1979	Bill Gorden, Jeff Horowitz,
	Larry Bausher, John Malley *(tied with)*
	Geof Brod, Harold Feldheim,
	Alan Schwartz, Josh Feldstein *(and)*
	William Ashford, Robert Woodard,
	Abbott Feren, Gilbert Munz
1980	Helen Lowenthal, John Lowenthal,
	Phillip Martin, Elizabeth Nelson
1981	Richard Hecht, Joel Friedberg, Luke Gillespie,
	David Ehler, Gene Saxe, Steve Ligas

NEW ENGLAND INDIVIDUAL

1945	Kenneth Hill
1946	Meyer Channen
1947	Stuart Thoits
1948	Milton Casson
1949	Robert Fels
1950	Archie Markson
1951	E. Farrington Abbott, Jr.
1952	Robert Fox
1953	Perley Weatherbee
1954	James Lee
1955	Ashlund Shaghalian
1956	Kenneth Edmunds
1957	Francis Rosen
1958	Cy Farell
1959	Dr. Alexander Ramer
1960	Ed Noyes
1961	John Hunt
1962	Jerry Bauer
1963	Harding Johnson, Jr.
1964	Dr. Sam Sheiman
1965	John Hunt
1966	Marshall Feld
1967	Kenneth Edmunds
1968	Elsie Mentuck
1969	Leo Weiner
1970	James Tang
1971	Doris Lenk
1972	Val Habicht
1973	David Silberstein
1974	Dennis Scott
1975	Josh Parker
1976	Gary Schwartz
1977	Jean White
1978	Mark Aguino
1979	Harry Shearer *(tied with)*
	Mrs. B. J. Ryan
1980	Clint Morrell
1981	Philip Lam *(tied with)*
	Paul Schmitt

KNOCKOUT TEAMS

1974	Dennis Dawson, Jackie Dawson, John Stiefel,
	James Bennett, Jr., Marian Keszycki, Bob Hughes
1975	Richard Zeckhauser, Arthur Waldmann, Bob Kehoe,
	Bob Cohen, Paul Brenner
1976	Mark Feldman, Allan Conkin, Ross Grabel,
	Charles Coon, Steve Sion
1977	Lou Reich, Bart Bramley, Jay Merrill,
	Arthur Waldmann, Merle Tom
1978	Bernie Miller, Leslie Popper,
	Clint Morrell, Harold Stengel
1979	Leslie Popper, Bernie Miller, Harold Stengel,
	Steve Biciocchi, Charles Coon
1980	Kathie Wei, Judi Radin, Ron Andersen,
	Dave Berkowitz, Chuck Lamprey
1981	Bob Feller, Bob Yellis,
	Emmett Pollenz, Jeff Hall

NEW ENGLAND KNOCKOUTS

KNOCKOUT TEAMS

(When two results are given, the first names represent the winners of the Boston Chess Club event, and the second the winners of the Cavendish Club event.)

1930 Nathan Kelly, J. Arnold Farrer,
     P. R. Ammidon, Frank Perkins
1931 P. Hal Sims, Willard Karn,
     David Burnstine, Walter Malowan
1932 F. M. Howe, Francis Harding,
     F. D. Pollard, Mrs. H. Mann
1933 Mrs. W. J. Lyons, Mrs. F. Merrill,
     Eli Brown III, Cecil Head
1934 Nathan Kelly, Frank Perkins,
     John Barry, Cecil Head
1935 J. Arnold Farrer, Ruth Chase,
     Sidney Wirt, Ralph Ells
1936 Walter Malowan, Sidney Rusinow,
     Richard Frey, Mabel Frey
1937 Mrs. Charles Harvey, Charles Harvey,
     Frank Perkins, Edward Marcus
1937 W. Towne, Paul McNulty,
     George Verde, James Silin
1938 Nathan Kelly, Lawrence Weiss,
     Jerome Scheuer, Charles Harvey
1938 J. Arnold Farrer, Robert Elzholz,
     George Verde, James Silin
1939 Cecil Head, Lawrence Weiss,
     Jerome Scheuer, Stephen Weiss
1939 Edward Marcus, Sidney Green,
     Minna Levine, Frank Perkins
1940 George Verde, Arthur Bell,
     J. Arnold Farrer, Paul McNulty
1940 George Verde, Sidney Wirt,
     Arthur Bell, J. Arnold Farrer
1941 Frank Perkins, Cecil Head, Lawrence Weiss,
     Jerome Scheuer, Edward Marcus
1941 Frank Perkins, Cecil Head, Lawrence Weiss,
     Jerome Scheuer, Edward Marcus
1942 Lawrence Weiss, Arthur Howard,
     Edward Marcus, Frank Perkins
1942 William Campbell, Bryan Ruiter, Paul McNulty,
     Warren Hopkins, Dr. J. F. Roberts
1942 William Campbell, Bryan Ruiter, Paul McNulty,
     Warrent Hopkins, Dr. J. F. Roberts
1943 Jerome Scheuer, Fredrick Solomon,
     Milton Casson, Albert Jacobson
1943 Peter Johnson, Richard Fisher, R. Martens,
     M. Marks, Y. Barkan
1944 Mrs. Herbert Ansin, Charles Goren,
     Edward Marcus, Harold Fagin
1944 Mrs. Herbert Ansin, Edward Marcus, Bernard Levin,
     Sidney Green, William Silver
1945 Mrs. Herbert Ansin, Lawrence Weiss, Edward Marcus,
     Robert Elzhoz, Bernard Levin
1945 Milton Casson, Jerome Scheuer,
     Cecil Head, Sidney Wirt
1946 Milton Casson, Jerome Scheuer,
     Cecil Head, Sidney Wirt
1946 Milton Casson, Jerome Scheuer,
     Cecil Head, Sidney Wirt
1947 Milton Casson, Jerome Scheuer,
     Cecil Head, Sidney Wirt
1948 Kenneth Hill, Richmond Skinner,
     Helen Zacks, Howard Zacks
1949 Ethel Keohane, H. Dean Baker,
     Royal Baker, Frank Westcott
1950 Milton Casson, John Liston, Albert Morehead,
     Jerome Scheuer, Sidney Wirt
1951 Jerome Scheuer, Sidney Wirt, John Liston,
     Albert Morehead, Cecil Head
1952 Murray Meltzer, Ivar Stakgold,
     Richard Lesser, Ludwig Katz
1953 H. Dean Baker, Helen Baker,
     Robert Cox, J. Walter Ryan
1954 Cecil Head, Edgar Kaplan,
     Jerome Scheuer, Ivor Stakgold
1955 Bernard Goldman, Fred Solomon,
     Milton Casson, Kenneth Hill
1956 Frank Westcott, Royal Baker,
     Robert Fox, Robert Starr
1957 Larry Weiss, William Grieve, Alex Tschekaloff,
     Charles Coon, George Durgin
1958 Constance Kemball, Phil Feldman, Charles Coon,
     Peter Johnson, Richard Sears
1959 Frank Westcott, Robert Fox,
     Robert Starr, Royal Baker
1960 William Butcher, Evelyn Garfield, Elsie Abrams,
     Dr. George Dorfman, William Passell

1961 William Levin, Dave Cliff, Charles Coon,
     Richard Sears, Larry Weiss
1962 Frank Westcott, Royal Baker, Robert Fox,
     Robert Starr, Harry Bernstrom, Milton Calder
1963 Frank Westcott, Royal Baker, Robert Starr,
     Robert Fox, Chester Davis
1964 Frank Goldring, Charles Coon, Richard Sears,
     Richard Zeckhauser, Larry Weiss
1965 Frank Silver, John Benoit, Joe Goldberg,
     Leslie Popper, Mike Cappelletti
1966 Ron Blau, Lester Sokolower,
     John Lowenthal, Paul Heitner
1967 Steve Labins, Chuck Sonnenschein, Mel Marcus,
     Marshall Spitz, Khris Bhavnani, Richard Schreitmueller
1968 Andy Bernstein, Harold Feldheim,
     Peter Weichsel, Tom Smith
1969 Chester Davis, Dr. Robert Tator, Larry Weiss,
     Leslie Popper, Norman Humer, Joseph Goldberg
1970 Bernie Chazen, Richard Budd,
     Chuck Lamprey, Stephen Labins
1971 Joe Silver, Eric Kokish,
     Mark Blumenthal, Robert Lipsitz
1972 Joe Silver, Eric Kokish,
     Mike Gurwitz, John Bookstaver
1973 Chester Davis, Norman Humer,
     Bernard Miller, Dr. Robert Tator
1974 Kathi Wei, Steve Goldstein, Tom Merle,
     Ken Lebensold, Ron Andersen, Mark Feldman
1975 Mike Cappelletti, Kathie Cappelletti,
     Stephen Labins, Chuck Lamprey
1976 Peter Weichsel, Alan Sontag, Allan Cokin,
     Steve Sion, Charles Coon
1977 Lou Reich, Bart Bramley, Jay Merrill,
     Arthur Waldmann, Merle Tom
1978 Ross Grabel, Josh Parker,
     Marc Nathan, Don Probst
1979 Jim Sternberg, Allan Cokin, Steve Sion,
     Alan Sontag, Peter Weichsel
1980 Kathie Wei, Ron Andersen, Judi Radin,
     Mark Feldman, Chuck Lamprey
1981 Mike Cappelletti, Kathie Cappelletti,
     David Hoffner, Glenn Lubin

MASTER PAIRS
1969 Paul Heitner, Bernard Chazen

OPEN PAIRS
1970 Ethel Keohane, Bob Thurrell
1971 Richard DeMartino, Harry Woodman
1972 Chuck Wallace, Marvin Schwalb
1973 James Tevis, Mildred Bonney
1976 Nat Gerstman, Mary Lou Cushner
1977 James Lee, Bill Cunningham
Smoking:
1978 James Scott, Peter Sugarman
1979 Jeff Juster, Mark Cohen
1980 Harry Widmer, Jake McDonald
1981 Julie Rowe, Patrick Home
Non-Smoking:
1978 Larry Simon, John Saxe
1979 Marty Bergen, Alan Schwartz
1980 Bruce Kayle, Ken Harris
1981 Stasha Wroblewski, Mark Cohen

BOARD-A-MATCH TEAMS
1968 Tom Griffin, Paul Heitner,
     John Lowenthal, Ronald Crown *(tied with)*
     Dorothy Hayden, Steve Becker,
     Mike Becker, B. Jay Becker *(and)*
     W. Adams, E. Delahanty,
     Robert Easterbrook, John Hunt *(and)*
     Ken Parker, Judy Parker, L. Schwartz,
     E. Segal, Ira Zippert

SWISS TEAMS
1974 Monty Kuka, Robert Gilbertson,
     Carl Moxey, Robert Hughes *(tied with)*
     Shirley Hewitt, Richard Hewitt,
     Genevieve Fernandez, William Fernandez *(and)*
     Michael Agranoff, Roger Briley,
     Steven Slitt, Howard Lawrence *(and)*
     Jim Logan, Anne Logan,
     Rennie Graham, Connie Graham
1975 Jay Merrill, Chip Martel,
     Arthur Waldmann, Harlow Lewis
1976 William Dubay, Jeff Klemm,
     Bob Clifton, Dave Peloguin
1977 David Beer, Abby Heitner, Paul Heitner,
     Steve Labins, Chuck Lamprey *(tied with)*
     Glen Lublin, Martin Nelson,
     Ron Sukoneck, Ely Solomon *(and)*
     Douglas Fraser, Harold Goldstein, Mark Molson,
     Robert Lebi, Renee Mancuso, Sam Kleinplatz

1978   Kathie Wei, Judi Radin, Ron Andersen,
Dave Berkowitz, Gerald Caravelli *(tied with)*
Paul Vickers, Bob Fiske,
Judi Cody, Bob Hughes *(and)*
Ken Kadis, Elayne Kadis,
James Lee, Anne Walkins
1979   Clint Morrell, Lewis Finkel,
R. Jay Becker, Robert Barr
1980   Ross Grabel, Ethan Stein,
Mark Cohen, Josh Parker
1981   B. Jay Becker, Lew Finkel,
Frank Mastrola, Richard Taube
Flight A:
1979   John Malley, Harold Feldheim,
David Ehler, Dick Hecht
1980   Richard Budd, Jackie Dawson,
John Batcheller, Dennis Dawson
1981   Frank Merblum, Howard Merblum,
Stephen Earl, Judith Merrill *(tied with)*
Dale Beers, Jeff Aker, Doug Doub, Geof Brod

MASTER SWISS TEAMS

1977   Marc Jacobus, Marvin Herbert, Harold Stengel,
Alan Applebaum, Allan Cokin
1978   Kathie Wei, Judi Radin, Ron Andersen,
Dave Berkowitz, Gerald Caravelli

NEW ENGLAND MASTERS

MASTER TEAMS

1948   Richmond Skinner, Philip Herrman,
Philip Katzenstein, Sam Gold
1949   Helen Zacks, Howard Zacks,
Kenneth Hill, Ethel Keohane
1950   Edward Marcus, Lawrence Weiss,
Florence Hootstein, Sidney Aronson
1951   H. Ballou, H. Dean Baker,
W. Offner, Paul Kerwick
1952   Edward Marcus, Peter Johnson,
Jack Kushner, Max Kelleher
1953   Howard Zacks, Helen Zacks,
Sandra Fox, Henry Mullaney
1954   Robert Fels, James Gildea,
Philip Herrmann, Howard Palmer
1955   Edgar Kaplan, Alfred Sheinwold,
Ivar Stakgold, Sol Rubinow
1956   Alex Tschekaloff, Charles Coon,
George Durgin, David Cliff
1957   Edgar Kaplan, Alfred Sheinwold,
Leonard Harmon, Ivar Stakgold
1958   Richard Lesser, Walter May,
Marvin Rosenblatt, Charles Coon *(tied with)*
Harry Bernstrom, Milton Calder,
Helen Baker, H. Dean Baker
1959   Peter Pender, Robert Sitnek,
John Moran, Robert Levine
1960   Norman Kay, Robert Jordan,
Arthur Robinson, Peter Pender
1961   Michael Engel, L. James Phillips,
Paul Trent, Marvin Altman
1962   Robert Mosher, Jeff Rubens,
David Kitzes, William Bradley
1963   Paul Heitner, Linda Heitner,
Ira Ewen, Eugene Prosnitz
1964   Marshall Feld, Rena Feld,
Irwin Boris, Paul Brenner
1965   James Bennett, Lt. Col. William Christian,
Gail Shane, Mike Moss
1966   Steve Labins, Chuck Lamprey, Marshall Spitz,
Mel Marcus, Chuck Sonnenschein
1967   Robert Lipsitz, Art Waldmann,
Marvin Rosenblatt, William Butcher
1968   Frank Merblum, Howard Merblum,
Monroe Magnus, David Corbin
1969   John Solodar, Henry Bethe,
Art Waldmann, Marvin Rosenblatt
1970   Marshall Feld, Rena Feld,
James Bennett, Marian Keszcki *(tied with)*
Mark Blumenthal, Robert Lipsitz,
Stephen Labins, Chuck Lamprey
1971   John Appleton, John McDermott,
Bill Braucher, Clint Morrell
1972   John Appleton, John McDermott,
Bill Braucher, Clint Morrell
1973   Bart Bramley, Chuck Lamprey,
Lou Reich, Steve Labins
1974   Ben Goldsmith, Richard Weiss,
Steve Ligas, Luke Gillespie
1975   Bill Butcher, Jim Bennett, Dave Cliff,
Leon St. Jean, Marian Keszycki
1977   Steve Biciocchi, Harry Stengel,
Leslie Popper, Clint Morrell

1978   George Caldwell, Bob Fiske, Rick Binder,
Paul Vickers, Bill Braucher, John McDermott *(tied with)*
Nancy Greer, Jim Greer,
Mike Charles, Steve Dunham

MASTER PAIRS

1942   Albert Jacobson, Sidney Aronson
1946   Fred Carpenter, Archie Markson
1947   E. Farrington Abbott, Jr., Stuart Thoits
1948   Albert Jacobson, Peter Johnson
1949   Edward Marcus, Sam Stayman
1950   Wilbur Johnson, Royal Baker
1951   W. Hopkins, Harry Williams
1952   Edward Marcus, Peter Johnson
1953   Perley Weatherbee, E. Farrington Abbott, Jr.
1954   Robert Ludwig, Ludwig Katz
1955   J. Mechutan, E. Van Cott
1956   William Lipton, Murray Schnee
1957   Sol Rubinow, Morton Rubinow
1958   Peter Pender, Robert Sitnek
1959   Richard Lesser, Walter May
1960   Sol Rubinow, Dave Strasberg
1961   Harry Bernstrom, Milton Calder
1962   Jeff Rubens, Robert Mosher
1963   Harry Bernstrom, Milton Calder
1964   Mike Cappelletti, John Benoit
1965   Betty Fourierzos, Monroe Magnus, Jr.
1966   Peter Pender, Jeremy Flint
1967   Richard Fleischman, Phil Leon
1968   Gail Moss, Sandra Roark
1969   Mary Lou Cushner, Garrett Nash
1970   Carol Krupp, Paul Trent
1971   Richard Freedman, Ed Krugman
1972   Alberta Albersheim, Charles Coon
1973   Russ Ekeblad, Robert Stone
1974   Ronald Newberg, Pat McDevitt
1975   Charles Coon, Steve Sion
1976   Jay Merrill, Lou Reich

MASTER MEN'S PAIRS

1967   Art Waldmann, Marshall Feld
1968   Bill Butcher, Bernie Chazen
1969   Robert Sidman, Eugene Spiegel
1970   William Henry, James Wadas
1971   Stephen Labins, Chuck Lamprey
1972   Roger.Stokey, Ed Sullivan

MASTER WOMEN'S PAIRS

1967   Sylvia Le Savoy, Mrs. S. Epstein
1968   Gladys Kransberg, Evelyn Garfield
1969   Betty Vail, Winnie Clark
1970   Pat Jones, Mildred Fromm
1971   Judi Solodar, Gail Moss
1972   Mary Campbell, Anne Cortner *(tied with)*
Elyse Katz, Polly Riggs

OPEN PAIRS

1977   Steve Sion, Allan Cokin
1978   Jerry Kuklinski, Roberto Serenyi
1979   Marvin Darter, Linda Kay Darter
1980   Ed Spear, Leonard Levy
1981   Steve Gladyszak, Ken Simpson

SWISS TEAMS

1976   Bill Butcher, James Bennett, Jr., John Stiefel
Marian Keszycki, Leon St. Jean, John Batcheller
1979   John McDermott, Bob Fiske, Rick Binder,
Bill Braucher, George Caldwell, Paul Lavallee
1980   Jim Bennett, Larry Bausher,
Jeffrey Horowitz, Chet Davis
1981   Richard Budd, John McDermott,
Dennis Dawson, Chet Davis

NEW ENGLAND SPRING

OPEN TEAMS

1948   Jack Kushner, Saul Wilson,
Robert Fels, David Goldschmidt
1949   Jack Kushner, Saul Wilson,
Robert Fels, David Goldschmidt
1950   Mrs. Fred Solomon, Jerome Scheuer,
John O'Donnell, Samuel Gottlieb
1951   Ethel Keohane, Kenneth Hill,
E. Farrington Abbot, Jr., Perley Weatherbee
1952   Frank Westcott, Robert Starr,
Robert Fox, Wilbur Johnson
1953   Earl Ackerman, Mabel Ackerman,
Frances Harding, Peter Johnson
1954   Frank Westcott, Royal Baker,
Robert Fox, Robert Starr
1955   Peter Johnson, Ludwig Katz,
Maurice Braunstein, Robert Ludwig
1956   Edgar Kaplan, Alfred Sheinwold,
Charles Coon, Ivar Stakgold

1957 William Grieve, Larry Weiss, George Durgin,
     William Levin, David Cliff
1958 Royal Baker, Robert Starr,
     Robert Fox, Frank Westcott
1959 Charles Coon, Richard Sears,
     William Levin, David Cliff
1960 David Cliff, William Levin,
     Charles Coon, Larry Weiss
1961 David Cliff, Charles Coon,
     William Levin, Larry Weiss
1962 Frank Westcott, Robert Fox,
     Royal Baker, Robert Starr
1963 Charles Coon, Larry Weiss,
     Sidney Aronson, William Levin
1964 James Carney, Peter Sorter,
     Mike Engel, Francis Lindon
1965 Agnes Gordon, Nat Gerstman,
     Michael Kassay, Raymond Brown
1966 Agnes Gordon, Nat Gerstman,
     Michael Kassay, Raymond Brown
1967 Ethel Keohane, Bob Thurrell,
     Al Oszy, Zavan Garabedian
1968 Ethel Keohane, Bob Thurrell,
     Al Oszy, Zavan Garabedian
1969 Ralph Cohen, Buddy Marsh, Peter Nagy,
     Eric Kokish, Joe Silver
1970 Art Waldmann, Marvin Rosenblatt,
     Mike Moss, Mark Blumenthal
1971 Chester Davis, Robert Tator,
     Charles Zegar, Harold Feldheim
1972 Selma Raphael, Howard Palmer,
     Sidney Cohen, Allan Thall
1973 Eric Kokish, Sharyn Kokish, George Mittelman,
     Joe Silver, Dianna Gordon
1974 Stephen Ligas, Luke Gillespie,
     Ben Goldsmith, Richard Weiss

OPEN PAIRS

1932 Dorothy Robinson, H.J. O'Meara
1933 Milton Casson, William Campbell
1934 Edward Marcus, William Silver
1935 Walter Malowan, Sidney Rusinow
1936 Rosamond Vahey, John Liston
1937 George Verde, James Silin
1937 Dr. Richard Ecker, Jack Cushing
1938 G. Tolman, Jr., A.L. Moeldner
1938 Albert Morehead, Geoffrey Mott-Smith
1939 Norman Bonney, Frank Edlin
1939 Everett Clarke, P. Sweet
1940 Wingate Bixby, Mrs. S.W. Peck
1940 George Verde, Arthur Bell
1941 Burton Linderman, Sidney Wirt
1941 Mrs. R.H. Mason, Dana Wilber *(tied with)*
     George Verde, Sidney Aronson
1942 Luke Goff, Raphael Hartley
1942 Milton Casson, Chester Kopelman
1943 Luke Goff, Raphael Hartley
1943 Lee Hazen, Edward Marcus
1944 Lt. Arnold Kauder, Mary Jane Kauder
1944 Meyer Channen, Archie Markson
1945 James Albert, Milton Wayner
1945 Bernard Goldman, Louis Plotkin
1946 Mary Hartley, Harry Cohn
1946 Eula Hill, Arthur Bell
1947 John O'Donnell, Albert Jacobson
1948 Sam Stayman, Edward Marcus
1949 Sumner Cotzin, Murray Meltzer
1950 Sidney Wirt, Milton Casson
1951 Mrs. Earl Ackerman, Earl Ackerman
1952 Robert Fox, Wilbur Johnson
1953 Sol Rubinow, Morton Rubinow
1954 Raphael Hartley, Mary Hartley
1955 Mary Cabral, Charles Coon
1956 Alan Leeds, Eugene Thumim
1957 Alan Leeds, Eugene Thumim
1958 Harvey Poock, Henry Francis
1959 Rena Talbot, Selma Raphael
1960 David Cliff, William Levin
1961 Kitty Creedon, Paul Kerwick
1962 Frank Goldring, Charles Coon
1963 William Butcher, Marvin Rosenblatt
1964 Robert Mosher, Jeff Rubens
1965 Ralph Cohen, Peter Pender
1966 Chester Davis, Dr. Robert Tator
1967 Art Waldmann, Marvin Rosenblatt
1968 John Solodar, Peter Weichsel
1969 Ralph Cohen, Buddy Marsh
1970 Frank Westcott, Robert Starr
1971 Steve Ekeblad, Mark Feldman
1972 Peter Hollander, Henry Cukoff
1973 Jean Roche, Andre Levesque
1974 Steve Sion, James Rosenbloom

WOMEN'S PAIRS

1964 Terry Michaels, Sallie Johnson
1967 Marietta Passell, Gail Shane
1974 Helga Reznikoff, Margaret O'Neal

MIXED PAIRS

1973 Les Roth, Esther Roth
1974 Mary Lehner, George Melikan

MEN'S PAIRS

1964 Charles O'Conner, Cartright Phillips
1967 Jerome Clark, Walter Nichols
1974 Divakar Bhargava, Don Probst

NEW ENGLAND SUMMER

KNOCKOUT TEAMS

1975 Mark Feldman, Marc Jacobus,
     Peter Nagy, Eric Kokish
1976 Mark Feldman, Bart Bramley,
     Eric Kokish, Peter Nagy
1977 Arthur Waldmann, Mark Rosenbloom,
     Marvin Rosenblattt, Ken Gorfkle
1978 Dale Beers, Steven Bloom, Betty Bloom,
     Jeff Juster, Jerry Ginsparg
1979 Steve Labins, Chuck Lamprey,
     Marty Bergen, Alan Schwartz
1980 Michael Rosmarin, Bruce Rogoff,
     Tom Abbott, Barry Goren
1981 Bill Pollack, Howard Chandross, Ron Gerard,
     Rozanne Marel Pollack, Ethan Stein, Larry Cohen

OPEN TEAMS

1975 Bill Russ, Luz Chandler,
     Eric Robinson, Harry Looks *(tied with)*
     Neil Silverman, Merle Tom, Peter Weichsel,
     Alan Sontag, Bart Bramley, Lou Reich
1976 Jim Bennett, Marian Keszycki, John Batcheller,
     John Stiefel, Larry Bausher, Jeff Horowitz
1977 Harry Staruk, Peg Staruk, Ken Bradford,
     Gary Bujaucius, Joe Steponavic
1978 Steve Sion, Allan Cokin,
     Jim Sternberg, Bart Bramley
1979 Paul Lavallee, John Malley, Joel Krug,
     Bill Gorden, Mark Rosenberg
1980 Alan Schwartz, Brian Glubok,
     Marty Bergen, Thomas Goodwin *(tied with)*
     Steve Shepard, Richard Graveman,
     Maurice Wong, Robert Klein
1981 Steve Weinstein, Fred Stewart,
     Stephen Sanborn, William Kreps

INDIVIDUAL

1975 Tom Lennon
1976 Elizabeth Beckett
1981 Frank Salamon

OPEN PAIRS

1975 Lewis Handelsman, Michael Rosmarin
1976 Lloyd Arvedon, Bob Feller
1977 Harold Feldheim, Steve Nellissen
1978 Dave Ehler, Dick Hecht
1979 Carol Salinger, David Brecher *(Smoking)*
     Ross Grabel, Josh Parker *(Non-Smoking)*
1980 Mark Cohen, Stasha Wroblewski
1981 David Ehler, Richard Hecht

MIXED PAIRS

1975 Pat Roy, Helene Beaulieu
1976 Harold Feldheim, Catherine Hall
1980 Evelyn Bernstein, Martin Bernstein
1981 C. Lebow, James Rosenbloom

APPENDIX III

International Championships

EUROPEAN CHAMPIONSHIPS

OPEN WINNERS	RUNNERS-UP
1932 Scheveningen, Holland	
Austria	Holland
Dr. Paul Stern	Ernst C. Goudsmit
Edmond R. H. Pollak	Frits W. Goudsmit
Louis Urvater	Bolo Einhorn
Simon Fleischmann	Jacques Borel
	J. R. Cor van Bemmel Suyck
1933 London, England	
Austria	Holland
Simon Fleischmann	Ernst C. Goudsmit
Walter Herbert	Frits W. Goudsmit
Dr. Paul von Kaltenegger	Bolo Einhorn
Edmond R. H. Pollak	Jean de Kuyper
Dr. Paul Stern	J.R. Cor van Bemmel Suyck
1934 Vienna, Austria	
Hungary	Holland
Emeric Alpar	Ernst Goudsmit
Rafael Cohen	Frits Goudsmit
Láslóo Decsi	Bolo Einhorn
Francis von Leitner	J.R. Cor van Bemmel Suyck
Andor Keleti	Sam van Houten
László Klór	Lion B. Zeldenrust
1935 Brussels, Belgium	
France	Hungary
Baron Robert de Nexon	Emeric Alpar
Pierre Albarran	Rafael Cohen
Adrien Aron	Lásló Decsi
Joseph Broutin	George Ferenczy
M. Georges Rousset	László Klor
Sophocles Venizelos	Andor Keleti
1936 Stockholm, Sweden	
Austria	Hungary
Hans Jellinek	Emeric Alpar
Dr. Paul von Kaltenegger	Rafael Cohen
Edmond R.H. Pollak	Lásló Decsi
Karl Schneider	Andor Keleti
	Lászlo Klór
1938 Oslo, Norway	
Hungary	Norway
G. E. Zichy	R. Abrahamsen
E. Bokor	Leif Christiansen
George Ferenczi	Ranik Halle
László Klór	Odd Larsson
A. Por	Jens Magnussen
Dr. Lajos Widder	Trygve Sommervelt
1939 The Hague, Holland	
Sweden	Yugoslavia
Rudolf Kock	Dr. Nicholas Singer
Jac Neumann	Dr. Josef Fischer
Tore Sandgren	Geza Klein
Dr. Einar Werner	Ing. Marjanovic
	G. Stern
	Julius Klein
1948 Copenhagen, Denmark	
Great Britain	Sweden
Leslie W. Dodds	Dr. Einar Werner
Kenneth W. Konstam	Rudolf Kock
Edward Rayne	Nils-Olof Lilliehöök
Boris Schapiro	Jan Wohlin
Terence Reese	K. Sundin
S. J. Simon	Tom Wennberg
Maurice Harrison-Gray (capt.)	
1949 Paris, France	
Great Britain	Sweden
Kenneth Konstam	Rudolf Kock
Adam Meredith	Dr. Einar Werner
Boris Schapiro	Jan Wohlin
Terence Reese	Nils-Olof Lilliehöök
S. J. Simon	P. Brome
Maurice Harrison-Gray (capt.)	J. Kjelldahl
1950 Brighton, England	
Great Britain	Sweden
John C.H. Marx	Rudolf Kock

Kenneth W. Konstam	Dr. Einar Werner
Leslie W. Dodds	Jan Wohlin
Nico Gardener	P. Brome
Louis Tarlo	J. Kjelldahl
Maurice Harrison-Gray (capt.)	
1951 Venice, Italy	
Italy	Austria
Paoli Baroni	Hans Eisler
Eugenio Chiaradia	Laszlo Gulyas
Pietro Forquet	Hans Gruber
Augusto Ricci	Karl Klimt
Mario Franco	Dr. Max Reithoffer
Guglielmo Siniscalco	Karl Schneider
Carl Alberto Perroux (npc)	William Marschner (npc)
1952 DunLaoghaire, Ireland	
Sweden	Italy
Gunnar Anulf	Eugenio Chiaradia
Rudolf Kock	Mario Franco
Robert Larsen	Michele Giovine
Dr. Einer Werner	Guglielmo Siniscalco
Nils-Olof Lilliehöök	Paolo Baroni
Jan Wohlin	Celestino Zeuli
Tore Ljungberg (npc)	Carl Alberto Perroux (npc)
1953 Helsinki, Finland	
France	Great Britain
Jacques Amouraben	Leslie W. Dodds
Marcel Kornblum	Kenneth W. Konstam
Dr. F. Hervouët	Nico Gardener
Pierre Ghestem	Albert Rose
Robert Schiltz	Peter F. Swimmerton-Dyer
René Bacherich	Dimmie Fleming
Baron Robert de Nexon (npc)	Reginald F. Corwen (npc)
1954 Montreux, Switzerland	
Great Britain	France
Leslie W. Dodds	Pierre Jaïs
Kenneth W. Konstam	F. Bodier
Boris Schapiro	P. Figeac
Terence Reese	P.J. Guerin
Adam Meredith	Henri Svarc
Jordanis Pavlides	Roger Trézel
Reginald F. Corwen (npc)	Baron Robert de Nexon (npc)
1955 Amsterdam, Holland	
France	Italy
Pierre Jaïs	Eugenio Chiaradia
Roger Trézel	N. Sabetti
Pierre Ghestem	Massimo d'Alelio
Robert Lattes	Mario Franco
René Bacherich	Michele Giovine
Bertrand Romanet	Augusto Ricci
Baron Robert de Nexon (npc)	Dr. Paolo V. Valenti (npc)
1956 Stockholm, Sweden	
Italy	France
Walter Avarelli	Pierre Ghestem
Giorgio Belladonna	René Bacherich
Eugenio Chiaradia	Henri Svarc
Massimo d'Alelio	Gerard Bourchtoff
Pietro Forquet	Pierre Jaïs
Guglielmo Siniscalco	Roger Trézel
Carl Alberto Perroux (npc)	Baron Robert de Nexon (npc)
1957 Vienna, Austria	
Italy	Austria
Walter Avarelli	Dr. Max Reithoffer
Giorgio Belladonna	Hans Eisler
Eugenio Chiaradia	Karl Klimt
Massimo d'Alelio	Hans Hartwich
Pietro Forquet	Dr. Erich Gluttig
Guglielmo Siniscalco	Karl Schneider (capt.)
Carl Alberto Perroux (npc)	
1958 Oslo, Norway	
Italy	Great Britain
Walter Avarelli	Terence Reese
Giorgio Belladonna	Boris Schapiro
Eugenio Chiaradia	James Sharples
Massio d'Alelio	Robert Sharples
Pietro Forquet	Maurice Harrison-Gray
Guglielmo Siniscalco	Alan Truscott
Carl Alberto Perroux (nps)	Reginald F. Corwen (npc)

1959 Palermo, Italy

Italy	France
Walter Avarelli	Pierre Jaïs
Giorgio Belladonna	Roger Trézel
Benito Bianchi	Gerald Bourchtoff
R. Manca	Claude Delmouly
Pietro Forquet	Dr. Jacques Pariente
Eugenio Chiaradia	Henri Svarc
Carl Alberto Perroux (npc)	Baron Robert de Nexon (npc)

1961 Torquay, England

Great Britain	France
Nico Gardener	Pierre Ghestem
Albert Rose	René Bacherich
Claude Rodrigue	Louis Malabat
Kenneth W. Konstam	Calude Deruy
R. Anthony Priday	J. Herschmann
Alan Truscott	Jacques Stetten
Louis Tarlo (npc)	Baron Robert de Nexon (npc)

1962 Beirut, Lebanon

France	Italy
René Bacherich	Giorgio Belladonna
Pierre Ghestem	Massimo d'Alelio
Gerard Desrousseaux	Benito Bianchi
Dr. Georges Théron	Giovan Battista Brogi
Jacques Stetten	Giuseppe Messina
Leon Tintner	Camillo Pabis-Ticci
Baron Robert de Nexon (npc)	Giovanni Pelucchi (npc)

1963 Baden-Baden, Germany

Great Britain	Italy
Jeremy Flint	Benito Bianchi
Maurice Harrison-Gray	Giovan Battista Brogi
Kenneth W. Konstam	Eugenio Chiaradia
Terence Reese	Massimo d'Alelio
Boris Schapiro	Dr. Giuseppe Messina
Joel Tarlo	Camillo Pabis-Ticci
Louis Tarlo (npc)	Sergio Osella (nps)

1965 Ostend, Belgium

Italy	The Netherlands
Piero Astolfi	Moritz Blitzblum
Giorgio Belladonna	Pieter Boender
Benito Bianchi	J. T. M. (Hans) Kreyns
Vito Gandolfi	C. Leo Oudshoorn
Dr. Giuseppe Messina	Anton Rijke
Renato Mondolfo	Cornelis (Bob) Slavenburg
Angelo Tracanella (npc)	Jut Kramer (npc)

1966 Warsaw, Poland

France	The Netherlands
Jean-Michel Boulenger	Martijn Cats
Henri Svarc	Cornelis Kaiser
Jean-Marc Roudinesco	Jacobus C. Kokkes
Jacques Pariente	Jut Kramer
Jacques Stetten	Cornelis (Bob) Slavenburg
René Huni (npc)	N. Jo Neelis (npc)

1967 Dublin, Ireland

Italy	France
Giorgio Belladonna	Henri Svarc
Renato Mondolfo	Jean-Michel Boulenger
Benito Bianchi	Jacques Pariente
Dr. Giuseppe Messina	Jean-Marc Roudinesco
Cesale Bresciani	Dr. Georges Théron
Oscar Bellentani	Gerard Desrousseaux
Angelo Tracanella (npc)	René Huni (npc)

1969 Oslo, Norway

Italy	Norway
Giorgio Belladonna	Erik Höie
Benito Bianchi	Tore Jensen
Paolo Frendel	Knut Koppang
Benito Garrozzo	Bjorn Larsen
Dr. Giuseppe Messina	Louis André Ström
Renato Mondolfo	Willy Varnäs
Umberto Barsotti (npc)	Baard Baardsen (npc)

1970 Estoril, Portugal

France	Poland
Jean-Michel Boulenger	Wit Klapper
Pierre Jaïs	Lukasz Lebioda
Jean-Marc Roudinesco	Janusz Nowak
Jean-Louis Stoppa	Janusz Pietruk
Henri Svarc	Andrzej Wilkosz
Roger Trézel	Adam Zimnielski
René Huni (npc)	

1971 Athens, Greece

Italy	Great Britain
Giorgio Belladonna	Jonathan Cansino
Benito Bianchi	Chris Dixon
Benito Garozzo	Jeremy Flint
Dr. Giuseppe Messina	R. Anthony Priday
Federico Meyer	Claude Rodrigue
Renato Mondolfo	Rob Sheehan
Umberto Barsotti (npc)	Louis Tarlo (npc)

1973 Ostend, Belgium

Italy	France
Giorgio Belladonna	Jean-Michel Boulenger
Dano de Falco	Charles Guiton
Arturo Franco	Pierre Jaïs
Benito Garozzo	Michel Lebel
Rodolfo Pedrini	Christian Mari
Antonio Vivaldi	Henri Svarc
Sandro Salvetti (npc)	Claude DeRuy (npc)

1974 Herzliya, Israel

France	Italy
Jean-Michel Boulenger	Oscar Bellentani
Michel Lebel	Benito Bianchi
François Leenhardt	Cesare Besciani
Christian Mari	Giorgio Matteucci
Henri Svarc	Carlo Mosca
Edmond Vial	Silvio Sbarigia
René Bacherich (npc)	Umberto Barsotti (npc)

1975 Brighton, England

Italy	Israel
S. Di Stefano	Julian Frydrich
Arturo Franco	Michael Hochzeit
Benito Garozzo	Schmuel Lev
Ottorino Milani	Yeshayha Levit
Carlo Mosca	Pinhas Romik
Silvio Sbarigia	Eliahim Shauffel

1976 No contest (after 1975 held only in odd years).

1977 Elsinore, Denmark

Sweden	Italy
Sven-Olov Flodqvist	Vittorio Fellegara
Per Olof Sundelin	Benito Garozzo
Hans Gothe	Giorgio Belladonna
Anders Morath	Vito Pittala
Anders Brunzell	Antonio Vivaldi
Jorgen Lingquist	Arturo Franco
Sven-Erik Berglund (npc)	Sandro Salvetti (npc)

1979 Lausanne, Switzerland

Italy	Denmark
Vito Pittala	Stig Werdelin
Loranzo Lauria	Steffen Steen Moller
Giorgio Belladonna	Peter Schaltz
Dano De Falco	Knud Aage Boesgaard
Benito Garozzo	Hans Werge
Arturo Franco	Erik Grande
Sandro Salvetti (npc)	Jens Kurrse (npc)

1981 Birmingham, England

Poland	Great Britain
Alexander Jeziro	Irving Rose
Julian Klukowski	Robert Sheehan
Tomasz Przybora	John Collings
Krzysztof Martens	Paul Hackett
Andrzej Milde	Tony Sowter
Marek Kukla	Steve Lodge
Marian Frenkiel (npc)	

WOMEN'S CHAMPIONSHIPS

1935 Brussels, Belgium

Austria
Gertrude Brunner
Marianne Boschan
Ethel Ernst
Gretl Joseffy
Hella Mandl
Rixi Markus

1936 Stockholm, Sweden

Austria
Gertrude Brunner
Marianne Boschan
Ethel Ernst
Gretl Joseffy
Hella Mandl
Rixi Markus

1938 Oslo, Norway

Denmark
Mrs. K. Kolle

1939 The Hague, Holland

France
Moussia Behr

Mrs. E. Lundsteen
Mrs. A. Hillerup
Demly Wilming

1948   Copenhagen, Denmark

Denmark

Else Dam
Rigmor Fraenckel
Gurli Kieldsen
Vera Thostrup
Demly Wilming

1950   Brighton, England

Great Britain

Mrs. N. Renshaw
Phyllis M. Williams
Penguin Evans
Fritzi Gordon
Alison B. Crisford
Mrs. A. N. Carr
Col. Gordon Walshe (npc)

1952   Dun Laoghaire, Ireland

Great Britain

Penguin Evans
Fritzi Gordon
Dimmie Fleming
Lady Doris Rhodes
Rixi Markus
Phyllis Williams
Ewart Kempson (npc)

1954   Montreus, Switzerland

France

Suzanne Baldon
Andrée Bourchtoff
Mrs. M. d Vries
Christianne Martin
Marie de Montaigu
Mrs. Morand
Maître Andreé Larrivoire (npc)

1956   Stockholm, Sweden

France

Mrs. C. Bedin
Christianne Martin
Mrs. M. de Vries
Simone de Temmermann
Esmerian Pouldjian
Andrée Sussel

1958   Oslo, Norway

Denmark

Annelise Faber
Rigmor Fraenckel
Gerda Ljungberg
Otti Damm
Mis Nyholm
N. Funding (npc)

1961   Torquay, England

Great Britain

Fritzi Gordon
Rixi Markus
Jane Juan
Dorothy Shanahan
Joan Durran
Marjorie Hiron
Peter F. Swinnerton-Dyer (npc)

1963   Baden-Baden, Germany

Great Britain

Dimmie Fleming
Fritzi Gordon
Jane Juan
Rixi Markus
Mary Moss
Dorothy Shanahan
Harold Franklin (npc)

1966   Warsaw, Poland

Great Britain

Joan Durran
Fritzi Gordon
Betty Harris
Jane Juan
Rixi Markus
Dorothy Shanahan
Harold Franklin (npc)

Marie de Montaigu
Christianne Martin
Esmerian Pouldjian

1949   Paris, France

Denmark

Rigmor Fraenckel
Otti Damm
Else Dam
Demly Wilming

1951   Venice, Italy

Great Britain

Penguin Evans
Fritzi Gordon
Dimmie Fleming
Rixi Markus
Lady Doris Rhodes
Phyllis M. Williams
Dr. Sidney Lee (npc)

1953   Helsinki, Finland

France

Suzanne Baldon
Mrs. M. de Vries
Andrée Bourchtoff
Mrs. Morand
Marie de Montaigu (capt.)

1955   Amsterdam, Holland

Denmark

Otti Damm
Lizzie Schaltz
Vibeke Peterson
Rigmor Fraenckel
Gulle Skotte

1957   Vienna, Austria

Denmark

Otti Damm
Mrs. Detlevsen
Rigmor Fraenckel
Vibeke Petersen
Gulle Skotte
Erik Varn (npc)

1959   Palermo, Italy

Great Britain

Fritzi Gordon
Dimmie Fleming
Rixi Markus
Marjorie Whitaker
Mary Edwards
Mrs. G.R. Higginson
Edward Leader-Williams (npc)

1962   Beirut, Lebanon

Sweden

Inga Lisa Larsson
Maj Rex
Rut Segander
Britta Werner
Elna Friberg
Lotty Saabye-Christiansen

1965   Ostend, Belgium

France

Mrs. de Gailhard
Christianne Martin
Esmerian Pouldjian
Andrée Sussel
Simone de Temmermann
Jacqueline Velut
M. Gadelle (npc)

1967   Dublin, Ireland

Sweden

Britt Blom
Mrs. G. Jarpner
May Moore
Rut Segander
Gunborg Silborn
Britta Werner
Lotty Saabye (npc)

1969   Oslo, Norway

France

Mrs. C. Brochot
Mrs. M. de Vries
Mrs. M. Kitabji
Marianne Serf
Andrée Sussel
Simone de Temmermann
Claude Demouly (npc)

1971   Athens, Greece

Italy

Marisa Bianchi
Rina Jabes
Maria Antonia Robaudo
Luciana C. Romanelli
Anna Valenti
Maria Venturini
Giovanni Pelucchi (npc)

1974   Herzliya, Israel

Italy

Marisa Bianchi
Luciana Capodanno
Marisa D'Andrea
Rina Jabes
Maria Antonia Robaudo
Anna Valenti
Giovanni Pelucchi (npc)

1976   No contest

(After 1975 held
only in odd years)

1979   Lausanne, Switzerland

Great Britain

Nicola Gardener
Rita Oldroyd
Sally Sowter
Sandra Landy
Michelle Brunner
Rosemary Hudson
Chris Dixon (npc)

1970   Estoril, Portugal

Italy

Marisa Bianchi
Rina Jabes
Antionetta Robaudo
Luciana C. Romanelli
Anna Valenti
Maria Venturini
Giovanni Pelucchi (npc)

1973   Ostend, Belgium

Italy

Marisa Bianchi
Luciana Canessa
Rina Jabes
Maria Antonia Robaudo
Anna Valenti
Maria Venturini
Giovanni Pelucchi (npc)

1975   Brighton, England

Great Britain

Charley Esterson
Nicola Gardener
Fritzi Gordon
Sandra Landy
Rixi Markus
Rita Oldroyd
G.O.J. Cooke (npc)

1977   Elsinore, Denmark

Italy

Marisa Bianchi
Luciana Capodanno
Marisa D'Andrea
Enrichetta Gut
Andreina Morini
Anna Valenti

1981   Birmingham, England

Great Britain

Pat Davies
Nicola Gardener
Sandra Landy
Sally Sowter
Maureen Dennison
Diana Williams
Derek Rimington (npc)

FAR EAST CHAMPIONSHIPS

OPEN WINNERS

1957   Manila, Philippines

Philippines

Stephen Chua
Antonio Zamora
Lionel de Silva
Robert Yap
Carmen Ballesteros
Florence Leung

1958   Tokyo, Japan

Philippines

Jose J. Reyes
Stephen Chua
Lionel de Silva
R. Hernandez
Eligio Teehankee
Vincent Reyes
Severo A. Tuason (npc)

1959   Taipei, Formosa

Hong Kong

Y. T. Fong
L. A. Ozorio
Henry S. Y. Kuai
Victor Zirinsky
George Tsiang
Y. M. Chu
David Miao (npc)

1960   Hong Kong

Hong Kong

Y. T. Fong
L. A. Ozorio
William Wong
Dodge Chen
Henry S. Y. Kuai

Andre Ouan
David Miao (npc)

1961 Bangkok, Thailand

Thailand

Kovit Suchartkul
Somboon Nandhabiwat
Thakerngdeji Sudasna
Reggie Gaan
Dr. Sanong Unakul
K. W. Shen
Thawee Raenkham (npc)

1962 Manila, Philippines

Indonesia

Oei Keng Hian
Tan Hok San
M. W. Hasnam
Mr. Djanwar
Thio Oen Gei
Tan Kiong Say
Sie Ban Hwei (npc)

1963 Taipei, Formosa

Thailand

Kovit Suchartkul
Boontham Nantaterm
Ua Isrankul
Somboon Nandhabiwat
Manoo Veeraburus
Benno Gimkiewicz
Sudasana Sirisuay (npc)

OPEN WINNERS

1964 Tokyo, Japan

Indonesia

Liem Hok Po
Boris Hutagalung
P. Sanbudhi
K. Sudianto
J. Alex Fransz
Oey Tek Goan
F. J. Inkiriwang (npc)

1965 Hong Kong

Thailand

Kovit Suchartkul
Ananta Boonsupa
Manoo Veeraburus
Vibal Rasmidatta
Patama Narabhallobh
Ua Israngkul

1966 Bangkok, Thailand

Thailand

K. W. Shen
Benno Gimkiewicz
Reggie Gaan
Somboon Nandhabiwat
Sara Pothisuwan
Prakorb Vanigbandhu
Dr. Mongkol Suebsaeng (npc)

1967 Manila, Philippines

Taiwan

Y. J. Hsi
Min-Fan Tai
Patrick Kuang-Hui Huang
Harry T. Lin
C. W. Liaw
Charles C. Wei (npc)

1968 Kuala Lumpur, Malaysia

Australia

Jessel Rothfield
Nat Rothfield
Tim Seres
Roelof Smilde
Wally Scott
Jim Borin

1969 Taipei, Taiwan

Taiwan

Conrad K. R. Cheng
V. Chow
C. Hsoia
Patrick Kuang-Hui Huang
C. Lee
Min-Fan Tai

WOMEN'S WINNERS

Thailand

Saisawart Chang
Gladys Huang
Promsri Pibulsonggram
Cherdsri Sooksawasdi

Malaysia

Gladys Loh
Dr. Lily Lim
Mrs. R. G. Fraser
Mrs. G. W. Arnott
Shirley Bradley
Doreen Peddie

Thailand

Saisawart Chang
Gladys Huang
Manee Dibavadi
Inthira Chandarasomboon
Cherdsri Sooksawasdi
Promsri Pibulsonggram
Ananta Boonsupa (npc)

Philippines

Mrs. M. Cacho
Helen Small
R. Cacho
Imelda Tubangui
Helen Tubangui
Margaut Yu
William Wong (npc)

Philippines

Carmen LaGuardia
Mrs. L. Galpert
Mrs. C. Palmer
Paz A. de Tuason
Imelda Tubangui
Severo A. Tuason (npc)

Singapore

Josephine Crain
Lotta Pahverk
Sybil Holloway
Emily Hee
Jenny Han

1970 Jakarta, Indonesia

Australia

Ron Klinger
Mary McMahon
Jessel Rothfield
Tim Seres
Roelof Smilde

Indonesia

Joan Shariff
Indra Widowo
Netty Suparto
E. Gontha
A. Raturandang
M. Djajawikadj

1971 Melbourne, Australia

Taiwan

C. Chen
Conrad Cheng
Ching-Po Huang
Harry Lin
C. Lu
Min-Fan Tai

Singapore

Josephine Crain
Lotta Pahverk
Sybil Holloway
Carmen Laguardia
Emily Hee
Jenny Han

1972 Singapore

Indonesia

Max Aguw
J. Alex Fransz
Hengky Lasut
Frank E. Manoppo
M. F. Manoppo
E. Najoan
Denny Sacul
Ferdinand Walujan
Dick Masengri (npc)

Singapore

Josephine Crain
Lotta Pahverk
Sybil Holloway
Carmen Laguardia
Emily Hee
Jenny Han

1973 Hong Kong

Indonesia

Hengky Lasut
Max Aguw
Frank E. Manoppo
M. F. Manoppo
B. Mutagalune

Australia

Felicity Beale
Ruth Eaton
Gerda Stern
Winsome Lipscomb
Mary McMahon
Gabay Tabak
Hans Rosendorff (npc)

1974 Manila, Philippines

Indonesia

Frank Manoppo
M. F. Manoppo
I. Arwin
Hengky Lasut
W. A. Moniaga
Denny Sacul
Dr. J. O. Wullur (npc)

Australia

P. Brown
Ruth Eaton
Gerda Stern
Winsome Lipscomb
Mary McMahon
Elaine Poulsen
Hans Rosendorff (npc)

1975 Hong Kong

Hong Kong

Leslie Sung
T. S. Lo
Anthony Chow
Raymond S. P. Chow
Derek Zen
Woo Tsing (npc)

Australia

Margaret Choate
Mary McMahon
Mrs. G. Reynolds
Cecile Miles
Val Cummings
Ivy Dahler
Hans Rosendorff (npc)

1976 Auckland, New Zealand

Taiwan

Min-Fan Tai
Harry Shien-Chu Lin
Patrick Kuang-Hui Huang
Che Hung Kuo
Conrad Cheng

New Zealand

Eileen Taylor
Zelda Morris
Val Bell
Nola Mather
Marion Hill
Frances Ewington
Cedric Friis (npc)

1977 Manila, Philippines

India

A. Brahmachari
S. Ganguly
S. K. Ghosh
S. R. Ghosh
Kamal Mukherjee
G. Singha
M. C. Mitter (npc)

Australia

Ivy Dahler
Elizabeth Havas
Fay Landy
Claire Lester
Barbara McDonald
Cecile Miles
Hans Rosendorff (npc)

1978 New Delhi, India

Taiwan

Patrick Kuang-Hui Huang
Dr. Chun Shan Shen
Che-Hung Kuo
Conrad Cheng
Harry Lin
Ya Pin Tu

India

Rita Choksi
Lina Mayadas
Suhhadra Krishna
Mrs. S. Thadami
Mrs. S. Mahajan
Jane Verma

1979 Tokyo, Japan

Indonesia	Philippines
Hengky Lasut	Helen Tubangui
Max Aguw	Rose Unson
Denny Sacul	Florence Yap
Munawar Sawirudin	Tina del Gallego
Ferdinand Waluyan	Rudi Santiago
Jasin Wijaya	Carmen LaGuardia
Amran Zamzami (npc)	Vic Santiago (npc)

1980 Not Contested

1981 Taipei, Taiwan

Taipei	New Zealand
Harry S. C. Lin	Kathy Boardman
Patrick K. H. Huang	Jane Evitt
Yin-Tzun Chang	Jan Cormack
Che-Hung Kuo	Jocelyn Kinsella
K. R. Chen	Stella Secker
H. T. Chang	Rosalie Cunningham
	Frank Lu (npc)

1982 Bangkok, Thailand

Indonesia	Phillippines
Denny Sacul	Tina del Gallego
Henky Lasut	Lydia Jalbuena
Ferdinand Waluyan	Carmel LaGuardia
Munawar Sawirudin	Rudi Santiago
Donny Tuerah	Helen Tubangui
	Florence Yap
	Rina Milhomme (npc)

SOUTH AMERICAN CHAMPIONSHIPS

OPEN WINNERS	WOMEN'S WINNERS

1948 Buenos Aires, Argentina

Argentina	Argentina
Ricardo M. Argerich	Celia M. de Basavilbaso
Alberto J. Blousson	Josefina M. de Crámer
Carlos Cabanne	Celia de Luro
Alejandro Castro	Sara R. de Piacentini
Carlos Ottolenghi	Etelvina S. de Vergara
Dr. Luis A. Schenone	Mercedes Guerrico

1949 São Paulo and Rio de Janeiro, Brazil

Brazil	
Milton Alvarenga	
Mauricio de Couver	
Renato Cusano	
A. Figueredo	
Alaerte Frugoli	
Dr. Samuel Leite Ribeiro	
A. Raúl Reis	
N. Schloman	
Adolfo Taubkin	
Armando Trompowsky	
Ulises Viana	

1950 Montevideo, Uruguay

Argentina	Argentina
Carlos Cabanne	Inés M. G. de Casado
Fernando de Corral	Mercedes Guerrico
Alejandro Zumarin Olmedo	Esther Pérez Mendoza
Julio Quesada	María Elvira Quesada
Marcos Ugarte	

1951 Santiago, Chile

Chile	Argentina
Alfonso Aguero	Inés M. G. de Casado
Antonio Carrasco	María Laura V. de Mihura
Carlos Doren	Etelvina S. de Vergara
Jorge Guzmán	Elsa C. de Vidal
Arturo Herrera	Mercedes Guerrico
Jorge Ovalle	Esther Pérez Mendoza
Jorge Suárez	
Julio Subercasseaux	

1953 Punta del Este, Uruguay

Argentina	Argentina
Ricardo M. Argerich	Inés M. G. de Casado
Carlos Cabanne	María Laura V. de Mihura
Alejandro Castro	Mercedes Guerrico
Alejandro Olmedo	Esther Pérez Mendoza
Dr. Luis A. Schenone	Leonor Vivot
	Etelvina S. de Vergara

1954 São Paulo, Brazil

Argentina	Brazil
Miguel Alfredo Benedit	France Estella
Carlos Cabanne	Doris Machado

Alejandro Castro	Sylvia Salles Godoy
Hector Crámer	Lucía Stefani
Carlos F. Dibar	Dolores Vasconcellos
Adolfo Gabarret	Margarita Villalobos

1955 Buenos Aires, Argentina

Brazil	Brazil
Eros Amaral	Marina Farias
Milton Alvarenga	Eddy Lessa Dos Santos
Lásló Desci	Doris Machado
Norberto Mandler	Rosa Figueira de Mello
João Murtinho	Lucía Stefani
Carlos Souto	Dolores Vasconcellos

1956 Lima, Peru

Brazil	Brazil
Milton Alvarenga	Marina Farias
Mario Giorgetti	Eddy Lessa Dos Santos
Caio Luis Pereira de Sousa	Doris Machado
Norberto Mandler	Luciá Stefani
Nelson Martins	Dolores Vasconcellos
João Murtinho	

1957 Santiago, Chile

Argentina	Argentina
Alberto J. Blousson	Inés M. G. de Casado
Carlos Cabanne	María Elena C. de Rodrigué
Alejandro Castro	Etelvina S. de Vergara
Hector Crámer	Esther Pérez Mendoza
Dr. Marcelo H. Lerner	María Elvira Quesada
Alejandro Olmedo	Leonor Vivot

1958 Punta del Este, Uruguay

Argentina	Brazil
Alberto Berisso	Sylvia Godoy
Alberto J. Blousson	Eddy Lessa Dos Santos
Alejandro Castro	Esther Rodrigues
Carlos F. Dibar	Regina Schmieder
Arturo Jaques	Lea Sigueira
Carlos Ottolenghi	Lucía Stefani

1959 Santos, Brazil

Argentina	Brazil
Alberto Berisso	Selda Almeida
Desiderio Blum	Marina Faria
Carlos Cabanne	Rosa Figueira de Mello
Richardo Calvente	Doris Machado
Arturo Jaques	Ria Petzold
Egisto Rocchi	Dolores Vasconcellos

1960 Not contested

1961 Lima, Peru

Argentina	Argentina
Luis Attaguile	Inés M. G. de Casado
Alberto Berisso	María Elena C. de Rodrigué
Carlos Cabanne	Mercedes G. de Schenone
Ricardo Calvente	Etelvina S. de Vergara
Arturo Jaques	Esther Pérez Mendoza
Egisto Rocchi	María Elvira Quesada

1962 Buenos Aires, Argentina

Argentina	Argentina
Luis Attaguile	Inés M. G. de Casado
Alberto Berisso	María Elena C. de Rodrigué
Desiderio Blum	Mercedes G. de Schenone
Carlos Cabanne	Etelvina S. de Vergara
Agustín Santamarina	Maria Teresa P. de Espinosa Paz
Marcos Santamarina	María Elvira Quesada

1963 Caracas, Venezuela

Venezuela	Peru
Edgar Lloynaz	Paulina de Alaez
Manuel González–Vale	Elena de Bozzo
Mario Onorati	Maruja de Foccaci
Renato Straziota	Elena de Carbone
Roger Rossignol	Zita de Fleischman
David A. Berah	Ana de Isnardi
Roberto Benaím (npc)	

1964 Montevideo and Punta del Este, Uruguay

Argentina	Argentina
Luis Attaguile	Esther Claret de Aguirre
Desiderio Blum	Inés M. G. de Casado
Carlos Cabanne	Adela N. de Engel
Egisto Rocchi	Hildegaard S. de Lippstadt
Agustín Santamarina	Etelvina S. de Vergara
Alfredo Saravia	María Elvira Quesada

1965 Santiago, Chile

Venezuela	Brazil

Roberto Benaím
David A. Berah
Mario Onorati
Roger Rossignol
Renato Straziota
Francis Vernon
Dr. Geraim Rodrigrez (npc)

1966 São Paulo, Brazil

Venezuela

Roberto Benaím
David A. Berah
Edgar Lloynaz
Roberto Romanelli
Roger Rossignol
Francis Vernon
Dr. José Coriat (npc)

1967 Lima, Peru

Brazil

Pedro Paulo Assumpção
Mario Giorgetti
George S. Golefarf
Eduardo Nahmias
Gabriel Pinheiro
Adelstano Porto D'Ave

1968 Bogota, Colombia

Brazil

Marcelo Castelo Branco
Roberto Figueira de Mello
Decio Martins Coutinho
Pedro Paulo Assumpção
Gabriel Pinheiro Chagas
Adelstano Porto D'Ave
Paulo S. de Barros Brum (npc)

1969 Buenos Aires, Argentina

Brazil

Pedro Paulo Assumpção
Pablo Plinio de Barros
Eduardo Bastos
Pedro Paulo Castelo Branco
Gabriel Pinheiro Chagas
Synesio Martins Ferreira

1970 Caracas, Venezuela

Brazil

Eros Amaral
Pedro Paulo Assumpção
Gabriel Pinheiro Chagas
Gabino Cintra
Christiano G. Fonseca
Tibor Kenedi

1971 Montevideo, Uruguay

Brazil

Pedro Paulo Assumpção
Adelstano Porto D'Ave
Sergio Barbosa
Marcelo Castelo Branco
Octavio G. de Faria
Christiano G. Fonseca

1972 Santiago, Chile

Brazil

Pedro Paulo Assumpção
Marcelo Castelo Branco
Pedro Paulo Castelo Branco
Gabriel Pinheiro Chagas
Gabino Cintra
Christiano G. Fonesca
Adelstano Porto D'Ave (npc)

1973 Rio de Janeiro, Brazil

Brazil

Pedro Paulo Assumpção
Marcelo Castelo Branco
Pedro Paulo Castelo Branco
Gabriel Pinheiro Chagas
Gabina Cintra
Christiano G. Fonesca

1974 Lima, Peru

Sybil Jung
María Elena Mirando
Jordao
Yolanda Paéz de Barros
Vera Sampaio
Lea Sequeira
Dolores Vasconcellos

Brazil

Tereza Chammas
Marina Farías
María Elena Mirando Jordao
Sylvia Figueira de Mello
Sylvia Salles Godoy
Dolores Vasconcellos
(tied with)

Uruguay

Marta Brito del Pino
Lola P. de Castillo
Esther M. de Ham
Raquel D. de Methol
Brígida Philipstal
Elena María G. de Zumarán

Uruguay

Marta Brito del Pino
Lola P. de Castillo
Esther M. de Ham
Raquel D. de Methol
Brígida Philipstal
Elena Maria G. de Zumarán

Colombia

Angela Echeverri González
Marta Marulanda de Ferrer
Marta Olga Vélez de Hortet
María Cristina Rivas de Rivas
Ana Pinzón de Soto
Emilia Osorio de Velez
R. Escobar npc

Peru

María Delfina de Denegri
Zita de Fleischman
Blanca de Magnani
Eda de Piana
Alicia de Flücker
Pilar de Velarde

Colombia

Tania de Mandowsky
Rosario de Nuñez
Marina de Prieto
María Cristina Rivas de Rivas
Ana P. de Soto
Olga de Zuloaga

Uruguay

Esther M. de Ham
Raquel D. de Methol
María del Carmen C. de Meyer
Marta Brito del Pino
Brígida Philipsthal
Lola de Piñeyrúa

Brazil

Lia Cintra
Gilda Leal
Doris Machado
Elizabeth Murtinho
María Helena de Oliveira
Dolores Vasconcellos

Brazil

Lia Cintra
Suzy Fujihura
Gerty Gramegna
Lucía Gil
Elizabeth Murtinho
Heloisa Nogueira

Brazil

Eros Amaral
Pedro Paulo Assumpção
Pablo Plinio de Barros
Gabriel Pinheiro Chagas
Nelson Martins Ferreira
Synesio Martins Ferreira

1975 Bogota, Colombia

Brazil

Pedro Paulo Assumpção
Gabriel Pinheiro Chagas
Pedro Castelo Branco
Marcelo Castelo Branco
Gabino Cintra
Christiano G. Fonseca

1976 Buenos Aires, Argentina

Argentina

Luis Attaguile
Jaime Braceras
Carlos Cabanne
Egisto Rocchi
Agustín Santamarina
Eduardo Scanavino

1977 Montevideo, Uruguay

Brazil

Pedro Paulo Assumpção
Gabriel Pinheiro Chagas
Gabino Cintra
Marcelo Castelo Branco
José Barbosa Oliveira
Roberto Figueira de Mello

1978 Isla Margarita, Venezuela

Brazil

Pedro Paulo Assumpção
Gabriel Pinheiro Chagas
Gabino Cintra
Marcelo Castelo Branco
José Barbosa Oliveira
Roberto Figueira de Mello

1979 Santiago, Chile

Argentina

Luis Attaguile
Héctor Camberos
Pablo Lambardi
Egisto Rocchi
Agustín Santamarina
Eduardo Scanavino

1980 Bahía, Brazil

Argentina

Luis Attaguile
Héctor Camberos
Pablo Lambardi
Egisto Rocchi
Agustín Santamarina
Eduardo Scanavino

1981 Lima, Peru

Argentina

Gustavo Alujas
Luis Attaguile
Héctor Camberos
Agustín Santamarina
Eduardo Scanavino
David Zanalda

Uruguay

Vera B. de Beer
Raquel D. de Methol
María del Carmen C. de Meyer
Marta Brito del Pino
Brígida Philipsthal
Lola de Piñeyrúa

Brazil

Sylvia Figueira de Mello
Gertie Gramegna
Heloisa L. Nogueira
Agota Mandelot
Maria Elizabeth Murtinho
Vera Schaffer

Colombia

Josefina de Bennet
Angela Echeverry Gónzalez
Marta Marulanda de Ferrer
Marta O. Velez de Hortet
Blanca de Jaramillo
Silvia de Vazquez

Argentina

Delia C. de Biquard
Matilde I. de Espiasse
Adriana C. Martinez de Hoz
Anke M. J. de Moirano
Mary Ann M. de Monsegur
Mercedes G. de Schenone

Chile

Adriana D. de Aguad
Odette Y. de Yanine
Samira B. de Awad
Dare Turenne
Carla P. de Parlatore
Sonia R. de Ready

Argentina

Ana María G. de Alonso
Martha J. Matienzo
Clara Monsegur
Lurecia T. Monsegur
Mercedes G. de Schenone
Cristina de Suaya

Brazil

Heloisa Nogueira
Gertie Gramegna
Ana Maria Assumpção
Agota Mandelot
Maria Elizabeth Murtinho
Sylvia Figueira de Mello

Brazil

Agota Mandelot
Sylvia Figueira de Mello
Maria Elizabeth Murtinho
Susy Powidzer
Alice Saade
Maria Elena Brito E. Silva
Lia Cintra (npc)

BIBLIOGRAPHY

KEY: Many thousands of books have been written on bridge; this bibliography attempts to list those which have permanent value, under 17 subdivisions. In this category the books are listed alphabetically by author. All publishers, unless otherwise indicated, are American. If no place of publication appears after the publisher, it was published in New York City. Where there has been more than one edition, the earliest and latest dates are given when known. There may be slight variations in number of pages in different editions. No distinction is made between hardcover and paperback books.

A HISTORY Whist, Auction Bridge, Bridge

B ANTHOLOGIES

C BIDDING (including systems)

D PLAY

E BIDDING AND PLAY (in combination)

F DUPLICATE BRIDGE (bidding, play, and tournament directing)

G MATCH AND TOURNAMENT RECORDS

H HAND COLLECTIONS

I FICTION

J PROBLEMS, QUIZZES, PUZZLES

K BIOGRAPHY

L HUMOR AND POETRY

M MATHEMATICS

N LAWS

O PERIODICALS

P ENCYCLOPEDIAS

Q BIBLIOGRAPHIES

Books of historic significance and books of importance for the purposes of a modern technical bridge library have been separately identified as follows:

    * Books marked thus made a major contribution to the technical development of the game.

† Books marked thus are optional requirements for a modern technical bridge library

‡ Books marked thus are mandatory requirements for a modern technical bridge library.

AUTHOR	TITLE	PUBLISHER	PAGES	DATES
A HISTORY Whist, Auction Bridge, Bridge				
Ames, Fisher	*A Practical Guide to Whist*	Scribner's	92	1891–1907
Benham, W. Gurney	*Playing Cards: History of the Pack*	Ward, Lock (London & Melbourne)	196	1931
		Spring Books (London)	196	1957
Bruelheide, F. E.	*Party Bridge*	Buzza Co. (Minneapolis)	102	1927
Burney, Admiral James	**Treatise on the Game of Whist*	Thos. & Wm. Boone (London)	87	1823
Butler, William	*The Whist Reference Book*	John C. Yorston Co. (Philadelphia)	568	1899
Cavendish (Henry Jones)	*Card Essays, Clay's Decisions, and Card-Table Talk*	Thos. De La Rue (London)	260	1879
Cavendish (Henry Jones)	**Cavendish on Whist*	Thos. De La Rue (London)	107	1862–1902
Cavendish (Henry Jones)	*Whist Developments*	Thos. De La Rue (London)	181	1885–1891
Chatto, William Andrew	*Facts and Speculations on the Origin and History of Playing Cards*	John Russell Smith (London)	343	1848
Cotton, Charles	*Compleat Gamester*	Henry Brome (London)	232	1674–1726
Dalton, W.	*Auction Bridge up to Date*	Thos. De La Rue (London)	210	1909
Daniels, David	*The Golden Age of Contract Bridge*	Stein & Day	212	1980
Deschappeles, Guillaume	*Traité du Whiste*	Perrotin (Paris)	328	1840
Elwell, Joseph B.	**Advanced Bridge*	Scribner's	297	1904–09
Elwell, Joseph B.	*Elwell on Bridge*	Scribner's	136	1902–11
Elwell, Joseph B.	**Auction Bridge*	Scribner's	170	1910–12
Emery, Sue	*No Passing Fancy — Fifty Years of Contract Bridge*	ACBL (Memphis)	128	1977
Ferguson, Wynne	*Auction Bridge*	Ferguson	64	1915–29
Foster, Robert F.	*Foster on Auction*	Dutton	384	1918–25
Foster, Robert F.	*Foster's Bridge Manual*	Brentano's	200	1900–08
Hargrave, Catherine	*A History of Playing Cards*	Houghton Mifflin	468	1930
		Dover (Paperback)	462	1966
Howell, Edwin	*Whist Openings — A Systematic Treatment of the Short-Suit Game*	Pinkham Press (Boston)	206	1896
Hoyle, Edmund	**A Short Treatise on the Game of Whist*	T. Osborne (London)	86	1743–50
Hyde-Wollaston, A (see Robertson, Edmond)	*Bridge Developments*			
Lenz, Sidney	**Lenz on Bridge*	Simon & Schuster	379	1926
Lenz, Sidney	*Lenz on Bridge*, volume II	Simon & Schuster	456	1927
Lenz, Sidney and Rendel, Robert	*How's Your Bridge?*	Simon & Schuster	224	1929
Manning-Foster, A. E.	*Auction Bridge for All*	Ernest Benn (London)	317	1928–30
Manning-Foster, A. E.	*Auction & Contract Bridge Made Clear*	Grayson & Grayson (London)	327	1933
Manning-Foster, A. E.	*Bridge — Plafond*	Ernest Benn (London)	93	1933

AUTHOR	TITLE	PUBLISHER	PAGES	DATES
Mathews, T.	*Advice to the Young Whist Player	Meyler & Son (England)	64	1806–25
Mitchell, John T.	Duplicate Whist — Its Rules and Methods of Play	McClurg (Chicago)	110	1891
Payne, William	*Maxims for Playing the Game of Whist with All Necessary Calculations	Payne & Son (England)	67	1773–90
Pole, William	Evolution of Whist	Longmans (London & NYC)	269	1895
Pole, William	*Philosophy of Whist	Thos. De La Rue (London)	218	1883–87
Portland (James Hogg)	The Whist Table	John Hogg (London)	472	1894
Reith, George	*The Art of Successful Bidding	Doubleday	227	1928
Rendel, Robert (see Lenz, Sidney)	How's Your Bridge?			
Rheinhardt, Rudolf	Whist Scores and Card-Table Talk with a Bibliography of Whist	Mc Clurg (Chicago)	310	1887
Robertson, Edmund and Hyde-Wollaston, A.	Bridge Developments	Brentano's	127	1904
Seymour, Richard	The Compleat Gamester	Curll & Wilford (London)	132	1734–54
Shepard, E. V.	Expert Auction	Harper & Bros.	245	1913–17
Shepard, E. V.	Scientific Auction Bridge	Harper & Bros.	241	1913–14
Singer, Samuel W.	Researches into the History of Playing Cards	Robert Triphook (London)	378	1816
Tilley, Roger	A History of Playing Cards	Crown	192	1973
Warren, Mrs. Prescott	Auction and Contract Bridge Condensed	Houghton Mifflin (Boston)	247	1927
Whitehead, Wilbur C.	*Auction Bridge Standards	Stokes	188	1921–26
Whitehead, Wilbur C.	Whitehead's Conventions of Auction Bridge	Stokes	243	1914
Work, Milton	*Auction Bridge Complete	J. C. Winston (Philadelphia)	500	1926–29

B ANTHOLOGIES

The Bridge World	The Bridge World: Best of the Sixties	The Bridge World	48	1982
Frey, Richard (Editor)	Bridge for Women	Doubleday	221	1967
		Funk & Wagnalls	224	1970
Goren, Charles H.	Bridge Is My Game: Lessons of a Lifetime	Doubleday	190	1965
Goren, Charles H.	The Sports Illustrated Book of Bridge	Time, Inc.	520	1961
Hart, Norman de V.	The Bridge Players' Bedside Book	Eyre & Spottiswoode (London)	160	1939
Hervey, George F.	The Bridge Players' Bedside Book	Faber & Faber (London)	116	1964
Jacoby, Oswald and Morehead, Albert	Fireside Book of Cards	Simon & Schuster	365	1957
Jaïs, Pierre et al	L'Artistocratie du Bridge	Balland (Paris)	317	1973
Kleinman, Danny	The Bridge Weird Anthology	Kleinman (Los Angeles)	160	1981
Le Dentu, José (see Jaïs, Pierre)	L'Artistocratie du Bridge			
Le Dentu, José	Bridge à La Une	Fayard (Paris)	428	1964
Le Dentu, José	‡Championship Bridge (trans. by Alan Truscott and Amalya Kearse)	Harper & Row	308	1974
Mackey, Rex	The Walk of the Oysters	W. H. Allen (London)	197	1964
Mollo, Victor	Bridge Immortals	Faber & Faber (London)	191	1967
		Hart	256	1968
Morehead, Albert (see Jacoby, Oswald)	Fireside Book of Cards			
Olsen, Jack	The Mad World of Bridge	Holt, Rinehart & Winston	239	1960
Ostrow, Albert	The Bridge Player's Bedside Companion	Prentice-Hall (Englewood Cliffs NJ)	391	1955
Reese, Terence (ed.)	Bridge Tips from the Masters	Crown	234	1981
Stern, Milton and the Experts	Expert Bridge (edited by Shirley Silverman)	Max Hardy (Inglewood CA)	136	1978
Truscott, Alan (see Jaïs, Pierre)	L'Aristocratie du Bridge			

C BIDDING (including systems)

Albano, Helen	Analysis and Practical Application of Goren Method	Albano	27	1970
Amsbury, Joe	Bridge: Bidding Naturally	Batsford (London)	152	1979
Amsbury, Joe	Control Asking	Bridge Players Handbooks (Nottingham, England)	32	1980
Amsbury, Joe (see Payne, Dick)	TNT and Competitive Bidding			
Andersen, Ron	Where and How High	Wisconsin Bridge Associates WI	92	1970
Andersen, Ron (see Wei, C. C.)	Bidding Precisely — Volume 2			
Andersen, Ron (see Wei, C. C.)	Bidding Precisely — Volume 3			
Andersen, Ron (see Wei, Katherine)	Action for the Defense — When the Enemy Opens the Bidding			
Anderson, Merrell (see Wolf, Murray)	The Subtle Club			

AUTHOR	TITLE	PUBLISHER	PAGES	DATES
Anstett, Charles (see Winslow, T. N.)	*Win With Winslow*			
Avarelli, Walter (see Belladonna, Giorgio)	*The Roman Club System of Distributional Bidding			
Baker, Bob	The Swiss Convention	Bridge Players Handbooks (Nottingham, England)	31	1980
Bangs, Fred T.	*Basic Bidding Contract Bridge*	Phoenix Publishers (Phoenix)	128	1955
Barclay, Shepard	*The Contract Bridge Guide*	Bobbs-Merrill (Indianapolis)	266	1931
Baron, Leo and Meredith, Adam	*Baron System of Contract Bridge	Contract Bridge Equipment Co. (Leeds)	180	1948
Baron, Randy et al	*Clobber Their Artificial Club*	Baron Bridge Supplies (Shelbyville KY)	20	1979
Barrow, Rhoda	*Acolites Quiz*	George Allen & Unwin Ltd. (London)	197	1970
Barton, Major F. P.	*The Barton System*	Farrar & Reinhart	80	1934
Barton, Major F. P.	*The "Barton" Variation*	Joiner & Steele (London)	88	1933–42
Beasley, Lt. Col. H. M.	*The Beasley Contract Bridge System*	Assoc. Newspapers (London)	128	1935
Becker, Mike et al	*The Ultimate Club	Ultimate Club (Livington NJ)	126	1981
Belladonna, Giorgio and Avarelli, Walter	*The Roman Club System of Distributional Bidding	Simon & Schuster	162	1959
Belladonna, Giorgio and Garozzo, Benito	‡Precision and Super Precision Bidding	G. P. Putnam's Sons	237	1975
Belladonna, Giorgio (see Wei, C. C.)	*Summary of Super Precision*			
Bissell, Harold	*The Bissell System: Distributional Method of Bidding*	Columbia University Press	316	1936
Blackwood, Easley	*Blackwood on Bidding*	Bobbs-Merrill (Indianapolis)	215	1956
Blackwood, Easley	*Blackwood on Slams*	Prentice-Hall (Englewood Cliffs NJ)	160	1970
Blackwood, Easley and Wallace, Charlton	*Blackwood Slam Bidding	Bruelheide (Minneapolis)	64	1941
Boland, Vincent and Law, John	*Accurate Contract Bidding*	Boland & Law (Cleveland)	84	1931
Borin, Jim	*Bridge Borin Style* (Baronized Acol)	Borin School of Bridge (South Yarra, Australia)		1978
Borin, Jim and Norma	*Our Precision Style*	D. W. Thorpe (West Melbourne, Australia)	72	1981
Bose Mullick, S. G.	*The Relay Club*	Allied (Bombay)	344	1975
Boyden, Elizabeth (see Warren, Mrs. Prescott)	*Contract Bridge of 1929*			
Braham, V. G. (see Smith, F. D.)	*The Victorian Blackwood Slam Convention*			
Brannon, Robert Means	*The Incomparable Club Convention*	News Printing House(Charlotte NC)	88	1935
Bridge Headquarters	*The Official System of Contract Bridge*	Winston (Philadelphia)	236	1931
Brown, John	*Bidding Craft*	Duckworth (London)	133	1962
Budin, Barnett and Kornfeld, Morris	*Bridge Players Digest of Conventions*	Budin Press (Philadelphia)	32	1962–63
Burgay, Leandro	*Bridge: The Burgay Diamond*	Burgay (Italy)	85	1979
Burns, Margery	*The Nottingham System of Contract Bridge*	Educational Productions (London)	107	1954–69
Burnstine, David (see Four Aces)	*The Four Aces System of Contract Bridge*			
Burnstine, David	*The Four Horsemen's One-over-One Method of Contract Bidding*	Walter J. Black, Inc.	118	1932
Butler, Geoffrey and Stern, Paul	*Two Club System of Bidding*	Faber & Faber (London)	300	1946
Cayley, Frank	*Contract Bridge-bidding*	Rigby (Australia)	64	1970
Champney, Ken (see Baron, Randy)	*Clobber Their Artificial Club*			
Chiaradia, Eugenio and Perroux, Carl'Alberto	*Il Fiori Napoletano*	Federazione Italiana Bridge (Milano)	96	1956
Churchill, S. Garton	*Churchill Natural Bidding Style at Contract Bridge*	Churchill (Great Neck NY)	743	1979
Churchill, S. Garton and Ferguson, Albert	*Contract Bidding Tactics at Match Point Play	Ad Press	323	1936
Coffin, George	*Acol and the New Point Count*	Duckworth (London)	56	1953
Coffin, George	*Natural Big Club*	Coffin (Parsonsfield ME)	192	1969
Coffin, George	*The Weak No Trump*	Eaton Press (Massachusetts)	32	1956
Coffin, George	*Winning Duplicate*	B. Humphries (Boston)	146	1933
Cohen, Ben and Lederer, Rhoda	*Current Conventions Made Clear*	Allen & Unwin (London)	161	1973
Cohen, Ben and Reese, Terence	*The Acol System of Contract Bridge* (3rd ed.)	Joiner & Steele (London)	84	1946
Cohen, Larry et al	†Breakthrough in Bridge	Breakthrough Enterprises (Monona WI)	186	1974
Collins, J. H.	*The Archer System*	Collins (Chicago)	303	1955
Courtenay, F. Dudley	*The Standardized Code of Contract Bridge Bidding*	Bridge Headquarters	108	1937
Courtenay, F. Dudley	*The System the Experts Play	Bridge Headquarters	94	1934
Cox, Jean	*Bridge With Jean Cox — The Bidding*	Cox (Pittsburgh)	66	1963
Crane, Joshua	*The Crane System of Modern Contract Bidding*	*East Anglian Daily Times* (London)	107	1948

AUTHOR	TITLE	PUBLISHER	PAGES	DATES
Criticus	Contract Simplicitas	Jenkins, Ltd. (London)	332	1933
Crowhurst, Eric	Acol in Competition	Pelham (London)	383	1980
Crowhurst, Eric	Precision Bidding in Acol	Pelham (London)	240	1974
Culbertson, Ely	*Contract Bridge Blue Book	The Bridge World	348	1930
Culbertson, Ely	Contract Bridge Blue Book of 1933	The Bridge World	599	1933
Culbertson, Ely	Culbertson's Summary	The Bridge World	47	1931
Culbertson, Ely	Point Count Bidding	J. C. Winston (Philadelphia)	171	1952
Culbertson, Josephine	Contract Bridge Made Easy the Point Count Way	J. C. Winston (Philadelphia)	148	1955
Danielson, Robert	Danielson's Precision	Danielson (Hackensack NJ)	26	1976
Danielson, Robert	Relay Precision (5 booklets)	Danielson (Hackensack NJ)	442	1977–79
Davis, Frank Maxie	Precision Bridge	Dorrance (Philadelphia)	425	1976
Dettman, H. V.	Simplified Precision Bidding	Dorrance (Philadelphia)	145	1972
Dewhurst, Victor	The Two-Club System	Faber & Faber (London)	220	1965
Disbrow, Bennett L. (see Solomon, Charles J.)	Slam Bidding and Point Count			
Dormer, Albert (see Reese, Terence)	The Acol System Today Blueprint for Bidding (American title)			
Dormer, Albert	†Powerhouse Hands	Prentice-Hall (Englewood Cliffs NJ)	223	1975
Drury, Douglas	The Drury Two Club Convention	Drury	46	1969
Duncan, John	New Dimension Bidding in Contract Bridge	Robert B. Luce Inc. (Washington DC)	308	1963
Eastgate, C. L. and McKillop, L. M.	Modern Gladiator System of Bidding	Whitcombe & Tomes (New Zealand)	67	1953
Ewen, Robert	‡Doubles for Takeout, Penalties and Profit	Prentice-Hall (Englewood Cliffs NJ)	278	1973
Ewen, Robert	‡Preemptive Bidding	Prentice-Hall (Englewood Cliffs NJ)	162	1975
Feldheim, Harold	†Weak Two-Bid in Bridge	Barclay Bridge Supplies	105	1971–73
Ferguson, Albert (see S. Garton Churchill)	*Contract Bidding Tactics at Match Point Play			
Fishbein, Harry	The Fishbein Convention	Crown	83	1960
Flannery, William	The Complete Flannery 2 Diamond Opener	Nella (Chicago)	16	1979
Forquet, Pietro (see Garozzo, Benito)	‡The Italian Blue Team Bridge Book			
Foss, Frank	*Simplified Contract Bidding	Gane & Son (Willimantic CT)	67	1935
Four Aces	*The Four Aces System of Contract Bridge	Random House	302	1935
Fox, G. C. H.	†Modern Bidding Systems in Bridge	The Penguin Press (London) 2nd rev. ed.	333 424	1967 1973
Fox, G. C. H.	Sound Bidding at Contract	E. Arnold (London)	254	1954
Frey, Richard L. (see Four Aces)	*The Four Aces System of Contract Bridge			
Garozzo, Benito (see Belladonna, Giorgio)	‡Precision and Super Precision Bidding			
Garozzo, Benito and Forquet, Pietro	‡The Italian Blue Team Bridge Book	Grosset & Dunlap	274	1969
Garozzo (see Wei, C. C.)	Summary of Super Precision			
Garozzo, Benito and Yallouze, Leon	†The Blue Club	Faber & Faber (London)	170	1969
Gerber, John	*The Four Club Bid: A Slam Convention	Gerber (Houston)	28	1942
Gerber, John	The Gerber Four Club Slam Convention	Texas Bridge (Houston)	24	1963
Gold, Don	Intermediate Two-Bids in Bridge	Exposition Press	128	1982
Goldman, Bobby	†Aces Scientific	Goldman Max Hardy (Inglewood CA)	250 169	1973 1978
Goodwin, Thomas	A Natural Relay System	Goodwin (Portland ME)	77	1982
Goren, Charles	Advanced Bidding: A Tutor Text	Doubleday	342	1963
Goren, Charles	Goren Settles the Bridge Arguments	Hart	429	1974
Goren, Charles	Goren Presents The Italian Bridge System	Doubleday	216	1958
Goren, Charles	†Point Count Bidding	Simon & Schuster	154	1949–58
Goren, Charles and Wei, C. C.	Precision Bridge for Everyone	Doubleday	155	1978
Goren, Charles	†The Precision System	Doubleday	228	1971
Goren, Charles	The Standard Book of Bidding	Doubleday	249	1944–49
Gottlieb, Michael (see Four Aces)	*The Four Aces System of Contract Bridge			
Hanna, William and Steen, Douglas	Precision Power Bidding: The Bulldog System	Coffin (Waltham MA)	104	1956
Hardy, Max	†Five Card Majors, Western Style	Hardy (Camarillo CA)	94	1974
Hardy, Max	*Two Over One Game Force	Hardy (Hawthorne CA)	147	1982
Hart, Norman de V. (see Kempson, Ewart)	The Quintessence of CAB			
Hart, Norman de V.	Slams à la Culbertson	Joiner & Steele (London)	99	1937
Hart, Norman de V. (see Stern, Paul)	The Vienna System of Contract Bridge			
Hayden, Dorothy	†Bid Better, Play Better	Harper & Row Award Books	196 254	1966 1967
Heath, Forrest	*Seven-Eleven: A Manual of the Heath System	Heath (Upper Montclair NJ)	55	1933

AUTHOR	TITLE	PUBLISHER	PAGES	DATES
Horn, A. C.	*Limited Opening Bids*	Horn (Dolthan AL)	167	1977
Horn, Stormy (see Reed, Dick)	*The System — Bidding Techniques of Reed–Horn*			
Horton, Mark	*Defences to a Strong Club*	Probray Press (Nottingham, England)	32	1982
Horton, Sally	*Responding to 2 NT*	Probray Press (Nottingham, England)	32	1982
Howard, Denis (ed.)	*The New South Wales System*	Howard (NSW)	83	1964
		Howard (NSW)	70	1970
Ingram, H. St. John	*The Ingram One Club*	Eyre & Spottiswoode (London)	96	1935
Irwin, Florence	*Contract Bridge*	Stokes	23	1927
Jacoby, Oswald (see Four Aces)	**Four Aces System of Contract Bridge*			
Jacoby, Oswald	*Point Count Bidding Made Easy*	Arrco (Chicago)	31	1960
Jacoby, Oswald	*What's New in Bridge*	Hanover House	158	1954
Jannersten, Eric	*†Precision Bridge*	Allen & Unwin (London)	224	1972
Kantar, Edwin	*Bidding*	Kantar (Los Angeles)	52	1965
Kantar, Edwin	*†Bridge Bidding Made Easy*	Wilshire Books (North Hollywood CA)	256	1972
Kantar, Edwin	*‡Bridge Conventions*	Wilshire Books (North Hollywood CA)	108	1972
Kantar, Edwin	*An Expert's Guide to Improving Your Bidding Skills*	Wilshire Books (North Hollywood CA)	151	1980
Kaplan, Edgar	*†Competitive Bidding in Modern Bridge*	Fleet	192	1965
Kaplan, Edgar	**†Complete Italian System of Winning Bridge*	Washburn	159	1959
Kaplan, Edgar	*Kaplan Sheinwold Updated*	The Bridge World	42	1972
Kaplan, Edgar and Sheinwold, Alfred	**‡How to Play Winning Bridge: Kaplan–Sheinwold System*	Fleet	256	1958–63
		Collier	224	1962–69
Karpin, Fred	**The Karpin Point Count System*	Kaufmann (Washington DC)	89	1949
Katz, Richard H. (see Cohen, Larry)	*†Breakthrough in Bridge*			
Kearse, Amalya	*‡Bridge Conventions Complete* (revised and expanded)	Hart	656	1975
Kelsey, H. W.	*Slam Bidding*	Faber & Faber (London)	200	1973
Kempson, Ewart and Hart, Norman de V.	*The Quintessence of CAB*	Nicholas Kaye (London)	160	1959
Kennedy, George	*The Kennedy System of Bridge*	Arco	281	1965
Kerr, R. P. and Jones, W. L.	*The Symmetric Relay*	Kerr & Jones (Australia)	98	1980
Kerwin, Madeleine	*One Over One for Everyone*	Kerwin Co.	116	1932
Kierein, John	*Kamikaze No Trump*	Kierein (Boulder CO)	45	1977
Kleinman, Danny	*Understanding Bidding — Volume I: Fundamentals*	Kleinman (Los Angeles)	177	1981
Kleinman, Danny	*Understanding Bidding — Volume 2: Ramifications*	Kleinman (Los Angeles)	144	1981
Kornfeld, Morris	*Bridge Player's Digest of Conventions*	Kornfeld (Warrington PA)	48	1962–68
Kushner, Jack	*The TNT System of Bidding*	Kushner	8	
Law, John (see Boland, Vincent)	*Accurate Contract Bidding*			
Lawrence, Mike	*†The Complete Book on Balancing in Contract Bridge*	Max Hardy (Hawthorne CA)	209	1981
Lawrence, Mike	*‡The Complete Book on Overcalls in Contract Bridge*	Max Hardy (Hawthorne CA)	202	1979
Lawrence, Mike	*The Jacoby & Texas Transfer Convention*	Texas Bridge Supplies (Baytown TX)	22	1982
Lawrence, Mike	*The Lebensohl Convention*	Texas Bridge Supplies (Baytown TX)	24	1983
Lea, Robert	*Bridge Is Easy with the Lea System*	R. H. Lea (Littleton CO)	144	1965
Lederer, Richard	**Lederer Bids Two Clubs*	Williams & Norgate (London)	220	1934
Lenz, Sidney	*My System of Contract Bidding*	Simon & Schuster	93	1930
Lindelof, E. T.	*COBRA: The Computerized Bidding System*	Victor Gollancz Ltd. (London)	280	1983
Lindsay, Kenneth	*3-D and the MAFIA Club*	AIGA Publications (Baton Rouge)	228	1981
Manning-Foster, A. E.	*Contract Bridge for All*	Ernest Benn (London)	221	1930
Marchione, Richard	*Power Precision Updated and Expanded*	Barclay (Port Chester NY)	138	1982
McKillop, L. M. (see Eastgate, C. L.)	*Modern Gladiator System*			
Meredith, Adam (see Baron, Leo)	*Baron System of Contract Bridge*			
Miller, Richard A.	*Point Count Bidding*	R. A. Miller (York PA)	32	1947
Mollo, Victor	*Bridge: Modern Bidding*	Faber & Faber (London)	124	1961–78
Mollo, Victor	**†Streamlined Bridge: or Bidding Without Tears*	Christopher Johnson (London)	256	1947–54
Monk, Charles	*Le Bridge: Système Complet des Enchères Modernes*	Albin Michel (Paris)	276	1970
Morehead, Albert	**‡Morehead on Bidding*	Macmillan	374	1964
Morehead, Albert	*‡Morehead on Bidding* (R. L. Frey, ed.)	Simon & Schuster	447	1974
Mott-Smith, Geoffrey	*Contract Bridge and Advanced Auction Bidding*	Minton, Balch	281	1927
Mundy, Lindsay	*The Direct British System of Contract Bidding*	Rich & Cowan (London)	176	1932

AUTHOR	TITLE	PUBLISHER	PAGES	DATES
Nail, G. R. and Stucker, Robert	*Revolution in Bridge*	Naylor (San Antonio)	325	1965
Noall, William	*Contract Bridge: The Australian One Club System*	Angus & Robertson (Sydney)	109	1959
Oakie, Don	*Simplified Standard American Bridge Bidding*	BPA (San Francisco)	339	1976
Pavlicek, Richard (see Root, William)	†*Modern Bridge Conventions*			
Payne, Dick and Amsbury, Joe	*Bridge: TNT and Competitive Bidding*	Batsford (London)	175	1981
Perkins, Frank	*Simplified Contract Standards*	Coffin (Fitzwilliam NH)	80	1939
Peterson, Olive (see Work, Milton)	*The Work–Peterson Accurate Valuation System*			
Radin, Judi (see Wei, Katherine)	*Precision's One Club Complete*			
Reed, Dick and Horn, Stormy	*The System — Bidding Techniques of Reed-Horn*	BPA (San Francisco)	51	1976
Reese, Terence	‡*Develop Your Bidding Judgement*	Sterling	254	1962
Reese, Terence	*Modern Bidding and the Acol System*	Nicholson & Watson (London)	128	1952–60
Reese, Terence (see Cohen, Ben)	*The Acol System of Contract Bridge*			
Reese, Terence and Dormer, Albert	*‡The Acol System Today	E. Arnold (London)	163	1961
Reese, Terence and Dormer, Albert	*‡Blueprint for Bidding (American title)	Sterling	163	1961
Reith, George	*Contract*	John Day	250	1929
Reith, George	*Contract Bidding*	John Day	37	1930
Reith, George	*One over One System of Contract Bidding*	Knickerbocker	50	1932
Richards, Ralph (see Work, Milton)	*Common Sense Contract Bridge*			
Root, William	*Introduction to Bidding*	Prentice-Hall (Englewood Cliffs NJ)	151	1967
Root, William and Pavlicek, Richard	†*Modern Bridge Conventions*	Crown	244	1981
Rosenkranz, George	*Bid Your Way to the Top*	Chancellor Hall/Barclay	212	1978
Rosenkranz, George and Truscott, Alan	†*Modern Ideas in Bidding*	Devyn Press (Shelbyville KY)	236	1982
Rosenkranz, George	*The Romex System of Bidding*	World Publishing	325	1970
Rosenkranz, George	†*Win With Romex*	Crown	402	1975
Roth, Al	*The Roth–Stone System	Melville (Washington DC)	176	1953
Roth, Alvin and Rubens, Jeff	†*Modern Bridge Bidding Complete*	Funk & Wagnalls	512	1968
Roth, Alvin and Stone, Tobias	*‡Bridge is a Partnership Game: the Roth–Stone System*	Dutton	237	1958
Rotzell, Peggy	*Bridge Bidding Complete*		43	
Rubens, Jeff (see Roth, Alvin)	†*Modern Bridge Bidding Complete*			
Ruminski, Stanislaw (see Slawinski, Lukose)	*Introduction to Weak Opening Systems and Regres System*			
Sands, Norma	*Standard American Bridge Updated — Five-Card Majors*	Rocky Mountain Books (Denver)	85	1980
Sapire, Max	*Accurate Slam Bidding at Contract (Asking Bids)*	*The Bridge World*	63	1949
Schenken, Howard	*‡Better Bidding in Fifteen Minutes*	Simon & Schuster	192	1963
Schenken, Howard (see Four Aces)	*The Four Aces System of Contract Bridge*			
Schenken, Howard	‡*Howard Schenken's Big Club*	Simon & Schuster	224	1968
Senior, Brian	*The Multi-Colored 2 ◊*	Probray Press (Nottingham, England)	32	1982
Sharif, Omar	*How to Play the Blue Team Club*	Stancraft Products (Minneapolis)	48	1969
Sheinwold, Alfred (see Kaplan, Edgar)	*Kaplan-Sheinwold System of Winning Bridge*			
Shepard, E. V.	*Correct Contract Bridge*	Doubleday	265	1929
Silodor, Sidney	*Silodor Says*	Pageant Press	240	1952
Silverman, Shirley (see Wei, C. C.)	*Official Precision Teacher's Manual*			
Simon, S. J.	*Design for Bidding*	Nicholson & Watson (London)	268	1949
Sims, Dorothy	*Psychic Bidding*	Vanguard Press	87	1932
Sims, P. Hal	*Master Contract	Simon & Schuster	348	1934
Sims, P. Hal	*Money Contract	Simon & Schuster	246	1932
Slawinski, Lukosz and Ruminski, Stanislaw	*Introduction to Weak Opening Systems and Regres System*	Slawinski (Warsaw, Poland)	102	1979
Slawinski, Lukosz	*The Singleton System "Delta"*	Slawinski (Warsaw, Poland)	30	1979
Smith, A. J. (see Stern, Paul)	*The Vienna System of Contract Bridge*			
Smith, Curtis	*Bidding Through Logic*	Curtis Smith (Houston)	185	1962
Smith, Curtis	*Bidding Through Logic — Completely Updated and Conventionalized*	Baxter (Jefferson LA)	174	1981

AUTHOR	TITLE	PUBLISHER	PAGES	DATES
Smith, F. D. and Braham, V. G.	*The Victorian Blackwood Slam Convention*	(Australia)	48	1939
Smokski, Roman	*Defenses to 1 NT*	Probray Press (Nottingham, England)	32	1982
Solomon, Charles	*No Trump Bidding*	7 Stars (Woodstown NY)	49	1946
Solomon, Charles and Disbrow, Bennett	*Slam Bidding and Point Count*	Macrae Smith (Philadelphia)	281	1951
Sontag, Alan	*Power Precision*	Morrow	319	1979
Sowter, Sally	*Transfers After One No Trump*	Bridge Players Handbooks (Nottingham, England)	32	1980
Sowter, Tony	*The Takeout Double*	Bridge Players Handbooks (Nottingham, England)	32	1980
Squire, Norman	*Bidding at Bridge*	Penguin (London)	191	1965
Squire, Norman	*A Guide to Bridge Conventions*	Duckworth (London)	138 100	1958 1979
Squire, Norman	*†The Theory of Bidding	Duckworth (London)	280	1957
Stallard, M. Berl	*Stallard's First Up* (presented by Terence Reese)	Berl & Helen Stallard (Miles City MT)	73	1978
Stayman, Samuel	*The Complete Stayman System of Contract Bidding	Rinehart	223	1956
Stayman, Samuel	‡*Do You Play Stayman?*	Odyssey	207	1965
Stayman, Samuel	*Expert Bidding at Contract Bridge*	Wellington	144	1951
Stayman, Samuel	*Highroad to Winning Bridge* (reprint of Do You Play Stayman?)	Cornerstone Library	192	1970
Steen, Douglas (see Hanna, William)	*Precision Power Bidding: The Bulldog System*			
Stern, Paul	*The Stern Austrian System	Harrap (London)	192	1938
Stern, Paul (see Butler, Geoffrey)	*Two Club System of Bidding*			
Stern, Paul et al	*The Vienna System of Contract Bridge*	Contract Bridge Equipment (Leeds)	249	1948
Stone, Tobias (see Roth, Alvin)	*Bridge Is a Partnership Game*			
Stucker, Robert (see Nail, G. R.)	*Revolution in Bridge*			
Sundby, Robert (see Cohen, Larry)	†*Breakthrough in Bridge*			
Truscott, Alan and Dorothy	*Teach Yourself Basic Bidding*	Arco	270	1976
Vanderbilt, Harold	†*The Club Convention*	Scribner's	186	1964
Vanderbilt, Harold	*Contract Bridge: Bidding and the Club Convention	Scribner's	251	1929
Vanderbilt, Harold	*The New Contract Bridge (Club Convention Bidding and Forcing Overbids)*	Scribner's	333	1930
Vickery, Ron	*The Hybrid Club, an Action System*	Vickery (Fountain Valley CA)	112	1981
Von der Porten, Ron	*Introduction to Defensive Bidding*	Prentice-Hall (Englewood Cliffs NJ)	151	1967
Wallace, Charlton (see Blackwood, Easley)	*Blackwood Slam Bidding*			
Walshe, G. G. J.	*Count to Win at Bridge*	Ernest Benn (London)	147	1948
Walshe, G. G. J.	*Let's Play CAB	Methuen (London)	71	1945
Warren, Mrs. Prescott and Boyden, Elizabeth	*Contract Bridge of 1929*	Garden City Press (Newton MA)	140	1928
Wei, C. C.	*Bidding Precisely*	Precision Headquarters	210	1974
Wei, C. C. and Andersen, Ron	*Bidding Precisely, Volume 2*	Monna Lisa Precision	159	1976
Wei, C. C. and Andersen, Ron	*Profits from Preempts: Bidding Precisely, Volume 3*	Monna Lisa Precision	162	1977
Wei, C. C. and Silverman, Shirley	*Official Precision Teacher's Manual*	Barclay (Port Chester NY)	65	1972
Wei, C. C.	†*Precision Bidding in Bridge*	Barclay (Port Chester NY)	112	1969
Wei, C. C. (see Goren, Charles)	*Precision Bridge for Everyone*			
Wei, C. C.	*The Simplified Precision System of Bridge Bidding*	Precision Headquarters	64	1972
Wei, C. C. et al	*Summary of the Super Precision System*	Precision Headquarters	28	1974
Wei, Katherine and Andersen, Ron	*Action for the Defense — When the Enemy Opens the Bidding*	Monna Lisa Precision	245	1980
Wei, Katherine and Radin, Judi	*Precision's One Club Complete*	Monna Lisa Precision	169	1981
Weiss, Lawrence	*Contract Bridge: The Bidding Structure	Garden Press (Newton MA)	376	1942
Winslow, T. N. and Anstett, Charles	*Win with Winslow*	Nascon	42	1933
Wolf, Murray and Anderson, Merrell	*The Subtle Club*	Wand Books (Chelmsford MA)	187	1974
Woodson, William	*Woodson Electronic Bidding System*	Greensboro Printing (NC)	63	1958
Woodson, William	*Woodson Two-Way No Trump*	Greensboro Printing (NC)	31	1953
Work, Milton et al	*Common Sense Contract Bridge*	J. C. Winston (Philadelphia)	369	1931
Work, Milton and Peterson, Olive	*The Work–Peterson Accurate Valuation System of Contract Bridge*	J. C. Winston (Philadelphia)	101	1934

AUTHOR	TITLE	PUBLISHER	PAGES	DATES
Wyman, Walter (see Work, Milton)	Common Sense Contract Bridge			
Yallouze, Leon (see Garozzo, Benito)	†The Blue Club			

D PLAY

AUTHOR	TITLE	PUBLISHER	PAGES	DATES
Andersson, Ivar and Coffin, George	†Sure Tricks	Coffin (Fitzwilliam NH) David McKay	255 255	1948 1950
Barrow, Rhoda (see Cohen, Ben)	Opening Leads to Better Bridge			
Barrow, Rhoda (see Cohen, Ben)	Your Lead, Partner			
Bellanger, Pierre and Roussiere, C.	*Les Impasses au Bridge: Étude Scientifique et Solutions Pratiques de'apres une Théorie Nouvelle	Librairie Plon (Paris)	424	1936
Berthe, Robert and Lébely, Norbert	Bridge: Step by Step Card Play — No-Trumps (trans. by Barry Seabrook)	Batsford (London)	167	1981
Blackwood, Easley	†The Complete Book of Opening Leads	Devyn Press (Shelbyville KY)	475	1983
Blackwood, Easley	Play of the Hand with Blackwood	Pinnacle Books	458	1978
Brown, John	*‡Winning Defense	Duckworth (London)	343	1952–60
Brown, John	Winning Tricks	Duckworth (London)	300	1947
Bruelheide, F. E.	Fundamentals of Play	Bruelheide (Minneapolis)	64	1939
Cayley, Frank	Bridge Play Made Easy	Reed (Sydney, Australia)	88	1980
Cayley, Frank	Contract Bridge — Play	Rigby (Australia)	64	1978
Cioffi, Raphael	Bridge Endings	Coffin (Boston)	127	1953
Coffin, George	†Bridge Play Four Classics	Duckworth (London)	960	1975
Coffin, George	Bridge Play from A to Z	Faber & Faber (London)	352	1954
Coffin, George	*End Plays	Duckworth (London)	212	1950
Coffin, George	Endplays at Bridge Explained	Bruce Humphries (Boston)	96	1932
Coffin, George (see Andersson, Ivar)	†Sure Tricks			
Cohen, Ben and Barrow, Rhoda	Opening Leads to Better Bridge (American Edition of Your Lead, Partner)	A. S. Barnes & Co.	96	1964
Cohen, Ben and Barrow, Rhoda	Your Lead, Partner	Allen & Unwin (London)	96	1964
Cohen, Ruth	The Elements of Play	Barclay	63	1958–61
Courtenay, F. Dudley	Standard Manual on Play	Methuen (London)	95	1938
Cox, Jean	Bridge with Jean Cox — The Play	Cox (Pittsburgh)	54	1964
Culbertson, Ely	*Contract Bridge Red Book on Play	J. C. Winston (Philadelphia)	616	1934
Culbertson, Ely	How to Lead and Play: Self Instructor	The Bridge World	64	1934
Donnelly, John	Happiness Is a Squeeze	Vantage	121	1972
Dormer, Albert (see Reese, Terence)	The Play of the Cards			
Eng, Fook	‡Bridge Squeezes Illustrated	Eng	185	1973
England, Frank and Reford, Hope	The Play of the Cards	Thos. De La Rue (London)	223	1934
Ewen, Robert	*‡Opening Leads	Prentice-Hall (Englewood Cliffs NJ)	226	1970
Flint, Jeremy and Greenwood, David	Instructions for the Defense	Bodley Head (London)	125	1980
Flint, Jeremy and North, Freddie	Match Your Skill against the Masters	Stein & Day	208	1972
Fox, G. C. H.	Bridge: The Elements of Play	Robert Hale (London)	176	1980
Freehill, H. G.	The Squeeze at Bridge	Faber & Faber (London)	126	1949
Gardener, Nico (see Mollo, Victor)	‡Card Play Technique			
Goren, Charles	Better Bridge for Better Players	Doubleday	538	1942
Goren, Charles	‡Goren on Play and Defense	Doubleday	489	1974
Hathorn, John (see Nail, G. R.)	How to Play the Hand			
Hathorn, John	It's Your Lead	Texas Bridge (Houston)	34	1958
Hathorn, John	Your Best Defense	Adams Press (Chicago)	40	1960
Hayden, Dorothy	Winning Declarer Play	Harper & Row	280	1969
Jannersten, Eric	†Cards on the Table Card Reading (American title)	Allen-Unwin (London) Hart	207 207	1972 1972
Jourdain, Patrick (see Reese, Terence)	Squeeze Play Made Easy			
Kantar, Edwin	‡Complete Defensive Bridge Play	Wilshire Books (North Hollywood CA)	528	1974
Kantar, Edwin (see Reese, Terence)	Defend with Your Life			
Kantar, Edwin	Defensive Play	Kantar (Los Angeles)	47	1965
Kantar, Edwin and Stanley, Jackson	Gamesman Bridge	Liveright	177	1972
Kantar, Edwin	Introduction to Declarer's Play	Prentice-Hall (Englewood Cliffs NJ)	147	1967
Kantar, Edwin	Introduction to Defender's Play	Prentice-Hall (Englewood Cliffs NJ)	153	1968
Kantar, Edwin	Play of the Hand Complete	Kantar (Los Angeles)	62	1965
Karpin, Fred	†The Art of Card Reading	Harper & Row	232	1973

AUTHOR	TITLE	PUBLISHER	PAGES	DATES
Karpin, Fred	*The Drawing of Trumps and Its Postponement*	Max Hardy (Hawthorne CA)	178	1981
Karpin, Fred	‡*The Finesse*	Prentice-Hall (Englewood Cliffs NJ)	273	1972
Karpin, Fred	*How to Play and Misplay Slam Contracts*	Harper & Bros.	171	1962
Karpin, Fred	*How to Play Slam Contracts* (reprint of *How to Play and Misplay Slam Contracts*)	Collier	191	1964
Karpin, Fred	‡*The Play of the Cards*	Bridge Quarterly (Chestnut Hill MA)	506	1958
Karpin, Fred	†*Winning Play in Contract Bridge: Strategy at Trick One*	Dell	288	1964
Kelsey, H. W.	*‡Advanced Play at Bridge*	Hart	192	1968
Kelsey, Hugh (see Ottlik, Géza)	*Adventures in Card Play*			
Kelsey, H. W.	*Bridge: The Mind of the Expert*	Faber & Faber (London)	160	1981
Kelsey, H. W. and Glauert, Michael	*Bridge Odds for Practical Players*	Victor Gollancz (London)	125	1980
Kelsey, H. W. and Matheson, John	*Improve Your Opening Leds*	Victor Gollancz (London)	124	1979
Kelsey, H. W.	*‡Killing Defense at Bridge*	Hart	192	1967
Kelsey, H. W.	†*More Killing Defense*	Hart	92	1972
Kelsey, Hugh	*The Tricky Game*	Max Hardy (Hawthorne CA)	198	1982
Kelsey, Hugh	*Winning Card Play*	Victor Gollancz (London)	234	1979
King, Jack	*Squeeze in Valhalla*	Carlton Press	300	1964
Klinger, Ron	*Bridge Without Error*	Victor Gollancz (London)	128	1981
Lavinthal, Hy	*†Defense Tricks*	Coffin (Waltham MA)	192	1963
Lawrence, Mike	†*Dynamic Defense*	Devyn Press (Shelbyville KY)	226	1982
Lawrence, Mike	‡*How to Read Your Opponent's Cards*	Prentice-Hall (Englewood Cliffs NJ)	175	1973
Lébely, Norbert (see Berthe, Robert)	*Bridge: Step by Step Card Play — No-Trumps*			
Love, Clyde	†*Bridge Squeezes Complete*	Barclay (Port Chester NY)	260	1959
		Dover	260	1968
Love, Clyde	*Squeeze Play in Bridge*	R. R. Smith	183	1951
Mallon, John	*How to Play Your Cards When You Are the Declarer at Contract Bridge*	Chilton Book Co. (Radnor PA)	119	1976
Mallon, John	*Opening Leads and Signals in Contract Bridge*	Collier (London)	158	1969
Miles, Marshall	*‡All 52 Cards*	Exposition Press	142	1963–83
Mollo, Victor and Gardener, Nico	‡*Card Play Technique*	Geo. Newnes, Ltd. (London)	381	1955–67
Nail, G. R. and Hathorn, John	*How to Play the Hand*	Texas Bridge (Houston)	73	1961
Nielsen, Aksel	*Focus on Bridge Defense*	Kaye & Ward (London)	196	1980
North, Freddie (see Flint, Jeremy)	*Match Your Skill against the Masters*			
Ottlik, Géza and Kelsey, Hugh	*Adventures in Card Play*	Victor Gollancz (London)	285	1979
Parson, Donald	*Fall of the Cards*	Little, Brown (Boston)	280	1959
Pavlicek, Richard	*Play and Defense at Bridge*	Pavlicek	20	1976
Perkins, Frank	*Vital Tricks at Contract Bridge*	Joiner & Steele (London)	96	1953
Reese, Terence and Trézel, Roger	*The Art of Defense in Bridge*	Frederick Fell	79	1979
Reese, Terence and Trézel, Roger	*Blocking and Unblocking Plays in Bridge*	Frederick Fell	64	1976
Reese, Terence and Kantar, Edwin	*Defend with Your Life*	Faber & Faber (London)	160	1981
Reese, Terence and Trézel, Roger	*Elimination Play in Bridge*	Frederick Fell	77	1977
Reese, Terence	*‡The Expert Game*	E. Arnold (London)	190	1958
	Master Play (American title)	Coffin (Waltham MA)	144	1960
Reese, Terence and Trézel, Roger	*Master the Odds in Bridge*	Frederick Fell	79	1979
Reese, Terence and Dormer, Albert	*The Play of the Cards*	Penquin (Middlesex, England)	269	1967
Reese, Terence	*‡Play Bridge with Reese*	Sterling	251	1960
Reese, Terence	*†Reese on Play*	E. Arnold (London)	232	1947–75
Reese, Terence and Trézel, Roger	*Safety Plays in Bridge*	Frederick Fell	63	1976
Reese, Terence and Trézel, Roger	*Snares and Swindles in Bridge*	Frederick Fell	64	1977
Reese, Terence and Jourdain, Patrick	*Squeeze Play Made Easy*	Sterling	145	1980
Reese, Terence and Trézel, Roger	*Those Extra Chances in Bridge*	Frederick Fell	64	1978
Reese, Terence and Trézel, Roger	*When to Duck When to Win in Bridge*	Frederick Fell	64	1978
Reford, Hope (see England, Frank)	*The Play of the Cards*			
Romanet, Bertrand	*Le Squeeze au Bridge*	Grasset (Paris)	414	1954

AUTHOR	TITLE	PUBLISHER	PAGES	DATES
Rosencrans	Squeezes, Coups, and End Plays	Rosencrans Publishing Co.	68	1965
Rotzell, Peggy	Bridge Play and Defense			
Roussière, C. (see Bellanger, Pierre)	Les Impasses au Bridge			
Rovere, Ernest	Leads, Signals and Discards in Contract Bridge	Call Bulletin (San Francisco)	36	1941
Schuld, Frank	The Simple Squeeze in Bridge	Drake	223	1974–77
Seabrook, Barry	Bridge: Expert Dummy Play	Batsford (London)	175	1981
Sheinwold, Alfred	Second Book of Bridge: The Play of the Hand	Sterling	159	1953
Sheinwold, Alfred	A Short Cut to Winning Bridge	Fleet	160	1961
Silverman, Shirley	Play of the Hand as Declarer and Defender	Barclay (Port Chester NY)	64	1980
Smith, A. J.	Handbook of Safety Plays	Smith (England)	78	
Sowter, Tony	Bridge: Improve Your Defense	Batsford (London)	168	1979
Squire, Norman	Contract Bridge Card Play Technique	Pitman (London)	145	1976
Squire, Norman	Contract Bridge — Squeeze Play Simplified	Duckworth (London)	184	1979
Stanley, Jackson (see Kantar, Edwin)	Gamesman Bridge			
Trézel, Roger (see Reese, Terence)	The Art of Defense in Bridge			
Trézel, Roger (see Reese, Terence)	Blocking and Unblocking Plays in Bridge			
Trézel, Roger	Cahiers de Bridge	Trézel (Paris)		1956–64
Trézel, Roger (see Reese, Terence)	Elimination Play in Bridge			
Trézel, Roger (see Reese, Terence)	Master the Odds in Bridge			
Trézel, Roger (see Reese, Terence)	Safety Plays in Bridge			
Trézel, Roger (see Reese, Terence)	Snares and Swindles in Bridge			
Trézel, Roger (see Reese, Terence)	Those Extra Chances in Bridge			
Trézel, Roger (see Reese, Terence)	When to Duck When to Win in Bridge			
Traub, Alec	†Trump Technique	Traub (Cape Town)	363	1981
Victor, A.	Effective Defense at Contract Bridge	Victor (New Delhi, India)	217	1982
Vinje, Helge	*Defensive Play in Bridge	Sterling	184	1980
Walshe, G. G. J.	Slams Made Simple — How to Use Cue Bids	Methuen (London)	67	1938
Watson, Louis	*Waton on the Play of the Hand at Contract Bridge	Copeland	492	1934
Watson, Louis	Watson's Classic Book on the Play of the Hand at Bridge (edited and modernized by Sam Fry, Jr.)	Sterling	475	1958
Wolfe, Edward	The Play of the Cards at Contract Bridge	J. C. Winston (Philadelphia)	251	1932–34
Woolsey, Kit	†Modern Defensive Signalling in Contract Bridge	Barclay (Port Chester NY)	64	1981
Woolsey, Kit	‡Partnership Defense in Bridge	Devyn Press (Shelbyville KY)	303	1980

E   BIDDING AND PLAY (in combination)

AUTHOR	TITLE	PUBLISHER	PAGES	DATES
Abrahams, Gerald	Brains in Bridge	Constable (London)	262	1964
		Horizon Press	261	1964
Adams, Charles True	Contract Bridge Standardized	Adams (Chicago)	73	1928
Albarran, Pierre	Encyclopédie du Bridge Moderne	Librairie Arthème Fayard (Paris)	800	1957
Albarran, Pierre and Jaïs, Pierre	How to Win at Rubber Bridge	Barrie Books (London)	191	1961
Albarran, Pierre and de Nexon, R.	Notre Methods de Bridge	Grasset (Paris)	313	1935
Bailey, Maureen O'Brien and Oeschger, Ivy	Bridge for the Joneses	Morrow	331	1947
Barclay, Shepard	Learn Bridge Fast	David McKay (Philadelphia)	125	1944–50
Barrow, Rhoda (see Cohen, Ben)	ABC of Contract Bridge			
Blackwood, Easley	Bridge Humanics	Droke House (Indianapolis)	255	1949
Blackwood, Easley	How You Can Play Winning Bridge with Blackwood	Pinnacle Books (Los Angeles)	281	1977
Bonney, Jack	Master Bridge Teaching Guide	Barclay	128	1957
Brannon, Robert Means	Fool Proof Contract	R. M. Brannon	169	1930–33
Buller, Lt. Col. Walter	How to Play Contract Bridge	The Star (London)	144	1932
Buller, Lt. Col. Walter	Reflections of a Bridge Player	Methuen (London)	197	1929
Cederborg, Warren (compiler)	Coffee with Mary Jane (Farell)	BPA (San Francisco)	142	1974
Chase, Stephen (see Gooden, George)	Contract Bridge Advanced Lesson Course			
Coffin, George	Learn Bridge the Easy Way	C. Branford (Boston)	128	1950
Cohen, Ben and Barrow, Rhoda	ABC of Contract Bridge	Anthony Blond (London)	288	1964

AUTHOR	TITLE	PUBLISHER	PAGES	DATES
Cook, D. J.	*Cook and Deal*	D. J. Cook (Vero Beach FL)	210	1982
Cook, D. J.	*Learn to Play Winning Bridge*	D. J. Cook (Wilmette IL)	85	1962–67
Cook, Mary	*Confessions of a Bridge Addict*	Mary Cook (Twin Falls ID)	215	1979
Cooper, Joan	*Bridge Basics*	Coles (Toronto)	152	1976
Cotter, E. P. C.	*The Financial Times Book of Bridge*	Robert Hale (London)	176	1977
Courtenay, F. Dudley	*Standardized Contract Bridge Complete*	Bartholomew	160	1941
Crawford, John	*Crawford's Contract Bridge*	Grosset & Dunlap	367	1953
Crawford, Richard	*Men, Women and Bridge*	Sterling	191	1978
Crawford, Richard	*People Play Bridge*	Vantage Press	167	1976
Cromelin, Paul	*Bridge Is Beautiful*	Cromelin (Savannah GA)	400	1977
Culbertson, Ely	*Contract Bridge Complete: Gold Book of Bidding and Play	J. C. Winston (Philadelphia)	603	1936–54
Culbertson, Ely	*Contract Bridge for Everyone*	J. C. Winston (Philadelphia)	118	1948
Culbertson, Ely	*The Official Book of Contract Bridge*	J. C. Winston (Philadelphia)	399	1944
Culbertson, Josephine	*Contract Bridge for Beginners*	J. C. Winston (Philadelphia)	221	1938–49
de Satnick, Shelly	*Bridge for Everyone: A Step-by-Step Text and Workbook*	Avon	152	1982
Dormer, Albert (see Reese, Terence)	*The Bridge Player's Alphabetical Handbook*			
Dormer, Albert (see Reese, Terence)	‡*Complete Book of Bridge*			
Dormer, Albert (see Reese, Terence)	†*How to Play a Better Game of Bridge*			
Erdos, Ivan	*Bridge-a-la-Carte*	American Press (Los Angeles)	232	1966
Ewen, Robert	*Contract Bridge: How to Improve Your Technique*	Franklin Watts	64	1975
Ewen, Robert	*The Teenager's Guide to Bridge*	Dodd, Mead	214	1976
Feldheim, Harold	*Negative and Responsive Doubles in Bridge*	Barclay (Port Chester NY)	64	1980
Flint, Jeremy	*Tiger Bridge*	Simon & Schuster	192	1970
Forquet, Pietro	*Bridge with the Blue Team*	A. B. Publications (Sydney, Australia)	384	1983
Foster, Robert F.	*Foster's Contract Bridge*	Greenberg	121	1927
Fox, G. C. H.	*Begin Bridge*	Elliot Rightway (Surrey, England)	125	1973
Fox, Gerald (see Lawrence, Mike)	*Introduction to Contract Bridge and Point Count Bidding*			
Franklin, Harold (see Reese, Terence)	*The Listener Book of Bridge — Best of Bridge on the Air*			
Frey, Richard	*How to Win at Contract in Ten Easy Lessons*	Fawcett Pub.	288	1961–72
Fry, Sam Jr.	*Better Bridge*	Leisure League	109	1935
Fry, Sam Jr.	*How to Win at Bridge with Any Partner*	Golden Press	144	1960
Gardener, Nico (see Mollo, Victor)	*Bridge for Beginners*			
Goldstein, Abraham	*Common-Sense Bridge for the Intermediate Player*	Arco	80	1959
Gooden, George et al	*Contract Bridge Advanced Lesson Course*	Int'l Society of Bridge Teachers (Carmel CA)	138	1972
Gooden, George	*Contract Bridge, Bidding and Play*	G. S. Gooden (Carmel CA)	150	1969
Gooden, George	*Contract Bridge Lesson Course*	G. S. Gooden (Carmel CA)	121	1960–78
Gooden, George	*Contract Bridge Teacher's Blue Book*	G. S. Gooden (Carmel CA)	200	1967
Goren, Charles	*Contract Bridge Complete*	Doubleday	498	1951–57
Goren, Charles	*Contract Bridge in a Nutshell*	Doubleday	128	1946–72
Goren, Charles	*Contract Bridge Made Easy*	Doubleday	96	1948
Goren, Charles	*The Elements of Bridge*	Doubleday	420	1960
Goren, Charles	‡*Goren's Bridge Complete*	Doubleday	562	1963
Goren, Charles (with Sharif, Omar)	*Goren's Bridge Complete*	Doubleday	706	1980
Goren, Charles	*Goren's Easy Steps to Winning Bridge*	Franklin Watts	287	1963
Goren, Charles	*Goren's Winning Partnership Bridge*	Random House	183	1961
Harkness, Kenneth	*Invitation to Bridge*	Simon & Schuster	306	1950
Hathorn, John	*The Secrets of Tactical Bridge*	Texas Bridge (Houston)	85	1961
Ingram, H. St. John	*How to Win at Bridge*	Eyre & Spottiswoode (London)	126	1950
International Bridge Academy	*Annals (trans. by Alec Traub) — Volume 1 — Volume 2	(Brussels)	88 103	1966 1969
Jacoby, Oswald and James	*Win at Bridge with Jacoby and Son*	G. P. Putnam's Sons	222	1966
Jacoby, Oswald and James	*Win at Bridge with Jacoby Modern*	Enterprise Publications	128	1970
Jaïs, Pierre	*Apprendez à Mieux Jouer au Bridge*	Julliard (Paris)	582	1957
Jaïs, Pierre (see Albarran, Pierre)	*How to Win at Rubber Bridge*			
Kantar, Edwin	*Beginner's Lessons*	Kantar (Los Angeles)	50	1965
Kantar, Edwin	*A Comprehensive Bridge Manual*	Kantar (Los Angeles)	143	1965
Kaplan, Edgar	*‡Winning Contract Bridge Complete*	Fleet	434	1964
Karn, Willard	*Karn's Bridge Service*	Long & Smith	361	1933
Karpin, Fred	*Psychological Strategy in Contract Bridge*	Harper	325	1960
Kearse, Amalya	‡*Bridge Conventions Complete*	Hart	624	1975
Kearse, Amalya	*Bridge at Your Fingertips*	Hart	320	1979

AUTHOR	TITLE	PUBLISHER	PAGES	DATES
Kelsey, H. W.	*Improve Your Bridge*	Hart	191	1971
Kempson, Ewart	*Contract Bridge, How to Play It*	Emerson Books (London)	164	1957
Kempson, Ewart	*Kempson on Contract — How to Win at Contract Bridge*	Hodder & Stoughton (London)	180	1935
Kerwin, Madeleine	*Partnership Contract*	Wm. Morrow	180	1934
Klinger, Ron	*Basic Bridge — A Guide to Good Acol Bidding and Play*	Ward Lock (London)	127	1978
Klinger, Ron	*Bridge Basics*	Reldt (Australia)	118	1971
Lagron, E. M.	*Defensive Bridge*	Bobbs-Merrill (Indianapolis)	162	1933
Lampert, Harry	*The Fun Way to Learn Serious Bridge*	Hardel (Roselyn NY) Cornerstone Library	136 160	1978 1980
Lawrence, Mike and Fox, Gerald	*Introduction to Contract Bridge and and Point Count Bidding*	Bridge-O-Matic (Inglewood CA)	32	1975
Lawrence, Mike	*Judgment at Bridge*	Max Hardy (Inglewood CA)	151	1976
Lawrence, Mike	*Play a Swiss Teams of Four with Mike Lawrence*	Max Hardy (Hawthorne CA)	99	1982
Le Dentu, José	*Bridge Analysis* (trans. & ed. by Amalya Kearse)	Hart	287	1978
Le Dentu, José	*Bridge Facile*	Fayard (Paris)	446	1970
Lederer, Richard	*Modern Contract & Duplicate*	Williams & Norgate (London)	149	1936
Lederer, Tony and Rhoda	*Learn Bridge with the Lederers*	Cassell (London)	202	1977
Lenz, Sidney	*Lenz on Contract Bridge*	Simon & Schuster	131	1927–29
Liggett, Winfield Jr.	*Contract Bridge Summary: Official System*	Stokes	20	1931
Lukacs, Paul (see Milnes, Eric)	*Learn to Play Bridge*			
MacLeod, Iain	*Bridge Is an Easy Game*	Falcon Press (London) Victor Gollancz (London)	244 215	1952 1980
Markus, Rixi	*Common Sense Bridge*	Random House	171	1973
Markus, Rixi	*Improve Your Bridge*	Bodley Head (London)	104	1979
Markus, Rixi	*Play Better Bridge*	Octopus Books (London)	157	1979
Mayer, Edward	*Money Bridge*	Van Nostrand	258	1954
Mayer, Edward	*Winning at Rubber Bridge*	Batsford (London)	195	1975
Miles, Marshall	†*Marshall Miles Teaches Logical Bridge*	Exposition Press	319	1967
Milnes, Eric and Lukacs, Paul	*Learn to Play Bridge*	Kaye & Ward (London)	153	1977
Mollo, Victor	*Bridge Basics and Beyond*	Hart	155	1976
Mollo, Victor and Gardener, Nico	*Bridge for Beginners*	Barnes & Co.	160	1960
Mollo, Victor	*Bridge Course Complete*	Faber & Faber (London)	237	1977
Mollo, Victor	*Bridge with a Master*	Barnes & Co.	102	1960
Mollo, Victor	*Bridge Psychology*	Duckworth (London)	127	1958
Mollo, Victor	*Bridge Saga*	Hart	210	1976
Mollo, Victor	*The Finer Arts of Bridge*	Faber & Faber (London)	201	1978
Mollo, Victor	*Success at Bridge*	Newnes (London)	125	1964
Morehead, Albert	*Bridge the Expert Way*	Bridge World Accessories	62	1943
Morehead, Albert	‡*Contract Bridge Summary*	Macmillan	126	1963
Oeschger, Ivy (see Bailey, Maureen)	*Bridge for the Joneses*			
Pavlicek, Richard	*Modern Bridge*	Pavlicek	21	1975
Pearson, N. W.	*Chicago Bridge*	Cricket Press	61	1963
Phillips, Hubert and Reese, Terence	*The Elements of Contract* 2nd Rev. Ed.	British Bridge World (London) Eyre & Spottiswoode (London)	271 266	1937 1948
Phillips, Hubert	*Making Bridge Pay — How to Win at Rubber Bridge*	Max Parrish (London)	448	1962
Phillips, Hubert	*Thorne's Complete Contract Bridge*	Eyre & Spottiswoode (London)	257	1948
Reese, Terence	‡*Advanced Bridge* (reprint of *Play Bridge with Reese* and *Develop Your Bidding Judgment*)	Sterling	464	1973
Reese, Terence	*Begin Bridge with Reese*	Sterling	128	1977
Reese, Terence	†*Bridge for Bright Beginners*	Sterling	151	1965
Reese, Terence and Shapiro Boris	*Bridge Card by Card*	Hamlyn (London)	88	1969
Reese, Terence and Dormer, Albert	*The Bridge Player's Alphabetical Handbook*	Faber & Faber (London)	223	1981
Reese, Terence and Dormer, Albert	‡*The Complete Book of Bridge*	Dutton	486	1974
Reese, Terence (see Phillips, Hubert)	*The Elements of Contract*			
Reese, Terence and Dormer, Albert	†*How to Play a Better Game of Bridge*	Stein & Day	181	1969
Reese, Terence and Franklin, Harold	*The Listener Book of Bridge — Best of Bridge on the Air*	BBC (London)	176	1965
Reese, Terence	†*Precision Bidding and Precision Play*	Sterling	153	1973
Reese, Terence	*Your Bridge Questions Answered*	Jordan & Sons (London)	136	1951
Rimington, Derek	*Learn Bridge from the Experts — 100 Lessons*	Pelham (London)	208	1981

AUTHOR	TITLE	PUBLISHER	PAGES	DATES
Romanet, Bertrand	*Les Bases du Bridge Moderne	Albin Michell (Paris)	368	1958
Roth, Alvin and Rubens, Jeff	Bridge for Beginners	Funk & Wagnalls	216	1970
Rovere, Ernest	†Contract Bridge Complete	Simon & Schuster	834	1965
			844	1973
Rovere, Ernest	Point Count Contract Bridge Complete	Random House	710	1954–64
Rubens, Jeff	*The Secrets of Winning Bridge	Grosset & Dunlap	241	1969
Rubens, Jeff (see Roth, Alvin)	Bridge for Beginners			
Seabrook, Barry	Bridge: From Average to Expert	Batsford (London)	175	1979
Shapiro, Boris (see Reese, Terence)	Bridge Card by Card			
Sheinwold, Alfred	Complete Bridge Course First Book of Bridge Second Book of Bridge — Play of the Hand Third Book of Bridge — How to Bid and Play In Duplicate Tournaments Fourth Book of Bridge — How to Improve Your Game	Sterling	640	1959
Sheinwold, Alfred	First Book of Bridge	Sterling	152	1952
		Barnes & Noble	153	1969
Sheinwold, Alfred	*‡Five Weeks to Winning Bridge	Pocket Books	498	1960–75
		Simon & Schuster	548	1959–64
Shepard, E. V.	Contract Bridge Standardized	Cosmopolitan Book Corp.	209	1931
Silodor, Sidney and Tierney, John	Contract Bridge According to Silodor and Tierney	Stanley Allan (Chester Hill NJ)	442	1961
Silverman, Shirley	Advanced and Duplicate Bridge Student Text	Barclay (Port Chester NY)	64	1976
Silverman, Shirley	Elementary Five Card Major Student Text	Barclay (Port Chester NY)	48	1976
Silverman, Shirley	Five Card Major Bridge Teacher's Manual	Barclay (Port Chester NY)	334	1976–80
Silverman, Shirley	Intermediate Bridge Five Card Major Student Text	Barclay (Port Chester NY)	64	1976
Simon, S. J.	*†Why You Lose at Bridge	Simon & Schuster	159	1946
Sobel, Helen	All the Tricks	Greenberg	245	1949
	Winning Bridge (British title)	Peter Davies (London)	253	1950
Solomon, Charles and Disbrow, Bennett	How to Bid and What to Lead	Macrae Smith (Philadelphia)	128	1953
Squire, Norman	Contract Bridge: How to Become a Champion	Vikas Publ. (Delhi, India)	118	1976
Sydnor, Caroline	Bridge Made Easy	Sydnor (Alexandria VA)		
	Book One		165	1975
	Book Two		207	1977
	Book Three		266	1981
Tait, J. W.	Bridge Challenge	Wolfe (London)	141	1974
Tait, J. W.	Bridge Match	Faber & Faber (London)	133	1976
Tierney, John (see Silodor, Sidney)	Contract Bridge According to Silodor and Tierney			
Thomas, Frank (see Gooden, George)	Contract Bridge Advanced Lesson Course			
Truscott, Alan	Bridge: Successful Play from First Principles	Oldbourne (London)	159	1961
Truscott, Alan	The New York Times Guide to Practical Bridge	Golden Press	220	1970
Vanderbilt, Harold	Contract by Hand Analysis	The Bridge World	165	1933
Watson, Louis	The Outline of Contract Bridge	Grosset & Dunlap	333	1934
Whitehead, Wilbur	Contract Bridge: What (to do) and Why	Frederick A. Stokes	183	1931
Woods, Jo	Little Green Book, Artificial Bids, Leads, Signals	Woods (Little Rock AR)	68	1968
Work, Milton	Contract Bridge for All	J. C. Winston (Philadelphia)	243	1929–31
Young, Ray	Bridge for People Who Don't Know One Card from Another	Follett (Chicago)	127	1964

F DUPLICATE BRIDGE (Bidding, Play, and Tournament Directing)

AUTHOR	TITLE	PUBLISHER	PAGES	DATES
Andersen, Ron (see Wei, C. C.)	†Match Point Precision			
Benjamin, Albert (see Kempson, Ewart)	Tournament Bridge for Everyone			
Beynon, George	‡Bridge Director's Manual (6th ed., rev.)	Coffin (Waltham MA)	192	1944
Beynon, George	*Tournament and Duplicate Bridge	Stuyvesant	270	1944
The Bridge World	How Would You Rule?	The Bridge World	52	1978
Bruelheide, F. E.	Duplicate Bridge Guide	Bruelheide (Minneapolis)	64	1938
Coffin, George	Perfect Plays and Match Point Ways	Coffin (Waltham MA)	160	1973
Culbertson, Ely	*Bidding and Play in Duplicate Contract Bridge	J. C. Winston (Philadelphia)	271	1946
Dormer, Albert (see Reese, Terence)	Bridge for Tournament Players			
Farrington, Frank	*Duplicate Bridge Movements	Farrington (England)	98	1960

AUTHOR	TITLE	PUBLISHER	PAGES	DATES
Feldheim, Harold	*Winning Swiss Team Tactics in Bridge*	Barclay (Port Chester NY)	236	1976
Fox, G. C. H.	*Duplicate Bridge*	St. Martin's Press	160	1974
Fox, G. C. H.	*Duplicate Bridge, Its Procedures and Tactics*	E. Arnold (London)	143	1955
Greenberg, Julie	*Duplicate Decisions, A Club Director's Guide for Ruling at the Table*	ACBL (Memphis)	52	1982
Greenwood, David	*The Pairs Game*	Cassell (London)	150	1978
Groner, Alex	‡*Duplicate Bridge Direction*	Barclay (Port Chester NY)	224	1967
Groner, Alex	‡*Duplicate Bridge Direction: A Complete Handbook*	Barclay (Port Chester NY)	224	1972
Gruenther, Alfred	**Duplicate Contract Complete*	The Bridge World	328	1933
Hardy, Max (see Roney, Bill)	*Play My Card*			
Harrison-Gray, Maurice (see Squire, Norman)	*†*Winning Points at Match-Point Bridge*			
Hasler, Alexander T.	*Duplicate Bridge Simplified*	Harrop (London)	134	ca.1935
Hathorn, John (see Nail, G. R.)	*How to Play Championship Duplicate Bridge*			
Hoffman, Martin	*Hoffman on Pairs Play*	Faber & Faber (London)	184	1982
Jannersten, Eric and Wohlin, Jan	*Winning Pairs Technique* (trans. by Hugh Kelsey)	Victor Gollancz (London)	160	1980
Jourdan, Catherine	*ABC of Duplicate Bridge Direction*	Coffin (Waltham MA)	96	1967
Kaplan, Edgar	*Director's Guide*	ACBL (Memphis)	32	1976
Kaplan, Edgar	†*Duplicate Bridge, How to Play, How to Win*	Bantam Books Hearthside Press	149 148	1966 1968
Karpin, Fred (see Kay, Norman)	‡*The Complete Book of Duplicate Bridge*			
Karpin, Fred	*Winning Play in Tournament and Duplicate Bridge: How the Experts Triumph*	New American Library	241	1968
Kay, Norman et al	‡*The Complete Book of Duplicate Bridge*	G. P. Putnam Sons Barnes & Noble	496 496	1965 1969–72
Kelsey, H. W.	†*Match Point Bridge*	Faber & Faber (London)	239	1970
Kempson, Ewart and Benjamin, Albert	*Tournament Bridge for Everyone*	Faber & Faber (London)	200	1963
Low, William	*Graphic Guide to Duplicate Bridge Directing* (charts, tables)	Low (NYC)	57	1978
McKinnon, Ian	*Bridge Directing Complete* (100 appendices)	Computer Accounting Services (Sydney, Australia)	182	1979
Miles, Marshall	*‡*How to Win at Duplicate Bridge*	Exposition Press	463	1957
Nail, G. R. and Hathorn, John	*How to Play Championship Duplicate Bridge*	Texas Bridge (Houston)	69	1963
Nail, G. R. and Hathorn, John	*Winning Duplicate*	Texas Bridge (Houston)	28	1962
Needham, Richard	*Tournament Tactics at Contract Bridge*	Needham	16	1934
Parker, Allan	*Let's Play Duplicate — Actual Duplicate in the Home*	Miller Quarles (Houston) vol. 1 vol. 2		1961 1962
Reese, Terence and Dormer, Albert	†*Bridge for Tournament Players*	Robert Hale (London)	173	1968
Roney, Bill and Hardy, Max	*Play My Card*	Max Hardy (Hawthorne CA)	136	1980
Sheinwold, Alfred	*Third Book of Bridge — How to Bid and Play in Duplicate Tournaments*	Sterling	157	1954
Silodor, Sidney (see Kay, Norman)	‡*The Complete Book of Duplicate Bridge*			
Squire, Norman and Harrison-Gray, Maurice	*†*Winning Points at Match-Point Bridge*	Faber & Faber (London)	151	1959
Wei, C. C. and Andersen, Ron	†*Match Point Precision*	Monna Lisa	195	1975
Wohlin, Jan (see Jannersten, Eric)	*Winning Pairs Technique*			
Woolsey, Kit	*Matchpoints	Devyn Press (Shelbyville KY)	343	1982

G MATCH AND TOURNAMENT RECORDS
Editor

Albarran, Pierre (see Bellanger, Pierre)	*Les 102 Donnes d'un Grand Match*			
Aron, Adiene (see Bellanger, Pierre)	*Les 102 Donnes d'un Grand Match*			
Beasley, H. M.	*Beasley v. Culbertson*	Hutchinson (London)	288	1933
Bellanger, Pierre et al	*Les 102 Donnes d'un Grand Match*	Bernard Grasset (Paris)	189	1933
Buller, Walter and Kempson, Ewart	*The Buller Almacks Bridge Contest*	Vail (London)	108	1934
Buller, Walter	*Colonel Buller on the Beasley–Culbertson Bridge Contest*	The Star (London)	128	1933
Buller, Walter	*International Bridge Test*	News-Chronicle (London)	222	1930
Culbertson, Ely	**Famous Hands of the Culbertson–Lenz Match*	The Bridge World	437	1932

AUTHOR	TITLE	PUBLISHER	PAGES	DATES
Culbertson, Ely	*300 Contract Bridge Hands — First World Bridge Championship* (England vs. U.S)	*The Bridge World*	380	1933
Culbertson, Ely	*The 1932 World Bridge Olympic Hands*	*The Bridge World*	96	1932
England, Frank and Harris, A.F. Stapleton	*Experts at Contract: Crockford's Club v. the Dutch and German Teams*	Bodley Head (London)	104	1932
Francis, Henry	*1973 World Bridge Champonships* (Brazil, Italy, North America, Indonesia, Aces)	ACBL (Memphis)	215	1973
Francis, Henry	*1974 World Bridge Championships* (Brazil, France, Indonesia, Italy, New Zealand, North America)	ACBL (Memphis)	192	1974
Francis, Henry	*1975 World Championship* (Brazil, France, Indonesia, Italy, North America)	ACBL (Memphis)	205	1975
Francis, Henry	*1976 World Championships* (Bermuda Bowl, Venice Trophy, Olympiad)	ACBL (Memphis)	191	1976
Francis, Henry	*World Championship '77* (Argentina, Australia, North America, Sweden, Taiwan, North America)	ACBL (Memphis)	187	1978
Francis, Henry	*V World Pair Olympiad* (Open Pairs, Women's Pairs, Mixed Pairs, Venice Trophy, Rosenblum Cup)	ACBL (Memphis)	159	1979
Francis, Henry	*1979 World Championship* (Australia, Brazil, Italy, North America, Panama-Venezuela, Taiwan)	ACBL (Memphis)	238	1980
Francis, Henry	*1980 World Bridge Team Olympiad* (Open Series, Ladies Series)	ACBL (Memphis)	190	1981
Francis, Henry	*1981 World Championships for the Bermuda Bowl* (Argentine, Australia, Great Britain, Indonesia, Pakistan, Poland, United States) *and the Venice Trophy* (Australia, Brazil, Great Britain, United States, Venezuela)	ACBL (Memphis)	255	1982
Franklin, Harold (see Reese, Terence)	*World Bridge Championship 1955*			
Frey, Richard	*International Team Playoff*	ACBL	96	1969
Frey, Richard	*Team Trials*	ACBL		1964
Frey, Richard	*Team Trials*	ACBL		1965
Frey, Richard	*Team Trials*	ACBL	144	1966
Frey, Richard	*World Championship* (United States, Italy, and Argentina)	ACBL	158	1958
Frey, Richard	*World Championship* (United States, Italy, and Argentina)	ACBL	160	1959
Frey, Richard	*World Bridge Olympiad* (France, Great Britain, Italy, and United States)	ACBL	136	1960
Frey, Richard	*World Championship* (Italy, North America France, and Argentina)	ACBL	132	1961
Frey, Richard	*World Championship* (Italy, North America Great Britain, and Argentina)	ACBL	118	1962
Frey, Richard	*World Championship* (Italy, North America, France, and Argentina)	ACBL	120	1963
Frey, Richard	*World Bridge Olympiad* (Italy, United States, Canada, Great Britain, and 25 others)	ACBL	192	1964
Frey, Richard	*World Bridge Championship* (Italy, North America, Great Britain, Argentina)	ACBL	192	1965
Frey, Richard	*World Bridge Championship* (Italy, North America, Thailand, Venezuela, The Netherlands)	ACBL	224	1966
Frey, Richard	*World Bridge Championship* (Italy, France, North America, Thailand, Venezuela)	ACBL (Greenwich CT)	224	1967
Frey, Richard	*World Bridge Olympiad* (Italy, United States, Canada, The Netherlands, and 29 others)	ACBL (Greenwich CT)	192	1968
Frey, Richard	*World Bridge Championship* (Italy, North America, France, Taiwan, Brazil)	ACBL (Greenwich CT)	224	1969
Harris, A. F. Stapleton (see England, Frank)	*Experts at Contract: Crockford's Club v. the Dutch and German Teams*			
Herts, B. Russell (see Kerwin, Madeleine)	*Expert Misbidding* (Culbertson-Lenz 1931)			
Hirsch, Tannah	*1970 World Championship* (Italy, North American, Norway, Taiwan, Brazil)	ACBL (Greenwich CT)	224	1970
Hirsch, Tannah	*1971 World Championship* (Aces France, Australia, Taiwan, Brazil, North America)	ACBL (Greenwich CT)	223	1971
Kempson, Ewart	*Bridge Match in Dublin*	Waddington (Leeds, England)	100	1958
Kempson, Ewart (see Buller, Walter)	*The Buller Almacks Bridge Contest*			
Kempson, Ewart	*Championship Hands*	Joiner & Steele (London)	59	1950
Kempson, Ewart	*Kempson versus Baron Exhibition Contest-100 Hands*	Newcastle Chronicle (Newcastle)	104	1946
Kerwin, Madeleine and Herts, B. Russell	*Expert Misbidding* (Culbertson-Lenz 1931)	Covice-Friede	140	1932

AUTHOR	TITLE	PUBLISHER	PAGES	DATES
Klinger, Ron	*The Australian Open Team at the Sixth World Team Olympiad (Valkenburg, 1980)*	Klinger (Australia)	50	1980
McKenney, William	*Par Bridge-Hands for Replay National Intercollegiate Bridge Tournaments*	Barclay & Assoc. of American Card Manufacturers		1938
Moyse, Alphonse Jr. and Sheinwold, Alfred	*World Championship, U.S. and Sweden*	ACBL	136	1953
	World Championship, U.S., France	ACBL	80	1954
	World Championship, U.S., Great Britain	ACBL	120	1955
	World Championship, U.S., France	ACBL	84	1956
	World Championship (United States, Italy)	ACBL	126	1957
Pigot, Peter	*Lausanne 1979 (Story of the Irish Bridge Team)*	Pigot (Ireland)	194	1979
Reese, Terence and Franklin, Harold	*World Bridge Championship (Great Britain v. United States)*	Thos. De La Rue (London)	106	1955
Richards, Ralph	*Championship Bridge*	Greenberg	114	1928
Smith, Thomas M.	*World Bridge Olympiad (Italy, United States, Canada, France and 35 others)*	ACBL	224	1972
Stern, Paul	*Beating the Culbertsons*	T. Werner Laurie (London)	128	1938
Sullivan, Michael and Williams, R. E.	*World Par Hands*	World Bridge Federation	40	1961–63
Venizelos, Sophocle (see Bellanger, Pierre)	*Les 102 Donnes d'un Grand Match*			
Williams, R. E. (see Sullivan, Michael)	*World Par Hands*			

H   HAND COLLECTIONS

Becker, B. Jay	*Becker on Bridge*	Grosset & Dunlap	128	1971
Bird, David (see Reese, Terence)	*Miracles of Card Play*			
Corn, Ira	*Play Bridge with the Aces*	Fawcett (Greenwich CT)	224	1972
Culbertson, Ely	*60 Contract Bridge Hands*	*The Bridge World*	160	1933
Darvas, Robert and Hart, Norman de V.	**Right Through the Pack*	Stuyvesant House	328	1947
Darvas, Robert and Lukacs, Paul	*†Spotlight on Card Play*	Barclay	160	1960
Fox, G. C. H.	*The Daily Telegraph Book of Bridge*	Robert Hale (London)	237	1975
Fox, G. C. H.	*Master Play — The Best of International Bridge*	Robert Hale (London)	186	1976
Goren, Charles	*The Best of Championship Bridge*	American Van Lines	25	
Goren, Charles	*Bridge Mystery Deals*	Heines (Minneapolis)	64	1964
Goren, Charles	*Championship Bridge with Charles Goren*	Doubleday	255	1964
Goren, Charles	*Charles H. Goren's 100 Challenging Bridge Hands for You to Enjoy*	Doubleday	100	1976
Griffiths, John	*The Golden Years of Bridge (Classic Hands from the Past)*	Victor Gollancz (London)	127	1981
Harrison-Gray, Maurice	*Country Life Book of Bridge*	Hamlyn Group (London)	160	1972
Hart, Norman de V. (see Darvas, Robert)	**Right Through the Pack*			
Havas, George	*The Australian Book of Bridge*	Horwitz Publications (Hong Kong)	128	1979
Jannersten, Eric (see Mollo, Victor)	*†The Best of Bridge*			
Jannersten, Eric	*Bridge Writer's Choice 1964*	IBPA (Sweden)	177	1965
Jannersten, Eric	*Bridge Writer's Choice 1968*	IBPA (Sweden)	240	1968
Jelks, Edward and Schmitt, Raymond	*Trick Taking Potential*	Jett (Normal IL)	80	1974
Kauder, James	*The Bridge Philosopher*	Kauder (Los Angeles)	144	1972
Kempson, Ewart	*Contract Bridge Hands*	Faber & Faber (London)	96	1950
Le Dentu, Jose	*120 Donnes et Problèmes du Bridge*	Presses Pocket (Paris)	189	1975
Lukacs, Paul (see Darvas, Robert)	*Spotlight on Card Play*			
Lukacs, Paul (see Milnes, Eric)	*Bridge Hands for the Connoisseur*			
Markus, Rixi	*Aces and Places*	Bodley Head (London)	140	1972
		Drake	140	1973
Markus, Rixi	*†Bid Boldly, Play Safe*	Blond (London)	212	1966
Markus, Rixi	*Bridge Around the World*	Bodley Head (London)	239	1979
McKenney, William	*Contract Bridge (Bidding and Playing of over 750 Hands from Championship Tournaments)*	American Merchandise Co.	108	1935
Miller, Richard A	*Bridge Brilliance and Blunders*	Dow Jones (Princeton NJ)	222	1974
Miller, Richard A.	*More Bridge Brilliance and Blunders*	Dow Jones (Princeton NJ)	217	1975
Milnes, Eric and Lukacs, Paul	*†Bridge Hands for the Connoisseur*	Barclay Bridge Supplies	127	1974
Mollo, Victor and Jannersten, Eric	*†The Best of Bridge*	Faber & Faber (London)	223	1973
Nielsen, Aksel	*Bridge with the Three Musketeers*	Kaye & Ward (London)	233	1978

AUTHOR	TITLE	PUBLISHER	PAGES	DATES
North, Freddie	*Bridge with Aunt Agatha*	Faber & Faber (London)	208	1983
Peterson, Olive (see Work, Milton)	*101 Celebrated Hands*			
Phillips, Hubert	*Bridge with Goren*	Citadel Press	128	1960
Phillips, Hubert	*Bridge at Ruff's Club*	Batchworth Press (London)	248	1951
Phillips, Hubert and Reese, Terence	*Bridge with Mr. Playbetter*	Batchworth Press (London)	219	1952
Phillips, Hubert	*Brush Up on Your Bridge*	Dent (London)	119	1939
Phillips, Hubert	*100 Contract Bridge Hands*	Faber & Faber (London)	146	1932
Phillips, Hubert and Westall, F. C.	*200 Hands from Match Play*	Thos. De La Rue (London)	401	1934
Reese, Terence (see Phillips, Hubert)	*Bridge with Mr. Playbetter*			
Reese, Terence and Bird, David	*Miracles of Card Play*	Victor Gollancz (London)	160	1982
Saunders, P. F.	*Bridge with a Perfect Partner*	Ward Lock (London)	127	1976
Schmitt, Raymond (see Jelks, Edward)	*Trick Taking Potential*			
Shapiro, Boris	*Bridge Analysis*	Sterling	187	1976
Simon, S. J.	*Cut for Partners*	Nicholson & Watson (London)	128	1950
Smith, A. J.	*Contract Chronicles*	Grayson & Grayson (London)	52	1936
Smith, A. J. (see Stern, Paul)	*Sorry Partner*			
Solomon, Charles and Wilson, Bert	*Hold Our Bridge Hands*	Lefax, Inc. (Philadelphia)	187	1976
Stern, Paul and Smith, A. J.	*Sorry Partner*	Faber & Faber (London)	141	1945
Truscott, Alan	†*Master Bridge by Question and Answer*	Quadrangle Books (Chicago)	252	1971
Tuite, Hugh	*Contract Bridge for Iris*	Geoffrey Bles (London)	125	1929
Tuite, Hugh	*Mrs. Pottleton's Bridge Parties*	Simon & Schuster	153	1928
White, Travis	*Odd Tricks* reprinted	*The Bridge World* GBC Press (Las Vegas)	104 141	1934 1978
Whitehead, Wilbur	*Championship Bridge Hands*	Stokes	120	1929
Wilson, Bert (see Solomon, Charles)	*Hold Our Bridge Hands*			
Work, Milton and Peterson, Olive	*101 Celebrated Hands*	J. C. Winston (Philadelphia)	215	1933

I FICTION

Cole, E. R. and Edwards, James (eds.)	*Grand Slam*	Putnam	224	1975
DeSerpa, Allan	*The Mexican Contract*	Max Hardy (Hawthorne CA)	148	1981
Edwards, James (see Cole, E. R.)	*Grand Slam*			
Flint, Jeremy (see Reese, Terence)	*Trick 13*			
Friedman, B. H.	*Yarborough*	World Publishing Co.	374	1964
Gooden, George and Thomas, Frank	*Sherlock Holmes, Bridge Detective*	Frank Thomas (Los Angeles)	122	1973
Herts, Russell	*Grand Slam: The Rise and Fall of a Bridge Wizard*	Pratt	288	1932
Nicolet, C. C.	*Death of a Bridge Expert*	Simon & Schuster	235	1932
Powell, Richard	*Tickets to the Devil*	Scribner's	306	1968
Quinn, Terry	*The Great Bridge Conspiracy*	St. Martin's Press	196	1979
Reese, Terence and Flint, Jeremy	*Trick 13*	Weidenfeld & Nicolson (London)	172	1979
Theimer, Ernst T.	*The Bridge Adventures of Androcles MacThick*	E. T. Theimer (Rumson NJ)	247	1981
Thomas, Frank (see Gooden, George)	*Sherlock Holmes, Bridge Detective*			
Thomas, Frank	*Sherlock Holmes, Bridge Detective Returns*	Frank Thomas (Los Angeles)	199	1975
Von Elsner, Don	*The Ace of Spies*	Award Books	192	1966
Von Elsner, Don	*The Best of Jake Winkman*	Max Hardy (Hawthorne CA)	117	1981
Von Elsner, Don	*Cruise Bridge*	Max Hardy (Hawthorne CA)	187	1981
Von Elsner, Don	*Everything's Jake with Me*	Max Hardy (Hawthorne CA)	105	1980
Von Elsner, Don	*The Jack of Hearts*	Award Books	188	1968
Von Elsner, Don	*The Jake of Diamonds*	Award Books	192	1963

J PROBLEMS, QUIZZES, AND PUZZLES

The Bridge World	*Bridge Movies & Post-Mortems*	*The Bridge World*	48	1979
The Bridge World	*Challenge the Champs* (Book I)	*The Bridge World*	52	1978
	(Book II)	*The Bridge World*	48	1974
	(Book III)	*The Bridge World*	48	1980
	(Book IV)	*The Bridge World*	48	1981
The Bridge World	*Rate Your Own Game*	*The Bridge World*	48	1981
Cohen, Ben	*Playing Better Bridge* (reprint of *Test Your Bridge*)	A. S. Barnes	227	1964

AUTHOR	TITLE	PUBLISHER	PAGES	DATES
Cohen, Ben	Test Your Bridge	Arco (London)	227	1962
Cotter, Pat and Rimington, Derek	Bridge Quiz from a New Angle	Paperfronts Elliot Right Way Books (Surrey, England)	159	1972
Darwen, Hugh	†Bridge Magic	Faber & Faber (London)	213	1973
Ewen, Robert	The Defensive Bidding Quiz Book	Monna Lisa Precision	105	1980
Foster, Robert F.	*Vanity Fair's Bridge Problems	Horace Liveright	198	1932
Fox, G. C. H.	The Daily Telegraph Bridge Quiz	Robert Hale (London)	115	1977
Fox, G. C. H.	The Second Daily Telegraph Bridge Quiz	Robert Hale (London)	122	1979
Goren, Charles	Bridge Quiz Book	Permabooks	184	1949
Jannerstein, Eric	Find the Mistakes: A Bridge Quiz (trans. & adapted by Hugh Kelsey)	Victor Gollancz (London)	160	1982
Jannersten, Eric	The Only Chance (trans. & adapted by Hugh Kelsey)	Bodley Head (London)	171	1980
Jannersten, Eric and Wohlin, Jan	Play Safe — and Win (trans. by Hugh Kelsey)	Victor Gollancz (London)	160	1981
Kantar, Edwin	Kantar for the Defense: Volume I	Wilshire (N. Hollywood CA)	200	1983
Kantar, Edwin	Test Your Bridge Play	Wilshire (N. Hollywood CA)	201	1974
Kantar, Edwin	Test Your Bridge Play: Volume II	Wilshire (N. Hollywood CA)	234	1981
Kelsey, Hugh	Test Your Card-Reading	Victor Gollancz (London)	80	1982
Kelsey, Hugh	Test Your Communications	Victor Gollancz (London)	80	1982
Kelsey, Hugh	Test Your Finessing	Victor Gollancz (London)	80	1981
Kelsey, H. W.	Test Your Match Play	Faber & Faber (London)	190	1977
Kelsey, Hugh	Test Your Trump Control	Victor Gollancz (London)	80	1981
Kelsey, H. W.	The Tough Game	Faber & Faber (London)	190	1979
Kempson, Ewart and Ritch, J. H.	Bridge Quiz	Contract Bridge Equipment Co, (Leeds)	215	1949
Kempson, Ewart	First Pocket Book of Bridge Problems	Nicholas Vane (London)	79	1961
Kempson, Ewart	More Bridge Quizzes	Wm. Jackson (London)	109	1952
Klinger, Ron	Playing to Win at Bridge—Practical Problems for the Improving Player	Ward Lock (London)	125	1976
Klinger, Ron	Winning Bridge — Trick by Trick	Victor Gollancz (London)	127	1980
Lederer, Rhoda Barrow	Acolites Quiz	Allen & Unwin (London)	197	1970–74
Lukacs, Paul (see Milnes, Eric)	Improve Your Dummy Play			
Lukacs, Paul and Rubens, Jeff	Test Your Play as Declarer	Hart	189	1977
Lukacs, Paul and Rubens, Jeff	Test Your Play as Declarer — volume 2	Devyn Press (Shelbyville KY)	222	1982
Martin, Emerson	Bridge Word Puzzles	White Arts (Indianapolis)	140	1973
Milnes, Eric and Lukacs, Paul	Improve Your Dummy Play	Barclay	80	1969
Mollo, Victor	Test Your Defense	Prentice Hall (Englewood Cliffs NJ)	311	172
Mollo, Victor and Nielson, Aksel	How Good Is Your Defense?	Hart	256	1976
Nielson, Aksel (see Mollo, Victor)	How Good Is Your Defense?			
Osborn, Florence	How's Your Bridge?	Faber & Faber (London)	212	1949
Osborn, Florence	How's Your Bridge Game? (American title)	McGraw-Hill	201	1948
Priest, Denis	Problems in Play: First Book of Bridge Problems	U. of Queensland Press (Australia)	167	1982
Reese, Terence	The Most Puzzling Situations in Bridge	Sterling	160	1978
Reese, Terence	Play These Hands With Me	W. H. Allen (London)	195	1976
Rimington, Derek (see Cotter, Pat)	Bridge Quiz from a New Angle			
Ritch, J. H. (see Kempson, Ewart)	Bridge Quiz			
Roudinesco, Jean-Marc	Play Bridge with me—Forty Problems in Card Play	Victor Gollancz (London)	95	1980
Rubens, Jeff (see Lukacs, Paul)	Test Your Play as Declarer			
Rubens, Jeff (see Lukacs, Paul)	Test Your Play as Declarer - volume 2			
Sheinwold, Alfred	The Pocket Book of Puzzles (Nos. 1-6) reprinted	Pocket Books (6 vols.) Devyn Press (Shelbyville KY) (3 vols.)	191 185	1970–71 1981
Wohlin, Jan (see Jannersten, Eric)	Play Safe — and Win			

K BIOGRAPHY

AUTHOR	TITLE	PUBLISHER	PAGES	DATES
Culbertson, Ely	*Strange Lives of One Man	J. C. Winston (Philadelphia)	693	1940
Dunne, J. Patrick and Ostrow, Albert	Championship Bridge as Played by the Experts	McGraw-Hill Bodley Head (London)	251 188	1949 1952
Mollo, Victor	Confessions of an Addict	Newnes (London)	199	1966
Ostrow, Albert (see Dunne, J. Patrick)	Championship Bridge as Played by the Experts			
Ramsey, Guy	Aces All	Museum Press (London)	204	1955
Reese, Terence	Bridge at the Top	Faber & Faber (London)	143	1977
Schenken, Howard	The Education of a Bridge Player	Simon & Schuster	286	1973

AUTHOR	TITLE	PUBLISHER	PAGES	DATES
Sheinwold, Patricia Fox	*Husbands and Other Men I've Played With*	Houghton Mifflin (Boston)	196	1976
Sims, Dorothy Rice	*Curiouser and Curiouser*	Simon & Schuster	203	1940
Sontag, Alan	*The Bridge Bum — My Life and Play*	Morrow	240	1977

L HUMOR AND POETRY

AUTHOR	TITLE	PUBLISHER	PAGES	DATES
Barclay, Shepard	*Bridge Fun Verse and Worse*	Walter Drey	95	1934
The Bridge World	*Bridge World Humor — 9 Short Stories*	*The Bridge World*	48	1980
Calhoun, Philo (see Webster, H. T.)	*Who Dealt This Mess?*			
Goldman, Bobby	*Winners and Losers at the Bridge Table* (illus. by Mary Grace)	Max Hardy (Hawthorne CA)	108	1979
Goodwin, Jude	*Table Talk*	Devyn Press (Shelbyville KY)	128	1982
Goren, Charles	*Bridge Players Write the Funniest Letters*	Doubleday	148	1968
James, Joe	*What the Hell Is Trumps?*	A. S. Barnes	91	1969
Johnston, William (see Webster, H. T.)	*Webster's Bridge*			
Kantar, Edwin	*Bridge Humor*	Wilshire (N. Hollywood CA)	151	1977
Lawrence, Mike	*True Bridge Humor*	Max Hardy (Hawthorne CA)	61	1980
Lind, Betty	*Psychotics, Neurotics and Bridge Players*	Simons Pub. (Santa Fe NM)	58	1961
Machlin, Jerome	*Tournament Bridge — An Uncensored Memoir*	Max Hardy (Hawthorne CA)	120	1980
Mollo, Victor	*Bridge in the Fourth Dimension*	Faber & Faber (London)	160	1974
Mollo, Victor	*Bridge in the Menagerie*	Hawthorn	152	1967
Mollo, Victor	*Masters and Monsters*	Faber & Faber (London & Boston)	242	1979
Phillips, Hubert	*You Can Play and Laugh*	Faber & Faber (London)	269	1934
Webster, H. T. and Johnston, William	*Webster's Bridge*	Stokes	112	1924
Webster, H. T. and Calhoun, Philo	*Who Dealt This Mess?*	Doubleday	174	1948

M MATHEMATICS

AUTHOR	TITLE	PUBLISHER	PAGES	DATES
Borel, Émile and Chéron, André	‡*Mathematical Theory of Bridge* (trans. by Alex Traub)	Monna Lisa Precision	434	1975
Borel, Émile and Chéron, André	*Théorie Mathématique du Bridge	Gauthier-Villars (Paris)	424	1940-55
Frost, Frederick	†*Bridge Odds Complete*	Coffin (Waltham MA)	96	1971
Goren, Charles	*Go with the Odds*	MacMillan	308	1969
Jacoby, Oswald	*How to Figure the Odds*	Doubleday	215	1947
Kibler, Robert et al	*Probabilities in Contract Bridge*	Frost	103	1963
Levinson,	*Science of Chance*	Faber & Faber (London)		1952
Northrop, Eugene and Stein, Arthur	*Mathematical Odds in Contract*	Vanguard	93	1933
Telfer, Roy	*Practical Odds at Bridge*	Traub (Capetown)	114	1961
Telfer, Roy (see Kibler, Robert)	*Probabilities in Contract Bridge*			
Traub, Alex (see Kibler, Robert)	*Probabilities in Contract Bridge*			

N LAWS

AUTHOR	TITLE	PUBLISHER	PAGES	DATES
Whist Club, N. Y.	*The Laws of Contract Bridge*	J. C. Winston (Philadelphia)	54	1932
ACBL Laws Commission	*The Laws of Duplicate Contract Bridge*	ABL, USBA (Philadelphia)	64	1933
Whist Club, N. Y.	*The Laws of Contract Bridge*	J. C. Winston (Philadelphia)	51	1935
ACBL Laws Commission	*The Laws of Duplicate Contract Bridge*	J. C. Winston (Philadelphia)	91	1935
ACBL Laws Commission	*The Laws of Contract Bridge*	J. C. Winston (Philadelphia)	62	1943
ACBL Laws Commission	*The Laws of Contract Bridge*	J. C. Winston (Philadelphia)	47	1948
ACBL Laws Commission	*The Laws of Duplicate Contract Bridge*	J. C. Winston (Philadelphia)	67	1948
ACBL Laws Commission	*The Laws of Contract Bridge*	Crown	62	1963
ACBL Laws Commission	*The Laws of Duplicate Contract Bridge*	Crown	78	1963
ACBL Laws Commission	‡*Laws of Duplicate Contract Bridge*	ACBL (Memphis)	102	1975
ACBL Laws Commission	*Laws of Contract Bridge*	ACBL (Memphis)	55	1981
Portland Club, EBL, ACBL, and WBF	*The International Laws of Contract Bridge 1981*	Bibliagora (Hounslow England)		1981

O PERIODICALS

AUTHOR	TITLE	PAGES	DATES
Dollar, Stanley	*The American Bridge Digest*	12	1962-63
Kent, Walter	(originally California Bridge Digest)		1962-63
Coffin, George	*American Bridge Teachers' Quarterly*	4	1961-63
Shaw, Harold	7250 Franklin Ave.		1963-69
Thomas, Frank	Los Angeles, CA 90046		1969-
Howard, Denis	*Australian Bridge*	6	1970-71
Klinger, Ron	Box 3805		1972-
	GPO Sydney, NSW 2001, Australia		
	Bridge	12	
Haremaker, R. N.	Nederlandse Bridge Bond		1930-34
Goudsmit, Frits	Emmapark 9		1935-41
Goudsmit, Frits	2595 Es Den Haag		1946-56
Filarski, Herman	The Netherlands		1956-63
Elffers, G.			1963-71

AUTHOR	TITLE	PUBLISHER	PAGES	DATES
Boekhorst, André				1971–
Schipperheyn, Ton				
de Togorco, Antonio	*Bridge*		4	1961–
Castellõn, Joaquin	Edicones Bridge			
Goded, Fredrico	Castello, 45			
Francos, Luis	Madrid–1, Spain			
Martorell, Juan				
Jaques, Arturo	*Bridge Argentino*		6	1952–66
Lerena, Raúl	Association del Bridge Argentino			1966–
	Lavalle 1145 4° Piso B			
	1048 Buenos Aires, Argentina			
Mardulyn, Jean	*Bridge Belgium*		6	1957–
	Avenue Louis Lepoutre, 57			
	1060 Bruxelles, Belgium			
Sachen, Bill	*Bridge Buffs' Bulletin*		4	1973–
	927 Grand Avenue,			
	Waukegan, IL 60085			
Firpo, Luigi	*Bridge D'Italia*		12	1943–75
Barbone, Guido	Largo Augusto 3			1975–
	20122 Milano, Italy			
Bruelheide, Frank	*Bridge Digest*		12	1937–39
	1645 Hennepin Avenue			
	Minneapolis MN			
Gokhale, Avinash	*Bridge Digest*		8	1978–
	Ram Krópra, 17 Deccan Gymkhana			
	Poona 414 004, India			
Sandsmark, Tommy H. S.	*Bridge I Norge*		8	
Stedding, Svein Thomas	Postboks 6765			
	St. Plass, Oslo 1, Norway			
Rubens, Jeff	*The Bridge Journal*			1963–67
	88–35 164 St.			
	Jamaica 2, NY			
Shaikh, Mohammed Aslam	*Bridge Kibitzer*			1983–
	108 Motan Building, 2nd Floor			
	M. A. Jinnah Road, Karachi-2, Pakistan			
Manning-Foster, Alfred Edye	*Bridge Magazine*		12	1926–39
	(not published during War)			
Kempson, Cpt. Ewart	Wakefield Rd.			1946–65
Milnes, Eric	Leeds 10, England			1965–80
Alder, Phillip				1980–
Jannersten, Eric	*Bridge Tidningen*		10	1943–80
Flodqvist, Sven-Olov	Box 45 774 01 Avesta			1980–
	Stockholm, Sweden			
Culbertson, Ely	*Bridge World*		12	1929–55
Moyse, Alphonse Jr.	39 W. 94th St.			1956–66
Kaplan, Edgar and Rubens, Jeff	New York NY 10025			1967–
Phillips, Hubert	*British Bridge World*		12	1932–39
Reese, Terrence	35 Dover St.			1956–62
Dormer, Albert	London, W.1 England			1962–64
Pomianowski, Jerzy	*Brydź*			
	Ul. Widok 22			
	00–023 Warszawa, Poland			
Zankay, Peter	*Bridzselet*		12	Current
	Buda 8 rsi ut 24			
	1118 Budapest, Hungary			
Cotzin, Sumner	*Communication*		12	1978–
	10 Jamesbury Drive			
	Worchester MA			
Mott-Smith, Geoffrey	*The Contract Bridge Bulletin*		12	1934–37
	American Contract Bridge League			
Huske, William J.	2200 Democrat Rd.			1937–39
Benyon, George W.	P.O. Box 161192			1939–52
Sheinwold, Alfred	Memphis TN 38186			1952–58
Frey, Richard				1958–70
Becker, Steve	Executive Editor			1970–72
Hirsch, Tannah	Editor			1970–72
Francis, Henry	Executive Editor			1972–
Emery, Sue	Editor			1972–
Harrison-Gray, Maurice	*Contract Bridge Journal*			1946–47
Stern, Dr. Paul	3 London Lane			1947–
Ramsey, Guy	Bromley, Kent, England			1947–50
Ingram, Henry St. John				1951–55
Nielsen, Aksel J.	*Dansk Bridge*		10	1941–47
Pedersen,Leo	Postboks 121			1947–58
Boeck, Jens	D-K 3400 Hillerød, Denmark			1958–64
Krause, Svend G.				1964–66
Boeck, Jens				1966–73
Lundby, Ib				1973–
Von Mutius, Erhard	*Deutsches Bridge Verbands-Blatt*		12	1952–64
Schubert, Fritz	Teckstrasse 27			1964–74
Schubert, Vilma	7238 Oberndorf, West Germany			1974–79
Borho, Volker				1979–
Jannersten, Eric	*European Bridge Review*		12	1949–54
	(in English)			
Neamtzu, Coriolan	*Expert Bridge*		4–6	Current
	Victoe Manu 42,			
	73314 Bucarest, Romania			

EDITOR	PERIODICAL	ISSUES	DATES
Jannerstein, Eric Barrow, Rhoda Dormer, Albert Jourdain, Patrick	*IBPA Bulletin* The International Bridge Press Association Flat 8, Felin Wen, Rhiwbina, Cardiff, Wales CF4 6NW	10	1958–67 1967–72 1972–82 1982–
Amsbury, Joe Sowter, Tony	*International Popular Bridge Monthly* 12 Beech Avenue, Sherwood Rise Nottingham NG7 7LL.	12	1974–80 1980–
Walsh, P. F.	*Irish Bridge Journal* Northgate Street Athlone, Co Westmeath, Ireland	6	1979–
Hirsch, Tannah Frydrich, Julian	*Israel Bridge Magazine* 41 Weizmann St. Tel Aviv, Israel		1963–65 1966–67
Birman, David	*The Israeli Bridge Bulletin* 5 Bugrashov Tel-Aviv, Israel		1980–
Wong, John Hikawa, Tetsuji	*Japan Contract Bridge League Bulletin* c/o Fudosan–Kaikan Room 705 3–5 Yotsuya Shinjuku-Ku, Tokyo 160		1963–80 1980–
Carruthers, John	*The Kibitzer* 65 Tiago Ave. Toronto ON, Canada M4B 2A2	4	Current
Kokish, Eric	*Melange de Bridge* 5050 Clanranald Ave., #406 Montreal PQ, Canada H3X 2S2	1	1975–
Freeman, Richard A.	*Modern Bridge* 1447 Peachtree St., N.E. Atlanta GA 30309	9	1964
Victor, Brig. A.D.J.	*News Bulletin* A–222 Defense Colony New Delhi 110 024, India	12	Current
Fenton, H. E. Adams, Lindsay	*New Zealand Bridge* 49 Argyle St. Herne Bay, Auckland 2, New Zealand	6	1965–75 1975–
Wolenik, Bob	*Popular Bridge* 17337 Ventura Blvd. Encino CA 91316	6	1967–
Frey, Richard L.	*Precision Newsletter* 277 Park Avenue New York NY 10017	12	1973–81
Cardoso, Alinda Aranha, Sérgio Barros, Ana C. M. Pinto, Sandra	*Revista Brasileira de Bridge* Caixa Postal 3334 São Paulo, Brazil	12	1975–
Bongrand, Michel Dreux, Emile Meyer, Jean-Paul	*Revue Française de Bridge, Bridgeur* 28 Rue de Richelieu 75001 Paris, France	11	1958–
Sapire, Leon	*The South African Bridge Bulletin* South African Bridge Federation P.O. Box 10849 Johannesburg, South Africa 2000	11	1954–
Hathorn, John B.	*Texas Bridge* (last issue National Bridge)		1959–64
Marraro, Francesco	*Tutto Bridge* Roma Via della Scrofa 14 Milano, Italy	11	1980–
Dormer, Albert	*World Bridge News* 151 Blackheath Park London S.E. 3 OHA England	5–6	1971–

P ENCYCLOPEDIAS

EDITORS

Cohen, Ben and Barrow, Rhoda	*The Bridge Player's Encyclopedia —* *International Edition* (British Edition of *The Official Encyclopedia of Bridge*)	Paul Hamlyn (London)	674	1967
Culbertson, Ely	*The Encyclopedia of Bridge*	*The Bridge World*	477	1935
Francis, Henry and Truscott, Alan	*The Official Encyclopedia of Bridge* Diane Hayward (editor) 4th ed.	Crown		1983
Frey, Richard and Truscott, Alan	*The Official Encyclopedia of Bridge* Thomas Smith (editor) 2nd ed. Amalya Kearse (editor) 3rd. ed.	Crown Crown Crown	691 793 858	1964 1971 1976

Q BIBLIOGRAPHIES

Horr, Norton	*A Bibliography of Card-Games and* *of the History of Playing Cards*	Charles Orr (Cleveland)	79	1892
Jessel, Frederic	*A Bibliography of Works in English* *on Playing Cards and Gaming*	Longman's, Green & Co.	311	1905
Parris, Leslie and Patricia	*Contract Bridge Books, an Annotated* *Bibliography for the British Isles* *1920–1969*	Wyvern House (Powys, Wales))	95	1975
Rather, John and Goldwater, Walter	*According to Hoyle . . . 1742–1850* *A Bibliography of editions by or* *based on the writings of Edmund Hoyle*	University Place Book Shop	18	1983